ASSOCIATION FOR CONSUMER RESEARCH

APPRECIATING DIVERSITY

2012

Volume XL
PROCEEDINGS

Editors
Zeynep Gürhan-Canli
Cele Otnes
Rui (Juliet) Zhu

Advances in Consumer Research, Volume 40

Zeynep Gürhan-Canli, Cele Otnes, Rui (Juliet) Zhu

International Standard Book Number (ISBN): 978-0-915552-70-2

Cover art: Scott Martin

Association for Consumer Research
Labovitz School of Business & Economics
University of Minnesota Duluth
11 East Superior Street, Suite 210
Duluth, MN 55802

www.acrwebsite.org

Preface

The ACR North American conference held in Vancouver, B.C. from October 4-7 2012 marked the 43rd consecutive year the association gathered in North America. Furthermore, it was the second meeting in Vancouver – with the 2012 conference occurring almost 20 years to the day since the last time it was held there.

This year, the conference theme was "Appreciating Diversity." Everyone who helped plan and execute the conference took this theme to heart. Sharon Shavitt, Past President, and Angela Lee, President-Elect, organized the plenary session on professional ethics that featured a variety of renowned scholars adopting different perspectives from which ethical issues needed to be considered. Likewise, the Conference co-chairs, as well as Executive Director Rajiv Vaidyanathan, Conference Manager Paula Rigling, Doctoral symposium co-chairs Jennifer Argo and Amna Kirmani, Poster Track co-chairs Maureen (Mimi) Morrin and Vanessa Patrick, Roundtable co-chairs Zeynep Arsel and Hope Jensen Schau, Film Festival co-chairs Marylouise Caldwell and Paul Henry, Meet the Editors Breakfast organizers Susan Dobscha and Katherine (Kay) Lemon and the hundreds of volunteer reviewers, worked to create a conference program that reflected the breadth and depth of our discipline. Specifically, several innovations at the 2012 conference were designed to reflect the myriad methodological, theoretical and topical approaches that exist within the consumer behavior discipline. These included:

*Increasing the number of concurrent sessions to 15, allowing almost 300 competitive papers to be presented, even as a record 773 were submitted due to the first-time shift to 1000 word-abstract submissions versus past requests for papers that could be a maximum of 20 pages.

*Including nine roundtables on the program, which represent highly innovative research topics, and/or methodological approaches to these topics.

*Making a balanced program our goal; e.g., by making sure certain topics did not dominate. At the same time, we offered "micro-tracks" so attendees could enjoy back-to-back sessions within similar research realms.

*Retaining not only the Thursday plenary session, but also including a "Meet the Editors" breakfast on Sunday, that featured representatives from a broader spectrum of journals than in the past.

Whether all of these innovations pleased each individual member, it was the case that attendance at this conference set an all-time high just shy of 1100. Furthermore, 239 were newcomers. We hope our choice of a Newcomers' Chocolate Dessert Buffet, (although perhaps contradicting all of the sessions on moderation and food consumption), as well as the many opportunities to socialize at the receptions and the Gala at the Vancouver Aquarium, made the newcomers—and all members – feel welcome.

We would like to take this opportunity to thank ACR President J. Jeffrey Inman for trusting us with the responsibility of organizing and executing ACR (although we had a lot of help from those mentioned above, to whom we express our deepest thanks). It was an honor and a privilege to strategize this event, and we enjoyed working on this "diverse" team (we are on three continents, were born in three different decades and work in three different areas of consumer behavior). However, we are of one mind that the experience was highly rewarding—and we hope those who attended ACR found the conference to be so as well.

We are also happy that on the following pages, we are able to formally acknowledge everyone who helped from the "global village" that comprises ACR. We hope you enjoy this volume and that it will prove useful in research and in creating lasting collaborations.

Zeynep Gürhan-Canli, Koç University
Cele Otnes, University of Illinois at Urbana-Champaign
Rui (Juliet) Zhu, University of British Columbia
ACR 2012 Conference Co-Chairs

PROGRAM COMMITTEE: COMPETITIVE PAPERS

Pankaj Aggarwal	Nidhi Agrawal	On Amir	Laurel Anderson
Eduardo Andrade	A. Selin Atalay	Nilufer Aydinoglu	Fleura Bardhi
Daniel Bartels	Russell Belk	Jonah Berger	Barbara Bickart
Baler Bilgin	Stefania Borghini	Anick Bosmans	Simona Botti
Jan Brace-Govan	Tonya Williams Bradford	Christie Brown	Frederic Brunel
Robin Canniford	Elaine Chan	Lan Chaplin	Amar Cheema
Suraj Commuri	Elizabeth Cowley	Elizabeth Crosby	Samantha N. Cross
Amy Dalton	Xiaoyan Deng	Kalpesh Kaushik Desai	Utpal Dholakia
Kristin Diehl	Brittany Duff	Adam Duhachek	Giana Eckhardt
Amber Epp	David Faro	Karen V. Fernandez	Rosellina Ferraro
A. Fuat Firat	Jeff Galak	Maria Galli	Roland Gau
Guliz Ger	Mary C. Gilly	Dhruv Grewal	Vladas Griskevicius
Kunter Gunasti	Jay Handelman	Kelly Haws	William Hedgcock
Kelly Herd	Ron Hill	JoAndrea Hoegg	Margaret Hogg
Ashlee Humphreys	Iris W. Hung	Caglar Irmak	Shailendra Jain
Annamma Joy	Eminegul Karababa	Anat Keinan	Uzma Khan
Dannie Kjeldgaard	Robert Kozinets	Thomas Kramer	John Lastovicka
Loraine Lau-Gesk	Leonard Lee	Xiuping Li	Wendy Liu
Kelley Main	Alan Malter	Le Gall Ely Marine	Shashi Matta
Mary Ann McGrath	A. Peter McGraw	Ravi Mehta	Arul Mishra
Cassie Mogilner	Alokparna (Sonia) Monga	Ashwani Monga	Andrea Morales
Anirban Mukhopadhyay	Michelle Nelson	Sharon Ng	Theodore Noseworthy
Nailya Ordabayeva	Jacob Ostberg	Nacima Ourahmoune	Karen Page Winterich
Mauricio Palmeira	Ji Kyung Park	Marie-Agnès Parmentier	Lisa Penaloza
Andrew Perkins	Hilke Plassmann	Cait Poynor	Linda Price
Stefano Puntoni	Suresh Ramanathan	Martin Reimann	Hila Riemer
Dennis Rook	Jose Antonio Rosa	Julie Ruth	Gad Saad
Ann Schlosser	Aner Sela	L. J. Shrum	Timothy Silk
Joydeep Srivastava	Vanitha Swaminathan	Kelly Tian	Carlos Torelli
Remi Trudel	Claire Tsai	Gulnur Tumbat	Linda Tuncay Zayer
Gülden Ülkümen	Rajiv Vaidyanathan	Koert Van Ittersum	Ekant Veer
Alladi Venkatesh	Peeter Verlegh	Madhu Viswanathan	Joachim Vosgerau
Melanie Wallendorf	Echo Wen Wan	Jing (Alice) Wang	Luk Warlop
Christian Wheeler	Katherine White	Tiffany White	Keith Wilcox
Patti Williams	Nancy Wong	David Wooten	Eugenia Wu
Lan Xia	Jing Xu	Catherine Yeung	Carolyn Yoon
Judy Zaichkowsky	Meng Zhang	Ying Zhang	Rongrong Zhou
Meng Zhu			

PROGRAM COMMITTEE: SPECIAL SESSIONS

Rashmi Adaval	Zeynep Arsel	Rajeev Batra	Lauren Block
Susan Broniarczyk	Merrie Brucks	James Burroughs	Margaret Campbell
Ziv Carmon	Amitav Chakravarti	Pierre Chandon	June Cotte
Peter Darke	Ron Faber	Eileen Fischer	Susan Fournier
Andrew Gershoff	Kent Grayson	Rebecca Hamilton	Elizabeth Hirschman
Aparna Labroo	Tina M. Lowrey	Nicholas Lurie	Pauline Maclaran
Naomi Mandel	Joan Meyers-Levy	Tom Meyvis	C. Page Moreau
Vicki Morwitz	Dhananjay Nayakankuppam	Leif Nelson	Steve Nowlis
Per Ostergaard	Michel Tuan Pham	Priya Raghubir	S. (Ratti) Ratneshwar
Aric Rindfleisch	Sankar Sen	Jaideep Sengupta	Dilip Soman
Zakary Tormala	Ana Valenzuela	Kathleen Vohs	Klaus Wertenbroch
Eric Yorkston			

WORKING PAPER REVIEWERS

Joshua Ackerman	Hamed Aghakhani	Tanvir Ahmed	Ezgi Akpinar
Nelson Amaral	Demetra Andrews	Susan Andrzejewski	Lalin Anik
Zachary Arens	Ashley R. Arsena	Laurence Ashworth	May Aung
Nilufer Aydinoglu	Ainsworth A. Bailey	Emma Banister	Sachin Banker
Denise Barros	Ernest Baskin	Rishee Batra	Julia Bayuk

Colleen Bee	George Belch	Imed Ben Nasr	Aronte Bennett
Delancy Bennett	Jonathan Berman	Mariam Beruchashvili	Arundhati Bhattacharyya
Simon J. Blanchard	Jeffrey Boichuk	Jean Boisvert	Andrea Bonezzi
Ruan Bowen	Neil Brigden	Nina Brosius	Christie Brown
Sabrina Bruyneel	Eva Buechel	Denise Buhrau	Clifford Butler
Oliver B. Büttner	Gwarlann Caffier De Kerviler	Colin Campbell	Stephanie Cantu
Benedetta Cappellini	Marina Carnevale	Stephanie Carpenter	Michal Carrington
Leah Carter Schneider	Cecilia Cassinger	Iana Castro	Moran Cerf
Elisa Chan	Eugene Chan	Fong Yee Chan	Pierre Chandon
Chia-Jung Chang	Patrali Chatterjee	Anne-Sophie Chaxel	Bo Chen
Rongjuan Chen	Sydney Chinchanachokchai	Pepukayi Chitakunye	Sunmyoung Cho
Yoon-Na Cho	Woo Jin Choi	Rojanasak Chomvilailuk	Cindy Chung
Bart Claus	Kevina Cody	Paul Connell	Amy Cox
Elizabeth Crosby	Samantha N. Cross	Kim Daniloski	Prakash Das
Sudipta Das	Meredith David	Derick Davis	Helene de Burgh-Woodman
Marjorie Delbaere	Berna Devezer	Kivilcim Dogerlioglu Demir	Ping Dong
Karolien Driesmans	Courtney Droms	Brittany Duff	Claudia Dumitrescu
Lea Dunn	Susan Dunnett	Kristina Durante	Hristina Dzhogleva
Amanda Earley	Jiska Eelen	Eric Eisenstein	Hounaida El Jurdi
Julie Emontspool	Basil Englis	Jordan Etkin	Douglas Ewing
Uchenna Cyril Eze	Tatiana Fajardo	R. Adam Farmer	Daniel Fernandes
Stacey Finkelstein	Jörg Finsterwalder	Greg Fisher	Rajani Ganesh Pillai
Aaron Garvey	Tarje Gaustad	Xin Ge	Markus Giesler
Brian Gillespie	Pierrick Gomez	Margarita Gorlin	Stephen Gould
Nina Gros	Aditi Grover	Yangjie Gu	Michael Guiry
Erin Younhee Ha	Henrik Hagtvedt	Eric Hamerman	Mitchell Hamilton
Sidney Su Han	Haiming Hang	Yoosun Hann	Philip Harris
Johannes Hattula	Stefan Hattula	Timothy Heath	Wendy Hein
Kelly Herd	Michal Herzenstein	Nico Heuvinck	Christian Hildebrand
Elizabeth Hirschman	Guy Hochman	Soonkwan Hong	Chun-Kai Tommy Hsu
Ming Hsu	Hao Hu	Lei Huang	Young Eun Huh
Jamie Hyodo	Sajna Ibrahim	Caglar Irmak	Mathew S. Isaac
Aarti Ivanic	Steffen Jahn	Narayan Janakiraman	Claudia Jasmand
Jennifer Jeffrey	Jenny Jiao	Zachary Johnson	Joshy Joseph
Sacha Joseph-Mathews	Kiju Jung	Andrew Kaikati	Bernadette Kamleitner
Esther Kang	Faye Kao	Sommer Kapitan	Carol Kaufman-Scarborough
Sarah Kelly	Ben Kerrane	Blair Kidwell	Eunice Kim
Hae Joo Kim	Joonkyung Kim	Moon-Yong Kim	Soo Kim
Eva Kipnis	Susan Kleine	Dongwoo Ko	Monika Koller
Jayoung Koo	Isabella Kopton	Goedele Krekels	Gachoucha Kretz
Ann Kronrod	Monika Kukar-Kinney	Atul Kulkarni	Sushant Kumar
Man Ching Kwan	JaeHwan Kwon	Robert Latimer	Kathryn LaTour
Fornia Law	Richard Leary	Crystal, T. Lee	Eun-Jung Lee
Jaehoon Lee	Sae Rom Lee	Seung Hwan (Mark) Lee	Yun Jung Lee
Gail Leizerovici	Marijke Leliveld	Christophe Lembregts	En Li
Yuan-Yuan Li	Jianping Liang	Elison Lim	Heejin Lim
Lily Lin	MengHsien (Jenny) Lin	Andrew Lindridge	Marc Linzmajer
Min Liu	Peggy Liu	Richie Liu	Yuanyuan Liu
Alison Lo	Sara Loughran Dommer	Fang-Chi Lu	Ji Lu
Cuauhtemoc Luna-Nevarez	Rhiannon MacDonnell	Robert Madrigal	Natalia Maehle
Virginie Maille	Kelley Main	Moutusy Maity	Igor Makienko
Anne-Flore Maman	Danielle Mantovani	Andre Marchand	Daniele Mathras
Pragya Mathur	Anna R McAlister	Morven G. McEachern	Sally McKechnie
Lindsay McShane	Katrien Meert	Philippe Merigot	Kathleen Micken
Kobe Millet	Adam Mills	Kate E. Min	Kyeong Sam Min
Mauricio Mittelman	Daniel Mochon	Risto Moisio	Sarah Moore
Maureen Morrin	Mehdi Mourali	James A. Mourey	Sarah Mueller
Ruth Mugge	Mudra Mukesh	Sayantani Mukherjee	Andrew Murphy
Frida Mwiti	Mohammed Nadeem	Anish Nagpal	Vanisha Narsey
Gergana Y. Nenkov	Marcelo V. Nepomuceno	Claudia Nicolai	Leonardo Nicolao
Mihai Niculescu	Valeria Noguti	Leigh Novak	Philippe Odou
Lale Okyay Ata	Fon Sim Ong	Yesim Ozalp	Gabriele Paolacci
Jihye Park	Jeffrey Parker	Marie-Agnès Parmentier	Vladimir Pashkevich

John Peloza	Andrew Perkins	Paula Peter	Bruce E. Pfeiffer
Nguyen Pham	Barbara J. Phillips	Joan Phillips	Matthew Philp
Meghan Pierce	Dante Pirouz	Kirk Plangger	Andreas Plank
Cécile Plaud	Maxim Polonsky	Ingrid Poncin	Siwarit Pongsakornrungsilp
Monica Popa	Sanne Poulsen	Keiko Powers	Cait Poynor
Cait Poynor Lamberton	Chloe Preece	Sonja Prokopec	Theeranuch Pusaksrikit
Martin Pyle	Simon Quaschning	Srividya Raghavan	Kaleel Rahman
Mike Reid	Renée Richardson Gosline	Hila Riemer	Pilar Rojas Gaviria
Joonas Rokka	Emily Rosenzweig	Spencer Ross	Caroline Roux
Himadri Roy Chaudhuri	Alberto Rubio	Laszlo Sajtos	Anthony Salerno
Geetanjali Saluja	Adriana Samper	Sridhar Samu	Kristen San Jose
Shelle Santana	Gülen Sarial-Abi	Daiane Scaraboto	Robert Schindler
Joachim Scholz	Stefanie Scholz	Laura Marie Schons	Heather Schulz
Steven Schulz	Irene Scopelliti	Maura Scott	Joon Yong Seo
Julio Sevilla	Avni Shah	Jingzhi Shang	Dhiraj Sharma
Daniel Sheehan	Luxi Shen	Sargent Shriver	Yvetta Simonyan
Bonnie Simpson	Andrew Smith	Lei Song	Zhuozhao Song
Robin Soster	Katherine Sredl	Antonios Stamatogiannakis	Mark Staton
Randy Stein	Sascha Steinmann	Eric Stenstrom	Jason Stornelli
Yixia Sun	Jill Sundie	Courtney Szocs	Babak Taheri
Chenying Tang	Chenying (Claire) Tang	Berna Tari Kasnakoglu	Marilyn Terzic
Mrugank Thakor	Kevin Thomas	Veronica Thomas	Maryam Tofighi
Valerie Trifts	Luiz Valerio Trindade	Ke (Christy) Tu	Yanping Tu
Mirjam Tuk	Gulnur Tumbat	Mine Üçok Hughes	Oleg Urminsky
Murat Usta	Rajiv Vaidyanathan	Anu Valtonen	Femke van Horen
Koert Van Ittersum	Anneleen Van Kerckhove	Valter Vieira	Akshaya Vijayalakshmi
Rohini Vijaygopal	Alexander Vossen	Benjamin Voyer	Fang Wan
Chen Wang	Kai-Yu Wang	Lili Wang	Ze Wang
Kimberlee Weaver	Caroline Wiertz	Jennifer Wiggins Johnson	Kim Willems
Elanor Williams	Andrew Wilson	Inga Wobker	Niklas Woermann
Markus Wohlfeil	Jiayun (Gavin) Wu	Na Xiao	Chunyan Xie
Qian Xu	Cagri Yalkin	Naoki Yamada	Chun Ming Yang
Haiyang Yang	Xiaojing Yang	Natalia Yannopoulou	E. Tacli Yazicioglu
Marie Yeh	Lia Zarantonello	Jennifer Zarzosa	Yael Zemack-Rugar
Charles Y.Z. Zhang	Dan Zhang	Kuangjie Zhang	Yinlong Zhang
Xin Zhao	Manja Zidansek		

FILM FESTIVAL REVIEWERS

Tanvir Ahmed	Russell Belk	Moran Cerf	Aleksey Cherfas
Laurel Cook	Gokcen Coskuner-Balli	Carolyn Costley	Sudipta Das
Amanda Earley	Giana Eckhardt	Basil Englis	Shelagh Ferguson
Lorraine Friend	Markus Giesler	Wendy Hein	Joel Hietanen
Eva Kipnis	Michael Korchia	Eric Li	Cuauhtemoc Luna-Nevarez
Mohammed Nadeem	Laura Oswald	Yesim Ozalp	Maria Eugenia Perez
Chloe Preece	Diego Rinallo	Joonas Rokka	John Sherry
Babak Taheri	Berna Tari Kasnakoglu	Marilyn Terzic	Gulnur Tumbat
Valter Vieira	Markus Wohlfeil		

Table of Contents

2012 ACR Presidential Address

The Elephant Not in The Room:
The Need for Useful, Actionable Insights in Behavioral Research. 1
J. Jeffrey Inman, ACR President, University of Pittsburgh

Special Session Summaries

Rituals Improve Emotions, Consumption, Interpersonal Relationships, and Even Luck 5
Chairs: Kathleen D. Vohs, University of Minnesota, USA
Yajin Wang, University of Minnesota, USA

> **Paper #1: Rituals Enhance the Experience of Consumption**
> *Kathleen D. Vohs, University of Minnesota, USA*
> *Yajin Wang, University of Minnesota, USA*
> *Francesca Gino, Harvard University, USA*
> *Michael I. Norton, Harvard University, USA*
> **Paper #2: Home and Commercial Hospitality Rituals in Arab Gulf Countries**
> *Rana Sobh, Qatar University, USA*
> *Russell W. Belk, York University, USA*
> *Jonathan Wilson, University of Greenwich, USA*
> *Karim Ginena, College of Graduate Islamic Studies, USA*
> **Paper #3: Rituals Alleviate Grieving for Loved Ones, Lovers, and Lotteries**
> *Michael I. Norton, Harvard University, USA*
> *Francesca Gino, Harvard University, USA*
> **Paper #4: Rituals for Reversing One's Fortune**
> *Jane L. Risen, University of Chicago, USA*
> *Yan Zhang, National University of Singapore, USA*
> *Christine Hosey, University of Chicago, USA*

Deepening our Understanding of Depletion: New Causes, Boundaries, and Processes 9
Chairs: Kathleen D. Vohs, University of Minnesota, USA
Yael Zemack-Rugar, Virginia Tech, USA

> **Paper #1: What You Don't Know Can Hurt You: Uncertainty Depletes Self-Regulatory Resources**
> *Jessica L. Alquist, Florida State University, USA*
> *Roy F. Baumeister, Florida State University, USA*
> *Dianne M. Tice, Florida State University, USA*
> **Paper #2: Haunts or Helps from the Past: How Does Recalling Past Self-Control Acts Affect Current Self-Control?**
> *Hristina Dzhogleva, University of Pittsburgh, USA*
> *Cait Poynor Lamberton, University of Pittsburgh, USA*
> *Kelly L. Haws, Texas A&M University, USA*
> **Paper #3: Motivation, Personal Beliefs, and Limited Resources All Contribute to Self-Control**
> *Kathleen D. Vohs, University of Minnesota, USA*
> *Roy F. Baumeister, Florida State University, USA*
> *Brandon J. Schmeichel, Texas A&M University, USA*
> **Paper #4: A Reexamination of the Role of Negative Affect in Resource Depletion Effects**
> *Yael Zemack-Rugar, Virginia Tech, USA*

To Ask or Not to Ask: When Charitable Appeals Are Most Effective 13
Chair: Emily N. Garbinsky, Stanford Graduate School of Business, USA

    Paper #1: Make Them Smile: The Temporal Effect of Emotions on Giving
    Emily N. Garbinsky, Stanford Graduate School of Business, USA
    Jennifer L. Aaker, Stanford Graduate School of Business, USA

    Paper #2: Donating in Recessionary Times: Resource Scarcity, Social Distance, and Charitable Giving
    Michal Herzenstein, University of Delaware, USA
    Deborah Small, University of Pennsylvania, USA

    Paper #3: Are the Rich or Poor the More Generous Ones? It Depends on the Way the Appeal is Framed
    Kathleen D. Vohs, University of Minnesota, USA
    Bob M. Fennis, University of Groningen, The Netherlands

    Paper #4: Prosocial Spending and Well-Being: Cross-Cultural Evidence for a Psychological Universal
    Michael I. Norton, Harvard Business School, USA
    Lara B. Aknin, University of British Columbia, Canada
    Chris P. Barrington-Leigh, University of British Columbia, Canada
    Elizabeth W. Dunn, University of British Columbia, Canada
    John F. Helliwell, University of British Columbia, Canada
    Robert Biswas-Deiner, Centre for Applied Positive Psychology, USA
    Imelda Kemeza, Mbarara University of Science and Technology, Uganda
    Paul Nyende, Makerere University Institute of Psychology, Uganda
    Claire Ashton-James, University of Groningen, Netherlands

Virgins, Mommies, and Hags: Women Buying into Change 18
Chairs: Julie L. Ozanne, Virginia Tech, USA
Emily Moscato, Virginia Tech, USA

    Paper #1: Red Flag: Inadequate Sanitary Care Derails the Transition to Secondary School in Africa
    Linda Scott, University of Oxford, UK

    Paper #2: Outsourcing Motherhood: Managing Assemblages of Care
    Amber M. Epp, University of Wisconsin, USA
    Sunaina R. Velagaleti, University of Wisconsin, USA

    Paper #3: The Social Construction of Womanhood in Middle Age: Menopause as a Rite of Passage
    Canan Corus, St. John's University, USA
    Bige Saatcioglu, HEC Paris, France

    Paper #4: Crones, Hags, and Biddies: How I Became a Burlesque Queen at Seventy
    Emily Moscato, Virginia Tech, USA
    Julie L. Ozanne, Virginia Tech, USA

An Integrative Perspective on Moral Judgments: Understanding the Emotional, Cognitive, Sensory,
and Genetic Antecedents of Consumers' Moral Judgments 22
Session Chairs: Gergana Y. Nenkov, Boston College, USA
Karen Page Winterich, Pennsylvania State University, USA

    Paper #1: All Sins Are Not Equal: The Moderating Role of Transgression Magnitude on the Effect of Disgust
    on Moral Judgments
    Karen Page Winterich, Pennsylvania State University, USA
    Andrea C. Morales, Arizona State University, USA
    Vikas Mittal, Rice University, USA

    Paper #2: Sense and Sensibility: The Impact of Sensory Input on Moral Judgments
    Gergana Nenkov, Boston College, USA
    Maureen (Mimi) Morrin, Rutgers University School of Business, USA
    Virginie Maille, Skema Business School, USA
    May O. Lwin, Nanyang Technological University, Singapore

    Paper #3: Short horizons and tempting situations: Lack of continuity to our future selves leads
    to unethical decision making and behavior
    Hal E. Hershfield, New York University, USA
    Taya Cohen, Carnegie Mellon University, USA
    Leigh Thompson, Northwestern University, USA

    Paper #4: The Genetic Contribution to Preference Consistency in Moral Judgments
    Nina Mazar, University of Toronto, Canada
    Christopher Dawes, New York University, USA
    Peter J. Loewen, University of Toronto, Canada
    David Cesarini, New York University, USA
    Magnus Johannesson, Stockholm School of Economics, Sweden
    Patrik K. E. Magnusson, Karolinska Institutet, Sweden

Making Places: Sensemaking and Sensegiving in Domestic, Communal and Retail Settings **28**
Chairs: Zeynep Arsel, Concordia University, Canada
Alain Debenedetti, Université Paris Est, IRG, France
Philippe Mérigot, INSEEC, France

    Paper #1: The Value of Atmosphere
    Jeppe Trolle Linnet, University of Southern Denmark, Denmark
    Paper #2: The Atmosphere of Cosmopolitanism: Mono- or Multi-cultural?
    Hanne Pico Larsen, Columbia University, USA
    Jonathan Bean, Parsons the New School for Design, USA
    Paper #3: The Dynamics and Continuity of Place Attachment: Cues from a Parisian Wine Bar
    Zeynep Arsel, Concordia University, Canada
    Alain Debenedetti, Université Paris Est, IRG, France
    Philippe Mérigot, INSEEC, France
    Paper #4: Creating Home and Community in Public Spaces: Vestaval in Tailgating
    John F. Sherry, Jr., Mendoza College of Business, USA
    Tonya Williams Bradford, Mendoza College of Business, USA

The Paradox of Memory **32**
Chair: Kathryn LaTour, Cornell University, USA

    Paper #1: Value of Memories
    Patrick Vargas, University of Illinois, USA
    Paper #2: Nostalgic Charity Appeals: Moderating Effect of Mood, Beneficiary, and Childhood Icons
    Kathryn LaTour, Cornell University, USA
    Altaf Merchant, University of Washington, USA
    John B. Ford, Old Dominion University, USA
    Michael S. LaTour, Cornell University, USA
    Paper #3: Memories Jogging at High Intensity: The Effect of Recollecting Past Hedonic Experiences on their Retrospective Evaluations
    Rajesh Bhargave, University of Texas, USA
    Antonia Mantonakis, Brock University, Canada
    Paper #4: Remembering the Best of Times or the Worst of Times? The Moderating Role of Brand Commitment on False Product Experience Memories
    Nicole Votolato Montgomery, College of William and Mary, USA
    Priyali Rajagopal, Southern Methodist University, USA

Come Eat With Us: Social Influences in the Food Domain. **37**
Chairs: Peggy J. Liu, Duke University, USA
Troy H. Campbell, Duke University, USA

    Paper #1: The (Ironic) Dove Effect: How Normalizing Overweight Body Types Increases Unhealthy Food Consumption and Lowers Motivation to Engage in Healthy Behaviors
    Lily Lin, University of British Columbia, Canada
    Brent McFerran, University of Michigan, USA
    Paper #2: Matching Choices to Minimize Offense: Avoiding Offending Stigmatized Group Members by Making Similar Choices for Them and for Us
    Peggy J. Liu, Duke University, USA
    Troy H. Campbell, Duke University, USA
    Gavan J. Fitzsimons, Duke University, USA
    Gráinne M. Fitzsimons, Duke University, USA
    Paper #3: Using Contextual Positioning to Bias Healthier Social Behavior
    Brennan Davis, Baylor University, USA
    Beth Vallen, Fordham University, USA
    Brian Wansink, Cornell University, USA
    Paper #4: Created Equal? The Morality of Food and the People Who Eat It
    Jenny Olson, University of Michigan, USA
    Brent McFerran, University of Michigan, USA
    Andrea C. Morales, Arizona State University, USA
    Darren W. Dahl, University of British Columbia, Canada

The Effects of Temperature on Consumers Cognitive and Affective Decisions 42
Chairs: Rhonda Hadi, Baruch College, USA
Dan King, National University of Singapore Business School, Singapore

    Paper #1: Warmer or Cooler: Exploring the Influence of Ambient Temperature on Cognitive Task Performance
    Luqiong Tong, Tsinghua University, China
    Yuhuang Zheng, Tsinghua University, China
    Ping Zhao, Tsinghua University, China
    Rui (Juliet) Zhu, University of British Columbia, China

    Paper #2: Influence of Warm (versus Cool) Temperatures on Consumer Choice: A Resource Depletion Account
    Amar Cheema, University of Virginia, USA
    Vanessa M. Patrick , University of Houston, USA

    Paper #3: Mental Thermoregulation: Affective and Cognitive Pathways for Non-physical Temperature Regulation
    Rhonda Hadi, Baruch College, USA
    Lauren G. Block, Baruch College, USA
    Dan King, National University of Singapore Business School, Singapore

    **Paper #4: Physical Warmth and Following the Crowd: The Effect of Ambient Temperature
    on Preference for Popularity**
    Xun (Irene) Huang, The Chinese University of Hong Kong, Hong Kong
    Meng Zhang, The Chinese University of Hong Kong, Hong Kong
    Michael K. Hui, The Chinese University of Hong Kong, Hong Kong
    Robert S. Wyer, The Chinese University of Hong Kong, Hong Kong

Signaling to the Self and Others:
Selective Use of and Connection with Brands 48
Chairs: Danielle J. Brick, Duke University, USA
Tarje Gaustad, BI Norwegian Business School, USA

    Paper #1: As Income Rises So Too Does Our Connection to "Tide"
    Danielle J. Brick, Duke University, USA
    Gavan J. Fitzsimons, Duke University, USA
    Tanya L. Chartrand, Duke University, USA

    **Paper #2: Benefits Offered by High-End Counterfeits Influence Intentions to Purchase Counterfeits
    – The Role of Self-Presentation**
    Gülen Sarial-Abi, Koc University, Turkey
    Zeynep Gürhan-Canli, Koc University, Turkey

    Paper #3: Taking More Money and Donating More Money: The Influence of Self-Threat on Goal-Pursuit
    Alison Jing Xu, University of Toronto, Canada
    Shirley Y. Y. Cheng, Hong Kong Baptist University, Hong Kong
    Tiffany Barnett White, University of Illinois at Urbana-Champaign, USA

    **Paper #4: Identity Change: The Effects of Actual and Ideal Self-Brand Connections on Consumers' Response
    to Brand Image Change**
    Tarje Gaustad, BI Norwegian Business School, Norway
    Bendik M. Samuelsen, BI Norwegian Business School, Norway
    Luk Warlop, BI Norwegian Business School / KU Leuven, Norway
    Gavan J. Fitzsimons, Duke University, USA

The Costs and Benefits of Consumer Labor 53
Session Chair: Daniel Mochon, Tulane University, USA
    Paper #1: Labor or Leisure?
    Christopher K. Hsee, University of Chicago Booth School of Business, USA

    Paper #2: The Influence of Identity on Creative Outcomes
    Kelly B. Herd, Indiana University, USA
    C. Page Moreau, University of Colorado-Boulder, USA

    Paper #3: Self-Customization Effects on Brand Extensions
    Ulrike Kaiser, Vienna University of Economics and Business, Austria
    Chezy Ofir, The Hebrew University of Jerusalem, Israel
    Martin Schreier, Vienna University of Economics and Business, Austria

    Paper #4: The IKEA Effect: Signaling and Restoring Feelings of Competence
    Daniel Mochon, Tulane University, USA
    Michael I. Norton, Harvard University, USA
    Dan Ariely, Duke University, USA

The Best of Times, The Worst of Times:
How Resource Abundance and Scarcity Shape Consumer Behavior 58
Chairs: Eugene M. Caruso, University of Chicago, USA
Nicole L. Mead, Erasmus University, The Netherlands

    Paper #1: Do the Worst of Times Increase Creativity?: Scarcity vs. Abundance Psychology and Creativity
    Ravi Mehta, University of Illinois at Urbana Champaign, USA
    Meng Zhu, The Johns Hopkins Carey Business School, USA
    Paper #2: Dealing with Uncertainty Through Haptic Sensations
    Femke van Horen, University of Cologne, Germany
    Thomas Mussweiler, University of Cologne, Germany
    Paper #3: Perceived Resource Scarcity Reduces Trust among Men but Increases Trust among Women
    Nicole L. Mead, Erasmus University, The Netherlands
    Evan Weingarten, University of Chicago, USA
    Eugene M. Caruso, University of Chicago, USA
    Paper #4: Mental Accounting in the Context of Poverty
    Crystal Hall, University of Washington, USA
    Eldar Shafir, Princeton University, USA

How Corporate Social Responsibility Influences Consumers 62
Chair: John Peloza, Florida State University, USA

    Paper #1: Is Corporate Social Responsibility Good For You? How Corporate-Level CSR Impacts Consumer
    Perceptions of Product-Level Attributes
    John Peloza, Florida State University, USA
    Christine Ye, Florida State University, USA
    Paper #2: Managing Charitable Giving: Cause Portfolio Dimensions And Their Impact
    on Stakeholder Evaluations
    A. Meike Eilert, University of South Carolina, USA
    Stefanie Rosen Robinson, North Carolina State University, USA
    Satish Jayachandran, University of South Carolina, USA
    Paper #3: Can Social Responsibility Backfire? The Role of Intentions in Times of Corporate Crisis
    Katie Kelting, University of Arkansas, USA
    Adam Duhachek, Indiana University, USA
    Durairaj Maheswaran, NYU, USA
    Paper #4: Is Less More When Communicating Sustainability? Consumer Response to Ambiguous
    versus Detailed Sustainability Product Labels
    Rebecca Walker Naylor, The Ohio State University, USA
    Remi Trudel, Boston University, USA

Construal Levels: New Antecedents, Insights and Implications 66
Chair: Dengfeng Yan, University of Texas at San Antonio, USA

    Paper #1: Why Does Psychological Distance Influence Construal Level? The Role of Processing Mode
    Dengfeng Yan, University of Texas at San Antonio, USA
    Jaideep Sengupta, HKUST, Hong Kong
    Jiewen Hong, HKUST, Hong Kong
    Paper #2: Do Lilliputians See the Big Picture? The Effect of Physical Level on the Level of Construal
    Pankaj Aggarwal, University of Toronto, Canada
    Min Zhao, University of Toronto, Canada
    Paper #3: When Proximity Prompts Abstraction: High-Level Construal as a Means of Counteractive Control
    Kentaro Fujita, Ohio State University, USA
    Karen MacGregor, Ohio State University, USA
    Paper #4: When Feeling Depleted Helps: The Positive Effect of Regulatory Depletion
    Echo Wen Wan, University of Hong Kong, Hong Kong
    Nidhi Agrawal, Northwestern University, USA

The Good, the Bad, and the Ugly of Consumer Spending within Close Relationships **70**
Chairs: Kristina Durante, University of Texas, USA
Scott Rick, University of Michigan, USA
  Paper #1: I Love You Both Equally, But...
  Parental Spending on Girls versus Boys in Economic Recessions
  Kristina Durante, University of Texas at San Antonio, USA
  Vladas Griskevicius, University of Minnesota, USA
  Joseph P. Redden, University of Minnesota, USA
  Andrew E. White, Arizona State University, USA
  Paper #2: Romantic Motives and Men's Conspicuous Consumption: The Role of Materialism
  Inge Lens, KU Leuven, Belgium
  Luk Warlop, KU Leuven, Belgium and Norwegian Business School (BI), Norway and Norwegian Business School (BI), Norway
  Mario Pandelaere, Ghent University, Belgium
  Paper #3: When is Saving Sexy? The Role of Construal Level in Shaping the Appeal of Savers and Spenders as Romantic Relationship Partners
  Jenny Olson, University of Michigan, USA
  Scott Rick, University of Michigan, USA
  Paper #4: Why is Materialism Bad for Marriage? Testing Pathways Linking Materialism to Divorce
  Jill Sundie, University of Texas at San Antonio, USA
  James Burroughs, University of Virginia, USA
  Daniel Beal, Rice University, USA

New Perspectives on Symbolic Brands and Reference Groups **76**
Chair: Silvia Bellezza, Harvard Business School, USA
  Paper #1: Connecting with Celebrities: The Therapeutic Function of Celebrity Endorsement
  Jennifer Edson Escalas, Vanderbilt University, USA
  James R. Bettman, Duke University, USA
  Paper #2: Brand-Tourists or Brand-Immigrants? How New Lower-Status Consumers Dilute or Enhance the Image of Symbolic Brands
  Silvia Bellezza, Harvard Business School, USA
  Anat Keinan, Harvard Business School, USA
  Paper #3: Brand Dilution: The Impact of the User of Counterfeits on Genuine Brand Perceptions and the Moderating Role of Social Class
  Nelson Amaral, University of Minnesota, USA
  Barbara Loken, University of Minnesota, USA
  Paper #4: When 'Your Brand' Changes the Terms of the Relationship: Vicarious Dissonance in the Context of Brand Attachment
  Eda Sayin, Koc University, Turkey
  Nilufer Aydinoglu, Koc University, Turkey
  Zeynep Gürhan-Canli, Koc University, Turkey

Understanding Diversity in Consumer Influence and Contextually Embedded Influencers. **81**
Chairs: Pierre-Yann Dolbec, York University, Canada
Andrew N. Smith, York University, Canada
  Paper #1: Consumer-Bloggers Mobilized in Marketing Campaigns: A Study of Opinion Leaders' Authenticity Management in a Streetwear Community
  Benoit-Mykolas Savignac, HEC Montréal, Canada
  Marie-Agnès Parmentier, HEC Montréal, Canada
  Jean-Sébastien Marcoux, HEC Montréal, Canada
  Paper #2: Institutional Dynamics when Consumers Coalesce in Aestheticized Product Markets
  Pierre-Yann Dolbec, York University, Canada
  Eileen Fischer, York University, Canada
  Paper #3: Never-Ending Stories: Opinion Leadership and Antenarratives in an Online Investment Community
  Andrew N. Smith, York University, Canada
  Paper #4: Learning the Language of the Market: Contextual Influence and the Use of Code Switching in Online Consumer Acculturation Platforms
  Hope Jensen Schau, University of Arizona, USA
  Yan Dang, Northern Arizona University, USA
  Yulei Zhang, Northern Arizona University, USA

Encouraging Healthier Food Consumption: The Role of Product Package Cues 85
Chairs: Paul M. Connell, City University London, UK
Elizabeth G. Miller, University of Massachusetts, Amherst, USA

    Paper #1: The Impact of Licensed Cartoon Characters on Children's Eating Choices
    Bridget Leonard, University of Colorado, USA
    Kenneth C. Manning, Colorado State University, USA
    Margaret C. Campbell, University of Colorado, USA
    Paper #2: Exposure to Advertising and Packaging Cues in Early Childhood Leads to Blurred Distinction
    Between Commercial and Entertainment Media That Persists into Adulthood
    Paul M. Connell, City University London, UK
    Merrie Brucks, University of Arizona, USA
    Jesper H. Nielsen, University of Arizona, USA
    Paper #3: Is That Healthy? The Influence of Information Type and Location on Nutritional Information Processing
    Kathleen Debevec, University of Massachusetts, USA
    Yana Andonova, University of Massachusetts, USA
    Elizabeth G. Miller, University of Massachusetts, USA
    Paper #4: Confronting the U.S. Obesity Conundrum: Assessing Front-of- Package Evaluative
    vs. Reductive Nutrition Information Disclosure Systems
    Christopher L. Newman, University of Mississippi, USA
    Elizabeth Howlett, University of Arkansas, USA
    Scot Burton, University of Arkansas, USA
    J. Craig Andrews, Marquette University, USA

The Control Dilemma: Pros and Cons of Perceived Control on Self-Regulation 90
Chair: Jaideep Sengupta, HKUST, Hong Kong

    Paper #1: Environmental Disorder Leads to Self-Regulatory Failure
    Boyoun (Grace) Chae, University of British Columbia, Canada
    Rui (Juliet) Zhu, University of British Columbia, Canada
    Paper #2: What's the Point of Temptation if You Don't Give in to It? The Positive Impact of Vice Consumption
    on Consumer Vitality
    Fangyuan Chen, HKUST, Hong Kong
    Jaideep Sengupta, HKUST, Hong Kong
    Paper #3: Let Freedom Ring? Divergent Effects of Free Choice on Goal Pursuit
    Jordan Etkin, University of Maryland, USA
    Juliano Laran, University of Miami, USA
    Paper #4: Kids in the Candy Store: The Motivational Consequences of Multiple Goals
    Szu-chi Huang, University of Texas at Austin, USA
    Ying Zhang, University of Texas at Austin, USA

Brands as a Means of Self-Expression:
Threatened, Unexpressed, Omnivorous, and Flexible Self 95
Chair: Jingjing Ma, Northwestern University, USA

    Paper #1: Being Mean to Keep 'Em Keen: Retail Rejection Increases Aspiring Consumers' Desire
    for the Rejecting Brand
    Morgan K. Ward, Southern Methodist University, USA
    Darren W. Dahl, University of British Columbia, Canada
    Paper #2: The Unexpressed Self: The Impact of Restricting Freedom of Self-Expression on Brand Preferences
    Jingjing Ma, Northwestern University, USA
    Ryan Hamilton, Emory University, USA
    Alexander Chernev, Northwestern University , USA
    Paper #3: Breaking Status Boundaries: When Interstatus Brand Collaborations Undermine Self-Expression
    by Omnivorous Consumers
    Renée Richardson Gosline, Massachusetts Institute of Technology, USA
    Jeffrey K. Lee, Harvard Business School, USA
    Paper #4: Will Broad Identity Make People Feel Stronger: The Impact of Identity Framing on Motivation
    and Self-Control Behavior
    Ying Ding, Peking University, China
    Jing Xu, Peking University, China
    Echo Wen Wan, University of Hong Kong, Hong Kong

**Countervailing the Effects of Poverty: Individual and Collective Strategies among Impoverished Consumers
for Sustainable Well-Being** **101**

Chairs: Fredah Mwiti, Lancaster University Management School, UK
Andres Barrios, Lancaster University Management School, UK and Universidad de los Andes, Colombia

    Paper #1: Single Mothers in Poverty: Consumption Paradoxes of Stigma Avoidance

    Kathy Hamilton, University of Strathclyde, Glasgow, Scotland

    **Paper #2: Integrating Resources via Practices within Consumer Networks: Subsistence Consumers Participating
    in 'Chama' Networks in Kenya**

    Fredah G Mwiti, Maria Piacentini and Andrew Pressey; Lancaster University, UK

    **Paper #3: Using Consumption Practices to Countervail Stigma Experiences and Transform Self-Identity among
    the Homeless**

    Andres Barrios, Lancaster University, UK and Universidad de los Andes, Colombia
    Chris Blocker, Baylor University, USA

    Paper #4: Vulnerable Consumers: Ethnography of the Consumption of French Farmers Facing Impoverishment

    Françoise Passerard, HEC Paris, France
    Kristine De Valck, HEC Paris, France
    Romain Laufer, HEC Paris, France

In Pursuit of Happiness:
Towards Understanding the Complex Relationship
Between Consumption and Happiness. **106**

Chairs: Jingjing Ma, Northwestern University, USA
Haiyang Yang, INSEAD, Singapore
Neal J. Roese, Northwestern University, USA

    Paper #1: Taking Advantage of Real and Perceived Differences between Material and Experiential Purchases

    Travis J. Carter, The University of Chicago, USA
    Emily Rosenzweig, Cornell University, USA
    Thomas Gilovich, Cornell University, USA

    Paper #2: More Possessions can Make You Less Happy

    Haiyang Yang, INSEAD, Singapore
    Ziv Carmon, INSEAD, Singapore
    Ravi Dhar, Yale University, USA

    Paper #3: The Countability Effect: Comparative versus Experiential Reactions to Reward Distributions

    Jingjing Ma, Northwestern University, USA
    Neal J. Roese, Northwestern University, USA

    **Paper #4: When Happiness Doesn't Seem Contingent on Material Goods: The Influence of Positive Affect on
    Materialism and Conspicuous Consumption**

    Jin Seok Pyone, Cornell University, USA
    Alice M. Isen, Cornell University, USA

Inside the Turk:
Methodological Concerns and Solutions in Mechanical Turk Experimentation **112**

Chair: Gabriele Paolacci, Erasmus University Rotterdam, The Netherlands

    Paper #1: Data Collection in a Flat World: Strengths and Weaknesses of Mechanical Turk Samples

    Joseph K. Goodman, Washington University in St. Louis, USA
    Cynthia E. Cryder, Washington University in St. Louis, USA
    Amar Cheema, University of Virginia, USA

    Paper #2: Screening Participants on Mechanical Turk: Techniques and Justifications

    Julie S. Downs, Carnegie Mellon University, USA
    Mandy B. Holbrook, Carnegie Mellon University, USA
    Emily Peel, Carnegie Mellon University, USA

    Paper #3: Under the Radar: Determinants of Honesty in an Online Labor Market

    Daniel G. Goldstein, Microsoft Research, USA
    Winter Mason, Stevens Institute of Technology, USA
    Siddharth Suri, Microsoft Research, USA

    Paper #4: Non-naïvety Among Experimental Participants on Amazon Mechanical Turk

    Jesse Chandler, Princeton University, USA
    Pam Mueller, Princeton University, USA
    Gabriele Paolacci, Erasmus University Rotterdam, The Netherlands

Gender and Family Identity **117**
Chairs: Paul M. Connell, City University London, UK
Hope Jensen Schau, University of Arizona, USA

    Paper #1: Gender and Family Identification in Television Narratives: Homophilization and Appropriation
    Hope Jensen Schau, University of Arizona, USA
    Cristel Russell, American University, USA
    David Crockett, University of South Carolina, USA

    Paper #2: Gender Norms, Family Identity, and the Performance of Motherhood Using Commercial Childcare
    Aimee Dinnin Huff, University of Western Ontario, Canada
    June Cotte, University of Western Ontario, Canada

    Paper #3: Negotiating "the new father": the consumption of technology within the contemporary family
    Shona M. Bettany, Hull University, UK
    Ben Kerrane, Bradford University, UK
    Margaret K. Hogg, Lancaster University, UK

    Paper #4: The Influence of Gendered Interfamily Coalitions on Intergenerational Transfer
    Paul M. Connell, City University London, UK
    Hope Jensen Schau, University of Arizona, USA

The Mere Idea of Money Alters Consumer Welfare, Preferences, and Morality **121**
Chairs: Avni Shah, Duke University, USA
Kathleen D. Vohs, University of Minnesota, USA

    Paper #1: Reminders of Money Focus People on What's Functional
    Kathleen D. Vohs, University of Minnesota, USA
    Cassie Mogilner, University of Pennsylvania, USA
    George Newman, Yale University, USA
    Jennifer L. Aaker, Stanford University, USA

    Paper #2: The Paradox of Payment: The Moderating Effect of Pain of Payment on Buying Behavior as the Number of Alternatives Increases
    Avni Shah, Duke University, USA
    James R. Bettman, Duke University, USA
    John Payne, Duke University, USA

    Paper #3: People Pay More When They Pay-It-Forward
    Minah H. Jung, University of California Berkeley, USA
    Leif D. Nelson, University of California Berkeley, USA
    Ayelet Gneezy, University of California San Diego, USA
    Uri Gneezy, University of California San Diego, USA

    Paper #4: Clean Versus Dirty Money Produce Wildly Different Effects on Behavior
    Kathleen D. Vohs, University of Minnesota, USA
    Qing Yang, Sun Yat-Sen University, China
    Xiaochang Wu, Sun Yat-Sen University, China
    Nicole L. Mead, Católica University Portugal, Portugal
    Roy F. Baumeister, Florida State University, USA

Doing Well vs. Doing Good:
The Interplay of Morality and Performance in Consumer Judgments **125**
Chair: Jonathan Berman, University of Pennsylvania, USA

    Paper #1: Redemption through Success: When Good Things Happen to Bad People
    Eric Hamerman, Tulane University, USA
    Jeffrey R. Parker, Georgia State University, USA

    Paper #2: Tip of the Hat, Wag of the Finger: How Moral Decoupling Enables Consumers to Admire and Admonish
    Amit Bhattacharjee, Dartmouth College, USA
    Jonathan Z. Berman, University of Pennsylvania, USA
    Americus Reed II, University of Pennsylvania, USA

    Paper #3: Double Standards in the Use of Enhancing Products by Self and Others
    Elanor F. Williams, University of California San Diego, USA
    Mary Steffel, University of Cincinnati, USA

    Paper #4: Actions Speak Less Loud Than Sentiments: A New Model of Moral Judgment
    Clayton R. Critcher, University of California Berkeley, USA
    Erik G. Helzer, Cornell University, USA
    David Tannenbaum, University of California, Los Angeles
    David A. Pizarro, Cornell University, USA

**Expanding the Theoretical Understandings of the Place of Consumption in
Market Formation and Transformation** **129**
Chair: Güliz Ger, Bilkent University, Turkey
> **Paper #1: The Creation and Transformation of an Illegal Market: Kurdish Music in Turkey**
> *Alev Kuruoğlu, Bilkent University, Turkey*
> **Paper #2: Myth Market Collaboration: Transforming a Culturally Contaminated Area into a Thriving Tourism
> Market**
> *Ela Veresiu, Witten/Herdecke University, Germany*
> **Paper #3: Beyond the Social System: Understanding Markets as Consumers**
> *Markus Giesler, York University, Canada*
> **Paper #4: Consumer Markets and Value Transformation in the Global Context**
> *Alladi Venkatesh, University of California Irvine, USA*
> *Lisa Peñaloza, Bordeaux Management School, France*
> *Özlem Sandıkcı, Bilkent University, Turkey*

Would Others be Gaga for Lady Gaga?
When Experience and Perspective Lead to (Mis)Predictions of Others' Preferences **134**
Chair: Troy H. Campbell, Duke University, USA
> **Paper #1: Why a Frying Pan is Better than Flowers: A Construal Level Approach to Gift Exchange**
> *Ernest Baskin, Yale University, USA*
> *Cheryl J. Wakslak, University of Southern California, USA*
> *Yaacov Trope, New York University, USA*
> *Nathan Novemsky, Yale University, USA*
> **Paper #2: Too Much Experience: Predicting Others' Emotive Reactions and Making Recommendations after
> Repeated Exposure**
> *Troy H. Campbell, Duke University, USA*
> *Ed O'Brien, University of Michigan, USA*
> *Norbert Schwarz, University of Michigan, USA*
> *Leaf Van Boven, University of Colorado, USA*
> *Peter A. Ubel, Duke University, USA*
> **Paper #3: From Personal Choices to Perceived Popularity: The Impact of Choice Difficulty on
> Estimated Consensus**
> *Mary Steffel, University of Cincinnati, USA*
> *Eldar Shafir, Princeton University, USA*
> **Paper #4: When My Pain is (Not) Your Pain: Self, Similarity, and Embodied Cognition in Social Predictions**
> *Ed O'Brien, University of Michigan, USA*
> *Phoebe C. Ellsworth, University of Michigan, USA*

Socio-Historical Change and Representations of Consumers in Ads **139**
Chair: Melanie Wallendorf, Eller College of Management, USA
> **Paper #1: Making the Changing Scene**
> *Sidney J. Levy, University of Arizona, and Marketing Department, Northwestern University (emeritus), USA*
> **Paper #2: Working Reality: Advertising Representations of Social Class and Race during a Time of Increasing
> Income Inequality, 1970-2010**
> *Erika Paulson, University of Wisconsin, USA*
> *Thomas O'Guinn, University of Wisconsin, USA*
> **Paper #3: "I am Canadian": The Rise of Canadian Identity in Canada's Censuses, 1981-2006**
> *Gillian Stevens, University of Alberta, Canada*
> **Paper #4: An Historical Analysis of Archetypical Shifts in Representations of Women in Luxury
> Product Advertising in the early 1960's**
> *Alyssa Travis, University of Arizona, USA*
> *Melanie Wallendorf, University of Arizona, USA*

At the Bottom of the Pyramid: How Consumers Cope with Low Status **143**
Chair: Nailya Ordabayeva, Erasmus University Rotterdam, The Netherlands

    Paper #1: Status, Race, and Money: The Impact of Racial Hierarchy on Willingness-to-Pay

    Aarti S. Ivanic, University of San Diego, USA

    Jennifer R. Overbeck, University of Southern California, USA

    Joseph C. Nunes, University of Southern California, USA

    Paper #2: When Diamonds are not the Poor's Best Friend: How the Poor Deal with Unaffordables

    Cara de Boer, Katholieke Universiteit Leuven, Belgium

    Siegfried Dewitte, Katholieke Universiteit Leuven, Belgium

    Wouter Vanhouche, Katholieke Universiteit Leuven, Belgium

    Paper #3: I'll Sell That for a Dollar: How Social Status Threats Devalue One's Possessions

    David Dubois, INSEAD, France

    Esta Denton, Northwestern University, USA

    Derek D. Rucker, Northwestern University, USA

    Paper #4: When Improving Equality Promotes Selfish Behavior

    Nailya Ordabayeva, Erasmus University Rotterdam, The Netherlands

    Pierre Chandon, INSEAD, France

Stereotypes, Memories and Nostalgia:
Contested States of Longing, Belonging, and Being Within Consumer Acculturation **148**
Chair: Andrew Lindridge, The Open University Business School, UK

    Paper #1: "Russians Always Wear Red Lipstick:" Acculturation, Identity and Stereotypes

    Natalia Tolstikova, Stockholm University, Sweden

    Susanna Molander, Stockholm University, Sweden

    Paper #2: Memories of Pre- and Post-Migration Consumption: Better Times or Embodiments of a
    Defensive Mental State?

    Andrew Lindridge, The Open University, UK

    Paper #3: Home Sweet Home: The Role of Home Country Nostalgia on Immigrants' Acculturation
    and Consumption

    Celina Stamboli-Rodriguez, Iseg,, France

    Luca M. Visconti, ESCP Europe, France

    Paper #4: 4. Social Status Implications of Transmigrants' Consumer Practices in Their Cultures of Origin

    Mine Üçok Hughes, Woodbury University, USA

Beyond Individualism and Collectivism: Novel Cultural Factors and
Their Influence on Consumer Behavior **153**
Chair: Carlos J. Torelli, University of Minnesota, USA

    Paper #1: The Interplay between Power Distance, Position in the Social Hierarchy, and Product Type:
    Consequences for Consumers' Preferences for Premium over Generic Brands

    Carlos J. Torelli, University of Minnesota, USA

    Ashok K. Lalwani, Indiana University, USA

    Jessie J. Wang, Indiana University, USA

    Yajin Wang, University of Minnesota, USA

    Paper #2: Equality Equals Efficacy: The Effect of Power Distance Belief on Charitable Giving

    Karen Page Winterich, Penn State University, USA

    Yinlong Zhang, University of Texas at San Antonio, USA

    Paper #3: Eye for an Eye: The Effect of Honor Values on Consumer Responses to Brand Failures

    Frank May, University of South Carolina, USA

    Alokparna (Sonia) Monga, University of South Carolina, USA

    Kartik Kalaignanam, University of South Carolina, USA

    Paper #4: Power Distance Belief and Brand Personality

    Xuehua Wang, Shanghai University of Finance and Economics, China

    Xiaoyu Wang, Shanghai University of Finance and Economics, China

    Xiang Fang, Oklahoma State University, USA

Experiencing and Evaluating in the Brain: fMRI and Single-Neuron Studies **158**
Chair: Moran Cerf, New York University, USA

> **Paper #1: 1. Identifying Emotions on the Basis of Neural Activation**
> *Moran Cerf, New York University and University of California Los Angeles, USA*
> *Vicki G. Morwitz, New York University, USA*
> *Tom Meyvis, New York University, USA*
> *Eric Greenleaf, New York University, USA*
> **Paper #2: 2. Risk and Attribute Framing: They're Different**
> *Hilke Plassmann, INSEAD, France*
> *Beth Pavlicek, École des Neurosciences de Paris, France*
> *Baba Shiv, Stanford University, USA*
> **Paper #3: 3. How incidental affect alters subsequent judgments: insights from a human fMRI study**
> *William Hedgcock, University of Iowa, USA*
> *Irwin Levin, University of Iowa, USA*
> *Kameko Halfman, University of Iowa, USA*
> *Jooyoung Park, University of Iowa, USA*
> *Natalie Denburg, University of Iowa, USA*
> **Paper #4: 4. Single-neuron correlates of emotion regulation in humans**
> *Karim Kassam, Carnegie Mellon University, USA*
> *Amanda Markey, Carnegie Mellon University, USA*
> *Vladimir Cherkassky, Carnegie Mellon University, USA*
> *George Loewenstein, Carnegie Mellon University, USA*
> *Marcel Just, Carnegie Mellon University, USA*

Of Carrots, Candy, & Self-Control: Decreasing and Increasing Food Consumption **163**
Chairs: Vladas Griskevicius, University of Minnesota, USA
Joseph P. Redden, University of Minnesota, USA

> **Paper #1: Interventions to Get School Children to Eat More Vegetables**
> *Joseph P. Redden, University of Minnesota, USA*
> *Traci Mann, University of Minnesota, USA*
> *Elton Mykerezi, University of Minnesota, USA*
> *Marla Reicks, University of Minnesota, USA*
> *Zata Vickers, University of Minnesota, USA*
> **Paper #2: In Control of Variety: How Self-Control Reduces the Effect of Food Variety**
> *Kelly L. Haws, Texas A&M University, USA*
> **Paper #3: Red, Ripe, and Ready: Effect of Food Color on Consumption**
> *Stephanie Cantu, University of Minnesota, USA*
> *Vladas Griskevicius, University of Minnesota, USA*
> **Paper #4: Mortality Threat Can Increase or Decrease Women's Caloric Intake Depending on Their Childhood Environment**
> *Sarah E Hill, Texas Christian University, USA*
> *Christopher D. Rodeheffer, Texas Christian University, USA*
> *Danielle J. DelPriore, Texas Christian University, USA*
> *Max E. Butterfield, Texas Christian University, USA*

Sooner Rather than Later?
The Implications of Delay on Enjoyment and Consumption. **168**
Chair: Min Zhao, University of Toronto, Canada

> **Paper #1: 1. The Immediate and Delayed Effects of Price Promotions on Post-Purchase Consumption Experience**
> *Leonard Lee, Columbia University, USA*
> *Claire I. Tsai, University of Toronto, Canada*
> **Paper #2: 2. Clock-time, Event-time and Consumer Decision-Making.**
> *Anne-Laure Sellier, HEC Paris, France*
> *Tamar Avnet, Yeshiva University, USA*
> **Paper #3: 3. What's Queuing Worth? Sunk Effort and the Value of A Queue Position**
> *Min Zhao, University of Toronto, Canada*
> *Dilip Soman, University of Toronto, Canada*
> *Adelle Yang, University of Chicago, USA*
> **Paper #4: 4. Is it Still Working? The Effects of Task Difficulty on Perceived Duration of Product Efficacy**
> *Veronika Ilyuk, Baruch College*
> *Lauren G. Block, Baruch College*
> *David Faro, London Business School*

What You Expect is Not Always What You Get –
The Effect of Consumer Biases on Food Intake **173**
Chairs: Darren Dahl, University of British Columbia, Canada
Nina Gros, Maastricht University, The Netherlands

> **Paper #1: Mix it Baby - the Effect of Self-creation on Perceived Healthiness**
> *Nina Gros, Maastricht University, The Netherlands*
> *Anne Klesse, Tilburg University, The Netherlands*
> *Valerie Meise, Maastricht University, The Netherlands*
> *Darren W. Dahl, University of British Columbia, Vancouver*
> **Paper #2: The Best of Both Worlds: Effects of Product Color Brightness on Hedonic Food Consumption**
> *Adriana V. Madzharov, Baruch College, the City University of New York, USA*
> *Suresh Ramanathan, Texas A&M, USA*
> *Lauren G. Block, Baruch College, the City University of New York, USA*
> **Paper #3: Red Bull versus Red Thunder - The Influence of Brand Labels on Consumption Amount**
> *Nina Gros, Maastricht University, The Netherlands*
> *Kelly Geyskens, Maastricht University, The Netherlands*
> *Caroline Goukens, Maastricht University, The Netherlands*
> *Ko de Ruyter, Maastricht University, The Netherlands*
> **Paper #4: The Low Intensity of Light: Behavioral and fMRI Insights into the Effects of "Light" and "Organic"**
> **Claims on Flavor Processing**
> *Hilke Plassmann, INSEAD, France*
> *Pierre Chandon, INSEAD, France*
> *Monica Wadhwa, INSEAD, Singapore*
> *Nicolas Linder, University of Bonn, Germany*
> *Bernd Weber, University of Bonn, Germany*

"Hell is Other People": When Others Make Us Impulsive,
Selfish and Judgmental and Factors that Help Us Fight This **178**
Chairs: Jin Youn, Northwestern University, USA
Kelly Goldsmith, Northwestern University, USA

> **Paper #1: Mo' Men, Mo' Problems: Sex Ratio, Impulsive Spending, and Conspicuous Consumption**
> *Vladas Griskevicius, University of Minnesota, USA*
> *Joshua Ackerman, MIT, USA*
> *Yajin Wang, University of Minnesota, USA*
> *Andrew White, Arizona State University, USA*
> **Paper #2: The Green Eyed Monster is Motivated: How Incidental Envy Triggers an Agentic Orientation**
> *Jin Youn, Northwestern University, USA*
> *Kelly Goldsmith, Northwestern University, USA*
> **Paper #3: (Secretly) Blowing out Candles to Make Ours Burn Brighter: The Relationship Between Self-Esteem,**
> **Malicious Envy, and Interpersonal Behaviors**
> *Cait Poynor Lamberton, University of Pittsburgh,*
> *Kirk Kristofferson, University of British Columbia, Canada*
> *Darren W. Dahl, University of British Columbia, Canada*
> **Paper #4: Do the Crime, *Always* Do the Time? Insights into Consumer-to-Consumer Punishment Decisions**
> *Lily Lin, University of British Columbia, Canada**
> *Darren W. Dahl, University of British Columbia, Canada*
> *Jennifer J. Argo, University of Alberta, Canada*

Not What I Expected: Unanticipated Consequences of Product Exposure and Use **182**
Chair: Adriana Samper, Arizona State University, USA

    Paper #1: Finding Brands and Losing Your Religion?
    Keisha M. Cutright, University of Pennsylvania, USA
    Tülin Erdem, New York University, USA
    Gavan J. Fitzsimons, Duke University, USA
    Ron Shachar, Interdisciplinary Center (IDC), Israel

    Paper #2: The Pride (and the Pain?, USA The Downstream Consequences of Using High End Products in Performance Situations
    Adriana Samper, Arizona State University, USA
    James R. Bettman, Duke University, USA
    Gavan J. Fitzsimons, Duke University, USA

    Paper #3: It's Smiling at Me: Satisfying Social Needs Through Consumer Products…At the Expense of Genuine Relationships
    James A. Mourey, University of Michigan, USA
    Jenny Olson, University of Michigan, USA
    Carolyn Yoon, University of Michigan, USA

    Paper #4: Exposure to Unattainable Luxury: Boomerang Effects on Extrinsic and Materialistic Goals
    Katrien Meert, Ghent University, Belgium
    Inge Lens, KU Leuven, Belgium
    Mario Pandelaere, Ghent University, Belgium

Goal-Driven Financial Decisions:
Understanding the Role of Consumer Goals in Financial Decision Making **187**
Chair: Gergana Y. Nenkov, Boston College, USA

    Paper #1: Helping Consumers Get Out of Debt Faster: How Debt Repayment Strategies Affect Motivation to Repay Debt
    Keri Kettle, University of Miami, USA
    Remi Trudel, Boston University, USA
    Gerald Häubl, University of Alberta, Canada

    Paper #2: Can Small Victories Help Win the War? Evidence from Consumer Debt Management
    David Gal, Northwestern University, USA
    Blake McShane, Northwestern University, USA

    Paper #3: The Influence of Debt Repayment Goals on Repayment Decisions and Perceived Progress
    Linda Court Salisbury, Boston College, USA
    Gergana Nenkov, Boston College, USA

    Paper #4: Consequence of Motivated Goal Setting on Sequential Goals in Investment Decision Making
    Cecile Cho, University of California, Riverside, USA

Narrative Persuasion:
Applications and Reflections on This Approach from Three Discplines. **191**
Chairs: David Brinberg, Virginia Tech, USA
Anne Hamby, Virginia Tech, USA

    Paper #1: Narrative Engagement across Media Forms and Levels of Interactivity
    Rick Busselle, Washington State University, USA

    Paper #2: Narratives in Cancer Prevention: A Review of a 10-Year Research Program
    Matthew Kreuter, Washington University, USA

    Paper #3: The Effects of Social Relationships on Narrative Persuasion
    Jing Wang, University of Iowa, USA
    Jennifer Edson Escalas, Vanderbilt University, USA

    Paper #4: A Framework of Narrative Persuasion
    Anne Hamby, Virginia Tech, USA
    Kim Daniloski, University of Scranton, USA
    David Brinberg, Virginia Tech, USA

Financial Incentives and Consumer Choice **195**
Chair: Boris Maciejovsky, Imperial College London, UK
> **Paper #1: Consumer Reactance to Conditional Price Promotions**
> *Aylin Aydinli, London Business School, UK*
> *Marco Bertini, London Business School, UK*
> **Paper #2: Placebo/Placui Effects of Marketing Actions: Consumers Get What They Pay/Paid For**
> *Bram Van den Bergh, Erasmus University Rotterdam, The Netherlands*
> *Bart de Langhe, University of Colorado, USA*
> **Paper #3: Macroeconomic Threat Increases Preference for Mainstream Products**
> *Stacey Finkelstein, Columbia University, USA*
> *Kimberly Rios, University of Chicago, USA*

Counterintuitive Effects of Mood, Environmental Cues, and
Lay-Beliefs in Food Consumption Contexts **198**
Chair: Rajagopal Raghunathan (UT, Austin; eclipse.raj@gmail.com)
> **Paper #1: How Sadness Signals Danger of Over-indulgence**
> *Anthony Salerno, University of Miami, USA*
> *Juliano Laran, University of Miami, USA*
> *Chris Janiszewski, University of Florida, USA*
> **Paper #2: Reducing Eating Motivation by Intensifying Prior Temptations**
> *Cara de Boer, University of Leuven, Belgium*
> *Siegfried Dewitte, University of Leuven, Belgium*
> **Paper #3: Encouraging Ideal Behavior by Imagining Luxury Consumption**
> *Keith Wilcox, Babson College, USA*
> *Henrik Hagtvedt, Boston College, USA*
> *Bruno Kocher, HEC Paris, France*
> **Paper #4: The Unhealthy = Filling Intuition**
> *Rajagopal Raghunathan, University of Texas at Austin, USA*
> *Jacob A. Suher, University of Texas at Austin, USA*

Online Social Networks:
Why Do We Use Online Social Networks and How Do They Affect Us? **203**
Chair: Eva Buechel, University of Miami, USA
> **Paper #1: Need Satisfaction from Interacting with People Versus Content: The Roles**
> **of Motivational Orientation and Identification with Social Media Groups**
> *Donna L. Hoffman, UC Riverside, USA*
> *Thomas P. Novak, UC Riverside, USA*
> **Paper #2: Facebook Therapy? Why People Share Self-Relevant Content Online**
> *Eva Buechel, University of Miami, USA*
> *Jonah Berger, Wharton, USA*
> **Paper #3: Are Close Friends the Enemy? Online Social Networks, Narcissism and Self-Control**
> *Keith Wilcox, Babson College, USA*
> *Andrew Stephen, University of Pittsburgh, USA*
> **Paper #4: The Facebook Effect: Are Judgments Influenced by the Knowledge That Others Are Also Evaluating?**
> *Claire I. Tsai, University of Toronto, Canada*
> *Min Zhao, University of Toronto, Canada*
> *Dilip Soman, University of Toronto, Canada*

Roll Out the Red Carpet:
The Impact of Customer Treatment on Judgment and Decision Making 209
Session Chair: Chen Wang, University of British Columbia, USA

    Paper #1: Consumer Reactions towards Preferential Treatment
    Lan Jiang, University of Oregon, USA
    JoAndrea (Joey) Hoegg, University of British Columbia, Canada
    Darren W. Dahl, University of British Columbia, Canada
    Paper #2: Status By Association
    Brent McFerran, University of Michigan, USA
    Jennifer A. Argo, University of Alberta, Canada
    Paper #3: Target-Observer Asymmetry in the Use of Persuasion Knowledge
    Guang-Xin Xie, University of Massachusetts Boston, USA
    Tracy Rank, Rutgers University, USA
    Kent Grayson, Northwestern University, USA
    Paper #4: The Impact of Sales Team's Perceived Entitativity on Customer Satisfaction
    Chen Wang, University of British Columbia, Canada
    JoAndrea (Joey) Hoegg, University of British Columbia, Canada
    Darren W. Dahl, University of British Columbia, Canada

Creativity at Different Times in Life 213
Chairs: Haiyang Yang, INSEAD, France
Amitava Chattopadhyay, INSEAD, Singapore

    Paper #1: Creativity and Aging: Positive Consequences of Diminished Inhibitory Control
    Stephanie M. Carpenter, University of Michigan, USA
    Carolyn Yoon, University of Michigan, USA
    Paper #2: Why Some Children Move and Groove So Well: A Look at Creative Performance and Theory of Mind
    Lan Nguyen Chaplin, Villanova University, USA
    Michael I. Norton, Harvard Business School, USA
    Paper #3: How Awareness of the End of Life Impacts Creativity
    Haiyang Yang, INSEAD, France
    Amitava Chattopadhyay, INSEAD, Singapore
    Paper #4: How Fashion Designers Develop New Styles: Creative Epiphany Versus Market Feedback
    Joseph C. Nunes, University of Southern California, USA
    Xavier Drèze, UCLA, USA
    Paola Cillo, Bocconi University, Italy
    Emanuella Prandelli, Bocconi University, Italy
    Irene Scopelliti, Carnegie Mellon University, USA

From the Field: New Research on Interventions, Commitments and Behavior Change 219
Session Chair: Ayelet Gneezy, University of California, San Diego, USA

    Paper #1: Taming Temptation: Targeting Self-Control Increases Healthy Food Behaviors
    Janet Schwartz, Tulane University, USA
    Jason Riis, Harvard University, USA
    Brian Elbel, New York University, USA
    Daniel Mochon, Tulane University, USA
    Dan Ariely, Duke University, USA
    Paper #2: Exercising to the Lowest Common Denominator
    Leslie John, Harvard University, USA
    Michael I. Norton, Harvard University, USA
    Paper #3: Commitment and Environmental Behavior Change: Evidence from the Field
    Katie Baca-Motes, Disney Research, USA
    Amber Brown, Disney Research, USA
    Ayelet Gneezy, University of California San Diego, USA
    Elizabeth Keenan, University of California San Diego, USA
    Leif D. Nelson, University of California at Berkeley, USA

A Variety of Views on Variety-Seeking. **223**
Chairs: Yanping Tu, University of Chicago, USA
Aner Sela, University of Florida, USA

    Paper #1: Preferring the Same, but Consuming Differently: Vicarious Satiation and Variety-seeking in groups
    Yanping Tu, University of Chicago, USA
    Ayelet Fishbach, University of Chicago, USA
    Paper #2: Less is More: Variety as a Preference Strength Signal
    Aner Sela, University of Florida, USA
    Michal Maimaran, Northwestern University, USA
    Paper #3: The "Visual Preference Heuristic" and the Influence of Visual versus Verbal Depiction
    on Perceived Assortment Variety
    Claudia Townsend, University of Miami, USA
    Barbara E. Kahn, University of Pennsylvania, USA
    Paper #4: Variety and the Spice of Life: The Effect of Spicy Gustatory Experiences on Variety-Seeking
    Sayantani Mukherjee, California State University, Long Beach, USA
    Thomas Kramer, University of South Carolina, USA
    Katina Kulow, University of South Carolina, USA

New Directions in Word-of-Mouth. **228**
Chairs: Ezgi Akpinar, Erasmus University, The Netherlands
Jonah Berger, University of Pennsylvania, USA

    Paper #1: When Controversy Begets Conversation
    Zoey Chen, Georgia Tech, USA
    Jonah Berger, University of Pennsylvania, USA
    Paper #2: Rating with Confidence: Rating Certainty and Word-of-Mouth Behavior
    Yu-Jen Chen, University of Maryland, USA
    David Godes, University of Maryland, USA
    Paper #3: Valuable Virality: The Effect of Advertising Appeals and Brand Integralness
    Ezgi Akpinar, Erasmus University, The Netherlands
    Jonah Berger, University of Pennsylvania, USA
    Paper #4: Does Paying For Online Product Reviews Pay Off? The Effects of Monetary Incentives
    on Content Creators and Consumers
    Andrew Stephen, University of Pittsburg, USA
    Yakov Bart, INSEAD, France
    Christilene Du Plessis, INSEAD, France
    Dilney Goncalves, IE Business School, Spain

Driving Diffusion: How Social Networks, Sender Motives, and
Item Characteristics Shape Social Epidemics. **232**
Jonah Berger, University of Pennsylvania, USA
Ezgi Akpinar, Erasmus University, The Netherlands

    Paper #1: Share and Scare: Solving the Communication Dilemma of Early Adopters with a High Need
    for Uniqueness
    Sarit Moldovan, Technion, Israel
    Yael Steinhart, University of Haifa , Israel
    Shlomit Ofen, Technion , Israel
    Paper #2: The Cultural Success of Sensory Metaphors
    Ezgi Akpinar, Erasmus University, The Netherlands
    Jonah Berger, University of Pennsylvania, USA
    Paper #3: Ideation and the Spread of Innovative Ideas in Social Networks
    Andrew Stephen, University of Pittsburgh, USA
    Peter Zubcsek, University of Florida, USA
    Jacob Goldenberg, Hebrew University, Israel
    Paper #4: Local Neighborhoods as Early Predictors of Innovation Adoption
    Jacob Goldenberg, Hebrew University, Israel
    Sangman Han, Sungkyunkwan University, Soeul, Korea
    Donald Lehmann, Columbia University, USA
    Jangyuk Lee, Sungkyunkwan University, Soeul, Korea
    Kyung Young Ohk, Sungkyunkwan University, Soeul, Korea
    Daniel Shapira, Sungkyunkwan University, Soeul, Korea

The Nosy Decision Maker: How the Sense of Smell Influences Consumers' Decisions. 236
Chairs: Meng-Hsien (Jenny) Lin, Iowa State University, USA
Terry L. Childers, Iowa State University, USA

> **Paper #1: The Smell Factor: Individual Differences in Olfaction Memory, Judgments and Decision-Making**
> *Meng-Hsien (Jenny) Lin, Iowa State University, USA*
>
> *Terry Childers, Iowa State University, USA*
>
> *Samantha Cross, Iowa State University, USA*
>
> **Paper #2: Exploring the Dark Side of Chocolate: Moral Cleansing and Licensing Among Restrained Eaters**
> *Maureen (Mimi) Morrin, Rutgers University, USA*
>
> *Nguyen Pham, Arizona State University, USA*
>
> *May Lwin, Nanyang Technological University, Singapore*
>
> *Mellisa G. Bublitz, University of Wisconsin - Oshkosh, USA*
>
> **Paper #3: Love at First Sight or at First Smell? Order Effects of Olfactory and Visual Cues**
> *Dipayan Biswas, University of South Florida, USA*
>
> *Lauren I. Labrecque, Loyola University Chicago, USA*
>
> *Donald Lehmann, Columbia University, USA*
>
> **Paper #4: Seeing What You Smell: An Eye-Tracking Analysis of Visual Attention**
> *May Lwin, Nanyang Technological University, Singapore*
>
> *Maureen (Mimi) Morrin, Rutgers University, USA*
>
> *Chiao Sing Chong, Nanyang Technological University, Singapore*
>
> *Su Xia Tan, Nanyang Technological University, Singapore*

New Insights into the Causes and Consequences of Unplanned Purchases 241
Chairs: Leonard Lee, Columbia University, USA
Scott Rick, University of Michigan, USA

> **Paper #1: Capturing the "First Moment of Truth": Understanding Point-of-Purchase Drivers of Unplanned Consideration and Purchase Using Video Tracking**
> *Yanliu Huang, Drexel University, USA*
>
> *Sam K. Hui, NYU, USA*
>
> *J. Jeffrey Inman, University of Pittsburgh, USA*
>
> *Jacob A. Suher, University of Texas at Austin, USA*
>
> **Paper #2: Boosting Promotional Effectiveness with Thoughtful Product Displays**
> *Marco Bertini, LBS, UK*
>
> *Mitja Pirc, A.T. Kearney, USA*
>
> *Ana Valenzuela, Universitat Pompeu Fabra, Spain*
>
> **Paper #3: The Temperature Premium: How Physical Warmth Increases Product Valuation**
> *Yonat Zwebner, Hebrew University, Israel*
>
> *Jacob Goldenberg, Hebrew University, Israel*
>
> *Leonard Lee, Columbia, USA*
>
> **Paper #4: The Benefits of Retail Therapy: Choosing to Buy Alleviates Sadness**
> *Scott Rick, University of Michigan, USA*
>
> *Beatriz Pereira, University of Michigan, USA*
>
> *Katherine Burson, University of Michigan, USA*

Anomalies in Goal Pursuit 246
Chairs: Luxi Shen, University of Chicago, USA
Ayelet Fishbach, University of Chicago, USA

> **Paper #1: Opportunity Cost Neglect in Goal Pursuit Under Uncertainty**
> *Derek Koehler, University of Waterloo, Canada*
>
> *Cade Massey, University of Pennsylvania, USA*
>
> **Paper #2: The Uniqueness Heuristic: A Preference for Unique Options for a Single Goal**
> *Luxi Shen, University of Chicago, USA*
>
> *Ayelet Fishbach, University of Chicago, USA*
>
> **Paper #3: Blind to All Else: The Role of Mindsets in Multiple-Goal Pursuit**
> *Anastasiya Pocheptsova, University of Maryland, USA*
>
> *Jordan Etkin, University of Maryland, USA*
>
> *Ravi Dhar, Yale University, USA*
>
> **Paper #4: Space, Time and Getting Things Done: The Role of Mindsets in Goal Pursuit**
> *Dilip Soman, University of Toronto, Canada*

Raising the Bar: New Insights into the Development of an Optimal Donation Solicitation **250**
Chair: Tatiana Fajardo, University of Miami, USA

    Paper #1: Construing Charity: Consumer Construal Level and Charitable Contributions of Time Versus Money.
Rhiannon MacDonnell, University of Calgary, Canada
Katherine White, University of British Columbia, Canada

    Paper #2: Empathy, Donation, and the Moderating Role of Psychological Distance.
Joseph Paniculangara, Lakehead University, Canada
Xin He, University of Central Florida, USA

    Paper #3: Splitting the Decision: Increasing Donations by Recognizing the Differential Impact of Internal and External Considerations
Tatiana M. Fajardo, University of Miami, USA
Claudia Townsend, University of Miami, USA

    Paper #4: For Charities not all Aesthetics are Created Equal: The Differential Effects of Aesthetics With and Without Cost Implications on Response to Donor Solicitations
Shweta Oza, University of Miami, USA
Claudia Townsend, University of Miami, USA

Consumer Sociality and Happiness **255**
Chair: Merrie Brucks, University of Arizona, USA

    Paper #1: What Are Others Thinking?: Hedonic Adaptation in Public Consumption Contexts
Sunaina Chugani, University of Texas at Austin, USA
Julie Irwin, University of Texas at Austin, USA

    Paper #2: Verbal Sharing: Purchase, Tell Others, and Be Happy
Wilson Bastos, University of Arizona, USA
Merrie Brucks, University of Arizona, USA

    Paper #3: On the Importance of Experiential Purchases to Defining and Preserving the Self-Concept
Thomas Gilovich, Cornell University, USA
Travis J. Carter, University of Chicago, USA

    Paper #4: It's the Company that Counts: Shared Experiences and Possessions Make People Happier than Experiences and Possessions Alone
Peter A. Caprariello, University of Rochester, USA
Harry T. Reis, University of Rochester, USA

Satisfaction Across the Consumption Experience: The Impact of Judgment Timing, Emotions and Interruptions on Consumer Enjoyment **261**
Chair: Patti Williams, University of Pennsylvania, USA

    Paper #1: The Road Not Taken: The Effect of Forming Pre-Choice Product Expectations and Making a Choice on Subsequent Consumption Enjoyment
Naomi Mandel, Arizona State University, USA
Stephen M. Nowlis, Washington University, USA

    Paper #2: Angry Avengers or Disappointed Deferrers: Consumers' Emotional Reactions to Stockouts
Nicole Verrochi Coleman, University of Pittsburgh, USA
Patti Williams, University of Pennsylvania, USA
Gavan J. Fitzsimons, Duke University, USA

    Paper #3: The Effect of Curiosity on Consumption Enjoyment
Elif Isakman, University of Southern California, USA
Lisa Cavanaugh, University of Southern California, USA
Deborah J. MacInnis, University of Southern California, USA
Gülden Ülkümen, University of Southern California, USA

    Paper #4: Waiter, There's a Fly in My Soup (and I Have an iPhone)! How Evaluation Timing can Impact Customer Reviews
Christine Ringler, Rutgers University, USA
Andrea C. Morales, Arizona State University, USA
Nancy J. Sirianni, Texas Christian University, USA

Conflicted Choices: New Perspectives on Choice Conflict **266**
Chair: Andrea Bonezzi, New York University, USA

    Paper #1: When Two is Better than One: Polarization and Compromise in Unrestricted Choice
    Andrea Bonezzi, New York University, USA
    Alexander Chernev, Northwestern University, USA
    Aaron R. Brough, Pepperdine University, USA
    Paper #2: By Tradeoff or by Criterion: Bottom-Up Construction of Constructive Decision Rules
    Aner Sela, University of Florida, USA
    Itamar Simonson, Stanford University, USA
    Paper #3: Blurring Similarities and Differences: The Role of Category Width on Salient Comparison Orientation
    Selin A. Malkoc, Washington University, USA
    Gülden Ülkümen, University of Southern California, USA
    Paper #4: Choice Overload with Repeated Choice Exposures: The Role of Preference Retrieval and Variety
    Simona Botti, London Business School, UK
    Sheena Iyengar, Columbia University, USA
    Yangjie Gu, London Business School, UK

The Egocentrist and the Stranger:
Conditional Inference When Making Sense of Others **271**
Chairs: Julia Minson, University of Pennsylvania, USA
Oleg Urminsky, University of Chicago, USA

    Paper #1: Conditional Projection: How Own Evaluations Impact Beliefs about Others Whose Choices Are Known
    Yesim Orhun, University of Michigan, USA
    Oleg Urminsky, University of Chicago, USA
    Paper #2: 'Tis Better to Give Than to Receive: Preference Estimates Conditioned on Own and Other's Preferences
    Andrew Gershoff, University of Texas at Austin, USA
    Susan Broniarczyk, University of Texas at Austin, USA
    Paper #3: Estimating Central Tendencies: Dead Reckoning vs. Decomposition
    Shane Frederick, Yale University, USA
    Paper #4: There is Such a Thing as a Stupid Question: Question Disclosure in Strategic Communication
    Julia Minson, University of Pennsylvania, USA
    Nicole E. Ruedy, University of Washington, USA
    Maurice E. Schweitzer, University of Pennsylvania, USA

Feeling Mixed? When, Why and To What End Do We Feel Mixed Emotions? **276**
Chair: Patti Williams, University of Pennsylvania, USA

    Paper #1: Finding Meaning in Mixed Affective Experiences
    Sayantani Mukherjee, California State University Long Beach, USA
    Thomas Kramer, University of South Carolina, USA
    Loraine Lau-Gesk, University of California Irvine, USA
    Paper #2: Putting the Consumer in the Picture: Visual Perspectives and Mixed Emotions in Advertising
    Iris Hung, National University of Singapore, Singapore
    Anirban Mukhopadhyay, Hong Kong University of Science and Technology, China
    Paper #3: Mixed Emotional Experience is Associated With and Precedes Improvements in Well-Being
    Hal E. Hershfield, New York University, USA
    Jonathan M. Adler, Franklin W. Olin College of Engineering, USA

Numerical Cognition:
Numbers and Their Downstream Consequences for Consumer Behavior **280**
Chair: Bart de Langhe, University of Colorado at Boulder, USA

 Paper #1: Numerical Cognition and a Mere-Looking Effect in Multi-Attribute Choice
 Ellen Peters, Ohio State University, USA
 Louise Meilleur, Ohio State University, USA
 Paper #2: Need for Speed?
 Bart de Langhe, University of Colorado at Boulder, USA
 Stefano Puntoni, Erasmus University Rotterdam, The Netherlands
 Paper #3: Tipping the Scale: Discriminability Effects in Measurement
 Katherine Burson, University of Michigan, USA
 Richard Larrick, Duke University, USA
 Paper #4: When to Put the Cart in Front of the Horse: How Presentation Order of Goal Reward and Effort
 Information Affects Goal Pursuit
 Derick F. Davis, Virginia Tech, USA
 Rajesh Bagchi, Virginia Tech, USA
 Yong Kyu Lee, Virginia Tech, USA

Mental Representations of Uncertainty and Risk. **284**
Chair: Bart de Langhe, University of Colorado at Boulder, USA

 Paper #1: Lay Understanding of the First Four Moments of Observed Distributions: A Test of Economic and
 Psychological Assumptions
 David Rothschild, Yahoo! Research, USA
 Daniel G. Goldstein, Yahoo! Research, USA
 Paper #2: Recency and Reference-Point Formation: The Effect on Risky Choice Behavior
 George Wu, University of Chicago, USA
 Michael Yeomans, University of Chicago, USA
 Paper #3: The Role of Payoff Ratio in Decision Making Under Uncertainty
 Bart de Langhe, University of Colorado at Boulder, USA
 Stefano Puntoni, Erasmus University Rotterdam, The Netherlands
 Paper #4: Outcome Neglect: How Guessing Heuristics Supersede Expected Value
 Oleg Urminsky, University of Chicago, USA
 Adelle Yang, University of Chicago, USA

Identity Structure and the Boundaries of Identity Marketing. **288**
Chairs: Bella Rozenkrants, Stanford University, USA
Christian Wheeler, Stanford University, USA

 Paper #1: Escaping the Crosshairs: Possibilities and Perils in Identity Marketing
 Amit Bhattacharjee, Dartmouth College, USA
 Geeta Menon, New York University, USA
 Americus Reed II, University of Pennsylvania, USA
 Jonah Berger, University of Pennsylvania, USA
 Paper #2: When Do Consumers Prefer Mistargeted Products? The Effect of Structure and Competition on
 Preference for Identity-(In)Consistency
 Julian Saint Clair, University of Washington, USA
 Mark Forehand, University of Washington, USA
 Paper #3: Repeated Exposure to the Thin Ideal and Its Implications for the Self: Two Weight-Loss
 Program Studies
 Anne Klesse, Tilburg University, The Netherlands
 Caroline Goukens, Maastricht University, The Netherlands
 Kelly Geyskens, Maastricht University, The Netherlands
 Ko de Ruyter, Maastricht University, The Netherlands
 Paper #4: Identity Cues in Product Rating Distributions? The Role of Self-Concept Clarity in
 Consumer Preferences
 Bella Rozenkrants, Stanford University, USA
 S. Christian Wheeler, Stanford University, USA
 Baba Shiv, Stanford University, USA

Beyond the "Pain of Paying:"
The Role of Specific Emotions in Consumers' Reactions to Prices and Payment Decisions 293
Chair: Shelle Santana, New York University, USA

Paper #1: Price Discounting for Emotional Impact
Aylin Aydinli, London Business School, UK
Marco Bertini, London Business School, UK

Paper #2: Do Emotions Increase or Decrease Present Bias in Monetary Decisions?
Manoj Thomas, Cornell University, USA
Joowon Park, Cornell University, USA

Paper #3: Emotional Effects of Purchase Price-Reference Price Divergence
Isabelle Engeler, University of St. Gallen, Switzerland, USA
Christian Laesser, University of St.Gallen, Switzerland, USA

Paper #4: Beyond Clarity and Confusion: Affective Responses to Price Framing in the Airline Industry
Shelle Santana, New York University, USA
Vicki G. Morwitz, New York University, USA

Designing Effective Choice Architectures 298
Chairs: Oleg Urminsky, University of Chicago, USA
Indranil Goswami, University of Chicago, USA

Paper #1: In Search of Optimally Effective Defaults
Indranil Goswami, University of Chicago, USA
Oleg Urminsky, University of Chicago, USA

Paper #2: Redundant Information as a Choice Architecture Tool: How Attribute Decomposition on Displays
can be used to Highlight Important Dimensions for Consumers
Christoph Ungemach, Columbia University, USA
Adrian Camilleri, Duke University, USA
Eric Johnson, Columbia University, USA
Richard Larrick, Duke University, USA
Elke U. Weber, Columbia University, USA

Paper #3: Product Level and Segment Level Differences in the Effectiveness of a Longitudinal Labeling and
Choice Architecture Intervention at a Large Hospital Cafeteria
Jason Riis, Harvard Business School, USA
Susan Barraclough, Massachusetts General Hospital, USA
Doug Levy, Massachusetts General Hospital, USA
Lillian Sonnenberg, Massachusetts General Hospital, USA
Anne Thorndike, Massachusetts General Hospital, USA

Paper #4: Why are Benefits Left on the Table? Assessing the Role of Information, Complexity, and Stigma on
Take-up with an IRS Field Experiment
Saurabh Bhargava, Carnegie Mellon University, USA
Day Manoli, University of California – Los Angeles, USA

Power and Decision Making: Exploring the Processes and Nuances 303
Chair: Selin A. Malkoc, Washington University in St. Louis, USA

Paper #1: Power and Unconventional Choice
Mehdi Mourali, University of Calgary, Canada
Frank Pons, Université Laval, Canada

Paper #2: The Power Switch: How Psychological Power Influences Brand Switching Decisions
Yuwei Jiang, Hong Kong Polytechnic University , Hong Kong
Lingjing Zhan, Hong Kong Polytechnic University , Hong Kong
Derek D. Rucker, Northwestern University, USA

Paper #3: Not All Power is Created Equal: Role of Social and Personal Power in Decision Making
Selin A. Malkoc, Washington University in St. Louis, USA
Michelle M. Duguid, Washington University in St. Louis, USA

Paper #4: Experience Versus Expectations of Power: A Recipe for Altering the Effects of Power
Miao Hu, Northwestern University, USA
Derek D. Rucker, Northwestern University, USA
Adam D. Galinsky, Northwestern University, USA

When It's What's Outside That Matters:
Recent Findings on Product and Packaging Design **308**
Chair: Julio Sevilla, University of Miami, USA

    Paper #1: Transparent Packaging and Consumer Purchase Decisions
    Darron Billeter, Brigham Young University, USA
    Meng Zhu, Johns Hopkins University, USA
    J. Jeffrey Inman, University of Pittsburgh, USA
    Paper #2: The Effect of Product Shape Closure on Perceptions of Quantity, Preference and Consumption
    Julio Sevilla, University of Miami, USA
    Barbara E. Kahn, University of Pennsylvania, USA
    Paper #3: Aesthetics versus Humor in Product Packaging: Their Impact on Ownership Pride
    Gratiana Pol, University of Southern California, USA
    C.W. Park, University of Southern California, USA
    Martin Reimann, University of Southern California, USA
    Paper #4: Where You Say It Matters: How Product Packaging Increases Message Believability
    Claudia Townsend, University of Miami, USA
    Tatiana M. Fajardo, University of Miami, USA
    Juliano Laran, University of Miami, USA

Disadoption **313**
Chair: Donald R. Lehmann, Columbia University, USA

    Paper #1: Disadoption
    Donald Lehmann, Columbia University, USA
    Jeffrey R. Parker, Georgia State University, USA
    Paper #2: Disadopting Unsustainable Consumption
    Min Ding, Pennsylvania State University, USA
    Paper #3: Disadoption through the Relationship Lens
    Susan Fournier, Boston University, USA
    Claudio Alvarez, Boston University, USA
    Jill Avery, Simmons School of Management, USA
    Paper #4: When Firms Disadopt Consumers: Exploring How Consumers Respond to Firm-Initiated
    Relationship Disengagement
    Martin Mende, University of Kentucky, USA
    Maura Scott, University of Kentucky, USA
    Katherine Lemon, Boston College, USA
    Scott Thompson, University of Georgia, USA

Competitive Papers—Full

Through Which Mechanisms Does Ambient Scent Affect Purchase Intention in Retail Settings? **319**
Silke Bambauer-Sachse, University of Fribourg, Switzerland

Appalachian Mountain Men-of-Action: Nascar at Bristol. **327**
Elizabeth Hirschman, Rutgers University, USA
Ayalla Ruvio, Temple University, USA
Russell W. Belk, York University, Canada

Do Price Promotions Lead to a Reduction of Consumers' Internal Reference Price and If So, under Which
Conditions Is this Effect Less Strong? **334**
Silke Bambauer-Sachse, University of Fribourg, Switzerland
Angélique Dupuy, University of Fribourg, Switzerland

How Relevant Is Marketing Scholarship? A Case History with a Prediction **342**
Edward McQuarrie, Santa Clara University, USA
Barbara Phillips, University of Saskatchewan, Canada
Steven Andrews, Roger Williams University, USA

The 'No Hard Feelings' Effect: Voters' Resolution of Ambivalence
to Make a Choice Between Candidates **349**
Robert D. Jewell, Kent State University, USA
Jennifer Wiggins Johnson, Kent State University, USA
Hyun Jung Lee, Kent State University, USA

When Motherhood is too Hard To Face: Anti-Consumption in Difficult Pregnancy **357**
Tonner Andrea, University of Strathclyde, UK

Revisiting Aaker's (1997) Brand Personality Dimensions: Validation and Expansion **363**
Renu Emile, Auckland University of Technology, New Zealand
Mike Lee, University of Auckland, New Zealand

The Product Choices of Young Adult Consumers: Does Gender Matter?. **371**
Renu Emile, Auckland University of Technology, New Zealand
Kenneth F. Hyde, Auckland University of Technology, New Zealand
Mike Lee, University of Auckland, New Zealand

The Before and After: A Study of Plastic Surgery Consumption with Young Women in Brazil. **379**
Fernanda Borelli, Universidade Federal do Rio de Janeiro, Brazil
Leticia Moreira Casotti, Universidade Federal do Rio de Janeiro, Brazil

Cyborg as Commodity: Exploring Conception of Self-Identity, Body
and Citizenship within the Context of Emerging Transplant Technologies **386**
Ai-Ling Lai, University of Leicester, UK

The Meaning of Nature and its Implications for Individual Consumption Behavior **395**
Vimala Kunchamboo, Monash University, Malaysia
Christina K.C Lee, Monash University, Malaysia

Correcting for Unconscious Experiential Processing **403**
Francine Espinoza, ESMT, Germany

Fooling Yourself:
The Role of Internal Defense Mechanisms in Unsustainable Consumption Behavior **408**
Alexander Stich, WHU-Otto Beisheim School of Management, Germany
Tillmann Wagner, WHU-Otto Beisheim School of Management, Germany

Utilising Consumer Introspection Theory to place the Culture of
Consumer Research into the Flow of Life **417**
Tim Stone, Universty of Aberdeen, UK
Fuat Firat, University of Texas - Pan American, USA
Stephen J. Gould, Baruch College, USA

The Impact of Internet Search on Price/Quality Correlations **422**
Ellen Garbarino, University of Sydney, Australia
Nelly Oromulu, Transystems, USA

Living Diversity: Developing a Typology of Consumer Cultural Orientations in
Culturally Diverse Marketplaces: Consequences for Consumption **427**
Eva Kipnis, Coventry Business School, UK
Julie Emontspool, University of Southern Denmark
Amanda J Broderick, University of Salford, UK

"Great Sleep" as a Form of Hedonic Consumption **436**
Anu Valtonen, University of Lapland, Finland
Johanna Moisander, Aalto University, Finland

The Forgotten Brand Personality Dimension **442**
Iftakar Haji, Aston University, UK
Heiner Evanschitzky, Aston University, UK
Ian Combe, Aston University, UK
Andrew Farrell, Aston University, UK

Globalization in the Less Affluent World:
The Moroccan Consumers' Acculturation to Global Consumer Culture in Their Homeland **454**
Delphine Godefroit-Winkel, Univ Lille Nord de France- SKEMA Business School, France
Marie-Hélène Fosse-Gomez, Univ Lille Nord de France- SKEMA Business School, France
Nil Özçaglar-Toulouse, Univ Lille Nord de France- SKEMA Business School, France

Understanding Sub-Cultural Identity and Consumption Among Indians in the United States:
From Desis to Coconuts **462**
Minita Sanghvi, University of North Carolina Greensboro, USA
Nancy Hodges, University of North Carolina Greensboro, USA

I Don't Need an Agreement on My Inconsistent Consumption Preferences:
Multiple Selves and Consumption in Japan **469**
Satoko Suzuki, Kyoto University, Japan
Akutsu Satoshi, Hitotsubashi University, Japan

Immersion in a New Commercial Virtual Environment:
The Role of the Avatar in the Appropriation Process **475**
Ingrid Poncin, SKEMA - Univ Lille Nord de France, France
Marion Garnier, SKEMA - Univ Lille Nord de France, France

'Because I'm Worth It' - Luxury and the Construction of Consumers' Selves **483**
Andrea Hemetsberger, University of Innsbruck, Austria
Sylvia von Wallpach, University of Innsbruck, Austria
Martina Bauer, University of Innsbruck, Austria

Social Curation in Consumer Communities
Consumers as Curators of Online Media Content **490**
Mikko Villi, Aalto University, Finland
Johanna Moisander, Aalto University, Finland
Annamma Joy, University of British Columbia, Canada

Cars for Sale! An Ethnography of the Collusion of Space and Consumption
in Power and Agency Struggles **496**
Helene de Burgh-Woodman, University of Notre Dame, Australia

In Pursuit of Being Different **502**
Andrea Hemetsberger, University of Innsbruck, Austria
Ralf Weinberger, University of Innsbruck, Austria

Cultural Brand Innovation within Emerging Economies:
A Tale of Two Campaigns from Modernising India **510**
Sudipta Das, University of Strathclyde, UK
Paul Hewer, University of Strathclyde, UK

An Exploratory Study of Collective Nostalgia **514**
Faye Kao, Eastern Michigan University, USA

'Granny Would be Proud': On the Labours of Doing Vintage, Practices and Emergent Socialities **519**
Katherine Duffy, University of Strathclyde, UK
Paul Hewer, University of Strathclyde, UK
Juliette Wilson, University of Strathclyde, UK

Consumption-Related Values and Product Placement: The Effect of Cultivating Fashion Consciousness on the
Appeal of Brands in Reality Television **526**
Claire Sherman, Zayed University, UAE
Damien Arthur, Zayed University, UAE

Cyber-Jihad: Islamic Consumer Activism on the Web **532**
Elif Izberk-Bilgin, University of Michigan-Dearborn, USA

How Do Social Capital-Driven Consumption Communities Conceal Their Economic Interests? **540**
Katharina C. Husemann, University of Innsbruck, Austria

The Effect of Dual Anchors on Numeric Judgments:
The Moderating Effects of Anchor Order and Domain Knowledge **547**
Devon DelVecchio, Miami University, USA
Timothy B. Heath, HEC Paris, France

Collective Authentication **553**
Sabrina Gabl, University of Innsbruck, Austria
Andrea Hemetsberger, University of Innsbruck, Austria

"A Coke is a Coke?" Interpreting Social Media Anti-Brand Rhetoric and Resolution **561**
E. Taçlı Yazıcıoğlu, Bogazici University, Turkey
Eser Borak, Bogazici University, Turkey

Brand Authenticity:
Towards a Deeper Understanding of Its Conceptualization and Measurement **567**
Manfred Bruhn, University of Basel, Switzerland
Verena Schoenmüller, University of Basel, Switzerland
Daniela Schäfer, University of Basel, Switzerland
Daniel Heinrich, Technische Universität Braunschweig, Germany

Competitive Papers—Extended Abstracts

Judging by Appearances: The Effect of Goal Pursuit on Product Preferences **577**
Tess Bogaerts, Ghent University, Belgium
Mario Pandelaere, Ghent University, Belgium

Effects of Narrative Transportation on Persuasion: A Meta-Analysis. **579**
Tom van Laer, ESCP Europe, United Kingdom
Ko de Ruyter , Maastricht University, the Netherlands
Martin Wetzels, Maastricht University, the Netherlands

Good Deeds, Risky Bids: Accessible Pro-Social Behavior Increases Monetary Risk Taking **582**
Maria Blekher, Ben-Gurion University of the Negev, Israel
Shai Danziger, Tel-Aviv University, Israel
Amir Grinstein, Ben-Gurion University of the Negev, Israel

When are Frugal Consumers NOT Frugal? It Depends on Who They Are With. **584**
Seung Hwan (Mark) Lee, Colorado State University, USA

From Bye-Bye to Buy Buy: Influence of Homophonic Primes on Judgment and Behavior **585**
Derick F. Davis, Virginia Tech, USA
Paul M. Herr, Virginia Tech, USA

Towards a Better Understanding of the Role of Social Media in the Processes of Independent and
Interdependent Identity Construction. **587**
Gachoucha Kretz, ISC, Paris
Benjamin G.Voyer, ESCP Europe, UK

Time and Context Dependencies in Consumer Behavior. **589**
Euehun Lee, Korea Advanced Institute of Science and Technology, Korea
Anil Mathur, Hofstra University, USA
Choong Kwai Fatt, University of Malaya, Malaysia
George P. Moschis, Georgia State University, USA

What Effect Does the Relationship Portfolio Have on Well Being?
Comparing the Impact of Brand, Service, and Interpersonal Relationships **590**
Seung Hwan (Mark) Lee, Colorado State University, USA
Allison Johnson, University of Western Ontario, Canada
Matthew Thomson, University of Western Ontario, Canada

Market Mavens and Networking: Benefits and Costs of Network Participation **593**
Seung Hwan (Mark) Lee, Colorado State University, USA
Gail Leizerovici, University of Western Ontario, Canada
Shuoyang Zhang, Colorado State University, USA

Is More Always Better? Examining the Effects of Highly Attentive Service **595**
Maggie Wenjing Liu, Tsinghua University, China
Hean Tat Keh, University of Queensland, Australia
Lijun Zhang, Peking University, China

"Shall We Share Our Clothes?":
Understanding Clothing Exchanges With Friends During Adolescence **598**
Elodie Gentina, University Lille Nord de France, France
Marie-Hélène Fosse-Gomez, University Lille Nord de France, France

Alliteration Alters: Its Influence in Perceptions of Product Promotions and Pricing **600**
Derick F. Davis, Virginia Tech, USA
Rajesh Bagchi, Virginia Tech, USA
Lauren G. Block, Baruch College, USA

The Secondary Contamination Effect of Luck **602**
Chun-Ming Yang, Ming Chuan University, Taiwan
Edward Ku, National Kaohsiung University of Hospitality and Tourism, Taiwan

Shifting Identities and Brand Preferences: How and When
A Malleable Identity Helps Individuals Differentiate, and the Role of Brands **604**
Sara Dommer, University of Pittsburgh, USA
Vanitha Swaminathan, University of Pittsburgh, USA
Rohini Ahluwalia, University of Minnesota, USA

Resistance to Persuasion: Minimizing Cognitive Effort by Implicit Forewarning **606**
Marieke L. Fransen, University of Amsterdam, The Netherlands

New Variables for the Brand Prominence Construct **608**
Heather M. Schulz, University of Nebraska at Kearney, USA
Steven A. Schulz, University of Nebraska at Kearney, USA

Preferred Persuasion:
How Self Construal Changes Consumer Responses to Persuasion Attempts **610**
Wenxia Guo, University of Manitoba, Canada
Kelley J. Main, University of Manitoba, Canada

Consumer Propensity to Resist (CPR): Measurement and Validation **612**
Annie Stéphanie Banikema, Groupe Sup de Co Amiens-Picardie, France
Dominique Roux, Université Paris Sud, France

Negative Consumption Episodes, Counterfactuals and Persuasion **614**
Kai-Yu Wang, Brock University, Canada
Xiaojing Yang, University of Wisconsin-Milwaukee, U.S.A.
Shailendra P. Jain, University of Washington, U.S.A.

The Mediating Role of the Built Environment in Family Consumption Practices **616**
Margaret K. Hogg, Lancaster University Management School, England
Pauline Maclaran, Royal Holloway University of London, England
Carolyn Folkman Curasi, Georgia State University, University Plaza, USA

Store Personality as a Source of Customer Value **618**
Kim Willems, Vrije Universiteit Brussel & Hasselt University, Belgium
Sara Leroi-Werelds, Hasselt University, Belgium
Sandra Streukens, Hasselt University, Belgium

Helping Others or Oneself: How Incidental Social Comparisons Affect Prosocial Behavior **620**
Ann Schlosser, University of Washington, USA
Eric Levy, Cambridge University, UK

Becoming a Mindful Eater: Improving Food Choices through Emotional Ability Training. **622**
Blair Kidwell, Ohio State University, USA
Jonathan Hasford, University of Kentucky, USA
David Hardesty, University of Kentucky, USA
Terry Childers, Iowa State University, USA

Political Ideology, Persuasive Appeals, and Sustainability **626**
Blair Kidwell, Ohio State University, USA
Adam Farmer, University of Kentucky, USA
David Hardesty, University of Kentucky, USA

Putting Your Eggs in One Basket: Sex Ratio Effects on Bet-Hedging **629**
Joshua Ackerman, Massachusetts Institute of Technology, USA
Vladas Griskevicius, University of Minnesota, USA

"How About Giving My Things Away Over The Internet?"
When Internet Makes It Easier To Give Things Away **630**
Valérie Guillard, Paris Dauphine University, France
Céline Del Bucchia, Audencia Business School, Nantes, France

From Luxury Counterfeits to Genuine Goods: Why Would Consumers Switch? **632**
Anne-Flore Maman Larraufie, INSEEC & SemioConsult, France

Friends Show the Forest Beyond the Trees:
Friendship Enhances Consumer Self-Control by Facilitating Global Processing **633**
Eline L.E. De Vries, University of Groningen, The Netherlands
Debra Trampe, University of Groningen, The Netherlands
Bob M. Fennis, University of Groningen, The Netherlands, and Norway Business School BI, Norway

The Perception of Two Types of
Corporate Social Responsibility on the Consumer-brand Relationship **635**
Lei Huang, Dalhousie University, Canada

All Numbers are Not Created Equal: Price Points, Price Processing and Price Rigidity **637**
Haipeng (Allan) Chen, Texas A&M University, USA
Avichai Snir, Bar-Ilan University, Israel
Daniel Levy, Bar-Ilan University, ISRAEL, Emory University, USA, and Rimini Center for Economic Analysis, Italy
Alex Gotler, Open University, Israel

In the Aftermath of an Earthquake: Interactive Effects of Self-construal and Victim Group-Status on
Charitable Behavior **640**
Rod Duclos, Hong Kong University of Science and Technology, Hong Kong
Alixandra Barasch, University of Pennsylvania, USA

Do Open Hands (Always) Open Wallets: The Influence of Gestures on Generosity **642**
Ellen Garbarino, University of Sydney, Australia
En Li, Central Queensland University, Australia

Leisure Consumption as Conspicuous Work **644**
Andre F. Maciel, University of Arizona, USA
Melanie Wallendorf, University of Arizona, USA

Influence of Future Time Perspective on Involvement:
An Approach with two Studies **646**
Stefanie Scholz, Otto-Friedrich-University Bamberg, Germany
Yvonne Illich, Friedrich-Alexander-University Erlangen-Nuremberg, Germany
Björn S. Ivens, Otto-Friedrich-University Bamberg, Germany
Martina Steul-Fischer, Friedrich-Alexander-University Erlangen-Nuremberg, Germany

Differential Discounting of Hedonic and Utilitarian Rewards:
The Effect of Outcome Related Affect on Time-Sensitivity **649**
Selcuk Onay, University of Waterloo, Canada
Valeria Noguti, University of Technology Sydney, Australia

Cooling Down or Heating Up with Emotions:
How Temperature Affects Customer Response to Emotional Advertising Appeals **651**
Pascal Bruno, University of Cologne, Germany
Valentyna Melnyk, University of Waikato, New Zealand
Franziska Völckner, University of Cologne, Germany

The Specificity Heuristic: Consumer Evaluation of Expert Recommendation **653**
Mauricio Palmeira, Monash Unviversity, Australia
Gerri Spassova, Monash Unviversity, Australia

Regulating Consumer Behavior by Refraining From Action **655**
Anneleen Van Kerckhove, Ghent University, Belgium
Maggie Geuens, Ghent University, Belgium

When Lower is Better: The Impact of Activated Magnitude Interpretation Frames on Reactions to
Alpha-numeric Brand Names 658
Anneleen Van Kerckhove, Ghent University, Belgium
Hendrik Slabbinck, Ghent University, Belgium
Mario Pandelaere, Ghent University, Belgium

In or Out of Focus? Subcategories Trigger In-group Heterogeneity and
Out-group Homogeneity Effects in Product Assortments 661
Erica van Herpen, University of Wagening, The Netherlands
Anick Bosmans, Tilburg University, The Netherlands

Together or Alone: How The Social Setting of Experiences Impacts
Preferences For Improving Versus Declining Sequences. 663
Rajesh Bhargave, University of Texas at San Antonio, USA
Nicole Votolato Montgomery, College of William and Mary, USA

On Higher Ground: Moral Thinking Leads to Abstract Processing. 665
Eugene Chan, University of Toronto, Canada
Eunice Kim Cho, University of Toronto, Canada

The Role of Gender Congruity for Anthropomorphized Product Perception 667
Ellis van den Hende, University of Amsterdam, The Netherlands
Ruth Mugge, Delft University of Technology, The Netherlands

Disclosure in Word-of-Mouth Marketing: The Role of Prior Agent Experience. 670
Lisa J. Abendroth, University of St. Thomas, USA

Exploring the Mythology of Viral Videos and the Epic Fail:
Why Video Communications Capture the Market's Imagination 672
Dante M. Pirouz, Ivey Business School, Western University, Canada
Allison Johnson, Ivey Business School, Western University, Canada
Raymond Pirouz, Ivey Business School, Western University, Canada
Matthew Thomson, Ivey Business School, Western University, Canada

When Excuses Backfire: The Ironic Effect of Excuses on Consumer Perceptions 673
Elise Chandon Ince, Virginia Tech, USA
Nora Moran, Virginia Tech, USA
Rajesh Bagchi, Virginia Tech, USA

When Losing Hurts Less:
How Spending Time versus Money Affects Outcome Happiness 675
Subimal Chatterjee, Binghamton University, USA
Chien-Wei (Wilson) Lin, Binghamton University, USA

Matching The Words to the Features in Persuasive Advertising:
A Construal-Matching Hypothesis. 678
Karthik Easwar, Ohio State University, USA
Lifeng Yang, University of Mississippi, USA

The Influence of Discrete Emotions on Strategic Goal-Setting. 680
Karthik Easwar, Ohio State University, USA
Patricia M. West, Ohio State University, USA

When the Message "Feels Right": When and How does Source Similarity Enhance Message Persuasiveness? 682
Ali Faraji-Rad, Columbia University, USA
Luk Warlop, KU Leuven, Belgium and BI Norwegian Business School, Norway
Bendik M. Samuelsen, BI Norwegian Business School, Norway

Using Construal-Level Theory to Deter Social Desirability Responding 684
Scott Wright, Providence College, USA

Conservative When Crowded: How Social Crowding Leads to Safety-Oriented Choices 686
Ahreum Maeng, University of Wisconsin - Madison, USA
Dilip Soman, University of Toronto, Canada
Robin Tanner, University of Wisconsin - Madison, USA

**When the Accessible Global Identity Leads to Unfavorable Evaluations of Global Products? The Roles of
Consumers' Lay Theory on Global and Local Cultures** **688**
Yinlong Zhang, University of Texas at San Antonio, USA
Ying-Yi Hong, Nanyang Technological University, Singapore

Moving On and Away: Closure Increases Psychological Distance Through Emotion **690**
Jae-Eun Namkoong, University of Texas at Austin, USA
Andrew Gershoff, University of Texas at Austin, USA

**Powerlessness-induced Compensatory Consumption:
The Preference for Experiential vs. Material Luxury Products** **691**
Ayalla Ruvio, Temple University, USA
David Dubois, INSEAD, France

**Can Brands Move In from the Outside:
How Moral Identity Enhances Out-group Brand Evaluations.** **693**
Woo Jin Choi, Texas A&M University, USA
Karen Page Winterich, Pennsylvania State University, USA

The Influences of Social Power on Social and Physical Distance **695**
Yanli Jia, Chinese University of Hong Kong, China
Robert S. Wyer, Chinese University of Hong Kong, China
Hao Hu, Chinese University of Hong Kong, China

The Effect of Package Shape on Consumer's Calorie Estimation **697**
Jieun Koo, Korea University, Korea
Kwanho Suk, Korea University, Korea

Anti-Consumption Lifestyles and Personal Debt **699**
Marcelo Nepomuceno, ESCP Europe, France
Michel Laroche, Concordia University, Canada

**Rebels Without a Clue:
Nonconscious Motivation for Autonomy Preservation Moderates Social Decision Biases** **701**
Randy Stein, University of California-Riverside, USA
Joshua Ackerman, Massachusetts Institute of Technology, USA
John A. Bargh, Yale University, USA

**The Difference Novelty Makes:
Incidental Exposure to Unfamiliar Stimuli Primes Exploratory Behavior** **703**
Gerri Spassova, Monash Unviversity, Australia
Alice M. Isen, Cornell University, Ithaca, USA

**Guilt Appeals as a Blessing or a Curse?
Influences of Sponsorship Identity and Sponsor-Issue Fit on Guilt Appeals in Charity-Related Advertising** **705**
Chun-Tuan Chang, National Sun Yat-sen University, Taiwan
Ya-Ting Yu, National Sun Yat-sen University, Taiwan
You Lin, National Sun Yat-sen University, Taiwan

Brand-Related Background Music and Consumer Choice. **707**
Arnd Florack, University of Vienna, Austria
Claudiu Dimofte, San Diego State University, USA
Rössler, Karin, University of Vienna, Austria
Susanne Leder, Zeppelin University, Germany

**Using Consumption in Everyday Resistance Practices to Contest Negative Stereotypes:
The Case of Teenage Mothers** **708**
Emma N. Banister, University of Manchester, United Kingdom
Margaret K. Hogg, Lancaster University, United Kingdom
Mandy Dixon, Lancaster University, United Kingdom

**Should I Get in Shape or Get Closer to "Mr. Health"?
The Effects of Goal Anthropomorphization on Goal Pursuit** **710**
Frank May, University of South Carolina, USA

Happiness from Actions versus Inactions 712
Priyali Rajagopal, Southern Methodist University, USA
Sekar Raju, Iowa State University, USA
Rao Unnava, Ohio State University, USA

Bonding Through Service Friendliness: A Potential Double-Edged Sword 714
Elison Ai Ching Lim, Nanyang Technological University, Singapore
Yih Hwai Lee, National University of Singapore, Singapore
Maw-Der Foo, University of Colorado, Boulder, USA

Over and Over Again: Negative Emotions,
Consumer Rumination and Post-Service Failure Outcomes 716
Yuliya Strizhakova, Rutgers University, USA
Julie A. Ruth, Rutgers University, USA

Seeking the Coherent Moral Self: A Process of Alignment 718
Michal J. Carrington, La Trobe University, Australia
Benjamin A. Neville, University of Melbourne, Australia
Robin Canniford, University of Melbourne, Australia

Family Quality Time and the Techno-Culture Food Environment 720
Pepukayi Chitakunye, University of KwaZulu-Natal, South Africa
Amandeep Takhar, University of Bedfordshire, United Kingdom

The Best and the Bizarre:
Prototype and Exemplar-based Retrospective Evaluations of Experiences 722
Robert Latimer, New York University, USA
Priya Raghubir, New York University, USA

Social Context as Price Information:
Social Density, Status Inferences, and Object Valuations 724
Ahreum Maeng, University of Wisconsin - Madison, USA
Thomas O'Guinn, University of Wisconsin - Madison, USA
Robin Tanner, University of Wisconsin - Madison, USA

An Examination of Social Collective Decision-Making 725
Julie Tinson, University of Stirling, UK
Pete Nuttall, University of Bath, UK

The Dead People Bias in Disaster Aid 727
Ioannis Evangelidis, Erasmus University Rotterdam, The Netherlands
Bram Van den Bergh, Erasmus University Rotterdam, The Netherlands

"Happiness Ain't Always Material Things" (Destiny by Michael Jackson) -- Or, Is It? 729
Lan Nguyen Chaplin, Villanova University, USA
Tina M. Lowrey, University of Texas at San Antonio, USA
Kristin Trask, University of Texas at San Antonio, USA
Ayalla Ruvio, Temple University, USA

My Heart Longs for More: The Role of Emotions in Assortment Size Preferences 731
Aylin Aydinli, London Business School, UK
Yangjie Gu, London Business School, UK
Michel Tuan Pham, Columbia University, USA

Me, Myself, and Ikea: Qualifying the Role of Implicit Egotism in Brand Judgment 733
Jacob H. Wiebenga, University of Groningen, the Netherlands
Bob M. Fennis, University of Groningen, the Netherlands, and Norwegian Business School BI, Norway

Trading off Health for Thrift in a Supersized World 735
Kelly L. Haws, Texas A&M University, USA
Karen Page Winterich, Pennsylvania State University, USA

Would You Purchase From A Seller in Alaska?
Preference for Differently Located Sellers in Online Marketplaces 737
Sae Rom Lee, Pennsylvania State University, USA
Margaret G. Meloy, Pennsylvania State University, USA

The Thrifty Meal: Re-creating Value in the Kitchen **739**
Benedetta Cappellini, Royal Holloway, University of London, UK
Elizabeth Parsons, Keele University, UK

Virtually Unhappy:
How Probability Neglect in Social Comparison Biases Judgments of Satisfaction with Life **741**
Mudra Mukesh, IE University, Spain
Dilney Goncalves, IE University, Spain

Slow Sinkers Are the Real Stinkers:
Why a Plummeting Stock Price Can Be Better for Investors Than a Gradual Decline **743**
Neil Brigden, University of Alberta, Canada
Gerald Häubl, University of Alberta, Canada

Shape Matters: How does Logo Shape Inference Shape Consumer Judgments **745**
Yuwei Jiang, Hong Kong Polytechnic University, Hong Kong
Gerald J. Gorn, University of Hong Kong, Hong Kong
Maria Galli, HKUST, Hong Kong
Amitava Chattopadhyay, INSEAD, Singapore

Predicting Consumer Preference:
Prediction Strategy and Data Presentation **747**
Jaewoo Joo, Kookmin University, Korea

Should Birds of a Feather Flock Together? Navigating Self-Control Decisions in Dyads **749**
Hristina Dzhogleva, University of Pittsburgh, USA
Cait Poynor Lamberton, University of Pittsburgh, USA

How do Adolescents Define Consumer Vulnerability? Toward A Youth-Centric Approach **751**
Wided Batat, University of Lyon 2, France

Focusing Attention on the Hedonic Experience of Eating and the
Changing Course of Hunger and Pleasure **753**
Jordan LeBel, Concordia University, Canada
Ji Lu, Dalhousie University, Canada
Laurette Dubé, McGill University, Canada

The Distributed Spirit of Consumerism:
How Consumers Inform and Defend Themselves in a Fragmented World **755**
Dominique Roux, Université Paris-Sud, France
Corinne Chevalier, Université Paris-Sud, France
Lydiane Nabec, Université Paris-Sud, France

The Red Sneakers Effect: Inferring Status from Signals of Nonconformity **757**
Silvia Bellezza, Harvard Business School, USA
Francesca Gino, Harvard Business School, USA
Anat Keinan, Harvard Business School, USA

Growing with Love:
Priming Attachment Security Enhances Exploratory Consumer Behaviors **759**
Yuan-Yuan Li, KU Leuven, Belgium
Sabrina Bruyneel, KU Leuven, Belgium
Luk Warlop, KU Leuven, Belgium

Low Batteries Make You Greedy: The Effect of Product States on Human Behavior **761**
Zoey Chen, Georgia Institute of Technology, USA
Nicholas H. Lurie, University of Connecticut, USA

Measuring Arousal in Consumer Research: A New EDA Signal Processing Method **763**
Mathieu Lajante, University of Rennes 1, and Center for Research in Economics and Management, France
Olivier Droulers, University of Rennes 1, and Center for Research in Economics and Management

When Making it Easy Leads to Working Harder:
The Effects of Popularity Cues on Consumer Decision Making **765**
Erin Younhee Ha, University of Illinois at Urbana-Champaign, USA
Tiffany Barnett White, University of Illinois at Urbana–Champaign, USA
Robert S. Wyer, Chinese University of Hong Kong, Hong Kong

How does Power Affect the Evaluations of Luxury Brand Extensions?. **767**
Youngseon Kim, Central Connecticut State University, USA
Yinlong Zhang, University of Texas at San Antonio, USA

Modelling Everyday Consumer Behavior: The Case of Restricted Consumption **769**
Justine Rapp, University of San Diego, USA
Ronald Paul Hill, Villanova University, USA
Donald Lehmann, Columbia University, USA

Consuming the Dead: Symbolic Exchange in Thai 'Hungry Ghost' Festivals **771**
Rungpaka Amy Tiwsakul, Queen Mary, University of London, UK
Chris Hackley, Royal Holloway University of London, UK

The Crossmodal Effect of Attention on Preferences **773**
Hao Shen, Chinese University of Hong Kong, Hong Kong
Jaideep Sengupta, Hong Kong University of Science and Technology, Hong Kong

Insights into Decisions from Neuroscience and Choice Experiments:
The Effect of Eye Movements on Choice **774**
Barbara E. Kahn, University of Pennsylvania, USA
Jordan J. Louviere, University of Technology Sydney, Australia
Claudia Townsend, University of Miami, USA
Chelsea Wise, University of Technology Sydney, Australia

Uncertainty Increases People's Reliance on Their Feelings **776**
Ali Faraji-Rad, Columbia University, USA
Michel Tuan Pham, Columbia University, USA

"Seeing" the Consumer-Brand Relationship:
How Relative Physical Position Influences Relationship Perceptions **777**
Irene Xun Huang, The Chinese University of Hong Kong, Hong Kong
Xiuping Li, National University of Singapore, Singapore
Meng Zhang, The Chinese University of Hong Kong, Hong Kong

Mere-Alignability of Alphanumeric Brand Names:
How Exposure To Mercedes C350 Affects The Choice Between BMW 335I and BMW 330I **779**
Kunter Gunasti, University of Connecticut, USA
Berna Devezer, Michigan State University, USA

Two-sided Messages for Health Risk Prevention:
The Role of Argument Type, Refutation and Issue Ambivalence **782**
Erlinde Cornelis, Ghent University, Belgium
Veroline Cauberghe, Ghent University, Belgium
Patrick De Pelsmacker, University of Antwerp, Belgium

Decrease or Enhance?
Assessment of the Effect of Shanzhai on the Original Products **784**
Liangyan Wang, Shanghai Jiao Tong University, Shanghai
Cornelia Pechmann, University of California, USA
Yitong Wang, Tsinghua University, Beijing

Actors Conform, Observers Counteract:
The Effects of Interpersonal Synchrony on Conformity **786**
Xianchi Dai, The Chinese University of Hong Kong, Hong Kong
Ping Dong, University of Toronto, Canada
Robert S. Wyer Jr., The Chinese University of Hong Kong, Hong Kong

Intertwined Destinies: How Subsistence Entrepreneurs and
Consumers Harness Social Capital to Overcome Constraints and Uncertainties **788**
Srinivas Venugopal, University of Illinois at Urbana-Champaign, USA
Madhu Viswanathan, University of Illinois at Urbana-Champaign, USA
Raj Echambadi, University of Illinois at Urbana-Champaign, USA
Srinivas Sridharan, Monash University, Australia

The Product-agnosia Effect: How Increased Visual Scrutiny Reduces Distinctiveness **790**
Jayson Jia, Stanford University, USA
Sanjay Rao, Stanford University, USA
Baba Shiv, Stanford University, USA

Exploding Turkeys and Shattered Reporters:
Comparative Ads and Their Unintended Affective Consequences **791**
Ozge Yucel-Aybat, Pennsylvania State University at Harrisburg, USA
Thomas Kramer, University of South Carolina, USA

What Did You Do To My Brand?
Consumer Responses to Changes in Brands Towards Which They are Nostalgic **793**
Alison B. Shields, Kent State University, USA
Jennifer Wiggins Johnson, Kent State University, USA

The Mere Presence of Money Motivates Goal Achievement **795**
Gülen Sarial-Abi, Koç University, Turkey
Kathleen D. Vohs, University of Minnesota, USA

Power Distance Belief, Status, and Charity Giving **796**
DaHee Han, Indiana University, USA
Ashok K. Lalwani, Indiana University, USA
Adam Duhachek, Indiana University, USA

When Does Personalization Really Pay Off? **798**
Isabelle Kes, TU Braunschweig, Germany
David M. Woisetschläger, TU Braunschweig, Germany

Two Paths from Boredom to Consumption **800**
Soo Kim, Northwestern University, USA
C. Miguel Brendl, Northwestern University, USA

Consumers' Search Intentions in Response to Conditional Promotions. **802**
Atul Kulkarni, University of Missouri, USA
Hong Yuan, University of Illinois, USA

When White Obscures Evaluations: The Influence of Automatic Color Preferences on Product, Race and
Spokesperson Evaluations **804**
Ioannis Kareklas, Washington State University, USA
Frédéric F. Brunel, Boston University, USA
Robin A. Coulter, University of Connecticut, USA

Sticking to Plan: How Concrete Mindsets Increase Reliance on Mental Budget **807**
Sonja Prokopec, ESSEC Business School, France
Francine Espinoza, ESMT, Germany
Vanessa M. Patrick, University of Houston, USA

Center of Shelf Attention: Understanding the Role of Visual Attention on Product Choice. **809**
A. Selin Atalay, HEC Paris, France
H. Onur Bodur, Concordia University, Canada
Dina Rasolofoarison, Aston University, UK

Spatio-Temporal Dimensions in Consumer-Oriented Activism **811**
Andreas Chatzidakis, Royal Holloway, University of London, UK
Pauline Maclaran, Royal Holloway, University of London, UK
Alan Bradshaw, Royal Holloway University of London, UK

Navigating the Waters: Regulating versus Using Feelings Toward Risky Choices **813**
Eugene Chan, University of Toronto, Canada
Najam Saqib, Qatar University, Qatar

The Impact of Goal (Non)attainment on Behavior through Changes in Regulatory Focus. **815**
Danielle Mantovani, Federal University of Parana, Brazil
Paulo Prado, Federal University of Parana, Brazil
Eduardo B. Andrade, University of California Berkeley, USA

The Ghosts of Information Past and Future:
Effects of Memory and Motivation on Reference Price **817**
Jolie M. Martin, University of Minnesota, USA
Tomas Lejarraga, University of the Balearic Islands, Spain
Cleotilde Gonzalez, Carnegie Mellon University, USA

**Thank You for the Music! A Working Memory Examination of
the Effect of Musical Elements on Verbal Learning** 819
Esther Kang, State University of New York, USA
Arun Lakshmanan, State University of New York, USA

Culture, Relationship Norms, and Perceived Fairness of Asymmetric Pricing 821
Haipeng (Allan) Chen, Texas A&M University, USA
Lisa Bolton, Pennsylvania State University, USA
Sharon Ng, Nanyang Technological University, Singapore

**Effects of Timing of Purchase and Perceived Proximity of
Climate Change on Green Product Purchase** 823
Kiju Jung, University of Illinois at Urbana-Champaign, USA
Madhu Viswanathan, University of Illinois at Urbana-Champaign, USA
Robert S. Wyer, Jr., Chinese University of Hong Kong, Hong Kong
Dolores Albarracin, University of Pennsylvania, USA

**Looking For Answers in the Forest Rather than the Trees:
Causal Uncertainty Increases Attraction to Abstraction** 825
Jae-Eun Namkoong, University of Texas at Austin, USA
Marlone Henderson, University of Texas at Austin, USA

**Love it or Leave it?
Diverging from Others Depends on Attachment** 826
Yajin Wang, University of Minnesota
Deborah Roedder John, University of Minnesota

**When Do Consumers Forgive? A Causal Attribution Model of
Marketer Transgression and the Moderating Effects of Self-Construal** 827
Jayati Sinha, University of Arizona, USA
Fang-Chi Lu, University of Iowa, USA
Narayan Janakiraman, University of Arizona, USA

Talking About the Ad Vs. Talking About The Product: What Works And When. 829
Rashmi Adaval, Hong Kong University of Science and Technology, Hong Kong
Maria Galli, Hong Kong University of Science and Technology, Hong Kong
Robert S. Wyer Jr., Chinese University of Hong Kong, Hong Kong

Competing Consumers and the Valuation of Products 830
Gerald Häubl, University of Alberta, Canada
Christian Schmid, University of Alberta, Canada
Hua (Olivia) Lian, University of Alberta, Canada

Humorous Consumer Complaints 834
A. Peter McGraw, University of Colorado, USA
Christina Kan, University of Colorado, USA
Caleb Warren, Universita Commerciale Luigi Bocconi, Italy

Improving Associative and Item Memory for Brands Among Elderly Consumers. 836
Praggyan (Pam) Mohanty, Governors State University, USA
S. (Ratti) Ratneshwar, University of Missouri, USA
Moshe Naveh-Benjamin, University of Missouri, USA

To Think or Not to Think: The Pros and Cons of Thought Suppression 837
Natalina Zlatevska, Bond University, Australia
Elizabeth Cowley, University of Sydney, Australia

Self-Affirmation Can Backfire For Experts: The Case Of Product Warning Messages 839
Valeria Noguti, University of Technology Sydney, Australia

Transformational Solutions of Self through Companion Animals 841
Jill Mosteller, Portland State University, USA

Increasing Serving-Size Increases Amount Consumed: A Catch-22 843
Natalina Zlatevska, Bond University, Australia
Chris Dubelaar, Bond University, Australia
Stephen Holden, Bond University, Australia

**Exploring African-American Women's
Lived Experiences with Stigma, Identity, and Consumption.** 845
Elizabeth Crosby, University of Wisconsin La Crosse, USA

**Don't Put All Your Green Eggs in One Basket:
Examining Self-monitoring and Environmentally Friendly Sub-branding Strategy.** 847
Jayoung Koo, University of Minnesota, USA
Barbara Loken, University of Minnesota, USA

Food Customization: How Decision Frame Influences Choice. 849
Anish Nagpal, The University of Melbourne, Australia
Jing Lei, The University of Melbourne, Australia
Adwait Khare, The University of Texas Arlington, USA

Social Support Style and Risky Behaviors in Everyday Life. 851
Lili Wang, Zhejiang University, China
Tanya L. Chartrand, Duke University, USA
Linyun Yang, University of North Carolina, USA

**Is Consumer Culture Good for Women?
A Study of the Role of Consumer Culture in Disadvantaged Women's Gender Role Negotiation** 854
Zuzana Chytkova, University of Economics, Czech Republic
Dannie Kjeldgaard, University of Southern Denmark, Denmark

Brand Perception: Influence of Gender Cues on Dimensions of Warmth and Competence 856
Alexandra Hess, the University of Waikato, New Zealand
Valentyna Melnyk, the University of Waikato, New Zealand
Carolyn Costley, the University of Waikato, New Zealand

**Self-Control Spillover:
Impulse Inhibition Facilitates Simultaneous Self-Control in Unrelated Domains** 858
Mirjam A. Tuk, Imperial College Business School, UK, INSEAD, France
Kuangjie Zhang, INSEAD, France
Steven Sweldens, INSEAD, France

Exploration vs. Exploitation Mindsets in Consumer Search. 860
Valerie Trifts, Dalhousie University, Canada
Gerald Häubl, University of Alberta, Canada

For Fun or Profit: How Shopping Orientation Influences the Effectiveness of Monetary and Nonmonetary Promotions 862
Oliver B. Büttner, University of Vienna, Austria
Arnd Florack, University of Vienna, Austria
Anja S. Göritz, University of Freiburg, Germany

**This Number Just Feels Right:
The Impact of Roundness of Numbers on Reliance on Feelings versus Cognition** 864
Monica Wadhwa, INSEAD, France
Kuangjie Zhang, INSEAD, France

**Easy Like a Sunday Morning:
How The Fluency of Analogies Affects Innovation Liking** 866
Antonia Erz, Copenhagen Business School, Denmark
Bo T. Christensen, Copenhagen Business School, Denmark
Torsten Tomczak, University of St. Gallen, Switzerland

**The Impact of Flow on Memory and Attitudes For In-Game Brand Placements:
The Moderating Role of Brand Congruence and Placement Prominence** 868
Iris Vermeir, University College Ghent and Ghent University, Belgium
Snezhanka Kazakova, Ghent University, Belgium
Tina Tessitore, Ghent University, Belgium
Veroline Cauberghe, Ghent University, Belgium
Hendrik Slabbinck, Ghent University, Belgium

Segmenting Consumer Reactions to Social Network Advertising 870
Colin Campbell, Monash University, Australia
Carla Ferraro, Monash University, Australia
Sean Sands, Monash University, Australia

Producing & Consuming Public Space: A 'Rhythmanalysis' of the Urban Park **873**
Morven McEachern, Lancaster University, UK
Gary Warnaby, University of Liverpool, UK
Fiona Cheetham, University of Salford, UK

Trajectories of the Self: A Phenomenological Study of Women's
Changing Faces Reflected in Cosmetics Consumption **875**
Chihling Liu, University of Manchester, UK
Debbie Keeling, University of Manchester, UK
Margaret K. Hogg, Lancaster University, UK

The BOP Metanarrative: A Critical Exploration **877**
Suparna Chatterjee, Xavier University, USA

The Effect of Social Networking Orientation on Risk Preference:
The Risk-Taking Capacity Hypothesis. **879**
Hakkyun Kim, Concordia University, Canada
Kyoungmi Lee, Yonsei University, Korea
Kiwan Park, Seoul National University, Korea

Minority Matters:
The Influence of Minority And Majority Descriptive Norms on Product Choice **881**
Erica van Herpen, Wageningen University, The Netherlands
Hans C. M. van Trijp, Wageningen University, The Netherlands
Mariette van Amstel, Schuttelaar & Partners and Vrije Universiteit, The Netherlands

Fashion Sense:
Chinese Women's Response to Feminine Appeals in Transnational Advertising **883**
Jie Gao Fowler, Valdosta State University, USA
Aubrey R. Fowler III, Valdosta State University, USA

When and How Price-Dropping Serves as a Coping Mechanism for Price-Jolts **885**
Aaron M. Garvey, The Pennsylvania State University, USA
Simon J. Blanchard, Georgetown University, USA
Karen Page, The Pennsylvania State University, USA

You Might not Get what You Ask for:
Evidence for and Impact of Non-WTP Reporting in Willingness-to-Pay Surveys **887**
Reto Hofstetter, University of St. Gallen, Switzerland
David Blatter, University of Bern, Switzerland
Klaus M. Miller, University of Bern, Switzerland

When Good Things Come to an End: Mispredicting Motivation for Unavailable Goods **889**
Yang Yang, Carnegie Mellon University, USA
Carey Morewedge, Carnegie Mellon University, USA
Jeff Galak, Carnegie Mellon University, USA

Forced Transformations and Consumption Practices in Liquid Times **890**
Andres Barrios, Lancaster University, UK and Universidad de los Andes, Colombia
Maria Piacentini, Lancaster University, UK
Laura Salciuviene, Lancaster University, UK

Dispositional Greed: Scale Development and Validation. **892**
Goedele Krekels, Ghent University, Belgium
Mario Pandelaere, Ghent University, Belgium
Bert Weijters, Vlerick Leuven Gent Management School, Belgium

From Commitment to Detachment:
A Historical Analysis of Gift Advertisements by Department Stores in Japan, 1963-2008. . . . . **894**
Takeshi Matsui, Hitotsubashi University, Japan
Yuko Minowa, Long Island University, USA
Russell W. Belk, York University, Canada

When Hopes are Dashed: Sour Grapes or Searching for Greener Pastures? **896**
Aaron M. Garvey, Pennsylvania State University, USA
Margaret G. Meloy, Pennsylvania State University, USA
Baba Shiv, Stanford University, USA

Consumer-Created Advertising:
Does Awareness of Advertising Co-Creation Help or Hurt Persuasion? 898
Debora Thompson, Georgetown University, USA
Prashant Malaviya, Georgetown University, USA

Pictures Versus Words in Changing Implicit Attitudes in Ambush Marketing Disclosure:
The Role of Valence of Mental Images 899
Olivier Trendel, Grenoble Ecole de Management, France
Marc Mazodier, University of South Australia, Australia
Kathleen D. Vohs, University of Minnesota, USA

"I Would Want a Magic Gift":
Desire for Romantic Gift Giving and the Cultural Fantasies of Baby Boomers in Japan 901
Yuko Minowa, Long Island University, USA
Takeshi Matsui, Hitotsubashi University, Japan
Russell W. Belk, York University, Canada

My LV bag is a Counterfeit:
The Role of Regulatory Focus on Consumer Deceptive Behavior 903
So Hyun Bae, Nanyang Technological University, Singapore
Sharon Ng, Nanyang Technological University, Singapore

Implicit Measures of Motivation: Convergent, Discriminant and Predictive Validity 905
Alexandra Kraus, Aarhus University, Denmark
Joachim Scholderer, Aarhus University, Denmark

Exposure to Food Temptation Improves
Children's Resistance to Similar Food Temptations 907
Aiste Grubliauskiene, KU Leuven, Belgium
Siegfried Dewitte, KU Leuven, Belgium
Luk Warlop, KU Leuven, Belgium and BI Norwegian Business School, Norway

Negative Scope Sensitivity:
The Collapse of Feeling-Based Valuation for Multiple Desirable Objects 909
Kuangjie Zhang, INSEAD, Singapore
Steven Sweldens, INSEAD, France
Monica Wadhwa, INSEAD, Singapore

A Penny Saved is Another Penny Spurned
The Effect of Promotions on Consumer Impatience 911
Franklin Shaddy, Columbia University, USA
Leonard Lee, Columbia University, USA

The Role of Personal Relevance in the Effect of Ad Repetition on Attitudes and Choice 913
Ann Kronrod, MIT, USA
Joel Huber, Duke University, USA

Is Extremeness Aversion Driven by Loss Aversion?
Contrasting Reference-Point Models of Durable Product Choice 915
Nico Neumann, University of New South Wales, Australia
Ashish Sinha, University of New South Wales, Australia
Ulf Böckenholt, Northwestern University, USA

Effects of Set Size, Scarcity, Packaging, and Taste on the Marketing Placebo Effect 917
Scott Wright, Providence College, USA
José Mauro da Costa Hernandez, Centro Universitário da FEI, Brazil
Aparna Sundar, University of Cincinnati, USA
John Dinsmore, University of Cincinnati, USA
Frank Kardes, University of Cincinnati, USA

From the Hands to the Mind: Haptic Brand Signatures 920
Mathias Streicher, University of Innsbruck, Austria

Getting (Ex)cited: The Role of Herding in Driving Citations 922
Simon Quaschning, University College Ghent/Ghent University, Belgium
Mario Pandelaere, Ghent University, Belgium
Iris Vermeir, University College Ghent/Ghent University, Belgium

Unintended Effects of Implementation Intentions on Goal Pursuit Initiation vs. Persistence:
Substitution and Acceleration **924**
Jelena Spanjol, University of Illinois at Chicago, USA
Leona Tam, University of Wollongong, Australia
José Antonio Rosa, University of Wyoming, USA

Do Higher Stakes Lead to Better Choices? **926**
Traci Freling, University of Texas - Arlington, USA
Ritesh Saini, University of Texas - Arlington, USA
Zhiyong Yang, University of Texas - Arlington, USA

Remembering Better or Remembering Worse: Age Effects on False Memory **928**
Priyali Rajagopal, Southern Methodist University, USA
Nicole Votolato Montgomery, College of William & Mary, USA

Dynamic Patterns of Intra-Shopping Spending for
Budget and Non-Budget Shoppers **929**
Daniel Sheehan, Georgia Institute of Technology, USA
Koert van Ittersum, Georgia Institute of Technology, USA

Effective Substitution: The Drawback of High Similarity **931**
Zachary G. Arens, Jesse H. Jones Graduate School of Business, USA
Rebecca W. Hamilton, Robert H. Smith School of Business, USA

The Effect of Message Credibility, Need for Cognitive Closure, and
Information Sufficiency on Thought-Induced Attitude Change **933**
Bruce E. Pfeiffer, University of New Hampshire, USA
Hélène Deval, Dalhousie University, Canada
David H. Silvera, University of Texas at San Antonio, USA
Maria L. Cronley, Miami University, USA
Frank Kardes, University of Cincinnati, USA

Diversity Appreciated?
A Visual Longitudinal Analysis of Ukraine's Nation Branding Campaigns. **935**
Luca M. Visconti, , ESCP Europe, France
Mine Üçok Hughes, Woodbury University, USA
Ruben Bagramian, Woodbury University, USA

Should You or Could You? The Effect of Social Influence in Text Warnings Against Product Placement and the
Moderating Role of Self-Monitoring. **937**
Tina Tessitore, Ghent University, Belgium
Maggie Geuens, Ghent University, Belgium

"I Apologize. I Understand Your Concerns": When an Empathetic Apology Works **939**
Kyeong Sam Min, University of New Orleans, USA
Jae Min Jung, California State Polytechnic University at Pomona, USA
Kisang Ryu, Sejong University, Korea

Monetary Incentives and Pro-Social Behavior in Idea Co-creation **941**
Christoph Ihl, RWTH Aachen University, Germany
Alexander Vossen, RWTH Aachen University, Germany

Targeted Marketing and Customer Search **943**
Nathan Fong, Temple University, USA

The Traffic Light Colors Red and Green in the Context of Healthy Food Decision-Making **945**
Joerg Koenigstorfer, Pennsylvania State University, USA
Andrea Groeppel-Klein, Saarland University, Germany
Friederike Kamm, Saarland University, Germany
Michaela Rohr, Saarland University, Germany
Dirk Wentura, Saarland University, Germany

The Importance of Warmth and Competence in the
Acquisition and Retention of New Customers. **947**
Iana A. Castro, San Diego State University, USA
Scott Thompson, University of Georgia, USA
James Ward, Arizona State University, USA

Gift Cards and the Social Relationship **949**
Kunter Gunasti, University of Connecticut, USA
Michelle F. Weinberger, Northwestern University, USA

The Construction of Cosmetics-Consuming Women Through Generational Families in
Brazil's "New Middle Class" Context **950**
Roberta Dias-Campos, Federal University of Rio de Janeiro, Brazil
Leticia Moreira Casotti, Federal University of Rio de Janeiro, Brazil

Cruising the Unadulterated Terrain of Consumption:
Rural Snowmobilers' Interpellation through Collective Simplicity **952**
Soonkwan Hong, Michigan Technological University, USA

Eat to Be Fit or Fit to Eat?
Restrained Eaters' Food Consumption in Response to Fitness Cues **954**
Joerg Koenigstorfer, Pennsylvania State University, USA
Hans Baumgartner, Pennsylvania State University, USA

How Accidents Can Be Good For the Brand: The Role of Accident-Brand Stereotype Match and
Self-Brand Congruity in User Accidents. **956**
Tarje Gaustad, BI Norwegian Business School, Norway
Jakob Utgård, BI Norwegian Business School, Norway
Gavan J. Fitzsimons, Duke University, USA

Tell Me What to Do When I am in a Good Mood,
Show Me What to Do When I am in a Bad Mood:
Mood as a Moderator of Social Norm's Influence **958**
Vladimir Melnyk, Maastricht University, The Netherlands
Erica van Herpen, Wageningen University, The Netherlands
Arnout Fischer, Wageningen University, The Netherlands
Hans C. M. van Trijp, Wageningen University, The Netherlands

Consuming the Cyborg **960**
Arundhati Bhattacharyya, York University, Canada
Richard Kedzior, Bucknell University, USA

Infectious Counterfeiting:
Labeling Products as Fakes can Contaminate Perceived & Actual Efficacy **962**
Moty Amar, OAC, Israel
Ziv Carmon, INSEAD, Singapore
Dan Ariely, Duke University, USA

Recovering From Ethical Failures:
Role of External Attribution and Monetary Compensation **964**
Sekar Raju, Iowa State University, USA
Priyali Rajagopal, Southern Methodist University, USA

Cultural Effects on Perception and Cognition:
Integrating Recent Findings and Reviewing Implications for Consumer Research **966**
Minas N. Kastanakis, ESCP Europe, UK
Benjamin G.Voyer, ESCP Europe, UK

An Exclusionary or Integrative Approach to Goal Conflict:
The Moderating Role of Mindset Abstraction. **968**
Fang-Chi Lu, University of Iowa, USA
Jooyoung Park, University of Iowa, USA
Dhananjay Nayakankuppam, University of Iowa, USA

Compliments Made Me Bolder: The Role of Self Construal and Brand Status in Brand Attachment and
Product Evaluation **970**
Fang Wan, University of Manitoba, Canada
Letty Kwan, Nanyang Technological University, Singapore
Amitava Chattopadhyay, INSEAD, France
Hesham Fazel, University of Manitoba, Canada
CY Chiu, Nanyang Technological University, Singapore

Mythologized Glocalization of Popular Culture: A Postcolonial Perspective 972
Soonkwan Hong, Michigan Technological University, USA
Chang-Ho Kim, Nam-Seoul University, South Korea

Different Ways of Saying Goodbye:
Outlining Three Types of Abandonment of A Product Category 974
Maribel Suarez, Federal University of Rio de Janeiro / COPPEAD, Brazil
Marie Agnes Chauvel, Federal University of São João del Rei, Brazil

Marketplace Performances in Emerging Economies:
Eliciting the Asymmetric Interactions Between Service Providers and Western Tourists 976
Nacima Ourahmoune, Reims Management School, France

Uppers and Downers: Conveying Product Activity Level with Diagonals 980
Ann Schlosser, University of Washington, USA
Ruchi Rikhi, University of Washington, USA

Who Made This Thing? How Designer Identity and Brand Personality
Impact Consumers' Evaluations of New Product Offerings 982
Matt O'Hern, University of Oregon, USA
Lan Jiang, University of Oregon, USA

I Think I Can, I Think I Can: Brand Use, Self-Efficacy, and Performance 984
Ji Kyung Park, University of Delaware, USA
Deborah Roedder John, University of Minnesota, USA

Beyond Seeing McDonald's Fiesta Menu:
The Role of Accent in Brand Sincerity of Ethnic Products and Brands. 985
Marina Puzakova, Oregon State University, USA
Hyokjin Kwak, Drexel University, USA
Monique Bell, Drexel University, USA

For Love of Brand and Community: Why Self-Brand Connection Changes the Nature of Social Comparisons
Involving Prestige Brands. 987
Jill Sundie, University of Texas at San Antonio, USA
Daniel Beal, Rice University, USA
Andrew Perkins, University of Western Ontario, Canada
James Ward, Arizona State University, USA

Do You Believe in Love at First Sight? I Do: Implicit Self-Theories and Attitude Strength 989
JaeHwan Kwon, University of Iowa, USA
Dhananjay Nayakankuppam, University of Iowa, USA

Good or Bad, We Want It Now:
Resolution Theory Explains Magnitude Reversal in Intertemporal Choice 991
David Hardisty, Stanford University, USA
Kirstin Appelt, Columbia University, USA
Elke U. Weber, Columbia University, USA

Accentuate the Positive: How Identity Affects Customer Satisfaction 993
Tilottama G. Chowdhury, Quinnipiac University, USA
Kalpesh K. Desai, State University of New York, Binghamton, USA
Lisa Bolton, Penn State University, USA

Cultures of Caring Consumption: Social Support and the Self in the Myeloma Community 995
Susan Dunnett, University of Edinburgh Business School, UK
Paul Hewer, University of Strathclyde, UK
Douglas Brownlie, University of Stirling, UK

Everyday Objects of Desire:
Dimensions of Design Innovation and the Centrality of Product Aesthetics 997
Harold Cassab, University of Auckland, New Zealand
Claudiu Dimofte, San Diego State University, USA

Inter-Racial Couples, Household Decision-Making and
Contextual Influences on Consumer Acculturation. 999
Wakiuru Wamwara-Mbugua, Wright State University, USA

Something to Chew on:
Mastication based on Food Haptics and its Impact on Calorie Estimation 1001
Dipayan Biswas, University of South Florida, USA
Courtney Szocs, University of South Florida, USA
Aradhna Krishna, University of Michigan, USA
Donald Lehmann, Columbia University, USA

Lies, Damned Lies, and Statistics:
Risk Reduction Framing and the Power of Prominent Brands 1003
Robert Madrigal, University of Oregon, USA
Catherine Armstrong Soule, University of Oregon, USA
Leslie Koppenhafer, University of Oregon, USA

Will Power Lead to Variety Seeking in Sexually Related Consumer Choices? 1005
Duo Jiang, University of Illinois at Urbana-Champaign, USA
Sharon Shavitt, University of Illinois at Urbana-Champaign, USA

Influenced by the Context: The Role of Thinking Systems in the Use of Contextual Cues 1007
Ryan Rahinel, University of Minnesota, USA
Rohini Ahluwalia, University of Minnesota, USA

In The Mood for Special Experiences:
The Impact of Day-to-day Changes On Consumers 1009
Jiska Eelen, University of Amsterdam, The Netherlands
Kobe Millet, VU University Amsterdam, The Netherlands
Luk Warlop, KU Leuven, Belgium and Norwegian Business School (BI), Norway and BI Norwegian Business School, Norway

Self-Construal and the Identifiable Victim Effect 1011
Tatiana M. Fajardo, University of Miami, USA
Jiao Zhang, University of Miami, USA

When Empathic Managers Become Consumers: A Self-Referential Bias 1013
Johannes Hattula, University of St. Gallen, Switzerland
Walter Herzog, WHU – Otto Beisheim School of Management, Germany
Darren W. Dahl, University of British Columbia, Canada
Sven Reinecke, University of St. Gallen, Switzerland

How to Persuade 100,000 Friends? Understanding Blogs as One-to-One Mass Media 1015
Soyean (Julia) Kim, Boston University, USA
Seema Pai, Boston University, USA
Frédéric F. Brunel, Boston University, USA
Barbara A. Bickart, Boston University, USA

Street Credibility:
What is it? Who has it? Why is it so Appealing to Diverse Consumer Groups? 1017
Delancy Bennett, University of Massachusetts, USA
William Diamond, University of Massachusetts, USA

Taking the Complexity Out of Complex Product Customization Decisions. 1019
Christian Hildebrand, University of St. Gallen, Switzerland
Jan R. Landwehr, Goethe University Frankfurt, Germany
Andreas Herrmann, University of St. Gallen, Switzerland
Gerald Häubl, University of Alberta, Canada

Two wrongs CAN make a right:
The influence of salient self-attribution on self-image and subsequent goal pursuit 1021
Nina Gros, Maastricht University, The Netherlands
Kelly Geyskens, Maastricht University, The Netherlands
Caroline Goukens, Maastricht University, The Netherlands
Ko de Ruyter, Maastricht University, The Netherlands

The Sleeper Framing Effect: The Influence of Frame Valence on Immediate and Retrospective
Experiential Judgments. 1023
Mathew S. Isaac, Seattle University, USA
Morgan Poor, University of San Diego, USA

An Examination of the Effects of Market Returns and
Market Volatility on Investor Risk Tolerance and Investment Allocation Decisions 1025
Courtney M. Droms, Butler University, USA
Kurt Carlson, Georgetown University, USA
William G. Droms, Georgetown University, USA

Shifting Away From Discomfort:
Managing Decision Difficulty Through Emotion Regulation 1027
Stephanie M. Carpenter, University of Michigan, USA
J. Frank Yates, University of Michigan, USA
Stephanie D. Preston, University of Michigan, USA
Lydia Chen, University of Michigan, USA

"That Ad's Been Retouched? – That Can Be Me!":
The Persuasive Impact of Advertising Disclosure and Body-Image Idealization 1029
Rania W. Semaan, American University of Sharjah, UAE
Stephen J. Gould, Baruch College/CUNY, USA
Bruno Kocher, HEC Paris, France

On the Impact of Prior Ideas on Ideation Performance in Ideation Contests 1031
Suleiman Aryobsei, University of St.Gallen, Switzerland
Reto Hofstetter, University of St.Gallen, Switzerland
Andreas Herrmann, University of St.Gallen, Switzerland

When the Crowd is Divided: Perceptions of Dispersion in Word-of-Mouth 1033
Stephen He, Georgia Institute of Technology, USA
Samuel Bond, Georgia Institute of Technology, USA

Consuming 'Media Trash:' When "Bad" Becomes "Good" 1035
Björn Bohnenkamp, University of Muenster, Germany
Caroline Wiertz, City University London, UK
Thorsten Hennig-Thurau, University of Muenster, Germany

But How Did You Expect To Feel?: The Motivated Misremembering of Affective Forecasts 1037
Mathew S. Isaac, Seattle University, USA
Alexander Fedorikhin, Indiana University, USA
David Gal, Northwestern University, USA

You Can't Always Forget What You Want:
Social Identity and Memory for Identity-based Advertising 1038
Amy N. Dalton, Hong Kong University of Science and Technology, Hong Kong
Li Huang, City University of Hong Kong, Hong Kong.

The Individual Propensity to Take a Smell at Products 1039
Monika Koller, WU Vienna, Austria
Thomas Salzberger, WU Vienna, Austria
Alexander Zauner, WU Vienna, Austria
Arne Floh, University of Surrey, UK
Maria Sääksjärvi, Delft University of Technology, The Netherlands
Hendrik Schifferstein, Delft University of Technology, The Netherlands

When Status Pulls You One Way and Another: A Dilemma for Sustainable Investments 1041
Hannah Winkler von Mohrenfels, Frankfurt University, Germany
Corinne Faure, Grenoble Ecole de Management, France
Daniel Klapper, Humboldt University Berlin, Germany

When More Leads to Less: Greater Attentional Bias for Emotional Information is Negatively Associated
with Self-Reported Feelings 1043
Daniel Fernandes, Erasmus University Rotterdam, The Netherlands
Bart de Langhe, University of Colorado, USA
Stefano Puntoni, Erasmus University Rotterdam, The Netherlands

Emotional Marketing:
How Pride and Compassion Impact Preferences for Underdog and Top Dog Brands .1045
Mark Staton, Western Washington University, USA
Neeru Paharia, Georgetown University, USA
Christopher Oveis, University of California San Diego, USA

Ridiculing the Working Class and Reinforcing Class Boundaries:
The Chav Myth and Consumption in the Night Time Space. 1047
Hayley L. Cocker, Lancaster University, UK
Maria Piacentini, Lancaster University, UK
Emma N. Banister, University of Manchester, UK

When Soft Drink Taxes Don't Work: A Comparative Study. 1049
Andrew Hanks, Cornell University, USA
Brian Wansink, Cornell University, USA
David Just, Cornell University, USA

A Weight On Your Shoulders Makes You Pull Your Weight 1051
Minkyung Koo, University of Illinois at Urbana Champaign, USA
Mina Kwon, University of Illinois at Urbana Champaign, USA
Sharon Shavitt, University of Illinois at Urbana Champaign, USA

A Meta-Analytic and Psychometric Investigation of the
Effect of Financial Literacy on Downstream Financial Behaviors. 1052
Daniel Fernandes, Erasmus University Rotterdam, The Netherlands
John G. Lynch, Jr., University of Colorado, USA
Richard Netemeyer, University of Virginia, USA

Gleaning Signals from Soldout Products 1053
Xin Ge, University of Northern British Columbia, Canada
Paul R. Messinger, University of Alberta, Canada
Yuanfang Lin, University of Alberta, Canada

Taking Dogs to Tourism Activities:
Examining a Pet-Related Constraints Negotiation Model 1055
Annie Chen, University of Westminster, UK
Norman Peng, University of Westminster, UK

Consuming Branded Stories:
A Netnography of Fashion and Luxury Blog Consumption 1057
Gachoucha Kretz, ISC Paris School of Management, France

False but Persuasive Information: The Automatic Success of Infomercials 1059
Claudiu Dimofte, San Diego State University, USA
Richard Yalch, University of Washington, USA
Kyra Wiggin, University of Washington, USA

Social Power and Financial Risk Taking: The Role of Agency-Communion .1061
Didem Kurt, Boston University, USA

When Up Is Down: Natural Height Congruency in Product Evaluation 1063
Michael Giblin, University at Buffalo, USA
Aner Tal, Cornell University, USA
Brian Wansink, Cornell University, USA

Sadder, but Not Wiser: The Myopia of Misery 1065
Jennifer S. Lerner, Harvard University, USA
Ye Li, Harvard University, USA
Elke U. Weber, Columbia University, USA

Walk A Mile In *My* Shoes: Psychological Ownership And Psychological Distance. 1067
Bart Claus, Iéseg School of Management, France
Wouter Vanhouche, Lessius University College, Belgium
Siegfried Dewitte, KU Leuven, Belgium
Luk Warlop, KU leuven, Belgium/ Bi Oslo, Norway

Reducing Majority Customers' Prejudiced Behavior in
Inter-Ethnic Service Encounters - Applying a Stress and Coping Framework. 1069
Simon Brach, Friedrich-Schiller-University of Jena, Germany
Gianfranco Walsh, Friedrich-Schiller-University of Jena, Germany
Arne Albrecht, Friedrich-Schiller-University of Jena, Germany
Patrick Hille, Friedrich-Schiller-University of Jena, Germany
David Dose, Friedrich-Schiller-University of Jena, Germany
Mario Schaarschmidt, Friedrich-Schiller-University of Jena, Germany

Inter-Consumer Competition:
When Consumers Compete in the Marketplace for Products, Services, and Prizes 1070
Derick F. Davis, Virginia Tech, USA
Kimberlee Weaver, Virginia Tech, USA

The Category Size Bias and Consumers' Perceptions of Risk 1072
Mathew S. Isaac, Seattle University, USA
Aaron R. Brough, Pepperdine University, USA

Choosing an Experience Over a Product:
Uncertainty, Holistic Processing and Price Sensitivity 1073
Iñigo Gallo, University of California Los Angeles, USA
Sanjay Sood, University of California Los Angeles, USA

Order Effects of Sampling Sequential Products with
Similar Versus Dissimilar Sensory Cues 1075
Dipayan Biswas, University of South Florida, USA
Lauren I. Labrecque, Loyola University Chicago, USA
Donald Lehmann, Columbia University, USA
Ereni Markos, Quinnipiac University, USA

Carrying the Torch for the Brand: Inferring Brand Attachment From Logo Signals .1077
Ted Matherly, Oklahoma State University, USA
Amna Kirmani, University of Maryland, USA

Balancing the Basket:
The Role of Shopping Basket Composition in Embarrassment 1079
Sean Blair, Northwestern University, USA
Neal J. Roese, Northwestern University, USA

Reading Smiles to Read Minds: Impact of Positive Facial Affective Displays on Perceptions 1081
Ze Wang, University of Central Florida, USA
Fan Liu, University of Central Florida, USA
Huifang Mao, University of Central Florida, USA

Film Festival 2012

Same Same but Even Better! 1083
Marylouise Caldwell, University of Sydney
Paul Henry, University of Sydney

Perceptions of Music Authenticity 1083
Paul Barretta, University of Texas - Pan American, USA
Yi-Chia Wu, University of Texas - Pan American, USA

Aging and the Changing Meaning of Consumption Experiences 1083
Raquel Castano, Tecnológico de Monterrey, EGADE Business School, Mexico
Claudia Quintanilla, Tecnológico de Monterrey, EGADE Business School, Mexico
Maria Eugenia Perez, Tecnológico de Monterrey, EGADE Business School, Mexico

Co-Creation and Co-Production of Value: The Emergence of Competing Brand Subcultures 1083
Jacob Hiler, Louisiana State University, USA

Parklife. 1084
Morven McEachern, Lancaster University, UK

Differing Days - Planning and Emergence in Contemporary Mundane Routines 1084
Karolus Vittala, Aalto University, Finland
Joel Hietanen, Aalto University, Finland

The Père-Lachaise Cemetery: Between Touristic Experience and Heterotopic Consumption 1084
Alain Decrop, University of Namur, Belgium
Stéphanie Toussaint, Université Catholique de Louvain, Belgium

Living Abroad and Coming Back to Brazil: Analysis of the Acculturation and Re-adaptation Process of Brazilian Consumers 1084
Simone Vedana, UFRGS, Brazil
Teniza da Silveira, UFRGS, Brazil

Arab Hospitality 1084
Russell W. Belk, York University, Canada
Rana Sobh, University of Qatar, Qatar

Spaces and Temporarility 1084
Joel Hietanen, Aalto University, Finland
Elina Koivisto, Aalto University, Finland
Pekka Mattila, Aalto University, Finland
Anastasia Seregina, Aalto University, Finland

Labour of Love: Reforging Community Ownership and Identity 1084
Matthew Alexander, University of Strathclyde, UK
Kathy Hamilton, University of Strathclyde, UK

Fear and Flow: Climbing the Bugaboos, British Columbia 1085
Tommy Chandler, Backcountry.com, Utah, USA
Jeff Foreman, North Georgia College and State University, USA
Aditi Grover, Plymouth State University, USA
Karen Hood, University of Arkansas at Little Rock, USA

Roundtable Summaries

**Different Methodological Approaches to Studying Transformative Consumer Research:
What Can We Learn from Each Other?Participants:** 1087
Julie L. Ozanne, Virginia Tech, USA
Ekant Veer, University of Canterbury, New Zealand
Paul M. Connell, City University London, UK
Michal Ann Strahilevitz, Golden Gate University, USA
Ekant Veer, University of Canterbury, New Zealand
Paul M. Connell, City University London, UK
Michal Ann Strahilevitz, Golden Gate University, USA
Cornelia Pechmann, University of California Irvine, USA
Stacey Mezel Baker, University of Wyoming, USA
Punam Anand Keller, Dartmouth University, USA
Linda Price, University of Arizona, USA
Alan Andreasen, Georgetown University, USA
Laura Peracchio, University of Wisconsin-Milwaukee
Rebecca Ratner, University of Maryland
Carlos J. Torelli, University of Minnesota, USA

**Consumption Addiction: Developing a Research Agenda to Understanding How Consumers Progress from
Normal to Maladaptive Consumption and Addiction** 1089
Dante M. Pirouz, Western University, Canada
Hieu Nguyen, California State University Long Beach, USA
Ingrid M. Martin, California State University Long Beach, USA
Merrie Brucks, University of Arizona, USA
Paul M. Connell, City University London, UK
June Cotte, Western University, Canada
Scott Davis, Texas A&M University, USA
Kelly L. Haws, Texas A&M University, USA
Michael Kamins, Stonybrook, USA
Ingrid M. Martin, California State University Long Beach, USA
Ann Mirabito, Baylor, USA
Hieu Nguyen, California State University Long Beach, USA
Dante M. Pirouz, Western University, Canada
Justine Rapp, University of San Diego, USA
Maura Scott, University of Kentucky, USA
Allison Johnson, Western University, Canada

Evolutionary Consumption:
Methodological Pluralism, Interdisciplinarity, and Consilience (Unified Knowledge) 1091
Gad Saad, Concordia University, Canada
Joshua Ackerman, MIT, USA
Sarah E. Hill, Texas Christian University, USA
Kristina Durante, University of Texas at San Antonio, USA
Jill Sundie, University of Texas at San Antonio, USA
Eric Stenstrom, Concordia University, Canada
Tripat Gill, Wilfred Laurier University, Canada
Bram Van den Bergh, Erasmus University Rotterdam, The Netherlands
Gad Saad, Concordia University, Canada

Journal of Consumer Research (JCR) Reviewer Workshop 1093
Darren W. Dahl, University of British Columbia, Canada
Eileen Fischer, York University, Canada
Rashmi Adaval, Hong Kong University of Science and Technology, China
Søren Askegaard, University of Southern Denmark, Denmark
Hans Baumgartner, Pennsylvania State University, USA
Lauren G. Block, Baruch College/CUNY, USA
James Burroughs, University of Virginia, USA
Margaret C. Campbell, University of Colorado, USA
Darren W. Dahl, University of British Columbia, Canada
Aimee Drolet, University of California, Los Angeles, USA
Jennifer Edson Escalas, Vanderbilt University, USA
Eileen Fischer, York University, Canada
Gavan J. Fitzsimons, Duke University, USA
Kent Grayson, Northwestern University, USA
Rebecca W. Hamilton, University of Maryland, USA
Joel Huber, Duke University, USA
Gita Johar, Columbia University, USA
C. Page Moreau, University of Colorado, USA
Brian Ratchford, University of Texas at Dallas, USA
Rebecca Ratner, University of Maryland, USA
Jaideep Sengupta, Hong Kong University of Science and Technology, China
Baba Shiv, Stanford University, USA
Craig Thompson, University of Wisconsin, USA

Conversations on the Sacred and Spirituality in Consumer Behavior 1094
Diego Rinallo, Bocconi University, Italy
Pauline Maclaran, Royal Holloway, University of London, UK
Pauline Maclaran, Royal Holloway, University of London, UK
Russell W. Belk, York University, Canada
Stephen J. Gould, Baruch College, USA
Elif Izberk-Bilgin, University of Michigan, USA
Richard Kedzior, Hanken School of Economics, Finland
Robert Kozinets, York University, Canada
Hope Jensen Schau, University of Arizona, USA
Linda Scott, University of Oxford, UK
John F. Sherry, University of Notre Dame, USA
Eric J. Arnould, University of Bath, UK

Market System Dynamics: The Value of and the Open Questions Associated with
Studying Markets in Consumer Culture Theory 1096
Anton Siebert, Witten/Herdecke University, Germany
Anastasia Thyroff, University of Arkansas, USA
Ashlee Humphreys, Northwestern University, USA
Eminegul Karababa, Middle East Technical University, Turkey
Gokcen Coskuner-Balli, Chapman University, USA
Ela Veresiu, Witten/Herdecke University, Germany
Dannie Kjeldgaard, University of Southern Denmark, Denmark
Melea Press, University of Bath, UK
Eric J. Arnould, University of Bath, UK
John W. Schouten, Aalto University, Finland
Jeff B. Murray, University of Arkansas, USA
Anastasia Thyroff, University of Arkansas, USA

"Death and All His Friends":
The Role of Identity, Ritual, and Disposition in the Consumption of Death 1098
Susan Dobscha, Bentley University, USA
Jenna Drenten, John Carroll University, USA
Kent Drummond, University of Wyoming, USA
Terrance Gabel, University of Arkansas, Fort Smith, USA
Chris Hackley, Royal Holloway, University of London, UK
Sidney J. Levy, University of Arizona, USA
Jeffrey Podoshen, Franklin and Marshall College, USA
Dennis Rook, University of Southern California, USA
Katherine Sredl, University of Notre Dame, USA
Rungpaka Amy Tiwsakul, Durham University, UK
Ekant Veer, University of Canterbury, NZ

Think Outside the Lab: Using Field Data in Behavioral Research 1100
Jonah Berger, University of Pennsylvania, USA
J. Jeffrey Inman, University of Pittsburgh, USA
Darren W. Dahl, University of British Columbia, Canada
Leslie John, Harvard University, USA
Ayelet Gneezy, University of California San Diego, USA
Uri Simonsohn, University of Pennsylvania, USA
Leif D. Nelson, University of California Berkeley, USA
Joe Simmons, University of Pennsylvania, USA
Sarah Moore, University of Alberta, Canada
Michael I. Norton, Harvard University, USA

Reading the Mind of the Consumer:
Promises and Challenges of Predictive Methods in Consumer Neuroscience 1102
Ming Hsu, University of California, Berkeley
Ming Hsu, University of California Berkeley, USA
Uma Karmarkar, Harvard Business School, USA
Karim Kassam, Carnegie Mellon, USA
Tom Meyvis, New York University, USA
Hilke Plassmann, INSEAD, France
Akshay Rao, University of Minnesota, USA
Baba Shiv, Stanford University, USA
Monica Wadhwa, INSEAD, France
Carolyn Yoon, University of Michigan, USA
Drazen Prelec, Massachusetts Institute of Technology, USA
William Hedgcock, University of Iowa, USA
Adam Craig, University of South Florida, USA
Mili Milosavljevic, Stanford University, USA
Angelika Dimoka, Temple University, USA
Nina Mazar, University of Toronto, Canada

Working Papers

1. Better Together or Alone? Joint vs. Individual Goal Pursuit 1105
Lauren Trabold, Baruch College/CUNY, USA
Stephen J. Gould, Baruch College/CUNY, USA

2. Planning to Fail? The Role of Implementation Intentions in Emotional Responses to Goal Failures 1105
Jason Stornelli, University of Michigan, USA
J. Frank Yates, University of Michigan, USA

3. Knowing What I Want: Alignability, Attentional Focus, and the Identification of Consumption Goals 1105
Michael Hair, Georgia Institute of Technology, USA
Samuel Bond, Georgia Institute of Technology, USA

4. Lay Theories in Consumer Goal Setting and Striving: The Case of Weight Loss 1105
Mariam Beruchashvili, California State University, Northridge, USA
Risto Moisio, California State University. Long Beach, USA
James Gentry, University of Nebraska-Lincoln, USA

5. **From Apples to Alcopops: The Forbidden Fruit Effect on Supersized Alcoholic Beverages** .1105
Cassandra Davis, University of Arkansas, USA
Elizabeth Howlett, University of Arkansas, USA

6. **Knowing When to Assimilate and When to Contrast: Self-Control and the Influence of Contextual Order** 1106
Kelly L. Haws, Texas A&M University, USA
Joseph P. Redden, University of Minnesota, USA
Scott Davis, Texas A&M University, USA

7. **All Things Considered: When the Budgeting Process Promotes Consumers' Savings** 1106
Min Jung Kim, Texas A&M University, USA
Haipeng (Allan) Chen, Texas A&M University, USA

8. **Implementation Intentions as Self-Regulation Tool for Low- and High-Level Impulsive Buyers:**
A Behavioral and Neurophysiological Investigation 1106
Isabella Kopton, Zeppelin University, Germany
Bruno Preilowski, Zeppelin University, Germany
Peter Kenning, Zeppelin University, Germany

9. **Joe vs. joe: Turning to One's Partner vs. Favorite Product in Emotion Regulation** .1106
Danielle J. Brick, Duke University, USA
Hannah Honey, Duke University, USA
Gráinne M. Fitzsimons, Duke University, USA
Gavan J. Fitzsimons, Duke University, USA

10. **The Influence of Social Relationships on Self-regulatory Focus in Buying for Others** 1106
Huimin Xu, The Sage Colleges, USA
Paul M. Connell, City University London, UK
Ada Leung, Pennsylvania State University Berks, USA
Cuiping Chen, University of Ontario Institute of Technology, Canada

11. **When Self-Serving Does Not Serve the Self: The Role of Serving-Style in Food Consumption** 1107
Anna Linda Hagen, University of Michigan, USA
Brent McFerran, University of Michigan, USA
Aradhna Krishna, University of Michigan, USA

12. **When Do Consumers Compromise on Calories? Exploring the Attraction and Compromise Effects**
in Food Choice. 1107
Ryall Carroll, St. John's University, USA
Beth Valen, Fordham University, USA

13. **Changing Implicit Beliefs through Advertising: Exploring One of the Origins of the**
"Unhealthy=Tasty" Intuition 1107
Carolina Werle, Grenoble École de Management, France
Olivier Trendel, Grenoble École de Management, France

14. **Toward a Gender-Specific Emotional Eating Model: The Role of Self-Esteem and Emotional Intelligence** 1107
Paula C. Peter, San Diego State University, USA
Sukumarakurup Krishnakumar, North Dakota State University, USA

15. **The Effect of Pictorial Cues of Food on Restrained vs. Unrestrained Eaters** 1107
Nguyen Pham, Arizona State University, USA
Maureen (Mimi) Morrin, Rutgers University, USA
May Lwin, Nanyang Technological University, Singapore
Melissa G. Bublitz, University of Wisconsin Oshkosh, USA

16. **Ironic Effects of Food Commercials: When More Food-Related Mental Images Make You Eat Less** 1108
Carolina Werle, Grenoble École de Management, France
Mia Birau, Grenoble École de Management, France

17. **Consumers' Alternative Dietary Lifestyles – A Narrative Approach** 1108
Anniina Luukkonen, Aalto University, Finland
Ilona Mikkonen, Aalto University, Finland
Elina Koivisto, Aalto University, Finland

18. Happy Fat or Staying Thin? Evolutionary Motives Underlying Consumer Food Choice. 1108
Rob Richerson, University of Kentucky, USA
Blair Kidwell, Ohio State University, USA
Virginie Lopez-Kidwell, University of Kentucky, USA

19. Food in Motion 1108
Michael Giblin, University at Buffalo, USA
Aner Tal, Cornell University, USA
Brian Wansink, Cornell University, USA

**20. Oh Dear, I'm So Confused: Cognitive and Affective Coping Strategies to Deal with Consumer Confusion
in the Food Market** 1108
Inga Wobker, Zeppelin University, Germany
Peter Kenning, Zeppelin University, Germany

**21. It's Not Just Numbers: Nutrition Information Disclosure is Perceived as a Social Identity Threat by
French Consumers** 1108
Pierrick Gomez, Reims Management School and Université Paris Dauphine, France

22. When Dieting in Your Mind Brings Cake in Your Mouth 1109
Jiah Yoo, Yonsei University, South Korea
Youngwoo Sohn, Yonsei University, South Korea

23. Self-Construal and Self-Affirmation Effects in Effortful Customer Experiences 1109
Prakash Das, University of Calgary, Canada
James Agarwal, University of Calgary, Canada

24. The Persuasiveness of Abstract vs. Concrete Language in Commercial and Non-Commercial Settings. 1109
Peeter Verlegh, University of Amsterdam, The Netherlands

25. Better in the (Near) Future: Biased Temporal Conceptions of Team Identification 1109
Jesse S. King, Oregon State University, Cascades, USA
Colleen C. Bee, Oregon State University, Cascades, USA

26. The Moderating Role of Construal Level on Effectiveness of Purchase-Contingent Donations 1109
Nara Youn, Hongik University, South Korea
Yun Lee, Virginia State University, USA

27. Activating Multiple Facets of the Self: Identity-Signaling and Brand Personality 1109
Marilyn Giroux, Concordia University, Canada
Bianca Grohmann, Concordia University, Canada
Frank Pons, Université Laval, Canada

**28. Impression Management Practices of Stigma-Conscious Communities: The Case of an Online
Pro-Smoking Forum** 1110
Navin Bahl, University of Hawaii, USA
Namita Bhatnagar, University of Manitoba, Canada
Rajesh V. Manchanda, University of Manitoba, Canada
Anne Lavack, Kwantlen Polytechnic University, Canada

29. Putting Myself in your Shoes: The Role of Identification in Persuasion 1110
Anne Hamby, Virginia Tech, USA
Meghan Pierce, Pontificia Universidad Católica de Chile, Chile
Kim Daniloski, University of Scranton, USA

30. Self-Construal as a Cultural Mindset and its Relevance for Automatic Social Behavior 1110
Geetanjali Saluja, HKUST, Hong Kong
Rashmi Adaval, HKUST, Hong Kong

31. Self-Construal Moderates the Effect of Fear of Failure on Donation Likelihood 1110
Lale Okyay-Ata, Koç University, Turkey
Baler Bilgin, Koç University, Turkey
Zeynep Gürhan-Canli, Koç University, Turkey

32. **Dynamic Co-Creation: Moving Beyond Foucault to Understand the Ideological Field of Parenting** 1110
Alexander S. Rose, University of Arkansas, USA
Robin L. Soster, University of Arkansas, USA
Kelly Tian, University of Wyoming, USA
Randall L. Rose, University of South Carolina, USA

33. **Children's Preferences of Package Design** 1111
Dan Zhang, City University of New York, USA
James Hunt, Temple University, USA
C. Anthony Di Benedetto, Temple University, USA
Richard Lancioni, Temple University, USA

34. **Innovation for Your Parents? The Impact of Lay Theories of Innovativeness on Upward Intergenerational
Gift Giving** 1111
Jianping Liang, Sun Yat-sen University, China
Hongyan Jiang, China University of Mining & Technology, China

35. **Who Spends More on Children's Education: "I" or "We"?** 1111
Lingjiang Tu, University of Texas at San Antonio, USA
Yinlong Zhang, University of Texas at San Antonio, USA

36. **Ethno-Culturally Diverse Social Ecosystems** 1111
Esi Abbam Elliot, University of Illinois at Chicago, USA
Joseph Cherian, George Washington University, USA

37. **Cultural Identity and Brand Relationships: Negotiating Brand Meanings in a New Cultural Context** 1111
Anna Jansson Vredeveld, University of Connecticut, USA
Robin A. Coulter, University of Connecticut, USA

38. **Style Reimagined: Exploring Fashion and Identity among South African Smarteez** 1112
Kevin Thomas, University of Texas at Austin, USA
Guillaume Johnson, University of the Witwatersrand, South Africa
Marike Venter, University of the Witwatersrand, South Africa
Kristin Stewart, University of Texas at Austin, USA

39. **A Cross-Cultural Comparison of the Impact of Consumers' Conspicuous Consumption Orientations on
Brand Attitude and Purchase Intention** 1112
Xia (Linda) Liu, Louisiana State University, USA
Alvin C. Burns, Louisiana State University, USA
HongYan Yu, Sun Yat-Sen University, China

40. **Does Accent Matter? The Impact of Ethnic Similarity and Product Congruence on Spokesperson Credibility
and Purchase Intention** 1112
Aarti S. Ivanic, University of San Diego, USA
Kenneth Bates, University of San Diego, USA
T. Somasundaram, University of San Diego, USA

41. **Acculturation, Brand Personality and Brand Preferences.** 1112
Umut Kubat, University of Pittsburgh, USA
Vanitha Swaminathan, University of Pittsburgh, USA

42. **Decoding BE-Commerce: The Invisible Hand of National Culture.** 1112
Lei Song, Drexel University, USA
Srinivasan Swaminathan, Drexel University, USA
Rolph E. Anderson, Drexel University, USA

43. **Disentangling Two Types of Country of Origin: The Interactive Effects of Brand Origin and Product Origin
on Persuasion** 1113
Sangwon Lee, Ball State University, USA
Xin He, University of Central Florida, USA

44. **Exposure to Chicken-Abuse Images Has More Impact than that of Cows on Targeted Meat Consumption
among a Sample of Japanese Consumers** 1113
Douglas Trelfa, Tamagawa University, Japan
Carolina Werle, Grenoble École de Management, France

45. Gender Identity Politics and Consumption: Mobilizing Scottish Masculinities through Relational
Consumption Practices 1113
Wendy Hein, University of London, UK

46. Constructing Ethnic Identity through Mealtime Rituals and Practices 1113
Amandeep Takhar, University of Bedfordshire, UK
Pepukayi Chitakunye, University of KwaZulu-Natal, South Africa

47. Hey Y'all: Exporting Southern Food Culture, Implications for Brand Meaning and Local Consumer Identity 1113
Catherine Coleman, Texas Christian University, USA

48. The Making of an Everyday Concubine: Accounting for Simultaneous Love of Modernity and the Recently
(Re-)Discovered Ottoman Heritage 1113
Cagri Yalkin, Kadir Has University, Turkey

49. Power over When: If Time is Human, Humans Act When They Want 1114
Frank May, University of South Carolina, USA
Ashwani Monga, University of South Carolina, USA

50. Gifting Lightly When Feeling Powerful: Self-Construal, Power, and Gifting Anxiety 1114
Fang Wan, University of Manitoba, Canada
Mehdi Akghari, University of Manitoba, Canada
Annika Sun, University of Manitoba, Canada
Yuwei Jiang, Hong Kong Polytechnic University, Hong Kong

51. Will Purchasing from Groupon Make A Lonely Consumer Feel Empowered? Loneliness and Preference for
Group-Buying Purchase Experiences 1114
Hangeun Lee, Yonsei University, South Korea
Junyoung Lee, Yonsei University, South Korea
Kyoungmi Lee, Yonsei University, South Korea
Hakkyun Kim, Concordia University, Canada

52. The Identifiable In-Group: Group Status Moderates the Identifiable Victim Effect 1114
Alixandra Barasch, University of Pennsylvania, USA
Rod Duclos, HKUST, Hong Kong
Emma Edelman, University of Pennsylvania, USA

53. The Effect of Significant Others' Perceived States on the Evaluation of Relevant Products 1114
Kiwan Park, Seoul National University, South Korea
Jiyoung Lee, Seoul National University, South Korea
Jerry Jisang Han, University of Texas-Austin, USA

54. Mark of Popularity or Distrust? The Role of "Peer Purchase Number" as a Cue Affecting Consumer Attitudes
in the Web-Based Retail Context. 1115
Eun-Jung Lee, Kent State University, USA
Robert D. Jewell, Kent State University, USA

55. Network Coproduction: The Role of Self-Presentational Persona in Electronic Word-Of-Mouth 1115
Shuling Liao, Yuan Ze University, Taiwan
Crystal Tzuying Lee, National Cheng-Chi University, Taiwan
Tzu Han Lin, Yuan Ze University, Taiwan

56. Examining Consumer Response to Preferential Treatment Practices 1115
Lan Xia, Bentley University, USA
Monika Kukar-Kinney, University of Richmond, USA

57. Burger or Yogurt? The Effect of Private vs. Public Consumption Contexts on Indulgent Behavior 1115
Shih-Chieh Chuang, National Chung Cheng University, Taiwan
Yin-Hui Cheng, National Taichung University of Education, Taiwan
Chien-Jung Huang, National Chung Cheng University, Taiwan
Yun Ken, National Yunlin University of Science and Technology, Taiwan

58. Marketplace Metacognition in Consumer-to-Consumer Inferences: I Buy for Quality, You Buy for Status 1115
Meghan Pierce, Pontificia Universidad Catolica de Chile, Chile
Kimberlee Weaver, VirginiaTech, USA
Kim Daniloski, University of Scranton, USA
Norbert Schwarz, University of Michigan, USA

59. **Dressed to Impress: When Images of Financial Success in Advertising Have an Inspirational vs. Detrimental Effect on Men** 1116
Abigail Schneider, University of Colorado, USA
Ethan Pew, Purdue University, USA
Susan Jung Grant, University of Colorado, USA

60. **Who Cares If It Is Deceptive, I Like It: The Effect of Social Exclusion on Advertising Deception** 1116
Hamed Aghakhani, University of Manitoba, Canada
Kelley J. Main, University of Manitoba, Canada

61. **Speed and Social Connection** 1116
Melanie Thomas, University of Pennsylvania, USA
Cassie Mogilner, University of Pennsylvania, USA

62. **Opening the Black Box: An Exploration of Consumer Production Influence on Marketplace Dynamics** 1116
Henri Weijo, Aalto University, Finland
Daiane Scaraboto, Pontificia Universidad Católica de Chile, Chile
Saara Könkkölä, Aalto University, Finland

63. **True Comeliness or Fake Beauty: Cosmetic Surgery as Mating Strategy** 1116
Sunyee Yoon, University of Wisconsin-Madison, USA
Nancy Wong, University of Wisconsin-Madison, USA

64. **Classification of the Factors Influencing Ethical Consumer Choice: The Framework** .1117
Natalia Maehle, Institute for Research in Economics and Business Administration, Norway
Nina Iversen, Institute for Research in Economics and Business Administration, Norway
Leif Hem, Norwegian School of Economics, Norway

65. **Whom to Trust? The Impact of Peer vs. Expert Opinions on Consumption Experiences** 1117
Travis Hancock, Brigham Young University, USA
Ryan Elder, Brigham Young University, USA

66. **The effect of Vertical Individualism on Status Consumption and Advertising Response** 1117
Michelle Nelson, University of Illinois at Urbana-Champaign, USA
Jing Zhang, San Jose State University, USA

67. **Emotional Intelligence, Giving, and Life Satisfaction: Some New Data and Conclusions** 1117
Rajani Ganesh Pillai, North Dakota State University, USA
Doug Rymph, North Dakota State University, USA
Sukumarakurup Krishnakumar, North Dakota State University, USA

68. **It's All About Me: Effects on Product Samples for Self vs. Other** 1117
Chelsea Johnson, University of Illinois at Urbana-Champaign, USA
Brittany Duff, University of Illinois at Urbana-Champaign, USA

69. **The Effect of Face Pressure on Chinese Consumer Decision-Making** 1117
Karthik Easwar, Ohio State University, USA
Robert Burnkrant, Ohio State University, USA

70. **Sense and Cents: Collective Consumer Sensemaking in an Online Investment Community** 1118
Andrew N. Smith, York University, Canada

71. **Consumer Creativity in Co-Creation: The Interaction between Default Product and Design Goal** 1118
Bo Chen, ESSEC Business School, France
Niek Althuizen, ESSEC Business School, France

72. **Bidirectional Consumer Friends' Knowledge Calibration —Overestimated or Underestimated? A Two-Stage Model** 1118
Joicey Jie Wei, National University of Singapore, Singapore
Iris Hung, National University of Singapore, Singapore
Gita Johar, Columbia University, USA

73. **What Drives Individual Purchase Decisions in a Network? A Consumer-Motivation Approach** 1118
Dongwoo Ko, University of Iowa, USA
Sanguk Jung, University of Auckland, New Zealand

74. Assimilation and Contrast in Web Product Reviews: Devaluing the Recommendation of a Proficient but Dissimilar Reviewer 1118
Michael Dorn, University of Bern, Switzerland
Claude Messner, University of Bern, Switzerland

75. A Typology of Crowdsourcing Participation Styles 1118
Eric Martineau, Concordia University, Canada
Zeynep Arsel, Concordia University, Canada

76. Exploring Consumer Attitudes toward Social-Network Advertising 1119
Cuauhtemoc Luna-Nevarez, New Mexico State University, USA
Jennifer Zarzosa, New Mexico State University, USA

77. It's Not All About Coffee: A Netnography of the Starbucks Brand Page on Facebook 1119
Heejin Lim, University of Tennessee, USA
Jewon Lyu, University of Tennessee, USA

78. Changing Consumption Habits: Does Personalization Really Work? 1119
Kirsikka Kaipainen, VTT Technical Research Centre, Finland
Brian Wansink, Cornell University, USA

79. Getting Lucky: When Loyalty Status Makes You Feel Lucky. 1119
Rebecca Walker Naylor, Ohio State University, USA
Kelly L. Haws, Texas A&M University, USA
Christopher Summers, Ohio State University, USA

80. Feeling Lucky while Feeling Good: The Relative Impacts of Superstitious Beliefs and Affect on Consumer Judgment and Choice. 1119
Thomas Kramer, University of South Carolina, USA
Meredith David, University of South Carolina, USA

81. Shame on You! Motivating Consumer Behavior with Shame Appeals 1119
Jennifer Jeffrey, University of Western Ontario, Canada
Juan Wang, University of Western Ontario, Canada
Dante M. Pirouz, University of Western Ontario, Canada
Matthew Thomson, University of Western Ontario, Canada

82. Corporate Communications in Uncertain Times: Messages of Hope or Pride? 1120
Anne Roggeveen, Babson College, USA
Anirban Mukhopadhyay, HKUST, Hong Kong
Dhruv Grewal, Babson College, USA

83. Affect and Consumer Behavior: A Meta-Analytic Review. 1120
Nancy M. Puccinelli, Oxford University, UK
Dhruv Grewal, Babson College, USA
Scott Motyka, Brandeis University, USA
Susan A. Andrzejewski, Franklin and Marshall College, USA

84. Hoarding and Consumer Anxiety: Understanding When Consumption Becomes Dysfunctional 1120
Gail Leizerovici, University of Western Ontario, Canada
Dante M. Pirouz, University of Western Ontario, Canada
Samantha Cross, Iowa State University, USA

85. All Kidding Aside: Humors Lowers Propensity to Remedy a Problem. 1120
A. Peter McGraw, University of Colorado, USA
Philip Fernbach, University of Colorado, USA
Julie Schiro, University of Colorado, USA

86. Asymmetries in the Impact of Action and Inaction Regret: When and Why Do They Occur?. 1120
Atul Kulkarni, University of Missouri-Kansas City, USA
Rashmi Adaval, HKUST, Hong Kong

87. The Effect of Aging on Consumer Regret. 1120
Li Jiang, University of California Los Angeles, USA

88. **Not Immediately Stupid: The Moderating Effects of Purchase Immediacy and the Mediating Effects of Regret on Self-Perceptions of Consumer Incompetence** 1121
Matthew Philp, Queen's University, Canada
Laurence Ashworth, Queen's University, Canada

89. **Assessment of Heterogeneity of Compulsive Buyers Based on Affective States Preceding Buying Lapses.** 1121
Sunghwan Yi, University of Guelph, Canada
Joowon Jung, Dongguk University, South Korea

90. **Do Hedonic Benefits Always Create "Hedonic" Feeling? The Impact of Two Factors on Consumer's Response to Hedonic Rewards Design of Loyalty Program** 1121
Sidney Su Han, University of Guelph, Canada
Lefa Teng, University of Guelph, Canada
Yiqiu Wang, Northeastern University, China

91. **Compulsive Buyers Show an Attentional Bias in Shopping Situations** 1121
Oliver B. Büttner, University of Vienna, Austria
Matthew Paul, University of Vienna, Austria
Arnd Florack, University of Vienna, Austria
Helmut Leder, University of Vienna, Austria
Anna Maria Schulz, University of Vienna, Austria

92. **Physical Temperature Effects on Consumer Decision Making** 1121
Tingting Wang, HKUST, Hong Kong
Rongrong Zhou, HKUST, Hong Kong

93. **"It's Cold in Here. I Need a Bowl of Soup to Warm Me Up!" The Effects of Incidental Sensory Frames on Conflicting Sensory Inputs** 1122
Sydney Chinchanachokchai, University of Illinois at Urbana-Champaign, USA
Rashmi Adaval, HKUST, Hong Kong

94. **"Size Matters!" The Effect of Floor Tile Size on Consumer Behavior in a Retail Environment** 1122
Nico Heuvinck, Ghent University and University College Ghent, Belgium
Iris Vermeir, Ghent University and University College Ghent, Belgium
Simon Quaschning, Ghent University and University College Ghent, Belgium

95. **Will People Express More or Less Conformity When They Feel Warm? The Moderating Role of Self-Construal** 1122
Xun (Irene) Huang, Chinese University of Hong Kong, Hong Kong
Meng Zhang, Chinese University of Hong Kong, Hong Kong
Michael K. Hui, Chinese University of Hong Kong, Hong Kong
Robert S. Wyer, Chinese University of Hong Kong, Hong Kong

96. **I Can Feel Your Pain: The Influences of Haptic Input on Donation Amount** 1122
Chun-Ming Yang, Ming Chuan University, Taiwan
Rong-Da Liang, National Kaohsiung University of Hospitality and Tourism, Taiwan

97. **Chi Ku: Bitter Taste Preferences and Responses to Unpleasant Experiences** 1122
Chun-Ming Yang, Ming Chuan University, Taiwan

98. **Detaching the Ties of Ownership: The Effects of Hand Washing on the Exchange of Endowed Products** 1123
Arnd Florack, University of Vienna, Austria
Janet Kleber, University of Vienna, Austria
Romy Busch, University of Vienna, Austria
David Stoehr, University of Vienna, Austria

99. **The Magic Touch: Psychological Drivers of the Discrepancy Between Traditional and Touchscreen Equipment** 1123
Ying Zhu, The University of British Columbia, Canad

Jeffrey Meyer, Bowling Green State University, USA

100. **The Effect of Tangibility on Desire.** 1123
Katrien Meert, Ghent University, Belgium
Mario Pandelaere, Ghent University, Belgium

101. **Visceral Vigor: The Effects of Disgust on Goal Pursuit** 1123
Sachin Banker, MIT, USA
Joshua Ackerman, MIT, USA

102. Do We Judge a Book by its Cover? Unwrapping the Role of Visually-Appealing Packaging in Product Evaluation 1123
Tanuka Ghoshal, Indian School of Business, India
Peter Boatwright, Carnegie Mellon University, USA
Jonathan Cagan, Carnegie Mellon University, USA

103. Implied Sensory Experiences in Product Designs Makes People Think Global 1123
Christophe Labyt, Ghent University, Belgium
Mario Pandelaere, Ghent University, Belgium

104. We're Gonna Need a Bigger Spoon: Spoon Size Effects on Product Perception 1124
Aner Tal, Cornell University, USA
Brian Wansink, Cornell University, USA

105. The Effects of Physical Constraints on Creativity 1124
Ke (Christy) Tu, University of Alberta, Canada
Jennifer A. Argo, University of Alberta, Canada

106. Multi-sensory Perception in Servicescapes: A Typology and Avenues for Future Research 1124
Bernd Frederik Reitsamer, University of Innsbruck, Austria
Nicola Stokburger-Sauer, University of Innsbruck, Austria

107. The Sweet Taste of Charity: Cause Branding Affects Product Experience 1124
Alyssa Niman, Cornell University, USA
Aner Tal, Cornell University, USA

**108. The Perils of an Expansive Posture: The Effect of Everyday, Incidental Posture on Stealing, Cheating and\
Parking Violations.** 1124
Andy Yap, Columbia University, USA
Abbie Wazlawek, Columbia University, USA
Brian Lucas, Northwestern University, USA
Amy Cuddy, Harvard Business School, USA
Dana Carney, University of California Berkeley, USA

109. Hormones and Prosocial Behavior: The Influence of the Menstrual Cycle on Gift-Giving Propensity. 1124
Eric Stenstrom, Concordia University, Canada
Gad Saad, Concordia University, Canada

110. What Are Consumers Afraid Of? Perceived Risk toward Environmentally Sustainable Consumption 1125
Jiyun Kang, Texas State University, USA
Sang-Hoon Kim, Seoul National University, South Korea

111. Sustainable Luxury: Oxymoron or Pleonasm? How Scarcity and Ephemerality Affect Consumers' Perceptions of Fit between Luxury and Sustainability. 1125
Catherine Janssen, Université Catholique de Louvain, Belgium
Joëlle Vanhamme, EDHEC Business School, France
Adam Lindgreen, University of Cardiff, UK
Cécile Lefebvre, IESEG School of Management, France

112. Born Out There: The Discursive Creation of Harmony between Humans and Nature 1125
Joachim Scholz, Queen's University, Canada
Jay M. Handelman, Queen's University, Canada

113. Doing Good While Looking Good: Consumer Perceptions of Sustainability in the Fashion Industry 1125
Rishtee Batra, Indian School of Business, India
Tonya Boone, College of William and Mary, USA

114. The Greening of Consumers: An Assimilation-Contrast Perspective for Product Sustainability Labeling. 1125
Yoon-Na Cho, University of Arkansas, USA
Scot Burton, University of Arkansas, USA

115. Going Green, Going Feminism: Stereotype about Green Consumption and Social General Role 1126
Yunhui Huang, Nanjing University, China
Echo Wen Wan, University of Hong Kong, Hong Kong

116. **Consumer Emotional Intelligence: Exploring Shades of Green and Grey** 1126
Sukumarakurup Krishnakumar, North Dakota State University, USA
Sonakshi Garg, North Dakota State University, USA
Christopher Neck, Arizona State University, USA

117. **The Moderating Role of Situational Consumer Skepticism towards Sustainability Claims in the**
Effectiveness of Credibility Signals 1126
Bonnie Simpson, University of Calgary, Canada
Scott Radford, University of Calgary, Canada
Mehdi Mourali, University of Calgary, Canada

118. **The Moderating Role of Perceived Consumer Effectiveness and Consumer Involvement on the Effect of**
Message-Framing on Intention to Purchase Organic Food Products 1126
Courtney Briggs, Purdue University, USA
Sejin Ha, Purdue University, USA
Richard Feinberg, Purdue University, USA

119. **From General vs. From Specific: Effects of Overestimating Future Engagement in General vs. Specific**
Green Behavior on Immediate Within-Domain and Across-Domain Green Behaviors 1126
Kiju Jung, University of Illinois at Urbana-Champaign, USA
Dolores Albarracin, University of Pennsylvania, USA
Madhu Viswanathan, University of Illinois at Urbana-Champaign, USA

120. **Mitigating Climate Change: The Role of Reasoning Errors, Ecological Knowledge, and Moral Positions** 1127
Christian Weibel, University of Bern, Switzerland
Ralph Hertwig, University of Basel, Switzerland
Sidonia Widmer, University of Basel, Switzerland

121. **In the Name of Environmental Friendliness: Effects on Attitudes toward the Service.** 1127
Ronnie (Chuang Rang) Gao, Drexel University, USA
Rajneesh Suri, Drexel University, USA

122. **The Restorative Nature of Nature: Improving Consumer Decision Making** 1127
Merrie Brucks, University of Arizona, USA
Kevin Newman, University of Arizona, USA
Caitlin Nitta, University of Arizona, USA

123. **Risky Decisions: Citing Sources in Print Advertisement Claims** 1127
Catherine Armstrong Soule, University of Oregon, USA
Leslie Koppenhafer, University of Oregon, USA

124. **"Is it Risky or Beneficial?" Analysis of Supplement-Type and Dosage Preferences in Terms of Risk-Benefit**
Tradeoffs and Epistemological Beliefs 1127
Zoe Rogers, Baruch College/CUNY USA
Stephen J. Gould, Baruch College/CUNY, USA

125. **Personal Death-Thought Accessibility: A Mediating Mechanism between Self-Esteem and Risky**
Consumer Behaviors?. 1128
Sandor Czellar, University of Lausanne, Switzerland
Charles Lebar, HEC Paris, France
Christian Martin, University of Lausanne, Switzerland
Russell H. Fazio, Ohio State University, USA

126. **Optimizing Targeting Effectiveness: The Reversed U-Shape Relationship between Target Market and**
Consumer Attitude 1128
Shuoyang Zhang, Colorado State University, USA
Ishani Banerji, Indiana University, USA
Eliot Smith, Indiana University, USA

127. **Vice vs. Virtue: How Compromise Phantom Alternatives Can Increase Indulgence.** 1128
Yuanyuan Liu, ESSEC Business School, France
Timothy B. Heath, HEC Paris, France
Ayse Önçüler, ESSEC Business School, France

128. Scare an Optimist and Reassure a Pessimist: Message Frames Adjusted to Individual Coping Styles Enhance Breast Cancer Screening Participation 1128
Laure Weckx, Katholieke University Leuven, Belgium
Anouk Festjens, Katholieke University Leuven, Belgium
Sabrina Bruyneel, Katholieke University Leuven, Belgium

129. To Trade or Not? Removing Trading Motivation Eliminates the Endowment Effect 1128
Laurence Ashworth, Queens University, Canada
Lindsay McShane, Queens University, Canada
Tiffany Vu, Queens University, Canada

130. Why Preference Stability of Certain Product Attributes are More Than Others: Disaggregating Stability (Instability) into Core and Supplementary Attributes 1129
Fangzhou Xu, University of Guelph, Canada
Juan Wang, Western University, Canada
Towhidul Ialam, University of Guelph, Canada

131. The Effect of the Change-Matching Heuristic on Consumer Purchase Decision Making 1129
Yin-Hui Cheng, National Taichung University of Education, Taiwan
Chia-Jung Chang, National Chung Cheng University, Taiwan
Shih-Chieh Chuang, National Chung Cheng University, Taiwan
Che-Hung Lin, Cheng Shiu University, Taiwan

132. The Effects of Consumption Goals and Assortment on Cross-Price Sensitivity 1129
Kiwan Park, Seoul National University, South Korea
Joonkyung Kim, Seoul National University, South Korea

133. The Effect of Price Discounts and Quantity Restrictions on Consumption Enjoyment 1129
Zhenfeng Ma, Wilfrid Laurier University, Canada
Guanfu Wang, University of International Business and Economics, China

134. Letting Go of Meaningful Goods: How the Voluntary vs. Involuntary Nature of Disposition Impacts Seller Pricing 1129
Kapitan Sommer, University of Texas at San Antonio, USA
David H. Silvera, University of Texas at San Antonio, USA

135. The Effects of Stackable Discounts on Consumers' Retail Price Image Perception 1129
Shan Feng, William Paterson University, USA
Jane Cai, Independent, USA

136. Presentation of Comparative Prices: Role of Working Memory 1130
Rajneesh Suri, Drexel University, USA
Shan Feng, William Patterson University, USA
Rajesh Chandrashekran, Farleigh Dickinson University, USA

137. Virtual Endowment: How Location and Duration of Virtual Ownership Influence Valuation 1130
Elisa K. Chan, Cornell University, USA
Aner Tal, Cornell University, USA

138. The Effects of Scarcity Claims on Consumers' Willingness to Pay 1130
Doreen Pick, Freie Universität, Germany
Peter Kenning, Zeppelin Universität, Germany
Felix Eggers, Zeppelin Universität, Germany

139. Don't Think Twice: The Effects of Decision Confidence on the Experienced Utility of Incidental Rewards 1130
Aaron Snyder, Stanford University, USA
Maya Shankar, Stanford University, USA
Baba Shiv, Stanford University, USA

140. Your Cheating Heart: The Negative Impact of Sales Promotions on Loyalty 1130
Olga (Olya) Bullard, University of Manitoba, Canada
Kelley J. Main, University of Manitoba, Canada
Jennifer J. Argo, University of Alberta, Canada

141. My Brand and I, and Others between Us: The Influence of Interpersonal Relationships on Consumer-Brand Relationships 1131
Marina Carnevale, Fordham University, USA
Lauren G. Block, Baruch College/CUNY, USA

142. **Revelatory Experiences: The Brand Backstory and its Impact on Consumers'**
Experience of Brand Narratives 1131
Vanisha Narsey, University of Auckland, New Zealand
Cristel Russell, University of Auckland, New Zealand
Hope Jensen Schau, University of Arizona, USA

143. **Who is the Brand Creator? The Effect of Different Brand Biographies on the Perception of**
Brand Personality 1131
Marc Linzmajer, Zeppelin University, Germany
Jana Hauck, Zeppelin University, Germany
Marco Hubert, Zeppelin University, Germany
Reinhard Prügl, Zeppelin University, Germany

144. **Consumer Persuasion Knowledge in Non-Conventional Marketplaces: The Case of Branded**
Prescription Drugs 1131
Marjorie Delbaere, University of Saskatchewan, Canada
Mei-Ling Wei, Saint Mary's University, Canada

145. **The Magic of Numbers and Letters in Alphanumeric Brand Names** .1131
Selcan Kara, University of Connecticut, USA
Kunter Gunasti, University of Connecticut, USA

146. **What is Brand Authenticity? An Exploration of the Concept** 1132
Amélie Guèvremont, Concordia University, Canada
Bianca Grohmann, Concordia University, Canada

147. **Brand Happiness: Scale Development and Validation** 1132
Sunmyoung Cho, Yonsei University, South Korea
Ae-Ran Koh, Yonsei University, South Korea

148. **Primacy of Acculturation Categories over Demographic Variables as Differentiators of Brand Preference** 1132
Rohini Vijaygopal, University of Bedfordshire, UK
Sally Dibb, Open University, UK
Maureen Meadows, Open University, UK

149. **Why Are Consumers Fans of Counterfeit Branded Products? Consumers' Psychological Motivations in**
Counterfeit Consumption. 1132
Xuemei Bian, University of Nottingham, UK
Natalia Yannopoulou, University of Newcastle, UK
Kai-Yu Wang, University of Brock, Canada
Shu Liu, University of Nottingham, UK

150. **Is Social Responsibility Beneficial for Private-Label Brands?** 1132
Maryam Tofighi, Concordia University, Canada
H. Onur. Bodur, Concordia University, Canada

151. **The Impact of Luxury Brand-Retailer Co-Branding Strategy on Consumers' Evaluation of Luxury**
Brand Image: The Case of the U.S. vs. Taiwan 1133
Shih-Ching Wang, Temple University, USA
Primidya K. Soesilo, Temple University, USA
Dan Zhang, City University of New York, USA
C. Anthony Di Benedetto, Temple University, USA

152. **My Brand and I: The Influence of Personal Pronouns on Brand Name Preference** 1133
Nicole Palermo, Fordham University, USA
Luke Kachersky, Fordham University, USA

153. **The Influence of Logo Design Elements on Perceptions of Brand Personality** 1133
Aditi Bajaj, Georgia Tech, USA
Samuel Bond, Georgia Tech, USA

154. **The Impact of Phonetic Symbolism on Stock Performance: Stocks with Stop-Consonant Ticker Symbols**
Perform Better Than Stocks with Fricative-Consonant Ticker Symbols during First Year of Trading. 1133
L.J. Shrum, University of Texas at San Antonio, USA
Tina M. Lowrey, University of Texas at San Antonio, USA
Sarah Roche, University of Texas at San Antonio, USA

155. **Phonetic Symbolism and Children's Brand Name and Brand Logo Preference** 1133
Stacey Baxter, University of Newcastle, Australia
Tina M. Lowrey, University of Texas at San Antonio, USA
Min Liu, University of Texas at San Antonio, USA

156. **Should Firms Apologize After a Crisis? The Moderating Role of Negative Publicity** 1134
Zack Mendenhall, McGill University, Canada
Ashesh Mukherjee, McGill University, Canada

157. **Does Identifying Ambushers as Non-Sponsors Help or Hurt Legitimate Sponsors? Memory and Attitudinal**
Consequences 1134
Clinton S. Weeks, Queensland University of Technology, Australia

158. **The Bad Side of Good: When More Experience Hurts Brands and Marketplace Agents** 1134
Jungim Mun, State University of New York Buffalo, USA
Charles Lindsey, State University of New York Buffalo, USA
Mike Wiles, Arizona State University, USA

159. **Hot Brands, Hot Cognition: The Effects of Incumbency and Negative Advertising on Brand Preference and**
Choice—A Longitudinal Field Experiment 1134
Joan Phillips, Loyola University Chicago, USA
Joel Urbany, University of Notre Dame, USA

160. **The Company or the Crowd? The Impact of Customer-Led Service Recovery on Satisfaction** 1134
Lan Jiang, University of Oregon, USA
Matt O'Hern, University of Oregon, USA
Sara Bahnson, University of Oregon, USA

161. **Don't Care about Service Recovery—Inertia Effects Buffer the Impact of Complaint Satisfaction** 1135
Christian Brock, Zeppelin University, Germany
Markus Blut, University of Dortmund, Germany
Heiner Evanschitzky, Aston University, UK
Peter Kenning, Zeppelin University, Germany
Marco Hubert, Zeppelin University, Germany

162. **Doing Worse and Feeling Better: Why Low Performance Can Increase Satisfaction** 1135
Dilney Goncalves, IE Business School, Spain
Antonios Stamatogiannakis, IE Business School, Spain
Jonathan Luffarelli, IE Business School, Spain

163. **New Insights on the Moderating Role of Switching Costs on the Satisfaction-Loyalty Link** 1135
Thomas Rudolph, University of St. Gallen, Switzerland
Liane Nagengast, University of St. Gallen, Switzerland
Heiner Evanschitzky, Aston University, UK
Markus Blut, TU Dortmund, Germany

164. **An Interruption Effect on Service Recovery** 1135
Fan Liu, University of Central Florida, USA

165. **Customer Satisfaction and Overall Rating: The Influence of Judgment Certainty** 1135
Eugene Sivadas, University of Washington, Tacoma, USA
John Kim, Oakland University, USA
Norman Bruvold, University of Cincinnati, USA

166. **Investigating the Positive Impact of Unexpected CSR** 1136
H. Onur Bodur, Concordia University, Canada
Bianca Grohmann, Concordia University, Canada
Ali Tezer, Concordia University, Canada

167. **A Research Paper on Process of Complaint Behavior Towards Social Commerce, Based on Attribution Theory** 1136
Yaeeun Kim, Korea Advanced Institute of Science and Technology, South Korea
Younghoon Chang, Korea Advanced Institute of Science and Technology, South Korea
Myeong-Cheol Park, Korea Advanced Institute of Science and Technology, South Korea

168. **The Difference of Satisfaction with the Second-Best Choice between Hedonic and Utilitarian Consumption** 1136
Yoonji Shim, University of British Columbia, Canada
Jinhyung Kim, Texas A&M University, USA
Incheol Choi, Seoul National University, South Korea

169. **The Role of Self-Congruence in Consumers' Responses to Service Failures** 1136
Shuqin Wei, Southern Illinois University Carbondale, USA
Tyson Ang, Southern Illinois University Carbondale, USA

170. **Does Complaining Really Ruin a Relationship? Effects of the Propensity to Complain on Positive
Consumer-Brand Relationships** 1136
Hongmin Ahn, West Virginia University, USA
Yongjun Sung, University of Texas at Austin, USA
Minette Drumwright, University of Texas at Austin, USA

171. **Grotesque Imagery in Fashion Advertising** 1137
Jennifer Zarzosa, New Mexico State University, USA
Cuauhtemoc Luna-Nevarez, New Mexico State University, USA

172. **A Meta-Analysis of Nonverbal Accuracy Outcomes in Consumer Research Settings** 1137
Susan A. Andrzejewski, Franklin & Marshall College, USA

173. **(Illusory) Distance of Exposure as a Moderator of the Mere Exposure Effect** .1137
Anneleen Van Kerckhove, Ghent University, Belgium
Maggie Geuens, Ghent University, Belgium

174. **The Effects of Perceived Product-Association Incongruity on Consumption Experiences** 1137
Sarah Clemente, Brock University, Canada
Eric Dolansky, Brock University, Canada
Antonia Mantonakis, Brock University, Canada
Katherine White, University of British Columbia, Canada

175. **The Effect of Menu Presentation Characteristics on Consumer Food Choices** .1137
Jing Lei, University of Melbourne, Australia
Ying Jiang, University of Ontario Institute of Technology, Canada
Catharinna Cao, Mars Australia, Australia

176. **The Impact of Category Labels on Perceived Variety** 1137
Tamara Ansons, University of Michigan, USA
Aradhna Krishna, University of Michigan, USA
Norbert Schwarz, University of Michigan, USA

177. **Illusion of Variety: The Effect of Metacognitive Difficulty on Variety Judgment** 1138
Zhongqiang (Tak) Huang, Chinese University of Hong Kong, Hong Kong
Y.Y., Jessica Kwong, Chinese University of Hong Kong, Hong Kong

178. **Coffee without Overchoice** 1138
Claude Messner, University of Bern, Switzerland
Michaela Wänke, University of Mannheim, Germany

179. **Hmm…What Did Those Ads Say? Reducing the Continued Influence Effect in Political Comparison Ads** 1138
Rebecca E. Dingus, Kent State University, USA
Robert D. Jewell, Kent State University, USA
Jennifer Wiggins Johnson, Kent State University, USA

180. **Holistic vs. Analytic Thinkers in the West: Differential Reliance on Logos in Cognition- and
Feelings-Based Product Evaluations** 1138
Alexander Jakubanecs, Institute for Research in Economics and Business Administration, Norway
Magne Supphellen, Norwegian School of Economics and Business Administration, Norway

181. **The Relative Importance of Advertising Elements and the Roles of Sex (Gender) and Involvement** 1138
Even J. Lanseng, Norwegian Business School, BI, Norway
Maarten L. Majoor, Norwegian Business School, BI, Norway and University of Groningen, The Netherlands

182. **Trivial Gets Central** 1138
Charan Bagga, Western University, Canada
Niraj Dawar, Western University, Canada

183. **Deception in Marketing: How the Source Influences Consumers' Responses to Deception and Its
Contagious Effect on Unrelated Immoral Behavior** 1139
Marijke Leliveld, University of Groningen, The Netherlands
Laetitia Mulder, University of Groningen, The Netherlands

184. Compassion for Evil but Apathy for Angels: The Interactive Effects of Mortality Salience and Just-World Beliefs on Donation Behavior 1139
Fengyan Cai, Shanghai Jiao Tong University, China
Robert S. Wyer Jr., Chinese University of Hong Kong, Hong Kong

185. All Types of Mortality Salience Are Not Equal: The Effect of Contemplating Natural vs. Unnatural Death on Materialism Behavior 1139
Zhi Wang, Chinese University of Hong Kong, Hong Kong

186. How Product Information Shapes Purchase Decisions: Behavioral and Functional Magnetic Resonance Imaging Studies 1139
Sargent Shriver, Temple University, USA
Uma Karmarkar, Harvard University, USA
Michael I. Norton, Harvard University, USA
Angelika Dimoka, Temple University, USA

187. New Notion of Nostalgia 1139
Keiko Makino, Seijo University, Japan

188. Constructing the Citizen-Consumer through Political Discourse in the U.S. 1139
Gokcen Coskuner-Balli, Chapman University, USA
Gulnur Tumbat, San Francisco State University, USA

189. When Nothing Means Everything: Consumer Evaluations of Specialized and Unspecialized Products 1140
Gabriela Tonietto, Washington University in St. Louis, USA
Brittney Dalton, Washington University in St. Louis, USA
Stephen M. Nowlis, Washington University in St. Louis, USA

190. Can't Finish What You Started? Consumption Following Climactic Interruption 1140
Daniella Kupor, Stanford University, USA
Taly Reich, Stanford University, USA
Baba Shiv, Stanford University, USA

191. Monotonous Forests and Colorful Trees. 1140
Hyojin Lee, Ohio State University, USA
Xiaoyan Deng, Ohio State University, USA
Rao Unnava, Ohio State University, USA

2012 ACR Presidential Address

The Elephant Not in The Room:
The Need for Useful, Actionable Insights in Behavioral Research

J. Jeffrey Inman, ACR President, University of Pittsburgh

INTRODUCTION

I am honored and humbled to serve as president of ACR. When I attended my first ACR conference as a doctoral student and didn't know a soul, it never occurred to me that someday I might be standing up here. And I have to tell you that looking out at over 1000 of you is a pretty intimidating sight! Now I wish I had practiced my talk more.

As I considered potential topics for this address, I tried to generate ones that (1) are important, (2) that I am passionate about, and (3) that I know something about. Due in particular to that third objective, finding this combination proved to be a little more difficult than I had hoped, but the epiphany finally struck.

Today, I want to talk to you about a topic that I suspect 1/3 of you will have strong feelings against, 1/3 of you will resonate with, and 1/3 of you may not realize that there was even an issue. I want to talk about the increasing need for useful insights in our work. I've heard many friends and colleagues increasingly lament the lack of contribution of our work to actual problems faced by public policy makers, industry, and consumers. A quick scan of the implications section of a lot of consumer behavior articles reveals that the implications offered there are often rather far removed from the findings.

This brings us to the title of my address, "The Elephant NOT in the Room." Since some of you may not be familiar with the metaphor I used in the title of my talk, I'll briefly define it. My favorite source of metaphorical definitions, Wikipedia, defines this term as "An obvious truth that is either being ignored or going unaddressed. The expression also applies to an obvious problem or risk no one wants to discuss." I think it will soon become clear why I slightly adapted this metaphor for the title of this address.

I'll use the venerable ACR logo to make my point. But first, I want you all to take a pop quiz. Consider the following four options describing what the three characters in the ACR logo stand for. If you didn't know that they represent something, just guess.

A) Theoretical, Methodological, and Empirical contributions
B) Academia, Government, and Industry
C) Ann McGill, Mary Frances Luce, and Laura Peracchio
D) Consumers, Academics, and Practitioners

The correct answer is B) Academia, government, and industry. I suspect that many of us did not know that.

Over a period of many years, ACR has become increasingly focused on research topics that are of interest primarily to the academic constituency, with lip service often paid to the potential implications to public policy makers and practitioners. To illustrate where this rather insular focus has led, I culled through the registrations for this year's ACR conference. As you know, this year's ACR has set a new record for attendance. Unfortunately, attendance across the three constituencies has grown quite lopsided, with attendance by academics dwarfing those from government and industry. In fact, academics comprise over 99% of this year's conference attendance. I don't know about you, but I find this alarming.

THE LYNCH ET AL. (2012) TYPOLOGY

In the October issue of *JCP*, John Lynch, Joe Alba, Aradhna Krishna, Vicki Morwitz, and Zeynep Gurhan-Canli (when she wasn't busy co-chairing this year's ACR conference) co-authored a very thought-provoking article discussing multiple paths by which consumer research can create knowledge. They present a 2x2 typology broken out by the intended contribution of the research (conceptual vs. substantive) and the focus on concepts vs. findings. They discuss each combination in turn and provide guidelines for reviewers based on the core criterion that the research results in a shift in beliefs about something deemed important. This is a very interesting paper and I encourage you to read it.

My take on the four cells of this typology is that our field has become overly fixated on theory building or nomological network construction, such that the lion's share of research being presented at ACR and being published in the top consumer behavior journals falls in the upper left-hand cell. Regarding the right-hand column (findings-focused research), while there are notable exceptions, including an article in the most recent issue of *JCR*, research of this type tends to face a strong headwind in the review process. Pejorative comments such as "atheoretical," "ad hoc," and "applied" often greet the author who submits such a paper. Given the decidedly daunting task of pursuing findings-focused research in the right-hand column, my hope today is that I can convince you or at least a substantial proportion of you to pursue more research of the bottom left-hand type that seeks to generate theory-based, useful insights.

EVALUATING SUBSTANTIVE CONTRIBUTION:
THE US PATENT OFFICE APPROACH

This begs the following question: what qualifies as a substantive contribution? "Substantive" is a rather vague term, so I searched for a more concrete set of criteria for evaluating theory-based substantive research. As is so often the case, the answer came from an unexpected source – in this case the United States government. More specifically, from the US Patent and Trademark Office.

It turns out that the US Patent and Trademark Office considers three criteria when evaluating a potential patent: the concept or invention needs to be novel, non-obvious, and USEFUL. Fortunate for me given the time constraints, the criteria of novelty and non-obviousness were the focus of last year's presidential address by Sharon Shavitt, so I will refer you to Sharon's fascinating discussion of those topics and spend my remaining time on the third criteria - usefulness.

Our behavioral colleagues in management and OB are also struggling with the issue of evaluating research. In a recent article in the *Academy of Management Review,* Corley and Gioia (2011) discuss what constitutes a theoretical contribution and argue a similar point: "Our synthesis reveals two dimensions – originality and utility – that currently dominate considerations of theoretical contribution." While I don't think that we in consumer research are ready to claim that useful insights necessarily constitute a theoretical contribution, this is consistent with the notion that useful insights increase the overall contribution of a research manuscript.

The idea of generating useful insights may seem appealing, but how can we judge whether our findings are useful? Let's return to the US Patent and Trademark Office. Its position is that in order to be useful, an invention must work and serve some type of purpose.

More specifically, the US Patent and Trademark Office Manual of Patent Examining Procedure, says that, "The claimed invention as a whole must be <u>useful</u> (emphasis added). The purpose of this requirement is to limit patent protection to inventions that possess a certain level of "real world" value, as opposed to subject matter that represents nothing more than an idea or concept, or is simply a starting point for future investigation or research."

THE GROWING CALL FOR USEFUL INSIGHTS

Lest you think that I am alone in calling for more useful insights in our research, I wanted to cite some examples that suggest there is a growing sense that change is needed.

First, 40% of the respondents to last year's ACR membership survey said that more substantive research is needed. Second, there are several efforts underway in marketing to reconnect academic research with the real world. For example, our modeling colleagues are struggling with their own demons. They have found that the arms race of increasing model complexity has diminished the actionability (and usefulness) of their work. To help counter this trend, they launched the ISMS practice prize a few years ago to recognize and reward research that makes a difference to practice. Of course, our field is fortunate to have MSI to help fund useful research with implications for practice, so I would be remiss not to mention them. The TCR initiative begun by David Mick has motivated researchers to examine important consumer-centric topics such as over-eating and financial decision making. Finally, in 2011, marketing faculty members from Columbia and Harvard held the inaugural Theory and Practice in Marketing conference at Columbia. The deans from Harvard, Columbia, and Wharton participated along with the editors of *JCR*, *JMR*, and *Marketing Science* and academics from several universities. I wasn't able to attend because of a conflict, but I did see the attendance list and I was happy to see that several other behavioral researchers attended, suggesting that others are concerned about this issue.

But how do we translate this notion of usefulness to consumer research? Useful research moves beyond nomological insights that are often the sole focus of theory development research. But I'll come back to that later. The findings should pass the "so what?" or "who cares?" test and offer useful insights to other constituencies: public policy makers, industry, and yes, consumers as well. Importantly, relevance to other constituencies should not be a stretch. We should all think carefully about how our findings offer useful, actionable insights to non-researchers rather than just adding this to the discussion as an afterthought or ignoring it altogether.

WHY CHANGE?

You may be sitting there wondering, this is all well and good, but why should I change what I'm doing? As an associate dean for research and faculty, I've learned that getting faculty to row in a different direction is often a huge undertaking. After all, most of us get into this field because we are attracted by the idea of studying what interests us.

Returning to the Lynch et al (2012) 2x2 typology, there are at least three good reasons that you should consider pursuing more research of the bottom left-hand type. First, there is a growing need for research that provides generalizable explanations for real world phenomena. Witness the conversion of market research departments at many profit and non-profit firms to "consumer insights" depart-

ments. There is growing agreement that an increased understanding of the consumer should be a central focus of the organization.

Second, research of this type is often easier to get published. Editors, AEs, and reviewers who are tired of reading the 100th submission seeking to extend a popular theory-of-the-moment that relies exclusively on self-report lab studies to test the authors' hypotheses may well be more positively disposed to a paper that uses theory in a novel, non-obvious way to inform a substantive topic and generate useful insights. Am I arguing that we should abandon research focused on theory-building? NO. In fact, I just had a paper accepted last week that is of this type. I am suggesting, in the theme of this year's ACR conference, that we embrace the need for diversity in terms of the mix of research that we pursue.

Third, as we are all painfully aware, acceptance rates at our top journals are about 10% and are not going up. So even if your manuscript is twice as good as average, you have an 80% chance of having it rejected. If you are in a marketing department at a business school, and my random sample of the ACR registrations indicates that most of us are, then you might be motivated to submit your manuscript to another marketing journal. Based on my experience as an author and as an AE at JMR and JM, your chances are better if your paper is of the lower left-hand type and generates useful, actionable insights.

DIFFERENCES IN MANUSCRIPTS PURSUING USEFUL INSIGHTS

So, how does the pursuit of useful insights change the way we go about conducting and writing up our research? In my experience, I have noticed three main differences. One is in the way we test our predictions, one is in the topics that we choose for research to begin with, and one is in the way we craft the introduction and discussion sections of our manuscripts. I will briefly discuss each of these.

Consequential Dependent Variables.

The first difference is that total reliance on self-reports just won't cut it anymore for substantive research. In my role as an associate editor at JMR and JM, I tend to receive mainly consumer behavior manuscripts. I have seen a trend over the past few years by reviewers to ask for at least one study with what I will call a consequential dependent variable. What's that?

A consequential dependent variable is one where the study participant invests a resource and/or experiences a consequence. That is, they put some skin in the game such as Money, Time, Choice, or Effort. The strength of a consequential dependent variable is that it increases confidence in the substantive usefulness of the research by demonstrating generalizability of the findings to a believable context. In short, a consequential dependent variable makes your research more compelling and much more difficult to dismiss.

The most obvious context for a study with a consequential dependent variable is a field test. A field test demonstrates that your thesis obtains in an actual setting. That is, beyond the obvious advantage of increased external validity, it demonstrates generalizability and shows that the effects make a difference. While field tests are great, I feel that a lab or online context is often suitable as well, depending on the particular research focus. I'll also note that field tests are not a panacea for useful insights.

Should every paper include a study with a consequential dependent variable? Of course not. The focal construct may not lend itself to operationalization as a consequential dependent variable. That said, a lot of theory-building research could benefit from the inclusion of at least one study with a consequential dependent variable in order to demonstrate the pertinence of the theory to manifested consumer behavior.

Topic Selection.

A second change in research toward theory-driven useful insights is topic selection. The consumer shouldn't just be a convenient context. I'll briefly overview two examples where I see great opportunity for theory-driven consumer research with potentially game-changing useful insights. The first is Mobile Consumer Research. The second is…Mobile Consumer Research! Actually, this is a double entendre.

One meaning of mobile consumer research is consumer research in the mobile domain. There is already a lot of interesting work underway on digital consumer research, but the increasing penetration of smartphones offers particularly interesting and theoretically rich research problems such as the role of social media in an "always on" environment, the effect of smartphones and apps on consumer choice, and mobile shopping.

The other meaning of mobile consumer research focuses on mobile as the method, either as a data collection medium or as a way to deliver theory-based interventions, such as gamification and consumer self-monitoring. By self-monitoring I mean contexts where consumers are motivated to track their own behavior in pursuit of a goal such as weight loss. For example, there is a consumer movement called "The Quantified Self". This movement began several years ago in the United States but now there are Quantified Self groups throughout the world, including one here in Vancouver. Consumers join clubs in their city and attend monthly meetings to learn about various ways of tracking their behavior. Several apps and stand-along products such as biometric monitoring equipment and sleep monitors have been developed to assist consumers in this endeavor. The apps run the gamut from mood tracking to calorie burn trackers. This context is hungry for behavioral interventions to aid consumers in achieving their goals. This is just a sampling and I could have devoted my entire address to this topic.

Manuscript Construction.

The third difference is in manuscript construction. These differences are most notable in terms of the introduction and the discussion. The introduction lays out the importance of the consumer-related problem being addressed, along with the theory base being brought to bear on it. The discussion then circles back to the theoretical take-aways and the actionable insights from the research.

One drawback of a 2x2 typology like that proposed by Lynch et al. (2012) is that it implies that a given research can only fall into a single cell. I would argue that nomologically-focused research can also generate useful insights and that substantively-focused research can generate theoretical insights. In fact, if you look at the award-winning consumer research articles, you will find that many of them tend to provide a combination of nomological and useful insights. Thus, I urge us to not be confined to one of these cells but, rather, to think about how our research speaks to both theory and substance. I firmly believe that this is not necessarily a case of either-or and that we can often have our cake and eat it too.

So what is ACR doing to help?, you might ask.

AN ACR JOURNAL

As a follow on to the 2011 Task Force on ACR Strategic Direction that was appointed by Sharon Shavitt, I appointed the 2012 ACR Task Force to study the question of whether ACR should launch its own journal. Many people think of JCR as the ACR journal but this is not the case. ACR is only one of 11 organizations that sponsor JCR. I want to thank all of the task force members who donated significant amounts of time to this effort.

The journal task force applied three main principles in generating a recommended positioning for a potential ACR journal. First, it should avoid duplication with existing journals, particularly *JCR*. Second, they sought a positioning that would enable the journal to achieve a premier standing viewed by promotion and tenure committees as comparable to current premier journals such as *JCR*. And third, it should focus on "real problems" and encourage external validity. This is a familiar theme!

The task force also considered several alternative positionings and generated three key recommendations. First, the journal should focus on substance vs. theory or method as the primary contribution. To quote, "These include issues of consumer welfare, public policy, as well as for-profit and not-for-profit businesses." Second, it should encourage thematic work. That is, issues focused on a particular topic. Third, the new journal should encourage the use of field studies and/or secondary data.

Yesterday, the ACR Board discussed the task force's report and unanimously approved their recommendations. The next step is to develop an implementation plan for launching an ACR journal. This work will continue into 2013 and your feedback and suggestions are of course welcome.

ACR'S POSITIONING

Speaking of positioning, I wanted to use a stylized positioning map to make my final point. Over the years, I've heard some ACR opinion leaders caution against research that is too closely tied to practice, lest we become so-called "Handmaidens of Business." I've never been exactly sure what they meant by that, but they make it sound like a really bad thing. Plus, this strikes me as a rather brassy comment if you work in a marketing department in a business school. Besides, based on the statistics I reported earlier in this talk, we aren't at risk of becoming handmaidens of business anytime soon. In fact, if anything, one could argue that much of our work has taken ACR in the opposite direction and moved us toward psychology. My caution is that we need to be careful not to become handmaidens of a different sort.

Actually, it seems to me that ACR is uniquely positioned between the social science disciplines and practice. We have an opportunity and, I would argue, an obligation, to play a critical role in not only contributing to the "mother disciplines" but also to provide useful insights to practice.

CONCLUSIONS

In closing, the ACR logo captures the central guiding principle of ACR: the need to form linkages – linkages with other disciplines and sub-disciplines, linkages between these disciplines and practice, and linkages between nomological insights and useful insights. The bad news is that, like Elvis, the elephant of practice has left the building. The good news is that it is not too late to re-engage. However, in order for that to happen, as authors, we need to submit manuscripts that generate useful insights. Especially for those of us in business schools – we fail to heed this call at our peril. Amidst the present environment of state budget cuts for higher education, concerns about research ethics, and growing calls for faculty research accountability by alumni, students, and taxpayers, the ball is in our court to demonstrate the value of our research. Useful insights and implications for practice will go a long way in that regard.

Am I saying that we should shift all our focus to research that generates useful insights? Absolutely not. I AM saying today that we need to achieve a sustainable equilibrium between research that builds theory and research that applies theory to substantive issues to generate useful insights. Through this, we can form touchpoints beyond our academic colleagues and truly make a difference to practice and to society. Thank you.

REFERENCES

Corley, Kevin G. and Dennis A. Gioia (2011), "Building Theory About Theory Building: What Constitutes a Theoretical Contribution?" *Academy of Management Review*, 36 (1), 12-32.

Lynch Jr., John G., Joseph W. Alba, Aradhna Krishna, Vicki G. Morwitz, Zeynep Gurhan-Canli (2012), "Knowledge Creation in Consumer Research: Multiple Routes, Multiple Criteria," *Journal of Consumer Psychology,* 22 (4),473-485.

Special Session Summaries

Rituals Improve Emotions, Consumption, Interpersonal Relationships, and Even Luck

Chairs: Kathleen D. Vohs, University of Minnesota, USA
Yajin Wang, University of Minnesota, USA

Paper #1: Rituals Enhance the Experience of Consumption

Kathleen D. Vohs, University of Minnesota, USA
Yajin Wang, University of Minnesota, USA
Francesca Gino, Harvard University, USA
Michael I. Norton, Harvard University, USA

Paper #2: Home and Commercial Hospitality Rituals in Arab Gulf Countries

Rana Sobh, Qatar University, USA
Russell W. Belk, York University, USA
Jonathan Wilson, University of Greenwich, USA
Karim Ginena, College of Graduate Islamic Studies, USA

Paper #3: Rituals Alleviate Grieving for Loved Ones, Lovers, and Lotteries

Michael I. Norton, Harvard University, USA
Francesca Gino, Harvard University, USA

Paper #4: Rituals for Reversing One's Fortune

Jane L. Risen, University of Chicago, USA
Yan Zhang, National University of Singapore, USA
Christine Hosey, University of Chicago, USA

SESSION OVERVIEW

This session will present research on the importance of rituals in consumption. The study of rituals have a long and rich history, with the use of rituals traced back to early humans – as well as other animals that use rituals in consumption acts (e.g., eating, attracting a mate). The papers in this session highlight the prevalence and power of rituals in consumer behavior. All data or materials have already been collected, and no work has been published.

This session speaks to the theme of diversity in the 2012 ACR conference in several ways. First is the diversity in the populations under study. Some work tested college and MBA students, whereas others studied community adults in Europe and Arab States.

Second, the methodology used in this work spans the breadth of approaches that consumer behavior scholars use. These presentations feature experimental, survey, and qualitative research.

Third, the way that rituals are conceptualized in these papers varies. Norton and Gino had consumers use their own personalized forms of rituals, whereas Risen et al. made use of popular rituals already known in the culture. Vohs et al. created novel rituals for consumers to use, whereas Sobh and colleagues observed naturalistic rituals being carried out.

Fourth, the breadth of the work on rituals and consumption is exceptionally diverse. Vohs and colleagues focus on the sensations and perceptions that accompany consumption under rituals, providing more of a bottom-up approach to understanding the effects of consumption rituals. Sobh and colleagues provide a top-down approach, focusing on cultural and religious identities as intertwined with rituals. In contrast still, Norton and Gino's as well as Risen et al focus on how people feel when events in life turn – or could turn – for the worse. Norton and Gino investigate how the use of rituals can soothe people's negative emotional state after a loss (from lotteries to lovers). Risen et al found that performing ritual actions provides a sense of psychological insurance that bad events will be kept at bay.

In summary, this is a session that consumer behavior scholars will want to see. It offers indepth, empirical, and theoretical advances featuring perceptual, cognitive, emotional, behavioral, and identity outcomes. To show that grieving, eating, hosting, and protecting are all made better by rituals illustrates why rituals are so common and, as the proposed session will highlight, so powerful.

Rituals Enhance the Experience of Consumption

EXTENDED ABSTRACT

Rituals mark many life events, big and small. From the sequences of activities around Thanksgiving dinner to the activities involved in opening a bottle of wine, people use systematized sequences of behaviors in order to signify an event, and quite often those are consumption experiences. We hypothesized that one reason that rituals are so tightly tied to consumption is that they amplify experiences. Four experiments tested and found support for this hypothesis.

In experiment 1, participants tasted a chocolate bar, before which they either performed or did not perform a ritual. In the *ritual* condition, participants were told that, "Before a consumption experience, people often engage in simple rituals (e.g., when opening a bottle of wine at a restaurant). Please follow these specific steps in unwrapping the chocolate: 1. Without unwrapping the chocolate bar, break it in half. 2. Unwrap one half of the chocolate bar and eat it. 3. Then, unwrap the other half and eat it." In the *no-ritual* condition, participants were told that, "Before you taste the chocolate, please spend a couple of minutes relaxing." We measured how much they savored the chocolate, as surreptitiously measured by duration spent consuming it. We also measured how much participants reported enjoying the chocolate, and how potent was its taste. We predicted and found that participants in the ritual condition spent longer eating the chocolate (i.e., savored it more), found the chocolate's taste to be more potent, and enjoyed the chocolate more than participants in the non-ritual condition.

Experiment 2 tested the hypothesis that rituals are effective in boosting consumption enjoyment and potency only when performed by the individual who is about to do the consuming. Experiment 2 tested whether rituals must be performed by the self in order to aid the consumption experience. Experiment 2 also included a measure of mood to examine whether engaging in rituals influences emotional state during the consumption experience. In the *self-ritual condition*, participants were given a series of steps that formed the ritual of making a glass of lemonade. They were told to pour half of a packet of lemonade powder and half glass of water into a glass, then to stir the mixture, and then wait for 30 seconds. After 30 seconds, they were told to pour the remainder of the lemonade mix and water into the glass, stir, and wait for 30 seconds. In the *other-ritual condition*, participants observed the experimenter perform the same steps as described above. The results demonstrated that rituals before consumption increase the potency of the consumption experience when performed by the individual who is about to consume rather than another person. We also ruled out mood, as there were no differences in positive or negative affect as a function of condition.

Experiment 3 compared ritualistic behaviors involving systematic movements to a control condition where participants engage in similar movements that are random and therefore not systematic. Second, the experiment included a control condition where no ritual was performed. Third, we measured both anticipated enjoyment before consumption and actual enjoyment. Last, we used an international sample of community adults. Participants were told that their task would involve consuming a specific beverage (of their choice), one that they drank at least five days a week in a typical week. They were given instructions to carry with them and perform wherever they consumed the drink. Participants assigned to the *ritual condition* were instructed to perform a distinct set of gestures before the first sip of the beverage. Then they rated their anticipated enjoyment of the beverage and willingness to pay, which occurred immediately before the first sip of the beverage that day. Participants assigned to the *non-ritual gesturing condition* performed hand gestures before consumption, but the gestures were randomized such that there was no consistent pattern. Participants assigned to the *no-ritual condition* were not given a ritual to perform before consuming the beverage. Results showed, as predicted, that anticipated enjoyment rose throughout each consumption experience for participants in the ritual condition but not so for participants in the other conditions. A similar pattern was found with actual enjoyment, and mediation analyses confirmed that the heightened anticipation of consumption led to heightened enjoyment upon consuming.

We designed a last study to further examine the relationship between potency, enjoyment and savoring in consumers' consumption experience, and test the role of fluency and intrinsic interest in explaining the beneficial effects of rituals. The study used the same product and procedure as in experiment 1. Participants were informed that they would be asked to taste a chocolate bar. The measures, as in Experiment 1, were enjoyment, and time spent savoring. In addition, we included measures of 5-item measure of fluency. The results showed that ritual condition participants enjoyed the chocolate more and spent more time savoring it, in a replication of experiment 1. Moreover, we found the same evidence for mediation through fluency for both enjoyment ratings and time spent savoring as dependent measures.

In summary, this work provides robust evidence that performing ritualized behaviors prior to consumption enhances the consumption experience. People who were randomly assigned to perform a ritual enjoyed that which they consumed more so than others. Meditational evidence suggested that anticipating the act of consumption is key, as is fluency. This work will be of interest to scholars who study motivated behavior, the regulation of intake (e.g., calories), as well as those interested in satiation. Because rituals are a lubricant for consumption, intervention implications are also suggested by this work.

"Home and Commercial Hospitality Rituals in Arab Gulf Countries"

EXTENDED ABSTRACT

Hospitality is so much a part of Arab Gulf heritage that a number of ethnographies of the region have titles like "'Ever a Guest in our House'" (Shryock and Howell 2001), "Guests of the Sheik (Fernea 1969), and "Culture-Middle East: Arab Hospitality Runs Deep" (Janardhan 2002). Arab hospitality is viewed as an expression of the high value placed by Arabs on generosity (Karam). Arab hospitality or karam al-arab is a traditional virtue of which Arabs are deliberately proud (Shryock 2004). There is a general consensus among Muslim scholars that hospitality and generosity towards guests are an integral part of faith in Islam. Many verses in the Q'uran as well as a significant number of ahadith (prophet Muhammad's sayings) provide such evidence.

The importance of hospitality to social relations in different regions of the Arab world has been documented by anthropologists (e.g., Young 2007). In the Gulf region hospitality rituals are attributed both to their traditional necessity in the harsh desert environment of the region's Bedouins and to their moral centrality in Islam. Hospitality in Arab Gulf countries is expressive of culture and an important part of the presentation of national identity. Yet, such rituals have been little studied in the social sciences either generally or in the Gulf region in particular. The concept of hospitality remains largely un-specified and un-examined. We believe that hospitality is a critical concept in a globalizing world and that the insights gained in the Gulf region can help inform theory and practice in other parts of the world. Due to petrowealth, Qatar and the UAE are the two wealthiest nations on earth and both are changing rapidly and dramatically. Despite such changes the society still requires strong adherence to traditional norms of hospitality. Urbanization has not eliminated these rituals and, if anything, may have increased their importance as a means for citizens who have become a minority in their own countries to assert their cultural identity in the face of broad immigration and visitation by guest workers, foreign business people, and tourists to the Gulf region.

Using depth-interviews and observations of hospitality rituals in Qatari households, we explore culturally constructed meanings of hospitality rituals in Gulf Arab States and examine associated performative constructions of ethnic identity as well as the multifaceted exchange of material and symbolic possessions (especially foods, perfumes, and incense) that take place between the host and guests. We also study commercial hospitality in high end hotels, restaurants and similar touristic sites in the Gulf region, focusing on the capitals of Doha in Qatar and Dubai in the UAE. Both commercial and home hospitality are forms of what Goffman (1959) called the presentation of self. That is, both are self-conscious acts performed for the guest in order to create a particular impression of the self, whether the self of relevance is the family or the culture. We show how contemporary hospitality rituals can help us better understand the concept of hospitality itself and how it differs from the hospitality of the Bedouin past, as well as what the possible futures of hospitality are between these minority hosts and majority guests. Ironically, this may be a future dependent more on commercial hospitality, inasmuch as few non-Qataris and non-Emiratis are visitors in Qatari and Emirati homes.

In the process, we discuss the process of commoditizing culture and its impact on both hosts and guests. Within the more public realm of paying guests, many of these rituals are transformed. The gracious hosts are now more like servants to the paying guests. This can occur, for example, from the moment of entering Qatar at the Doha airport. For a fee (often arranged by local hosts), rather than stand in lines to get a visa and have passports inspected and stamped, the visitor will be escorted to a lounge and asked to relax while a young woman takes the passport and does all required processing. When she returns, she delivers the passport and escorts the guest through the airport to transportation or another local contact person. Because service workers in Qatar are almost inevitably foreigners themselves, this is one of the first evident differences from hospitality within Qatari homes. Even at Bedouin and Arabian themed hotels, restaurants, oases, and other representations of local culture, the workers and performers are not likely to be Qataris. This may raise issues of authenticity (Bruner 2005), but authenticity is a socially constructed concept and as with going to the theater, the guests seem willing to either suspend disbelief or adopt a questioning gaze rather than a more critical rejection of the representation (Kasfir 1999). After all, the tourist, business visitor, or non-Arab local has chosen this place rather than another that is part of the indistinguishable global chains that Augé (1995) calls non-places and Ritzer (2004) calls nothingness. And rather than being impartial observers of their experiences in the Gulf states, these visitors are likely to be affected by lingering Orientalism (De Botton 2002; Said 1978). At least to a certain degree, we see what we expect to see, even if this means reinforcing stereotypes. In addition, as with tourists in Dubai (Junemo 2004), tourists in Doha have a liminal attitude toward what they see and experience that is more playful than analytic. They likely take their role as guests quite differently than guest workers who have come to Qatar in order to remit money to their families in their original cultures.

We believe that there are potential lessons for the hospitality industry in terms of the specific meanings of the concept in the Gulf region. The transition, which has been described by some as, Arabs moving from the camel to the Cadillac, has transformed the region into a globally recognised hub of activity, ranging from finance, sports, and tourism to art, architecture, and education -- each of which has been infused with the imagery of hospitality and pluralism. Symbols of hospitality rituals and Bedouin generosity become attractive sources of ethnic identity and are prominently displayed in the public domain and in sites of commercial hospitality such has restaurants and hotels. Simply put, hospitality plays a major role in publicly marketing Qatar and the UAE as nations on the world stage.

Rituals Alleviate Grieving for Loved Ones, Lovers, and Lotteries

EXTENDED ABSTRACT

Rituals of mourning in the face of loss – from the death of loved ones to the end of meaningful relationships to losses in wars and competitions – are ubiquitous across time and cultures (Ashenburg, 2004; Durkheim, 1912; Stroebe, Hansson, Stroebe, & Schut, 2001). The most frequently studied rituals are those surrounding religion; people turn to prayer after negative life events such as September 11th, for example, and prayer has been associated with improved coping (Ai, Tice, Peterson, & Huang, 2005; Pargament, 1997; Sherkat & Reed, 1992). So common is this instinct to devise rituals in the face of negative events that the wide variety of known mourning rituals can even be contradictory: crying near the dying is viewed as disruptive by Tibetan Buddhists but as a sign of respect by Catholic Latinos; Hindu rituals stress the removal of hair when mourning while growing hair (a beard) is the preferred ritual for Jewish males (Clements, 2003; Kemp & Bhungalia, 2002). Ritualistic behavior manifests not just in religious practice, but is ubiquitous across domains of human life, providing order and stability while marking change – especially in times of chaos and disorder (Romanoff, 1998; Turner, 1969).

Why are rituals so ubiquitous, and why do they seem to improve coping? Despite the variance in the form that rituals take, we propose that a common psychological mechanism underlies their effectiveness: a restoration of feelings of control that losses impair. Indeed, people who suffer losses often report feeling "out of control" (Low, 1994) and actively try to regain control when they feel it slipping away (Brehm, 1966); feeling in control in turn is associated with increased well-being, physical health, and coping ability (Glass & Singer, 1972; Klein, Fencil-Morse, & Seligman, 1976; Rodin & Langer, 1977). Some qualitative data offer initial evidence for the link between rituals and control; for example, the extent to which athletes and fisherman engage in rituals is related to the unpredictability of their jobs (Gmelch, 1971; Malinowski & Redfield, 1948; see Whitson & Galinsky, 2008). We suggest that the use of rituals serves as a compensatory mechanism designed to restore feelings of control after losses, and that this increased feeling of control contributes to improved coping.

We propose that people turn to rituals after diverse kinds of losses – in the experiments below, of loved ones, lovers, and lotteries – in order to reestablish their feelings of control and mitigate their general negative feelings, such that the feelings of control brought about by rituals will mediate the relationship between ritual use and reduced grief. Although we recognize the many differences in the rituals people use after experiencing a loss and the diversity of emotions that accompany different types of losses, we propose that a common psychological mechanism – perceived control – underlies the effectiveness of rituals. Engaging in rituals mitigates grief by restoring the feelings of control that are impaired by both life-changing (the death of loved ones) and more mundane (losing lotteries) losses, and rituals are particularly effective when participants are convinced of the efficacy of those rituals.

We tested our hypotheses in two experiments in which we explored the impact of mourning rituals after losses – of loved ones, lovers, and lotteries – on mitigating grief. Participants who were directed to reflect on past rituals (Experiment 1) or who were assigned to complete novel rituals after experiencing losses (Experiment 2) reported lower levels of grief. Increased feelings of control after rituals mediated the link between use of rituals and reduced grief after losses, and a belief in the effectiveness of rituals enhanced their positive effects.

In Experiment 1, we relied on participants' self-definitions of what constitutes a "ritual" – as a result, our investigation encompasses a broad definition of the term, including both actions prescribed by a religion or a community of reference as well as behaviors chosen arbitrarily by participants (and the experimenters). This choice is consistent with evidence that mourning rituals across cultures and religious are often contradictory, suggesting that the effectiveness of rituals on grief and coping after a loss is driven primarily by the act of engaging in a ritual and not by the specific actions involved in the ritual. Future research, however, is needed to explore at a more granular level the impact of specific types of rituals on mourning.

Finally, we note that our participants were drawn from non-clinical samples, and our conclusions therefore must be qualified in light of research suggesting that overly ritualistic behavior can negatively impair psychological functions, as in the case of obsessive-compulsive disorder (Tolin, Abramowitz, Przeworski, & Foa, 2002). Clearly, further research is needed to understand which rituals benefit which individuals. Still, our results offer initial support for Durkheim's contention that "mourning is left behind, thanks to mourning itself" (Durkheim, 1912, p. 299); the rituals of mourning in which our participants engage hasten the decline of the feeling of mourning that accompanies loss.

Rituals for Reversing One's Fortune

EXTENDED ABSTRACT

Across cultures, people try to "undo" bad luck with superstitious rituals such as knocking on wood, spitting, or throwing salt. We suggest that these superstitious rituals have more in common than just being actions that offer a sense of control. Instead, these superstitious rituals for reversing one's fortune all seem to involve avoidant motor movements that exert force away from the self. Thus, even though at first glance these rituals may appear to be unrelated cultural traditions, we suggest that these particular rituals may have developed and been passed on, in part, because these avoidant actions create a sense that bad luck is being pushed away from the self.

This hypothesis is based on two streams of embodied cognition research. First, recent work suggests that people use bodily movements to understand and simulate their experience with abstract concepts (Barsalou, 2008; Niedenthal et al., 2005). Second, research has shown that pulling something towards one's representation of self is associated with approaching desired stimuli, and pushing something away from the represented self is associated with avoiding undesired stimuli (Cacioppo, Priester, & Bernston, 1993; Chen & Bargh, 1999; Markman & Brendl, 2005). We suggest that, because avoidant motor actions help avoid negative objects and reduce risk, engaging in an avoidant action may simulate the experience of avoiding bad luck. Consequently, after engaging in an avoidant action, people may feel less pessimistic about the likelihood of anticipated negative outcomes.

Four experiments test this hypothesis by having participants tempt fate and then engage in avoidant actions. In all four studies, participants were lead to tempt fate by having a scripted conversation with the experimenter. The experimenter asked questions and participants were provided with three answers that had the same meaning, but were phrased differently. They were asked to choose the one that sounded the most like them. For example, in Study 1, the experimenter said, "A friend of mine recently got into a car accident… it got me thinking about how dangerous it can be on the road, especially when the snow starts to fall. Do you think that there is a possibility that you or someone close to you will get into a horrible car accident this winter?" Participants in the control condition selected from one of three neutral options (e.g., "I can't believe it's going to start snowing soon"). Participants in the tempting fate condition chose from one of three options designed to express presumptuousness (e.g., "No way. Nobody I know would get into a bad car accident. It's just not possible"). Participants in Study 2a tempted fate about getting the swine flu and participants in Study 2b and 3 tempted fate about being mugged.

Based on previous findings (Risen & Gilovich, 2008), we expected that negative outcomes would seem especially likely after people tempted fate. We predicted, however, that the effect of the jinx would be reduced if people engaged in avoidant actions that exerted force away from the self. Critically, according to our hypothesis, even non-superstitious avoidant actions should be effective for reversing the effect of a jinx. Thus, we tested our prediction with a superstitious action (Study 1, knocking on wood) and a non-superstitious action (Studies 2a, 2b, and 3, throwing a ball).

In Study 1, after the conversation, the experimenter told participants that they should clear their thoughts before continuing to the next part of the study. To help, he would slowly count to 5. In the knocking-down condition, participants were instructed to knock down on the table with each number (away from themselves). In the knocking-up condition, participants were told to knock up on the underside of the table (towards themselves). In the no-knocking condition, the experimenter counted to five with no instructions to knock. Participants then rated how likely they believed it was that they or someone close to them would get into a horrible car accident. As predicted, participants who tempted fate were more pessimistic in the no-knocking and knocking-up conditions than those who did not tempt fate, but the effect of the jinx was eliminated when participants knocked down on the table and away from themselves.

Study 2 tested whether other movements that exert force away from self–even those that are not ingrained as superstitious rituals–also reduce the subjective likelihood of a bad outcome after people tempt fate. After the conversation with the experimenter, participants in Singapore (2a) and the United States (2b) were asked to either hold a ball in their hand or toss it away. After doing so, they rated the likelihood of becoming seriously ill or being mugged, respectively. We found that after tempting fate, participants who tossed the ball away were less concerned about getting sick and getting mugged than those who held the ball in hand.

Finally, in Study 3, we distinguished between exerting force away from the self and creating physical distance from an object in one's environment, and tested whether each was sufficient for undoing the effect of the jinx. All participants tempted fate and then engaged in an action that either created distance or not and either exerted force or not. We found that pretending to throw a ball (an action that does not create distance, but does simulate pushing something away) was as effective for reducing the effect of the jinx as actually throwing the ball.

The present research suggests that knocking (down) on wood is a successful strategy for reducing the heightened concern that typically follows a tempting fate behavior. Moreover, our results suggest that the success is due, at least in part, to the avoidant nature of the act. After tempting fate, avoidant actions—even those that are not part of a superstitious belief system—effectively undo the effect of the jinx. Although superstitions are often culturally defined, our results suggest that the underlying psychological processes that give rise to them may be shared across cultures.

Deepening our Understanding of Depletion: New Causes, Boundaries, and Processes

Chairs: Kathleen D. Vohs, University of Minnesota, USA
Yael Zemack-Rugar, Virginia Tech, USA

Paper #1: What You Don't Know Can Hurt You: Uncertainty Depletes Self-Regulatory Resources

Jessica L. Alquist, Florida State University, USA
Roy F. Baumeister, Florida State University, USA
Dianne M. Tice, Florida State University, USA

Paper #2: Haunts or Helps from the Past: How Does Recalling Past Self-Control Acts Affect Current Self-Control?

Hristina Dzhogleva, University of Pittsburgh, USA
Cait Poynor Lamberton, University of Pittsburgh, USA
Kelly L. Haws, Texas A&M University, USA

Paper #3: Motivation, Personal Beliefs, and Limited Resources All Contribute to Self-Control

Kathleen D. Vohs, University of Minnesota, USA
Roy F. Baumeister, Florida State University, USA
Brandon J. Schmeichel, Texas A&M University, USA

Paper #4: A Reexamination of the Role of Negative Affect in Resource Depletion Effects

Yael Zemack-Rugar, Virginia Tech, USA

SESSION OVERVIEW

Resource depletion theory has been a prominent theory of self-regulation since its inception, and has been a source of great interest and much research in both the psychology and consumer behavior fields. Resource depletion theory argues that the resources that underlie self-regulation are limited and that using these resources for an initial self-regulation task leaves less of them available for use at a later time. Moreover, such resource depletion causes decrements in self-regulation performance. Much of existing research has focused on demonstrating the wide variety of self-regulation tasks that can be depleting, and the wide variety of subsequent tasks that can be affected.

The four papers in this session provide new insights into the causes, boundaries, and processes underlying self-regulatory resource depletion. The first two papers demonstrate that initial exertion of self-regulation efforts is not required in order for depletion effects to arise; instead, the authors identify two new causes of self-regulatory depletion.

In the first paper, Alquist, Baumeister, and Tice show that uncertainty is depleting. The authors show that individuals need not exert self-control in an initial task in order for depletion effects to emerge. Instead, the authors either measure or manipulate uncertainty, and show that when an initial task brings about a state of high uncertainty, later performance on self-regulation tasks suffers. Five experiments demonstrate this effect. For example, the authors show that when participants were uncertain (certain) as to whether they were providing correct responses on an initial task, they persisted less (more) at a subsequent puzzle task. Similarly, participants who were unsure as to whether they would be asked to give a speech at the end of the study solved fewer anagrams than participants who knew whether or not they would be required to give a speech. In fact, even participants who knew they were going to give a speech (an unpleasant outcome) persisted longer at the anagrams than participants who were uncertain about whether they would have to give a speech. The authors further show that these effects are not driven by construal level or time orientation, and that the effects can be erased by the consumption of glucose.

This research demonstrates the inherent difficulty underlying self-regulation under uncertainty. This is a central point for a wide range of decisions and their implications, such as how much to gamble on a risky prospect, whether to buy shares of a stock with variable performance, and how a consumer regulates her consumption behavior in days when she awaits the results of an important health test.

The second paper by Dzhogleva, Lamberton, and Haws describes how recalling past acts of self-regulation can be depleting, depending on both the nature of the previous self-regulation and the ease of recall. This paper extends existing work which shows that depletion can occur vicariously (that is, without actually exerting effort; Ackerman et al., 2009) in several ways. First, previous research suggests that thinking about exerting self-regulation, that is, imagining successful self-regulation is depleting; the paper presented here shows that imagining *unsuccessful* self-regulation is also depleting, sometimes more so than thinking about successful regulation.

Dzhogleva et al. report three studies that show that participants who recalled instances of prior self-control failure were more likely to fail at a subsequent task than participants who recalled instances of prior self-control success. The authors found evidence for depletion, as self-reports of subjective fatigue mediated the results (Finkel et al. 2006). Moreover, the authors show that when self-control success is recalled, this is helpful (hurtful) for subsequent self-regulation when the recall process itself is easy (difficult). For example, the authors show that when participants were either under cognitive load or under no load (varying the difficulty of recall), recalling past failure was always depleting, leading to subsequent decrements in self-control. However, recalling past success was only depleting under load, such that when recall of success was difficult it lead to more depletion (and less subsequent self-control) than when recall of success was easy.

This research shows the power of mental simulation to impel consumers to fail at self-control, while also demonstrating that simulating self-control exertion can sometimes lead to self-control success. Moreover, this research identifies two new moderators of depletion: the valence of previous self-regulation efforts (i.e., success or failure) and the ease of retrieval of these past events.

The third paper in this session pushes forward our understanding of depletion effects by re-examining previously identified boundary conditions. Specifically, previous research has shown that intrinsic motivation can undo the effects of depletion (Muraven and Slessareva, 2003), as can the belief that self-control resources are unlimited (Job, Dweck, and Walton, 2010). Some have interpreted these findings as suggesting that depletion is "all in one's head." To examine this claim Vohs, Baumeister, and Schmeichel look at the effects of belief and motivations following either no depletion, mild depletion, or severe depletion.

Across two studies the authors found that when depletion is absent or mild, intrinsic motivation and beliefs in unlimited resources can overcome depletion hold. However, when depletion is severe, motivation and beliefs do not help mitigate the effects of depletion on behavior. For example, the authors show that when participants believed self-regulation resources were unlimited, they performed similarly well on a self-regulation task following no depletion or mild depletion, but significantly worse following severe depletion. This findings show that depletion is not simply "in one's head", but rather is a real phenomenon.

This research more clearly delineates the boundaries of depletion effects, bringing together existing research under one parsimonious umbrella, while extending our understanding of how and when depletion operates. This research demonstrates that beliefs about willpower and motivation sometimes moderate depletion effects and sometimes do not.

The final paper in this session provides a look at a possible process underlying depletion. In this paper, Zemack-Rugar shows that, contrary to previous theory and findings, depletion procedures can increase negative affect. Specifically, previous research has repeatedly shown a null effect of depletion conditions on both the PANAS and BMIS affect measures. Instead of these measures, the author uses a more sensitive measure of affect: stimuli evaluations. Previous research shows that negative affect leads to reduced stimuli evaluations. Accordingly, the author predicts that depletion will lead to reduced stimuli evaluations/increased negative affect.

Across two studies the data shows that depletion increased negative affect. Moreover, as predicted, this effect is moderated by trait self-control, such that it is stronger (weaker) for individuals low (high) on trait self-control. Most importantly, as predicted, the data shows that measured negative affect significantly mediates the effects of depletion on subsequent behavior.

This research furthers our understanding of how depletion might operate to impact such a wide variety of behaviors. This research is unique in that it examines the process underlying depletion, and is novel, in that, contrary to a wide stream of findings, it demonstrates that depletion does lead to an increase in negative affect, and that this increase is at least partially responsible for post-depletion behavior.

In sum, across four papers and 12 studies, this session provides new insights into the causes, boundaries, moderators, and processes underlying depletion. The presenters will report novel findings showing that initial exertion of self-regulation is not required for depletion; instead, the experience of uncertainty and the recall of past self-regulation failures (i.e., of a lack of self-regulation exertion) are also depleting. Moreover, this session shows that depletion is real, and that when it is severe, it cannot be overcome simply through beliefs or motivation. Finally, the session provides novel insight into on possible process underlying depletion – negative affect.

All papers included in this session contribute to the diversity theme of the conference as they present a variety of research methods, manipulations, and measures. The studies involve correlational data, measured and manipulated independent variables, a variety of dependent variables, as well as process measures. Based on the prominence of this theory and the vast interest in self-regulation, we the authors expect this session will appeal to a wide variety of audiences – most specifically scholars interested in self-control, ego depletion, goal pursuit, motivation, executive functioning, self and identity, and emotion regulation.

What You Don't Know Can Hurt You: Uncertainty Depletes Self-Regulatory Resources

EXTENDED ABSTRACT

The present research tested the hypothesis that uncertainty impairs self-control performance on unrelated tasks. Previous research has shown that people think more and remember more about situations that are uncertain than about situations that are certain (Wilson, Centerbar, Kermer, & Gilbert, 2005). Other research shows that certain kinds of mental effort, such as logical reasoning and decision-making can also deplete self-regulatory resources (Schmeichel, Vohs, & Baumeister, 2003; Vohs, Baumeister, Schmeichel, Twenge, Nelson, & Tice, 2008). Given these findings, we predicted that the extra mental effort uncertainty requires will lead to impairment in self-control.

We tested this hypothesis across 5 studies. In study 1 we asked participants to report how uncertain their job, social relationships, financial situation, and life overall had been over the past week. We then asked participants to report how often, over the past week, they engaged in a variety of behaviors that commonly require self-control (Oaten & Cheng, 2005). We found that participants who reported having more uncertain weeks did less housework, did less personal grooming, controlled their emotions less, managed their time less well, smoked more cigarettes, and drank more alcohol than less uncertain participants.

In study 2, we manipulated uncertainty by varying how uncertain/certain participants were about whether they were responding correctly. We then measured the amount of time spent and number of tries made on unsolvable puzzles. We found that participants in the uncertain condition made significantly fewer attempts and spent marginally less time working on the puzzle than participants in the certain condition. We also found that participants' self-reported uncertainty mediated the relationship between condition and persistence on the unsolvable puzzles.

In study 3 participants were either told whether or not they would be giving a speech or told that their experimenter had misplaced their condition sheet and would have to tell them their assigned condition later in the study. We then measured participants' self-regulation by asking them to solve as many anagrams as possible in ten minutes (Muraven et al., 1998). We found that participants in the uncertain condition attempted and solved significantly fewer anagrams than participants who were certain they wouldn't have to give a speech. This was true even for participants who were certain they *would* have to give a speech. Uncertainty resulted in less self-control than being certain of an undesirable outcome.

Study 4 was designed to rule out explanations based on construal level (Trope & Liberman, 2003) or time orientation (Mischel, Shoda, & Rodriguez, 1989; Twenge, Catanese, & Baumeister, 2003). We used the same manipulation as in study 3 and measured self-control using the game Operation (DeWall, Baumeister, & Vohs, 2008); construal level and time orientation were also measured. Participants in the uncertain condition made significantly more errors than participants in the speech and no speech conditions. However, there were no differences between conditions on construal level or time orientation.

Study 5 sought to test a moderator for our effects. Previous research has shown that glucose plays an important role in the limited resource model of self-control (Gailliot et al., 2007). People's glucose levels are lowered after engaging in self-control and when glucose is low, people's self-control performance suffers. An infusion of glucose can restore people's ability to exercise self-control after a previous act of self-control. After the uncertainty manipulation (from Study 3), we gave participants lemonade that was sweetened with either real sugar or a sugar substitute. We then measured participants' self-control using solvable anagrams. We found that among participants in the uncertain condition, participants who were given real sugar (restoring glucose) performed significantly better than participants who were given Splenda (not restoring glucose). In the control condition, there were no differences between participants who were given real sugar and participants who were given Splenda. Sugar improved the performance of participants whose self-control resources had previously been depleted by uncertainty but did not improve the performance of participants who had not been uncertain. This provides evidence that uncertainty impairs self-control by reducing self-control resources (mainly glucose).

The present research provides evidence that uncertainty can impair individuals' ability to exercise self-control. Uncertainty impaired self-control whether participants were uncertain about what they were doing (Study 2) or what would happen to them (Studies 3-5) and glucose restored participants' self-control performance (Study 5).

Haunts or Helps from the Past: How Does Recalling Past Self-Control Acts Affect Current Self-Control?

EXTENDED ABSTRACT

Recollections of one's past can be an invaluable source of information for future decisions (Aarts and Dijksterhuis 1999). Across three studies, we explore two dimensions of consumers' recall of past self-regulation behaviors: (1) the valence of the recalled acts (past successes or failures at self-control) and (2) the metacognitive experience accompanying the recall (subjective ease or difficulty of retrieval). We show that recalling failures prompts consumers toward indulgence no matter how difficult the recall of the past behavior is. However, when recalling successes, metacognitive information matters: easily-recalled successes prompt consumers to demonstrate increased self-restraint, but difficult recall of past successes leads to reduced self-control.

We argue that the interplay of valence of recalled acts and subjective difficulty of retrieval creates different levels of depletion, which, in turn, influences consumers' likelihood to indulge in the present. We argue that the interplay of the valence of recalled acts and subjective difficulty of retrieval creates different levels of depletion. We demonstrate that consumers are likely to be most depleted by one of two experiences: the recall of failures, whether easy or difficult, or the recall of successes, when doing so is particularly hard for them. The momentary sense of depletion felt in such recall situations is integrated into consumers' self-perceptions, such that these more depleted consumers feel they are worse at self-control and behave accordingly. However, when consumers find that recalling successes is easy, doing so does not create depletion. Therefore, they are able to use the recall of successes to bolster their own faith in their self-control ability and to restrain themselves in the present.

In Experiment 1, we used cognitive load (number memorization task: 7-digit vs. 2-digit number) to create different levels of subjective difficulty of retrieval. Participants were asked to retrieve either past self-control successes or failures within the spending domain. Then, participants completed a monthly household budgeting task, in which they allocated \$2,500 among three categories: necessities, luxuries, and savings. Our results reveal that when participants reflected on their past self-control successes, those in the difficult recall condition allocated more money to luxuries in comparison to necessities than those in the easy recall condition ($p = 0.01$). In contrast, when participants recalled their past self-control failures, there was no significant difference between the recall conditions ($p = 0.96$).

In Experiment 2, participants were presented with one of two advertisements designed to cue recall of either past self-control failures or successes in the spending domain. The subjective difficulty of retrieval was measured. Subsequently, participants were asked to indicate their likelihood of contributing to a 401(k) program. We find that when recalling past self-control success is easy, consumers were more likely to contribute to their 401k than when recall was difficult ($p < .001$) or when failure was recalled; the effects of failure recall were the same regardless of difficulty ($p = 0.49$).

In Experiment 3, we used a range of the number of self-control acts (1 to 7 acts) to manipulate the subjective difficulty of the recall task with higher number of acts expected to induce greater perceived difficulty. Participants were randomly asked to retrieve either past

self-control successes or failures within the spending domain. They were then asked to indicate how much debt they were willing to incur to purchase an attractive item. We found a significant interaction ($p = .02$) between difficulty and valence such that when consumers recall their past self-control successes, the greater difficulty of the retrieval task led to increased indulgence ($p < .001$), whereas when recalling failures, task difficulty did not impact amount of indulgence ($p = .42$). Furthermore, participants indicated their level of depletion by responding to two established measures (Finkel et al. 2006). Results indicated that reported depletion fully mediated these effects (Sobel test $z = -2.52$, $p = .01$).

The present work contributes new insights to the self-regulation literature. Our research suggests that recall of self-regulation acts alone can deplete consumers and inhibit their ability to restrain themselves in the present. This occurs even (or more so) when the recall is of past failure, that is, the recalled event involves no exertion of self-control. Furthermore, our work reveals that recalling failures is more detrimental to present self-control than is recalling successes: in the domain of self-control, thinking positively may be a better strategy than is dwelling on past failures. However, this advice should be given with a caveat: recalling success is only beneficial for long-term goal pursuit when the retrieval of those acts is subjectively easy.

Motivation, Personal Beliefs, and Limited Resources All Contribute to Self-Control

EXTENDED ABSTRACT

Is self-control a matter of managing a limited energy supply or does it depend more on subjective beliefs and motivations? Contrary to the findings of depletion theory (Baumeister, Vohs, & Tice, 2007; Vohs & Heatherton, 2000) some research suggests self-control might be caused more by beliefs, motivation, or mindsets than limited resources. For example, Muraven and Slessareva (2003) showed that offering incentives can overcome depletion. Job, Dweck, and Walton (2010) showed that people who believed in unlimited willpower were immune to ego depletion. They provocatively proposed that ego depletion is "all in your head."

The present research integrates the findings of Job et al. (2010) and Muraven and Slessareva (2003) with the broader set of ego depletion findings. We hypothesized that personal beliefs and motivations can have significant effects on self-regulation under conditions of moderate depletion, but not at more profound levels of depletion.

Experiment 1 was a 2 (belief: willpower limited/unlimited) by 3 (depletion: none, moderate, severe) between subjects design. The first task comprised the manipulation of willpower beliefs and consisted of having participants rate their agreement with biased questionnaire items that either promoted belief in unlimited willpower or promoted belief in limited willpower (Job et al., 2010).

For the depletion manipulation the no depletion condition participants viewed products on a computer screen for four minutes and wrote phrases or words that occurred to them. They were told that in the end, they would receive one of the products they viewed. In the moderate depletion condition, participants viewed the same products as in the zero-task condition but made choices. Making such choices has been shown to cause ego depletion (Vohs et al., 2008). They also performed the Stroop task for two minutes.

In severe depletion condition, participants first completed the choice and Stroop tasks as in the two-task condition. Next, they watched an excerpt from a comedy video and told to stifle their facial and emotional reactions (Gross, 1998; Schmeichel et al., 2003). Last, they were given two pages of text and challenging instructions on when to cross out appearances of the letter *e*.

We assessed two dependent measures of self-control. First, participants made six intertemporal choices. These started with the choice between $10 now and $10 a week hence, ending with the choice of $10 now versus $15 in a week. Second came the Cognitive Estimation Test (CET), which is comprised of 20 questions that require active, logical thinking to generate plausible estimates (e.g., How much do a dozen apples weigh?; Schmeichel, Vohs, and Baumeister 2003).

Results revealed the predicted interaction between extent of depletion and willpower belief. On both outcomes, performance was unaltered by willpower theory condition when participants had performed no initial self-control tasks. Under mild depletion (two self-control tasks), participants' self-regulation was improved when they regarded willpower as unlimited rather than limited. However, as predicted, the effect of willpower belief disappeared among the severely depleted participants. In fact, in the case of CET scores, we found a significant reversal such that participants who were severely depleted and were induced to believe in unlimited willpower performed worse than their counterparts who were induced to believe in limited willpower.

Experiment 2 used a similar design, manipulating motivation rather than beliefs. The 3 depletion manipulations were similar to those in experiment 1. The motivation manipulation was similar to Muraven & Slessereva (2003). Participants in the high motivation condition read that their participation would help improve the well-being of consumers. Participants in the neutral motivation condition were not told that this experiment had special implications. The dependent measures were the same as in experiment 1.

The results were replicated. Participants in the no-depletion condition were unaffected by the motivation condition. Performance by participants in the mild depletion condition was benefited by extra motivational, relative to participants in the neutral-motivation condition. However, at extreme levels of depletion, extra motivation did not boost performance, which was equivalent between motivated and neutral-motivated participants.

In summary, ego depletion is a real, potentially powerful condition, but that at mild and moderate levels its impact competes with other variables such as subjective beliefs and motivations. However, as the extent of energy depletion increases, the scope for influence by other variables diminishes too. By analogy, a slightly tired person could perform well when bolstered by subjective motivation or self-confidence — but severe exhaustion would take its toll regardless of such factors.

A Reexamination of the Role of Negative Affect in Resource Depletion Effects

EXTENDED ABSTRACT

Depletion and negative affect are both deleterious to self-regulation. However, depletion theory posits that negative affect plays no role in depletion effects (Baumeister, Bratslavsky, Muraven, & Tice, 1998). Empirics largely support this stance. In a literature review 73 studies showed a null effect of depletion on negative affect. Yet, 5 studies showed that depletion increases negative affect, and a meta-analysis (of 36 studies) found a small but significant effect (Hagger et al. 2010).

We propose that this inconsistency occurs not because depletion does not influence negative affect, but because of measurement issues. Specifically, affect has been measured using either the BMIS (Mayer & Gaschke, 1988) or the PANAS (Watson, Clark, & Tellegen, 1988). Instead, we use more sensitive measures: stimuli evaluations. We argue stimuli evaluations will more consistently capture the effects of depletion on negative affect, showing reduced stimuli evaluations (i.e., increased negative affect; Winkielman & Berridge, 2004) for depleted individuals.

This prediction is supported by various parallels between depletion and negative affect. Both have similar effects on self-regulation (Baumeister et al., 1994; Tice et al., 2001) and time perception (Droit-Volet & Meck, 2007; Vohs & Schmeichel, 2003). Both have similar causes, for example, difficult tradeoffs (Luce, Payne, & Bettman, 1999; Wang, Novemsky, Dhar, & Baumeister, 2010), and both have similar moderators such as positive affect (Tice, Baumeister, Shmueli, & Muraven, 2007), glucose (Benton 2002; Gailliot et al. 2007), and cash incentives (DeWall, Baumeister, & Vohs, 2008; Meloy, Russo, & Miller, 2006). Finally, because depletion tasks are effortful and tiring (Hagger et al., 2010) they may increase negative affect.

Given these similarities we predict that depletion will increase negative affect. We expect this increase will not be detectable when using the BMIS or PANAS, however, it will be detectable using stimuli evaluations. We further predict that trait self-control will moderate this effect. Trait self-control operates like a muscle, where "stronger" individuals are more resistant to the effects of depletion (Baumeister et al., 2006). Thus, individuals will be more (less) likely to reduce stimuli evaluations when they are low (high) on trait self-control. We also examine the mediating role of negative affect in post-depletion behavior, predicting that negative affect will be a significant mediator of depletion's effects on behavior.

Across two studies participants were depleted using established depletion tasks (study 1: Stroop, Wallace & Baumeister, 2002; study 2: text typing, Muraven et al., 2008) followed by either the established affect scales (PANAS, BMIS) or stimuli evaluations (study 1: music, study 2: Chinese ideographs, Winkielman, Zajonc, & Schwartz, 1997). Participants then completed an established self-regulation task (study 1: time spent on open ended math problems, Schmeichel, Vohs, & Baumeister, 2003; study 2: time spent on unsolvable anagrams, Baumeister et al., 1998) and the self-control scale (Tangney, Baumeister, & Boone, 2004).

In both studies depletion, self-control, and their interaction did not affect any of the PANAS or BMIS subscales; PANAS and BMIS also did not predict behavior (p's .11-.85). In contrast, in both studies, depletion and depletion by self-control significantly predicted behavior ($ps < .05$; consistent with prior research) and also predicted music evaluations (consistent with our predictions; $ps < .05$). Simple effects were such that depletion had no effect on evaluations when self-control was high (+1 SD; $ps > .50$), and a significant effect when it was low (-1 SD; $ps < .05$), reducing music evaluations for depleted participants low in self-control.

Also as predicted (in both studies) music evaluations significantly predicted behavior ($ps < .05$). Most importantly, when both depletion by self-control and music evaluations were included in the models, both remained significant (study 1: music evaluation: $t(145) = 2.18$, $p < .05$; depletion by self-control: $t(145) = 2.04$, $p < .05$; study 2: evaluations: $t(52) = 4.75$, $p < .0001$; depletion by self-control: $t(52) = 2.24$, $p < .05$). In both cases, evaluations were a significant mediator of the effects of depletion on behavior (Study 1: $Z = -2.16$, $p < .05$; Study 2: $Z = 4.55$, $p < .05$; Sobel, 1982).

These findings explore and identify the role of negative affect in depletion. It appears that the similarities in causes, moderators, and effects of depletion and negative affect arise because negative affect partially explains depletion effects. Negative affect provides a parsimonious explanation for previously unrelated depletion moderators and provides some insight into the processes underlying depletion. Importantly, we do not argue that negative affect is the sole explanation for depletion. Instead, our findings suggest that other mechanisms are also at play.

To Ask or Not to Ask: When Charitable Appeals Are Most Effective
Chair: Emily N. Garbinsky, Stanford Graduate School of Business, USA

Paper #1: Make Them Smile: The Temporal Effect of Emotions on Giving

Emily N. Garbinsky, Stanford Graduate School of Business, USA
Jennifer L. Aaker, Stanford Graduate School of Business, USA

Paper #2: Donating in Recessionary Times: Resource Scarcity, Social Distance, and Charitable Giving

Michal Herzenstein, University of Delaware, USA
Deborah Small, University of Pennsylvania, USA

Paper #3: Are the Rich or Poor the More Generous Ones? It Depends on the Way the Appeal is Framed

Kathleen D. Vohs, University of Minnesota, USA
Bob M. Fennis, University of Groningen, The Netherlands

Paper #4: Prosocial Spending and Well-Being: Cross-Cultural Evidence for a Psychological Universal

Michael I. Norton, Harvard Business School, USA
Lara B. Aknin, University of British Columbia, Canada
Chris P. Barrington-Leigh, University of British Columbia, Canada
Elizabeth W. Dunn, University of British Columbia, Canada
John F. Helliwell, University of British Columbia, Canada
Robert Biswas-Deiner, Centre for Applied Positive Psychology, USA
Imelda Kemeza, Mbarara University of Science and Technology, Uganda
Paul Nyende, Makerere University Institute of Psychology, Uganda
Claire Ashton-James, University of Groningen, Netherlands

SESSION OVERVIEW

Charitable giving is a $290 billion industry in the United States (Giving USA Foundation 2011). With over 800,000 charitable organizations in the United States alone, charities must compete for limited donation dollars (Small and Verrochi 2009). As a result of this competition, nonprofit organizations claim that encouraging donations is their single most important challenge (West 2004). For this reason, charities have begun to spend significant amounts of money on marketing (Watson 2006). In addition to helping charities increase their donation rates, understanding what makes people likely to donate is important for consumer welfare as giving has been tied to increases in happiness and life satisfaction (Lyubomirsky, Tkach and Sheldon 2004, Meier and Stutzer 2008) as well as decreases in anxiety and depression (Field, Hernandez-Reif, Quintino, Schanberg and Kuhn 1998). This raises the important question: Why do people give and under what conditions are they more likely to do so?

With four papers, this session addresses this question as it integrates various research perspectives to identify factors that lead to charitable giving. Garbinsky and Aaker examine the effectiveness of emotional donation appeals over time. While past research has shown that inducing a negative emotion (sadness) results in greater willingness to give immediately following advertisement exposure, they show that inducing a positive emotion (happiness) results in greater donation amounts if solicitation occurs at a later point in time. Herzenstein and Small focus on how situational factors affect willingness to give by examining the effects of scarcity, showing that when financial resources are scarce, people are more likely to give to charities concentrated on local as opposed to global causes. This outcome is a result of social myopia whereby financial scarcity causes

them to more heavily discount the lives of distant others relative to close others. Vohs and Fennis investigate how reminders of money affect donation behavior depending upon the frame. Interestingly, they find that when appeals are framed in terms of others, people reminded of money are less generous than others, but when appeals are framed in terms of the self, people reminded of money are more generous than others. Finally, Norton et al. focus on the positive consequences of giving by providing the first evidence for a psychological universal: people around the world experience emotional rewards from using their financial resources to benefit others. This emotional benefit was observed not only in countries with plentiful resources, but also in impoverished nations.

Make Them Smile:
The Temporal Effect of Emotions on Giving

EXTENDED ABSTRACT

Charity advertisements often display a picture of a victim in order to obtain prosocial responses. These advertisements are effective because the victim's facial expression has the power to elicit the same emotion in the observer by means of emotional contagion (Hatfield, Cacioppo and Rapson 1992, 1994, Neumann and Strack 2000). For this reason, the emotional response that is elicited by the charity appeal depends heavily on the nature of the accompanying picture. Past research has shown that advertisements evoking sadness are more effective than advertisements evoking happiness if the donation is solicited immediately after exposure (Small and Verrochi 2009). However, it remains unclear if the same pattern holds over time.

Knowing that positive emotions are better remembered than negative ones (Walker, Vogl and Thompson 1997), we hypothesize that the immediate advantage of sadness-inducing advertisements will fade over time, and as a result, if a donation is solicited long after advertisement exposure, happiness-inducing advertisements will result in greater giving. Furthermore, we hypothesize that individuals' reasons for donating differ depending on whether the donation is solicited immediately after advertisement exposure vs. a later point in time and that these differential reasons also play an important role in the amount of money that people ultimately decide to give.

To test the first hypothesis, experiment 1 examined whether manipulating the emotion evoked while reading an advertisement would affect donation rates at a later point in time. Thus, participants were asked to evaluate an advertisement for St. Jude Children's Research Hospital that depicted a child with a happy or sad facial expression and then asked two weeks later about their likelihood of donating to this organization if they were to win a $50 lottery. Thus, experiment 1 utilized a single-factor between-subjects design where the emotion evoked while reading an advertisement was manipulated (advertisement: happy vs. sad) and where the donation rate two weeks later was the key dependent variable.

Follow-up survey results revealed no significant differences in the propensity to donate if the $50 lottery was won ($\chi^2 = .54, p = .46$). However, there were significant differences in the amount of money participants would be willing to donate if they won ($t(30) = -2.36, p = .025$). Participants that viewed the happy advertisement two weeks ago indicated that they would be willing to donate a greater portion of their $50 winnings ($M = 20.67, SD = 14.25$) than participants that viewed the sad advertisement ($M = 10.65, SD = 9.60$). While sadness-inducing advertisements cause increased giving in the short-term, these results reveal that this pattern reverses over time.

To test the second hypothesis, experiment 2 examined the differential reasons for why individuals donate immediately after advertisement exposure or at a later point in time when sadness vs. happiness was induced while viewing the advertisement. After rating their current emotional state, participants were exposed to an advertisement for St. Jude Children's Research Hospital that depicted either a happy-faced child or a sad-faced child. Then, half of the participants were asked whether they would donate money to St. Jude if they were to win a $50 lottery while they were viewing the ad while the other half were asked whether they would donate money to St. Jude one week later. Those who indicated that they would donate were asked to provide an amount in addition to reasons why they would donate. Thus, experiment 2 utilized a 2 (ad: happy vs. sad) x 2 (donate: now vs. later) between-subjects design.

Follow-up survey results revealed no significant differences in the propensity to give for the donate now ($\chi^2 = 1.045$, $p = .307$) vs. donate one week later conditions ($\chi^2 = .436$, $p = .509$). However, there were significant differences in the amount of money participants would be willing to donate if they won. In the donate now condition, participants that viewed the sad advertisement indicated that they would be willing to donate a greater portion of their $50 winnings ($M = 30.23$, $SD = 14.92$) than participants that viewed the happy advertisement ($M = 20.00$, $SD = 14.83$), $t(46) = 2.37$, $p = .022$. Conversely, in the donate later condition, participants that viewed the happy advertisement indicated that they would be willing to donate a greater portion of their $50 winnings ($M = 25.00$, $SD = 13.96$) than participants that viewed the sad advertisement ($M = 15.79$, $SD = 8.04$), $t(38) = -2.52$, $p = .016$.

These temporal effects of donation solicitation then translated into differential reasons for giving based on the emotion that was evoked while viewing the advertisement. Participants were provided with a list of 8 statements and asked to indicate the extent to which the statement would be true for them if they were to win the lottery and donate. In the donate now conditions, one's current emotions (the emotions evoked by the ad) seemed to play a critical role in the decision to donate. Those in the sad ad condition indicated greater agreement with the statement that they would donate in order to feel happy than those in the happy ad condition, $t(46) = 2.054$, $p = .046$. In the donate later conditions, one's current emotions do not seem to play a large role, with participants in the happy ad condition indicating greater agreement with the statement that they would donate to feel important than those in the sad ad condition, $t(38) = -2.318$, $p = .026$. Furthermore, this desire to feel important mediates the relationship between ad condition and amount donated for the donate later participants, with a 95% confidence interval excluding zero (.488, 9.743).

Our studies are one of the first to integrate a temporal perspective on donating, with the results suggesting that the reasons why people give differ across time. Furthermore, the findings illustrate that eliciting negative emotions (sadness) may not always be advantageous and it is important to consider when donations will be solicited when designing charity advertisements. In follow-up investigations, we hope to shed more light on why time differentially affects emotions that were elicited during appeals and how charities can effectively use these mechanisms to increase their donation rates.

Donating in Recessionary Times: Resource Scarcity, Social Distance, and Charitable Giving

EXTENDED ABSTRACT

We examine whether perceptions of financial scarcity affect the allocation of resources to charity. A common sense assumption is that donations will decrease when resources are scarce. Indeed, charitable giving in the U.S. declined by seven percent during the global economic crisis in 2008. Interestingly, however, during that time, donations to national charities decreased more than to local ones (Rosenblum 2010). Thus, in addition to any main effect decrease in financial giving when resources are scarce, it appears that people choose differently—directing resources toward different causes. The present research examines this phenomenon in the laboratory with tighter controls and attempts to understand the psychology behind resource scarcity and donation choices.

Our main hypothesis is that people direct resources toward more socially proximate causes when resources are scarce than when they are abundant. In general, people are more empathic and helpful when they feel closer to others. Research on intergroup relations consistently finds that people care more about others in their in-group than in the out-group (e.g., Dovidio et al. 1997) and are less caring as anonymity between people increases (Bohnet and Frey 1999).

We expect that this tendency is amplified under conditions of resource scarcity and diminished under conditions of resource abundance. Why? From an evolutionary perspective, when resources are scarce, shifting focus to one's own group is necessary for survival. However, when financial resources are abundant, people may feel less concerned about in-group protection and more empowered to help others, regardless of their psychological distance.

In a recent paper, Shah, Shafir, and Mullainathan (2011) find that people behave more myopically when resources are scarce—heavily discounting the future. These findings help explain why the poor, compared with other populations, are more likely to take short-term high-interest loans, which help in the short run but are clearly damaging in the long run. People may likewise be *socially* myopic under conditions of scarcity—more heavily discounting the lives of distant others relative to close others. Indeed, Jones and Rachlin (2006) found that generosity declines with social distance in a "hyperbolic" pattern that resembled the hyperbolic function observed in studies of time discounting. Thus, there are fundamental similarities between temporal and social distance and that may translate to corresponding patterns under conditions of scarcity.

To test this hypothesis, we conducted three experiments involving actual monetary donations. In all experiments participants arrived at a lab, were seated in private cubicles, and received $5 compensation for their participation. In all experiments we induced feelings of financial scarcity or abundance by asking participants to estimate how much money they have in their combined bank accounts (following Nelson and Morrison (2005)). In the scarce resource condition, the scale for this question ranged from $0 to over $50,000 with increments of $5,000. Almost all participants checked the first tier of this scale. In the abundant resource condition, the scale ranged from $0 to over $500 with increments of $50, and almost all participants checked the last tier of the scale. In an ostensibly unrelated experiment participants read about a "great way to help children" and a description of UNICEF followed.

In the first two experiments, the donation targets were UNICEF in the U.S. ("helping children in our local community") and Africa ("helping children in a faraway community"). In experiment 1 (n = 107) we employed a within-participant design such that all participants could donate to UNICEF U.S., UNICEF Africa, or not donate at all. They could also decide the amount to be donated. Donations were made in private to reduce any social pressure. We calculated the difference between the donation each participant allocated to the U.S. and Africa and subjected this variable to an ordered logit. Results show that resource scarcity significantly impacts where the money was donated: as resources become scarce, donations to the U.S. fund increased compared with Africa.

In experiment 2 (n = 158) we used a between-participants design such that roughly half of the participants read about UNICEF U.S. and the other half about UNICEF African. A 2(scarcity) × 2(donation target) ANOVA revealed only a significant interaction such that donations to the U.S. fund are higher than to the Africa fund when resources are perceived as scarce, but when resources are abundant there is no significant difference between the amounts donated to each country.

In experiment 3 (n = 131) we attempted to generalize our finding to another natural in-group/out-group dichotomy. Half of participants were asked to donate to "help improve the living conditions of business students like you" and the other half was asked to donate to "help improve the living conditions of agriculture students". A 2(scarcity) × 2(donation target) ANOVA revealed a significant interaction. Donations to business students are higher than to agriculture students when resources are perceived as scarce, but when resources are abundant there is no significant difference between the amounts donated to each group.

In sum, three experiments show that resource scarcity leads to socially-myopic donation choices. The results have important implications for understanding public aid in recessionary times. They suggest that beyond a simple decrease in generosity when financial resources are tight, there is also a shift in *where* people donate.

Are the Rich or Poor the More Generous Ones? It Depends on the Way the Appeal is Framed

EXTENDED ABSTRACT

Are the rich or poor the more generous ones? Confusingly, there are supportive findings on both sides. Two studies investigated how money reminders produce differential donation behavior. Our results in fact suggest that both states can lead people to donate more (or less), depending on the way that the appeal is framed.

Research has documented that having money can result in more and less donation behavior. Longitudinal research by Schervish and Havens (2001) has found that the wealthiest 7% of U.S. households contribute over 50% of the money to charitable causes. Experimental studies demonstrated the existence of a "noblesse oblige" social norm that prompts high status individuals, and not their low status counterparts, to behave prosocially (Fiddick and Cummins 2007). But the reverse also seems to be true, in that people without much money tend to donate more than their richer counterparts. For instance, household incomes of greater than $100,000 donate a lower proportion of their incomes than those of less than $25,000 (Gardyn 2003).

Because people who possess many or few financial resources might be inherently different types of people and, accordingly, such individual differences might be driving differences in donation behavior, we first sought to study the effects of mere exposure to the idea of money on donation behavior. In study 1, participants were brought into the laboratory and given 8 quarters ($.25) for their participation, a device that also allowed us to be sure that participants possessed money for the donation opportunity to follow. Next came a manipulation of the idea of money: Participants were either reminded of money or nonmoney (neutral) concepts via a phrase de-

scrambling task. After completing filler questionnaires, participants were told that the experiment was over and given a false debriefing. While participants gathered their belongings, the experimenter pointed to a covered box in the back of the room and commented that the lab was taking donations for the University Student Fund if the participant wished to donate. Participants were given a private opportunity to donate, which was the dependent measure.

The results showed that money-reminded participants donated less than participants in the neutral condition. In fact, money reminded participants donated on average 57% of what others did.

Study 1's results indicated that people reminded of money were less generous than others. A broader conclusion from this and other work is that people reminded of having money appear to be driven by a focus on the self (Vohs et al. 2006). Yet most donation appeals focus explicitly on others, not the self. We hypothesized that when an appeal for donations is framed in terms of others, people reminded of money would be less generous than others, as in study 1. Yet when framed in terms of the self, people reminded of money were predicted to be more generous than others.

We predicted the opposite effect for people reminded of lacking money. Recent work has depicted low socioeconomic individuals as more generous, charitable, trusting, and helpful compared to their high social class counterparts (Piff et al. 2010). By implication, we predicted that when in a mindset of lacking money, donations would rise if participants were reminded of others and fall if they were reminded of the self.

We tested our hypotheses using a field experiment assessing actual monetary donations to an existing charitable cause. The design was a 2 (prime: having money vs. lacking money) x 2 (reminder: own behavior vs. others' behavior) between-subjects factorial design. Participants first performed a descramble task designed to prime the sense of either having versus lacking money.

Then the experimenter indicated that she was soliciting monetary donations for the World Wildlife Fund (WWF). Participants in the self condition were asked if they agreed that thought the WWF was a worthy organization (all agreed). Then the experimenter reminded them of their support of the WWF and asked for a donation. In the other condition, participants were told that many other people had already supported the WWF by donating. Then the experimenter asked for a donation.

Results showed the expected pattern, that prime and reminder conditions interacted to predict donation behavior. In support of hypotheses, participants primed with the idea of having money donated more when the call for charity reminded them of their own behavior than when it highlighted the behaviors of others. Among participants who had been primed with the idea of lacking money, the pattern reversed — these participants donated more of their own money when the charitable request reminded them not of themselves but of the behavior of others.

Previous work has shown that people who have money display more charitable giving than do people lacking money — but, perturbingly, the reverse also has ample support. The present research shows that both outcomes depend on the way the appeal for generosity is framed.

Prosocial Spending and Well-Being: Cross-Cultural Evidence for a Psychological Universal

EXTENDED ABSTRACT

Warren Buffett, one of the richest people in the world, recently pledged to give away 99% of his wealth, saying that he "couldn't be happier with that decision" (Buffet 2010). Consistent with Buffett's claim, recent research suggests that financial generosity may indeed promote happiness (e.g., Dunn, Aknin and Norton 2008). For Buffett, this striking act of generosity necessitated little self-sacrifice; he noted that "my family and I will give up nothing we need or want by fulfilling this 99% pledge," whereas for other people, "the dollars [they] drop into a collection plate or give to United Way mean forgone movies, dinners out, or other personal pleasures" (Buffett 2010). Of course, in many parts of the world, spending one's limited financial resources on others may mean sacrificing more than just movies and dinners out. Does spending money on others promote happiness even in relatively impoverished areas of the world?

To examine the correlation between prosocial spending and subjective well-being within a large number of countries, we use data collected from 136 countries between 2006-2008 as part of the Gallup World Poll (GWP; total $N = 234{,}917$, $M_{age} = 38$, $SD = 17$; 49% male). The sample represents over 95% of the world's adult population (aged 15 and older) and provides an exceptionally large and diverse snapshot. The data are collected using randomly selected, nationally representative samples with a mean size of 1321 individuals per country ($SD = 730$, range = 141- 4437). The relationship between prosocial spending and SWB is positive in 120 out of 136 countries included in the Gallup World Poll, with this relationship reaching traditional levels of significance ($p < .05$) in some 59% of these 120 countries. In a pooled global estimate, the prosocial spending coefficient, b = .27, $p < .03$, exceeds half the coefficient of log income, b = .41, $p < .03$. Thus donating to charity has a similar relationship to SWB as a doubling of household income. Importantly, although rates of prosocial spending are higher in wealthier countries, $r(134) = 0.54$, $p < .001$, the size of the relationship between prosocial spending and SWB that emerges within countries is unrelated to rates of donation, $r(134) = -.10$, $p = .23$, or to the countries' mean incomes, $r(134) = -.09$, $p = .31$, suggesting that generous financial behavior is linked to well-being in poor and rich countries alike.

In Study 2a, we tested the causal impact of prosocial spending on happiness, randomly assigning participants in Canada (N = 140) and Uganda (N = 680) to write about a time they had spent money on themselves (*personal spending*) or others (*prosocial spending*). As predicted, there was a significant main effect of spending type, whereby participants randomly assigned to recall a purchase made for someone else ($M = .09$, SD = 1.00) reported significantly higher happiness than participants assigned to recall a purchase made for themselves ($M = -.09$, SD = 0.99), $F(1, 784) = 8.21, p = .004$. The interaction of spending type and country was not significant, $F(1, 784) = 1.88$, $p = .17$. Thus, participants in Canada and Uganda reported higher levels of happiness when they thought about spending money on others rather than themselves. In Study 2b, participants in India (N = 101) were assigned to recall a recent purchase in which they spent money on themselves (personal spending condition) or someone else (prosocial spending condition); those in the control condition proceeded directly to our happiness measures without recalling a past spending experience. A one-way ANOVA revealed significant between-group differences in positive affect, $F(2, 96) = 3.44, p < .04$. Using LSD contrasts, we found that positive affect levels reported by participants in the control condition ($M = 3.72$, $SD = .72$) and personal spending condition ($M = 3.64$, $SD = .49$) were not significantly different from each other, $p > .65$; most importantly, participants in the prosocial spending condition reported higher levels of PA ($M = 4.11$, $SD = .54$) than participants in either of the other conditions, p's $< .04$.

In Study 3, participants in both Canada (N = 60) and Uganda (N = 95) engaged in a version of the "dictator game," a widely-used economic paradigm in which generous financial behavior can be observed in a controlled setting. We entered trait happiness, donation

amount, country, and a donation amount X country interaction term into a linear regression equation predicting post-task positive affect. Supporting our hypothesis, donation size was the only significant predictor of post-task PA, such that larger donations were associated with higher levels of positive affect ($\beta = .27$, $p < .001$). The interaction of donation amount and country ($\beta = -.06$, $p > .45$) did not approach significance, such that donation amount predicted dictators' post-task positive affect in both the Ugandan ($\beta = .19$, $p < .04$) and Canadian ($\beta = .35$, $p < .005$) samples.

Taken together, the present studies provide the first evidence for a possible psychological universal: human beings around the world experience emotional rewards from using their financial resources to benefit others. From an evolutionary perspective, the emotional rewards that people experience when they help others may serve as a proximate mechanism that evolved to facilitate prosocial behavior, which may have carried short-term costs but long-term benefits for survival over human evolutionary history. The robustness of this mechanism is supported by our finding that people experience emotional benefits from sharing their financial resources with others not only in countries where such resources are plentiful, but also in impoverished countries where scarcity might seem to limit the possibilities to reap the gains from giving to others. In highlighting the potential universality of emotional benefits stemming from prosocial spending, the present work adds to the chorus of recent interdisciplinary research on the importance of generosity for human well-being.

REFERENCES

Bohnet, Iris and Bruno Frey (1999), "The Sound of Silence in Prisoner's Dilemma and Dictator Games," *Journal of Economic Behavior and Organization, 38,* 43–57.

Buffet, Warren (2010), "My Philanthropic Pledge." Retrieved from http://money.cnn.com/2010/06/15/news/newsmakers/Warren_Buffett_Pledge_Letter.fortune/index.htm.

Dovidio, John, Samuel Gaertner, Ana Validzic, Kimberly Matoka, Brenda Johnson and Stacy Frazier (1997), "Extending the Benefits of Recategorization: Evaluations, Self Disclosure, and Helping," *Journal of Experimental Social Psychology, 33,* 401–420.

Dunn, Elizabeth, Lara Aknin and Michael Norton (2008), "Spending Money on Others Promotes Happiness," *Science,* 319, 1687-1688.

Fiddick, Laurence and Denise Cummins (2007), "Are Perceptions of Fairness Relationship-Specific? The Case of Noblesse Oblige," *The Quarterly Journal of Experimental Psychology,* 60, 16-31.

Field, Tiffany, Maria Hernandez-Reif, Olga Quintino, Saul Schanberg and Cynthai Kuhn (1998), "Elder Retired Volunteers Benefit from Giving Massage Therapy to Infants," *Journal of Applied Gerontology*, 17, 229-239.

Gardyn, Rebecca (2003), "Generosity and Income," *American Demographics, December 2002-January 2003,* 46-47.

Giving USA Foundation (2011), "Annual Report on Philanthropy 2010." Retrieved from http://www.givingusareports.org/products/GivingUSA_2011_ExecSummary_Print.pdf.

Hatfield, Elaine, John Cacioppo and Richard Rapson (1992), "Primitive Emotional Contagion," In *Emotion and Social Behavior*, Margaret S. Clark (Ed.), Thousand Oaks, CA: Sage Publications, 151-177.

Hatfield, Elaine, John Cacioppo, and Richard Rapson (1994), *Emotional Contagion*, New York: Cambridge University Press.

Jones, Bryan and Howard Rachlin (2006), "Social Discounting," *Psychological Science, 17,* 283–286.

Lyubomirsky, Sonja, Chris Tkach and Kennon Sheldon. (2004), "Pursuing Sustained Happiness through Random Acts of Kindness and Counting One's Blessings: Tests of Two Six-Week Interventions," Unpublished data, Department of Psychology, University of California, Riverside.

Meier, Stephan and Alois Stutzer (2008), "Is Volunteering Rewarding in Itself?" *Economica*, 75, 39-59.

Nelson, Leif and Evan Morrison (2005), "The Symptoms of Resource Scarcity," *Psychological Science*, 16(2), 167-173.

Neuman, Roland and Fritz Strack (2000), "Mood Contagion: The Automatic Transfer of Mood between Persons," *Journal of Personality and Social Psychology*, 79(2), 211-223.

Piff, Paul, Michael Kraus, Stephanie Côté, Bonnie Cheng and Dacher Keltner (2010), "Having Less, Giving More: The Influence of Social Class on Prosocial Behavior," *Journal of Personality and Social Psychology, 99,* 771-784.

Schervish, Paul and John Havens (2001), "The New Physics of Philanthropy: The Supply-Side

Vectors of Charitable Giving—Part 1: The Material Side of the Supply Side," *The CASE International Journal of Educational Advancement*, 2, 95-113.

Shah, Anuj, Eldar Shafir and Sendhil Mullainathan (2011). "A Simple Look at Having Less," Working paper, Princeton University.

Small, Deborah and Nicole Verrochi (2009), "The Face of Need: Facial Emotion Expression on

Charity Advertisements," *Journal of Marketing Research*, 46, 777-787.

Rosenblum, Christine (2010) "Organizations Tighten Belts as Local, National Donations Down," *Centre Daily*, December 12 (Accessed February 23, 2012).

Vohs, Kathleen, Nicole Mead and Miranda Goode (2006), "The Psychological Consequences of Money," *Science*, 314, 1154-1156.

Walker, W. Richard, Rodney Vogl and Charles Thompson (1997), "Autobiographical Memory: Unpleasantness Fades Faster than Pleasantness Over Time," *Applied Cognitive Psychology*, 11, 399-413.

Watson, Tom (2006), "Consumer Philanthropy: Nonprofits Spend Billions to Reach Consumers," Retrieved from http://www. huffingtonpost.com/tom-watson/consumer-philanthropy-non_b_36261.html.

West, Lori (2004), "Non-profits Face Funding Pressures," *Journal of Accountancy*, 198(September), 1-2.

Virgins, Mommies, and Hags: Women Buying into Change

Chairs: Julie L. Ozanne, Virginia Tech, USA
Emily Moscato, Virginia Tech, USA

Paper #1: Red Flag: Inadequate Sanitary Care Derails the Transition to Secondary School in Africa

Linda Scott, University of Oxford, UK

Paper #2: Outsourcing Motherhood: Managing Assemblages of Care

Amber M. Epp, University of Wisconsin, USA
Sunaina R. Velagaleti, University of Wisconsin, USA

Paper #3: The Social Construction of Womanhood in Middle Age: Menopause as a Rite of Passage

Canan Corus, St. John's University, USA
Bige Saatcioglu, HEC Paris, France

Paper #4: Crones, Hags, and Biddies: How I Became a Burlesque Queen at Seventy

Emily Moscato, Virginia Tech, USA
Julie L. Ozanne, Virginia Tech, USA

SESSION OVERVIEW

This special session is unified by a focus on women managing significant life transitions. Each of the four papers examines how women struggle across diverse life stages, the successful and unsuccessful use of goods and services during this transition, and how gendered roles constrain action as women negotiate to create spaces in which they can maneuver and thrive. The papers traverse across the life stages of virginity, motherhood, and middle age (van Gennep 1960).

Linda Scott examines the problem of retaining girls in secondary education in economically developing countries. In three field studies, she explores the viability of providing girls sanitary menstrual products to increase their attendance. Feminist discourses have traditionally argued that the same social structures oppressing women also dominate nature (Plumwood 1993). Thus, ecofeminists argue that researchers should align to dismantle the underlying dualisms (e.g., masculine/culture/developed vs. feminine/nature/developing). Ironically, global discourses in this context force a false choice between either protecting at-risk young women or the environment, all the while ignoring the environmental contradictions of Western women's practices.

Shifting to the challenges of motherhood, Amber Epp and Sunaina Velagaleti explore how Western women who have an abundance of opportunities manage motherhood through outsourcing. Mothers face new services aimed at families that extend beyond the traditional dilemma of selecting childcare to more nontraditional services. Mothers create assemblages of care that seek to balance control, intimacy, and substitutability as they explore the boundaries between private family life and public marketplace exchanges.

The final two papers explore later life stages as women transition through menopause and into the life stage of old age. Given the negative stereotypes and stigmas associated with being an older woman, these stages are associated with the assertion of new positive identities. Canan Corus and Bige Saatcioglu explore how menopausal women construct the meaning of womanhood and beauty as they go through this transitional life stage. Highlighting the relationship between women's consumption practices and these constructed meanings, they find that women evolve new identities aided by consumption practices in the domains of beauty, health care, and leisure.

Emily Moscato and Julie Ozanne examine the brand community of the Red Hat Society, which is a group of women over fifty who meet socially for friendship, fun, and laughter. The 'red hatters' are best known for their outlandish costumes of red hats, purple dresses, and dazzling accessories, as well as their penchant for shopping and dining out. Yet a deeper analysis suggests that, consistent with situated learning and theories on communities of practice (Wenger 2000), these women use this social support to learn and practice the skills needed for aging.

This session highlights diversity by examining the negotiation of gender both across life stages as well as across developing and developed economies. This session should be of relevant to researchers interested in consumer socialization, aging, rites of passage, feminist theory, gender, and issues of discrimination and social justice.

Red Flag: Inadequate Sanitary Care Derails the Transition to Secondary School in Africa

EXTENDED ABSTRACT

Retaining girls in secondary school is thought to be key to solving problems that block economic prosperity in poor nations: high fertility rates, high infant and maternal mortality, and rapid spread of disease, for instance (Hausmann et al. 2007). Yet drops in female enrollment after puberty continue to be dramatic and often prove intractable in the face of NGO and government efforts to encourage girls' education (World Bank 2011).

Local custom often takes a "coercive pronatalist" stance (Folbre 2009), even where official exhortations discourage early marriage and large families. Among other practices, habits and attitudes surrounding the onset of menstruation, such as unhygienic care and limited personal privacy, push girls into early motherhood even when they wish to continue in school. At the same time, menstrual taboos inhibit frank discussion of the problem, while rites of passage trumpet the sexual "ripeness" of even very young post-pubescent girls (Buckley and Gottlieb 1988; van de Walle et al. 2001).

This talk will focus on three studies, two completed and one ongoing, in east and west Africa, that investigate sanitary pads provision in educational settings, within the context of girls' transition into adulthood. However, sources and experiences from other developing nations will also be brought to bear on what is believed to be a widespread problem (for instance, El-Gilany et al. 2005; Mahon and Fernandes 2010; Nabar et al. 2006).

Two completed investigations of the impact of free sanitary pads provision will be described, one in Ghana and one in Uganda. Initial data, collected in Ghana, show that providing ordinary disposable sanitary pads increases not only attendance in school, but the ability to concentrate, levels of confidence, and engagement in activities from sports to household chores. An extension of this work, among a larger sample and with a longer time horizon, is now underway in Uganda.

After years of silence, menstrual provision has now emerged as a topic of keen interest in Africa, with nations such as Ghana and Kenya leading initiatives to guarantee adequate sanitary care, in order to protect girls' rights to equal education (for instance, Cherono 2011). Yet this welcome attention to a long-neglected problem has brought new challenges: toilet facilities are woefully inadequate and disposable pads may cause costly backups. At the same time, Western environmental activists, who are often unaware of the nature of the material constraints, are pushing against the provision of disposable pads, arguing instead for menstrual cups and cloth pads (see, for instance, "Danish Company Gets Sida Grant to Sell Menstrual Cups in Kenya" 2011; Oster and Thompson 2007).

Thus, the third study, expected to conclude in July 2012, looks into the acceptability of various eco-preferable alternatives in the secondary and primary schools of a remote community in Uganda. Three locally sourced cloth pads are being tested alongside a paper pad made from papyrus in local cottage factories. In addition, an innovative incinerator for disposables (including the papyrus pad) is being tested. This incinerator burns without fuel at medical waste temperatures and can be attached directly to a latrine closet. The reasons for omitting menstrual cups, which pose a substantial public health threat, will also be outlined.

Distributing free sanitary pads may help improve girls' attendance and, perhaps, their performance and retention. But the world community also balks at giving girls these consumer products, particularly because of environmental concerns surrounding disposal of pads. Thus, this talk will end by describing the conflicting agendas of women's rights activists and environmental advocates in the context of puberty and education in the developing world.

Outsourcing Motherhood:
Managing Assemblages of Care

EXTENDED ABSTRACT

Increasingly, mothers are choosing to outsource some of their most intimate parental practices to the marketplace. Outsourcing refers to "the transfer of intimate tasks historically or normatively seen as being performed within the family and by family members to formal commercial establishments located outside of the family" (Lair 2007, p. 32-33). Although questions about whether to enroll children in daycare or place an elderly parent in a nursing home have long been at the center of public and academic debates, examples of outsourcing everyday family life have begun to proliferate in the media. Services exist for everything from teaching your child to ride a bike to taking your kids on college tours (Leider 2009). These emergent services blur the boundaries between family and the marketplace, and prompt new questions about what is acceptable to outsource and how families make these sometimes contentious decisions.

Family life incorporates a range of everyday practices of care, which range from daily rhythms to our most sacred milestones (Epp and Price 2008, 2010). Beyond acknowledging that "consumption is a moment in every practice" (Warde 2005), some scholars argue that the marketplace has become *too* close to family life. Prior research sets up an oppositional dichotomy between the realms of love/family/sacred and money/market/profane (Hochschild 2003). This strict dichotomy positions the marketplace as an intrusion in family life, propagated by overbooked lifestyles that force families to substitute paid care for family-produced practices (Hochschild 2003). Rather than accept this dichotomy as given, we allow families to reveal their own assumptions about how the marketplace should or should not be integrated into family life. This alternate perspective examines how intimacy and the marketplace coexist and draw upon one another in both conflict and partnership (Thompson 1996; Zelizer 2005).

Consumer researchers have only recently entered the academic debate on outsourcing and they tend to focus on major family decision contexts such as daycare or eldercare (Bradford and Sullivan 2010; Huff and Cotte 2011). Our study extends this research by investigating how mothers make choices about outsourcing everyday practices, where boundaries about what is acceptable to outsource

are challenged. Practices of care are not limited to major life decisions, but rather manifest in a range of everyday activities such as grocery shopping and preparing dinner, often heralded as sites for the expression of love and sacrifice (Miller 1998; Thompson 1996). Mothers express guilt and anxiety over outsourcing certain activities to make time for others (Daly 2001; Leider 2009), especially when there is fear of missing milestones or questions about whether the market can provide the same personalization of care (Hochschild 2003). Other mothers express pride in being able to provide their children with rewarding experiences delivered by professionals (Thompson 1996), but perhaps all practices are not equally up for negotiation. The potential for tension exists as practices considered sacred to some might be traded off for other practices (Epp and Price 2010, 2011).

We adopted a grounded theory approach based on in-depth interviews with 25 couples with children. Participants varied in their views, practices, and constraints related to outsourcing based on factors such as income or social class, availability of kin networks, and family structure. In order to ensure diversity with regard to access to outsourcing services, we interviewed families in multiple cities.

Our primary contribution is a framework for how mothers make decisions about outsourcing everyday practices of care. Specifically, mothers generate complex assemblages of care that incorporate heterogeneous resources to assert control, preserve intimacy, and approximate substitutability. Clear tensions exist around how and when to enlist outside resources that move beyond considerations of expertise. For example, following Hochschild (2003), mothers often expressed desires for service providers to customize care for their children to mirror the care she would provide herself. This might include sharing details about birthday traditions or rewards given during potty training. However, despite the sense of control and peace of mind gained from being able to customize, it also presented drawbacks. Facilitating perfect substitution engendered feelings of irrelevance: "if it could be substituted by any other adult, then what sets you apart as a parent?" (Lorna, Mother). Instead, care assemblages must include at least some practices that are "just ours," even if the meanings of practices or what these accomplish shift from some practices to others. That is, mothers weigh the entire assemblage of care when making outsourcing decisions, rather than thinking about a particular service in isolation. Further, attempts to substitute focus mostly on the child's experience, but mothers find it difficult to miss out: "Tara [care provider] has those memories [firsts], and I won't" (Allison, Mother). In addition to customization tensions, many service providers attempt to preserve intimacy by making children's experiences more accessible. Examples such as texting updates, online video feeds, or reports on the child's activities were prevalent. Tensions also surfaced with this strategy, as mothers who missed milestones attempted to redefine them ("it'll be a first time for *us* when we see her walk, too... *that* will be our first... We'll count that one, not the other one"—Allison, Mother). Mothers found it more difficult to reframe the milestone when providers tried to include them ("She [care provider] caught her steps with her camera"—Allison, Mother). Across families, we observed variation in the extent to which mothers' assemblages of care were intentional or emergent, but considering questions of control, intimacy, and substitutability often shaped which resources mothers incorporated.

The Social Construction of Womanhood in Middle Age: Menopause as a Rite of Passage

EXTENDED ABSTRACT

Middle age is considered a prominent rite of passage in a person's life whereby physical appearances change, new roles are adapted, and identities are negotiated (van Gennep 1960). Much of consumer research on aging focuses on the elderly (Price, Arnould, and Curasi 2000; Bonsu and Belk 2003; Schau, Gilly, and Wolfinbarger 2009), even though middle age is a major life transition that poses multiple physical, psychological, and social challenges (Hollis 1993). Middle age is experienced very differently by women than by men since the physiological change of menopause marks the beginning of midlife. As they become middle-aged, women not only undergo bodily and emotional changes but they also are at times subject to negative stereotypes related to aging, beauty, and their sexual attractiveness.

Middle-aged women are an understudied population in consumer research (see, for exceptions, Hill 1991; Thompson 2004; Ustuner and Holt 2007). Understanding women better and exploring their changing marketplace practices as they enter midlife is important for several reasons. First, women constitute a fairly large consumer segment with diverse needs and expectations (Huddleston and Minahan 2011). Second, women take an active role when it comes to consumption; for example, they are often the primary decision makers in much of the familial consumption practices (McIntosh and Zey 1989). In addition, exploring the depth and richness of the female world would contribute to the research on diversity and marketplace inclusion (Williams and Henderson 2012).

The purpose of this study is to explore middle-aged women's social construction of womanhood as they go through menopause. We study menopause as a transition that triggers changing definitions of self and womanhood. We seek to address questions regarding women's identity construction as they experience this transition: How are women's experiences of menopause colored by specific cultural and contextual constructions? What are the roles of social others (e.g., family, healthcare staff) in women's construction of their experiences? How do women's interpretations of their bodily changes shape their identity negotiations? We explore the ways menopausal women construct the meaning of womanhood and beauty as they go through this transitional life stage. Further, we try to understand the nature of the relationship between women's consumption practices and these constructed meanings.

Menopause is a rich context to explore the shaping and negotiation of womanhood in midlife for several reasons. First, menopause is a unique transition in that it is "strictly a female passage" that marks the beginning of several changes, challenges, and transitions in women's lives (Coulbrooke 2002, p. 170). As compared to men, women's bodies are more central to their social interactions, negotiations of power, and self-definitions. As such, there is much to learn through examining transitions in the way women's bodies are treated and imagined. Second, women who enter the menopausal period experience bodily changes that trigger different health and self-care consumption practices (Herrick, Douglas, and Carlson 1996; Lyons and Griffin 2003). Finally, menopause is often viewed as a woman's loss of her attractiveness and sexual appeal; in a society that worships youth and beauty, these perceptions highlight the challenges faced by midlife women (Martin 2001).

Although menopause is a natural hormonal transformation, it is sometimes treated as a "process of breakdown, failure, and decline" (Martin 2001, p. 43). In this definition of menopause, the female body is seen as a system that breaks down and loses its reproductive capabilities (Martin 2001, p. 42). Within this narrow and largely negative depiction of the female body in transition, menopause is described as a problem of hormone deficiency, a pathological state, which needs to be treated (i.e., the medicalization of menopause) [Conrad 2007]. In opposition to the medical discourse, feminist discourse constructs menopause as a natural physiological transformation that brings along new roles and freedoms in women's lives (Kaufert 1983).

Preliminary findings based on in-depth interviews with women across menopausal phases hint at multiple distinct constructions of menopause and middle age. For example, while few of our informants perceive menopause as a medical condition that needs to be cured via medical procedures (e.g., hormone replacement therapy) and thus, adhering to the medical discourse, others see it as a positive transition that motivates new beginnings (i.e., engaging in new hobbies, negotiating roles, and challenging societal norms about womanhood). Consistent with van Gennep's (1960) and Schouten's (1991) descriptions of rites of passage, we find that our informants go through the "separation" phase during which they distance from their previous social construction of womanhood. Menopause becomes the triggering event to start this separation phase. However, our initial findings highlight more complex versions of the two subsequent phases of rites of passage (i.e., transition and incorporation) than the ones conceptualized by van Gennep (1960) and Schouten (1991). Furthermore, our findings point to a variety of coping strategies with menopause and midlife transitions as well as newly acquired consumption practices in various domains such as beauty, healthcare, and hobbies. As such, our data highlights the diversity in both individual and social identities of women going through midlife.

Crones, Hags, and Biddies: How I Became a Burlesque Queen at Seventy

EXTENDED ABSTRACT

The stigmas of aging–unattractiveness, frailty, and dependency–are often amplified by gender expectations for women. For instance, looks are traditionally a source of social capital for women and, thus, women are judged harshly as their "looks fade." Women grow old while men become distinguished; men are seldom accused of "sagging" (Calasanti 2005). Against this backdrop, the members of the Red Hat Society (RHS) perform gender by parodying traditional expectations that women look pretty and act demurely. The RHS encourages its members to wear gaudy attire, buy branded merchandise, and consume loudly and hedonistically. The Red Hat community provides an opportunity to enhance our understanding of how older women negotiate culturally embedded standards of aging and beauty.

The Red Hat Society is an organization for women fifty years and older dedicated to celebrating aging through "fun, friendship, and freedom." The RHS boasts 80,000 registered members embracing the advice from Jenny Joseph's poem, *Warning*: "When I am an old woman, I shall wear purple, with a red hat that doesn't go…" They attend local chapter meetings at restaurants wearing their regalia of red and purple and accessorizing with feathers, flowers, beads, and sparkles. RHS members are known for their loud laughter, spontaneous singing, and frequent playing of red and purple kazoos. RHS is a brand community heavily focused on buying and consuming from their outlandish costumes to their monthly feasting rituals in which cocktails and desserts are consumed before the main meal.

Corporate headquarters states that "the official sport of Red Hat Society is shopping."

Emergent findings, based on interviews and fieldwork, suggest that beneath the surface silliness, these women both support and challenge traditional notions of what it means to be an older woman. The RHS highlights the dynamic tensions between conformity and resistance in consumption communities of marginalized individuals seeking mainstream recognition without assimilation. The RHS members coalesce around consumption of the RHS brand, sharing rituals, traditions, and a sense of responsibility to community members and potential members (Muniz and O'Guinn 2001). RHS prides itself on contradicting traditional gender roles. Publically, members are loud and boisterous and they focus on themselves and pleasure (rather than attending to family or social obligations). They support other gendered roles such as shopping, gift giving, and being beautiful. Yet, ironically, their performance of beauty is over-the-top like the garishness of burlesque queens as they don feathered boas, velvet dresses, and plenty of bling. "I saw this hat and I was just flabbergasted by it... it was so great I just had to have that hat so I bought it... and immediately wore that one and it was a hoot. Everybody just oohed and awed over it and it was great. I loved it" (Dana, 12/17/11).

Their focus on having fun and drawing attention is also a direct challenge of societal norms about appropriate behavior and appearance of older women, who are expected to "fade into the woodwork" (Stalp, Williams, Lynch, and Radina 2008, 247). Violating social expectations introduces RHS members to a new type of social performance, as one informant stated, "it's okay to laugh and be silly and make noise in a restaurant and do things that I've been socialized and condition not to do all these years" (Macey 10/24/11). Consistent with situated learning and theories on communities of practice (Lave 1991; Wenger 2000), RHS members acquire knowledge and skills for coping with the aging process through their community involvement. Through sharing, laughter, and community these women reframe their discomfort over growing old and affirm their worth and entitlement in a culture focused on youth, speed, and independence.

SELECTED REFERENCES

Buckley, Thomas and Alma Gottlieb (1988), *Blood Magic: The Anthropology of Menstruation*, Berkeley, CA: University of California.

Calasanti, Toni (2005), "Ageism, Gravity, and Gender: Experiences of Aging Bodies," *Generations*, 29 (3), 8-12.

El-Gilany, Abdel-Hady, Karima Badawi and Sanaa El-Fedawy (2005), "Menstrual Hygiene among Adolescent Schoolgirls in Mansoura, Egypt," *Reproductive Health Matters,* 13 (26): 147-52.

Folbre, Nancy (2009), *Greed, Lust, and Gender: A History of Economic Ideas*, Oxford: Oxford University Press.

Hausmann, Ricardo, Laura D. Tyson and Saadia Zahidi (2007), *The Global Gender Gap Report 2007*, Geneva: World Economic Forum.

Hochschild, Arlie Russell (2003), *The Commercialization of Intimate Life*, University of California Press.

Martin, Emily (2001), *The Woman in the Body: A Cultural Analysis of Reproduction*, Boston, MA: Beacon Press.

Oster, Emily and Rebecca Thompson (2011), "Menstruation, Sanitary Products, and School Attendance: Evidence from a Randomized Evaluation," *American Economic Journal: Applied Economics*, 3 (1), 91-100.

Schouten, John W. (1991), "Selves in Transition: Symbolic Consumption in Personal Rites of Passage and Identity Reconstruction," *Journal of Consumer Research*, 17 (March), 412-25.

Thompson, Craig J. (1996), "Caring Consumers: Gendered Consumption Meanings and the Juggling Lifestyle," *Journal of Consumer Research,* 22 (March), 388-407.

Van Gennep, Arnold (1960), *The Rites of Passage*, London: Routledge.

Zelizer, Vivianna (2005), *The Purchase of Intimacy*, Princeton, NJ: Princeton University Press.

An Integrative Perspective on Moral Judgments: Understanding the Emotional, Cognitive, Sensory, and Genetic Antecedents of Consumers' Moral Judgments

Session Chairs: Gergana Y. Nenkov, Boston College, USA

Karen Page Winterich, Pennsylvania State University, USA

Paper #1: All Sins Are Not Equal: The Moderating Role of Transgression Magnitude on the Effect of Disgust on Moral Judgments

Karen Page Winterich, Pennsylvania State University, USA

Andrea C. Morales, Arizona State University, USA

Vikas Mittal, Rice University, USA

Paper #2: Sense and Sensibility: The Impact of Sensory Input on Moral Judgments

Gergana Nenkov, Boston College, USA

Maureen (Mimi) Morrin, Rutgers University School of Business, USA

Virginie Maille, Skema Business School, USA

May O. Lwin, Nanyang Technological University, Singapore

Paper #3: Short horizons and tempting situations: Lack of continuity to our future selves leads to unethical decision making and behavior

Hal E. Hershfield, New York University, USA

Taya Cohen, Carnegie Mellon University, USA

Leigh Thompson, Northwestern University, USA

Paper #4: The Genetic Contribution to Preference Consistency in Moral Judgments

Nina Mazar, University of Toronto, Canada

Christopher Dawes, New York University, USA

Peter J. Loewen, University of Toronto, Canada

David Cesarini, New York University, USA

Magnus Johannesson, Stockholm School of Economics, Sweden

Patrik K. E. Magnusson, Karolinska Institutet, Sweden

SESSION OVERVIEW

Understanding moral judgments is critical for society at large as well as businesses given an increasing level of moral uneasiness (Mills 2000) and growing dissention regarding judgments of right and wrong (or moral versus immoral) among political ideologies as well as religion and culture (Haidt and Joseph 2004). In seeking to understand moral judgments, a growing body of research has started to examine the role of various antecedents to moral judgments. For example, to date, research has examined how moral judgments are influenced by emotions and moral intuitions (Pizarro, Inbar, and Helion 2011; Ugazio, Lamm, and Singer 2012), individual differences such as sensitivity to bodily sensations and disgust (Inbar et al. 2009; Schnall, Haidt, Clore, and Jordan 2008), sensory experiences such as taste and physical cleanliness (Eskine, Kacinik, and Prinz 2011; Inbar et al. 2009), and even hypnotism (Wheatley and Haidt 2005). Nonetheless, the discord surrounding morality and moral judgments in society suggests that there is much yet to be understood.

The goal of this session is to gain better understanding of the various antecedents of consumers' moral judgments. Each of the four papers examines a different factor and thereby takes an integrative approach to understanding the precursors of the consumer moral judgment process. In doing so, this session draws on several different fields of study, addressing the conference mission of appreciating diversity to the extent that the series of papers offers interdisciplinary insights into moral judgments.

The first paper by Winterich, Morales, and Mittal presents four studies examining nuances of the extensive findings on affective antecedents of the moral judgment process. The authors explore how specific emotions (disgust, happiness, sadness) affect the severity of consumers' moral judgments. An important insight offered in this paper is the role of transgression magnitude in reversing the effect of emotions on moral judgments with both positively and negatively valenced emotion having similar effects on the severity of moral judgments based on other cognitions associated with the specific emotion.

Moving from the affective antecedents to the sensory determinants of the moral judgment process, the second paper by Nenkov et al. features six studies. The authors show that sensory input (i.e., seeing, touching, smelling, or hearing a product) lowers consumers' level of construal, which leads to less harsh moral judgments, less sophisticated moral reasoning, and more motivated moral reasoning.

The third paper by Hershfield, Cohen, and Thompson explores the cognitive determinants of moral judgment. In a series of five studies, this paper establishes consumers' ability to project one's self into the future as an important determinant of moral decision making. Specifically, whether measured or manipulated, similarity to one's future self not only decreases the severity of moral judgments, but also increases the likelihood of engaging in immoral behaviors such as lying and cheating.

Finally, after considering nuances of the affective, sensory, and cognitive antecedents of moral judgments, the fourth paper by Mazar et al. employs a large-scale twin study to explore the genetic determinants of the consistency of consumers' moral judgments. Their findings suggest that genetic structure can predict consistency in moral judgments, but, notably, genetics do not seem to underlie consistency in other judgments such as religious or economic decisions.

This set of papers not only considers a diverse set of antecedents to moral judgments ranging from heritable genetics to situational factors such as sensory inputs, but also offers insights from a total of 16 studies, some of which are field studies and others examining actual immoral behavior in addition to judgments. All four projects included in this session are at a very advanced stage of completion, and the manuscripts for all four of the papers, as well as the cited references, will be available upon request.

By studying various determinants (i.e., emotional, sensory, cognitive, and genetic aspects) of the moral judgment process, which includes the harshness and consistency of moral judgments, the sophistication of moral reasoning, as well as consumers' (un)ethical conduct, this symposium brings together diverse perspectives on the moral judgment process and is a model of "appreciating diversity" in keeping with the 2012 ACR conference theme. The projects presented in this session span multiple scholarly domains, various methodological approaches, as well as sample characteristics. Data were gathered from multiple countries around the globe (USA, France, Singapore, Sweden) such that diverse populations are represented and findings are not limited to potential cultural differences in moral judgments (Haidt and Joseph 2004). Moreover, the diversity of this session suggests it will be of interest to a wide range of scholars, with the following audiences finding this work to be of particular interest: scholars of moral judgment, researchers examining the nuances of specific emotions, academics interested in sensory and genetic influences on consumer behavior, along with scientists interested in understanding influences of future-oriented thinking.

In short, the findings being presented embody a wide range of approaches, and we believe offer an integrative study of the diverse factors that affect the consumer moral judgment process. In doing so, this session not only offers theoretical insights, but also provides important considerations for individuals, business, and society facing increasing levels of moral unrest.

REFERENCES

Eskine, Kendall J., Natalie A. Kacinik, and Jesse J. Prinz (2011), "A Bad Taste in the Mouth Gustatory Disgust Influences Moral Judgment," *Psychological Science*, 22 (3), 295-299.

Haidt, Jonathan and Craig Joseph (2004), "Intuitive Ethics: How Innately Prepared Intuitions Generate Culturally Variable Virtues," *Daedalus: Special Issue on Human Nature*, 133 (4), 55–66.

Inbar, Yoel, David A. Pizarro, Joshua Knobe, and Paul Bloom (2009), "Disgust Sensitivity Predicts Intuitive Disapproval of Gays," *Emotion*, 9 (3), 435-439.

Pizarro, David, Yoel Inbar, and Chelsea Helion (2011), "On Disgust and Moral Judgment," *Emotion Review*, 3 (3), 267-268.

Schnall, Simone, Jonathan Haidt, Gerald L. Clore, and Alexander H. Jordan (2008), "Disgust as Embodied Moral Judgment," *Personality and Social Psychology Bulletin*, 34 (8), 1096-109.

Ugazio, Giuseppe, Claus Lamm, and Tanis Singer (2012), "The Role of Emotions for Moral Judgments Depends on the Type of Emotion and Moral Scenario," *Emotion*, 12 (3), 579-590.

Wheatley, Thalia and Jonathan Haidt (2005), "Hypnotic Disgust Makes Moral Judgments More Severe," *Psychological Science*, 16 (10), 780-84.

All Sins Are Not Equal:
The Moderating Role of Transgression Magnitude on the Effect of Disgust on Moral judgments

EXTENDED ABSTRACT

We do not judge all sins equally: most would consider stealing a laser printer to be a more severe transgression (i.e., more wrong) than stealing a few sheets of printer paper. How do people make such judgments and how do they vary based on emotions? Disgust has been found to influence judgments of immoral behaviors (Horberg, Oveis, Keltner, and Cohen 2009; Schnall, Haidt, Clore, and Jordan 2008; Wheatley and Haidt 2005), but the mechanism responsible for the impact of disgust on moral judgments is underdeveloped. Interestingly, a careful investigation reveals the positive relationship between disgust and moral judgments may be stronger when the magnitude of the transgression is high whereas the association may be weaker when the transgression is of low magnitude (Schnall et al. 2008; Wheatley and Haidt 2005). Why would this be the case?

We propose disgust and its corresponding cognitive appraisals of rejection (Rozin et al. 2000; Smith and Ellsworth 1985) may influence construal level (Trope and Liberman 2003 2010; Vallacher and Wegner 1987) such that perceived transgression magnitude moderates the association between disgust and moral judgments. Specifically, the abstract construal from disgust motivates people to examine the "why" of the behavior being evaluated. When judging high magnitude transgressions, disgusted individuals consider why one would engage in such a behavior and find it relatively harder to provide justifications for such high magnitude transgressions and judge the transgression more severely. In contrast, disgusted individuals

considering why one would engage in low magnitude transgressions are able to think of numerous justifications, resulting in less severe judgments than those not making an evaluation based on "why" (i.e., neutral state). This pattern results in divergent effects of disgust on moral judgments depending on transgression magnitude.

The first study is a 2 (emotion: disgust vs. neutral) x 2 (transgression magnitude: high vs. low) mixed design with emotion manipulated between-subjects and transgression magnitude within-subjects. Disgust was induced with a product evaluation task, and then participants evaluated a subset of high and low magnitude immoral behaviors used in past research (Detert et al. 2008; Eyal et al. 2008; Horberg et al. 2009; Schnall et al. 2008). A pretest confirmed that participants perceived the four high transgression magnitude scenarios to be of higher magnitude than the low transgression magnitude scenarios. Participants judged the wrongness and immorality of each scenario. Repeated-measures analysis revealed a two-way interaction of disgust and transgression magnitude. For the high (low) magnitude transgressions, disgusted participants evaluated the immoral behavior more (less) severely than the neutral participants. Thus, disgust *increases* the perceived severity of judgments when the behavior is of high magnitude, whereas disgust *decreases* perceived severity of judgments when the transgression is of low magnitude. A second study replicated this effect when the high and low magnitude immoral financial scenarios were identical except for the monetary value of the immoral behavior (i.e., embezzling $10 million vs. $100).

Next, we examine whether differences in construal level underlies this moderating effect. We propose that in an abstract construal the "why" processing that occurs results in more severe judgments for high magnitude behaviors (Eyal et al. 2008), but for low magnitude behaviors, justifications occur such that behaviors are not immoral in the "big picture." First, we demonstrate the disgust does indeed elicit an abstract construal. Study 3A elicits disgust through a video clip and finds participants in the disgust condition construed activities more abstractly than those in the neutral condition (Vallacher and Wegner 1989). Study 3B elicited disgust through a writing task and found disgust condition participants created fewer (i.e., broader) categories than those in the neutral condition (Liberman, Sagristano, and Trope 2002; Smith and Trope 2006), again indicating disgust results in a more abstract construal than a neutral state.

Study 4 adds two additional features to the experimental design. First, we examine sadness and happiness in addition to disgust. We include these additional emotional states to demonstrate that the effect of disgust on moral judgments is distinct from other negative emotions (Chapman et al. 2009; Lerner et al. 2004) and the process is driven by construal level since happiness is opposite of disgust in valence, but is characterized by the same abstract construal level (Labroo and Patrick 2009). Thus, the abstract construal resulting from both disgust and happiness should lead to similar effects on moral judgments. We also examine participants' thoughts regarding their moral judgments to determine the level of abstract processing (Malkoc, Zauberman, and Bettman 2010).

Participants were randomly assigned to one cell in a 4 (emotion: happy, sad, disgusted, neutral) x 2 (transgression magnitude: high vs. low) between-subjects design. Disgust was elicited through a writing task, and then participants evaluated either the four low magnitude or four high magnitude immoral financial behaviors used in study 2. Participants also listed their thoughts when making the evaluations, which were coded for justification of why one would engage in the behavior. The interaction of emotion and transgression magnitude was significant such that for high transgression magnitude behaviors, disgusted and happy participants made more severe moral judgments than neutral or sad participants. The opposite pattern occurred for low transgression magnitude behaviors, such that disgust and happiness reduced the perceived severity of low magnitude immoral behaviors relative to neutral and sadness participants. Bootstrapping analysis revealed that justification thoughts mediated the relationship between emotion and transgression magnitude and severity of moral judgments. These results suggest that the effect of disgust on moral judgments is not accounted for by "gut feelings." Rather, it is the abstract construal associated with the affective state that influences moral judgments, allowing for disgust to both increase and decrease the perceived severity of the behavior depending on the transgression magnitude.

These results provide important insights into the nuances of the relationship between disgust and moral judgments, enhance our understanding of the affect and construal level relationship, and indicate how justifications may reduce the perceived severity of immoral behaviors, which has important societal implications.

REFERENCES

Chapman, Hanah A., David A. Kim, Joshua M. Susskind, and Adam K. Anderson (2009), "In Bad Taste: Evidence for the Oral Origins of Moral Disgust," *Science*, 323 (Feb), 1222-6.

Detert, James R., Linda K. Treviño, and Vicki L. Sweitzer, (2008), "Moral Disengagement in Ethical Decision Making: A Study of Antecedents and Outcomes, *Journal of Applied Psychology*, 93 (2), 374-91.

Eyal, Tal, Nira Liberman, and Yaacov Trope (2008), "Judging Near and Distant Virtue and Vice," *Journal of Experimental Social Psychology*. 44 (July), 1204-09.

Horberg, E. J., Christopher Oveis, Dacher Keltner, and Adam B. Cohen (2009), "Disgust and the Moralization of Purity," *Journal of Personality and Social Psychology*, 97 (6), 963-76.

Lerner, Jennifer S., Deborah A. Small, and George Loewenstein (2004), "Heart Strings and Purse Strings: Carry-Over Effects of Emotions on Economic Transactions," *Psychological Science*, 15 (5), 337-41.

Labroo, Aparna A. and Vanessa M. Patrick (2009), "Psychological Distancing: Why Happiness Helps You See the Big Picture," *Journal of Consumer Research*, 35 (February), 800-9.

Liberman, Nira, Michael D. Sagristano, and Yaacov Trope (2002), "The Effect of Temporal Distance on Level of Mental Construal," *Journal of Experimental Social Psychology*, 38 (November), 523-34.

Malkoc, Selin A., Gal Zauberman, and James R. Bettman, (2010), Unstuck from the Concrete: Carryover effects of Abstract Mindsets in Intertemporal Preferences," *Organizational Behavior and Human Decision Processes*, 113, 112-126.

Rozin, Paul, Jonathan Haidt, and Clark McCauley (2000), "Disgust," in *Handbook of Emotions*, ed. Michael Lewis and Jeannette M. Haviland, New York: Guilford, 637-53.

Schnall, Simone, Jonathan Haidt, Gerald L. Clore, and Alexander H. Jordan (2008), "Disgust as Embodied Moral Judgment," *Personality and Social Psychology Bulletin*, 34 (8), 1096-109.

Smith, Craig A. and Phoebe C. Ellsworth (1985), "Patterns of Cognitive Appraisal in Emotion," *Journal of Personality and Social Psychology*, 48 (4), 813-38.

Trope, Yaacov and Nira Liberman (2010), "Construal-level Theory of Psychological Distance," *Psychological Review*, 117 (2), 440-63.

Trope, Yaacov and Nira Liberman (2003), "Temporal Construal," *Psychological Review*, 110 (3), 403-21.

Vallacher, Robin R. and Daniel M. Wegner, (1987), "What Do People Think They're Doing? Action Identification and Human Behavior," *Psychological Review*, 94, 3-15.

Vallacher, Robin R. and Daniel M. Wegner (1989), "Levels of Personal Agency: Individual Differences in Action Identification," *Journal of Personality and Social Psychology*, 57 (February), 660-71.

Wheatley, Thalia and Jonathan Haidt (2005), "Hypnotic Disgust Makes Moral Judgments More Severe," *Psychological Science*, 16 (10), 780-84.

Sense and Sensibility:
The Impact of Sensory Input on Moral Judgments

EXTENDED ABSTRACT

Prior research has not examined how individuals associate their concrete sensory experiences of sound, color, touch, or odor with higher-level abstract concepts such as morality. The purpose of the current research is to explore the effects of sensory input on several aspects of the moral judgment processes. We propose and subsequently show that sensory modality inputs (i.e., seeing, touching, smelling, or hearing a product) lower consumers' level of construal, which then leads to less harsh moral judgments, less sophisticated moral reasoning, and more motivated moral reasoning.

A product is more directly experienced when consumers can see, feel, hear, or smell it. We argue that products experienced with fewer sensory modality inputs (i.e., products described verbally) will be mentally construed at a more abstract level because they are less directly perceived in terms of the constellation of their sensory properties (Kardes, Cronley, and Kim 2006; Stephan, Liberman, and Trope 2010). No prior research we are aware of has directly tested whether the various modalities of sensory input alone or in combination reduce the level at which objects such as consumer products are mentally construed.

We further predict that sensory input, by reducing mental construal level, would lead individuals who encounter moral dilemmas to mentally represent these dilemmas at a more concrete level, with more specific, contextual details. As such, consumers' moral judgments would be more likely to reflect context-specific considerations, rather than simply follow general moral principles (e.g., it is wrong to steal).

We explore the effects of sensory input on several aspects of the moral judgment process. First, we show that sensory input reduces the level of moral reasoning, leading consumers to use lower-level moral intuition, which is more automatic, concrete, and context-dependent, as opposed to higher-level moral reasoning, which is more controlled, abstract, and context-independent (Haidt 2001). Second, sensory input is shown to lead consumers to take into consideration the context in which a moral violation occurs, reducing the harshness of their moral judgments (Agerstrom and Bjorklund 2009; Eyal, Liberman, and Trope 2008). Third, sensory input makes consumers more likely to engage in motivated moral reasoning by ignoring or selectively applying general moral principles depending on the context in which a moral transgression occurs (Ditto, Pizarro, and Tannenbaum 2009). We further explore the underlying process and show that the effects of sensory input on the moral judgment process are driven by changes in consumers' level of mental construal.

We test our predictions in six studies (total n = 918). We conduct three studies that demonstrate the effect of sensory input (visual, haptic, and olfactory) on construal level and three studies that explore the effects of sensory input (visual, olfactory, and auditory) on the moral judgment process and demonstrate the mediating role of construal level. In all six studies we utilize sandpaper as the focal object, as it provides the opportunity to manipulate all of the sensory modalities except for taste (i.e., vision, audition, olfaction, and touch), but has a generally low level of familiarity among the target (manipulation checks confirmed generally low levels of category and brand awareness). We avoided products involving taste (i.e., the gustatory sense) due to the interactive effects of olfaction and taste and to avoid potentially strong differences in taste preferences.

Overall, our predicted effects of sensory experiences on morality emerge consistently when: using different measures of construals level used in past literature (Fujita et al. 2006; Semin and Fiedler 1988; Trope and Liberman 2003); manipulating different modalities of sensory input (visual, haptic, olfactory, and auditory); and examining different aspects of the moral judgment process (level of moral reasoning, the harshness of moral judgments, and the likelihood of engaging in motivated moral reasoning).

The current research shows that sensory input affects several aspects of the moral judgment processes by lowering consumers' mental construal level. In doing so, this research makes several important contributions to the literature. First, it sheds light on the effects of individuals' sensory experiences on the moral judgment process, contributing to recent literature on embodied cognition, which has largely focused on motor-driven rather than sensory-driven processes (Reimann et al. 2012). Second, it provides evidence for the effects of construal level on moral judgments, adding to recent research that has started to explore this issue (Agerstrom and Bjorklund, 2009; Eyal, et al., 2008). Third, it makes important contributions to construal level theory (Trope and Liberman 2003), as it broadens the conceptualization of psychological distance by demonstrating the effect of sensory input on construal level.

REFERENCES

Agerstrom, Jens and Fredrik Bjorklund (2009), "Moral Concerns Are Greater for Temporally Distant Events and Are Moderated by Value Strength," *Social Cognition,* 27 (2), 261-282.

Ditto, Peter H., David A. Pizarro, and David Tannenbaum (2009), "Motivated Moral Reasoning," in *Moral judgment and decision making: The psychology of learning and motivation,* ed. Daniel M. Bartels, Chistopher W. Bauman, Linda J. Skitka and Douglas L. Medin, Elsevier, 307– 338.

Eyal, Tal, Nira Liberman, and Yaacov Trope (2008), "Judging Near and Distant Virtue and Vice," *Journal of Experimental Social Psychology,* 44 (July), 1204-09.

Fujita, Kentaro, Marlone Henderson, Juliana Eng, Yaakov Trope, and Nira Liberman (2006), "Spatial Distance and Mental Construal of Social Events," *Psychological Science,* 17 (April), 278-282.

Haidt, Jonathan (2001), "The Emotional Dog and its Rational Tail: A Social Intuitionist Approach to Moral Judgment," *Psychological Review,* 108, 814-834.

Kardes, Frank R., Maria L. Cronley, and John Kim (2006), "Construal-Level Effects on Preference Stability, Preference-Behavior Correspondence, and the Suppression of Competing Brands," *Journal of Consumer Psychology,* 16 (2), 135-144.

Reimann, Martin, Wilko Feye, Alan J. Malter, Josh Ackerman, Raquel Castaño, Nitika Garg, Robert Kreuzbauer, Aparna A. Labroo, Angela Y. Lee, Maureen Morrin, Gergana Y. Nenkov, Jesper H. Nielsen, Maria Perez, Gratiana Pol, José Antonio Rosa, Carolyn Yoon, and Chen-Bo Zhong (2012), "Embodiment in Judgment and Choice," *Journal of Neuroscience, Psychology, and Economics,* 5 (2), 104-123.

Semin, Gun R. and Klaus Fiedler (1988), "The Cognitive Functions of Linguistic Categories in Describing Persons: Social Cognition and Language," *Journal of Personality and Social Psychology,* 54 (4), 558-568.

Stephan, Elena, Nira Liberman, and Yaacov Trope (2010), "Politeness and Psychological Distance: A Construal Level Perspective," *Journal of Personality and Social Psychology,* 98 (2), 268-280.

Trope, Yaacov and Nira Liberman (2003), "Temporal Construal," *Psychological Review,* 110 (3), 403-421.

Short Horizons and Tempting Situations: Lack of Continuity to Our Future Selves Leads to Unethical Decision Making and Behavior

EXTENDED ABSTRACT

In this paper, we suggest that one underlying cause of unethical conduct is a fundamental inability to project one's self into the future. Our thesis is that feeling disconnected from one's future self is intimately linked to unethical decision making. Just as sense of shared connection with another person can lead to shared emotional and physiological states (Cwir, Carr, Walton, and Spencer 2011), feeling continuity with the future self may provide better access to that future self's feelings. If I am about to act in a potentially unethical way, but I can access the feelings that my future self will feel (e.g., guilty, ashamed) – because I maintain a sense of continuity with that self – I will recognize that I will be better off in the long run if I do not act in such a way. On the contrary, if my future self feels like a stranger to me – if I lack continuity with it and I do not have a good sense of how my self will feel in the future – then I might be more tempted to act in an unethical way in the present.

In five studies, we tested this hypothesis by exploring whether perceived continuity with one's future self is associated with unethical judgments and decision making. Studies 1a and 1b show that individual differences in future self-continuity predict unethical decision making in business contexts (as measured by the Unethical Business Decisions Scale), and rule out potential alternative accounts. Namely, we show that future self-continuity has a distinct effect on unethical decision making independent of relationships other types of selves (e.g., the ideal self, the past self) may have on unethical decision making. Study 2 extends this finding to attitudes toward inappropriate negotiation strategies (using the Self-reported Inappropriate Negotiation Strategies Scale) and establishes the mediating role of consideration of future consequences.

Study 3 extends the first two studies by showing that individual differences in future self-continuity are related to two different types of unethical behavior: lies and false promises. Study 3 was a two-part study. In the first phase, we administered the future self-continuity scale. In the second phase, we invited participants who scored in the upper and lower quartile of the future self-continuity scale to attend a lab session in which we directly examined the relationship between future self-continuity and lying. We administered Cohen, Gunia, Kim-Jun, and Murnighan's (2009) modified version of Gneezy's (2005) deception game—a "sender-receiver" decision making task in which participants have a monetary incentive to lie (see also Cohen et al., 2011). The design of Study 3 also allowed us to assess the relationship between future self-continuity and the propensity to make false promises. By signing up for the voluntary lab session, participants were, in effect, making a promise to attend it. Given that almost no research study has perfect attendance rates, we were able to determine whether participants high in future self-continuity were more likely to attend the lab session, and thus, uphold a promise they had made. Here, we find that individuals who are low in future self-continuity are significantly more likely to lie on the deception game, and also less likely to follow through on their promise to attend the laboratory session.

In Study 4, we sought to replicate and extend the results of Study 3. First, we employed a different behavioral measure of unethical behavior: cheating. Second, although in Study 1b we ruled out one set of alternative explanations for our finding (i.e., different types of relationships between selves), in Study 4 we wanted to control for another alternative explanation. Namely, it is possible the unethical intentions and behaviors we observed in Studies 1-3 were not necessarily a function of continuity with the future self per se, but rather, were a result of a general lack of self-control. Indeed, recent research has shown that individuals whose self-control resources are depleted are more likely to engage in unethical behavior (Barnes et al. 2011; Gino et al. 2011; Mead et al. 2009). To what extent, then, are future self-continuity and self-control distinct constructs, and to what extent does each of these constructs independently explain unethical behavior? To address these questions, in Study 4 we assessed the relationships among self-control, future self-continuity, and the propensity to cheat on a laboratory task. Results indicated a negative correlation between future self-continuity and the propensity to cheat, even when controlling for trait levels of self-control, as well as the other Big 5 personality traits.

Results from Studies 1 through 4 demonstrate a robust significant relationship between low future self-continuity and unethical choices, even when controlling for a host of potentially relevant personality variables. These studies, however, rely on correlational evidence and thus, cannot necessarily speak to the causal relationship between low future self-continuity and unethical behavior. Thus, in Study 5, we examined whether a direct experimental manipulation of future self-continuity would affect subsequent endorsement of unethical behavior (measured by the SINS II scale, as in Study 2). In the experimental condition, we instructed participants to write about how they would remain similar over time—specifically, in ten years' time. We compared their behavior to those in a control condition in which participants wrote about what the world would be like in ten years. Given that both the experimental and control condition involved thinking about the future, this comparison is a stringent test of our hypothesis that feeling similar to one's future self, rather than just the future per se, leads to disapproval of unethical behavior. In line with our main hypothesis, participants in the experimental condition were significantly less likely to advocate inappropriate negotiation strategies than were participants in the control condition.

REFERENCES

Barnes, Christopher M., John Schaubroeck, Megan Huth, and Sonia Ghumman (2011), "Lack of Sleep and Unethical Conduct," *Organizational Behavior and Human Decision Processes, 115* (July), 169-80.

Cwir, David, Priyanka B. Carr, Gregory M. Walton, and Steven J. Spencer (2011), Your Heart Makes My Heart Move: Cues of Social Connectedness Cause Shared Emotions and Physiological States Among Strangers," *Journal of Experimental Social Psychology,* 47 (January), 661-664.

Cohen, Taya R., Brian C. Gunia, Sun Young Kim-Jun, J. Keith Murnighan (2009), "Do Groups Lie More Than Individuals? Honesty and Deception as a Function of Strategic Self-Interest," *Journal of Experimental Social Psychology,* 45 (November), 1321-24.

Gino, Francesca, Maurice E. Schweitzer, Nicole L. Mead, and Dan Ariely (2011), "Unable to Resist Temptation: How Self-Control Depletion Promotes Unethical Behavior," *Organizational Behavior and Human Decision Processes,* 115 (July), 191-203.

Gneezy, Uri (2005), "Deception: The Role of Consequences," *American Economic Review,* 95 (1), 384-94.

Mead, Nicole L., Roy R. Baumeister, Francesca Gino, Maurice E. Schweitzer, and Dan Ariely (2009), "Too Tired to Tell the Truth: Self-Control Resource Depletion and Dishonesty," *Journal of Experimental Social Psychology,* 45 (3), 594-97.

The Genetic Contribution to Preference Consistency in Moral Judgments

EXTENDED ABSTRACT

Human behavior is guided not only by self-interest but also by social motivations as manifested in our moral intuitions and capacity for moral reasoning. While morality may be universal, many social and political controversies in which harm is inevitable invoke a conflict between individual rights and the greater good, and it is known that there is heterogeneity in how such tradeoffs are resolved. For example, a focus on the cost-benefit analysis of the ends of an action and the goal to promote the greater good is more likely to result in utilitarian moral judgments. Putting more weight on the means rather than the ends of an action and striving to respect the inherent rights of all individuals is more likely to result in deontological moral judgments. Interestingly, however, individuals do not always show consistent preferences for one goal over the other. That is, they sometimes display inconsistent patterns of moral judgment (or "preference reversals"), and little is known about why some individuals' ethical convictions appear more stringent than others'.

The prototypical example-pair for a preference reversal in moral judgments are the trolley and footbridge dilemma. In the trolley dilemma, a runaway trolley is headed for five people, who will be killed if it proceeds on its present track. The only way to save them is to hit a switch that will turn the trolley onto an alternate set of tracks where it will kill one person instead. The question is whether it is morally right to sacrifice one person to save five others by hitting the switch. Most people faced with this dilemma say yes, it is morally right. That is, they give a utilitarian answer. In the similar footbridge dilemma, the runaway trolley again threatens to kill five people. In this scenario, however, the only way to save the five people is to push a stranger that is standing on a footbridge onto the tracks below. The stranger will die if this is done, but his body will stop the trolley from reaching the others. The question in this dilemma is whether it is morally right to sacrifice one person to save five others by pushing the stranger. Most people in this dilemma say no, it is not morally right.

The reason for these different outcomes has been suggested to lie in the extent to which a moral dilemma engages automatic emotional processing versus deliberate cognitive processing (Greene et al. 2001). What is not sufficiently understood, however, are the individual differences underlying the degree to which individuals exhibit stable preferences in moral judgments and the sources of that variation. In particular, individuals can either exhibit consistency across the trolley and footbridge dilemmas or appear sensitive to the differences in those dilemmas' emotional content and switch between utilitarian and deontological responses, exhibiting a preference reversal. Based on a classic twin study-design with Swedish twins (the largest twin-registry in the world) this paper shows that almost 40% of the individual differences can be explained by genetic variation. In addition, recent studies suggest that gender, religiosity, and cognitive reflection play a role in explaining individual-level variation in type of moral judgments (Banerjee, Heubner, and Hauser 2010; Paxton, Ungar, and Greene 2011); and indeed we find that women and people low on cognitive reflection are more likely to give consistent responses (Lee, Amir, Ariely 2009). Thus, we also examine whether there is a shared genetic architecture between those factors and the tendency to make consistent moral judgments but find no statistical evidence for that.

The findings reported in this paper contribute to our understanding of individual differences in moral judgments. While the heritable variation of a trait should not be considered rigid across age and environmental conditions, similar to uncovering the forces of more economic behavioral anomalies such as loss aversion or procrastination (Cesarini, Johannesson, Magnusson, and Wallace 2011), the knowledge of the forces that generate perhaps undesirable patterns in the consistency of moral judgments may provide cues for policy on how to reduce them. Furthermore, our findings might motivate the search for reliable biological predictors of these individual differences such as genetic markers or hormone levels. For example, genetic variation in candidate genes that has shown to account for phenotypic variation in related behaviors could be tested for association to the consistency of moral judgments. This, in turn, may shed light on deeper biological processes (e.g., particular hormone regulations and other neurological processes). In addition, our findings about the consistency in moral judgments do not seem to generalize to consistency in any types of judgments. In particular, the survey asked respondents two questions to capture the fungibility of money across different frames. While the monetary outcomes described in the two scenarios are objectively the same, people tend to give inconsistent answers due to psychological accounting (Tversky and Kahneman 1981). Interestingly, we found no significant correlation between the consistency in those monetary judgments and the consistency in the moral judgments. Together our results underline the importance of genetic differences as a source of variation in the stability of preferences in moral judgments.

REFERENCES

Banerjee, Konika, Bryce Huebner, and Marc Hauser (2010), "Intuitive Moral Judgments are Robust Across Variation in Gender, Education, Politics and Religion: A Large-Scale Web-based Study," *Journal of Cognition and Culture*, 10 (3-4), 253–281.

Cesarini, David, Magnus Johannesson, Patrik KE Magnusson, and Bjorn Wallace (2012), "The Behavioral Genetics of Bhavioral Anomalies, *Management Science*, 58 (1), 21-34.

Greene, Joshua D., R. Brian Sommerville, Leigh E. Nystrom, John M. Darley, and Jonathan D. Cohen (2001), "An fMRI Investigation of Emotional Engagement in Moral Judgment," *Science*, 293 (5537), 2105–2108.

Lee, Leonard, Om Amir, and Dan Ariely (2009), "In Search of Homo Economicus: Cognitive Noise and the Role of Emotion in Preference Consistency," *Journal of Consumer Research*, 36 (August), 173–187.

Paxton, Joseph M., Leo Ungar, and Joshua D. Greene (2011), "Reflection and Reasoning in Moral Judgment," *Cognitive Science*, 36 (1), 163-177.

Tversky, Amos and Daniel Kahneman (1981), "The Framing of Decisions and the Psychology of Choice," *Science*, 211, 453–458.

Making Places: Sensemaking and Sensegiving in Domestic, Communal and Retail Settings

Chairs: Zeynep Arsel, Concordia University, Canada
Alain Debenedetti, Université Paris Est, IRG, France
Philippe Mérigot, INSEEC, France

Paper #1: The Value of Atmosphere

Jeppe Trolle Linnet, University of Southern Denmark, Denmark

Paper #2: The Atmosphere of Cosmopolitanism: Mono- or Multi-cultural?

Hanne Pico Larsen, Columbia University, USA
Jonathan Bean, Parsons the New School for Design, USA

Paper #3: The Dynamics and Continuity of Place Attachment: Cues from a Parisian Wine Bar

Zeynep Arsel, Concordia University, Canada
Alain Debenedetti, Université Paris Est, IRG, France
Philippe Mérigot, INSEEC, France

Paper #4: Creating Home and Community in Public Spaces: Vestaval in Tailgating

John F. Sherry, Jr., Mendoza College of Business, USA
Tonya Williams Bradford, Mendoza College of Business, USA

SESSION OVERVIEW

Physical spaces become places when we ascribe meanings to them (Williams et al 1992). Following Sherry's (2000) call to researchers to further investigate the issue, we propose to bring together a session that explores how a sense of place is constructed. The ways consumers attach meanings to their environment has primarily been studied in branded servicescapes such as malls (Haytko and Baker 2004; Maclaran and Brown 2005; Sandikci and Holt 1998) or flagship stores (Borghini et al. 2009; Kozinets et al. 2002), or extraordinary retail spectacles (Hollenbeck, Peters, and Zinkhan 2008; Kozinets et al. 2004). Yet, we argue that these studies focus more on how consumers interact with these settings than the act of place making. In other words the ways spaces become places, via sensemaking by marketers and sensegiving by consumers, has been relatively understudied. We suggest that consumer researchers need to better explore these processes.

Our session aims to contribute to consumer research by looking at how marketplace practices imprint a setting with a sense of place. Ranging from the experience of atmosphere in homes Linnet), to the establishment of a sense of place in servicescapes (Linnet; Larsen and Bean; Arsel, Debenedetti, and Mérigot), or constructing interiority via outdoor rituals (Sherry and Bradford), all four presentations in the session aim to unpack how places are constructed in marketplace and how consumers make sense of these places. All presentations also deal with the stability and dynamics of sensegiving and sensemaking activities in the marketplace. Whether a sense of place is built with a specific cosmopolitan ideology in mind (Larsen and Bean), or is imbued with a culturally specific sense of atmosphere (Linnet), or interrupted with servicescape discontinuities (Arsel, Debenedetti, and Mérigot), or even just temporally constituted through encampments (Sherry and Bradford), places are dynamic entities that are contextualized into a network of marketplace activities.

Linnet will start the session with a broader discussion of interiority in the marketplace and how marketplace sensemaking enables the subjective experience of *hygge*—the Danish equivalent of cosiness. Larsen and Bean will follow up this with their study of the commercial emplacement of cosmopolitanism in two New York restaurants. Arsel, Debenedetti and Mérigot will then discuss interruption and change by their work on a defunct Parisian restaurant

and its two spatially, symbolically and socially connected spinoffs. Finally, Sherry and Bradford will discuss the case of a transient place through their analysis of tailgating.

This session will appeal to a broad range of ACR members. The presentations should attract those scholars that are interested in culturally grounded and interpretivist work in general. However, we also aim to attract an interdisciplinary set of researchers investigating retail and retail atmospherics, rituals, domestic consumption, and food. The session also aims to contribute to the conference mission of *appreciating diversity* in multiple ways. First of all, we explore the diversity in the ways the sense of place can be constructed, emphasizing the role of mundane marketplace experiences: rituals, strategic emplacements, atmospherics, and social connections. Second, our researchers investigate a diverse range of cultural and geographical contexts: Small college towns, metropolitan cities, USA, Denmark, and France. Third we incorporate a diverse range of scholars: consumer researchers, sociologists, anthropologists and design scholars. Fourth, we study places where diverse people gather and share experiences.

All four projects are at the advanced stage, with complete data sets and substantial theoretical development. However, none of the papers have been accepted for publication elsewhere.

The Value of Atmosphere

EXTENDED ABSTRACT

Providing consumers with a sense of atmosphere is regarded as a competitive advantage in marketing. An added value that distinguishes, in the experience of consumers, a provider from competitors, even if products or services are in themselves quite similar. Atmosphere is seen as a subjective consumer experience that arises through a network-effect among a wide range of factors: Sensory, interactional and symbolic (Kotler 1973). In these two ways, atmosphere as it was first described in marketing research bears a close resemblance to another concept that has later received a great deal of attention in attempts to analyze and control the complex field of factors that constitute consumer experience: The brand. In spite of these conceptual similarities, at the level of everyday experience atmosphere differs from brand in being inherently site-bound.

The value of atmosphere is undeniable, but seems to figure in marketing literature on atmosphere as a commonplace observation in need of no further explanation; a black box assumption unopened by theory. Yet the constitution of perceived atmosphere is, from a theoretical viewpoint, a contested issue that invites very different and mutually contradictory explanations which ultimately rest on different ontological assumptions about how man relates to his surrounding world. Can material settings be seen as having inherent qualities that afford a certain experience, or should the factors that constitute the latter be sought in human subjectivity? On the side of subjectivity, should we look to culture and social group for an explanation, or to the human species´ sensory apparatus and neurological wiring? This paper brings those discussions into the arena of consumer research, asking *why* the experience of atmosphere is valuable. Suggesting an answer demands connecting atmosphere to what we know both about human faculties of sensory appreciation, ways of cultural interpretation, and existential needs. The paper presents empirical examples of how atmosphere comes about, drawn from several years of ethnographic research into the Danish cultural phenomenon of *hygge*, a form of atmosphere that will be referred to here as simply coziness.

The perception of atmosphere arises through a subtle interaction between subject and object (Böhme 1992). In a consumption perspective "subject" refer to those subjective psychological and cultural factors that prime the consumer for seeking, perceiving and appreciating a certain type of atmosphere. "Object" refers to those material and symbolic conditions that impinges upon the consumer's experience of a specific site, mainly those experienced there, which marketers try to control, although memories or anticipations of factors not immediately present (e.g. a stressful working day) can also exert influence. This perspective resonates with Kotler's (1973) classic on the subject. Using the subject – object distinction, this paper presents empirical examples of how atmosphere arises in both homes and commercial venues like 3rd places and retail sites. The analytical goal is to isolate certain principles, across these different realms, for the creation of atmosphere, hereby shedding light on the issue of *why* the experience of atmosphere is valuable.

Based on empirical findings the discussion revolves around two main principles: Interiority and authenticity. Interiority concerns the experience of being sheltered, of being allowed to turn one's back on discipline, sharing the here and now with others co-present (McCarthy 2005). It has to do with concrete arrangements of spaces, light, sounds etc. as well as symbols that communicate to people what this scene is about, what it allows and what kind of behavior it suggests. Authenticity concerns the singularity and rootedness of products or services that defies serial production and purely economic transactions. The paper argues that atmosphere essentially denotes the experience of being present at a site, through an awareness of its boundaries and of balanced interactions across those boundaries with the social and material world that surrounds the site. Such aspects are characteristic of the concept of interiority, of which atmosphere can be seen as an example, and which is useful in conceptualizing the fact that while atmosphere constitutes an inward-turning dynamic, it also relies upon a subjective awareness of spatial, temporal and symbolic contrasts to external realms, at least when we consider pleasurable forms of atmosphere like coziness. The subjective awareness of a spatial, temporal or symbolic contrast to the outside world facilitates the experience of pausing in a pleasurable, safe and invigorating environment. Authenticity is part and parcel of this dynamic since it further effects a localization of the experience, a rooting in the biographies of the site and the people present, including owners and those delivering the service.

The value of atmosphere then is predicated upon the symbolic needs of modern men and women who seek a temporary refuge from the control and discipline of work and gym, as well as the encounter with authenticity. However it also speaks to the preference of our neurological system for spaces that offer symbols of prospect and refuge, and amounts of visual information that can be decoded with a speed that pleases the brain, as neuro-architectural research shows (Rostrup 2011).

In the final instance of the interpretation offered in this paper, the value that is created for the subject (e.g. a consumer) of atmosphere is that in social and cultural terms it facilitates a focus on the here and now. This experience is shared with other people and relies for its effect upon their co-presence, but to a balanced extent, or else the atmosphere becomes claustrophobic. This interpretation may suggest what propels consumers to seek 3rd place sociality in places like cafés as a repetitive, ritual consumption act e.g. on Friday afternoon. The atmospheric immersion into a here and now is effective as a marker of transition, e.g. from the working week to the weekend.

Atmospheric establishments therefore afford the successful execution of certain consumer rituals (Rook 1985).

The Atmosphere of Cosmopolitanism: Mono- or Multi-cultural?

EXTENDED ABSTRACT

In this paper we analyze two new restaurants in New York City: The Red Rooster, Harlem, and Aamanns Copenhagen, located in Tribeca. The Red Rooster, owned by celebrity chef Marcus Samuelsson, is post-national, while Aamanns, backed by Sanne Ytting, a Dane residing in New York, strongly references Denmark. These restaurants were chosen for their opposing approach to cosmopolitanism. Both are trying to transcend the category of mere eateries by positioning their spaces as "community centers." We develop the concept of consumer-friendly cosmopolitanism by referencing the way this type of enterprise unproblematically serves up ideas of culture, ethnicity, and heritage. Through interviews, participant observation, and visual analysis of these two spaces, we develop the idea that cosmopolitanism can be expressed in the commercial sphere in at least two ways: either through mono- or multi-culturalism.

Restaurants are a constituent part of the genre of servicescapes (Bittner 1992, Sherry 1998) and are loaded with meanings useful to the study of place (Sherry 2000). They are valuable sites for research because they function as the nexus for sociality. As Kirschenblatt-Gimblett notes, "entire scenes form around a particular food… or beverage…. These scenes are distinguished by their architecture, décor, ambience, social style, equipage, schedule, music, fashion, and cuisine, and by the close attention paid to the details of the provisioning, preparation, presentation, and consumption of the defining food or drink" (2007: 78). Furthermore, in the US, food often becomes the medium used to engage with one's cultural roots or those of others while providing a way to gloss over differences. This mode of ethnicity is connected with middleclass North America, a segment of society to whom engagement with ethnic identity tends to be voluntary and associated with positive connotations (Alba 1990, Waters 1990). By disconnecting ethnicity from discrimination, it becomes a mode of enjoyment for the privileged (Larsen and Österlund-Pötzsch forthcoming). In addition to these ideas, the concept of American Plus is a useful way to underline the element of flexibility in the context in which this ethnic identity is performed. American Plus includes all the advantages (and disadvantages) of American identity, plus the potential advantages presented by the ethnic identity. This particular approach to ethnic identity emphasizes the aspect of choice and suppresses many problematic aspects connected with ethnicity. (Österlund-Pötzsch 2003).

We build on the idea of American Plus to suggest that restaurants such as the two we study are primary spaces in which people partake in consumable cosmopolitanism. Cosmopolitanism, as defined by Hannertz, is "a stance towards diversity itself, toward the coexistence of cultures in the individual experience… cosmopolitanism is first of all an orientation, a willingness to engage with the Other. It is an intellectual and aesthetic stance of openness toward divergent cultural experiences, a search for contrasts rather than uniformity" (1990, 237). Whereas Thompson and Tambyah (1999) highlight the tension between cosmopolitan identity and local culture, our work illuminates the construction of a local culture designed to make cosmopolitians feel at home. Recent work builts on Hannertz's thesis and theoretical tools from actor-network theory to distinguish different kinds of cosmopolitanism and to better understand the role objects play in cosmopolitanism (Saito 2011).

In our case studies we detect two very different kinds of consumable cosmopolitanism, namely that of mono- and and multi-culturalism, which are differentiated by the consumption of only one other culture or by an assemblage of many others. Samuelsson's approach is multi-cultural. A business writer attributes Samuelsson's success to his multi-ethnic background, claiming that "Samuelsson's background hits on almost every point of cultural diversification researchers say helps open a person to unusual associations" (Johansson 2006). Upon the opening of the Red Rooster Harlem the New York Times reviewer nodded to the food but effused about the cosmopolitan scene:

> *The racial and ethnic variety in the vast bar and loft-like dining room are virtually unrivaled. The restaurant may not be the best to open in New York City this year (though the food is good). But it will surely be counted as among the most important. It is that rarest of cultural enterprises, one that supports not just the idea or promise of diversity, but diversity itself. (Sifton 2011)*

This review and other similar media representations of Samuelsson and his restaurant raise the question of how an atmosphere catering to a cosmopolitan audience is consciously constructed. Samuelsson weaves his own identity and multi-ethnic background into the environment of the restaurant, which includes a bar made of three colors of wood meant to denote skin color, a series of curated, but anonymous vintage photos of multicultural families, and wallpaper custom-printed with family recipes illustrating his culinary heritage.

In contrast, Sanne Ytting, the Danish entrepreneur opening a franchise of Aamanns Copenhagen in New York, has chosen to include only the Danish reference. In her mono-cultural project everything from food to utensils needs to be Danish. The chef explained the decision to stick with *rugbrød*, the Danish word for the restaurant's signature dish, because he thinks something gets lost in the translation to "open faced sandwiches," and stands behind this decision to keep an "unpronounceable word unpronounceable" (Eater 2011). The all-white interior of Aamanns, designed by a Danish designer living in Denmark, is filled with potent symbols of Danish culture that have been provided by leading Danish design interests, including Anne Black ceramics, Bang and Olufsen speakers, and Arne Jacobsen chairs (Øllgaard 2001).

These two examples illuminate two different kinds of cosmopolitanism. At Aamanns established ideas of Danishness are being retold through place and the composition of this particular consumer narrative is kept tight. The Red Rooster reflects only Samuelsson's ideas about multiculturalism, wheras Ytting's role is akin to a curator organizing an exhibition of all things Danish. One is expansive and multicultural. It draws others in and refigures them into a new and coherent total experience. The other is exclusive and monocultural. It draws only one kind of other in and re-configures an existing category of atmosphere in a new place. This work contributes to knowledge on the relationship between cosmopolitanism and consumption within the field of consumer research.

The Dynamics and Continuity of Place Attachment: Cues from a Parisian Wine Bar

EXTENDED ABSTRACT

Place attachment corresponds to the emotional aspect of a sense of place (Hummon 1992; Jorgensen and Stedman 2001) which includes meaning systems, experiences, and social interactions with a spatial setting. Existing research on place attachment mainly focuses on either residential settings (e.g. Fried 1963) or outdoor recreation places (e.g. Williams and al. 1992) but not commercial spaces. While research on retail frequently touch on the notion of place, these scholars either treat one dimension of retailscapes, such as the social (e.g. Price and Arnould 1999; Rosenbaum et al. 2007), as the central point of investigation, or consider place holistically (e.g. Maclaran and Brown 2005) without explicating how these different elements come together. Building on Altman and Low (1992) who suggest that a combination of different elements contributes to establishing an emotional sense of place, we argue that it is important for researchers to better explicate the dynamics between these elements.

Furthermore, existing consumer research hasn't looked at the continuity of attachment through time and space. Kleine and Baker (2004) show the similarities between attachment to possessions and place attachment, yet acknowledge that material possessions are portable whereas places are immovable due to the unique characteristics of spatial settings. Places are embedded in a geographical landscape: moving an establishment disconnects it from its original spatial context. Yet, in the context of multi-outlet stores—where the original setting may contain specific meanings (for example brand history and legacy)—successful continuity of a brand across new branches seems to prove that place attachment could be transferred to some extent. Understanding the elements of continuity is also crucial to manage transitions such as moves, transfers of ownership, or dissolutions that are recurrent in small business servicescapes. We argue that constraining place to one specific dimension, considering it only as a non-separable entity, or ignoring the changes in these elements through time and space oversimplify the complex retail dynamics and the attachment processes.

With this paper, we aim to unpack two issues: 1. What are the servicescape elements that contribute to the attachment that consumers develop towards a commercial setting? 2. To what extent this attachment is maintained in case any of these elements change?

We address these questions using a longitudinal ethnographic approach, based on the investigation of one defunct Parisian wine bar—Le Coin de Verre—and the two interrelated institutions that emerged after the bar's closure. The first one, Café Epicerie, has only kept the physical envelope of the original wine bar even though the new owners claim the legacy of Le Coin de Verre on their website. The location, as well as the path that leads to the setting (address and phone number), remain the same, but the place has been physically (through rebuilding, decoration) and socially (managers, employees, new customer profile) changed. Furthermore symbolic activities and rituals (e.g. ringing a bell to get access to the setting) as well as differentiating offerings (e.g. recipes) that once made the place special are no longer present. The second spinoff is Coin de Table, which opened one block away from original setting. It is managed by a former waitress of Le Coin de Verre and claims the heritage of the original setting through the consultancy and recurrent presence of former manager of the original place. In contrast to Le Café Epicerie, this setting has tried to keep the spirit of Le Coin de Verre through atmosphere, social elements and activities, while many physical elements changed.

We conducted 20 interviews with customers of Le Coin de Verre, some of which now frequent the spinoff establishments. We also conducted three interviews with managers of these institutions. The interview data amounts to a total of 26 hours of recordings. In addition, we made extended participant observation recording diaries, fieldnotes and photos. These were supplemented by secondary data from gastronomy chronicles in newspapers and customer reviews gathered from the Internet.

In our findings, we discuss three main servicescape dimensions that establish place attachment: social, physical and activity-based. Social elements are the staff, other customers, and the relationships consumers build within these spaces. Physical elements relate to the aesthetics of the place as well as the spatial belongingness such as terroir and locale. We also argue the physical trajectory, the geographic path that a consumer takes to reach the place is relevant. Lastly, activity based elements include product and service assortment, and specific procedures—rituals, scripts and norms—that are embedded in these activities.

Our next set of findings concerns the transfer and continuity of place attachment. Our informants, who were originally attached to Le Coin de Verre, indicate a sense of detachment from Café Epicerie, claiming that "the soul has been lost" because of many reasons: the spatial environment has been altered through rebuilding, and the commercial proposal is quite different from Le Coin de Verre where only artisanal products were sold. Most importantly, the social relationship has been altered and customers of the original setting lost their social connections. Conversely, in Coin de Table, even though the spatial setting is not be the same (new locale, new trajectory to reach the place, new decor), some key differentiating elements have been kept: the social atmosphere (the waitress, the bell, the special welcome, the lack of table settings); the service concept and the commercial proposal are also similar to those of Le Coin de Verre. As a result, loyal Coin de Verre customers feel like they have found their home again.

Preserving the emotional attachment to a service establishment goes beyond claiming the same heritage, and needs to be orchestrated using multiple servicescape dimensions. Even though physical elements are easier to preserve (location, trajectories, or elements like the fireplace in the case of Café Epicerie), this does not result in the same sense of place. On the contrary, while places are theoretically impossible to move, when spatial elements are altered but social elements and activities are kept, consumers experience the same sense of place in a different setting. Thus we argue that while it is impossible to completely replicate places due to their ontology, place attachment can be preserved with careful management of servicescapes.

Creating Home and Community in Public Spaces: Vestaval in Tailgating

EXTENDED ABSTRACT

Consumption encampments are ephemeral phenomena of varying duration and composition, whose closest commercial analogs are periodic markets such as swap meets (Belk, Sherry, and Wallendorf 1988; Sherry 1990), farmers' markets (McGrath, Sherry, and Heisley 1993), and art fairs. Consumption encampments have been the focus of previous inquiry into dwelling sites such as Wrigley Field (Holt 1995), Burning Man (Kozinets 2002), and Mountain Man Rendezvouses (Belk and Costa 1998). Tailgates are consumption encampments that occur in conjunction with sporting events or music concerts, and provide a stage for the convergence of such American cynosures as automobility, overindulgence and voluntary association. Tailgates, with one notable exception (St. John 2005), have gone largely unexamined, and are the context we explore to explain public enactments of consumer chorography.

Consumption encampments share a "dwelling" aspect that is different from the simpler "visiting" aspect attaching to most of their commercial cousins. Themed flagship brandstores (Diamond et al. 2009), coffee shops (Simon 2009) and brandfests (McAlexander and Schouten 1998; McAlexander, Schouten, and Koenig 2002) have occasionally sought to tap the dwelling ethos. However, a sense of dwelling is largely confined to populist constructions unfolding at a site of consumption, whether private or public, where managerial intention may guide rather than direct consumer agency. In a very tangible sense, in the duration of a tailgate, a city is raised (and ultimately razed), replete with ersatz homes, a grid of streets with ingenious address coordinates, playing fields, and channels of information exchange.

Place making at the tailgate begins with the deployment of material culture. The stuff of tailgating is distributed in a way that defines macro and micro zones of consumption. Discrete places are constructed for the performance of particular activities and the enactment of the genres of tailgating. Generally speaking, we find three kinds of place established by tailgaters in their deployment of material objects: personal, tribal, and commercial. The most common and deeply appreciated place is close and personal. Nomads establish a minimalist home on the grounds of the larger encampment. This is a domestic place, configured like its counterparts in the everyday world. Within this place, we can discern kitchens, dining rooms, family rooms, and living rooms. Bars and patios are also in evidence. Yards are a figurative presence, detectable n the play spaces between tailgates. It is as if the walls of the domicile have been removed, leaving many of the household's everyday practices exposed to the surrounding world. This public performance of domesticity is a hallmark of the tailgate.

The structure and dynamics of tailgating reveal an interesting interaction between the hestial and hermetic dimensions of experience (Sherry 2001; Sherry et al. 2001) . The quintessentially domestic activities of the household are put on public display, giving the polity a collective opportunity to examine the interior world of the household, even as that display contributes to the emergence of that polity in real time. A community of tailgaters arises through the many public performances of domestic practice which encourage interaction within and across individual tailgates. This performance in plain sight of thousands of individual acts of hospitality, the public enactment of generosity (as well as such dark side behaviors as invidious comparison and theft), and the forging of community through the sacred-celebratory vehicle of the party (Kozinets 2003) brings hestial and hermetic into intimate association. As household dramas unfold in the agora of lots and fields, against the backdrop of the gridiron drama staged in the agon of the stadium, the ethos of tailgating is manifested. On the one hand, even if males do not completely appropriate quintessentially female space, their vigorous participation is blessed by women. On the other, to the extent that tailgating is construed as "extreme picnicking" or "camping lite," women are welcomed onto the masculine terrain of living rough. Either way, males are domesticated, and publicly valorize their taming.

Tailgating is a ritual act of eversion that turns the household inside out, putting its interior workings on public display. While it shares elements of the carnivalesque, carnival is more properly a ritual act of inversion, which turns social conventions upside down. Similarly, tailgating incorporates elements of the festal, but festival is more clearly a ritual act of obversion, which reveals a ludic dimension to quotidian life, turning the outside in. Finally, tailgating enjoys some contiguity with the spectacular, but spectacle is better considered a ritual of subversion, which saps authentic participatory agency in the service of political pacification, and structures social relations hegemonically, right-side up. Carnival, festival and spectacle are recognized social forms to which we would add "vestaval," (Vesta + levāre), after the goddess of the hearth. To the literature, we contribute a description of how a vestaval celebrates household values, dramatizing them in hermetic space, publicly proclaiming the importance of a shared sense of domesticity to the life of a culture. In terms of the semiotic square, the vestaval is in a relation of contradiction to spectacle, of contrariety to carnival, and complementary to festival.

The Paradox of Memory

Chair: Kathryn LaTour, Cornell University, USA

Paper #1: Value of Memories

Patrick Vargas, University of Illinois, USA

Paper #2: Nostalgic Charity Appeals: Moderating Effect of Mood, Beneficiary, and Childhood Icons

Kathryn LaTour, Cornell University, USA

Altaf Merchant, University of Washington, USA

John B. Ford, Old Dominion University, USA

Michael S. LaTour, Cornell University, USA

Paper #3: Memories Jogging at High Intensity: The Effect of Recollecting Past Hedonic Experiences on their Retrospective Evaluations

Rajesh Bhargave, University of Texas, USA

Antonia Mantonakis, Brock University, Canada

Paper #4: Remembering the Best of Times or the Worst of Times? The Moderating Role of Brand Commitment on False Product Experience Memories

Nicole Votolato Montgomery, College of William and Mary, USA

Priyali Rajagopal, Southern Methodist University, USA

SESSION OVERVIEW

On one hand most Americans believe that "memory works like a video camera" (Simons & Chabris, 2011, p. 1) laying down representations of events that are accurate and accessible. Consumers value these memories enormously, and yet we know as consumer researchers that these memories to be highly malleable and subject to distortion. Broadly this session will be about this memory paradox. This session will contribute to the diversity call of the conference through these different views of memory and the role memory plays in consumer decision making. Marketers need to understand why consumers value memories if they want to build on them with their communication efforts as well as to what degree they can frame memories and at what point should they expect "push back" if their influence attempts become too apparent.

In my own research I have studied the two extremes of this paradox-- how early childhood memories frame current preferences (Braun-LaTour, LaTour and Zinkhan 2007), and the fragility of these memories (Braun, Ellis and Loftus 2001). This session is designed to dig deeper into that memory paradox. While these papers were selected to highlight one side over the other (value vs. distortion), the paradox is implicit in all the work because if we didn't value the memories, then having them distorted wouldn't be important, nor would we value the memories as much if we thought they would never be forgotten.

The session will start off with Patrick Vargas highlighting the extreme value consumers place on their memory experiences. He will discuss research he has done asking people to provide dollar values to certain memories and the astronomical numbers they attach to even negative experiences. Then Altaf Merchant will discuss some research we have done on nostalgic advertising and developing a nostalgic advertising scale. These studies look at how marketers can bank on the value of consumer memories but there are aspects, like icons, that they shouldn't messed with when trying to appeal to the past, such as PBS' move to promoting Cookie Monster as Veggie Monster.

Then we move to the malleability side of things—Rajesh Bhargave will present his work looking at under what conditions memories are more positively recalled. This research identifies a basic factor that can distort memories—the act of recollecting an episode provides information on how memorable the experience was, which in turn can influence evaluations. Thus, while people value memories and seek to recollect past events, they may distort these memories each time they recall them in great detail.

Nicole Votolato Montgomery will end by presenting her paper on the moderating role of brand commitment on false product experience memories. Hence, while the first two papers focus on the value attached to memories by consumers, the latter two papers focus on the malleability of these memories. The paper on brand commitment and false memories further highlights this paradox by demonstrating that consumers can be motivated through brand commitment to distort their memories.

On The Often Outrageous Value of Memories

EXTENDED ABSTRACT

Try to recall your first kiss, or the time you bought your first car and drove it home. Now imagine that I am both willing and able to buy those memories from you. If you agree to sell me those specific, episodic memories those events will no longer exist in your mind; however, you will have cash money that I pay you, and you can do whatever you like with the cash. If a memory is particularly valuable to you, you would place a high price on it; if it is not valuable to you, you would place a low price on it. If it is a painful memory (e.g., your first heartbreak) perhaps you would even be willing to pay me to extract that memory.

People asked to value their memories via this thought experiment placed astronomically high dollar values on their memories. In one study people averaged $1x1036 per memory. To put this into perspective, the wealthiest man in the world, Carlos Slim Helú, is estimated to be worth $74 billion, or 74x109. The number of atoms in the observable universe is estimated at 1080. Values in the neighborhood of $1036 are most likely symbolic, to be interpreted as "this memory is exceptionally important to me."

In a second study I asked people to constrain themselves, and I reminded them of Carlos Slim's net worth. Even then, the mean dollar values for individual memories were around $5 million. By eliminating some of the ultra-high values I still ended up with mean values ranging from $11,000 to $1.9 million per memory.

From these two simple studies I arrived at several tentative conclusions. First, people value their memories a lot. Second, there is remarkable variability in the extent to which people value their memories. The values placed on "memory of first heartbreak," for example, ranged from $-1 million (i.e., willingness to pay me a million to remove the memory) to $100 million. Third, for negative memories, such as first heartbreak, there was a nearly symmetrical distribution of values around zero, suggesting that some people really value negative life events and others would much rather get rid of negative memories.

This is an investigation of the extent to which, and reasons why, people feel that their memories of specific life events are valuable. What makes some memories more valuable than others? Inspired by Katz's (1960) work on attitude functions, I propose several possible reasons why memories are so valuable. First, the commonly held illusion that our memories are accurate, like a video recorder (Simons & Chabris, 2011), probably accounts for some of the value people place on their memories. Memory is not like a video camera, it is

Advances in Consumer Research
Volume 40, ©2012

not accurate. Memory is reconstructive, and easily manipulated; our memories for life events are most likely full of large errors (Braun, Ellis & Loftus, 2002; Talarico & Rubin, 2003). If people learn that their memories are inaccurate, they should place lower values on them. People are not rational, and this prediction – that people would devalue their memories if they learned about the frailty of human memory – requires further empirical testing.

Second, the valence of the memory matters; presumably happy memories would be worth more, on average, than aversive memories. So memories might be valuable to the extent that they help us to regulate our emotions. One surprising example of the importance of memory for emotion regulation is in a study of amnesiac patients v. "normal" controls. Both groups were shown a sad movie. Amnesiacs showed poorer recall of the film than controls; however amnesiacs showed greater persistence of sad feelings than controls because only the "normal" group was able to recall the sad film and attribute their sadness to the film (Feinstein, Duff, & Tranel, 2010).

Third, some negative memoires might be valuable, if the memory represents some kind of lesson learned. If I no longer had the memory of getting food poisoning, I wouldn't know to avoid eating Maryland crabs that had been sitting out in the sun all afternoon. Memories might be valuable because they serve a knowledge function (Katz, 1960; Shavitt, 1990).

Fourth, and perhaps most importantly, people may feel that losing a valuable memory might somehow fundamentally change them. Our intuition is that our memories make us who we are; with a different set of memories, or minus a few critical memories, you or I might be a very different person. So memories might be valuable because they serve an essential, existential function. Related to this idea, people's willingness to take enhancing drugs is inversely related to the extent to which that drug will affect a trait perceived as fundamental. For example, most everyone would benefit from being kinder, but only nine to ten percent of people would be willing to take a drug that improves kindness because kindness is perceived as a fundamental trait. On the other hand, 45-51 percent of people would be willing to take a drug that improves rote memory, because rote memory is not perceived as a fundamental trait (Riis, Simmons, & Goodwin, 2008). There may be other reasons we value memories, as well. This project will help us understand the psychology of self-perception and self-knowledge.

REFERENCES

Braun, K.A., Ellis, R., and Loftus, E.F. (2002). Make my memory: How advertising can change our memories of the past. *Psychology & Marketing*, 19, 1–23.

Feinstein, J. S., Duff, M. C., & Tranel, D. (2010). Sustained experience of emotion after loss of memory in patients with amnesia. *Proceedings of the National Academy of Sciences*, 1–6.

Katz, D. (1960). The functional approach to the study of attitudes. *Public Opinion Quarterly*, 24, 163-204

Riis, J., Simmons, J. P., & Goodwin, G. P. (2008). Preferences for Enhancement Pharmaceuticals: The Reluctance to Enhance Fundamental Traits. *Journal of Consumer Research*, 35(3), 495–508.

Shavitt, S. (1990). The role of attitude objects in attitude functions. *Journal of Experimental Social Psychology*, 26(2), 124–148.

Simons, D. J., & Chabris, C. F. (2011). What people believe about how memory works: A representative survey of the U.S. population. *PLoS ONE*, 6(8), e22757.

Talarico, J., & Rubin, D. (2003). Confidence, not consistency, characterizes flashbulb memories. *Psychological Science*, 14(5), 455.

Nostalgic Charity Appeals: Moderating Effect of Memory Processing, Beneficiary, and Childhood Icons

EXTENDED ABSTRACT

Individuals donated about $217.8 Billion to charity in 2011. This represented about three quarters of all philanthropic giving (Giving U.S.A., 2012). Charitable organizations have increasingly realized that their fundraising communications need to have a credible and engaging message. Appeals to donate are often designed to emotionally stir consumers, attempting to influence their donations (Basil, Ridgway & Basil, 2008; Dillard & Peck, 2000). Some of the emotions that have been studied in the context of appeals for charities are sadness, anger, fear and guilt. Recently, Merchant, Ford and Rose (2011) found that nostalgia could be one of the reasons why people donate to charity. Moreover, Ford and Merchant (2010) and Zhou, Wildschut, Sedikides, Shi and Feng (2011) posit that nostalgia based fundraising appeals promotes charitable giving.

Nostalgia has been found to influence preferences for certain products and services (Braun-LaTour, LaTour & Zinkhan, 2007). In a content analysis of a thousand U.S. television advertisements, Unger, McConocha and Faier (1991) found that nostalgia was used via theme, copy or music in ten percent of all of the U.S. advertisements analyzed. This reuniting of the individual with a longed-for past (Bassin, 1993) can be seen in the use of the songs of the 1960s and 1970s to evoke strong emotional connections with such products as automobiles, foods and beverages. It is a particularly promising mechanism for companies that claim a long and storied history since it is possible that multiple generations of consumers have past experiences that can be connected to happy periods in their lives which would potentially enhance their emotional orientation towards the company involved.

In the current inquiry we add to the emerging research (Ford & Merchant, 2010; Merchant et al., 2011; Zhou et al., 2011) on the influence of nostalgia on charitable donations, by examining three boundary conditions of this effect. First, we argue that the effect of nostalgic charity appeals is moderated by the consumer's memory processing. Next, we posit that they are more efficacious when consumers feel communal connections with the beneficiary of the charity. Lastly, we contend that nostalgic appeals work better when they evoke important consumer memories using childhood icons.

In the first study we employed a 2X2 experimental design among 201 consumers. Attitude towards the ad (Aad) was the dependent variable; memory processing (personal/generic) and type of charity appeal (nostalgic/non-nostalgic) were the independent variables. The findings reveal that nostalgic appeals for charity work especially well when the consumer is primed with generic childhood memories. It appears than when the consumer is primed for personal childhood memories, he/she is any way emotionally engaged and hence even non-nostalgic ads perform as well.

Belk (2010) postulates that when someone shares with family or the extended family, the act of sharing expands the sense of self for the individual; sustaining feelings of community with the receiver. Thus, past research has found that donors are more likely to donate to people with whom they can relate to and feel they have a communal relationship with (Small and Simonsohn, 2008). In study two we employed a 2X2 experimental design among 65 consumers. The dependent variable was Aad; the independent variables were communal connections with beneficiary of the donation (manipulated – high or low) and nostalgic memories evoked (measured-high or low). The findings reveal that when consumers feel that they have communal connections with the beneficiary of the charity, increasing nostalgic memories would result in higher attitudes towards the ad.

Lastly, in study three, we argue that nonprofits can depend on the consumer's nostalgic memories for raising donations but there are aspects, like icons, that they shouldn't messed with when trying to appeal to the past, such as PBS' move to promoting Cookie Monster as Veggie Monster. Here we employed a 2X2 experimental design among 67 consumers. The dependent variable was nostalgic memories evoked and the independent variables were ad character (manipulated – familiar or changed) and need to belong (measured-high or low) (Loveland, Smeesters and Mandel, 2010). The results from study three indicate that changing iconic characters of nonprofits may have an effect on how consumers process charitable appeals. This especially has an effect in the high need to belong consumers and tends to deflate the ability of the ad to evoke nostalgic memories.

In summary, we build on recent research on the influence of nostalgia on charitable donations by suggesting more nuances to these effects.

REFERENCES

Basil D., N. Ridgway & M. Basil, (2008), "Guilt and Giving: A Process Model of Empathy and Efficacy," *Psychology and Marketing*, 25(1), 1-23.

Bassin, D (1993), "Nostalgic Objects Of Our Affection: Mourning, Memory And Maternal Subjectivity," *Psychoanalytic Psychology*, 10 (3), 425-436.

Belk, R. (2010), "Sharing," *Journal of Consumer Research*, 36, 715-734.

Braun-LaTour, K., M. LaTour & G. Zinkhan (2007), "Using Childhood Memories to Gain Insight into Brand Meaning," *Journal of Marketing*, 71, 45-60.

Dillard, J. P., and E. Peck (2000), "Emotional Responses to Public Sector Announcements," *Communication Research*, 27 (4), 461-495.

Giving U.S.A. Giving USA Foundation Reports (accessed 14 February 2012), [available at http://www.givingusareports. org/)

Ford, J.B. & A. Merchant (2010), "Nostalgia Drives Donations: The Power of Charitable Appeals Based on Emotions and Intentions," *Journal of Advertising Research*, 50(4), 450-459.

Loveland, K.E., D.Smeesters, & N.Mandel (2010), "Still Preoccupied with 1995: The Need to Belong and Preference for Nostalgic Products," *Journal of Consumer Research*, 37(4), 393-408.

Merchant, A., J. B. Ford & G.Rose (2011), "How Personal Nostalgia Influences Giving to Charity," *Journal of Business Research,* 64(6), 610-16.

Small, D. & U Simonsohn (2008), "Friends of Victims: Personal Experience and Prosocial Behavior," *Journal of Consumer Research*, 35, 532-542.

Unger, L. S., D.M. McConocha & J.A. Faier (1991), "The Use of Nostalgia in Television Advertising: A Content Analysis," *Journalism Quarterly*, 68, 345-353.

Zhou, X., T. Wildschut, C. Sedikides, K. Shi & C. Feng (2012), "Nostalgia: The Gift That Keeps on Giving," *Journal of Consumer Research*, 39(1), 39-50.

Memorability and Retrospective Evaluations: The Social Function of Autobiographical Memory in Evaluations of Experiences

EXTENDED ABSTRACT

Consumers are often prompted to remember details from past hedonic experiences. A patron may recollect a dish she ate at a restaurant in order to write a recipe. Alternatively, she may remember such details to share a story with a friend. We suggest that such reminiscence can impact the episode's retrospective evaluations; if the event seems very memorable, it is evaluated at higher intensity. In our work, we also explore how the function of memory moderates the relationship between remembering the episode and its evaluations.

Recently evoked information can contaminate consumers' memories of past experiences through reconstructive processes. For instance, consumers incorporate information from post-experience advertising in their experiential memories (Braun, 1999). Imagery-evoking ads can also produce false memories, whereby consumers mistakenly believe that they have experienced the advertised brand (Rajagopal & Montgomery, 2011). These results suggest that consumers' memories are malleable, shaped by lay theories and inferences.

We argue that people may form their inferences about past experiences on memorability itself. When a past event is recalled, the act of reminiscence provides new information: the subjective experience of ease or difficulty of remembering the event (Schwarz et al, 1991). Given that more intense experiences generally produce more vivid memories (Talarcio, LaBar, & Rubin 2004), consumers may learn the positive association between memorability and intensity across various experiential domains. As such, we predict that consumers will infer that if they can vividly recall the sensory details of a past experience, it was more intense. Thus, this inference is based on a lay theory concerning how memory operates. Importantly, although intense experiences are typically more memorable, other factors can influence the ability to remember a past episode, thereby dissociating this relationship.

We further argue that this effect—inferring intensity from memorability—will be more pronounced when the memory is generated for social purposes—to communicate with others—and less pronounced for directive purposes—when using the past experience to guide one's own future behavior (Bluck et al., 2005). The ability to recall an episode with vivid sensory details is more diagnostic for social uses of memory than directive uses, because describing the event to others requires concrete information to ensure a smooth and fluent interaction (Schlosser & Shavitt, 1999). Indeed, one of Grice's (1975) conversational maxims is that speakers must be clear, avoiding obscurity—a principle served by retrieving specific sensory details when recalling a hedonic episode.

We tested these predictions in three studies. In study 1, student participants (N = 69) engaged in a blind taste test of a wine through a series of sips. After a filler task, participants were asked to think about serving the wine at a future social gathering. Next, as a between-subjects manipulation of ease-of-retrieval for sensory details, they were asked to recall and write about either two sensory aspects about the wine—an easy task, or six such aspects—a more difficult task. The study also had a control condition in which participants did not recall any sensory aspects. They were then asked how interested and likely they would be in serving the wine at a social gathering and how successful and memorable it would be with guests. As predicted, ratings of intensity were higher when few sensory aspects ($M = 5.64$) were recalled versus no ($M = 5.22$) or many sensory aspects (M

= 5.22). Participants in the few sensory aspects condition also valued the wine $3 per bottle higher than the other two conditions. Notably, recalling six aspects was perceived to be more difficult than recalling two sensory aspects, consistent with an ease-of-retrieval effect.

In study 2, mTurk participants (N = 133) were asked to retrieve a past autobiographical dining experience that took place between two weeks and two months ago. First, they wrote basic information about the experience: where they ate and who accompanied them on the meal. Next, they were asked to recall two, six, or no sensory aspects from the experience in a similar between-subjects manipulation of ease-of-retrieval as in study 1. They were then asked to rate the experience on its overall positivity, how much they enjoyed it, and how likely they would be to return to the restaurant. Ratings were higher in the few aspects condition (*M* = 6.32) than the many (*M* = 5.75) or no sensory aspects (*M* = 5.9) condition. Follow-up analyses revealed that the types of sensory aspects listed in the few and many conditions did not differ in their valence. However, writing more sensory aspects was perceived as more difficult.

In study 3, we examined the role of memory function. We propose that the emphasis on either social versus directive functions of autobiographical memory can differ incidentally according to how people perceive themselves in relation to others when recalling a past episode. Study 3 (N = 166 mTurk participants) primed whether participants would construe themselves as primarily independent from others or interdependent with others after writing about the target experience (Trafimow et al, 1991). Examining our key dependent measures of perceived intensity, we found a significant ease-of-retrieval X self-construal interaction ($p < .01$); greater memorability enhanced perceived intensity in the interdependent self-construal condition, but not the independent self-construal condition. Taken together, our work offers new insights on the role of memorability in consumers' evaluations and the functions of autobiographical memory.

REFERENCES

Bluck, S., Alea, N., Habermas, T., & Rubin, D. (2005). "A tale of three functions: The self-reported uses of autobiographical memory." *Social Cognition, 23(1)*: 91-117.

Braun, K.A. (1999). "Postexperience advertising effects on consumer memory." *Journal of Consumer Research, 25*, 319–334

Grice, P. (1975). "Logic and conversation". In Cole, P. and Morgan, J. (eds.) *Syntax and semantics, Vol 3*. New York: Academic Press.

Rajagopal, P. & Mongtomery, N.V. (2011). "I imagine, I experience, I like: The false experience effect." *Journal of Consumer Research, (38)*.

Schlosser, Ann and Sharon Shavitt (1999), "Effects of an Approaching Group Discussion on Product Responses," *Journal of Consumer Psychology*, 8 (4), 377–406.

Schwarz, N., Bless, H., Strack, F., Klumpp, G., Rittenauer-Schatke, H., & Simons, A. (1991). "Ease of retrieval as information: Another look at the availability heuristic." *Journal of Personality and Social Psychology, 61*:195–202.

Talarcio, J., LaBar, K., & Rubin, D. (2004), "Emotional intensity predicts autobiographical memory experience." *Memory and Cognition, 32(7)*:1118–1132.

Trafimow, D., Triandis, H.C., & Goto, S.G. (1991). "Some tests of the distinction between the private self and the collective self." *Journal of Personality and Social Psychology*, 60, 649-655.

Remembering the Best of Times or the Worst of Times? The Moderating Role of Brand Commitment on False Product Experience Memories

EXTENDED ABSTRACT

According to the reconstructive view of memory (Braun, 1999; Braun-LaTour et al, 2004), people may inadvertently recreate a recent experience (e.g., a visit to a favorite restaurant) by integrating information obtained from multiple sources, both internal (e.g., past experiences dining at the restaurant) and external (e.g. reviews of the restaurant, word of mouth from friends). Thus, consumers may erroneously recall entire experiences or details about experiences that did not occur. Such mistaken beliefs about an event are termed as *false memories (*Loftus 1997, 2003*)*.

We extend the literature on false memory by suggesting that consumers' commitment to a brand moderates their false memories about that brand. Specifically, we show that brand commitment can both increase as well decrease the incidence of false memories, depending on the valence of the experience. Thus, highly committed consumers are less susceptible to the creation of negative false memories, but are *more* susceptible to the creation of positive false memories about prior brand experience. This is because negative experiences are likely to be atypical for high commitment consumers, thus lowering the plausibility of a false negative experience for these consumers. On the other hand, we suggest that positive and negative experiences are likely to be equally typical and hence, equally plausible for low commitment consumers. Therefore, low commitment consumers will not differ in their susceptibility to positive versus negative false memories. We find these effects of brand commitment across two different communication routes: advertising (study 1) and word of mouth (studies 2 and 3). Exposure to vivid experiential information either through marketing communications like advertising or exposure to vicarious experiences appear to result in memory distortion.

In our first study we found that a significantly larger proportion of consumers who were highly committed to Pizza Hut (48.3%) reported having tried a fictitious brand variant (Pizza Hut "Naturals" pizza) than consumers who were not as committed to Pizza Hut (17.8%, $\chi^2(1) = 6.12$, $p < .05$). Further the highly committed consumers were also more confident in their false memories (3.97) than the low commitment consumers (2.36, $t (102)= 2.93, p < .05$). Thus, when the product experience was neutral/positive, highly committed consumers were more susceptible to the creation of false memories.

In our second study, we found that consumers who were not highly committed to Subway reported higher negative false memories (2.2 on a 4-point scale) after exposure to vivid, negative online experience reviews, as compared to exposure to vivid and positive online reviews (1.6, $t = 2.12$, $p < .05$). Thus, low commitment consumers' false memories varied with the valence of the reviews. On the other hand, consumers who were highly committed to Subway did not exhibit any significant difference in their incidence of false negative memories across exposure to negative (1.44) or positive reviews (1.77, t < 1). We also found that false memories impacted brand attitudes such that negative (positive) false memories lowered (increased) brand attitudes for the low commitment consumers, but not for the high commitment consumers. Thus, in addition to strategically using memories as a defense mechanism against vivid negative information, high commitment consumers are also unlikely to allow memories to change their favorable brand evaluations. Finally, a mediation analysis revealed that false memories mediated the effect of review valence on brand attitudes.

In our final study, we extend these findings from study 2 by documenting a similar pattern of results when the target brand varies across respondents (respondents selected the brand of athletic shoes they most preferred and were committed to) and a fictitious variant of the target brand is advertised (e.g., Nike Altra athletic shoes). Further, we examine the effect of commitment across several additional dependent measures including brand experience recall, the likelihood of other consumers' negative experiences with the brand variant, brand variant quality assessment and brand variant purchase intentions, and find similar results across all these measures.

We contribute to the false memory literature in several ways. First, we document a new moderator of false memory effects – brand commitment and show that brand commitment interacts with experience valence to affect the incidence of false memories. Second, we add to the emerging research on false memories in marketing (Lakshmanan and Krishnan 2009; Schlosser 2006) by exploring a previously unexamined route by which false beliefs about product experience may arise – word of mouth. Finally, we explore how the valence of presented information affects the nature of the false beliefs about past product experience and, hence, product evaluations.

We also contribute to the literature on brand commitment by demonstrating that memory can be used as a strategic defense by highly committed brand consumers. Previous research has shown that highly committed consumers refute negative information through the generation of counterarguments and limiting the spillover of negative information to unrelated attributes (e.g. Ahluwalia et al. 2001). Our research suggests that highly committed consumers may also indulge in memory distortion to reduce the effect of negative brand information.

REFERENCES

Ahluwalia, R., H. R. Unnava, & R.E. Burnkrant(2001)"The Moderating Role of Commitment on the Spillover Effect of Marketing Communications"*Journal of Marketing Research* 38, 458-471

Braun, Kathryn A. (1999), "Post-Experience Advertising Effects on Consumer Memory," *Journal of Consumer Research*, 25(March), 319-334.

Braun-LaTour, K. A., M. LaTour, J. E. Pickrell, & E. F. Loftus (2004), "How and When Advertising Can Influence Memory for Consumer Experience,"*Journal of Advertising*,33,7-25.

Lakshmanan, A. & S. H. Krishnan (2009), "How Does Imagery in Interactive Consumption Lead to False Memory? A Reconstructive Memory Perspective," *Journal of Consumer Psychology*, 19(3), 451-62.

Loftus, E. F. (1997), "Creating childhood memories,"*Applied Cognitive Psychology*,11,S75-S86.

Loftus, E. F. (2003), "Make-Believe memories," *American Psychologist*, 58(11), 867-73.

Schlosser, A. E. (2006), "Learning through Virtual Product Experience: The Role of Imagery on True versus False Memories,"*Journal of Consumer Research*, 33(3), 377-83.

Come Eat With Us: Social Influences in the Food Domain

Chairs: Peggy J. Liu, Duke University, USA

Troy H. Campbell, Duke University, USA

Paper #1: The (Ironic) Dove Effect: How Normalizing Overweight Body Types Increases Unhealthy Food Consumption and Lowers Motivation to Engage in Healthy Behaviors

Lily Lin, University of British Columbia, Canada

Brent McFerran, University of Michigan, USA

Paper #2: Matching Choices to Minimize Offense: Avoiding Offending Stigmatized Group Members by Making Similar Choices for Them and for Us

Peggy J. Liu, Duke University, USA

Troy H. Campbell, Duke University, USA

Gavan J. Fitzsimons, Duke University, USA

Gráinne M. Fitzsimons, Duke University, USA

Paper #3: Using Contextual Positioning to Bias Healthier Social Behavior

Brennan Davis, Baylor University, USA

Beth Vallen, Fordham University, USA

Brian Wansink, Cornell University, USA

Paper #4: Created Equal? The Morality of Food and the People Who Eat It

Jenny Olson, University of Michigan, USA

Brent McFerran, University of Michigan, USA

Andrea C. Morales, Arizona State University, USA

Darren W. Dahl, University of British Columbia, Canada

SESSION OVERVIEW

Prior research has examined social and interpersonal influences in the food environment (Herman, Roth, & Polivy 2003). This session advances existing research by exploring a wide range of different types of social influences in the food domain. Specifically, through these four papers, we examine: 1) how the societal normalization of being overweight affects people's food choices and consumption [paper 1], 2) how the body type of social others affects people's choices for themselves and for social others [paper 2], 3) how people make food choices for themselves in social settings in which social others' food choices are not easily observable [paper 3], and 4) how people judge low-income versus non-low income consumers as a function of their food choices (paper 4).

In the first paper, Lin and McFerran show that exposing women to societal images that normalize being overweight leads them to engage in more unhealthy behavior. The paper was inspired by actual large-scale advertising campaigns such as Dove's "Real Beauty" campaign, which feature images of normal weight and overweight women. The authors conducted two studies that exposed participants to ads featuring an overweight model in which being overweight was either normalized (through the addition of an ad tagline "For Normal Women" or "For Real Women") or not normalized (with the ad tagline "For Plus-Size Women"). They found that exposure to an ad normalizing being overweight led participants to consume more of an unhealthy snack (study 1), to choose higher calorie meals (study 2), and to be less motivated to live a healthier lifestyle (study 2). In sum, Lin and McFerran show that the social normalization of being overweight leads to an increase in unhealthy food choices and consumption.

In the second paper, Liu et al. examine how consumers choose foods for themselves and for social others, as a function of the social other's body type. In four studies, the authors show that people are more likely to choose the same foods for themselves and an over-

weight recipient than they are for themselves and a normal weight recipient. Furthermore, they show that this effect is driven by people's desire to minimize negative inferences that overweight recipients might make if different foods were selected. Specifically, they find that people choose the same foods more for themselves and an overweight recipient, but only when choosing different foods might lead the recipient to make negative inferences (such as if the different foods differed on the dimension of healthiness). In addition, they find that the effect of the recipient's weight on choosing the same foods is mediated by a desire to avoid making the recipient feel bad about her weight, but only for an overweight recipient. Therefore, unlike past research showing contrast from dissociative group members, such as the overweight (Berger and Heath 2007), the authors find that in social consumption settings, people are more likely to choose the same foods for themselves and an overweight other when different foods could lead to negative inferences being drawn.

In the third paper, Davis et al. show that how much people base their food choices on the contextual positioning of the dining venue is a function of whether the food choices of their dining companions are initially observable or ambiguous. In five studies, including a field study, the authors find that when individuals are dining with friends (versus alone), they make healthier choices at venues positioned as healthy and unhealthier choices at venues positioned as unhealthy. This reliance on contextual cues does not occur when the venue is ambiguous in its health positioning or when dining companions send clear cues about the healthiness of their food choices. Furthermore, the authors show that when making consumption choices, people elaborate on thoughts that reflect the venue's health positioning when they eat with friends versus alone; these positioning-related thoughts mediate the relationship between contextual positioning and social context on choice. In sum, the authors find that in the absence of cues regarding peers' foods choices, individual choices become overly biased by contextual cues as a means of reducing social risk.

In the fourth paper, Olson et al. examine how an individual's personal income level and food choices jointly shape others consumers' moral judgments of the individual. In four studies, the authors find that whereas people perceive non-low income consumers to be more moral when they purchase organic foods, they perceive low-income consumers to be *less* moral when they purchase organic foods. These effects are driven by people's perceptions that organic foods are an unnecessary indulgence when purchased by low-income consumers. Accordingly, the authors find that lower-income consumers' morality can be partially repaired when they purchase organic food (1) on sale rather than at regular, premium prices or (2) for children. In sum, Olson et al. show that food choices and income status are important determinants of people's judgments of other consumers.

Across four papers and 15 studies, this session investigates both social influences on people's food choices and consumption for themselves and others as well as the effects of food choices on others' impressions of them. This session is expected to appeal to a wide audience including those interested in social influences on consumer choice, food choices, choices for others, and moral judgments. This work relates to the conference theme of "appreciating diversity" both because the four papers explore a breadth of different types of social influences in the food domain and because two of the papers address an often-overlooked group of consumers that is becoming more prevalent (the overweight and obese). Full references for articles cited in this submission are available upon request.

Advances in Consumer Research

Volume 40, ©2012

The (Ironic) Dove Effect: How Normalizing Overweight Body Types Increases Unhealthy Food Consumption and Lowers Motivation to Engage in Healthy Behaviors

EXTENDED ABSTRACT

In 2004, Dove introduced the "Real Beauty" campaign, which featured overweight models with the tagline, "Real women with real curves." Similarly, The Body Shop's "Love Your Body" campaign featured the image of an overweight Barbie doll and the tagline, "There are 3 billion women who don't look like supermodels and only 8 who do." Although these campaigns set out to enhance women's body-esteem and have been both commercially successful and widely applauded, they also suggest that an overweight or obese body is normal, prevalent, and acceptable. Promoting healthy body-esteem is an important goal; however, given the rise in obesity rates, it is equally important to examine whether "normalizing" larger body types might also be detrimental to people's health and wellness.

Overweight or obese individuals are at a heightened risk for serious health problems such as heart disease, diabetes, and cancer (Bianchini, Kaaks, & Vainio, 2002). Over two-thirds of adults and one-third of preschoolers in the U.S. are either overweight or obese (NHANES, 2004), which validates a report entitled, "Is Overweight the New Normal Weight?" (Gray, 2011). Normalizing a behavior or concept can decrease the stigma or negativity associated with it, which in turn can have detrimental consequences. For example, normalizing personal debt (because "everyone does it") enhances people's justification to make poorer financial decisions (Peñaloza & Barnhart, 2011). Similarly, we suggest that a belief that overweight bodies are the norm reduces people's desire to (1) lower their caloric consumption and (2) be in better shape. Past research has examined how different body types (thin vs. overweight) affect self-perceptions (Mills, Herman, & Tiggemann, 2002) and food consumption (McFerran et al., 2010). We diverge from this research by asking how—holding body type constant—normalizing an overweight body type affects people's consumption of an unhealthy food item (study 1), the calorie counts of their meals (study 2), and motivation to live a healthier lifestyle (study 2).

Study 1

The study had a one-way between-subjects design with three conditions (advertisement: normalization vs. plus size vs. control), and 80 participants (M_{age} = 19.90). All participants were female students because females are especially susceptible to the influences of stimuli related to body image (Häfner, 2009; Halliwell & Dittmar, 2005). Upon arriving for the experiment, all participants were given an opaque cup containing seven individually-wrapped chocolates, purportedly "left over from a prior experiment" and told that they were free to snack on as many or as few as they wished. Participants next viewed an ad for a fictitious female clothing store. The ad contained a photo of an overweight female model, accompanied by the tagline "*For Normal Women*" (normalization condition), "*For Plus Size Women*" (plus size condition), or "*For Women*" (control condition). The model was removed in the control ad. (A pretest confirmed that exposure to the normalization (vs. plus size) ad resulted in more agreement that being obese or overweight was "normal.") Before leaving the study, participants also completed several unrelated measures designed to mask the purpose of the research. The dependent measure of the study was the number of chocolates consumed during the session (approximately 45 minutes).

An ANOVA revealed a significant effect of advertisement condition, $F(2, 79)$ = 6.44, p = .003. Participants in the normalization condition consumed more chocolates (M = 4.59) than participants in the plus size (vs. M = 3.05, $t(77)$ = -1.98, p = .05), and control (vs. M = 2.03, $t(77)$ = -3.58, p = .001) conditions. The latter two conditions did not differ ($t(77)$ = -1.34, *ns*), thus supporting our postulation that normalizing the overweight body type *increased* consumption of an unhealthy food item.

Study 2

Participants of both genders (N = 162) were recruited from a national online survey panel (M_{age} = 32.99; females = 60.6%). The manipulation was similar to study 1, but we removed the tagline completely in the control condition and changed the tagline from "*For Normal Women*" to "*For Real Women*" in the normalization condition. This manipulation is subtler and is consistent with the message promoted in Dove's "Real Beauty" campaign. Pretesting again confirmed the efficacy of the advertisement manipulation.

After viewing the advertisement and answering filler questions, participants created their ideal meal from a list of 15 food items. Pictures and calorie counts were given for each item, and the total calorie count for the meal was summed. Participants also rated the extent to which they "want to be in better shape" (-3 = not at all, +3 = very much). Significant effects were found for calorie count ($M_{normalization}$ = 625.00 vs. $M_{plus\,size}$ = 448.21 vs. $M_{control}$ = 503.46, $F(2, 161)$ = 4.25, p = .01) and motivation ($M_{normalization}$ = 1.53 vs. $M_{plus\,size}$ = 2.02 vs. $M_{control}$ = 2.16, $F(2, 161)$ = 3.77, p = .03). The pattern of results replicated those observed in study 1, suggesting that normalizing an overweight body *increased* the selection of foods with higher calories, and *decreased* people's motivation to be in better shape.

Discussion

The present research demonstrates that a mere media suggestion regarding the normality of overweight body types has adverse consequences for healthy intentions and behaviors. Our experimental paradigm suggests one reason why obesity has been shown to be socially contagious (Christakis & Fowler, 2007). The prevalence of a condition is associated with its normality and in many cultures today, being overweight places one in the majority. As being overweight or obese becomes normalized (in a literal sense or simply via manipulations such as ours), individuals subsequently make poorer health choices.

Matching Choices to Minimize Offense: Avoiding Offending Stigmatized Group Members by Making Similar Choices for Them and for Us

EXTENDED ABSTRACT

Consumption situations in which people choose products both for themselves and for others to consume together are common. For instance, people may find themselves responsible for buying drinks at the bar for themselves and another, picking up take-out dinner entrees for themselves and a colleague, or packing snacks for a social event. What happens when people need to choose products for themselves and stigmatized others? Given that we are increasingly encountering consumers who are members of stigmatized groups, we examine the interpersonal challenges that arise in such communal consumption scenarios in which people choose for and consume together with stigmatized group members. Specifically, we focus on overweight others as a special case of a stigmatized group.

Past research suggests that we may choose different products for ourselves versus for members of stigmatized groups (Berger & Heath, 2007). However, this and other related research examined choices in isolation (i.e., when one is choosing to consume alone) (Berger & Heath, 2007; McFerran et al., 2010). However, there are often situations in which people choose for both themselves and a stigmatized group member and consume together with them. In such situations, we propose that a new factor comes into play: the potential for the stigmatized group member to make negative inferences about different choices. We argue that people may worry about the inferences the other person would make about differing choices and that this concern would therefore influence them to make more similar choices for themselves and a stigmatized group member.

We examine this phenomenon of making the same choice for yourself and a stigmatized group member in the context of choosing foods for yourself and an overweight person. We predict that people have the intuition that choosing non-matching foods for an overweight recipient can lead to the recipient making negative inferences. Furthermore, we predict that people act on this intuition by being more likely to choose the same foods for themselves and for a recipient when the recipient is overweight than when the recipient is normal weight. Results from four studies supported our hypotheses.

In the first study, which had a within-subjects design, participants predicted the inferences that an overweight versus normal weight recipient would make if the selector made matching choices (the same unhealthy or healthy option for both persons) versus non-matching choices (a healthy option for one person and an unhealthy option for the other). Participants predicted that recipients would make more negative inferences if the selector made non-matching choices for an overweight recipient. This study suggests people believe they can prevent overweight recipients from forming negative inferences by matching choices.

The second study tested this intuition with a between-subjects design in which half of participants chose salad or fries for an overweight recipient and themselves, and half made selections for a normal weight recipient and themselves. We confirmed the intuition, finding that people chose matching foods more often with an overweight recipient than a normal weight recipient.

The third study tested whether the second study's findings were due to a strategy to avoid the recipient making negative inferences, rather than a tendency to always select matching options for themselves and an overweight other. Specifically, we used a 2x2 between-subjects design in which participants chose between fries and salad or fries and onion rings, for themselves and either an overweight or normal weight recipient. We found that when dining with an overweight recipient, increased matching occurred when choosing different food options might lead to negative inferences (i.e., when the items differed in healthiness: salad/fries), but not when choosing different food options would not readily lead to negative inferences (i.e., when the items were of the same healthiness: onion rings/fries).

Finally, the fourth study tested our hypothesis that increased matching occurred when eating with an overweight recipient because people did not want the overweight recipient to feel bad. Specifically, we used a between-subjects design similar to that used in study 2, in which half of participants chose a healthy or unhealthy food for an overweight recipient and themselves and half of participants chose between a healthy or unhealthy food for normal weight recipient and themselves. Participants were then asked to indicate to what extent they chose the foods to make the recipient feel positive (not negative) about her weight. We hypothesized and found that there was moderated mediation, such that for an overweight recipient but not a normal weight recipient, the effect of the recipient's weight on matching was mediated by whether the participant chose the options to make the recipient feel positive, not negative, about her weight.

The present research therefore examined the choices that selectors make for themselves and for overweight versus normal weight recipients in scenarios in which recipients are aware of both choices. First, we found that people think that making non-matching choices that differ in healthiness will lead an overweight person to make more negative inferences than a normal weight person (study 1). In line with these beliefs, we found that people are more likely to choose the same choices for themselves and a recipient if the recipient is overweight than if the recipient is normal weight (studies 2-4). Importantly, we found that people are only more likely to choose the same choices for themselves and an overweight recipient than a normal weight recipient if the non-matching choices differ in healthiness (study 3). Finally, we found that people make matching choices to make an overweight recipient feel positive (not negative) about her weight (study 4).

Thus, in four studies, we identify a novel choice strategy of matching to avoid offending others. Unlike past research that shows divergence from the choices of undesirable groups, we found that in communal consumption scenarios, people select the same products when choosing for oneself and a member of a stigmatized group. More broadly, we argue that people may use a general matching strategy when choosing for oneself and for others if non-matching choices could lead the recipient to make negative inferences.

Using Contextual Positioning to Bias Healthier Social Behavior

EXTENDED ABSTRACT

Consumers tend to model their own behavior on observations of their peers' behavior (Feunekes, de Graaf, & Van Staveren, 1995; Herman, Roth, & Polivy, 2003; Kulviwat, Bruner, & Al-Shuridah, 2009), such as selecting an alcoholic beverage at a lunch outing after observing others doing the same or choosing food based on what others are eating. Yet there are situations in which the behavior of others is not observable or predictable, such as placing a food or beverage order before all others in a group. In these situations, individuals would often like to avoid eating a salad when everyone else has chosen a burger or drinking beer when everyone else has selected water,

In this research, we explore the cues to which consumers turn in social settings when the behavior of others is not easily inferred. We focus on food-related consumption decisions because they often are associated with social risk. Social risk could arise in the form of embarrassment for consuming an unhealthy product among those who typically consume healthily, or judgment from others who observe a loss of willpower when breaking a promise of abstinence (e.g., a pledge to avoid alcoholic beverages or fattening foods). Conversely, social risk could also arise in the form of embarrassment for consuming a healthy product among those who consume unhealthily or appearing to be prudish or judgmental while everyone else is letting loose. In the absence of information about others, we propose that consumers use cues in the external environment to serve as standards for consumption and infer social behavior. Past research has demonstrated that environmental cues have a wide-ranging influence on consumption behavior (Wansink, 2004). This research investigates instances in which individuals use such environmental cues to compensate for the lack of explicit information about social behavior. Specifically, we investigate how consumer choice and consumption are impacted by contextual positioning (e.g., healthy versus unhealthy restaurants) and social context (e.g., consuming with friends versus alone). When friends' behavior is unobservable, people may be likely to eat healthfully at a restaurant positioned as healthy or to eat unhealthfully at a restaurant positioned as unhealthy. When eating alone, however, individuals are free from the evaluative concerns that drive them to behave in line with social behavior and therefore are less likely to rely on contextual cues. In this situation, food preferences may be more important than the restaurant's positioning.

To explore the role of contextual positioning in a social context, this paper includes a field study and a series of lab experiments. In Studies 1 and 2, we find that individuals dining with friends make more healthful choices at venues positioned as healthy (e.g., Chipotle) than individuals dining alone. Conversely, individuals make less healthful choices when they dine with friends at venues positioned as unhealthy (e.g., Taco Bell) than individuals dining alone. These results suggest that individuals dining alone do not model their choices on a venue's positioning. Furthermore, when a venue's positioning is ambiguous, there is no observed difference between choices made while eating with friends versus alone (Study 3). In this situation, there are no environmental cues from which individuals are able to infer relevant information about the expected behavior of others. In addition, Study 4 demonstrates that, when dining with friends whose food choices are unambiguously healthy or unhealthy, individuals do not model the healthfulness of their food choices on a restaurant's health positioning. In this case, individuals use the behavior of their friends to gauge their own consumption. Finally, in Study 5 we show that when eating with friends, people make consumption choices and elaborate on thoughts that reflect the venue's health positioning. These positioning-related thoughts mediate the relationship between contextual positioning and social context on choice.

In sum, our findings illustrate that people look to venue positioning in a social context when actual social behavior is not observable. This finding carries important implications for food manufacturers and retailers, because it demonstrates the importance of positioning for consumption of healthy foods. To illustrate, although many "unhealthy" restaurants have added more nutritious selections to their menus (e.g., salads at McDonald's) and many food manufacturers have created healthier versions of snack foods (e.g., 100 calorie packs), prior research has shown that these efforts do not always lead consumers to engage in more healthful eating behaviors (e.g., Scott et al., 2008; Wilcox et al., 2009). Based on our research, we propose that consumers may select these healthy options more frequently if the producers' positioning is more healthful. However, the role of contextual positioning in a social consumption setting reaches far beyond the food domain to include various consumption behaviors and scenarios. Given the joint impact of social context and contextual positioning on consumption, parties involved in marketing exchanges will be well-served to investigate the outcomes associated with these effects.

Created Equal?
The Morality of Food and the People Who Eat It

EXTENDED ABSTRACT

In light of growing environmental concerns, food safety issues, and rising obesity rates, many consumers are seeking out healthier, more sustainable alternatives to conventional agriculture. A trip to one's local grocery store will highlight the increasing availability of products possessing organic, fair-trade, and green-friendly labels. The organic industry alone has experienced tremendous growth in recent years. For example, in 2010, U.S. sales grew to nearly $29 billion, with 78% of families reporting that they have purchased organic foods in the past (Organic Trade Association, 2011a, 2011b). However, foods possessing these ethical attributes (such as organic food) tend to come with a higher price tag, which makes purchasing them less feasible for low-income segments of the population. If low-income consumers purchase these items, others may view these consumers as being wasteful or overly indulgent. The present research explores how an individual's personal income level and food choices jointly shape how other consumers judge his/her morality.

Beginning with Haire's (1950) seminal grocery list study, prior literature reveals that individuals judge others based upon their food choices. More recently, Stein and Nemeroff (1995) demonstrated that individuals judge others who consume unhealthy, fattening foods as more immoral than those who eat healthy, noncaloric foods. In addition to ascribing social meanings and values to specific food choices (Barker, Tandy, & Stookey, 1997), individuals also attribute specific qualities to members of different social classes. Low-income groups are often perceived as "other" and lesser in moral values, character, work ethic, and motivation (Bullock, Wyche, & Williams, 2001; Cozzarelli, Wilkinson, & Tagler, 2001; Lott, 2002). We propose that consumers also hold strong associations between "moral" and choosing "organic" but that this association may not be present or even reverse when the target shopper is low in socioeconomic status. That is, when purchased by low-income shoppers, organic food may be perceived as an unnecessary indulgence.

Study 1 utilized a 2(organic label: yes, no) × 3(annual income: $85,000, $25,000, welfare) between-subjects design. Participants were presented with a grocery list featuring eight items that belonged to a target individual where three of the foods (i.e., carrots, 2% milk, and cereal) were labeled organic or not. The remaining five foods were held constant across conditions. An overall morality index was created by averaging responses from four items: unethical/ethical, cruel/kindhearted, immoral/moral, and uncaring/caring (α = .90). As expected, analysis revealed a significant interaction between income and organic labeling (p = .016). Specifically, individuals earning $85,000 were perceived as significantly *more* moral when they choose organic foods versus conventional equivalents, whereas those receiving welfare benefits were perceived as significantly *less* moral. Moderated mediation tests demonstrated that the effects of organic labelling on moral judgment were mediated by differences in perceptions of the grocery shopper's Puritan work ethic, but only when the shopper was described as receiving welfare benefits or earning $25,000. It appears purchasing organic food is viewed as selfish and irresponsible among lower-income groups, which results in perceptions of immorality.

Study 2 builds upon these findings by manipulating health value directly, rather than controlling for its effect. Study 2 used a 2(organic label: yes, no) × 2(health: healthy, unhealthy) × 2(annual income: $85,000, welfare) between-subjects design. A similar 8-item grocery list paradigm was used with either three healthy items [i.e., extra-lean (3% fat) beef, whole wheat bread, and skim milk cheese] or three unhealthy items [i.e., regular (30% fat) beef, white bread, and whole milk cheese]. These same three items either contained the organic label or not, while the remaining five filler items were held constant across conditions. Participants completed the same series of measures as in Study 1. A significant three-way interaction was found on the morality index (p = .046). Higher-income consumers were seen as more moral when purchasing healthy and organic food versus unhealthy and conventional food. In contrast, low-income consumers were seen as immoral when purchasing organic food. However, they were not seen as more immoral when the food was merely healthy but not organic.

To address the potential role of price, Study 3 utilized a 2(price: premium, discount) × 2(annual income: $85,000, welfare) between-subjects design. In the discounted pricing condition, organic items appeared with prices that were 30% lower than the prices appearing in the premium condition. Again, a significant interaction was found on the morality index (p = .026). Whereas wealthy consumers were not judged differently depending upon whether or not the organic items were on sale, perceptions of lower-income consumers' morality were significantly higher when they purchased organic items for a discount. This pattern suggests that lower-income consumers' morality can be partially repaired when they purchase organic food on sale rather than at regular, premium price points.

Study 4 manipulated who the food was to be consumed by, adults versus children, and featured a 2(label: child, no label) × 2(household income: $140,000, welfare) between-subjects design. All participants viewed a portion of a grocery list belonging to a family consisting of two children and two adults. Three items were always organic, but half of the participants were presented these items with a children's label [e.g., (kids') organic yogurt; (children's) organic crackers]. Results showed two significant main effects (both

p's < .001). Individuals were perceived as more moral when the organic food was for children (vs. not) and when purchased by wealthy (vs. poor) individuals. Interestingly, a family receiving welfare buying organic food for children was viewed as equally moral compared to a wealthy family buying organic food for adults. These findings suggest that the negative stigma that comes from buying organic food when one is low-income can be eliminated if the organic food is purchased for children.

In conclusion, results from four studies demonstrate for the first time that consumers not only make moral judgments of each other based merely on food choice, but that these judgments are based on a sliding scale depending on the target's income.

The Effects of Temperature on Consumers Cognitive and Affective Decisions

Chairs: Rhonda Hadi, Baruch College, USA

Dan King, National University of Singapore Business School, Singapore

Paper #1: Warmer or Cooler: Exploring the Influence of Ambient Temperature on Cognitive Task Performance

Luqiong Tong, Tsinghua University, China

Yuhuang Zheng, Tsinghua University, China

Ping Zhao, Tsinghua University, China

Rui (Juliet) Zhu, University of British Columbia, China

Paper #2: Influence of Warm (versus Cool) Temperatures on Consumer Choice: A Resource Depletion Account

Amar Cheema, University of Virginia, USA

Vanessa M. Patrick , University of Houston, USA

Paper #3: Mental Thermoregulation: Affective and Cognitive Pathways for Non-physical Temperature Regulation

Rhonda Hadi, Baruch College, USA

Lauren G. Block, Baruch College, USA

Dan King, National University of Singapore Business School, Singapore

Paper #4: Physical Warmth and Following the Crowd: The Effect of Ambient Temperature on Preference for Popularity

Xun (Irene) Huang, The Chinese University of Hong Kong, Hong Kong

Meng Zhang, The Chinese University of Hong Kong, Hong Kong

Michael K. Hui, The Chinese University of Hong Kong, Hong Kong

Robert S. Wyer, The Chinese University of Hong Kong, Hong Kong

SESSION OVERVIEW

Consumers are continuously exposed to fluctuations in temperature. Some fluctuations happen gradually (e.g. changing seasons), while others happen more suddenly (e.g. stepping inside an air-conditioned store). While previous research documents that consumers' physical surroundings significantly affect their decisions (Belk 1975), temperature remains an understudied atmospheric variable. Despite widespread agreement that temperature influences consumer behavior, the literature is rife with mixed results, partly driven by a lack of consensus on the theoretical mechanism by which temperature exerts its effects. This session addresses the gap in our understanding and reconciles mixed findings by examining in more detail why, when, and how temperature impacts consumer decision-making.

We bring together four papers that explore the impact of ambient temperature on different outcome variables and behaviors: task performance, complex decision-making, social conformity, and processing strategy. Importantly, each paper relies on diverse theoretical bases to investigate the temperature conundrum. Tong and colleagues explore the impact of ambient temperature on task performance using a thermal stress account. While previous literature reported mixed findings regarding the effect of temperature on cognitive task performance, they reconcile the inconsistent findings by showing that the nature of the task interacts with temperature to jointly determine performance level.

Building on the thermal stress paradigm, Cheema and Patrick narrow the theoretical underpinnings by proposing a resource-depletion explanation: warm temperatures increase thermal load, resulting in resource depletion. The authors extend the effects to a different behavioral domain: complex decisions; and postulate

boundary conditions under which warm (vs. cool) temperatures lead to System 1 vs. System 2 processing. The next paper continues exploring the effects of warmer/cooler temperatures on processing style by introducing the notion of "mental thermoregulation." Using a regulatory lens, Hadi, Block and King examine the effect of experienced temperature on individuals' use of cognitive versus affective processing. They find that reliance on emotions/cognitions can function as warming/cooling mechanisms, and thus individuals may alter their decision-making style according to their thermoregulatory objectives. Finally, Huang and colleagues complete the session by exploring the social consequences of ambient temperature independent of affect. Applying a social distance paradigm to the study of ambient temperature, Huang and colleagues explore the effect of ambient temperature on consumers' preferences for popularity (vs. uniqueness). All the papers in this session are in advanced stages of completion, with multiple studies and full papers available.

All these papers explore the impact of temperature on consumer behavior. However, consistent with the conference's theme of appreciating diversity, they draw from various theoretical underpinnings and come to results that may seem conflicting on the surface. We plan to discuss the systematic differences across papers to reconcile these findings. Due to this interesting juxtaposition and general interest in the burgeoning area of temperature, we expect this symposium to stimulate much discussion and appeal to a large group of conference attendees.

Warmer or Cooler: Exploring the Influence of Ambient Temperature on Cognitive Task Performance

EXTENDED ABSTRACT

Although both practitioners and academics agree that temperature affects human cognition in important ways (Hancock, Ross, and Szalma 2007; Williams and Bargh 2008), there is no consensus in terms of how temperature exerts its effect. In fact, mixed results have been observed in the literature (Hancock and Vasmatzidis 1998). While some research suggests that warmer temperatures enhance cognitive task performance (Ramsey 1995; Wyon, Anderson, and Lundqvist 1979), other studies suggest just the opposite (Givoni and Rim 1962; Hancock 1981). We aim to reconcile this discrepancy in the literature by suggesting that task complexity moderates the impact of temperature on task performance. While for simple tasks, cool (vs. warm) temperatures help, the opposite is true for complex tasks. Support for our hypothesis comes from three lines of research.

First, prior research on temperature suggests that heat, which can induce thermal stress, competes for cognitive resource and consequently hurts task performance (Hancock and Warm 1989). Thus, compared to individuals in a cool temperature condition, those in a warm temperature condition should have limited cognitive resource towards the focal task (Ramsey et al. 1983).

Second, a separate line of research suggests that different levels of cognitive resources can prompt alternative information processing modes. When individuals have limited cognitive resource for the focal task, they are likely to engage in less systematic and more heuristic processing (Todorov et al. 2002). Thus, we expect that those in the warm (cool) temperature condition, due to their limited (abundant) cognitive resources, are likely to engage in primarily heuristic (systematic) processing (Cheema and Patrick 2011).

Finally, past research has shown that while systematic processing benefits simple tasks (Frisch and Clemen 1994), heuristic processing is more beneficial for complex tasks (Rieskamp and Hoffrage 1999). Systematic processing is extensive and compensatory, whereas heuristic processing involves limited and selective information processing. The comprehensive nature of systematic processing makes it particularly suited to simple tasks (i.e., tasks that require individuals to process a small amount of information). However, a different pattern of results is expected for complex tasks. Decision makers have limited information-processing capacity. Thus, as task complexity increases (i.e., as the task requires individuals to process a larger amount of information), systematic processing suffers from computational errors and limited memory capacity (Bettman, Luce, and Payne 1998), leading to worse decisions. Heuristic processing, because it relies on less information and is less subject to computational errors, does not lead to worse decisions as task complexity increases. Relatively speaking, then, heuristic (vs. systematic) processing should lead to better performance on complex tasks. Summarizing our theorizing so far, we hypothesize that cool (vs. warm) temperature should prompt greater systematic processing, and consequently lead to better performance on simple tasks; and that, in contrast, warm (vs. cool) temperature activates primarily heuristic processing, and thus leads to better performance on complex tasks.

Our first two studies (1A & 1B) test the above hypothesis. Study 1A used 3 (temperature: warm vs. moderate vs. cool) * 2 (task complexity: simple vs. complex) between-subject design. The focal task was a classic choice task, which requires participants to select their preferred lottery from four different options (Payne et al., 2008). Options were defined by payoffs for 12 equiprobable events defined by drawing 1 of 4 numbered balls (simple condition) or 1 of 12 numbered balls (complex condition) from a bingo cage. Among the four options, one option had the highest expected value, which represents the correct answer. The study was run with no more than four people per session. The same lab was used, but the temperature was set to be warm (25-26 Celsius), moderate (21-22 Celsius), or cool (16-17 Celsius). Results confirmed our hypothesis, such that when the task was complex, a significantly higher percentage of individuals in the warm temperature condition chose the correct option than that in the cool or moderate temperature condition. However, when the task was simple, participants in the cool (vs. warm) temperature performed better. Study 1B was a theoretical replication of study1A by using a different task.

Study 2 aims to shed light on the underlying mechanism. If, as we argue, heuristic processing underlies the beneficial effects of warm temperature on complex task performance, then we should observe equally good performance from those in the cool temperature condition if we prompt them to engage in heuristic processing. To induce heuristic processing, we manipulated participants' available cognitive resource by having them remember either a 2-digit or an 8-digit number (Gilbert and Hixon 1991). In line with prior research, we expect that those being asked to remember the short (long) number would have ample (limited) cognitive resources for the focal task, and thus engage in primarily systematic (heuristic) processing (Chen and Chaiken 1999). The study employed a 2 (temperature: warm vs. cool) * 2 (available resources: high vs. low) between subject design. The focal task was always the complex lottery task as used in study 1A. As anticipated, when participants had ample resources for the focal task, we replicated prior result such that those in the warm (vs. cool) temperature performed better on the complex lottery task. However, for those with low available resources, they performed equally well regardless of whether they were in the warm or cool temperature condition, presumably.

Study 3 extends our theorizing to the domain of creative cognition. We theorize that warm temperatures, due to its activation of heuristic processing, can enhance creativity. Prior research suggests that the carefree nature of heuristic processing prompts individuals to think freely and thus facilitate creative cognition (Friedman and Förster 2000). In three separate tasks (studies 3A, 3B, and 3C), we found support to this hypothesis.

Influence of Warm (versus Cool) Temperatures on Consumer Choice: A Resource Depletion Account

EXTENDED ABSTRACT

Across four studies, we find that relative to people who are cool, people who are warm are (1) less likely to gamble, especially for difficult gambles, (2) less likely to purchase an innovative product, (3) more likely to rely on System 1 processing, and, (4) more likely to perform poorly on complex cognitive tasks.

OVERVIEW OF STUDIES

Pilot Study

This study provided preliminary evidence that warm temperatures can impact lottery sales, but only for difficult lotteries. We used daily lottery sales over a one-year period from a large metropolitan county in the USA. Pre-tests revealed that multiple-option lotteries were judged to be more complex relative to single-option lotteries. We find that temperature has a significant negative effect on lottery sales, but only for complex (difficult) lotteries.

Study 1

replicate in the laboratory the basic effect found in the pilot study. We manipulate the temperature to be either warm (77 degrees Fahrenheit) or cool (67 degrees). Participants are asked how likely they will be to make a series of gambles. We manipulate gamble difficulty by either providing (easy) or not providing (difficult) the expected values of gambles. We find that for difficult gambles, warm (versus cool) individuals are less likely to gamble. However, temperature does not affect likelihood of making easy gambles.

Study 2

This study implicates resource depletion as the process underlying the effect of temperature. We manipulate temperature to be warm or cool. We manipulate depletion with a procedure used by Baumeister et al. (1998). Participants see a silent video clip of a woman being interviewed. The video also includes common words that appear on one side of the screen. Participants in the depleted condition are told to ignore the words and, if their attention is drawn to the words, to consciously focus it back on the interviewee. Participants in the non-depleted condition are not provided these instructions. The dependent measure is participants' proof-reading performance. We find that for non-depleted individuals, warm participants have lower cognitive performance (the number of correctly identified typos) than cool participants. However, temperature doesn't affect depleted individuals' performance.

Study 3

This study has two objectives. First, it shows that warm (versus cool) temperatures are depleting. Second, it demonstrates the moderating role of task complexity: warm temperatures lower willingness to adopt an innovative new product, but don't influence adoption of an established product. As before, we manipulate temperature to be warm or cool. We use a complex estimation task to measure performance. The cognitive estimation task requires participants to provide

10 estimates that are typically difficult to generate (for example, one item asks participants to estimate the height of the empire state building, in feet). Each estimate is scored in terms of its variation from a norm determined on the basis of typical responses. More extreme estimates, that are too high or too low, get a higher score (1 or 2) while estimates within the norm are scored as a zero. A higher score on this task has previously been used as evidence of decreased System 2 processing, being inhibited by depletion (Schmeichel et al. 2003). We find that warm participants perform worse (score higher) relative to cool participants. As a control, performance on a 10-item general knowledge task (such as asking people about the capital of a country) is not affected by temperature. As general knowledge responses are likely retrieved from memory rather than constructed, System 2 inhibition doesn't affect performance on this task.

Following the cognitive estimation and general knowledge tasks, participants see a product purchase opportunity. All participants read that they have been looking for an affordable voice recorder to take notes. Half the participants saw an established product (a box-shaped voice recorder) while the remaining saw a new, innovative product (a voice recorder in a pen). We find that among participants who saw the innovative recorder, cool (versus warm) participants were more likely to buy. However, among participants who saw the regular voice recorder, warm (versus cool) participants were more likely to buy.

Study 4

This study juxtaposes the effects of depletion and temperature to show that warm temperatures hamper performance on complex tasks because of an increased reliance on System 1 (heuristic) processing. We manipulate temperature to be warm or cool. We manipulate depletion using the video attention task from study 2 (Baumeister 1998). We use the complex estimation task from study 3 to test for the effects of depletion on cognitive performance. We find that for non-depleted participants, warm (vs. cool) temperatures lead to poorer performance with more varied answers. However, the effect of temperature is attenuated for depleted participants. Similar to study 3, neither temperature nor depletion affects performance on the general knowledge task.

We measure propensity for System 1 processing using a task from Mishra et al. (2007), with participants choosing between two cell phone plans (A and B). A cursory examination of the charges associated with above-plan usage suggests Plan A (which is actually the more expensive plan) is superior to Plan B (the frugal plan). However, closer examination reveals that Plan B is more frugal because it gives the user more free in-plan minutes. Mishra et al. (2007) demonstrate that individuals using System 1 are more likely to choose the expensive plan compared to individuals using System 2. We find that among non-depleted participants, warm (versus cool) participants are more likely to choose the expensive plan. By contrast, temperature doesn't affect plan choice among depleted participants.

Mental Thermoregulation: Affective and Cognitive Pathways for Non-physical Temperature Regulation

EXTENDED ABSTRACT

In the behavioral sciences, the term "cool" processing typically refers to those processes which involve cognitions and critical analysis, while "warm" processing alludes to those systems involving feelings, desires, and emotions (Metcalfe & Mischel 1999). This terminology suggests that at least semantically, each of these processes encompasses a distinct thermoregulatory tone. However, if reliance on emotions can indeed function as a psychologically warming process and reliance on cognitions functions as a psychologically cooling process, individuals may alter their decision-making style according to their thermoregulatory objectives, without conscious awareness. It is precisely this notion that we address in the current research.

The mammalian tendency to physically thermoregulate is well documented in the biological sciences (Kirkes 1899, Alberts & Brunjes 1978). Mammals seek warm stimuli when their body temperature drops below normal, and seek cooling stimuli when their body temperature rises above normal. For humans, however, physical thermoregulation may not be the only way in which regulation can occur. Thermoregulation might be possible via non-physical mechanisms. For example, some research suggests individuals may consume stimulating products and partake in interpersonal activities in response to physical cold (Parker & Tavassoli 2000, Tavassoli 2000, Zhang & Risen 2010). Collectively, such research seems to imply that humans can engage in thermoregulation through non-physical and largely mental means, a process we term "mental thermoregulation." We assume this is indeed the case, and further propose that the use of a particular decision-making style (using either an affective or cognitive pathway) can also serve as a thermoregulatory mechanism.

Thus, we propose that an individual may embody a particular decision-making process that is metaphorically consistent with his or her thermoregulatory *objective* (and thus inconsistent with his or her thermoregulatory *state*), whenever the current state is non-optimal. Our specific hypotheses are as follows:

Hypothesis 1a: *Cooler temperatures lead individuals to rely more on emotions when making decisions.*

Hypothesis 1b: *Warmer temperatures lead individuals to rely less on emotions when making decisions.*

In study 1, participants were assigned to either a cold or warm temperature condition, and were given a binary choice task in which one alternative, chocolate cake, was superior on the affective dimension but inferior on the cognitive dimension compared to the other alternative, fruit salad (procedure borrowed from Shiv & Fedorikhin 1999). Results confirmed a significant main effect of temperature on choice in the hypothesized direction: the cake was chosen more often in the cold temperature condition than in the warm temperature condition. A 4-item decision basis scale ($\alpha = .84$) measured whether decisions across different conditions were based on respondents' affective reactions or cognitions. Specifying a confidence interval of 98%, with 5000 bootstrap resamples, the indirect effect of temperature on choice through decision basis was significant, with a confidence interval excluding zero, suggesting that reliance on emotions mediated the relationship of temperature on choice of cake.

Study 2 was a 2 (temperature: cold vs. warm) x 2 (object description: low sentiment vs. high sentiment) between-subjects design, and examined the degree to which individuals were relying on affect by measuring their WTP for insurance for an object (an antique clock). Presumably, if one is not relying on emotions, there should be no difference between WTP under the two object descriptions. However, if one *is* relying on emotions, we expect WTP to be higher for the object with a high sentiment description. Results revealed a significant temperature by object description interaction. In the cold temperature condition, the difference between the low sentiment and high sentiment conditions was indeed significant, with individuals' WTP higher in the high sentiment condition than in the low sentiment condition. In the warm temperature condition however, the difference between the two object description conditions was not significantly different.

The third study was a 2 (temperature simulation: cold vs. warm) x 2 (number of pandas: one vs. four) between subjects design. We adapted our procedure from Hsee and Rottenstreich (2004), who argue that when individuals rely on affect in making decisions, they become insensitive to scale. Thus, individuals relying on their emotions are willing to donate as much money to save one panda as to save four pandas, but those using cognitive processing are willing to donate more to save more pandas. Results revealed a significant temperature x number of pandas interaction. In the warm condition, the difference between the one-panda and four-pandas conditions was indeed significant- participants were more likely to donate when there were four pandas in the scenario than when there was only one panda in the scenario). In the cold temperature condition however, subjects appeared to indeed be insensitive to scale- the difference between the one-panda and four-pandas conditions was not significant.

The purpose of our fourth study was to support the thermoregulation explanation by suggesting that the mere use of cognitive versus affective pathways can indeed alter an individual's perception of physical temperature. After the temperature manipulation, participants were given explicit instructions to use either their feelings or evaluative thoughts in assessing a series of scenarios (adapted from Pham 2001), and then asked to indicate how cold/warm they felt, as well as how comfortable they felt temperature-wise. Results indicated that participants in the affective pathway condition felt warmer than those individuals in the cognitive pathway condition, regardless of their initial temperature condition. Further, results produced a significant temperature x processing interaction on comfort: in the cold condition, affective respondents were more comfortable than cognitive respondents, but the reverse was true in the warm condition, supporting our mental thermoregulation account.

Our research suggests that instead of merely reacting to the physical temperature in a metaphorically consistent manner, physical sensations might instead activate a thermoregulatory goal, thus motivating individuals to embody a process with a metaphorically-opposite thermoregulatory tone. This research encourages more research to explore instances in which physical sensations may lead to goal-driven behavior in a pattern that is metaphorically inconsistent with one's current physical state.

Physical Warmth and Following the Crowd: The Effect of Ambient Temperature on Preference for Popularity

EXTENDED ABSTRACT

The effect of ambient temperature on consumer behavior has seldom been investigated. Furthermore, most prior research has focused on the adverse effects of uncomfortable (very hot or very cold) temperatures (e.g., Anderson et al., 2000). We argue, however, that temperatures within a comfortable range can influence consumers' preferences and behaviors independently of the affect that the temperatures elicit. This possibility is especially relevant to marketing, as most retail stores set the ambient temperature within this range (Baker and Cameron 1996).

We propose that warm ambient temperatures increase consumers' preferences for choice alternatives that are preferred by others. Other research indicates that ambient warmth increases perceptions of social proximity (IJzerman and Semin 2009). We show that these perceptions influence the propensity to follow others' decisions in two different ways.

First, people who experience warm temperatures tend to perceive others as friendlier (Williams and Bargh 2008). When people view themselves as close to others, they experience a sense of "we-ness." As a consequence, they may consider conformity to others' decisions to be more socially desirable independently of the validity of these decisions (Gardner, Gabriel and Hochschild 2002). Such social approval-based conformity may facilitate people's fulfillment of their need for affiliation (Baumeister and Leary 1995, Martin, Hewstone and Martin 2003). This motive generally holds for decisions that reflect primarily the decision maker's personal values and lifestyle.

Second, relative to socially distant others, socially close others are also believed to hold more reliable and accurate opinions (Naylor, Lamberton and Norton 2011). To this extent, the adoption of others' views and decisions may occur not only when individuals' primary goal is to gain social approval but also when their financial well-being is at stake (Cialdini 2001, Castelli, Vanzetto, Sherman and Arcuri 2001, Quinn and Schlenker 2002).

We tested the above predictions in four laboratory experiments and a field study of the betting behavior at the racetrack. In the laboratory experiments, participants were seated in a room in which the temperature was either warm (75-77°F) or cool (61-63°F), but in each case was within the comfortable range (Anderson et al. 2000; Baker & Cameron, 1996; Baron & Bell, 1976; IJzerman & Semin, 2009). Experiment 1 examined conformity when decisions were a matter of personal taste. Participants were shown an ad for a museum and asked to report their attitude towards it. In some cases, the ad emphasized popularity ("Visited by Over a Million People Each Year") and in other cases, it stressed uniqueness ("Stand Out from the Crowd"). Participants evaluated the first ad more favorably, but evaluated the second ad less favorably, when they were in a warm room than when they were in a cool room.

Experiment 2 replicated these findings and, in addition, confirmed that the effects were mediated by the impact of ambient temperature on perceptions of social closeness. However, participants' affective reactions did not differ as a function of temperature, indicating that differences in affect were not a contributor to the effects we observed.

The next three studies extended our findings to decisions in which the primary consideration was financial. In Experiment 3, participants were given six graphs, each depicting changes in the price of a stock, and were asked in each case whether they would buy the stock or sell it. In some conditions, participants were shown the predictions that the majority of previous participants in the experiment had made. In control conditions, this information was not provided. Participants who received information about others' predictions were more likely to conform to them when the temperature was high than when it was low. In the control conditions, participants' choices did not depend on temperature.

Experiment 4 further examined the mediation of perceived social closeness in the domain of financial decisions. Participants in both warm and cool temperature conditions were told to imagine they were at the race track and had an opportunity to place bets on each of seven races. For each race, the distribution of "winning odds" (a function of the amount of money that was bet on each horse) was provided. Participants were more likely to bet on the favorite (i.e. the horse with lowest odds) when the temperature was warm than when it was cool. These effects were mediated by the effects of ambient temperature on participants' perceptions of their social closeness to other betters. However, the positive and negative affect that participants reported experiencing, their risk propensity, involvement, arousal, relaxation and tiredness, did not depend on temperature.

A field study was then conducted in the context of horse racing data in Hong Kong over a period of three consecutive years

(2007 - 2009). Horse races are only held in seasons during which the temperature is comfortable. The extent to which bets on each race converged on the favorite over the hour before each race was averaged over the races run on each day and correlated with the average temperature on that day. This correlation was significantly positive ($r = .20$; $n = 204$). Furthermore the mean standard deviation of the odds associated with the horses in each race (a second indication of the convergence of bets on the favorite) was also significantly correlated with temperature ($r = .11$, $n = 224$). Thus, these data confirm the effects we observed in the laboratory and indicate that the impact of ambient temperature on the adoption of others' opinions is motivated by a desire to make money and is not restricted to conditions in which conformity is motivated by social desirability concerns.

REFERENCES

Alberts, J. R. & Brunjes, P. C. (1978). "Ontogeny of Thermal and Olfactory Determinants of Huddling in the Rat," *Journal of Comparative and Physiological Psychology*, 92, 897-906.

Anderson, C. A., Anderson, K. B., Dorr, N., DeNeve, K. M., & Flanagan, M. (2000). Temperature and aggression. In M. P. Zanna (Ed.), *Advances in experimental social psychology* (pp. 63-133). New York: Academic Press.

Baker, J. & Cameron, M. (1996). "The Effects of the Service Environment on Affect and Consumer Perception of Waiting Time: An Integrative Review and Research Propositions," *Journal of the Academy of Marketing Science*, 24 (4), 338-49.

Baron, R. A. & Bell. P. A. (1976). "Aggression and Heat: The Influence of Ambient Temperature, Negative Affect, and a Cooling Drink on Physical Aggression," *Journal of Personality and Social Psychology*, 33(3): 245-55.

Baumeister, R., Bratslavsky, E., Muraven, M., & Tice, D. (1998). Ego depletion: Is the Active Self a Limited Resource? *Journal of Personality and Social Psychology*, 74, 1252-65.

Belk, R. W. (1975). "Situational Variables and Consumer Behavior," *Journal of Consumer Research*, 2 (December), 157-64.

Bettman, J. R., Luce, M. F., & Payne, J. W. (1998). "Constructive Consumer Choice Processes," *Journal of Consumer Research*, 25(3), 187-217.

Brewer, M. B. (1991). "The Social Self: On Being the Same and Different at the Same Time," *Personality and Social Psychology Bulletin,* 17 (5), 475-82.

Brewer, M. B., & Roccas, S. (2001). "Individual Values, Social Identify, and Optimal Distinctiveness," in *Individual Self, Relational Self, and Collective Self*, Constantine Sedikides and Marilynn B. Brewer, eds, Philadelphia: Psychology Press, 219-237.

Castelli, L., Vanzetto, K., Sherman, S. J. & Arcuri, L. (2001). "The explicit and implicit perception of in-group members who use stereotypes: Blatant rejection but subtle conformity," *Journal of Experimental Social Psychology*, 37, 419–26.

Cialdini, R. B. (2001). *Influences: Science and Practice*, 4th ed. New York: Allyn & Bacon.

Cheema, A. & Patrick, V. M. (2011). "Influence of Warm (versus Cool) Temperatures on Consumer Risk-Taking: a Resource Depletion Account," working paper.

Chen, S. & Chaiken, S. (1999). "The Heuristic-systematic Model in Its Broader Context," in *Dual-process theories in social and cognitive psychology*, ed. Shelly Chaiken and Yaacov Trope, New York: Guilford Press, 73-96.

Friedman, R. S. & Förster, J. (2001). "The Effects of Promotion and Prevention Cues on Creativity," *Journal of Personality and Social Psychology*, 81(6), 1001-013.

Frisch, D. & Clemen, R. T. (1994). "Beyond Expected Utility: Rethinking Behavioral Decision Research," *Psychological Bulletin*, 116(1), 46-54.

Gardner, W. L., Gabriel, S., & Hochschild, L. (2002). When you and I are" we," you are not threatening: The role of self-expansion in social comparison. *Journal of Personality and Social Psychology*, *82*, 239-251.

Gilbert, D. T. & Hixon, G. J. (1991). "The Trouble of Thinking Activation and Application of Stereotypic Beliefs," *Journal of Personality and Social Psychology*, 60(4), 509-17.

Giovani, B. and Y. Rim (1962). "Effect of the Thermal Environment and Psychological Factors upon Subject's Responses and Performance of Mental Work," *Ergonomics*, 5(1), 99-114.

Hancock, P. A. (1981). "Heat Stress Impairment of Mental Performance: A Revision of Tolerance Limits," *Aviation, Space and Environmental Medicine*, 52(3), 177-80.

Hancock, P. A. & Vasmatzidis, I. (1998). "Human Occupational and Performance Limits under Stress: the Thermal Environment as a Prototypical Example," *Ergonomics*, 41(8), 1169-191.

Hancock, P. A., Ross, J. M., & Szalma, J. L. (2007). "A Meta-analysis of Performance Response under Thermal Stressors," *Human Factors*, 49(5), 851-77.

Hancock, P. A. & Warm, J. S. (1989). "A Dynamic Model of Stress and Sustained Attention," *Human Factors*, 31(5), 519-37.

Hsee, C. K., & Kunreuther, H. C. (2000). The affection effect in insurance decisions. *Journal of Risk and Uncertainty*, 20, 141–159.

Hsee, C. K., & Rottenstreich (2004). Music, Pandas and Muggers: On the Affective Psychology of Value. *Journal of Experimental Psychology*, 133, 23-30.

IJzerman, H., & Semin, G. R. (2009). The thermometer of social relations: Mapping social proximity on temperature. *Psychological Science*, *20*, 1214-1220.

Kirkes, W. S. (1899). *Handbook of Physiology*, Philadelphia, PA: Blakiston.

Lakin, J. L., & Chartrand, T. L. (2003). Using nonconscious behavioral mimicry to create affiliation and rapport. *Psychological Science*, *14*, 334-339.

Lynn, M., & Snyder, C. R. (2002). Uniqueness seeking. In: C. R. Snyder and S. J. Lopez (Eds.), *Handbook of positive psychology* (pp. 395-410). London: Oxford University Press.

Kim, H., & Markus, H. R. (1999). "Deviance or Uniqueness, Harmony or Conformity? A Cultural Analysis," *Journal of Personality and Social Psychology,* 77 (4), 785-800.

Martin, R., Hewstone, M., & Martin, P. Y. (2003). "Resistance to persuasive messages as a function of majority and minority source status," *Journal of Experimental Social Psychology*, 39, 585-93.

Metcalfe, J., & Mischel, W. (1999). A hot/cool system analysis of delay of gratification: Dynamics of willpower. *Psychological Review*, 106, 3-19.

Mishra, H., Mishra, A., & Nayakankuppam, D. (2007). "Seeing Through the Heart's Eye: The Interference of System 1 in System 2," *Marketing Science*, 26 (5), 666-78.

Naylor, R. W., Lamberton, C. P., & Norton, D. A. (2011). Seeing ourselves in others: Reviewer ambiguity, egocentric anchoring, and persuasion. *Journal of Marketing Research*, 48, 617-631.

Panksepp, J. (1998). *Affective Neuroscience: The Foundations of Human and Animal Emotions,* New York, NY: Oxford University Press.

Parker, P., & Tavassoli, N. (2000). Homeostasis and Consumer Behavior Across Cultures. *International Journal of Research in Marketing*, 17, 33–53.

Payne, J. W., Samper, A., Bettman, J. R., & Luce, M. F. (2008). "Boundary Conditions on Unconscious Thought in Complex Decision Making," *Psychological Science*, 19(11), 1118-123.

Pham, M. T., Cohen, J. B., Pracejus, J. W., & Hughes, G. D. (2001). Affect monitoring and the primacy of feelings in judgment. *Journal of Consumer Research,* 28(2), 167-188.

Quinn, A. & Schlenker, B. R. (2002). "Can Accountability Produce Independence? Goals as Determinants of the Impact of Accountability on conformity," *Personality and Social Psychology Bulletin*, 23, 472–78.

Ramsey, J. D. (1995). "Task Performance in Heat: A Review," *Ergonomics*, 38(1), 154-65.

Ramsey, J. D., Burford, C. L., Beshir, M. Y., & Jensen, R. C. (1983). "Effect of Workplace Thermal Conditions on Safe Work Behavior," *Journal of Safety Research*, 14(3), 105-14.

Rieskamp, J. & Hoffrage, U. (1999). "When Do People Use Simple Heuristics and How Can We Tell?" in *Simple Heuristics that Make Us Smart,* ed. Gerd Gigerenzer, Peter M. Todd, and the ABC Research Group, Oxford: Oxford University Press, 141-67.

Schmeichel, B., K. Vohs and R. Baumeister (2003), "Intellectual performance and ego depletion: Role of the self in logical reasoning and other information processing," *Journal of Personality and Social Psychology*, 85, 33-46.

Shiv, B. & Fedorikhin, A. (1999). Heart and mind in conflict: The interplay of affects and cognition in consumer decision making. *Journal of Consumer Research,* 26(3), 278-292.

Steinmetz, J. & Mussweiler, T. (2011). "Breaking the ice: How physical warmth shapes social comparison consequences," Journal of Experimental Social Psychology, 47, 1025-1028.

Snyder, C. R. & Fromkin, H. L. (1977). "Abnormality as a Positive Characteristic: The Development and Validation of a Scale Measuring Need for Uniqueness," *Journal of Abnormal Psychology,* 86 (5), 518-527.

Tavassoli, N. (2009). Climate, Psychological Homeostasis and Individual Behaviors Across Cultures. In R. Wyer, C. Chiu, Y. & Hong N. (Eds.), *Understanding culture: theory, research, and application.* (pp. 211-221). New York: Psychology Press.

Todorov, A., Chaiken, S., & Henderson, M. D. (2002). "The Heuristic-systematic Model of Social Information Processing," in *The Persuasion Handbook: Developments in Theory and Practice,* ed. James Price Dillard and Michael Pfau ,Thousand Oaks, CA: Sage Publications, 195-211.

Williams, L. E., & Bargh, J. A. (2008). Experiencing physical warmth promotes interpersonal warmth. *Science, 322,* 606-607.

Wyon, D. P., Andersen, M. D., & Lundqvist, G. R. (1979). "The Effects of Moderate Heat Stress on Mental Performance," Scandinavian Journal of Work, Environment & Health, 5(4), 352-61.

Zhang, Y. & Risen, J. (2010). Staying Warm in The Winter: Seeking Psychological Warmth to Reduce Physical Coldness, in *Advances in Consumer Research* Volume 38.

Signaling to the Self and Others:
Selective Use of and Connection with Brands

Chairs: Danielle J. Brick, Duke University, USA

Tarje Gaustad, BI Norwegian Business School, USA

Paper #1: As Income Rises So Too Does Our Connection to "Tide"

Danielle J. Brick, Duke University, USA

Gavan J. Fitzsimons, Duke University, USA

Tanya L. Chartrand, Duke University, USA

Paper #2: Benefits Offered by High-End Counterfeits Influence Intentions to Purchase Counterfeits – The Role of Self-Presentation

Gülen Sarial-Abi, Koc University, Turkey

Zeynep Gürhan-Canli, Koc University, Turkey

Paper #3: Taking More Money and Donating More Money: The Influence of Self-Threat on Goal-Pursuit

Alison Jing Xu, University of Toronto, Canada

Shirley Y. Y. Cheng, Hong Kong Baptist University, Hong Kong

Tiffany Barnett White, University of Illinois at Urbana-Champaign, USA

Paper #4: Identity Change: The Effects of Actual and Ideal Self-Brand Connections on Consumers' Response to Brand Image Change

Tarje Gaustad, BI Norwegian Business School, Norway

Bendik M. Samuelsen, BI Norwegian Business School, Norway

Luk Warlop, BI Norwegian Business School / KU Leuven, Norway

Gavan J. Fitzsimons, Duke University, USA

SESSION OVERVIEW

Individuals use brands to construct their self-concepts and their identities. Once individuals have incorporated their brands into their self-image, individuals often use these brands as signals to others. These signals often function as status symbols. However, the use of brands as signals may also function as self-verification or self-enhancement tools (Escalas and Bettman 2003). In this session we explore beyond the many ways individuals use brands as signals to others. We examine ways in which individuals use brands as signals to themselves, and by doing so fulfill needs, including relational, functional, and identity relevant. In the first part of the session we examine how individuals use brands commonly thought of as status symbols to fulfill other, more basic needs. We then examine the ways in which individuals, who have fulfilled identity needs by incorporating brands into their self-image, react to a threat to the brand. Taken together, these papers present a novel, multicultural picture of the antecedents and consequences of the selective use of brands as a means of need fulfillment.

In the first part of the session, we examine situations in which many would expect brands to be used merely as status signals to others and yet, instead, are also being used to fulfill other, basic needs. In the first paper, Brick, Fitzsimons and Chartrand explore how wealthy individuals are using their favorite brands not to demonstrate their wealth, but rather to serve as relationship partners. Although many individuals often associate high-end, luxurious brands with the wealthy, they find that wealthy individuals report stronger brand relationships with brands that are less expensive, less publically consumed and more likely to be consumer packaged goods.

They also find that it is connection with these brands that contributes to the strong brand relationships.

In the second paper, Sarial-Abi and Gürhan-Canli examine another, related area in their examination of who purchases high-end counterfeits. Intuitively, one might think that high-end counterfeits are only used as self-enhancement signals. However, Sarial-Abi and Gürhan-Canli find that this is not always the case, and that high-end counterfeits can fulfill other, practical needs. They examine how the functional and symbolic benefits offered by high-end counterfeits influence purchasing intentions, and that self-presentation goals determine on which aspects of the product individuals will place the most value.

Next, we move to consequences of the use of brands as a signal, particularly once those brands have been used to fulfill an identity-relevant need. Once individuals have incorporated brands into their identity, threats to the brand, including brand failure or changes in brand image, may be felt as a threat to the self. Xu, Cheng, and White support this theory in the third paper by their examination of the consequences of brand failure on self-esteem and subsequent attempts to restore the "shaken" self-view. They show that after a brand threat, consumers with high (but not low) self-brand connections are more motivated to pursue salient goals in an effort to correct the threat to their self-esteem.

Finally, Gaustad, Samuelsen, Warlop, and Fitzsimons expound upon the role that a change in the brand image can have on one's esteem in their paper. In particular, they show that highly connected consumers experience brand, and self-identity threat, not only as a result of the introduction of new traits to a brand image, but also, counter intuitively, as a result of reinforcement of current traits. The threat response is contingent upon the degree to which the brand primarily relates to consumers' actual or ideal self.

Besides offering an in-depth view, through the examination of antecedents and consequences, of the selective use of brands, this session also offers a broad view of this topic through the inclusion of multi-cultural studies. Submitters represent schools from a variety of nations, and this variety creates a large, diverse sampling population. As a result, this session presents a number of theoretical and practical contributions appealing to a broad audience, and should attract researchers with interests in topics as far ranging as consumer-brand relationships, goal pursuit, social identity, behavioral predictions (including charitable giving), and life satisfaction. In sum, this session has implications for a large, multicultural audience, and will further the conference's mission of appreciating diversity.

All speakers (Brick, Sarial-Abi, White, and Gaustad) have agreed to participate if the proposal is accepted. Of note, all papers in this session are advanced and extensive data collection, including multiple studies for each paper, has been completed. We anticipate allowing 15 minutes for each presentation and 15-20 minutes of discussion regarding the session topic and individual presentations.

As Income Level Rises,
So Too Does Our Connection with "Tide"

EXTENDED ABSTRACT

Individuals use brands to signal identity and self-concept; individuals also use brands as self-verification and self-enhancement tools (Escalas and Bettman 2003). As such, one might think wealthy individuals would be most loyal to high-end, luxury brands that, in effect, serve as status verification and self-enhancement signals to the self and others. However, we find this is not the case. Instead, we argue, that wealthier individuals are using brands for another reason – to serve as relationship partners. Instead of signaling status to others or even to themselves, wealthier individuals are choosing and using brands that fulfill basic relationship needs. As a result, wealthier individuals form stronger brand relationships, the strength of which is mediated by self-brand connection.

Why might wealthier individuals form stronger brand relationships? Past research has demonstrated that having money makes people more self-sufficient, less likely to turn to others for support (Vohs, Meade and Goode 2006), and that the mere presence of money can make people more distant, cold, and less willing to help others (Vohs, Meade and Goode 2008). These effects extend beyond the immediate context; higher socioeconomic status has been associated with signs of weaker social connections (Kraus and Keltner 2009). As the need for social relationships is fundamental to human psychology (Baumeister and Leary 1995), we argue that instead of turning to others, wealthier individuals are turning to their brands to fulfill this need. They are developing stronger brand relationships than less wealthy individuals, who are more likely to form stronger interpersonal relationships (Kraus, Côtè and Keltner 2010).

In a first study, we examined whether wealthier individuals form stronger brand relationships and the types of brands they are forming these relationships with. Although there have been a few scales designed to measure relationship quality (e.g., Park, Kim and Kim 2009), some of these scales are relatively long and most do not contain all of the characteristics commonly found in interpersonal relationships we intended to study. Therefore, in order to test brand relationship strength we devised a Brand Relationship Measure for this study. The seven-item measure (α=0.87) was rated on a 1 (not at all) to 7 (very much) scale. In order to evaluate the brands individuals were reporting on, two independent coders rated each of the brands reported on several characteristics (interrater reliability α=.98). If they are fulfilling an intrinsically-motivated, fundamental relationship need, we hypothesized the brands to which wealthier individuals are reporting as being most loyal would not be expensive, "keeping up with the Joneses" brands, often associated with social jockeying (Christen and Morgan 2005) or status signals. Instead, we hypothesized these brands would be less expensive, more privately consumed, and more likely to be consumer packaged goods (CPGs) than the brands to which less wealthy individuals are reporting as being most loyal.

One hundred six individuals (N=71 females, Mage=41.2 years, SDage=13.5) from an online source participated in this study. In line with our hypothesis, we found that wealthier individuals, as characterized by income, report a significantly stronger brand relationship with their brands. Providing additional support that wealthier individuals are forming relationships with brands that are not serving as a status signal, the brands wealthier individuals reported were significantly less expensive, less publically consumed, and more CPGs than less wealthy individuals.

Study 2 sought to replicate the findings from study 1 that wealthier individuals form stronger brand relationships, and also to explore our prediction that connection with the brand mediates the effect. One hundred one individuals were recruited and participated in this study from an online source (N=68 females, Mage=35.7 years, SDage=13.8). We used the same Brand Relationship Measure from study 1, and in order to test connection with the brand, we used Escalas and Bettman's (2003) self-brand connection scale.

Replicating our initial findings, individuals with greater wealth, as measured by income level, reported significantly stronger brand relationships. Next, we examined our contention that connection with the brands mediates the effects of wealth on brand relationships. In line with our hypothesis, wealth significantly and positively predicted self-brand connection. Furthermore, brand connection positively predicted relationship strength. When self-brand connection is added to the model predicting wealth on the brand relationship measure, self-brand connection remains a significant predictor, but wealth is no longer significant. In order to test whether connection with the brand mediates the effect of wealth on brand relationship strength, we used a 5,000 resamples bootstrapping approach (Preacher and Hayes 2008). The bootstrapping technique did not contain zero, suggesting connection with the brand mediates the relationship between wealth and brand relationship strength.

Study 3 enhances the above findings by manipulating perceptions of wealth, and then asking participants to report on their brand relationships and connection with their brands. Supporting our hypothesis we find that individuals who feel wealthier report significantly stronger brand relationships, and that this is again mediated by connection with the brand. In study 4, we provide further evidence that wealthier individuals are not using their brands just to signal status to others or themselves. We again manipulate perceptions of wealth, but in this study we introduce a new set of brands and measure strength of the brand relationship and connection with the new brand. In addition, we expand upon the prior studies by evaluating the effects of the prior findings on consumer behavior outcomes. The theoretical and practical implications are discussed.

Benefits Offered by High-End Counterfeits Influence Intentions to Purchase Counterfeits–The Role of Self-Presentation

EXTENDED ABSTRACT

In today's economy, counterfeits are estimated to account for 7% of the whole world trade (World Customs Organization 2004). Previous research mainly investigates why consumers buy cheap knockoffs of the genuine brands (Wilcox et al. 2009). However, with increased technology, a new generation of counterfeits is emerging that is often more convincing than the cheap knockoffs with much higher prices (Holmes 2011). In this research, we investigate who would buy these high-end counterfeits and why.

Counterfeiting: Demographic factors influence intentions to purchase counterfeits. For example, females are more likely to be heavy buyers of counterfeit clothing and accessories (Cheung and Prendergast 2006). Social factors such as the presence of a friend buying a counterfeit influence one's intention to buy counterfeits (Penz and Stöttinger 2005). Product and brand-related factors such as the selling price also enhances willingness to buy counterfeits (Lau 2006).

Functional Versus Symbolic Benefits: Individuals buy things for what they can do with them and for what those things mean to them (Keller 1993). Brand features or brand associations refer to attributes or benefits that consumers link to a brand and that, in their minds, differentiate it from competitors (Dillon et al. 2001). Extant literature has focused on functional benefits (Domzal and Kernan 1992), as well as symbolic benefits offered by brands (Drolet and Aaker 2002).

Functional benefits are related to the more intrinsic aspects of product consumption and usually correspond to product attributes. High-end counterfeits offer high functional benefits. For example, they are made of high-quality materials, which increase their durability (Holmes 2011). On the other hand, symbolic benefits are related to the extrinsic advantages of product consumption. They usually correspond to non-product-related attributes and relate to underlying needs for social approval and personal expression (Park et al. 1986). Because symbolic benefits relate to underlying needs for social approval and personal expression, individuals who have high need for self-presentation should be more likely to purchase high-end counterfeits. However, are individuals who have low need for self-presentation ever likely to purchase high-end counterfeits?

Self-Presentation: Self-presentation is the goal-directed process of people controlling information about the self to influence the impression others form of them (Schlenker et al. 1996). Social actions required for self-presentation are consumption-oriented and depend upon individuals' brands (Williams and Bendelow 1998). Consumers may self-present by purchasing high-end counterfeits because counterfeits help them create identities and impress others (Hoe et al. 2003). This suggests that individuals who have high need for self-presentation should be more likely to purchase high-end counterfeits when these counterfeits offer them symbolic benefits. However, they should be less likely to purchase high-end counterfeits if these counterfeits offer them high functional benefits (e.g., quality) but low symbolic benefits (e.g., no logo).

Individuals who have low need for self-presentation are less concerned with impressing other people. Because they are less concerned with impressing others, what they expect from a brand is more likely to be related to the functional benefits. Given the possibility that some high-end counterfeits may offer as many functional benefits as the original brands, these individuals who need low self-presentation should be more likely to purchase high-end counterfeits when these counterfeits offer them high functional benefits. However, they should be less likely to purchase high-end counterfeits if these counterfeits offer them high symbolic benefits, but low functional benefits.

Study 1(N=100): Participants first received the self-presentation manipulation. Afterwards, they randomly received the functional and symbolic benefits manipulations. Dependent variables and control variables were then measured.

An ANOVA on intentions to purchase counterfeits yielded a significant self-presentation by benefits interaction ($F(1, 96) = 13.26$, $p < .001$). Participants who have high (vs. low) need for self-presentation have higher intentions to purchase counterfeits when they think about symbolic brand benefits (3.76 vs. 2.43; $F(1, 96) = 7.9$, $p < .05$). On the other hand, participants who have low (vs. high) need for self-presentation have higher intentions to purchase counterfeits when they think about functional brand benefits (3.22 vs. 1.89; $F(1, 96) = 7.82$, $p < .05$).

Study 2 (N=200): Participants first received the self-presentation manipulation. Afterwards, they randomly received the functional and symbolic benefits manipulations. The order of the benefits manipulations was counterbalanced. Dependent variables and control variables were then measured.

An ANOVA on intentions to purchase counterfeits revealed a significant three-way interaction of self-presentation, functional benefits, and symbolic benefits ($F(1, 192) = 5.56$, $p < 0.05$). When func-

tional benefits are high, individuals who have low (vs. high) need for self-presentation are more likely to purchase high-end counterfeits if these counterfeits offer low symbolic benefits (3.96 vs. 2.89, $F(1, 192) = 7.24$, $p < .05$). However, intentions to purchase high-end counterfeits did not vary as a function of low (vs. high) need for self-presentation when high-end counterfeits offer high functional and symbolic benefits (3.74 vs. 3.82, $F(1, 192) = .13$, $p > .72$).

Moreover, when functional benefits of high-end counterfeits are low, individuals who have low (vs. high) need for self-presentation are less likely to purchase high-end counterfeits if these products offer high symbolic benefits (2.72 vs. 3.86, $F(1, 192) = 7.69$, $p < .05$). However, intentions to purchase high-end counterfeits did not vary as a function of low (vs. high) need for self-presentation when high-end counterfeits offer low functional and symbolic benefits (2.61 vs. 2.53, $F(1, 192) = .12$, $p > .73$).

General Discussion: In this research, we extend the literature on intentions to purchase counterfeits by examining high-end counterfeits specifically. Second, we extend the literature by demonstrating that functional and symbolic benefits offered by high-end counterfeits influence purchase intentions. Finally, we demonstrate that those individuals who have low need for self-presentation are also likely to purchase high-end counterfeits when these counterfeits offer them functional benefits. Focusing on how improvements in functional (vs. symbolic) benefits offered by high-end counterfeits influences brands' long-term profitability would be an important research focus. More research with different methodologies is required to understand the impact of counterfeit consumption on consumers.

Taking More Money and Donating More Money: The Influence of Self-Threat on Goal-Pursuit

EXTENDED ABSTRACT

Believing that the self is a capable and lovable person is a basic human need (Branden 1969) and is essential to individuals' subjective wellbeing (Taylor and Brown 1988). However, it seems inevitable for us to encounter incidents that threaten this belief, even in consumption contexts. For example, consumers may feel shame about their appearance when they view an ad featuring attractive models (Gulas and McKeage 2000) or feel incompetent when they realize that they paid more than others for an identical item (Argo, White, and Dahl 2006). Having a favorite brand could also be a source of self-threat when the beloved brand fails (Cheng, White, and Chaplin 2012). For those who want to be unique, realizing one's favorite brand is also liked by a large number of consumers could also pose a threat (Imak, Vallen, and Sen 2010).

Of course, human beings are not passive victims of various threats. In response to these threatening incidents, individuals are often motivated to restore a positive self-view through biased information processing or biased attributions (for a review, see Sherman and Cohen 2006). Unfortunately, many of these defensive responses are maladaptive because they promote an inaccurate understanding of the self and the world. We propose and test a beneficial consequence of experiencing self-threat. Specially, we suggest that self-threat can elicit a general motivation that urges people to pursue salient goals that they consider to be important. Moreover, pursuing important goals can boost individuals' threatened self-esteem.

Experiment 1 was a 2 (*Self Threat*: Threat vs. No-Threat) x 2 (*Salient Goals*: Help Others vs. Pursue Self-Interest) between-participant design. Self-threat was manipulated using a RAT task and the salient goal was manipulated through participating in either a "Buyer-Seller Game" (the "self-interest" condition) or a "Doner-Donee Game" (the "help others" condition). The results of Experiment 1 are consistent with our hypothesis that self-threat motivates individuals to pursue the goal that was made salient by the context (significant goal by self-threat interaction, $F(1, 75) = 6.06$, $p < .02$). Significant planned contrasts revealed that when the goal to pursue self-interest was made salient in the Seller-Buyer Game, self-threat increased the amount of money that participants decided to keep for themselves ($M_{threat} = 9.00$ vs. $M_{no-threat} = 7.96$). However, when the goal to help others was made salient by the Doner-Donee Game, self-threat increased the amount of money that participants decided to give to others themselves ($M_{no-threat} = 4.73$ vs. $M_{threat} = 6.06$). Moreover, even though the manipulation of self-threat decreased participants' self-esteem, this effect was completely eliminated following successful goal pursuit.

Experiment 2 used a 2 (*Self Threat:* Threat vs. No threat) x 3 (*Salient Goals:* Saving Money vs. Spending Money on Luxurious Products vs. control) between-subjects design. Participants were given an opportunity to pursue a more important goal (i.e., saving money; $M_{importance} = 6.06$) or a less important goal (i.e., spending money on luxury products; $M_{importance} = 3.93$). When the goal was [not] important, threatened participants [did not] save[d] a greater amount of money than did control participants (threat x goal importance interaction = $F(1, 201) = 4.40$, $p < .04$). Moreover, only pursuing important an goal was self-affirming.

In Experiments 4 and 5, we induced self-threat exposing participants to negative brand information for brands with for which they had a high vs. low self brand connection (SBC). Cheng, White, and Chaplin (2012) found that consumers with high self-brand connections to certain brands experienced a threat to their positive self-view upon receiving negative brand information. Extending these findings, we suggest that negative brand information should motivate high SBC consumers to pursue irrelevant goals (e.g., helping others) that are made salient by the situation. To test this possibility, we used the brand Adidas, which was one of the major business sponsors of 2008 Beijing Olympic Games. After getting information about Adidas' sponsorship, participants read either a negative commentary or a neutral commentary on this sponsorship. In Experiment 4, we found a significant brand information x SBC interaction ($\beta = .49$, $t = 2.46$; $p < .02$). Simple slope analysis revealed that when participants received negative information about Adidas, those who felt highly connected with the brand took more money for themselves ($\beta = .30$; $t = 2.01$; $p = .05$). However, when participants received neutral information about Adidas, the effects of SBC on the amount money that participants took was not significant ($\beta = -.26$; $t = -1.54$; $p > .10$). In Experiment 5, we manipulated self-threat by providing negative brand information about Blackberry to high vs. low SBC respondents and measured their willingness to donate to UNICEF. As expected, the effect of SBC on the amount of donation was significant ($\beta = .51$, $t = 2.86$, $p < .02$), indicating that when participants received negative information about Blackberry, those who were highly connected to the brand donated more money to UNICEF. We also measured self-esteem in this study. As expected, receiving negative information about Blackberry decreased participants' self-esteem when they were highly connected to the brand Blackberry. Moreover, it appears that this self-threat motivated participants to donate more to charity, which, in turn, boosted (restored) their self-esteem.

Conclusion. Individuals often take actions to self-affirm following threats to their positive-self view. We propose that: 1) self-threat can cultivate a general motivation to pursue salient goals; 2) this tendency could lead to behaviors with divergent implications when opposing goals are activated; and 3) goal importance moderates this effect. We tested the implications of this framework in the context of self-brand connections; we show that negative brand information

poses a self-threat to consumers with a high self-brand connection (but not to those with a low self-brand connection) and motivates them to pursue the goals highlighted in the subsequent situation. In particular, following exposure to negative brand information, high SBC consumers donated more money when the goal to help was made salient, yet took more money when the salient goal was to pursue self-interest.

Identity Change: The Effects of Actual and Ideal Self-Brand Connections on Consumers' Response to Brand Image Change

EXTENDED ABSTRACT

In contrast to the extant literature (MacInnis et al. 2009), we investigate a potential disadvantage of strong of consumer-brand bonds. Consumers sometimes incorporate brands into their self-concept to construct and/or signal identity (self-brand connection, Escalas and Bettman 2003). We argue that for those consumers who have incorporated the brand into their self-concept, change in brand image can represent an identity-threat. Consumers cope with this threat, not only by reacting negatively to the change, but also by reducing their felt brand connection.

Study 1 applies brand acquisitions as the context. We propose that consumers' reactions to an acquisition are contingent on whether or not it changes target brand image. Further, we expect self-brand connection to moderate this effect. Since strongly connected consumers incorporate the brand in their self-concept, a change in brand image is a forced change in the self and represents an identity-threat. Thus, we expect these consumers to reduce their connection if brand image change.

Seventy undergraduate students participated in a 2 (no change/change) $\times$ self-brand connection (measured) mixed design experiment. First, we measured attitude and self-brand connection to Nike and other filler brands. Then (one hour later), participants read a newspaper article about the acquisition of Nike. The acquirer was a fictitious venture capital company. Statements in the article manipulated no change/change in brand personality due to the acquisition (the change condition entailed Nike becoming more glamorous, sophisticated and upper class). Last, we measured the dependent variables and manipulation checks.

We conducted multiple regressions with the experimental conditions (no change/change), self-brand connection (continuous), and their interaction as independent variables.

The results showed an interaction between the experimental conditions and self-brand connection on attitude to the acquisition ($\beta = -.40$, $t = -2.44$, $p < .02$) and, more interestingly, also on both change in attitude ($\beta = -.38$, $t = -2.03$, $p < .05$) and change in self-brand connection ($\beta = -.26$, $t = -.194$, $p = .057$) to the target brand. Investigations of the interactions confirmed the predicted significance of slopes, as well as contrasts between no change/change at high levels of self-brand connection.

The results indicate that consumers react more negatively to change in brand image the greater connection they have with the brand. Further, strongly connected consumers experience brand image change as a threat to their self and withdraw from the brand relationship.

The first experiment investigated brand imagechange through the introduction of new traits. However, brand image can also change by reinforcement of existing traits. There is some evidence that consumers are reluctant to enhance existing traits that are fundamental to their self-concept (Riis et al. 2008). Hence, we expect consumers with strong self-brand connection to react negatively to every deviation from the existing brand image, even to reinforcement of existing salient traits.

Based on pretests, we chose 'Diesel' as the target brand for study 2. The traits most strongly associated with Diesel were rugged, tough, masculine and daring (pretest). We therefore used these strongly associated traits to examine reactions to change through reinforcement of established traits. Except for the use of established (vs. new) traits, the procedure was similar to study 1. Thirty-six undergraduate students completed the study.

Multiple regression revealed an interaction between the experimental conditions and self-brand connection on attitude to the acquisition (β=-.71, t=-2.70, p<.02), as well as on change in attitude (β=-.68, t=-2.05, p<.05) and change in self-brand connection (β=-.37, t=-2.51, p<.02). Investigations of the interactions confirmed the predicted significance of slopes, as well as contrasts at low and high levels of self-brand connection.

The results indicate that strongly connected consumers react negatively and show threat response, not only to introduction of new traits, but also to change through reinforcement of existing brand associations. Next, we investigate whether this effect is valid for all brand connections or whether it depends on which part of the self-concept the brand primarily connects (actual or ideal self).

In study 3, we investigate the hypothesis that whether the brand is primarily connected to consumers' actual or ideal self influences reactions to brand image change. We hypothesize that for consumers' feeling congruence between their actual self and the brand, all brand image changes are negative because they decrease the felt congruence between the self and the brand. However, for consumers feeling congruence between their ideal self and the brand, reinforcement of the existing brand image can be positive as it increases the brands ability to signal an ideal identity.

One hundred and seventy-two participants completed a survey on an online web panel (American participants age_{mean} = 35.1, 56 % females). First, we measured brand attitude, actual and ideal self-brand congruity, as well as brand personality. After some filler tasks, participants read a hypothetical scenario about the re-positioning and change in Nike's brand image. Lastly, we measured participants' attitudes to change in different personality traits of Nike.

We conducted multiple regressions with an index of attitude to change in the five most descriptive traits (based on the personality evaluation in the first part of the survey: successful, leader, winner, confident, and up-to-date) as a dependent measure, with degree of actual self-brand congruity (continuous) and degree of ideal self-brand congruity (continuous) as independent variables.

The results revealed a negative effect of actual self-brand congruency (β=-.15, t=-2.16, p<.04) and a positive effect of ideal self-brand congruency (β=.26, t=4.65, p<.01).The results indicate that consumers' response to reinforcement of existing salient traits depends on whether the brand is connected to the consumers' actual self or ideal self.

Overall, we find support for the hypothesis that consumers who use the brand to construct and/or signal their identity demonstrate identity-threat responses to brand image change. They are more negative to brand image change (than those who are less connected to the brand) and react by withdrawing from the relationship. We also demonstrate that if the connection is based on congruence between the actual self and the brand, all changes in brand image are perceived as negative. However, if the brand connection is based on congruence between the ideal self and the brand, changes through reinforcement of existing brand traits are perceived as positive.

The Costs and Benefits of Consumer Labor

Session Chair: Daniel Mochon, Tulane University, USA

Paper #1: Labor or Leisure?
Christopher K. Hsee, University of Chicago Booth School of Business, USA

Paper #2: The Influence of Identity on Creative Outcomes
Kelly B. Herd, Indiana University, USA
C. Page Moreau, University of Colorado-Boulder, USA

Paper #3: Self-Customization Effects on Brand Extensions
Ulrike Kaiser, Vienna University of Economics and Business, Austria
Chezy Ofir, The Hebrew University of Jerusalem, Israel
Martin Schreier, Vienna University of Economics and Business, Austria

Paper #4: The IKEA Effect: Signaling and Restoring Feelings of Competence
Daniel Mochon, Tulane University, USA
Michael I. Norton, Harvard University, USA
Dan Ariely, Duke University, USA

SESSION OVERVIEW

Consumers are increasingly acting as co-creators of value, rather than as just passive recipients of it (e.g. Prahalad and Ramaswamy 2002; Vargo and Lusch 2004). Numerous companies have emerged that allow customers to design their own products, both through mass-customization toolkits and crowdsourcing sites. Moreover, firms continue to expand the involvement of customers in the promotion of their products, by encouraging them to create and distribute brand related content. This trend has lead to an unprecedented amount of labor being outsourced to the firms' costumers. In this session we present diverse perspectives on the costs and benefits of consumer labor for both the firms, and the consumers themselves.

The first paper examines some of its costs, by showing that people may be insensitive to their earning rate, and thus work to the point where they are tired, rather than when they have maximized their overall utility. As such, constraints on the amount people can earn can lead to higher well-being. The second paper looks at the effect of constraints in creative tasks. It shows that constraints can influence the evaluation of self-created products and the effort devoted to these, and that this is moderated by the identity primed. The third paper shows how labor not only affects the evaluation of the product created, but also how it can affect the overall relationship with the brand. Finally, the last paper examines the mechanism behind the value customers derive from their own labor, and shows how this can be used to increase the involvement of customers in co-creation. As a whole, this session provides novel and varied views on the consequences of consumer labor.

Labor or Leisure?

EXTENDED ABSTRACT

This research studies how people allocate their time between labor and leisure, a question that is relevant to every consumer who needs to work in order to earn what she/he wants to consume. Do people ever overwork – endure unpleasant labor to earn more than what they believe they can possibly consume?

Although these questions are apparently important, they are hardly answerable in the real world, because the real world is too complex for researchers to determine what the right amount of work or the right amount of earning is; hence to define what overworking or over-earning is.

Instead of studying overworking or over-earning in the real world, the current research seeks to achieve the following more modest and specific objectives: to introduce a minimalistic paradigm that allows researchers to define and study overworking and over-earning in a controlled laboratory setting, and to use this paradigm to demonstrate when and why people overwork and over-earn.

The Paradigm

Participants are run individually using a personal computer, and each participant is required to wear a set of headphones. The experiment consists of two consecutive phases, each lasting five minutes. During phase I, the participant can either listen to music and earn nothing (leisure) or listen to noises and earn chocolates (work). The default is listening to music. At any time she can press a dedicated key on the computer keyboard to disrupt the music and listen to a short, 0.2 sec, beep-like noise, and for every certain number of times she listens to the noise, she will earn one piece of chocolate. The noise is pretested as less pleasant than the music. Throughout phase I, the computer screen displays the number of chocolates earned and the time elapsed. The participant may not eat the earned chocolates in phase I.

Once phase I ends, phase II commences. The computer instructs the participant to take the number of chocolates she has earned in phase I from a jar on the table and start to eat them. She does not have to eat all the earned chocolates, and if there are any remaining ones, she has to leave them on the table and cannot bring them home. The participant may not listen to more noises or earn more chocolates in this phase.

Every aspect of the procedure is explained to the participant before the experiment starts; she knows what type of chocolate she will earn and what type of noise she will hear. In addition, the participant is told that it is entirely up to her how many chocolates to earn in phase I and how many to eat in phase II, and that her only objective is to make herself as happy as possible in the entire experiment. The main dependent variables are how many chocolates she earns in phase I and how many she eats in phase II.

We define *overworking* as forgoing leisure (music) to earn more chocolates in phase I than the predicted optimal amount. (In this paradigm, overworking and overearning are the same, and we will use these terms interchangeably.) We define *predicted optimal amount* as the number of chocolates the participant herself or somebody in the same situation as the participant *predicts* that she will eat in order to make her most satisfied, and we empirically establish this level in pretests.

Findings

Using this method, we have conducted a series of studies to explore when and why participants overwork (or underwork). Because we already introduced the method above and also because of the space limit, we will not elaborate on each study. Instead, we will summarize the main empirical findings below:

- When the earning rate was low (e.g., earning 1 chocolate every 10 times one listened to the noise), participants underworked, i.e., stopped working and earning before they earned the predicted optimal amount. When the earning rate was high (e.g., earning 1 chocolate every time one listened to the noise), participants overworked, i.e., continued to work and earn after they had earned the predicted optimal amount. These results imply that low-income people tend to underwork relative to what they need and high-income people tend to overwork relative to what they need

- The above effects occurred, because participants were insensitive to the earning rate or to the utility of their earning; they worked until they felt tired, rather than until they had enough.

- Predicted optimal amount was quite accurate, that is, quite similar to the actual consumption amount. Note that this similarity was not due to participants' desire to be consistent between prediction and behavior, because the predicted optimal amount was elicited from a separate group of participants and the main participants were not aware.

- Participants who overworked were less happy than participants who did not. It suggested that people overworked, not because they enjoyed working.

- Finally, we tested a paternalistic intervention method – not allowing participants to earn more chocolates after a certain point, though still allowing them to work (listen to noise) if they wished. This method produced two effects: First (less interesting), it curtained overworking. Second (more interesting), it increased participants' happiness. It suggested that (high-income) people lack the self control to stop working and stop earning after they have already earned more than what they can possibly consume and not allowing them to make excessive earning can reduce their tendency to overwork and, more importantly, can make them happier.

The Influence of Identity on Creative Outcomes

EXTENDED ABSTRACT

While much of creative consumption involves creating a product for personal use, the bulk of work on consumer creativity focuses on "objective" evaluations of an outcome by someone other than the individual who created it. When creating for oneself, we propose that identity motives interact with constraints provided at the time of design to influence consumers evaluations of their own creative outcomes.

Prior literature has shown that constraints both enhance and inhibit creativity (e.g., Dahl and Moreau 2007; Moreau and Dahl 2005; Sellier and Dahl 2012). Through three studies all involving actual creative tasks, we show that identity motives influence the relationship between constraints and evaluations of self-created outputs. Importantly, this relationship also depends on the structured nature of the creative task itself (i.e., an unstructured drawing task vs. customization via a structured toolkit).

Identity, what comes to mind when we think of ourselves, includes two major components: a personal identity related to the independent self and a social identity related to the interdependent self (Kirmani 2009; Oyserman 2009). Cheng et al. (2008) suggest that activating an identity makes related knowledge structures accessible for creative tasks. This knowledge structure accessibility may make creative tasks easier, but it can also lead to more habitual and less objectively creative outcomes (e.g., Aarts and Dijksterhuis 2000). Across three studies, we examine how priming identity-related knowledge influences both effort expended and evaluations of one's own creative outcomes.

In Study 1 all participants (N =97) receive a blank piece of paper along with colored pencils (high constraint = 6 colors, low constraint = 12 colors) and are asked to draw a picture that could be used on a customized product. Those in the "identity" condition are told to draw something that represents something interesting or important to them (participants in the "no identity" condition are simply asked to

think about products that could have customized designs). We find a significant interaction of the two manipulated factors on evaluations $(F(1,96) = 3.81, p = .05)$. When identity is primed, participants with high constraints evaluate their drawings more positively than those with low constraints ($M_{\text{Identity, Low Constraints}} = 4.08$ vs. $M_{\text{Identity, High Constraints}} = 4.96$; $F(1, 96) = 4.87$, $p < .03$). When identity is not primed, input constraints do not have a significant influence on evaluations ($M_{\text{No Identity, Low Constraints}} = 4.29$ vs. $M_{\text{No Identity, High Constraints}} = 4.19$; $F(1, 96) = .06$, n/s). We find that effort expended mediates design evaluations such that when participants are not primed with identity, they exert more effort when constraints are low. However, when primed with identity, they report exerting more effort when constraints are high. From this study, we conclude that in an unstructured task environment, when identity motives are not active, participants prefer low constraints. But when motivated by identity, participants prefer higher constraints.

In the following studies, we examine the interaction between constraints and identity motives using online customization toolkits. Like other constraints, we propose that the structured nature of these task environments make participants less reliant on their own memories and accessible knowledge structures, leading them off the Path of Least Resistance (e.g., Fink et al. 1992; Moreau and Dahl 2005; Ward et al. 2002). To test this theory in our next two studies, all participants engage in creative tasks using online customization toolkits. We capture product evaluations both at the time of design and several weeks later at delivery.

In Study 2, all participants (N = 89) design a "skin" cover for a cell phone or MP3 player. Again we manipulate identity motive (absent vs. present) and input constraints (low = option to upload images or use library, high = library images only). We find that consumers evaluate their designs more favorably when constraints are low ($M_{\text{Low Constraints}} = 5.41$ vs. $M_{\text{High Constraints}} = 4.37$; $F(1, 88) = 13.57$ $p < .001$). This difference is enhanced when an identity goal has been activated and the interaction is significant ($F(1, 88) = 3.92, p = .05$). This pattern holds 10 days later when we deliver the product. As in Study 1, we find that effort (captured as time taken) mediates the effect of the manipulated factors on evaluations at the time of design.

Study 2 demonstrates that in a structured task environment, consumers given greater design freedom evaluate their designs higher and are more satisfied at delivery than those given less design leeway. In our next study, rather than broadly motivating identity, we independently motivate two competing identity-based motivations: personal identity and social identity (e.g., Oyserman 2009).

In Study 3, all participants (N = 82) design a customized travel mug (all participants actually receive the product they design, allowing us to capture satisfaction measures 6 weeks later at delivery). Two factors are manipulated across participants: input constraints (high vs. low, as in Study 2) and identity motives (social vs. personal). A two-way ANOVA reveals a significant interaction ($F(1,81) = 3.70, p = .05$). Participants reported higher evaluations of their designs when constraints were low (vs. high). This effect was more pronounced for those primed with personal identity motivations ($M_{\text{Personal, Low Constraints}} = 5.43$ vs. $M_{\text{Personal, High Constraints}} = 4.23$; $F(1,81) = 10.14, p < .01$) than with social identity motivations ($M_{\text{Social, Low Constraints}} = 5.15$ vs. $M_{\text{Social, High Constraints}} = 4.93$; $F(1, 81) = .38$, n/s). These results hold 6 weeks later at delivery.

By engaging participants in real creativity tasks, these three studies examine the influence that identity-related motivations have on consumers' evaluations of their own creations. These studies demonstrate that simply making salient an identity motivation prior to design can significantly influence design evaluations, product satisfaction and the effectiveness of the input constraints.

Self-Customization Effects on Brand Extensions

EXTENDED ABSTRACT

Mass customization (i.e., letting consumers customize their own products) is considered central to current marketing strategies and is gaining growing popularity in practice. So far, the main finding in the literature has been that self-customized products deliver superior value to customers (Franke et al. 2010; Norton et al. 2012; Randall et al. 2005). Four studies in the current research demonstrate that self-customization also positively affect the more general customer-brand relationship, conceptualized as brand attachment (Fedorikhin et al. 2008; Thomson et al. 2005; Park et al. 2010). The resulted brand attachment affects customers' intention to buy and willingness to pay for a *noncustomized* brand extension.

Study 1 was a scenario-based experiment to test effects of self-customization on brand attachment. We used scenarios to control for the most common reported outcome of self-customization, namely preference fit (defined as the fit between customer preferences and product characteristics). Following scholars like Bendapudi and Leone (2003), we developed two graphic scenarios to portray different purchasing situations. To allow participants to identify easily, we used a hypothetical figure named Pat. 159 participants were randomly assigned to one of the following conditions: (1) self-customization group, in which Pat was designing an individual PC with a mass-customization toolkit, and (2) the standard choice condition, in which Pat chose one option. All participants were informed that Pat was very satisfied with the self-customized (chosen) PC. The brand attachment measure focused on participants' connection to the brand (Thomson et al. 2005). We also included questions assessing preference fit and reactions to the graphic scenarios. Manipulation checks suggest that, as intended, preference fit was perceived to be constant (i.e. high) across conditions. Our results indicate that, as hypothesized, self-customization has a significant effect on brand attachment.

In Study 2 and 3 we show that feelings of autonomy and competence that result from self-customization mediate the processes leading to higher brand attachment. This effect is also found to depend on the design freedom granted to consumers: in case of a large (small) solution space the effects are amplified (attenuated) (Study 2). Study 2 was a one-way between subject random design with three conditions. 259 students were randomly assigned to either the standard condition or one of the two self-customization conditions. Those in the standard choice condition were asked to select a pair of casual shoes; participants in the self-customization groups were asked to design their own pair of shoes in a real customization task. In the high solution space condition, participants had a great deal of options; in the low solution space condition, the number of available options was much more limited. The collection of standard shoes and also the modules and options in the customization tool were pretested and developed by a professional designer. Following executing the task, respondents rated items measuring the main variables: brand attachment, autonomy and competence. Autonomy is defined as people's need to believe that their activities are self-chosen, self-governed, self-determined, and self-organized. Competence is the need to feel capable and effective and to have a sense of achievement. It refers to the anticipated satisfaction derived from completing a creative task successfully. We also measured preference fit and some other control variables (perceived effort of the design / choice tasks and product category involvement).

Manipulation checks suggest that actual solution space significantly affected perceived solution space. An Anova model applied to the brand attachment measure resulted in a significant effect of customization. In particular, mass-customization in the high solution space resulted in a significantly higher brand attachment than in the other conditions. There is no significant difference, however, between the standard choice and the low customization conditions (i.e. effects are attenuated in the customization low solution space condition). Bootstrapping results suggest that feelings of autonomy and competence mediate this effect. Results are robust when including our control variables.

We designed another scenario-based study (Study 3; n = 444) to deepen our understanding of psychological processes and would contribute to the understanding of processes that underlie the formation of brand attachment. Method and procedure was very similar to Study 1. In a 2 (self-customization vs. standard condition) x 2 (preference fit high vs. average) factorial design, we show that both self-customization and preference fit have an independent and positive impact on brand attachment. We again show that feelings of autonomy and competence mediate the main effect of customization on attachment.

Finally, Study 4 demonstrates the mediating role of brand attachment on the effect of mass customization on the acceptance of brand extension of a *noncustomized* product – highlighting the importance of incorporating brand attachment in the theory and practice of mass customization and brand extensions. We conducted between-subject experiment that involved a real customization (choice) task. Participants (n = 126) were randomly assigned to one of the following two conditions: (1) The self-customization group was asked to design its own muesli mix (using the mass-customization toolkit of the company Mymuesli [www.mymuesli.com]) and (2) the standard choice condition was given the task of choosing one of 10 ready-made mixes. To add realism, participants were delivered the exact breakfast cereal mix they had self-customized (chosen). After product delivery – and after some time allowing for product trial – we measured preference fit, brand attachment, and willingness to pay (WTP) for a moderately dissimilar brand extension (muesli bars). In order to avoid any "cheap talk", we conducted an incentive-compatible BDM lottery to assess WTP for a brand extension. In line with our previous studies, we find that self-customization positively affects brand attachment. The effect of self-customization on WTP for a noncustomized brand extension is also significant and positive. Customers are willing to pay, on average, 35% more for the brand extension (package of muesli bar). We conducted a product-of-coefficients test to establish our proposed mediation.

In sum, our contributions are as follows: First, we extend the literature on brand attachment to mass customization research; second, we demonstrate the mediating role of brand attachment on the effect of mass customization on the acceptance of brand extension of a *noncustomized* product. Theoretical implications for mass-customization, brand attachment and brand extension along with managerial implications are discussed.

The IKEA Effect:
Signaling and Restoring Feelings of Competence

EXTENDED ABSTRACT

Prior work has shown that consumers are willing to pay more for self-made products than for identical products made by someone else (Franke, Schreier, and Kaiser 2010; Norton, Mochon, and Ariely 2012), an effect labeled the IKEA effect (Norton et al. 2012). In the current work we examine the underlying process behind this effect. We suggest that this premium is due to the role that self-created products have in fulfilling two deep identity-related desires of consumers: their desire to signal to themselves an identity that they are competent and have effectance, and their desire to display that identity to others. Self-assembly of products fulfills both of these needs: by building things myself I am controlling and shaping my environment, proving my own competence, and by displaying my creations I am demonstrating my competence to others. In support of this theory, we demonstrate that feelings of competence mediate the premium attached to self-made products (Study 1); that allowing consumers to affirm their competence another way reduces the magnitude of this effect (Study 2); and that threatening people's sense of competence in one domain, increases their desire to assemble goods, and thus reestablish their competent self-view (Study 3).

In study 1 we examine whether feelings of competence mediate the IKEA effect. In this study participants were presented with a Lego car. *Builders* were given the pieces for the car with the instructions that come with the product, and were asked to assemble it accordingly. *Non-Builders* were given the car already assembled, and were asked to examine it. Participants were then asked to give their maximum willingness to pay using an incentive compatible BDM procedure. We then measured the feelings of competence associated with the product, as well as participants' overall mood. Replicating prior work on the IKEA effect, the builders were willing to pay more for their car ($M = \$1.20$, $SD = 1.35$) than the non-builders ($M = \$0.57$, $SD = .76$; $p < .05$). Builders also associated higher feelings of competence with their creations ($M = 4.39$, $SD = 1.48$) than non-builders ($M = 2.81$, $SD = 1.34$; $p < .001$). Importantly, the feelings of competence associated with the product fully mediated the effect of build condition on WTP (Sobel $Z = 2.08$, $p < .05$). Moreover, while builders ended up with a more positive mood than non-builders, mood did not mediate the IKEA effect.

In study 2, we test our account by both measuring, and also directly manipulating participants' need to feel competent. If our theory is correct, participants who are allowed to affirm the self another way (Aronson, Cohen, and Nail 1999; Steele 1988) may no longer need to signal competence through the products they create, and therefore should not show the IKEA effect. Participants in this study were randomly assigned to one of four conditions of a 2 self-affirmation condition (no affirmation vs. self-affirmation) x 2 build condition (pre-built vs. build) between-subjects design. Participants were first presented with a manipulation where they either did or did not affirm their values (Sherman, Nelson, and Steele 2000). Following the self-affirmation manipulation, participants were presented with an IKEA Kassett storage box. *Builders* were given the parts necessary to assemble the box, as well as the instructions from IKEA to assemble it, and assembled the box. *Non-Builders* were presented with a box that was already built, and were asked to examine it. We then measured participants maximum WTP using an incentive compatible procedure as well as the feelings of competence associated with the product.

The results showed no significant main effect of the self-affirmation or build conditions. However, we found the predicted significant interaction between these two factors ($F(1,115) = 3.90$, $p = .05$). In the no affirmation condition, we replicated the standard IKEA effect: builders ($M = \$0.72$, $SD = .45$) were willing to pay significantly more than those who received a box pre-built ($M = \$0.46$, $SD = .50$; $p = .05$). This effect was eliminated for participants in the self-affirmation condition, where there was no significant difference between builders ($M = \$0.49$, $SD = .46$) and those who received a pre-built box ($M = \$0.58$, $SD = .46$; $p = .48$). Thus, providing participants with an opportunity to affirm the self eliminated the IKEA effect. We further tested a model of moderated mediation to examine whether the indirect effect of competence on WTP depends on self-affirmation (Preacher, Rucker, and Hayes 2007). The results suggest

that, as in the previous study, competence acts as a mediator of the effect of building on WTP, but that this effect was moderated by the self-affirmation manipulation. Indeed, the analyses revealed a significant conditional indirect effect of the competence mediator in the no affirmation condition ($Z = 2.80$, $p < .01$), and a non-significant conditional indirect effect of the mediator in the self-affirmation condition ($Z = 1.34$, $p = .18$).

In study 3 we examined whether threatening people's sense of competence would increase their propensity to want to create their own products. In this study participants were first presented with a short math test which was either very difficult (*Low Competence Condition*) or easy (*Control Condition*). Participants were then asked to imagine that they had just bought a bookcase from IKEA, and were asked whether they would prefer to assemble it themselves, or would prefer for it to come pre-assembled. While only 33% of participants in the control condition said that they would prefer to assemble the bookcase themselves, 58% of participants in the low competence condition indicated that they would prefer to do so ($p < .05$).

The above results provide convergent evidence that the IKEA effect is driven by consumer's desire to signal competence to themselves and others. Moreover, these results suggest important practical implications for firms, by demonstrating that customers can be encouraged to participate in co-creation by appealing to their desire to signal competence.

SESSION CONCLUSION

This session helps further the conference's mission of diversity by drawing attention to a growing area in consumer research that views consumers in a novel way: rather than just being passive recipients of goods, under the perspective of this session, consumers are active creators of value. The diverse perspectives presented here should offer a good starting point for the discussion of the advantages and costs of this new model of consumer behavior.

REFERENCES

Aarts, Henk and Ap Dijksterhuis (2000), "Habits as Knowledge Structures: Automaticity in Goal-Directed Behavior," *Journal of Personality and Social Psychology*, 78 (1), 53-63.

Aronson, Joshua, Geoffrey Cohen, and Paul R. Nail (1999), "Self-Affirmation Theory: An Update and Appraisal," in *Cognitive Dissonance: Progress on a Pivotal Theory in Social Psychology*, ed. Eddie Harmon-Jones and Judson Mills, Washington, DC: American Psychological Association, 127-47.

Bendapudi, Neeli and Robert P. Leone (2003), "Psychological Implications of Customer Participation in Co-Production," *Journal of Marketing*, 67 (January), 14–28.

Cheng, Chi-Ying, Jeffrey Sanchez-Burks, and Fiona Lee (2008), "Connecting the Dots Within: Creative Performance and Identity Integration," *Psychological Science*, 19 (11), 1178-84.

Dahl, Darren W. and C. Page Moreau (2007), "Thinking Inside the Box: Why Consumers Enjoy Constrained Creative Experiences," *Journal of Marketing Research*, 44 (3), 357-69.

Fedorikhin, Alexander, C. W. Park, and Matthew Thomson (2008), "Beyond Fit and Attitude: The Effect of Emotional Attachment to Brand Extensions," *Journal of Consumer Psychology*, 18 (October), 281–91.

Finke, Ronald, Thomas Ward, and Steven Smith (1992), "Creative Cognition: Theory, Research, and Applications," Cambridge, MA: MIT Press.

Franke, Nikolaus, Martin Schreier, and Ulrike Kaiser (2010), "The 'I Designed It Myself' Effect in Mass Customization," *Management Science*, 56 (1), 125–40.

Kirmani, Amna (2009), "The Self and the Brand," *Journal of Consumer Psychology*, 19 (3), 271-75.

Moreau, C. Page and Darren W. Dahl (2005), "Designing the Solution: The Impact of Constraints on Consumers' Creativity," *Journal of Consumer Research*, 32 (1), 13-22.

Norton, Michael I., Daniel Mochon, and Dan Ariely (2012), "The Ikea Effect: When Labor Leads to Love," *Journal of Consumer Psychology* 22 (3), 453-60.

Oyserman, Daphna (2009), "Identity-Based Motivation: Implications for Action-Readiness, Procedural-Readiness, and Consumer Behavior," *Journal of Consumer Research*, 19 (3), 250-60.

Park, C. W., Deborah J. MacInnis, Joseph R. Priester, Andreas B. Eisingerich, and Dawn Iacobucci (2010), "Brand Attachment and Brand Attitude Strength: Conceptual and Empirical Differentiation of Two Critical Brand Equity Drivers," *Journal of Marketing*, 74 (6), 1-17.

Prahalad, C. K. and Venkatram Ramaswamy (2002), "The Co-Creation Connection," *Strategy and Business,* 27 (2), 50-61.

Preacher, Kristopher J., Derek D. Rucker, and Andrew F. Hayes (2007), "Addressing Moderated Mediation Hypotheses: Theory, Methods, and Prescriptions," *Multivariate Behavioral Research*, 42 (1), 185-227.

Randall, Taylor, Christian Terwiesch, and Karl T. Ulrich (2007), "User Design of Customized Products," *Marketing Science*, 26 (March/April), 268–80.

Sellier, Anne-Laure and Darren W. Dahl (2011), "Focus! Creative Success Is Enjoyed Through Restricted Choice," *Journal of Marketing Research*, 48 (6), 996-1007.

Sherman, David K., Leif D. Nelson, and Claude M. Steele (2000), "Do Messages About Health Risks Threaten the Self? Increasing the Acceptance of Threatening Health Messages Via Self-Affirmation," *Personality and Social Psychology Bulletin*, 26 (9), 1046-58.

Steele, Claude M. (1988), "The Psychology of Self-Affirmation: Sustaining the Integrity of the Self," in *Advances in Experimental Social Psychology*, Vol. 21, ed. Leonard Berkowitz, New York: Academic Press, 261-302.

Thomson, Matthew, Deborah J. MacInnis, and C. W. Park (2005), "The Ties That Bind: Measuring the Strength of Consumers' Emotional Attachments to Brands," *Journal of Consumer Psychology*, 15 (1), 77–91.

Vargo, Stephen L. and Robert F. Lusch (2004), "Evolving a New Dominant Logic for Marketing," *Journal of Marketing,* 68 (January), 1-17.

Ward, Thomas B., Merryl J.Patterson, Cynthia M. Sifonis, Rebecca A. Dodds, and Katherine N. Saunders (2002), "The Role of Graded Category Structure in Imaginative Thought," *Memory & Cognition*, 30 (2), 199-216.

The Best of Times, The Worst of Times:
How Resource Abundance and Scarcity Shape Consumer Behavior

Chairs: Eugene M. Caruso, University of Chicago, USA
Nicole L. Mead, Erasmus University, The Netherlands

Paper #1: Do the Worst of Times Increase Creativity?: Scarcity vs. Abundance Psychology and Creativity

Ravi Mehta, University of Illinois at Urbana Champaign, USA
Meng Zhu, The Johns Hopkins Carey Business School, USA

Paper #2: Dealing with Uncertainty Through Haptic Sensations

Femke van Horen, University of Cologne, Germany
Thomas Mussweiler, University of Cologne, Germany

Paper #3: Perceived Resource Scarcity Reduces Trust among Men but Increases Trust among Women

Nicole L. Mead, Erasmus University, The Netherlands
Evan Weingarten, University of Chicago, USA
Eugene M. Caruso, University of Chicago, USA

Paper #4: Mental Accounting in the Context of Poverty

Crystal Hall, University of Washington, USA
Eldar Shafir, Princeton University, USA

SESSION OVERVIEW

In order to survive, consumers depend on a several key resources, including food and money. Yet in any given day, these resources can be seen as threatened (e.g., short-term financial crisis) or experienced as lacking (e.g., chronic poverty). Despite the centrality of resources in daily human life, relatively little research has investigated how actual or perceived scarcity can shape consumer mindsets, product preferences, and daily decisions, such as tradeoffs between time and money. The proposed session aims to highlight the newest research from around the globe that tackles these questions and more using a diverse range of methods, population samples, and measures. Broadly, the first two papers examine how resource scarcity (compared to resource abundance) changes consumers' mindsets and product preferences, whereas the final two papers examine resource scarcity among different populations. Specifically, Mehta will begin by showing that resource scarcity changes the way that people approach problems in a way that leads them to think outside in the box, thereby heightening consumer creativity. Van Horen will continue by examining how consumers use products with specific haptic sensations to restore a sense of comfort when resources are perceived as uncertain. Mead will then focus on how scarcity affects monetary trust decisions, showing that scarcity differentially impacts men and women's trust. Hall will close the session by demonstrating and discussing how and why low-income consumers differ in everyday financial decisions from high-income consumers. Taken together, the diverse approaches, methods, and populations represented in the four papers provide a broad yet deep view into emerging research on the implications of resource scarcity and abundance for consumer behavior. Particularly in the current climate of economic and political uncertainty, the novelty of the topic and diversity of the research will surely draw a large audience and stimulate a lively dialogue among these researchers.

Do the Worst of Times Increase Creativity?: Scarcity vs. Abundance Psychology and Creativity

EXTENDED ABSTRACT

The face of human society is constantly changing. As humans moved into the late modern era as an industrialized society, consumerism and over-acquisition of resources started to become the way of living (Côté 1993, 1996; Riesman 1950). Abundance started to supplant scarcity, especially in first world societies. Simultaneously, creativity has taken on a relatively more central and important role in consumption environments. On the demand side of the equation, consumers engage in everyday creative behavior such as home décor and fashion (Burroughs and Mick 2004; Burroughs, Moreau and Mick 2008). On the supply side of the equation, many businesses thrive on consumers' ability and desire to be creative.

One question that arises, then, is whether and how perceived availability of resources affects creativity in consumption environments. Or more specifically, how might a scarcity (vs. abundance) mindset influence consumers' creativity? In the current work, we conceptualize scarcity as the perception of an insufficient supply of resources, and abundance as the perception of an excessive supply of resources (Zhu and Kalra 2012). Past research has shown that the existence of constraints induces novel problem solving (Moreau and Dahl 2005). That is, constraints make people move away from the path of least resistance (POLR), thereby increasing their creativity. Hence, we argue that perceptions of scarcity will cause consumers to approach problems from multiple perspectives. That is, when scarcity cues are salient, individuals will overcome functional fixedness (Ward, Smith, & Finke, 1999) and explore solutions more broadly, leading to heightened creativity. However, when abundance cues are salient, individuals may not have sufficient motivation to move away from the POLR. Thus, among abundance participants, we predict a higher degree of functional fixedness, narrower exploration of solutions, and relatively lower creativity.

Experiment 1 tested our basic hypothesis that inducing a scarcity (vs. abundance) mindset will lead to higher creativity. To manipulate mindset, we had some participants write a paragraph about "Growing up in a society with scarce resources" (scarce condition), and other participants write a paragraph about "Growing up in a society with abundant resources" (abundance condition). Then all participants were presented with 10 Remote Associate Test items; their responses were assessed as a measure of creativity (Mednick 1962). As expected, participants primed with abundance cues demonstrated lower creativity as compared to participants primed with scarcity cues and participants in the control condition.

In experiment 2, we examined the mechanism through which perceived resource availability affected creativity. Specifically, we assessed whether abundance (vs. scarcity) mindset led to lower creativity because it increased functional fixedness. To induce perceptions of abundance and scarcity, we used the same manipulation used in experiment 1. All participants were then asked to generate creative uses of a brick (Friedman and Forster 2001). To assess the creativity of the uses generated, a panel of 12 judges rated the creativity of participants' responses. A second independent panel of 12 judges rated each of the uses on functional fixedness (i.e., how different the idea was from the usual use of a brick). As predicted, uses for the brick generated by scarcity participants were judged to be more creative as compared to those generated by abundance participants. Also, we observed that functional fixedness mediated the effect, such that a scarcity mindset led to lower functional fixedness, which in turn led to more creative uses for the brick.

Experiment 3 provided further support for functional fixedness as the underlying mechanism. In this experiment, we manipulated functional fixedness salience in addition to manipulating perceived resource scarcity. To manipulate functional fixedness, participants were asked to generate ideas for a new kind of a computer keyboard. Those in the functional fixedness salient condition were told specifically to generate ideas for a new type of a "computer keyboard (the one you are using to type now)," whereas those in the control condition were simply asked to generate ideas for a new type of "computer keyboard." A two-way analysis of variance (ANOVA) revealed an interaction between functional fixedness and scarcity. Participants in the control condition demonstrated the same pattern of results observed in experiments 1 and 2: an abundance (vs. scarcity) mindset lowered creativity. However, when functional fixedness was induced experimentally, the effect disappeared: creativity did not differ between abundance and scarcity participants.

In summary, three experiments indicate perceived availability of resources has important consequences for consumer creativity and problem solving. Whereas a scarcity mindset induces the psychological processes necessary to stimulate creativity, an abundance mindset causes people to engage in a narrow exploration of solutions, thereby impairing creativity. Implications for consumer behavior and managerial practices will be discussed.

Dealing with Uncertainty Through Haptic Sensations

EXTENDED ABSTRACT

How do consumers adapt to a world that is fundamentally uncertain? For example, how do consumers react and cope with the prospect of financial scarcity during a financial crisis or after job loss? Or, how do consumers respond to profound shifts in a country's political climate?

Much research has focused on uncertainty regarding people's preferences or choices, which may be reduced by active information search (Kohn-Berning and Jacoby 1974; Urbany, Dickson, and Wilkie 1989). Uncertainty, however, is often externally rather than internally imposed (Kahneman and Tversky 1982). Uncertainty is thus a characteristic inherent in the environment and hence out of people's control, making it nearly impossible to reduce uncertainty by simply searching for information (Smithson 2008). Some research has suggested that people combat such external uncertainty by reestablishing a sense of order and structure, for instance through perceiving meaningful patterns among random stimuli (Whitson and Galinsky 2008) or by increasing faith in governmental institutions or in God (Kay, Gaucher, Napier, Callan, and Laurin 2008). In the current work, we suggest that people may deal with such uncertainty on a more basic experiential level – through seeking specific haptic sensations.

Touch is the first sense to develop and is critical in understanding and dealing with the world. Early haptic sensations importantly shape our memories and drive our future behavior (Gallace and Spence 2010). Interpersonal touch forms the foundation for beliefs about caring and comfort. Research shows that such learned beliefs can affect our behavior. For instance, in one study a simple pat on the back increased people's sense of security and led them to make riskier financial decisions (Levav and Argo 2010). Even touching non-

personal objects, such as a teddy bear, influenced people's behavior and affective experiences by making them act more prosocially after social exclusion (Tai, Zheng, and Narayanan 2011) or by reducing their negative mood (King and Janiszewski 2011).

As touch is associated with comfort, we hypothesize that simply touching, holding, or feeling something soft may be an effective way to deal with uncertainty. More specifically, we propose that, when feeling uncertain, consumers will seek such haptic sensations and choose products with softer as compared to harder properties. In addition, we predict that softness is functional and that it reduces feelings of uncertainty. Three experimental studies tested these hypotheses.

In experiment 1, participants read and wrote about life events that were characterized by either high levels of uncertainty (e.g., financial scarcity, job loss) or high levels of certainty (e.g., financial stability, good health services). Subsequently, participants unobtrusively experienced softness by drawing two pictures with two pens – one with a soft-grip and one with a hard-grip (counterbalanced). As a token of appreciation, participants were then asked to choose one of these pens. The results showed that participants who had earlier read about certainty were no more likely to choose the soft or hard pen (18, 18). Uncertain consumers, however, chose the soft-grip pen more often (27) than the hard-grip pen (9). There were no differences in mood between conditions. Hence, the effect of certainty on preference for softness cannot be attributed to mood.

In experiment 2, we conceptually replicated the results of experiment 1 using a different behavioral measure – namely, the choice between a hard and soft sweet. Additionally, we incentivized choice of the hard candy by making the hard candy more attractive than the soft one. (Pre-test results confirmed that the hard candy was indeed more attractive than the soft candy.) Thus, not surprisingly, certain participants chose the soft candy much less often (2) than the hard candy (21). Uncertain participants, however, chose the soft candy about as often (9) as the hard candy (11). Thus, across two experiments, uncertain consumers deviated from certain consumers by switching towards a softer commodity.

In the last experiment, we demonstrate that consumers do not only deal with uncertainty through touching something soft, but that softness also has the capability to *restore* certainty. After uncertainty/certainty was induced, participants were asked to write down the objects they believed were hidden in a Snowy Picture Task (SPT, Ekstrom, French, Harman, and Dermen 1976) while writing either with a soft-grip pen or with a hard-grip pen. Importantly, for each object they were asked to indicate how uncertain/certain they felt about their answers. In addition, participants were asked right after the manipulation (time point 1) and right after the SPT (time point 2) how uncertain/certain they felt at the time. As expected, uncertain consumers felt more certain about their answers on the SPT after writing with a soft-grip pen than after writing with a hard-grip pen, whereas there were no differences between conditions for certain consumers. Furthermore, uncertain consumers felt, as predicted, more certain at time point 2 than at time point 1 after using a pen with a soft-grip, whereas using a pen with a hard-grip did not change feelings of uncertainty. For certain consumers, on the other hand, using a soft-grip pen induced uncertainty, whereas using a hard-grip pen kept their level of certainty equally high over time.

Across three experiments, using two different behavioral measures, results indicate that feelings of uncertainty induce a preference for soft products. Furthermore, we found that softness can mollify feelings of uncertainty. This finding indicates that, in the face of uncertainty (e.g., prospect of financial scarcity), solace can be found and uncertainty can be reduced through the experience of soft haptic sensations.

Perceived Resource Scarcity Reduces Trust among Men but Increases Trust among Women

EXTENDED ABSTRACT

Trust plays a crucial role in both economic and social transactions (Fehr 2009). In this research, we examined whether merely altering people's perception of available resources can affect their trust, and whether perceived resource scarcity has different effects among men and women. From an evolutionary perspective, times of resource scarcity should have differentially affected men and women. In particular, when resources were relatively scarce, competition for dominance might have increased among men (Daly and Wilson 1988), but attempts to affiliate with others for social support might have increased among women (Taylor 2002). We therefore predicted that perceived resource scarcity would decrease trust among men, but increase trust among women. We tested this prediction in two experiments by manipulating the amount of two separate resources (food and money) that participants felt were available to them and measuring their trusting attitudes and actual trusting behavior.

In experiment 1, forty-seven undergraduate students read a scenario in which they were asked to imagine traveling to a new country they had never visited before. We manipulated the perceived scarcity of food by telling some participants to imagine that, upon arriving in a small village, they discovered that it was a national holiday and all the stores and restaurants were closed until the next morning. They were further told that they only had a small amount of food with them, which would have to last until the stores reopen in the morning. Participants in the abundance condition read the same story but were told that they had more than enough food in with them to last until the morning. As a manipulation check, we asked all participants the extent to which they felt they had enough food to last until the next day. This measure confirmed that participants in the scarcity condition reported having less than enough food to last them until the next day, relative to the abundance condition; the manipulation was equally successful for men and women (i.e., the interaction was not significant).

After reading this scenario, participants completed the Interpersonal Trust Scale (Rotter 1967), which is designed to measure an individual's propensity to trust other people (e.g., "Most people can be counted on to do what they say they will do.") A 2 (resources: scarcity vs. abundance) X 2 (gender: male vs. female) ANOVA on the Interpersonal Trust Scale revealed no main effects. However, there was a significant Resources X Gender interaction, whereby women in the scarcity condition trusted significantly more than women in the abundance condition, whereas men in the scarcity condition trusted relatively (but not significantly) less than men in the abundance condition.

In experiment 2, sixty-six undergraduate students participated in a "trust game" for real money (Berg, Dickhaut, and McCabe 1995). All participants played the role of sender, in which they had the option of keeping a €5 endowment for themselves (not trust) or sending it all to an anonymous partner (trust). If sent, the money would be quadrupled to €20 and the receiver then had the option of returning half the money to the sender or keeping it all for him/herself. We induced feelings of financial scarcity or abundance by changing the categories on a scale asking participants how much money they had in their checking and savings account, such that most respondents either placed themselves in the lowest (scarcity condition) or highest (abundance condition) category (for a similar manipulation, see Nelson and Morrison 2005). We then measured their decision to trust and their beliefs about the trustworthiness of their partner.

We regressed the decision to trust on resources condition, gender, and the interaction between resources and gender. The only significant effect that emerged from this model was a Resources X Gender interaction. Men in the scarcity condition trusted less than men in the abundance condition, whereas women in the scarcity condition trusted more than women in the abundance condition. We also found a Resources X Gender interaction on perceived trustworthiness of their partner. Mirroring the pattern from the decision to trust data, scarce men thought that their partner would be less likely to split the money evenly with them compared to abundant men, whereas scarce women thought that their partner would be relatively more likely to split the money evenly with them compared to abundant women.

Taken together, the results of two experiments suggest that the perceived availability of critical resources such as food and money can have different effects on trust beliefs and behavior among men and women. These findings suggest that changes in macroeconomic conditions—such as the recent global financial crisis—might lead men and women to adopt different strategies for coping with the resulting threat to their personal resources.

Mental Accounting in the Context of Poverty

EXTENDED ABSTRACT

While the mental accounting literature has contributed to the understanding of general consumer behavior, no work to date has examined these phenomena with respect to low-income consumers. In terms of simple, everyday decisions regarding buying and saving, low- and high-income decision makers make many of the same choices. Deciding whether to spend more time to save a certain amount of money is a common choice for both groups, but these choices might be more consequential for lower-income individuals. In addition, low-income individuals might be more used to focusing on smaller amounts, amounts that may carry less meaning for those with greater incomes. Saving a modest amount on a pair of shoes might seem appealing to both groups, but the lack of a financial buffer experienced by low-income individuals might make them more sensitive to the absolute amount saved rather than the proportion of the total amount saved.

We hypothesize that low-income individuals might not replicate the traditional topical accounting pattern observed in previous experiments that examine the willingness to travel to save a fixed amount of money on either a large or a small purchase (Tversky and Kahneman 1981). Specifically, because they live in a context where modest sums of money matter more, low-income individuals may not be as sensitive to different proportional amounts to be saved. The scenarios presented represent reasonable choices that both groups may face, but the context of poverty may cause low-income individuals to be more sensitive to absolute amounts. Overall, the main goal is to argue that, for some mental accounting scenarios, generalizing from findings demonstrated with high-income groups does not accurately describe the behavior of low-income decision makers. Low-income individuals do not show the same pattern of preference for relative over absolute savings (for modest amounts), resulting in a different pattern of results than what has traditionally been described by the literature.

In these surveys, we show that low-income individuals do not replicate the traditional pattern of topical accounting results. Study 1 uses adapted versions of Tversky and Kahneman's (1981) stimuli, examining willingness to travel to save money. Study 2 more rigorously extends this using a novel, within-subjects design which forces participants to choose between saving scenarios. In study 3, explore the relationship between numeracy and these effects.

In Study 1, low-income participants did not replicate the usual findings consistent with a strong preference for proportional saving. High-income participants demonstrate the expected preference reversal, while low-income participants seem more concerned with the absolute amount in these cases. In Study 2, this finding is supported using a novel, within-subjects design. When asked to decide between two saving options, high-income participants prefer the savings option that reflects the greater proportion. When the amount saved is not identical, high-income participants still choose the greater proportion, even when it is a lower absolute amount. Low-income participants do not replicate this; instead, they appear to rely more on absolute values. These findings may suggest that low-income individuals are more sensitive to modest amounts; without the buffer enjoyed by individuals in a higher-income context, low-income individuals may be more sensitive to absolute amounts, even under similar types of choice scenarios. The third study examines the rela-

tionship between numeracy and willingness to save. Previous studies have shown that individuals higher in numeracy are more likely to show the preference for a higher amount of proportional savings. This study replicates this pattern for the high-income consumers, but does not hold for the low-income participants. Lower-class consumers show the same pattern as in the previous studies, regardless of their level of numeracy.

Across this set of studies, the results for high-income individuals are consistent with previous findings in the literature. Of greater interest are the responses by low-income individuals. The data suggest that, relative to the high-income respondents, low-income respondents are more sensitive to absolute savings. Low-income participants do not show a clear preference for saving the greater absolute amount. They appear to be influenced by smaller relative sums that generate greater proportional savings. In contrast, high-income individuals appear to focus on the absolute amount at these moderate levels of saving.

How Corporate Social Responsibility Influences Consumers

Chair: John Peloza, Florida State University, USA

Paper #1: Is Corporate Social Responsibility Good For You? How Corporate-Level CSR Impacts Consumer Perceptions of Product-Level Attributes

John Peloza, Florida State University, USA
Christine Ye, Florida State University, USA

Paper #2: Managing Charitable Giving: Cause Portfolio Dimensions And Their Impact on Stakeholder Evaluations

A. Meike Eilert, University of South Carolina, USA
Stefanie Rosen Robinson, North Carolina State University, USA
Satish Jayachandran, University of South Carolina, USA

Paper #3: Can Social Responsibility Backfire? The Role of Intentions in Times of Corporate Crisis

Katie Kelting, University of Arkansas, USA
Adam Duhachek, Indiana University, USA
Durairaj Maheswaran, NYU, USA

Paper #4: Is Less More When Communicating Sustainability? Consumer Response to Ambiguous versus Detailed Sustainability Product Labels

Rebecca Walker Naylor, The Ohio State University, USA
Remi Trudel, Boston University, USA

SESSION OVERVIEW

A recent survey shows that when marketers invest in corporate social responsibility (CSR) initiatives, enhancing relationships between consumers and brands is the number one objective (BCG/ MIT Sloan Management Review). Consumers report higher intentions to purchase goods and services from companies known for CSR, and willingness to pay higher price for those goods and services (e.g., Cotte and Trudel 2009). However, market data suggests that these intentions do not materialize in consumer behavior, since many products marketed by firms with strong CSR reputations remain niche products. Recent research suggests that the relationship between CSR and consumer behavior is complex, and CSR initiatives sometimes lead to *decreased* consumer preference (e.g., Luchs et al., 2010). The objective of the proposed session is to more deeply examine how, when and why CSR initiatives influence consumer behavior. The research presented here addresses calls from previous researchers to "unpack" the causal mechanisms by which CSR can lead to enhanced business performance and/or social and environmental outcomes (e.g., Margolis, Elfenbein, and Walsh 2009; Peloza 2009).

The proposed session includes four papers that are completed works, or all in advanced stages of completion including data collection in multiple studies. Across four papers, CSR's impact on consumer behavior is examined in new ways. For example, the session will provide important insights into the conditions under which consumers support or resist CSR (all presentations), the equivocal role of perceived corporate intentions (presentations 1 and 3), how consumer behavior can lead to improved firm financial performance (presentation 2), and how the means by which CSR is communicated to consumers influences their support (presentations 1 and 4). In particular, Presentation 1 demonstrates that a reputation for CSR at a corporate-level leads consumers to overestimate the ability for the firms products to provide health and safety benefits. Presentation 2 suggests that firms benefit from increased consumer support when philanthropy is focused among a small portfolio of charitable causes. Presentation 3 examines how consumers attribute blame for corporate crises, with the counterintuitive finding that perceptions of social (versus financial) motivations by the firm increase attributed blame. Finally, Presentation 4 examines how marketers can use either ambiguous or detailed product labels to more effectively gain consumer support for environmental initiatives. Although these four papers highlight different aspects of CSR and its ability to shape consumer attitudes and behaviors, they provide an integration of current research in a topic area that is of critical importance to the field of consumer behavior. In order to accommodate four papers in 75 minutes, we intend to allocate 15 minutes of presentation time for each paper with a 15-minute group Q&A session at the end.

Each of these papers make a strong contribution in its own right, and the collection of these papers in a special session allows for a highly focused discussion of the relationship between CSR and consumer behavior. However, although highly focused, the papers in this session represent a diverse range of perspective on CSR, and include a focus on both consumer and corporate outcomes, positive and negative aspects of CSR, a variety of forms of CSR, examined using a diverse set of theoretical bases. We therefore expect relatively broad interest from researchers interested in transformative consumer research, CSR, sustainability, prosocial behavior, consumer well-being, public policy and branding to name a few. We believe that our understanding of how CSR impacts consumer behavior is in its infancy, and this session will serve as a catalyst for future research initiatives and a basis for valuable discussion at the conference.

Is Corporate Social Responsibility Good For You? How Corporate-Level CSR Impacts Consumer Perceptions of Product-Level Attributes

EXTENDED ABSTRACT

Early research in corporate social responsibility (CSR) demonstrated that it leads to benefits for marketers through corporate level, as opposed to product level, effects. For example, activities such as charity donations lead to enhanced consumer-company identification (e.g., Bhattacharya and Sen 2003). Brown and Dacin (1997, p. 70) argue that a positioning based on CSR "offers consumers little information that is directly associated with the products and services it provides." More recently, researchers have examined the potential for CSR to directly influence perceptions of product performance. For example, Luchs et al. (2010) find that when products are positioned with attributes that make environmental sensitivity a priority (e.g., detergents and soaps made from eco-friendly ingredients), consumers may infer product performance trade-offs. In this more recent stream of research, although CSR impacts consumers' product performance evaluations, CSR is conceived in a fashion that makes it highly salient to product performance (e.g., source ingredients).

The current research posits a third route to consumer influence through CSR, and bridges the gap between these two literatures by examining the potential for corporate-level CSR initiatives such as philanthropy to impact perceptions of product attributes and performance. Specifically, this research posits that when companies position themselves as compassionate and caring through activities such corporate philanthropy, it leads consumers to over-estimate product attributes related to their own well-being (e.g., healthiness, calorie content, etc.). The theory behind this effect is derived from the literature on consumer inference-making. Kardes, Posavac, and Cronley (2004) demonstrate that consumers form inferences about missing information by making connections between the missing information and other available information. This research proposes that perceptions of product attributes related to consumer well-being are influenced by consumer inferences of stakeholder stewardship by the firm.

We demonstrate these effects across four studies. In Study 1, participants estimated a lower number of calories, saturated fat and trans fat in granola bars marketed from a company described as highly involved in corporate level CSR activities (e.g., donations to charity, treatment of employees) than a company with a neutral CSR reputation. Triangulating these nutrition estimates were concurrent estimates of better taste of the product marketed by the firm with a neutral CSR reputation (i.e., unhealthy=tasty, Raghunathan et al. 2006). Study 2 examines the role of firm intentions behind the CSR and finds that when firms engaged in CSR activities are viewed as motivated by community concern versus public image management, their products are perceived as healthier. This effect is consistent across calories, saturated and trans fat and sodium, as well as a general measure of product healthiness. We again find that perceptions of taste are higher for the firm not motivated by community concern.

In Study 3 we demonstrate that products marketed by firms with strong corporate level CSR reputations are particularly attractive to health conscious consumers, who state higher purchase intentions for such products compared to consumers low in health consciousness. Further, we find that health conscious consumers demonstrate higher purchase intentions to products advertised using CSR appeals versus more direct health appeals. We show that skepticism toward the more informational approach of health appeals is behind these effects. Finally, in Study 4 we replicate our findings with a parent sample examining perceived sunscreen safety. We demonstrate that parents are more likely to purchase sunscreen marketed by a firm with a strong (versus weak) corporate level CSR reputation, and that this effect is mediated through perceived product safety.

This research extends previous studies that examine the perceived trade-off between product performance and ethics (e.g., Sen and Bhattacharya 2001), and contributes to the literature examining the business case for CSR (e.g., Peloza 2009). The research also extends prior research examining inference-making with product-level attributes (e.g., how perceptions of taste are altered by labeling (Allison and Uhl 1964) or product color (Hoegg and Alba 2007)). Elder and Krishna (2009, p. 755) note that impacts of heuristic-based cognition on perception is a "fruitful area for future research" and that "thoughts generated by other extrinsic cues could be equally as intriguing." The proposed corporate-level examination represents an extension on this basis.

Managing Charitable Giving: Cause Portfolio Dimensions And Their Impact on Stakeholder Evaluations

EXTENDED ABSTRACT

Firms donate a substantial amount of their profit to non-profit organizations. According to the Foundation Center (2010), giving of corporate foundations rose by 3.9 percent in 2008 to $4.6 billion. As charitable giving increases, firms shift their focus to the profitable management of these activities. Recent studies have highlighted the complexity of the charitable giving – performance relationship (Wang, Choi, and Li 2008; Lev, Petrovits, and Radhakrishnan 2010) and the objective of this research is to understand whether and when a firm's giving activities create value for the firm. To date, most studies focus on the impact of the *amount of giving* on firm value but little is known about the impact of the *allocation of giving*.

To investigate how allocation decisions create value for the firm, we develop the concept of cause portfolios which we define as all relationships a firm builds with non-profits as part of its day-to-day business activities. The size and diversification of the cause portfolio should be guided by brand and market considerations (Varadarajan and Menon 1988) and take into consideration the different stakeholder groups of the firm (e.g., consumers). A firm can promote the varying interests of these stakeholder groups through their charitable giving activities (Drumwright 1996) which can result in improved performance, such as higher perceptions about the firm and its brands, higher satisfaction, stronger identification with the firm, and higher purchase intentions (Brown and Dacin 1997; Creyer and Ross 1997; Luo and Bhattacharya 2006; Marin and Ruiz 2007; Sen and Bhattacharya 2001). To obtain these benefits from its cause portfolio investments, firms have to manage the relationships within the cause portfolio properly. Depending on how portfolio characteristics, such as size and diversification, are managed, firms may or may not be able to attain the same level of return.

We base our predictions on relationship management theory to propose a mechanism that explains why these cause portfolio characteristics (e.g., size and diversification) have a differential impact on stakeholder evaluations and thus firm value. We propose that diverse cause portfolios are more strongly associated with positive outcomes for the firm when the portfolio is small rather than large. Stakeholders make assessments about the firm's motivation to give to charities and non-profits. If a cause portfolio appears to be stretched too far in both size and scope, then stakeholders should have lower perceptions of the firm. As firms donate to a large number of non-profits associated with various causes, it should become more difficult for the stakeholders to identify the focus of the firm's giving activities. This, in turn, should lower the perceptions that the firm is committed to the causes in the cause portfolio. Furthermore we propose that perceived commitment mediates the relationship between cause portfolio characteristics and performance outcomes.

In Study 1, we address our hypotheses using an experimental setting. Participants (n=86) were asked to read about Company Y, a bath company that makes shampoos, hand and face soaps, and lotions. Participants were told that Company Y was selling a new body wash and were provided a brief description of it. Further, participants were told that Company Y is helping the community through its support of certain causes. Participants were shown one of four conditions in a 2 (Size: Small [5 charities] vs. Large [20 charities]) X 2 (Diversification: Diverse vs. Focused) between-subjects design. After reading the scenario, participants rated the body wash on the following variables of interest: purchase likelihood and perceived commitment of the company to the causes. The results showed a significant interactive effect of size and diversification ($F(1, 85) = 3.99, p < .05$). The results show that for a diverse portfolio, purchase likelihood is greater when it only includes five charities compared to twenty charities ($p < .05$). We do not see such a difference in perceptions for a focused portfolio. Therefore, the findings of the experiment confirm our prediction that diverse portfolios are more likely to lead to better performance when they are small as compared to large. Furthermore, we tested for mediated moderation and in line with our prediction we find that perceived commitment of the firm to the cause portfolio mediates the relationship between cause portfolio characteristics and performance.

Data from secondary sources confirm our findings from our experimental study and show that both a large and a diverse cause portfolio that targets different giving areas, such as education, health, or the environment, can be beneficial but the simultaneous pursuit of a large and diverse cause portfolio is not rewarded by the firm's stakeholders. We find that this pattern of results holds for different stakeholder groups evaluating a firm's charitable giving activities including both consumers and investors. Finally, we examine whether a stakeholder's perception of the firm's charitable engagement is in line with the actual social impact of the firm. Using information on the firm's community social performance, we also find evidence that firms with diverse portfolios are not better at meeting stakeholder expectations regarding community impact when the portfolio is large compared to a diverse and small portfolio.

This present paper provides some initial insights into the structural management of charitable giving. We show that, besides the overall amount of giving, characteristics of the cause portfolio, such as size and diversification, matter to consumers (and other stakeholder groups) and thus influence the likelihood that firms receive a return on their charitable giving. In summary, our results show that in order to appeal to consumers, cause portfolios have to be properly managed.

Can Social Responsibility Backfire? The Role of Intentions in Times of Corporate Crisis

EXTENDED ABSTRACT

The purpose of the current research is to examine the impact of a corporate crisis on consumer perceptions of a firm involved in the crisis. We advance prior research on corporate crises (Brown and Dacin, 1997; Gorn, Jiang and Johar, 2008; Luchs et al., 2010; Palmatier et al., 2009; Sen and Bhattacharya, 2001; Yoon, Gurhan-Canli and Schwarz, 2006) by incorporating the role of counterfactual thinking. Specifically, in this paper, we theorize how consumer perceptions of a firm embroiled in a crisis are driven not only by thoughts about what the firm has done wrong but also by thoughts about what the firm could have done differently to prevent the crisis. We theorize that such processing is affected by the intentions that a firm states for actions taken preceding the crisis. In this research, we focus on two different types of intentions that firms state for corporate decisions (socially-motivated versus profit-driven) and find evidence to support the counter-intuitive notion that a socially-motivated as opposed to a profit-driven intention leads consumers to think more about what the firm could have done differently to prevent the crisis and as a result to deem the firm more blameworthy for the crisis. In this paper, we also identify factors surrounding corporate crises (i.e., outcome of a default event and emotions) that not only amplify the degree of blame that consumers bestow on a firm but also isolate the process through which consumer perceptions of a firm are formed in times of crisis.

In Study 1, we asked a total of 135 undergraduate students to participate in a 2 (stated intention for a focal corporate decision: socially-motivated versus profit-driven) x 2 (outcome of the default event: different versus similar) between-subject study for course credit. The study involved participants reading an article about the financial bailout of *General Motors (GM)*. Thus, information about our two factors as well as information about a corporate crisis involving *GM* was communicated to participants via the article. For clarity, we believe that it is important to define the term default event. In the counterfactual thinking literature, a default event is defined as "a highly available counterfactual mutation to the factual event; it is the event that readily comes to mind as an alternative to the factual event that preceded some to-be explained outcome" (Wells and Gavanski 1989, p.162). Notably, the outcome of a default event is commonly used in the counterfactual thinking literature as a way to either accentuate or attenuate the degree of counterfactual thought processing. For example, prior research has shown that more

(less) counterfactual thinking occurs when the outcome of a default is different (similar) than that of the actual event. Thus, in Study 1, we posit and show a significant interaction between stated corporate intentions and the outcome of a default event. Specifically, we find that when consumers read about *GM's* corporate crisis and learn that a default event existed which would have yielded a different (versus similar) outcome than the actual event, knowledge that *GM* had a socially-motivated as opposed to a profit-driven intention leads to more counterfactual thoughts implicating *GM* and as a result to more negative consumer perceptions of *GM* (i.e., mediation supported). Thus, these results support the proposed theorizing.

Next, we garner additional support for our counterfactual thinking perspective by examining the role of emotions, which is another factor shown to produce counterfactual thinking (Meyers-Levy and Maheswaran, 1992). While a number of negative emotions exist, we focus on the effects of two - anger and sadness - because they are relevant to the context of corporate crises and appraisal theory suggests differential implications for counterfactual thinking. Specifically, anger tends to arise out of an attribution that others are responsible for the situation, whereas sadness tends to be associated with the attribution that events are beyond anyone's control (Han, Lerner and Keltner, 2007). Also, anger (sadness) increases (decreases) the tendency to blame others, as consumers have been shown to direct attributions outward as they attempt to resolve a violation (Maheswaran and Chen, 2006). Thus, we theorize anger (sadness) will accentuate (attenuate) Study 1 effects.

To test this notion, we asked a total of 209 undergraduate students to participate in a 2 (emotion: anger versus sadness) x 2 (stated intention for focal corporate decision: socially-motivated versus profit-driven) x 2 (outcome of the default event: different versus similar) between-subject study for course credit. The procedure was identical to that used in Study 1 except for the following: prior to presenting an article about *GM*, participants in the *anger (sadness)* condition were asked to recall an event that made them angry (sad) and to describe their emotions in a personal essay (Maheswaran and Chen, 2006). As expected, we found a significant three-way interaction. Specifically, we find that when consumers feel angry, read information about *GM's* corporate crisis, and learn that a default event existed which would have yielded a different (versus similar) outcome than the actual event, knowledge that *GM* had a socially-motivated as opposed to a profit-driven intention leads to more negative consumer perceptions of *GM*. Notably, sadness did not exhibit this pattern of results.

This research contributes to the literature on product and service failure, social responsibility, emotions and counterfactual thinking. The findings suggest firms stating socially responsible intentions expose themselves to additional risk once crises occur. This hypothesis differs from predictions made using attribution theory perspectives to corporate crises. This research accounts for this divergence by providing evidence of an additional mechanism through which assessments of blame arise via counterfactual thinking. The research also conjoins emotions and counterfactual thinking to reveal theoretical linkages between these important consequences of corporate crises.

Is Less More When Communicating Sustainability? Consumer Response to Ambiguous versus Detailed Sustainability Product Labels

EXTENDED ABSTRACT

As more sustainable products flood the marketplace each year (Luchs et al. 2010), consumers are faced with the increasing challenge of trying to discern which products positioned as "sustainable" actually deliver on this promise. To do so, an increasing number of consumers are turning to various on-product labels designed to communicate sustainability. Although ample past research in marketing has explored how consumers respond to product labels, much of this research has focused on consumer response to nutrition labels (e.g., Block and Perrachio 2006). Unlike nutrition labels, which are mandated by the Nutritional Labeling and Education Act (NLEA), labels designed to communicate sustainability can take almost any form. New standards for water use, packaging, recyclability, and carbon impact are competing for attention and space, and multiple versions of the same label are in use (e.g., detailed vs. ambiguous versions of the Carbon Reduction Label). This situation creates a challenge for marketers since it is an open question how best to communicate sustainability to a broad audience that varies in their interest in sustainability.

Our research seeks to provide guidance on this issue, focusing specifically on how consumers respond to different variations in detail on sustainability labels. We hypothesize that the consumer response to sustainable products will depend both on the level of detail in labeling and on consumers' level of concern for the environment. Specifically, we hypothesize that consumers with relatively low levels of concern for the environment will respond more positively to ambiguous than to detailed sustainability labels. Ambiguous labels that do not provide detail about a sustainable product's characteristics are more appealing to these consumers because they do not lead the consumer to think in-depth about the environmental issue behind the label (e.g., the consequences of global warming when reading a Carbon Reduction Label). More detailed labels can lead consumers who would not normally think about environmental issues to do so in greater detail than they wish to, making them feel less hopeful about the issue, resulting in negative affect that transfers to the product itself. Conversely, specific labels do not negatively impact consumers who care a great deal about environmental issues because these consumers are already inclined to think about these issues in detail regardless of the amount of information featured on a label.

To test this hypothesis, we conducted two studies using the Carbon Reduction Label, an on-pack sustainability label that consumers can use to check whether products are working with the Carbon Trust to reduce their carbon emissions. The label exists in multiple versions, all with a footprint graphic; in addition to this graphic, the ambiguous version reads "Reducing with the Carbon Trust," while the detailed version includes this wording plus specific information about the carbon footprint. Our studies used t-shirts as stimuli, so the detailed version of the label showed the carbon footprint (in kg) per garment.

Study 1 employed a 2 (label type: ambiguous vs. detailed) x green personal identity design where green personal identity was a measured variable (GREEN scale; Haws, Winterich, and Naylor 2012). All participants viewed a webpage about a brand of sustainable t-shirts called "Green Label T's" that was purportedly working with the Carbon Trust to reduce carbon emissions. The label shown was either ambiguous or detailed, depending on condition. After viewing the t-shirts and label, all participants then indicated how much they liked the t-shirts. Participants subsequently completed a questionnaire that included the GREEN scale. The results support our hypothesis with a significant interaction between label condition and score on the GREEN scale ($F(1, 62) = 9.86, p < .01$). Follow-up analyses indicated that participants with low scores on the GREEN scale liked the product more when the sustainability label was ambiguous ($F(1, 62) = 3.71, p = .06$), while participants with high scores on the GREEN scale liked the product more when the sustainability label was more detailed ($F(1, 62) = 6.43, p < .05$).

Study 2 employed a 2 (label type) x 2 (prime: green vs. neutral) design where level of environmental concern was manipulated by a sentence unscramble task designed to prime a "green" mindset. Participants once again indicated how much they liked the t-shirts after viewing the shirts and label. After doing so, all participants completed a follow-up questionnaire. One of the questionnaire items measured our hypothesized mediator, "When you think about the problem of carbon emissions negatively impacting the environment, how *hopeful* do you feel about the chance of correcting this issue". Results revealed a significant label x prime interaction ($F(1, 212) = 3.65, p = .06$). Participants in the neutral prime condition (i.e., participants not primed to have high levels of environmental concern) liked the shirts better when they saw the ambiguous (vs. detailed) label ($F(1, 212) = 6.50, p < .05$). Label condition did not impact liking for participants primed to have a high environmental concern ($F(1, 212) = 0.13$, NS). To provide support that label and environmental concern influence how much consumers like the t-shirt through hopeful, we conducted a moderated mediation analysis (Preacher, Rucker, and Hayes 2007; model 2). The first, mediator model revealed a significant main effect of label ($\beta = -.54, p < .05$) and a significant environmental concern x label interaction ($\beta = .79, p < .05$) on hopeful. The second, dependent variable model examined the effects of label, environmental concern, hopeful, and the interaction between label and environmental concern on how much participants liked the t-shirts. The dependent variable model showed a significant effect of hopeful ($\beta = .15\ p < .05$), and label ($\beta = -.67\ p < .05$) on how much participants liked the t-shirt while all other effects proved to be non-significant ($ps > .10$). Bootstrapping techniques employed to test conditional indirect effects confirmed the mediating role of hopeful for consumers low in environmental concern (95% confidence intervals excluding zero; -.25 to -. 01) but not for consumers high in environmental concern (95% confidence interval includes zero; -.02 to .18) (Preacher et al., 2007; Zhao et al., 2010).

Construal Levels: New Antecedents, Insights and Implications

Chair: Dengfeng Yan, University of Texas at San Antonio, USA

Paper #1: Why Does Psychological Distance Influence Construal Level? The Role of Processing Mode

Dengfeng Yan, University of Texas at San Antonio, USA
Jaideep Sengupta, HKUST, Hong Kong
Jiewen Hong, HKUST, Hong Kong

Paper #2: Do Lilliputians See the Big Picture? The Effect of Physical Level on the Level of Construal

Pankaj Aggarwal, University of Toronto, Canada
Min Zhao, University of Toronto, Canada

Paper #3: When Proximity Prompts Abstraction: High-Level Construal as a Means of Counteractive Control

Kentaro Fujita, Ohio State University, USA
Karen MacGregor, Ohio State University, USA

Paper #4: When Feeling Depleted Helps: The Positive Effect of Regulatory Depletion

Echo Wen Wan, University of Hong Kong, Hong Kong
Nidhi Agrawal, Northwestern University, USA

SESSION OVERVIEW

Since the publication of Liberman and Trope (1998), considerable work has been devoted to the theme of construal level theory. Despite the large amount of research in this area, some critical gaps remain. The objective of this session is to address these underexplored questions. Below, we briefly describe these gaps and how each paper seeks to bridge them.

First, while it is now well established that psychological distance influences construal levels, the fundamental question of why this is so has received limited attention. The paper by Yan et al. suggests one possible mechanism, arguing for an intervening role of mode of processing (visual vs. verbal). Consistent with this argument, their studies reveal that people tend to process psychologically near events visually by forming mental images, while processing distant events verbally. In turn, visual (vs. verbal) processing leads to more concrete, lower level construals, thus explaining the oft-observed impact of psychological distance.

Second, extant research on the antecedents of construal level has primarily focused on the four dimensions of psychological distance (e.g., temporal, social, etc.). Surprisingly little attention has been devoted to identify other possible drivers (for exceptions, see Labroo and Patrick 2009; Lee, Keller, and Sternthal 2010). Drawing on perspectives on grounded cognition, the paper by Aggarwal and Zhao identifies a novel antecedent: the physical height at which people are currently imagining themselves to be. This paper proposes and shows that locations higher up (e.g., a hot-air balloon ride) are associated with a big-picture perspective and induce a higher level of construal, while locations lower down (e.g., a deep-sea diving trip) are associated with a detail-oriented perspective, inducing lower levels of construal.

Third, research on the antecedents of construal level has typically adopted a cognitive perspective, arguing in terms of existing, overgeneralized associations between antecedent factors such as psychological distance, and the evoked level of construal (Trope and Liberman 2003); indeed, the paper by Aggarwal and Zhao above, while it identifies a novel antecedent, also draws on an association-based perspective. Much less is known, however, about motivational factors underlying the activation of construal levels. The paper by Fujita and MacGregor, to our knowledge, is among the first to exam-

ine this possibility. Specifically, the authors propose and find that in order to resist proximal temptations (which break down defenses by activating low-level construals), people deliberately activate high-level construals, which in turn facilitates self-control.

Finally, in addition to exploring novel questions regarding the antecedents of construal level, this session also provides new insights into the consequences end of the spectrum. A large body of empirical studies in psychology and marketing has shown a negative impact of regulatory depletion: performing a prior self-control task impairs performance on a subsequent task. In contrast, the paper by Wan and Agrawal draws on construal level theory to predict and demonstrate the reverse: experiencing regulatory depletion shifts individuals' construals to lower levels, and therefore enhances performance on subsequent tasks that require attending to lower-level, contextual details.

Why Does Psychological Distance Influence Construal Level? The Role of Processing Mode

EXTENDED ABSTRACT

Construal level theory proposes that people tend to construe psychologically distant (proximal) events at higher (lower) levels. Much empirical evidence has since been obtained for the proposition (Trope and Liberman 2010). Surprisingly little, however, is known about the mechanisms underlying the effect of psychological distance on construal levels. The objective of the present research is to fill this gap by proposing and testing such a mechanism.

Our argument conjoins two premises: a) proximal (vs. distal) events are more likely to induce imagery-based (vs. verbal) processing; b) visual (verbal) processing leads to relatively concrete, low-level construals (vs. abstract, high-level construals). The paper on which this abstract is based reviews several lines of thought supporting each premise; here, we report one such supportive argument for each. The first premise is consistent with research showing that when an event is temporally closer or more likely to happen (vs. distant or less likely to happen), people are more likely to form implementation intentions (Trope and Liberman 2003); in turn, forming implementation intentions usually involves mentally imagining the steps that must be taken to achieve a goal (Gollwitzer 1999). The second premise is consistent with definitions of "concrete", which comprise ideas such as "capable of being perceived by the senses", "real", "actual", etc. Because visualized information (as opposed to verbal information) can be directly perceived by the senses, it should induce a more concrete construal. Relatedly, much research suggests that imagining an event makes it more "real" (Carroll 1978; Rajagopal and Montgomery 2011) – again, this argues for a link between visual/verbal processing on the one hand, and concrete/abstract construals on the other.

We tested our proposition in four studies. Study 1 used a 2 (task orientation: visual vs. verbal) x 2 (temporal distance: proximal vs. distant) design. Participants were first asked to write a short essay about "this weekend" or "a weekend in 2020". They then tried to solve a puzzle that involved either a hidden figure or a hidden word. Consistent with the premise that near (far) events induce visual (verbal) processing, participants in the proximal condition performed better in the hidden figure task ($M_{proximal} = 6.68$ vs. $M_{distant} = 5.27$; $t = 2.80$, $p < .01$), but worse in the hidden word task ($M_{proximal} = 2.09$ vs.

$M_{distant} = 3.06$; $t = 1.94$, $p = .06$; 2-way interaction $F(1, 125) = 11.23$, $p = .001$).

In study 2, participants were first asked to imagine that a friend was visiting Hong Kong either tomorrow or a year from now and they were to show her around. Then they were shown a list of 40 tourist attractions in Hong Kong and asked to categorize them into groups. Participants also responded to two items that measure their extent of mental imagery while completing the categorization task. Participants generated more categories ($M_{proximal} = 5.59$ vs. $M_{distant} = 4.17$; $F(1, 65) = 10.43$, $p < .01$) and were more likely to form mental imagery when the event was proximal vs. distant ($M_{proximal} = 3.72$ vs. $M_{distant} = 2.64$; $F(1, 65) = 128.37$, $p < .001$). Importantly, a mediation analysis showed that the extent of mental imagery mediated the effect of temporal distance on construal level.

Study 3 tested our proposition by examining theoretically-derived boundary conditions for the impact of psychological distance. If processing mode indeed mediates the effect of distance on construal level, this effect should attenuate both for chronic visualizers and verbalizers. That is, visualizers (verbalizers) should construe *both* distant and proximal events at a lower (higher) level. Hypothetical distance was used to operationalize psychological distance. Participants were asked to imagine that their friend was planning to visit Hong Kong, with a likelihood of either 95% or 5%. They then completed the same categorization task as in study 2, before filling out the Style of Processing Scale (SOP; Childers, Houston & Heckler 1985), which assesses the chronic tendency to form visual images. As expected, lower hypothetical distance ($t = 2.80$, $p < .01$) and higher scores on SOP ($t = 6.92$, $p < .001$) both led to more categories being formed. More importantly, spotlight analyses revealed that the effects of hypothetical distance on construal level became non-significant for chronic verbalizers, and also for chronic visualizers (p's > .10).

Study 4 replicated these findings while manipulating processing mode and examining the social dimension of psychological distance. A 2 (social distance) x 3 (visualizing vs. verbalizing vs. control) between-subject design was employed. Participants first completed either a hidden figure or word puzzle (visualizing vs. verbalizing conditions). Those in the control condition did not perform any task. Afterwards, participants received information about a target person, described as being very similar or very dissimilar to them. All respondents then completed the BIF measure (Behavioral Identification Form; Vallacher and Wegner 1989), which is a standard assessment of activated construal level; higher means indicate more abstraction. The control condition obtained the usual effect of social distance on construal level: distance produced more abstract construals ($M_{proximal} = 14.77$ vs. $M_{distant} = 16.59$; $F(1, 187) = 3.45$, $p = .07$). Further, those in the visualizing condition reported more concrete construals than those in the verbalizing condition ($M_{visualizing} = 14.73$ vs. $M_{verbalizing} = 16.32$; $F(2, 187) = 2.97$, $p = .05$). Most importantly, the visualizing condition led to relatively concrete construals irrespective of social distance ($Ms = 14.52$ vs. 14.94, $t < 1$, $p > .60$), while the verbalizing condition produced abstract construals irrespective of distance ($Ms = 15.95$ vs. 16.79, $t < 1$, $p > .30$). These findings are consistent with the proposition that the effect of social distance on construal level was indeed driven by the processing mode.

Our paper contributes to the construal level literature by identifying one possible mechanism that underlies the effects of psychological distance on construal level. We also add to the mental imagery literature by identifying a new factor (psychological distance) that can influence the tendency to engage in visual versus verbal processing.

Do Lilliputians See the Big Picture? The Effect of Physical Level on the Level of Construal

EXTENDED ABSTRACT

We often use terms like big-picture view or broad perspective to suggest a higher level of thinking, and limited vision or narrow view to describe a lower level of thinking. Clearly, vision is associated not just with the physical act of seeing but also with perspective in the metaphorical sense, that is, how one thinks. Is it possible that these two meanings of vision are linked to each other such that a person's physical location could influence the way in which that person thinks?

In this research, we draw upon prior work on grounded cognition (Barsalou 1999, 2008) and construal-level theory (Liberman and Trope 1998) to examine the interesting proposition that the physical level at which people imagine themselves to be affects their level of thinking. Specifically, locations higher up lead to a higher level of thinking, with a big-picture perspective, while locations lower down lead to a lower level of thinking, with a detail-oriented perspective. Recent work on grounded cognition suggests that people tend to associate their physical experiences, whether bodily or simulated, with more abstract conceptual meanings, and that changes in one tend to be associated with changes in the other (Barsalou 2008). For example, people who are primed with the physical experience of warm temperature (holding a warm cup of coffee) judge an unknown person as more likeable and friendly (socially warm) than do people who hold a cold cup of coffee (Williams and Bargh 2008). The key premise underlying these findings is that bodily states can be used to generate cognitive activity (Barsalou 2008). These findings are also consistent with prior work on metaphorical representations, which suggests that metaphors reflect something deeper about our ability to represent knowledge (Lakoff and Johnson 1980), and that the representation of abstract concepts might function in a similar manner, with metaphors being a manifestation of how we ground abstract thought (Barsalou 2008). For example, height is associated with affect (Meier and Robinson 2004), power (Meier and Dionne 2009), divine (Meier et al. 2007) and prosocial behavior (Sanna et al. 2011).

Extending this stream of research, we propose that physical level can affect people's construal level since physical view and mental view are metaphorically related. Because being physically higher up gives people a broad view of a situation, we believe that this physical experience is linked to the metaphorical meaning of taking a big-picture view, that is, a high level of construal, with greater focus on the central aspect of a decision. Thus, a higher physical level gives people the ability to see the forest without being distracted by the trees. Similarly, a physically lower level gives people a more detail-oriented view, which is linked metaphorically to a low level of construal, resulting in a greater focus on the peripheral aspects—resulting in the classic situation of not being able to see the forest for the trees. Put more formally, the main proposition is that physical level will influence level of construal such that a physically higher level leads to a high-level construal and a physically lower level will lead to a low-level construal. And this effect of level on construal occurs because individuals on a physically higher level are more likely to have big-picture orientation compared to those on a physically lower level.

We test our predictions through four studies using different manipulations of physical level and different dependent variables to assess level of construal. In Study 1 we compare people imagining a ride in a hot-air balloon with those imagining a deep-sea diving trip. Consistent with our hypothesis, participants in the high (hot-air balloon) condition were more likely to choose the LL (larger-later) rewards over the SS (smaller-sooner) rewards compared to those in the low (scuba diving) condition (Ms = 86% vs. 63%, $\chi2$ (1) = 7.92, $p < .01$). Study 2 adapts a scenario from the children's classic Gulliver's Travels (Swift 2001) to demonstrate that participants who put themselves in the shoes of Gulliver (a tall person) indicate a greater preference for a higher-payoff, lower-odds gamble than are those who take the view of the Lilliputians (tiny people) (Ms = 6.77 vs. 5.69, $F(1, 91)$ = 5.24, $p < .05$), and use more abstract terms to describe what they imagine seeing (Ms = 3.61 vs. 3.03, $F(1, 91)$ = 9.19, $p < .01$). Further, participants' big-picture orientation score mediates the effect of height on the level of construal. Study 3 extends these findings to a real behavioral measure using a lottery. Physical level was manipulated by displaying locations on a map north and south of a city representing higher and lower physical levels (Meier et al. 2011). Results showed that those in the high condition (north) prefer receiving LL (larger later) rewards relative to those in the low condition (south) (Ms = 6.69 vs. 4.63, $F(1, 40)$ = 4.37, $p < .05$). Finally, in Study 4, we take a more direct measure of the underlying process and find that those located on the upper level of a building prefer a job requiring a big-picture orientation relative to those on the lower level of the building (Ms = 5.32 vs. 7.39, $F(1, 44)$ = 4.58, $p < .05$). Across the four studies, we rule out alternative explanations, including affect, perceived power, and physical distance.

This research contributes theoretically to growing research on embodied cognition, metaphorical representation and construal level theory. It also suggests itself to future investigation linking physical height (across gender, cultures, etc.) to their perspectives. In addition, the findings provide some very interesting managerial implications for industries such as real estate, airlines and subways.

When Proximity Prompts Abstraction: High-Level Construal as a Means of Counteractive Control

EXTENDED ABSTRACT

The allure of salient concrete and immediate rewards frequently tempts people to forgo the attainment of abstract and delayed goals. Research on counteractive control theory has revealed a number of cognitive and behavioral means by which people counteract the negative impact of proximal temptations on goal pursuit (e.g., Fishbach and Trope 2007). The present research proposes that high-level construal can serve a counteractive control function to promote self-control.

Construal level theory (CLT) suggests that one way that proximal temptations undermine self-control is by prompting low-level construal. CLT proposes that psychological distance impacts the way people subjectively represent or construe events (Liberman and Trope 2008; Trope and Liberman 2003; 2010). Psychological distance refers to the removal of an event from direct experience of the here-and-now. People often lack detailed information about distant events. To prepare and plan for such events, people engage in high-level construal, using cognitive abstraction to extract the central, primary, and goal-relevant features likely to be present in all possible manifestations of the events. As detailed specifics become increasingly available and reliable with greater proximity, people are able to engage in low-level construal, incorporating this information into concrete representations that highlight those secondary features that render a particular event unique. This association between distance and construal is over-generalized, apparent even when equivalent information about psychologically near and distant events is available.

Research indicates that the low-level construal that the proximity of temptations triggers is deleterious to self-control (e.g., Fujita 2008). The focus on concrete and idiosyncratic features promoted

by low-level construal may distract one from one's abstract and distal goals. Supporting this assertion, for example, female undergraduate students, a population generally concerned about their weight, are more likely to prefer candy bars over apples as a snack when engaged in low-level rather than high-level construal (Fujita and Han 2009). This and other research suggests that proximal temptations promote self-control failure by prompting low-level construal (Fujita 2008).

The present research proposes that people have mechanisms that allow them to counteract the tendency for proximal temptations to trigger low-level construal, and to engage instead in high-level construal. If indeed high-level construal serves as a means of counteractive self-control, it should be evident when people anticipate temptations will undermine valued goals (Study 1) and have no alternative means of control available (Study 2). Engaging in counteractive high-level construal should promote successful self-control (Study 3).

Study 1 tested the hypothesis that people engage in high-level construal when they anticipate temptations will undermine valued long-term goals. Undergraduate students were recruited a week prior to a midterm examination. Those in the high threat salience condition were asked to list upcoming exams along with temptations that interfere with exam, whereas those in the low threat condition were not. Participants then reported which of two paired abstract and concrete descriptions of studying best corresponded to their own thoughts as an assessment of construal (e.g., "reading chapters in my textbook" vs. "mastering course material"). Participants also reported their academic achievement motivation. Threat salience condition had no effect on academic achievement motivation, $t(86)$ = .67, $p = .51$. As predicted, however, threat salience and goal motivation interacted to predict construal level, $b = .32$, $SE = .15$, $p = .04$. Salient threats led undergraduates to prefer more abstract descriptions of studying as their academic goal motivation increased, $b = .57$, $SE= .21$, $p = .01$. By contrast, academic goal motivation was not related to construal when threats were not made salient. People thus appear to engage in counteractive high-level construal to the extent that they anticipate temptations will undermine valued goals.

The availability of alternative means of control should reduce the need to engage in counteractive high-level construal (Fishbach & Trope, 2005). To test this, participants were led to believe that they would be sampling a new cookie product that was tasty yet unhealthy and fattening. Half were told that it was up to them to decide how many cookies they desired to eat (self-control condition), whereas the other half were told that the experimenter would decide how many cookies they could eat (other-control condition). As an assessment of construal, participants were asked to what extent their thoughts about the upcoming cookie taste test took the form of words versus pictures. Research indicates that whereas words are associated with high-level construal, pictures are associated with low-level construal (Amit, Trope, and Algom 2009; Yan, Sengupta, and Hong, this symposium). As predicted, those in the self-control condition reported using words more than pictures, as compared to those in the other-control conditions, $F(1, 106)$ = 3.86, $p = .05$. People appear to engage in counteractive high-level construal, then, to the extent that they have no alternative means of control.

Study 3 sought to demonstrate that counteractive high-level construal promotes successful self-control behavior. Undergraduate students were recruited a week prior to their final exam. All participants were asked to list their exams and temptations that interfered with exam preparation. They then reported whether their thoughts about studying took the form of words versus pictures as an assessment of construal. Students also reported their academic goal motivation. We used students' grade improvement between their midterms and final exams as an indicator of successful self-control in their final exam preparations. As predicted, increasing goal motivation was associated with greater use of words over pictures, $\beta = .56$, $SE = .28$, $t(39) = 1.98$, $p = .05$, suggesting high-level construal. The use of words over pictures, in turn, predicted greater grade improvement from the midterm to the final, $\beta = .02$, $SE = .01$, $t(38) = 2.39$, $p = .02$. The 95% confidence interval for the indirect path through word over picture representation, as predicted, did not include zero (.0009 to .03), indicating a significant indirect effect of goal motivation on grade improvement through high-level construal. Thus, counteractive high-level construal appears to promote successful self-control behavior.

When Feeling Depleted Helps: The Positive Effect of Regulatory Depletion

EXTENDED ABSTRACT

Past research on regulatory depletion theory posits that exerting self-control consumes regulatory resource (Muraven and Baumeister 2000), and predicts a negative impact of regulatory depletion: performing a prior self-control task impairs the performance on a subsequent task that also involves volitional action, a phenomena termed as the depletion effect (Baumeister et al. 1998; Muraven and Baumeister 2000). A large body of empirical studies in psychology and marketing has demonstrated the depletion effect in diverse domains. For example, Baumeister et al. (1998) found that participants who exerted regulatory resources to resist the temptation of food, compared with those who did not engage in this self-control act, were less persistent on trying to solve a challenging puzzle subsequently. Likewise, suppressing thoughts undermines individuals' control on impulse purchases (Vohs and Faber 2007). Other studies have documented this effect in the contexts such as alcohol consumption (Muraven, Collins, and Nienhaus 2002), processing health-risk information (Agrawal and Wan 2009), and making deliberative choices (Vohs et al. 2008; Wang et al. 2010).

The current paper bridges the research on regulatory depletion and the literature on construal level theory to propose a new case in which depletion might exert a positive effect on task performance. Recent research on self-control has suggested that exerting self-control alters the way in which individuals construe information. Wan and Agrawal (2011) suggest that engaging in self-control systematically shifts individuals' construals to lower levels. Their studies showed that highly depleted (vs. less depleted) participants relied on feasibility (vs. desirability) attributes, favored secondary (vs. primary) features, and chose products framed in a proximal (vs. distal) perspective. Similarly, Bruyneel and Dewitte (2006) showed that depletion leads to a narrow attention span and breadth of categorization which are consistent with the mental representations at lower-level construals.

The literature on construal levels suggests that construal levels influence individuals' cognitive style and information processing (e.g., Liberman and Trope 1998; Trope and Liberman 2003). At lower-level construals, individuals are likely to attend to subordinate, incidental features, and concrete and contextual details, whereas being at higher-level construals emphasize superordinate features, and abstract and global pictures. If experiencing depletion shifts indi-

viduals' construals to lower levels, we predict that regulatory depletion will enhance the performance on tasks that require attending to low-level and contextual details.

Three experiments tested our proposition. In experiment 1, participants first completed a cross-off-letter task adopted from past research to manipulate regulatory depletion (Baumeister et al. 1998). Then participant performed the picture completion subtest of the Wechsler task (Wechsler 1991), a task used to examine people's ability to observe contextual details (Wakslak and Trope 2009). Specifically, all participants were presented with thirty pictures, each of which contains a missing part. Their task was to identify the missing parts within three minutes. Our results showed that highly depleted participants identified more missing objects than did less depleted participants ($p < .05$), supporting our prediction that depletion enhances the performance on tasks that require the attention to details.

In experiment 2, participants first performed the same cross-off-letter task that manipulated depletion, followed by an Embedded Figure Test (Witkin et al. 1971) in which eleven objects are embedded within a more complex big figure. Participants' task was to identify the embedded objects. Past research has shown that, to identify the embedded objects, people need to focus on the contextual details and ignore the big picture. Participants were given five minutes to perform the task. The results showed that highly depleted participants identified more embedded objects than did less depleted participants ($p < .05$), replicating the finding in experiment 1 and again supporting our prediction.

Experiment 3 tested our prediction in a product evaluation context with a 2 (high vs. low depletion) x 3 (information omission with cue vs. information omission without cue vs. full information) between-subject design. Participants first performed a thought suppression task adopted from past research (Vohs and Faber 2007) to manipulate depletion, followed by reading the message about a laptop computer. In the full information condition, the message described the computer on five major attributes. In the information omission without cue condition, the important attribute of memory size was omitted from the attribute list. In information omission with cue condition, the memory size information was omitted but was listed as "information unavailable to customer." Participants evaluated the computer, and recalled if any attributes were missing from the message. A 2 x 3 ANOVA on product attitudes indicated a significant interaction ($p < .05$). When there was a missing attribute without the omission cue, highly depleted participants evaluated the product less favorably than did less depleted participants ($p < .01$). However, participants in the full information did not differ in their attitudes whether they were highly or less depleted ($F < 1$). Similarly, in the omission with cue condition highly depleted and less depleted participants did not differ in their attitudes ($F < 1$). We also found the same pattern on the number of recalled missing attributes. Moreover, in the information omission conditions the number of recalled missing attributes mediated the effect of depletion on product evaluation. These results suggest that depletion enhances performance on detecting details, which has influenced their evaluation of the target products.

The current research contributes to the literature by identifying novel effects of regulatory depletion through the lens of variations in construals, and enhances the understanding the psychological processes underlying self-control.

The Good, the Bad, and the Ugly of Consumer Spending within Close Relationships

Chairs: Kristina Durante, University of Texas, USA
Scott Rick, University of Michigan, USA

Paper #1: I Love You Both Equally, But... Parental Spending on Girls versus Boys in Economic Recessions

Kristina Durante, University of Texas at San Antonio, USA
Vladas Griskevicius, University of Minnesota, USA
Joseph P. Redden, University of Minnesota, USA
Andrew E. White, Arizona State University, USA

Paper #2: Romantic Motives and Men's Conspicuous Consumption: The Role of Materialism

Inge Lens, KU Leuven, Belgium
Luk Warlop, KU Leuven, Belgium and Norwegian Business School (BI), Norway and Norwegian Business School (BI), Norway
Mario Pandelaere, Ghent University, Belgium

Paper #3: When is Saving Sexy? The Role of Construal Level in Shaping the Appeal of Savers and Spenders as Romantic Relationship Partners

Jenny Olson, University of Michigan, USA
Scott Rick, University of Michigan, USA

Paper #4: Why is Materialism Bad for Marriage? Testing Pathways Linking Materialism to Divorce

Jill Sundie, University of Texas at San Antonio, USA
James Burroughs, University of Virginia, USA
Daniel Beal, Rice University, USA

SESSION OVERVIEW

It begins with dinner and a movie. With any luck, an engagement ring follows. Before we know it we are buying our first home, deciding on vacation destinations, saving for our children's college tuition, and eventually retirement. Spending decisions permeate our close relationships and often form the basis for their long-term success or ultimate failure. However, little is known about the factors that can impact (for better or for worse) the financial decisions we make in our dating, marriage, and family life and how those decisions affect the overall health of our close relationships.

The four papers in this session all present emerging research on spending behavior within close relationships – from dating partners and marriage partners to parents and children – and the critical factors that shape the financial decisions that we make within them. The first paper uses both archival and experimental methods to investigate the environmental factors that shift parental consumer choice. The next two papers examine spending behavior within the context of initial attraction and dating – including when and why spending behavior influences the mate attraction dynamics of potential dating and marriage partners. The final paper focuses on critical factors linking materialism to marital discord and divorce.

Durante and colleagues draw on theory and research in animal behavior to investigate how the economic climate can influence whether parents spend more money on daughters versus sons. Consistent with the effects of resource scarcity on parental investment across species, they find – in a series of experiments – that economic recessions lead parents to spend more on daughters than on sons.

Lens and colleagues examined conditions under which men conspicuously consume to attract dating partners. They use both real and experimentally-induced dating situations to investigate materialism's influence on men's conspicuous consumption. Materialism predicts the extent to which men consider their wealth a tool to at-tract a romantic partner, as well as the type of partner these men desire.

Olson and Rick examined whether and why construal level influences how savers and spenders are viewed as potential dating partners. While lavish spending is sometimes used to attract romantic partners, they find that people induced to have a concrete mindset are more attracted to savers than to spender. The reverse is true for those evaluating dating partners under an abstract mindset.

Sundie, Burroughs, and Beal investigated the factors that lead materialism to erode a marriage. Using survey data from married couples collected at multiple time points, they find a three-pathway model that links materialism to divorce. Additional findings reveal important mediators of materialism's influence on marital discord.

Overall, this session focuses on the factors that influence our spending behavior within the context of close relationships and how these spending patterns can impact attraction and relationship maintenance. This session aims to celebrate diversity by introducing research lines that have received little to no empirical attention to date and by presenting novel avenues for future consumer research. As such, the session would be of interest to a breadth of consumer researchers, including those interested in family spending, motivation, social perception, nonconscious processes, romantic relationships, and biological and evolutionary approaches to consumer behavior.

I Love You Both Equally, But...Parental Spending on Girls versus Boys in Economic Recessions

EXTENDED ABSTRACT

Do economic conditions influence how parents spend money on their children? While past research has revealed important insights into children's consumer behavior and the consumption patterns of spouses (e.g., Rick, Small, and Finkel 2011), much less is known about how parents make spending decisions regarding sons versus daughters. Drawing on theory in animal behavior, we use both archival and experimental methods to examine how spending on boys versus girls is influenced by economic recessions.

Theory and research in animal behavior shows that parental investment in male versus female offspring depends on environmental conditions (Clutton-Brock 1991; Trivers and Willard 1973). When conditions are favorable, parents invest relatively more in male offspring. By contrast, when conditions are bad, parents invest more in female offspring. This gender-specific difference stems from the difference in reproductive variance between males and females. Across the animal kingdom, males have *higher* reproductive variance: Whereas some high-status males attract a large number of females and, as a result, produce high numbers of offspring, a substantial portion of lower-status males attract no mates and produce zero offspring (Dittus 1998). By contrast, females have *low* reproductive variance: As long as a female is healthy enough for reproduction, almost all females are able to attract a mate and tend to produce some moderate number of offspring.

Environmental conditions alter how parents invest in male versus female offspring because an offspring's likelihood of reproduction depends on their status and health. However, whereas under good conditions parental investment is focused on achieving a *maximum amount of status* (e.g., large size and dominance) for offspring, in bad conditions parental investment is focused on maintaining a *minimum level of health* needed for reproduction. When conditions are good, investing in male offspring has higher reproductive benefits because a high-status male will out-reproduce any female. When conditions are bad, however, this pattern reverses. In bad conditions, investing in a female ensures that there will be at least some offspring. Accordingly, animal research shows that when environmental conditions are favorable (e.g., abundant food resources), parents invest more in male offspring. But when environmental conditions are poor (e.g., scarce food resources), parents invest more in female offspring (Krist 2006).

In the current research, we examine whether humans might show similar types of patterns by examining how economic recessions infleunce investment in daughers versus sons. Based on theory and research in animal behavior , we hypothesized that economic recessions should be associated with higher spending on girls versus boys.

Study 1 examined how household spending on girls' versus boys' apparel in the US relates to fluctuation in the US Gross Domestic Product (GDP) from 1984 to 2010. We focused on apparel because it is a child consumer product category that is clearly separated by gender. Consistent with predictions, findings showed that GDP growth was negatively related to the ratio of spending on apparel for girls relative to boys ($r=-.55$, $p=.003$). This means that downturns in GDP over the last 26 years are associated with spending more money on girls' relative to boys' clothing.

Study 2 used experimental methods. Participants (both parents and non-parents) first read a news story either about an economic recession, an economic upswing, or a neutral story. Participants then imagined that they have two school-aged children (a boy and a girl) and answered questions about allocating resources to either their son or daughter. For example, "You have the funds to put one child in a special healthy lunch program at school. Which child will get the lunch program?" Responses were provided on 8-point scales (no midpoint) with "Definitely Son" and "Definitely Daughter" at the endpoints. Participants also indicated how they would divide their assets to bequeth either to their son or daughter. Consistent with predictions, people invested more resources in daughters in the economic recession condition ($p=.011$). Economic recessions also led people to bequeth more assets to daughters than to sons ($p=.036$).

Both studies thus far find that economic recessions are associated with increased allocation of resources to daughters versus sons. Study 3 investigated whether mothers and fathers might invest different types of resources in their children. Because "resources" include both money and time, we examined whether economic conditions influence how fathers and mothers invest time versus money in their children.

In Study 3, participants again read a news story either about an economic recession or an economic boom. They then answered a question about allocating money ($100) and a question about allocating time (10 hours) between a son and a daughter. As in the first two studies, people invested more in daughters than sons in the economic recession condition ($p=.01$). However, the specific nature of the investment – time or money – depended on the gender of the parent. Economic conditions altered *monetary investment* primarily for fathers. Fathers allocated 8% more money to daughters in recessions ($p=.037$). However, economic conditions altered *time investment* primarily for mothers. Mothers allocated 7% more time to daughters in recessions ($p=.032$).

These findings highlight how theory and research in animal behavior can provide insight into consumer behavior. Just as resource scarcity leads animals to invest more in female offspring, we find

that the resource scarcity (as indexed by economic recessions) leads people to invest more resources in daughters relative to sons.

Romantic Motives and Men's Conspicuous Consumption: The Role of Materialism

EXTENDED ABSTRACT

Men's conspicuous consumption may fulfil an important communicative function in a mating context (Griskevicius et al. 2007). Indeed, in response to women's preference for men with status, men in a mating mindset show an increased interest in status-signaling products (Griskevicius et al. 2007). However, little research has investigated the consequences of materialism for (men's) mating goals and partner preferences. The current research examines links between men's reliance on conspicuous consumption to attract women and materialistic values.

Research suggests that materialistic men may desire partners who are sexy or highly attractive, characteristics which are especially important in a short-term mating context rather than long-term, mating interest. Indeed, the fact that materialists tend to display little empathy and to experience poor interpersonal relationships could be interpreted as signals of low ability or willingness to commit. Materialism is related to extrinsic goal pursuit. As such, materialistic men may place greater emphasis on characteristics (e.g., attractiveness) that afford social approval.

Three studies examined materialism's influence on conspicuous consumption in mating contexts. Studies 1 and 2 investigated whether materialistic men particularly rely on conspicuous consumption to attract mates. Study 3 explores a) whether materialism predicts a preference for socially visible and attractive partners, and b) whether extrinsic goal pursuit (e.g., striving for the approval of others) mediates materialistic men's partner preferences.

In Study 1, 40 men indicated to what extent they relied on eight characteristics (wealth, humor, intelligence, attractiveness, masculinity, caretaking abilities, faithfulness, status) to attract women. Materialism (Richins 2004) was positively correlated with reliance on wealth and status to attract women, and negatively correlated with promoting one's caretaking abilities.

Study 2 assessed more explicitly whether the activation of men's mating motives, induced by a real-life encounter with an attractive woman, increased materialistic men's interest in *products* which *signal status*. 117 men were welcomed in the lab by a female experiment leader who was either plainly (control) or sexily dressed (mating condition). Next, participants rated the attractiveness of 5 status-signaling gadgets and 5 inconspicuous products (all pretested), then completed the materialism measure. GLM analysis yielded a significant interaction between Materialism, Condition, and Product Type (within subjects), $p=.048$. Mating goal activation increased interest in status-related products (but not in functional products) among more materialistic men.

In study 3, 150 men read descriptions of two hypothetical romantic partners. Description A depicted a woman who scored high on characteristics related to social visibility (attractive, admired by others), but low on characteristics typically valuable in the long run (responsible, faithful); vice versa for description B. Participants indicated which type (A or B) corresponded best to their ideal partner. They completed a measure of extrinsic goal pursuit (Kasser and Sheldon 2000) assessing their motivation to gain social approval, and the materialism measure.

Logistic regression analyses revealed that the probability of preferring partner B (over A) decreased with increasing levels of materialism, $p=.03$. Extrinsic goal pursuit significantly mediated the relationship between materialism and partner preference, *p*=.81. Hence, a need for social approval underlies materialistic men's pursuit of socially visible, attractive partners.

In sum, this paper investigated the role of materialistic values play in mating-relevant behaviors such as conspicuous consumption, and advanced our understanding of the consequences of materialism for romantic partner choice. Materialistic men prioritized socially desirable, surface partner characteristics (e.g., attractiveness), even when those qualities come at the expense of faithfulness and conscientiousness in a forced choice scenario. Materialistic men's partner preferences appear to be more in line with short-term (as opposed to long-term) mating criteria. Interestingly, men's conspicuous consumption may draw women's attention, in particular when women are ovulating and ovulation temporarily increases women's short-term mating interests (Lens et al. 2012). Hence, ovulating women may be most receptive to the conspicuous consumption displays of materialistic men. In addition, ovulating women may more strongly resemble materialists' ideal partners. Together, this seems to imply that materialism, from a short-term mating perspective, could be considered as a beneficial trait. This idea is novel given the abundance of research documenting the negative consequences of materialism, yet requires further testing.

When is Saving Sexy? The Role of Construal Level in Shaping the Appeal of Savers and Spenders as Romantic Relationship Partners

EXTENDED ABSTRACT

Among all the possible sources of conflict in romantic relationships, financial disagreements are some of the most prevalent (e.g., Amato and Rogers 1997). Different attitudes toward spending money among spouses can be a common source of such arguments (Rick, Small, and Finkel 2011). Are some spending habits initially more appealing than others in prospective mates? Lavish spending can signal desirable information about one's resources, and thus help to attract mates (Griskevicius et al. 2007). But are there situations in which chronic savers are initially more appealing than spenders?

Given that "saver" and "spender" labels could bring to mind abstract or more concrete outcomes (e.g., retiring comfortably vs. avoiding daily indulgences), we considered this question from a construal level theory (CLT) perspective (Trope and Liberman 2003). CLT suggests that the same event, behavior, or individual can be represented at multiple levels. High-level construals are relatively simple, abstract representations that capture the primary essence of available information. Low-level construals, by contrast, are more concrete and detail-oriented.

Competing predictions based on CLT are plausible. On the one hand, recent work suggests that priming a high-level (versus low-level) construal leads to better self-control, which reduces preference for immediate gratification and encourages a focus on long-term benefits (Fujita et al. 2006). Because birds of a feather flock together in relationships (e.g., Watson et al. 2004), these results suggest that a high-level construal might increase the appeal of potential mates who are also responsible. On the other hand, Kivetz and Keinan (2006) find that virtuous choices also lead to stronger regret over time. From this perspective, people who take a global, more abstract perspective may seek spenders to avoid a future filled with regret over missed opportunities. Savers, who potentially miss out on many expensive but fulfilling experiences, may be considerably less attractive to people thinking abstractly.

We conducted two studies to examine whether and why construal level influences how desirable chronic savers and spenders are

as relationship partners. In Study 1, participants were first induced to have either a high-level or low-level construal mindset using a word categorization task validated by Fujita et al. (2006). Following manipulation checks, a second, seemingly unrelated study examining perceptions of local singles was introduced. Participants were presented an opposite-sex target who was either a self-described saver or spender. Targets were rated for their attractiveness as both short-term and long-term relationship partners.

Because the attractiveness items correlated highly and previous research points to a single dimension underlying mating strategies (Simpson and Gangestad 1991), we averaged the two items to form an overall index of attractiveness. Analyses revealed a significant interaction between construal level and the target's spending habits. When participants were thinking concretely, savers were significantly more appealing as relationship partners than spenders. When participants were thinking abstractly, the attraction "gap" between savers and spenders disappeared.

Thus, the initial evidence is consistent with the regret-avoidance hypothesis. Of course, many questions about the underlying process remain unanswered. For example, does one's construal level change the inferences made based upon the saver/spender label? It is possible that a saver is viewed as especially practical by low-level construers, while a spender is viewed as especially idealistic? Another possibility is that priorities change as construal level is varied, with low-level construers valuing responsibility more than high-level construers.

Study 2 sought to replicate the initial findings and gain insight into how construal level shapes the information conveyed by the monetary labels. Participants were randomly assigned to have either a high-level or low-level construal mindset before evaluating a potential mate (a "saver" or "spender"). Targets were again rated on the attractiveness index, but also in terms of various personality traits. Two indices were formed by averaging responses to five items each: an excitement index (adventurous, fun, exciting, confident, and outgoing) and a responsibility index (timid, careful, cautious, practical, and responsible). Results again revealed an interaction on the attractiveness index, suggesting that savers are especially appealing to low-level construers but not to high-level construers. More importantly, we found that responsibility was a significant predictor of attractiveness among low-level construers, but excitement was not. Conversely, excitement was a significant predictor of attractiveness among high-level construers, but responsibility was not. Construal level did not influence the inferences drawn from the saver/spender label (e.g., spenders were always viewed as more exciting than savers, by both low-level and high-level construers).

In conclusion, results from two studies demonstrate that the effect of a potential partner's monetary habits on attractiveness depends upon construal level. Because savers are viewed as more responsible than spenders, and low-construal increases the extent to which responsibility is valued, low-construers prefer savers to spenders. High-construers value excitement more than responsibility, and thus do not show a preference for savers. Thus, saving can be sexy, as long as the search for love is accompanied by a concrete mindset.

Why is Materialism Bad for Marriage? Testing Pathways Linking Materialism to Divorce

EXTENDED ABSTRACT

In 2009, Jamie McCourt filed for divorce from her former business partner and husband of thirty years, L.A. Dodgers owner Frank McCourt. Amid rumors the McCourts misused Dodgers assets to fund their posh billionaire lifestyle, the team was taken over by Major League Baseball. In a May 2011 ABC News interview, Frank McCourt accepted blame for the "unhealthy" and "unsustainable" lifestyle he felt contributed to the demise of his marriage. Stories such as that of the McCourt's highlight a downside of "living the high life"—rampant materialism may undermine the viability of close relationships. Surprisingly little research has sought to understand how institutions of social connection, such as marriage, are influenced by materialistic values and the rise of consumer culture. Prior research shows materialism correlates with poor individual-level outcomes. Materialists report lower personal well-being, and people who emphasize extrinsic goals (e.g., financial success) report having shorter, more negative friendships and romantic partnerships (Kasser and Ryan 2001). We examined how materialism influences marital viability, investigating three pathways by which material values may negatively influence marital dynamics:

Household Finances. As a predictor of marital quality, household money management is surprisingly under-studied despite ample popular press claiming its leading role in divorce. Materialism is linked to poor money management (Richins 2011). Rick and colleagues (2011) did not investigate materialism's role in marital finances, but did find that larger *differences* between spouses in tight versus loose spending tendencies predicted financial conflict and lower marital satisfaction. We examined whether poor outcomes on key household financial benchmarks (retirement savings, emergency savings, credit card debt, and credit rating) mediate the relation between couples' materialism and divorce intentions.

Relationship Investment. Materialists may invest more in things than they do relationships. People prioritizing extrinsic goals characterize their relationships in more negative terms (e.g., more emotional extremes and jealousy, less trust; Kasser and Ryan 2001). Reasons for the correlation between materialism and poor relationships are not well understood. A person's developmental environment may play a role--young adults rating financial success as an important life goal also reported experiencing low maternal nurturance (Kasser et al. 1995). Attachment theorists suggest that people developing avoidant attachment styles–deactivation of the need to rely on close others for support–may turn to money and the acquisition of objects to foster identity and self-worth (Mikulincer and Shaver 2008). Furthermore, materialistic pursuits are linked to other traits emphasizing a lack of interest in others' well-being, such as Machiavellianism (McHoskey 1999). These factors may lead materialists to invest less in close relationships. We examined whether relationship investment mediates the relation between materialism and divorce intentions.

Coping with Marital Conflict. Disagreements occur routinely within even healthy partnerships, and the way partners handle conflicts can serve to resolve (or magnify) the problems, and solidify (or harm) the relationship over time. Two forms of problematic coping seem likely for materialists: hostile/argumentative, and depressive/self-blaming. Several findings suggest that materialism is connected to hostile reactions to social problems. Materialism is linked to disagreeable and ungracious reactions to others (McCullough et al. 2002). Materialists exhibit narcissism and avoidance, which manifests in manipulative, defensive, and aggressive conflict coping

Table 1. Standardized path coefficients for Couple-Level Model of the marital outcomes of happiness and success materialism

Predictors	Income	Credit Score	Relationship Investment	Self-Blame	Conflict Coping
Happiness Materialism	-.27*	-.38*	-.23*	.43*	.29*
Success Materialism	-.05	.07	.21*	-.07	.19
Outcome					
Divorce Intentions		-.10	-.24*	-.03	.46*

Note: Income was specified as an exogenous variable (correlating with materialism) that influenced credit score. *$p < .05$.

Table 2. Standardized path coefficients for Actor-Partner Interdependence Model of the marital outcomes of happiness and success materialism

Predictors	Husband's RI	Wife's RI	Husband's Conflict Coping	Wife's Conflict Coping
Husband's Happiness Materialism	-.34*	-.35*	.00	.12
Wife's Happiness Materialism	.05	.06	.36*	.13
Husband's Success Materialism	.21	.45*	.24	.22
Wife's Success Materialism	.00	-.16	-.12	.09
Outcomes				
Husband's Divorce Intentions	-.25*	-.07	.32*	.18*
Wife's Divorce Intentions	-.18*	-.10	.23*	.23*

Note: Income was specified as an exogenous variable (correlating with materialism) that influenced credit score.
RI = Relationship Investment. *$p < .05$.

(e.g., Bushman and Baumeister 1998). Regarding the self-blaming response, Wachtel and Blatt (1990) found that materialists scored higher on the self-criticality dimension of a depression inventory. This tendency for materialists to focus inwardly and negatively suggests that they may self-blame during disagreements. Since neither coping style is considered constructive in resolving conflicts, these poor coping mechanisms may erode relationships. We examined whether poor coping with conflict mediates the materialism--divorce intentions link.

180 socioeconomically and demographically diverse married couples participated. Two surveys were administered at least 5 days apart to separate constructs that could contaminate one another or produce common method bias. Concerns of method bias were further alleviated by having spouses rate the materialism (Richins 2004) of their partner.

Given previous findings of divergent validities between the happiness and success facets of materialism and well-being outcomes (e.g., Deckop et al. 2005), we examined separate models for the overall materialism construct and these two facets. We also examined separate models for couple-level effects (scores on materialism, financial health, relationship investment, coping styles, and divorce intentions, averaged across husband and wife) and intra-couple effects (Actor-Partner Interdependence Models). All of these models provided good fit to the data (CFIs ranged from .93-.96). A close examination revealed several interesting findings. First, the model collapsing across materialism facets revealed small to moderate effects through the financial and hostile coping pathways, but did not support self-blame or relationship investment pathways. Once success and happiness facets of materialism were split out, an interesting pattern emerged revealing support primarily for the relationship investment and hostile coping pathways, as these were the only predictors of divorce intentions (Table 1). Happiness materialism predicted unfavorable outcomes across the board, whereas success materialism predicted increases in relationship investment.

We expanded the final model to include husband and wife paths (allowing for separate influences, and cross-partner effects), but focused on the relationship investment and conflict coping mediators. Model 2 bore both similarities and differences to the above effects. First, though husbands' materialism affected wives' relationship investment (happiness decreased it, and success increased it), wives' relationship investment did not predict divorce intentions (Table 2). A similar pattern was found for husbands, but their relationship investment *did* predict divorce intentions. A final path linked wives' happiness materialism to both husband and wife divorce intentions by increasing husbands' hostile coping. Happiness materialism increased divorce intentions of both husbands and wives, but did so primarily through a decrease in husbands' relationship investment and an increase in husbands' hostile coping. In addition, some evidence supports a positive role for success materialism by increasing perceptions of relationship investment.

REFERENCES

Amato, Paul R. and Stacy J. Rogers (1997), "A Longitudinal Study of Marital Problems and Subsequent Divorce," *Journal of Marriage and the Family*, 59 (August), 612–24.

Bushman, Brad J. and Roy F. Baumeister (1998), "Threatened Egotism, Narcissism, Self-Esteem, and Direct and Displaced Aggression: Does Self-Love or Self-Hate Lead to Violence?," *Journal of Personality and Social Psychology*, 75(1), 219-229.

Clutton-Brock, Tim H (1991), *"The Evolution of Parental Care,"* Princeton, NJ: Princeton Univ Press.

Deckop, J. R., Jurkiewicz, C. L., & Giacalone, R. A. (2010). Effects of materialism on work-related personal well-being. Human Relations, 63(7), 1007–1030. doi:10.1177/0018726709353953

Dittus, W. P. J. (1998), "Birth Sex Ratios in Toque Macaques and Other Mammals: Integrating the Effects of Maternal Condition and Competition," *Behavioral Ecology and Sociobiology*, 44, 149-60.

Fujita, Kentaro, Yaacov Trope, Nira Liberman, and Maya Levin-Sagi (2006), "Construal Levels and Self-Control," *Journal of Personality and Social Psychology*, 90, 351–67.

Griskevicius, Vladas, Joshua M. Tybur, Jill M. Sundie, Robert B. Cialdini, G. F. Miller, and Douglas T. Kenrick (2007), "Blatant Benevolence and Conspicuous Consumption: When Romantic Motives Elicit Strategic Costly Signals," *Journal of Personality and Social Psychology*, 93, 85–102.

Janssens, Kim, Mario Pandelaere, Bram Van den Bergh, Kobe Millet, Inge Lens, and Keith Roe (2011), "Can Buy Me Love. Mate Attraction Goals Lead to Perceptual Readiness for Status Products," *Journal of Experimental Social Psychology*, 47 (1), 254-58.

Kasser, Tim, Richard M. Ryan, Melvin Zax, and Arnold J. Sameroff (1995), "The Relations of Maternal and Social Environments to Late Adolescents' Materialistic and Prosocial Values. *Developmental Psychology*, 31(6), 907-914.

Kasser, Tim and Kennon M. Sheldon (2000), "Of Wealth and Death: Materialism, Mortality Salience, and Consumption Behavior," *Psychological Science*, 11 (4), 348-51.

Kasser, Tim, & Ryan, R. M. (2001), "Be Careful What You Wish For: Optimal Functioning and the Relative Attainment of Intrinsic and Extrinsic Goals," In P. Schmuck & K. M. Sheldon (Eds.), *Life Goals and Well-Being: Towards a Positive Psychology of Human Striving*, Seattle: Hogrefe & Huber.

Kivetz, Ran and Anat Keinan (2006), "Repenting Hyperopia: An Analysis of Self-Control Regrets," *Journal of Consumer Research*, 33 (September), 273–82.

Krist, Milo (2006), "Should Mothers in Poor Condition Invest More in Daughter Than Son?" *Ethology, Ecology, and Evolution*, 18, 241-146.

Lens, Inge, Karolien Driesmans, Mario Pandelaere, & Kim Janssens (2012), "Would Male Conspicuous Consumption Capture the Female Eye? Menstrual Cycle Effects on Women's Attention to Status Products," *Journal of Experimental Social Psychology*, 48, 346-49.

McCullough, Michael E., Robert A. Emmons, and Jo-Ann Tsang (2002), "The Grateful Disposition: a Conceptual and Empirical Topography," *Journal of Personality and Social Psychology*, 82(1), 112-27.

McHoskey, John W. (1999). Machiavellianism, Intrinsic Versus Extrinsic Goals, and Social Interest: A Self-Determination Theory Analysis. *Motivation and Emotion*, 23(4), 267-283.

Mikulincer, Mario, and Phillip R. Shaver (2008), "Can't Buy Me Love": An Attachment Perspective on Social Support and Money as Psychological Buffers," *Psychological Inquiry*, 19(3-4), 167-173.

Richins, Marsha L. (2004), "The Material Values Scale: Measurement Properties and Development of a Short Form," *Journal of Consumer Research*, 31(1), 209-219.

Richins, Marsha L. (2011), "Materialism, Transformation Expectations, and Spending: Implications for Credit Use," *Journal of Public Policy and Marketing*, 30 (Fall), 141-56.

Rick, Scott I., Deborah A. Small, and Eli J. Finkel (2011), "Fatal (Fiscal) Attraction: Spendthrifts and Tightwads in Marriage," *Journal of Marketing Research*, 48 (April), 228–37.

Sheldon, Kennon M. and Tim Kasser (1995), "Coherence and Congruence: Two Aspects of Personality Integration," *Journal of Personality and Social Psychology,* 68, 531-43.

Simpson, Jeffry A. and Steven W. Gangestad (1991), "Individual Differences in Sociosexuality: Evidence for Convergent and Discriminant Validity," *Journal of Pers and Social Psych,* 67, 870–83.

Trivers, Robert L. and Dan E. Willard (1973), "Natural Selection of Parental Ability to Vary the Sex Ratio Of Offspring," *Science,* 179, 90-92.

Trope, Yaacov and Nira Liberman (2003), "Temporal Construal," *Psychological Review*, 110, 403–21.

Wachtel, Paul L. and Sidney J. Blatt (1990), "Perceptions of Economic Needs and of Anticipated Future Income," *Journal of Economic Psychology*, 11 (September), 403-415.

Watson, David, Eva C. Klohnen, Alex Casillas, Ericka N. Simms, Jeffrey Haig, and Diane S. Berry (2004), "Match Makers and Deal Breakers: Analyses of Assortative Mating in Newlywed Couples," *Journal of Personality*, 72, 1029–68.

New Perspectives on Symbolic Brands and Reference Groups

Chair: Silvia Bellezza, Harvard Business School, USA

Paper #1: Connecting with Celebrities: The Therapeutic Function of Celebrity Endorsement

Jennifer Edson Escalas, Vanderbilt University, USA

James R. Bettman, Duke University, USA

Paper #2: Brand-Tourists or Brand-Immigrants? How New Lower-Status Consumers Dilute or Enhance the Image of Symbolic Brands

Silvia Bellezza, Harvard Business School, USA

Anat Keinan, Harvard Business School, USA

Paper #3: Brand Dilution: The Impact of the User of Counterfeits on Genuine Brand Perceptions and the Moderating Role of Social Class

Nelson Amaral, University of Minnesota, USA

Barbara Loken, University of Minnesota, USA

Paper #4: When 'Your Brand' Changes the Terms of the Relationship: Vicarious Dissonance in the Context of Brand Attachment

Eda Sayin, Koc University, Turkey

Nilufer Aydinoglu, Koc University, Turkey

Zeynep Gürhan-Canli, Koc University, Turkey

SESSION OVERVIEW

Consumers use symbolic products and brands to express who they are and to make inferences about the identities of others (Escalas and Bettman 2005). Symbolic brands are markers of in-group identity and signal membership to a specific brand community. The dynamic group of users of the brand shapes the associations and attitudes that consumers hold with respect to their symbolic brands (Berger and Heath 2007; White and Dahl 2006). The papers in this session examine the roles of brands as symbols and means of self-expression for consumers, as individuals and as members of specific in-groups.

Besides contributing to the main conference theme of appreciating diversity by providing novel theoretical insights into the particular domain of symbolic brands, the proposed session contributes to the understanding of several topics that are of great interest to ACR conference attendees, including conspicuous consumption, brand attachment, brand extensions and dilution, and in-group and out-group dynamics.

In the first paper, Escalas and Bettman propose that consumers appropriate brand symbolism that comes from celebrity endorsement to construct and communicate their self-concepts and that consumers with compromised identities look to celebrities to a greater extent than those with less insecurity. Across three studies, the authors demonstrate that consumers are more likely to look to celebrities for meaning when their self-esteem is threatened (1), have low levels of social complexity (2), and are under high life stress (3).

The second paper by Bellezza and Keinan examines how current users of symbolic brands react to new lower-status users of the brand. Contrary to the shared notion that lower-status consumers are by definition a threat to the brand, five lab and field studies demonstrate the conditions under which lower-status consumers enhance rather than dilute the brand image. This research shows that positive brand enhancement is mediated by the impact on the pride of current users of the brand and moderated by self-brand connection level.

In the third paper, Amaral and Loken investigate brand dilution for prestige brands and the moderating role of the users' group

social class. In four studies, the authors examine the effects of using counterfeit luxury products on the perceptions of observers regarding the genuine brand. Results show more favorable beliefs toward and attitudes regarding prestige when the counterfeit product is used by an in-group (versus an out-group) social class member.

Finally, the fourth paper by Sayin, Aydinoglu and Gurhan-Canli examines how consumers' evaluations of incongruent brand extensions differ depending on the level of attachment to the symbolic brand. Building on vicarious dissonance theory in social psychology, this research shows in a series of studies employing symbolic brands that strong consumer-brand attachment leads to vicarious dissonance and can positively affect consumer attitudes toward the brand extension and the product category.

All speakers (Escalas, Bellezza, Amaral, Sayin; indicated by asterisk below) have agreed to serve if the proposal is accepted.

Connecting with Celebrities: The Therapeutic Function of Celebrity Endorsement

EXTENDED ABSTRACT

With the rise of social media and reality television, some refer to our times as the social era of celebrity (adly.com). Given the prevalence of celebrity endorsements, it is important to understand their effects. We propose that consumers appropriate brand symbolism that comes from celebrity endorsement to construct and communicate their self-concepts and that consumers with compromised identities look to celebrities to a greater extent than those with less insecurity. Three studies show that consumers whose identities are compromised are more likely to look to celebrities for meaning: the effect of celebrity endorsement on self-brand connections is augmented when consumers' self-esteem is threatened (study 1), for consumers with low levels of social complexity (study 2), and for consumers who are experiencing life stress (study 3).

McCracken (1986) asserts that brand meaning originates in the culturally constituted world, moving into goods via the fashion system, word of mouth, reference groups, and, importantly for our purposes, celebrities. A celebrity endorser may provide a bundle of cultural meanings that becomes associated with the brands s/he endorses. Meaning moves to consumers as they construct their identities through brand choices based on congruency between brand meaning and desired self-image. Thus, the meaning and value of a brand is not just its ability to express the self, but also its role in helping consumers create and build their self-identities (McCracken 1986). Additionally, research has shown that source congruence, that is, the match between the celebrity's image and the brand's image, is an important influence on brand beliefs and attitudes under conditions of high involvement/elaboration (Kirmani and Shiv 1998).

In our research, we examine the therapeutic function of celebrity as a source of meaning in modern consumer culture. We propose that celebrities play the role of modern heroes, where heroes have historically helped people make sense of their lives and form connections with others (Campbell [1949] 2008). Although this may be true for society in general, it is particularly relevant for individuals with compromised identities. When consumers' have a compromised identity, in response to stressful events, life changes, lack of a complex social network, or some other self-esteem threat, they are motivated to repair their self-identity (Leary et al. 1995). We argue that these vulnerable consumers are more likely to look to modern heroes (celebrities) to make sense of who they are and their role in society.

Our assertion that consumers with compromised identities seek meaning from celebrities is supported by research into why some people become more obsessive about celebrities in general. Some social psychological analyses link celebrity worship with shyness, loneliness, lack of cognitive flexibility, fantasy proneness, and substandard mental health (e.g., Maltby et al. 2006). A compromised identity also may lead to obsession with celebrities that enables such individuals to establish an identity and sense of fulfillment. In this research tradition, celebrities have a therapeutic function; people look to celebrities to repair their compromised identity. Thus, we expect to find that consumers with greater active self-concept concerns or insecurities (i.e., more compromised identities) will be more likely to look to celebrities for meaning in the consumption domain, augmenting the effects of celebrity endorsement.

In study 1, we found that a compromised identity augments the influence of celebrity endorsement on self-brand connections by threatening self-esteem. We presented participants with an article criticizing the US, which threatened the self-esteem of those participants who had a high US national identity. We found a significant interaction of self-esteem threat by celebrity aspiration level (F (1, 277) = 4.07, $p < .05$). People whose self-esteem had been threatened formed connections to brands that were endorsed by celebrities that they aspired to be like. They also rejected brands that were endorsed by celebrities with images that did not match their desired self-image. Participants whose self-esteem was not threatened did not form differential self-brand connections based on celebrity aspiration level.

Study 2 examined a second source of compromised identity, social complexity, defined as joining and maintaining membership in diverse groups. By providing social support, social complexity provides a buffering effect against stress and loneliness and enhances personal and collective self-esteem. In this study, we found a significant three-way interaction of social complexity, source congruency, and participant congruency on self-brand connections (F(1, 109) = 5.47, $p < .05$). Consumers who were not socially complex (thus, have compromised identities) looked to celebrities for meaning more than consumers who had highly complex social networks. This effect was augmented by source congruence (that is, the celebrity image matches the brand image, Kirmani and Shiv 1998) and consumer congruence (the consumer's self-image matches the brand image – in this study, athletic watches).

Study 3 examined yet a third vulnerability for consumers' personal identity: life stressors. As people deal with loss of a spouse, a job, or go through other periods of stress, they are often in a transitional or liminal state with regards to their self-identity. Here, we found a significant three way interaction of life stressors, source congruence, and participant congruence on self-brand connections (F(1, 335) = 6.09, $p = .01$): consumers whose identities are compromised by dealing with stress in their lives look to celebrities for meaning more than consumers who have fewer life stressors. This effect is also augmented by source congruence and consumer congruence (in this study – a Syrah wine).

In sum, our studies show celebrity plays a therapeutic function for consumers in our culture, with consumers with compromised identities being more likely to look to celebrity endorsers as a source of meaning. We find this effect whether we threaten self-esteem, measure social complexity, or measure the number of life stressors present in consumers' lives. In all three cases, the effect of celebrity endorsement on self-brand connections is stronger, compared to consumers who do not have similarly compromised identities.

Brand-Tourists or Brand-Immigrants? How New Lower-Status Consumers Dilute or Enhance the Image of Symbolic Brands

EXTENDED ABSTRACT

There is an inherent trade-off in managing symbolic and luxury brands. Brand managers need to generate growth by extending the customer base to new segments and new markets; yet, this increased popularity and prevalence can paradoxically hurt the brand and threaten its symbolic value. Indeed, marketing research warns managers of brand dilution risks (Loken and Roedder John 2009). Contrary to the shared view that new lower-status consumers are a threat to symbolic brands, we investigate the conditions under which new lower-status users and downward brand extensions can enhance rather than dilute the image of the brand.

We introduce a distinction between two types of new consumers based on how they are perceived by current brand users. We define "*brand immigrants*" as those who are perceived by current brand users to claim "in-group status" they do not fully deserve (i.e., consider themselves as part of the in-group of brand users), and define "*brand tourists*" as those who buy the new branded products but do not claim any in-group membership (i.e., do not claim to be part of the brand users' in-group). We propose that new consumers who are perceived by the current users as claiming but not fully deserving in-group status (brand immigrants) will have a negative impact on the brand. However, when these new consumers are not perceived to claim membership status, but just show their admiration for the brand (brand tourists), they will not dilute the image but rather enhance the symbolic value of the brand.

These predictions build on research examining attitudes toward out-groups (Berger and Heath 2007; White and Dahl 2006) and immigration (Lee and Fiske 2006). Immigrants are often treated with hostility by national residents due to economic and symbolic threats. Similarly, in the context of symbolic brands, we predict that brand immigrants can threaten the exclusivity of the brand. In contrast, tourists, who do not demand any privileges or citizenship rights, are often welcomed and encouraged to visit host countries. In a pilot study with 210 American citizens, we confirm that citizens hold more favorable attitudes towards tourists than towards immigrants. Tourists boost the pride of citizens. Likewise, brand tourists, as fans of the brand, are expected to have a positive effect on the symbolic value of the brand and the pride of current customers.

Five lab and field studies explore the responses of current symbolic and luxury brand consumers to new customers and new brand extensions. To ensure high external validity of our findings, all our studies examine the reactions of real consumers to brands they actually own or use, and are based on real branding dilemmas and brand extension scenarios. We explore diverse consumer populations and symbolic brands representing a wide variety of ways to obtain in-group status, such as monetary investment and product knowledge (owners of Ferrari cars or luxury bags), passing admission tests (students at Harvard University), or even training for an activity (yoga practitioners who wear Lululemon, or participants of the "Tough Mudder" race).

We demonstrate that the negative responses to brand immigrants and positive responses to brand tourists are mediated by feelings of pride and moderated by brand ownership and level of self-brand connection (Escalas and Bettman 2005).

Study 1a examines the responses of Harvard Undergraduates to a Harvard part-time online undergraduate program. We manipulate the description of the part-time students between-subjects in three conditions by providing testimonials claiming in-group status (brand immigrants), testimonials not claiming membership (brand tourists), or no testimonials at all (control condition). We find that Harvard students have positive reactions when part-time students are perceived as brand tourists and that pride mediates the reactions.

In Study 1b, we recruited owners of Prada and Marc Jacobs's products and followed the same experimental paradigm of study 1a (i.e. description of new lower-status consumers of the brand). We find that the prestige image of the brand is significantly higher in the brand tourist condition than in the control and brand immigrant conditions.

Study 2 examines the responses of participants of the endurance run "Tough Mudder." We test how participants react to offering non-participants the opportunity to buy a ticket to watch the run and take part in the festivities. We describe these non-participants as brand tourists or immigrants. We find that while brand immigrants are perceived as a threat to the symbolic value of the brand, tourists reinforce and enhance the brand's desirability and status. This effect is mediated by the impact on pride and it moderated by level of self-brand connection.

Study 3 investigates how and where the product is being used by examining Ferrari car owners' reactions to Ferrari car renters. We find that owners react negatively when renters intend to drive the car on the streets of Miami and could be mistaken for real owners, but react positively when the renters' intention is to experience the car on a Miami racing track.

Study 4 identifies boundary conditions for the brand tourism effect by comparing the responses of owners of a symbolic (Lululemon) vs. non-symbolic (Gap) brand and investigate yet another way of depicting brand tourists and immigrants by manipulating the ability and the potential of the new consumer to claim in-group status (i.e., a toddler vs. an adult). We demonstrate that while Lululemon owners are very sensitive to non-members' ability to claim in-group status, Gap owners are less sensitive to these concerns.

Finally, we discuss theoretical and managerial implications, including additional studies and demonstrations of how some of our findings have been applied in the field.

Brand Dilution: The Impact of the User of Counterfeits on Genuine Brand Perceptions and the Moderating Role of Social Class

EXTENDED ABSTRACT

Traditionally, brands of luxury goods or status goods are defined as those for which the mere use or display of the branded product brings prestige on the owner, apart from any functional utility. Many firms spend significant portions of their revenue, and top management's time, on building such strong brands by communicating positive and unique identities to consumers. These efforts, however, can be undermined by the unauthorized use of trademarks through counterfeit products, offering consumers some of the symbolism of the brand for a fraction of the cost of the genuine name brands ($20 Rolex watches or $40 Prada bags). Despite the magnitude of the problem, little attention has been devoted to counterfeits in the literature (for exceptions see Wilcox, Min Kim and Sen 2009). Specifically, research on the effects of counterfeit goods on perceptions of the brands they imitate is lacking (Loken and John 2009). We examine the nature of people's inferences about others using counterfeit brands and how these perceptions interact with social class in affecting a brand's equity.

People compare themselves to both in-group and out-group members to maintain in-group distinctiveness. Consumers aspire to buy products of their associative reference groups, and presti-

gious brands, in particular, come to symbolize an individual's social class position (Martineau 1968). Research on dissociative reference groups suggests that people avoid or even abandon brands that are linked to disliked groups (White and Dahl 2006, Berger and Heath 2007).

The consumer's use of a counterfeit product, such as a counterfeit "Louis Vuitton" bag, could change the symbolism of that brand, depending on the social class of the counterfeit user and the social class of the observer. Specifically, persons should be more likely to accept counterfeit product usage by persons from a similar than a different social class as them. Perceptions of the genuine brand should be negatively (positively) affected when a counterfeit product is used by a member of one's out (in)-group social class. We investigate this hypothesis through four experiments in which this match between social classes is either implied (studies 1 and 2) or manipulated (studies 3 and 4).

Experiments were conducted in a variety of settings. In studies 1 and 3 experiments were conducted in a laboratory setting with female undergraduates at a large University in the Midwest. Study 2 data were collected from inner-city high-school aged females in local community centers. Study 4 was conducted using a popular online survey provider. In studies 1 and 2, participants viewed a photo of a consumer using a luxury handbag and subsequently reported their prestige beliefs and attitudes about the genuine brand. The luxury handbag shown in the photo was described as either a counterfeit luxury brand or a real luxury brand, and the woman in the photo (using the handbag) was described in terms that reflected either a higher or a lower social class. In Studies 3 and 4, we provided a more direct investigation of the role of social group similarity on brand beliefs. In study 3 we manipulated the class of both the consumer and the observer (i.e. the participants) and in study 4 we manipulated the perceived similarity between the consumer and the observer.

The results from the first two studies suggest that, for prestige products, the use of counterfeit products can change people's perceptions of the genuine brand but that this effect is limited by the match between the social class of the observer (i.e. participant) and the perceived social class of the consumer. Specifically, study 1 participants, drawn from a relatively high-class population, rated Prada and Louis Vuitton as more prestigious and more likeable when the counterfeit was being used by a higher than a lower class consumer . For study 2 participants, drawn from a relatively lower social class, the reverse effect occurred. The genuine brands were rated as more prestigious and less likeable when the counterfeit was used by a *lower* than a *higher* social class consumer.

Study 3 manipulated participants' perceptions of their own social class by framing questions about income and education with relatively high or low choice options. Results demonstrated that a match in the social classes of the observer and the consumer resulted in higher beliefs and attitudes towards the original brand than a mis-match between the social classes, for both high and low class observers.

Study 4 manipulated participants' perceptions of overall similarity between the user of the counterfeit and the observer by asking participants to imagine someone who was very much un/like them and then to imagine that person using a counterfeit prestige product. Corroborating our hypothesis, the brand was rated as more prestigious and likeable when the user of the counterfeit was similar rather than dissimilar to the participant.

Together, these studies provide compelling empirical evidence for the effects of counterfeit usage by social class in-groups and outgroups on perceptions of the genuine brand. That is, the effects of observing counterfeit use on beliefs of prestige and overall brand attitudes depend significantly on the social class of the observer and the consumer. Importantly, the perceptions of people who observe the use of counterfeits of luxury brands are more positively (negatively) disposed to liking the genuine brand when the counterfeit product is used by an in-group (out-group) member.

When 'Your Brand' Changes the Terms of the Relationship: Vicarious Dissonance in the Context of Brand Attachment

EXTENDED ABSTRACT

Consumers see brands as legitimate relationship partners (Fournier 1998). When consumers have strong personal connection (attachment) with a brand, they incorporate the brand into their own sense of self (Park et al. 2009). Attachment to a particular brand influences one's allocation of emotional, cognitive and behavioral resources towards the object of attachment and induces a readiness to evaluate it positively. Consumers follow the brands that they feel attached to, know them very well and have expectations from them. They have a tendency to see these brands as extensions of self and members of their in-groups.

Consumers rely on their relationships with a brand when they are evaluating brand extensions (Aaker and Keller 1990). Consumers evaluate brand extensions according to their established perceptions of a family brand and the similarity with the extension categories. Such evaluations build on the terms of the brand-self relationship (i.e., characteristics of the brand perceived by the individual as part of self-concept). Accordingly, consumers might experience dissonance when these brands do not behave in line with their expectations.

Vicarious dissonance theory in social psychology suggests that when people witness a discrepant behavior (contradictory to already established expectations) from a person that they have a bond with and regard as a member of their in-group, they experience a dissonance. As the behavior cannot be undone, individuals have a tendency to change their own attitudes toward the discrepant behavior in order to reduce the dissonance. Applying the vicarious dissonance theory to the marketing context, we suggest that people who feel connected to specific brands will have certain expectations regarding how these brands should behave. When these brands do not behave in line with expectations, specifically within the context of brand extensions, consumers will experience vicarious dissonance and then change their attitudes towards the unexpected behavior. In order words, consumer attitudes toward the brand extension and its product category will become more positive compared to their first reaction due to the vicarious dissonance felt.

For example, a person who identifies himself with the Porsche brand may associate the brand personality (young, exciting sports cars) of Porsche with himself, and therefore feel vicarious dissonance when Porsche decides to produce an SUV, a product category that is incongruent with the established brand personality of Porsche. In an effort to reduce the dissonance, the consumer may amend his own attitude towards the SUV product category. Hence, a person who has a bond with the Porsche brand may develop a positive attitude toward SUVs as a product category (not only to the Porsche SUV) after Porsche's decision to produce SUVs. To sum up, we suggest that strong consumer-brand attachment will lead to vicarious dissonance and affect the attitudes toward the brand extension and the product category.

Additionally, we suggest that not only different attachment levels, but also the different functions of the brands may impact the attitudes of consumers. Park and his colleagues (2009) specify three functions that brands serve; entertaining the self, enabling the self and enriching the self. In order to create consumer-brand attachment, brands need to serve all three of these resources. However, the prominence of each of these resources may be different for various brands. We assume that consumers identify themselves more with brands that have more enriching resources. Hence, we believe that different resources of brands such as enriching, enabling and entertaining the individuals, affect the level of brand-self-identification and impact the vicarious dissonance felt by the consumers when an incongruent behavior occurs. Thus, we expect that the prominence of different functions of brands will moderate the vicarious dissonance felt by the consumers. Negative impact of incongruent brand extensions on consumer attitudes toward the brand will be lower for brands with enriching resources in comparison to brands with entertaining and enabling resources.

Three pretests were conducted to choose the brands to be studied, to identify the congruent and incongruent brand extensions that these brands have, the type of attachment consumers feel for these brands and the baseline evaluations for the product categories of incongruent brand extensions. Based on these pretests, we selected two well-known brands; one luxury car brand and one fashion clothing brand.

In the first laboratory experiment, we demonstrated that participants felt vicarious dissonance when a brand that they were highly attached to introduced an incongruent brand extension. We first measured the evaluations for the unbranded product categories. Participants' evaluations for these unbranded product categories were significantly increased after they were informed that brands that they were highly attached to launched them. In contrast, there was no change in the evaluations of the participants who did not feel attached to the brands. These findings are replicated for both brands and product categories.

In the second study, we have examined the same effects using hypothetical scenarios with fictitious brands. Hence, attachment levels were manipulated. Consistent with study 1, we found that participants' evaluations increased for the unbranded product categories, even though they found them incongruent with the brands explained in the scenarios. In the third study that we are currently conducting, we are collecting data to measure the effect of different attachment types on vicarious dissonance and product evaluations.

Our research contributes to the work on attitudes toward atypical brand extensions. We extend the vicarious dissonance literature by demonstrating its effect on the incongruent extensions of brands that consumers feel attached to.

REFERENCES

Aaker, D. A. and Keller, K. L. (1990), Consumer evaluations of brand extensions. *Journal of Marketing, 54*(1), 27-41.

Berger, Jonah, and Chip Heath (2007), "Where Consumers Diverge from Others: Identity Signaling and Product Domains," *Journal of Consumer Research*, 34(August), 121–35.

Campbell, J. ([1949] 2008), *The Hero with a Thousand Faces*, Novato, CA: New World Library.

Escalas, Jennifer E., and James R. Bettman (2005), "Self-Construal, Reference Groups, and Brand Meaning," *Journal of Consumer Research*, 32, 378–89.

Fournier, S. (1998), Consumers and their brands: Developing relationship theory in consumer research. *Journal of Consumer Research, 24*, 343-373.

Kirmani, A., and Baba Shiv (1998), Effects of Source Congruity on Brand Attitudes and Beliefs: The Moderating Role of Issue-Relevant Elaboration, *Journal of Consumer Psychology,* 7(1): 25-47.

Leary, M. R., Tambor, E. S., Terdal S. K. and Downs, D. L. (1995), Self-Esteem as an Interpersonal Monitor: The Sociometer Hypothesis, *Journal of Personality and Social Psychology*, 68 (3), 518-530.

Lee, Tiane, and Susan Fiske (2006), "Not an outgroup, not yet an ingroup: Immigrants in the Stereotype Content Model," *International Journal of Intercultural Relations*, 30(6), 751–68.

Loken, Barbara, and Deborah Roedder John (2009), "When Do Bad Things Happen to Good Brands? Understanding Internal and External Sources of Brand Dilution," in *Brands and Brand Management: Contemporary Research Perspectives*, B. Loken, R. Ahluwalia, and M. J. Houston, eds., Routledge, 233–63.

Maltby, J., Day, L., McCutcheon, L. E., Houran, J. and Ashe, D. (2006), Extreme Celebrity Worship, Fantasy Proneness, and Dissociation: Developing the Measurement and Understanding of Celebrity Worship within a Clinical Personality Context, *Personality and Individual Differences*, 40, 273-283.

Martineau, P. (1968), Social Class and Spending Behavior. *Journal of Marketing*, 23, 274-278.

McCracken, G. (1986), Culture and Consumption: A Theoretical Account of the Structure and Movement of the Cultural Meaning of Consumer Goods, *Journal of Consumer Research*, 13 (June), 71-84.

Park, C. W., Priester, J. R., MacInnis, D. J. and Wan, Z. (2009), The Connection-prominence attachment model. *in Handbook of Brand Relationships,* Eds. MacInnis, D. J., Park, C. W. and Priester, J. R. 327-341, New York: Society for Consumer Psychology.

White, Katherine, and Darren W. Dahl (2006), "To Be or Not Be? The Influence of Dissociative Reference Groups on Consumer Preferences," *Journal of Consumer Psychology*, 16(4), 404–14.

Wilcox, K., Min Kim, H. and Sen S. (2009), Why Do Consumers Buy Counterfeit Luxury Brands? *Journal of Marketing Research, 46 (April),* 247–59.

Understanding Diversity in Consumer Influence and Contextually Embedded Influencers

Chairs: Pierre-Yann Dolbec, York University, Canada
Andrew N. Smith, York University, Canada

Paper #1: Consumer-Bloggers Mobilized in Marketing Campaigns: A Study of Opinion Leaders' Authenticity Management in a Streetwear Community

Benoit-Mykolas Savignac, HEC Montréal, Canada
Marie-Agnès Parmentier, HEC Montréal, Canada
Jean-Sébastien Marcoux, HEC Montréal, Canada

Paper #2: Institutional Dynamics when Consumers Coalesce in Aestheticized Product Markets

Pierre-Yann Dolbec, York University, Canada
Eileen Fischer, York University, Canada

Paper #3: Never-Ending Stories: Opinion Leadership and Antenarratives in an Online Investment Community

Andrew N. Smith, York University, Canada

Paper #4: Learning the Language of the Market: Contextual Influence and the Use of Code Switching in Online Consumer Acculturation Platforms

Hope Jensen Schau, University of Arizona, USA
Yan Dang, Northern Arizona University, USA
Yulei Zhang, Northern Arizona University, USA

SESSION OVERVIEW

For decades, the topic of how consumers influence other consumers has been of vital interest to consumer behavior and marketing strategy scholars. They have explored it through studies of word of mouth (e.g. de Matos & Rossie 2008; Dichter 1966), of the flow of product information through networks (e.g. Lee, Cotte, and Nosworthy 2010), of opinion leaders and opinion followers (e.g. Silk 1966; Coulter et al 2002), of market mavens (e.g Feick and Price 1987), of leader users (e.g. Kratzer and Lettl 2009; Schreier, Oberhauser, Prugl 2007) and of peer influence (e.g. Watts and Dodds 2007). Indeed, more than 190 consumer and marketing research studies have been published in the 28 peer-reviewed journals and conference proceedings reviewed for this session. Not surprisingly, a considerable amount of knowledge has accumulated. Relatively little attention has been paid, however, to understanding the diverse ways in which influence is (co) produced, especially within different kinds of consumption communities. Moreover, we lack understanding of the diverse ways that consumers come to have and to maintain influence and what the effects of their influence practices may be. This oversight is particularly problematic given the explosive growth in online communities in which consumers with shared consumption interests may congregate. Our objective in this session is to shed new light on the very nature of consumer influence and on factors and processes that make some consumers more influential than others in online contexts.

The general orientation of this session is toward seeing influence as a contextually embedded and collectively co-constructed phenomenon. We anticipate some similarity across contexts, but we seek to understand the diversity, both in what influence means, and in what makes consumers influential in online communities that have differing norms and practices, that interact on different kinds of platforms and that share interests in products, practices, and problems with differing characteristics.

Likely audience

Scholars interested in word of mouth, opinion leaders and followers, peer influence, and consumption communities will all find fresh insights in this session.

Issues and topics to be covered

In the first two papers of the session, a primary issue of concern is how influential consumers produce and maintain their influence. Savignac, Parmentier, and Marcoux, study the authenticity management tactics of lead bloggers in a somewhat countercultural community focused on skateboards and the street-wear that skateboarders favor. Dolbec and Fischer highlight how curatorial practices are crucial in an aesthetic community. The latter study, as well as the final two in the session, illuminate the diverse means by which influence can be co-created. Dolbec and Fischer highlight the emergence of an alternative taste structure that deviates from that of mainstream fashion, Smith focuses on how opinion leaders in an online investing community provide antenarratives with which followers engage to help make sense of unstable markets, and Schau, Dang and Zhang analyze "code switching" in the influence process in a community populated by migrants seeking to understand US markets and marketing practices.

Why the session is likely to make an important contribution

The session will make an important contribution because it complements and moves beyond previous work that has studied influence in the form of encouraging or discouraging new product acceptance, or general psychological, demographic and socio-graphic characteristics of those whose transmit word of mouth or who are regarded as lead users, influencers or opinion leaders. It does so by focusing on contextually situated and materially shaped practices within diverse communities, where new product adoption is but one of many issues relevant to participants. Together the papers in this session will broaden and deepen our understanding of the concept of influence, of the ways in which consumers can come to be influential, and of how influence is sustained.

Furthering the conference mission of appreciating diversity

This session furthers the mission of appreciating diversity first by focusing on online communities that involve consumers from diverse countries, ranging from China (in the community studied by Schau et al) to French Canada (in that studied by Savignac et al) to regions as disparate as the Philippines, France, the UK, and Japan (in that studied by Dolbec and Fischer). The session also furthers the conference mission by involving researchers who originate in multiple countries: Canada, China, and the United States. Diversity is also represented in the mix of scholars, from masters and doctoral students, to junior faculty, to senior faculty. Finally, diversity is reflected in the mix of quantitative (see Schau et al) and qualitative methods and in the varied theories used across the papers.

Stage of Completion of Each Paper

All data has been collected and analyzed for each paper, and working versions of each have been drafted.

Consumer-Bloggers Mobilized in Marketing Campaigns: A Study of Opinion Leaders' Authenticity Management in a Streetwear Community

EXTENDED ABSTRACT

Recent research (Thompson 2006; Kozinets et al. 2010) has shown that consumer-bloggers, acting as opinion leaders in online communities, can have a substantial influence on their audience. Prior research efforts have been concerned with identifying optimal narrative strategies that can be used by bloggers when participating in a WOM campaign (Kozinets et al. 2010), and with the perceived credibility of bloggers as information sources (Kumkale et al. 2010; Eisend 2010). In contrast, our research focuses on how influential bloggers manage their authenticity through their online presentation of self as they participate in marketing campaigns. We ask: Do influential consumer-bloggers feel their authenticity threatened by the commercial pressures they face? And if so, what practices do they engage in to build and maintain authenticity, with what effect?

We know from previous research efforts that the concept of authenticity relies on perception of others (Beverland 2006; Rose et Wood 2005). More precisely, an individual may be perceived as authentic if his or her actions reveal his "real" self (Arnould and Price 2000). We argue that the literature has yet to address how influential consumers perceive the social construction of their influence within a community and, as a consequence, how they build and manage an authentic self. We find, in particular, a paucity of research about the processes and practices of authenticity management online. We are particularly interested in the context of consumer-bloggers acting as opinion leaders in their virtual community of consumption as they increasingly face potential communal-commercial tensions when getting involved in marketing campaigns (Kozinets et al. 2010). Our paper addresses these gaps by focusing on consumer-bloggers' perspectives on online authenticity and their strategies to maintain an authentic self.

The qualitative methodology used for this research project follows Kozinets (2010) recommendations about the netnographic approach. Specifically, data was collected through combining a netnography of six influential blogs with offline in-depth interviews with each consumer behind these blogs. The participants were all members of Montreal's streetwear community, i.e. an on- and off-line community formed around a common interest in streetwear fashion (e.g., sneakers), urban art, and skateboarding. The first author, a member of the community, engaged in offline observation of the community as well. Our netnography was concerned with these opinion leaders' approaches in discussing products and brands on their blogs (both sponsored and non-sponsored products) and their presentation of self as influential members of the community. Through the in-depth interviews, the first author investigated further the relationships between these consumer-bloggers and their audience, made of community members, outsider-consumers and marketers.

Schau and Gilly (2003) argue that the Internet offers the opportunity for web users to plan, refine and even rebuild their presentation of self. Our results show that consumers acting as opinion leaders are greatly preoccupied with conveying an authentic self to their audience. To that effect, our research findings show five main practices mobilized by consumer-bloggers in order to construct an authentic self. First, by adopting an informal tone (1) in the writing process of their blog entries, and thus remaining true to the communal norms, our bloggers felt they improved the authenticity of their online self. Also, by publishing original content as opposed to simply sharing existing content (2) and contextualizing in detail the subjects of their blog entries (3), our bloggers perceived that they were

strengthening the authenticity of their self-presentation. Publishing blog entries that reflected their offline reality (4) was also perceived by bloggers as instrumental to the construction of an authentic self, as was displaying field-specific capital and expertise around the subjects discussed on their blogs (5). These strategies seem to be effective considering the increase attention these influencers received from both consumer and marketing manager audiences. In conclusion, this research extends consumer behavior knowledge by demonstrating that consumer-bloggers evolving in a virtual community of consumption are not only concerned with the perception of their readers, but also attempt to maintain their influence by actively managing what they perceive as their authentic self.

Institutional Dynamics when Consumers Coalesce in Aestheticized Product Markets

EXTENDED ABSTRACT

Consumer researchers are increasingly interested in marketplace dynamics – understanding what leads to the creation of new markets (Ansari and Philips 2010; Humphreys 2010a, 2010b) or to significant changes in existing markets (Giesler 2008, 2012; Scaraboto and Fischer forthcoming; Thompson and Coskuner-Bali 2007). Prior market level research has examined the role of consumers to a limited extent, often emphasizing marketers as the main agents of market dynamics (e.g. Giesler 2012; Humphreys 2010a). Research that has looked at consumers' roles in market dynamics has largely focused on those who want to challenge the market, either based on ideology or unmet needs (e.g., Coskuner-Bali 2007; Scaraboto and Fischer forthcoming). Little attention has been paid to the unintended consequences for markets that may ensue when 'contented' consumers, not seeking any particular form of market change, interconnect with one another because of their shared interests in and enthusiasm for a product category. Interconnected consumers have been presented as value creators for particular brands (Schau, Jensen and Muniz 2009) and as brand co-producers (Fuller et al. 2008), but no prior research has examined the market-level implications of interactions by avid, interconnected consumers. We aim to fill this gap, focusing on an aestheticized market, where aesthetics *are* the products (Entwistle 2002), and inquiring about the processes by which the actions and interactions of interconnected consumers leads to institutional level changes in the market.

The context of this study is the fashion industry. We used a multi-method qualitative approach. Our data set is composed of field notes and observation following an 18-month long netnography on an outfit sharing website, lookbook.nu, combined with interviews with 13 fashion bloggers and participants in lookbook.nu, journal articles from major fashion magazines and websites, leading world journals and interviews with industry actors, and data gathered from leading online fashion forums and fashion bloggers. We employed institutional theory (e.g., Greenwood et al. 2008) as our theoretical lens to facilitate a market-level analysis, which we combined with field theory (Bourdieu 1984; 1991). We draw on concepts such as institutional logics, institutional work, mimetic isomorphism and concepts of symbolic capital derived from Bourdieu's perspective to make sense of the marketplace dynamics and sources of changes we observed. Our findings provide a process-oriented analysis which identifies different, inter-related processes and institutional impacts for each.

First, consumers need an easily accessible platform through which they can connect and share their passion for products in a category. Platforms such as online forums, sharing and curating websites, and easily self-publishable discussion sites (e.g., blogs), are first created by enthusiasts. When multiple such platforms have been created and are widely embraced by consumers who share their tastes and opinions, a new type of institution can be said to have emerged in the field. These institutions allow consumers to emulatw practices engaged in by other categories of actors in the institutional field,(e.g. consumer-produced photo shoots), ultimately re-distributing the locus of institutional work. Second, some consumers, through their creative contributions in such forms as fashion critiques, fashion creations, street photography, and outfit photo shoots, and through the "fans" they accrue, gain greater symbolic capital in the eyes of other actors in the field. Such consumers may convert their existing capital to enter the field of fashion in producerly roles. Others may develop "bridging" capital, combining high and low fashion, acting as facilitators between those two subfields by translating high fashion looks into everyday fashion. Third, platforms where consumers congregate can become important institutional players,as a growing range of institutional actors, such as designers, model agencies and industry publications, are influenced by what is being said and done on those platforms, and, in the case of publications, citing the interventions of consumers on those platforms. More, companies begin to mimic the platforms created by consumers to appropriate the latter under their own brand. Fourth, powerful market actors further contribute to the legitimation of consumer-created trends by sponsoring those who started them, emulating the platforms consumers created, using consumer-generated pictures to sell their own products, inviting influential consumers to industry events, featuring influential consumers in mainstream fashion publications, and citing them as inspiration. Fifth, a niche economy develops around the new tastes represented by interconnected consumers. A growing number of online retailers are now catering to those, answering to the rapid changes for new tastes and emerging trends. Ultimately, some of these trends get diffused in mainstream fashion.

Our research shows the unintended consequences which can alter an aesthecized market when interconnected consumers increase the level and the visibility of their participation in the market. While consumers cannot escape markets when they wish to do so (Kozinets 2001) they can profoundly alter those they wish to participate in.

Never-Ending Stories: Opinion Leadership and Antenarratives in an Online Investment Community

EXTENDED ABSTRACT

Consumer researchers have studied opinion leadership for decades (c.f. Silk 1966), investigating aspects including characteristics and dimensions of the concept (e.g. King and Summers 1970; Flynn, Goldsmith, and Eastman 1996), its relationship with network structure (e.g. Kratzer and Lettl 2009; Lee, Cotte, and Noseworthy 2010) motivations and antecedents (e.g. Feick, Price, and Higie 1986; Stokburger-Sauer and Hoyer 2009) and its effects, especially on the diffusion of innovations (e.g. Leonard-Barton 1985; Iyengar, Van den Bulte and Valente 2011). Researchers have also identified activities in which opinion leaders engage: the acquisition of knowledge about categories of interest, word-of-mouth behavior, and advice-giving on product search, purchase, and use. However, few studies actually observe opinion leaders in action; one exception is Kozinets et al. (2010), who focus on word of mouth involving online product seeding. The dearth of research that observes how opinion leaders interact with others suggests there is an opportunity to refine our understanding on what opinion leaders actually do.

This study seeks to broaden our understanding of what opinion leadership entails.

It does so by investigating opinion leaders and other participants in an online investment community, Seeking Alpha. Investing is an increasingly important consumer research topic (c.f. Morrin et al. 2002; Hirsto 2011). Seeking Alpha positions itself as "the premier website for actionable stock market opinion and analysis, and vibrant, intelligent finance discussion." It hosts more than 300,000 blog posts, written by more than 4,000 contributing investors. The site tracks and publicizes "opinion leaders," deemed as such based on how many page views their posts received during the preceding 90-day period. This study draws on more than 3,000 blog posts, and all ensuing discussion, from 26 contributing investors posted over the 90-day period of November 28, 2011 to February 26, 2012. These investors were the "opinion leaders" over this time period for the most read category in the community, "Long & Short Ideas." This category includes 7 subcategories (e.g. long ideas, IPO analysis, options, etc.). All "opinion leaders" in the sample ranked in the top 5 most read authors in at least one of these 7 subcategories.

Based on my analysis, I offer some novel answers to the question *'what do opinion leaders do?'* Specifically, I find that they construct and facilitate the evolution of "antenarratives." Antenarratives are "non-linear, incoherent, collective, unplotted, and pre-narrative speculations, a bet, that a proper narrative can be constituted" (Boje 2001: 1)." They differ from traditional narratives, possessing neither plot nor coherence, and being inherently speculative since they arise in the flow of experience that occurs before narrative closure (Boje 2001; Barge 2004). Collectively drafted, antenarratives emerge in a variety of contexts (e.g. organizations (Vaara and Tienari 2011); advertising campaigns (Grow 2008)). Investing appears to be a context in which antenarratives that help to make sense of unfolding events are particularly welcome, perhaps because 'the market' is constantly evolving, presenting itself as a "continuous knowledge project for consumers" (Zwick and Dholakia 2006) and because one purpose of investing is to speculate on 'the market', and make a bet on one's mastery of its logic. In an online community context, these bets are proposed – and sometimes taken up – as well as collectively debated, refined, reformed, discarded and resuscitated with the next analyst upgrade, quarterly report, management shake-up, economic forecast, rate cut, etc.

My analysis also indicates that opinion leadership is not strictly about influencing product decisions, but also about influencing others' participation in marketplace storytelling, a phenomena that is important both to those who are interested in value co-creation and those who are interested in the movement of the stock market, which rises and descends with the information and stories that envelop it. My analysis reveals that participants in Seeking Alpha – who only infrequently admit to being influenced in terms of stock buying or selling – are regularly enticed by the "opinion leaders" to participate in the authoring of antenarratives through commenting and unique posts. The factors that appear to be associated with this type of influence (revealed through higher reader participation) in this context include a content focus on "cult stocks" (e.g. Apple, Sirus XM, Annaly Capital Management) within the community, the use of inter-textual referencing, and the inclusion of personal investing anecdotes and positions.

My paper offers a significant complement to the extant literature on opinion leaders and the ways in which they exert influence over others. It elaborates on antenarrative storytelling as one key behavior of online opinion leaders and discusses how influence pertains to activities like storytelling and not just purchase decisions. It also explains how opinion leaders in such a community exert influence. It thus enhances our understanding of online consumer influence and influencers.

Learning the Language of the Market:
Contextual Influence and the Use of Code Switching in
Online Consumer Acculturation Platforms

EXTENDED ABSTRACT

The US marketplace is governed by a host of contradictory situational norms that can, at times, confuse even the savviest American consumers. For example, in some circumstances you pay full asking price (i.e., groceries, clothing, and department stores), haggle (i.e., automobiles, second hand goods, and domiciles), bid (i.e., antiques and eBay), barter (i.e., co-operatives), donate (i.e., Goodwill and Toys for Tots), and tip (i.e., hair salons, restaurants, and cabs). You may pay in advance, pay at the time of purchase or service, pay in installments, pay a third party over time, or even lease. A consumer is unlikely to have perfect market information, therefore, the most favorable price or "best deal" on a given product or service across stores is virtually unknown (Urbany et al. 2000). Consumers less familiar with the rules and norms of the American marketplace (i.e., immigrants, temporary residents and tourists) are at a severe disadvantage.

Immigration is a cornerstone of American society. In 2010, 1,042,625 people were granted legal permanent residency in the United States (Monger and Yankay 2011), 619,913 became naturalized citizens (Lee 2011), 73,293 were given refugee status, and 21,113 were granted asylum (Martin 2011). Homeland Security reports 160 million nonimmigrant admissions to the United States in 2010 (Monger and Mathews 2011). And these figures only reflect legal, documented entrants. Nearly 11 million "unauthorized immigrants" were estimated to reside in the US in 2010 (Hoefer et al. 2011). Regardless of formal status, these immigrants, refugees and foreign nationals must all learn to navigate American marketplaces.

Peñaloza (1994) provides a complex model of immigrant consumer acculturation, demonstrating that the process requires specific types of influential consumer acculturation agents, who know both the culture of origin and the culture of immigration (Peñaloza 1994, 36, 48). Part of this influence is language facility that enables the transmission of complex cultural logics from one culture to another. Consumer acculturation agents are highly influential because their dual language competencies can help them impart the requisite cultural logics to new consumers, thus teaching consumers to navigate new marketplaces. Drawing from sociolinguistics, we demonstrate that code switching is a common consumer acculturation strategy. Influencing agents educate new migrants through thick descriptions of market practices in the language of origin and directly import terms from the host language as labels for the practices.

Codes are defined in the sociolinguistics literature as community-level communication systems (Gumperz 1982) and code switching as a communicator's systematic and deliberate shifting between codes during a single communicative episode (Coulmas 2005; Heller 1988). The most common community-level communication system is a language and code switching occurs between languages. For example, immigrants from China may switch between speaking Chinese and speaking English in a single communication event such as a face-to-face conversation in a grocery store. We show that code switching allows the cultural entrant to both understand market phenomenon of the host locale and recognize it when it appears in host language communications. Interestingly, we also find that code switching may persist beyond the initial learning stages to become the manner in which influential communications about brands, price discounts and bundling promotions are conveyed.

Our study is situated in an online forum, MITBBS (http://www.mitbbs.com/) which serves as an influential acculturation platform where Chinese immigrants and foreign nationals interact to discuss the rules and norms of the American marketplace.

We combine netnography, a qualitative method of manual thematic forum analysis (Kozinets 2009) with an established computational linguistics method to trace the discourse on the acculturation platform MITBBS specifically, the market-oriented sub-board, "PennySaver." The netnographic method is used to obtain the general patterns in the data; the computational linguistics method is used to generate quantitative analysis results to determine the magnitude of the phenomenon. The data reveal that the message board is an influential acculturation tool. We demonstrate that one specific linguistic strategy dominates the process of learning the market: code switching. Code switching behavior occurs at the language-level and at a subcultural level with a shared code developed among participants on the acculturation platform regarding American retail protocols and marketing promotions. This discovery of a shared code on the acculturation platform echoes a recent study that discovered language, dialect and brand level codes operating in quick service restaurants and beverage bars (Schau et al. 2007). We illustrate the manner in which code switching is used by contextually embedded influentials to teach market rules and collaboratively strategize ways of extracting maximum value in market transactions. We also show that code switching, while expected in early learning stages, becomes a robust norm for these influentials to communicate market-level phenomenon to susceptible novice consumers.

Encouraging Healthier Food Consumption: The Role of Product Package Cues

Chairs: Paul M. Connell, City University London, UK
Elizabeth G. Miller, University of Massachusetts, Amherst, USA

Paper #1: The Impact of Licensed Cartoon Characters on Children's Eating Choices

Bridget Leonard, University of Colorado, USA
Kenneth C. Manning, Colorado State University, USA
Margaret C. Campbell, University of Colorado, USA

Paper #2: Exposure to Advertising and Packaging Cues in Early Childhood Leads to Blurred Distinction Between Commercial and Entertainment Media That Persists into Adulthood

Paul M. Connell, City University London, UK
Merrie Brucks, University of Arizona, USA
Jesper H. Nielsen, University of Arizona, USA

Paper #3: Is That Healthy? The Influence of Information Type and Location on Nutritional Information Processing

Kathleen Debevec, University of Massachusetts, USA
Yana Andonova, University of Massachusetts, USA
Elizabeth G. Miller, University of Massachusetts, USA

Paper #4: Confronting the U.S. Obesity Conundrum: Assessing Front-of- Package Evaluative vs. Reductive Nutrition Information Disclosure Systems

Christopher L. Newman, University of Mississippi, USA
Elizabeth Howlett, University of Arkansas, USA
Scot Burton, University of Arkansas, USA
J. Craig Andrews, Marquette University, USA

SESSION OVERVIEW

This session brings together four papers that explore an influential element of marketing communications, a product's packaging, on consumer health and well-being. Because a product's packaging is the final aspect of the marketing communications mix that consumers are confronted with (at point of sale), the influence of packaging on judgment and decision making has important implications. In particular, because overweight and obesity are widespread public health problems, effects of packaging elements on nutrition judgments and food choices are particularly important from a practical perspective.

The first two papers in the session (Leonard, Manning, and Campbell; Connell, Brucks, and Nielsen) investigate the role of visual packaging elements such as licensed characters and spokescharacters from a developmental perspective. Leonard et al. investigate how the presence of licensed characters on packaging influence children's food preferences and the amount of food consumed. Building on this theme, Connell et al. investigate how children's cognitive constraints in recognizing and defending against product packaging and advertising elements lead to a blurred distinction between commercial and entertainment content that persists into adulthood and potentially leads to biased judgments of associated food products.

The second two papers in the session (Debevec, Andonova, and Miller; Newman, Howlett, Burton, and Andrews) investigate how the portrayal of nutrition packaging information enhances or thwarts consumers' ability to process this information. Debevec et al. investigate how placement and portrayal of nutrition information on a product's package influences the extent to which consumers recall and process this information. Newman et al. demonstrate that the combination of nutrition facts disclosures available to consumers impacts their ability to process this information.

Thus, as a whole, these papers provide new insights into how different packaging elements influence consumers' food judgments

and decisions. They investigate this question from a variety of perspectives – examining influences on both children (Leonard et al.) and adults (Debevec et al., Newman et al.) as well as how these influences vary over time (Connell et al.). They also consider the impact of both health (Debevec et al., Newman et al.) and non-health related information (Leonard et al., Connell et al.) and have important implications for improving consumers' food choices.

The findings should be of interest to diverse constituencies at ACR, including researchers interested in information processing, judgment and decision making, child development, and consumer health and well-being. The four papers represent work at advanced stages of conceptual development and data collection. This session contributes to the ACR conference's theme of diversity by integrating a diverse set of perspectives (developmental, information processing, and judgment and decision making) under one overarching theme (product packaging's effects on consumer health). In addition, these papers present data from both children (an important at-risk group) as well as adult participants. (Note: * denotes speaking author. Each speaker has agreed to present at the ACR conference in the event the session is accepted.)

The Impact of Licensed Cartoon Characters on Children's Eating Choices

EXTENDED ABSTRACT

The incidence of overweight and obesity among children in the U.S. has shown a dramatic increase over the past 40 years. For instance, obesity rates among preschool-aged children have more than doubled since the 1970s, and have more than tripled among 6-11 year old children. During this period, food and beverage companies have increased the amount spent on marketing to children. Including licensed characters on packaging is a prevalent part of marketing to children, with licensed characters and tie-ins with children's entertainment accounting for 13% ($208 million) of all youth marketing, and up to 50% of youth marketing in some food categories, such as restaurant foods and fruits and vegetables (Kovacic et al 2008). While advertising to children has declined, the incidence of cross-promotions such as licensed characters increased by 78% between 2006 and 2008 (Harris et al 2009). Some advocates have argued that companies should not use characters to promote food products to children, and some companies have agreed to only use licensed characters to promote food products that meet a minimum nutritional standard. However, several questions about the impact of package-based licensed characters on children's preferences, choices, and consumption behavior remain unanswered.

Recently, studies have shown that the presence of brands and licensed characters on food product packaging can affect the perceived taste of the foods among young children. When children were asked to taste pairs of identical foods presented in packaging that differed only in terms of whether it was branded as McDonald's (Robinson and Matheson 2007) or included a sticker of a licensed character (Roberto et al 2010), children indicated that the food from the branded/ stickered package tasted better than the food from the plain package, and that they would prefer food in the branded/stickered package as a snack. In a between-subjects design, children indicated that an ostensibly healthy cereal tasted better when it came from a package with a licensed character than without, but there was no perceived taste difference when the cereal was purportedly unhealthy (Lapierre et al 2011). While these studies find that the presence of licensed characters or branding elements on the food product package improved the perceived taste of the food among young children, none of the studies gave the children the opportunity to actually choose a snack or to consume as much as they wanted. Based on research showing that positive arousal leads to increased consumption in adults (Macht et al 2002; Kenardy et al 2003), we propose that the presence of a licensed character will, among children, increase positive arousal and thereby influence product selection and the amount consumed. The subsequently described studies extend existing research by examining whether the inclusion of popular licensed characters on packaging affects (1) the choices children make, and (2) the amount that children choose to consume and/or what foods they choose to consume. In a yet to be completed study, we will also seek to understand why the presence of a licensed character on a food package affects choice and consumption.

The goal of Studies 1a and 1b was to confirm the common belief that children are more likely to choose food in packaging that includes a licensed character over packaging that does not. For both studies, children between 4 and 10 years old were approached in public spaces and offered a choice between a free sample of two fruit gummy snacks, one with a licensed character, and one without. Study 1a (n=26), used the same brand of fruit gummy snacks, one with a sticker of a Spongebob character attached. Study 1b (n=26) used two different brands of fruit gummy snacks, one that included Scooby Doo characters on the package, and the other with pictures of fruit, but no character. Children were significantly more likely to choose the option with the licensed character than expected by chance in both Study 1a (77%; (χ^2= 7.54, p=.006) and 1b (69%; χ^2 = 3.85, p=.05).

Considering that children choose food packages that include a licensed character over food packages that do not, the goal of study 2 was to examine the effects of a licensed character on consumption amount of healthy and unhealthy foods. Eighty children aged 4 to 7 were asked to participate in a taste test. They saw a package of either cookies or dried apricots that either included an image of Scooby Doo or the same package, but without Scooby Doo. They were offered a bowl of the cookies or dried apricots, purportedly from that package, and asked to taste at least one and to complete a survey. Afterwards, the amount of the food the child consumed during the survey was measured. Results show a main effect of character, controlling for hunger, such that for both healthy and unhealthy foods, children consume more when Scooby Doo is on the package ($M_{Character}$ = 0.68, $M_{No\ Character}$ = 0.54, p=.05). There were no other significant effects.

Overall, this set of studies contributes to the literature on the effects of marketing techniques on children by examining the effects of including popular licensed characters on food packaging. We find that children are more likely to choose food with licensed characters on the package and importantly, to consume more of both healthy and unhealthy foods when the package includes a licensed character. A fourth study examines why these effects occur, specifically examining the role of arousal.

Exposure to Advertising and Packaging Cues in Early Childhood Leads to Blurred Distinction Between Commercial and Entertainment Media That Persists into Adulthood

EXTENDED ABSTRACT

Previous research has found that children incrementally learn how to recognize and cope with marketing communications as they age. It is now well-established that children first learn how to distinguish commercial from entertainment content (Butter et al. 1981), then later recognize the persuasive intent of marketing communications (Ward, Wackman, and Wartella 1977), and finally learn to utilize cognitive defenses against marketing communications (Brucks, Armstrong, and Goldberg 1986). However, the question remains as to whether these developmental constraints lead to effects that persist into adulthood. Across four studies, we demonstrate that distinction between commercial and entertainment stimuli from early childhood is blurred. In contrast, we do not observe this blurred distinction for stimuli that is initially encountered later in life, after full development of marketing communications knowledge. This blurred distinction, along with hedonic associations with early childhood advertising stimuli, results in subsequent judgment biases favoring associated products on unrelated utilitarian (e.g., nutrition) attributes that can persist into adulthood. These biases are likely to be activated by advertising/product packaging elements (e.g., spokescharacters), are difficult to correct, and can even extend to brand extensions supported by the same advertising/packaging elements (Bousch and Loken 1991).

The purpose of study 1 was to provide evidence that memory representation of commercial stimuli experienced first in early childhood remain influenced by the initial encoding as entertainment. Fifty-one U.S.-born and raised participants completed an Implicit Association Test (IAT; Greenwald 2008), where they classified stimuli as either entertainment or advertising. We selected eight entertainment (four "earlier" and four "later") and eight advertising/packaging characters (four "earlier" and four "later") to be used as visual stimuli. The "earlier" stimuli had all been widely used for decades, thus ensuring that participants likely would have been exposed to them initially in early childhood. "Later" stimuli were chosen so that they were nonexistent in early childhood for older participants, but were extant and commonplace in early childhood for younger participants. Participants were classified as "older" or "younger" based on the age the participant would have been at the time the later stimuli were introduced so that "older" participants could have experienced only half the stimuli in early childhood. In contrast, "younger" participants would have likely experienced all of the stimuli in early childhood, before advertising knowledge would have been fully developed. Results supported the predicted interaction between participant age group, stimulus chronology, and stimulus type (F(1,50)=3.81,p=.056). Exploring the older group of participants further revealed a two-way interaction of stimuli type by stimuli chronology (F(1, 50)=3.78, p=.056) which, as predicted, is driven by an enhanced ability to categorize advertising stimuli where initial exposure came after full development of advertising knowledge ($M_{Earlier}$=1078.64, M_{Later}= 942.45, F(1,50=17.34), p<.001). In contrast, there were no differences in this age group in their ability to categorize the stimuli (F(1,50)=1.83, p = .18). Importantly, this two-way interaction did not replicate for younger participants (F(1,50)<1).

The purpose of study 2 was to provide evidence to show that the blurred distinction documented in study 1 can lead to biased nutrition judgments for products associated with the advertising, due to the hedonic nature of children's advertising. As a visual stimulus, we selected a well-recognized mascot used for advertising and packaging since its associated pre-sweetened cereal's launch in 1979. One hundred and fifteen participants from the United States were recruited from Amazon mTurk. As in study 1, participants were divided into younger and older groups based upon the age they would have been when this product was launched. After viewing the stimulus, the associated product was rated on health-related items embedded among other measures on 7-point scales. As expected, the younger group rated the product as healthier than the older group ($M_{Younger}$=4.31,M_{Older}=4.00,$F(1,112)$=2.61,p=.05).

The purpose of studies 3 and 4 was to demonstrate that nutrition-related biases for early childhood products are resilient and difficult to correct, and can be done so only when both motivation and ability to correct bias are high (Wegener and Petty 1985) and when highly positive affect does not serve as a motivational deterrent to attend to negative attributes (e.g., high sugar) in a product (Ahluwalia, Burnkrant, and Unnava 1998). In both studies, we selected a visual stimulus that has been heavily and continuously used in advertising and packaging since 1951, making it highly likely that U.S.-born participants would have been exposed to this mascot at a very early age. In study 3, 150 U.S.-born undergraduate participants were randomly assigned to a between-subjects design where motivation (prime:health/control per Bargh et al. 2001) and ability (source of bias made salient/not salient) were manipulated and affect toward the stimulus image was measured. The presweetened cereal product endorsed by the relevant stimulus was then rated on health-related items embedded among other measures, as in study 1, on 7-point scales. We observed the hypothesized interaction between motivation, ability, and positive affect ($F(1,141)$=4.23, p<.05). When both ability and motivation to correct were enhanced, there was a significant linear relationship, with the effect of a decreasing likelihood to correct bias as positive affect toward the relevant stimulus increased (t=3.14,β=.46, p <.01). Judgments did not change regardless of level of felt affect in the other three conditions (all $t < |1|$). In study 4, we replicated this pattern of results on a product extension with different ability manipulation (passage read on advertising's effects on children/elderly) and with motivation measured by assessing how interested participants were with the information in the ability manipulation with 78 U.S.-born participants ($F(1,69)$ =5.10, p< .05). As in study 3, higher levels of positive affect interfered with bias correction when ability to correct was enhanced and participants were motivated to attend to the message (t = 2.94, β = .55, p < .01). Also replicating the pattern in study 3, judgments did not change regardless of level of felt affect in the other three conditions (all $t < |1|$).

This research provides evidence that early exposure to advertising and packaging elements can lead to effects that persist for years, even decades, into adulthood. Furthermore, these effects have the potential to adversely impact consumer health and well-being.

Is That Healthy? The Influence of Information Type and Location on Nutritional Information Processing

EXTENDED ABSTRACT

Rising obesity rates and a resulting increase in health consciousness has led to increased interest in how to better communicate nutritional information on packaging. Several systems (e.g., traffic light, Facts Up Front, NuVal, Smart Choices) have been introduced. In this paper, we focus on two such systems – Facts Up Front (FF), which typically places icons with calorie, total fat, sodium and sugar information in the top corner of the package, and NuVal, which rates products on a 1-100 scale based on 30-plus nutrients and nutrition

factors. Although NuVal has not been used on packages to date (they provide information on shelf tags and at their website), we selected it for study due to its summary nature, in contrast to FF's inclusion of more specific information about individual nutrients.

We examine how the type of information (FF, NuVal) and its location influence consumer awareness of the information as well as the degree to which they prompt self-referencing (i.e., whether consumers process this information relative to their own experiences). Self-referencing was chosen as a key focus of our investigation because self-referencing has been shown to lead to greater learning and recall of information (e.g., Klein and Loftus 1988), increased message elaboration and persuasion when message arguments are strong (Burnkrant and Unnava 1995), more favorable attitudes toward ads and products, and increased purchase intention (Debevec and Iyer 1988). Further, given research reporting that females tend to be more health-focused than men, we also sought to understand how the effectiveness of the nutritional information varied by gender. Specifically, we examine: (1) whether consumers are more likely to pay attention to the nutritional labels when they are overlapping the product, in close proximity to the product, or at the top right corner; (2) whether consumer self-referencing varies based on the location and type of the nutritional information; and (3) whether gender moderates these effects.

To examine these questions, we conducted a 3 (location: top, overlapping, proximal) x 2 (type of information: FF, NuVal) x 2 (gender) between-subjects experiment with an additional control group; 247 students (42.5% female) participated for course credit. Participants were presented with a picture of the front of a box of WhoNu cookies which contained the product name, image of the cookies, and four health-related manufacturer claims (e.g., "as much fiber as a bowl of oatmeal"). In the NuVal and FF conditions, the box also contained the NuVal logo and score or the 4 FF boxes in one of three different locations on the package – overlapping the cookies, above the cookies (proximal), or in the top right corner of the package. After viewing the package, participants were asked questions to assess their recall and processing of the nutritional information.

As expected, location influenced the degree to which consumers paid attention to the nutritional information. We expected recall to be highest for information overlapping the product image since information in this location would be more likely to fall within the consumers' focal view when examining the product. Consistent with this hypothesis, NuVal information yielded the highest recall when it overlapped the cookies (54% correct vs. 15% in top right (p = .02) and 11% when proximal (p = .01)). However, results suggest that the optimal location of information may vary by information type. Recall was highest for FF when it was placed in the top right corner (68% correct compared to 54% and 30% when it was overlapping and proximal to the cookies, respectively). There were no differences in recall by gender.

Also, as expected, location, type of information, and gender influenced the degree to which consumers engaged in self-referencing. A 3 (location) x 2 (type of information) x 2 (gender) ANOVA on self-referencing revealed a main effect of location (F(2, 199) = 3.14, p < .05) and a main effect for gender (F(1, 199) = 6.08, p < .02). Nutritional information placed on the top right resulted in marginally higher self-referencing (M = 4.45) than when the information was overlapping (M = 3.74, p = .06), but did not differ from when it was proximal to the cookies (M = 4.10, p > .4). As expected, females had higher levels of self-referencing than males (M_f = 4.45, M_m = 3.84, p < .01). There was also a significant three-way interaction among location, type of information, and gender (F(2, 199) = 3.22, p < .05). This interaction appeared to be driven by differences in how men and women responded to the information when it overlapped the cookies. Men were significantly more likely to self-reference the NuVal information (M = 3.86) than the FF information (M = 2.94, p < .05), while women were (directionally) more likely to self-reference the FF information (M = 4.52) than the NuVal information (M = 3.61, p = .1).

Our research contributes to the literature on consumer processing of nutrition information by identifying the optimal placement of different types of nutritional information (specifically, FF and Nu-Val). Follow-up studies will seek to enrich our understanding of these findings by exploring why males and females differ in the type of information seen as most relevant to them and why the optimal location varies by information type. Further, our research contributes to an understanding of how consumers use front-of-package nutritional information. Despite grocery store efforts to promote the NuVal measure, consumers' knowledge of this system is still limited. Eighty percent of our respondents indicated they were not familiar with the NuVal scoring system, even though 59% shop at a store that displays the information. Overall recall of nutritional information on packages (regardless of information type) was also low, suggesting efforts should be directed at raising consumer awareness of these systems if they are to be effective. In addition, marketers and policy makers should consider where the information is placed on the package and how its placement relates to other information on the package if they want to maximize the likelihood that consumers perceive the information and use it in their choices.

Confronting the U.S. Obesity Conundrum: Assessing Front-of- Package Evaluative vs. Reductive Nutrition Information Disclosure Systems

EXTENDED ABSTRACT

Some two-thirds of all U.S. adults are overweight and 33% are considered "obese." It has been estimated that by 2015, 75% of all U.S. adults will be overweight and 41% will be obese (Wang and Beydoun 2007). Obesity, largely driven by food and beverage consumption, is a major cause of heart disease (CDC 2012) – a disease that accounts for approximately 29% of all U.S. deaths. While consumers may be bombarded with considerable nutrition information in facts panels and with claims on the front of packages, in today's retail environment, consumers are faced with literally thousands of choices that they make in a very restricted amount of time. While many consumers are interested in making healthier food choices at the retail shelf, each package presents various types of information, and this package and product category 'clutter' makes decisions more difficult for consumers.

To help address consumer welfare and health issues by simplifying the task consumers face at the shelf, a number of initiatives have been implemented recently. These include 'reductive' systems that present some subset of calorie and nutrient information found in the Nutrition Facts panel (e.g., the GMA/FMI Facts Up Front labeling system with calories, saturated fat, sodium, and sugar), as well as evaluative systems that integrate nutrient information (e.g., Walmart's Great For You icon, the Institute of Medicine's (IOM) multiple 'stars' rating system). While there is a common goal of for these various approaches (i.e., to help consumers more easily determine if a particular food item is a healthful choice), each system has certain potential strengths and weaknesses (Andrews, Burton, and Kees 2011; IOM 2011; Cooper 2012). While much of the research on FOP provision supports the basic premise that *some form* of simplified or summarized FOP nutrition information can be useful, the literature is unclear with regard to what *specific* information or format will be most effective (IOM 2011).

In this research, we employ a processing fluency theoretical framework to develop and test hypotheses concerning effects of different FOP labeling approaches (Winkielman and Cacioppo 2001; Schwarz 2004; Winkielman et al. 2003). Of particular interest is the influence of package disclosures on consumer evaluations of perceived package and category retail shelf processing fluency, consumer evaluations (healthfulness, purchase intentions), and choice when FOP information is presented in isolation and when it is combined. Data have been collected from a series of four experiments that are a mix of retail lab studies and internet-based experiments. The first two studies are internet-based between subject experiments (with 300+ adult consumers). Results show that the presence of a FOP interpretive icon moderates the effect of a Facts Up Front reductive (multi-nutrient) disclosure on both perceived fluency (F $(3,355)$ = 9.53, p <.01) and trustworthiness (F $(3,355)$ = 11.41, p <.01) of FOP health information. Additional results reveal a moderating effect of consumer skepticism toward FOP labeling on perceived organization trustworthiness (F $(3,355)$ = 4.74, p <.05). The pattern of results across the two studies shows how alternative FOP disclosure systems can potentially complement one another by compensating for weaknesses of the individual systems (Andrews et al. 2011).

Studies 3 and 4 are retail lab experiments where participants are exposed to FOP information on packages for different categories with multiple brands on retail store shelving. Experiment 3 is a 2 (interpretive FOP system: (IOM stars vs. control) x 2 (reductive system: Facts Up Front vs. control) x 2 (healthfulness: more healthful vs. less healthful product options) across two product categories: soup and granola bars. The first two factors are between subjects and the latter is a within subjects (i.e., participants are exposed to multiple products and categories). Results indicate that a FOP interpretive icon (IOM 'stars') moderates the effect of objective product healthfulness on purchase intentions in both the granola category (F $(1,96)$ = 15.59, p < .001) and the soup category (F $(1,96)$ = 11.85, p < .01). Addition of the IOM 'stars' strengthen effects of product healthfulness on purchase intentions. Results also reveal that the FOP interpretive icon (IOM 'stars') moderates objective product healthfulness on perceptions of product nutritiousness for both the granola category (F $(1,96)$ = 17.88, p < .001) and the soup category (F $(1,96)$ = 17.25, p < .001), as well. The fourth experiment replicates the design for Study 3 but varies the product categories (to include granola bars and macaroni and cheese) and uses 121 adult consumers with children living at home as participants. Analysis suggests that a FOP interpretive icon moderates objective product healthfulness on product attitudes in both the granola category (F $(1,110)$ = 21.66, p < .001) and the macaroni and cheese category (F $(1,110)$ = 25.15, p < .001). In addition, inclusion of the FOP icon strengthens parents' intentions to purchase the more healthful food product for their children in both the granola category (F $(1,110)$ = 13.68 p < .001) and the macaroni and cheese category (F $(1,112)$ = 7.01, p < .01).

An additional study will use a large internet-based experiment (n=600) to further address adult consumers with children at home. The between subjects experiment assesses the effect of two recently announced evaluative FOP systems (IOM 'stars' vs. Walmart 'Great for You' vs. FOP control), in conjunction with a reductive FOP system (Facts Up Front vs. control) across brands and product healthfulness levels.

From a conceptual perspective, findings extend our knowledge and understanding of conceptual fluency in a packaging context, and they demonstrate how the fluency conceptualization can be extended to a full product category retail shelf context. These findings, taken cumulatively, have important theoretical implications as well as practical implications relevant to policy makers and promotion and brand managers.

The Control Dilemma: Pros and Cons of Perceived Control on Self-Regulation

Chair: Jaideep Sengupta, HKUST, Hong Kong

Paper #1: Environmental Disorder Leads to Self-Regulatory Failure

Boyoun (Grace) Chae, University of British Columbia, Canada
Rui (Juliet) Zhu, University of British Columbia, Canada

Paper #2: What's the Point of Temptation if You Don't Give in to It? The Positive Impact of Vice Consumption on Consumer Vitality

Fangyuan Chen, HKUST, Hong Kong
Jaideep Sengupta, HKUST, Hong Kong

Paper #3: Let Freedom Ring? Divergent Effects of Free Choice on Goal Pursuit

Jordan Etkin, University of Maryland, USA
Juliano Laran, University of Miami, USA

Paper #4: Kids in the Candy Store: The Motivational Consequences of Multiple Goals

Szu-chi Huang, University of Texas at Austin, USA
Ying Zhang, University of Texas at Austin, USA

SESSION OVERVIEW

Objectives and Overview

A greater sense of control over one's decisions and choices is usually viewed to be desirable (Kelly 1963; Ryan and Frederick 1997). Thus, consumers in general appreciate making their own decisions (Markus and Kitayama 2003), and companies strive to offer as many alternatives as possible in order to enhance perceptions of choice freedom (Levav and Zhu 2009). There is, however, relatively scant research on the possible downsides of perceived control and autonomy (for an exception, see Botti, Orfali, and Iyengar 2009). The papers in this session offer new insights into the nature and effects of perceived control, with a particular emphasis on how it may exert either a positive or negative influence on self-regulation, depending on aspects of the context and the task. In putting together this work, we hope to spark an interest in new directions of inquiry into perceived control and its effects.

Topics

The first two papers in the proposed session identify, respectively, a negative and a positive influence of perceived control on self-regulation. The next two papers then use the goal pursuit context to identify moderating factors for when either a positive or a negative effect may be obtained.

First, Chae and Zhu, while documenting the negative impact of low perceived control, identify an entirely novel antecedent of such perceptions. The authors examine the impact of environmental orderliness on consumers' self-regulation. Across four studies, they propose and find that a disorganized (vs. organized) environment threatens individuals' sense of personal control, causing them to spend substantial cognitive resources to cope with this threat. Consequently, people are resource depleted and exhibit more self-regulatory failures in a disorganized (vs. organized) environment. In the second paper, Chen and Sengupta demonstrate the beneficial effects of consuming vices, and in so doing, identify a context in which lower perceived control actually produces a positive influence on self-regulation. Across four studies, they find that giving in to temptations (e.g., eating indulgent food, or impulsively buying hedonic products) increases subjective vitality – defined as the positive energy available

to oneself. Increased vitality, in turn, produces better self-regulation. Of importance, these effects only obtain when vice consumption can be justified – such as when it can be explained away on the grounds of relatively low personal control. For example, greater vitality and improved self-regulation obtain when eating an unhealthy but tasty snack is perceived as complying with the experimenter's instructions, rather than resulting from one's own free choice. Thus, in the specific context of vice consumption, lower perceived control actually produces beneficial effects. The next two papers focus on how perceived control in the sense of choice freedom influences self-regulation, as manifested in goal pursuit. Etkin and Laran propose that freedom (vs. restricted freedom) in an initial goal-consistent choice can increase or decrease goal-directed motivation, depending on the level of goal activation prior to choice. Across three studies, they show that when a goal is highly active at the time of choice, increased (vs. restricted) freedom in making a goal-consistent choice leads to that choice being interpreted as having fulfilled the goal. Ironically, this then hinders subsequent goal pursuit. For example, having the freedom to choose between several healthy products (vs. having to pick the only available product) in pursuit of an active self-control goal induces the inference that one has at least partly satisfied the goal, lessening the motivation to engage further in it. On the other hand, when the goal is less active at the time of choice, free (vs. restricted) choice simply increases goal activation, which then increases subsequent goal pursuit. Finally, Huang and Zhang also propose both positive and negative effects on goal pursuit as a result of increased choice freedom, operationalized in their work as the number of reward options available upon task completion (e.g., having the freedom to choose between many different rewards after completing a certain number of frequent flyer miles, as opposed to having just one possible reward). The critical moderator identified in their work is stage of goal pursuit. At an early stage, the multiple available rewards are construed as substitutable for one another; these substitutes, combined, create a greater perceived likelihood that one will eventually get something desirable. Therefore, freedom of choice increases goal pursuit motivation. On the other hand, when nearing goal attainment, multiple available rewards (vs. an assigned reward) are conversely construed as competitive against one another – the consumer now has to decide which one to pick. Because it highlights the fact that some attractive rewards will have to be foregone, this produces a demotivating effect on goal pursuit.

General Orientation and Likely audience

Together, the four papers in this proposed session enhance our understanding of the nature of personal control, and also of how it may influence self-regulation. We believe that this session, if accepted, will attract scholars interested in the diverse yet related areas of motivation, goals, vitality, and self-regulation. Given the overlap as well as the distinctions between the four papers, we hope that they will, as a set, provoke illuminating discussion and debate.

Fit with Conference Theme

Finally, we believe that this session proposal fits with the theme of this year's ACR – appreciating diversity – along two aspects. First, while all the presentations will touch upon two common themes (perceived control, and self-regulation) each of them offers distinct insights on a diverse set of topics, such as vitality, environmental disorder, option availability, and reward programs. Second, the authors involved in the different papers represent schools across Canada, Hong Kong and the US; thus, this session, if accepted, would serve to further facilitate interaction among a far-flung group of scholars.

Environmental Disorder Leads to Self-Regulatory Failure

EXTENDED ABSTRACT

A common theme in many popular home organizations TV shows is that environmental disorganization is associated with a number of negative outcomes, such as deteriorating health and self-regulatory failures. As such, better organization or de-cluttering can improve life quality. Despite these beliefs in practice, our theoretical understanding of how environmental organization or orderliness can affect cognition and behavior remains limited (Keizer, Lindenberg, and Steg 2008). We address this question in this research by focusing on the impact of environmental orderliness on self-regulation.

Research on personal control (Kelly 1963) suggest that humans have a fundamental need to control their environment (Kelly 1963; White 1959). Among various factors such as choice freedom and predictability of outcomes that are known to affect personal control, we focused on the impact of characteristic of physical environment on personal control and consequently self-regulation. Previous literature documents that characteristics of a physical environment, such as physical confinement, can threaten individuals' sense of freedom, a very important component for people to maintain their sense of personal control (Baum, Singer, and Baum 1981; Edney and Buda 1976; Levav and Zhu 2009). For instance, Levav and Zhu (2009) showed that, just like restriction on choice freedom, physical confinement also increases reactance behaviors. Extending on this line of research, we suggest that environmental orderliness can threaten individuals' sense of personal control, because people in messy homes often feel that their lives are also out of control (Belk, Seo, and Li 2007; Cwerner and Metcalfe 2003) and people tend to attribute a messy home to the person's lack of ability to manage her time and life (Bitner 1990). Furthermore, research on resource depletion theory suggests that coping with a threat demands cognitive resources, and subsequently increases self-regulatory failures (Glass, Singer, and Friedman 1969; Inzlicht and Kang 2010). Combining the above theorizing, we propose that a disorganized environment threatens individuals' sense of personal control, causing them to spend substantial cognitive resources to cope with this threat. As a result, these people are resource depleted and exhibit more self-regulatory failures in subsequent tasks.

Across four studies, we show that individuals who were exposed to a disorganized (vs. organized) environment exhibited more self-regulatory failures in subsequent tasks, such as impulsive buying, less persistence on challenging tasks, and unhealthy eating. We also validate our process explanation by showing that: (1) the negative impact of environmental disorder on self-regulation is more acute for people who are highly sensitive to control threats (study 2), (2) the control motivation mediates the relationship between environmental orderliness and self-regulation (study 3), and (3) self-affirmation, which helps recoup cognitive resources, moderates the relationship between environmental orderliness and self-regulation (study 4a and 4b).

Study 1 showed that a disorganized (vs. organized) environment leads to poorer performance on a challenging task. The study was run with one participant at a time. Upon arrival, the participant was guided to the room where environmental orderliness was manipulated. Specifically, she was exposed to either an organized or a disorganized environment. In the disorganized environment condi-

tion, office supplies (e.g., paper, file folders, and paper cups) were scattered all over the place in a cluttered manner. In contrast, in the organized environment condition, the same amount of items was placed in a very structured and ordered manner. Then, the participant was escorted to the second room where no orderliness manipulation was present and was asked to complete an unsolvable puzzle (Baumeister et al. 1998). We found that participants who were exposed to the disorganized (vs. organized) environment earlier gave up sooner on the unsolvable puzzle.

Study 2 provided a theoretical replication in an impulsive buying context, and illuminated the process by showing that this effect is more salient among individuals who are chronically motivated to react to control threats. The environmental orderliness manipulation and the procedure were similar to those in the study 1. After exposure to either an organized environment or a disorganized environment, participants were asked to indicate Willingness-To-Pay (WTP) for a number of products (Vohs and Faber 2007). Individuals' chronic reactance were assessed via the Hong Psychological Reactance Scale (Hong and Faedda 1996). The result provided the replication on impulsive buying: participants in the disorganized environment indicated higher WTP than those in the organized environment. Furthermore, the impact of environmental orderliness on WTP was only salient among participants who were chronically high in reactance.

Study 3 tested the proposed process explanation by demonstrating that the control motivation mediates the effect of environmental orderliness on unhealthy eating behavior. Adopting a lexical decision task to assess the implicit activation of control motivation, we showed that people in a disorganized (vs. organized) environment responded faster to control-related words, indicating the increased activation of control motivation (as measured by response time to control-related words) mediated the effect of environmental orderliness on chocolate consumption.

Finally, Study 4 provided further evidence for the underlying process. Based on the finding that self-affirmation counteracts resource depletion and facilitates subsequent self-control behaviors (Schmeichel and Vohs 2009), we expected that self-affirmation will counteract the resource depletion induced by a disorganized environment, and thus attenuate self-regulatory failures in subsequent tasks. Results from two studies (4A and 4B) supported our hypothesis.

What's the Point of Temptation if You Don't Give in to It? The Positive Impact of Vice Consumption on Consumer Vitality

EXTENDED ABSTRACT

Vice consumptions are characterized by immediate pleasures, which have negative later consequences (Rook 1987). Therefore, such behaviors, e.g., eating a rich but fattening piece of cake, or buying an expensive sweater that one can't quite afford – are typically viewed as being normatively "bad". This research takes a different tack: we examine how vice consumption can actually have beneficial effects – specifically, by increasing vitality – as long as the consumption can be explained away on grounds of relatively low perceived control.

Arising from self-determination theory (SDT; Deci and Ryan 1991), subjective vitality refers to the positive experience of having energy and feeling alive (Christianson et al. 2005; Nix et al., 1999). Vitality arises from the feeling of behaving in fulfillment of intrinsic motivations rather than norm-based rewards and punishments (Deci and Ryan 1991). Thus, tasks that are inherently enjoyable (e.g., jogging for the sheer pleasure of it) typically produce more vitality than tasks that are performed as a means to an end (e.g., jogging in order to lose weight; Ryan and Deci 2000). Viewed from this perspective, since vices are associated with immediate hedonic pleasure, yielding to the temptation to consume a vice (vs. a virtue) should produce enhanced subjective vitality.

Vice consumption should also exert a countervailing force on vitality, however. Given its negative normative connotations, consuming a vice typically produces guilt. Because vitality is characterized by the absence of conflict (Ryan and Frederick 1997), the tension produced by these feelings of guilt should dampen the vitality that would otherwise be induced by vice consumption. We argue, therefore, that vice consumption will enhance vitality only when the accompanying guilt can be reduced by justifying the behavior. For example, if eating a chocolate cake can be justified on the grounds of complying with instructions (as opposed to freely choosing to do so), it should improve vitality. Support for this argument would inform SDT, which posits that autonomous (i.e., freely-chosen) behaviors produce more vitality than behaviors that are externally mandated. While this positive effect of autonomy has received wide support in the context of regulatory behaviors (Muraven, Gagne, and Rosman, 2008; Nix et al. 1999), we argue that the vice consumption context is qualitatively different: here lower autonomy actually leads to increased vitality. Finally, our research also examines downstream consequences of the increased vitality produced by vice consumption. Drawing on the idea of vitality as an enabling resource (e.g., Muraven et al. 2008), we propose that as long as accompanying guilt can be attenuated, the increase in vitality produced by consuming a vice should lead to enhanced creativity, as well as improved self-control.

Results from four studies provide convergent support for these arguments. Experiment 1 required participants to sample either a chocolate cake (vice) or baby carrots (virtue), and vitality was measured using a standard scale (Ryan and Frederick, 1997). Higher vitality obtained for the former ($M_{chocolate}$ = 4.46 vs. M_{carrot} = 3.74, $F(1, 82)$ =11.92, $p < .01$). A corresponding effect was obtained on creativity as measured on an alien-drawing task (8.73 vs. 6.96, respectively, F =38.78, $p < .01$); vitality fully mediated this effect.

Experiment 2 provided a more complete picture by examining the interaction between type of behavior and external justification. Participants were either explicitly instructed to sample the snack they were exposed to (either chocolates or carrots) as part of the experiment, or were asked to choose between eating the snack and writing an aversively long essay – eating the snack was more under one's control and accordingly less "justified" in this condition. The vitality benefit accruing from eating a chocolate (vs. a carrot) was greater in the justified condition (M's: 4.78 vs. 3.79, $F(1, 76)$ = 13.71, $p < .01$) than in the not-justified condition (M's: 3.95 vs. 3.78, $F(1, 76)$ = 0.57, $p > .50$). Note that these results argue against a simple physiological account (eating chocolates increases vitality because of higher sugar/calorific intake); this argument would not explain the effect of justification. Results from a control condition (M = 3.88) showed that the vitality difference observed in the justified conditions was due to increased vitality obtaining in the chocolate condition, rather than a dampening in the carrots condition. Guilt was also measured in this study, and as expected, indulgent behavior led to higher guilt in the no-justification condition ($M_{chocolate}$ = 5.22 vs. M_{carrot} = 2.62, $F(1, 76)$ = 7.23, $p < .01$), but not in the justification condition (M's: 2.96 vs. 2.89). This study included a new measure of creativity, as manifested in advertising slogans generated by participants, and adjudged by independent observers. The creativity of these slogans was greater given justified (vs. not-justified) vice consumption (M's: 7.16 vs. 5.24, $F(1, 76)$ = 32.46, $p < .01$); inter-

estingly, justification had the reverse effect for virtue consumption (M's: 5.15 vs. 6.07, $F(1, 32)$ = 7.08, $p = .01$).

Experiment 3 used the same design as Experiment 2 and found evidence for another downstream consequence of the vitality induced by consuming vices: i.e., self-control performance, as measured in a concentration task. Individuals who consumed a vice performed significantly better at this task when the vice was justified (vs. not); no such difference obtained for virtue consumption. Experiment 4 replicated these results using a different operationalization of vice vs. virtue behaviors (impulsively buying a hedonic product vs. deliberatively buying a utilitarian product), and also of justification (mentally accounting the purchase as a gift from another person). Exactly the same significant pattern of results on vitality, guilt, and self-control was obtained as in previous studies (not detailed here for reasons of space).

Thus, in opposition to the view that one should not give in to the temptation of consuming a vice, we find evidence for its beneficial effects – vice consumption heightens a resource, vitality, which then benefits consumers' creativity and self-control performance. We also inform self-determination theory: contrary to extant findings in this literature, in the vice-consumption context, lower autonomy may actually benefit vitality.

Let Freedom Ring?
Divergent Effects of Free Choice on Goal Pursuit

EXTENDED ABSTRACT

There is a generalized belief that freedom of choice is beneficial to consumers. Companies strive to offer as many product lines as possible, shopping malls are popular for having many different stores available, and consumers appreciate making their own decisions, without the influence of others. The current research looks at freedom of choice from a goal pursuit perspective. Our focus is on understanding the conditions under which perceiving freedom in an initial goal-consistent choice (e.g., being able to choose without any restrictions, making decisions without the influence of others) helps versus hinders subsequent goal pursuit. For example, when will healthy grocery-shoppers feel more motivated to be healthy? After making healthy snack choices with freedom, or after their freedom to choose has been restricted?

We propose that the impact of freedom in an initial goal-consistent choice on subsequent goal pursuit will depend on the level of activation of the goal at the time of choice. Specifically, we predict that having freedom in goal-consistent choice when a goal is highly active at the time of choice will reduce subsequent goal pursuit, whereas having freedom in goal-consistent choice when a goal is not highly active at the time of choice will increase subsequent goal pursuit. We base our predictions on the following reasoning. When people have freedom in choosing products associated with a goal, we expect that they will perceive their behavior as pursuing their goal to a greater degree relative to when they do not have as much freedom. For instance, going to the supermarket and being free to choose several different healthy items is perceived to be a stronger exertion of self-control than when one is able to choose only one type of item (the number of options is restricted), even if in the same quantity.

The impact of this perceived stronger act of goal pursuit on subsequent motivation will depend on the level of goal activation prior to choice. When the goal is highly active, for example, if people have been exposed to environmental cues associated with the goal (Chartrand et al. 2008), a strong act of goal pursuit will satisfy the goal to a greater degree. As a result, the goal will be less active following freedom versus restricted goal-consistent choice (Bargh and Ferguson

2004), decreasing subsequent goal pursuit. In contrast, when the goal is not highly active prior to choice, a strong act of goal pursuit will not satisfy the goal, but increase the activation of the goal (Bargh 2006; Laran and Janiszewski 2009; Shah and Kruglanski 2002). As a result, having freedom versus restricted freedom in initial goal-consistent choice should increase subsequent goal pursuit in this case.

Across three studies we find support for our propositions. In each study, we invite participants to make several healthy snack choices, varying whether a health goal is highly active (vs. not active) prior to choice, as well as whether participants have freedom (vs. restricted freedom) in choosing snacks. Having participants choose among healthy snacks ensures that they all have the opportunity to pursue a health goal, with or without freedom. Study 1 provides an initial test of our reasoning regarding the effect of freedom versus restricted freedom in goal-consistent choice on goal activation. Consistent with our argument, when a health goal was not activated prior to choice, free (vs. restricted) choice increased the level of goal activation, as measured by a word-stem completion task ($M_{freedom} = 3.52$, $M_{restricted} = 2.28$; $F(1, 121) = 15.77$, $p < .001$). In contrast, when a health goal was activated prior to the snack choice task, free (vs. restricted) choice satisfied the goal, decreasing its level of activation as measured by a word-stem completion task ($M_{freedom} = 3.03$, $M_{restricted} = 3.67$; $F(1, 121) = 3.84$, $p = .05$).

Study 2 demonstrates the divergent effects of choice freedom on goal pursuit following an initial goal-consistent choice. Supporting our predictions, when a health goal was not activated prior to choice, free (vs. restricted) choice among the healthy snacks increased participants' subsequent likelihood of engaging in a healthy behavior, as measured by their propensity to participate in an unrelated study involving eating raisins (health goal-consistent) versus M&Ms (health goal-inconsistent; $M_{freedom} = 58.3\%$, $M_{restricted} = 23.1\%$; $\chi^2(1) = 9.70$, $p < .01$). In contrast, when a health goal was activated prior to choice, free (vs. restricted) choice decreased participants' subsequent likelihood of engaging in a healthy behavior ($M_{freedom} = 38.9\%$, $M_{restricted} = 71.1\%$; $\chi^2(1) = 7.74$, $p < .01$). Finally, study 3 provides another demonstration of these effects, with different goal activation and choice freedom manipulations. Again supporting our predictions, when a health goal was not activated prior to choice, free (vs. restricted) choice among the healthy snacks increased participants' subsequent likelihood of making a healthy choice, as measured by their propensity to choose an apple (health goal-consistent) versus a candy bar (health goal-inconsistent) as a thank you for participating in the study ($M_{freedom} = 63.3\%$, $M_{restricted} = 31.8\%$; $\chi^2(1) = 4.46$, $p < .05$). In contrast, when a health goal was activated prior to choice, free (vs. restricted) choice decreased participants' subsequent likelihood of making a healthy choice ($M_{freedom} = 26.9\%$, $M_{restricted} = 56.0\%$; $\chi^2(1) = 4.45$, $p < .05$).

In sum, this research demonstrates divergent effects of experiencing freedom in goal-consistent on subsequent goal pursuit; freedom (vs. restricted freedom) can increase or decrease goal-directed motivation, depending on the level of goal activation prior to choice. As such, our findings contribute to the literature on goal pursuit by showing that motivation to pursue a goal is not simply dependent on whether consumers make a goal-consistent choice or not, but on the degree of freedom associated with this choice. In addition, we contribute to the literature on the benefits of offering consumers freedom by showing that freedom of choice is not always beneficial and may in fact be detrimental to people's motivation to pursue a goal.

Kids in the Candy Store:
The Motivational Consequences of Multiple Goals

EXTENDED ABSTRACT

A goal is the mental representation of a desirable end state, and could influence not only the direction of people's behavior, but also the intensity of such behavior (Locke & Latham, 1990; Pieters et al., 1995). While prior research has mainly focused on the pursuit of a goal in isolation, recent efforts have been made to extend our understanding toward "goal structure" that comprises a network of interrelated goals (Kruglanski et al., 2002). In practice, marketers often offer multiple goals for customers to choose from (e.g., offering multiple rewards for customers who have accumulated 10,000 miles in a frequent flyer program), under the assumption that such freedom of choice would lead to greater motivation and participation. In this research, we ask the question: Is the offering of multiple goals always more motivating? For companies that try to encourage repeat purchases, should they design a loyalty program that allows consumers to choose a prize from multiple options? Also, should companies use the same reward structure to motivate customers who just joined a loyalty program as those who are getting close to redemption?

We posit that people view the relations among multiple goals that can be served by a single means differently as they move from earlier stages to later stages of the pursuit, and thus the freedom of choice could either be motivating or demotivating, depending on one's current stage in the pursuit. Specifically, when people first begin the pursuit and are still far away from the end-point at which they would need to make a decision on the final reward, the freedom of choice among multiple goals (vs. an assigned goal) elicits greater motivation. This is because, at this early stage, multiple goals are construed as *substitutable* for one another; therefore, these potential substitutes, combined, create a greater perceived likelihood that one would eventually attain something one desires, which leads to greater motivation in the pursuit.

However, when people have made substantial progress and are approaching the end of the pursuit, the need to make a decision on the reward becomes imminent and people begin to compare among options; at this advanced stage of pursuit, the freedom of choice among multiple goals (vs. an assigned goal) conversely becomes demotivating. This is because, when people begin to contemplate and compare among options, multiple goals would conversely be construed as *competitive* against one another (i.e., one would have to let go some equally attractive options), which leads to lower perceived value in the pursuit and thus lower motivation.

Two studies provided supportive evidence for the proposed hypothesis and the underlying mechanisms. In Study 1, we asked participants to memorize price information of products in different categories, and to type down these prices in question sections to earn points for the reward. We provided participants either one assigned reward or four different rewards (of equal market value) to choose from, and tracked how their motivation naturally progressed throughout the pursuit. This study allowed us to obtain the trend of participants' motivation when given the freedom of choice among multiple goals. We found that when there was only one assigned reward offered for attaining the target number of points, participants' motivation constituted a linearly increasing trend as they accumulated more progress. In contrast, when given the freedom to choose from multiple rewards, participants' motivation instead fitted a cubit trend; further analyses showed that, although participants who had the freedom of choice among multiple rewards became slightly more motivated from stage1 to stage 2, their motivation did not increase as they moved across the mid-point of the pursuit (i.e., as they advanced into the later stage and started comparing among different options).

In Study 2, we provided prospective customers of a school-based debit-card loyalty program either one assigned reward or four different rewards to choose from, and directly manipulated the loyalty points they have accumulated so far in the semester (based on their accumulated expenditure on campus and school-related businesses) as their progress level in the program when they joined. We measured these prospective customers' thoughts about the loyalty program and the reward system (e.g., the perceived goal competitiveness, goal attainability, and goal value) to capture the underlying mechanisms, and we also measured their sign-up rate for the loyalty program as a proxy for their motivation to continue the pursuit of the reward. Three moderated mediation models provided supportive evidence for the proposed mechanisms. We found that when people were at the initial stage of the pursuit, having the freedom to choose among multiple goals led to higher perceived likelihood to attain something one desired, which elicited greater motivation to sign up for the loyalty program (conditional indirect effect: $\beta = .07$, $z = 2.74$, $p < .01$); however, when people were at the advanced stage of the pursuit, the freedom to choose among multiple goals conversely led to lower perceived value of the program, which led to lower motivation to sign up (conditional indirect effect: $\beta = -.04$, $z = -1.65$, $p < .10$); this is because the perceived goal competitiveness (i.e., the perception that some options were more attractive than others) led to lower perceived value for people at this advanced stage of pursuit (conditional indirect effect: $\beta = -.05$, $z = -2.88$, $p < .01$).

Brands as a Means of Self-Expression:
Threatened, Unexpressed, Omnivorous, and Flexible Self
Chair: Jingjing Ma, Northwestern University, USA

Paper #1: Being Mean to Keep 'Em Keen: Retail Rejection Increases Aspiring Consumers' Desire for the Rejecting Brand
Morgan K. Ward, Southern Methodist University, USA
Darren W. Dahl, University of British Columbia, Canada

Paper #2: The Unexpressed Self: The Impact of Restricting Freedom of Self-Expression on Brand Preferences
Jingjing Ma, Northwestern University, USA
Ryan Hamilton, Emory University, USA
Alexander Chernev, Northwestern University , USA

Paper #3: Breaking Status Boundaries: When Interstatus Brand Collaborations Undermine Self-Expression by Omnivorous Consumers
Renée Richardson Gosline, Massachusetts Institute of Technology, USA
Jeffrey K. Lee, Harvard Business School, USA

Paper #4: Will Broad Identity Make People Feel Stronger: The Impact of Identity Framing on Motivation and Self-Control Behavior
Ying Ding, Peking University, China
Jing Xu, Peking University, China
Echo Wen Wan, University of Hong Kong, Hong Kong

SESSION OVERVIEW

The goal of the proposed session is to build on the existing literature to further the understanding how self-identity affects consumers' brand preferences. Research papers to be presented investigate this topic from multiple theoretical perspectives, offering a broader view of the role of brands in self-expression. Given the relevance of the topic to central issues in consumer behavior, this session is likely to have significant effect on future identity research and, in particular, the role of brands as a means of self-expression. Apart from providing theoretical insights into how identity influences brand preferences, the proposed session will contribute to the understanding of several content areas of great interest to ACR conference attendees, including brand extension, attitudes, self-concept, and compensatory consumption. Specifically, this special session will address the following issues:

Research presented by Ward and Dahl explores the effect of threats to self on brand preferences. They extend past research which has established that when one's self-concept is threatened, s/he is more likely to acquire objects to reaffirm the self. Ward and Dahl investigate this proposition in a luxury retail context and examine how a rejection from the sales staff impact consumers' brand perceptions. The authors show that, contrary to conventional wisdom that a welcoming sales staff will attract consumers, rejecting consumers may actually enhance retailers' appeal to some consumers. Specifically, they conclude that when an individual is rejected by a salesperson from brand that is relevant to his/her ideal (vs. actual) self, s/he is likely to increase (decrease) his/her assessments of the brand and willingness to consume in ways that enable him/her to affiliate (disassociate) with the rejecting brand.

Research by Ma, Hamilton, and Chernev examines how restricting self-expression in the social and political domains (e.g., being forbidden to comment on political leaders; inability to express feelings toward others) impacts consumers' brand preferences. They

show that the unexpressed self in the social domain leads to an increased need for self-expression and conspicuous consumption, strengthening individuals' preferences for self-expressive brands. They attribute this effect to the compensatory nature of self-expression, whereby restricting self-expressive means in one domain leads to a greater desire to self-express in an unrelated domain.

Adding to the counterintuitive findings that the threatened self and unexpressed self can lead to increased brand preferences, research by Gosline and Lee examines another counterintuitive hypothesis that omnivores (consumers who mix high and low status brands) find interstatus brand collaborations less appealing than univores (owners of only the high or the low status brands). They test this hypothesis using various experiments that feature hypothetical and actual interstatus co-branding collaborations. They find that the greatest damage to brand prestige is actually amongst current owners of both the high and lower status brands. These findings contribute to the longstanding brand extension literature, particularly the literature that addresses symbolic status brands, which suggests that these brands could dilute their image and reputation when engaging in some form of downward extension.

Lastly, Ding, Xu, and Wan examine the impact of identity framing on motivation and self-control. They show that consumers with a broad identity (vs. a narrow identity) perceive themselves as having more social resources, which in turn enhances motivation for social tasks and improves their self-control. They further demonstrate that this effect is apparent in communal relationships but attenuated in exchange relationships. Moreover, the findings confirm that perceived social resource mediate the effect of identity framing on consumers' motivation and self-control.

Our proposed session can contribute substantively to the theme of ACR 2012—appreciating diversity. The research papers in this session investigate the relationship between self-identity and brand preference in diverse range of contexts, such as in-store purchasing, restricted social and political environment, co-branding collaborations, and social tasks. These research projects involved a wide array of consumers, including those from both East and West, and in the lab and the field. This session will contribute both to basic theory development in the realm of identity and branding, and as well will suggest implications for marketing strategy.

Each presenter will be given 15 minutes to present. This will leave 15 minutes for discussions between the presenters and audience. The discussion will aim at facilitating a broader understanding of the role of brands as a means of self-expression and the implications of this understanding on expanding the field of consumer behavior.

Being Mean to Keep 'Em Keen:
Retail Rejection Increases Aspiring Consumers' Desire for the Rejecting Brand

EXTENDED ABSTRACT

Consumers often feel intimidated by unfriendly sales staff at luxury retailers and cite this as a reason they avoid shopping in these venues. Indeed, a former employee of Yves Saint Laurent admits that sales people size up a customer by looking at his watch and his shoes and 'if the accessories are not expensive, the customer is not worth the effort of even a simple hello' (Wilson 2009). However, as luxury sales have declined in recent years, retailers endeavor to become approachable in an effort to attract new consumers and increase sales (Odell 2009).

Yet, contrary to conventional wisdom that a welcoming sales staff will attract consumers, we demonstrate that rejecting consumers may actually enhance retailers' appeal to some consumers. The extant research supports this conjecture: individuals who have been rejected have been found to endeavor to ingratiate themselves with the rejecter (Romero-Caynas et al. 2010). Indeed, when aspects of the self-concept are threatened, people become more materialistic (Chang and Arkin 2002), are subsequently more likely to acquire objects that make a good impression on the rejecting party (Meade et al 2010) and bolster the threatened the self (Rucker and Galinsky 2008)

Building on the prior research on social rejection, we contend that people differentially respond to rejection. Individuals' sense of who they currently are and who they want to be is largely dependent on and reinforced by the groups they belong to. While one's actual self is fairly stable, one's ideal self is less certain and thus more vulnerable to threat (Swann1983). Consequently, our prediction is that when we an individual is rejected by a brand that is relevant to his/ her ideal (vs. actual) self, s/he is likely to increase (decrease) his/her assessments of the brand and willingness to consume in ways that enable him/her to re-affiliate (disassociate) with the rejecting brand. Luxury brands are a domain that consumers are likely turn to when they are seeking affirmation and self-expression and as such, provide an excellent context to examine our hypotheses.

In the first study we investigate how consumers' self-concepts affect their brand assessments and desire to purchase from brands to which they aspire but feel rejected by. In a 2 (brand: Gucci vs.. Louis Vuitton) x 2 (salesperson behavior: rejecting vs. neutral greeting) experiment, participants first indicate their level of identification with and degree to which they aspire toward the brand. Next, they read a scenario describing a hypothetical shopping experience in which they are directed to some clothing items in a store by a rejecting (vs. neutral) salesperson.

After reading the scenario participants answered a series of questions about their brand perceptions and desire to buy and wear the clothing from the brand.

We examined how the rejecting (vs. control) salesperson affected participants' assessments of the products from that brand. We observe an self-concept X salesperson behavior interaction (F(1, 100) = 4.78, p < .03) indicating that when consumers who possess ideal vs. (actual) identities relative to the brand, are rejected (vs. control) by the brand representative, they evaluate the products sold by the brand more positively.

The results show that not all rejection causes consumers to ingratiate via consumption but rather these behaviors are most likely when the rejection is threatening to the individual's tenuous ideal self. In the next study, we further investigate how self-control affects consumers' responses to rejection by manipulating their self-concept rather than measuring it.

In our second study we controlled self-views by priming participants' ideal vs. actual identity with a sentence rearranging technique in which participants rearranged words relevant to one's aspiration (vs. actual) identity. Next, participants completed an ostensibly unrelated study using the same scenario as the prior study. Finally, participants answered the same questions described in study 1.

We replicated the self-concept x salesperson behavior interaction (F(1, 121) = 4.28, p < .05) indicating that when consumers who aspire toward (versus identify with) the brand, are rejected by (vs

have a neutral interaction) with the brand representative, they evaluate the products sold by the brand more positively.

In study 3, we created a situation that mimics the experience of rejection in a retail environment. Participants participated in a 2 (brand: Gucci vs. Louis Vuitton) x 2 (salesperson behavior: rejecting vs. neutral) x 2 (prime self-concept: ideal vs. actual identity) x 2 (pre-experimental self-verification: self-verify vs. control) "product assessment study" in which participants interacted with a brand representative. Prior to the study half of the participants participated in a fashion knowledge tool (vs. neutral questions) enabling participants to express their fashion expertise enabling them to preemptively self-verify their fashion identity. Next, half of the participants were primed with an ideal vs. actual identity prime (see study 2). Finally, participants interacted with brand representatives who followed either a rejecting or neutral script. In rejecting conditions brand representatives appeared skeptical of the participant's knowledge of the brand, and disapproving of his/her appearance (versus neutral). Participants then rated bags from the brand on how variables from prior studies. Two weeks after the study, participants again rated their views about of the brand.

The data reveal a salesperson behavior x prime self-concept x pre-experimental self-verification interaction (F(2, 172) = 6.61, p < .01) indicating that consumers who aspire towards (vs. feel affiliated with) the brand and have not (vs. have) been allowed to self-verify prior to interacting with a rejecting (vs. control) brand representative evaluate the products sold by the brand more positively.

Finally, we show that participants who had a rejecting (vs. neutral) interaction with the brand representative had significantly less positive perceptions of the brand two weeks after the interaction (M Rejecting= 4.82 vs. M Neutral = 5.60, F(1, 121) = 4.09, p < .04).

The findings from three studies show that retailer rejection may drive consumers to prefer products that enable them to ingratiate themselves to the rejecting group when the group is one which they aspire to belong. However, these effects can be mitigated if they are able to self-verify prior to rejection.

REFERENCES

Chang, LinChiat and Robert M. Arkin (2002), "Materialism as an Attempt to Cope with Uncertainty," *Psychology and Marketing*, 19, 389-406.

Mead, Nicole L., Roy F. Baumeister, Tyler F. Stillman, Catherine D. Rawn, and Kathleen D. Vohs (2011), "Social Exclusion Causes People to Spend and Consume Strategically in the Service of Affiliation," *Journal of Consumer Research*, 37 (February), 902–19.

Odell, Amy (2009), "Salespeople at Snooty Stores Won't Be Snooty to You This Holiday Shopping Season" http://nymag.com/daily/fashion/2009/12/salespeople_at_snooty_ stores_w.html#comments

Romero-Canyas, Rainer , Geraldine Downey, Kavita S. Reddy, Sylvia Rodriguez, Timothy J. Cavanaugh, and Rosemary Pelayo (2010), "Paying to Belong: When Does Rejection Trigger Ingratiation?" *Journal of Personality and Social Psychology*, 99(5): 802–823.

Rucker, Derek D. and Adam D. Galinsky (2008), "Desire to Acquire: Powerlessness and Compensatory Consumption," *Journal of Consumer Research*, 35 (August), 257–67.

Swann, William B., Jr. (1983), "Self-Verification: Bringing Social Reality into Harmony with the Self," in *Social Psychological Perspectives on the Self*, Vol. 2, Jerry Suls and Anthony G. Greenwald, eds. Hillsdale, NJ: Lawrence Erlbaum Associates, 33–66.

Wilson, Eric (2009), "Economy adjusts store relations on Madison Avenue," http://www.nytimes.com/2009/02/18/style/18iht-18shopping.20274101.html?_r=1

The Unexpressed Self: The Impact of Restricting Freedom of Self-Expression on Brand Preferences

EXTENDED ABSTRACT

Individuals frequently have a desire to express aspects of the self. This desire to self-express stems from one of the most basic human needs—the need to belong and to be accepted and valued by others (Baumeister and Leary 1995; Fiske 2010; Maslow 1970). Despite the fundamental nature of self-expression, individuals are not always free to express their values, opinions, and beliefs. The limits to self-expression can be caused by a variety of factors. One is the restriction on free expression imposed by various government and regulatory entities. Such suppression of one's ability to express views typically involves the domains of politics and public policy, often extending to related domains that include religion, communications, the media, and use of the Internet. In addition to being restricted by government, individuals' self-expression also can be limited by social context, such as an imbalance of power in interpersonal relationships (e.g., an employee arguing with the boss). One's need for self-expression can further be curbed by social norms, such as restrictions imposed by traditions (e.g., not speaking ill of the dead), as well as by norms of politeness (e.g., not telling a friend how she really looks in skinny jeans). On many occasions, individuals' ability to express their views can be limited by a variety of factors that physically restrict one's ability to reach an audience (e.g., when access to one's social network is temporarily disrupted).

The ubiquity of possible impediments to self-expression raises the question of how restricting one's ability to express values, opinions, and beliefs influences subsequent behavior. Because of its importance, the topic of restricting self-expression has been the focus of numerous studies that for the most part have focused primarily on the implications of restricting self-expression in social or political domains. In this context, it has been shown that suppressing social or political self-expression is likely to produce perceptions of injustice (Stevens 1992), as well as trigger oppositional social movements (Andersen 2006; Fetner 2008; Polletta 2004).

Building on prior research, we take a different approach and examine whether and how restricting one's ability to express opinions in socio-political domains influences individuals' preferences and behaviors in domains unrelated to the views being suppressed, in particular, the domain of product consumption. In this context, we investigate how the impact of restricting individuals' ability to express their socio-political views influences their brand preferences.

We argue that restricting individuals' ability to express their socio-political views can have a significant impact on brand preferences and that this impact tends to strengthen their need for self-expression through brands. This proposition builds on previous findings in the goal literature suggesting that when the means of pursuing a goal or fulfilling a need are restricted, people frequently experience a rebound effect, such that the restriction leads to a subsequent increase in need-related behavior (Lewin 1951). For example, suppressing thoughts about colors (Liberman and Förster 2000), stereotypes (Macrae et al. 1994) or white bears (Wegner et al. 1987) leads to increased thoughts of these constructs relative to a condition in which these thoughts were not suppressed. Likewise, when the means to fulfill a goal are removed, the desire to complete the goal becomes stronger (Förster and Liberman 2001; Förster, Liberman,

and Higgins 2005). This is consistent with Lewin's (1926) tension system theory of goals, which states that when a goal has been activated, the person feels a tension until the goal is completed.

Applied to self-expression, these findings imply that restricting the means to self-express can increase people's motivation to express themselves. Since brands can serve as a non-restricted means of self-expression when other avenues are closed off, we propose that restricting one's ability to express in social or political domains can strengthen one's preference for self-expressive brands. Thus, we predict that curbing one's ability to share their views of a major political or social event—such as opining about the performance of the president, commenting on major world news events, even sharing opinions about celebrities—will strengthen individuals' preferences for ostensibly unrelated brands such as Nike, Oakley, or Levi's. We propose that individuals' need for self-expression is compensatory in nature and that consumers tend to offset their inability to self-express in one domain by seeking opportunities to express in other, unrelated domains.

We test this prediction in a series of five empirical studies. Experiment 1 shows that restricting self-expression in various social domains (opinions about celebrities, countries, universities, pop stars, etc.) strengthens consumer preferences for self-expressive brands. Experiment 2 further shows that restricting freedom of speech (commenting on a newsworthy current event) strengthens consumer preferences for self-expressive brands. Building on the findings of the first two studies, Experiment 3 further documents the compensatory nature of self-expression in cases when the restriction of self-expression is internally imposed (e.g. voluntarily controlling one's feelings toward others). Experiments 4 and 5 aim to shed more light on the compensatory nature of self-expression. Specifically, Experiment 4 shows that the effects observed in the first three studies are attenuated when consumers have a channel other than brand evaluation in which to express themselves. Experiment 5 provides further support for our account by showing that conspicuous consumption, such as choosing a self-expressive brand, decreases individuals' need for self-expression in the original, restricted domain (e.g. inability to comment on Obama's performance).

In sum, this research investigates how curbing one's ability to express an opinion in non-consumption domains subsequently increases one's preferences for self-relevant brands. We show that this effect is due to the compensatory nature of self-expression—the unexpressed self in one domain can be expressed by self-expressive means from other domains, such as brands. This research adds to the literature on self-expression by demonstrating the compensatory nature of self-expression. It also adds to the literature on branding by documenting that brands can help consumers express the unexpressed self in non-consumption domains.

REFERENCES

Andersen, Ellen (2006), *Out of the Closets & into the Courts: Legal Opportunity Structure and Gay Rights Litigation*: Ann Arbor, MI: University of Michigan Press.

Baumeister, Roy and Mark Leary (1995), "The Need to Belong: Desire for Interpersonal Attachments as a Fundamental Human Motivation," *Psychological Bulletin*, 117, 497.

Fetner, Tina (2008), *How the Religious Right Shaped Lesbian and Gay Activism*, Minneapolis, MN: University of Minnesota Press.

Fiske, Susan (2010), *Social Beings: Core Motives in Social Psychology*, 2nd ed, Hoboken, NJ: John Wiley & Sons Inc.

Förster, Jens and Nira Liberman (2001), "The Role of Attribution of Motivation in Producing Postsuppressional Rebound," *Journal of Personality and Social Psychology*, 81, 377.

Förster, Jens, Nira Liberman, and Edward T. Higgins (2005), "Accessibility from Active and Fulfilled Goals," *Journal of Experimental Social Psychology*, 41, 220-39.

Lewin, K. (1951), "Intention, Will and Need," in *Organization and Pathology of Thought*, ed., New York Columbia University Press, 95-153.

Lewin, Kurt (1926), "Vorsatz, Wille Und Bedürfnis," *Psychological Research*, 7, 330-85.

Liberman, Nira and Jens Förster (2000), "Expression after Suppression: A Motivational Explanation of Postsuppressional Rebound," *Journal of Personality and Social Psychology*, 79, 190.

Macrae, Neil, Galen Bodenhausen, Alan Milne, and Jetten Jetten (1994), "Out of Mind but Back in Sight: Stereotypes on the Rebound," *Journal of Personality and Social Psychology*, 67, 808.

Maslow, Abraham H. (1970), *Motivation and Personality* (2d ed.), New York,: Harper & Row.

Polletta, Francesca (2004), *Freedom Is an Endless Meeting: Democracy in American Social Movements*: University of Chicago Press.

Stevens, John (1992), "The Freedom of Speech," *The Yale Law Journal*, 102, 1293.

Wegner, D. M., D. J. Schneider, S. R. Carter, and T. L. White (1987), "Paradoxical Effects of Thought Suppression," *Journal of Personality and Social Psychology*, 53 (July), 5-13.

Breaking Status Boundaries: When Interstatus Brand Collaborations Undermine Self-Expression by Omnivorous Consumers

EXTENDED ABSTRACT

Past research has shown that symbolic brands serve as a means for consumers to express their identities and social status, and to differentiate from dissociative outgroups (Chernev, Hamilton, Hal 2011; Berger and Heath 2007; White and Dahl 2006, 2007; Holt 1998; Shavitt 1990; Belk 1981; Veblen 1899). It may be quite surprising then that, recently, fashion brands have witnessed a growing phenomenon: co-branding partnerships between high and lower status brands. High status luxury brands (such as Jimmy Choo, Karl Lagerfeld, Stella McCartney, Roberto Cavalli, and Vera Wang), have entered into collaborations with lower status companies like Target, Kohls, J.C. Penney, Wal-Mart, and Payless Shoes. These status boundary violations (Lamont 1996) support recent research that has shown that many high status persons are not cultural snobs, but in fact eclectic and "omnivorous," in their tastes (Erickson Peterson and Kern 1996; Erickson 1996; Peterson and Simkus 1992). Previous literature has explained this as a generational shift, due to cohort replacement and changes in social structure, values, and art-world dynamics. We introduce a new perspective on this phenomenon: that omnivorous status boundary-violating behavior is based on a need for self-expression. This leads us to a counterintuitive hypothesis that omnivores (consumers who mix high and low status brands) should find interstatus brand collaborations less appealing than univores (owners of only the high or the low status brands). We test this hypothesis using various experiments that feature hypothetical and actual interstatus co-branding collaborations. We find that the greatest damage to brand prestige is actually amongst current owners of both the high and lower status brands. These findings contribute to the longstanding brand extension literature, particularly the literature that addresses symbolic status brands, which suggests that these brands could dilute their image and reputation when engaging in some form of downward extension.

Our first study focuses on univores, and shows that owners of either the high status brand or the low status brand penalize their brands for collaboration. We recruited undergraduate students at Harvard to complete an online survey on a potential co-branding effort between Harvard and the University of Phoenix, and to browse the beta-website of the Harvard-Phoenix Online University to "get a sense of what the joint initiative would look like." This collaboration was seen as an affront to owners of the high status brands (Harvard undergraduates), as the Harvard brand was deemed highly symbolic and used as a means of identity expression. We show that these subjects feel that their Harvard brand suffers lowered status (t(29) = -10.770, p < 0.001) and prestige points (t(29) = -7.324, p < 0.001), due to this collaboration. For non-Harvard subjects, who did not use the brands as self-expressive symbols, we saw no such penalty for the interstatus collaboration. Additionally, our Study 1 shows that Harvard subjects believed that the lower status school's brand would increase in status and prestige due to the inter-status co-branding initiative with their school (t(29) = 12.245, p < 0.001). This indicates that the high status consumers are not merely trying to dissociate from or punish the lower status consumers.

Study 2 shows that, surprisingly, that the greatest damage to the collaborating brands is amongst consumers who currently own both the high status and lower status brands. These types of consumers, called omnivores, consume high and lower status brands simultaneously – this mixing behavior is a means of self-expression that is undermined by interstatus brand collaborations. Study 2 demonstrates this with an experiment featuring a hypothetical collaboration between the high-status Prada brand and the lower-status Banana Republic brand. We find that actual univore owners of Prada and actual univore owners of Banana Republic are quite similar to non-owners, in that their ratings of the prestige level of their respective brands experience little to no change. However, we find that actual omnivore owners of both Prada and Banana Republic penalize the high status brand (t(83) = -1.73, p = 0.087). These omnivores also rate the prestige of the collaboration significantly lower (t(84) = -2.22, p = 0.029), while univore owners of either the high status or the lower status brand are not significantly different from non-owners in their prestige ratings of the collaboration. We find that omnivores seek to make self-expressive statements with their status boundary violations. Despite the fact that these omnivore consumers currently own both the high and lower status brands simultaneously in their wardrobes, they also have a significantly lower rating of the fit of these same brands for a co-branding collaboration (t(84) = -3.254, p = 0.002). We argue that these consumers are motivated by a need for self-expression, and that omnivore behavior conveys a boundary spanning behavior that speaks to distinctive taste (Bourdieu 1984). As a result, when high and lower-status brands collaborate, they obviate the self-expressive nature of omnivore consumption.

In Study 3, we test whether interstatus collaborating brands may escape penalty if self-expression is aided by a "moral alibi" -- an alternative explanation provided by the manufacturer that allows omnivore consumers to impute a moral meaning, like a charity or goodwill effort, to their consumption behavior. This moral alibi may create a means for self-expression for the brand owners that could defray the perceived negative consequences of the co-branding on the higher-status brand. However, though we find that it can significantly reduce the prestige or status lost compared to when a moral alibi is not proffered, the higher-status brand in the co-branding collaboration still suffers a penalty (t(32) = -3.922, p < 0.001).

The results of these three studies indicate the importance of preserving opportunities for self-expression amongst consumers of symbolic products. Interstatus collaborations may seem most appropriate for people who already mix brands of differing status, but pre-fabricated omnivrous brand offerings undermine the ability of consumers to express themselves via omnivorous consumption.

REFERENCES

Belk, R. W. (1988). "Possessions and the Extended Self." *Journal of Consumer Research* 15(2):139-168.

Berger, J. and C. Heath (2007). "Where Consumers Diverge from Others: Identity Signaling and Product Domains." *Journal of Consumer Research* 34(2): 121-134.

Berger, J. and M. Ward (2010). "Subtle Signals of Inconspicuous Consumption." *Journal of Consumer Research* 37.

Bourdieu, P. (1986). Distinction : a social critique of the judgement of taste. London, Routledge & Kegan Paul.

Bryson, B. (1996). "Anything but Heavy Metal: Symbolic Exclusion and Musical Dislikes." *American Sociological Review* 61: 16.

Chernev, Alexander, Ryan Hamilton, and David Gal (2011) "Competing for Consumer Identity: Limits to Self-Expression and the Perils of Lifestyle Branding," *Journal of Marketing* (May).

Duesenberry, J. S. (1949). Income, saving, and the theory of consumer behavior. Cambridge, Harvard University Press.

Erickson B H (1991) 'What is good taste for?', *Canadian Review of Sociology and Anthropology*, 28(2), 255-278.

Erickson B H (1996) Culture, class and connections', *American Journal of Sociology* 102(1), (1996), 217-251.

Escalas, J. E. and J. R. Bettman (2003). "You Are What They Eat: The Influence of Reference Groups on Consumers' Connections to Brands." *Journal of Consumer Psychology* (Lawrence Erlbaum Associates) 13(3): 339.

Frank, R. H. (1985). Choosing the right pond : human behavior and the quest for status. New York ;Oxford [Oxfordshire], Oxford University Press.

Han, Y. J., J. C. Nunes, et al. (2010). "Signaling Status with Luxury Goods: The Role of Brand Prominence." *Journal of Marketing* 74 (July): 17.

Holt, D. B. (1998). "Does Cultural Capital Structure American Consumption?" *Journal of Consumer Research* 25(1): 1-25.

Lamont, Michèle and Virág Molnár. 2002. "The Study of Boundaries in the Social Sciences." *Annual Review of Sociology* 28: 167-195.

Leibenstein, H. (1950). "Bandwagon, Snob, and Veblen Effects in the Theory of Consumers' Demand." *The Quarterly Journal of Economics* 64(2): 183-207.

Peterson R A (1992) Understanding audience segmentation: from elite and mass to omnivore and univore, Poetics ,21, 243-58

Peterson R A (1997) The rise and fall of highbrow snobbery as a status marker, Poetics, 25 75-92

Peterson R & Kern R (1996) Changing highbrow taste: from snob to omnivore, *American Sociological Review*, 61, 900-907

Peterson R A & Simkus A (1992) How musical tastes mark occupational status groups in Lamont M & Fournier M (eds) Cultivating Differences: symbolic boundaries and the making of inequality Chicago IL University of Chicago Press, 152-86

Richins, M. L. (1994). "Valuing Things: The Public and Private Meanings of Possessions." *Journal of Consumer Research* 21(3): 504-521.

Tajfel, H. and J. C. Turner (1979). An integrative theory of intergroup conflict. Differentiation between social groups: Studies in the social psychology of intergroup relations. H. Tajfel. London and New York, Published in cooperation with European Association of Experimental Social Psychology by Academic Press.

Veblen, T. (2006). Conspicuous consumption. New York, Penguin Books.

White, K. and D. Dahl (2007). "Are All Out-Groups Created Equal? Consumer Identity and Dissociative Influence." *Journal of Consumer Research* 34: 525-536.

Will Broad Identity Make People Feel Stronger: The Impact of Identity Framing on Motivation and Self-Control Behavior

EXTENDED ABSTRACT

Prior research has suggested that identities are situation-sensitive and that a shift in identities can lead to differences in information processing and actual behavior (Oyserman 2009). For example, Mandel (2003) finds that individuals primed with the interdependent (vs. independent) self-identity were more likely to take financial risks. Shih et al. (1999) found that Asian-American women performed better on a mathematics test when their ethnic identity was activated, but worse when their gender identity was made accessible.

Although a sizable research has examined the effect of different types of social identities on judgment and behavior (Aaker and Lee 2001), so far little research has examined the impact of different levels of social identity on behavior. According to self-categorization theory (Turner et al. 1987), people have multiple social identities with multiple levels of inclusiveness: the superordinate level based on similarities among human beings, the intermediate level emphasizing interdependence, and the subordinate level emphasizing independence. Based on this theory, we posit that social identities can be defined either broadly or narrowly. A broad identity defines a member in a superordinate group (e.g., an employee in P&G China), which combines heterogeneous features, and focuses on the similarities among subgroups. Conversely, a narrow identity defines a member in a subgroup (e.g., an employee in the Beijing Center in the R&D Department of P&G China), which constrains individuals to a specific domain, and focuses on the differences among subgroups. We further hypothesize that making the broad or narrow identity accessible to individuals will alter their cognitions and behaviors accordingly. Specifically, we propose that individuals with a more accessible broad identity (vs. narrow identity) will perceive belonging to a bigger group and having more social resources to spare, which in turn increase their motivation in social tasks. Moreover, prior literature has indicated that social support could attenuate job-stress and enhance self-efficacy (Viswesvaran et al. 1999). So we posit that a broad identity will enhance individuals' perception about their self-regulation strength and improve self-control.

We also examine the boundary condition for the effects of identity framing on motivation and self-control. Building on the differences between communal and exchange interpersonal relationship (Aggarwal 2004), we hypothesize that a broad identity (vs. a narrow identity) will increase individuals' motivation and self-control in subsequent tasks only when people perceive the interpersonal relationship as communal but not when they perceive it as exchange, and that this moderation effect would be mediated by the perceived social resources.

To tests the proposed hypotheses, we conducted three experiments. In Experiment 1, the identity framing was manipulated by presenting either the whole organization chart of HP (broad condition) or the same chart but with the highlight that they belong to the "Engineering Management" subdivision (narrow condition). Following this task, participants responded to the perceived social resource scale adopted from Zimet et al. (1988). Afterwards, they were instructed to read the description of environmental protection campaign which required them to collect signatures among their friends to support the campaign. Then participants estimated how many signatures they could get, and returned the collected signatures one week later. The results indicated that participants primed with a broad identity (vs. a narrow identity) reported having more social resources, estimated that they could collect more signatures, and actually returned more signatures. These results provided initial evidences for our proposed effect of the identity framing on self-perception and motivation.

Experiment 2 tested the moderation effect of interpersonal relationship on the impact of identity framing. The manipulation of identity framing was similar to that used in experiment 1. The interpersonal relationship was manipulated in the form of an idiom understanding task. In the communal condition, participants read the idiom as "Between friends all is common" which implied that people should care about others and show a genuine concern. Conversely, in the exchange condition, "Even reckoning makes long friends" was presented which emphasized that interpersonal relationship should be quid-pro-quo and that people should try to keep things even with others. We then measured participants' motivation in social tasks by estimating how many signatures they could get to protect endangered animals. The performance on self-control was measured using a task of processing useful but threatening health message (Agrawal and Wan 2009). The findings demonstrated that among the participants in the communal condition, those primed with broad identity estimated they could get more signatures than those primed with narrow identity. However, for the participants in the exchange condition, the estimation of signature numbers did not differ between participants primed with broad identity and those primed with narrow identity. A similar pattern was found on the amount of time spent on reading the health message which reflected the participants' self-control.

Experiment 3 explored the process underlying the moderating effect of interpersonal relationship on the impact of identity framing. We also aimed to replicate the results of experiment 2 in a marketing relevant context. Specifically, the identity framing was manipulated by priming participants as members of one parent brand fans club (broad identity) or one sub-brand fans group (narrow identity). Then participants moved on to the idiom task which manipulated the interpersonal relationship. Next, participants read the brochure of one new product trial campaign, and estimated the number of friends they could invite to join the campaign. Afterwards, participants proceeded to a product evaluation survey involving a series of binary choice, a task adopted from Vohs et al. (2008) to assess self-control. They were told to do as many as they could, with the understanding that they could stop anytime when they "want to quit." The amount of time spent on doing the survey served as the dependent measure of self-control. Consistent with our predictions, the positive effect of broad identity on performance for both social and self-control tasks were only replicated in the communal relationship condition. Furthermore, we found that this moderation effect was mediated by perceived social resource.

This research contributes to the literature of social identity, prosocial behavior, and self-control. In addition, our findings provide insightful implications for marketing practice and organization behavior.

REFERENCES

Aaker, Jennifer L. and Angela Y. Lee (2001), ""I" Seek Pleasures and "We" Avoid Pains: The Role of Self-Regulatory Goals in Information Processing and Persuasion," *Journal of Consumer Research*, 28 (1), 33-49.

Aggarwal, Pankaj (2004), "The Effects of Brand Relationship Norms on Consumer Attitudes and Behavior," *Journal of Consumer Research*, 31 (1), 87–101.

Aggarwal, Nidhi and Echo Wen Wan (2009), "Regulating Risk or Risking Regulation? Construal Levels and Depletion Effects in the Processing of Health Messages," *Journal of Consumer Research*, 36 (3), 448-62.

Mandel. Naomi (2003), "Shifting Selves and Decision Making: The Effects of Self-Construal Priming on Consumer Risk-Taking," *Journal of Consumer Research*, 30(1), 30-40.

Oyserman, Daphna (2009), "Identity-Based Motivation: Implications for Action-Readiness, Procedural-Readiness, and Consumer Behavior," *Journal of Consumer Psychology*, 19 (3), 250-60.

Shih, Margaret, Todd L. Pittinsky and Nalini Ambady (1999), "Stereotype Susceptibility: Identity Salience and Shifts in Quantitative Performance," *Psychological Science*, 10 (1), 80-3.

Turner, John C., Michael A. Hogg, Pamela J. Oakes, Stephen Reicher, and Margaret S. Wetherell (1987), *Rediscovering the Social Group: A Self-Categorization Theory*, Oxford: Basil Blackwell.

Viswesvaran, Chockalingam, Juan I. Sanchez, Jeffrey Fisher (1999), "The Role of Social Support in the Process of Work Stress: A Meta-Analysis," *Journal of Vocational Behavior*, 54 (2), 314-34.

Vohs, Kathleen D., Roy F. Baumeister, Brandon J. Schmeichel, Jean M. Twenge, Noelle M. Nelson and Dianne M. Tice (2008), "Making Choices Impairs Subsequent Self-Control: A Limited-Resource Account of Decision Making, Self-Regulation, and Active Initiative," *Journal of Personality and Social Psychology*, 94 (5), 883-98.

Zimet, Gregory D., Nancy W. Dahlem, Sara G. Zimet and Gordon K. Farley (1988). "The Multidimensional Scale of Perceived Social Support," *Journal of Personality Assessment*, 52(1), 30-41.

Countervailing the Effects of Poverty: Individual and Collective Strategies among Impoverished Consumers for Sustainable Well-Being

Chairs: Fredah Mwiti, Lancaster University Management School, UK
Andres Barrios, Lancaster University Management School, UK and Universidad de los Andes, Colombia

Paper #1: Single Mothers in Poverty: Consumption Paradoxes of Stigma Avoidance

Kathy Hamilton, University of Strathclyde, Glasgow, Scotland

Paper #2: Integrating Resources via Practices within Consumer Networks: Subsistence Consumers Participating in 'Chama' Networks in Kenya

Fredah G Mwiti, Maria Piacentini and Andrew Pressey; Lancaster University, UK

Paper #3: Using Consumption Practices to Countervail Stigma Experiences and Transform Self-Identity among the Homeless

Andres Barrios, Lancaster University, UK and Universidad de los Andes, Colombia
Chris Blocker, Baylor University, USA

Paper #4: Vulnerable Consumers: Ethnography of the Consumption of French Farmers Facing Impoverishment

Françoise Passerard, HEC Paris, France
Kristine De Valck, HEC Paris, France
Romain Laufer, HEC Paris, France

SESSION OVERVIEW

Douglas (2007) defines poverty as the inability to maintain the exchanges that define one as a member of the society. Such exchanges are not however limited to economic domains, and as such the effects of poverty on consumers – as well as the mechanisms that impoverished individuals employ to countervail the hardships in their lives – are multifaceted. This special session draws inspiration from the TCR agenda to address substantive issues facing consumers around the world and synthesizes four studies that explore the effects of poverty and impoverished consumers' efforts to improve their lives.

Each of the papers to be presented relates to completed research projects, and fits with the conference mission of appreciating diversity as they not only explore the effects of poverty from different situational contexts (rural farmers in France, the homeless in the US and UK, slum-dwellers in Kenya, and single mothers in the UK), but also utilize different units of analysis (individual, family, and their broader networks). The papers draw on discussions within the poverty track at a recent TCR dialogical conference, in which the scholars identified five research streams with implications for impoverished consumption including: consumption choice amidst the burdens of poverty, product and service experiences, the effects of consumer culture, adverse marketplace forces, and consumption capabilities (Blocker et al 2011, 2012).

Kathy Hamilton (University of Strathclyde) explores consumption paradoxes of stigma avoidance with single mothers living in poverty in the UK. Fredah Mwiti, Maria Piacentini, (Lancaster University) and Andrew Pressey (Birmingham University) use ethnography to examine the integration of resources within subsistence consumer networks in Kenya. Andres Barrios (Lancaster University) and Chris Blocker (Baylor University) explore the consumption practices that homeless individuals use to countervail the experience of stigma and transform their self-identity in the UK and US. Françoise Passerard investigates the consumption vulnerability of French farmers. Beyond the implications that each individual study poses for

poverty-related TCR, together these four studies contribute to dialogue on consumer surprise, irony, and ambivalence. In particular, a 2011 JCR editorial highlights the idea that research could explore ways that consumers are made better or worse off when they experience and act upon surprising thoughts or behaviors (Hsee et al. 2003). The studies in this proposed session make salient consumers' varying strategies for countervailing the effects poverty, and in doing so, the collective findings reveal paradoxical tensions and feelings of ambivalence. Thus, we anticipate interesting dialogue as to how consumer strategies may ultimately help mitigate their vulnerabilities or exacerbate them. Speakers will have a maximum of 15 minutes each to present their papers. This will ensure that sufficient time is allocated for general audience engagement and discussion.

In sum the session provides a platform for those interested in the intersection of poverty and transformative consumer research to discuss and gain major understanding over the 4 billion plus consumers who live in impoverished conditions. Beyond this, the session will appeal to a wide audience including those who have a theoretical interest in consumer vulnerability, consumer disadvantage, social exclusion, consumer coping, stigma and emerging markets.

Single Mothers in Poverty: Consumption Paradoxes of Stigma Avoidance

EXTENDED ABSTRACT

This presentation will focus on single mothers in poverty and the paradoxical nature of their quest to avoid stigmatization and social disapproval. At previous ACR conferences, I have concluded that single mothers can improve their situations and develop self-esteem through initiating various creative strategies to respond to their family's demands (Hamilton and Catterall 2007, 2008). A re-interpretation of this research reveals that coping strategies which seem functional and effective at the micro level may have unanticipated outcomes if considered within the wider societal context. Thus the coping strategies employed to disguise poverty and aid the portrayal of a socially acceptable image can actually create further stigmatization. This highlights the importance of moving beyond only focusing on the stigma management strategies employed by consumers to also incorporate sociocultural understandings.

This study consists of 24 in-depth interviews in single mother households. A family approach was adopted for the study meaning that children aged 11 and over also participated in interviews. Therefore in 9 households, a family interview was conducted with the mother and her child(ren) and in 16 households the mother was interviewed alone. Interviews were conducted in respondents' homes and interview topics included everyday life, budgetary strategies, hopes for the future, family background information and financial circumstances. Hermeneutics was used to interpret the data. In this paper, the data interpretation is advanced by using macro social discourse to gain a deeper and more complete understanding of individual experiences. To do so, the lived experience of low-income consumers is considered within the context of exclusion and single mother discourse.

Poor consumers are often defined in relation to marketplace exclusion. For example, Bauman (2005, 38, 112-113) argued that 'a "normal life" is the life of consumers" with the poor described as 'inadequate,' 'unwanted,' 'abnormal,' 'blemished, defective, faulty and deficient,' 'flawed consumers' and 'non-consumers.' However, recent popular discussion "focuses not on the inability to consume, but on the *excessive* participation in forms of market-oriented consumption which are deemed *aesthetically* impoverished" (Hayward and Yar 2006, 14).

Coping through consumption is a strategy that extends to almost all the families in the study, and there is emphasis placed on ensuring children have access to the 'right' brands to facilitate identity construction. Many strategies focused on minimizing expenditure are strictly followed to ensure budget allocation towards more conspicuous forms of consumption including clothing, footwear, jewellery, home decor and gifts for others. The purchase and display of brand names is viewed as a way of avoiding stigma and could be considered as a disconfirmation of the stereotype (Miller & Major, 2000) aimed at disguising restricted class positions. By attempting to contest and resist the stigmatizing regime, low-income consumers seek consumer normalcy (Baker, 2006) through their marketplace transactions. According to Bourdieu (1984, 56) the 'refusal of tastes' plays a key role in consumer choice as people avoid the purchase of goods and services that may be detrimental to their social self-concept. Within the current context, this includes the rejection of low-cost clothing in favour of visible brand names and logos. Evidence suggests that coping efforts may be empowering for lone mothers and can result in higher self-esteem. This interpretation provides an optimistic image of the low-income consumer as an active individual coping victoriously within the challenging context of consumer culture to improve the standard of living for themselves and their family.

However, by interpreting such consumption activity in relation to "a new vocabulary of social class" (Tyler 2008) it becomes apparent that those who follow a strategy of conspicuous consumption in efforts to mask poverty ultimately encounter the very stigmatization that they set out to avoid in the first instance. In recent years, exclusion discourse in the UK has focused on 'chav' culture (alongside regional variations in semantics). Often believed to stand for 'Council Housed and Violent,' popular media representations and discourse surrounding chav culture is overwhelmingly negative. The stigmatisation of single mothers is particularly prevalent in chav discourse as articulated in Tyler's (2008) article entitled 'Chav Mum Chav Scum.' As Tyler (2008, 26) suggests "whilst young unwed working-class mothers have always been a target of social stigma, hatred and anxiety, the fetishisation of the chav mum within popular culture has a contemporary specificity and marks a new outpouring of sexist class disgust." The chav single mother is heavily criticised for vulgar consumption choices, in particular dressing her children "with expensive and thus apparently wholly inappropriate designer clothing and jewellery" (Hayward and Yar 2006, 22). In a cruel irony, some of the brand names that low income consumers purchase to escape stigmatization are the same brands that have particular negative user stereotypes associated with them.

Research on stigma is often based on either micro-individual or macro-social analysis. However, as Campbell & Deacon (2006, p. 412) suggested, there are problems with both these approaches because stigma is both a psychological and a social process. By focusing on the stigmatized individual, 'existing social relations are usually taken as given' and by focusing on macro-social analysis, one risks overlooking the 'individual psychological dimensions of stigma.' The current research contributes by combining both approaches. By highlighting individual lived experiences of poverty and coping with stigma in relation to discourse on chav culture and

single mothers, this study has highlighted the paradoxical nature of consumption.

Integrating Resources via Practices within Consumer Networks: Subsistence Consumers Participating in 'Chama' Networks in Kenya

EXTENDED ABSTRACT

Subsistence consumers are portrayed as being characterized by a scarcity of economic resources, but rich in social ties formed through networks (Viswanathan et al., 2008). Such networks give them opportunities to interact with one another and generate various forms of resources which enable them to enact their life projects and meet their goals (Arnould, Price and Malshe 2006; Sewell, 1992). The kinds of resources generated and employed vary, as do the terms used to categorize them. Bourdieu's (1986) categorizes resources in terms of capital, including economic, social, cultural and symbolic capital. More recent studies using the service dominant logic categorize resources as either operand (tangible resources such as material objects) or operant (intangible resources such as social resources) (Arnould, Price and Malshe 2006). A number of other classifications exist, but despite the different terminologies used, resources constitute accumulative assets that consumers can use to achieve their goals and basically to satisfy their needs (Bristow and Mowen, 1998: 2). Within consumer research there have been calls for researchers to consider the resources that the poor have and not just deficits (Moser 1998). This paper explores how subsistence consumers in Kenya integrate and (re) configure their resources by engaging in consumer collectives (Chama), and concludes that through the practices enacted within such collectives the integration of resources is perpetuated with varying outcomes.

The term 'Chama' is used to refer to collectives very similar to the Rotating Savings and Credit Associations (ROSCAs), and is the term to be used in this paper to refer to ROSCAs and other similar collectives. The emergence of such groups in Kenya started in the 1970s and 1980s (Johnson, 2004), predominantly organized and run by women. The prevalence of women participants has been attributed to the patrilineal nature of the communities they live in, where inheritance and ownership arrangements are often biased against them (Kimuyu, 1999). This makes it hard to access lump-sum financial resources offered by banks and other lenders who usually require collateral in form of property rights to extend such credit to them (Johnson, 2004). Consequently, many of them form Chama to access informal credit easily in order to meet their consumption goals. Given the view that Chamas are formed primarily for purposes of accessing credit and for saving, Chamas have largely been studied within economic disciplines, where they are depicted as forms of informal financial markets that fill in gaps left by formal financial markets (Siamwalla et al., 1990; Bouman, 1995). However, they also serve non-financial roles as they are avenues in which societal roles are enacted (Johnson, 2004). This implies that other non-financial resources may be activated, accumulated and shared there as well. Furthermore, Chamas also play important consumption–related roles, as they enable participants to pool funds together in order to meet consumption goals (Kimuyu, 1999). In this paper therefore, Chamas are considered as consumer-constituted collectives which enable various forms of resources to be employed and integrated with various outcomes for the participating consumers.

Methodology and Findings

The study employed an ethnographic approach and was carried out in two slums in the capital city of Kenya (Nairobi) over a period of 5 months. Living in the slum is characterized by what has been conceptualized as "poor living" (Sen 2000) where consumers face a shortage of income, insecurity, limited social amenities, poor infrastructure among others. In order to experience the lived worlds of these consumers, the first author spent a significant amount of time in the slums with the participants as they went on with their daily activities such as shopping and attending Chama meetings. Six different Chamas, each consisting of an average of 15 women were visited on several occasions. The researcher would sit in during their meetings and take notes, and whenever consent was given the proceedings would be audio-recorded and photographs taken. Group interviews were conducted during these meetings, and individual interviews also followed on different dates with at least 3 different people from each of the Chama. Other data collection methods were also employed such as observations, document analysis as well visits to the sites (like markets) that these participants frequented within the slum.

Findings from the study reveal that subsistence consumers do indeed possess various resources which they employ within their contexts. Consistent with other studies focusing on impoverished communities (e.g. Lee, Ozanne and Hill 1999), social capital was found to be prevalent within the Chamas, and engendered norms like mutual support, reciprocity and trust. Drawing on these norms, the participants were able to leverage this capital and achieve certain goals such as assisting one another to educate their children or acquiring consumer durables that they would not otherwise afford individually. Chama hence endows them with capabilities that enable them to perform their consumer (as well as other societal) roles.

The findings further reveal that consumers engaged in several practices in Chama, and were consequently able to accrue various forms of resources, as well as convert them to other forms through these practices. In one of the main practices named 'merry-go-round' for instance, participants meet in one of their homes primarily to pool financial resources together for various consumption purposes (integration of economic capital). Such meetings are in some instances characterized by feasting, providing participants opportunities for social interaction (accruing social capital) as well as enabling the hosts to demonstrate their hospitality skills, gaining respect through their adroit performances (demonstration of cultural capital and possible accumulation symbolic capital). For these women, the ability to perform this 'merry-go-round' practice effectively (e.g. by consistently providing the funds to be pooled, cooking the 'right' foods) demonstrates possession of context-specific cultural capital, and women who do not demonstrate this capability may sometimes find themselves excluded from engaging in future Chama activities. So important is it to be part of Chama that some of the participants consider women who do not belong to Chama 'abnormal'. As such, exclusion from Chama would marginalize them socially, further exacerbating the vulnerabilities they face.

Literature on resource integration has been presented largely within consumer-supplier exchange contexts (e.g. McGrath and Otnes 1995), and even when done outside such contexts, the emphasis has been on financial resources (e.g. Ruth and Hsiung, 2007). This current research makes contributions by focusing on a variety of resources integrated by consumers collectively outside the market exchange interface. It is envisaged that much can be learnt about resource integration outside such contexts especially amongst impoverished consumers whose resource constraints have wider implications beyond those experienced within the consumer-supplier exchange interface. This research also addresses recent calls to focus on the practices involved in integrating resources (e.g. Kleinaltenkamp, 2012) and highlights how collective practices act as the catalysts that determine how resources are integrated, accumulated and even lost.

Using Consumption Practices to Countervail Stigma Experiences and Transform Self-Identity among the Homeless

EXTENDED ABSTRACT

Becoming homeless is a stressful event that society stigmatizes (Phelan et al. 1997). Homeless individuals experience a threat to their self as a result of not only stress-inducing events such as loss of their economic resources, but also the stigma experience and social disapproval of their social identity (Dovidio et al. 2000). Link and Phelan (2001) reviewed various definitions and conceptualized stigma as a convergence of components that develop with the co-occurrence of social labelling, stereotyping, separation, status loss and discrimination, as well as the existence of an adverse power structure that allows these factors to facilitate stigmatization. In short, "it takes power to stigmatize" (Link and Phelan 2001, p. 375). This implies that the social production of stigma on an individual or group depends on social, economic, political, and cultural power to activate stereotypes, stimulate discrimination, and link them to undesirable characteristics in society.

Beyond the presence of power structures, scholars argue that the effects of stigma on individuals are shaped by the extent to which those individuals internalize the stigma (Veer, 2009, Alonzo and Reynolds, 1995). In particular, Miller and Major (2000, p.247) suggest that stigmatized individuals will not necessarily "suffer from reduced well being if they use coping strategies that are effective at managing the internal or external demands posed by the appraised threat." Individuals can use coping strategies to protect the threatened individual self, and generate cognitive and behavioral efforts to countervail the stigma threat. In other words, the stigma threat perceived by individuals depends on not only the socio-culturally produced stigma prevalent in society, but also how they manage the stigmatization.

One critical realm for coping with the experience of stigma threat is community. According to Swanson (1985), stigmatized individuals that live in a supportive community can draw vital material and spiritual support from other community members to help them adapt to the social world. Part of this adaption involves challenging the legitimacy of social stigma and re-appropriating cultural meanings that bring harm. An example from a consumer behavior perspective is found in Scaraboto and Fischer (2010), who investigated the "Fat Acceptance Movement" and demonstrated how the action of collectives helps consumers fight stigma and promote social change.

Goffman (1963) posits that stigma is developed through social interaction, and the marketplace is one of the social spaces in which individuals perform and develop their social identities. In recent years, studies have focused on analyzing different groups that suffer from discrimination in the marketplace. Scholars have identified the way individual and collective practices can become instruments that consumers use to not only cope with a stigmatized experience, but also promote a positive self-conception (Adkins and Ozzane 2005, Crosby and Otnes 2010, Hamilton and Catterall 2008, Hamilton and Hassan 2008). However, most studies focus on stigma and coping strategies when people are already stigmatized. Few studies have explored how a stigmatized characteristic is developed and its trajectory over time (e.g Sandikci and Ger 2010), or have used a process-oriented approach to analyze individuals' response strategies while the stigma characteristic is being constructed (see Alonzo and Reynols, 1995 for an exception in the medical literature, who described the stigma trajectory on HIV patients).

The present study analyzes different consumption-related strategies that homeless individuals, and communities related to them, use to alter the power relationship that influences their stigma experience (Link and Phelan 2001). To do so, the study draws upon ethnographic methods including observation, immersion experiences, and depth interviews in two contexts: a shelter dedicated to offer different services to the homeless individuals in the UK, and a US organization that seeks to develop community among homeless people through weekly religious services.

In the first context, the inquiries focus on identifying the different types of stigma that UK and US individuals experience and the consumption-related coping strategies they employ along their pathways to homelessness (Clapham, 2003). Findings reflect how individuals experience different types of stigma during their path into homelessness, as well as the different coping strategies they develop and modify during the time they spend on the streets. We find that informants initially fight their stigma, however, they embrace it during periods of chronic homelessness. Interestingly, we find that some individuals learn to use stigma to their own benefit (e.g. Hiding or highlighting the their stigmatized label to obtain money by begging). Participants range from passive victims to active challengers, and individuals found alternatives in their everyday lives to change the power dynamics and resist the experience of stigmatization

In the second scenario, inquiries are directed to explore the role that collective action and the sense of community with people who do not share the stereotyped characteristic plays in the stigma experience. Findings in this scenario reveal that collective action and the sense of community become the individual's authoritative performances (Arnould and Price 2000), in which the community creates and sustains shared collective traditions that enable individuals to gain power and agency to face the difficult situation they are experiencing. The participation of non-stigmatized individuals within the community experience (i.e. religious service) brings a legitimating view from outsiders that re-orients the social sphere and minimizes focus on stereotypes/status (i.e. "*I don't care if you're homeless or a CEO, in this place all are children of God*").

In conclusion, the study reflects an overlap between manifestations of consumer resistance and coping strategies employed to reduce disadvantages in the marketplace. This phenomenon is consistent with Firat and Venkatesh's (1995) view that in postmodernity, consumption processes have an emancipatory potential.

Vulnerable consumers: Ethnography of the Consumption of French Farmers Facing Impoverishment

EXTENDED ABSTRACT

When Time magazine has a cover title about "France's Rural Revolution: Traditional French farms are dying", we can read between the lines and ask ourselves about the farmers whose farms are dying. Who are those farmers? How does this context impact their life, their family life? How are they facing this transition, this "revolution"? A closer look at this specific population of smallholding farmers (a total of 328.000 families) gives striking figures for the year 2011 showing that more than 39.000 impoverished families of farmers are eligible for welfare assistance such as income support and food bank. The paradoxical phenomenon is such that farmers, who are supposed to feed the people, can no longer feed themselves.

The current research consists of an ethnography of the consumption culture of vulnerable and impoverished consumers. The originality of this study lies in the singularity of farmers as a community, and as a professional group, that is facing a multi-level crisis (international, European, national, regional, departmental, professional, familial, individual).

Within the domain of consumer vulnerability, we have identified calls for research to study unique and specific populations to develop the field of consumer vulnerability (Baker, Gentry, Rittenburg, 2005), and to study impoverished vulnerable consumers in rural areas of developed countries (Hill 2008). Our literature review is three-fold: Marketing and poverty researchers (Townsend 1962, Caplovitz 1962, Andreasen 1993, Alwitt 1995, Adkins and Ozanne 2005, Hill 2008) have first looked at what poor people consume, before looking at the behavior and culture of consumption of those impoverished consumers. Social scientists see poverty as an issue related to the lack of social links and to the inability to express oneself through consumption goods and rites (Douglas 2007). Transformative Consumer Researchers take the approach that research should shed light on consumer issues, and help to improve consumers' lives (Mick 2006).

We propose two research questions. First, how can we characterize and describe the notion of consumer vulnerability in the context of the rural and agricultural space? Second, if we consider that one function of consumer goods is to make culture tangible, then how can we characterize poor farmers' culture of consumption? More specifically, we look at how the experience of vulnerability shapes consumers' response and adaptation to the consumption context. Mary Douglas (2007) describes the cultural theory of apathy as a long-lasting state that emerges when the freedom to choose is suppressed, when socialization networks are destroyed, when despair is stronger than hope. We hypothesize that a way out of this dead end occurs when vulnerable consumers engage in a project of creating new social links through consumption practices.

To follow the tradition inherent to the stream of research on poverty and vulnerability issues, we rely on ethnographic methods such as interviews and observation: individual in-depth unstructured and semi-structured follow-up interviews, group interviews, (Arnould and Wallendorf, 1994); participant observation and analysis of documents (diaries, blogs, forums). Our unit of analysis is the family, i.e three generations (the farmer, the farmer's parents, and the farmer's children). In order to integrate farmers' children, we use children's drawing (Chan, 2006) as a support for the interview.

A French association, dedicated to help farmers facing difficulties, helped us get in touch with their members and access our field of research. During the year 2011, fifteen interviews were conducted, resulting in a focus on three families. We met each family in their farm, and we spent full days with them. Thus, we could observe and share several moments of their daily life in order to develop an in-depth understanding of the material and social world in which our informants live.

From the findings, we have established a typology of farmers that allows us to identify their different reactions and adaptation to vulnerability as consumers. For example, farmers who see themselves as "entrepreneurs" initiate networks of barter economy. Those who continuously redirect their production also experience a lack of stability in their daily consumption. Farmers who remain on the fringe of development inevitably adopt a way of life similar to voluntary simplicity. Over-indebted farmers tend to deny their state of impoverishment and refuse to ask for resources allowances or to go to the food bank.

"Before the mad cow disease, our life was a life of constraints, for sure, and it was ok for us. Being a farmer means having a life of constraints. But today, we suffer from new constraints which we haven't chosen and we drown. We don't know when this will end.

Every day we wake up for work but we lose more money than what we earn. We have given up some habits. We go back to former practices; we live next to nothing, like our grandparents did."

Considering poor farmers' culture of consumption, this quote highlights how families experience vulnerability as a specific period of time which is remembered as a strong event. Then, any single tool or good represents a memory of the family's former and more elaborate material culture: an old coffee mill, the reuse of old sheets to sew up curtains or dresses, the familial hair scissors to avoid the cost of a hairdresser. Staying in touch with their familial roots help those farmers keep the faith in their future. Their motto is henceforth: "*If everyone took care of the little they have, the world would feel bet-*

ter." This peasant common sense par excellence introduces a sensitizing theoretical framework for how families elaborate a system of values underlying their world of consumption.

The findings of this ethnography have the potential to inform social marketing and social business by elaborating a specific knowledge of one kind of hidden poverty. We portray a typology of consumption processes within a vulnerable population, and enhance knowledge of the role of consumption goods in their strategies of identity survival. We also help social marketing actors better target this population of impoverished farmers when preventing bankruptcy, social isolation or suicide.

In Pursuit of Happiness:
Towards Understanding the Complex Relationship Between Consumption and Happiness

Chairs: Jingjing Ma, Northwestern University, USA
Haiyang Yang, INSEAD, Singapore
Neal J. Roese, Northwestern University, USA

Paper #1: Taking Advantage of Real and Perceived Differences between Material and Experiential Purchases

Travis J. Carter, The University of Chicago, USA
Emily Rosenzweig, Cornell University, USA
Thomas Gilovich, Cornell University, USA

Paper #2: More Possessions can Make You Less Happy

Haiyang Yang, INSEAD, Singapore
Ziv Carmon, INSEAD, Singapore
Ravi Dhar, Yale University, USA

Paper #3: The Countability Effect: Comparative versus Experiential Reactions to Reward Distributions

Jingjing Ma, Northwestern University, USA
Neal J. Roese, Northwestern University, USA

Paper #4: When Happiness Doesn't Seem Contingent on Material Goods: The Influence of Positive Affect on Materialism and Conspicuous Consumption

Jin Seok Pyone, Cornell University, USA
Alice M. Isen, Cornell University, USA

SESSION OVERVIEW

The pursuit of happiness is a fundamental goal consumers have. However, the relationship between consumption and happiness is not well understood (e.g., Mick et al. 2011). In this proposed session, we present four research projects that shed light on the complex and surprising effects of consumption on consumer well-being. These four research projects not only offer different theoretical perspectives on the drivers of happiness but also explore a diverse range of consumption contexts. In the first paper, Carter, Rosenzweig, and Gilovich show that consumers can take advantage of the ambiguous nature of the boundary between material and experiential purchases to increase their happiness. That is, happiness is a function of how an acquisition is subjectively categorized by consumers. The second paper by Yang, Carmon, and Dhar challenges the widespread belief that having more material possessions necessarily makes consumers happier. They show that owning multiple goods in the same product category can ironically dampen satisfaction when important attributes of the goods are negatively correlated. Further, the third paper by Ma and Roese shows that fewer material rewards may produce the same amount of happiness as more material rewards. This effect occurs when the reward format involves less easily counted units. In the fourth presentation, Pyone and Isen explore how affect impacts materialistic tendencies. They show that under positive affect, people are less likely to pursue material goods as means to achieve happiness. Each presenter will have 15 minutes to present their paper, leaving 15 minutes for discussions between the presenters and audience.

Our proposed session can contribute substantively to the theme of ACR 2012—appreciating diversity. The research papers in this session investigate the relationship between consumption and happiness in a diverse range of consumption contexts such as consumer choice, post-choice consumption, pre-choice decisions, and responses to reward distributions. These research projects involved a wide array of consumers, including those from the East and West, and in the lab and the field. This session will contribute to theoretical development in the areas of well-being and consumption, and yield important implications for consumers and firms. Further, this session will appeal to a large segment of ACR members interested in judgment and decision making, happiness, and consumer well-being, qualities of lives, materialism, affect, and value sensitivity. This session will also foster discussions of diverse range of topics relating to consumption and happiness, sparking new future research directions.

Taking Advantage of Real and Perceived Differences Between Material and Experiential Purchases

EXTENDED ABSTRACT

A growing body of work suggests that there are genuine benefits to purchasing experiences, intangible purchases such as vacations and concerts, instead of purchasing material possessions, tangible goods such as clothes, trinkets, and electronics (Carter & Gilovich, 2010, 2012; Howell, Pchelin, & Iyer, in press; Nicolao, Irwin, & Goodman, 2009; Rosenzweig & Gilovich, 2011; Van Boven & Gilovich, 2003). Experiences, compared with possessions, appear to be ultimately more satisfying because they are less likely to suffer from invidious comparisons to unchosen options or new information (Carter & Gilovich, 2010), and are more central to one's self-concept (Carter & Gilovich, 2012). What's more, the general tendency to choose experiences over possessions is associated with well-being and life satisfaction (Howell et al., in press). However, as all of this work acknowledges, the categories are not very clearly defined. What makes an experience an experience? What makes a possession a possession? While there are certainly purchases that are clearly experiential (e.g. concerts) or material (e.g. clothes), there are also quite a few that cannot be so easily categorized. An mp3 player is a tangible object, but it also allows one to enjoy the experience of listening to music. How do these ambiguous purchases fit into the overall pattern of findings? What's more, what does such ambiguity say about the underlying properties that define the categories?

To start, we endeavored to examine the types of purchases that participants generated when prompted to recall a material or an experiential purchase. In Study 1, we found that independent raters were easily able to guess, based on the description provided by the participant, which type of purchase they had been assigned to recall. This suggests that, regardless of any fuzziness in the categories, most participants seemed to have little trouble using them. There were some purchases, however, that fell somewhere in the middle, and also appeared to be somewhat middling in terms of their satisfaction. Would it be possible to take advantage of that ambiguity, to take those same purchases and emphasize aspects of one category or the other, to produce the same psychological effects?

In Study 2, we again had participants recall either a material or an experiential purchase, and again found that participants in the experiential condition were more satisfied with their purchases. However, we also asked a third group of participants to recall a material purchase, but we asked them to take a moment to think about its experiential qualities. As expected, we found that this group was just as satisfied as participants in the experiential condition. While the previous study suggested that there are real differences between the categories, this finding indicates that there is a certain amount of latitude in how one thinks about a given purchase.

In the next three studies, we examined that very latitude. We took the same purchase, one that was smack in the middle of that fuzzy boundary between the two types of purchases, and emphasized either its material or its experiential qualities. Participants in Study 3 were asked to think about a boxed set of music either as part of a music collection, something one puts on a shelf, or as an experience, something one listens to. Participants who had been led to think of it as an experience were less bothered by negative comparative information (learning it was now available for a lower price), and thought it would be more satisfying than participants who framed it as a possession.

In Study 4, participants were asked to think about a new 3-D TV as either a possession, emphasizing where it would go in their home and fit in with their other possessions, or as an experience, emphasizing experiencing television in a whole new way and how it would fit with their other activities. We then showed participants several sets of overlapping circles, as in the Inclusion of the Other in the Self scale (Aron, Aron, & Smollan, 1992), and asked them to choose which matched how much they thought the TV would be a part of their self-concept. As predicted, participants in the experiential framing condition chose circles that overlapped to a greater degree, thinking that the more experiential television would be more closely associated with their self-concept.

In Study 5, we looked at the flip side of satisfaction: regret. People tend to feel regrets of inaction about their experiences (i.e. missed opportunities) and regrets of action about their possessions (i.e. buyer's remorse). Would framing a purchase as an experience or possession produce similar patterns of regret? When a 3-D TV was described as an experience, participants felt that the regret of a missed opportunity would be stronger than the regret of buyer's remorse, but not when it was framed as a possession.

It's worth noting that reframing ambiguity may be asymmetric. That is, it may be fairly easy to think of a tangible object in terms of the experiences it affords, but rather difficult, if not impossible, to think about an intangible experience in terms of its material qualities. Fortunately, turning possessions into experiences appears to be the reframing that is most psychologically beneficial.

These studies taken together suggest the differences between the categories appear to have something to do with real, tangible differences between possessions and experiences, but also with certain psychological processes, such as comparison and regret, and perhaps it is those psychological processes that underlie what makes an experience an experience. What's more, the ambiguity in category definitions can actually be taken advantage of – producing greater satisfaction and reduced susceptibility to negative comparative information. In sum, although it's possible that the categories are largely in the mind, it may be the mind that matters.

REFERENCES

Aron, A., Aron, E. N., & Smollan, D. (1992). Inclusion of other in the self scale and the structure of interpersonal closeness. *Journal of Personality and Social Psychology, 63*(4), 596-612. doi:10.1037/0022-3514.63.4.596

Carter, T. J., & Gilovich, T. (2010). The relative relativity of material and experiential purchases. *Journal of Personality and Social Psychology, 98*(1), 146-159. doi:10.1037/a0017145

Carter, T. J., & Gilovich, T. (2012). I am what I do, not what I have: The centrality of experiential purchases to the self-concept. *Journal of Personality and Social Psychology, 102(6)*, 1304-1317.

Howell, R. T., Pchelin, P, & Iyer, R. (2012). The preference for experiences over possessions: Measurement and construct validation of the experiential buying tendency scale. *The Journal of Positive Psychology, 7(1)*, 57-71. doi: 10.1080/17439760.2011.626791.

Nicolao, L., Irwin, J. R., & Goodman, J. K. (2009). Happiness for sale: Do experiential purchases make consumers happier than material purchases? *Journal of Consumer Research, 36*(2), 188-198. doi:10.1086/597049

Rosenzweig, E., & Gilovich, T. (In press). Buyer's remorse or missed opportunity? Differential regrets for material and experiential purchases. *Journal of Personality and Social Psychology*. doi: 10.1037/a0024999

Van Boven, L., & Gilovich, T. (2003). To do or to have? that is the question. *Journal of Personality and Social Psychology, 85*(6), 1193-1202. doi:10.1037/0022-3514.85.6.1193

More Possessions can Make You Less Happy

EXTENDED ABSTRACT

A fundamental tenet of consumerism is that owning more is more desirable than owning less. The yearning for additional possessions is reflected in such impressive statistics as American women on average owning 27 pairs of shoes, and men, 12 pairs (TIME 2006), and average households having 2.9 TV's—more TV's than people (Neilsen 2009). In this research, we challenge that belief, identifying a common condition under which owning more can dampen rather than boost consumption satisfaction.

While prior research sheds important light on how judgments and choices are affected by options being viewed jointly or in isolation (e.g., Botti and Iyengar 2006; Bazerman et al. 1992; Brenner et al. 1999; Hsee and Leclerc 1998; Nowlis and Simonson 1997; Schwartz 2004), the effect of owning multiple goods on consumer satisfaction is not well understood. The current research advances the notion of competing advantages—each good in a set being perceived as better than others on some dimensions yet worse on other dimensions. When the set is consumed, differences between the attributes (e.g., one TV has USB ports; the other, 3D graphics) and attribute values (e.g., one TV has a larger screen but inferior sound quality than the other) become salient. This induces an upward shift of the comparison standard for assessing satisfaction, making each good in the set appear deficient on some dimensions. Because deficiencies tend to be more salient and attention-grabbing (e.g., Pratto and John 1991) and weighted more heavily in evaluations (e.g., Fiske 1980; Mittal et al.1998) than positive attributes, the deficiencies loom larger than sufficiencies. Thus, compared with owning just one good where a comparison standard naturally present in consumers' mind (e.g., the expected consumption experience) is applied to assess satisfaction, owning multiple goods can, ironically, be less satisfying.

The degree to which competing advantages alters comparison standards should depend on the extent to which consumers' standards are developed and stable. Those with high need-to-evaluate (NTE) chronically make more judgments (Jarvis and Petty 1996), possess more developed and stable internal standards (Federico 2004), and are less likely to alter their established views when they encounter additional information pertaining to those views (Albarracín et al. 2004). Consumers with low-NTE are thus likely to be more affected by competing advantages, as their comparison standards for satisfaction assessment are more malleable.

We tested our propositions in the lab and field. In Study 1, participants were randomly assigned one of three consumption sets (Set_{TV1}, $Set_{TV1\&2}$, and $Set_{TV1\&3}$) and asked to imagine owning the good(s). $Set_{TV1\&2}$ had competing advantages—TV1 had both better and worse attributes than TV2. $Set_{TV1\&3}$ did not—TV1 dominated TV3 on all dimensions. Though a pretest established that participants strongly preferred $Set_{TV1\&2}$ over the alternatives in a choice task, those who had this set were significantly less satisfied than those had Set_{TV1} or $Set_{TV1\&3}$. That owning $Set_{TV1\&3}$ was more satisfying than owning the superior $Set_{TV1\&2}$ nicely illustrates the detrimental impact of competing advantages, as TV3 was, by design, objectively inferior to TV2. Further, as an indirect measure of the comparison standard used to assess satisfaction, participants were asked rate the extent to which they thought their TV(s) were imperfect.

As predicted, participants with $Set_{TV1\&2}$ were less satisfied than those who had Set_{TV1}. This negative effect of owning more disappeared when the competing advantages were removed by downgrading the attributes of one of the TV's (downgrading from TV2 to TV3). This suggests that the competing advantages were a cause of the lowered satisfaction, and that the negative effect of owning more could not be accounted for by an averaging mechanism—participants simply averaged their satisfaction with each TV when assessing their overall satisfaction with two TV's. If averaging were driving the effect, those who with an inferior set of two TV's ($Set_{TV1\&3}$) should have been less satisfied than those who with the superior set ($Set_{TV1\&2}$). Finally, the changes in participants' comparison standards mediated the differences in satisfaction.

Study 2 investigated the negative impact of owning more in the field. Consumers took home either multiple framed pictures with competing advantages, or just one. After owning the product(s) for a few days, they responded to measures similar to those in Study 1. They also answered an open-ended question about an ideal framed photo, another measure of changes in the comparison standard. Although a pretest revealed that owning more was clearly preferred in a choice task, participants who owned more were significantly less satisfied. Further, compared to participants who had one good, those who owned multiple goods described significantly more product attributes on the ideal-product measure, and perceived their goods as significantly more imperfect. These changes in comparison standards mediated the effect of owning more on satisfaction.

Study 3 examined whether dispositional differences in Need-to-Evaluate (NTE) moderate the negative effect of owning more, and whether competing advantages reduce satisfaction with individual goods in the consumption set. Accordingly, the Set_{TV1} and $Set_{TV1\&2}$ conditions were identical to those of Study 1, and, in a third condition ($Set_{TV1|TV1\&2}$), participants were given TV1 and TV2 but asked to assess their satisfaction with only TV1. In addition to responding to measures used in Study 1, participants also completed the NTE scale (Jarvis and Petty 1996). As expected, those with low NTE were significantly more affected by competing advantages—they altered their comparison standard more and reported lower satisfaction than those with high NTE. Further, compared to participants with Set_{TV1}, those who received $Set_{TV1|TV1\&2}$ reported significantly lower satisfaction with TV1. Finally, the satisfaction differences across the three conditions were mediated by the changes in comparison standards.

Altogether, our findings cast doubt on whether overflowing closets of clothes and shoes or multiple TV's, necessarily provide higher satisfaction than having fewer possessions. Contrary to popular belief, owning more can, in fact, be less gratifying. Further, our research advances the notion of competing advantages and explicates their impact on comparison standards used to assess satisfaction. Finally, our research yields transformative advice for consumers—owning and consuming less can help the environment and, in and of itself, be more satisfying.

REFERENCES

Albarracín, Dolores, Harry M. Wallace, and Laura R. Glasman (2004), "Survival and Change in Judgments: A Model of Activation and Comparison," in *Advances in Experimental Social Psychology* (Vol. 36), ed. Mark P. Zanna, San Diego: Academic Press, 251-315.

Bazerman, Max H., George F. Loewenstein, and Sally Blount White (1992), "Reversals of Preference in Allocation Decisions: Judging an Alternative versus Choosing among Alternatives," *Administrative Science Quarterly*, 37 (June), 220–240.

Bizer, George Y., Jon A. Krosnick, Allyson L. Holbrook, S. Christian Wheeler, Derek D. Rucker, and Richard E. Petty, (2004), "The Impact of Personality on Cognitive, Behavioral, and Affective Political Processes: The Effects of Need to Evaluate," *Journal of Personality*, 72, 995-1027.

Botti, Simona and Sheena S. Iyengar (2006), "The Dark Side of Choice: When Choice Impairs Social Welfare," *Journal of Public Policy and Marketing*, 25, 24–38.

Brenner, Lyle, Yuval Rottenstreich, and Sanjay Sood (1999), "Comparison, Grouping, and Preference," *Psychological Science*, 10 (May), 225–29.

Federico, Christopher M. (2004), "Predicting Attitude Extremity," *Personality and Social Psychology Bulletin*, 30, 1281-1294.

Fiske, Susan T. (1980), "Attention and Weight in Person Perception: The Impact of Negative and Extreme Behavior," *Journal of Personality and Social Psychology*, 38 (6), 889-906.

Hsee, Christopher K. and France Leclerc (1998), "Will Products Look More Attractive When Presented Separately or Together?" *Journal of Consumer Research*, 25 (2), 175–86.

Jarvis, Blair and Richard E. Petty (1996), "The Need to Evaluate," *Journal of Personality and Social Psychology*, 70(1), 172-194.

Mittal, Vikas, William T. Ross, and Patrick M. Baldasare (1998), "The Asymmetric Impact of Negative and Positive Attribute-Level Performance on Overall Satisfaction and Repurchase Intentions," *Journal of Marketing*, 62 (January), 33-47.

Nielsen (2009), "More than Half the Homes in U.S. Have Three or More TV's," retrieved August 30, 2011, from http://blog.nielsen.com/nielsenwire/media_entertainment/more-than-half-the-homes-in-us-have-three-or-more-tvs/.

Nowlis, Stephen M. and Itamar Simonson (1997), "Attribute-Task Compatibility as a Determinant of Consumer Preference Reversals," *Journal of Marketing Research*, 34 (May), 205–218.

Pratto, Felicia and Oliver John (1991), "Automatic Vigilance: The Attention-Grabbing Power of Negative Social Information," *Journal of Personality and Social Psychology*, 61 (September), 380-391.

Schwartz, Barry (2004), *The Paradox of Choice: Why More is Less*. New York: Harper Collins.

TIME (2006), "TIME Style and Design Poll," retrieved August 30, 2011, from www.time.com/time/arts/article/0,8599,1169863,00.html.

The Countability Effect: Comparative versus Experiential Reactions to Reward Distributions

EXTENDED ABSTRACT

There is general agreement in the fairness literature that people who are under-benefitted are less satisfied than those who are over-benefitted (Adams 1963; Homans 1973; Walster et al. 1978). For example, when compensated for precisely the same work, an employee receiving $10 / hr will be less satisfied than another employee receiving $15 / hr. However, it has become increasingly clear that other factors may moderate the impact of inequity on satisfaction. A key perspective centers on value sensitivity, or evaluability, which reflects the extent to which the magnitude of subjective value is influenced by the magnitude of objective value (e.g., Hsee 1996; Hsee 1998; Hsee et al. 1999; Hsee et al. 2009). As summarized in the recent General Evaluability Theory, the construct of evaluability is defined as "the extent to which a person has relevant reference information to gauge the desirability of target values and map them onto evaluation" (Hsee and Zhang 2010, p. 344).

In the present research, we argue that countability feeds into evaluability, and as such will operate as a powerful moderator of the impact of inequity on satisfaction. When a reward can be easily counted in numerical terms, the effect of inequity on satisfaction is relatively straightforward: those who receive less than they ought to feel less satisfied than those who received more than they ought to. However, when rewards are not so easily counted, people cannot rely so easily on a simple numerical indicator of relative value. Instead, they focus on idiosyncratic aspects of how the reward might be enjoyed at a purely experiential level.

More generally, countability reflects the powerful role that numbers play in our lives. People associate numbers with cardinal values, such that numbers act as representations of internal magnitudes or quantitative values (e.g., Diester and Nieder 2007; Rubinsten et al. 2002). Once these associations are established in mind, they provide a foundation for estimation and comparison that is indispensible in people's lives (e.g. Girelli, Lucangeli, and Butterworth 2000). Research on numerical information processing (e.g., $32 dollars, 20 calories, 500 mg) consistently finds that numerical information is processed relatively rapidly and efficiently (Dehaene and Akhavein 1995; Girelli, Lucangeli, and Butterworth 2000; Tzelgov, Meyer, and Henik 1992; Viswanathan and Childers 1996). This literature thus provides support for our contention that when distributions can be counted in numerical terms, people are more likely to make comparisons and to be more sensitive to inequity than when distributions cannot be counted. Hence, we propose two main hypotheses:

Hypothesis 1:   *Countability moderates the effect of inequity on satisfaction. Although an easily counted over-benefit will evoke greater satisfaction than an easily counted under-benefit, a less easily counted over-benefit and under-benefit will evoke similar degrees of satisfaction.*

Hypothesis 2:   *The underlying mechanism for H1 is that countable rewards evoke comparisons within the reward distribution, whereas uncountable rewards evoke a focus on the experiential aspects of one's own reward.*

With a 2 (benefit: under-benefit vs. over-benefit) x 2 (countability: countable vs. uncountable) between-subjects design, six experiments consistently demonstrated that when rewards can be counted in numerical terms (e.g. two vs. three slices of cake), the under-benefited are less satisfied than the over-benefited, whereas when rewards cannot be counted in numerical terms (e.g. small vs. large cake), the under-benefited are just as satisfied as the over-benefited. This effect was demonstrated across different product categories, across different demographic groups, and across the East vs. West.

Moreover, we examined the underlying cognitive mechanism for the role of countability. Specifically, when participants were prompted to think comparatively (i.e., calculate the numerical amounts of rewards), those in the uncountable condition behaved as though they were in the unprompted countable condition, and when participants in the countable condition were prompted to focus on their consumption experience, they behaved as though they were in the unprompted uncountable condition. Thus, uncountable rewards mitigate the sting of unfair reward distributions in part because they push people to focus more on the experiential aspects of their own reward, while pulling them away from unfavorable upward comparisons to those who received more.

This research extends General Evaluability Theory (Hsee and Zhang 2010) by proposing a new powerful factor – countablility – influencing value sensitivity. It also adds to the literature on how information display influences people's perception by demonstrating that the numerical format of rewards can make people focus more on face value and ignore the possible emotional elements. Moreover, it proposes a new way to mitigate unfairness perception and unhappy feelings in unfair distributions. Making the world an objectively fair place is important, but when unfairness is unavoidable, we should be able to find a way to increase our subjective happiness in unfair situations. Unfair distributions do not necessarily lead to subjective perceptions of unfairness that affect our emotions and behaviors (Weiner 1995). We are a species that relies on emotions and perceptions as inputs into judgments and behaviors, we should learn to deal with potentially negative situations and nonetheless derive eventual happiness from them. This idea of subjective approaches to unfair situations is one contribution of this article. Although the cake distributions are objectively unfair, we may still enjoy our small cake if we do not count it!

REFERENCES

Adams, Stacy (1963), "Towards an Understanding of Inequity," *The Journal of Abnormal and Social Psychology*, 67 (5), 422-36.

Dehaene, Stanislas and Rokny Akhavein (1995), "Attention, Automaticity, and Levels of Representation in Number Processing," *Journal of Experimental Psychology: Learning, Memory, and Cognition*, 21 (2), 314-26.

Diester, Ilka and Andreas Nieder (2007), "Semantic Associations between Signs and Numerical Categories in the Prefrontal Cortex," *PLoS Biology*, 5 (11), 2684-95.

Girelli, Luisa, Daniela Lucangeli, and Brian Butterworth (2000), "The Development of Automaticity in Accessing Number Magnitude," *Journal of Experimental Child Psychology*, 76 (2), 104-22.

Hatfield, Elaine, G. William Walster, and Ellen Berscheid (1978), *Equity: Theory and Research*, Boston, MA: Allyn and Bacon.

Homans, George (1961), *Social Behaviour: Its Elementary Forms*, Oxford: Harcourt, Brace.

Hsee, Chrisopher, George Loewenstein, Sally Blount, and Max Bazerman (1999), "Preference Reversals between Joint and Separate Evaluations of Options: A Review and Theoretical Analysis," *Psychological Bulletin*, 125 (5), 576-90.

Hsee, Christopher (1996), "The Evaluability Hypothesis: An Explanation for Preference Reversals between Joint and Separate Evaluations of Alternatives," *Organizational Behavior and Human Decision Processes*, 67 (3), 247-57.

Hsee, Christopher (1998), "Less Is Better: When Low Value Options Are Valued More Highly Than High Value Options," *Journal of Behavioral Decision Making*, 11 (2), 107-21.

Hsee, Christopher, Yang Yang, Naihe Li, and Luxi Shen (2009), "Wealth, Warmth, and Well-Being: Whether Happiness Is Relative or Absolute Depends on Whether It Is About Money, Acquisition, or Consumption," *Journal of Marketing Research*, 46 (3), 396-409.

Hsee, Christopher and Jiao Zhang (2010), "General Evaluability Theory," *Perspectives on Psychological Science*, 5 (4), 343-55.

Rubinsten, Orly, Avishai Henik, Andrea Berger, and Sharon Shahar-Shalev (2002), "The Development of Internal Representations of Magnitude and Their Association with Arabic Numerals," *Journal of Experimental Child Psychology*, 81 (1), 74-92.

Tzelgov, Joseph, Joachim Meyer, and Avishai Henik (1992), "Automatic and Intentional Processing of Numerical Information," *Journal of Experimental Psychology: Learning, Memory, and Cognition*, 18 (1), 166-79.

Viswanathan, Madhubalan and Terry Childers (1996), "Processing of Numerical and Verbal Product Information," *Journal of Consumer Psychology* (4), 359-85.

Weiner, Bernard (1995), *Judgments of Responsibility: A Foundation for a Theory of Social Conduct*, New York: The Guilford Press.

When Happiness Doesn't Seem Contingent on Material Goods: The Influence of Positive Affect on Materialism and Conspicuous Consumption

EXTENDED ABSTRACT

Much of the previous research has investigated how materialism influences happiness (e.g., Belk 1984; Van Boven and Gilovich 2003). On the other hand, relatively little research has been conducted on the reverse, the influence of positive affect on materialism. In the present research, we examine how mild positive affect that people experience in everyday life influences materialistic and conspicuous consumption behavior.

Based on the affect literature suggesting that positive affect leads to more flexible thinking (Isen 2008) and broadened scope of attention and cognition (Fredrickson and Branigan 2005), we hypothesize that positive affect enables people to think about aspects of their life and their happiness more flexibly (i.e., they can think of various ways of pursuing happiness other than acquiring material goods), and thus they are less likely to rely on material goods as a primary source of happiness or self-worth, while neglecting its other sources.

First, in order to examine a lay theory of materialism, in a pilot study we asked participants to describe materialism in their own words. They defined materialism broadly in two ways: 1) valuing material goods over other, or abstract, values in life (e.g., family or friendship), and 2) engaging in consumption behavior in order to "show off" or signal status. In five studies, we tested the influence of positive affect on materialism as represented in prior research and the lay ideas generated above.

Study 1: What Makes You Happy? Participants were randomly assigned to either a positive or a neutral affect condition. Affect was manipulated using a video clip: a mildly amusing clip (showing a dancing hippo) or a neutral clip (showing moving color bars). After the affect induction task, materialism was measured in a way similar to that used by Chaplin and John (2007). Participants were asked to list things that make them happy using six categories: Hobbies, Material Things, Achievements, Sports, People, Other. A ratio index of materialism was obtained by dividing the number of material items by the total number of items, for each participant. The results revealed that people in positive affect reported lower materialism ratios than did those in neutral affect.

Study 2: Money Allocation II -Material vs. Experiential Purchase. In Study 3, following the research by Van Boven and Gilovich (2003), we measured materialism in terms of the type of purchases people pursue (material or experiential). After the affect induction task (as in Study 1), participants were asked what specific things they would like to buy or do with the $500, and to indicate the amount of money they allotted to each item. A materialism index was created for each subject, by subtracting the amount allocated to experiential purchases (e.g., going out to dinner with friends, skiing) from that to material purchases (e.g., new clothing, handbags). Results showed that people in positive affect allocated a smaller portion of the money to material purchases (relative to experiential purchases), than did the controls.

Study 3: Conspicuous Consumption I. In Studies 4 and 5, we measured materialism in terms of the underlying motive for buying material goods: the degree to which people want to signal wealth or social status. Participants (all female) were randomly assigned to a 2 (affect) x 2 (signal: high, low) between-subjects design. After the affect induction task, participants were told that they would evaluate a high-end product. Half of the participants saw an image of a Gucci handbag with a salient brand-logo (high signal), and the other half saw a Gucci bag with no logo (low signal). Results revealed that people in neutral (vs. positive) affect perceived the good with the salient logo as more attractive, wanted to own it more, and were willing to pay more for it.

Study 4: Conspicuous Consumption II. In Study 5, Conspicuous consumption was measured among male subjects. Participants (all male) read product descriptions about cars from two different brands: a Low-end model from BMW and a Premium model from Mazda. The BMW model was described so that participants could see that its performance (e.g., engine, fuel efficiency, horsepower, etc) was inferior to that of the Mazda, but as superior as a status symbol. Participants then were asked to make a choice between the two models. The results showed that positive-affect people were more likely to choose the high-end Mazda (performance) over the low-end BMW (status) than were controls.

In sum, results of four studies suggest that under mild positive (vs. neutral) affect, people are less likely to rely on material goods as a primary source of happiness, while neglecting its other sources, and also less likely to engage in conspicuous consumption (i.e., signal status through material goods).

REFERENCES

Belk, Russell W. (1984), "Three Scales to Measure Constructs Related to Materialism: Reliability, Validity, and Relationships to Measures of Happiness," in *Advances in Consumer Research*, Vol. 11, ed. Thomas Kinnear, Provo, UT: Association for Consumer Research, 291–97.

Chaplin, Lan Nguyen and Deborah Roedder John (2007), "Growing Up in a Material World: Age Differences in Materialism in Child and Adolescents," *Journal of Consumer Research*, 34 (4), 480-93.

Fredrickson, Barbara L. and Christine Branigan (2005), "Positive emotions broaden the scope of attention and thought-action repertoires," *Cognition and Emotion,* 19 (3), 313-32.

Isen, Alice M. (2008), "Some ways in which positive affect influences problem solving and decision making," in *Handbook of Emotions*, eds. Michael Lewis, Jeannette M. Haviland-Jones, and Lisa Feldman Barrett, NY: Guilford, 548-73.

Van Boven, Leaf and Thomas Gilovich (2003), "To do or to have? That is the question," *Journal of Personality and Social Psychology*, 85, 1193-202.

Inside the Turk:
Methodological Concerns and Solutions in Mechanical Turk Experimentation
Chair: Gabriele Paolacci, Erasmus University Rotterdam, The Netherlands

Paper #1: Data Collection in a Flat World: Strengths and Weaknesses of Mechanical Turk Samples

Joseph K. Goodman, Washington University in St. Louis, USA
Cynthia E. Cryder, Washington University in St. Louis, USA
Amar Cheema, University of Virginia, USA

Paper #2: Screening Participants on Mechanical Turk: Techniques and Justifications

Julie S. Downs, Carnegie Mellon University, USA
Mandy B. Holbrook, Carnegie Mellon University, USA
Emily Peel, Carnegie Mellon University, USA

Paper #3: Under the Radar: Determinants of Honesty in an Online Labor Market

Daniel G. Goldstein, Microsoft Research, USA
Winter Mason, Stevens Institute of Technology, USA
Siddharth Suri, Microsoft Research, USA

Paper #4: Non-naïvety Among Experimental Participants on Amazon Mechanical Turk

Jesse Chandler, Princeton University, USA
Pam Mueller, Princeton University, USA
Gabriele Paolacci, Erasmus University Rotterdam, The Netherlands

SESSION OVERVIEW

Online labor markets allow "requesters" to recruit "workers" for the completion of computer-based tasks. One such market, Amazon Mechanical Turk (AMT), offers a convenient means of accessing a relatively diverse population. The speed and ease with which data can be collected on AMT has led to considerable interest in using it to collect experimental data, as indicated by the large and growing number of publications that rely on AMT data over the past few years (>400 in the social sciences alone) and self-reports by researchers subscribed to the major mailing lists in social psychology and decision-making (>50% have used AMT).

Initial evaluations of AMT as a source of data have emphasized its compelling strengths, notably the comparatively diversity of workers and the possibility of conducting research on a common population. In a nutshell, these studies have found that AMT workers produce quality data, and are more representative than other convenience samples.

Fewer efforts have been made to explore and quantify potential unique drawbacks and limitations of using AMT to collect social science data. This special session focuses on some of the issues that threaten experimental validity on AMT and on providing easily implementable solutions to avoid these problems.

The four papers included in the session deal with diverse issues. Joe Goodman discusses differences between AMT workers and more traditional subject populations that are of high relevance to consumer behavior research. Julie Downs discusses strategies for restricting data collection and data retention to attentive participants, together with their implications for the generalizability of AMT data. Dan Goldstein addresses issues of participant honesty, including the results of experiments designed to detect dishonest behaviors among AMT participants and identify some of their predictors. Gabriele Paolacci addresses the issue of non-naïvety among AMT workers by presenting studies about cross-talk and duplicate participation and provide simple remedies to attenuate this concern.

The special session contributes to the conference mission of appreciating diversity by focusing on a research method – web experimentation – that expands diversity in two important ways. First, it allows researchers to access a more representative, and certainly more heterogeneous population that traditional subject pools. Second, it democratizes science, by making these populations available to all researchers at a low cost and with minimal technical knowledge, eliminating geographic constraints and reducing financial constraints on research. Taken together, the four proposed contributions will provide attendees with a comprehensive view of how to make the best use of this resource, while avoiding common, but not widely discussed threats to data quality.

Data Collection in a Flat World: Strengths and Weaknesses of Mechanical Turk Samples

EXTENDED ABSTRACT

Mechanical Turk (AMT), an online labor system run by Amazon.com, provides quick, easy, and inexpensive access to online research participants. As use of AMT has grown, so have questions from behavioral researchers about its participants, reliability, and low compensation. A main concern about using AMT for research is that participants who are willing to participate in a study for well below the minimum wage must be unusual. And, most importantly, they might be unusual in ways that challenge the validity of research investigations. Researchers have verified that AMT demographic responses are accurate (Rand, 2012), validated the psychometric properties of AMT responses (Buhrmester, Kwang, & Gosling, 2011), and replicated some of the classic findings in behavioral economics (Horton, Rand, & Zeckhauser, 2011; Suri & Watts, 2010) and decision-making research (Paolacci. Chandler, & Ipeirotis, 2010). However, research has not thoroughly investigated differences between AMT participants and traditional samples on attention, personality, financial, and consumption dimensions. In this paper we review recent research on using AMT and compare AMT participants to community (Study 1) and student (Study 2) samples on several dimensions, finding many similarities between AMT participants and traditional samples, but also finding important differences that are relevant to consumer research.

In Study 1 we examine whether AMT participants are less attentive to study instructions than college student samples. We measured the rate at which participants pay attention by administering an attention test or Instructional Manipulation Check (IMC; Oppenheimer, Meyvis, & Davidenko, 2009) requiring careful reading of study materials. Similarly, we investigated whether AMT participants have different cognitive capabilities compared to non-AMT participants by administering the Cognitive Reflection Test (CRT; Frederick, 2005). Our results showed that AMT participants performed more poorly on the IMC and CRT compared to student participants. More importantly, we found that simply administering the attention test and filtering participants by whether they correctly answered the IMC or not reduced statistical noise; including participants who failed the IMC reduced the likelihood of finding statistically significant differences between groups on other dimensions. Though we found that IMC failure was correlated with a participant being from outside the US or a non-native speaker of English, the results suggest the IMC was the most efficient filter as it both excluded fewer people and reduced Type II error.

For consumer behavior researchers, it is especially important to examine whether AMT participants differ in terms of how they value and spend money and time. Given that AMT participants are willing to complete tasks for little money, some have questioned their valuation of money and time. To address this issue, in Study 2 we compared AMT participants, college students and a community sample on their preferences for time and money (Cryder & Loewenstein, 2010), their material values (using the Material Values Scale; Richins, 2004), and how averse they are to spending money (using the Tightwad-Spendthrift scale; Rick, Cryder, & Loewenstein, 2008). We also compared AMT and non-AMT participants on the Big Five dimensions of personality (Gosling, Rentfrow, & Swann Jr., 2003) and global self-esteem (Robins, Hendin, & Trzesniewski, 2001).

Our results showed that compared to non-AMT participants, AMT participants were significantly (p's < .05) less extraverted, less emotionally stable, and had lower self-esteem. AMT participants also exhibited attitudes about money and time that were more similar to student participants than to community participants, valuing money more than time, reporting more materialistic values and feeling more averse to spending money (p's < .05) than the community sample. Compared to students, AMT participants were equivalent on all these dimensions. It seems that AMT participants may be similar to students in terms of their financial outlook.

Given the low compensation of AMT participants, AMT participants might also respond unusually to decision tasks involving money and risk. We explored this proposition by testing for present bias and discounting asymmetries (Loewenstein, 1988; Malkoc & Zauberman, 2006), risk aversion for gains, risk seeking for losses, and the certainty effect (Kahneman and Tversky, 1979). Our results showed that AMT participants exhibited the same effects as the student population. AMT participants were present-biased, showed delay/expedite asymmetries, were risk averse for gains, risk seeking for losses, and showed the certainty effect—but no more so than other samples.

Recent research about the use of AMT for behavioral research has concluded that AMT has many benefits, making it suitable for a wide range of behavioral research. We agree: We found that AMT participants generally produced reliable results that are consistent with previous decision making research and we found many commonalities between AMT participants and our traditional samples, contributing to this growing literature (Buhrmester et al., 2011; Paolacci et al., 2010; Rand, 2012). However, we also found important differences between AMT participants and community and student participants. To mitigate concerns that may arise from these differences, we discuss and recommend to researchers the use of screening procedures to measure participants' attention levels and acknowledge that AMT participants may vary from non-AMT participants on social and financial traits.

Screening Participants on Mechanical Turk: Techniques and Justifications

EXTENDED ABSTRACT

Concerns about the quality of Amazon Mechanical Turk (AMT) participants have led researchers to use a variety of screening techniques. Some researchers use screening data to disqualify participants in real time, punishing them for their poor performance, and some use it to omit suspicious data at the time of analysis. We assess several strategies for restricting data collection and data retention, evaluating them according to their discriminant power to identify observations contributing only noise.

We evaluated four categories of screening techniques: 1) meta-data from typical surveys, such as time on task, and depth of responses; 2) pre-screening of participants, such as limiting participation to those meeting a threshold of performance in the AMT system; 3) integral aspects of survey design, such as incentives and required responses; and 4) responses to questions included specifically to identify "poor" participants, such as gold standard questions (for which there is an objectively correct answer, unlike most survey responses). Some gold standard questions are unobtrusive, whereas others communicate their purpose to participants (e.g., by asking participants to give non-standard answers). The latter type, sometimes called Instructional Manipulation Checks (IMC; Oppenheimer, Meyvis, & Davidenko, 2009) has the potential to change participant responses in systematic ways. By randomizing whether these questions appeared at the beginning or end of the task, we created a measure of the impact of obtrusive gold standard questions on responses (conditional on passing). We included two types of criteria to assess the effectiveness of each screening technique: reliability of measures, and effect sizes of established psychological phenomena. For reliability, we used classic individual difference scales (e.g., Need for Cognition, with a Cronbach's alpha in the mid-90s; Caciopppo & Petty, 1982), as well as measures of internal consistency on behavioral tasks (e.g., choosing between lotteries that varied along dimensions of risk). For phenomenological effect sizes, we used classic demonstrations of cognitive performance and bias in judgment and decision making, such as the Stroop task and the framing effect. In addition to assessing the level of noise in the data between the screened-out and retained populations, we examined responses from these populations for evidence of systematic differences on our measures. Participants located in the US were recruited into five different surveys on AMT, each paying the equivalent of about $8 per hour, to approximate minimum wage, plus a possible bonus in some cases, to incentivize performance. For most surveys (except where noted) we required 500 or more completed AMT tasks and an approval rating of 95% or higher.

Each category of screening technique will be reviewed in turn. Simple meta-data did not prove to be useful in identifying noisy observations. The fastest 8% of respondents performed no worse than the population as a whole (N = 302, z = 0.08, p = .936), and the fastest 3% (10 of 302 participants, who performed remarkably fast with a slight discontinuity from the rest of the sample) performed only very slightly worse (z = 0.73, p = .465). The slowest 3% of the sample performed slightly better than the rest of the sample, although not significantly so. Although the faster and slower respondents did not produce notably noisier data than their more average peers, these respondents did differ along certain individual difference measures, with faster responders scoring lower in Need for Cognition and slower responders scoring higher. Removing standard pre-screening criteria did not reduce reliabilities compared to those who were required to have a large number of completed tasks and a high approval rating (N = 403; z = 0.58, p = .562). Requiring responses did not significantly improve reliabilities (N = 303; z = 1.18, p = .238). Reducing the payment rate to one-quarter of minimum wage (25¢ for an 8-minute task) had no notable effects on reliabilities (N = 346; z = 0.10, p = .920). Participants who failed gold standard questions did not perform any worse in reliabilities than those who passed (N = 178; z = 0.27, p = .787), although other differences in performance did emerge. Measures of bias did differ in some of the populations that would be omitted based on the various screeners, and obtrusive gold standard questions had moderate effects on some outcome measures, including changing the effect sizes of some measures of judgment bias. These effects will be discussed in more detail.

Consistent with other research, data quality in this sample was reasonable. Furthermore, screening strategies failed to identify meaningful subsets of the population who were contributing mere noise to the data. Although these findings cannot attest to full engagement of all participants in the tasks, they also cannot support the practice of omitting participants based on screener performance without concern about biasing the sample (at least in US populations). For example, although time stamps are a popular technique that can be used without adding to participant burden to omit people taking too little (or too much) time, these individuals' data did not warrant exclusion from analyses. Indeed, the systematic differences between high and low performance on many screening tools suggest that omitting participants based on these indicators would likely bias the sample rather than merely reduce noise. We suspect that the internal reputation system used by Amazon is effective in dissuading participants from attempting to game the system.

Under the Radar: Determinants of Honesty in an Online Labor Market

EXTENDED ABSTRACT

Many institutions and social systems depend upon some degree of honesty to function as intended. The legal system, for example, is predicated on honest testimony, and oaths are used with the goal of promoting truth-telling. Moreover, many economic transactions assume a truthful description of what is being sold or a promise that an agreement will result in a payment.

For online labor markets like AMT, honesty between the employers and employees helps the market to be efficient. Employers who trust the work of the employees, and employees who trust that payment will be rendered by the employer, both benefit from an environment in which honest dealing is the norm. Consumer behavior research, which relies heavily on self-report, is hard to verify, meaning that under prevalent dishonesty, such markets would be of limited interest to researchers.

Standard economic models capture the belief that people trade off the benefits of cheating with the costs of getting caught (Allingham & Sandmo, 1972; Becker, 1968). On AMT the costs of getting caught at any individual time are arguably low–a worker might only have their work rejected. However, consistently dishonest behavior can lead workers to be banned from the site. The frequency of cheating is an open question, determined both by the hassle of creating a new account, and recultivating the reputation necessary to complete much of the more lucrative work. Additionally, The pragmatic benefits of cheating sit in tension with people's intrinsic motivation to avoid feeling like they are dishonest (e.g., Mazar, Amir, & Ariely, 2008) and to maintain the appearance of honesty to others (Hao & Houser, 2011). Thus, it is not a priori clear how much dishonesty would be exhibited by workers in an online labor market.

The central focus of this work is measuring the degree to which workers on AMT are honest and determining which factors affect their honesty. Fischbacher and Heusi (2008) conducted a study which is the inspiration for this work. In a series of offline laboratory experiments, the authors had participants roll a die in private and report their roll. Participants were paid proportionally to the value they reported (with the exception of rolling six, which paid nothing). Since the experimenter could not see the roll, the participant could report any number. While each number would be expected 17% of the time, the subjects reported a roll of four 27% of the time and reported a roll of five 35% of the time. A roll of six, the lowest paying

roll, was only reported 6.4% of the time, suggesting dishonest reporting. In addition to this baseline treatment, the authors conducted additional treatments where they increased the stakes (by a factor of three), ensured the anonymity of the participants, and changed the victim of the lie from the experimenter to another subject. These treatments did not have a large impact on the distribution of reported rolls.

In this work, we seek to understand the determinants of dishonesty in experiments in which payment can be affected by lying. We asked participants on AMT to roll die (at home or using a randomizer website, as they wished) and to report the values of the rolls, which gave them both ample opportunities to lie and no chance of being caught lying on any single roll (since we, as experimenters, could not observe the participants).

In the first experiment, we replicate the basic effect. Participants report a die roll between one and six and are paid 25 cents per pip (spot on the die). The average roll, under honest reporting, would be 3.5. The average of the reported rolls was 3.91, significantly higher than chance (p < .0005), with the distribution of rolls heavily favoring fives and sixes.

The second experiment asked whether people would report more honestly if there were less to be gained by lying. In the first experiment, the ratio of payouts between the worst and best roll (taking the flat fee into account) was 3.5, giving a strong incentive to cheat. In the second study, this ratio was reduced to merely 1.24. However, despite having less to gain, participants cheated as much in this condition as in the baseline, showing surprising insensitivity to what can be gained through dishonesty. Furthermore, participants from India and the US cheated by the same amount, again suggesting that the stakes are not a key determinant of cheating.

Given that cheating seems relatively unrelated to the magnitude and variance of the payouts, the third and fourth experiments ask whether the probability of detection may drive the decision to cheat. In all studies reported above, including those by other researchers, participants rolled a die just one time before reporting their answer. In such a situation, a six is just as likely as a one. However, when reporting, for example 10 rolls, it is less likely that the sum of these rolls would equal 60 by chance as it would equal, say, 35. If participants have a grasp of intuitive statistics, they would realize the experimenter could reject the null of honest reporting over multiple rolls if the sum of the die exceeds a certain number (or if the distribution of values reported deviates significantly from uniformity). In a large randomized experiment, participants rolled a die either 2, 3, 5, 10, or 20 times and were paid proportional to the sum of the result. Consistent with the view of people as intuitive statisticians, participants continued to cheat in a way that was easily detectable at the aggregate level, but undetectable at the individual level.

Non-naïvety Among Experimental Participants on Amazon Mechanical Turk

EXTENDED ABSTRACT

Certain experimental paradigms strongly rely on participant naïvety, either as a precondition for an effect to emerge, or to prevent experimental demand effects. Prior knowledge about the purpose of an experiment, familiarity with an experimental manipulation, or reason to suspect deception, can influence participant responses. While traditional subject pools offer a continuous supply of naïve participants, this is less true of AMT, where workers can complete an unlimited number of experiments. Given the popularity of AMT among consumer researchers, it is important to know whether concerns of non- naïvety among AMT workers are negligible or not.

Further, if non- naïvety is prevalent, it is pressing to come up with solutions that can be implemented by single researchers or scientific communities to mitigate this problem. In this work, we discuss two potential sources of non-naivety on AMT.

One important phenomenon that affects participant naïvety is cross-talk between participants. Empirical research on college undergraduate populations has demonstrated that participants do share information with each other, at least when sufficiently motivated (e.g., when incentives are offered for a correct response; Edlund, et al., 2009). The web offers great opportunities for cross-talk: Indeed, AMT workers maintain online forums where they share information and opinions, which could potentially lead to foreknowledge in experimental participants.

A second concern is participation in experiments that share independent or dependent measures. AMT automatically prevents workers from completing a single task multiple times. However, it is still possible that participants are recruited for experiments that are conceptually or methodologically related to experiments they have previously completed. Our survey data (Study 1, N = 300) show that cross-talk is not a critical issue on AMT. Only 26% of participants reported knowing personally someone else who used AMT, and only 28% reported reading forums and blogs about AMT. Further, when asked to rank the reasons why they discuss or read about AMT, the actual purpose or contents of the tasks are far less important than pragmatic considerations such as the amount requesters pay or their reputation. Only half of the respondents who actually read blogs (about 13% of the overall sample) reported ever seeing a discussion about the contents of a social science research study online. Such low levels of reported cross-talk can hardly contribute substantially to participant non- naïvety. However, researchers should probably monitor discussion boards that refer a lot of respondents, and conclude their experiments by asking workers how they found the task. We also highlight the less tangible effects of workers discussing the reputations of individual experimenters and research institutions.

Duplicate participation is a more serious concern. 55% of our worker sample from Study 1 reported having a list of favorite requesters and monitoring their tasks (indeed, browser plug-ins are available that do this automatically), and 58% of the time this list included academic researchers. Data from a follow up conducted one year later showed that these percentages became 63% and 71% respectively, suggesting that this is a growing concern. Moreover, a substantial proportion of workers reported participating in some of the more common and easily describable experimental paradigms (e.g., 52% of Study 1 participants played an Ultimatum Game, becoming 83% one year later).

In order to obtain more reliable information about duplicate participation, we pooled the data from several researchers who had received a total of 16,408 completed submissions (Study 2). The tasks included in this sample had been completed by a total of 7,498 workers. The average worker completed more than two studies, with the most prolific 10% of the workers (N = 750) responsible for 41% (N = 5,864) of the completed submissions. Taken together, these results suggest that duplicate participation is a potential source of non-naïvety that cannot be neglected by researchers who use AMT. At a minimum, experimenters should ask participants whether they have completed similar experiments before and treat prior participation as an additional factor in their data analysis. We offer several practical solutions that allow duplicate workers to be filtered out before they participate, saving money, and eliminating the concern that excluding duplicate workers may contribute additional researcher degrees of freedom.

The very features that make online labor markets appealing to researchers, such as its accessibility, lead to some concerns about whether experimental participants are naïve enough to participate in all experiments. Whereas participant cross-talk seems not to constitute a problem, care is required to deal with duplicate participants.

REFERENCES

Allingham, M. G., & Sandmo, A. (1972), "Income tax evasion: A theoretical analysis," *Journal of Public Economics*, 1, 323-338.

Becker, G. (1968), "Crime and punishment: An economic approach," *Journal of Political Economy*, 76(2), 169-217.

Buhrmester, M., Kwang, T., & Gosling, S.D. (2011), "Amazon's Mechanical Turk: A new source of cheap, yet high-quality, data?," *Perspectives on Psychological Science, 6,* 3-5.

Cacioppo, J. T. & Petty, R. E. (1982), "The Need for Cognition," *Journal of Personality and Social Psychology*, 42 (January), 116-31.

Cryder, C., & Loewenstein, G. (2010), "The time versus money scale," Unpublished data, Olin Business School, Washington University in St. Louis.

Edlund, J. E., Sagarin, B. J., Skowronski, J. J., Johnson, & S. J., Kutter, J. (2009), "Whatever

happens in the laboratory stays in the laboratory: The prevalence and prevention of participant crosstalk," *Personality and Social Psychology Bulletin, 35,* 635-642.

Fischbacher, U., & Heusi, F. (2008), "Lies in disguise: An experimental study on cheating (Research Paper Series No. 40)," *Thurgau Institute of Economics and Department of Economics at the University of Konstanz.*

Frederick, S. (2005), "Cognitive reflection and decision making," *Journal of Economic Perspectives, 19,* 25-42.

Gosling, S.D., Rentfrow, P.J., & Swann Jr., W.B. (2003), "A very brief measure of the big-five personality domains," *Journal of Research in Personality, 37,* 504-528.

Hao, L., & Houser, D. (2011), "Honest lies," *Discussion Paper, Interdisciplinary Center for Economic Science, George Mason University.*

Horton J.J., Rand D.G., & Zeckhauser R.J. (2011), "The online laboratory: Conducting experiments in a real labor market," *Experimental Economics*, 14, 399-425.

Loewenstein, G. (1988), "Frames of mind in intertemporal choice," *Management Science*, 34, 200-214.

Malkoc, S. A., & Zauberman G. (2006), "Deferring versus expediting consumption: The effect of outcome concreteness on sensitivity to time horizon," *Journal of Marketing Research*, 43, 618-627.

Mazar, N., Amir, O., & Ariely, D. (2008), "The dishonesty of honest people: A theory of self-concept maintenance," *Journal of Marketing Research*, 45, 633-644.

Oppenheimer, D., Meyvis T., & Davidenko N. (2009), "Instructional manipulation checks: Detecting satisficing to increase statistical power," *Journal of Experimental Social Psychology*, 45, 867-872.

Paolacci, G., Chandler, J., & Ipeirotis, P. G. (2010), "Running experiments on Amazon Mechanical Turk," *Judgment and Decision Making, 5,* 411-419.

Rand, D.G. (2012), "The promise of Mechanical Turk: How online labor markets can help theorists run behavioral experiments," *Journal of Theoretical Biology, 299*(4), 172-179.

Richins, M. L. (2004), "The material values scale: Measurement properties and development of a short form," *Journal of Consumer Research, 31,* 209-219.

Rick, S. I., Cryder, C. E., & Loewenstein, G. (2008), "Tightwads and spendthrifts," *Journal of Consumer Research, 34,* 767-782.

Robins, R. W., Hendin, H. M., & Trzesniewski, K. H. (2001), "Measuring global self-esteem: Construct validation of a single-item measure and the Rosenberg Self-Esteem Scale," *Personality and Social Psychology Bulletin, 27,* 151-161.

Suri, S., & Watts, D. J. (2011), "Cooperation and contagion in webbased, networked public goods experiments," *PLoS One, 6*(3).

Gender and Family Identity

Chairs: Paul M. Connell, City University London, UK
Hope Jensen Schau, University of Arizona, USA

Paper #1: Gender and Family Identification in Television Narratives: Homophilization and Appropriation
Hope Jensen Schau, University of Arizona, USA
Cristel Russell, American University, USA
David Crockett, University of South Carolina, USA

Paper #2: Gender Norms, Family Identity, and the Performance of Motherhood Using Commercial Childcare
Aimee Dinnin Huff, University of Western Ontario, Canada
June Cotte, University of Western Ontario, Canada

Paper #3: Negotiating "the new father": the consumption of technology within the contemporary family
Shona M. Bettany, Hull University, UK
Ben Kerrane, Bradford University, UK
Margaret K. Hogg, Lancaster University, UK

Paper #4: The Influence of Gendered Interfamily Coalitions on Intergenerational Transfer
Paul M. Connell, City University London, UK
Hope Jensen Schau, University of Arizona, USA

SESSION OVERVIEW

This session brings together four papers that examine an important but neglected area in consumer research: gender roles and family identity. Because the growth of non-traditional families frequently violates traditional gender roles and norms as defined by society, investigating the interplay of gender identity and family identity is of crucial importance in understanding consumption in modern families. All of the papers in the session take a consumer culture theory (CCT) perspective and use ethnographic data, specifically interviews and observation, to examine these nuances of gender and family identity.

The first paper in the session (Schau, Russell, and Crockett) investigates how family and gender representations within television narratives are appropriated by consumers and linked to their consumption choices. The second and third papers in the session examine unique challenges to family identity for mothers (Huff and Cotte) and for fathers (Bettany, Kerrane, and Hogg). The final paper (Schau and Connell) investigates how gender roles within families influence intergenerational transfers between mothers and fathers and their children.

Collectively, the papers' findings should have broad appeal for attendees interested in consumer culture. The session will be of particular interest to researchers examining the roles family identity and gender identity play in consumption. In addition, given that several of the papers in the session examine constraints consumers face or conflicts within families, the session will also have appeal to members of the transformative consumer research community.

This session is particularly well-suited for the conference's mission on appreciating diversity. The research not only examines gender roles and unique identity challenges faced by both female and male consumers, but also includes changing family roles and nontraditional families. Furthermore, attendees to this session will be exposed to consumer perspectives from Canada, the United Kingdom, and the United States. The four papers in this session offer completed work by scholars who are esteemed for their work on family and gender identity

Gender and Family Identification in Television Narratives: Homophilization and Appropriation

EXTENDED ABSTRACT

We explore how family and gender representations within television narratives are appropriated by consumers and linked to their consumption choices. In contemporary culture, family and gender have multiple, highly contested meanings (Spigel 1992). Television instantiates reigning cultural logics; it is a prime medium for acculturation (Morley 1988), where consumers observe and adopt the cultural logics and consumption practices depicted in the narratives. Consumers must engage and reconcile polysemic texts as they construct and communicate their family and gender identities (McKinley 1997). We posit that television viewing is uniquely important in addressing questions about how family and gender take on meaning and impact consumption.

We asked 137 young adults (19-39 years) to create a collage centered on a TV-based character's consumption choices and to complete an online semi-structured questionnaire about their collage. A subset of these collage creators (N = 22) also participated in an interview about their collage: using the collage in a manner analogous to Heisley and Levy's (1991) autodriving, participants were asked to walk the researcher through their collages discussing the meanings they attributed to the brands, the significance of their inclusion and placement within the collage, and how the collages related to the participants' own consumption constellations (Solomon and Englis 1992) and identities.

Our data reveal that consumers identify with television narratives through a process we term "homophilization": they actively envision various features of television narratives as similar to their own lived experience, even if the similarities are not readily apparent to a casual observer. The data show that homophilization is enacted primarily by customizing the narrative, or textual poaching (Jenkins 1992), where consumers insert themselves into the narrative, at times bending both the narrative and their own lived experience to achieve resonance, and further that consumption choices serve as primary mechanisms for poaching. Interestingly, our data show that the consumers relate to the media text primarily through the lens of family of origin (their childhood family), rather than as a family of procreation (romantic partner and children), friends, colleagues, or neighbors. The consumers consistently draw on gendered roles within families of origin to anchor their identification.

Our informants describe the myriad narratives available in the mediascape and the lengths they go to identifying with the characters as members of their family of origin. This may best be shown using a specific data example. One informant described a void in the mediascape to explain her choice of a classic television program, *The Cosby Show* because, "I love the premise: a strong black upper middle class family talking about morals, education, ethics and music." When asked if she was like the characters in the show, she responded, "Well, no... I'm a 34 year old black woman... I'll never be a doctor like he was on the show, or a lawyer like Clair, his wife on the show. I'll just never be. My family was not middle class. We lived pay check to pay check. We still do... It kept me in school." She notes her gender difference from Bill Cosby, as well as a wide social class gulf between family life as she experiences it and as portrayed on *The Cosby Show*. Yet, she indicates that when she watches the show she identifies Cosby as a father figure. She cites the exceptional nature of the depiction of middle class black family life as her main motivation for watching the show which she still accesses to fuel her identification. She credits the show's emphasis on education and Cosby's father figure depiction with encouraging her to remain in college, to consume higher education.

Consumers revise, or retrofit media narratives to coalesce with their own lives, seamlessly merging the depictions and their idiosyncratic lived experience. In the example, this occurs even though the defunct *The Cosby Show* narrative is quite different in family and gender depiction from her own family of origin which contained a single mother and a mostly absent father. Here, our informant, as a 34 year old woman with two children of her own could have identified with the narrative as a family of procreation (she in the role of mother). Instead she draws discrete comparisons between the media text and her life, and actively identifies with the television family the Huxtables as members of her family of origin.

At times the homophilization may be attributed to aspirations (as in the above) but need not be. For example, a 21 year old informant sees Monica of *Friends* as a "mother" to the rest of the group. As such, she references the brands that symbolize, based on her family experience, an inviting home. She imagines Monica would use Kitchen Aid, stating "One of my first memories regarding this product is when I was 10 years old and my father bought me my first mixer, it [the one in the Monica collage] was the one that he got me." The informant's own family experiences shape how she envisions both Monica and motherhood. Here, the homophilization occurs, consumption is implicated, and the textual poaching to make that happen bends both the narrative and her own experience of family: Monica is not a mother in the narrative and the informant's experience with the consumption object is actually through her father. The same informant also imagines Monica uses a specific brand of coffee, Maxwell House, though it is never depicted on the show because her parents served it to household guest.

Our data reveal consumers engaging in active homophilization through textual poaching that bends the narrative and/or their lived experience until there is a tenable perceived similarity and implicates consumption as a tangible signifier of identification. Consumers consistently opted to identify with the narrative through the lens of family of origin as opposed to a family of procreation, or no familial identification at all (friends, colleagues, neighbors) and cite gendered roles within the family as explicit points of connection.

Gender Norms, Family Identity, and the Performance of Motherhood Using Commercial Childcare

EXTENDED ABSTRACT

Gender and identity are heavily implicated in consumption. Prior research has established that consumption can facilitate gender performance and identity work by providing symbols and resources to enact gendered identity (e.g., Holt and Thompson 2004; Thompson 1996). More recent work has revealed that consumption can complicate gender performance and identity work, particularly for consumers in a period of transition; competing discourses, ideologies, and gender norms can create new tensions for consumers as they engage in identity projects (The VOICE Group 2010a, b; Zayer et al. 2012). Consumption can also be problematized by gender discourses that are no longer dominant (Fischer, Otnes, and Tuncay 2007), which raises questions about how traditional and contemporary gender roles shape and are shaped by consumption. Further, questions remain about how family identity – a family's subjective sense of itself – is influenced by individual members' identity work

and consumption practices (Epp and Price 2008). In this research, we focus on mothers' experiences using commercial childcare as they pursue careers. Our goal is to understand how childcare consumption facilitates and problematizes mothers' identity work, influences how motherhood is performed in relationships between mother and children, and is co-constitutive of collective family identity.

Much of the current consumer research on gender and family identity focuses on the consumption of products, particularly those of importance, such as the integration of a special heirloom into a family home (e.g., Epp and Price 2010; Thomsen and Sørensen 2006). We build on this body of research by exploring the consumption of a service in everyday life. In foregrounding the routine use of a service, we are able to examine the ways that motherhood is both produced and consumed, and the ways that the marketplace influences family identity at individual, relational, and collective levels (Epp and Price 2008; Hogg, Curasi, and Maclaran 2004).

Motherhood plays a prominent role in women's gender performance (Christopher 2012). We focus on mothers with careers because these women are likely to experience strong tensions between the dominant logic of the marketplace, which emphasizes productivity and self-interest, and the dominant logic of motherhood, which emphasizes selflessness (Friedan 1963/2001; Hays 1996; Zelizer 2005). On a daily basis, these women encounter competing gender norms, including norms for contemporary working women, and more traditional norms associated with motherhood (Collins 2009). Consequently, mothers need to reconceptualize how they perform motherhood, because the daily caregiving of their children is outsourced to a service provider (Christopher 2012).

To address our research goal, we conducted depth interviews with four women who have young children in childcare and who classify themselves as professional. The interviews were conducted face-to-face in informants' homes, and lasted approximately 90 minutes. We sampled purposively for mothers who were eager to return to work after taking maternity leave from their careers. Our data included 93 single-spaced pages of transcripts and field notes. We used a hermeneutic approach to analyze and interpret the data (Thompson, Pollio, and Locander 1994), and engaged in peer debriefing.

In our sample, each informant is married, a loving mother, and has a career that required post-secondary education and a professional designation. Informants are very pleased with the quality of childcare they are currently using, and note that their children enjoy going. Further, each informant reveals that they did not enjoy their maternity leaves (ranging from 1 to 12 months) as much as they had expected; they found themselves unfulfilled by the mundane tasks of full-time childcare, and sought the feelings of achievement and productivity that came from their careers.

Following the framework of family identity put forth by Epp and Price (2008), we examine the intersection of gender and family identity in the context of commercial childcare consumption. We begin by revealing how mothers' individual identity work is shaped by competing conceptions of fulfillment, which plays a prominent role in the lives of professional women. Our informants reveal that fulfillment can be conceptualized in traditional ways, wherein fulfillment is achieved through intensive mothering and domestic work, and in more contemporary ways, wherein fulfillment must include some degree of productivity in the marketplace. These opposing perspectives of fulfillment complicate women's gender performance (Tropp 2006; Zayer et al. 2012).

Next, we demonstrate that the use of commercial childcare reframes our informants' relationships with their children. This relational identity is reconstructed as mothers outsource daily childcare. Our informants demonstrate gender fluidity as they draw on traditional and contemporary norms to perform motherhood in the time they do share with their children. Unscripted, child-focused leisure time takes precedence over domestic labour, and women re-conceptualize motherhood to involve managing childcare rather than providing it (Christopher 2012; Epp and Price 2012; Johnston and Swanson 2006), which has implications for the identity enactments of this relational group.

Last, we uncover the ways that family identity is shaped by use of childcare. Our data are somewhat limited in this regard, but we sketch out how families enact collective identity when young children are in commercial care during regular working hours. Our informants contrast their own families' activities with those of families with stay-at-home mothers, and reveal that nonmaternal childcare challenges and reinforces the family's sense of itself (Epp and Price 2008).

This work contributes to our understanding of gender, family identity and consumption. We begin to tease apart the traditional and contemporary gender roles, and reveal how they influence mothers' identity, mothers' relationships with their children, and collective family identity. By foregrounding childcare consumption, we are able to shed some light on the ways that routine, everyday consumption facilitates and complicates gender performance and family identity.

Negotiating "The New Father": The Consumption of Technology Within the Contemporary Family

EXTENDED ABSTRACT

In consumer research, the negotiation of the relation between fatherhood and masculinity as expressed and reproduced through consumption practices and processes has been identified as a research area in need of further investigation (Gentry *et al.,* 2003; Davies *et al.,* 2009). In this research we undertake such an investigation using the specific case of fathers engaging in their first transition into fatherhood. We focus on the inextricably linked negotiation processes of first time fatherhood and masculinity around the choice, consumption, and use of technological consumption objects typically purchased during this period.

It has been documented in the wider social sciences and consumer research that the relation between masculinity and fatherhood is contested, complex and contentious (Davies *et al.,* 2009; Gentry *et al.*, 2003; Miller, 2011). Specifically, the discourses which frame men's transitions into first time fatherhood sit uneasily between more traditional expressions of hegemonic masculinity (Connell, 1995) (for example, father as breadwinner and economic provider), and more recent articulations of the involved and nurturing fatherhood (Gatrell, 2007; Wall and Arnold, 2007). Hegemonic masculinity, the ability of the dominant group to obtain consent from those being subjugated, frames fatherhood within certain conceptions of masculinity (Williams, 2008) as bound up in the breadwinner model. Such cultured stereotypes of masculinity are suggested to inhibit care-giving or nurturing behaviour (Russell, 1986) in favour of economic fatherhood alone (Townsend, 2002). Whilst some maintain that there has been relatively little change in the input of fathers into family life (see, for example, Demos and Acock, 1993; Jamieson, 1999), others argue that men *are* becoming more involved in family life, challenging traditional notions of hegemonic masculinity (O'Brien and Shemilt, 2003; Warin *et al.*, 1999). At the nexus of these conflicting discourses, the important contemporary cultural figure of "the new father" has emerged.

The new father emerges, it is argued, as an effect of a range of policy, economic, demographic and cultural shifts, rendering this figure as both responsible financially for his offspring (Townsend, 2002) and, in addition, as an important and (ideally) equal caregiver and nurturer within the family dynamic (Miller, 2011). Implicated and entwined in this emergence of "the new father" are both reproductions of, and challenges to, gender norms, including the negotiation of what masculinity and fatherhood means, reproductions of hegemonic masculinity and the emergence of new, competing masculinities (Connell, 1995).

Utilising Laclauian discourse analysis, we examine how "the new father" emerges as an "empty signifier" within the field of discursivity around the transition to fatherhood; and how chains of equivalence emerge and are maintained within the family setting which allow for the simultaneous challenging and reaffirmation of hegemonic masculinity within the negotiations of consumption (and other) family practices and processes during this transitional period.

Laclauian discourse analysis has been used to examine the intersections of culture, politics and cultural identity and to examine the formation of hegemonies within cultural and political settings. As such, we suggest, it is well positioned to provide a theoretical framework and toolkit to examine the multiple articulations of masculinity implied in this study (Carpentier and Spinoi, 2008). The power dynamics of familial relations at this specific time in family formation, and the implications for gendered identity formation, utilisation and reinforcement suggest the requirement for a theoretical framework that can not only explain identity formation but also expose the complex political machinations and power struggles within the family that ultimately conclude in the reproduction of common sense of "what it is to be a man" at this crucial transitional time.

Utilising ethnographic data, we examine how three "must have" technological consumption objects, "the baby buggy", "the baby monitor" and "the baby car seat" emerge as important nodal points around which power and gender relations within and around the family are negotiated, and hegemonic gender norms are simultaneously challenged and reaffirmed. We found key episodes around the consumption and use of these products where these processes of "gender trouble" are played out. We conclude that although the purchase and use of technological products provide a refuge for new fathers within this challenging transitional period, allowing expressions of hegemonic masculinity, that the figure of the new father allows the expression of newer discourses of caring masculinity and nurturance to be appropriated. We demonstrate how these technology-suffused products become symbols of masculine power and domination over women and nature within the family but, in addition, how they simultaneously become important nodes for contestation of patriarchal gender relations.

The Influence of Gendered Interfamily Coalitions on Intergenerational Transfer

EXTENDED ABSTRACT

Intergenerational transfer is a pervasive yet poorly understood consumer behavior. The small amount of research in the field has acknowledged and/or observed gendered patterns of intergenerational transfer. For example, Fournier (1998) finds evidence of brand preferences that are passed down from mother to daughter. Similarly, other research has observed disposition of special possessions to subsequent generations in gender-stereotypic ways, such as fishing poles to male family members and dishes to female family members (Curasi, Price, and Arnould 2004; Price, Arnould, and Curasi 2000). Perhaps recognizing the impact of gender in intergeneration transfer, Moore, Wilkie and Lutz (2002) conducted their study on intergenerational transfer entirely within the context of mother-daughter dyads.

However, gender roles have not been the focus of this research, leaving a major gap in understanding this widespread phenomenon.

Because one's gender is a culturally persistent part of one's identity, we believe it plays a profound role in how intergenerational transfers manifest themselves within families. Epp and Prices (2008) describe how family identity operates at individual (each person within the family), relational (interfamily coalitions), and collective (the entire family) levels. We believe that gender roles within the family are likely to particularly influence the nature of intrafamily coalitions as they relate to intergenerational transfers. Thus, in this research we specifically examine how coalitions within families are formed around identity-centered consumption that is passed down from one generation to the next.

In the spirit of discovery-oriented consumer research to develop new theories (Wells 1992), we used depth interviews to draw on key themes that emerge from the data (Glaser and Strauss 1967). Depth interviews allow us to gain emic understanding through detailed discussion and probing the informant about complex inspirations and experiences (McCracken 1988). To locate relevant field sites and recruit informants, we opted for theoretical sampling (Glaser and Strauss 1967; Miles and Huberman 1994). We interviewed 27 informants about practices they had either adopted from their parents or had passed along to their children. Sixteen of these informants belonged to one of five families where we interviewed multiple family members that represented different generations within the family. Three key patterns emerged from our data: (1) a parent tended to favor engaging in intergenerational transfers with same-sex child in gender-stereotypic ways that exclude opposite-sex children, (2) a parent tended to disengage from intrafamily identity projects that were aligned in gender-stereotypic ways with their opposite-sex family members, even if they supported these identity projects, and (3) a parent tended to engage in gender-neutral intergenerational transfer with opposite-sex children if same-sex children were not in the household.

We will first examine the instances in which a parent tended to favor engaging in intergenerational transfers with same-sex child in gender-stereotypic ways that exclude opposite-sex children. We observed this pattern in nearly all of our interviews that involved dyads or networks of individuals within families that belonged to the same sex. As gender is a pervasively salient part of one's identity in Western culture (Eagly and Wood 1999), it is not surprising that parents would seek to instill those aspects of their gender identity in their same-sexed children. When intergenerational transfer attempts were well-received by same-sex children, the frequent result was a synergistic relational family identity project involving the parent and his/her same sex child(ren). We observed that even with consumption that could be construed as gender-neutral (e.g., collecting Disney movies and merchandise or sports), this was often defined along gender lines (e.g., Disney "princesses" among mother and daughter or football among father and son). Thus, opposite-sex children were excluded from these intrafamily coalitions. We observed that these consumption coalitions, while facilitating relational family identity among same-sex family members, often created tension between the coalition and opposite-sex family members. Sadly, these tensions that often involved feelings of isolation, jealousy, and resentment were seldom recognized by members of the coalition. Interestingly, excluded family members seemed less concerned about their inability to participate in the consumption in question, but rather felt that it served as an impediment to building family identity with their opposite-sex family members. We did observe exceptions where opposite-sex children chose to engage in the coalitional practice anyway (e.g., a daughter playing sports when it was clearly identified in the family as a male activity). When this was the case, it often resulted in open conflict among the parent and the opposite-sex child that potentially drove them farther apart.

Next, we will examine when a parent tended to disengage from intrafamily identity projects that were aligned in gender-stereotypic ways with their opposite-sex family members. In contrast to the situation when a child was excluded from gendered intergenerational transfers, we did not observe cases where a parent felt resentful or envious of such consumption in our data. Rather, the parent was often supportive of these identity projects if they felt it facilitated relational family identity-building among their spouse and opposite-sex child(ren). However, in cases where intergenerational transfer attempts strongly encouraged by the spouse but were met with resistance from the child(ren), then support for these intergenerational transfers among opposite-sex parents began to wane because they no longer viewed the consumption as facilitating family identity-building.

Finally, in many families a parent does not have any same-sex children, and is not content with merely playing supporting role to their spouse's gendered intergenerational transfers to the family's children. In this case, the parent tended to engage in what they viewed as gender-neutral intergenerational transfer with their opposite-sex children. For example, one informant described wanting to share his love of Lego building blocks with his daughter because "Legos are for everyone."

While intergenerational transfer is a pervasive behavior, and is clearly influenced by gender, research on this phenomenon has been practically nonexistent. When it has been addressed in the literature, it has typically been relegated to the sidelines. We hope that our research, as the first in-depth investigation into the influence of gender roles on intergenerational transfers within families, will spur additional inquiry into this important phenomenon.

The Mere Idea of Money Alters Consumer Welfare, Preferences, and Morality

Chairs: Avni Shah, Duke University, USA
Kathleen D. Vohs, University of Minnesota, USA

Paper #1: Reminders of Money Focus People on What's Functional

Kathleen D. Vohs, University of Minnesota, USA
Cassie Mogilner, University of Pennsylvania, USA
George Newman, Yale University, USA
Jennifer L. Aaker, Stanford University, USA

Paper #2: The Paradox of Payment: The Moderating Effect of Pain of Payment on Buying Behavior as the Number of Alternatives Increases

Avni Shah, Duke University, USA
James R. Bettman, Duke University, USA
John Payne, Duke University, USA

Paper #3: People Pay More When They Pay-It-Forward

Minah H. Jung, University of California Berkeley, USA
Leif D. Nelson, University of California Berkeley, USA
Ayelet Gneezy, University of California San Diego, USA
Uri Gneezy, University of California San Diego, USA

Paper #4: Clean Versus Dirty Money Produce Wildly Different Effects on Behavior

Kathleen D. Vohs, University of Minnesota, USA
Qing Yang, Sun Yat-Sen University, China
Xiaochang Wu, Sun Yat-Sen University, China
Nicole L. Mead, Católica University Portugal, Portugal
Roy F. Baumeister, Florida State University, USA

SESSION OVERVIEW

Money is crucial to surviving and thriving in modern life. Most obviously is its use as a tool, but perhaps more intriguing is its far-ranging ramifications for the self, interpersonal relationships, and morality. This session features cutting-edge research on the psychology of money, showing how it not only affects spending (and how to aid consumer welfare in the process) but also how it affects moral judgments and interpersonal behavior.

The first talk by Mogilner will discuss three experiments demonstrating that reminders of money shift people's focus toward functionality. Prior work has shown that reminders of money harm interpersonal connectedness, but Mogilner's talk will discuss how to reverse that effect. People plan to socialize more and actually socialize better (as rated by their partners) after socializing is framed as a functional behavior – i.e., a networking opportunity. Even more telling is the additional finding that money reminders shift moral judgments in a classic "trolley problem" game, whereby money primed participants are more likely to say they would push one person off of a bridge to save five others. Money and functionality are tied together in a much more basic way, of course, namely through spending money to obtain desired goods and services. Yet spending situations in which the choice size is large can be stressful, leading people to exit the spending situation without purchasing. The second talk by Shah will discuss how to assuage consumer feelings during a spending situation with a large choice size, using several clever manipulations that reduce the pain of paying. In doing so, her findings show that not only does spending increase but consumers report feeling less decision conflict and being more satisfied than otherwise.

Spending is also a part of the story that the third talk, by Nelson, will discuss — but not spending in a traditional way. Nelson's work attempts to understand how people think about how much money to

spend when it is completely up to them to price the product. Using a novel manipulation, consumers entering a museum are told that another customer already has paid for his or her entry and they are given the opportunity to pay for a future customer. The question is how much will consumers then pay when they are paying for a future customer in this Pay-It-Forward pricing scheme. The results show that in comparison with Pay-What-You-Wish pricing (which is economically identical), Pay-It-Forward pricing scheme yields higher revenue. Last, the interpersonal and moral dimensions of money are at the forefront of Vohs's presentation. In her work, money that is crisp, clean, banknotes or money that has been soiled in dirt for several days is used as a manipulation to activate notions of fairness or greed. Using these manipulations, she finds consistent evidence that clean money produces fair trade and honest responding, whereas dirty money elicits moral violations, greed, and dishonesty.

In summary, this session tackles some of the big questions about money's effects on consumer psychology. How do various forms of money affect spending, relating, and moral behavior? The answers to these questions and many more will be revealed in the current session. The issues examined in this session have important implications for policy and societal well-being, as well as basic scientific understandings of the psychology of money. As a result, this session will appeal to researchers interested in the self, interpersonal relationships, morality, judgment and decision making, as well as those interested in policy or managerial decision-making. This session speaks to the theme of diversity in several ways. First, the papers presented collectively embrace a diverse set of research methodologies, using field and laboratory experimental methods, as well as survey and qualitative methodologies. Second, the diverse population of those studied, undergraduate students, graduate students, and the general public. Finally, money is as close to a universal uniter as any contemporary cultural construction. As a consequence we expect that a diverse set of scientists, policymakers, and scholars will find value in the session.

Reminders of Money Focus People on What's Functional

EXTENDED ABSTRACT

A growing body of research has shown that thinking about money makes people less socially inclined. Reminders of money lead people to be less likely to help others, less likely to ask others for help, more likely to maintain physical distance from others (Vohs, Mead, and Goode 2006), more impervious to social rejection (Zhou, Vohs, and Bauemeister 2009), more threatened by affiliation attempts (Liu, Vohs, and Smeesters 2011), and less motivated to socialize (Mogilner 2010). These results have been explained by the observation that money serves as a supremely functional resource that allows individuals to be self-sufficient, not relying on others to obtain what they want and need (Lea and Webley 2006; Vohs et al. 2006). Here, we explore the possibility that, beyond money serving as a tool, merely focusing on money may increase people's own functionality. That is, reminders of money may lead individuals to behave more functionally. Furthermore, this functionality may result in individuals behaving more prosocially—when it serves a functional benefit.

Across three studies we test this hypothesis that money makes people functional. The results show that, compared to neutral primes, money primes increase individuals' tendencies to choose behaviors that are more functional in nature. Furthermore, in instances where prosocial behaviors are functional, these findings demonstrate that thinking about money can make individuals *more* socially inclined, rather than less.

Experiment 1 tested whether participants primed with money would be better able to make a tough, emotionally-laden moral decision in order to benefit a greater number of people. First, participants were asked to complete a "guessing task" in which they were shown a series of eight magazine covers and were asked to guess the year and month that the particular cover appeared. For participants in the money prime condition, the magazine covers were from Money magazine and the word "money" appeared in large block letters on all of the covers. For participants in the control condition, the covers were all from Scientific American magazine.

Next, participants were asked to respond to an ostensibly unrelated dilemma – the moral dilemma posed by the Trolley Problem. Two common variants of the trolley problem were used. In the flip-the-switch variant, participants were told that there was a runaway trolley headed toward five people and the only way to save them was by flipping a switch, which would divert the trolley on to a second track that contained one person. In the push-the-man variant, participants were again told about a trolley headed toward five people. However, in this case the only way to save them was to push an overweight man onto the track. Participants were asked, "How likely would you be to flip the switch [push the man] in order to save 5 people?" The results showed that priming money increased participants' likelihood of diverting the trolley to save five people, particularly in a situation in which people are less likely to endorse this option (the push-the-man variant).

Previous research has shown that priming money makes people less motivated to socialize when it is solely for the sake of interpersonal connection (Mogilner 2010). Experiment 2 thus tested whether participants primed with money would be *more* motivated to socialize when socializing was framed as functional (i.e., good for one's health). First, participants read a short newspaper article and were told that they would subsequently be asked related questions. Participants were randomly assigned to read either an article that espoused the health benefits of spending time with friends or a control article about jellyfish. Then, half of the participants completed a sentence unscramble task that surreptitiously exposed them to money-related words. Participants who did not complete this task comprised the control condition. All participants then went on to complete a survey about how they planned to spend their day. The results showed that after reading the control article, participant primed with money planned to socialize less than the control participants; however, after reading the article that highlighted the functional health benefits of socializing, participants primed with money planned to socialize more.

Experiment 3 tested whether participants primed with money actually socialized better when socializing was framed as being functional (i.e., a networking opportunity). First, participants completed a sentence unscramble task that exposed them to money-related words or all neutral words. Then, participants were informed that they would have the opportunity to interact with another student for 10 minutes. For some, this interaction was framed as a networking opportunity, and for the rest it was simply framed as an opportunity to get to know someone. The participants were then paired up and given 10 minutes to talk. Following the interaction, participants rated their partner in terms of how much they would like to interact with them in the future, etc. We relied on each participant's partner's ratings to assess the quality of participants' socializing. The results

revealed that in the normal social frame, participants primed with money were worse at socializing than those in the control condition; however, when the interaction was framed as a networking opportunity, participants primed with money were more charming.

Together, these results suggest that reminders of money make people behave more functionally and, in some cases, more prosocially—when doing so has serviceable benefits.

The Paradox of Payment: The Moderating Effect of Pain of Payment on Buying Behavior as the Number of Alternatives Increases

EXTENDED ABSTRACT

In an economy with increasing product variety and mounting financial debt, we ask how the number of alternatives affects consumer behavior and well-being and how the pain of payment influences this relationship. There is accumulating evidence that as the number of alternatives increases, buying initially increases and then decreases (Shah & Wolford, 2007). Two processes account for this function. First, as the number of alternatives increases, there is a positive monotonic effect of choice size on matching consumer preferences. However, as choice increases, there is a negative monotonic effect of choice size and cognitive load. As the number of alternatives increases, consumers are more likely to have two or more alternatives that meet their criteria and are close in subjective value, resulting in increased effort and search cost (Schwartz, 2000, 2004; Shugan, 1980), lower choice accuracy (Payne, 1976), lower decision satisfaction (Malhotra, 1982), increased post-decision regret (Schwartz, 2004), and greater choice avoidance (Dhar, 1997; Dhar and Simonson, 2003; Iyengar & Lepper, 2000). An U-shaped function describes how buying as the number of options increases as a result of these two forces. Across three studies, we examine whether attenuating the pain of payment through either payment mechanism (credit/debit card versus cash) or by reducing the price moderates the inverted-U finding. That is, reducing the pain of payment may lead to increased buying and higher post-decision satisfaction as the number of alternatives increases.

When people make purchases, the pain they feel from giving away a piece of their wealth reduces the pleasure they feel about purchasing a product (Prelec & Loewenstein, 1998). Furthermore, the 'pain of payment' varies for different payment mechanisms. Money in the form of legal tender conjures more thoughts of payment than other payment mechanisms (Raghubir & Srivastava, 2008). Attenuating the pain of payment associated with a purchase (e.g., paying with a credit or debit card versus cash) leads consumers to not think as much about the negative attributes of their purchase resulting in more positive evaluations overall (Chatterjee and Rose, 2011). We hypothesize that reducing the pain of payment through payment mechanism will increase buying and satisfaction as the number of alternatives increase by lowering the cognitive costs, affective costs, and decision conflict associated with purchase.

Experiment 1 tested whether reducing the pain of payment by paying with a credit or debit card increased buying as the number of alternatives increased. Experiment 1 had a 2 (mode of payment: cash, student 'plastic' card) X 10 (number of alternatives: 2, 4, 6, 8, 10, 12, 14, 16, 18, 20) between subjects design. The price for each pen varied from $0.70 to $1.50. In a field experiment, students were invited to purchase a pen from a given choice set using their own money in order to elicit true buying behavior. Half of the participants could only pay with cash while a different set of participants could only pay with a student debit/credit card commonly used on campus. As predicted, for cash consumers, buying behavior was a curvilinear function of the number of alternatives, resulting in an inverted U-shape consistent with previous research (Shah and Wolford, 2007; Iyengar and Lepper, 2000). For card consumers, initially buying increased as a function of the number of alternatives. However, in contrast to cash consumers, buying did not significantly decrease for choice sets with more alternatives. For those who bought across conditions, consumers paying with plastic bought more pen units overall than consumers paying with cash.

Study 2 sought to replicate the findings of Experiment 1, gain greater insight into potential processes driving the effects, and also rule out an alterative explanation. Experiment 2 had a 2 (mode of payment: cash, student 'plastic' card) X 2 (purchase restriction: unlimited pen purchase, single pen purchase) X 5 (number of alternatives: 2, 6, 10, 14, 18) between-subjects design. Students passing through common areas were invited to purchase a pen from a set of alternatives using their own money and were restricted to purchasing only one pen if they so desired. We also sought to rule out an alternative explanation that budget constraint differences could be driving the effect by restricting consumers to purchasing at most one pen. Plastic card consumers may have responded to tradeoff difficulties between options by purchasing all suitable options because they were less constrained. With a purchase restriction, consumers could spend no more than $1.50 regardless of the payment mechanism. As predicted, pain of payment via payment mechanism moderated the effect of an increasing choice set on buying regardless of restriction level. Buying behavior as the number of alternatives increased was described by an inverted U-shape function for cash consumers, while plastic card consumers did not significantly decrease buying. In addition, plastic card consumers spent less time making a purchase decision (lowered cognitive costs) and reported higher levels of post-purchase satisfaction (lowered affective costs) than cash consumers.

In Study 3, we examined whether an alternative method for reducing the pain of payment, manipulating the cost of the items would moderate the choice overload effect. Study 3 had a 2 (mode of payment: cash, student 'plastic' card) X 3 (number of alternatives: 4, 10, 16) X 3 (price per pen: $0.25, $1.00, $2.00) between-subjects design. Again, students were restricted to one pen per purchase from a given choice set using their own money. Consistent with our theory, reducing the price of the pen to $0.25 moderated the inverted U-shape, with individuals buying more in higher choice sets. For plastic card consumers, increasing the price of the pen to $2.00 led to an inverted U-shape, with individuals buying less in the higher choice sets.

In summary, reducing the pain of payment associated with the purchase through payment mechanism or price moderates buying behavior as the number of alternatives increases. This research advances our understanding of choice overload. Furthermore, these results provide evidence that the pain of payment can significantly influence consumer decision-making and welfare.

People Pay More When They Pay-It-Forward

EXTENDED ABSTRACT

In daily economic transactions, people often follow the norms of market exchange: seeking the lowest possible prices in order to find the highest possible value. This narrative neglects the fundamental social forces at play in an exchange. Our research considers the consequences for a shift from market-determined fixed prices, to customer-dictated flexible prices. What happens when a company asks its customers to simply pay whatever price they want? That shift – from a pure market transaction to one steeped in fairness, donation, and giving – upends established knowledge about consumer behav-ior, and opens questions about how such a market could work, and when it could thrive.

Pay-what-you-want pricing has grown in popularity, and is most frequently seen in its basic format: a company offers a good or service and the customer can pay any price he or she would like (typically including $0). Past research highlighted how much small variants can influence the success of such a program. For example, in one large experiment, when people learned that half of their payment would go to charity, people paid six-times as much (Gneezy et al. 2010). That treatment offered a better product to the customer, was maximally profitable for the firm, and also yielded a substantial charitable surplus. This small pricing tweak uniformly increased total social welfare.

Our research considers an even more fundamental change to pay-what-you-want (PWYW) pricing. What if payments were all gifts? What happens when people have an option to pay for someone else (and are told that someone has already paid for them)? Such pay-it-forward (PIF) pricing has identical commercial features (e.g., the option to pay $0), but invokes a very different set of social norms. We predict that people's willingness-to-pay is higher when they pay forward than pay what they want. In three studies we test this prediction and investigate some of the factors that might explain higher payments in the PIF pricing model.

In our first study, museum visitors (N = 311) saw either PWYW or PIF admission prices. As we predicted, people paid a higher amount for their admission to the museum under PIF pricing than PWYW pricing (M = $3.12 vs. $1.89). This field study suggests that when people pay what they want, they pay more for someone else than they do for themselves.

Perhaps people paid more because they felt something of an obligation for the other customers? Consistent with this possibility, prior research has shown that social preferences are heavily influenced by knowledge of, and experience with, the givers and recipients of prosocial acts (Small & Loewenstein, 2003; Roth,1995; Hoffman et al., 1996; Bohnet & Frey, 1999; Xiao & Houser, 2005). In Study 2, we tested the role of social interaction in people's willingness-to-pay in PWYW and PIF pricing in a controlled lab setting. Perhaps increased social interaction would differentially influence PWYW and the comparatively socially-oriented PIF pricing schemes. Participants (N = 294) interacted with the previous participant (the gift giver in PIF conditions), the next participant (the gift receiver in the PIF conditions), or no one, immediately prior to the experiment. At the end of the session, participants were presented with a coffee mug and asked to either pay-what-they-want or pay-it-forward to the next participant.

People paid more for a coffee mug under pay-it-forward than under pay-what-you-want (M = $1.79 vs. $1.27). However, contrary to our predictions, social interaction did not influence payments in the PIF conditions. Interestingly, there was a persistent effect that across all conditions people thought that the previous participant and the next participant paid more than they did. Furthermore, those estimates of the payments of others were particularly heavily influenced by the payment manipulation: people think that others will pay more under PIF than PWYW.

These results suggested that PIF operated in two stages. Something about the manipulation led participants to believe that other people were paying more. Based on that assessment, participants raised their own payments to match their new perceived norms. If that is true, we reasoned, then we should be able to eliminate the influence of PIF by simply informing participants about the payments of others. We tested this prediction by telling approximately half of the participants (N = 198) that the previous participant had paid $1.50, whereas the remainder were not told this.

Consistent with our prediction, and with the previous findings, when people did not know how much the previous participant had paid, they paid more under PIF than under PWYW (M = $2.48 vs. $1.19). When participants learned how much the previous person had paid this effect was eliminated and people paid about the same amount under PIF and PWYW (M = $1.21 vs. $1.23).

In summary, Pay-it-Forward leads to higher payments than does Pay-What-You-Want. This effect was not influenced by social interaction with the giver or the receiver of the gift. However, the effect was entirely eliminated when participants had a clear reference price of others' payments. People appear to believe that, because PIF must increase the payments of others, they should increase their own payments to match.

Clean Versus Dirty Money Produce Wildly Different Effects on Behavior

EXTENDED ABSTRACT

The present research began with the view that many people hold two distinct sets of associations about money. On one hand, money may evoke ideas of greed, exploitation, selfishness, corruption, and other unsavory, antisocial patterns, especially because many such antisocial actions have been performed throughout history in order to obtain money. Money may therefore elicit immoral sentiments and harmful behavior. Yet, money facilitates culture, fair trade, philanthropy, caring for loved ones, science and art, and many other social goods, and so it may be associated in people's minds with norms of fair exchange and positive treatment of others. Therefore, it may elicit morally commendable sentiments and prosocial actions.

We sought to evoke these different patterns of associations using clean and dirty money. We predicted that clean money would evoke the positive associations (and attendant behaviors) toward fair exchange, whereas dirty money would evoke the unsavory and antisocial associations. The prediction was that money and dirt would interact to influence how people treat others.

Experiment 1 was a field experiment designed to show the differential effects of clean versus dirty money on actual financial behavior. In a farmer's market, experimental confederates purchased vegetables and paid initially with either clean or dirty money. The confederates then ostensibly decided to purchase an additional vegetable, so they asked for the original money back. After collecting the (second) vegetables that constituted the main dependent measure, the experimenter actually paid for all their purchases with typical circulating money. Therefore, clean and dirty money acted as naturalistic primes. The dependent measure was the actual weight of the additional vegetable. In all cases, the customer ordered and paid for 500 grams of the last vegetables, and so fairness and reciprocity would dictate giving the customer precisely 500 grams.

We computed a fairness index for each sale by dividing the actual weight by the amount for which the vendor had charged (i.e., normally 500 grams but occasionally slightly more or less). As predicted, the dirty money prime caused vendors to short-change and thus cheat the customer by giving them less (in weight) than they paid for. In comparison, the clean money prime led to transactions that were in line with what consumers paid for.

Experiment 2 used a 2x2 between-participants design in which participants first performed a finger dexterity task. As a function of condition, they counted out dirty or clean money or dirty or clean sheets of paper. Then participants played the trust game, which has two distinct roles. The sender is given a certain stake of money and can send any part of it to the other person (the receiver), while keeping the rest. The sender is told that whatever money is sent will be tripled by the experimenter and given to the receiver, who then is free to divide the enriched amount between self and the sender. Thus, the receiver can keep all the (tripled) money that the sender donated.

All participants believed they were playing the role of receiver, and it was up to them to decide how to divide the money. Thus, someone else had trusted them, and they could decide whether to repay that trust or keep most of the money for themselves. We predicted an interaction effect, such that participants who had handled clean money would tend toward making a fair and even division of the money, whereas those who had handled dirty money would keep more money for themselves. We predicted an interaction effect, such that participants who had handled clean money would tend toward making a fair and even division of the money, whereas those who had handled dirty money would keep more money for themselves.

Results were in line with expectations. The clean money group returned significantly more money than the dirty money group. The paper conditions did not differ from one another.

Experiment 3 used the most basic of economic games, the dictator game. The participant is given a stake of money to divide between self and another person. The participant's decision is final, and both players get whatever that allocation is. The other person has no vote and no power. Hence it constitutes a relatively pure measure of how well the participant wishes to treat the other person.

This study also changed the manipulation. There were 3 conditions. All participants counted ordinary and thus not notably clean or dirty money (and no one counted paper). Control participants went to the next task. For dirty and clean money manipulations, participants read an ostensible news item about how clean or how dirty is the nation's money supply. Then they performed a lexical decision task in which they rated the positivity of words related to fairness and reciprocity. Last, they played the dictator game and allocated money to an anonymous partner.

Dictator game results: As expected, the clean money group was significantly more generous and fairer to the others than the clean paper group. Meanwhile, the dirty money group was less fair than the control group.

Word rating results: As predicted, the clean money group rated reciprocity words more positively than the control group. The dirty money group rated these words as worse than the control group. We found mediation on the part of word ratings to explain the relationship between the manipulation of dirty money vs clean money vs control on dictator game generosity. Participants in the dirty money condition evaluated fairness words less positively than participants in the control and clean money condition, who rated those words most positively. This accounted for their low and high generosity in the dictator game.

Money is a pervasive aspect of modern life, and the idea of money crosses the average person's mind many times every day. The present findings suggest that there may be more than one set of associations to money. In particular, we found that clean money and dirty money had radically different effects. Despite the negative associations that money can evoke, the idea of clean money can improve people's tendencies to behave in positive, prosocial, culturally beneficial ways.

Doing Well vs. Doing Good:
The Interplay of Morality and Performance in Consumer Judgments

Chair: Jonathan Berman, *University of Pennsylvania, USA*

Paper #1: Redemption through Success: When Good Things Happen to Bad People

Eric Hamerman, Tulane University, USA

Jeffrey R. Parker, Georgia State University, USA

Paper #2: Tip of the Hat, Wag of the Finger: How Moral Decoupling Enables Consumers to Admire and Admonish

Amit Bhattacharjee, Dartmouth College, USA

Jonathan Z. Berman, University of Pennsylvania, USA

Americus Reed II, University of Pennsylvania, USA

Paper #3: Double Standards in the Use of Enhancing Products by Self and Others

Elanor F. Williams, University of California San Diego, USA

Mary Steffel, University of Cincinnati, USA

Paper #4: Actions Speak Less Loud Than Sentiments: A New Model of Moral Judgment

Clayton R. Critcher, University of California Berkeley, USA

Erik G. Helzer, Cornell University, USA

David Tannenbaum, University of California, Los Angeles

David A. Pizarro, Cornell University, USA

SESSION OVERVIEW

Moral beliefs are among the strongest beliefs that consumers hold, and are deeply tied to how individuals view themselves. However, in the real world, successful performance is not always associated with morally upstanding behavior. For example, individuals sometimes resort to immoral behavior in order to perform better and achieve success, and successful individuals sometimes behave as if they are exempt from certain moral standards. The present session seeks to examine the complex and fascinating interplay of morality and performance in consumer judgments. Specifically, the four papers presented here examine how consumers make moral judgments about others, and how these judgments influence subsequent purchase decisions and brand evaluations.

Virtually every week, new examples emerge of public figures that have been accused of immoral behaviors, and the first two papers concern the relation between performance and morality when evaluating these cases. First, Hamerman and Parker show that a public figure's good performance can be as redemptive as an apology for bad behavior. Next, Bhattacharjee, Berman and Reed investigate a new reasoning process that consumers use to support public figures that have transgressed. Similarly, the latter two papers broadly concern moral judgments of performance. Williams and Steffel show that consumers display an ethical double standard in judging their own versus others' use of products that enhance performance (e.g. sports drinks, medication). Finally, Critcher et al. propose a new model of moral judgment: instead of focusing on the performance of good or bad deeds per se, individuals instead focus on an actor's moral sentiments. The first three papers are currently in review process, and the fourth will be submitted for review shortly.

Together, these papers highlight various ways in which consumers combine and reconcile dimensions of performance and morality in their judgments. Given the breadth of these issues and the primacy of moral beliefs as a driver of consumer decision making (e.g., Brinkmann 2004; Smith 1990), we expect that the session will be well attended by researchers with interests in brand management,

motivated reasoning, social cognition, CSR, and morality and ethics to name a few. However, despite the pervasiveness of moral concerns in consumption contexts, it is striking to note the dearth of sessions dealing with moral judgments at recent ACR conferences. In the spirit of the conference theme of appreciating diversity, we hope that this session can offer a special opportunity to open the field to investigating the moral consumer.

Redemption through Success: When Good Things Happen to Bad People

EXTENDED ABSTRACT

Media reports are filled with instances of pop stars, athletes, and corporate executives being linked to immoral or illegal acts. However, these misdeeds seem to be ignored after the transgressors recapture professional success (e.g., by winning a big game). This paper demonstrates that because people infer the morality of others based on their professional performance, success can be as effective as an apology in redeeming one's reputation. Demonstrating that this is not merely a halo effect, three experiments show that seeing an immoral person achieve professional success is upsetting, which leads to a discounting of the immoral act in a manner consistent with cognitive dissonance. When participants were provided with the tools to cope with threatening information (via self-affirmation) or were no longer threatened by this information (such as when the actor was punished for his or her misdeed), they ceased to discount the transgression.

Experiments 1A and 1B investigated the influence of professional success on the evaluations that participants made about a real protagonist: Michael Vick, an NFL quarterback who served time in federal prison for running a dog-fighting ring. The good-play scenario described Vick's on-field success during the 2010 NFL regular season. The poor-play scenario described Vick's poor play during the 2010 NFL playoffs. Finally, the apology condition simply quoted the apology on his website and made no mention of his on-field performance. Participants indicated their general perceptions of Vick (1 = negative, 8 = positive), how trustworthy they perceived him to be (1 = not trustworthy at all, 7 = extremely trustworthy), and how likely they would be to purchase two products endorsed by Vick (Experiment 1A). The perception and trustworthiness items were combined into a single measure of participants' evaluations of Vick's moral character (the same measures were used in experiments 2 and 3).

As predicted, the evaluation of Vick in the apology condition (M = 3.73) did not differ from the good-play condition (M = 3.16). More importantly, evaluations in the apology and good-play conditions were significantly more positive than in the poor-play condition (M = 2.03; p < .05). Participants were also asked to evaluate Vick's on-field football performance. It is important to note that while perceptions of Vick's football performance in the apology condition were higher than those in the poor-play condition, they were also lower than those in the good-play condition. Thus, perceptions of Vick's performance did not map directly onto respondents' evaluations of Vick as a person. In other words, participants were not simply using Vick's professional success as a proxy for evaluating him as a person.

Experiment 1B used conditions identical to those in experiment 1. However, experiment 1A allowed participants to enter either: (i) a lottery for Michael Vick jersey, or (ii) a lottery for Kevin Kolb (described as being an "average" NFL quarterback) jersey. As expected, participants were more likely to enter a lottery for a Michael Vick jersey (vs. a Kevin Kolb jersey) when Vick was successful (29/38 (76%)) versus unsuccessful (18/37 (49%)), p < .05. Further, those participants in the apology condition were just as likely to choose the Vick jersey (22/37 (59%)) as were those in the successful condition (29/38 (76%)), $\chi^2(2) < 1$.

To explore the process behind this finding, two additional experiments were conducted. We hypothesized that the results of experiments 1A and 1B were related to cognitive dissonance. Specifically, because people are upset by the idea of an immoral person achieving professional success (shown in a pretest), we hypothesized that individuals discount the severity of a moral transgression ascribed to someone who subsequently becomes successful, thereby leading to more positive evaluations of this actor. Accordingly, manipulations that either (i) increase participants' ability to handle such threatening information, or (ii) alleviate the upsetting nature of this apparent conflict should attenuate the documented effect.

In experiment 2, a subset of participants was given the tools to cope with threatening information via self-affirmation. After reaffirming core values, people are better able to handle threatening information without resorting to rationalizations seen in cognitive dissonance (Harris, Mayle, Mabbott, & Napper, 2007; Steele & Liu, 1983; Steele, Spencer, & Lynch, 1993). Accordingly, completing a self-affirmation exercise should reduce the need to rationalize or discount transgressions committed by successful individuals, reducing the influence of professional success (vs. failure) on evaluations of others. After completing either a self-affirmation or an unrelated control task, participants read a scenario describing a banker who was arrested for drunk driving and subsequently made successful or unsuccessful investments. We found a main effect of success for evaluations of the banker (p < .01), qualified by an interaction between success and self-affirmation (p < .01). As predicted, there was no effect of professional success in the self-affirmation condition ($M_{Successful} = 3.62$ vs. $M_{Unsuccessful} = 3.69$), F < 1, but the attitudes of the participants in the no-affirmation condition were strongly affected by the banker's level of professional success ($M_{Successful} = 4.17$ vs. $M_{Unsuccessful} = 2.99$), p < .001).

In experiment 3, we expected that punishing the banker would alleviate the threatening nature of his post-transgression success. Punishment ensures that transgressors receive their "just deserts" (Carlsmith, 2002; Darley & Pittman, 2003). Therefore, it should be less upsetting to discover that an immoral person has been successful after learning that he or she has (vs. has not) been punished. Using the same "drunk driving" story from experiment 2, we manipulated the banker's investment success and whether he was punished for his actions.

As expected, we found a main effect of success on participants' evaluations of the banker (p < .001), qualified by a significant interaction between success and punishment (p < .01). Participants' attitudes in the not-punished condition were strongly affected by professional success ($M_{Successful} = 5.13$ vs. $M_{Unsuccessful} = 2.92$), p < .001, while success played no role in the attitudes of those in the punished condition ($M_{Successful} = 3.84$ vs. $M_{Unsuccessful} = 3.50$), F < 1. Moreover, respondents' evaluation of the seriousness of the act (drunk driving) fully mediated their judgments of the banker's moral character.

Tip of the Hat, Wag of the Finger: How Moral Decoupling Enables Consumers to Admire and Admonish

EXTENDED ABSTRACT

Bill Clinton, Roman Polanski, Tiger Woods, and Martha Stewart all share something in common: they are public figures whose immoral actions have threatened their professional reputations. How do consumers reason to support public figures who have acted immorally? We propose that when motivated to support a public figure who has transgressed, consumers engage in *moral decoupling*, a psychological separation process by which they selectively dissociate judgments of morality from judgments of performance.

Though moral beliefs are among the strongest beliefs that people hold, they are particularly subject to motivational biases (Ditto, Pizarro and Tannenbaum 2009). Current research emphasizes moral rationalization processes, by which consumers reconstrue transgressions as less immoral when motivated to do so (e.g., Mazar, Amir and Ariely 2008; Paharia and Deshpande 2009). However, because rationalization requires people to implicitly condone an immoral behavior, and because such judgments are deeply tied to the self (Aquino and Reed 2002), this mechanism may threaten consumers' moral self-image. We propose that people also engage in moral decoupling, a distinct moral reasoning strategy that enables consumers to support a transgressor while still condemning the transgression. Moral decoupling works by altering an individual's view of the relevance of moral actions to performance in a given domain. By dissociating performance from morality, an individual can support an immoral actor without being subject to self-reproach for condoning immoral behavior.

Five studies demonstrate that, relative to moral rationalization, moral decoupling is psychologically distinct, easier to justify, and more predictive of consumer support in one real world context.

A pilot study provides initial evidence that moral decoupling is distinct from moral rationalization. After reading a scenario describing an Olympic gold medalist who has physically abused his wife, participants rated their agreement with moral decoupling and moral rationalization items and rated the player on performance and degree of immorality. Regression analysis found that only decoupling significantly positively predicted performance ratings ($t(95) = 7.59$, $p < .001$), while only rationalization significantly reduced judgments of immorality ($t(93) = -3.55$, $p < .001$), suggesting that these constructs are distinct.

In study 1, we sought to gain causal insight by priming specific moral reasoning strategies. Participants wrote statements related to moral decoupling, moral rationalization, or humor (as a control). In an ostensibly different study, they then read about a CEO of a consumer electronics firm who has supported discriminatory hiring policies. Participants primed with a moral decoupling or a moral rationalization reasoning strategy reported being more likely to purchase the company's products than those in a control condition ($F(2, 118) = 9.93$, $p < .001$). More importantly, participants in the moral decoupling condition rated the performance of the CEO higher than the moral rationalization and control conditions ($F(2, 118) = 9.87$, $p < .001$), while those in the moral rationalization condition rated the immorality of the CEO's actions to be less severe than the other two conditions ($F(2, 118) = 7.00$, $p < .001$), reinforcing the difference between these psychological pathways.

In study 2, we examined the process of moral decoupling by directly varying the relevance of a transgression to performance. Participants read a scenario in which either a baseball player or a governor was found to have either taken steroids or engaged in tax evasion. As expected, participants were more supportive when transgressions were less relevant ($F(1, 83) = 22.2$, $p < .001$). Multiple-step mediation analysis found that relevance directly influenced moral decoupling, which increased performance judgments, leading to greater consumer support (indirect effect = -0.82; 95% C.I. = [-1.25, -0.44]). However, relevance had no effect on the degree of moral rationalization or the degree of immorality (ts < 1), clarifying our proposed process and better establishing discriminant validity.

Study 3 investigates consumers' choice of a moral reasoning strategy as well as the implications for the self. Participants read the above scenario involving a baseball player or governor, and selected a supportive statement (reflecting either moral rationalization or moral decoupling) that best reflected their own beliefs. They then wrote an argument justifying their beliefs. Consistent with our previous findings, participants were more likely to select a decoupling (vs. rationalization) statement when the transgression was low (vs. high) in relevance ($\chi^2(1) = 8.20$, $p = .004$). In addition, a two-way ANOVA revealed a main effect of strategy choice on ease of justification ($F(1, 58) = 7.60$, $p = .008$): regardless of relevance, participants who chose a moral decoupling felt that their argument was easier to justify than those who selected a moral rationalization argument.

Finally, we looked for field evidence of moral decoupling using a sample of online comments about Tiger Woods before his return to golf in April 2010. From a random subset of 400 comments posted on major news sites, we eliminated those that were irrelevant, retaining 124 comments for analysis. Three coders blind to hypotheses rated the degree to which each comment supported or opposed Tiger Woods. In addition, they rated each comment on the extent of moral rationalization, the extent to which participants separated performance and morality (i.e., moral decoupling). Regression analysis shows that the degree of moral decoupling ($t(120) = 6.18$, $p < .001$) was a strong significant predictor of expressed support, while the degree of moral rationalization was only marginally significant ($t(120) = -1.84$, $p = .067$). Further, both the degree of moral decoupling ($t(120) = -3.48$, $p < .001$) was a strong significant predictors of opposition, while the degree of moral rationalization did not significantly predict expressed opposition ($t(120) = -1.03$, $p = .30$).

Thus, we outline the existence and nature of a new psychological mechanism—moral decoupling—by which consumers selectively dissociate judgments of morality from judgments of performance in order to support public figures that have transgressed. Doing so allows consumers to admire immoral actors while still admonishing their immoral actions, simultaneously tipping their hats and wagging their fingers.

Double Standards in the
Use of Enhancing Products by Self and Others

EXTENDED ABSTRACT

Products can improve their users' lives in many ways, allowing them access to experiences, traits, and abilities they would not be able to achieve on their own. These types of product benefits raise questions about such products' ethical use, and how their use is perceived. One factor that may determine perceptions of their ethicality is how the effect of such products is construed, whether they are seen as helping to enable a person to reveal their true abilities or enhance them beyond their true abilities; further, this construal may differ depending on who benefits from them.

We suggest that the same product will have different ethical implications depending on whether oneself or another person is using it. People think their own potential ability is a part of who they are but not a part of others (Williams, Gilovich, and Dunning 2012), and consequently, products that seem to enable the self appear to enhance others. Because people are less comfortable with products and interventions that enhance a consumer's standing than ones that enable it (Lowery, Chow, and Crosby 2009; Riis, Simmons, and Goodwin 2008), people may see the same product as morally acceptable for the self to use but less so for others.

To establish that people see the same product as enabling themselves but enhancing others, and to show this effect with actual product use, in study 1 we had participants consume Jelly Belly Sport Beans, which work like sports drinks do to improve performance. Participants were supposedly paired with another student on an intellectual task to examine the effects of the beans on performance. They completed a baseline round of the task, consumed the jellybeans, and then completed the second target round. Next, they received feedback about their own or the other participant's performance in both rounds; the feedback was identical for both, such that the player improved his/her ranking on the task after consuming the jellybeans. When asked to what extent the Sport Beans helped reveal the player's true abilities (= 0; an enablement interpretation) versus helped them perform above and beyond them (=100; an enhancement interpretation), participants indicated that the Sport Beans were more enhancing of the other participant (M = 30.4) than they were of the self (M = 22.5; t(147) = 2.22, p < .05). This suggests that people do have different interpretations of the effects of the same potentially enhancing product when it is used by the self or another person.

In study 2, we connected this difference to ethical double standards. Participants imagined an interview for a much-wanted job. Ideal candidates were to be easy-going and relaxed, capable of dealing calmly with issues on the job. Participants then imagined that the candidate on this interview believed they had the potential to be the ideal candidate, but were worried that the interview situation would make them appear more tense than they actually are. The candidate took an anti-anxiety medication, Zatex, for the interview, and they got the job. Importantly, half the participants imagined that they were the job candidate, and half imagined that they were the interviewer.

Participants indicated that Zatex helped the candidate's true abilities show (= 1; versus making them appear to have abilities they don't actually possess = 7) to a greater extent when they themselves were the candidate (M = 3.5) than when they were interviewing the candidate (M = 4.4; F(1,119) = 11.29, p = .001). They also believed that the use of Zatex was more acceptable when they used it (M = 4.4) than another person (M = 3.8; F(1,119) = 6.51, p = .01). Participants' interpretation of the effects of the drug significantly mediated how acceptable its use was perceived to be. Namely, the more enhancing the drug seemed, the less fair its use. And because the drug seemed more enhancing when another person took it than the self, people held double standards for the use of Zatex. Further, how acceptable the use of the drug seemed to be determined how deserving of the job the candidate seemed to be, and whether the candidate should have to disclose that they took Zatex.

Finally, in study 3, we tested some consequences of these interpretations for how participants would choose to regulate the marketplace for such products. Student participants considered a potential new policy at their university that would forbid students from using non-prescribed attention-enhancing drugs like Ritalin or Adderall. This policy was framed as something the participant would need to agree to, or something that students in general (of whom the participant is logically a part) would need to agree to. Participants considering the effects of such a policy on themselves, rather than students in general, were more likely to believe that the drugs enabled (= 1; versus enhanced = 7) their users ($M_{self} = 3.8$ vs. $M_{students} = 4.4$; F(1,74) = 4.12, p < .05). They also believed that the policy was more fair when framed as affecting students (M = 5.1) rather than themselves (M = 3.9; F(1,74) = 4.38, p < .05). Participants' interpretation of the effects of a product's effects predicted how unfair they perceived the policy to be, suggesting that interpretations of a product's effects influence how consumers think the product should be regulated. Further, the fact that mere framing could lead to these differences suggests that this goes beyond a simple self-favoring bias. The consequences for the self were constant between framing conditions; if participants were solely trying to give themselves flexibility to use the product, simply changing their focus from self to a group that still includes the self would be unlikely to bring about the difference in perceived fairness.

Our research thus indicates that who is using a potentially enhancing product, oneself or someone else, can alter how moral a person perceives the use of that product to be. This work suggests that marketers, organizations, and citizens in general should carefully consider who uses such products, who will know, and what that means.

Actions Speak Less Loud Than Sentiments: A New Model of Moral Judgment

EXTENDED ABSTRACT

Consumers frequently form moral evaluations of others. They may question whether a celebrity spokesperson is an upstanding role-model, ask themselves whether a company's executive has solid moral values, or assess the moral character of other consumers. One may think the simple answer to such questions lie in the target's deeds—after all, "Actions speak louder than words". In fact, a long tradition in moral psychology has asked what it is that makes an action praiseworthy or blameworthy (e.g., Kohlberg, 1969; Gilligan, 1982; Greene, 2009).

Previous research in social and moral psychology has noted one obvious caveat: People should not get credit for doing the "right thing" for the "wrong reason" (Malle, 2004). Consumers are known to be suspicious of the ulterior motives of others (Fein, 1997). For example, after reflecting on businessmen-philanthropists identified by *Slate* as among the most altruistic people in America, participants became increasingly cynical about the philanthropists' motives (Critcher & Dunning, 2011). In total, work in this tradition suggests that consumers are quick to decide that good actions do not merit praise.

Instead, we propose that this approach to moral judgment is fundamentally flawed. In assessing others' moral character, it is not the case that people give others credit for good actions as long as they cannot be explained away by ulterior motives. In fact, we contend that it may not even make sense to talk about certain actions as good or bad at all. Instead, consumers try to make sense of what moral sentiments others experience and judge them positively to the extent that they act consistently with them. As a concrete example, when people praise a consumer for returning an item that was accidentally shoplifted, people do not praise the consumer for the action, but for acting in accordance with a moral sentiment (here, an assumed tinge of guilt the consumer likely experienced when seeing the unpaid-for item). Without the sentiment, praise is not offered.

In the way that moral judgment has typically been studied, these two possibilities—praising others' for good actions versus for acting on moral sentiment—have not been distinguishable, in large part because of the decontextualized scenarios in which moral judgment effects are examined. This is particularly troubling for consumer behavior researchers who draw on moral psychology perspectives and theory in motivating our research. In this talk, we offer four studies that distinguish between these competing possibilities and find consistent support for our perspective (praise for acting on sentiments) instead of the typical perspective (praise for doing good)

or a motives perspective (praise for having good intentions). Our studies show the importance of perceived moral sentiments not as praiseworthy or blameworthy cues in themselves (as motives are), but as part of a sentiment—action chain on which moral evaluation is actually based.

In Studies 1a-1c, participants considered (different) moral dilemmas: the Nazi-baby dilemma, a moral quandary in which a Jewish townsperson must decide whether to smother a crying child to death so Nazi soldiers will not find Jewish villagers' hiding spot'; the sick Johnny scenario (Tetlock et al., 2000) in which a hospital director must decide whether to use hospital funds to save the life of a sick seven-year-old or instead update hospital infrastructure; and a novel moral dilemma in which an American military commander must decide whether or not to order a strike on a rural Ukrainian inn where high-level Al Qaeda terrorists as well as innocent civilians are staying. First, participants indicated to what extent the decision-maker was likely experiencing each of two competing moral sentiments (e.g., "finds it morally wrong to let the child die" vs. "realizes many more lives could be saved by diverting the funds elsewhere"). After then learning what the moral agent decided, participants judged his character. In all three studies, analogous meditational models showed that participants praised the moral agent to the extent he was assumed to appreciate the moral sentiment that would lead to the action. This provided initial support for the acting on sentiments perspective.

Our model makes the unique prediction that factors that change the likelihood that a decision-maker will appreciate one moral sentiment or another also change the praise that different actions will receive. Studies 2-4 used the earlier-described dilemmas but varied an action-unrelated feature that we assumed (and empirically confirmed) would change the moral sentiments a target would be assumed to appreciate: a neurological disorder the agent was said to have (Study 2); the time the agent had to make the decision (Study 3); and the arbitrary visual perspective of the agent (Study 4). In each case, these manipulations had the predicted effect: They changed the moral sentiments the target was assumed to appreciate, which changed the praise the agent received for each action. For example, in Study 3, participants assumed that if the Jewish townsperson was rushed, he would have an immediate impulse to not kill a child but would not fully appreciate the utilitarian justification for the opposite course of action. Only in this case did people praise the townsperson for not smothering the child. In Study 4, even though participants knew that the military commander was aware of who all was in the hotel, participants assumed his moral sentiments would shift depending on whether he happened to see an al Qaeda operative or an innocent civilian through a window. Thus, even though the decision-maker confronted the same moral dilemma, he was praised for ordering the strike when he could actually see the terrorist, but was praised for instead not ordering the strike when he could actually see the innocent civilian.

Behavioral researchers from consumer, social, and cognitive psychology have spent considerable effort asking what makes behavior morally (im)permissible. The present research suggests that such an approach may be misguided. We instead show the real question to be what moral sentiments people assume others will appreciate. By understanding how (frequently arbitrary) features of a decision-making context shift what sentiments are assumed to be salient to moral decision-makers, we can then predict when and why actions receive moral praise.

Expanding the Theoretical Understandings of the Place of Consumption in Market Formation and Transformation

Chair: Güliz Ger, Bilkent University, Turkey

Paper #1: The Creation and Transformation of an Illegal Market: Kurdish Music in Turkey

Alev Kuruoğlu, Bilkent University, Turkey

Paper #2: Myth Market Collaboration: Transforming a Culturally Contaminated Area into a Thriving Tourism Market

Ela Veresiu, Witten/Herdecke University, Germany

Paper #3: Beyond the Social System: Understanding Markets as Consumers

Markus Giesler, York University, Canada

Paper #4: Consumer Markets and Value Transformation in the Global Context

Alladi Venkatesh, University of California Irvine, USA
Lisa Peñaloza, Bordeaux Management School, France
Özlem Sandıkcı, Bilkent University, Turkey

SESSION OVERVIEW

The goal of this proposed session is to examine how markets are formed and transformed, and the ways in which markets constitute – and are constituted by – transformations in their environments. Embedded within dynamic social, cultural, legal, and historical environments (Giesler 2008; Ger and Karababa 2011), markets are constituted by – and constitutive of - internal and external actors, who have different roles in facilitating/hindering formation, legitimation (Humphreys 2010b), signification/valuation (Peñaloza and Mish 2011) and evolution (Giesler 2008) of the market. This session builds up on, and would like to push forward, an important stream of research on *market*s, and offers new perspectives by discussing multiple facets and transformative potentials of marketplace activities. Markets are conceptualized by the authors as actors attempting to create social change; mythmakers transforming contaminated space; signifying and value-creating enterprises; or consuming entities. What is common to these arguments is the potential of markets to transform norms, ideals, legislations, and socio-cultural dynamics. These discussions contribute to a further understanding of how market actors mobilize resources and discourses, engage in strategic alliances, create different types of values, and also shape academic discourse; in attempting to transforming and legitimating both themselves and their environments. We believe this session also provides valuable discussions for other research initiatives on the relationship(s) between consumers and markets.

The papers in this session extend, but also question and contest previous arguments on market creation, evolution and transformation; providing a diversity of perspectives on these important topics. The first two papers are perspectives on transformations of illicit/contaminated markets, with Kuruoglu's paper exploring market creation and transformation in a restricted environment and questions whether legitimation is sufficient in explaining the processes of formation and transformation. Veresiu on the other hand draws upon assemblage theory to theorize the transformation of a previously "contaminated" space into a thriving market via mythmaking. Venkatesh et al. contribute with a conceptual piece which argues that transformation can be understood through the conceptualization of value co-production. Giesler, on the other hand, challenges existing conceptualizations of markets, arguing that markets are consumers, and that strategical "mythmakers" not only effectively reshape so-

cial realities, but also influence the way researchers conceptualize markets. For all four studies in our session, data collection (when relevant), and analyses are complete. The last 15 minutes of the session will be devoted to discussions guided by Güliz Ger.

The Creation and Transformation of an Illegal Market: Kurdish Music in Turkey

EXTENDED ABSTRACT

Market creation has been described as a process of legitimation wherein social networks, financial resources, territorial structures, and legitimating discourses are mobilized by multiple actors (Humphreys 2010a), including "firms, consumers, policymakers, and financial stakeholders" (Peñaloza and Mish 2011: 26). The social and cultural structure within which these actors are embedded shapes the processes through which a market is created, but in turn, this larger structure is also prone to change through strategic actions of "coalitions of actors" that propote or oppose its legitimation (Humphreys 2010a: 14; cf. Ger and Karababa 2011; Peñaloza and Gilly 1999).

Marketplace interactions have been the context for the negotiation of illegal, immoral, stigmatized, or transgressive practices (Ger and Karababa 2011; Giesler 2008; Goulding et al 2009; Humphreys 2010 a,b). Competing ideologies frame these practices in different lights (Giesler 2008) – drinking coffee at the Ottoman coffeehouse, for instance, was deemed an immoral practice by orthodox Sunni Islam, whereas the heterodox Sufi sect, saw coffee as carrying health and moral benefits. Coffeehouse owners and the public were complicit in tactical resistance, and collaborated in effecting changes in legislations (Ger and Karababa 2011). Humphreys (2010a, b) also shows how different actors – including the state - come together in bringing about change in public opinions as well as legislations with regards to gambling at casinos in the USA. This paper seeks to extend previous research on the creation of a market that is initially illegitimate; and focuses on the marketplace performances of multiple actors in striving to attain legitimacy and effect social change, through practices with regards to both use and exchange (Venkatesh and Peñaloza 2006).

The legitimacy of the market for Kurdish music has been rendered problematic (and to this day remains so) in connection to a longstanding history of ethnic tension and armed conflict, particularly between the Turkish state and the Kurdish terrorist organization PKK (Marcus 2007), as well as prohibitive state policies and practices of social exclusion. Broadcasting and publishing in Kurdish were prohibited by constitution in Turkey until 1991; owning and playing music recordings in Kurdish language at the time could lead to several years of imprisonment. An amendment in 1991 legalized Kurdish music production, but an informal market for music had long existed. Cassettes were smuggled across borders, and home-made recordings of the live performances were exchanged among social networks, and transported to other cities. This circulation of cassettes formed an informal marketplace, and was instrumental in the creation of an imagined community (Anderson 1983) characterized by Kurdish ethnicity. The experience of listening to the music was heightened by a fear of getting caught as well as the aura of enacting a resistive performance of ethnicity.

Post-1991, many companies started producing music albums in Kurdish, but strict state-imposed surveillance and censorship prevailed in the market throughout the 1990s. The firms and other actors, including artists, politicians, publishing houses and broadcasters engaged both legitimating discourses, and also other resistive and discursive acts in trying to attain a less restricted environment for Kurdish music production – framing the music as cultural heritage or as a part of Turkey's ethnic and cultural multiplicity; engaging in activities such as selling cassettes off the records, educating and engaging audience to join the Kurdish movement, drawing international attention to the legal restrictions, and joining illegal organizations (including the PKK). The 2000s have been characterized by a somewhat more relaxed atmosphere, with local and multinational companies producing many albums each year, but the legitimacy of the market for Kurdish music is still ambiguous, with celebratory accounts of music and performances coexisting with discriminatory practices such as lack of shelf space or opportunities for advertisement in mass media. Thus, despite having undergone a transformation from illegal and informal to a legal, institutionalized marketplace, with sophisticated production and distribution channels, the Kurdish music market has attained legitimacy only in the regulatory sense, but not in the normative or cultural-cognitive sense (Suchman 1995), when examined in the whole of Turkey.

This analysis is based on an ethnography of the market for Kurdish music in Turkey. Data that I gathered from interviews with producers, artists, cultural producers in other fields, and audience; participant observation at relevant events; as well as a survey of newspaper articles and other secondary texts have contributed to the emergent account I present here.

Myth Market Collaboration: Transforming a Culturally Contaminated Area into a Thriving Tourism Market

EXTENDED ABSTRACT

How can culturally contaminated areas be transformed into successful tourism markets? A dominant research stream unpacking the relationship between market creation and culture is the literature on myth markets. This research commonly conceptualizes the formation of myth markets – the markets for goods, services, or experiences created from culturally resonant, and thus consumer identity-enhancing stories – as a process of ideological and cultural competition and conflict among multiple stakeholders (e.g., Arsel and Thompson 2011; Giesler 2008; Holt 2004; Luedicke, Thompson, and Giesler 2010; Peñaloza 2001; Thompson 2004; Thompson and Tian 2008). Consequently, little theoretical attention has been devoted to the strategic alliances and symbiotic relationships that can form among stakeholders to shape a myth market's cultural meanings and consumer identity value.

This paper examines the collaborative mythmaking practices involved in transforming a culturally contaminated area into a thriving tourism myth market. Drawing on assemblage theory in sociology (De Landa 2006), I describe myth markets as assemblages of actors and develop a process model of myth market collaboration. According to De Landa (2006, 4), "[a]ssemblages are wholes whose properties emerge from the interaction between parts." In particular, De Landa (2006) characterizes assemblages along three dimensions: (1) defining the roles that an assemblage's parts may play, (2) defining the processes in which these parts become involved and, (3) defining processes in which specialized expressive media (genetic or linguistic) intervene to provide the assemblage with more flexibility or rigidity. Building on these characteristics, I theorize that an assemblage of actors (e.g., business owners, governments, the media, celebrities, consumers, etc.) can strategically coordinate their myth-making activities to confine the negative cultural meanings associated with an area and establish their desired definitions of a market.

To illustrate myth market collaboration, I conducted a two-year ethnographic and netnographic (Kozinets 2002) investigation of the ongoing transformation project of a place popularly dubbed "Hitler's Hill" in the German Alps (Obersalzberg, Bavaria) that was historically associated with the Nazi Party. Since 2001, several actors including the Bavarian and German governments, the InterContinental hotel, the national media, historians, intellectuals, and celebrities, as well as local museums, restaurants, ski resorts, tourist promoters, and residents, have joined forces to establish a successful tourism market. I conducted up to three interviews with five international tourists, four InterContinental hotel staff, six local business owners, and three government officials, where we discussed topics ranging from the area's origins, to Hitler's domination, to current tourism business opportunities, challenges, and future directions. I analyzed the complete data-set, which includes 34 in-depth, semi-structured interviews ranging from 20 minutes to two hours in length, as well as 160 pages of online materials and historical data, using the established hermeneutical analysis mode of tacking back and forth between data and theory (Thompson 1997).

My findings reveal the decontamination strategies actors use to displace the negative cultural meanings associated with an area and to remythologize it as an idyllic touristic landscape. The collaborative mythmaking practices focus on creating and maintaining a clear distinction between the area's violent past and peaceful present. This idea is aptly summarized by German historian Volker Dahm (2005), who argues, "the best way to demystify places associated with the Nazis is to allow normal life to go on there." Thus, similar to assemblage theory, I find that each involved actor has specifically assigned roles and processes that stabilize the contemporary tourism myth market. As a few examples, two new touristic destinations (the InterContinental Hotel and the Documentation Centre) have been established on the very site where Hitler and his generals had their homes in order to create a strategic duality. The five-star hotel's role is to represent the relaxing and luxurious Alpine touristic experience, while the area's main museum is responsible for containing the only reminders of the past. Even the "Eagle's Nest," Hitler's 50th birthday present by the Nazi Party, has been transformed into a restaurant highlighting local cuisine. The Bavarian government, which owns the majority of the land, has the watchdog role to ensure that all tourism business initiatives follow the overarching mythic storyline of classy Alpine retreat with the past of an innocent mountain village.

Overall, these findings advance the growing research on myth markets, and the nascent literature on market system dynamics – the social processes involved in market creation and evolution (Giesler 2008; Humphreys 2010; Karababa and Ger 2011). Myth market collaboration can better help us understand the co-creative role of multiple evolving interests in shaping and transforming the cultural meanings and myths associated with tourism markets.

Beyond the Social System: Understanding Markets as Consumers

EXTENDED ABSTRACT

The worldwide soft drinks market consumes more than 1.4 trillion liters of fresh water to produce 392 billion liters of soft drinks per year (Chamberlain 2008). A rapidly growing global seafood market has led to an overexploitation of 25% of world fisheries to the point where their current biomass is less than the level that maximizes their sustainable yield (Grafton et al 2007). Each year, the global tourism market consumes nearly as much energy as Japan, produces the same amount of solid waste as France, and consumes as much fresh water as is contained in Lake Superior (Krantz 2007).

Markets - not countries - are now the largest consumers of the world's energy, resources, and life. And yet surprisingly little theoretical attention has been devoted to understanding markets *as* consumers. Perhaps this oversight stems from the ways in which markets have been previously theorized. From within the marketing discipline, consumer researchers have referred to markets as "institutionalized arenas of conflict and compromise" (Giesler 2008), "performative stages" (Deighton 1992), or "concrete exchange structures" (Humphreys 2010).

The goal of this paper is to offer a theorization that conceptualizes markets as consumers. I argue that markets are successful to the extent to which they can mask their identity as consumers and instead position themselves at the center for the production of consensus, freedom, empowerment, creativity, and community.

In the first part of the analysis, I explore the relationship between consumer culture theory and a certain branch of economic thought referred to as neoliberalism to better understand the existing perspective on markets and consumers. I offer three methodological neoliberalisms that have prevented consumer researchers from approaching markets as consumers. First is the tendency to uncritically adopt rather than interrogate the traditional economic distinction between "consumer" and "market." Second is the tendency to understand markets as structural stage or spaces on/in which agents productively interact rather than as macro-actors who have the potential to reshape interests and identities. And third is the tendency to view the distribution of resources, their meanings (e.g., music, gambling, coffee), and their production and consumption as if they were naturally situated within the borders of individual market systems.

After that, I analyze the rhetorical masking practices involved in expanding what has been referred to as the "global market system" (Schiller 2000). To understand this market system, I conducted a multi-year ethnographic investigation of the World Economic Forum (WEF) in Davos, Switzerland. The WEF was founded in 1971 and includes the most prominent transnational corporations.

I conducted in-depth interviews with 14 WEF delegates to document how they tailored global, national, and regional, territories, resources, social and political problems, and the needs and wants of individuals in relation to their competitive and ideological consumption needs and to combat criticisms rendering the global market as an inequitable, volatile, ecologically wasteful, and all-consuming villain (George 2010; Klein 2009; Chomsky 2011; Vertovec 2009; Sassen 1998). To track changes in their evolving global market representations, each informant was interviewed up to four times between 2004 and 201. To analyze the data, I used an iterative, part-to-whole process of hermeneutic analysis (Thompson 1997; Giesler 2008). To contextualize the interview data, I also collected WEF communiqués and annual competitive reports published between 1987 and 2010, as well as other cultural materials available through mass media channels and on the Internet.

This research makes two contributions. First, it contributes to prior studies on market system dynamics (Humphreys 2010; Giesler 2008). This stream of research has studied how concrete exchange structures between producers and consumers are established and evolve. My analysis complements and extends this body of research by theoretically explicating the agency markets mobilize to reshape social realities and subjectivities in relation to their ideological and competitive goals as well as the resistance against this marketization process.

Second, I demonstrate how the import of rhetorical conventions from marketing and economics, while lending legitimacy to earlier

CCT generations, also brought in a number of neoliberal biases. These manifest in the tendency to either concentrate on an autonomous, entrepreneurial consumer-subject or the creation of a marketplace structure instead of asking how the latter reshaped the former so that the former can sustain the latter. In doing so, some of the worst volatilities, contradictions, and excesses of contemporary market consumption are erased from the analytical radar. Theorizing markets as consumers - how they systematically tailor societies, territories, resources, and living beings in relation to their economic and ideological agendas - may help address some of these theoretical blind spots.

Consumer Markets and Value Transformation in the Global Context

EXTENDED ABSTRACT

Recently, there has been a growing interest among consumer and marketing researchers in examining the study of "markets" as our disciplinary focus especially in the current global context (Humphreys 2010, Venkatesh and Peñaloza 2006, Domegan et. al Forthcoming). As noted by Sandıkcı and Rice (2011), one main shortcoming of contemporary consumer/marketing theories is that they are very US centric and are applied to various contexts without examining differing cultural conditions. In this study, we propose to study more broadly *markets as value creating enterprises* and examine their transformational characteristics in terms of their value creation potential.

Our focus in this proposal is on the constitution of particular subject positions within "consumer markets" as the social and economic institutional arrangements within which value is created by and for various constituencies which include customers, stakeholders and other agents/participants, and the society at large. In the global context where markets transcend national boundaries, truly global markets extend beyond such boundaries (Ger 1999) and give us an opportunity as researchers to examine and develop a value system appropriate for such a study.

As noted by Peñaloza and Mish (2011), the concept of value in consumer marketing has been viewed in terms of the material, instrumental and psychological benefits (e.g. satisfaction) derived by the customer through engagement with the product or service.

Typically, the field of consumer marketing has focused primarily on Exchange Value and Use Value as its primary focus. We broaden this binary conceptualization of value framework in working through four distinct types of value: Exchange Value, Use Value, Sign/Cultural Value and Societal Value. It is the integration of different value systems that presages global transformational possibilities.

Exchange Value

One fundamental notion of value discussed in our discipline is that there is a value producer and intended value recipient – the former creates value (i.e. confers value on an object or engages in an action that embodies value) and the recipient is the beneficiary (Bagozzi 1975). If the value recipient performs something in return, this is an example of exchange value.

Use Value

The concept of use value stems from the notion that the offering that has been produced through exchange is *useful* (and usable) and is therefore put to use by the customer (Holbrook 1999). Use value refers to the direct usefulness of an object or service. It can also be called the functional value and is inextricably tied to the tangible or intangible property of the offering. A use-value can be both subjective and objective. A major focus of the field of consumer research may be said to concentrate on use value.

Sign/Cultural Value

Broadly speaking, the concept of sign refers to the symbolism and meanings within the significatory system in which the product is embedded (Levy 1981). The meanings attributed to physical objects, or broadly, company offerings, are well documented in cultural and anthropological studies (Lash and Urry 1994). For example, Ger (1999) provided symbolic notions of glocalization (1999) in marketing practices, Holt (2004) detailed the incorporation of social trends and group language by firms in advertisements for "iconic" brands. Scott (2004) elaborated the intricate interrelations between cultural and economic development in tracing feminist consumption sensibilities to the changing place of women in the workforce. Venkatesh (1995) proposed the notion of ethnoconsumerism as incorporating sign systems in the global/cultural contexts. The implications of this for sign value are that in the global economy, signs are created, transferred, controlled, expressed and consumed in relation to other sets of signs that encompass consumers' identities in ways that negotiate their interests and relations with other constituencies.

Societal Value

Here the simple question is, when does the market system through its product offerings and activities benefit a society and when does it compromise the latter? Of interest here are the pragmatic and societal questions that have become very central in the contemporary environmentally conscious world.

In looking at the market as a value-based economy, the above framework t integrates the four systems of value: exchange value, use value, sign value and societal value into the market system.

Summary and Conclusions

The goal of this proposed session is to examine the transformational potential of markets and market formations. In this study, we have proposed a framework that examines consumer markets as value creating enterprises in a dynamic global context. Our framework integrates four systems of values in markets – exchange value, use value, sign/cultural value and societal value, with implications for consumption practices and theories.

REFERENCES

Arnould Eric J. and Craig Thompson (2005), "Consumer Culture Theory (CCT): Twenty Years of Research," *Journal of Consumer Research*, 31 (March), 868-82.

Arsel, Zeynep, and Craig J. Thompson (2011), "Demythologizing Consumption Practices: How Consumers Protect Their Field-Dependent Identity Investments from Devaluing Marketplace Myths," *Journal of Consumer Research,* 37 (February), 791-806.

Anderson, Benedict (1983) *Imagined Communities* NY: Verso

Bagozzi, R. (1975), "Marketing as Exchange," *Journal of Marketing*, Vol. 39, No. 4: 32-39.

Bryce, Robert (2011), *Power Hungry: The Myths of "Green" Energy and the Real Fuels of the Future.* New York: Public Affairs.

Chamberlain, Gary (2008), Troubled Waters: Religion, Ethics, and Global Water Crisis. Lanham: Rowman & Littlefield Publishers Inc.

Chomsky, Noam (2011), *A New Generation Draws the Line: Humanitarian Intervention and the "Responsibility to Protect" Today.* Boulder: Paradigm Publishers.

Clark, Jayne (2005), "Hitler Hotel' courts controversy," USA Today, March 10.

De Landa, Manuel (2006), *A New Philosophy of Society: Assemblage Theory and Social Complexity.* London: Continuum.

Deighton, John (1992), "The Consumption of Performance," *Journal of Consumer Research*, 19 (December), 362–72.

Devine, N. (2004), *Education and Public Choice: A Critical Account of the Invisible Hand in Education.* Westport: Praeger Press.

Domegan, Christine, Michaela Haase, Kim Harris, Carol Kelleher, Willem-Jan van den Heuvel, Paul Maglio, Timo Meynhardt, Andrea Ordanini, and Lisa Peñaloza (forthcoming), "Value, Values, Symbols and Outcomes," *Marketing Theory.*

Dorn, Walter (1999), *World Order for a New Millennium: Political, Cultural, and Spiritual Approaches to Building Peace.* New York: St. Martin's Press.

George, Susan (2010), *Whose Crisis, Whose Future.* Cambridge: Polity Press.

Ger, G (1999), "Localizing in the Global Village: Local firms Competing in Global Markets," California Mangement Review, 41 (4), 64-83.

Giesler, Markus (2008), "Conflict and Compromise: Drama in Marketplace Evolution," *Journal of Consumer Research*, 34 (April), 739-754.

Goulding, Christina, Avi Shankar, Richard Elliot, Robin Canniford (2009) "The Marketplace Management of Illicit Pleasure", *Journal of Consumer Research*, Vol. 35(Feb): 759-771

Grafton, R. Q., T. Kompas, and R. W. Hilborn (2007), "Economics of Overexploitation Revisited," Science, 318 (December), 1601.

Holbrook, M. (1999), *Consumer Value: A Framework for Analysis and Research*, London: Routledge.

Holt, D. (2004), *How Brands Become Icons: The Principles of Cultural Branding*, Boston, MA: Harvard Business School.

Humphreys, Ashlee (2010a), "Megamarketing: The Creation of Markets as a Social Process" *Journal of Marketing* Vol. 74: 1-19

Humphreys, Ashlee (2010b), "Semiotic Structure and the Legitimation of Consumption Practices: The Case of Casino Gambling", *Journal of Consumer Research* Vol. 37 (October): 490-510

Karababa, Eminegül and Güliz Ger (2011) "Early Modern Ottoman Coffeehouse Culture and the Formation of the Consumer Subject" Vol. 37(5): 737-760

Klein, Naomi (2009), *No Logo: No Space, No Choice, No Jobs.* New York: Picador.

Krantz, David (2007), Global Trends in Coastal Tourism, Washington, DC: Center on Ecotourism and Sustainable Development.

Kozinets, Robert V. (2002) "The Field Behind the Screen: Using Netnography for Marketing Research in Online Communities," *Journal of Marketing Research*, 39 (1): 61-73.

Lash, S. and Urry, J. (1994) *Economies of Sign & Space*, Sage Publications.

Levy, S. J, (1981), "Interpreting Consumer Mythology," *Journal of Marketing*, 45(3), 49-61.

Marcus, A. (2007) *Blood and Belief: PKK and the Kurdish Fight for Independence*, NY: NYU Press

Peñaloza, L. and M. C. Gilly (1999) "Marketer Acculturation: The Changer and the Changed" *Journal of Marketing* Vol. 63(3) 84-104

Peñaloza, Lisa (2001), "Consuming the American West: Animating Cultural Meaning at a Stock Show and Rodeo," *Journal of Consumer Research,* 28 (December), 369–98.

Peñaloza, Lisa and Jenny Mish (2011) "The Nature and Processes of Market Co-Creation in Triple Bottom-Line Firms: Leveraging Insights from Consumer Culture Theory and Service Dominant Logic" *Marketing Theory* 11(1): 9-34

Sandıkcı, O and G. Rice (2011) *Handbook of Islamic Marketing*, Edward Elgar Publishing.

Sassen, Saskia (1998), *Globalization and Its Discontents.* New York: The New Press.

Schiller, D. (2000), *Digital Capitalism: Networking the Global Market System.* Cambridge: MIT Press.

Scott, L. (2004), *Fresh Lipstick: Redressing Fashion and Feminism,* Palgrave Macmillan.

Suchman, M. C. (1995) "Managing Legitimacy: Strategic and Institutional Approaches" *Academy of Management Review* 20(3): 571-610

Thompson, Craig J. (1997) "Interpreting Consumers: A Hermeneutical Framework for Deriving Marketing Insights from the Texts of Consumers' Consumption Stories," *Journal of Marketing Research*, 24 (4), 438-455.

Thompson, Craig J. (2004), "Marketplace Mythology and Discourses of Power," *Journal of Consumer Research*, 31 (June), 162–180.

Thompson, Craig. J, and Kelly Tian (2008), "Reconstructing the South: How commercial myths compete for identity value through the ideological shaping of popular memories and coutermemories," *Journal of Consumer Research*, 34 (February), 595-613.

Venkatesh A. (1995), "Ethnoconsumerism: A New Paradigm to Study Cultural and Cross-cultural Consumer Behavior," in J.A.Costa and G. Bamossy (eds.) *Marketing in a Multicultural World*, SAGE Publications, 26-67.

Venkatesh, A. and L. Peñaloza (2006) "From Marketing to the *Market:* A Call for a Paradigm Shift" in Jagdish N. Sheth and Rajendra S. Sisodia (ed.) *Does Marketing Need Reform?: Fresh Perspectives on the Future* NY; London: M.E. Sharpe

Venkatesh, A. and L. Peñaloza (forthcoming), *"The Study of Consumer Markets: A Proposal"*

Vertovec, Steven (2009), *Transnationalism.* New York: Routledge.

Would Others be Gaga for Lady Gaga? When Experience and Perspective Lead to (Mis) Predictions of Others' Preferences

Chair: Troy H. Campbell, Duke University, USA

Paper #1: Why a Frying Pan is Better than Flowers: A Construl Level Approach to Gift Exchange

Ernest Baskin, Yale University, USA
Cheryl J. Wakslak, University of Southern California, USA
Yaacov Trope, New York University, USA
Nathan Novemsky, Yale University, USA

Paper #2: Too Much Experience: Predicting Others' Emotive Reactions and Making Recommendations after Repeated Exposure

Troy H. Campbell, Duke University, USA
Ed O'Brien, University of Michigan, USA
Norbert Schwarz, University of Michigan, USA
Leaf Van Boven, University of Colorado, USA
Peter A. Ubel, Duke University, USA

Paper #3: From Personal Choices to Perceived Popularity: The Impact of Choice Difficulty on Estimated Consensus

Mary Steffel, University of Cincinnati, USA
Eldar Shafir, Princeton University, USA

Paper #4: When My Pain is (Not) Your Pain: Self, Similarity, and Embodied Cognition in Social Predictions

Ed O'Brien, University of Michigan, USA
Phoebe C. Ellsworth, University of Michigan, USA

SESSION OVERVIEW

Accurately predicting how and when consumers, peers, colleagues, and citizens will react to content (advertisements, gifts), share items (e.g. word of mouth), feel in situations (e.g. thirst, physical pain), and make decisions (e.g. investments, purchases) is a fundamental requirement for some of the most important consumer, social, and policy decisions. The research presented in these four papers demonstrates that often a person's state (e.g. experiences, construal) can threaten the accuracy of the social cognitions necessary for these important decisions.

In this special session we identify factors that influence when people are likely and unlikely to use their own perspectives and metacognitions to inform their predictions of others' preferences and reactions. Importantly, we also identify when reliance on these perspectives and metacognitions will facilitate accurate predictions and when the same reliance will lead to costly mispredictions. In addition to these theoretical contributions on choices and predictions for others, metacognition, and psychological distance, the session makes substantial contributions to the topics of word of mouth, gift giving, and investing, and demonstrates how a few popular lay beliefs (e.g. indulgent items are better gifts and more experience leads to wiser predictions) can lead consumers astray. In summary, each paper tells a piece of a larger narrative about how and when consumers (inaccurately) rely on their own perspectives and feelings when making predictions for similar and dissimilar others.

In the first paper, Baskin and colleagues examine a construal level (Trope & Liberman, 2010) mismatch between gift givers and gift receivers. The authors find that givers tend to conceptualize their gift choices abstractly due to their high distance from the consumption experience. Therefore, givers choose gifts higher on desirability attributes to the detriment of gifts higher on feasibility attributes. Gift recipients, in contrast, conceptualize received gifts more con-cretely, and care more about feasibility aspects (how easy a game is to learn versus the quality of the game). This difference leads gift givers to mispredict how much a receiver will enjoy certain gifts and to mistakenly overpay for desirable items. Further, gift givers mistakenly expect giving an item high on desirability will increase social bonds with the receiver and will result in more social reciprocity. The findings of this paper contradict the popular lay belief that the best gift for someone is an indulgent, highly desirable gift. Instead the results suggest that givers may save a lot of money and trouble by putting themselves in the shoes of the receivers and that marketers who are motivated to encourage successful gift giving should try to bring gift givers down to a lower construal level.

One potential way to improve predictions of others' reactions to content is to acquire concrete experience with the content or to ask someone who has had a lot of concrete experience. However in the second paper, Campbell and colleagues find people can quickly gain too much experience. Individuals can rapidly become desensitized (Dijksterhuis & Smith, 2002) to content after repeated or extended exposure such that their current tastes and sensitivities to emotive content become vastly different from people who have not been as thoroughly exposed to the content. Importantly, the authors find that people are largely unaware of the effect that repeated exposure has had on their personal emotive reactions, even when prompted to consider the influence. Accordingly, they overweight their own current dulled sensitivities in their predictions for others' emotive reactions and preferences (e.g. for comedy, art, sports photography, painful noises). This leads consumers to mispredict others' reactions and at times to choose to share bad content that others will not enjoy. Finally, the authors find that when consumers are searching for quality emotive experiences, they tend to seek out a person who has had more versus less repeated experience. The authors experimentally demonstrate how this behavior can doom consumers to receive inappropriate recommendations and ultimately can lead consumers to have worse experiences.

Similarly to Campbell et al., Steffel and Shafir investigate how people use their own feelings to infer others' preferences. Specifically, the researchers examine how the metacognitive feeling of choice difficulty impacts estimated consensus. They find that participants' estimates of the proportion of other people who shared their preferences in a series of choices were correlated with their subjective ratings of choice difficulty. Further, they find in an initial study that subjective difficulty was a valid cue of actual consensus. However, even though choice difficulty can serve as a valid cue for consensus, the authors found that when choice difficulty is manipulated in a manner that does not actually influence consensus (e.g. font readability), reliance on choice difficulty can lead to systematic mispredictions of consensus. Similarly to Campbell et al. focus on repeated experience, Steffel and Shafir find that the common experience of repeated exposure to a choice can reduce the metacognitive feeling of difficulty and lead to increased predictions of consensus. In a final study, the authors identify a boundary condition to this phenomenon such that when one is dissimilar to the target population, one does not use subjective difficulty to judge consensus in the target population.

In the first three studies, the authors examined how people's experiences and perspectives influenced their judgments. In the last paper, similarly to the final study in Steffel et al., O'Brien and colleagues examine when people are likely to rely on their own state, particularly their metacognitive feelings, when making predictions for others. A wealth of research suggests that people use their own visceral states to inform their social judgments, such as predicting others are thirstier when oneself is dehydrated (Van Boven & Loewenstein, 2003). The authors find that these typical egocentric influences on social predictions (replicated in the prior papers in this session) are at times undermined by incidental knowledge of the target. Cold and thirsty participants judged others as more sensitive to cold and thirst, but only when those in question shared their ideological values (e.g. same stance on same sex marriage). This suggests that internal cues in general may simply be less (or not) influential when predicting the responses of dissimilar others. For instance, while at a hot baseball game one might not use their own feeling of thirst to determine whether a dissimilar other would enjoy a cold drink. In general, this is one of the first studies to find identify a boundary in embodied cognition.

Across four papers and 17 studies, this session investigates when people are likely to rely on their own states to predict others' preferences, and when reliance on their own states is likely to benefit or bias their predictions of others' preferences. Data has been collected for all reported studies and all papers are very advanced or complete. This session relates to the theme of "appreciating" diversity as it tells a narrative of consumer interaction interwoven between theoretical perspectives. The session should appeal to a wide audience including those with theoretical interests in choosing for others, metacognition, embodied cognition, perspective taking, psychological distance, outgroup perception, and social cognition in general. Additionally, the session will appeal to those with substantive interests in word of mouth, gift giving, and investment. This session also directly relates to the theme of "appreciating diversity" as all four papers deal with how people predict others' responses, and the latter three papers specifically examine how people predict the reactions of others who have explicitly different beliefs or have had explicitly different experiences. Full references for articles cited in this submission are available upon request.

Why a Frying Pan is Better than Flowers: A Construal Level Approach to Gift Exchange

EXTENDED ABSTRACT

The tradition of gift giving is as old as culture itself. From the circular gift exchange formed by the Trobriand islanders (Malinowski, 1922) to today's frenzied holiday shopping, gift-giving rituals have played a central cultural role. Indeed, evolutionary psychologists have suggested that gifts are a natural way to establish, create and maintain order in a group of social beings (Cosmides & Tooby, 1992). Additionally, anthropologists have focused on the role of gift exchange in building and maintaining social bonds (Gouldner, 1960; Mauss, 1925). Thus, due to the importance of gifts, givers have a large stake in making sure their gifts are well received and then reciprocated in order to ensure the continuity of their social relationships.

The importance of gift-giving raises the question of how one decides on the perfect gift. In this research, we look at differences in giver/receiver gift evaluation using construal level theory (CLT) as a framework (Trope & Liberman, 2010). We propose that givers conceptualize their choices abstractly due to their high distance from the receiver and the eventual use of the gift. Therefore, they choose gifts higher on desirability attributes to the detriment of attributes higher on feasibility dimensions. Gift recipients, in contrast, conceptualize received gifts more concretely, and care more about

feasibility aspects (e.g., how easy is the gift to use?). This difference in construal between givers and receivers creates an important asymmetry between what givers care about and what recipients care about that leads to a mismatch in the kinds of gifts the two parties prefer to give/receive and reciprocate. Our findings also stand in contrast to the typical folk wisdom that givers should always seek to maximize gifts' desirability.

We explored this asymmetry in a series of studies. In Study 1a, we asked participants to assume a gift giving or receiving mode by respectively writing about a time they gave or received a gift. Those in giving mode scored higher on the Behavioral Identification Form (Vallacher & Wegner, 1989), a measure of abstract orientation. This study establishes that a giving mode activates a more abstract orientation than a receiving mode. Study 1b corroborates the link to construal by showing that gift givers can be induced to give more feasible gifts by giving gifts to people in nearby locations while receivers show no effect based on distance from givers. This suggests that givers are imagining the receiver using the gift such that the psychological distance from the consumption experience decreases with the spatial distance. However, receivers imagine their own consumption, so they are unaffected by these changes in spatial distance.

Studies 2a and 2b examined tradeoffs people make when giving gifts. By using items that require tradeoffs between abstract/desirability and concrete/feasibility dimensions (e.g., a high resolution 3D videogame that takes 10 hours to learn vs. a poor looking videogame that one can pick up and play), we show that givers evaluated high desirability gifts as better than high feasibility gifts. However, receivers do not exhibit this preference. We assigned participants to either the giver or the receiver role and asked them to evaluate gifts in a variety of domains (e.g. restaurant gift certificates, newspaper subscriptions, etc.). Participants evaluated gifts using a scale consisting of the following questions: "How much did you like the item as a gift?", "How good is this gift?", "How appropriate is this gift?" and "How positive is this gift?" Study 2b extended these finding by eliciting participants' willingness to pay (WTP). Givers reported their WTP for the gift while receivers reported their WTP as if they were buying the item for themselves. While receivers were willing to pay significantly more for desirable gifts than feasible gifts, givers had a significantly higher WTP difference than receivers between high desirability and high feasibility gifts. From this study, we show that there is a mismatch in willingness to pay for desirable goods in that givers are willing to pay a comparatively higher price than receivers for highly desirable gifts. The results of Studies 2a and 2b combined show that givers place more value on desirability attributes over and above that placed by receivers, and literally pay for this error.

Study 3 examined implications of these differences for social bonds between exchange partners. Participants were told about two different movie offers, one of which was more desirable, but relatively inconvenient (access to view *Harry Potter and the Deathly Hallows (HP7): Part 2* online during an inconvenient five-hour window) and the other less desirable, but more convenient (access to view the less novel and widely available *HP7: Part 1* online during a convenient 30-day window). Participants believed they were either giving a gift to, or had received a gift from, another participant in the study. As predicted, givers preferred to give other participants in the study the more desirable/less convenient *HP7: Part 2*, but receivers preferred to receive the less desirable/more convenient *HP7: Part 1*. More importantly, givers thought that if they picked *HP7: Part 2*, receivers would be more likely to reciprocate their gift in the future. Receivers, on the other hand, were willing to reciprocate both gifts equally suggesting that their opinions of the giver were not affected by the choice of gift. Instead, givers are mistaken in their prediction that desirable gifts will increase social bonds.

Since gift giving is primarily about relationships, we are conducting future research to examine how various gifts change the relationship between gift givers and gift receivers and how people's awareness of biases in selecting gifts may improve their relationship with the other person. Overall, the results of this current research suggest that givers may save a lot of trouble and at times money by putting themselves in the shoes of the receivers and think about the kind of gift they would prefer to receive. The findings further suggest that the conventional wisdom of always maximizing gift desirability, rather than other gift features, may be incorrect since givers generally underweight concrete/feasibility aspects of the gift as compared to receivers.

Too Much Experience: Predicting Others' Emotive Reactions and Making Recommendations after Repeated Exposure

EXTENDED ABSTRACT

People often seek out individuals who are distinguished by their repeated experience with emotive content (e.g. art, comedy, freeway noise). Consumers seek out these individuals for recommendations, corporations hire these individuals to design products for the public, and governments employ these individuals to craft policy for the public. Additionally, when trying to predict others' reactions to emotive content, people often make an effort to become a well exposed person. For instance, a person may deliberately watch a YouTube video multiple times to decide whether it is funny or appropriate enough for sharing. Both lay intuition and empirical research suggest this gaining experience can help people predict others' emotive reactions by closing empathy gaps (Nordgren, McDonnell, & Loewenstein, 2011).

However, individuals can quickly gain too much experience and become desensitized to content after repeated or extended experiences (Dijksterhuis & Smith, 2002). Although much research has examined how desensitization affects judgments of one's own tastes and preferences (e.g., Loewenstein, O'Donoghue, & Rabin, 2003; Wilson & Gilbert, 2003), we examined downstream consequences for prediction of others' judgments.

We hypothesized that people will not only desensitize to an emotive experience after repeated exposure, but also incorrectly use their desensitized sensitivities to make predictions of how someone else would react to an emotive experience. Our framework is rooted in the dual judgment model of emotional perspective taking (Van Boven & Loewenstein, 2005). This model posits people predict others' emotions by first considering their own (simulated) emotions and often fail to adequately adjust for differences between self and other. Thus, rather than realizing that one's own current state (e.g., subjective desensitization) may be different from someone else who lacks a high level of exposure, people who desensitize to an emotive experience might falsely assume that the experience is less arousing for others. This should lead them to mispredict others' preferences and emotive reactions and lead to error when they recommend and share content with others. We tested this desensitization bias in social judgment hypothesis across six studies using various emotive content ranging in valence, complexity, and repeated exposure method.

In the first study, we exposed participants to twenty images of a dramatic style of astrological art called "Digital Blasphemy." After the exposures, we asked participants to remember from a written description the first and last images they had seen and to indicate which

image would be better for publically consumed Space Art media. We counterbalanced the first and last picture between subjects, and found that participants showed a bias to select the image that was presented at the start of the exposure (before they became desensitized) rather than the image at the end.

In study 2, after viewing a slideshow of motorcycle tricks, we presented participants with two images, each featuring a different thrilling stunt performed on a motorcycle. Participants were asked to select which image would be more impressive as a single promotional image to people viewing motorcycle stunts for the first time in their lives. We found that participants were more likely to choose the image of a specific stunt type if that stunt type had been featured *less often* in a slideshow that preceded the choice.

In study 3, people were repeatedly exposed to one of two shocking pictures of Lady Gaga.

We found participants were more likely to predict others previously unexposed to both images would be less shocked by the image participants themselves were repeatedly exposed to compare to the image participants were not repeatedly exposed to.

Additionally, a variety of indirect and direct probes in studies 2 and 3 found that participants were largely unaware of the desensitization bias and unable to retrospectively correct for the bias. In sum, the breadth of the first three studies distinguishes the desensitization bias as a unique phenomenon separate from related phenomena such as primacy effects (Carpenter & Nakamoto, 1989) and peak-end biases (Kahneman et. al, 1993).

In studies 4 and 5, we tested the underlying process and potential downstream consequences. In study 4, we found that repeated exposure to a joke (writing it five versus one time) lead participants to find the joke personally less humorous, predict the joke would be less humorous to others, and report lower likelihood to share the joke. As predicted, we found the effect of repeated exposure on one's own feelings fully mediated the effect of repeated exposure on predictions of others' feelings and likelihood to share. In study 5, we found that after extended versus shorter exposure to a painful noise, participants predicted an additional very short sound burst would be less painful for themselves, predicted it would be less painful for others never exposed to the sound, and reported they would feel less guilty using the sound burst to punish other participants in a game. Similar to study 4, the effect of exposure on the latter two other-regarding variables was fully mediated by predictions of how painful a short noise burst would be for oneself.

In the final study, we tested whether this desensitization-bias could lead high-exposure consumers to make very poor recommendations for unexposed others. Participants were given an objectively better joke and an objectively worse joke (based on pre-test ratings). We found that participants who were repeatedly exposed to the good joke (writing it down five times) were about 3x less likely to choose to share it with someone else compared to participants who were not repeatedly exposed (presumably because the extra exposure desensitized them to its funniness). Moreover, we described the study to a separate group of participants and asked them who they would rely on to choose them the funnier joke: a person in the control condition or a person in the repeated exposure condition? A majority chose the person in the repeated exposure condition, thus dooming themselves to a worse experience.

These studies suggest that repeated exposure can dramatically and negatively influence sharing, recommendations, and social behavior. The lay intuition to seek out those with more exposure and to acquire more exposure to better predict others' reactions may often steer consumers in the wrong direction. At times, high-exposure "experts" might be in the *worst* position to connect with someone who lacks any exposure at all.

From Personal Choices to Perceived Popularity: The Impact of Choice Difficulty On Estimated Consensus

EXTENDED ABSTRACT

Effective decision-making often depends on accurately gauging others' preferences. Manufacturers try to forecast consumer preferences, politicians try to gauge public opinion, and most people try to anticipate how their peers will react to what they say and do. Incorrect predictions of others' preferences can lead to detrimental behaviors, like investing in a product that fails to generate interest, or campaigning on an issue that triggers unexpected reactions.

Although psychologists have well documented the impact of choices – conceived as binary outcomes – on predictions of others' preferences (e.g., Ross, Greene, and House 1977), relatively little is known about the impact of the metacognitive experiences that accompany those choices. This research explores how the feeling of choice difficulty impacts people's predictions of others' preferences and how it impacts judgmental accuracy.

We hypothesize that people perceive greater consensus when choice feels easy than when it feels difficult. In a pretest, participants' estimates of the proportion of other people who shared their preferences in a series of choices between monetary lotteries were correlated with their subjective ratings of choice difficulty, (b = -0.91, t = 8.88, p < .001). Further, in these initial situations, subjective choice difficulty served as a valid cue for predicting consensus, as it was highly correlated with consensus (β = -0.77, t = 4.91, p < .001). Thus, at least in some cases, the metacognitive feeling of choice difficulty can guide people to correct estimates of consensus.

However, there are many cases in which choice difficulty may be misleading. Many factors that are not indicative of actual consensus can influence subjective choice difficulty. For example, factors such as font readability, mere exposure, reason listing, and brow furrowing, can all increase perceptions of choice difficulty (Alter and Oppenheimer 2009). We show that, when choice difficulty is manipulated independently from the relative attractiveness of the choice alternatives, reliance on choice difficulty can lead to systematic mispredictions of consensus.

We first tested when holding actual consensus constant, would manipulating choice difficulty influence estimated consensus? Participants were presented with a hypothetical choice about whether or not to tip a waitress who provided fast service (easy condition) or slow service (difficult condition). Although participants were equally likely to tip the waitress across conditions, participants estimated greater consensus in the easy condition (M = 81%) than in the hard condition (M = 74%; t(156) = 2.84, p = .005). Choice difficulty fully mediated the relationship between the manipulation and estimated consensus, (95% CI = -7.85 to -2.62).

Study 2 sought to isolate the feeling of choice difficulty as the mechanism underlying consensus estimates by holding constant the content of the choice options and manipulating choice difficulty via fluency. In this study, a target lottery was presented either several times (fluent condition) or only once (disfluent condition; for a review of repetition as a form of fluency, see Alter and Oppenheimer, 2009). As predicted, estimated consensus was greater when the choice was repeated (M = 62%) than when the choice was novel (M = 53%; t(123) = 4.28, p < .001), regardless of which option was chosen. Choice difficulty served as a significant partial mediator of the relationship between the fluency manipulation and estimated consensus, (95% CI = -4.90 to -.83). Within the repeated condition, there

was a linear trend such that participants estimated greater consensus with increased repetition (first presentation: M = 59%; second presentation: M = 60%; third presentation: M = 62%; F(1, 67) = 5.44, p = .02). The difference in choice difficulty between the first and final presentation mediated this effect, (β = -4.17, SE = .54, t = -7.78, p < .001).

An additional aim of study 2 was to illustrate a consequence of relying on choice difficulty to predict consensus: since estimated consensus should increase with repetition regardless of which lottery is chosen, then false consensus (as measured by the sum of estimated consensus for the lottery chosen by the majority and the lottery chosen by the minority) is more likely to emerge when choices are repeated than when choices are novel. Indeed, false consensus was 125.3% when the choice was repeated and 105.2% when the choice was novel. Within the repeated condition, the sum of estimated consensus for the lottery chosen by the majority and the lottery chosen by the minority increased with repetition (first presentation: 117%; second presentation: 120%; third presentation: 125%).

Study 3 explored whether perceived similarity moderates the extent to which people rely on choice difficulty to gauge consensus by priming participants to think of ways in which they were similar to or different from the target population. Indeed, there was a significant interaction between the priming condition and choice difficulty, (b = -0.20, t = 2.35, p = .02), such that participants who were primed to think of similarities relied on choice difficulty to predict consensus (b = -0.39, t = 4.51, p < .001) but those primed to think of dissimilarities did not (b = -0.11, t = 1.18, p = .24).

People gauge consensus, not just based on their own choices, but also based on the metacognitive experiences that accompany choosing. People infer greater consensus when choice feels easy than when it feels difficult. Although subjective choice difficulty can sometimes serve as a valid indicator of consensus, many factors that are not indicative of consensus can affect choice difficulty and lead to systematic mispredictions. We will discuss implications for real-world decisions: for example, an investor who has had greater exposure to the stocks in his portfolio may expect greater buy-in from other investors than is borne out in the stock market, or a politician who repeatedly reevaluates his platform may expect more unified support from his constituents than is borne out in the actual election. We will also discuss moderators of reliance on choice difficulty – e.g., perceived dissimilarity to the target population and attributions for choice difficulty – and directions for future research.

When My Pain is (Not) Your Pain: Self, Similarity, and Embodied Cognition in Social Predictions

EXTENDED ABSTRACT

Predictions of others' thoughts, feelings, and preferences do not occur in a bubble. Rather, people predict the internal states of others differently depending on whether those in question are perceived as similar or dissimilar to them on the surface.

People typically judge similar others egocentrically – they put themselves in the others' shoes by first thinking, "How would *I* feel in their situation?" (Dunning & Hayes, 1996; Epley et al., 2004). Thus, one's own states are often projected onto similar others. Obama-supporting Democrats might overconfidently assume that Obama likes the same wine that they do.

However, people are less likely to use their own experience as an anchor when judging others who seem very different from them (Ames, 2004; Robbins & Krueger, 2005). In these cases, the self becomes a poor proxy to figure out very dissimilar people. Obama-supporting Democrats might have little reason to assume Sarah Palin shares their wine preference.

In our experiments, we examined how far the effect of dissimilarity extends. We focused on the influence of one's visceral states on how people perceive similar versus dissimilar others' feelings and preferences.

Visceral states refer to strong transient states of arousal (e.g., hunger, threat). These feelings are typically so strong that they assimilate with perceptions of others who may not even be experiencing the same state. For example, when people are dehydrated they perceive others as thirsty (Van Boven & Loewenstein, 2003), and when people are frightened they perceive others as afraid (Van Boven, Loewenstein, & Dunning, 2005). Might the effect of even these powerful states dissipate when judging others who seem very different?

In Experiment 1, we explored this question by assigning participants to read a story about a hiker who gets lost with no food, no water, and no extra clothes (adapted from Van Boven & Loewenstein, 2003). Participants rated the hiker's feelings and their own feelings. To manipulate similarity, the hiker was described as either a left-wing, pro-gay rights Democrat or a right-wing, anti-gay rights Republican, who went hiking on a break from a political campaign (a strong dissimilarity manipulation: Mitchell, Macrae, & Banaji, 2006). At the end of the study, participants answered a forced-choice item about whether they were similar or dissimilar to the hiker, confirmed by their own political values. We used this forced-choice to group participants into "similar" or "dissimilar" conditions. To manipulate visceral experience, all participants were recruited during winter in Michigan (M_{temp}=6° Fahrenheit). We tested people who were indoors in the university library ("warm" condition) or outdoors at a nearby bus stop ("cold" condition).

Did being in the freezing cold influence social judgment? Yes – but only when judging similar others. When asked whether hunger, thirst, or cold was most unpleasant for the hiker, a significant interaction was obtained between similarity and location (β=-2.75, p=.005). Participants who perceived the hiker as similar were more likely to choose "cold" when they were outdoors (94%) than indoors (57%), replicating standard assimilation effects. However, judgments of dissimilar hikers were uninfluenced by location (55% outdoors, 63% indoors). The same interactions were obtained for whether the hiker most regretted not packing food, water, or *extra clothes* (β=-2.05, p<.01), and for how cold the hiker felt on a continuous scale (β=2.21, p<.001). These patterns were further reflected by regression-based mediation: participants' coldness mediated judgments of how cold similar others felt (β=−0.71, p=.004)—but not how cold dissimilar others felt (β =0.06, p=.86).

In Experiment 2, participants were induced to feel thirsty by eating salty snacks either with or without water. The same patterns from Experiment 1 were observed. When asked whether hunger, thirst, or cold was most unpleasant for the hiker, a significant interaction was obtained between similarity and thirst (β =-1.81, p<.02). Participants who perceived the hiker as similar were more likely to choose "thirsty" when they were thirsty (71%) versus quenched (20%); judgments of dissimilar hikers were uninfluenced by participants' own thirst (37% thirsty, 26% quenched). The same interactions were obtained for whether the hiker most regretted not packing food, extra clothes, or *water* (β=-1.88, p<.03), and for how thirsty the hiker felt on a continuous scale (β=1.72, p<.01). Again, participants' thirstiness mediated judgments of how thirsty similar others felt (β=0.54, p=.02) – but not how dissimilar others felt (β=0.04, p=.89).

Although physical feelings powerfully shape our predictions of others' thoughts, feelings, and preferences, these findings suggest that their influence is eliminated when judging dissimilar others. This observation may have far-reaching consequences. In other studies, for example, people who held a warm cup of coffee judged a target person as more socially "warm" (Williams & Bargh, 2008), and those who held a resume on a heavy clipboard thought it was more "weighty" and "important" (Ackerman, Nocera, & Bargh, 2010). These embodiment effects may be inhibited by dissimilar targets; liberal undergraduates holding a warm drink may not think Republicans are nicer.

More importantly, predicting how others feel is vital for everyday interactions between bosses and employees, relationship partners, and sellers and consumers. One way to more accurately understand others' situations is to find one's self in their shoes. For example, actually catching a sickness or feeling pain can help people better empathize with others' needs (Loewenstein, 2005). But the success of this strategy might be inhibited if one perceives others as different, even on a superficial level. For instance, while shopping for Christmas gifts on a cold New York City night, a woman may be inspired by her own cold feelings to purchase a winter jacket if she was shopping for a close cousin, but *not* if she were shopping for a distant mother in-law.

In sum: egocentric processes underlying how people make predictions of others' states are undermined by incidental knowledge about those in question. Such knowledge appears to prevent environmental stimuli (e.g. a hot coffee cup, the weather, hunger) from influencing social predictions, which at times may inhibit people's ability to make optimal predictions of others' needs and preferences.

Socio-Historical Change and Representations of Consumers in Ads

Chair: Melanie Wallendorf, Eller College of Management, USA

Paper #1: Making the Changing Scene
Sidney J. Levy, University of Arizona, and Marketing Department, Northwestern University (emeritus), USA

Paper #2: Working Reality: Advertising Representations of Social Class and Race during a Time of Increasing Income Inequality, 1970-2010
Erika Paulson, University of Wisconsin, USA
Thomas O'Guinn, University of Wisconsin, USA

Paper #3: "I am Canadian": The Rise of Canadian Identity in Canada's Censuses, 1981-2006
Gillian Stevens, University of Alberta, Canada

Paper #4: An Historical Analysis of Archetypical Shifts in Representations of Women in Luxury Product Advertising in the early 1960's
Alyssa Travis, University of Arizona, USA
Melanie Wallendorf, University of Arizona, USA

SESSION OVERVIEW

Session objective

To bring together diverse yet similar papers examining change in advertising depictions over time employing a cultural lens to address the relation between socio-cultural change and advertising representations of various social categories of consumers.

General orientation

The session's orientation is socio-cultural rather than psychological and covers broad temporal change in representations of social categories in advertising.

Likely audience

The likely audience is consumer researchers with an interest in advertising and its relation to larger society. It will also draw CCT scholars and consumer researchers with social science interests outside psychology, particularly those with interests in historical analysis, sociological interpretation, and anthropological approaches. It will attract those with an interest in social class, gender, and ethnicity. And, given the focus of the Stephens paper, we anticipate that it will attract many Canadians at the conference.

Issues and topics to be covered

Advertising, cultural change, historical analysis, gender, race, class, immigration, and inequality.

Importance of contribution to CB

On average, biology grants us the opportunity to understand a time span of 78.49 years (81.48 years for Canadians) through direct experience. Historical analysis expands our range of understanding beyond that granted by biology, and deepens our understanding beyond what can be directly experienced.

The conference mission of appreciating diversity in approaches

The topics covered that are often not covered in ACR presentations are gender as a social category, social inequality, relations between immigrants and host culture, international relations through advertising, and most importantly, a broad historical perspective. The presenters include several first time ACR presenters, including an award winning senior scholar from sociology. The presentations draw from the perspectives of three different generations of consumer researchers, each of whom approaches these time periods in a different way.

Stage of completion

All projects are fully complete.

Making the Changing Scene

EXTENDED ABSTRACT

The basic goal of the presentation is to observe and analyze how advertising expresses a society's values. The themes to be discussed are these: Society moves generally from mass consumption to making increasingly individual choices serving subgroup and personal choices. There is the large development that starts with the struggle to feed, clothe, and house masses of poor people. I term this *obligatory marketing*. This mass consumption is accompanied by relative scarcity, the central role of commodities, problems of distribution, an emphasis on economics, and pressure toward low prices as well as the importance of commodity companies, non-profit agencies, and government.

Movement toward economic success increases opportunities for the expression of subgroup lifestyles and personal distinction; that is, both to belong and to stand out. I term this *permissive marketing*. Individualized and niche consumption goes with branding, higher prices, and the creation of distinction for products through artistic means. A key artistic achievement is the creation of brand images. Brand images are created by all marketing means, but especially by advertising. Planning and executing advertising is a rich, complex, and challenging activity. To do it well requires awareness of cultural changes in values. Sometimes advertising leads the way with innovation and anticipation of where society is going. Commonly it follows where the people are going.

Three JIF Peanut Butter commercials from three historical periods are used as exemplars of advertising's process of adaptation to changing values and roles in American life. The first commercial shows a traditional emphasis on being a good mother. It assumes the mother stays at home and takes care of the children. The second commercial is one in which JIF brand represents women as working women rather than "just mothers." However, despite their job related concerns, their concern with good food for the family is depicted as still being of primary importance. The third commercial includes the father of the family doing the shopping and being the one who chooses JIF while the woman is evidently off doing something else.

Taken across time, these advertisements point to important questions about the ways advertising reflects and/or provokes cultural change. As such, the presentation is intended as an opening to the discussion on this topic that the other papers take up.

Working Reality: Advertising Representations of Social Class and Race during a Time of Increasing Income Inequality, 1970-2010

EXTENDED ABSTRACT

We will present the results of a systematic analysis of American general interest magazine advertising, 1970-2010. We will focus on representations of the middle class, the working class, and race.

The ads are a subsample (n=213 for all general interest) of a larger data collection (n=1200) covering the period 1900 to 2010 and coded along multiple dimensions of stratification including age, race, gender, and social class by three trained coders (Krippendorff's alpha = 0.78). We focus on the 1970-2010 period due to its sociological and economic significance. It is during this period that the U.S. exits a post-World War II period of increasing equality, equitable income growth and economic wellbeing. From the mid 1970s forward the U.S. experiences increasing inequality on virtually every dimension, rending the class divide ever wider. This reversal of fortunes that occurred in the 1970s is widely known to sociologists as the Great U-Turn (Harrison and Bluestone 1988). The presentation will overlay our content analysis with other empirical social indicators, such as measures of income inequality and public opinion. We will investigate whether this trend holds only in general interest advertising or whether the same class message is conveyed differently to consumers occupying different social classes. We will also identify, describe, and report the frequency and nature of one common visual trope within each of the social class representations. In each case we examine how the trope deftly leverages social stratifications to sell products, and presents a world consistent with advertising's institutional goals.

The overwhelming majority of individuals who appear in general interest advertising are drawn from the middle class. The period begins in 1970 with 45.2 % of pictured individuals identified as middle class. They average 55.9% of the sub-sample. While this level over-represents the middle class compared to the 32% of the population that is objectively middle class, it is the astonishing growth of images of the middle class until 2000 that is particularly striking, at which point the middle class comprises 73.3 % of the individuals in our subsample. Advertising insists that the middle class is stable, secure, even growing. This trend becomes particularly interesting and counterintuitive when overlaid with popular press and public opinion data that suggest a significantly threatened, shrinking, or even disappearing middle class. The distance between advertising images and public perception is investigated along multiple dimensions: an artifact of the target market of mass advertising, a "safe" and desirable way to sell products, as part and parcel of the "egalitarian myth" that has been an ever present and defining theme in American politics (Pessen 1971), and the institutional environment in which a foreshortened class structure is present (Marchand 1985).

In examining the portrayal of the middle class in general circulation advertising, we go beyond numeric representations and investigate the common tropes or tableau in which the middle class is placed. We find that the middle class plays a unique role in advertising. The modal ad shows the middle class to be overworked and over-committed (Schor 1993). In this trope, which we label the "consumer drama," a simple narrative unfolds. These narratives are unbalanced and dramatic; women scramble up on chairs when they see a mouse, fall off clumsy step stools, and are escorted off beaches by police officers. All tell a simple narrative in which something goes wrong and a branded consumer good or service is used to solve the problem. The function of this style of trope and its relationship to the stratification of society is suggested.

The end of this counter-empirical reality comes in 2010. Abruptly, representations of the middle class fall from 73.3% to 36.6% in just ten years. Why? We propose a number of possible hypotheses. We examine alternative social stratifications and hierarchies as well as popular opinion and populist sentiment as potential drivers of this shift. By 2010 income inequality had become common a common media meme, a mid-term election issue, and part of several left and right populist movements.

In accounting for the decline of the middle class in the final decennial year, 2010, we expand our analysis to the intersections of social class with race and ethnicity. The proportion of Blacks, Latinos, and other minority ethnic groups portrayed in ads averages a combined 8.0% from 1970 to 2000, never exceeding 20%. However, in 2010 the number of non-whites portrayed in general interest advertising crescendos to a remarkable 47.5% of all individuals. Not only is the increase sharp, 2010 represents the first year when racial and ethnic minorities are overrepresented as compared to the actual population. We consider multiple causes of this dramatic shift including demographic shifts in the American populace, the powerful effect of Obama's presidency, and the emergence of a "post-racial America." Because class, race and ethnicity are often confounded, we also consider socioeconomic shifts such as the Great Recession. When these explanations are found lacking, we turn to the final crucial factor – the institutional environment. Our analysis reveals that the most compelling explanation for this shift is less about demography or ideology than the institutional environment. Many minorities pictured in 2010 appear in ads that emphasize a firm's corporate social responsibility and charitable activities across the world including China, India, and Africa.

A large body of empirical work has consistently shown that media representations significantly impact people's beliefs about the composition of the social world (Gerbner et al. 2002). Our world is increasingly mediated by social representations brought by advertising supported television, paid search, and entertainment. Advertising is the most explicit in its purpose: to get consumers to want and buy things. Yet, social class, inextricably tied to consumption, has remained largely unexamined. As theorists have argued, the information in ads is never random (Schudson 1984; Goffman 1976) or mundane, but rather goes well beyond copy and product demonstration to comment on the fabric of social life. Our investigation of class and stratification images reveals crucial processes of social representation and the interplay of forces such as institutions that have not been apparent in previous research.

REFERENCES

Gerbner, George, Larry Gross, Michael Morgan, Nancy Signorielli, James Shanahan (2002), "Growing up with Television: Cultivation Process," in *Media Effects: Advances in Theory and Research*, 2nd edition, ed. Jennings Bryant and Dolf Zillman, Mahwah, NJ: Lawrence Erlbaum Associates, 43-67.

Goffman, Erving (1976), *Gender Advertisements*, Washington: Society for the Anthropology of Visual Communication.

Harrison, Bennett and Barry Bluestone (1988), *The Great U-Turn: Corporate Restructuring and the Polarizing of America*, New York: Basic Books.

Marchand, Roland (1985), *Advertising the American Dream: Making Way for Modernity, 1920-1940*, Berkeley: University of California Press.

Pessen, Edward (1971). "The Egalitarian Myth and the American Social Reality: Wealth, Mobility, and Equality in the 'Era of the Common Man,'" *The American Historical Review* 76(4): 989–1034.

Schor, Juliet (1993), *The Overworked American: The Unexpected Decline Of Leisure*. New York: Basic Books.

Schudson, M. (1984), "Advertising as Capitalist Realism," in *Advertising, The Uneasy Persuasion: It's Dubious Impact on American Society,* New York: Basic Books, 209-3

"I am Canadian": The Rise of Canadian Identity in Canada's Censuses, 1981-2006

EXTENDED ABSTRACT

The "I am Canadian" commercial for Molson's *Canadian* beer, first aired in 2000, became an overnight phenomenon in Canada. In "The Rant," as it was known, an actor listed stereotypical characteristics of Canadians and ended with the emphatic declaration "I am Canadian." This ad was interpreted by many as an expression of national pride and an emblem of Canadian patriotism (MacGregor, 2003); its success quickly led to numerous spin-offs and spoofs, and increased beer sales for Molson's Beer Co. The campaign was perfectly timed: it occurred after two decades of change in how Canadians identified themselves. In 1981, less than 1% of the Canadian population identified their origins on the federal census as "Canadian" or "Canadien". By 2001, the number describing their origins as at least partly Canadian or Canadien had grown to 40%.

The rapid growth of the numbers and percentages of people in Canada identifying themselves as Canadian in response to the census questions on race and ethnic "origins" between 1981 and 2006 is the result of several different sets of processes. The first set consists of demographic processes: immigration, racial and ethnic intermarriage, and generational aging. Immigrant origins such as "Ukrainian" or "Italian" fade in salience by the third and later generations. As intermarriage between origin or ancestry groups increases, the complexity of origins of the next generation increases and the salience of any one ancestral thread decreases.

A second set of processes consists of methodological issues that helped shaped the conversation between the premier data-gathering organization of the country, Statistics Canada, and the nation's population. Details of the operationalization and design of the questions and the responses for racial and ethnic "origins" in the censuses, first discouraged, then allowed, then reacted to, and finally encouraged people to declare that their racial or ethnic origins were "Canadian" or "Canadien" or included a Canadian component. In this regard, both Statistics Canada and the respondents to the censuses worked in concert to produce an upswing in the numbers of people declaring themselves, at least in part, as Canadian.

A third set of issues concern the ambiguity and complexity of the concepts–nationality, race, ethnicity–that underlay ancestral origins and the phenomena that shape people's choice of a particular discourse describing their origins. Because these concepts are complex and overlapping, contemporaneous and extraneous phenomena such as advertising campaigns for beer or a clothing chain can bring a specific discourse to the forefront at a time when respondents must confront the need to choose a particular answer on a federal form.

Scholars have argued that the tenor of Canadian nationalism changed in the mid-1980s. During the 1980s and 1990s, several commercial enterprises became important actors in the expression of Canadian patriotism. These included Roots, a Canadian clothing store, Tim Horton's chain of coffee and donut shops, as well as Molson's beer company. The proclivity of Canadians to drape themselves in clothing branded with beavers, canoes and maple leaves, and to drink coffee in shops associated with a hockey player, blossomed during these two decades. Carstairs (2006) argues that these consumer purchases allowed Canadians the ability to be "proudly Canadian" while imagining an idealized life of wilderness parks and successful athletes. The success of Molson's nationalistic and forceful "I am Canadian" campaign, which was particularly evident at the very beginning of the 21st century, may well have helped produce the crest in the numbers of individuals who chose to opt for the response most evocative of a nationalistic stance in the 2001 census,

fielded only a year after the beginning of the campaign. It is also possible that the Canadian Government's extensive advertisements for the 1998 Winter Olympics in Nagano, Japan (Rose, 2003) fueled nationalistic responses on the 2001 census.

However, five years later, in 2006, the year of the next census, the percentage of respondents declaring themselves as Canadian/Canadien dropped back slightly to 35%. But by then the novelty and prominence of Molson's very forceful campaign had faded and so the other options, discourses centered on race or ethnic origins, may have moved back into the forefront for some individuals as they confronted the need to choose one or two words to describe their origins on the federal census form.

REFERENCES

Carstairs, Catherine. 2007. Roots Nationalism: Branding English Canada Cool in the 1980s and 1990s. *Histoire sociale/Social History* 2006(1): 235-255.

Dittmer, Jason and Soren Larsen. 2007. *Captain Canuck*, Audience Response, and the Project of Canadian Nationalism. *Social & Cultural Geography* 8(5): 735-753.

MacGregor, Robert M. 2003. I am Canadian: National Identity in Beer Commercials. *The Journal of Popular Culture* 37(2): 276-286.

Rose, Jonathan. 2003. "Government Advertising and the Creation of National Myths: The Canadian Case. *International Journal of Nonprofit and Voluntary Sector Marketing* 8(2): 1153-165.

An Historical Analysis of Archetypical Shifts in Representations of Women in Luxury Product Advertising in the early 1960's

EXTENDED ABSTRACT

This study zooms in on a particularly noteworthy moment in U.S. history to closely examine how socio-historical events reverberate in advertising representations of social categories of consumers. It follows the work of Marchand (1985) and others focused on advertising's cultural meanings within a particular socio-historical context (Scott 1994; Stern 1989, 1996; O'Guinn, Pracejus, Olsen 2006). We examine the temporal relationship between political and social change and advertising representations of consumers. We began our research wanting to consider whether a single traumatic event in U.S. history could significantly alter advertising conventions for luxury products not directly connected to the event. That is, can changes in advertising representations of consumers be traced to distinct social disruptions, even in ads for luxury products that usually show little change over time?

Method. We examine a set of 800 magazine ads for women's perfume and cologne appearing from 1962 – 1965, a period that brackets the assassination of President John F. Kennedy on November 22, 1963. In this presentation we examine changes in representations of women in these ads. Our data is a comprehensive set of such ads contained in the J. Walter Thompson Competitive Advertisements Collection at the Hartman Center at Duke University. Our data set provides broad inclusion of perfume and cologne advertisements found in a structured sample of major distribution magazines including *Mademoiselle, The New Yorker, Harper's Bazaar, Seventeen, Good Housekeeping, Ladies' Home Journal,* and *Life.*

Perfume and cologne advertisements were chosen because they often utilize abstract messages to sell the product. Like automobile, soft drink, and cigarette advertisements, perfume ads seek to associate the product with culturally framed aspirations such as success, romance, youthfulness, or adventure (Zelman 1992). However, unlike automobiles, soft drinks, and cigarettes, there is no commonly understood vocabulary to fully express the particular compositional qualities of fragrance. Consequently, perfume and cologne advertisements rely on abstract symbolism to sell the product and to link a particular scent to elements of an American dream (Zelman 1992). Because perfume and cologne advertisements employ symbolism rather than information about functional product attributes, their advertising conventions are perhaps more flexible in their ability to change with shifts in cultural meanings.

The advertisements in the data set were coded on many executional dimensions, but in this presentation we focus on the representations of women in the ad. By closely examining the implied viewer, surroundings, eye contact, clothing, and social setting, women appearing in the ads were coded as representing archetypal images. Eight archetypal images of women were frequently featured: Femme Fatale/Woman as Animal, the Girl-Next-Door, the Sophisticated Upper-Class Woman, the Bathing Beauty, the Young Lover, the Pretty Woman, the Passively Seductive Woman, and the Hand. Of the 500 ads that featured women rather than just product packaging, 438 of the women represented one of these eight archetypal images.

Results. The results focus on decreases in the prevalence of the Sophisticated Upper-Class woman after the assassination, increases in both the Femme Fatale/Woman as Animal and the Passively Seductive Woman, and a later-period resurgence in representations of the Girl-Next-Door.

In the analysis, these shifting representations of the social category of women are interpreted not just with respect to the assassination of JFK and the disappearance of Jackie Kennedy from the public eye (Perry 2004), but also with respect to other social disruptions that occurred in parallel during the time period under study. In particular, FDA approval of the birth control in 1960 (Watkins 1998), the publication of Betty Friedan's *The Feminine Mystique* in the spring of 1963, and the appearance of the Beatles on the Ed Sullivan television show in late 1963 all had important consequences for American culture's complex construction of the symbolic meanings of gender. Our analysis traces each of these social disruptions in the ongoing cultural conversation about gender that takes place even in the pages of magazines that feature advertisements for perfume and cologne.

Conclusion. Nuanced cultural analysis of shifting archetypical representations of women in perfume and cologne ads during this period point to the complex conversations that constitute cultural change, even when focusing simply on ads for luxury products. By identifying each strand in this conversation, our understanding of the moving collective consensus and conflict around gender is given dimensionality and dynamism.

Thus, the primary contribution of this research is not in its details about this particular time period or these particular ads. Instead, its contribution to consumer research is in highlighting the importance of moving beyond research that is insensitive to temporal change, and instead finding explanations of the microscopic, yet profound, steps in the processes of cultural change.

REFERENCES

Marchand, Roland (1985), *Advertising the American Dream: Making Way for Modernity, 1920-1940*, London: University of California Press.

O'Guinn, Thomas C., John W. Pracejus, and G. Douglas Olsen (2006), "How Nothing Became Something: White Space, Rhetoric, History, and Meaning," *Journal of Consumer Research*, 33 (June), 82-90.

Perry, Barbara A. (2004), *Jacqueline Kennedy: First Lady of the New Frontier*, Lawrence, KS: University Press of Kansas.

Scott, Linda A (1994), "Images in Advertising: The Need for a Theory of Visual Rhetoric," *Journal of Consumer Research*, 21 (September), 252-273.

Stern, Barbara B. (1989), "Literary Criticism and Consumer Research: Overview and Illustrative Analysis," *Journal of Consumer Research*, 16 (December), 322-334.

Stern, Barbara B. (1996), "Deconstructive Strategy and Consumer Research: Concepts and Illustrative Exemplar," *Journal of Consumer Research*, 23 (Sept), 136-147.

Watkins, Elizabeth S. (1998), *On the Pill: A Social History of Oral Contraceptives 1950-1970*, London: The John Hopkins University Press.

Zelman, Thomas (1992) "Language and Perfume: A Study of Symbol-Formation" in *Advertising and Popular Culture: Studies in Variety and Versatility*, ed. Sammy R. Danna, Bowling Green, Ohio: Bowling Green State University Popular Press, 109-114.

At the Bottom of the Pyramid: How Consumers Cope with Low Status

Chair: Nailya Ordabayeva, Erasmus University Rotterdam, The Netherlands

Paper #1: Status, Race, and Money: The Impact of Racial Hierarchy on Willingness-to-Pay

Aarti S. Ivanic, University of San Diego, USA
Jennifer R. Overbeck, University of Southern California, USA
Joseph C. Nunes, University of Southern California, USA

Paper #2: When Diamonds are not the Poor's Best Friend: How the Poor Deal with Unaffordables

Cara de Boer, Katholieke Universiteit Leuven, Belgium
Siegfried Dewitte, Katholieke Universiteit Leuven, Belgium
Wouter Vanhouche, Katholieke Universiteit Leuven, Belgium

Paper #3: I'll Sell That for a Dollar: How Social Status Threats Devalue One's Possessions

David Dubois, INSEAD, France
Esta Denton, Northwestern University, USA
Derek D. Rucker, Northwestern University, USA

Paper #4: When Improving Equality Promotes Selfish Behavior

Nailya Ordabayeva, Erasmus University Rotterdam, The Netherlands
Pierre Chandon, INSEAD, France

SESSION OVERVIEW

Record numbers of consumers found themselves at the bottom of the pyramid in the past few years. Job loss, foreclosures, and wage cuts in the recent economic recession drove countless middle-class families below the poverty line (Yen, 2011). In 2009 alone, more than 170,000 US families were pushed out of their homes and into the homeless shelters. At the same time, the amount of time spent at the shelters and the number of consumers moving into shared dwellings with other families soared compared to the preceding years (Pugh, 2010). In the midst of these alarming trends a question that is often raised is, what is the reality of being at the bottom of the distribution?

Previous research found that low-status individuals—those who are inferior to others on a socially relevant dimension (Ridgeway & Walker, 1995)—often feel shame, dissatisfaction, and envy towards others (Frank, 2007; Goffman, 1982). As a result, they save less (Dynan, Skinner, & Zeldes, 2004), spend more (Charles, Hurst, & Roussanov, 2007), eat more high-calorie foods (McLaren, 2007), and take more risks (Haisley, Mostafa, & Loewenstein, 2008) than high-status individuals. This limits their ability to accumulate wealth and to improve well-being in the long run (Bagwell & Bernheim, 1996). Such troubling patterns of behavior, paired with increasing numbers of low-status individuals in the population (Cohen, 2010), have made it critical for researchers and policy makers to understand how consumers experience and cope with low status. This session addresses these issues.

Four papers examine the strategies that consumers use to cope with low status and ways to mitigate their negative outcomes. Ivanic, Overbeck and Nunes start off by showing that African Americans, assumed to have lower endowed status than Caucasians, will pay more voluntarily for certain products in order to assert status. The saliency of race during the transaction and the strength of one's racial identification moderate this tendency. De Boer, Dewitte and Vanhouche continue by arguing that low-status consumers do not always give in to the temptation to spend money on high-status products. In fact, individuals, who have low status due to their restrained financial resources, may strategically reduce the attractiveness of unaffordable products after autonomously refraining from purchasing them.

Next, Dubois, Denton and Rucker find that a similar devaluation effect extends to consumers' valuations of *owned* possessions, leading low-status consumers to sell their possessions for less than their actual value. Finally, Ordabayeva and Chandon find that low-status individuals are motivated to improve their rank even if it means demoting others and hurting the welfare of the group, especially when equality is high. This effect disappears when the status gain is costly.

These findings advance our understanding of relative deprivation in several important ways. First, they demonstrate the diverse nature of behaviors that individuals adapt in response to low status (all papers). Second, they show that the effects of low status extend far beyond simple spending decisions (all papers) and consumers' individual welfare (all papers), but that they also impact the welfare of the group (papers 1 and 4) and efficiency of market transactions (papers 2 and 3). Third, the papers propose strategies to curb the negative outcomes of low-status responses (papers 3 and 4), and in doing so uncover surprising findings that suggest some effects established in the previous literature do not hold at the bottom of the pyramid (e.g., endowment effect and benefits of equality in papers 3 and 4).

The papers complement each other and respond to the call for diversity in many ways. First, the papers draw on diverse theories (status, stereotypes, self-determination theory, attitude change, behavioral decision theory, group processes). Second, they employ complementary views of status (perceived and actual availability of financial resources, the endowed status of race, relative position within a group), and consequently examine diverse samples of low-status individuals (those who actually experience low status due to their resource constraints or race as well as unsuspecting individuals who are put in a low status position in an experimental task). Finally, the papers demonstrate the effects of low status on a diverse set of outcomes (willingness to pay, product attitudes, purchase decisions, the endowment effect, other-directed behaviors within a social group). Needless to say, the session brings together scholars with diverse backgrounds in terms of geography as well as stage in the career.

Overall, the session offers novel insights on status processes and encourages a debate on the rationality of compensatory behaviors and their effectiveness as coping mechanisms. The session will appeal to a vast audience interested in consumer psychology, stereotypes, group processes, and behavioral economics.

Status, Race, and Money: The Impact of Racial Hierarchy on Willingness-to-Pay

EXTENDED ABSTRACT

Status affects one's opportunities, relationships, and self-concept. Regardless of whether people choose to acknowledge this, society is vertically stratified on several dimensions (e.g., income, education, race), and status hierarchies persist. Whether based on achievement (merit) or endowment (birth), status hierarchies are socially imposed, and manifested in the way certain groups are treated. Consequently, status perceptions affect how group members behave. We examined how the ingrained status hierarchy between African Americans and Caucasians affects individuals' spending behavior. Specifically, we explored whether, when, and why African Americans willingly pay more for products and services than they would otherwise, and more than Caucasians.

Advances in Consumer Research
Volume 40, ©2012

Historically, African Americans have had lower endowed status than Caucasians, which has led to persistent discrimination. African Americans are often stereotyped as being poor, lazy, and uneducated and thus treated as inferior (Wittenbrink, Judd, & Park, 1997). In the marketplace, African Americans feel categorized as "low value" customers because of the perception that they cannot afford purchases at upscale stores (Ainscough & Motley, 2000) and frequently report being skipped over by sales associates who serve Caucasian customers first.

Past work has demonstrated that members of racial minorities respond by consuming status-related goods as a way of asserting high status (Fontes & Fan, 2006). More generally, individuals purchase products that convey high status to restore a sense of power or to repair self-integrity (Rucker & Galinsky, 2008). Our work goes beyond high-status goods as we propose paying more money itself constitutes a strategy for asserting status.

The ability to spend money represents success, wealth, and high social status (Veblen, 1899). Spending money engenders feelings of equality because money begets respect (Goldberg & Lewis, 1978). In the early 1980s, the NAACP created "Black Dollar Days," encouraging African Americans to spend money to demonstrate the strength of African Americans' purchasing power (Boyer, 1985). By extension, we predict that African Americans would increase their WTP (for both status- and non-status-conveying products) in an attempt to assert high status. We expect this would be particularly true for African Americans who are concerned that their social standing is seen as inferior— a concern that may arise from a chronic sense of status disadvantage or from explicit awareness of race (and associated low-status stereotypes).

We also propose that the manner in which race, or endowed status, is made salient can affect African Americans' WTP. When a stereotype is implicitly activated, the automatic response is to confirm the stereotype (Bargh & Pietromonaco, 1982). With explicit activation, individuals become more mindful of the stereotype and may behave in stereotype-inconsistent ways (Wheeler & Petty, 2001). We argue, when race is explicitly activated, African Americans are reminded of the stereotype that they are poor and low status. Consequently, they elevate their WTP to fight against the stereotype and assert high status—particularly if they perceive themselves to be disadvantaged with regard to status. Conversely, implicit activation should lead African Americans to decrease their WTP, because implicit activation occurs outside awareness and thus does not prompt stereotype resistance. We anticipated that individual differences in racial identification might moderate the effect of identity salience: More highly identified African Americans who feel a greater sense of pride in group membership may counteract societally imposed status stereotyping reducing their need to pay more to assert status.

We tested our predictions in several studies. Study 1 examined the differential effect of race salience on WTP for African Americans versus Caucasians. The study used a 2 (race: African American, Caucasian) × 3 (race salience: explicit, implicit, control) between-subjects design. When the concept of race was not activated, the difference between African Americans' and Caucasians' WTP was not significant. When the concept of race was activated explicitly, African Americans were willing to pay significantly more than Caucasians as well as more than in the control condition. Conversely, African Americans were willing to pay less in the implicit activation condition than in the control condition.

The data suggest that when the concept of race is explicitly activated, African Americans become sensitized to stereotypes of being poor and inferior, and hence increase their WTP in what we argue is an attempt to assert their status. Conversely, these stereotypes and related behaviors are so ingrained that implicit activation of the concept of race leads African Americans to decrease their WTP, as they do not feel a need to assert their status.

Study 2 examined the role of two possible moderators of this effect: perceived status disadvantage (PSD) relative to others and racial identification. We reasoned that greater PSD should heighten WTP, given the greater experience of threatened status. Conversely, we expected that stronger racial identification would lower WTP. As predicted, PSD and racial identification yielded opposing effects on WTP. Greater feelings of status disadvantage resulted in a higher WTP as African Americans tried to assert high status when race was salient. In contrast, stronger racial identification resulted in a lower WTP among African Americans when race was salient.

In Study 3, we explored how differences in WTP result from feelings of threat, by introducing a common overt status threat and examining its interaction with race and race salience. Key findings include: African Americans who received inferior treatment in the marketplace and for whom race was made salient reported higher WTP than poorly treated African Americans whose race was not salient, and well-treated African Americans whose race was made explicitly salient. They also reported higher WTP than did Caucasians in any of the conditions in this study.

Findings from the three studies support our claim that African Americans who feel disadvantaged use payment behavior as a way to assert high status. Additional studies underway explore how racial diversity in the presence of others at the time of purchase impacts willingness to pay. Our work raises awareness that some individuals may sometimes support an unfair system through their own behavior. By underscoring how an entrenched status hierarchy can create internalized imperatives for African Americans to pay more, our studies provide insight into race-based status dynamics and how they affect consumption patterns.

When Diamonds are not the Poor's Best Friend: How the Poor Deal with Unaffordables

EXTENDED ABSTRACT

Governmental, judicial, and bank policies tend to reduce the poor's financial freedom by either giving them allowances for specific purchases or by limiting their credit options (Ruelens & Nicaise, 2002). The rational for the autonomy reducing approach is endorsed by research suggesting that the poor lack sufficient regulatory skills to control their expenses (Green et al., 1996), which might boost excess spending behavior as a way to attenuate their lower class status. We question if autonomy reducing measures help consumers to deal with, and resist, luxury products. We explore how the degree of autonomy shapes attitudes of luxurious products. The term "luxury" is taken to refer to the situation in which buying a certain good, although physically possible in some circumstances, would put undue strain on the buyer's budget.

A wide array of research suggest that (high) autonomy increases a consumer's ability to deal with challenging situations (Ryan & Deci, 2001), and one way to deal with the temptation of luxury products, is to downplay their value ("The grapes are too sour"). Importantly, research in the self-control domain suggests that self-control is exerted only when external control is absent (Fischbach & Trope, 2005), i.e. when autonomy is high. Findings in the food domain suggest that exposure to food without consumption leads to a reduced attractiveness of the tempting food items (Dewitte et al., 2009). Reduced attractiveness seems to be observed under high autonomy conditions. Hence, this evidence suggests that high autonomy can decrease the attractiveness of luxury products. But, as people are motivated to regulate their behavior in function of the necessity of that behavior (Vohs et al., 2008), the effect should be specific to the poor or to people harboring another self-based motivation to refrain from buying the luxury product.

We distinguish three possible processes that may be responsible for attitude changes. Attitude reduction may be product specific, implying a devaluation that is limited to the currently encountered luxury product (Myrseth et al., 2009). Attitude reduction can also be attribute specific, implying that the attitude reduction of the luxury product spreads towards related products (e.g. from candies to M&Ms, Geyskens et al., 2008). Lastly, attitude reduction, may be driven by a generalized inhibition effect (Tuk et al., 2011), implying that after encountering a luxury product all attractive products devalue. We test these hypotheses in three studies.

In the first experiment we explored the influence of autonomy and financial scarcity (both manipulated) during restrained purchase of a luxury product (a concert ticket) on one's subsequent attitude toward that product. We asked participants about their finances by means of 3 questions on a 10-point scale and varied the scale anchor points to manipulate financial scarcity (Nelson & Morrison, 2005). Participants then read a scenario where they had the opportunity to buy a concert ticket of their favorite band. In the low autonomy condition, it was announced the concert tickets were sold out. Participants then rated the attractiveness of the concert ticket (4 items on a 7-point scale). The attitude towards the luxury product, the concert ticket, was significantly lower among the autonomous poor (M = 3.48) relative to non-autonomous poor (M = 4.02, p < 0.05). For the non-poor, no differences between the autonomous and the non-autonomous were obtained (respectively, M = 3.87 vs. 3.73, p > .05).

The second study aimed at testing whether devaluation is driven by a product specific, attribute specific, or generalized devaluation process. We pre-exposed participants (all in financial scarcity conditions) to a physically present gadget (a penguin fan) and either helped them decide not to buy it or made the "not buy" decision for them (high versus low autonomy). We then had them rate the gadget and products that varied in relatedness to the gadget (strong relation: ice bear headphone, an igloo tent, and refrigerator poetry; weak relation: an egg cup, an i-pod holder, and a small helicopter with remote control). We replicated the devaluation of the target product in the autonomous group (M = 3.31) relative to the non-autonomous (M = 4.64, $F(1, 60)$ = 11.87, p < .01). Devaluation expanded only to products related to the non-purchased item: The related products were considered as significantly less attractive in the autonomous group (M = 2.90) relative to the non-autonomous group (M = 3.58, p < .05). For the unrelated products no significant differences emerged between the autonomous and non-autonomous (M = 4.46 vs. 4.35, p > .05). Both study 1 and study 2 demonstrated the causal relationship between autonomously refraining from the purchase of a luxury product, and its subsequent devaluation. Study 2 extends these findings by illustrating how this devaluation might be attribute specific.

To complement the internal validity of our lab study, we conducted a field study with actual poor consumers, who had either a history of high or low financial autonomy. We compared them to a matched sample of non-poor consumers. Assuming that pre-exposure is cumulative and that the devaluation operates via attribute attitudes, we predict that the autonomous poor will devalue luxury products more than non-autonomous poor. We don't expect this difference for the moderately expensive and cheap products. A significant interaction between poverty category and price level emerged ($F(4, 60)$ = 2.62, p < .05), and was consistent with the predicted pattern. Attitudes towards the products did not vary much, except for

the attitude towards luxury products among the autonomous poor, which were significantly lower than the other attitudes.

Together, the results suggest that the poor, provided that they autonomously manage their budget, may develop a coping mechanism that helps them deal with products that are not within their budget. The findings suggest that if public policy wants to help the poor to resist luxury products, it may be unwise to deny poor consumers access to luxuries or to control their expenses for them.

I'll Sell That for a Dollar: How Social Status Threats Devalue One's Possessions

EXTENDED ABSTRACT

One feature of many unprivileged consumers' daily experience is their repeated encounter with psychological threats in social situations (Marmot, 2004). And, it is well documented that a variety of status threats to consumers have far-reaching effects on consumer behavior (for reviews see Lee & Shrum, in press). The majority of this literature, however, has focused solely on consumers as *buyers* and investigated how threats impact consumers' willingness to spend on products based on whether they have the potential to alleviate the threat or not.

This research investigates how status threats affect consumers as *sellers*. Specifically, we propose that experiencing a threat has the potential to spillover to the valuation of one's possessions. Past research has posited that one's possessions are often evaluated in relation to the self (Belk, 1988). For example, an individual for whom football is a large part of his identity is likely to value an autographed football more than an individual who has little passion for the game. Building on this idea, we propose that when the self is threatened, changes to the self may affect the value of one's possessions. Specifically, when threats diminish *social worth* or *status—one's value relative to others—* we hypothesize that the experienced loss in social worth might spillover onto their possessions. Consequently, although past research on the endowment effect has shown that owning an object increases its value (Kahneman, Knetsch, & Thaler, 1990), this work proposes that threatened sellers might price owned possessions as lower than objects they do not own.

Furthermore, we propose our devaluation effect should be moderated by whether people encounter a social status vs. personal threat. For example, an individual's intelligence might be under threat because she is focused on the fact she performed poorer than her classmates (i.e., a social status threat) or because she received a grade on a test that was below her own personal standard (i.e., a personal threat). Although each instance reflects a threat to one's intelligence, the loss in social worth, and subsequent devaluation of one's possessions should be greater when the threat is social in nature.

Finally, we predict that social status threats do not devalue every possession an individual owns. In particular, when possessions have the potential to help alleviate the threat, we hypothesize that its value to cope with the threat *increases* the product's value in the eyes of the consumer. For example, an individual whose intelligence is threatened may part with their favorite science fiction novel for less, but sell their encyclopedia collection for even more.

We test these hypotheses across three experiments.

Experiment 1: Can Social Status Threats Devalue One's Possessions? Undergraduates were randomly assigned to a 2 (mug ownership: owned, non-owned) × 2 (threat condition: none, social) between-subject design. Participants were first given a mug to own or to use just for the session. Threat was manipulated by instructing participants to recall a time they went to the grocery store (no threat) or performed poorly relative to others (social status threat).

Subsequently, all subjects were asked at what price they would sell their mug. A significant interaction emerged, $p < .01$. In the no threat condition, participants owning the mug set a higher selling price than participants who did not own the mug, $p < .01$, consistent with findings from the endowment literature. Of greater novelty, threatened participants set a lower selling price when they owned the mug than when they did not own the mug, $p < .01$.

Experiment 2: Social Status Threats versus Personal Threats. Undergraduates were randomly assigned to a 2 (ownership of a pen: owned, non-owned) × 3 (threat condition: none, social, personal) between-subject design. Participants were given a pen to own or simply to use for the session. Threat was manipulated using a recall task, where participants were asked to recall a list of items they purchased the last time they were at a grocery store (no-threat), performed poorly relative to others (status threat), or performed worse than their personal standard (personal threat). Finally, participants had the opportunity to set the price of the pen. An ANOVA revealed a significant 2-way interaction, $p < .001$. Replicating Experiment 1, participants in the social threat condition set a lower selling price when they owned the pen compared to when they did not own the pen, $p < .05$. However, participants in the personal and no-threat conditions set higher prices when they owned the product compared to when they did not. Furthermore, participants' loss of social worth mediated the effect of social status threat on selling price.

Experiment 3: The Value of Possessions that Alleviate Threat. Undergraduates were assigned to a 2 (ownership: owned, non-owned) × 2 (threat condition: none, social) × 2 (product relevance: threat irrelevant, threat relevant) between-subject design. Participants were given a new pen to own or to use momentarily. The pen was described to participants as an opportunity to display one's intelligence to others in the threat relevant condition (i.e., it was capable of alleviating the threat), and as just a pen in the threat-irrelevant condition. Threat was subsequently manipulated using the recall task in former experiments. Finally, participants were asked to set the price they would sell the pen for. An ANOVA revealed a significant 3-way interaction, $p < .01$. When products were threat-irrelevant, threatened participants devalued products they owned. However when products were threat-relevant, there was a significant ownership × threat interaction, $p < .05$. Threatened participants owning the threat-relevant pen set an even higher selling price than threatened participants who did not own the pen, $p < .01$.

Conclusion and Contributions: Social status threats led consumers to set the selling price of an item they owned lower than non-threatened consumers. This effect was moderated by whether threats were personal versus social, and reversed when the owned product had the potential to alleviate the threat. Implications for the threat and endowment literatures, as well as for social policy as discussed.

When Improving Equality Promotes Selfish Behavior

EXTENDED ABSTRACT

Increasing equality is expected to bring a host of social benefits in a group (Frank, 1985). In particular, it is expected to reduce conspicuous consumption by people who feel threatened by their low status (Becker, Murphy & Werning, 2005). More generally, equality is expected to improve social cohesion and cooperation and to promote welfare-enhancing behaviors within a group (Zizzo, 2003).

However, recent research has demonstrated that increasing equality may not always be beneficial. Ordabayeva & Chandon (2011) showed that greater equality actually increases, rather than decreases, conspicuous consumption among people at the bottom of the hierarchy because it increases how status gains (the number

of people that can be surpassed) provided by consumption. Interestingly, much of the previous literature focused on conspicuous consumption as a means to enhance status, thus overlooking other methods that individuals may use to improve their relative position. We propose that aside from conspicuous consumption, which improves one's rank by enhancing own performance, people may also improve their rank by pulling other people down. For example, they can "burn" other people's money (Zizzo, 2003) or sabotage others' performance in order to improve rank. Whereas conspicuous consumption directly affects only one's own well-being, demoting others hurts the well-being of others and the total welfare of the group.

This research therefore examines whether, counter to existing arguments (Wilkinson & Pickett, 2010), equality promotes selfish behaviors that low-status individuals use to cope with a status threat. We hypothesize that increasing equality will increase status-seeking among low-status individuals by encouraging behaviors that demote others and the group. Furthermore, the effect should be moderated by status level (low vs. high) and status desirability. We expect that equality effects should be stronger for low-status individuals than for high-status individuals (because for high-status individuals, increasing equality has the opposite effect of reducing position gains) and when status gain is positive (vs. negative). We tested our hypotheses in four studies, which measured selfish tendencies of low-ranked individuals in the context of salespeople. This context was chosen because salespeople are commonly assessed based on their ranking and low ranking poses tangible threats such as withheld commissions and job loss.

A pilot study examined whether a low-status individual was evaluated more negatively and hence had stronger reasons to engage in status-seeking behaviors when the distribution of performance was equal (vs. unequal). A group of MBAs read a scenario about managing 20 salespeople at an electronics store. They read that to evaluate the salespeople's performance they monitored the distribution of monthly sales. They saw an equal or an unequal distribution of previous month's sales and indicated how likely they would be to fire a salesperson with a low sales rank (19th out of 20). The results indicated that the low-ranked salesperson was evaluated more positively and faced a lower threat of being fired in the equal than in the unequal distribution.

In study 1, we examined whether equality would encourage selfish status-seeking behaviors among low-ranked individuals despite higher performance evaluation by managers. The participants read the same scenario as in the pilot study, except that they imagined that they were a salesperson (vs. a manager in study 1). The participants imagined having attained low rank (19th out of 20) or high rank (9th out of 20) in the equal or the unequal distribution of sales. They were then asked to indicate how likely they would be to help a new colleague, who could improve the store's overall sales, but reduce the performance of individual salespeople. The results revealed that the low-status salesperson was less likely to help a new colleague than the high-status salesperson. More importantly, equality reduced the likelihood of helping among low-status salespeople but not among high-status salespeople.

Study 2 examined the moderating role of individual selfish tendencies. The participants read the same scenario as in the low-status condition of study 1 and answered three questions about the low-ranked individual's selfish status-seeking behaviors. The first behavior involved refusing to train a new colleague (as in study 1). The second behavior involved directly sabotaging a colleague's sales, and the third behavior involved directing customers to the competing store in exchange for a higher commission from the competitor. We measured the individual propensity to endorse selfish, devious, and manipulative behaviors using the Machiavellian attitudes scale (Christie & Geis, 1970). Whereas people with strong Machiavellian attitudes indicated high likelihood of engaging in selfish status-seeking behaviors regardless of equality, individuals with weak Machiavellian attitudes were more likely to engage in selfish behaviors when the distribution of performance was equal (vs. unequal).

Study 3 sought to replicate the findings in the context of real behaviors and tested the moderating role of status desirability. Throughout the experiment, the participants earned tickets for a lottery that was conducted at the end of each session for a €10 cash prize. In the first stage, the participants earned tickets in a general knowledge test. At the end of the test, everyone was assigned low performance rank (2 correct answers out of 10 = 10 tickets) and saw the distribution of everyone's test scores (high vs. low equality). In the second stage, the respondents participated in a public goods game (in which they could multiply everyone's tickets by initially contributing tickets to the common pool) and a burning game (in which they could spend some of their tickets to burn the tickets of others). Status desirability was manipulated by informing half of the participants that the winner would pay a tax on the lottery earnings and help a research assistant, which reduced the benefits of ticket accumulation. The results showed that high equality reduced contributions to the common pool and increased spending to burn others' tickets when the lottery earnings were free, but not when the lottery winnings were taxed.

Overall, our findings demonstrate that the effects of equality go beyond consumption decisions and may encourage status seeking so much that people resort to selfish behaviors that hurt others and the group. More generally, the results have implications for understanding the adverse effects of equality and the dark side of social comparisons.

Stereotypes, Memories and Nostalgia:
Contested States of Longing, Belonging, and Being Within Consumer Acculturation
Chair: Andrew Lindridge, The Open University Business School, UK

Paper #1: "Russians Always Wear Red Lipstick:" Acculturation, Identity and Stereotypes

Natalia Tolstikova, Stockholm University, Sweden

Susanna Molander, Stockholm University, Sweden

Paper #2: Memories of Pre- and Post-Migration Consumption: Better Times or Embodiments of a Defensive Mental State?

Andrew Lindridge, The Open University, UK

Paper #3: Home Sweet Home: The Role of Home Country Nostalgia on Immigrants' Acculturation and Consumption

Celina Stamboli-Rodriguez, Iseg,, France

Luca M. Visconti, ESCP Europe, France

Paper #4: 4. Social Status Implications of Transmigrants' Consumer Practices in Their Cultures of Origin

Mine Üçok Hughes, Woodbury University, USA

SESSION OVERVIEW

The theme of this year's ACR conference is "Appreciating Diversity". In congruence with this theme, this session explores various stages of consumer acculturation as they relate to the experience of immigrants both in the country of re-rooting and in their home country. Consumer acculturation then is viewed as a manifestation of wider interactions and power play between the dominant host society, the immigrant populations, and their ethnic networks in the home countries, as these groups negotiate inevitable cultural and societal changes. Extant acculturation research has tended to be either American centric favouring comparative studies of assimilation amongst different ethnic groups (Waters 2005) or focuses mostly on the way immigrants confront the consumption practices of the host nation (Wamwara-Mbugua, Cornwell, and Boller 2007). The four presentations together address these criticisms through illustrating the varying stages in the consumer acculturation process, ranging from initial immigrant contact, through to negotiating feelings of loss and dislocation, culminating in consumer acculturation problems related to the migrants' return to their original home country. By drawing upon research from a European centric perspective we illustrate the complex roles that consumption undertakes in how immigrants negotiate and construct their sense of identity, self-esteem and place in the world.

The first paper explores the role of consumption in stereotyping and stigmatising amongst Russian immigrants living in Sweden. To handle the stereotypes ascribed to them the Russian informants seemed inclined to conform to the stereotypes they ascribed to the Swedes and to thus consume accordingly. The sense of dislocation inferred in this paper is continued in the next paper, which explores the role of real and re-created memories amongst immigrants. Negative acculturation experiences lead to migrants recalling and re-creating pre-migration memories and making these memories real through consumption cues. In doing so immigrants tended to split their memories distinctly between pre- and post-migration, recreating pre-migration consumption memories as a defence mechanism against acculturation stress. The third paper continues the theme of dislocation and recreating pre-migration through understanding the role of nostalgia within consumer acculturation. In particular, this paper deconstructs the nostalgia of Turkish immigrants living in France into four categories indicative of their acculturation process-

es, including a nostalgia based around the desire to identify with the country of their ancestral origin. Nostalgia and the desire to return to Turkey by Turkish immigrants are discussed in our final paper, which also touches upon stereotypes and stigma among those who do return to visit Turkey. Exposure to Western European culture and consumer acculturation renders these returning Turks as foreigners in a country that they feel a close connection with. The four papers in this session thus firmly locate the migrant not as a welcomed, integrated embodiment of wider society, but forever a group in transition and constantly adapting, recreating and reconstructing a sense of identity. Notably, migrant identity practices implicate consumption to simultaneously integrate into the dominant culture, while yielding protection from the wider pressures of acculturation.

Three of the session papers are completed projects, with one representing an ongoing project, and all present differing theoretical perspectives. Methodologically, the papers adhere to the interpretivist approach and provide empirical knowledge based on ethnographic data. This special session is then expected to appeal to an audience interested in the interactions between culture, ethnicity, identity and consumption, whilst being of interest to those academics with an interest in memories and nostalgia.

Finally, the focus of the proposed session on immigrants and the role of consumer acculturation from a European centric perspective addresses the diverse audience of ACR and resonates with Vancouver's diverse population.

"Russians always wear red lipstick": Acculturation, Identity and Stereotypes

EXTENDED ABSTRACT

During the last few decades the world has experienced migration on a global scale resulting in a growing number of consumers with a foreign background living in Sweden; something which has put acculturation on the political agenda. Immigrants both forge and are subjected to various processes of acculturation and previous consumer acculturation research has documented the play of multiple cultures: the host, the migrant, and the transnational.

Since the acculturation process is a mutual adjustment where the parties are learning to co-exist, it is important to study the ways in which migrants and hosts develop understandings of each other. Both the migrant and the host are often a subject of mutual stereotyping where particular traits and values are ascribed to them. Those stereotypes can be positive but are more often biased and oversimplified. The stereotyping has to do with normative expectations regarding conduct or character of people "who are passing strangers to us" (Goffman 1963, p. 68). The concept of stereotyping has been well developed in other disciplines but not in literature dealing with acculturation through consumption (i.e. Askegaard et al. 2005, Luedicke 2011). This study intends to fill this literature gap by exploring how stereotyping affects the process of acculturation through consumption. The analysis will be based on the multi-disciplinary literature on stereotypes (e.g., Hinton 2000), as well as on stigma (Goffman 1963).

We have chosen to study Russian immigrants in Sweden and conducted a pilot study consisting of three in-depth interviews with young Russian females living in Stockholm. The informants were asked about why they came to Sweden, what they do now and what their everyday life looks like. In the course of these "oral stories" the goal was to identify stereotypes as well as the coping practices. The main study consists of 20 interviews with Russians of diverse ages and backgrounds. Complimenting this, a critical review was undertaken of Swedish media portrayals of Swedish stereotypes of Russians connected to historic-political developments. From the data, three main stereotypes are highlighted:

- A cultivated culture: refined, formed through literature, music, theater: pre-revolutionary Russia;
- A feared culture: characterized by strong 'bullying' power, military domination: a Communist ideological stronghold throughout, especially during the cold war;
- A materialist culture: non-sophisticated consumption, nouveau rich: post-Communism.

When summarizing the interviews we found that, remarkably, only negative stereotypes, similar to those propagated by Swedish popular culture, were identified by the interviewees:

"Russians can always be identified as Russians. [They] *always* [wear] *red lipstick and too much eye make-up, stiletto heels. The colors* [of their dress and make-up] *are always standing out"* (interview with A). The same woman was eager to point out that she did not belong to this category and was similar to a Swede who dressed more "low key."

The preliminary analysis of the interviews show that the emerging stereotypes are "the extreme materialist" (Russian stereotype of Russians) and "the rational functionalist" (Russian stereotype of Swedes). These stereotypes could be partially explained by the power dynamics between the groups, where Swedishness holds the dominating position and Russianness is perceived an abnormality, a deviant expression, and a stigma (Goffman 1963). Stigma is a mark of distinction and articulation of distinctions and is a social construct, not an inherent quality (ibid). As an ascribed way of behavior and appearance it renders Russians to be socially inferior. All three interviewees, both verbally and in their appearance, were inclined to conform to the Swedish cultural ideology of "lagom" or "just enough". "Lagom" propagates moderation which seems to diametrically oppose the Russian materialist stereotype – the garishness and the tendency to "show off". We hope to develop this finding further at a later research stage.

Our preliminary research also demonstrates that although created externally, stereotypes are internalized by those subjected to them, so a Russian can always recognize another Russian. Furthermore, Russians also seem to use stereotyping as part of a power play. For example, *"It is easy to recognize a Russian... In Russia ... we dress on our best when* [going out]. *Swedes can show up in a pajama, it is considered normal"* (interview with N).

The stereotypes presented here can be seen as subject positions mutually constructed by Swedes and Russians; positions that operate as a reference points from which people compare/distinguish themselves. The analysis shows that these stereotypes seem to play a major part in the acculturation process and mostly manifest themselves through consumption.

Memories of pre- and post-migration consumption: Better times or embodiments of a defensive mental state?

EXTENDED ABSTRACT

Previous migration studies tend to draw an implicit line between the place and time of migration (past) and the current place and time (present). Yet this approach fails to address how pre-migration memories emerge and appear in migrants' daily lives. In particular, research has not addressed: (i) how migrants present lives evoke memories of their past, or how consumption may reproduce pre-migration routines and knowledge, and (ii) how consumption is used in recalling past memories into the present, even if this leads to conflict between what is remembered and what is experienced. We explore these questions through migrants' pre- and post-migration memories, and how they manifest through consumption. In doing so we address research calls to understand how people encode and retrieve memories (Hastie and Dawes, 2001) and identity-based consumer memories (Mercurio and Forehand (2011).

The concept of memories and consumption, extensively addressed within consumer literature, offers interesting insights into the relationship between migration memories and consumption. For example, migrants' consumption of products indicative of pre-migration, such as food, may reinforce positive memories (Schlosser, 2006), yet such consumption acts may be undertaken to create false pre-migration memories. Indeed, Schlosser (2006, p. 377) notes that object interactivity may lead to "the creation of vivid, internally generated recollections that pose as real memories". Real experiences of a pre-migration life subsequently may become modified based around autobiographical events into false memories (Loftus and Pickerell, 1995) or be induced by product consumption that the individual has not previously used (Rajagopal and Montgomery, 2011). Hence, Aaker, Drolet and Griffin (2008), drawing upon the psychological theory of memory, argue that memories are not a direct copy of the individual's past but instead are reconstructed and re-imagined, brought alive through a variety of cues that assist individuals in making inferences about their past. The extent then that acculturation produces stress and this stress is managed through positive real and re-imagined memories of a pre-migration through consumption cues forms the basis of this research.

A sample group (n=8) of first generation Indian immigrants living in Britain were repeatedly interviewed to gather their pre- and post-migration experiences, lived lives, memories and consumption behaviors. Interviews were recorded, transcribed and analysed.

Data analysis revealed a clear splitting in participants' memories between their pre- and post-migration experiences, and consequently their memories. Of interest was how consumption featured in these memories and the sensory aspects of these memories differed.

Migration memories for participants were vividly recalled in terms of colours, smells and textures. For example, Margey describes her childhood memories of life in India as '*...bright and warm and very real almost...the colours are more vivid and alive, the smells I can recall are like I am actually there* [in India]'. References are made to cultural symbolisms such as brightly coloured bracelets and cloth being purchased to make clothes. In contrast, Margey's post-migration life in Britain, one where acculturation stress manifested in family tensions, is described as feeling '*...a bit cold because it's wintery quite a lot. Maybe I felt the cold more because I was from a warm place, but it felt cold ... and me wearing ...a grey duffle coat I used to have...so it feels like a black and white film.*' The association of memories of life in Britain in black and white terms is later associated with consumption experiences, such as collecting the coal for the lounge fire, the brown lino floor covering and so on. Similar findings were shared with other participants.

The recall of memories in sensory terms is somewhat similar to Aaker, Drolet and Griffin's (2008) and Loftus and Pickerell's (1995) work on reconstruction of memories. The focussing on pre-migration memories predominately represented happier times for participants, when issues of identity difference and related stresses were less pronounced. Consequently, participants appear to be engaging in a process of re-imagining pre-migration memories and related experiences, as suggested by Rajagopal and Montgomery (2011). Participants achieved these re-imagining symbolic consumption experiences, such as their mother's cooking, indicative of pre-migration. Whilst clothing and religious artifacts, to some extent supported these memory recalls, food production and consumption was seen as central to memory recall. For instance, Tracey commented how she recreates childhood pre-migration memories through consuming potato poratas (a potato-bread dish): '*When my older sister makes it* [potato poratas]*, it does take you back. You remember her* [participant's sister] *making it for you and putting it on your plate, you used to think, 'Oh, I remember this, eating this on* [this pre-migration date]*', call it the baby turn...reminds you of old times'*. These consumption experiences tended to occur during moments of heightened stress levels.

The question then arises why do participants split their pre- and post-migration memories so distinctly? We suggest that the answer may lie in the psychodynamic term 'splitting', where traumatic events are separated and compartmentalised by the individual between good and bad events. In this instance, participants effectively were splitting their migration memories between pre-migration (colourful and positive) and post-migration (black and white, and negative). This act of splitting then represents a psychological defence mechanism to protect the individual's self-identity. Participants' pre-migration memories tended to be provoked during stressful experiences (feelings surrounding acculturation stress, such as ethnic difference) or illness (comforting). In the former, consumption was actively used to recall pre-migration memories to relieve symptoms of acculturation stress, whilst in the latter consumption invoked positive, comforting, pre-migration memories.

For those migrants who migrated as children, post-migration is reflected in various acculturation stresses, suggesting a wider sense of disempowerment arising from migration. Recreating consumption experiences based on pre-migration memories offered a means of relieving acculturation stresses, offering a sense of empowerment. For example, Peter watching old Bollywood films remembered from his childhood in India. The extent that these memories are re-imagined is inferred by the participants themselves, which may explain the contrasting colours used in memory recall. In contrast, only one participant differed in her memory narratives. A woman who actively sought out and chosen migration to emancipate herself from Indian cultural patriarchy.

Home Sweet Home: The Role of Home Country Nostalgia on Immigrants' Acculturation and Consumption

EXTENDED ABSTRACT

Nostalgia has been defined as a psychological obsession "to be back", that is, "a sentimental longing for the past", which people may develop with reference to things, significant-others, places or experiences that are no longer existing or at direct reach.

Acculturation studies and nostalgia research have developed quite independently. While extant works on nostalgia have largely advanced, and identified various facets of this emotion and its implications on consumption, acculturation studies have only marginally addressed nostalgia. Within the body of works investigating nostalgia, it has been argued that nostalgia can be either a state of *personal* (Holbrook and Schindler 1991) or *social* emotion (Zauberman, Ratner, and Kim 2009). Also, it has been proved that nostalgia can be activated from: (i) an idealization of direct memories (*true or real nostalgia*), (ii) from an indirect experience via the memories of the people close to us (*simulated nostalgia*) and, (iii) from the collective evocation of some pretended origins (*collective nostalgia*) (Baker and Kennedy 1994). Finally, (iv) time orientation marks the distinc-

tion between retrospective (*"if only" fantasies*) versus prospective forms of nostalgia (*"someday" fantasies*) (Akhtar 1996).

Whilst nostalgia recurs within acculturation studies this is mostly as a side-effect. Immigrants developing new cultural competences in the host culture are described as nostalgic individuals who indulge in the consumption of artifacts (food, media, novels, clothes, etc.). These artifacts are dense in memories of their "other life" and, for many of them, of the "dreamed future life" once back to the country of origin (i.e., the myth of return) (Akhtar 1996). As such, nostalgia is seen as an effect or an implication of acculturation.

Our work argues that nostalgia is not only an *outcome* of immigration and the related pains of integrating in a frequently hostile, resisting, culture, but also plays a major role in the way immigrants acculturate to the host culture. Nostalgia then may be a *constituent* of the acculturation process that extant research has undervalued. In detail, this paper aims at answering to two main research questions: (i) what is the role of home country nostalgia in the processes of immigrants' acculturation? and (ii) what is the connection between immigrants' nostalgia for their home country and their consumption behaviors?

This study is based on an ethnographic research, conducted in France, on 18 Turkish immigrants (seven first generation and 11 second generation participants) followed during a period of 18 months. Data were mainly collected by means of in-depth interviews and participant observation, and complemented by factual data on the narrators, indirect indicators (e.g., social capital indicators captured during the interviews), and photography, in order to increase the richness of the data set. During the semi-structured interviews, questions covered the interviewees' life histories, their feelings about their host and the home society, their food and media consumption habits, and more. Data were analyzed iteratively consistently with interpretive research logics and through a circular theory-field process.

Our findings are two-fold. First, we detect four main nostalgia consumption strategies deployed by immigrants' along their process of acculturation: shelter, tribute, solidarity, and reculturation. More expectedly, when immigrants are dissatisfied with their extant life due to isolation, negative stereotypes or marginality (cfr. Tolstikova and Molander's, Lindridge's, and Ucok Hugh's papers in this session), they may indulge in nostalgic consumption — typically of food, given its pervasive capability of activating various senses and Turkish soap operas — so to build a *shelter* in which to escape the arduousness of their life. More notably, nostalgic consumption can be used as a *tribute* to the home country. The largest majority of Turkish immigrants in France, including our informants, migrated for economic reasons looking for better job opportunities. As a consequence, many of these migrants later developed a sense of guilt because they felt they had abandoned their country for personal financial gain. Paradoxically, the perceived betrayal of a beloved Turkey, due to personal materialistic reasons, is emended through materialistic purchase and consumption of nostalgic goods (cultural products as DVDs, albums, decoration objects, etc.). These purchases then become a tribute to their home country where their achieved economic capital is transformed into symbolic and cultural capital (cfr. Üçok Hughes' paper in the session).

Nostalgic consumption may also serve at a social level, and notably within the local ethnic community, as an expression of *solidarity*. Our data shows that Turkish immigrants are evaluated and sanctioned by relatives and other Turkish acquaintances living in France. As such, the decision of indulging in nostalgic consumptions (folklore, food, narratives, etc), as a form of reciprocal support, testifies to their common belongingness; the celebration of an "ideal us", as opposed to the dominating French society. Finally, and especially for second generations, nostalgic consumptions serve as means of *reculturation*. Food, Turkish art, media, and ethnic retailing shops respond to the quest of yearning and understanding of Turkish culture for Turks living in France, who have grown up in a different cultural context. Reculturation applies also to first generation immigrants, but in this case nostalgic consumptions are used to revisit, revise, and groom their pristine cultural background.

A second order of findings illustrates the nature of the connection between home country, nostalgia and consumption. Empirical evidence demonstrates a *circular, self-feeding process* through either the exposure of Turkish immigrants to nostalgic consumptions activates nostalgic feelings, or the search for nostalgic consumptions is guided by a pre-existing nostalgic emotion for the home country.

This work helps advance acculturation research by locating immigrant's nostalgia for the home country in the middle of the acculturation process. Nostalgic consumption then is not only an effect of acculturation but also a powerful part of it. A part that is capable of increasing/reducing immigrants' chances to succeed in their double integration into the host culture and the local ethnic community.

Social Status Implications of Transmigrants' Consumer Practices in Their Cultures of Origin

EXTENDED ABSTRACT

While substantial research focuses on the consumption practices and identity projects of immigrants in their cultures of settlement, this phenomenon is largely ignored with regards to transmigrants' cultures of origin. Rooted in ethnographic empirical research, this paper explores the consumption practices, experiences, perceptions and identity negotiations of Turkish transmigrants, living in Denmark, during their annual visits to Turkey and the subsequent implications on their social status.

Research literature abounds with studies of acculturation patterns of people moving into a new culture, including patterns of immigrant consumer acculturation from one extreme (hyper identification) to the other (rejection). Recently, integration of transmigrant studies (Basch et al., 1994) have analyzed immigrants as being global, transnational, consumers whose lives and consumption practices are affected not only by interactions with their cultures of migration, but also with their cultures of origin (Üçok and Kjeldgaard 2005). These transmigrants are described as immigrants who continue to forge and sustain ties with their home/host cultures, implying connections to their countries of origin (Basch et al. 1994).

Transmigrants often acquire several identities, as their social status and class varies across social and national contexts. Many carry their possessions with them, often as status symbols. Yet, these possessions may connote different meanings in different contexts. For example, Caglar (2002) found that the decoration and organization of Turkish immigrants' homes, in Germany and Turkey differed strikingly, due to German Turks' quest for recognition. Being stigmatized in Germany as a foreign, non-European group, they suffer from a lack of social recognition. In contrast to their low status in Germany, working class German Turks find themselves economically closer to the middle class in Turkey. However, because Turkey is a class structured society, with invisible barriers to class mobility, transmigrants experience resistance from the Turkish middle class who find German Turks' symbolic capital to be insufficient for inclusion.

Beginning in the early 1960s, Turkey has witnessed major migratory movements, domestically and internationally. Üstüner and Holt (2007) researched the social status struggles of domestic migrants and their descendants who settled in big city squatters, and found that their efforts at social mobility were restricted by their lack of capital.

Turkish immigrants in Denmark constitute a heterogeneous group with regards to age, gender, education level, and occupation. For example, Üçok and Kjeldgaard (2005) found that within one group, savings accumulated in Denmark are transferred to Turkey to buy status-symbol goods, whilst in another group, economic capital is transferred, within Denmark, into social and cultural capital to facilitate successful integration. Typically, first-generation immigrants are likely to invest in Turkey by accumulating houses, land and shops in their hometown, and summer houses in coastal towns. They continue to support their relatives financially and contribute to the local community by donating towards the building of mosques or other communal buildings. Vacationing at five star holiday resorts on the Turkish Riviera also is popular, especially among the descendants (ibid).

Data for the current research were collected in Turkey and Denmark, amongst Turkish transmigrants, in five towns, over a period of two years. Semi-structured and in-depth interviews were conducted with members of Turkish immigrant communities in Denmark, as well as with their families living in Turkey. The author also participated in several cultural events in both countries and documented her observations via a research journal. Photographs were taken to document immigrants' homes (inside and outside), personal possessions and their cultural functions. Secondary data was also collected, mainly, through Turkish and Danish print media. All immigrants interviewed still held strong ties with their friends and families living in Turkey. This paper focuses then on the consumption practices of the immigrants during their annual visits to Turkey.

Vedat, a male, first generation immigrant informant, is typical of participants when he spoke about the *stigmatization* Turks living in Denmark encounter in their "home" town/country: "*When we go to Turkey they say we are tourists, they don't look at us. We have become strangers. The villagers . . . they look at us and call us gavur-cusun [you are a foreigner] . . . everywhere! Once you are in Turkey, everywhere*". *Gavur,* meaning "an infidel", is a term, heavily laden with negative connotations, applied by Turks to Islamic disbelievers, especially Christians. Similarly, the word *Almancı*, "Germanite", connotes that the emigrants are non-Turkish "foreigners", associated with Europeans and Christians. Thus, Turks visiting Turkey are seen as tourists in a place they consider their home. This stigmatization is common among the upper-middle class Turks, who often perceive Turkish immigrants as *nouveau rich*, working class, peasants.

Üstüner and Holt's (2007) description of second-generation squatter women in Turkey, also applies to the second-generation informants in this study, whose relation to their parents' villages is one of *deterritoralization*, lacking in a natural connection. Many of these informants migrated to European cities, often having never experienced the consumer acculturation that they would have gained had they lived in large Turkish cities. Upon arriving in Europe, they lived in immigrant enclaves and stuck to their roots, thus severely affecting their acculturation process, resulting in lower cultural and social capital.

In summary, in a less industrialized country, such as Turkey, where socio-cultural structures create barriers for social mobility, Turkish transmigrants may hold economic capital but this does not necessarily transfer into cultural and social capital, necessary to allow them to be accepted and participate in Turkish society. This can manifest itself as stigmatization of the consumers, which then can result in them feeling alienated from the community of which they consider themselves to be a part. The transmigrants' identity positionings in various national and socio-cultural contexts are problematic because they are far from being fluid. Building on previous literature (Caglar 2002; Üstüner and Holt 2007; 2010) the contributions suggest conceptualization of transmigrant identity positionings in the cultures of origins similar to those that have been conceptualized in the cultures of destination.

REFERENCES

Aaker, Jennifer, Drolet, Aimlee and Griffin, Dale (2008), "Recalling Mixed Emotions," *Journal of Consumer Research,* 35 (2), 268-78.

Akhtar Salman (1996), "'Someday…' and 'If Only…' Fantasies: Pathological Optimism and Inordinate Nostalgia as Related Forms of Idealization," *Journal of the American Psychoanalytic Association*, 44 (November), 723-53.

Askergaard, Søren (et al) (2005), "Postassimilationalist Ethnic Consumer Research: Qualifications and Extensions," *Journal of Consumer Research*, vol. 31, no. 1: 160-170

Baker, Stacey M. and Patricia F. Kennedy (1994), "Death by Nostalgia: A Diagnostic of Context-specific Cases," *Advances in Consumer Research*, Vol. 21, 169-174.

Basch, L., Glick Schiller, N., & Szanton Blanc, C. (1994), *Nations Unbound: Transnational projects, postcolonial predicaments, and deterritorialized nation states*, Amsterdam: Gordon and Breach.

Çağlar, A. S. (2002), "A Table in Two Hands," in *Fragments of Culture. The Everyday of Modern Turkey,* ed. D. Kandiyoti & A. Saktanber. New Brunswick, New Jersey: Rutgers University Press.

Goffman, Erving (1963), *Stigma: Notes on the Management of Spoiled Identity*, Penguin Books.

Hastie, Reid and Dawes, Robyn M. (2001), *Rational Choice in an Uncertain World*, Thousand Oaks, CA: Sage.

Hinton, Perry (2000), *Stereotypes, cognition and culture*, Psychology Press.

Holbrook, Morris B. and Robert M. Schindler (1991), "Echoes of the Dear Departed Past: Some Work in Progress on Nostalgia," *Advances in Consumer Research*, Vol. 16, 330-333.

Loftus, Elizabeth F. and Pickerell, Jacqueline E. (1995), "The Formation of False Memories," *Psychiatric Annals,* 25 (12), 720-25.

Luedicke, Marius K. (2011), "Consumer Acculturation Theory: (Crossing) Conceptual Boundaries," *Consumption, Markets and Culture*, Vol. 14, No. 3, September. pp. 223-244.

Mercurio, Kathryn and Forehand, Mark R. (2011), "An Interpretive Frame Model of Identity-Dependent Learning: The Moderating Role of Content State Association," *Journal of Consumer Research,* 38 (October), 555-77.

Pries, Ludgar (1999), "New Migration in Transnational Spaces," in *Migration and Transnational Social Spaces*, ed. L. Pries, Aldershot, Brookfield, Sydney, Singapore: Ashgate.

Pries, Ludgar (2001), "The approach of transnational social spaces: Responding to new configurations of the social and the spatial," in *New Transnational Social Spaces* ed. Ludgar Pries, London, New York: Routledge.

Rajagopal, Priyali and Montgomery, Nicola V. (2011), "I Imagine, I Experience, I Like: The False Experience Effect," *Journal of Consumer Research,* 38 (October), 578-94.

Schlosser, Ann E. (2006), "Learning through Virtual Product Experience: The Role of Imagery on True versus False Memories," *Journal of Consumer Research,* 33(December), 377-83.

Üçok, Mine and Askegaard Søren (2008), "Capital Build-up and Transfer: The Case of Turco-Danish Transmigrants", in *Advances in Consumer Research.* Association for Consumer Research, Vol. 35, eds. A. Lee, D. Soman, Memphis, TN.

Üçok, Mine and Dannie Kjeldgaard (2005), "Consumption Practices in Transnational Social Spaces: A Study of Turkish Transmigrants", in *European Advances in Consumer Research*, vol. 7, eds. Karin Ekström and Helene Brembeck.

Üstüner and Holt (2007), "Dominated Consumer Acculturation: The Social Construction of Poor Migrant Women's Consumer Identity Projects in a Turkish Squatter," *Journal of Consumer Research*, 34, 41-56.

Üstüner and Holt (2010), "Toward a Theory of Status Consumption in Less Industrialized Countries," *Journal of Consumer Research*, 37, 37-56.

Wamwara-Mbuga, L. W Wakiuru, Cornwell, T. Bettina and Boller, Gregory (2008), "Triple acculturation: The role of African Americans in the consumer acculturation of Kenyan immigrants," *Journal of Business Research*, Vol. 61 No. 2, pp 83-90.

Waters, Mary C. (2005) "Assessing Immigrant Assimilation: New Empirical and Theoretical Challenges", *Annual Review of Sociology*, Vol. 31 August, pp. 105-125.

Zauberman, Gal, Rebecca K. Ranter, and B Kyu Kim (2009), "Memories as Assets: Strategic Memory Protection in Choice over Time," *Journal of Consumer Research*, 35 (February): 715-28.

Beyond Individualism and Collectivism: Novel Cultural Factors and Their Influence on Consumer Behavior

Chair: Carlos J. Torelli, University of Minnesota, USA

Paper #1: The Interplay between Power Distance, Position in the Social Hierarchy, and Product Type: Consequences for Consumers' Preferences for Premium over Generic Brands

Carlos J. Torelli, University of Minnesota, USA
Ashok K. Lalwani, Indiana University, USA
Jessie J. Wang, Indiana University, USA
Yajin Wang, University of Minnesota, USA

Paper #2: Equality Equals Efficacy: The Effect of Power Distance Belief on Charitable Giving

Karen Page Winterich, Penn State University, USA
Yinlong Zhang, University of Texas at San Antonio, USA

Paper #3: Eye for an Eye: The Effect of Honor Values on Consumer Responses to Brand Failures

Frank May, University of South Carolina, USA
Alokparna (Sonia) Monga, University of South Carolina, USA
Kartik Kalaignanam, University of South Carolina, USA

Paper #4: Power Distance Belief and Brand Personality

Xuehua Wang, Shanghai University of Finance and Economics, China
Xiaoyu Wang, Shanghai University of Finance and Economics, China
Xiang Fang, Oklahoma State University, USA

SESSION OVERVIEW

A great deal has been learned in recent years about the role of culture in consumer psychology. However, despite the rapidly accumulating evidence of culture as a determinant of consumer behavior, nearly all of the evidence has dealt with a broad-based cultural distinction – the distinction between individualist (IND) and collectivist (COL), or independent and interdependent, cultural classifications (Shavitt et al. 2006). This distinction is profoundly important, and thus represents the most broadly used dimension of cultural variability for cross-cultural comparison (Gudykunst & Ting-Toomey, 1988). However, there are limitations on the insights afforded by any broad dimension. This session unites under a common theme of investigating novel cultural dimensions that can afford a more nuanced understanding of cultural patterns in consumer behavior. Specifically, the papers in this session focus on power distance beliefs (PDB), or the extent to which a society accepts human inequality in the distribution of power, wealth, or prestige (Hofstede 1980), and on honor cultures, or those in which a person's claim to virtue is the value of the person in his own eyes and the eyes of his society (Cohen 1998). Although both of these dimensions have emerged as reliable predictors of a variety of patterns in social behavior (e.g., reliance on fair processes or violence for resolving disputes, Brockner et al. 2001; Cohen 1998), relatively less is known about their role in consumer behavior. This session is aimed at filling this gap.

The first paper by Lalwani, Torelli, J. Wang, & Y. Wang investigates the effects of the interplay between consumers' PDB and their position in the social hierarchy (i.e., low vs. high social standing) on preferences for premium over generic brands. In a first multi-country study using actual purchases of national (more premium) brands and private labels (more generic brands), they find that, after controlling for other cultural dimensions in Hofstede (1980) framework (e.g., IND) and other relevant country-level factors (e.g., level of devel-

opment of private labels), high (vs. low) PDB was associated with *higher* preference for premium (national) brands over generic (private label) brands. This effect was stronger for functional (vs. symbolic) products. In a second study using priming procedures, low (vs. high) status consumers exhibited higher preferences for premium over generic brands of functional products, but only under high (and not low) PDB. In contrast, high (vs. low) status individuals exhibited higher preferences for premium over generic brands of symbolic products, but only under low (and not high) PDB. These findings are interpreted in terms of the instrumentality of premium brands for conveying social status, something of value in high (vs. low) PDB contexts, and particularly so for low status individuals when buying common functional products.

The second paper by Winterich and Zhang explores the effects of the link between PDB and perceived outcome efficacy on charitable giving. Because people in high (vs. low) PDB cultures are more likely to accept social inequalities and to believe that everyone should have a defined place within the social order, they are hypothesized to have lower outcome efficacy (i.e., the expectation that one can contribute to effective solutions), which in turn should decrease their charitable giving to aid others (i.e., aiding others will not change the social order). An exploratory study using multi-country data on charitable giving showed that PDB negatively predicted percentage of giving, private philanthropy, and volunteering at the country-level, even after controlling for other cultural (e.g., IND) and country-level factors (e.g., GNP). A series of studies measuring PDB at the individual-level or using priming procedures further showed that high (vs. low) PDB resulted in less charitable giving via lower perceptions of outcome efficacy. These findings have important implications for understanding cross-cultural patterns in charitable giving beyond predictions using the IND-COL distinction.

The third paper by May, Monga, and Kalaignanam focuses on an unexplored variable in consumer research—endorsement of honor values, and its effect on responses to brand failures. Across three lab studies and one archival data study on real consumer complaints across different U.S. states (known to vary in ascription to honor values), the authors find that endorsement of honor values positively predicts retaliatory behavior in the case of a brand failure. They also find that this relationship is stronger in the event of a process (vs. outcome) failure and is attenuated when high-honor consumers are given the opportunity to personally punish the service person responsible. Perceptions of abuse were found to mediate the effects. These findings contribute to our understanding of the cultural factors that can trigger vengeful behavior and consumer satisfaction.

The final paper by Wang, Wang, and Fang investigates the effect of PDB on consumers' assessments of desirable personality traits ascribed to brands. In a series of studies, the authors find that high (vs. low) PDB increases the likelihood of associating favorably-evaluated personality traits with in-group (vs. out-group) brands (i.e., rating in-group brands higher in terms of desirable personality traits than out-group brands). They further demonstrate that consumers' tendencies to categorize brands according to the social groups they represent mediate the relationship between PDB and ascribing desirable personality traits to in-group (vs. out-group) brands.

The papers share several important linkages on affording a more nuanced understanding of cultural patterns in consumer behavior beyond the IND-COL classification, while adding slightly different perspectives. Collectively, the papers provide evidence for the effects of power distance beliefs and culture-of-honor values on consumption decisions both at the cultural group level (i.e., entire countries or regions within a country) as well as at the individual level, which highlights the usefulness of these novel cultural factors. The papers also illuminate on some of the psychological processes associated with these cultural dimensions (e.g., low outcome efficacy in high PDB cultures, perceptions of being abused in cultures of honor, or brand social categorization). In keeping with the theme of the conference (Appreciating diversity), the papers in this special session investigate a diverse set of consumption-related outcomes (e.g., brand preferences and choices, charitable giving, brand evaluations, complaining behavior) that are culturally-patterned when considering the dimensions of power distance and honor values. The findings in this session should appeal specifically to scholars interested in cross-cultural consumer behavior, donating behavior, advertising, branding and more generally to those interested in the psychological processes underlying product evaluation.

The Interplay between
Power Distance, Position in the Social Hierarchy, and
Product Type: Consequences for Consumers' Preferences
for Premium over Generic Brands

EXTENDED ABSTRACT

In his celebrated treatise on the "leisure class," Veblen (1899) introduces the notion of conspicuous consumption as a way of conveying one's wealth and social status to others. This observation has spawned considerable research explaining why and when consumers' prefer premium or luxury brands that are instrumental for symbolizing high-status (e.g., Rucker and Galinsky 2008; Han, Nunes, and Dreze 2010). As judged by the global growth of these brands, consumers in every culture appear to rely on these brands for enhancing their status. Nevertheless, some researchers suggest that there seems to be a higher need for premium brands as status symbols in cultures that accept and expect power differences between citizens (i.e., those that are high in power distance belief or PDB) (de Mooij & Hofstede 2010; Kim & Zhang 2011). In these cultures, people emphasize status, prestige, and wealth as these form the basis of their standing in society (Hofstede 2001), which in turn leads these people to prefer premium (vs. generic) brands. However, the empirical evidence for this premise is mixed at best. Although some small-scale studies suggest that consumers high (vs. low) in PDB attach more importance to products' brand names (Bristow and Asquith 1999; Robinson 1996), other large-scale studies show no relationship between power distance and the role of brands as signals (Erdem, Swait, and Valenzuela 2006). We propose that past research on the topic has neglected to consider important factors that moderate the link between PDB and preference for premium brands. Specifically, we investigate in this research the impact of one's position in the social hierarchy (high vs. low) and the type of product under consideration on the link between PDB and preference for premium brands.

One's position in the social hierarchy can be a strong determinant of consumer behavior. Because high-status individuals often accumulate wealth and acquire power (Magee and Galinsky 2008), research suggests that they develop preferences for products offering utility (e.g., performance, quality, Rucker and Galinsky 2009), rather than for the sake of ascertaining status. However, high-status consumers facing choices of luxury products can still choose high-status products that only those "in the know" can recognize (i.e., most expensive products with 'quieter' logo designs, Han et al. 2010).

In other words, high-status individuals can be quite discerning in their product choices and can choose functional, performance based products in one context, and high-prestige products in another. This is consistent with the view that high power/status individuals engage in situation-specific judgment and behavior (Guinote & Vescio 2010). In contrast, low status/power individuals tend to respond in less situation-specific ways (Guinote & Vescio 2010), and to base their choices more on status affordances than on performance-based reasons (Rucker and Galinsky 2009). Because in high (vs. low) PDB societies prestige and wealth shape vertical relationships between socio-economic classes, the tendencies just described should be particularly strong in high (vs. low) PDB contexts. We thus propose that under high PDB, and when choosing among functional products that offer utility, low- (vs. high-) status individuals should be more likely to prefer premium brands associated with status over generic brands promoted on the basis of performance. However, because for symbolic products most people would rely on social identity criteria like prestige and status, both high and low-status consumers would prefer premium over generic brands. These effects should be weaker (or absent) in low PDB contexts that do not emphasize prestige and wealth in shaping social relationships.

Based on the notion that private labels are commonly positioned as generic brands that offer a price discount for lower or comparable quality, relative to national brands (Vaidyanathan & Aggarwal 2000), study 1 operationalized the relative preference for generic (vs. premium) brands as the market share of private labels in the country. We estimated a linear model with the country-level share of private label brands (from Euromonitor database; N = 519) for different product categories varying along the functional-symbolic continuum (e.g., hair care, household care, or apparel) as the dependent variable, and country-level scores for power distance, uncertainty avoidance, masculinity, and individualism (Hofstede, 2001), the GINI coefficient (a measure of country's income inequality), the level of private label development in the country, the level of product symbolism, and the interaction between this last term and the power distance score as predictors. As expected, power distance emerged as a significant negative predictor of private label share, suggesting that in high (vs. low) PDB countries consumers prefer less private label than premium brands. Furthermore, this effect was qualified by a significant PDB x product symbolism interaction, such that the negative relationship between PDB and private label share was higher for functional compared to symbolic products. Considering that the sample in the study comprised low and middle status consumers, these findings support the hypothesis that in high PDB contexts, low and mid-status consumers prefer premium over generic brands, and particularly so for functional products.

In study 2, we manipulated power distance belief (high vs. low) and status (high vs. low) between –subjects and asked participants about their preferences for premium over generic brands of functional and symbolic products (within-subjects). Results showed that in the high PDB condition, low (vs. high) status participants exhibited greater preferences for premium (over generic) brands of functional products. In contrast, they showed similar higher preferences for premium brands of symbolic products. These differences were not observed in the low PDB condition.

The findings in this research are consistent with the notion that, in high (vs. low) PDB contexts, people low (vs. high) in status prefer premium (over generic) brands due to their instrumentality for conveying social status, something of value in high PDB contexts. Furthermore, this is particularly the case with functional products that are often more likely to be impacted by cultural factors (Lee and Shavitt 2006; Monga and John 2010). A third study for which data collection is underway explores the mediating role of the instrumentality of premium brands for fulfilling status concerns on the reported effects.

Equality Equals Efficacy: The Effect of Power Distance Belief on Charitable Giving

EXTENDED ABSTRACT

Charitable giving differs significantly across cultures, with Australia and New Zealand found to be the most generous countries in the world (Charities Aid Foundation 2010). Though not among the wealthiest countries, these countries are both characterized by low power-distance belief. Power-distance belief (PDB hereafter) has been defined as the degree of power disparity the people in a culture expect and accept (Hofstede 1984, 2001; Oyserman 2006). Can such a belief impact consumers' charitable giving? Though much attention has been given to individualism/collectivism (Aaker and Lee 2001; Oyserman and Lee 2007), Oyserman (2006) notes that PDB was the first cultural factor identified by Hofstede (1984). We theorize that the accepted inequality among those with high PDB results in lower perceptions of outcome efficacy, which represents the evaluation of the extent to which one can contribute to effective solutions (e.g., Stern et al. 1999; Van Liere and Dunlap, 1978). In turn, those with higher PDB donate less.

The central difference between high- and low-PDB cultures does not lie in actual power disparity per se, but in people's attitudes toward power disparity. Consumers in high PDB cultures tend to be more likely to accept inequality. Accordingly, high PDB cultures facilitate a norm that everyone should have a "defined" place within the social order. Consumers who are aware of these social orders feel the existing social order should be well respected and any effort in altering this order tends to be regarded as fruitless (Bourdieu 1984; Miller et al. 1993). Thus, we expect consumers in this social order-salient mindset to believe that aiding others will not change the social order, or, in other words, have low outcome efficacy.

In contrast to high PDB cultures, the norm in low PDB cultures is to maintain and respect the equality inherent in social interactions (Hofstede 1984, 2001). Even though an actual disparity in power may exist, individuals in these cultures do not believe that differences in power, wealth, and prestige are inevitable (Oyserman 2006). As such, consumers may seek out opportunities to achieve equality and should believe that aiding others will make a difference in changing the unjust social order. Given the expectation and acceptance of (in) equality in (high) low PDB cultures, we theorize that PDB influences 1) perceptions of outcome efficacy when aiding others (due to unavoidable social order) to achieve equality, and 2) charitable giving. Specifically, high PDB consumers will have lower perceptions of outcome efficacy and donate less to charities to aid others than low PDB consumers.

Exploratory analysis revealed that country-level power-distance belief (Hofstede 2011) predicted percentage of giving, private philanthropy, and volunteering at the country-level, even after controlling for collectivism, education, GNP, and income inequality. Therefore, we conducted a series of studies to examine this pattern at the individual level and demonstrate causality. In the first study, we measured PDB of online survey participants and, after a filler task, asked them to choose between a donation to a charity or a bonus payment for themselves. PDB predicted choice of donation, regardless of self-construal, such that those with higher PDB were less likely to choose the donation. Study 1B replicated this finding when PDB was made temporarily accessible using a sentence-scrambling task (Zhang, Winterich, and Mittal 2010). We next examined the underly-

ing mechanism of outcome efficacy (Steg and de Groot 2010). As in Study 1, measured PDB predicted donation intentions, but, importantly, this effect was mediated by outcome efficacy such that those with higher PDB had lower outcome efficacy which led to lower donation intentions.

In Study 3, we examined the moderating role of charity recipient to causally test our proposed psychological process of outcome efficacy (Spencer, Zanna, and Fong 2005). If consumers with higher PDB choose not to donate because they believe inequality will exist regardless of their efforts to aid less fortunate others, then these consumers should not differ from those with lower PDB in their donations when the donation benefits others regardless of social class. This study considered recipients to be the general public or specifically the poor and needy. The study was a 2 (PDB prime: high vs. low) X 2 (charity recipient social class: lower vs. higher) between-subjects design with a non-profit organization described as advocating art for everyone and improving communities versus advocating art for families in poverty. Results revealed a significant interaction between PDB and charity recipient such that PDB predicted donation likelihood for lower social class charity recipients but not for higher social class charity recipients. Moreover, outcome efficacy mediated this effect on donation likelihood, supporting our theorizing.

A final study sought to identify a boundary condition for the effect of PDB on charitable giving such that consumers, regardless of PDB, would donate to a charity aiding those in the low social class at the same rate that those with low PDB do. We focus on cause involvement as the potential moderator. PDB was primed between-subjects and involvement with the arts was measured continuously with participants asked to allocate 50 cents to a charity for the arts versus a bonus payment to themselves. A significant interaction revealed that PDB only predicted donation allocation for those with low cause involvement. When cause involvement was high, donation allocations did not differ by PDB. Again, outcome efficacy mediated this effect such that those with greater cause involvement had higher perceptions of outcome efficacy even when in the high PDB condition.

These results have important theoretical implications for understanding the drivers of charitable giving, particularly cultural factors beyond collectivism. By understanding the role of outcome efficacy in this effect, we can suggest ways in which this effect of PDB can be overcome to increase donations, which may be particularly important given the increasing standard of living among consumers from developing countries such as BRIC. We hope this research advances understanding of factors influencing charitable giving, moving from individual and cultural level variables beyond those of self-construal or collectivism.

Eye for an Eye: The Effect of Honor Values on Consumer Responses to Brand Failures

EXTENDED ABSTRACT

Brand failures are becoming increasingly common and publicized. Examples include the recent recall of Tylenol products from the market place, the unreasonable increase in Netflix prices, and the listing of Bank of America and AOL in MSN money's "customer service hall of shame." Compounding these problems, huge advancements in social media allow consumers to exact revenge on businesses that have wronged them. Social networking websites (e.g., Facebook) and anti-business websites (e.g., walmartsucks.com) allow consumers to retaliate with far more ease and speed than ever before. Despite the vast amount of research which has been done in the area of brand failures (Ahluwalia et al. 2000; Dawar and Pillutla,

2000; Folkes 1984; Klein and Dawar, 2004; Pullig, Netemeyer, and Biswas, 2006), there is no research that addresses the role that honor values may play in consumers' response to such failures.

People who endorse honor values believe that one's worth or value is not necessarily a given; it must be earned and acknowledged by others (Pitt-Rivers 1966). Honor values are important because they vary not only across individuals, but also across geographic regions and cultures. People who endorse honor values are particularly sensitive to abuse (Ijzerman et al. 2007; Cohen et al. 1996). Cohen et al. (2006) found that people who do not endorse honor values were relatively unaffected by a person bumping into them and muttering an insult, while people who do endorse honor values were more likely to perceive abuse. Drawing upon this research, we propose that, people who strongly endorse honor values are more sensitive to brand failures, and therefore more likely to engage in retaliatory behaviors, such as complaining to the firm, spreading negative word of mouth, or posting negative online reviews.

In study one, participants were primed with either high or low honor and then exposed to a scenario that depicted a restaurant service failure. As expected, the participants in the high honor condition expressed a greater desire for vengeance than the participants in the low honor condition did.

In study two, we examine the effects of regional variations in honor. For example, residents of some states in the American South are more likely to endorse honor values (Cohen and Nisbett 1994; Nisbett and Cohen 1996). We examined transactional data spanning a twelve year period (1997-2009) from a U.S. catalog retailer. The database provides information on issuance of special coupons given to pacify angry customers (who were wronged by the retailer). We consider issuance of such coupons as a proxy for customer complaining to the firm because consumers who express their anger and complain are given these special coupons. Complaining is an important kind of vengeful behavior (Bechwati and Morrin 2003). No other coupons were issued in this period. We supplemented this database with demographic data, state-level honor scores (Nisbett et al. 1996), and individualism scores (Vandello and Cohen 1999). We estimated a probit model that links coupons issued to honor scores. We also controlled for several factors (e.g., individualism/collectivism, income, age, years of schooling, and population). We predicted and found that honor is positively related to issuance of coupons. Individualism is not significantly related to the likelihood of coupon issuance.

In study three, we examine the effects of honor on retaliatory behavior across process and outcome failure situations. An outcome failure refers to when an aspect of the promised product or service is not performed, resulting in an economic loss (e.g., a restaurant that served poor quality food). A process failure refers to a situation in which the product or service is not delivered in a satisfactory manner, resulting in a social loss (e.g., status, esteem) (e.g., a restaurant where the waiter ignores the customer) (Chan and Wan 2008). We used a 2 (ascription to honor values: high vs. low) X 2 (failure type: outcome failure scenario vs. process failure scenario) between subjects design. We used a different stimulus in this study, consisting of a computer service failure scenario. Honor was measured using an honor scale (Cohen and Nisbett 1994). Because process failures tend to be more social in nature, and honor values are associated with social situations, we predicted that a stronger effect of honor values on vengeful behavior would emerge in the process failure than in the outcome failure conditions. Our results supported our prediction and perceptions of abuse by the firm mediated the effects of honor on retaliatory behavior.

In study four, we examine the process mechanism. We used a 2 (ascription to honor values: Republicans vs. Democrats) X 2 (punishment: present, absent) between subjects design. In this study, honor was operationalized using political party identification. In general, the Republican Party endorses issues that are important to high honor consumers (e.g., gun ownership, strong national defense; Cohen 1996) A pretest confirmed this intuition, as Republicans scored higher on an honor scale than Democrats did. Since people who endorse honor values believe that honor is something that can be both lost and regained, and are driven to maintain honor, giving these people an opportunity to restore lost honor should attenuate the desire to retaliate against the brand. We predicted that for people high in honor, desire to engage in retaliatory behavior against the brand after the service failure would be lower when allowed to have a hand in punishing the offending service employee vs. when not allowed, whereas for people low in honor there would be no significant difference across conditions. Our results supported our prediction and perceptions of abuse mediated the effects of honor and punishment on retaliatory behavior.

Our findings make important contributions to the area of branding, brand failures, and cultural values.

Power Distance Belief and Brand Personality

EXTENDED ABSTRACT

Brands, as consumption symbols, carry important cultural meanings in consumers' minds. Past research has showed that different cultures influence consumers' perceptions of various brand personality dimensions (e.g., Aaker et al. 2001). In this research, we investigate the effect of power distance belief (PDB hereafter) on brand personality evaluations. PDB refers to the extent to which people "accept and expect that power is distributed unequally" (Hofstede 2001, p. 83). Though marketing scholars gradually recognize the importance of examining the influence of PDB on consumer behavior, only a handful of studies have done so (e.g., Zhang, 2011). We extend the current stream of research on PDB to variations in consumers' assessments of personality traits ascribed to brands and identify the underlying mechanism of these variations.

People with high PDB expect to see unequal power distribution in a society and attend to differences among various classes within the social hierarchy (Gaertner et al. 1989). Therefore, we argue that they are more aware of in-group--out-group differences and thus tend to regard in-group members as more superior than out-group members. In this research, we extend this social categorization concept to the brand level. Since brands carry important symbolic meanings, we expect that consumers may also arrange brands into a hierarchy according to the groups that these brands symbolize. We refer to this as an individual's brand social categorization tendency. People high in PDB, who accept power disparity in a society and believe that power should be distributed unequally, should cognitively develop a high tendency to arrange objects such as brands in a hierarchy according to the groups associated with these brands. In contrast, people with low PDB would perceive relatively equal power distribution in a society, which should lower their tendency to categorize brands in this manner. Therefore, we expect that high (vs. low) PDB should increase the likelihood of associating favorably-evaluated personality traits with in-group (vs. out-group) brands. More importantly, we propose that brand social categorization tendency mediates the relationship between PDB and ascribing desirable personality traits to in-group (vs. out-group) brands.

We conducted a series of studies to test our hypotheses. Study 1 explored the relationship between PDB and brand personality traits.

The sample consisted of 926 coffee consumers in three major cities in Mainland China. Participants were instructed to think about a coffee store brand they frequently go to (in-group brand). Power distance beliefs (PDB) and five dimensions of brand personality were measured. The results showed that PDB exerted a significantly positive influence on the ratings for the five brand personality traits (all ps < .05).

Study 2 used two experiments to test the potential mediation effect of brand social categorization tendency. In Study 2A (N = 64), participants were either primed with high or low PDB. They were then given ten brands of sportswear and were asked to imagine each brand as a person and categorize the brands as in-group members, out-group members, and those with no clear associations with either group. Brand social categorization tendency was measured by three items, adapted from Gaertner et al. (1994) (e.g., I usually feel that the brands belong to different social classes). The main dependent variable was the perceived difference between in-group and out-group brands. Results showed that individuals with high PDB displayed greater brand social categorization tendencies than those with low PDB. Furthermore, participants in the high-PDB condition perceived a greater difference between in-group and out-group brands (M = 5.82) than those in the low-PDB condition (M = 4.41, F = 16.92, p < .05). To enhance generalizability and the robustness of our finding, we conducted Study 2b using a different categorization measure in a different product category.

In Study 2b (N = 62), Chinese participants followed a similar procedure with a few exceptions. Ten familiar brands of cell-phones were used as stimuli, and participants were asked to categorize these ten brands by drawing circles including the brands they thought belonged to the same group. We expected that the stronger the social categorization tendency participants have, the more circles that they should draw. The results showed that participants in the high-PDB condition drew more circles (M = 3.47) than those in the low-PDB condition (M = 2.56; F = 16.31, p < .05), indicating that individuals with high (vs. low) PDB tend to categorize brands more in terms of their associations with social groups . Next we conducted Study 3 to directly test brand social categorization tendency as mediator of the relationship between PDB and the extent to which desirable personality traits are ascribed to brands.

In Study 3, upon the completion of the PDB priming task, participants were asked to imagine Adidas (an in-group brand, from a pretest) and XTEP (an out-group brand) as individuals and to rate the two brands on the "competence" dimension (rated as the most important brand personality trait in sportswear category based on the pretest). Results indicated that individuals in the high-PDB condition associated Adidas more with the desirable "competence" dimension (M = 5.44) than those in the low-PDB condition (M = 4.79, p < .05). In contrast, individuals in the high-PDB condition associated XTEP less with the same dimension (M = 3.19) than those in the low-PDB condition (M = 3.70, p < .05). Further, participants in the high- (versus low-) PDB condition perceived the difference between the desirable trait ascribed to the in-group and the out-group brand as significantly larger ($M_{\text{high-PDB}}$ =2.24, $M_{\text{low-PDB}}$ =1.10, p < .05). In sum, these findings suggest that high (vs. low) PDB increases the likelihood of associating favorably evaluated personality trait with in-group (vs. out-group) brands. Furthermore, our mediation analysis showed that this effect was mediated by participants' tendency to categorize brands according to their associations with social groups.

Our research makes important contributions to the current brand personality literature by investigating the link to a less-researched cultural dimension: power distance beliefs. Brand social categorization tendency was found to mediate the relationship between PDB and the difference in desirable personality traits ascribed to in-group and out-group brands.

REFERENCES

Aaker, Jennifer L. (1997), "Dimensions of Brand Personality," *Journal of Marketing Research*, 34 (3), 347-56.

Cohen, Dov, Richard Nisbett, Brian Bowdle, and Norbert Schwartz (1996), "Insult, Aggression, and the Southern Culture of Honor: An "Experimental Ethnography", *Journal of Personality and Social Psychology*, 70(5), 945-960.

Hofstede, Geert H. (2001), *Culture's Consequences : Comparing Values, Behaviors, Institutions and Organizations across Nations*. Thousand Oaks, Calif.: Sage.

Magee, Joe C. and Adam D. Galinsky (2008), "Social Hierarchy: The Self-Reinforcing Nature of Power and Status," *The Academy of Management Annals*, 2 (1), 351-98.

Oyserman, Daphna (2006), "High Power, Low Power, and Equality: Culture Beyond Individualism and Collectivism," *Journal of Consumer Psychology*, 16 (4), 352-256.

Rucker, Derek D. and Adam D. Galinsky (2008), "Desire to Acquire: Powerlessness and Compensatory Consumption," *Journal of Consumer Research*, 35 (2), 257-67.

Experiencing and Evaluating in the Brain: fMRI and Single-Neuron Studies

Chair: Moran Cerf, New York University, USA

Paper #1: 1. Identifying Emotions on the Basis of Neural Activation

Moran Cerf, New York University and University of California Los Angeles, USA

Vicki G. Morwitz, New York University, USA

Tom Meyvis, New York University, USA

Eric Greenleaf, New York University, USA

Paper #2: 2. Risk and Attribute Framing: They're Different

Hilke Plassmann, INSEAD, France

Beth Pavlicek, École des Neurosciences de Paris, France

Baba Shiv, Stanford University, USA

Paper #3: 3. How incidental affect alters subsequent judgments: insights from a human fMRI study

William Hedgcock, University of Iowa, USA

Irwin Levin, University of Iowa, USA

Kameko Halfman, University of Iowa, USA

Jooyoung Park, University of Iowa, USA

Natalie Denburg, University of Iowa, USA

Paper #4: 4. Single-neuron correlates of emotion regulation in humans

Karim Kassam, Carnegie Mellon University, USA

Amanda Markey, Carnegie Mellon University, USA

Vladimir Cherkassky, Carnegie Mellon University, USA

George Loewenstein, Carnegie Mellon University, USA

Marcel Just, Carnegie Mellon University, USA

SESSION OVERVIEW

When experiencing daily interactions we often think of the momentary evaluation of an experience and its following evaluations as one. However, we now have mounting evidence to the contrary from psychology and neuroscience studies. Eating the chocolate or remembering its taste an hour later are distinguishably different experiences. We trust our memories and evaluation of past events and attach high confidence to them. Our evaluation of past experiences is often shaped by their encoding in our brains and the momentary emotional state we are at upon recalling them. Remembering, therefore, is just another form of evaluation – prone to many failures.

In this session we will address the notion of experience versus its following recount through evaluation, and focus on its effects on consumer decisions. In a sequence of four talks, we will address multiple facets of the problem and suggest methods to assess the difference between experience and reappraisal, as well as evidence for its direct effects on choice and decision-making.

To address these notions, Karim Kassam will initiate the session by showing a novel imaging study that proposes evidence for identifiable emotions signatures that generalize across individuals. That is, a method by which we can isolate a certain emotion by reading brain activity when a subject is experiencing a certain feeling. The emotions tested vary and include complex emotions such as pride, embarrassment and shame. Presumably, these emotions, which are not necessarily accessible to the subjects themselves or to a direct survey can then be read using this method in order to infer consumer evaluation of current experience and of past experiences.

Following this emotional evaluation introduction, William Hedgcock will show the results of a series of studies, which focus on a type of emotional difference between the experience and its evaluation. Dr. Hedgcock's work focuses on a type of decisions prone to

what s known as the framing effect, where decision makers respond differently to problems that are described in positive or negative terms despite the fact that the outcomes are objectively identical. In terms of evaluation of past choices, the framing effect provides evidence to the fact that our evaluations are not only likely to be mistaken but can easily be manipulated by the choice of question asked during the evaluation process. Additionally, Dr. Hedgcock will introduce the notion of emotion suppression as a tool that is often used by subjects to regulate their choices based on emotions.

The third project, presented by Hilke Plassmann, will look at the manifestation of the problem in effective consumer choices. In Dr. Plassmann's work, subjects are asked to evaluate a preference based on their past experience – in the particular case, the taste of wine - and are showing biased choice based on monetary rewards received earlier. This direct manipulation of the choice acts as another evidence for the difference between the pure objective taste, which we deem the experience, and the following modified evaluation.

While the previous three presentations addressed the choice and the evaluation mainly using imaging techniques and behavioral responses, the fourth presentation will target the question using an alternative method, which is proven more precise yet less spatially distributed and quite invasive: directly recording of the activity of single neurons in the brains of humans undergoing neurosurgery. Moran Cerf's presentation will demonstrate the ability to identify signature correlates of emotions similar to the work shown in the first presentation, only at the level of individual neurons. Dr. Cerf demonstrates the ability to identify single-neuron correlates of the experience and the regulation of a given emotion while patients are either empathizing with emotional content expressed, or while the patients are regulation the emotions and trying to change their evaluation of it. Regulation of the emotion will be demonstrated both using internal manipulation by the patients, or external biases of decision making as shown in the third work.

The four talks will address the ability to exhibit emotion and experiences in the lab, and scientists the ability to measure these emotions using various methods ranging from surveys, to imaging and invasive recordings of single neurons in the brains. The talks will show evidences for the differences between the direct experiences and the following evaluation of it over time, with evidence for the ability to bias decisions under certain conditions of reward or framing. Finally, the four presenters will show alternative methods used to regulate or enhance such biases and will address their potential usage in consumer psychology.

Audience and level of Completeness

The potential ACR audience for this session is quite broad. This session will be of interest to researchers in the following areas: attitudes and intentions, affective and emotional processing, and decision making. In addition, it will be of interest to practitioners who use survey research methodologies, and researchers interested in exposure to imaging techniques and the novel single-neuron recording in humans.

All four presentations will present the results of completed studies.

Discussion

Moran Cerf will be the leading a discussion at the end of the session. Dr. Cerf is has been involved in both neuroscience and marketing research, and has published papers in both fields as well as decision-making studies. Method-wise, his work has involved both imaging works and single-neuron recordings, which are the main methods discussed in the session. He therefore has a unique perspective for discussing these papers and leading a discussion about an appropriate research agenda for continued work in this area.

Plan for the Session

Each work will be presented for 15 minutes, followed by 5 minutes of question and answer. We will leave 15 minutes at the end for a general audience discussion.

Identifying Emotions on the Basis of Neural Activation

EXTENDED ABSTRACT

Development of reliable measures of specific emotion has proven difficult. Self-report, still the gold standard, is vulnerable to deception and demand effects. Physiological measures such as heart rate and skin conductance show some ability to discriminate between broad categories of emotion but have limited ability to make finer classifications. Facial expressions have also been used to categorize a subset of emotions, but emotions can occur in the absence of facial expressions and facial expressions can occur in the absence of emotion. Neural circuits that mediate certain emotion-related behaviors (e.g. freezing) have been identified, but researchers have yet to achieve reliable identification of emotions on the basis of neural activation. In short, existing methods of emotion measurement suffer from a variety of limitations.

Neuroimaging data has held the promise of providing more powerful methods for identifying emotions, but the promise of fMRI has yet to be realized. The search for neural correlates of emotion may have been hampered by the use of statistical methods not well suited to the task of identifying spatially-distributed activation signatures from very large data sets. Indeed, recent meta-analyses of fMRI studies using univariate analyses failed to find any region that was specifically and consistently activated by a single emotion.

Rather than search for neural structures associated with specific emotions, we applied recently developed multi-voxel pattern analysis techniques to identify distributed patterns of activity associated with specific emotions. These techniques relax linearity assumptions and acknowledge the fact that neural responses to emotional stimulation occur in many brain areas simultaneously. These algorithms frequently result in increased predictive power, and recent research suggests that they hold promise for classifying emotion using neurological and physiological data.

We applied a Gaussian Naïve Bayes pooled variance classifier to neurological data to classify a broad variety of emotional experiences. Participants were method actors experienced with entering and exiting emotional states on cue. Prior to the neuroimaging session, each wrote scenarios that had made them feel or would make them feel emotional states denoted by 18 words grouped into nine emotion categories: anger (angry, enraged), disgust (disgusted, revolted), envy (envious, jealous), fear (afraid, frightened), happiness(happy, joyous), lust (lustful, horny), pride (proud, admirable), sadness (sad, gloomy), and shame (ashamed, embarrassed). Participants also wrote a calm scenario that was used as a baseline. In the scanner, participants were given nine seconds to imagine the scenario and enter the appropriate emotional state, followed by eleven seconds to exit that state, rate their emotional intensity, and prepare for the next trial. Once this portion of the session was complete, participants viewed 12 disgusting images and 12 calm/neutral images in random order.

We first examined the ability of our classifier to identify a participant's emotion on a particular trial on the basis of his/her neural activation during the other trials. In the cross-validation procedure used to assess emotion identification accuracy, the classifier was trained on four of the six presentations of a word and tested on the average of the two presentations held out. We report the mean rank accuracy of the classification performance, that is, the percentile rank of the correct emotion category in the classifier's posterior-probability-ordered list of emotions, averaged across the 15 ways of choosing two of six presentations. If the classification were operating at chance level, one would expect a mean normalized rank accuracy of 0.50, indicating that the correct emotion appeared on average in the fifth position in the classifier's output of a ranked list of all nine emotions. The rank accuracies for this within-subject analysis ranged from 0.72 to 0.90, with an average of 0.84, well above the chance classification rate of 0.5 (a mean accuracy greater than .51 would be significant at the $p = .05$ level). Thus, a participant's neural activation patterns on one subset of trials could be used to reliably identify their emotions on a separate subset of held-out trials, indicating that participants exhibited consistent patterns of neural activation for all emotion categories.

Next we examined whether a participant's specific emotions could be identified on the basis of other participants' activation patterns. For these tests, the emotions experienced by each participant were identified using a classifier trained on the activation data from the other nine participants. Despite the challenges presented by individual variability in functional organization and methodological difficulties in normalizing morphological differences, the classifier achieved a mean rank accuracy of 0.70, well above chance levels (accuracy of 0.56 significant at the $p = .01$ level). Our classifier predicted the emotions experienced using activation patterns of other participants at significantly better than chance levels for eight of ten participants, suggesting that the neural correlates of emotional experience share significant commonality across individuals.

Finally, we investigated whether patterns of activation observed in self-induced emotion trials could predict the emotional content of a stimulus of an entirely different modality. We trained a classifier using participants' neural activation during word-cued self-induced emotions, and tested whether it could identify the emotional content of a visual image. Successful classification would indicate that the activations observed correspond to emotional experience in general, rather than remembered or imagined emotional experiences specifically. This classification identified responses to disgust pictures with a rank accuracy of 0.91, well above chance rates (accuracy of 0.74 significant at the $p = .01$ level). Thus, even though the classifier had not encountered neural activation in response to pictures, it was able to accurately identify the emotional content of pictures. The results demonstrate a consistency in the neural representation of emotional response to qualitatively different stimuli.

In sum, we show that specific emotional states can be identified on the basis of their neural signatures, and that these signatures are reliably activated across episodes, across individuals, and across different types of emotional experiences. The results inform our understanding of emotional processes, highlight the predictive value of specific emotions, and suggest the potential to infer a person's emotional reaction to an arbitrary stimulus – a flag, a brand name, or a political candidate, for example – on the basis of neural activation.

Risk and Attribute Framing: They're Different

EXTENDED ABSTRACT

Framing effects occur when decision makers respond differently to problems that are described in positive or negative terms despite the fact that the outcomes are objectively identical. Framing effects are most often treated as homogenous phenomenon, though some research suggests there may be several distinctive types of frames (Levin, Schneider, and Gaeth, 1998). Two of the most common framing types that have been identified are risk and attribute framing. Risk frames involve a choice between a risky and a riskless option, and individuals typically have a higher preference for risky options when the problems are described in negative terms. In contrast, attribute frames involve evaluations where options are either risky or riskless and attribute descriptions, such as quality, are manipulated. Individuals typically give higher evaluations for options when the attributes are described in positive terms (e.g., % chance of being successful) and lower evaluations when the attributes are framed in negative terms (e.g., % chance of being unsuccessful).

Critically, these different framing effects may be caused by independent processes (Levin, Gaeth, Schreiber, 2002; Van Schie & Van der Pligt, 1995). In fact, within subject measurements of risk and attribute framing have not been significantly correlated (Levin et al., 2002). Additionally, risk framing and attribute framing correlate with different personality traits. Risk framing preference reversals correlate with high neuroticism, low openness, high conscientiousness, and low agreeableness (Levin et al., 2002). In contrast, individual differences in attribute framing correlate with low conscientiousness and high agreeableness (Levin et al., 2002). Note that though these two personality traits are correlated with risk framing as well, the correlations are in opposite directions.

There is some evidence that risk framing is associated with emotional processes (De Martino, Kumaran, Seymour, Dolan, 2006); though the evidence is mixed (Talmi, Hurlemann, Patin, Dolan, 2010). De Martino et al. (2006) found a correlation between "rational" decision making and activity in the ventromedial prefrontal cortex (VMPC). They further found that the anterior cingulate cortex (ACC) and the amygdala were involved in framing. In contrast, Talmi and colleagues (2010) did not find any differences between patients with amygdala damage and controls.

We conducted a series of behavioral and functional magnetic resonance imaging studies to investigate processing differences in risk and attribute framing using a within subject valence manipulation. The studies reported here examined (1) which personality traits were correlated with risk and attribute framing, (2) how risk and attribute framing effects were affected by emotion suppression instructions, and (3) the neural correlates of risk and attribute framing. We predicted:

Risk and attribute framing would have different personality trait correlates.

Attribute framing would be affected by emotion suppression instructions while risk framing would not be affected by emotion suppression instructions.

Risk and attribute framing would show distinct patterns of neural activation. Specifically, we predicted attribute framing effects would be more strongly associated with activity in regions of the brain such as the amygdala and VMPFC (regions associated with emotional processing) than risk framing.

Here we provide a series of studies demonstrating that independent processes likely govern attribute and risk framing.

Risk and Attribute Framing Correlate Study

Participants responded to risk and attribute framing questions as well as filling out the Big 5, and questions designed to measure their levels of risk and loss aversion. Attribute framing effects were not correlated to risk aversion, loss aversion, or any of the Big 5 personality traits (all $ps > 0.15$). On the other hand, risk framing effects were correlated with loss aversion ($p < .05$), neuroticism ($p < .05$), and numeracy ($p < .05$). This provides some preliminary evidence that risk and attribute framing may be caused by independent mechanisms.

Emotion Suppression Study

Participants responded to risk and attribute framing questions. Some of the participants received standard instructions to choose options they preferred the most while others received additional instructions to adopt a detached an unemotional attitude when choosing their preferred alternative. Participants in the control condition had the standard set of results. Negative risk framing increased risk seeking ($p < 0.01$) while negative attribute framing increased quality seeking ($p < 0.05$). However, results were different when participants received emotion suppression instructions. In this case, risk framing still lead to risk seeking ($p < 0.01$) but attribute framing did not lead to quality seeking ($p = 0.41$). Thus, emotion suppression did not affect risky framing but it did affect attribute framing.

fMRI Framing Study

Participants responded to risk and attribute framing questions while we measured brain activation with functional magnetic resonance imaging (fMRI). As expected, negative risk frames resulted in risk seeking ($p < 0.01$) while negative attribute framing resulted in quality seeking ($p < 0.05$). Preliminary analyses indicated the attribute framing effect was associated with activity in the amygdala and prefrontal cortex, whereas the risk framing effect was associated with activity in the parietal lobe. Moreover, there is very little overlap in activity between attribute framing and risk framing.

We provide considerable evidence that risk and attribute framing effects have different causes. We find risk framing is correlated with loss aversion, neuroticism and numeracy while attribute framing is not correlated to any of these measures. Further, we find emotion suppression affects attribute framing but not risk framing. Finally, we show risk and attribute framing have different neural correlates. Our results suggest researchers shouldn't assume risk and attribute framing are driven by the same processes.

How Incidental Affect Alters Subsequent Judgments: Insights from a Human fMRI Study

EXTENDED ABSTRACT

People do not have stable, coherent and readily accessible preferences that can be reliably measured through self-report. Instead, judgments are constructed on the spot and recent, contextual factors exert a disproportionate influence on judgments (Payne, Bettman, and Johnson, 1992; Slovic, 1995). These contextual influences include feelings that are unrelated to the judgment (such as moods, emotions, and expectation of receiving a reward, Schwarz & Clore 1996). Why is the brain susceptible to these types of rewards that engender such changes in revealed preferences? To address this question, we discuss the impact of incidental affect on the neural representation of experienced value, an essential computation in the process of value-based decision-making.

We scanned human subjects' brains (N=19, 6f, aged 21-46 years) using fMRI while engaging in a task that first involved the receipt of a monetary reward ($0, $50, $200) for real using a one-armed bandit task and subsequently the receipt of a food reward (two different liked wines). During the tasting task, subjects were instructed to evaluate how much they liked the taste of each wine.

Behavioral analysis showed that the incidental rewards (i.e. amounts won from the slot machine) significantly biased participant's judgments of how much they enjoyed the wines (F(1, 18) = 7.46, p<.01). No effect on reaction times was found.

We ran a set of different univariate fMRI analysis. First, we looked for brain areas correlating with the size of monetary reward and found that the size of incidental rewards triggered activity changes in different brain areas previously found to be involved in reward processing (i.e. vStr, dStr, amydala, insula, inferior OFC). Second, we investigated brain areas that correlate with the size of reported experienced value (EV) and found that EV was encoded in brain areas that also have been previously found to encode EV (i.e. vmPFC, the inferior lateral OFC, anterior insula). Third, we analyzed the neural correlates of how the judgement of the consumption experience is biased by the size of the incidental reward. Interestingly, we found that incidental rewards affect EV through a negative correlation in two of the EV areas mentioned above, the insula and the inferior lateral OFC. Our own data and also previous studies could show that activity in these brain areas correlate negatively with taste pleasantness.

Our results show that incidental rewards have an effect of reported OV. Interestingly, our fMRI results reveal that incidental affect bias taste processing on an earlier stage as compared to more cognitive cues (i.e. the price of the wine, semantic label of an odor, Plassmann et al. 2008). Finally, it seems that incidental affect "make subjects dislike the wines less" instead of liking them more as compared to other papers that have looked at a cognitive modulation of EV.

Single Neuron Correlates of
Emotion Regulation In Humans

EXTENDED ABSTRACT

Adult humans have the ability to regulate their emotions, an ability that emerges late in development and breaks down in some psychiatric diseases. A leading neurological model of emotional representations in the brain hypothesizes that the amygdala modulates prefrontal cortex activity by top-down influences. The basis of emotion regulation, however, has never been investigated in humans at the single neuron level. This research provides the first extensive study of what happens to the activity of individual neurons in the human brain as people experience and regulate their emotions while viewing emotional moving images.

In order to test participants' ability to control and regulate their emotions we used a novel technique: recording the activity of single neurons directly from the brains of humans, while they were exhibiting emotions or regulating them.

Participants were 8 epilepsy patients undergoing brain surgery for possible clinical resection of the seizure foci, who agreed to participate in research studies during their hospital stay. During a clinical procedure, up to 128 electrodes were implanted in the exposed brain of each patient. These electrodes allow for the continuous recording of single neuron activity. This ability to record the brain's activity in its highest resolution allows us to examine how thoughts and emotions are expressed using the brain's own language of electrical spiking in individual neurons (Cerf et al., 2010; Kreiman et al., 2000; Gelbard et al., 2008) rather than imaging activity related to oxygenation in areas each containing many thousands of neurons, as in the method used in fMRI research, which is of significantly lower temporal and spatial resolution (Mukamel et al., 2005).

Participants viewed a number of short video clips, including excerpts from films, public-service ads, and political ads, intended to prompt emotional reactions. We also included neutral control clips designed not to induce emotional reactions. Participants were instructed first to view all of the clips and to let their feelings flow naturally. Following the viewing of the clips participants rated each clip on scales measuring emotion, engagement, and arousal. Next, participants were instructed to again view both the emotional and the control clips, but this time were instructed to regulate their emotions. That is, participants were instructed to suppress their positive or negative emotions such that the feelings they felt during the first viewing would not manifest during the second viewing. Patients also reported whether they had been able to successfully regulate their emotions.

In order to determine the timing of the onset and offset of emotional content in the clips, a set of healthy participants (n = 44) first independently rated the clips continuously for their emotional content (positive/negative). Participants watched the clips in real-time and were instructed to rate them using a moving dial continuously. We used their ratings to estimate the moments of the onset and duration of emotional content while testing the neurological patients.

In trials where participants subjectively reported successfully regulating their emotions, we compared the spiking activity of single neurons in their brains in the two conditions. Cells in the amygdala – part of the brain which is commonly implicated with emotions, primarily negative ones such as fear and disgust – showed increased activity when participants viewed film clips during the first exposure. That is, when participants viewed the film clips naturally. However, during the second viewing, when the participants reported successful regulating of their emotions, we observed a gradual decrease in the amygdala firing over time, controlled by activity in the Orbito-Frontal Cortex (OFC), which is commonly said to be the seat of top-down executive control of emotions. These results show direct neuronal evidence for humans' ability to regulate emotions.

Effectively, we found that neurons in the amygdala were modulated not only by emotional content in the stimuli, but also by the patients' volitional regulating of emotions. Participants' initial response to the stimuli occurred within an early temporal epoch, followed by a later epoch where responses were modulated by the regulation instruction, suggesting an early and mostly bottom-up response within the amygdala followed by a later response that is driven by top-down influences.

Using the activity of OFC neurons alone, we could predict a) how the content of the films affected participants (i.e., whether they would report feeling specific discrete emotions while watching the content), and b) whether they let these emotions naturally manifest, or whether they suppressed them. Decoding performance was above 90% during the first 3s of exposure to the emotional clips. Negative emotions were decoded within 1s from the onset of the emotional moment in the clip and were reflected by a change of 5STD above or below (dependent on the neurons excitatory or inhibitory properties) the baseline firing rate. Baseline was established during passive viewing of the screen without content.

These results should be of interest to consumer psychologists who study emotions, as they provide direct evidence of emotions in single-neuron activity in the human brain, and show the mechanisms underlying emotion regulation at the single-neuron level. The results also demonstrate the direct effect of the viewing of different types of emotional content on the human brain. They suggest that it is possible to use single-neuron activity to monitor the effect of different kinds of emotional content on consumers – whether they are reacting emotionally to the content, whether they are reacting positively or negatively to the content, what specific emotions they are feeling, and whether they are able to control their emotional reactions.

The novel method of direct recording of neuronal activity from human brains will be of great interest to consumer psychologists, and we believe this conference is a perfect forum for exposing consumer psychologists, for this first time, to this new and unique method of measurement. We believe that this method could be used to examine a wide range of topics of interest to consumer psychologists, including how memories are formed in real-time, and how people form associations between one piece of information and another – such as a brand and its associations. Ultimately, this method can be used to examine how people form judgments and make choices in real-time, while directly examining the brain's own coding mechanism.

Of Carrots, Candy, & Self-Control: Decreasing and Increasing Food Consumption

Chairs: Vladas Griskevicius, University of Minnesota, USA
Joseph P. Redden, University of Minnesota, USA

Paper #1: Interventions to Get School Children to Eat More Vegetables

Joseph P. Redden, University of Minnesota, USA
Traci Mann, University of Minnesota, USA
Elton Mykerezi, University of Minnesota, USA
Marla Reicks, University of Minnesota, USA
Zata Vickers, University of Minnesota, USA

Paper #2: In Control of Variety: How Self-Control Reduces the Effect of Food Variety

Kelly L. Haws, Texas A&M University, USA

Paper #3: Red, Ripe, and Ready: Effect of Food Color on Consumption

Stephanie Cantu, University of Minnesota, USA
Vladas Griskevicius, University of Minnesota, USA

Paper #4: Mortality Threat Can Increase or Decrease Women's Caloric Intake Depending on Their Childhood Environment

Sarah E Hill, Texas Christian University, USA
Christopher D. Rodeheffer, Texas Christian University, USA
Danielle J. DelPriore, Texas Christian University, USA
Max E. Butterfield, Texas Christian University, USA

SESSION OVERVIEW

Each year Americans spend $700 billion on food. Whether it's in a store, restaurant, school cafeteria, or at home, each day consumers are confronted with myriad food options. The choices that people make, both about what to eat and how much to eat, play a large role in determining their health, obesity, and well-being. But while people generally recognize the importance of their diet, they often don't appreciate the drivers of eating behavior.

In this proposed session, we consider various factors that shape food choices and consumption. Two of the papers focus on how food choices are influenced by environmental factors such as social norms and food color. The two other papers focus on person variables, including self-control and childhood environment. All four papers provide insight into how these factors influence food preferences. Importantly, each paper goes beyond mere measures of food liking and presents findings for the actual quantity of food consumed. It is only with measures of intake that we can make stronger claims about subsequent effects on health and well-being.

In the first paper, Redden and colleagues present three field experiments in elementary school cafeterias testing different interventions for increasing kids' consumption of vegetables. They find that placing photos of specific vegetables on lunch trays increased carrot and green bean intake by 178%. They also show that serving school children carrots at the table as they waited to be called to enter the cafeteria line increased carrot intake by 430%.

In the next paper, Haws examines how individual differences in self-control influence the "variety effect" – the notion that the presence of variety leads people to eat higher quantities of food. In a series of experiments, she shows that trait self-control plays a critical role in how variety influences eating. For people low in trait self-control, for example, the presence of variety increased snack consumption by 73%. But for people high in trait self-control, the presence of variety increased snack consumption by only 14%.

The third paper by Cantu and Griskevicius investigates how food color affects consumption. Drawing on the idea that the color red has reliably served as an indicator of a food's (e.g., fruit and berries) ripeness, sweetness, and adaptive value, they present three experiments testing how cues to redness affect consumption. They find that people eat about twice as many chocolates when the candies are wrapped in red wrappers.

In the final paper, Hill and colleagues investigate how morality stressors influence women's food consumption. Drawing on theory in biology, they propose that mortality stress should have different effects depending on women's childhood environment. Across three experiments, they show that whereas mortality cues *increase* food consumption for women who grew up poor, mortality stress *decreases* food consumption for women who grew up wealthy.

The papers in this session highlight two types of factors driving food consumption the person and the situation. Across the four research projects, there is consistent evidence that both types of factors play a central role in what people eat and how much they consume. By using a diversity of perspectives (behavioral economics, evolutionary psychology, consumer traits), and a variety of methods (lab studies and field experiments), this session delivers a rich understanding of factors driving food consumption. This approach and the importance of the core topic of food will appeal to a wide range of audiences, including those interested in food preferences and consumption, consumer health, public policy interventions, variety, self-control, and evolutionary approaches.

Interventions to Get School Children to Eat More Vegetables

EXTENDED ABSTRACT

Childhood obesity remains a significant public health concern in the United States, especially among minority populations. Eating behaviors that include low intakes of fruits and vegetables and high intakes of energy-dense foods are risk factors for childhood obesity. According to national dietary intake data (NHANES 2007-2008), approximately 90% of children 8 years-old and older do not meet the current recommendation for total daily vegetable intake. In this research, we test the effectiveness of three interventions to increase vegetable intake at an elementary school cafeteria with approximately 800 students.

The relatively new field of behavioral economics has increased awareness of the effectiveness of small environmental changes to alter behavior. These so-called "nudges" have been effective in a range of settings (Thaler and Sunstein 2010), with the notion that people are more likely to engage in behaviors they feel like they "freely" chose. We propose that interventions will be more effective when they make children actively choose and consume the vegetables for themselves (i.e., without being coerced). Specifically, we test how much the following three small interventions (or nudges) will increase vegetable intake at an elementary school cafeteria: (1) increasing the portion size, (2) providing photos on lunch trays to suggest that taking vegetables is the norm, and (3) serving vegetables before the rest of the meal.

Prior research has shown that the quantity people consume increases as they are served larger servings of food (Wansink 2004). People tend to infer from the portion size what a typical person eats. People then subsequently follow this consumption norm, leading to a positive relationship between portion size and quantity consumed.

People have a tendency to finish the entire serving in front of them (Siegel 1957), suggesting that portion size largely determines the quantity consumed.

Study 1 tested whether increasing the portion size for a vegetable (carrots) and a fruit (oranges) by 50% would increase intake in an elementary school cafeteria. Compared to a control day with an identical menu, school children ate 12% more carrots and 24% more oranges. However, a limiting factor of this intervention for vegetables was that less than 10% of the school children placed carrots on their school tray (versus 33% for oranges). Therefore, the consumption norm for vegetables could not have any effect for 90% of the children.

In Study 2, we developed an intervention to more directly address the fact that very few school children would take the necessary first step of putting carrots on their plate. Here, we employed a nudge based on social norms, which have long been recognized as a particularly powerful way to shape behavior. Norms reflect both what most people think should be done and what most people actually do (Cialdini, Reno, and Kallgren 1990; Deutsch and Gerard 1955), and people often use them as a cue to infer the best course of action (Cialdini 2001). In the school cafeteria setting, we created a norm to eat vegetables by adhering a photo of green beans and a photo of carrots in two separate compartments on the lunch tray. We expected these photos would indicate that others typically select and place vegetables into those compartments and that they should do so too. Compared to a control day with an identical menu, this intervention increased the percentage of students taking green beans from 6% to 15%, and the percentage taking carrots from 12% to 37%. More importantly, those putting the vegetables on their trays subsequently ate them as overall consumption per student in the cafeteria increased by 133% for green beans and 178% for carrots. Furthermore, this intervention required minimal time and cost (about 20 minutes and $0.03 per 100 trays).

In Study 3, we tested how we could make children willingly choose to consume vegetables by making them more attractive. Given that liking depends on how a stimulus compares to a reference point (Helson 1964; Parducci 1995), a vegetable will generally be unappealing when compared to more tasty unhealthy foods like pizza and chicken nuggets. To combat these contrast effects in liking, we propose that healthy foods will be more appealing when eaten in isolation. This would give a moderately liked healthy food a "fighting chance" to be chosen, liked, and ultimately consumed more. Furthermore, when it is the only food present, people may be more likely to clean their plate and eat all of it (Geier, Rozin, and Doros 2006; Siegel 1957). We therefore predict that, when both a healthy and an unhealthy food will be eaten, intake of the healthy food will increase when it is consumed first by itself without the unhealthy food present. Study 3 tested this prediction by first serving the school children carrots at the table as they waited to be called to enter the cafeteria line. Compared to a control day with an identical menu, this intervention increased the intake of carrots per student by 430%.

Overall, we show that three interventions each increase vegetable intake from 12% to 430%. The most effective interventions were those focused on encouraging children to simply put vegetables on their tray. Thus, future research should concentrate on designing small "nudges" that encourage children to be open to and select vegetables. Once children get past this initial hurdle of avoidance, they appear open to subsequently eating the vegetables on their tray. Finally, future efforts to improve the dietary habits of children and increase vegetable intake may benefit from simpler interventions like ours rather than expensive educational efforts.

REFERENCES

Cialdini, Robert B. (2001), *Influence: Science and Practice,* 4th, Boston, MA: Allyn & Bacon.

Cialdini, Robert B., Raymond R. Reno, and Carl A. Kallgren (1990), "A Focus Theory on Normative Conduct: Recycling the Concept of Norms to Reduce Littering in Public Places," *Journal of Personality and Social Psychology,* 58 (6), 1015-26.

Deutsch, Morton and Harold Gerard (1955), "A Study of Normative and Informational Social Influence Upon Individual Judgment," *Journal of Abnormal and Social Psychology,* 51, 629-36.

Geier, Andrew B., Paul Rozin, and Gheorghe Doros (2006), "Unit Bias: A New Heuristic That Helps Explain the Effect of Portion Size on Food Intake," *Psychological Science,* 17 (6), 521-25.

Helson, Harry (1964), *Adaptation-Level Theory,* New York: Harper & Row.

Parducci, Allen (1995), *Happiness, Pleasure, and Judgment: The Contextual Theory and Its Applications,* Mahwah, NJ: Lawrence Erlbaum Associates.

Siegel, P. S. (1957), "The Completion Compulsion in Eating," *Psychological Reports,* 3, 15-16.

In Control of Variety:
How Self-Control Reduces the Effect of Food Variety

EXTENDED ABSTRACT

Variety typically leads to increased consumption. A recent review refers to this phenomenon as the *variety effect* (Remick, Polivy, and Pliner 2009). Using a meta-analytic approach, Remick et al. (2009) conclude that while situational factors influence the variety effect, internal factors including gender, BMI, and dietary restraint do not. This work proposes that an overlooked moderator of the variety effect is general self-control.

Self-control has been linked with numerous long-term positive life outcomes, including better grades and job performance, healthier interpersonal relationships and higher self-esteem (Tangney, Baumeister, and Boone 2004). Given the pervasiveness of variety in our daily food options, I anticipate that the long-term nature of self-control will influence patterns of consumption in a healthy way, in this case through reducing the variety effect, consistent with the tendency of those higher in self-control to better monitor their behavior and be less susceptible to environmental influences. In a series of three studies, I examine the impact that variety has on preferences for various types of foods as well as the resulting influence on the quantity consumed.

In Study 1, 266 participants were asked how many candies they wanted to eat for an afternoon snack. In the variety condition, participants were shown a variety of snacks (Hershey's, Kit Kat, and/ or Reeses miniatures), whereas the single snack condition offered only one of the three snacks. We later assessed general self-control. Consistent with prior research, the variety effect emerged such that participants who saw the various snacks indicated they wanted more overall. However, an interaction between the variety condition and self-control also emerged ($p < .01$), such that the effect of self-control on quantity desired was more than four times larger in the variety condition than in the single snack condition. As well, self-control matters in the variety case ($p < .01$), as low self-control people showed a 40% higher quantity than those with high self-control in a spotlight analysis.

Study 2 used consumption of assorted snacks as the dependent measure. As in the first study, participants were either in a variety or no variety condition, with each group receiving 3 separate servings of miniature cookies (Chips Ahoy, Nutter Butters, and/or Oreos). Participants received these snacks in three rounds, with the order of snacks randomized in the variety condition. They performed unrelated, but timed tasks after receiving each snack in order to allow time for consumption. Following the study, consumption was measured and recorded. As in study 1, there was again evidence of the variety effect overall, but also the interaction with self-control. For those low in self-control, the variety effect led to about 73% more consumption than a single snack whereas this increase was only 14% for those high in self-control. As such, this study demonstrates the interaction between variety and self-control by extending our findings to differences in actual consumption.

In Study 3, all participants actually consumed a variety of snacks. Specifically, participants were given a plate with small samples of nine common snack foods representing three each of healthy, medium, and unhealthy snacks. Participants rated their enjoyment of each snack in random order. Participants then received a plate with five chocolate chip cookies and were told to enjoy them while watching a video. Our purpose was to create a level of satiation with unhealthy snacks to see how this satiation would impact subsequent liking for the variety of snacks. Participants then rated the same nine snacks again, and separately completed the general self-control scale. I predict that people high in self-control would show a greater drop in liking across all of the snacks, demonstrating that their satiation spread further, thereby reducing the appeal afforded by variety. This would provide additional evidence of a weakening of the variety effect. The drop in liking ratings for each of the three food types were submitted to a repeated-measures ANCOVA with the snack type as a within-subjects factor, and trait self-control as a continuous covariate. I found the predicted interaction between food type and trait self-control, such that those with high trait self-control seem to satiate spontaneously on all of the foods while those with low trait self-control satiated little on the other food types (especially on the unhealthy foods), suggesting that the variety increased satiation across the board for those high in self-control but not for those low in self-control.

Overall, three studies using different approaches, including actual food consumption, to demonstrate an important factor in understanding the influence of variety on patterns of preference and consumption. Specifically, this work identifies general self-control as an internal factor that moderates the variety effect, which may help explain positive health outcomes over time as those with higher self-control are less susceptible to dramatically increasing their consumption of or preference for foods in the presence of variety.

REFERENCES

Remick, Abigail K., Janet Polivy, and Patricia Pliner (2009), "Internal and External Moderators of the Effect of Variety on Food Intake," *Psychological Bulletin*, 153 (3), 434-451.

Tangney, June P., Roy F. Baumeister, and Angie Luzio Boone (2004), "High Self-Control Predicts Good Adjustment, Less Pathology, Better Grades, and Interpersonal Success," *Journal of Personality*, 72, 271-324.

Red, Ripe, and Ready:
Effect of Food Color on Consumption

EXTENDED ABSTRACT

People are confronted with multiple food choices every day. How do they decide which foods to eat – and how much to consume? Building on past research showing that environmental cues can influence food consumption (Wansink 2004), we examine how food color influences food desirability and consumption.

All of our ancestors successfully solved the challenge of determining which foods to eat. As omnivorous generalists, humans can obtain nutrients from a wide variety of foods. However, some foods have always been more adaptive than others. For example, our ancestors would have benefitted more from consuming foods that were calorie-rich and easy to digest rather than eating foods that contained few calories and were difficult to digest (Rozin 1999).

We propose that an important cue that helps determine a food's adaptive value is its color. Research in biology shows a link between a species' diet and the nature of that species' vision (Smith et al. 2003). Specifically, meat-eating carnivores such as dogs and tigers tend not to have trichromatic color vision and often see in black and white. By contrast, omnivores such as humans and other primates have trichromatic color vision that differentiates between green and red colors. Biologists have argued that because omnivores consume plants (e.g., fruits and berries), color vision may have evolved to help determine the adaptive value of food (Dominy & Lucas 2000). For example, the color of fruits and berries, which universally vary on a green-to-red spectrum, reliably serves as an indicator of their adaptive value, whereby redness is associated with high adaptive value: Redness tends to signal ripeness, a desirable sweet taste, easy digestibility, and higher nutritional value (Goff & Klee 2006).

Given the association between the color red and the adaptive value of food, we examined how the color red relates to food psychology and consumption. We hypothesized that the color red in the context of food should be associated with (1) automatic tendencies to approach red-colored foods, and that (2) people should consume higher quantities of red-colored foods.

Experiment 1 tested people's automatic tendencies to physically approach the color red versus the color green. We used an established behavioral task, in which people made physical movements using a joystick to approach stimuli presented on a computer screen, whereby the speed of the movements was the dependent measure (Chen and Bargh 1999). The experiment had two between-subjects conditions that manipulated the context in which people saw the color red and green: Colors were presented either in a food context or in a non-food context (control). Context was manipulated by priming people either with food-related thoughts or with neutral control thoughts before assessing the speed at which people approached the color green and the color red.

Results showed that in the control condition people were slightly (non-significantly) slower to approach the color red than green. However, when people were first primed with food-related thoughts, they were significantly faster to approach the color red, $F(1,57)=8.94$, $p=.004$; $M_{Control}=778$ ms, $M_{Food}=687$ ms. Thus, in the context of food, people were faster to approach the color red.

Experiment 2 tested how food color influenced the quantity of actual food consumption. The study had two between-subjects conditions, whereby all participants watched a video, but they were provided with one of two different types of snacks (chocolate candies): The candies were either wrapped in red wrappers or in green wrappers. We measured the quantity of candies eaten during the movie. Results showed that participants who were given snacks wrapped in red ate nearly twice as many candies as participants who were given snacks wrapped in green, t(93)=-2.707, p=.008; M_{Green}=1.84 candies, M_{Red}=3.46 candies.

Experiment 3 sought to identify a condition when the color red exerts the strongest effect on food consumption by testing a theoretically-derived moderator of the effect. Because the color red has been a reliable indicator of food ripeness and sweetness throughout evolutionary history (Goff & Klee 2006), we hypothesized that the color red would have the strongest effect for the consumption of sweet foods rather than non-sweet foods (e.g., salty foods). Experiment 3 therefore had a 2 (food color: red vs. green) X 2 (food type: sweet vs. salty) between-subjects design. All participants watched a video and were given either candies or tortilla chips as snacks. However, the foods were either red or green. We measured the quantity of food eaten. Findings showed an interaction (p < .05). Conceptually replicating Study 2, people ate more candies in the red than in the green condition. However, color did not influence the consumption quantity of salty foods.

Across three studies, we find the consistent pattern that consumers have a natural attraction to red foods. We attribute this behavior to the adaptive value of food signaled by the color red: it has ripened and can be enjoyed when eaten. Therefore, when encountering an ideally sweet food, consumers approach the food faster and subsequently consume more of it when it is red (versus green). Our research establishes these basic effects, and it highlights the importance of color for food palatability. We believe this knowledge can assist food marketers in making their products more attractive and more importantly more enjoyable.

REFERENCES

Chen, Mark and John A. Bargh (1999), "Consequences of Automatic Evaluation: Immediate Behavioral Predispositions to Approach or Avoid the Stimulus," *Personality and Social Psychology Bulletin*, 25 (February), 215-24.

Dominy, Nathaniel J. and Peter W. Lucas (2000), "Ecological Importance of Trichromatic Vision to Primates," *Nature*, 410 (March), 363-66.

Goff, Stephen A. and Harry J. Klee (2006), "Plant Volatile Compounds: Sensory Cues for Health and Nutritional Value," *Science*, 311 (February), 815-19.

Rozin, Paul (1999), "Food is Fundamental, Fun, Frightening, and Far-Reaching," *Social Research*, 66, 9-30.

Smith, Andrew C., Hannah M. Buchanan-Smith, Alison K. Surridge, Daniel Osorio, and Nicholas I. Mundy (2003), "The Effect of Color Vision Status on the Detection and Selection of Fruits by Tamarins," *Journal of Experimental Biology*, 206 (September), 3159-65.

Wansink, Brian (2004), "Environmental Factors That Increase the Food Intake and Consumption Volume of Unknowing Consumers," *Annual Review of Nutrition*, 24 (July), 455-79.

Mortality Threat Can Increase or Decrease Women's Caloric Intake Depending on Their Childhood Environment

EXTENDED ABSTRACT

Why do some women obsess over calories and go to extreme measures to prevent weight gain, while others eat without thought, having little concern for how their food choices affect their body weight? In this research, we draw on an evolutionary perspective on eating, which suggests that women's caloric intake is related to fertility. Importantly, because female fertility across animal species is

known to be regulated by environmental conditions indicating high mortality, we propose that women's eating behavior might be influenced by perceptions of mortality dangers. In three experiments, we examine if, when, and why mortality dangers influence women's eating psychology and food consumption.

From an evolutionary perspective, all organisms, including humans, vary on whether they follow a 'Fast' or a 'Slow' evolutionary strategy (Ellis et al. 2009). *Fast strategies* are associated with more rapid sexual development, earlier ages of reproduction, and higher quantity of offspring. *Slow strategies*, by contrast, are associated with slower sexual development, later ages of reproduction, and lower quantity of offspring. This means that whereas fast strategists behave in ways to facilitate immediate reproduction, slow strategists delay reproduction.

Whether organisms, including humans, adopt fast versus slow strategies depends on the stressfulness of their early-life environment (Ellis et al. 2009). For example, whereas people growing up in stressful low-SES environments tend to adopt faster strategies, people growing up in less-stressful high-SES environments tend to adopt slower strategies. Importantly, research shows that behavioral tendencies associated with fast versus slow strategies are especially prominent when individuals are facing mortality dangers (Griskevicius et al. 2011). Specifically, mortality threat leads people from low-SES background to exhibit fast strategy behaviors such as wanting to start a family sooner. In contrast, the same mortality threat leads people from high-SES background to exhibit slow strategy behaviors such as delaying reproduction.

Because fast and slow strategies differ in the timing of reproductive activity, these strategies also directly relate to women's caloric consumption. This is because women's ability to reproduce depends on having substantial amounts of body fat (Anderson and Crawford 1992). Because female reproductive timing and capacity depend on body fat, this means that reproductive timing and capacity can be sped up *or* slowed down by adjusting body fat levels (Salomon et al 2008; Wasser and Barash 1983). That is, whereas increasing caloric intake increases the likelihood that a woman is physically able to reproduce, decreasing caloric intake suppresses female reproduction.

Because fast strategies are associated with immediate reproduction, they might be associated with *increased* caloric intake to facilitate this immediate reproduction. By contrast, because slow strategies are associated with delaying reproduction, they might be associated with *decreased* caloric intake to delay reproduction. Given that behavioral tendencies associated with fast versus slow strategies is most prominent under mortality threat (Griskevicius et al. 2011), in three experiments we investigated how mortality threat influences women's eating psychology and behavior. Building on past research, we predicted that mortality cues should have different effects on depending on whether women grew up in low-SES versus high-SES environments. Whereas those from *low-SES* backgrounds should respond to mortality by *increasing* fatty food intake to facilitate body fat accumulation (consistent with a fast strategy), women from *high-SES* childhoods should respond to mortality by *decreasing fatty food intake* to hinder body fat accumulation (consistent with a slow strategy).

In Study 1, we experimentally manipulated mortality cues by having people read a news article about increasing rates of violent crime or having them read a control article. We then examined women's (and men's) desire for food by measuring the size of their drawing of cookies, which were drawn from memory viewed earlier in the session. Results revealed that for women growing up in more stressful, lower SES environments, the mortality news articles *increased* desire for food. In contrast, among women growing up in more advantaged high-SES environments, mortality cues *decreased* desire for food. No such effects were found for men.

In Study 2, mortality cues were manipulated by having women view a slideshow with visual images of escalating violent crime or control images. Women were then offered snacks (cookies and pretzels) that they could take with them when leaving the laboratory. Findings conceptually replicated the results of Study 1. Specifically, women who grew up in more stressful, lower-SES environments, mortality cues significantly *increased* the number of food items taken. Among women growing up in more advantaged environments, however, these same cues significantly *decreased* the number of food items taken.

Study 3 examined whether mortality cues would influence women's beliefs about calorie regulation and desire to prevent weight gain. Consistent with the results from Studies 1 and 2, Study 3 found that for women growing up in lower SES environments, morality cues significantly *decreased* desire to restrict calories and prevent weight gain. Among women growing up in more advantaged environments, however, these cues significantly *increased* desire to restrict calories and prevent weight gain. Additionally, the changes in calorie restriction were found to be fully mediated by the changes in weight regulation desires.

These studies provide important new insights into the complex relationship between environmental cues and women's food regulation behavior and have important implications for understanding women's consumption behaviors.

REFERENCES

Anderson, J. L., & Crawford, C. B. (1992). Modeling costs and benefits of adolescent weight control as mechanism for reproductive suppression. *Human Nature, 3,* 299-334.

Ellis, Bruce J., A.J. Figueredo, B.H. Brumbach, and Gabriel L. Schlomer (2009), "Fundamental dimensions of environmental risk: The impact of harsh vs. unpredictable environments on the evolution and development of life history strategies," *Human Nature*, 20, 204-268.

Griskevicius, V., Delton, A. W., Robertson, T. E., & Tybur, J. M. (2011). Environmental contingency in life history strategies: The influence of mortality and socioeconomic status on reproductive timing. *Journal of Personality and Social Psychology, 100,* 241-254.

Salmon, C., Crawford, C., Dane, L. & Zuberbier, O. (2008). Ancestral mechanisms in modern environments: Impact of competition and stressors on body image and dieting behavior. *Human Nature, 19,* 103-117.

Wasser, S. K., & Barash, D. P. (1983). Reproductive suppression among female mammals: Implications for biomedicine and sexual selection theory. *Quarterly Review of Biology, 58,* 513–538.

Sooner Rather than Later?
The Implications of Delay on Enjoyment and Consumption
Chair: Min Zhao, University of Toronto, Canada

Paper #1: 1. The Immediate and Delayed Effects of Price Promotions on Post-Purchase Consumption Experience
Leonard Lee, Columbia University, USA
Claire I. Tsai, University of Toronto, Canada

Paper #2: 2. Clock-time, Event-time and Consumer Decision-Making.
Anne-Laure Sellier, HEC Paris, France
Tamar Avnet, Yeshiva University, USA

Paper #3: 3. What's Queuing Worth? Sunk Effort and the Value of A Queue Position
Min Zhao, University of Toronto, Canada
Dilip Soman, University of Toronto, Canada
Adelle Yang, University of Chicago, USA

Paper #4: 4. Is it Still Working? The Effects of Task Difficulty on Perceived Duration of Product Efficacy
Veronika Ilyuk, Baruch College
Lauren G. Block, Baruch College
David Faro, London Business School

SESSION OVERVIEW

Time delay is a ubiquitous phenomenon in consumer life. Prior research has shown that delay discounts the peripheral aspects of a consumption scenario and increases the importance of central aspects of the decision (e.g., Trope and Liberman 2003). In the waiting literature, research has shown that people's experiences with a consumption episode are usually negatively correlated with delay because sooner is better (Taylor 1994). Yet other research suggests that more negative experience during waiting can also increase goal desirability (Koo and Fishbach 2010). Furthermore, different consumers might use different strategies to regulate their time and decisions (Lauer 1981). How does delay and time elapse play a role in consumer behaviour? This session tries to expand our understanding of the effect of time delay and duration by systematically examining the effect of delay/time elapse on consumption enjoyment and decisions across diverse domains, and conversely, how consumers form duration perception as a result of their ongoing consumption experience.

The session begins with a paper by *Lee and Tsai* that examines how price promotions influence hedonic consumption experience immediately after payment versus after a delay. The findings suggest that discounts make instant consumption more enjoyable; however, this pattern reverses when consumption is delayed due to consumers' changed feelings and involvement. *Sellier and Avnet* further investigate how consumers with different temporal regulation strategies react to different promotion strategies offering different time flexibility. For example, they demonstrate that clock-time style results in higher preferences towards delayed services with more waiting than immediate service, compared with event-time style, because clock-time consumers can shift tasks around more easily. Following up these findings, *Zhao, Soman and Yang* propose and show that more waiting time and a greater number of people behind during waiting lead consumers to value the delay more highly and to consume at higher levels because they need to compensate for their perceived sunk cost. Finally, while the first three papers examine the effect of delay/duration of waiting on consumption decisions and experi-

ence, *Ilyuk, Block and Faro* take a reversed direction and investigate how current consumption experience impacts the perceived efficacy duration of a product, a previously neglected construct. Their findings suggest that higher difficulty of the current experience leads to shorter perceived efficacy duration of the product and thus increases the frequency of intake of the product.

The papers in this session proposal are all in advanced stages of completion, with multiple studies conducted and full papers available. Taken together, the session is designed to provide an integrative overview of new research aimed at enhancing our understanding of the role of delay in consumption enjoyment, consumer spending and other aspects of consumer decisions. In this sense, the session helps to further the conference mission of appreciating diversity by examining the role of delay in these diverse areas. Besides their theoretical contributions, the findings in this session also provide important implications to enhance consumption experiences in situations involving delay and waiting, and to increase consumers' health and welfare by changing their perceived efficacy duration of drugs. The likely audience for this session will be consumer researchers in general and specifically those who are interested in consumers' decision-making related with time and duration. Thus we expect to draw the interest of a wide range of researchers.

The Immediate and Delayed Effects of Price Promotions on Post-Purchase Consumption Experience

EXTENDED ABSTRACT

Consumers generally believe that getting a good deal for a product would enhance their hedonic experience of consuming the product. The present research examines this intuition. We find that getting a price discount can make consumption more enjoyable. However, contrary to lay beliefs, when consumption is decoupled from payment with a time delay, price promotions actually diminish consumption enjoyment over time. While prior research has documented the effects of price promotions on sales and perceived quality (e.g., the placebo effect in which discounts have been found to decrease perceived efficacy of *utilitarian* products – Shiv, Carmon, and Ariely 2005), we systematically investigate the effect of price promotions on post-purchase *consumption experience of hedonic products* over time.

On the one hand, getting a good bargain can elevate moods (Heilman, Nakamoto, and Rao 2002), which spills over to consumption experience and makes consumption more enjoyable. On the other hand, paying a lower price may reduce the psychological need to recover one's expenditure (Gourville and Soman 2002); thus, the less a consumer has paid for a product, the less relevant the consumer perceives the product to be, and the less involved he/she becomes during consumption. The resulting lower involvement thus makes evaluation less extreme (Petty and Brinol 2010) and diminishes the intensity of consumption enjoyment. Given that mood effects are often transient while involvement effects might be more persistent, we propose that if a product is consumed immediately after payment, price promotions should enhance consumption enjoyment. However, if the consumption is delayed, the negative effect of price promotions (due to lower involvement) will dominate.

To test our hypotheses, we conducted four experiments (three of which involving real spending and product consumption) in which

Advances in Consumer Research
Volume 40, ©2012

we manipulated how much participants paid for a product and when they consumed the product after payment. Experiment 1 employed a 2 (discount: 0% vs. 50%) x 2 (consumption: immediate vs. delayed) between-subjects design. Specifically, participants first earned a wage by completing an unrelated study. Then, in the main "shopping study," they used (some of) that money to purchase one of two given music recordings either at the full price or a (50%) discounted price. After paying for their chosen recording, participants were given the recording on an iPod either immediately or after a 25-minute delay, asked to listen to the recording, and then evaluate how much they enjoyed listening to it. To control for perceived quality, the music recording was the same in all conditions unbeknownst to the participants. As expected, for immediate consumption, price promotions increased consumption enjoyment, whereas for delayed consumption, the effect was reversed. More important, mediation analysis showed that mood mediated the effect of promotions for immediate consumption but not for delayed consumption. We replicated these findings in Experiment 2 using a different sensory stimulus (chocolates) with an extended time delay (1 week).

In Experiment 3, we attempted to gain insight into consumers' affective and cognitive reactions to price promotions using a similar consumption context as Experiment 1, and therefore, to obtain process evidence for the hypothesized dual factors—positive feeling and involvement—in accounting for the observed interaction effect. The results demonstrate that while consumers may be insensitive to the transient nature of feelings (due primarily to affective misforecasting; Gilbert et al. 1998), their insight into the persistent effect of price-induced involvement is consistent with the results of experiments 1 and 2.

Nonetheless, to further demonstrate the role of involvement in the delayed-consumption results, we manipulated stimulus valence in Experiment 4. Specifically, the proposed involvement account predicts that, over time, price promotions should weaken consumption experience, making the experience of consuming a liked product (i.e., orange juice with honey) less enjoyable, and conversely, a disliked product (i.e., orange juice with vinegar) less unpleasant. Indeed, for immediate consumption, price promotions enhanced consumption experience regardless of stimulus valence. However, for delayed consumption, price promotions made the tasty juice less enjoyable and the sour juice less unpleasant. Mediation analysis confirmed that involvement during consumption mediated the effect of price promotions for delayed consumption. The results also ruled out perceived quality as an alternative explanation, suggesting that these effects of promotions can operate above and beyond price-quality associations.

Our work provides new insight to the literature on the psychological effects of price promotions on hedonic consumption experiences over time. Contrary to lay beliefs, getting a good deal actually reduces consumption enjoyment if consumption is decoupled from payment with a time delay. Besides the placebo effect, our findings also complement prior work on the psychology of payment that examines the difference between pre-payment and post-payment on consumption experience (Prelec and Loewenstein 1998) by investigating the effect of promotions on consumption experience at different points in time *after* payment Further, our empirical findings may offer a potential alternative explanation for the extant finding that price promotions can have negative long-term effects on customer satisfaction and brand loyalty.

Clock-time, Event-time and Consumer Decision-Making

EXTENDED ABSTRACT

Time is a continuum on which consumption activities occur in succession from past to present to the future. Two ways in which individuals schedule tasks over time have been documented (e.g., Lauer 1981; Levine 1997): 1) "clock-time," where individuals divide time into objective and quantifiable units, and let an external clock dictate when tasks begin/end; and (2) "event-time," where tasks are planned relative to other tasks, and individuals transition from one to the next when they internally sense that the former task is complete (Lauer, 1981). To illustrate, clock-time individuals may have breakfast at 8 am, work from 9 am to 5 pm, dine at 6.30 pm. Event-time individuals begin work after breakfast, linger at the market for however long it takes to have one's basket full, and leave work when they can "call it a day". Recent research suggests that people's adoption of a clock-versus event-time scheduling style is related to successful self-regulation (Avnet and Sellier 2011).

This research documents two critical ways in which these scheduling styles differ in their influence on consumers' decision-making. A first difference is that clock-time consumers slice time into quantifiable, independent units, which provides them with the ability to switch tasks around more easily than event-time consumers, who view time as a sequence of events following one another, and are therefore relatively more captive of their task ordering. This greater flexibility of clock-time consumers leads to three predictions: first, they should value consumption contexts enabling them to rearrange tasks more than event-time consumers (H1). Second, a reliance on clock-time implies two costs, which influence decisions about impulsive consumption opportunities: (1) one is that of being used to incurring "empty" time whenever a task takes less time to complete than anticipated. Clock- (vs. event)-time consumers should better respond to opportunities taking place during empty time because they fill an otherwise wasted slot (H2); (2) in the context of an unscheduled opportunity appearing outside of empty time, clock-time consumers should require more time to think about the rearrangement of tasks than event-time consumers, because the latter only postpone all their tasks to later (H3). A second difference is that clock-time consumers are concerned with efficiency (getting things done) whereas event-time consumers are focused on effectiveness (doing things well). From this, we derived the prediction that clock-time (vs. event-time) consumers are generally likely to purchase discounted items independent of whether they need those items at the time of purchase. In sharp contrast, event-time consumers should seek to purchase items when they can use them (H4).

Across five studies, we either measured participants' chronic reliance on clock- (event-) time (Studies 1-4) or primed them with these scheduling styles (Study 5). Consistent with H1, clock-time (vs. event-time) participants in a first study were more likely to buy products online rather than at a brick-and-mortar store, p < .05, presumably because shopping online is possible any time.

A second study involved 111 participants reading consumption scenarios. In a first scenario, participants imagined that they saw that a designer store is running a 30% one-day sale. A salesperson further explained that they could buy a coupon extending the 30% discount for two months. Again supportive of H1, we found that clock-time participants showed a higher preference and willingness to pay for coupons they could use later but had to pay for, compared to a free coupon they could only use immediately, both p < .05.

In a second scenario, participants reported their readiness to seize an unexpected discount opportunity during empty time. Participants imagined they were purchasing items at a department store and could get 20% off if they used coupons they could request at the other end of the store. Imagining their next scheduled task was 15 minutes later, clock-time participants indicated they were willing to spend more time getting the coupons than event-time participants, one-tailed p < .05 (H2).

In a third scenario, participants were unexpectedly offered to leave the next day for a 3-day trip to a secluded beach resort, all expenses paid, provided the decision was made right away, we found that – compared to event-time participants - clock-time participants were significantly less ready to immediately go on the trip, needed time to think about it more, and would be more likely to only go on the trip if it were at least a week later (all p's < .05, H3).

A third study had 55 students react to a reservation service for restaurants that normally have a "no reservation" policy, allowing consumers to book a table in exchange for a fee. Indicating that clock-time consumers are more comfortable around empty time than event-time consumers (H3), we found that clock-time participants liked the idea less than event-time participants (p < .03) and intended to tell others about it less (p = .05).

A fourth and fifth study tested H4. In both studies, participants imagined that the season was winter (or summer) and that some stores at their mall are offering up to 50% off. We told them to assume that they were thinking of buying the products on sale at some point anyway. Their time scheduling style was either measured (Study 4) or primed (Study 5). Subjects reported their likelihood of buying the discounted summer (e.g., sunglasses) and winter products (e.g., boots). The key replicated finding is that clock-time consumers are more likely to purchase discounted items off-season than event-time consumers, who prefer to buy discounted items during the season in which the items can be used. Together, these findings suggest profound ways in which task scheduling styles shape decision-making.

What's Queuing Worth?
Sunk Effort and the Value of A Queue Position

EXTENDED ABSTRACT

Consumers routinely have to wait in queues to obtain a product or service. In this research, we examine the manner in which people value their position in a queue and the effect of this valuation on their subsequent consumption decisions. Specifically, we investigate the effect of two cues in the queuing environment: the time spent in the queue and the number of people behind. We hypothesize that more time spent in the queue and a greater number of people behind lead people to value the wait more highly and to consume at higher levels because of the perceived sunk cost.

Our predictions are based on prior research on mental accounting (Thaler, 1985) and the psychology of queuing (Koo and Fishbach, 2010; Zhou and Soman, 2003). Research on mental accounting suggests that when people prepay to purchase an experience such as a ski pass, they open a mental account for the purpose and tag it with a negative balance – the disutility of the payment they have just made. The only way in which they can satisfactorily close their mental account "in the black" (i.e., without a loss) is by consuming what they paid for (Prelec and Loewenstein, 1998), even if it rains on the ski day. We propose that people think about the queuing experience much like how they think about the utility of a transaction, following the same principles of mental accounting. As such, people in queues value the effort/psychological cost they have expended to achieve their position in the queue, and they seek to be compensated for it through product purchase or other form of reimbursement so that they can close the mental account in the black. Because the longer people have to wait, the more effort is involved and the

greater their negative emotional reactions are (Taylor 1994), we predict that greater time of wait leads to greater valuation of the queue and hence greater consumption required to make up for the wait. Second, because pervious research has demonstrated that number of people behind in a queue impacts people's queuing behavior (Koo and Fishbach, 2010; Zhou and Soman, 2003), we predict that people would also take number of people behind as a cue to evaluate their effort expended so far. Therefore, when the number of people behind is larger, people perceive higher psychological cost. Consequently, they need a higher level of benefit to compensate for their efforts, and consume at a higher level.

Our findings in three studies largely supported our hypotheses. While Study 1 examined the interaction between time of wait and number of people behind, Study 2 further investigated the effect of waiting time and Study 3 further investigated the effect of number of people behind. In Study 1, we asked participants to imagine that they were waiting in queue in a popular restaurant. During waiting they were told that the restaurant will be closing due to unforeseen circumstances and they will receive a gift certificate to compensate for the waiting. Across different conditions, participants were either told that they have been waiting for 20 minutes or for 45 minutes, and that there were either 5 vs. 10 groups behind them. Participants were asked to indicate the amount of compensation they would request. Consistent with our prediction, we found that people requested a higher amount of gift certificate after waiting for longer time (45 min.) compared with waiting for shorter time (20 min.). However, this effect was attenuated when there were 10 groups of people behind them: Participants requested higher amount of compensation regardless how long they have waited, presumably because they used number of people behind (10 groups) as an additional cue for their perceived effort of waiting. A mediation analysis supported our proposition that the perceived cost of waiting drove the observed interaction between time of wait and number of people behind on the valuation of the queue position.

In Study 2, we directly manipulated personal waiting cost (high vs. low) and examined its interaction with time of wait on people's consumption decisions in a restaurant. We found that when people had to undergo a wait themselves and thus perceived high wait cost, they tended to order a more expensive meal after spending more time waiting. However, when they did not have to wait themselves and thus the perceived psychological cost of the wait was low, this effect was attenuated. In Study 3, we examined the effect of number of people behind in a field setting and found that when the cue of the number of people behind was salient, consumers at a car wash chose the more upgraded and expensive car wash options when the number of people (cars) behind was large, but this effect was attenuated when the cue was difficult to observe.

These findings contribute to the literature on queuing and value perception. Our research represents the first piece of work to apply mental accounting to an investigation of how waiting time and number of people behind in a queue impact the value perception of the queue, and how this valuation is translated into different consumption levels.

Is it Still Working? The Effects of Task Difficulty on
Perceived Duration of Product Efficacy

EXTENDED ABSTRACT

As consumers, we often wonder how long products will last or, alternatively, how long before they "wear off." How long will the morning brew give you energy? How long will the headache medicine relieve pain and keep the excruciating headache from coming back? Despite the pervasiveness of such questions and their importance in determining consumption—namely intake frequency—there has been no research on consumers' judgments of product efficacy duration.

In the present research, we take a neglected construct—perceived duration of product efficacy—and propose that contextual factors, namely the tasks consumers perform during and after product consumption, affect such judgments. Specifically, we demonstrate the consumer belief that duration of product efficacy depends on the difficulty level of a cognitive task one performs.

Importantly, evidence supports that this lay belief has no basis in scientific fact. There is no increased energy utilization during tasks that require more vs. less cognitive effort (Clarke and Sokoloff 1998; Gibson and Green 2002; Lennie 2003; Gibson 2007; Kurzban 2010). The efficacy duration of a product's active ingredients (e.g., half life of medication, glucose metabolism) is determined by factors such as genetics and body weight; for the average, healthy individual who is not glucose depleted, no physical or cognitive task that he/she performs can change its kinetics. Despite the scientific evidence to the contrary, across three studies we demonstrate that consumers hold the belief that product efficacy duration is shorter (vs. longer) when they perform a difficult (vs. easy) cognitive activity.

In study 1, we obtain evidence that perceived duration of product efficacy—measured by actual consumption in real-time—depends on the difficulty of the task one performs. We administered a reading task and manipulated task difficulty by adjusting font style, using degraded font in the difficult condition. Participants were placed in either the difficult or easy task condition and given Jelly Belly Sport Beans® (note that the short-term energy enhancing jelly beans have an actual onset time of 30 minutes, which experimentally controls for any glucose entering the system) to eat while they worked on the task. They were instructed to eat another Sport Bean® whenever they felt the effects wearing off and to press [SPACE BAR] each time they did so. These key presses captured perceived efficacy duration. As hypothesized, perceived efficacy duration was shorter for those in the difficult font condition ($M_{difficult}$ = 6.25 minutes) than for those in the easy, standard font condition (M_{easy} = 8.15 minutes; $F(1, 100)$ = 6.16, p < .05). While our main dependent variable was an on-line judgment of product efficacy duration, retrospective judgments of product efficacy duration showed an identical pattern of results such that those in the difficult font condition judged the Sport Beans® to have a shorter efficacy duration than those in the easy font condition ($M_{difficult}$ = 2.90 vs. M_{easy} = 3.41; $F(1, 109)$ = 4.24, p < .05). Additional measures collected in this study ruled out the alternative explanation that results were due to differences in negative affect, decreased alertness, fatigue, or motivation across conditions.

In study 2, we manipulated perceived rather than actual task difficulty. In this study, we also varied consumers' beliefs about efficacy duration via a priming technique that either reinforced the belief that duration depends on context, or countered the belief with evidence that duration is context-independent. Participants were given the same instructions to eat Jelly Belly Sport Beans®, this time while working on identical GMAT reading comprehension questions that were supposedly either difficult or easy. When participants read that efficacy duration is often dependent on contextual factors, the effect from study 1 replicated ($F(1, 162)$ = 4.80, p < .05). In contrast, when they read that efficacy duration is not dependent on contextual factors, they did not exhibit the pattern of results found in our previous study (F < 1).

In study 3, we find that the presentation mode of manufacturer's "suggested intake" (interval vs. fixed time format) affects duration judgments such that an interval (vs. fixed) format yields duration estimates in line with the malleable intuitive belief. When instructions for medication (Advil) are presented in an interval format (e.g., "Take every 2 – 4 hours") versus a fixed time (e.g., "Take every 3 hours"), the same interactive effect with task difficulty emerges as in the previous study, such that participants in the interval format condition estimate efficacy duration to be shorter when anticipating to perform a difficult (vs. easy) task ($M_{difficult}$ = 2.89 vs. M_{easy} = 4.28; $F(1, 166)$ = 5.97, p = .02). However, those presented with intake instructions in a "fixed" format show no significant difference in duration estimates across difficult and easy conditions (F < 1).

Across three studies, we demonstrate that consumers hold an intuitive belief that product efficacy duration is context dependent; duration judgments are shorter (vs. longer) when consumers engage in cognitive tasks perceived to be difficult (vs. easy). These findings have important implications for product (mis)use. A potential consequence of the documented belief includes product over- and under-consumption which, undoubtedly, affects consumer health and well-being.

REFERENCES

Avnet, Tamar and Anne-Laure Sellier (2011), "Clock-Time Versus Event-Time: Temporal Culture or Self-Regulation?" *Journal of Experimental Social Psychology*, 47(3), 665-67.

Clarke, Donald D. and Louis Sokoloff (1998), "Circulation and Energy Metabolism of the Brain," in *Basic Neurochemistry: Molecular, Cellular, and Medical Aspects*, ed. G. Siegel, B. Agranoff, R. Albers, S. Fisher, and M. Uhler, 6th Ed., Philadelphia, PA: Lippincott Raven, 637-69.

Gibson, E. Leigh (2007), "Carbohydrates and Mental Function: Feeding or Impeding the Brain?" *Nutrition Bulletin, 32,* 71-83.

Gibson, E. Leigh and Michael W. Green (2002), "Nutritional Influences on Cognitive Function: Mechanisms of Susceptibility," *Nutrition Research Reviews, 15,* 169–206.

Gilbert, Daniel T., Elizabeth C. Pinel, Timothy D. Wilson, Stephen J. Blumberg, and Thalia P. Wheatley (1998), "Immune Neglect: A Source of Durability Bias in Affective Forecasting," *Journal of Personality and Social Psychology*, 75(3), 617-38.

Gourville, John and Dilip Soman (2002), "Pricing and the Psychology of Consumption," *Harvard Business Review*, September, 90-6.

Heilman, Carrie, Kent Nakamoto, and Ambar Rao (2002), "Pleasant Surprises: Consumer Response to Unexpected In-Store Coupons," *Journal of Marketing Research*, 39(2), 242-52.

Kurzban, Robert (2010), "Does the Brain Consume Additional Glucose during Self-Control Tasks?" *Evolutionary Psychology*, 8 (2), 244-59.

Koo Minjung and Ayelet Fishbach (2010), "A Silver Lining of Standing In Line: Queuing Increases Value of Products," *Journal of Marketing Research*, 47, 713–24.

Lauer, Robert (1981), *Temporal Man: The Meaning and Uses of Social Time*. New York, Praeger.

Lennie, Peter (2003), "The Cost of Cortical Computation," *Current Biology, 13,* 493-97.

Levine, Robert (1997), *A Geography of Time: The Temporal Misadventures of a Social Psychologist, or How Every Culture Keeps Time Just a Little Bit Differently*. New York, NY, Basic Books.

Petty, Richard E. and Pablo Brinol (2010), "Attitude Change," in *Advanced Social Psychology: The State of the Science*, ed. Roy F. Baumeister and Eli J. Finkel, Oxford: Oxford University Press, 217-59.

Prelec, Drazen and George Loewenstein (1998), "The Red and the Black: Mental Accounting of Savings and Debt," *Marketing Science*, 17, 4–28.

Shiv, Baba, Ziv Carmon, and Dan Ariely (2005), "Placebo Effects of Marketing Actions: Consumers Get What They Pay For," *Journal of Marketing Research*, 42(4), 383-93.

Thaler, Richard H. (1985), "Mental Accounting and Consumer Choice*," Marketing Science*, 4, 199-214.

Taylor, Shirley (1994), "Waiting for Service: The Relationship between Delays and Evaluations of Service," *Journal of Marketing*, 58, 56–69.

Trope, Yaacov and Nira Liberman (2003), "Temporal Construal," *Psychological Review*, 110 (3), 403-21.

Zhou, Rongrong and Dilip Soman (2003), "Looking Back: Exploring the Psychology of Queuing and the Effect of the Number of People Behind," *Journal of Consumer Research*, 29, 517–30.

What You Expect is Not Always What You Get –
The Effect of Consumer Biases on Food Intake

Chairs: Darren Dahl, University of British Columbia, Canada
Nina Gros, Maastricht University, The Netherlands

Paper #1: Mix it Baby - the Effect of Self-creation on Perceived Healthiness

Nina Gros, Maastricht University, The Netherlands
Anne Klesse, Tilburg University, The Netherlands
Valerie Meise, Maastricht University, The Netherlands
Darren W. Dahl, University of British Columbia, Vancouver

Paper #2: The Best of Both Worlds: Effects of Product Color Brightness on Hedonic Food Consumption

Adriana V. Madzharov, Baruch College,
the City University of New York, USA
Suresh Ramanathan, Texas A&M, USA
Lauren G. Block, Baruch College, the City University of New York, USA

Paper #3: Red Bull versus Red Thunder - The Influence of Brand Labels on Consumption Amount

Nina Gros, Maastricht University, The Netherlands
Kelly Geyskens, Maastricht University, The Netherlands
Caroline Goukens, Maastricht University, The Netherlands
Ko de Ruyter, Maastricht University, The Netherlands

Paper #4: The Low Intensity of Light: Behavioral and fMRI Insights into the Effects of "Light" and "Organic" Claims on Flavor Processing

Hilke Plassmann, INSEAD, France
Pierre Chandon, INSEAD, France
Monica Wadhwa, INSEAD, Singapore
Nicolas Linder, University of Bonn, Germany
Bernd Weber, University of Bonn, Germany

SESSION OVERVIEW

All too often, consumers find themselves making decisions deviating from their initial expectations. Indeed, product perceptions are often biased by the incorrect but also unintended and unconscious use of perceptual aspects in consumers' decision making (Kahn, Luce, & Nowlis 2006). These biased perceptions might lead to suboptimal decisions (Hoegg & Alba 2007). In fact, extrinsic factors such as price and irrelevant product attributes have been identified to bias consumers in this manner. For example, it has been shown that visual cues can be more instrumental in driving taste perceptions than actual taste (Hoegg & Alba 2007) and that consumers incorrectly rely on assortment aspects rather than inherent hunger or diet restrictions to derive the appropriate consumption amount (Kahn & Wansink 2004). These findings demonstrate that consumers' consumption decisions are often influenced by factors that bias their expectations and in turn might influence their behavior. Especially in the context of food consumption, investigating how and why consumption biases influence expectations and consumed amount is timely, since obesity rates are rising.

Therefore, it is important to understand these types of consumer biases such that one can mitigate their negative impact (Kahn et al. 2006). The papers in this session fit this need as they all provide insight into potentially biasing factors in the consumption environment. Indeed, these papers provide new findings with respect to the nature of consumer biases, and simultaneously offer consumers strategies that may help them to avoid suboptimal decisions or even

unwanted behavior (i.e. increased consumption). In doing so, this session adds to existing research (e.g., Chandon & Wansink 2007a; Raghunathan, Naylor, & Hoyer 2006; Shiv, Carmon, & Ariely 2005) that has sought to identify negative biases on consumption.

In the first paper, Gros, Klesse, Meise and Dahl show that customization can be a source of bias in consumers' product perceptions (i.e. healthiness perception). They establish the counterintuitive finding that selecting your own ingredients as compared to receiving a prepared product decreases its perceived healthiness. In the second paper, Madzharov, Ramanathan and Block focus on the unexamined biasing factor that color brightness might have on food consumption. Not only do they show that people consume more from food products in light colors than from food products in dark colors but they also investigate the relevant role of the cognitive and affective reactions to food color that lead to this biased consumption. The third paper by Gros, Geyskens, Goukens and de Ruyter investigates the effects of brand labels on the consumed amount of snacks. Three studies show that the consumed amount of branded versus private label products depends on the consumption goal/context. The last paper by Plassmann, Chandon, Wadhwa, Linder, and Weber investigates how different nutrition claims associated with health perceptions of foods influence expectations about taste. Behavioral studies suggest that people perceive light vs. organic food claims to be lower in flavor pleasantness and intensity. However, fMRI data shows it is only experienced intensity, but not pleasantness that differs.

Taken together, these papers (all in advanced stage) disclose four unobtrusive factors that foster consumer biases in a food consumption context. This session does not only demonstrate that subtle cues might lead to counterintuitive consumers' product evaluations but, more importantly, they might even, unexpectedly, alter consumption behavior. As this session integrates diverse paradoxical phenomena in a food consumption context and integrates a diversity of research techniques (behavioral data and neuroscience data), we believe it contributes to the topic "Appreciating Diversity". We believe that this session will draw attention from a diverse audience. More specifically, it is expected to appeal to those interested in consumer biases, food consumption, self-control, and self-regulatory processes.

Mix it Baby - the Effect of Self-creation on Perceived Healthiness

EXTENDED ABSTRACT

Nowadays consumers are often given the opportunity to customize a certain product (Bendapudi & Leone 2003). Even companies in the food industry (e.g., M&Ms, Chocomize or Mymuesli) engage customers in the production process. That is, consumers have the possibility to select between different chocolate toppings or cereal ingredients and can create their individual product.

The primary purpose of this research is to explore whether the mere act of selecting one's own ingredients for a given food/drink influences its perceived healthiness. Considering the increasing trend for customization as well as the rising rates of obesity, it is relevant to investigate whether customizing food products could bias consumers' healthiness perceptions. In doing so, this research intends to add to existing research that identifies factors, such as price (Shiv et al. 2005), health positioning (Chandon & Wansink 2007a), and healthiness (Raghunathan et al. 2006) which bias consumers' product perceptions. We present three studies to demonstrate that the mere act of selecting one's own ingredients as compared to buying the complete product decreases its perceived healthiness. Further, we show that this effect occurs independently of whether individuals perform the mixing action themselves or merely select the ingredients of their choice.

Study 1 fulfills the purpose to investigate whether students that mix their own juice and those that obtain a ready-made juice differ in their healthiness perceptions of the drink. For this purpose we asked students (N=85) entering the university whether they would like to have a free glass of juice in exchange for answering a questionnaire. Depending on the condition the student either saw one carafe containing a mixture of juices (non-creators) or three different carafes (self-creators), each containing a different juice. Since we want to test whether the mere act of selecting ingredients influences individuals' healthiness perceptions, we need three juices that do not differ in perceived healthiness. Based on a pre-test (N=38) we selected cranberry, lemon and orange juice since these juices were rated as equally healthy and tasty. After participants mixed their juice or obtained the prepared mix they were given a short questionnaire. The dependent variable was the perceived healthiness of the juice measured on a 7 points semantic differential scale (1=healthy and 7=unhealthy). An ANOVA with the healthiness ratings of the juice as dependent variable revealed that self-creators ($M_{self-creators}$=2.88, SD=0.21) rated the juice as significantly less healthy than non-creators ($M_{non-creators}$=2.12, SD=0.21; $F(1,83)$=6.58, $p<0.05$).

Study 2 replicates these findings in a laboratory setting. For generalizability of our findings, we make use of food (i.e., cereal). In line with study 1 we intend to explore whether selecting your own cereal ingredients as compared to obtaining a prepared mix decreases the perceived healthiness of the cereal. Participants (N = 62) were assigned to a self-creator condition or non-creator condition. While the self-creators selected the cereal ingredients of their choice (dried strawberries, dried apples, hazelnuts and almonds; pre-tested to be equal in perceived healthiness and taste), the non-creators obtained a prepared mix of ingredients. Before participants were allowed to eat the cereal, they indicated its perceived healthiness on an 11 point Likert scale (0=unhealthy, 10=very healthy). An ANOVA with the healthiness ratings of the cereal as the dependent variable revealed that self-creators ($M_{self-creators}$=6.39, SD=0.32) rated the cereal as significantly less healthy than non-creators ($M_{non-creators}$=7.29, SD=0.32; $F(1,60)$=4.07, $p<0.05$).

Study 3 fulfills the purpose to explore whether this effect is dependent on the physical act of mixing the ingredients together oneself. To test this we manipulate whether participants (N = 114) can create their own cereal (self-creators vs. non-creators) and whether they perform the action of mixing themselves (yes vs. no). We make use of cereal but use different ingredients (i.e., walnuts, pumpkin seeds and dried strawberries; pre-tested to be equally healthy and tasty). The set-up for study 3 is similar to study 2. However, we manipulate whether participants perform the act of mixing their ingredients themselves or whether a researcher assistant takes care of this. That is, self-creators can either fill the ingredients of their choice together themselves or tell a researcher which ones to mix. Similarly, non-creators can either fill the pre-determined ingredients together themselves or a researcher takes care of this. Before participants were allowed to eat the cereal, they indicated its perceived healthiness. A two-way ANOVA with healthiness ratings of the cereal as the dependent variable revealed a statistically significant main effect for creating your own cereal with self-creators rating the cereal as less healthy ($M_{self-creators}$=7.29, SD=0.23) than non-creators (M_{non-}

$_{creators}$=7.93, SD=0.22; $F(1,110)$=4.02; $p<0.05$) irrespective of who performs the action of mixing the ingredients.

Our studies reveal customization as a factor that biases consumers' healthiness perception: The mere act of selecting ingredients oneself decreases consumers' healthiness perception. We believe that this decrease in perceived healthiness could be due to altered variety perceptions. Extant research revealed that consumers' perceptions of variety are not necessarily contingent on the actual number of options present but can be influenced by assortment structure (Kahn & Wansink 2004) or categorizations (Mogilner, Rudnick, & Iyengar 2008). In line with this, we argue that selecting ingredients oneself might alter individuals' variety perceptions because it draws individuals' attention to the separate ingredients (i.e., sub-categories) rather than the product as a whole. Consequently, we argue that self-creators are more likely to recognize high- or low variety, i.e. three/four different ingredients than non-creators as in our experiments. In line with this argumentation study 3 demonstrates that self-creators rate the perceived variety as lower than non-self-creators. Further, we argue that individuals associate product variety with healthiness. That is, we predict that self-creators perceive the product as less healthy because they perceive it to contain less variety than non-creators. In a follow-up experiment, we intent to test this argumentation explicitly by manipulating the variety of ingredients participants choose from. If our effect is indeed caused by the fact that self-creators perceive the choice set to offer less variety, the effect should be blocked or even reversed if they can choose from a high variety of ingredients.

The Best of Both Worlds: Effects of Product Color Brightness on Hedonic Food Consumption

EXTENDED ABSTRACT

Color of food is essential for the consumption experience as it forms expectations about the food's flavor, freshness and taste (Chandon and Wansink 2010). In modern days, more and more foods are created in colors that do not necessarily match their natural color or have little relation to flavor (e.g., Gatorade drinks, Goldfish crackers, M&Ms). Advances in food coloring technology have made it possible for food companies to use color in innovative ways in order to differentiate their products, add variety to their assortments, and even to bring more fun and excitement to the food experience. Despite a dramatic increase in the variations and shades of colors and the corresponding increase in consumers' acceptance of them, scant attention has been paid to the topic of color in a food context in the consumer research literature (Labrecque and Patrick 2012).

Much of the consumer behavior research on color has looked at the effects of specific hues or hue categories (e.g., red vs. blue), while it has neglected the effects of color brightness, defined as the degree of lightness or darkness of the color (Labrecque and Patrick 2012). However, extant research from psychophysics and psychology posits that color brightness can produce strong systematic effects on people's emotions, perceptions and behavior (Meier, Robinson, and Clore 2004). For instance, previous research has found that lighter vs. darker colors evoke more positive affect and carry more positive meaning, and that people automatically perceive light objects positively and dark objects negatively (Meier et al. 2004). In the present research, we build on these findings, and propose that color brightness of the food will serve as an implicit perceptual and affective cue that ultimately biases food consumption.

Over a series of five studies, we present evidence that the color brightness of a hedonic food serves both as an automatic evaluative cue about its taste and healthiness and as an input to in-the-moment emotions that ultimately bias the volume of food consumed. We demonstrate that light-colored foods are seen as both healthier and tastier, and are consumed more than dark-colored snacks. In addition, we show that the increased consumption of light-colored foods is due to a heterogeneous emotional response, with some people doing so due to increasing positive emotions and others due to decreasing negative emotions.

In study 1a we begin an investigation of the effect of food color brightness on consumption volume with two colors that vary on brightness but not on hue and chroma in order to control for these two properties of color. Study 1a was run as a single factor (product color brightness: light vs. dark color vs. control) between-subject design where respondents were given white M&Ms in the first condition, black M&Ms in the second, and gray M&Ms in the control condition. Respondents consumed more of the white M&Ms than the gray and black M&Ms. These effects were robust even after controlling for factors such as color preference, product liking, hunger and dietary restraint. In Study 1b we replicated these effects of increased consumption of the light-colored food with a different food product and shades of color, namely Golden Oreos which have a light, beige color, and Original Oreos which have a dark, black-brown color.

In study 2a, we used an IAT test to investigate the nature of the evaluations that people have of food that differs on color brightness. The results show that light-colored snacks are automatically seen as healthier, but also as tastier than dark-colored snacks. Thus, light-colored foods develop a positive halo that is deeply internalized, thereby evoking an automatic positive response among consumers, in terms of both the short-term hedonic and the long-term functional consequences of consumption. In study 2b we use a process-dissociation test and show that the health-related evaluations are stronger than the taste-related evaluations.

In Study 3 we examine how color brightness affects the dynamics of both positive and negative emotions over time as people consume the food. The results revealed that the effect of product color on emotions is heterogeneous. Two distinct latent classes of individuals were identified from the emotion data: a) High positive, Low negative, and b) High positive, High negative. In the first class, light-colored foods caused a strong ramp-up in positive emotions compared to dark colored foods, but had no effect on negative emotions. In the second class, light colored foods caused a significantly reduced level of negative emotions over time compared to dark colored foods, but had no effect on positive emotions. In addition, the analysis revealed that these emotion trajectories mediated the effect of color on consumption.

In the present paper we identify a new food halo, namely the effect of color brightness as a perceptual cue that automatically influences evaluations, in-the-moment emotions and actual consumption. We contribute to the literature on stimulus-based effects on food consumption by being the first to show that the color of the food itself influences consumption volume. This work also represents the first research in consumer behavior to provide an in-depth exploration of the effects of color brightness. In doing so, we also contribute to the consumer behavior and color psychology literatures by providing a moment-to-moment analysis of the effect of color during actual consumption.

Red Bull versus Red Thunder - The Influence of Brand Labels on Consumption Amount

EXTENDED ABSTRACT

Existing literature illustrates and supports that marketing actions can affect consumers' judgments, expectations and behavior. Studies investigating the influence of branding information on be-havior showed, for example, that the energy brand displayed on cars in video games can affect the driving style (e.g. speed (Brasel & Gips 2011)), and that the pricing of an energy drink can impact objective performance metrics, also referred to as the placebo effect (Shiv et al. 2005). However, none of them investigated the effects of brand information on the consumed amount of that specific product. This is however an urgent matter given that the number of consumers switching from national brands to private label brands is drastically increasing (Steenkamp, Van Heerde, & Geyskens, 2010).

Based on the placebo effect literature in marketing, we assume that branded products are perceived to be more effective and of higher quality compared to private label brands. These differences in perception might affect the consumed amount of these products in two opposing ways. On the one hand, the higher effectiveness and quality signaled by a branded product might lead consumers to consume more of the branded product to generate more added value. On the other hand, previous research has shown that consumers trade off taste reductions for increased consumption. That is, labeling food as "healthy" reduces consumers' taste expectations (Raghunathan et al. 2006) and labels such as "low-fat" increase food intake (Wansink & Chandon, 2006). Following this reasoning, it might be that consumers compensate for the perceived lower quality of private label products by consuming more of them.

This research intends to shed some insight in these opposing predictions. Interestingly, we see that the answer is not as univocal as previously thought. Across three studies, we see that the relationship between branding and consumption depends on the consumption context. More specifically, if a product (e.g., candy) is consumed for a purpose in line with the general positioning of the brand (e.g., pleasure), consumption is expected to be higher for the branded product since this product is of higher quality and therefore expected to be more effective in contributing to reach the purpose. In other words, attributes communicated through the branding of a product become more relevant and thus consumers will consume more of the product to derive those benefits. However, interestingly, if a product (e.g., candy) is consumed for no particular purpose (e.g. recognition task), consumption is expected to be higher for the private label product since consumers want to compensate the lower quality by consuming more.

Study 1 (N=182) investigates the effect of brand information on the consumed amount of cola candies in two different consumption contexts. Cola candies are advertised as a product to enjoy. Participants were given a bowl of cola candies[1], preceded by a text with either no specific brand information, a "well-known and internationally recognized brand", or a "private label" information, and were asked to rate the candy either on taste enjoyment (Product Related context) or taste recognition (Product Unrelated context). A two-way ANOVA with consumption amount as the dependent variable revealed a statistically significant interaction effect ($F_{(2,176)}=5.700$, $p < .05$), indicating that in the Related Context condition more of the "branded" cola candies is consumed compared to the "private label" cola candies or the cola candies without any brand information. However, in the Unrelated Context condition, participants ate more of the "private label" cola candies compared to the "branded" cola candies or the cola candies without any brand information.

Study 2 (N=78) replicates these findings with another hedonic product (i.e. chocolate spread) and with an adjusted manipulation in which the consumption time was kept constant (exactly 12 minutes). Chocolate spread is also positioned as a product to enjoy. The results of the 2 (Label: Nutella vs Private label) x 2 (Product Related con-

---

1   In all three studies the branded product was used. All products were pre-tested on their hedonic/functional perception.

text: enjoyment of a movie vs Product Unrelated context: remembering details of a movie) design indicate a significant interaction effect on consumption ($F(1,71)=5.470$, $p < 0.05$). In the Related Context condition, more is consumed "Nutella" chocolate spread compared to "private label" chocolate spread. However, in the Unrelated Context condition, more is consumed of the "private label" chocolate spread compared to the "Nutella" chocolate spread.

Study 3 (N=92) intends to rule out an alternative hypothesis for the above-found effect. That is, in the two previous studies, the product related context was always an hedonic context, while the product unrelated context was a utilitarian one. This might drive the results. In this study we therefore used a product that is positioned as a product that is consumed for utilitarian reasons (i.e., Red Bull). A 2 (Label: Red Bull, Private Label) x 2 (Product Related context: non-verbal reasoning test vs Product Unrelated context: watching a movie) design reveals a significant interaction effect on consumption amount ($F(1,88) = 10.192$, $p < 0.01$), replicating the findings of the previous studies. When doing a non-verbal reasoning test (Product Related context), participants consume significantly more of the Red Bull energy drink compared to the energy drink labeled as a private label. When the consumption does not have a particular purpose (Product Unrelated context), participants consume significantly more of the energy drink labeled as a private label compared to the energy drink labeled as Red Bull if the consumption.

Throughout three studies, we show that the consumed amount of branded versus private label products depends on the consumption goal/context. Interestingly, when the product does serve the consumption purpose, people consume more of the product if it is labeled as a well-known brand. However, if the product does not serve the consumption purpose, people consume more of the product if it is labeled as a private label. These findings imply that positioning branded products as serving a particular purpose seems to be a profitable strategy since it increases consumption of the branded product.

The Low Intensity of Light: Behavioral and fMRI Insights into the Effects of "Light" and "Organic" Claims on Flavor Processing

EXTENDED ABSTRACT

Why has people's weight kept increasing even though "healthy" foods have become more popular? One explanation is that people eat more when foods are positioned as healthy (Chandon & Wansink 2007a; Provencher, Polivy, & Herman 2009; Wansink & Chandon 2006). However, other studies (Raghunathan et al. 2006) have shown that people expect healthy food to taste less good. How can we reconcile these two findings and understand why people eat more when they expect the food to taste less good?

One reason is that people eat more when the food is presented as "healthy" (either as "diet," or "organic") because they expect that it contains fewer calories and hence that they can eat more of it without gaining weight (Chandon & Wansink 2007b; Provencher et al. 2009; Wansink & Chandon 2006; Schuldt & Schwarz 2010). On the other hand, these healthfulness claims differ with respect to consumers' expectations about the tastiness of the food. Unlike light foods, organic foods are perceived to be both healthy AND tasty (Niewold 2010).

Exploring answers to these conflicting findings about health associations, we examine how claims that the food is "light," "organic," or "regular" influence flavor perceptions using behavioral, self-reported, and neuro-imaging data. By doing this, we test another explanation of the "low fat food and high fat people" phenomenon, which is that people expect food positioned "light" to have a less intense flavor, and hence consume more of it to achieve the desired levels of hedonic satisfaction.

In the first study, 57 participants were asked to sample a regular version of a drink and then to match the flavor pleasantness or flavor intensity of this drink with another (not sampled) drink that was either labeled as "healthy" or "organic". To do this, they were provided with concentrated pure flavor extracts, which they were asked to add to either the "regular" drink they had just sampled or the other drink. Participants added more flavor to the "light" drink than to the "regular" drink ($F(1, 56) = 77.61$, $p<.001$), regardless of whether they were asked to match them on pleasantness ($M_{light}=4.85$ SEM=.49 vs. $M_{regular}=0.58$, SEM=.26) or on intensity ($M_{light}=5.63$, SEM=.73; $M_{reg}=0.68$, SEM=.26). As predicted, the organic claim had opposite (though weaker) effects ($F(1, 56) = 7.46$, $p<.01$): People added more flavor to the regular drink in both the pleasantness matching task ($M_{organic}=1.01$, SEM=.31 vs. $M_{reg}=2.05$, SEM=.47) and the intensity matching task ($M_{organic}=1.43$, SEM=.39 vs. $M_{reg}=3.06$, SEM=.71). Overall, the study showed, from behavioral data, that people expect "light" to be worse than "regular", which is in turn worse than "organic", in terms of both flavor pleasantness and intensity.

In the second study (N=58), we investigated how flavor expectations induced by health claims affect how the flavor is actually experienced using both self-reported and functional magnetic resonance (fMRI) data. Consistent with the expectations obtained in Study 1, experienced pleasantness was higher in the "regular" ($M_{reg}=5.62$; SEM=0.21) than in the "light" condition ($M_{light}=5.27$; SEM=0.21; $T(1,28)=2.93$; $p<.005$). Another comparison also showed that pleasantness was higher in the organic condition ($M_{organic}=6.09$; SEM=0.16) than in the regular condition regular ($M_{reg}=5.58$; SEM=0.17; $T(1,28)=3.74$; $p<.001$). Ratings of experienced intensity were also consistent with the expectation results found in study 1 for light claims ($M_{reg}=5.83$; SEM=0.17 vs. $M_{light}=5.19$; SEM=0.19; $T(1,28)=3.66$; $p<.001$) but not for organic claims, which did not significantly affect experienced flavor intensity ($M_{organic}=5.68$; SEM=0.14 vs. $M_{reg}=5.68$; SEM=0.14; $T(1,28)=0.04$; $p=.52$).

Analyses of the brain activity while people were consuming these identical foods were consistent with the reported ratings for intensity, but not for pleasantness. The "light" label reduced activity in the brain area encoding flavor intensity (i.e. the ventral striatum, amygdala), and activity in this area was similar in the "organic" and "regular" conditions. The "organic" label increased brain activity in the area encoding flavor pleasantness (i.e. the orbitofrontal cortex), which was consistent with the ratings. However, activity in the area encoding pleasantness was similar in the "light" and "regular" conditions, contrary to what the self-reports indicated. These results support earlier findings about the unreliability of self-reported measures of flavor intensity, which did not adequately represent brain activity, and demonstrate the value of measuring brain activity to understand the effects of food claims. More importantly, they show that people actually experienced similar taste pleasantness for light food.

Given the interesting pattern of results for the "light" claims, in a third study, we focused on

the effects of "light" claims. We asked 34 participants to add milk to a drink powder that either claimed to be "light" or "regular". People added less milk when the powder was labeled as "light" (M = 294.26 ml, SEM = 36.85ml) than "regular" (M = 327.08 ml, SEM = 49.09 ml; $F(1,32)= 8.52$, $p<.01$). Yet, they expected to need to drink more of a pre-mixed version of the

drink to feel full for three hours when the powder was labeled "light" (M =675.23 ml, SEM = 55.01 ml) vs. "regular" (M=403 ml, SEM = 36.03 ml; $F(1,32)= 3.19$, $p<.08$).

Overall, our results show that "light" and "organic" claims, while both seen as improving the healthfulness of the food, have mostly opposite effects in terms of the flavor of the food. Organic claims improve expected flavor intensity and both expected and experienced pleasantness, and these results are consistent across all measures.

Our results about the effects of "light" claims reveal an intriguing pattern. People think that "light" foods have a less pleasant and less intense flavor, before and after consuming them, which is why they expect that they have to drink more of it to be satiated. However, fMRI data shows that "light" claims only influence experienced intensity, but not pleasantness. Thus, people may overeat light products because of reduced perception of flavor intensity—yet may misattribute it to lower taste pleasantness. This may explain the paradoxical phenomenon that people overeat light products even though they expect to like them less. It also offers a potential solution: Let people compensate for the lower expected intensity of light products by increasing the dosage of the flavor component, rather than by eating more of it.

REFERENCES

Bendapudi, Neeli & Robert P. Leone (2003), "Psychological Implications of Customer Participation in Co-Production," *Journal of Marketing*, 67 (January), 14-28.

Brasel, S. Adam, & James Gips (2011), "Red Bull "Gives You Wings" for better or worse: A double-edged impact of brand exposure on consumer performance," *Journal of Consumer Psychology*, 21(1), 57-64.

Chandon, Pierre & Brian Wansink (2007a), "The Biasing Health Halos of Fast-Food Restaurant Health Claims: Lower Calorie Estimates and Higher Side-Dish Consumption Intentions," *Journal of Consumer Research, 34*(3), 301-314.

Chandon, Pierre & Brian Wansink (2007b), "Is obesity caused by calorie underestimation? A psychophysical model of meal size estimation," *Journal of Marketing Research*, 44(1), 84–99.

Chandon, Pierre & Brian Wansink (2010), "Is Food Marketing Making Us Fat? A Multi disciplinary Review," *Foundations and Trends in Marketing*, 5 (3), 113-96.

Hoegg, JoAndrea, & Joseph W. Alba (2007), "Taste Perception: More than Meets the Tongue," *Journal of Consumer Research*, 33(4), 490-498.

Horsky, Sharon & Heather Honea (2009), "Do We Judge a Book by its Cover and a Product by its Package? How Affective Expectations are Contrasted and Assimilated into the Consumption Experience," *Advances in Consumer Research*, 36.

Howard, Meagan A. & Cecile A. Marczinski (2010), "Acute effects of a glucose energy drink on behavioral control," *Experimental and Clinical Psychopharmacology*, 18(6), 553.

Kahn, Barbara E., Mary Frances Luce & Stephen M. Nowlis (2006), "Debiasing Insights from Process Tests," *Journal of Consumer Research*, 33(1), 131-138.

Kahn, Barbara E. & Brian Wansink (2004), "The Influence of Assortment Structure on Perceived Variety and Consumption Quantities," *Journal of Consumer Research*, 30(4), 519-533.

Koenigs, Michael & Daniel Tranel (2008), "Prefrontal cortex damage abolishes brand-cued change in cola preference," *Social cognitive and affective neuroscience*, 3(1), 1.

Labrecque, Lauren & Vanessa M. Patrick (2012), "The Marketers' Prismatic Palette: a Review of Color Research and Future Directions, working paper.

Meier, Brian P., Michael D. Robinson & Gerald L. Clore (2004),"Why Good Guys Wear White Automatic Inferences About Stimulus Valence Based on Brightness," *Psychological Science*, 15, 82-87.

Mogilner, Cassie, Tamar Rudnick & Sheena S. Iyengar (2008), "The Mere Categorization Effect: How the Presence of Categories Increases Choosers' Perceptions of Assortment Variety and Outcome Satisfaction," *Journal of Consumer Research*, 35 (August), 202-215.

Niewold, Theo A. (2010), "Organic more healthy? Green shoots in a scientific semi-desert," *British Journal of Nutrition*, 103(05), 627. Provencher, Véronique, Janet Polivy & C. Peter Herman (2009), "Perceived healthiness of food. If it's healthy, you can eat more!" *Appetite*, 52(2), 340–344.

Raghunathan, Rajagopal, Rebecca Walker Naylor & Wayne D. Hoyer (2006), "The Unhealthy = Tasty Intuition and Its Effects on Taste Inferences, Enjoyment, and Choice of Food Products," *Journal of Marketing, 70*(4), 170-184.

Schuldt, Jonathon & Norbert Schwarz (2010), "The "organic" path to obesity? Organic claims influence calorie judgments and exercise recommendations," *Judgment and Decision Making*, 5(3), 144–150.

Shiv, Baba, Ziv Carmon & Dan Ariely (2005), "Placebo Effects of Marketing Actions: Consumers May Get What They Pay For," *Journal of Marketing Research, 42*(4), 383-393.

Steenkamp, Jan-Benedict E. M., Harald J. Van Heerde & Inge Geyskens (2010), "What Makes Consumers Willing to Pay a Price Premium for National Brands over Private Labels?" *Journal of Marketing Research*, 47(6), 1011-1024.

Wansink, Brian & Pierre Chandon (2006), "Can "low-fat" nutrition labels lead to obesity?" *Journal of Marketing Research*, 43(4), 605–617.

"Hell is Other People": When Others Make Us Impulsive, Selfish and Judgmental and Factors that Help Us Fight This

Chairs: Jin Youn, Northwestern University, USA
Kelly Goldsmith, Northwestern University, USA

Paper #1: Mo' Men, Mo' Problems: Sex Ratio, Impulsive Spending, and Conspicuous Consumption

Vladas Griskevicius, University of Minnesota, USA
Joshua Ackerman, MIT, USA
Yajin Wang, University of Minnesota, USA
Andrew White, Arizona State University, USA

Paper #2: The Green Eyed Monster is Motivated: How Incidental Envy Triggers an Agentic Orientation

Jin Youn, Northwestern University, USA
Kelly Goldsmith, Northwestern University, USA

Paper #3: (Secretly) Blowing out Candles to Make Ours Burn Brighter: The Relationship Between Self-Esteem, Malicious Envy, and Interpersonal Behaviors

Cait Poynor Lamberton, University of Pittsburgh,
Kirk Kristofferson, University of British Columbia, Canada
Darren W. Dahl, University of British Columbia, Canada

Paper #4: Do the Crime, *Always* Do the Time? Insights into Consumer-to-Consumer Punishment Decisions

Lily Lin, University of British Columbia, Canada*
Darren W. Dahl, University of British Columbia, Canada
Jennifer J. Argo, University of Alberta, Canada

SESSION OVERVIEW

The question of how we are affected by the others around us is one that has preoccupied philosophers and psychologists, among others. Humans are commonly characterized as "social animals" and conventional wisdom often dictates that lives enriched with social interactions are more rewarding. Indeed, findings show that people who spend more quality time with others (per day) tend to be more satisfied with their lives (Goldsmith and Goldsmith 2010). Further, social isolation, or loneliness, which results from a dissatisfaction with the quality or quantity of one's social relationships can have a variety of negative cognitive, behavioral and physiological consequences (for review see Hawkley and Cacioppo 2010). However, conventional wisdom and prior research notwithstanding, this session will demonstrate that there are a variety of contexts in which "hell is other people" (Sartre 1944) illustrating the dark side of consumer behavior that can come as a result of social interactions and social comparisons.

Specifically, this session contains three papers that highlight when and how others can promote more impulsive and selfish consumer behaviors and concludes with a fourth paper that highlights important moderators to this pattern. The first paper by Griskevicius and colleagues examines how sex ratio (the ratio of men to women in the social environment) can affect consumer decision making. The authors find that when men perceive a relative abundance of men (or a shortage of women) their spending behavior becomes more impulsive and they are more likely to engage in conspicuous consumption. Building on this work, the second paper by Youn and Goldsmith tests how priming envy, an emotion rooted in social comparison, affects subsequent unrelated decisions. These authors find priming envy towards others leads consumers to become more selfish, more hard working, and more prone to conspicuous consumption due to an underlying shift towards an agentic orientation. Next Lamberton,

Kristofferson and Dahl explore the consequences of envy in an interpersonal context. These authors find that consumers with high self-esteem will congratulate envied others, but covertly sabotage them; however, those with low self-esteem will either react overtly against the envied other or take their negative feelings out on the envied product rather than the envied person. Having shown the negative ramifications that social interactions and social comparisons can bring, the final paper by Lin, Dahl, and Argo rounds out the session by examining the factors that make consumers more forgiving towards others. Specifically, this paper explores a variety of variables that increase the likelihood that consumers will make excuses for the others' violations (e.g., when they violate social norms) as opposed to condemning them. All projects are in advanced stages of completion.

Because these projects approach the topic of how social interactions and social comparisons affect consumer behavior from very different perspectives (e.g., theory is drawn from evolutionary psychology, social psychology, the emotions literature and marketing) we expect that this session will be of interest to a wide audience. Further, because these four papers all feature research that makes substantial theoretical contributions to the existing work on how others influence consumer behavior while being grounded in phenomenon that are marketing relevant, we expect that the practical insights each paper suggests will make this session appealing to many.

Mo' Men, Mo' Problems: Sex Ratio, Impulsive Spending, and Conspicuous Consumption

EXTENDED ABSTRACT

How does the ratio of men to women influence consumer behavior? We show that an abundance of men leads other men to become more impulsive, save less, and borrow more. A scarcity of women also led men to increase conspicuous consumption, including spending more money on engagement rings.

Macon and Columbus are two cities in the U.S. state of Georgia. Despite being less than a hundred miles apart, the residents of each city have drastically different spending habits: The consumer debt of people living in Columbus is an astounding 2.7 standard deviations higher than that of people living in Macon—a difference of $3,479 per consumer. What might account for this staggering divergence in borrowing and spending across the two nearby cities?

We suggest that this difference in debt might be linked to an often overlooked difference between the two cities: the ratio of single men to women in each area. Whereas in fiscally-responsible Macon there are only 0.78 single men for every woman, in debt-heavy Columbus there are 1.18 single men for every woman. In the current research we use both archival data and some of the first experimental manipulations of perceived sex ratio to examine how sex ratio influences financial decisions and spending.

The ratio of males to females is known to be an important factor in determining animal behavior. Animal research shows that imbalanced sex ratios tend to have the strongest effects on male behavior. When females become scarce (male-biased sex ratio), males intensify mating and competition behavior. For example, as sex ratio shifts from female-biased to male-biased, male grey mouse lemurs allocate more effort on mate search and courtship (Eberle and Kappeler

2004), and male European bitterlings intensify intra-sexual competition (Mills and Reynolds 2003).

Sex ratio also varies in human populations. For example, whereas Las Vegas, Nevada, has 1.16 men per every woman, Birmingham, Alabama, has 0.88 men per every woman (Kruger 2009). Sex ratios can also vary between nations. China, for example, will soon have a surplus of over 40 million men (Hesketh 2009).

Given that sex ratio influences mating and competition behavior in animals, we hypothesize that sex ratio may affect people's consumer behavior. Mating effort and intra-sexual competition in humans is associated with increased men's conspicuous consumption (Griskevicius et al., 2007; Sundie et al., 2011) and increased men's desire for immediate financial rewards (Van den Bergh, Dewitte, & Warlop, 2008). Given that a scarcity of women should amplify men's mating and competition behavior, we predicted that a male-biased sex ratio should lead men to become (1) more impulsive, (2) save less and borrow more, and (3) spend more money on mating and status-related products.

Study 1 examined the relationship between sex ratio in 120 US cities and two behavioral measures of economic impulsivity: (a) average number of credit cards owned by residents in each city and (b) average amount of debt carried by people in each city. Results revealed a positive correlation between sex ratio and number of credit cards, $r(134) = .24$, $p = .005$, and amount of debt, $r(134) = .19$, $p = .025$. A scarcity of women in American cities is related to owning more credit cards and having a higher amount of debt.

Study 2 used an experiment approach. Participants first viewed photo arrays of men and women that were ostensibly indicative of the local population. The arrays either had more men, more women, or equal sex ratio (control). Then, participants made a series of inter-temporal financial choices involving real monetary incentives. For example, people chose between receiving $37 tomorrow versus $54 in 33 days. Findings showed that sex ratio had no effect on women's inter-temporal choice. For men, however, sex ratio produced a large effect. As predicted, a male-biased ratio led men to opt for immediate financial rewards, $t(199) = 3.26$, $p = .001$. This means that as women became scarce, men desired immediate monetary rewards.

In Study 3 participants read news articles describing the local population as either having more single men or more single women. Participants then indicated how much money they would save each month from a paycheck, as well as how much money they would borrow each month for immediate expenditures. Findings showed that sex ratio again had no effect on women's saving or borrowing. However, male-biased sex ratios led men to save less money, $t(95) = 2.90$, $p = .005$, cutting their monthly savings by 42%. A scarcity of women also led men to want to borrow 84% more money for use toward immediate expenditures, $t(95) = 2.29$, $p = .025$.

Study 4 investigated how sex ratio influences spending. The study focused on two types of expenditures: (1) *mating-related* expenditures (Valentine's Day gift, dinner date, engagement ring) and (2) *status-related conspicuous* products (new car, designer handbag/wallet, and designer sunglasses). Findings showed that a scarcity of women led men to pay more for both mating-related and status-related products, $t(143) = 3.18$, $p = .001$. When the sex ratio was male-biased, for example, men paid $6.01 more for a Valentine's Day gift and $278 more for an engagement ring.

Our findings highlight people's sensitivity to a particular feature of the social environment—the ratio of men to women. Just as sex ratio has important effects on animal behavior, we find that sex ratio has theoretically consistent effects on human behavior. In addition, the current studies suggest that sex ratio might have far-reaching consequences for many economic decisions and, potentially, whole economies.

The Green Eyed Monster is Motivated: How Incidental Envy Triggers an Agentic Orientation

EXTENDED ABSTRACT

We live in a world where others (ranging from celebrities to peers) have things that we want yet we do not or cannot own. For this reason, envy is common among consumers. Envy is an emotion that results from upward social comparisons, which can be made deliberately or unintentionally (Mussweiler, Ruter, and Epstude 2004). It activates mixed emotions: causing both longing and wishfulness along with self-criticism and dissatisfaction (Smith, Kim, and Parrott 1988). Prior research demonstrates that envy causes consumers to focus on the person or object that arouses the emotion (e.g., showing that we are willing to pay more for products that we envy, Van de Ven, Zeelenberg, and Pieters 2011). However, far less is known about how the incidental activation of envy can affect judgments and behaviors in unrelated domains.

We hypothesize that incidental feelings of envy will affect unrelated judgments and behaviors by way of activating a more agentic orientation (Hogan 1982). Prior work has distinguished between agentic and communal motivations, defining agency as the desire to "get ahead" in a given context, even if this comes at the expense of others. Conversely, communion refers to the desire to "get along" by incorporating others in one's goal pursuits (e.g., Rucker, Galinsky and Dubois 2012). We will test if incidentally activating envy increases agentic behavior in subsequent, unrelated decisions (e.g., resource distribution, self-regulation, and consumption). Furthermore, we posit that this agentic behavior will only emerge when people feel envious toward others, but not when they feel envied by others. Said differently feeling dissatisfied with oneself in comparison to others will cause consumers to act in a more self-focused way, however, priming the concept of envy, more generally, will not. We test this prediction across three studies.

In our first study, incidental envy was activated through an episodic recall task (Malatesta and Izard 1984), which asked participants to recall a time they felt envy towards others (other-envy condition). Results from this condition were then compared to two control conditions, one in which participants were asked to recall their activities from last week (control condition) and a second in which participants were asked to recall a time someone else felt envy towards them (self-envy condition).

After completing the incidental envy manipulation, participants were asked to participate in a dictator game (i.e., asked how much they would want to keep for themselves and how much they would want to allocate to a hypothetical other that they were paired with in the game, total amount = $5). In line with our prediction that incidentally activating envy toward others will produce a more self-focused, agentic orientation, we observe that those primed with other-envy kept significantly more money for themselves (allocating less to others) than those in either the control condition or in the self-envy condition (amount allocated to others: $M_{other-envy}$=$2.37; $M_{control}$=$2.89; $M_{self-envy}$=$3.00; p's<.05). Not only do these results provide preliminary support for our hypothesis that envy promotes an agentic orientation (seen here in retention of resources at the expense of others), but we also observe that merely priming the concept of envy does not produce this pattern. This suggests that the role of the self, particularly perceptions of the self as inferior compared to others, in the experience of envy is vital to generate the agentic response.

Study 2 was designed to test more directly for the role of envy as a motivational force to "get ahead." For this study, participants were randomly assigned to the other-envy versus control conditions described previously. After completing the episodic recall task, they were then asked to solve a series of anagrams that were presented as part of an unrelated task. The final anagram was unsolvable, and the time spent persisting on this task was used as the dependent measure, as time spent persisting on unsolvable tasks is often used as a proxy for motivation (Shah and Higgins 1997; Shah, Higgins, and Friedman 1998). In line with our predictions, the results demonstrate that the activation of incidental envy increased motivation on the task (seconds spent on the unsolvable task: $M_{other\text{-}envy}$=83.62; $M_{control}$=41.89; p<.05).

Study 3 was designed to build on the results of studies 1 and 2 by testing for the role of incidental envy more directly on consumption decisions. Because flaunting material resources is instrumental to gaining social status (Veblen 1899), we argue that an agentic orientation (here, caused by envy) should increase consumers' desire for such goods. In this study, participants were assigned to one of the three conditions described in Study 1, then presented with an array of luxury products (e.g., Hermes belt, Prada sunglasses, Louis Vuitton bag etc.), and instructed to answer what percentage of its retail price they were willing to bid on an auction, ranging from 0 to 120% (in line with prior research, this measure was used to reduce the variance that might occur with open-ended responses; Rucker and Galinsky 2008). The results support our prediction: when people recalled experiences of envying others, they were willing to pay more for conspicuous goods than either the control condition or the self-envy condition (% of retail: $M_{other\text{-}envy}$=54.76; $M_{self\text{-}envy}$=43.10; $M_{control}$=43.17; p's<.05)

Taken together, these studies suggest that experiencing envy towards others, and not merely activating the concept of envy, triggers an agentic mindset that leads to distinct behaviors in various domains. Specifically, other-envy lead people to be more selfish with resources (Study 1), work harder (Study 2), and engage more in conspicuous consumption (Study 3). We are in the process of conducting additional studies to demonstrate: (1) that the activation of an agentic orientation mediates the effect of envy on these behavioral outcomes and (2) that the increase in consumption is specific to domains where one could gain social status. We conclude with a discussion of the theoretical and practical implications for these findings.

(Secretly) Blowing out Candles to Make Ours Burn Brighter: The relationship between self-esteem, malicious envy, and interpersonal behaviors

EXTENDED ABSTRACT

Intuition suggests that self-confident individuals respond to difficult social situations with magnanimity. For example, on seeing others succeed where they have failed, the high-self esteem individual claps the victor on the back with a smile, while the low self-esteem individual bitterly retreats to a corner to lick their wounds. Such observations lead us to equate high self-esteem with stronger moral character in the face of painful social emotions like envy.

We argue that this relationship may not hold true if one looks beyond overt actions or considers multiple types of envy experiences. To challenge this intuition, the present research documents the behavior of individuals of varying level of self-esteem when experiencing envy. We consider both benign and malicious envy (following Van deVen et al. 2011), create real envy situations, and examine both overt and covert behaviors toward the envied individual.

Study 1 followed a 2 (malicious or benign envy) x 2 (no winner, winner) x self-esteem (continuous) between-subjects design. Self-esteem was collected approximately 3 weeks prior to the session, using the Rosenberg (1979) scale. Participants visited the lab in groups of 4 or 5 with one confederate. They were told that their business school was offering an opportunity to interview for a marketing internship at a popular company (Lululemon athletic clothing). However, only a few students would be able to interview. In the *benign envy* sessions, award was dependent on relevant work experience provided to career services earlier in the semester via an in-class survey. In the *malicious envy* sessions, participants read that envelopes had been placed under the seats in the room. The envelopes indicated who would be selected for the interview. Further, in some sessions, the confederate was simply another participant and there was no winner. In others, the confederate won and celebrated appropriately.

After learning if anyone had won the internship opportunity, we captured both overt and covert behaviors toward the winner. Overt behavior was captured by allowing participants to help the interview winner prepare. Willing individuals would be contacted immediately after the session to set up a coaching meeting. Willingness to help was captured on a 1 (not at all willing) to 7 (very willing) scale. Covert behaviors were captured by asking participants to anonymously provide 5 practice interview questions for the winner. Quality of these questions as determined by two condition-blind judges constituted our covert behavior measure.

An ANOVA was estimated using envy type condition, winner/no-winner condition, and participants' self-esteem scores to predict both overt and covert behavior. We first note results consistent with intuition: higher self-esteem individuals were significantly (p < .05) more likely to overtly help the interview winner than lower self-esteem individuals. No other interactions or main effects emerged.

However, analyzing covert behavior provided yields a three-way interaction of benign/malicious envy, whether the winner was present or not, and self-esteem (p = .01). When the interview recipient deserved to win the internship (benign envy condition), none of our manipulated or measured factors influenced question quality (p > .3). This supports the findings of van de Ven (2011) regarding the non-hurtful tendencies of benign envy. By contrast, when the award was random (malicious envy condition), higher self-esteem individuals provided significantly lower-quality interview questions than lower self-esteem individuals when the confederate was a winner as opposed to when the confederate was simply another participant. Thus, higher self-esteem individuals were willing to covertly sabotage undeserving victors.

Study 2 focused on malicious situations and tested for that meditational role of envy. We also wanted to see if covert harm to the envied other bled over onto the envied product. This study followed a 2 (winner-present, no winner present) x self-esteem (continuous) design. Participants had the opportunity to win a set of Vancouver Canucks tickets. A confederate was once again present in all conditions, and in the winner-present conditions, was awarded the tickets during the session based on a random seat assignment.

As part of a presumably unrelated task, participants later read that they would be randomly assigned another individual about whom to form "thin-slice" judgments. In reality all participants were assigned the confederate. Their evaluation of the confederate on various positive personality traits (e.g., hardworking, intelligent, etc.) formed our measure of covert behavior. We also collected willingness-to-pay for the Canucks tickets in a list of other event tickets in the area. Embedded in a battery of measures at the close of the session were three questions asking participants to rate how much they felt envious, jealous, or as though someone was better off than they were during the session, indexed to form an envy measure.

Mirroring study 1, higher self-esteem individuals showed a significantly worse evaluation of the confederate when the confederate had won the tickets as opposed to when they had not won (p < .05). Envy mediated effects on evaluations of the confederate. Surprisingly, we found that this relationship was inverted for WTP for the envied product (but saw no effects on other ticket prices): Lower self-esteem individuals showed significant *decreases* in value for the tickets when a winner had been in their session, in those cases valuing it significantly less than did the higher self-esteem individuals.

Thus, it appears that while higher self-esteem individuals express envy via covert actions toward the envied person, lower self-esteem individuals exhibit a sour grapes effect, taking out their frustration on the product and overtly refusing help. Thus, it may be that our equation of moral strength and self-esteem exists because this sour grapes effect is expressed publicly. Still, high self-esteem responses may be no less damaging, though better-hidden, and warrant further research and intervention.

Do the Crime, *Always* Do the Time? Insights into Consumer-to-Consumer Punishment Decisions

EXTENDED ABSTRACT

Social order can be disrupted by norm violations in consumption contexts (e.g., cutting the line, hovering), and previous research has established the theoretical conceptualization that restoration of social order that was disrupted by norm violations can be demonstrated through a victim's (or bystander's) decision to punish the norm violator (Bernhard et al. 2006; Golash 2005; Miethe and Meier 1994). Diverging from the conventional conceptualization that the restoration of social order is achieved through punishment, the current research investigates whether consumers can also achieve social order through the excusing of norm violators in various consumption contexts.

While previous literature has focused on defining the purpose of punishment (e.g., whether the intent of punishment is to seek retribution or to teach the norm violator a lesson; Kolber 2009), and identifying individual difference factors that enhance punishment tendencies (e.g., justice sensitivity, Gollwitzer et al. 2009), little is known about the boundary conditions of the punishment decision. We address this research gap by identifying factors that can influence the level of punishment delivered by consumers. Specifically, we investigate whether consumers can achieve social order by mitigating punishment against another consumer who has violated a consumption norm. The specific instances we explore are a) if social order has already been restored by the actions of other parties in the consumption environment (Study 1), b) if a norm violator has experienced an unjustified adversity (Studies 2a/b), and c) if the violator holds a position that is aspirational (Study 3). In our studies, we consider two categories of punishment (Skinner 1953): positive (i.e., punishment which involves the presentation of an undesirable stimulus such as scolding or a physically demanding task) and negative (i.e., punishment which involves the removal of a desirable stimulus from the norm violator such as withholding assistance).

Study 1. This study employed a 2 (norm violation: present vs. absent) x 2 (action by another party: yes vs. no) + (control) between-participants design. The context of the study was a product evaluation task, in which participants were asked to evaluate a shirt at a display table. To manipulate norm violation, the confederate either created a mess (vs. did not create a mess) at a store display table. To manipulate action by another party, the experimenter verbally scold-ed (vs. did not scold) the confederate. The confederate then "accidently" knocked over a pile of papers in front of the participant, and the punishment measure was determined by whether the participant refrained from helping the confederate pick up the papers. We show that when social order was restored by the punishment delivered to the norm violator by another party, i.e., store employee in the retail context, consumers mitigated the likelihood of punishment.

Study 2a. This study employed a 2 (norm violation: present vs. absent) x 2 (adversity: yes vs. no) between-participants design. To manipulate adversity, the participant either witnesses another passenger experiencing a computer failure (vs. no failure) at an airline counter. To manipulate norm violation, the passenger in the scenario either cut in line (vs. did not cut in line) later on at the security checkpoint. Results show that when a norm violator faced an unjustified adversity that disrupts the perceived social order, i.e., negative consumption event, social order is achieved by excusing the norm violator.

Study 2b. This study employed a 2 (norm violation: present vs. absent) x 3 (adversity: yes – personal control vs. yes – no personal control vs. no) between-participants design. The context of the scenario involved the participant witnessing a norm violation at a post office. To manipulate norm violation, a consumer who arrived at the same time as a woman with the baby stroller either moved in front (vs. did not move in front) of the woman as she made her way through the door with the stroller. To manipulate adversity, the consumer was either of average weight (vs. obese). Additionally, the obese target was described as someone who lives a sedentary lifestyle (vs. had a medical condition that causes weight gain). The results show that when a norm violator experienced an unjustified adversity that is beyond personal control, i.e., negative physical attribute due to medical condition, social order is again achieved by excusing the norm violator.

Study 3. This study employed a one cell (aspirational position: yes vs. no) + control between- participants design, and business students participated. The context of the study was the evaluation of a personal training service whereby the participants were asked to design a physical exercise routine for the confederate who was posing as a participant. Norm violation was held at a constant for the aspirational position conditions, so the confederate arrived 5 minutes late for the study. To manipulate aspirational position, the confederate either casually mentioned that he had a job interview with a large marketing company (vs. café on campus). To measure punishment, participants indicated the number of push-ups (range from 0-50 repetitions) the confederate should be asked to complete. We find the aspirational position held by the norm violator changes the subsequent punishment required to restore social order. Here, justification for the norm violation mediates this relationship between the aspirational position and the level of punishment delivered.

Discussion. Previous work in consumer behavior has focused on identifying important consumption norms and determining how the promotion of these norms can change people's behaviors (e.g., Goldstein et al. 2008). Our research diverges from this line of work by exploring how consumers react toward those who violate norms in the consumption context. Based on the theoretical conceptualization that disrupted social order can be restored through punishment of the norm violators, the current research contributes to our understanding of consumers' reactions toward norm violators by providing new insight into how consumers use the level of punishment delivered as a means to address a norm violation that has occurred in the consumption context.

Not What I Expected: Unanticipated Consequences of Product Exposure and Use

Chair: Adriana Samper, Arizona State University, USA

Paper #1: Finding Brands and Losing Your Religion?

Keisha M. Cutright, University of Pennsylvania, USA
Tülin Erdem, New York University, USA
Gavan J. Fitzsimons, Duke University, USA
Ron Shachar, Interdisciplinary Center (IDC), Israel

Paper #2: The Pride (and the Pain?, USA The Downstream Consequences of Using High End Products in Performance Situations

Adriana Samper, Arizona State University, USA
James R. Bettman, Duke University, USA
Gavan J. Fitzsimons, Duke University, USA

Paper #3: It's Smiling at Me: Satisfying Social Needs Through Consumer Products…At the Expense of Genuine Relationships

James A. Mourey, University of Michigan, USA
Jenny Olson, University of Michigan, USA
Carolyn Yoon, University of Michigan, USA

Paper #4: Exposure to Unattainable Luxury: Boomerang Effects on Extrinsic and Materialistic Goals

Katrien Meert, Ghent University, Belgium
Inge Lens, KU Leuven, Belgium
Mario Pandelaere, Ghent University, Belgium

SESSION OVERVIEW

Consumers often seek out products or brands in the service of satisfying personal goals, and marketers may try to stimulate consumption by making these goals salient. For example, consumers may believe that by purchasing specific products or brands, they can express unique aspects of themselves (Berger and Heath 2007), close gaps in identity (Wicklund and Gollwitzer 1982), affiliate with others (Mead et al. 2011) or even feel more powerful (Rucker and Galinsky 2008) and marketers may strengthen this perceived link through promotional campaigns or messages. In this session, we examine contexts where consumer and marketer intuitions about brand and luxury exposure may boomerang; when seeking out or promoting products may have unintended, and sometimes even deleterious, consequences.

First, Cutright and colleagues demonstrate that by using products and brands to the end of expressing the self, consumers may actually be suppressing their overall religiosity. In this manner, subtle exposure to brands through choice or trial can actually cause people to "lose their religion." Samper, Bettman and Fitzsimons show that consumers, in an effort to put their best foot forward by choosing a higher end item for a high-stakes task(e.g., Armani Suit for a job interview, Odyssey Golf Club for a putting task), may actually polarize their self-perceptions of success and failure. While consumers using a high end branded item who succeed on a task feel significantly more skilled than those using a neutral item, these consumers also feel significantly more frustrated and less skilled when using this branded item if their performance was unsuccessful. Mourey, Olson and Yoon examine this phenomenon in the domain of affiliation, where they show that while social exclusion increases desire for brands that may fulfill interpersonal needs, using these anthropomorphized products can actually lead consumers to be less likely to seek out human connections. Finally, Meert, Lens and Pandelaere examine this phenomenon through a marketer's lens, showing that standard practices of trying to persuade consumers and encourage materialistic goal pursuit by showing images of luxury can actually

backfire when consumers are presented with *unattainable* luxury. Specifically, the salience of unattainable luxury can lead to reduced interest in material goods and even increased prosocial behaviors. The fourth paper facilitates an integration of these unintended consequences across consumer and marketer-related goals.

Given its unique, counterintuitive focus, this session is expected to appeal to a broad segment of ACR members. The four papers, all at advanced stages, are expected to generate interest among individuals with interests in anthropomorphism, branding, goal pursuit and motivation, luxury goods, priming, product use, religion, consumer welfare and marketing applications. All speakers (Cutright, Samper, Mourey and Meert, indicated by asterisk, below) have agreed to serve if the proposal is accepted.

In sum, this session brings together a diverse set of papers examining the unintended effects of brand or product exposure in religious, aspirational, affiliative and luxury contexts. By combining a breadth of papers that address this similar phenomenon, we underscore the importance of understanding the downstream consequences of consumption and shed greater insight into how the goals of consumers and marketers may be undermined by exposure to initially desirable products or brands.

Finding Brands and Losing Your Religion?

EXTENDED ABSTRACT

Whether you consider it to be a source of deadly extremism or the pathway to humanity's highest potential (Pargament, 2002), few will deny the power of religion. In this research, however, we ask whether religiosity (i.e., the centrality of religion in one's life) can be undermined by the presence of brand name products. We reason that when brands are salient, religion will be devalued, given that people often use brands to satisfy similar self-expressive needs as religion (e.g., Shachar, Erdem, Cutright, & Fitzsimons, 2011). However, we expect that the salience of brands will lead to lower levels of religiosity only when individuals are able to incorporate the brands as meaningful extensions of themselves. When brands do not allow individuals to communicate a part of "self", they are unlikely to be viewed as acceptable substitutes for religion.

Study 1 tested our basic hypothesis that the salience of brands leads to lower levels of religiosity. The experiment contained two between-subject conditions: high brand salience versus low brand salience. In the high brand salience condition, participants chose between two branded products, 10 different times. For example, in one choice, they decided between a red Adidas shirt and a green Adidas shirt. In the low brand salience condition, participants chose between the same pairs of products except the brand names were removed. After making their choices, participants completed the Religious Commitment scale (Worthington et al., 2003, e.g., "My religious beliefs lie behind my whole approach to life"). Consistent with hypotheses, results indicated that the high brand salience condition reported significantly lower religious commitment than the low brand salience condition.

In Study 2, we explored the breadth of the hypothesized effect by investigating how brand salience would impact items indirectly related to religion. In particular, we were interested in how brand salience would influence attitudes towards malls that resembled churches versus those that did not. We expected that high brand salience would cause people to devalue religion and apply these attitudes towards malls that resembled churches. The experiment's design was a 2(brand salience: high vs. low; between subjects) x 2(mall type: high church resemblance vs. no church resemblance; within subjects).

Participants were randomly assigned to a high brand salience condition or low brand salience condition as in Study 1. After making their choices, participants evaluated a series of six malls, half of which strongly resembled churches while the others did not. Participants then indicated how much they liked each mall (7pt scales).

Results revealed no significant main effects, but there was a significant interaction of brand salience and mall type on liking. When evaluating the malls that resembled churches, the high brand salience condition liked the malls less than the low brand salience condition. When evaluating the malls that did not resemble churches, the two conditions did not differ from one another. This study therefore suggests that brands not only impact basic reports of religiosity, but even color individuals' perceptions of objects that are loosely associated with religion.

In the studies reported thus far, we have used an inherently self-expressive context to reveal the hypothesized effect of brands: choice exercises that allowed people to express themselves with the brands to which they were exposed. In the next study, we wanted to more explicitly demonstrate that the relationship between brands and religiosity exists only when brands are incorporated into one's expression of self. Thus, Study 3 was designed to manipulate the degree to which products are incorporated into the self by altering individuals' physical relationship with the product. We hypothesized that wearing a brand would provide a strong opportunity for individuals to incorporate the brand into one's expression of self (e.g., Gino, Norton, & Ariely, 2010), while simply looking at a product would not. Accordingly, we expected that when individuals wore a branded product (versus a non-branded product), religiosity would decline. We did not expect this relationship to exist when individuals simply looked at the brand. In other words, we expected "wearing" a brand to have similar effects as "choosing" a brand since each of these contexts allows people to say something about themselves with brands. We expected that simply "looking at" a brand would be less likely to aid self-expression.

The design was a 2(brand salience: high vs. low) x 2(self-expressive context: high vs. low). In half of the sessions participants came into the lab and were given an Apple-branded lanyard (high brand salience). In the remaining sessions, participants were given a plain black lanyard (low brand salience). After receiving their lanyards, half of the participants were told to wear and evaluate the lanyard (high expression). The remaining participants were told NOT to wear it; just to look at it and evaluate it (low expression). Participants then completed the Religious Commitment scale.

There were no main effects of brand salience or self-expressive context on religious commitment. However, a significant interaction of the two conditions emerged. In the high self-expression condition (i.e., wearing the lanyard), individuals in the high brand salience condition (Apple) reported lower religious beliefs than individuals in the low brand salience condition. Within the low self-expression condition (i.e., looking only), the high and low brand salience groups were not significantly different from one another. This study therefore reiterates the notion that brands only lead to lower levels of religiosity when incorporated into expressions of the self.

In summary, these studies have demonstrated that beliefs about God waver when brands take center stage in individuals' minds. We've found that this is most likely to be true when brands are incorporated into the self and serve as a tool for self-expression. This

research offers not only an understanding of the power of brands in shaping individuals' most sacred beliefs, but also sheds light on the value that many individuals assign to religiosity. It seems that what many consider sacred is often treated as merely a means to an (expressive) end.

Rolling the Dice with Premium Products: Using a High End Product Polarizes Self-Perceptions of Performance

EXTENDED ABSTRACT

Phrases like "dress for success," or "you've got to look the part" suggest that having the right accoutrements for a performance task (fancy golf equipment on the course; a new tailored interview suit) can be beneficial to success. Importantly, while we may purchase elite branded products in the hopes that these products will help us perform well, sometimes we may succeed, while other times we may still fail. In the current research, we examine how a performance outcome interacts with the type of product used to influence self-perceptions. That is, if we use products to pose as the ideal self that we have not quite arrived at, how does this affect how we feel when we succeed or fail?

We draw from work on priming and self-concept (DeMarree, Petty and Wheeler 2005) to examine this question. Research has shown that objects can serve as primes to increase the accessibility of related aspects in self-concept (Kay et al. 2004). In this sense, the use of a high end golf club may make the construct of a skilled golfer more accessible. Success with a high end golf club assimilates to this construct, thereby strengthening the link between the self and elite golfer, resulting in greater self-perceptions of skill and talent. However, if the construct of "skilled golfer" was initially accessible through choice of a high end club, failure with a high end club contrasts even more starkly against this construct, thus making self-perceptions seem even poorer. In this manner, individuals should feel more skilled following success with a high-end (vs. low-end) product, and importantly, they should also feel even less skilled following failure with this same high-end (vs. low-end) product. This should be particularly pronounced for individuals who are more reliant on accessible inward beliefs to guide their self-perceptions, specifically, for low self-monitors (Snyder & Tanke 1976). Thus, we suggest that there may be both pride and pain associated with posing, and test this across three studies.

Study 1 used a two-cell design to test the basic effect of product type in a failure situation. Twenty-eight undergraduates read a first-person scenario about purchasing a new interview suit in which they were randomly assigned to choose an Armani or Dockers suit. Depending on condition, participants were then told that their interview was successful (unsuccessful). Participants then rated their self-perceptions of how skilled they would feel at interviewing. Results revealed that individuals who had chosen the high end Armani (vs. low end Dockers) suit felt less qualified for the interview position. Thus, this study reveals preliminary evidence that using a high end product can make failure feel more extreme.

In Study 2, we tested this effect in an actual golfing performance context, looking at the effects of product use on both failure and success, and examining the role of the self by comparing situations in which one is assigned to (non self-relevant) vs. chooses (self-relevant) to use a high end product. Four hundred and twenty eight participants were randomly assigned to the conditions of a 2 (product: high end Odyssey club vs. low end Basic club) x 2 (selection: choice vs. assignment) design. Participants were informed that they would be evaluated on their putting skills from a distance of 4.25 ft. and presented with two clubs: the high end Odyssey or the low end Basic. Participants were either assigned to use a high (low) end Odyssey (Basic) putter, or were allowed to choose their putter. Participants completed one putt, and either succeeded or failed. Neither the choice vs. assignment of a putter nor the use of a Basic vs. Odyssey putter influenced success or failure. As such, we crossed these two factors with success vs. failure to yield a 2 (product: high end vs. low end) x 2 (selection: choice vs. assignment) x 2 (success vs. failure) between-subjects design. All cells had at least 21 participants. Participants then rated their self-perceptions of how skilled they felt at putting. Results revealed a significant selection x club x outcome interaction and showed that for individuals assigned to a putter, there was no difference in self-perceptions across putters following failure, and no difference across clubs following success. In the choice conditions, however, following failure, individuals felt more negative self-perceptions of skill if they had chosen the Odyssey vs. Basic putter. Following success, individuals felt more positive self-perceptions if they had chosen the Odyssey vs. Basic putter. Thus, high end (vs. low end) product choice makes one feel even more skilled after success, but even less skilled after failure. Importantly, the role of choice suggests that the linking of the product to one's self-concept must be present for these effects to hold. In Study 3, we probe the role of self-concept more deeply by examining the impact of self-monitoring.

In Study 3, we examined the role of self-monitoring in this phenomenon to further understand the process by which product use drives changes in self-concept and hence self-perceptions. Because we wanted to look at a domain that was particularly important to undergraduate business students, we returned to the interview scenario. One hundred and seventy-six undergraduates were randomly assigned to a 2 (product: high end vs. low end) x 2 (outcome: success vs. failure) x self-monitoring (measured) design. Participants read a scenario in which they were debating whether to purchase an Armani or H&M suit for a highly anticipated job interview. Participants were randomly assigned to "ultimately decide" on the Armani (H&M) suit and read a short passage describing their interview as highly successful or highly unsuccessful. Participants then rated their self-perceptions of interviewing skills and completed the revised self-monitoring scale (Lennox and Wolfe 1984), which was unaffected by the manipulations. Results revealed that as before, following failure, using a high end (vs. low end) suit made people feel worse about their interviewing skills, while following success, using this high end (vs. low end) suit made people feel better about their interviewing skills. Measures of positive and negative emotion also paralleled these results. Most importantly, these effects were driven by low self-monitors, suggesting that low self-monitors' greater reliance on the mental contents associated with the high end suit, as well as the success or failure that may assimilate or contrast to this content, likely drives changes in self-perceptions.

Thus, these results suggest that using high end products can have unanticipated consequences on self-perceptions. While individuals typically gravitate toward choosing higher end goods to emulate the individuals they aspire to be, their use may have polarizing effects resulting in sweeter success, but sourer failure.

It's Smiling at Me: Satisfying Social Needs Through Consumer Products...At the Expense of Genuine Relationships

EXTENDED ABSTRACT

Beginning with imaginary friends and teddy bears in childhood, human beings demonstrate a fundamental need for belonging that continues across the lifespan (Baumeister & Leary, 1995; Maslow,

1943). Although social needs are often fulfilled through contact with other people, it seems plausible that consumer products could fulfill similar needs. For example, consumers might purchase goods and services hoping to attain love, affection, and emotional pleasure. Seeking social need fulfillment through products may, paradoxically, serve as a detriment to interpersonal relationship development and maintenance. The objective of the current research is to explore how the consumption of products, in general, can come at the cost of social relationships when products satisfy the needs customarily fulfilled by other people.

Just how far people supplement human interactions with product interactions is a matter warranting careful study. Research suggests the possibility of consumers developing relationships with nonsocial objects that mirror interpersonal relationships (Aggarwal, 2004; Fournier, 1998). Further evidence indicates that individuals readily perceive objects as gendered (Guthrie, 2007), brands as having personality (Aaker, 1997), and brand-related characters as human (Rook & Levy, 1999). Social exclusion may play a role in these findings, however, such that those craving human contact may more readily "see" people in their products. Research by Epley, Waytz, Akalis, and Cacioppo (2008) shows that people who feel more chronically disconnected from others anthropomorphize more than those who feel more connected. Indeed, individuals who are well integrated in their social networks are less likely to seek additional bonds relative to their more deprived counterparts (Baumeister & Leary, 1995).

We propose that when a social need exists, products may satisfy it in a way similar to people, which reduces the likelihood of seeking interpersonal fulfillment. Baumeister and Leary (1995) propose, but never empirically test, that social relationships "...should substitute for each other, to some extent, as would be indicated by effective replacement of lost relationship partners and by a capacity for social relatedness in one sphere to overcome potential ill effects of social deprivation in another sphere." We seek to demonstrate that consumers who perceive a void in affiliative bonds may be able to derive similar social benefits from product consumption.

Study 1 involved a 2(words: control, negative social) x 2(Roomba: anthropomorphized, non-anthropomorphized) between-subjects design. Undergraduate students completed a computerized word task where they identified the number of syllables in words flashed on the screen. Participants viewed 40 randomly presented words: 20 control words (e.g., guitar, banana, lampshade) and either 20 negative social words (e.g., excluded, unaccepted, unloved) or 20 neutral words. Following this priming task, participants completed an ostensibly unrelated task in which they were told a company was interested in the shopping behavior of young adults. Participants were shown a Roomba vacuum, but half were randomly assigned to see a version in which the product's features resembled a smiling face (anthropomorphized) while the other half saw the same Roomba turned 90-degrees clockwise so that the product was identical but did not resemble a smiling face (non-anthropomorphized). Participants then answered several questions regarding their impressions of the Roomba including their familiarity with the product, willingness to pay, how attached or dependent they might become on the product, and a series of ratings regarding the following characteristics: attractive, desirable, efficient, high-maintenance, reliable, stylish, unsafe, and has a mind of its own.

Results revealed a significant interaction between prime and Roomba condition showing that participants primed with negative social words and shown an anthropomorphized Roomba were willing to pay more and become attached to the product. Interestingly, these participants were also more likely to see the product as both more attractive and as having a mind of its own, suggesting greater sensitivity to the product's humanistic attributes.

To see whether this sensitivity would influence consumption decisions, Study 2 utilized a 2(social exclusion, non-social negative control) × 2(anthropomorphized, non-anthropomorphized product) between-subjects design. Undergraduates were randomly assigned to one of two essay conditions: social exclusion ("a time you felt very excluded by other people") or a nonsocial negative control ("a time you did worse than expected on an academic assignment"). Participants were then presented a version of iRobot's Roomba as done in Study 1. A series of rating scales followed the Roomba presentation to assess product perceptions.

Results revealed a significant interaction between the two independent variables for purchase likelihood, after controlling for Roomba ownership: the anthropomorphized version was preferred among socially excluded individuals but not control participants. More importantly, socially excluded participants expressed a greater likelihood of buying the anthropomorphized Roomba over its non-anthropomorphized counterpart. Additionally, results replicated the finding in Study 1 showing that socially excluded participants were willing to spend more money on an anthropomorphized Roomba than the control group.

Study 3 replicated Study 2 with a more heterogeneous sample and focused on social behaviors rather than product perceptions. A similar design was used: 1) individuals wrote about a time they felt either socially included or excluded (no control group), 2) viewed either an anthropomorphized or nonanthropomorphized Roomba, and 3) responded to a series of items including whether they wanted to wait alone or with others for subsequent tasks. Results yielded a significant interaction between the two independent variables in desire for social contact. Means indicate that those made to feel excluded were more likely to prefer waiting alone when presented with an anthropomorphized version of the Roomba compared to those also made to feel excluded who were presented with a nonanthropomorphized version. Presumably, the excluded individuals were able to "fill the void" when presented a humanlike product.

In sum, we find initial evidence for the idea that perceptions of social exclusion 1) make consumers more sensitive to humanistic attributes of products, 2) influence the kinds of products they might buy, and 2) those products influence social behavior. We hope future results will further support our central argument: If social needs can be satisfied through products, consumers may not seek fulfillment through other people and, therefore, increase their risk of negatively impacting real social relationships.

Exposure to Unattainable Luxury: Boomerang Effects on Extrinsic and Materialistic Goals

EXTENDED ABSTRACT

While ample research has investigated consumers' motives to buy luxury products (e.g., Vigneron & Johnson, 2004), it is less clear whether exposure to luxury influences people's values and goals. As luxury consumption is related to materialism (e.g., Belk & Pollay, 1985), it seems obvious to assume that exposure to (images of) luxury increases materialistic and related extrinsic (Kasser, 2002) goal pursuit. Indeed, advertising exposure – which frequently displays images of luxuries – is linked to materialism (e.g., Paek & Pan, 2004); however, studies are correlational or quasi-experimental at best, precluding causal inferences. In addition, results of our pilot study show that people generally think that exposure to luxury induces materialism.

At first sight, one may expect that exposure to *unattainable* (i.e. unaffordable) luxury produces a similar outcome. A second pilot study confirmed this. However, based on goals literature, we propose that the influence of exposure to luxury is much more complex than is usually assumed.

People tend to commit to a goal that is likely to be achieved and to disengage from goals that are difficult to attain (Kruglanski et al., 2002). When the likelihood of attainment is deemed too small, one may even abandon the goal (Baumgartner & Pieters, 2008). We propose that the affordability of consumer goods serves as a signal of the likelihood that one may successfully attain one's extrinsic and material goals. Hence, we propose that exposure to attainable luxuries might strengthen the endorsement of extrinsic and materialistic goals while exposure to unattainable luxuries might decrease it.

Study 1 tests this prediction. 152 students were asked to either decorate a highly expensive villa (i.e. unattainable luxury) versus a mainstream house. Specifically, participants received a floor plan of a villa versus smaller house and sets of photos with possible interiors per room to choose from (luxurious versus common interiors). Participants placed the pictures of their choice on the floor plan. A pretest measured the attainability of the villa/mainstream house (i.e., the likelihood of living in the decorated type of home within ten years from now). As expected, participants believed that the villa would be significantly less attainable within ten years than the mainstream house.

As an additional manipulation of attainability, participants were encouraged (versus not) to imagine themselves owning the home they decorated (the imagination procedure aims to render the luxurious villa less unattainable). Overall, participants were randomly assigned to one of four conditions (type of home: expensive villa vs. mainstream house; simulation: imagination vs. no imagination). Subsequently, we measured materialism (Richins & Dawson 1992) and extrinsic goal pursuit (Aspiration Index; Kasser & Sheldon 2000).

For both dependent variables, type of home interacted significantly with simulation. In contrast to prior intuitions (cf. pilot study), participants were significantly *less* materialistic after decorating the expensive villa versus the mainstream house in the condition without explicit imagination. However, imagining (versus not) owning the villa significantly increased materialistic values, while no such effect was found with regard to the mainstream house. A fairly similar data pattern was found for extrinsic goal pursuit.

These results suggest that consumers try to cope with their inability to own the exposed luxuries by downplaying the importance of material wealth. After all, participants only indicate attaching less importance to materialistic and extrinsic values when being exposed to *unattainable* luxuries, not when the same luxuries seem less unattainable as a result of simulating owning them.

Study 2 tests this assumption more explicitly by also assessing the role of self-esteem. Rather than manipulating attainability, we now measured participants' perception of their own ability to afford the advertised products. Forty-two students either saw six print ads for moderately expensive products (to allow for variation in participants' feelings of affordability; e.g., Hugo Boss clothing) or no ads (control condition). Next, we measured extrinsic goal pursuit (like in Study 1) and self-esteem (Rosenberg 1965). After a number of unrelated tasks, participants in both conditions judged for each ad whether they could afford the advertised product. An index of perceived affordability was computed. Affordability was measured at the end of the experiment to assess whether these concerns affected self-esteem and goal pursuit without being actively cued (as in Study 1).

Both for extrinsic goal pursuit and for self-esteem, we found a significant interaction between condition and perceived affordability. Advertising exposure increased extrinsic goal pursuit and self-esteem of participants who believed they could afford the promoted luxuries, but decreased it for participants who felt they could not afford them. Finally, a mediated moderation analysis showed that self-esteem partially mediated the effect of condition and affordability on extrinsic goal pursuit.

These results raise the question whether exposure to unattainable luxuries merely causes people to *say* that materialism and extrinsic goal pursuit are less important, or whether they also *intend to act* upon this belief. Hence, study 3 examines the impact of luxury consumption on prosocial behavior in the context of a dictator game (Hoffman et al., 1994). Fifty-seven respondents were exposed to either 30 exclusive luxury pictures (e.g., private jet; unaffordable luxury condition), 30 photos depicting functional products (e.g., cal-culator; functional condition) or to no pictures (control condition). Next, all respondents evaluated different organizations and indicated their favorite charity. Subsequently, participants were asked to allo-cate €10 between themselves and their favorite good cause.

Consistent with the previous studies, the amount of money do-nated to a good cause was significantly higher after exposure to unat-tainable luxury than after exposure to functional products or in the control condition.

In sum, common intuition (cf. pilot study) suggests that *any* exposure to luxury would increase materialism. However, our re-sults show that exposure to extreme and *unattainable* luxury (e.g., through reruns of *MTV Cribs*) may decrease how important consum-ers find such luxury, and extrinsic goals, more generally. Interest-ingly, exposure to unattainable luxury may potentially even instigate prosocial behavior. To conclude, our results may contribute to the debate on advertising exposure and increased materialism.

Goal-Driven Financial Decisions:
Understanding the Role of Consumer Goals in Financial Decision Making
Chair: Gergana Y. Nenkov, Boston College, USA

Paper #1: Helping Consumers Get Out of Debt Faster: How Debt Repayment Strategies Affect Motivation to Repay Debt

Keri Kettle, University of Miami, USA
Remi Trudel, Boston University, USA
Gerald Häubl, University of Alberta, Canada

Paper #2: Can Small Victories Help Win the War? Evidence from Consumer Debt Management

David Gal, Northwestern University, USA
Blake McShane, Northwestern University, USA

Paper #3: The Influence of Debt Repayment Goals on Repayment Decisions and Perceived Progress

Linda Court Salisbury, Boston College, USA
Gergana Nenkov, Boston College, USA

Paper #4: Consequence of Motivated Goal Setting on Sequential Goals in Investment Decision Making

Cecile Cho, University of California, Riverside, USA

SESSION OVERVIEW

Reports abound throughout the media regarding a plethora of financial hardships being faced by consumers. Regardless of recent turmoil in various economic markets, a consistent factor contributing to lowered consumer financial well-being resides in the debt repayment and investment decisions consumers make individually. One underexplored question is the role that consumers' goals play in their financial decisions. The purpose of this session is to provide insight into consumers' goal-driven financial decisions and each of the four papers examines a different aspect of this question.

The first paper by Kettle, Trudel, and Häubl reports three studies that examine how debt repayment strategies influence consumers' motivation to repay debt and show that paying down debt accounts sequentially (versus simultaneously) increases the motivation of low self-control consumers, who are most likely to have debt in the first place. The second paper by Gal and McShane analyzes data from a leading U.S. debt settlement company to show that completing discrete debt management subgoals motivates overall goal attainment. These authors find that closing debt accounts early in a debt management program, regardless of the size of the debt accounts, is predictive of eliminating one's debts. The third paper by Salisbury and Nenkov presents two studies featuring US adult consumers, which examine how borrowers' future- versus present-oriented debt repayment goals interact with credit card information disclosures to influence debt repayment behavior and perception of progress toward paying off debt. They find that the effects of repayment goals on perceived progress differ from the effects on repayment behavior, even when accurate goal-related information is provided. Finally, the fourth paper by Cho offers four experiments that provide evidence that setting a minimal, conservative financial goal (vs. high goal) and achieving it leads to a spike in the level of risk taken in subsequent financial decisions due to a persistent loss frame. All four projects included in this session are at advanced stages of completion, and the working manuscripts for all four of the papers, as well as all of the cited references, are available upon request.

This symposium is a model of "appreciating diversity," and therefore embodies the theme of 2012 ACR, because the researchers featured in the session study the role of goals in financial decisions

by spanning various theoretical domains, multiple methodological approaches, and sample characteristics. Researchers will discuss lab-based experiments as well as large-scale studies with real US consumers, and actual field debt settlement data to provide insight into consumers' goal driven financial decisions and choices.

Beyond being of interest to academic researchers studying financial decision making and goal pursuit and motivation, the work presented in this session will have important implications for individual consumers repaying their debts, individual investors managing their portfolios, public policymakers, financial services firms, as well as the fiduciaries responsible for structuring financial instruments and investment options in general.

Helping Consumers Get Out of Debt Faster: How Debt Repayment Strategies Affect Motivation to Repay Debt

EXTENDED ABSTRACT

Consumers with multiple debts can choose among different strategies for paying down their debt accounts (Amar et al. 2011). In particular, they can repay their accounts sequentially (one at a time) or simultaneously (allocating the same amount to each account). We propose that paying down accounts sequentially (versus simultaneously) differentially affects the motivation of individuals with low (versus high) trait self-control.

By closing down individual accounts, a sequential strategy enhances the appearance of progress toward the long-term goal of becoming debt-free, and can thus increase goal commitment and motivation (Kivetz, Urminsky, and Zheng 2006). We predict that using a sequential strategy will increase motivation - and thus lead to people becoming debt-free sooner - but only for individuals who chronically lack self-control.

Results from three studies support this prediction. Participants began each study in debt (divided into 5 equal accounts). They earned money in a word-generation task, and had to first pay off their debt before they could keep any earnings. Participants completed 10 performance rounds; accounts were updated after each round.

In study 1, half of the participants were randomly assigned to a debt repayment strategy, and the other half chose a strategy. Low self-control individuals earned more money when paying off their debt accounts sequentially (versus simultaneously) whether they were randomly assigned to a strategy or chose it.

We tested our goal-pursuit account in study 2 by manipulating the amount that individuals earned per word. In the attainable-goal condition (in which all participants were able to get out of debt), we replicated the results of study 1. However, in the unattainable-goal condition (in which it was nearly impossible to get out of debt), debt repayment strategy did not affect the motivation of low self-control individuals.

In study 3, participants received a recommendation for either the simultaneous or sequential strategy (82% followed it). Low self-control individuals performed better when paying off their debts sequentially (versus simultaneously), and they also performed better when they followed the recommendation. Thus, the motivation of low self-control consumers was greatest when they followed the recommendation to repay accounts sequentially.

This research is the first to examine how debt repayment strategies influence consumers' motivation to repay debt. Paying down debt accounts sequentially (versus simultaneously) increases the motivation of low self-control consumers - precisely those who have difficulty achieving long-term goals (Baumeister, Vohs, and Tice 2007) and are most likely to have debt in the first place (Meier and Sprenger 2010).

REFERENCES

Amar, Moty, Dan Ariely, Shahar Ayal, Cynthia E. Cryder, Scott I. Rick (2011), "Winning the Battle but Losing the War: The Psychology of Debt Management," *Journal of Marketing Research*, 48 (Special Issue), S38–S50.

Baumeister, Roy F., Kathleen D. Vohs, and Dianne M. Tice (2007), "The Strength Model of Self-Control," *Current Directions in Psychological Science*, 16 (6), 351-355.

Kivetz, Ran, Oleg Urminsky, and Yuhuang Zheng (2006), "The Goal-Gradient Hypothesis Resurrected: Purchase Acceleration, Illusionary Goal Progress, and Customer Retention," *Journal of Marketing Research*, 43 (February), 39-58.

Meier, Stephan and Charles Sprenger, (2010), "Present-Biased Preferences and Credit Card Borrowing*," American Economic Journal: Applied Economics*, 2 (1), 193-210.

Can Small Victories Help Win the War? Evidence from Consumer Debt Management

EXTENDED ABSTRACT

Globally, consumer debt is measured in the trillions of dollars, with U.S. credit card debt alone amounting to approximately $1 trillion and with U.S. residents, on average, holding five credit cards each (Experian 2009). How best to reduce and eliminate debt is therefore an important question for consumers in a modern economy.

The popular and influential American personal finance guru Dave Ramsey advocates an approach to reducing and eliminating debt that involves paying off small debt balances before larger ones because he believes that paying off the smaller balances can motivate an individual to subsequently pay off the larger balances. Ramsey terms this approach the "snowball method," arguing that consumers need "some quick wins in order to stay pumped enough to get out of debt completely" (Ramsey 2009b,a). Ramsey is not alone in this view, with advocacy of this approach common among consumer financial advisors (Hamm 2007; Think Money, Ltd. 2009).

However, from a normative perspective, the size of the account balance consumers pay off first should not matter to their ability to reduce or eliminate their debt. Rather, consumers should focus on paying higher interest balances first regardless of the size of the account balance (after making minimum payments on all accounts to avoid penalties and surcharges). This approach is thus advocated by the U.S government.

We obtained a highly unique data set that allows us to examine this question on a time horizon measured in years with real world behavior and high stakes consequences for the individuals concerned. In particular, we obtained data from a leading U.S. debt settlement company that allow us to examine the question of whether closing accounts early in a debt management program predicts whether consumers succeed in eliminating their debts independent of the size of the closed account balances. That is, is closing a greater number of outstanding balances early in a debt repayment program predictive of debt elimination regardless of the size of the closed account balances?

Our main finding was that closing off debt accounts—independent of the dollar balances of the closed accounts—was predictive of eliminating one's debts at any point in time during participation in a debt settlement program. In fact, the fraction of debt accounts paid off appeared to be a more powerful predictor of whether or not one eliminates one's debts than the fraction of the total dollar debt paid off, despite the latter being a relatively more objective measure of progress towards the debt elimination goal. More striking still, the dollar balance of closed debt accounts was not predictive of debt elimination when accounting, nominally, for closed debt accounts.

In addition to specific implications for how different forms of goal progress affect goal pursuit, our findings make a more general contribution to research on goals by highlighting possible temporal shifts in the importance of different determinants of goal pursuit in the short run versus the long run. Specifically, whereas prior research has identified important psychological processes whereby attainment of a subgoal demotivates individuals from persisting in pursuit of their goal (Amir and Ariely 2008; Fishbach, Dhar, and Zhang 2006; Khan and Dhar 2006), our research suggests that the impact of these processes might be attenuated over a longer time horizon. Given that many important goals are pursued over long periods of time, our findings call for more research examining how psychological processes affect goal pursuit over long time horizons.

REFERENCES

Amir, On and Dan Ariely (2008), "Resting on Laurels: The Effects of Discrete Progress Markers as Subgoals on Task Performance and Preferences," *Journal of Experimental Psychology: Learning, Memory, and Cognition*, 34 (5), 1158–71.

Fishbach, Ayelet, Ravi Dhar and Ying Zhang (2006), "Subgoals as Substitutes or Complements: The Role of Goal Accessibility," *Journal of Personality and Social Psychology*, 91 (2), 232–42.

Khan, Uzma and Ravi Dhar (2006), "Licensing Effect in Consumer Choice," *Journal of Marketing Research*, 43 (May), 259–66.

Experian (2009), "Marketing Insight Snapshot," (accessed April 24, 2012), [available at http://www.experian.com/decision-analytics/ market-insight-snapshot-june09-form.html].

Ramsey, Dave (2009a), "Get out of Debt with the Debt Snowball Plan," DaveRamsey.com, (August 1), (accessed April 24, 2012), [available at http://www.daveramsey.com/article/get-out-of-debtwith-the-debt-snowball-plan].

——— (2009b), *The Total Money Makeover: A Proven Plan for Financial Fitness*. Nashville, TN: Thomas Nelson.

The Influence of Debt Repayment Goals on Repayment Decisions and Perceived Progress

EXTENDED ABSTRACT

Managing personal debt is an ongoing challenge for many consumers. Average credit card debt amongst U.S. consumers was approximately $6,600 per household in mid-2011. Managing that debt load can be difficult, and it can be very expensive – U.S. consumers paid $94 billion in credit card interest in 2009 alone (Meijer et al. 2011).

A recent study by the U.S. Federal Reserve Bank suggests that many Americans underestimate how much credit card debt they owe, with an estimated 34% gap in aggregate (Brown et al. 2011). This is likely to have adverse effects on the debt repayment goals consumers set for themselves, as well as on their actual repayment behavior. For instance, this gap in perceptions could lead consumers to underestimate the time needed to pay off their debt as well as the amount they will pay in interest, causing them to adopt present-oriented goals and spend more instead of repaying their debt, potentially incurring more debt than they can comfortably shoulder

Public policymakers encourage lenders to disclose loan cost information to enable borrowers to make more informed debt repayment decisions (e.g., the CARD Act). In the current research we examine how the presence of information about loan interest cost and payoff time interacts with consumers' repayment goals to influence debt repayment decisions and perceptions of debt repayment progress.

Two experimental studies, with 570 adult U.S. consumers, examined the effect of repayment goals and loan information on repayment decisions and perceived debt payoff progress. In both studies, participants were shown a hypothetical credit card bill and asked how much of the credit card balance they would repay. Study 1 included three experimental conditions in which we manipulated the loan payoff time information participants received on their credit card bill: 1) only loan balance, interest rate, and minimum payment required information, 2) additional information about how much time it will take to pay off the loan if the minimum required amount were repaid each month, and 3) additional information about how much time it will take to pay off the loan if an amount larger than the minimum were repaid each month. Study 2 used a similar procedure, but had seven information conditions presenting information about either the interest cost participants would incur if the minimum required or some larger amount were repaid each month, and/or loan payoff time information similar to study 1. We further measured whether borrowers had a future-oriented (i.e., pay off debt balance fast to have more money for other purposes in the future) or a present-oriented (i.e., pay the least amount possible to have more money for other purposes in the present) repayment goal. Finally, we assessed participants' repayment decisions as well as their perceived progress toward paying off the loan balance. A series of analyses were conducted to test the effects of goal type and information type, controlling for participants' income, financial knowledge, attitude toward debt, temporal orientation, and credit card repayment habits.

Results indicate that repayment goals had a robust effect on repayment amount. Participants with a future-oriented goal to pay off the balance fast tended to repay *more*, while participants with a present-oriented goal to repay the least amount possible repaid *less*. Interestingly, the negative effect of holding a present-oriented goal was larger when payoff time information was present. The loan cost information and payoff time information manipulations had little direct impact on repayment amount.

Repayment goals also influenced participants' perceived progress toward paying off their loan, and these effects were moderated by the type of information present on the credit card statement. A future-oriented goal to repay the loan balance fast had a significant positive effect on perceived progress, after controlling for repayment amount, suggesting a kind of optimism toward achieving loan payoff. This positive effect on perceived progress was further enhanced by the presence of payoff time information on the credit card bill. This suggests that, while disclosing payoff time information may not increase repayment amount (and therefore speed up loan repayment), it has the potential to increase consumers' perceptions of progress toward paying off the loan. In other words, for borrowers with a future-oriented payoff goal, providing loan payoff time information does not change goal-oriented behavior, but it does change (i.e., increase) perceptions of goal progress.

We found no significant main effects of payoff time information on perceived progress. On the other hand, the presence of loan cost information had a significant negative effect on perceived progress (after controlling for repayment amount); this was the case regardless of repayment goal type. Thus, disclosing loan cost information may lead borrowers to feel more pessimistic about making progress toward loan payoff.

Finally, a present-oriented goal to repay the least amount possible had significant effects on perceived progress, after controlling for repayment amount, but the valence of the effect varied across information conditions. Having a present-oriented goal had a significant *positive* effect on perceived progress in all conditions, except one: when participants were provided with information about the loan payoff time associated with repaying only the minimum each month, a present-oriented goal had a significant *negative* effect on perceived progress. Thus, having a present-oriented goal to pay the least amount possible *decreased* perceived loan payoff progress when time information was present and *increased* perceived progress otherwise.

Our findings regarding the effects of repayment goals and information disclosure on perceived debt repayment progress are noteworthy because past research has shown that perceptions of goal progress (even progress that is illusory and artificial) increase consumers' effort toward achieving the goal (e.g., Kivetz, Urminsky, and Zheng 2006; Nunes and Dreze 2006). We add to this literature stream by providing insight into the differential effects of having present- versus future-oriented goals and receiving time- versus money-related information on perceived goal progress.

A third follow-up study is planned, aimed at clarifying the theoretical mechanisms underlying the effects observed in studies 1 and 2. In this study participants' future- and present-oriented goals, as well as actual progress towards debt repayment, will be manipulated. Perceived progress toward goal achievement, as well and perceived feasibility and desirability of goal achievement, will be measured.

The key contributions from these studies will inform our understanding of how consumer goals interact with information disclosure to influence consumer debt repayment behavior and perception of progress toward paying off debt. These findings have important implications for consumers, public policy makers, as well as for lenders. They are particularly timely given recent legislation (e.g., CARD Act) related to the types of disclosure information that must be revealed to consumers of credit, which often involves the provision of cost- and time-related loan payoff information.

REFERENCES

Brown, Meta, Andrew Haughwout, Donghoon Lee, and Wilbert van der Klaauw (2011), "Do We KNow What We Owe? A Comparison of Borrower- and Lender-Reported Consumer Debt," *The Federal Reserve Bank of New York*, Staff Report No. 523.

Kivetz, Ran, Oleg Urminsky, and Yuhuang Zheng (2006), "The Goal-Gradient Hypothesis Resurrected: Purchase Acceleration, Illusionary Goal Progress, and Customer Retention," *Journal of Marketing Research*, 43 (February), 39-58.

Meijer, Erik, Michael A. Zabek, Scott Schuh, and Kevin Foster (2011), "The 2009 Survey of Consumer Payment Choice," *The Federal Reserve Bank of Boston*, Public Policy Discussion Paper No. 11-1.

Nunes, Joseph C. and Xavier Dreze (2006), "The Endowed Progress Effect: How Artificial Advancement Increases Effort," *Journal of Consumer Research*, 32 (4), 504–12.

Consequence of Motivated Goal Setting on Sequential Goals in Investment Decision Making

EXTENDED ABSTRACT

Imagine that you have decided to invest in the financial stocks of emerging markets. Markets have been rather volatile with much fluctuation. Given the uncertainty of the financial markets, you decide that you would be happy as long as it returns a little over what you would get from a bank deposit, and allocate your money into the conservative stocks with low risk. At the year's end you find that your portfolio has done better than the bank rates, but also finds out that many other stocks have done even better, achieving double the rate of return. For the next period, what would be the level of risk you take? Would you take on greater risk? Stay the course with the same set of stocks? Or take on less risk since you achieved your goal? Given how often decisions are made in a sequence of decision periods, surprisingly little attention has been given to understanding investment decisions and judgments within its sequential decision making context.

In this research, we examine the relationship between what we term "strategic goal setting," confirmation of the goal, and the subsequent level of risk taken, in the domain of investment decision making. More specifically, our research investigates the consequence of setting a minimal, conservative performance goal (vs. high goal) on the subsequent target setting for a risky decision when the goal is successfully obtained. Whereas individuals often set lower investment targets assuming they will be happy if only the target is met, this assumption is often unfulfilled because the reference point is no longer the initial goal but a higher, "could-have-been" performance level (Cho and Johar 2011). We predict and find that, due to the upward shifting reference standard, low-goal setters are likely to find themselves in the domain of losses, and become more risk seeking in their subsequent investment decisions. Our hypothesized process model is as follows:

Goal Level → Feedback (confirmed) → Outcome compared to higher reference point than goal → domain of losses → Risk at T2

Across four studies involving investment decisions, we asked individuals to set return goals for their investment portfolios, pick three stocks in a simulated investment task, confirm their goals (feedbacks which match the performance to their return goals), then ask them to set another goal for the next period. Respondents were induced to pick low or high goals via priming tasks (approach-avoidance orientation, delight vs. disappointment) then were told

that their investment goals were met for that period (goals confirmed for all conditions), followed by satisfaction measures, then the key measure: target goal for the next investment period. We found that the low-goal setters set target performances that were consistently higher (greater magnitude of increase) than the high-goal setters (studies 1 and 4). This pattern was observed even when the actual performance level was controlled for (studies 2 and 3).

We adopt the framework of prospect theory to conceptualize our finding (Kahneman and Tversky 1979). A central concept within prospect theory is the framing effect: individuals tend to avoid risks when perceiving an outcome as gains or exceeding a reference point, and they seek risks when an outcome is perceived as losses or performing below a reference point. In other words, when one achieves the goal one set out to achieve, or when one's targeted performance has been obtained, this should put the person in a domain of gains. Based on this model, a corresponding prediction would be that on the subsequent risk-taking decision, one would be less inclined to risk the gain already obtained (Heath, Larrick and Wu 1999). In short, confirmation of goal should lead to risk-aversion. We demonstrate that confirmation of goal leads to greater risk seeking in the subsequent decision among those who set conservative goals due to the tendency to upward compare. Because individuals tend to compare their outcome to a higher reference standard, and this upward comparison process creates a loss frame in which the low-goal setter perceives a more intense loss frame than the high-goal setter. Our finding is consistent with the literature on misprediction of future affect and more broadly, lend insight into the topic of unstable risk preferences.

REFERENCES

Cho, Cecile and Gita V. Johar (2011), "Attaining Satisfaction," *Journal of Consumer Research*, 38 (4), 622-631.

Heath, Chip, Richard P. Larrick and George Wu (1999), "Goals as Reference Points," *Cognitive Psychology*, 38, 79-109.

Kahneman, Daniel and Amos Tversky (1979), "Prospect Theory: An Analysis of Decisions under Risk," *Econometrica*, 47 (2), 263-91.

Narrative Persuasion:
Applications and Reflections on This Approach from Three Disciplines

Chairs: David Brinberg, Virginia Tech, USA
Anne Hamby, Virginia Tech, USA

Paper #1: Narrative Engagement across Media Forms and Levels of Interactivity

Rick Busselle, Washington State University, USA

Paper #2: Narratives in Cancer Prevention: A Review of a 10-Year Research Program

Matthew Kreuter, Washington University, USA

Paper #3: The Effects of Social Relationships on Narrative Persuasion

Jing Wang, University of Iowa, USA
Jennifer Edson Escalas, Vanderbilt University, USA

Paper #4: A Framework of Narrative Persuasion

Anne Hamby, Virginia Tech, USA
Kim Daniloski, University of Scranton, USA
David Brinberg, Virginia Tech, USA

SESSION OVERVIEW

The objective of this session is to gain a greater appreciation of the persuasive value of narratives. A traditional social science approach to persuasion has focused on how individuals respond to rhetoric, or argument-driven messages, such as those captured by dual-route perspective models (e.g., Petty and Cacioppo 1986). This approach is in contrast to daily practice, where individuals exist in, and readily engage with, an environment saturated with narratives.

Scholars in a number of fields recognize the persuasive value of narratives and, importantly, that narratives invoke a form of processing that is different from a traditional, argument-oriented approach. These stories (or narratives) depict events and consequences for characters, in contrast to informational and expository communication that presents reasons and arguments in favor of a particular focus. Green and Brock (2000) introduced the concept of "transportation" to the social science literature, which describes the experience of immersing in a narrative and involves processes such as emotional involvement, the generation of imagery, and suspension of disbelief.

A growing number of studies anchored in academically-oriented, consumer-related domains have demonstrated that narratives affect the attitudes and behavior of their audiences. Researchers in the consumer domain are likely to benefit from a deeper understanding of the processes involved in and the impact of narrative transportation, particularly given the wide array of consumer-oriented stimuli that use a narrative format, such as advertisements, consumer reviews, brand narratives, and WOM communications. Consumers often actively seek narratives, and routinely underestimate the persuasive impact they have on their attitudes and behaviors.

Previous work has identified a range of narrative effects that impact both health and social behaviors (Green, Strange, and Brock 2002). These studies have identified a number of relevant theoretical mechanisms (emotional and cognitive engagement, identification, reduced counter-arguing, imagery) and have established their effect on behavioral and pre-behavioral outcomes, but the causal mechanisms and relative importance of these relationships are not yet well understood (Moyer-Guse 2008). An objective of this session is to introduce consumer researchers to the as-of-yet unexplored potential of narrative persuasion. We anticipate that further research in this area is likely to make a contribution to the consumer field, given the

frequency and willingness with which people engage with narratives, the extent to which they pervade our daily environment.

The study of narratives has a long tradition within literary analysis and communication, which acknowledge that stories are central to how humans think and make choices. This topic area allows a variety of intellectual vantage points to converge, both fostering the appreciation of academic diversity and promoting scholarly work between disciplines. Buselle introduces a conceptual overview of narrative persuasion from a communications perspective, organizing the different genres and media platforms that induce narrative processing. Kreuter presents a review of 10 years of health-oriented research that applies narratives to address breast cancer. Escalas applies narratives in a consumer context, and Hamby presents a framework that integrates determinants, mediators, and moderators that have been examined in narrative research.

Narrative Engagement across
Media Forms and Levels of Interactivity

EXTENDED ABSTRACT

The recognition that telling audiences about events and characters dates back to Aristotle (Herrick 1997). However, only within the past half-century have social scientists focused on stories as tools of persuasion (Green and Brock 2000), and even more recently, explored the relations between the narrative experience and its outcomes (Busselle and Bilandzic, forthcoming). Research into communication, entertainment-education, and advertising has incorporated both theoretical and methodological elements of narrative processing and persuasion (e.g., Durkin and Wakefield 2008; Moyer-Gusé 2008). This work has been extended to the influence of narrative elements in videogame experiences (Ip 2011).

Central to narrative persuasion research is the premise that information presented in a narrative form is not only different in structure – based on characters and events rather than claims and evidence – but also produces a fundamentally different experience. Further, the nature and quality of that experience mediates the influence of the narrative on the reader, viewer or player. Specifically, the more engrossing the narrative experience the greater the narrative's influence (e.g., Green & Brock 2000; Moyer-Gusé and Nabi 2010). Currently, narrative persuasion research is challenged by competing conceptualizations of what it means to be engaged, absorbed, or transported. This challenge is complicated further by the different media forms narratives may take, such as a medical-drama program, a drama-advertisement on TV or in YouTube. These varying forms, genres and levels of interaction offer opportunities for narrative experiences that may be quite different from each other and may require different methodological and measurement tools. The focus on narrative across different media forms raises questions about the extent to which narrative experiences are similar or different depending on the nature of the message and the characteristics of the media platform.

The present paper describes a conceptual structure to organize narrative experiences across genres and media platforms based on the extent to which they approximate real life experiences. The paper reviews the theoretical and conceptual explanation used to describe and understand narrative experiences, such as mental model construction, flow experiences, and imagery production and outlines theoretically separate dimensions, such as attention, comprehension, identification, and presence (Busselle and Bilandzic 2009) and how those experiential processes may manifest across different media forms, formats and genres.

Narratives in Cancer Prevention: A Review of a 10 year Research Program

EXTENDED ABSTRACT

This presentation will summarize findings from a decade-long research program examining audience effects of personal experience narratives. The narratives studied in this research are breast cancer survivor stories collected on video from African American women and shown to other African American women without breast cancer. Outcomes of interest across a series of independent studies include beliefs, perceptions, recall, and health behaviors.

The promise and appeal of narrative lies in its familiarity as a basic mode of human interaction. People communicate with one another and learn about the world around them largely through stories. Kreuter et al. (2007) have proposed a typology of narrative application in cancer control that has four distinctive capabilities: (1) overcoming resistance; (2) facilitating information processing; (3) providing surrogate social connections; and, (4) addressing emotional and existential issues, and are applicable to outcomes across the cancer control continuum (e.g., prevention, detection, diagnosis, treatment, survivorship).

The breast cancer survivor stories were collected in St. Louis, MO. We elicited stories from 36 African American women who had been diagnosed with breast cancer and 13 family members of these women. Survivors ranged in age from 35-67, had been survivors for <1 to >23 years, and 91% were members of one of five different African American breast cancer survivor support groups in St. Louis, MO.

African American women (n = 489) ages 40 and older were recruited from low-income neighborhoods in St. Louis, MO and randomly assigned to watch the narrative or informational video. Effects on mammography use, cancer-related beliefs, recall of core content and a range of reactions were measured immediately post-exposure and at 3- and 6-month follow-up. The narrative was better liked, enhanced recall, reduced counter-arguing, increased breast cancer discussions with family and was perceived as more novel. Women who watched the narrative also reported fewer barriers to mammography, more confidence that mammograms work, and were more likely to perceive cancer as an important problem affecting African Americans. Use of mammography at six month follow-up did not differ for the narrative versus informational groups overall (49% vs. 40%), but did among women with less than a high school education (65% vs. 32%, $p < .01$), and trended in the same direction for those who had no close friends or family with breast cancer (49% vs. 31%, $p = .06$) and those who were less trusting of traditional cancer information sources (48% vs. 30%, $p = .06$). The findings suggested that narrative forms of communication may increase the effectiveness of interventions to reduce cancer health disparities, and may have particular value in certain population sub-groups (Kreuter et al. 2010).

One consistent finding across studies was the role of affect, or emotional responses to the videos. A community-based convenience sample of African American women (n = 59) used an audience response device to report the intensity of their emotional reaction while watching the video. We assessed the correspondence between video content and emotional responses, types of emotion experienced, and recall of video content. Strong emotions were more likely to correspond to contextual information about characters in the video and less likely to correspond to health content among women who watched the narrative compared to those who watched the informational video (p < .05). Both videos elicited strong emotional responses, but the type of emotion differed. Women who watched the narrative video were more likely than those who watched the informational video to report feeling attentive (41% vs. 28% respectively), inspired (54% vs. 34%) and proud (30% vs. 18%), and less likely to feel upset (8% vs. 16%) (*p* < .05). Women in the narrative group were also more likely to mention the women's personal stories than health information in open-ended recall questions. Lessons learned from this research program are discussed as well as directions for future research.

The Effects of Social Relationships on Narrative Persuasion

EXTENDED ABSTRACT

Americans feel more socially isolated than two decades ago—10% of respondents in a social science survey had no one to discuss important matters with in 1985, as opposed to 24.6% in 2004 (McPherson et.al. 2006). Socially isolated people tend to behave more aggressively, are less prosocial, and less cooperative with others (Twenge et.al. 2007). Despite a rich psychology literature on how social isolation affects people in terms of interpersonal social behaviors and physiological reactions, there is limited research on how loneliness, the subjective feeling of social isolation (Hawkley and Cacioppo 2007), affects consumers.

We examine how loneliness affects consumers' responses to narratives. Consumers encounter various forms of narratives daily. They read books, watch movies, listen to stories, and are constantly exposed to narrative marketing communications, such as advertisements (Escalas 1998). Although abundant evidence suggests that narratives can be highly persuasive through the process of narrative transportation (e.g., Green and Brock 2000), it is not clear whether lonely consumers are more or less likely to be transported into narratives.

Lonely people not only have a strong desire to form meaningful connections with other human beings, they are also more likely to create human connections with nonhuman gadgets (Epley et al. 2008). For example, lonely (vs. non-lonely) people think that a wheeled alarm clock that "runs away" has its own mind and can experience emotions. These findings suggest that lonely people might be more likely to be transported into narratives. On the other hand, stories often portray human interaction to which socially isolated individuals might not relate well. In three studies, we examine whether lonely consumers will be more or less transported into narrative contents and how such transportation affects persuasion.

The first study examines the relationship between loneliness and narrative transportation. One hundred participants read a short story taken from Chicken Soup for the College Soul. The four-page story is about a college student and a depressed customer who help cheer each other up by being considerate and caring. The story has been used in previous research to generate various levels of transportation (Wang and Calder 2006). Participants' transportation was measured by a 15-item transportation scale (Green and Brock 2000). After reading the story and responding to the transportation scale, participants also responded to the revised UCLA loneliness scale (Russell 1996). Participants' responses to the scales were summed into transportation scores ($\alpha = .84$) and loneliness scores ($\alpha = .90$). A regression analysis showed that the more lonely the participants, the more they were transported to the story ($\beta = .41$, $t = 2.65$, $p = .01$).

The second study examined whether the effect of loneliness on transportation will occur in advertisements rather than a story. Participants (n = 238) evaluated two ads. The print ad featuring a young man and woman showed a jar of Borghese Fango mud mask and a product description. The story board of a TV commercial for Folgers coffee consisted of 10 snapshots of a family enjoying the coffee during the holidays. Each participant evaluated both ads, with order counterbalanced. Participants evaluated each ad (1 = unfavorable, bad, uninteresting, poor quality; 7 = favorable, good, interesting, good quality) and responded to the ad transportation scale and the loneliness scale.

Regression analyses showed that, consistent with results of the first study, lonely participants were more likely to be transported into the print ad ($\beta = .21$, $t = 2.87$, $p < .01$). In addition, highly transported participants showed more favorable attitude toward the ad ($\beta = .06$, $t = 11.2$, $p < .001$). However, loneliness did not affect ad attitude directly.

The same set of analyses on the commercial story board revealed a different pattern. Lonely participants were less likely to be transported into the story board ($\beta = -.22$, $t = -2.84$, $p < .01$). Whereas transportation into the story board led to more favorable ad attitude ($\beta = .07$, $t = 13.37$, $p < .001$), loneliness also had a marginal effect on ad attitude ($\beta = -.01$, $t = -1.78$, $p = .08$). Mediation analyses support transportation's mediating role between loneliness and ad attitude.

Two potential explanations might account for the different patterns between print and story board. Modality may moderate feeling transported; that is, lonely people are more easily transported into print ad but less into TV commercials. This is consistent with the findings of study 1, which used a text-only medium. Alternatively, the warm family interaction in the Folger's ad was more social than the Borghese ad, making it difficult for a socially isolated individual to relate to the story. We are conducting a third study to further examine these alternative explanations using a 2 (modality: print vs. TV) × 2 (ad focus: social vs. non-social) design. Participants will again evaluate one print ad and one TV ad story board. However, some participants will see the social version of ads (featuring more people) whereas others will see the nonsocial version (featuring no human interaction). The study is underway and we will be able to present the results at ACR.

A Framework of Narrative Persuasion

EXTENDED ABSTRACT

Researchers in social psychology and related fields have studied persuasion based on rhetoric for the past 70 years, yielding a detailed understanding of factors that enhance or diminish the effectiveness of argument-driven, persuasive communications. In contrast, the study of narrative persuasion has gained momentum only within the past 15 years, and researchers are still working toward a full understanding of the factors that influence narrative persuasion and the psychological mechanisms responsible for these effects.

Researchers from a variety of disciplines such as psychology (Green and Brock 2000), education (Slater and Rouner 2002), communication (Hinyard and Kreuter 2007), advertising (Phillips and McQuarrie 2010) and marketing (Escalas 2007) have contributed to the area of narrative persuasion. The recent growth in the study of narratives from different social science orientations highlights the need for an overview of how extant research interrelates and contributes to our understanding of narrative persuasion mechanisms. We present a framework that integrates narrative persuasion research relevant to consumer behavior.

We organize this literature drawing in part from McGuire's Communication Matrix (1989), a popular theory that considers both input and output variables pertaining to the persuasive communication process. A number of studies have demonstrated that a narrative format (input) can impact a number of persuasion-related outputs; e.g., the audience's beliefs about narrative-related topics (Fazio and Marsh 2008) and behavior consistent with messages contained in a narrative (Durkin and Wakefield 2006).

More recent studies have examined mediators of this narrative effect (primary and secondary processes, as conceptualized in our model). For example, Kreuter et al. (2010) found that women who viewed a narrative video (compared with an informational video) experienced more positive and negative affect, identified more with the message source, and were more engaged. This, in turn, lead to reduced counter-arguing, which influenced the behavioral correlates of perceived barriers, cancer fatalism, and message recall.

In our framework, the initial category of "inputs" includes structural factors such as narrative format, a fact or fiction label (Green et al. 2006), and the quality of the text in terms of sequence coherence and message production elements (Kreuter et al. 2007).

After exposure to a narrative, several mediating mechanisms are evoked, including the experience of emotion (Appel and Richter 2010), production of imagery (Phillips and McQuarrie 2010), telepresence (Slater and Rouner 1996), cognitive engagement (Chang 2009) identification with the characters portrayed in the narrative (Cohen 2001). Many authors label the occurrence of these factors as "transportation" (Green and Brock 2000) or "narrative engagement" (Busselle and Bilandzik 2009).

Research indicates these initial steps involved in processing narratives lead to a second set of mental processes, such as reduced levels of counter-arguing against assertions embedded in the narrative (Moyer-Guse and Nabi 2010), increased levels of self-referencing (Escalas 2007), perceived narrative realism (Busselle and Bilandzik 2009), elevated levels of story-relevant risk perception (Moyer-Guse and Nabi 2010), and the willing suspension of disbelief such that a reader temporarily accepts the constructed story world as reality (Chang 2009).

The outcomes commonly examined include belief change, behavioral intention, enjoyment, knowledge, and attitude change. The primary and secondary processes are mediators that link the "input" factors with the "output" factors.

Many studies indicate that this sequence has several moderators. For example, need for affect moderates the relationship between transportation and outcome beliefs, such that people with higher levels of need for affect are more persuaded (Appel and Richter 2010). Expertise appears to moderate the relationship between narrative format and transportation, contingent on the context (Green 2004). Other moderators examined in the context of narrative persuasion include need for cognition (Appel and Richter 2007), transportability (Mazzocco et al. 2010), sensation seeking (Jensen, Imboden, and Ivic 2011), and persuasion knowledge (Escalas 2007).

We anticipate this framework will facilitate a systematic discussion of past research on narrative persuasion and to highlight areas in which more research is needed, working toward a more complete understanding of the factors that influence narrative persuasion and the psychological mechanisms responsible for these effects.

REFERENCES

Appel, Markus (2008), Fictional narratives cultivate just-world beliefs, *Journal of Communication*, 58(1), 62-83.

Appel, Markus and Tobias Richter (2007), Persuasive effects of fictional narratives increase over time, *Media Psychology*, 10(1),113-34.

_____ (2010), Transportation and need for affect in narrative persuasion, A mediated moderation model, *Media Psychology*, 13(2), 101-35.

Braverman, Julia (2008), Testimonials versus informational persuasive messages: The moderating effect of delivery mode and personal involvement, *Communication Research*, 35(5), 666-94.

Busselle, Rick and Helena Bilandzic (2009), Measuring narrative engagement, *Media Psychology*, 12(4), 321-47.

_____ (Forthcoming), "Narrative Persuasion," In *The Persuasion Handbook*, eds. James Dillard and Lijiang Shen, Thousand Oaks, CA: Sage.

Chang, Ching Ching (2009), "Being Hooked" By Editorial Content: The Implications for Processing Narrative Advertising, *Journal of Advertising*, 38(Spring), 21-34.

Cohen, Joel (2001), Defining identification: A theoretical look at the identification of audiences with media characters, *Mass Communication and Society*, 4(3), 245-64.

Durkin, Sarah and Melanie Wakefield (2008), Interrupting a narrative transportation experience: Program placement effects on responses to antismoking advertising, *Journal of Heath Communication*, 13(7), 667-680.

Epley, Nicholas, Scott Akalis, Adam Waytz, and John Cacioppo (2008), Creating social connection through inferential reproduction: Loneliness and perceived agency in gadgets, gods, and greyhounds, *Psychological Science*, 19(2), 114–120.

Escalas, Jennifer Edson (1998), "Advertising Narratives? What are they and how do they work?" In *Representing Consumers: Voices, Views and Visions*, ed .Barbara Stern, London: Routledge, 267-89.

_____ (2007), Self-referencing and persuasion: Narrative transportation versus analytical elaboration, *Journal of Consumer Research*, 33(March), 421-9.

Fazio, Lisa and Elizabeth Marsh (2008), Slowing presentation time increases, rather than decreases, errors learned from fictional stories, *Psychonomic Bulletin and Review*, 15(1), 180-5.

Gabriel, Shira and Ariana Young (2011), Becoming a Vampire Without Being Bitten: The Narrative Collective-Assimilation Hypothesis, *Psychological Science*, 22(8)*, 990-4.*

Garro, Cheryl and Linda Mattingly (2000), Narrative and the Cultural Construction of Illness and Healing. Berkeley and Los Angeles: University of California Press.

Green, Melanie and Timothy Brock (2000), The role of transportation in the persuasiveness of public narratives, *Journal of Personality and Social Psychology*, 79(5), 701-21.

Green, Melanie, Jennifer Garst, Timothy Brock, and Sungeun Chung (2006), Fact versus fiction labeling: Persuasion parity despite heightened scrutiny of fact, *Media Psychology*, 8(3), 267-85.

Green, Melanie, Jeffrey Strange, and Timothy Brock (2002), *Narrative impact: Social and cognitive foundations,* Mahwah, NJ: Erlbaum.

Hawkley, Louise and John Cacioppo (2007), Aging and Loneliness: Downhill Quickly? *Current Directions in Psychological Science,* 16(4), 187-91.

Herrick, James (1997), *The history and theory of rhetoric: An introduction*, Scottsdale, AZ: Gorsuch Scarisbrick.

Hinyard, Leslie, and Matthew Kreuter (2007), Using narrative communication as a tool for health behavior change: A conceptual, theoretical, and empirical overview, *Health Education and Behavior,* 34(5), 777-92.

Ip, Barry (2011), Narrative structures in computer and video games: Part 1: Context, definitions, and initial findings, *Games and Culture,* 6(2), 103-34.

Jensen, Jakob, Kristen Imboden, and Rebecca Ivic (2011), Sensation seeking and narrative transportation: High sensation seeking children's interest in reading and writing outside of school. *Scientific Studies of Reading, 15* (6), 541-558.

Kreuter, Matthew, Melanie Green, Joseph Cappella, Michael Slater, Meg Wise, Doug Storey, Eddie Clark, Daniel O'Keefe, Deborah O. Erwin, Kathleen Holmes, Leslie J. Hinyard, Thomas Houston, and Sabra Woolley (2007), Narrative Communication in Cancer Prevention and Control: A Framework to Guide Research and Application, *Annals of Behavioral Medicine,* 33(3), 221–235.

Kreuter, Matthew, Kathleen Holmes, Kassandra Alcaraz, Bindu Kalesan, Suchitra Rath, Melissa Richert, Amy McQueen, Nikki Caito, Lou Robinson, Eddie M. Clark (2010), Comparing narrative and informational videos to increase mammography in low-income African American women, *Patient education and counseling*, 81(December), S6-S14.

Mazzocco, Philip, Melanie Green, Jo Sasota, Norman Jones (2010), This Story Is Not for Everyone: Transportability and Narrative Persuasion, *Social Psychological and Personality Science,* 3(2), 361-8.

McPherson, Miller, Lynn Smith-Lovin, and Matthew Brashears (2006), Social Isolation in America: Changes in Core Discussion Networks over Two Decades, *American Sociological Review,* 71(3), 353-375.

Moyer-Gusé, Emily (2008), Toward a theory of entertainment persuasion: Explaining the persuasive effects of entertainment-education messages, *Communication Theory,* 18(3)*,* 407-25.

Moyer-Gusé, Emily and Nabi, Robin (2010). Explaining the effects of narrative in and entertainment television program: Overcoming resistance to persuasion, *Human Communication Research,* 36(January), 26-52.

Petty, Richard and John Cacioppo (1986), *Communication and persuasion: Central and peripheral routes to attitude change*: Springer.

Phillips, Barbara and Edward McQuarrie (2010), Narrative and Persuasion in Fashion Advertising, *Journal of Consumer Research,* 37(October), 368-92.

Russell, Daniel (1996), UCLA Loneliness Scale (Version 3): Reliability, Validity, and Factor Structure, *Journal of Personality Assessment,* 66(1), 20-40.

Slater, Michael and Deborah Rouner (1996), How message evaluation and source attributes may influence credibility assessment and belief change, *Journalism and Mass Communication Quarterly*, 73(4), 974-91.

_____ (2002), Entertainment-education and elaboration likelihood: Understanding the processing of narrative persuasion, *Communication Theory*, 12(2), 173-91.

Twenge, Jean, Roy Baumeister, Nathan DeWall, Natalie Ciarocco and J. Michaels Bartels (2007), Social Exclusion Decreases Prosocial Behavior, *Journal of Personality and Social Psychology,* 92(1) 56–66.

Wang, Jing and Bobby Calder (2006), Media transportation and advertising, *Journal of Consumer Research*, 33(September), 151-62.

Financial Incentives and Consumer Choice
Chair: Boris Maciejovsky, Imperial College London, UK

Paper #1: Consumer Reactance to Conditional Price Promotions
Aylin Aydinli, London Business School, UK
Marco Bertini, London Business School, UK

Paper #2: Placebo/Placui Effects of Marketing Actions: Consumers Get What They Pay/Paid For
Bram Van den Bergh, Erasmus University Rotterdam, The Netherlands
Bart de Langhe, University of Colorado, USA

Paper #3: Macroeconomic Threat Increases Preference for Mainstream Products
Stacey Finkelstein, Columbia University, USA
Kimberly Rios, University of Chicago, USA

SESSION OVERVIEW

The objective of this session is to highlight the differential effects of financial incentives on consumer behavior. The session is comprised of three papers that show the negative (Aydinli & Bertini), the time-dynamic (Van den Bergh & de Langhe), and the macroeconomic (Finkelstein & Rios) effect of financial incentives.

Aydinli & Bertini show the boundary conditions of contingent price promotions by demonstrating that these promotions may provoke reactance when consumers' perceive them as constraining their freedom. Van den Bergh & de Langhe examine the time-dynamic effects of price promotions and show that such promotions may lead to specific product efficacies. And finally, Finkelstein & Rios show that incentives in the form of a macro-economic threat that potentially restricts financial resources promotes domestic products over fair trade products.

The main contribution of the session is to demonstrate that a single marketing variable, in this case, *financial incentives*, can lead to different effects that range from positive to negative, and that vary across time, thereby affecting choice. The likely audience for this session are scholars who work on pricing, promotion, consumer choice, and behavioral decision-making. All three papers in this session have been completed and provide important implications for the design of financial incentives that may have repercussions beyond the realm of consumer behavior.

Consumer Reactance to Conditional Price Promotions

EXTENDED ABSTRACT

The marketplace is replete with promotional offers that are conditional on certain additional behaviours. Basically, the motivation of the firm is to have conditions on their promotions to ensure that certain behaviours take place in exchange for the discount. However, in this paper we point out that such conditional price promotions can sometimes backfire, resulting in more cautious decision-making by the consumer.

Building on reactance theory (Brehm 1966) and adding to the growing literature on reactance within consumer contexts (e.g. Fitzsimons 2000; Fitzsimons and Lehmann 2004; Kivetz 2005) as well as to the recent interest in the broader affective and cognitive implications of price promotions (Aydinli and Bertini 2012; Chandon et al. 2000), we propose that consumers may perceive conditional promotions as intended to influence their purchase behaviour, thereby constraining their freedom and self-determination. In order to reassert their freedom, consumers may act more cautiously in terms of their

product choices through selection of cheaper and fewer options than they otherwise would.

Consistent with our hypothesis, we found that compared to unconditional promotions, conditional promotions reduce consumers' overall spending with the firm as they shift consumer preferences towards cheaper and fewer options as well as lower their commitment with the firm. Further, the results of our experiments underscore the role of reactance in this process.

In Experiment 1, the participants were asked to choose among three types of rental options that were differently priced based on the features of the available cars. They were also asked to select several additional products and services that were charged separately from the rental fee. The experiment employed a single factor (no promotion vs. unconditional promotion vs. conditional promotion) between subjects design. The conditional promotion had the sentence "... conditional on the person picking up the car from the branch of the company at the central train station" added to the description in the unconditional promotion condition. Consistent with our hypothesis, we found that participants' total spending was lower in the conditional promotion than in the unconditional promotion ($p < .01$) and in the no promotion condition ($p < .05$). Participants in the conditional promotion preferred cheaper rental options and were willing to spend less on additional services than participants in the unconditional promotion ($p < .01$ and $p < .04$, respectively). Importantly, participants evaluated the two types of promotional offers as equally attractive, ruling out a value-based response ($F < 1$).

In Experiment 2, we looked for evidence for the role of reactance in driving the observed effects. Prior research suggests that reactance is less likely to occur when the restriction of freedom is justifiable or legitimate (Brehm 1966). Thus, we predicted that the conditional promotion would arouse less reactance if the firm's behaviour is perceived as legitimate, mitigating consumers' cautious behaviour. The type of conditional promotion we used was a channel discount. Participants were randomly assigned to the no promotion, high reactance promotion, or low reactance promotion conditions in the context of purchasing a cable TV and Internet service. Participants in the high reactance promotion condition were told that the firm was offering a discount for using an online channel to sign up for the service. In contrast, participants in the low reactance promotion condition were told that the firm was offering the discount for using an online channel because Internet subscriptions were cheaper to process, which in turn allowed them to share the savings with customers. Participants were asked to choose between two TV packages (Base Pack, Max Pack) and among three Internet connection speed (2MB, 4MB, Max Speed). They were also asked if they would add a separately charged telephone service to their chosen bundle. As expected, in the high reactance promotion condition participants' overall expenditure was lower than in the low reactance promotion condition ($p < .01$) and in the no promotion condition ($p < .05$). As such, the former preferred more basic TV packages with lower speed of Internet and were less likely to add a telephone service to their chosen bundle.

Due to difficulties in measuring situational reactance, in Experiment 3, we used a trait-level measure to provide evidence of a reactance process. We examined whether our effects are stronger among individuals who are more likely to experience reactance. We predicted that the conditional promotions would induce cautious decision making more among high reactance (vs. low reactance) consumers.

The experiment utilized a 2 (Promotion: unconditional vs. conditional) x 2 (Trait Reactance) mixed design. Participants were asked to choose among three differently priced gym membership options as well as three different contract terms available for membership. They also indicated the additional services they were most likely to purchase during their membership. The conditional promotion was framed as a referral discount with the sentence "…conditional on the new customer joining with a second person" added to the discount offer description in the unconditional promotion condition. As predicted, high reactance participants were willing to spend less on membership and additional services when the gym offered a conditional promotion than when no condition was attached to the promotion ($p < .01$). However, there was no corresponding effect among low reactance participants ($p = .73$).

Overall we demonstrate that promotions that are conditional on certain additional behaviours can sometimes backfire. Our findings delineate the situational and dispositional conditions under which conditional promotions are and are not effective, while also shedding light on the mechanism behind our effects. As such, we provide an important counterpoint to the notion that consumers respond favourably to economic incentives.

Placebo/Placui Effects Of Marketing Actions: Consumers Get What They Pay/Paid For

EXTENDED ABSTRACT

Marketing actions can produce placebo effects. For instance, the efficacy of a product may decrease when the price of a product is lowered (Shiv, Carmon, and Ariely 2005). The placebo effect results from consumers' reliance on marketing activities to form expectations about product quality (e.g., "*you get what you pay for*"). However, when consumers learn about product efficacy through first-hand experience, the relative reliance on extrinsic aspects to evaluate product quality may decrease in favor of using intrinsic cues (Levin and Gaeth 1988; Rao and Monroe 1988). In the present research, we investigate whether consumers continue to rely on information extracted from marketer controlled sources after product experience. In addition, we investigate to what extent the placebo effect persists over time. As the placebo effect is largely unconscious (Shiv et al. 2005), (un)favorable product experiences may unknowingly sustain expectancies in subsequent product experiences. Current price promotions could therefore affect product efficacy at future consumption episodes. In two 'longitudinal' experiments, we address the role of product experience in the placebo effect and investigate whether the placebo effect is a transient or persistent phenomenon.

In the first experiment, individuals' mental performance was tested after consuming a cup of coffee from an unknown brand. Consistent with the placebo effect (Shiv et al. 2005), individuals who consumed regularly priced coffee (€2, high price condition) found more words in a word search puzzle than individuals who consumed the same coffee at a price discount (€0.9, low price condition). Two weeks later, these same individuals consumed the same coffee as before and were again randomly assigned to a high (€2) and a low (€0.9) price condition, yielding 4 conditions (price$_{time1}$: high vs. low × price$_{time2}$: high vs. low). Those in the "high$_{t1}$&low$_{t2}$"condition were told that "*the product is now on sale*", whereas those in the "low$_{t1}$&high$_{t2}$" condition were told that "*the price promotion ended*". Participants in the "high$_{t1}$&high$_{t2}$" and "low$_{t1}$&low$_{t2}$" conditions were told that the price was the same as before. Individuals who consumed high priced coffee at time2 found more words in the word search puzzle than individuals who consumed low priced coffee at time2. Current marketing activities seem therefore capable of pro-

ducing *tenacious* placebo effects ("you *still* get what you pay for"): Even after product experience, individuals continue to use an extrinsic cue as a signal for product quality. Interestingly, the price of time1 exerted a significant influence on the performance at time2: Participants who consumed high priced coffee two weeks earlier performed better at time2 than participants who consumed low priced coffee two weeks earlier. We refer to this phenomenon as a *placui* effect of marketing actions (Latin for "*I have pleased*" rather than placebo, Latin for "*I shall please*"): Prior marketing activities affect current product efficacy.

In the second experiment, we aimed to uncover the mechanism behind the placui effect. Individuals' mental performance was tested after consuming an energy drink with a high price, low price or "for free". Consistent with the placebo effect, individuals who consumed a regularly priced energy drink (€2, high price condition) found more words in a word search puzzle than individuals who consumed the energy drink at a price discount (€0.69, low price condition). Importantly, individuals who believed that "*the university received the energy drink in bulk as free samples*" (€0, zero price condition) performed better than individuals in the low price condition and not significantly different from those in the high price condition (performance$_{t1}$: high$_{t1}$ ≈ zero$_{t1}$ > low$_{t1}$). This suggests that not all price promotions instigate placebo effects. One week later, the same participants consumed the same energy drink as before, after being randomly assigned to the high (€2) or low (€0.69) price condition, yielding 6 conditions (price$_{t1}$: high vs. low vs. zero × price$_{t2}$: high vs. low). Replicating experiment 1, individuals who consumed a high priced energy drink at time2 found more words in the word search puzzle than participants who consumed a low priced energy drink at time2 (i.e., a tenacious placebo effect, as individuals continue to use price as a cue for quality, even after product experience). The price at time1 also exerted a significant influence on the performance at time2 (i.e., a placui effect): Participants who consumed a high priced energy drink one week earlier performed better than participants who had consumed a low priced drink one week earlier. Most importantly, the placui effect seemed to be driven by prior marketing rather than by prior performance. Indeed, although the performance of zero$_{t1}$-individuals was similar to the performance of high$_{t1}$-individuals at time1 (performance$_{t1}$: zero$_{t1}$ ≈ high$_{t1}$ > low$_{t1}$), the performance of zero$_{t1}$-individuals was significantly lower than the performance of high$_{t1}$-individuals at time2 (performance$_{t2}$: high$_{t1}$ > low$_{t1}$ ≈ zero$_{t1}$). That is, prior marketing (i.e., price discounts), not prior performance, instigates the placui effect.

Across experiments, we obtain evidence for three variations on the placebo effect: 1) a *regular* placebo effect (the effect of price$_{t1}$ on performance$_{t1}$); 2) a *tenacious* placebo effect (the effect of price$_{t2}$ on performance$_{t2}$); and 3) a *placui* effect (the effect of price$_{t1}$ on performance$_{t2}$). The tenacious placebo effect suggests that current marketing activities may at times overrule expectations based on prior experience. The placui effect suggests that product performance is not only affected by current marketing actions, but by prior marketing activities as well. Therefore, we can conclude that consumers not only get what they *pay* for (placebo effect), but also that they get what they *paid* for (placui effect).

Macroeconomic Threat Increases Preference for Mainstream Products

EXTENDED ABSTRACT

Previous research has explored the role of individual differences in consumer ethnocentrism (Shimp & Sharma, 1987; Shimp et al, 1995; Watson & Wright, 2000) and sensitivity to value-based claims

(Shuldt, Muller, & Schwarz, 2011) to explain preferences for mainstream and fair trade options, respectively. In the present research, we examine the role of intergroup threat in people's preferences for mainstream relative to fair trade products. Intergroup threat can take several different forms (for reviews, see Riek, Mania, & Gaertner, 2006; Stephan, Ybarra, & Morrison, 2009). These forms include realistic threats to a group's power, material resources, and safety (Maddux, Cuddy, Galinsky, & Polifroni, 2008; Morrison & Ybarra, 2008), symbolic threats to a group's values and way of life (Morrison & Ybarra, 2009; Pereira, Vala, & Leyens, 2009), and social identity threats to a group's reputation (Ellemers, Spears, & Doosje, 2002) or morality (Cameron, Duck, Terry, & Lalonde, 2005). Here, we focus on a particular form of realistic threat that we refer to as *macroeconomic threat* – threat to a group's economic position and resources. We do so because macroeconomic threat is especially relevant to evaluations of material goods and products. Broadly speaking, macroeconomic threat is an important contextual variable to study because the state of the economy is constantly in flux. As such, understanding how consumer's attitudes, preferences, and behaviors shift as a function of changing economic times is crucial.

Under conditions of realistic threat, desirable material resources are seen as scarce, and people will take steps to assert the power and status of their own group over other groups (Levine & Campbell, 1972). Recent research has begun to investigate the specific effects of macroeconomic threat. This research attests that macroeconomic threat activates attempts to restore and maintain the ingroup's equality relative to outgroups (Butz & Yogeeswaran, 2011).

Although realistic (e.g., macroeconomic) threat has been shown to increase intergroup biases like prejudice, much less is known about other effects of such threat. In the context of macroeconomic threat, one possible effect could be differential evaluations of material resources that benefit the ingroup versus outgroups. Specifically, a threat to the macroeconomic climate may lead people to choose products that are made domestically and cater to the masses ("mainstream products") over products that are made internationally and promote global social justice ("fair trade products"). This preference for domestic products would reflect a desire to safeguard the national economy against threat.

We conducted two studies to test the role of macroeconomic threat in preferences for mainstream and fair trade products. To explore the unique impact of macro-economic threat on preferences for mainstream products, we compared participants who read an article about the instability of the current macroeconomic climate to those who read a threatening article not related to the economy (i.e., an article about global warming) and those who read a neutral article (see Butz & Yogeeswaran, 2011 for this manipulation of macro-economic threat). Next, participants evaluated a series of mainstream and fair trade products (e.g., Tazo Tea versus Zhena's Gypsy Tea). The mainstream and fair-trade products were pre-tested to ensure that they were equally desirable and attractive to our subject population with the only difference being how common/mainstream the products were viewed by our subject population. We predicted and found that compared to those who read the neutral article (control condition) or those who read the threatening article about the environment (non-macroeconomic threat condition), those who read about a threatening macroeconomic climate evaluated mainstream products more favorably. Importantly, this effect was not driven by differences in affect after reading the threatening articles. Interestingly, participants' evaluations of fair trade products did not shift as a function of which article they read (macroeconomic threat vs. environmental threat vs. control), possibly because participants might have experienced social desirability concerns that prevented them from derogating products that are marketed in such an inclusive way. In study 2, we had participants choose between earning a mainstream or fair-trade product for compensation. By having participants choose which product they would like, versus evaluating both products, we attempted to alleviate social desirability concerns.

In study 2, participants read an essay about either the instability of the macroeconomic climate or a control topic, prior to choosing a product as compensation for taking place in the study. As compensation, participants chose between earning a $10 gift certificate for Hickory Farms (mainstream option) or Global Exchange (fair-trade option). Pre-testing indicated both gift certificates were equally desirable and that consumers inferred they could get a similar value for their money at both websites; the only difference was that one option (Hickory Farms) was perceived to be a more mainstream brand than the fair-trade option (Global Exchange). After indicating which product they wanted to consume, participants completed the Social Dominance Orientation (SDO; Pratto et al., 1994) scale as a measure of their support for inequality and hierarchy in society. We found that macroeconomic threat increased consumers' preferences for mainstream products. We also predicted that this effect was strongest among people high in SDO, who are especially sensitive and responsive to threats to their group's position.

Two studies demonstrate that perceived macro-economic threat impacts preferences for mainstream options. Specifically, those who feel their economic livelihood is threatened shift towards preferring mainstream options. These studies have implications for marketers of mainstream (fair trade) products, who could heighten (decrease) consumers' sense of economic instability to boost sales of their products.

CONCLUSION

This session will further the conference's mission of appreciating diversity by providing a forum that discusses how a single marketing variable, in this case, *financial incentives*, can lead to entirely different effects that range from positive to negative, and that vary across time, thereby affecting choice.

Counterintuitive Effects of Mood, Environmental Cues, and Lay-Beliefs in Food Consumption Contexts

Chair: Rajagopal Raghunathan (UT, Austin; eclipse.raj@gmail.com)

Paper #1: How Sadness Signals Danger of Over-indulgence

Anthony Salerno, University of Miami, USA
Juliano Laran, University of Miami, USA
Chris Janiszewski, University of Florida, USA

Paper #2: Reducing Eating Motivation by Intensifying Prior Temptations

Cara de Boer, University of Leuven, Belgium
Siegfried Dewitte, University of Leuven, Belgium

Paper #3: Encouraging Ideal Behavior by Imagining Luxury Consumption

Keith Wilcox, Babson College, USA
Henrik Hagtvedt, Boston College, USA
Bruno Kocher, HEC Paris, France

Paper #4: The Unhealthy = Filling Intuition

Rajagopal Raghunathan, University of Texas at Austin, USA
Jacob A. Suher, University of Texas at Austin, USA

SESSION OVERVIEW

Explorations into the various influences that promote or mitigate consumption of unhealthy food has yielded important, and sometimes counter-intuitive, theoretical insights. For instance, we now know that consumers often "eat with their eyes" rather than with their stomachs; that is, they stop eating when their plate is empty rather than when they feel full (Wansink 2007). We also know that obesity can be an epidemic and spread like a disease (Christakis and Fowler 2007).

For those interested in regulating their food consumption, at least three major lessons have emerged. The first lesson is that we should watch out for moments in which we are vulnerable to over-consumption of unhealthy food. Findings reveal that we have a predilection for such food when we are feeling sad or when our ego is depleted. The second lesson is that we should stay away from tempting stimuli whenever possible: avoidance is the best policy (Hoch and Loewenstein 1991). The third lesson is that we should watch out for sub-conscious influences that steer us toward unhealthy food. Raghunathan et al. (2006) show that most of us aren't even aware of the influence of the unhealthy = tasty intuition—which steers us toward unhealthy food when we want something tasty—on our food choices.

The set of four papers in this special session report findings that challenge each of these three themes from past research. The first paper, by Salerno, Laran and Janiszewski, suggests that, although sadness or the presence of indulgent environmental cues may individually promote unhealthy eating, together, they steer people toward healthy choices. In their first study, the authors show that the tendency to consume healthy food is higher when an indulgence prime is combined with sadness, but not when it is combined with anger. The next two studies provide evidence for the proposed underlying mechanism: sadness cues increase vigilance against danger of over-indulgence.

The second paper, by Boer and Dewitte, suggests that people are sometimes more likely to choose healthy food when temptation levels are more (vs. less) intense. In study 1, the authors use construal level to manipulate intensity of temptations. In studies 2 and 3, they use hot vs. cold imagination to do the same. Across all three studies and across various measures of temptations (including amount

of saliva secreted), the authors find evidence for their thesis: that the greater the temptation, the greater the tendency to resist consumption of tempting food.

The third paper, by Wilcox, Hagtvedt, and Kocher, explores the influence of luxury primes on eating. At first blush, one may expect the influence of luxury primes to be similar to that of the presence of indulgent environmental cues. However, these authors find that luxury primes actually have the opposite effect: they steer people toward healthy (vs. unhealthy) choices. Studies 1 and 2 establish the basic effect, while studies 3 and 4 document evidence for the proposed mediating mechanism. Specifically, these studies document evidence that exposure to luxury primes results in lower indulgence of food because of a reduction in discrepancy between the actual and ideal selves.

The final paper, by Raghunathan and Suher, explores the influence of the unhealthy = filling intuition. They find that people infer unhealthy food to be more filling and, therefore, feel that they can go longer without eating if they have just consumed less (vs. more) healthy food. The first study uses the IAT procedure to document that people implicitly subscribe to the unhealthy = filling intuition. Study 2 provides evidence that subscription to the intuition leads people to rate a food item portrayed as less (vs. more) healthy as more filling. The study also shows that people feel that they would need to consume less of an unhealthy (vs. healthy) item to stay away from getting hungry for the same period of time. A study in progress aims to show that actual consumption of unhealthy (vs. healthy) food lowers hunger levels to a greater extent.

Together, these papers make a compelling case for how the lessons we appear to have learned from past research must be applied with caution. Specifically, although it may generally be a good idea to watch out for the effect of sadness on the tendency to indulge, it turns out that this may not always be the case. Those feeling sad may actually be quite "safe" when surrounded by indulgent cues. Similarly, although it may generally be a good idea to avoid being tempted, it turns out that intense temptations can actually stimulate an even stronger self-control mechanism such that we are more capable of avoiding temptations when we are more (vs. less) intensely tempted. There is another reason why indulgent cues may lead to lower consumption of indulgent food: they lower the discrepancy between actual and ideal selves. Finally, while many lay-beliefs may have a detrimental effect on food consumption, it turns out that the unhealthy = filling intuition may actually have a beneficial effect. Those who subscribe to this intuition feel that they can go for longer without consuming food when they have just consumed less (vs. more) healthy food.

Researchers interested in the topic of food and obesity, as well as those interested in the topic of self-control are our primary audience. However, we expect the session to be of general interest as well, given the breadth of theoretical constructs covered.

The proposal contributes to the theme of diversity by bringing together various theoretical perspectives—from motivational and cognitive to perceptual—together to shed light on a topic (food consumption) of universal interest and appeal.

How Sadness Signals Danger of Over-indulgence

EXTENDED ABSTRACT

The act of indulging can be a precarious experience for many consumers. Oftentimes, the margin for error is small in terms of exercising self-control and indulging in moderation versus experiencing self-control failure and over-indulging. This balancing act is complicated by the fact that consumers can be led to indulge by factors such as indulgent environmental cues (Geyskens et al. 2008; Laran and Janiszewski 2009) and the experience of negative emotion (Garg, Wansink, and Inman 2007; Gross 1998). Because indulgent food consumption represents a self-control dilemma, even an initial indulgent act by consumers can be perceived as a complete self-control failure, resulting in excessive indulgence (Cochran and Tesser 1996; Polivy and Herman 1985). This risk of over-indulgence is a concern for many consumers, as it can lead to maladaptive consequences such as weight gain and obesity (Wang and Beydoun 2007). Our current research investigates how this potential risk of over-indulgence is ironically what causes indulgent environmental cues and sadness, two factors that have been shown to increase indulgent consumption in isolation, to result in increased healthy consumption when experienced concurrently. We find that this effect occurs because sadness exerts an informational function on consumers' goal-directed behaviors. Where an indulgent cue would normally signal to indulge, we find that sadness increases the sensitivity for harm to occur and signals the risk of over-indulgence. This perceived risk of over-indulgence leads consumers to the seeking of protection in the form of virtuous consumption. As a result, this protective function of sadness, in the presence of an indulgence goal, allows consumers to better regulate their behavior and ultimately aid in consumers' pursuit of wellbeing.

In study 1, we tested our proposed effect and found that virtuous consumption only occurs when an indulgence prime is combined with sadness and not other negative emotions such as anger. Participants were randomly assigned into either an indulgence or neutral prime in combination with the induction of either anger or sadness. The priming task had participants unscramble sentences, where each sentence contained one word that was related to either indulgence or a neutral construct. Then participants read and responded to a hypothetical scenario that either evoked anger or sadness. Lastly, participants completed a purportedly unrelated food preference task. In this task, participants rated the desirability of 20 equally liked foods, half of which were perceived as healthy and the other half as indulgent but unhealthy. In the neutral prime groups, angry and sad participants were both significantly more likely to prefer tasty food to healthy food, a finding consistent with emotion regulation research (Andrade and Cohen 2007). More importantly, within the indulgence prime, we found that only participants experiencing sadness were significantly more likely to prefer healthy over tasty foods, showing that other emotions do not trigger the same sense of danger towards over-indulgence that sadness does.

In study 2, we established process evidence and found that the virtuous consumption observed within the indulgence and sadness combination is driven by an increased sense of danger towards over-indulgence. We also tested whether this sense of danger is specific to cues that signal to indulge or if it applies to other environmental cues such as exercising self-control. If the threat of over-indulgence is also present with cues signaling self-control, this should lead to increased danger-related cognitions and decreased indulgent consumption. Study 2 used the same sentence unscrambling task as study 1 to create indulgence, self-control, or neutral priming groups in combi-

nation with the induction of no emotion or sadness. Mediation was assessed using a scrambled word task previously shown to be an implicit measure of mental construct accessibility (Arndt et al. 2007). Participants solved 25 incomplete words in total (e.g., "w_r_", for which the solution is "word"), where six words had the potential to be either neutral or danger-related constructs (e.g., "_anger" for which the solution is "ranger" or "danger"). Participants completed the same food preference task from study 1. While both self-control and indulgence priming groups experiencing sadness displayed an increased desirability for healthy foods, only the indulgence and sadness condition constructed a significantly greater number of danger-related words and indicated a significantly lower preference for tasty foods.

In study 3, we investigated whether the sense of danger observed within the indulgence and sadness combination becomes stronger as the initial cues to indulge strengthen. Research in the area of priming and goal pursuit has shown that stronger priming effects can lead to stronger motivated behavior (Dijksterhuis and van Knippenberg 1998). Using the same manipulations from study 2, participants were assigned to either a neutral, indulgence, or strong indulgence prime and then induced to feel sadness or no emotion. The strong indulgence prime required that participants completed an additional task of viewing pictures of indulgent foods and clicking on the foods they liked most (Geyskens et al. 2008). Participants were then asked to choose between two gift card options, one being a virtuous "grocery store gift card" and the other being an indulgent "trendy restaurant gift card". We found evidence of an amplified indulgence prime, where participants in the no emotion groups were more likely to select the trendy restaurant as the indulgence prime became stronger. More importantly, we found that the people experiencing sadness in these same indulgence primes were significantly more likely to choose the virtuous grocery store as the indulgence cues became stronger.

Reducing Eating Motivation by Intensifying Prior Temptations

EXTENDED ABSTRACT

Nowadays, a common practice at schools or at home is to restrict physical access to temptations, such as candys, potato chips and soft drinks. But the short term success that this protective, but artificial, environment entails may not lead to long term success (e.g. Fisher & Birch, 1999). When children leave home or school, they enter an environment of easily accessible temptations . In this research, we explore how exposure to temptations can in some circumstances reduce consumption in a durable way (e.g. Fischbach et al. 2003, Geyskens et al 2008, Kroese et al 2009).

Past research has shown that behavioral conflict is associated with self-control failure (e.g. Boon et al. 1998; Meltcafe & Mischel 1999). However, other research has illustrated the involvement of behavioral conflict in the activation of brain areas associated with enhanced self-regulation (Bush, 2001), which, in turn, might induce behavioral change (e.g. Miller and Cohen, 2001). In line with this, it has been shown that exposure to temptations in situations where the consumer cannot succumb, reduces free consumption of similar temptations in subsequent situations (Geyskens, Dewitte, Pandelaere, & Warlop 2008; Dewitte, Bruyneel, & Geyskens 2009). Based on cognitive control theory, we suggest that the process underlying this behavioral change is the spontaneous and durable change in incentive value of the temptation (see Russo et al 1996) . Thus, the primary contribution of this paper is to explore if alterations in the incentive value to consume (e.g. Russo, Medvec and Meloy 1996) are a plausible process underlying behavioral change. We also test our underlying assumption that the exposure-induced behavioral change (Geyskens et al. 2008) replicates in pre-adolescent children (aged 8-11).

We build on Michel's (1970) delay of gratification paradigm to create a situation where children are exposed to temptation but simultaneously autonomously decide not to consume, with a view to obtaining a larger reward. In study 1, we look at the effects of this exposure on behavior. In study 2, we demonstrate the importance of behavioral conflict during exposure for the effect to occur and the role of changes in the incentive value to consume, as measured by saliva and self-reported attitudes . The secondary contribution of this paper is to shed some light on the emergence of the substantial gender differences in eating behavior and the processes governing it (e.g. Cooke & Wardle 2005; Wansink, Cheney and Chan 2003). For that reason, we include boys and explore to what extent their behavior and the underlying processes can be distinguished from that of girls.

In study 1, we designed an earning game where pre-adolescents were repeatedly asked to choose between having one candy/marble now, or earn three candies/marbles later. We boosted the manipulation power by repeating the exposure on four consecutive days based on cognitive literature suggesting that high frequencies of behavioral conflicts enhances people's ability to deal with behavioral conflict (Logan and Zbrodoff, 1979). By tripling the reward, we made sure children would chose to delay. On the fifth day, we measured self-regulation through consumption of candies (Schachter, Goldman and Gordon 1986). We expected that those who had been in the candy condition would consume less than in the marble condition. Indeed, girls consumed less in the candy condition relative to the control condition. For boys, consumption did not differ between the candy and the control condition. Across gender, there was no difference between girls and boys in the candy condition. In the control condition, girls consumed more relative to boys.

Our first aim for Study 2 was to assess changes in the incentive value to consume in response to behavioral conflict. For this, we used an explicit, self-report measure and, to reduce possible demand effects, a saliva measure. Salivary response is a preconsummatory, physiological and uncontrollable response to food palatability and related to the motivation to acquire food. Second, to demonstrate the importance of behavioral conflict in the pre-exposure effect, we added a condition, where we exposed participants to temptation but suppressed behavioral conflict. Specifically, we created two instruction sets for the delay of gratification procedure. In the hot imaginary condition, we intensified the appetitive aspects of the candy and thereby boosted behavioral conflict by directing participants' attention to the hot features of the candy. In the cool imaginary condition in contrast, we reduced the intensity of the temptation, and thereby the behavioral conflict, by emphasizing the non-tempting, cool aspects of the candy. For the control condition, we used two different experimental versions. Both were designed to let participants do a similar task without exposure to actionable food temptations and without ideation instructions. As none of the analyses yielded differences between these two versions of the control condition, they were merged into one condition in the remainder of the paper. Findings suggest that for girls, salivary flow after delay decreases in the hot imagination condition relative to the cool imagination condition. A similar pattern can be observed between the hot imagination condition and control condition, but this difference did not reach statistical significance. Likewise, no differences in salivation were found between the cool imagination condition and the control condition. A different pattern emerged for boys: they salivate more in the hot

imagination condition and the cool imagination condition (the two condition with exposure to temptation) than in the control condition (no exposure to temptation). The two exposure conditions did not differ. Viewed from a different angle, boys salivate more relative to girls in the hot imagination condition, but not in the cool imagination or control condition, illustrating a profound gender difference when temptation intensity is increased during pre-exposure. For the self-report measure the pattern was consistent with that of saliva for girls: They considered the candy to be less tasty in the hot imagination condition relative to the cool imagination condition and the no imagination condition. Boys did not evaluate the tastiness differently between the hot imagination, the cool imagination and the control condition. Again in line with the results on saliva, girls found the chosen candy less tasty than boys in the hot imagination condition. No other gender differences were found in the cool imagination condition and the control condition.

In line with our expectations, we show that a boost of behavioral conflict during past exposure without consumption reduces pre-adolescents consumption over a time span. In addition, our findings suggest that this is driven by a reduced physical and psychological incentive to consume. Moreover, we show that it is not necessarily exposure to temptations in itself, but behavioral conflict that triggers behavioral adaptation processes. However, we find this only for girls. Further research needs to investigate gender differences in food regulation and how this process might lead to hyperopic behavior in the food domain.

REFERENCES

Cooke, L.J., Wardle, J. (2005). Age and Gender Differences in Children's Food Preferences. *British Journal of Nutrition (2005), 93, 741–746.*

Dewitte, S., Bruyneel, S.D., & Geyskens, K. (2009). Self-regulation Enhances Self-regulation in Subsequent Consumer Decisions Involving Similar Response Conflicts. *Journal of Consumer Research, 36, 394-405.*

Fischer, J.O. & Birch, L.L. (1999). Restricting Access to Foods and Children's Eating. *Appetite, 32, 405-419.*

Fishbach, A., Friedman, R. S., & Kruglanski, A. W. (2003). Leading Us Not Unto Temptation: Momentary Allurements Elicit Overriding Goal Activation. *Journal of Personality and Social Psychology, 84, 296–309.*

Fischbach, A., Trope, Y. (2005). The Substitutability of External Control and Self-control, *41 (3), 256-270.*

Geyskens, K., Dewitte S., Pandelaere, M., Warlop, L. (2008). Tempt Me Just a Little Bit More: The Effect of Prior Food Temptations Actionability on Goal Activation and Consumption. *Journal of Consumer Research, 35 (12), 600-610.*

Logan, G.D. & Zbrodoff, N.J. (1979). When it Helps to be Misled: Facilitative Effects of Increasing The Frequency of Conflicting Stimuli in a Stroop-like Task. *Memory and Cognition, 7 (3) , 166-174.*

Miller, E.K. & Cohen, J.D. (2001). An Integrative Theory of Prefrontal Cortex Function. *Annual Review of Neuroscience, 24, 167-202.*

Mischel, W. & Ebbesen, E. B.(1970). Attention in Delay of Gratification. *Journal of Personality and Social Psychology, Vol 16(2), 329-337.*

Meltcafe, J. & Mischel, W. (1999). A Hot/Cool system Analysis of Delay of Gratification: Dynamics of Willpower. *Psychological Review, 106 (1), 3-19.*

Russo, J.E., Medvec, V.H., Meloy, M.G. (1996). The Distortion of Information during Decisions. *Organizational Behavior and Decision , 66 (1), 102-110.*

Schachter, S. , Goldman; R., Gordon, A. (1968). Effects of Fear, Food Deprivation and Obesity On Eating, *Journal of Personality and Social Psychology, 10, pp. 91–97*

Wansink, B., Cheney M.M., Chan N. (2003). Exploring comfort food preferences across age and gender. *Physiology & Behavior, 79, 739– 747.*

Encouraging Ideal Behavior by Imagining Luxury Consumption

EXTENDED ABSTRACT

People maintain a set of traits that they ideally would like to possess, such as wealth, good health and physical fitness. This idealized version of the self, representing people's hopes and aspirations, serves as a key source of motivation (Higgins 1987). For example, many people ideally would like to maintain a thin physique. In order to achieve or maintain this ideal, they may eat lighter meals, choose healthier foods and avoid behaviors that would create a discrepancy between their actual state (i.e., the actual self) and ideal state (i.e., the ideal self).

Much of the previous research on the ideal self has focused on the negative effects of ideal self discrepancies on behavior. It is generally assumed that making people aware of ideal self discrepancies results in negative emotions, antisocial behavior and less motivation (Strauman and Higgins 1987). Ways to reduce ideal self discrepancies and encourage ideal behavior has been largely unexplored.

In this research, we explore the relationship between luxury consumption and the ideal self. We introduce luxury consumption as one mechanism for reducing ideal self discrepancies to encourage behavior consistent with the ideal self. Specifically, we show that, because luxury products are linked to people's hopes and aspirations, imagining the consumption of luxury products increases the perception that the actual self is aligned with the ideal self. This leads people to subsequently engage in behaviors that are consistent with the ideal self (e.g., making healthier food choices). Additionally, we demonstrate that this effect is moderated by public self-consciousness. Public self-consciousness increases people's attention to discrepancies between their actual and ideal self (Scheier 1976). Thus, we show that making people publicly self-conscious while imagining luxury consumption leads them to subsequently engage in behaviors that are more inconsistent with the ideal self.

In study 1, participants were randomly assigned to one of three conditions. In the luxury condition, participants chose their favorite brand from a list of ten luxury brands (e.g., Louis Vuitton, Gucci) before writing about the experience of consuming a product by the selected brand. In the everyday condition, participants were asked to choose their favorite everyday brand (e.g., American Eagle, The Gap) before writing about the experience of consuming a product by the selected brand. In the control condition, participants were asked to choose their favorite luxury brand before writing about their typical day. Afterwards, all participants were given an unrelated study examining food choices. Participants in the luxury condition were more likely to make a healthier choice than those in the everyday and control conditions.

In study 2, participants were randomly assigned to the same consumption conditions as study 1. Afterwards, they were administered an unsolvable anagram task purportedly as a short-test of their verbal abilities. Consistent with the results of study 1, participants

in the luxury condition persisted longer at the task than those in the everyday or control conditions.

In study 3, we investigated the moderating effect of public self-consciousness. In the low self-consciousness conditions, participants wrote about consuming a luxury or everyday brand using the same procedure as prior studies. In the high self-consciousness conditions, participants also wrote about the experience of consuming a luxury or everyday brand, but were encouraged to write about the experience of consuming the product in public. Participants were then given two unrelated studies on food consumption and charity involvement. Participants in the low self-consciousness conditions were more likely to make a healthy choice and more willing to donate their time to charity in the luxury condition than in the everyday condition. Additionally, participants in the high self-consciousness luxury condition were less likely to make a healthy choice and less willing to donate their time to charity compared to those in the low self-consciousness luxury condition. These results were mediated by public self-consciousness.

In study 4, we examined the effect of luxury consumption on ideal self discrepancies. Participants were assigned to the same writing conditions from study 3. Afterwards, they were administrated the Integrated Self Discrepancy Index (Hardin and Lakin 2009), which is as a measure of ideal self discrepancies. As expected, in the low self-consciousness conditions, participants who wrote about luxury indicated that there was less of a discrepancy between their actual and ideal self in the luxury condition than in the everyday condition. Participants in the high self-consciousness luxury condition indicated that there was a greater ideal self discrepancy compared to those in the low self-consciousness luxury condition.

Although previous research has focused on the negative effects of ideal self discrepancies, this current research demonstrates the positive effects of reducing ideal self discrepancies on behavior. Specifically, we show that reducing ideal self discrepancies by imagining luxury consumption encourages healthier food choices, greater motivation and more altruistic behavior. Thus, an understanding of ways to tap into the ideal self is of substantial importance for understanding consumer behaviour at the individual level, as well as broader issues like the U.S. obesity epidemic.

The Unhealthy = Filling Intuition" (Rajagopal Raghunathan and Jacob Suher)

EXTENDED ABSTRACT

An important theme to emerge from research on decision-making is that we are often unaware of the forces that shape our judgments and choices. In the context of food, for example, most of us are unaware of the influence of the unhealthy = tasty intuition on our enjoyment and choices of food. In the present research, we investigate the influence of a related intuition, the "Unhealthy = Filling" intuition on food choice. Interestingly, unlike the unhealthy = tasty intuition, which steers consumers toward unhealthy food, and therefore appears to have a detrimental influence, we report findings which suggest that the unhealthy = filling intuition may actually have a beneficial impact on food choices. Specifically, because people consider unhealthy food to be more filling, we find that people feel that they can go longer without consuming any additional food if they feel that they have consumed unhealthy (vs. healthy) food. Given that the primary cause for obesity is over-consumption of food, this suggests that people may be better off when they believe that they have just consumed unhealthy (vs. healthy) food.

We report results from two studies below. Our first study uses the implicit association test (IAT) to establish that people implicitly assume an inverse relationship between healthiness and fillingness. The second experiment confirms our prediction that less (vs. more) healthy food is: (1) inferred to be less filling and (2) participants feel they can go longer without feeling hungry if they have just consumed less (vs. more) healthy food. We obtained these patterns regardless of explicitly reported belief in the unhealthy = filling intuition, suggesting that, like the unhealthy = tasty intuition, the influence of the unhealthy = filling intuition is also implicit.

The objective of the first study was to assess whether people implicitly subscribe to the unhealthy = filling intuition. Using standard IAT procedure, participants were asked to categorize relevant stimuli into categories that were either congruent with the intuition, or incongruent with it. A second condition was created to show that unhealthy food is associated with filling rather than with nourishing or sustaining concepts. In this condition, participants categorized stimuli into categories that were congruent and incongruent with an unhealthy = nourishing intuition. Findings revealed support for implicit belief in the unhealthy = filling intuition, but not the unhealthy = nourishing intuition. Specifically, response latencies were smaller when participants categorized stimuli into categories that were congruent (vs. incongruent) with the unhealthy = filling intuition. In contrast, response latencies were larger when participants categorized stimuli that were congruent (vs. incongruent) with the unhealthy = nourishing intuition. These results show that people implicitly believe that unhealthy food is more filling; even as they implicitly believe that unhealthy food is less sustaining or nourishing.

The second study was a controlled lab experiment in which we asked participants to compare healthy and unhealthy versions of the same food item on dimension of healthiness, tastiness and fillingness. We also ask participants to tell us how much of the healthy and unhealthy versions of the food they would have to eat to feel full for a set period of time. Finally, we asked participants to report how strongly they believed in the unhealthy = filling intuition, using a 1 – 7 scale. Two main findings emerged from this study. First, we found that the healthier a food item is perceived to be, the lower its inferred fillingness. This relationship held regardless of explicitness of belief in the unhealthy = filling intuition, conceptually replicating the IAT results in suggesting that subscription to the intuition is implicit. Second, participants reported that they would need to consume a smaller quantity of the unhealthy (vs. healthy) item in order to not get hungry for a set period of time.

In a proposed third study, which is in progress, we will observe the influence of perceived unhealthiness on actual consumption levels. Participants will be given either a healthy snack or a less healthy version of the same snack in compensation for participating in the experiment. In reality, the snack will be the same across the two conditions. At the end of the experiment, we will measure the amount of the snack consumed, and the extent of hunger reported while leaving the experiment. We expect to find the following pattern of results: controlling for the actual amount of snack consumed, and other relevant variables (such as gender, how hungry they were when coming into the experiment, and BMI), those led to believe that the snack was healthy will report feeling hungrier and will also report a desire to eat sooner than those led to believe that the snack was unhealthy. We expect this pattern to be particularly pronounced among those who report stronger explicit belief in the unhealthy = filling intuition.

Taken together, these studies show that people implicitly subscribe to the unhealthy = filling intuition, and that, unlike the unhealthy = tasty intuition, this intuition has a beneficial impact on food consumption, at least from a caloric standpoint.

Online Social Networks:
Why Do We Use Online Social Networks and How Do They Affect Us?
Chair: Eva Buechel, University of Miami, USA

Paper #1: Need Satisfaction from Interacting with People Versus Content: The Roles of Motivational Orientation and Identification with Social Media Groups

Donna L. Hoffman, UC Riverside, USA

Thomas P. Novak, UC Riverside, USA

Paper #2: Facebook Therapy? Why People Share Self-Relevant Content Online

Eva Buechel, University of Miami, USA

Jonah Berger, Wharton, USA

Paper #3: Are Close Friends the Enemy? Online Social Networks, Narcissism and Self-Control

Keith Wilcox, Babson College, USA

Andrew Stephen, University of Pittsburgh, USA

Paper #4: The Facebook Effect: Are Judgments Influenced by the Knowledge That Others Are Also Evaluating?

Claire I. Tsai, University of Toronto, Canada

Min Zhao, University of Toronto, Canada

Dilip Soman, University of Toronto, Canada

SESSION OVERVIEW

Online social networks (OSNs), such as Facebook and Twitter have experienced exponential growth in membership in recent years. As of 2010, 74% of American internet users visit social networks regularly and an average user spends one quarter of the time online on these sites. The most popular online social network is Facebook with 155 million users in America and 845 million users worldwide. Surveys show that 48% of 18-34 year old users check their Facebook account right when they wake up, 28% of which report doing so before even getting out of bed. These numbers demonstrate that online social networking sites have become a part of our everyday lives, revolutionizing the way we spend our time, the way we communicate and the way we maintain relationships. But why do people use these sites in the first place? And how does using these sites impact consumer behavior and well-being? While it is clear that online social network usage is frequent and important, questions about what drives people to use them, and the general impact they have on its users are not well understood. Focusing on both, the antecedents and consequences of online social networks, this session aims to answer these questions. The session unifies four complementary papers that examine the motivators for online social networking, as well as the consequences they have for consumer well-being, their judgment and decision making, and marketers more generally.

The first paper examines the antecedents of online social networking. Using multilevel linear modeling with a large sample of social media users, Hoffman and Novak investigate why people use online social networks. Compared to previous research, which has mainly stressed social connections as a motivation to engage in OSN, they examine how both, social goals and content goals can interact with dispositional tendencies and motivational orientation to satisfy needs of relatedness, autonomy and competence.

The second paper looks at both, a motivator for, and a consequence of online social networking. Many OSNs allows users to share short messages about their thoughts, feelings and actions (e.g., Facebook status updates) with their online social network. Buechel and Berger examine why people post such self-relevant content on-

line. Using survey and experimental data they suggest that sharing such messages is driven in part by emotionally instability. In particular emotionally unstable individuals use this feature to express their emotions, and doing so helps boost their well-being by increasing perceived social support after negative emotional experiences.

The next two papers focus on the consequences of online behavior. Wilcox and Stephen show some surprising and important negative consequences of using Facebook. Experimental data shows that browsing Facebook (as opposed to a neutral website) leads to an increase in spending and a decrease in performance on a persistence self-control task. A correlational study establishes the relationship between Facebook usage and a number of negative health and financial well-being markers. These negative consequences, they argue, result from an increase in self-esteem after exposure to Facebook, which can activate a narcissistic state and result in self-control failure. Finally, Tsai, Zhao and Soman investigate the influence of online social networks on consumers' judgment. In four studies they show that the mere knowledge of virtual others leads to less extreme objective and subjective judgments. The reason for this, they propose, is that virtual others increase the uncertainty about the accuracy of their judgments, which leads to a decrease in judgment confidence and consequently the need to conform. This need to conform then reduces the extremity of judgments. Consistent with their theorizing, they find that making conforming undesirable mitigates the virtual others effect, leading to judgments that resemble a control condition with no knowledge of virtual others.

Taken together, this set of complete papers provides a deeper understanding of the motivators to engage in online social networking and its consequences for consumer decision making, self-control and well-being. Given the novelty and the timeliness of the session topic, its practical importance, as well as its theoretical relevance for many areas of consumer behavior, such as emotion regulation, self-control, goal pursuit and judgment and decision making, the session is expected to appeal to a large audience in the field of consumer research. The session is thus likely to produce a fruitful interdisciplinary discussion that will lead to more research on online social networks and online consumer behavior more generally.

Need Satisfaction from Interacting with People versus Content: The Roles of Motivational Orientation and Identification with Social Media Groups

EXTENDED ABTRACT

As social media use continues to increase, it is critical for consumer behavior researchers to gain a deep understanding of what motivates consumer use and leads to need satisfaction. Using the self-determination theory framework which stresses that *autonomy, competence,* and *relatedness* foster motivation and engagement for activities, we evaluate how motivational orientation and the importance to identity of one's online social groups (ISM) influence how relatedness, autonomy and competence (Deci and Ryan 2000) need satisfaction may emerge from one's interactions with either other people or content. Although it may seem obvious that social media use can drive the experience of feeling related, consumers may seek additional fundamental experiences from social media goal pursuit, including competence and autonomy (Deci and Ryan 1985).

In the Web's early days, Hoffman and Novak (1996) noted that computer-mediated communication was differentiated from traditional mass media because it incorporated both person-interactivity and machine-interactivity. While the likelihood of satisfying basic needs through person-interactivity is fairly obvious, the satisfaction of such needs through machine- (i.e. via social media technology) interactivity, or interactivity with social media *content*, is less clear. Researchers examining social media usage tend to consider social media goals as those for which the primary objective is to connect with other people (e.g. Sheldon, Abad and Hinsch 2011), but in addition to interacting with other people when using social media, people also engage in behaviors focused primarily on either consuming or creating social media content (Hoffman and Novak 2011). We denote the former goals, social goals, and the latter goals, content goals.

In our framework, whether or not these fundamental needs are satisfied depends on the goal-specific motivations underlying goal pursuit, along with dispositional tendencies. For example, a person high in a dispositional need for relatedness may be particularly motivated to use social media to experience the satisfaction of relatedness needs. But as social media interactions take place in a social context involving other groups of people, a disposition uniquely relevant to the context is also likely to play an influential role. We argue that such a disposition involves the importance to one's identity of one's online social groups, a construct we refer to as identification with social media (ISM). This construct is adapted from the identity aspect of collective self-esteem (Luhtanen and Crocker 1992) and derives from the idea that individuals are motivated to maintain and enhance their collective or social identity, not just their personal identity (Rosenberg 1979). As such it captures the importance of one's social groups to one's self-concept.

Our conceptual model predicts how the type of social media goal individuals pursue while engaging in social media behavior is likely to moderate the relationship between 1) need satisfaction and intrinsic motivational goal orientation (hypotheses 1a, 1b and 1c), 2) need satisfaction and introjected (a form of extrinsic) motivational goal orientation (hypotheses 2a, 2b, and 2c), and 3) need satisfaction and the individual difference ISM (hypotheses 3a, 3b and 3c).

Multilevel data were collected at both person and goal levels in a web-based study of 338 participants. At the goal level (Level 1), participants identified their five most important objectives when using social media and rated each objective on goal importance, need satisfaction (relatedness, autonomy and competence), intrinsic and introjected motivation, and two process measures (direct experience and control). At the person level (Level 2), we collected four dispositional measures (ISM, relatedness, autonomy and competence) and five types of social media usage. The 1690 goals were classified by two independent judges into three categories: social goals, content goals, or not classifiable due to insufficient information (Krippendorf's alpha =.865, see Hayes and Krippendorff 2007). Disagreements were resolved by consensus and 40 goals that could not be classified were eliminated.

To test our three sets of hypotheses, multilevel linear models were estimated using maximum likelihood, using the sample of all social and content goals (n=1650). Separate models were fit for each of the three dependent goal-level variables, relatedness, autonomy and competence. The model for each dependent variable included the following fixed effects: main effect for goal type (Level 1), main effects for intrinsic and introjected motivation (Level 1), main effect for ISM (Level 2), interaction of goal type-by-intrinsic motivation (hypotheses 1a and 1b), interaction of goal type-by-introjected motivation (hypotheses 2a and 2b), and the cross-level interaction of goal type-by-ISM (hypotheses 3a and 3b). In addition, the hypoth-

esis model included three control variables – goal importance (Level 1), social media usage (Level 2), and need disposition (Level 2). For need disposition, the Level 2 dispositional covariate was used that corresponded to the Level 1 goal-specific dependent variable (i.e, relatedness, autonomy, or competence). Goodness-of-fit tests, parameter estimates and tests of significance are omitted in the interests of space.

Hypotheses were tested by evaluating conditional slopes. All hypotheses were supported. Higher intrinsic motivation led to greater relatedness need satisfaction for social goals compared to content goals (hypothesis 1a), higher intrinsic motivation increased autonomy more for content goals than for social goals (hypothesis 1b), and intrinsic motivation equally increased competence for both social and content goals hypothesis 1c). Hypotheses 2a and 2b predicted the reverse pattern of results for introjected motivation for relatedness and autonomy need satisfaction. Content goals, compared to social goals, led to higher relatedness when motivation was introjected (hypothesis 2a) and autonomy increased more for social goals compared to content goals when introjected motivation was high (hypothesis 2b). Similar to hypothesis 1c, introjected motivation increased competence for content goals, as well as social goals (hypothesis 2c).

Identification with social media boosted the experience of relatedness need satisfaction for content goals (hypothesis 3a) and amplified the experiences of autonomy and competence need satisfaction for social goals (hypotheses 3b and 3c). Multilevel structural equation modeling tested the hypothesized processes. ISM was found to increases relatedness need satisfaction for content goals by strengthening the experience of a more direct online social connection and ISM increased autonomy and competence need satisfaction for social goals by facilitating feelings of control in online social contexts. These results establish several fundamental effects that may be useful as consumer behavior researchers work to increase fundamental understanding of why people use social media.

Facebook Therapy?
Why People Share Self-Relevant Content Online

EXTENDED ABSTRACT

The Internet has become a pervasive part of everyday life, yet its impact on well-being is not well understood. Researchers (Kraut et al. 1998; Tonioni et al. 2012) and cultural critics (Yoffe 2009) argue that the Internet is addictive and that it reduces face-to-face interaction, leaving people depressed, anxious, and lonely. Further, sites based on social interaction (i.e. Facebook) are said to be merely "havens…for people with poor self-image…and narcissists demanding the world's attention," (DiSalvo 2010, p. 53), oftentimes leading to disapproval by other users (Buffardi and Campbell 2008; Forest and Wood 2012). They are associated with negative health and financial behaviors (Wilcox and Stephen 2012) and expose users to physical and cyber risk (Gross and Acquisity 2005). Given these downsides, why is online social networking so popular?

We suggest that certain online behaviors may improve well-being short-term. One of most popular features of many online social networks is micro blogging, a feature that gives users the opportunity to post short messages (e.g. status updates) about their thoughts, feelings, or actions for their online friends to read and potentially respond. Though one might argue that these "updates" are driven by vanity or by the need for extraverts to maintain existing social ties (Gosling et al. 2011) we argue that the sharing of such information with online friends can have another function. In particular, we suggest that users frequently share emotions through status updates and that this type of sharing can aid emotion regulation, boosting well-being after negative emotional experiences by eliciting expected social support (Rimé 2009).

This "social buffer" we hypothesize is of particular importance for low emotionally stable individuals. Low emotionally stable individuals experience emotions more intensely (Barr, Kahn, and Schneider 2008) and negatively (Costa and McCrae 1980) and are less adept at regulating their emotion on their own (Gross and John 2003). Although this leaves them with a heightened need to share their emotions with others (Saxena and Mehrotra 2001), low affiliation and their tendency to be socially apprehensive (Luminet et al. 2000) makes it difficult for these individuals to do so offline. Consequently, we argue that they are more likely to rely on their online social network to help them deal with their emotions. After all, their online friends increase their perceived social capital (Ellison, Steinfield, and Lampe 2007) and the online setting makes emotional sharing less threatening (Bargh and McKenna 2004). In tree studies we test this possibility.

In study 1 we examine whether low emotionally stable individuals update their status more frequently and share more emotions when doing so. Participants in this study were asked to report how often they updated their Facebook status. In addition they were asked to copy their 10 most recent status updates into the survey. They then reported the extent to which they used OSNs to interact with people, share experiences, share emotions, display identity, or to seek information from other users. They also completed the Big Five Personality Inventory (Gosling, Rentfrow, and Swann 2003). Regression analysis revealed that emotional stability was the only personality factor significantly related to status updating, whereby less emotionally stable participants reported updating their status more frequently. This relationship was mediated by their self-reported motivation to use online social networks to express emotion. Furthermore, content analysis of their status updates revealed that less emotionally stable individuals expressed more emotions in their updates.

In study 2 we test whether this increased emotional sharing is unique to online social networks. Participants randomly assigned to an offline condition reported the frequency of sharing their emotions in person. Participants in an online condition reported the frequency of sharing their emotions through status updates. Participants in this condition also reported how often they updated their Facebook status, as well as their preference for online vs. offline sharing. Finally the Big Five personality factors were assessed. As expected, a significant interaction revealed that while low emotionally stable individuals shared more emotions online than emotionally stable ones, this tendency was not observed in offline sharing, making this tendency unique to online sharing. Replicating the findings of study 1 with a different population, the results also again demonstrate that less emotionally stable people post more status updates and further, that this relationship is mediated by their preference for online over offline emotion expression.

In Study 3 we examined the consequences of such emotional sharing. First, negative affect was induced through false feedback on a performance task (Forgas 1991). Participants also provided a known other's email address to ensure that a known other was similarly activated across conditions. Next, they completed a "writing study". Some participants wrote about a control topic (office products). The other three conditions wrote about their current emotions, either (1) in private, or (2) to be shared with the known other who they were told would not be able to respond or (3) who might respond. Finally, participants reported their current well-being, perceived social support (Metzler 2003), and emotional stability (McCrae and Costa 2004). Results demonstrated that emotional writing

to a known other who might respond helped low emotionally stable individuals repair well-being after negative experiences. These benefits did not accrue for participants writing in general (control), writing about emotions (i.e. venting), or sharing emotion with a known other alone. Instead, the notion that a known other would read what they had written and potentially respond (as on OSNs) boosted well-being. Finally, consistent with our theorizing, this boost in well-being from sharing with potential response was mediated by perceived social support.

These results of the three studies provide insight into a motivator for, and benefit of, online social networking. Emotional unstable individuals are more likely to post status updates and write about their emotions when doing so. Further, such emotional writing, paired with the potential to receive social support – as on social networking sites – helps them repair well-being after negative experiences.

Are Close Friends the Enemy?
Online Social Networks, Narcissism and Self-Control

EXTENDED ABSTRACT

Online social networks are having a fundamental and important influence on society. Facebook, the largest social network, has over 750 million active users (www.facebook.com). Despite their popularity, a systematic understanding of the effect of social networks on consumer behavior remains elusive. Does using a social network, for instance, impact the choices consumers make in their daily lives? If so, what effect does social network use have on consumers' well-being?

People use social networks to fulfill a variety of social needs, including affiliation, self-expression, and self-presentation. Consequently, social network use can have a positive effect on how people feel about themselves and their well-being. For instance, when adolescents receive positive feedback on their social network profile, it enhances their self-esteem and well-being (Valkenburg, Peters, and Schouten 2006). Importantly, people tend to share mostly positive information about themselves to others on social networks (Gonzales and Hancock 2011). Thus, simply browsing a social network has been shown to momentarily increase users' self-esteem (Gonzales and Hancock 2011).

While high levels of self-esteem are often associated with positive social behavior, there also is a "dark side" to high self-esteem, particularly when it comes in the form of narcissism. Narcissism is often conceptualized as a personality trait that is associated with high levels of self-esteem and self-promoting tendencies. We propose that narcissism may not only be a personality trait, but also a state that can be activated by social network use. Specifically, we argue that since social networks facilitate self-presentation and boost self-esteem, the use of a social network should lead people to adopt a narcissistic mindset. We further propose that this mindset will remain active after social network use and affect behavior after the users have logged-off the network.

These predictions were tested in four studies. We demonstrate that browsing a social network lowers self-control, thereby reducing performance in subsequent tasks requiring self regulation. Additionally, we demonstrate that browsing a social network can lead people to display other narcissistic tendencies, such as defensive self-enhancement. Importantly, these effects emerge only for consumers who maintain relatively strong ties to their friends on the social network.

In study 1, one hundred sixty-nine Facebook users from an online panel participated. The study was comprised of three parts that were disguised a separate studies. In the first part, participants answered several general questions about their Internet use including how close they are to their friends on Facebook, which served as a measure of tie strength. Next, participants were administered a website viewing task where they either browsed Facebook or a popular news website (CNN.com) for five minutes. Finally, respondents participated in an online auction for a new Apple iPad. As expected, participants submitted higher bids (i.e., displayed less spending control) during the auction after browsing Facebook compared to CNN. com. However, the effect emerged only in people with strong ties to their Facebook friends.

Study 2 was designed to rule out the possibility that Facebook use simply makes people more impulsive by examining how Facebook use influences persistence in an unsolvable anagram task, which is a more general measure of self-control (Vohs and Heatherton 2000). Additionally, we measured self-esteem after the task. As expected, participants with close ties to their Facebook friends gave up quicker at the unsolvable task after browsing Facebook. Conditional indirect effects analyses using a bootstrap method (Preacher, Rucker and Hayes 2007) found that the effect of browsing Facebook on persistence is mediated by self-esteem for those with strong ties to their Facebook friends.

The purpose of study 3 was to demonstrate that browsing a social network can lead people to adopt a narcissist mindset. Consequently, we had people browse or not browse Facebook before having them complete the 40-item Narcissistic Personality Inventory. The findings demonstrate that those with strong ties to their Facebook friends report higher levels of narcissism after browsing Facebook. Conditional indirect effects analyses found that the effect of browsing Facebook on narcissism is mediated by self-esteem for those with strong ties to their Facebook friends.

In study 4, we examine the relationship between social network use and longer-term well-being. Five hundred forty-three Facebook users from an online panel covering the general population of U.S. Internet users participated in an online survey. They survey included several questions about social network use and behaviors related to poor self-control in eating and financial decision-making. The findings demonstrate that greater Facebook use is associated with a higher body-mass index (BMI), a greater likelihood of binge eating, more credit card debt and a lower credit score. However, the effect emerges primarily in people with close connections to their Facebook friends.

Social networks, such as Facebook, are now part of the daily lives of hundreds of millions of people around the world. Indeed a number of psychological benefits can be derived from social network use. However, this research demonstrates that using a social network (Facebook) may have a detrimental effect on behavior by lowering consumers' self-control. These results are concerning given the increased time people spend using social networks, as well as the worldwide proliferation of access to social networks anywhere anytime (i.e., via mobile smartphones, smart TVs, tablet computers, etc.). Given that self-control is important for maintaining social order and personal well-being, this subtle effect could have widespread impact. This is particularly true for adolescents and young adults who are the heaviest users of social networks and have grown up using social networks as a normal part of their daily lives.

The Facebook Effect: Are Judgments Influenced by the Knowledge That Others Are Also Evaluating?

EXTENDED ABTRACT

As web-based social networks proliferate, companies increasingly rely on virtual social communities to conduct market research and promote products. To encourage participation, companies often inform respondents that members of their virtual community are also evaluating the same products ("100 of your friends are also participating in this survey"). The present work examines how the knowledge of virtual others influences judgments. Specifically, we propose that the mere knowledge of virtual others highlights the uncertainty in the correctness of judgment (compared with social norm or consensus). The decrease in confidence, in turn, activates a need to conform and thus systematically reduces the extremity of judgments.

Results of four experiments provided support for this hypothesis in various domains including financial forecasting, movie box office revenues, and art work. Unlike previous research on social influence, we developed a new paradigm that allows us to test how knowledge of virtual others influences judgments without having to provide any consensus information to respondents. This feature increases the generality of our work as this information is often difficult to verify or observe in virtual communities.

To test the effect of virtual others, we first conducted a field experiment on Facebook. Participants were recruited into a social community on Facebook and asked to participate in a trivia game in which they were asked to estimate future and past events, including stock prices, currency exchange rate, and movie box-office revenues. In the virtual-other condition, we told participants that members of their community on Facebook were also participating in the study. In the control condition, we skipped this instruction. To demonstrate the role of need to conform, we added a consensus condition in which participants predicted the judgments of the members of the Facebook community about the same events. We offered performance-based incentives to control for effort and motivation. Consistent with our hypothesis, the results showed that participants in the virtual-other condition were less extreme (closer to the midpoint of the scale) in their estimation than were control participants. The results from the virtual-other condition also more closely tracked the perceived consensus than the results from the control condition, confirming the role of need to conform. Furthermore, we observed that participants in the virtual-other condition were less confident in the correctness of their estimation than were the control participants, which increased their need to conform to (perceived) consensus and reduced the extremity of judgments.

In study 2, we further tested the extremity hypothesis by manipulating the valence of judgment targets and using art work as the stimulus, which provides a conservative test for the effect of virtual others. Art is often perceived as a matter of personal taste and should be less prone to the need to conform. However, consistent with the Facebook study, we found that participants were less extreme in their evaluation of art work such that they were less positive about an attractive poster but more positive about an unattractive poster.

In the next two studies, we tested the moderating role of need to conform directly. Specifically, we manipulated need to conform by varying the similarity of members of a virtual community (peer vs. senior citizens; study 3) and activating a lay belief that being different from others is desirable or undesirable (study 4). Results of these two studies consistently showed that need for conformity is a key driver for the effect of virtual others. When participants perceived members of their virtual community as dissimilar to them (i.e., senior citizens) and thus need for conformity was low, or when they were primed with a lay belief that conformity is undesirable, their judgments were as extreme as the control group. The similarity manipulation also allowed us to rule out priming as an alternative explanation. That is, if the knowledge of virtual others reduced judgment extremity by simply priming participants to behave in a way that was similar to their community members without increasing their motivation to conform, then exposure to senior citizens should cause participants to be more conservative in their financial forecasts as senior citizens often do. However, we found the opposite. Participants in the dissimilar (senior citizen) condition were as extreme in their forecasts as the control group. Further, in study 3, we tested the mediating effect of confidence. We found that the knowledge of virtual others reduced confidence in judgments, which mediated the extremity of judgments.

Our findings contribute to the literatures on social influence by extending the effect of need for conformity to virtual communities and examining the role of confidence in the mechanism that underlies the effect of virtual others. Imagine that a person, alone in a closed room, is evaluating a new product, advertisement, or another person. Clearly, whether or not a virtual community is also evaluating the same object has no bearing on whether and how this person would be judged by the community (it would not have access to his/her response), unlike when community members are physically present. However, across four studies, we found that the mere knowledge of virtual others reduces the extremity of judgments. As virtual social communities proliferate, the present research also raises important issues concerning potential biases in data collected via virtual social networks for academic researchers, policy makers, and practitioners. In the virtual world, consumer evaluations of delight or disgust may be dampened and reported as a mild liking or a mild disliking.

REFERENCES

Bargh, John A. and Katelyn Y. A. McKenna (2004), "The Internet and Social Life," *Annual Review of Psychology*, 55 (February), 573-90.

Barr, Leah, Jefferey H. Kahn, and W. Joel Schneider (2008),"Individual Differences in Emotion Expression: Hierarchical Structure and Relations with Psychological Distress," *Journal of Social and Clinical Psychology*, 27 (December), 1045-77.

Buffardi, Laura E. and W. Keith Campbell (2008), "Narcissism and Social Networking Sites," *Personality and Social Psychology Bulletin, 34 (October),* 1303-14.

Costa, Paul T. and Robert R. McCrae (1980), "Influence of Extraversion and Neuroticism on Subjective Well-being: Happy and Unhappy People," *Journal of Personality and Social Psychology*, 23 (April), 668-78.

Deci, E. L., & Ryan, R. M. (1985). *Intrinsic motivation and self-determination in human behavior.* New York: Plenum.

Deci, E. L., & Ryan, R. M. (2000). The "what" and "why" of goal pursuits: Human needs and the self-determination of behavior. *Psychological Inquiry, 11*, 227-268.

DiSalvo, David (2010), "Are Social Networks Messing With Your Head?" *Scientific American Mind*, 20 (January/February), 48-55.

Ellison, Nicole B., Charles Steinfield, and Cliff Lampe (2007), "The Benefits of Facebook 'Friends:' Social Capital and College Students' Use of Online Social Network Sites," *Journal of Computer-Mediated Communication*, 12 (July), 1143-68.

Forest, Amanda L. and Joanne Wood (2012), "When Social Networking Is Not Working: Individuals With Low Self-Esteem Recognize but Do Not Reap the Benefits of Self-Disclosure on Facebook," 23 (March), *Psychological Science*, 296 - 305.

Forgas, Joseph F. (1991), "Affective Influences on Partner Choice: Role of Mood in Social Decisions," *Journal of Personality and Social Psychology,* 61 (November), 708-20.

Gonzales, Amy L. and Jeffrey T. Hancock (2011), "Mirror, Mirror on my Facebook Wall: Effects of Exposure to Facebook on Self-Esteem," *Cyberpsychology, Behavior, and Social Networking*, 14 (February), 79-83.

Gosling, Samuel D., Adam A. Augustine, Simine Vazire, Nicholas S. Holtzman, and Sam Gaddis (2011), "Manifestations of Personality in Online Social Networks: Self-reported Facebook-related Behaviors and Observable Profile Information," *Cyberpsychology, Behavior, and Social Networking*, 14 (September), 438-88.

Gosling, Samuel. D., Peter J. Rentfrow, and William B. Swann Jr. (2003), "A Very Brief Measure of the Big-Five Personality Domains," *Journal of Research in Personality,* 37 (December), 504-28.

Gross, Ralph and Allesandro Acquisti (November 2005), "Information Revelation and Privacy in Online Social Networks,' paper presented at ACM workshop on Privacy in the Electronic Society, Alexandria, VA.

Gross, James J. and Oliver P. John (2003), "Individual Differences in Two Emotion Regulation Processes: Implications for Affect, Relationships, and Well-being," *Journal of Personality and Social Psychology*, 85 (August), 348–62.

Hayes, Andrew F. and Klaus Krippendorff (2007), "Answering the Call for a Standard Reliability Measure for Coding Data," *Communication Methods and Measures*, 1 (1), 77-89.

Hoffman, Donna .L. and Tomas P. Novak (1996), "Marketing in Hypermedia Computer-Mediated Environments: Conceptual Foundations," *Journal of Marketing*, 60 (July), 50-68.

Hoffman, Donna L. and Thomas P. Novak (2011), "Social Media Strategy," in *Handbook on Marketing Strategy*, Venkatesh Shankar and Gregory S. Carpenter (eds.), Edward Elgar Publishing, Ltd.

Kraut Robert, Michael Patterson, Vicki Lundmark, Sara Kiesler, Tridas Mukophadhyay, and William Scherlis (1998), "Internet Paradox: A Social Technology that Reduces Social Involvement and Psychological Well-being?" *American Psychologist*, 53(September), 1017-31.

Luhtanen, Riia and Jennifer Crocker (1992), "A Collective Self-Esteem Scale: Self-Evaluation of One's Social Identity," *Personality and Social Psychology Bulletin*, 18 (June), 302-318.

Luminet, Oliver, Emanuelle Zech, Bernard Rimé, and Hugh Wagner (2000b), "Predicting Cognitive and Social Consequences of Emotional Episodes: The Contribution of Emotional Intensity, the Five Factor Model, and Alexithymia," *Journal of Research in Personality,* 34 (December), 471–97.

McCrae, Robert R. and Paul T. Costa (2004), "A Contemplated Revision of the NEO Five-Factor Inventory," *Personality and Individual Differences*, 36 (February), 587–96.

Meltzer, H. (2003), "Development of a Common Instrument for Mental Health," In *EUROHIS: Developing Common Instruments for Health Surveys*, ed. Anatoliy Nosikov and Claire Gudex, Amsterdam: IOS Press, 35-61.

Preacher, Kristopher J., Derek D. Rucker, and Andrew F. Hayes (2007), "Assessing Moderated Mediation Hypotheses: Strategies, Methods, and Prescriptions," *Multivariate Behavioral Research*, 42, 185–227.

Rimé, Bernard (2009), "Emotion Elicits the Social Sharing of Emotion: Theory and Empirical Review," *Emotion Review*, 1 (January), 60-85.

Saxena, Priya and Seema Mehrotra (2010), "Emotional Disclosure in Day-to-Day Living and Subjective Well Being," *Psychological Studies*, 55 (September), 208-18.

Sheldon, Kenneth M., Neetu Abad and Christian Hinsch (2011), "A Two-Process View of Facebook Use and Relatedness Need Satisfaction: Disconnection Drives Use, and Connection Rewards It," *Journal of Personality and Social Psychology*, 100 (4), 766-775.

Tonioni Federico, Lucio D'Alessandris, Carlo Lai, David Martinelli, Stefano Corvino, Massimo Vasale, Fabrizio Fanella, Paola Aceto, and Pietro Bria (2012),"Internet Addiction: Hours Spent Online, Behaviors and Psychological Symptoms," <u>*General Hospital Psychiatry,*</u> 34 (January), 80–7.

Valkenburg, Patti M., Jochen Peter, and Alexander P. Schouten (2006), "Friend Networking Sites and their Relationship to Adolescents' Well-Being and Social Self-Esteem," *Cyberpsychology & Behavior*, 9 (5), 584-90

Vohs, Kathleen D. and Todd F. Heatherton (2000), "Self-Regulatory Failure: A Resource Depletion Approach," *Psychological Science*, 11 (3), 249-54.

Wilcox, Keith and Andrew T. Stephen (2012), "Are Close Friends the Enemy? Online Social Networks, Narcissism, and Self-Control," Working Paper, Babson College, Babson Park, MA 02457.

Yoffe, Emily (2009), "Seeking: How the Brain Hard-wires us to Love Google, Twitter, and Texting. And Why that's Dangerous", *Slate,* <u>*http://www.slate.com/id/2224932/*</u>

Roll Out the Red Carpet:
The Impact of Customer Treatment on Judgment and Decision Making

Session Chair: Chen Wang, University of British Columbia, USA

Paper #1: Consumer Reactions towards Preferential Treatment

Lan Jiang, University of Oregon, USA

JoAndrea (Joey) Hoegg, University of British Columbia, Canada

Darren W. Dahl, University of British Columbia, Canada

Paper #2: Status By Association

Brent McFerran, University of Michigan, USA

Jennifer A. Argo, University of Alberta, Canada

Paper #3: Target-Observer Asymmetry in the Use of Persuasion Knowledge

Guang-Xin Xie, University of Massachusetts Boston, USA

Tracy Rank, Rutgers University, USA

Kent Grayson, Northwestern University, USA

Paper #4: The Impact of Sales Team's Perceived Entitativity on Customer Satisfaction

Chen Wang, University of British Columbia, Canada

JoAndrea (Joey) Hoegg, University of British Columbia, Canada

Darren W. Dahl, University of British Columbia, Canada

SESSION OVERVIEW

One of the most important elements in sales success lies in customer treatment in a retail setting (Crosby et al. 1990; Dwyer et al. 1987). It has been suggested that how consumers are treated and served during their purchase experiences greatly influences their subsequent judgment and decision making (Crosby et al. 1990). Despite its significance in practice, customer treatment has received little attention in consumer research. Existing research on consumer behavior in a sales context has primarily focused on the consumption outcomes as well as the outcomes' impact on consumers' future decisions (Keillor et al. 2000). However, much remains to be learned about how the means (e.g., how consumers are treated and served during a sales experience) influence various outcomes (e.g., consumers' judgment and decision making).

In an attempt to advance our understanding of the impact of customer treatment, this session brings together four papers that provide insights on how consumers are treated and served during a sales experience may influence their judgment and decision making. Specifically, this session investigates the following questions: How do consumers' responses towards the service change when they are treated with extra benefits during a purchase? How do consumers' evaluations of persuasion tactics change when they are confronted with salespeople's persuasion attempts? How does consumers' satisfaction towards a shopping experience change if they are served by a salesperson versus a sales team, and further, a coordinated team versus an uncoordinated team?

In the first paper, Jiang, Hoegg, and Dahl investigate consumers' responses towards the service when they are receiving extra benefits from a salesperson. They show that such preferential treatment can produce social discomfort when the treatment is experienced in a public environment. This effect is moderated by whether the treatment is witnessed, as well as how justified it is.

In the second paper, McFerran and Argo also explore consumers' responses towards preferential treatment by focusing on another beneficiary group – guests of VIPs. They demonstrate a "status by association" effect, such that the preferential treatment makes the guests experience the same (or more) status than their sponsor. Further, this effect is moderated by the ambiguity of the true identity of the status holder, and the guest's social distance from the VIP.

In the third paper, Xie, Rank, and Grayson examine consumers' evaluations of persuasion tactics when they are confronted with salespeople's persuasion attempts. They find that consumers' persuasion knowledge can moderate the target-observer asymmetry regarding perceived effectiveness of persuasion tactics. The moderation effect is mitigated when consumers are motivated to maintain or enhance positive self-perception.

Finally, in the fourth paper, Wang, Hoegg, and Dahl investigate consumers' satisfaction when they are treated with team service. They show that either a behavioral entitativity cue (e.g., coordinated behaviors among team members) or a physical entitativity cue (e.g., wearing the same uniform) of a sales team may enhance customer satisfaction. However, a sales team that lacks perceived coherence may undermine customer satisfaction, compared to a sales individual. Further, they demonstrate that the two entitativity cues may jointly determine customer satisfaction towards the service.

We believe that this session will appeal to a wide audience at ACR. There has been a relative dearth of consumer research on the impact of customer treatment. This session advances the literature by investigating various topics in customer treatment (e.g., preferential treatment, persuasion attempts, team service), and by providing insights on how each treatment may affect consumers' judgment and decision making. All research is in advanced stages – sixteen studies in total with three to five studies in each paper. Further, this session echoes the conference mission of appreciating diversity by including a variety of topics while maintaining a coherent theme, and by embracing research collaborated by researchers across the U.S. and Canada.

Consumer Reactions towards Preferential Treatment

EXTENDED ABSTRACT

Preferential treatment, where some people but not others are offered extra benefits, is a common phenomenon in consumption contexts, such as shopping in a store or dining in a restaurant. If you were the beneficiary in these contexts, how would you feel about receiving such preferential treatment in front of other people who do not receive the benefits? Conventional wisdom, management practice, and prior research would suggest you should be more satisfied (Lacey, Suh and Morgan 2007; Homburg, Droll and Totzek 2008; Dreze and Nunes 2009). However, we suspect that satisfaction with receiving preferential treatment may be a function of the context in which the treatment is received. In particular, we argue that the nature of the environment in which preferential treatment is offered and the basis on which the customer is selected can dramatically alter consumer evaluation of the experience.

We propose that customers' feelings and behaviors when they are treated preferentially in a public environment would be different from the outcomes in a private environment. More specifically, when preferential treatment is received in the presence of other consumers who do not receive such treatment, concerns about unfavorable evaluations from other individuals could lead to feelings of social discomfort (Miller and Leary 1992; Dahl et al. 2001). These feelings would accompany any positive emotions associated with receiving special treatment, potentially lowering satisfaction and altering consumption behavior. When no other consumers are present, however, these negative consequences should not materialize. Moreover, we argue that consumers will feel concern about negative impressions from others and experience the subsequent feelings of social discomfort when they receive a preferential treatment that lacks justification and is offered in a setting with a social audience that witnesses the behavior.

Studies 1A and 1B tested the idea that although consumers believe that they will feel only positive emotions after receiving preferential treatment, the actual experience can involve a mix of both positive and negative emotions when the preferential treatment is offered in the presence of others. The two studies utilized the same 2 (treatment: preferential vs. common) x 2 (environment: social presence vs. no social presence) between-subjects design, and the same shopping scenario, with the only difference being that Study 1A was a hypothetical case but Study 1B was a real experience. Social presence was manipulated by whether there were other customers in the shopping environment. In this shopping scenario, participants received a 25% discount through a random "scratch and save" draw. In the preferential condition, they were told that they are the only customer getting the deal, but in the common condition, everybody got the deal. Results from the hypothetical study (1A) showed that people assume that receiving preferential treatment will increase their satisfaction, whether in public or private. Interestingly, when actually experiencing the preferential treatment (1B) in a social environment, participants reported both negative and positive emotions and the negative feeling of social discomfort mitigated their overall satisfaction and reduced actual purchase.

Study 2 tested two factors that moderate the negative outcomes of preferential treatment, i.e., witness and justification of preferential treatment. In this study, participants visited a booth, where a local retailer was giving away three personal care product samples. The preferential treatment was the extra sample offered. In the justified condition, extra samples were offered because of their loyalty status. In the non-justified condition, they were offered without any explanations. We also distinguished two types of social presence, i.e., witness and no witness. Results showed that an individual who accepts preferential treatment without justification bears the risk of appearing undesirable, and when being witnessed by people who do not receive the same benefits, can feel socially uncomfortable. However, the feeling of social discomfort diminishes when there is no witness, even though there may still be other people present.

In study 3, we revisited the discrepancy between Studies 1A and 1B, and examined why people cannot predict the social discomfort when asked to imagine receiving preferential treatment in a social environment. We proposed that the failure to recognize these negative emotions is due to a processing mindset that results in a tendency to overlook background or contextual information when making predictions about an event. In the study, we manipulated people's processing mindsets to process events in either a holistic or analytic manner. Results showed that when people imagined a scenario and made an appraisal, their responses resembled the case when they were prompted to adopt an analytic mindset. When promoted to adopt a holistic mindset, their appraisal of the situation was closer to the real experienced responses.

This research contributes to the literature on preferential treatment, social influence, and focalism bias. We demonstrated that social discomfort can emerge when preferential treatment is experienced in a public environment. Moreover, adopting a holistic mindset enables people to capture the social elements and predict more accurate responses.

Status By Association

EXTENDED ABSTRACT

Status and social hierarchies are ubiquitous in human societies. In marketing, status is commonly signalled by brand names, but it can also by endowed by loyalty program rewards, where certain customers receive a disproportionate share of a firm's attention or resources. This preferential treatment can take for example the form of dedicated check-in lines, special discounts, and exclusive lounges for profitable/loyal customers – treatments which are designed to make these individuals feel special. While research has examined the implications of consumers receiving versus not receiving preferential treatment (i.e., VIPs vs. non-VIPs), the present research diverges by examing a third group of consumers: *guests* of VIPs. Guests are individuals who share in the preferential treatment received by VIPs not because they have earned this right due to their brand loyalty or purchase volume, but rather because many loyalty programs entitle a VIP to bring others (e.g., family member, friends, colleagues). For example, such guests might include a spouse of a frequent flyer receiving lounge access or working-class staff receiving an opportunity to enjoy the corporate box at a sporting event. Do these guests feel "special" and what consumption implications does this have? When should reward programs allow consumers to bring guests?

We propose a "status by association (SBA)" effect, such that status can extend from a "true deserver" to the individual's associates. Support for why status may rub off on those around them comes from research on emotional contagion (Hatfield et al. 1994; Neumann and Strack 2000; Ramanathan and McGill 2007), spontaneous trait transference (Argo and Main 2008; Winter and Uleman 1984) and contagion effects (Argo et al. 2006; 2008). We conduct four studies to demonstrate both *how* and *when* status contagion is likely to occur, and its impact on the likelihood of spreading positive word-of-mouth.

In Study 1, we demonstrate the tendency for the status by association effect (SBA) to occur. This study used a one-factor design with four between-subject levels. Participants read a scenario indicating that they are planning on attending a nightclub [a common service experience for this population, as well as one that frequently has benefits of status (e.g., VIP sections, free beverages, special entrances)]. In the scenario, participants read that upon arrival they notice that there is a long line at the nightclub. In the *self* condition, participants read that they have a VIP card that allows them to jump the line. In the *friend* condition participants read that their friend has a VIP card that allows both of them to skip the line. In the *same benefit control* condition, the participant knows someone who is already at the front of the line so the participant will get in right away and will not have to wait (i.e., no status but still get to cut the line). In the *no benefit control* condition, participants arrive before the line forms, so access is gained into the club without waiting (i.e., no status but no special and/or negative treatment). Results demonstrate that individuals feel more status in both the self and friend conditions (which do not differ from one another) as compared to the two control conditions.

Study 2 identifies a boundary condition for the effect, namely the ambiguity of the true identity of the status holder. Specifically, we predict that when the identity of the true status holder is unclear, greater SBA should occur. This is because we derive satisfaction from the exhibition of goods rather than mere ownership (Veblen 1899; Mason 1981). A 2 (holder of the status marker: self vs. friend) x 2(ambiguity of the true identity of the status holder: high vs. low) between-subjects design tested our predictions. The procedure mirrored the "self" and "friend" conditions from Study 1, with the following exception: in the scenario when the other patrons in line see the participant entering ahead of them, it was made either *ambiguous* or *unambiguous* to other patrons as to who is the true cardholder. We also assess positive WOM intentions as an additional dependent measure. Results revealed an interaction, where the greatest status was (equally) felt by VIPs in the unambiguous condition and guests in the ambiguous condition. Further, greater status mediated increased WOM intentions.

Study 3 was similar to study 2, except that we also manipulated social distance of the guest (close friend vs. distant acquaintance), in a 2x3 design. Results revealed an interaction, where ambiguity mattered for both VIPs and socially distant guests (same pattern as Study 2), but ambiguity had no effect for socially close guests: they felt equal status regardless. Again, increased WOM intentions were mediated by felt status.

Study 4 is a field study of status contagion involving both the owner and guests in real luxury suites at a professional football game. Respondents self-identified as either owners or guests of the suite in a survey. We also assessed a different type of social distance (friends of friends). Results reveal that guests feel more status than owners, regardless of whether they were actual friends or merely friends of friends. Again, higher felt status mediates higher WOM intentions. Moreover, this effect is negatively related to the number of games people have watched from the suite (i.e., more games, lower felt status and low WOM intentions), suggesting that status decays over time and that WOM is harder to cultivate among long-standing status holders. Finally, results also reveal that guests use marginally fewer of the suite's perks, suggesting that they are not more expensive to service. Collectively, our results show that frequent status holders may require more and more perks to feel the same felt status over time as a person who only experiences VIP treatment on a single (or very few occasions).

In sum, our research suggests that there may be a significant return in the form of positive WOM from status contagion without the incurrence of a large cost. Thus, allowing VIPs to bring guests may be more beneficial than firms might think.

Target-Observer Asymmetry in the Use of Persuasion Knowledge

EXTENDED ABSTRACT

Persuasion knowledge (PK) aids consumers when responding to persuasion attempts as "targets" or "observers" (Friestad and Wright 1994). Research has documented the "target-observer asymmetry" of perceived sincerity of marketers due to consumer suspicion of marketers' ulterior motives (Campbell and Kirmani 2000). That is, consumer "targets" are cognitively busier than "observers", and therefore the former become less suspicious when persuasion knowledge is not accessible. When persuasion knowledge is accessible, the asymmetry becomes less salient.

The purpose of this research is to examine the target-observer asymmetry in regard to consumer judgment about the effectiveness of persuasion tactics. In five studies, we find consumers with *low PK* rate persuasion tactics as more effective as an observer than a target. In contrast, *high PK* consumers, rate the tactics effective despite the target/observer perspective. However, when the notion of "being influenced by tactics" is activated, consumers are motivated to maintain or enhance positive self-perception. As a result, PK-induced moderation effect is mitigated.

In study 1, participants were presented with a scenario in which a consumer is shopping for wine. They were asked to evaluate the scenario from either a target or an observer perspective. The store

employee presents the consumer with a more expensive bottle of wine, while warning that is the last bottle. Next, participants rated the extent to which the tactic would affect the consumer's purchase decision, followed by an individual difference scale of PK (Bearden et al. 2001). Results suggest *low-PK* participants rated the tactic more effective as an observer than as target. *High-PK* participants' rated the tactic equally effective as an observer or target. In study 2 and 3, we examined if accessibility of persuasion knowledge and cognitive business account for the observed PK moderation effect.

In study 2, participants read the same scenario with accessibility of persuasion knowledge being primed (or not). Prior to the scenario, half of the participants saw a screen shot of a website that suggested a discount offer would be expiring (primed). They then saw the same screen shot suggesting the offer would be ending on a different day, after the pervious deadline had passed. The other half participants read the scenario directly (not primed). Results replicated the moderation effect of PK; but the priming had no significant effect on perceived effectiveness.

In study 3, participants read the scenario from the observer perspective. Cognitive capacity was manipulated by asking participants to remember a set of numbers (or not) while reading the scenario. The results suggest both *high-PK/busy* and *high-PK/non-busy* participants rated the tactics as equally effective. The pattern remains the same for the *low-PK* participants. These results suggest accessibility or cognitive busyness does not necessarily account for the observed PK moderation effect. In study 4 and 5, we further explored a motivational account based on self-concept enhancement.

In study 4, participants first completed a "persuasion IQ test" (i.e., ten ambiguous multiple-choice questions about the knowledge of persuasion tactics). Right after the test, they were given feedbacks that they were very knowledgeable (i.e., 9 out of 10 correct) or not knowledgeable (i.e., 4 out 10 correct). Next, they read the same scenario from study 1. A 2 (Feedback: positive vs. negative) X 2 (Perspective: target vs. observer) X 2 (PK: high vs. low) three-way interaction was significant. Specifically, when feedback was positive, both high- and low- PK participants rated tactics as more effective as an observer than as a target. When the feedback was negative, the observed pattern in study 1 and 2 was reversed: *high-PK* participants rated the tactic more effective as an observer than target; *low-PK* participants rated the tactic equally effective as an observer or target.

In study 5, participants were presented with a different scenario in which a store employee flatters a consumer for his/her choice of clothing before or after the purchase decision (Campbell and Kirmani 2000). A 2 (Flattery: before vs. after purchase decision) X 2 (Perspective: target vs. observer) X 2 (PK: high vs. low) three-way interaction was significant. When flattery was made before the purchase decision, both high- and low- PK participants rated the tactic more effective as an observer than target. When flattery was made after the purchase decision, the moderation effect of PK was replicated. Combined, these results suggest PK can moderate the target-observer asymmetry in the perceived effectiveness of persuasion tactics. The effect can be mitigated when consumers are motivated to maintain or enhance positive self-perception. This research extends the literature by revealing a motivational account underlying the target-observer asymmetry in the use of PK.

The Impact of Sales Team's Perceived Entitativity on Customer Satisfaction

EXTENDED ABSTRACT

Team-based selling has been a growing sales strategy (Cummings 2007). Surprisingly, although the team approach is highly prominent in industry, academic research on team selling is sparse (Ahearne et al. 2010). This research seeks to fill this gap by investigating *whether* and *how* the perceived entitativity of a sales team can affect customer satisfaction.

Entitativity refers to the degree to which a social collection is perceived as having "the nature of an entity" (Campbell 1958). Prior research has suggested two distinct cues to entitativity perception. Behavioral-based entitativity contends that coordinated collective behaviors among group members imply common goals, leading to increased entitativity perceptions (Ip et al. 2006). Physical-based entitativity posits that similarity in physical characteristics indicates common traits, also resulting in greater perceived entitativity (Dasgupta, Banaji, and Abelson 1999). Building on these findings, we hypothesize that either a behavioral-based entitativity cue (e.g., coordinated behaviors among team members) or a physical-based entitativity cue (e.g., wearing the same uniform) results in enhanced customer satisfaction.

Further, we predict that the interaction between the two entitativity cues is multiplicative. Specifically, the team produces the greatest customer satisfaction when both cues indicate high entitativity. However, customer satisfaction is undermined if either cue suggests low entitativity. We argue that such effects occur because a low (versus high) entitativity cue is more diagnostic in making entitativity judgment. According to schematic processing (Reeder and Brewer 1979), whenever a low entitativity cue exists, perceivers would use it as diagnostic information to conclude that the group is no longer cohesive and unified, leading to lower customer satisfaction. Further, such interaction on customer satisfaction is mediated by the team's perceived entitativity.

Study 1 tested the impact of the behavioral entitativity cue on customer satisfaction. We operationalize the behavioral cue by a salesperson's rationalized referral (e.g., lack of expertise) of another salesperson. We employ a 2 (indication of low expertise: yes vs. no) x 2 (referral: yes vs. no) between-subjects design. Participants read a scenario in which they went to purchase an e-book reader and asked one of the two salespeople for product information. In the indication-of-low-expertise conditions, the salesperson said, "I'm sorry that I'm no good at the e-book reader." In the referral-to-another-salesperson conditions, he said, "Let me introduce you to Ben." Participants were asked to indicate their satisfaction towards the team. Results are consistent with our hypothesis. Specifically, when a team referral was present, a rationalized referral (i.e., indicating low expertise in the product category) enhanced customer satisfaction relative to a non-rationalized referral. Moreover, our findings suggest the circumstances under which an individual's service might be advantageous

compared to a team's service. Specifically, when the salesperson did not indicate his capabilities beforehand, proceeding with individual service increased customer satisfaction, compared to involving another team member without reason.

Study 2 examined the impact of physical entitativity cue on customer satisfaction. We employed a one factor between-subjects design (same uniform vs. different uniforms vs. one salesperson-control condition). Participants read a similar scenario in which they went to purchase an electronics product. The salesperson either introduced another salesperson for further service (team conditions) or served the customer himself (control condition). The physical cue of the salespeople was manipulated by presenting their pictures in the narrative. Participants were asked to indicate their satisfaction with the service. As predicted, results revealed that the sales team in the same uniform produced higher customer satisfaction than the team in different uniforms, and the individual salesperson. The contrast between the latter two conditions was also significant, indicating that the team in different uniforms actually impaired customer satisfaction, compared to the individual.

Study 3 investigated the interaction between physical and behavioral cues on customer satisfaction. We used a 2 (indication of low expertise: yes vs. no) x 2 (uniform: same vs. different) between-subjects design. We shot a video featuring a similar scenario, in which a salesperson either indicated his low expertise in the product before introducing the second salesperson, or directly referred the customer to the second salesperson without any rationale, and the team wore either the same or different uniforms, depending on condition. Participants were asked to indicate their satisfaction towards the team and each salesperson. Entitativity was measured by the extent to which the two salespeople were perceived as a coherent group. Results revealed a significant interaction between physical and behavioral cues on customer satisfaction. Consistent with the multiplicative effect, the team produced the greatest customer satisfaction when both cues indicated high entitativity. However, customer satisfaction was undermined if either cue suggested low entitativity. Mediation analysis confirmed the mediating role of perceived entitativity. More interestingly, a super-additive effect was found when both cues suggested high entitativity. Specifically, when the team employed rationalized referral *and* wore the same outfit, customer satisfaction towards the team was greater than the average satisfaction towards the individuals.

This research contributes to the team-selling literature as well as advances entitativity research by examining the impact of sales team's perceived entitativity on customer satisfaction, and by demonstrating a multiplicative effect when the two entitativity cues interact.

Creativity at Different Times in Life

Chairs: Haiyang Yang, INSEAD, France
Amitava Chattopadhyay, INSEAD, Singapore

Paper #1: Creativity and Aging: Positive Consequences of Diminished Inhibitory Control

Stephanie M. Carpenter, University of Michigan, USA
Carolyn Yoon, University of Michigan, USA

Paper #2: Why Some Children Move and Groove So Well: A Look at Creative Performance and Theory of Mind

Lan Nguyen Chaplin, Villanova University, USA
Michael I. Norton, Harvard Business School, USA

Paper #3: How Awareness of the End of Life Impacts Creativity

Haiyang Yang, INSEAD, France
Amitava Chattopadhyay, INSEAD, Singapore

Paper #4: How Fashion Designers Develop New Styles: Creative Epiphany Versus Market Feedback

Joseph C. Nunes, University of Southern California, USA
Xavier Drèze, UCLA, USA
Paola Cillo, Bocconi University, Italy
Emanuella Prandelli, Bocconi University, Italy
Irene Scopelliti, Carnegie Mellon University, USA

SESSION OVERVIEW

From the zealous adoption of innovative products to the widespread passion for do-it-yourself goods, today's consumers not only value creative aspects of the goods they consume but also enjoy engaging in creative activities themselves (Dahl and Moreau 2007). To win the hearts of these consumers and thrive in a competitive global market, firms have to constantly innovate and develop creative products and services. Thus, understanding psychological processes underlying creative ingenuity is important for both consumer satisfaction and corporate success (e.g., Burroughs and Mick 2004; Moreau and Dahl 2005). The purpose of this proposed special session is to interest and attract more consumer researchers to this domain, by presenting a diverse set of recent research findings on people's creativity at different times in life, and by fostering a discussion of potentially interesting questions regarding theoretical developments in this domain, thereby sparking future research.

The four papers in this proposal each discusses creativity in a different stage of life. In the first presentation, Carpenter and Yoon show that while aging has long been thought to negatively affect cognitive ability, it can facilitate creativity performance. This effect is driven by the elderly's vulnerability to distracting information. Further, young individuals who are more vulnerable to distractions are also more creative. The second presentation by Chaplin and Norton focuses on children, 3-12 years in age, and shows that younger children are more creative than their somewhat older counterparts: Younger children (ages 3-6) are more likely to exhibit creative, carefree behaviors than older children (ages 7-12) because the development of children's 'Theory of Mind' increases their sensitivity to criticism from others.

In the third presentation, Yang and Chattopadhyay show that awareness of the end of life inhibits diverse exploration of ideas and impairs creativity, and that locus-of-control moderates this effect—while high internal locus-of-control individuals can be more creative problem solvers in many situations, their creative ability is inferior to those with moderate levels of locus-of-control under mortality salience. Finally, in the fourth presentation, Nunes, Drèze, Cillo, Prandelli, and Scopelliti examine, through a large scale empirical investi-

gation, how the designs of fashion designers—who are at the prime of their creative careers—evolve over time. Refuting the notion that iconic fashion designers are independent creative visionaries, the researchers show that the designs by fashion designers themselves and their competitors in prior years significantly affect the designers' creativity and designs in the current year. Each presenter will have 15 minutes to present their project, leaving 15 minutes for discussions between the presenters and audience.

This special session contributes substantively to the theme of the ACR 2012 conference—appreciating diversity. The session brings together creativity researchers from different parts of the world, who have explored the impact of time and age on creativity in different contexts involving participants from a diverse range of age, demographic, and cultural groups. The four presentations highlight a wide range of theoretical perspectives on creativity and yield implications for consumers, firms, and society. Through the session, we hope to bring consumer researchers' attention to creativity research, initiate discussions on a wide set of factors that impact creativity, and spark future research on creativity in consumer contexts. Finally, this session would appeal to a diverse range of consumer researchers, such as those interested in creativity, fashion and design, aging, cognition, memory, motivation, developmental psychology, and mortality salience.

Creativity and Aging: Positive Consequences of Diminished Inhibitory Control

EXTENDED ABSTRACT

Consumers of all ages often make decisions about products and services in complex and busy consumption environments. In such environments, consumers have to ignore or inhibit a vast amount of distracting information in order to make more effective and satisfying choices. One theory of information processing suggests that as people age, they become more vulnerable to the effects of distracting information due to normal age-related declines in inhibitory control (Hasher, Zacks, and May 1999). While this has typically been discussed as a negative feature of normal cognitive aging, the current line of research seeks to investigate positive outcomes associated with vulnerability to distraction. Past research suggests that distracting information can prime older adults with concepts that improve performance on the Remotes Associates Task (RAT; Kim, Hasher, and Zacks 2007). Better performance on the RAT is thought to be associated with cognitive flexibility and convergent thinking. In addition, research on creativity suggests that when the goal is complex, such as a creative or artistic goal, divergent thinking is enhanced, in part, by an attention to distracting (and often seemingly irrelevant) information (Kasof 1997).

The present line of research seeks to merge the separate literatures on inhibitory processes and on creativity by investigating how greater disinhibition of seemingly distracting information can enhance performance on subsequent tasks requiring divergent thinking. We hypothesize that enhanced vulnerability to distracting information will lead to greater creativity in both young and older adults. We reason that a difficult inhibition task will cause features of the distracting information to remain activated and enhance performance on an unrelated creativity task. In two studies we test our hypothesis

Advances in Consumer Research
Volume 40, ©2012

that difficulty in inhibiting distracting information leads to the generation of more original recipe ideas.

Study 1: One hundred and ninety-four undergraduates (mean age = 19; 93 females) at the University of Michigan were recruited to participate in a study on reading comprehension. Participants were randomly assigned into one of two distraction conditions, or a control condition. All participants read a mundane passage about a person going on a regular trip to the grocery store. Participants in the control condition read the passage in italicized font without any distracting information. Participants in the first distraction condition were asked to read the italicized passage with irrelevant food related words (e.g., avocado, chicken) periodically embedded in upright font. Their task was to "read all of the italicized words" in the passage. In the second distraction condition, participants read the same italicized passage with food related words periodically embedded in upright font, but the task was to "ignore all of the upright words." These instructions were adapted from pre-existing distraction paradigms (Kim et al. 2007). After completing the reading task, participants answered a few short comprehension questions. They then completed a creativity task where they were given 5 minutes to generate and write down as many cooking recipes as possible.

Following a coding procedure developed by Cheong, Burks, and Lee (2008), the recipes were scored by two blind judges who were self-identified "cooking connoisseurs." Each recipe was judged on 3 items --dish creativity, deliciousness, and potential popularity-- on a 5-point scale ranging from 1 (low) to 5 (high). These three items were then averaged together to create an "originality composite" score. Results indicated that young participants in the two distraction conditions generated recipes with significantly higher originality composite scores than those in the control condition (p = .031). Participants in the two distraction conditions also generated significantly more recipes in the allotted 5 minutes than those in the control condition (p < .001).

Study 2: Twenty-three community-dwelling older adults (mean age = 76; 12 females) were recruited to participate in a reading comprehension task. Older adults are a population with declining inhibitory control, which is generally viewed as having negative consequences for attention and memory. If, however, we find that vulnerability to distraction enhances performance on subsequent tasks requiring divergent thinking, this would provide further support for the idea that declines in inhibitory control may have benefits for tasks requiring creativity. The procedure in this study was identical to that described in Study 1. Results indicated that older adult participants in the two distraction conditions also generated recipes with significantly higher originality composite scores than those in the control condition (p = .001).

Overall, the results of two studies provide initial support for our theory that reduced inhibitory control can have positive consequences for creativity on tasks that require divergent thinking. Importantly, these facilitative effects occur for both young and older adults. In contrast to the well-documented detrimental effects of declines in inhibitory control associated with normal cognitive aging, our findings suggest positive consequences for creativity. Additional research is underway to further decompose the relationship between inhibitory mechanisms and creative processing. This includes determining what relationship a vulnerability to distracting information has to both divergent and convergent forms of thinking. Better understanding the relationship between disinhibition and creativity is important because consumers of all ages are faced with complex decision environments that require inhibition of distracting information in order to make more satisfying consumption choices. Our results suggest one context in which greater vulnerability to distraction may actually be beneficial.

Why Some Children Move and Groove So Well: A Look at Creative Performance and Theory of Mind

EXTENDED ABSTRACT

Chaperoning a middle school dance – with girls and boys in their early teens slouched against the bleachers, carefully monitoring their peers and refusing to dance despite the booming music – inevitably leads adults to comment: "Why aren't they dancing?" This refusal to dance is particularly notable because many of these same children, just a few years earlier, were prone to dance, sing, and more generally *perform* constantly – in school, at home, in the backseat of the car, and while watching television – with huge smiles and obvious relish. Why do people lose this willingness to perform – to sing and dance – as they age? We suggest that it is the very development of children's awareness that their peers might be judging them – itself an offshoot of the generally positive development of an ability to take the perspective of others – that robs them of the joy of getting out on the dance floor when the latest Lady Gaga track starts playing. We gave children the opportunity to behave in a creative, carefree manner – asking them to perform impromptu singing and dancing – and measuring their willingness to do so, as well as their ability to adopt the perspectives of those who might be watching (and judging) them.

The development of theory of mind (ToM) over the course of childhood is generally viewed as representing a positive development – allowing people to understand social norms and to "fit in" to social groups (Gauvain 1998; Liddle and Nettle (2006); Walker 2005; Walker and Shore 2011). Typically, ToM begins to develop around age 4; by age 5 or 6, success at ToM tasks becomes common, with some further development throughout school-age years (Chandler, Sokol, and Hallett 2001; Perner and Wimmer 1985; Wellman, Cross, and Watson 2001; Wimmer and Perner 1983). We predicted that increases in ToM deprive older children of the joy that comes with creative behaviors – like singing and dancing – due to the heightened sensitivity to criticism that ToM engenders (Dunn 1995). We chose singing and dancing since these behaviors have been shown to have significant benefits for health and well-being (Bonilha 2008; Brown et al. 2005; Clift et al. 2008; Bungay, Clift, and Skingley 2010; Verghese 2003); unfortunately, these are also behaviors that are subject to scrutiny by others, as evidenced by television shows like "American Idol."

One hundred fifty-nine children (81 girls, 78 boys) aged 3 through 12 participated in the experiment, and completed two tasks: a creative performance task and a task assessing ToM. The tasks were counterbalanced; order did not influence our results. In the performance task, we presented four options in a random order: sing a song, perform a dance, circle specific shapes on a page, or fill a square with a predefined color. (The first two tasks are associated with creative expressions, while the latter two tasks involve little creativity). Participants selected two tasks to complete in front of the experimenter. We assessed ToM with three measures: "Sally and Anne" false belief task (Baron-Cohen, Leslie, and Frith 1985); "Cookie Box" misleading container test (Gopnik and Astington, 1988); "Duck and Lion" social test (Nguyen and Frye 1999). Following McAlister and Peterson (2006), we summed the responses to form a composite measure of ToM (range: 0 to 3).

Based on previous research suggesting pervasive competency on ToM tasks by age 6 (Wellman et al. 2001), we divided children into two groups for analysis: younger children (ages 3-6) and older children (ages 7-12). As expected, older children ($M = 2.59$, $SD = .76$) had a more developed ToM compared to younger children ($M = .87$, $SD = 1.17$), $t(157) = 11.24$, $p < .001$.

More than twice as many younger children chose the creative tasks (singing or dancing) than older children: 59.7% of younger children selected singing and 50% dancing, compared to just 25.8% and 21.5% of older children, χ^2s$(1) > 13.81$, $ps < .001$. Similarly, younger children were less likely to choose the non-creative tasks (circling and coloring; 41.9% and 48.4%) than older children, who overwhelmingly preferred these tasks (70.1% and 82.5%), χ^2s$(1) > 12.42$, $ps < .001$. Put another way, only 11.3% of young children passed up the chance to sing and dance, whereas 55.7% of older children avoided both of these creative behaviors.

ToM mediated these differences in creative behaviors: The effect of age on the total number of sing and dance was significantly reduced (from $\beta = -.48$, $p < .001$, to $\beta = -.03$, $p = .72$) when ToM was included in the equation, and ToM significantly predicted singing and dancing ($\beta = -.67$, $p < .001$), such that ToM fully mediated the impact of age on willingness to sing and dance, Sobel's $Z = 6.83$, $p < .01$. (This analysis also holds when treating age as a continuous variable, Sobel's $Z = 6.36$, $p < .01$.)

These results suggest that the development of ToM comes with costs, by decreasing people's willingness to engage in creative, carefree tasks that bring them joy due to the heightened concern with evaluation that ToM engenders. While some research has documented the link between ToM and negative behaviors such as antisocial deception (Repacholi, Slaughter, Pritchard, and Gibbs 2003), our results suggest that ToM can also decrease the prevalence of positive behaviors. Our results are also relevant to understanding "savant syndrome" in people with autism, who lack ToM (Baron-Cohen, Leslie, and Frith 1985; Treffert 2009). Our results suggest that one reason for the extraordinary creative abilities of some autistic may be the absence of the performance anxiety experienced by children without autism.

How Awareness of the End of Life Impacts Creativity

EXTENDED ABSTRACT

From natural disasters (e.g., earthquakes, hurricanes) to terrorism and wars (e.g., September 11) to social unrest (e.g., riots, murders) to accidents (e.g., car/plane crashes, train derailments), we are constantly exposed to information that makes our own mortality salient. At times, we may even be quite close to such misfortunes (e.g., living in New Orleans during Hurricane Katrina, working in Japan during the Fukushima nuclear emergency). This research explores how awareness of death affects creative ability and what type of individuals are more sensitive to this effect.

Extant research shows that mortality salience, or awareness of one's death, elicits existential anxiety and, to buffer against this paralyzing anxiety, people deploy terror management strategies to create a sense of meaning and order, seeking to transcend death (e.g., Solomon, Greenberg, and Pyszczynski 1991; Greenberg, Solomon, and Pyszczynski 1997). Because cultural values provide meaning and structure to one's world and represent permanence beyond any individual's demise, mortality salience intensifies people's adherence to their cultural values and worldviews (e.g., Greenberg et al. 1990; Rosenblatt, Greenberg, Solomon, Pyszczynski, and Lyon 1989). This effect has been shown to be unique to death (as opposed other aversive events) and occurs outside of consciousness (Greenberg, Pyszczynski, Solomon, Simon, and Breus 1994).

While numerous studies on terror management theory have focused on the impact of mortality salience on evaluations of self and others (see Burke, Martens, and Faucher 2010 for a review), the current understanding of how mortality salience impacts creativity is limited (Routledge, Arndt, Vess, and Sheldon 2008). Seeking to fill this gap in the literature, the current research proposes that mortality salience inhibits access to information outside of one's conventional knowledge, as a means to protect the coherence and stability of one's core cultural values and worldviews. This inhibition occurs because access to peripheral information that may conflict or cast doubt on one's core values and worldviews, can make adherence to them more difficult, reducing the effectiveness of this terror-management strategy. Thus, mortality salience is likely to hamper assess to divergent information in memory, impairing creative ingenuity.

Further, given that death represents the ultimate form of loss of control for human beings—we cannot prevent our eventual demise nor exert any control over post-mortal events (Becker 1973)—mortality salience may impact people with different control beliefs differently. While individuals with high internal locus-of-control believe that event outcomes are primarily controlled by their own efforts and actions, those with moderate internal locus-of-control believe that they have control over only some events (Rotter 1966). The first group's beliefs are irreconcilable with the notion of death, leading to the elicitation of stronger terror-management behaviors under mortality salience. This, in turn, impairs their creative ability more. Consequently, while individuals with high internal locus-of-control can be more creative problem solvers in many situations (e.g., Burroughs and Mick 2004), their creativity ability is likely to be inferior to those with moderate level of internal locus-of-control under mortality salience.

Our propositions were tested in three experimental studies. Study 1a examined whether mortality salience (MS) inhibits assess to divergent knowledge. Participants first responded to a locus-of-control scale (Rotter 1966). Following a widely used TMT paradigm (Burke, Martens, and Faucher 2010), participants were then asked to write down thoughts regarding either their own death (MS condition) or viewing TV programs (control condition). Next, they completed the Positive and Negative Affect Schedule (Watson, Clark, and Tellegen 1988), which captured participants' affective states and served as a delay task (cf. Pyszczynski, Greenberg, and Solomon 1999). Thereafter, participants in both conditions were asked to write down all the place names they could think of with "A" as the first letter. Consistent with the hypothesis that mortality salience inhibits access to divergent information in memory, participants in the MS condition wrote down significantly fewer foreign place names (e.g., Algeria, Antarctica, Australia) than those in the control condition. Further, a significant interaction effect between the locus of control measure and mortality salience manipulation was found. Analysis of the interaction revealed that, in the MS condition, participants with high internal locus-of-control wrote down significantly fewer foreign place names than those with moderate internal locus-of-control; however, the opposite was true in the control condition.

The experimental procedure for Study 1b and 2 was similar to that of Study 1a. In Study 1b, a set of Remote Associate Test (RAT; Mednick 1962) questions was utilized to investigate the impact of MS on participants' ability to connect disparate semantic concepts. In Study 2, participants were given a managerial decision making task—deciding what new business should go into a commercial property where a restaurant had just gone bankrupt (adapted from Goncalo and Staw 2006). Providing further support for our hypotheses, participants in the MS condition correctly answered fewer RAT questions (Study 1b) and were more likely to follow the precedence, i.e., using the space for a restaurant again (Study 2). Locus-of-control moderated the effect of MS on participants' responses in both studies. While those with high internal locus of control exhibited better performance in the control condition, they were outperformed by those with moderate locus of control in the MS condition. Finally, ruling out an affect-based account of the results we found in the three studies, including the PANAS scores in the analyses did not change the findings.

Overall, these results not only shed light on the impact of mortality salience on information accessibility and creative problem solving, but also illuminate the role of control beliefs in terror management theories. Further, our findings contradict lay intuitions: A survey of mid to senior level executives at a large logistics firm revealed that the majority (67%) would put high locus-of-control managers in charge of problem solving, in crisis scenarios (e.g., natural disasters or terrorist attack that resulted in a major loss of life). Our results, however, suggest that those with moderate locus-of-control may be more creative problem solvers in those dire scenarios.

How Fashion Designers Develop New Styles: Creative Epiphany Versus Market Feedback

EXTENDED ABSTRACT

The fashion world is characterized by change. Like other creative industries including music, theater, and publishing, the public appetite for something novel in fashion seems insatiable. Fashion thrives on change, and the success of the industry as a whole depends on its ability to introduce new styles. World renowned design houses such as Chanel, Prada, Gucci, and Balenciaga and their top designers Karl Lagerfeld, Miuccia Prada, Frida Giannini, and Nicolas Ghesquière are devoted to introducing distinctive, original styles each season. But how fashion designers derive their inspiration is often shrouded in mystery. Like musicians, actors, and authors, designers are prone to see themselves as visionaries and creativity as an epiphany, impervious to outside influence. For example, Karl Lagerfeld, creative director at the helm of Chanel since 1983, claims his best work is effortless, coming to him in his sleep.

Despite ongoing research in fashion within many disciplines, data driven research on style changes across time is conspicuously absent in the literature. To the best of our knowledge, there exist no systematic empirical investigations regarding how styles change over time. As such, no research examines whether and how innovation in fashion depends on influences outside of the firm, such as market feedback and competitors' behavior. This research sets out to determine whether fashion designers are indeed immune to caprices of the market. Specifically, we investigate whether fashion designers attend to market feedback. In doing so, we empirically test if and how the relative success or failure of styles introduced in the past affects new styles that are subsequently introduced. If designers are immune to criticism, we should observe no relationship. If, however, designers are shrewd marketers attuned to what critics say, the styles they introduce each season should be more similar to those styles that were reviewed more positively in the past and less similar to less positively received styles. Thus, we would expect to observe a systematic relationship between what they do and what they have done, as well as what their competitors, have done.

Our data collection occurred in multiple stages. We obtained a listing of all brands that were included in the catwalk calendars of Milan and Paris from 1999-2007 (fall/winter and spring/summer). Only those companies that put on runway shows with their seasonal collections during Fashion Week for at least five years were included in our data set. This resulted in 38 companies, with 22 from Milan and 16 from Paris. To develop a metric to gauge the extent to which each designer's style changed from year to year, we compared prototypical pieces that were offered commercially following each show. To this end, we collected every ad published in Vogue Italia, Vogue France, Elle Italia, and MarieClaire France for all of the design houses each year. We used these ads to assess the change in style for a specific designer or design team. We focused on 11 primary types of garments (e.g., dresses, pants, etc.). Judges coded each garment on some subset of 13 style elements that were appropriate for the particular type of apparel. For example, tops were evaluated on sleeve length while pants were not. Six elements were evaluated using continuous measures (e.g., sleeve length, neckline), while seven elements were comprised of multiple discrete measures (e.g., color, fabric). Our data therefore included information on styles introduced by 38 design houses across nine years for two seasons derived from 5,343 advertisements. Taken together, this created what we refer to as the style genome for each of the 38 designers for each of the 18 seasons in our sample.

We label the difference between any two style genomes (across time but either within or across designers) as the style distance. A style distance measure reflects the relative change in styles and was constructed by calculating the Euclidean distance in a 61-dimensional space based on the 61 style measures using the 13 style elements for the 11 garment types. The style distance is a single number that is indicative of the relative change in styles across time, but is always calculated within season (fall/winter, spring/summer). We also collected critical reviews of the catwalk shows for each major season (spring/summer, fall/winter) for each year in the sample (1999-2007). We took differences in reviews as an indicator of relative success or failure in the market and consider more positive reviews as greater acceptance of a style by the marketplace.

Our main focus was to explore how new styles were affected by reviews of past styles. First and foremost, we observe a tendency for designers to move away from styles that were reviewed less favorably in the past. Designers, intentionally or unintentionally, stick closer to styles that have been well-received in the past and shy away from those not as well-liked. Empirically, we demonstrate that designers distance themselves further from previous styles over time, exactly how far they move is moderated by how the market responded to specific styles in the past. This result dispels the long-held myth of the designer as dictator unfettered by how the market responds to his or her creations.

We also observe a tendency for designers to move away from styles introduced by other designers' that were reviewed less favorably in the past. This suggests that not only do designers' attend to how the market responds to the designs they introduced previously, but they are keenly aware of, and respond to, what the market says about other designers' previous styles. These results provide the first empirical evidence that styles evolve based on market forces as well as creative forces, documenting the dynamic interaction between fashion houses and their customers in a recurring feedback loop.

Our data and our results suggest that fashion designer, as commercial artists, are not only sensitive to their own past successes and failures when deciding what new designs to introduce, but shows they also consider competitors' past work and how those styles have fared in the marketplace. Ours is the first empirical evidence of market feedback impacting new product introductions in an industry based on aesthetic innovation. The paradox of fashion is the conflict between looking distinctive while giving the impression of a certain degree of uniformity. Understanding how aesthetic innovation occurs, and what drives its acceptance or rejection is an important area that should garner a lot of attention in the future.

REFERENCES

Baron-Cohen, Simon, Alan M. Leslie, and Uta Frith (1985), "Does the Autistic Child have a Theory of Mind?" *Cognition*, 21, 37-46.

Becker, Ernest (1973), *The Denial of Death*. New York: Free Press.

Bonilha, Amanda Gimenes, Fernanda Onofre, Maria Lucia Vieira, Maria Yuka Almeida Prado, and José Antônio Baddini Martinez1 (2008), "Effects of Singing Classes on Pulmonary Function and Quality of Life of COPD Patients," *International Journal of COPD*, 4, 1-8.

Brown, William M., Lee Cronk, Keith Grochow, Amy Jacobson, C. Karen Liu, Zoran Popovic, and Robert Trivers (2005), "Dance Reveals Symmetry Especially in Young Men," *Nature*, 438, 1148-1150.

Burke, Burke L., Andy Martens, and Erik H. Faucher (2010), "Two Decades of Terror Management Theory: A Meta-analysis of Mortality Salience Research," *Personality and Social Psychology Review*, 14, 155–95.

Burroughs, James R. and David G. Mick (2004), "Exploring Antecedents and Consequences of Consumer Creativity in a Problem Solving Context," *Journal of Consumer Research*, 31 (2), 402-411.

Chandler, Michael J., Bryan W. Sokol, and Darcy Hallett (2001), "Moral Responsibility and the Interpretive Turn: Children's Changing Conceptions of Truth and Rightness," in *Intentions and Intentionality: Foundations of Social Cognition*, eds. D.A. Baldwin, L.J. Moses, and B.F. Malle, Cambridge, MA: MIT, 345-66.

Cheng, Chi-Ying, Jeffrey Sanchez-Burks, and Fiona Lee (2008), "Connecting the Dots Within: Creative Performance and Identity Integration," *Psychological Science*, 19, 1178-1184.

Clift, Stephen, Grenville Hancox, Ian Morrison, Bärbel Hess, Don Stewart, and Gunter Kreutz (2008), *Choral Singing, Wellbeing and Health: Findings from a Cross-National Survey*. Canterbury: Canterbury Christ Church University.

Dahl, Darren W. and Page C. Moreau (2002), "The Influence and Value of Analogical Thinking During New Product Ideation," *Journal of Marketing Research*, 39 (February), 47-60.

Gauvain, Mary (1998), "Culture, Development, and Theory of Mind: Comment on Lillard," *Psychological Bulletin*, 123, 37-42.

Goncalo, Jack A. and Barry M. Staw (2006), "Individualism-Collectivism and Group Creativity," *Organizational Behavior and Human Decision Processes*, 100, 96-109.

Gopnik, Alison and Janet W. Astington (1988), "Children's Understanding of Representational Change and its Relation to the Understanding of False Belief and the Appearance-Reality Distinction," *Child Development*, 59, 26-37.

Greenberg, Jeff, Tom Pyszczynski, Sheldon Solomon, Abram Rosenblatt, Mitchell Veeder, Shari Kirkland, and Deborah Lyon (1990). "Evidence for Terror Management Theory II: The Effects of Mortality on Reactions to those who Threaten or Bolster the Cultural Worldview," *Journal of Personality and Social Psychology*, 58, 308–318.

Greenberg, Jeff, Tom Pyszczynski, Sheldon Solomon, Linda Simon, and Michael Breus (1994), "Role of Consciousness and Accessibility of Death-Related Thoughts in Mortality Salience Effects," *Journal of Personality and Social Psychology*, 67, 627-637.

Greenberg, Jeff, Sheldon Solomon, and Tom Pyszczynski (1997), "Terror Management Theory of Self-Esteem and Cultural Worldviews: Empirical Assessments and Conceptual Refinements," in *Advances in Experimental Social Psychology*, Vol. 29, ed. Mark P. Zanna, San Diego, CA: Academic Press, 61–139.

Hasher, Lynn, Rose T. Zacks, and Cynthia P. May (1999), "Inhibitory Control, Circadian Arousal, and Age," in *Attention and Performance XVII: Cognitive Regulation of Performance: Interaction of Theory and Application*, eds. Daniel Gopher and Asher Koriat, Cambridge, MA: MIT Press, 653-675.

Kim, Sunghan, Lynn Hasher, and Rose T. Zacks (2007), "Aging and a Benefit of Distractability," *Psychonomic Bulletin & Review*, 14, 301-305.

Kasof, Joseph (1997), "Creativity and Breadth of Attention," *Creativity Research Journal*, 10. 303-315.

Liddle, Bethany and Daniel Nettle (2006), "Higher-order Theory of Mind and Social Competence in School-age Children," *Journal of Cultural and Evolutionary Psychology*, 4, 231–246.

Mednick, Sarnoff A. (1962), "The Associative Basis of the Creative Process," *Psychological Review*, 69 (3), 220–32.

Moreau, C. Page and Darren W. Dahl (2005), "Designing the Solution: The Impact of Constraints on Consumer Creativity," *Journal of Consumer Research*, 32 (June), 13-22.

Nguyen, Leanh and Douglas Frye (1999), "Children's Theory of Mind: Understanding of Desire, Belief and Emotion with Social Referents," *Social Development*, 8, 70-92.

Perner, Josef and Heinz Wimmer (1985), "'John thinks that Mary thinks that…' Attribution of Second-Order Beliefs by 5- to 10-year-old Children," *Journal of Experimental Child Psychology*, 39, 437-71.

Pyszczynski, Tom, Jeff Greenberg, and Sheldon Solomon (1999), "A Dual Process Model of Defense against Conscious and Unconscious Death-related Thoughts: An Extension of Terror Management Theory," *Psychological Review*, 106, 835-845.

Repacholi, Betty, Virginia Slaughter, Michelle Pritchard, and Vicki Gibbs (2003), "Theory of Mind, Machiavellianism, and Social Functioning in Childhood," in *Individual Differences in Theory of Mind*, eds. B. Repacholi and V. Slaughter, New York: Psychology Press, 67–94.

Rosenblatt, Abram, Jeff Greenberg, Sheldon Solomon, Tom Pyszczynski, and Deborah Lyon (1989), "Evidence for Terror Management Theory I: The Effects of Mortality Salience on Reactions to Those Who Violate or Uphold Cultural Values," Journal of Personality and Social Psychology, 57 (October), 681–90.

Rotter, Julian B. (1966), "Generalized Expectancies for Internal Versus External Control of Reinforcement," *Psychological Monographs*, 80, 609.

Routledge, Clay, Jamie Arndt, Matthew Vess, and Kennon M. Sheldon (2008), "The Life and Death of Creativity: The Effects of Mortality Salience on Self versus Social-directed Creative Expression," *Motivation & Emotion*, 32, 331–338.

Solomon, Sheldon, Jeff Greenberg, and Tom Pyszczynski (1991), "A Terror Management Theory of Social Behavior: The Psychological Functions of Self-Esteem and Cultural Worldviews," in *Advances in Experimental Social Psychology*, Vol. 24, ed. Mark E. P. Zanna, San Diego, CA: Academic Press, 93–159.

Treffert, Darold A. (2009), "The Savant Syndrome: An Extraordinary Condition. A Synopsis: Past, Present, Future," *Philosophical Transactions of the Royal Society B: Biological Sciences* 364 (1522): 1351–1357.

Verghese, Joe, Richard B. Lipton, Mindy J. Katz,Charles B. Hall, Carol A. Derby, Gail Kuslansky, Anne F. Ambrose, Martin Sliwinski, and Herman Buschke (2003), "Leisure Activities and the Risk of Dementia in the Elderly," *New England Journal of Medicine*, 348, 2508-2516.

Walker, Cheryl L. and Bruce M. Shore (2011), "Theory of Mind and Giftedness: New Connections," *Journal for the Education of the Gifted*, 34, 644-668.

Walker, Sue (2005), "Gender Differences in the Relationship between Young Children's Peer-related Social Competence and Individual Differences in Theory of Mind," *The Journal of Genetic Psychology*, 166, 297–312.

Watson, David, Lee A. Clark, and Auke Tellegen (1988), "Development and Validation of Brief Measures of Positive and Negative Affect: The PANAS Scales," *Journal of Personality and Social Psychology*, 53 (June), 1063–70.

Wellman, Henry M, David Cross, and Julanne Watson (2001), "Meta-analysis of Theory of Mind Development: The Truth about False Belief," *Child Development*, 72, 655-84.

Wimmer, Heinz and Josef Perner (1983), "Beliefs about Beliefs: Representation and Constraining Function of Wrong Beliefs in Young Children's Understanding of Deception," *Cognition*, 13, 103-28.

From the Field: New Research on Interventions, Commitments and Behavior Change

Session Chair: Ayelet Gneezy, University of California, San Diego, USA

Paper #1: Taming Temptation: Targeting Self-Control Increases Healthy Food Behaviors

Janet Schwartz, Tulane University, USA
Jason Riis, Harvard University, USA
Brian Elbel, New York University, USA
Daniel Mochon, Tulane University, USA
Dan Ariely, Duke University, USA

Paper #2: Exercising to the Lowest Common Denominator

Leslie John, Harvard University, USA
Michael I. Norton, Harvard University, USA

Paper #3: Commitment and Environmental Behavior Change: Evidence from the Field

Katie Baca-Motes, Disney Research, USA
Amber Brown, Disney Research, USA
Ayelet Gneezy, University of California San Diego, USA
Elizabeth Keenan, University of California San Diego, USA
Leif D. Nelson, University of California at Berkeley, USA

SESSION OVERVIEW

The research described here shows how relatively small, yet well-planned interventions can lead to significant changes in behavior. Influencing behavior change is an ongoing challenge in today's society. In response, psychology, economics and consumer behavior researchers have been trying to find effective ways to induce new habits (e.g., Choi et al. 2004; Cialdini 2003). Recently, Thaler & Sustein (2009) proposed that it is possible to change behavior by manipulating the context in which individuals make decisions (i.e., nudges). The four papers included in this session take the nudge approach and provide new evidence for behavior change in applied settings.

The papers focus on three domains of social concern: health, wealth and the environment, which consumer research is poised to address. Consequently, the present work provides practical strategies for improving practices in these areas, via the use of economic and psychological theories. All papers included in this session involved field experimentation, and spanned the globe. As such they appeal broadly to both those who conduct randomized experimental work as well as those who are interested in exploring behavior change in diverse real world settings.

The first two papers apply concepts of self-control, commitment and normative feedback to address overeating and sedentary behavior. The paper by Schwartz et al. shows that urging self-control through simple prompts and pre-commitment can significantly improve nutrition behavior. For instance, consumers accept offers to reduce their calorie intake by taking smaller portions of side-dishes in a fast food restaurant. Taking a different approach to health, the paper by John and Norton addresses how to increase activity (i.e., reduce sedentary behavior) in a work setting through the use of walk-stations – treadmills attached to elevated workspaces – while also giving employees feedback on their own and coworkers' walkstation usage. Results show that walkstation usage declines over time, and that this decline is greater when participants are given information on peers' usage levels, presumably due to a tendency to converge to the lowest common denominator.

The final paper by Baca-Motes et al. highlights the potential use of a commitment device to increase individuals' compliance with environmental appeals. Results show that guests who make a specific commitment to environmental behavior and are given the chance to strengthen this commitment with a publicly displayed symbol (an environmental pin) are more likely to reuse their towels during their hotel stay, arguably via signaling.

We are convinced this session will be of broad interest to the ACR community, as it addresses important topics and provides insights regarding the ways we can change behavior (for the better). Finally, this session complements the theme of this year's ACR conference, "appreciating diversity", in that the interventions tested were applied to a diverse set of contexts with diverse sets of populations.

Taming Temptation: Targeting Self-Control Increases Healthy Food Behaviors

EXTENDED ABSTRACT

The obesity epidemic lacks a clear and actionable solution. Some communities have taken first steps towards healthier diets with interventions that require prominent nutritional information. Such interventions rely on information to encourage healthier food choices. Behavioral science research has shown, however, that while information-based interventions (e.g., mandatory calorie labeling) can effectively change attitudes, they often fail to change actual behavior. As an alternative, we propose tackling the problem from a different angle. Specifically, we have targeted the temptation to make unhealthy food decisions through a series of field and web-based experiments that specifically focus on activating self-control. Our results show that this strategy is effective, easily implemented and especially welcomed by consumers.

First, we conduct a series of field experiments were at a Chinese fast-food restaurant. In Study 1 participants were asked by restaurant staff if they wanted to "cut over 200 calories from their meal" by taking a half-portion side dish (ranging in calories from 440-570). In one condition the participants were merely prompted to cut back, in a second condition they were offered a nominal (25 cent) discount along with the prompt and the third condition was a baseline condition. One-third of the participants accepted the offer, enough to lower the overall number of calories served not only to downsizers, but over the entire restaurant population. Study 2 replicated and extended these findings by demonstrating the same pattern of results and showing that the downsizing prompt was better than calorie labeling at reducing the number of calories served. Study 3 once again replicated this pattern of results, and demonstrated that meal downsizing resulted in significantly fewer calories served. Moreover, an analysis of leftovers in Study 3 showed that meal downsizing not only led to fewer calories being served, but also to fewer calories being consumed.

All three studies took place over multiple day blocks that alternated several days each of baseline activity, the downsize prompt (with and without either a small incentive or calorie labeling), and another baseline. Customers were unaware that a study was taking place and all data were recorded through daily cash register receipts.

Table 1 shows that while customers almost never spontaneously ask for a half portion side dish, anywhere from 18-33% were willing to take one when it was suggested ($p < .05$ in all studies)—even without an incentive (Study 1). In addition calorie labels were not effective—either before and after it was introduced and especially compared to the downsize prompt (Study 2). Study 3 also assessed the weight of patrons' leftovers and found that regardless of how much food consumers started out with, everyone left an average of 2oz of food on their plates. This allowed us to determine that meal downsizing not only influences the amount of food purchased, but the amount of food eaten. Finally, the cash register receipt data also revealed there was no evidence of compensation whereby participants who downsized then opted for more highly caloric entrees.

Next, we examined the effectiveness of pre-commitment on shoppers at a popular grocery store in South Africa. Members who ordinarily receive a 25% discount on their healthy food purchases were asked if they would be willing to put their discount on the line by pledging to increase the number of healthy food items by a certain percentage. For example, members were asked if they would pledge to increase their percentage of healthy food items from 25% to 30% in order to maintain their 25% discount. Those who reach the goal get the healthy food discount on all items, but those who fail to reach the goal lose the discount on ALL healthy food items. The data showed that 2/3 of the incentive program members said they were willing to put their discount on the line and pre-commit to buying healthier food at the grocery store. We are now running a field experiment with members from the same population to determine how effective this program is in an actual shopping environment. These data will be presented.

We close by noting that public health interventions often focus on giving information to help consumers make better choices. In reality, this information may have limited ability to change behavior. Our research takes a different approach—one that targets self-control as the primary contributor to poor eating habits. These strategies are effective, easy to implement and are often welcomed by both consumers and retailers. As such, these findings have significant implications for both marketing and public policy.

Exercising to the Lowest Common Denominator

EXTENDED ABSTRACT

Sedentary behavior has been on the dramatic rise in the United States in recent decades. Half of occupations required at least moderate physical exercise in the 1960s; just one fifth did so in 2010 (Church et al., 2011). As a result, average daily occupation-related energy expenditure has decreased by more than 100 calories over the same time period, a reduction that alone can account for a significant portion of the increase in average body weight (Church et al., 2011). In a field study, we attempted to reduce sedentary workplace behavior by introducing walkstations – slow-moving treadmills attached to elevated workspaces enabling employees to walk while working – giving employees feedback on their own and their coworkers' walk-

station usage, and measuring the impact of the health behaviors of coworkers on usage over time.

People's desire to align their behavior with descriptive norms can lead to positive behavior change if the target behavior is positive and people are underperforming relative to the descriptive norm, but also to "boomerang" effects if the target behavior is positive and people are outperforming the descriptive norm (Cialdini et al., 1990; Schultz et al., 2007). While some previous research has documented the positive effects of social support on health behavior (e.g., Berkman, 1986; Cohen & Syme, 1985), recent research suggests that peers can exert more downward than upward pressure on health behaviors, such as research demonstrating that obesity can "spread" though social networks (Christakis & Fowler, 2007); in one study of United States Air Force Academy students, being randomly assigned to squadrons with peers who were less fit in high school predicted the probability of failing the academy's fitness requirements, and these downward effects were driven in particular by exposure to the least physically fit students (Carrell et al., 2011).

But through what proximal mechanism do these distal effects occur? How do the health behaviors of one's peers in the short term create these longer-term health outcomes? Social facilitation suggests that group behavior tends to converge upon the dominant response (Zajonc, 1965); in one study, many participants who had agreed to volunteer their time stopped volunteering as soon as someone else had stopped: once anyone exhibited the dominant response – in this case, *not* volunteering – others followed suit (Linardi & McConnell, 2011). The obesity epidemic and increase in sedentary workplace behavior suggest that with respect to physical activity, the dominant response is *not* to exercise. As a result, feedback on others' walkstation use could cause dyad and group behavior to converge to the dominant response – sitting down – such that people's exercise would converge to the lowest performing member of the group: the lowest common denominator.

Employees (*N*=224) at a US company participated in a six month between-subjects randomized field experiment. In the "hold-out" control condition, participants could not use the walkstations. In three experimental conditions, participants were asked to use the walkstations and sent a personalized weekly email. In the *solo* condition the email summarized the participant's walkstation usage for the previous week; in the *duo* condition – in which each participant was randomly paired with another participant – the email summarized the participant's and their partner's usage. In the *quintet* condition – in which each participant was randomly grouped with four others – the email summarized each participant's and the other four participants' usage. The study was conducted with employees from three differ-

Table 1: Calories per customer (SE)

		No Calorie Labels		t/F	Calorie Labels		t/F	
		Baseline	Downsize		Baseline	Downsize		
Study 1 33% accept	Side dish	480 (9)	396 (11)	5.7***	-	-	-	
(N = 283)	Entrees	530 (21)	516 (17)	<1	-	-	-	
Study 2 18% accept	Side dish	484 (5)	437 (10)		478 (6)	456 (9)	21.8***	
(N = 992)	Entrees	536 (13)	508 (16)		555 (14)	560 (17)	<1	
Study 3 22% accept	Side dish				462 (9)	419 (12)	2.8**	
(N = 263)	Entrees				465 (17)	483 (19)	<1	
Leftover weight (oz)					2.1 (0.2)	1.7 (0.2)	<1	

*p < .05, **p<.01, ***p<.001.

ent work sites of the same company in the same city; randomization was stratified by work site. To use the walkstations, employees entered their unique employee ID; our primary outcome measure was walkstation usage assessed by these login data, which allowed us to assess how often and for how long each employee used the machine.

Walkstation use declined over time ($F(1, 2896)=86.8, p<.0005$) – in general, participants reverted to the dominant response over time – but this main effect was qualified by an interaction between time and feedback condition ($F(2, 2896)=4.62 p=.01$). In both the *duo* and *quintet* conditions, usage declined faster than in the *solo* condition ($F(1, 2898)=5.11, p=.02$). This greater decline in usage in duos and quintets was driven by the fact that usage converges to that of the least frequent user – the lowest common denominator. We first identified each quintet's top performer (the participant with the highest usage), worst performer (the lowest common denominator), and the three "middling" performers in month one, then tracked their behavior in months 2-5 and month 6. Middling performers converge over time to the lowest common denominator, rather than being pulled upward by the top performer. For duos, the same pattern is apparent: over time the top performer is pulled more toward the bottom performer than the reverse. When we randomly group solo participants into post-hoc "quintets," we see no evidence of similar convergence; the same holds true when we group solos into post-hoc "duos." This lack of convergence in these synthetic groups offers further support for the specific impact of social feedback on convergence to the lowest common denominator.

We showed that the impact of social feedback on walkstation usage was to decrease health behaviors: usage declined more in the *duo* and *quintet* conditions than in the solo condition, due to a tendency for people to converge to the lowest common denominator. Our results do not suggest that social feedback always leads to worse behavior; social support can be beneficial in improving people's health (Berkman, 1986; Cohen & Syme, 1985); they do suggest, however, that when the dominant response for a behavior is the negative one (from not exercising to overeating) that social feedback is likely to reinforce rather than ameliorate. Given the power of the dominant response in shaping social behavior, future research should explore the impact of framing behaviors as the dominant response – even when they are not – on health behaviors; in our paradigm, we could have shown participants in quintets *only* data from the top performer, changing the ostensible dominant response, decreasing the salience of the lowest common denominator, and perhaps changing behavior for the better.

Commitment and Environmental Behavior Change: Evidence from the Field

EXTENDED ABSTRACT

Influencing sustainable behavior is an ongoing challenge in psychology and consumer behavior research. One example is that of hotel towel reuse programs, which typically ask guests to "do their part" for the environment by reusing their towels. It is hoped this will trigger conservation minded behavior, but data shows participation rates are generally low (30-38%) (Goldstein et al. 2008). Normative appeals can increase participation (e.g., Goldstein et al. 2008), yet an estimated 50% of hotel patrons remain unresponsive. Furthermore, the "social norm" solution relies on communicating a typically false social "norm"—the majority of guests in most hotels do not reuse their towels.

In this paper we propose a novel approach for increasing guests' participation in hotel towel reuse programs. Specifically, we suggest that allowing guests to actively express their interest in joining hotels' environmental efforts by reusing their towels would consequently increase the likelihood they would do so. In order to test this proposition, we ran a large, intensive field experiment (N = 4,345) in a California hotel to examine how committing to practice sustainable behavior at check-in would influences guests' subsequent compliance with eco-friendly behavior during their stay. Results show that specific commitments coupled with a publicly displayed symbol (environmental pin) increased towel reuse, arguably via signaling and dissonance avoidance.

We predict that guests' participation in towel reuse programs would increase if they initially choose to commit to do so, presumably because *choosing* to commit sends a signal to the individual that she cares about the environment, which should promote consistent behavior (self signaling; see Ariely & Norton 2008; Bem 1972; Bénabou & Tirole 2011). Additionally, we argue that allowing guests to express their commitment to the environment publicly would reinforce their commitment and further increase sustainable behavior (e.g., Ariely et al. 2009). Finally, we expect that guests' participation would be positively affected if their commitment *specifies* the steps required to achieve such behavior (e.g., Wright & Kacmar 1994).

Guests were randomly given the option at check-in to join the hotel's environmental efforts through two types of commitments: General (commitment to be environmentally friendly during stay) or Specific (commitment to reuse towels during stay). To reinforce signaling, some guests received a "Friend of the Earth" pin. This resulted in a two (Commitment Specificity: general, specific) by two (Symbol: pin, no pin), between-participants, design. We also included three external control conditions: "Message Only"—guests were only exposed to the hotel's environmental message, "Pin Only"—guests only received a pin, and "No Manipulation". Our main measure of compliance was the likelihood of towel reuse—hanging towels to be reused the next day.

A logistic regression analysis showed Specific Commitment guests were more likely to hang a towel relative to General Commitment guests ($M_{Specific} = 66.6\%$ vs. $M_{General} = 61.0\%$; $Wald(1) = 4.49, p = .034$). The regression further revealed a significant effect of Symbol: guests that received a pin were more likely to hang a towel ($M_{Pin} = 68.0\%$, $M_{NoPin} = 59.6\%$), $Wald(1) = 10.02, p = .002$). The interaction was not significant. A comparison to the three control conditions revealed that Specific Commitment plus Pin guests were more likely to hang a towel than guests in any of the control conditions (p's < .001), while General Commitment plus Pin guests were only more likely to hang a towel than Pin Only guests ($p = .016$). When using a Bonferoni correction for multiple comparisons, the Specific Commitment plus Pin condition differed from all other conditions, and there were no other significant differences.

Overall, we found that a commitment alone is relatively ineffective in motivating behavior—the increase in desired behavior occurred only when the commitment was detailed and action-oriented. Based on past work, we propose that an abstract, diffused, commitment requires very little effort to be fulfilled. In contrast, a more specified commitment promotes subsequent behavior consistent with the desired change. In addition, guests signing this specific contract further signal to themselves that they in fact care about the environment, which increases the likelihood that they will behave consistently with that identity. When coupled with a symbol to reinforce their commitment, guests were most likely to practice sustainable behavior, supporting our proposition that adding a social component would further promote behavior change. Notably, the commitment itself was entirely symbolic—once guests completed the check-in process they were able to exist in anonymity and behave as they wished, since they were unaware that their behavior would be monitored. From the perspective of hotels, and other entities attempting to motivate certain behaviors, our approach offers a simple alternative that hinges on individuals' self-identity. Adding one small step to the check-in process significantly increased guests' eco-friendly behavior leading to savings of both scarce resources and money.

REFERENCES

Ariely, Dan, Anat Bracha, and Stephan Meier (2009), "Doing Good or Doing Well? Image Motivation and Monetary Incentives in Behaving Prosocially," *The American Economic Review*, 99 (1), 544–555.

Ariely, Dan and Michael I. Norton (2008), "How Actions Create–Not Just Reveal–Preferences," *Trends in Cognitive Sciences*, 12 (1), 13–16.

Bem, Daryl J. (1972), "Self-Perception Theory," in *Advances in Experimental Social Psychology*, Vol. 6, ed. Leonard Berkowitz, New York, NY: Academic Press, 1–62.

Bénabou, Roland and Jean Tirole (2011), "Identity, Morals, and Taboos: Beliefs as Assets," *The Quarterly Journal of Economics*, 126 (2), 805–855.

Berkman, Lisa F. (1986), "Social Networks, Support, and Health: Taking the Next Step Forward," *American Journal of Epidemiology*, 123(4), 559-562.

Carrell, Scott E., Mark Hoekstra, and James E. West (2011), "Is Poor Fitness Contagious? Evidence From Randomly Assigned Friends," *Journal of Public Economics*, 95, 657-663.

Choi, James J., David Laibson, Brigitte Madrian, and Andrew Metrick (2004), "For Better or For Worse: Default Effects and 401(K) Savings Behavior," In *Perspectives in the Economics of Aging*, ed. David Wise, 81-121, Chicago, IL: University Press.

Christakis, Nicholas A. and James H. Fowler (2007), "The Spread of Obesity in a Large Social Network Over 32 Years," *New England Journal of Medicine, 357*, 370-379.

Church Timothy S., Diana M. Thomas, Catrine Tudor-Locke, Peter T. Katzmarzyk, Conrad P. Earnest, et al. (2011), "Trends Over 5 Decades in U.S. Occupation-Related Physical Activity and their Associations With Obesity," *PLoS ONE* 6(5): 1-7.

Cialdini, Robert B. (2003), "Crafting Normative Messages to Protect the Environment," *Current Directions in Psychological Science*, 12, 105-109.

Cialdini, Robert B., Raymond R. Reno, and Carl A. Kallgren (1990), "A Focus Theory of Normative Conduct: Recycling the Concept of Norms to Reduce Littering in Public Places," *Journal of Personality and Social Psychology*, 58(6), 1015-1026.

Goldstein, Noah J., Robert B. Cialdini, and Vladas Griskevicius (2008), "A Room with a Viewpoint: Using Social Norms to Motivate Environmental Conservation in Hotels," *Journal of Consumer Research*, 35 (3), 472–482.

Linardi, Sera and Margaret A. McConnell (2011), "No Excuses for Good Behavior," *Journal of Public Economics*, 95(5-6), 445-454.

Schultz, P. Wesley, Jessica M. Nolan, Robert B. Cialdini, Noah J. Goldstein, and Vladas Griskevicius (2007), "The Constructive, Destructive, and Reconstructive Power of Social Norms," *Psychological Science*, 18(5), 429-434.

Thaler, Richard H. and Cass R. Sustein (2009), *Nudge: Improving Decisions about Health, Wealth, and Happiness*, New York, NY: Penguin Books.

Wright, Patrick M. and K. Michele Kacmar (1994), "Goal Specificity as a Determinant of Goal Commitment and Goal Change," *Organizational Behavior and Human Decision Processes*, 59, 242–260.

Zajonc, Robert B. (1965), "Social Facilitation," *Science*, 149(3681), 269-274.

A Variety of Views on Variety-Seeking

Chairs: Yanping Tu, University of Chicago, USA
Aner Sela, University of Florida, USA

Paper #1: Preferring the Same, but Consuming Differently: Vicarious Satiation and Variety-seeking in groups

Yanping Tu, University of Chicago, USA
Ayelet Fishbach, University of Chicago, USA

Paper #2: Less is More: Variety as a Preference Strength Signal

Aner Sela, University of Florida, USA
Michal Maimaran, Northwestern University, USA

Paper #3: The "Visual Preference Heuristic" and the Influence of Visual versus Verbal Depiction on Perceived Assortment Variety

Claudia Townsend, University of Miami, USA
Barbara E. Kahn, University of Pennsylvania, USA

Paper #4: Variety and the Spice of Life: The Effect of Spicy Gustatory Experiences on Variety-Seeking

Sayantani Mukherjee, California State University, Long Beach, USA
Thomas Kramer, University of South Carolina, USA
Katina Kulow, University of South Carolina, USA

SESSION OVERVIEW

People often exhibit a preference for variety in choice: we buy an assortment of cereals, yogurt flavors, and beverages rather than pick our favorite option multiple times. Variety-seeking behavior is fundamentally intriguing because, although people can usually select their favorite options repeatedly, they often choose to include less-preferred options (McAlister and Pessemier 1982). Perhaps not surprisingly, variety-seeking has generated a considerable amount of research focusing on the reasons for this behavior (Kahn and Ratner 2005 for review), such as uncertainty about future preferences (Read and Loewenstein 1995; Simonson 1990), a preference for varied experiences (Ratner, Kahn, and Kahneman 1999), and social norms favoring variety (Ratner and Kahn 2002).

But while it is clear that people tend to incorporate variety in their choices for various reasons, new insights suggest that variety may serve additional purposes, and have further antecedents and consequences, than previously considered. Can variety-seeking be driven by vicarious satiation from products that others choose to consume? Might variety serve as a self-presentation instrument, through which consumers convey information about their preferences? Can perceptions of variety be influenced by solely altering the presentation format? And is the notion of variety as "the spice of life" actually related to physical spiciness?

The current session addresses these and related questions as it offers cutting-edge insights into the role of variety-seeking in consumer behavior. The first paper (Tu and Fishbach) finds that the variety of products a group of people would choose to consume is larger than the variety of products an equivalent group of people would identify as their favorite. This is because people's desires for certain products can be vicariously satiated by others' consumption-oriented choices, but not from others' stated preferences The second paper (Sela and Maimaran) shows that people use variety as a means of conveying information about the strength of their preferences, choosing less variety to signal strong preferences for socially-desirable options (e.g., highbrow products) and more variety to signal weak preferences for socially-undesirable options (e.g., lowbrow products).

Whereas the first two papers focus on novel antecedents and roles of variety-seeking, the next papers examine perceptions of variety and the embodied underpinnings of variety seeking. The third paper (Townsend and Kahn) illustrates how visual versus verbal presentation format differentially influences perceived variety. While visual presentation is beneficial in small choice-sets, in larger ones it increases perceived variety and complexity, ultimately leading to greater choice overload and deferral, compared to a verbal presentation format. Finally, the fourth paper (Mukherjee, Kramer, and Kulow) takes an embodied cognition perspective and shows that people choose more variety after eating spicy food, reflecting the adage that "variety is the spice of life".

Taken together, the papers illuminate the social, informative, structural, and physical aspects of variety and variety-seeking. Considering the ubiquity of variety-seeking behavior, and the breadth of topics these papers cover, the session should be of interest to a broad set of audiences. Not only should it appeal to researchers working on judgment, decision making, and choice, but also to those who study satiation, self-presentation, processing styles, and embodied cognition more generally.

Preferring the Same, but Consuming Differently: Vicarious Satiation and Variety-seeking in groups

EXTENDED ABSTRACT

A key finding in previous research is that people tend to seek variety. Whereas most of the research examined variety-seeking at the individual level (Kahn and Lehmann 1991; McAlister 1982; Ratner and Khan 2002; Read and Loewenstein 1995; Simonson 1990), consumers also seek variety at the group level (Ariely and Levav 2000). In fact, lots of consumption related decisions are made in groups, where each consumer's decision can be viewed as part of a group's decision. Therefore it is imperative to understand the driving forces of variety-seeking behaviors at the group level.

Ariely and Levav (2000) showed that the variety of products chosen by a group is larger when group members announce their choices sequentially rather than making choices individually, mainly due to information-gathering motivation and self-presentational concerns. In this paper, we propose vicarious satiation as a novel factor that can account for this effect, and base our hypothesis on two separate lines of research. Firstly, experiencing or anticipating satiation from consumption (McAlister 1982; Read and Loewenstein 1995) is one major reason that people seek variety. Secondly, research on vicarious effects showed that people could vicariously share others' experience, such as goal fulfillment (McCulloch et al. 2011; Wilcox et al. 2009), depletion (Ackerman et al. 2009), loneliness (Wesselmann, Bagg, and Williams 2009), cognitive dissonance (Norton et al. 2003). Therefore we argue that other's choice of consumption goods can vicariously satiate one's own desire for them, resulting in variety-seeking in choice at group level.

To test this hypothesis, we directly compared variety-seeking in choice with variety-seeking in preference at the group level across four studies. Specifically, we asked participants to either choose products that they wanted to consume or identify products that they preferred, after learning about others' choices or preferences. We predict that people would seek more variety in making choices than stating preferences. This is because, although both others' choices and preferences can provide positive information about the chosen or preferred items, only the former can vicariously satisfy one's own desire, leading to greater variety-seeking.

In study 1, we used dyads, and showed participants several pairs of products (e.g., bookends, chairs, water bottles). Depending on conditions, we asked participants to either make a choice ("which one will you choose?") or state their preference ("which one do you like better?") regarding each product pair sequentially. We measured the variety of products chosen or preferred by these dyads, and found that the variety in "making choice" condition is larger than that in "stating preference" condition.

Because preference sometimes implies choice and choice indicates preference, in study 2, we used a stronger manipulation to better distinguish these two constructs. Specifically, we used several pairs of gendered-products that matched the gender of our target participants (e.g., men's shoes/wallets/belts for male participants, and women's shoes/wallets/belts for female participants). We asked participants to either make consumption-oriented choices or state preferences after a confederate did the same thing. In "making choice" condition, the gender of the confederate was the same as that of the products (i.e., the confederate was male/female when the products were men's/women's); whereas in "stating preference" condition, the gender of the confederate was different from that of the products (i.e., the confederate was male/female when the products were women's/men's). The logic is that, when the gender of the confederate does not match that of the products, his/her preferences can no longer imply choice (or consumption). We measured the variety of products chosen or preferred by these dyads, and again found that the former is greater than the latter.

Study 3 extended the context of vicarious satiation from between two individuals to between an individual and a group. Specifically, we showed participants several pairs of products (e.g., lamps, clocks, napkin holders) and told them that these products have recently been tested among a panel of consumers. In the "making choice" condition (vs. "stating preference" condition), we randomly picked one item from each product pair and told participants that this item was the most-chosen one (vs. the most-preferred one) by the consumer panel. We asked participants to either make choices or state preferences regarding each product pair and then measured the variety of products incorporated by the "grand group", which consisted of our target participant and the consumer panel (fake group members). The variety index for this grand group would be higher if our target participants don't follow the consumer panel's decisions. Results showed that people indeed were less likely to follow the consumer panel's decisions (i.e., greater variety-seeking) in making choices than in stating preferences.

Having shown the basic effect, we further explored whether vicarious satiation and the tendency that people seek variety in choice can translate into purchase intentions. We reason that because other's choice of a consumption item can vicariously satisfy one's own desire for it, people should exhibit lower purchase intentions when a product is chosen by others than preferred by others, although both others' choice and preference can provide positive information about the product. Therefore in study 4, we showed participants a series of food items – for example, Quaker oatmeal (Raisin & Spice), Orville popcorn (Movie Theater Butter) - and asked about their intentions to purchase the items. Before they made their decision, we told participants that these products were either the "most-chosen items", or "most-liked items", of a large group of people we recently surveyed. We found that people's purchase intentions were lower after knowing that a product was chosen by most people, than preferred by most people.

Across four studies, we found the consistent pattern that the variety of products a group of people choose to consume is larger than the variety of products they identify as their preferred ones. By merely manipulating decision type (i.e., choices or preferences), we held factors such as self-presentational concern, need for uniqueness, pressure to conform, etc. constant. By directly comparing variety-seeking in choice with variety-seeking in preference, we provided evidence for the vicarious satiation account.

Less is More: Variety as a Preference Strength Signal

EXTENDED ABSTRACT

People often exhibit a preference for variety when selecting multiple items from a category on a single occasion. We buy an assortment of yogurt flavors, snacks, and herbal teas rather than pick our favorite option multiple times, even though doing so forces us to include less-preferred options (McAlister and Pessemier 1982). This preference for variety is explained in terms of uncertainty about future preferences (Read and Loewenstein 1995; Simonson 1990), a tendency to prefer varied experiences (Drolet 2002; Ratner, Kahn, and Kahneman 1999), and social norms favoring variety (Ariely and Levav 2000; Ratner and Kahn 2002).

Although most prior work has focused on factors that lead people to increase the amount of variety in their selections, are there situations in which less, rather than more variety would be preferred? We propose that people selectively choose smaller or larger amounts of variety to convey information, both to others and to themselves, about the strength of their preferences. We demonstrate that choosing a small variety is often perceived as an indication of strong and identity-related preferences for the selected options, whereas choice of a large variety is perceived as an indication of weaker and identity-unrelated preferences.

This proposition leads to novel predictions that are unexplained by previous accounts. Specifically, we predict and demonstrate that people often vary the amount of variety they choose as a means of conveying desirable information about the strength or weakness of their preferences for options in socially-desirable vs. undesirable domains. Four experiments support this prediction and demonstrate that when self-presentation cues are present (e.g., when expecting to be evaluated by others), they incorporate less variety in choices among socially-desirable options (e.g., healthful and highbrow products), thereby expressing strong preferences for such options, and more variety in choices among socially-undesirable options (e.g., unhealthful and lowbrow products), thereby expressing weak preferences for such options.

Experiment 1 demonstrates that people rely on the association between smaller variety and stronger preferences as a guide when trying to convey information to others through their choices. Specifically, we asked participants to imagine they either wanted others to infer that they had strong, identity-relevant preferences for the selected options or did not want others to make such an inference. Participants then indicated whether they would choose a small or a large variety of options, in various domains. The results show that participants explicitly said they would choose a small variety when they wanted others to think they had stronger and more identity-relevant preferences and a large variety when they did not want other to make this inference about them.

Experiment 2 examined conditions that lead people to strategically choose different amounts of variety, as a means of conveying information about the strength of their preferences. Participants were asked to choose 3 snacks from a healthful versus unhealthful assortment. Using an expected evaluation manipulation (Ratner and

Kahn 2002; Simonson and Nowlis 2000), we manipulated whether healthful options were perceived as socially-desirable in that situation. The results show that participants who expected their choice to be evaluated by nutritionists and health-professionals (for whom healthful snack was socially-desirable, based on a pretest) chose *less* variety among healthful snacks, thereby signaling stronger preferences for these options, and *more* variety among unhealthful snacks, thereby signaling weaker preferences for these options, compared to participants who expected their choices to be evaluated by academics (pretested to be less healthfulness-neutral) or participants who did not expect to be evaluated at all.

Experiment 3 demonstrates the process underlying the effect of anticipated evaluation on variety-seeking by directly manipulating social desirability. If people choose different amounts of variety to signal the strength of their preferences for socially-desirable versus undesirable options, then the effect of anticipated evaluation should *reverse* depending on which type of options are perceived as more versus less socially-desirable in a given context. College students selected among movies starring either highbrow or lowbrow actors, but we manipulated whether highbrow versus lowbrow options were perceived as more socially-desirable in that particular context (we did that by varying the evaluators' identity). The results show that participants chose less variety among movies starring highbrow actors when expecting to be evaluated by faculty members, whom we manipulated to be seen as having a highbrow taste. However, this effect reversed when participants expected to be evaluated by students, whom we manipulated to be seen as having a lowbrow taste. That is, they chose more variety among movies starring highbrow actors and less variety among movies starring lowbrow actors.

Experiment 4 demonstrates that people use variety to convey information not only to others but also to themselves, as a means for bolstering their self-view. Participants were first primed to feel either certain or uncertain about their own level of sophistication. Then, they selected three movies starring either highbrow or lowbrow actors. Consistent with our theory, they selected less variety among highbrow options and more variety among lowbrow options after being primed with sophistication-*uncertainty* than with sophistication-certainty. Moreover, choosing a smaller variety among highbrow options boosted participants' sophisticated self-perceptions.

Taken together, these findings provide a novel explanation for variety-seeking behavior and support our hypothesis that people choose variety strategically, to signal their preferences for options with socially (un)desirable traits. The results suggest that people choose less (vs. more) variety to signal stronger, more identity-relevant (vs. weaker, identity-irrelevant) preferences for socially-desirable (vs. undesirable) options. Further, although prior work has focused on consumers' tendency to incorporate *more* variety in their selections, the current findings suggest that a small variety is often more diagnostic than a large variety as an indicator of underlying preferences.

The "Visual Preference Heuristic" and the Influence of Visual versus Verbal Depiction on Perceived Assortment Variety

EXTENDED ABSTRACT

Variety in choice options tends to be an attractive feature (Sellars 1991 as cited in Kahn 1995) and variety-seeking is understood to be a common consumer behavior (McAlister and Pessemier 1982). And yet, variety can increase perceived complexity and, moreover, too much variety can be overwhelming leading to decreased motivation to choose and harming subsequent satisfaction (Jacoby, Speller,

and Berning 1974; Iyengar and Lepper 2000). Therefore, it seems a balance must be struck between providing enough variety so as to attract consumers, without overwhelming them with options.

A natural question that arises from this discussion is to consider how variety is perceived. We investigate this by focusing on the presentation form of the options, whether products are presented visually in pictures or verbally in words. We examine what type of presentation form is preferred and also whether presentation form influences the decision-making process including perceptions of variety and choice.

Specifically we look to inherent differences in the processing of images and words to form our hypotheses. Prior research describes images processed in a quick gestalt manner where all attributes are generally processed in parallel. In contrast, the processing of words requires a piecemeal approach which is slower and sequential in nature (Hart 1997; Paivio 1986). We hypothesize and find a decreased effectiveness of visual depiction for large choice sets occurs because of this difference in processing. The gestalt processing used to examine individual images carries over to affect the manner in which the entire choice set is considered resulting in a faster and less systematic approach. Additionally, because gestalt processing allows for easier identification of attribute interactions (Holbrook and Moore 1981; Veryzer and Hutchinson 1998), visual depiction of choice options increases the perceived variety of the choice set. While increased perceived variety is generally positive in smaller choice sets, in larger choice sets it can be accompanied by increased perceived complexity. In contrast, the more deliberate and systematic piecemeal processing necessary with verbal depiction increases processing time, which is helpful in larger choice sets and further explains the observed differences in choice behavior resulting from the two presentation forms. Moreover, because this more automatic and holistic processing of words likely feels easier than that of text, we predict decision-makers will prefer visual depiction over verbal even when it is not ideal. Indeed, in an initial pretest, we provide evidence for a "visual preference heuristic;" consumers overwhelmingly choose visual over verbal depiction 81%, $t(97) = 7.63$, p < .01) and this preference exists regardless of choice set size (x^2 (1, N= 46) = 2.71, p=.10).

Then in five studies we examine the impact of presentation format on assortment processing, perception, and choice behavior. Study 1 shows that in larger choice sets image depiction can lead to greater perceived complexity (M_{visual} = 6.1, M_{verbal} = 4.6, $F(1,117)$ = 16.04, $p < .001$) and a higher likelihood to abstain from choice (visual = 16%, verbal = 3%, $\chi^2(1)$ = 6.15, p = .01) than text depiction. Study 2 examines option recall to offer further evidence for an interaction of choice set size and presentation format on processing efficacy. We find a significant interaction between presentation format and number of options ($F(1,201)$ = 57.82, p < .001). Among 8 options, respondents who saw images perform better on an aided recognition task than those who saw verbal descriptions (M_{verbal} = 1.9, M_{visual} = 2.9, $F(1,97)$ = 46.59, $p < .001$). However among 27 options, respondents who saw images perform worse on the aided recognition task than those who saw verbal descriptions (M_{verbal} = 8.1, M_{visual} = 7.5, $F(1,102)$ = 6.14, p = .02).

The final three studies examine whether in fact the difference in processing of images and words are causing both the visual preference heuristic as well as the differences in assortment perception and choice behavior observed in the prior studies. In study 3, we use eye-tracking software to observe the actual process with which options are examined. We find no systematic differences in processing styles in small choice sets between visual and verbal depictions, but in larger choices sets verbal depiction causes respondents to use a more systematic, piecemeal process whereby they spend longer examining each option, use a pattern similar to reading, and as such skip fewer options than when presented with visual depiction.

In study 4, we find further evidence that the differences inherent in piecemeal and gestalt processing cause the variations in assortment perceptions choice behavior between verbal and visual depiction observed. Specifically we show that if we force participants to process more systematically, as they do with verbal stimuli, the negative effects of visual depiction for larger choice sets are diminished; for both verbal and visual depiction choice overload and propensity to opt out of choice decreases with an increase in choice options (27 rather than 8) (options = 12.0%, 27 options = 2.0%, $\chi^2(1) = 3.63$, $p = .057$) and there is no effect of presentation format (visual = 6.0%, verbal = 8.0%, $\chi^2(1) = .08$, $p = .78$).

Finally, in study 5, we consider a more realistic boundary condition to our findings by employing existing familiar products and depicting them with either brand names or photographs. Consistent with all of our previous studies, the photographic visual stimuli result in more perceived variety than do the brand name verbal stimuli ($M_{visual} = 8.0$, $M_{verbal} = 7.4$, $F(1,101) = 6.42$, $p = .01$). However, unlike our previous studies, because of familiarity with the products, participants to do not take longer to review the text choice set ($M_{visual} = 18.9$, $M_{verbal} = 20.6$, $F(1, 100) = .64$, $p = .42$) nor rate the image choice set as more complex ($M_{visual} = 4.2$, $M_{verbal} = 5.2$, $F(1,101) = 8.05$, $p = .01$). We conclude with a discussion of the implications of our findings for managers and researchers.

Variety and the Spice of Life: The Effect of Spicy Gustatory Experiences on Variety-Seeking

EXTENDED ABSTRACT

Consumers often seek variety in their choices (McAlister and Pessemier 1982; Ratner, Kahn, and Kahneman 1999; Simonson 1990). Reasons for variety-seeking that have been identified include uncertainty about future preferences (Kahn and Lehman 1991) and anticipated satiation (McAlister 1982). Interestingly, and consistent with the idiom that variety is the spice of life – that is, that one's life will be more interesting if it includes a variety of experiences – consumers also engage in variety-seeking to make a positive impression on others (Ratner and Kahn 2002), given that choosing greater variety is reflective of being a more interesting person. The current research takes the expression that variety "spices up" one's life and provocatively examines the reverse. Specifically, adding to emerging findings on embodied cognition, we test if gustatory sensations of greater spiciness will lead to increased variety in consumers' choices.

Theories of embodied cognition suggest that not only does the mind control the body, but that the body also influences the mind (e.g., Barsalou 2008). Much research in the area of embodied cognition has investigated the effect of bodily movement on cognition. For example, Labroo and Nielsen (2010) find that movement towards aversive stimuli results in more favorable evaluations of them. As well, firming one's muscles increases willpower and ability to withstand temptations (Hung and Labroo 2011). Recent research has also explored the cognitive consequences of sensory experiences, such as touch and smell. For example, holding a warm versus cold cup results in a target person to be judged warmer versus colder (Ijzerman and Semin 2009; Williams and Bargh 2008; Zhong and Leonardelli 2008). Interestingly, a fishy smell tends to arouse suspicion in people (Lee and Schwarz 2011), showing that a sensory experience can indeed influence cognitions that include metaphors. Our research tests if tasting more (vs. less) spicy food results in greater variety-seeking

behavior, based on the association between variety and spicing up one's life.

In study 1, 72 participants were assigned to a more (vs. less) spicy taste condition in a one-factor between-subjects design. Respondents were informed that they were participating in a series of unrelated studies, the first of which would be a taste test for a tortilla chip. After tasting either the more or less spicy chip, they completed the variety-seeking task. Specifically, following Levav and Zhu (2009), participants chose three highlighter pens out of six possible colors, which constituted our main dependent variable. Participants were told that they could choose the highlighters in any combination of colors, which they would receive following the experiment.

Next, they evaluated their tortilla chip experience, rated the extent to which they liked spicy food and tortilla chips, and how often they ate spicy food. None of the means differed between conditions; $Fs < 1$.

Manipulation checks confirmed that our manipulation worked as intended: participants who ate the more spicy tortilla chip judged it to be spicier ($M = 5.07$) than those who ate the less spicy chip ($M = 1.43$; $F(1, 69) = 109.52$, $p < .001$). Importantly, and consistent with our hypothesis, participants who tasted the relatively more spicy chip chose more variety in the color of their highlighters, as compared to those who tasted the less spicy chip; $M = 2.92$ versus 2.62, respectively; $F(1, 69) = 6.24$, $p < .05$.

Thus, we found that a spicy gustatory sensation increases variety-seeking. However, if indeed spiciness brings to the fore the benefits of variety, then – once variety has been chosen and thus life has been made more interesting – it should have less of an effect on a subsequent, second variety-seeking task. We test this hypothesis, and an alternative explanation based on positive affect (Kahn and Isen 1993), in study 2.

In study 2, 68 participants were assigned to conditions in a 2 (chips: more vs. less spicy) X 2 (intervening task: variety-seeking vs. control) between-subjects design. Similar to study 1, the current study ostensibly consisted of a series of unrelated tasks, the first of which was a taste test for a tortilla chip. After tasting the more or less spicy chip, participants in the control conditions completed a filler task, while those in the variety-seeking intervening task conditions were asked to list three ice creams flavors they would choose for the next three weeks. Finally, all participants completed the focal variety-seeking task, choosing three chocolates to take home in any combination out of six possible brands.

Manipulation checks and ancillary measures identical to those of study 1 confirmed that our manipulation worked as intended and that the both chips were enjoyed equally. Further, no effects on positive affect were obtained. A 2 (chips: more vs. less spicy) X 2 (intervening task: variety-seeking vs. control) ANOVA on the number of different chocolates chosen yielded the expected interaction; $F(1, 64) = 4.10$, $p < .05$. Specifically, participants in the control condition chose more variety when they had tasted the more ($M = 2.88$) versus less ($M = 2.28$) spicy chip; $F(1, 64) = 7.51$, $p < .05$. Conversely, when provided the opportunity to express variety in the intervening task by selecting ice cream flavors, participants no longer differed in the variety of the chocolates chosen after tasting the more ($M = 2.38$) versus less ($M = 2.41$) spicy chip; $F(1, 64) < 1$.

A third study, currently underway, tests priming as an alternative explanation. Specifically, participants are presented with 'Hot Tamales' spicy candy in a study that ostensibly consists of two parts. Participants in the experimental condition will first complete a candy taste study, which consist of eating and evaluating the spicy candy, before the second study consisting of a variety-seeking task. Those in the control condition will receive the candy at the beginning of the study, but will be told not to eat it until they have completed the first study consisting of the variety-seeking task. Greater variety-seeking when participants receive and consume the candy, as compared to when they receive but do not consume the candy, will be consistent with our embodied cognition-based explanation, but inconsistent with a priming account.

New Directions in Word-of-Mouth

Chairs: Ezgi Akpinar, Erasmus University, The Netherlands
Jonah Berger, University of Pennsylvania, USA

Paper #1: When Controversy Begets Conversation

Zoey Chen, Georgia Tech, USA
Jonah Berger, University of Pennsylvania, USA

Paper #2: Rating with Confidence: Rating Certainty and Word-of-Mouth Behavior

Yu-Jen Chen, University of Maryland, USA
David Godes, University of Maryland, USA

Paper #3: Valuable Virality: The Effect of Advertising Appeals and Brand Integralness

Ezgi Akpinar, Erasmus University, The Netherlands
Jonah Berger, University of Pennsylvania, USA

Paper #4: Does Paying For Online Product Reviews Pay Off? The Effects of Monetary Incentives on Content Creators and Consumers

Andrew Stephen, University of Pittsburg, USA
Yakov Bart, INSEAD, France
Christilene Du Plessis, INSEAD, France
Dilney Goncalves, IE Business School, Spain

SESSION OVERVIEW

Talking with others is a fundamental consumer motive. People tell friends about new restaurants, forward online content to co-workers, and post online reviews about products they like (or hate). Further, these behaviors have a large impact on consumer behavior. Word-of-mouth influences the products people buy, movies they watch, and online communities they join (Chevalier and Mayzlin 2006; Trusov, Bucklin and Pauwels 2009; Huffaker et al. 2011). Consequently, there has been lots of recent interest in word-of-mouth and social media (e.g., Facebook and Twitter). Firms spend a good deal of effort trying to generate word-of-mouth (e.g., encouraging people to write reviews) and create content that consumers will share.

But while it is clear that word-of-mouth is both frequent, and important, less is known about how firm activities shape WOM generation and its consequences. Intuition suggests that more controversial ads will be talked about more, but is that really the case? Companies often ask consumers to rate their experiences, but could using a 5 vs. 100 point scale affect consumer's propensity to share WOM? How can brands create valuable virality, or content that is not only shared but also has positive downstream consequences for the brand (e.g., boosts evaluation or purchase)? How does paying people to write reviews impact review quality and how does disclosure of payment influence consumer evaluations?

This session examines these, and related questions, as it integrates various research perspectives to examine how firm activities affect both the generation and outcomes of word-of-mouth. **Chen and Berger** show that while controversy makes topics more interesting to talk about, it also reduces comfort. Consequently, the effect of controversy on conversation depends on how aspects of the situation (e.g. identity disclosure) and the audience (friends vs. strangers) shape these complementary mechanisms. **Chen and Godes** show that rating an experience on a 5-pt (vs. 100-pt) scale leads to higher WOM intention. These results reflect a rating-certainty effect where the rater believes that her rating captures accurately her underlying utility. **Akpinar and Berger** provide evidence that while soft sell ad appeals (e.g., stories or cool content) are more likely to be shared than hard sell appeals (e.g. emphasizing product features), they

less likely to have a positive impact on purchase likelihood and brand evaluation. Consequently, to create valuable virality, brands must make soft appeal ads where the brand in an integral part of the narrative. Finally, **Stephen et al.** show how paying for reviews and disclosing payment impacts actual and perceived review quality. While paying consumers actually leads to higher quality reviews and does not negatively impact perceptions of review quality, disclosure can either increase or decrease perceptions of product quality because of the contrast between expectations and actual experience.

Consistent with ACR 2012's theme, this session offers diversity in several ways. First, while prior work usually examines the drivers and effects of word-of-mouth separately, this session bridges the gap to simultaneously examine the causes and consequences of word-of-mouth. Second, rather than focusing solely on one methodological approach, this session brings together a variety of methods (e.g., experiments and empirical analysis of field data) to address the questions at hand. Third, each paper attacks these phenomena from a unique perspective, delivering diverse but complementary insights. The co-chairs (Ezgi Akpinar and Jonah Berger) will integrate the talks and open discussion about potential directions for future work in this exciting area.

Given how fundamental word-of-mouth and social transmission is to our daily lives, and recent interest in social media, we expect this session will be of substantial interest to a host of contingencies. Not only should it appeal to researchers working on word of mouth and attitude change, but also to those who study advertising, social influence, consumer-generated content, persuasion and the effects of rating scales. This should produce a fruitful interdisciplinary discussion that will encourage more research in the area.

When Controversy Begets Conversation

EXTENDED ABSTRACT

Conversation topics vary on how controversial they are, or whether they are marked by opposing views (Merriam-Webster 2003). Some advertisements, topics and brands are relatively non-controversial while others are more divisive. GoDaddy.com, for example, often makes risqué Super Bowl ads, while Chevy's ads tend to be less contentious. Topics like the weather are less controversial than gay marriage.

But how does controversy impact conversation? The lay belief among marketers and consumers is that controversy increases conversation (Steel 2011). But is that actually the case?

Further, people engage in all types of conversations. They post anonymously on online discussion boards or have conversations on Facebook; they chat face-to-face with friends or converse with strangers. Might these different contextual factors impact the relationship between controversy and conversation, and if so, how?

We theorize that the impact of controversy on conversation will depend on two countervailing forces. On the one hand, controversy can boost conversation because it is interesting. Differences in opinion can liven things up, and people talk about interesting things to entertain others (Heath et al. 2001) or fulfill self-enhancement goals (e.g., signal that the speaker is interesting, Berger and Schwartz 2011). On the other hand, controversy can decrease conversation by making people uncomfortable. People want to be socially accepted, and interpersonal conflicts, such as those generated by controversial topics, can jeopardize acceptance. How controversy shape conversation, then, will depend on the strength of the two underlying processes.

Contextual factors such as identity disclosure and conversation partner (e.g., friend vs. stranger) should moderate the relationship between controversy and conversation by acting upon these underlying processes. The effect of interestingness is likely to remain static across situations since interesting topics are likely to remain interesting across settings. However, if discomfort reflects concerns about social acceptance, then it should be weaker in contexts when social acceptance concerns are less salient (e.g., when there is no identity disclosure) or less threatened by discussion of controversial issues (e.g., when talking to friends).

Three studies examine (1) how controversy affects conversation, (2) the underlying drivers, and (3) how this relationship varies in different conversation contexts.

Field Study 1: Our first study uses articles from a real news website to look at how the amount of controversy an article evokes impacts the number of comments it receives. We collected over two hundred articles as well as the number of comments each received (~5,000 comments overall. Two independent coders then rated each article on controversy (1 = not at all controversial, 7 = very controversial). Regressing the number of comments articles received on both the linear and squared controversy ratings shows an inverted-U relationship between controversy and conversation. Low levels of controversy increase conversation. But past a moderate controversy, additional controversy fails to increase (and even decreases) conversation. This is particularly noteworthy given the moderate level at which the effects of controversy start to reverse.

Study 2: In our second study, we experimentally manipulate controversy to observe directly examine its causal impact on conversation. We also test the underlying processes of interest and comfort and also explore how identity disclosure moderates the relationship between controversy and conversation by affecting comfort.

Participants were randomly assigned to condition in a 2 Disclosure (No disclosure vs. disclosure) x 3 Controversy (low vs. moderate vs. high) design. They listed a broad topic in current events (e.g., "taxes") and then listed three subtopics, one that is high, middle, and low in controversy (e.g., "corporate bailout", "taxing the rich", and "sales tax"). Participants were asked to imagine having an online conversation with a stranger in which everyone was either using aliases (No Disclosure condition) or real names (Disclosure condition). Then, they were randomly given one of the subtopics they listed and asked to rate how likely they would be to talk about the subtopic in that conversation. They also rated how interesting they found the subtopic to be and how (un)comfortable they would feel talking about the subtopic.

Results show that disclosure moderate the relationship between controversy and conversation. In the no disclosure condition, controversy has an inverted-U relationship with conversation where moderate level of controversy increases conversation ($M_{low} = 4.24$ vs. $M_{moderate} = 5.61$, $p = .02$). However, additional controversy decreases conversation ($M_{moderate} = 5.61$ vs. $M_{high} = 4.04$, $p < .01$). In the disclosure condition, controversy doesn't increase conversation (low same as middle same as high, $ps > .23$) and appears to decrease conversation ($M_{high} = 3.58$ vs. $M_{low} = 4.87$, $p < .05$). Mediation analyses show that when people do not disclose identity, conversation is driven primarily by interestingness. When identity is disclosed, however, conversation is driven by both interestingness and comfort.

Study 3: In our third study, we further test our framework and examine how conversation partner (friend vs. stranger) affects people's propensity to talk about controversies.

We again asked participants to list a general topic and three subtopics that varied in level of controversy. Then we manipulated the audience by asking them to imagine having a face-to-face conversation with either a friend or stranger. Then, they rated each of the three subtopics they listed on likelihood of talking (main DV), interestingness, and discomfort.

Results reveal that conversation partner moderates the relationship between controversy and conversation. When talking to friends, controversy increases conversation. A move from low to moderate levels of controversy increases conversation ($M_{low} = 3.65$ vs. $M_{moderate} = 4.81$ $p = .02$). Beyond that point, however, additional controversy fails to further increase conversation ($M_{moderate} = 4.81$ vs. $M_{high} = 5.00$, $p = .68$). When talking to strangers, conversation is flat across the three controversy conditions ($M_{low} = 3.78$ vs. $M_{moderate} = 3.52$, and $M_{high} = 3.48$, pairwise comparisons all insignificant). Mediation analyses reveal that when talking to friends, conversation is driven primarily by interestingness; however, when talking to strangers, the positive effect of interesting is canceled out by discomfort.

Taken together, result show that (1) controversy doesn't necessarily increase conversation, (2) interesting and comfort drive the effects, and that (3) situational factors moderate the outcome by affecting the underlying processes.

Rating with Confidence: Rating Certainty and Word-of-Mouth Behavior

EXTENDED ABSTRACT

Online product ratings represent a common outlet for consumers to express their post-consumption (dis)satisfaction about product performance. Consumers, as product reviewers, evaluate products based on their consumption experience via ratings and reviews on retailer websites such as Amazon.com and Yelp.com or manufacturer websites such as Apple.com and dominos.com. It has been consistently shown that product ratings, as a part of WOM, have a significant impact on product sales (Chevalier and Mayzlin 2006; Chintagunta et al 2011; Zhu and Zhang 2010). While most research has focused on the impact of product reviews on those reading them, little attention has been paid to their impact on those providing them. We address this question here by investigating a product reviewer's subsequent WOM behavior after writing a review or rating a product.

In a pilot study, we found that different rating scales led to different levels of WOM. Respondents asked to rate an experience on a 5-pt scale report higher WOM intention compared with those rating on a 100-pt scale. To our knowledge, no existing theory explains this effect. We hypothesize that the result is driven by a general psychological construct which we label "rating certainty." According to this theory, a product reviewer's "true" utility must be mapped to the platform's chosen rating scale. The fidelity of the mapping process in communicating the rater's true utility varies across contexts. This fidelity – the extent to which one's chosen rating captures accurately her underlying utility – is the essence of rating certainty. Finally, when a consumer has higher rating certainty, we argue that she is more likely to transmit WOM.

While our theory is based on rating certainty, it is also entirely plausible that attitude certainty may play a similar role. That is, when people are more certain about their attitude, the likelihood of performing attitude-associated behavior, such as engaging in WOM, will increase (Bassili 1996; Tormala and Petty 2002). However, we stress that rating certainty differs from attitude certainty in that the former captures one's certainty toward the rating while the latter captures certainty toward the attitude target. To demonstrate that these two constructs are distinct, we present the results of a discriminant validity analysis. Moreover, we control for attitude certainty in all analyses.

Next, we examined the impact of rating scale on WOM and the mediating role of rating certainty. One hundred and twenty two adults from Amazon Mechnical Turk participated in a video rating study. The study design was a 2 (rating scale: 2pt or 5pt) x 2 (certainty measure order: rating certainty first (RC) or attitude certainty first (AC)). Participants first watched a 2-minute video and then rated the video on either a 2-point or 5-point rating scale anchored from awful to excellent. In the RC condition, we measured rating certainty via four 9-point items which had been chosen based on a previous scale development study. These included: "How sure are you that the rating score you assigned is precise?", "How definite is your rating score of the video?", "The rating score I assigned was clear", and "The rating score I assigned was precise." We combined these four items to generate a rating certainty index (Cronbach's α= .95). Next, we measured participants' attitude toward the video and their certainty with respect to the attitude measure (Barden and Petty 2008). In the AC condition, we first measured participants' attitude certainty and then their rating certainty. We counterbalanced the question order of RC and AC to control for any order effect. Since the results show no order effect, we combined these two conditions in our analysis. Finally, we assessed WOM likelihood on a 7-point scale.

We found the predicted rating-scale effect: participants were more likely to transmit WOM in the 5-pt condition than in the 2 pt condition (M_{2pt}=2.2, M_{5pt}=2.8, $p < .04$). Moreover, rating certainty was higher in the 5 pt condition than in the 2 pt condition (M_{2pt}=6.4, M_{5pt}=7.6, $p < .04$). Notably, we find no effect of rating scale on attitude certainty: participants in the two scale conditions are equally certain about their attitude toward the video (M_{2pt}=8.0, M_{5pt}=7.9, $p = .69$). This suggests that rating scale is not a source of attitude certainty and, thus, that attitude certainty does not explain the effect of scale on WOM. Finally, we perform a mediation test which supports the hypothesis that the effect of rating scale on WOM can be explained by rating certainty. The five-point scale induces higher levels of rating certainty leading to higher levels of WOM.

In sum, we develop and validate a measure of rating certainty and demonstrate its discriminant validity with respect to attitude certainty. Finally, we demonstrate that rating certainty can be affected by the chosen rating scale and that, in turn, it may be an antecedent to WOM intention.

Valuable Virality: The Effect of Advertising Appeals and Brand Integralness

EXTENDED ABSTRACT

What influences whether ads are not only highly shared (i.e., viral) but also increase product evaluation and sales of the brands that create them (i.e., valuable)?

Recent research has shown that word-of-mouth can boost diffusion and sales (e.g., Godes and Mayzlin 2004, 2009; Goldenberg et al. 2009). Consequently, many organizations and brands have invested lots of resources in trying to craft content that consumers will talk about and share. But there are two difficulties with this approach. On the one hand, most people don't like to share things that look like ads, so companies try to create outrageous or funny content (e.g., Subservient Chicken or Old Spice). On the other hand, while it's great to make viral content, the content will only help the brand if it changes downstream consumer behavior, such as increasing brand evaluation or purchase. How can companies craft content that is not only viral, but also valuable?

We suggest that valuable virality depends on two key factors: ad appeal (hard vs. soft sell) and brand integralness (whether brand is integral to the advertising plot or not). While *hard sell* appeals focus on product features using a sales orientation, *soft sell* appeals convey a story through indirect mechanisms (i.e. showing beautiful scenes or evoking affective reactions such as humor and surprise, Okazaki, Mueller and Taylor 2010). As noted above, people don't like to share things that look like direct persuasion attempts and soft sell appeals might be shared more because they provide more interesting content.

That said, soft sell appeals are not very useful if they don't boost product evaluation or choice. Further, consumers realize advertisers are trying to persuade them and may dislike ads that they know are trying to trick them (Friestad and Wright 1994). Consequently, we suggest that to generate valuable virality, the ad must not only be interesting content but the brand must be integral to the narrative - woven in so deeply that it's directly connected to the underlying story.

We test this possibility in two studies. In Study 1, we exposed participants to either (1) a soft sell-brand integral ad; (b) a soft sell-brand not integral ad or (c) a hard sell ad (brand integral by default). Then they reported their evaluation of the ad and likelihood of sharing it, as well as their evaluation of the brand, and likelihood of purchase.

Results show how appeal type and brand integralness influence different dependent variables differently (Figure 1). As predicted, soft sell appeals boosted sharing and ad evaluation. Compared to the hard sell appeal, participants said they would be more likely to share either of the soft sell appeals and evaluated them more favorably.

The effects differed, however, for brand evaluation and purchase. As predicted, while hard sell appeals boosted brand evaluation and purchase above soft sell appeals where the brand was not integral, soft sell appeals where the brand was integral had the most positive effects.

In Study 2, we rule out alternative explanations and provide deeper insight into the mechanism behind the effects. While the results of Study 1 are supportive, one might wonder whether it was something about the ads themselves, rather than the integralness of the brand, that drove the effects. To rule out this possibility, we created two versions of each ad. The ad content itself was the same, but we varied what type of product the ad was for to manipulate integralness. So across conditions, the same ad was either integral or not depending on whether the product it was for fit with the ad content. We also tested why non integral soft sell appeals reduce brand evaluation and choice by measuring how participants feel about persuasive attempts.

A 2 (product category) × 3 (ad type) ANOVA was conducted on the various dependent measures. As expected, and extending the results of Study 1, the manipulations had different impacts on different

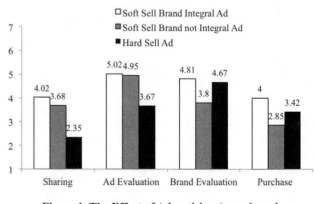

Figure 1. The Effect of Advertising Appeals and Brand Integralness

dependent variables. While soft sells boosted sharing and ad evaluation compared to hard sells, only integral soft sell appeal boosted brand evaluation and purchase. Further, mediation analyses show that these effects are driven by the extent to which consumers find the ad persuasive attempts as acceptable and not very manipulative. When the brand is integral to the ad, persuasive attempts seemed more acceptable and less manipulative and therefore those brands receive more favorable evaluations and purchase intentions.

Taken together, these results show how content (e.g., ads) can be crafted so that it is both highly shared and beneficial to the brand or organization that made it. While soft sell appeals are more likely to be shared, the brand must be integral to the ad to receive the benefits of brand evaluation and purchase. This is driven by consumers' perceptions of advertiser's persuasive attempts. Overall the findings suggest how to generate virality that is also valuable to the brand.

Does Paying For Online Product Reviews Pay Off? The Effects of Monetary Incentives on Content Creators and Consumers

EXTENDED ABSTRACT

This research considers whether offering incentives to encourage consumers to write online product reviews is beneficial for firms. We propose that paying customers will result in more helpful reviews because offering content creators an explicit incentive may encourage them to take a more professional approach to the review-writing task. Paradoxically if content consumers know that the content creator was paid they may form less favorable expectations of product quality based on the review. Specifically, when incentive provision is disclosed, review consumers doubt the quality of the reviewed product. The doubt induced by payment disclosure is hypothesized to distort product judgments resulting in a shift of evaluations toward a neutral or indifferent attitude when the review is valenced. Paying content creators may therefore ironically decrease review-based product evaluations even though the review itself is more helpful.

We test our predictions in four experiments. In all experiments, participants were members of a large online panel in the U.S. In the first part of Study 1, participants were content creators who played an online game and then wrote a review about it. Participants were randomly assigned to either receive no incentive or a $1 incentive for writing their review. We find that paying an incentive had no impact on perceived effort, or difficulty related to writing the review.

In part 2 of Study 1, subjects were content consumers. Each was randomly assigned one of the reviews generated in part 1 and asked questions about the helpfulness, positivity, and objectivity of the review. Using random effects regression, we find a significant positive effect of incentive provision on helpfulness ($b = .18$, $t = 2.16$, $p = .03$), but not positivity ($p = .78$) or objectivity ($p = .73$). We also show that increasing review helpfulness (through incentive provision) may lead to content consumers being more interested in product trial.

Using a similar procedure, Study 2 examined how content consumers' product evaluations are affected by incentive disclosure. Participants were randomly assigned to one of four conditions in a 2 (no disclosure vs. disclosure) x 2 (no incentive vs. $1 incentive) between-subjects design. In the disclosure (no-disclosure) conditions, participants were (were not) given information about whether the content creator was paid to write the review. The incentive manipulation was the same as that used in Study 1.

We tested how incentives and disclosing them affected content consumers' product evaluations (1 to 5 stars) and their willingness to pay for the game as an app download ($0 to $0.99). We find that product evaluations are *lower* when content creators are incentivized and content consumers are aware of this. In addition, willingness to pay dropped from 81 cents to 25 cents when the reviewer was incentivized and incentive provision was disclosed.

In Study 3 we replicate the Study 2 findings in a different product category (music) and rule out the possibility that consumer-generated reviews are only influential in the absence of more reliable information.

Participants were randomly assigned to one of six conditions in a 3(silent vs. not paid vs. paid) x 2(no additional information vs. additional information) between-subjects design. The first factor manipulated the specificity of the incentive disclosure (silent: no information regarding incentives provision; not paid: "the person who wrote this review was not paid"; paid: "the person who wrote this review was paid"). This new manipulation allowed us to check whether our results hold when disclosure is ambiguous.

The second factor manipulated the inclusion of information from a more realistic source in the participant's information set (no additional information: basic description of the band whose music video was the subject of the review; additional information: basic description of the band and a three page *Rolling Stone* magazine article that positively described the band's history and was created for this study).

We replicate our prior findings by showing that disclosure has a significant main effect on product evaluation ($F(2, 212) = 3.94$, $p = .02$). The main effect of additional information and the two-way interaction were not significant ($p > .6$). The mean product evaluation was lower when the participants thought the content creator had been paid ($M_{paid} = 3.38$) than when nothing was disclosed ($M_{silent} = 3.69$) or when receiving no payment was disclosed ($M_{not-paid} = 3.62$). The evaluation-lowering effect therefore holds despite changes to how incentive disclosure is conveyed and whether or not additional product information is available to content consumers.

Study 4 shows that the effect of incentive disclosure on content consumers' product evaluations is mediated by an increase in doubt in product quality and that this process only occurs when reviews are positive. Additionally, this study examines whether changes in review-based product evaluations caused by incentive disclosure carry over to affect post-experience evaluations.

The product used in this study was the game from the first two studies. Participants were randomly assigned to one of six conditions in a 3 (paid $0 vs. paid $0.75 vs. paid $1.25) x 2 (positive review vs. negative review) between-subjects design. The incentive-disclosure manipulation was similar to that used in the previous studies except that we used two non-zero conditions ($0.75 and $1.25) to show that our previous results were not specifically due to disclosure of a $1 incentive. The valence manipulation involved randomly presenting participants with either a positive or a negative review.

Using the procedure for testing moderated mediation detailed in Preacher, Rucker, and Hayes (2007), we find that the effect of incentive disclosure on pre-experience product evaluation was mediated by doubt when the review was positive. Furthermore, we find that the effect of incentive disclosure on product evaluations through doubt carries over to affect product evaluations when additional experiential information is available.

This research shows that information related to whether a content creator is incentivized can make a difference not only to how the generated content is interpreted by a consumer but also in their assessment of the focal product in both the short-term (at the stage of forming expectations of product quality) and long-term (lowering product evaluations even after having first-hand product experience).

Driving Diffusion: How Social Networks, Sender Motives, and Item Characteristics Shape Social Epidemics

Jonah Berger, University of Pennsylvania, USA
Ezgi Akpinar, Erasmus University, The Netherlands

Paper #1: Share and Scare: Solving the Communication Dilemma of Early Adopters with a High Need for Uniqueness
Sarit Moldovan, Technion, Israel
Yael Steinhart, University of Haifa , Israel
Shlomit Ofen, Technion , Israel

Paper #2: The Cultural Success of Sensory Metaphors
Ezgi Akpinar, Erasmus University, The Netherlands
Jonah Berger, University of Pennsylvania, USA

Paper #3: Ideation and the Spread of Innovative Ideas in Social Networks
Andrew Stephen, University of Pittsburgh, USA
Peter Zubcsek, University of Florida, USA
Jacob Goldenberg, Hebrew University, Israel

Paper #4: Local Neighborhoods as Early Predictors of Innovation Adoption
Jacob Goldenberg, Hebrew University, Israel
Sangman Han, Sungkyunkwan University, Soeul, Korea
Donald Lehmann, Columbia University, USA
Jangyuk Lee, Sungkyunkwan University, Soeul, Korea
Kyung Young Ohk, Sungkyunkwan University, Soeul, Korea
Daniel Shapira, Sungkyunkwan University, Soeul, Korea

SESSION OVERVIEW

Why do some products, ideas, and behaviors catch on? Some products become popular, some innovations spread, and some catchphrases or sayings become successful. Others never seem to get traction and fade quickly. What makes certain things diffuse more than others?

These questions have been investigated from a number of research perspectives. Sociologists and marketing scientists have examined how social network structures impact diffusion (Christakis and Fowler 2009, Goldenberg, Libai, and Muller 2001). Behavioral researchers have examined how psychological motives influence what people decide to share (Cheema and Kaikati 2011; Wojnicki and Godes 2008). Others have looked at how characteristics of the cultural items themselves, such as whether stories are more or less emotional, shapes what goes viral (Heath, Bell and Sternberg 2001; Berger and Milkman 2012). But while each of these research streams has separately examined diffusion, little work has integrated these perspectives.

This session brings together diverse work on social networks, sender characteristics motives, and item characteristics to shed light on the behavioral processes behind diffusion. While early adopters are seen as the key to diffusion, might their psychological motives actually lead them to share less, reducing diffusion? Might sensory phrases (e.g., "bright student" rather than 'smart student") be more likely to diffuse over time? How do social network structures impact both the creativity of ideas people generate, and their diffusion? How can success in certain local neighborhoods be used to predict overall success in the broader social network?

This session addresses these, and related questions, as it integrates multiple research perspectives to shed light on what drives social contagion. The first two papers focus on psychological drivers of transmission. Moldovan, Steinhart, and Ofen demonstrate that

while early adopters are motivated to share word-of-mouth to boost their social status, sharing information can also reduce their uniqueness. Consequently, they often adopt a tactic of sharing while scaring, or telling others about how difficult the product is to use. Using both experiments, and 200 years of data from 5 million books, Akpinar and Berger show that phrases which create a metaphorical link to the senses (e.g., bright student or warm welcome) diffuse more widely than their semantic analogues (i.e., smart student or kind welcome) because they are more memorable.

The next two papers examine the role of social networks in diffusion. Stephen, Zubcsek, and Goldenberg show that having more sources of inspiration (i.e., higher degree and thus more neighbors) does not necessarily improve one's ideas. Rather, it depends on how interconnected (i.e., clustered) one's neighbors are, and the nature of the idea generation task (general vs. specific task). Goldenberg et al. use a social networks database to show that large and dense clusters in a social network are better predictors of success of innovative adoption than other clusters and random samples.

Taken together, these talks illuminate the psychological and sociological processes that shape diffusion and cultural success. Given recent interest in social networks, social media, and social contagion, the session should appeal to broad range of researchers including those who study user-generated content, diffusion and new product adoption as well as those interested in social influence, attitude change, needs for distinction, social networks, and embodied cognition more broadly. The co-chairs (Jonah Berger and Ezgi Akpinar) will integrate the talks and open discussion about potential directions for future research.

Further, as highlighted in this year's program, the session also brings a diversity of methodological perspectives to address these important research questions. The papers cover a wide span of methodologies from experiments and social network analysis to analytic modeling, and empirical analyses of large datasets. As a whole, the talks will deliver diverse but complementary insights on what factors shape diffusion and social epidemics. While sociologists, physicists, and marketing scientists have begun to pay more attention to social contagion, this session integrates a variety of perspectives to examine how psychology and consumer behavior shape these important phenomena.

"Share and Scare": Solving the Communication Dilemma of Early Adopters with a High Need for Uniqueness

EXTENDED ABSTRACT

Early adopters are frequently discussed in the literature as individuals who play an essential role in new product success (Rogers 1995). Early adopters are the first to adopt an innovation, and are therefore the first to recommend it to later adopters. The literature (and practice) consequently treats early adopters as "social salespeople" of new products (Goldsmith and Flynn 1992; Mahajan, Muller, and Srivastava 1990; Midgley and Dowling 1993; Rogers 1995). This, however, may not always be the case. In this research we explore the unwillingness of early adopters to "spread the word" about innovations they adopt. Specifically, we propose that early adopters often face a communication dilemma. While they are inherently motivated to share information about the innovation to others, and reinforce their social status as early adopters, they are aware that this status is diluted as the number of adopters increases. To remain among a selected few who use or possess the innovation, they may intentionally scare others from adopting it too. We therefore name the solution of this dilemma as "share and scare".

The current research reveals the underlying mechanism that drives this dilemma among the early adopters. This mechanism is a product of consumers' need for uniqueness; namely, a positive need to be different relative to other people (Tepper and Hoyle 1996; Tian, Bearden and Hunter 2001). Need for uniqueness is strongly tied to the adoption of unusual and scarce products (Tian et al. 2001). By definition, innovations are scarce, since it is possessed by few or none in its early stages in the market. Therefore, we claim that this dilemma is experienced by early adopters who are driven by elevated need for uniqueness and thus value the uniqueness of the innovation as one of its most beneficial utilities. Early adopters with a high need for uniqueness will therefore desire to express their uniqueness in the presence of a group. However, by "showing off" their new adoption, early adopters increase the risk that other consumers will also adopt the innovation, thereby diminishing early adopters' uniqueness.

Study 1 demonstrates the existence of the dilemma among early adopters with a high need for uniqueness and for different product categories.

Study 2 identifies a possible boundary condition for the dilemma. This study demonstrates that the dilemma would be experienced only when the innovation faces an immediate public launch, and is not experienced for innovations for which launch is expected to be in the future. Results show that when the innovation is not anticipated to be available on the market in the near future, early adopters with a high need for uniqueness are less likely to be concerned that others will imitate them, and therefore report on lower dilemma levels. However, in the future launch condition, there is not a significant difference within the levels of the dilemma across consumer groups.

Study 3 explores how the dilemma is affected by the type of audience that is exposed to the early adopters' word of mouth. Its findings reveal that when the target audience is less likely to imitate the early adopter (i.e. laggard audience), or when the early adopters wish to be imitated by the target audience (i.e. super ordinate audience), early adopters report on lower levels of the dilemma compared to when facing a peer audience.

Studies 4 and 5 shed more light on the "share and scare" solution of the dilemma by showing that early adopters with a high need for uniqueness are more likely recommend the product but at the same time to warn others about it. Study 4 shows that while all consumer groups are willing to recommend both innovative and non-innovative products, early adopters with a high need of uniqueness also intend to scare others from adopting an innovative, but not an existing, product. Study 5 explored additional aspects of the "share and scare" communication and showed that this behavior is relevant for a privately consumed product as well.

The communication dilemma and the "share and scare" solution indicate that, unlike what is "expected" from them, early adopters may not always be willing to spread the word about innovations they adopt, and may intentionally delay or even derail the diffusion process.

This research also integrates into and extends the chasm theory. The chasm is a break in the diffusion process between early and later adopters, presumably because of a lack of communication between the two markets (Moore 1999, Goldenberg, Libai and Muller 2002). However, we suggest that communications in fact exists between the two markets, as early adopters "share" information about the product. Yet, the nature of the information they provide may not acceler-

ate the adoption of the innovation, as they sometimes "scare" others from adopting it.

Managers should be aware of the existence of the communication dilemma when launching innovative products and consequently execute campaigns that overcome this reluctance.

The Cultural Success of Sensory Metaphors

EXTENDED ABSTRACT

Language varies over time (Lieberman et al. 2007; Nowak, Komarova and Niyogi 2002; Pagel, Atkinson and Meade, 2007). There are often many ways to convey the same thing and linguistic variants often act as substitutes. In 1800s, for example, people used the phrase "popular topic" but now the phrase "hot topic" is more en vogue. Why are certain linguistic variants more culturally successful than others?

We suggest that linguistic variants which relate to senses in metaphoric ways should be more successful. A kind person can be described as "warm", an unpleasant note as "sour". Sensory experiences serve as analogical basis for expressing abstract concepts with metaphors (Gibbs and Tendhal 2006; Lakoff and Johnson 1980). Calling a person "warm" suggests the person is inviting, just like a warm shower might be.

Sensory metaphors have important consequences for human thought and behavior (Lee and Schwarz 2010; Zhong and Leonardelli 2008). Humans scaffold abstract concepts onto existing knowledge acquired through sensory experiences with the physical environment. So when an abstract concept is encountered (e.g. feeling socially excluded at a reception), the sensory neural cues associated with the formation of that concept are triggered (e.g. feeling cold), and downstream behaviors (e.g. desire for warm foods and drinks) or expression of the concept (e.g. chilly reception) are based on the activated sensory cues. Thus, abstract concepts can be processed using cues of sensory experiences, even without physically interacting with any sensory stimuli.

Sensory metaphors (e.g., warm person) should be more culturally successful in part, because they are more likely to be remembered. Sensory metaphors may be easier to remember because they activate the same brain regions as sensory experiences (Stilla, Sathiana and Sathian 2012). Further, retrieval of sensory experience knowledge (e.g. "cat has fur") is more automatic, and involves less processing than semantic knowledge (e.g. "cat needs training"; Golberg et al. 2007). Consequently, compared to semantic analogues, there should be stronger associations between sensory metaphors and sensory experiences which should make them easier to retrieve.

Sensory metaphorical phrases may also be easier to remember because they have multiple and accessible linkages with memory. While non-sensory phrases are only stored with their semantic meaning, sensory metaphors are stored both in semantic and sensory codes. Further, the sensory cues are prevalent in the environment. Thus, we expect that increased number of associative cues, some of which are more accessible in the environment may boost memory.

Two studies investigate whether sensory metaphors are (1) more culturally successful over time and (2) more memorable.

In first study, we examined the cultural success of sensory metaphors. First, we compiled an extensive list of sensory metaphors (e.g. bright student) and their semantic analogues (e.g. intelligent student and smart student). Then we recorded the success of each phrase over time using the Google Books corpus. This dataset allowed us to track the number of times phrases were mentioned every year in over 5 million digitized books from 1800 to today. We compared the use of sensory metaphors and semantic analogues using a Poisson model with linear and quadratic effects.

As illustrated in Figure 1, rigorous modeling results show that sensory metaphors are more successful over time, with an increasing quadratic trend ($\beta_{Time*Sensory\ Metaphors}$ = .024, p < .001; β_{Time}^{2} *Sensory Metaphors = -3.55E-5, p < .001; higher than zero for all value of time).

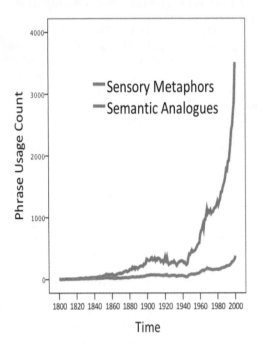

Figure 1- Sensory Metaphors are Used More Frequently over Time

Study 2 experimentally examines whether sensory metaphors are more memorable. Further, we test the underlying role of relation to the senses and greater prevalence of associative cues.

Participants received 32 randomly selected phrases from the pool used in Study 1. Some participants rated each phrase on the extent to which it relates to senses while others rated each phrase on the number of associations it has with other words and ideas. After filler tasks, participants completed an unaided-recall task where they wrote down as many of phrases as they could remember.

The results support our theorizing. First, compared to semantic analogues, sensory metaphors were more likely to be remembered. Second, as predicted, sensory metaphors were rated as more related to the senses and having more associative links. Third, a multiple mediation analysis shows that the effect of phrase type on memory is partially driven by the combination of their sensory nature and prevalence of associative cues.

Alternative mechanisms have difficulty explaining these effects. More emotional (Mackay and Ahmetzanov, 2005), interesting, or descriptive phrases might be more memorable, and concrete, visualizable information may be easier for people to retrieve (Rubin 1995). The sensory metaphorical phrases used here, however, did not differ from the semantic analogues on any of these dimensions. Also, Study 1 still holds if we only look at non-visual sensory metaphors.

Taken together, these findings illustrate how senses shape cultural success in language. Compared to linguistic variants with similar meanings, sensory metaphors are more (1) memorable and (2) culturally successful over time. These findings not only speak to the reciprocal influence between individual psychological processes and collective outcomes (Gureckis and Goldstone 2009) but also em-

bodied cognition, and neural linkages between sensory processing and language.

Ideation and the Spread of Innovative Ideas in Social Networks

EXTENDED ABSTRACT

A growing trend in marketing involves firms using crowd sourcing as part of the product development process. Firms tap the apparent wisdom of consumers to solicit ideas for new products and suggestions for how to improve or extend existing product. In practice, crowd sourced product ideation has led to a proliferation of firm-specific online communities where consumers can submit ideas. Typically the consumer community then discusses, criticizes, elaborates on, and votes on ideas, and firms use this information to help them decide which ideas to develop further. Firms using this approach include BMW, Dell, Delta Air Lines, Google, Kraft, Lego, P&G, and Starbucks. A challenge, however, is soliciting high-quality *innovative* ideas from consumers. Like any social network, information (in this case idea) can diffuse throughout these communities. While this may facilitate the propagation of good ideas that leads to even better ideas, it may also result in mediocre or even bad ideas spreading and negatively impacting the quality of the ideas provided by other members of the networked community.

This research examines the role played by network structure and an individual's network position in product ideation networks/communities in affecting their ability to produce innovative ideas. A novel experimental approach was taken whereby participants were linked to each other through a custom-built online product ideation platform. The platform allowed us to manipulate the network structure, thereby allowing us to vary specific parameters related to participants' positions and connectivity in their networks. We focused on manipulating participants' numbers of neighbors (i.e., their degree), which influenced how many sources of inspiration they were exposed to, and how interconnected participants' neighbors were (i.e., their clustering coefficient), which influenced how independent their sources of inspiration were. Our main hypothesis was that while being exposed to many sources of inspiration can potentially help participants produce highly innovative ideas, this would only happen when their neighbors were not tightly interconnected. In other words, we predicted an interaction between degree and clustering such that idea innovativeness is higher when participants have high degree but low clustering.

In four studies, participants were assigned to networks and various positions (nodes) in networks and contributed product ideas over multiple rounds. Participants could see ideas submitted by other participants to whom they were directly connected. Network structures were predetermined and varied between groups to allow us to examine how properties of individuals' local networks (size/degree and interconnectedness/clustering) affected (1) social contagion and idea diffusion processes within each network over time and (2) ultimately the innovativeness of the ideas.

Our main hypothesis was supported across four studies. Having more sources of inspiration (higher degree) does not necessarily improve one's ideas. In fact, more sources of inspiration can lower one's innovativeness when their neighbors are connected to each other (i.e., a negative interaction between degree and clustering). This effect is moderated by the nature of the ideation task with respect to how general or specific it is. In more specific (and structured) ideation tasks, ideas diffuse over the network and, provided that individuals are exposed to multiple sources of inspiration with whom they are not tightly interconnected (i.e., lower clustering); good ideas will spread and be improved upon, resulting in higher levels of output idea innovativeness. However, when the task is more general (and unstructured) initial ideas tend to be more eclectic, thus making it harder for any single concept to "catch on" and spread throughout the network. These effects were found in a variety of contexts, including generating ideas for mobile banking smartphone apps, ways to improve the air travel experience for commercial airline passengers, and ideas for making Facebook more useful to people.

Overall, this research shows that social networks and consumers' positions in them can influence their ability to influence others and be influenced by others in the context of crowd sourced product ideation. While having connections indeed can facilitate the spread of ideas, those connections do not always facilitate the spread of innovative ideas.

Local Neighborhoods as Early Predictors of Innovation Adoption

EXTENDED ABSTRACT

"As Maine goes, so goes the nation". This proverb of U.S. politics suggests that what happens in a particular neighborhood can be a good predictor of a much larger population (in this case the United States, or more precisely who wins the presidential election). More generally, both political scientists and managers spend considerable effort trying to find ways to predict the behavior of large populations. This paper focuses on predicting innovation adoption based on what we term predictive neighborhoods (groups of connected individuals whose adoption patterns evolve similarly to, yet earlier than, overall population behavior). We demonstrate that some neighborhoods can indeed be used to predict overall adoption and that their predictions are superior to those of random samples.

Previous research has shown that product adoption decisions are influenced by social peers and relationships (see Godes et al. 2005; Goldenberg et al. 2009; Libai 2005; Libai et al. 2009; Trusov et al. 2008b; Valente 1995; Van den Bulte and Joshi 2007; Watts and Dodds 2007). Research also provides evidence of the benefits garnered from an advantageous network position and the structural properties of one's local network. These properties include the resources of one's direct network (Burt 1997; Lin 2001), the number and strength of ties (e.g., Granovetter 1973) and closure or local clustering (Coleman 1990; Lin 2001).

A few studies have found that the individual adoption process is driven by group adoption (Jones and Ritz 1991; Kim and Srivastava 1998). However, these studies focus on cases where group adoption precedes individual adoption within that group. Here we consider the case of social networks characterized by a high clustering coefficient (Watts and Strogatz 1998). This paper first investigates how the individual adoption decisions within a neighborhood are influenced by the properties of the clusters to which they belong, and second, whether certain local neighborhoods can be reliable predictors of overall network adoption (i.e., are predictive neighborhoods).

We first show analytically that for success-failure predictions, random samples (the common standard in marketing) are less useful than specific clusters in the network. If correct, this means that using a random sample may not be the best way if a network structure exists, and if it is known. We predict that large and dense clusters that have high betweenness centrality (at the cluster level) should be better predictors of success than other clusters and random samples.

We then tested empirically this conjecture using a network data with multiple diffusion processes over it (the Korean Cyworld newtrok).

In the period of this study, the number of members in the Cyworld database grew from 2,492,036 in December 2003 to 12,685,214 in July 2005. In October 2006, there were about 22 million registered members and an average of 20 million monthly unique visitors. Many people considered Cyworld a part of their everyday life and as a tool for building relationships and sharing information about their lives on their homepages. A key aspect of the service, for our purpose, allows people to customize their homepages by including documents, photos, and other "goodies" at no charge. Members can also decorate their minihompy (personal homepage) with paid items such as virtual household items—furniture, electronics, wallpapers. People can also adopt items such as pictures or video clips directly from the minihompies they visit (called "scrapping" in Cyworld.). This study focuses on this latter type of adoption, using data from December 2003 to July 2005.

We examine a set of 114 neighborhoods analyzed earlier. We identified the number of scraps (adoptions) for each item and eliminated those with fewer than 20 adoptions (i.e., niche products and abject failures which had very sparse data on which to base analyses). Of the remaining products, the top 10 items (in effect the "mega hits") were adopted by between 104 and 7952 people while the bottom 30 were adopted by 20-25 individuals, meaning highly successful items were adopted at a rate of at least four times greater, and in many cases at an order of magnitude greater, than less successful ones.

As a measure of how well a local neighborhood predicts adoption in the total network, we used the correlation between adoption in a neighborhood at the time 5%, 16%, and 50% of the eventual market had adopted it (i.e., early adoption in the neighborhood), and eventual total network adoptions after the adoption process is completed. Using these 40 items, (the top 10 plus the bottom 30), we then compared the ability to predict total adoption in the overall market based on a) a random sample (the "gold standard" of market research) of size 200, similar to the average cluster size of 214, b) the average of all the neighborhoods in the network, and c) the 20 clusters with the highest correlation between their adoption at the time 16% of the market had adopted and eventual market adoption.

The empirical results show that certain neighborhoods do predict adoption better than random and stratified samples as well as samples of innovators. Further, they predict about as well as samples of social hubs whose use requires knowledge of the entire network structure.

The Nosy Decision Maker: How the Sense of Smell Influences Consumers' Decisions

Chairs: Meng-Hsien (Jenny) Lin, Iowa State University, USA
Terry L. Childers, Iowa State University, USA

Paper #1: The Smell Factor: Individual Differences in Olfaction Memory, Judgments and Decision-Making

Meng-Hsien (Jenny) Lin, Iowa State University, USA
Terry Childers, Iowa State University, USA
Samantha Cross, Iowa State University, USA

Paper #2: Exploring the Dark Side of Chocolate: Moral Cleansing and Licensing Among Restrained Eaters

Maureen (Mimi) Morrin, Rutgers University, USA
Nguyen Pham, Arizona State University, USA
May Lwin, Nanyang Technological University, Singapore
Mellisa G. Bublitz, University of Wisconsin - Oshkosh, USA

Paper #3: Love at First Sight or at First Smell? Order Effects of Olfactory and Visual Cues

Dipayan Biswas, University of South Florida, USA
Lauren I. Labrecque, Loyola University Chicago, USA
Donald Lehmann, Columbia University, USA

Paper #4: Seeing What You Smell: An Eye-Tracking Analysis of Visual Attention

May Lwin, Nanyang Technological University, Singapore
Maureen (Mimi) Morrin, Rutgers University, USA
Chiao Sing Chong, Nanyang Technological University, Singapore
Su Xia Tan, Nanyang Technological University, Singapore

SESSION OVERVIEW

While sensory marketing has recently gained a lot of attention in the realm of consumer research, most studies in this domain have focused on visual and auditory aspects (Krishna 2009, 2012). In contrast, olfaction has received relatively less attention in the consumer literature. In that regard, this special session focuses on olfaction and our main objective is to present a series of studies exploring the influences of olfactory cues on consumption-related decisions and behaviors. This session also seeks to encourage discussion on the broader theme of sensory influences in consumer decision making and attract participation from researchers with a common interest in different aspects of sensory marketing.

Past research in the consumer literature has examined how scent impacts memory (Krishna, Lwin and Morrin 2010; Morrin and Ratneshwar 2003). What are rarely considered in these studies are individual differences in the sense of smell and the interaction of other senses with that of the sense of smell. In line with the conference's "Appreciating Diversity" theme, the first paper by Lin, Childers and Cross takes into consideration individuals' varying abilities to smell (ranging from a heightened sense of smell to a diminished or even absent sense of smell) and investigates its impact on consumer-related decisions for products and ads. Thus, this paper examines the role of olfaction in consumer behavior and how individual differences in olfaction ability and preference affect memory, judgment, and decision making.

Exploring the relationship between olfaction and vision, Lwin, Morrin, Chong and Tan investigate the manner in which olfactory cues attract and increase a person's attention to ad information using eye-tracking methods. Another paper in this session (Biswas, Labrecque and Lehmann) focuses on the sequential order effects of olfactory and visual stimuli and how the outcomes translate into food taste perceptions. Morrin, Pham, Lwin and Bublitz also explore the

complementary sensory relationship between olfaction and taste, and how dietary restraint moderates the effects. The extent to which olfaction affects taste expectations and actual eating behavior is thus explored in two of the studies (Biswas et al.; Morrin, Pham, Lwin and Bublitz).

The four papers comprising this special session on sensory influences all focus on olfaction and its role on consumer's information processing and decision-making. However, each paper embraces diversity by taking into account different dimensions of individual differences. Lin et al focus on individual differences in sense of smell, and examine how this varying ability influences their decisions in product purchase, judgment and scent memory. They also investigate the concerns individuals with either heightened or diminished sense of smell may have in the marketplace and household and methods of coping. Morrin et al examine restrained eaters and non-restrained eaters and find that there are individual differences in the effect of moral cleansing on chocolate consumption. Studying another dimension of food consumption, Biswas et al find that individuals under different states of hunger form opposite expectations for taste, depending on the order of encountering olfaction and visual cues. Finally, in Lwin et al's paper, they find that only when scent is congruent with the object in the ad, will people pay more attention to the information presented to individuals. Further, they find this effect is enhanced when the ad element is concrete versus abstract in nature.

In addition to the variety of topics related to the sense of smell, these papers use a variety of research methods to investigate their research questions. Lin et al take a multi-method approach, with a combination of surveys, in-depth interviews, experimental designs and neuroscience methods to address their broad research objective of understanding the impact of individual differences in olfactory ability. Lwin et al approach their research using eye-tracking methodologies. Morrin et al and Biswas et al use behavioral experiments to address food consumption decisions.

This session therefore contributes to the conference theme by embracing a diversity of approaches to the topic, a range of methods, with researchers from several areas of the world (Singapore, Hong Kong and the U.S.) with diverse cultural and geographic origins. Given the relatively nascent state of this topic domain, it is likely to lead to discussions for future research ideas.

Completion stage: Data have been collected and analyzed for all papers.

The Smell Factor: Individual Differences in Olfaction Memory, Judgments and Decision-Making

EXTENDED ABSTRACT

Olfaction is often a subtle, but important, tool used by consumers in their memory associations, social and marketplace interactions and their judgments and evaluation of product and consumption choices. Yet, although there are a growing number of studies on the loss of smell, primarily in medical journals (Miwa et al 2001; Aschenbrenner et al 2007), this is still a greatly under-researched area in the marketing and psychology literature. In addition, very little, if any, research has been done looking at individual differences in smell based on the level of olfactory sensitivity in consumers. This research examines individual differences in olfaction on consumer memory, judgments and decision making. We specifically study the impact of olfaction in consumers with a complete loss of smell (anosmia) or a diminished olfactory sensitivity (hyposmia); those with an enhanced olfactory sensitivity (hyperosmia) and those who have a normal sense of smell.

Stevenson (2010) identifies three main functions of the olfactory system: to aid or complement ingestive behavior; to avoid environmental hazards; and to facilitate social communication. In their research on anosmics, Miwa et al (2001) noted that olfactory loss primarily affected food and safety related activities, but also had an effect on quality of life. Aschenbrenner et al (2007) discussed the social implications, noting that individuals with olfactory loss avoid mealtime interactions with friends, showing a reluctance to comment on food they can't really experience and also reported going out to eat at restaurants less often. Thus, there is an impact both on social interactions and purchase behavior. However, research on hyperosmics has even been more limited with a focus on odor intolerance (Nordin et al 2003; Dalton 1999). Thus, we know little about how smell fits into the everyday lives and shopping patterns of individuals with elevated olfactory abilities.

Thus our research questions are as follows. 1) What is the role of olfaction in consumer behavior? 2) What are the individual differences in olfaction ability and preference? 3) How do these differences affect olfaction memory, judgments and decision making?

To answer these questions, we use a multi-phase design approach, which incorporates a mix of qualitative and quantitative studies, both sequential and embedded (Creswell and Clark 2011). There are four phases in the overall study. In phases 2 to 4, individuals differing in olfactory sensitivity (diminished, sensitive, normal) were specifically recruited. Part 1 is a questionnaire study with approximately 700 undergraduate student participants, using a mix of existing olfactory scales (c.f., Wrzeniewski et al 1999; Martin et al 2001). In the 2nd phase, based on the survey responses in phase 1, 240 undergraduate participants, differing in reported olfactory sensitivity were selected for behavioral experiments. These were extensions of studies by Krishna et al (2010) and Bulsing et al (2007). In the 3rd phase, in-depth interviews incorporating two olfaction tests (UPenn BSIT; Sniffin' Sticks) were conducted with 35 mature participants (ages ranged from 25 to 70 years old). In these interviews, the researchers explored issues of safety, food consumption, social and marketplace interactions and overall consumer well-being. The final phase of the project is an ERP study with 60 participants where the neuro-responses to olfactory related words are recorded.

Across the scales used, we see a similar pattern of results: a U-shaped relationship with hyperosmics a little higher than normals and the decreased group (hyposmics and anosmics) in the middle. This is the pattern for the different scales testing the use of smell, the dispensability of smell, liking through smell, emotions and smell and attention to odors. Findings across the studies also illustrate that not only do those in the heightened group see smell as a more important aspect of life than those in the diminished group, but odors and scents are shown as better able to elicit memories for this group versus the diminished group. This is potentially disturbing as smell is considered very important for its ability to facilitate recall of past experiences (Stevenson 2010).

Olfactory sensitivity is also seen to impact where, how and why individual consumers make purchase decisions and what consumption choices they make. The sense of smell is a taken for granted, but heavily relied upon, sense that often becomes a salient factor when it is seen as deviating from the norm or affects social, workplace or marketplace interactions. Coping strategies used to counteract these effects are both cognitive and experiential and fall into the categories of avoidance, compensation, removal and deliberation. The authors

explore the nuances of olfactory sensitivity and develop a typology of smell-related triggers and phases. Results indicate that olfactory-related responses are often involuntary, context-driven, complement our other senses and perceived in relation to others.

Based on our studies (n = 781), approximately 10% of the population sampled has no ability or a diminished ability to smell (which mirrors the existing literature), 19% fall into the heightened category and 71% fall into a normal range. This research thus makes a theoretical contribution to our existing knowledge of individual differences and sensory influences, by exploring the impact of olfaction across all three groups and fostering appreciation for the sensory aspects of consumer diversity. Level of olfactory sensitivity is seen to affect memory, judgment and decision making. It also has an impact not just on consumption choice, but also on the purchase decision process and the overall shopping experience. Yet, unlike other sensory stimuli (vision, touch, taste, hearing), consumers' expectations of marketplace accommodation are low and marketplace responses to consumer concerns are unconsidered, low or misguided. Finally, this study uses a mixed method approach to understanding individual differences in olfaction, triangulating across methods with a scope that has not been previously used in the consumer behavior literature. The authors show that a diversity of approaches and perspectives serves to highlight and illuminate the importance and implications of olfaction on consumption.

Exploring the Dark Side of Chocolate: Moral Cleansing and Licensing Among Restrained Eaters

EXTENDED ABSTRACT

The obesity rate in the U.S. has doubled since 1980, and now stands at about a third of the adult population, with another third classified as overweight. Overeating can have negative consequences not only for one's health, but also for one's psyche, in terms of the social stigma associated with it. Dietary restraint refers to the chronic effort to restrict food intake, especially of forbidden foods or those considered fattening. Individuals who score high on measures of dietary restraint (e.g., Herman and Polivy 1980) have greater concerns about their shape and weight and exhibit a strong desire for thinness. We argue that for many dieters, overeating or eating "forbidden" foods is associated with acting contrary to social norms, and thus has a negative impact on their moral identity. One's moral identity is typically measured in terms of beliefs that one is caring, compassionate, fair, friendly, generous, helpful, hardworking, honest and kind (Aquino and Reed 2002; Hart et al. 1998). For dieters it can also involve food consumption behavior. We argue here that in addition to environmental cues impacting dieters' eating behavior, their dynamic moral self-worth also plays a role. Both moral cleansing (remunerative moral strivings) and moral licensing (relaxed moral strivings) have been observed in other domains (Jordan, Mullen and Murningham 2011) and we expect to observe them in the domain of food consumption.

Embodied cognition theory suggests that metaphors are used to link abstract concepts to physical and sensory experiences (Barsalou 2008, Lakoff and Johnson 1980). In this way, physically cleansing the body can lead to beliefs about moral purity. Smelling a citrus scent activates concepts related to cleanliness (Holland, Henriks and Aarts 2005; Schnall, Benton and Harvey 2008). Hand washing has been shown to not only physically clean but also to psychologically cleanse an individual of past moral transgressions (Zhong & Liljenquist 2006). We explore here the potential ability of physical cleansing to morally cleanse dieters of their misdeeds in terms of forbidden food consumption, which will be evident in their feeling licensed to re-indulge in forbidden food consumption. The physically cleansing products in this study contain scents strongly associated with cleansing activities (mint, citrus).

Two hundred and three undergraduate students participated for a small cash payment. The design consisted of a 2 (tasting condition: eat chocolate, resist eating chocolate) x 3 (cleansing condition: groom with haircomb; cleanse with handwipe, cleanse with toothbrush) full factorial. Participants were randomly assigned to one of the six cells. All participants were provided with a sample of chocolate. They were instructed to look at, smell, and touch the chocolate and either eat it [or not] and to provide an evaluation of the product. Participants then evaluated a haircomb (i.e., were groomed but not cleansed), a citrus-scented handwipe (i.e., were cleansed), or a toothbrush with mint-scented toothpaste (i.e., were cleansed). After completing various closed items in a survey, participants chose a gift from a selection of chocolates, pencils, and erasers, arranged randomly on a table, on the way out of the experiment. Their gift choice was covertly recorded.

We conducted a logistic regression on whether or not chocolate was chosen on the way out of the experiment (yes, no) as a function of tasting condition, cleansing condition, dietary restraint, and all possible interactions. Two effects were significant: the 2-way interaction between dietary restraint and cleansing condition, and the 3-way interaction between dietary restraint, cleansing condition, and tasting condition. We find that among those low in dietary restraint, there are no significant differences in likelihood of taking chocolate on the way out of the experiment within cleansing conditions as a function of whether the participant had eaten or resisted chocolate. However, among those high in dietary restraint who were not cleansed (i.e., used the haircomb), significantly fewer took chocolate on the way out if they had tasted versus resisted chocolate. Among restrained eaters, cleansing with either a citrus-scented hand wipe or toothbrush with minty toothpaste compared to grooming with a comb significantly increased the likelihood of taking chocolate on the way out of the experiment, if chocolate had been tasted. We thus find that physical cleansing absolves only restrained eaters from what only they perceive as moral transgression associated with forbidden food consumption.

Love at First Sight or at First Smell?
Order Effects of Olfactory and Visual Cues

EXTENDED ABSTRACT

Prior research, across multiple disciplines, has documented the effects of different types of sensory stimuli inputs on the evaluation of products. These studies have typically examined the effects of sensory stimuli such as color, scent, touch, and taste. Some studies have also examined the effects of multiple sensory stimuli such as touch and taste or vision and touch (Krishna 2012). However, no study has examined how the *sequential order* in which multiple sensory stimuli are encountered influence product evaluations. This is especially relevant since in many real world situations, consumers can encounter multiple sensory stimuli sequentially (and not simultaneously, especially since different sensory cues are acquired differently. For example, visual stimuli can be evaluated with a greater degree of non-proximity than olfactory or haptic stimuli. That is, objects can usually be seen from a further distance than they can be smelled. On the other hand, for visual stimuli processing, one needs to have the object in the line of vision, whereas olfactory stimuli can be evaluated omnidirectionally. Hence, cases can be made for different sensory stimuli to be encountered in sequentially different orders. As an illustrative example, suppose a consumer enters a chocolate

shop, and smells the chocolates first before she actually sees them versus if the consumer first sees the chocolates (e.g., through the store window) before she smells them. Would the consumer's evaluation of the chocolates be influenced by the sequential order in which she sees versus smells the chocolates? The present research attempts to make an important first step in trying to answer this research question.

Our propositions and hypotheses are influenced by recent work in the domain of interaction and carryover effects between sensory stimuli and the related sensory-neurological reactions (Krishna 2012; Rolls et al. 2010), along with research on order effects (Biswas et al. 2010). We test our propositions/hypotheses with the help of five experiments. First, Study 1 examines the sequential order effects of evaluating a beverage's visual aspects such as color (henceforth referred to as "V") versus olfactory/scent aspects (henceforth referred to as "O"). Study 1 used a single-factor (sequential order of sensory stimuli: V-O vs. O-V) between-subjects design experiment. A concocted beverage was used as the product in Study 1, with the beverage color and scent determined through a series of pretests. Participants were given the beverages in cups with lids and were asked to take off the lids after receiving the beverages. In the V-O condition, participants received the beverages in transparent cups, whereby they could see the color first before they could smell the beverage. In the O-V condition, participants received the beverages in opaque cups of similar quality, with the odor dissipating through the porous lid. As a result, they could smell the scent of the beverage first before they could see the beverage color. To ensure that the quality of the cups did not influence consumer taste perceptions (e.g., Krishna and Morrin 2008), the quality and price of the cups were identical, with the only difference of the cups being opaque versus transparent. The results of Study 1 showed that a beverage's taste is more favorably evaluated when participants encounter the visual aspects of the product prior to the olfactory aspects (that is, the sequence of V–O leads to more favorable evaluations than the sequence of O–V).

Study 2 then provides additional process evidence and also examines sensory cue order effects across a non-food context and the moderating effects of individual visual processing tendency (e.g., Wyer, Hung, and Jiang 2008). The results show that overall product evaluations are higher when the visual stimulus is earlier in a sequence of sensory stimuli, with the effects primarily being driven by those who are high on visual processing tendency.

Although the results of Studies 1 and 2 support our theoretical premises related to sensory carryover interactions and the sequential dominance of the visual cues over olfactory or auditory cues, there can be a potential alternative explanation of the results related to the role of short term working memory (e.g., Biswas et al. 2010). Hence, in order to further investigate which of the two underlying processes (sensory carryover versus role of working memory) is more dominant, Studies 3A and 3B were conducted. These studies examine the order effects of evaluating a food's visual and olfactory aspects when the visual color is desirable but the olfactory aspect (scent/odor) is undesirable (henceforth referred to as O') or when the olfactory aspect is desirable but the visual color is undesirable (henceforth referred to as V'). The results of Study 3A show that taste perceptions are higher for V-O' than for O'-V and the results of Study 3B show that taste perceptions are higher for O-V' than for V'-O.

Finally, Study 4 identifies a boundary condition (by examining the moderating effects of hunger) whereby the effects of Study 1 are reversed. Under low hunger, consumers have more favorable product taste perceptions for the V-O than the O-V sequence, consistent with the results observed in Study 1. However, under high levels of hunger, the effects get reversed, whereby consumers' taste perceptions were higher for the O-V, than the V-O, sequence. This occurs because the odor/scent of a food has stronger sensory impact under high levels of hunger.

Taken together, the results of the five experiments reveal interesting theoretical and practical insights regarding the effects of sequential presentation of sensory stimuli (e.g., olfactory and visual) on consumer product evaluations.

Seeing what you Smell:
An Eye Tracking Analysis of Visual Attention

EXTENDED ABSTRACT

Interest in sensory marketing is on the rise, with growing evidence that sensory inputs such as scent can enhance consumer both product evaluations (Spangenberg, Crowley and Henderson 1996) and memory for product information (Krishna, Lwin and Morrin 2010; Morrin and Ratneshwar 2003). Most studies to date have investigated such effects using relatively distal measures such as self-reported attitudes and/or delayed recall. The present research investigates the effect of scent on visual attention to elements in print advertisements with eye-tracking technology. We explore whether the presence or absence of a pleasant scent increases attention generally, or only when objects in the ad are semantically congruent with the odors being smelled.

In this research we manipulate not only the presence or absence of scent, but also the congruency between the scent (if present) and objects in the ad. Cue congruity refers to the degree to which a particular cue, such as a product's scent, complements a target stimulus (Bone and Ellen 1999). In the present research we operationalize congruency in terms of the semantic associations between the scent and product or service promoted in a print advertisement.

The literature on scent and attitudes suggests congruent odors often increase consumer evaluations (Spangenberg, Sprott, Grohmann and Tracy 2006), but the literature on scent and memory is mixed. Morrin and Ratneshwar (2003) found that incongruent ambient scents were just as effective as congruent ambient scents at enhancing recall and recognition of brand names and packaging. Nevertheless, Bone and Ellen (1999) argue that incongruent scents, which are those that are perceived by the consumer as not fitting with the product, may interfere with the processing of relevant brand information. Do only congruent scents facilitate the processing and storage of product information and enhance accessibility to stored information and elaboration through the process of attention? We seek to explore this issue by examining the effect of scent on visual attention to elements in print advertisements.

The use of eye-tracking technology has been relatively scarce in consumer research, although studies are beginning to emerge (e.g., Wedel and Pieters 2000). In the current set of studies, a Tobii T60 Eye Tracker (integrated into a 17" TFT monitor) was used to record the visual activity of participants. Upon entering the laboratory, participants were seated at a desk where several scent stimuli, a canister of coffee grounds, and the eye-tracking monitor had been set up. Each of the scent stimuli contained filter paper that had been infused [or not] with an essential oil. The eye tracker was calibrated according to each individual's height and position. Participants sniffed five scent packets, one at a time, as they viewed each of five advertisements. The participants were exposed to five randomly ordered ads for hypothetical brands in different product categories, one of which was the target ad. For the target ad we measure eye fixation count, which indicates degree of drawing attention to stimulus, and eye gaze fixation length, which indicates overall interest in the stimulus. Pre-determined areas of interest (AOI's) representing the location

of a manipulated ad element (word or picture) were mapped out. In between each ad, coffee grounds were sniffed to clear out nasal passages. After viewing the ads, participants completed a survey booklet with other measures.

Three studies were conducted using this procedure. In study one, a strawberry scent was [or was not] sniffed while viewing a full color advertisement for a hypothetical brand of food coloring. The ad contained pictures of four bottles of colored liquid. The bottle in the upper right quadrant appeared either in grey or red to manipulate color congruency with the strawberry scent. In study 2, a lemon scent was [or was not] sniffed while viewing an ad for a juice bar. The advertisement contained pictures of four different smoothie ingredients. The item in the upper right quadrant was either a lemon or banana to manipulate congruency with the lemon scent (controlling for color congruency). In study 3, a citrus scent was [or was not] sniffed while viewing either a pictorial ad for a retail superstore or a text-based ad for taekwondo services. In the upper right corner of each ad was a woman cleaning a kitchen sink [or placing a book on a shelf] in the visual ad; or the word "clean" [or "walk"] in the verbal ad.

We conducted analyses of variance on mean fixation count and fixation length as well as other measures captured in the survey booklet as a function of scent (yes, no) and ad element congruency (yes, no). Across the studies we find that sniffing a scent increases both eye fixation count and length of eye gaze on the area of interest *only* when the scent is congruent with an object in the ad. Moreover, we find that the size of the enhanced attention effect is larger when the ad element is concrete versus abstract in nature. Implications for consumer multi-sensory processing are discussed.

REFERENCES

Aquino, K., and A. Reed (2002). "The Self-Importance of Moral Identity," *Journal of Personality and Social Psychology*, 83 (6), 1423-1440.

Aschenbrenner, K., C.Hummel, K.Teszmer, F.Krone, T.Ishimaru, H.Seo, and T.Hummel (2007). "The Influence of Olfactory Loss on Dietary Behaviors," *The Larygoscope*, 118, 135-144.

Barsalou, L. W. (2008), "Grounded Cognition," *Annual Review of Psychology*, 59, 617-45.

Baumeister, R. F. (2002), "Yielding to Temptation: Self-Control Failure, Impulsive Purchasing, and Consumer Behavior," *Journal of Consumer Research*, 28(4), 670-676.

Biswas, D., D. Grewal, and A. Roggeveen (2010), "How the Order of Sampled Experiential Products Affects Choice," *Journal of Marketing Research*, 47 (3), 508-519.

Bone, P. F. and P. S. Ellen (1999), "Scents in the Marketplace: Explaining a Fraction of Olfaction," *Journal of Retailing*, 75(2), 243-262.

Bulsing, P. J., M. A. M. Smeets, and M. A. van den Hout (2007). "Positive Implicit Attitudes toward Odor Words," *Chemical Senses*, 32(6), 525-534.

Creswell, John W. and Vicki L. Plano Clark (2011), *Designing and Conducting Mixed Methods Research*, Thousand Oaks, CA: SAGE Publications, Inc.

Dalton, P. (1999). "Cognitive Influence on Healthy Symptoms from Acute Chemical Exposure," *Health Psychology*, 18(6), 579-590.

Herman, C.P., & Polivy, J. (1980). Restrained Eating. In A.J. Stunkard (Ed.), *Obesity* (pp. 208-225). Philadelphia: Sauders.

Holland, R. W., M. Hendriks, and H. Aarts (2005) "Smells Like Clean Spirit: Nonconscious Effects of Scent on Cognition and Behavior," *Psychological Science,* 16(9), 689-693.

Jordan, J., E. Mullen and J. K. Murningham (2011), "Striving for the Moral Self: The Effects of Recalling Past Moral Actions on Future Moral Behavior," *Personality and Social Psychology Bulletin*, 37(5), 701-713.

Krishna, Aradhna (2009), *Sensory Marketing: Research on the Sensuality of Products*, New York, NY: Taylor & Francis Group.

Krishna, A. (2012), "An Integrative Review of Sensory Marketing: Engaging the Senses to Affect Perception, Judgment, and Behavior," *Journal of Consumer Psychology*, forthcoming.

Krishna, A., M. Lwin, and M. Morrin (2010). "Product Scent and Memory," *Journal of Consumer Research*, 37, 57-67.

Krishna, A. and M. Morrin (2008), "Does touch affect taste? The perceptual transfer of product container haptic cues," *Journal of Consumer Research, 34* (April), 807-818.

Lakoff, George and Mark Johnson (1980), *Metaphors We Live By*, Chicago: University of Chicago Press.

Martin, G.N., F. Apena, Z. Chaudry, Z. Mulligan, and C. Nixon (2001). "The Development of an Attitude Towards the Sense of Smell Questionnaire (SoSQ) and a Comparison of Different Professions" Responses," *North American Journal of Psychology*, 3(3), 491-502.

Mattila, A. S. and Wirtz, J. (2002). "Congruency of Scent and Music as a Driver of In-Store Evaluations and Behavior," *Journal of Retailing, 77*, 272-289.

Miwa, T., M. Furukawa, T. Tsuakatani, R. Costanzo, L. DiNardo, and E. R. Reiter (2001). "Impact of Olfactory Impairment on Quality of Life and Disability," *Arch Otolaryngol Head Neck Surg*, 127 (May), 497-503.

Morrin, M., and S. Ratneshwar (2003), "Does it Make Sense to Use Scents to Enhance Brand Memory," *Journal of Marketing Research*, 40, 10-25.

Nordin, S., E. Millqvist, O. Lowhagen, and M. Bende (2003). "The Chemical Sensitivity Scale: Psychometric Properties and Comparison with the Noise Sensitivity Scale," *Journal of Environmental Psychology*, 23, 359-367.

Rolls, E.T., H. D. Critchley, J.V. Verhagen and M. Kadohisa (2010), "The Representation of Information about Taste and Odor in the Orbitofrontal Cortex," *Chemosensory Perception*, 3, 16-33.

Schnall, S., J. Benton and S. Harvey (2008). "With a Clean Conscience: Cleanliness Reduces the Severity of Moral Judgments," *Psychological Science,* 19(12), 1219-1222.

Spangenberg, E.R., A.E.Crowley and P.W.Henderson (1996). "Improving the store environment: do olfactory cues affect evaluations and behaviors?" *Journal of Marketing, 60*, 67–80.

Spangenberg, E.R., D. E. Sprott, B. Grohmann, and D. L.Tracy, (2006). "Gender Congruent Ambient Scent Influences on Approach and Avoidance Behaviors in a Retail Store," *Journal of Business Research*, *59*, 1281-1287.

Stevenson, R. J. (2010). "An Initial Evaluation of the Functions of Human Olfaction," *Chemical Senses*, 35(1), 3-20.

Wedel, M., & Pieters, R. (2000). "Eye Fixations on Advertisements and Memory for Brands: A Model and Findings," *Marketing Science*, *19*(4), 297-312.

Wrzesniewski, A., C. McCauley, and P. Rozin (1999)."Odor and Affect: Individual Differences in the Impact of Odor on Liking for Places, Things and People,"*Chemical Senses*,24,713-721.

Wyer, R. S., I. W. Hung, and Y. Jiang (2008). "Visual and Verbal Processing Strategies in Comprehension and Judgment," *Journal of Consumer Psychology*, 18, 244-257.

Zhong, CB and K. Liljenquist (2006), "Washing Away Your Sins: Threatened Morality and Physical Cleansing," *Science*, 313, 1451-1452.

New Insights into the Causes and Consequences of Unplanned Purchases

Chairs: Leonard Lee, Columbia University, USA
Scott Rick, University of Michigan, USA

Paper #1: Capturing the "First Moment of Truth": Understanding Point-of-Purchase Drivers of Unplanned Consideration and Purchase Using Video Tracking

Yanliu Huang, Drexel University, USA
Sam K. Hui, NYU, USA
J. Jeffrey Inman, University of Pittsburgh, USA
Jacob A. Suher, University of Texas at Austin, USA

Paper #2: Boosting Promotional Effectiveness with Thoughtful Product Displays

Marco Bertini, LBS, UK
Mitja Pirc, A.T. Kearney, USA
Ana Valenzuela, Universitat Pompeu Fabra, Spain

Paper #3: The Temperature Premium: How Physical Warmth Increases Product Valuation

Yonat Zwebner, Hebrew University, Israel
Jacob Goldenberg, Hebrew University, Israel
Leonard Lee, Columbia, USA

Paper #4: The Benefits of Retail Therapy: Choosing to Buy Alleviates Sadness

Scott Rick, University of Michigan, USA
Beatriz Pereira, University of Michigan, USA
Katherine Burson, University of Michigan, USA

SESSION OVERVIEW

According to a recent 2010 study by Booz & Co., 83% of Consumer Packaged Goods companies planned to boost their spending on shopper marketing in the next three years, and 55% of the companies ranked shopper marketing as their top investment. These efforts are increasingly focused on stimulating unplanned purchases.

The proposed session brings together four papers that provide new insights into the causes and consequences of impulse buying and shopping more broadly. The session begins with Huang, Hui, Inman, and Suher, who use advanced portable video-tracking technology to track the in-store behavior of 250 shoppers. They propose and test a comprehensive framework of shopping-trip-level and point-of-purchase drivers of unplanned purchases. This is followed by two papers that delve into specific situational factors that influence what shoppers buy in a store. Specifically, Bertini, Pirc, and Valenzuela investigate how different shelf-space arrangements in the retail environment (i.e., vertical vs. horizontal vs. random) influence shoppers' propensity to buy hedonic versus utilitarian products. Zwebner, Goldenberg, and Lee examine the effect of a sensory factor—temperature—on shoppers' valuation of a variety of products. Both groups of researchers also study and discuss the psychological mechanisms that underlie their respective effects. Finally, Rick, Pereira, and Burson examine a phenomenon that drives many unplanned purchases—retail therapy—and explore whether and why shopping when distressed actually helps to alleviate distress.

Overall, these papers highlight several new insights into the causes and consequences of unplanned purchases using a diverse set of research methodologies (surveys, field and incentive-compatible lab experiments, video-tracking) and explore a variety of cognitive and affective processes (fluency, congruency, emotional attachment, emotion regulation). Given the relevance of these effects to consumers' daily lives and marketers' bottom lines, this session should be of interest to a wide range of psychologically- and managerially-minded consumer researchers who are interested in retail environments, sensory marketing, fluency, emotion and decision-making, and anyone who is fascinated by the factors that can affect their shopping and buying behavior.

Capturing the "First Moment of Truth": Understanding Point-of-Purchase Drivers of Unplanned Consideration and Purchase Using Video Tracking

EXTENDED ABSTRACT

The majority of grocery purchases are unplanned at the category level (Inman et al. 2009). Because of the economic importance of unplanned spending, manufacturers and retailers alike are very interested in understanding in-store drivers of unplanned purchases in order to optimize their shopper marketing strategies (Grocery Marketing Association study, 2007). They are especially interested in understanding shopping behavior at the point of purchase, termed by Procter & Gamble as "the first moment of truth". In particular, given the importance of product consideration in product purchase (Hauser and Wernerfelt 1989), retailers try to identify trip- and point-of-purchase- level factors that lead shoppers to make more unplanned considerations, and raise the likelihood that these considerations will turn into actual purchases.

With a few notable exceptions (e.g., Stilley et al. 2010), previous academic research on unplanned purchases often relies on scanner data (e.g., Inman et al. 2009). Typically, a shopper's purchase, as recorded by scanner data, is compared to an entrance survey to identify whether a certain purchase is planned or unplanned. What happens *during* the trip (e.g., how a shopper considers and purchases from each product category), however, is not recorded. As such, previous studies are typically limited to studying the influence of demographic (e.g., gender) and psychographic (e.g., impulsivity) factors on unplanned purchases. Point-of-purchase behaviors along the shopping path are rarely considered. In this research, we address two important questions about unplanned considerations and purchases. First, what shopping trip-level characteristics are related to a higher number of unplanned considerations? Second, for each unplanned consideration, what aspects of point-of-purchase behavior are related to a greater likelihood of conversion to purchase?

We first hypothesize that both the length of the shopper's travel path and the extent to which she follows the most efficient path to obtain her planned items are associated with the number of unplanned considerations she will make. Specifically, the longer the distance that a shopper travels in the store, the more in-store stimuli she will get exposed to, which may in turn trigger forgotten needs and lead to unplanned purchases (Granbois 1968). Thus, we hypothesize that a longer in-store travel distance is associated with more unplanned considerations. We then predict that when grocery shoppers do not plan forward efficiently to take the shortest path connecting all the products they plan to buy, they may focus on the actions that maximize immediate utility rather than ones that maximize utility over a relatively longer time horizon (Hutchinson and Meyer 1994). This diminished regard for future consequences is often hedonically driven and correlates with a powerful and persistent urge to buy immediately (Rook 1987). Thus, we hypothesize that shoppers who take a less efficient shopping path through the store are likely to engage in more unplanned considerations.

Advances in Consumer Research
Volume 40, ©2012

We then predict that a few consideration characteristics can be related to whether an unplanned consideration will convert into an actual unplanned purchase. First, the wide variety of sensory stimuli presented in grocery shoppers' decision environment might activate their important shopping goals and therefore increase their engagement in a product purchase (Celsi and Olson 1988). Since this heightened product engagement generally leads to greater purchase intentions (Bloch and Richins 1983), we expect that the more engaged a shopper is during an unplanned consideration, the more likely it is to result in a purchase conversion. Specifically, we hypothesize that longer consideration duration and more product touches, both of which are indicative of higher engagement (Peck and Childers 2003), is associated with a higher likelihood of a purchase conversion.

We then hypothesize that a "deep" consideration where fewer products are considered in greater amount of detail may be more likely to result in a purchase conversion than a "wide" consideration where more products are considered within the same amount of time. By focusing their attention on a small number of products, shoppers may feel more involved with the specific product, which makes them more likely to purchase it (Bloch and Richins 1983). In contrast, by having more products in the field of view, shoppers could easily suffer from "choice overload" and become less likely to make a purchase (Iyengar and Lepper 2000). Therefore, the fewer shelf displays viewed by the shoppers allow them to be more focused on certain products (i.e., a "deep" type of consideration) and thus more likely to make an unplanned purchase. In addition, by physically standing closer to the product shelf, the shopper's field of vision will necessarily contain fewer products.

Finally, shoppers may reference in-store circular, coupons, or interact with store employees while they are engaged in an unplanned consideration. Shoppers' ongoing information search during a particular decision results from different motives such as obtaining tangible consumer benefits or seeking hedonic feelings (e.g., Punj and Staelin 1983). Since outcomes of both motives lead to a higher likelihood of product purchase (Rook 1987), we hypothesize that referencing external information relevant to the current product under consideration relates to greater purchase conversion.

We tested these hypotheses in a field study that was conducted in a medium-sized grocery store located in a northwestern U.S. city, where we had around 250 shoppers wear portable video cameras to observe each incidence of their point-of-purchase decision making process. We also collected their shopping intentions, and gathered relevant demographic and psychographic information by asking them to complete both an entrance and an exit survey. Eyecam videos were then coded and analyzed. Consistent with our hypotheses, we find that longer in-store travel distance and lower shopping "efficiency" lead to more unplanned considerations. We further show that an unplanned consideration is more likely to develop into an actual purchase if a shopper (i) spends more time in consideration, (ii) touches more products, (iii) references external information (e.g., circular, coupon, smart phone), (iv) stands closer to the shelf, (v) views fewer product shelf displays, and (vi) interacts with the store staff. Managerial implications of our findings are discussed.

Boosting Promotional Effectiveness with Thoughtful Product Displays

EXTENDED ABSTRACT

Options available to consumers are typically displayed in a two-dimensional "canvas." Prior research shows that there is indeed a difference in consumers' reactions to displays in which products are oriented vertically or horizontally (Valenzuela and Raghubir 2009). However, despite the importance of shelf placement in consumers' decisions, consumer researchers have paid little attention to it (but see Chandon et al. 2009; Drèze, Hoch, and Purk 1994). This paper adds to the literature by showing that firms can improve the effectiveness of promotional campaigns by managing the orientation of product displays. Key to our theory is the distinction between goods with a high hedonic or utilitarian content. We find that any orientation, vertical or horizontal, boosts the sales lift of a good that is primarily hedonic, while only vertical orientation is desirable when the discounted good is mostly utilitarian in nature.

We propose that product display orientation, horizontal or vertical, influences decisions through two different mechanisms: fluency and congruity (Hsee and Rottenstreich 2004). Fluency is linked to the psychological cost of the decision making process. The experience of difficulty accompanying a decision process may influence consumers' evaluation of the decision outcome (Novemsky et al. 2007). If consumer decision-making is fluent, the positive experience that accompanies the process of choosing becomes an input to the evaluation of the choice itself making choice more likely. We believe that the mere existence of order in a display of choice options will enhance fluency as consumers find it easier to access information before making a decision. Congruity, by contrast, is related to the feeling that the obtained information is right. The literature shows that when consumers find schema-consistent information they tend to use simple heuristics instead of engaging in more systematic processing (Sujan, Bettman and Sujan 1986). For example, a possible simple heuristic identified by Inman, McAlister and Hoyer (1990) was that products placed at the end of the aisle are considered a good deal, even when they are not.

This paper investigates whether product display orientation effects are different for products with high hedonic and utilitarian content (Dhar and Wertenbroch 2000). Consumers deciding on hedonic goods are expected to be processing more affectively and may favor perceptual inputs in their decision-making such as the feeling of fluency. If an ordered display by itself is able to enhance feelings of fluency, we would expect display order (independent of its orientation) to enhance sales and, thus, the size of the promotional lift. By contrast, when consumers buy utilitarian goods, they tend to process information more analytically, and cognitive determinants such as congruency may become relevant. In this context, we expect that only display order that is consistent with consumer shelf schemas would lead to a larger promotional lift. The literature supports consumers are most aware of the vertical shelf schema, which accounts for "top-bottom" or vertical order (Valenzuela, Raghubir and Mittakakis 2012). We test this pattern of effects using an in-store field experiment and then explore the proposed underlying mechanism using a controlled lab experiment.

A field experiment tested the hypothesized pattern of effects at a large European grocery retailer. It was conducted as an end of aisle promotion with 58 SKUs from a regular assortment of 17 product categories at 10 test stores together with 10 control stores to enable comparison of stores of similar type, size, traffic, location and presence of competitors. The field test was implemented as regular promotional activity, and the orientation of the products on the promotional display represented three conditions: random, horizontal or vertical (Figure 1). We measured quantities sold in the pre-promotion period, during promotion and after promotion period. All three periods had equal lengths of 13 days. Analysis corresponds to the variable *Promotional Lift* or the ratio of the quantity sold during the promotional period and the quantity sold before the promotional period. Prior to the field test we pre-tested consumers' perceptions of the extent of hedonic and utilitarian content of the 17 different categories. Product type variable was defined as *(Hedonic – Utilitarian) ratings* and named *HU*.

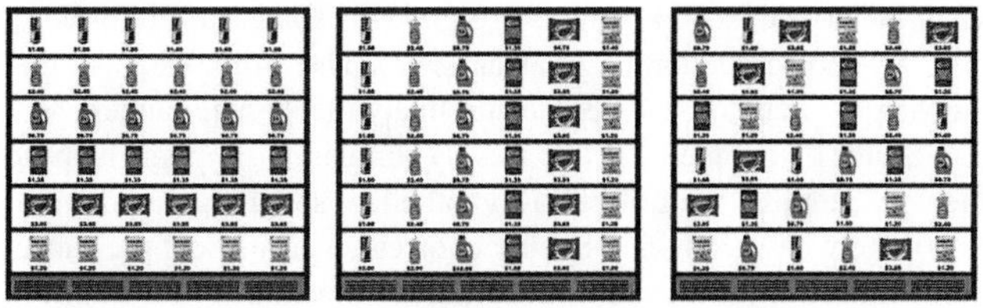

Figure 1: Orientation conditions, from left to right: vertical, horizontal, random

We performed three spotlight analyses exploring the difference in promotional lift in the three order conditions and two product types: more hedonic (mean centered *HU* + one standard deviation) and less hedonic goods (mean centered *HU* – one standard deviation). Results revealed that utilitarian products (-1 SD) enjoyed a larger promotional lift when displays were ordered vertically than horizontally or randomly ($M_{vertical}$= 3.04, $M_{horizontal}$= 2.16, M_{random}= 2.40). On the other hand, in the case of hedonic products (+1 SD) both vertical and horizontally ordered displays provide larger promotional lifts than random displays ($M_{vertical}$= 3.73, $M_{horizontal}$= 3.50, M_{random}= 2.87). We performed a nested regression providing simultaneous test for all the proposed patterns of results controlling for additional variables influencing promotional lift such as expenditure in other promotional elements: Hedonic goods have higher promotional lift compared to utilitarian goods. Vertical orientation increases promotional lift for both hedonic and utilitarian goods. Horizontal orientation increases promotional lift only for hedonic goods.

Overall, when decisions involve hedonic goods, consumers process more affectively. Any ordered display despite its orientation generates fluency, which enhances promotional sales. On the other hand, when the decision involves utilitarian goods, consumers process more analytically and congruity matters. In that case, it is only the more prevalent vertical orientation that enhances promotional sales.

The Temperature Premium: How Physical Warmth Increases Product Valuation

EXTENDED ABSTRACT

A variety of environmental factors in a store can influence how consumers shop and what they buy (Bitner 1992; Kotler 1973; Krishna 2011). However, the impact of an important dimension of our physical surroundings—temperature—on consumer behavior has been relatively little examined (for an exception, see Hong and Sun 2012). In the present research, we focus on this topic and, in particular, examine the influence of temperature on consumers' product valuation.

Recent research has shown that temperature is an important factor in interpersonal relationships (Kang et al. 2010; Williams and Bargh 2008). The findings in this literature share the main idea that it is warmth, and not coldness, which leads to an individual's favorable attitudes towards others. Given this association between physical warmth and positive feelings, it is likely that warmth will also increase favorable attitudes in the consumption arena. Drawing on this idea, we suggest that warmth generates favorable emotions which in turn increase product valuation.

The first two experiments were designed to test the basic effect of temperature on product valuations. In experiment 1A, 98 participants were seated in either a pre-warmed or a pre-cooled room (ad-

justed to 26°C or 18°C respectively). Next, they evaluated a varied set of 11 consumption products (i.e., a pack of M&Ms candy, a wireless computer mouse, a can of Coca Cola, a six-pack of Duracell batteries, a pampering massage, a CD of a popular singer, a two-liter jug of milk, a cup of coffee, a container of popcorn, Dove bath gel, and a Gap t-shirt). We found that participants who evaluated these products in ambient warm temperature were willing to pay more for the products (standardized *M*'s of .13) than those who evaluated them in cool temperature (standardized *M*'s of -.11; $t(96) = 2.26, p = .026$).

In experiment 1B, we used a different temperature manipulation, asking 46 participants to touch a warm (vs. cool) therapeutic pad as part of an initial study in which they had to evaluate a new product. Next, in a second purportedly unrelated study, participants were asked to indicate their willingness-to-pay for both a hedonic product (a slice of chocolate cake) and a utilitarian product (batteries). Again, those who had experienced physical warmth were willing to pay significantly more for both products, as compared to those who had experienced physical coolness ($M_{warm} = 16.13$ vs. $M_{cool} = 11.85$; $t(44) = 3.41, p = .001$). Together with experiment 1A, this experiment shows that physical warmth increases product valuation, demonstrating the existence of a *temperature premium*.

The purpose of the next two experiments was to examine the underlying process for this temperature premium. Experiment 2 was designed as a mediation study which involves real consequential choice, hence examining the external validity of the temperature premium phenomenon. Sixty participants touched a warm (vs. cool) pad as in experiment 1B, and then evaluated a real pen and rated their current affective reactions towards the pen (using a seven-item scale [Derbaix 1995]; $\alpha = .85$). Finally, to thank them for their participation, participants were given a choice between receiving the pen and receiving 3 NIS. The results again suggest that valuation of the pen increased in the warm condition: 77% of participants in the warm condition chose the pen over money, compared to 47% in the cool condition ($c^2 = 5.71, p = .017$). Importantly, participants' affective reactions mediated the positive effect of warmth on product valuation as indicated by a bootstrap mediation analysis (95% CI: .02, 1.43).

Experiment 3 was designed to further test the role of affect in the temperature premium phenomenon by employing the findings of recent research indicating that emotional reaction is associated with reduced perceived distance (Van Boven et al. 2010). Specifically, we investigated whether physical warmth would also affect distance perception, which would implicate the role of emotions in the observed effects. An online pretest demonstrated that participants experiencing warmth estimated their distance from Paris to be closer than the control group ($M_{warm} = 3439.9$ km vs. $M_{control} = 4130.2$ km; $t(120) = -2.44, p = .016$). The results of experiment 3 revealed a similar pattern in a more controlled (lab) setting. Specifically, 66 participants were first exposed to a warm versus cool pad as before, and were then asked to estimate their distance from a pen that was placed 40 centimeters in front of them. We found that exposure to warm (vs. cool) temperatures reduced participants' perceived distance to the pen ($M_{warm} = 26.19$ cm vs. $M_{cool} = 38.28$ cm; $t(76) = -3.86, p < .001$), further supporting the affect-based account. Additionally, physical warmth again increased valuation of the pen ($M_{warm} = 8.56$ NIS vs. $M_{control} = 7.31$ NIS; $t(76) = 2.02, p = .047$), replicating our previous findings.

In summary, using a variety of products and temperature manipulations, the current work shows that physical warmth increases product valuation, demonstrating the existence of a temperature premium. Importantly, the findings suggest that consumers' positive emotional response to target products in the presence of physical warmth underlie these results. Besides contributing to the atmospherics and sensory marketing literature, our findings also add to the growing literature on embodiment effects. Finally, we offer practical implications by demonstrating the positive influence of appropriate physical warmth in the buying environment.

The Benefits of Retail Therapy: Choosing to Buy Alleviates Sadness

EXTENDED ABSTRACT

How do people regulate their negative affect? Psychologists have documented several common (and often ineffective) responses to negative affect (e.g., rumination). Consumer researchers have also argued that negative affect encourages shopping, a phenomenon commonly known as "retail therapy." We examine whether and why retail therapy is an effective way to regulate negative affect. We focus on shopping's potential to alleviate sadness in particular, as previous research has demonstrated that sadness can increase the desire to buy (Cryder et al. 2008; Lerner, Small, and Loewenstein 2004).

Qualitative research supports the notion that retail therapy can help to alleviate sadness (e.g., Atalay and Meloy 2011). While suggestive, prior research on the effectiveness of retail therapy is plagued by at least two important limitations that cloud interpretation of the findings. First, research in this area has not utilized random assignment. Instead, this work has relied on surveys and interviews with people who chose to engage in retail therapy. Without randomly assigning participants to shopping or equally engaging "control" activities, it is unclear whether shopping conveys benefits above and beyond those produced by distraction or the mere passage of time.

Second, research in this area has relied entirely on retrospective reports of how shopping influenced affect. For example, Faber and Christenson (1996, p. 809) administered a questionnaire that assessed the "frequency of feeling each of nine different mood states immediately before deciding to go shopping and how often they were experienced while shopping." Because "shopping" has many components, including browsing, choosing, paying, acquiring, and consuming, retrospective reports of the effects of "shopping" cannot shed light on which component(s) are necessary for healing to occur.

This is not merely a descriptive shortcoming. Instead, differences in the effectiveness of different components could shed light on why shopping helps to alleviate sadness. To develop hypotheses about why some components will be more influential than others, we consider sadness from an appraisal theory perspective (e.g., Lerner and Keltner 2000). Appraisal theory suggests that the way people cognitively appraise their environment can be both a cause and consequence of different emotions. Smith and Ellsworth (1985) identified six dimensions that best characterize the appraisals that differentiate emotions: the extent to which the current situation is pleasant, predictable, demanding of attention, demanding of effort, under human (versus situational) control, and under one's own or other people's control.

Smith and Ellsworth (1985) found that sadness, more than any other investigated emotion, was associated with a perceived lack of personal control. People who are sad are especially likely to view personally relevant outcomes as governed by some combination of other people's desires and chance. To the extent that these appraisals create or maintain the experience of sadness, aspects of shopping that help to restore a sense of personal control may in turn alleviate sadness.

The ability to choose tends to enhance one's sense of personal control (e.g., Langer 1975). Because choices are inherent to shopping (e.g., choosing what to buy), shopping may help to restore a sense of control and thus alleviate sadness. In particular, there is reason to expect that choosing to buy will be more likely to restore a sense of control than choosing not to buy. People do not buy the vast majority of products they encounter, so arguably choosing not to buy is the default action in shopping environments. In fact, choosing not to buy when faced with several alternative goods is sometimes referred to as a "no-choice" option (e.g., Dhar 1997). Therefore, we posit that choosing an item to buy is especially likely to alleviate sadness.

Study 1 examined whether merely simulating shopping helps to alleviate sadness. We utilized a hypothetical shopping paradigm to determine whether making buying choices (even without the subsequent attainment of a good) was sufficient to help alleviate sadness.

We collected a baseline measure of affect and then showed a sad video to all participants. Participants were then randomly assigned to either choose which of several products they would (hypothetically) buy (Buyers) or judge which of those products would be most useful for travelling (Browsers). (The buying and browsing tasks lasted the same amount of time.) We then took a final measure of affect.

We found no significant difference between final and baseline levels of sadness among Buyers. Browsers, however, were significantly sadder at the end of the experiment than at baseline. Thus, Buyers were more likely to be "healed" by the end of the experiment.

Study 2 examined whether the benefits of choosing to buy persist when participants must actually part with money to obtain a good (that is, when shopping for real). We also examined whether making a buying decision helps to alleviate anger. Anger is generally as unpleasant as sadness, but is associated with a much greater sense of personal control (Keltner, Ellsworth, and Edwards 1993). Thus, we did not anticipate that making a buying decision, which should help to restore a sense of personal control, would help to alleviate anger.

We paid participants up front for participating and then took a baseline measure of affect. Participants then watched a video previously demonstrated to induce both anger and sadness. We then randomly assigned participants to Shopping or Browsing conditions. In the Shopping condition, participants either bought one of several snacks (Buyers) or did not buy one (Non-Buyers). Buyers did not consume their snack in the lab. In the Browsing condition, participants inspected the same set of snacks and ranked them based on perceived amount of food-coloring (Browsers). We then took a final measure of affect.

Consistent with Study 1, there was no significant difference between final and baseline levels of sadness among Buyers. Non-Buyers and Browsers were significantly sadder at the end of the experiment than at baseline. All participants were significantly angrier at the end of the experiment than at baseline, consistent with our theoretical account.

Taken together, our results do not support the broad notion that shopping alleviates negative affect. Instead, our evidence suggests that buying helps to restore control and alleviate sadness.

REFERENCES

Atalay, A. Selin and Margaret G. Meloy (2011), "Retail Therapy: A Strategic Effort to Improve Mood," *Psychology and Marketing*, 28(6), 638–59.

Bitner, Mary Jo (1992), "Servicescapes: The Impact of Physical Surroundings on Customers and Employees," *Journal of Marketing,* 56(April), 57–71.

Bloch, Peter H. and Marsha L. Richins (1983), "A Theoretical Model for the Study of Product Importance Perceptions," *Journal of Marketing*, 47(3), 69-81.

Celsi, Richard L. and Jerry C. Olsen (1988), "The Role of Involvement in Attention and Comprehension Processes," *Journal of Consumer Research*, 15(September), 210-24.

Chandon, Pierre, J. Wesley Hutchinson, Eric T. Bradlow, and Scott Young (2009), "Does In- Store Marketing Work? Effects of the Number and Position of Shelf Facings on Brand Attention and Evaluation at the Point of Purchase," *Journal of Marketing*, 73(6), 1-17.

Cryder, Cynthia, Jennifer Lerner, James Gross, and Ronald Dahl (2008), "Misery is not Miserly: Sad and Self-Focused Individuals Spend More," *Psychological Science,* 19(6), 525-30.

Derbaix, Christian M. (1995), "The Impact of Affective Reactions on Attitudes toward the Advertisement and the Brand: A Step toward Ecological Validity," *Journal of Marketing Research*, 32(November), 470–9.

Dhar, Ravi (1997), "Consumer Preference for a No-Choice Option," *Journal of Consumer Research*, 24(2), 215-31.

_____ and Wertenbroch, Klaus (2000), "Consumer Choice between Hedonic and Utilitarian Goods," *Journal of Marketing Research*, 37(1), 60-71.

Drèze, Xavier, Stephen J. Hoch, and Mary E. Purk (1994), "Shelf Management and Space Elasticity," *Journal of Retailing*, 70(4), 301-26.

Faber, Ronald J. and Gary A. Christenson (1996), "In the Mood to Buy: Differences in the Mood States Experienced by Compulsive Buyers and Other Consumers," *Psychology and Marketing*, 13(8), 803-19.

Granbois, Donald H. (1968), "Improving the Study of Customer In-Store Behavior," *Journal of Marketing*, 32(4), 28-33.

Hauser, John R. and Birger Wernerfelt (1989), "The Competitive Implications of Relevant-Set Response Analysis," *Journal of Marketing Research*, 26(November), 391-405.

Hong, Jiewen and Sun, Yacheng (2012), "Warm It Up with Love: The Effect of Physical Coldness on Liking of Romance Movies," *Journal of Consumer Research*, forthcoming.

Hsee, Christopher K. and Rottenstreich, Yuval (2004), "Music, Pandas, and Muggers: On the Affective Psychology of Value," *Journal of Experimental Psychology*, 133(1), 23-30.

Hutchinson, J. Wesley and Robert J. Meyer (1994), "Dynamic Decision Making: Optimal Policies and Actual Behavior in Sequential Choice Problems," *Marketing Letters*, 5(4), 369-93.

Inman, Jeffrey J., Leigh McAlister, and Wayne D. Hoyer (1990), "Promotion Signal: Proxy for a Price Cut?" *Journal of Consumer Research*, 17(June), 74-81.

Inman, J. Jeffrey, Russell S. Winer, and Rosellina Ferraro (2009), "The Interplay between Category Characteristics, Customer Characteristics, and Customer Activities on In- Store Decision Making," *Journal of Marketing,* 73(September), 19-29.

Iyengar, Sheena S. and Mark R. Lepper (2000), "When Choice Is Demotivating: Can One Desire Too Much of a Good Thing?"*Journal of Personality and Social Psychology*, 79(6), 995–1006.

Kamenica, Emir (2008), "Contextual Inference in Markets: On the Informational Content of Product Lines," *American Economic Review*, 98(5), 2127-2149.

Kang, Yoona, Williams, Lawrence E., Clark, Margaret S., Gray, Jeremy P., and Bargh, John A. (2011), "Physical Temperature Effects on Trust Behavior: The Role of Insula," *Social Cognitive and Affective Neuroscience*, 6(4), 507-15.

Keltner, Dacher, Phoebe C. Ellsworth, and Kari Edwards (1993), "Beyond Simple Pessimism: Effects of Sadness and Anger on Social Perception," *Journal of Personality and Social Psychology*, 64, 740-52.

Kotler, Philip (1973), "Atmospherics as a Marketing Tool," *Journal of Retailing,* 49(Winter), 48–64.

Krishna, Aradhna (2012), "An Integrative Review of Sensory Marketing: Engaging the Senses to Affect Perception, Judgment and Behavior," *Journal of Consumer Psychology*, forthcoming.

Langer, Ellen J. (1975), "The Illusion of Control," *Journal of Personality and Social Psychology*, 32, 311-28.

Lerner, Jennifer and Dacher Keltner (2000), "Beyond Valence: Toward a Model of Emotion-Specific Influences on Judgment and Choice," *Cognition and Emotion*, 14, 473-93.

Lerner, Jennifer, Deborah Small, and George Loewenstein (2004), "Heart Strings and Purse Strings: Carryover Effects of Emotions on Economic Decisions," *Psychological Science*, 15(5), 337-41.

Novemsky, Nathan, Dhar, Ravi, Schwarz, Norbert, and Itamar Simonson (2007). "Preference Fluency in Choice," *Journal of Marketing Research*, 44(3), 347-56.

Peck, Joann and Terry L. Childers (2003), "To Have and To Hold: The Influence of Haptic Information on Product Judgments," *Journal of Marketing*, 67(April), 35–48.

Punj, Girish N. and Richard Staelin (1983), "A Model of Consumer Information Search Behavior for New Automobiles," *Journal of Consumer Research*, 9(March), 366-80.

Rook, Dennis W. (1987), "The Buying Impulse," *Journal of Consumer Research*, 14(September), 189-96.

Smith, Craig A. and Phoebe C. Ellsworth (1985), "Patterns of Cognitive Appraisal in Emotion," *Journal of Personality and Social Psychology*, 48, 813-38.

Stilley, Karen M., J. Jeffrey Inman, and Kirk L. Wakefield (2010), "Spending on the Fly: Mental Budgets, Promotions, and Spending Behavior," *Journal of Marketing*, 74(May), 34-47.

Sujan, Mita, James R. Bettman, and Harish Sujan (1986), "Effects of Consumer Expectations on Information Processing in Selling Encounters," *Journal of Marketing Research*, 23, 346-53.

Valenzuela, Ana and Priya Raghubir (2009), "Position-based Beliefs: The Center-Stage Effect," *Journal of Consumer Psychology*, 19(2), 185-96.

Valenzuela, Ana, Priya Raghubir, and Chrissy Mitakakis (2012), "Shelf Space Schemas: Myth or Reality?" *Journal of Business Research*, forthcoming.

Van Boven, Leaf, Kane, Joanne, McGraw, Pete A., and Dale, Jeannette (2010), "Feeling Close: Emotional Intensity Reduces Perceived Psychological Distance," *Journal of Personality and Social Psychology*, 98, 872–85.

Williams, Lawrence E. and Bargh, John A. (2008), "Experiencing Physical Warmth Promotes Interpersonal Warmth," *Science*, 322(5901), 606–7.

Anomalies in Goal Pursuit

Chairs: Luxi Shen, University of Chicago, USA
Ayelet Fishbach, University of Chicago, USA

Paper #1: Opportunity Cost Neglect in Goal Pursuit Under Uncertainty

Derek Koehler, University of Waterloo, Canada
Cade Massey, University of Pennsylvania, USA

Paper #2: The Uniqueness Heuristic: A Preference for Unique Options for a Single Goal

Luxi Shen, University of Chicago, USA
Ayelet Fishbach, University of Chicago, USA

Paper #3: Blind to All Else: The Role of Mindsets in Multiple-Goal Pursuit

Anastasiya Pocheptsova, University of Maryland, USA
Jordan Etkin, University of Maryland, USA
Ravi Dhar, Yale University, USA

Paper #4: Space, Time and Getting Things Done: The Role of Mindsets in Goal Pursuit

Dilip Soman, University of Toronto, Canada

SESSION OVERVIEW

People generally make purchases with a specific goal in mind. But can they effectively attain the goal? While economists believe that consumers have stable and well-defined preferences about desired ends and act in ways that reliably achieves these ends, psychologists find that people do not always pursue goals in a rational and effective manner. In this session, we explore such anomalies in goal pursuit. We aim to highlight findings that demonstrate instances when consumers' choices and behaviors violate normative theories and reveal the cognitive mechanism underlying these anomalies. Specifically, the first two papers show that consumers' goal pursuit behaviors appear inconsistent with rational behavior axioms, whereas the last two papers focus on how contextual cues drive consumers to behave differently under similar goal pursuit situations.

The first paper, by Derek Koehler and Cade Massey, asks whether consumers seek to maximize their ultimate utility from goal pursuit. In particular, the authors study goal abandonment and investigate whether consumers neglect opportunity costs in a pursuit of a goal with uncertainty. Normatively, if goal attainment is uncertain, consumers should consider giving up their current goal pursuit at some point in order to maximize their gain and minimize their loss. However, they found that consumers tend to over-persist on their goals, forging opportunities offered by alternative pursuits.

The second paper, by Luxi Shen and Ayelet Fishbach, examines choice consistency and focuses on consumers' preference for uniqueness in a goal-based choice. They identified the uniqueness heuristic such that consumers choose unique options for one single goal but defer from that option when choosing for multiple goals. This heuristic leads to a preference reversal: Consumers prefer a unique option either for Goal A or for Goal B, but when choosing for both Goal A and B together, they prefer an ordinary option.

The third paper, by Anastasiya Pocheptsova, Jordan Etkin, and Ravi Dhar, considers how goal-related mindsets affect the approach that consumers adopt for multiple-goal pursuit. Although previous literature suggests that consumers faced with multiple goals usually switch between pursuing their multiple goals, their findings showed that consumers at times prefer to highlight the pursuit of one of their goals at the expense of other co-active goals. They further identified

the role of implemental mindset (vs. deliberative mindset) in driving this effect.

The last paper, by Dilip Soman, takes an integrative perspective on how incidental contextual cues effect consumers' initiation of goal pursuit. In one of his studies, he found that the patience (commitment) of consumers in a queue depends on whether they were already inside a queue guide area (a visual boundary of the task system) regardless of the length of the area, though normatively the decision of dropping a queue should be a function of the absolute time/distance expected to wait. Based on consistent findings across the domains of space and time, the author develops a new framework for understanding the interplay between incidental contextual cues and the implemental mindset.

Together, these four interconnected papers provide interesting perspectives on when consumers' goal pursuit decisions and behaviors appear inconsistent, explore the cognitive structure underlying the goal pursuit anomalies, and specify when the anomalies may help consumers effectively attain their goals and when they may not. The papers yield insights into consumer goal pursuit across a wide range of settings, and carry theoretical as well as practical implications for consumer research. Data collection in all papers is complete and all participants have agreed to present, should the session be accepted. The chairs will facilitate audience discussion drawing connections between the session topic, anomalies in goal pursuit, and other areas of consumer research.

Opportunity Cost Neglect in Goal Pursuit Under Uncertainty

EXTENDED ABSTRACT

Consumer choices are often made in the context of goal pursuit. Weight-loss products are purchased on the basis of their anticipated contribution to progress toward a weight-loss goal; financial investment products are selected in the context of a retirement or other savings goal; subscriptions to online dating services are made with the goal of establishing a romantic relationship. One notable feature these examples have in common is that the goal's achievability is uncertain.

Much of the recent work on decision making in goal pursuit has focused on self-regulatory mechanisms that influence trade-offs between short-term expenditures (e.g., of effort) and long-term rewards associated with goal achievement (e.g., Heath, Larrick, and Wu 1999; Fishbach and Dhar 2005). A simplifying assumption typically made in such research is that the goal in question can be achieved and is worth achieving (i.e., benefits of goal achievement outweigh its costs). On such analyses, the primary implications of goal proximity or rate of progress are motivational, in that willingness to expend effort to make further progress toward a goal may vary with its proximity and how progress toward it is construed (e.g., Fishbach, Dhar, and Zhang 2006).

In many decisions we face, however, there is uncertainty about a goal's achievability. There may come a point at which a goal may not be worth continued pursuit because the anticipated benefits of goal achievement are outweighed by its costs. Often such uncertainty can be at least partly resolved over time as progress toward the goal is made: One can calculate whether, in light of this progress and the cost at which it was attained, the expected returns of achieving the goal justify the costs of its continued pursuit. Optimal decision making, on this account, relies on belief revision, i.e., reassessment of whether the current goal should be continue to be pursued, or should instead be abandoned. Suboptimal goal pursuit behavior, then, can arise from miscalculation of cost and benefits of continued goal pursuit (i.e., leading to adoption of a suboptimal goal-pursuit strategy), as well as from the more familiar self-regulation challenges the underlie failure to execute an otherwise optimal goal-pursuit strategy. We suggest that the problem-solving aspect of goal pursuit, that is, how costs and benefits are and ought optimally to be integrated in decisions about whether to continue to pursue a goal, has been relatively understudied.

In the present research, therefore, we investigate decisions about whether to abandon or continue pursuit of a goal whose achievability is uncertain. Typically, decisions of this type are faced sequentially, as progress toward the goal is made and can be used to update the likelihood and value of goal achievement (e.g., an entrepreneur who faces continual decisions about whether to make further investments in a business project). Appropriate responsiveness to progress feedback is needed for optimal decisions -- one must balance the risk of abandoning the goal too early against pursuing it too long.

A challenge in studying this issue is identifying optimal decision-making. We build on the classic ball-and-urn paradigm to develop a task allowing the quantification of goal pursuit's costs and benefits. With this approach it is possible to gauge any systematic bias toward over-persistence or under-persistence. In each round, one of two urns containing red and green balls is randomly selected. Participants--who know the composition of each urn but not which one was selected for the current round--choose whether or not to draw balls from it. If the participant draws a target number of green balls (the "goal"), he or she receives a payoff. Draws are made without replacement, at a fixed cost deducted from an initial endowment for the round. The challenge is that only one of the two urns contains enough green balls to achieve the goal. The participant may quit the round at any time and keep what remains of the initial endowment. Thus, the participant must continually assess whether to persist or, alternatively, to abandon the goal. Multiple rounds of the game are played (with one randomly-selected round played for real money), allowing assessment of whether goal pursuit decisions improve with experience.

In multiple studies we investigate the impact of reward size and probability on participant behavior. We also evaluate performance in a variation of the paradigm in which participants can abandon urns in exchange for draws from other urns, rather than for a fixed payment. Across all studies we find a strong tendency to over-persist. That is, participants invest too much in trying to achieving success on the current urn, relative to an optimal benchmark suggesting that expected returns of goal achievement are outweighed by the anticipated cost of achieving it. This tendency is exacerbated by insufficient sensitivity to reward size and probability, and is worse in studies in which the foregone benefit is additional opportunity rather than a fixed payment.

Across studies we find the largest bias when a decision-maker receives "bad news" (makes relatively slow progress) in the early stages of goal pursuit. Optimal play requires abandonment in such circumstances. As a result, a Bayesian player is certain to sometimes abandon (ex-post) achievable goals (favorable urns), making up for it via more future opportunities. Our participants, on the other hand, rarely mistakenly abandon an achievable goal (favorable urn), but at the cost of leaving themselves far fewer opportunities for future goal achievement. There is no evidence from our studies that this bias is attenuated with task experience. We suggest that cost-benefit trad-

eoffs between current (or focal) and future (or alternative) opportunities is a fundamental tension in goal pursuit and ripe for additional psychological investigation.

The Uniqueness Heuristic:
A Preference for Unique Options for a Single Goal

EXTENDED ABSTRACT

When painting their bedroom, will homeowners select spring tulip red or beige? Would they make a different choice when painting their living room? This research explores people's preferences for unique versus non-unique choice options.

Previous research has examined several factors that contribute to a preference for non-unique options, including a desire to reduce risk (Simonson and Tversky 1992), to make an easily justifiable choice (Shafir, Simonson, and Tversky 1993; Simonson 1989), and to conform to a perceived social norm (Asch 1955; Simonson and Nowlis 2000). In contrast, other research has documented people's need for uniqueness (Ariely and Levav 2000; Berger and Heath 2007; Tian and McKenzie 2001), which leads to a preference for unique options.

In light of the existing research, we identify a "uniqueness heuristic" -- a stronger preference for unique options when choosing for a single goal than when choosing for multiple goals. We explain the uniqueness heuristic as the trade-off between multi-finality (i.e., how many goals one option serves) and instrumentality (i.e., how well one option serves each of the goals) in the cognitive network of goal system (Kruglanski et al. 2002; Zhang, Fishbach, and Kruglanski 2007). According to our analysis, unique options appear highly instrumental to a few goals, whereas non-unique options appear less instrumental but can serve many goals.

We further predict a preference reversal: What people choose for each single goal alone differs from what they choose for all the single goals together. For example, people may choose a unique restaurant either to dine with friend A or to dine with friend B, but choose a non-unique restaurant for dinner with both A and B.

In six studies involving different choice contexts, we tested the uniqueness heuristic with subtle and naturalistic goal activation, ruled out alternative explanations such as risk aversion, and explored the underlying mechanism.

In Study 1, we adopted the conceptual definition of uniqueness -- atypicality, that is, how remote one option is from the prototype of its category. Specifically, we designed a list of ice-creams with unique flavors (orange dark chocolate ice-cream and rosy vanilla ice-cream) and non-unique flavors (chocolate and vanilla). In the weeks around the Valentine's Day, we asked customers at a campus café to think of a friend who might be telling her felling to her crush and choose an ice-cream for one of the following purposes: (single goal a) to celebrate she entered a new relationship, (single goal b) to comfort her because she was rejected by her crush, and (multiple goals) to either celebrate or comfort because they were still waiting for her. We found that the atypical (unique) ice-cream flavors were preferred in both single goal cases but the typical (non-unique) ice-cream flavors were preferred in the multiple goal case.

The rest of the studies experimentally manipulated the uniqueness of an option by configuring different choice sets. The same option can be of low frequency and thus appears unique in one choice set (e.g., a French restaurant among many Italian restaurants), but be of high frequency and thus appears non-unique in another choice set (e.g., the French restaurant among many other French restaurants). In Study 2, participants chose a restaurant for dinner with one friend (single goal) or five friends (multiple goals). We found a preference for the unique restaurant in the choice set (either one French restaurant among Italian restaurants or one Italian restaurant among French restaurants) for one friend but not for five friends.

Similarly, in Study 3, participants preferred a unique suitcase (either soft-sided among hard-sided, or hard-sided among soft-sided) for one upcoming trip (single goal) but not for multiple upcoming trips (multiple goals).

In Study 4, we examined choices with real consequence. Participants chose and sent a card to their family members. This experiment again confirmed the uniqueness heuristic and suggested a preference reversal: Participants preferred the uniquely-shaped card for their aunt alone and for their uncle alone, but not for both their aunt and uncle.

In Study 5, we ruled out an alternative explanation, risk aversion, by comparing choice for one goal versus one out of multiple goals. Participants selected the unique wine (either Californian among Australian or Australian among Californian) when shopping for one future occasion (single goal) but not when shopping for one out of four potential future occasions (multiple goals). The real outcome risk for experiencing a unique option was equal in both conditions and thus our finding suggested that the uniqueness heuristic cannot be explained by risk aversion.

Finally, in Study 6, we examined the underlying mechanism of the uniqueness heuristic. Participants chose apples, either red among green or green among red, for one experimenter (single goal) or for one of six experimenters (multiple goals) and made predictions on how much the apples would be enjoyed either before or after choosing. We found that participants used the uniqueness heuristic when choosing before predicting but not after. We also found that participants based their choice for single goals on their predictions regardless of whether they chose before or after predicting and their choice for multiple goals on their predictions only when they make predictions first. These findings confirmed the uniqueness heuristic, revealed its mechanism, and suggested that thinking about the instrumentality of each option before choosing can prevent the preference reversal by the uniqueness heuristic.

Blind to All Else:
The Role of Mindsets in Multiple-Goal Pursuit

EXTENDED ABSTRACT

It is now well established that consumer behavior is goal-driven (Bargh and Gollwitzer 1994; Kruglanski et al. 2002; Markman and Brendl 2005). Consumers typically have multiple goals that they try to pursue at the same time, for example, simultaneously wishing to be fit and to eat tasty foods, and to socialize with friends and achieve greater success in the workplace. When consumers maintain multiple goals, they will often temporarily disengage from initial pursuit of one goal to attend to their other co-active goals, a dynamic referred to as balancing (Dhar and Simonson 1999; Fishbach and Dhar 2005; Kivetz and Simonson 2002).

In contrast, the present research focuses on situations when consumers may instead selectively focus on the pursuit of only one of their multiple goals, a dynamic referred to as highlighting (Dhar and Simonson 1999). We propose that the propensity to highlight in multiple-goal pursuit is moderated by the cognitive orientation that consumers naturally adopt during different phases of goal pursuit. Mindsets theory (Gollwitzer 1990; Heckhausen and Gollwitzer 1987) demonstrates that goal pursuit can be construed via two different cognitive orientations: deliberative and implemental mindset. The deliberative mindset consists of evaluating the pros and cons of pursuing an intended goal whereas the implemental mindset consists

of deciding where, when, and how to act in order to implement the intended goal (Gollwitzer, Heckhausen and Steller, 1990; Chandran and Morwitz 2005).

We argue that being in an implemental mindset for one of multiple co-active goals will lead consumers to inhibit the activation level of alternative pursuits, decreasing the likelihood of deviating from target goal pursuit (goal shielding; Shah et al. 2002). Consequently, consumers will highlight pursuit of a single goal at the expense of their other co-active goals, affecting choice of goal-related products, or means, to multiple-goal attainment. Specifically, we predict that consumers will repeatedly select means related to the goal associated with an implemental mindset, forgoing opportunities to balance multiple-goal pursuit by alternating between means related to several of their co-active goals. We further argue that implemental mindsets will affect consumers' preferences for products that would allow them to simultaneously pursue multiple co-active goals (i.e., "multifinal means"). While previous literature has shown increased preference for such means in multiple-goal contexts (Chun et al. 2011, Kopetz et al. 2011), we propose that consumers in implemental mindset would be less likely to prefer multifinal means as a consequence of highlighting the pursuit of only one of their several co-active goals.

Five studies provide support for these propositions. Study 1 shows that being in an implemental (vs. deliberative) mindset for one of two co-active goals results in a decrease in the accessibility of other co-active goals. In a word search task designed to measure goal accessibility, participants in an implemental (vs. deliberative) mindset for one of two goals (i.e., the target goal) found fewer words related to their non-target goal ($M_{implemental} = 1.31$, $M_{deliberative} = 1.01$; $F(1, 138) = 8.89$, $p < .01$). Studies 2a and 2b examine the effect of mindsets on highlighting in the sequential choice of products. In study 2a we show that participants in an implemental (vs. deliberative) mindset for one of two co-active goals were more likely to repeatedly choose products consistent with only that goal, disrupting the process of balancing in multiple-goal pursuit (preference for second product: $M_{implemental} = 78.9\%$ vs. $M_{deliberative} = 33.3\%$; $\chi^2 = 7.84$, $p < .01$). Study 2b extends this finding by demonstrating that consumers in an implemental mindset for one of their multiple co-active goals decline opportunities to pursue their other goals, even when such opportunities do not affect the pursuit of the target goal. Specifically, we show that participants in an implemental (vs. deliberative) mindset are more likely to postpone choice than to choose an option consistent with their other co-active goal ($M_{implemental} = 95\%$ vs. $M_{deliberative} = 69\%$, $\chi^2 = 4.07$, $p < .05$).

The next two studies demonstrate the effect of mindsets on preference for multifinal means. Study 3a shows that in a simultaneous choice paradigm, consumers in an implemental mindset are less likely to prefer multifinal product assortments than are consumers in a deliberative mindset. Specifically, when given the option to construct a balanced product assortment to pursue two co-active goals (health and indulgence), participants in an implemental mindset favored their target health goal (number of products selected: $M_{healthy} = 6.52$ vs. $M_{indulgent} = 4.30$; $F(1, 135) = 25.97$, $p < .001$), whereas participants in a deliberative mindset favored a more balanced product assortment ($M_{healthy} = 6.01$ vs. $M_{indulgent} = 5.36$; $F(1, 135) = 2.06$, $p > .1$). Finally, study 3b extends this finding to a consequential choice setting by showing that consumers in an implemental (vs. deliberative) mindset for one goal are less likely to select an option that allows for the simultaneous pursuit of their multiple co-active goals ($M_{implemental} = 37\%$ vs. $M_{deliberative} = 62.5\%$; $\chi^2 [1] = 4.18$, $p = .04$).

This research makes several contributions to past work on goal-related mindsets and the dynamics of multiple-goal pursuit. First, we identify implemental mindset as an important boundary condition to previously established dynamics of balancing in multiple-goal pursuit. Second, we show that consumer mindsets moderate the established preference for means that help consumers pursue multiple goals at the same time; despite having multiple co-active goals, consumers in an implemental mindset for one of those goals are less likely to use multifinal means. Taken together, our research extends current knowledge of the dynamics of multiple-goal pursuit and of the role played by goal-related mindsets in influencing consumer choice.

Space, Time and Getting Things Done: The Role of Mindsets in Goal Pursuit

EXTENDED ABSTRACT

The achievement of most behavioral goals is preceded by a phase in which consumers approach the goal over space and time. In this stream of research, I study goal pursuit during this phase of approach and address the question of how consumers' goal commitment and implementation activity is affected by their proximity to the goal. Results from both the domain of time (Tu and Soman 2012) and space (Zhao, Lee, and Soman 2012) show that consumers tend to partition the approach into distinct categories – a "later and there" category in which the outcome is spatially and temporally distant and a "now and here" category in which it is proximal. The categorization process can be facilitated by any cues in the environment that facilitate perceptual, semantic or conceptual similarities. In the domain of space, for example, we find that a space that is labeled "inside," or space that is demarcated by the use of area rugs and queue guides is more likely to be categorized as proximal to the goal. In the domain of time, categorization is facilitated by duration markers – events like the end of the month or year, or other salient episodes in consumers' lifetimes (e.g., a birthday, the end of an academic term) such that outcomes that happen before the salient marker are categorized as "now" and those that will happen after the marker are categorized as "later."

Prior research has also documented that consumer's cognitive processing changes as a function of their distance from the goal. For instance, Lewin (1926), Heckenhausen (1987) and Gollwitzer (2012) have all made the distinction between the motivation phase [a phase where the consumer plans and strategizes] and the volition phase [when tactics are executed to get the desired outcome]. Gollwitzer (2012) and others (e.g., Xu and Wyer 2010) use the term mindset to capture these differences. In a deliberative mindset, the consumer plans; in an implemental mindset, the consumer does. An implemental mindset can be characterized by the willingness to make and commit to a choice, by a sense of optimism about achieving the desired outcome, and by heightened action orientation more generally. Xu and Wyer (2010) argue that implemental mindsets are triggered by the activation of procedural knowledge, but not much else has been written about when during goal pursuit does a consumer switch from a deliberative mindset to an implemental one.

I propose that categorical processes provide a key input into determining when the mindstate transition happens. The physical and temporal movement from the "there and later" to the "here and now" triggers a mindset change. In particular, the urgency associated with the "here and now" puts people in an implemental mindset and hence they are more likely to work to accomplish the final outcome.

Two completed papers provide empirical evidence on which this framework is based. In the domain of time, we find (Tu and Soman, 2012) that when a task that is due D-days from now is due this period as opposed to the next, participants invest greater effort to achieve the task. Likewise in the domain of space, we (Zhao, Lee and Soman 2012) observed people waiting to check into a flight or use an ATM machine, and found that they were very likely to keep all of their documentation (e.g. tickets, passport, ATM card) ready as soon as they stepped onto an area rug in front of the service area. Across 12 experiments in both domains, we find evidence for goal accomplishment, commitment, effort and optimism when consumers are "here and now".

In this talk, I will

- Develop a new theoretical framework of goal pursuit and mindsets
- Present some selected evidence from two completed papers; Tu and Soman (2012) in the domain of time and Zhao, Lee and Soman (2012) in the domain of space.
- Discuss additional ways of categorization that may produce counter-intuitive results, for example situations in which people who are physically or temporally distant could be more action oriented by the activation of another categorization cue. For example, a professor is more motivated to work on next Tuesday's class on the preceding Tuesday when s/he is teaching her previous class because all Tuesdays may be categorized as "teaching days."
- Integrate the findings and discuss implications for consumer behavior, marketers, and policy makers and for the theory of goal pursuit more generally.

Raising the Bar: New Insights into the Development of an Optimal Donation Solicitation

Chair: Tatiana Fajardo, University of Miami, USA

Paper #1: Construing Charity: Consumer Construal Level and Charitable Contributions of Time Versus Money.

Rhiannon MacDonnell, University of Calgary, Canada
Katherine White, University of British Columbia, Canada

Paper #2: Empathy, Donation, and the Moderating Role of Psychological Distance.

Joseph Paniculangara, Lakehead University, Canada
Xin He, University of Central Florida, USA

Paper #3: Splitting the Decision: Increasing Donations by Recognizing the Differential Impact of Internal and External Considerations

Tatiana M. Fajardo, University of Miami, USA
Claudia Townsend, University of Miami, USA

Paper #4: For Charities not all Aesthetics are Created Equal: The Differential Effects of Aesthetics With and Without Cost Implications on Response to Donor Solicitations

Shweta Oza, University of Miami, USA
Claudia Townsend, University of Miami, USA

SESSION OVERVIEW

Charities service very diverse populations and provide for many vital services, such as health care, education, housing and disaster relief. However, they are continually confronted with growing competition for resources. Increased need for charitable support has necessitated that nonprofit organizations utilize the most effective means of communicating with the consumer (White and Peloza 2009). The objective of this session is to provide new insights into how non-profit organizations can more effectively construct their donation solicitations. A major contribution of this session will be its implications for how non-profit organizations (or companies interested in pro-social activities) should manage their fundraising efforts.

Recognizing the importance of charitable contributions, researchers have worked rigorously to identify factors influencing donation behavior (Bendapudi, Singh and Bendapudi 1996; Reed, Aquino and Levy 2007). The projects in the session extend this work, examining factors which have generally been overlooked or understudied by previous research. Broadly speaking, influences on donation behavior can be categorized into (1) those integral to the donor (e.g. donor's gender identity: Winterich, Mittal and Ross Jr. 2009) and (2) those external to the donor, contextual or situational factors (e.g. the presence of incentives: Bénabou 2005). Importantly, the projects in this session consider these two types of factors both separately and as they interact.

MacDonnell and White demonstrate how an internal factor, donor's construal orientation, interacts with an external factor, type of donation solicited, to influence donation behavior. Similarly, Paniculangara and He show how the interaction between an internal factor, donor's sense of empathy, and an external factor, donor's distance from the recipient, effects contributions. Fajardo and Townsend identify two parts to the donation decision and examine how they are differentially influenced by internal and external considerations. They build on this knowledge to develop a more effective donation solicitation with internal appeals addressing the decision to donate and external appeals addressing the quantity decision. Then, in contrast to these three papers and the majority of the work in this area, Oza and Townsend consider an entirely external consideration – aesthetics of a donation appeal – to offer additional insights on solicitation

optimization above and beyond the informational persuasions used to motivate donation.

Individually, each project offers recommendations for how to optimize donation. Taken together, the papers in this session provide a blueprint for an effective donation appeal including when to present the appeal, how it should be designed, structured and specifically worded. Researchers interested the non-profit sector and/or pro-social behavior in general would be interested in the session. Given the diverse range of substantive topics to be covered, we also hope to draw attendees who are interested in research on advertising, persuasion techniques, public policy issues, construal level theory and aesthetics. By identifying and examining a diverse range of factors influencing donation behavior and making specific recommendations on how to optimize donation appeals, the session makes great contributions to the fields of persuasion and consumer behavior in general and pro-social marketing in particular.

All of the papers in this symposium are in a very advanced stage. They all have well-developed theoretical frameworks and have completed substantial empirical work. Notably, all these projects include at least one measure of real donation behavior. The working manuscripts for all of the papers in this session (as well as all of the cited references) will be available upon request.

Construing Charity: Consumer Construal Level and Charitable Contributions of Time Versus Money

EXTENDED ABSTRACT

According to construal level theory (Trope and Liberman 2003), mental representations of events influence how individuals process information (Fujita et al. 2006), and these construals, in turn, guide choices, preferences, and behaviors (Trope, Liberman, and Wakslak 2007). A low-level construal is characterized as being more concrete in terms of specific, subordinate, and contextualized features, whereas a high-level construal is one that is more abstract in that it represents events in terms of general, superordinate, and decontextualized features (1989; Liberman and Trope 1998). The current research proposes that while money might be commonly viewed at a relatively concrete level, time might be construed as being more abstract. Further, it is posited that this has implications for marketers requesting charitable support on the part of consumers.

Past research demonstrates that the level at which the consumer construes a particular action can indeed influence various consumer outcomes including brand extension evaluations (Kim and Roedder John, 2008), product attitudes (Lee et al. 2010), and recycling behaviors (White, MacDonnell and Dahl 2011). For example, White et al. (2011) find that a "match" of construal-level with message frame (e.g., abstract messages with gain frames; concrete messages with loss frames) leads to the most positive consumer recycling behaviors and intentions.

Research does suggest that the manner in which consumers perceive time and money do indeed differ (Leclerc et al. 2005; Okada and Hoch 2003). Here, we forward the novel hypothesis that money (time) might be viewed more concretely (abstractly). This is because money is often considered in a concrete, lower-level manner as it serves as a "common currency" that many goods, services, and experiences must be broken down to in order to evaluate. Time, on the other hand, is a more experiential, general, and abstract concept. Given this, we propose that utilizing congruent messaging (concrete vs. abstract) with donation request (paired with money vs. time, respectively) will lead to the most positive charitable support. These predictions were examined across two pretests and three studies. In two pretests, we show that thinking about money (time) leads to more concrete (abstract) thoughts when considering product usage (i.e., an iPod) and recalling a consumption experience (i.e., a date). Next, we turn to the prediction that a match of message (concrete vs. abstract) to the type of charitable support requested (money vs. time) will lead to the most positive charitable responses.

The first study utilized a 2(message: concrete vs. abstract) x 2(donation type: money vs. time) mixed-model design, with donation type as the within-subjects factor. Participants ($N = 86$) read one of two charitable appeals asking for contributions to a hunger-related cause (both with the same branding elements). The first appeal pretested as being more concrete in nature ("contribute to serving breakfasts to children"), and the second pretested as being more abstract ("contribute to addressing hunger for children"). Participants then reported how many dollars and hours (in counterbalanced order) they were willing to contribute to the charitable cause. These measures were standardized for comparison. A mixed-model ANOVA revealed a significant message x donation interaction ($F(1,83)=4.28$, $p<.05$). When presented with a more concrete appeal, consumers were more apt to give money ($M=.442$) than time ($M=.081$; $t=2.94$, $p<.05$). When provided with an abstract appeal, consumers intended to give more time ($M=.296$) than money ($M=-.133$; $t=2.41$, $p<.05$).

To provide converging evidence for our construal level account, study 2 examined individual differences on construal level. Participants (N=60) were then asked to indicate how many dollars and hours they were willing to contribute to the cause communicated in a marketing message. Each measure was converted to a z-score for analysis. Construal preferences were assessed using Vallacher and Wegner's (1989) 25-item "action identification" scale and these were averaged such that lower (higher) scores represented a more concrete (abstract) construal preference. For analysis, a difference score between time and money donations was calculated, with higher numbers indicating greater time donations. Linear regression revealed that the continuous mean-centered action identification scale significantly predicted charitable contributions of time versus money ($\beta = .30$; $t(58)=2.16$, $p<.05$). Thus, those disposed to more abstract construals were more likely to donate time (vs. money).

In the third study, we examined real consumer behaviors. The construal level of the message was varied to be more concrete or abstract (as in study 1). Participants ($N = 72$) were run individually and were asked to contribute either time or money and their actual behavioral contributions were observed. The z scores of actual dollar and hour contributions were used as the dependent measure. In addition, participants completed measures of positive moods. The appeal (concrete vs. abstract) by donation type (money vs. time) between-subjects interaction on actual contributions was significant ($F(1,68)=8.65$, $p<.01$). When the cause was presented as being concrete consumers were more likely to donate money ($M=.39$) versus time ($M=-.21$; $t=2.15$, $p<.05$), whereas when the cause was presented in more abstract terms consumers were more likely to donate time ($M=.13$) versus money ($M=-.49$; $t=2.24$, $p<.05$). Bootstrapping analysis revealed that the effects were mediated by positive mood states (confidence interval .0020 to .1598; $p < .03$). The pattern of results showed that the most positive moods emerged when there was a match of construal-level of the message with the donation type.

Taken together, the results have implications for both theory and practice. Theoretically, the findings that money is viewed more concretely, while time is viewed more abstractly build upon past work both examining consumer construal-level and consumer dif-

ferences in perceptions of time vs. money. Practically, the results suggest that charitable organizations wishing to generate monetary support might profitably make more concrete appeals to consumers. For example, appeals that highlight how the money would be used, along with the specific programs that will be supported might be particularly successful. Conversely, when the goal is to recruit individuals to donate their time, broader appeals that discuss the general cause might be more successful.

Empathy, Donation, and the Moderating Role of Psychological Distance

EXTENDED ABSTRACT

It is well-established that empathy has a positive effect on charity, both in psychology (Eisenberg and Miller, 1987) and marketing (Bagozzi and Moore, 1994). We show that the effect of empathy on donation is contingent on psychological distance between donor and recipient.

Empathy is defined as "Einfühlung" the original German word roughly translated as "to feel one's way into." In other words, "being cognitively aware of another person's internal states and/ or putting oneself in the place of another and experiencing his or her feelings" (Bagozzi and Moore, 1994, p.58) or "one's ability to experience and understand another person's affective or psychological state" (Argo, Zhu, and Dahl, 2008, p. 615). Bagozzi and Moore (1994) found a partial mediation of empathy on a decision to help while Eisenberg and Miller (1987) used a meta-analytic approach to reveal significant positive effects of empathy on prosocial behavior. We argue that the effect of empathy on donation is moderated by psychological distance (Liberman, Trope and Stephan, 2007), with the role of dispositional empathy magnified by closer psychological distance between donor and recipient. Dispositional empathy is a stable trait and its *effect* depends on how easy it is to envision another's situation. Decreased distance between donor and recipient would facilitate such a process and therefore enhance the effect of dispositional empathy on donations.

Hypothesis: Psychological distance will moderate the effect of dispositional empathy on donations. The beneficial effect of greater empathy will be exacerbated when the donor and recipient are separated by lesser distance (physical, temporal, and hypothetical) and attenuated when there is greater distance.

The above hypothesis was tested in four experiments, with psychological distance manipulated between subjects and dispositional empathy measured. The first three experiments studied the donation of time in the form of extra credit points. Participants were students of an introductory marketing course and could participate in research to earn ten additional course credit points (in a 1000-point class). They read that another student could not participate due to illness or work. Participants were asked how many of their points would they donate to this unfortunate student. Barring the manipulation of psychological distance, no other information about the needy student was provided. It must be emphasized that when completing the questionnaire, participants committed to making an actual donation and they were debriefed following submission of the questionnaire. Within the questionnaire, participants completed a measure of dispositional empathy (Davis, 1980), for which Cronbach's α was found to be acceptable. Manipulation checks indicated the success of the distance manipulation in each experiment.

In the first experiment, we studied the moderating role of physical distance. Seventy undergraduate students were assigned to one of the two levels of physical distance. All participants were enrolled in the introductory marketing section on the main campus of the university. There was a similar section at a satellite campus about one hundred miles away. Half the participants considered a recipient enrolled in the satellite campus (farther physical distance) and the rest considered a recipient enrolled in the main campus (closer physical distance). The results revealed a significant interaction between dispositional empathy and physical distance in participants' donation of their extra credit points ($F(1, 66) = 6.44$, $p < .05$). Planned comparisons indicated that dispositional empathy was significant in predicting donation only at closer physical distance but not at farther physical distance.

The second experiment documented the moderating effects of temporal distance. Sixty-eight participants were assigned to one of two levels of temporal distance. The experiment was conducted in the first half of the semester. The scenario indicated that the unfortunate student would either receive the donation within a week (closer temporal distance) or at the end of the semester (farther temporal distance). There was a marginally significant interaction between temporal distance and dispositional empathy on the likelihood of donating extra credit points ($F(1, 65) = 3.16$, $p < .10$). Planned comparisons indicated that dispositional empathy was a significant predictor of likelihood of donation only in the condition of closer temporal distance but not at farther temporal distance.

Hypothetical distance was manipulated in the third experiment. Sixty-nine participants considered a scenario portraying one of two levels of hypothetical distance. Participants read that a student had been chosen to receive their donation (closer hypothetical distance) or read that a student would be chosen (farther hypothetical distance), a manipulation used previously (Small and Loewenstein, 2003). We found a significant interaction between dispositional empathy and hypothetical distance in determining actual donation of extra credit points ($F(1, 65) = 4.91$, $p < .05$). This interaction arose from the significant effect of dispositional empathy at closer hypothetical distance but not at farther hypothetical distance.

In experiment four, we studied the donation of money and endowed sixty participants with five one-dollar notes in an envelope. Our dependant variable was the number of notes they transferred to an envelope meant for a student at lesser or greater hypothetical distance, manipulated in the same fashion as in experiment three. We found a marginally significant interaction between dispositional empathy and hypothetical distance on donations of actual dollars ($F(1, 56) = 2.69$, p = .1). As shown previously, this interaction arose from the significance of dispositional empathy in predicting dollar donations at closer hypothetical distance but not at greater hypothetical distance. In this experiment we also ruled out a possible confound of Inclusion of Others in Self using a previously validated measure (Winterich, Mittal and Ross, 2009).which yielded no significant difference. We discount the possibility of our distance manipulation leading to feelings of "oneness."

To sum up, the role of dispositional empathy in charitable donation depends on psychological distance between the donor and the recipient. Consistent results are observed using different manipulations of psychological distance and different measures of donation. Our findings contribute to a better understanding of charitable behavior, particularly with respect to the interactive effects of empathy and psychological distance. Not-for-profit organizations may better plan fundraising efforts by taking into account the various forms of psychological distance existing between the donor and the recipient.

Splitting the Decision: Increasing Donations by Recognizing the Differential Impact of Internal and External Considerations

EXTENDED ABSTRACT

When considering a charitable donation, the decision-maker decides whether to make a donation (choice) and then how much to donate (quantity). Building off the idea of two-stage valuation models (Kleindorfer and Kunreuther 1988; Slovic and Lichtenstein 1968; Winter and Fried 2001) researchers interested in pro-social behavior have suggested that these decisions are driven by different factors (e.g. Smith, Kehoe, and Cremer 1995; Smith and Berger 1996; Dickert, Sagara, and Slovic 2011). Considering such findings in aggregate we hypothesized and found that donation choice is determined primarily by considerations internal to the decision-maker (e.g. self-identity, self-relevance) while donation quantity is determined primarily by external factors (e.g. neediness of victims, effectiveness of organization).

Additionally, we extended our findings by applying them to a different context and testing a new optimal structure for solicitations. Prior work has demonstrated that providing excessive information may cause anxiety and poor decision-making (Reuters 1996; Shenk 1997). Thus, we hypothesized that an optimal solicitation structure would be one that explicitly separates the two decisions and enables different persuasive arguments to be offered for the choice and quantity decisions. Indeed we find that this solicitation structure maximizes both number and amount of donations.

In study 1a we manipulated moral-identity, an internal factor, and hypothesized that our manipulation would influence donation choice but not donation quantity. Participants first completed a brief questionnaire and received false feedback identifying them as having either a high or low moral-identity. They were then shown a hypothetical donation appeal for a fictitious non-profit organization, Foster Support, described as providing clothing and toys to foster children. As expected, a larger percentage of participants in the high moral-identity condition selected to make a donation than in the low moral-identity condition (High moral identity = 91.7%, Low Moral Identity = 50%, $X^2 = 6.84$, $p < .01$). Donation quantity, however, remained unaffected by moral-identity; participants in the high moral-identity condition did not estimate a higher donation amount than participants in the low moral-identity condition (M_{high} = \$35.51 vs. M_{low} = \$26.91, $F(1, 58) = 1.02$, $p = .32$). In study 1b we manipulated self-relevance of the charitable cause, another factor internal to the decision-maker, by describing Foster Support as operating either within the participant's state-of-residence or across the nation. Results replicated study 1a; self-relevance affected donation choice (High Self-Relevance = 81%, Low Self-Relevance = 52%, $X^2 = 4.22$, $p < .05$) but not donation quantity (M_{high} = \$24.93 vs. M_{low} = \$23.24, $F < 1$).

Having shown that two different internal factors influence the decision of whether to donate but not donation amount, in study 2 we considered two external factors and predicted that the opposite would be true, that donation quantity would be affected but not donation choice. First, in study 2a we manipulated seriousness of the cause. All participants saw a donation appeal for Project No Isiolo, a fictitious organization providing mosquito nets to individuals at risk of contracting Isiolo Fever. We manipulated seriousness of the cause between subjects by describing Isiolo Fever as resulting in either short-term discomfort (low seriousness) or death (high seriousness). In accordance with our predictions donation choice was not affected by the seriousness of the cause (High Seriousness = 74%, Low Seriousness = 63%, $X^2 = 1.19$, $p > .10$). In contrast, the decision of how much to donate was significantly influenced; participants reading the high seriousness appeal offered a higher donation amount than participants reading the low seriousness appeal ($M_{\text{high seriousness}}$ = \$28.58 vs. $M_{\text{low seriousness}}$ = \$16.64, $F(1, 139)$ = 8.46, $p < .01$). In study 2b we manipulated the efficiency of the charitable organization by including information about Project No Isiolo's overhead expenditure. As in study 2a, donation choice was not influenced by our manipulation (High Efficiency = 73.7%, Low Efficiency = 61.1%, X^2 = 0.67, $p >$ .10), while donation quantity was (M_{high} = \$44.45 vs. M_{low} = \$28.48, $F(1, 56)$ = 5.52, $p < .05$).

Having separately examined the influence of internal and external factors on donation behavior, in study 3 we combine the two by offering both types of persuasions and varying which type is paired with which donation decision, choice or quantity. Participants considered one of two versions of a donation solicitation for a nonprofit, Community-in-Schools (CIS). The two versions of the appeal letter varied in terms of the *order* of information presented while holding actual information content constant. In one version of the appeal, internal factors – self-relevance and donors' self-view – were emphasized as participants considered whether to make a donation. The decision of how much to donate was then accompanied by information on external factors. In the other version of the appeal the order in which the information was presented was reversed; external factors were emphasized prior to donation choice and factors internal to the donor were emphasized prior to the quantity decision. In accordance with our predictions the former version of the appeal led to both a higher rate of donations (54% vs. 37%, X^2 = 4.32, $p < .05$) and a higher average donation amount (M = \$12.43 vs. M = \$9.37, $F(1, 65)$ = 4.27, $p < .05$). Study 4 was a field replication of study 3 where we varied the actual solicitation letter sent by CIS to potential donors. Indeed, in the context of real dollar donations, the effects both on donation choice and donation quantity replicated prior studies.

Having established the discreet and differential effects of internal and external factors on the decisions whether and how much to donate, in study 5 we extended our findings by testing the impact of explicitly splitting the decisions. Additionally, we applied our theory to a new context, willingness to participate in an online educational program. We found that compared to the traditional solicitation structure which offers all information upfront, splitting the two decisions and aligning the arguments with the decision they most influence maximized both adoption rate (choice) and predicted amount of effort (quantity). Thus, this research offers an optimal set-up for a broad range of persuasive solicitations.

For Charities not all Aesthetics are Created Equal: The Differential Effects of Aesthetics With and Without Cost Implications on Response to Donor Solicitations

EXTENDED ABSTRACT

Many of the findings in judgment and decision-making have been tested or applied in the context of charitable direct marketing (e.g. donation solicitations or requests for volunteer work). Prior work has considered concepts such as providing an anchor (Fraser, Hite, and Sauer 1988), framing in positive or negative valence (Stone 1992), or utilizing the availability heuristic (Smith and Berger 1996) in an effort to optimize the language used by non-profit organizations to gain support. An area where less research has occurred is in consideration of the overall look of the solicitation. Holding the text and information constant, can a solicitation be made more effective? In line with prior work, an initial hypothesis might suggest that, what applies in advertising or other persuasive techniques will apply in this context as well. As such one might predict that the bet-

ter looking or aesthetically pleasing something is, the more effective and persuasive it will be (e.g. DeBono and Harnish 1988).

However, better aesthetics likely come at a price, literally, that is, there are some aspects of making a solicitation more attractive that likely cost more. And when the context is non-profit organizations cost perceptions come into play. Non-profits are judged by their efficiency and frugality with sites such as charitywatch.org and charitynavigator.org set up to do exactly this. Charitable organizations must justify extra expenses (Marchand and Lavoie 1998). Indeed, prior work suggests that in contrast to for-profit organizations, for non profits a higher price tag can actually turn off rather than entice patrons (Griffiths 2005). Spending too much may make patrons feel their money is being used improperly and result in negative evaluations of the organization's competence. In fact research by Aaker et al. (2010) reveals that, at a baseline, non profits are considered less competent than for-profit organizations and they must use subtle cues connoting credibility to garner the same willingness to pay for products as would be offered to for-profit organizations.

As such we hypothesize that not all aesthetics cues are equally beneficial in increasing response to a charitable direct marketing solicitation. Specifically we separate aspects of aesthetics that imply something about the cost of the solicitation from those that do not. We predict that these two classes of aesthetic will have differential and interacting effects on solicitation response such that, donation amounts are higher when the solicitation mailers are aesthetically pleasing and perceived to have lower costs associated with them as compared to when the solicitation mailers are aesthetically pleasing and perceived to have higher costs associated with them. We examine this in two lab studies and one field study.

Study 1 was a 2 ("Aesthetics"- aesthetics separate from cost: high, low) by 2 ("Perceived Cost" - aesthetics related to cost: high, low) design lab study where undergraduate students were shown a solicitation from a hypothetical non-profit and asked whether and how much they would be willing to donate. Aesthetics separate from cost was manipulated by varying the alignment of the text and border, type of border, fonts, and color of the cardstock. Perceived cost was manipulated by varying the thickness of the cardstock, whether the mailer was a postcard or letter and envelope, and whether it included a pre-paid return envelope. Pretests confirm our manipulations. Examining amount donated we find a significant main effect of Aesthetics ($M_{\text{Low Aesthetics}}$ = \$11.28, $M_{\text{High Aesthetics}}$ = \$21.83; $F(1, 236)$ = 3.65, $p = .05$) and no effect of Perceived Cost ($M_{\text{Low Cost}}$ = \$19.88, $M_{\text{High Cost}}$ = \$13.23; $F(1, 236)$ = 1.375, $p = .24$). Importantly, there is a significant interaction of the two ($F(1, 236)$ = 3.67, $p = .05$). Among the Low Aesthetics conditions there is no difference between the two Perceived Cost conditions ($M_{\text{Low Cost}}$ = \$9.35, $M_{\text{High Cost}}$ = \$13.21, $F(1,230)$ = .26, $p = .60$). However among the High Aesthetics conditions there is a significant benefit of the low Perceived cost ($M_{\text{Low Cost}}$ = \$30.40, $M_{\text{High Cost}}$ = \$3.25, $F(1,230)$ = 4.32, $p = .039$).

Next, we tested our predictions in a real world context using a field study. We partnered with a non-profit organization and created four versions of the invitation to be sent to their mailing list for their annual benefit gala. The invitations varied in appearance in line with the design of study 1. Examining the amount spent on tickets we find no main effect of Aesthetics ($M_{\text{Low Aesthetics}}$ = \$44.14, $M_{\text{High Aesthetics}}$ = \$53.69; $F(1, 288)$ = .15, $p = .70$) nor of Perceived Cost ($M_{\text{Low Cost}}$ = \$58.83, $M_{\text{High Cost}}$ = \$38.99; $F(1, 288)$ = .65, $p = .42$). However, there is a significant interaction of the two ($F(1, 288)$ = 4.01, $p = .04$). Among the Low Aesthetics conditions there is no difference between the two Perceived Cost conditions ($M_{\text{Low Cost}}$ = \$29.51, $M_{\text{High Cost}}$ = \$58.77, $F(1,148)$ = .37, $p = .54$), though directionally in line with study 1. However among the High Aesthetics conditions there is a marginal benefit of the low Perceived cost ($M_{\text{Low Cost}}$ = $88.16, $M_{\text{High Cost}}$ = $19.21, $F(1,139) = 3.71$, $p = .056$).

The results of the first two studies demonstrated the differential effects of aesthetics with and without cost implications and support our hypothesis. In the last study we examined a boundary condition for this effect. We posited that perceptions of cost associated with aesthetics cues could act as a proxy for organization's competence and as such influence the donation amounts. As such in study 3, in addition to varying aesthetics and cost as in study 1, we also varied competence of the organization by providing information about the organization's overhead expenditure. The results indicated that competence moderates the effect of aesthetics and perceived cost on donation amounts. Taken together the results of these studies have a potential to help non-profit organizations optimize their donation solicitation mailers and avoid unnecessary expenses.

Consumer Sociality and Happiness

Chair: Merrie Brucks, University of Arizona, USA

Paper #1: What Are Others Thinking?: Hedonic Adaptation in Public Consumption Contexts

Sunaina Chugani, University of Texas at Austin, USA

Julie Irwin, University of Texas at Austin, USA

Paper #2: Verbal Sharing: Purchase, Tell Others, and Be Happy

Wilson Bastos, University of Arizona, USA

Merrie Brucks, University of Arizona, USA

Paper #3: On the Importance of Experiential Purchases to Defining and Preserving the Self-Concept

Thomas Gilovich, Cornell University, USA

Travis J. Carter, University of Chicago, USA

Paper #4: It's the Company that Counts: Shared Experiences and Possessions Make People Happier than Experiences and Possessions Alone

Peter A. Caprariello, University of Rochester, USA

Harry T. Reis, University of Rochester, USA

SESSION OVERVIEW

Aristotle described happiness as "the best, noblest, and most pleasant thing in the world...the highest good (Aristotle. Nichomachean Ethics, 1925)." Additionally, we know that individuals place great weight on the acquisition of products and experiences in their pursuit of happiness (Pelletier, 2009). Despite the relevance of happiness and the widespread pursuit of happiness through consumption, the factors that influence consumer happiness are still vastly unknown.

The present papers, which are either completed works or are at an advanced stage of completion, demonstrate that social factors associated with purchases not only deserve more attention but also figure as potential explanations for certain purchases' ability to advance happiness. Such factors are especially important given that they are often the backdrop against which much of our behaviors as consumers occur. We know, for example, that our purchases are often exposed to or shared with (i.e., told to) others, that we often use our purchases to reflect our social self, and that many of our purchases involve social interaction. Accordingly, this session presents four papers illustrating that consumer happiness is enhanced when a purchase is exposed to others (Chugani and Irwin), shared with others (Bastos and Brucks), reflective of one's social self (Gilovich and Carter), or conducive to social interaction (Caprariello and Reis).

Together, these investigations make several valuable contributions. First, they enlarge our understanding of the relationship between purchases and happiness. Second, they help to demystify the distinction between experiential and material purchases by examining different purchases' ability to reflect (Carter and Gilovich) and enhance (Bastos and Brucks) the self, and to facilitate social interaction (Caprariello and Reis). Finally, they add to the literature on the effects of social forces by investigating the different roles those forces play in consumption—e.g., a silent spectator of a consumption experience (Chugani and Irwin), an active audience for a recounted consumption (Bastos and Brucks), a component of the constructed social self (Gilovich and Carter), or a partner in a consumption experience (Caprariello and Reis).

The first paper highlights the powerful role of social factors by examining the effect of social presence on consumption happiness. Chugani and Irwin examine this relationship through the lens of hedonic adaptation: the process by which the magnitude of the happi-

ness derived from product purchases diminishes over time so that positive (negative) purchases tend to become less positive (negative) over time. The researchers gather real-time adaptation data and find that when consumers are cognizant of social contexts, the presence of others slows down the process of hedonic adaptation: consuming a product in the presence of others keeps consumers happy with positive purchases and unhappy with negative purchases for longer periods of time than consuming a product in isolation. This impeding of adaptation results from consumers viewing their possessions through the eyes of others, keeping the initial affective intensity of the possession fresh in their minds.

In accordance with Chugani and Irwin's findings on the importance of the social environment in facilitating happiness with purchases, Bastos and Brucks show that post-purchase sharing (i.e., telling others) mediates the effect of purchase type on happiness. Precisely, they find that the superiority of experiential purchases over material purchases in advancing happiness (Van Boven and Gilovich, 2003) can be explained by people's greater inclination to share the former with others. Additionally, they show that people expect to be more highly regarded by others as a result of sharing their life experiences versus their material objects. This expectation, in turn, explains people's stronger inclination to share experiences (vs. objects). The authors limit the long abstract to one study in order to offer a deeper explanation of procedures and findings (which replicate across all studies). For conference presentation purposes four studies will be presented.

Next, Carter and Gilovich strengthen the premise that the link between a purchase and the social self is critical for consumer happiness. They argue that, due to their intangibility, experiences exist in our collection of memories instead of in the physical world, as do objects. Accordingly, they present empirical support for the proposition that experiences form a larger part of the self (i.e., people see them as being closer and more representative of the self), and that this aspect explains why experiential purchases are more satisfying than material purchases. Thus, this research suggests that life experiences (vs. material goods) contribute more to the social self and, consequently, afford greater rewards.

Lastly, Caprariello and Reis provide further evidence for the importance of considering the relationship context of consumption in understanding consumer happiness with purchases. Specifically, the authors find that the ability of a purchase to promote social interaction predicts the amount of happiness generated, and that this factor helps explain the experiential vs. material distinction found in prior literature (Van Boven and Gilovich, 2003). These findings suggest that spending money to do or have things with others may be one method for promoting happiness.

In summary, this research suggests that social factors play an important role in consumer happiness from the perspectives of consumption setting, post-purchase interpersonal sharing, construction of a social self, and interpersonal relatedness. Separately these works shed light on nuanced processes, and together they provide a broad and coherent understanding of the happiness phenomenon. As such, they should be well-received by a wide audience and especially valuable to researchers interested in consumer happiness and the related concepts of the social environment, social sharing, social self, and social relationships.

This session embraces diversity by 1) suggesting a diverse set of novel constructs that affect happiness, 2) illuminating different

Advances in Consumer Research
Volume 40, ©2012

perspectives through which to define sociality, 3) presenting a rich variety of experimental approaches, and 4) including a geographically and culturally diverse team of researchers.

What Are Others Thinking?:
Hedonic Adaptation in Public Consumption Contexts

EXTENDED ABSTRACT

Happiness (and unhappiness) with purchases generally diminishes over time: positive purchases become less positive and negative purchases become less negative (Frederick & Loewenstein, 1999); this process is often termed "hedonic adaptation". We examine the effect of an everyday social force on adaptation by asking how the presence of others while experiencing a product affects adaptation to that product. Four studies show that public contexts impede adaptation by inducing consumers to consider what others think of their product. Consumers who like their product assume others view their product favorably, and this enjoyable experience impedes adaptation over time.

Study 1

Study 1 tracked real-time adaptation to a product in lab. Participants were either (1) out of view from each other with dividers between lab stations (private condition) or (2) allowed to be seen by others, with no dividers (public condition). We manipulated cognizance of public context by asking participants either to report on an experience where they were the center of attention (priming cognizance of public context) or to describe a picture of a mundane fish or lamp (neutral prime). We then gave participants one of 9 products and tracked adaptation by measuring initial happiness and happiness at two other subsequent points.

There was an interaction between consumption context, public context cognizance, time period, and initial happiness $(F(1,188)=7.95, p<.01)$. For those who were primed with public context cognizance (but not for those who received the neutral prime), a public context kept those who were initially happy with their product happy for a longer period of time $(F(1,188)=6.75, p=.01)$ and those who were initially unhappy with their product unhappy for a longer period of time $(F(1,188)=3.21, p=.07)$ than a private context. In sum, in a public context, with a public prime, adaptation was impeded.

Study 2:

Study 2 replicated the methodology of Study 1. However, rather than priming cognizance of public contexts, we measured participants' Self Monitoring scores. High self monitors are more chronically cognizant of being observed in public than are low self-monitors (Lavine & Snyder, 1996; Snyder & DeBono, 2008). Thus, we would expect SM scores to operate similar to the prime used in Study 2, providing triangulating evidence for our public cognizance moderator. We collected happiness at two time points.

There was a significant interaction between SM score, consumption context, and initial happiness with the product on happiness at Time 2 $(F(1,299)=4.23, p<.05)$. Consumption context had a significant effect among high self monitors (fitting model at high SM score: consumption context X Time 1 happiness interaction, $(F(1,299)=4.25, p<.05)$ but not among low self monitors (fitting model at low SM score: consumption context X Time 1 interaction, $(F(1,299)=.91, NS)$. For instance, a public consumption context kept high (but not low) self monitors who were initially happy with their products happier for a longer period of time $(F(1,299)=7.27, p<.01)$ than did a private context. Thus, Study 2 again showed, using a combination of our manipulated public/private variable and a measured

variable, that the more consumers are cognizant of public contexts the more slowly they adapt to products.

Study 3

Study 3 tests our mechanism directly by manipulating whether participants are cued to see their products through others' eyes (others' eyes manipulation). We placed all participants in a public context and asked them to report initial happiness with one of 8 products we gave them. Then, half reported how happy they thought *others* in the room thought they were with their product (others' eyes prime), and the other half answered filler questions (neutral prime). Participants then reported their happiness with the product two more times throughout the session so that we could track adaptation.

There was a significant "others' eyes" manipulation X time period X initial happiness interaction on happiness at a given time period $(F(1,136)=5.22, p<.05)$. Participants in the neutral prime condition experienced adaptation to their products over time (significant time period X initial happiness interaction, $(F(1,136)=15.44, p<.001)$ but participants who were cued to look at their product through others' eyes did not exhibit adaptation at all (non-significant time period X initial happiness interaction, $(F(1,136)=.95, NS)$.

Summary

Three studies provide evidence that public (vs. private) consumption contexts impede adaptation among individuals who are aware of being in a public context by causing consumers to view their products not only through their own eyes but also through the eyes of others.

REFERENCES

Frederick, Shane and George Loewenstein (1999), Hedonic Adaptation, In D. Kahneman, E. Diener & N. Schwarz (Eds.), Well-Being: The Foundations of Hedonic Psychology (pp. 302-329), New York: Russell Sage Foundation.

Lavine, Howard and Mark Snyder (1996), "Cognitive Processing and the Functional Matching Effect in Persuasion: The Mediating Role of Subjective Perceptions of Message Quality, "*Journal of Experimental Social Psychology*, 32(6), 580-604.

Snyder, Mark and Kenneth K. DeBono (2008), Appeals to Image and Claims about Quality: Understanding the Psychology of Advertising, In R. H. Fazio & R. E. Petty (Eds.), Attitudes: Their structure, function, and consequences, (pp. 231-242), New York: Psychology Press.

Verbal Sharing: Purchase, Tell Others, and Be Happy

EXTENDED ABSTRACT

Recently, the relation between purchases and happiness has received increased attention from academics and the popular press (Flatow, 2009; Pelletier, 2009). A common finding is that experiential purchases are better than material purchases at advancing happiness (Van Boven & Gilovich, 2003). A question that deserves further attention, however, is: What mechanism(s) underlies such effect?

Aiming to address that question, we drew on the disclosure and social sharing literatures to argue that consumers of experiences (e.g., taking a kayaking trip) are more likely than consumers of objects (e.g., buying a kayak) to share (i.e., tell others about) their purchases and to, in turn, enjoy the benefits of such activity (hypothesis 1 below). To provide support for this proposition, two questions should be addressed: 1) Why would people be more inclined to share experiential than material purchases?, and 2) How beneficial is sharing?

With regards to the first question, previous research (Van Boven, Campbell & Gilovich, 2010) shows that individuals form less favorable impressions of people associated with material (vs. experiential) purchases, and enjoy having conversations about experiential purchases more than about material purchases. Van Boven et al. thus conclude that "being associated with materialistic rather than experiential pursuits can pose a barrier to successful social relationships (p. 560)." Accordingly, we expect that people are more inclined to share their experiential (vs. material) purchases; and that such behavioral difference is driven by their expectations that sharing experiential (vs. material) purchases will lead others to form more favorable impressions about them (hypothesis 2 below).

Answering the second question, research suggests that sharing leads to far-reaching benefits. For example, sharing provides the teller with greater positive affect and well-being (Gable, Reis, Impett, & Asher, 2004). Additionally, it brings interpersonal rewards in the form of teller's greater liking for the listener as a result of having disclosed to him/her (Collins & Miller, 1994). Lastly, sharing benefits the disclosed event itself. It helps one achieve a better understanding of the shared event (Finkenauer & Rime, 1998), "creates an opportunity for reliving and reexperiencing the event" (Gable et al. 2004, p. 229), and "make[s] the event both more memorable to oneself and to others (Langston, 1994, p. 1113)." Harrigan (2001) summed the relevance of sharing by stating, "Happiness held is the seed; happiness shared is the flower". So, compelling evidence indicates various benefits of sharing. What remains unknown, however, is whether post-purchase sharing affects a purchase's ability to advance happiness.

Based on the above-mentioned findings, we argue that consumers of experiential (vs. material) purchases are more inclined to share the details of their purchase with others and, in turn, more likely to draw rewards (i.e., happiness) from doing so (H1), and that those consumers' expectations for how they will be regarded by others explain the difference in inclination to share (H2). This mediated-mediation can be formally hypothesized as:

Hypothesis 1: *Sharing will mediate the effect of purchase type on happiness.*

Hypothesis 2: *Regard will mediate the effect of purchase type on sharing.*

Experimental Design

To test our two hypotheses, we conducted an experiment with 95 participants who were randomly assigned to one of two conditions: material vs. experiential purchase. Participants were given instructions of what constitutes a material (or experiential) purchase and were asked to recall and write about a fifty-dollar personal purchase that reflected the condition they were in. Next, participants answered, on 7-point Likert scales, questions related to happiness (e.g., When you think about this purchase, how happy does it make you?), sharing behavior (e.g., I would feel excited about sharing the details of my object/experience; I would want to share with others the details of my object/experience), and regard (I think the person listening to me would regard me more highly after learning about my object/experience).

Results

Our results supported hypothesis 1. Specifically, we conducted four regressions (*a-d*) and a Sobel (1982) test of mediation and found that (*a*) experiential purchases advanced significantly more happiness than did material purchases ($F(1, 94) = 3.97$, $p = .04$). Further,

significant effects were found when (*b*) the mediator (i.e., sharing) was regressed on the IV (i.e., purchase type) ($F(1, 94) = 8.73$, $p = .004$), and (*c*) the DV (i.e., happiness) was regressed on the mediator ($F(1, 94) = 18.49$, $p < .001$). Importantly, (*d*) when happiness was regressed on both purchase type and sharing the previously significant main effect of purchase type on happiness became nonsignificant ($p = .36$). In line with this, our Sobel test showed a significant result ($z = 2.34$, $p = .01$). As hypothesized, these results suggest that sharing mediates the effect of purchase type on happiness.

To test hypothesis 2, we conducted a similar set of analyses and found significant effects for (a) purchase type on sharing ($F(1, 94) = 8.73$, $p = .004$), (b) regard (i.e., the mediator) on sharing ($F(1, 94) = 10.75$, $p = .001$), and (c) purchase type on regard ($F(1, 94) = 3.92$, $p = .05$). Revealingly, when both purchase type and regard were included in the model, the relation between purchase type and sharing was attenuated ($F(1, 94) = 2.40$, $p = .01$). Finally, the Sobel test indicated a marginally significant effect ($z = 1.66$, $p = .09$). These results support the premise that regard plays at least a partial mediating role in the effect of purchase type on sharing.

According to these analyses, the following picture emerges from our research: Experiential purchases are better than material purchases at advancing happiness (replicating Van Boven & Gilovich, 2003), and sharing mediates that effect. The difference in sharing is explained, in turn, by how people expect to be regarded as a result of their sharing. To our knowledge, this is the first research in marketing that examines the role of sharing in advancing consumer happiness. Moreover, these findings illustrate how important post-consumption events are for happiness. This is especially relevant given previous evidence suggesting that pre-consumption states (e.g., a sense of anticipation), but not post-consumption ones, are effective in generating happiness (Nawijn, Marchand, Veenhoven, & Vingerhoets, 2010).

REFERENCES

Collins, Nancy L. and Lynn Carol Miller (1994), "Self-Disclosure and Liking: A Meta-Analysis Review, *Psychological Bulletin,* 116 (3), 457-475.

Finkenauer, Catrin and Bernand Rime (1998), "Socially Shared Emotional Experiences Vs. Emotional Experiences Kept Secret: Differential Characteristics and Consequences," *Journal of Social and Clinical Psychology,* 17 (3), 295-318.

Flatow, I. (2009, February 13). Buying into life instead of things. *National Public Radio.* Retrieved from http://www.npr.org/ templates/story/story.php?storyId=100673355

Gable, Shelly L., Harry T. Reis, Emily A. Impett, and Evan R. Asher (2004), "What Do You Do When Things Go Right? The Intrapersonal and Interpersonal Benefits of Sharing Positive Events," *Journal of Personality and Social Psychology,* 87 (2), 228-245.

Harrigan, John (2001), BrainyQuote, Retrieved from http://www. brainyquote.com/quotes/authors/j/john_harrigan.html

Langston, Christopher A. (1994), "Capitalizing On and Coping With Daily-Life Events: Expressive Responses to Positive Events," *Journal of Personality and Social Psychology,* 67 (6), 1112-1125.

Nawijn, Jeroen, Miquelle A. Marchand, Rutt Beenhoven, and Ad J. Vingerhoets (2010), "Vacationers Happier, but More not Happier After a Holiday," *Applied Research Quality Life,* 5, 35-47.

Pelletier, Jillian (2009), ""*Money Does Not Buy Happiness*" Using the Sociological Imagination to Move Beyond Stressful Lives," *Journal of the Sociology of Self-Knowledge,* 7 (Summer), 173-80.

Sobel, Michael E. (1982). Asymptotic intervals for indirect effects in structural equations models. In S. Leinhart (Eds.), *Sociological methodology* (pp. 290-312). San Francisco, California: Jossey-Bass.

Van Boven, Leaf, Margaret C. Campbell, and Thomas Gilovich (2010), "Stigmatizing Materialism: On Stereotypes and Impressions of Materialistic and Experiential Pursuits," *Personality and Social Psychology Bulleting,* 36, 551-563.

Van Boven, Leaf and Thomas Gilovich (2003), "To Do or to Have? This Is the Question," *Journal of Personality and Social Psychology,* 85 (6), 1193 – 1202.

On the Importance of Experiential Purchases to Defining and Preserving the Self-Concept

EXTENDED ABSTRACT

Can money buy happiness? Generally, the answer is thought to be no. However, it may simply be that people are not spending their money wisely. Previous research suggests that greater happiness can be found in experiential purchases (e.g. meals at restaurants, vacations, and concerts) than with material purchases (e.g. clothes, jewelry, and gadgets; Carter & Gilovich, 2010; Van Boven & Gilovich, 2003). One of the cited reasons for this difference in satisfaction is that experiences make a greater contribution to the "social self" than do material possessions. So far this has not been empirically demonstrated. The present research aims to do just that, as well as to examine whether this is qualified by trait materialism.

Why might experiential purchases form a greater part of the social self than material possessions? We believe there are several reasons, but one of the most important is that experiences, being largely intangible, exist primarily in memory, whereas possessions are largely tangible objects that persist in the physical world. It is partly because they persist in memory that experiences become more truly part of who we are, as it is our collection of memories and experiences that define us.

If experiences do form a larger part of the social self, why would they be more satisfying than possessions? First, being physical objects, material possessions are subject to the ravages of time. Clothes get dingy and torn, mp3 players become obsolete, cars break down. Experiences, on the other hand, may actually see their greatest benefit over time (Carter & Gilovich, 2010). Indeed, people tend to take the "rosy view" of experiences over time, even though the actual experience might be fraught with disappointing moments (Mitchell et al., 1997; cf. Nicolao, Irwin & Goodwin, 2009).

Second, and related to the first, as part of the social self, memories of purchased experiences can be embellished using the same sorts of motivated biases that allow people to maintain positive self-views (e.g. Dunning, 2005). Being intangible, experiences may be more open to construals or (re)interpretation than possessions, an essential part of the process of motivated reasoning (Kunda, 1990). It may be that evaluating the quality of one's experiences is, in essence, evaluating aspects of oneself, and as a result, people are motivated to see those experiences in a positive light, particularly over time.

We first wanted to test whether people do, in an almost literal sense, think of their experiential purchases as being closer to their social self than their material purchases. Participants were first asked to briefly describe 8 important purchases they had made, four material, and four experiential. Borrowing a page from work on the

different conceptions of self in independent and interdependent cultures (Markus & Kitayama, 1991), we showed participants a sample diagram where circles representing different family members were plotted around a Self-circle such that the proximity of the family member represented the degree of overlap with the self. Participants were asked to follow a similar logic in plotting each of the eight purchases around a central Self-circle. We measured the distance from the center of each purchase's circle to the center of the Self-circle. As predicted, participants plotted their experiences closer to the Self than they did their possessions, paired $t(47) = 2.09$, $p < .05$. This result was not qualified by participants' trait materialism.

Next, we wanted to know if people would choose to use their experiential purchases more than their material purchases when describing themselves. Again, participants were asked to recall and briefly describe 10 purchases, five material, and five experiential. They were then asked to tell their life story, and were encouraged to incorporate into the narrative the purchases they had previously listed where appropriate. As predicted, participants included more of their experiential purchases (40%) than their material purchases (22%) into their life narrative, paired $t(89) = 5.94$, $p < .001$. Again, participants' level of materialism did not qualify these findings.

Most importantly, we wanted to know whether these findings could help explain why experiences tend to be more satisfying than possessions. We asked one sample of participants whether a stranger would have greater insight into their "true self" as a result of knowing about their experiential or material purchase history. As predicted, participants believed that knowledge of a their experiences was the clearer window to their self, $t(120) = 4.08$, $p < .001$. This belief was also significantly correlated with participants' greater satisfaction with a specific experience over a specific possession ($r = .19$, $p < .05$).

One consequence of experiences being a greater part of the self is that people would be less willing to give up those memories, as it would mean deleting a part of the self (Gilovich, 1991). In a final study, participants were asked to recall and briefly describe either a material or experiential purchase, and then to imagine that they could go back in time and swap out their memories of that purchase for memories of a different purchase. Participants were more satisfied with their purchases in the experiential than in the material condition. Participants in the material condition were both less satisfied with their purchases, $t(58) = 2.22$, $p < .04$, and more willing to exchange their memories than participants in the experiential condition, $t(58) = 2.88$, $p < .01$. This difference in how closely participants clung to the memories of their purchase mediated the difference in satisfaction between conditions, Sobel $z = 1.99$, $p < .05$.

These results, taken together, suggest that people do indeed hold their experiences more closely to their social self than their possessions, and that this tendency helps to explain why, ultimately, experiences tend to be more satisfying than possessions. What's more, it was not only those low in materialism who show this tendency, suggesting that there may be a disconnect between what materialists believe will be meaningful to them, and what actually is. Indeed, from many angles, it seems that purchasing experiences will ultimately prove a better investment for one's well-being.

REFERENCES

Carter, Travis and Thomas Gilovich (2010), "The Relative Relativity of Material and Experiential Purchases," *Journal of Personality and Social Psychology*, 98, 146–159. doi:10.1037/a0017145

Dunning, David (2005), Self-Insight: Roadblocks and Detours on the Path to Knowing Thyself, New York, NY: Psychology Press. doi:10.4324/ 9780203337998

Kunda, Ziva (1990), "The Case for Motivated Reasoning," *Psychological Bulletin*, 108, 480–498. doi:10.1037/0033-2909.108.3.480

Markus, Hazel Rose and Shinobu Kitayama (1991), "Culture and the Self: Implications for Cognition, Emotion, and Motivation," *Psychological Review*, 98, 224–253. doi:10.1037/0033-295X.98.2.224

Mitchell, Rerence R., Leigh Thompson, Erika Peterson, and Randy Cronk (1997), "Temporal Adjustments in the Evaluation of Events: The "rosy view."," *Journal of Experimental Social Psychology*, 33, 421–448. doi:10.1006/ jesp.1997.1333

Nicolao, Leonardo, Julie R. Irwin, and Joseph K. Goodman (2009), "Happiness for Sale: Do Experiential Purchases Make Consumers Happier than Material Purchases?," *Journal of Consumer Research*, 36, 188–198. doi:10.1086/ 597049

Rosenzweig, Emily and Thomas Gilovich (2012), "Buyer's Remorse or Missed Opportunity? Differential Regrets for Material and Experiential Purchases," *Journal of Personality and Social Psychology*, 101(2), 215-223. doi: 10.1037/ a0024999

Van Boven, Leaf and Thomas Gilovich (2003), "To Do or to Have? That is the Question," *Journal of Personality and Social Psychology*, 85, 1193–1202. doi:10.1037/0022-3514.85.6.1193

It's the Company that Counts:
Shared Experiences and Possessions Make People Happier than Experiences and Possessions Alone

EXTENDED ABSTRACT

One reliable way to elevate happiness appears to be spending money on life experiences over material possessions (Van Boven & Gilovich, 2003). Van Boven and Gilovich defined experiential purchases as "events or series of events that a person lives through" (2003, p. 1194). In a series of studies, they found that people reported greater happiness by spending their discretionary money – money spent with the intention of increasing happiness – on experiences rather than on material possessions. Importantly, this effect replicated in a nationally representative sample and has been documented in retrospective, concurrent, and longitudinal reports of well-being (Howell & Hill, 2009; Nicolao, Irwin, & Goodman, 2009).

The present research proposes that distinguishing spending along a materialism-experientialism dimension overlooks another important difference between life experiences and material possessions: Typically, experiences are more likely than material things to involve other persons. Extensive research shows that social relations, especially those that foster feelings of connectedness, are influential sources of happiness (e.g., Argyle, 1999; Berscheid & Reis, 1998; Baumeister & Leary, 1995; Reis, Clark, & Holmes, 2004). We suggest that the *sharing* involved in experiences is central to their benefits relative to material possessions. If correct, happiness would be obtained indirectly from experiential activities, and directly from sharing the activities interpersonally.

On the other hand, material possessions tend to be associated with self-oriented motives, such as a desire to signal uniqueness (Berger & Heath, 2007), status (Griskevicius, Tybur, Sundie, Cialdini, Miller, & Kenrick, 2007), and identity (Belk, 1988), or to bolster self-esteem (Escalas & Bettman, 2003). Thus material possessions in and of themselves tend to lack the central quality of experiences

that make them amenable to improving happiness – the involvement of others.

In Study 1, we tested how the happiness benefits of experiential buying varied as a function of social involvement. Here, 327 participants were randomly assigned to pick between 1 of 2 kinds of purchases – between material objects and social experiences, material objects and solitary experiences, and solitary and social experiences. When comparing material purchases to social experiences, participants were significantly more likely to indicate that social experience would make them happier, $M = .70$, $\chi^2(1) = 151.36$, $p < .001$. When comparing material purchases to solitary experiences, participants were significantly *less* likely to indicate that solitary experiences would make them happier, $M = .38$, $\chi^2(1) = 54.22$, $p < .001$. Finally, when comparing solitary to social experiences, participants were significantly more likely to indicate that social experiences would make them happier, $M = .85$, $\chi^2(1) = 465.08$, $p < .001$. These results make clear that sharing experiences with others is necessary for deriving happiness from the experience. In fact, when presented with the option of a material possession or an experience *without* others, participants favored the material good over the experience.

Nevertheless, these results raise the question: Can the value of material possessions be enhanced by involving others? Some material possessions can certainly *facilitate* social interactions (e.g., board games, sports equipment, and stereo systems for family rooms). Furthermore, people strategically act on this knowledge by spending money for this purpose (e.g., to re-affiliate following rejection; Mead, Baumeister, Stillman, Rawn, & Vohs, 2011). If social interactions are as critical to happiness as research suggests, then material possessions obtained in the service of enhancing social interaction may make people happier than material objects obtained primarily for personal use. From this reasoning, we propose that proper understanding of the happiness benefits of life experiences versus material possessions requires consideration of whether one's purchases are meant to be shared or solitary. Crossing these two dimensions results in four possibilities: Shared experiences, shared possessions, solitary experiences, and solitary possessions. We hypothesize that the social-solitary dimension better predicts anticipated happiness from spending than the materialism-experientialism dimension.

In Study 2, 308 participants were given definitions of discretionary spending and were asked to think about the last time they spent their discretionary money to further their happiness. No other leading instructions were given. After describing the purchase and rating their happiness with it, participants self-coded the purchases into experiential-material and social-solitary categories. Based on this four-category conceptualization, we found evidence for the effects of social involvement on happiness but not for experientialism. In other words, we found that, collapsing across self-coded material and experiential purchases, the effect of sharing purchases on happiness was significant, $F(1, 295) = 10.76$, $p < .001$, such that social purchases were recalled as making people happier ($M = 3.89$) than purchases for solitary consumption ($M = 3.45$). Neither the main effect of experiential-material consumption nor the interaction were significant $F < 1.0$, $F(1, 295) = 2.11$, *ns*, respectively.

To ensure that our results were not biased by participants rating themselves, three coders, blind to conditions, rated every purchase along the same two dimensions as before. We found the same results with coder ratings as we had found with participant ratings, $F_{social-solitary}(1, 297) = 6.29$, $p = .01$, all other Fs < 1.0, with social experiences ($M = 3.77$) trumping solitary experiences ($M = 3.45$). In this study, therefore, we extended prior research by showing that the happiness benefits of social involvement, whether for experiential or materialistic purchasing, trump the happiness benefits of experiential buying per se. Furthermore, these results can not be explained by socially desirable responding, because participants were not led to think about the potential value or drawbacks of presenting themselves either experientially or materialistically (Van Boven, Campbell, & Gilovich, 2010).

Overall, these results are consistent with recent findings that spending money on others makes people happier than spending money on oneself (Dunn et al., 2008). Although evidence suggests that merely reminding people of money distances the self from others (Vohs, Mead, & Goode, 2006), overcoming a self-reliant mindset to spend money to do or have things with others, rather than to do or have things strictly for oneself, may be an important outlet for promoting sustainable happiness (Lyubomirsky, Sheldon, & Schkade, 2005).

REFERENCES

Argyle, Michael (1999), Causes and Correlates of Happiness, In D. Kahneman, E. Diener, & N. Schwarz (Eds.), Well-being: The foundations of hedonic psychology, New York: Russell Sage Foundation.

Baumeister, Roy and Mark Leary (1995), "The Need to Belong: Desire for Interpersonal Attachments as a Fundamental Human Motivation," *Psychological Bulletin*, 117, 497-529.

Belk, Russell W. (1988), "Possessions and the Extended Self," *Journal of Consumer Research*, 15, 139-167.

Berger, Jonah and Chip Heath (2007), "Where Consumers Diverge from Others: Identity Signaling and Product Domains," *Journal of Consumer Research*, 34, 121-134.

Berscheid, E., & Reis, H. T. (1998), Attaction and Close Relationships, In D. T. Gilbert, S. T.

Fiske, & G. Lindzey (Eds.), The handbook of social psychology (4th ed., pp. 193-281), New York: McGraw-Hill.

Dunn, E., Aknin, L., & Norton, M. (2008), "Spending Money on Others Promotes Happiness," *Science*, 319, 1687-1688.

Escalas, J. E., & Bettman, J. R. (2003), "You Are What They Eat: The Influence of Reference Groups on Consumer Connection to Brands," *Journal of Consumer Research*, 13, 339-348.

Griskevicius, V., Tybur, J. M., Sundie, J. M., Cialdini, R. B., Miller, G. F., & Kenrick, D. T. (2007). Blatant Benevolence and Conspicuous Consumption: When Romantic Motives Elicit Strategic Costly Signals," *Journal of Personality and Social Psychology*, 93, 85-102.

Howell, Ryan and Graham Hill (2009), "The Mediators of Experiential Purchases: Determining the Impact of Psychological Needs Satisfaction and Social Comparison," *The Journal of Positive Psychology,* 4 (6), 511-522.

Lyubomirsky, Sonja, Kennon M. Sheldon, and David Schkade (2005), "Pursuing Happiness: The Architecture of Sustainable Change," *Review of General Psychology*, 9, 111-131.

Mead, N. L., Baumeister, R. F., Stillman, T. F., Rawn, C. D., & Vohs, K. D. (2011), "Social Exclusion Causes People to Spend and Consume in the Service of Affiliation," *Journal of Consumer Research*, 37, 902-919.

Nicolao, Leonardo, Julie R. Irwin, and Joseph K. Goodman (2009), "Happiness for Sale: Do Experiential Purchases Make Consumers Happier than Material Purchases?," *Journal of Consumer Research,* 36 (August), 188–189.

Van Boven, Leaf, Margaret C. Campbell, and Thomas Gilovich (2010), "Stigmatizing Materialism: On Stereotypes and Impressions of Materialistic and Experiential Pursuits," *Personality and Social Psychology Bulleting,* 36, 551-563.

Van Boven, Leaf and Thomas Gilovich (2003), "To Do or to Have? This Is the Question," *Journal of Personality and Social Psychology,* 85 (6), 1193–1202.

Vohs, K., Mead, N., & Goode, M. (2006), "The Psychological Consequences of Money," *Science*,314, 1154-1156.

Satisfaction Across the Consumption Experience: The Impact of Judgment Timing, Emotions and Interruptions on Consumer Enjoyment

Chair: Patti Williams, University of Pennsylvania, USA

Paper #1: The Road Not Taken: The Effect of Forming Pre-Choice Product Expectations and Making a Choice on Subsequent Consumption Enjoyment

Naomi Mandel, Arizona State University, USA

Stephen M. Nowlis, Washington University, USA

Paper #2: Angry Avengers or Disappointed Deferrers: Consumers' Emotional Reactions to Stockouts

Nicole Verrochi Coleman, University of Pittsburgh, USA

Patti Williams, University of Pennsylvania, USA

Gavan J. Fitzsimons, Duke University, USA

Paper #3: The Effect of Curiosity on Consumption Enjoyment

Elif Isakman, University of Southern California, USA

Lisa Cavanaugh, University of Southern California, USA

Deborah J. MacInnis, University of Southern California, USA

Gülden Ülkümen, University of Southern California, USA

Paper #4: Waiter, There's a Fly in My Soup (and I Have an iPhone)! How Evaluation Timing can Impact Customer Reviews

Christine Ringler, Rutgers University, USA

Andrea C. Morales, Arizona State University, USA

Nancy J. Sirianni, Texas Christian University, USA

SESSION OVERVIEW

These papers focus upon the process of consumption in a variety of ways: by jointly investigating the discrete stages of the choice process, considering the emotions consumers feel when confronted with a stockout during a choice situation, assessing the impact of interruptions on consumption and exploring how the timing of evaluations impact the overall positivity of those evaluations. Broadly, each of the papers examines consumer satisfaction across the consumption process, predicting high levels of dissatisfaction depending upon the timing of judgment, the emotions felt or interruptions experienced during the consumption experience. The first paper (Mandel and Nowlis) emphasizes the distinction between satisfaction after choice but before consumption, compared with satisfaction after consumption. The second paper (Coleman Williams and Fitzsimons) focuses upon emotional reactions during the consumption process and their implications for decision satisfaction and downstream behaviors. The third paper (Isakman, Cavanaugh, MacInnis and Ülüman) focuses upon how curiosity-evoking interruptions to consumption can influence satisfaction levels. The fourth paper (Ringler, Morales and Sirianni) examines how the timing of when consumers provide evaluations influences consumer satisfaction. Together these papers suggest that the way in which the consumption process unfolds, rather than simply the moment of consuming the chosen item, influences consumer satisfaction in substantial ways.

The first paper in this session (Mandel and Nowlis) examines the separate and joint effects of forming expectations, making a choice and actually consuming the chosen item on consumption enjoyment. Results show that consistent with the cognitive dissonance literature, participants who formed expectations and chose, but did not consume, bolstered their choices by showing a divergence of alternatives after forming expectations. However, participants who formed expectations, made a choice, and then consumed their choice experienced lower consumption enjoyment than those in other conditions, due to the convergence of option attractiveness after consump-

tion. This research offers implications for the many studies published on the topic of dissonance, examining the degree to which the frequently obtained effect of spreading of alternatives persists after consumers have consumed their selections.

The second paper in this session (Coleman, Williams and Fitzsimons) examines the emotions consumers feel in response to experiencing a stockout. Previous research has shown that stockouts reduce decision satisfaction and lead to store or brand-switching behaviors and negative word of mouth. In this paper, the authors suggest that the effect of stockouts on satisfaction is mediated by their immediate emotional reactions to the stockout situation. Results show that consumers often feel anger and disappointment in response to a stockout and that these emotions differentially predict the actions consumers take in response to a stockout. Results suggest that consumers nearly always feel disappointed in response to a stockout but that they are likely to feel angry when the stockout affects an item they are highly committeed to or when the stockout feels personal. Three studies demonstrate that consumers naturally experience anger and disappointment in response to stockouts, and that anger leads to greater levels of damaging retaliatory behaviors (e.g., store switching) while disappointment predicts choice deferral.

The third paper (Isakman, Cavanaugh, MacInnis and Ülkümen) examines the impact of increasingly common curiosity-arousing contexts on consumption experiences. Daily occurrences of ringing cell phones, incoming email notifications, or unopened mail can evoke curiosity about who is calling or writing, what they have to say, and whether there is good or bad news to be learned. Defining curiosity as a feeling of deprivation that arises when there is a gap between what one knows currently (i.e., someone is trying to get in touch with me) and what wants to know (who is it and what do they want to tell me), the paper suggests that individuals in a state of curiosity feel deprived because the resolution of the curiosity-evoking event is self-relevant but unknown to them, and may interrupt consumption in order to attend to these events. Results show that that curiosity-evoking events evoke a feeling of deprivation and a state of discomfort that motivates an impulsive search for resolution. Such information seeking behavior disrupts the consumption experience and undermines its enjoyment.

The fourth paper in this session (Ringler, Morales and Sirianni), in contrast, suggests that taking time to provide evaluations during consumption can lead to more favorable reviews and higher levels of satisfaction than evaluations provided after a delay. Results demonstrate that these effects are driven by higher levels of negative emotions at the time of delayed evaluation, suggesting that merely asking customers for feedback one week after their experiences creates negative feelings that then color consumer evaluations. Consumers find delayed evaluations to require a greater expenditure of effort as they work to recall their real-time feelings and experiences. This extra effort leads to more negative affect and thus decreased evaluations and satisfaction.

This session is likely to be of interest broadly to ACR members, including those interested in consumer satisfaction, those who study emotions, and those interested in how new technologies might influence consumer behavior. The session furthers the conference's mission of appreciating diversity in a variety of ways. While all the papers in this session focus broadly upon consumer satisfaction or dissatisfaction as the consumption process unfolds, they approach that topic from different directions.

The Road Not Taken: The Effect of Forming Pre-Choice Product Expectations and Making a Choice on Subsequent Consumption Enjoyment

EXTENDED ABSTRACT

Consumers often form expectations about products before choosing and consuming an option. For example, a consumer attending a wine-tasting might form detailed expectations about the attributes of each wine, such as whether it will be fruity, earthy, pungent, or resinous. Will this person enjoy consuming the chosen wine more or less than someone who does not form such detailed expectations? While prior research has examined how the acts of forming expectations, choosing, and consuming can independently influence satisfaction or consumption enjoyment, this paper is the first to demonstrate that the combination of all three is both necessary and sufficient to systematically lower consumption enjoyment.

One line of prior research, based on the theory of cognitive dissonance (Festinger 1957) suggests that forming expectations prior to choice may increase consumption enjoyment, because consumers may want to defend their choice by increasing their stated preference for the chosen option. This phenomenon is known as "spreading of alternatives," because individuals indicate a higher attractiveness differential between the options after choice, compared to before choice (Brehm 1956). Although thousands of studies have been published on the topic of cognitive dissonance since the 1950s, to our knowledge not a single study has investigated whether such spreading of alternatives persists after consumers have consumed their selections. We examine this question in our studies.

A second line of prior research suggests that thinking too hard about the available options (which may occur while forming such expectations) may lower product satisfaction (Wilson and Schooler 1991). In attempt to reconcile these disparate prior findings, we propose that when consumers form expectations, consistent with the cognitive dissonance literature, the attractiveness of the two product options diverge after choice (but only when the product is not in fact consumed, as is typical in this literature). However, consistent with more recent literature (Litt and Tormala 2010), we also predict that after forming expectations, choice, *and* consumption, the attractiveness of those same two options converge; that is, the chosen option becomes less attractive and the unchosen option becomes more attractive (Carmon et al. 2003). This convergence of alternatives leads to regret and ultimately reduces consumption enjoyment.

The purpose of study 1 was to examine the joint effects of forming expectations, making a choice, and consuming that choice on option attractiveness and consumption enjoyment. We conducted a 2 (Formed expectations: Yes vs. No) x 2 (Made a Choice: Yes vs. No) x 2 (Product Consumed: Yes vs. No) between-subjects design with 436 participants who chose between two equally attractive flavors of jelly beans: Very Cherry and Green Apple. Participants in the formed expectations condition provided ratings for of how much they expected each option to be sweet, tart, refreshing, flavorful, sour, chewy, and good tasting. Participants in the no expectations condition did not give any such ratings. Participants in the choice condition chose between the two jelly beans, and participants in the no choice condition received an assigned jelly bean. Participants in the consumption condition consumed the chosen or assigned jelly bean, while participants in the no consumption condition did not consume a jelly bean.

We calculated the attractiveness differential as the difference in attractiveness between the chosen/assigned and unchosen/unassigned option. Consistent with prior research on the spreading of alternatives, the attractiveness differential was significantly larger when participants made a choice than when they did not make a choice. Furthermore, in support of our predictions, participants who formed expectations, made a choice, and consumed that choice enjoyed the product significantly less than participants who did not form expectations, but did make a choice and consume that choice. Consistent with the cognitive dissonance literature, participants who did not consume bolstered their choices by showing a divergence of alternatives after forming expectations. However, as predicted, participants who formed expectations, made a choice, and then consumed their choice experienced lower consumption enjoyment than those in other conditions, due to the convergence of option attractiveness after consumption.

One limitation of study 1 is that, unlike in classic cognitive dissonance studies, we did not look at the change in attractiveness ratings over time within a single participant. Our preliminary findings suggest a timing component; that is, consumers' ratings of two options diverge after choice, but then they converge after consumption due to regret or disappointment. In order to establish these changes over time, we implemented an experiment (otherwise similar to study 1) in which each participant rated the two product options (jelly beans) at three different time periods: after forming expectations (when applicable), after choosing, and after consuming their choice.

Our analysis revealed a replication of study 1, in which the combination of forming expectations, making a choice, and consuming that choice reduced consumption enjoyment. More specifically, participants enjoyed consuming their choices significantly less when they had first formed expectations than when they had not. Second, participants who formed expectations indeed demonstrated a significant spreading of alternatives when rating the attractiveness of the chosen option after choice (M = 4.55 after expectations vs. M = 5.33 after choice) and a significant convergence of attractiveness after consumption (M = 4.74 after consumption). This finding provides further support for the idea that the product options shift in attractiveness at various stages in the decision process.

We are currently running additional studies to uncover the cognitive process underlying these results. It is possible that consumers who bolster their choices feel disappointed after consumption due to expectation disconfirmation. Alternatively, because demonstrating spreading alternatives in preferences reduces cognitive dissonance and thus psychological discomfort (Elliot & Devine 1994; Galinsky et al. 2000), it is possible that the act of consumption reduces such discomfort, rendering this bias no longer necessary. To tease apart these alternative explanations, study 3 (ongoing) measures how well consumption of the products matched participants' expectations and their disappointment and psychological discomfort levels, as well as individual differences in regret tendencies. Study 3 also extends the findings of the first two studies to an additional product category (music).

Angry Avengers or Disappointed Deferrers: Consumers' Emotional Reactions to Stockouts

EXTENDED ABSTRACT

Stockouts are a common retail experience, with estimates in the range of an average of 10-20 percent of items being unavailable on a typical afternoon (IHL Group 2008). Given the practical importance and general prevalence of stockouts, understanding consumer responses to out-of-stocks and the costs of product unavailability has been an area of considerable interest both in marketing and supply chain management.

The behaviors consumers engage in following a stockout can vary considerably, thus impacting key players in the chain differently: from buying another brand in the same store (hurting the manufacturer, but not the retailer) or switching to another store altogether (hurting the retailer, but not the manufacturer), to long-term effects such as negative word of mouth and reduced attitudes toward the store and the brand. Few papers have examined the underlying causes of consumer response to stockouts, or what drives consumers to choose one behavioral response over another. In this research, we seek to better understand when and why consumers retaliate with specific behaviors when encountering a stockout.

In four experiments we examine when and why stockouts impact consumers' retaliatory behaviors, focusing upon the mediational role of emotions and satisfaction jointly. We predict that two emotions will be important for stockouts: anger and disappointment. Anger tends to arise when an individual's goal progress is impeded: feels caused by another person, perceived as controllable by that other person, and seems personally directed (Frijda, Kuipers, & ter Schure 1989). Anger typically leads to active retaliation and an antagonistic response. This is in contrast to disappointment, which is caused by the situation, is perceived as uncontrollable, and is impersonal. Disappointment leads to more passive retaliation, where the individual attempts to change the situation (Zeelenberg et al. 1998).

We examine when consumers are likely to experience anger versus disappointment in response to a stockout and how those discrete emotions lead to different patterns of retaliatory behaviors toward a retailer or brand. With this focus, we look more deeply at the psychological processes that mediate stockout experiences on consumer evaluations and reactionary behaviors. Results demonstrate that consumers naturally experience anger and disappointment in response to stockouts, and that anger leads to greater levels of damaging retaliatory behaviors (e.g., store switching) while disappointment predicts choice deferral.

In a first exploratory study, we examine whether consumers naturally discuss stockout experiences in emotional terms, and specifically if anger and disappointment are innate reactions to an out-of-stock situation. Participants were asked to recall and describe their most recent stockout experience. Participants described a variety of stockout situations, across different retailers, for items at different price levels. Across their open-ended responses, 60% of respondents mentioned experiencing an emotion in response to a stockout: specifically, 40% of respondents experienced disappointment, while 16% mentioned feeling angry or furious, and two respondents (4%) mentioned another emotion—panic. Thus, more than half of the respondents mentioned emotions in their discussion of stockouts.

The second study sought to manipulate aspects of the stockout situation in order to determine the underlying causes of the different emotional reactions—and whether each emotion predicts a specific punitive response. Participants completed an engaging online shopping task in which they were purchasing a cake to take to a dinner party. Two factors were manipulated: the availability of their preferred cake (in-stock, out-of-stock), and their commitment to the preferred cake (high, low). Following the cake purchase situation, participants completed a variety of measures, including: emotion ratings, their satisfaction with the decision process, likelihood of returning to the bakery in the future (store switching), and what they would tell their friends about the bakery (word-of-mouth). Participants' feelings of anger were affected by availability, such that participants who experienced a stockout were significantly angrier than those whose cake was available; this result is qualified by a significant interaction of

availability and commitment, such that when their cake was out-of-stock, highly committed participants were angrier than those with low commitment to the out of stock item. On the other hand, disappointment was only affected by availability—commitment did not amplify consumers' feelings of disappointment. Similarly, decision satisfaction was also only impacted by availability; unsurprisingly, participants whose preferred cake was out-of-stock experienced lower satisfaction with their decision.

In the third study, the personalization of the stockout announcement was manipulated such that participants entered their name at the beginning of the study, and then—upon reaching the checkout counter—the baker told them that he would never sell their preferred cake to a person with the subject's name (personal), or simply that he had already sold the last one of their preferred cake (impersonal). Participants were more angry when the stockout was personal (M = 5.56) than impersonal (M = 4.50; F(1, 254) = 14.659, p < .001), yet disappointment was equal across the two conditions (Mpersonal=4.43, Mimpersonal=4.06, p > .75). Similarly, individuals who felt personally targeted for the stockout were less likely to return to the bakery (M = 30.01) than those who received an impersonal stockout (M = 51.91; F(1, 254) = 27.196, p < .001), and this result was mediated by feelings of anger (z = -2.48, p < .05). This study demonstrates that with higher commitment comes greater anger, which then leads to retaliatory behaviors; while disappointment remains constant.

In Study 4 participants complete the same cake shopping scenario but we manipulate their commitment level by having them first specify what cake they would buy (chocolate, carrot, or fruit) and, in the high commitment condition, write about why that cake would make a good gift. Also, in this study, after experiencing a stock-out of their preferred cake participants were given the option of either choosing another in-stock cake or indicating they would choose to go to another bakery altogether. As in the previous studies, highly committed participants were more angry (M = 4.39) than low commitment (M = 3.44; F(1, 145) = 7.622, p < .01). Interestingly, disappointment was also higher in the high commitment condition (M = 3.88) than the low (M = 3.28; F(1, 145) = 5.154, p < .05). Commitment also affected the likelihood that an individual would choose to go to a different store, such that high commitment led to a higher likelihood of store switching (β = 1.519, p < .001). Anger ratings partially mediated the effect of commitment on store switching (z = -1.817, p = .062), while disappointment ratings did not (z = 1.54, p > .15).

These studies tell a consistent story of emotions in reactions to stockouts: anger and disappointment are integral to the experience of stockouts. In particular, as an individual becomes more committed to a particular option, the likelihood of experiencing anger increases. Importantly, experiencing anger predicts whether the individual will switch stores—seen in the repeated mediation of commitment on store switching by anger. Interestingly, disappointment seems to be a relatively invariant component of stockout experiences: few aspects of the stockout situation changed the experience of disappointment, suggesting that *any* stockout will lead to disappointment. Understanding what emotions a consumer will experience upon encountering a stockout has implications for predicting the downstream retaliatory behaviors, as well as suggesting courses of action that stores can take to reconcile with consumers.

The Effects of Curiosity on Consumption Enjoyment

EXTENDED ABSTRACT

Consumers increasingly face curiosity-arousing contexts. For example, daily occurrences of ringing cell phones, incoming email notifications, or unopened mail can evoke curiosity about who is calling or writing, what they have to say, and whether there is good or bad news to be learned. Consistent with Loewenstein (1994), we define curiosity as a feeling of deprivation that arises when there is a gap between what one knows currently (i.e., someone is trying to get in touch with me) and what wants to know (who is it and what do they want to tell me). Individuals in a state of curiosity feel deprived because the resolution of the curiosity-evoking event is self-relevant but unknown to them. .

Despite the prevalence of curiosity evoking events in consumers' lives, limited consumer behavior research has focused on the effects of curiosity. We ask the novel question of whether and to what extent the interruption of a consumption episode (i.e., a dinner, a nice drive, a movie, a massage, a concert, a book) by a curiosity-evoking event (i.e., a ringing cell phone) impacts enjoyment of the consumption experience.

On the one hand, prior research shows that interruption can increase consumption enjoyment. Specifically, (Nelson and Meyvis 2008) showed that breaks increase enjoyment with positive experiences and decrease enjoyment with negative experiences. Their theorizing is based on the notion that breaks disrupt hedonic adaptation and intensify the consumption experience. Based on this research, one might expect that a curiosity-evoking event that interrupts a consumption experience might enhance consumption enjoyment.

However, we predict the opposite. Our theoretical framework suggests that curiosity-evoking events do more than interrupt. By evoking a feeling of deprivation they create a state of discomfort about the gap between what one knows and what wants to know. They motivate an impulsive search for resolution. Indeed, prior research confirms that when in a state of curiosity, consumers seek information and are more responsive to that which is received (Menon and Soman 2002; Steenkamp and Baumgartner 1992). Such information seeking behavior disrupts the consumption experience and may undermine its enjoyment. Moreover, social forces (norms against answering phones or emails while dining with others), legal forces (laws against texting while driving) or physical limitations (phones that are out of reach during a massage) may prohibit information resolution. Under such circumstances we anticipate that individuals ruminate about the curiosity-evoking event and that such rumination further undermines consumption enjoyment.

One field study and two experiments provide preliminary evidence consistent with these predictions. In study 1, Three hundred individuals completed a short survey immediately following movie screenings. Respondents were asked to evaluate their enjoyment of the movie and whether or not they received calls, emails or texts during the movie itself. The results indicated that participants enjoyed the movie significantly less, if they checked their phones or received a phone call during the movie. Although correlational, this study provides some preliminary evidence that a curiosity-evoking event reduces consumption enjoyment.

Study 2 provided a more rigorous test of the link between curiosity and consumption enjoyment. Specifically, study 2 was designed to determine whether the observed effects were attributable to curiosity and not merely distraction. Seventy-seven individuals were randomly assigned to one of three experimental conditions (curiosity, distraction, or control). All respondents were seated in a comfortable chair and asked to evaluate a foot massager by having a 3-minute foot massage. Respondents' belongings, including their cell phones, were placed nearby but beyond reach. In the curiosity condition, we called participants' cell phones during the massage experience. In the distraction condition, we remotely operated a fan located near the participant. Respondents in the control condition heard no inter-

ruption. At the conclusion of the massage, participants rated their enjoyment. As hypothesized, enjoyment of the foot massage was significantly lower in the curiosity condition than in the distraction and control conditions, which were equivalent. The results of study 2 suggest that curiosity-evoking events can decrease consumption enjoyment, and this effect is not driven by pure distraction.

Study 3 was designed to provide a conceptual replication and extension our findings by examining the process underlying the relationship between curiosity and consumption enjoyment. Study 3 offers an initial test of whether curiosity's effect on enjoyment is explained by attention to and rumination about the curiosity evoking event. Eighty-six participants were randomly assigned to curiosity, distraction or control condition. Participants were asked to play a Mario Kart Nintendo Wii driving game for four minutes. In the curiosity condition, respondents placed their cell phones on a table next to the chair at which they were seated. To evoke curiosity, we called respondents on their cell phone once while they played. In the distraction condition, we placed an iPod on the same table by respondents' chairs and created a distraction by remotely starting the iPod. Immediately following the game, respondents were asked to rate their enjoyment of the game. Consistent with study 2, we found that enjoyment with the videogame experience was significantly lower in the curiosity than in the distraction and control conditions, which did not differ. To measure attention, we coded participant behavior, i.e, whether and how frequently they looked at their cell phones or iPod. Meditation analyses showed that attention mediated the effect of curiosity on enjoyment.

Although work in progress aims to further explore the mechanism driving our results, the current findings add to our understanding of the effects of curiosity. Importantly our work suggests that curiosity negatively impacts consumption enjoyment, has different effects on consumption experiences compared to simple distractions or interruptions, and that its effects are driven by a rumination mechanism that takes attention away from the consumption experience. To the best of our knowledge, this work is the first to examine curiosity in a context independent of the focal consumption experience. Hence, our findings also contribute to the incidental emotion literature by showing how curiosity that is unrelated to the focal task impacts overall enjoyment.

Waiter, There's a Fly in My Soup (and I Have an iPhone)! How Evaluation Timing can Impact Customer Reviews

EXTENDED ABSTRACT

Mobile technology and reviewer-driven applications like Yelp!, Citysearch and Amazon.com enable customers to evaluate products and services in real-time. According to the head of mobile applications at Citysearch, the practice of real-time reviewing is beneficial for customers because it empowers them to express what they are currently feeling as they use products and receive services. Further, Citysearch views immediate evaluations as more honest and informative than those written after a delay, thereby increasing their value to consumers who use posted reviews in their own decision-making (Miller 2009). While immediate evaluations can prove beneficial to consumers, what does this mean for the companies being reviewed and whose reputations are at stake? Generally speaking, how does timing affect the valence of consumers' product, service and brand evaluations? Are ratings more positive (negative) when they are written in the heat of the consumption experience, or after a delay, when the experience has ended and customers have had some time to cool off?

Across four studies, we provide strong evidence supporting our theory about the role of delayed feedback timing and its negative effect on consumer attitudes. When consumers give feedback about a product or service consumed after a time delay has occurred (vs. in real-time), they should report more negative evaluations of the experience, lower levels of satisfaction, and more negative affect. In contrast, when products or services are evaluated in real-time, overall evaluations and satisfaction are higher, regardless of product or service quality.

The goal of study 1 is to investigate how evaluation timing impacts consumer evaluations regardless of the quality of the consumer's actual service experience. As such, in study 1, a quasi-field study (using a pizza delivery company), we ran a 2x3 between-subjects experimental design with feedback timing (immediate vs. delayed) and quality of the service delivered (substandard vs. standard vs. above standard) as the experimental factors. We randomly assigned participants to one of the six conditions for a total of 164 undergraduate students who received course credit for their participation. We uncover evidence to support a delayed feedback effect whereby participants report lower satisfaction with their service experiences and more negative attitudes toward the company that delivered those experiences when feedback was submitted one week after the service encounter as compared to instances when feedback was submitted immediately following the service encounter.

The main objective of the second study is to extend our findings beyond service contexts to the lower involvement consumption context of everyday consumer packaged goods (paper towels). In Study 2, we ran a 2x2 between-subjects experimental design with feedback timing (immediate vs. delayed) and quality of the paper towel (low vs. high) as the experimental factors. Specifically, in study 2 we seek to determine whether the same findings are observed with the evaluation of something as basic as a paper towel, while broadening our investigation to look at whether affect is also affected in the delayed feedback conditions. The findings of study 2 provide additional support for the existence of a delayed feedback effect. Consistent with study 1, we found that when feedback was elicited after a delay, evaluations of the product and likelihood to purchase that product were lower than when feedback was elicited immediately following the product sampling experience. We are able to demonstrate that it is not the baseline mood at the time of product interaction that is coloring the evaluation. Rather, Study 2 demonstrates that the negative emotions reported by study participants were significantly more prevalent at the time of the delayed evaluation (time 2) over what was reported at the baseline (time 1). This lends support to the idea that merely asking customers for feedback one week after their experiences creates negative feelings and these color consumer evaluations.

The primary goal of Study 3 is to gain a better understanding for why, when soliciting customer feedback after a delay, a decrease in product and service evaluations occurs. Namely, we are interested in the amount of perceived effort by the consumer when completing the evaluation at time 2. Study 3 also extends our contribution by examining the effectiveness of incentives offered to customers for taking part in follow-up surveys, such as nominal gift cards. We randomly assigned seventy-three undergraduate participants to a one-factor (incentive: no incentive vs. gift card) between-subjects experimental design. Evaluation timing was held constant in this study in that all participants were asked to evaluate products after a delay. Consistent with studies 1 and 2, results indicated that evaluation and satisfaction at time 1 were significantly higher than at time 2. Additionally, results indicated that the perceived effort at time 1 was significantly lower than the perceived effort at time 2. Thus, as hypothesized, participants perceived there to be more effort expended when they were asked to complete a survey one-week after the consumption experience as compared to when they were asked to complete a survey during the experience. This resulted in decreased satisfaction and decreased evaluations of the product. Additionally, it appears that participants expect some type of incentive when completing a follow-up survey, but by offering a small two-dollar gift card, participants' need for an additional incentive decreases significantly.

The main objective of study 4 was to gain a better understanding of the underlying process. We test evaluation of the paper towels via a quality manipulation in either real-time or after a delay. Additionally, we measure perceived effort as a potential mediator for those in the delayed feedback condition. Consistent with the previous studies, we find evaluations of the product to be lower in the delayed feedback condition, regardless of paper towel quality. Additionally we find perceived effort to be higher when feedback is delayed versus immediate. In the open-ended portion of the survey, participants indicated that they perceived effort to be higher in the delayed feedback condition because it was difficult to recall the exact feeling and experience of the product when it wasn't directly in front of them. Together this set of results confirms our proposed theory that by asking for feedback after a delay, perceived effort increases, resulting in lower evaluations and decreased levels of satisfaction for products, services, and firms.

Conflicted Choices: New Perspectives on Choice Conflict

Chair: Andrea Bonezzi, New York University, USA

Paper #1: When Two is Better than One: Polarization and Compromise in Unrestricted Choice

Andrea Bonezzi, New York University, USA
Alexander Chernev, Northwestern University, USA
Aaron R. Brough, Pepperdine University, USA

Paper #2: By Tradeoff or by Criterion: Bottom-Up Construction of Constructive Decision Rules

Aner Sela, University of Florida, USA
Itamar Simonson, Stanford University, USA

Paper #3: Blurring Similarities and Differences: The Role of Category Width on Salient Comparison Orientation

Selin A. Malkoc, Washington University, USA
Gülden Ülkümen, University of Southern California, USA

Paper #4: Choice Overload with Repeated Choice Exposures: The Role of Preference Retrieval and Variety

Simona Botti, London Business School, UK
Sheena Iyengar, Columbia University, USA
Yangjie Gu, London Business School, UK

SESSION OVERVIEW

In many everyday decisions consumers experience choice conflict, stemming from the need to make difficult trade-offs between the available choice alternatives. Understanding how consumers chose when faced with decision conflict is important because their choices ultimately influence their happiness and well being. Prior research suggests that experiencing choice conflict might lead consumers to choose a compromise option that provides moderate levels of performance on all desired attributes (Simonson 1989; Simonson and Tversky 1992), defer choice and avoid purchasing any of the available options (Dhar 1997; Tversky and Shafir 1992), or seek variety and purchase multiple options (Simonson 1990). This special session aims to advance our understanding of how consumers deal with decision conflict. The four papers offer a diversity of innovative perspectives that enhance the breadth of our knowledge in this area of research, providing a coherent yet diverse set of findings.

The first paper, by Bonezzi, Chernev and Brough, argues that the strategy consumers use to resolve decision conflict is contingent on purchase quantity restrictions. In particular, this paper shows a polarization effect, whereby, when purchase quantity is not restricted to a single option, consumers tend to resolve decision conflict by choosing multiple options with extreme attribute values rather than a single compromise alternative. This polarization effect in unrestricted choice is attributed to consumers' desire to resolve decision conflict by maximizing gains rather than minimizing losses.

The second paper, by Sela and Simonson, argues that certain features of a choice problem can prompt consumers to deal with choice conflict by adopting either compensatory (trade-off based) or lexicographic (criterion-based) decision strategies. In particular, attribute frames that appear generic and not unique to the choice-set being evaluated induce criterion-based decision-making. In contrast, attribute frames that make the attributes seem local and relevant to the particular problem at hand induce tradeoff-based decision-making. Notably, while criterion-based decision strategies lead to selection of compromise alternatives, tradeoff-based decision strategies lead to selection of extreme alternatives.

The third paper, by Malkoc and Ülkümen, argues that the degree of decision conflict consumers experience when choosing among two or more products can be influenced by the comparison focus adopted. In particular, focusing on the similarities among the available choice alternatives increases decision conflict, compared to focusing on the differences among the available choice alternatives. Importantly, this paper shows that the width of the categories to which consumers are exposed before making a choice influences the comparison focus they will adopt for the choice at hand, thus influencing decision conflict.

The fourth paper, by Botti, Iyengar and Gu argues that psychological conflict stemming from choosing from larger versus smaller choice sets can be mitigated by repeated choice exposures. Repeated choice exposures reduce conflict by increasing familiarity with the choice task and allowing consumers to retrieve previously-established preferences, thus decreasing the cognitive and emotional conflict associated with perusing a great number of options in larger choice sets. However, when consumers cannot retrieve their initially established preferences, the choice overload effect reverses and choosing from smaller sets generates less decision confidence than choosing from larger sets.

Taken together, these four papers advance our understanding of how consumers make decisions under conflict. Overall this session offers a coherent set of innovative perspectives that enhance the breadth of our knowledge in an established area of research. We expect this session to appeal to a broad audience, and be of particular interest to researchers studying choice and decision making. Data collection in all papers is complete, or at an advanced stage of completion. All participants have agreed to present, should the session be accepted.

When Two is Better than One: Polarization and Compromise in Unrestricted Choice

EXTENDED ABSTRACT

When faced with a decision involving tradeoffs between the available choice alternatives, consumers often attempt to resolve decision conflict by selecting a compromise option (Simonson 1989; Simonson and Tversky 1992). In particular, prior research on the compromise effect has shown that the choice share of an option increases when it becomes the middle alternative in a choice set, rather than one of the extremes (Kivetz, Netzer, and Srinivasan 2004). Choosing a compromise option resolves conflict by enabling consumers to minimize tradeoffs between attributes of the available options by avoiding the lowest levels of performance on any single attribute (Simonson and Tversky 1992).

Most of the existing research on the compromise effect, however, has investigated situations in which consumers are restricted to choosing a single alternative from a given set of options (Benartzi and Thaler 2002; Dhar and Simonson 2003; Simonson and Nowlis 2000). In reality, however, purchase quantity is often discretionary and consumers frequently choose multiple items. This raises the question of whether and how removing the single-option restriction from the choice task will influence consumer preferences for how to resolve decision conflict.

In this research, we argue that when choice is unrestricted, consumers tend to resolve decision conflict by choosing multiple options with extreme attribute values rather than a single compromise alternative. We propose that this polarization effect is a function of the degree of decision conflict experienced by consumers. In particular, we argue that preference for multiple extreme options is more pronounced when decision conflict is high rather than low, a prediction opposite to previous findings in the context of restricted choice, which show that heightened decision conflict increases preference for the compromise option at the expense of the extremes. We attribute this polarization effect to consumers' desire to maximize gains on each attribute, rather than settling for intermediate performance on both.

We documented this polarization effect in unrestricted choice across three empirical studies. In experiment 1, we documented the polarization effect by showing that that when choice is unrestricted, choice share of the compromise option declines as consumers opt to resolve decision conflict by selecting multiple extreme options rather than a single intermediate one. Consistent with the compromise effect, choices across four product categories showed that when participants could select only one of three available options (ABC), preference for B was higher than when the set consisted only of AB or BC. However, when participants were permitted to select two options, preferences shifted toward the combination AC rather than B. For example, in the headache medications category, participants were shown three options which varied in how quickly they relieved pain (onset) and how long they lasted (duration). In restricted choice, people preferred medication B, which had a moderate onset and moderate duration. However, in unrestricted choice, preference for B declined and instead people preferred a combination of two extreme medications—A, which had the shortest onset but shortest duration, and C, which had the longest onset but longest duration. This polarization effect was consistent across each of the four categories tested.

In experiment 2, we provided evidence that choice conflict drives this polarization effect by showing that the polarization effect becomes more pronounced as decision conflict increases. We manipulated conflict by varying the range of attribute values of the two extreme options (A and C) while holding constant the attribute values of the compromise option (B). For example, in the sunscreen category, the difference in UVA protection between the two extreme options A and C was 40% in the low conflict condition but 80% in the high conflict condition. These results are consistent with our theory that the polarization effect occurs as consumers attempt to resolve conflict differently in unrestricted versus restricted choice.

In experiment 3, we provided further evidence for the underlying process by showing that the polarization effect is more likely to occur when consumers focus on maximizing gains rather than minimizing losses. Prior to articulating their preferences, participants in one condition listed the advantages of each option in the choice set, whereas participants in another condition listed the disadvantages of each option. Results indicated that the polarization effect in unrestricted choice was attenuated among participants who focused on the disadvantages rather than on the advantages of each option.

The present research provides an important contribution to the literature on choice conflict and the compormise effect. Contrary to prior findings that in restricted choice consumers attempt to resolve decision conflict by selecting a compromise option, we show that in unrestricted choice, consumers are less likely to select the compromise option and instead display a preference for extreme options. Our results further suggest that the greater the conflict a consumer experiences when deliberating about the different choice options, the more likely he is to choose multiple extreme options rather than a single intermediate one when choice is unrestricted. From a conceptual standpoint, our findings lend support to the notion that the polarization effect occurs because people wish to resolve conflict by maximizing gains; polarization is likely to occur when people focus

on the advantages of having both options, but is likely to be attenuated when people recognize the disadvantages of choosing extreme options.

By Tradeoff or by Criterion: Bottom-Up Construction of Constructive Decision Rules

EXTENDED ABSTRACT

When faced with a choice problem, decision makers often engage in tradeoffs to identify the best option. Alternatively, they may first identify the more important attribute(s) and then proceed to select the best option given these criteria. These strategies roughly correspond to compensatory and lexicographic decision strategies, respectively, which have been discussed extensively in the JDM literature (Bettman, Luce, and Payne 1998).

However, whereas the traditional view sees the choice between such decision strategies as a top-down process, largely determined by people's information processing goals (e.g., balancing accuracy vs. cognitive effort, minimizing negative emotion, or maximizing ease of justification; Bettman et al. 1998), we propose that the tendency to focus on tradeoffs versus criteria can be driven by bottom-up features of the choice problem itself. That is, certain problem domains and attribute frames may cause decision makers to focus on tradeoffs, whereas others call for use of generic criteria.

Moreover, choice based on criteria (i.e., the lexicographic strategy) itself has generally been treated as contingent on people's ability to recruit relevant beliefs and preferences in a top-down manner, either from memory or from other available sources (e.g., a consumer may choose based on the belief that reliability is the most important attribute for a car). However, we demonstrate that people may use the lexicographic strategy and choose based on criteria even when they cannot retrieve or otherwise rely on meaningful preferences and values. Namely, criterion-based decision making may be driven not only by the availability of relevant criteria but by a metacognitive belief that one should have consistent priorities in a certain domain.

We identify two bottom-up factors that influence the choice between tradeoff- and criterion-based decision-making. First, we argue that attribute descriptions or frames that appear generic and not unique to the choice-set being evaluated, tend to induce criterion-based decision-making. In contrast, attribute frames that make the attributes seem local and relevant to the particular problem at hand induce tradeoff-based decision-making. In addition, we show that dispositional and situational influences (e.g., nonconscious primes) can induce tradeoff- versus criterion-based decision-making, causing people to use lexicographic strategies even in the absence of applicable criteria.

We demonstrate these propositions in five studies using the compromise effect (Simonson 1989; Simonson and Tversky 1992). Prior research has demonstrated that selection of the compromise (i.e., middle) alternative typically reflects compensatory tradeoff-making (Dhar, Nowlis, and Sherman 2000; Khan, Zhu, and Kalra 2011). In contrast, choice of an extreme option is more likely to reflect criterion-based selection (i.e., the belief that one attribute is more important).

In study 1, we show that three-option choice problems involving generic attributes tend to produce extreme choices whereas problems in which the attributes seem more local and relevant only to the specific product at hand lead people to choose the middle option. Further, we show that the tendency to compromise is stronger among people high in self-monitoring (Snyder 1987), whereas the tendency to select an extreme option is stronger among low self-monitors. This suggests that the tendency to use a tradeoff versus criterion-based strategy may be influenced by general individual dispositions that affect the tendency to base decisions on situational cues versus inner attitudes and beliefs.

In study 2, participants were primed with words related to either calculation (e.g., compute, exchange), principles (e.g., faith, opinion), or neutral words (e.g., birds, fabulous). Then, they made choices from a number of three-option choice-sets. The results indicate that, whereas the calculation prime increased the tendency to select the middle option compared to the control condition, the principles prime increased the tendency to select an extreme option. Thus, a mere "principles mindset" caused people to employ a criterion-based decision strategy.

One might argue that a principles prime and low self-monitoring decrease the tendency to choose the middle option because they lead people to reflect on their preexisting attitudes for familiar options. However, study 3 demonstrates that these effects are independent of existing attitudes by using a truly hypothetical product with hypothetical attributes. We first primed half of the participants with principles by having them write about a situation in which their decision was strongly influenced by personal values and principles. The other half served as control group. We then asked participants to choose among three made-up options differing on two made-up attributes. Whereas 82% chose the middle option in the control condition, this decreased to 64% in the principles prime condition (p < .06). Taken together, these results suggest that criterion-based decision-making may be driven in part by a metacognitive notion that one has or should have relevant criteria in a certain domain, independent of the actual availability of such criteria.

Study 4 demonstrates how specific task characteristics can activate one mode of preference construction versus the other. Before making choices, some participants rated the importance of each of the two attributes that define the choice set on two separate scales (one for each attribute), which highlights the distinct goal underlying each polar dimension. Others rated the attributes on a single bipolar scale, which highlights the tradeoff between them. The results indicate that participants who rated the attributes separately were more likely to choose an extreme option compared to a control condition, whereas those using a single bi-polar scale were more likely to choose the middle option.

Our last study (in progress) examines how the framing of attributes as generic (e.g., capacity and portability for a BBQ grill) versus local (e.g., cooking area and weight) induces criterion- versus tradeoff-based decision-making, respectively, resulting in increased choice of extreme options versus an increase in the choice of the compromise option.

Taken together, the studies make an important contribution by demonstrating that the choice of decision strategies itself may be constructed, based on bottom-up factors rather than top-down information processing goals.

Blurring Similarities and Differences: The Role of Category Width on Salient Comparison Orientation

EXTENDED ABSTRACT

Almost all purchase decisions consumers make involve a comparison between two or more products. When purchasing a car, computer, or even a wristwatch, consumers focus on either the similarities or differences between options. Retailers often strategically sway what consumers pay attention to (e.g., a salesclerk pointing out similarities or differences), hoping to influence their ultimate choice. We suggest that the adopted comparison focus have important implications for whether two products are perceived to be similar or

different - regardless of their objective similarity. Furthermore, consumers' perceptions of product similarity have other important consequences on decision conflict and preference strength. For instance, to the extent that consumers view options as similar, they would have a harder time differentiating them and thus increasing their choice difficulty, decreasing their strength of preference and influencing their willingness to pay for options.

Previous literature suggests that certain contexts make similarities or differences relatively more salient and the decision makers are likely to adopt this salient comparison focus in their evaluations. However, this research is mute on whether there is any factor that would lead consumers to deviate from this salient focus. We argue that while important, contextual salience might not be sufficient in understanding why consumers adopt or not adopt a salient comparison focus. In particular, we examine how the width of categories consumers have been previously exposed to (Ulkumen, Chakravarti, and Morwitz 2009) would influence the adaptation of salient comparison focus.

Our theory suggests that being exposed to narrower (broader) categories leads to use of more (less) dimensions in evaluations and decisions (Ulkumen et al. 2009). Accordingly, we argue that while the uni-dimensional broad categorizers will follow the cues given by the context and adopt the salient comparison focus, while the multi-dimensional narrow categorizers will attend to both similarities and differences – regardless of the salient cues in the environment. We also show that this shift in comparison focus alters perceptions of similarity, and influence choice conflict, evaluations of a new product offering, and preference strength.

In study 1 (N = 86) participants first completed the category width (CW) manipulation, where they responded to questions about themselves that had either many, narrow response categories (narrow condition), or few, broad response categories (broad condition). Next, they considered two backpacks, which were described by a salesclerk as either similar to or different from each other. Participants made a choice and reported their relative consideration of the similarities and differences between these products while making their choice. We found that CW moderates the effect of salient orientation on consideration of similarities and differences. That is, while the broads adopt the focus (similarities *or* differences) suggested by the context, narrows are less sensitive to the context and consider both similarities *and* differences.

Study 2 (N = 108) extended this effect to similarity perceptions as it pertains to multi attribute products. Participants first completed the same CW manipulation. Next, they made choices between two target products in three categories (beer, TV, car). Target products were presented together with two additional products that either had more extreme attribute values (designed to make the target products more similar) or fell between the target products (and made the target products appear more different). Participants indicated their perceived similarity of the two products, both on attribute level and overall. We find that while broad categorizers adopted the salient cue and thus found the options more similar (dissimilar) when the surrounding options were extreme (in between), the similarity judgments of the narrow categorizers were uninfluenced by the salient cues.

In study 3 (N = 92), we explored the downstream consequences of this effect to consumers' strength of preference and decision conflict. Participants first completed the same CW manipulation. Next, they saw a furniture catalog and made a choice between two target chairs. We manipulated salient comparison focus by visually varying the background chairs to be either similar or different from target chairs. Participants reported their decision confidence and conflict, preference strength, and their relative consideration of similarities and differences. As expected, we found that board categorizers who focus on the salient similarities (differences) experienced higher (lower) decision conflict, and lower (higher) confidence and preference strength. As expected, this was not the case for narrow categorizers. Moreover, these effects were mediated by the relative consideration of similarities and differences.

Lastly, in study 4 (N = 84) we investigate a different context where similarity perceptions are of utmost importance. We explore consumer's responses to a stock out, where the new alternative offered is either similar to or different from their original selection.

Participants completed a different manipulation of CW, followed by a choice among several backpacks. They were told their selection was out of stock and were offered an alternative backpack, which was either objectively similar to or different from their selection. We measured participants' attitudes toward the new backpack, and their consideration of similarities and/or differences while choosing. As before, we found that the focus manipulation influenced attitudes only for broad categorizers, such that participants liked the new offering more when they focused on its similarity to the original backpack, than when they focused on its difference. Moreover, as in study 3, relative consideration of similarities and differences mediated the effect.

In four studies we show that the experienced choice conflict, preference strength and product evaluations are significantly influenced not only by the salient comparison orientation, but also by the width of categories consumers are previously exposed to in an unrelated context. Using multiple manipulations of similarity orientation, we demonstrate that consumers exposed to broad categorizations experience more choice conflict when a similarity (vs. difference) orientation is made salient. In contrast, consumers exposed to narrow categorizers consider both similarities and differences between products regardless of the salient comparison orientation.

Choice Overload with Repeated Choice Exposures: The Role of Preference Retrieval and Variety

EXTENDED ABSTRACT

Research on choice overload has shown that the psychological conflicts involved in choosing from larger, versus smaller, sets can decrease satisfaction and decision confidence (Iyengar and Lepper 2000). And yet, in real life consumers seem able to cope with large assortments better than researchers would expect, as they not only regularly make choices from these assortments, but also demand more choices and variety. How can we reconcile consumers' apparent ability to handle extensive choice with the evidence for its detriments? One possibility is that participants in choice overload studies are typically asked to make one-shot decisions, whereas in real life consumers often have the option to make repeated choices over time. One may expect that repeated choice exposures mitigate choice overload. Larger sets, relative to smaller ones, increase the likelihood of finding the option that best matches individual preferences because of their greater variety. In the one-shot decisions investigated in choice overload, this benefit is overwhelmed by the higher level of cognitive and emotional conflict associated with perusing numerous, versus fewer, options, which results in lower decision confidence. In contrast, it is plausible that repeated choice exposures reduce conflict by increasing familiarity with the choice task (Alba and Hutchinson 1987), and therefore enhance consumers' confidence with decisions made from larger sets.

In this paper, however, we hypothesize a more complex relationship between repeated choices and decision confidence, and specifically that this relationship depends on the interaction between preference retrieval and variety. When the preferences expressed in an initial choice cannot be retrieved in a subsequent choice, lower variety will progressively reduce the confidence of consumers choosing from smaller, relative to larger, sets and reverse the choice overload effect. In contrast, when these preferences can be retrieved, these consumers' original greater confidence will persist over time despite lower variety.

We build this hypothesis on two findings. First, consumers construe their preferences based on the available alternatives and tend to retrieve these initial preferences when making subsequent choices (Hoeffler and Ariely 1999). Second, variety is less important when preferences are more clearly established, as in the case of small-set choices, than when they are more uncertain, as in the case of large-set choices (Simonson 1990). If consumers cannot retrieve their preferences in subsequent choices, for example because the initial selection becomes unavailable, they need to re-engage in the choice task and re-construct their preferences. For consumers choosing from smaller, relative to larger, sets, repeated exposures to the choice task are unlikely to further reduce the already low level of decision-related conflicts; rather, reiterated attempts to preference construal will just heighten the disadvantages of limited variety (Chernev 2003) and gradually reduce their higher initial confidence. Conversely, if the preferences initially construed can be retrieved at a later time, these consumers' original greater confidence is unlikely to be negatively affected by low variety. Consumers choosing from smaller, versus larger, sets will be more likely to simply retrieve those preferences without re-engaging in the choice task, thereby maintaining their initial relative superior confidence over time.

We test these predictions in two studies. In the first study, we prevented participants from retrieving their preferences and expected a reversal of the choice overload effect. Participants were exposed for 10 subsequent days to the same selection of iTunes, either 300 songs (large-set condition) or 30 songs (small-set condition). Each day, participants were emailed a survey. The first part of the survey assessed their satisfaction with the song chosen in the previous day, the second part required them to choose another song, and the third part included questions about the choice-task difficulty. Because each selected iTune was downloaded on participants' computers, they had to re-engage in the choice task at each exposure. Consistent with choice overload, on the first exposure participants reported greater difficulty and stress, and lower decision confidence, in the large-, versus small-, set condition. Over the subsequent nine exposures, the choice process became easier and less stressful for participants confronted with a larger, relative to a smaller, set. As predicted, decision confidence decreased in the small-, as compared to the large-, set condition, and on the last exposure choosing from a smaller set generated lower confidence than choosing from a larger set.

In the second study we allowed participants to repeat their choices. This study involved five choice exposures on five consecutive days to the same selection of chocolates that was either large (large/same: 50) or small (small/same: five), such that participants were free to choose the same chocolate in different days. We confronted these two conditions with a third one that, similar to the large-set condition in study 1, offered greater variety but no possibility for preference retrieval. In this third condition, participants were also exposed to a small set of five chocolates, which however changed every day, forcing participants to re-engage in the choice task at each exposure (small/different). Each day participants chose a chocolate from one of the three sets, tasted it, and answered a questionnaire similar to the one employed in study 1.

Consistent with choice overload, on the first exposure choosing from both smaller sets was considered easier, less stressful, and conducive to greater decision confidence than choosing from the larger set. Over repeated exposures, choosing became increasingly easier and less stressful for participants in the large-set condition than for those in both small-set conditions. As we predicted, however, decision confidence remained higher in the small/same condition relative to the large/same condition, indicating that the choice overload effect persisted over time. In addition, in line with previous results, participants in the small/different condition became increasingly less confident relative to those in the other two conditions, indicating that variety is less important when preferences can be retrieved.

In conclusion, these results suggest that choice overload can be mitigated by repeated choice exposures, but only when consumers cannot settle on the preference they have construed within the initial choice-set boundaries.

The Egocentrist and the Stranger:
Conditional Inference When Making Sense of Others

Chairs: Julia Minson, University of Pennsylvania, USA
Oleg Urminsky, University of Chicago, USA

Paper #1: Conditional Projection: How Own Evaluations Impact Beliefs about Others Whose Choices Are Known

Yesim Orhun, University of Michigan, USA
Oleg Urminsky, University of Chicago, USA

Paper #2: 'Tis Better to Give Than to Receive: Preference Estimates Conditioned on Own and Other's Preferences

Andrew Gershoff, University of Texas at Austin, USA
Susan Broniarczyk, University of Texas at Austin, USA

Paper #3: Estimating Central Tendencies: Dead Reckoning vs. Decomposition

Shane Frederick, Yale University, USA

Paper #4: There is Such a Thing as a Stupid Question: Question Disclosure in Strategic Communication

Julia Minson, University of Pennsylvania, USA
Nicole E. Ruedy, University of Washington, USA
Maurice E. Schweitzer, University of Pennsylvania, USA

SESSION OVERVIEW

Beliefs about others' preferences, attitudes, and valuations are an important element in consumer decision-making (West 1996). We rely on these beliefs in a variety of strategic situations, from gift giving to pricing, from product adoption to voting, from word of mouth to bidding and negotiations. A large literature on social projection finds that people egocentrically estimate positions they themselves endorse as more common than positions they don't endorse (Lord, Lepper & House, 1979; Marks & Miller, 1987; Mullen, et al., 1985).

However, beyond this basic effect, little research has attempted to illuminate the interplay between one's own preferences versus what is known, hypothesized or inferred about others, when estimating others' preferences and making strategic choices. This represents a critical gap in our understanding, as our choices and decisions are rarely formed in a vacuum but instead usually involve incorporating our (incomplete) knowledge of others. The papers in this session investigate this important emerging topic and find that prior research on beliefs about others does not account for the ways that reasoning about others changes when taking into account what is known or assumed about others.

In the first paper, Orhun and Urminsky investigate estimates of others' evaluations of the choice options, when others' choices are known (e.g., for others making the same or opposite choice relative to the self). They find evidence of conditional projection, such that a person's evaluation of the option she chose influences her beliefs about how others evaluated either the same or opposite options that they, respectively, chose. This projection of corresponding evaluations to opposite choosers, in particular, suggests a process of analogical reasoning about others that is incompatible with prior accounts of social projection and false consensus.

In the second paper, Gershoff and Broniarczyk look at conditional inferences in advice giving. They find that the influence of what is known about others on one's own preferences and the influence of one's own preferences on estimates of others can be confounded in people's minds. As a result, consumers are prone to systematic errors in conditional probability estimates involving their own preferences consistent with differences in the accessibility and diagnosticity of

the relevant sample space for the task. Consumers are more accurate when making probability judgments associated with giving recommendations (compared to receiving them), particularly when the conditioning information was not attribute based.

In the third paper, Frederick investigates the effect of aggregating hypothetical conditional estimates about different types of others, when making judgments regarding aggregate quantities or group means – such as the number of pieces of sushi needed for a party. Imputed quantities were calculated by eliciting subsidiary judgments: how many people would enjoy the focal good ("not much", "somewhat", "a lot", or "I'd love it!") and the average willingness to pay among people in each category. These imputed quantities were more accurate than direct "dead reckoning" estimates.

In the fourth paper, Minson, Ruedy and Schweitzer demonstrate a novel way in which others may unwittingly reveal the kind of information that informs conditional inferences in strategic settings: the questions they ask. They compared three types of questions. *General* questions lack a specific line of investigation and convey the impression that the asker is not knowledgeable. *Positive Assumption* questions ask about a specific issue, but communicate the assumption while problems are possible, no concerns currently exist. *Negative Assumption* questions ask about a specific issue with an implicit assumption that a problem exists. The inferences participants made about their negotiation counterparts based on their questions dramatically affected their level of honesty during the negotiation.

These papers go beyond the existing literature on general social projection, to investigate the pervasive but understudied phenomenon of conditional inferences about others across different inference contexts, including product valuation, voting, advice giving and word of mouth, and negotiation. These papers present a new and more sophisticated understanding of the manner in which what we know or infer about others, how we relate those others to ourselves, and even how we hypothetically segment others all systematically influence our beliefs, and inform strategic decisions. We anticipate that this session will generate interest among a diverse group of ACR attendees, including those who are interested in interpersonal interactions, inference and belief formation and strategic decision-making. We believe that this session will suggest important new directions for future research into social inference and influence.

Conditional Projection: How Own Evaluations Impact Beliefs About Others Whose Choices Are Known

EXTENDED ABSTRACT

In this paper, we investigate how people's ratings of their choice options impact their beliefs about others' ratings, both for others making the same as well as the opposite choice. Consider, for example, a consumer who has chosen a Sony camera over a Panasonic camera. How will her own evaluations of both cameras influence her beliefs about how those who also chose Sony (*same-choosers*) or those who instead chose Panasonic (*opposite choosers*) evaluated both cameras? Contrary to existing theories of false consensus, we find *conditional preference projection*: beliefs about others are based on the assumption that their choices arose from corresponding preferences to one's own. Thus, for example, the higher the Sony-chooser rated Sony, the more she would believe that *opposite choosers* (e.g.

271

Advances in Consumer Research
Volume 40, ©2012

Panasonic choosers) would rate their own preferred camera (Panasonic) highly. Conversely, the less negatively the Sony-chooser rated the one she did not choose (Panasonic), the more she would believe that opposite-choosers would likely not be as negative about their rejected camera (Sony).

Our conditional projection account is distinct from three alternative accounts that arise by extending existing models of social projection to estimating the evaluations of opposite choosers:

I. Direct negative projection of one's own evaluation of an option. In this case (suggested by the differentiation account, Mullen, Davidio, Johnson and Copper 1992), a person with high evaluations of her chosen option is expected to believe opposite-choosers to have lower evaluations of that same option (compared to another person with lukewarm evaluations). Evaluations of Sony among Panasonic choosers would be *lower* for Sony choosers with higher evaluations of Sony.

II. Direct positive projection of one's own evaluation of an option. In this case (suggested by the induction account; Dawes 1989, Hoch 1987), a person with higher evaluations of her chosen option would be more likely to believe that opposite-choosers have more positive evaluations of this option (albeit lower than their evaluations of the other option, which they chose). Evaluations of Sony among Panasonic choosers would be *higher* for Sony choosers with higher evaluations of Sony.

III. Lack of projection to opposite-choosers, since opposite choosers are an out-group. In this case, (suggested by the selective anchoring account, Clement and Krueger 2002), everyone would on average have the same beliefs about opposite-choosers' evaluations. Sony choosers' estimated evaluations of Sony among Panasonic choosers would not depend on the Sony choosers' own evaluations.

Across five studies, we examine people's beliefs about the evaluations of same-choosers and opposite-choosers. In particular, the proposed pattern of projection to opposite-choosers distinguishes our account of conditional projection from the extensions of existing choice projection theories to evaluations discussed above. We provide evidence for our predictions using across-people differences in ratings of choice options, within-person changes in ratings, as well as manipulated differences in participants' ratings. In Study 1, we focus on political decision making as a particularly appropriate context to study the formation and implications of one's beliefs about others. In data collected right before the 2008 Presidential election, we explored if and how a person's own evaluations about Obama and McCain shaped her beliefs about others' evaluations, conditional on knowing which candidate they support. For both general voters (N=351) and a sample of lab participants incentivized for accuracy (N=72), we confirm our conditional projection account. Obama voters' evaluations of their chosen candidate, Obama, primarily influenced their estimates of McCain voters' evaluations McCain. Likewise, Obama voters' evaluations of their rejected candidate, McCain, primarily influenced their estimates of McCain voters' evaluations Obama. Moreover, in a recontact study conducted before and after the first presidential debate, we confirm the same pattern of results for how *changes* in one's own candidate evaluations corresponded to changes in beliefs about opposite-choosers' candidate evaluations.

In Study 2 (N=159), we replicated our results in the context of technology adoption (evaluations of the Nintendo Wii and Sony PS3 videogame consoles), another context in which people's beliefs about others can be important for understanding their own choices. In Study 3 (N=151), we use the context of art posters to replicate the findings and rule out the possibility of reverse causation as an explanation. We show that learning about opposite-choosers' evaluations of two posters does not influence one's own evaluations. However,

participants' own evaluations did affect their estimates of the corresponding evaluations of opposite-choosers.

In Study 4 (N=65), we further address causality concerns by experimentally manipulating evaluations of digital cameras (Sony and Panasonic), by either making participants aware of additional unavailable information about the cameras, or not. We find that those in the unaware condition rate their chosen camera higher, and the differences in own evaluations is conditionally projected to both same- and opposite-choosers. In Study 5 (N=274), we investigate the effect of spontaneous changes in post-choice evaluations of digital cameras over time (absent new information) on beliefs about others. We found that ratings for the rejected camera were lower in the second wave (one week later) when participants no longer had detailed information in front of them. Correspondingly, they estimated that evaluations of both same and opposite choosers' respective rejected cameras would be lower as well.

Across the studies, we identify belief in similar decision processes as moderators, confirm that people endorse our account of "analogical projection" as a descriptor of their own decision process and rule out reverse causation (e.g. preferences influenced by beliefs) and belief in negative correlations as explanations.

'Tis Better to Give Than to Receive: Preference Estimates Conditioned on Own and Other's Preferences

EXTENDED ABSTRACT

Consumers are both givers and receivers of advice. Sometimes they recommend products to others. Sometimes they seek out recommendations from others (Gershoff, Broniarczyk, West 2001). Since information is neither perfect nor costless, and the future is uncertain, the recommendations that they give and receive are not always accurate. Therefore, both when giving and receiving advice, consumers often must make estimates about own and others' preferences (Loewenstien and Schkade 1999; West 1996).

Frequently these estimates are conditional probabilities involving both one's own and another's preferences or evaluations (Gershoff et al. 2001). For example, for the task of giving a recommendation to a friend, you might consider the conditional probability that your friend will like an alternative given that you liked it; P(other +|self +). For the task of receiving a recommendation, you might consider the conditional probability that you will like what your friend liked; P(self +|other +). Although both tasks require consideration of both one's own and other's preferences, the conditional probabilities to be estimated differ in that one is the inverse of the other.

This research presents three studies that explore accuracy in estimates of probability of liking conditioned on one's own another's preferences Prior work has shown that that people's ability to assess conditional probabilities depends on the task (Gershoff et al. 2001) and information presentation (Gigerenzer and Hoffrage 1995). One error that has been observed is the occasional mistaking of P(A|B), with its inverse, P(B|A) (Bar-Hillel 1983). An explanation for this finding is that a category that is more accessible or perceived to be more diagnostic tends to be adopted as the denominator, or sample space, for the conditional probability estimate (Sherman, McMullen, Gavanski 1992; Brase Cosmides, and Tooby 1999). Depending on whether a consumer is giving or receiving a recommendation, the appropriate sample space for assessing the conditional probability differs. When giving a recommendation it is the set of alternatives that the consumer has given a positive rating. When receiving a recommendation, it is the set of alternatives that the other individual has given a positive rating.

Where a categorization schema for the relevant sample space is difficult to access, people may rely on a more accessible schema that may appear diagnostic because it is related to the task at hand and or is relevant for similar tasks (Hilton and Fein 1989). Compared to information about another's preferences, information about one's own preferences is likely to be more accessible, and generally more relevant. Indeed, information that is self-relevant has been shown to be easier to recall and to be perceived as more important than information that is not self-relevant (Bower and Gilligan 1979). Categorizing a set of alternatives in terms of one's own likes and dislikes is likely to be a more natural way to categorize the alternative space than in terms of another's likes and dislikes. Thus, it is predicted that people will be less accurate when assessing P(self+|other+) (assessing a received recommendation), compared to assessing P(other+|self+) (assessing a given recommendation), but task characteristics that influence categorization in terms of one's own versus others' preferences will moderate this effect.

Study one asked 146 participants to examine and rate 50 posters while simultaneously learning the ratings of another participant. Next participants estimated P(self +| other +) and P(other +| self +). The order was counterbalanced. As predicted, the correlation between estimates of P(self +| other +) and actual (r = .271; z = 1.96, p = .05) was significantly less than the correlation between estimates of P(other +| self +) (r = .467). There was also more absolute error estimates of P(self +| other +) (M = .2215) than P(other +| self +) (M = .1825; F(1,145) = 7.002, p < .01).

Study 2 manipulated organization of information. Eighty participants sorted posters into those they liked and disliked or into those a partner liked and disliked. In the self-sort condition, accuracy echoed that of study 1. There was greater correlation for estimated and actual P(partner+|self+) (r = .81) than for P(self+|partner+) (r = -.08; Z = 5.42; p < .001). Sorting by partners' preferences attenuated this. The correlation between estimated and actual P(partner+|self+) (r = .41) was not significantly different from P(self+|partner+) (r = .44; Z = .135, p > .1). The same pattern of results held for measures of absolute values of accuracy.

Study 3 explored boundaries on accuracy in conditional probability estimates involving one's own preferences. One hundred and twenty four participants made estimates of the probability that they would like an alternative conditioned on an attribute of the alternative (either the subject of the poster, or the catalog where it is sold) rather than conditioned on another's preference. Because thinking about a set of alternatives in terms of commonly used descriptive attributes is likely to be a natural way to categorize the alternative space, in study 3 it was predicted that estimates of P(self+|attribute) would show less error than estimates of P(attribute|self+). As predicted, correlation of estimates and actual for P(self +| attribute) (r = .632, p < .001) were greater than for P(attribute| self +) (r = .104, p = .250; z = 4.981, p < .001). Likewise there was less absolute error for P(self +| attribute) (M = .1338) compared to P(attribute| self +) (M = .1617) (F(1,122) = 3.870, p = .051).

In three studies we found that consumers are prone to systematic errors in conditional probability estimates involving their own preferences consistent with differences in the accessibility and diagnosticity of the relevant sample space for the task. Probability estimation errors were consistent with better accuracy associated with the task of giving compared to receiving recommendations (Study 1 and 2). However the errors could be attenuated by categorization of information at the time of exposure (Study 2) and the presence of other more salient natural level categories (Study 3).

Estimating Central Tendencies: Dead Reckoning vs. Decomposition

EXTENDED ABSTRACT

Predicting aggregate quantities, such as the number of pieces of sushi needed for a party can be done either by "dead reckoning" or by decomposing the global judgment into subsidiary elements (How many people will come?; How many pieces will the typical person eat?) I find that the large systematic biases found by Frederick (2012) in judgments of average valuation for products and services can be attenuated, or even eliminated by decomposing the task of dead reckoning a central tendency of some focal group into subsidiary judgments about the distribution of some other trait (such as liking) followed by the conditional judgments of valuation based on levels of liking.

In the focal study, 663 picnickers in Boston were shown two "goods" – DVDs of the first four seasons of *The Sopranos* and a two hour cheese tasting event held at a local cheese store. All respondents first indicated the most that they would be willing to pay for the presented good. Thereafter, respondents were randomly assigned to one of two prediction groups. The direct prediction group then simply predicted the mean valuation among all others taking the survey. By contrast, the "decomposed" prediction group first indicated how much they, themselves, would enjoy the focal good ("not much", "somewhat", "a lot", or "I'd love it!"), then estimated the percentage of other respondents in each of these four response categories, and then estimated the average willingness to pay among people in each categories (which, of course, includes the category in which they placed themselves). Although respondents in the decomposed prediction group were never directly asked to estimate the mean willingness to pay of the population, their subsidiary estimates entail such a prediction, and a predicted mean can be *imputed*.

As shown in Tables 1 and 2, among the *direct* prediction group, estimates of the mean valuations significantly exceeded the actual mean for both the Sopranos DVDs ($85.80 vs. $46.05; paired t(336) = 11.72; p<0.0001) and the cheese tasting event ($64.30 vs. $46.13; t(339) = 3.89; p<0.001). For the decomposed group, the bias was diminished for the Sopranos DVDs ($70.35 vs. $46.13; t(258) = 11.72; p<0.0001), and eliminated for the cheese tasting event (Estimates = $35.11 vs. Actual = $33.19; t(260) = 1.17; p>0.24).

The judgments rendered by the decomposed prediction group help distinguish two potential sources of the overestimation bias reported by Frederick (2012): an exaggerated sense of how much the target population likes the focal product, and an exaggerated sense of how much others would be willing to pay conditional on their stated level of liking. For the *Sopranos* DVDs, both quantities were exaggerated, such that the bias remained substantial, even in the decomposed prediction group. However, for the cheese tasting event, respondents underestimated how much people would like it, but overestimated how much people of a given liking level would be willing to pay. These errors roughly cancelled such that imputed estimates were very close to the true mean.

The bottom four rows of each table report estimates for respondents with different levels of liking for the good. Consistent with other work on projection, the imputed estimates of "fans" (those who loved the good or liked it a lot) exceeded the imputed estimates of "non fans" (those in the lower two liking groups). Note, though, that aside from helping to disentangle various elements of the "X effect" (Frederick, 2012), this study also helps distinguish different kinds or levels or "depths" of projection. For example, a *Sopranos* fan may project their enthusiasm for the show onto either their estimate of the frequency of fellow fans or onto the monetary valuations of those who are lesser fans, or both. These results suggest that projection is predominantly of the first type. If one looks down any of the columns, the bottommost four rows are often strikingly similar. When asked to make predictions *conditioned on* another feature known to vary (in this case liking), participants were *not* anchored on their own valuations. For instance, though cheese lovers would pay an average of $54 for a ticket to the cheese tasting event, compared to just $7 among those with the lowest level of expressed liking, those two different groups made identical predictions of the valuation of the low interest group ($8).

There *is* Such a Thing as a Stupid Question: Question Disclosure in Strategic Communication

EXTENDED ABSTRACT

Consumers require information from others to guide decisions. Situations ranging from home purchases, to medical decisions, to investment choices are characterized by information dependence (see Adair & Brett, 2005; Galinsky, Maddux, Gilin & White, 2008; Gino & Moore, 2008). For example, in evaluating a used car buyers are dependent, at least in part, on the seller providing accurate information about the vehicle's condition. In these settings, individuals seek information from counterparts who often have incentives to conceal unfavorable facts. We term interactions characterized by asymmetric information and motivated disclosure *strategic information exchanges*.

In strategic information exchanges scholars advise individuals to ask questions (e.g. Malhotra and Bazerman, 2007; Nierenberg, 1986; Shell, 1999; Thompson, 2005). This advice, however, is predicated on an incomplete conceptualizations of questions. Specifically, prior work has overlooked the critical role questions play in *revealing* information. In this paper, we develop the following thesis: the questions individuals ask not only solicit information, but also disclose information. We define the previously unexplored phenomenon of questions revealing information as *question disclosure*. We develop a new theory, the Question Disclosure Model, for organizing related findings and report experimental results that demonstrate question disclosure and its consequences.

We characterize responses to questions with respect to (a) the attributes respondents mention, and (b) the overall valence (positive/negative) of the information. For example, in replying to a question about an apartment, a landlord could describe attributes such as the neighborhood, the amenities, or the building. The valence of those features might be positive (e.g. lively restaurant scene) or negative (e.g. noisy neighbors), affecting the overall valence of the description. According to our model, the inferences that individuals make based on questions they receive influence the valence of the response and the features mentioned.

In our experiment, we tested the predictions of the QDM by introducing three types of questions that lead to different inferences about the asker's knowledge structures and intentions. We expect these different types of questions to influence the content, valence,

Table 1. Estimates of others' values conditioned on own and others' liking (DVDs)

Valuation of Sopranos DVDs [direct] and decomposed not much		Liking $_{frequency}$			
		some what	a lot	I'd love it!	
Actual	[$46] $46	$16 $_{27\%}$	$43 $_{37\%}$	$65 $_{28\%}$	$92 $_{8\%}$
Estimated (overall)	[$86] $70	$18 $_{15\%}$	$41 $_{23\%}$	$71 $_{31\%}$	$112 $_{31\%}$
by "not much" group	$62	$15 $_{17\%}$	$25 $_{22\%}$	$62 $_{30\%}$	$99 $_{32\%}$
by "somewhat" group	$71	$18 $_{14\%}$	$30 $_{23\%}$	$71 $_{31\%}$	$113 $_{32\%}$
by "a lot" group	$74	$22 $_{14\%}$	$31 $_{24\%}$	$78 $_{33\%}$	$117 $_{28\%}$
by "I'd love it!" group	$86	$20 $_{15\%}$	$23 $_{20\%}$	$83 $_{28\%}$	$131 $_{37\%}$

Table 2. Estimates of others' values conditioned on own and others' liking (Cheese)

Valuation of cheese tasting event [direct] and decomposed not much		Liking $_{frequency}$			
		some what	a lot	I'd love it!	
Actual	[$46] $35	$7 $_{13\%}$	$25 $_{27\%}$	$44 $_{34\%}$	$54 $_{26\%}$
Estimated (overall)	[$64] $33	$9 $_{24\%}$	$22 $_{31\%}$	$41 $_{27\%}$	$71 $_{19\%}$
by "not much" group	$27	$8 $_{33\%}$	$19 $_{31\%}$	$42 $_{22\%}$	$63 $_{14\%}$
by "somewhat" group	$31	$9 $_{23\%}$	$23 $_{36\%}$	$41 $_{25\%}$	$67 $_{16\%}$
by "a lot" group	$33	$11 $_{23\%}$	$23 $_{31\%}$	$45 $_{31\%}$	$76 $_{15\%}$
by "I'd love it!" group	$38	$8 $_{20\%}$	$21 $_{25\%}$	$40 $_{27\%}$	$73 $_{28\%}$

and consequently the veracity of responses. We term these questions types: *General* questions, *Positive Assumption* questions, and *Negative Assumption* questions.

General questions pose a broad inquiry about a situation, a good or a service (e.g. "How is the project going?"). General questions lack a specific line of investigation and convey the impression that the asker might not be knowledgeable about the topic of discussion. *Positive Assumption* questions ask about a specific issue, but communicate the assumption that no problems exist (e.g. "The project is not likely to run over budget, is it?"). These questions reveal an awareness of a possible issue, but either a lack of concern or interpersonal discomfort with pursuing an assertive line of questioning. *Negative Assumption* questions ask about a specific issue, and communicate an implicit assumption that a problem exists (e.g. "How much over budget is this project likely to run?"). Negative Assumption questions communicate knowledge of potential problems and comfort with pursuing an assertive line of questioning.

In our study, participants negotiated with a confederate regarding the sale of a used iPod. We assigned every participant to the role of "Seller" and randomized them into one of three conditions. Across conditions, the confederate asked a General, a Positive Assumption, or a Negative Assumption question. The participants were provided several pieces of information about the iPod including color, age, memory capacity, and working condition. In particular, we were interested in whether participants would reveal to their counterpart that the iPod has a history of undiagnosed crashes, which in the past have resulted in the loss of all stored music.

In line with the predictions of the Question Disclosure Model, participants judged negotiation counterparts who asked a Positive Assumption or Negative Assumption question to be more knowledgeable than counterparts who asked a General question. They also judged counterparts who asked a Negative Assumption question to be more determined to gather accurate information than those who asked either a General or a Positive Assumption question. Consequently, the content of the responses and the valence of the responses differed across conditions, and these differences were mediated by the inferences participants made.

Most importantly, the information revealed in the question dramatically affected the likelihood that participants revealed the truth about the working condition of the iPod. Participants were much more likely to inform the buyer that the iPod had a history of crashing when they were asked a Negative Assumption question (89.0%) than when they were asked a Positive Assumption question (61.1%), *chi squared*(1) = 15.2, $p < .001$, or a General question (8.1%), *chi squared*(1) = 95.2, $p < .001$, (comparing Positive Assumption and General question conditions, *chi squared*(1) = 45.5, $p < .001$). Supporting the QDM, participants changed both the content and valence of the response as a function of questions they received.

Our work suggests that consumers readily draw inferences about others based on the questions they ask. Furthermore, such inferences lead to changes in important behaviors, such as revealing unfavorable information in the course of a transaction. Prior research has considered questions strictly as a tool for gathering information. The Question Disclosure Model provides a framework for investigating the manner in which questions reveal information and the effects of this phenomenon on consumer behavior.

Feeling Mixed? When, Why and To What End Do We Feel Mixed Emotions?

Chair: Patti Williams, University of Pennsylvania, USA

Paper #1: Finding Meaning in Mixed Affective Experiences

Sayantani Mukherjee, California State University Long Beach, USA

Thomas Kramer, University of South Carolina, USA

Loraine Lau-Gesk, University of California Irvine, USA

Paper #2: Putting the Consumer in the Picture: Visual Perspectives and Mixed Emotions in Advertising

Iris Hung, National University of Singapore, Singapore

Anirban Mukhopadhyay, Hong Kong University of Science and Technology, China

Paper #3: Mixed Emotional Experience is Associated With and Precedes Improvements in Well-Being

Hal E. Hershfield, New York University, USA

Jonathan M. Adler, Franklin W. Olin College of Engineering, USA

SESSION OVERVIEW

Over the past decade, scholars in marketing and psychology have investigated whether individuals can experience mixed emotions, the psychological processes associated with such experiences and the individual differences and situational factors that make them more or less likely. The majority of this work has focused on understanding when individuals are likely to experience discomfort in response to mixed emotions (e.g. Williams and Aaker 2002), with findings suggesting young, Caucasian Americans and those with a concrete construal mindset (Hong and Lee 2010) likely to experience discomfort and thus to find mixed emotions aversive.

Building upon, and yet in contrast to this previous work, the papers in this session suggest that mixed emotions are frequent experiences, even among those for whom past research has suggested they might be aversive. Mixed emotions may, in fact, even be deliberately sought. The papers in this session suggest that mixed emotions may be integral to goal pursuit and personal achievement, can be an essential component in meaning making, particularly in the face of adversity, may be perceived as reflecting reality, and can be processed fluently depending upon an individual's perspective toward them.

The first paper in this session (Mukherjee, Kramer & Lau-Gesk) suggests that consumers may not always want to avoid mixed affective experiences, particularly in the domain of goal pursuit and personal achievement, because a combination of positive and negative experiences is associated with the creation of meaning. In particular, the addition of some negative affect to goal pursuit can enhance feelings of accomplishment through hardship. This research suggests that while mixed-ness can be aversive when individuals are focused on the process of goal achievement, a focus on the outcome links mixed-ness to meaning-making and to more enjoyment of the experience itself.

The second paper (Hung and Mukhopadhyay) examines the impact of visual perspectives on the fluency with which consumers process advertising evoking mixtures of hedonic and self-conscious emotions, and hence on attitudes to products featured in the appeals. Results show that consumers who adopt a third-person, observer perspective process self-conscious emotional ads more fluently and evaluate them more favorably, while consumers adopting a first-person, actor perspective process ads that highlight hedonic emotions more fluently and evaluate them more favorably.

The third paper (Hershfield and Adler) suggests that concurrent experiences of conflicting emotions in times of adversity can ultimately lead to greater well-being over time. Individuals who sought therapeutic treatment for a wide variety of life events were asked to write about their experiences. These narratives were coded and results show that blends of happiness and sadness in response to therapy were associated well-being over time. As in the first paper, this research suggests that the blends may not have been pleasant at the time of their experience, but are shown to have a prospective influence, such that the impact of mixed emotions on well-being unfolds over time.

This session is likely to be of interest to ACR members studying emotions generally as well as those studying mixed emotions and those who are investigating well-being and how consumers find meaning in consumption experiences. The session furthers the conference's mission of appreciating diversity in a variety of ways. First, the papers investigate mixed emotions in a variety of settings, from the more traditional advertising context, to video game playing and to coping with life-stressors and therapeutic interventions. The papers in the session also examine a variety of different types of mixed emotions, from happiness and sadness to mixtures of hedonic and self-conscious emotions. Previous work on mixed emotions has focused upon when mixed emotions can be construed as more or less negative and aversive. This session, in contrast to that previous literature, focuses upon when mixed emotions might actually be processed fluently, actively pursued and associated with meaning-making and enhanced well-being, which is a substantial contribution to the current literature on mixed emotions.

Finding Meaning in Mixed Affective Experiences

EXTENDED ABSTRACT

Past research has shown that mixed affective experiences generally are aversive unless consumers find a way to cope with their associated discomfort (Williams and Aaker 2002). Yet consumers often knowingly seek out experiences that elicit both positive and negative affect. For example, skydivers find enjoyment from feeling intense happiness and fear during their jump (Celsi, Rose, and Leigh 1993). Thus, many mixed affective experiences are those that consumers actually wish for rather than wish to avoid. Responding favorably to this type of mixed affective experience seems not a function of coping with unpleasantness, but rather enjoying its pleasantness. Departing from past research which examines mixed affective experiences that consumers want to avoid, we investigate those that consumers actually desire. Specifically, we address two interrelated questions. First, can mixed affective experiences be more enjoyable than pure positive ones? And second, what makes such mixed affective experiences enjoyable to consumers?

We propose that in the context of mixed affective experiences that involve goal pursuit and personal achievements, mixed affective experiences can be more enjoyable than pure positive ones because consumers derive more meaning from the experience. This is based on past research which has discussed the importance of goal pursuit in deriving meaning where meaning is defined as having a sense of purpose and attainment of goals that are important to an individual (King et al. 2006). Thus, mixed affective experiences that involve goal pursuit not only are associated with mixed affect but are also likely to be linked with meaningfulness. In turn, consistent with research showing that meaningfulness is often associated with greater levels of enjoyment (Csikszentmihalyi 1990), we suggest that consumers may seek out and enjoy mixed experiences from which they derive meaning. Further, we argue that mixed affective experiences can be enjoyed more than pure positive ones. This is because when engaged in goal pursuit, consumers may infer that detriments, such as negative affect, are necessary evils to experience on the way to success, as popularized by the expressions of "no pain, no gain," or "the road to accomplishment is through hardship." For example, Kramer et al. (2011) found that consumer responses to medications with severe, as compared to mild, side effects were more favorable. Further, a bad-tasting cough syrup was judged to be more effective at fighting colds than a good-tasting one. Likewise, Loewenstein (1999) found that the pain endured during mountain climbing reveals one's strength under harsh conditions to others.

To test our proposition, we directly examined mixed affective experiences that involve goals and personal accomplishments, such as mastering a videogame or a challenging mountain bike ride. We conducted a field study in a videogame arcade where 41 patrons played a videogame of their choice. After playing the game, participants reported their affective intensity and overall evaluations. As expected, results showed that participants evaluated the experience as significantly more enjoyable when it was mixed versus pure positive (6.09 vs. 5.5; $F(1, 39) = 4.64$, $p < .05$). In our second study, we examined the mediating role of meaningfulness. We also included felt discomfort measures to rule it out as an alternate mediator to demonstrate the novelty of desirable mixed affective experiences. Further, since we suggest that consumers obtain meaning from mixed affective experiences when such experiences are associated with goals and personal achievement, we theorized that this effect should emerge when consumers focused on the end goal (of accomplishment). Thus, in the next study, we manipulated the focus of participants' thoughts to either emphasize the end goal of achievement (outcome-focus) or emphasize the process or steps that lead to the goal (process-focus) (Escalas and Luce 2003).

One hundred and fifteen undergraduate students participated in a study on mountain-biking. A 2 (affective experience: mixed vs. pure positive) X 2 (focus: outcome vs. process) ANOVA on participants' enjoyment yielded the expected affective experience X focus interaction ($F(1, 111) = 4.62$, $p < .05$). Enjoyment of the mixed affective experience was significantly greater than the pure positive one (6.53 vs. 6.00; $F(1, 111) = 5.49$, $p < .05$). However, type of affective experience did not impact the level of enjoyment for participants in the process focus condition (6.15 vs. 6.26; $F(1, 111) = .31$, $p > .10$). To examine whether meaningfulness mediated the interaction between affective experience and focus on enjoyment ratings, a mediated moderation analysis was conducted (Muller, Judd, and Yzerbyt 2005). Results showed that the effect of type of affective experience on enjoyment is mediated by meaningfulness. However, and as expected, the observed effects only emerged for consumers who were focused on the outcome or end goal of the experience, as compared to the process. Further, findings showed that felt discomfort did not mediate the joint influence of type of affective experience and focus on enjoyment.

Together, the findings from our two studies show that mixed affective experiences are not only enjoyable but they can even provide more enjoyment than pure positive affective experiences. This adds to research across different domains of mixed experiences such as mixed affect (Williams and Aaker 2002) and cognitive dissonance (Elliott and Devine 1994).

Putting the Consumer in the Picture:
Visual Perspectives and Mixed Emotions in Advertising

EXTENDED ABSTRACT

Advertising appeals that describe a consumption experience often elicit mixed emotions. Typically, such advertisements portray cognitively complex stimuli or phenomena (Larsen, McGraw, and Cacioppo 2001). For example, Williams and Aaker (2002) studied responses to an ad for a brand of photographic film, where a person was ostensibly commenting on a photograph of themselves as a baby posed with their now deceased grandmother. The commentary here was in the first person. ("My Nana, Emma, passed away this past year... I loved sharing time with her. I miss her...".) What factors influence the effectiveness of such mixed-emotional advertising? In this research, we investigate how the use of different visual perspectives, e.g., first versus third person, might influence consumers' responses to such mixed appeals. In so doing, we aim to identify one important factor that facilitates the processing of appeals that elicit mixtures of emotions, and therefore influences attitudes towards the advertised products.

Consumers viewing advertising such as the above may visualize the advertised situation and transport themselves into it in one of two ways. They may view the situation in the first person as if they are living it, as in William's and Aaker's stimuli, or they may observe the situation as if they are watching a movie of themselves. In either case, they may use the elicited emotions as bases for evaluating the product (Sujan, Bettman and Baumgartner 1993; Escalas 2007). Hung and Mukhopadhyay (2012) demonstrated that the visual perspectives people take to view a given situation influence the intensity of the emotions people experience, such that people who take an actor's (i.e., first person) perspective feel stronger hedonic emotions whereas those who take an observer's perspective experience stronger self-conscious emotions. Based on this, we argue that when depicting mixed emotions, ads that use an actor's (observer's) perspective facilitate the processing of the hedonic (self-conscious) emotions involved. The ease with which the emotion is processed should consequently increase evaluations of the advertisement as well as the advertised product.

Product consumption often involves simultaneous experiences of different specific emotions (Larsen et al. 2001; Williams and Aaker 2002). For example, an ad portraying the consumption of a late-night snack because one has to study for an exam thereby foregoing a concert by one's favorite band might elicit both the hedonic emotion of sadness (for missing out on the concert) and the self-conscious emotion of pride (for studying hard). Hedonic emotions such as excitement and sadness are relatively spontaneous and can be elicited without much cognitive deliberation whereas self-conscious emotions such as pride and guilt are characterized as being accompanied by thoughts about how others might evaluate me/the desirability of my behavior (Leary 2007). Given the difference in the nature of these emotions, recent findings show that visual perspectives, which dispose people to focus on different aspects of information (Jones and Nisbett 1972), might influence people's experience of these emotions (Hung and Mukhopadhyay 2012). Actors, who pay more attention to situational circumstances, might respond more fluently to aspects of events that elicit hedonic emotions. Observers, who pay more attention to the 'me' in the situation (i.e., as if one is seeing a movie of oneself), might respond more fluently to aspects of events that elicit self-conscious emotions.

Building on these findings, we examine the role of visual perspectives in responses to advertising appeals which feature product consumption experiences that typically elicit mixed emotions. We propose that actors' (observers') perspectives should facilitate the processing of an appeal that highlights a hedonic (self-conscious) emotion in a product consumption experience that typically elicits a mixture of hedonic and self-conscious emotions. Consequently, the ease with which actors (observers) process the appeal should increase evaluations of the appeal itself as well as the advertised products.

Three experiments support these propositions. Participants took either an actor's or an observer's perspective to process an appeal that described a product consumption experience eliciting a mixture of hedonic and self-conscious emotion (experiments 1 and 3). Regardless of the valence of the emotion highlighted, actors evaluated the ad and the advertised product more favorably when the ad highlighted a hedonic emotion than observers did. In contrast, observers evaluated the ad and the advertised product more favorably when the ad highlighted a self-conscious emotion than actors did. Experiments 2 to 3 further examined whether similar effects of visual perspectives occur when the use of visual perspectives were subtly manipulated by the appeal. Participants processed an ad describing a mixed-emotional experience that elicits a positive (negative) hedonic emotion of excitement (sadness) and a negative (positive) self-conscious emotion of guilt (pride). The mixed-emotional experience involved either studying in the library while one's favorite band was in concert (simultaneous sadness and pride), or attending the concert despite an exam the next day (simultaneous excitement and guilt). The visual for the ad featured a photograph of a library scene or a concert scene, as viewed on a mobile phone. The text in the ad however highlighted only one of the four emotions involved: positive hedonic (excitement), negative hedonic (sadness), positive self-conscious (pride), or negative self-conscious (guilt). Visual perspectives were manipulated integrally, using tag-markers on the photograph itself. Participants reported their attitudes towards the ad, and the advertised products. Across three studies, results consistently showed that the ad and the advertised product were evaluated more favorably when participants took an actor's (observer's) perspective to view a mixed-emotional situation that highlighted a hedonic (self-conscious) emotion. This effect was mediated by the ease of processing the appeal, and was observed when the visual perspective was induced incidentally as well as integrally by the advertisement, and whether the advertisement was viewed subsequently or simultaneously.

Overall, this research contributes to the understanding of the conditions under which mixed emotional appeals are likely to be fluently processed, thereby increasing consumers' evaluations of advertised products. This research also sheds new light on the role of visual perspectives in the impact of appeals that depict integral and mixed emotions, by examining the relative impact of mixed emotions that might typically be elicited in product consumption experiences portrayed in emotional appeals. Theoretical and practical implications will be discussed in the session.

Mixed Emotional Experience is Associated With and Precedes Improvements in Well-Being

EXTENDED ABSTRACT

The respective benefits and drawbacks of positive and negative emotional experience on well-being have been well documented (e.g., Lyubomirsky, King, & Diener, 2005). Yet, considerably less attention has been given to the ways in which the experience of mixed emotions – that is, the concurrent experience of positive and negative emotions – can affect well-being. A notable exception is the co-activation model of health proposed by Larsen and colleagues (2003), which holds that experiencing positive emotions concurrently with negative emotions may detoxify them, transforming a negative emotional experience into fodder for meaning-making and subsequently enhanced well-being. Although recent work has tested the postulates of Larsen's model on physical health (Hershfield, Scheibe, Sims, & Carstensen, Under review), very little research to date has directly examined the connection between mixed emotional experience and enhanced well-being. In the present study, we investigated whether mixed emotional experience – specifically the concurrent experience of happiness and sadness - prospectively benefits improvement in well-being. The context for this investigation was a naturalistic longitudinal study of psychotherapy in an outpatient clinic. Psychotherapy is fundamentally concerned with emotional experience (Greenberg & Safran, 1987) and provided an opportunity to assess the unfolding relationships between mixed emotional experience and well-being. The present study aims to demonstrate that concurrent happiness and sadness may temporally precede improvements in well-being.

When facing negative events in the course of one's life, people may choose to either suppress negative emotions (Gross & John, 2003) or express them (e.g., Pennebaker, 1997). There are benefits and drawbacks to both approaches, but failing to confront negative events can ultimately lead to increased stress levels (Pennebaker, Kiecolt-Glaser, & Glaswer, 1988). Larsen and colleagues (2003) propose that a third strategy, one of "taking the good with the bad", might actually benefit individuals during difficult times by allowing them to confront adversity and ultimately find meaning in life's stressors (a eudaimonic outcome), as well as to feel better in their wake (a hedonic outcome). In their co-activation model, allowing for the experience of positive emotion alongside negative emotion prompts individuals to face negative life events and gain insight into them. Larsen and colleagues' model thus suggests that during difficult situations, a mix of positive and negative emotions may be optimal for well-being. For instance, when experiencing the loss of a loved one, allowing positive memories to be experienced alongside sadness could potentially lead to a healthier bereavement process (Folkman & Moskowitz, 2000). As Davis and colleagues (Davis, Zautra, & Smith, 2004) note, one key to resilience across the adult life span, may be the "ability to maintain affective complexity in the face of life's inevitable difficulties" (p. 1155).

Although prior work offers preliminary evidence for the positive role that the blending of positive and negative emotion can play in well-being, none has systematically examined the *prospective* benefits that mixed emotions may have on well-being over time in a fine-grained way. Thus, in the present study, we sought to examine whether mixed emotional experiences are prospectively linked to enhanced well-being.

Forty-seven adults (M_{age} = 36 years) who sought treatment at a major outpatient clinic for a wide variety of problems, ranging from significant psychopathology to more typical life events such as divorce or the transition to parenthood, were enrolled in the present study prior to beginning treatment. In order to tap a broad conception of well-being encompassing both hedonic and eudaimonic elements (Ryan & Deci, 2001), the Systemic Therapy Inventory of Change was selected as the primary outcome measure (STIC; Pinsof & Chambers, 2009). To assess the emotional content of participants' experiences in psychotherapy, we collected private narratives about participants' perspectives on treatment. The present study asked participants to reflect in writing on their thoughts and feelings associated with being in therapy, including the way they saw the treatment fitting into their overall life or sense of self. As such, the narratives discussed both participants' life events as well as their experiences in treatment.

A team of two trained raters (undergraduate research assistants, trained by the first author, who were blind to the hypotheses of the study and unfamiliar with the coactivation model) coded the narratives for their emotional content. Previous theoretical and empirical work on mixed emotional experience has taken a broad approach to operationalizing the construct, including generic categories of "positive" and "negative" emotional experience. In contrast, in the present study we sought to empirically identify the specific blend of positive and negative emotions that are associated with improvements in well-being. Given that happiness and sadness were the only specific emotions to show a significant relationship with well-being over time, the six other specific emotions were dropped from subsequent analysis and a composite variable, representing instances when happiness and sadness co-occurred, was created.

The primary analytical strategy applied growth curve modeling to the data. This technique is well-suited to accommodate missing data and unbalanced spacing of assessment points, both of which are inevitable in data collected from a naturalistic sample. The results indicate that participants who experienced a concurrent mixture of happiness and sadness during the course of treatment enjoyed subsequent improvements in their well-being. This finding remained significant when controlling for the impact of the passage of time as well as that of dispositional personality traits associated with affect. In addition, the results suggest that the significant association between the experience of concurrent happiness and sadness is uniquely related to well-being at the following assessment point, but not concurrently, when controlling for the independent impacts of happiness and sadness themselves. In other words, mixed emotional experience was seen to have a prospective influence on well-being, but its concurrent association with well-being was explained by the independent effects of happiness and sadness. This suggests that mixed emotional experience may have a distinct prospective potency; its association with well-being unfolds over time. Thus, while the concurrent experience of happiness and sadness in the face of adversity might not provide immediate benefit, it may signal enhancements in well-being in the near future.

Numerical Cognition:
Numbers and Their Downstream Consequences for Consumer Behavior

Chair: Bart de Langhe, University of Colorado at Boulder, USA

Paper #1: Numerical Cognition and a Mere-Looking Effect in Multi-Attribute Choice

Ellen Peters, Ohio State University, USA
Louise Meilleur, Ohio State University, USA

Paper #2: Need for Speed?

Bart de Langhe, University of Colorado at Boulder, USA
Stefano Puntoni, Erasmus University Rotterdam, The Netherlands

Paper #3: Tipping the Scale: Discriminability Effects in Measurement

Katherine Burson, University of Michigan, USA
Richard Larrick, Duke University, USA

Paper #4: When to Put the Cart in Front of the Horse: How Presentation Order of Goal Reward and Effort Information Affects Goal Pursuit

Derick F. Davis, Virginia Tech, USA
Rajesh Bagchi, Virginia Tech, USA
Yong Kyu Lee, Virginia Tech, USA

SESSION OVERVIEW

Numerical stimuli in marketing are ubiquitous. For example, they are used by companies to communicate the performance of products or information about product attributes, they facilitate the interpretation of rating scale anchors, and they are used by consumers to monitor goal progress. Examining how consumers extract meaning from numbers is therefore crucial to understanding consumer decision making. This symposium consists of four papers that interconnect at different levels. Together, they provide new perspectives on numerical cognition and, more generally, the psychology of consumer decisions.

The first paper, by **Peters and Meilleur**, shows that numerical information drives early attention and subsequent choices. They argue that low Arab numerals are associated with a focus of visual attention to the left and that high Arab numerals are associated with a focus of visual attention to the right. Presenting a low (1) versus high (9) digit between two decision options also impacts choice in line with the authors' selective attention account.

The second paper, by **de Langhe and Puntoni**, draws attention to a factor contributing to consumers' willingness to pay for technological progress. The performance of many technologies is expressed in terms of speed (e.g., Internet bandwidth). Four studies show that consumers misunderstand the relationship between increases in speed and time savings. They hold the belief that the same increment in speed provides the same time saving regardless of whether the initial speed is low or high, even though time savings become in fact smaller as speed increases. The studies also show how to reduce this bias by drawing attention to time (e.g., via experience or by restructuring numerical information).

The third paper, by **Burson and Larrick**, examines how perceptions of magnitude affect conclusions about attribute importance that are inferred from conjoint studies. By multiplying a ratio scale by an arbitrary factor, numerical scales that are used to describe product attributes can be contracted (e.g., 1-10) or expanded (e.g., 1-100). The relative importance of attributes inferred from conjoint studies is greater when the scale is expanded, but decreasingly so because of decreasing sensitivity.

The fourth paper, by **Davis, Bagchi, and Lee**, investigates how the order of presentation of effort and reward information affects goal pursuit and examines the role of numerosity in this effect. In three studies, they manipulate the numerosity of the metric used to express the amount of effort required to meet a goal and found that in the presence of large number (connoting high effort requirements), presenting the rewards before the effort reduces effort salience and energizes consumers.

Because of the fundamental importance of numerical cognition for understanding consumer psychology, we expect this special session to be of interest to a wide audience. The session will appeal to researchers on topics as diverse as (1) motivation and goal achievement, (2) marketing research, scaling, and conjoint analysis, (3) attention, (4) decision making, and (5) innovation. Data collection in all papers is complete and the session features a total of 13 studies using a variety of paradigms and methods (e.g., choice, conjoint, priming). All participants have agreed to present, should the session be accepted. The chair will facilitate audience discussion drawing further connections between the new perspectives introduced in this session and other areas of consumer research.

In sum, we believe that this proposal fits both the spirit of ACR special sessions and the theme of the conference—appreciating diversity. In addition to the diversity of approaches to numerical cognition that the papers exemplify, the session also brings together researchers from different areas of research, including marketing, management and psychology. The participation of Ellen Peters, a leading psychologist and numeracy researcher, is especially noteworthy.

Numerical Cognition and a Mere-Looking Effect in Multi-Attribute Choice

EXTENDED ABSTRACT

Selective attention has been a long-standing theme in decision research (Einhorn & Hogarth, 1981; Weber & Johnson, 2009), but studies have not manipulated early attention in complex, multi-attribute decisions outside of awareness and independent of participant goals. In the present paper, we take advantage of symbols learned in early childhood – integers from 1 to 9 – that are not obviously directional but have been shown to have a left-to-right spatial orientation that can subtly shift attention (Dehaene, Bossini, & Giraux, 1993; Fischer, Castel, Dodd, & Pratt, 2003).

In four studies, we used these incidental attentional shifts to test their influence on high-level cognitive processes involved in multi-attribute binary choices. Of course, just because individuals look in the direction of information does not mean that they process or use it in decisions. However, some evidence exists for a disproportionate influence of early information on decisions (Weber & Johnson, 2009; DeKay et al., 2009; Russo et al., 2006). Thus, we hypothesized that presentation of an incidental small or large Arabic digit (physically located between two choice options) would shift visual attention to the left and right options, respectively, and information attended earlier would disproportionately influence information processing and choice – a mere-looking effect.

Results of the present four studies provided converging evidence, across diverse decision paradigms, to support the causal role of covert and overt shifts of attention in influencing the processing and valuation of decision options. In Study 1, the attention shift created by implicit cues – a "1" or "9" – located between two real choice options produced preference reversals. Faced with a simple choice between two identical erasers, "1" participants were more likely than "9" participants to choose the left-side eraser (65.2% and 33.3%, respectively; $\chi^2(df=1)=4.5$, p=0.03, $\varphi=.32$). Study 1 provided evidence that the presentation of Arabic integers activated magnitude and shifted early attention to information that influenced choice. The effect occurred despite spatial attention being driven exogenously, from a normatively irrelevant and incidental source.

In Study 2, participants chose between two hypothetical vacation spots – one with average attributes; the other with both positive and negative attributes (materials adapted from Shafir et al., 1993). In a 2x2 between-subjects design, participants were shown either a large "1" or "9" in the middle column, with enriched Spot B's positive or negative attributes on top. When the enriched option was attended early, top-to-bottom attribute order significantly influenced choices; when the average option was attended early, the top-to-bottom order of attributes for the enriched option had little influence (interaction: Wald $\chi^2(df=1)=9.1$, p=0.003, f=.22). In particular, when attention was directed left ("1"), B's attribute order did not influence choice; 60% versus 62% of participants chose Spot A when B's negative versus positive attributes, respectively, were on top. However, among "9" participants (attention directed rightward), significantly more participants chose left-side Spot A when B's negative attributes were on top (85%) than when its positive attributes were (47%). Mere looking did not produce simple liking of whatever is looked at first; instead, it biased choices based on processing the first-attended information.

Studies 1 and 2 provided initial evidence that the spatial orientation of the mental number line can orient attention and alter choices when no real difference exists between options (Study 1) or when the choice is hypothetical (Study 2). Study 3 provided evidence that "mere looking" at information matters in choices among consumer goods, specifically when choosing between a decision of the head and a decision of the heart. In this case, participants chose between two snacks – one that tasted better and another that was healthier. Such choices involve a tradeoff between perceived taste and healthiness; how individuals process these tradeoffs is unclear, however. Previous studies have indicated that decreasing available cognitive capacity can increase choices of the less healthy option (Shiv & Fedorikhin, 1998). In the present Study 3, cognitive capacity was not altered; instead, attention was simply directed first at one option or the other. Participants chose between Regular and Baked Lays (counterbalancing their left/right order) with "1", "9", or nothing between them. When nothing was in between the snacks, 69% and 19% of participants, respectively, chose Baked Lays, respectively, when it was on the left or the right. This result is congruent with previous eye-tracking results indicating that about 75% of participants in a binary choice look at the option on the left first (Krajbich et al., 2010). With Baked Lays on the left and using the attention manipulation, participants were more likely to choose them in the "1" condition compared to the "9" condition (60% and 31%, respectively, chose Baked Lays). With Baked Lays on the right, the effect reversed, with participants significantly less likely to choose them in the "1" than the "9" condition (47% and 75%, respectively, chose Baked Lays).

Finally, in Study 4, choices between 41 food pairs that varied in perceived healthiness and tastiness were made with "1", "9", or "5" between options in each pair. Our prior choice effects were replicated. Preliminary analysis of eye tracking data supported the hypothesized information-processing mechanisms.

That the attentional effects of conventional, overlearned symbols can guide attention and influence choices suggests a strong link between visual attention and choice. Broader implications of this and other research also further highlight the constructive nature of choice (Lichtenstein & Slovic, 2006; Payne, Bettman, & Schkade, 1999), and, importantly, point towards some of the subtle influences that marketers and other information providers can exert on choices.

Need for Speed?

EXTENDED ABSTRACT

Technology often advances by increasing the speed of specific processes and, consequently, by reducing the time required to perform a particular task. Marketers tend to express the performance of time-saving technologies in terms of their speed. For example, the performance of computers' CPU is expressed in megahertz (MHz = cycles per second), Internet bandwidth is expressed in megabits per second (Mbps), the performance of printing technologies is expressed in pages per minute (ppm), and the performance of kitchen robots is expressed in rotations per second (rps). Increases in speed result in time savings. The speed of a product is thus a diagnostic *feature* allowing consumers to assess the *benefit* they receive in terms of time saved.

Marketing theory suggests that, to maximize sales, in their communication to consumers marketers should focus on benefits as opposed to features. This suggests that marketers' focus on speed may negatively affect consumers' willingness to pay for technological progress. Our research shows that, in fact, consumers are willing to pay more for time-saving technologies when marketers highlight speed rather than time. This result occurs because consumers misunderstand the relationship between speed increases and time savings. They think this relationship is linear (i.e., an increase in speed has the same effect on time saved regardless of whether speed is low or speed is high), while in fact the relationship between speed and time is nonlinear (i.e., an increase in speed has a larger effect on time saved when speed is low than when speed is high).

In a first study, participants indicated how much they were willing to pay for 5 data transfer speeds (1MBps; 2 MBps; 3 MBps; 4 MBps; 5 MBps). Before indicating their willingness to pay, about half of participants were given the opportunity to actually experience how long it takes to download a 30 MB file with each transfer speed. For participants without actual experience, willingness to pay was linearly related to increases in data transfer speed. For participants with actual experience, willingness to pay was linearly related to time savings.

In a second study, participants rank-ordered five increases in printer speed (ppm) in terms of time saved (A: 15 ppm to 30 ppm; B: 5 ppm to 15 ppm; C: 18 ppm to 26 ppm; D: 12 ppm to 17 ppm; E: 7 ppm to 10 ppm). Participants' rank-order reflected increases in speed (A > B > C > D > E). That is, participants believed that larger increases in terms of ppm also result in larger time savings, while the correct ordering in terms of time saved should have been: B > E > A > D > C.

In a third study, participants were asked to choose between four kitchen robots that differed in terms of speed and price (A: 2.50 rps for $200; B: 3.33 rps for $250; C: 4.17 rps for $300; D: 5 rps for $350). For half of participants, we also highlighted the performance of the kitchen robots in terms of time savings. These participants were also presented with the performance of each kitchen robot in terms of seconds per rotation (A: 0.4 spr; B: 0.3 spr; C: 0.24 spr; D:

0.2spr). Participants receiving restructured numerical information in terms of seconds per rotation were more likely to choose a less expensive kitchen robot. While rotations per second highlights speed, seconds per rotations facilitates mental calculations regarding time saved.

To extend our findings to a setting where "slower is better", we also examined a situation where consumers pay a certain amount of money for a service per unit of time. In the context of mobile phone plans, for instance, consumers pay a specific rate where a lower cost per unit of time (i.e., a slower outflow of money) is preferred over a higher cost per unit of time (i.e., a faster outflow of money). In a fourth study, participants were asked to imagine they were willing to spend $50 per month on their mobile phone plan. We told participants that their current provider considered increasing their rate. Participants were asked how likely they were to switch to another provider if their current provider decided (a) to increase their rate from $0.10 to $0.15 per minute and (b) to increase their rate from $0.20 to $0.30 per minute. If participants accurately assess how the rate increase affects the number of minutes they can call for $50 per month, they should be more likely to switch when their rate increases from $0.10 to $0.15 (i.e., a loss of 167 minutes) than when their rate increases from $0.20 to $0.30 (i.e., a loss 83 minutes). However, participants indicated they would be more likely to switch when their rate increased from $0.20 to $0.30, again reflecting the erroneous mapping of speed on time.

In sum, companies' focus on communicating speed when promoting time-saving technological improvements of existing products leads consumers to overvalue technological progress. We will discuss the importance of our findings for marketers, but also for public policy makers.

Tipping the Scale: Discriminability Effects in Measurement

EXTENDED ABSTRACT

In Ireland, a District Court judge reduced the speeding charge of a driver who had been clocked going 180 kilometers per hour in a 100 kilometer per hour zone. Looking at this decision, an outside observer might conclude that the court believed the driver's speed was less important in the decision than, say, his previous driving record. However, the judge's explanation for the decision was that the speed did not look "as bad" when converted into 112 miles per hour in a 62 mile per hour zone (Associated Press, 2007). Objectively, speeding by 80 kph is still violating the law by the same proportion as speeding by 50 mph and thus warrants the same penalty. Any scale with ratio properties can be converted from one scale to another (without changing the information provided by the scale) by multiplying the original values by some constant factor. However, this trivial transformation is psychologically consequential, as is clear in this example: The expanded scale highlights the difference between the speed limit and the driver's speed, making that difference seem large. In contrast, the contracted scale minimizes the difference (Pandelaere, Briers, & Lembregts, 2011).

There are decades of research on how people perceive and interpret numerical attributes in psychology and in marketing. In summarizing these traditions, Mellers and Cooke (1994) propose a three-stage sequence by which a perceiver evaluates a multi-attribute object. First, there is a perceptual stage in which specific attribute levels are translated into internal representations. Then, there is a weighting stage in which different internal representations of attributes are combined into an overall judgment. Finally, there is a response stage in which an overall judgment is expressed as a judg-

ment or choice. Market researchers attempting to understand consumer behavior often try to back attribute weighting (the second stage) out of observed preferences or choices (the final stage). For example, conjoint researchers infer participants' attribute importance from their responses. We argue that, like an outside observer of the Irish court decision, conjoint researchers may inappropriately attribute observed choices to attribute importance when what is actually guiding choice is the internal representation of the difference in products.

To test this hypothesis, we expand and contract attribute scales in a conjoint design and observe the impact on choice and inferred attribute importance. We propose that these manipulations directly influence internal representations because people focus on the attribute value and neglect the attribute's scale magnitude—alternatives seem more different on that expanded attribute and are encoded as such. This leads to shifts in choice, and thus in attribute importance inferred using the usual conjoint method. We go on to verify that the *actual* importance of attributes to participants is *not* influenced by scale expansion, only the internal representation. In addition, we show that because of diminishing sensitivity to scale expansion, extreme scale expansion does not continue to influence that internal representation.

Specifically, in each of two studies, we find that participants' choices closely track the expanded attribute in the conjoint design, replicating past research (Burson, Larrick, & Lynch, 2009). Because conjoint analysis determines the relative importance of a particular attribute by observing its impact on choices relative to the impact of other attributes, the natural conclusion of a market researcher examining one of our conditions in isolation would be that the attribute using an expanded scale is a very important attribute to consumers. Critically, however, our experiments show that this cannot be the case because that importance seems to vary from condition to condition. For example, in Study 1 one attribute appeared to be the most important attribute in choice when it was presented on an expanded scale (54%), but appeared to become less and less influential when it was contracted (44%). A similar pattern was revealed in Study 2 (relative importance of expanded conditions = 62% vs. contracted condition = 46%). These results are a statistical artifact. Just as the Irish judge in our opening example did not suddenly discount the importance of speeding in his penalty decision, participants in our studies are not revising the importance of product attributes. Rather, attribute expansion directly influences internal representations of products—exaggerating differences in products—but importance of an expanded attribute is no greater than that of a contracted attribute.

We confirm that relative importance is a statistical artifact by examining the rated importance of each feature. There was no change in these ratings in response to scale expansion. Furthermore, scale expansion was found to impact mental representations of the alternatives: Participants believed that an attribute had larger differences in the expanded conditions.

These findings have important implications for market researchers as our studies show that attributes represented on expanded attributes only *appear* to have inflated importance in consumer choice. The interpretation of a conjoint analysis will be sensitive to attribute expansion, thus marketers should take care when they choose how to infer preferences or how to describe their products. Furthermore, Study 2 also reveals that, due to diminishing marginal utility, scale expansion has its limits: Expanding an attribute from a 100 point to a 1000 point scale did not increase preference for the product that performed well on that attribute, nor the inferred importance of the attribute. Therefore, market researchers should also recognize the boundaries of scale effects.

When to Put the Cart in Front of the Horse: How Presentation Order of Goal Reward and Effort Information Affects Goal Pursuit

EXTENDED ABSTRACT

Why do consumers often fail to begin working towards a beneficial goal? One possibility may be that while effort has to be invested immediately, the benefits occur later. Thus, effort may be more salient at the outset and may overweigh perceptions of the benefits to be accrued from the outcome later. How can effort perceptions (effort salience) be altered to initiate action and/or goal-pursuit? We suggest that changing the presentation order of goal outcome and effort may influence how salient the effort is and may affect goal-pursuit.

Most research has focused on how motivation to pursue goals can be increased as the reward gets proximal. For instance, animals and humans have been shown to move faster when approaching a reward (Hull 1932; Kivetz, Urminsky, and Zheng 2006). Endowing consumers with progress at the outset can also increase acceleration (Nunes and Dreze 2006). However, it is not always possible to endow progress (e.g., when preparing for an exam, it is not possible to tell students that they have already reviewed a few chapters). We show one way in which consumers can be motivated to pursue goals at the initial stages of goal-pursuit.

We argue that when the effort involved in attaining a goal is perceived to be large (e.g. expressed via high numerosity; To get an "A" review 300 pages), presenting the reward first (To get an "A") followed by effort (review 300 pages) reduces effort salience relative to when effort is presented first followed by reward (Review 300 pages to get an "A") and has beneficial effects on goal-pursuit. This effect of information presentation order on effort is attenuated when smaller numerosities are used to express effort (To get an "A" review 10 (30 page) chapters). We demonstrate this effect in three studies. In study 1 we show the basic effect. In study 2, we show that this effect only occurs when the outcome is far (and thus effort required is large) and provide process support. Finally, in study 3, we prime focus (outcome vs. process), and show that the order effects persist when focus is on outcomes (vs. process), and show meditational support.

Study 1: Reviewing Course Materials for a Grade

We used the scenario described above. We told undergraduates the requirements to get an "A" in a class and manipulated presentation order and numerosity, as described above. Thus, we used a 2 Order (reward-effort vs. effort-reward) x 2 Numerosity (high vs. low) full factorial between-subjects design. Participants indicated the likelihood of pursuing an "A", effort perceptions, and the likelihood of recommending this class to friends. An ANOVA revealed the predicted order x numerosity interaction ($F (1, 96) = 4.01, p < .05$) for pursuit likelihood. Participants were more likely to pursue an "A" when reward was presented first in the high numerosity condition ($M_{reward-effort} = 5.71$ vs. $M_{effort-reward} = 4.64; p < .02$), but no difference emerged when numerosity was lower ($M_{reward-effort} = 6.19$ vs. $M_{effort-}$

$_{reward} = 6.25; p > .85$). Similar patterns emerged for perceptions of effort (interaction: $F (1, 96) = 4.31, p < .05$) and recommendation likelihood (interaction: $F (1, 96) = 5.33, p < .05$).

Study 2: Pursuing a Loyalty Reward

Participants learned that they could earn a reward upon accruing a certain number of points (effort). We manipulated presentation order by stating the reward first or the effort first. In the high (low) numerosity condition, 1,000 (100) points were needed. However, the step-sizes were also higher (10 vs. 1 point(s) per dollar). Therefore, the amount needed to earn the reward was constant ($100). Participants were either close to or far away from the reward. We thus used a 2 Order (reward-effort vs. effort-reward) x 2 Numerosity (high vs. low) x 2 Reward Distance (far vs. near) design.

Analysis revealed three-way interactions with consistent patterns of means across a range of dependent variables; program attractiveness ($F(1,335) = 4.72, p < .04$), likelihood of earning the reward ($F(1,335) = 5.38, p < .03$), satisfaction ($F(1,335) = 2.78, p < .10$), positive store perceptions ($F(1,335) = 3.03, p < .09$), recommendation likelihood $F(1,335) = 4.55, p < .04$, store loyalty ($F(1,335) = 6.76, p < .009$). Presenting reward first had a positive effect on the aforementioned variables relative to presenting the effort first when numerosity was high and the reward was far. Order effects did not emerge in other conditions. We also found that progress perceptions mediated the three-way interactions reported above.

Study 3: Priming Focus on Outcome or Process

Study 3 used a scenario similar to that used in study 2. We only used the far conditions and primed participants to focus on the outcome of achievement or on the process involved in achievement. We used a 2 Order (reward-effort vs. effort-reward) x 2 Focus (outcome vs. process) between-subjects design. Analysis revealed two-way interactions for program attractiveness ($F(1,152) = 5.64, p < .02$), satisfaction ($F(1,152) = 6.44, p < .02$), positive store perceptions ($F(1,152) = 4.78, p < .04$), and loyalty ($F(1,152) = 3.41, p < 0.07$). A consistent pattern of means appeared for these variables; the presentation order of reward and effort influenced perceptions with outcome-focus, but not with process-focus. Thus, when focusing on the process, effort is salient regardless of order. Although, priming people to focus on the outcome reduces the salience of effort, this salience is restored when effort is presented first. Progress perceptions mediated the effects of the variables reported above.

Conclusions

Findings are consistent across three studies—the presentation order of goal reward and effort information influences perceptions when the effort required to attain the goal is expressed in a high numerosity medium and the goal is distant. When goal reward is presented first, individuals see the goal in a more positive light relative to when the effort is presented first. We argue that presentation order influences the salience of the effort required, which in turn, influences perceptions related to the goal. We discuss implications and future research.

Mental Representations of Uncertainty and Risk
Chair: Bart de Langhe, University of Colorado at Boulder, USA

Paper #1: Lay Understanding of the First Four Moments of Observed Distributions: A Test of Economic and Psychological Assumptions

David Rothschild, Yahoo! Research, USA

Daniel G. Goldstein, Yahoo! Research, USA

Paper #2: Recency and Reference-Point Formation: The Effect on Risky Choice Behavior

George Wu, University of Chicago, USA

Michael Yeomans, University of Chicago, USA

Paper #3: The Role of Payoff Ratio in Decision Making Under Uncertainty

Bart de Langhe, University of Colorado at Boulder, USA

Stefano Puntoni, Erasmus University Rotterdam, The Netherlands

Paper #4: Outcome Neglect: How Guessing Heuristics Supersede Expected Value

Oleg Urminsky, University of Chicago, USA

Adelle Yang, University of Chicago, USA

SESSION OVERVIEW

Dealing with uncertain decision outcomes is a paramount challenge in consumer decision making. Consumers choose between brands while having imperfect knowledge about product quality; they participate in lotteries with different probabilities and outcomes; they choose between financial products with great uncertainty about future returns. Despite the complexity of dealing with uncertain prospects, consumers make decisions like this on a daily basis, and strikingly, most often they do this relying on judgment only. This session consists of four papers that provide new perspectives on consumer choice by showing how consumers' mental representations of risky prospects deviate from central assumptions made by standard psychological and economic models of decision making.

The first paper, by Rothschild and Goldstein, examines whether laypeople can comprehend and estimate the statistical moments (mean, variance, skewness, and kurtosis) of observed numerical information. The survey tradition in economics assumes only aggregated responses are useful and the behavioral literature suggests individual estimates are biased (e.g., the overconfidence and related literatures). Rothschild and Goldstein, however, show that laypeople's understanding of these subtle statistical moments is more accurate than is currently believed. New methods based on graphical interfaces allow non-experts to produce accurate estimates of all four moments of a distribution.

The second paper, by Wu and Yeomans, examines how people form reference points when choosing between risky decision alternatives. Most empirical tests of prospect theory either use the status quo as the reference point or code the outcomes relative to some pre-determined reference point. Wu and Yeomans show, however, that reference point formation is affected by very basic attentional processes. Because people use the most recent outcome as a reference point (a recency effect), they are more likely to choose a risky gamble when outcomes are revealed in an ascending rather than descending order. This is because individuals are typically risk-averse when gambles are framed as gains, but risk-seeking when the same outcomes are coded as losses.

The third paper, by de Langhe and Puntoni, examines how people mentally integrate uncertain gains and losses. Landmark norma-

tive and descriptive theories of decision making (like expected value theory and prospect theory) assume that people integrate, or combine, uncertain gains and losses using an additive integration rule (gain − loss). De Langhe and Puntoni show, however, that people show the pervasive tendency to rely on the payoff ratio (gain/loss), implying multiplicative integration of gains and losses. Reliance on the payoff ratio when choosing between mixed gambles leads to (1) suboptimal monetary outcomes when payoff ratio and expected value are dissociated and (2) to risk seeking (aversion) when choosing between mixed gambles with a negative (positive) expected value. The latter finding qualifies prospect theory's prediction of general risk aversion for mixed gambles.

The fourth paper, by Urminsky and Yang, shows that the maximization of expected utility can best be seen as one of many potential heuristics available to people. Depending on the goal that is activated by the context (e.g., accurately guessing a number in a lottery), people may rely on many other potential heuristics. They show that in both lab and field studies, when people have to guess an amount they could win, they neglect the fact that higher guesses represent the same probability of winning but a higher conditional payoff. They label this effect "outcome neglect".

The mental representation of uncertainty and risk is a fundamental topic that is likely to appeal to a wide audience, for instance, researchers interested in behavioral decision theory, behavioral economics, attention, numerical cognition, and consumer financial decision making. In line with the spirit of ACR special sessions and the theme of the conference—appreciating diversity—the session also brings together research scientists with different backgrounds such as marketing, management, and business (Yahoo!). The participation of George Wu, a world-renowned expert on decision making under uncertainty, is especially noteworthy. All participants have agreed to present, should the session be accepted. The chair will facilitate audience discussion drawing further connections between the new perspectives introduced in this session and other areas of consumer research.

Lay Understanding of the First Four Moments of Observed Distributions: A Test of Economic and Psychological Assumptions

EXTENDED ABSTRACT

Numbers abound in everyday life; laypeople regularly observe prices, sizes, distances, and beyond. Mental representations of this information can inform decision making, much as statistical summaries inform scientific inference.

Economic theory suggests that people coordinate subjective expectations with subjective utilities to determine what actions are undertaken. A fairly standard assumption in modeling is that individuals have perfect expectations. When generalizing from empirical data, it is similarly standard to only trust revealed behavior as the expression of both expectations and utility. Thus, economists study utility by assuming perfect expectations and study expectations by assuming rational utility calculations.

The practice of surveying assumes that, in aggregate, individual estimates of the first moment are unbiased. However, the individual decision making tradition has long reported biases that affect individual-level expectations, such as anchoring effects, primacy effects, recency effects, and attention to local maxima (e.g., peak-end biases).

While expected to be unbiased in aggregate, the view that individual-level estimates of expected value are accurate has no champions. Indeed, the "wisdom of the crowd" logic is based on that idea that estimates are inaccurate, though in symmetrical ways.

In survey research, it is common to ask laypeople what they believe to be an "average" value. However, there are many measures of central tendency, such as mean, median, and mode, and it is not clear which definition respondents assume.

The psychological literature assumes that estimates of the second moment are too narrow, the so-called overconfidence effect, which is moderated by various question formats that lead to better calibration and discrimination. We test, under the various elicitation techniques, whether estimates of distributions exhibit systematic overconfidence. Finally, there has been little research in any discipline on lay intuitions of third and fourth moments: skewness and kurtosis. Our tests of understanding the third and fourth moments help establish a baseline and gauge human sensitivity to higher moments.

In this research, we control the statistical information presented to decision makers and then gauge the degree to which people's perceptions of the first four moments are accurate. In order to simulate the natural flow of numerical information that decision makers might encounter in watching the news or observing prices over time, we provide participants with sequences of 100 numbers, drawn from six distinct beta distributions of varying shapes. Randomly assigned groups use one of multiple elicitation techniques to express beliefs about the quantities they observed.

At the start of the experiment, the participants are told "Imagine we have a bag with a million ping pong balls in it. Each ball has a value between 1 and 20 written on it. In the next 100 seconds, we will randomly choose 100 balls from the bag and show you their values." When the presentation begins, each number appears on screen for 3/5 of a second so that the participant sees 100 numbers in one minute. Participants are told "Now imagine we are throwing the 100 balls back into the bag and mixing them up. We will now draw 100 balls at random from the bag. We will refer to this as our *second draw*." After this, participants are randomly assigned to one of four main question sequences.

In the first condition we ask the respondents to create a full probability distribution that would describe the second draw. We do this by providing a graphical user interface with which the respondent can distribute 100 balls into buckets representing the 20 possible numbers of the distribution.

The second condition elicits fractiles of a distribution by asking respondents to "think about our second draw of 100 balls [and] imagine they were arranged in front of [the respondent] with the smallest values on the left and the largest values on the right. " We then ask them to provide the likely values of the 5th, 25th, 50th, 75th, and 95th balls from the left.

The third and fourth conditions address the first moment directly. In the third condition we ask the respondent to provide the mean of the second draw, providing the definition of a mean. This contrasts with the fourth condition, in which we ask for the "average" of the second draw, leaving the participants free to interpret the term as they wish, with the purpose of gaining insight into how people understand the term "average".

The fifth condition addresses the second moment directly. Participants are asked to provide the value they are 90% certain a random ball would be greater than and, in addition, a value they are 90% certain a random ball would be less than.

The sixth and seventh conditions take a step back and address the full distributions, rather than the moments that define them. In the sixth condition, participants try to identify the distribution they observed in a forced-choice task involving two histograms. The seventh condition is identical, except that participants choose between tables of numbers.

By way of results, we find that laypeople are able to produce accurate estimates of all four moments of a distribution: point-estimates -- including distinctions between the mean, median, and mode -- confidence ranges, and representations of the skewness and kurtosis. We show how the "average" relates to these different measures and that laypeople are able to make meaningful distinctions between these different kinds of average when they utilize a graphical elicitation method. Using new methods, including graphical interfaces that allow the specification of an entire distribution, we allow non-experts to expressed information that they have, but would be unable to communicate in ordinary surveys.

Recency and Reference-Point Formation: The Effect on Risky Choice Behavior

EXTENDED ABSTRACT

Prospect theory posits that outcomes are evaluated relative to a reference point (Kahneman & Tversky, 1979), with individuals typically risk-averse when gambles are framed as gains, but risk-seeking when the same outcomes are coded as losses. However, most empirical studies either use the status quo as the reference point or code the outcomes relative to some pre-determined reference point (for exceptions, see Abeler et al., 2011; Camerer et al, 1997; Heath Huddart & Lang, 1999; Heath, Larrick & Wu, 1999). Until recently, there has been almost no empirical or theoretical literature on how reference points are determined and updated.

Recently, Koszegi & Rabin (2006, 2007, 2009) proposed a theoretical model in which reference points are "rational expectations" of future outcomes (see Arkes et al. (2008) and Baucells & Weber (2011) for two recent empirical studies of reference point formation). We suggest that Koszegi and Rabin's theory is an incomplete account of the process of reference point formation. Consider, for example, an investor who has seen a series of prices for a stock. Beliefs may not be rational because an investor believes in momentum or regression effects. Moreover, there may also be attentional or memory biases that may influence how individuals weight information and hence make decisions.

In this paper, we examine how a very basic attentional bias, recency, influences reference point formation and ultimately whether participants choose a risky gamble. We control explicitly for beliefs by providing participants with objective information about the choices involved. We nevertheless find that participants are more likely to choose the gamble over a sure thing if the highest value of the gamble is revealed last, rather than first. We argue that this result is consistent with a recency-based reference point account. If the largest outcome serves as a reference point, then outcomes will be viewed as losses, a domain in which individuals are most likely to be risk-seeking.

Study 1

Study1 used a 2 x 2 between-subjects design in which participants saw outcomes either in an ascending or descending sequence and were either endowed with a gamble or the expected value of a gamble. The three possible outcomes were $2, $3, and $10. Participants who were endowed with the gamble were given the option to switch to a sure thing of $5, while others were given the option to switching from a sure thing of $5 to the gamble. To increase the possibility of an attentional bias, participants completed 3 minutes of anagrams as a distraction after revealing each of the first two outcome values. After participants saw the final outcome, they were given the choice between the gamble or a sure thing (at EV).

Results

One hundred and forty participants were recruited through a downtown community sample. We analyzed the between-subjects effects of order and endowment in a binary logistic regression and found that both main effects are significant, with no interaction between the two. Participants gambled more when they were given the payments in ascending order (48.6%) than in descending order (33.3%). Participants also gambled more when they started with the lottery (50%) than when it was the sure thing (31.9%).

Discussion

We replicated Sprenger & Andreoni's (2011) finding of an endowment effect for risk, which could be the result of either an effect on risk preferences (Koszegi & Rabin, 2007), or a possession-based endowment effect (Brenner et al., 2007). We also find that participants gamble more when the last value was the highest than when it was the lowest, consistent with a recency-based account of reference point formation. One alternative explanation is that there is an effect of affect on risk preferences (Loewenstein et al., 2001) rather than an effect of attention on reference point formation. That is, participants may have felt happy after getting a high final value and which led them to be more risk-seeking. To rule out this alternative explanation, we must test multiple value sets, varying both the final value (low or high) and the relative order (ascending or descending).

Study 2

We conducted a second study to examine the robustness of our effect and to minimize the effect of positive affect. We implemented a within-subjects design and simplified the design from Study 1: the gambles had two rather than three outcomes and participants were always endowed with the gamble. We used 6 different gambles, ($1,$3), ($1,$6), ($1,$9), ($4,$6), ($4,$9), and ($7,$9), with each gamble shown in either ascending or descending order. To test for the ascending series as affect account, we used gambles in which the highest outcome was relatively low or relatively high.

During each of the 12 rounds of the study, participants learned the "heads" value of a coin, then spent 45 seconds doing anagrams as a distractor, then learned the "tails" value of the same coin, and finally chose between staying with the gamble or switching to a sure expected. After all 12 rounds, one of the 12 coins was randomly chosen from a bag and flipped "for real."

Results

Overall, participants were more likely to gamble when the same value pair was presented in ascending order (45.1%) than in descending order (40.3%). We found this directional pattern for 5 of the 6 series. A logistic regression, controlling for the fixed effects of value pair and participant, confirms this effect. A separate logistic regression that includes the value of the final outcome replicates this finding and shows no effect of that final value on risk preferences.

Discussion

We replicate the recency effect in a within-subjects design in another paradigm where beliefs are held constant. Note that we do not find evidence that the absolute level of the second value has an effect on risk preferences, which would be predicted by an affect account. Rather, we argue that increased attention on the second value, through both recency and the built-up anticipation during the anagrams, caused it to be a more salient comparison standard for the

choice. Consequently it received more weight as a reference point for evaluating the attractiveness of the gamble.

The Role of Payoff Ratio in Decision Making Under Uncertainty

EXTENDED ABSTRACT

Many decisions involve the possibility of financial gains and losses. Our understanding of decision making under risk is based on Expected Value Theory (Pascal, 1670/1966), Expected Utility Theory (von Neumann & Morgenstern, 1944), and Prospect Theory (Kahneman & Tversky, 1979). These landmark theories share the fundamental assumption that people integrate, or combine, expected gains and losses using an additive integration rule.

To illustrate, imagine that you are asked to choose between two gambles. With gamble A, you either win $5 or lose $9. With gamble B, you win $15 or lose $20. Which gamble should you choose, gamble A (+5, .50; -9, .50) or gamble B (+15, .50; -20, .50)? Additive integration implies subtracting expected losses (or a transformation thereof) from expected gains (or a transformation thereof). According to Expected Value Theory, for instance, the value of gamble A is -2 (i.e., EV_A = 2.5 - 4.5) and the value of gamble B is -2.5 (i.e., EV_B = 7.5 - 10). According to Prospect Theory, the value of gamble A is -5.72 (i.e., PT_A = 2.06 – 7.78)[1] and the value of gamble B is -10.29 (i.e., PT_B = 5.42 – 15.71). Both normative and descriptive theories of decision making therefore predict a preference for gamble A. We presented 109 college students trained in economics and statistics with this choice and 68% opted for gamble B ($\chi^2(1)$ = 10.96, p < .001). We claim that people prefer gamble B because it has a more attractive gain/loss ratio, or payoff ratio (i.e., 15/20 = 0.75), than gamble A (i.e., 5/9 = 0.56).

In general, additive integration is suitable when the quantities to be integrated are commensurable—that is when they have a common standard or belong to the same category—but is not suitable when the quantities to be integrated are not commensurable. For example, when choosing between two jobs differing in workload (measured in hours) and salary (measured in dollars), to compute a summary statistic that jointly considers time and money, one does not subtract the number of hours worked from total dollars earned. In situations where the quantities to be integrated are not commensurable, multiplicative integration is appropriate. For example, a useful statistic to compare the two jobs could be dollars per hour.

Additive integration thus assumes that gains and losses are commensurable. From a normative point of view, this is of course warranted because gains and losses are typically measured with the same standard (e.g., money). From a psychological point of view, however, the assumption that gains and losses, even when measured with the same standard, are perceived as commensurable is not straightforward. Recent developments in emotion research (Cacioppo, Gardner, and Berntson 1999, Larsen, McGraw, and Cacioppo 2001) and neuropsychology (Yacubian et al. 2006; Zhong et al. 2009) suggest that losses are not merely the opposite of gains, but that they are experienced as something different altogether. When evaluating risky decision alternatives, people may therefore have a natural tendency to integrate gains and losses using a multiplicative rule. If so, the payoff ratio is a summary statistic that people may be especially sensitive to.

In a theoretical analysis, we analytically derive the conditions under which payoff ratio, expected value, and prospect theory are

---

[1] Consistent with Tversky and Kahneman (1992), these estimates are based on a value function with an exponent of .88 and a loss aversion parameter of 2.25.

dissociated. This analysis also predicts that reliance on the payoff ratio as a proxy for expected value leads to risk aversion (seeking) for mixed gambles with a positive (negative) expected value, whereas prospect theory predicts general risk aversion for mixed gambles. Five empirical studies support the payoff ratio as an important driver of risky choice.

In our first study, participants rated one of four gambles on a scale from -10 (*extremely unattractive*) to +10 (*extremely attractive*): A(+4, .50; -2, .50), B(+8, .50; -5, .50), C(+2, .50; -4, .50), and D(+5, .50; -8, .50). Across both the positive (A and B) and the negative domain (C and D), participants rated the gambles with the higher payoff ratio, gambles A and D, as more attractive than the gambles with the lower payoff ratio, gambles B and C, although the gambles with the lower payoff ratio had a higher expected value.

In our third study, participants were asked to choose two times between pairs of gambles. The first pair of gambles was: A(+300, .50; -150, .50) and B(+500, .50; -200, .50). According to expected value, prospect theory, and payoff ratio, participants should favor gamble B. We constructed the second pair of gambles by adding a sure gain of $100 to all payoffs of the first pair of gambles: C(+400, .50; -50, .50) and D(+600, .50; -100, .50). Similar to the first pair, gamble D is superior to gamble C in terms of expected value and prospect theory. However, adding a sure gain of $100 reversed the rank of the two gambles in terms of payoff ratio. If individuals rely on payoff ratio to choose between gambles, we should observe a preference reversal across the two gamble pairs. Consistent with reliance on the payoff ratio, 78% of participants chose gamble B over gamble A and 64% of participants chose gamble C over gamble D.

In our fifth experiment, all participants are presented with a gamble A (+60, .50; -30, .50). Half of participants are presented with another gamble B (+80, .50; -__, .50) for which the loss is missing. The other half of participants are presented with a gamble C (+__, .50; -40, .50) for which the gain is missing. Participants are asked to match the two gambles in terms of attractiveness. We find that most participants match the payoff ratio of both gambles, but not the expected value.

We will discuss the implications of multiplicative integration for multi-attribute evaluations and attitude formation.

Outcome Neglect:
How Guessing Heuristics Supersede Expected Value

EXTENDED ABSTRACT

In decision-making, we often face situations where the goal of "getting it right" is highly salient, but the differences in consequences if we succeed may be more easily overlooked. Consider a common radio call-in contest: a winning number, representing the prize amount, has been selected within some known range, and the caller has to guess it. If the caller guesses correctly, she will win exactly that amount. Thinking in terms of expected utility (or any utility-maximization approach which incorporates probabilities and outcomes), the right strategy is to guess the highest possible number, as long as all payoffs have equal probability. However, we show that people very rarely use this strategy.

In the first study, participants made a single guess, for an amount drawn from a uniform distribution between $1 and $20, in increments of $.50. They were told that if they guessed correctly, they would win that amount of money, and that they would see the distribution of everyone's prize amounts at the end, to enable them to confirm. While the optimal guess was $20, 85% of participants gave a lower guess. The average guess was $13.11, significantly lower than $20.

In the second study, participants in a classroom setting played a sequential game. A prize amount was drawn at random from a pack of cards numbered between $1 and $10.95, in increments of $.05, in front of the participants. They then took turns guessing, and after each person's guess, all the participants were told whether the actual amount was higher or lower. When a participant guessed correctly, a new number was drawn, until all the participants had the opportunity to make one guess (4 rounds). Participants' guesses were scored from 1 (highest valid guess) to 0 (lowest valid guess). The average guess was .67, significantly lower than 1. While participants gave significantly higher guesses earlier in each round, there was no evidence of learning from observing others' outcomes (better guesses in later rounds). We also found some evidence that round numbers were more likely to be guessed.

In the third study, we analyzed 154 valid guesses made by callers to an actual radio contest, over the course of two months. In each game, a number between $750 and $2012 was chosen and callers made a guess. Similarly to Study 2, if the guess was correct, they won the guessed amount, but if not, whether their guess was too high or too low was announced on-air for the benefit of subsequent callers. Across 36 games, the first caller's guesses averaged $1381, significantly lower than the optimal guess of $2012. Rescaling all guesses to the interval between 1 (highest valid guess) and 0 (lowest valid guess), the average guess was .5, significantly lower than the optimal guess of 1. This did not vary with the time, number of elapsed guesses in that game, or the expected value of the best guess. These findings were confirmed with data from a second radio station contest with the same general format but a different audience demographic.

The field data confirms the presence of outcome neglect in a real-world setting with high potential stakes. It is important to note that callers' behavior could be explained by several alternative accounts, including not believing that the numbers were randomly drawn, wanting to help others by "narrowing down" the range of valid numbers or thinking that doing so might even benefit oneself in the future. However, the lab studies rule out any of these accounts.

Our findings have important implications for several lines of research. Our results suggest that maximizing utility is best seen as one of many potential heuristics available to people, which can be easily overlooked when the goal (e.g. "accurately guessing a number") suggests other heuristics as potentially more relevant. We will discuss the potential for re-framing manipulations to make utility maximizing heuristics more salient and thereby eliminate the effect.

While the irrationality of participants' behavior is clearly demonstrable in the specific setting we use, we argue that the basic notion of outcome neglect generalizes to many other goal-pursuit settings where the negative impact may be more difficult to identify. Arguably, a common mistake is to overinvest in low-payoff tasks because we want to "get it right", or to choose lower-payoff tasks strictly because of their feasibility, failing to adjust for the expected value. In these settings, outcome neglect may be an important cause. Lastly, we note that our findings represent a fairly strong failure of "wishful thinking", as participants' guesses did not reflect wishful thinking, even though it was in their interest to do so in this setting.

Identity Structure and the Boundaries of Identity Marketing

Chairs: Bella Rozenkrants, Stanford University, USA
Christian Wheeler, Stanford University, USA

Paper #1: Escaping the Crosshairs: Possibilities and Perils in Identity Marketing

Amit Bhattacharjee, Dartmouth College, USA

Geeta Menon, New York University, USA

Americus Reed II, University of Pennsylvania, USA

Jonah Berger, University of Pennsylvania, USA

Paper #2: When Do Consumers Prefer Mistargeted Products? The Effect of Structure and Competition on Preference for Identity-(In)Consistency

Julian Saint Clair, University of Washington, USA

Mark Forehand, University of Washington, USA

Paper #3: Repeated Exposure to the Thin Ideal and Its Implications for the Self: Two Weight-Loss Program Studies

Anne Klesse, Tilburg University, The Netherlands

Caroline Goukens, Maastricht University, The Netherlands

Kelly Geyskens, Maastricht University, The Netherlands

Ko de Ruyter, Maastricht University, The Netherlands

Paper #4: Identity Cues in Product Rating Distributions? The Role of Self-Concept Clarity in Consumer Preferences

Bella Rozenkrants, Stanford University, USA

S. Christian Wheeler, Stanford University, USA

Baba Shiv, Stanford University, USA

SESSION OVERVIEW

The powerful influence of identity on consumer behavior has captivated scholars and practitioners alike for decades (e.g., Belk, 1988; Levy, 1959). Identities that are salient (i.e., currently activated by context cues) guide behavior, and research demonstrates that consumers prefer products and messages that match their salient identity (Aaker, 1990; Wheeler, Petty, & Bizer; Reed, 2004). Accordingly, identity marketing has become a cornerstone of marketing theory and practice. But is simply seeking to match consumer identity enough? The present session presents evidence for the role of the consumer identity structure in preference and effectiveness of identity marketing. Specifically, we provide a deeper understanding of identity marketing by investigating the influence of identity clarity and identity structure on consumers' motivation to regulate and protect their identities.

The first two papers examine how features of the self-concept representation itself (specifically its clarity and integration) affect preferences and behavior. Rozenkrants, Wheeler, and Shiv examine the role of self-concept clarity, or the extent to which people have clearly defined identities or self-views. Results show that people with low-self concept clarity prefer products with bimodal rating distributions as opposed to unimodal rating distributions. This is because products with polarizing (liked by some and hated by others) ratings are seen as more self-expressive. Similarly, Saint Claire and Forehand examine inter-identity structure. They show that people approach identity mismatching when they hold an associated (highly integrated) inter-identity structure and inter-identity competition is low or when they hold a disassociated (weakly integrated) inter-identity structure and inter-identity competition is high. Effects are driven by inter-identity associations or by identity-valence associations depending on whether inter-identity competition is low or high, respectively. The latter two papers examine how features of identity marketing (specifically its explicitness and extremity) affect consum-

er preferences and behavior. Bhattacharjee, Menon, Reed, and Berger show that people who have a clear definition of an identity and high identity relevance are turned off by marketing that defines the terms of identity expression. Instead, these consumers prefer identity marketing that merely references their identity and does not threaten their freedom in identity expression. Klesse, Goukens, Geyskens, and de Ruyter examine the structure of current and ideal identities. They show that when women are primed with extremely idealized identities, such as skinny models, they ironically behave in ways that run counter to the ideal, and actually gain weight. These findings suggest that identities that are made salient through exaggeration are seen as unattainable because of the large discrepancy between the current and ideal selves.

Together, these papers[1] emphasize the importance of identity clarity and structure, and provide a more complete and integrative view of how self-concept and identity marketing interact to shape preferences and behavior. Given the fundamental nature of these concepts, we expect that the session will be well attended by researchers interested in branding, advertising, persuasion, social cognition, attitudes, and consumer backlash, as well as in self and identity. In highlighting both the diversity of consumer identities and diversity in the way those identities are represented, our session complements this year's theme of "Appreciating Diversity."

Escaping the Crosshairs: Possibilities and Perils in Identity Marketing

EXTENDED ABSTRACT

Marketing messages often appeal to consumers based on identities they possess. Jif peanut butter targets mothers by suggesting that, "Choosy Moms choose Jif." DirecTV advertises, "If you call yourself a sports fan, you gotta have DirecTV!" Similarly, Gamefly.com urges, "You call yourself a gamer? You have to have it!" Such approaches are consistent with decades of consumer research suggest that identity marketing leads to increased purchase and deeper loyalty (e.g., Berger and Heath 2007; Escalas and Bettman 2005; Levy 1959; Reed 2004).

In contrast, we propose that messages that explicitly connect consumer identity expression to the purchase of a particular product can backfire. Specifically, while marketing messages that merely reference consumer identity (*identity-referencing* messages) are beneficial, we argue that messages that explicitly define the terms of consumer identity expression (*identity-defining* messages) actually reduce purchase. The persuasive intent of identity-defining messages is especially salient, and thus, they may be perceived as an attempt to influence consumers and limit options for identity expression. Because autonomy is especially crucial in the context of identity expression (Deci and Ryan 1985; Kivetz 2005), these messages are likely to backfire. In order to reassert their autonomy, consumers may avoid products that would otherwise naturally resonate with their identity.

Five studies test this theorizing. An initial study sought to assess whether managers can anticipate consumers' need for autonomy in identity expression and craft messages accordingly. We expected that managers would prefer identity-defining messages,

---

1   All the papers are in advanced stage: either in the last stages of data collection or under review.

since they are more explicit and more clearly intended for the target segment. A panel of actual executives selected one of three messages to advertise an environmentally friendly, biodegradable soap to a segment of "green" consumers: "Charlie's: A good choice for consumers." (non-identity), "Charlie's: A good choice for green consumers." (identity-referencing), and "Charlie's: The only good choice for green consumers!" (identity-defining). As expected, managers preferred the identity-defining message ($\chi^2(2) = 7.36, p < 0.03$), and predicted that it would lead to higher purchase than both the non-identity baseline ($t(57) = 7.59, p < 0.001$) and the identity-referencing message ($t(57) = 2.06, p < 0.05$). Confirming our expectations, ratings of explicitness in targeting were highly correlated with predicted purchase and perceived consumer freedom in identity expression ($rs(58) > .67, ps < .001$).

A second study tested the accuracy of managerial predictions by testing these same messages in a consumption scenario. We also tested the mechanism underlying these effects in two ways. If these effects are driven by identity, as we suggest, then they should occur only among consumers whose target identity is salient (e.g., Reed 2004). Accordingly, we primed participants with a green versus neutral identity. Moreover, we tested the proposed mediating mechanism of freedom in identity expression. As expected, message type had no influence among neutral participants. However, among green participants, contrary to managerial predictions, the identity-defining message decreased purchase relative to the identity-referencing message ($t(68) = 6.54, p < .001$) and even relative to the non-identity baseline ($t(66) = 2.24, p < .03$). This effect was mediated by reduced perceptions of consumer freedom in identity expression ($b = -0.29, z = -3.61, p < .001$), supporting our theorizing.

A third study using the same stimuli built on these findings by measuring instead of manipulating identity. We also tested a real behavior: actual choice of a sample of the target versus a neutral soap. As predicted, these effects held for actual soap choice, and were moderated by identity centrality (i.e. the extent to which an identity is deeply important). Message type had a significant effect on soap choice among high-centrality participants ($\chi^2(1) = 9.94, p < .01$), but no effect among low-centrality participants ($\chi^2(1) = 2.29, p > .13$).

A fourth study examined our proposed mechanism using a different moderator: individual sensitivity to constraint (Hong and Faedda 1996). Moreover, to establish external validity, we used a sample of mothers and actual identity marketing messages from the marketplace: "Moms like you choose Jif" (identity-referencing) versus "Choosy moms choose Jif!" (identity-defining). Mothers reacted increasingly against the identity-defining message as individual sensitivity to constraint increased ($\chi^2(1) = 4.49, p < .04$), further clarifying the mechanism.

Finally, a fifth study investigated an instance in which autonomy might be undesirable: when consumers are highly uncertain about what an identity means to them. According to our theorizing, greater identity definition is likely to be preferred in such cases. To test our predictions, we primed parent identity certainty versus uncertainty (Gao, Wheeler and Shiv 2009). While certain parents reacted against identity-defining messages (vs. identity-referencing; $F(1,142) = 4.59, p < .04$), uncertain parents welcomed identity definition and actually increased purchase ($F(1, 142) = 5.98, p < .02$), supporting our theoretical account.

While the literature has focused exclusively on the possibilities of identity marketing, our findings highlight its perils. Together with the drive to construct and define the self, the need for a sense of autonomy in doing so is one of the fundamental motivations of

the self. Hence, considering consumer autonomy appears particularly crucial in the context of identity expression. Our findings simultaneously offer a caveat to the identity marketing literature and validate the power of the identity construct.

When Do Consumers Prefer Mistargeted Products? The Effect of Structure and Competition on Preference for Identity-(In)Consistency

EXTENDED ABSTRACT

A working-parent may prefer work-oriented products or family-oriented products depending on whether her employee or parent identity is active. Although the literature supports the notion that consumers have multiple identities and that priming a given identity can prompt approach toward identity-consistent (and avoidance of identity-inconsistent) preferences and behaviors (Forehand and Deshpande 2001; Forehand, Deshpande, and Reed 2002; Grier and Deshpande 2001; Zhang and Khare 2009), attention to the situations or factors that facilitate such response is sparse. We argue that two critical determinants of preference for identity (in)consistency are 1) The underlying inter-identity structure and 2) The level of inter-identity competition.

Past research within the Bicultural Identity Integration (BII) literature has shown that biculturals with a highly integrated, or "associated," inter-identity (II) structure demonstrate the typical identity priming effect whereby individuals approach behaviors consistent with the primed identity and avoid behaviors inconsistent with the primed identity. Alternatively, biculturals with a weakly integrated, or "disassociated," II structure demonstrate a contrastive effect wherein they avoid (approach) identity-consistent (-inconsistent) behaviors (Benet-Martinez et al. 2002; Cheng, Lee, and Benet-Martinez 2006; Mok and Morris 2009, 2010; see also Sacharin, Lee, and Gonzalez 2009; Zou, Morris, and Benet-Martinez 2008). These effects are argued to occur due to the positive and negative valence associations with cultural identity held by high and low BII consumers respectively (Benet-Martinez et al. 2002; Cheng et al. 2006; Mok and Morris 2009).

The above valence-driven effects are well established within the literature on cultural identity. However, it has also been suggested that consumers cognitively organize multiple identities within an associative network where identities may be associated or disassociated in a more benign, valence-neutral way (Amiot et al. 2007; Greenwald et al. 2002; Luna, Ringberg, and Peracchio 2008). As such, spreading activation suggests that priming one identity should inhibit the activation of disassociated identities (e.g., Hugenberg and Bodenhausen 2004) and facilitate the activation of associated identities. In this case, one would expect the typical priming effect in the presence of *disassociated* identities as individuals approach (avoid) the activated (inhibited) identity. Alternatively, when consumers possess associated identities one would expect dual approach of both the activated identity and the associated identity. These novel predictions are contrary to those of BII theory and are driven simply by the inter-identity association rather than by valence.

To reconcile the competing predictions regarding the influence of II structure on preference for identity (in)consistency, we propose that the predictions of BII will hold when II competition is high but not when II competition is low. The valence-driven effects of BII may be especially prevalent when two identities have a high degree of direct competition and associated stressors (Benet-Martinez and Haritatos 2005; Cheng et al. 2006). However, across the broader realm of consumer identities (e.g., student, female, sister, tennis player), high direct competition need not necessarily be the case. Thus, identities may be associated or disassociated in a more benign, valence-neutral way facilitating the predicted II association-driven effects.

We tested the foregoing predictions in three experiments. Across experiments we used scenarios to manipulate II structure and II competition between undergraduate participants' "student" and "friend" identities. We varied whether participants rated identity-consistent or identity-inconsistent products by priming an identity (student vs. friend) and presenting them with the same product targeted toward a matching or mismatching identity (student vs. friend).

In experiment 1 (n = 78), the interaction between Inter-Identity Competition and Identity-Product Consistency was significant ($p < .01$) such that when II competition was high (low), participants in a disassociated II structure had higher (lower) attitude ratings for the identity-inconsistent product relative to the identity-consistent product; $M = 5.78$ vs. 4.92 (5.03 vs. 5.93). This supported the notion that valence-driven BII effects are found under high competition but the novel II association-driven effects are found under low competition. In experiment 2 (n = 77) we further explored II structure's influence under low II competition. The interaction between II Structure and Identity-Product Consistency was significant ($p < .05$) such that participants in a disassociated II structure again had a lower relative preference for the identity-inconsistent (vs. –consistent) product; $M = 5.02$ vs. 5.80. Critically, participants in an associated II structure had no difference in relative preference between products, supporting the proposed dual approach model; $M = 5.86$ vs. 5.35. Experiment 3 (n = 109) further explores the counter-intuitive effect where an associated II structure leads to approach toward identity-inconsistent behavior. The interaction between II Structure and Identity-Product Consistency was significant ($p < .05$). Participants in a disassociated II structure rated an identity-inconsistent product equally to a control product which did not target a specific identity; $M = 5.27$ vs. 5.39. Participants in an associated II structure counterintuitively rated the identity-inconsistent product higher than the control product; $M = 5.92$ vs. 4.91. This pattern also held for a measure of purchase intentions ($p < .05$). The effects on preference were mediated by perceived product fit (Sobel $ps < .01$; Bootstrap $ps < .05$). When primed with their friend identity, for example, participants in an associated II structure actually felt that a *student*-targeted product fit their needs. This supports the notion that priming a given identity also activates associated identities and their inherent needs and preferences.

In sum, the present research provides an important update to identity theory by demonstrating that consumer preference for identity (in)consistency depends on both inter-identity structure and inter-identity competition. Under high II competition consumers demonstrate the typical preference for identity-consistency only with an associated II structure; consumers actually counter-intuitively approach identity-*in*consistency under a disassociated structure. Under low II competition, the typical preference for identity-consistency is found only under a disassociated structure; the counterintuitive approach toward identity-consistency is found under an associated structure. Considering that the broader realm of identity is likely to have low II competition, marketing campaigns should encourage an associated II structure to facilitate approach.

Repeated Exposure to the Thin Ideal and its Implications for the Self: Two Weight Loss Program Studies

EXTENDED ABSTRACT

Body image is an important part of our identity (Harter 1999). Through comparing ourselves to others we become aware of our self-image and of how we would (or should) want to look like (Festinger 1954). Nowadays, the media bombards us with models that are considerably thinner than the majority of the female population (Levine & Smolak 1996) and, hence, constitute an ideal out of reach for most women. The consequences of this exposure have been researched abundantly, primarily demonstrating that self-esteem and body satisfaction decrease when dieters are exposed to thin media images (Grabe, Ward, & Hyde 2008).

Surprisingly, existing research on the behavioral consequences has been limited to a single exposure and assessment of eating behavior right afterwards. Our research adds to and advances existing research by taking a goal perspective and exploring how constant exposure to thin models influences dieters' desire to reach a thinner self over time. We believe a longer time perspective is needed during which the motivation to reach the desired ideal and eating behavior is concurrently investigated. Accordingly, we explore over time whether being constantly confronted with the thin ideal motivates or demotivates dieters to obtain a thinner self.

On the one hand, exposure to thin models could motivate dieters to obtain a thinner self: Specifically, research on the nonconscious effects of subtle cues on behavior suggests that primes activate more enduring effects when the prime is perceived as distant form the active self-concept (Sela & Shiv 2009). In this context, a perceived discrepancy between individuals' active self-concept and the cue signals that the goal has not been attained and, hence, functions as a motivator (Dijksterhuis, Chartrand, & Aarts 2007). However, on the other hand, according to the goal gradient hypothesis (Hull 1934) or the 'goals loom larger' effect (Brendl & Higgins 1995) the motivation to attain a certain goal increases as the desired end state approaches. That is, if a goal becomes closer and easier to attain, individuals become more confident (Tubbs, Boehe, & Dahl 1993) and allocate more effort in order to reach the desired end state.

We conducted two weight loss program studies (each lasted for one week) in order to explore whether constant exposure to the thin ideal increases or decreases individuals' motivation to reach a thinner self and fosters goal consistent or inconsistent behavior over time. For both studies we invited female students that wanted to lose weight. They received an eating diary enabling them to note down exactly what they ate after every consumption occasion (i.e., breakfast, lunch, dinner, and snacks in between). For half of the participants the cover of the diary featured an extremely thin model while for the other half of the participants the cover featured a neutral dieting-related image (study 1) or a moderately thin model (study 2). Participants were weighted at the begin and the end of the weight loss program.

The findings of study 1 (N= 48) demonstrate that constant exposure to the thin ideal while trying to lose weight backfires: participants who were exposed to the thin model (Mt = 4.08) perceived a thinner self as significantly less attainable than participants in the control condition (Mc = 5.08; $F(1,46) = 6.29$, p < .05). Further they (Mt = 1284.75) consumed snacks higher in calorie content than the control condition (Mc = 754.15; $F(1, 46) = 4.92$, p < .05) and gained weight (Mt = -.23) rather than lost weight as the control condition ($F(1, 46) = 5.24$, p < .05; Mc = .87)[2].

---

2   We express the weight gain/loss not in absolute terms but in relation to participants' initial weight. A negative value implies

In study 2 (N = 42) both conditions are exposed to a model. However, while the treatment condition is confronted with an extremely thin model the control condition is exposed to the same but normal-sized (photoshoped) model. This enables us to test whether particularly the exposure to an unrealistically thin model triggers the perception that the thinner self is unattainable and causes individuals to give up. Study 2 reveals a significant difference in weight loss success: while participants exposed to the moderately thin model manage to lose weight (Mc = .013), participants confronted with the extremely thin model did not lose weight (Mt = .003; F(1, 40) = 6.56, p < .05). Following Zhao, Lynch, and Chen (2010) we applied a bootstrap test to establish whether perceived attainability mediates this effect. The results reveal the mean indirect effect to be positive and significant (a x b = .0022), with a 95 % confidence interval excluding zero (.0051 to .0001).

While existing research has demonstrated that exposure to thin models influences dieters' motivation to diet and eating behavior, the assessment was limited to behavioral consequences right afterward. In this research, we show that it is important to explore the consequences of exposure to thin model cues over time: although the omnipresence of thin models in our environment fosters the desire for a thinner self, it at the same time, hampers individuals' attempt to reach this ideal identity. By this, an individual realizes that the thin ideal is, for her, not that easy to attain which results in disengagement from the goal.

Existing research on self-identity has shown that several activities help to build a stock of knowledge about oneself. For instance, individuals develop several self-schemata (Markus 1977), which are specific ideas or pieces of information about the self and its characteristics. In forming these self-schemata individuals think of recent experience of success or failure they have had (Baumeister 2010). We add to this by showing that exposure to thin models changes the importance that individuals attach to certain self-schemata and the willingness to engage in actions needed to obtain their ideal self. That individuals engage in goal inconsistent behavior, i.e. eating unhealthy snacks (study 1), to a greater extent after repeated exposure to a thin model implies that this constant confrontation with their ideal self, decreased individuals' motivation to achieve it.

Identity Cues in Product Rating Distributions: The Role of Self-Concept Clarity in Consumer Preferences

EXTENDED ABSTRACT

Online retailers like Amazon synthesize consumer reviews in terms of means and distributions of star ratings. Whereas the mean rating conveys the average liking for the product, the distribution conveys the level of agreement among consumers. The present research probes how the shape of rating distributions and levels of agreement among reviewers affect consumer preferences.

Distinctiveness theory posits that people selectively focus on traits that emphasize their peculiar and unique characteristics (McGuire, McGuire, Child, & Fujioka, 1978; McGuire & McGuire, 1988). The need to establish distinctiveness is particularly salient when people feel uncertain about themselves (Baumgardner, 1990). Frequently, this uncertainty is addressed by adherence to firm and extreme attitudes (Sherman, Hogg, & Maitner, 2009). Hence, people have a heightened need to achieve distinctiveness and clarify their self-concept when they are uncertain about who they are.

One indicator of self-certainty is self-concept clarity. Self-concept clarity reflects the extent to which people hold clearly defined self-beliefs (Campbell, 1990). Generally, it is the sense of knowl-

edge about who you are and what you stand for. Because lacking certainty and clarity in one's self-views is aversive (McGregor & Marigold, 2003), those with low self-concept clarity are motivated to establish a consistent self-view. Because choice of products with identity-relevant characteristics helps maintain a well-defined identity through time (Kleine, Kleine, & Allen, 1995), one way to rectify a compromised self-concept is to choose products to re-establish and clarify a certain identity (Englis & Solomon, 1995; Gao, Wheeler, & Shiv, 2009). We propose that another way to satisfy this need is by choosing polarizing products, because products that are not homogenously liked help consumers differentiate themselves.

The shape of rating distributions signals the degree of consensus regarding product appeal and allows consumers to assess their preferences relative to others. Unimodal distributions are clustered around a particular rating, decline in the tails, and convey a clear consensus on the level of appeal. On the other hand, bimodal distributions have two clusters, with one cluster in the high ratings and the other one in the low ratings. Because bimodal distributions indicate a lack of consensus about a product, products with bimodal rating distributions can make one more distinctive, and hence be more self-defining.

Because preference for products with bimodal distributions suggests disagreement with a larger share of people than in the unimodal condition, people who are motivated to hold a clearer self-view should favor products with bimodal distributions. Thus, we predict that as compared to high self-concept clarity consumers, those with low self-concept clarity should find products with bimodal distributions more appealing.

In experiment 1, we examined people's lay theories about rating distributions. Participants chose the product types (generally liked, generally disliked, or polarizing) that they perceived to be the most informative about one's identity and most self-expressive. These measures created a single factor of identity relevance, with polarizing products seen as the most identity relevant, $c^2(2) = 101.87$, $p <.01$.

In experiment 2, we examined the influence of self-concept clarity and rating distributions on product evaluations. Participants saw a movie poster ("Contagion"), along with the movie synopsis, and were randomly assigned to see the bimodal or unimodal distribution (same mean rating). Ratings of the perceived quality, likelihood of enjoyment, and likelihood of seeing the movie were consolidated into a desirability factor. We measured self-concept clarity using a validated scale (Campbell et al., 1996). A significant interaction emerged, $b = -0.74$, $t(145) = -2.41$, $p = .017$, such that participants with low self-concept clarity preferred movies with bimodal distributions, whereas participants with high self-concept clarity preferred movies with a unimodal distribution.

The purpose of experiment 3 was to manipulate self-concept clarity. Participants were randomly assigned to complete a task designed to lower or heighten self-certainty (Hogg, Sherman, Dierselhuis, Maitner, & Moffit, 2007). They then completed the self-concept clarity scale. Next, participants were asked to imagine they were considering movie purchase and were provided with ratings (unimodal or bimodal) from previous viewers. This was done to ensure that the use of the specific movie in experiment 2 did not drive the results, because of genre or other confounding factors. This was followed by the experiment 2 desirability questions. Although the certainty manipulation did not have a direct effect on movie preferences, a moderated mediation path was significant, 95% CI [-0.2123, -0.250]. Participants in the uncertainty condition had lower self-concept clarity scores, and this led them to have higher preferences for the movie with a bimodal, relative to unimodal, distribution.

weight gain.

We conducted experiment 4 to explore whether group polarization was driving this effect. To clearly convey polarization, we simplified our distributions into three categories: like, dislike, or neutral. The procedure mimicked experiment 3, except that the feedback from previous consumers was polarizing [neutral], "65% really enjoyed the movie" and "35% really disliked [had neutral feelings about] the movie." Results revealed a significant interaction, $b = -0.41$, $t(162) = -2.04$, $p = 0.04$. Although participants high in self-concept clarity preferred the movie with the neutral ratings, this effect was attenuated for participants low in self-concept clarity, despite the fact that the polarizing movie had an objectively lower rating than the neutral movie.

Our examination of the role of product rating variance in product evaluation shows an influence of self-concept clarity. Surprisingly, this need to clarify one's identity persists despite the negativity bias. Adding to the identity driven consumption literature, the results suggest that polarizing products may provide a way for self-uncertain consumers to feel a sense of certainty and assert their identity. This implies that retailers should look to rating distributions to understand their customers, and attempt to appeal to self-uncertain consumers (e.g. adolescents) with polarizing products.

Beyond the "Pain of Paying:"
The Role of Specific Emotions in Consumers' Reactions to Prices and Payment Decisions

Chair: Shelle Santana, New York University, USA

Paper #1: Price Discounting for Emotional Impact
Aylin Aydinli, London Business School, UK
Marco Bertini, London Business School, UK

Paper #2: Do Emotions Increase or Decrease Present Bias in Monetary Decisions?
Manoj Thomas, Cornell University, USA
Joowon Park, Cornell University, USA

Paper #3: Emotional Effects of Purchase Price-Reference Price Divergence
Isabelle Engeler, University of St. Gallen, Switzerland, USA
Christian Laesser, University of St.Gallen, Switzerland, USA

Paper #4: Beyond Clarity and Confusion: Affective Responses to Price Framing in the Airline Industry
Shelle Santana, New York University, USA
Vicki G. Morwitz, New York University, USA

SESSION OVERVIEW

Apart from Prelec and Loewenstein's (1998) "pain of paying," research on the specific role that emotions play in consumer reactions to prices and to payment decisions has been sparse. The papers presented in this session aim to close this gap by examining how affect and emotions influence reactions to price promotions, the present value of money, discrepancies between reference prices and purchase prices, and price framing. Although pricing has received considerable attention from marketing researchers, the approach has been almost exclusively from a cognitive perspective. The goal of this proposed session is to expand our current understanding of the role that emotions play in pricing and payment situations. Each paper investigates this research objective from a unique theoretical perspective using different methodological approaches.

The first paper by Aydinli and Bertini examines the relationship between consumers' emotional responses and price promotions. Applying a dual process account of decision making, the authors posit and show that price promotions reduce the motivation for thinking and pave the way for affective decision making. As a result, price discounting results in stronger preference for emotionally-laden products as well as valuations that are scope insensitive and more polarized. Results from five experiments support the authors' hypotheses and shed new light on the emotional implications of price promotions.

The second paper by Thomas and Park shows that negative emotions can have a positive effect on consumer financial decision making. In contrast to the widely held view that emotions are detrimental to rational decision-making, the authors show that emotional decision making can reduce the present bias in consumers—especially for those who are predisposed to regret spending money (Tightwads). Three experiments show that when consumers are primed with feelings (vs. calculation), they exhibit reduced levels of present bias in financial decisions. Results from a third study using skin conductance to measure arousal provide further support.

The third paper by Engeler and Laesser posits that specific emotions arise from discrepancies between a consumer's purchase price and various reference prices. Specifically, when a purchase price is lower than a consumer's maximum WTP, consumers will experience pride in themselves about their positive consumer surplus. However,

when a purchase price is lower (higher) than their expected reference price, consumers will experience gratitude (anger) toward the seller. Three field studies widely support these predictions. Furthermore, these emotional states related to self- versus seller attributions predict post-purchase behavior such as positive WOM and repurchase intentions.

The fourth paper by Santana and Morwitz examines consumers' emotional responses to different ways airlines present prices that include fees. This topic has received considerable attention in both the popular press and from government agencies in the wake of new regulatory requirements calling for more price clarity and transparency from airlines. Three laboratory studies show that some common ways that fees are framed (e.g., drip and a la carte fee listing) can result in high negative emotions and low positive post-purchase behavior. These negative emotional reactions stem from consumers' reactions to the additional fees (versus higher total prices or base prices). However, the authors also show that these negative emotions can be reduced when fees are presented as a mixed bundle (where a la carte and equivalent package prices are shown concurrently).

Audience: The potential ACR audience for this session is quite broad. Apart from providing new theoretical insights for researchers interested in behavioral pricing, the session will attract a cross-section of ACR conference attendees who are interested in diverse areas of research such as general affect, specific emotions, mental accounting, and multi-method research.

Level of Completeness: For all four papers, the theorizing has been completed and multiple studies have already been conducted. Since all four papers are close to completion, we expect this to be an interesting and high quality session.

Plan for the Session: Our goal for the session is to give each presenter sufficient time to clearly present his or her findings, to encourage audience interaction with the presenters, and to facilitate a discussion about future research. We plan to allocate the session time in the following manner. Each paper will be presented for 15 minutes, followed by 2-3 minutes of question and answer.

Summary: In sum, while each of the papers examines the role that emotions play in consumers' reactions to prices and payment decisions, each provides different conceptual and methodological contributions. We believe that examining the range of affective, attributional, and physiological responses that consumers experience in response to purchase and payment decisions will not only appeal to a broad cross-section of ACR members, but also make an important contribution to theory. By highlighting the synergy in our research questions, we hope to provide significant insight and lay the foundation for future research on emotions, price, and payment.

Price Discounting For Emotional Impact

EXTENDED ABSTRACT

The process by which consumers respond to price promotions is generally thought to be a cognitive process (Inman, McAlister, and Hoyer 1990). Emotions are seldom considered, unless they are the outcome of a process that is still deliberate (Chandon, Wansink, and Laurent 2000) or evoked spontaneously without the mediation by cognitive processes (Naylor, Raghunathan, and Ramanathan 2006). We propose a more parsimonious view of consumer response to price promotions, acknowledging that consumer decisions are guided by a combination of affective and deliberative processes (Loewenstein and O'Donoghue 2007).

We suggest that a price promotion is likely to influence the relative dominance of the two processes by lowering the stakes in the decision environment and therefore reducing the motivation of consumers to engage in effortful deliberation. As the relative influence of cognitions diminishes, affect takes control of behavior, and feelings are more relied on as inputs in judgments and decisions. This process produces a series of related effects, including shift in preferences towards goods with higher emotional content and valuations that are scope insensitive and more polarized.

In Experiment 1, participants were asked to purchase an affectively superior or a cognitively superior snack. These snacks were sold at full price or at a 50% discount. As predicted, the presence of a price discount shifted preference toward the former option. Importantly, participants in the discount condition performed worse on a recall task and reported relying more on their feelings when deciding. We tested for two plausible confounds, a mood and a justification mechanism, but found no evidence of these accounts.

In Experiment 2, we tested a promotional setting in which only one brand was discounted at a time. Participants were asked to indicate their preference between two brands, one that was affectively superior compared to the other brand, in three different product categories: cars, mobile phones and watches. The experiment manipulated a single between-subjects factor, price promotion, across three levels: baseline (no promotion), promotion on more emotional brand vs. promotion on less emotional brand. Participants' relative preferences were analyzed in a 3 X 3 mixed factorial ANOVA with price promotion as the between-subjects factor and product category as the repeated measure. Consistent with our prediction, we found that a price discount offered on the more emotional brand increased participants' preferences for it ($p < .000$), whereas the same promotion offered on the less emotional brand did not change participants' relative preferences ($p = .531$).

Experiment 3 expanded our investigation to consumer valuations by capitalizing on a judgmental correlate of feeling-based evaluations. Based on prior research that suggests that feeling-based evaluations are relatively insensitive to the scope of the target stimulus (Hsee and Rottenstreich 2004), we predicted that the scope insensitivity should be more pronounced in the presence of a price promotion than in its absence. Consistent with this prediction, we found that in their willingness to pay for a bundle of music CDs, participants were significantly less sensitive to the number of CDs in the box set when the box set was on promotion than when it was not on promotion.

In order to garner further process evidence, Experiment 4 examined whether an individual's need for cognition (NFC) moderates the proposed impact of a price promotion. Based on prior research suggesting that the NFC is a determinant of processing motivation and that reliance on feelings is greater when NFC is low, we proposed that a price promotion is likely to increase preference for the affectively superior option for low NFC individuals who are less motivated to think, while high NFC individuals' preferences are likely to be unaffected by the promotion. The experiment utilized a 2 (promotion) x 2 (NFC) mixed design. Participants were asked to indicate their preference between an affectively superior resort room and a cognitively superior resort room which were similar in price. The rooms were offered at full price or at a 30% discount. As predicted, the price promotion increased preference for the affectively superior room only for low NFC individuals ($p < .001$), while high NFC individuals' preferences were unaffected by the promotion ($p = .737$). A second objective of this experiment was to document another facet

of reliance on feelings (Ratner and Herbst 2005), testing the prediction that a price promotion would lead to more extreme and polarized evaluations of the target object. We found support for our prediction.

Finally, Experiment 5 manipulated the weight attached to feelings vs. cognitions. We examined whether our effect would be mitigated by instructing participants to use their cognitions as the basis for their decisions. Participants were instructed to use either feeling-based processing or reason-based processing as they were creating a list of DVDs from a sample of 'highbrow' and 'lowbrow' movies belonging to an online DVD rental service that either did or did not offer a price promotion. The experiment thus employed a 2 (price promotion) x 2 (judgment process) between-subjects factorial design. As expected, analyses revealed a 2-way interaction (p < .03). When instructed to rely on their feelings, participants preferred the affectively superior movies more strongly in the presence of a price promotion than in its absence ($p = .032$). However, when instructed to rely on their reason and logic, participants' relative preferences were not affected by the price promotion ($p = .260$).

Overall, these experiments demonstrate the impact of price promotions on consumers' reliance on affective vs. deliberative processes and how this would influence their preferences and valuations. Our findings highlight the importance of understanding the guts of consumers' reactions to price promotions.

Do Emotions Decrease or Increase Present Bias in Monetary Decisions?

EXTENDED ABSTRACT

For a long time, it has been argued that emotions are detrimental to rational decisions. However, the past few decades of research has provided support for the proponents of the other side of the debate. For example, patients with damage in the ventromedial prefrontal cortex (vmPFC) of the brain, who are not able to use emotions to aid in decision making, often engaged in behaviors that were detrimental to their well-being even though their reasoning and problem-solving abilities were unaffected by the brain damage (Damasio 1994). Furthermore, recent findings suggest that it is not only the excess of emotions but also the lack of emotions that is causing some of the most serious problems that mankind is facing.

The present research extends this debate in the context of the present bias – the propensity to focus on the present value of money rather than its future value. A typical study on the present bias employs a delay of gratification paradigm, wherein an individual has to choose between a smaller but immediate reward and larger but delayed reward. For example, a person might be asked to choose between $1000 a year later and $750 now. Generally, it has been found that most people tend to exhibit a preference for smaller present rewards than larger future rewards. Several scholars have argued that relying on emotions exacerbates the present bias (e.g., Van den Bergh, Dewitte, and Warlop 2008).

We challenge this view and argue that certain types of emotions – namely anticipated regret – can reduce the present bias. Therefore, people who are prone to anticipate regret are likely to benefit from relying on emotions when making financial decisions. Our conceptualization posits that the delay of gratification paradigm can be reframed as a battle between two different emotions: a positive visceral reaction to the immediate reward versus the anticipated regret from foregoing the larger delayed reward. Following other researchers, we assume that in terms of consequentiality and neurophysiological substrates, anticipation of regret is akin to the experience of regret (Camille, Coricelli, Sallet, Pradat-Diehl, Duhamel, and Sirigu 2004; Zeelenberg and Pieters 2007). Three studies demonstrate how dispositional traits and situational primes can interact to increase the anticipated regret that reduces the present bias. Across the studies, we find that when primed to rely on emotions, tightwads – who are predisposed to anticipate regret from spending money – become less present biased. This effect did not manifest for spendthrifts who are predisposed to experience less regret.

Study 1 tests the hypothesis that relying on emotions/feelings helps people to make loan prepayment decisions. Loan prepayment decision can be framed as a decision between keeping money to spend now versus prepaying money to save on interest payments and spend more in the future. 299 participants were randomly assigned to one of the three different priming conditions: feeling prime, calculation prime, or control. The priming task was adopted from Hsee and Rottenstreich (2004). After the priming task, participants were told to imagine that they had a loan and that the bank is considering giving them the option to prepay. All participants saw six different loan prepayment scenarios that varied in the prepayment amount and future interest. For each scenario, they indicated whether they want to prepay the amount given in the scenario to reduce their monthly payment amount or not to prepay and stay with the current monthly payment amount. After that, participants were administered a scale that captures dispositional propensity to be a tightwad or a spendthrift (Rick, Cryder, & Loewenstein 2008). Results show that priming participants to rely on their emotions reduced the present bias for tightwads but not for spendthrifts. Tightwads were most likely to prepay their loans when they were primed to rely on their emotions.

Study 2 tests the hypothesis using the standard present bias paradigm (Rachlin, Raineri, and Cross1991). 131 participants went through the same priming procedure as in Study 1. Then they were asked to make a series of choices between smaller money delivered in the present and larger money delivered in the future. In line with the Study 1 results, priming participants to rely on their emotions reduced the present bias for tightwads but not for spendthrifts. Additionally, the effect was mediated by participants' anticipated regret such that when primed to rely on their emotions, tightwads anticipated strong regret but spendthrifts did not.

Study 3 was designed to provide additional support for the hypothesized role of emotions by using skin conductance response data, which have often been used as a measure of physiological arousal. 87participants went through the same priming and choice tasks as in study 2 while wearing a sensor on their palm that measures their skin conductance responses. Results replicate the effects found in previous studies such that tightwads were less present biased and experienced greater arousal when primed to rely on emotions.

In sum, we argue that emotions can help in the financial decision and failure to anticipate regret can result in suboptimal financial decisions.

Emotional Effects of Purchase Price-Reference Price Divergence

EXTENDED ABSTRACT

Although the ability of price outcomes to elicit (un)happiness has long been postulated (Thaler 1985), empirical research on price affect (O'Neill and Lambert 2001) and particularly on the formation and impact of qualitatively different price-related emotions is relatively young (e.g., Gelbrich 2011). This research investigates consumers' discrete emotional responses to discrepancies between the actual market price of a product and (i) consumers' internal reference price (i.e., transaction utility), or (ii) their maximum willingness to pay (i.e., consumer surplus). Our results provide insight into how the general happiness or pleasure of relative gains and the pain of losses (Thaler 1985) relates to specific emotional reactions to prices, which can have implications for long-term customer-seller relationships.

Consumer surplus has been defined as the difference between the actual market price and consumers' maximum willingness to pay (Frank and Bernanke 2001). Transaction utility incorporates a more psychological perspective. It depends on the difference between the actual market price and a consumer's reference price, that is, a consumer's conception of a fair or normal price the seller is expected to charge (Thaler 1985). The different standards considered (i.e., self-related vs. social norm-based) are expected to induce distinct evaluations in a purchasing context. Appraisal theories of emotion assume that such distinct appraisals about an event can elicit different discrete emotions (Lazarus 1991). Specifically, we expect that a consumer's surplus is evaluated in a self-attributional way ("I could beat the market!"), while a given transaction (dis)utility is appraised as related to the seller ("That was a really (un)fair price the seller charged me!"). This project focuses on consumers' emotional responses after having purchased a product (i.e., actual price ≤ maximum willingness to pay). Hence, we hypothesize that a positive consumer surplus will generate feelings of personal pride, while transaction (dis)utility is expected to trigger feelings of gratitude toward (anger about) the seller (Roseman, Spindel, and Jose 1990; Weiner 2000). Further, consumers are expected to cope with these emotions in specific ways (Lazarus 1991). Seller-related feelings of gratitude and anger are hypothesized to more strongly influence consumers' post-purchase behavioral intentions toward that seller than self-related feelings of pride about one's personal achievement (Soscia 2007; Nyer 1997).

We conducted three field surveys to test the hypotheses with consumers who had purchased a public transportation product (fare ticket, leisure product, etc.). In Study 1, a short online questionnaire was part of a diary study yielding 717 purchase observations. Maximum willingness to pay was measured by asking the respondents to indicate the highest price they would be willing to pay (Suri and Monroe 2001). The internal reference price was calculated based on the respondents' estimate of a fair price, normal market price, past price paid, as well as their highest and lowest price willing to pay (Chandrashekaran and Grewal 2003; Klein and Oglethorpe 1987; Suri and Monroe 2001). Multiple linear regression results indicate that transaction utility significantly triggers a consumer's attitude toward the price paid (p < .001) while consumer surplus does not (p = .402).

To further examine the role of discrete emotions, Study 2 was conducted online with 415 customers who were asked about their latest purchase of a public transportation product. As expected, multiple linear regressions revealed that a consumer's surplus triggers pride (p = .013), while gratitude (anger) toward the seller increases, the higher (lower) a consumer's transaction utility (ps < .01). 95% bootstrap confidence intervals on the significance of the specific indirect effects (Preacher and Hayes 2008) indicate that the effect of transaction utility on price attitude is mediated by gratitude and anger, while pride was not found to provide a significant indirect path from consumer surplus to price attitude.

Study 3 investigates the distinct behavioral coping responses associated with each discrete emotion. The sample included 803 consumers who just purchased a discounted ticket that was only available online and for specific fares. Again, transaction utility was found to trigger seller-related feelings of gratitude (p < .001) and anger (p = .028). However, it also had a positive effect on pride (p = .001), while the partial effect of consumer surplus on pride could not be replicated (p = .309). The latter may be due to using a newly introduced product category for which consumers' might not yet have constructed a concise idea about the value. Nonetheless, 95% bootstrap confidence intervals indicate that anger, gratitude, and pride significantly mediate the effect from transaction utility on positive word-of-mouth and gratitude also explains repurchase intentions.

In sum, the results demonstrate that existing discrepancies in the actual price paid and various reference prices can elicit a portfolio of different emotional responses. Our findings emphasize the importance of investigating specific discrete price-related emotions beyond consumers' general (un)happiness as they distinctively impact consumers' behavioral responses to prices.

Beyond Clarity and Confusion: Affective Responses to Price Framing in the Airline Industry

EXTENDED ABSTRACT

Price framing ranges from the clear and simple (penny candy) to the opaque and confusing (many wireless service plans), with a wide range of effects on consumer judgment and decision-making. Prior research shows that price presentation affects price recall (Morwitz, Greenleaf, and Johnson 1998), purchase intention (Gilbride, Guiltinan, and Urbany 2008; Morwitz, Greenleaf and Johnson 1998), perceived deal value (Bertini and Wathieu 2008), perceived fairness (Sheng, Bao, and Pan 2007), and perceived savings (Krishna, Briesch, Lehmann, and Yuan 2002), just to name a few.

Our paper examines the effect of price presentation on consumers from a new perspective. We explore how consumers respond emotionally to different price presentation formats in the airline industry, and then predict post-purchase behavior based on the experienced emotion. This is a question of considerable public policy importance, as new regulations in both the U.S. and the UK require airlines to change how they display their prices to consumers. These price presentation requirements were imposed, in part, to increase clarity and transparency of pricing. However, our results show that they can also trigger emotional responses from consumers—an unforeseen consequence of this protective legislation.

We include three common pricing formats in our analysis—a la carte pricing, where sellers present a price for a basic product as well as a listing of fees or charges for optional add-ons; mixed bundle pricing, where an a la carte listing of prices for optional add-ons is presented alongside a bundle that includes some of the optional add-ons priced as a unit; and drip pricing, a pricing tactic related to partitioned pricing that has not been researched before. In drip pricing, consumers only see a portion of the total price up-front, with optional or mandatory fees revealed only as a consumer progresses through the buying process.

Our first study examined how consumers shopping for an airline ticket respond to a la carte pricing of optional fees relative to an all-inclusive combined price (control) and a partitioned price where the additional fees were for mandatory taxes and surcharges. The base price in the a la carte and partitioned conditions were the same, and the total price was kept constant across all conditions. We included the partitioned price condition to rule out the alternative explanation that consumers simply respond negatively to multiple fees versus one fee. A strict "pain of paying" view of consumer response would predict that, assuming each fee was mentally processed as a separate payment, negative affect in the a la carte and partitioned conditions should be comparable, and that both should be higher than that in the combined condition. However, our results did not confirm this prediction. A self-reported measure of anger with the total price and with surcharges (recorded post-purchase) was significantly higher in the a la carte condition than in either the partitioned or control con-

ditions (p < .001). Participants in the a la carte condition were also marginally more likely to complain after a mild service failure (p < .10) and were least likely to recommend the airline again (p < .01). Mediation analysis showed that these differences in post-purchase behavior across price presentation conditions were completely mediated by feelings of anger.

Our second study was designed to examine whether anger could be alleviated if the optional fees were offered in a mixed bundle. Thirty subjects shopping for an airline ticket were randomly assigned to either a mixed bundle fee condition or to an a la carte fee condition. The mixed bundle condition showed an a la carte listing of several optional fees as well as a bundle which included a subset of the same options. The bundle price was simply the sum of the a la carte fees for the included items (i.e., not discounted). As in Study 1, consumer anger about additional fees was significantly higher in the a la carte condition, but was reduced in the mixed bundle condition, even though the bundle price offered no discount (p < .05). Additionally, the additional fees were perceived to be fairer in the mixed bundle condition versus the a la carte condition (p < .05).

Our third study (in progress) examines consumers' emotional responses to drip pricing—an understudied pricing format, that is currently of much interest to government regulators in the U.S. and the UK. In this experiment we manipulate the timing (early versus late) and manner (drip versus combined) in which consumers are informed about additional fees during their purchase process. Preliminary results suggest that consumers exposed to drip pricing are more likely to purchase an airline ticket, are less accurate in price estimation and price recall tasks, and they experience higher negative emotional reactions than their combined price counterparts.

In summary, we show that the manner in which a price is presented affects consumers' emotions and their subsequent post-purchase behavior. Our findings also highlight how protective actions taken by government agencies should consider the affective as well as the cognitive impacts on consumers.

REFERENCES

Bertini, Marco and Luc Wathieu (2008), "Attention Arousal Through Price Partitioning," *Marketing Science,* 27 (2), 236-246.

Camille, Nathalie, Giorgio Coricelli, Jerome Sallet, Pascale Pradat-Diehl, Jean-Rene Duhamel, and Angela Sirigu (2004). The involvement of the orbitofrontal cortex in the experience of regret. Science, 304, 1167- 1170.

Chandon, Pierre, Brian Wansink, and Gilles Laurent (2000), "A Benefit Congruency Framework of Sales Promotion Effectiveness," *Journal of Marketing,* 64(4), 65-81.

Chandrashekaran, Rajesh and Dhruv Grewal (2003), "Assimilation of Advertised Reference Prices: The Moderating Role of Involvement," *Journal of Retailing,* 79 (Spring), 53-62.

Chen, Shih-Fen S., Kent B. Monroe, and Yung-Chien Lou (1998), "The Effects of Framing Price Promotion Messages on Consumers' Perceptions and Purchase Intentions," *Journal of Retailing,* 74(3), 353-372.

Damasio, A. R. (1994). Descartes' error: Emotion, reason, and the human brain. New York: Putnam.

Frank, Robert H. and Ben S. Bernanke (2001), *Principles of Economics*, New York, NY: McGraw-Hill/Irwin.

Gelbrich, Katja (2011), "I Have Paid Less Than You! The Emotional and Behavioral Consequences of Advantaged Price Inequality," *Journal of Retailing,* 87 (June), 207-24.

Gilbride. Timothy J., Joseph P. Guiltinan, and Joel E. Urbany (2008), "Framing Effects in Mixed Bundle Pricing," *Marketing Letters,* 19 (2), 125-139.

Hsee, Christopher K. and Yuval Rottenstreich (2004), "Music, Pandas, and Muggers: On the Affective Psychology of Value," *Journal of Experimental Psychology: General*, 133 (1), 23–30.

Inman, J. Jeffrey, Leigh McAlister, and Wayne D. Hoyer (1990), "Promotion Signal: Proxy for a Price Cut?" *Journal of Consumer Research*, 17 (June), 74-81.

Klein, Noreen H. and Janet E. Oglethorpe (1987), "Cognitive Reference Points in Consumer Decision Making," in *Advances in Consumer Research*, Vol. 14, ed. Melanie Wallendorf and Paul Anderson, Provo, UT: Association for Consumer Research, 183-87.

Krishna, Aradhna, Richard Briesch, Donald R. Lehmann, and Hong Yuan (2002), "A Meta-Analysis of the Impact of Price Presentation on Perceived Savings," *Journal of Retailing,* 78, 101-118.Lazarus, Richard S. (1991), *Emotion and Adaptation,* New York, NY: Oxford University Press.

Loewenstein, George and Ted O'Donoghue (2007), "The Heat of the Moment: Modeling Interactions Between Affect and Deliberation," working paper, Carnegie Mellon University.

Morwitz, Vicki G., Eric A. Greenleaf, and Eric J. Johnson (1998), "Divide and Prosper: Consumers' Reactions to Partitioned Prices," *Journal of Consumer Research,* 35(4), 453-463.

Naylor, Rebecca W., Rajagopal Raghunathan, and Suresh Ramanathan (2006), "Promotions Spontaneously Induce a Positive Evaluative Response," *Journal of Consumer Psychology*, 16 (July), 295–305.

Nyer, Prashanth U. (1997), "A Study of the Relationships between Cognitive Appraisals and Consumption Emotions," *Journal of the Academy of Marketing Science,* 25 (Fall), 296-304.

O'Neill, Regina M. and David R. Lambert (2001), "The Emotional Side of Price," *Psychology and Marketing,* 18 (March), 217-37.

Preacher, Kristopher J. and Andrew F. Hayes (2008), "Asymptotic and Resampling Strategies for Assessing and Comparing Indirect Effects in Multiple Mediator Models," *Behavior Research Methods,* 40 (August), 879-91.

Rachlin, H., Raineri, A., and Cross, D. (1991). Subjective probability and Delay. Journal of the Experimental Analysis of Behavior, 55, 233-244.

Ratner, Rebecca K. and Kenneth C. Herbst (2005), "When Good Decisions Have Bad Outcomes: The Impact of Affect on Switching Behavior," *Organizational Behavior and Human Decision Processes, 96,* 23–37.

Rick, S., Cryder, C. and Loewenstein, G. (2008). Tightwads and spendthrifts. Journal of

Consumer Research, 34, 767-782.

Roseman, Ira J., Martin S. Spindel, and Paul E. Jose (1990), "Appraisals of Emotion-Eliciting Events: Testing a Theory of Discrete Emotions," *Journal of Personality and Social Psychology,* 59 (November), 899-915.

Sheng, Shibin, Yeqing Bao, and Yue Pan (2007), "Partitioning or Bundling? Perceived Fairness of the Surcharge Makes a Difference,"*Psychology and Marketing,* 24(12), 1025-1041.

Soscia, Isabella (2007), "Gratitude, Delight, or Guilt: The Role of Consumers' Emotions in Predicting Postconsumption Behaviors," *Psychology and Marketing,* 24 (October), 871-94.

Suri, Rajneesh and Kent B. Monroe (2001), "The Effects of Need for Cognition and Trait Anxiety on Price Acceptability," *Psychology and Marketing,* 18 (January), 21-42.

Thaler, Richard (1985), "Mental Accounting and Consumer Choice," *Marketing Science,* 4 (Summer), 199-214.

Van den Bergh, B., Dewitte, S., and Warlop, L. (2008). Bikinis instigate generalized impatience in intertemporal choice. Journal of Consumer Research, 35 (1), 85-97.

Weiner, Bernard (2000), "Attributional Thoughts about Consumer Behavior," *Journal of Consumer Research,* 27 (December), 382-87.

Zeelenberg, M. and Pieters, R. (2007). A theory of regret regulation 1.0. Journal of Consumer Psychology, 17 (1), 3-18.

Designing Effective Choice Architectures

Chairs: Oleg Urminsky, University of Chicago, USA
Indranil Goswami, University of Chicago, USA

Paper #1: In Search of Optimally Effective Defaults

Indranil Goswami, University of Chicago, USA
Oleg Urminsky, University of Chicago, USA

Paper #2: Redundant Information as a Choice Architecture Tool: How Attribute Decomposition on Displays can be used to Highlight Important Dimensions for Consumers

Christoph Ungemach, Columbia University, USA
Adrian Camilleri, Duke University, USA
Eric Johnson, Columbia University, USA
Richard Larrick, Duke University, USA
Elke U. Weber, Columbia University, USA

Paper #3: Product Level and Segment Level Differences in the Effectiveness of a Longitudinal Labeling and Choice Architecture Intervention at a Large Hospital Cafeteria

Jason Riis, Harvard Business School, USA
Susan Barraclough, Massachusetts General Hospital, USA
Doug Levy, Massachusetts General Hospital, USA
Lillian Sonnenberg, Massachusetts General Hospital, USA
Anne Thorndike, Massachusetts General Hospital, USA

Paper #4: Why are Benefits Left on the Table? Assessing the Role of Information, Complexity, and Stigma on Take-up with an IRS Field Experiment

Saurabh Bhargava, Carnegie Mellon University, USA
Day Manoli, University of California – Los Angeles, USA

SESSION OVERVIEW

A large literature has established that people's preferences are often malleable and are influenced by context and environmental cues. Much of the research along these lines has provided "existence proofs" – demonstrating factors which can consistently have some effect on decisions. Therefore, a natural question is how to best structure the decision context (e.g., the "choice architecture", Thaler and Sunstein 2008) such that the impact on outcomes is maximal. Answering this question not only has immense practical implications, but also poses an important theoretical challenge to decision researchers. In most choice environments, there are multiple potential influences and existing theories often provide either no prediction or competing predictions of when contextual factors will be most impactful. Hence, to generate recommendations for designing "optimally effective" choice architecture, we need to pit all the competing forces against one another, identify the influences that yield differential effectiveness and come up with a deeper understanding that can generate simple principles to guide choice architecture decisions. This session is aimed both at providing some answers to such questions, but even more so, to demonstrate the usefulness of this approach for consumer research, both practically and theoretically, spurring related future research.

Pre-set defaults have very robust effects on choices, and have been used effectively in various consequential domains, such as organ donation and retirement savings. Different extant research, however, has implied that defaults that are either too high or too low might have detrimental consequences. Hence it is unclear how to maximize the impact of a default policy, and whether setting a default might sometimes have negative effects relative to no default. Across a range of domains (pricing, charitable donation, savings goals) that differ in the decision maker's motivations and implica-

tions of being amenable to the default, Goswami and Urminsky find that high defaults generally have a greater impact on increasing 'participation amount' than low defaults, without any difference in participation rate. Evidence for immediate downstream consequences of high versus low default on goal disengagement and rejection of subsequent defaults seem to be limited. These findings suggest an important principle of choice architecture, that setting low defaults might have negative consequences, but there is little risk of setting too high a default.

Another common approach to choice architecture is to provide (or mandate) detailed information for consumers. Research has indicated that consumers tend to undervalue the importance of long-term savings factors such as fuel economy, even when provided with detailed information about it in their car purchasing decisions. Ungemach, Camilleri, Johnson, Larrick and Weber show that a simple attribute decomposition intervention, communicating the fuel economy information multiple times and in different formats (e.g. miles per gallon, annual fuel cost etc.,) can increase the weight decision makers assign to this attribute irrespective of the purchase motivations. The efficacy is not driven by changing inferences about superiority on the most salient dimension, since even redundant information on the attribute influenced assigned weights. Rather, these findings suggest that optimizing choice architecture involves taking into account the weight and emphasis placed on information by considering the distribution of attributes across the key dimensions.

Along similar lines, recent attempts to improve consumers' food choices by providing calorie information have yielded largely disappointing results. In a large scale field study in a hospital cafeteria, Riis, Barraclough, Levy, Sonnenberg, and Thorndike demonstrate that labeling foods as red, yellow, or green, coupled with interventions to make the green food items more visible and accessible, had a dramatic impact. Specifically, the sale of bottled water increased 26%, seemingly driven by consumers' desire to make a healthy choice on a complimentary item in their meal without making sacrifices on the taste of focal component of the meal. These findings demonstrate that optimizing choice architecture may occur when information is made as easy to process and as accessible as possible, even at the expense of detail, and when it is offered on complementary items rather than focal items.

In another large scale field study, Bhargava and Manoli show how Earned Income Tax Credit (EITC) claims can be increased among eligible taxpayers (the working poor). They find that simplifying the program information meant to address issues like lack of awareness, misunderstanding of EITC rules including eligibility, and underestimation of benefit size substantially increases claims. More importantly, they test these interventions against competing interventions, including attempts to reduce perceived transaction cost and social stigma and risk of audit, which did not have any effect. Overall, the successful interventions reduced incomplete take-up from 25% to 22%, with a cumulative effect measured in millions of dollars. Their field study (and accompanying survey) findings further demonstrate that optimizing choice architecture involves maximizing comprehension and confidence with the information provided, rather than maximizing the quantity or detail of information.

Taken together, the four papers suggest that equally plausible interventions in the decision context can often have profoundly different effects, across many consequential domains. We expect that this session would be of interest to a broad audience including consumer and decision researchers, economists, and policy practitioners. This session will also contribute to the diversity of types of research at ACR, by presenting data from two large scale field studies. We believe that our understanding of how to use choice architecture most effectively is under-developed, and that attempting to identify the conditions that yield optimal effectiveness is of crucial importance for both theoretical and practical reasons. We hope that this session will stimulate ideas and promote future research in the optimal effectiveness of choice architecture design.

In Search Of Optimally Effective Defaults

EXTENDED ABSTRACT

Pre-set default options are a key element of choice architecture. However, recommendations and defaults might yield a behavioral backlash if they are inconsistent with initial impressions (Fitzsimons and Lehmann 2004), invoke negative assessment of motives (Brown and Krishna 2004), or if the individual or group setting the default option is distrusted (Liersch and McKenzie 2011). Companies often set a fairly low default 401(k) contribution rate relative to chosen rates of saving, partly out of a concern that a higher default rate could reduce enrollment (WSJ, 7/2011). Thus, a critical unanswered question is how to set optimally effective defaults and whether setting defaults too low or too high is likely to have a greater impact.

In six completed studies, we set out to empirically test the potential for negative backlash effects of high defaults and anchoring effects of low defaults on active choices (i.e. not passive enrollment). To answer this question, we investigated the impact of default size on total amounts, as well as average 'amounts' among participants, participation rate, and immediate downstream consequences on goal disengagement and response to subsequent defaults. In order to generalize our findings, we use a range of domains, from savings to pricing, where the decision makers' motivations are very different and hence defaults are likely to be operating via different routes. In addition, we specifically investigate the effect of psychological reactance (Brehm 1966; Hong and Faedda 1996) and trust on different levels of default.

In Study 1 (n=502), we tested default policies on consumers' choices of savings goals (defaults of 7%, 5%, 3%, 1% or no default; b/w/s). The default was calculated from data attributed either to the U.S. Government (a well-known source) or U.S. Bureau of Economic Analysis (a lesser known source). Overall, the average savings goal increased monotonically with increasing default. When Government was the source, the savings rate was significantly increased by a high (7%) default and significantly decreased by a low (1%) default, relative to no default. Furthermore, high default did not increase drop-out rates (not setting any savings goal at all) relative to other conditions. Reactance reduced the overall efficacy of defaults, but did not differentially impact high defaults. In a follow-up study, Study 2 (n=443), we replicated our findings with unrealistically high default savings goals (defaults of 40%, 20%, 5%, 1% or no default; b/w/s). Even for these extreme rates, we found no evidence of backlash for high defaults (relative to no default), even among high reactance participants. In addition, non-participation rates, self-reported confidence and decision satisfaction did not differ.

In the next two studies, Study 3 (n=241) and Study 4 (n=453) we tested these results with participants facing real stakes. In study 3 we used a setting where 'higher' choice is not intrinsically desirable for the participants. Participants picked their own price to buy academic planners from a menu of prices with a default of $40, $5, $1, or no defaults b/w/s. Inexperienced participants, who did not

use planners in the previous year, valued the product significantly more when the default was higher. The effect could not be explained by increased attractiveness of the planners for inexperienced buyers, or default acting as a signal of information. Also, there was no difference in the participation rates across conditions. The high defaults ($40, $5) were effective in increasing willingness to pay, even though no one selected the defaults.

In Study 4, participants decided on how much they would be willing to donate from a real lottery award which every participant had an equal chance to win. High defaults (but now low defaults) significantly increased intended donations when participants had low information (resulting in low trust) about the charitable organization. Defaults did not have an effect on participants with high information. The pattern was true for participation rate as well. Therefore, in the absence of credibility bolstering information, high defaults helped to increase both average amounts as well as participation rates.

In two other hypothetical studies we tested people's response to defaults in a choice of how many promotional emails to allow a company to send them. In both Study 4 (n=192) and Study 5 (n=71), the average number of emails permitted did not vary significantly based on the default, and there were no negative consequences of high defaults. Also, across all studies we find very limited evidence of immediate downstream consequences of encountering high versus low defaults in a prior decision task.

Our findings suggest minimal potential for backlash against high defaults, particularly in multi-option choices. Even when a high default is rejected, it can influence choices by anchoring the participant on a high value. In contrast, we find that deviation from maximal defaults occurs primarily when defaults are too low, rather than too high. While psychological reactance reduces the impact of defaults, we find little evidence that high reactance leads to a backlash against high defaults. Trust is an important factor in the absence of defaults, but defaults can improve outcomes when trust is low.

Redundant Information as a Choice Architecture Tool: How Attribute Decomposition on Displays can be used to Highlight Important Dimensions for Consumers

EXTENDED ABSTRACT

Among the scientific community there is no doubt that climate change is a reality and that we must act immediately to reduce CO_2 emissions (Karl, Melillo, & Peterson, 2009). While purely economic solutions have already been leveraged, it has been increasingly recognised that insights from psychology and behavioural economics are crucial to initiate and maintain the changes required to combat the threat (Johnson et al., 2012; Weber & Stern, 2011). One of the most promising psychology-based approaches to producing behavioural change is through the development of "choice architecture".

The choice architecture approach to behavioural change rests on the established finding that individuals often construct their preferences in the immediate choice context (Slovic, 1995; Lichtenstein & Slovic, 2006) and that decision context often influences the choice that is made (Thaler & Sunstein, 2008). A key principle of this approach is that there is no neutral choice context and any framing can and will affect what is chosen. Examples of nudges that have been shown to be effective include the selection of defaults (Johnson, Bellman, & Lohse, 2002), the number of alternatives presented (Payne, Bettman, & Johnson, 1993), the partitioning of options and attributes (Fox, Ratner, & Lieb, 2005), and rescaling (Burson, Larrick, & Lynch, 2009). A related observation with potential choice architecture implications is "attribute splitting", describing the phenomenon that decomposing an attribute into several sub-attributes can increase the psychological weight assigned to that dimension (Jacobi & Hobbs, 2007; Weber, Eisenfuehr & von Winterfeldt, 1988). Attribute splitting has been demonstrated within weighting tasks but it remains unclear how the distribution of attribute values affects preferences.

The inherent goal of the presented series of experiments is to further understand the impact of and mechanisms behind attribute decomposition, and develop a new choice architecture tool within the domain of environmental decisions.

Experiment 1. A primary source of human-induced CO2 emissions is transportation, contributing approximately 27% of total U.S. greenhouse gas emissions in 2008 (http://www.epa.gov/otaq/climate/basicinfo.htm). However, prior research seems to indicate that consumers presented with relevant information undervalue fuel economy information in their car-purchasing decisions (e.g. German, 2002; Maples, 2003; Patterson, 2002). An interesting feature of the new fuel economy labels launched by the Environmental Protection Agency is that the fuel economy information is presented in a number of different, but highly correlated, metrics (e.g. MPG, GPM, annual fuel cost). In order to test whether repetition of the same attribute potentially reduces undervaluation of fuel cost information, as implied by the findings on attribute decomposition, we conducted a discrete choice experiment. 200 online respondents were asked to choose between pairs of cars for which EPA fuel economy labels (7 correlated metrics of fuel economy) and the prices of the car (one single price) were provided. The choice pairs were created using three MPG levels (High, Medium, Low) and three Price levels (High, Medium, Low). Each participant had to make 4 choices in 2 different scenarios: In the 'Capability' scenario, participants helped a friend select the car with the lowest overall cost (i.e, price and operating cost) given a fixed yearly mileage of 15,000 miles and 5 years before replacing the car; In the 'Preference' scenario, participants could choose the car they personally preferred assuming the same mileage and driving period. The label presentation format was also manipulated such that each pair of labels was either presented simultaneously or sequentially.

Discrete choice analysis showed that when using the label with multiple fuel efficiency metrics, participants tended to slightly overweight the fuel economy information relative to the car price. This tendency was observed in both scenarios and was not affected by the order the scenarios were presented in.

Experiment 2. In order to investigate whether people actually make use of all the highly correlated information on the label, we conducted a second experiment in the laboratory (n=10) where we tracked participant's eye movements while going through the same choice task as in Experiment 1. Although the calculation of the overall cost on the 'Capacity' task only required the combination of two numbers (one fuel economy metric and the price) the process tracing data revealed that most participants did indeed allocate attention to all of the available metrics, including the redundant information. Furthermore, the gaze paths show that redundant information was not merely scanned initially as part of the search process but participants repeatedly transitioned between similar attributes across labels, indicating that this information was used as part of the choice process itself.

Experiment 3. The observations made in Experiment 1 and 2 suggest that the presentation of multiple, highly correlated attributes may cause decision-makers to psychologically weigh this attribute more heavily. Our investigation is also related to the "majority rule" heuristic, which asserts that decision-makers tend to choose the option superior on most of the available cues (Zhang et al., 2005). However, this heuristic is applicable only to alternatives with more

than two attributes and it is unclear whether the heuristic can apply to multiple redundant attributes.

Our aim in Experiment 3 was to systematically manipulate the proportion of redundant attributes for a given dimension and observe the impact on the psychological weight assigned to that dimension. To fulfil this aim, we carried out a 2 (Upfront Cost Information: 1 metric vs. 4 metrics) x 2 (Running Cost Information: 1 metric vs. 4 metrics) x 3 (Upfront Cost: High, Medium, Low) x 3 (Running Cost: High, Medium, Low) between-subjects discrete choice experiment. 400 online respondents were presented with nine decision problems that each required a choice between two vehicles that varied in Upfront and Running costs, as in the 'Capability' scenario in Experiment 1 and 2. We found that, in general, presentation of multiple redundant attributes shifted the psychological weight assigned to that dimension.

Together, the results from these studies show that redundant information is utilized in the formation of preferences and that it might be overweighted. This observation offers choice architects a new tool to help decision-makers identify the important dimensions in a choice problem and nudge people towards buying more energy efficient cars.

Product Level and Segment Level Differences in the Effectiveness of a Longitudinal Labeling and Choice Architecture Intervention at a Large Hospital Cafeteria

EXTENDED ABSTRACT

Although many food retailers are trying to encourage their customers to make healthier choices, few of their interventions have been studied formally, and few are able to claim much success. The current study incorporated a two-phase retail intervention in a large hospital cafeteria. In the first phase, a simplified menu labeling system was applied throughout the cafeteria. Since calorie labeling interventions have shown limited success in changing customer purchase behavior, this study implements a simpler and more meaningful labeling scheme whereby all foods in the cafeteria were labeled as red, yellow, or green (with green being the healthiest). The second phase of the study altered the choice architecture of the food and beverages in the cafeteria, making it easier for customers to see and find the healthier food items. We compared the purchase patterns made during these two 3-month intervention phases with purchase patterns during a 3-month baseline period.

The setting for the study was the main cafeteria at large hospital in Massachusetts. More than 5000 individuals visit the cafeteria during a typical weekday and daily revenues exceed $30,000. Just over a quarter of the revenues come from employees who use a "meal card" which allows purchases to be directly deducted from their paychecks. The purchases of these individuals can hence be tracked over time.

The first phase of the intervention involved a point-of-purchase labeling intervention designed to educate the employees, patients, and visitors about the nutritional value of the foods and beverages of the cafeteria. All foods and beverages in the cafeteria were labeled as red, yellow, or green based on criteria that reflect USDA healthy eating recommendations. Displays around the cafeteria informed customers that Red items should be consumed rarely, as they are high in calories or unhealthy fat while Green items, which feature fresh fruits and vegetables, whole grains, and healthy proteins, should be consumed often. Yellow items are intermediate. The red-yellow-green categories were developed by a team of nutritionists at the hospital.

Following the three months of Phase 1, the second phase of the cafeteria intervention began. The labeling scheme did not change from Phase 1; food and beverages continued to be labeled red, yellow, and green; but choice architecture changes were made.

The intervention at Phase 2 involved a series of changes to the layout of the cafeteria and the standard servings of some items. These changes were designed to increase the purchase rates of green items by making them more salient and more convenient to select. Examples include the following: a) Bottled water and diet soda (both green items) appeared at many more locations around the cafeteria, including several prominent, easy-access baskets near each food service station; b) Pre-packaged side salads became available beside the pizza and grill stations, where previously customers who wanted a side salad must make a separate trip to the salad bar, and c) Healthier snack items and sandwiches were moved to the most visible and accessible shelves, while less healthy items in these categories were moved to less visible and less accessible shelves.

Cash register data recorded all purchases for the 9 month study period. In addition to analyzing cafeteria-wide purchase trends, we followed a cohort of 5000 meal card users. For each user in the cohort, we knew their age, sex, race/ethnicity, and job type, in addition to their purchase history.

The labeling intervention led to large reductions in the consumption of unhealthy foods and beverages, but this paper will focus on the choice architecture intervention. Some analyses of category effects and segment interactions are pending, but some results are clear. By far the largest single product category change due to choice architecture was for bottled water which showed a 26% increase in sales during the choice architecture period. Changes in other categories were less than half that. We believe that this is because beverages are complements to meals, and taste sacrifices here will seem relatively modest compared to taste sacrifices on a meal entrée or on a food favorite.

In terms of segment differences, there were very large differences in purchase patterns at baseline: For example, Black and Latino employees purchased 31% red items while, white employees consumed just 18%. Reductions of red item purchases and increases in green item purchases were however largely uniform across ethnic and income groups. All groups showed similarly substantial improvements in healthy purchasing. For example, the average reduction in calories per beverage was about 15% for each group, from baseline to Phase 2.

Finally, cafeteria revenues were consistent through the three periods, suggesting that such interventions may be sustainable. The interventions are ongoing at the hospital and we are currently looking at the second year of register and panel data.

Why are Benefits Left on the Table? Assessing the Role of Information, Complexity, and Stigma on Take-up with an IRS Field Experiment

EXTENDED ABSTRACT

A well-recognized, and perhaps surprising, feature of transfers to the economically and socially disadvantaged is that many targeted individuals fail to take-up their benefits (Currie 2006). The Earned Income Tax Credit (EITC), the nation's largest means-tested cash transfer program, is a prime example with an estimated 25 percent rate of incomplete take-up that amounts to 6.7 million non-claimants each year (Plueger 2009).

The policy consequences of incomplete take-up are significant. A typical EITC non-claimant forgoes credits equivalent to 33 days of income. Moreover, non-claimants forfeit other advantages, such as those related to family health, education, or consumption, that may be linked to transfers (Hoynes, Miller, and Simon 2011; Dahl and Lochner 2011; Smeeding, Phillips, and O'Connor 2001). The problem may be even more severe for other means-tested programs.

Several explanations are generally cited for incomplete take-up: lack of information, stigma, transaction costs, and complexity (Currie 2006). In this paper, we test the effect of a set of novel interventions on take-up with a unique field experiment administered in collaboration with the Internal Revenue Service (IRS). In addition to identifying strategies to improve take-up, our experiment allows us to evaluate leading theories as to its causes. Specifically, we test the role of information (regarding program benefits, costs, and rules), the complexity of such information, and program stigma on the take-up of the EITC.

We implement the experiment by modifying the informational content and complexity of IRS tax mailings and distributing these to the universe of over 35,000 tax filers from California who failed to claim their TY 2009 EITC despite presumed eligibility and the receipt of an initial reminder notice. Each mailing communicates likely eligibility for the program, and includes a worksheet which a recipient can complete and return to claim a credit. We use the differential response across mailings to adjudicate among the tested mechanisms. To maximize statistical efficiency, and to permit tests of treatment interactions, we assign and distribute the mailing elements---that is, the reminder notice, claiming worksheet, and an experimental envelope---with three independent randomizations to blocks defined by zip code and dependent status. The packets were published, assembled and mailed by the IRS in a single batch in mid-November of 2010. All told, we inform individuals of $26 million in unclaimed government benefits, of which about $4 million is ultimately claimed.

The experiment offers five main findings. First, we observe that the mere receipt of the experimental "control," just months after the receipt of a first, similar, IRS reminder mailing, prompts 0.14 of the residual non-respondents to take-up (this compares to an initial notice response of 0.41). Second, the experiment suggests that informational complexity influences response. Relative to the control notice and worksheet (0.14), a notice with a simplified layout and less repetition improves take-up by 0.06 ($p < .01$), while a shorter worksheet, without the inclusion of criteria that does not substantively screen for eligibility, increases response by 0.04 ($p < .01$). Importantly, the basic information conveyed by the control notice and worksheet, and the complexity treatments, is equivalent. Third, providing benefit information also raises take-up. Displaying the upper bound of a potential benefit improves take-up by 0.08 relative to the 0.23 response of the baseline notice in which no benefit is displayed ($p < .01$). Fourth, we find that attempts to clarify the time and penalty costs associated with completing and returning the worksheet do not improve response. Finally, our attempts to reduce program stigma do not improve take-up.

By integrating the results from the experimental findings and randomized surveys of tax-filer beliefs, we can arbitrate between competing explanations for incomplete take-up in the literature. Our findings suggest that incomplete take-up in the specific context of EITC filers is due primarily to low program awareness, incomplete information regarding benefits and eligibility, as well as the high complexity of information. We do not find evidence to implicate direct transaction costs, the likelihood of an audit, or program stigma. A set of psychometric surveys offers additional insight into why take-up is so sensitive to modest changes in informational content and presentation. The evidence suggests that information, and informational complexity, may shape behavior by prompting both direct and indirect inferences regarding program parameters, as well by, possibly, changing the degree to which readers attend to the information.

Overall, the potential policy impact of the tested interventions is large. We calculate that the most effective experimental treatments, if applied to the entire population of filing non-claimants, could reduce incomplete take-up among filers from 10% to 7%, and overall incomplete take-up from an estimated 25% to 22%. The increase in response due to our context-based interventions is equivalent to that which would be produced by expanding benefits by up to 101% for this population.

Power and Decision Making: Exploring the Processes and Nuances

Chair: Selin A. Malkoc, Washington University in St. Louis, USA

Paper #1: Power and Unconventional Choice

Mehdi Mourali, University of Calgary, Canada
Frank Pons, Université Laval, Canada

Paper #2: The Power Switch: How Psychological Power Influences Brand Switching Decisions

Yuwei Jiang, Hong Kong Polytechnic University , Hong Kong
Lingjing Zhan, Hong Kong Polytechnic University , Hong Kong
Derek D. Rucker, Northwestern University, USA

Paper #3: Not All Power is Created Equal: Role of Social and Personal Power in Decision Making

Selin A. Malkoc, Washington University in St. Louis, USA
Michelle M. Duguid, Washington University in St. Louis, USA

Paper #4: Experience Versus Expectations of Power: A Recipe for Altering the Effects of Power

Miao Hu, Northwestern University, USA
Derek D. Rucker, Northwestern University, USA
Adam D. Galinsky, Northwestern University, USA

SESSION OVERVIEW

Power is arguably one of the most fundamental features of our social world. As such, it has been the focus of a substantial amount of academic inquiry in the past decade (e.g., Briñol et al. 2007; Galinsky, Gruenfeld, and Magee 2003), which identified a variety of important consequences of feeling powerful versus powerless. However, to date, examination of the consumption decisions of the powerful has been rather scarce (for notable exceptions see Rucker and Galinsky 2008, 2009). These omissions are somewhat surprising because consumers routinely find themselves in the position of power, like when a mother makes decisions for the family dinner, when a leader of a department chooses the locations of a retreat or when a graduating college student finally having the money to buy the computer she would like. As such, it is crucial to examine the consequences of feeling powerful and its effects on subsequent consumption decisions. The four papers in this session not only identify important consequences of power in the consumption domain, but also extend the current literature on power by identifying new processes, moderators and nuances that have not been previously proposed or demonstrated.

In particular, the first two papers in the session explore important outcomes of feeling powerful in the consumption domain by examining whether consumers who feel powerful make different choices (Mourali and Pons) and whether they are more or less likely to stick to their previous choices (Jiang et al). The remaining two papers introduce additional nuances above and beyond the dichotomy of powerful versus powerful, by distinguishing between personal and social power (Malkoc and Duguid) and experiences versus expectations of power (Hu et al).

The first paper by Mourali and Pons examines how the choices made by the powerful and powerless might be systematically different. To that end, they demonstrate that consumers who feel powerful are more likely to choose unconventional options. Their results indicate that this tendency is caused by the powerful wanting to signal their power to others. Accordingly, they show that if the choices are made in private or if the unconventional items are deemed popular, powerful consumers no longer prefer these options as they lose their signaling value.

The second paper by Jiang, Zhan and Rucker studies how consumers' likelihood to switch away from their current brands is influenced by their sense of power. They demonstrate that while powerless consumers stick with their brands more, powerful consumers opt to switch more frequently. They argue that this tendency is due to an increased inclination of the power holders to take action. Supporting this idea, they show that if consumers take physical action before the switch/stay choice, the effect of power is eliminated.

In the third paper, Malkoc and Duguid critically distinguish between social power (over others) and personal power (over the self) and show the important implications of this distinction on a variety of context effects. In particular, their results demonstrate that personal (vs. social) power holders defer choice more and compromise less, while showing no difference with respect to the attraction effect. Furthermore, they theorize and show that these effects can be accounted by the increased level of freedom experienced by personal power holders compared to social power holders.

Finally, the fourth paper by Hu, Rucker and Galinsky introduces the important distinction between the experience of power and the expectation of power. Replicating prior research, they show that when focused on the experience of power, those who lack it show increased preference for status and process information to a greater extent. However, shifting people's attention to what others expect of them in situations of power (vs. no power) reverses these findings by leading them to behave in a manner that meets those expectations.

Studying power across a variety of consumption contexts (unconventional choices, switching decisions, compromise and attraction effects, choice deferral and status products), the four papers in this session extend the boundaries of research on power by introducing previously unstudied consequences (unconventional choices (Mourali and Pons), switch/stay decision (Jiang et al), context effects (Malkoc and Duguid)), psychological mechanisms (signaling (Mourali and Pons), freedom (Malkoc and Duguid), expectation confirmation (Hu et al)) and moderators (private vs. public consumption (Mourali and Pons), physical actions (Jiang et al), personal vs. social nature of power (Malkoc and Duguid), experience vs. expectation of power (Hu et al)).

Taken together, these papers present new directions in power research. Given the growing impact of power in consumer research, we expect this session to generate a high level of interest among ACR attendees and spark future research directions, as well as engaging the audience to debate nuances of power in interpretation of its many consequences.

Power and Unconventional Choices

EXTENDED ABSTRACT

Despite a relatively late start, consumer researchers have recently shown considerable interest in the study of power and its influence on consumption behavior (see Rucker, Galinsky, and Dubois 2011 for a review). This follows a decade of extremely fertile psychological research on the consequences of having versus lacking power. At least three influential research streams currently describe power's influence on decision making. One stream (Guinote 2007, 2008) argues that power affects process-related aspects of information processing, which in turn affect behavior. According to the Situated Focus Theory of Power (Guinote 2007), power increases the ability to process information selectively. Selective processing in turn increases the ability to behave in more focused and prioritized ways. A second stream of research focuses on content-based effects of power (Anderson and Berdahl 2002; Galinsky et al 2003; Keltner et al. 2003). The approach/inhibition theory of power (Keltner et al. 2003) maintains that elevated power increases sensitivity to certain contents such as rewards and positive features, and signals to the individual that the environment is benign. Low power increases sensitivity to other types of contents (e.g., punishments, threats in the environment, and negative features). As a result, high power activates the behavioral approach system, leading to more positive affect, automatic information processing, and disinhibited behavior, whereas low power activates the behavioral inhibition system, leading to more negative affect, controlled information processing, and inhibited social behavior (Keltner et al. 2003). A third stream of research emphasizes the motivational effects of power (e.g., Rucker and Galinsky 2008, 2009; Rucker et al. 2011). The compensatory consumption model suggests that powerlessness is an aversive state that people are motivated to alleviate. As a result, when consumers feel powerless, they tend to exhibit a strong preference for acquiring and displaying status-related products to compensate for their lack of power.

We propose a fourth way in which power may influence decision making. We offer that powerful consumers often make unconventional choices to signal their power to others. Our conceptualization draws on Berger and Heath's (2007) identity-signaling model, which posits that people often diverge in their choices to communicate a desired identity. We submit that high power is a desirable state that individuals feel compelled to communicate to others. One way to signal one's power is to show that one is not afraid to make bold, unconventional, choices. We examine the signaling hypothesis in decision contexts involving choices between extreme vs. compromise options, safe vs. risky options, and gambles with known vs. unknown (ambiguous) probabilities. Consider the choice between compromise and extreme options. Maimaran and Simonson (2011) reasoned that selecting a compromise option represents a conventional choice because compromise options are seen as safer and less likely to be criticized. In contrast, selecting an extreme option represents a bold and unconventional choice because it reflects a willingness to take a stand and express one's view. Similarly, selections of risky options and gambles with unknown probabilities reflect unconventional behavior to the extent that safe options and gambles with known probabilities are seen as the conventional defaults (Maimaran and Simonson 2011; Einhorn and Hogarth 1986).

We tested the signaling hypothesis in three experimental studies. Study 1 was designed to assess the general idea that power increases preference for unconventional options. We manipulated participants' power using a role-based procedure adapted from Galinsky et al. (2003). Participants then responded to a total of 6 choice scenarios reflecting decisions between compromise and extreme options; risky and safe options; and gambles with known vs. unknown probabilities. The results indicate that across all six scenarios, participants in the high power position selected the unconventional options significantly more frequently than those in the low power position.

Study 2 was designed to test an important implication of the signaling hypothesis, namely that the effect of power on choice of unconventional options should be stronger when choices are public than when they are private. Study 2 consisted of a 3 (low power vs. control vs. high power) x 2 (public choice vs. private choice) x 3 (extreme vs. risky vs. ambiguous scenarios) mixed design, with choice scenarios manipulated within subjects. Power was primed using a writing task (Galinsky et al. 2003). The results indicate that high power led to increased preference for unconventional options

when choices were public, but not when choices were private. There was no difference in choice patterns between the three scenarios, and between the low power and control groups.

Finally, study 3 was designed to test another important implication of the signaling hypothesis. We reasoned that power increases preference for unconventional options because of these options' signaling value not their inherent qualities. Thus, these options should become less attractive to powerful consumers if selecting them no longer reflects a bold, unconventional choice. We tested this hypothesis by presenting half of the respondents with information suggesting that risky and ambiguous options are in fact popular options (i.e., options that most people choose). Indeed, suggesting that risky and ambiguous options are chosen by most people makes selecting them a rather conventional and timid behavior because they may now seem safer and less likely to be criticized. Study 3 found that presenting nominally unconventional options as popular not only reduced their perceived attractiveness in the eyes of powerful consumers, but also made them seem more attractive to consumers with less power.

The Power Switch: How Psychological Power Influences Brand Switching Decisions

EXTENDED ABSTRACT

Consumers' brand switching is an inevitable, and represents a serious problem for most companies. Recent research finds that up to 33% of the unit sales increase is attributable to brand switching (Van Heerde, Gupta, and Wittink 2003). Surprisingly, there still remains much to understand with respect to consumers' behavioral motivations to switch to new brands. To add a novel perspective on switching behavior, the current research examines the impact that incidental states of power have on brand switching decisions.

Defined as an individual's ability to control own and others' resources (Galinsky, Gruenfeld, and Magee 2003), power is a force that touches on most social interactions. Power also shapes consumer values in a variety of consumption decisions (Rucker, Galinsky, and Dubois 2011). A finding particularly relevant to the current research is that states of high power increases individuals' action orientation. Keltner, Gruenfeld, and Anderson (2003) proposed that power activates a behavioral approach system. Specifically, high-power individuals possess more resources and pay more attention to rewards and opportunities in the environment, and thus show an approach-related tendency to pursue and obtain goals. Supporting this hypothesis, Galinsky, et al. (2003) showed that high-power participants were more likely to take an additional card in a simulated blackjack game, or to turn off an annoying fan in a room.

Sometimes consumers consider new options to replace the current product or service. For instance, an individual might think about changing their television provider when seeing an alternative cable package advertised. In this case, the consumer is facing two options involving different levels of action. Sticking with the current television provider requires minimal action, while changing to a new brand is associated with more action in the form of making a phone call, cancelling the current service, etc. Based on the linkage between power and action orientation, we propose that a state of high power will naturally lead to a tendency to engage in switching behavior as this allows people to fulfill the action orientation of a high-power state. We test this hypothesis in three experiments.

In experiment 1, participants were first asked to recall a past event during which they felt either powerful or powerless, a power-priming process used in past power literature (e.g. Galinsky et al. 2003). Participants then read a scenario and imagined that they just moved to a new apartment and needed to install internet service.

They were told that most residents in the building were using the default internet service provided by brand A and the residents were in general satisfied with brand A's service. There was also another company (brand B) available, but detailed information about brand B was unknown. Participants were then asked to indicate whether they would use brand A (the default) as the internet service provider, or reject brand A and consider switching to brand B. We found that more participants in the high-power condition (54%) considered switching to a new brand than in the low-power condition (40.6%; $p < .05$). Additional data showed that both perceptions of the current brand and expectation of the new brand did not differ across power conditions.

Experiment 2 replicated study 1's findings in a real behavior context. At the beginning of experiment 2, all participants received a new pen and were asked to answer all the questionnaires using the pen. They were also told that they could keep the pen after the study. Feeling of power was then manipulated using the same recall task as in experiment 1. After the recall task, participants were told to decide either to keep their current pen, or to exchange it for a different but equally-priced pen. Consistent with our hypothesis, more participants in the high-power condition (40%) switched the pen than in the low-power condition (20.4%; $p < .05$). Again, additional data confirmed that this effect was not caused by different perceptions of the two pens.

If the previously observed effect of power on brand switching is indeed caused by a heightened action orientation, we proposed that real physical actions taken prior to the brand switching decision might sate the action orientation, and thus mitigate the effect of power on brand switching. Participants in experiment 3 were randomly assigned to conditions in a 2 (power: high vs. low) × 2 (physical action: action vs. no action) between-subject design. Similar to experiment 2, participants first received a new pen upon arrival. After a short demographics questionnaire, we manipulated participants' feeling of power following the manager-subordinate role playing procedures adapted from Anderson and Berdahl (2002). While waiting for the task materials, participants completed an ostensibly unrelated task portrayed as evaluating a product, but in actuality introduced the manipulation of physical action. In the action conditions, each participant received a small rubber massage ball and was instructed to squeeze it for 30 seconds to test this product. In the control conditions, participants instead observed the same ball in a transparent, plastic box for 30 seconds without touching. After the squeezing/observing, participants evaluated the ball. Then as in experiment 2, participants were asked to indicate their intention of exchanging the current pen for another new and equally-priced pen by answering the question "how much do you want to change the current pen" using a 9-point scale. As shown in Figure 1, we found a significant interaction effect of power and physical action ($F (1, 157) = 4.34, p < .05$). Planned comparisons confirmed that high-power participants showed higher preferences for pen switching ($M_{high-power} = 4.95$ vs. $M_{low-power} = 4.03$; $F (1, 157) = 4.65, p < .05$) in the no-action control conditions. However, the effect disappeared in the physical action conditions ($M_{high-power} = 3.55$; $M_{low-power} = 3.93$; $n.s.$).

In summary, we examine a behavioral motivation that propels brand switching behavior in the form of psychological power. In doing so, we demonstrate that the action orientation associated with high power can be sated by a prior opportunity to engage in action. This has potentially important implications in better understanding psychological antecedents of brand switching.

Not All Power is Created Equal: Role of Social and Personal Power in Decision Making

EXTENDED ABSTRACT

Power has been the focus of much academic inquiry in the past decade (e.g., Briñol et. al., 2007; Galinsky et. al., 2003). Extant literature, however, primarily focuses on social power and overlooked personal power. In this paper, we empirically differentiate between personal and social power and examine its effects on commonly reported context effects.

Power is generally defined as the ability to control resources for oneself and others without interference. This definition has two distinct components: social and personal power. Social power is individuals' ability to exercise control over others (French & Raven, 1959). Alternatively, personal power is the ability to control one's own outcomes, without being influenced and constrained by others (Van Dijke & Poppe, 2006). Even though some researchers have acknowledged the existence of the social power and personal power distinction (Galinsky et al., 2003; Van Dijke & Poppe, 2006), most studies have treated power as a single construct (for an exception see Lammers, Stoker, & Stapel 2009).

We argue that one important distinction between social and personal power is the sense of freedom the power holder feels. High personal power individuals act independently, with little or no consideration of their social environment. As such, they have a high sense of freedom. Alternatively, social power is associated with interdependence (Fiske & Depret, 1996), which is associated with connection to others (Cross, Bacon & Morris, 2000), which presumably limits their sense of freedom. Therefore, we hypothesize that having personal power, compared to social power, leads to higher sense of freedom.

We further suggest that this sense of freedom (or lack thereof) has important implications for a host of context effects. We theorize that those who feel powerful have a desire to maintain this sense of freedom and they make decision that helps them achieve this goal. As such, we would expect feeling personal power to highlight a sense of freedom, making consumers wanting to maintain their freedom. Thus, we expect them to be more likely to choose extreme options that allow them to exercise their freedom, thus diminishing the compromise effect. One might suggest power, instead of operating through a need to maintain freedom, operates through an increased ability to cope with conflict. If this is the case, then we would expect those with personal (vs. social) power to also defer less and be less prone to the attraction effect. However, our theory predicts that since feeling personal (vs. social) power highlights freedom and the need to maintain it, those with personal power would be morel more likely to defer choice in an attempt to maintain their freedom. Similarly, since the choice of a dominating or dominated option does not allow for the maintenance of freedom, we would expect social versus personal power distinction to not influence the attraction effect.

A pilot study tested the basic premise our theory by having participants recall an event where they had social or personal power, and having an independent coder examining the written responses. We found that while those with personal power had more thoughts relating to freedom than those with social power, their responses did not differ in their stated confidence or mood.

Study 1 was designed to examine the compromise effect. Participants (N=113) first completed the power-inducing task. Next, they made a choice for a wine from three options. We varied the set composition so that option B would either be a compromise {ABC} or an extreme alternative {BCD}. We found that participants with social power chose option B more when it was the compromise option (79%) in set {ABC} than when it was the extreme option (38%) in set {BCD}. However, this compromise effect (difference of option B choice) was present only for those with high social power and not for those with personal power.

Study 2 examined the mediating role of experienced freedom. Participants (N = 89) completed the power-inducing task and then made a choice for an investment among three options, one of which was compromise. As predicted, we found that high personal power individuals chose the compromise option (57%) less than those with social power (77%). More importantly, we find that the feelings of elicited freedom mediated the effect of power type on the choice of compromise option.

Study 3 was designed to rule salience of others as an alternative explanation and examined the role of power type on attraction effect. Participants (N = 220) completed the power-inducing task and then made a choice between three cell phone plans. We varied the set composition so that the third option was either dominated by option A (A') or by option B (B'). As predicted, we found that choice share of option A was higher (82%) in set {A'AB} than set {ABB'} (47%). More importantly, power type did not interact with decoy location and attraction effect was observed for both for personal power ({A'AB} = 69%; {ABB'} = 54%) and for social power ({A'AB} = 67%; {ABB'} = 47%)

In Study 4, participants (N = 138) completed a power-inducing task. Next, they made a choice between two CDs and had the option to either choose one of these CDs or to defer choice and search more. As predicted, we found participants who recalled an incident of personal power chose to defer their choice more (41%) than those who recalled an incident of social power (19%) or those in the control condition (28%). An examination of the verbal protocols revealed that having personal power increased the thoughts relating to freedom and that this heightened sense of freedom mediated the effect of power type on deferral.

Five studies demonstrate that the effect of power on context effects depends on its type: while personal power attenuates the compromise effect, it augments the choice deferral, having no effect on the attraction effect. We further demonstrate that it is the heightened sense of freedom those with personal power feel that drives these effects.

Experience Versus Expectations of Power: A Recipe for Altering the Effects of Power

EXTENDED ABSTRACT

The current research explores how both consumers' state of power and a focus on the experience of power versus how others expect them to behave jointly influence their behavior in the forms of desire for status and information processing.

When focused on the experience of lacking power, as opposed to possessing power, consumers are known to exhibit an increased desire for status-related products (Rucker and Galinsky 2008, 2009) and greater information processing (Briñol et al. 2007). However, we put forth a novel hypothesis that, when focused on the expectations of power (i.e., characteristics and stereotypes associated with power), a state of high power may lead to a greater willingness to acquire status-related products. Similarly, when focused on the expectations of power, it is predicted that the powerful people might process information more carefully compared to powerless people.

An expectation-confirmation perspective is offered as the foundation of this novel prediction. Specifically, it seems that people develop and hold different expectations of people who have low versus high power (Magee and Galinsky 2008). Elsewhere it has been shown that expectations shape people's interpretation of social events and also people's behaviors to conform to existing expectations and stereotypes (Kipnis 1972). In a similar vein, we suggest that focusing people who are in a low or high power state on the expectations associated with the low- or high- power position might lead them to behave in a manner that meets those expectations. Five experiments test our novel hypotheses.

Experiment 1: The Expectations of Power. The first experiment assessed the expectations people naturally hold with respect to how power should affect people's behaviors. Participants saw descriptions of behaviors related to status consumption and information processing and were asked to identify if these behaviors were something they expected from either powerful or powerless people. Results showed that participants rated the behaviors of purchasing status products and processing information carefully as more consistent with powerful people compared to powerless people ($ps < .01$). Our remaining experiments examine whether focusing people on the expectations of others could shift their behavior to align with these expectations.

Experiment 2a and 2b: Power and Status Products. Experiment 2a adopted a 2 (level of power: high vs. low) × 2 (focus: experience vs. expectations) between-subject design. Participants' level of power and focus were manipulated through an episodic recall task adapted from Galinsky et al. (2003). Subsequently, participants were asked to evaluate two status-related products. Results revealed a significant power × focus interaction ($p = .002$) such that, when focused on the experience of power, low-power participants had a higher willingness to pay for the status products compared to high-power participants ($p = .02$). In contrast, when focused on the expectations of power, high-power participants had a higher willingness to pay compared to low-power participants ($p < .001$), consistent with people's expectations reported in experiment 1.

Experiment 2b adopted a 2 (level of power: high vs. low) × 2 (focus: experience vs. expectations) × 2 (brand status: high- vs. non- status) between subject design. Participants' level of power and focus were manipulated in a role-playing task (Dubois et al. 2010; Rucker et al. 2011). Subsequently, participants were asked to identify their purchase intentions for either a BMW or a Toyota. Results revealed a significant three-way interaction between power, focus, and brand status ($p = .004$). For participants evaluating a high-status brand (BMW), there was a significant two-way interaction between power and focus ($p < .001$) such that among participants focused on the experience of power, low-power participants showed a higher purchase intention compared to high-status participants ($p = .009$). In contrast, among participants who focused on the expectations of power, high-power participants had a higher purchase intention compared to low-power participants ($p = .008$). No effects were found for participants who evaluated a Toyota ($F < 1$).

Experiment 3a and 3b: Power and Information Processing. Experiment 3a adopted a 2 (level of power: high vs. low) × 2 (focus: experience vs. expectations) between-subject design in which power and focus were manipulated as in experiment 2a. After manipulating power and focus, participants rated two job candidates that differed in the strength of their profiles. A discrimination score was calculated by subtracting participant's evaluation of the weak candidate from that of the strong candidate. Results revealed a significant power × focus interaction ($p < .001$) such that when focused on the experience of power, low-power participants showed greater discrimination compared with high-power participants ($p = .01$). In contrast, when focused on the expectations of power, high-power participants showed greater discrimination than low-power participants ($p = .03$).

Experiment 3b adopted a 2 (power: high vs. low) × 2 (focus: experience vs. expectations) × 2 (argument strength: strong vs. weak) between-subject design in which power and focus were manipulated as in experiment 2b. Participants evaluated an ad for a snack that differed in argument strength. Results revealed a significant three-way interaction between power, focus, and argument strength ($p = .008$). In the experience conditions, low-power participants liked the snack more after receiving strong compared to weak arguments ($p < .001$) while high-power participants did not show any difference ($F < 1$). In the expectation conditions, high-power participants liked the snack more after strong compared to weak arguments ($p = .02$) while low-power participants showed no difference ($F < 1$).

Conclusion and Contributions. Across experiments, the focus associated with power created different effects on consumers' desire for status products and the depth of information processing. These findings add another important dimension to the research of power and consumption by suggest a new and critical moderator for understanding how states of power affect consumption.

REFERENCES

Anderson, Cameron and Jennifer L. Berdahl (2002), "The Experience of Power: Examining the Effects of Power on Approach and Inhibition Tendencies," *Journal of Personality and Social Psychology*, 83, 1362-77.

Berger, Jonah and Chip Heath (2007), "Where Consumers Diverge from Others: Identity Signaling and Product Domains," *Journal of Consumer Research*, 34 (August), 121-34.

Briñol, Pablo, Richard E. Petty, Carmen Valle, Derek D. Rucker, and Alberto Becerra

(2007), "The Effects of Message Recipients' Power Before and After Persuasion: A Self-Validation Analysis," *Journal of Personality and Social Psychology*, 93 (6), 1040-53.

Cross, Susan E., Pamela L. Bacon, and Michael L. Morris (2000), "The Relational- Interdependent Self-Construal and Relationships," *Journal of Personality and Social Psychology*, 78 (4), 791-808.

Einhorn, Hillel J. and Robin M. Hogarth (1986), "Decision Making under Ambiguity," *Journal of Business*, 59 (4), 433-61.

Fiske, Susan T. and Eric Depret (1996), "Control, Interdependence and Power: Understanding Social Cognition and Its Social Context," *European Review of Social Psychology*, 7, 31-61.

French, John R. P., Jr. and Bertram Raven (1959), "The Basis of Social Power," in *Studies in Social Power*, ed. Dorwin Cartwright, Ann Arbor, MI: Institute for Social Research, 118-49.

Galinsky, Adam D., Deborah H. Gruenfeld, and Joe C. Magee (2003), "From Power to Action," *Journal of Personality and Social Psychology*, 85 (September), 453-66.

Guinote, Ana (2007), "Power Affects Basic Cognition: Increased Attentional Inhibition and Flexibility," *Journal of Experimental Social Psychology*, 43 (July), 685-97.

Guinote, Ana (2008), "Power and Affordances: When the Situation Has More Power over Powerful than Powerless Individuals," *Journal of Personality and Social Psychology,* 95 (August), 237-52.

Keltner, Dacher, Deborah H Gruenfeld, and Cameron Anderson (2003), "Power, Approach, and Inhibition," *Psychological Review*, 110(2), 265-284.

Kipnis, David (1972), "Does Power Corrupt?," *Journal of Personality and Social Psychology, 24,* 33-41.

Lammers, Joris, Janka I. Stoker, and Diederik A. Stapel (2009), "Differentiating Social

and Personal Power: Opposite Effects on Stereotyping, but Parallel Effects on Behavioral Approach Tendencies," *Psychological Science*, 20 (12), 1543-48.

Magee, Joe C. and Adam D. Galinsky (2008), "Social Hierarchy: The Self-Reinforcing   Nature of Power and Status," *Academy of Management Annals*. 2: 351-398.

Maimaran, Michal and Itamar Simonson (2011), "Multiple Routes to Self- Versus Other-Expression in Consumer Choice," *Journal of Marketing Research*, 48 (4), 755-66.

Rucker, Derek D. and Adam D. Galinsky (2008), "Desire to Acquire: Powerlessness and Compensatory Consumption," *Journal of Consumer Research*, 35 (August), 257-67.

Rucker, Derek D. and Adam D. Galinsky (2009), "Conspicuous Consumption Versus Utilitarian Ideals: How Different Levels of Power Shape Consumer Behavior," *Journal of Experimental Social Psychology*, 45, 549-55.

Rucker, Derek D., Adam D. Galinsky, and David Dubois (2011), "Power and Consumer Behavior: How Power Shapes Who and What Consumers Value," *Journal of Consumer Psychology*, doi: 10.1016/j.jcps.2011.06.001.

Van Dijke, Marius and Matthijs Poppe (2006), "Striving for Personal Power as a Basis for Social Power Dynamics," *European Journal of Social Psychology*, 36 (4), 537-56.

Van Heerde, Harald J., Sachin Gupta, and Dick R. Wittink (2003), "Is 75% of the Sales Promotion Bump Due to Brand Switching? No, Only 33% Is." *Journal of Marketing Research*, 40(4), 481-91.

When It's What's Outside That Matters:
Recent Findings on Product and Packaging Design

Chair: Julio Sevilla, University of Miami, USA

Paper #1: Transparent Packaging and Consumer Purchase Decisions

Darron Billeter, Brigham Young University, USA
Meng Zhu, Johns Hopkins University, USA
J. Jeffrey Inman, University of Pittsburgh, USA

Paper #2: The Effect of Product Shape Closure on Perceptions of Quantity, Preference and Consumption

Julio Sevilla, University of Miami, USA
Barbara E. Kahn, University of Pennsylvania, USA

Paper #3: Aesthetics versus Humor in Product Packaging: Their Impact on Ownership Pride

Gratiana Pol, University of Southern California, USA
C.W. Park, University of Southern California, USA
Martin Reimann, University of Southern California, USA

Paper #4: Where You Say It Matters: How Product Packaging Increases Message Believability

Claudia Townsend, University of Miami, USA
Tatiana M. Fajardo, University of Miami, USA
Juliano Laran, University of Miami, USA

SESSION OVERVIEW

More than half of purchase decisions are made at the retail place (Inman and Winer 1998) and manufacturers are aware of this. This phenomenon has spawned a new emphasis on "shopper marketing," which entails examining consumer's in-store decision making from the store back and identifying what might influence the shopper. One of the key ways a product can stand out from others is through its package or shape, as it has been shown that functional and aesthetic appearance is an imperative factor in determining a product's appeal (Bloch 1995). Despite the growing awareness of the importance of product packaging, it is only fairly recently that we as consumer researchers have begun to develop theory to understand how consumers respond to the appearance of a product or package (Patrick and Peracchio 2010). This session is designed to help fill that gap.

This session offers four research papers that study the area of packaging from four separate but complementary view points. All of these projects are in very advanced stages, as they combine for a total of 18 completed experiments. Three of these projects are either under review or being prepared for submission. The first paper in the session, "Transparent Packaging and Consumer Purchase Decisions," by Darron Billeter, Meng Zhu and J. JeffreyInman, shows that consumers prefer transparent packages as these enhance perceptions of product trustworthiness even in cases where product quality and freshness are controlled for. This finding clearly demonstrates how physical aspects of a product design can affect higher level perceptions such as consumer trust of the product and the manufacturer. Additionally this research reveals consumers to be extremely responsive to the environmental cues perceived in the retail environment, especially to those related to the physical aspects of the product.

Consistent with this notion, the second paper, "The Effect of Product Shape Closure on Perceptions of Quantity, Preference and Consumption," by Julio Sevilla and Barbara E. Kahn demonstrates how consumer perceptions of product size, purchase intentions, and actual consumption can be altered by another seemingly irrelevant external aspect of a product, such as the degree of closure or completeness evoked by its shape. In this research, the authors keep the size and weight of the products constant and found the effect to be so robust that it trumps other well documented packaging phenomena such as the primary dimension and the attention attraction effect, and can be extended to other aspects of a product such as its label.

The third paper of the session, "Aesthetics versus Humor in Product Packaging: Their Impact on Ownership Pride," by Gratiana Pol, C.W. Park and Martin Reimann, looks at the effect that more global aspects of a package's appearance, such as its aesthetic or humorous properties, can have on product preference. The authors go beyond the first two papers by showing that a product package can transmit its socially desirable or undesirable aspects to the consumer, which will in turn impact product preference through feelings of ownership pride.

The last paper of the session, "Where You Say It Matters: How Product Packaging Increases Message Believability," by Claudia Townsend, Tatiana Fajardo and Juliano Laran, reveals another important benefit that a product package may convey. Specifically, the authors show that product claims are perceived as more effective, more credible and psychologically closer when presented on a package than when present in an advertisement. The implication of this research is that findings related to advertisements cannot necessarily be applied to packages and therefore there is an entire area of important research on product packaging to be explored.

We believe that a special session on product packaging that deals with diverse, current, fresh and substantive topics such as the ones we propose, should draw a great deal of attention from a diverse group of researchers coming from areas such as marketing strategy, psychophysics and environmental cues, retailing, product design, nutrition and public policy, hedonic consumption, aesthetics, social psychology, advertising, among others. A session that could attract such a diverse crowd would be likely to spawn a synergic, unique and fruitful discussion that could potentially lead to collaboration among researchers from these different areas. Finally, the currently proposed session benefits from the unique and diverse insights of its authors, as three of them come from different countries of Latin America, two of them from different countries of Asia, and one from Europe, while the rest are from the United States.

Transparent Packaging and Consumer Purchase Decisions

EXTENDED ABSTRACT

Due to limited processing capacity, consumers are frequently uncertain about their own preferences and the value of product offerings (e.g. Bettman, Luce and Payne 1998), and they often make inferences and construct meaning based on information that is salient in the immediate purchase context, such as product packaging. Existing literature confirms that consumers make inferences about product unit cost, capacity and consumption norms based on packaging size (Wansink 1996), packaging shape (Wansink and van Ittersum 2003) and packaging servings (Geier, Rozin and Doros 2006, Cheema and Soman 2008, Scott, Nowlis, Mandel, and Morales 2008, Coelho do Vale, Pieters, and Zeelenberg 2008).

In the current work, we study the impact of packaging transparency on consumer purchase decisions. Firms can select to encase a product in many different levels of packaging transparency, yet firms often choose to present their products in non-transparent packaging. We suggest that consumers will exhibit greater preference for products in transparent as compared non-transparent packaging even when explicitly controlling for product freshness and quality. We argue this is the case because that (1) people associate the notion of "transparent" with honesty, openness, candidness, and forthcoming behavior (2) they often make inferences and judgment about products based on non-diagnostic packaging cues that are salient in the purchase context (such as transparency) rather than diagnostic product information (such as ingredients) that is not salient in the local decision context (e.g. Wansink and Van Ittersum 1999; Zhu, Billeter and Inman 2012). Thus, products covered in transparent packaging will be viewed as more trustworthy as compared to the exact same products presented in non-transparent packaging, leading to greater purchase intention for and higher choice of transparent products.

Experiment 1a tests whether transparent packaging increases perceptions of the products trustworthiness. To do so, we first exposed participants to a picture of a bottle of orange juice in either a transparent or a non-transparent package. Then, we asked participants to rate the product's trustworthiness using the trustworthiness scale developed by De Wulf, Schroder, and Iacobucci (2001). Consistent with our theory, we find that consumer's perceive the orange juice as being more trustworthy when it is in a transparent as opposed to a non-transparent package.

The natural question that follows is how perceptions of freshness and quality are impacted by the transparent packaging. To address this, we conducted Experiment 1b. Participants were presented with a variety pack of well-known wrapped chocolate bars (Hershey's, Reeses, Kit Kats) that were altogether wrapped in either a transparent, cellophane wrapping or wrapped with a picture on the top of the packaging that depicted the exact same information shown through the transparent packaging. After viewing the variety pack, participants rated the product's trustworthiness (using the same scale from Experiment 1a) and find greater brand trust for the transparent packaging even after controlling for freshness (the expiration dates on the packages were highlighted and identical) and quality expectations (these are well known chocolate bars with consistent quality expectations). This test demonstrates that even when consumers know that the products are identical, consumers still rely on the non-diagnostic cue of transparent packaging in determining how much they trust the product.

In experiment 2, we investigate the next step in our conceptual framework by testing whether transparent packaging impacts purchase intention. In Experiment 2, participants view either a transparent or a non-transparent bottle of liquid laundry detergent. Then, participants rate their purchase intention for the laundry detergent on a scale developed by Baker and Churchill (1977). Confirming our hypothesis, we find greater purchase intention for the product in transparent packaging.

In Experiment 3, we return to the orange juice category and test the entire framework by testing whether transparent packaging increases purchase intention; and whether that increase in purchase intention is mediated by brand trust. Participants were shown either the transparent or non-transparent orange juice bottle (as in Experiment 1a). Then, they were asked to rate the product's trustworthiness (using the De Wulf, Schroder, and Iacobucci 2001 scale) and their purchase intention (using the Baker and Churchill 1977 scale). Consistent with our hypothesis we find greater purchase intention for the product in the transparent orange juice bottle. Additionally, we find that the relationship between transparent packaging and purchase intention is (complementary) mediated by brand trust (Preacher and

Hayes, 2004; Zhao, Lynch and Chen 2010). This result is consistent with our conceptual framework.

In Experiment 4 we investigated whether people prefer transparent to non-transparent packaging. 181 students were asked to choose between an actual transparent shampoo bottle and an actual non-transparent shampoo bottle of the same color as the shampoo. 77% of participants selected the transparent package confirming consumer preference for transparent packaging.

Finally, in Experiment 5, we propose and investigate a boundary condition for the effect. Unappealing products, rotting products, or products that do not meet consumer expectations would likely not benefit from transparent packaging. The inferences made about products in transparent packaging would likely not overcome the actual, observed negative attributes inherent in viewing rotting or unappetizing products or even icy, pale, frozen French fries. To test this, participants began Experiment 5 by looking at either a puke green transparent laundry detergent package or a non-transparent package. Then, participants rated the trustworthiness of the product. Consistent with the notion that inferences made about transparent packaging cannot overcome the judgments made when viewing unappealing products, we find that participants viewing the non-transparent laundry detergent have greater trust in the product than participants viewing the puke green transparent package.

To summarize, results from five experiments suggest that transparent (vs. non-transparent) leads to higher purchase intention and increased product choice, even when explicitly controlling for product freshness and quality. We identify perceptions of product trustworthiness as the mediator and physical appeal of products as an important boundary condition for this effect.

The Effect of Product Shape Closure on Perceptions of Quantity, Preference and Consumption

EXTENDED ABSTRACT

Consumers attend to environmental cues in the retail place in order to make inferences about the properties of a product (Zeithaml 1988). One of the most important indicators of a product's characteristics is its external aspect, including its shape. A product's shape has been shown to influence perceptions of size (Raghubir and Krishna 1999; Krider, Raghubir and Krishna 2001; Folkes and Matta 2004), preference (Raghubir and Krishna 1999; Krider, Raghubir and Krishna 2001; Folkes and Matta 2004) and consumption (Raghubir and Krishna 1999; Krider, Raghubir and Krishna 2001; Wansink and Van Ittersum 2003).

Past research on product shapes has demonstrated that people estimate products that have a longer (Raghubir and Krishna 1999) or more prominent primary dimension to be bigger (Krider, Raghubir and Krishna 2001). This is because consumers make effort-accuracy trade-offs that lead to heuristic processing of area estimations and size judgments biases. Moreover, research by Folkes and Matta (2004) has reversed this effect by showing that a product's ability to attract attention affects size perceptions due to mental contamination.

In this research, we introduce "product shape closure" as an even more robust determinant of perceptions of size judgments, preference and food consumption. Psychological closure refers to the feeling that a life experience is past or complete (Beike, Adams, and Wirth-Beaumont 2007). Past research has also defined need for closure as the desire to quickly reach firm answers that allow closing the door on a matter (Kardes et al. 2004, 2007; Kruglanski and Webster 1996). Reaching psychological closure allows individuals to pursue other goals and avoid negative affect (Beike, Markman, and Karadogan 2009; Beike and Wirth-Beaumont 2005).

In the current research, we tested if perceptions of the physical closure associated to the shape or the design of a package could have an effect on people size estimations and preference for a product. We manipulate product shape closure by keeping the size and weight of a product constant and by altering physical aspects of its design. For example, we compare cheese slices which surfaces include holes or not, sandwiches which are cut in halves or offered in their complete form, a shampoo bottle which possesses an overture on its package against one that does not, etc. Our results showed that products whose shapes evoked feelings of closure against those who did not were perceived as bigger and were preferred. This effect persisted in cases where the product that evoked the most feelings of closure and completeness did not have a larger primary dimension and did not attract more attention.

We ran seven studies to test the robustness and generalizability of this phenomenon, its underlying mechanism, and explore some boundary conditions for it. Study 1 was a field study held during a business lunch attended by medical doctors and healthcare executives. In this field experiment, subjects located in two different rooms ate equal weight snack sandwiches. Subjects in each group were invited to serve themselves snack size sandwiches which shape was complete (evoked closure) or incomplete (did not evoke closure). Despite the group that was assigned to the incomplete sandwiches condition had significantly less males (50%) than the other (70.7%), we found that subjects in that condition ate more sandwiches than those in the other group ($M_{unclosed}$ = 3.23 vs. M_{closed} = 2.38; t (44) = 3.96, $p < .0001$). As we expected, participants in the incomplete condition probably found the sandwiches to be smaller, which led them to eat more.

Study 2A demonstrated the phenomenon in a more controlled laboratory experiment and extended the findings from food consumption to size perceptions. This study showed that a bread bun and a cheese slice are considered to contain more quantity when their shape is closed or complete as opposed to unclosed or incomplete, even if the latter has a larger primary dimension. However, this effect will be reversed if the incomplete stimuli are assigned names of products for which an incomplete shape is representative of the product category (i.e. bagel and swiss cheese). In this case, the incompletely shaped products will be estimated to contain more quantity, as their incompleteness will not be used to adjust down consumer estimations, and instead participants will anchor on their prominent primary dimension and estimate them to be bigger. Study 2B used a similar design to demonstrate that the closure effect is mediated by the extent to which consumers perceive that a product corresponds to a full unit, as they will use this "unity heuristic" to estimate size perceptions and will ignore the fact that a product which is a fraction of a unit may be bigger than one which corresponds to a full unit, if the unit from which the former is a fraction is considerably larger. This bias is similar to the numerosity heuristic (Pelham, Sumarta and Myaskovsky 1994).

Studies 3A and 3B employed choice tasks to demonstrate that when participants compare products they will estimate that the completely shaped ones contain more quantity, are bigger, and will be more likely to be bought than the incomplete ones. Study 3A used sandwiches and packages of Babybel cheese to demonstrate that the effect will reverse the primary dimension heuristic, while Study 3B used bread buns and cheese slices to show that the phenomenon will also trump the attention attraction effect.

Study 4 used a similar design as the one used in Studies 3A and 3B to provided additional evidence in favor of the shape closure ef-

fect by showing that the phenomenon will be significantly stronger among participants who have high versus low Need for Cognitive Closure (NFCC). Finally, Study 5 demonstrated the robustness of the closure effect by showing that it can be extended to package labels and is not limited to package shapes. This experiment replicated the effect for cases where two products (juice galloons) have the same shape and size but one of them contains a more closure evoking label image than the other (i.e. a complete versus an incomplete apple picture).

Aesthetics versus Humor in Product Packaging: Their Impact on Ownership Pride

EXTENDED ABSTRACT

Product designers often strive to create designs whose sight elicits a positive emotional reaction in consumers (Desmet, 2003). To accomplish this, two of the most frequently used approaches consist in creating either an aesthetically appealing (Bloch, 1995; Coates, 2003) or a humorous-looking design (Doyle, 1998). Yet, while consumers' reactions to aesthetically appealing designs have garnered substantial attention in consumer research (Patrick & Peracchio, 2010), we know little to nothing about responses to humorous-looking designs. Aside from triggering a smile or a giggle, does a humorous-looking design provide any other value to consumers—most importantly, social value? Prior research has found aesthetically appealing designs to generate social value in the form of enhanced ownership pride (e.g., Townsend & Shu, 2010), but has not yet shown similar responses for humorous-looking designs. If such designs do indeed provide social value, how does it compare to that offered by a functionally equivalent, yet aesthetically appealing design? The present research will address these questions.

A visually attractive appearance represents a socially valued characteristic in interpersonal relationships (e.g., Sigall & Landy, 1993), but also in a consumption context, where aesthetically appealing products instill pride in their owners (Pol & Park, 2012; Townsend & Shu, 2010), who are often eager to display such products to the world (Bloch, 1995). Humor, on the other hand, while a highly socially desirable trait (Apte, 1978), can also evoke negative social connotations, such as impressions of inappropriateness or low source credibility (Eisend, 2008; Bressler & Balshine, 2006). In the context of a utilitarian product, such connotations may cause one to dismiss a humorous-looking product as a gimmick because of a perceived disconnect between its appearance and its functional purpose (Buchanan, 1989). This should, in turn, negatively affect the social benefits of owning such a product, potentially even triggering embarrassment rather than ownership pride in consumers. We hence propose that, between an aesthetically appealing and a humorous-looking product that are functionally equivalent and equally pleasant to look at, the humorous item should provide significantly lower social benefits to consumers, as evidenced through lower expectations of ownership pride. We tested this hypothesis in Study 1.

Visually appealing products have been associated with a host of desirable social connotations, most notably impressions of tastefulness (Cziksentmihalyi & Robinson, 1990; Wagner, 1999). Consistent with a self-signaling account (Bodner & Prelec, 2001), owning a visually attractive product should hence convey to oneself (and also to others) that one possess good taste, which in turn is conducive to instilling feelings of pride in consumers (Chang & Wu, 2007). A humorous-looking item, on the other hand, is unlikely to provide signals about one's level of taste (provided, of course, that the humor is not perceived as blatantly distasteful). It should, however, be perceived as interesting and original (Ludden, Schifferstein, & Hekkert,

2008), such that its ownership would convey that one possesses a unique and distinctive personality—a social signal that typically enhances individuals' sense of self-worth (Kim & Markus, 1999). We hence propose that aesthetically appealing products provide social value (i.e., elicit pride) because they signal that their owner has good taste, while humorous-looking products do so because they signal uniqueness. This second hypothesis was tested in Study 2.

In Study 1, we verified that humorous-looking product designs create less social value than humorous-looking ones do. The study employed a one-way (visual appearance: aesthetically appealing vs. humorous-looking vs. neutral-looking) within-subjects design. Each participant in the study saw a total of nine computer speakers (three in each category), which were described as identical in terms of price, manufacturer, quality, and functionality. Afterwards, participants indicated how proud they would be to own each item. The manipulation check confirmed that the aesthetically appealing products were significantly more attractive than all the other items, while the humorous products were perceived as the funniest. Respondents further reported the same degree of pleasure when looking at the attractive and the humorous-looking items. Consistent with our hypothesis, a repeated-measure ANOVA with planned contrasts revealed that the humorous-looking items did indeed trigger lower expectations of ownership pride compared to the aesthetically appealing products ($p < .05$). Interestingly, however, they elicited higher pride expectations than the neutral-looking ones (the latter of which served as a control group) ($p < .05$). These results show that, while an aesthetically appealing product offers stronger social benefits than a humorous-looking item does, humor may bring some social value to a product's design after all.

In Study 2, we examined whether aesthetically appealing and humorous-looking designs create social value through different mechanism. The study employed a one-way (visual appearance: aesthetically appealing vs. humorous-looking vs. neutral-looking) between-subjects design. We showed participants a range of household products (such as teapots, desk lamps, and alarm clocks) and asked them to the select three items they would best describe as beautiful, funny, and neutral-looking, respectively. Each participant was then presented with one of the three items based on the group he or she belonged to. We chose household items as stimuli because they are traditionally designed for private consumption, and would allow for a rather conservative replication of our previous results. In line with Study 1, we again found that the pride expectations elicited by the humorous-looking products were lower than those triggered by the aesthetically appealing products ($p < .05$), yet higher than those associated with the neutral-looking items ($p < .05$). Consistent with our hypothesis, two mediation analyses based on bootstrap further suggested that, while good taste best explained the impact of visual attractiveness on ownership pride, the relationship between humor and pride was explained by uniqueness ($p < .001$).

This research shows that a humorous-looking product design does provide social value to consumers, though to a lesser extent than an equally pleasant, yet aesthetically appealing design would. Moreover, aesthetics is socially valuable because it signals good taste, while humor providing social value because it connotes uniqueness. These findings provide initial evidence for how consumers' responses to hedonically appealing product designs vary across hedonic characteristics.

Where You Say It Matters:
How Product Packaging Increases Message Believability

EXTENDED ABSTRACT

For a message to have any effect it must be believed. Broadly speaking, persuasion research has identified three factors which influence message believability: source (Hovland and Weiss 1951), audience (Petty, Cacioppo, and Schumann 1983), and context (Oppenheimer 2006). In addition to this, proximity of the message to its audience may also influence believability (Latané et al. 1995). In effect, spatial distance can be considered part of a larger concept, that of psychological distance, the subjective experience of something being close or far away from the self. In the context of believability this is particularly relevant as there is a strong connection between psychological distance and construal level and moreover there is evidence to suggest construal level also influences believability (Wright et al. 2012).

Building on this work, we propose a new determinate of believability - psychological proximity of a message to its subject. Specifically we hypothesize that, all else equal, the closer a message seems to its object, the more believable it will be. We consider this in a consumer decision-making context by examining how product message placement (whether on a package versus in an advertisement) influences believability. Across three studies, we demonstrate that decision-makers consider product claims more (less) believable when presented on a package (advertisement) and that this effect is mediated by perceived proximity of the claim to the product.

Study 1a establishes the basic effect of presentation material on message believability and the moderating role of claim strength. Participants were shown a product description for an electric kettle with a claim that it boils water in either two or eighteen seconds. We manipulated whether the message was presented on a package or in an advertisement through introductory language and simple graphic variations. Analysis of believability ratings revealed a significant two-way interaction between claim strength and presentation material ($F(1, 159) = 7.73, p = .01$). When presented with a strong product claim, participants rated it as more believable if presented on a package than in an advertisement ($M_{strong\ claim,\ package} = 4.00$, $M_{strong\ claim,\ advertisement} = 3.23$, $F(1, 79) = 4.37, p = .04$). There was no effect of presentation material on message believability in the weak claim conditions ($F < 1$) suggesting that this effect is only relevant with strong claims where believability may be called into question.

Some consumers may be immune to the effect of presentation material; study 1b tested this possibility be examining the role of product knowledge. We used nail polish as our product category and gender as an indicator of product knowledge. All participants were shown either an advertisement or package for a nail polish top coat. Analysis of believability ratings revealed a significant two-way interaction between gender and presentation material ($F(1, 178) = 4.60, p = .03$). Men rated the product claim as more believable when presented on a package ($M_{male,\ package} = 4.06$, $M_{male,\ advertisement} = 3.22$, $F(1, 99) = 8.50, p < .01$). Presentation material did not influence the believability ratings of female participants ($F < 1$). We find, therefore, that the effect of claim placement, and presumably closeness, is stronger when participants have less knowledge of the product category.

Studies 2 and 3 examined the mechanism through which package messages seem more believable than those in advertisements. If the proximity of the product to the message is indeed the key difference between an advertisement and a package in terms of believability, then varying alternative forms of psychological distance should moderate our effect. In study 2 we primed different degrees of spatial distance. Additionally, we tested our theory using a new product, digital video recorders (DVRs). We used current DVR ownership as an indicator of product knowledge. Analysis of believability ratings revealed a significant three-way interaction between presentation material, distance prime, and ownership ($F(2, 347) = 3.59$, $p = .03$). Under control conditions, presentation material did not influence perceived believability among participants who own a DVR ($F < 1$) but did affect believability among those who do not; these participants rated the product claim as more believable when presented on a package than in an advertisement ($M_{control, package, do not own} = 5.97$, $M_{control, advertisement, do not own} = 4.91$, $F (1, 347) = 4.92$, $p = .03$). Furthermore, among these participants there was an effect of distance prime on package claim believability; this effect was driven by decreased believability in the far distance conditions ($M_{control, package, do not own} = 5.97$, $M_{far, package, do not own} = 4.98$, $F (1, 76) = 4.46$, $p = .04$; $M_{near, package, do not own} = 5.75$, $M_{far, package, do not own} = 4.98$, $F (1, 80) = 2.93$, $p = .09$). There was no significant effect of the distance prime on advertisement claim believability, however we did see that the near prime slightly increased the believability of an advertisement claim ($M_{control, advertisement, do not own} = 4.91$, $M_{near, advertisement, do not own} = 5.68$, $F (1, 71) = 2.55$, $p = .12$).

In study 3 we considered varying psychological distance in a third manner, narrative voice. We found a significant three-way interaction between presentation material, narrative voice, and ownership ($F(2, 251) = 4.98$, $p < .01$). Results replicated prior findings and were mediated by perceptions of the proximity between the product and the product information. Once presented in a first-person (third-person) voice the claim was perceived as close to (far from) the product regardless of presentation material and thus relatively believable (unbelievable).

Across three operationalizations of psychological proximity we see that presenting a claim as closer to its subject will increase believability. These findings extend our knowledge of psychological distance and its effects on persuasion. Beyond the current context of advertisements and packages, our results are relevant in any situation where message-to-subject proximity may be manipulated and of particular use in situations where a claim appears improbable (e.g. fundraising campaigns where need is extreme) or where the consumer's best interest is in complying with the stated message (e.g. usage of OTC pharmaceuticals or public safety campaigns). Furthermore, our results challenge the implicit notion that consumer responses to advertisements and packaging are the same.

Disadoption

Chair: Donald R. Lehmann, Columbia University, USA

Paper #1: Disadoption
Donald Lehmann, Columbia University, USA
Jeffrey R. Parker, Georgia State University, USA

Paper #2: Disadopting Unsustainable Consumption
Min Ding, Pennsylvania State University, USA

Paper #3: Disadoption through the Relationship Lens
Susan Fournier, Boston University, USA
Claudio Alvarez, Boston University, USA
Jill Avery, Simmons School of Management, USA

Paper #4: When Firms Disadopt Consumers: Exploring How Consumers Respond to Firm-Initiated Relationship Disengagement
Martin Mende, University of Kentucky, USA
Maura Scott, University of Kentucky, USA
Katherine Lemon, Boston College, USA
Scott Thompson, University of Georgia, USA

SESSION OVERVIEW

The purpose of this session is to focus attention on a fundamental and understudied area: disadoption. While considerable effort has been focused on the adoption of innovations (e.g., Rogers 1995), stopping doing something is an equally intriguing topic. While various specific disadoptions have been studied and or encouraged (e.g., churn /customer defection, health behaviors related to smoking and eating), little effort has been directed toward studying disadoption as a general topic and integrating perspectives into a unified "theory" of disadoption. The purpose of this session is to make progress in that direction.

The session will begin with a paper by Lehmann and Parker which discusses disadoption as a general phenomenon. Aspects discussed will include reasons for disadoption (including whether it is voluntary or forced and long or short term), which forces speed or retard it, how to model it, and what consequences arise (e.g., is it accepted or resisted?) Then three very different types of disadoption will be discussed.

Specifically, Min Ding will discuss cessation of behaviors that relate to sustainability. Susan Fournier will take a different tack, viewing disadoption from the lens of a relationship breakup. Finally, Kay Lemon will focus on modeling forced disadoptions in the area of customer defections, e.g., when companies decide to delete a customer and how the customer responds. The session will conclude with a general discussion aimed at integrating the talks and creating an agenda for future research.

Disadoption

EXTENDED ABSTRACT

The breadth of studies investigating diffusion and adoption processes is impressively extensive (for excellent reviews, see Majay, Muller, and Bass 1990; and Sultan, Farley, and Lehmann 1990). For instance, factors affecting product and/or innovation adoption that have been investigated include, but are not limited to, advertising (Dockner and Jorgensen 1988; Horsky and Simon 1983; Kalish 1985), word of mouth and social influence (Godes and Mayzlin 2009; Iyengar, Van den Bulte, and Valente 2011) consumer expertise (Moreau, Lehmann, and Markman 2001), product categorization (Moreau, Markman, and Lehmann 2001), product warranties

(Bearden and Shimp 1982), and price and product benefits (Horsky 1990).

Needless to say, product/innovation adoption has received a great deal of attention. While the variety of topics covered under the adoption umbrella has been vast, they have all contributed to a systematic investigation and understanding of when, why, and how fast individuals adopt products and innovations. In other words, adoption is considered a unified, unique, and general process with many inputs, moderators, and consequences.

By contrast, the opposite process, disadoption (i.e., the discontinuance of use of a product or behavior), has yet to be considered as a stand-alone, general phenomenon and has received relatively little systematic attention. While specific disadoption related behaviors have been studied (e.g., smoking cessation, dieting, product disposal, etc.), the focus has been on the specific activity rather than the general process of disadoption. The purpose of this paper is to consider disadoption as a general phenomenon and outline its antecedents, process, and consequences in the spirit of Greenleaf and Lehmann's (1995) analysis of reasons for decision delay. In contrast to that work, however, we consider a broader range of instances in our conceptualization and include a more diverse population in our experiments.

One perspective on disadoption is that stopping doing something is merely the adoption of a new (or non-) behavior, which suggests that disadoption and adoption can be characterized, conceptualized, and modeled in the same way (e.g., a Bass model can be used to model disadoption as well as adoption). From this perspective, choosing to quit smoking is identical to choosing to live a smoke free life functionally, behaviorally, and psychologically. At first glance, this seems to be a reasonable position. After all, given a choice between A and B, choosing "A" is equivalent to choosing "not B."

However, there are several aspects of disadoption which are unique. First, when a person disadopts something, there is relatively little uncertainty about what they are foregoing, in contrast to adoption processes where uncertainty in inherent. Second, while adoption is generally modeled in a binary fashion (yes or no), disadoption can be gradual and partial, occurring over time or in steps or stages. Third, whereas adopting a product requires taking possession of it, it is possible to disadopt a product without disposing of it. Fourth, giving something up brings into play several psychological processes such as loss aversion and possession utility which play less of a role in adoption decisions. Further, the psychology of choice has been shown to differ significantly from the psychology of rejection (Chernev 2009; Laran and Wilcox 2011; Park, Jun, and MacInnis 2000; Shafir 1993). Consequently, a broad examination of disadoption seems warranted.

Broadly described, we define disadoption as the process of cessation or substantial reduction in the use of a previously valued behavior or possession. This process can be fairly complex. Disadoption can occur either abruptly ("cold turkey") or over the course of a long period of time. It can be triggered by a variety of external (e.g., availability or social pressure) and internal (e.g., a new or increasingly salient goal) factors, whose effects may be cumulative. It may be a permanent or temporary change. And, importantly, the subsequent reaction to the disadoption may be positive and reinforcing or negative and regret inducing.

This paper takes four major steps toward formalizing the concept and investigation of disadoption. First, we propose a conceptual

Advances in Consumer Research
Volume 40, ©2012

model of the disadoption process. This model illustrates how a large variety of factors including (i) internal and external influences (triggers), (ii) the perceived ease and permanence of the disadoption, and (iii) the ultimate response to the disadoption can impact the likelihood that a consumer will consider (at all) and ultimately choose to disadopt.

Second, we draw from and integrate a wide array of literature that addresses impactful disadoption triggers. This conceptual analysis is supplemented with empirical data on disadoption triggers collected from over 600 student and non-student participants across two studies. Study 1 presents preliminary evidence that the reasons for disadoption are fairly consistent within subpopulations (e.g., students), but can vary significantly across different populations (e.g., students vs. a more diverse national sample). Study 2 factor analyzes consumers' reasons for disadoption and finds evidence that a wide variety of specific reasons for disadoption can be explained by five factors (general reasons): (i) life transitions, (ii) negative aspects/ social pressure, (iii) irritation, (iv) variety seeking, and (v) future viability.

Third, we present an initial discussion on the opportunities and challenges of modeling disadoption. Fourth, and finally, we outline a research agenda for studying disadoption. It is our hope that this paper and session will stimulate conversation and research on the topic of disadoption, a largely ignored yet very important general phenomenon.

Disadopting Unsustainable Consumption

EXTENDED ABSTRACT

Sustainable development (SD) has now become a guiding force in policy making at various government levels, from township to city to state to country, and to inter-nation organizations. For example, many city governments now approve new development with sustainability in mind, and demand their contractors to practice sustainable development. Firms, in turn, have incorporate sustainable development in their strategic planning and daily operation, and further demand their own suppliers and distributors to practice sustainable development. Walmart, for example, asks its suppliers to complete a sustainability report and a supplier that fares badly on this report might lose their business with Walmart. Most importantly, citizens are demanding it and practicing it. In the words of a senior executive at a major consumer product company, "customers will punish us if we don't do it".

The modern definition of SD is proposed in the 1987 World Commission on Environment and Development (WCED, also known as the Brundtland Commission). This commission enriched the definition to include both social and environmental concerns and this modern definition is the most important contribution from its report, Our Common Future (a.k.a. the Brundtland Report). Specifically, it defines SD as "the kind of development that meets the needs of the present without compromising the ability of future generations to meet their own needs." In 1992, UN Conference of Environment and Development in Rio de Janeiro (also known as Earth Summit) published Agenda 21, in which almost all nations committed to implement specific items consistent with SD. In 2002, World Summit on Sustainable Development in Johannesburg, South Africa, heads of state agreed to implement Agenda 21. This year (2012), the United Nation Conference on Sustainable Development (also called Rio+20) will review the progress of SD and set agenda for the future.

The biggest challenge in SD is to change our behavior, change how we normally do things. Government needs to change their policies, firms need to change their practice, and individuals need to change their consumption habits. We study how individuals change their behavior in this paper.

The behavioral change involves disadoption of routines an individual is practicing now, even already habitualized. Such disadoption requires a different theoretical understanding of the process than adoption. To the best of our knowledge, there is no systematic study of disadoption behavior driven by concern on SD. The closest research to this is the disadoption of behaviors that are not healthy, such as smoking, drinking, or uncontrolled eating.

However, there are at least three major differences between the SD driven disadoption and existing disadoption behavior:

- Existing disadoption research studies behavior that will have an effect on oneself, for example, one's chance of dying of lung cancer will decrease substantially if he stops smoking. On the other hand, SD related disadoption research studies behavior that has no effect on oneself, instead, it studies behavior that will have an effect on future generation whom the individual will not even meet. For example, if one uses less energy now, the future generation will have more energy reserve (e.g., oil).
- Existing disadoption research studies behavior that will have an effect independent of what other people will do. Again, for smoking, if one stops smoking, the benefit of this disadoption is assured regardless of what other people do. On the other hand, SD related disadoption research studies behavior where the effect depends on other people doing the same thing. If only one person reduces energy use, and the other people do not, future generation will unlikely benefit from this person's action. Furthermore, there is a free riding concern. If enough people save energy, future generation will have enough reserve even if one doesn't do it.
- The third difference is that we study willingness to disadopt, in terms of quantitative measures ($). This will provide a more rigorous understanding of this behavior, and provide more actionable guidelines to managers and policy makers, in addition to individuals.

The types of SD related disadoption behavior we are interested in include the following examples (but not limited to). We will not study duel-purpose disadoption, where disadoption has benefit for SD as well as for oneself (e.g., reducing energy use can save money as well). Here are some examples in SD related disadoption:

- Disadoption of leather cloth/accessories (to contribute to biodiversity, and reduce animal cruelty).
- Disadoption of plastic bags as much as one can (to contribute to low landfill)
- Disadoption of disposable plastic water bottles (to contribute to low landfill)
- Disadoption of less SD friendly (to environment, to their employees, to the community they are in) business' products (to contribute to both environment and society)
- Disadoption of products with fancy packages (to reduce waste)
- Disadoption of eating unnecessary meat (it takes substantial environmental resource to produce meat)
- Disadoption of showering too long and too often

Our research should help understand how consumers make SD related disadoptions, and may help us develop more effective communication strategies to encourage individuals to disadopt such behavior.

Disadoption through the Relationship Lens

EXTENDED ABSTRACT

This presentation offers an expanded perspective on disadoption as viewed through the relationship theoretic lens. Our inquiry builds from three brand relationship tenets (Fournier 1998): relationships as processes; relationships as contextualized and meaning-laden experiences involving a person, his/her social networks, and a product, service, or brand; and relationships as multiplex phenomena that vary in strength and kind. These principles stand in stark contrast to the frame of diffusion theory typically applied to the disadoption problem and thus offer the potential to extend our understanding of disadoption in meaningful ways.

First, relationship theory forces us to move beyond popular conceptualizations of disadoption as a yes/no brand decision to consider the process aspects of the experience at hand. Relationships, at their core, are dynamic phenomena that evolve and change in response to reciprocating signals exchanged over time. The process of ending a relationship has been variously described as separation, termination, dissolution, withdrawal, disengagement, divorce, break-up, discontinuity, decline, exit, and rejection—each possessing a process phenomenology worthy of investigation in its own right (Duck 1982). While relationship discontinuity has received attention in consumer research (Aaker, Fournier and Brasel 2004; Aggarwal 2004; Fournier 1998), theory is limited by a focus on brand transgressions as precipitators of relationship decline. Clearly, the transgression-recovery process is important to an understanding of relationship dissolution, but this event-based and brand-centric framework far from exhausts the processes whereby consumers and brands are driven apart. Even within the transgression framework, certain frames have yet to be fully leveraged. Rich constructs from relationship contracting theory including opportunistic contracting (MacNeil 1985) or contract drift and misalignment (Rousseau and McLean Parks 1992) can help explain the deterioration of relationships between consumers and brands. Disadoption viewed through a relationship theory lens can shift basic conceptions of a process that is not always constituted as termination and dissolution, but rather gradual separation or a more liminal state of disengagement and detachment over time.

Second, relationship theory forces deeper acknowledgement of the person and how the experience of disadoption flows from and affects that person's life. One of the major criticisms of diffusion research concerns its source bias: the tendency to examine diffusion phenomena almost exclusively from the perspective of the change agency itself (Rogers 1995). Despite noteworthy exceptions (Johnson, Matear and Thomson 2011; Lastovicka and Fernandez 2005; Price, Arnould and Curasi 2000), not enough consumer research has explored what happens when something is dis-adopted: we lack a comprehensive exposition of the lived experience and consequences of disadoption through the person's eyes. Of interest is the implicit assumption that a discontinued relationship is a "failed" relationship, and that breakups are inherently bad. But dissolution may rescue a person from an abusive relationship or provide paths for growth not possible when a particular relationship is engaged. Recent approaches (Specher and Fehr 1998) treat dissolution holistically as an integral part of a person's life projects and activities, not as a separate process. Moreover, disadoption can be a very social process that implicates not only the person but also networks of family and friends. A relationship always takes place within a set of other relationships and yet we know little of the role, experience and influence of third parties on the disadoption process itself.

A third relationship principle highlights the diversity of relationships and the variability of processes relating to these different relationship forms. Although there are literally hundreds of types of relationships, consumer research applications of relationship theory designed to enrich our understanding of disadoption focus on but one relationship type: the marriage between consumer and brand. Within this implicit framing, our understanding of relationship dissolution is conceptualized metaphorically as divorce (Dwyer, Schurr and Oh 1987). Perrin-Martinenq (2004) depicts relationship dissolution as a multi-phased exit process similar to Duck's (1982) four-phased model of breakdown, decline, disengagement and dissolution in divorce (Perrin-Martinenq, 2004). Still, consumer researchers have yet to unpack the complexity of the divorce phenomenon as illuminated through relationships research (Baxter 1984; Duck 1982; Simpson 1987). Divorce is a messy, protracted, and embedded experience through which a relationship other becomes dis-integrated from a person and his/her social life.

Still, few brand engagements qualify as marriages (Miller, Fournier and Allen 2012), and emotionally-laden divorces are likely rare. Brand relationships research supports a range of valid templates (Fournier 1998) that are not yet accommodated in theories of disadoption of brands. The character of the dissolution experience will be fundamentally different depending on the type of brand relationship disengaged. For certain relationship types, disadoption plays a different role altogether. For example, separation of brand and person serve not as the ending of a given relationship, but rather as the qualifier for relationship initiation in the case of adversaries, brand enemies and former friends (Johnson, Matear and Thomson 2011).

This study uses findings from three qualitative datasets that collectively enliven the lived experience of disadoption as viewed through a relationship lens. First is a two-year longitudinal inquiry involving twenty-five consumers' experiences with an Internet grocery service, fifteen of whom eventually disadopt the service. A second database includes comments posted by consumers on blogs, discussion boards and social media sites in response to controversial brand decisions, and focuses on those who disengage from the brand. Lastly, we consider interview data from sixteen loyal, "best customers" whose relationships were terminated unexpectedly at the company's hands. Collectively these studies allow multiple perspectives on disadoption as manifest in different contexts, thereby addressing our exploratory research goals.

In this presentation we leverage the above theories of relationship deterioration and our data to present alternate conceptualizations of disadoption for five different brand relationships: marriages, flings, adversaries, abusive partnerships, and functional business exchange. Stress factors precipitating breakdown, patterns of break-up, processes of dissolution, and consumer responses to dissolution are considered as they vary by relationship type. We close with propositions intended to improve the accuracy of our disadoption predictions and stimulate research on disadoption through the relationships lens.

REFERENCES

Aaker, Jennifer, Susan Fournier, and S. Adam Brasel (2004), "When Good Brands Do Bad," *Journal of Consumer Research,* 31 (1), 1-16.

Aggarwal, Pankaj (2004), "The Effects of Brand Relationship Norms on Consumer Attitudes and Behavior," *Journal of Consumer Research*, 31 (1), 87-101.

Baxter, Leslie (1984), "Trajectories of Relationship Disengagement," *Journal of Social and Personal Relationships*, 1, 29-48.

Duck, Steven (1982), *Personal Relationships 4: Dissolving Personal Relationships*. London: Academic Press.

Dwyer, F. Robert, Paul H. Schurr, and Sejo Oh (1987), "Developing Buyer-Seller Relationships," *Journal of Marketing*, 51 (2), 11.

Fournier, Susan (1998), "Consumers and Their Brands: Developing Relationship Theory in Consumer Research," *Journal of Consumer Research*, 24 (March 1988), 343-73.

Johnson, Allison R., Maggie Matear, and Matthew Thomson (2011), "A Coal in the Heart: Self-Relevance as a Post-Exit Predictor of Anti-Brand Actions," *Journal of Consumer Research*, 38 (1), 108-125.

Lastovicka, John L., and Karen V. Fernandez (2005), "Three Paths to Disposition: The Movement of Meaningful Possessions to Strangers," *Journal of Consumer Research*, 31 (4), 813-823.

MacNeil, I.R. (1985), "Relational Contracts: What We Do and Do Not Know," *Wisconsin Law Review*, 483-525.

Miller, Felicia, Susan Fournier and Chris Allen (2012, forthcoming), "Exploring Relationship Analogues in the Brand Space," to appear in *Consumer-Brand Relationships: Theory and Practice*, S. Fournier, M. Breazeale, and M. Fetscherin (eds.), London: Routledge/Taylor & Francis Group.

Perrin-Martinenq, Delphine (2004), "The Role of Brand Detachment on the Dissolution of the Relationship between the Consumer and the Brand," *Journal of Marketing Management*, 20 (9-10), 1001-1023.

Price, Linda, Eric Amould, and Carolyn Curasi (2000), "Older Consumers' Disposition of Valued Possessions," *Journal of Consumer Research*, 27 (September), 179-201.

Rogers, Everett M. (1995), *Diffusion of Innovations* (4th ed.). New York: The Free Press.

Rousseau, Denise M. and Judi McLean Parks (1992), "The Contracts of Individuals and Organizations," *Research in Organizational Behavior*, Vol. 15: JAI Press Inc.

Simpson, J. A. (1987), "The Dissolution of Romantic Relationships: Factors Involved in Relationship Stability and Emotional Distress," *Journal of Personality and Social Psychology*, 53 (4), 683-692.

Specher, Susan, and Barbara Fehr (1998), "The Dissolution of Close Relationships," in *Perspectives on Loss: A Sourcebook*, J. H. Harvey (ed.), Philadelphia: Brunner/Mazel.

When Firms Disadopt Consumers: Exploring How Consumers Respond to Firm-Initiated Relationship Disengagement

EXTENDED ABSTRACT

Firm-initiated consumer disadoption (firms choosing to disengage from or end a relationship with a consumer) is increasingly common. For instance, in 2007, telecommunications firm Sprint terminated more than 1,000 consumers who called customer service ("too") frequently. Two studies reveal how mechanisms of blame attribution, judgments of deservingness, and social exclusion influence consumer responses to disadoption (e.g., in terms of perceived firm integrity, anger, negative attitude).

Because companies are concerned about their reputation and perceived integrity when abandoning consumers, Study 1 (field study) examines how *non-targeted, observing* consumers respond. Grounded in deservingness and attribution theories, this study shows

that observers' responses to the firm (Sprint) are influenced by whether they believe targeted consumers deserve being disadopted.

Study 2 (experiment), examines how *targeted* consumers respond to distinct configurations of disadoption. Grounded in social exclusion theory, it shows that the interaction between how firms disadopt consumers (via direct dissolution vs. costly inclusion) and why firms disadopt them (via dispositional vs. non-dispositional blame) influences consumer response. This study suggests that consumer-perceived firm integrity and anger play mediating roles in consumer response to firm-initiated consumer disadoption.

Study 1

The study context is a popular consumer website which posted two stories on Sprint's decision to terminate consumers in July 2007. The stories described Sprint's actions and policies around the disadoption of some of its customers, and included a copy of Sprint's termination letter blaming those consumers for excessive complaining. Commenting on these stories, observing consumers posted a total of 173 comments. These consumer reactions were content analyzed. Coders rated each message from –3 to +3 based on two variables: the poster's portrayal of the firm's (Sprint's) integrity and the poster's emotional response. Scores at the extreme (-3, +3) indicate the message portrayed firm integrity negatively (-3, e.g., dishonest, unethical, greedy) or positively (+3, honest, ethical, not greedy).

The ANOVA on firm integrity revealed a significant main effect of blame attribution, $F(1, 172) = 168.80$, $p < .01$. When Sprint was blamed, perceived firm integrity was negative ($M = -1.46$). However, when observers blamed the fired consumers, firm integrity was portrayed positively ($M = .78$). An example posting: *"I think many people would disagree with me, but I think this is an honorable way for them [Sprint] to end this."*

The ANOVA on emotional responses revealed a significant blame main effect, $F(1, 172) = 86.97$, $p < .01$. Messages blaming Sprint contained negative emotional responses ($M = -1.20$). An example posting: *"Sprint sucks and I hope this idiotic decision hurts their bottom line."* However, when observers blamed the terminated consumers, the messages reflected a slightly positive emotional response ($M = .23$).

We conducted a bootstrapping analysis (Zhao, Lynch, and Chen 2010) with blame attributions as the IV, firm integrity as a potential mediator, and emotional response as the DV. Confidence intervals with 5000 bootstrap samples at the 95% level excluded zero ($a \times b = -1.24$; 95% CI = -1.60 to -.91), indicating an indirect effect of firm integrity.

Study 2

Study 2 was a 2(blame content: dispositional, non-dispositional) × 2(approach: direct dissolution, costly inclusion) between subjects experiment. We asked participants to imagine being a member of a bookstore discount club similar to a large U. S. bookstore. Participants were told they intended to renew their membership ($25 annual fee), but one month before the membership expiration the bookstore sent a letter informing them of the disadoption. In this letter, we manipulated two factors. Because excessive complaining and lack of profitability are major reasons for disadoption, we manipulated the (non-)dispositional *blame* accordingly. We manipulated the disadoption *approach* by specifying either direct dissolution or costly inclusion through a price increase. Participants then indicated their attitude toward the firm, their perception of the firm's integrity, and their feelings of anger.

Negative Attitude. ANOVA of negative attitude revealed a blame content main effect ($F(1, 177) = 13.44, p < .001$), qualified by its interaction with the disadoption approach ($F(1, 177) = 8.30, p < .005$), see Figure 1. The disadoption approach main effect was non-significant ($F<1$). Contrasts revealed that when the blame is dispositional, negative attitudes were greater under costly inclusion ($M_{CI} = 6.43$) than under direct dissolution ($M_{DD} = 5.94; F(1, 177) = 3.84, p < .05$). The reverse pattern was present when blame was non-dispositional; negative attitudes were greater for a direct dissolution ($M_{DD} = 5.80$) than costly inclusion ($M_{CI} = 5.23; F(1, 177) = 4.46, p < .05$).

Firm Integrity. ANOVA of firm integrity ($\alpha = .70$) revealed a blame content main effect ($F(1, 177) = 12.45, p < .001$), qualified by its interaction with the disadoption approach ($F(1, 177) = 11.96, p < .001$), see Figure 2. The disadoption approach main effect was non-significant ($F < 1$). Contrasts revealed that for dispositional blame, firm integrity was higher with direct dissolution ($M_{DD} = 1.90$) than costly inclusion ($M_{CI} = 1.38; F(1, 177) = 3.96, p < .05$); for non-dispositional blame, firm integrity was lower with direct dissolution ($M_{DD} = 1.91$) than costly inclusion ($M_{CI} = 2.71; F(1, 177) = 8.26, p < .005$).

Using a bootstrapping procedure (Preacher and Hayes 2008), our model included the blame-by-disadoption interaction as the independent variable, blame content and disadoption approach as covariates, and negative attitude as the dependent variable. Potential mediators were firm integrity and anger. Confidence intervals with 5000 resamples at the 95% level excluded zero for firm integrity ($a \times b = -.59$; 95% CI = -1.10 to -.26) and anger ($a \times b = -.15$; 95% CI = -.44 to -.01), indicating an indirect effect of firm integrity and anger.

Discussion:

Study 1 suggests that the allocation of blame and judgments of deservingness influence how non-targeted consumers respond to relationship dissolution. Observers who feel that targeted consumers deserved their firing tend to portray the firm positively. Study 2 suggests that the interaction between *why* and *how* firms disadopt consumers determines their response. The results show that costly inclusion – under certain circumstances – can be superior to direct dissolution for consumers and firms.

Figure 1:

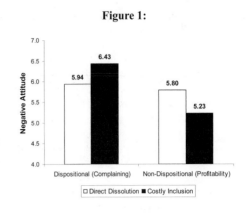

Figure 2:

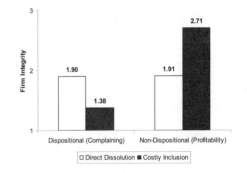

Competitive Papers—Full

Through Which Mechanisms Does Ambient Scent Affect Purchase Intention in Retail Settings?

Silke Bambauer-Sachse, University of Fribourg, Switzerland

ABSTRACT

In this paper, the effect of ambient scent on purchase intention is examined in a retail setting. The theoretical arguments suggest and the empirical analysis confirms that this effect is mediated by variables such as mood, ambiance evaluation, salesperson evaluation, and assortment evaluation.

INTRODUCTION

Ambient scents that are often considered as extraneous environmental cues (Bosmans 2006) evoke more powerful reactions than does addressing the other senses (Hirsch 1992). Although individuals may have difficulty recognizing a scent, scent identification is not a necessary condition for scent effects to occur (Ellen and Bone 1998). Thus, scents can have effects on consumers even if they do not pay attention to scents as they do with regard to other environmental stimuli (Ward, Davies, and Kooijman 2007). Consequently, effects of ambient scents are interesting from a consumer research perspective.

This study consists of a detailed examination of the mechanisms by which ambient scent effects occur in a real retail environment. Thus, it is the objective of this study to integrate the variables derived from previous research that might play a role in the considered context into one research model and to examine the specific relations between these variables in terms of rather direct or indirect ambient scent effects. The variables derived from previous studies are: mood, ambiance evaluation, salesperson evaluation, assortment evaluation, and purchase intention. In order to create a research model containing these variables, two research streams are brought together: research on ambient scent effects and research on mood effects. Following the argument of Morrin and Ratneswar (2003) that unpleasant scents have little practical relevance in marketing efforts, this study focuses on pleasant scents. Furthermore, the product category studied here represents a high involvement product category because especially the purchase of high involvement products often requires the recommendation of a salesperson. Thus, choosing such a product category for the empirical study made it possible to examine effects of ambient scent on the evaluation of the salesperson.

The study presented here goes beyond previous research because previous studies only examined single effects of ambient scent, but did not consider the broader context of possible other effects. Furthermore, although there is a comparatively large body of research on effects of product scents (Gulas and Bloch 1995), much less research was conducted on effects of ambient scents on consumer response variables such as product evaluations (Bosmans 2006) or purchase intentions. In addition, the study presented here fills three further gaps of previous research. First, the study was conducted in a real retail store whereas most of the previous studies were conducted in a laboratory setting (e.g., Morrin and Ratneshwar 2000; Spangenberg, Crowley, and Henderson 1996). Second, this study is based on a real customer sample whereas previous studies often used student convenient samples (e.g., Morrin and Ratneshwar 2000). Third, many previous studies looked at direct effects of ambient scent on purchase intention without examining these effects and underlying processes in detail. This study will do so by analyzing the role of relevant mediator variables.

In addition, by providing insights in the processes underlying the effects of ambient scent on purchase intention, this study helps retailers to better understand the mechanisms by which they are able to motivate customers to purchase (Davies, Kooijman, and Ward 2003).

EMPIRICAL BACKGROUND

Despite the large number of studies on scents, the number of studies that examine effects of ambient scents in a consumer research context is limited. The existing studies often look at direct links between ambient scent and consumer response variables such as product evaluation and purchase intention, but do not examine several effect paths in detail. Table 1 gives a chronological overview of the objectives and most important findings of studies on effects of ambient scent on consumer response variables.

The studies summarized in table 1 point out variables that play a role in the context of ambient scent effects. The variables that were analyzed in different studies and that repeatedly proved to be important are ambient evaluation, assortment evaluation, mood, and purchase intention. Although single studies examined some of these variables, studies that integrate all of these variables in a holistic framework and analyze their effects simultaneously do not exist. This paper will fill this gap and present a model containing these variables that is developed by bringing together the partial relations that were identified in previous studies.

With regard to the variable mood it is important to note that although Morrin and Ratneshwar (2000) did not find an effect of ambient scent on mood, this variable will still be considered in the study presented below. A possible explanation why Morrin and Ratneshwar (2000) did not find effects might be associated with the fact that they conducted a laboratory experiment. In a laboratory experiment mood induction might be less authentic and thus, mood might have weaker effects than in a real purchase situation.

The studies presented in table 1 also suggest that ambient scent might have effects on consumer memory. However, in a real purchase situation where a retail store is scented, scent-induced memory does not play a role because the purchase decision is usually made before memory effects can occur.

In addition to the variables derived from research on ambient scent effects, another variable that has not been mentioned yet in this stream of research but that has proved to play an important role in the context of the effectiveness of sales conversations (DeShields, Kara, and Kaynak 1996; Gierl and Bambauer 2006; Woodside and Davenport 1974) and thus might be relevant for a study conducted in a real retail store, is the evaluation of the salesperson.

DEVELOPMENT OF THE RESEARCH HYPOTHESES

Below, the partial relations that can be derived from previous research will be looked at in detail and be brought together in order to build up a holistic framework that contains assumptions on direct and indirect relations between the considered variables.

Effect of Ambient Scent through Ambiance Evaluation on the Evaluation of the Salesperson

Prior research found that ambient scents work as affective and contextual cues that affect consumers' subsequent evaluations

Advances in Consumer Research
Volume 40, ©2012

Table 1
Empirical Background

Study	Objective	Major findings
Mitchell, Kahn, and Knasko (1995)	examining how the congruency of ambient scent affects brand choice, decision processes, and memory	when ambient scent is congruent, people spend more time processing the data, are more holistic in their processing, and are more likely to go beyond the information given, relying more on inferences and self-references
Spangenberg, Crowley, and Henderson (1996)	investigating whether the presence of an inoffensive ambient scent versus no ambient scent affects intentions to visit the store, purchase intentions, evaluations of the store, the store environment, the merchandise in general	the presence of an ambient scent consistently enhanced evaluations, behaviors, and the subjective experience for retail shoppers
Morrin and Ratneshwar (2000)	examining the impact of ambient scent on mood, evaluation, attention, and memory for familiar and unfamiliar brands	the presence of a pleasant ambient scent led to additional processing efforts and superior re-call of the unfamiliar brands (rather than for familiar brands); no effect of ambient scent on mood
Fiore, Yah, and Yoh (2000)	studying the impact of ambient scent on attitude toward the product and purchase intention	positive effects of ambient scent on attitude and purchase intention
Mattila and Wirtz (2001)	examining effects of ambient scent on consumers' perceptions of retail environments	scent led to descriptively (but not significantly) more positive evaluations of the store environment than no scent
Morrin and Ratneshwar (2003)	investigating effects of ambient scent on brand memory	positive effect of ambient scent on brand memory only at the brand encoding stage, but not at the brand retrieval stage
Chebat and Michon (2003)	examining the impact of ambient scent in shopping malls on perceptions of the shopping environment and product quality	a light and pleasing ambient scent positively affects consumers' perceptions of the shopping environment and of product quality
Spangenberg, Grohmann, and Sprott (2005)	studying interaction effects between scent and music on consumer evaluations of the store and the merchandise	consistency between ambient scent and music produces more favorable shop and merchandise evaluations
Bosmans (2006)	analyzing the impact of ambient scent on product evaluation	significant positive effect of ambient scent on product evaluation
Spangenberg, Sprott, Grohmann, and Tracy (2006)	exploring congruity between gender-based product offerings and perceived femininity/masculinity of ambient scents	positive effects of ambient scent on store and merchandise evaluation if the ambient scent is congruent with gender-based products
Ward, Davies, and Kooijman (2007)	examining effects of ambient scent on perceptions of the retail environment and mood	positive effects of ambient scent on perceptions of the retail environment and mood
Krishna, Lwin, and Morrin (2009)	exploring the relative effectiveness of product scent versus ambient scent at improving memory for product information	product scent is more effective than ambient scent at enhancing memory for product-related information

(Aggleton and Waskett 1999; Bosmans 2006; Cann and Ross 1989). More specifically, ambient scents have direct effects on customers' perception of the environment (Bone and Ellen 1999; Chebat and Michon, 2003). Thus, it can be assumed that pleasant ambient scents have positive effects on customers' evaluations of the store ambiance. This argument leads to the first hypothesis:

Hypothesis 1: *The evaluation of the store ambiance is more positive in the ambient scent condition than in the no scent condition.*

Furthermore, based on the finding of Sharma and Stafford (2000) that a "prestige store ambiance" leads to significantly higher salesperson credibility than a "discount store ambiance", it can be argued that a positive evaluation of the store ambiance that is caused by a pleasant ambient scent has positive effects on the evaluation of

the trustworthiness and the competence of the salesperson working in this store. Thus:

Hypothesis 2: *The more positive customers' evaluation of the store ambiance, the more positive is their evaluation of the salesperson.*

Note that the causality assumed in H2 specifically refers to the effect of store ambiance on the evaluation of a salesperson's *trustworthiness and competence* and is due to the following order effect. A customer entering a store forms an impression of the store ambiance first and then starts an interaction with a salesperson. After having talked to the salesperson, the customer is able to evaluate the salesperson's trustworthiness and competence (Bitner 1992). On the contrary, effects of the evaluation of a salesperson on the perception of store ambiance might occur if perceptions rather refer to the salesperson's appearance (e.g., well-dressed). Such effects are not considered here.

Effect of Ambient Scent through Mood on the Evaluation of the Salesperson

Studies conducted in several fields of research found positive effects of a pleasant ambient scent on mood (social sciences: Baron and Thomley 1994, chemistry: Knasko 1992, medical science: Lehrner, Eckerberger, Walla, Pötsch, and Deecke 2000). The qualitative findings of a study on effects of ambient scent in retail environments (Ward et al. 2007) also support the notion that a pleasant ambient scent can produce a more positive mood (compared to the no scent condition). These considerations lead to the next hypothesis:

Hypothesis 3: *Mood is more positive in the ambient scent condition than in the no scent condition.*

In their study on mood effects in personal sales conversations, Gierl and Bambauer (2006) showed that mood is positively related to the evaluation of a salesperson. Thus, a comparatively positive mood is supposed to lead to a comparatively positive evaluation of the salesperson. Two theoretical approaches can be used to explain such an effect. According to the affect priming mechanism (Fazio, Sanbonmatsu, Powell, and Kardes 1986; Klauer, Rossnagel, and Musch 1997) which postulates that an emotion produced by a context stimulus affects the evaluation of a subsequently perceived stimulus, a positive mood state which is generated by a pleasant ambient scent has a positive effect on the perception of the salesperson with whom a customer is interacting. In addition, the mood maintenance theory (Isen, Means, Patrick, and Nowicki 1982) suggests that people in a positive mood judge objects or other people less rigorously (Cunningham et al. 1990) and with less cognitive effort in order to maintain their positive mood (Bower 1991; Cunningham 1988; Forgas 1995; Forgas 1998, Greenberg and Pyszczynski 1986; Milberg and Clark 1988). Thus, positive mood induced by the ambient scent is supposed to influence customers' evaluations of the salesperson's competence and trustworthiness:

Hypothesis 4: *The more positive customers' mood, the more positive is their evaluation of the salesperson.*

Note that a customer's evaluation of the salesperson might in turn influence his mood. There are two plausible effects. First, the customer's mood that is positive due to the ambient scent becomes even more positive because the customer is delighted about the salesperson's competence and trustworthiness. From a retailer's perspective, this is the optimal case because positive effects of a positive mood are even intensified. The second effect is that the customer's disappointment about a lack of competence and trustworthiness of the salesperson might deteriorate the customer's initial positive mood. This effect is not considered here because retailers should have a high motivation to have highly competent and trustworthy salespeople.

Effects of Mood and Ambiance Evaluation on the Evaluation of the Assortment

Several studies show that mood has positive effects on attitudes and evaluations (Batra and Stayman 1990; Batra and Stephens 1994; Gorn, Goldberg, and Basu 1993; Groenland and Schoormans 1994; Holbrook and Batra 1987; Isen and Shalker 1982). In addition, studies in a retail context provide the notion that store-induced mood strongly influences customers' in-store responses (Donovan and Rossiter 1982; Sherman, Mathur, and Smith 1997). These arguments lead to the assumption that customers' mood induced by the ambient scent has a positive effect on their evaluation of the store assortment. Thus:

Hypothesis 5: *The more positive customers' mood, the more positive is their evaluation of the assortment.*

The causality assumed in H5 is plausible because the mood induction takes place when entering the store and (un)consciously smelling the ambient scent, thus *before* forming an evaluation of the assortment which can only be done after having spent a while in the store. A negative evaluation of the assortment might in turn influence the initial positive mood, but this particular case is not considered here.

Direct effects of mood on purchase intention are not expected because the study presented here is on high involvement products and previous research has shown that direct mood effects on product evaluation are less important for high involvement products than for low involvement products (Bambauer-Sachse and Gierl 2009) and thus should have an even weaker effect on purchase intention which represents a consequence of product evaluation.

Regarding the effect of ambiance evaluation on assortment evaluation, previous research provides the notion that environmental elements affect consumer evaluations of merchandise quality (Baker, Grewal, and Parasuraman, 1994). More specifically, Sharma and Stafford (2000) found that product evaluation is more positive for "prestige ambiance" stores than for "discount ambiance" stores. Thus, it can be argued that the evaluation of the store ambiance has positive effects on the evaluation of the store assortment. Therefore:

Hypothesis 6: *The more positive customers' evaluation of the store ambiance, the more positive is their evaluation of the assortment.*

It can further be assumed that ambiance evaluation does not have any direct effects on purchase intention because ambiance represents a contextual cue that is not directly linked to the high involvement products offered in a store.

Effects of Salesperson and Assortment Evaluation on Purchase Intention

Findings of previous research provide the notion that customers' satisfaction with the salesperson positively influences satisfaction with the retailer (Goff, Boles, Bellenger, and Stojack 1997) as well as anticipation of future interaction with the salesperson and purchase intention (Ramsey and Sohi 1997). Furthermore, the studies of Swinyard (1993) as well as of Lam and Mukherjee (2005) provide the notion that merchandise evaluation positively influences purchase intention in retail settings. Thus:

Hypothesis 7: *The more positive customers' evaluations of the salesperson and the assortment, the higher are their purchase intentions.*

Research Model

The above presented theoretical considerations are summarized in the research model presented in figure 1. The paths shown in the model will be tested in the empirical study presented below.

Figure 1
Research Model

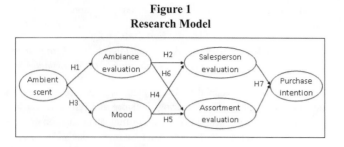

EMPIRICAL STUDY

Product category

As it was intended to conduct the empirical study in a real shopping environment, several stores selling high involvement products in a midsize town in the south of Germany were contacted. The stores were selected on the basis of the following criteria. They should not be too large because otherwise it would have been difficult to diffuse the ambience scent in a sufficient way. In addition, they should have a manageable number of customers per day so that it was possible to administer the questionnaires without disturbing the normal business activities too much. Moreover, it should be plausible to use ambient scent for the considered product category. Furthermore, it was important that the products sold in these stores were unscented so that it was possible to clearly isolate the effect of the ambient scent. Finally, the stores should have attractive assortments in order to avoid negative effects of assortment perceptions. Among the contacted stores, the owner of a jewelry store agreed to participate. Thus, this store, which was not an upscale, luxurious jewelry store, but rather a store offering affordable silver jewelry, was chosen as the test store. The choice of the test store is in line with the notion provided by Fiore, Yah, and Yoh (2000) that ambient scents work best for products that are associated with pleasure and that have moderate prices.

Pretest

A scent that is intended to have positive effects should be perceived as pleasant (Fiore et al. 2000) and should fit to the object studied (Bone and Ellen 1999; Bone and Jantrania 1992) because only in this case, ambient scents continue to affect product judgments, even when they become salient or when consumers are motivated to discount their potential influences (Bosmans 2006). Thus, the purpose of the pretest was to identify an ambient scent for the main study that was judged as likable by the majority of customers and that was characterized by a high fit to the product category chosen for the main study (jewelry). In the first step, six commonly used ambient scents were selected (lavender, rose, cedarwood, green tea, ocean breeze, jasmine). The high percentage of floral scents among the scents selected was in line with the notion provided by Spangenberg et al. (1996) that floral scents are generally perceived as inoffensive scents and thus are likely to generate positive affective responses, and are considered pleasant by most people.

Thirty pretest participants evaluated the first three scents and another 30 participants evaluated the remaining three scents. Thus, 30 evaluations resulted per scent. Following the procedure proposed by Bosmans (2006), small glass bottles that contained a cotton ball with some drops of the tested fragrances were presented to the pretest participants and the participants were asked to sniff the bottles and then to evaluate likeability and scent-store-fit of the fragrances. The order of the scents was varied from respondent to respondent to counterbalance possible order effects. The pretest participants evaluated the likeability of the scents on the basis of four items (pleasant, agreeable, attractive, stimulating, $\alpha = .82$) that were taken from previous literature (Bone and Jantrania 1992; Ellen and Bone 1998; Morrin and Ratneshwar 2000, Spangenberg et al. 1996). The fit of the respective scent to a jewelry store was measured using the single item "this ambient scent is appropriate for a jewelry store" following the recommendation of Bone and Jantrania (1992). The results of the pretest (mean values) that are summarized in table 2 show that the lavender scent was evaluated most positively and was at the same time characterized by the highest fit to the considered store type. Thus, lavender was chosen as ambient scent for the main study. This choice is also consistent with previous literature that characterizes lavender as having a pleasant smell (Bosmans 2006) as well as having positive effects on dwell time and money spent (Soars 2009).

Measures

In the main study, scent likeability and scent-store fit were measured again in order to do manipulation checks. The same items as in the pretest were used ($\alpha_{likeability} = .77$).

In addition, measures were needed for the following model variables: mood, evaluations of the ambiance, the store assortment, and the sales person as well as purchase intention. The mood measures were derived from the studies of Baron and Thomley (1994), Chebat and Michon (2003), Ellen and Bone (1998), Mehrabian and Russell (1974), and McGoldrick and Pieros (1998). The ambiance evaluation was measured following the recommendations of Chebat and Michon (2003) as well as of Spangenberg et al. (1996). The evaluation of the store assortment was operationalized based on statements similar to those used by Chebat and Michon (2003), Morrin and Ratneshwar (2000), and Spangenberg et al. (1996). The evaluation of the salesperson was measured using statements that were derived from the work of Gierl and Bambauer (2006), and purchase intention was measured using the item "I can imagine buying an item from this store". Table 3 gives an overview of the items used, the factor loadings, the corresponding *t*-values per item as well as the α-values per variable.

Table 2
Results of the Scent Pretest

Ambient scent	Lavender	Rose	Jasmine	Green tea	Ocean breeze	Cedarwood	ANOVA results
Likeability	4.99	4.02	4.28	4.68	3.31	3.61	$F = 7.51$ ($p < .001$)
scent-store fit	4.40	3.60	2.53	4.17	2.73	3.67	$F = 4.32$ ($p < .01$)

Table 3
Measures, Factor Loadings, and Reliability

Variable	Item	PLS factor loadings (t-values)	Alpha
Mood	feel good	.85 (*t* = 24.54)	.86
	happy	.56 (*t* = 6.74)	
	pleased	.87 (*t* = 32.74)	
	cheerful	.88 (*t* = 35.05)	
	aroused	.67 (*t* = 8.96)	
	energetic	.86 (*t* = 25.25)	
Ambiance evaluation	stimulating	.78 (*t* = 14.72)	.86
	lively	.76 (*t* = 16.20)	
	interesting	.79 (*t* = 16.10)	
	favorable	.76 (*t* = 17.49)	
	attractive	.75 (*t* = 15.04)	
	motivating	.79 (*t* = 16.70)	
Assortment evaluation	high quality	.79 (*t* = 18.03)	.83
	favorable	.78 (*t* = 19.45)	
	adequate selection	.82 (*t* = 19.99)	
	attractive	.77 (*t* = 9.31)	
Salesperson evaluation	much knowledge about the product	.74 (*t* = 10.75)	.84
	competent	.64 (*t* = 7.17)	
	qualified	.62 (*t* = 8.19)	
	provided helpful information	.74 (*t* = 16.52)	
	honest	.63 (*t* = 6.72)	
	straightforward	.82 (*t* = 22.48)	
	trustworthy	.79 (*t* = 16.77)	

Note: all items were measured on 7-point rating scales ranging from 1 (strongly disagree) to 7 (strongly agree)

The sufficiently high factor loadings, the highly significant *t*-values and the high *α*-values show that the chosen items are appropriate to reliably measure the model variables. Thus, for the data analyses, overall variable values were calculated as mean values of the single items that were intended to measure the respective variable.

Main Study

Sample, Experimental Design, and Procedure

Hundred twelve people who entered the jewelry store participated in the main study (participation rate: 75%). The sample consisted of 83% women and 17% men. The age of the participants ranged from 16 to 75 years, the average age was 35.1 years.

The study participants were assigned to two different groups (56 respondents per group) that were based on the ambience scent manipulation (lavender ambient scent vs. no ambient scent). During one month of the data collection period (April), there was no ambience scent in the jewelry store and during another month (May), lavender ambient scent was diffused. The test months were comparable with regard to weather conditions, outside temperature etc. The two groups resulting from the scent manipulation were comparable with regard to average age (group 1: 35.2, group 2: 34.8, *t* = .44, *p* > .10) as well as with regard to gender distribution (chi-square = .69, *p* > .10).

The procedure of the data collection was as follows. The people entered the store and were approached and assisted by a salesperson. Note that the salesperson was trained before the start of the experiment in order to behave in a competent and trustworthy way. After the sales conversation the customers were asked whether they would like to fill in a questionnaire. The questionnaire contained in the first place the measures for mood, than the measures for purchase intention, the evaluation of the salesperson, the assortment, and the store ambiance. At the end of the questionnaire, the respondents were asked to indicate their age and gender. Those respondents who were assigned to the ambient scent condition were additionally asked to evaluate the likeability of the scent and to judge the scent-store fit.

Data Analysis and Results

Before discussing the results of the main study, the results of manipulation checks for scent likeability and the scent-store fit that were conducted on the basis of the main study data will be presented. The results show that scent likeability and the fit between the lavender scent and the jewelry store are evaluated as significantly more positive than the scale midpoint (scent likeability: *M* = 4.68, *t* = 8.66, *p* < .001, scent-store fit: *M* = 4.60, *t* = 2.62, *p* < .05), which means that the manipulation was successful.

Figure 2
Pls Model

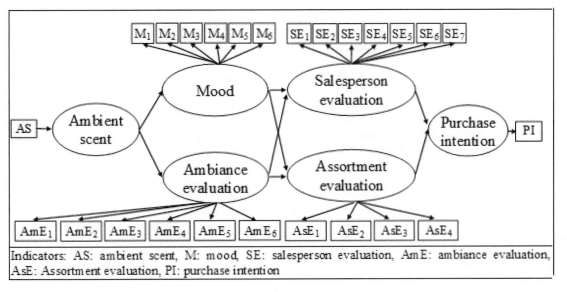

Indicators: AS: ambient scent, M: mood, SE: salesperson evaluation, AmE: ambiance evaluation, AsE: Assortment evaluation, PI: purchase intention

Now, the results of testing the research model presented in figure 1 will be presented. The research model was transformed into the structural model shown in figure 2 and the model structures were estimated using the SmartPLS procedure.

Possible direct effects of ambient scent on salesperson evaluation, assortment evaluation and purchase intention as well as of mood and ambiance evaluation on purchase intention or effects of mood on ambiance evaluation (or vice versa) were tested in the first step and proved to be non-significant. Therefore, in a second step, only the model paths shown in figure 2 were estimated. The path coefficients and the *t*-values estimated with the PLS procedure are summarized in table 4.

Table 4
PLS Path Coefficients and T-Values

Effect	Path coefficient	*T*-value (*p*-value)
Ambient scent → mood	.60	9.81 ($p < .001$)
Ambient scent → ambiance evaluation	.39	5.23 ($p < .001$)
Mood → salesperson evaluation	.55	4.38 ($p < .001$)
Mood → assortment evaluation	.47	3.97 ($p < .001$)
Ambiance evaluation → salesperson evaluation	.18	1.22 ($p > .10$)
Ambiance evaluation → assortment evaluation	.39	3.29 ($p < .001$)
Salesperson evaluation → purchase intention	.46	5.49 ($p < .001$)
Assortment evaluation → purchase intention	.45	5.37 ($p < .001$)

The path coefficients and the associated *t*-values show that the effect of ambiance evaluation on the evaluation of the salesperson is not significant whereas all other effects are significantly positive. Thus, hypotheses 1, 2, 3, 5, 6, and 7 are supported, whereas hypothesis 4 is not supported. In more detail, the results indicate that customers' mood and their evaluation of the general store ambiance are more positive when a likeable ambient scent that fits to the store assortment is diffused than in the case where no ambient scent is present. In addition, the results show that the more positive customers' mood, the more positive is their evaluation of the salesperson and of the assortment. Furthermore, a comparatively positive ambiance evaluation leads to a comparatively positive evaluation of the assortment, but does not affect the evaluation of the salesperson. Finally, customers' purchase intentions increase with an increasingly positive evaluation of the salesperson and the assortment.

CONCLUSION

The starting point of this paper was the observation that although there is a broad body of research on scent effects, research on effects of ambient scent on purchase intention in real retail settings is limited, and research looking at the detailed mechanisms underlying scent effects does not exist. Consequently, from both a retailer's and a consumer researcher's perspective, it stood to reason to develop an integrated research model reflecting possible mechanisms underlying effects of ambient scent and testing this model in a real retail setting.

The findings of the empirical study show that the effects of ambient scent on purchase intention in retail settings result from much more complex processes than previous research suggested. More specifically, the results provide the notion that ambient scent basically triggers two effects: one of them through mood and the other through ambiance evaluation. Mood in turn has effects through salesperson evaluation and assortment evaluation on purchase inten-

tion, whereas ambiance evaluation only has effects on purchase intention through assortment evaluation.

These findings do not only provide a valuable contribution to existing research in the field of ambient scent in retail settings but also suggest that retailers should profit from the diffusion of appropriate ambient scents to generate higher purchase intentions. Furthermore, the results provide a better understanding to retailers with regard to where the positive effects of ambient scent come from. Thus, the results indicate what retailers can do to enhance positive effects of ambient scent on purchase intention. For example, retailers could work with additional mood induction procedures beyond ambient scent (e.g., music, offering coupons etc.) to enhance the effect of ambient scent through mood on salesperson evaluation and assortment evaluation. In addition, retailers could hire well-trained, highly motivated, and professional salespeople to enhance effects of mood through salesperson evaluation on purchase intention. Finally, retailers could try to present their assortments in a way that is attractive from the perspective of potential customers in order to additionally support effects of ambient scent through ambiance and assortment evaluation on purchase intention.

For future research, it might be interesting to replicate the study presented here for other store types and product categories. In addition, effects of further variables, such as the gender of the salesperson, the influence of accompanying relatives or friends, or person-specific differences in mood states could be analyzed. Finally, it might be interesting to examine which specific measures might contribute to more positive perceptions of variables such as assortment or store ambiance in order to support effects of ambient scent.

REFERENCES

Aggleton, John P. and Louise Waskett (1999), "The Ability of Odours to Serve as State-Dependent Cues for Real-World Memories: Can Viking Smells Aid the Recall of Viking Experiences," *British Journal of Psychology*, 90 (1), 1-7.

Baker, Julie, Dhruv Grewal, and A. Parasuraman (1994), "The Influence of Store Environment on Quality Inferences and Store Image," *Journal of the Academy of Marketing Sciences*, 22 (4), 328-339.

Bambauer-Sachse, Silke and Heribert Gierl (2009), "Can a Positive Mood Counterbalance Weak Arguments in Personal Sales Conversations?," *Journal of Retailing and Consumer Services*, 16 (3), 190-196.

Baron, Robert A. and Jill Thomley (1994), "A Whiff of Reality. Positive Affects as a Potential Mediator of the Effects of Pleasant Fragrances on Task Performance and Helping," *Environment and Behavior*, 26 (6), 766-784.

Batra, Rajeev and Douglas M. Stayman (1990), "The Role of Mood in Advertising Effectiveness," *Journal of Consumer Research*, 17 (2), 203-214.

Batra, Rajeev and Debra Stephens (1994), "Attitudinal Effects of Ad-Evoked Moods and Emotions: The Moderating Role of Motivation," *Psychology & Marketing*, 11 (3), 199-215.

Bitner, Mary Jo (1992), "Servicescapes: The Impact of Physical Surroundings on Customers and Employees," *Journal of Marketing*, 56 (April), 57-71.

Bone, Paula F. and Swati Jantrania (1992), "Olfaction as a Cue for Product Quality," *Marketing Letters*, 3 (3), 289-296.

Bone, Paula F. and Pam S. Ellen (1999), "Scents in The Marketplace: Explaining a Fraction of Olfaction," *Journal of Retailing*, 75 (2), 243-262.

Bosmans, Anick (2006), "Scents and Sensibility: When Do (In) Congruent Ambient Scents Influence Product Evaluations?," *Journal of Marketing*, 70 (3), 32-43.

Bower, Gordon H. (1991), "Mood Congruity of Social Judgments," in *Emotion and Social Judgments,* ed. Joseph P. Forgas, Oxford: Pergamon Press, 31-53.

Cann, Arnie and Debra A. Ross (1989), "Olfactory Stimuli as Context Cues in Human Memory," *The American Journal of Psychology*, 102 (1), 91-102.

Chebat, Jean-Charles and Richard Michon (2003), "Impact of Ambient Odors on Mall Shoppers' Emotions, Cognition, and Spending. A Test of Competitive Causal Theories," *Journal of Business Research*, 56 (7), 529-539.

Cunningham, Michael R. (1988), "What Do You Do When You're Happy or Blue? Mood, Expectancies and Behavioral Interest," *Motivation and Emotion*, 12 (4), 309-331.

Cunningham, Michael R.; David R. Shaffer, Anita P. Barbee, Patricia L. Wolff, and David J. Kelley (1990), "Separate Processes in the Relation of Elation and Depression Helping Social versus Personal Concerns," *Journal of Experimental Social Psychology*, 26 (1), 13-33.

Davies, Barry J., Dion Kooijman, and Philippa Ward (2003), "The Sweet Smell of Success: Olfaction in Retailing," *Journal of Marketing Management*, 19 (5-6), 611-627.

DeShields, Oscar W. Jr., Ali Kara, and Erdener Kaynak (1996), "Source Effects in Purchase Decisions: The Impact of Physical Attractiveness and Accent of Salesperson," *Journal of Research in Marketing*, 13 (1), 89-101.

Donovan, Robert J. and John R. Rossiter (1982), "Store Atmosphere: An Environmental Psychology Approach," *Journal of Retailing*, 58 (1), 34-57.

Ellen, Pam S. and Paula F. Bone (1998), "Does It Matter If It Smells? Olfactory Stimuli as Advertising Executional Cues," *Journal of Advertising*, 17 (4), 29-39.

Fazio, Russel H., David M. Sanbonmatsu, Martha C. Powell, and Frank R. Kardes (1986), "On the Automatic Activation of Attitudes," *Journal of Personality and Social Psychology*, 50 (2), 229-238.

Fiore, Ann M., Xinlu Yah, and Eunah Yoh (2000), "Effects of a Product Display and Environmental Fragrancing on Approach Responses and Pleasurable Experiences," *Psychology and Marketing*, 17 (1), 27-54.

Forgas, Joseph P. (1995), "Mood and Judgement: The Affect Infusion Model (AIM)," *Psychological Bulletin*, 117 (1), 39-66.

Forgas, Joseph P. (1998), "Asking Nicely? The Effects of Mood on Responding to More or Less Polite Requests," *Personality and Social Psychology Bulletin*, 24 (2), 173-185.

Gierl, Heribert and Silke Bambauer (2006), "Effects of Consumers' Mood in a Personal Sales Conversation," *Marketing Journal of Research and Management*, 28 (1), 30-42.

Goff, Brent G., James S. Boles, Danny N. Bellenger, and Carrie Stojack (1997), "The Influence of Salesperson Selling Behaviors on Customer Satisfaction with Products," *Journal of Retailing*, 73 (2), 171-183.

Gorn, Gerald J., Marvin E. Goldberg and Kunal Basu (1993), "Mood, Awareness and Product Evaluation," *Journal of Consumer Psychology*, 2 (3), 237-256.

Greenberg, Jeff and Tom Pyszczynski (1986), "Persistent High Self-Focus after Failure and Low Self-Focus after Success: The Depressive Self-Focusing Style," *Journal of Personality and Social Psychology*, 50 (5), 1039-1044.

Groenland, Edward A. and Jan P. Schoormans (1994), "Comparing Mood-Induction and Affective Conditioning as Mechanisms Influencing Product Evaluation and Product Choice," *Psychology & Marketing*, 11 (2), 183-197.

Gulas, Charles S. and Peter H. Bloch (1995), "Right Under Our Noses: Ambient Scent and Consumer Responses," *Journal of Business and Psychology*, 10 (1), 87-98.

Hirsch, Alan R. (1992), "A Scent of Well Being," *Successful Attitudes*, 10 (2), 27-47.

Holbrook, Morris B. and Rajeev Batra (1987), "Assessing the Role of Emotion as Mediators of Consumer Responses to Advertising," *Journal of Consumer Research*, 14 (3), 404-420.

Isen, Alice M. and Thomas E. Shalker (1982), "The Effect of Feeling State on Evaluation of Positive, Neutral, and Negative Stimuli: When You "Accentuate the Positive," Do You 'Eliminate the Negative'?," *Social Psychology Quarterly*, 45 (1), 58-63.

Isen, Alice M., Barbara Means, Robert Patrick, and Gary Nowicki (1982), "Some Factors Influencing Decision-Making Strategy and Risk-Taking," in *Affect and cognition*, eds. Margaret S. Clark & Susan T. Fiske, Hillsdale, NJ: Erlbaum, 243-261.

Klauer, Karl C., Christian Rossnagel, and Jochen Musch (1997), "List-Context Effects in Evaluative Priming," *Journal of Experimental Psychology: Learning, Memory, and Cognition*, 23 (1), 246-255.

Knasko, Susan C. (1992), "Ambient Odor's Effect on Creativity, Mood, and Perceived Health," *Chemical Senses*, 17 (1), 27-35.

Krishna, Aradhna, May O. Lwin, and Maureen Morrin (2010), "Product Scent and Memory," *Journal of Consumer Research*, 37 (1), 57-67.

Lam, Shun Yin and Avinandan Mukherjee ((2005), "The Effects of Merchandise Coordination and Juxtaposition on Consumers' Product Evaluation and Purchase Intention in Store-Based Retailing," *Journal of Retailing*, 81 (3), 231-250.

Lehrner, Johann, Christine Eckersberger, Peter Walla, G. Pötsch, and Lüder Deecke (2000), "Ambient Odor of Orange in a Dental Office Reduces Anxiety and Improves Mood in Female Patients," *Physiology & Behavior*, 71 (1-2), 83-86.

Mattila, Anna S. and Jochen Wirtz (2001): "Congruency of Scent and Music as a Driver of In-Store Evaluatioins and Behavior," *Journal of Retailing*, 77 (2), 273-289.

McGoldrick, Peter J. and Christos P. Pieros (1998), "Atmospherics, Pleasure and Arousal: The Influence of Response Moderators," *Journal of Marketing Management*, 14 (1-3), 173-197.

Mehrabian, Albert and James A. Russell (1974), *An Approach to Environmental Psychology*, Cambridge: MIT Press.

Mitchell, Deborah J., Barbara E. Kahn, and Susan C. Knasko (1995), "There's Something in the Air: Effects of Congruent or Incongruent Ambient Odor on Consumer Decision Making," *Journal of Consumer Research*, 22 (2), 229-238.

Morrin, Maureen and Srinivasan Ratneshwar (2000), "The Impact of Ambient Scent on Evaluation, Attention, and Memory for Familiar and Unfamiliar Brands", *Journal of Business Research*, 49 (2), 157-165.

Morrin, Maureen and Srinivasan Ratneshwar (2003), "Does It Make Sense to Use Scents to Enhance Brand Memory?," *Journal of Marketing Research*, 40 (1), 10-25.

Ramsey, Rosemarie P. and Ravipreet S. Sohi (1997), "Listening to Your Customers: The Impact of Perceived Salesperson Listening Behavior on Relationship Outcomes," *Journal of the Academy of Marketing Science*, 25 (2), 127-137.

Sharma, Arun and Thomas F. Stafford (2000), "The Effect of Retail Atmospherics on Customers' Perceptions of Salespeople and Customer Persuasion: An Empirical Approach," *Journal of Business Research,* 49 (2), 183-191.

Sherman, Elaine, Anil Mathur, and Ruth Belk Smith (1997), "Store Environment and Consumer Purchase Behavior: Mediating Role of Consumer Emotions," *Psychology & Marketing*, 14 (4) 361-378.

Soars, Brenda (2009), "Driving Sales through Shoppers' Sense of Sound, Sight, Smell and Touch," *International Journal Retail and Distribution Management*, 37 (3), 286-298.

Spangenberg, Eric R., Ayn E. Crowley, and Pamela W. Henderson (1996), "Improving the Store Environment: Do Olfactory Cues Affect Evaluations and Behaviors?," *Journal of Marketing*, 60 (2), 67-80

Spangenberg, Eric R., Bianca Grohmann, and David E. Sprott (2005), "It's Beginning to Smell (and Sound) a lot like Christmas: The Interactive Effects of Ambient Scent and Music in a Retail Setting," *Journal of Business Research*, 58 (11), 1583-1589.

Spangenberg, Eric R., David E. Sprott, Bianca Grohmann, and Daniel L. Tracy (2006), "Gender-Congruent Ambient Scent Influences on Approach and Avoidance Behaviors in a Retail Store," *Journal of Business Research*, 59 (12), 1281-1287.

Swinyard, William R. (1993), "The Effects of Mood, Involvement, and Quality of Store Experience on Shopping Intentions," *Journal of Consumer Research*, 20 (2), 271-280.

Ward, Philippa, Barry J. Davies, and Dion Kooijman (2007), "Olfaction and the Retail Environment: Examining the Influence of Ambient Scent," *Service Business*, 1 (4), 295-316.

Woodside, Arch G. and William J. Jr. Davenport (1974), "The Effect of Salesman Similarity and Expertise on Consumer Purchasing Behavior," *Journal of Marketing Research*, 11 (2), 198-202.

Appalachian Mountain Men-of-Action: Nascar at Bristol

Elizabeth Hirschman, Rutgers University, USA
Ayalla Ruvio, Temple University, USA
Russell W. Belk, York University, Canada

ABSTRACT

Southern white masculinity is often said to be distinctive. Scholarly treatments of the subject attribute the characteristics of conservatism, patriotism, independence, racism, a disdain for centralized authority and a tendency toward violence to southern white men (see e.g., Friend 2009; Watts 2008). The crucible for these traits is usually said to be the Civil War and Reconstruction which (partially) emancipated black males, while shattering the foundation of white southern masculinity, leading to a "crisis in gender" (Whites 1992; Wyatt-Brown 1982). As Friend (2009, p. viii) observes "the war's outcome did not eradicate mastery and honor as the primary axes about which white southern manhood formed, but it did force a reconfiguration of how those ideals could be met."

Both E. Anthony Rotundo's (1994) *American_Manhood* and Michael Kimmel's *Manhood in America* (1996) largely ignored or disparaged white southern men as suitable cultural models of American masculinity, as did Gail Bederman's (1995) *Manliness and Civilization.* Across these treatises, white southern men are described as drinkers, brawlers and racists who are most comfortable hunting, fishing, and driving around in pick-up trucks. We are not going to quibble with this characterization, as in broad form, aspects of it are accurate. Even southern white male scholars describe their own regional masculine culture as one which is "beholden to a code of honor that... encouraged violence – martial, retributive or vigilante – gambling, blood sports, sowing wild oats, hunting and...by the early twentieth century, organized sports "(Creech, p. 25). What we do intend to argue, however, is that this same template has served as a model for masculinity since the region's origins, well prior to the Civil War, and indeed prior to the Revolutionary War.

Just as whiteness is typically positioned in opposition to "ethnicity" in scholarly treatises (see Burton 2009 a, b) and masculinity is positioned as counter to femininity (see e.g., Martin, Schouten and McAlexander 2006), southern white male culture is positioned in opposition to that of the southern white female (Watts 2008; Whites 1992; Wilson and Ferris 1989), though both are said to be grounded in Fundamentalist Christianity. Indeed, the Bible is often cited as an authoritative source justifying the secondary status of women within southern white culture, generally (Cash 1941; McPherson 1982). Southern white masculinity is also said to be strongly linked to activities evidencing independence and self-sufficiency (see e.g., Littlefield and Ozanne 2011 for a discussion of hunting in the rural south). According to Watts (2009, p. 10). "The ideal of independent, performative white manhood … continues in real and fictional varieties such as the rough frontiersman…moonshiners, many NASCAR drivers and fans, and pickup truck enthusiasts displaying gun racks and the Confederate flag".

To date, there have been two detailed studies of American masculinity put forward in consumer research – that of the Mountain Man, as developed by Belk and Costa (1998) and that of the Action-Hero Man, developed by Holt and Thompson (2004).Our intention is to compare the white southern masculine ideology, as described above, with these two prior models in order to identify similarities and discontinuities among these three different perspectives on masculinity. Further, our study will also survey *boundary conditions* for the more recent of these two studies (Holt and Thompson 2004).

SETTING AND METHOD

The setting for our study is the area in and around Bristol VA/TN -- a location referred to by MSNBC commentator Andrea Mitchell as the "Redneck Capital of the World" during the 2008 US presidential campaign (statement made on-air June 5, 2008). Bristol TN/VA was founded in the late 1800s as a railroad terminal for the Norfolk and Southern Railway. It was during this period of time that coal mining became central to the economy of the Southern Appalachian region and a freight train system was established linking Kentucky, Tennessee, Virginia and West Virginia in order to transport coal to the steel manufacturing centers of western Pennsylvania and the Great Lakes region (LaLone, 1997;Solomon and Yough 2009;). The entry of large-scale industrialization, organized labor and corporate businesses dramatically impacted the social ecology of the region, shifting men and machinery from working on the land to working in the mine and on the railroad (Bensel 2000; LaLone 1997 Solomon and Yough 2009).

For many men in the region, personal independence and self-reliance – which had sprung from their independent yeoman status -- became more difficult to maintain, as jobs and skills were increasingly dependent upon distant factories and external sources of capital (Lalone 1997; Williams 2002). As a result, personal expertise at activities such as hunting, fishing, carpentry, engine maintenance, sports and other outdoor activities became increasingly relied upon as signals of masculine competency (Watts 2008; Williams 2002; Wilson and Ferris 1989).

Despite its remote Appalachian location, Bristol VA/TN is the origin point for two significant events in Southeastern regional history. The first is that Bristol was the site of some of the earliest commercial country music recordings. The so-called "Bristol Sessions" recordings of the Carter Family were produced there in 1927; Jimmie Rodgers also made early recordings in Bristol during the 1920s, as did Tennessee Ernie Ford during the 1950s (Williams 2002). The entrepreneurism and willingness of the local people to re-shape their production activities to match external commercial and technological opportunities demonstrated by the country music business are also characteristic of the primary research site of our study; the Bristol Motor Speedway.

Bristol Motor Speedway As Belk (2004, p. 273) writes, "love of automobiles, motorcycles and trucks is an overwhelmingly male preoccupation [due to] … the association of such vehicles with power, danger, mobility, status competition, and industrial dominance over nature…" Belk (2004) further observes that male car enthusiasts will often undertake long distance pilgrimages to seek *communitas* with like-minded males in order to celebrate the power and glory that is the automobile. Perhaps no destination on Earth is more revered in these annual pilgrimages than the trio of August NASCAR races at Bristol Motor Speedway (BMS).

The week of August 16-21, 2010 was the fiftieth anniversary of the Bristol Motor Speedway and the 100th running of the NASCAR Sprint Cup Race. Thus it served as an ideal venue at which to observe southern white male culture in full flower. The primary researcher attended the three NASCAR-sponsored races during that week, taking photographs, making field notes, and collecting written materials available at the track and in the surrounding communities relevant to the races. A three person interpretive team with multi-year ethnographic research experience was responsible for developing the collected materials into a comparative structure using *socio-semiotic analysis* (see Schroeder and Zwick, 2004, for a discussion of this method using advertising images of masculinity). Each document, individually, and the set as a whole was subjected to *close reading* by the three researchers using the two models of masculinity proposed in the consumer behavior literature (e.g., Belk and Costa 1998; Holt and Thompson 2004) and the southern white masculinity model described earlier. Thus, the methodology used in the present study is consistent with that of Belk and Costa (1998), but extends beyond ethnography to incorporate socio-semiotics (Schroeder and Zwick 2005). The present methodology differs from that of Holt and Thompson (2004). The latter study utilized experiential-phenomenological interviews – a method which has received recent criticism for its lack of cultural grounding (see e.g., Moisander, Valtonen and Hirsto 2009). We turn now to a detailed discussion of the two prior models of masculinity against which a comparison of the present data will be made.

MOUNTAIN MAN MASCULINITY

The Belk and Costa (1998) study focused upon modern-day mountain men who "adopt grooming, clothing and manners that appear strikingly countercultural, rustic and unique. They live for a time in … teepees or tents at a variety of remote locations near sites of original [mountain men] rendezvous. Clothing and conveniences that did not exist in 1840 are banished, including cars, plastics, prepared foods, flashlights, radios… (pp. 218-219)."

In their study, the authors found a form of white male masculinity intended to "invoke a mythic and heroicized past" (p. 219). "The original mountain men they seek to emulate engaged in dangerous, often violent, activities, struggling against wild animals and hostile Indians. Their present-day imitators desire to partake of this mythology, while also merry-making, trading, and consuming large quantities of alcohol." Notably though most of Belk and Costa's participants were working class, some were middle class. Yet external social status hierarchies were abandoned at the campsite to "form a communal, homogeneous social structure…."

Belk and Costa found that most mountain men participants have atypical personal appearances including long hair, pierced ears, and full beards and/or moustaches. They propose that these signal rebellion against prevailing cultural norms that continue into their everyday lives (Belk and Costa 1998). Meat is heavily consumed during the rendezvous, as is beer and liquor. Several of the men are overweight due to these dietary patterns. Belk and Costa (1998) interpret much of this as a "celebration of the power and passion of the primitive; because [the mountain men] believe these qualities have disappeared from contemporary urban life (p. 230)."

Man of Action Heroes The 2004 article by Holt and Thompson critiques contemporary scholarly writings on masculinity, e.g., Ehrenreich (1983) and Kimmel (1996), as well as earlier work on masculinity published in the consumer behavior literature (e.g., Belk and Costa 1998). They propose that a central thesis in this literature is the social emasculation of American men during the twentieth century brought about by the industrialization of the American workplace and the increasing economic independence and political emancipation of women. This drove American men to engage in compensatory consumption in order to reinforce their manhood.

Holt and Thompson propose that masculine cultural models such as the cowboy, Harley rider, and big game hunter are instantiated in mass media portrayals by actors such as Clint Eastwood, Bruce Willis and John Wayne. These circulating cultural icons are used as touchstones for a romantic model of masculinity which they

term the Rebel Model. This ideology of masculinity "harkens back to the settling of the American West….Hunters and trappers were represented as uncivilized, anarchic and fiercely independent men who survived through courage, physical skills and cunning… (p. 428)." The negative aspect of the Rebel Model is that such men can be viewed as "immature boys…men who refuse to grow up, taking flight from adult responsibility" (p. 428).

In contrast to this, Holt and Thompson describe the Breadwinner Model which is "grounded in the American myth of success… That America is a land of boundless opportunity…" (p. 427). As the country became professionalized and industrialized, men had to "soften the combative edges of individual achievement….[and] peaceably coexist within an ethos of teamwork and the rules of hierarchy…In the breadwinner model, men work hard and are dependable collaborators in a corporate environment…They are reserved, dependable, and devoid of self-aggrandizing flamboyance…" Holt and Thompson propose that "the most celebrated men in American culture are neither breadwinners nor rebels. Instead they draw from the best of both models…[They] embody the rugged individualism of the rebel, while maintaining their allegiance to collective interests… (p. 429)."

The sample Holt and Thompson used to construct their man-of-action hero model was "15 [heterosexual] white men from both working- and middle-class backgrounds…recruited from a Midwestern city of 250,000 and a small eastern city of 60,000 (p. 430)." Each respondent was interviewed in-depth using the existential-phenomenological method. Ultimately, two men, Robert and Donney, served as the middle-class and working class exemplars of how this model of masculinity is enacted in everyday consumption behavior. A shortcoming of this method is that, when used without supplemental cultural data, E-P interviews may render an overly mentalistic view of the subject of the inquiry (see Moisander, Valtonen and Hirsto 2009 for a review of these criticisms). We now turn to a historically-grounded evaluation of these models of masculinity vis a vis that of white southern manhood.

CONTINUITY, PERMEABILITY AND WHITE SOUTHERN MASCULINITY

The region surrounding Bristol TN/VA has a significant history not only with regard to the formation of southern white masculinity, but also that of American masculinity, generally. Daniel Boone and his extended family settled in the area in 1774. Violent confrontations with Native Americans in the Cumberland Gap area next to Bristol were a frequent occurrence for Boone and the other early settlers (Beeman 1984; Williams 2002). David Crockett, hero of the Texas militia at the Alamo, was born and raised in Limestone, TN, approximately 30 miles away. The direct descendants of these early settlers still live throughout the region (Kephardt 1976; Williams 2002).

Thus, we propose argue that this region was the primary cauldron within which American ideals of masculinity were first formed – and mythologized -- and that an undercurrent of this original masculine ideology has been present in the area since Colonial times (Watts 2008). We also propose that this southern white masculinity has existed symbiotically and comfortably with external sources of capital and has consistently participated in the larger U.S. economy and corporate structures, as they developed (see e.g., Bensel 2000; Solomon and Yough 2009).

This suggests that the out-of-bounds Rebel icon, which Holt and Thompson (2004) see Boone and Crockett representing as frontiersman, did not exist historically. This factual discrepancy brings into question the hybridized model which they present. For example,

Crockett and Boone both were family men whose historic exploits and expeditions were primarily undertaken to support their families (Williams 2002). Boone was employed by the Hendersons, a regionally powerful set of brothers who engaged in trading with the Indians and land speculation (Draper 1998). Together with other Long Hunters, Boone engaged in fur trading and land speculation (Draper 1998). The famous Wilderness Road, scouted and constructed by Boone and 35 other early settlers though the Cumberland Gap, was a commercial project whose purpose was to open up the area of Kain-tuck (Kentucky) for the lucrative fur trade and land speculation (Draper 1998; Williams 2002).

Analogously, Crockett's stand at the Alamo was intrinsically linked to a commercial venture. The initial American settlers in central Texas had journeyed there from eastern Tennessee during the early 1800s in search of agricultural and trading opportunities with Mexico (Williams 2002). They arrived and settled as extended families, engaging not only in agriculture, but also in trading and mercantile dealings with corporations "back East" (Williams 2002). Thus, the presentation of the Rebel ideal and the Family Man ideal as oppositional foundations of American masculinity would seem to be factually inaccurate, at least in the Appalachian region.

We propose that the present day Bristol NASCAR fans and drivers are cut from the same cloth as the region's early pioneer-breadwinner-entrepreneurs. We also document the fluidity and interchangeability between the drivers and fans/consumers. We propose that what is actually occurring is not compensatory consumption, rather it is *participatory consumption* in which fans/consumers participate as drivers/producers and driver/producers participate as fans/consumers. A common sense of Southern white masculinity, manhood and manliness is shared between them.

Stock Car Racing Origins Just as with early farming and hunting activities in the area, stock car racing was born of economic necessity and entrepreneurism During Prohibition and the Great Depression, the rural Southeastern U.S. region was one of the poorest areas of the country (much as it is now). Seeking to supplement their meager farming incomes, enterprising residents began turning a portion of their corn crops into distilled liquor (Hirschman, Brown and Maclaran 2006; Howell 1997: Kellner 1971). Such activities were illegal and "moonshiners" were targeted by Federal tax revenue agents (Miller 1991). To outrun these "revenuers", farmers used their ample mechanical skills to increase the speed and road handling ability of their family automobiles, using them to haul gallons of illicit corn liquor over the Appalachian mountains to central distribution points such as Atlanta, GA and Charlotte, NC (Hirschman, Brown and Maclaran 2006; Kellner 1971; Miller 1991)).

In support of the thesis that entrepeneurism and undertaking risky activities may form a nexus of cohering values within white southern masculinity is an advertisement appearing in the BMS race program, which shows one of the "winningest" drivers at the Bristol Motor Speedway, Junior Johnson. Born in North Carolina to a farming family, Johnson is (in)famous for beginning his racing career using cars that he "ran shine" in during the week. Notably, the body copy blends references to the authenticity and illicitness of Johnson's off-track activities, as well as those of the product, a mythologizing motif discussed by Tian and Thompson (2007) as characterizing the 'hillbilly'.

Direct entry to the sport of stock car racing is still available today, just as it was in Johnson's era of the 1940s and 1950s. For example, a full page newspaper advertisement (August 18, 2010) from the *Bristol Courier* invites residents to come to the Volunteer Speedway in Bull's Gap, TN to both watch and compete in local races. This speedway is about an hour's drive west of Bristol and serves as

an 'entry point' for local men to try their hand at racing. Additional documentation of apprenticeships enabling young local men entry to the sport is provided in a BMS press release (Bristol Motor Speedway, 2010). The narrative valorizes stockcar racing as a signal of manhood and masculine pride in the region. Also notable is another article in the BMS Program about Chase Elliott, son of local NASCAR veteran driver Bill Elliott, who is competing professionally in an "entry-level" race at the age of 14. In order to possess a Tennessee Driver's License, one must be at least age 17. Obviously, these requirements are being 'bent' to permit boys to pursue this career.

Other communications in the BMS Race Week program (Bristol Motor Speedway 2010) reiterate the message of fan/driver interchangeability and father/son legacy. For example, an article on rookie driver, Trevor Bayne, age 19 and from Knoxville, TN emphasizes his being a racing fan since childhood, having been taken from school on race days by his parents to watch the competitions. However, perhaps the most iconic exemplar of the fan/driver and father/son racing legacy is Dale Earnhardt, Jr., the son of Dale Earnhardt, one of NASCAR's most spectacular (and aggressive) drivers. A print advertisement appearing in the BMS program carries the headline "Real Men Let their Right Foot do the Talking"; it assumes the readers' knowledge of this father/son linkage and equates Earnhardt, Jr. with authentic manhood. Only Earnhardt Jr's face is used as an identity marker, there is deemed to be no need to use text to identify who is being pictured.

WARRIORS, WEAPONS AND PATRIOTISM

Historically, the region surrounding Bristol VA/TN was the origin point for the Overmountain Men (Williams 2002), a colonial-era paramilitary force composed of farmers and longhunters who won the Battle of King's Mountain, a critical turning point in the Revolutionary War (Alderman 1986). The specifics of the militia and the battle, itself, are valuable in creating a deeper understanding of the current ideology of masculinity within the region and its exhibition in the events observed at Bristol Motor Speedway in August 2010.

The Overmountain Men and their families had taken up residence on lands west of the Appalachian Mountains in areas now comprising northeastern Tennessee and Southwestern Virginia. Alderman (1986, p153), reports that, "they settled on land believed to be in Virginia, but which was actually issued to Lord Granville of North Carolina...., leaving the Watauga settlers without legal claim to the land..." Thus, the Watauga settlers, who included Daniel Boone and John Crockett, the ancestor of David Crocket, had only a tentative hold on their lands. With the assistance of the Hendersons (mentioned earlier), the settlers purchased a large tract of land from the Cherokee in 1775. Comprising a total of 20,000,000 acres, this was the largest land transaction in North America prior to the Revolutionary War (Alderman 1986); it was called the Watauga Settlement. Notably, the settlers chose *not* to declare themselves part of the British colonies and similarly refused to commit their allegiance to the nascent US colonial government, declaring themselves to be an independent nation (Alderman 1986).

In 1780, the British threatened to attack the area. The Watauga Settlement militia organized itself and a force of 1,000 men marched through North Carolina, picking up an additional 350 volunteers. Though largely untrained and completely unauthorized, the volunteer militia traveled overnight to arrive at King's Mountain. According to an eye-witness account, they "circled the mountain and then charged straight toward the British" (Alderson 1986, p. 217). An hour later, the British commander, Patrick Ferguson, and the majority of his British force lay dead on the battlefield. The Watauga men then returned home. This display of colonial-era American masculinity did become the stuff of legend, being replayed most recently in Mel Gibson's 1999 film, *The Patriot*.

The commitment to patriotic sacrifice as a source of white southern masculine pride was very visible at the Bristol Motor Speedway during August race week. The opening ceremonies before each of the three races included displays of American military prowess and power: Honor guards accompanied by veterans, often disabled, from the current Iraq and Afghanistan conflicts marched onto the track and up to the ceremonial platform. The Pledge of Allegiance was recited by the entire audience of 165,000 persons, as 3 military jet fighters flew overhead. On Saturday night, the capstone of the week's events, six paratroopers were dropped by military aircraft onto the race track, as a giant American flag was unfurled in the stands. Fireworks went off and the Star Spangled Banner played.

Reinforcing this patriotic theme was an article in the BMS race program for the "Impact a Hero" public service program which provides financial and social support to disabled veterans. These soldiers were described as "fighting the War on Terror and keeping Americans safe:" Because self-sacrifice is seen within this worldview as one's *obligation* to the community, those who are killed or injured while fulfilling public service duties are considered heroes and martyrs.

The working man ethos was also given voice during the BMS race event through a Tradesman Challenge sponsored by Irwin Tools. This contest pits mechanics, welders, carpenters and other manual workers against one another in speed and performance competitions. The common thread across the races and these competitive events is *physical and mechanical competence*, combined with speed and withstanding challenges from others. A print ad for Irwin Tools found in the BMS race program depicts the mechanic in a heroic pose – competent and in control of a much larger machine.

THE CONFLUENCE OF MASCULINE HONOR, VIOLENCE AND CHRISTIANITY

We next consider a sermon to the mustered Watauga Overmountain men discussed earlier. The region, then as now, is viewed as the Bible Belt (Williams 2002), a bedrock of fundamentalist Christianity. Consistent with this characterization, the minister invokes a clear linkage between *God's will* and the *right to use violence*. This religious justification for aggressive actions has been – and continues to be – a core element of white southern masculinity.

My countrymen, you are about to set out on an expedition which is full of hardships and dangers, but one in which the Almighty will attend you. The Mother Country {England} has her hand upon you...and takes that for which our fathers planted their homes in the wilderness – our liberty... The enemy is marching hither to destroy your homes. Brave men, you are not unacquainted with battle... You have wrested these beautiful valleys of the Holston and Watauga from the savage hand... Go forth in the strength of your manhood to the aid of your brethren, the defense of your liberty and the protection of your homes. Oh, God of Battle, arise in Thy might. Avenge the slaughter of Thy people... Help us as good soldiers to wield the sword of the Lord."

We additionally glimpse in this text strong ideological support for vigilantism and 'taking the law into one's hands', even to the extent of waging war against an existing government, if God's law is believed to differ from it. This value is very much in evidence in the contemporary politics of the region, with the area strongly supporting John McCain in 2008 and 'Tea Party' libertarian and conserva-

tive candidates in the 2010 elections. Regional residents remain both suspicious of the Federal Government and skeptical of its ability to improve their lives. Although the Civil War was the battleground where the ideological divide between white southern male honor and the Federal government played out most vividly (Wyatt-Brown 1982), the same sense of honor and retributive justice led to decades' long feuds between men in various family groups (e.g., the Hatfields and McCoy, see Waller 1988). In several of the documents we collected, honor was said to underlie on-track feuds between individual drivers. The same sense of "giving him what's coming to him" is felt among the fans, who boo and throw cups at drivers whom they believe act unfairly on the track, e.g., by cutting off other drivers, wrecking competitors' cars or pushing them against the wall.

On Friday night, a man-to-man conflict occurred between two drivers. This is described by BMS (Bristol Motor Speedway, August 2010) as follows: "Sparks flew, fenders crunched ...A tangle between Brad Keselowski and Kyle Busch saw Keselowski spin off the nose of Busch's machine. Busch was welcomed with a shower of boos in Victory Lane". A discussion of the moral necessity created by the underlying white southern male ideology leading to such events is given below, taken from a local newspaper: "You know it when you see it...the right way and wrong way to get aggressive on the race track...Naked aggression, but done in a way that allows (the other driver) to stay on the race track; it comes down to racing somebody with respect" (Dave Ongie, *Kingsport Times News*, "Speaking in code", August 2010, p. B1)

WHITE SOUTHERN MALE STATUS: SUPREMACY OR SEPARATION?

We turn now to considering one of the key points said to differentiate white Southern masculinity from that found elsewhere in the country: do white southern males set themselves in dominant positions over women and non-whites, particularly blacks? Does the pre-Civil War tradition of white male supremacy continue? We propose that what is currently practiced is not so much an ideology of *supremacy*, but rather one of *separation*. In the photographic materials collected before, during and after NASCAR race week and from observations made of the spectators who attended the races, there was clearly a predominance of white men. The local sports writers covering the race were white males; the BMS executives whose photographs were shown in the program were white males. The CEO of the companies, e.g. Food City, Irwin Tools, sponsoring the races were white males. The pit crews were composed of white males. The race drivers – with *one* exception – were white males; (the sole exception being Juan Pablo Montoya, who is Hispanic).

However, comparing race and gender as separate bases for classification, racial separation seemed more marked than gender separation (and see Burton 2009 for a discussion of whiteness and social separation). For example, the spectators were virtually all white. However, the percentage of woman ranged between 20% to 30% across the three events. Similarly, an examination of the BMS employee photographs shown as a group in the race program found about 30% to be female, but only one non-white person (a black female) among the set of 109 BMS employees. Although the region around Bristol has only a 6% presence of blacks and a 2% Latino population, this would still suggest a lack of inter-racial representation at the raceway.

We believe this obvious disproportionality in race and gender grows more from the desire of Southern white males to *separate* or *distance* themselves from females and non-whites, than from an ideology of supremacy. Supremacy requires that the subordinate gender or race be present and publicly displayed in a subordinate position to the master (Dollard 1937). Yet women and especially non-whites of either gender were neither highly visible nor placed in subordinate positions. The more justifiable interpretation would seem to be that BMS represents a refuge, haven or 'turf' in which southern white males can share ideological camaraderie. It is a place where "[white] boys can be [white] boys".

DISCUSSION

We now discuss the areas of agreement, disagreement and extension between the present study and the Belk and Costa (1998) and Holt and Thompson (2004) models of masculinity.

Belk and Costa 1998: The Mountain Man We found three points of overlap with the Mountain Man study. First, the dietary habits exhibited by the modern-day Mountain Men and the Bristol Motor Speedway NASCAR race fans are virtually identical. At BMS the commercial vendors supplied meat, especially pork, several brands of beer, hard liquor and tobacco products, including snuff, chewing tobacco and cigarettes. These were accompanied by white bread, cornbread, baked beans and French fries. Fans consumed large quantities of these foodstuffs; approximately half of the fans observed were overweight or obese.

However, although copious quantities of liquor and beer were consumed, most attendees did not appear intoxicated. Drunkenness would have made climbing up the steep concrete steps to one's seat very difficult, and some who had over-imbibed did fall down in the attempt. Personal coolers and foods were allowed in the stands and occasionally empty cans would be thrown toward the race track to express displeasure at a driver's performance, but this behavior was not

Typical

Extending Belk and Costa's recounting of these dietary practices, we suggest that they evidence a celebration of masculine food ways. 'Real men' are expected to eat large quantities of meat (i.e., the muscles of prey animals) in order to construct their own body muscle mass. They are also expected in the southeastern U.S. to be able to drink large amounts of alcohol, but not to lose control or become ill while doing so. The notion that a real man can 'hold his liquor' is embedded in the regional culture (see e.g., Miller 1991; Watts 2008). Consistent with prior findings on gendered meanings of foods, virtually no green vegetables or dairy products were available for consumption at the track. This is consistent with our interpretation of the events as representing a gender-segregated site.

A second consistency with Belk and Costa was the suspension of status hierarchies at the race track, especially with regard to apparel display. No one was dressed in business attire or even 'business casual'. There was a virtual absence of prestige brands. Instead, attendees wore shorts and t-shirts, jeans and tank tops. Both men and women wore trucker-style caps. Footwear included sneakers, flip flops, and sandals. The only apparent status identifiers were shirts and jackets emblazoned with a specific driver's image or car number. There were several men wearing Dale Earnhardt's image on their apparel, Earnhardt being viewed as a heroic martyr to the sport

A third similarity with the work of Belk and Costa is a strong sense of community and comaraderie among the BMS fans. There is a large and mobile 'NASCAR nation' which travels from race to race across the country by camper as the season progresses. This 'nation' was strongly in evidence at Bristol, stretching for miles along all access roads near the Speedway.

There were two major *dissimilarities* between the expressions of masculinity we found, as compared to the study by Belk and Costa. First, their study noted a consistent preference among the Moun-

tain Men for items dating from the Native American cultures of the late 1800s. The Mountain Men typically construct their own clothing, equipment and camp housing, and spurn modern commercial manufactured items. Almost the complete reversal is found among the male attendees, drivers and pit crews at BMS.

Technological advantage is avidly sought in the racetrack setting. Male fans often wear radio-receiver headgear which permits them to listen to communications between each driver and his pit-crew chief. Prior to each race, a sheet of radio frequencies is distributed to the fans and those equipped with ear phone receivers (which can be purchased or rented on-site) are able to listen to drivers' conversations throughout the race. The drivers and crew also display a high level of technological competence, discussing turning and banking ratios, wear levels on brakes and tires, steering stability and other aspects of performance. Military/police style language is used and communications between driver and pit crew are unemotional and pragmatic. We propose that this is an outgrowth of the manual labor-based entrepreneurism of the region. Men of the region are comfortable with and competent at operating machines and employing technologies to achieve their goals (Hirschman, Brown and Maclaran 2006).

A second dissimilarity between the present study and that of Belk and Costa is one identified as well by Holt and Thompson. The performance-consumption model does not appear to be compensatory, but rather woven into everyday life practice. It is a safe bet that most of the men attending the BMS race can and do conduct primary maintenance on their own vehicles (Williams 2002). Observations made around the Bristol area indicate that local men can change oil, change tires, adjust brakes, fix headlights, tune engines, replace spark plugs and windshield wipers, and some are capable of rebuilding entire engines. Thus it is not surprising that they may closely identify with the drivers and crew on the track. However, male competence at manual labor in the region extends well beyond automobiles. Most local men can also perform electrical, carpentry and plumbing tasks, repair washers and dryers, replace gutters and repair lawnmowers, motorcycles and farm equipment. It is accurate to say these would be among the *culturally-expected* competencies for a man living in or around Bristol.

Thus when these same men arrive at BMS to watch the races, they come with a mindset and skill set largely comparable to the men driving the cars around the track and those re-fueling and re-tiring them when they come in for a pit-stop. It is this *overlap between producer and consumer competencies* that enables permeability between these roles for individual men. Fans can and do become drivers or pit crew members; drivers and pit crew members can and do begin their interest in the sport as fans.

Let the Circle be Unbroken: Holt and Thompson (2004)

In "Man of Action Heroes" (2004), Holt and Thompson challenge the masculinity as-compensatory-consumption thesis and critique as inadequate two models of American manhood, labeled the Rebel and the Breadwinner. Our study strongly supports Holt and Thompson's assertion that much of contemporary American masculinity does not represent *compensatory consumption*, but rather *participatory consumption*. That is, significant aspects of masculine ideology are enacted daily in men's lives. Their consumption choices and attitudes incorporate both the Rebel and Breadwinner models of manhood, as described by Holt and Thompson.

Where our analysis differs from the Holt and Thompson study is that we present historical documentation challenging the notion that the Rebel and Breadwinner models were *separate* ideologies within the southeastern United States. In our analysis, these two ways of being men were *always* intrinsically interwoven. When the ancestors of the men now living in Bristol and environs arrived in the mid-1700s, they were competent to hunt, shoot, fight, make liquor, skin animals, fell trees, build houses, cure meat, plant and harvest crops, ride horses, forge iron and herd cattle and hogs (Hirschman et al, 2006; Williams 2002).

Further, while they did not seem to exhibit the negative traits Holt and Thompson ascribe to Rebels (e.g., being selfish, juvenile), they often did rebel against authority, as witness their participation in both the Revolutionary and Civil Wars. The point we wish to make is that their behaviors may indeed be the stuff of which myth was (and is) made, but their actions were genuine, not fictional. More recently, the stockcar racing-moonshining mythos has been used to add dramatic flair to Southern speedways such as Bristol (see e.g., Thompson and Tian 2008), but these activities too have authentic, historical roots in the region. Though this may now be used as an advertising motif to sell liquor, the foundations are factual.

A second lacuna between the present study and that of Holt and Thompson is that the "Man of Action Hero" analysis takes as its initial foundation earlier social theorist treatises on masculinity, e.g. Kimmel, which are themselves culturally-constructed narratives about macro-cultural phenomena such as industrialization, economic stratification, and mass media products.. While this approach is quite appropriate when addressing socio-cultural trends on a national level, it risks glossing over vital specifics at a regional and local level. For example, although the majority of contemporary American men learned of Daniel Boone, Davy Crockett, the Revolutionary War, the Civil War, moon-shining and stockcar racing from films and TV shows, the men of the southeastern region *additionally* learned about them through family histories and direct personal experience. Roadsides in the region are dotted with topographical and human reference points; e.g., here is Crockett Tavern, here is Boone's Creek, here is the Overmountain Men mustering site, here is the cemetery for the Civil War dead. This is an altogether different form of 'grounding' than images received via digital media. These constitute the tangible, familiar markers that give rise to an in-the-blood and in-the-soul sense of regional manhood. Factors such as these suggest that there is a strong need to address masculinity at a more organic, local level, rather than to rely solely upon grand-scale analyses that may mute regional differences.

A final variation found in the present study is the seemingly self-contradictory notion of blue collar entrepreneurism, which was not detected either by Holt and Thompson (2004) or Belk and Costa (1998). Perhaps the central performative feature of the southeastern region's white male culture is its unique form of yeoman labor. Virtually all social theories of working class labor view it as a non-hegemonic mode of production (Bensel 2000). Craftsmen and laborers are depicted as interchangeable cogs in a much larger productive machine. For many industries in the Northeast, this was historically true (Bensel 2000).

However, the Appalachian region is the site of only one large-scale industrialized labor context, coal mining (Caudill 1963; LaLone 1997). Yet with the exception of men employed full-time as miners, the majority of southeastern regional male residents work either on their own farms or as skilled laborers, e.g., as mechanics, carpenters, electricians, plumbers, and truck drivers. Though most of these men do not earn incomes in any way approaching affluent, they are financially independent.

Many grow their own vegetables, raise hogs and chickens for meat, hunt and fish, and maintain their own cars (and see Williams 2002). This provides a sense of self-sufficiency, dignity and personal worth that serves as a significant reservoir of manhood and masculinity.

We believe this sense of individual self-worth may be what men in many other parts of the country – whether factory workers or upper middle class service professionals – are seeking.

REFERENCES

Alderman, Pat, (1986), *The Overmountain Men*, Johnson City, TN: The Overmountain Press.Ayers, Edward L. (1992) *The Promise of the South*, New York: Oxford University Press

Bederman, Gail (1995), *Manliness and Civilization: A Cultural History of Gender and Race in the United States*, 1880 – 1917, Chicago: University of Chicago Press

Beeman, Richard R. (1984), *The Evolution of Southern Backcountry*, Philadelphia, Liberty Press.

Belk, Russell W. (2004), "Men and Their Machines", in *Advances in Consumer Research*, Vol. 31, Barbara Kahn and Mary Frances Luce, eds., Valdosta , GA, Association for Consumer Research, 273 - 278

Bensel, Richard Franklin, (2000), *The Political Economy of American Industrialization, 1877 – 1900*, Cambridge: Cambridge University Press.

Blackman, Marion Cyrenus, (1971), *Look Away! Dixie Land Remembered*, New York:McCall.

Bristol Motor Speedway, (2010) *100ᵗʰ Cup Race Program*, August, Bristol, TN.

Bultman, Stephanie, (1996), *Redneck Heaven: Portrait of a Vanishing Culture*, New York, Bantam

Burton, Dawn, (2009a), "Reading Whiteness in Consumer Research", *Consumption, Markets and Culture*, Vol. 12, 2, June, 171 – 201.

Caudill, Harry M. (1963), *Night Comes to the Cumberlands*, Boston, Little & Brown

Cash, W. J. (1941), *The Mind of the South*, New York: Vintage

Dollard, John, (1937), *Caste and Class in a Southern Town*, New Haven: Yale University Press

Draper, Lyman, (1998), *The Life of Daniel Boone*, Mechanicsburg, PA, Stackpole

Ehrenreich, Barbara, (1983), *The Hearts of Men: American Dreams and the Flight from Commitment,* Garden City, NY: Doubleday.

Friend, Craig T. (2009), "Introduction", *Southern Masculinity*, Athens: University of Georgia Press.

Goad, Jim (1997), *Redneck Manifesto: How Hillbillies, Hicks and Rednecks Became America's Scapegoats*, New York : Simon & Schuster

Graham, Michael, (2002), *Redneck Nation*, New York: Warner.

Hirschman, Elizabeth C., Stephen Brown and Pauline Maclaran, (2006), *Two Continents, One Culture: The Scotch-Irish in Southern Appalachia*, Johnson City, TN: The Overmountain Press.

Howell, Mark D. (1997), *From Moonshine to Madison Avenue: A Cultural History of the NASCAR Winston Cup,* Bowling Green Ohio, Bowling Green University Popular Press

Kephart, Horace, (1976), *Our Southern Highlanders*, Knoxville: University of Tennessee Press

Killian, Lewis M., (1970), *White Southerners*, New York: Random House.

Kimmel, Michael, (1996), *Manhood in America: A Cultural History*. New York: The Free Press.

Kirwan, Albert, (1951), *Revolt of the Rednecks: Mississippi 1876 – 1925*, Lexington: University of Kentucky Press.

Kellner, Esther, (1971), *Moonshine: Its History and Folklore*, New York: Weathervane Books.

Killian, Lewis M. (1970), *White Southerners,* New York: Random House

LaLone, Mary B. (1997), *Appalachian Coal Mining Memories: Life in the Coal Fields of Virginia's New River Valley*, Blacksburg, VA: Pocahontas PressLittlefield, Jon and Julie L. Ozanne, (2011), "Socialization into Consumer Culture: Hunters Learning to be Men", *Consumption, Markets and Culture*, Vol. 14, 4, December, 333 – 360.Martin, Diane, John W. Schouten and James H. McAlexander, (2006), Claiming the Throttle: Multiple Femininities in a Hyper-Masculine Subculture", *Consumption, Markets and Culture*, Vol. 9, 3, September, 171 – 205.

McGee, David M. and Sonya A. Haskins, (2006), *Bristol Motor Speedway*, Charleston, S.C. Arcadia

McPherson, James M. (1982), *Ordeal by Fire: The Civil War and Reconstruction*, New York: Knopf.

Miller, Wilbur R. (1991), *Revenuers and Moonshiners: Enforcing Federal Liquor Laws in the Mountain South,* Chapel: University of North Carolina Press

Moisander, Johanna, Anu Valtonen, and Heidi Hirsto, (2009), "Personal interviews in cultural consumer research – post-structuralist challenges", *Consumption, Markets and Culture*, Vol. 12, 4, December, 329 – 348.

Rotundo, Anthony (1993), *American Manhood: Transformations in Masculinity From the Revolution to the Modern Era*, New York : Basic Books.

Schroeder, Jonathan E. and Detlev Zwick, (2004), Mirrors of Masculinity: Representation and Identity in Advertising Images", *Consumption, Markets and Culture*, Vol. 7, 1, March, 21 – 52.

Solomon, Brian and Patrick Yough, (2009), *Coal Trains: The History of Railroading and Coal in the United States*, New York: Voyageur Press.

Thompson, Craig and Kelly Tian, (2008)," Reconstructing the South", *Journal of Consumer Research*, Vol. 34, February, 595 – 613.

Watts, Trent, (2008), *White Masculinity in the Recent South,* Baton Rouge: Louisiana University Press

Whites, LeeAnn, (1992), "The Civil War as a Crisis in Gender", in *Divided Houses: Gender and the Civil War*, Catherine Clinton and Nina Silber (eds.), New York: Oxford University Press.

Waller, Altina L. (1988), *Feud: Hatfields, McCoys and Social Change in Appalachia*, 1860 – 1900, Chapel Hill, University of North Carolina Press.

Watts, Trent, (2008), *White Masculinity in the Recent South*, Baton Rouge: Louisiana University Press.

Whites, LeeAnn, (1992), "The Civil War as a Crisis in Gender", in *Divided Houses: Gender and Civil War*, Catherine Clinton and Nina Silber (eds.) New York: Oxford University Press.

Williams, John Alexander, (2002), *Appalachia: A History*, Chapel Hill: University of North Carolina Press.

Wilson, Charles Reagan and William Ferris, (989), *Encyclopedia of Southern Culture*, Chapel Hill: University of North Carolina Press.

Wyatt-Brown, Bertram, (1982), *Southern Honor: Ethics and Behavior in the Old South*, Oxford: Oxford University Press.

Do Price Promotions Lead to a Reduction of Consumers' Internal Reference Price and If So, under Which Conditions Is this Effect Less Strong?

Silke Bambauer-Sachse, University of Fribourg, Switzerland
Angélique Dupuy, University of Fribourg, Switzerland

ABSTRACT

This paper examines effects of price promotions on changes of internal reference prices by analyzing moderator effects of price confidence, involvement, and the saving presentation. The results of the empirical study show how marketers should communicate price promotions to avoid strong reductions of consumers' internal reference prices.

INTRODUCTION

In recent time, an increase of price-related advertising campaigns, specifically price promotions or price comparisons, can be observed (Chandrashekaran and Grewal 2006; DelVecchio, Krishnan, and Smith 2007; Howard and Kerin 2006; Tsiros and Hardesty 2010). Such advertising campaigns aim to positively influence consumers' purchase intentions and many studies provide empirical support for this effect (Ailawadi and Neslin 1998; Chen, Monroe, and Lou 1998; Grewal et al. 1998; Gupta 1988; Gupta and Cooper 1992; Kumar and Leone 1988; Sun 2005). However, these studies only look at positive effects of price-related advertising and neglect the fact that intensively highlighting information about reduced prices can at the same time have negative effects through other paths. One such negative effect could be that providing people with information about reduced prices might lead to a reduction of consumers' internal reference prices which in turn could lead to a lower willingness to pay as well as to a lower willingness to purchase products at the regular price. Such effects have not yet been covered by many studies. In addition, the existing studies analyzed rather basic effects and did not look at conditions under which a reduction of consumers' internal reference prices might be more or less strong.

Thus, the first objective of this study is to examine effects of price promotions (displaying the amount of the saving and the reduced price) on consumers' internal reference prices. The second objective is to identify conditions under which the reduction of the internal reference price is less strong. In this study, three variables, which represent such conditions and proved to play an important role in the formation of internal reference prices in previous studies (Chandrashekaran and Grewal 2003, 2006; Grewal et al. 1998; Thomas and Menon 2007), are analyzed: involvement, price confidence, and the saving presentation format ("% off" vs. "amount off").

Product involvement refers to the consumers' degree of personal interest into or personal relevance of a product category (McQuarrie and Munson 1992). Consumers have a higher motivation to process product-related information (e.g., price information) about high-involvement products than about low-involvement products (Laurent and Kapferer 1985). Price confidence refers to the idea that consumers are more or less confident with their price estimates and as a consequence, such consumers are more or less likely to use these estimates in order to evaluate an actual price (Mazumdar and Monroe 1992).

These conceptualizations suggest that price confidence and involvement are independent constructs. Whereas price confidence is a rather person-specific variable, product involvement is a rather product category-specific variable. Furthermore, independently of the extent of information processing, consumers can be more or less confident about the result of the information processing. Thus, with regard to the context considered here, it can be argued that more or less intensive processing of price information in the case of high or low involvement can result in the formation of a reference price the consumers are more or less confident about.

The study presented here adds to the existing body of research by analyzing interaction effects that were not examined in the context of effects of price promotions on changes of internal reference prices before. From a consumer research perspective, such a simultaneous analysis of these interaction effects is important because the results of such an analysis enable consumer researchers to better understand consumers' adaptions of their internal reference prices depending on their individual level of price confidence as well as depending on product category-related involvement under the alternative conditions of being faced with a "% off" versus an "amount off" saving presentation format.

In addition to covering research gaps left by previous studies, the paper addresses marketers by showing which saving presentation format ("% off" vs. "amount off") should be used under which involvement and price confidence conditions in price promotion ads in order to avoid a strong reduction of consumers' internal reference prices.

EMPIRICAL BACKGROUND

Despite the considerable number of studies on internal reference prices, the number of studies that examine moderator effects of price confidence, involvement, and saving presentation format in the context of effects of price promotions on changes of the internal reference price is limited.

Previous studies rather examined the formation or the type of the internal reference price (Briesch et al. 1997; Rajendran and Tellis 1994), the use of the internal or external reference prices (Chandrashekaran and Jagpal 1995; Liefeld and Heslop 1985; Mayhew and Winer 1992; Moon, Russell, and Duvvuri 2006), the impact of the level of the external reference price (Biswas and Blair 1991; Biswas et al. 1999; Burman and Biswas 2004; Compeau and Grewal 1998; Frankenberger and Liu 1994; Lichtenstein and Bearden 1989; Urbany, Bearden, and Weilbaker 1988), or the impact of semantic cues (Lichtenstein, Burton, and Karson 1991).

There are only a few studies that analyzed effects of price promotions on internal reference prices. Table 1 gives an overview of the objectives and most important findings of these studies in a chronological order.

Most of the studies summarized in table 1 support well the assumption that price promotions lead to a reduction of internal reference prices. However, these studies focused on very few variables and did not examine conditions (e.g., consumers' price confidence and involvement) under which price promotions with different saving presentation formats have more or less strong effects on internal reference prices. Furthermore, only a few studies (Chandrashekaran and Grewal 2003, 2006; Sinha and Smith 2000) measured the internal reference price before and after exposure to the price promotion, thus the change of the internal reference price that can be unambiguously assigned to the examined independent variable. These research gaps will be closed by the new study presented below.

Three other studies examined the moderating role of involvement (see table 2), but in slightly different contexts.

Table 1
Studies on Effects of Price Promotions on Internal Reference Prices

Study	Objective	Major findings
Diamond and Campbell (1989)	Examined the effect of different types of promotions on reference prices (RP).	The monetary promotion (discount) reduces the RP while the non-monetary promotion (premium attached, extra product) does not.
Lattin and Bucklin (1989)	Analyzed, among other questions, the formation of consumers' reference prices after exposure to a brand promotion.	High exposure to a brand's promotional activity reduces the accordingly formed reference price.
Grewal et al. (1998)	Examined, among other aspects, effects of price discounts on consumers' internal reference prices.	The promotions reduce the consumers' internal reference price.
Sinha and Smith (2000)	Examined, among other questions, the effects of three deal types on internal reference prices.	Consumers' internal reference prices are not affected after seeing the deal once.

Table 2
Studies on the Moderating Role of Involvement

Study	Objective	Major findings
Chandrashekaran and Grewal (2003)	Examined effects of the advertised reference price (ARP) and the moderating role of involvement on the change of internal reference price.	Low involvement consumers show a stronger change of the internal reference price into the direction of the ARP than high involvement consumers.
Chandrashekaran (2004)	Examined, among other questions, effects of the advertised reference price (ARP) and the moderating role of involvement on consumer evaluations (transaction value, acquisition value and purchase intention).	Under high involvement, consumer evaluations are not influenced by the ARP. Under low involvement, consumer evaluations are positively influenced by the ARP.
Howard and Kerin (2006)	Examined, among other questions, effects of the advertised reference price (ARP) (absent vs. present) and the moderating role of involvement on price attitudes.	Under high involvement, consumers' price attitudes are more favourable if the ARP is present. Under low involvement, there is no difference in consumers' price attitudes depending on whether the ARP is present or absent.

Table 3
Studies on the Role of the Saving Presentation Format

Study	Objective	Major findings
Chandrashekaran and Grewal (2006)	Examined, among other effects, the impact of the saving presentation format on changes of the internal reference price (IRP).	The change of the IRP is stronger if the saving information is provided as "% off" than in the case where the saving presentation is provided as "amount off".
DelVecchio et al. (2007)	Examined, among other questions, the effect of promotion framing ("% off" vs. "amount off") on price expectations.	An "amount off" format leads to a stronger reduction of the price expectation than a "% off" format.

The first study presented in table 2 shows that, under low involvement, consumers' formation of reference prices is more strongly influenced by available price information than under high involvement. The other two studies show that the effects of reference prices on evaluations or attitudes are somehow mixed under different involvement conditions. The findings, specifically of the first study, provide support for the importance of the involvement in the context of the formation of reference prices. However, none of the previous studies specifically examined the role of involvement in the context of effects of price promotions on internal reference prices or interactions of involvement and other moderator variables. Thus, it is necessary to examine such effects in the new empirical study presented below.

In addition, two studies on effects of the saving presentation format can be found (see table 3).

The conclusion that can be drawn from the two studies summarized in table 3 is that the "% off" format leads to greater reduction of the internal reference price/the price expectation than the "amount off" format, whereas the opposite effect occurs when price expectation is considered as target variable. Thus, it will be interesting to examine the role of the saving presentation format, and more specifically, possible interactions between the saving presentation format, involvement, and price confidence in the more complex context of effects of price promotions on internal reference prices.

Up to our knowledge, no study has yet examined the moderating role of consumers' price confidence in the context of effects of price promotions on internal reference prices.

The gaps identified in the existing studies presented above will be addressed in the new study presented below. The research hypotheses that represent the basis of the empirical study will be developed in the next section.

DEVELOPMENT OF THE RESEARCH HYPOTHESES

For the situation of being faced with new price information, it can be assumed that consumers – consciously or unconsciously - revise their internal reference price by including the new price information (Yadav and Seiders 1998). More specifically, when faced with a reduced price and/or the amount of the saving, consumers are believed to incorporate the new price information into their internal reference price. As internal reference prices are usually formed through complex mechanisms considering several types of price information (Briesch et al. 1997; Mayhew and Winer 1992; Mazumdar and Papatla 2000; Rajendran and Tellis 1994; Winer 1986), it can be assumed that encountering one single piece or a few pieces of new price information leads to a rather heuristic incorporation into the internal reference price (Chandrashekaran and Grewal 2003; Frankenberger and Liu 1994; Yadav and Seiders 1998). A heuristic which is appropriate to explain how consumers incorporate a single/a few piece(s) of new price information into their internal reference price, is anchoring and adjustment. The new price information encountered serves as an anchor toward which the internal reference price is adjusted. As one single/a few piece(s) of price information is/are not able to change the internal reference price completely, this adjustment will be insufficient. The type of the price information that represents the anchor value and the extent of the adjustment of the internal reference price into the direction of the anchor are believed to depend on consumers' price confidence because price confidence plays an important role in price judgments (Mazumdar and Monroe 1992; Thomas and Menon 2007), on involvement (Chandrashekaran and Grewal 2003; Vaidyanathan and Aggarwal 2001) as well as on the saving presentation format (Chandreshekaran and Grewal 2006; DelVecchio et al. 2007).

Highly price-confident consumers are less influenced by price promotions (Bearden, Hardesty, and Rose 2001) and less likely to considerably change their internal reference price because of encountering a single piece of new price information (Yadav and Seiders 1998). *Less* price-confident consumers are more likely to be influenced by environmental information (Bearden et al. 2001; Yadav and Seiders 1998) and pay high attention to additional price information provided (Dutta 2011), such as the saving information and the reduced price in a price promotion ad and incorporate such information to a larger extent into their internal reference price than highly price confident consumers. These arguments lead to the first hypothesis:

Hypothesis 1:   *Price promotions lead to stronger reductions of the internal reference for less than for highly price-confident consumers.*

Beyond the effect of price confidence, possible effects of involvement and the saving presentation format need to be explained theoretically. In the case of *low* involvement, consumers generally show an effortless and context-driven processing, and are open to promotional signals in ads (Chandrashekaran 2004; Howard and Kerin 2006; Petty, Cacioppo, and Schumann 1983). In the case of *high* involvement, consumers are motivated to spend a considerable effort to intensively process information (Petty et al. 1983). Consequently, consumers form internal reference prices on the basis of logically relevant facts (Lichtenstein, Bloch, and Black 1988; Zaichkowsky 1988) that they carefully process because, due to their high involvement, they are more skeptical of advertised price claims (Chandrashekaran and Grewal 2003).

If *less* involved consumers are faced with a price promotion ad that contains the saving information in the "% off" format, the only

clearly available price information that can be easily processed is the reduced price. As the "% off" information is more difficult to process than the "amount off" information (DelVecchio et al. 2007; Lee and Han 2002; Morwitz, Greenleaf, and Johnson 1998), less involved customers are not motivated to further process the percentage indicating the saving amount. Thus, in this case, the reduced price represents the anchor toward which the internal reference is adjusted.

If less involved consumers encounter a price promotion ad that contains the "amount off" saving presentation format, two types of price information are available: the reduced price and the amount of the saving. Although the saving amount represents irrelevant information with regard to the internal reference price, this price information is likely to be considered because even irrelevant anchors can have effects on consumers' judgments (Brewer and Chapman 2002; Switzer and Sniezek 1991; Wilson et al. 1996) and such effects might specifically exist in the case of low involvement. Particularly under these conditions, the so-called "illusion of knowledge effect" according to which additional information reduces the accuracy of the estimation (Hall, Ariss, and Todorov 2007) is likely to occur. Thus, less involved consumers being faced with two types of price information (saving amount, reduced price), tend to rely on all types of available information, even on less relevant information. When incorporating the two types of price information into their internal reference price, consumers perceive this price information in terms of a partitioned price. This phenomenon can be explained as follows: when forming internal reference prices, consumers try, if possible, to consider several regular prices. When faced with a price promotion ad that displays the amount of the saving and the reduced price, the regular price is provided in terms of a partitioned price that consists of a larger price component (the reduced price) and a smaller price component (the saving). Research on the processing of partitioned prices (Gierl and Bambauer-Sachse 2007) as well as research on willingness to pay for product bundles (Gaeth et al. 1990) suggests that consumers who are not motivated to engage in exact processing tend to come up with price estimates/levels of willingness to pay that result from an averaging procedure that assigns about equal weights to the components to be processed. Thus, for the case considered here, it can be argued that less involved consumers who are faced with the reduced price and the amount of the saving, are not motivated to fully process the partitioned price information and rather build an average value out of the two components that represents the anchor toward which they adjust their internal reference price. As the anchor value resulting in this case is lower than the anchor value used in the "low involvement, '% off'" condition, the reduction of the internal reference price is expected to be stronger in the "amount off" than in the "% off" condition. These arguments lead to the following hypothesis:

Hypothesis 2a: *In the case of low involvement, reductions of the internal reference price are stronger if the "amount off" format is used (compared to the "% off" format).*

If *highly* involved consumers are faced with a price promotion ad containing the reduced price and the "% off" saving information, it is, as already argued for low involvement, comparatively difficult to calculate the regular price (DelVecchio et al. 2007; Lee and Han 2002; Morwitz et al. 1998), even if highly involved consumers might be motivated to do so. Thus, the only available price information that can serve as an anchor toward which the internal reference price is adjusted is the reduced price.

If highly involved consumers encounter a price promotion ad displaying the reduced price and the amount of the saving, they are highly motivated to calculate, based on the price information provided, the regular price because this is the most diagnostic type of price information they can use in order to modify their internal reference price. Thus, when incorporating the new price information into their internal reference price, consumers are likely to either use the calculated regular price or the range of plausible values from the reduced price to the regular price as an anchor. The latter is plausible because consumers generally tend to show a downward bias in their price estimates if faced with price promotions (Krishna et al. 2002). Note that highly involved consumers will not consider the amount of the saving as independent price information, but they will rather use it to calculate the regular price.

Thus, comparing the anchor used by highly involved consumers when faced with the "% off" saving format presentation to the anchor used when encountering the "amount off" saving format presentation, it can be concluded that the stronger reduction of the reference price can be expected for the "% off" condition. These arguments lead to the following hypothesis:

Hypothesis 2b: *In the case of high involvement, reductions of the internal reference price are stronger if the "% off" format is used (compared to the "amount off" format).*

The above derived hypotheses will be tested in the empirical study presented below.

EMPIRICAL STUDY

Product Category

In order to examine whether price promotions have different effects on consumers' internal reference prices for low and high involvement products, two appropriate test products had to be chosen. The products used were T-shirts and jeans which have the advantage that they differ with regard to product involvement, but can both be assigned to the same product category (clothing).

MEASURES

In order to make manipulation checks, product involvement was measured by four items such as "is important to me" (Alpha = 0.81) following the suggestions of Laurent and Kapferer (1985) as well as of McQuarrie and Munson (1992). The internal reference price was measured using eight dimensions (normal/fair/average/minimum/maximum/appropriate price, last price paid, price expected for the next purchase, Alpha = 0.97) recommended by Chandrashekaran and Grewal (2003) as well as Chandrashekaran (2004). Price confidence was measured using two statements such as "I am confident about my price estimation" ($r = 0.71$) following the recommendations of Biswas and Sherrell (1993) as well as of Thomas and Menon (2007).

The high α-values and the high correlation show that the chosen items are appropriate to reliably measure the model variables. Thus, the overall variable values used in the data analyses were calculated as mean values of the single items that were intended to measure the respective variable.

SAMPLE, EXPERIMENTAL DESIGN, AND PROCEDURE

The sample of the empirical study consisted of 240 respondents (54% women, 46% men). The age of the participants ranged from 16 to 61 years, the average age was 28.3 years.

The study was based on a 2 (saving presentation format: "% off" vs. "amount off") x 2 (product involvement: low vs. high) design. Note that the variable price confidence that was also consid-

ered in the data analyses was not manipulated, but measured. Table 4 gives an overview of the test ads that were used to implement the experimental design.

Table 4
Test Ads

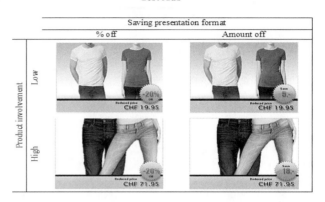

The procedure of the data collection was as follows. The respondents were assigned to one of the four groups resulting from the experimental design and were asked to fill in the respective questionnaire. The questionnaire contained in the first place a battery of measures that aimed to capture the initial reference price. Afterwards, the respondents had to indicate their price confidence as well as their involvement in the respective product category. In the next step, the respondents were presented with an ad displaying the product and the price information and they were then asked to fill in the reference price measures a second time. At the end of the questionnaire, the respondents had to indicate their age and gender.

DATA ANALYSIS AND RESULTS

Before discussing the main results of the study, the results of the manipulation check for involvement will be presented. The results of a t-test show that the measured involvement is significantly higher for jeans ($M = 4.48$) than for T-shirts ($M = 3.81$; $t = 3.91$, $p < .001$). Thus, the involvement manipulation based on choosing jeans (T-shirts) as high (low) involvement products was successful. In addition, it is important to show that the variables involvement and price confidence are not too highly correlated because otherwise, it would not be possible to treat these variables as independent conditions. The correlation between these variables is rather low ($r = 0.34$).

Now, the main results will be presented. Figure 1 gives an overview of the changes of the reference prices depending on the saving presentation format, involvement, and consumers' price confidence. The results are simultaneously differentiated according to all variables because, on the basis of this type of result presentation, it is possible to test all hypotheses.

The results presented in figure 1 basically show that providing information about a price promotion leads to a considerable reduction of the internal reference price (main effect of the information about the price promotion: $F = 11.83$, $p < .01$). This result is consistent with the finding of Grewal, Monroe, and Krishnan (1998) that there is a positive relation between the advertised selling price and the internal reference price. This finding is specifically remarkable because the participants of the study were faced only once with this information.

In order to test the first hypothesis, the results for low and high price confidence are compared for all four experimental conditions. As assumed in hypothesis 1, the reduction of the reference price is stronger for less price-confident consumers in three out of the four cases (low involvement, "% off": $\Delta_{\text{low price confidence}} = 9.88$, $\Delta_{\text{high price confi-}}$

Figure 1
Effects of Saving Presentation Format, Product Involvement,
and Consumers' Price Confidence on Internal Reference Prices

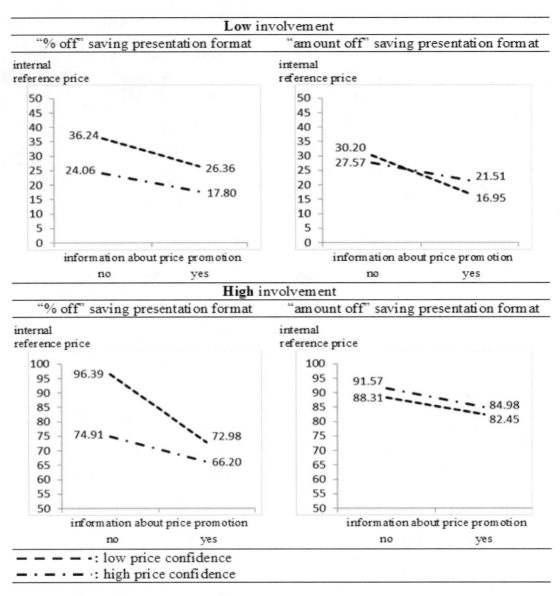

dence = 6.26, t = 3.31, p < .001; low involvement, "amount off": $\Delta_{low\ price\ confidence}$ = 13.25, $\Delta_{high\ price\ confidence}$ = 6.06, t = 7.63, p < .001; high involvement, "% off": $\Delta_{low\ price\ confidence}$ = 23.41, $\Delta_{high\ price\ confidence}$ = 8.71, t = 4.96, p < .001). Only in the case of high involvement and the "amount off" format, there is no difference in the reduction of the reference price between more and less price-confident consumers (high involvement, "amount off": $\Delta_{low\ price\ confidence}$ = 5.86, $\Delta_{high\ price\ confidence}$ = 6.59; t = -0.24, p > .10). Thus, hypothesis 1 is widely supported. A possible explanation for the finding that the reference price is reduced to about the same extent in the "high involvement, 'amount off'" condition for more and less price confident consumers could be that in this condition, consumers are provided with the reduced price and the amount of the reduction so that they can estimate the total price comparatively easily. Thus, independently of their price confidence, consumers are motivated to process the information provided in order to get a price estimate that is close to the regular price. Consequently, in both conditions, they will use a similar anchor and thus end up with a similar reduction of the internal reference price.

Moreover, the findings indicate for less involved and less price-confident consumers that the reduction of the internal reference price (IRP) is stronger if the saving presentation format "amount off" is used ("amount off": Δ_{IRP} = 13.25 vs. "% off": Δ_{IRP} = 9.88; t = 3.52, p < .001). However, for less involved, but highly price-confident consumers, this result pattern cannot be observed ("amount off": Δ_{IRP} = 6.06 vs. "% off": Δ_{IRP} = 6.26; t = -0.19, p > .10). Thus, hypothesis 2a is only supported for less price-confident consumers. A possible explanation for the non-significant effect for highly price-confident consumers could be that these consumers are, due to their high price confidence, less influenced by price promotions and thus, assign a lower weight to the saving amount than to the reduced price when processing these pieces of price information through averaging in the "amount off" format condition. Consequently, the resulting anchor is not (much) different from the anchor in the "% off" condition and thus the reductions of the internal reference price are of about the same extent.

Furthermore, the results show for highly involved, but less price-confident consumers that the reduction of the internal reference price is stronger if the saving presentation format "% off" is used ("% off": $\Delta_{IRP} = 23.41$ vs. "amount off": $\Delta_{IRP} = 5.86$; $t = 5.57$, $p < .001$). Although the same pattern results for highly involved and highly price-confident consumers, this difference is not significant ("% off": $\Delta_{IRP} = 8.71$ vs. "amount off": $\Delta_{IRP} = 6.59$; $t = 0.74$, $p > .10$). Thus, hypothesis 2b is only supported for less price-confident consumers. A possible explanation for the non-significant effect for highly price-confident consumers could be that these consumers are generally less influenced by price promotions than less price-confident consumers. Thus, if they realize that it is not possible to calculate the regular price out of the price information provided, they might adjust their internal reference price to a lesser extent into the direction of the reduced price than less price-confident consumers.

CONCLUSION

The starting point of this paper was the observation that, due to an increasing competition in many consumer product categories, marketers increasingly promote price reductions with the intention to increase purchase intentions. This observation brought up the idea that beyond having such positive effects, advertising reduced prices might at the same time have negative effects through reducing consumers' internal reference prices. Such effects would be negative from the marketer's perspective because previous research has shown that the internal reference price is linked to the price people are willing to pay (Ranyard, Charlton, and Williamson 2001). Consequently, from both a consumer researcher's and a marketer's perspective, it stood to reason to examine effects of price promotions on consumers' internal reference price. In order to go beyond what was analyzed in previous studies, the study presented here looked in more detail at such effects by differentiating between low and high involvement, low and high price confidence and different presentation formats of the saving information ("% off" vs. "amount off").

The findings of the empirical study show that being faced with a price promotion leads to a downward correction of the internal reference price, even after only one contact with the information about the price reduction and even if consumers are highly price-confident. However, for highly price-confident consumers, the reduction of the reference price is less strong than for less price-confident consumers. In addition, the results show that if less price-confident consumers encounter a price promotion, the effects depend on involvement and the saving presentation format. If less involved consumers are addressed, the "amount off" saving presentation format has the most detrimental effects, whereas in the case where highly involved consumers are targeted, the reduction of the internal reference price is strongest when the "% off" format is used.

These findings do not only provide a valuable contribution to existing research in the field of effects of price promotions on reference prices, but also suggest that marketers should be aware of the fact that already one contact with a reduced price leads to a reduction of consumers' internal reference prices independently of their price confidence or the product category. Thus, marketers should carefully consider the advantages and disadvantages when deciding on a price promotion. Furthermore, the results provide a better understanding of how marketers should communicate saving information to consumers in a way that reduces the observed effects of price reductions on internal reference prices. Specifically if marketers of low (high) involvement products target less price-confident consumers, they should choose the "% off" ("amount off") saving presentation format in order to minimize negative effects on consumers' internal reference prices.

For future research, it might be interesting to examine effects of an increasing number of contacts with price promotions in order to know whether consumers could be desensitized to the price promotion information due to the repetition effect. Furthermore, it might be interesting to add willingness to pay and purchase intentions to the research model in order to know to what extent the change of internal reference price influences such typical consumer response variables. Moreover, it might be of interest to simultaneously examine positive and negative effects of price promotions through different paths. Finally, it could be interesting to examine whether a price promotion in combination with the comparison with a related or unrelated low- or high-price product can influence the internal reference price as it was examined for willingness to pay by Adaval and Wyer Jr. (2011) in a slightly different context.

REFERENCES

Adaval, Rashmi and Robert S. Wyer Jr. (2011), "Conscious and Nonconscious Comparisons with Price Anchors: Effects on Willingness to Pay for Related and Unrelated Products," *Journal of Marketing Research*, 48 (2), 355-65.

Ailawadi, Kusum L. and Scott A. Neslin (1998), "The Effect of Promotion on Consumption: Buying More and Consuming It Faster," *Journal of Marketing Research*, 35 (3), 390-98.

Y. Lee, Dilip Soman, Duluth, MN: Association for Consumer Research, 262-68.

Bearden, William O., David M. Hardesty, and Randall L. Rose (2001), "Consumer Self-Confidence: Refinements in Conceptualization and Measurement," *Journal of Consumer Research*, 28 (1), 121-34.

Biswas, Abhijit and Edward A. Blair (1991), "Contextual Effects of Reference Prices in Retail Advertisements," *Journal of Marketing*, 55 (3), 1-12.

Biswas, Abhijit, Chris Pullig, Balaji C. Krishnan, and Scot Burton (1999), "Consumer Evaluation of Reference Price Advertisements: Effects of Other Brands' Prices and Semantic Cues," *Journal of Public Policy & Marketing*, 18 (1), 52-65.

Biswas, Abhijit and Daniel L. Sherrell (1993), "The Influence of Product Knowledge and Brand Name on Internal Price Standards and Confidence," *Psychology & Marketing*, 10 (1), 31-46.

Brewer, Noel T. and Gretchen B. Chapman (2002), "The Fragile Basic Anchoring Effect," *Journal of Behavioral Decision Making*, 15 (1), 65-77.

Briesch, Richard A., Lakshman Krishnamurthi, Tridib Mazumdar, and S.P. Raj (1997), "A Comparative Analysis of Reference Price Models," *Journal of Consumer Research*, 24 (2), 202-14.

Burman, Bidisha and Abhijit Biswas (2004), "Reference Prices in Retail Advertisements: Moderating Effects of Market Price Dispersion and Need for Cognition on Consumer Value Perception and Shopping Intention," *Journal of Product & Brand Management*, 13 (6), 379-89.

Chandrashekaran, Rajesh (2004), "The Influence of Redundant Comparison Prices and Other Price Presentation Formats on Consumers' Evaluations and Purchase Intentions," *Journal of Retailing*, 80 (1), 53-66.

Chandrashekaran, Rajesh and Dhruv Grewal (2003), "Assimilation of Advertised Reference Prices: The Moderating Role of Involvement," *Journal of Retailing*, 79 (1), 53-62.

_____ (2006), "Anchoring Effects of Advertised Reference Price and Sale Price: The Moderating Role of Saving Presentation Format," *Journal of Business Research*, 59 (10), 1063-71.

Chandrashekaran, Rajesh and Harsharanjeet Jagpal (1995), "Is There a Well-Defined Internal Reference Price?", in *Advances in Consumer Research*, Vol. 22, ed. Frank R. Kardes, Mita Sujan, Provo, UT: Association for Consumer Research, 230-35.

Chen, Shih-Fen S., Kent B. Monroe, and Yung-Chien Lou (1998), "The Effects of Framing Price Promotion Messages on Consumers' Perceptions and Purchase Intentions," *Journal of Retailing*, 74 (3), 353-372.

Compeau, Larry D. and Dhruv Grewal (1998), "Comparative Price Advertising: An Integrative Review," *Journal of Public Policy & Marketing*, 17 (2), 257-73.

DelVecchio, Devon, H. Shanker Krishnan, and Daniel C. Smith (2007), "Cents or Percent? The Effects of Promotion Framing on Price Expectations and Choice," *Journal of Marketing*, 71 (3), 158-70.

Diamond, William D. and Leland Campbell (1989), "The Framing of Sales Promotions: Effects on Reference Price Change," in *Advances in Consumer Research*, Vol. 16, ed. Thomas K. Srull, Provo, UT: Association for Consumer Research, 241-47.

Dutta, Sujay (2011), "Vulnerability to Low-Price Signals: An Experimental Study of the Effectiveness of Genuine and Deceptive Signals," *Journal of Retailing*, forthcoming.

Frankenberger, Kristina D. and Ruiming Liu (1994), "Does Consumer Knowledge Affect Consumer Responses to Advertised Reference Price Claims?", *Psychology & Marketing*, 11 (3), 235-51.

Gaeth, Gary J., Irwin P. Levin, Goutam Chakraborty, and Aron M. Levin (1990), "Consumer Evaluation of Multi-Product Bundles: An Information Integration Analysis," *Marketing Letters*, 2 (1), 47-57.

Gierl, Heribert and Silke Bambauer-Sachse (2007), "Effects of Price Partitioning on Product Evaluation," *Marketing – Journal of Research and Management*, 3 (2), 61-74.

Grewal, Dhruv, R. Krishnan, Julie Baker, and Norm Borin (1998), "The Effect of Store Name, Brand Name and Price Discounts on Consumers' Evaluations and Purchase Intentions," *Journal of Retailing*, 74 (3), 331-52.

Grewal, Dhruv, Kent B. Monroe, and R. Krishnan (1998), "The Effects of Price-Comparison Advertising on Buyers' Perceptions of Acquisition Value, Transaction Value and Behavioral Intentions," *Journal of Marketing*, 62 (2), 46-59.

Gupta, Sunil (1988), "Impact of Sales Promotions on When, What, and How Much to Buy," *Journal of Marketing Research*, 25 (4), 342-55.

Gupta, Sunil and Lee G. Cooper (1992), "The Discounting of Discounts and Promotion Thresholds," *Journal of Consumer Research*, 19 (3), 401-11.

Hall, Crystal C, Lynn Ariss, and Alexander Todorov (2007), "The Illusion of Knowledge: When More Information Reduces Accuracy and Increases Confidence*," Organizational Behavior and Human Decision Processes*, 103 (2), 277-90.

Howard, Daniel J. and Roger A. Kerin (2006), "Broadening the Scope of Reference Price Advertising Research: A Field Study of Consumer Shopping Involvement," *Journal of Marketing*, 70 (4), 185-204.

Krishna, Aradhna, Richard Briesch, Donald R. Lehmann, and Hong Yuan (2002), "A Meta-Analysis of the Impact of Price Presentation on Perceived Savings," *Journal of Retailing*, 78 (2), 101-18.

Kumar, V. and Robert P. Leone (1988), "Measuring the Effect of Retail Store Promotions on Brand and Store Substitution," *Journal of Marketing Research*, 25 (2), 178-85.

Lattin, James M. and Randolph E. Bucklin (1989), "Reference Effects of Price and Promotion on Brand Choice Behavior," *Journal of Marketing Research*, 26 (3), 299-310.

Laurent, Gilles and Jean-Noël Kapferer (1985), "Measuring Consumer Involvement Profiles," *Journal of Marketing Research*, 22 (1), 41-53.

Lee, Yih Hwai and Cheng Yuen Han (2002), "Partitioned Pricing in Advertising: Effects on Brand and Retailer Attitudes," *Marketing Letters*, 13 (1), 27-40.

Lichtenstein, Donald R. and William O. Bearden (1989), "Contextual Influences on Perceptions of Merchant-Supplied Reference Prices," *Journal of Consumer Research*, 16 (1), 55-66.

Lichtenstein, Donald R., Peter H. Bloch, and William C. Black (1988), "Correlates of Price Acceptability," *Journal of Consumer Research*, 15 (2), 243-52.

Lichtenstein, Donald R., Scot Burton, and Eric J. Karson (1991), "The Effect of Semantic Cues on Consumer Perceptions of Reference Price Ads," *Journal of Consumer Research*, 18 (3), 380-91.

Liefeld, John and Louise A. Heslop (1985), "Reference Prices and Deception in Newspaper Advertising," *Journal of Consumer Research*, 11 (4), 868-76.

Mayhew, Glenn E. and Russell S. Winer (1992), "An Empirical Analysis of Internal and External Reference Prices Using Scanner Data," *Journal of Consumer Research*, 19 (1), 62-70.

Mazumdar, Tridib and Kent B. Monroe (1992), "Effects of Inter-store and In-store Price Comparisons on Price Recall Accuracy and Confidence," *Journal of Retailing*, 68 (1), 66-89.

Mazumdar, Tridib and Purushottam Papatla (2000), "An Investigation of Reference Price Segments," *Journal of Marketing Research*, 37 (2), 246-58.

McQuarrie, Edward F. and J. Michael Munson (1992), "A Revised Product Involvement Inventory: Improved Usability and Validity," in *Advances in Consumer Research*, Vol. 19, ed. John F. Sherry, Jr., Brian Sternthal, Prove, UT: Association for Consumer Research, 108-15.

Moon, Sangkil, Gary J. Russell, and Sri Davi Duvvuri (2006), "Profiling the Reference Price Consumer," *Journal of Retailing*, 82 (1), 1-11.

Morwitz, Vicki G., Eric A. Greenleaf, and Eric J. Johnson (1998), "Divide and Prosper: Consumers' Reactions to Partitioned Prices," *Journal of Marketing Research*, 35 (4), 453-63.

Petty, Richard E., John T. Cacioppo, and David Schumann (1983), "Central and Peripheral Routes to Advertising Effectiveness: The Moderating Role of Involvement," *Journal of Consumer Research*, 10 (2), 135-46.

Rajendran, K.N. and Gerard J. Tellis (1994), "Contextual and Temporal Components of Reference Price," *Journal of Marketing*, 58 (1), 22-34.

Ranyard, Rob, John P. Charlton, and Janis Williamson (2001), "The Role of Internal Reference Prices in Consumers' Willingness to Pay Judgments: Thaler's Beer Pricing Task Revisited," *Acta Psychologica*, 106 (3), 265-83.

Sinha, Indrajit and Michael F. Smith (2000), "Consumers' Perceptions of Promotional Framing of Price," *Psychology & Marketing*, 17 (3), 257-75.

Sun, Baohong (2005), "Promotion Effect on Endogenous Consumption," *Marketing Science*, 24 (3), 430-43.

Switzer, Fred S. and Janet A. Sniezek (1991), "Judgment Processes in Motivation: Anchoring and Adjustment Effects on Judgment and Behavior," *Organizational Behavior and Human Decision Processes*, 49 (2), 208-29.

Thomas, Manoj and Geeta Menon (2007), "When Internal Reference Prices and Price Expectations Diverge: The Role of Confidence," *Journal of Marketing Research*, 44 (3), 401-9.

Tsiros, Michael and David M. Hardesty (2010), "Ending a Price Promotion: Retracting It in One Step or Phasing It Out Gradually," *Journal of Marketing*, 74 (1), 49-64.

Urbany, Joel E., William O. Bearden, and Dan C. Weilbaker (1988), "The Effect of Plausible and Exaggerated Reference Prices on Consumer Perceptions and Price Search," *Journal of Consumer Research*, 15 (1), 95-110.

Vaidyanathan, Rajiv and Praveen Aggarwal (2001), "Use of Internal Reference Prices for Deal Evaluations: Decision Structure and Role of Involvement," *The Marketing Management Journal*, 11 (2), 108-22.

Winer, Russell S. (1986), "A Reference Price Model of Brand Choice for Frequently Purchased Products," *Journal of Consumer Research*, 13 (2), 250-56.

Wilson, Timothy D., Christopher E. Houston, Kathryn M. Etling, and Nancy Brekke (1996), "A New Look at Anchoring Effects: Basic Anchoring and Its Antecedents," *Journal of Experimental Psychology: General*, 125 (4), 387-402.

Yadav, Manjit S. and Kathleen Seiders (1998), "Is the Price Right? Understanding Contingent Processing in Reference Price Formation," *Journal of Retailing*, 74 (3), 311-29.

Zaichkowsky, Judith Lynne (1988), "Involvement and the Price Cue," in *Advances in Consumer Research*, Vol. 15, ed. Micheal J. Houston, Provo, UT: Association for Consumer Research, 323-27.

How Relevant Is Marketing Scholarship? A Case History with a Prediction

Edward McQuarrie, Santa Clara University, USA
Barbara Phillips, University of Saskatchewan, Canada
Steven Andrews, Roger Williams University, USA

ABSTRACT

Debate over whether marketing scholarship ought to be more relevant has a long history. This paper takes a positive rather than a normative approach to the issue, and provides an empirical examination of the degree of relevance achieved in a sub-discipline of consumer behavior: marketing communications. A content analysis of 485 laboratory experiments published in six marketing journals over the last twelve years was conducted. Results show little concern for relevance in the design of advertising print experiments, and a longitudinal comparison suggests that relevance has decreased over time. The paper concludes by considering sociological explanations for why the relevance of marketing scholarship may not improve.

The online Oxford English dictionary defines 'academic' as "not of practical relevance." This definition squares poorly with the oft-heard injunction to marketing scholars that their research needs to become more relevant, an exhortation that has appeared regularly for more than thirty years (e.g., Ferber 1977; McQuarrie 1998; Preston 1985), and most recently in Reibstein, Day, and Wind (2009). In this paper, we do not attempt to resolve the normative issue of whether marketing scholarship ought to be relevant, or needs to become more relevant; rather, we aim at a positive account of the degree of relevance currently achieved. The goal is to document the extent to which laboratory work in one consumer behavior area of marketing scholarship—marketing communications—has or has not been relevant.

In what follows we define the criteria for relevance used in this paper and distinguish various aspects of relevance within the context of marketing communication research. We apply these criteria to twelve years of experimental research on print advertising published in six marketing journals from 1998 to 2009. This produces a tabulation of the number and proportion of published studies that are relevant to one or another causal factor characteristic of the real consumer behavior phenomenon. We find sustained low levels of relevance, and no difference in relevance across advertising, consumer behavior, or general marketing journals. We conclude, again in a positive rather than normative mode, by sketching out a theory that could explain why relevance has been minimal in this area of marketing scholarship and is likely to remain so, no matter how many exhortations in the vein of Reibstein et al. (2009) may appear.

CRITERA FOR RELEVANCE

Proximal Similarity

We define relevance in terms of Campbell's (1986) concept of proximal similarity. On this criterion, a marketing communication experiment may be judged relevant to the extent its stimuli and procedures reproduce the distinctive characteristics of consumer advertisements (McQuarrie 2004). Of course, similarity is never absolute, and laboratory experiments can never provide the same setting or the same event matrix as any particular advertising exposure in the field. Hence for Campbell, similarity functions as a threshold—that is the meaning of the modifier 'proximal'. The issue is whether experimental stimuli and procedures incorporate *enough* of those aspects of the phenomenon that are important for understanding cause and effect. That is, does the experiment go far enough to produce *ad-*

vertisements and *consumer behavior*, or do its conditions actually capture some other kind of human behavior?

The power of Campbell's concept of proximal similarity can be illustrated by re-considering the hoary debate over the use of student subjects (Sears 1986). From Campbell's standpoint, use of student subjects is neither here nor there. If the purchase domain is potato chips and 20 year olds are substantially represented among the buying population for chips (as they are *not* among the population that rents cars or purchases fur coats), then an experiment that exposed students to ads for potato chips would not be irrelevant thereby.

But now suppose these students don't actually purchase any potato chips during the experiment. Suppose further they don't choose a brand; in fact, suppose there are no brands in the experiment at all, but only labels heading up a written description of a 'snack product'. Suppose that what these students do after reading these descriptive paragraphs is carefully examine a few additional sentences describing the object to which the labels refer, and check boxes in response. Is this checking of a box 'consumer behavior'? Is this picture-free text an 'ad'? Under Campbell's analysis, the answer in both cases probably would be no. The experiment does not reproduce 'buying behavior', nor does it reproduce 'magazine advertisement'; there is insufficient similarity. The stimuli used, and the nature of the responses gathered, are distal rather than proximal to the advertising domain.

The real issue for Campbell, in judging whether an advertising experiment is relevant, would not be whether the experimental subjects are students, but whether these students are exposed to *advertisements,* as that term is commonly understood, and then have the opportunity, after a suitable interval, to *choose* from among advertised brands and *buy*. Advertisements, within the larger domain of persuasive messages, are distinguished by being highly crafted amalgams of visual and verbal elements embedded in particular sorts of mass-media contexts, where consumers can (and often do) ignore those ads. A written paragraph whose scrutiny is mandated would lack most of these elements. Likewise, purchases involve choice, real monetary cost, the subtler loss of foregone alternatives, and the risk of remorse. Checking a box on a paper form need not involve any of these elements. Thus, by Campbell's criterion of proximal similarity, an experiment in which a written paragraph is administered and subjects check boxes on paper forms in response, may contribute to scientific knowledge of text comprehension or communication, but is not likely to be relevant to understanding cause and effect in the *advertising* domain of consumer behavior—the experimental set up is too dissimilar.

Conversely, if one was a political scientist concerned with the phenomenon of voting, that same experiment might be sufficiently proximal. Voting behavior *is* a matter of indicating a preference by checking a box on a form. Voters *do* learn about candidates by reading extended written text. The criteria for proximal similarity *are* met if the experiment seeks to understand how written communication influences voting behavior.

By necessity, laboratory experiments are highly artificial (Petty and Cacioppo 1996; Wells 1993), but this doesn't matter in Campbell's view, as long as the artifice reproduces elements important for determining how an advertisement can cause a desired effect. The real question, in determining whether an experiment is relevant to the consumer behavior domain of advertising, is whether the stimulus exposed is something like an advertisement, and whether the reception environment is something like that in which ads are encountered, and whether the responses measured are something like purchase behavior.

Decomposition of Relevance

The goal of this paper is to examine published marketing scholarship and count the number of studies that address a set of causal factors prototypical of advertising and advertising reception environments. If it can be documented that numerous experiments exist that manipulate a particular factor as present or absent, or there exist numbers of experiments with the factor present and numerous others with it absent, then meta-analysis can ultimately reveal whether that factor is causal, and to what extent. But if a factor is excluded from most published experiments, then just that much of the domain of consumer behavior remains terra incognita (Armstrong 2010).

As a case in point, if there were no studies in which ad stimuli were repeated, then we could not know how level of repetition might alter the impact of a particular persuasive appeal. Absence of evidence concerning repetition effects is not evidence for the absence of repetition effects. We might assume that anything that is effective in a single repetition would be as effective, or more so, if repeated; but there would be no empirical foundation for this position. And to the extent there was any evidence that some appeals only work after wear-in, while others are vulnerable to wear-out, we would be on very thin ice in assuming that some other appeal that had failed (succeeded) in a single repetition would be just as (in)effective if repeated.

To focus the analysis, we examine experiments that use print advertisements, as discussed subsequently. In 2012 in North America, the typical magazine ad directed at consumers is dominated by its picture, containing few words; will be exposed repeatedly; will be embedded in a media vehicle whose articles are the primary focus for the consumer, who is in no way forced to look at the ad or dwell on it; and this consumer will, after a delay, have an opportunity to act in connection with the ad, often by making a choice between brands, with which s/he was already familiar, at some economic cost.

Almost any field experiment would include all of these factors, and any 'single source' data set would likewise include them all (e.g., Lodish et al. 1995). More important, it is feasible to reproduce any one of these conditions in an artificial laboratory experiment—or not. The balance of pictures and words in an ad, whether it is embedded in other material, whether exposure is forced, whether response is measured with a delay, and so on, are all choices that individual scholars make in the course of designing an experiment. An experimenter could instead type out a paragraph containing attribute claims and staple it to a sheaf of pages containing rating scales, with the overt or covert statement that experimental credit will not be given to participants unless the written paragraph is carefully attended to and the ratings diligently made (Allen 2004). Arguably, neither 'advertising' nor 'consumer behavior' are present in such a situation. The empirical question, then, is how many marketing scholars have chosen the written paragraph, check-a-box design, with forced exposure and immediate response, versus the number of scholars who chose to reproduce pictorial aspects, or unforced exposure, or any of the other prototypical elements of the advertising phenomenon.

Again, we do not contest the contribution of the written paragraph, check-a-box experiment to the rigorous testing of scientific theories of human persuasion (Calder, Phillips and Tybout 1981). A long stream of research in social psychology exactly fits this template. Rather, we set out to review twelve years of published marketing communications experiments in marketing journals and count how many laboratory experiments incorporate one of more relevance conditions, versus how many approximate the written paragraph, check-a-box template inherited from the older discipline of social psychology. There is no expectation that any given laboratory experiment will incorporate all the causal factors, and with at least 2^n possible combinations of factors, it might be impossible for any one experiment to vary all the factors simultaneously. But it is certainly fair to hold up twelve years of the *collective* product of marketing, consumer behavior, and advertising scholarship, and estimate the degree of relevance achieved, net. What do the facts show?

METHOD
Journal and Study Selection

From 1998 to 2009 inclusive, we examined each issue of the following leading journals: *Journal of Advertising, Journal of Advertising Research, Journal of Consumer Psychology, Journal of Consumer Research, Journal of Marketing,* and *Journal of Marketing Research.* These journals contained the majority of published research on advertising. The table of contents and abstracts were reviewed to identify articles containing laboratory experiments that purported to be about advertising, as indicated by title or abstract. 'Laboratory experiments' were defined broadly as non-field studies where a set of treatments were administered; hence a study in which subjects were recruited at a shopping mall or airport and randomly assigned to different treatments would be included. Any laboratory study where the authors referred to its stimuli or topic as 'ads' or 'advertising' was deemed admissible.

An initial perusal showed that print advertising stimuli dominated the population of studies (approximately 3:1 ratio), so only experiments using printed stimuli were retained for further examination[1]. The computer presentation of still images accompanied by text was accepted as 'print'. This focus on print ad studies had the further advantage of simplifying the set of relevance criteria, and also of maximizing the availability of stimuli for inspection (print stimuli are often reproduced in article appendices, while television and radio stimuli, before the age of Web appendices, could not be). A total of 485 laboratory experiments in 289 articles were identified, as described in Table 1. The 122 articles reporting multiple experiments accounted for 2/3 of the experiments in the dataset.

Scoring Criteria for Relevance

The authors scored each experiment for the presence or absence of: 1) a real (as opposed to fictitious brand; 2) embedded, non-focal exposure; 3) repeated exposure; 4) inclusions of competitive advertising; 5) measurement of responses after a delay or one day or more; 6) inclusion of choice as one of these responses. These six criteria allow for a longitudinal comparison to the analysis of pre-1998 experiments reported in McQuarrie (1998). The sum of these six dichotomous criteria will be referred to as the relevance score.

Experiments also were scored as to whether they manipulated the verbal element, the visual element, or both. Pollay (1985) and McQuarrie and Phillips (2008) show a drastic decrease in the number of words appearing in magazine ads over time. Increasingly, magazine ads no longer have any body copy, as traditionally defined.

---

[1] Of the ~150 excluded experiments, approximately half used television ads, a third used digital stimuli of some kind, and the remainder were scattered across other media. Hence, none of these would have produced a large enough sample to be meaningfully analyzed, especially at the journal or discipline level.

TABLE 1
Incidence of Individual Relevance Criteria in Advertising Experiments

	1998-2009 N = 485		1990-1997a N = 231
	N	%	%
Relevance Criterion			
Real brand	168	34.6	28
Embedded, non-focal exposure	39	8.0	17
Repeated exposure	30	6.2	16
Competitive advertising present	23	4.7	20
Delayed measurement	35	7.2	5
Choice measured	19	3.9	14
Frequency distribution			
Zero criteria present	249	51.3	40
One	174	35.9	32
Two	49	10.1	19
Three	10	2.1	9
Four	3	0.6	0
Five	0	0.0	1
Manipulation of:			
Visual element	61	12.6	--
Verbal element	209	43.1	
Both	96	19.8	
Neither	119	24.5	
WIRIWS Incidence (written immediate response to isolated written stimulus)	316	65.2	--

a From Table 3 of McQuarrie (1998). The *Journal of Consumer Psychology* was not included in his study, nor was the manipulation of visual or verbal elements tabulated.

Do recent laboratory experiments reflect this ongoing de-emphasis on words?

Measured responses were also classified as behavioral (e.g., response latency, successful recognition) or written. Experiments with only written responses, measured immediately, in isolation, with no manipulation of visual elements, repetition or competitive interference, were coded as such. These will be referred to as 'WIRIWS' studies (written immediate responses to isolated written stimuli). Finally, when an article included the stimulus used, these were examined and compared to actual magazine ads for the same product, to get a sense of which components of actual magazine ads were being incorporated into lab stimuli.

RESULTS

Relevance

Real brands were not uncommon in academic experimental research on advertising during 1998-2009, appearing in about a third of all experiments. However, all of the other relevance criteria were conspicuous by their absence, omitted from between 92% and 96% of experiments (Table 1). Few researchers during this period felt it necessary to arrange unforced exposure to ads, or to study the effects of repetition, delay, or competitive interference, or to make subjects choose a brand following ad exposure, as opposed to completing rating scales.

In terms of a relevance score, just over half the experiments scored zero; the mean incidence of relevance criteria was .65 out of a possible 6.0. The overall results are measurably worse than those reported by McQuarrie (1998) for 154 print ad experiments published in 1990-97, which in turn he found to be measurably worse than those reported for pre-1990 print ad experiments. Some individual relevance criteria were more common in the present study (real brands), others less so (competition, choice); others stayed at the same low level as seen in both the earlier time periods studied by McQuarrie (unforced exposure).

Finally, studies that manipulate only verbal elements, unrepeated and without competitive interference, while taking an immediate written response, were the norm during these twelve years, accounting for 65% of these experiments. WIRIWS studies represent the modal print ad experiment. In summary, laboratory experiments currently reported in marketing journals appear not to be much concerned with relevance, defined in terms of proximal similarity to advertising and consumer behavior. The longitudinal data suggests that, if anything, relevance has declined over time.

Turning to other aspects of relevance, manipulation of visual elements of the advertising stimulus was half as common as manipulation of verbal elements (Table 1); whereas the nature of the verbal manipulations is extremely diverse, most of the visual manipulations consist of a change in the object depicted, rather than a change in the style or manner of depiction (for the distinction, see Scott and Vargas [2007]). The incidence of visual manipulations did not increase over the twelve year period, in marked contrast to what was happening during this era to print advertisements outside the laboratory (McQuarrie and Phillips 2008).

Some sense of the gap that separates the verbal stimuli described as 'ads' within marketing scholarship, as compared to real and now primarily visual ads directed at consumers, can be gleaned from Figures 1 and 2. The left panel of Figure 1 reproduces the stimulus used in 1999 *JMR* paper, which purports to be an advertisement for toothpaste. In the right panel of Figure 1 an actual toothpaste ad is reproduced. The differences are stark. The Dazzle ad is almost entirely composed of words, with no visual element other than a border. The actual Crest ad contains few easily visible words, consisting otherwise of a highly stylized picture that fills the page. No actual toothpaste ad appearing in today's mass media would use such a densely packed volume of verbal text as the Dazzle stimulus; one has to go back over a century to find an era where such word-heavy, picture-light ads were the norm (Pollay 1985). Is the Dazzle stimulus really an instance of 'advertisement'—the everyday phenomenon to which consumers are exposed? A case can be made that the Dazzle experiments, however internally valid, lack construct validity—if proffered as research on *consumer response to advertising,* as opposed to comprehension of written text.

The same problem can be seen in Figure 2, where the experimental stimulus used in a 2007 *JA* paper appears in the left panel, and an actual ad for jeans appears in the right panel. This time the experimental ad does contain a large picture, but what is manipulated and tested is the attribute list that appears in a large font at the lower left. For comparison, the actual jeans ad reproduced in the right panel of Figure 2 makes no verbal claim to possess any attribute, much less a list. In fact, the actual jeans ad has no headline or body text at all. Such an absence of verbal text is the norm in contemporary ads for fashion clothing (Phillips and McQuarrie 2011); it is difficult to see how the results of such marketing experiments can be relevant to a fashion advertiser who is constrained to accomplish his or her promotional purpose without the use of any verbally stated attribute claim.

Relevance by Discipline

It might be argued that consumer researchers, whose journals are sponsored by multiple disciplines outside of marketing, don't have the same obligation or opportunity for relevance as do marketing scholars publishing in AMA journals, who are taxed with providing managerial implications. Likewise, one might suppose that advertising researchers might be more oriented to reproducing the distinctive characteristics of advertising, relative to scholars concerned with more general questions of consumer behavior or marketing action. To this end, we grouped journals by discipline and compared relevance scores and WIRIWS scores across discipline. As Table 2 shows, there were no differences across journal discipline (χ^2 (2) = 2.86 and 1.21 for relevance and WIRIWS scores respectively, both *ns*). In sum, none of the three disciplines appears any

FIGURE 1
Academic Toothpaste Ad (Left) Versus an Actual Toothpaste Ad (Right)

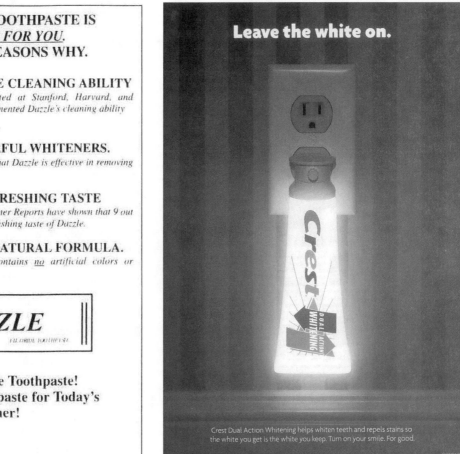

FIGURE 2
Academic Jeans Ad (Left) Versus an Actual Jeans Ad (Right)

more or less concerned with relevance in the design of advertising experiments.

DISCUSSION

We examined one specific area within marketing scholarship where a high volume of publications and a lengthy history of publication exist: laboratory experiments on advertising. This consumer behavior sub-domain is also attractive because it features experimental design alternatives that are equally feasible (e.g., manipulate pictures or words, repeat or not repeat stimuli) along with straightforward criteria for judging any given design alternative as more or less relevant to actual marketing practice. What we found does not make us optimistic that the call for institutional change of Reibstein et al. (2009) will be answered anytime soon.

A tabulation of 485 published laboratory experiments on print advertising published in six journals over the preceding twelve years showed little concern with relevance. A majority of studies consisted of immediate paper-and pencil ratings taken in response to single forced exposures to written text. Measurement of purchase behavior was the exception, and even choice measurements were rare. Delayed response after incidental exposure was vanishingly rare. There were no significant differences across disciplines, and no evidence of improvement in relevance relative to earlier accounts (McQuarrie 1998; Preston 1985).

TABLE 2
Incidence of Relevance across Journals and Disciplines

	Zero Relevance		WIRIWS Design	
	N	*%*	*N*	*%*
Discipline				
AMA journals (*JM, JMR*)	38	45.2	59	70.2
Consumer (*JCP, JCR*)	119	50.2	153	64.6
Advertising (*JA, JAR*)	92	56.1	104	63.4

Note. See text for the definition and calculation of the relevance and WIRIWS scores. The percentages reflect the proportion of studies in a journal group that had zero relevance or used a WIRIWS design; e.g., 59 of 84 experiments in the AMA journals used this design.

Must Academic Scholarship Be Irrelevant?

It is traditional to lament findings of the sort presented in this paper. This tradition predates Preston (Ferber 1977) and continues to the present day (Reibstein et al. 2009). Often this lament issues in an exhortation: scholars could, and should, do better—should endeavor to make their research *more* relevant. We essay an alternative response, in order to understand why academic scholarship may never move in the direction of greater relevance. The idea is that any trend as strong and well-established as the trend to irrelevance, as documented by Preston (1985), McQuarrie (1998), and the present effort, is likely underpinned by enduring philosophical, institutional and structural factors.

Within academia, the tradition of lamenting the lack of relevance is opposed by an alternative philosophical tradition, of equal age and diffusion, which explicitly denies the value of relevance (Calder et al. 1981). The formulation runs something like this: "the data don't generalize—it's the theory that generalizes" (Mook 1983). Because the scholar is not concerned with predicting some particular causal sequence outside the laboratory, the details of the causal sequence selected for use in the laboratory do not matter. On this reasoning, if one avoids using a familiar real brand, with all its troublesome specificity, the theoretical explanation can potentially be generalized to both real and fictitious brands. The emptier the data are of specifics—the more the causal sequences studied in the laboratory consist only of widespread, multi-context human behaviors such as reading and writing—the wider the span of contexts within which the theoretical explanation can be generalized. The rebuttal—that research conducted with diligent readers might only generalize to similar contexts, and not to advertising contexts, where diligent reading cannot be assumed—is not considered. Since diligence was not manipulated, there is no reason to suppose that theoretical predictions are limited to diligent readers (Lynch 1982). On this view, imposing a requirement of relevance—of proximal similarity— would restrict rather than enhance the generalizability of the research, and reduce the contribution to Theory. What makes some set of concepts a Theory, and potentially generalizable across contexts, is precisely their remoteness from any specific context.

The necessary separation of Theory from data, as laid out above, is the gold standard for academic rejection of the need for proximal similarity in experimental design. Unfortunately, decades ago the logician Quine (1953) put the kibosh to this argument. Quine's challenge, in simplified form, can be captured as follows: (1) if the theory generalizes but the data do not, then the theory must be fundamentally separate from the data; (2) but if the theory is really separate from the data, in what sense can it be said to explain that data, or be tested by it? An early response to this conundrum, associated with logical empiricism (see Hunt [2007] for an account), was that auxiliary concepts can be used to tie the theory to the 'plane of observation'. Quine's rebuttal was that any causal knowledge obtained empirically must then always take the form of a test of Theory + Auxiliaries, and its generalizability would accordingly be limited to circumstances where both the theoretical concept(s) and the auxiliary concept(s) are again conjoined. But since the auxiliary concepts are connected to the data—that's their purpose—then it cannot be true to say that the data don't generalize, only the theory. To close the loop, an example of an auxiliary concept would be whether a brand is familiar or unfamiliar, whether exposure is single or repeated, whether response is immediate or delayed—i.e., the sorts of things that were earlier described in terms of proximal similarity, or relevance.

Given the age of Quine's (1953) essay, one may reasonably ask why the phrase, 'the data don't generalize, it's the theory that generalizes' continues to be advanced as the rationale for ignoring considerations of proximal similarity. In the next section we advance a sociological explanation for why scholars in advertising, consumer and marketing have chosen to ignore Quine's debunking of the separateness of theory and data.

A Social Theory Perspective on Marketing Scholarship

Insights from the French social theorist, Pierre Bourdieu (1984), may help us to derive an explanation of what marketing scholarship is really about, if not the search for relevant, practical marketing knowledge. If we apply Bourdieu's perspective, marketing scholar-

ship represents a social field in which participants compete to obtain elite status, and elites act to maintain their status by enforcing a distinction between elite and non-elite. More specifically, the elite maintains its distinction by valorizing success in difficult practices, and individual members of the elite maintain and improve their personal distinction by repeatedly demonstrating success in these practices—the more difficult and exclusive, the better.

Stepping back, a key mistake in the Reibstein et al. (2009) worldview was to assume that marketing academics as a group care much about acquiring knowledge of real marketing phenomena. There are some who certainly do; but the prediction from Bourdieu is that as a rule, individual marketing scholars will primarily care about publishing papers in journals perceived as elite by peers they esteem. Success in this difficult practice confers and sustains elite status. In a Bourdieusian world, obtaining and maintaining the regard of one's aspirational group would be the primary motivation governing the scholarship activities of marketing academics.

The prediction from Bourdieu, then, is that marketing academics will gravitate toward scholarship that gets published in the leading journals of the field. If these journals do not insist on relevance, and if arranging for relevance is in any way more costly than letting it slide, then marketing scholars as a group will dispense with relevance in their work. It isn't important to the goal of getting published.

There is a circularity here which is important to tease apart because it reflects the fact that elites are 'sticky'; that is, they are generally able to reproduce themselves through time. Thus, we may suppose that journals mostly publish articles that members of their Editorial Boards esteem; in turn, publishing enough such articles gets one appointed to Editorial Boards, where one tends to esteem the kind of articles that earned one that elite status. Since any elite journal will do, authors who publish in *JMR* may also publish in *JCR*, and vice versa, so that appointment to one Editorial Board may co-occur with appointment to the other, leading to a homogenization of journal acceptance criteria, despite the very different mandates of their sponsors. From this perspective, irrelevance in marketing scholarship becomes *self-sustaining,* despite being entirely contingent in historical terms.

There may be some readers who recoil from this Bourdeusian account as a grotesque parody of the collaborative, peer-reviewed quest for scientific knowledge to which they have devoted their lives and honor. Nevertheless, the Bourdeusian account has the virtue of predicting the facts on the ground. It explains why the relevance of advertising experiments hasn't improved despite decades of exhortation, and it explains why advertising experiments in consumer behavior journals aren't any more relevant than those in advertising journals.

It also makes falsifiable predictions about the future. A reasonable prediction from this study is that the Reibstein et al. (2009) initiative will slowly drop from view, as did each of its predecessors, and that a decade from now, and any number of decades from now, relevance will continue to be ignored in judging the merits of individual instances of academic marketing scholarship. That is, the alternative intellectual tradition laid out in Petty and Cacioppo (1996) will prevail and continue to govern the actual conduct of research. It also predicts that years from now there will be another editorial in a marketing journal, pursuing the same plaints, and similarly neglectful of the lengthy ancestry of such screeds, going back to Preston (1986) and Ferber (1977). The thrust of marketing scholarship isn't going to change in the direction of greater relevance until a critical mass of its elite, who gained their status when relevance was irrelevant, come to see the Calder et al. (1981) and Petty and Cacioppo (1996) position as untenable.

Mea Culpa and Ex Culpa

It is important to acknowledge that several of our own experiments appear in the data and, on the whole, do not score terrifically higher with respect to relevance. We acknowledge living in a glass house and can only plead that we wanted to be published, too. Second, although there was good reason to focus on laboratory experiments on advertising, the tables show these to be less numerous in the AMA marketing journals as compared to the consumer journals. A follow-up analysis also might show, for instance, that field experiments, with their automatic relevance, are more common in marketing than in consumer journals. In addition, marketing communication is only one small piece of marketing, and it may be that non-advertising articles appearing in marketing journals are rather more relevant on the whole than the experimental advertising studies examined here. But if that is so, why were Reibstein et al. (2009) and their predecessors motivated to write as they did? Regardless of relative frequency, why would a journal publish any article whose relevance to marketing phenomena was suspect?

The answer, of course, is that Editorial Boards are primarily concerned with maintaining standards of internal validity, and for vetting the caliber of the statistical analysis deployed. Again, for the record, we are not questioning the internal validity of any of the 485 experiments examined or the correctness of the statistical inferences made. Our concern is with the construct validity of the stimuli and procedures used. And ultimately that is the theoretical importance of relevance; for if relevance cannot be established, there can be no assurance that a theory of *advertising and consumer behavior* has been tested—as opposed to a theory of something else.

In conclusion, we sought to contribute to the ongoing discussion of the relevance of relevance to marketing scholarship by taking a positive rather than a normative approach. Regardless of how relevant marketing scholarship should be, how relevant is it and has it been? This required a focus on a specific sub-domain of consumer behavior, and a statement of the criteria to be applied in assessing relevance. This positive approach allowed us to show both the prevalence of irrelevance, and its stasis over time. These positive facts then provided the grounds for a theoretical account of marketing scholarship as a social practice, grounded in Bourdieu, which explains both the genesis and maintenance of irrelevance, and predicts its continuance.

REFERENCES

Allen, Chris T. (2004), "A Theory-Based Approach for Improving Demand Artifact Assessment in Advertising Experiments," *Journal of Advertising*, 33 (2), 63-73.

Armstrong, J. Scott (2010), *Persuasive Advertising*. NY: Palgrave MacMillan.

Bourdieu, Pierre (1984), *Distinction: A Social Critique of the Judgment of Taste*. Cambridge, MA: Harvard University Press.

Calder, Bobby J., Lynn W. Phillips, and Alice M. Tybout (1981), "Designing Research for Application," *Journal of Consumer Research*, 8 (September), 197-207.

Campbell, Donald T. (1986), "Relabeling Internal and External Validity for Applied Social Scientists," *Advances in Quasi-Experimental Design and Analysis*, William M. K. Trochim, (ed.), San Francisco, CA: Jossey-Bass, 67-78.

Ferber, Robert (1977), "Research by Convenience," *Journal of Consumer Research*, 4 (June), 57-8.

Hunt, Shelby D. (2007), *Controversy in Marketing Theory*. Armonk, NY: M.E. Sharpe.

Lodish, Leonard M., Magid Abraham, Stuart Kalmenson, Jeanne Livelsberger, Beth Lubetkin, Bruce Richardson, and Mary Ellen Stevens (1995), "How TV Advertising Works: A Meta-Analysis of 389 Real World Split Cable T.V. Advertising Experiments," *Journal of Marketing Research*, 32 (May), 125-39.

Lynch, John G. (1982), "On the External Validity of Experiments in Consumer Research," *Journal of Consumer Research*, 9 (December), 225-39.

McQuarrie, Edward F. (1998), "Have Laboratory Experiments Become Detached from Advertiser Goals? A Meta-Analysis," *Journal of Advertising Research*, 38 (6), 15-26.

McQuarrie, Edward F. (2004), "Integration of Construct and External Validity by Means of Proximal Similarity: Implications for Laboratory Experiments in Marketing," *Journal of Business Research*, 57, 142-53.

McQuarrie, Edward F. and Phillips, Barbara J. (2008) "It's Not Your Father's Magazine Ad: Magnitude and Direction of Recent Changes in Advertising Style," *Journal of Advertising*, 37 (3), 95-106.

Mook, Douglas G. (1983), "In Defense of External Invalidity," *American Psychologist*, 38 (April), 379-87.

Petty, Richard E. and John T. Cacioppo (1996), "Addressing Disturbing and Disturbed Consumer Behavior: Is It Necessary to Change the Way We Conduct Behavioral Science?" *Journal of Marketing Research*, 33 (February), 1-8.

Phillips, Barbara J. and McQuarrie, Edward F. (2011), "Contesting the Social Impact of Marketing: A Re-Characterization of Women's Fashion Advertising," *Marketing Theory*, 11 (2), 99-126.

Pollay, Richard W. (1985), "The Subsidizing Sizzle: A Descriptive History of Print Advertising, 1900-1980," *Journal of Marketing*, 48 (Summer), 24-37.

Preston, Ivan L. (1985), "The Developing Detachment of Advertising Research from the Study of Advertiser Goals," *Current Issues and Research in Advertising*, 7, 1-15.

Quine, W. V. (1951), "Main Trends in Recent Philosophy: Two Dogmas of Empiricism," *The Philosophical Review*, 60 (1), 20-43.

Reibstein, David J., George Day, and Jerry Wind (2009), "Guest Editorial: Is Marketing Academia Losing Its Way?" *Journal of Marketing*, 73 (July), 1-3.

Scott, Linda M. and Patrick Vargas (2007), "Writing with Pictures: Toward a Unifying Theory of Consumer Response to Images," *Journal of Consumer Research*, 34 (October), 341-56.

Sears, David O. (1986), "College Sophomores in the Laboratory: Influences of a Narrow Database on Social Psychology's View of Human Nature," *Journal of Personality and Social Psychology*, 51 (3), 515-30.

Wells, William D. (1993), "Discovery-Oriented Consumer Research," *Journal of Consumer Research*, 19 (March), 489-504.

The 'No Hard Feelings' Effect: Voters' Resolution of Ambivalence to Make a Choice Between Candidates

Robert D. Jewell, Kent State University, USA
Jennifer Wiggins Johnson, Kent State University, USA
Hyun Jung Lee, Kent State University, USA

ABSTRACT

This paper examines how voters resolve their ambivalence and polarize their attitudes in order to make a choice between candidates. These effects are tested with a longitudinal natural experiment examining voters' choices between candidates in the 2004 and 2008 presidential elections. The results show that voters reduce their ambivalence and polarize their attitudes toward the candidates as the deadline to make their choice becomes more imminent, while nonvoters do not exhibit this pattern over the same time frame. This research further examines the stability of these attitude changes after the vote has taken place and finds that attitudes and ambivalence toward the unchosen candidate exhibit a rebound pattern, the "no hard feelings effect," while attitudes toward the chosen candidate continue to become more positive after the choice has been made. Implications for communicating with voters during the 2012 presidential election campaign are considered.

"In an election, you have to highlight the differences and minimize the commonalities so that people can make a choice."
Former U.S. President Bill Clinton
The Daily Show with John Stewart, September 21, 2009

Researchers have long understood that voters in an election make their decisions as to which candidate to vote for at different times leading up to the date of the election (Chaffee and Choe 1980). This has created a challenge for those who try to communicate with voters through political advertising, as they must adapt their messages to different voters at different times. To complicate matters, over the past twenty years, voters have been observed to be making their decisions later and later in the campaign season, with an increasing number of voters making their decisions at the last minute, on or right before Election Day (Nir and Druckman 2008). Voters who make their decisions later in the campaign season are more likely to consider information that they are exposed to during the campaign when making their decisions (Chaffee and Choe 1980). Late deciders have been found to be more heavily influenced by political advertising (Bowen 1994), campaign events such as conventions and debates (Hillygus and Jackman 2003; Fournier et al. 2004), and campaign media coverage (Fournier et al. 2004), making communications with last-minute deciders even more important to political campaigns. This has led to a need to better understand what leads voters to choose at the last minute and how they make their decision as Election Day approaches.

Nir (2005) finds that voters are more likely to delay their decision when their attitudes toward the candidates are more ambivalent. Nir measures ambivalence by examining voters' ratings of both leading candidates in a presidential election and classifying voters as low in ambivalence if their attitudes are one-sided, regardless of which of the candidates they prefer, and high in ambivalence if their attitudes toward the two candidates were mixed. Voters who were more ambivalent were found to make their decisions later in the campaign season than less ambivalent voters (Nir 2005). This effect was found to be particularly strong when highly ambivalent voters were facing an environment in which they were exposed to mixed information that included similar positive or negative information about both candidates, as opposed to one-sided information that favored one candidate or the other (Nir and Druckman 2008).

Adding to the complexity of this decision is the likelihood that voters are not only ambivalent between the candidates in an election, but also hold mixed or conflicting beliefs and/or emotions toward each candidate as an individual. It is common for individuals to have a mix of positive and negative feelings towards each particular alternative in a choice, as well as mixed feelings between the alternatives (Kaplan 1972). The degree to which an individual's attitude toward a particular object is characterized by a mix of positive and negative components has been referred to as attitudinal ambivalence (Kaplan 1972; Priester and Petty 1996; Thompson, Zanna and Griffin 1995). This mix of positive and negative attitude components contributes to a sense of conflict or mixed emotions that has been termed subjective ambivalence (Kaplan 1972; Priester and Petty 1996). Voters who have a mix of positive and negative feelings toward each of the candidates in an election are likely to experience this type of emotional conflict.

Although holding ambivalent attitudes does not cause ongoing conflict in everyday life, such attitudes may create a problem for the individual when he or she has to make a choice, as when the individual must choose which candidate to vote for. The problem occurs because individuals are motivated to hold correct attitudes toward each of the candidates (Petty and Cacioppo 1986) and to make a correct choice that is consistent with their evaluations of and attitudes toward the candidates (Ajzen and Fishbein 1980; Fazio 1986). The voting task becomes difficult when an individual must select a candidate for whom he or she holds some negative evaluations or select against a candidate with some perceived positive aspects. Luce, Jia and Fischer (2003) suggest that a mix of positive and negative evaluations of a candidate could lead to an approach-avoidance conflict that would increase the individual's preference uncertainty. This feeling of uncertainty and mixed emotions has been linked to discomfort (Williams and Aaker 2002) and dissatisfaction (Olsen, Wilcox and Olsson 2005) with the choice.

Given the complex situation of a voter who may hold ambivalent attitudes toward each of the candidates, may be ambivalent between the candidates, and may be in an environment of mixed information about the candidates, how is a voter to come to a decision before Election Day? We suggest that an individual who intends to vote in an election will be motivated to resolve his or her conflicting attitudes in order to make the voting task easier, reduce his or her feelings of uncertainty, and avoid negative emotions. How the voter accomplishes this resolution in order to make a choice has not been examined in the literature.

This paper extends the research on voter decision-making by examining the way voters resolve their ambivalence to reduce their uncertainty and make a choice. We propose that voters will change their attitude structure by reducing their attitudinal and subjective ambivalence and polarizing their attitudes toward the candidates. These changes in attitude structure are expected to occur as the deadline to vote becomes imminent. Once the vote has passed, the motivation to resolve one's ambivalence and make a correct choice dissipates. In the absence of this motivational force, the voter's attitudes are expected to return to a more ambivalent state as the pressure to polarize his or her attitudes recedes, which we term the "no hard feelings effect." Individuals who do not plan to vote are not expected to be motivated to modify their attitude structure over the same time frame.

IMMINENT DEADLINES AND AMBIVALENCE

One of the unique aspects of the voting decision is that voters have a deadline by which they must make their choice of candidates, as they must vote on the day of the election. Researchers have repeatedly found that individuals who must make a decision with a deadline are influenced by how far in the future the decision will take place. Individuals have been found to make more simple evaluations of alternatives for decisions that are temporally distant, and more specific and detailed evaluations of alternatives for decisions that are temporally imminent (Wright and Weitz 1977). Individuals become less concerned with the desirability of alternatives and more concerned with their feasibility and practicality as the decision grows temporally closer (Vallacher and Wegner 1989). Individuals have also been found to more easily comprehend and process abstract information about alternatives when a decision is temporally distant and concrete information about alternatives when a decision is temporally imminent (Reber, Schwarz and Winkielman 2004; Kim, Rao and Lee 2009). Temporal construal theory suggests that this is due to temporally distant events being conceptualized in more abstract terms and processed at a higher level of abstraction, while temporally imminent events are conceptualized in more concrete terms and processed at a lower level of abstraction (Trope and Lieberman 2000; 2003). As a result, individuals are likely to focus more on a concrete, detailed evaluation of alternatives when the decision is temporally imminent than when it is temporally distant.

In addition to processing information more concretely, individuals who are facing an imminent decision are likely to be more sensitive to negative information than individuals who are facing a temporally distant decision (Loewenstein and Prelec 1991; Wright and Weitz 1977). Individuals considering a decision in the future have been shown to be able to anticipate how they will feel if their decisions yield negative or positive results and the extent to which they will regret their choice (Simonson 1992). Individuals who anticipate future outcomes have also been found to be more sensitive to potential negative outcomes or losses than to positive outcomes or gains (Kahneman and Tversky 1984). These potential negative outcomes become more salient as the decision, and therefore the risk of regret, becomes more temporally imminent (Eyal, Liberman, Trope and Walther 2004; Shelley 1994). Individuals therefore become less optimistic about being able to fulfill their goals (Gilovich, Kerr and Medvec 1993; Nisan 1972; Sanna 1999; Savitsky, Medvec, Charlton and Gilovich 1998; Shepperd, Ouellette and Fernandez 1996) and more prevention-focused (Mogliner, Aaker and Pennington 2008) as the potential for making an incorrect choice grows closer. This should increase the individual's motivation to make a correct choice and avoid the potential negative feelings associated with making a choice that is based on mixed or ambivalent attitudes (Olsen et al. 2005; Williams and Aaker 2002).

This suggests that voters who hold both positive and negative evaluations of the candidates will not experience conflict when the vote is in the distant future due to the more abstract nature of evaluation versus choice. However, as the deadline for an election becomes temporally imminent, will likely become more sensitive to conflicts or ambivalence within the specific components of their evaluations. Therefore, unlike when the choice is temporally distant, the voter is likely to be motivated to resolve his or her ambivalence as the vote

grows more imminent and his or her processing and evaluation of the alternatives becomes more concrete.

As a result, individuals who anticipate voting in the election are expected to alter the positive and negative components of their attitude structures in order to reduce their attitudinal ambivalence and polarize their attitudes toward the candidates as the deadline for the vote becomes more imminent. Such polarization will make the candidates more distinct and thus the choice easier. Voters have been found to exhibit a pattern of attitude polarization as the date of the election approaches (Meffert et al. 2006; Taber and Lodge 2006). This has been attributed to voters' tendency to pay more attention to information about their preferred candidate and to focus on positive information about their preferred candidate and negative information about their non-preferred candidate (Meffert et al. 2006). In addition, voters have been found to seek out information that confirms their preexisting beliefs, uncritically accept information that supports their beliefs, and counterargue information that is contrary to their beliefs (Taber and Lodge 2006). This leads voters to develop more positive attitudes toward their preferred candidate and more negative attitudes toward their non-preferred candidate as the election approaches, thus reducing their ambivalence. This change in their attitude structure should contribute to reducing their feelings of mixed emotions or subjective ambivalence. Individuals who do not anticipate voting, however, will not be motivated to change their attitude structure and should be unaffected by the approaching deadline. This leads to Hypothesis 1:

Hypothesis 1a: *As the election approaches, voters will reduce their attitudinal ambivalence toward the candidates more than nonvoters.*

Hypothesis 1b: *As the election approaches, voters will polarize their attitudes toward the candidates, becoming more positive about their chosen candidate and more negative about their unchosen candidate, more than nonvoters.*

Hypothesis 1c: *As the election approaches, voters will reduce their subjective ambivalence toward the candidates more than those nonvoters.*

POST-CHOICE AMBIVALENCE

If it is the pressure of the imminent deadline that motivates the voter to resolve his or her ambivalence, then this motivation will no longer apply once the election has passed. This would suggest that the voter's attitudes and ambivalence would return to their pre-vote level. However, individuals have been repeatedly found to be motivated to believe that their behaviors are consistent with their attitudes (Azjen and Fishbein 1980; Fazio 1986). In a post-choice setting, the motivation to be consistent is still present, and can lead the voter to change his or her attitudes toward the candidates to be more consistent with the alternative that was chosen (see Petty, Unnava and Strathman 1998 for a review). This would suggest that the attitude polarization that occurs as the deadline for the election approaches would remain after the election has passed.

Which of these outcomes occurs may depend on whether the relevant attitude components are positive or negative. Previous research suggests that the negative components of an attitude may increase in salience as the individual approaches a choice setting (Eyal et al. 2004; Jewell 2003; Mogliner et al. 2008). This is consistent the well-documented "positivity offset" and "negativity bias" that occur when individuals are in a choice setting (Cacioppo and Bernston 1999; Cacioppo, Gardner and Bernston 1997). The positivity offset effect suggests that when a goal is distant, individuals place more weight on positive aspects of a behavior and less weight on the negative aspects. However, as the goal becomes more imminent, the negative aspects of the behavior become more salient. The negativity bias predicts that in addition to this increase in salience as the goal approaches, individuals tend to give more weight to negative information in general than they do to positive information. This negativity bias has been found to influence voters' processing of political information during a campaign (Meffert et al. 2006).

If it is the negative components of voters' attitudes toward the candidates that are increasing in salience and being given more weight as the deadline for the election becomes more imminent, these changes are likely to be temporary increases in salience that do not persist after the election has passed. However, changes in the positive components of voters' attitudes toward the candidates are not likely to be subject to the positivity offset and negativity bias, suggesting that these changes may be more persistent than their negative counterparts. In order to polarize their attitudes to make a choice, voters need to increase the positive components of their attitudes toward the chosen candidate and the negative components of their attitudes toward the unchosen candidate. Thus, ambivalence and attitudes toward the unchosen candidate are expected to rebound after the choice has been made, returning to their pre-choice levels, while ambivalence and attitudes toward the chosen candidate should not exhibit this rebound effect. We term this the "no hard feelings" effect, as the voter is becoming less negative toward the unchosen candidate after the choice has been made. This leads to Hypotheses 2 and 3:

Hypothesis 2:   *After the election passes, voters' (a) attitudinal ambivalence toward their unchosen candidate will increase, (b) attitudes toward their unchosen candidate will become less negative, and (c) subjective ambivalence toward their unchosen candidate will increase.*

Hypothesis 3:   *After the election passes, voters' (a) attitudinal ambivalence toward their chosen candidate will continue to decrease, (b) attitudes toward their chosen candidate will continue to become more positive, and (c) subjective ambivalence toward their chosen candidate will continue to decrease.*

METHOD

These hypotheses were tested using a longitudinal natural experiment conducted during the 2004 and 2008 presidential elections. The same procedure was used for both elections. Participants completed a questionnaire about their election decision three times: the first, six weeks before the election, the second, one week before the election, and the third, one week after the election. In each questionnaire, participants' attitudes, attitudinal ambivalence, and subjective ambivalence were measured toward each of the two presidential candidates. In the first and second questionnaires, participants were then asked if they were registered to vote, if they intended to vote, and which of the candidates they intended to vote for in the upcoming election. In the third questionnaire, participants were asked if they

had voted and, if so, which of the candidates they had voted for in the recent election.

Participants were classified as voters if they participated in all three questionnaires, reported an intention to vote in the election in the pre-election questionnaires, and voted in the presidential election on Election Day. The nonvoter group was defined as individuals who participated in all three questionnaires and were eligible to vote (e.g. U.S. citizens over the age of eighteen), but did not vote in the election. Participants who voted via absentee ballot prior to Election Day were excluded because of the lack of a consistent deadline for their decision.

Each voter's chosen and unchosen candidate was coded based on his or her reported voting behavior. This analysis was only concerned with the two major party candidates (Republican and Democrat), and not with any third party candidates. The major party candidate for whom the participant voted was coded as the chosen candidate and the major party candidate for whom the participant did not vote was coded as the unchosen candidate. Measures of voting intention were used in place of actual voting behavior to code chosen and unchosen candidates for nonvoters. No participants reported voting for a candidate other than the major party candidates in either election.

Participants' attitudinal ambivalence toward each of the candidates was measured using the six-item measure developed by Thompson et al. (1995; see Appendix for items). Each item was measured on a 9-point scale. Three of the items capture the positive components of the individual's attitude, and three capture the negative components. The items were combined using the formula developed by Thompson et al. (1995), as follows:

$$\text{Ambivalence} = [(\text{Positive} + \text{Negative})/2] - |\text{Positive} - \text{Negative}|$$

This calculation is considered to be preferable to analyzing the positive and negative components of attitude separately because it captures both the magnitude (the first term) and the extremity (the second term) of the individual's positive and negative attitudinal components.

Participants' overall attitude toward each of the candidates was measured using four semantic differential items in response to the statement, "As President of the United States for the next four years, [*candidate*] would be…" with endpoints good/bad, desirable/undesirable, superior/inferior, and satisfactory/unsatisfactory. Participants' subjective ambivalence toward each of the candidates was measured using the three semantic differential items used by Priester and Petty (1996) and Thompson et al. (1995; see Appendix for items). All items were measured on a 9-point scale.

RESULTS

Sample Description

A total of two hundred ninety-one undergraduate students at a midwestern university completed all three parts of this study in exchange for course credit, one hundred forty-nine in 2004 and one hundred forty-two in 2008. All of the participants were old enough to vote in the upcoming presidential election. The participants were 58.3% female and had an average age of 21. One hundred seventy-eight (61.2%) of the participants were in their junior year of college, sixty-one (21.0%) were in their senior year, and fifty-one (17.5%) were in their sophomore year, with one participant not reporting his or her class. Two hundred fifty-five (87.6%) of the participants were Caucasian, nineteen (6.5%) were African-American, five (1.7%) were of Asian or Pacific descent, three (1.0%) were of Hispanic or

Latino descent, and eight (2.7%) had an ethnic background other than these four, with one participant not reporting his or her ethnic background.

Thirty participants (10.3%) considered themselves conservative republicans, forty-three (14.8%) were moderate republicans, forty (13.7%) were independent but leaned toward the republican party, forty-six (15.8%) considered themselves neither a republican nor a democrat, thirty-nine (13.4%) were independent but leaned toward the democratic party, forty-six (15.8%) were moderate democrats, and forty-five (15.5%) were liberal democrats with one participant not reporting his or her political affiliation.

Two hundred seventeen (74.6%) voted on Election Day and seventy-four (25.4%) did not vote in the election. This higher than average percentage of voters is likely due to the unusually high turnout of young voters to support the Democratic candidates during both the 2004 and 2008 elections. Indeed, of the two hundred seventeen participants who voted in the election, one hundred thirty-six (62.7%) voted for the Democratic candidate (John Kerry or Barack Obama) and eighty-one (37.3%) voted for the Republican candidate (George W. Bush or John McCain). Since the candidates were coded as chosen and unchosen for each individual participant, this did not affect the results.

Measure Validation

The measures were checked for reliability before any further analysis was conducted. The six-item measure of attitudinal ambivalence contains three positively worded items and three negatively worded items that are not expected to correlate with each other (Thompson et al., 1995). Therefore, reliability coefficients were calculated for the positive and negative items separately. The positive items had acceptable reliability for both the chosen candidate ($\alpha = 0.91$) and the unchosen candidate ($\alpha = 0.92$), and the negative items had slightly lower but still acceptable reliability for both the chosen candidate ($\alpha = 0.82$) and the unchosen candidate ($\alpha = 0.80$). The formula developed by Thompson et al. (1995) was used to calculate participants' attitudinal ambivalence toward each of the candidates.

The four-item attitude measure had acceptable reliability for both attitude toward the chosen candidate ($\alpha = 0.94$) and attitude toward the unchosen candidate ($\alpha = 0.97$). The three-item subjective ambivalence measure also had slightly lower but acceptable reliability for both the chosen candidate ($\alpha = 0.82$) and the unchosen candidate ($\alpha = 0.70$). The attitude and subjective ambivalence measures were averaged to create composite measures. No differences across the 2004 and 2008 elections were found on any of the ambivalence and attitude measures.

Tests of Pre-Choice Hypotheses

Hypothesis 1 was tested using a 2 (voter status: voter, nonvoter) x 2 (time) doubly multivariate repeated measures ANOVA on participants' ambivalence and attitudes toward their chosen and unchosen candidates, as recommended by Stevens (1996). The multivariate analysis revealed a significant interaction effect between voter status and time ($F (6, 275) = 2.52$, $p < .05$), and significant main effects of both time ($F (6, 275) = 5.29$, $p < .001$) and voter status ($F (6, 275) = 3.25$, $p < .005$).

Participants' attitudinal ambivalence toward their chosen candidates did not produce a significant interaction effect ($F (1, 280) = 0.01$, $p > .10$), but the main effects of both time ($F (1, 280) = 6.79$, $p = .01$) and voter status ($F (1, 280) = 6.99$, $p < .01$) were significant. Separate analyses revealed that voters' attitudinal ambivalence toward their chosen candidates decreased significantly as the deadline for the election approached ($M_1 = 4.63$, $M_2 = 4.12$, $F (1, 211) = 7.33$,

$p < .01$), while nonvoters' attitudinal ambivalence did not decrease significantly ($M_1 = 5.48$, $M_2 = 5.01$, $F (1, 69) = 2.17$, $p > .10$). Participants' attitudinal ambivalence toward their unchosen candidates did reveal a significant interaction effect ($F (1, 280) = 4.72$, $p < .05$) and a significant main effect of voter status ($F (1, 280) = 7.51$, $p < .01$). The main effect of time, however, was not significant ($F (1, 280) = 2.63$, $p > .10$). Separate analyses again revealed that voters' attitudinal ambivalence toward their unchosen candidates decreased significantly as the deadline for the election approached ($M_1 = 4.65$, $M_2 = 3.96$, $F (1, 211) = 14.27$, $p < .001$), while nonvoters' ambivalence did not decrease significantly ($M_1 = 5.17$, $M_2 = 5.27$, $F (1, 69) = 0.11$, $p > .10$), providing support for Hypothesis 1a.

Univariate tests on participants' attitudes toward their chosen candidates found a significant interaction effect between voter status and time ($F (1, 280) = 4.28$, $p < .05$) as well as significant main effects of both time ($F (1, 280) = 6.99$, $p < .01$) and deadline ($F (1, 280) = 17.36$, $p < .001$). Separate analyses revealed that voters' attitudes toward their chosen candidates became significantly more positive as the deadline for the election approached ($M_1 = 6.80$, $M_2 = 7.33$, $F (1, 211) = 42.52$, $p < .001$), while nonvoters' attitudes toward their chosen candidates did not show a significant change ($M_1 = 6.17$, $M_2 = 6.24$, $F (1, 69) = 0.05$ $p > .10$), supporting Hypothesis 1b. The interaction effect for participants' attitudes toward their unchosen candidates was not significant ($F (1, 280) = 2.14$, $p > .10$), but the analysis revealed significant main effects of both time ($F (1, 280) = 8.29$, $p < .005$) and voter status ($F (1, 280) = 9.45$, $p < .005$). Although the interaction effect did not reach conventional levels of statistical significance, separate analyses revealed that voters' attitudes toward their unchosen candidates became significantly more negative as the deadline for the election approached ($M_1 = 3.18$, $M_2 = 2.80$, $F (1, 211) = 17.30$, $p < .001$), while nonvoters' attitudes toward their unchosen candidates did not change ($M_1 = 3.74$, $M_2 = 3.61$, $F (1, 211) = 0.951$, $p > .10$), supporting Hypothesis 1b.

Finally, participants' subjective ambivalence toward their chosen candidates also did not produce a significant interaction effect ($F (1, 280) = 2.33$, $p > .10$), but the main effects of both time ($F (1, 280) = 20.43$, $p < .001$) and voter status ($F (1, 280) = 8.89$, $p < .005$) were significant. Separate analyses revealed that voters' subjective ambivalence toward their chosen candidates decreased significantly as the deadline for the election approached ($M_1 = 4.00$, $M_2 = 3.28$, $F (1, 211) = 34.63$, $p < .001$), while nonvoters' ambivalence did not decrease significantly ($M_1 = 4.50$, $M_2 = 5.01$, $F (1, 69) = 4.15$, $p > .05$). Participants' subjective ambivalence toward their unchosen candidates did exhibit a significant interaction effect ($F (1, 280) = 6.84$, $p < .01$) as well as significant main effects of both time ($F (1, 280) = 7.02$, $p < .01$) and voter status ($F (1, 280) = 4.38$, $p < .05$). Separate analyses again revealed that voters' subjective ambivalence decreased significantly as the deadline for the election approached ($M_1 = 4.35$, $M_2 = 3.65$, $F (1, 211) = 27.97$, $p < .001$), while nonvoters' ambivalence did not decrease significantly ($M_1 = 4.50$, $M_2 = 4.50$, $F (1, 69) = 0.00$, $p > .10$). Overall, these findings provide support for Hypothesis 1c. These results are summarized in Table 1.

Tests of Post-Choice Hypotheses

Hypotheses 2 and 3 were tested using a multivariate repeated measures ANOVA on 2004 and 2008 voters' attitudinal ambiva-

Table 1
Pre-Election Results: Voters and Nonvoters

	Voters' Evaluations N = 217		Nonvoters' Evaluations N = 74	
	Time 1	Time 2	Time 1	Time 2
Attitudinal Ambivalence Toward the Chosen Candidate	4.63[a]	4.12[a]	5.48	5.01
Attitudinal Ambivalence Toward the Unchosen Candidate	4.65[b]	3.96[b]	5.17	5.27
Attitude Toward the Chosen Candidate	6.80[c]	7.33[c]	6.17	6.24
Attitude Toward the Unchosen Candidate	3.18[d]	2.80[d]	3.74	3.61
Subjective Ambivalence Toward the Chosen Candidate	4.00[e]	3.28[e]	4.50	5.01
Subjective Ambivalence Toward the Unchosen Candidate	4.35[f]	3.65[f]	4.50	4.50

Means with the same superscript are significantly different from each other at $p < .05$.

lence, attitude, and subjective ambivalence toward the chosen and unchosen candidates using data from all three questionnaires. Based on the hypothesized effects, participants' attitudes and ambivalence were expected to produce a linear effect for their chosen candidates and a quadratic effect for their unchosen candidates. Due to missing data, this analysis was performed on a sample of two hundred and eleven voters from the combined data set. The multivariate analysis revealed a significant main effect of time ($F (12, 199) = 10.73, p < .001$). Univariate tests revealed significant changes over time for all six variables: Attitudinal Ambivalence Chosen ($F (2, 420) = 21.30, p < .001$), Attitudinal Ambivalence Unchosen ($F (2, 420) = 10.88, p < .001$), Attitude Chosen ($F (2, 420) = 49.63, p < .001$), Attitude Unchosen ($F (2, 420) = 9.82, p < .001$), Subjective Ambivalence Chosen ($F (2, 420) = 35.53, p < .001$), and Subjective Ambivalence Unchosen ($F (2, 420) = 17.36, p < .001$).

Voters' attitudinal ambivalence toward the unchosen candidate exhibited both a significant linear effect ($F (1, 210) = 14.08, p < .001$) and a significant quadratic effect ($F (1, 210) = 5.53, p < .05$). It appears that rather than fully rebounding, voters' attitudinal ambivalence toward the unchosen candidate leveled off after the election had passed ($M_1 = 4.65, M_2 = 3.96, M_3 = 3.90$), so Hypothesis 2a is not supported. Voters' attitudes toward their unchosen candidates, however, exhibited a significant quadratic effect, becoming more negative as the election approached and less negative after the election passed ($M_1 = 3.18, M_2 = 2.80, M_3 = 2.93, F (1, 210) = 13.64, p < .001$), supporting Hypothesis 2b and demonstrating the "no hard feelings effect." Voters' subjective ambivalence toward the unchosen candidate also exhibited both a significant linear effect ($F (1, 210) = 20.03, p < .001$) and a significant quadratic effect ($F (1, 210) = 13.76$,

$p < .001$). Subjective ambivalence, however, did show the rebound effect, paralleling the results for attitude toward the unchosen candidate ($M_1 = 4.35, M_2 = 3.65, M_3 = 3.73$) and supporting Hypothesis 2c. This suggests that attitudinal and subjective ambivalence may exhibit different patterns after the deadline for the decision has passed.

As predicted, voters' attitudinal ambivalence toward their chosen candidates exhibited a significant linear effect, steadily decreasing as the election approached and then passed ($M_1 = 4.63, M_2 = 4.12, M_3 = 3.42, F (1, 210) = 35.64, p < .001$), supporting Hypothesis 3a. Voters' attitudes toward their chosen candidates also exhibited a significant linear effect, with attitudes steadily becoming more positive ($M_1 = 6.80, M_2 = 7.33, M_3 = 7.59, F (1, 210) = 76.34, p < .001$), supporting Hypothesis 3b. Voters' subjective ambivalence toward their chosen candidates also followed the predicted pattern ($M_1 = 4.00, M_2 = 3.28, M_3 = 3.05, F (1, 210) = 56.57, p < .001$), supporting Hypothesis 3c. These results are summarized in Table 2.

DISCUSSION

The analysis of the 2004 and 2008 presidential election data found that voters did reduce their attitudinal and subjective am-

Table 2
Post-Election Results: Voters Only

	Voters' Evaluations n = 217		
	Time 1	Time 2	Time 3
Attitudinal Ambivalence Toward the Chosen Candidate	4.63[a]	4.12[a]	3.42[a]
Attitudinal Ambivalence Toward the Unchosen Candidate	4.65[b]	3.96[b]	3.90[b]
Attitude Toward the Chosen Candidate	6.80[c]	7.33[c]	7.59[c]
Attitude Toward the Unchosen Candidate	3.18[d]	2.80[d]	2.93[d]
Subjective Ambivalence Toward the Chosen Candidate	4.00[e]	3.28[e]	3.05[e]
Subjective Ambivalence Toward the Unchosen Candidate	4.35[f]	3.65[f]	3.73[f]

Means with the superscripts a, c, and e exhibited a significant linear effect at $p < .001$. Means with the superscripts d and f exhibited a significant quadratic effect at $p < .001$. Means with the superscript b exhibited a significant quadratic effect at $p < .05$.

bivalence and polarize their attitudes toward the candidates as the election approached. The significant changes observed in voters' ambivalence and attitudes as the election approached were not observed among nonvoters over the same time period. This supports our prediction that voters reduced their ambivalence and polarized their attitudes due to the imminent deadline of the election.

The analysis also provided evidence that voters' attitudes and subjective ambivalence toward their unchosen candidates rebounded in the direction of their original levels after the election had passed. Interestingly, voters' attitudinal ambivalence did not rebound, but simply leveled off after the election had passed. This may suggest that the rebound effect is more of an affective response than an actual change in beliefs or attitudinal ambivalence. Voters' attitudes toward their chosen candidates, in contrast, continued to become more positive after the election had passed, while their attitudinal and subjective ambivalence toward their chosen candidates continued to decrease. This effectively preserves the gap between the chosen and unchosen alternatives after the election passes, which enables the individual to maintain an attitude that is consistent with his or her choice.

These findings contribute to our understanding of voter decision-making by demonstrating how ambivalent voters resolve the conflict in their attitudes in order to make a choice by the deadline of Election Day, beyond simply extending their decision time. We further show how voters adjust their attitudes and ambivalence toward the candidates after the election has passed in order to maintain attitudes that are consistent with their choice.

It is interesting to note that this effect holds not only across two elections with different results in terms of the winning candidate's party affiliation and incumbency, but also regardless of whether the voter's chosen candidate won the election. This was not a case of sympathy for the losing candidate or confirmation of the winner as the correct choice. Participants' attitudes toward the candidate they had voted for continued to become more positive and less ambivalent after the election had passed whether their chosen candidate had won or lost the election. Their attitudes toward the candidate they

had not voted for became more positive and *more* ambivalent after the election had passed whether that candidate had won or lost the election. This suggests that the continued change in ambivalence and attitude acts as a confirmation of the voter's decision, and is not a response to the result of the election.

These findings suggest several recommendations for the use of advertising to provide voters with information during the 2012 campaign season. First, since ambivalent voters are delaying their decisions and resolving their ambivalence so close to the date of the election, information communicated to voters during the last few weeks before the election is clearly very important. The need for voters to polarize their attitudes further suggests that candidates would benefit from providing voters with information that will help them to distinguish between the candidates and see the positive aspects of their preferred candidate and the negative aspects of their non-preferred candidate. Previous research has found that ads with a negatively framed message can lead to greater image discrimination between the candidates and greater attitude polarization among voters (Garramone et al. 1990). While negative political advertising has been associated with voters developing more negative attitudes toward political campaigns in general, Pinkleton, Um and Austin (2002) find that when negative ads are comparative in nature, they are perceived less negatively by voters. As comparative ads would also help to highlight the differences between the candidates, this suggests that candidates would be well served by using advertising that is negatively framed but emphasizes comparisons between the candidates during the last few weeks of the campaign season.

REFERENCES

Ajzen, Icek and Martin Fishbein (1980), *Understanding Attitudes and Predicting Social Behavior*, Englewood Cliffs, NJ: Erlbaum.

Bowen, Lawrence (1994), "Time of Voting Decision and Use of Political Advertising: The Slade Gorton-Brock Adams Senatorial Campaign," *Journalism Quarterly* 71(3), 665-675.

Cacioppo, John T., Wendi L. Gardner and Gary G. Bernston (1997), "Beyond Bipolar Conceptualizations and Measures: The Case of Attitudes and Evaluative Space," *Personality and Social Psychology Review,* 1(1), 3-25.

Cacioppo, John T. and Gary G. Bernston (1999), "The Affect System: Architecture and Operating Characteristics," *Current Directions in Psychological Science,* 8 (October), 133-137.

Chaffee, Steven H. and Sun Yuel Choe (1980), "Time of Decision and Media Use During the Ford-Carter Campaign," *Public Opinion Quarterly,* 44(1), 53-69.

Eyal, Tal, Nira Liberman, Yaacov Trope, and Eva Walther (2004), "The Pros and Cons of Temporally Near and Distant Action," *Journal of Personality and Social Psychology,* 86 (June), 781-795.

Fazio, Russell H. (1986), "How do attitudes guide behavior?" in *The Handbook of Motivation and Cognition: Foundation of Social Behavior*, ed. Richard M. Sorrentino, and E. Tory Higgins. New York: Guilford Press, 204-243.

Fournier, Patrick, Richard Nadeau, André Blais, Elisabeth Gidengil and Neil Nevitte (2001), "Validation of Time of Voting Decision Recall," *Public Opinion Quarterly* 65(1), 95-107.

Garramone, Gina M., Charles K. Atkin, Bruce E. Pinkleton and Richard T. Cole (1990), "Effects of Negative Political Advertising on the Political Process," *Journal of Broadcasting & Electronic Media,* 34(3), 299-311.

Gilovich, Thomas, Margaret Kerr and Victoria Husted Medvec (1993), "Effect of Temporal Perspective on Subjective Confidence," *Journal of Personality and Social Psychology,* 64 (April), 522-560.

Hillygus, D. Sunshine and Simon Jackman (2003), "Voter Decision Making in Election 2000: Campaign Effects, Partisan Activation, and the Clinton Legacy," *American Journal of Political Science,* 47(4), 583-596.

Jewell, Robert D. (2003), "The Effects of Deadline Pressure on Attitudinal Ambivalence," *Marketing Letters,* 14(2), 83-95.

Kahneman, Daniel and Amos Tversky (1984), "Choices, Values, and Frames," *American Psychologist,* 39(4), 341-350.

Kaplan, Kalman J. (1972), "On the Ambivalence-Indifference Problem in Attitude Theory and Measurement: A Suggested Modification of the Semantic Differential Technique," *Psychological Bulletin,* 77 (May), 361-372.

Kim, Hakkyun, Ashkay R. Rao and Angela Y. Lee (2009), "It's Time to Vote: The Effect of Matching Message Orientation and Temporal Frame on Political Persuasion," *Journal of Consumer Research,* 35 (April), 877-889.

Loewenstein, George and Drazen Prelec (1991), "Negative Time Preference," *American Economic Review,* 81 (May), 347-352.

Luce, Mary Frances, Jianmin Jia and Gregory W. Fischer (2003), "How Much Do You Like It? Within-Alternative Conflict and Subjective Confidence in Consumer Judgments," *Journal of Consumer Research,* 30 (December), 464-472.

Meffert, Michael F., Sungeun Chung, Amber J. Joiner, Leah Waks and Jennifer Garst (2006), "The Effects of Negativity and Motivated Information Processing During a Political Campaign," *Journal of Communication* 56(1), 27-51.

Mogilner, Cassie, Jennifer L. Aaker and Ginger L. Pennington (2008), "Time Will Tell: The Distant Appeal of Promotion and Imminent Appeal of Prevention," *Journal of Consumer Research,* 34 (February), 670-681.

Nir, Liliach (2005), "Ambivalent Social Networks and Their Consequences for Participation," *International Journal of Public Opinion Research,* 17(4), 422-442.

Nir, Liliach and James N. Druckman (2008), "Campaign Mixed-Message Flows and Timing of Vote Decision," *International Journal of Public Opinion Research,* 20(3), 327-346.

Nisan, Mordecai (1972), "Dimension of Time in Relation to Choice Behavior and Achievement Orientation," *Journal of Personality and Social Psychology,* 21 (February), 175-182.

Olsen, Svein Ottar, James Wilcox and Ulf Olsson (2005), "Consequences of Ambivalence on Satisfaction and Loyalty," *Psychology & Marketing,* 22 (March), 247-269.

Petty, Richard E. and John T. Cacioppo (1986), *Communication and Persuasion: Central and Peripheral Routes to Attitude Change,* New York: Springer/Verlag.

Petty, Richard E., Rao H. Unnava and Alan J. Strathman (1998), "Theories of Attitude Change," in *Handbook of Consumer Behavior*, ed. Thomas S. Robertson and Harold H. Kassarjian, Upper Saddle River, NJ: Prentice-Hall, 241-280.

Pinkleton, Bruce E., Nam-Hyun Um and Erica Weintraub Austin (2002), "An Exploration of the Effects of Negative Political Advertising on Political Decision Making," *Journal of Advertising,* 31(1), 13-25.

Priester, Joseph R. and Richard E. Petty (1996), "The Gradual Threshold Model of Ambivalence: Relating the Positive and Negative Bases of Attitudes to Subjective Ambivalence," *Journal of Personality and Social Psychology,* 71 (September), 431-449.

Reber, Rolf, Norbert Schwarz and Piotr Winkielman (2004), "Processing Fluency and Aesthetic Pleasure: Is Beauty in the Perceiver's Processing Experience?" *Personality and Social Psychology Review,* 8(4), 364-382.

Sanna, Lawrence J. (1999), "Mental Simulations, Affect, and Subjective Confidence: Timing is Everything," *Psychological Science,* 10 (July), 339-345.

Savitsky, Kenneth, Victoria Husted Medvec, Ann E. Charlton and Thomas Gilovich (1998), "What, Me Worry? Arousal Misattribution and the Effect of Temporal Distance on Confidence," *Personality and Social Psychology Bulletin,* 24 (May), 529-536.

Shelley, Marjorie K. (1994), "Gain/Loss Asymmetry in Risky Intertemporal Choice," *Organizational Behavior and Human Decision Processes,* 59 (July), 124-159.

Shepperd, James A., Judith A. Ouellette and Julie K. Fernandez (1996), "Abandoning Unrealistic Optimism: Performance Estimates and the Temporal Proximity of Self-Relevant Feedback," *Journal of Personality and Social Psychology,* 70 (April), 844-855.

Simonson, Itamar (1992), "The Influence of Anticipating Regret and Responsibility on Purchase Decisions," *Journal of Consumer Research,* 19 (June), 105-118.

Stevens, James (1996), *Applied Multivariate Statistics for the Social Sciences*, Third Edition, Mahwah, NJ: Erlbaum.

Taber, Charles S. and Milton Lodge (2006), "Motivated Skepticism in the Evaluation of Political Beliefs," *American Journal of Political Science*, 50(3), 755-769.

Thompson, Megan M., Mark P. Zanna and Dale W. Griffin (1995), "Let's Not Be Indifferent About (Attitudinal) Ambivalence," in *Attitude Strength: Antecedents and Consequences*, ed. Richard E. Petty and Jon A. Krosnick, Hillsdale: Erlbaum, 361-386.

Trope, Yaacov and Nira Liberman (2000), "Temporal Construal and Time-Dependent Changes in Preferences," *Journal of Personality and Social Psychology,* 79 (December), 876-889.

Trope, Yaacov and Nira Liberman (2003), "Temporal Construal," *Psychological Review,* 110 (3), 403-421.

Vallacher, Robin R. and Daniel M. Wegner (1989), "Levels of Personal Agency: Individual Variation in Action Identification," *Journal of Personality and Social Psychology,* 57 (October), 660-671.

Williams, Patti and Jennifer L. Aaker (2002), "Can Mixed Emotions Peacefully Coexist?" *Journal of Consumer Research,* 28 (March), 636-649.

Wright, Peter and Barton Weitz (1977), "Time Horizon Effects on Product Evaluation Strategies," *Journal of Marketing Research,* 14 (November), 429-443.

APPENDIX: AMBIVALENCE MEASURES

Attitudinal Ambivalence

1. Think about your overall impression and opinion about [*candidate*]. Considering only the favorable qualities of [*candidate*] and ignoring the unfavorable characteristics, how favorable is your evaluation of [*candidate*]? (endpoints not at all favorable/very favorable)

2. Think about your feelings or emotions about [*candidate*]. Considering only your feelings of satisfaction with [*candidate*] and ignoring your feelings of dissatisfaction, how satisfied do you feel about [*candidate*]? (endpoints not at all satisfied/very satisfied)

3. Think about your thoughts or beliefs about [*candidate*]. Considering only the beneficial qualities of [*candidate*] and ignoring the harmful characteristics, how beneficial do you believe [*candidate*] would be as president? (endpoints not at all beneficial/very beneficial)

4. Think about your overall impression and opinion about [*candidate*]. Considering only the unfavorable qualities of [*candidate*] and ignoring the favorable characteristics, how unfavorable is your evaluation of [*candidate*]? (endpoints not at all unfavorable, very unfavorable)

5. Think about your feelings or emotions about [*candidate*]. Considering only your feelings of dissatisfaction with [*candidate*] and ignoring your feelings of satisfaction, how dissatisfied do you feel about [*candidate*]? (endpoints not at all dissatisfied/very dissatisfied)

6. Think about your thoughts or beliefs about [*candidate*]. Considering only the harmful qualities of [*candidate*] and ignoring the beneficial characteristics, how harmful do you believe [*candidate*] would be as president? (endpoints not at all harmful, very harmful)

Subjective Ambivalence

1. How conflicted (e.g. in conflict with each other) are your impressions and opinions regarding [candidate]? (endpoints feel no conflict at all/feel maximum conflict)

2. How indecisive (e.g. not that sure) are you about your impressions and opinions regarding [candidate]? (endpoints feel no indecision at all/feel maximum indecision)

3. How mixed (e.g. both good and bad) or one-sided (e.g. only good or bad) are your impressions and opinions regarding [candidate]? (endpoints completely one-sided/ completely mixed)

When Motherhood is too Hard To Face: Anti-Consumption in Difficult Pregnancy

Tonner Andrea, University of Strathclyde, UK

ABSTRACT

This paper presents a narrative study of pregnancy, considering anti-consumption as instrumental to liminal identity. Focussed upon pregnancies at odds with motherhood ideals it finds that avoiding consumption is central to managing women's resultant 'othered' state and therefore that anti-consumption must be considered within conceptualisations of liminal consumption.

INTRODUCTION

New motherhood has been considered to be a liminal (mid-transition) period in a woman's life (The Voice Group, 2010a and 2010b; Thomsen and Sorensen, 2006; Taylor et al, 2004; Prothero, 2002). One in which the liminar is particularly vulnerable since she must negotiate the establishment of her own 'mothering' identity and practices against the norms and expectations of 'motherhood' as an institutional form and define her "parenthood as a human construction and a social institution" Prothero (2002: 399). This negotiation of social norms and individual preference is suggested by the Voice Group (2010a) to give rise to ambivalence: "the simultaneous or sequential experience of multiple emotional states as a result or the interaction between internal factors and external objects" (Otnes et al, 1997:82). This paper considers that there is a need to understand consumption in liminality as a means of coping with this ambivalence; particularly it considers how liminars employ anti-consumption. It begins, therefore, by discussing the institution of motherhood; exploring how social dimensions of motherhood are derived; and exposing their complexity. It considers anti-consumption with a focus upon expressive anti-consumption and it relationship with consumer coping and asks how this may be understood particularly within the liminal context. The empirical findings seek to meet the research aim of exploring new mothers' ambivalence and how they employ anti-consumption as a means of consumer coping. They show the limited range of coping mechanism at women's disposal and identify the breadth of anti-consumption practices employed by women in this respect arguing for the inclusion of delay as an underexplored form of anti-consumption practice. They finally show that anti-consumption is not only a means of consumer coping but also achieves positive identity outcomes. The impact of these is then considered to both liminal and anti-consumption theory.

Motherhood ideals and realities

'Motherhood' is differentiated from 'mothering' as distinctive aspects of the same life stage phenomenon. Contemporary scholarship follow Rich's (1977) proposal that 'mothering' is the experience individuals have in their roles as mothers while 'motherhood' may be considered as the institutional expectation of how mothering may appropriately be done. The voice group (2010a) suggest that as these two aspects interact, women experience both vulnerability and ambivalence. Ambivalence is experienced when individuals are required to manage conflict between demands and expectations externally extant within 'motherhood' and their internal preferences of 'mothering'. Sevin and Ladwein (2007) discuss that this conflicted state is strongly felt by new mothers as they negotiate unfamiliar, liminal terrain.

Discourses have been classified into two types: life-project framing and culturally pervasive (Fischer et al. 2007). Considering these in the context of motherhood Banister et al (2010) argue that life-project discourse emphasizes mothers as natural and instinctive while the main culturally pervasive discourse relates to self-management with expectation that mother's become expert in responding to a multiplicity of expert (e.g. medical) discourses. Discourses of motherhood are suggested to emanate from multiple social institutions, the Voice Group (2010b) argue for four major sources: medical, legal and political, sociocultural, and media. Amplifying mothers' vulnerability these discourses are marked by both intra and inter-source conflict making 'motherhood' a difficult concept for mothers to deconstruct and perform against (Elvin-Nowak and Thomsson, 2001). Miller (2005) for example argues that medicalization of childbearing has given rise to appropriate ways of preparing to become a mother. Health professionals have the cultural authority for obstetrics and hospital births are dominant form of child birth in UK: only 2.5% of births in England and Wales are home births (Office of National Statistics, 2012). Against this context there is a strong cultural discourse of natural childbirth where mothers are expected to resist the medical interventions inherent within the system (Voice Group, 2010b) having a utopian pregnancy and birth devoid of the sullying influence of medics (Frost et al, 2006) .

Media discourses too provide evidence of the inherent complexity of motherhood definitions. These have been argued to show motherhood as biologically and socially simple; with well-paid women enjoying easily conceived children (Woodward, 1999), yet against this ideal there is recognition of the changing nature of contemporary motherhood (Goodwin & Huppatz, Porter & Kelso, 2006). Demographic trends, in western societies, show later motherhood is increasingly the norm, with a significant minority of teen mothers and of women remaining childless (Hadfield et al, 2007) therefore traditional conceptions of motherhood and family, as encompassing young nuclear families no longer fit many mothers experience (Finch, 2007). Yet within media the enduring moral discourses remains of the good mother (Gillespie, 2000) who is young, fertile and committed to full-time mothering: a powerful socio-cultural construction of motherhood against which individual women must interpret and understand their mothering choices (Voice Group, 2010a). Thus choices women make regarding pregnancy and motherhood involve negotiating many conflicting social expectations. This paper considers how as these discourses become more complex, more women find their circumstances place them at odds with the norms of motherhood.

Against this backdrop of institutional motherhood the embodied experience of becoming a mother and establishing a mothering identity is intrinsically one of vulnerability for women. This liminal state is agreed to be characterised by ambiguity and uncertainty (Voice Group, 2012b), an identity which is in flux: "liminal entities are neither here nor there; they are betwixt and between the [established] positions." (Turner, 1969: 95). Since such states of flux and uncertainty are contrary to human preference for stability and continuity, liminars are argued to engage in coping strategies to increase certainty (Duhachek and Kelting, 2009) and consumption activity has been theorised as part of this consumer coping (Sneath et al, 2009).

Consumption avoidance and anti-consumption

Kozinets et al (2010) argue that "whole area of anti-consumption is about as foggy as a November morning on the Scottish Moors." While encompassing a range of motivations and practices what binds its different forms together is a challenge the ideological primacy of consumption. They map the territory based upon the dimensions of situational specificity and motivational frame giving rise to a suggestion of four anti-consumption types: activist, utopian, transformative and expressive. This paper bound as it is the situational specificity of pregnancy and personal context of mothering consumption it is perhaps best situated as expressive anti-consumption and consideration is given to it thus.

Anti-consumption is often associated with concepts of consumer resistance which question the current capitalistic system, reduce consumption and resist oppressive forces (Penaloza and Price, 1993) but Kozinets et al (2010) suggest neither is necessarily typified by active and collective action. Penaloza and Price (1993) identify that individual consumer resistance may be appropriate where benign motives drive consumers to appropriate and subvert symbols and practices in response to structures of domination. As a form of action anti-consumption can include behaviours such as rejecting a brand, organisation or resisting and entire marketplace (Lee et al, 2009) and minimization of consumption has also been considered an appropriate form of anti-consumption. The drivers of anti-consumption are considered to be based either in unsatisfactory consumer experience or incongruence based upon identity or ideology (Lee et al, 2009) though consumer coping (Luce, 1998) and identity creation (Kleine and Kleine, 2000) may also be appropriate.

Hogg et al (2009) reflect specifically upon identity relevant anti-consumption. Utilising a symbolic consumption frame they discuss how at a subordinate level consumers can engage in consumption avoidance associated with the disposition of old identities or construction of new ones (Kleine and Kleine, 2000). Anti-consumption of this type is argued by Hogg (1998) to be preceded by aversion (dislike, disgust, revulsion) leading either to avoidance or abandonment behavioural response. Lee et al. (2009) too have established disassociation with particular brands, products or services as associated with identity avoidance.

Yet anti-consumption at a micro-level need not only be situated in symbolic consumption, it is also identified as a means of consumer coping. It may be used to alleviate emotional or cognitive impacts of stress and as a means of solving associated problems (Luce, 1998). Lazarus and Folkman (1984) identify three main coping strategies: problem-focused coping; emotion-focused coping including distancing oneself from the threat or avoiding thinking about the threat; and cultivating, seeking and using social support. Duhachek and Kelting (2009) suggest that rather than employing only a single coping mechanism that consumers typically employ a coping repertoire integrating appropriate responses to their situation and that anti-consumption can incorporate aspects of all three coping strategies. Piacentini & Banister (2008) have shown anti-consumption as a means of coping with identity at odds with a heavy drinking culture encompassing cognitive, emotive and social coping strategies and Nuttall and Tinson (2009: 1726) in avoiding high-school prom attendance have reflected particularly upon anti-consumption during liminality encompassing motivations of: non-choice, risk aversion, passive disengagement and intentional disengagement.

METHOD

In recognising the existing scholarship suggesting the ambivalence creating nature of negotiating mothering identity and motherhood ideals and the role of consumption in negotiating the uncertainty of life transitions the aim of this study is to explore further the experience of new-mother's ambivalence and how anti-consumption is utilised as a means of consumer coping. It seeks to explore two research questions: how mothers situate their mothering experiences against expectations of motherhood; and how they use (anti)con-

sumption as a means of negotiating the terrain between motherhood and mothering.

For this study a purposive homogeneous sample allowing representativeness and comparability was recruited (Miles and Huberman, 1994). Cody (2012) discuss how in exploring liminal experiences one must select an instance in time "to capture lived experience of 'betwixt and between' at its most lucid". Therefore the researcher has worked with a sample of women, pregnant or with youngest children of no more than one year. Twenty women in total participated; they are all white, middle class, range in age from 25 to 40. The voice group (2010a) note that such women are relevant to consumer research because they have the greatest opportunity to determine their consumption activity. The group were recruited using snowballing methods, similar recruitment strategies are reported in other studies of motherhood (The Voice Group 2010a, Miller, 2005). While the women had a variety of pregnancy experiences ten of the women had pregnancies which they considered at odds with good 'motherhood' as discussed within the literature and it is their accounts which form the core data for this paper. These ten women were not recruited because their pregnancies were pre-established as difficult rather their accounts are demonstrative of the prevalence of mothers' ambivalence and the difficulty in meeting motherhood ideals.

The analysis presented in this article is based upon narrative interviews with informants of between one and two hours in-home and via Skype to suit the constraints of mothering. With permission the interviews were audio-recorded and later transcribed; the identity of the participants is protected by use of pseudonyms. The data was analyzed using Thompson's (1997:441) hermeneutic framework seeking to be "open to possibilities afforded by the text" in exploring anti-consumption.

FINDINGS

The findings of this paper are structured around its research questions and therefore it seeks to explore women's understanding of the ideals of 'motherhood' and the situation of their own mothering identity against these standards and how consumption is employed as a means of negotiating the terrain between.

Mothering experiences situated against expectations of motherhood

All the women in this study discussed awareness of motherhood ideals and difficulty in meeting the expectation inherent within them. The matters embraced by motherhood discourses were diverse and while Banister et al's (2010) forms (life-project discourse emphasizing mothers as natural and instinctive and culturally pervasive discourse relating to self-management) were evident, they were not sufficient to fully explore consumers understanding and experience of motherhood ideals. A comment by one of the respondents, Elaine, has been useful in extending Banister et al (2010) and conceptualizing motherhood within this paper, she said:

> R: Well there's the just accepted things that everyone does [culturally pervasive] and then the stuff you do depending on the kind of mum you want to be [life-project] and then the everyday stuff which folk still have opinions about [minutia]

While not all the women the women had segmented their accounts thus it proved a useful means of negotiating the diverse and multi-layered nature of 'motherhood' since such differentiations were implicit across accounts. (particularly when considering life-project discourses and their dichotomous nature). Half of the women interviewed considered that their pregnancy circumstances meant that many of these ideals became not only challenging but simply unattainable. These women recounted pregnancies which were at odds with at least one and in some case multiple of the ideals of motherhood discussed above and as a result they felt excluded from the mainstream and 'other' than their peers. Othering has been defined as a process that identifies those that are thought to be different from the mainstream, and which produces positions of domination and subordination (Johnson et al, 2004).

In their accounts women drew upon a range of factors, which they considered to be, explanatory of their feelings that motherhood ideals were beyond their grasp. While not exhaustive in exploring potential othering factors this paper is reflective of the range of matters drawn upon by informants. These included physiological, psychological and social aspects. Many of the women's accounts focused upon the culturally pervasive motherhood ideal that pregnancy is joyful and planned. Ashley, whose sister Coleen has the genetic condition Down syndrome, discusses her pregnancies:

R: I don't know but I get the feeling other people do a pregnancy test and they're delighted. I can't really do that 'cause I know I've got quite a lot of worrying to do before things are all right. We've got to have the genetic counseling and tests and that does make things different.

Ashley's account contains specific issues and a relatively rare condition (Down's accounts for 1 of every 691 babies born in the United States each year (CDC, 2007) and 1.2 per 1000 births in the UK (Morris and Alberman, 2009) (in considering the prevalence of other factors considered by informants England and Wales data only will be utilized. While recognizing that whole UK and USA data will contain differences, the England and Wales data is demonstrative of the scale of the impact of these factors). This make her pregnancies a time of particular worry and isolation but other, much more common, factors made women feel equally removed from the culturally pervasive motherhood ideal of joy. Previous miscarriage, prenatal depression, being over 35 at conception and uncertain relationships were all cited as reasons why pregnancies were outside the mainstream. Marie's account contains perhaps the most widespread and benign of conditions to lead to this othered state:

R: I had a really rubbish pregnancy I was so worried all the way through. I was 36 when I got pregnant and right from the start it was just all about the risks of being an older mother. I've never felt so old.. We were getting all this advice to have tests and I was getting special monitoring …so stressful. I hear stories about other people's pregnancies and mine just wasn't like that.

Marie's condition (35+) is, of the othering factors cited by informants, perhaps the most prevalent within the population with 20% of births in England and Wales (Office for National Statistics, 2012) being among mothers 35 and older. Marie should therefore perhaps have a large cohort of peers providing support yet she characterizes her experience as isolated.

Two areas were evident as the matters of life project motherhood typologies with dichotomous schools within: medical vs. natural birthing and stay at home vs. working mothers, here too women related unresolvable ambivalence and othering. This was particularly evident where women considered circumstances had removed their individual control over their motherhood type. Lack of agency, they considered, had an isolating, othering effect. On the natural- medical motherhood antinomy Lorraine, who had experienced 3 previous miscarriages, discusses her lack of voice regarding her motherhood type:

R: I really liked the idea of being in the water during labour but it was just like no way… Most people in my hospital never even saw their consultant [senior doctor but I was consultant every visit. He was so clear "you'll be brought in early and it'll be a cesarean"… It was like there was no point in me going to the parenting classes bit 'cause when people were talking about how they'd like their birth I couldn't join in.

Miscarriage, like older motherhood, is relatively common; between 10 –25% of pregnancies end in miscarriage (NHS, 2012), yet both have clearly had wide ranging impacts upon the pregnancy experience of the Lorraine and Marie. Rather than their widespread nature opening supportive networks they are perhaps considered too commonplace to require special consideration.

Considering the other life-project antinomy of working vs. stay at home mothers, women also felt most othered from the mainstream when they lacked agency. Carrie talks about her pregnancy thus:

R: well it was really not ideal. Jack and I hadn't been together very long at all. I was still getting divorced. There was no way we could even talk about me giving up work, we weren't even living together… we had to have a big conversation about if we even had the baby. I mean I'm 33 I thought my life was past that but….no I had to plan that it might just be me and the baby..

Again Carrie's circumstances are prevalent with contemporary society, using England and Wales data, 46% of births are to parents living outside of marriage or civil partnership within which 16% are non-cohabiting (Office of National Statistics, 2012), yet she considers that as a result she is presented with a false-choice within this discourse. Staying at home would make her welfare dependent another potential good motherhood transgression, though this discourse wasn't widely reflected in informants narratives perhaps because of the middle class sample.

Motherhood ideals are not however limited to these relatively large matters, informants discussed how their tyranny is often inherent in the micro context; the minutia of daily practices which become laden with meaning about mothering status. While these ideals clustered around the topics of feeding, sleeping and soothing informants reflected that there was little that was not the subject of advice and controversy. Here too othering was evident emerging particularly as women sought communitas with other new mothers. The Voice Group's (2010a) have reflected upon the negative aspects of communitas, that camaraderie while potentially positive and supportive can also lead to the emergence of group norms among liminars and expectations at odds with women's experiences leaving them conflicted and othered. Valerie discusses her 'othered' feelings of attending a sling meet, where new mother socialize because of their use of sling carriers:

R: I don't know all those women and their chat can really get you down. You go along to these sling meets and I liked the sling when Maria was wee but they were all the 'knit your own lentils' kind and still breast feeding massive toddlers…. that's not me. I just liked using a sling so they weren't really my kind of folk.

Micro forms of othering were less impactful upon the women's mothering identities than the more encompassing motherhood discourses. Valerie's account however shows that in coping, even with this lesser form of othering, anti-consumption is employed. Having been othered in the sling meet setting she rejects this consumer culture group and distances herself from their expectations a form of anti-consumption noted by Hogg et al (2009).

The impact of the unresolvable ambivalence, evident in women's accounts of interactions with both culturally pervasive and life-project motherhood ideals, is evidenced in their resulting negative emotional states particularly of isolation and guilt. By characterizing their conflict as unresolvable women also considered themselves limited in their problem solving and coping strategies. As outlined, coping has been considered to contain three dimensions: problem-focused coping; emotion-focused coping; and cultivating, seeking and using social support (Lazarus and Folkman, 1984). Yet these women discussed an inability to access either the problem-focused or social support forms. Marie, whose account of being an older mother is considered above, discusses her inability to engage in problem focused coping:

R: Well there's so little you can do.. I mean my only risk is being over 35. I can lie I suppose but other than that what?... I mean I can't turn back time so I have to sort of accept that my pregnancy is risky.

Lack of agency inherent in many of the accounts, including Marie's, makes it difficult for informants to identify cognitive or behavioral approaches which may mitigate their ambivalence or its impact.

In considering themselves other than their peers and isolated from their social networks women also discussed an inability to engage in coping through social support. They discussed their liminal identity not as collegiate with those in a similar state but uniquely difficult. Elaine discusses the isolation of her infertility:

R: I know it's more common and people tell you about their own problems afterwards but never at the time….. you just feel like you're the only one, everyone else is just popping them out and then there's me injecting and what not.. just not the picture perfect way

Elaine's account also makes a point about the nature of social support among mothers, which all the informants reflected in their accounts. Only after pregnancy, and for these women successful births, did other mothers' experiences become readily shared. This is perhaps reflexive of other liminal rites such as hazing (Johnson, 2011) where liminars have an uncertain place within the hierarchical structure of the group and only successful completion brings membership and access to resultant support.

(Anti)-consumption which negotiates the terrain between motherhood and mothering.

In answering the first research question there is abundant evidence of ambivalence caused by irreconcilability between motherhood ideals and women's mothering identities and compelling accounts of the associated negative emotional consequences of isolation and guilt. Yet women also dismissed two identified coping strategies, cognitive and social support. This leaves informants reliant upon emotional forms of coping, which have been identified as: distancing oneself from the threat; and avoiding thinking about the threat (Lazarus and Folkman, 1984). These forms of coping have been associated with anti- consumption (Piacentini & Banister, 2008) yet anti-consumption is conceptually more dense that just a form of emotional coping. Some aspects of anti-consumption are not evident within the data of this study there are no accounts of collective action nor active rebellion. So, in considering this final research question, consideration is given to a form of anti-consumption which is: based upon individual action; which encompasses both single or-

ganization and whole market rejection; avoidance and minimizing behavior; and a combination of non-choice, passive and active disengagement, to explores women's accounts of consumer coping but also their positive construction of mothering identities.

Beginning in consumer coping all women discussed some form of anti-consumption in the uncertain early months of pregnancy; avoiding buying items for fear of 'jinxing' the pregnancy. For those women who considered themselves othered anti-consumption was more extensive. As Piacentini & Banister (2008) suggest, anti-consumption can both allow informants to avoiding thinking about the ideal which is unattainable and aid them in resisting the expectations of the ideal. In the first of these forms of coping informant showed clear cognitive and behavioral congruence; avoiding thinking about motherhood ideals and engaging in consumption avoidance behavior contemporaneously. Emily's account, while relatively extreme demonstrates this congruence. Emily identified herself as suffering from pre-natal depression which is estimated to affect up to 10% of pregnant women (Bennett et al, 2004) and says:

R: Well I wasn't in the best way at all… I couldn't think about buying anything.. seriously I had like my partner saying don't we need things and I was yeah yeah we will… We had nothing.. I was waiting to be let out of hospital while Chris went to and bought a car seat so we could take Kyla home (laughs).

This account of anti-consumption, which avoids the entire pregnancy marketplace, is routed within the psychologically othered nature of Emily's pregnancy. Unable to feel the socially pervasive motherhood ideal of joy Emily withdrew from all mothering domains including its associated consumer culture, this is akin to the passive disengagement Nuttall and Tinson (2011) found in their study with teens.

Implicit in Emily's account and evident in many women's stories was delay. This is form of anti-consumption not particularly evident in extant literature but relevant in liminal accounts because of the transient nature of liminal identity. Elaine's account of returning to work and her non-choice and lack of agency in this decision are considered above and here she considers her anti-consumption, in the form of delay, in this regard:

R: I think I said… I was always going to go back to work, no question but I left it really late to get a nursery. People kept saying you need to do these things really early and, I suppose, I thought I was.. I started phoning when she was 6 months and some places were, like, no chance we've got places for this time next year… so I had to keep looking

Elaine regains some agency through her anti-consumption while engaging in resistance of the working mother ideal she feel bound to. This form of coping is not without impact however and Elaine's account shows how in delaying consumption, so intrinsically linked to her inevitable identity, she limited her resultant market choices.

For most women these extremes of avoidance were neither reasonable nor desirable. Many discussed minimization of consumer culture interactions. Lorraine, whose account of miscarriage is considered above, discusses how ambivalence to the culturally pervasive motherhood ideals of maternal joy made her resistant to consumerist approaches to pregnancy and her disengagement from consumer culture:

R: I just thought about basics, so much can go wrong and I didn't want anything jinxing this pregnancy….. so we used this shop where you can buy your things but they don't deliver them till your baby's born…. so god forbid…. You know you've not got all this stuff. Anyway I didn't want it, I just wanted this baby… here.

Lorraine employs the delay strategy and uses the structure of the marketplace to achieve this without the consequent marketplace limitation encountered by Elaine. Lorraine's account goes further however, beyond delay she also engages in market rejection. She questions the need for the pervasive consumer items of maternity and her othered nature leads her to reject some of the structures of consumerist domination (Penaloza and Price, 1993).

Women did not however only engage in whole market anti-consumption for some specific brands, organizations and consumer culture resources were singled out for rejection. This rejection was both as a result of their own brand experiences, as in Carrie's account of the NCT and Valerie's rejection of sling meets considered above, and because of the symbolic associations which women considered them to have. Lisa's experience in selecting and obstetrician has been considered earlier and another US informants Christine discussed her active rejection of an obstetrician based upon reputation:

R: my gynecologist had a list of local obstetricians she had worked with before, she didn't do both so I had to look around… so I started asking friends and researching on their websites and things.. I'd had a difficult birth with my first child and I wasn't doing all the hours of breathing again and there was one obstetrician that everyone said was really reluctant to intervene…so he was quickly off the list.

Christine's experience of having a previous child and her belonging in mother networks equipped her more than other informants to engage in rejection. Others such as Lisa found this process much more liminality inducing, as the voice group (2010b) suggest, engaging with unfamiliar consumer culture (selecting an obstetrician in this case) can be a source of considerable consumer vulnerability.

Finally many of the women discussed lack of agency in various forms, Elaine, Lorraine, Carrie and Marie's agency stories are within this paper, but for some of these women anti-consumption acted as a form of regaining control of their mothering identity. Marie, whose account of being an older mother (36) is contained above, discussed how through anti-consumption she created a positive dimension to her story:

R: I can't change my age but I can beat the stats… I've seen some pretty unhealthy 28 year olds so through my pregnancy I was just really as careful as I could be. I didn't drink at all (alcohol) and I cut out all the bad food, no junk – really none a really balanced diet, no hair colouring nothing which could cause a problem.

Marie's anti-consumption while minimizing risk, an established form of anti-consumption in its own right (Nuttall and Tinson, 2011), was also a form of positive identity creation through her consumer culture sacrifices. She was engaged in care-work of the type other disciplines have long associated with motherhood (DeVault, 1991).

THEORETICAL IMPLICATIONS

This paper adds to the small but dynamic body of work considering the potential 'dark' (Turner, 1969) side of maternity and motherhood. It makes specific contributions to scholarship upon consumer coping and anti-consumption applying these specifically to liminal transition. First it extends understanding the nature, matter and sources of motherhood discourses as proposed by Banister et al (2010) by considering emic interpretation of these typically etic forms. Specifically it considers minutia as an impactful motherhood discourse the tyranny of this discourse is in the seemingly infinite scope of its matter.

It agrees with the Voice Group (2010b) that motherhood is a time of particularly vulnerability for women. It considers too that consumer ambivalence is likely to become increasingly prevalent among contemporary mothers and supplements the conditions the Voice Group (2010a) suggest for this state. Perhaps women with rare complicating factors such as family genetic conditions have always been prone to isolation but as motherhood discourse fail to adapt to demographic and social changes in parenthood increasing numbers of ambivalent women emerge, driven by evermore commonplace transgression such as older maternity. The lack of agency women identified in determining their mothering is little discussed in extant literature and provides direction for further research since it impacts both progress through liminality and access to established cognitive and social coping mechanisms.

This paper develops understanding of consumption during transitions particularly within the 'dark' (Turner, 1969) matters of liminal identity. It shows that anti-consumption becomes central as women, through their lack of agency, are denied the traditional repertoire of coping strategies (Luce, 1998). Emotional coping, through anti-consumption which avoids consideration of the whole marketplace and which is resistant to consumerist ideals, is confirmed within liminars (Lazarus and Folkman, 1984). The paper also demonstrates the fuller scope of anti-consumption as means of coping, with evidence of rejection and minimisation alongside the underexplored anti-consumption form of delay which is particularly relevant in time-bound identities associated within transition. It considers that anti-consumption can be theorised beyond coping and symbolic rejection and demonstrates it to be positively identity creating. Sacrifice within consumption can act as a form of mothering identity; building agency and engaging in care-work (DeVault, 1991).

Finally by bringing distinct strands of scholarship together this paper identifies underexplore aspects of each. It proposes delay as a form of anti-consumption particularly relevant to transitions and demonstrates that the liminal experience may be impacted by consumer avoidance as much as consumer engagement.

REFERENCES

Banister, Emma .N, Margaret Hogg,, Dixon, M. (2010), " Becoming a mother: negotiating discourses within the life framing identity project of motherhood", *Advances in Consumer Research* 37

Bennett, Heather A., Adrienne Einarson, Anna Taddio, Gideon Koren, and Thomas R. Einarson. (2004). Prevalence of Depression During Pregnancy: Systematic Review. *Obstetrics & Gynecology, 103*(4), 698-709.

CDC (2007) *Birth Defects Research Part A: Clinical and Molecular Teratology*, 79(2), 66-93

Cody Kevina (2012) 'No Longer, but not yet' Tweens and the mediating of threshold selves through liminal consumption. *Journal of Consumer Culture* 12(1): 41-65

De Vault, Marjorie .L. (1991), *Feeding the Family Chicago*: Chicago University Press

Duhachek, Adam and Katie Kelting (2009) Coping repertoire: Integrating a new conceptualization of coping with transactional theory, *Journal of Consumer Psychology* 19, 473–485

Elvin Nowak, Ylva. and Helene Thomsson (2001) Motherhood as idea and practice: a discursive understanding of employed mothers in Sweden *Gender and Society* 15(3),407-428

Finch, Janet (2007) Displaying Families, *Sociology,* 41(1), 65-81

Fischer, Eileen, Cele Otnes and Linda Tuncay (2007) "Pursuing Parenthood: Integrating Cultural and Cognitive Perspectives on Persistent Goal Striving" Journal of Consumer Research 34 (Dec) 425-440

Frost, Julia, Catherine Pope, Rachel Liebling, and Deirdre Murphy (2006). Utopian Theory and the Discourse of Natural Birth, *Social Theory & Health*, 4(4), 299-318

Gillespie, Rosemary (2000) When no means no: disbelief, disregard and deviance as discourse of voluntary childlessness *Women's studies International Forum* 23 (2), 223-234

Goodwin, Susan and Kate Huppatz (2010) *The Good Mother: Contemporary Motherhoods in Australia* Sydney: Sydney University Press

Hadfield, Lucy, Naomi Rudoe and Gillian Sanderson-Mann (2007) Motherhood, choice and the British media: a time to reflect. *Gender and Education,* 19 (2), 255-263

Hogg, Margaret.K. (1998), "Anti-constellations: exploring the impact of negation on consumption", *Journal of Marketing Management*, 14 (1), 133-58.

Hogg, Margaret K., Emma N Banister, and Christopher A Stephenson (2009). Mapping symbolic (anti-) consumption. *Journal of Business Research,* 62 (2), 148-159.

Johnson, Joy L., Joan L. Bottorff, Annette J. Browne, Sukhdev Grewal, B. Ann Hilton, and Heather Clarke (2004). Othering and Being Othered in the Context of Health Care Services. *Health Communication*, 16(2), 255-271

Kleine, Robert.E and Susan S Kleine (2000), Consumption and self-schema changes throughout the identity project life cycle, *Advances in Consumer Research* 27, 279-285.

Kozinets, Robert. V., Jay M Handelman and Michael SW Lee (2010). Don't read this; or, who cares what the hell anti-consumption is, anyways? *Consumption Markets & Culture, 13*(3), 225-233

Lazarus, Richard.S. and Susan Folkman (1984) *Stress, Appraisal and Coping.* New York: Springer Publishing Company;

Lee, Michael S. W., Judith Motion and Denise Conroy (2009). Anti-consumption and brand avoidance. *Journal of Business Research, 62*(2), 169-180

Luce, Mary F. (1998). Choosing to Avoid: Coping with Negatively Emotion-Laden Consumer Decisions. *Journal of Consumer Research, 24*(4), 409-433.

Miles Matthew and A Michael Huberman (1994) *Qualitative data analysis: an expand*ed *sourcebook* Thousand Oaks: Sage

Miller Daniel (2004) How Infants Grow Mothers in North London In Taylor JS, Layne LL and Wozniak DF (Eds) *Consuming Motherhood* New Brunswick: Rutgers University Press: 211-248

Miller Tina (2005) *Making Sense of Motherhood: A Narrative Approach* Cambridge: Cambridge University Press

Morris, Joan K, and Eva Alberman (2009). Trends in Down's syndrome live births and antenatal diagnoses in England and Wales from 1989 to 2008: analysis of data from the National Down Syndrome Cytogenetic Register. *British Medical Journal, 339*

NHS (2012) Miscarriage http://www.nhs.uk/Conditions/ Miscarriage/Pages [accessed 1.7.2012]

Nuttall,Peter and Julie Tinson (2011) "Resistance to ritual practice: exploring perceptions of others", *European Journal of Marketing*, 45 (11/12), 1725 - 1735

Office for National Statistics (2012) Live births, stillbirths and infant deaths: babies born in 2010 in England and Wales.

Otnes, Cele, Tina M Lowrey, and L. J Shrum (1997) Toward an Understanding of Consumer Ambivalence. *Journal of Consumer Research* 24, 80-93.

Penaloza Lisa and Linda L Price (1993) Consumer resistance: a conceptual overview. Advances in Consumer Research 20, 123–8.

Piacentinini, Maria.G. and Emma N Banister (2009), "Managing anti-consumption in an excessive drinking culture", Journal of Business Research, 62 (2), 279-88.

Porter, Marie and Julie Kelso (2006) *Theorising and representing maternal realities* Newcastle: Cambridge Scholars Publishing

Prothero Andrea (2002) Consuming Motherhood: An Introspective Journey on Consuming to be a Good Mother *Proceedings of the 6th Conference of gender Marketing and Consumer Behaviour* Dublin, June: 211-225

Rich Adrienne (1977) *Of Woman Born* London: Virago

Sevin Elodie and Richard Ladwein R (2007) To start being… The anticipation of a social role through consumption in life transition: the case of the first-time pregnancy. *Associaltion of Consumer Research Conference* Memphis.

Taylor Janelle S, Linda Layne and Danielle Wozniak (2004) *Consuming Motherhood* New Brunswick: Rutgers University Press: 211-248

The VOICE Group (2010a) Motherhood, Marketization and Consumer Vulnerability, *Journal of Macromarketing* 30(4) 384-397

The VOICE Group, (2010b) Buying into Motherhood? Problematic consumption and ambivalence in transitional phases*, Consumption Markets and Culture*, 13 (4), 373-397

Thompson, Craig. J (1997), Interpreting consumers: A hermeneutical framework for deriving marketing insights from the texts of consumers' consumption stories. *Journal of Marketing Research*, 34 (4) 438-455

Thomsen, Thyra. U. and Elin B Sorensen (2006) The First Four-wheeled Status Symbol: Pram Consumption as a Vehicle for the Construction of Motherhood Identity*, Journal of Marketing Management*, 22, 907-927

Turner, Victor.W. (1969) *The Ritual Process: Structure and Anti-Structure.* Ithica: Cornell University Press

Woodward, Kathryn. (1999) *Identity and Difference* Milton Keynes: Open University Press

Revisiting Aaker's (1997) Brand Personality Dimensions: Validation and Expansion

Renu Emile, Auckland University of Technology, New Zealand
Mike Lee, University of Auckland, New Zealand

ABSTRACT

Using qualitative data from 230 respondent descriptions of four consumers' auto-photographical product selections, this paper examines whether Aaker's model of brand personality should be expanded; and if the concept of brand personality is also transferable to products not clearly identified or presented to respondents as recognisable brands.

INTRODUCTION

Brand personality remains an important area of concern for marketing scholars and practitioners alike because of the impact on product evaluation and consumer choice (see, for e.g., Aaker, 1997; Batra, Lehman & Singh, 1993; Maehle, Ones & Supphellen, 2011; van Rekom, Jacobs & Verlegh, 2006). Though a number of studies share consensus upon Aaker's widely recognised brand personality model, scholars offer various perspectives on brand personality. Some studies attempt to define or refine and develop measures of brand personality (see, for e.g., Austin, Siguaw & Mattila, 2003; Azoulay & Kapferer, 2003; Geuens, Weijters & Wulf, 2009; Sung & Tinkham, 2005) or test the predictive role of brand personality in consumer behaviour (Chu & Sung, 2011; Freling & Forbes, 2005; Govers & Schoormans, 2005). Austin, Siguaw and Mattila (2003), for example, examine the potential boundary conditions to ascertain the generalisability of Aaker's (1997) framework. Freling and Forbes (2005) study the motivations and consequences characterising brand personality; consumers are likely to perceive a product with a strong, positive brand personality as more familiar and less risky compared to products with no distinct brand personality, or a negative brand personality. A few identify sources and specific product or brand characteristics that influence perceptions of brand personality (Maehle & Supphellen, 2008; Maehle, Otnes & Supphellen, 2011).

What is noticeable, however, is the relative lack of empirical investigation on consumers' perceptions of brand personality. Such investigation is important to gain an understanding of the different personality dimensions consumers perceive as typical of products. Aaker (1997, p. 347) defines brand personality as "the set of human characteristics associated with a brand". Aaker's definition takes anchor in McCracken's (1989) proposition that personality traits associated with product or brand users are transferred to the product or brand itself, and that consumers' choices of products or brands symbolise or communicate the same characteristics to others. Brands, thus, carry symbolic meaning (Arnould & Thompson, 2005; Belk, 1988; O'Cass & McEwen, 2004; Souiden & M'saad, 2011; Wang & Wallendorf, 2006).

Aaker's brand personality model takes root in the "Big Five" framework of human personality, namely extraversion or surgency (talkative, assertive, energetic, enthusiastic), agreeableness (good-natured, cooperative, trustful), conscientiousness (orderly, responsible, dependable, control, constraint), emotional stability versus neuroticism (calm, negative affectivity, or nervousness), and openness or intellect (intellectual, imaginative, independent minded) (Goldberg, 1992, 1993; John & Srivastava, 1999). Aaker's model encapsulates human characteristics in terms of five broad brand personality dimensions: sincerity, excitement, competence, sophistication, and ruggedness. While three dimensions - sincerity, excitement and competence relate with agreeableness, extroversion, and conscientiousness in the

human personality framework; Aaker also introduces two additional dimensions - sophistication and ruggedness.

Personality traits associated with sincerity include down-to-earth, honest, wholesome, cheerful, genuine, domestic, warmth, acceptance; excitement is associated with daring, spirited, imaginative, up-to-date, sociability, energy and activity; competence with reliable, intelligent, responsible, dependable, and efficient; sophistication with upper class, charm; and ruggedness with outdoorsy, tough, strength (Aaker, 1997). Although Aaker (1997) recognizes demographics such as gender, age and class as relevant in personality constructs of scholars such as Levy (1959), she does not include these aspects in her own model as do some others (e.g., Grohmann, 2009) via explicit recognition of personality dimensions such as masculinity and femininity.

Taking Aaker's definition of brand personality model as a starting point, this paper examines the extent to which consumers' perceptions of product or brand personality accord with those identified by Aaker (1997). The study directed young adult consumers between the ages of 18 to 21 to take photographs of products or brands that communicated aspects of their selves to their peer groups. Four sets of photograph collages belonging to four participants were presented to a sample of 230 respondents (observers) who were instructed to infer characteristics associated with products/brands from the photograph collages they saw.

Specifically, this paper addresses two key questions - first, whether and to what extent respondents' inferences validate Aaker's model in terms of personality dimensions; and second, whether the concept of brand personality is also transferable to products not clearly identified or presented to respondents as recognisable brands.

METHOD

The study focuses on young adult consumers between the ages of 18 and 21 as they make a transition from adolescence to full-fledged adulthood, a period in which they are highly cognisant of the symbolic value of the products they consume and make active investments to construct or communicate their selves (e.g., Erikson, 1968, 1975; Galican, 2004; Johnson, Berg, & Sirotzki, 2007; Moschis & Churchill, 1978; Piacentini & Mailer, 2004; Stokes & Wyn, 2007). The study employed auto-photography (Noland, 2006; Ziller, 1988, 1990) and directed 28 young adults to photograph products that they considered said something about their self to their peers. Photograph sets belonging to four participants (Kate, John, Abby, and Peter, refer to Figure 1-4 in Appendix) were selected on the basis of gender, range of photographs, and the ability of participants to speak of their self-related characteristics in relation to selected products in sufficient depth. Data was collected via an online survey. Respondents were invited to view the four sets of photographs and then directed to write a paragraph to describe the characteristics of the person to whom the products or brands belonged. All respondents were residents of Auckland, New Zealand and between 18 to 21 years of age. A total of 230 receivers completed the survey. The study undertook a content analysis (Kassarjian, 1977; Kolbe & Burnett, 1991; Krippendorff, 2004; Sillars, 1986) of the entire set of receiver descriptions of the four profiles. The content analysis procedure involved identifying thought units (words or expressions) that communicated who or what the sender was like, or what the word or phrase said about the sender. Extracted words and phrases were studied to iden-

Advances in Consumer Research
Volume 40, ©2012

tify cluster themes. That is, those words or phrases that expressed a similar focus in thought or meaning were grouped together. The researcher conducted an initial content analysis of five sample paragraph descriptions for each sender, and checked on the same with experienced marketing academics and practitioners. Once there was consensus on the process, she proceeded with the remaining data set of observer descriptions for each sender.

FINDINGS AND DISCUSSION

This section provides an overview of photograph collages, where the results of the content analysis are discussed in terms of the key characteristics attributed to each sender by receivers. These are then compared across the four participants and conclusions drawn.

An overview of respondent descriptions of participants shows that respondents describe sender characteristics from the product portfolios they view, in two key ways - in a holistic story-like manner, or by relating characteristics attributed to senders with specific products. In holistic story-like descriptions, the focus tends to be on the conglomerate of products in each sender's portfolio rather than

on any single product or brand. This is evident in representative quotes below (See, for example, Table 1, Quotes 1, 3 and 5).

On the other hand, when receivers relate specific products to senders, they tend to refer to specific self-related characteristics the products symbolise. (See, for example, Table 1, quotes 2, 4 and 6). In quote 2, for instance, the *scuba diving equipment* and *fishing gear* communicate that the owner is someone who is male, very fit and adventurous. The *alcohol* suggests that John likes to have a good time socialising. The design of the *shoes* in quote 4 communicates that Kate is fashion-conscious; the *fruit* clearly suggests health-consciousness, and this in turn is linked to her body figure. The *barbeque table* communicates that she is sociable, and possibly has a good amount of disposable income. The colour pink and products such as the *Yves Saint Laurent (YSL) Baby Doll perfume* and the *Sony Vaio* in quote 6 are associated with someone who is 18-25. The *Get Shaky Flyer* and *alcohol* (quote 6) communicate that the person is social and loves partying.

In both cases, in story-like descriptions and in the linkages of sender characteristics with specific products, respondents lend cre-

Table 1: Representative Quotes

(Quote 1 - Description of Kate) Mid 20s female, living in Auckland. Working in a good job, well off, probably from a wealthy family. Confident, very social, a lot of entertaining, eats healthy and most likely goes to the gym/works out.

(Quote 2 - Description of John) This person is male, very fit and very adventurous by scuba diving equipment, fishing gear... likes to have a good time socialising by the alcohol and look good and be clean while out referencing shampoo and deodorant...

(Quote 3 - Description of Abby) Very social, bubbly female, in her early 20s. Very social, likes to go out clubbing and drinking with friends. Girly and takes pride in appearance. Works out and tries to take care of her health/fitness. Organised and technology savvy.

(Quote 4 - Description of Kate) The choice of shoes being a very 'in' design suggests to me she's quite up to date in her fashion. The fruit tells me that she's quite healthy and likes to look after her body which can be supported by the size of clothing displayed. The barbeque table could mean she's social and likes to entertain people. Or it could be linked to her amount of disposable income which to afford a luxury item like that at that age would mean she's well paid.

(Quote 5 - Description of Peter) Brought up in Onehunga this young male has had an average upbringing. He is loyal to his family and background. He is possibly Maori or Pacific Islander. His interests are Rugby, working out, reggae music and cars.

(Quote 6 - Description of Abby) This person looks that they it's obviously a Woman who would be in the 18- 25 age range, this suggests that it is a woman because of the colour of the products such as Perfume Yves Saint Laurent (YSL) Baby Doll Pink and the Laptop (Sony Vaio) is pink...The Flyers such as Get Shaky dance party suggest she is young and is a party goer just loves partying and is suggested by the alcohol.

dence to the notion that products symbolise self-related characteristics and these in turn are transferred to product owners or senders.

The process of content analysis of receiver descriptions resulted in the identification of key characteristics as in Table 2.

A comparison across identified characteristics for all four senders (see Table 2) shows that receivers attribute senders with two characteristics (***gender*** and ***age or life stage***) relatively consistently, and with ***income, class, status and spending*** and ***role and profession*** to a lesser extent. For example, 93 phrases specifically identify Kate in terms of ***gender*** - as a *female, girl* or *woman;* 114 refer to John as a *male, guy* or a *boy;* 133 to Abby as a *female, woman, lady* or *girl.* Similarly, 82 expressions comment on the ***age and life stage*** of Kate. A majority of the receivers comment on the sender as *young,* with age estimates ranging from late teens, through the twenties. A total number of 139 words or phrases refer to John as someone in his *late teens or early 20s, in their early 20s,* and *early 20s to early 30s.* 126 expressions describe Abby as being *young; quite young* and *someone in her teenage years or early twenties;* similarly 89 refer to Peter as someone who is *young,* or a *teenager.* Most refer to the age group of late teens to early or late twenties. A total of

145 phrases relate to ***income, class, status and spending*** for Kate. The vast majority describe Kate as a person who is *upper middle class, relatively affluent, wealthy, has high income, high disposable income,* or *substantial income,* of *mid to high socio economic status,* and someone who *can afford to host parties, can afford things this expensive, doesn't mind spending lots of money on accessories* and has *earned a reasonable income in order to purchase some of the items.* However, in the case of John, only 21 expressions describe John as *would be middle class; has an average income; does not have enough money; not enough money to buy branded clothing.* Similarly, a small number of descriptions (19) refer to ***income, class, status and spending related*** characteristics for Abby. These include has *an average income; is a middle income person; not very rich; aren't very wealthy* and *not really affluent* dominate. 20 expressions such as *must be wealthy* to *aren't well to do; not too wealthy; belong to a middle to lower income family* and *mid-high income* are ***income, class, status and spending related*** in the case of Peter.

Some clusters refer to ***role and profession related*** aspects of senders. For example, 70 expressions refer to Abby's ***role and profession*** as *probably a university student; studies health care* and

Table 2: Key Characteristics Attributed to Each Sender and the Number of Times Identified by Receivers

Kate		John		Abby		Peter	
Income, class, status and spending related	145	Enjoys certain sports	147	Sociable	160	Gender	113
Gender	93	Age or life stage	139	Gender	133	Miscellaneous	104
Fashion related	91	Gender	114	Age or life stage	126	Guitar, music and art related interests	103
Age or life stage	82	Sociable	83	Fashion related	81	Ethnicity and culture related	95
Miscellaneous	75	Values sports and fitness	82	Miscellaneous	80	Age or life stage	89
Brand or label conscious	57	Ethnicity and culture	68	Health conscious	75	Likes sports, works out and goes to the gym	88
Sociable	50	Miscellaneous	65	Role and profession related	70	Role and profession related	50
Health conscious	49	Role and profession related	58	Busy and organized	66	Tough yet soft	39
Cares about appearance	41	Technology related	56	Sports and exercise related	38	Alcohol related	38
Eats healthy	31	Alcohol related	46	Cares about appearance	27	Rugby player	34
Role and profession related	31	Hobbies and personal interests	43	Music and dance as recreation	26	Car related interests	34
Image conscious	23	Active	41	Alcohol related	24	Brand or label conscious	27
Enjoys the outdoors	16	Fashion related	38	Technology friendly	22	Sociable	25
Outgoing	12	Cares about Appearance	32	Gender stereotypes	21	Patriotic and proud of their country	25
Outdoors lifestyle	11	Health related problems and allergies	28	Income, class, status and spending related	19	Gender and cultural stereotypes	25
Residence or location	11	Income, class, status and spending related	21	Eating healthy	16	Income, class, status and spending related	20
Sports and exercise	10	Outgoing	20	Image conscious	11	Health conscious	20
Ethnicity and culture related	9	Easy going, and laid back	20	Politically conscious	10	Proud of their school	17
Enjoys outdoor meals	8	Brand or label conscious	19	Outgoing	10	Cares about Appearance	14
Materialistic	8	Loves the outdoors	19	Brand or label conscious	9	Fashion related	13
Loves the summer and the beach	6	Hygienic	18	Takes care of herself	7	Outgoing	7
Gender stereotypes	5	Gender or ethnicity related stereotypes	14			Image conscious	8
		Music and dancing as recreation	14			Residence or location related	8
		Humour and fun	13				

studying and following politics. A reasonable consensus (50 phrases) emerges on Peter's status as a student. Most describe Peter as a *secondary school student, college student, has just finished his college* or as *university student*.

Respondents also attribute **ethnicity and culture** related aspects to participants. For example, three expressions identify Kate as *Asian*, one as *someone from the Chinese/East Asian origin*, one as European, another as *Western in culture*, while still another said *should/would be a White person*. Two are open in terms of *any eth-*

nicity and *any New Zealand home owner*. 68 words/phrases refer to John's **ethnicity and culture** as someone of *Maori or Pacific Island heritage* (30), as *simply Kiwi or New Zealand guy* (16), or in terms of *cultural affiliations* (22). Expressions include *Maori ethnicity; possibly Maori; Maori heritage; Maori/Kiwi; New Zealander; most likely to be a Kiwi; takes pride in their culture and country of origin; likes cultural symbols; love for New Zealand culture* and *identifies with his culture well*. Similarly, 95 expressions refer to Peter as someone of New Zealand or Kiwi ethnicity (30), of Maori or Pacific

Island ethnicity (29), or as someone who is proud of their country, culture and ethnicity (36).

Clearly, there is general consensus amongst respondents on **gender, age and life stage, income, class, status and spending** and **role** related characteristics. In the case of **ethnicity and culture**, however, there is a range of comments. This means products/brands cannot be clearly linked to **ethnicity and culture** related aspects. A noticeable aspect is the differential attribution of meaning across participants. For example, receivers attribute **income, class, status and spending** more frequently to Kate than to the other three senders. Most descriptors in the **income, class, status and spending** category for Kate refer to high income, upper middle or upper class, and also high status; this suggests that Kate's choice of products communicates these aspects more strongly in comparison to others.

In sum, this study provides support and substantiates the inclusion of demographic related characteristics such as gender, age or life stage, income, class, status and spending, and role and profession as part of brand personality. Even though Aaker does not include the same in her model, this study provides evidence that respondents perceive products and brands in terms of such characteristics, in some cases, more saliently than classic 'personality' traits. Thus, from a consumer perspective, excluding these characteristics from the brand personality model may limit the validity of the concept.

Receivers also attribute some other self-related characteristics in relation to product choices to all four senders. These include the recognition of aspects relating to **sociability** and **outgoing nature, health consciousness, valuing sports and exercise, fashion and image conscious.** 83 expressions, for example, suggest the *sociable* nature of John. These include *enjoys socialising; enjoys going out and partying; social* and *enjoys hanging out with mates.* 20 refer to John as *outgoing,* for example, *very outgoing* and *outgoing person.* Several phrases describe Kate as a person who is **health conscious** (49), is someone who **eats healthy** (31), and also **pursues sport and exercise** (10). The range of comments include *healthy; healthy habits; healthy lifestyle; health conscious; most likely goes to the gym/works out; eats healthily;* and *quite petite who likes multi grain bread and enjoys tea rather than coffee.* 156 phrases refer to Peter as a **rugby player** (34), **likes sports, works out and goes to the gym** (88), **health conscious** (20) and **cares about appearance** (14). These include - *keeps fit to maintain his figure and to keep fit for rugby training; loves his rugby; probably very into rugby; goes to gym quite often; dedicated sports person; enjoys working out; cares about his health and body; takes care of his looks; health conscious person; tough and strong; fit and athletic* and *playing sports and the gym.*

Respondents also identify *fashion* and *image* related aspects in product portfolios. For example, 91 receivers describe Kate in terms of **fashion-related** expressions such as *fashion oriented; fashion conscious; all her clothes and accessories are up to date;* and *very into fashion.* Related to the *'fashion'* cluster is **image-conscious, cares about appearance** and **brand conscious.**

Clearly, there is general consensus amongst respondents on several characteristics such as sociability and outgoing nature, health conscious, values sports and exercise, fashion, and image conscious. This means products are communicating similar meanings in terms of personality characteristics to the respondents in this study. These aspects in turn relate with Aaker's dimensions of excitement, sophistication and ruggedness. For example, sociability and outgoing aspects relate with excitement; fashion and image related aspects with sophistication, and sports and exercise related aspects with ruggedness.

A significant category is that of **miscellaneous.** Most **miscellaneous** characteristics tend to be personal, inward oriented, and not strongly socially observable. For example, participants attribute a range of **miscellaneous** characteristics (75 terms) such as - *most likely a politically positioned citizen; loves cleanliness and tidiness; very cute and cool;* and *modern* to Kate. A relatively large number of characteristics (80) such as *laid back; balances out her youth party life with responsible things such as health care book, running and Labour Party meetings; not a get out in the mud and gumboots girl* and *quite innocent* are included under **miscellaneous** for Abby. A range of 104 characteristics appear on the **miscellaneous** list for Peter. These include *may have a slightly nerdy side; creative; down to earth; likes to be part of a team; not materialistic; has no fears but big dream; loyal to his family background; rasta man,* and *has experienced the tough times of life and has come through successfully.* 65 expressions refer to John's **miscellaneous** characteristics such as *eloquent* and *confident.*

Some clusters refer to participants' personal interests, likes and dislikes. These include expressions relating to interests such as those of technology, recreational activities, and love for alcohol. For example, 56 expressions refer to John in terms of **technology related** expressions; as someone who is **into technology (12), someone up to date with technology (16), someone who is techno savvy (3), and someone who enjoys technology (25).** Examples include *very much into technology; technology is what he lives on; up to date with the technology; keeps up with technology; catches up with technology; loves to surf the internet, texting; kind of tech savvy with the electronics,* and *enjoys accessing the internet.* 14 phrases such as *enjoys music and dancing* and *involved in music and jazz* refer to John's interests in **music and dance as recreation**; 46 expressions refer to John as someone who *likes to drink alcohol; loves drinking especially spirit and beer; enjoys drinking* and *drinks lover.* Several (43) expressions refer to John's **hobbies and personal interests** such as *likes to travel; might like lifestyle living; has many different hobbies and interests; all rounder;* and *has many sides to him.* A smaller number of phrases (22) such as *up to date on the latest electronics; likely to text frequently* and *likes technology* describe Abby as someone who is **technology friendly.** Some other clusters are - **music and dance as recreation** (26), **alcohol related** (24), and **politically conscious** (10). Some clusters refer to Peter's **car related interests** (34), and **guitar, music and art related interests** (103). These include *enjoys his toys; hobby for cars; enjoys working on cars; interested in cars, likes to jam reggae on his guitar; a Bob Marley fan; interested in music, the guitar, art; respects classic idols such as Bob Marley* and *likes to paint, listen to old school music as well as playing the guitar.* A cluster of **alcohol-related** expressions (38) such as *enjoys to drink; probably likes to have a drink; he is a drinker but not an alcoholic; social drinker* indicate that Peter enjoys drinking.

As noted above, receivers attribute a range of self-related characteristics to each sender in the miscellaneous category. There is meagre evidence of two dimensions in Aaker's brand personality model - sincerity and competence - as in expressions such as *down to earth; loyal to his family;* and *may have a slightly nerdy side.* Some characteristics such as *confident; modern; independent; has no fears but big dreams* seem to be close to Aaker's excitement dimension. Importantly, miscellaneous characteristics such as most *likely a politically positioned person; loves cleanliness and tidiness; very cute and cool; likes to be part of a team; not materialistic* do not seem to fit into any of the five dimensions identified by Aaker. Nor do those relating to demographics, personal interests, likes and dislikes such as those of technology, recreational activities and love for alcohol relate with any of the personality dimensions identified by Aaker.

Table 3: An Expanded Version of Aaker's (1997) Model

Aaker's Dimensions (1997)	Demographic Characteristics	Personal interests	Miscellaneous characteristics
Sincerity; excitement; competence; sophistication; ruggedness	E.g., Gender; Age or life stage; Role and profession; Income, class, status	E.g., Orientation towards technology; love for music and dance; love for travel; lifestyle living	E.g., most likely a politically positioned person; loves cleanliness and tidiness; likes to be part of a team; not materialistic

The findings of this study suggest that miscellaneous characteristics, demographic factors, personal interests, likes and dislikes are part of the brand personality gestalt and any arbitrary exclusion of the same may not be theoretically or practically reasonable. Accordingly, this study proposes a more expansive model as below:

CONCLUSION

This study set out to examine two key questions - first, whether respondents validate Aaker's model in terms of brand personality dimensions; and second, whether the concept of brand personality is also transferable to products not clearly identified or presented to respondents as recognisable brands.

The study provides strong evidence in favour of three of Aaker's brand personality dimensions - excitement, sophistication and ruggedness. However, there is limited evidence on the remaining two - sincerity and competence. Further, if brand personality is the set of human characteristics associated with a brand, then respondents identify a number of other characteristics as well. These include demographics such as gender, age or life stage, income, class, status and spending, and role and profession; miscellaneous characteristics such as personal interests, likes and dislikes such as those of technology, recreation activities, and love for alcohol. In part, this study supports previous assertions (e.g., Grohmann, 2009; Levy, 1959) that brand personality, similar to human personality, is multidimensional and should also include masculinity and femininity. It further suggests that consumers do indeed infer a range of characteristics from brands. From a consumer perspective, categorizations such as those noted in this study may well be included within the set of human characteristics associated with a brand. Accordingly, this paper calls for the recognition of the same especially in terms of impact on consumer behaviour, thereby proposing an extension and expansion of Aaker's brand personality model.

Further, as noted in the photo collages, some products are recognisable brands, yet others are not clearly identified as brands. Yet receivers/observers speak of both brands and products in similar ways. This means personality dimensions are equally applicable to products as they are to brands. In sum, brand personality dimensions do not generalise to individual brands alone, rather the same can be mapped on to both products and brands within and across product categories. This study suggests avenues for further research which include generating more inclusive personality frameworks and identifying key dimensions for differentiating competitive brands within product categories.

In closing, consumers use brands and products to express more about themselves than the established set of five personality traits. In order to truly appreciate the diversity of human characteristics that consumers communicate via their product or brand choice/s, consumer researchers need to revisit and expand the classic notions of brand personality in consumers' product or brand choices.

REFERENCES

Aaker, Jennifer L. (1997), "Dimensions of brand personality", Journal of Marketing Research, 34 (3), 347-356.

Aaker, Jennifer L. (1997), "Dimensions of brand personality", *Journal of Marketing Research,* 34 (3), 347-356.

Arnould, Eric J and Thompson, Craig J. (2005); "Consumer culture theory (CCT): Twenty years of research", *Journal of Consumer Research*, 31 (4), 868-882.

Austin, Jon R., Siguaw, Judy A. and Mattila, Anna S. (2003), "A re-examination of the generalizability of the Aaker brand personality measurement framework", Journal of Strategic Marketing, 11 (June), 77-92.

Azoulay, Audrey and Kapferer, Jean-Noel (2003), "Do brand personality scales really measure brand personality?", *Journal of Brand Management,* 11 (2), 143-155.

Batra Rajeev, Lehman, Donald R. and Singh, Dipinder (1993), "The brand personality component of brand goodwill: some antecedents and consequences", in *Brand Equity and Advertising: Advertising's Role in Building Strong Brands,* eds. David A. Aaker and Alexander L. Biel, Erlbaum Associates: Hillsdale, NJ.

Belk, Russell W. (1988), "Possessions and the extended self", *Journal of Consumer Research,* 15 (2), 139-168.

Chu, Shu-Chuan and Sung, Yongjun (2011), "Brand Personality Dimensions in China," *Journal of Marketing Communications,* 17 (3), 163-181.

Erikson, Erik H. (1968), Identity: Youth and crisis, New York: Norton.

Erikson, Erik H. (1975), Life history and the historical moment, New York: Norton.

Freling, Traci H. and Forbes, Lukas P. (2005), "An examination of brand personality through methodological triangulation", *Brand Management,* 13 (2), 148-162.

Galican, Mary-Lou (2004), *Handbook of product placement in the mass media: New strategies in marketing theory, practice, trends, and ethics,* Toronto: The Haworth Press.

Geuens Maggie, Weijters, Bert and Wulf, Kristof De (2009), "A new measure of brand personality", *International Journal of Research in Marketing,* 26, 97-107.

Goldberg, Lewis R. (1992), "The development of markers for the Big-Five factor structure", *Psychological Assessment,* 4, 26-42.

Goldberg, Lewis R. (1993), "The structure of phenotypic personality traits", *American Psychologist,* 48 (1), 26-34.

Govers PCM, Schoormans, JPL (2005), "Product personality and its influence on consumer preference", *Journal of Consumer Marketing,* 22 (4), 189-197.

Grohmann, Bianca (2009), "Gender dimensions of brand personality", *Journal of Marketing Research*, Vol. XLVI (February), 105-119.

John, O.P., & Srivastava, S. (1999), "The Big Five trait taxonomy: History, measurement and theoretical perspectives", in *Handbook of Personality,* eds. Lawrence A. Pervin, and Oliver P. John, The Guilford Press, New York, 102-138.

Johnson, Monika K., Berg, Justin A. and Sirotzki, Toni (2007), "Differentiation in self-perceived adulthood: Extending the confluence model of subjective age identity", *Social Psychology Quarterly,* 70 (3), 243-261.

Kassarjian, Harold. H. (1977), "Content analysis in consumer research", *Journal of Consumer Research,* 4 (1), 8-18.

Kolbe, Richard H. and Burnett, Melissa S. (1991), "Content-Analysis Research: An examination of applications with directives for improving research reliability and objectivity", *Journal of Consumer Research,* 18 (2), 243-250.

Krippendorff, Klaus (2004), *Content Analysis: An introduction to its methodology* (2nd ed.), Thousand Oaks, CA: Sage.

Levy, Sidney J. (1959), "Symbols for sale", *Harvard Business Review,* 37 (4): 117-124.

Maehle Natalia and Supphellen, Magne (2008), "Sources of brand personality: a survey of ten brands", in *Advances in Consumer Research,* Vol. 35, eds. AY Lee, D Soman, Association for Consumer Research: Duluth, MN: 915-916.

Maehle, Natalia, Otnes, Celes, and Supphellen, Magne (2011), "Consumers' perceptions of the dimensions of brand personality", *Journal of Consumer Behaviour,* 10, 290-303.

McCracken, Grant (1989), "Who is the celebrity endorser? Cultural foundations of the endorsement process", *Journal of Consumer Research,* 16, 310-321.

Moschis, George P., and Churchill, Jr., Gilbert A. (1978), "Consumer socialization: A theoretical and empirical analysis", *Journal of Marketing Research,* 15 (4), 599-609.

Noland, Carey M. (2006), "Auto-photography as a research practice: Identity and self-esteem research", *Journal of Research Practice,* 2 (1), Article M1.

O'Cass, Aron and McEwen, Hmily (2004), "Exploring consumer status and conspicuous consumption", *Journal of Consumer Behaviour,* 4 (1), 25-39.

Piacentini, Maria and Mailer, Greig (2004), "Symbolic consumption in teenagers' clothing choices", Journal of Consumer Behaviour, 3 (3), 251-262.

Sillars, A. L. (1986), "Procedures for coding interpersonal conflict: The verbal tactics coding scheme (VTCS)", http://www2.umt.edu/dcs/pdf%20files/alan/conflict%20codingman.pdf (accessed March 23, 2008).

Souiden, Nizar and M'saad, Bouthaina (2011), "Adolescent girls from a modern conservative culture: The impact of their social identity on their perception of brand symbolism", *Psychology & Marketing,* 28 (12), 1133-1153.

Stokes, Helen and Wyn, Johanna (2007), "Constructing identities and making careers: Young people's perspectives on work and learning", *International Journal of Lifelong Education,* 26 (5), 495-511.

Sung, Yongjun and Tinkham, Spencer F. (2005), "Brand personality structures in the United States and Korea: Common and culture-specific factors", *Journal of Consumer Psychology,* 15 (4), 334-350.

Van, Rekom J., Jacobs-Belschak, Gabriele and Verleigh, Peeter W. J. (2006). Measuring and managing the essence of a brand personality. Marketing Letters, 17, 181-192.

Wang, Jeff and Wallendorf, Melanie (2006), "Materialism, status signaling, and product satisfaction", *Journal of the Academy of Marketing Science,* 34 (4), 494-505.

Ziller, Robert C. (1988), "Orientations: The cognitive liking person-situation interactions", *Journal of Social Behaviour and Personality,* 1, 1-18.

Ziller, Robert C. (1990), *Photographing the self: Methods for observing personal orientations,* Newbury Park, CA: Sage.

APPENDIX

Figure 1 Kate, the photo collage comprised of: a barbeque table, a bag (Louis Vuitton), a handbag, fruit, a pair of jeans (Ksubi), a pair of sunglasses (Gucci), perfumes (Lancome and Christian Dior), a pair of shoes, a pair of shorts (Ksubi), and a car (VW Golf).

Figure 2 Peter, photo collages comprised of: a soft toy (with motto "Born to Fly"), a painting, a perfume (Ralph Lauren), a T-shirt (Ralph Lauren), a belt (Bob Marley), a guitar, a car (Holden Commodore), another car (Honda), a Rugby jersey (De La Salle School), the New Zealand flag, and alcohol (42 below).

Figure 3 John, the photo collage comprised of: dance sports gear (dress, shirt, dance shoes, dance jacket and the Trombone), necklaces (with Maori symbols), a T-shirt (with Maori symbol), a pair of jandals (with Maori pattern), a bag (Billabong), a belt (QuickSilver), Shorts (Mossimo), shampoo, deodorant, asthma and hay fever pills, scuba tank for diving, diving watch, a fishing rod and a map of hits in Fiordland, Vodka (Smirnoff) and Beer (Tui), IPod, computer and a mobile phone, and two T-Shirts.

Figure 4 Abby, the photo collages comprised of: a health care book, a pair of running shoes (Nike), alcohol (Lindauer and Malibu), cellphones, a dress, a high waisted skirt, a wall planner, a pair of sunglasses, a pair of shoes, an Ipod, flyers, a pair of earrings, strawberries, and perfume (Yves Saint Laurent Baby Doll).

The Product Choices of Young Adult Consumers: Does Gender Matter?

Renu Emile, Auckland University of Technology, New Zealand
Kenneth F. Hyde, Auckland University of Technology, New Zealand
Mike Lee, University of Auckland, New Zealand

ABSTRACT

Through content analysis of 266 product photos from 28 participants, this paper aims to ascertain the influence of gender on the product choices that young adult consumers make, and whether females and males employ products to communicate aspects of the self in similar or different ways.

INTRODUCTION

The use of products and/or brands to communicate aspects of the self is well recognised in the consumer behaviour literature (Arnould & Thompson, 2005; Belk, 1988; McCracken, 1986). Consumers use products and/or brands to communicate a range of aspects such as class, status and lifestyle; ethnicity and culture; membership of reference groups or belongingness to communities; uniqueness; age; and cosmopolitanism or global affiliation (see, for e.g., Auty & Elliott, 1998; Crane, Hamilton, & Wilson, 2004; Elliott, 1994; Escalas & Bettman, 2005; Franke & Schreier, 2008; Fung, 2002; Hogg & Michell, 1996; Lamont & Molnar, 2001; Leigh & Gabel, 1992; Lindridge, Hogg, & Shah, 2004; O'Cass & Frost, 2002, O'Cass & McEwen, 2004; Tian, Bearden, & Hunter, 2001; Thompson & Tambyah, 1999; Wang & Wallendorf, 2006; Wattanasuwan, 2007; White & Dahl, 2006, 2007). Typically, studies tend to focus on researcher driven pre-selections of product categories or brands to examine how participants use the same to communicate specific aspects of the self. However, the empirical examination of consumers' self-selection of products, and their self-identification of self-related aspects these products communicate remains relatively unaddressed. This paper attempts to address this gap and specifically focuses on self-selected product choices of young adult consumers between the ages of 18 and 21. The aim of this paper is twofold - First, to specifically examine the nature and type of product choices young adult consumers make, and whether such choices are a function of gender. The question of the diverse product category or brand choices that consumers make, when given the opportunity to do so, in an undirected manner, has so far not been addressed in the literature, nor the role of gender in young adult consumers' product/brand choices, when given free rein to select products/brands that communicate aspects of their selves. Second, to identify aspects of the self these choices represent or emphasize and examine whether female and male participants employ products and/or brands to communicate aspects of their selves in similar or different ways. So far, to the best of the authors' knowledge, no research has addressed these diverse self-related aspects in product selection together, within a single study. In doing so, the study endeavours to add new knowledge to the understanding of the role of gender in self-selected product or brand choices, and also contributes to the understanding of salient self-related aspects in young adult consumers' product or brand choices when communicating the self.

THE ROLE OF GENDER IN PRODUCT AND/OR BRAND CHOICE

Empirical literature suggests that gender can have an impact on the product and/or brand choices consumers make. Gender in the marketing and consumer behaviour literature tends to signify the biological sex, gender roles, or the degree to which an individual identifies with masculine or feminine personality traits (Caldwell, Kleppe, & Henry, 2007; Kolyesnikova, Dodd & Wilcox, 2009; Palan, 2011). Typically, studies investigate differences between males and females

on processes underlying judgment (Dube & Morgan, 1996; Myers-Levy & Sternthal, 1991); information search and processing (Barber, Dodd, & Kolyesnikova, 2009); product perception and self image (Gentry, Doering, & O'Brien, 1978) or gift giving (Garbarino & Strahilevitz, 2004; Laroche, Saad, Cleveland, & Browne, 2000; Thompson, 1996). A stream of literature examines female role portrayals and stereotypes in advertising (e.g., Lysonski, 1985; Plakoyiannaki & Zotos, 2009; Wiles, Charles, & Tjernlund, 1995). A more recent study by Tuncay, Sredl, Parmentier, and Coleman (2009) examines discourses of gender and consumption in the media, specifically in two television shows, 'Entourage' and 'Sex and the City'.

Only a few empirical studies outside the realm of advertising and media studies examine gender related aspects in consumers' product choices (e.g., Allison, Golden, Mullet, & Coogan, 1980; Dittmar, Beattie, & Friese, 1995; Fugate & Philips, 2010; Goulding & Saren, 2009; Morris & Cundiff, 1971; Patterson & Hogg, 2004; Vitz & Johnson, 1965), and the majority involve researcher selected products. A cluster of studies specifically examine gender related stereotypes in the symbolic value of products; such stereotypes are appropriated by consumers to communicate specific gender related aspects of the self. Vitz and Johnson (1965), for example, demonstrate the symbolic value of products to communicate masculinity or femininity. They found that males were likely to smoke cigarettes with masculine images; and females were likely to smoke cigarettes with feminine images. Similarly, Allison et al. (1980) observe that masculinity and femininity are separate constructs, that product images tend to be gendered, and these in turn have a bearing on consumer behaviour. Morris and Cundiff's (1971) study shows males are inhibited in buying hair spray because of the perceived feminine appeal of the product. In other words, they are reluctant to buy the product as it does not communicate desired gender related aspects of the self. Dittmar et al. (1995) suggest that men tend to buy items that are instrumental or leisure related to express independence and activity, whereas women tend to buy products that express appearance and emotional aspects of the self. Along similar lines, Fugate and Philips's (2010) study focuses on gender related aspects in product consumption. The researchers asked participants to indicate the masculinity or femininity of 41 pre-selected products. Items such as beer, cars, SUVs, coffee, athletic shoes, lawnmowers, and potato chips were considered masculine in nature, whereas other researcher selected products such as shampoo, bath soap, wine, digital cameras, facial tissue, food processors, frozen vegetables and hair spray were considered feminine. These studies suggest that consumers consider the gender images of their product choices to express gender related aspects of the self.

Along similar lines, Patterson and Hogg (2004), in a study with two males and females aged between 18 and 24, report that one male participant did not buy books by female authors because he perceived them as 'girly' books aimed at girls. Similarly, a female participant was particularly conscious of what her clothes symbolized in terms of her femininity. Gould and Stern (1989) used pre-selected items such as dresses, shoes, blouses, hats, hairstyle, jewellery in a fashion consciousness scale and note that women were more conscious of fashion related products in relation to gender than men. Goulding and Saren's (2009) study shows how participants, in the context of the Whitby Goth festival, express various gender related aspects. Straight men, for example, express their feminine side by wearing lace, ruffles, and velvet associated with the Gothic dandy. These studies, together, suggest that gender has an impact on product or brand choice, that is, both males and females are conscious of the gender related stereotypes they communicate via the product choices they make. However, in the majority of previous work, researchers have selected or driven the product or brand selections, which may not necessarily be ideal representations of consumers' product choices to communicate their selves. Thus, by virtue of allowing participants the autonomy to self-select the products that communicate aspects of their selves, this study allows a more authentic and realistic view of young adult consumers' product or brand choices to communicate the self. Therefore, the intent of this study is twofold. First - when given free rein, are young adult consumers' product or brand choices indeed a function of gender? That is, whether there are noticeable differences in young adult consumers' product or brand choices, based on gender. Second, do the aspects of the self that young adult consumers choose to communicate, validate or confirm those identified in the literature (as discussed in the following section)?

Representation of aspects of the self in product choice: Proposition formulations

That consumers use products to communicate aspects of the self is well recognized in the consumer behavior literature. Based on a review of the literature on the use of products and/or brands to communicate aspects of the self, this paper formulates seven propositions (P1 to P7 - See Table 1) to examine whether and the extent to which these aspects are identified when consumers self-select products and brands to communicate aspects of the self. It is hoped that such examination of propositions would add to the current understanding of the relationship between product/brand choice and specific aspects of the self, and would also provide a commentary on the relative significance of specific self-related aspects in young adult consumers' product or brand choices. The study formulates propositions as follows:

Extant research indicates strong evidence for product choice to denote group membership or affiliation (e.g., Berger & Heath, 2007, 2008; Escalas & Bettman, 2005; Hogg & Michell, 1996; White & Dahl, 2006, 2007). It is expected that participants in this study would reflect this behaviour:

P1: Young adult discourses are characterised by evidence of the use of products to express affiliation, association, or belongingness with reference groups or community.

The literature provides evidence for individuals' use of products to denote status (e.g., Lamont & Molnar, 2001; O'Cass & Frost, 2002; O'Cass & McEwen, 2004; Vigneron & Johnson, 1999). It also provides evidence that consumers use products to indicate ethnicity (e.g., Chattaraman & Lennon, 2008; Lindridge et al., 2004; Oswald, 1999; Penaloza, 1994). It is expected that respondents in this study would reflect these behaviours, and accordingly Propositions Two and Three are set out:

P2: Young adult discourses are characterised by evidence of the use of products to indicate status.

P3: Young adult discourses are characterised by evidence of the use of products to indicate ethnicity.

There is some empirical evidence for the notion that individuals use products to establish differentiation from others in terms of uniqueness (e.g., Chan et al., 2009; Franke & Schreier, 2008). Accordingly, the following proposition is set out.

P4: Young adult discourses are characterised by evidence of the use of products to communicate uniqueness.

Existing studies suggest consumers' product choices indicate cosmopolitanism-related characteristics of the self (e.g., Caldwell et al., 2006; Wattanasuwan, 2007). The following proposition follows.

P5: Young adult discourses are characterised by evidence of the use of products to communicate cosmopolitanism related characteristics of the self.

Consumers' product choices reflect and support age and life stage related characteristics (e.g., Auty & Elliott, 1998; Elliott, 1994). It is expected that the same characteristics will be reflected in young adult consumer discourses.

P6: Young adult discourses are characterised by evidence of the use of products to communicate age and life stage related characteristics.

Empirical studies suggest the use of products to communicate gender related aspects of the self (e.g., Fugate & Philips, 2010; Goulding & Saren, 2009; Patterson & Hogg, 2004; Vitz and Johnson, 1965). Accordingly, this study sets out the following proposition:

P7: Young adult discourses are characterised by evidence of the use of products to communicate gender related characteristics.

METHOD

This paper comprises two parts. The first examines the types of products and/or brands young adults self-select to communicate aspects of their selves and whether and to what extent gender (male versus female) plays a role in such choices. The second, the aspects of the self these choices represent relative to aspects identified in the literature, and whether both female and male participants employ products and/or brands to communicate aspects of their selves in similar or different ways. Such understanding is relevant to scholars and practitioners with a specific interest in young adult consumers, their choices and behaviors, especially so to develop appropriate gender segmentation, targeting and promotional strategies.

SAMPLE

Twenty-eight young adults (18-21 years of age) participated in the study, 13 male and 15 female. All participants were university students at Auckland, New Zealand. Participants were instructed to take photographs of products and/or brands they owned and which said something about them to their peers.

PROCEDURE

The first part of the study involves identification of products selected by participants. Identification of the self-selected products and brands was undertaken by examining the contents of the photographs supplied. This was done in conjunction with the participants as an aspect of the interviews was the clarification of any ambiguity associated with the items selected for inclusion. Once each interview was transcribed, the researcher identified and listed all product categories (and brands) through two sample transcripts, and confirmed the findings with two independent judges who undertook the same task for the two sample transcripts. There was complete agreement on identified product categories (and brands), following which the researcher repeated the process for all 28 transcripts. This paper analyses 266 photographs taken by 28 participants and categorized into seven broad product groupings (see Table 2).

The second part of the study involved the use of content analysis techniques. In qualitative research, the term content analysis is used in two ways; as an umbrella term for both quantitative and qualitative approaches to text (words and/or pictures) analysis, or to only describe the process of quantifying data (Kassarjian, 1977; Krippendorff, 2004; Neuendorf, 2002; Smith, 1992). Where the term *content analysis* is used to denote qualitative content only, terms such as *words, phrases, thematic* or *discourse analysis* are used to denote the qualitative condition. In the case of quantified output, the researcher systematically assigns measurable codes to specific elements (e.g. words, phrases, objects) in the text; where applicable, descriptive statistics can be used to identify patterns in the data (Kassarjian, 1977; Krippendorff, 2004; Neuendorf, 2002; Smith, 1992). In this study, the data is subjected to both quantitative and qualitative content analysis. Inferences about the set of propositions are based on a quantitative content analysis of the themes and word frequencies linked to each photograph within each of the 28 transcribed interviews. This approach allows an indication of the scope and substance of the associations and provides indicative evidence.

The first step in the quantification process is the creation of key terms and operationalisations pertaining to specific propositions as described in Table 1. The essence of each proposition, key term and operationalisation was established by agreement and discussion between three judges.

As noted in Table 1, each proposition related to key terms, for e.g., P1 to affiliation, P2 to status, P3 to ethnicity, and so on. While specific procedures for analysing quantitative data are well-established and accepted, methods for analysis of qualitative data are diverse and often subject to variability (Holsti, 1969; Kassarjian, 1977; Krippendorff, 2004; Neuendorf, 2002; Smith, 1992). Analyses of qualitative data can also be ad-hoc and emergent, however, the use of measurement and formal tables can assist in pattern-identification. Analysis tables, summarizing and synthesizing information from diverse sources in a standardized format can also serve as reporting tools (Krippendorff, 2004; Neuendorf, 2002). Quantification in this study is based on unit counts and provides a basis for inference.

A unit was defined as "the specific segment of content that is characterised by placing it into a given category" (Holsti, 1969, p. 116). In this study, Holsti's use of the word *category* is also applicable to propositions. Categorisations of content could comprise of a single sentence or multiple sentences referring to a specific proposition in relation to one photograph. If a participant spoke of one or more propositions in relation to a photograph, then a count was recorded for all identified propositions. In other words, each of the

Table 1: Propositions and operationalisation

Propositions	Key term	Operational definition
P1: Young adult discourses are characterised by evidence of the use of products to express affiliation, association, or belongingness with reference groups or community (e.g., Berger and Heath 2007, 2008; Escalas and Bettman 2005; Hogg and Michell 1996; White and Dahl 2006, 2007).	Affiliation	Reference to an actual or imaginary group conceived of having significant direct or inverted relevance upon an individual's evaluations, aspirations, or behaviour (Park & Lessig, 1977).
P2: Young adult discourses are characterised by evidence of the use of products to indicate status (e.g., Lamont and Molnar 2001; O'Cass and Frost 2002; O'Cass and McEwen 2004; Vigneron and Johnson 1999)	Status	Reference to prestige, honour or deference accorded to an individual by others (Burn, 2004); reference to class, wealth or the lack of it (Coleman, 1983; Vigneron & Johnson, 1999).
P3: Young adult discourses are characterised by evidence of the use of products to indicate ethnicity (e.g., Chattaraman and Lennon 2008; Lindridge et al. 2004; Oswald 1999; Penaloza 1994).	Ethnicity	Reference to a sense of common ancestry based on shared individual characteristics and/or shared socio-cultural experiences (Driedger, 1978).
P4: Young adult discourses are characterised by evidence of the use of products to communicate uniqueness (e.g., Chan et al. 2009; Franke and Schreier 2008).	Uniqueness	Seeking to express difference through the purchase, use or display of original, novel or unique consumer goods; avoidance of similarity (Tian et al., 2001); references to product or brand choices in terms of not being particularly socially acceptable (Simonson & Nowlis, 2000; Snyder & Fromkin, 1977).
P5: Young adult discourses are characterised by evidence of the use of products to communicate cosmopolitanism related characteristics of the self (e.g., Caldwell et al. 2006; Wattanasuwan 2007)	Cosmopolitanism	Reference to notions of world citizenship (Cannon & Yaprak, 2002).
P6: Young adult discourses are characterised by evidence of the use of products to communicate age and life stage related characteristics (e.g., Auty and Elliott 1998; Elliott 1994)	Age & life stage	Reference to age, e.g., in terms of young, old or middle aged; life stage.
P7: Young adult discourses are characterised by evidence of the use of products to communicate gender related characteristics (e.g., Fugate and Philips 2010; Goulding and Saren 2009; Patterson and Hogg 2004; Vitz and Johnson 1965)	Gender	Reference to gender - male or female; masculine or feminine.

seven propositions could be counted only once for a given photograph, fulfilling the criteria of "existence (existent) or nonexistence (nonexistent)" (Kassarjian, 1977, p. 11), applicability or non-applicability of propositions. Further, if a participant referred collectively to a set of photographs in terms of one or more key terms, then the same proposition/s would apply to each photograph. For example, in this study, Participant 28 refers to two dresses, a Latin shirt, a pair of ballroom Latin shoes, and a sports jacket in terms of *uniqueness* (P4) and *age and life stage* (P6) - so both propositions (P4 and P6) were applied to each of the five photographs he referred to - a total of five counts for P4 and five counts for P6. All three judges (the researcher, J1 and J2) were requested to highlight and extract proposition related statement(s) in relation to each photograph for both sample transcripts (Participant 1 and Participant 28). They were to record if one or more propositions (coded as P1 to P7) were applicable to a photograph. They were to enter all data in columns - the first, noting the product or brand in photograph (or photographs if spoken of as a cluster); the second, noting the applicable proposition; the third, comprising of proposition related statements.

Following this task, comparisons were made on the bases of evidence identified in support of each proposition for each photograph. Comparisons amongst the three judges were made on the applicability or non-applicability of each of the seven propositions to each photograph. There was more than 90% agreement amongst the three judges. Where disagreements occurred, differences were resolved through discussion. A total count of 34 and 25 propositions applied, respectively, to sample transcript 1 and sample transcript 2. On the basis of the high figure of inter-coder reliability, the researcher proceeded to analyze the remaining 26 transcripts.

FINDINGS AND DISCUSSION

This paper analyses 266 photographs taken by 28 participants (see Table 2). The photographs were categorised into seven broad product groupings:

- **Clothing and accessories** (clothing, bags & wallets, hats & belts, shoes, jewellery, sunglasses and reading glasses, watches);
- **Cosmetics**: (make up, perfumes and deodorants, and personal cleaning and grooming products);
- **Electronics**: (cell phones, computers, iPods, domestic appliances, LCD TVs, hair straighteners, cameras, play station/X-box, music systems, CDs/DVDs, miscellaneous electronic/electrical (GPS, CD rewritable);
- **Food and Drinks (non-alcoholic)**;
- **Drinks (alcoholic)**;
- **Cars**;
- **Miscellaneous** (barbeque table, soft toy, painting, sporting equipment (chess & cards, gym equipment, scuba tank, diving watch, fishing rod, map of huts in Fiordland, hockey stick bag, cricket bat and soccer ball), trombone, books, magazines, books, stationery, wall planner, flyer for dance party (Get Shaky), flyer (Young Labour Party), flyer for entertainment show (Rhythm & Vines), movie posters, photograph wall, photograph frame, flat (door), computer tablet (to draw on), bus card, car keys, Kleenex tissues, items of cultural significance, Flag of NZ)

Table 2 shows the total number of photographs per product category. Both female and male participants most commonly link aspects of their self to clothing/ accessories (36% of photographs) and electronics (25% of photographs).

The dominance of the product categories of *clothing and accessories* and *electronics* may be explained in a number of reasons. It could be young adult consumers find these product categories most relevant to their selves and that these product categories most readily assist them to communicate self-related characteristics. Interestingly, in this study young adult male consumers (43% of all male photos) use clothing and accessories to express themselves approximately 1.4 times more than young adult female consumers (30% of all female photos). It could be that young adult male consumers tend to place greater emphasis on clothing and accessory items such as bags and wallets, hats and belts, and watches as markers of the self compared to young adult female consumers.

The interest in *clothing and accessories* and *electronics* could also reflect a concern with aspects relating to self-image and status. As Wilska (2003) notes, information and communication technologies are a very important part of the everyday life of young people. Svoen's (2007) study suggests that young adults use technologies to construct self-directed identities.

Several reasons may explain the interest in the product categories of *magazines and books* and *sporting equipment* within the miscellaneous product category. It could be that such products help manage and communicate aspects of the self to others, for example, by communicating belongingness to a certain social set, supporting or contesting stereotypes of masculinity or femininity, and providing information on self-related aspects, such as the relative roles and attitudes of men and women (Kim & Ward, 2004; Moore, Earless, & Parsons, 1992; Shannon, 2004). Photographs of food and drinks suggest that these categories are of significance to young adult consumers as communicators of the self. However, the difference in percentage of photographs taken by young female (12% of all female photos) and male (7% of all male photos) adult consumers for the food and drinks category suggests that females emphasise food and drinks, as communicators of the self, 1.7 times more than males.

There is nearly double the percentage (1.86) of photographs taken by female participants (13% of all female photos) than by male participants (7% of all male photos) in the cosmetics product category. The same holds true for the miscellaneous product category which suggests that miscellaneous items are of much greater interest (1.67) to females (15% of all female photos) than males (9% of all male photos). It could be that cosmetics and miscellaneous products such as the barbeque table, soft toys, planners and flyers, photographs and items of cultural significance are of greater value as communicators of the self for young adult female consumers than they are for young adult male consumers. The sample for this study does not provide evidence of choices involving high investments such as real estate, luxury vehicles or top of the line luxury goods. This could be due to the life stage and financial constraints of the participant sample.

The next part of the study examines the use young adult consumers put the products and/or brands to, and whether both female and male participants employ products and/or brands to communicate aspects of their selves in similar ways. Table 3 presents the number of instances in support of the study propositions, with data presented separately for males and females by product category.

As seen in Table 3, *group affiliation* (P1), *status* (P2) and *age* (P6) are the dominant aspects of self that participants seek to communicate. It can be concluded that

Proposition 1 - Young adult discourses are characterised by evidence of the use of products to express affiliation, association, or belongingness with reference groups or community, and

Proposition 2 - Young adult discourses are characterised by evidence of the use of products to indicate status can be accepted.

Similarly, though not as substantial, there is some evidence across product categories that participants are interested in communicating that they are young. So

Table 2: Number of Photographs per Category per Gender

Product Category	Females	Males	% Difference	No. Photographs
Clothing & Accessories: clothing, bags & wallets, hats & belts, shoes, jewellery, sunglasses and reading glasses, watches	43(30%)	53(43%)	43/30=1.43	**96 = 36%**
Electronics: cell phones, computers, iPods, domestic appliances, LCD TVs, hair straighteners, cameras, play station/X-box, music systems, CDs/DVDs, miscellaneous electronic/electrical, GPS, CD rewritable	36(25%)	31(25%)	25/25=1	**67 = 25%**
Miscellaneous: barbeque table, soft toy, painting, sporting equipment (chess & cards, gym equipment, scuba tank, diving watch, fishing rod, map of huts in Fiordland, hockey stick bag, cricket bat and soccer ball), trombone, books, magazines, books, stationery, wall planner, flyer for dance party (Get Shaky), flyer (Young Labour Party), flyer for entertainment show (Rhythm & Vines), movie posters, photograph wall, photograph frame, flat (door), computer tablet (to draw on), bus card, car keys, Kleenex tissues, items of cultural significance, Flag of NZ.	**22(15%)**	**11(9%)**	**15/9=1.67**	33 = 12.5%
Cosmetics: make up, perfumes and deodorants, and personal cleaning and grooming products	**18(13%)**	**9(7%)**	**13/7=1.86**	27 = 10%
Food/Drink	**17(12%)**	**9(7%)**	**12/7=1.71**	26 = 9.7%
Cars	5(3%)	5(4%)	4/3=1.33	10 = 4%
Alcohol	3(2%)	4(3%)	3/2=1.5	7= 2.6%
	144 (100%)	122 (100%)		266 (100%)

Table 3: Evidence in Support of Propositions from each Product Category - Females (F) and Males (M)

Product categories	P1 Affiliation		P2 Status		P3 Ethnicity		P4 Uniqueness		P5 Cosmopolitanism		P6 Age		P7 Gender	
	F	M	F	M	F	M	F	M	F	M	F	M	F	M
Clothing / accessories	17	20	29	29	4	6	16	4	0	0	16	11	6	4
Cosmetics	9	6	10	2	0	0	2	0	0	0	7	1	3	3
Electronics	21	15	12	11	0	0	2	0	0	0	13	10	3	2
Food / non alcohol drinks	10	6	3	2	2	0	0	0	0	0	3	2	0	0
Alcoholic drinks	2	2	1	4	0	0	0	0	0	0	0	1	0	1
Cars	2	0	5	5	0	1	0	0	0	0	1	2	1	1
Miscellaneous	14	8	3	0	2	2	2	3	0	0	3	1	1	1
Total	75	57	63	53	8	9	22	7	0	0	43	28	14	12

Proposition 6 - Young adult discourses are characterised by evidence of the use of products to communicate age related characteristics,

can also be accepted.

Though some participants seek to communicate *ethnicity* (Proposition 3), *uniqueness* (Proposition 4) or *gender* (Proposition 7), the number of instances is fewer. Yet, even though weaker, each of the three propositions -

Proposition 3: Young adult discourses are characterised by evidence of the use of products to indicate ethnicity.

Proposition 4: Young adult discourses are characterised by evidence of the use of products to communicate uniqueness.

Proposition 7: Young adult discourses are characterised by evidence of the use of products to communicate gender related characteristics

is accepted.

There is no evidence for Proposition Five, that

Young adult discourses are characterised by evidence of the use of products to communicate cosmopolitanism related characteristics of the self.

This could be due to a number of reasons - for example, physical location, specific socio-cultural context, or insufficient global experience. The bulk of the cosmopolitan literature includes a sample population of adults (e.g., Caldwell et al., 2006; Thompson & Tambyah, 1999), although a few studies that involve young adults specifically examine the link between geographical location and cosmopolitanism (e.g., Kjeldgaard, 2003; Wattanasuwan, 2007).

Table 3 shows that (with the exception of cosmopolitanism) both male and female participants use products and brands to express affiliation, association, or belongingness with reference groups or community, status, age, ethnicity, uniqueness and gender.

The final part of this study compares female and male participants' use of products to communicate specific aspects of their selves. This paper restricts discussion to only those instances where one gender was seen to emphasise some aspect of the self at double (or more) the frequency of the other gender. We also refrain from drawing conclusions where incidences were coded less than two times for both females and males.

As Table 3 displays, for *Affiliation* (P1) there are no substantial overall differences between genders, nor are there any note worthy product level differences. For *Status* (P2), while there are no overall differences, females are three times more likely to use cosmetics and miscellaneous items to denote status, whereas males (in this study) prefer to use alcoholic drinks to express status. There are no marked gender differences at the overall or product level for *Ethnicity* (P3). *Uniqueness* (P4) seems to provide the most contrast. Here, females are three times more likely to use products to communicate uniqueness, with most of this difference stemming from the use of clothing and accessories. Females are also more likely to use cosmetics and miscellaneous items to communicate aspects of *Age* (P6). Last, although much literature espouses the influence of gender on product choice, we find no marked differences between male and female young adult consumers' use of products to convey *Gender* (P7).

The findings suggest that aspects of the selves that young female and male consumers intend to communicate seem to be associated with the nature of the products selected. The selection of common product categories by both female and male consumers and the emphases on specific aspects could also be attributed to the influence of social media. Over the past decade or so, social media has become increasingly popular in influencing consumers, especially from the standpoint of communicating the self (Kietzmann et al., 2012; Pan & Thomas, 2012; Utz, 2010). As consumers construct profiles, view and traverse connections in online environments, they share information about their interests and choices. Such sharing influences product selections as a basis for impression formation and identity construction. This paper suggests that social media may well stimulate the construction of the self in off-line environments too, and that it may be worthwhile to explore this aspect further in future research.

CONCLUSION

To conclude, this paper set out to examine the role of gender in the nature and types of product choices young adult consumers make, and whether females and males employ products and/or brands to communicate aspects of the self in similar or different ways. The paper extends current knowledge by focusing attention on specific product categories relevant to female and male young adult consumers, and aspects most salient in the use of products to communicate the self. Cosmetics, followed by food/drink, and then the miscel-

laneous category accounted for the main differences in product use based on gender. Females appear to use a variety of products to express themselves, more so than males. −However, more interesting, is the diversity in terms of how female and male participants use products to communicate aspects of their selves. Females are more conscious of communicating age, uniqueness and status compared to males. In view of the sample size for this study, while it may be inappropriate to generalise, some plausible implications for practitioners lie in focusing on aforementioned aspects of self representation when promoting specific products to women. For example, when directing advertising and promotional material to women, emphasizing more than chronology, age as a state of mind and heart, uniqueness as being special in some ways, status and affiliation in terms of roles or ways of thinking and perceiving the world.

REFERENCES

Allison, Nell K., Golden, Linda L., Mullet, Gary M. and Coogan, Donna (1980), "Sex-typed product images: The effects of sex, sex role self-concept and measurement implications", *Advances in Consumer Research, 7,* 604-609.

Arnould, Eric J. And Thompson, Craig J. (2005), "Consumer culture theory (CCT): Twenty Years of Research", *Journal of Consumer Research,* 31 (4), 868-882.

Auty, Susan and Elliott, Richard (1998), "Fashion involvement, self-monitoring and the meaning of brands", *The Journal of Product and Brand Management* 7 (2), 109-123.

Barber, Nelson, Dodd, Tim H. and Kolyesnikova, Natalia (2009), "Gender differences in information search: Implications for retailing", Journal of Consumer Marketing, 26 (6), 415-426.

Belk, Russell W. (1988), "Possessions and the extended self", *Journal of Consumer Research,* 15, 139-168.

Berger, Jonah and Heath, Chip (2007), "Where consumers diverge from others: Identity signaling and product domains", *Journal of Consumer Research,* 34, 121-134.

Berger, Jonah and Heath, Chip (2008), "Who drives divergence? Identity signaling, outgroup dissimilarity, and the abandonment of cultural tastes", *Journal of Personality and Social Psychology,* 95 (3), 593-607.

Burn, Shawn M. (2004), *Groups: Theory and practice,* Belmont, CA: Thomson Wadsworth.

Caldwell, Marylouise, Blackwell, Kristen and Tulloch, Kirsty (2006), "Cosmopolitanism as a consumer orientation: Replicating and extending prior research", *Qualitative Market Research: An International Journal,* 9 (2), 126-139.

Caldwell, Marylouise, Kleppe Ingborg Astrid and Paul. Henry, Paul (2007), "Prosuming multiple gender role identities: A multi-country written and audio-visual exploration of contemporary mainstream female achievers", *Consumption, Markets and Culture,* 10, 96-116.

Cannon, Hugh M. and Yaprak, Attila (2002), "Will the real-world citizen please stand up! The many faces of cosmopolitan consumer behaviour", *Journal of International Marketing,* 10 (4), 30-52.

Chan, Cindy, Berger, Jonah and Boven, Leaf Van (2009), *"Differentiating the "I" in "In-Group": How identity-signaling and uniqueness motives combine to drive consumer choice",* Paper presented at the Advances in Consumer Psychology Conference.

Chattaraman, Veena and Lennon, Sharron J. (2008), "Ethnic identity, consumption of cultural apparel, and self-perceptions of ethnic consumers", *Journal of Fashion Marketing and Management,* 12 (4), 518-531.

Coleman, Richard P. (1983), "The continuing significance of social class to marketing", *Journal of Consumer Research,* 10 (3), 265-280.

Crane, Tara Christopher, Hamilton, Jean A. and Wilson, Laurel E. (2004), "Scottish dress, ethnicity and self-identity", *Journal of Fashion Marketing & Management,* 8 (1), 66-83.

Dittmar, Helga, Beattie, Jane and Friese, Sussane (1995), "Gender identity and material symbols: Objects and decision considerations in impulse purchases", *Journal of Economic Psychology,* 16 (3), 491-511.

Driedger, Leo (1978), *The Canadian ethnic mosaic,* Toronto: McClelland and Stewart.

Dube, Laurette and Morgan, Michael S. (1996), "Trend effects and gender differences in retrospective judgments of consumption emotions," *Journal of Consumer Research,* 23 (Sept.), 156-162.

Elliott, Richard (1994), "Exploring the symbolic meanings of brands", *British Journal of Management,* 5, S13-S19.

Escalas Jennifer E, and Bettman James R. (2005), "Self-construal, reference groups, and brand meaning", *Journal of Consumer Research,* 32 (3), 378-389.

Franke, Nikolaus and Schreier, Martin (2008), "Product uniqueness as a driver of customer utility in mass customization", *Marketing Letters,* 19 (2), 93-107.

Fugate, Douglas L. and Philips, Joanna (2010), "Product gender perceptions and antecedents of product gender congruence", *Journal of Consumer Marketing,* 27 (3), 251-261.

Fung, Anthony (2002), "Women's magazines: Construction of identities and cultural consumption in Hong Kong", *Consumption, markets and culture,* 5 (4), 321-336.

Garbarino, Ellen and Strahilevitz, Michal (2004), "Gender differences in the perceived risk of buying online and the effects of receiving a site recommendation", *Journal of Business Research,* 57, 768- 775.

Gentry, James W., Doering, Mildred, and O'Brien, Terrence V. (1978), "Masculinity and femininity factors in product perception and self image", *Advances in Consumer Research,* 5.

Gould, Stephen J., and Stern, Barbara B. (1989), "Gender schema and fashion consciousness", *Psychology & Marketing,* 6 (2), 129-145.

Goulding, Christina and Saren, Michael (2009), "Performing identity: An analysis of gender expressions at the Whitby Goth festival", *Consumption Markets & Culture,* 12 (1), 27-46.

Hogg, Margaret K. and Michell, Paul C.N. (1996), "Identity, self and consumption: A conceptual framework", *Journal of Marketing Management,* 12, 629-644.

Holsti, Ole R. (1969), *Content analysis for the social sciences and humanities,* Reading, MA: Addison-Wesley.

Kassarjian, Harold H. (1977), "Content analysis in consumer research", *Journal of Consumer Research,* 4 (1), 8-18.

Kietzmann, Jan H.; Silvestre, Bruno S.; McCarthy, Ian P. and Pitt, Leyland (2012), "Unpacking the social media phenomenon: towards a research agenda", *Journal of Public Affairs.*

Kim, Janna L. and Ward, L. Monique (2004), "Pleasure reading: Associations between young women's sexual attitudes and their reading of contemporary women's magazines", *Psychology of Women's Quarterly,* 28, 48-58.

Kjeldgaard, Dannie (2003), "Youth identities in the global cultural economy: Central and peripheral consumer culture in Denmark and Greenland", *European Journal of Cultural Studies,* 6 (3), 285-304.

Kolyesnikova, Natalia, Dodd, Tim H. and Wilcox, James B. (2009), "Gender as a moderator of reciprocal consumer behaviour", *Journal of Consumer Marketing,* 26 (3), 200-213.

Krippendorff, Klaus (2004), *Content Analysis: An introduction to its methodology (2nd ed.),* Thousand Oaks, CA: Sage.

Lamont, Michele and Molnar, Virag (2001), "How Blacks use consumption to shape their collective identity", *Journal of Consumer Culture,* 1 (1), 31-45.

Laroche, Michel, Saad, Gad, Cleveland, Mark and Browne, Elizabeth (2000), "Gender Differences in Information Search Strategies for a Christmas Gift," *Journal of Consumer Marketing,* 17 (6), 500-524.

Leigh, James H. and Gabel, Terrance G. (1992), "Symbolic interactionism: Its effects on consumer behavior and implications for marketing strategy", *The Journal of Consumer Marketing,* 9 (1), 27-38.

Lindridge, Andrew M, Hogg, Margaret K. and Shah, Mita (2004), "Imagined multiple worlds: How South Asian women in Britain use family and friends to navigate the "border Crossings" between household and societal contexts", *Consumption, Markets and Culture,* 7 (3), 211-238.

Lysonski, Steven (1985), "Role portrayals in British magazine advertisements", *European Journal of Marketing,* 19, 37-55.

McCracken, Grant (1986), "Culture and consumption: A theoretical account of the structure and movement of the cultural meaning of consumer goods", *Journal of Consumer Research,* 13 (1), 71-84

Moore, Jacqueline, Earless, Anne and Parsons Tony (1992), "Women's magazines: Their influence on nutritional knowledge and food habits", *Nutrition & Food Science,* 92 (3), 18-21.

Morris, George P. and Cundiff, Ed W. (1971), "Acceptance by males of feminine products", *Journal of Marketing Research,* 8 (3), 372-374.

Myers-Levy, Joan and Sternthal, Brian (1991), "Gender differences in the use of message cues and judgments", *Journal of Marketing Research,* 28 (Feb.), 84-96.

Neuendorf, Kimberly A. (2002), *The content analysis guidebook.* Thousand Oaks, CA: Sage.

O'Cass, Aron and McEwen, Hmily (2004), "Exploring consumer status and conspicuous consumption", *Journal of Consumer Behaviour,* 4 (1), 25-39.

O'Cass, Aron and Frost, Hmily (2002), "Status brands: Examining the effects of non-product-related brand associations on status and conspicuous consumption", *Journal of Product & Brand Management,* 11 (2), 67-88.

Oswald, Laura R. (1999), "Culture swapping: Consumption and the ethnogenesis of middle-class Haitian immigrants", *Journal of Consumer Research,* 25 (3), 303-318.

Palan, Kay M. (2001), "Gender identity in consumer behavior research: A literature and research agenda", *Academy of Marketing Science Review,* 10 (1), 1-26.

Pan, Yue, and Thomas, John (2012), "Hot or not: A qualitative study on ecological impact of social media & fashion consumption", *Proceedings of the ACM 2012 conference on Computer Supported Cooperative Work Companion,* 293-300.

Park, Whan C.., and Lessig, Parker V. (1977), "Students and housewives: Differences in susceptibility to reference group influence", *Journal of Consumer Research,* 4 (2), 102-110.

Patterson, Claudine E. and Hogg, Margaret K. (2004), "Gender identity, gender salience and symbolic consumption", in *Gender and consumer behavior,* Scott LM, Thompson CJ (eds). Association for Consumer Research: Madison, WI.

Penaloza, Lisa (1994), "A critical ethnographic exploration of the consumer acculturation of Mexican immigrants", *Journal of Consumer Research,* 21 (1), 32-54.

Plakoyiannaki, Emmanuella and Zotos, Yorgos (2009), "Female role stereotypes in print advertising: Identifying associations with magazine and product categories", *European Journal of Marketing,* 43, 11/12, 1411-1434.

Shannon, Brent (2004), "ReFashioning men: Fashion, masculinity, and the cultivation of the male consumer in Britain, 1860-1914", *Victorian Studies,* 46 (4), 597-630.

Simonson, Itamar and Nowlis, Stephen M. (2000), "The role of explanations and need for uniqueness in consumer decision making: Unconventional choices based on reasons", *Journal of Consumer Research,* 27 (1), 49-68.

Smith, Charles P. (1992), *Motivation and personality: Handbook of thematic content analysis,* New York: Cambridge University Press.

Snyder, Charles R. and Fromkin, Howard L. (1977), "Abnormality as a positive characteristic: The development and validation of a scale measuring need for uniqueness", *Journal of Abnormal Psychology,* 86 (5), 518-527.

Svoen, Brit (2007), "Consumers, participants, and creators: Young people's diverse use of television and new media", *ACM Computers in Entertainment,* 5 (2), 1- 16.

Thompson, Craig J. (1996), "Caring consumers: gendered consumption meanings and the juggling of lifestyle", *Journal of Consumer Research,* 22 (Mar.), 388-407.

Tian, Kelly T., Bearden, William O. And Hunter, Gary L. (2001), "Consumers' need for uniqueness: Scale development and validation", *Journal of Consumer Research,* 28 (1), 50-66.

Thompson, Craig J. and Tambyah, Siok Kuan (1999), "Trying to be cosmopolitan", *Journal of Consumer Research,* 26 (3), 214-241.

Tuncay, Linda, Sredl, Katherine, Parmentier, Marie-Agnes and Coleman, Catherine (2009), "Exploring discourses of Gender and consumption in the Media", *Advances in Consumer Research,* 36, 797-798.

Utz, Sonja (2010), "Show me your friends and I will tell you what type of person you are: How one's profile, number of friends, and type of friends influence impression formation on social networking sites", *Journal of Computer-Mediated Communication,* 15 (2), 314-315.

Vigneron, Franck and Johnson, Lester W., (2004), "Measuring perceptions of brand luxury", *The Journal of Brand Management,* 11 (6), 484-506.

Vitz, Paul C. and Johnson, Donald (1965), "Masculinity of smokers and the masculinity of cigarette images", *Journal of Applied Psychology,* 49 (3), 155-159.

Wang, Jeff and Wallendorf, Melanie (2006), "Materialism, status signaling, and product satisfaction", *Journal of the Academy of Marketing Science,* 34 (4), 494-505.

Wattanasuwan, Kritsadarat (2007), "Balancing the hybrid self in the competing landscapes of consumption", *The Journal of American Academy of Business,* 11 (1), 9-17.

White, Katherine, Dahl Darren W. (2006), "To Be or *Not* Be: The influence of disassociative reference groups on consumer preferences", *Journal of Consumer Psychology,* 16 (4), 404-13.

White, Katherine and Dahl Darren W. (2007), "Are all out-groups created equal? Consumer identity and dissociative influence", *Journal of Consumer Research,* 34 (4), 525-536.

Wiles, Judith A., Wiles, Charles R., and Tjernlund, Anders (1995), "A comparison of gender role portrayals in magazine advertising: The Netherlands, Sweden and the USA", *European Journal of Marketing,* 29 (11), 35-49.

Wilska, Terhi-Anna (2003), "Mobile phone use as part of young people's consumption styles, *Journal of Consumer Policy",* 26, 441-463.

The Before and After: A Study of Plastic Surgery Consumption with Young Women in Brazil

Fernanda Borelli, Universidade Federal do Rio de Janeiro, Brazil
Leticia Moreira Casotti, Universidade Federal do Rio de Janeiro, Brazil

ABSTRACT

As the body assumes a central dimension of identity, plastic surgery becomes increasingly common. Using in-depth interviews, this study extends the understanding of the relation between body-related consumption and identity construction by examining young women's decision and experience of transforming their identity and their body through plastic surgery.

INTRODUCTION

As Vigarello's (2006) historical account shows, the fascination with beauty is not a recent matter. Ideals of beauty have moved according to social, political and cultural shifts of each period. Vigarello (2006) points to the growing importance of the body and the act of beautification over the centuries.

Over the last century, beauty and wellbeing became related. Beauty came to mean to feel good about one's body. Wellbeing became a fundamental rule of beautification (Vigarello 2006).

The years 1950 and 1960 have witnessed the body becoming an object of consumption (Vigarello 2006). From the second half of the twentieth century on, the body cult gained a more important social dimension and entered the era of the masses. The body cult combines the esteem for youthfulness with the pursuit of bodily perfection, and brings in tow a range of bodily activities such as exercise and specialized treatments (Goldenberg 2002).

Body appearance became an essential dimension of contemporary identity (Askergaard et al. 2002; Goldenberg 2002; Lipovetsky 2000). Beautification has been diversifying and disseminating rapidly. The profusion of beautifying devices democratized beauty–until then merely the result of nature or exception. This becomes even stronger in a society in which individual wellbeing is an endless pursuit and an affordable and mandatory ideal. Since wellbeing and beauty are related, the idea of investing in one's individual image/body gained strength and became norm (Vigarello 2006).

It is in this context that the consumption of plastic surgery has grown and become increasingly commonplace (Askergaard et al. 2002). Malysse (2002), comparing individuals from Brazil (Rio de Janeiro) and France, indicated that Brazilians seemed more concerned with bodily aesthetics than Europeans. This high esteem of the body – attributed by some to the tropical climate and miles of beach that encourage the use of light clothing and exposed skin – seems to add to the professionalism of the school established by the recognized plastic surgeon Dr Pitanguy to favor the uptake of plastic surgery in Brazil (Goldenberg 2002; 2007; Malysse 2002).

Brazil is one of the largest plastic surgery markets in the world. Between September 2007 and August 2008, according to Brazilian Society for Plastic Surgery[1], 547,000 cosmetic plastic surgeries were performed; being the most common types the silicone prosthesis implants and the liposuction, and the major consumers, women. Those levels are not really surprising in a marketplace where firms advertise plastic surgery operations payable in up to 36 installments.

This exploratory study aims to extend the understanding of the relation between body-related consumption and identity construction by examining young women's decision and experience of transforming their identity and their body through plastic surgery – a phenomenon still overlooked by consumer research. To do that we gather together a range of interpretations and viewpoints that can help us better understand the phenomenon of plastic surgery consumption among young women. We chose to focus on young women in order to explore the consumption of plastic surgery that is unrelated to issues of aging or attenuation of the effects of pregnancy.

THEORETICAL BACKGROUND

Identity is based on difference and similarity, where neither can exist without the other. Identities are not given; rather, they are continually created and recreated by each individual in their interaction – and negotiation – with others; as such, the individual and the collective are interrelated and act jointly. Positive feedback of others belonging to the same social group of reference is essential for the successful expression of identity. Thus, identity is seen as a self-reflective process based on the monitoring of past actions and modification of future behavior (Giddens 2002; Jenkins 2005; Ransome 2005).

As Giddens (2002) points out, in modernity, the process of identity construction is influenced by the new type of relationship that emerges: the *pure relationship*. In it, there are no external anchors, such as moral obligations, social and economic issues. Thus, the *pure relationship* is maintained only while each of those involved views it as satisfying and rewarding and perceives its benefits. As such, the relationship has an open and reflective character and can end at any moment. This lack of permanence makes individuals more self-centered and preoccupied with their attractiveness in terms of aesthetic characteristics.

In the literature on consumer research, it's not uncommon to find identity treated from the perspective of personal narrative (Ahuvia 2005; Kleine, Kleine, and Allen 1995; Sirgy 1982). Such narrative has a reflexive nature (Giddens 2002) inasmuch as it assumes that the history of the consumer is built based on who the individual was, is, or wishes to become.

Thompson and Hirschman (1995) believe that whereas identity used to be defined by work activities, in postmodernity this occurs through consumption. The fluid and reflective nature of identity (Bauman 2005; Giddens 2002) seems to render the act of consumption a means of producing the desired self, based on images and styles transmitted through possessions (Thompson and Hirschman 1995). Consumption assists individuals in the acquisition, maintenance, alteration, reconstruction and disposal of the individual's identity or identities (Kleine et al. 1995; McAlexander 1991; Schouten 1991; Young 1991) – to the point that goods can even be considered our *extended-self* (Belk, 1988). Consumption also acts in reducing or resolving identity conflicts as, for example, tensions between the consumer's past identity and the person one wishes to become (Ahuvia 2005; Mittal 2006).

The concepts of identity and self-concept are bound to the concept of self-esteem. Banister and Hogg (2004) claim marketing managers recognize the pursuit of self-esteem as one of the most important motivational drivers of consumer behavior and decision making. Consumption activities have a major role in enhancing or protecting self-esteem (Sirgy, Grewal, Mangleburg, Park, Chon, Claiborne, Johar, and Berkman 1997). Self-esteem refers to the evaluation of a person in relation to oneself (James 1890 cited in Pyszczynski, Greenberg, Solomon, and Arndt 2004). Giddens (2002) stresses the social nature of self-esteem, which relates strongly with responses

---

[1] Sociedade Brasileira de Cirurgia Plástica (see www.cirurgiaplastica.org.br).

by others. The non-conformance of the body to prevailing media and social standards tends to reduce the individual's self-esteem (Goldenberg and Ramos 2002).

Identity, consumption and body

There is no way to develop identity without embodiment (Mead 1934 cited in Jenkins 2005). Thus, the body can be seen as the continuation of the individual, as an element of identification with the collective and as a means of giving form to identity. Body appearance is, therefore, decisive in the acquisition of identity and socialization (Malysse 2002). For the self is exhibited to others via its embodiment (Giddens 2002). In a social context in which consumption gains strength as a definer of identity (Ransome 2005; Thompson and Hirschman 1995), the body – main billboard for expressing one's identity – assumes increasing importance. Its role is even exalted with the promotion of the body cult, from which appearance becomes a fundamental part of people's identity (Goldenberg 2002; 2007).

Vigarello (2006) suggests that the pursuit of body beauty is disguised as individual choice and self-realization, so that each one is responsible for one's own beauty. But this subjectivity or the idea of individual choice seems illusory. Normalization is still present, reinforced by the duality of wellbeing and malaise.

Individuals are bombarded by media images of the normalized body and, perceiving themselves as falling short of such a norm, come to be dissatisfied or reject their own appearance (Lipovetsky 2000). Thenceforth people who might be perfectly healthy start to see their body as defective, as needing improvements (Malysse 2002), and go on to develop extreme self-criticism in relation to their body. Any deviation from the idealized body becomes a problem, including low self-esteem, against which they must struggle (Thompson and Hirschman 1995).

The current array of *corrective treatments* for the body – from makeup or cosmetics to exercises, plastic surgery, hair/facial treatments, etc. – operates an apparent democratization of beauty (Vigarello 2006), getting the body *in shape*, young and beautiful for everyone, through hard work and willpower, rendering the individual as solely responsible for their own appearance. The body comes to symbolize the individual's moral character – it is not sufficient to merely maintain such continuous control; it is necessary to be noticed by others when so doing. Being *in shape* becomes an indicator of personal success, while a body that's *out of shape*, sickly or poorly looking becomes synonymous with lack of willpower, laziness, indiscipline or lack of control (Bouzón 2008; Goldenberg 2002; Goldenberg and Ramos 2002; Giddens 2002; Lipovetsky 2000; Thompson and Hirschman 1995).

But despite beauty being seen as the result of work and willpower, it is strongly related to purchasing power. In becoming an object of consumption (Baudrillard 1995), the body gains a classificatory, hierarchical function, communicating symbols and rendering differences between social groups visible (Bouzón 2008; Goldenberg 2002; Goldenberg and Ramos 2002). Thus, the physical appearance is actively changed in order to provide the other with the desired information (Malysse 2002).

The body cult brings in tow a sense of permanent dissatisfaction with one's figure (Sabino 2000) – that relates to the impossibility of satisfaction discussed by Bauman (2001) – which becomes evident when Edmonds (2002) shows that plastic surgery seems to transcend mere compliance with a standard, and becomes the endless pursuit of an ever-more elusive goal. Edmonds (2002) attributes the growing acceptance of plastic surgery to the democratization of beauty and the belief in a link between self-esteem and physical appearance. So,

plastic surgery appears both as a need for conformity with cultural mores and as a means of bridging the gap between how women are viewed, and how they actually are or feel.

Schouten (1991), in a study of men and women in the US, suggests one reason for plastic surgery is dissatisfaction with a particular feature or part of the body. Negative body self-images can appear during adolescence or be triggered by critical remarks of a child's body. He also finds evidence that plastic surgery led to improved self-esteem and feelings of enhanced physical attraction and self-confidence. Furthermore, plastic surgery appeared to act in the transition of roles. In the study by Askegaard et al. (2002), with women aged 30 to 60, the respondents are divided according to their goals as to the plastic surgery: some cited personal wellbeing; others cited the desire to become more attractive to others. The respondents demonstrated conflicts and contradictions when expressing their true motivations for surgery.

The quantitative study of Pentina et al. (2009) highlights the motivational role of perceived discrepancies between actual and ideal self in choosing cosmetic surgery by young women. The authors also point out to social support as a moderating effect in their decisions – being the support of friends an encouragement to the enhancement of the body. Mowen et al. (2009) investigated the trait predictors of cosmetic surgery. One of their findings is that individuals tending to plastic surgery may view their bodies as like any other resource – it can be molded in order to achieve their goals, as anticipated by Le Breton (2003).

METHODOLOGY

This study aims to extend the understanding of the relation between body-related consumption and identity construction by examining young women's decision and experience of transforming their identity and their body through plastic surgery. To do that, we seek to understand, among other things, how they use plastic surgery in order to make sense of themselves in their world; what they seek to get out of plastic surgery; how the cultural context influences their choice of transforming their body through plastic surgery.

Since the research topic required an understanding of "detailed individual experiences, choices and personal biographies," (Gaskell 2002, 78) and due to the sensitive nature of the subject matter, which could cause anxiety or discomfort in respondents (Gaskell 2002), we opted for semi-structured, in-depth individual interviews. The research objectives required a broader understanding of the women interviewed, of the decision-making process involving surgery, and of changes experienced by them post-surgery. So, we use a life-history narrative approach (Atkinson 1998; Woodruffe-Burton and Elliott 2005) in the script.

Fourteen interviews were conducted. Data collection was halted when it was deemed to be close to saturation point (Gaskell 2002). All interviews were conducted in Rio de Janeiro and were recorded, generating 912 minutes of material, the equivalent to 215 typed pages of transcripts. The interviewees were selected via personal recommendations. The selection criteria parameters were a) female gender; b) age between 20 and 35; c) underwent plastic surgery prior to having children. The option for exploring women's issues exclusively was due to differences regarding gender vis-à-vis motivations, needs and ways to use the body as a means of expression (Goldenberg and Ramos 2002; Sabino 2000). The age group and the issue of motherhood are related to the goal of understanding the consumption of plastic surgery separately from issues of aging and body changes caused by pregnancy. The option for residents of Rio de Janeiro was to be able to hear women inserted in the same context of bodily esteem and subjected to similar aesthetic standards, as well as to facilitate the researchers' access to respondents.

The following figure profiles each of the young women interviewed:

The interview protocol was developed primarily based on the findings of Schouten (1991) and Askegaard et al. (2002). The interview script was used as a device for the analysis of transcripts (Gaskell 2002), dividing the interviews in major areas of analysis.

Data analysis was inspired by the technique of discourse analysis (Gill 2002).

In the next sections, we present the findings divided into three topics: *the before*, life stories influenced by the other and by the context; *the moment*, which deals primarily with the motivations and incentives behind the decision for surgery; and *the after*, which examines transformations experienced by the women after the surgery.

Table 1. Profile of women interviewed

Name	Age	Surgery
Alice	30	Liposuction + Breast implants
Ana	27	Breast implants
Angela	25	Breast Reduction
Antônia	31	Breast Reduction
Camila	30	Rhinoplasty + Breast implants
Carla	24	Liposuction + Breast implants
Celeste	32	Liposuction and Liposculpting + Breast implants

Name	Age	Surgery
Fátima	22	Breast implants
Ilda	30	Liposuction
Luana	23	Breast implants
Monica	28	Breast implants
Monique	26	Liposuction of the buttocks
Nadia	25	Liposuction
Tânia	26	Breast implants

The before: life stories influenced by the other and by the context

If identity is based on differences and similarities and depends on the validation of others (Jenkins 2005; Ransome 2005), and the body is the means of exhibiting one's identity, it follows that the body seems extremely susceptible to comparison and to influence of others' gazes. Examination of the life stories points to bodily changes experienced during adolescence as possible sources of dissatisfaction that somehow drove these women to plastic surgery (Schouten 1991). It seems possible to relate the requirements of body modification expressed by respondents to the reflective nature that the body assumes in modernity (Giddens 2002), that is, the constant questioning of one's own body, the medium through which identity is displayed. Body shape seems to have a decisive role in forging the identity of these young people: the absence of breasts during adolescence can lead them to resemble either the male gender or younger children; overly large breasts or excess weight may distance them from the female standard they seek to emulate and that the media pushes; finally, the others may be the mirror of their dissatisfactions, as the following accounts suggest:

"I looked like a little boy, completely flat-chested. I didn't feel feminine. Not just a little boy, also a kid." (Ana, 27)

"I was always a chubby child. And being chubby when you enter adolescence becomes annoying. Women don't like being chubby; woman want to be skinny. Even more so because of the stereotypes we see on television, in magazines." (Alice, 30)

Ana, Alice and Luana speak of adolescence and dissatisfaction with their bodies, perceiving them as different or outside the standard. They also speak of the influence of the vision of the body of the other on the perception that each has of her own body, and suggesting that the difference can lead to an inferiority complex, shamefulness, hate of one's own body (Lipovetsky 2000; Malysse 2002).

The importance of the body's appearance is described in the context of the socialization process, that is, to the other. Interestingly, the other appears in the narratives of interviewees' life stories

in several ways: as city, neighborhood, girl-friends, sisters, cousins, lovers, boys.

The concern with the gaze of others is evidenced, for instance, by the strategies of concealing/displaying (Thompson and Hirschman 1998) used by the interviewees to manage their image. They hide or disguise what made them unhappy with their body ("I'd wear looser clothes that wouldn't draw attention to my figure and a tight bra to try to make my bust appear smaller") and divert attention to their favorite parts using tricks such as clothing, hairstyles, or even making them the focus of the workout ("since my upper body bothered me, I always valued the lower part").

Monica's report exemplify how moving to another city changed the way she saw about her body. She reports on the difference of "aesthetic standards" between Porto Alegre, where it "was far more cool to be slim" and "uncool to have a big butt," and Rio de Janeiro, where the ideal is the woman to be "all babe." With her move to Rio, she relates how she became accustomed to the city's aesthetic standards and stopped thinking her "butt" was "so big."

Carla's story shows how a change of place of residence led her to seek aesthetic changes to adapt her body to fit in with the new social group. She moved from Nova Iguaçu to Barra da Tijuca. Nova Iguaçu is one of 13 municipalities in the Rio de Janeiro metropolitan area. It is a 830,000 inhabitants city densely populated and heavily dominated by low-income residents. During the interview, Carla explained that this neighborhood comprises a group of high-income residents to which his family belonged to, and that its members are well acquaintance to each other. Barra da Tijuca is a district of Rio de Janeiro that has undergone rapid urbanization starting in the 1980s, and is known for its influx of emerging social groups. Carla acknowledges that after moving to Barra da Tijuca she ceased to be herself ("I was me") in order to be the other in this new place with different aesthetic standards.

"My family is from Nova Iguaçu – I lived there until I was 16. In Nova Iguaçu I was *the* Carla Marques. Everybody knew my dad and my older brothers. Being chubby didn't bother me too much. Because I was *myself*. So, it was never a problem in that context. Perhaps it began to bother me [when I moved to Barra da Tijuca]. When you're off the curve, just go to the beach or open up a magazine, you'll see: the standard of beauty is being thin, to work out. I was just another Carla. I'm not going to tell I do it [work out and diet] for other people. It's for me, but it's influenced by the environment I live in. I think if I lived some place where it was irrelevant, I don't really know if I'd find it so important" (Carla, 24)

Her report also suggests that in changing social context from Nova Iguaçu to Barra da Tijuca, her social capital lost its importance to her body capital (Bourdieu 1984: 194): she became just another Carla. At her new neighborhood, the body seems to strongly mark social position replacing social capital. In order to improve her position in social space, Carla needed to revise her identity, rebuilding her body.

The moment of plastic surgery: exploring motivations

The influence of the time of life of the interviewees in deciding to undergo surgery also appears in several accounts. Some reported they were having a difficult and stressful time. Difficulties with the marriage, in dating, in relationships and work, as well as personal problems, insecurity, heartness and sadness were also mentioned by interviewees. Thus, surgery appears as a kind of compensatory consumption (Woodruffe-Burton and Elliott 2005) in less-than-favorable life situations.

As pointed by Askegaard et al. (2002), it seems possible to associate some of these feelings to the anxieties caused by the lack of permanence of contemporary relationships (Giddens 2002). Fátima (22) associates plastic surgery with the fear of losing her far-away boyfriend, or even the fear of the fragile nature of her relationships, as the following testimony indicates:

"I don't think it [silicone implant surgery] was to try to hold on to him. It was to make me feel better, to value myself more. I think, when women lose the person they like, they believe they won't find anybody else. They think he's the last man in the world and they won't find anyone better. And it's exactly the contrary: you always find someone much better than him. So I think it wasn't at all a case of his thinking 'oh! she got implants, so I'm not going to cheat on her'. Rather, it was so that, if, by chance, he did not want me anymore, I would still be happy enough with myself to find someone else just as good or better."

In this report, Fátima suggests that a new body would render her a better position in a 'relationship' market, so that if her present relationship did not work out, her new boobs would enhance her chances to find a new (better) man.

In contexts described as difficult, that include the possibility of losses, fears and stress, plastic surgery seems to be driven by a consumer expectation to make peace with self-esteem or to boost self-confidence (Askegaard et al. 2002; Schouten 1991). Thus, the experience is described as a way to "value myself," to "feel more beautiful," as an "investment in me," a "self-compensation," a "self-indulgence," or even an "incentive" to overcome difficulties or to find someone "even better." These findings are consistent with Le Breton (2003), who pointed to the use of plastic surgery by individuals in crisis – those who sought the possibility of modifying the way people saw them, their life and their relationship with the world.

The bad or difficult time of interviewees life seem to put their identities in check, thus restoring feelings present since their adolescence, and demanding an urgent answer / attitude. The plastic surgery comes as a way to modify the shape of the body and thus, rebuilt their identities and transform how others see them, and therefore their life and their relations with the world.

Transition of roles or identity (Schouten 1991) also appears as another form of incentive in this study. Celeste (32), for example, living a process of separation and, therefore, ruling out the possibility of being a mother at that time, starts the review process of her self-concept through working out, massage, greater care with her appearance and, finally, liposuction, in order to incorporate a new identity: that of an unmarried woman "back into the market."

The incongruity between physical aspects and self-concept (Schouten 1991) also appears in the discourse of some interviewees when they talk about their life stories. Plastic surgery can mark the transition between childhood (child's body) and adult life (women's body) in some cases, and may be part of a larger process of transition, as the last stage of transformations sought. Antonia (31) explains:

"I was in the process of feeling better; I'd already completed my treatment [the medication she took for hormonal disorder during early adolescence]; I was already thinner; my hair looked great. But then I discovered that the shape and the size of my breasts were not what I wanted."

Most women interviewed made it clear that they had undergone plastic surgery for themselves, regardless of others' opinions. They needed to deny the concern with the gaze of others but tended to fall into contradiction during the interview. Tania (26), a good example, contradicts herself throughout the interview. She explains that "the average Brazilian" has no bust; so, her lack of breasts was seen as "normal" in the eyes of others. Yet, in other moments during the interview, she admits that her small breasts made her "the shame of the group." Shame, according to Giddens (2002), is a result of insecurity regarding social acceptability. Tania also reveals several suggestions from others before the surgery to insert silicone breast implants, but then seems oblivious to the shame revealed when attempting once again to explain that the surgery was for her only, denying the influence of others' gazes.

Contact with a girl friend who has recently undergone plastic surgery appears in the testimonies as another factor responsible for driving respondents to make a decision regarding surgery. Some of the women admit they were "scared to death" of the procedure. Thus, proximity with a successful plastic surgery served as encouragement, a "light shove," a "breath," a sign that what they wanted to achieve "was possible," as Camila (30) revealed:

"It was already something I had wanted to do, and then, just before I did, this friend got implants. I saw hers looked good, so then I got enthused and plucked up the courage to go ahead. It was just the smallest push I needed."

This may put some light on findings from Pentina et al. (2009) regarding the moderating role of peer support. A successful surgery patient, besides allaying fears related to the procedure, seems to operationalize plastic surgery within the realm of real possibilities and out of the field of dreams.

In addiction, the accounts indicate a sort of rule or hierarchy among the types of care and control of the body. Plastic surgery – in particular, liposuction – appears in the testimonies collected here as a "last resource," something you do after "having tried everything else:" "dieting," "working out," "eating healthy." For some interviewees, women seeking directly the last level of the hierarchy – plastic surgery – are seen in poor light and judged as lazy, since they failed to spend the energy required to get their bodies in shape. Control of the body is not sufficient; it is necessary that this fact be perceived by others (Giddens 2002).

"Before getting the lipo, after I had lost weight and so on, I still didn't go to the beach because there were still fat parts on my body that refused to go away. (...) I think [plastic surgery] is perfectly valid if something is bothering you like crazy, to the point where it prevents you from going to the beach, as was my case. And, when you've tried everything else, to no avail … I don't think plastic surgery should be used as a quick-fix for every little thing you don't like." (Carla, 24)

The interviewees also describe the behavior of other women with respect to plastic surgery as overkill. They relate this overkill with an "obsession with perfection," an "unhealthy" behavior, even the "loss of sense of danger." But, after all, where might the boundary lie between overkill and acceptable? Interestingly, the overkill mindset is always ascribed to others, never to themselves. This is the case even when it comes to those who show an almost obsessive preoccupation with their few extra kilos such as Carla (24) in the previous account.

The after: experienced transformations

When asked about others' reaction toward their post-surgery, the respondents show difficulties in claiming differences were indeed perceived in their appearance and, on occasions, would end up contradicting themselves during the interview. As in the case of the Tania (26), who initially said that "many people don't know because I put in very small implants"; however, later in the interview, she comments on how "several people" told her "Wow, aren't you the big sexy woman!" Such a contradiction seems to have something to do with the concern in affirming they had undergone surgery for themselves and not for others.

Many reported that expectations regarding the expected benefits of surgery are confirmed when they relate what happened *after*. They emphasize the effects of plastic surgery on their self-esteem and self-confidence, which was also found by previous works (Schouten 1991; Askegaard et al. 2002; Edmonds 2002). However, discrepancies were apparent in the testimonials. While some said they did not believe surgery had had any effect on their social relations (i.e., relations with others), other women spoke of changes in perceived self-esteem and self-confidence and reported profound changes in their social relations and even their sexuality after surgery: "I began to feel like socializing more"; "I stopped feeling shameful of getting close to men"; "I became much more comfortable sexually." The following account by Antonia (31) is quite illustrative of the benefits admitted to:

"My life has changed: I became more confident; I was no longer embarrassed about getting close to men. I got a boyfriend right away. I became more popular among my friends. I think people saw how I was prettier, more secure. I was no longer embarrassed about going out ... people would ask me out more, and I began socializing more, too. I started feeling more sociable than before. At work, the collateral effect of self-confidence from surgery was tremendous. Got a great job soon thereafter."

Those reports suggest that plastic surgery allowed an identity renegotiation. It seems to work as an "investment", improving body capital. Their improved body capital granted them a new and more valuable position in social space. For some, this identity and position change acquired through their body transformation was so vigorous that they even state that "the surgery has changed my life!" and report feeling "like another person after the surgery".

The interviewees also recount becoming vainer after surgery. This enhanced vanity intensifies previous body care and triggers a whole constellation of body and beauty-related consumption, such as buying clothing that displayed the new body; exercise and diets with specialized professionals; massage; lymphatic drainage; cosmetics to combat cellulite and sagging; pharmaceutical drugs (cellular nutrition).

Both new consumption and beauty treatments that were stepped up after surgery indicate an effort to maintain or leverage the investment made in their body capital. Plastic surgery enhances their body capital, however maintaining it requires continuing effort and investment.

Besides mentions to improved self-esteem and self-confidence, the interviewed women commonly used words such as happiness, enthusiasm, lively and excitement to describe feelings engendered by plastic surgery. It is interesting to notice that those psychological or emotional effects of surgery are far more frequent and more emphasized during the interviews than changes in physical appearance. However, when physical effects are mentioned, they appear as harmony, proportionality, a cool or great body. The interviewees seem to avoid words with overt links to beauty. This might allude to some fear of appearing futile (Casotti et al. 2008). The testimonials suggest that the quest for self-confidence would be more legitimate than the search for beauty, as exemplified by Angela (25):

"I think people are divided into two groups. The group of people who get it [plastic surgery] because they really do have something that calls attention, that really bothers them – then they do plastic surgery. And there are the people who want to have the perfect body, and then go overboard." (Angela, 25)

FINAL DISCUSSION

By exploring young women's decision and experience of transforming their identity and their body through plastic surgery, this work extends the understanding of the relation between body-related consumption and identity construction.

The decision of undergoing a plastic surgery by the interviewees seems the result of a conjunction of elements: a longtime deep dissatisfaction or discomfort with one's body or particular body parts; a specific stressful or difficult time of life; influence of someone who had experienced a successful plastic surgery; and, finally, having tried everything else unsuccessfully, exhausting any other way of *fixing* the body.

Some of the results support the findings of Schouten (1991) and Askegaard et al. (2002), pointing similarities in consumption of plastic surgery undergone by Brazilian – specifically residents of Rio de Janeiro – Danish and US women: adolescence as a source of dissatisfaction with the body that was sought to be corrected with surgery; the role of surgery in the transition of social roles, or as complementary agent or catalyst for change; the improving self-esteem and confidence; surgery as an act of self-determination (undergone for the sake of personal wellbeing).

However the accounts seem to put the body in a higher value place in the city of Rio de Janeiro, as suggested in other studies (Malysse 2002). In Rio, body capital seems to trump social capital. And that does not work only for the 'relationship' or "marriage market" (Bourdieu 1984: 126), enhanced body capital also grants a better position in the labor market and in friendships and other social relations. Plastic surgery thus works as an investment to enhance the value of body capital so as to gain better social standing.

But it does not exhaust the efforts for a body that contributes to a successful identity and a better social position. This new position requires continued investment and effort to be sustained. These begin way before the surgery – with exercising, dieting and so on – and must be intensified and expanded after it.

The interviewees' narratives uncover the relation between plastic surgery and identity construction. The body, as part of identity and thus to its self-reflective project, is central to a successful expression of identity. But its construction depends upon interaction and negotiation with others so that, in order to create a successful expression of identity, body must conform to the reference group or the cultural norms. Although each of the interviewees has her own history regarding plastic surgery and explains the plastic as something done to herself, this body change seems fundamental to them as a means of negotiating their identities with others, as a fundamental part in the process of building a successful identity and conquering a improved position in their social space.

Interaction and negotiation with others appear repeatedly in the interviewees' narratives. They are clear in their feeling of being different and their wiliness to belong; in their concealing/displaying strategies; in their very attempt to adequate their bodies to standards through plastic surgery; when they announce their decision to peers and can access their opinions – even denying their worries about it; and, of course, when they consider their surgeon's opinion (as the girl who got a second rhinoplasty when intended to get only breast implants).

Their non-normalized body becomes a source of anxiety, dissatisfaction and reduced self-esteem. It seems they seek not for the body they dream of, but to the body cultural norms made them want to. However, this young, beautiful and *fit* body must be pursued through hard work and willpower, so as it becomes an indicator of personal success.

There's why the interviewees seem to identify the existence of a hierarchy of beauty treatments, where plastic surgery figures as a last resource. If personal success depends on a body achieved by hard work, the plastic body seems to reduce personal merit. So, the plastic surgery must be legitimized and justified! Otherwise it can be regarded as cheating and overkill, putting them in a poor light.

Legitimization is carried out through hard work previously to the surgery – as engaging in dieting, weight-loss programs and exercising. In other words, they must work hard to deserve the body in shape. But previous hard work is not enough. It's imperative to justify the plastic surgery. First of all, it's only justified only when nothing else seems to placate body dissatisfaction. But the real justification seems to occur when the interviewees describe their dissatisfactions. They present a long rationalization – that seemed aimed to themselves and to others, represented by the researchers – their "unbearable complex" or "trauma," "absolute shamefulness," and "unreasonable hassle" that can cause even a "psychological problem." It requires a lot of work to undergo plastic surgery and still cope with cultural prescriptions.

REFERENCES

Ahuvia, Aaron C. (2005), "Beyond the Extended Self: Loved Objects and Consumers' Identity Narratives," *Journal of Consumer Research*, 32 (June), 171–184.

Askegaard, Søren, Martine C. Gertsen, and Roy Langer (2002), "The Body Consumed: Reflexivity and Cosmetic Surgery," *Psychology & Marketing*, 19 (10), 793-812.

Atkinson, Robert (1998), *The life story interview*, Londres: Sage.

Banister, Emma N., and Margareth K. Hogg (2004), "Negative Symbolic Consumption and Consumers' Drive for Self-Esteem: The Case of the Fashion Industry," *European Journal of Marketing*, 38 (7), 850-868.

Baudrillard, Jean (1997), *A sociedade de consumo*, Lisboa: Edições 70.

Bauman, Zygmunt (2001), *Modernidade líquida*, Rio de Janeiro: Jorge Zahar.

Bauman, Zygmunt (2005), *Identidade*, Rio de Janeiro: Jorge Zahar.

Belk, Russell W. (1998), "Possessions and the Extended Self," *Journal of Consumer Research*, 15 (2), 139-168.

Bourdieu, Pierre (2008), *A Distinção: Crítica Social do Julgamento*, São Paulo: Edusp.

Bouzón, Patricia (2008), "Cabelos e Construção de Identidades: Incursão Antropológica em um Salão de Beleza," in *O tempo da beleza: consumo e comportamento feminino, novos olhares*, ed. Leticia M. Casotti, Maribel C. Suarez, and Roberta D. Campos, Rio de Janeiro: Senac Nacional, 228-251.

Campos, Roberta D., Maribel C. Suarez, and Leticia M. Casotti (2006), "Me Explica o que é Ser Feminina? Um Estudo sobre a Influência entre Gerações no Consumo de Cosméticos", paper presented at the 30th ANPAD meeting, Salvador, BA.

Casotti, Leticia M., Maribel C. Suarez, and Roberta D. Campos (2008), *O tempo da beleza: consumo e comportamento feminino, novos olhares*, Rio de Janeiro: Senac Nacional.

Edmonds, Alexander (2002), "No universo da beleza: notas de campo sobre cirurgia plástica no Rio de Janeiro," in *Nu & Vestido: Dez Antropólogos Revelam a Cultura do Corpo Carioca*, ed. Mirian Goldenberg, Rio de Janeiro: Record, 189-262.

Gaskell, George (2002), "Entrevistas individuais e grupais," in *Pesquisa Qualitativa com Texto, Imagem e Som: um Manual Prático*, ed. Martin W. Bauer, and George Gaskell, Petrópolis: Vozes, 64-89.

Giddens, Anthony (2002), *Modernidade e Identidade*, Rio de Janeiro: Jorge Zahar.

Gill, Rosalind (2002), "Análise de discurso," in *Pesquisa Qualitativa com Texto, Imagem e Som: um Manual Prático*, ed. Martin W. Bauer, and George Gaskell, Petrópolis: Vozes, 244-270.

Goldenberg, Mirian, ed. (2002), *Nu & Vestido: Dez Antropólogos Revelam a Cultura do Corpo Carioca*, Rio de Janeiro: Record.

Goldenberg, Mirian, ed. (2007), *O Corpo como Capital: Estudos sobre Gênero, Sexualidade e Moda na Cultura Brasileira*. Barueri, SP: Estação das Letras e Cores.

Goldenberg, Mirian, and Marcelo S. Ramos (2002), "A Civilização das Formas: O Corpo como Valor," in *Nu & Vestido: Dez Antropólogos Revelam a Cultura do Corpo Carioca*, ed. Mirian Goldenberg, Rio de Janeiro: Record, 19-40.

Goldenberg, Mirian, ed. (2007), "O Corpo como Capital,"in *O Corpo como Capital: Estudos sobre Gênero, Sexualidade e Moda na Cultura Brasileira*, ed. Mirian Goldenberg, Barueri, SP: Estação das Letras e Cores, 17-31.

Jenkins, Richard (2005), *Social Identity*, Londres: Routledge.

Kleine, Susan S., Robert E. Kleine III, and Chris T. Allen (1995), "How is a Possession "Me" or "Not Me"? Characterizing Types and an Antecedent of Material Possession Attachment," *Journal of Consumer Research,* 22 (December), 327-343.

Le Breton, David (2003), *Adeus ao corpo: Antropologia e Sociedade*, Campinas, SP: Papirus.

Lipovetsky, Gilles (2000), *A Terceira Mulher: Permanência e Revolução do Feminino*, São Paulo: Cia das Letras.

Malysse, Stéphane (2002), *"Em Busca dos (H)alteres-ego: Olhares Franceses nos Bastidores da Corpolatria Carioca,"* in *Nu & Vestido: Dez Antropólogos Revelam a Cultura do Corpo Carioca,* ed. Mirian Goldenberg, Rio de Janeiro: Record, 79-138.

McAlexander, James H. (1991), "Divorce, the Disposition of the Relationship, and Everything," *in Advances in Consumer Research,* Vol. 18, eds. Rebecca H. Holman and Michael R. Solomon, Provo, UT : Association for Consumer Research, 43-48.

McCracken, Grant (1986), "Culture and Consumption: A Theoretical Account of the Structure and Movement of the Cultural Meaning of Consumer Goods," *Journal of Consumer Research*, 13 (June), 71–84.

Mittal, Banwari (2006), "I, Me, and Mine – How Products Become Consumer's Extended Selves," *Journal of Consumer Behavior,* 5 (Nov-Dec), 550-562.

Mowen, John C., Adelina Longoria, and Amy Sallee (2009), "Burning and Cutting: Identifying the Traits of Individuals with an Enduring Propensity to Tan and to Undergo Cosmetic Surgery," *Journal of Consumer Behavior,* 8 (5), 238-251.

Pentina, Iryna, David G. Taylor, and Troy A. Voelker (2009), "The Roles of Self-Discrepancy and Social Support in Young Females' Decisions to Undergo Cosmetic Procedures," *Journal of Consumer Behaviour,* 8 (4), 149-165.

Pyszczynski, Tom, Jeff Greenberg, Sheldon Solomon, and Jamie Arndt (2004), "Why Do People Need Self-Esteem? A Theoretical and Empirical Review," *Psychological Bulletin,* 130 (3), 435-468.

Ransome, Paul (2005), *Work, Consumption & Culture: Affluence and Social Change in the Twenty-First Century,* Londres: Sage.

Sabino, Cesar (2000), "Musculação: Expansão e Manutenção da Masculinidade," in *Os Novos Desejos: das Academias de Musculação* às *Agências de Encontros,* ed. Mirian Goldenberg, Rio de Janeiro: Record, 61-104.

Schouten, John W. (1991), "Selves in Transition: Symbolic Consumption in Personal Rites of Passage and Identity Reconstruction," *Journal of Consumer Research*, 17 (March), 412-425.

Sirgy, M. Joseph (1982), "Self-Concept in Consumer Behavior: a Critical Review," *Journal of Consumer Research*, 9 (December), 287-300.

Sirgy, M. Joseph, Dhruv Grewal, Tamara F. Mangleburg, Jae-ok Park, Kye-Sung Chon, C.B. Claiborne, J.S. Johar, and Harold Berkman (1997), "Assessing the Predictive Validity of Two Methods of Measuring Self-Image Congruence," *Journal of the Academy of Marketing Science*, 25 (3), 229-241.

Thompson, Craig J., and Elizabeth C. Hirschman (1995), "Understanding the Socialized Body: a Poststructuralist Analysis of Consumers' Self-Conceptions, Body Images, and Self-Care," *Journal of Consumer Research*, 22 (September) 139-153.

Thompson, Craig J., and Elizabeth C. Hirschman (1998), "An existential analysis of embodied self in postmodern consumer culture," *Consumption Markets & Culture*, 2 (4), 401-447.

Vanzellotti, Caroline A. (2007), "A esperança no consumo de cosméticos anti-sinais," unpublished dissertation, Programa de Pós-Graduação em Administração, Universidade Federal do Rio Grande do Sul, Porto Alegre, RS, 90010-460.

Vigarello, Georges (2006), *História da Beleza: o corpo e a arte de se embelezar, do Renascimento aos dias de hoje,* Rio de Janeiro: Ediouro.

Woodruffe-Burton, Hellen, and Richard Elliott (2005), "Compensatory Consumption and Narrative Identity Theory," *in Advances in Consumer Research*, Vol. 32, eds. Geeta Menon and Akshay R. Rao, Duluth, MN : Association for Consumer Research, 461-465.

Young, Melissa M. (1991), "Disposition of Possessions During Role Transitions," *in Advances in Consumer Research*, Vol. 18, eds. Rebecca H. Holman and Michael R. Solomon, Provo, UT: Association for Consumer Research, 33-39.

Cyborg as Commodity: Exploring Conception of Self-Identity, Body and Citizenship within the Context of Emerging Transplant Technologies

Ai-Ling Lai, University of Leicester, UK

ABSTRACT

This paper explores how advances in transplant technologies shape conceptions of self-identity, embodiment and citizenship. Drawing on the posthuman writing of Donna Haraway and from phenomenological interviews, I explore ambivalence towards the commodification of the cyborg-body, suggesting that biotechnology may potentially lead to a dystopian posthuman consumer society.

INTRODUCTION

Recent developments in transplant technologies open up exciting areas of study where the amalgamation of human, animal, and automaton spawn a proliferation of cyborgic couplings and chimeras. According to Haraway (1991: 149), a cyborg is a cybernetic organism, whose hybridity obfuscates Western conception of the body and selfhood. From *restorative* transplantation (i.e. the rejuvenation of lost bodily functions through organ replacements derived from xenotransplantation[1] and artificial organs) to *regenerative medicine* (e.g. the engineering of organs through stem cell therapy and cloning), the body are becoming increasingly *plastic* (Shilling 1993), *bionic* and *engineered* (Synnott 1993; Williams 1997). Consequently, we are "thrown into radical doubt" (Shilling 1993: 3) as to what the body is, who owns it, how we should treat it and what it might become (Williams 1997). The cyborg emerges as a socio-political battlefield where boundaries between the self and 'other', human and non-human, the automaton and the organism, nature and culture, subject and object are valiantly contested (Haraway 1991). Gray (2002) argues that cyborgs are political bodies, whose corporeal status dictates the extent to which they are granted civil rights, protection, equalities and freedom in a democratic posthuman society.

This paper seeks to explore how perceptions of emerging transplant technology are shaped by conceptions of self-identity, embodiment and citizenship among the British lay public. Specifically, I consider how individuals construct embodied meanings surrounding emerging transplant technologies. In addition, this paper analyses how individuals draw on cultural resources to help them negotiate meanings pertaining to (1) personhood (*what it means to be a person*), (2) technological embodiment (*what it means to have and be cyborg-bodies*), (3) posthuman citizenship (*how technology mediates social relations between human and non-human*) and (4) body commodification (*can the cyborg-body be reified as an object for consumption*).

In doing so, this paper endeavors to answer the call to theorize posthuman identity and body in consumer research (Venkatesh et al 2002; Giesler and Venkatesh 2005; Buchanan-Oliver 2008; Campbell et al 2005). This paper recognizes the need to embrace consumers as 'embodied cyborgs' (Giesler and Venkatesh 2005: 661), whose lifeworld and social existence is intricately woven with the materiality of technology (Giesler 2004). Following Featherstone and Burrow (1995), Venkatesh (2004) envisions posthuman consumer society as 'new cultures of technological embodiment' (pp. 400), which is constituted by 'a hybrid marketplace matrix' (Giesler and Venkatesh 2005: 1). This paper illustrates how marketplace myths and cultural metaphors are appropriated by individuals to help them make sense of the relationship between nature and

---

[1] Xenotransplantation involves the incorporation of living organs and tissues from a different species (usually animals such as pigs) to another (human beings).

technology (Thompson 2004). In doing so, I aim to contribute to previous writings by Johnson and Roberts (1997) and Belk (1990). Most notably, these scholars observe how the marketing of organ transplantation has previously been predicated on the 'mechanistic' metaphor of the body (Belk 1990). This metaphor is consistent with the 'technocratic' view, which presents technology as progressive and optimistic (Johnson and Roberts 1997). I now review the theoretical underpinning of cyborg embodiment and the slippery slope of its commodification within the context of emerging transplant technology.

Cyborg Embodiment and Commodification in Emerging Transplant Technology

Seale et al (2006) contend that body fragmentation and commodification are prominent themes in biomedicine, as it involves the disintegration of the body into isolated parts, which concurrently renders it susceptible to the process of objectification. Such mechanistic view of the body is grounded in the dualistic philosophy of Cartesianism, which privileges the mind over the body. For Descartes, the mind constitutes the seat of consciousness (*res cogitans*) that defines one's personhood (soul). Conversely, the body is a palpable material object that extends into space (*res extensa*) – and as such, is divisible and subjected to the laws of physics (Sawday 1996). As a machine that houses the conscious mind/soul, the body is deemed to be lacking in intentionality and intellect.

Elsewhere, Sharp (2000) argues that "commodification insists upon objectification in some form, transforming persons and their bodies from a human category into objects of economic desires" (pp. 293). According to Hogle (1995), advances in transplant technologies can potentially erase the cyborg-body of its personal history and cultural trappings; thereby objectifying it as a valuable commodity for exchange (Marx 1867/1976). As such, the medical cyborg is devoid of *intentionality* as a purposeful being (Heidegger 1927/1962). Instead, biomedicine transforms cyborg into a new category of species that are equipped with a new purpose or what Aristotle calls *telos* – i.e. "different categories of biological species has its own form of flourishing, of being true to itself" (Bowring 2003: 133). For Heidegger, treating a 'living organism' in an objectifying manner is tantamount to an act of depersonalization, which withdraws from them, their rights to dignity, mystery and humanity.

Fox and Swazey (1992) argue that the widening gap in the supply and demand of organs has fuelled medical and cultural fervour towards 'spare part pragmatism', which is predicated on the vision of the "replaceable body and limitless medical progress, and the escalating ardor about the life-saving goodness of repairing and remaking people in this fashion" (pp. xv). In *Human Body Shop: The Cloning, Engineering and Marketing of Life*, Kimbrell (1993) documented how the growing market for 'human products' (including blood, organs, tissues and reproductive cells) have alienated individuals from their bodies and from others, leading to disputes over ownership, distribution of profits and exploitations of the disenfranchised. As Bowring (2003) argues, the body is already a form of commodity in the modern world. Within the context of emerging transplant technology, the commodification of the body takes different forms – namely artificial organs, xenotransplantation and regenerative transplantation – which I will now discuss in turn.

The Bionic Body –
The Manufacturing of Artificial Organs

Langer and Vacanti (1995) advocate the need to close the gap in organ shortages by moving towards the 'manufacturing' of organs. Heart valves, pacemakers, artificial hip joints, prosthetic arms and legs, and synthetic lenses are now regularly implanted in human bodies (Sharp 2000: 311). As Haraway (1991) argues, "we *are* all hybrids of machine and organism, in short we are all *already* cyborgs" (pp. 150). More recently, the pioneering trial of AbioCor artificial heart in 2001 raises many ethical questions concerning its commodifying potentials. Fox and Swazey (2004) witness how an industry has mushroomed around the manufacturing and maintenance of mechanical hearts. Similarly, Gray (2002) contends that due to the mythological and metaphorical resonance of the heart (Manning-Steven 1997), promotion of artificial organ research by companies (usually established by researchers and medical corporations) is likely to generate profit due to its publicity alone.

Dumit and Davis-Floyd (1998) observe the paradoxical nature of cyborg as an *enhancer* as well as a *mutilator*. As cyborgs are potentially 'better than human', it holds great promises in enhancing our lives (life-saving) while at the same time harbouring destructive potential that threatens 'the loss of our identity' (pp. 13). The cyborg-as-machine invokes images of technological determination (Haraway 1991), in which man is rendered inert, dependent and de-skilled in relation to the powerful and self-regulating machine (Holland 1995). However, Haraway (1991) urges us to recognize the emancipatory potential of such fusion, claiming that how we define our relationship to cyborgs is predicated on an instinct for survival (pp. 153).

Chimera and Organ Pharming – Xenotransplantation

More recently, breakthroughs in genetic engineering has made possible the 'manufacturing' of body parts through organ 'pharming' – which involves the transfer of human genes into animal DNA to produce medically desirable substances (Bowring 2003). The hybrid genes are then inseminated into surrogate animals that carry the embryo to term, and in doing so, give birth to chimeric offspring known as transgenic animals. Gray (2002) suggests that the cloning of Dolly the Sheep has served as a factory prototype towards subsequent organ pharming. Clark (1999) warns that xenotransplantation can potentially lead to the production of organs on an industrial scale as it has the potential to reduce organ shortages by turning transgenic animals into a 'bioreactor' and 'pharmaceutical factory' of organs (Bowring 2003). The use of pig heart valves for transplantation has become common practice (Clark 1999). Indeed pigs are often regarded as ideal donors as their organs are of similar size to humans and more importantly, they can be bred on a larger scale and thus, providing an unlimited source of organs (Gallagher 2011). Gallaher postulates that there will be a shift from cadaveric transplantation towards 'growing your own organs'. The customizing of organs is a promising prospect as 'replacement' body parts can be 'pharmed' using personalized stem cells from the patient to reduce chances of organ rejection. In 1997, Dr. Jay Vacanti shocked the world by growing a human ear from cartilage cells on the back of a mouse (now famously known as the Vacanti Mouse). This leads scientists to believe that similar techniques can be applied to pave the way towards the tissue engineering of livers and hearts that are tailor-made to work with the patient's immune system (BBC News 2002).

Xenotransplantation is controversial because it destabilizes our conception of 'what is natural' (Williams 1997). According to Haraway (1991) "transgenic border-crossing signifies serious challenges to the 'sanctity of life' for many members of Western cultures" (pp.

217). This is not surprising as Douglas (1902/1966) argues; the solidarity of human society is modeled on corporeal solidarity and purity, which is impermeable by 'others'. Consequently, the violation of body boundaries signifies 'danger' since it "transgresses the symbolic boundaries of broader body politic" (Grosz 1994: 194). Haraway (1997) explains that Western culture has historically been preoccupied with racial purity, categories sanctioned by nature and the integrated self. She went on to explain that the distinction between nature and culture is sacred to Western society. The breaching of the human body by non-human species threatens to defile the purity of mankind (Douglas 1902/1966), disrupt the lineage of nature and potentially compromise the integrity of species (Haraway 1997). Following Deitch (1992), Featherstone and Burrows (1995) speculate that as genetic engineering and nanotechnology become routinized, "the next generation could very well be the last 'pure' human" (pp. 3). I now review the implications of genetic engineering in transplant technology.

The Engineered Body - Regenerative Transplantation

While the prospect of organ manufacturing and 'pharming' are fast becoming a reality, recent developments in genetic engineering, stem cell therapy and cloning push the frontier further towards the *engineering, regeneration* and *propagation* of bodies (Williams 1997). Stem cell research has created a possibility for cultivating tissues and organs from embryonic stem cells to be used for organ transplantation. More controversially, the propagation of embryonic stem cells may potentially lead to the cloning of human embryos for medical purposes. Therapeutic cloning has already been clinically trial to treat diabetes, Parkinson's and Alzheimer's disease. Therapeutic cloning involves the fusing of a human egg cell with the DNA of the person to be cloned. The fusion then cultivates embryonic stem cells that can then be used to generate transplant-ready tissues that are identical to the recipient's DNA, while the embryo is destroyed (Bowring 2003). Meanwhile reproductive cloning involves the implantation of a cloned embryo into a woman's uterus to facilitate the birth of a cloned child. The UK legislation has relaxed its rule concerning therapeutic cloning since 2001 but has maintained its prohibition against reproductive cloning (Human Fertilisation and Embryology Act 2008). However, Bowring doubts that such measures will be sustainable in the longer run as this involves global coalition against human cloning. He believes that therapeutic cloning will eventually lead down the slippery slope of reproductive cloning in countries where cloning for medical research is permitted. Bowring questions whether the eventual legalization of reproductive cloning may erupt in a political dispute over body ownership and create a 'monstrous caste system, one in which an entire category of persons, while perhaps labeled untouchable, is marginalized as not fully human." (pp. 203).

In addition, Gray (2002) is concerned that the trend toward human cloning may be perpetuated by reproductively challenged parents, who are already fervent advocates for *in vitro* fertilization and surrogacy. Most notably, he observes a worrying trend of parents attempting to conceive children in the hope that their newborn would be a compatible donor for their sick children. In a widely publicised case, the Ayala family made medical history for donating the bone marrow of their child Marissa, who was born to save the life of her sister Anissa. The Times Magazine featured the case in a cover story in June 1991, constructing it as a moral dilemma involving the 'tyranny of the gift-of-life' (Fox and Swazey 1992). The Times coverage generated outrage among the public who felt that the Ayala's case evoked 'baby farming, cannibalizing for spare parts' (Morrow 2001). The controversy surrounding the birth of Marissa centres on concerns over the violation of the sanctity of life, where 'the baby was ordered up to serve a means, as a biological supply vehicle' (Morrow 2001). In 2000, a couple from Denver, Lisa and Jack Nash, gave birth to Baby Adam, who is genetically screened and conceived through IVF to ensure his tissues matches with that of his sister (BBC News 2000). Baby Adam is hailed as the world's first 'designer baby', whose story become popularised in Jodi Picoult's novel, My Sister's Keeper.

The genetic manipulation and cloning of cyborg-babies inadvertently evokes eugenic discourse among critics (Gray 2002; Bowring 2003). Bowring envisions a posthuman society that upholds the breeding and engineering of superior children (positive eugenics) while eliminating and destroying 'inferior' gene lines (negative eugenics). Western history is steeped in the anxiety of negative eugenics, which constitutes the central ideology of Nazism to preserve the purity of the Aryan race. Consequently, race and class prejudices become intensified through high technologies (Schmidt and Moore 1998). However, Kimbrell (1993) argues that the extermination of inferior embryos is likely to be executed through 'commercial eugenics'. He foresees the growth of a new industry specialising in the marketing of designing and selecting desirable genetic traits of children, thereby preventing the birth of those who do not fit the 'perfect baby' mold. Mentor (1998) contends that the marketisation of 'designer babies' is likely to emphasise consumer choice as a proponent to humanise the logic for 'wanting the best for my baby':

> "Contemporary moves to eugenics will look less like *Brave New World's* state control and more like niche marketing and consumer choice. Postmodern eugenics will involve boundary-shifting discourses that import breeding logic into medicine, cloaked in the language of technology that mediates and 'humanizes' this logic. This will happen partly because current discourses on pregnancy and birth already include elements of eugenics and market language, so that 'I want what's best for my baby' moves easily into a demand for medicalised versions of 'the best.'" (pp. 83)

In short, breakthroughs in emerging transplant technologies are redefining corporeal boundaries leading to a proliferation of cyborgs, chimeras and hybrids, whose liminality problematizes traditional meanings of personhood, embodiment and citizenship. It is therefore at the border that these meanings are being negotiated. As Haraway (1991) maintains, "the cyborg is a kind of disassembled and reassembled, postmodern collective and personal self" (pp. 163). She calls for the need to create a *politicoscietific community* as a mean to achieve participatory public action towards the democratization of technoscientific liberty (Haraway 1997). Similarly, Davies and Burgess (2004) argue that the legitimization of medical knowledge and public policy should be achieved through a deliberative dialogue that is inclusive of the citizens. This is important as public trust in medical knowledge relies on individuals actively reflecting on their perception of risks, which is "intimately bound up with cultural beliefs, moral values, personal feelings and the social and material circumstances of their lives" (Williams and Calnan 1996: 1614). Through a phenomenological perspective, this paper seeks to explore lay perceptions among the British Public by understanding how conceptions of self-identities, the body and citizenship are implicated in negotiating the paradox between the life-saving promises and commodifying potentials of emerging transplant technologies.

METHODOLOGY

A phenomenological approach (Thompson et al 1997) is adopted to explore how participants construct meanings of posthuman

embodiment in the context of emerging transplant technologies. As Bates et al (2005) suggest public understanding and acceptance of scientific knowledge need to be translated into personally meaningful information. As such, a phenomenological approach is useful as it considers the multiplicity of participants' socio-cultural and historical frame of reference to reveal personal yet ethically complex meanings surrounding these technologies.

14 phenomenological active interviews were conducted with members recruited from the British public. Exploring lay perception is important as consumption of medical knowledge and technology are often legitimized and given credentials through citizen activity (Haraway 1997). This can be achieved using participatory dialogue (Davies and Burgess 2004). This study therefore adopted the active interviewing technique (Holstein and Gubrium 1995), which involves the researcher collaborating with the interviewee to develop a mutually engaging dialogue concerning a particular topic. Here, the interviewer acts as a co-author to facilitate participants' reflexivity on the socio-historical processes that shape their personal views on emerging transplant technology.

In order to derive a fine-grained analysis of participants' narratives, interview excerpts from 5 participants are presented in this paper. In particular, I analyse how participants use language to 'perform' and 'construct' meanings surrounding transplant technology and cyborg embodiment (Holstein and Gubrium 1995). I consider how these meanings are expressed through culturally familiar metaphors, myths, ideologies and common expressions/euphemisms, which reflect common sense beliefs as well as folk knowledge (Thompson 1997). This paper is derived from a broader study, which explores meanings and experiences of embodiment and organ donation among young adults (aged 21-30)[2]. As participants would be expected to discuss intimate experience of how they relate to their bodies, it was deemed more appropriate to interview only female participants as the researcher is also female.

ANALYSIS AND DISCUSSION

An analysis of participant's narratives reveals 3 emerging themes. The participants in this study recognize that the cyborg-body conceived through new transplant technologies is at once an *enhancer* and a *mutilator* (Dumit and Davis-Floyd 1998). While acknowledging the life-saving potential of emerging transplant technologies, the participants question the extent to which such developments (1) violate the purity of their humanness and self-identity that may in turn leads to the (2) objectification of the cyborg-body as a medical commodity. Consequently, they envisage how these new form of transplant technologies may bring about the (3) inclusion/exclusion of these posthuman cyborgs in posthuman society.

Theme 1: Violation of Human Purity - Embodying Integrated/Fragmented Identities

For the participants in this study, emerging transplant technologies challenges their assumption about what it means to be human, which is grounded in *having* and *being* a bounded body (Seale et al 2006; Douglas 1902/1966). They are perturbed by the hybridity of the human/machine/animal coupling, fearing that such union may eradicate their personhood and compromise their sense of humanity (Hallam et al 1999; Douglas 1902/1966; Haraway 1991). For ex-

---

[2] Young adults (aged 21-30) were interviewed because they are considered as a salient group to the marketing of organ donation. They are more likely to be confronted with the request to join the donor registry when obtaining their driving licence or registering with a GP when attending university (Prottas 1983; Thukral and Cummins 1987). Further research is now being conducted among wider members of the British public to include participants from different demographics.

ample, the cyborg is described as '*not a real person*', '*less human*' and '*degraded*', as Neve explains below:

> *There is a film. Can't remember what it is called now. He is a robot....well...it is a set in the future where he is basically a robot but I think that one day he gets a real organ put inside him. And cause he always felt like he is not a real person cause ....he is like 'I haven't got a real heart'......So maybe if I have got a mechanical heart I'd feel that I wasn't a real person. Yeah I think I might feel like that. Yeah I wouldn't feel like I'm a real person maybe or like a less of a human or something was missing or something wasn't quite right.* (Neve, Interview 1)

Drawing on the popular genre of a cyborg film, Neve envisions how the merging of organism with machine has reinforced her conviction that the body, and specifically the heart, is the seat of one's humanness (Manning-Steven 1997). For Neve, the film romanticizes the supremacy of human beings over machines (robots), which are built as an inferior replica of the human body. The absence of a '*real human heart*' renders the robot 'incomplete' as '*he always felt like he is not a real person*'. The capacity to 'feel' is invoked as a signifier of humanness in cyborg films (Holland 1995: 162). Here, Neve depicts the emotional anguish of the robot as he laments that '*he hasn't got a real heart*' and thus euphemizes the monstrosity and callousness of the cyborg-machine. Hence, the transplantation of a human heart into the robotic body is significant as it humanizes the robot as a sentient machine, and concurrently, fetishizes the heart as an indubitable source of emotion (Manning-Steven 1997). This theme has consistently foregrounded cyborg films. Most notable of which is the 2009 movie, Terminator Salvation. In the film, Marcus Wright, the humanoid protagonist solemnly ponders, "*What is it that makes us human? It's not something you can program. You can't put it into a chip. It's the strength of the human heart. The difference between us and machines.*" Such a narrative privileges the materiality of the body over the immateriality of the mind (programmable consciousness), thus inverting the Cartesian dictum from '*I think therefore I am*' to '*I feel therefore I am*'. Such a view merely fortifies the boundary that separates the body from the mind instead of dissolving it. Haraway (1991) argues that as technology progressively encroaches on our body, we are recalled to embrace an imagined organic body as a form of resistance. By occupying an embodied perspective, Neve expresses her ambivalence towards the incorporation of a mechanical heart, claiming that this would dehumanize her (*like a less of a human)* and potentially lead to the mechanization of her body. Neve envisages that the 'replacement' of an organic heart with a mechanical device will render her incomplete (*something was missing*) and artificial (*I wouldn't feel like I'm a real person*). The view that the transplantation of a mechanical heart necessarily eradicates one's capacity for emotion is not shared by all participants, as epitomized by Willa below:

> *I don't like the idea of organs being ...from somebody else's body. It is a sort of intrusion of somebody else's body part I suppose. It's not mine; it's not natural to my body. The idea of actually receiving somebody's blood, I don't like it. If they could sort of manufacture blood, in a laboratory, that would be much better than the idea of having out of some person. Um, you know, if they could sort of build them, you know, like a mechanical heart, I would rather have them, than either the human heart or the pig heart, um, yeah Mechanical organs? Yeah, absolutely no problem. Yes, I mean that would be my happiest option or the option that I would have...the least difficulty with. Although, I don't know how it would feel if it was a heart,*

> *you know, whether one would somehow at some level feel less of a human. I'm just thinking of the Tin Man from....erm...The Wizard of OZ..... when he said, "If I only had a heart". I think I'd feel fine about having a mechanical heart cos I know that my heart is not really where my feelings are coming from Erm... there's much for me there's much less emotional issue around mechanical organs. With a pig's heart...it's just like a very basic level feeling of rejection, you know, that it would be like I was somehow less human. And I think I wouldn't want anybody to know I had a pig's heart. I think I might feel ashamed on some level. You'd be the girl with the pig's heart, you know. Erm..... you'd be part pig. Pigs have always been a symbol of dirtiness and uncleanliness, unclean pigs. You dirty pig.* (Willa, Interview 1)

In her narrative, Willa espouses the optimistic promise afforded by the 'manufacturing' of body parts (Langer and Vacanti 1995), claiming that this will reduce the emotional resonance of sourcing organs from a 'living' being (human and animal/pig). Here, Willa adopts a technocratic viewpoint (Johnson and Roberts 1997) suggesting that the spare-part pragmatism (Fox and Swazey 1992) of '*manufacturing blood*' and '*building mechanical heart*' will resolve the need for '*intruding*' the bodies of '*others*'. For Willa, human and animals are 'living' organisms with intentionality or *telos* (Heidegger 1945/1962; Bowring 2003) and therefore are entitled to the ownership of their bodies. As such, the thought of incorporating a 'living' organ into her body is 'unnatural' as this constitutes an infringement of body ownership (*it's not mine*) and dissolves the 'natural' boundaries between the self and others (*somebody else's body*).

Like Neve, the heart occupies a metaphorical space as a signifier of personhood and humanness for Willa. When considering the prospect of receiving a mechanical heart, Willa enacts the cultural representation of the Tin Man (or Tin Woodman in the novel), a character created by Frank Baum, which was later popularized in the film The Wizard of Oz. According to Ritter (1997), the Tin Man is a symbolic allegory of a dehumanized industrial worker, who was transformed from a loving being into a 'heartless' machine by the Wicked Witch of the East. Baum depicts how the Tin Man was gradually divested of his body parts, which were then replaced by tin. His mechanical body increases the efficiency and productivity of his work. As such, Ritter suggests that the Tin Man's life is a cautionary tale depicting the mechanization of the body by technology. The tale warns of the 'dehumanizing effects of industrialism and the machine age' (pp. 181). More significantly, The Tin Man is deprived of a heart (*If I only had a heart*), which symbolizes 'the loss of soul' and his capacity to love (Ritter 1997). Drawing on these cultural meanings, Willa briefly entertains the possibility that receiving a mechanical heart may compromise her sense of humanness (*feel less of a human*). However she later shifts her interpretive standpoint, claiming that the heart is "*not really where my feelings are coming from.*"

For Willa, the thought of incorporating a pig's heart into her body is deemed more problematic as this does not only dehumanize her (*I was somehow less human*) but on symbolic level, it constitutes a degradation of her personhood. She does not only *own* a pig's heart (*having*) rather she *is* '*part pig*' (*being*). The prospect of embodying a 'pig/human' self (*chimera*) therefore evokes in her a feeling of '*shame*' as she feels '*rejected*' by a society that has symbolically demean pigs as '*dirty*' and '*unclean*'. Xenotransplantation therefore defiles the purity of her human lineage and reduced her to her animality (Haraway 1991).

Theme 2: Spare Parts Factory - Cyborg-Body as Medical Commodity

As evident in Theme 1, participants fear the dehumanizing aspect of emerging transplant technology. Specifically, they question whether the body will be stripped of its human trappings and thus renders it suitable for mass-production (Sharp 2000). In light of this, my participants are concerned with the social benefit and cost of emerging transplant technology, specifically with regards to issues of animal and human/cyborg welfare. Images of '*transgenic animal and robot factories*', '*spare parts industry*', '*stocked cupboard of body parts*' and '*organ farming*' dominate participants' imagination, as evident in Michaela's narrative below:

If you see kind of like....a pyramid, you know, animals being right at the bottom and then humans....Although I'm kind of .....believe in animal's rights..... like you shouldn't farm animals just to cut them up and put them in another people. I kind of take an overall belief I suppose. If it can feel pain...then I shouldn't do it. But you SHOULD if it's going to save our lives, you know. Obviously humans come as a priority over animals any day. And even though I am vegetarian, I still really appreciate that. When they farm animals especially for organ donation, I suppose, erm......they are not.....that's....that's their purpose....(it's) giving them a purpose....they are not....their only purpose in life is to be cut up and put inside us, if you see what I mean. Erm.....I suppose...this isn't particularly nice. But then again, I won't ever put the life of say, a pig over the life of a human even if I don't know them. You know, when it comes to weighing up your priorities, humans are much more important than say pigs or anything else. (Michaela, Interview 1, emphasis by participant)

For Michaela, the relationship between human and animals are organized in a pyramidal hierarchy, whose social position is predicated on their moral status. Singer (1990) calls this 'moral hierarchy', where sentient animals (such as human and primate) are accorded higher moral consideration as they are conscious of their existence and demonstrate *intentionality* for living (Heidegger 1927/1962). Meanwhile, organisms which are not self-aware and lack the *intentionality* for living occupy a lower status within the hierarchy (Singer 1990). For Michaela, the consciousness and intentionality that define one's being is founded on one's ability to '*feel pain*'. For Singer (1990), the pain and suffering of farm animals outweigh the pleasure of meat-eating by human. Such a view is largely grounded in the consequentialist (teleological) paradigm of ethics (Bowring 2003). Michaela is careful when justifying her support for xenotransplantation. On the one hand, she adopts a consequentialist standpoint, explaining that the farming of animals for transplantation is unjustifiable as the indignity and pain inflicted on animals (*if it can feel pain*) are tantamount to their objectification as commodities (*to cut them up and put them in another people*). On the other hand, Michaela emphasizes that the life of a human 'should' take precedence over the lives of animals (*humans come as a priority over animals*). For her, the farming of animals for organ transplantation is in itself an ethical act since it ennobles transgenic animals with a new *telos* (Bowring 2003), whose purpose in life is to save the lives of human beings. Michaela express her view in a 'matter-of-fact' manner, acknowledging that though organ farming is '*not nice*', it is nevertheless fundamental to the preservation of the human species. However, such a view is contested by other participants, as Willa's narrative shows:

Oh yes, and my concern also is that the animals, that if that became a normal thing to do, you know, the animals would be bred for it. I mean to me that's similar to animals who are being bred for meat on a large scale....erm....and you know, I have an issues with that, and I would have an issue also really with....I don't think that humans should be living at the expense of a species like that. I think....to me that is unnatural. I hate the idea of factories of animals being bred to be taken apart. The pig hadn't chosen to be a donor. Erm.....and...I don't know, you know that...I don't like the idea of animals being bred just to be donors. (Willa, Interview 2)

Willa fears that the routinization of xenotransplantation will lead to the '*breeding of animals*' on an industrial scale, which she contends is akin to the '*factory farming of animals*' in meat production. Unlike Michaela, Willa adhered strictly to the consequentialist paradigm of ethics, claiming that '*human should not live at the expense of animals*' as it disrespects the sanctity of other life forms (Haraway 1991). For Willa, animals (pigs) are living beings who has an inherent right to be free (Bowring 2003). The farming of animals for the purpose of transplantation is '*unnatural*' as it is a violation of their freedom since '*the pig hadn't chosen to be a donor.*' By reassigning their *telos* as organ donors (*just to be donors*), xenotransplantation potentially transforms animals into medical by-products or spare parts within the biomedical machine. This sentiment is shared by other participants, as Chloe's narrative demonstrates:

Well first when you hear cloning, it's like warning bells going off and you think, "No! That's all wrong." Yeah...erm...it does sound scary. I think there's like a taboo that goes with the word 'cloning' and the kind of like meaning that goes with it. Erm... yeah, it's tricky business, this cloning. If you can sort it out yourself like you say, can have a clone...erm...then you are probably more guaranteed obviously the match and you don't have to rely on somebody...somebody else's lost of life. So it's almost very BIZZARRE. Like a film where you can see these people kind of like, cloning themselves and fill in like a little stock cupboard of "just-in-case" you know, you need a spare parts (laugh). There was a case about parent wanting to clone one of their child to give life ....just to save the other one. And now that I really couldn't get my head around. There are a lot of moral questions that underpin it really. You just see people cloning themselves wholly or cloning their children because they want the child in a specific way. I don't really agree with that because I feel that you know, you are individual and you should be individual. Erm...but if...if there's a way of. Like when I said earlier, if I couldn't have children then I am not meant to have children. Sometimes people just aren't meant to live. And I don't know. Cloning babies and stuff like that just doesn't sound right to me. It sounds like we have taken it too far. (Carmen, Interview 2)

Carmen's narrative can be considered as a cautionary tale against reproductive cloning. For her, the cloning of a human for the purpose of transplantation is a social '*taboo*' since it crosses the line (*taken it too far*) of what is 'natural' (Haraway 1991) or in Carmen's words '*meant to be*'. On the one hand, Carmen acknowledges the therapeutic promise of organ cloning, claiming that this will ensure a '*guaranteed match*' of tissues that will prevent the transplanted organs from being rejected by the patient's immune system. In addition, the cloning of organs circumvents the need for 'cannibalizing' on the death of another. However, Carmen remains perturbed by the absurdity of reproductive cloning as this conjures up '*bizarre*' images of cloned-body-parts being '*stocked up*' as '*spare parts*' ready for the production line of organ transplantation. Though misguided, Carmen is aghast by stories of parents who opted to 'clone' their children to save the life of a sick sibling (Gray 2002). For her, this raises moral questions concerning the inherent value of the cloned child as a living being. More importantly, Carmen is concerned that the cloning of children for transplantation will lead to the creation of 'designer babies' (*because they want the child in a specific way*). For Carmen, such a practice is depersonalizing as it withdraws from the cloned-child, his '*individuality*' as a unique being (Haraway 1991; Mentor 1998). For Carmen, medical technology (such as reproductive cloning) disturbs the 'natural order of life' as '*sometimes people just aren't meant to live.*'

Theme 3: Cyborg Citizenship - Inclusion and Exclusion in Human Society

As demonstrated in Theme 2, most participants are adamant that the rights of posthuman cyborgs (eg. the cloned child and xenospecies/animals) should be respected as they are deemed as living 'subjects' with '*unique personality*' and '*human qualities*'. This leads participants to ponder the social ramification of transplant technologies as it has the potential to alter family dynamics and kinship. At its extreme, participants envisage that such technologies, in particular, organ cloning will inadvertently breed a new class of '*cloned race*', whose social position is subordinated to the '*pure human race*'. Consequently, they will be marginalized as the '*underclass*', '*half-bred*' or '*underdog.*' This is illustrated in Estelle's narrative below:

That's another debatable thing. Like the couple that had....was it a clone....a clone embryo inserted....so they had a baby that had the matching tissue for their son to cure him. Err...and it could be brilliantly... just the fact that it is brilliant the one son get to obviously live longer. And you celebrate....you'd worship the son where it came from cause they save your life and you would almost always think of them really fondly. But that could be really damaging. The fact that they could think, "Oh! I was just produced to help my brother. I wasn't born out of love."...like when a child was being born out of a one night stand. The whole idea of that is horrible... I think that could cause problems cause they really might be like, "oh what's the point of me being here if it was just for them." And then they would always possibly see themselves as the underdog to their siblings or something. That's a bit scary because erm... the fact with cloning ....one always just die early and it is just....the fact that they are being used for organ transplant rather than having just a great life as the person they were cloned from. The chances are that they do die or they have like.... a mutation and they are not...they are not quite right (laugh). I think that's a bit sad because you are producing something when you know the risks are really high that it's going to have a low quality of life. (Estelle, Interview 1)

In this narrative, Estelle questions the gifting dynamics underpinning a clone-sibling donation, claiming that this will marginalize the cloned child to a secondary status as an '*underdog to his sick sibling.*' Fox and Swazey (1992) call this the 'tyranny of the gift'. In other words, the cloned child is 'obligated' to donate lifesaving tissues for his sibling, whose sickness brought about his conception in the first place. As such, the identity of the cloned child is inextricably bound to his sibling as they become entangled in each other's lives. Such a bond alters the dynamics of sibling relationships, where the cloned child may be '*worshipped*' and '*celebrated*' for his lifesaving sacrifice. However, Estelle argues that such sacrificial ideal also

reveals a '*damaging*' burden for the cloned child, whose purpose in life (*telos*) centres on being his brother's keeper (*I was just produced to help my brother*). As such, the inherent value of the cloned child as an individual becomes eclipsed by his sibling, whose well-being takes precedence over his (*oh what's the point of me being here if it was just for them*). Estelle equates the cyborgic conception of human clones to being '*born out of a one night stand*', a birth that is bereft of love. Here, the cloned child is depicted as a '*product*' of science, engineered by medical technology to provide valuable commodities that can be '*used*' for transplantation (Morrow 2001). Estelle further observes that reproductive cloning may produce new forms of risk, such as genetic mutation, that science has yet to have the capacity to deal with. Giddens (1991) calls this 'manufactured risks'. Not only will cloning compromise the life expectancy of these cloned children, they will also be deprived of a '*great quality of life*' enjoyed by the siblings they saved. As such, the cloned child is merely an 'inferior' copy of their 'original' siblings. The perceived 'inferior' status accorded to cloned children raises question as to whether the normalization of reproductive cloning may fuel society towards the practice of eugenics, as Willa's explains below:

There's this book that Kazuo Ishiguro's just written. It's called Never Let Me Go. Have you heard about that? There are these teenagers there, and it's about them and gradually you realise that they're clones, and that they've been bred to give organ transplant. Um, they've been reared to be clones, um specifically for organ transplants for humans. Basically um, by the time they're 40 most of them are dead, and this girl is in her 30's and she's looking back on her school days and most of her friends have died now because gradually they've had all their organs removed. Bit by bit they have to go and have operations, and give away a bit, and they become ill. But for some reason a state experiment is going on where they decide to give these people a good education, and um, I mean obviously the book is really about you know...dangers of cloning, but it really upset me. Perhaps, you know, I'd end up, in some sort of cloning test laboratory, um, I have a lot of theoretical doubts about... various sorts of genetic screening because throws up issues, um...you can't help think of the sort of Nazi camp experiments and things, and, the idea that some people you know could be screened out because of perceived irregularities or imperfections that actually make them themselves. I wouldn't particularly want my body to be used as a testing ground for those sorts of things. I don't know who is to decide which are the, you know, which is the perfect gene solution, and you know, who is to be preserved and who isn't...um. It would be impossible to preserve life indefinitely because we would then have to breed a clone, a clone race to take the organs out, because if nobody was going to die, where would we be getting the body parts, and the answer is we'd be breeding some unfortunate underclass of half-people. Um, it would be like the Ishiguro book. (Willa, Interview 2)

Drawing on popular and historical discourses surrounding eugenics, Willa is concerned that the cloning of human may pave the way towards the elimination of '*imperfection*' through genetic screening. Willa foresees how the drive towards '*preserving*' human lives may necessitate the need to '*breed a clone race*' to supply body parts for organ transplantation. This reminded her of the dystopian novel by Kazuo Ishigoro, Never Let Me Go (2005), which poignantly depicts the lives of cloned children who are '*bred*' and '*reared*' to support the state-run organ donation programme. Willa is upset by the powerlessness of these cloned children, who are compelled by the donation system (that has primarily brought them into existence) to gradually '*give away their organs*' in fulfillment of their moral duty as 'donor-citizen'. As such, the cloned-bodies are regarded as 'living vessels' containing valuable commodities, which effectively transforming these children into routine donor-cyborgs (Hogle 1995). Such a gifting system is 'tyrannical' (Fox and Swazey 1992) as the well-beings of these clones are grossly disregarded (*they become ill*), which often leads to their death (*most of her friends have died*). Indeed, their death is often euphemized in the novel as '*completion*', effectively masking the unspoken 'guilt' of society for capitalising on a 'living' source.

Despite being '*given an education*', these cloned children are disenfranchised as the '*underclass*'. Their hybridity as '*half-people*' renders them monstrous (Haraway 1991). They are at once promising (*life-saving*) yet potentially destructive (*loss of humanity*). In the novel, Ishigoro portrays how the existence of these cloned children is often shrouded in silence, signifying their exclusion from human society. Their exclusion hints at the widespread prejudice of human society to accept the 'cloned race' as fully human (Schmidt and Moore 1998). Such a dystopian view of posthuman culture reflects Gray's (2002) fear of a divided cyborgian society, which is made up of the underprivileged 'technopeasants' and the privileged 'technocrats'. For Willa, the cloned children are the '*unfortunate underclass of half-people*' whose enfeebled bodies (*weakened through organ removal*) enslave them as 'peasants' within the posthuman workforce. Indeed, Ishigoro seems to suggest that the career options open to these cloned children are limited to being a 'donor' or a 'carer'[3]. In turn, the cloned-donor nourishes the body of the human race, who are granted privilege access, control and knowledge to lifesaving technologies. In other words, human's ability to command medical technologies cement their social position as the powerful 'technocrats' (Gray 2002), hence, widening the gap between the 'have' and the 'have not'.

Willa also warns of '*the danger of cloning*', stating that this may manifest into the practice of eugenics akin to the Nazi's racial cleansing movement in World War II (Bowring 2003). She is cautious that the quest for the '*perfect gene solutions*' may culminate into negative eugenics, in which '*irregularities*' and '*imperfections*' that make up the uniqueness of individuals (*that actually make them themselves*) are eliminated (Mentor 1998). Willa is apprehensive that her body may be used as a '*testing ground*' for genetic experimentations. She is concerned that genetic coding may be used to '*screen out*' individuals who are socially perceived to be 'deficient' while '*preserving*' individuals that fit into the social mold of the '*perfect gene*'. She raises an interesting question as to who has the power to make decisions concerning genetic screening and eugenics. Considering the cultural significance of eugenics in Western history, Willa implies that the genome project may well lead us towards a dystopian posthuman society, where such genetic screening are governed by the state (Gray 2002). Meanwhile, other participants worry that the cloning of 'designer babies' may accentuates consumer 'choices' in a posthuman society, where individuals (couples) are free to exercise their decisions concerning the reproduction of 'desirable' genes (Mentor 1998).

CONCLUSION

The narratives my participants constructed around emerging transplant technologies demonstrate that conceptions of posthuman

identity, body and citizenship are complex and their meanings are often contested within the political, historical, cultural and moral framework that contains it. Emerging transplant technologies challenges Western understanding of the 'integrated self', which is predicated on the ideal of the 'bounded body'. For individuals to accept emerging transplant technologies as a legitimate practice in biomedicine, they need to come to terms with their joint kinship with machines, animals and their clones, and be comfortable with embracing the partiality of 'fractured identities' (Haraway 1991). Concurrently, individuals must contemplate embodying a *permeable* body, where boundaries are continuously shifting, collapsing, regenerating and fusing with collective 'others'. One must therefore envisage a posthuman society where technoscientific liberty is endorsed (Haraway 1997) to include a diversity of cyborgs, chimeras, transgenics, bionics and clones as equal citizens. Gray (2002) argues that this calls for a 'democratic technological order' (pp. 198) where cyborg citizens are empowered through freedom in accessing knowledge and technologies. For Gray, citizenship is grounded in our embodiment and ability to exercise constructive power, which enables individuals to control technologies for their own cyborgization.

Haraway (1991) contends that current political climate precludes such democracy so long as grand narratives pertaining to the 'integrity of the Western selves', 'the sanctity of human purity' and 'the sacred division between nature and culture' continue to dominate socio-cultural discourse. For the participants in this study, the cyborg is an embodiment of paradox, whose technocratic optimism (Johnson and Roberts 1997) is intertwined with the monstrosity of unimaginable and dangerous couplings (Gray 2002; Haraway 1991). Their liminality and transgression destabilize cultural understanding of 'naturally-sanctioned' categories. While acknowledging its transcendental value as life-enhancing and life-saving, the participants are concerned that emerging transplant technologies may alienates the organic body from its rootedness in humanity, which subsequently leads to its commodification. Market metaphors pertaining to the '*mechanization of the body*', '*factory farming of spare parts*', '*engineering of customized cyborgs*' are ubiquitous in their narratives.

Popular media (such as films and novels) and historical stories (e.g. Nazism) provide cultural resources for participants to construct dystopian narratives of (1) technological determinism (*destruction of humanity by medical technology*), (2) techno-slavery (*the subordination of animals and non-human species*) and (3) negative eugenics (*elimination of imperfections*). These narratives resonate with Thompson's (2004) observation of the Romantic Myth in the natural health marketplace. The *Romantic Mythos* is an allegorical tale depicting the alienation of human by modern technology. According to Thompson, such allegory is a critique of scientific progress on modern society, which culminates in the disenchantment and dehumanization of man. The 'Tin Man' epitomizes the tragic character of the Romantic Mythos, whose natural body is displaced by the mechanistic forces of industrialization. The 'heart' emerges as a potent symbol in romantic myth, signifying the return to the organic body and the articulation of emotion (Venkatesh et al 2002). By enacting the romantic myth of the 'organic' and 'emotive' body, my participants are able to articulate their ambivalent relationship with emerging transplant technologies. For them, cyborgs are illegitimate offsprings (clones, transgenic animals) born out of transplant technologies (Gray 2002). Their conception is not predicated on metaphors of *rebirth* but on cyborg *regeneration* (Haraway 1991). As such, the cyborg has no origin story (Edenic Myth) in a Western sense, as Haraway poignantly reflects:

---

[3] In Kazuo Ishigoro's Never Let Me Go, a carer is a clone who is temporarily relieved from their duty as donor to care and support other cloned-donors as they give up their organs.

"A cyborg is not innocent; it was not born in a garden; it does not seek unitary identity and so generate antagonistic dualisms without end; it takes irony for granted" (pp. 180).

REFERENCES

Bates, B.R., Lynch, J.A., Bevan, J.L. and Condit, C.M. (2005), 'Warranted concerns, warranted outlooks: a focus group study of public understandings of genetic research', *Social Science and Medicine*, Vol. 60, 2, 331-344.

BBC News (2000), 'Baby created to save older sister', *http://news. bbc.co.uk/1/hi/health/954408.stm*. Accessed on 1 June 2012.

BBC News (2002), 'Artificial liver 'could be grown'', *http://news. bbc.co.uk/1/hi/health/1949073.stm*. Accessed on 1 June 2012.

Belk, R.W. (1990), 'Me and Thee Versus Mine and Thine: How Perceptions of the Body Influence Organ Donation and Transplantation', *in* Shanteau, J. and Harris, R.J. (eds.), *Organ Donation and Transplantation: Psychological and Behavioral Factors*, Washington, DC, American Psychological Association, 139-149

Bowring, F. (2003), *Science, Seeds and Cyborgs: Biotechnology and The Appropriation of Life*, London, Verso.

Buchanan-Oliver, M., Cruz, A. and Schroeder, J. (2008), 'Shaping the body and technology: discursive implications for the strategic communication of technological brands', *European Journal of Marketing*, Vol. 44, 5, 635-652.

Campbell, N., O'Driscoll, A. and Saren, M. (2005), 'Cyborg Consciousness: A Visual Culture Approach to the Technologised Body ', *in* K.M. Ekstrom and H. Brembeck (eds.), *European Advances in Consumer Research* Goteborg, Association for Consumer Research, 344-351

Clark, M.A. (1999), 'This Little Piggy Went to Market: The Xenotransplantation and Xenozoonose Debate', *The Journal of Law, Medicine and Ethics*, Vol. 27, 2, 137-152.

Davies, G. and Burgess, J. (2004), 'Challenging the 'view from nowhere': citizen reflections on specialist expertise in a deliberative process', *Health and Place*, Vol.10 4, 349 - 361.

Deitch, J. (1992), *Post Human*, Amsterdam, Idea Books.

Douglas, M. ([1902]1966), *Purity and Danger: An Analysis of Concepts of Pollution and Taboo*, London, Routledge and Keegan Paul.

Dumit, J. and Davis-Floyd, R. (1998), 'Introduction: Cyborg Babies - Children of the Millennium', *in* R. Davis-Floyd and J. Dumit (eds.), *Cyborg Babies: From Techno-Sex to Techno-Tots*, New York, Routledge.

Featherstone, M. and Burrows, R. (1995), *Cyberspace/ Cyberbodies/Cyberpunk*, London, Thousand Oaks and New Delhi, Sage Publications.

Fox, R.C. and Swazey, J.P. (1992), *Spare Parts: Organ Replacement in American Society*, New York and Oxford, Oxford University Press.

Fox, R.C. and Swazey, J.P. (2004), 'He Knows That Machine Is His Mortality: Old and New Social and Cultural Patterns in The Clinical Trial of the AbioCor Artificial Heart', *Perspectives in Biology and Medicine*, Vol. 47 (1), Winter, 74-99.

Gallagher, J. (2011), 'Animal Transplants Coming 'Soon'', *BBC News*, http://www.bbc.co.uk/news/health-15385648. Accessed on 1 June 2012.

Giddens, A. (1991), *Modernity and Self-Identity: Self and Society in the Late Modern Age*, Cambridge, Polity Press.

Giesler, M. (2004), 'Consuming Cyborgs: Posthuman Consumer Culture and Its Impact On The Conduct of Marketing', *in* B.E. Kahn and M.F. Luce (eds.), *Advances in Consumer Research*, Valdosta, GA, Association for Consumer Research, 400-402.

Giesler, M. and Venkatesh, A. (2005), 'Reframing the Embodied Consumer as Cyborg A Posthumanist Epistemology of Consumption', *in* G. Menon and A.R. Rao (eds.), *Advances in Consumer Research*, Duluth, MN, Association for Consumer Research, 661-669.

Gray, C.H. (2002), *Cyborg Citizen: Politics in the Posthuman Age* New York, Routledge.

Grosz, E. (1994), *Volatile Bodies: Toward a Corporeal Feminism*, Indianapolis, Indiana University Press.

Haraway, D.J. (1991), *Simians, Cyborgs, and Women: The Reinvention of Nature*, London, Free Association Books.

Haraway, D.J. (1997), 'Mice into Wormholes: A Comment on the Nature of No Nature', *in* G.L. Downey and J. Dumit (eds.), *Cyborgs and Citadels*, Santa Fe, School of American Research Press, 209-244.

Heidegger, M. ([1927]1962), 'Being and Time', *in* J. Macquarrie and E. Robinson (eds.), Oxford, Blackwell.

Hogle, L.F. (1995), 'Tales from the Cryptic: Technology Meets Organism in the Living Cadaver', *in* C.H. Gray, H.J. Figueroa-Sarrierra and S. Mentor (eds.), *The Cyborg Handbook*, New York, Routledge, 203-217.

Holland, S. (1995), 'Descartes Goes to Hollywood: Mind, Body and Gender in Contemporary Cyborg Cinema', *in* M. Featherstone and R. Burrows (eds.), *Cyberspace, Cyberbodies, Cyberpunk: Cultures of Technological Embodiment*, London, Sage.

Holstein, J.A. and Gubrium, J.F. (1995), *The Active Interview*, Thousand Oaks, CA, Sage.

Ishigoro, K. (2005), *Never Let Me Go*, London, Faber and Faber.

Johnson, K.A. and Roberts, S.D. (1997), 'The Role of the U.S. Medical Complex and the Media in Value Transformation: The Case of Viable Organ Transplant', *Consumption, Markets and Culture*, Vol. 1, 3, 197-302.

Kimbrell, A. (1993), *The Human Body Shop: The Engineering and Marketing of Life*, San Francisco, Harper San Francisco.

Langer, R. and Vacanti, J.P. (1995), 'Artificial Organs', *Scientific American*, September, 100-103.

Manning Stevens, S. (1997), 'Sacred Heart and Secular Brain', *in* Hillman, D. and Mazzio, C. (eds.), *The Body In Parts: Fantasies of Corporeality in Early Modern Europe*, London and New York, Routledge.

Marx, K. ([1867]1976), *Capital. Volume 1*, New York, Penguin Books.

Mentor, S. (1998), 'Witches, Nurses, Midwives and Cyborgs: IVF, ART and Complex Agency in the World of Technobirth', *in* R. Davis-Floyd and J. Dumit (eds.), *Cyborg Babies: From Techno-Sex to Techno-Tots*, New York, Routledge, 67-89.

Morrow, L. (2001), Cover Stories: When One Body Can Save Another', *Time Magazine,* http://www.time.com/time/ magazine/article/0,9171,157259,00.html. Access 2 June 2012.

Ritter, G. (1997), 'Silver Slippers and a Golden Cap: L Frank Baum's "The Wonderful Wizard of Oz" and Historical Memory in American Politics', *Journal of American Studies*, Vol. 31, 2, 171-202.

Sawday, J. (1996), *The Body Emblazoned: Dissection and the Human Body in Renaissance Culture*, London and New York, Routledge.

Schmidt, M. and Moore, J. (1998), 'Constructing a 'Good Catch' Picking A Winner', *in* R. Davis-Floyd, and J. Dumit (eds.), *Cyborg Babies: From Techno-Sex to Techno-Tots*, New York, Routledge, 21-39.

Seale, C., Carvers, D. and Dixon-Woods, M. (2006), 'Commodification of Body Parts: By Medicine or by Media?' *Body and Society*, Vol.12, 1, 25-42.

Sharp, L.A. (2000), 'The Commodification of the Body and Its Parts', *Annual Review in Anthropology*, Vol. 29, 287-328.

Shilling, C. (1993), *The Body and Social Theory*, London, Sage.

Singer, P. (1990), *Animal Liberation*, London, Jonathan Cape.

Synnott, A. (1993), *The Body Social: Symbolism, Self and Society*, London and New York, Routledge.

Thompson, C.J. (1997), 'Interpreting Consumers: A Hermeneutical Framework for Deriving Marketing Insights From The Text of Consumers' Consumption Stories', *Journal of Marketing Research*, Vol. XXXIV, 438-455.

Thompson, C.J. (2004), 'Marketplace Mythology and Discourses of Power', *Journal of Consumer Research*, Vol. 31, 6, 162-180.

Thompson, C.J., Locander, W.B. and Pollio, H.R. (1997), *The Phenomenology of Everyday Life*, Cambridge, Cambridge University Press.

Venkatesh, A. (2004), 'Posthumanism and the Sciences of the Artificial: Some New Directions for the Epistemologies of Consumption', *in* Kahn, B.E. and Luce, M.F. (eds.), *Advances in Consumer Research*, Valdosta, GA, Association for Consumer Research, 400-402.

Venkatesh, A., Karababa, E. and Ger, G. (2002), 'The Emergence of The Posthuman Consumer and the Fusion of The Virtual and The Real: A Critical Analysis of Sony's Ad for Memory Stick', *in* U.M. Broniarczyk and K. Nakamoto (eds.), *Advances in Consumer Research*, Valdosta, GA, Association for Consumer Research, 446-452.

Williams, S.J. (1997), 'Modern Medicine and The "Uncertain Body": From Corporeality to Hyperreality?' *Social Science and Medicine*, Vol. 45, 7, 1041-1049.

Williams, S. J., and Calnan, M. (1996). The 'Limits' of Medicalization? Modern Medicine and The Lay Populace in 'Late' Modernity'. *Social Science and Medicine,* Vol. 42, 12, 1609-1620.

The Meaning of Nature and its Implications for Individual Consumption Behavior

Vimala Kunchamboo, Monash University, Malaysia
Christina K.C Lee, Monash University, Malaysia

CONTRIBUTION STATEMENTS

There is a plethora of studies on nature related behavior from social psychology providing useful insights, especially on the impact of connectedness to nature in developing ecological behavior; however with minimum attempt to theorize why individuals engage with the natural world. This research presents a theoretical framework suggesting progress towards sustainability is only achievable if individuals see themselves as part or in total oneness with nature. Deeper insights into bloggers' thoughts, memories and experiences reflect their views of nature as extended self, their engagement with nature spirituality and their co-existence with nature as part of God's creation. This research has the potential to offer transformative insights on sustainable consumption behavior and contributes to consumer research by providing an avenue towards understanding individual experiences that may change sustainable consumption attitudes and behavior.

Nature may hold different meanings to different individuals. Therefore, each individual's experience with nature is unique and this translates into personal expression and meanings. Previous studies suggest connectedness to nature fosters ecological behavior, however, these studies lacked the theoretical foundation on *why* consumers engage with the natural world. This study explores what motivates consumers to be a part of nature. An interpretative approach is used and the data is based on an environmental blog over three years to explore the meaning of nature among those who are strongly inclined towards nature and its preservation. The results include the consideration of nature as an extension of self, spirituality and religion. Overall, the results suggest that viewing nature as one with self is a key motivational driver of ecological behavior and sustainable consumption. This article contributes to knowledge in consumer research by addressing the root-cause driving sustainable consumption behavior.

INTRODUCTION

Despite an overall increase in ecological awareness and concern, getting individuals to engage in actual conservation behavior is a major hurdle. Yet, there are individuals who are extreme lovers of nature, choosing to live differently by confirming to their ecological self and engaging in services to protect the environment (Craig-Lees and Hill 2002; Dobscha and Ozanne 2001). What makes these individuals unique and what drives them to be deeply involved with nature? An appropriate strategy to understand this unique relationship is to identify the root cause of individual ecological behavior by exploring their views and meanings attached to their personal experiences with nature. How individuals view nature and how we view our place within it has implications on nature related behavior (Hoffman and Sandelands 2005).When looking at the rainbow or the sunset, or feeling a drizzle of rain, what do individuals experience? Are there strong individual meanings attached to these experiences with nature?

Studies initiated to address our current environmental problems reveal that intimate contact with the natural world fosters ecological behavior and is critical to healthy human development (e.g. Beringer 2010; Gosling and Williams 2010; Mayer and Frantz 2004). Although fruitful, these studies only explored the extent individuals associate with nature without any theoretical foundation on *why* they engage with the natural world. Despite the emphasis given on developing nature-related behavior, only a small number of studies have attempted to theorize its findings. Therefore, differing from past studies, current research theorizes on the intense individual motivation towards nature, which is more consequential for sustainable behavior. Research on human-nature relationship would benefit from a more explicit understanding of reasons motivating humans to identify nature as part of their self. Therefore, if connection to nature influences our ecological behavior, it becomes critical to have an in-depth understanding on how humans view nature.

An interpretive approach, using grounded theory method is used to explore how individuals view nature based on their individual experiences, backgrounds and memories. The goal is to provide a more holistic and grounded perspectives on peoples' thoughts, feelings and images about nature to address "why people engage with nature and how their engagement with nature influences their consumption behavior". This study reveals the motivations for humans to connect with nature. The results contribute to the discussion on the root cause of ecological behavior. The study also provides an explanation on how an individual's motivation to connect with nature influences consumption behavior.

LITERATURE REVIEW

There are three world views encompassing human-nature relationship–anthropocentrism, ecocentrism and theocentrism. "Anthropocentrism considers the human as the most important life form, and other forms of life to be important only to the extent that they affect, or can be useful to humans" (Kortenkamp and Moore 2001, 262). This approach places human as central and is regarded as the most significant entity in the universe and places nature as an object for human to use and exploit. Hence the conclusion that "there is only man-the-subject and nature-the-object and between them, there is only the question of which of the two has priority" (Hoffman and Sandelands 2005, 147). Ecocentrism takes the opposite view of the world and promotes the idea of a living earth and nature is perceived as alive, sensitive and possessing intrinsic value thus nature can be, but ought not to be harmed (Brown 1995). Between these two views there is the question of dominance, that is, human over nature or nature over human.

Additionally, Hoffman and Sandelands (2005, 147) offer a modified view of nature called theocentrism, an environmentalism based on God, in which they argue;

> "Must the interest of human and nature be seen as separate and in conflict? Just as politicians are caught between the rock of meeting human needs for resources and the hard place of preserving nature's integrity and beauty, religious commentators are torn between the idea of man's God-given dominion over nature and the idea to respect God's creation of nature".

Theocentrism requires valuing what has been created by God by applying humility, selflessness, moderation and responsibility in every act human take towards nature (Hoffman and Sandelands 2005). The adoption of this theocentric paradigm shifts the environmental perspective to view nature and human as one.

Human-nature relationship is complex and can be viewed from many dimensions, such as, affective connection (Hinds and Sparks 2008; Mayer and Frantz 2004, Shultz et al. 2004), place identity (Fried 2000; Gosling and William 2010; Stedman 2002), spirituality

Advances in Consumer Research
Volume 40, ©2012

(Worthington et al. 2011) and well-being (Beringer 2010; Dobscha and Ozanne 2001). These studies have generally explored the effect of nature connection on ecological behavior. To promote sustainable behavior requires a fundamental understanding of an individual's psychologically driven personal relationship with the natural word.

In summary, the purpose of this study is to further understand how the meanings individuals attach to nature influence ecological behavior. The next section addresses the methodology used in this study, followed by the interpretative findings and discussion of the emergent themes. We conclude with implications for consumer research.

METHODOLOGY

An interpretivist approach, using grounded theory method is used to investigate how individuals view nature based on their experiences, backgrounds and memories. Data is collected from an eco-psycology blog called "Seeds for Thought" (http://thoughtoffering.blogs.com/ice_seeds/). The data compiled is grounded in the ideas and comments from the interaction between the bloggers. Bloggers share their thoughts, ideas and feelings using the "comment" function at the bottom of each post by the writer. Several studies have employed a similar method of collecting data from online communities such as Cova and Pace (2006) and Shaw et al. (2011). The ecopsychology blog "Seeds for Thought" was initiated in 1999 as an extension of public communication and is a collective blog by different members of the international community for ecopsychology. The blog addresses the idea of relationship between humans and the natural world. Data for this study is based on a period of three years, between 2005 to 2007, which includes 30 articles and 100 individual comments. This provides a deeper understanding on the evolution of human-nature relationship over the past three years. Although initial data collection was targeted up to 2010, data saturation was reached by the year 2007. The focus of the research is on understanding the meaning and interpretations of consumers towards nature and to understand their world from their points of view.

Data is interpreted using the following procedure. The codes were allowed to emerge from the data set. The comments of the bloggers were read as a whole to have a basic understanding of the essence of their thoughts. Additionally data was coded based on metaphors and key words in context. To generate initial categories, each article and comments were read and coded to generate as many themes as possible (Charmaz 2006; Strauss and Corbin 1998). These themes were later grouped to develop categories to understand the meanings individuals attach to nature and how these meanings implicate on their nature related behavior. Finally, the themes and emerging theoretical framework were weaved into the existing literature on environmental behavior.

It should be noted that the participants in the blog are particularly concerned about environmental and sustainability issues. Therefore, the insights provided by the blog members represent views of people who are genuinely concerned about nature. These insights provide a foundation to explore the extent ordinary consumers engage with nature and its influence on sustainable consumption. The focus on nature related behavior necessitates the importance of illustrating how nature is defined from the perspective of the participants and their relevant intentions to involve with nature. Therefore, the discussion of the themes generated from the data is organized into four sections below. We begin with (1) what is nature?; (2) categorizing nature-lovers; (3) nature and self; and finally (4) influence on sustainable consumption.

WHAT IS NATURE?

Human and all elements in nature are interconnected through a universal web. Similar to individuals, each element in nature has its own characteristics. Meaning is derived as an individual's traits intermingle with nature. Therefore, each individual's experience with nature is unique and this translates into personal expression and meanings. This personal experience with nature explains why some people feel relaxed as they walk through a willow, feel happy to hear the chirping of birds or delight in seeing the blooming of flowers. Interaction with nature opens the door to our inner self and we subconsciously interact to develop this intimate association and deeper meaning. To some, nature may simply mean a distant object, awesomely larger and more powerful than themselves, such as the ocean or mountains, and to others the meaning may run deeper, associated with elements of nature that is in proximate contact, for example a flower in their home garden. The data analysis reveals various places and things individuals classify as nature.

Participants in the blog addressed nature to resemble mountains, lakes, forest, sea, stars, sun, sky and to others nature simply means objects that is a part of their daily lives such as insects, pets, lawn, rocks, animals, yards, flowers, trees, parks, beach, potted plants, vegetable and flower garden. As nature lovers, these blog participants perceive nature as alive, real, sensitive and evolving. They voiced their disapproval on the usage of virtual reality as substitutes such as a simulated fire place instead of real fire;

> "It's sad to see people being so willing to settle for 'virtual reality' rather than natural reality". I know just what you mean about the blessings of the real thing".

> "Human artifacts and humanly created environments are just not complicated enough to provide the finely detailed, multisensory experience necessary for proper development".

CATEGORIES OF NATURE LOVERS

Additionally, the results show the intention to engage with nature is driven by the differing goals of individuals; the differing goals identified include, to seek, to honour or to nurture nature. The blog participants can be categorized into nature-seekers, nature-honours and nature-nurturers. Nature seekers are inclined to appreciate and enjoy nature as they hike, take walks in parks, or beaches. This exposure to nature nurtures a sense of belonging and contributes to knowledge building;

> "I have two nature aware kids, they have been exposed to nature since babies, they know that the birds are the eyes of the forest, and can tell you what is happening in our neighbourhood by listening to birds".

> "I just spend a long weekend on a mountain ridge in the middle of forest land and experienced some of this serenity and simplicity myself".

The nature-honors are moved by its beauty and power and they dwell in nature as a way to feel its wonders, accepting them as a part of universe. They acknowledge their co-existence with nature and its intrinsic value;

> "There's certainly something about the rose that reaches deep into the human heart and psyche with a healing grace. Just gazing at them, smelling them, talking with others about them is profoundly relaxing and delightful".

The nature-nurturers, through their deep involvement and strong compassion towards the natural world, are strongly motivated to protect and nurture it. These individuals engage in simple activities such as growing roses, feeding the ravens, growing organic food which they regard as contributing to the health of nature;

"Having a garden alive with food for me and for other creatures is a profoundly satisfying feeling".

Individuals' affiliation with nature triggers their interest to know nature, leading to increased ecological awareness. This awareness gradually progresses to the next stage of higher involvement with nature, to admire, appreciate and eventually develop a strong compassion with their natural surroundings. In summary, through the process of evolving with nature, nature-seekers develop into nature-honors and ultimately into nature-nurturers accepting their well-being and nature's as one. This is represented by the following thoughts of this blogger;

"Before taking up gardening seriously, I was a mainstream psychotherapist for many years. Like so many of us, I was oblivious to the larger context within which we live. I took up gardening as a "hobby"- a sort of exterior decoration. But soon my garden was "working" me even more than I was working my garden. Just kneeling on the earth, with sound of bees and birds in my ears as I touched plants started softening up some of the cultural armour that separates so many of us from our wild natures....so I understood that no individual exists in a vacuum... the ultimate context is the earth".

NATURE AND SELF

The notion of nature being viewed as self emerged from our data interpretation. The results reveal the intensity of the relationship between the individual and nature, to the extent that nature is seen as one with self. Three main themes that explained the relationship between human beings and the natural world were identified, that is, extended self, spirituality and religion. These themes are discussed next.

Nature as Extended Self

The self is a sense of who and what we are (Kleine, Kleine, and Kernan 1993). Accordingly Aron et al. (1991) argues that the extent to which one includes another person as part of the self is a core operationalization of relationship closeness. The term extended self refers to how human extend themselves to include their surroundings. Major categories of extended self includes body, internal process, ideas, experiences and those places to which one feels attached (Belk 1998). As such our perception towards nature as a distant object or as our extended self has implications to the way we treat nature.

Individuals who are deeply concerned with environmental and sustainability issues (that is the blog members) have a strong sense of self with nature, and perceive nature as part of the extended self. Belk suggests (1988) that external objects can be viewed as part of self when we are able to exercise power or control over them. "The more we believe we possess or are possessed by an object, the more a part of self it becomes. By claiming that something is mine we also come to believe that the object is me" (Belk 1988, 140). The concept of extended self has been applied to studies concerning sense of place (Stedman 2002), organizational self-identity (Tian and Belk 2005) and self-brand connection (Escalas and Bettman 2005). Additionally, Kuhn (2001, 13) states that individuals build psychological relationship with the environment through the process of self-actualization,

developing a "personal sense of self beyond one's encapsulated self to an extended larger self" incorporating nature. This deepening of one's ecological self brings forth sense of oneness with nature. This article explores the extent the self is viewed as one with nature.

Participants used phrases such as *"to allow the natural world into us"* to indicate the inclusion of nature into their self. Usage of metaphors describing nature as *"our womb"*, *"our mother"* and *"our root"* denotes the sense of oneness with nature and to view it as their origin. The bonding experience with nature is described as having a sense of belonging. Hence the individuals view self as a part of a bigger pattern of life. The comment below from a participant clearly acknowledges the inclusion of nature as his/her extended self.

"One might even say nature was our womb. We have been on planet Earth in our present form for one hundred thousand years. That's a long, long time! And throughout that time, we were immersed in living nature. It was there when we went to sleep, it was there all night, it was there when we awoke. We depended on living nature—and on each other as part of living nature—for everything".

Additionally, the more one experiences nature the higher the likelihood for it to become a part of themselves, thus strengthening the bond;

"Every Friday I walk at the beach not far from my house. The water, birds, passing dolphins and whales have become like members of my family. Every time I stroll along this stretch of sand, I become more bonded with it".

Perceiving a strong bond with nature and accepting nature as self, the bloggers self-reflect the feeling of empathy through expressive words such as *"my heart breaks"*, *"pain"*, *"suffering"*, *"anger"* and *"guilt"*, indicating hurting nature also means to hurt one's self. According to Kuhn (2001) empathy is experienced by individuals as they identify with the natural world through their sense of expanded ecological self.

"What does it mean that my heart breaks every time I hear of another species becoming extinct, every time I see emaciated people across the world, see ugly buildings where healthy, wild places once stood? Surely it *means* something. It means, doesn't it, that something is wrong if everything we've been taught to do and believe leads us to more of these things that breaks my heart? Surely mine isn't the only heart breaking...?"

"It was good to have a place to express my grief as well as my guilt in how I contribute to the pollution and contamination of the biosphere".

"It's painful to see what we are doing to the place we love (humans are the only species that actively and consciously "fouls its nest") and to see the wholesale killing of rare and endangered mega fauna".

As such, in the study of environmental behavior, the role of extended self cannot be ignored. Our perception towards nature as our extended self has implications for the way we treat nature. This perception elicits the awareness of interdependency with nature, leading to an emotional bonding. This bonding develops the view that nature has an intrinsic value. The sense of inclusion encourages people to view nature as "being" in their self, thus developing a strong need to value and protect it. As such, viewing nature as extended self encourages consumer ecological behavior which leads to a positive attitude towards sustainable consumption. However excluding it encourages the anthropocentric view that treats nature as an object and hence the tendency to exploit it. Therefore, the development of ecological behavior requires consumers to link themselves closely with nature.

Nature as Spirituality

The second theme that explains the participants' sense of oneness with nature is spirituality. Spirituality is defined as "a general feeling of closeness and connectedness to the sacred" (Worthington et al. 2011, 205). Krishnakumar and Neck (2002) referred spirituality as "an inner search for meaning or fulfillment that may be undertaken by anyone regardless of religion". "Individuals develop a sense of spiritual self in relation to a higher power or God and by recognizing the sacred and divine within them" (Klenke 2007, 82-83). It is a concept that originates from inside an individual. Spirituality, then, can be defined as the "core or inner life of the person and is found in all human societies through an individual experience of the divine, a connection to nature, and/or through religious practice" (Beverly 2010, 21). *Nature spirituality* involves "a sense of closeness and connection to the environment or to nature" (Worthington et al. 2011, 205). For example one's feeling of serenity and calmness while witnessing the wonders of nature. The potential importance of spirituality as a variable in explaining human-nature relationship is still neglected in the literature.

From the perspective of ecopsychology, individuals look towards nature as a source of nature-spirituality. It includes a sense of connectedness between the individual's inner self and the external world. This connectedness encourages the individual to identify self with nature and as an individual's nature-spirituality develops, their mind and body becomes one with nature.

The findings revealed close connection with spirituality and nature where many shared their views of experiencing a deeply moving and pleasurable sense with nature. Nature spirituality can be explained through shared thoughts of the blog members such as *" I became more what I call my 'authentic self' after experiencing with nature"*, in which this particular blogger claims finding her true and genuine self as she experiences nature.

Spiritual engagement with nature awakens the individual's true-self and encourages behavior consistent with their belief of self. Klenke (2007, 85) introduced the concept of self-disclosure to mean "opening oneself to a higher power, admitting to spiritual needs and struggles". Hence, with nature spirituality people are deeply aware of how they think and behave towards nature. Members recount their experiences with nature as deeply moving and pleasurable suggesting a sense of spiritual connectedness.

> "I only knew that I felt relief. During the period I went regularly to the creek and I can truly say that it felt as if I was going to visit a trusted and loving friend or beloved and wise teacher. Due to a shift in awareness away from my thoughts and towards a deeper sense of being that was free of mental process. There was a sense of being mute and I wanted no human interaction. The solace I received just by being there was truly astounding and there is no doubt this solace did indeed emanate from nature itself."

To this participant, the tree has meaning, symbolizing wisdom, hope, endurance and calmness. By connecting with the creek, the participant allowed the traits of the creek to flow into self, witnessing and accepting its calmness, comfort and wisdom leading to the experience of nature-spirituality.

An interesting area of discussion on spirituality relates to the role of sensory qualities of nature which aid the transfer of spiritual qualities from nature to individuals. The data reveals that nature's sensory qualities leads individuals to experience a deeply moving and pleasurable sense of oneness with nature which evokes a sense of spiritual wellbeing. "The smell of spring, sound of waves on the rock, sound of bees and humming birds, being caressed by a dewy overhanging willow, watching geese flying north for summer and seeing roses popping on bushes in the garden" inspires the individuals in this study to deepen their connection with their inner self and the external world. As highly involved individuals, bloggers are found to be highly sensitive to these sensory qualities in their surroundings;

> "But what caught me off guard when I stopped the car in my driveway was the smell... the smell of the sea, that wonderful salty air which my nostrils had forgotten during a short vacation. I ran up to my deck, looked at the sea, breathing in all the air I could, listening for the sounds of the waves on the rocks. I could have stayed there forever".

> "I gazed at the rugged coastline when I could, watched the exposed rocks at low-tide, observed formation of Canada geese flying north for the summer and wondered how my pile of snow was doing".

> "I dropped to my knees and started tending my plants, touching the earth. Within a couple of minutes the anxiety drained away, absorbed into the rich, dark soil. I started to breathe deeply again. I had a sense of serenity".

Besides, the acceptance of nature as something larger and more powerful than human, its magnificence, miracles, timelessness and solitude encourages individuals to immerse in deeper thoughts, evolving an emotional dependence on nature and developing strong individually driven internally bonding which leads to nature spirituality.

> "It's rare to find a person who hasn't experienced a deeply moving and pleasurable sense with something awesomely larger than themselves just through looking at the stars on a clear night"

> "During my visits I would just sit on the boulders along the creek or walk in the water. There was a sense of being mute and I wanted no human interaction. I was aware of the creek and woods as having a very distinct and palpable presence. The solace I received just by being there was truly astounding and there is no doubt this solace did indeed emanate from nature itself".

Nature based spirituality plays an important role in developing human well-being. There is evidence from previous studies that human benefit emotionally and physically by connecting to nature (Martens, Gutscher, and Bauer 2011; Ryan et al. 2010), for example, experiencing more positive feelings by merely being around, relaxing or walking in natural favorite places (Korpela and Yle'n 2007). Our results resonate past studies, that those who are in-tuned with nature view it as an essential source of emotional and physical well-being;

> "I still go to the mountain twice a week, the personal healing has been incredible".

"There are no words to describe what happens to people who start mixing mud with their feet, allows people to personally experience the earth in such a different way."

"Watching the endless subtle changes of the garden as the season passes grounds and relaxes me".

A spiritual connection with nature also leads to psychological and physical healing, this theme is conveyed through bloggers' comments of *"sense of serenity"*, *"happiness"*, *"inner peace"*, as they connect with nature.

Through nature-spirituality, individuals develop compassion, respect and inspiration to preserve and value nature. Embracing nature spiritually evokes emotional dependency, thus nature becomes a source of ecospirituality. Incorporating nature-spirituality into self alters the view that nature is an object and encourages the view that it is alive and therefore requires to be treated with care. It encourages viewing nature as a person to connect to where human finds solace and healing.

"We depended on living nature—and on each other as part of living nature—for everything. It is thus hardly surprising that we evolved an emotional dependence on nature, that it is our medicine, that we need it for our emotional well-being".

"By opening to spirit whenever we find it –in a forest, in art, in planting seeds in a garden, in meditation or prayers- we can let compassion and inspired action lend their strength to our fragile, small selves, empowering us to join with others to be part of Gaia's healing, not her destruction".

Nature as Religion

Anthropocentric view and ecocentric view involves the element of dominance. In the former view human is said to dominate nature, whereas the latter view encourages nature dominance over human. Hoffman and Sandelands (2005) argues that there is an alternative environmentalism, that is theocentric, which is an environmentalism centered on God. They argue that in the theocentric view, human do not dominate over nature or vice versa. On the contrary, it promotes the view that God rules over both human and nature thus human and nature are joined in God. This view joins human and nature as one and to perceive creation as a "totality of life" (Hoffman and Sandelands 2005, 152). This argument suggests the need to assess religion as a factor influencing individual behavior towards nature.

While spirituality is said to originate from within an individual and is more personal and private, religion tend to be more of an external connection with a higher being. Based on the Oxford definition, religion is a belief in supernatural power and involves a more structured form of belief, tradition and ritual. Spirituality can be said to emanate from religion. While spirituality preaches to love God and adopts the view that God is omnipresent and resides in oneself, religion engages believers to fear and obey God and that God is far from reach of human (Pettinger 2007). Theocentric view which argues the dominance of god over individual and nature, engages individuals to love and protect what has been created by the almighty.

Hence, theocentrism encourages sense of oneness with nature through eliminating the existence of dominance, that is, human over nature or nature over human. It signals the awareness of strong bonding, interconnection and oneness between human and nature. The awareness that both oneself as a human and nature is created by God emphasizes interdependency for mutual survival.

The blog data analysis captured religion as a theme in explaining our relationship with nature. This particular theme was derived through codes such as love, respect, beliefs, value and gratitude. Theocentric view is emphasized through expressions such as "to love what God loves" and "the farther we are separated from nature the farther we are separated from God".

'As we come to understand the interconnectedness of all things we realize that we share the earth, air, water and sunlight with a "web of life" on earth and in that realization is perhaps the most profound expression of our spiritual nature and the religious beliefs that give rise to that revelation".

"I have taken to a daily laying of my hand on the trunks of several trees in my apartment complex and speaking with them of my love and gratitude for what they are bringing to my life - strength, grace, beauty, wisdom. In the Holy Quran, we are encouraged to live in harmony with nature".

"But for the longest time my relationship with God was inversely proportional to the amount of steel around me. Inside the sanctuary, I heard but did not feel. Step outside and see the blue sky above me and I could "feel" the message take hold".

When an individual views oneself as embedded in nature and not separated from it, mistreating nature would mean to mistreat oneself. This encourages individuals to live in harmony with nature, using nature responsibly to satisfy individual needs and at the same time preserving it for future generation. Nature and human moves beyond merely coexisting, nature is viewed as human, as reflected in the following quote;

"A curious thing I've noticed about us rose nuts is that we always talk about roses as if they were people. Mostly "she" and sometimes "he" but never "it." I love this deep understanding that plants are relatives with whom we humans have shared the Cenozoic era".

"I understood that no individual exists in a vacuum, but within the context of family, community, culture. But why stop there? I began to understand that the ultimate context is the Earth".

INFLUENCE ON SUSTAINABLE CONSUMPTION

The deep realization of mutual existence through the incorporation of these views on nature encourages the development of positive attitude and intention to engage with nature. The more an individual relates to nature, believing in their coexistence and dependency for survival, the greater the intensity to engage in conservation behavior. It shifts the perspective that nature is an object whose resources are to be exploited by human to a paradigm that cultivates conservation. That is, the more meaningful nature is to an individual the stronger is the connection and intention to protect nature through consuming responsibly.

The intention to preserve nature is clearly indicated from the reported activities by bloggers such as engaging in organic gardening, simplifying diets and eating habits, using fireplace to heat their houses, cancelling cable TV and reducing paper printing. The bloggers intimate relationship with nature clearly translates into sustainable behavior as witnessed through the following comments from the bloggers;

"Some people don't realize how easy it is now to be more eco-friendly. Biodegradable cleaning products are the same price as beloved Hertel and Pinesol, clean just as well if not better, and with a much more refreshing smell. Plastic bags are wasteful.

Cars are useless when you have two legs, or even a bicycle. Use public transit or carpool. I sold my car last year and haven't really missed having it".

"The idea that energy conservation, recycling, car-pooling and other "sustainable" activities is an expression of one's religious values is an idea whose time has come".

Additionally, total self-engagement with nature impacts the level of appreciation and gratitude towards nature which was expressed through the act of saying grace, feelings of emotion (thankfulness) and appreciating blessings for nature's provision to human;

"Healthy foods are grown locally in tune with the seasons by people happy in their work. The simplicity of such meals is a form of the "abundance" that reflects the creativity of the cosmos and for which the word of "grace" is named".

"Once I sat down before this humble meal, I felt a surge of emotion. I paused and thanked the hare for this sustenance. I fought tears during the whole meal and it changed something in me with respect to this "free food" that is available in this community. I picked a few quarts of partridge berries last week and engaged in another "thanking" ritual".

In conclusion, individuals become highly sensitive of the actions towards nature as they attach meaningful connection with their surroundings.

DISCUSSION AND IMPLICATIONS

This article addresses a need for a revised theoretical framework that recognizes a deeper level of internally driven motivation as the key driving force of sustainable behavior. It alters the previous conception of human-nature relationship towards incorporating nature into self. Viewing self as one with nature has important implications which are discussed in the following sections; shift in focus and challenges in changing consumer views on nature.

Shift in Focus

This study suggests the need to rethink our strategies to encourage environmental friendly behavior. A pressing challenge facing NGOs, local governments and social marketers is how to encourage sustainable consumption as a step toward building a more sustainable society. Numerous policies and strategies have been developed and implemented; these, however, have had little impact on effectively changing existing environmental behavior. Current policies and strategies to encourage sustainability tend to focus on behavioral change through understanding and changing attitude, lifestyle and habits. These views are based on the assumption that consumers have to be encouraged, cajoled or coerce to look after our natural resources for the next generation. This article suggests that progress towards sustainability is only achievable if individuals see themselves as part of or in total oneness with nature. Viewing sustainability and consumption from this perspective suggests that policy makers and social marketers need to rethink their strategies to encourage sustainable behavior.

Mayer and Frantz (2004) emphasize that by connecting to nature, individuals experience subjective well-being and this sense of well-being increases the intention to engage in ecological behavior. While there is truth in this statement, our findings imply that mere connection does not necessarily engage individuals into actions of preservation. Consumers who merely express their ecological and societal concern may have different attitudes and may behave dif-

ferently to those who totally immersed in ecological living (Robert 1995). Additionally, Mayer and Frantz (2004) claim if an individual is unaware of their destructive action on the environment then increasing their connectedness to nature will have little impact. Hence, we argue that the motivation to connect to nature runs deeper than mere connection to nature, instead, it needs to be embedded in one's self. The ability to view self and nature as one is the central inspiration that leads a person to pay attention to nature. These meaningful connections to nature elicit an emotional attachment which drives the inner desire to protect and preserve nature. The results clearly demonstrate that the more one views self as one with nature, the stronger the intensity to engage with it. This type of motivation is intrinsically driven and has a deepening effect on the behavior of individuals, that is, individuals who view nature as self are more likely to engage in sustainable behavior. As such, pro-environmental behavior can be stimulated by encouraging the formation of a deeply rooted, internally and altruistically driven desire to be part of nature. Policies and strategies may be more effective in developing positive nature related behavior when supported by an aim to inspire people to embrace the co-existence of people and nature and the need to respect nature as a living resource. The present study demonstrates that understanding and addressing the root cause of individual behavior towards the environment is an essential step in developing nature-related behavior.

Thus, promoting sustainability requires changing the current view of individuals on nature as a distant object to be manipulated, towards viewing nature as being closer, as embedded in self. A deeper understanding of sustainable consumption behavior or the reasons for the apathy among some consumers can be gained from studying consumers' views on meaning of nature and their relationship with nature. Even as we now have some understanding of the motivation towards drawing closer to nature and its influence on consumption behavior, it is important to understand what repels others from avoiding nature and its effect on consumption behavior. The development of policies and strategies to encourage sustainability consumption are better informed with both sides of story.

Challenges in Changing Individual View on Nature

The aim to develop a sense of oneness with nature in individuals may prove to be a challenge. The internal desire to embrace nature as part of self is developed through unique individual psychological experiences, thoughts and emotional connections. For example nature-spirituality is exclusively an individual's experience. Individuals who regard themselves as part of nature are sensitive to its existence and clearly demonstrate selflessness as well as concern – these qualities reflected in their activities to nurture nature. Therefore, prompting such deeply rooted motivation requires a gradual process.

Past findings reveal individuals engage in conservation behavior by anticipating personal current benefits such as incentives (Stern 1999) or to avoid punishment (Sharp, Hoj, and Wheeler 2010). Individualistic behavior predominate care for the environment. For individuals with a hostile view of nature, changing their inner-self and stimulating altruistic behavior in their association with nature may not be easy. Nevertheless, this article uncovers the psychological root of understanding the reasons behind human disconnection from nature. An effective strategy may be to begin nature exposure at a young age with the goal of instilling a sense of ecological self, that is, "how we extend our sense of self in relationship to the world of nature"(Wilson 1996, 122). As such, social marketing and government policies may aim at the young minds, for example include nature exposure and interaction as part of the school curriculum.

The results of this study are based on bloggers who see themselves as lovers of nature and feel strongly connected to it. Hence, the interpreted data consist of views from extreme environmentalist and may not reflect the views of ordinary individuals. However, understanding these individuals' engagement with nature is necessary and provides a good starting point for future research to explore this notion with consumers who may be less extreme than these bloggers in their connection and bonding with nature.

For a deeper and more generalizable explanation of how an individual's view of nature affect sustainable consumption, future research should employ a broader study with additional data sources to examine various groups of participants with differing characteristics. This could be expanded to address whether the appreciation of nature experiences differ across diverse populations and cultures. A comparative study of different meanings of nature between urban and rural participants may provide guidelines in tackling the environmental problem. As we were unable to find support from the data to link the types of nature lovers to sustainable consumption behavior, future research may explore how the different categories of nature lovers (seekers, honors and nurturers) relationships with nature affect their consumption behavior. In addition, our understanding of nature-spirituality may be enriched by exploring the types of nature experiences sought by the different groups of nature lovers for spiritual renewal. Future studies may run experiments, using neuroscience to trace the impact of nature stimuli on the functioning of the brain. Another interesting avenue for research involves the exploration of the boundaries between nature and the virtual-nature constructed by the technological world.

This research has the potential to transform our perspective on sustainable consumption behavior by shifting the focus to explore people-nature relationship and nature connectedness. It contributes to consumer research by providing an avenue towards understanding individual experiences that may change sustainable consumption attitudes and behavior.

REFERENCES

Aron, Arthur., Elaine N. Aron., Michael Tudor, and Greg Nelson (1991), "Close Relationships as Including Other in the Self", *Journal of Personality and Social Psychology,* 60 (February), 241–53.

Belk, Russell W. (1988), "Possessions and the Extended Self", *Journal of Consumer Research*, 15 (September), 139-68.

Beringer, Almut (2010), "Sustainability and the Human Nature Relationship", in *State of the World, Transforming Cultures; From Consumerism to Sustainability, The WorldWatch Institute*, New York, W.W. Norton & Company, 58.

Beverly, Lanzetta (2010), "Spirituality", <u>*Alternative Therapies in Health and Medicine*, 16, (Jan/Feb), 20-5.</u>

Brown, Charles S. (1995), "Anthropocentrism and Ecocentrism: The Quest for a New Worldview", *The Midwest Quarterly,* 36, http://go.galegroup.com.ezproxy.lib.monash.edu.au

Charmaz, Kathy (2006), "Constructing Grounded Theory", London, Sage Publication.

Cova, Bernard, and Stefano Pace (2006), "Brand Community of Convenience Products: New forms of Customer Empowerment – the Case My Nutella the Community", *European Journal of Marketing*, 40, 1087-105.

Craig-Lees, and Margaret Hill (2002), "Understanding Voluntary Simplifiers", *Psychology & Marketing*, *19* (February), 187–210.

Dobscha, Susan, and Julie L. Ozanne (2001), "An Ecofeminist Analysis of Environmentally Sensitive Women Using Qualitative Methodology: The Emancipatory Potential of an Ecological Life", *Journal of Public Policy & Marketing*, 20 (Fall), 201-14.

Escalas, E. Jennifer, and James R. Bettman (2005), "Self-Construal, Reference Groups, and Brand Meaning", *Journal of Consumer Research*, 32 (December), 378-89.

Fried, Marc. (2000), "Continuities and Discontinuities of Place", *Journal of Environmental Psychology,* 20 (September), 193-205.

Gosling, Elizabeth, and Kathryn J.H. Williams (2010), "Connectedness to Nature, Place Attachment and Conservation Behavior: Testing Connectedness Theory Among Farmers", *Journal of Environmental Psychology*, 30 (September), 298-304.

Hinds, Joe, and Paul Sparks (2008), "Engaging with the Natural Environment: The Role of Affective Connection and Identity", *Journal Of Environmental Psychology*, 28 (June), 109-20.

Hoffman, Andrew J. and Llyod E. Sandelands (2005), "Getting Right with Nature", *Organization & Environment,* 18 (June), 141-62.

Kleine, Robert E., Susan S. Kleine, and Jerome B. Kernan (1993), "Mundane Consumption and the Self. A Social-Identity Perspective", *Journal of Consumer Psychology,* 2, 209-35.

Klenke, Karin (2007), "Authentic Leadership: A Self, Leader, and Spiritual Identity Perspective", *International Journal of Leadership Studies*, 3, 68-97, http://www.regent.edu/

Korpela, Kalevi M. and Matti Yle'n (2007), "Perceived Health is Associated with Visiting Natural Favourite Places in the Vicinity", *Health & Place,* 13 (March) 138–51.

Kortenkamp, Katherin V. and Colleen F. Moore (2001), "Ecocentrism and Anthropocentrism: Moral Reasoning about Ecological Commons Dilemmas", *Journal of Environmental Psychology*, 21(September), 261-72.

Krishnakumar, Sukumarakurup, and Christopher P. Neck (2002), "The "What", "Why" and "How" of Spirituality in the Workplace", *Journal of Managerial Psychology,* 17(Jan), 153-64.

Kuhn, L. James (2001), "Towards an Ecological Humanistic Psychology", *Journal of Humanistic Psychology, 41*(Spring*)*, 9-24.

Martens, Dorte., Heinz Gutscher, and Nicole Bauer (2011), "Walking in "Wild" and "Tended" Urban Forests: The Impact on Psychological Well Being", *Journal of Environment Psychology*, 31(March), 36-44.

Mayer, Stephan F. and Cynthia M. Frantz (2004), "The Connectedness to Nature Scale: A Measure of Individuals' Feeling In Community with Nature", *Journal of Environmental Psychology*, 24 (December), 503-15.

Pettinger, Tejvan (2007), "Religion vs Spirituality", http://www.biographyonline.net/spiritual/articles/religion_vs_spirituality.html

Roberts, James A. (1995), "Profiling Levels of Socially Responsible Consumer Behavior: A Cluster Analytic Approach and Its Implications for Marketing", *Journal of Marketing Theory and Practice*, 3(Fall), 97–117.

Ryan, Richard M., Netta Weinstein ., Jessey Bernstein, and Kirk Warran (2010), "Vitalizing Effects of Being Outdoors and in Nature", *Journal of Environmental Psychology*, 30 (June), 159–68.

Seeds for Thought: An Ecopscyhologhy Blog, http://thoughtoffering.blogs.com/ice_seeds/.

Shaw, Jing C., Pei W. Wang., Meng L.Shih., Jian J.Huang, and Li F.Tsai (2011), "Analysis of Online Word-of-Mouth of Blogs-Taking the Best-Selling Facial Masks", *Journal of Global Business Management*, 7 (April), 1-6.

Sharp, Anne., Stine Høj, and Meagan Wheeler (2010), "Proscription and its Impact on Anti-consumption Behavior and Attitudes: The Case of Plastic Bags", *Journal of Consumer Behavior*, 9 (November/December), 470–84.

Shultz, Wesley P., Chris Shriver., Jennifer J. Tabanico, and Azar M. Khazian (2004), "Implicit Connection with Nature", *Journal of Environmental Psychology,* 24 (March), 31-42.

Stedman, Richard C. (2002), "Toward a Social Psychology of Place: Predicting Behavior from Place-Based Cognitions, Attitude, and Identity", *Environment and Behavior*, 34 (September), 561-81.

Stern, Paul C. (1999), "Information, Incentives, and Proenvironmental Consumer Behavior, Journal of Consumer Policy 22 (December), 461–78.

Strauss, Anselm, and Juliet Corbin (1998), "Basic of Qualitative Research: Techniques and Procedures for Developing Grounded Theory", California: Sage Publication.

Tian, Kelly, and Russell W. Belk (2005), "Extended Self and Possessions in Workplace", *Journal of Consumer Research*, 32 (September), 297-310.

Wilson, Ruth A. (1996), "The Development of Ecological Self", *Early Childhood Education Journal*, 24 (December), 121-123.

Worthington Jr., Everett L., Joshua N. Hook., Davis E. Don. and Michael A. McDaniel (2011), "Religion and Spirituality", *Journal of Clinical Psychology*, 67 (February), 204–14.

Correcting for Unconscious Experiential Processing

Francine Espinoza, ESMT, Germany

ABSTRACT

Previous research is inconclusive about whether consumers can correct their judgments for the influence of unconscious subjective experiences. We manipulated the subjective experience of certainty associated with a persuasive message using subliminal priming and found that participants corrected their judgments in opposite directions depending on whether they were subliminally primed with certainty or uncertainty. These results demonstrate that consumers can correct for unconscious experiential processing.

Previous research has shown that subjective experiences that remain outside the consumer's awareness (e.g., visual stimuli presented faster than eye perception levels or audio stimuli played below audible volumes) may influence judgments. For example, an individual's judgment of a condo in a magazine ad may be negatively influenced by pictures of a terrorist attack placed in the parafoveal vision area. If this person is prompted to correct her judgments about the product in ad, would she be able to account for a potential influence of the unconscious experiential processing?

The correction literature has focused on situations in which people are or can become aware of potential influences (Wegener and Petty 1995). If people are aware of an influence, they must have processed the information either systematically, when considerable resources and motivation are present, or heuristically, when at least moderate resources and motivation are available (Petty and Cacioppo 1986). Research has shown that correction may happen under both of these types of processing if enough cognitive resources are available for correction (Petty, Wegener, and White 1998). In such situations, the direction of the correction effect depends on the perceived initial influence. Thus, judgments that were perceived to be positively influenced by the stimulus should become more negative after correction, and judgments that were perceived to be negatively influenced by the stimulus should become more positive (Wegener and Petty 1995).

In a third type of processing, experiential processing, judgments are formed based on immediate sensations and feelings prompted by the situation and that are often outside of people's awareness (Meyers-Levy and Malaviya 1999). Experiential processing happens automatically, unconsciously, and independently from conscious resources. It occurs when exposure to stimuli is subliminal or extremely brief. For instance, people tend to like unknown stimuli (e.g., Chinese ideographs) more when these follow positive subliminal primes (e.g., smiling faces) than when they follow negative primes (e.g., frowning faces; Murphy and Zajonc 1993).

The literature suggests that judgments based on experiential processing are the result of two sequential processes (e.g., Jacoby, Kelley, and Dywan 1989; Strack 1992). First, general cues about the target are evaluated automatically and unconsciously to produce a global feeling. These cues include cognitive, affective, and/or bodily reactions to the stimulus, such as, for example, feelings of fluency (Schwarz 2004), positive affect (Zajonc and Markus 1982) or perceptions of smell (Lee and Schwarz 2012). Second, this subjective experience is used as the default basis for judgment and may remain outside of consumers' awareness (Strack 1992). Thus, in the previous example, people with familiar, more fluent faces are judged as famous, objects associated with positive affect are more liked, or an argument associated with a smell of fish is judged as suspicious. When subliminal priming produces an influence, this influence is represented by a change in judgments or behavior (Aarts, Custers, and Marien 2008; Clore and Parrott 1994; Winkielman and Berridge

2004). For example, Clore and Parrot (1994) manipulated the feeling of certainty unconsciously (through hypnosis) and found that certain people understood a poem better than uncertain people.

Although experiential processing and its influence on judgments has been extensively shown in the literature (Schwarz and Clore 1996; Winkielman and Berridge 2004; Zajonc 1994), current evidence suggests that people may not be able to correct for an unconscious influence. In a series of experiments involving subliminal priming, Winkielman, Zajonc, and Schwarz (1997) found no evidence for judgment correction as predicted. Although the authors listed several potential methodological limitations, they generally concluded that correction may not happen when the stimulus does not produce consciously experienced feelings even though it has produced measurable influences on judgments. We integrate literatures on correction and experiential processing to build our hypothesis.

We propose that people can correct for unconscious experiential processing. According to correction theories, when people are prompted to correct their judgments, they will think back of that situation and appraise their initial reactions (Wegener and Petty 1995). We posit that when people appraise their reactions, they may also take into consideration their global and subjective reactions towards the target, even if these are not completely accessible to consciousness. Consumers will evaluate their judgments for accuracy and adjust them if they believe their judgments were biased for some reason. Consistent with the correction literature, we predict that the direction of correction should be the opposite of that of the initial influence. Nevertheless, our perspective deviates from the traditional view in a key way. Whereas the traditional view implies that people must consciously perceive an influence, we argue that people may correct for the influence of an unconscious subjective experience.

Experiential processing may be mediated by low-level systems that do not produce any accompanying conscious feeling (Winkielman et al. 1997; Zajonc 1994) but increase the accessibility of prime-related mental content (Loersch and Payne 2011). When affect is primed subliminally, it generates a diffuse and nonspecific sensation whose origin is not accessible (Murphy and Zajonc 1993). Based on such previous research, we expect that when an affective stimulus is presented subliminally, the unconsciously elicited feelings will be automatically associated with and interpreted as nonspecific affective reactions to the target (Bargh et al. 1992; Fazio et al. 1986). Thus, although the subliminal stimulus cannot produce identifiable feelings, we expect that people should be able to intuitively access their global feelings or an overall subjective experience that is attributed to their reactions to the target, and correct for this experiential processing.

METHOD

Design and Participants

The study employed a 2 subliminal prime (certain vs. uncertain) x 2 correction (no-correction vs. correction) between-subjects design. We subliminally primed participants with certainty or uncertainty-related words during a lexical decision task. One hundred sixty-seven university students participated in the experiment as part of a one-hour session in exchange for extra credit.

PROCEDURE

Prime manipulation. To prime the feeling of (un)certainty, we subliminally exposed participants to certainty or uncertainty-related

Advances in Consumer Research
Volume 40, ©2012

words. Participants were told that they were participating in two unrelated studies. Participants completed a lexical decision task in which they had to identify as quickly and accurately as possible whether a stimulus presented on a desktop computer was a word (using the "z" and the "/" keys). Before the actual task, participants completed six practice trials with no prime. At the beginning of each trial, a fixation point ("***") appeared at the center of a white screen for 2 seconds to focus their attention. The fixation point was replaced by a 16-point-black-font prime word. Primes consisted of certainty or uncertainty-related words and were presented in randomized order. Certainty-related primes were: confident, sure, convinced, certain, positive, definite, correct, and decisive. Uncertainty-related primes were: insecure, unsure, doubtful, uncertain, hesitant, vague, wrong, ambivalent. The primes were presented for 50 ms and then were replaced by a masking letter string (xvxvxvxv) that did not convey any additional meaning and was at least equal in length to the prime to ensure that the prime would not reach the threshold of conscious perception. The mask was then replaced by the target word, which appeared in the same location after a very brief delay (SOA-Stimulus Onset Asynchrony) varying randomly in duration (from 250 to 750 ms) to avoid participants anticipating the target's appearance. Targets were neutral words (e.g., house, planet, carpet, river, building, hat, window, ranch) or non-words (e.g., blater, campure, dight, lench, measing, nesion, poit, reesy) and appeared until participants registered their response. A combination of two blocks, eight primes, four words and four non-words yielded 32 trials (each prime was presented twice, once with a word and once with a non-word).

After exposure to the certainty primes, participants proceeded to the next task and read a scenario in which they were looking for an apartment to rent. They were told that they had narrowed their options down to two apartments and that a realtor had recommended the nicer but more expensive apartment (Appendix).

A pretest was conducted to test the efficacy of the priming (N = 32). Consistent with previous research, given that certainty was induced subliminally we found no significant effect of the primes on a measure of reported certainty ($p > .48$; "how certain are you about your attitude towards the recommended apartment?"). Therefore, to test whether the certainty primes were effective, we looked at participants' reaction times in the lexical decision task. Previous research indicates that certainty is related to faster responses (Gross, Holtz, and Miller 1995). We found that participants primed with certainty (vs. uncertainty) related words responded faster in the lexical decision task ($M_{certainty}$ = 821.95 ms, SD = 317.34 vs. $M_{uncertainty}$ = 1150.30 ms, SD = 536.47; $F(1, 28)$ = 4.00, p = .05, η^2 = .12), after accounting for outliers with an excessive number of error rates and cases with latencies faster than 300 ms or slower than 2000 ms (Bargh and Chartrand 2000). As an awareness check, we presented five of the subliminal stimuli again at the end of the pretest, told participants that words were being presented, and asked them to guess what those words were (Bargh and Chartrand 2000). None of the participants could identify any of the primed words, indicating that the subliminal priming was indeed subliminal.

Correction manipulation. In the no correction condition, participants answered the questions immediately after reading the scenario. In the correction condition, participants first read an instruction adapted from Wegener and Petty (1995): "In the next section, please be sure that the realtor's opinion will not influence your own opinion. It is very important that your answers be based on your own opinion of the apartments."

Measures. To capture judgments, we asked participants to rate their relative preference to the apartments ("1 = I prefer apartment one/ 7 = I prefer apartment two"). We did not measure certainty in

the study for two reasons. First, consistent with our pretest and with previous research (Winkielman and Berridge 2004), we did not expect an effect on a reported measure of certainty but on participants' judgments. Second, measuring certainty might affect the nature of the judgment process and create a demand for participants to respond according to their certainty judgments (Petrusic and Baranski 2003). If participants must be aware of their feelings for its effects on judgments to emerge, the generalizability of the findings would be limited and we could be observing a demand effect. By manipulating certainty subliminally and not including a reported measure of certainty, the study provides a compelling test of the effect with a clean manipulation. Finally, to help rule out participants' mood as an alternative explanation, we included thirteen mood measures adapted from the PANAS (Watson, Clark, and Tellegen 1988) ranging from 1 ("does not describe my current feeling at all") to 7 ("describes my current feelings very well").

RESULTS

After removing participants who had an exceptionally high error rate on the lexical decision task and the remaining cases with latencies faster than 300 ms or slower than 2000 ms (Bargh and Chartrand 2000), our final sample was one hundred twenty-three participants. Neither the error rate (χ^2 = .19, $p > .4$) nor the latencies beyond acceptable speed (χ^2 = 5.00, $p > .2$) were related to participants' assigned conditions, meaning that the removed cases were well distributed across conditions. Differences in degrees of freedom are due to missing values.

Manipulation check. Consistent with the pretest and confirming the efficacy of the certainty manipulation, a one-way (certainty vs. uncertainty) ANOVA ($F(1, 121)$ = 3.60, $p < .06$, η^2 = .03) shows that participants primed with certainty-related words responded marginally faster to the lexical decision task than participants primed with uncertainty-related words ($M_{certainty}$ = 816.71 ms, SD = 221.73; $M_{uncertainty}$ = 902.07 ms, SD = 276.20).

Judgments. A 2 (subliminal prime) x 2 (correction) ANOVA shows a significant interaction between subliminal prime and correction ($F(1, 119)$ = 11.83, $p < .001$, η^2 = .09). In the no-correction condition ($F(1, 119)$ = 9.64, $p < .01$, η^2 = .12), participants primed with certainty words ($M_{certainty}$ = 5.13, SD = 1.50) had more favorable judgments towards the recommended apartment than participants primed with uncertainty words ($M_{uncertainty}$ = 3.97, SD = 1.71). Providing support for the predicted effect of correction on judgments (figure 1), planned contrasts show that correction decreased preferences for the recommended apartment when certainty was primed ($F(1, 119)$ = 6.53, $p < .01$, η^2 = .11) but increased preferences for the recommended apartment when uncertainty was primed ($F(1, 119)$ = 5.31, $p < .02$, η^2 = .08).

Mood. Based on a factor analysis we created indices of positive mood (α = .86; happy, enthusiastic, excited, and proud), negative mood (α = .84; afraid, sad, depressed, upset, and irritable), and anxiety (α = .83; anxious, tense, distressed, and nervous). None of these indices showed significant effects (all $ps > .47$) when entered as dependent variables in a 2 (subliminal prime) x 2 (correction) ANOVA.

DISCUSSION

The results suggest that people can correct for the influence of stimuli that was presented subliminally and was not found to produce conscious feelings that participants could deliberately report even though we observe a subliminal priming effect on judgments. Our results suggest that changes in mood cannot explain the reported findings, and the fact that the effect of certainty on judgments was marginally reversed in the correction condition rules out regression

Figure 1. Judgements corrected for subliminal priming.

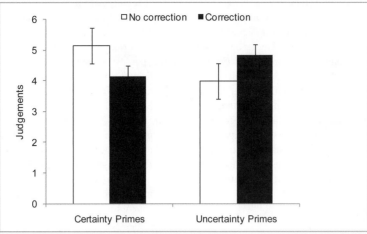

Note: Standard errors are represented in the figure by the error bars attached to each column.

to the mean as a potential explanation. This overcorrection suggests that individuals are adjusting their judgments based on their miscalibrated perceptions (Wilson and Brekke 1994) instead of simply reporting more moderate views.

GENERAL DISCUSSION

We present evidence for correction for unconscious experiential processing. Although most theories of correction assume that people will correct when they become aware that a given factor is influencing their judgments, we show that people can correct for the influence of a stimulus that was presented outside of their conscious awareness. In our study, there is no evidence that participants became aware of the influence. If anything, participants thought that the recommender was possibly influencing their opinion but they were neither aware of what about the recommender was influencing them nor were they told about the direction of the influence. Although the stimuli was primed subliminally and there was no evidence that participants were aware of them or of the feelings they convey, participants were able to intuitively access their global evaluation and correct in the direction opposite of their initial reactions, as correction models would predict.

Though the present study was not designed to test a specific explanation for the effect, it is useful to consider a few alternatives of processes underlying the effect. There are at least two explanatory accounts that could be explored in future research. Our results seem to be consistent with the feelings-as-information model for influence of consciously experienced affect on judgments (Schwarz 1990). This model predicts that judgments positively affected by, for example, positive mood, should become less favorable when people become aware that mood was influencing their judgments. Although unconscious, it is possible that the subliminally primed feelings were thought to be global reactions to the recommender, leading to discounting of these feelings from judgment.

It is also possible that the results here reported are not limited to affective priming but could be explained by semantic priming. One may wonder whether the effect would hold if the subliminal priming involves nonaffective stimuli. According to semantic priming findings people would discount the perceived influence according to the perceived meaning of the priming, which would lead to similar results. However, there is also evidence that affective and semantic priming involve different processes (Murphy and Zajonc 1993). If nonaffective semantic subliminal priming is less intuitively

accessible than affective priming, correction for subliminal semantic priming might be hindered.

A relevant agenda for future research includes not only to reveal what is driving the correction for experiential processing but also to determine when this effect is more or less prominent. Contrary to our results, Winkielman and colleagues (1997) did not find evidence for correction for subliminal affective priming as predicted by the correction literature, which raises the question of when we should observe persistence of subliminal priming and under what circumstances people should be able to correct for an influence they cannot consciously report. Perhaps key to obtain correction of unconscious experiential processing is the presence of an identifiable object to which the subjective experience can be attributed. Correction requires identification of a source of bias, which can be the recommender associated with the unconscious feelings.

Another possibility is that the way that correction is instigated matters. Winkielman and colleagues (1997) induced correction by making a potential source for the feelings salient and telling participants about the direction of influence. This manipulation has been proved successful in several studies using the feelings-as-information paradigm (Schwarz 1990). Our manipulation, on the other hand, was modeled closely after a traditional correction manipulation used in the correction literature (e.g., Wegener and Petty 1995). We have not explicitly told participants that there was an influence, but asked participants to not let the recommender influence their opinions. One key difference is that instead of calling attention to the source of feelings of which participants were unaware, our correction manipulation called attention to a potential (more general) influence by the recommender. The absence of correction in the predicted direction in Winkielman et al.'s (1997) study may have occurred because participants did not perceive the source of the feelings as a potential source of bias given that they were unaware of the feelings. Our manipulation, on the other hand, allows them to access their global reactions to the recommender and correct for that. Moreover, it is possible that telling participants about the source of the feeling (vs. prompting them to correct) did not motivate participants enough to correct.

A potential limitation of our study is that the primed feelings were accessible to consciousness somehow. This is still possible although we carefully developed the subliminal priming after methods used in previous research and the pretest has indicated that participants could not report conscious feelings consistent with the primes nor guess any of the words that were primed. To shed light on this issue, future research could examine how feelings that are primed subliminally manifest consciously or behaviorally.

In conclusion, the present results suggest that awareness of a biasing factor and naïve theories about how this factor influences one's judgments may not be necessarily consciously present for correction to occur, unlike assumed by traditional correction models (Martin 1986; Schwarz and Bless 1992; Wegener et al. 2004; Wilson and Brekke 1994). Given the pervasiveness of the influence of factors of which consumers are unaware, these results call for further testing and for updating of correction theories to include correction for subjective experiences in addition to conscious assessments. From a consumer welfare perspective, it is interesting that correction may serve as a tool to defend consumers from the influence of marketing stimuli, given that consumers are often unaware of the stimulus and of its influence.

APPENDIX

Stimuli

Imagine that you are looking for an apartment to rent. You have looked at a few apartments, but haven't found what you really want. Although you have seen several different apartments, nothing has seemed just right. You head into an apartment rental agency.

Picture yourself walking into the agency and looking at pictures and ads of apartments. There are pictures of different styles of apartments in various sizes and locations. A realtor walks up to you and says, "Hi, my name is Chris. Let me know if I can answer any questions for you."

Imagine that after looking through the pictures of several apartments, you narrow it down to two choices. The first is a nice, fairly standard apartment. The second apartment looks a little nicer, but it costs quite a bit more than the first. You look over the pictures one more time, looking carefully at the floor plans of each apartment. As you look at the picture of the second apartment, the realtor walks up to you and says, "That's a great apartment. I think it's a better option than the other one. Besides, it is very attractive." You look at the pictures and the floor plans one more time, wondering whether you should get the second apartment.

REFERENCES

Aarts, Henk, Ruud Custers, and Hans Marien (2008), "Preparing and motivating behavior outside of awareness," *Science,* 319(5870), 1639.

Bargh, John A., Shelly Chaiken, Rajen Govender, and Felicia Pratto (1992), "The generality of the automatic attitude activation effect," *Journal of Personality and Social Psychology Bulletin,* 62(6), 893-912.

Bargh, John A., and Tanya Chartrand. (2000), "The mind in the middle: A practical guide to priming and automaticity research," in *Handbook of Research Methods in Social and Personality Psychology*, ed. Harry T. Reis and Charles M. Judd, Cambridge, UK: Cambridge University, 253-85.

Clore, Gerald L., and W. Gerrod Parrott (1994), "Cognitive feelings and metacognitive judgments," *European Journal of Social Psychology,* 24(1), 101–15.

Fazio, Russell H., David M. Sanbonmatsu, Martha C. Powell, and Frank R. Kardes (1986), "On the automatic activation of attitudes," *Journal of Personality and Social Psychology,* 50(2), 229–38.

Gross, Sharon R., Rolf Holtz, and Norman Miller (1995), "Attitude Certainty," in *Attitude Strength Antecedents and Consequences*, ed. Richard E. Petty and Jon A. Krosnick, Mahwah, NJ: Laurence Erlbaum Associates, 215-46.

Jacoby, Larry. L., Colleeen M. Kelley, and Jane Dywan (1989), "Memory Attributions," in *Varieties of Memory and Consciousness: Essays in Honor of Endel Tulving*, ed. Endel Tulving, Henry L. Roediger and Fergus I. M. Craik, Hillsdale, NJ: Erlbaum, 391–422.

Lee, Spike W. S., and Norbert Schwarz (2012), Something smells fishy: On the bidirectional nature and cognitive mediation of metaphoric influence. Unpublished manuscript. University of Michigan.

Loersch, Chris, and B. Keith Payne (2011), "The situated inference model: An integrative account of the effects of primes on perception, behavior, and motivation," *Perspectives on Psychological Science,* 6(3), 234-52.

Martin, Leonard L. (1986), "Set/reset: Use and disuse of concepts in impression formation," *Journal of Personality and Social Psychology,* 51(3), 493-504.

Meyers-Levy, Joan, and Prashant Malaviya (1999), "Consumers' processing of persuasive advertisements: An integrated framework of persuasion theories," *Journal of Marketing,* 63, 45-60.

Murphy, Sheila T., and Robert B. Zajonc (1993), "Affect, cognition, and awareness: Affective priming with optimal and suboptimal stimulus exposures," *Journal of Personality & Social Psychology,* 64(5), 723-39.

Petrusic, William M., and Joseph V. Baranski (2003), "Judging confidence influences decision processing in comparative judgments," *Psychonomic Bulletin and Review,* 10(1), 177-83.

Petty, Richard E., and John T. Cacioppo (1986), "The elaboration likelihood model of persuasion," *Advances in Experimental Social Psychology,* 19, 123-62.

Petty, Richard E., Duane T. Wegener, and Paul H. White (1998), "Flexible correction processes in social judgment: implications for persuasion," *Social Cognition,* 16(1), 93-113.

Schwarz, Norbert (1990), "Feelings as Information: Informational and Motivational Functions of Affective States," in *Handbook of Motivation and Cognition: Foundations of Social Behavior*, Vol. 2, ed. E. Tory Higgins and Richard M. Sorrentino, New York: Guilford Press, 527-61.

——— (2004), "Metacognitive experiences in consumer judgment and decision making," *Journal of Consumer Psychology,* 14(4), 332–48.

Schwarz, Norbert, and Herbert Bless (1992), "Constructing Reality and Its Alternatives: An Inclusion/Exclusion Model of Assimilation and Contrasteffects in Social Judgment," in *The Construction of Social Judgments*, ed. Leonard L. Martin and Abraham Tesser, Hillsdale, NJ: Erlbaum, 217-45.

Schwarz, Norbert, and Gerald L. Clore (1996), "Feelings and Phenomenal Experiences," in *Social Psychology: Handbook of Basic Principles*, ed. E. Tory Higgins and Arie W. Kruglanski, New York: Guilford, 433-65.

Strack, Fritz (1992), "The Different Routes to Social Judgments: Experiential Versus Informational Strategies," in *The Construction of Social Judgments*, ed. Leonard L. Martin and Abraham Tesser, Hillsdale, NJ: Erlbaum, 249-76.

Watson, David, Lee A. Clark, and Auke Tellegen (1988), "Development and validation of brief measures of positive and negative affect: The PANAS scales," *Journal of Personality and Social Psychology,* 54(6), 1063-070.

Wegener, Duane T., and Richard E. Petty (1995), "Flexible correction processes in social judgment: The role of naive theories in corrections for perceived bias," *Journal of Personality and Social Psychology,* 68(1), 36-51.

Wegener, Duane T., Richard E. Petty, Natalie D. Smoak, and Leandre R. Fabrigar (2004), "Multiple Routes to Resisting Attitude Change," in *Resistance and Persuasion*, ed. Eric S. Knowles and Jay A. Linn, Mahwah, NJ: Lawrence Erlbaum, 13-38.

Wilson, Timothy D., and Nelson Brekke (1994), "Mental contamination and mental correction: Unwanted influences on judgments and evaluations" *Psychological Bulletin,* 116, 117-42.

Winkielman, Piotr, and Kent C. Berridge (2004), "Unconscious emotion," *Current Directions in Psychological Science,* 13, 120-23.

Winkielman, Piotr, Robert B. Zajonc, and Norbert Schwarz (1997), "Subliminal affective priming resists attributional interventions," *Cognition and Emotion,* 11, 433-65.

Zajonc, Robert B. (1994), "Can Emotions Be Unconscious?," in *The Nature of Emotion: Fundamental Questions*, ed. Paul Ekman and Richard J. Davidson, New York: Oxford University Press, 293-97.

Zajonc, Robert B., and Hazel Markus (1982), "Affective and Cognitive Factors in Preferences," *Journal of Consumer Research,* 9(2), 123-31.

Fooling Yourself:
The Role of Internal Defense Mechanisms in Unsustainable Consumption Behavior

Alexander Stich, WHU-Otto Beisheim School of Management, Germany
Tillmann Wagner, WHU-Otto Beisheim School of Management, Germany

ABSTRACT

Unsustainable consumption offers a fertile ground for the rise of intrapsychic conflicts. A series of 20 in-depth interviews was conducted to investigate people's inner conflicts in the field of sustainability and how consumers deal with them. After the development of a sustainability classification from a consumer's point of view, we led consumers to talk about their inner conflicts in the sustainability context. In particular, these conflicts emerge when long-term sustainability-related motives contrast with short-term motives. Results show that especially sustainability-oriented consumers show intrapsychic conflicts of varying degree when consuming unsustainably. Notably, consumers use a wide range of psychological defense mechanisms to continue unsustainable consumption behavior. Only in case of intense conflicts, actual behavior is modified. In general, this research proposes a theoretical framework of how consumers deal with their inner conflicts.

INTRODUCTION

The majority of consumers claim sustainability to be of high subjective importance. For instance, people state that it is essential to reduce waste and to be economical with natural resources like water, oil, or the tropical rain forest. Nevertheless, at the same time, many consumers also engage in unsustainable consumption behavior, for example taking the car instead of public transport or purchasing products based on a very resource-intensive production process. Therefore, the question arises why even sustainability-oriented consumers show unsustainable consumption behavior. Under the umbrella of the so-called attitude-behavior gap (Carrigan, Moraes, and Leek 2011) this question has been and still is controversially discussed in the area of consumer research (Eckhardt, Belk, and Devinney 2010). However, we speculate that there are also intrapsychic consumer conflicts involved. To the best of the authors' knowledge, the underlying psychological mechanisms of whether and how consumers solve the resulting inner conflicts have not yet been examined. Therefore, this approach tries to make a first step towards an understanding of how consumers solve their inner conflicts in the field of sustainability.

Due to the complex and explorative nature of the present research question, the authors decided to follow a qualitative approach using in-depth interviews (Bengtsson and Ostberg 2006). In-depth interviews are combined with pre-existing theoretical knowledge to propose a new theoretical framework, trying to explain how inner conflicts emerge and how different conflict types are resolved by consumers. This paper is structured as follows: First, a brief theoretical background about the concept of sustainability as well as about psychological defense mechanisms is provided. Second, method and findings of the conducted in-depth interviews are described. Finally, implications, limitations, and future research directions are discussed.

THEORETICAL BACKGROUND

Sustainability

Sustainability is an "emerging megatrend" (Lubin and Esty 2010, 44) which is also considered to be the essential and most important challenge for modern marketing (Kotler 2011; Sheth 2011). The common core of sustainability definitions is that a sustainable system is a "system [...] which survives or persists" (Costanza and Patten 1995, 193). However, there are many different definitions of sustainability.

Sustainability can, for example, be described as the use of resources in a way which enables future generations to live with the same or larger amount of resources (World Commission on Environment and Development 1987). Recent conceptual research proposes not only ecological and social aspects but also the importance of personal well-being in the context of consumer sustainability (Sheth, Sethia, and Srinivas 2011). Nevertheless, there is not much research about the consumer's understanding of the sustainability term and which facets it consists of. Therefore, this aspect will need to be explored first, thereby creating the basis for further investigation of inner conflicts in the field of unsustainable consumption.

But why do even sustainability-oriented consumers behave unsustainably? Recent studies investigate this issue by focusing on the gap between consumer attitudes and actual behavior (Bray, Johns, and Kilburn 2011). In doing so, current research systematizes the reasons consumers provide to justify unsustainable consumption (Banbury, Stinerock, and Subrahmanyan 2012; Eckhardt et al. 2010; Öberseder, Schlegelmilch, and Gruber 2011). One of these reasons is said to lie in local infrastructure (Banbury et al. 2012). Specifically, consumers who live in rural areas claim bad local infrastructure, in particular limited public transport opportunities, to account for an impossibility to live and consume sustainably. Consumers also state their own institutional dependency (Eckhardt et al. 2010), that is, they emphasize the responsibility of institutions such as the government to regulate which products are allowed to be sold or not. Furthermore, high prices of sustainable products are said to be a major reason for not buying them (Öberseder et al. 2011). To sum it up, there is a high need to know which reasons consumers point out regarding their unsustainable consumption behavior. However, it seems equally important to gain knowledge about the underlying psychological mechanisms of whether and how consumers solve their suspected inner conflicts when consuming unsustainably. Therefore, this paper focuses on the investigation of consumers' intrapsychic conflict resolution strategies.

Defense Mechanisms

The psychoanalytic concept of unconscious or semiconscious defense mechanisms is commonly used in everyday language. In particular, specific defense mechanisms like denial, suppression, repression, or projection are well-known terms for many people. These mechanisms enable individuals to encounter their inner conflicts (Freud 1936/1946). Although there are also voices who emphasize that some defense processes can be conscious to a certain degree (Erdelyi 2001), defense mechanisms are for the most part considered to be rather semiconscious or unconscious (Cramer 1998). However, it is important to note that individuals can use and elaborate on defense mechanisms without being conscious as to why they use them (Bond 1995).

In contrast to psychoanalysts, non-clinical researchers focused more on conscious processes like coping strategies so far (Cramer 2000), nevertheless, today there is a handful of empirical research outside the clinical context (Baumeister, Dale, and Sommer 1998). Defense mechanisms are also an emerging theme in marketing, but do not seem to have been investigated much (Homburg and Fürst 2007). Following this, our research takes a first step to empirically investigate defense mechanisms in consumer research. Building on in-depth interviews, this research develops a framework, revealing different types of inner conflicts and corresponding mechanisms employed for conflict resolution in the context of unsustainable consumption.

METHOD

We conducted 20 in-depth interviews with German consumers in an open and unstructured way. Participants were chosen according to demographic criteria, thereby varying according to age, gender, occupation as well as levels of education (table 1). To get a picture of average German consumers, very ecologically-minded individuals were not part of the sample. Interviews were audio-taped and transcribed verbatim. The data analysis was executed by two researchers using the standard procedure of coding and clustering the codes into higher-order categories (Creswell 2009). Comments from interviews were double-back translated. A general framework was built combining the qualitative data with theoretical background knowledge (Workman, Homburg, and Gruner 1998).

FINDINGS

In a first step, it seems important to get a better understanding of consumer sustainability to identify areas of potential inner conflicts. Therefore, we asked participants to reflect on sustainability from a consumer's point of view. Building on Sheth et al. (2011), we also asked them about their self-understanding of personal sustainability. Altogether, results reveal ecological (economic conservation, environmental preservation), social (family protection, occupational justice, social justice), and also individual facets of sustainability (physical health, mental health, economic health). Most notably, our data contribute to a first classification of consumers' sustainability objectives and issues (table 2).

Afterwards, we directed consumers to talk about their inner conflicts in the sustainability context. Our research leads to a theoretical framework (figure 1). The results suggest that conflicts, varying in terms of strength, emerge from the simultaneous presence of opposing

Table 1
Profiles of Interview Participants and Interview Facts

Pseudonym	Age	Occupation	Type of interview	Interview duration
Benjamin	53	Administration secretary	Phone	50 minutes
Bert	30	Fundraiser	Video	106 minutes
Charlene	27	Teacher (academic high school)	Phone	46 minutes
Clarissa	43	Electrician	Phone	60 minutes
Denice	27	Unemployed	Phone	81 minutes
George	82	Retiree	Phone	120 minutes
Jack	50	Marketing assistant	Phone	87 minutes
Jessica	34	Occupational health and safety practitioner	Video	68 minutes
Jonathan	44	Kitchen worker	Face-to-face	60 minutes
Kristie	38	Administrative assistant	Face-to-face	49 minutes
Maria	77	Housewife	Phone	85 minutes
Martin	27	Plasterer	Phone	52 minutes
Monica	48	General practitioner & housewife	Phone	54 minutes
Peter	25	Research assistant (marketing)	Face-to-face	146 minutes
Rebecca	58	Child care worker	Phone	75 minutes
Sadie	20	Hairdresser	Face-to-face	50 minutes
Thomas	27	Research assistant (sociology)	Phone	87 minutes
Todd	29	Glassblower	Phone	54 minutes
Tony	48	Sales manager	Phone	66 minutes
Ursula	58	Teacher (junior high school)	Phone	122 minutes

Table 2
Consumers' Sustainability Objectives and Issues: Examples from Interviews

Sustainability dimension	Sustainability objective	Most important issues
Ecological sustainability	Economic conservation	Resources, energy, consumption rate, waste, recycling, packaging, transport, organic food
	Environmental preservation	Climate, animals, pollution, damaging, mutilation
Individual sustainability	Economic health	Saving, debt, retirement provisions
	Mental health	Work-life balance, stress, recreation, spirituality
	Physical health	Balanced diet, exercise, sports, alcohol & cigarettes
Social sustainability	Family protection	Responsibility toward family, education, children's children
	Occupational justice	Working conditions, exploitation, minimum wages, child labor
	Social justice	Fairness, poverty, social engagement, peace

Figure 1
Framework for Inner Conflicts: Emergence, Types, and Management

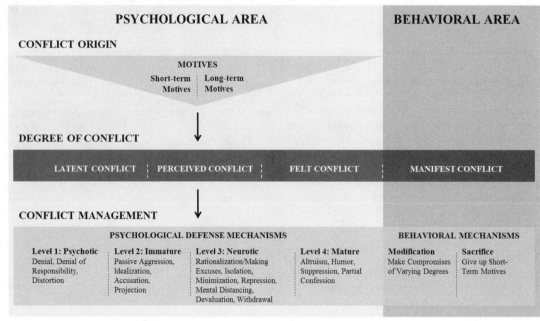

consumption motives. Depending on the degree of conscious awareness, there is a tendency to use specific defense mechanisms to resolve conflicts for the sake of continuing unsustainable consumption behavior, or, if conflict resolution was not successful, change actual behavior. In the following, the nature of this framework will be elaborated in more detail.

Intrapsychic Conflicts

We draw on common motive, need, and goal classifications (Reiss 2004) as well as consumer research about people's conflicts (Bahl and Milne 2010; Lee and Shrum 2012; Ratneshwar, Pechmann, and Shocker 1996). Motives can be divided into short-term and long-term motives (Schweitzer 2005), whereby sustainability refers by definition to the long-term perspective (Costanza and Patten 1995). Basically, we find that conflicts emerge in situations where long-term sustainability-related motives contrast with short-term motives.

Depending on salience and severity of specific motives clusters, the type of inner conflict can vary. For classification purposes, we used the terms latent conflict (people are not aware of a conflict at all), perceived conflict (people recognize a conflict without having bad feelings about it), felt conflict (people recognize a conflict while having bad feelings about it), and manifest conflict (people recognize a strong conflict which has immediately to be resolved), which have been labeled in organizational conflict research (Pondy 1967, 1989; Maltz and Kohli 2001), introducing these labels to intrapsychic conflicts. Our study provides initial evidence of these different consumer conflicts (table 3). It is important to note that conflict types can overlap, for example containing both cognitive and emotional conflict aspects at the same time (Luce 1998).

An example for perceived conflict comes from Jessica. Her long-term motive idealism (in the form of human orientation) is opposed to the short-term motive well-being (in the form of enjoyment). In contrast, Bert has to deal with a more severe conflict (felt conflict), where his short-term motives financial security, personal well-being (in the form of comfort), and acceptance by others (in the form of self-expression) contrast with idealism.

Even though one rather should not eat chocolate, because I believe that cultivating chocolate heavily relies on child labor, but, unfortunately, I always melt at the sight of chocolate myself. (Jessica, 34)

Sometimes, when I'm conscious of [using unsustainable products] and I think that's mostly the case for clothes, then indeed, I have a bit of a bad conscience. This is crap, yes, I should really do better, but I don't. Because it's too demanding for me, because it's too expensive, because I would look stupid in such clothes. (Bert, 30)

These two examples illustrate different degrees of inner conflicts in the field of unsustainable consumption behavior. Especially when conflicts become more severe, people show a bad conscience and tend to feel guilty. Therefore, it seems obvious that people heavily rely on certain strategies to deal with their inner conflicts.

Defense Mechanisms

Furthermore, we investigated consumers' semiconscious or unconscious processes. There is much research about conscious processes (Levav, Kivetz, and Cho 2010; Ratneshwar, Mick, and Huffman 2000) and recently, consumer researchers have started to show interest in the examination of unconscious processes (Chartrand et al. 2008; Laran and Janiszewski 2009). In particular, unconscious internal defense mechanisms can help people, at least in the short term, to solve their inner conflicts (Freud 1936/1946). We find that people use a wide range of defense mechanisms to face their inner conflicts for the sake of continuing unsustainable consumption behavior. Vaillant (1977, 1992) proposes a hierarchical classification of defense mechanisms into psychotic (mainly altering reality), immature (mainly altering distress), neurotic (mainly mastering acute distress), and mature (mainly mastering general distress). In our research, we identify established mechanisms by prior researchers as well as new ones which we allocate to the aforementioned hierarchi-

Table 3
Consumers' Inner Conflicts: Citations from Interviews

Type/degree of conflict	Working definition	Excerpt from interviews
Latent conflict	People do not recognize a conflict at all, despite the presence of conflicting motives.	[Talking about her reasons for consuming sustainably] . . . sometimes I have a critical look at the whole economic development. Well, at school we have learned 'economy only works if there is a steady growth'. And well, I think, in terms of pure logic, this isn't possible without destroying the environment, too. And for me personally, this is actually important, that I do not mindlessly consume and that means I am maybe to a certain degree unproductive with regard to economic interests. Well, actually sustainability is of higher importance. . . . I do not feel bad [*emphasized*], no [talking about consuming or using unsustainable products, for example owning two cars which are both used every day]. . . . No [asked if having sometimes a bad conscience]. *(Monica, 48)*
Perceived conflict	People recognize a conflict which they can describe without having bad feelings about it.	Well, it happens, and this is how I make many of my decisions concerning consumption, that I buy something and consume it or use it, let it be food or something else, and that I think to myself 'well, practically it is not quite correct what I'm doing'. *(Jack, 50)*
Felt conflict	People recognize a conflict which they can describe while having bad feelings about it.	Erm, often I do not think anything of it, it just hits the spot. But sometimes I have a bad conscience as I said before. When I see such animals [*suffering*] which look so faithful and gentle and which are really innocent, doing no harm to anybody, and when I know that they are being slaughtered, that they get killed. *(George, 82)*
Manifest conflict	People recognize a strong conflict which has to be resolved immediately.	And in the end I really felt shitty in doing so [wasting of resources]. And in the end, now when I care more about it, I don't feel necessarily much better, but simply not much worse, either, because I worry about certain resources and I am economical with them. *(Todd, 29)*

cal classification. Table 4 outlines definitions and examples of all the defense mechanisms employed by the participants.

Although every defense mechanism serves the common goal to solve inner conflicts, the extracted mechanisms vary in nature and frequency of use. In our study, among the most used defense mechanisms are denial of responsibility, rationalization, and suppression. In the following examples, Todd uses denial of responsibility in order to avoid negative feelings, Ursula excuses or rationalizes her behavior by time pressure, and George admits that he is actively suppressing his negative feelings.

And well, sometimes I even think if I take care or not, in my opinion in the end the whole caboodle will go down the drain anyway, such being the case [*pauses*]. Now, this is my personal opinion. (Todd, 29)

To be honest, I do have these noble goals, in some areas I reach them and I act more consciously. On the other hand, I would have to inform myself a lot about every single product that I buy [*emphasized*]. And I would have to question every single product, erm, and this might also be a self-serving declaration, I do not like to completely reject this, this might be a self-serving declaration when I claim 'I don't have the time for this'. It's too bad when you have to say 'I don't have the time for this', maybe this does also mean 'I don't want to take the time'. (Ursula, 58)

Well, I can say that in this case I'll suppress this. . . . I'm not aware of this bad conscience all the time, well, then I block it out. . . . Once the bad conscience has disappeared, the feeling

has disappeared, too. Then I'm not thinking about it, I don't think about it all the time. Then the problem has disappeared for the moment. (George, 82)

Besides several new subcategories, our findings provide initial evidence of the mechanisms accusation, mental distancing, and partial confession. First, accusation encompasses a direct allegation of somebody. This is in contrast to projection, which depends on comparisons with other people (Baumeister et al. 1998). Second, mental distancing characterizes the dissociation from others without devaluing them, whilst the latter one is defined as the attribution of exaggerated negative characteristics to others (Kernberg 1967, 1987). Third, partial confession describes the confession of minor own weaknesses in order to mask more severe weaknesses or to preempt arguments against oneself. As shown below, Jonathan accuses others to be responsible for his own wrongdoing, whilst Sadie uses projection to whitewash her behavior by comparison with others. Bert relies on mental distancing and Thomas uses devaluation to strengthen his own position. Finally, Monica is confessing one of her minor weaknesses in order to distract from her total consumption level which can be suspected to be very high (her family owns two cars which are both used every day, lives in a huge mansion, and goes on vacation at least four times a year).

Then of course I am thinking 'why did you do this again [dumping a cigarette end]?'. But sometimes this happens, then I just dump it. Because [*loud*] there is no container where you can put this cork top when you are on your way, there is none! Where have you seen a cigarette container here in V. [city name] where

Table 4
Defense Mechanisms for Dealing with Inner Conflicts: Citations from Interviews

Defense mechanism (Level)	Short definition	Excerpt from interviews
Denial (Psychotic)	Refusal to admit certain aspects of reality (Bovey and Hede 2001)	. . . the long-term effects, I'm sure that is something no one could imagine 20 or 30 years before that we would have these problems with emissions and that actually the global warming would be coming. If global warming actually exists. There you have also, erm, reports saying the opposite. . . . And because of this uncertainty about the actual existence, it is absolutely no buying criterion for me so far. *(Peter, 25)*
Denial of responsibility* (Psychotic)	Refusal to admit own responsibility for sth. (Bierhoff, Klein, and Kramp 1991)	Yeah okay, in most cases they [clothes made through child labor] are 'made in Japan', when you have a close look, right? . . . Or China is the most frequent one. But what can I do against this here in Germany?! I cannot do anything against it any more [*emotional*]. *(Rebecca, 58)*
Distortion (Psychotic)	Reshaping of reality to meet inner needs (Vaillant 1992)	Yeah, well, but I would really not define coffee as semiluxury food but as a necessity. *(Thomas, 27)*
Passive aggression (Immature)	Indirect or passive aggression towards others (Vaillant 1992)	I don't have a bad conscience [*tricksy*]. I have not killed anyone, I treat the environment well, I treat my fellow men well. Why should I have a bad conscience [*without understanding/ aggressive*], eh?! If I can give something, I give it to someone who has less than me, so why do I have to have a bad conscience [*emotional/aggressive*]?! *(Rebecca, 58)*
Idealization (Immature) • General* • Comparative*	Attribution of exaggerated positive characteristics to the self or to others (Kernberg 1987; Pauchant and Mitroff 1988)	Well, if everyone would do this, just to say, somewhat living like me, myself, my husband, just to say, then we would live in an almost ideal world, here, right?! *(Rebecca, 58)*
Accusation** (Immature)	Direct allegation that someone is guilty of sth.	There are people who think they have to drive directly into the post office, who don't walk a single footstep. Some people, who live here in O. [village name], drive to the mailbox just a few houses down the street, post a letter, and drive back. Yeah, here I am thinking 'they are nuts'. Isn't it just possible to walk there?! First, this would have been good for them. And also these short distances are no good for the car and they would have prevented the environment from harm a little bit, too, right?! *(Rebecca, 58)*
Projection (Immature)	Refusal to accept own weaknesses by comparison with others' weaknesses (Baumeister, Dale, and Sommer 1998)	When it comes to electricity, there I also try to be economical. This is a product where I really try to behave appropriately. For example when I go out of the house, I take care that not all the lamps are turned on everywhere and that the TV is off, yeah, that I don't have electrical devices on standby. Here, I try to behave in a certain way, in order to assure this. Well, there are families in which I have friends who don't pay attention to this. . . . everyone has his own TV and his own computer, these things run around the clock, and everyone has his own car. *(Todd, 29)*
Rationalization/making excuses (Neurotic) Complexity* • History/education* • Opportunity* • Material pressure* • Mental pressure* • Temporal pressure*	Justification of impulses, motives, or behaviors in order to make them plausible and tolerable (Brown and Starkey 2000)	. . . one knows that a big part of the coffee is simply made under conditions of exploitation in the southern hemisphere, in South America. And after all, there is then also, so to say, the presence of the normative consciousness, that practically fair trade coffee, if any, would be the good solution, but I have also to admit that I normally reach for the normal coffee due to the limited budget. *(Thomas, 27)*

*New mechanism subcategory/categorization.
**Newly discovered mechanism (including own working definition).

Table 4 (*continued*)

Defense mechanism (Level)	Short definition	Excerpt from interviews
Isolation (Neurotic)	Creation of a psychological distance between unpleasant issues and oneself (Homburg and Fürst 2007)	Erm, well, with cigarettes this is clearly an addiction. Here I'm totally fair and square, you can label this as addiction. . . . This is something, I would say, this is just an independent small issue, this addictive behavior. *(Ursula, 58)*
Minimization (Neurotic)	Trivialization of the wrongdoing (Hoyk and Hersey 2008)	Also, I sometimes think 'oh my God, another cancer stick'. This might be true. And I also think 'if I am smoking more and more now, I will die some day, I will die earlier'. . . . But I think 'as long as I can reduce it' [*pauses*]. For example, I can resist smoking a cigarette for 4 to 5 hours, I don't have to smoke then [*emphasized*]. *(Jonathan, 44)*
Repression (Neurotic)	Unconscious decision to exclude unpleasant thoughts or feelings (Vaillant 1977)	Well shit, actually this is shit. But well, that's just the way it is. *(Bert, 30)*
Mental distancing** (Neurotic)	Dissociate oneself from others' opinions, attitudes, or behaviors	I don't wanna be like that [extremely ecological], I cannot be like that, and maybe there's also no need for it. *(Thomas, 27)*
Devaluation (Neurotic) • Cynical* • Skeptical*	Attribution of exaggerated negative characteristics to the self or to others (Kernberg 1967, 1987)	Well, for example my girlfriend likes to watch consumer protection programs on TV. And this is again something to which I say ironically and cynically that this is 'the worst thing in the world, which I absolutely dislike'. *(Thomas, 27)*
Withdrawal (Neurotic)	Avoidance of threatening situations (Constantinides and Beck 2010)	Or take for example Takko Fashion [discount clothing store]: There, I don't go in that store as a matter of principle and for the purpose of not being tempted. *(Charlene, 27)*
Altruism (Mature)	Instinctively helping others in a constructive way (Vaillant 1992)	I don't know which country this was about, the one with the civil war problem, well there we have also donated something. . . . We are lucky to live in a country without suffering from hunger and now I have donated money for that. *(Clarissa, 43)*
Humor (Mature)	Outright expression of thoughts and feelings without discomfort (Vaillant 1992)	While eating, I don't think 'oh, this animal happily bounced around and has been slaughtered for me' [*travesties her words*]. *(Maria, 77)*
Suppression (Mature) • General* • Temporal*	Semiconscious or conscious decision to delay paying attention to sth. (Vaillant 1977)	But, so to say, then after all with the ulterior motive 'there are so many starting points where one should live sustainably', in a way, that it is always [*pauses*] difficult to say where to start and to condemn everything. Well, there I really caught myself how I totally suppressed this. *(Thomas, 27)*
Partial confession** (Mature)	To confess own weaknesses in order to mask more severe weaknesses or to preempt arguments against oneself	Sometimes if things are just incredibly cheap, then it doesn't matter to me. Well, there is a certain threshold, not for every product, but for some of them. If it falls below that threshold, I will just buy [*pauses*]. Okay, I know, that I do not always buy ecological and biological, this would be a lie, I cannot leave this behind me completely. *(Jessica, 34)*

*New mechanism subcategory/categorization.
**Newly discovered mechanism (including own working definition).

you can put the end, never [*pauses*]?! There the population has to intervene more, but that's not the case. Or the city government, it doesn't do anything either. (Jonathan, 44)

Okay, people always tell me 'you are way too posh'. I would spend so much money on clothes, everything, but when I see others compared to me, what a shoe cabinet or wardrobe they have, compared to them I am really modest [*pauses*]. This is nuts, when I have a look at my friends [*slightly bewildered*]. (Sadie, 20)

When it comes to clothes it is really difficult to get true healthy clothes. And then I would really walk around completely in eco-style, which is something that I don't like to do. (Bert, 30)

But at the same time, I sometimes realize that I'm not as consequent as I should be, and that I find myself sometimes provoking other people, who are very sustainable, a little . . . also that I sometimes realize that I take the opposite standpoint, and that I satirize so to say excessive sustainable thinking in a cynical way. (Thomas, 27)

Well, this is maybe impulse buying, which you do rather without thinking. That something in the shop is attracting you, let it be a T-shirt, there I don't have a look if it's 'made in Taiwan' or somewhere else. This can definitely happen, that in a certain moment I do not take care of sustainability. (Monica, 48)

In general, we find that more severe conflicts tend to be resolved by more advanced mechanisms. For example, participants with felt conflicts rely on mature rather than on psychotic defense mechanisms, while the latter suggest the existence of latent conflicts. Only when inner conflicts cannot be sufficiently resolved, people change actual consumption behavior. According to Ekins (1994), people use modification and/or sacrifice to feel like living a sustainable life. Indeed, participants report making minor compromises in order to resolve their manifest conflicts. As a consequence, they report having reduced their negative feelings or even produced positive ones.

I had ordered something for my kids, shipping order. And when I had the products [T-Shirts] later in my hands, I had a look at the label, then there was written 'made in Bangladesh'. There I wrapped them up and sent them back. . . . there I've thought 'no'. I've sent them back. This was a thing I somehow couldn't do, because I thought that there is child labor behind it, one-hundred percent. (Kristie, 38)

Kristie's example shows that she needed to change her actual behavior in order to overcome the underlying manifest conflict. To sum it up, participants sometimes tend to make compromises on behalf of sustainability issues, nonetheless in many cases psychological defense mechanisms prevent them from changing unsustainable consumption pattern.

DISCUSSION

This research tried to address the important question of why even sustainability-oriented consumers show unsustainable consumption behavior. We undertook a first step to develop a theoretical framework describing consumers' underlying psychological mechanisms. Notably, the concept of semiconscious defense mechanisms

was introduced as one possible explanation of the aforementioned phenomenon. In-depth interviews revealed that there is a wide range of different defense mechanisms which people use to continue unsustainable consumption behavior.

In addition to the specific results above, defense mechanisms show some general aspects which should be discussed. To begin with, defense mechanisms are often said to be rather unconscious (Cramer 1998). Indeed, there is a continuum between unconscious and semiconscious defenses. In particular, first level (psychotic) mechanisms like denial or distortion are mainly unconscious, that is, people use them to resist their bad conscience without being aware of using them. Therefore, it is sometimes difficult for researchers to detect psychotic defenses. Nevertheless, our research is indicative of some of these first level mechanisms. Second level (immature) mechanisms such as accusation or projection tend to be rather unconscious at the moment of their use, but under certain circumstances people might become aware of their utilization when reflecting about their own past behavior (Bond 1995). Mechanisms on the third level (neurotic) like rationalization or devaluation contain more semiconscious processes compared to immature mechanisms. Especially rationalization is a mechanism which participants use in different subtypes (complexity, history/education, opportunity, material pressure, mental pressure, temporal pressure). It is important to note that most of these rationalizations take the short-term, not sustainability-related, motive (personal comfort, enjoyment, acceptance by others etc.) as a default. In other words, participants are not willing to make any compromises at the cost of their short-term motives. This is why they start searching for arguments that justify their negligence of sustainability-related motives. Finally, fourth level (mature) mechanisms are used in a more semiconscious way (Vaillant 1992). For instance, general and temporal suppression constitute a promising way for consumers to overcome inner conflicts.

Furthermore, psychological defense mechanisms stem from psychoanalytic therapy and have often been connected with mentally ill individuals. However, mature defenses are common for healthy individuals to solve psychological conflicts (Vaillant 1992), as is supported by the conducted in-depth interviews. Moreover, neurotic defenses are well-established when healthy individuals have to master acute distress. Again, this seems obvious when having a look at the wide range of rationalizations used by our interview partners when being confronted with potential intrapsychic conflicts. Whilst clinicians consider immature (age 3 to 15) and psychotic defenses (age before 5) to be typical for children and adults in psychotherapy (Vaillant 1992), other researchers claim most defense mechanisms to have normal as well as pathological manifestations (Baumeister et al. 1998). Therefore, it is no surprise that people continue to use primitive defense mechanisms which they have learnt during childhood and adolescence. Our interviews indicate that individuals rather unconsciously rely on those mechanisms which have been successful for them in the past. Interestingly, results point in the direction that higher (vs. lower) levels of education are connected with more advanced defense mechanisms (neurotic, mature) and vice versa, therefore, individuals' intellectual age might play a role in this context.

Last but not least, there is some debate about the efficiency of specific defense mechanisms, building on the differentiation between adaptive and maladaptive defenses (Segal, Coolidge, and Mizuno 2007). Whilst adaptive mechanisms such as humor and suppression are said to help individuals solving their inner conflicts, maladaptive mechanisms like projection and withdrawal should even worsen the situation in the midterm. Even though we also found evidence that higher level defenses seem to be more helpful for individuals to reduce negative feelings in general, there is also a strong subjective preference for the use of specific mechanisms. We speculate that this originates from the individual's successful use of these mechanisms in the past.

LIMITATIONS AND FUTURE RESEARCH

For the purpose of classifying participants' degree of inner conflict, we draw on Pondy's systematization into latent, perceived, felt, and manifest conflicts (Pondy 1967, 1989). It hardly needs mentioning that in reality there is no clear-cut differentiation including four separated conflict types, but rather a continuum of inner conflicts according to strength. Nevertheless, we regard the terms 'latent', 'perceived', 'felt', and 'manifest' to be appropriate reflections of conflict strength. In particular, 'latent' as an indicator that the individual is not yet aware of the conflict at all, 'perceived' as the unemotional recognition of the conflict, 'felt' as the emotionally laden conflict perception, and 'manifest' as a very strong and apparent conflict, seem to be helpful criteria to classify inner conflicts.

In this research, several previously identified defense mechanisms as well as three new mechanisms (accusation, mental distancing, partial confession) could be identified. However, there are several additional defense mechanisms (Vaillant 1992), for example anticipation, somatization, sublimation, acting out, hypochondriasis, or displacement, which have been found inside the clinical context but were not supported in the conducted in-depth interviews. The possible reasons for this are threefold. First, there are some defenses like sublimation which are very difficult to detect via in-depth interviews. Maybe projective techniques might be an additional method to address this shortcoming. Second, the framework of unsustainable consumption behavior might lead to certain preferences concerning the selection of specific defense mechanisms whilst other defenses might not be very appropriate in this context. Third, the reason might also lie in the specific sample.

Finally, the detailed results concerning the evolution of inner conflicts and its respective conflict resolution strategies cannot be generalized to every human in every country in the same way. Not only do individuals have an inconsistent understanding what sustainability means, they also show huge differences concerning the subjective importance of particular sustainability aspects. Especially preferences, personality characteristics, and cultural aspects might play a role. For instance, there might be individual differences in altruism, materialism, or long-term orientation. These factors might shape the intensity of an intrapsychic conflict or the frequency of use of certain psychological defense mechanisms. However, they should by no means change the general theoretical framework which has been developed in this research approach.

Our theoretical contribution may be a starting point for further research to explore the nature and effectiveness of several conflict reduction strategies. Especially, additional knowledge about different degrees of intrapsychic conflicts and the corresponding internal defense mechanisms would help to further understand why consumers can continue to consume unsustainably although at the same time realizing the importance of living a sustainable life. As a matter of fact, defense mechanisms vary in nature. Therefore, building on experimental designs, it might be difficult to investigate the complete range of defense mechanisms in a single study. We suggest that future experimental research should concentrate on the examination of discrete defense mechanisms. Most interestingly, the effectiveness of a specific defense mechanism (denial of responsibility, rationalization, accusation, partial confession, or suppression) could be tested.

Finally, social desirability is an issue of high relevance (Dalton and Ortegren 2011; Mick 1996), thereby being especially dangerous for biasing results in research dealing with issues of unsustainable consumption. Consequently, we strongly advise to control for this bias when further investigating psychological defense mechanisms in the field of sustainability.

REFERENCES

Banbury, Catherine, Robert Stinerock, and Saroja Subrahmanyan (2012), "Sustainable Consumption: Introspecting across Multiple Lived Cultures," *Journal of Business Research*, 65 (April), 497-503.

Bahl, Shalini and George R. Milne (2010), "Talking to Ourselves: A Dialogical Exploration of Consumption Experiences," *Journal of Consumer Research*, 37 (June), 176-95.

Baumeister, Roy F., Karen Dale, and Kristin L. Sommer (1998), "Freudian Defense Mechanisms and Empirical Findings in Modern Social Psychology: Reaction Formation, Projection, Displacement, Undoing, Isolation, Sublimation, and Denial," *Journal of Personality*, 66 (December), 1081-124.

Bengtsson, Anders and Jacob Ostberg (2006), "Researching the Cultures of Brands," in *Handbook of qualitative research methods in marketing,* ed. Russell Belk, Aldershot, UK: Edward Elgar, 83-93.

Bierhoff, Hans W., Renate Klein, and Peter Kramp (1991), "Evidence for the Altruistic Personality from Data on Accident Research," *Journal of Personality*, 59 (June), 263-80.

Bond, Michael P. (1995), "The Development and Properties of the Defense Style Questionnaire," in *Ego Defenses: Theory and Measurement*, ed. Hope R. Conte and Robert Plutchik, New York: John Wiley & Sons, 202-20.

Bovey, Wayne H. and Andrew Hede (2001), "Resistance to Organisational Change: The Role of Defence Mechanisms," *Journal of Managerial Psychology*, 16 (7/8), 534-48.

Bray, Jeffery, Nick Johns, and David Kilburn (2011), "An Exploratory Study into the Factors Impeding Ethical Consumption," *Journal of Business Ethics*, 98 (February), 597-608.

Brown, Andrew D. and Ken Starkey (2000), "Organizational Identity and Learning: A Psychodynamic Perspective," *Academy of Management Review*, 25 (January), 102-20.

Carrigan, Marylyn, Caroline Moraes, and Sheena Leek (2011), "Fostering Responsible Communities: A Community Social Marketing Approach to Sustainable Living," *Journal of Business Ethics,* 100 (May), 515-34.

Chartrand, Tanya L., Joel Huber, Baba Shiv, and Robin J. Tanner (2008), "Nonconscious Goals and Consumer Choice," *Journal of Consumer Research*, 35 (August), 189-201.

Constantinides, Prometheas and Stephen M. Beck (2010), "Toward Developing a Scale to Empirically Measure Psychotic Defense Mechanisms," *Journal of the American Psychoanalytic Association*, 58 (December), 1159-88.

Costanza, Robert and Bernard C. Patten (1995), "Defining and Predicting Sustainability," *Ecological Economics,* 15 (December), 193-96.

Cramer, Phebe (1998), "Coping and Defense Mechanisms: What's the Difference?" *Journal of Personality*, 66 (December), 919-46.

_____ (2000), Defense Mechanisms in Psychology Today: Further Processes forAdaptation," *American Psychologist*, 55 (June), 637-46.

Creswell, John W. (2009), *Research Design. Qualitative, Quantitative, and Mixed Method Approaches*, Vol. 3, Thousand Oaks, CA: Sage Publications.

Dalton, Derek and Marc Ortegren (2011), "Gender Differences in Ethics Research: The Importance of Controlling for the Social Desirability Response Bias," *Journal of Business Ethics*, 103 (October), 73-93.

Eckhardt, Giana M., Russell Belk, and Timothy M. Devinney (2010), "Why Don't Consumers Consume Ethically?" *Journal of Consumer Behaviour*, 9 (November/December), 426-36.

Ekins, Paul (1994), "The Environmental Sustainability of Economic Processes: A Framework for Analysis," in *Toward Sustainable Development: Concepts, Methods, and Policy*, ed. Jeroen C. J. M. van den Bergh and Jan van der Straaten, Washington, DC: Island Press, 25-56.

Erdelyi, Mathew Hugh (2001), "Defense Processes Can Be Conscious or Unconscious," *American Psychologist*, 56 (September) 761-62.

Freud, Anna (1936/1946), *The Ego and the Mechanisms of Defense*, trans. C. Baines, New York: International Universities Press.

Homburg, Christian and Andreas Fürst (2007), "See no Evil, Hear no Evil, Speak no Evil: A Study of Defensive Organizational Behavior towards Customer Complaints," *Journal of the Academy of Marketing Science*, 35 (Winter), 523-36.

Hoyk, Robert and Paul Hersey (2008), *The Ethical Executive*, Stanford, CA: Stanford Business Books.

Kernberg, Otto F. (1967), "Borderline Personality Organization," *Journal of the American Psychoanalytic Association*, 15 (July), 641-85.

――――――― (1987), "Projection and Projective Identification: Developmental and Clinical Aspects," *Journal of the American Psychoanalytic Association*, 35 (August), 795-819.

Kotler, Philip (2011), "Re-Inventing Marketing to Manage the Environmental Imperative," *Journal of Marketing*, 75 (July), 131-35.

Laran, Juliano and Chris Janiszewski (2009), "Behavioral Consistency and Inconsistency in the Resolution of Goal Conflict," *Journal of Consumer Research*, 35 (April), 967-84.

Lee, Jaehoon and L. J. Shrum (2012), "Conspicuous Consumption versus Charitable Behavior in Response to Social Exclusion: A Differential Needs Explanation," *Journal of Consumer Research*, 39 (October), forthcoming.

Levav, Jonathan, Ran Kivetz, and Cecile K. Cho (2010), "Motivational Compatibility and Choice Conflict," *Journal of Consumer Research*, 37 (October), 429-42.

Lubin, David A. and Daniel C. Esty (2010), "The Sustainability Imperative," *Harvard Business Review*, 88 (May), 42-50.

Luce, Mary Frances (1998), "Choosing to Avoid: Coping with Negatively Emotion-Laden Consumer Decisions," *Journal of Consumer Research*, 24 (March), 409-33.

Maltz, Elliot and Ajay K. Kohli (2000), "Reducing Marketing's Conflict with Other Functions: The Differential Effects of Integrating Mechanisms," *Journal of the Academy of Marketing Science*, 28 (Fall), 479-92.

Mick, David Glen (1996), "Are Studies of Dark Side Variables Confounded by Socially Desirable Responding? The Case of Materialism," *Journal of Consumer Research*, 23 (September), 106-19.

Öberseder, Magdalena, Bodo B. Schlegelmilch, and Verena Gruber (2011), "'Why Don't Consumers Care about CSR?': A Qualitative Study Exploring the Role of CSR in Consumption Decisions," *Journal of Business Ethics*, 104 (December), 449-60.

Pauchant, Thierry C. and Ian I. Mitroff (1988), "Crisis Prone Versus Crisis Avoiding Organizations: Is Your Company's Culture Its Own Worst Enemy in Creating Crises?" *Organization & Environment*, 2 (March), 53-63.

Pondy, Louis R. (1967), "Organizational Conflict: Concepts and Models," *Administrative Science Quarterly*, 12 (September), 296-320.

――――――― (1989), "Reflections on Organizational Conflict," *Journal of Organizational Change Management*, 13 (May), 257-61.

Ratneshwar, S., David Glen Mick, and Cynthia Huffman (2000), "Consumer Goal Structures and Goal-Determination Processes: An Integrative Framework," in *The Why of Consumption: Contemporary Perspectives on Consumer Motives, Goals, and Desires*, ed. S. Ratneshwar, David Glen Mick, and Cynthia Huffman, London: Routledge, 9-35.

Ratneshwar, S., Cornelia Pechmann, and Allan D. Shocker (1996), "Goal-Derived Categories and the Antecedents of Across-Category Consideration," *Journal of Consumer Research*, 23 (December), 240-50.

Reiss, Steven (2004), "Multifaceted Nature of Intrinsic Motivation: The Theory of 16 Basic Desires," *Journal of General Psychology*, 8 (September), 179-93.

Schweitzer, Lars (2005), "Organizational Integration of Acquired Biotechnology Companies into Pharmaceutical Companies: The Need for a Hybrid Approach," *Academy of Management Journal*, 48 (December), 1051-74.

Segal, Daniel L., Frederick L. Coolidge, and Hideaki Mizuno (2007), "Defense Mechanism Differences between Younger and Older Adults: A Cross-Sectional Investigation," *Aging & Mental Health*, 11 (July), 415-22.

Sheth, Jagdish N. (2011), "Impact of Emerging Markets on Marketing: Rethinking Existing Perspectives and Practices," *Journal of Marketing*, 75 (July), 166-82.

Sheth, Jagdish N., Nirmal K. Sethia, and Shanti Srinivas (2011), "Mindful Consumption: A Customer-Centric Approach to Sustainability," *Journal of the Academy of Marketing Science*, 39 (February), 21-39.

Vaillant, George E. (1977), *Adaptation to Life*, Boston: Little, Brown.

――――――― (1992), *Ego Mechanisms of Defense: A Guide for Clinicians and Researchers*, Washington, DC: American Psychiatric Press.

Workman, John P., Jr., Christian Homburg, and Kjell Gruner (1998), "Marketing Organization: An Integrative Framework of Dimensions and Determinants," *Journal of Marketing*, 62 (July), 21-41.

World Commission on Environment and Development (1987), *Our Common Future*, Oxford: Oxford University Press.

Utilising Consumer Introspection Theory to place the Culture of Consumer Research into the Flow of Life

Tim Stone, Universty of Aberdeen, UK
Fuat Firat, University of Texas - Pan American, USA
Stephen J. Gould, Baruch College, USA

ABSTRACT

This article takes initial inspiration from the disciplinary pioneers of humanistic/cultural consumer research (especially Belk 1987, 1988; Belk, Wallendorf and Sherry 1989; Firat 1985; Firat and Dholakia 1982; Hirschmann and Holbrook 1982; Holbrook 1987; McCracken 1986; Mick 1986) who "encouraged investigation of the contextual, symbolic, and experiential aspects of consumption... from a macro, meso and micro theoretical perspective" (Arnould & Thompson 2005: 871). Such esteemed scholars often reflected insight from macroeconomics, microeconomics, psychology, sociology, anthropology, philosophy and the humanities into their accounts of consumer research. In this sense, and as Holbrook (1987) suggests, consumer researchers' have often adopted a multidisciplinary stance in attempting to view such constructs as acquisition, consumption, possession and disposition through different theoretical lenses. In this vein, and to paraphrase Belk (1987), *the aim of this paper is to reflexively examine the relationship between the culture of consumer research and the rest of life.* As Dholakia (2012: 221) suggests, this is important as it may allow us to better appreciate the "intertwined and not-so-visible rhizomes, linkages, influences, and flows" within our discipline.

With the preceding aim in mind, we specifically position ourselves alongside marketing and consumer researchers who have either attempted to provide a critical perspective (see Dholakia 2012, 2009; Dholakia and Firat 2006; Firat 2009; Firat and Dholakia 1982, 2003, 2006; Firat and Venkatesh 1995) or those scholars who have adopted an emotionally sensitised and close view of consumer research in relation to, for example; jazz consumption (e.g. Holbrook 1987), introspection (e.g. Gould 1991, 1995, 2008a, 2008b, 2012), place, technology and representation (e.g. Sherry 2000), poetry (e.g. Sherry and Schouten 2002), embodied imagination (e.g. Joy and Sherry 2003), videography (e.g. Belk and Kozinets 2005), post-humanism (e.g. Venkatesh, Karababa and Ger 2002) and transcendental consumption (e.g. Minowa 2011). Indeed, as Joy and Sherry (2003) in line with Pham, Cohen, Pracejus and Hughes (2001) suggest, feelings play a central role in consumers' (and consumer researchers) day-to-day lives and merit serious investigation. Following on from this, and as Joy and Sherry (2003) posit, studies of embodied realism (conscious and unconscious) have generated some of the most exciting consumer research as it allows us to get closer to the cultural context, atmospherics, texture and undercurrents that surround and permeate day-to-day life (Sherry and Schouten 2002).

THEORETICAL REFECTION (1) – HUMANISTIC CONSUMER RESEARCH AND CULTURAL DISCOURCE

Following Stone, Hewer and Brownlie (2011) we argue that, within the context of humanistic inspired consumer culture research, it has become relatively commonplace to draw upon, for example, the interpretive anthropology of Geertz (1973) to theoretically ground a broad range of empirical insight. Such scholarship as Stone et al. (2011) suggests, more often than not, either explicitly or implicitly, acknowledges that studies of "consumer culture" tend to fall in line with an anthropological tradition that views "culture" as a system of inherited conceptions and symbolic forms that enables men and women to communicate and further develop their knowledge and attitudes toward life (Geertz 1973). Following on from this, culture, combined with genetic predisposition (Ingold 2011), can be seen to play an important role in continually enabling a coherent and intelligible system of symbols and material artefacts to emerge within and throughout day-to-day lived experience.

Such a theoretical proposition might enable a question to appear in the reader's mind: How do people inherit symbolic symbols within a cultural context? Geertz (1973) suggests that when human beings are very young; a gap exists between emerging bodily knowledge and meaningful day-to-day functioning. Commenting on this gap, Ingold (2011) forwards the proposition that the fundamental aspects of cultural systems are genetically passed from one generation to the next. From this perspective, some consumer researchers (either implicitly or explicitly) tend to acknowledge that culture is thereby acquired through observation learning and practice (Warde 2005) rather than being innate. As Stone et al. (2011), in line with Ingold (2011) further suggest, freshly encultured individuals are then subsequently faced with a diverse range of environmental conditions which ensure that knowledge is constructed in such a way that enables individualised expression and subtle variations in observed behaviour. Reflecting upon such a proposition, the notion emerges whereby culture can either be thought of as a relatively natural and subtle "system of inherited conceptions and semiotic signs" (Geertz 1973) or a "significant web of meaning" (ibid.) that organises a wide range of meaningful consumption practices (Warde 2005), individual and shared symbolic experiences and knowledge generation activities.

THEORETICAL REFLECTION (2) – ANTHROPOLOGY AND CULTURAL DISCOURCE

With such thoughts in mind, we attempt to add nuance to scholarly debate surrounding the theorisation of culture within consumer research by offering an alternative anthropological perspective which suggests that a perspective of culture that is based on an assumed, coherent and static cultural boundary is problematic (Ingold 2011, 1992; Kottak 2008; Palsson 1993; Rapport and Overing 2007; Stone et al. 2011). Such a school of thought, we argue, is problematic because these particular theoretical building blocks seem to have been constructed on the basis that beliefs about the external world are converted into attitudes and behaviour that, in turn, become manifest in terms of outward appearance and verbal expression. Such a distinctive process appears to be shaped (and shape) by a wide range of cognitive rules which situate the person within the world and subsequently enable them to identify differences between the "self" and "others". By "others" we also refer to material artefacts, the earth beneath our feet, animals, birds, insects and so on. From this perspective, people can't attend to the world directly but have to figure it out along cognitive pathways that reflect upon a wide and diverse variety of integrated patterns of semiotic signs and material artefacts that come to the attention of the body's senses (Kottak 2008; Ingold 1992). As a consequence of such embodied mindfulness it is not entirely surprising that people divide and enwrap their understandings of the external world into discrete and meaningful cognitive parcels of knowledge.

From such a dualistic perspective, people are philosophically framed in such a way that suggests that individual and/or communal meaningful activities come into being within inverted, closed and static cultural boundaries (Ingold 2011). However, in practice, "what we do *not* find are neatly bounded and mutually exclusive bodies of thought and custom, perfectly shared by all who subscribe to them, and in which their lives and works are fully encapsulated" (Ingold 2008: 330). In other words, contemporary society could be thought of in terms of the sheer messy complexity that seems to circumnavigate traditional cultural boundaries. As Rapport and Overing (2007: 298) state, "[t]here is no longer traditional, bounded cultural worlds in which to live – pure, integrated, cohesive, place rooted – from which to depart and which to return, for all is situated and all is moving." From this we argue that cultural life "does not begin here or end there, or connect a point of origin with a final destination, but rather it keeps on going, finding a way through the myriad of things that form, persist and break up its currents" (Ingold 2011: 4). Life, in short, as Ingold (ibid.) reveals, is a movement of opening, not of closure. We therefore argue, that there is significant value in trying to recover that original openness to the world within consumer research in an attempt to revive and recover the things that make cultural life less structured and more sublime (Lacoue-Labarthe 1986; Lyotard 1986), magical (Buck 1936), liberatory (Durkheim 1915; Firat and Venkatesh 1995), free (Marcuse 2002), rich (Midgley 2003), impetuous, refined and enjoyable (Nietzsche 1990). Such an open epistemological and ontological perspective may enable us, as consumer researchers, to probe the complexities and nuances of context and environment in a deeper sense, thereby allowing more "disciplined enquiry into the conditions and potentials of human life" (Ingold, 2011: xi).

METHODOLOGY: EMPLOYING CONSUMER INTROSPECTION THEORY (CIT) TO OPEN UP CULTURAL DISCOURCE

Reflecting upon the preceding text enables an interesting question to emerge; how do we, as consumer researchers, open ourselves up in order to better appreciate the conditions of human life? In order to address this question it is necessary to align this paper with the way of the contemplative philosopher to propose methods that can be shared in order to experience reflexive revelations. Gould (2012: 455) suggests that we should consider employing Consumer Introspection Theory (henceforth, CIT) to extend the reach of cultural theory "by "excavat[ing] the dynamic of self-culture liminality and co-creation." Such a methodological approach can help to map the gestalt of experience by sensitising like minded consumer researchers to reflect upon dominant ideologies, obfuscations and mystifications playing out within the discipline. Our proposed methodological approach is similar to central Buddhist meditational techniques that explore the realms of consciousness, mind and the phenomenal world (Gould 1995; Wilber 2001). More specifically, we offer you three engaging introspective exercises or thought experiments - (1) You; (2) You and Your Work; and (3) Culture:

Introspective Exercise (1) – You

Consider all that makes up you; body parts, mind, thoughts, your name, relationships, aspects of identity such as gender, ethnicity or age, or consciousness and unconsciousness. Are any of these you? If not, what is you? Are you the sum of the parts, more than the sum of the parts, or are you multiple, i.e. each part is you – there are many yous. This may strike you as strange at first though it is not unlike deconstructing the self in postmodern terms. This way digs down in very specific ways. How does it make you feel? Is there a you? Or are you empty of you are you-ness? Perhaps the metaphor of the onion skin would be helpful here – you peel away layer after layer and in the end nothing remains. Is this true about you? How does this thought process make you feel? Are you empty or in emptiness? Continue by considering how you relate to your environment; physical, social and cultural. Are you part of it or separate from it? In any case, how are you connected to it? Is there a you that exists apart from it? Are you empty of existence with or without the environment?

This exercise should help you to think about and deconstruct theories of the self (e.g., extended and multiple selves; self-image and concept) in new and very personal ways. It can also help you to further engage with (your)self and your and our consumer research projects in new and stimulating ways. The next exercise is illustrative of one such further engagement with the self.

Introspective Exercise (2) – You and Your Work

Take a piece of your writing (it may be a current piece and at other times you may look retrospectively at your own published work) and read it through with special attention to the personal feelings and thoughts it brings up. Sometimes do this with more intention, that is, look for these things. Other times, let them arise spontaneously as you read and/or in other situations, such as post-reading. What do these feelings and thoughts tell you about the work and yourself? Does your work take a position and attempt to open up theoretical discourse or seek in some way to improve the world? Do these points matter to you? Does looking in this way change your understandings and perceptions? Certainly in literary criticism, we consider the idea of authorial intent. What were/are you as author intending in your writings? At the same time, you are a reader of your own work here – reader response. How do you respond to what you have said? How do you feel when you think of others reading your work? How have your views and therefore reading of any particular piece of yours changed? Read the work of others who cite/discuss your work. Do they get it? Does your authorial intent have any connection to their reader response, even to your own? (this exercise is adapted from Gould 2008b: 325).

Based on this reflexive introspection we attempt to suggest how various discursive inversions that present themselves to (and are used by) consumer researchers can be opened up. As such, we hope to sensitise you, the reader, to the role of boundaries in shaping you and your work though reflections that could relate (but necessarily be limited) to the following constructs; internal, external, introspective, extrospective, personal, cultural, narrative, meta-cognitive, objective, subjective, authorial intent, reader response and so on. Next, we provide an exercise which looks at and helps to deconstruct the boundaries of self and culture.

Introspective Exercise (3) – Culture

Is the self an outpost of culture? Watch your reactions to various manifestations of culture, such as everyday discourse; various practices in which you engage, especially as contrasted with those of others; and media use. Do you merely reproduce culture in these particular manifestations and expressions, i.e. being more produced than producing? Or do you actually produce culture, i.e. something new and different? Are your self and culture simultaneously produced, synchronously reflexive in relation to each other? Consider (cross)cultural phenomena such as hybridisation. When you encounter something new from another culture such as a new perspective or discourse, where does it go within you? Does it hybridize or does it somehow manifest as another of your multiple selves? Which selves express themselves when you critically access something? (this exercise is adapted from Gould: 2008b: 324).

As consumer researchers, we are all perhaps too familiar with the idea of cultural construction which indicates that meaning is produced by culture, that culture, itself, is produced and that there is no particular essence to be found, it would seem that the concept of personal cultural construction, allowing for the idea that there are such things as personal cultures, would be a parallel, if intermeshed universe. Our personal cultures consist of the meanings, discourse, rituals and practices we hold and engage in. They link to other levels of culture so seamlessly that we do not think of ourselves as 'a culture'.

THEORETICAL REFLECTION (3) – THE FLOW OF LIFE

Such introspective epistemological and ontological exercises have been carefully designed to sensitise you, the reader, to the proposition that cultural life issues forth through open, complex, dynamic, transformative, interdependent, never ending, cyclical currents of a world-in-formation that are never the same from one moment to the next (Ingold 2011; Stone et al. 2011). Such becomings bring forth the appearance of people as entangled beings that are ontologically incomplete (Minowa 2012). It is within such holistic, atmospheric, textured tangles, "continually ravelling here and unravelling there, that people grow or 'issue forth' along the lines of their relationships" (Ingold 2011: 71). Unbounded, people are united in shared and liberating beliefs of a way of knowing and being that is alive and open to a world in continuous birth. Life, seen in this way, flows though complex, fluid, textured atmospheric relationships. Moreover, and by way of clarification, we forward the proposition that our perspective goes beyond stressing the importance of beliefs and attitudes in shaping (and being shaped by) a particular worldview to warmly embrace the notion of dwelling (Ingold 2000) within a world of potential and possibility. Such a proposition is heightened by an increased sensitivity to a world in motion that continually changes from one moment to the next (Ingold 2011).

Lestel, Brunois and Gaunet (2006: 160) further develop this discussion by stating that "this is a shared complexity in the sense that a complex situation is complex in different ways for the different agents involved, whose representations of it are not reducible to those of other agents". Critical reflection of such a proposition enables what we would argue to be a worthy question to emerge: i.e. set within the context of such philosophical discussions, how can we attempt to gain yet deeper understandings of the culture of consumer research and the rest of life? A logical move might be to suggest that meaning is diluted everywhere and nowhere (ibid.) and that, perhaps to a greater or lesser extent, a kind of mutual affective co-operation exists between people and material artefacts, the earth beneath our feet, animals, birds, insects and soon. Thus, according to this perspective, an ontological position emerges in a complex, heterogeneous field of open connections that consist of continual and reciprocal relationships that are actively and constantly being (re)assembled, (trans)formed and (dis)placed within energetic flux (Bateson 1973).

From such an epistemological and ontological perspective, life in is not instantiated within a pre-ordained cultural framework, rather, as Ingold (2011: 83) poetically suggests, it is forever becoming, always moving like the "crest of a wave that overflows any boundaries that might be thrown around it, threading its way like the roots and runners of rhizome through whatever clefts and fissures leave room for growth and movement." From this perspective, people become meaningful as a consequence of their "patterns of activity and movement signatures" (ibid.) that can be found inscribed into particular identities, relationships, communities, sensitivities, things and so on (Stone et al. 2011 in line with Rapport and Overing 2007).

"As walking, talking and gesticulating creatures, human beings generate lines [of movement] wherever they go" (Ingold 2007: 1). From this nomothetic perspective, people can be thought of as being immersed in evolving patterns of atmospheric and dynamic movements along ways of life (Ingold 2011). Thus, bodily movement becomes a critical vista for enabling the world to endlessly renew itself (Ingold 2011, 2007; Stone et al. 2011). However, the complexities of movement cannot be simplified in our efforts to make them graspable. That is, expression may be simplified but not the nature of the complexity of the relationships that produce movement. In effect, there is a connection to the sublime-the evocation of that which is not representable (Lacoue-Labarthe 1986; Lyotard 1986)-here, in the sense that the unrepresentable completeness of the complexities of movement need to be represented in an imaginative (artistic?) way that triggers a sense of the whole.

Developing the emerging discussion still further, in line with Stone et al. (2011) the authors argue that bodily movement is responsible for the becoming, growth and reproduction of inter-place cultural knowledge. For example, the development of a knowledge system within consumer research is attributed to "the work that goes into moving its diverse components – including practitioners, their know-how and skills, technical devices and standards of evaluation – from one local site of knowledge production to another" (Turnbull 1993: 30 in Ingold 2000: 229). Ingold (2000: 227) further suggests that knowledge "comes from a history of previous flights, of take-offs and landings, and of incidents and encounters en-route. In other words it is forged in movement, in the passage from place-to-place and the changing horizons along the way". Thus, far from being copied, ready-made, into the mind in advance of its encounter with the world, knowledge is perpetually becoming within an open field of (sublime) relations established through the immersion of the sensitive actor-in-the-world (Minowa 2011). Knowledge, in this view, is not transmitted as a complex structure (Geertz 1973) but is the ever emergent product of a complex process of atmospherics and bodily movement.

In the light of the preceding discussion, the notion is forwarded that embodiment is a necessary condition of a natural, open, (sub) conscious, atmospheric life of movement. Moreover, we argue, embodiment is necessary and natural condition for sensuous life/lives of becoming (Turner 2008). Ingold (2011: 12) furthers this discussion by claiming that "since the living body is primordially and irrevocably stitched into the fabric of the world, our perception of the world is no more, and no less, than the world's perception of itself – in and through us." Or, in other words, the inhabited world is a sublime (Lacoue-Labarthe 1986; Lyotard 1986), unbounded (Ingold 2011, 2008, 1992; Kottak 2008; Palsson 1993; Rapport and Overing 2007), rich (Midgley 2003), magical (Buck 1936), liberatory (Firat and Venkatesh 1995), rhythmic, affective and sentient body. Viewed in this way, to be sensitive is to be open to the world, to yield to its embrace and to resonate in one's inner being to its illuminations, reverberations and to be aware of signifiers within, and throughout a world-of becoming (Ingold 2011). By utilising CIT to push back epistemological boundaries, consumer researchers can be thought of as being immersed in atmospherics of light and sound and that these fundamental aspects of day-to-day life are affectually experienced by sentient bodies along pathways of becoming that continually contribute to the ongoing renewal of the world (ibid.).

From this perspective, we argue, the cultural life of consumer research does not present itself (as any one truth) until it is encountered. Yet, every encounter is embodied and from a point of origin and at an angle. This means that as points of origin (or departure) and angles vary, so will the embodied truths that are encountered. That is, if there is such a thing as reality, it is likely to reveal itself in different ways to different people. The truth that presents itself is therefore in the encounter and is accumulated through the bodies' senses (seeing, hearing, smelling, tasting, feeling-touch; including interoception, proprioception) and subsequently contributes to the ongoing renewal of the world. Set within this context, the centrality of the senses in human understanding, consciousness and bodily movement cannot be underestimated. If a human being where unable to move and/or lack all of her/his senses she/he would have no experience of existence as we know it, nor would there be any consciousness as we know it. Thus, bodily sensing and, by extension, making sense are indeed central to human existence as the body is in a constant state of cultural (re)construction. The distinction so thoroughly made in modern thought between the body and the mind, therefore, needs to be re-thought. Rather than build our insights on the basis of the mutual influences of the body and the conceptual world of humans upon each other, we have to recognize the complex unity of the body that dwells (Ingold 2000) within an atmospheric world in-formation which gives impulse to the desire for movement and the essential organisation of life.

While consumer research on embodiment provides some useful insight in this regard, our approach takes a more holistic perspective such that these particular manifestations of embodiment are embedded in the (re-)production of cultural practices and meaning. Thus, sensing and by extension, bodily knowledge, movement and atmospherics are central to existence within a world in constant formation. Moreover, when we, as consumer researchers, can sense that we are no longer impeded or constrained by inverted ideologies through a realization that no reality has presence without atmospheric encounters, movement and bodily knowledge; and that different atmospheric encounters, movements and bodily knowledge are possible, we are burdened with a greater responsibility than simply discovering the truth. There is no longer a fundamental to show the way once discovered; no ready formula for life pre-exists to be discovered; no responsibility can be shirked or attributed to something beyond how we encounter a world-in-formation. Whatever truth we encounter is normally (but not always) constituted by our inverted conventions and perspectives.

Following on from this, the purpose of our particular brand of holistic consumer research is to open up the possibility of enabling people to get a deep, yet (in)expressible, understanding of a world-in-formation, an insight into the rich constellation of multiple truths, and, similar to Eastern philosophical approaches, make possible a meaningful recognition of the (in)significance of humanity. That is not to deny humanity of its position or place, but to make a greater sense of it through combining insights from an ever unfolding world-in-formation._

CONCLUSION

By way of a contribution, we have tried to provide the reader with insight into how our introspectively derived view of the culture of consumer research relates to the atmospheric linkages, influences and flows of life (Dholakia 2012; Ingold 2011) within an order of multiple orders (Firat 2009). Our current journey has not only reified the importance of feelings in cultural life (Joy and Sherry 2003 in line with Pham et al. 2001) but has also shown that studies of embodied realism (ibid.) hold the potential to more deeply access the flow of life (Ingold 2011). Moreover, we argue that such fundamental issues should be studied alongside atmospherics of movement and bodily knowledge (ibid.) in order to enable more sublime/holistic and sensitive understandings of consumption to emerge. Thus, and in keeping with the spirit of this paper, we call open-minded people towards the study of more holistic consumer research. Such a movement could seek to further illuminate, for example, the generation of knowledge that relates to the search for the sublime (Lacoue-Labarthe 1986; Lyotard 1986), the weather world (Ingold 2010), earth energies and ley lines, the availability and use of personal energy (Bateson 1972; Gould 1991), states of consciousness, what constitutes personhood, cybernetics (see craphound.com for thought provoking insight) and so on and so forth...

Viewed from this more holistic, and arguably critical-radical perspective (Dholakia 2012; Firat 2009), consumer research becomes the eclectic, open-ended (sub)conscious study of intertwined trajectories of human becomings and doings as they unfold through an atmospheric world-in-formation. In this sense, "there are no insides or outsides, no enclosures or disclosures, only openings and ways through" (Ingold 2011: 168). In short, we argue that the aim of holistic consumer research should be to visualise, sense and reveal the emancipatory and transformative flows (Dholakia 2012) and movements that contribute toward our ongoing formation.

ACKNOWLEDGEMENT

The authors of this work would like to take this opportunity to sincerely thank Tim Ingold (Professor of Social Anthropology at the University of Aberdeen, Scotland.) for providing the lead author with an advance copy of his unique and thought provoking book entitled *Being Alive. Essays on Movement, Knowledge and Description* published by Routledge.

REFERENCES

Arnould, Eric and Craig Thompson, (2005), Consumer Culture Theory (CCT): Twenty Years of Research, *Journal of Consumer Research*, 31 (March), 868-882.

Bateson, G. (1973), *Steps to an Ecology of Mind*, London: Paladin.

Belk, Russell (1987), Presidential Address: Happy Thought, Advances *in Consumer Research*, 14, 1–4.

_____ (1988), Possessions and the Extended Self, *Journal of Consumer Research*, 15 (September), 139-168.

Belk, Russell and Robert Kozinets (2005), Videography in marketing and consumer research, *Qualitative Market Research*, 8 (2), 128 – 141.

Belk, Russell, Melanie Wallendorf and John Sherry (1989), The Sacred and the Profane in Consumer Behavior: Theodicy on the Odyssey, *Journal of Consumer Research*, 16 (June), 1–39.

Buck, Peter (1936), *Regional Diversity In The Elaboration Of Sorcery In Polynesia*, in Yale University Publications in Anthropology, Numbers One to Seven, USA: Yale University Press.

Dholakia, Nikhilesh (2009), Marketing theory: Breaking the siege of incrementalism, *Journal of Marketing Management*, Vol. 25 (7 – 8), 825 – 829.

_____ (2012), Being Critical in Marketing Studies: The Imperative of Macro Perspectives, *Journal of Macromarketing*, 32 (2), 220 - 225.

Dholakia, Nikhilesh and Fuat Firat (2006), Global Business Beyond Modernity, *Critical Perspectives on International Business*, 6 (2), 147 – 162.

Durkheim, Emile. (1915), *The Elementary Forms of Religious Life*, London: Allen & Unwin.

Firat, Fuat (1985), A critique of the orientations in theory development in consumer behaviour: Suggestions for the future, *Advances in Consumer Research*, 12, 3 – 6.

_____ (2009), Beyond critical marketing, *Journal of Marketing Management*, 25 (7 – 8), 831 -834.

Firat, Fuat and Nikhilesh Dholakia (1982), Consumption Choices at the Macro Level, *Journal of Macromarketing*, Fall, 6 – 15.

____ and ____ (2003), *Consuming People: From Political Economy to Theatres of Consumption*, London and New York: Routledge.

____ and ____ (2006), Theoretical and Philosophical Implications of Postmodern Debates: Some Challenges to Modern Marketing, *Marketing Theory*, 6 (2), 123 – 162.

Firat, Fuat and Alladi Venkatesh (1995), Liberatory Postmodernism and the Reenchantment of Consumption, *Journal of Consumer Research*, 22 (December), 239 – 267.

Geertz, Clifford (1973), *The Interpretation of Culture*, Fontana Press.

Gould, Stephen (1991), The Self-Manipulation of My Pervasive, Perceived Vital Energy through Product Use: An Introspective-Praxis Perspective, *Journal of Consumer Research*, 18 (September), 194 – 207.

____ (1995), Researcher Introspection as a Method in Consumer Research: Applications, Issues and Implications, *Journal of Consumer Research*, 21 (March), 719 – 722.

____ (2008a), An introspective genealogy of my introspective genealogy, *Marketing Theory*, 8 (4), 407 – 424.

____ (2008b), Introspection as Critical Marketing Thought, Critical Marketing Though as Introspection, in Tadajewski, Mark and Douglas Brownlie (Eds.), *Critical Marketing. Issues in Contemporary Marketing*, 311 – 327.

____ (2012), The emergence of Consumer Introspection Theory (CIT): Introduction to JBR special issue, *Journal of Business Research*, 65 (4), 453 - 460.

Hirschman, Elizabeth and Morris Holbrook (1982), "Hedonic Consumption: Emerging Concepts, Methods, and Propositions, *Journal of Marketing*, 46 (Summer), 92–101.

Holbrook, Morris (1987), What Is Consumer Research? *Journal of Consumer Research*, 14 (June), 128–32.

Ingold, Tim (1992), The art of translation in a continuous world, in Palsson, Gisili (Ed.), *Beyond Boundaries. Understanding, Translation and Anthropological Discourse*, Oxford: Berg, 210 - 230.

____ (2000), *The Perception of the Environment. Essays in Livelihood, dwelling and skill*, Great Briton: Routledge.

____ (2008), *Lines. A Brief History*, Great Briton: Routledge.

____ (2010), Footprints through the weather-world: walking, breathing, knowing, *Journal of the Royal Anthropological Institute*, 121 – 139.

____ (2011), *Being Alive. Essays on Movement, Knowledge and Description*, Great Briton: Routledge.

Joy, Annamma and John F. Sherry (2003), Speaking of Art as Embodied Imagination: A Multisensory Approach to Understanding Aesthetic Experience, *Journal of Consumer Research*, 30 (September), 259 – 282.

Kottak, Conrad (2008), *Anthropology. Exploring Human Diversity*, McGraw Hill Higher Education.

Lacoue-Labarthe, Philippe (1986), On the Sublime, in *ICA Documents 4: Postmodernism*, Appignanesi, L. (Ed.), London: Institute of Contemporay Arts, 7 – 10.

Lestel, D., Brunois, F. and Gaunet, F. (2006), Etho-ethology and ethno-ethology, *Social Science Information*, 45 (2), 155-177.

Lyotard, Jean-Francois (1986), Complexity and the Sublime, in *ICA Documents 4: Postmodernsim*, Appignanesi, L (Ed.) London: Institute of Contemporary Arts, 10 -12.

Marcuse, Herbert (2002), *One-Dimensional Man*, United Kingdom: Routledge.

McCracken, Grant (1986), Culture and Consumption: A Theoretical Account of the Structure and Movement of the Cultural Meaning of Consumer Goods, *Journal of Consumer Research*, Vol. 13 (June), 71–84.

Mick, David (1986), Consumer Research and Semiotics: Exploring the Morphology of Signs, Symbols, and Significance, *Journal of Consumer Research*, 13 (September), 196–213.

Midgley, Mary (2003), *Heart and Mind: The Varieties of Moral Experience*, London and New York: Routledge.

Minowa, Yuko (2011), Practicing Qi and consuming Ki: Folk epistemology and consumption rituals in Japan, *Marketing Theory*, 12 (1), 27 - 44.

Nietzsche, Friedrich (1990), *Beyond Good and Evil*, London: Penguin Classics.

Palsson, Gisli (1992), *Beyond Boundaries. Understanding, Translation and Anthropological Discource*, Oxford: Berg.

Pham, Michael, Joel B. Cohen, John W. Pracejus and G. David Hughes (2001), Affect Monitoring and the Primacy of Feeling, *Journal of Consumer Research*, 28 (September), 167 – 188.

Rapport, Nigel & Joanna Overing (2007), *Social and Cultural Anthropology. The Key Concepts*, New York and London: Routledge.

Schouten, John and James McAlexander (1995), Subcultures of Consumption: Ethnography of the New Bikers, *Journal of Consumer Research*, 22 (June), 43-61.

Sherry, John (2000), Place, Technology, and Representation, *Journal of Consumer Research*, 27 (September), 273 – 278.

Sherry, John and John W. Schouten (2002), A Role for Poetry in Consumer Research, Journal of Consumer Research, 29 (September), 218 – 234.

Stone, Tim, Paul Hewer and Douglas Brownlie (2011), Movement, Knowledge and Consumption within Elderly Care Environments, *Advances in Consumer Research*, 39, 385 – 391.

Turnbull, David (1993), Local knowledge and comparative scientific traditions, *Knowledge and Policy*, 6, 29 – 54.

Turnbull, David (1989), *Maps are territories: science is an atlas*, Geelong: Deakin University Press.

Venkatesh, Alladi, Eminegul Karababa and Guliz Ger (2002), The emergence of the posthuman consumer and the fusion of the virtual and the real: A critical analysis of Sony's ad for a memory stick, *Advances in Consumer Research*, 29, 446 – 452.

Warde, Alan (2005), Consumption and Theories of Practice, *Journal of Consumer Culture*, 5 (2), 131 – 153.

Wilber, Ken (2001), *Eye to Eye: The Quest for the New Paradigm*, Boston: Shambhala.

The Impact of Internet Search on Price/Quality Correlations

Ellen Garbarino, University of Sydney, Australia

Nelly Oromulu, Transystems, USA

ABSTRACT

The price-quality correlation is typically low, suggesting market inefficiency. Information is a necessary condition for market efficiency and the Internet has radically increased information. This should lead to improved p-q correlations, at least for searched goods. Using secondary and survey data, we demonstrate this improvement, but only for durable goods.

EXTENDED ABSTRACT

Background: In an efficient market, products with low quality should only be able to survive by offering low prices and products with high quality should be able to command a price premium. Therefore, there should be a positive correlation between price and quality. The numerous empirical studies in consumer markets, however, consistently find weak correlations between price and objective quality, inviting the conclusion that market efficiency is the exception rather than the norm (Oxenfeldt 1950; Morris and Bronson 1969; Curry and Fauld 1986; Kirchler, Fischer and Hölzl 2010). Access to information is one of the necessary conditions for market efficiency (Ratchford 1980, Ratchford and Gupta 1990, Kamakura, Ratchford and Agrawal 1988). In support of this notion, Tellis and Wernerfelt (1987) demonstrate that the correlation between price and quality generally increases with the level of information in the market. Access to information has been growing steadily with the growth in Internet resources and penetration. This reduced cost of search should increase market efficiency, which should be reflected in improved p-q correlations.

Based on the premise that the advent of the Internet decreased the cost of search, we hypothesize that the p-q correlation should have increased in the post-Internet marketplace relative to the pre-internet marketplace. Given the central role of search in the expected improvement in the post-Internet marketplace, we also hypothesize that the effects will be stronger for durable goods than for non-durables goods due to the more limited search that is typically done for non-durable goods. In addition, we test directly whether the improvements in p-q correlation are driven by increases in the amount of online and/or offline search. The above hypotheses are tested using a combination of secondary source data (drawn from Consumer Reports) and primary survey data (drawn from an online panel).

Methods: The Pearson correlation between price and quality was calculated using data from *Consumer Reports* (pre-internet data from 1995-1998, post-Internet data from 2002-2005). 14 categories were chosen that had reviews in both time periods (7 durable, 7 non-durables). The following categories were used: top-loading washing machines, upright vacuum cleaners, supermarket cheese pizza, blenders, raisin bran breakfast cereal, built-in dishwashers, laundry detergent, self-propelled lawn mowers, crunchy peanut butter, large countertop microwave ovens, canned chicken noodles soup, non-stick cookware, corded steam irons and tortilla chips.[1]

Search habits and the judgement of the searchability of the 14 categories were measured through an online survey. 206 subjects

from a US online research panel responded to a survey concerning their online and offline search time for the 14 product categories (various versions counterbalanced order and categories; only half the categories were asked of each respondent to avoid fatigue). Additional questions addressed whether info available online was sufficient to purchase, whether the product needed to be experienced physically to purchase, ability to evaluate product before purchase, ability to evaluate product after purchase, the importance of price in purchase decisions, and the importance of quality in purchase decisions. These measures were included as covariates in our analyses; only the importance of price showed a significant effect (B=.856, p<.04), the more important price was in the category, the more improvement was seen in the p-q correlation. Search time was collected in hours and minutes, while all other items were measured using 7-point rating scales.

Results: Pearson correlations between price and quality for each category were computed using the prices and quality ratings in the *Consumer Reports*. The change in the p-q correlation was computed as the difference between the correlation post-internet and pre-internet for that category. Category-level search was coded as the average amount of time (in minutes) spent searching based on the responses from the survey. As expected, durable goods were searched more (both online and offline) than non-durable goods (Online Search: Durable Mean = 106.06 vs. Non-durable Mean=41.96, p<.003; Offline Search: Durable Mean=144.41 vs. Non-durable Mean=58.90, p<.001).

Across all 14 categories, the p-q correlation went up in 9 and down in 5 categories (binominal test probability 21%). Further analysis showed that this improvement in correlation was evident only for durable goods (6 out of 7 durable categories show improvement vs. 3 out 7 non-durable categories show improvement; $\chi^2 = 2.80$ p<.094), which was consistent with our expectation that the improvement in p-q correlation would be greater for durable goods for which consumers searched more. Examination of the direct influence of search time on the change in the p-q correlation showed a significant interaction between online search and durability of good (p<.008). A further exploration of this interaction showed that time spent searching online drives the change in p-q correlation only for durable goods. Specifically, for durable goods the more time spent searching a category the larger the improvement in the correlation (B=.008, p<.012). However, for non-durable goods the time spent searching does not led to an improvement in p-q correlation (B=-.005; p>.48). Time spent searching the category offline shows a similar but weaker effect (Durables: B=.005, p<.10; Non-durables: B=-.014, p>.19).

Summary: Using a combination of secondary and survey data, we show that the increase in information search with the advent of the Internet has lead to an improvement in the price-quality correlations for durable goods, but has had no effect on the price-quality correlations for less commonly searched non-durable goods.

If a market is efficient, products with low quality should only be able to survive by offering lower prices and products with high quality should be able to command a price premium. As stated in Geistfeld review of the price-quality literature, "If the relationship between price and quality is poor, markets are not working well and consumers are not making efficient use of their resources" (1988, p.144). This logic implies that in well functioning markets, price should be positively related to quality. However, the numerous empirical studies

---

[1] Little research has examined the changes in p-q correlation over time, however, based on the product life cycle theory, Curry and Reisz (1988) argue that p-q correlation should decline as products mature due to price compression and reduced spending on quality improvements. To minimize the effect of product life cycle we examine only mature products.

in consumer markets consistently find only a weak correlation between price and objective quality, with the average correlations for durable goods ranging from 0.25-0.30 and closer to zero correlation for nondurable goods (Oxenfedlt (1950), Morris and Bronson (1969), Sproles (1977), Riesz (1978), Gerstner (1985), Curry and Fauld 1986; Kirchler, Fischer and Hölzl (2010)). While these studies show an amazing consistency across countries, categories and decades, it is worth noting that, with the exception of the Kirchler et al. paper, all of these findings come from the pre-Internet age.

One of the hallmarks of the Internet age has been the explosion in available information. As noted by the literature, access to information is one of the necessary conditions for market efficiency (Ratchford 1980, Ratchford and Gupta 1990, Kamakura, Ratchford and Agrawal 1988, Maynes 1992). In support of this idea, Tellis and Wernerfelt (1987) demonstrate analytically that the correlation between price and quality should increase as the amount of information acquired increases. As we are all well aware, access to information has been growing steadily with the growth and penetration of Internet resources. These resources are now cheaply and easily accessible to most consumers. This reduced cost of search should be reflected in improved price-quality correlations.

There has been little study of how the price-quality correlation changes over time. In one of the few longitudinal studies, Curry and Riesz (1988) argue, using the product life cycle theory, that over time real prices decline and tend to converge and this is what they find. They initially hypothesized the price-quality correlation to increase as the market matured due to rising information levels, but they actually found that the correspondence between price and quality tended to decline over time. They speculate that this is caused by a shift toward spending on advertising rather than quality improvements as the market matured, although it could also be caused by a narrowing of the range of price and/or quality across the category as the market matures. In a similar market growth explanation, Hjorth-Andersen (1992), argues that low or negative price-quality correlations could be due to product improvements leading to inexpensive but higher quality alternatives being introduce to markets that are still rapidly evolving. To minimize the potential influence of the product life cycle on the change in the price-quality correlation, we will examine only mature product categories.

Hence, using secondary measures of price and quality from Consumer Reports from 1995-1998 and 2002-2005 for a selections of 14 mature categories (7 durable and 7 nondurable), we explore whether the price-quality correlation has increased for both durables and non durable goods with the advent of the Internet as a search tool. In addition, we explore whether consumers' stated level of category search predicts the expected improvement in price-quality correlation.

HYPOTHESES

Based on the premise that the advent of the Internet has decreased the cost of search, along with the fact that the cost of search is an established determinant of market efficiency (Ratchford 1980, Ratchford and Gupta 1990, Kamakura et al. 1988, Manyes 1992) and that the price-quality correlation is at least a partial indicator of market efficiency (Ratchford et al. 1996), we hypothesize that the p-q correlation should have increased in the post-Internet marketplace relative to the pre-Internet marketplace.

Hypothesis 1:   *Price-Quality correlations will increase in the post-Internet period relative to the correlations in the pre-Internet period.*

Stigler's (1961) model of the economics of information argues that the cost of search relative to its benefit will be lower for nondurable goods and hence one would expect lower search for nondurable goods. Given this more limited search for nondurables and the central role of search in the expected improvement in price-quality correlation in the post-Internet marketplace, we hypothesize that the increase in price-quality correlation will be more pronounced among durable goods than among non-durables goods.

Hypothesis 2:   *A post-Internet increase in price-quality correlation will be more common for durable goods than nondurable goods.*

Based on information economics, the hypothesized mechanism underlying the predicted increase in the correlation of price and quality is that the decreased cost of search with the rise of the Internet has lead to increased search for goods where the benefits of search are higher (i.e., more involved and risky goods). Hence we will more directly test whether the amount of time spent searching positively predicts the increase in the price-quality correlation. Given that the Internet is the new channels of search, the expectation is that any improvement seen will be most strongly related to the increase in online searching. However, it is also interesting to explore the effects in regards to the amount of offline searching. It is possible that online searching is such a strong substitute for offline searching, that offline search might even have a negative correlation with an improvement in price-quality correlation. However, it is also possible that the two forms of search are complimentary and that both will show the predicted positive relationship.

Given their small ticket price and generally low risk, the benefits to search for nondurables are modest. Additionally, the low involvement and low value of most nondurables leads there to be less readily available information on the Internet. Hence, the smaller changes in the search costs and benefits due to the Internet for nondurables should lead to little or no increase in price-quality correlation for these goods.

Hypothesis 3:   *The amount of search done (especially online search) should be positively related to the level of increase in the price-quality correlation.*

Hypothesis 4:   *The role of search increase of the price-quality correlation should be larger for durable goods than nondurables goods.*

METHODS

The above hypotheses are tested using a combination of secondary source data for price and quality ratings (drawn from *Consumer Reports*) and primary survey data on category specific search habits and impressions based on a survey (drawn from an online panel). *Consumer Reports* data has been used in most studies of the price quality relationship (e.g. Tellis and Wernerfelt 1987; Gerstner 1985, Morris and Bronson 1969). While Consumer Reports data has been criticized for over-simplifying objective quality and not including many factors that consumers use in purchase valuation (Hjorth-Andersen 1984, 1992), it is still the common standard for studies of this kind (Boyle and Lathrop 2009) due to it objectivity and comparability cross studies. In addition, any bias would not have a differential impact on durable or nondurable goods.

The Pearson correlation between price and quality is calculated using data from *Consumer Reports Magazine*. Price was represented by the dollar amount per unit of product and the overall satisfaction rating scaled from 0-100 was used as a measure of quality. The pre-Internet data was chosen from paperback issues between 1995-1998, while the post-Internet counterparts were selected from the online database from between 2002 and 2005.

The actual category selection was dictated by the availability of data on the same product categories and subcategories in both periods of time. To limit the influence of product life cycle stage on the price-quality correlation (Curry and Riesz, 1988), we examine only mature products. Hence, 14 mature categories were chosen that had reviews in both time periods (7 durable, 7 non-durables). The following categories were used: top-loading washing machines, upright vacuum cleaners, supermarket cheese pizza, blenders, raisin bran breakfast cereal, built-in dishwashers, laundry detergent, self-propelled lawn mowers, crunchy peanut butter, large countertop microwave ovens, canned chicken noodles soup, non-stick cookware, corded steam irons and tortilla chips.

The primary data consisted of a survey to assess category specific search habits and perceptions of each category. Pilot testing ascertained that judging 14 separate categories was too fatiguing for respondents, hence people were only asked to judge seven categories. Four versions were created that varied in the categories seen, order of the categories and balanced the number of durable and nondurable goods (the four versions showed no significant differences in evaluation and hence were collapsed across). A total of eight questions were asked for each category: time typically spent searching (in hours and minutes) online and offline, whether info available online was sufficient to purchase, whether the product needed to be experienced physically to purchase, ability to evaluate product before purchase, ability to evaluate product after purchase, the importance of price in purchase decisions, and the importance of quality in purchase decisions. Time searching was collected using open-ended questions about hours and minutes spent searching in

this category, while all other items were measured using 7-point rating scales ("agree very strongly" to "disagree very strongly"). 1400 requests were emailed out to an established commercial research panel designed to represent the US population, 206 valid responses were collected, for a response rate of 15%.

RESULTS

The dependent variable is the change in correlation between price and quality pre- and post-Internet. The change in the price quality correlation was computed as the difference between the Pearson correlations post-Internet and pre-Internet for that category using the prices and quality ratings in the *Consumer Reports*.[2] Category-level search was coded as the average amount of time (in minutes) spent searching online or offline aggregated from the responses to the survey. As expected, durable goods were searched more (both online and offline) than non-durable goods (Online Search: Durable Mean = 106.06 minutes vs. Non-durable Mean = 41.96 minutes, p<.003; Offline Search: Durable Mean = 144.41 minutes vs. Non-durable Mean = 58.90 minutes, p<.001). The scale items describing consumer beliefs about the characteristics of the categories were used as potential covariates. Analysis showed that only, the importance of price in category purchase showed a significant effect (B = .856, p<.04) on the change in the price-quality correlation; the more important price was in the category, the more increase was seen in the p-q correlation. Hence, only this covariate was retained.

Across all 14 categories, the price-quality correlation went up in nine and down in five categories (binominal test probability 21%), thus there is at least directional support for the expected improvement in price-quality correlation (H1, see Table 1). More detailed analysis showed that the hypothesized increase in correlation was evident only for durable goods (6 out of 7 durable categories show increased correlation vs. 3 out 7 non-durable categories show posi-

[2] Spearman rank correlations lead to substantively similar results.

Table 1
Changes in Price-Quality Correlation

Category	Post-Internet Correlation	Pre-Internet Correlation	Change in Correlation
Nondurables:			
Canned Chicken Noodle Soup	.1974	.6234	-.4260
Raisin Bran Cereal	-.7835	-.4043	-.3792
Non-Stick Cookware	.3305	.6801	-.3496
Crunchy Peanut Butter	-.2941	-.0050	-.2891
Tortilla Chips	-.1860	-.2790	.0930
Laundry Detergent	.6473	.0145	.6328
Frozen Cheese Pizza	.3010	-.3617	.6627
Average Price-Quality Correlation	.0304	.0382	-.0079
Durables:			
Steam Iron	.2528	.7278	-.4750
Upright Vacuum	.3101	.2851	.0250
Large Counter-Top Microwave	-.0089	-.0505	.0416
Top Loader Washing Machine	.8318	.6356	.1962
Blender	.1143	-.0837	.1980
Self-Propelled Lawn Mower	.5849	.2135	.3714
Built-in Dishwasher	.5080	.1050	.4030
Average Price-Quality Correlation	.3704	.2618	.1086

tive change; $\chi^2 = 2.80$ p<.094; supporting H2), which is consistent with our expectation that the increase in the post-Internet price-quality correlation would be more common for durable goods.

Table 1 shows the category specific correlations to assess not only the direction but magnitudes of the effects. Similar to prior studies (e.g., Gerstner 1985), the pre-Internet price-quality correlation for durables was .26 and nondurable was basically zero ($r = .04$). The average change in the correlation in the post-Internet period was an increase of .11 for durables and basically no change for nondurables ($\Delta = -.01$). This improvement in the price-quality correlation for durables represents over a 40% increase in the price-quality correlation for durable goods on average. Thus, not only do almost all of durable categories show the hypothesized increase in correlation but also the magnitude of the change is quite substantial.

Examination of the direct influence of search time on the change in the price-quality correlation shows no significant main effect of search on the change in price-quality correlation for either online or offline search (Online: p>69; Offline p>.69; not supporting H3). However, the interaction between online (and offline) search and durability of good is significant (Online: p<.008; Offline p<.023; supporting H4). A further exploration of these interactions shows that the time spent searching drive the change in price-quality correlation but only for durable goods. Specifically (see Figure 1), for durable goods the more time spent searching a category online the larger the improvement in the correlation (B = .008, p<.012). However, for non-durable goods the time spent searching online does not led to a change in price-quality correlation (B = -.005; p>.48). Time spent searching the category offline shows a similar but weaker effect (Durables: B = .005, p<.10; Non-durables: B = -.014, p>.19).

DISCUSSION

Using a combination of secondary and survey data, we test whether the advent of the Internet with its much broader and easier access to product and price information has lead to improved market efficiency as proxied by an improvement in the price-quality correlation. Even with only 14 categories (7 durable and 7 nondurable), we find the post-Internet price-quality correlation has improved, but only for durable goods. Using survey data of category specific search habits, we further show that information search (both online and offline) is the driver of this improvement in correlation amongst durable goods. These findings are consistent with the premise that the Internet has made search less costly, allowing consumers to better monitor the markets, leading to a better correspondence between price, at least for durable goods.

Nondurable goods present a different picture. Although in our data the results are not significant, it is curious to note that the direction of change and the effect of search on nondurable goods tends to be negative. We are uncertain why this may be true, it is possible that the quality and/or amount of information in regards to nondurables is poor and hence search is not leading to improved outcomes. Alternatively, it could be that the higher benefits to be gained from searching durables crowds out the more modest benefits to be gained from searching nondurables and hence consumers are substituting durable search for nondurable search. The finding does suggest that further and more extensive testing maybe needed to ascertain whether it is generally true or just an artifact of this sample.

Like all studies, this one is not without significant limitations. First, we use only fourteen categories (and only 7 in each subtype) and these were chosen only somewhat randomly. The strong results even with the tiny sample, however, suggest it is well worth extending the sampling to see if this improvement in correlation for durables is widespread. A larger study with more rigorously chosen categories is called for. Secondly, we can only assess category specific search for the post-Internet period and this only from retrospective self-report of search. It would have been much stronger to have a real time search behavior measure for both pre- and post- Internet periods, however such measures are not readily available and would not likely be available for a wide range of categories for both time

Figure 1
Effects of Search on Change in Price-Quality Correlation

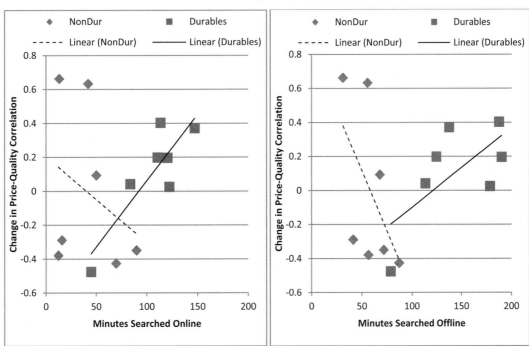

periods. Future research might use online search term frequency (e.g., Goolge trends) to better estimate category specific search. Our high search numbers across all categories suggest a strong upward bias in how much people claim to search, given that prior research finds actual search to be quite limited (Johnson et al. 2004). Thirdly, it is also possible that the product offerings have changed so much that comparison across the pre- and post- Internet periods are not valid. We consciously picked mature categories to minimize this concern, but it is still a limitation of any longitudinal study.

In sum, we demonstrate that the increase in information search with the advent of the Internet has lead to an increase in the price-quality correlations for durable goods, but has had no effect on the price-quality correlations for less commonly searched non-durable goods.

REFERENCES

Boyle, Peter J. And E. Scott Lathrop (2009), "Are consumers' perceptions of price-quality relationships well calibrated," *International Journal of Consumer Studies*, 33, 58-63.

Curry, David J. and David J. Faulds (1986), "Indexing Product Quality: Issues, Theory, and Results," *Journal of Consumer Research*, 13 (June), 134- 145.

Curry, David J. and. Peter C. Riesz (1988), "Prices and Price/ Quality Relationship: A Longitudinal Analysis," *Journal of Marketing*, (January), 36-51.

Geistfeld, L.V. (1988), "The price-quality relationship: The evidence we have, the evidence we need," In E.S. Maynes and the ACCI Research Committee (Eds.), *The Frontier of Research in the Consumer Interest*, Columbia, MO: American Council on Consumer Interests, 143-172.

Gerstner, Eitan, (1985), "Do Higher Prices Signal Higher Quality," *Journal of Marketing Research*, 22:2 9May), 209-215.

Hjorth-Andersen Christian. (1984), "The concept of quality and the efficiency of markets for consumer products," *Journal of Consumer Research*, 11, 708-718.

Hjorth-Andersen C. (1992), "Alternative interpretations of price-quality relations," *Journal of Consumer Policy*, 15, 71-82.

Johnson, Eric J., Wendy w. Moe, Peter S. Fader, Steven Bellman and Gerald L. Loshe (2004), "On the Depth of Dynamics of Online Search Behavior," *Management Science*, 50:3 (March), 229-308.

Kamakura, Wagner A., Brian T. Ratchford and Jagdish Agrawal (1988), "Measuring Market Efficiency and Welfare Loss," *Journal of Consumer Research*, 15:3 (December), 289-302.

Kirchler, Erich, Florian Fischer, and Erik Hölzl (2010) ; "Price and its Relation to Objective and Subjective Product Quality: Evidence from the Austrian Market," *Journal of Consumer Policy,* 33(3), 275.286.

Maynes, E. Scott (1992), "Salute and critique: A review of Ratchford and Gupta," *Journal of Consumer Policy*, 15, 83-96.

Morris, Ruby Turner and Claire Sekulski Bronson (1969), "The Chaos in Competition Indicated by Consumer Reports," *Journal of Marketing*, 33 (July), 26-43.

Oxenfeldt, Alfred R. (1950), "Consumer Knowledge: Its Measurement and Extent," *Review of Economics and Statistics*, 32, 300-314.

Ratchford, Brian T. (1980), "The Value of Information for Selected Appliances," *Journal of Marketing Research*, 17 (February), 14-25.

Ractchford, Brian T. and Gupta, Pola (1990), "On the interpretation of price-quality relations," *Journal of Consumer Policy*, 13:4, 389-411.

Ractchford, Brian T., Jagdish Agrawal, Pamela E. Grimm and Narasimhan Srinivasan (1996), "Toward Understanding the Measurement of Market Efficiency," *Journal of Public Policy & Marketing*, 15:2 (Fall), 167-184.

Riesz, Peter C. (1978), "Price versus quality in the marketplace: 1961-1975,", *Journal of Retailing*, 54, 253-264.

Sproles, G.B. (1977), "New evidence on price and product quality," *Journal of Consumer Affairs*, 11, 63-77.

Stigler, George (1961), "The Economics of Information," *Journal of Political Economy*, 69:3 (June), 213-225.

Tellis, Gerald J. and Wernerfelt, Birger (1987), "Competitive Price and Quality under Asymmetric Information," *Marketing Science*, 6:3 (Summer), 240-253.

Living Diversity: Developing a Typology of Consumer Cultural Orientations in Culturally Diverse Marketplaces: Consequences for Consumption

Eva Kipnis, Coventry Business School, UK

Julie Emontspool, University of Southern Denmark

Amanda J Broderick, University of Salford, UK

ABSTRACT

This paper argues that in culturally diverse environments cultural identity transitions are more complex than conceptualized by previous research and pertain equally to locally-born (mainstream) and migrant populations. We conceptualize a Typology of Consumer Cultural Orientations as explanatory framework for ethnic consumption and subsequently apply it in an empirical study. The findings indicate that through differential deployment of local, global and foreign cultures affinities for identity negotiation, mainstream and migrant consumers alike can develop or maintain uni-, bi- and multicultural orientations and use these orientations as informants of their consumption choices. Our findings suggest that the study of consumption implications of cultural diversity should be extended beyond mainstream/migrant differentiation which loses its significance in today's globalized world.

Complexities of cultural identity have been identified in studies on mainstream (i.e., locally born) populations (Jamal 2003) and migrant groups (Askegaard, Arnould, and Kjeldgaard 2005). In today's global world, mainstream and migrant individuals can develop affinities (i.e., affective attachment) with cultures and lifestyles through direct (travel, co-residence) and indirect (media, trade) experiences with these cultures' representatives. These affinities can take form of attachment to specific foreign cultures (Oberecker and Diamantopoulous 2010; Luna, Rindberg and Perraccio 2008) or general openness to foreign experiences as representations of global living (Thompson and Tambyah 1999), positively affecting consumption decisions towards products associated with the affinity culture (Oberecker et al, 2008).

While previous studies provide valuable insights into how a specific type of culture (local, global or foreign) is internalized in identities of either mainstream or migrant consumers, we argue that to broaden our understanding of the cultural drivers of consumption, research needs to move away from a mainstream/migrant paradigm. In culturally diverse environments (i.e., societies where multiple cultures co-exist) a large diversity of cultural influences as lifestyle options is opened to and experienced simultaneously by both mainstream and migrant consumers alike. This leads individuals from both groups to negotiate their identities through concurrent evaluation of these options' plurality (Kjeldgaard and Askegaard 2006). Perceptions of the surrounding cultural experiences evolved through this evaluation transform cultural orientations such that one, two or more types of cultures can be internalized by individuals irrespective of their ethnic belonging and have a differential affect on their consumption choices (Cayla and Eckhardt, 2008; Askegaard et al 2005). Hence, a broader conceptualization of cultural identity development in culturally diverse environments is required to account for the multilateral nature of cultural adaptation (Luedicke 2011).

In this paper we explore what forms of cultural identities emerge through individuals' contacts with multiple cultures in culturally diverse environments, and whether the diversity of cultures internalized by individuals leads to differential effects in people's perception and interpretation of consumption experiences. We developed a Typology of Consumer Cultural Orientations integrating research on cultural identities of mainstream consumers with that on cultural identity transitions of migrant consumers. The typology posits seven hypothesized types of uni-, bi- and multicultural orientations individuals may develop through simultaneous evaluation of three main types of cultures (local, global and foreign) as distinct options of being in a marketplace. To support our theoretical extrapolations, we then conducted a multi-country exploratory study, which indicates that cultural orientations of individuals in culturally diverse environments may take forms that are different from and more complex than those identified by past research.

CONCEPTUAL FRAMEWORK

Local, Global, and Foreign cultures' affinities as components of cultural orientations

Before developing a typology of consumer cultural orientations, we engaged in clarifying the meanings of its three main components, local, global and foreign cultures, to ensure applicability to both mainstream and migrant consumer contexts. In societies with an increasingly heterogenic demographic make-up, the meaning of 'locality' and 'local' is difficult to grasp (Murray, 2007). A general understanding has evolved that the meaning of localness is required to be grounded with the culture originating from the locale of one's residence (Roudometof, 2005; Korff 2003). Consumption-wise, the meaning of 'localness' has been identified to derive either from a given brand being perceived as produced within the boundaries of a give locale, or as adopting cultural symbols that originate from and uniquely characterize a given locale (Kipnis et al., 2012).

Conceptions of 'foreignness' and 'globalness' also call for clarification. Whilst the meaning of 'global' takes its origins in *"Western imaginary"* (Cayla & Arnould, 2008, p.88), it evolved from Western cultural reality gaze into a truly-global gaze (Iwabuchi 2002), and is equally deployed by Western and non-Western entities. For example, Cayla and Eckhardt (2008) show that global culture referents are deployed by regional Asian brands, while Steenkamp et al. (2003) demonstrate that a Western-origin (Dutch) Frito-Lay changed the name of the *"leading potato chip brand from Smiths to Lay's"* (p.53) to generate the meaning of globalness. At the same time, Leclerc et al. (1994) give examples of Western brands that encapsulate meanings of particular 'foreignness' (i.e., Giorgio St. Angelo – Italian culture; Häagen Dazs – Danish culture). Individuals may consume a range of Western and non-Western foreign produce assigned with the meaning of 'globalness' to draw from global standards of lifestyle excellence and/or materialize attachment to a particular Western and non-Western foreign cultures through consumption of produce assigned with a meaning of particular 'foreignness' (Cannon and Yaprak 2002; Eckhardt and Mahi 2004). We argue that to understand how foreign and global culture(s) affinities are internalized as distinct facets of identity, it is important to clarify that in culturally diverse societies the meaning of 'foreignness' can encapsulate cultures which, although represented in a given locale by media, residing ethnic groups, brands, are distinctly different from the local culture originating from this locale. Thus, we define the focal types of cultural influences present in the culturally diverse environment as:

1. Global culture (GC) – a homogenic set of values, beliefs, lifestyle and symbols shared in a unified manner by individuals across countries.

2. Local culture (LC) – ways of life and systems of values, beliefs and symbols considered originating from, unique to and mainstream in the country of residence (for example, in France – French culture).

3. Foreign culture(s) (FC) – a system of values, beliefs and symbols that comes from a definable cultural source(s) (country or cultural group) and is different from local culture.

Conceptualizing a typology of Uni, Bi- and Multi Cultural Orientations

To account for consumers' interaction with a multitude of cultural influences while jointly considering mainstream and migrant consumers, we integrated the existing evidence on cultural affiliations of mainstream and migrant individuals from a perspective of all key cultural influences (Global, Local and Foreign) and developed a Typology of Consumer Cultural Orientations (CCO Typology presented in Table 1). The Typology posits uni-, bi- and multicultural orientations that may be developed by individuals that formed basis of our empirical study. Our theoretical extrapolations through which orientations were hypothesized are briefly discussed below.

Unicultural orientations. Migrant consumption literature reports strong LC affinities as 'assimilation', the rejection of the culture of ethnic origin over the new culture of residence (Peñaloza, 1989; Palumbo & Teich, 2003). Strong LC affiliations of mainstream populations are also identified in the international marketing literature as 'localizm' (Crane, 2002; Reardon, Miller, Vida, & Kim, 2005). Hence, LC affinities are defined as Local Orientation in our Typology. Similarly, the Global Orientation encompasses GC affinities described by both streams of research (Alden et al., 2006; Strizhakova et al., 2008, Thompson & Tambyah, 1999). When considering affiliation with foreign culture(s), literature on mainstream groups notes that some individuals hold affinities with a culture of a particular foreign country due to this culture's positive, at times idealistic, stereotyping (Perlmutter, 1954; Kent & Burnight, 1951). Similarly, Jimenez (2010) identifies that individuals may develop affinities with a culture of a particular ethnic group that is not connected to one through heritage or ancestry. In parallel, literature on migrants refers to such processes as 'separation', individuals rejecting all other types of culture that surround them and maintaining a strong affiliation with the culture of their ethnic origin (Wallendorf and Reilly, 1983; Luna & Peracchio, 2005). Notably, many migrants, once established in a new country of residence, may be engaged in cultural exchange with non-heritage cultures similarly to mainstream population, through direct and indirect contact with these cultures'

Table 1 Consumer Cultural Orientations Typology

Type of Cultural Orientation	Definition	Literature sources	
		Mainstream (non-migrant) groups	Migrant and Ethnic groups
Local Orientation	Individual's affiliation with his mainstream culture of residence only, combined with no or low interest and involvement with other types of cultures.	Crane, 2002; Reardon, Miller, Vida, & Kim, 2005:	Peñaloza, 1989; Palumbo & Teich, 2003
Global Orientation	Individual's affiliation with global culture, as means to live 'global lifestyle' and feel citizen of the world.	Alden et al., 2006; Strizhakova et al., 2008	Thompson & Tambyah, 1999; Askegaard et al., 2005; Wamwara-Mbugua et al., 2008
Foreign Orientation	Individual's affiliation with specific foreign culture(s), combined with no or low interest and involvement with local and global cultures.	Perlmutter, 1954; Kent & Burnight, 1951	Wallendorf and Reilly, 1983; Luna & Peracchio, 2005
Local-Global Orientation	Individual's integrated affiliation with his culture of residence and global culture, combined with no or low interest and involvement in experiences with foreign cultures.	Kjeldgaard & Askegaard, 2006; Kjeldgaard & Ostberg, 2007	
Local-Foreign Orientation	Individual's integrated affiliation with his culture of residence and specific foreign culture(s), combined with no or low interest and involvement with global culture.	Luna & Peracchio, 2005; Luna et al., 2008; Oberecker et al., 2008; Jamal, 2003; Chattaraman et al. 2010; Sparrow, 2000; Sharma et al., 1995;	Cockburn, 2002; Peñaloza, 1994; Oswald, 1999; Askegaard et al., 2005
Global-Foreign Orientation	Individual's integrated affiliation with specific foreign culture(s) and global culture, combined with no or low interest and involvement with culture of residence.		
Full Integration	The individual internalizes all types of cultural influences (local, global and foreign) around him and integrates them in his lifestyle.	Holliday 2010; Sharma et al. 1995	Askegaard et al., 2005

representatives (travel, media, trade). Through participating in this exchange, migrants can develop liking of a particular foreign culture different from that of their origin, for the same reasons as the non-migrant mainstream populations (Oberecker and Diamantopoulos 2010). Therefore, we conceptualize Foreign Orientation as including FC affinities that evolve irrespectively of whether a given foreign culture is linked to an individual through heritage or not.

Bi-cultural Orientations. Less clarity and consistency can be found in the literature on bi- and multicultural orientations. While the body of literature focusing on non-migrants evidences that individuals can maintain affiliations with both local and global cultures (Kjeldgaard & Askegaard, 2006; Kjeldgaard & Ostberg, 2007), less is known about whether and how migrants integrate GC affiliations with their affiliation for culture of residence (LC). It is however reasonable to propose that such orientations are developed, as assimilated migrants exchange cultural knowledge with non-migrant individuals and are exposed to the global culture to the same extent and in the same environment as the non-migrants. Hence, the first type of bi-cultural orientation is identified as Local-Global Orientation in the Typology. The conceptualized Local-Foreign Orientation is grounded in the studies stemming from both bodies of literature whereby, similarly to glocalized individuals, individuals holding strong affiliations with local culture may develop/maintain affiliations with particular foreign cultures (Luna et al., 2008; Oberecker et al., 2008; Jamal, 2003; Chattaraman et al. 2010; Sparrow, 2000; Cockburn, 2002; Peñaloza, 1994). The final bicultural orientation type, Foreign-Global Orientation, conceptualizes individuals opposing or distancing themselves from their local culture on one hand, and distinguishing between Foreign and Global cultures on the other. Indeed, one may aspire to the global community and at the same time maintain a particular liking of a Foreign culture (for example, an individual residing in Poland may have a strong liking of Indian culture and at the same time identify with the Global culture). Similarly, one may be interested in participating in the global community and at the same time be eager to integrate authentic foreign cultural experiences in the lifestyle.

Multicultural Orientations. The final proposed orientation, Full Integration, stems from research on individuals within particular ethnocultural groups internalizing all three types of cultures (Local, Global, and 'other' Foreign) and integrating their elements in lifestyle (Wamwara-Mbugua et al. 2008; Askegaard et al. 2005). We apply the same reasoning to considering cultural orientations of the mainstream consumers, in line with authors like Holliday (2010) and Sharma et al (1995). For individuals in Full Integration, all types of cultures will be important, and they can be assumed to consciously integrate products and brands associated with Global, Local culture and specific Foreign culture(s).

METHOD

To add insight to our theoretical extrapolations, we conducted a multi-country study in Russia, Ukraine and Belgium. We sought to empirically test the uni-, bi- and multi-cultural orientations established in the CCO Typology and explore whether and how these orientations affect consumption choices. In view of the nature of the research objectives, a qualitative approach was deemed applicable. By sampling one Western country and two Eastern European countries, we aimed to supplement a predominantly Western body of knowledge on multi-cultural consumers with insights about multi-cultural orientations of consumers in emerging markets. In addition, all three sampled countries present an attractive field for research into cultural orientations in culturally-diverse environments as in all of them, mainstream (non-migrant) groups of population co-reside

with multiple sizeable ethnic migrant groups (Belgium Department of Federal Immigration 2009; All-Ukrainian Population Census 2001; All-Russian Census of Population 2002). Finally, all selected countries participate in the contemporary globalized consumption-scape (Ger and Ostergaard 1998; Appadurai 1996). The program of study was designed to comprise several steps and methods, in order to triangulate our research approach (Bryman 2003), and to provide a thorough understanding of both the respondents' attitude towards different cultures and of the consumption behavior that results from it. Specifically, data collection involved in-depth interviews complemented by accompanied shopping trips, which aided the respondents' reflections about cultural affiliations and consumption preferences. The interviews lasted on average 60 to 90 minutes, and were audio-recorded with the participants' consent. All participants' names used in this paper are pseudonyms to ensure their anonymity.

We selected 20 respondents of diverse ages, gender, and ethnic backgrounds for our study (8 in Russia, 8 in Ukraine and 4 in Belgium; full demographic characteristics of all respondents are presented in Table 2). The participants were selected based on the theoretical sampling method, which planned for each selected respondent to bring additional diversity and response elements to the study (Glaser and Strauss 1967). In order to take into account the concurring cultural influences and types of consumers, our selection was guided by our conceptualization: we ensured that both mainstream and migrant individuals were represented in the sample. To ensure participants' knowledge about the culture and product landscape in the country of residence, all solicited participants have been residing in the indicated country for no less than the last three years.

The interview transcripts and lists of participants' purchases formed the basis for data analysis. While prior coding structure was set by the CCO Typology, open coding was also allowed to inform analysis, as proposed by Strauss and Corbin (1998). To ensure within- and across-sample rigor (Miles & Huberman, 1994), two coders coded the data independently; the transcripts and coding structures were then cross-compared and analyzed following Berry's (1979) recommendation of combining single culture (emic) study with transcultural (etic).The findings for the different countries were therefore first analyzed separately following a meaning condensation approach (Kvale 1996), and subsequently combined to contrast the findings across countries.

FINDINGS

The CCO Typology hypothesizes that, along with 'glocal' cultural orientations adopted by individuals internalizing global and local cultures, other forms of bi-cultural (i.e., Local-Foreign and Global-Foreign) and multi-cultural (i.e., Full Integration) orientations exist. Our empirical findings support this proposition, indicating that multicultural orientations maintained by individuals take forms other than glocalizm. The findings are summarized in Table 3. The findings on uni-cultural orientations (Local Orientation, Foreign Orientation, and Global Orientation) and Local-Global Orientation are consistent with prior research (for details, see Oberecker et al. 2008; Alden et al. 2006; Kjeldgaard and Askegaard 2006). Due to space constraints, we focus on reporting the findings that shed new light on bi- and multi-cultural orientations.

Local-Foreign Orientation

As defined in the the typology, the Local-Foreign Orientation relates to joint affiliation with the local culture of residence and specific foreign culture(s), combined with no or low interest and involvement with global culture. Traditionally attributed to migrants negotiating between their culture of heritage and new culture of residence (see for example Abdel's quote in table 3), our findings demonstrate different forms of this orientation. The following excerpt indicates that Aniva, a Russian-origin citizen of Ukraine, considers US lifestyle desirable, less in order to migrate there permanently, but rather in order to take in this culture and then come back to Ukraine, while not displaying close links with her (Russian) heritage culture.

"Of course there is difference between global culture and foreign cultures... **I like how they live in America** *(USA). I watch 'A window to the US' [a local Ukrainian television program] and I think that they in America have a very good culture: people there are more valued and protected than anywhere else... I would like to live there...to have a good look at and learn more about how they live but not live forever, you know [laughs], like a long visit and then* **by all means come back home.***"* (Aniva, Ukraine)

Nadia, a Flemish Belgian, similarly aims at integrating local with foreign culture. As opposed to Aniva however, her foreign orientation does not focus on one particular culture, but on multiple cultures.

"I have travelled a lot, and there are **good things everywhere**, *or things that you think are strange, not like you expected, so there is positive and negative everywhere, but there is no country where I say 'that's it. [...] I think there is also a risk in it [globalisation], it's possible that certain things, which are very traditional and culturally important for people, will be sup-*

pressed [...] in fact it neutralizes everything, everything becomes the same, and I think we should keep the things that make a region special and typical, otherwise we are going to lose all these things." (Nadia, Belgium)

Consumers distancing themselves from global culture while internalizing local and foreign culture(s) appeared to translate this likewise in their consumption experiences. Indeed, they integrate brands perceived to create local and specific 'foreign culture living', while rejecting brands assigned with 'global' meanings. Nick (Russia) for example, who projects affiliation with local (Russian) culture and also affective aspirations toward America and Japan, identifies his purchased brands as Russian and American, and offers the following explanation for his choice:

"I buy our [Russian] brands because it is important that they are grown or made here [Interviewer: why is it important?] Because they are **made in my country**, *and now they are as* **good as best brands from abroad***...I would not want products from abroad to disappear from our shops like it used to be, I think it is great we have them...America is a very developed country, I think they know how to make things pleasant for you... [Interviewer: so how do you feel when you buy American products?] ...Don't know...[thinks] I suppose I like that I can now afford and access these nice things..."* (Nick, Russia)

Likewise, Nadia's orientation towards multiple foreign cultures is also manifested in what she considers important in driving her

Table 2. Summary demographics of all respondents

Name	Gender	Age	Country of Residence	Cultural Origin	Occupation
Alexandra	F	24	Ukraine	Ukrainian	Employee at estate agents
Aniva	F	57	Ukraine	Russian	Professional skilled worker but unemployed
Vebmart	M	21	Ukraine	Ukrainian	Manager in IT company
Alice	F	34	Ukraine	Ukrainian	Lecturer at a university and works for an MNC
Udana	F	21	Ukraine	Russian/Ukrainian	Student
Eveline	F	43	Ukraine	Russian	Music teacher
Dan	M	38	Ukraine	Russian	Artist
Max	M	65 + 1-5 years (uncomfortable giving his age)	Ukraine	Russian	Pensioner
Angela	F	60	Russia	Russian	Financial analyst
Erin	F	21	Russia	Russian	Student
Kate	F	40	Russia	Russian	Psychologist
Nick	M	20	Russia	Russian	Student
Tanie	F	23	Russia	Reports as mixed Eastern European origin but does not specify	Employee in multimedia company
Cancer	M	23	Russia	Russian	IT engineer
Dennis	M	31	Russia	Russian	Economist
Nikoo	M	49	Russia	Russian	Head of Innovation department in education software producing company
Nadia	F	36	Belgium	Flemish	Chemist
Thierry	M	29	Belgium	Walloon	Production manager
Abdel	M	30	Belgium	Malian	Designer/dressmaker
Christine	F	25	Belgium	French	Communication agent

Table 3 Summary table of findings on bi- and multi-cultural orientations

Type of cultural orientation[1]	Illustration	
	Example quotes - identity	Example quotes – consumption
Local-Global Orientation	*"Life is about change [...] I think we live when we change but other people may think differently. Personally, I find it **important to be part of the world culture** because we all live on one planet and the borders are historical givens [...] We [...] [Interviewer: Russia?] yes, can take good things from others but should **stay individual** and not become same as everyone else"* (Nikoo, Russia)	*"I either buy the **Ukrainian producer's brands or good big brands**. [...] It may be a stereotype but I think that the best brands come from the West...And I kind of like when our [Ukrainian] brands work to **Western technologies and standards**."* (Udana, Ukraine)
Local- Foreign Orientation	*"Thanks to my friends, I like it in Belgium, in Europe. But I always keep in mind Africa to see the other side"* (Abdel, Belgium) *"Of course there is difference between global culture and foreign cultures... **I like how they live in America** (USA). I watch 'A window to the US' [a local Ukrainian television program] and I think that they in America have a very good culture: people there are more valued and protected than anywhere else... I would like to live there...to have a good look at and learn more about how they live but not live forever, you know [laughs], like a long visit and then **by all means come back home**."* (Aniva, Ukraine) *"I have travelled a lot, and there are **good things everywhere**, or things that you think are strange, not like you expected, so there is positive and negative everywhere, but there is no country where I say 'that's it. [...] I think there is also a risk in it [globalisation], it's possible that certain things, which are very traditional and culturally important for people, will be suppressed [...] in fact it neutralizes everything, everything becomes the same, and I think we should keep the things that make a region special and typical, otherwise we are going to lose all these things."* (Nadia, Belgium)	*"I buy our [Russian] brands because it is important that they are grown or made here [Interviewer: why is it important?] Because they are **made in my country**, and now they are as **good as best brands from abroad**...I would not want products from abroad to disappear from our shops like it used to be, I think it is great we have them...America is a very developed country, I think they know how to make things pleasant for you... [Interviewer: so how do you feel when you buy American products?] ...Don't know...[thinks] I suppose I like that I can now afford and access these nice things..."* (Nick, Russia) *"When I arrived in Brussels I saw all those little shops, Tunisian, Moroccan, and they were full of vegetables and herbs I didn't know, so I went into the shops, bought these things, bought some cook books and I tried to see what I could do with this. I actually wanted to **taste the tastes of the world**, and I wanted to use what you could buy, and this opened me up to a bigger world"* (Nadia, Belgium)
Global-Foreign Orientation	*"I want to be in Europe [Interviewer: anywhere in Europe?] [thinks] Well, possibly not everywhere. Most likely not everywhere even [smiles]. If I could choose it would probably be **Germany or Great Britain**. [...] I think it is important to **be in touch with the rest of the world** these days, my daily routine is to check several websites to see what's going on. [Interviewer: what kind of websites you visit?] Several. News, business, product releases, others. I also look to see what kind of jobs abroad are on offer."* (Vebmart, Ukraine)	*"This is **the first Ukranian brand** [Roshen chocolate] **that is putting itself in one line with European brands**. It can be mistaken for Western or European brand: the name is foreign and the quality of packaging and design is far better than of other [Ukrainian] brands."* (Vebmart, Ukraine)
Full Integration	*"I think I should be a part of the **civilized global world**, my daughter is taught this at school. I like **Sweden**; I like monarchy, the way they live and the charitable deeds of their Queen, and also their developed economy... But I am also a patriot of my country, I even gave some money to a boy who was reciting the **Ukrainian national anthem** in a bus. **Russia is also an important part of my life, I think their culture is very close to mine**."* (Evelyne, Ukraine) *"**I feel close and comfortable with Italian culture**. It is terrible but the Italians' love for good food, good wine and good clothes got me hooked, it is more expensive to live like this and not always healthy (laughs).[...] I travel to visit friends in America [USA] a lot, they are very progressive with technology there. [...] **I think I am a bit of a world person**, no everyone enjoys travelling in my age but I find it very stimulating. [...] **I like the feeling of coming back home** [to Russia]."* (Angela, Russia)	*"Shall I show you what I carry around with me? [opens handbag and produces Hello! Magazine] I keep it because it has all the glamour, and this one also has pictures of the Queen [of Great Britain]".* *"I only buy the best and I have my collection of **favorites from around the world** [...] If you ask me, **the Italian brands are one of the best**, their cakes are divine! But at the moment **our [Russian] cakes are nice too**... My friend and I love to go to France, we try to go every year and we love go to a French patisserie here [in Russia], buy some nice cakes and then get a bottle of nice French wine – just wonderful!"* (Angela, Russia)

[1] Due to space constraints, we only report findings on bi- and multi-cultural orientations. We also identified participants of uni-cultural orientations (Local Orientation, Foreign Orientation, and Global Orientation), findings on these consumers are not reported in this paper as they were consistent with prior research.

consumption choices; she describes in the following quote her desire to *taste the tastes of the world*.

> *"When I arrived in Brussels I saw all those little shops, Tunisian, Moroccan, and they were full of vegetables and herbs I didn't know, so I went into the shops, bought these things, bought some cook books and I tried to see what I could do with this. I actually wanted to **taste the tastes of the world**, and I wanted to use what you could buy, and this opened me up to a bigger world"* (Nadia, Belgium)

Global-Foreign Orientation

Global-Foreign Orientation, defined in our Typology as "individual's integrated affiliation with specific foreign culture(s) and global culture, combined with no or low interest and involvement with culture of residence", has not been addressed in consumer research until now. We found this orientation extends beyond migrant groups. While among migrants Global-Foreign Orientation could have been expected due to the importance of global culture in migrant acculturation (Askegaard et al 2005), mainstream individuals also appeared to project this orientation, describing their local culture as of *'very low importance'*. In the following quote, Vebmart, a native Ukrainian, talks about his orientation towards particular foreign cultures, such as the German or British one, but also indicates that he wants to connect with the world.

> *"I want to be in Europe* [Interviewer: anywhere in Europe?] [thinks] *Well, possibly not everywhere. Most likely not everywhere even* [smiles]. *If I could choose it would probably be **Germany or Great Britain**.* [...] *I think it is important to **be in touch with the rest of the world** these days, my daily routine is to check several websites to see what's going on.* [Interviewer: what kind of websites you visit?] *Several. News, business, product releases, others. I also look to see what kind of jobs abroad are on offer."* (Vebmart, Ukraine)

Respondents reporting strong affiliations with Global and/or Foreign culture(s) but low affiliation with local culture predominantly base their consumption decisions on brand associations with these types of cultures and interestingly, while rejecting local-only perceived brands, favor local brands perceived to carry 'global' meanings and being of equal standard to 'truly-global' products. For example, Vebmart, while reporting a strong orientation toward the Western Europe and the global community, selected a local chocolate brand Roshen and explained his choice as follows:

> *"This is **the first Ukranian brand** [Roshen chocolate] **that is putting itself in one line with European brands**. It can be mistaken for Western or European brand: the name is foreign and the quality of packaging and design is far better than of other* [Ukrainian] *brands."* (Vebmart, Ukraine)

Full integration

Individuals reporting orientations towards local, foreign and global culture, refer to global and nationalistic affiliations while also acknowledging strong links to particular foreign cultures. For instance, Evelyne, an ethnic Russian born in Ukraine, mentions the global world, her attachment to Sweden and its culture, her pride of Ukrainian culture as local culture of her country, as well as importance of Russian as her heritage culture in her discourse, attributing high importance to all of them.

> *"I think I should be a part of the **civilized global world**, my daughter is taught this at school. I like **Sweden**; I like monarchy, the way they live and the charitable deeds of their Queen, and also their developed economy... But I am also a patriot of my country, I even gave some money to a boy who was reciting the **Ukrainian national anthem** in a bus. **Russia is also an important part of my life, I think their culture is very close to mine.**"* (Evelyne, Ukraine)

Consumption choices and brand perceptions of those respondents reporting orientation towards local, global and foreign cultures overall reflect their multi-cultural orientation and indicate that perceptions of consumed brands tend to differentiate between global-perceived brands and brands originating from favored foreign culture, a differentiation already highlighted in Nadia's quote earlier.

Similarly to glocalized consumers described earlier in the literature (Kjelgaard and Ostberg 2007; Kjelgaard and Askergaard 2006; Sandikci and Ger 2002), the multi-cultural individuals integrate both local and global brands in their consumption but also incorporate brands associated with favored foreign culture(s) that are of importance to them in their lifestyles. These consumers aim at maintaining a perceived balance of global and foreign brands in their consumption. Similarly to the "Best-of-both-worlders" described by Askegaard et al (2005), Angela, a native Russian reporting affinities with Italy, France and global culture, depicts her preference for the best products from the *whole* world, while also favoring products she places as local (Russian) and those associated with her foreign affinity cultures.

> *"I only buy the best and I have my collection of **favorites from around the world** [...] If you ask me, **the Italian brands are one of the best**, their cakes are divine! But at the moment our* [Russian] *cakes are nice too... My friend and I love to go to France, we try to go every year and we love go to a French patisserie here* [in Russia], *buy some nice cakes and then get a bottle of nice French wine – just wonderful!"* (Angela, Russia)

DISCUSSION

Our findings shed light on an important tendency; in culturally diverse environments, individuals may develop one or more cultural affiliations and integrate these cultures of importance in their lifestyles, mixing and combining objects and symbols perceived as representative of these cultures. Some of these tendencies were observed earlier in ethnic and/or migrant consumer behavior research (Askegaard et al. 2005; Penaloza 1989; Oswald 1999). However, our findings highlight that ethnic consumers can also develop affiliations with foreign cultures either in addition to, or instead of that of their heritage. Similarly, mainstream individuals presented with varying links to their local culture along with diverse and at times multiple links with cultures perceived external to their locale of origin (global and/or multiple foreign cultures). These insights have important implications for consumer behavior research: they showcase that the traditional divide in considering ethnic migrant consumers' identities within heritage-residence-global cultures milieu and mainstream consumers' identities within local(residence)-global milieu does not capture the complexity of cultural affinities within both these groups. These complexities subsequently elicit complexities in consumption, whereby individuals deploy their diverse cultural orientations as informing frames for interpreting and assigning meanings to brands, and other consumption choices.

In addition, our findings indicate that individuals clearly distinguish 'foreign' and 'global' meanings and differentially deploy them in materializing identity projects. For instance, consumers in Global-Foreign orientation deploy both foreign and global cultures simultaneously but not interchangeably. On the contrary, Local-Foreign oriented persons, whilst remaining open to 'outside' cultural experiences display a tendency of distancing themselves from global culture as in their view it encompasses the risk of attenuating diversity and uniqueness of external cultural experiences, a tendency that is not captured by the 'glocal' orientation established by prior research (Kjeldgaard and Askeggard 2006).

These findings extend current knowledge on anti-global consumer attitudes and necessitate further scholarly research into such theories as cultural openness (Sharma et al. 1995), cosmopolitanism (Cannon and Yaprak, 2002) and world-mindedness (Hannerz 1990). A number of current conceptualizations in the field of international marketing suggest intrinsic links between these psychological traits and acceptance of global-perceived brands as material symbols of global culture (Cleveland and Laroche 2007; Alden et al. 2006). Our findings indicate however that while welcoming inter-cultural exchange and consumption experiences from different foreign cultures one may strongly resist global culture.

Such a differentiation may be explained by consumers' quest for authenticity, defined as "against modern, mass culture" (Pratt 2007 p.293). Not only indifference or frustration with global culture may lead to consumers to turn to their own traditional norms and products but it may also lead them to seek more "authentic" foreign brands that have a clear association with particular cultures. As these consumers view global culture and products as threat to the individuality of cultures all over the world that leads to traditions and norms becoming blurred and similar (or 'mass'), preference for products that are assigned with *foreign but not global* meanings is logical. Similarly to Thompson and Tambyah's (1999) depiction of expatriates 'trying to be cosmopolitan' by immersing in authentic cultural experiences beyond tourist sites, consumers' differentiation between foreign and global products in this article points thus to a desire to express cultural affinities in an authentic way, outside of globalised consumer culture. Therefore, further research is needed to differentiate consumption choices of global- and foreign-oriented individuals explore whether these choices are performed as authenticating acts or in order to affiliate to particular communities (Arnould and Price, 2000). Although both groups will display a positive disposition toward cultures from 'outside' the locale, products and brands assigned with 'global' meanings would only be favored by the first group while avoided by the second group due to a polar affiliation with global culture itself. In addition, unexpected findings of our study provide some initial indication that consumers opposing local culture per se may hold positive attitudes to selected locally-produced brands that demonstrate an openness and engagement with the 'outside' cultures favoured by consumers themselves.

To sum up, our findings clearly suggest that dramatic diversification of the cultural landscapes brings to the fore the need for new approaches to the analysis of culturally-informed consumption and to consumer segmentation. To advance our understanding of cultural drivers of diversity in consumption preferences and behaviors, it is critical to shift from selectively sampling consumer groups either on the basis of their ethnic heritage or on the basis of their willingness to engage with external cultures, to appreciating the full diversity of cultural affiliations consumers may develop and categorizing them on the basis of their cultural orientations.

CONCLUSIONS

Our study investigates how the multiple cultural influences present in modern culturally diverse environments affect consumer lifestyle choices. It argues that the exchange between multiple cultures leads to complexities of cultural orientations among ethnic migrants and mainstream consumers alike. The proposed Consumer Cultural Orientation Typology, brings together the findings on mainstream individuals developing varying affiliations with local, global and foreign cultures stemming from the body of international marketing research on one hand (Oberecker et al. 2008; Kjelgaard and Askergaard 2006; Alden et al. 2006; Sandikci and Ger 2002; Crane 2002; Perlmutter 1954; Kent and Burnight 1951) and the findings on individuals integrating multiple cultures in their identities emerging from the body of ethnic consumer behavior research on the other hand (Kim et al. 2009; Wamwara-Mbugua et al. 2008; Askegaard et al. 2005; Luna and Peracchio 2005). The CCO Typology distinguishes uni-, bi- and multi-cultural orientations that accounts for overlaps in these bodies of literature and contributes to knowledge by presenting a more complete picture of diverse multi-cultural identities developed by mainstream and migrant consumers. Our study therefore extends consumer behavior theory by proposing an alternative consumer segmentation framework that takes into account the increasing numbers of consumers with multiple ethnic, national and cultural affiliations, which cannot be captured by ethnicity and nationality.

Since our study is limited by its relatively small sample size and geo-demographic characteristics, further research is required that will extend the multi-cultural orientations' enquiry into larger and more diverse samples. Future studies should attempt to validate the findings presented in this paper in other countries and analyze whether demographic characteristics (such as age, gender, education etc) have an effect upon multiculturalism. The study of identity switching described by immigrant research (Oswald 1999; Luna et al., 2008) should also involve the mainstream multicultural consumers, to determine how multi-cultural mainstream individuals navigate their new reformed identities. Finally, it would also be of interest to apply the typology developed in this article to analyze how multi-cultural orientations inform consumer interpretations of cultural meanings of brands and their usage. A better understanding of the way multi-cultural identities are derived and expressed through consumption would particularly assist marketers when segmenting consumers and developing branding strategies targeting multicultural consumers. A more sophisticated and in-depth understanding of consumption consequences of uni-, bi- or multicultural orientations is pertinent for a successful adaptation of marketing theory and practice to the new multicultural world.

REFERENCES

Alden, Dana L., Steenkamp, Jan-Benedict E. M., and Batra, Rajeev (1999), "Brand Positioning Through Advertising in Asia, North America, and Europe: The Role of Global Consumer Culture," *Journal of Marketing, 63*(1), 75/87.

Alden, Dana L., Steenkamp, Jan-Benedict E. M., and Batra, Rajeev (2006), "Consumer attitudes toward marketplace globalization: Structure, antecedents and consequences," *International Journal of Research in Marketing, 23*(3), 227-239.

Appadurai, Arjun. 1996, *Modernity at Large: Cultural Dimensions of Globalization*. Minneapolis, Minnesota University of Minnesota Press.

Arnould, Eric J. and Linda L. Price (2000), "Authenticating Acts and Authoritative Performances: Questing for Self and Community," in *The Why of Consumption: Contemporary Perspectives on Consumer Motives, Goals, and Desires*, ed. S. Ratneshwar, David Glen Mick, and Cynthia Huffman, London: Routledge, 140–63.

Askegaard, Soren R., Arnould, Eric J., and Kjeldgaard, Dannie. (2005), "Postassimilationist Ethnic Consumer Research: Qualifications and Extensions," *Journal of Consumer Research, 32*(1), 160-170.

Berry, John W. (1979), "Research in Multicultural Societies: Implications of Cross-Cultural Methods," *Journal of Cross-Cultural Psychology, 10*(4), 415-434.

Bryman, Alan (2003). Triangulation. *Encyclopedia of Social Science Research Methods*. London: Sage.

Cannon, Hugh M. and Yaprak, Attila (2002), "Will the Real-World Citizen Please Stand Up! The Many Faces of Cosmopolitan Consumer Behavior," *Journal of International Marketing, 10*(4), 30-52.

Cayla, Julien and Arnould, Eric J. (2008), "A Cultural Approach to Branding in the Global Marketplace," *Journal of International Marketing, 16*(4), 86-112.

Cayla, Julien and Eckhardt, Giana M. (2008), "Asian Brands and the Shaping of a Transnational Imagined Community," *Journal of Consumer Research, 35*(2), 216-230.

Chattaraman, Veena, Sharron J. Lennon, and Nancy A. Rudd (2010), "Social Identity Salience: Effects on Identity-based Brand Choices of Hispanic Consumers," *Psychology and Marketing*, 27(3), 263–284.

Cleveland, Mark and Laroche, Michel (2007), "Acculturation to the global consumer culture: Scale development and research paradigm," *Journal of Business Research, 60*, 249-259.

Cockburn, Laura (2002), "Children and Young People Living in Changing Worlds: The Process of Assessing and Understanding the 'Third Culture Kid'," *School Psychology International, 23*(4), 475-485.

Crane, Diana (2002), Culture and globalization, in *Global culture: Media, arts, policy and globalization,* ed. Diana Crane, Nobuko Kawashima, and Kenichi Kawasaki, New York: Routledge, 1-25.

Department of Federal Immigration Belgium (2008), *La population étrangère en Belgique*, http://www.dofi.fgov.be/fr/statistieken/statistiques_etrangers/Stat_ETRANGERS.htm.

Eckhardt, Giana M. and Mahi, Humaira (2004), "The Role of Consumer Agency in the Globalization Process in Emerging Markets," *Journal of Macromarketing, 24*(2), 136-146.

Ger, Guliz and Ostergaard, Per (1998), "Constucting Immigrant Identities in Consumoption: Appearance Among the Turko-Dane," *Advances in Consumer Research 25*(1), 48-52.

Glaser, Barney G. and Strauss, Anselm L. (1967), *The Discovery of Grounded Theory: Strategies for Qualitative Research*. New York: Aldine Publishing Company.

Hannerz, Ulf (1990), Cosmopolitans and Locals in World Culture, *Global Culture. Nationalism, Globalization and Modernity*, ed. Michael Featherstone, London: Sage, 237-252.

Holliday, Adrian (2010), "Complexity in cultural identity," *Language & Intercultural Communication 10*(2), 165-77.

Iwabuchi, Koichi (2002), From western gaze to global gaze, in *Global culture: Media, arts, policy and globalization,* ed. Diana Crane, Nobuko Kawashima, and Kenichi I. Kawasaki, London: Routledge, 256-270.

Jamal, Ahmad (2003), "Marketing in a multicultural world: the interplay of marketing, ethnicity and consumption," *European Journal of Marketing*, 37(11/12), 1599-1620.

Jiménez, Tomas R. (2010), "Affiliative ethnic identity: a more elastic link between ethnic ancestry and culture," *Ethnic and Racial Studies* 33(10), 1756-75.

Kent, Donald P. and Burnight, Robert G. (1951), "Group Centrism in Complex Societies," *American Journal of Sociology 57*(3), 256-59.

Kim, Chankon, Yang, Zhiyong, and Lee, Hanjoon (2009), "Cultural differences in consumer socialization: A comparison of Chinese-Canadian and Caucasian-Canadian children," *Journal of Business Research, 62*(10), 955-962.

Kipnis, Eva, Kubacki, Krzysztof, Broderick, Amanda J., Siemieniako, Dariusz, and Pisarenko, Nataliya L. (2012), "'They don't want us to become them': Brand Local Integration and consumer ethnocentrism," *Journal of Marketing Management, 28*(7-8), 836-864.

Kjeldgaard, Dannie and Askegaard, Soren R. (2006), "The Glocalization of Youth Culture: The Global Youth Segment as Structures of Common Difference," *Journal of Consumer Research, 33*(2), 231-247.

Kjeldgaard, Dannie and Ostberg, Jacob (2007), "Coffee Grounds and the Global Cup: Glocal Consumer Culture in Scandinavia," *Consumption, Markets & Culture, 10*(2), 175-187.

Kvale, S. (1996). *Interviews, an Introduction to Qualitative Research Interviewing*. London: Sage.

Leclerc, France, Schmitt, Bernd. H., and Dube, Laurette (1994), "Foreign Branding and Its Effects on Product Perceptions and Attitudes," *Journal of Marketing Research, 31*(2), 263-270.

Luedicke, Marius K. (2011), "Consumer acculturation theory: (crossing) conceptual boundaries," *Consumption, Markets & Culture, 14*(3), 223-244.

Luna, Davidand Peracchio, Laura A. (2005), "Advertising to Bilingual Consumers: The Impact of Code-Switching on Persuasion," *Journal of Consumer Research, 31*(4), 760-765.

Luna, David, Ringberg, Torsten, and Peracchio, Laura A. (2008), "One Individual, Two Identities: Frame Switching among Biculturals," *Journal of Consumer Research, 35*(2), 279-293.

Miles, M. B., and Huberman, A. M. (1994). *Qualitative Data Analysis: An Expanded Sourcebook*. Thousand Oaks, CA: Sage.

Oberecker, Eva M. and Diamantopoulos, Adamantios (2011), "Consumers' Emotional Bonds with Foreign Countries: Does Consumer Affinity Affect Behavioral Intentions?," *Journal of International Marketing, 19*(2), 45-72.

Oberecker, Eva M., Riefler, Petra, and Diamantopoulos, Adamantios (2008), "The Consumer Affinity Construct: Conceptualization, Qualitative Investigation, and Research Agenda," *Journal of International Marketing, 16*(3), 23-56.

Oswald, Laura R. (1999), "Culture Swapping: Consumption and the Ethnogenesis of Middle-Class Haitian Immigrants," *Journal of Consumer Research, 25*(4), 303-318.

Palumbo, Frederick A. and Teich, Ira (2003), "Market segmentation based on level of acculturation," *Marketing Intelligence and Planning, 22*(4), 472-484.

Penaloza, Lisa N. (1989), "Immigrant Consumer Acculturation," *Advances in Consumer Research, 16*(1), 110-118.

Penaloza, Lisa N. (1994), "Atravesando Fronteras/Border Crossings: A Critical Ethnographic Exploration of the Consumer Acculturation of Mexican Immigrants," *Journal of Consumer Research, 21*(1), 32-54.

Perlmutter, Howard V. (1954), "Some characteristics of the xenophilic personality," *Journal of Psychology, 38*, 291-300.

Pratt, Jeff (2007), "Food Values: The Local and the Authentic," *Critique of Anthropology, 27*(3), 285-300.

Reardon, James, Miller, Chip, Vida, Irena, and Kim, Irina (2005), "The effects of ethnocentrism and economic development on the formation of brand and ad attitudes in transitional economies," *European Journal of Marketing,* 39(7-8), 737-754.

Roudometof, Victor (2005), "Transnationalism, Cosmopolitanism and Glocalization," *Current Sociology, 53*(1), 113-135.

Russian Federal Deparmetn of State Statistics (2002), *All-Russian Census of Population,* http://uk.msn.com/?ocid=iehp

Sandikci, Ozlem and Ger, Guliz (2002), In-between modernities and postmodernities: theorizing Turkish consumptionscape, in *Advances in consumer research,* 29, ed. S.Broniarczyk and K.Nakomoto. Valdosta, GA: Association for Consumer Research., 465-470.

Sharma, Subhash, Shimp, Terence A., and Jeongshin, Shin (1995), "Consumer Ethnocentrism: A Test of Antecedents and Moderators," *Journal of the Academy of Marketing Science, 23*(1), 26-37.

Sparrow, Lise M. (2000), "Beyond multicultural man: complexities of identity," *International Journal of Intercultural Relations,* 24(2), 173-201.

Steenkamp, Jan-Benedict E. M., Batra, Rajeev, and Alden, Dana L. (2003), "How perceived brand globalness creates brand value," *Journal of International Business Studies, 34*(1), 53-65.

State Statistics Committee of Ukraine (2001), *All-Ukrainian Population Census,* http://2001.ukrcensus.gov.ua/eng/

Strauss, A. L. and Corbin, J. (1998). *Basics of qualitative research: Techniques and Procedures for developing grounded theory* (2nd ed.). London: Sage.

Strizhakova, Yuliya, Coulter, Robin A., and Price, Linda L. (2008), "Branded Products as a Passport to Global Citizenship: Perspectives from Developed and Developing Countries," *Journal of International Marketing, 16*(4), 57-85.

Thompson, Craig J. and Tambyah, Siok K. (1999), "Trying to Be Cosmopolitan," *Journal of Consumer Research, 26*(3), 214-241.

Wallendorf, Melanie and Reilly, Michael D. (1983), "Ethnic Migration, Assimilation, and Consumption," *Journal of Consumer Research, 10*(3), 292-302.

Wamwara-Mbugua, L. Waikiuru, Cornwell, T. Bettina, and Boller, Gregory (2008), "Triple acculturation: The role of African Americans in the consumer acculturation of Kenyan immigrants," *Journal of Business Research, 61*(2), 83-90.

"Great Sleep" as a Form of Hedonic Consumption

Anu Valtonen, University of Lapland, Finland
Johanna Moisander, Aalto University, Finland

ABSTRACT

While hedonic and experiential consumption is an established area of research, the "great sleep" as a new form of hedonic consumption has been largely overlooked in this literature. We will address this gap by, firstly, bringing together existing literature on hedonic and experiential consumption and socio-cultural studies on sleep, and secondly, by developing a practice-based narrative perspective that enables us to conceptualize how "great sleep" is commodified within the field of practices that constitutes consumer culture. In this process, a specific mode of being, sleep-as-consumption, is constructed.

INTRODUCTION

The contemporary consumer culture offers a wide range of cultural and material resources for consumers pursuing for "great sleep", either as an experience in itself, or as an enabler for better wakeful experiences. One example is sleep tourism, a form of tourism in which sleeping takes place in extraordinary places like in ice hotels or caves (Keinan and Kivetz 2011; Valtonen and Veijola 2011). In an on-line page entitled "The world's best places to catch some shut-eye" (www.slate.com/id/2220293), one sleep tourist tells about his experiences. He had constructed an igloo with the help of the guide, and after having poked a small air in the roof, he wore a wool hat, climbed to a double sleeping bag – and had the best sleep he had ever had. In his words, it "was the mythical supersleep, deeper than any other, the Atlantis of the unconscious. It was a heavy dose of what scientists call slow-wave sleep". The sleep tracker provides another example (www.sleeptracker.com). The web-page of this gadget, which looks like a wrist watch, tells us that it "monitors your sleep stages throughout the night and then uses that data to determine the exact moment when you should be awoken helping you feel refreshed and energetic". At the same page, a customer writes about her user experiences saying that "My first night with it was great – I woke up completely fresh and rested".

These market-driven narratives about "great sleep" illuminate developments in the contemporary discursive and material landscape of sleeping (Valtonen and Veijola 2011; Williams 2005). Accordingly, sleeping is no longer, or not merely, aligned with laziness and passivity but rather with entertainment, excitement, and experience. It also is aligned with new kinds of physical devices, and symbolic repertoires of knowledge, that allow consumers to control, and perhaps even maximize, their attempts to sleep well, and to wake up rested and energized. We treat these narratives (Moisander and Eriksson 2006) as one way through which "great sleep" is constructed as a culturally acceptable and an attractive experience.

In this paper, our focus is on exploring how "great sleep", as a culturally regulated practice, is commodified within the field of practices that constitutes consumer culture. Thus, instead of providing a phenomenological account on consumers' experiences of "great sleep", we are interested in how the consumption and marketing practices of sleep-related products and services attach particular meanings and values, which are often complex and contradictory, to the notion of "great sleep", and thereby commodify it (Penaloza 2000,83). We argue that through this commodification (a) "great sleep" is rendered a legitimate object of consumer desire, and thus subsumed under the dynamics and logics of consumer culture, and b) a specific mode of being, sleep-as-consumption, is constructed. This commodification structures and directs the way consumers enact their sleep, conceive of sleep and of themselves as sleeping consumers, and directs consumer desires toward new kinds of sleep-related fantasies, feelings and fun (Hirschman and Holbrook 1982).

On the level of theory, our aim is to work towards a new perspective on studying the commodification of sleep into an object of hedonic consumption. The practice-based narrative perspective that we here develop, draws upon cultural accounts on sleep (Mauss 1973; Taylor 1993; Valtonen and Veijola 2011; Williams 2005), theories of practice (Reckwitz 2002; Schatzki 2002; Schatzki et al. 2001; Warde 2005), and consumer culture theory discussing how cultural meanings and values are narrated in the marketplace (Penaloza 2000; Moisander and Eriksson 2006; Moisander and Valtonen 2006; Shankar, Elliott, and Goulding 2001). By way of conclusion, we suggest a tentative research agenda for studying sleeping as a form of hedonic consumption from this particular perspective.

The contributions of this paper are threefold. First, it extends the current understanding of the distinct 'states of being' involved in hedonic and experiential consumption. While previous studies have documented the way hedonic and experiential consumption practices bring about an alternative state of being – conceptualized, for instance, in terms of "flow", "liminality", or "losing it" – they have always assumed a waking subject in their investigations (Arnould and Price 1993; Belk and Costa 1998; Goulding, Shankar, Elliott, and Canniford 2009). We add the state of being asleep to these debates. By comparing it with the wakeful states we offer a fuller picture of the states of being associated to hedonic and experiential consumption. By drawing attention to the commodification of this state of being asleep, in turn, we provide one novel example of the way specific modes of being are constructed in the fields of practices that constitute consumer culture. Second, this paper articulates a practice-based narrative perspective on the commodification of sleeping into an object of hedonic and experiential consumption. This perspective provides one alternative to the recent anthropological (Tumbat and Belk 2011) and biosocial (Goulding et al. 2009) streams of research that have elaborated on the complex relationship between hedonic and experiential consumption and consumer and marketplace cultures. Third, this paper highlights the ways in which the practices of contemporary consumer culture shape and structure notions of sleep, rendering it an object of desire. In doing so, our study introduces sleeping, an under-researched yet burgeoning consumption phenomenon, to the research agenda of hedonic and experiential consumption, and suggests future directions for its theoretical and empirical exploration.

The paper starts by reviewing the key conceptual developments made in the research area of hedonic and pleasurable consumption. Then it turns to develop a practice-based narrative perspective on studying the commodification of sleep into an object of hedonic consumption. To conclude, the paper outlines areas for future research. While our exploratory paper is conceptual, it makes references to empirical examples for illustrative purposes.

Earlier research on hedonic and experiential consumption

In their seminal article Holbrook and Hirschman (1982) critiqued the then popular notion of the consumer as a rational and utilitarian decision-maker, and argued for an alternative perspective that would better capture types of consumption in which experiences, aesthetic enjoyment and emotional responses are central. Since that a distinctive body of theoretical knowledge about this type of consumption has been generated. Consumers scholars have taken different theoretical perspectives – phenomenological (Celsi, Rose, and Leigh 1993), anthropological (Belk and Costa 1998; Tumbat and Belk 2011), and biosocial (Goulding et al. 2009) – and empirically explored this phenomenon in a range of consumption settings from leisure activities (Arnould and Price 1993; Celsi et al. 1993; Joy and Sherry 2003; Tumbat and Belk 2011), festivals and carnivals (Belk and Costa 1998; Kozinets 2002), commercially created thematized spaces (Maclaran and Brown 2005; Kozinets et al. 2004), to the context of passionate consumption (Belk, Ger, and Askegaard 2003), to mention a few.

While these studies differ in their theoretical assumptions and empirical foci, they nevertheless appear to share an idea that the pleasurable and experiential consumption practices bring about a distinctive *state of being* – commonly figured as liminal, euphoric, child-like, magical, fantastic, flow state, or communitas – that provides for consumers a temporarily disengage from the demands, rules and roles of the quotidian life. Contemporary consumer culture offers a wide range of virtual or non-virtual "alternative realities", such as clubs, theme parks, or games, where this disengage is facilitated, and where consumers are invited to throw for strangeness, novelty, and excitement, and to enjoy of their imaginative capacities - occasionally also with the help of substances such as drugs or alcohol. Consumers can thereby transcend the social categories that normally define them and move beyond mundane subjectivities. It is precisely this temporal transcendence of normal mundane life, facilitated by the co-creative consumption and marketing practices, that is thought to produce the re-vitalization of the self thus to be the key source of pleasurable and hedonic consumption. To illustrate, Goulding et al. describe their findings of the clubbing experience in the following way:

> We find that the effects of the deafening music, the ingestion of ecstasy, the energetic dancing, and the management and organization of space combine to produce a calculated, highly sought-after shared experience and a temporary suspension of the rules and norms of everyday life. (Goulding et al. 2009)

This existing literature has, nevertheless, focused almost exclusively on exploring the waking life of consumers, making only occasional references to the realm of sleeping. For instance, Belk and Costa (1998) and Arnould and Price (1993) in their seminal articles on consumer fantasies and extraordinary experiences – both taking place in the nature – start their ethnographic research when the research subjects crawl from their tents or tepees and leave them when they retire. What happens in between *that* time is unknown – only notes to the silence of the night or a wet sleeping bag are being made: 'sleep seeps in with the growing dark; the camp quiets, and the night's rest is the most beautiful of all' (House via Belk and Costa 1998, 238-9). Recent studies show, however, that sleeping outdoors, in tents, tepees or igloos, might be an experience in itself (Valtonen and Veijola 2011). As Keinan and Kivetz (2011, 948) point out, sleeping in places such as ice hotels provides an opportunity for contemporary consumers to collect novel, sometimes non-pleasurable, experiences to be added to their experiential CV.

We thus suggest that the existing literature on hedonic and experiential consumption remains inadequate if it keeps neglecting the phenomenon of sleeping. Sleeping is not only an emerging form of hedonic and experiential consumption whose on-going commodifi-

cation remains under-theorized, but also a theoretically intriguing case for developing the existing body of knowledge on the states of being associated to hedonic and experiential consumption. Therefore, we start to bring together the existing studies on hedonic and experiential consumption and the growing body of socio-cultural literature on sleep. This latter body of research, generated in various cultural disciplines such as anthropology, sociology, and history, provides us an important contextual basis for understanding sleeping as a culturally regulated practice. It offers insights into the cultural nature of the state of 'being asleep' as well as of the social, symbolic, corporeal and aesthetic standards, norms and criteria guiding the way the sleep is 'done' (Taylor 1993).

The human *state of 'being asleep'* has given ground for a range of cultural myths and beliefs, as anthropological and historical studies well illustrate (Steger and Brunt 2003; Tedlock 1987). In the West, it has commonly been conceived as an irrational and mystified sphere of life associated with the death and darkness. The phenomenological accounts, in turn, let us know how this state, involving distinct states of consciousness and will, provides a cyclical, momentary and partial withdrawal from the self and from the world (Bergson 1958; Merleau-Ponty 1962). During this state the sleeper passes through various stages – ones during which dreams are seen (the so call REM sleep, Aserinsky and Kleitman 1953) and not seen, 'deep sleep' representing the most inactive state (Härmä and Sallinen 2004).

The state of dreaming – the focus of many cultural inquiries (Tedlock 1987) – is commonly seen to liberate the mind from the ordinary world, though only partly, and to open up a fantasy world that might be experienced as enjoyable as such (Valtonen 2011). The 'deep sleep', thus the state during which dreams are not seen, has received less attention within cultural scholarship, the work of Paul Harrison (2009) representing one exception. For him, this state is a way to offer a critique for contemporary studies focused on studying (merely) the active part of human life. For us, this state – as well as other states involved in sleep – is of interest because they are targets in the commodification of "great sleep". For instance, there are packaged holidays whose core offering is based upon the appreciation of the world of dreams, and the state of 'deep sleep' is, in turn, referred to as *the* state essential for having "supersleep" (www.slate.com/id/2220293).

Moreover, although the past research has provided important insights into how specific states of being are involved, for instance, in daydreaming (Belk, Ger, and Askegaard 2003), contemplating of art (Sherry and Joy 2003), or use of ecstasy (Goulding et al. 2009), we suggest that the recognition of the state of being asleep complements this existing understanding. As we discussed above, 'being asleep', like the states identified earlier, represents an altered state of consciousness, a state in which the mind is "switched off", enabling consumers thus to "lose it", "it" referring to the mind (Greenfield 2000 via Goulding et al 2009, 767), and falling asleep provides, in a way, one way to throw to the "thrill of the unknown" (Arnould and Price 1993). Thus, in this sense the state of being asleep might enrich existing understanding, and point to the importance of other states such as vulnerability or drowsiness.

'Doing sleep' refers to the wide range of the social, symbolic, material, corporeal and aesthetic standards, norms and criteria that are related to human attempts fall asleep, to sleep, and to wake up. In every culture and society there is large repertoire of implicit and explicit rules and ideals that designate when, where, with whom, and how to sleep. For instance, the commonplace sleep pattern of today is to have an eight-hour unbroken nocturnal sleep, lying in a horizontal position in a private bed located in a bedroom. While

it is tempting to consider this prevalent Western sleep practice as 'natural', it is the result of long socio-historical civilization process (Elias 1978). In history, bi-phasic nocturnal sleep patterns have been common (Ekrich 2003), all sorts of techniques of sleep have been practiced (Mauss [1934] 1973, 80–81), and sleeping has taken place in public places with other people (Elias 1978).

The seminal article of Marcel Mauss (1973) "Techniques of the Body" – where he introduced the notion of "techniques of sleep" – offers us a fruitful basis for understanding these 'doings'. It leads us to conceive sleeping as an *embodied skill, habit and technique* bearing imprints of culture, society, and economy. This means that the way we sleep is an outcome of cultural and social education which, through time, becomes habituated and normalized. The embodied practice of sleeping provides one example. It is commonly held that this form of experience and pleasure calls for specific bodily techniques (such as breathing for relaxation), embodied postures of staying still and lying down, and a number of material and sensory affordances (Valtonen and Veijola 2011). The sociability of sleeping provides another example. The widely-spread cultural belief of the privatization of sleeping easily shadows the socio-pleasures of sleeping – sharing pleasures is commonly discussed as an essential part of the experiential and hedonic consumption (Goulding et al.2009) – and sleeping together, with the closest ones, may provide an significant source of enjoyment.

The culturally shaped skills, habits and techniques of sleep are subject to change. In the recent decade, some sort of change can be identified in the way the sleep is discussed and practiced in Western societies (Williams 2005, 2011). This is reflected, for instance, in the proliferation of sleep-related media talks. Contemporary consumers thus are surrounded by a discourse, in which the sleep, or the lack of it, is commonly casted either as a major crisis of our time, or alternatively as a vital opportunity to revitalize and energize people. The rapidly growing 'sleep aids market' (Williams 2011, 145) and the emerging products and services aiming at offering better sleep illustrate the case.

Moreover, the rapid increase of recent neuro-scientific and physiological research on sleep has expanded contemporary languages and knowledge pertaining to sleep, shaping thereby the way sleep is thought of, conceived and practiced. These discursive and material shifts together with the establishment of physical realities (see Humphreys 2010), such as sleep spas or hotels in trees, play a role in the creation of "great sleep" as a culturally acceptable means of seeking entertainment, excitement, and experiences.

Practice-based narrative approach to commodification of sleep as a form of hedonic consumption

In building our practice-based theoretical perspective on the commodification of sleep into a marketable entity, a practice of hedonic consumption, we draw primarily on the literature on practice theory (Reckwitz 2002; Schatzki 2002; Schatzki, Cetina, and Savigny 2001) and post-structuralist narrative approach to consumer culture theory (Davies 2003a; Davies and Harré 1990; Marion and Nairn 2011; Moisander and Eriksson 2006b; Shankar, Elliott, and Goulding 2001). From this perspective consumption is viewed and conceptualized as something that occurs within and is part of a field of practices (Schatzki et al. 2001) that are socially instituted and brought about in the marketplace through processes and practices of narration (Shankar, Elliott, and Fitchett 2009) and dialogue between marketers and consumers (Peñaloza and Gilly 1999). And it is this field of practices—the total nexus of interconnected consumption practices—that constitutes consumer culture (Moisander and Valtonen 2006).

By the term 'practice' we refer here to the "embodied, materially mediated arrays of human activity" that are centrally organized around a shared practical understanding" (Schatzki et al. 2001: 2). Practice is a "routinized type of behavior which consists of several elements, interconnected to one other: forms of bodily activities, forms of mental activities, 'things' and their use, a background knowledge in the form of understanding, know how, states of emotion and motivational knowledge" (Reckwitz 2002: 249). It thus consists of not only patterns of bodily behavior but also a set of particular routinized ways of understanding, knowing how, and desiring, which are essential elements of the practice in the sense that they constitute the "logic" of the practice through which the practice gets its meaning and purpose in the marketplace.

From this perspective, we conceptualize commodification in terms of the market-mediated processes and practices of narration through which sleep, as an everyday consumer experience and bodily practice, is transformed into a marketable entity with economic value. Economic value is assigned to sleep by endowing it with particular cultural meanings that have symbolic or sign value (Venkatesh and Peñaloza 2006) and by producing particular service-providing offerings that are designed to deliver this value as consumers use these offerings when engaging in their sleeping-related practices. Through these practices of commodification, sleep is thus transformed into a practice of consumption, in the sense that the activity of consumption—the appropriation and appreciation of goods, services, performances, information and ambiance (Warde 2005: 137)—becomes a constitutive element of the practice of sleeping.

As a result, sleeping becomes a culturally regulated practice that can be perfected with the help of particular products and services that are exchanged in the market. Through commodification, consumers are offered and encouraged to draw upon on particular socially instituted practices and cultural narratives about sleeping. By cultural narratives we refer to socially constructed storylines through which people make sense of their everyday lives and achieve social order (Davies 2003a, b). They are *cultural* in the sense that they emerge and are constructed out of a socio-cultural ensemble of stories, storytelling and reading practices that are embedded in a complex formation of discourse, knowledge and power (Nakagawa 1993; Rappaport 2000).

In the field of practices that constitutes consumer culture, these cultural narratives about great sleep that marketers construct and reproduce thus make available particular ways of making sense of the world and sanction particular behaviors as appropriate, worthwhile, and desirable in particulars contexts. In this sense, narratives are constitutive of social reality. As Shankar et al. (2009) argue, "the process of telling stories is an act of creation and construction and not simply an act of remembering or retelling (Shankar et al. 2009)"

To illustrate, the following story of "supersleep" – that we have already quoted in the introduction – is an act of creation and construction of sleep. The story is, thus, not only a way to share the sleeping experiences with other consumers (Keinan and Kivetz 2011), but plays a role in the creation of sleeping as an experience.

A snow cave was a good place to start [the search for super-sleep]. In retrospect, it combines several elements likely to lead to deep sleep. A full day of hard exercise. A firm bed (snow). The sense of being buried under several feet of insulation. And most of all, the cold. As Herman Melville wrote in *Moby Dick*, "a sleeping apartment should never be furnished with a fire, which is one of the luxurious discomforts of the rich." To find the best sleep, he said, you must "have nothing but the blanket between you and your snugness and the cold of the outer air.

Then there you lie like the one warm spark in the heart of an arctic crystal."

Science helps explain what we're looking for in the search for supersleep. Sleep researchers classify sleep into four different stages, including the well-known REM, or "rapid eye movement," stage, and three stages of non-REM sleep. During the night, you cycle down through the stages and back up to REM-sleep, which is actually the closest to being awake. Most writers and scientists seem interested in REM sleep, because that's when Freud-style dreams take place. But a sleep connoisseur seeks something different: the bottom of the cycle, known as "slow-wave," or N3, sleep. Slow-wave is the deepest and most dreamless of sleeps, a form of sleep that makes neurons shut down. How much slow-wave you actually get varies quite a bit. Hence the search for more of it.

In search of big doses of that slow wave, it's worth traveling to some places for the sleep alone—"sleep tourism." With a drowsy fondness I recall Turkey's Capadocia region, where you can rent a room carved out of stone—a cave really—to pass out in. It can make you start to think this whole house thing may have been a big mistake. There is something about lying in a cave that is hard to replicate in an urban apartment or even the suburbs. The Turkish caves form the ultimate bedroom community: darker than night, deliciously cold, with blankets that are thick and beds that are firm. (They are built, after all, on solid limestone.) No wonder cavemen always looked so vigorous.

Another recommendation for the sleep-tourist is the Japanese *onsen* inn. Imagine a day spent hiking through the Japanese countryside, climbing volcanoes, perhaps communing with the local monkeys. You return, change into Yukata robes, proceed to soak yourself in hot, sulfurous water for an hour or so, then retreat to your tatami room for a lavish meal of duck stew and fish. If, after that, you don't fall into a deep sleep, you might as well give up.

For most people, the American road trip is all about national parks and roadside kitsch, but it can also be a good opportunity for sleeping, if you take it slow. There is something about the wide-open landscape of the West that can lure you into a calm drowsiness. A brisk hike each day, dull stretches of driving, and quiet, empty roadside motels can add up to some good sleep. (www.slate.com/id/2220293)

This narrative indicates that the state of being asleep is created as knowable, and thereby consumable entity, by way of making references to the lexicon provided by the sleep science ("N3 sleep") and by the practice of wine tasting ("sleep connoisseur"). The 'doing of sleep' is in turn created by way of making references to various embodied activities preceding sleeping, material qualities of the surroundings of sleep (e.g. thick blankets, firm bed), and the sensory and affective qualities of the space of sleep (e.g. quietness, darkness, cold). Thereby the narrative offers cultural elements of "great sleep" as well as guidelines for their appropriate orchestration.

The practice-based narrative perspective that we develop here continues and complements the existing theorizations of hedonic and experiential consumption in a number of ways. Namely, while the phenomenological accounts – treating the subjective meanings as

determinant of experiences – have dominated this area of research, the recent studies have put more emphasis on understanding how the marketplace culture, and the various practices, rules and tensions it involves, frames and shapes the production and consumption of experiences. For instance, the bio-social perspective on pleasure developed in the context of clubbing by Goulding and her colleagues (2009), situates the use of drugs to the contemporary dynamics of marketplace. They thus analyze a marketplace culture that is legally sanctioned while supporting a range of illegal practices. Through the construct of contained illegality they offer new insights of the functioning and management of pleasure and the operation of marketplace cultures (ibid. 769). They conclude that through the marketplace processes and practices of 'contained illegality' the morally contentious pleasures are rendered more controllable – and economically valuable for club owners.

In a similar fashion, a recent anthropologically informed study of mountaineering conducted by Tumbat and Belk (2011) grounds its analysis of extraordinary experiences to the dynamics of marketplace culture. Their argue that the structure-antistructure dichotomy – originally offered by Victor Turner – that has become a widely accepted model for understanding extraordinary experiences in consumer research, is problematic due to its romantic and essentialist claims. Their analysis brings to the fore how commercialism and competition for uniqueness within individual performance ideology create numerous tensions that invert this standard dichotomy (Tumbat and Belk 2011, 43).

As we conceptualize commodification in terms of the market-mediated processes and practices of narration, through which the social reality is created, we are able to offer a better understanding of how the tensions, rules, moralities, and values – identified by the prior literature – are constructed and distributed through the marketplace by narratives within and as part of the field of practices that constitute consumer culture. By way of analyzing the commodification of an emerging, and under-researched, consumption and marketing phenomenon, sleeping, we are able to show how it is rendered legitimate object of consumer aspiration and desire, and thus subsumed under the dynamics and logics of consumer and marketplace culture (Humphreys 2010). Our approach also points to the way the practices and process of commodification construct not only a consumable and marketable entity, sleeping in our case, but a specific mode of being, sleep-as-consumption, that shapes the way consumers relate to, value, and conceive of, this part of human existence.

Concluding thoughts for building the research agenda

In this paper, we have begun to argue that the inclusion of sleeping into the research agenda of hedonic and experiential consumption has the potential to complement and extend the existing knowledge generated in this area of research. We thus promote an enlarged view that avoids the focusing on the sphere of the (active) waking life only when enjoyable and experiential aspects are theorized and empirically investigated. To develop this broadened agenda we have tried to bring together existing literature on hedonic and experiential consumption and socio-cultural studies on sleep. We also have worked toward a practice-based narrative perspective that enables us to conceptualize how "great sleep" is commodified within the field of practices that constitutes consumer culture. To conclude we point to the issues, or themes, that we find vital in studying the way "great sleep" is constructed as an attractive and sought-after experience.

(1) To expand on the points made in this paper, an empirical investigation of the production and consumption of "great sleep" in the emerging sleep market seems necessary. There is, thus, a need to collect a wide corpus of on-line and off-line narratives distributed by

the new services and products such as sleep spas, nap bars, and extraordinary hotels. This would help us to better understand how the commodification of sleeping occurs through a complex universe of competing meanings and practices, and resulting perhaps in various notions of what "great sleep" is all about.

(2) Focusing on analyzing the commodification of the state of 'being asleep' in these narratives, that is, how this state is represented and 'known', and thus created as a specific mode of being. Methodologically, such an analysis may employ the wide range of analytical tools and principles developed by cultural consumer scholars (Moisander and Valtonen 2006). Namely, while the phenomenological state of being asleep itself is not (necessarily) empirically accessible for a cultural scholar, the cultural aspects that surround this state, and thus assign meanings to it, can be analyzed by the existing narrative and discursive methods. The same concerns, obviously, the doings of sleep.

(3) Focusing on analyzing the commodification of 'doing sleep' in these narratives by way of identifying the range of social, material, sensory, embodied, and emotional elements that are offered as central in the pursuit of "great sleep". How these elements are weaved together in the implicit or explicit guidelines inscribed in the narratives? What kinds of fantasies and imagery are aligned with "great sleep"?

(4) Situating the analysis of "great sleep" to the contemporary marketplace dynamics in which socio-historically constructed sleep-related myths, beliefs and patterns meet and compete with the ongoing discursive and material shifts brought about by recent techno-scientification of sleeping.

REFERENCES

Arnould, Eric, J. and Linda Price (1993), "River Magic: Extraordinary Experience and the Extended Service Encounter," *Journal of Consumer Research,* 20 (June), 24–45.

Aserinsky, E. and Kleitman, N. (1953), "Regularly Occurring Periods of Eye Motility, and Concomitant Phenomena, during Sleep", Science, 118, 273-74.

Belk, Russell, W. and Janeen A. Costa (1998), "The Mountain Man Myth: A Contemporary Consuming Fantasy," *Journal of Consumer Research*, 25 (December), 218–240.

Belk, Russell, W., Guliz Ger and Soren Askegaard (2003), "Fire for desire. A Multisited Inquiry into Consumer Passion," *Journal of Consumer Research*, 30 (December), 326-351.

Bergson, Henry (1958), Henkinen Tarmo (Finnish translation of L'énergie Spirituelle), Porvoo: WSOY.

Celsi, Richard, Randall Rose, and Thomas Leigh (1993), "An Exploration of High-Risk Leisure Consumption through Skydiving," *Journal of Consumer Research*, 20 (June), 1–21.

Davies, Bronwyn (2003a), *Frogs and Snails and Feminist Tales: Preschool Children and Gender*, Cresskill, NJ: Hampton Press.

Davies, Bronwyn (2003b) *Shards of Glass. Children reading & writing beyond gendered identities*, Cresskill, NJ: Hampton Press.

Davies, Bronwyn and Rom Harré (1990), Positioning: The Discursive Production of Selves. *Journal for The Theory of Social Behaviour*, 20, 43-63.

Ekrich, A. R. (2001) *The sleep we have lost: Pre-industrial slumber in the British Isles*. American Historical Review, 343, 386.

Elias, Norbert (1978), *The civilizing process*. The history of manners (Vol. 1), Oxford: Basil Blackwell.

Goulding, Christina, Avi Shankar, Richard Elliott, and Robin Canniford (2009), "The Marketplace Management of Illicit Pleasure," *Journal of Consumer Research*, 35(5), 759-771.

Harrison, Paul (2009), "In the absence of practice," *Environment and Planning D: Society and Space* 27, 987–1009.

Holbrook, Morris B. and Elisabeth Hirschman (1982), "The Experiential Aspects of Consumption: Consumer Fantasies, Feelings, and Fun," *Journal of Consumer Research*, 9 (September), 132–140.

Humphreys, Ashlee (2010), "Semiotic Structure and the Legitimation of Consumption Practices: The Case of Casino Gambling," *Journal of Consumer Research*, 37 (October), 490-510.

Härmä, Mikael and Sallinen, M. (2004), Hyvä uni – hyvä työ. Työterveyslaitos. Helsinki. [Good sleep-good work, publications of the Finnish Institution of Occupational Health].

Joy, Annamma and John Sherry Jr. (2003), "Speaking of Art as Embodied Imagination: A Multi-Sensory Approach to Understanding Aesthetic Experience," *Journal of Consumer Research*, 30 (2), 259-282.

Keinan, Anan and Ran Kivetz (2011), "Productivity Orientation and the Consumption of Collectable Experiences," *Journal of Consumer Research*, 37 (April), 9-12.

Kozinets, Robert (2002), "Can Consumers Escape the Market? Emancipatory Illuminations from Burning Man," *Journal of Consumer Research*, 29 (June), 20–38.

Kozinets, Robert, John F. Sherry Jr., Diana Storm, Adam Duhachek, Krittinee Nuttavuthist, and Benet DeBerry-Spence (2004), "Ludic Agency and Retail Spectacle," *Journal of Consumer Research*, 31 (December), 658–72.

Maclaran, Pauline and Stephen Brown (2005), "The Center Cannot Hold: Consuming the Utopian Marketplace," *Journal of Consumer Research*, 32 (September), 311-23.

Marion, Gilles and Agnes Nairn (2011), "We Make the Shoes, You Make the Story" Teenage Girls Experiences of Fashion: Bricolage, Tactics and Narrative Identity," *Consumption, Markets & Culture*, 14 (1), 29-56.

Moisander, Johanna and Päivi Eriksson (2006), "Corporate Narratives of Information Society: Making up the Mobile Consumer Subject," *Consumption, Markets & Culture*, 9 (4), 257-75.

Mauss, Marcel (1974), "Techniques of the Body," *Economy and Society*, 2(1), 70–85.

Merleau-Ponty, Maurice (1962), *The phenomenology of perception*, London: Routledge.

Moisander, Johanna and Anu Valtonen (2006), *Qualitative Marketing Research: A Cultural Approach*, London: Sage.

Nakagawa, Gordon (1993), Deformed Subjects, Docile Bodies: disciplinary practices and subject-constitution in stories of Japanese-American internment. In *Narrative and Social Control: Critical Perspectives*, edited by D. K. Mumby. Newbury Park, CA: Sage.

Peñaloza, Lisa (2000), "The Commodification of the American West: Marketers' Production of Cultural Meanings at the Trade Show", *Journal of Marketing*, 64 (October), 82-109.

Peñaloza, Lisa and Mary C. Gilly (1999), "Marketer Acculturation: The Changer and the Changed," *Journal of Marketing*, 63 (July), 84-104.

Rappaport, Julian (2000), "Community Narratives: Tales of Terror and Joy", *American Journal of Community Psychology* 28 (1), 1-24.

Reckwitz, Andreas (2002), "Toward a Theory of Social Practices. A Development in Culturalist Theorizing," *European Journal of Social Theory*, 5 (2), 243-63.

Schatzki, Theodore R. (2002), *The Site of the Social: A Philosophical Account of the Constitution of Social Life and Change*, University Park, PA: The Pennsylvania State University Press.

Schatzki, Theodore R., Karin Knorr Cetina, and Elke von Savigny, eds. (2001), *The Practice Turn in Contemporary Theory*, London and New York: Routledge.

Shankar, Avi, Richard Elliott, and James A. Fitchett (2009), "Identity, Consumption and Narratives of Socialization," *Marketing Theory*, 9 (1), 75-94.

Shankar, Avi, Richard Elliott, and Christina Goulding (2001), "Understanding Consumption: Contributions from a Narrative Perspective," *Journal of Marketing Management*, 17 (3-4), 429-53.

Steger, B., and Brunt, L. (2003), *Night-time and sleep in Asia and the West*. Exploring the dark side of life, London and New York: Routledge Curzon.

Taylor, B. (1993), "Unconsciousness and society: The sociology of sleep," *International journal of Politics, Culture and Society*, 6 (3), 463–471.

Tedlock, Barbara (1987), Dreaming and Dream Research. In *Dreaming*. Anthropological and Psychological Interpretation, ed. B. Tedlock, 1-30. UK: Cambridge University.

Tumbat, Gülnur and Russell W. Belk (2011), "Marketplace Tensions in Extraordinary Experiences," *Journal of Consumer Research*, 38 (June), 42-61.

Valtonen, Anu and Soile Veijola (2011), "Sleep in Tourism", *Annals of Tourism Research*, 38 (1), 175-192.

Valtonen Anu (2011), We Dream as we Live – Consuming, in Russell W. Belk, Kent Grayson, Albert M. Muñiz, Hope Jensen Schau (ed.) *Research in Consumer Behavior (Research in Consumer Behavior, Volume 13)*, Emerald Group Publishing Limited, pp. 93-110

Venkatesh, Alladi and Lisa Peñaloza (2006), "From Marketing to the Market: A Call for a Paradigm Shift," in *Does Marketing Need Reform: Fresh Perspectives on the Future*, ed. Jagdish Sheth and Rajendra Sisodia, New York: Sharpe Publishers, 134-50.

Warde, Alan (2005), "Consumption and Theories of Practice", *Journal of Consumer Culture* 5 (2), 131-53.

Williams, Simon J. (2005), *Sleep and Society: Sociological Ventures into the (Un)Known*, London: Routledge.

Williams, Simon, J. (2011), *Politics of Sleep*, London: Routledge.

The Forgotten Brand Personality Dimension

Iftakar Haji, Aston University, UK
Heiner Evanschitzky, Aston University, UK
Ian Combe, Aston University, UK
Andrew Farrell, Aston University, UK

ABSTRACT

Aaker's (1997) brand personality framework has become influential across many streams of brand personality research, but it fails to capture an important dimension that reflects consumer's anxious feelings towards brands. Consumers are increasingly evaluating brands through expressions of negative emotive language. For example, the BP oil spillage in the Gulf of Mexico stimulated negative emotions among consumers. This paper is the first to thoroughly incorporate a brand personality dimension reflective of consumer anxious tense and frustrated feelings towards brands. From the extant literature we propose and define negative brand personality. Four adjacent studies were conducted to explore, purify and refine in what form negative brand personality traits exist among consumers. This paper concludes with a conceptual model detailing the antecedent constructs to negative brand personality and behavioral consequences.

INTRODUCTION

Building on the importance of self-expression through brands, Aaker (1997) developed the brand personality framework to understand brand-consumer relationships. This framework has become influential across many streams of brand personality research (Aaker, Benet-Martinez and Garolera 2001; Sung and Kim 2010; Geuen, Weijters and Wulf 2009; Grohmann 2009; Smith 2009; Lee and Back (2010); Venable et al. 2005; Freling and Forbes 2005) and is based on the big five-factor human personality model.

However, Aaker's (1997) current brand personality framework only offers a positively-framed approach to brand personality. To date, there has been neither conceptual nor empirical research which has thoroughly incorporated a dimension reflective of negative brand personality, despite the fact that almost all researchers are in agreement that dimensions akin to 'Extraversion' and 'Neuroticism' need to be included in a comprehensive personality scale (Cattell 1943; Allport 1961; Popkins 1998; Waller and Zavala 1993; Borgatta 1964; Conley 1985; Hakel 1974; John 1989; Lorr and Manning 1978; McCrae and Costa 1985; Noller, Law and Comrey 1987; Norman 1963; Smith 1967).

While the dimension 'Extraversion' has been accommodated to an extent in brand personality frameworks (Aaker 1997; Aaker et al. 2001; Smith 2009; Kaplan et al. 2010; Venable et al. 2005), no dimension reflects 'Neuroticism' in a branding context.

Importantly, the presence of negative feelings towards a brand is not the same as a mere absence of positive traits. Negative traits are expressions that capture the importance of consumers' interpretations that are susceptible to being influenced by emotions of anxiety or frustration, and are, therefore, more aligned with the 'Neuroticism' dimension of human personality. Hence, it is important to explore negative traits that reflect a dissonant state. To this end, we define negative brand personality as:

A set of characteristics ascribed to a brand by the consumer which reflect emotions associated with tension, anxiety or frustration.

The purpose of this paper is to address the importance of developing a better understanding of brand personality by introducing negative brand personality traits to the literature. More precisely, four adjacent studies were conducted to first develop a measure for negative brand personality traits and, secondly, to identify their antecedents as well as consequences. The proposed model will be discussed with implications for marketing management and theory.

LITERATURE REVIEW

A review of the extant brand personality literature reveals that the current conceptualization of brand personality focuses on a positively valenced approach to the concept. This is probably due to the fact that current knowledge of brand personality has been displayed in specific contexts where it has not been treated as a characteristic expressed by consumers; instead, it has often been used synonymously with, or to explain, desired attributes marketers want to project about their brand.

For example, Aaker's (1997) work, as well as subsequent research (Aaker 2000; Aaker, Bene-Martinez and Garolera 2001; Sung and Kim 2010; Grohmann 2009), acknowledges the brand-consumer relationship but stresses marketers desired attributes, such as a brand being 'exciting' or 'down to earth'. Other researchers have attempted to build on the existing brand personality framework and have developed new observations by looking at ways to provide a more reflective measure of the big five personality factors (Phau and Lau 2000; Caprara, Barbaranelli and Guido 2001; Venable et al. 2005; Grohmann 2009). For example, Geuen, Weijters and Wulf (2009) developed a brand personality measure in an attempt to embrace all big five personality dimensions. Although the five dimensions identified are relevant to brand personality, the model fails to capture consumers' negative emotions that are prone to causing a cognitive strain on their intuitive processes (See Table 1).

Apparently, existing brand personality frameworks fail to capture consumers' anxious and frustrated feelings towards brands. Consumers are often aware of their own predispositions to tension, anxiety and frustration in the same sense as they have an awareness of their own propensity for becoming anxious and frustrated in response to different situations. Consumers are likely to classify their anxious or angry emotions with expressions that reflect their resentment of, or their insecure feelings towards, a brand to resolve the internal conflict and anxious feelings they may be experiencing. Other researchers have indicated the importance of this observation (see, for example, Sweeney and Brandon 2006; Geuen, Weijters and Wulf 2009). Importantly, these expressions are not indicative of the absence of positive traits, such as 'undependable' or 'unsuccessful' - they are, in fact, expressions that capture the importance of consumers' interpretations that are susceptible to being influenced by emotions of anxiety or frustration and are more aligned with the 'Neuroticism' dimension of human personality. It is, therefore, important to explore the universally accepted personality dimensions within the brand personality framework to reflect characteristics of a dissonant state.

Therefore, this research acknowledges the importance of understanding brand personality from a consumer perspective; that is, consumers are provided with a vehicle for self-expression (Azoulay

Table 1: Reflection of how Aaker's (1997) and Geuens, Weijters and Wulf's (2009) brand personality framework corresponds to the Human Personality framework.

Human Personality	Aaker's (1997) Brand Personality frame-work	Geuens et al (2009) Brand Personal-ity framework
Extraversion	Excitement	Simplicity
Agreeableness	Sincerity	Aggressive
Conscientiousness	Competence	Responsibility
Openness to Experience	-	Aggressive?
Neuroticism	-	-
Dimensions relevant to brand personality but not part of the Big Five Factors	Sophistication	Emotionality
	Ruggedness	Simplicity

and Kapferer 2003) which allows them to assign the brand personality traits based on the information received. This is unlike other research propositions that suggest brand personality is created by how marketers and advertisers intend to project a brand (Batra et al. 1993; Levy 1959; Plummer 1984).

Awareness and knowledge of negative brand personality traits is relevant to successful marketing because consumers that assign negative brand personality traits to brands are less likely to make rational buying decisions. The importance of negative brand personality traits to companies is based on the consequences and the economic impact that follows. For example, cognitive dissonance, dissatisfaction and negative word of mouth can negatively impact the economic performance of the company. Moreover, providing a measure that addresses negative brand personality traits will provide a more realistic and balanced view of the brand by increasing source credibility, which should, in turn, help retain consumer loyalty.

However, very little is known about negative brand personality as a construct as no research to date has empirically investigated in what form negative brand personality traits exist. This study, therefore, first concentrates on using interview data to explore in what form negative brand personality traits exist; it then purifies and refines the items explored through three subsequent studies. Based on the exploratory findings, a conceptual model is proposed and discussed by identifying the antecedents, potential moderators and behavioral consequences.

METHOD

It is likely that each consumer has an individual tension, anxiety and frustration proneness threshold, which when activated will lead consumers to express their emotions through negative brand personality traits. As with other multidimensional constructs of brand personality, such as Aaker (1997), that have been found to have separate but correlated factors, negative brand personality traits are expected to interrelate because negative expressions are likely to result from a dissonant state between the brand and the consumer (Festinger 1957). By adopting a four adjacent studies approach, a comprehensive foundation for negative brand personality was provided by means of the following: firstly, use of interview transcripts to explore in what form negative brand personality traits exist; secondly, use of a separate questionnaire to clarify and ascertain whether the traits identified are perceived in a negative light; thirdly, use of a free and a fixed sorting task to partition the interrelated negative brand personality traits into related dimensions to provide an insight into the underlying dimensions; and, fourthly, use of a substantive validity task to judge whether traits reflected the dimensions of interest.

A convenience sample of male and female consumers from a range of age groups was drawn to represent active consumer shoppers within the context of fashion and food retail brands. Under-

graduate students represented the majority of the sample within each study (Maehle and Supphellen 2011). Table 2 summarizes the procedure employed in each of the four studies to assess negative brand personality traits.

EXPLORATION OF NEGATIVE BRAND PERSONALITY TRAITS

Study 1

The initial study was contextualized to the fashion and food brand categories to provide a more holistic representation of brands that capture both symbolic and functional attributes of users' values and lifestyles (Ratchford 1987). The study consisted of a total of 52 in-depth interviews (42 of the respondents were presented with 12 fashion brands and 10 respondents were presented with seven food brands) to ensure data validation and saturation (Silverman 2004). Each respondent was presented with a stimulus in the form of a brand to activate their interpretations of brands in order to access the meanings they ascribe to brands. To eliminate subject fatigue and boredom, a male dominated brand was presented first and then followed by a neutral (unisexual) brand and a female dominated retail brand. Similarly, food brands were organized so that a confectionary brand was followed by a savory brand.

The interviews were conducted with students and non-students who were asked questions such as 'What is your perception of this brand?', 'What human characteristics would you assign to this brand?', 'Would you like to associate yourself with this brand?', and 'Do you hold any conflicting views towards the brand?' By identifying the conflicting views, respondents were given the opportunity to describe any negative traits the brand holds. This helped identify the personality traits and the rationale behind respondents' answers.

Negative traits were not only obtained from the interview text but further analysis was undertaken by assessing the content of the interviews (Krippendorff 2004). This was achieved by examining the interview transcripts and interpreting what negative characteristics are inferred through negative accounts of emotional distress. After developing the initial pool of items, 71 negative brand personality traits were obtained.

The traits were then cleaned systematically by deleting items that had a similar approximation of synonyms (Aaker 1997; Sung and Tinkham 2005). Following within-case and cross-case analysis, traits were grouped into emerging dimensions as an initial phase for the scale development. Such grouping was performed by the researcher to assist in item elimination (See Figure 1).

Eliminated items were validated using three expert judges (Bearden et al. 1989). The expert judges were carefully selected based on their education: they were either a PhD holder in human personality research or a PhD student in the Marketing field. Each

Table 2: A summary of the four adjacent studies conducted to investigate negative brand personality.

Study	Method	Objective	Data Sample	Gender	Analysis Method
Study 1.0	In-depth interview 12 Fashion retail brands 7 Food brands	To explore in what form negative traits exist and the antecedents behind the traits by analyzing data to provide a more integrative conceptual model of the negative brand personality traits, antecedents and behavioral consequences.	Consumers (N=42) interviewed with fashion retail brands. Consumers (N=10) interviewed with food brands.	Fashion Retail: Male: 45% Female : 55% Food Retail: Male: 60% Female : 40%	Content analysis Data cleaning by separating positive traits from negative traits and reading transcripts to identify the rationale for the traits assigned.
Study 1.1	Separation of positive traits from negative traits. Assessment task to ensure the traits were not just antonyms of Aaker's (1997) traits.	Ensure negative brand personality traits are distinguished from existing measures of positive brand personality traits.	The researcher and 3 independent consumer reviewers (N=4)		Content analysis with the aid of a Collins English Dictionary.
Study 1.2	Frequency count and eliminating traits that had similar approximate synonyms. 4 distinct negative dimensions were identified.	Capture, at the broad level of abstraction, the commonalities among the most frequent negative traits consumers can identify a brand with.	Three expert judges (N=3) Face Validity.		Content analysis
Study 2	Questionnaire	To assess the refined negative traits from the interview transcripts and see if they are perceived in a negative light by other consumers not involved in the initial interview study. Also, to enhance internal validity of the qualitative research.	37 Undergraduate students (N=37)	Male: 62% Female: 38%	Mean scores were assessed for the rate of significance.
Study 3	Free/Fixed Sorting task	To discover dimensions that are likely to result from the list of traits from a consumer's perspective without any contamination from the researcher's preconceptions.	Free Sorting Task: 9 consumers (N=9) Fixed Sorting task: 6 consumers	Free Sorting Task Male: 56% Female: 44% Fixed Sorting task Male: 33% Female: 66%	Sorting the brand personality traits into dimensions with an overall category name identified by the consumer.
Study 4	Substantive Validity task	The substantive validity assessment conducted for the purpose of pretesting of items (negative brand personality traits).	30 undergraduate students (N=30)		Filled out questionnaires to assess content validity of the dimensions obtained from the sorting task.

expert judge was provided with 71 negative brand personality traits; they were then given instructions to eliminate items with similar synonym approximations to other traits within the list, and to eliminate items that were not perceived as negative traits in light of branding. The list provided by the expert judges was then assessed against the traits eliminated by the researcher. A review was then taken to assess which items were suggested to be in need of deletion due to the

approximation of traits. Twenty-one items to be deleted were agreed upon by at least two out of the three judges.

To further purify the items, an assessment was undertaken to ensure the remaining 50 items were not the direct antonyms of the positive traits established in Aaker's (1997) brand personality framework. The assessment was conducted by looking up the traits mentioned in the interview transcripts and looking up the direct ant-

Figure 1: Exploration of Negative Brand Personality traits represented in four dimensions.

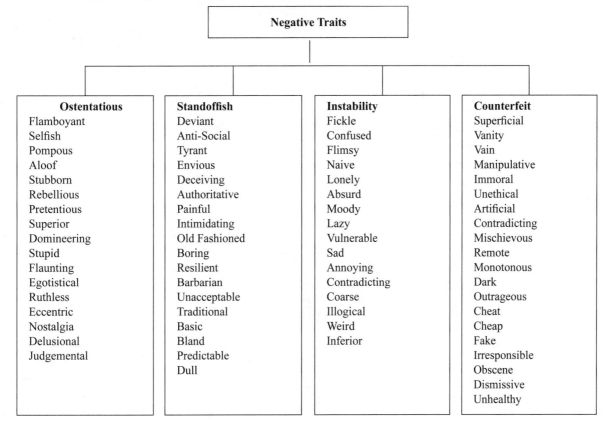

Negative Traits

Ostentatious	Standoffish	Instability	Counterfeit
Flamboyant	Deviant	Fickle	Superficial
Selfish	Anti-Social	Confused	Vanity
Pompous	Tyrant	Flimsy	Vain
Aloof	Envious	Naive	Manipulative
Stubborn	Deceiving	Lonely	Immoral
Rebellious	Authoritative	Absurd	Unethical
Pretentious	Painful	Moody	Artificial
Superior	Intimidating	Lazy	Contradicting
Domineering	Old Fashioned	Vulnerable	Mischievous
Stupid	Boring	Sad	Remote
Flaunting	Resilient	Annoying	Monotonous
Egotistical	Barbarian	Contradicting	Dark
Ruthless	Unacceptable	Coarse	Outrageous
Eccentric	Traditional	Illogical	Cheat
Nostalgia	Basic	Weird	Cheap
Delusional	Bland	Inferior	Fake
Judgemental	Predictable		Irresponsible
	Dull		Obscene
			Dismissive
			Unhealthy

Table 3: Direct antonyms of Aaker's brand personality traits.

Aaker's Brand Personality Traits	Direct Antonyms from Collins English Dictionary and Word 2007
Down to Earth	Unreasonable, foolish
Honest	Dishonest
Wholesome	Unpleasant, Distasteful
Cheerful	Sad, Depressing
Daring	Cowardly
Spirited	Pathetic, Spineless
Imaginative	Unimaginative, Dull
Up to date	Old Fashioned, Out of Date
Reliable	Undependable
Intelligent	Stupid
Successful	Unsuccessful, Failure
Upper Class	Lower class, Working Class
Charming	Repulsive
Outdoorsy	Indoor activity
Tough	Weak

onyms of the trait (See Table 3). The list was then given to an independent expert judge to assess the face validity of the traits presented, which provided further purification of negative brand personality items. The findings provide a diversified and meaningful representation of brand personality through the assessment of negative traits. The negative brand personality traits that manifested in respondents' expressions reflect their tense or anxious emotions towards brands. By identifying the negative and inferred negative brand personality traits, a frequency count of the negative traits was undertaken to summarize the negative traits mentioned within the sampled popu-

lation; this also provided an indication of inferences regarding the construct (Berelson and Lazarsfeld 1948, 6).

A frequency count was conducted to ensure emphasis was placed on the importance of using simple, straightforward language that is appropriate for the reading level of the scales' target population and for avoiding colloquial expressions (DeVellis 2003). Some respondents inferred a trait but used another form of expression; for example, the statement 'I don't find the brand interesting' infers the trait 'Boring'. All expressions that did not explicitly mention the trait but were inferred through the syntactical analysis of the inter-

Table 4: Frequency count of Negative brand personality traits obtained from interview transcripts.

Negative Brand Personality	Frequency	Negative Brand Personality	Frequency
Absurd	10	Intimidating	8
Aloof	9	Judgmental	8
Annoying	2	Lonely	11
Antisocial	38	Manipulative	38
Arrogant	19	Mischievous	4
Barbarian	22	Monotonous	29
Boring	56	Naive	18
Brash	12	Nostalgic	30
Cheap	55	Pompous	27
Coarse	8	Predictable	24
Confused	16	Pretentious	6
Contradicting	3	Rebellious	18
Deceiving	33	Repulsive	15
Delusional	4	Resilient	2
Deviant	18	Selfish	8
Dull	44	Snobby	15
Eccentric	17	Stubborn	16
Envious	5	Stupid	1
Fake	49	Superficial	31
Fickle	11	Traditional	16
Flamboyant	38	Tyrant	20
Flaunt	14	Unstable	9
Flimsy	13	Vain	24
Immoral	39	Vanity	13
Inferior	3	Weird	25

view transcripts were reviewed by an independent researcher in the marketing field to ensure consistency in assigning the implied traits. This is to further ensure that a clarified and appropriate list is distinct from existing measures of brand personality and, at the same time, reflects the negative brand personality dimension (See table 4).

A high frequency for a trait illustrates an agreement in item clarity and a common trend in traits expressed amongst the sampled population. However, few traits were scored relatively low in comparison to other traits such as 'Inferior' and 'Stupid'. A total of seven traits were eliminated at this stage as the items may be relevant to the study of brand personality but lack familiarity within the sampled population.

Study 2

Some traits mentioned by respondents from interviews were perceived in a positive light whilst other respondents perceived traits in a negative light. For example, some respondents referred to 'Flamboyant' as positive while others referred to it as negative. The perspective from which the traits were addressed was based on the syntactical rationale. Therefore, Study 2 sought to confirm whether traits assigned were perceived in a positive or a negative light. Structured questions were asked, such as 'Is this trait seen in a positive or negative light?', since traits were seen by some respondents as positive and by others as negative - these are referred to as 'ambiguous traits'. In order to clean the ambiguous traits obtained from the transcripts, a separate questionnaire was employed asking consumers to rate all perceived negative traits as either positive or negative by ticking a box. This questionnaire formed part of the triangulation

procedure to verify and strengthen the findings (Miles and Huberman 1994).

From the initial pool of 43 items, four items were predominantly perceived (i.e., by more than 50% of respondents) as positively associated rather than negative. These four traits are 'Flamboyant', 'Eccentric', 'Traditional' and 'Nostalgic', and were eliminated from the study of negative brand personality traits. No expert judgment was involved at this stage as this study investigated negative brand personality from a consumer perspective.

Study 3

The objective of Study 3 was to further purify and refine negative brand personality traits. The card sorting task conducted in this study is grounded in Kelly's personal construct theory that utilizes different types of objects or stimuli (for example, pictures, personality traits and colors) (Fincher and Tenenberg 2005; Green and Manzi 2002; Rosenberg and Kim 1975; Rugg and McGeorge 2005). "In a typical application of the sorting method, the respondent is asked to partition a set of inter-related objects or terms into different groups on the basis of their 'similarity,' 'relatedness,' or 'co-occurrence' depending on the particular application" (Rosenberg and Kim 1975, 489). In line with the application of the free card sorting task (Giguere 2006), stimuli in the form of traits and definitions of traits were presented in a card format to respondents.

The respondents were asked to partition the cards (each card contained one trait and its definition) into groups they felt they could be categorized into. No predefined categories or number of categories were given to respondents; instead, they were encouraged to formulate as many categories as they felt were necessary (Giguere 2006). Respondents were instructed to categorize the cards by creating mutually exclusive piles comprised of conceptually similar statements. Thus, statements in the same pile were more conceptually similar to each other compared with those that made up the other piles. Participants were also encouraged to bind the cards with paper clips to ensure accurate recording of traits in each pile. Once categories were formulated, the respondents were encouraged to name the category. Traits which respondents were unable to categorize provided an indication of irrelevant (or potentially cross-loading) negative brand personality traits.

The purpose of the free sorting method is not to uncover underlying cognitive processes; rather, it serves as a means to discover dimensions likely to result from the list of traits from a consumer perspective without any contamination from the researcher's preconceptions (Rosenberg and Kim 1975). Therefore, the free sorting task helps identify relevant categories by investigating commonalities and differences between consumers in the use of categorization.

Five categories emerged based on what traits consumers put together in a single pile. However, the name of each pile differed from respondent to respondent. Table 5 details the category names that respondents created alongside the common negative brand personality traits. As a result, the traits in each category were collated to form a list of traits. The list of traits was formed on the basis of obtaining 50% or more agreement within each pile. The names of the piles were categorized together to assess the similarity of the category group names to reflect the respondents' group labels.

Although some traits are commonly categorized in each dimension, there still remains variance in some of the dimensions. For example, in Group One, nearly all consumers placed 'Pompous' as an important trait to be classified within the same pile as other similar traits such as 'Vain'. However, not all consumers agreed that 'Selfish' should be classified within the same pile as 'Pompous' and 'Vain'. As a result, further data cleaning was conducted by adopting a fixed sorting method (Giguere 2006). Giguere's (2006) fixed card sorting method is similar to the free associated task, except that a restricted number of groups are generated during the card sorting task.

For the fixed card sorting task, the names for each dimension were finalized. Therefore, the group labels identified by consumers were collated to form an overall group name by summing up what consumers initially labeled each group. Three independent expert judges reviewed the overall category names in light of each category label identified by consumers. Expert judges were a PhD holder in personality research, and two PhD students (one carrying out their PhD in English Language and one in Marketing). All three expert judges agreed on the overall category dimensions as: Group One 'Egotistical'; Group Two 'Boring'; Group Three 'Socially Irresponsible'; Group Four 'Critical'; and Group Five 'Lacking Logic'.

Six additional respondents were requested to group all 39 traits into the five established groups to assess consistency in traits within each group. Respondents were also given the opportunity to either create a new category or to omit traits if they felt trait(s) did not fall into the category or could not be seen in light of the branding. All other instructions were the same as the free card sorting task detailed above.

The card sorting task data was analyzed by visually assessing the frequency of traits occurring in each dimension[1]. Traits that achieved 80% or more in frequency by respondents were shortlisted

---

[1] Multidimensional scaling is one statistical technique that historically has been used to analyze card sort tasks. However, the focus of this research is on identifying common negative brand personality traits and potential dimensions; therefore, a visual-frequency-of-traits-occurrence technique was applied to analyze the data.

to reflect the common traits amongst respondents. Table 6 details the overall results that show some consistency with respondents' classification of traits within each of the five groups.

The results indicate that consistency in negative brand personality traits emerged from both the free sorting task and the fixed sorting task with high frequency loadings assigned by consumers. Overall, the results of the free and fixed card sorting methods provided an indication of negative brand personality dimensions and traits that are likely to result from a factor analysis. Subsequent to the sorting task, a further assessment was undertaken to assess the content validity of the negative brand personality dimensions.

Study 4

Study 4 was a content validity assessment which follows the procedure suggested by Anderson and Gerbing (1991), and complements the sorting task. The substantive validity measure is defined as the extent to which a measure is judged to reflect the construct of interest (Holden and Jackson 1979), and was applied in this study to reflect the traits and dimensions of negative brand personality. The substantive validity assessment is particularly suited for the pretesting of items due to the small-sample nature as opposed to "assessments involving correlations, which suffer from the obfuscating effects of sampling error in small samples" (Anderson and Gerbing 1991, 732).

Respondents were provided with a list of 39 items (negative brand personality traits) and the five dimensions obtained from the card sorting task (Egotistical, Boring, Socially Irresponsible, Critical, and Lacking Logic). The definitions of the five dimensions were also provided. The respondents were instructed to read each of the items (traits) and assign it to the most closely reflected construct (dimension). The items were then analyzed using the content validity ratio proposed by Anderson and Gerbing (1991).

The substantive validity assessment was first calculated by the proportion of substantive agreement (P_{sa}), which is defined as "the proportion of respondents who assign an item to its intended construct" (Anderson and Gerbing 1991, 734). The proportion of substantive agreement is calculated as:

$$(P_{sa} = n_c / N)$$

Here, n_c represents the number of respondents assigning an item to its posited construct and N represents the total number of respondents. The range of values for P_{sa} is between 0.0 and 1.0, where high values indicate greater substantive validity of the item.

The second index reflects the *substantive-validity coefficient*, which reflects the extent to which respondents assign an item to its posited construct more than to any other construct (Anderson and Gerbing 1991, 734). The calculation for this index is:

$$C_{sv} = (n_c - n_o) / N$$

Here, n_c and N are defined as before and n_o indicates the highest number of assignments of the item to any other construct. The values for this index range from -1.0 to 1.0, where high positive values indicate greater substantial validity. Negative values indicate that an item is perceived by respondents as better reflecting a construct different to that which was originally supposed. A recommended threshold for the C_{sv} index is 0.5 (Anderson and Gerbing 1991, 734). Once the P_{sa} and C_{sv} scores had been calculated for each item, they were then calculated for each of the negative brand personality dimensions.

It should also be noted that initially there was a sixth construct termed 'Does not fit in any of the dimensions'. This construct was

Table 5: Details of the five main categories that emerged from the sorting task alongside the names of each of the groups identified by respondents.

Name of Categories	Traits					
GROUP ONE (Egotistical)						
High Self Opinion	Pompous	Pretentious	Vain	Snobby	Stubborn	
Egotistical	Pompous	Brash	Vain	Judgmental	Flaunt	Tyrant
Resentment	Pompous	Immoral	Unethical	Antisocial	Snobby	Tyrant
	Selfish	Pretentious	Vain	Arrogant	Flaunt	Fake
	Aloof	Coarse	Stubborn			
Self-Centered	Pompous	Selfish	Vain	Judgmental	Snobby	Tyrant
	Flaunt	Brash	Pretentious	Superficial	Manipulative	Intimidating
	Stubborn	Arrogant				
Superior	Stubborn	Selfish	Vain	Arrogant	Snobby	Tyrant
	Pretentious	Judgmental	Manipulative	Intimidating		
Self-Important	Pompous	Selfish	Vain	Arrogant	Snobby	Aloof
	Aloof	Absurd	Flaunt	Intimidating		
GROUP TWO (Boring)						
Boring	Dull	Deviant	Anti-Social	Aloof	Lonely	Cheap
Boring	Dull	Boring	Monotonous	Cheap		
Lack of Spirit	Dull	Boring	Cheap			
Tedious	Dull	Boring	Monotonous	Cheap		
Sad	Dull	Boring	Monotonous	Superficial	Mischievous	Cheap
Unpredictable	Dull	Boring	Monotonous	Superficial	Predictable	Cheap
GROUP THREE (Socially Irresponsible)						
Low Minded	Deceiving	Unethical	Immoral	Rebellious	Snobby	Repulsive
	Selfish	Arrogant	Stubborn	Mischievous		
Bad Faith	Deceiving	Unethical	Immoral	Fake		
Resentment	Pompous	Immoral	Unethical	Antisocial	Snobby	Tyrant
	Selfish	Pretentious	Vain	Arrogant	Flaunt	Fake
	Aloof	Coarse				
Operating outside established code of conduct	Deceiving	Unethical	Immoral			
Wrong		Unethical	Immoral			
Without Task	Deceiving	Unethical	Immoral	Coarse	Brash	Repulsive
	Deviant	Manipulative	Anti-Social	Mischievous		
GROUP FOUR (Critical)						
Anti-Establishment	Barbarian	Rebellious	Deviant	Tyrant	Antisocial	Judgmental
Selfish	Repulsive	Rebellious	Mischievous	Predictable	Cheap	Coarse
	Confused	Judgmental				
Low minded	Repulsive	Rebellious	Mischievous	Stubborn	Arrogant	Snobby
	Immoral	Selfish	Judgmental			
Unclear	Immoral	Rebellious	Selfish	Mischievous	Vain	Weird
	Lonely	Confused	Unstable	Naive	Aloof	Judgmental
Forceful	Stubborn	Rebellious	Tyrant	Judgmental		
Envious	Repulsive	Selfish	Superficial	Unstable	Pretentious	Predictable
	Vain	Mischievous	Weird	Judgmental		
Critical	Repulsive	Stubborn	Rebellious	Judgmental		
GROUP FIVE (Lacking Logic)						
Irrational/lacking Logic	Weird	Delusional	Unstable	Absurd	Naive	Superficial
Unreal	Fake	Delusional	Predictable	Superficial		
Different	Weird	Delusional	Unstable	Absurd	Deviant	
Ingenious	Lonely	Delusional	Naive	Superficial		
Unusual	Weird	Rebellious	Mischievous	Absurd	Deviant	Superficial
Shallow Mindedness	Weird	Delusional	Unstable	Superficial	Naive	Pretentious
	Confused	Lonely	Monotonous			
Different	Brash	Coarse	Naive	Absurd		

not theorized by the researcher but was included to provide respondents the opportunity of not assigning an item to any of the five constructs. It is worth noting that the sixth construct 'Does not fit in any of the dimensions' is not the focus of this research and is constructed as a means to aid item elimination at a later stage. Some respondents gave an indication that they felt items such as 'Delusional' and 'Lonely' belonged to the construct 'Does not fit in any of the dimensions'. These items were eliminated from further analysis whereby the P_{sa} and C_{sv} results scores for the items were deleted. The results of this substantive validity test are referred to as Test One for the purposes of subsequent discussion.

In addition, some items were classified as ambiguous, which was indicated by a low C_{sv} score (i.e., between -0.1 and 0.1). A low C_{sv} means that there is considerable ambiguity among respondents regarding the construct the item best describes. For an item to provide a low C_{sv} value, respondents must have assigned it a similar number of times to two or more dimensions.

For example, the item 'Lonely', which was posited to be part of the 'Boring' dimension of negative brand personality, was assigned nine times to 'Boring' and nine times to 'Socially Irresponsible'. Another item that was dropped based on item ambiguity was 'Mischievous', which was posited to be 'Socially Irresponsible'. 'Mischievous' was assigned ten times to the 'Socially Irresponsible' construct and six times to 'Egotistical'. The high scores in both the 'Socially Irresponsible' and 'Egotistical' constructs resulted in a low C_{sv} value of 0.1 for the item 'Mischievous'. These items were dropped from the analysis between Test One and Test Two.

Items classified as ambiguous warrant further theoretical investigation and should be closely examined during later data analysis via, for example, exploratory factor analysis. For the purposes of the substantive validity test, items with a low C_{sv} value were excluded, and further calculations were done in an attempt to increase the validity of the items under review. The results of this second stage of substantive validity testing are referred to as Test Two for

the purposes of subsequent discussion. Test Two involved only 35 of the original 39 items. Table 7 illustrates the findings of Test One and Test Two.

This method of triangulation provided an insight into consumers' emotional expressions and their perceptions of brands. The systematic combination of various types of data collection/analysis for the study of negative brand personality is an important step in validating the negative brand personality traits. The preceding methods are likely to aid in the interpretation of trait elimination in subsequent quantitative phases.

THE CONCEPTUAL FRAMEWORK

The results from the initial study - the interviews - and associated literature identify four particular antecedent constructs for Negative Brand Personality: Corporate Social Irresponsibility, Self-Incongruence, Brand Confusion, and Price Unfairness (See Figure 2). Together, these four constructs summarize the dissonant state between corporate brand communication and consumers' interpretations. Each of these antecedent constructs are dominated through implicit perceptions that consumers formulate through cues in order to locate consumers' discrepant self-meaning (Lau and Phau 2007).

Corporate Social Irresponsibility underpins consumers' perceptions of the brands' moral values (Du Bhattacharya and Sen 2007). Hollenbeck and Zinkhan (2010) illustrated the importance of this observation by acknowledging that media reports of brands using child labor may hold consumers back from purchasing a company's products. This meta-knowledge, whether accurate or not, guides consumers' perceptions of moral practices by setting examples of corporate wrongdoing (Brown and Dacin 1997, 80). Such findings were also demonstrated in consumers' responses that were unforgiving of the socially irresponsible behavior of a company; as a result, the respondents evaluated the brand by assigning negative traits based on brand ethics.

Table 6: Details of the traits consumers assigned from the fixed card sorting task.

Name of Dimension	Traits				
Egotistical	Pompous	Snobby	Brash	Vain	Arrogant
	Pretentious	Flaunt	Stubborn		
Boring	Boring	Monotonous	Dull	Lonely	Anti-Social
	Cheap				
Socially Irresponsible	Immoral	Unethical	Deceiving	Deviant	Fake
	Manipulative				
Critical	Confused	Mischievous	Rebellious	Selfish	Barbaric
	Judgmental				
Lacking Logic	Delusional	Weird	Unstable	Naive	Superficial

Table7: Illustration of the overall findings of Test One and Test Two.

	Test One			Test Two		
	Item	P_{sa}	C_{sv}	Item	P_{sa}	C_{sv}
Lacking Logic	12	0.671	0.560	12	0.671	0.560
Critical	4	0.773	0.675	3	0.858	0.793
Socially Irresponsible	8	0.753	0.665	7	0.809	0.733
Boring	4	0.833	0.767	4	0.833	0.767
Egotistical	8	0.858	0.783	8	0.858	0.783
Does Not fit in Either of the Dimensions	2	0.516	0.323			
Total/Average	**38**	**0.734**	**0.629**	**34**	**0.806**	**0.727**

Figure 2: A conceptual framework summarizing the results of the four studies conducted so far.

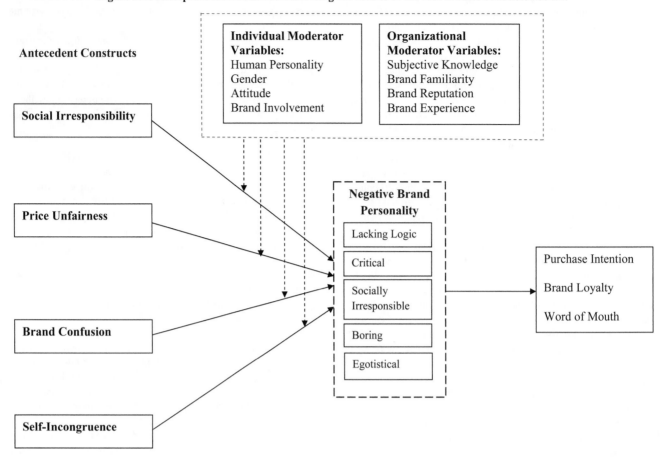

The findings from the interviews, which are also in line with the self-identity literature, have shown that a non-matching advertising appeal is likely to conflict with consumers' brand schemas, causing a cognitive strain on consumers' intuitive processes when trying to assimilate the information with their self-concept (Sirgy et al. 1997; Helgeson and Supphellen 2004). However, the *incongruence* between the advertisement and the self-concept of an individual increases the dissonant state. Coupling incongruence with cognitive dissonance provides further rationalization for negative brand personality traits. As a result, respondents experience tension, guilt arousal, and anxiety and doubt (Menasco and Hawkins 1978; Ghingold 1981).

The findings from the interview transcripts also reveal consumers' proneness to brand *confusion*. This is in line with other researchers who show that brand confusion results from perceived similarity of the product through brand imitations, information overload, and ambiguity in consumers' tolerance for processing unclear or misleading product information (Walsh, Hennig-Thurau and Mitchell 2010). Information overload, similarity and ambiguity arise when the information supply, due to its volume, exceeds consumers' processing capability. Consequently, consumers begin to exhibit symptoms of anxiety and frustration due to their limited processing capacity (Hafstrom et al. 1992; Mitchell and Papavassiliou 1999; Sproles and Sproles 1990).

Furthermore, the findings show that consumers' psychological reactions to *price unfairness* (Campbell 1999) often leads them to punish the brand by looking at alternative brands (Kahneman et al. 1986a, 1986b), or to attack the brand by assigning a discrepant self-meaning. The psychological reaction to what is perceived as a fair

price (Kamen and Toman 1970; Monroe 1973) is likely to stimulate anger, which is considered to be the strongest negative emotional response compared to disappointment and regret.

Significantly, the findings of the four antecedent constructs capture the multidimensionality of consumers' perceptions of negative brand personality.

Further potential moderating variables that are likely to affect the link between the antecedents and negative brand personality traits are broadly categorized into two groups - personal characteristics and organizational characteristics. Individual characteristics, such as gender, human personality traits, attitude and involvement (enduring and processing), are likely to exert a moderating influence because they are often linked to consumers' ability to rationalize and process brand stimuli.

Gender differences may be related to the experience framework since women tend to have more experiences of different brand products than men. Dimensions in *human personality* such as Consciousness and Neuroticism are more prone to negative emotions and are likely to strengthen the link between the antecedents' constructs and negative brand personality (Barick and Mount 1991). *Brand involvement* (enduring and processing) is likely to be associated with differences in sensitivity to brand stimuli, in that those who are highly motivated are interested and driven to evaluate brand cues (Zaichkowsky 1985; Kapferer and Laurent 1993). Similarly, consumers' overall *attitude* determines their beliefs (MacKenzie and Lutz 1986) and feelings (Olney, Halbrook and Batra 1991) towards brands. According to Day (1970), consumers' low confidence levels reflect uncertainty about the brand judgment or increase ambiguity about the meaning of the brand, thus increasing undesirable attributes.

The organizational characteristics consist of subjective brand knowledge, brand familiarity, brand reputation and brand experience. Each will be discussed briefly in turn.

Subjective knowledge is self-perceived knowledge based on pre-existing knowledge primarily accumulated through readily available information from media sources (Park, Jaworski and MacInnis 1994). It is likely that consumers who are less confident about their subjective knowledge are more likely to assign negative brand personality traits due to low tolerance levels for processing new information. Similarly, consumers are likely to be more prone to negative reactions with low levels of *brand familiarity* as a result of the discrimination between brand choices (Campbell and Keller 2003). *Brand reputation* is the aggregate perceptions formulated by consumers based on the salient characteristics producers send to the market to establish their brands (Fombrun 1996). Therefore, a brand that fails to fulfill its stated intentions or marketing signals is likely to develop a negative reputation.

Brand experience is induced from exposure to attributes that result from consumer interaction with brands. Experienced consumers are likely to be more prone to discriminating on hedonic evaluations grounded in their direct or indirect consumption (Hirschman and Holbrook 1982; Laroche, Kim and Zhou 1996). Although no study has investigated the outcome of negative brand personality, it is likely to be associated with low purchase intention (Laroche, Kim and Zhou 1996), and low brand loyalty and negative word of mouth (Richins 1983). These are likely to relate to the immediate effect of negative brand personality.

CONCLUSION AND IMPLICATIONS

Key findings from this study provide strong support for the existence of negative brand personality, which is consistent with the interpersonal domain of the *Big Five* human personality dimension. Furthermore, by building on Aaker's (1997) current conceptualization of brand personality, the findings contribute to a more complete understanding of brand personality through acknowledgement of negative brand personality. It is not enough to interpret negative traits as the absence of positive traits. Negative traits are a reflection of consumers' anxious and frustrated feelings The findings further contribute to the brand relationship literature by capturing consumers' emotions of frustration and anxiety; these are emotions which can impact on brand dissolution and consequently dissolve the brand-self relationship, an area that has been relatively under researched. Furthermore, the conceptual model provides marketers with guidance on how to communicate their brand(s) to consumers by acknowledging a more balanced view of the brand. By acknowledging and reducing negative brand personality traits, cognitive clarity among consumers should increase, which could be a major source of competitive advantage.

REFERENCES

Aaker, Jennifer. (1997), "Dimensions of Brand Personality," Journal *of Marketing Research*, 34 (August), 347-56.

Aaker, Jennifer, L. Veronica, Benet-Martinez. and Jordi Garolera. (2001), "Consumption Symbols as Carriers of Culture: A Study of Japanese and Spanish Brand Personality Constructs," *Journal of Personality Social Psychology*, 81 (April), 492-508.

Allport, Gordan, W. (1961), "Pattern and Growth in Personality," Holt, Rinehart and Winston, New York.

Anderson, James C. and David Gerbing (1991), "Predicting the Performance of Measures in a Confirmatory Factor Analysis with a Pretest Assessment of their Substantive Validities," *Journal of Applied Psychology*, 76 (May), 732-740.

Azoulay, Audrey and Jean-Noël Kapferer (2003), "Do Brand Personality Scales Really Measure Brand Personality?," *Brand Management*, 11 (November) 143-155.

Barrick Murray R and Michael K Mount (1991), "The Big Five Personality Dimensions and Job Performance: A Meta-Analysis," Personnel *Psychology*, 44 (March), 1-26.

Batra, Rajeev., Donald. R. Lehmann, and Dipinder Singh (1993), "The Brand Personality Component of Brand Goodwill: Some Antecedents and Consequences," in *Brand Equity and Advertising*, ed. David. A. Aaker & Alexander. L. Biel, Hillsdale, NJ: Lawrence Erlbaum Associates, 83-97.

Bearden, William O, Richard G. Netemeyer and Jesse E. Teel (1989). "Measurement of Consumer Susceptibility to Interpersonal Influence," *Journal of Consumer Research*. 15 (March), 473-481.

Berelson, Bernard and Lazarsfeld, Paul F. (1984), *The Analysis of Communication Content*. Chicago: University of Chicago Press.

Borgatta, Edgar. F. (1964), The Structure of Personality Characteristics. *Behavioral Science*, 12, 8-17.

Brown, Tom J. and Peter A. Dacin (1997), "The Company and the Product: Corporate Associations and Consumer Product Responses," *Journal of Marketing*, 61 (January), 68-84.

Campbell, Margret C. (1999), "Pricing Strategy & Practice ``Why Did You Do That?'' The Important Role of Inferred Motive in Perceptions of Price Fairness," *Journal of Product & Brand Management*, 8 (2), 145-52.

Campbell, Margaret C. and Kevin L. Keller (2003), "Brand Familiarity and Advertising Repetition Effects," *Journal of Consumer Research*, 30 (September) 292-30.

Caprara, Gian V., Claudio Barbaranelli, and Gianluigi Guido (2001), "Brand personality: How to Make the Metaphor Fit?," *Journal of Economic Psychology*, 22, (June) 377-395.

Cattell, Raymond B. (1943), "The Description of Personality: Basic Traits Resolved into Clusters," *Journal of Abnormal. Social, Psychology, 3*8 (October), 476-506.

Conley, James J. (1985), "Longitudinal Stability of Personality Traits: A Multitrait-Multimethod Multioccasion analysis," *Journal of Personality and Social Psychology*, 49 (November), 1266-82.

Day, George S. (1972), "Evaluating Models of Attitude Structure," *Journal of Marketing Research*, 9 (August), 279-286.

DeVellis, Robert F. (1991), *Scale Development, Theory and Application*, New Bury Park CA: Sage Publications.

Du, Shuili, Bhattacharya, C. B. and Sen, Sankar. (2007), "Reaping Relational Rewards from Corporate Social Responsibility: The Role of Competitive Positioning," *International Journal of Research in Marketing*, 24 (July), 224-41.

Festinger, Leon (1957), *A Theory of Cognitive Dissonance*, Stanford, CA: Stanford University Press.

Fincher, Sally and Josh Tenenberg (2005), "Making Sense of Card Sorting Data," *Expert Systems*, 22 (July), 89-93.

Fombrun, Charlls (1996), *Reputation: Realizing Value from the Corporate Image*. Cambridge, MA: Harvard Business School Press.

Freling, Traci H and Lucas P. Forbes (2005), "An Empirical Analysis of the Brand Personality Effect," *Journal of Product and Brand Management*, 14 (7), 404 – 13.

Geuens, Maggie., Weijters Bert and De Wulf Kristof. (2009), "A New Measure of Brand Personality," *International Journal of Research in Marketing*, 26 (April), 97-107.

Ghingold, Morry (1981), "Guilt Arousing Marketing Communications: An Unexplored Variable," *Advances in Consumer Research*, 8, 442-448.

Giguère, Gyslain (2006), "Collecting and analyzing data in multidimensional scaling experiments: A guide for psychologists using SPSS," *Tutorial in Quantitative Methods for Psychology*, 2 (April), 27-38.

Green, Raymond J and Robert Manzi Jr. (2002), "A Comparison of Methodologies for Uncovering the Structure of Racial Stereotype Subgrouping," *Social Behavior and Personality*, 30 709-728.

Grohmann Bianca. (2009), "Gender Dimensions of Brand Personality," *Journal of Marketing Research*, 46 (February), 105-19.

Hafstrom, Jeanne L., Sook J. Chae, and Sook Y. Chung (1992), "Consumer Decision- Making Styles: Comparison between United States and Korean Young Consumers," *The Journal of Consumers Affairs*, 26 (Summer), 146-158.

Hakel, Milton D. (1974), "Normative Personality Factors Recovered from Ratings of Personality Descriptors: the beholder's eye," *Personnel Psychology*, 27 (September), 409-21.

Helgeson, James G. and Magne Supphellen (2004), "A conceptual and Measurement Comparison of Self-Congruity and Brand Personality," *International Journal of Market Research*, 46 (April) 205-34.

Hirschman Elizabeth C and Morris B. Holbrook (1982), "Hedonic Consumption: Emerging Concepts, Methods and Propositions," Journal *of Marketing* 46 (Summer), 92-101.

Hollenbeck, Candice R and George Zinkhan M. (2010), "Anti-Brand Communities Negotiation of Brand Meaning, and the Learning Process: the Case of Wal-Mart," *Consumption Markets & Culture*, 13 (September), 325-45.

John, Oliver P. (1989), "Towards a Taxonomy of Personality Descriptors." In Buss, David. M., Cantor Nancy (ed.) *"Personality Psychology: Recent trends and Emerging Directions"* New York: Springer-Verlag.

Kahneman, Daniel., Jack, Knetsch and Richard Thaler (1986a), "Fairness as a Constraint on Profit Seeking: Entitlements in the Market," *The American Economic Review*, 76 (September), 728-41.

——— (1986b), "Fairness and the Assumptions of Economics," *Journal of Business*, 59 (October), S285-S300.

Kamen, Joseph M. and Robert J. Toman (1970), "Psychophysics of Prices," *Journal of Marketing Research*, 7 (February), 27-35.

Kapferer, Jean-Noël and Laurent Gilles (1993), "Further evidence on the consumer involvement profile: Five antecedents of involvement," *Psychology and Marketing*. 10 (July/August), 347-355.

Kaplan, Melike. D., Oznur Yurt, Burcu Guneri, and Kemal, Kurtulus. (2010), "Branding Places: Applying Brand Personality Concept to Cities," *European Journal of Marketing*, 44 (9/10), 1286-304.

Krippendorff, Klaus. (2004). *Content analysis: An introduction to its methodology (Second Edition)*, Thousand Oaks, CA: Sage.

Laroche Michel., Chankon Kim and Lianxi Zhou (1996), "Brand Familiarity and Confidence as Determinants of Purchase Intention: An Empirical Test in a Multiple Brand Context," *Journal of Business Research*, 37 (October), 115-120.

Lau, Kong C. and Ian Phau (2007), "Extending Symbolic Brands using their Personality: Examining Antecedents and Implications Towards Brand Image Fit and Brand Dilution," Psychology *and Marketing*, 24 (May), 421-444.

Lee, Jin-Soo and Ki Joon Back. (2010), "Examining Antecedents and Consequences of Brand Personality in the Upper-Upscale Business Hotel Segment," *Journal of Travel and Tourism Marketing*, 27 (March), 132-45.

Levy, Sidney J. (1981), "Interpreting Consumer Mythology: A Structural Approach to Consumer Behavior," *Journal of Marketing*, 45 (Summer), 49-61.

Lorr, Maurice and Tracey. Manning T. (1978) "Higher Order of the Personality Factors of the ISI," *Multivariate behavioral Research*, 13 (June), 3-7.

Mackenzie, Scott. B., Richard J. Lutz (1989), "An empirical examination of the structural antecedents of attitude toward the ad in the advertising pretesting context," *Journal of Marketing*, 53 (April), 48-65.

Maehle, Natalia and Magne Supphellen. (2010), "In Search of the Sources of brand Personality," *International Journal of Market Research*, 53 (January), 95-114.

McCrae, Robert.R and Paul Costa T. Jr. (1985), "Updating Norman "Adequate taxonomy" Intelligence and Personality Dimensions in Natural Language and in Questionnaires," *Journal of Personality and Social Psychology*, 49 (September), 710-21.

Menasco, Michael B., Del I. Hawkins (1978), "A Field Test of the Relationship between Cognitive Dissonance and State Anxiety," *Journal of Marketing Research*, 15 (November), 650-655.

Miles, Mathew B. and Michael A. Huberman (1994), *Qualitative Data Analysis*, (Second Edition), Thousand Oaks, CA: Sage Publications.

Mitchel, Vincent-Wayne and Vassilios Papavassiliou, (1999), "Marketing Causes and Implications of Consumer Confusion," *Journal of Product & Brand Management*, 8 (4), 319-339.

Monroe, Kent B. (1973), "Buyers' Subjective Perceptions of Price," *Journal of Marketing Research*, 10 (February), 70-80.

Noller, Patricia., Law, Henry & Comrey Andrew L. (1987), "Cattell, Comrey, and Eysenck Personality Factors Compared: More Evidence for the Robust Five Factors," *Journal of Personality and Social Psychology*, 53 (October), 775-82.

Norman, Warren T. (1963), "Towards an adequate taxonomy of personality attributes: replicated factor structure in peer nomination in personality ratings," *Journal of Abnormal and Social Psychology*, 56 (June), 574-583.

Olney, Thomas J., Morris B. Holbrook and Rajeev Batra (1991), "Consumer Responses to Advertising: The Effects of Ad Content, Emotions, and Attitude toward the Ad on Viewing Time," *Journal of Consumer Research*, 17 (March), 440-453.

Park, Whan C., Bernard J. Jaworski and Deborah J. MacInnis (1986), "Strategic Brand Concept-Image Management," *Journal of Marketing*, 50 (October), 135-145.

Phau, Ian and Kong C. Lau (2000), "Conceptualising Brand Personality: A review and Research Propositions," *Journal of Targeting, Measurement and Analysis for Marketing*, 9 (August) 52-69.

Popkins, Nathan. C. (1998), "The five-factor model: Emergence of a Taxonomic Model for Personality Psychology," Retrieved January 12, (2004) from http://www.personalityresearch.org/papers/popkins.html.

Plummer, Joseph T. (2000), "How Personality makes a difference," *Journal of Advertising Research*, 40 (November) 79-83.

Ratchford, Brian T. (1987), "New Insights About the FCB Grid," *Journal of Advertising Research,* 27 (August/September), 24-38.

Richins, Marsha L. (1983), "Negative Word of Mouth by Dissatisfied Consumers: A Pilot Study," *Journal of Marketing,* 47 (Winter), 68-78.

Rosenberg, Seymour and Moonja P. Kim (1975), "The Method of Sorting as a Data-Gathering Procedure in Multivariate Research," *Multivariate Behavioral Research.* 10 (October), 489-502.

Rudell, Fredrica (1979), *Consumer Food Selection and Nutrition Information*, New York: Praeger.

Rugg, Gordon and Peter McGeorg (2005), "The Sorting Techniques: A Tutorial Paper on Card Sorts, Picture Sorts and Item Sorts," *Expert System,* 22 (July) 94-107.

Silverman, David (2004) Qualitative research: Theory, Method and practice (Second Edition), Sage: London.

Sirgy, Joseph M., Dhruv Grewal., Tamara Mangleburg F., Jae-Ok, Park., Kye-Sung Chon., C. B Claiborne., J. S. Johar and Harold, Berkman. (1997), "Assessing the Predictability Validity of 2 Methods of measuring self image congruence," *Journal of the Academy of Marketing Science*, 25 (3), 229-41.

Smith, Gareth (2009), "Conceptualizing and Testing Brand Personality in British politics", *Journal of Political Marketing,* 8 (July), 209-32.

Smith, Gene M. (1967), "Usefulness of Peer Ratings of Personality in Educational Research," *Educational and Personality Measurement*, 27, 967-84.

Sproles, Elizabeth K. and George B. Sproles (1990), "Consumer Decision-Making Styles as a Function of Individual Learning Styles," *The Journal of Consumer Affairs*, 24 (Summer), 134-147.

Sung, Jongjun and Kim Jooyoung . (2010), "Effects on Brand Personality on Brand Trust and Brand Affect", *Psychology and Marketing,* 27 (June), 639-661.

Sung, Yongjun. and Spencer F. Tinkham (2005). "Brand Personality Structures in the United States and Korea: Common and Culture-Specific Factors." *Journal of Consumer Psychology*, 15 (April), 334-350.

Sweeney, Julian C. and Carol Brandon (2006), "Brand personality: Exploring the Potential to Move from Factor Analytical to Circumplex Models," *Psychology and Marketing*, 23 (June) 639-663.

Venable, Beverly T., Gregory, Rose M., Victoria, Bush D and Faye, Gilbert W. (2005), "The Role of Brand Personality in Charitable Giving: An Assessment and Validation," Journal *of the Academy of Marketing Science*, 33 (June), 295-312.

Waller, Neils, G and Joe, Zavala D. (1993), "Evaluating the Big Five," *Psychological Inquiry,* 4 (April), 131- 34.

Walsh, Gianfranco and Vincent–Wayne. (2010), "The Effects of Consumer Confusion Proneness on Word of Mouth, Trust, and Customer Satisfaction," *European Journal of Marketing,* 44 (6), 838-59.

Zaichkowsky, Judith L. (1985), "Measuring the Involvement Construct," *Journal of Consumer Research*, 12 (December), 341-352.

Globalization in the Less Affluent World:
The Moroccan Consumers' Acculturation to Global Consumer Culture in Their Homeland

Delphine Godefroit-Winkel, Univ Lille Nord de France- SKEMA Business School, France

Marie-Hélène Fosse-Gomez, Univ Lille Nord de France- SKEMA Business School, France

Nil Özçaglar-Toulouse, Univ Lille Nord de France- SKEMA Business School, France

ABSTRACT

Studies have highlighted the difficulty to build a typology of LAW consumers' behaviors in their increasingly global environment. In this observational and interview based research, The authors identified four consumptions modes in Casablanca which are related to the postassimilationist model, suggesting that acculturation is not restricted to migrants' experience.

The global consumer culture is currently part of the global world (Arnould and Thompson 2005) and many studies have been devoted to understand the way it has emerged. However it impacts around the globe with significant differences. In the Less Affluent World (LAW), the global consumer culture increasingly affects local consumers who have to adapt to a new environment (Ger and Belk 1996; Varman and Belk 2008). Despite several interesting contributions in different countries (see, Wilk in Belize, Ger in Turkey or Arnould in Niger), building a general typology of LAW consumer behaviors seems to be difficult, due to the diversity of cultural settings (Arnould 2002). This paper aims to identify different consumption modes in a LAW, by using acculturation framework.

This research considers the global consumer culture as a new culture -one that inhabitants of an economically developing country are forced to affront. Such inhabitants are confronted to this new consumer culture in the same way as immigrants discovering another culture in their host country. To some extent, they can experience "acculturation" in their own homelands. This research is limited to Morocco: this country has experienced remarkable economic growth, an exponential increase in quantities of available products and international brands, and numbers of new retail channels have soared over the last ten years.

THEORETICAL ISSUES

The links between consumer culture and capitalism have long been investigated (e.g. Ritzer 2004) and consumer culture has been considered in very different ways, from a control mechanism aimed at reducing individual freedom (Marcuse 1964) to a emancipatory opportunity (Firat and Venkatesh 1995). During the last decades, attention has been directed to the spear of a global consumer culture. The global consumer culture is defined as a "cultural entity not associated with a single country, but rather a larger group generally recognized as international and transcending individual national cultures" (Alden, Steenkamp and Batra 1999, 80). The arising of this global consumer culture has suggested new directions of research. First the question of homogenization of consumption patterns all over the world has been addressed. According to the proponents of the homogenization thesis, local cultures are colonized by transnational corporations, through the spreading of global brands. As the global consumer culture is rooted in the Western consumer culture, the question of western values' implementation in all the other cultures has also been considered. This global culture was suspected to crush the local ones and to generate a new form of domination. However, it seems that global brands are producing diversity, as people from different cultures re-interpret them in different ways and incorporate them in their own lifestyle (Ger and Belk 1996; Miller 1998). According to Thompson and Arsel "the intersection of global brands and local cultures produces cultural heterogeneity" (2004, 631).

The increasing marketization and globalization of local economies have impacted on much consumers in the Less Affluent World (LAW). The consumption modes observed in the LAWs differ from Western patterns and they are considered numerous and hybrid (Sandikçi and Ger 2002). Results emphasize their differences from Western societies and suggest that any generalization of phenomena observed in the West must be carefully undertaken (Ger and Belk 1996). They also provide evidence of the major role played by the media, television in particular (Varman and Belk 2008) and advertising (Zhao and Belk 2008) in developing a new consumption ideology. However, if the forces that drive globalized consumerism and global consumption homogenization and the consequences on consumers have been investigated (Ger and Belk 1996), the way people in LAW live the global consumer culture as a new culture is not enough studied.

Considering the large differences between global consumer culture and local cultures in the LAW, we suggest to consider global consumer culture as a new culture, which inhabitants of an economically developing country are forced to affront. Inhabitants of a LAW are confronted to the global consumer culture in the same way than immigrants discovering another culture in their host country; they experience "acculturation" in their own homelands. Indeed, consumers who were raised in traditional societies discover consumer society, like immigrants discover host culture on reaching the host country. It may be hard for migrants to adapt, mainly because of differences between the host and original culture. This lens suggests to consider acculturation theories as a frame to approach people reactions to the global consumer culture in the LAW.

The works of Berry (1997) is considered as a starting point for the development of acculturation theories in consumer research. According to Berry, individuals in a multi-cultural society hold attitudes based on their orientation with regards to two central issues: cultural maintenance of own group, and desirability of intergroup contact. In his model, individuals choose one of four acculturation modes: assimilation, integration, separation, or marginalization. But assimilation is, more or less, the expected goal for migrants, who are supposed to adopt the host culture. Post-assimilationist theories have focus mostly on identity (*e.g.* Oswald 1999; Askegaard, Arnould and Kjeldgaard 2005). The focus is on individuals, and consumption is considered as a resource that helps migrants to build their identity project. Oswald (1999), for example, developed a model of hybrid identity and of swapping culture. Üstüner and Holt (2007) introduced the sociocultural context to explore the identity project of poor migrants in Turkey, far from a postmodern view. Practices are explored mostly in an instrumental way, in order to analyse how migrants use consumption to pursue their identity project with the exception of Peñaloza's work on Mexican migrants (Peñaloza 1994). Peñaloza sets up four consumer acculturation practices: assimilation (adopt the host practices), resistance (favor home practices over host practices), acculturation (adopt both host and home practices), and segregation (a spatial form of separation). Later, Askegaard et al. (2005) point out the rise of transnational consumer culture as a third acculturating agent. They also show with the case of Greenlanders of Danish nationality and their integration in Danish society that acculturation should not be limited to migration movements between two different countries.

Advances in Consumer Research
Volume 40, ©2012

DEVELOPMENT OF A GLOBAL CONSUMER CULTURE IN MOROCCO

Belk defined consumer culture as a "culture in which the majority of consumers avidly desire (and some noticeable portion pursue, acquire and display) goods and services that are valued for non-utilitarian reasons, such as status seeking, envy provocation, and novelty seeking" (Belk 1988, 105). Such a culture was not prevalent in Morocco thirty years ago, when Geertz explored the Moroccan souks and retail channels (Geertz 1978). A short presentation of the Moroccan recent history can highlight its evolution towards consumer culture and especially towards global consumer culture.

After the Independence in 1956, a protectionist policy was adopted with high trade tariffs - 45% in 1982 - and many state owned companies. In the 80s, the Moroccan authorities decided to be part of the global world and started slowly the economic liberalization. Over the last decade, the Moroccan openness increased drastically - from 43.5% in 1998 to 70% in 2008 - and the foreign investments doubled - 18 billions MAD in 1999 and 42 billions MAD in 2007. In the following, we describe factors that have assisted the development of global consumer culture: availability of many products in the market, sufficient purchase power to buy them, and actual purchase willingness among the targeted consumers.

Availability of products in the market: Moroccan inner supply and retailing

In addition to local products, the Moroccan market is currently provided with many imported products as a result of custom taxes. During late 1980s, the Moroccan government implemented reforms, including economical liberalization and privatization of several state-owned enterprises. The Moroccan financial sector was acutely reformed in 1993 to meet international standards. As investments were made in order to increase quality levels, Moroccan industries signed several contracts to supply well-known foreign brands with textile and leather products. Moroccan expertise in terms of luxury products spread to smaller workshops, raising quality standards. Even in less prestigious sectors, local products increased in quality and numbers. However, some Moroccan people still think that local products are synonymous with bad quality.

The Moroccan distribution experiences drastic changes since the first hypermarket in 1990. For instance, some specialized megastores such as Bricoma - for tools - or Kitea - for home furnishings - have opened their doors and the largest shopping mall in Africa was inaugurated in Casablanca in December 2011. But, like in other LAW - e.g. Tunisia (Mejri and Lajili 2007) - according to USAID (2006[1]) to the Moroccan retail environment is dominated by traditional forms - the average distribution channel counts 4 to 5 intermediaries; the small retailers represents 91% of the retail sector with 1,27 million stores. On the other hand, the retail industry is moved by a drastic growth - 11% per year while contributing to the global consumer culture spread in Morocco.

Purchasing power

The development policy was accompanied by a social dialogue, which resulted among others in an improvement of the average household income; meanwhile, relative poverty has decreased (from 15% in 2001 to 9% in 2007). But, only 3% of the households have a saving account. Besides, the purchasing power has increased through the availability of credit in the last ten. 3 Moroccans on 4 have a short term credit (HCP 2009[2]) and half of them are given in Casablanca and Rabat. The household expenses concern mainly food

- 80% of the Moroccan households still spend half of their income in food (HCP 2009).

Readiness to consume

30 years ago, the poor diversity of the Moroccan supply was constraining the Moroccan willingness to consume. Today, the Moroccan market experiences a remarkable growth in consumption. Three reasons are to be given. Firstly, food abundance within the home reflects wealth of the host. Secondly, consumption appears to be indelibly linked to modern society. Ever-increasing consumption has begun. Furthermore, mass communication nourishes consumption desire (Varman and Belk 2008). Many foreign TV-channels are now available through satellite dissemination . Viewers, restricted to two Moroccan channels until the 1990s - and to one TV-channel before 1989 -, learn about global consumer culture through multiple TV-programs; the press is another developing media.

Importance of global culture in Morocco

Global consumer culture can be conceptualized in terms of "the proliferation of transnational corporation producing and marketing consumer goods" (Ger and Belk 1996, 274). Before the 90s, shopping facilities were inaccessible because of Moroccan protectionism and geographical distances. Obtaining global products, required traveling abroad - e.g. the Moroccan elite - or waiting for migrants to 'come back home' in vehicles brimming with Western manufactured products. With economic liberalization, the Moroccan market welcomed introduction of global products - 40% of the consumption concerns imported products - and the openings of distribution channels such as supermarkets, hypermarkets and franchises. Global brands have sold in supermarket, competing Moroccan ones.

However, there is still much disparity between the global and the Moroccan consumer cultures. In Morocco, the swift market evolution is observed but this rapid evolution entails issues and trauma. Moroccan consumers experience acculturation within their home country. Therefore, we advocate considering the urban Moroccan consumers as migrants affronting a previously distant culture.

METHODOLOGY

Among our research objectives were: 1) understanding the contact between the local and the global consumer culture and the resulting change for consumers in consumption practices ; 2) addressing whether the acculturation frame is relevant to analyze consumers' reactions to global consumer culture in a LAW.

We conducted an interpretive study in Casablanca, the Moroccan economic capital because even if consumption has increased drastically, its growth is larger in Casablanca than in any other parts of the country. In order to gain meaningful understanding of settings, distinct cultural shopping contexts were chosen, ranging from traditional markets to modern super and hypermarkets for food represent the most important household expenses. We privileged data collection and recording of human experience in natural settings, with non participant and participant observation as it facilitates access to backstage areas (Goffman 1959).

The first author collected the data. She has been living in Casablanca during her childhood and she settled back in Casablanca 14 years ago. She has a privileged access to the field, an understanding of local languages and customs while she is aware of the danger of being too much insider (Arnould and Wallendorf 1994).

The notes were taken during the observations and enriched a few hours after the observations (Corbin and Strauss 2008). Thick descriptions (Geertz 1973) helped in describing observed phenomena in order to assure an holistic rendu. The first author paid attention

---

[1] http://pdf.usaid.gov/pdf_docs/PNADH519.pdf

[2] http://www.hcp.ma/

to her emotional responses and she noted down her own reactions and interpretations during observations in order to reveal personal biases (Wallendorf, Belk and Heisley 1988).

Observations were complemented with 35 in-depth interviews to gain deep emic understanding of the phenomenon under study. Informants' profiles were diversified according to several demographical and sociological characteristics including age and education level.

Interviews were conducted with informants living in Casablanca, and varied from 34 minutes to one hour 47 minutes. They took place in different places, the choice of location was dictated by convenience, in informants' living room or kitchen or in cafés. Interviews were conducted either in French or Moroccan dialect. The interviewer used both French to comfort informants, because Moroccans gain in identity assertion and negotiation while they use French (Sadiqi 2003) and dialect to ensure proximity. In order to give an emic perspective and credibility to the data, 6 cultural mediators helped in interviewing 6 informants. A participant list is presented in table 1. The interviews were integrally translated and transcribed. An expert in Moroccan dialect and French checked the translations for accuracy.

The first author's experience as a migrant ensured an analytical perspective. The second author, a French woman has observed the Moroccan market evolution, during her frequent visits in Morocco. The second and third author provided analytical distance for data collection, coding, and interpretation. The three authors analyzed the data using an interpretative approach, first separately and then together, according to the themes which had emerged. By alternating between the specific case of each interviewee and the interviews as a whole, and by making use of field notes, pictures and literature, as in the final stages of the analysis, we have attained findings showing the relation modes of Moroccan consumers to global consumer culture.

FINDINGS

Through the various stories told by respondents, four relation modes with global consumer culture were identified. Each mode can be related to one of the acculturation modes identified in post-assimilationist literature. The first mode, "Adoption", meaning acceptance of the new consumer culture, is similar to "Assimilation". "Rejection" is similar to the "Hyperculture" suggested by Askegaard et al. (2005). "Negotiation" is close to "Pendulum", as people sometimes accept some traditional consumption modes and, in other circumstances, adopt new behaviors. Finally, we found evidence of "Best of both worlders" who value the two cultures. The data presented below evinces the dialogue of rejection and acceptance, marking this acculturation.

Adoption

Consumers who adopt markets do not question market mechanisms: they accept market rules; they conform to and find benefits, such as self-expression. Majd, a single male informant, is excited when he tells about shopping in the supermarket.

> In supermarkets, you always end up with something that you did not need. You know what they call gondolas, it is treacherous! You end up being taken in! You always end up taken in! [Laugh]… They tell you 'Price was 40'; they cross it and write 38. So you tell yourself 'What a good deal!'. You don't count. It's only when you go out that you realize. It's after… But you come back… and you do it with pleasure. You do your shopping in good conditions (Majd, 54, high school teacher)

If Majd buys more than expected, he still has a good image of his shopping experience in the retail industry. The adaptation process may generate problems with regards to integrating market logic but Majd accepts market rules and he quickly acculturated. He likes the ambiance and the products supplied in the retail industry. For instance, he buys ready-to-cook chicken breasts and abandoned the whole warm just-killed chickens, which are sold in the traditional markets. He reminds without any regrets the time when he would go to the traditional sellers : "I don't have to sit anymore on an empty box [...] watching the cockroaches or the mice walking around the food [laughs]".

Besides, the Moroccan retail industry provides consumers with a new space where they can express their self. Saida is a female student in Arabic law at the public University of Casablanca. She feels "special", "posh", when she goes to the hypermarket with her mother every month. "The only fact of having a trolley and walking through the alleys, makes me feel different. It's not like at the hanout [small next-door shop] or the souk where it is crowded and you have to shout: give me that!". And she admits that hypermarkets are an arena where definition of one's group is negotiated.

> In our country, there are people with low incomes who go to Marjane [hypermarket] to have a walk. Some of them don't even buy. Others buy a single pack of cheese. They wait in line at the cashier and then they leave but they leave with a plastic bag! They carry Marjane plastic bags! This means that they were at Marjane! They want to show that they went to a supermarket, that they are able to shop in supermarkets! We, Moroccan folk, focus on appearances. It is like that! This is how we are. (Saïda, 20, student)

Being a hypermarket' client is a way to approach one's social reference group. Leila chooses the hypermarket regarding to the clients.

> People who go to Marjane Californie [hypermarket] are different from those who go to Marjane Derb Soltan [hypermarket]. In Marjane Californie, people are more civilized. They are better dressed. Some women are smart, they carry Louis Vuitton bags; in their hands, they have car keys. (Leila, 36, school teacher)

Market rejection

Some Moroccan consumers refuse to buy certain items in supermarkets or in contemporary shops; they cook instead of buying prepared dishes, and so on. Two causes have been identified for such market avoidance: faith in tradition and protection of Moroccan identity.

Time perception and orientation is one of the most salient characterisics of consumer action (Bergadaà 1990). Fatima, a young housewife, points out the difference in the value of time in the traditional distribution and in the retail industry.

> In a hypermarket, you don't enjoy it at all because it is like a duty that you have to do. That's it! You are supposed to know how long you will stay in each section. And don't forget how long it will take to scan all your products! And when it's going to be your turn! When you go to the [permanent] souk, you don't watch the clock: you wander, asking each seller the price of any product. You walk with your basket, chickens cackle, there is a nice atmosphere. (Fatima, 36, housewife)

Table 1: Informants' List

name	age	marital situation	household excluding informant	occupation	spouse or father's occupation	home rental cost	sex	education
Abdelhamid	54	married	3 (spouse, 2 children)	professor	manager	high	m	phd
Abdellatif	21	single	3 (parents, 1 brother)	student	employee	medium	m	bachelor
Aicha	45	married	4 (spouse, 3 children)	housewife	retired	medium	f	high school
Amina	43	married	3 (spouse, 2 children)	secretary	employee	medium	f	bachelor
Btissam	37	married	3 (spouse, 2 children)	anaesthetist	manager	high	f	doctor
Charaf	51	married	1 (spouse)	professor	doctor	high	m	master
Farida	39	married	2 (spouse, 1 child)	housewife	mechanic	medium	f	high school
Fatiha	36	married	2 (spouse, 1 child)	housewife	salesman	low	f	high school
Fatima	36	married	3 (spouse, 2 children)	housewife	salesman	medium	f	high school
Fatima-Ezzahra	45	married	3 (spouse, 2 children)	teacher	manager	high	f	bachelor
Hasnaa	30	single	3 (parents, 1 brother)	employee	employee	medium	f	master
Hassan	42	married	3 (spouse, 2 children)	delivery boy	housewife	low	m	bachelor
Khadija	46	married	4 (spouse, 3 children)	housewife	manager	low	f	high school
Khadija	80	married	1 (spouse)	retired	retired	low	f	illiterate
Lakbira	40	married	5 (spouse, 4 children)	housewife	housekeeper	low	f	illiterate
Leila	36	married	3 (spouse, 2 children)	teacher	lawyer	medium	f	bachelor
Majd	54	single	2 (mother, helper)	teacher		high	m	bachelor
Malika	36	married	3 (spouse, 2 children)	housecleaner	housekeeper	low	f	illiterate
Mina	46	married	3 (spouse, 2 children)	housekeeper	retired	low	f	illiterate
Nabila	28	married	1 (spouse)	civil servant	employee	medium	f	bachelor
Naïma	57	married	8 (spouse, 3 children, 2 in laws, 3 grand children)	employee	retired	medium	f	high school

name	age	marital situation	household excluding informant	occupation	spouse or father's occupation	home rental cost	sex	education
Najia	36	married	4 (spouse, 3 children)	housewife	manager	medium	f	high school
Nour	22	single	4 (parents, 2 brothers)	student	retired	medium	f	bachelor
Saida	23	single	3 (parents, 1 brother)	employee	employee	low	f	master
Siham	32	married	2 (spouse, 1 child)	manager	employee	medium	f	bachelor
Saida	20	single	4 (parents, 2 brothers)	student	employee	low	f	bachelor
Sanaa	46	married	3 (spouse, 2 children)	manager	manager	medium	f	bachelor
Selma	22	single	4 (parents, 2 sisters)	student	salesman	medium	f	bachelor
Soumaya	36	single	3 (parents, 1 brother)	aesthetician	retired	medium	f	high school
Soumiya	35	married	1 (spouse)	manager	manager	high	f	master
Wafaa	40	married	4 (spouse, 3 children)	housewife	manager	low	f	bachelor
Walid	28	married	1 (spouse)	manager	manager	high	m	master
Yasmine	40	married	4 (spouse, 3 children)	civil servant	employee	medium	f	high school
Youssef	42	married	3 (spouse, 2 children)	teacher	employee	medium	f	bachelor
Zahra	40	single	3 (mother, 2 sisters)	translator		medium	f	bachelor

Fatima perceives shopping in souks as a timeless leisure activity, whereas shopping in hypermarkets is a stressful pursuit where time is a valuable resource. She expresses the change between traditional Moroccan and modern day perception of consumption. She values interpersonal relations over time, showing her attachment to the traditional shopping mode.

In the Moroccan exchange tradition, personal relationships between sellers and buyers are very important. Forging relation of trust is a primary Moroccan market strategy (Kapchan 1996) while in global consumer culture, trust is inspired by brands (Holt 2002). As an example, trust in the vendor is highly important for meat and poultry purchase in Morocco. Most informants refuse to buy such products in supermarkets. "I have the feeling that they sell old cows, really!" says Naïma, 57, employee. Naïma goes to the same butcher for many years. Informants like Naima do not trust ready-to-cook chicken from supermarkets, even if it is sold under a slaughterhouse's stamp and has a best before date printed on packaging.

Going to the hanout is also very important in the Moroccan everyday life, where people ties strong interpersonal relationships based on trust. Youssef enjoys his hanout, who allows him to buy on credit.

I have a notebook [at the hanout]. THE famous notebook, the one which permits to buy on credit and to pay at the end of the month. I wish that these hanouts don't disappear with all the supermarkets! They are friendly, and close to the people. We all have a souvenir with a hanout. I remember so well when we lived in the countryside: there was Hamid! .... then I moved to Casablanca... I wish that there will always be the hanouts. (Youssef, 50, merchant)

Youssef is deeply attached to the Moroccan traditions and to the hanouts which are socially rooted in the Moroccan identity. He perfectly knows that they don't represent the ideal stores which he would dream of: "they have warm yoghurts and flies on the bread". But, he is attached to them with their pros and cons and can't imagine a Morocco without them. The Moroccan culture is socially constructed through the stores.

Negotiation

The negotiation mode is an oscillation between cultures; assimilation with global consumer culture with simultaneous maintenance of Moroccan consumption behaviours. In the Moroccan retail industry, many consumers have traditional behaviours to proceed to shopping, at the cashier or during the decision making process.

A woman arrives at one express cashier, where "Fewer than 10 items" is written in French and in Arabic. She has a full trolley. In one plastic bag which is usually used for vegetables and fruits, she has put several yoghurts. She puts the plastic bag on the conveyer belt. The employee tells her in polite dialect that his cashier is limited to ten items maximum per client. The female client pouts and asks if the yoghurts in the plastic (of different brand and size) constitute one item. The employee explains slowly and gently to her the definition of an item. The woman doesn't move. A monologue begins: the employee tries to demonstrate that he cannot make any exception without the risk of being invaded by thousands of other packed trolleys. The female client doesn't answer, and doesn't look at him, no anger can be read on her face. The employee turns back and finishes to scan the former client's purchase. During that time, the female client empties her trolley on the conveyer belt. No more contestations: the employee scans her purchase and the next ten-item clients don't say anything.

The employee, who has total understanding of traditional culture, doesn't seem to show particular interest in forcing respect this specific hypermarket norm, which is a global norm. The express cash till is meant to save time, which is not a valued resource in traditional Moroccan culture. The cashier privileges harmonious interpersonal relations with the female client who is penetrated with the traditional habit of bargaining (Kapchan 1996). In this specific case, she negotiates the norm in order to be served.

Bargaining is in a traditional consumer behavior in the Moroccan souks (Geertz 1978). A Moroccan consumer always bargains in a souk to get a better offer. But Sarah has noticed that she can use her bargaining skills in the supermarket as well.

One day, I was watching the fishes on the shelf in the supermarket. The employee asked me if he could be of any help. I told him that I was hesitating, that I didn't know if I really wanted to have fish, that they were quite expensive fishes. After a while, he proposed me to trust him: he would give me a good fish for a good price. And you know what he did? He took a fish, cleaned it, emptied it and only then weighted it! In the supermarket, the prices that are for uncleaned fishes! [...] So of course, I gave him a good tip. He made me spare a huge amount of money: almost half of the price! Now, I always buy fish from him! (Sarah, 38, housewife)

Sarah, without any specific intention, has reproduced the traditional link which exists between a seller and a buyer in the traditional marketplace. She likes to shop in a supermarket, she has an accurate understanding of what can be and can't be done in the retail industry. But she doesn't want to get away from the traditional shopping behaviors and her home consumer culture.

The Best-of-both-world mode

The consumers take the best part of each culture. They value the positive side of their traditional culture while enjoying the incoming global culture. In our research, many informants consider shopping as a leisure activity (Tauber 1972). In the traditional Moroccan society, shopping is a masculine activity and the periodic souks are the best example of the male dominated Moroccan institutions (Kaplan 1996). Like many men in Casablanca, Hassan likes to go to the periodic souk every Sunday morning. He describes these shopping experiences as an important tradition. He leaves early in the morning with his father, his brother and his cousin. They buy several kilos of vegetables and meat to "feed the whole family" during a week. Then, they

return back home, and give their wive the purchased goods. In the afternoon, Hassan goes to the hypermarket: he buys cans of tomato paste, oil, flour, sugar or green tea, which can't be found in the souk. In Hassan's family, the women have the duty to prepare meals with what the men have brought back. Women don't write any wishing list for their husband nor ask for special items. They conform with what is purchased. However, the opening of hyper and supermarkets offered an additional opportunity for Hassan's wife and children to participate more actively in the shopping activity.

We go [to the supermarket] with the kids, to please my wife. Otherwise, she is not happy. She claims that I go out and that she always stays at home. (Hassan, 42, delivery boy)

Hassan's wife doesn't work and doesn't drive. During the week, she is busy with their three sons and her in-laws who live next door. So, she wants to have "fresh air", to go out on week ends, and the retail industry is attractive to her. Hassan is happy to drive his wife and children to the hypermarket. He perfectly knows that she would be angry if he doesn't bring her.

In the hypermarket, the eldest children run and the baby sits in the caddie. Hassan's wife watches the novelties or buy a pair of slippers for her. It's like a mini-trip for the family.

Each informant has been affected to one of the four modes described in the post assimilationist literature, suggesting that acculturation is a relevant frame to analyze Casablanca consumption behaviors in their increasingly global environment.

DISCUSSION

Our results confirm some of the already known consequences of the spearing of the global consumer culture in LAW. For example, shopping and consuming provides pleasure and gratification to many individuals; but as conspicuous consumption is very important, keeping up with the Joneses leads people to compete and to increase inequalities and tensions (Ger and Belk 1996).

A less expended result concerns the shift in roles within the family. Traditionally, men were the sole breadwinners in the West (Falk and Campbell 1997) and in Morocco (Kapchan 1996). They were both the decision maker and the shopper, as they attempted souks on a regular basis. Cultural norms gave husbands the legitimacy to make the decision, even in the food and cooking sphere. Today, urban Moroccan women gain in power while having access to shopping and become an more active agent in the family decision making. The encounter between a traditional family model and a more modern one (to use Rodman's terms) could have given ride to tensions. But thanks to global consumer culture, it seems to happen without drastic tensions within the family. Supermarkets and new retail channels turned to be more female ones, or at least family retailing channels. They have become a place where a woman can buy by their own, or where the all family can have a ride on Saturday or Sunday afternoon. Males do not feel hurt by the lost power, as their own territory – souk- is not threatened. Contrary to previous results (Ger and Belk, 1996), there is no clash between traditional and modern models, the ideology underlying the global consumer culture helps husbands and wife adapting to this new model. And an acculturation mode such as " best of both world" – souks for men hegemony and supermarket for women freedom- facilitates the shift from one family model to another one. More generally, consumers in a LAW are embedded in their changing cultural context and construct their roles through adopting or rejecting the new context (Miller 1995). The relation modes to the global culture do not necessarily arise only out of historical trajectory nor from a local cultural context (Arnould 1989). Consumers in a LAW elaborate individually their relation modes to the global culture while choosing to paste, to abandon or to negotiate their individual behaviors inherited from the traditional lifestyle.

Our results also contribute to the today debate about frontiers. Frontiers are at the heart of the first acculturation theories in social sciences, as their purpose was to understand how a migrant coming from a foreign county, crossing a physical frontier, could adapt to his host culture that involves crossing cultural ones. In post-assimilationist studies, the seminal work of Peñaloza about Mexican-Americans introduces in its title the notion of "frontiers" (Peñaloza 1994). Frontiers can be either tangible (a body, a country) or intangible (a social class, a category). They can fulfill a functional value (be a reference point) or a symbolic value (providing re-assurance) (Regany, Visconti and Fosse-Gomez 2012). More recently, the idea has been introduced that an acculturation process could occur inside the same country (internal migration of peasants to cities) without crossing any national border: Üstüner and Holt (2007) analyzed the identity project of poor migrant women leaving the countryside to settle in Istanbul. In this case the frontier lies between village and city. But in the case of global consumer culture spreading into a LAW as Morocco is, it seems to be no usual frontier at all. Using a frame as acculturation to analyze this case suggests some new uses of frontier. For some Moroccan people, frontiers do exist. People rejecting the global consumer culture, and the market ideology, build in their mind a clear frontier between traditional culture and this new one. Reifying such a frontier helps them to separate the two worlds and to manage their segregation. As Curtright (2012) pointed it recently, human individuals need to rely on boundaries, and sometime have to build them in their mind. For people using the three other modes – *adoption*, *negotiation* and *best-of-the both* modes- frontiers do exist but are more fluid. They have to be understood as in a world perceived as dominated by fluidity and global flows (Appadurai 1996).

CONCLUSION

Our work supports the use of the post assimilationist model as a relevant frame to analyze consumer culture in a LAW. Morocco appears to be a relevant county to conduct such a study. The retail industry creates a new space opportunity for LAW consumers to negotiate with the global culture while offering more choice in the sphere of everyday life (Holt 2002). LAW consumers benefit from the retail industry; they use consumption practices to negotiate differences between cultures. However, the actual fluid context gives LAW consumers no other choice than a creative activity of *bricolage* (Bouchet 1995). LAW consumers "bricolent" their behaviors to achieve their goals. They adopt, reject, negotiate or enjoy the global culture and the Moroccan culture to navigate in their increasingly globalized world. As a result, regular border boundary crossing dissolve clear-cut boundaries between Moroccan and global culture.

This work suffers from several limitations. One of the most prevalent one is the lack of socioeconomic perspective. We decided to focus on urban middle class consumers, as they were more concerned than any other ones by the spreading of a global consumer culture. Any generalization to another context must be carefully considered.

REFERENCES

Alden, Dana L., Steenkamp, Jan-Benedict E.M. & Rajeev Batra (1999), «Brand positioning through advertising in Asia, North America, and Europe: The role of global consumer culture», *Journal of Marketing*, 63, 1, 75- 87.

Appadurai, Arjun (1996), *Modernity at large: Cultural dimensions of globalization, Minneapolis*, University of Minnesota Press.

Arnould, Eric J. (1989), "Toward a Broadened Theory of Preference Formation and the Diffusion of Innovations: Cases from Zinder Province, Niger Republic," *Journal of Consumer Research*, 16 (September) 239-267.

Arnould, Eric J. (2002), "The Paradoxical Presence and Absence of Consumer Culture in a Third World Context", *Advances in Consumer Research*, 29, 463-4.

Arnould, Eric J. and Melanie Wallendorf (1994) "Ethnography: Interpretation Building and Marketing Strategy Formulation", *Journal of Marketing Research*, 31 (November), 484-504.

Arnould, Eric. J. and Craig J. Thompson (2005), "Consumer Culture Theory, Twenty Years of Research", *Journal of Consumer Research*, 31 (March), 868-82.

Askegaard, Søren, Eric J. Arnould, and Dannie Kjeldgaard (2005), "Postassimilationist Ethnic Consumer Research: Qualifications and Extensions," *Journal of Consumer Research*, 32(June), 160-70.

Belk, Russell W. (1988), "Possessions and the Extended Self", *Journal of Consumer Research*, 15 (September), 139-68

Bergadaà, Michelle (1990), "The Role of Time in the Action of the Consumer", *Journal of Consumer Research*, 17 (December), 289–302.

Berry, John W. (1997), "Immigration, Acculturation and Adaptation", *Applied Psychology: an International Review*, 46, 5-68

Bouchet, Dominique (1995), Marketing and the Redefinition of Ethnicity. In: *Marketing in a Multicultural World. Ethnicity, nationalism, and cultural identity*, Janeen Arnold Costa and Gary J. Bamossy (eds), 68–114, Thousand Oaks/London/New Delhi: Sage.

Corbin, Juliet and Anselm Strauss (2008), *Basics of Qualitative Research, 3e*. CA: Sage Publications.

Cutright, Keisha M. (2012), The beauty of boundaries: When and why we seek structure in consumption. *Journal of Consumer Research* 38, 5, 775-795.

Falk, Pasi and Colin Campbell (1997), *The Shopping Experience*, Sage Publications, London.

Firat A. Fuat and Alladi Venkatesh (1995), "Liberatory Postmodernism and the Reenchantment of Consumption," *Journal of Consumer Research*, 22 (December), 239-66.

Ger, Güliz and Russell W. Belk (1996), "I'd Like to Buy to buy the World a Coke: Consumptionscapes of the "Less Affluent World"", *Journal of Consumer Policy*, 19, 271-304.

Geertz, Clifford (1973), *The Interpretation of Cultures*. NY: Basic Books.

Geertz, Clifford (1978), "The Bazaar Economy: Information and Search in Peasant Marketing", *American Economic Review*, 68, 2 (May), 28-32.

Goffman, Erving (1959), *The Presentation of Self in Everyday Life*, Garden City. NY: Doubleday.

Kapchan, Deborah (1996), *Gender on the Market, Moroccan Women and the Revoicing of Tradition*, University of Pennsylvania Press, Philadelphia.

Holt, Douglas B. (2002) "Why Do Brands Cause Trouble? A Dialectical Theory of Consumer Culture and Branding", *Journal of Consumer Research* 29 (June): 70–90

Marcuse, Herbert (1964), *One-Dimensional Man: Studies in the Ideology of Advanced Industrial Society*, Beacon Street Press: Boston.

Mejri, Mohammed and Mohammed Lajili (2007), *Recherche sur la distribution moderne*, l'Univers Du Livre.

Miller, Daniel (1995) (Ed.), *Worlds Apart - Modernity Through the Prism of the Local*, Routledge: London.

Oswald, Laura R. (1999), "Culture Swapping: Consumption and the Ethnogenesis of Middle-Class Haitian Immigrants", Journal of Consumer Research, 25 (March), 303-18

Peñaloza, Lisa (1994), "Border Crossing: A Critical Ethnographic Exploration of the Consumer Acculturation of Mexican Immigrants", *Journal of Consumer Research*, 21 (June), 32-54.

Regany, Fatima, Luca Visconti and Marie-Helene Fosse-Gomez (2012) A Closer Glance at the Notion of Boundaries in Acculturation Studies: Typologies, Intergenerational Divergences, and Consumer Agency, Consumer Culture Theory Conference, Oxford, 16-19 august 2012

Ritzer, Georges (2004), *The Globalization of Nothing*, California: Pine Forge Press, Thousand Oaks

Sadiqi, Fatima (2003), "Women and Linguistic Space in Morocco", *Women Language*, 26 (Spring), 35-43.

Sandikci, Ozlem and Guliz Ger (2002), "In-between modernities and postmodernities : theorizing turkisch consumptionscape", in *Advances in Consumer Research*, 29, eds. Susan M. Broniarczyk and Kent Nakamoto, Valdosta, 465-470.

Tauber, Edward M. (1972), Why do people shop?, *Journal of Marketing*, 36, October, 46-59.

Thompson, Craig. J. and Zeyned Arsel (2004), "The Starbucks Brandscape and Consumers' (Anticorporate) Experiences of Glocalization," *Journal of Consumer Research,* 31 (December). 631-42**.**

Üstüner, Tuba and Douglas. B. Holt (2007), "Dominated Consumer Acculturation: The Social Construction of Poor Migrant Women's Consumer Identity Projects in a Turkish Squatter », *Journal of Consumer Research*, 34 (June), 41-56

Varman, Rohit and Russell W. Belk (2008), "Weaving the web: subaltern consumers, rising consumer culture and television", *Marketing Theory*, 8 (3), 227-252

Wallendorf, Melanie, Russell Belk, and Deborah Heisley (1988), "Deep Meaning in Possessions", *Advances in Consumer Research*, 15, 528-530.

Zhao, X. and Russell W. Belk (2008), "Politicizing consumer culture: Advertising appropriation of political ideology in social China transition", *Journal of Consumer Research*, 35 (August), 231-44

Understanding Sub-Cultural Identity and Consumption Among Indians in the United States: From Desis to Coconuts

Minita Sanghvi, University of North Carolina Greensboro, USA
Nancy Hodges, University of North Carolina Greensboro, USA

ABSTRACT

Much has been written regarding the multifaceted, fragmented relationship between ethnicity, identity and consumption (Burton, 2009), especially since Belk's (1988) seminal piece on possessions and the extended self. Consumption among wide-ranging subcultural groups has been investigated, including fundamental Christians (O'Guinn & Belk, 1989), Harley Davidson aficionados (Schouten & Alexander, 1995), gays (Kates, 2002), Burning Man constituents (Kozinets, 2005), and many others. Consumption is a critical piece in the formation of subcultural identities and a site where common values and meanings related to brands and products are shared (Kates, 2002; Mehta & Belk, 1991). Belk (1988) suggests that shared consumption helps identify group membership and define group self. Specific brands are intrinsically related to subcultural identities and help create boundaries from the dominant culture that foster group identity. However, consumption in contemporary subcultural contexts is often fraught with countervailing and ever shifting meanings (Kates, 2002).

Kates (2002 p. 384) defines a subculture "as a way of life expressing shared meanings and practices different from or oppositional to dominant, mainstream culture." Members share a common goal, an area of interest or band together because they are in minority to a dominant culture. There are voluntary subcultures based on interest or brand consumption as well as subcultures based on race, ethnicity or sexuality where the members group together because of lack of power or discrimination issues. Race and ethnicity, as cultural conditions play a pivotal role in the consumption practice of various individuals, and especially immigrants (Sekhon, 2007; Venkatesh, 1995). Immigrants often choose to hold on to certain patterns of culture and identity that connect them to their culture of origin through consumption (Sekhon, 2007).

This study looks at the interplay of ethnicity, identity and consumption within the Indian sub-culture living in the United States. While there have been some studies about the consumption habits of the Indian diaspora within the British-Indian milieu (Lindridge, 2010; Lindridge & Dhillon, 2005; Lindridge & Hogg, 2006; Sekhon, 2007; Sekhon & Szmigin, 2011), as well some among the American-Indian diaspora (Bhatia, 2007; Mehta & Belk, 1991) there is often a propensity among researchers to lump ethnic minorities having common ancestry as an analogous group (Lindridge, 2010). However, the Indian diaspora is diverse, comprised of a multitude of languages, religions, and ethnicities, making it difficult to combine them into one homogenous group. Thus, Lindridge (2010) suggests that it is critical to uncover and understand the various subcultures within a diaspora who have their own unique consumption habits and rituals. Our study identifies and explains the continuum of identities within subcultures of the Indian diaspora, specifically from *Desis* to *Coconuts*. *Desi* is a neutral term used by Indians to refer to their compatriots in the Indian diaspora. On the other end is the *Coconut,* a derogatory term used to describe Indian immigrants who act contrary to the parent culture's norms and group expectations by aligning themselves to the dominant, white culture. That is, they are brown on the outside but white on the inside.

Consumption is a critical aspect within the Indian diaspora and members often use consumption to showcase the degree of acceptance or rejection of cultural norms within the community (Lindridge

& Hogg, 2006; Sekhon, 2007). Our study reveals how consumption patterns are the primary mode of identifying and delineating *desis* and *coconuts*.

LITERATURE REVIEW

In this section, we begin with a historical analysis of the Indian diaspora, after which we analyze intersections of culture, ethnicity and identity as related to consumer culture to build a foundation for delving specifically into identity and consumption within the subculture of the Indian community residing in United States.

Indians in the United States

While the first known records of Indians entering the United States date back to 1820 most researchers have concluded it was that the Immigration and Nationality act in 1965 that brought a wave of Indian immigrants to the United States (Bhatia, 2007; Jacoby & Bal, 2007; Mehta & Belk, 1991). These individuals were mostly doctors, engineers, scientists, university professors or graduate students (Bhatia, 2007).

The Indian population's higher education levels and elevated job profiles afforded them a successful start (Mehta & Belk, 1991) and they have continued to succeed ever since. Indians account for less than 1% of the total US population yet they constitute 3% of engineers and 8% of physicians and surgeons in the U.S. (Richwine, 2009). They are considered the model minority for their academic, economic and social success as compared to the Latino and African-American minorities (Bhatia, 2007). It is no surprise that Indians consider achievement and success to be an intrinsic part of their identity and culture (Bhatia, 2007).

Identity, ethnicity and culture

Identity is a complex phenomenon that involves several parts of self. Factors such as culture, ethnicity, race, religion, sexuality, and language contribute towards a sense of self. To support the various parts of self, people consume an assortment of brands and products that they utilize to piece together and showcase their identity (Ahuvia, 2002; Belk, 1988). These products and brands are consumed not just for their functional value but also because they are symbolic and communicate cultural meaning (McCracken, 1986). The products and brands may represent different and sometimes even countervailing parts of the person's identity (Belk, 1988; Thompson & Haytko, 1997). Thus people may associate (or disassociate) with certain products and brands based on the cultural meanings they want to associate with. Consequently elements that contribute to a sense of self such as culture and ethnicity factor into a consumer's product and brand choices.

Identity is not a fixed construct, rather it is dynamic in nature, evolving continuously to integrate new possibilities and forms with old traditions and creating a dialogical model that is often conflicted, contested and countervailing (Bhatia, 2007; Lindridge, Hogg & Shah, 2004). There are several elements, both inherent and acquired, that influence identity. Among them race and ethnicity are inherent and unchangeable. However, culture is not inherent, rather it is acquired, often from family or members of society that the individual is attached to or inclined toward (Wallendorf & Reilly, 1983). Culture is a product of history as well as present day practices and evolves constantly to combat and inculcate various aspects of old and new traditions simultaneously. Culture represents a critical context for identity formation as well as identification, and provides a framework for social life and consumption (Lindridge, Hogg & Shah, 2004). An individual's identity is a part of the culture in which the individual chooses to exist. However, for an immigrant that often involves spanning at least two or more cultures comprising often disjointed and conflicting expectations within one identity. It is no surprise then that Belk (1988) suggests not just one product, rather an ensemble of consumption objects, represent the various, protean and countervailing aspects of the self.

An individual's identification with a specific culture is also identifiable by ethnicity, where an individual organizes themselves and others into specific groups by using ethnic labels (Lindridge & Dhillon, 2005). In other words, sometimes culture and ethnicities are interchangeable. For example, an individual may be white (ethnicity), but being southern comprises his or her culture. The dominant society assumes that because one belongs to a certain race or ethnicity; one must emulate the culture and traditions associated with it (Kibria, 2002). Belonging to a certain ethnicity automatically associates an individual with the culture of that particular ethnicity. That is, the values, religion, etiquette, language and customs inherent to that ethnicity (Lindridge, Hogg & Shah, 2004; Venkatesh, 1995). While ethnicity encompasses several identifiers such as race, religion, nationality, and language and is used to define the social identity of a person or group, it is not just a summation, rather a complex interplay of identifiers, especially within sub-ethnic groups (Lindridge, Hogg & Shah, 2004; Venkatesh, 1995). Cultures are constantly negotiating the past and the present, as well as contemporary versus traditional values and particularly within diasporic communities (Lindridge & Hogg, 2006). Individuals, families and communities as a whole are involved in this process as they evolve and adapt to their surroundings.

Indian identity

India is an amalgamation of various religions, languages, traditions and customs with Persian, Arabic, Tibetan, Portuguese, and English influences enmeshed over several centuries. India encompasses over 22 official languages and is home to several religions such as Hinduism, Islam, Buddhism and Sikhism. Thus, the Indian immigrant comes from a land that is as varied as it is vast, making it difficult to establish a single, homogenous Indian identity.

For the Indian immigrant, the question of identity is directly related to how the nation is remembered in the minds of individuals within a diasporic community (Bhatia, 2007). Thus, what it means to be an Indian depends on what the population deems Indian behavior or Indian culture. However, identities are shaped by personal memories and connotations that are not necessarily universal. Moreover, identities are often in a state of constant flux as cultures mix and move creating a myriad of experiences, some of which may be conflicting (Bhatia, 2007; Meamber & Venkatesh, 2001).

Bhatia (2007) writes, "the migrant community imagines and stitches together diverse notions of 'Indianness,' which are shaped by the members' class positions back home, nostalgia, memories, emotions, and longing for the original *desi* nation and culture of their homeland" (emphasis in original) (p. 14). Moreover, there is significant variation within the Indian sub-culture based on language, religion, ethnicity, etc., and this variation is rarely addressed in research. For example, a south Indian's perspective of what it means to be an Indian may be drastically different from that of someone from the north (Cardon, 2010).

Being Indian is not based on skin color alone, but by the way a person talks or behaves. Being Indian is measured by others via the norms within the culture. Thus, the community decides how "Indian" someone is and can pass judgment on that person's "Indianness" regardless of whether or not the individual agrees. The person who embraces the group ideal of Indianness is known as a *desi*, while for someone who deviates from the norm, the term *coconut* is often applied. Indian migrants have a complicated relationship with their ethnic identity. Although they are proud of their Indian culture and heritage, many shy away from displaying their Indianness in the United States for fear of negative effects on their social and professional lives (Bhatia, 2007). This largely stems from a feeling of inferiority about being brown skinned after nearly two hundred years of British rule, when race was employed as a cultural product used to dominate people in colonies like India (Singh, 2007).

After studying the relationships between the White and Black races in French colonies, Fanon (1967) theorized that the White colonizers consider themselves superior to people of color and that the people of color "want to prove to White men, at all costs, the richness of their thought, the equal value of their intellect" (Fanon, 1967 p. 10). Gaining approval from colonizers often lead to economic success and social standing, for which one had to give up their original culture and act white (Fanon, 1967). Acting white meant, among other things, talking English instead of the native language, adopting white customs and habits such as eating with a fork and knife versus eating with hands or with a spoon as is popular in India, and so forth. According to Fanon, this leads to an inferiority complex, wherein one internalizes these values while suffering from dislocation with one's native culture, and results in a feeling of separation from one's compatriots (Fanon, 1967). Fanon (1967) suggests the inferiority complex is particularly intense among the most educated who have to deal with the perceived 'betrayal' to their race, culture and identity on a day-to-day basis.

Although India gained independence in 1947, traces of internalization after approximately two hundred years of being colonized still exist. For example, many Indians still use creams such as *Fair and Lovely* to lighten their skin in an attempt to improve social standing and marriage prospects in the community. Indian immigrants who choose to leave their country for the ways of the west have a more agitated sense of identity. They adopt western customs in the workplace in order to succeed but resist assimilating by creating close-knit ties to the *desi* community in the USA whereby they try to keep the native culture alive (Bhatia, 2007). A certain resistance to western culture is thus expected from all Indian immigrants. An Indian immigrant who adapts to western culture too easily is seen as someone who has betrayed their race and can be ostracized within the *desi* community.

Thus, there are values about what an Indian migrant must "be like" to remain Indian enough in the eyes of the other Indians. *Coconuts*, or Indians who do not act Indian enough, are usually rejected by the broader Indian community. Consequently, some *coconuts* seek to align themselves with the dominant culture. By embracing white culture, they effectively distance themselves from the Indian sub-culture. However, their acceptance in the mainstream culture is not necessarily guaranteed, and as Lindridge and Dhillon (2005) point out, marginalization, or the rejection of the individual by the dominant culture as well as their own ethnic sub-culture, can lead to self-destructive behaviors such as substance abuse or isolation.

Consumption in the Indian community

Our possessions help create and communicate our identity and are often linked to our past as well as our present (Belk, 1988; Lindridge & Dhillon, 2005; Mehta & Belk, 1991). Objects produce a shared sense of belonging to a specific time, place or culture. Shared consumption defines group membership (Belk, 1988), and aids in ethnic group formation, as well as creating and maintaining boundaries, especially in the context of social interactions with other groups (Lindridge, Hogg & Shah, 2004). Moreover, consumption can be used as a symbolic marker providing instant non-verbal identification with a certain ethnic group and a mode of creating a culturally derived self-identity (Lindridge & Dhillon, 2005).

Within the diaspora, the Indian ethnic sub-culture uses consumption as a means of negotiating the multiple identities that an individual must use to traverse the various cultures he or she encounters on a daily basis. The relative variability of consumption within the sub-culture reflects the degree to which the individual relies on the group for identification (Belk, 1988). Thus an individual can use consumption to assimilate into, as well as disassociate from, the dominant culture as well as their own ethnic sub-culture (Lindridge & Dhillon, 2005).

Since the Indian community strongly values achievement and success, members often seek external validation within society through conspicuous consumption. Consumption is therefore used proactively as a tool to indicate rank and position, a way to gain respect, approval and even offers of marriage (Sekhon, 2007). For this reason the literature suggests that conspicuous consumption is important within the Indian community (Lindridge & Dhillon, 2005; Lindridge & Hogg, 2006; Sekhon, 2007). A person's cultural worth or status can often be deciphered through brands of clothes, cars, and so on (Lindridge & Dhillon, 2005; Lindridge & Hogg, 2006). Status is showcased and maintained via material possessions and is considered a natural part of being Indian (Sekhon, 2007). The opposite is also true wherein strong disassociations with certain brands are equally important.

An ideal balance of identity is difficult to achieve, as it is a moving target, created by the members of the sub-culture based on locally defined expectations and norms. As such, Indians who stray too far out of that ideal sub-cultural norm are deemed *coconuts* (not Indian enough) while people who identify themselves firmly with the ethnic sub-culture are considered too *desi* (too Indian).

METHOD

The goal of this study is to identify and understand the subcultures within the Indian diaspora by delving into the experiences of members of the Indian-American community and investigating their consumption patterns vis-à-vis the dominant Indian sub-culture. We use the ethno-consumerist methodology espoused by Meamber and Venkatesh (2001) as a basis for our research design in order to ensure that the various voices in this study are interpreted within their own multi-cultured context. Meamber and Venkatesh (2001) argue that it is imperative that culture be studied not as a backdrop to consumer behavior but rather to position consumption as a culturally constituted activity. The ethno-consumerist framework relies on the following tenets: (a) behavior is grounded in culture; (b) cultural categories are dependent upon both historical and socio-cultural forces as well as current practices; and (c) culture is constantly changing and, therefore so are the categories of culture (Lindridge & Hogg, 2006 p. 985).

The research was undertaken in two concurrent stages. The first consisted of review and analysis of relevant concepts in the literature providing a foundation for the study purpose. The second consisted of primary data collection in the form of focus groups and interviews with ten first generation immigrant men and women from India. Participants represent Indian immigrants in diverse regions across US

and differing socio-economic backgrounds, including working professionals, housewives, and students. Participants were from both large and small towns, with some having lived in the United States for several decades and others coming relatively "fresh off the boat" (also known as "FOB"). In as much as participants immigrated after the economic liberalization of India, they come from a rapidly developing economy, therefore their experiences and viewpoints are probably divergent from the Indians who left the impoverished third world country that India was in the 1960s. Participants come from both northern and southern India. Participants were recruited via a purposive sample approach to ensure a holistic study of identity, culture and consumption as experienced among the Indian community living in the United States.

Interviews were semi-structured to ensure that the participant had enough latitude to express him or herself while remaining on topic (Lindridge & Hogg, 2006). This approach allowed us to capture the participant's own viewpoints, understand the cultural nuances in their own words and glean insights from their particular experiences (Lindridge & Hogg, 2006). Interviews lasted from 1-2 hours each and were audio recorded with their consent. Once focus groups and interviews were complete, each was transcribed verbatim and the transcripts were read and re-read to establish preliminary codes. The process of coding, categorizing, and iteration as outlined by Spiggle (1994) was followed.

The following interpretation provides a window into the Indian immigrant's worldview. Excerpts from the data help illustrate the major findings. Pseudonyms are used to protect participant identity. As consumption is a critical aspect within the Indian diaspora and because members often use consumption to showcase the degree of acceptance or rejection of cultural norms within the community, we use consumption as the primary mode of identifying and delineating *coconuts* and *desis*. A thematic interpretation of the data resulted in the identification of four themes, (a) *bridging the gap*, (b) *communal influence*, (c) *breaking away*, and (d) *evolution of the immigrant identity*.

FINDINGS AND INTERPRETATION

Before we analyze the consumption patterns of *desis* and *coconuts*, we need to first understand how pre-immigration contact with the United States through word-of-mouth, media, and tourism affects the immigrant's worldview (Peñaloza, 1994). Shortly after economic liberalization in 1991 many Indians saw brisk economic growth in India and an influx of western brands. As one participant, Manpreet, explains, "And then mid-90's to late 90's the American brands started popping up (in India). I think Bollywood cinema was also influenced by that. You would see film stars were wearing designer shoes and big brands." Moreover, this generation grew up around movies such as *Kuch Kuch Hota Hai* (1997) and *Mohabbatein* (2000) in which Bollywood film stars portraying cool college kids were sporting brands such as Gap, Nike and Ralph Lauren Polo. Brands such as Levis and Nike, which had set up shop in India, quickly became the cool brands. Brands such as Gap and Ralph Lauren Polo gained prestige and status since they could be acquired on trips abroad by the wealthy and ultimately became aspirational brands for the middle-class urban Indian who did not have access to them in India. Beyond a few specific brands, knowledge of brands and brand culture remained fairly limited in India by the late 1990's.

Bridging the gap

Coming from this mind-set, when Indian immigrants land in the United States, they often feel overwhelmed in the American consumerscape. Suddenly they are exposed to a plethora of brands that they have never heard of and many participants indicated feeling lost when they first arrived. They found that brands that were popular in India were not popular here. As Sanjana explains,

> After coming here, we face sometimes an identity conflict. You know, like Levis was my [favorite] product in India. Levis, I would wear Levis jeans. I would go to the store, buy Levis. But when I came here [there were] all these different brands. Levis, nobody wears Levis. Levis was like OK here. So first, it took me a while to actually explore what brands do people wear, what is higher, what is lower. Still I'm learning, because still I don't fit into that...In India you know what is good, what is bad, you just know what brands [are cool], but here brands have different meaning. You just get lost sometimes.

Newly arrived immigrants will often seek out brands that help to bridge the gap between the two cultures. Similar to Peñaloza's (1994) experience with Mexican immigrants, Indian immigrants also use brands to maintain ties to their previous cultures even as they work on building a new identity in the United States. They do so in different ways based on brands or styles, as Priyanka says, "When an Indian consumer comes to US they try to fit in between US and India...You try to be little modern as well as you have to maintain a little conservative culture of India. So like instead of deep [cut] neck [line], you will buy sleeveless but make sure it's not very deep. You know you just try to maintain a balance."

Some bought brands that had name recognition within the Indian diaspora. Nikita suggests, "Indians...often lean towards brands that are also prestigious/ recognizable in India...like Nike over Puma, Gap over Eddie Bauer." Nandini furthers the point, "Brands which are visible to others, Indians love. Like a Harvard degree! Those [brands] which are not visible, I think, they are less interested in." Manpreet adds, "When you wear these [well-known] brands or shop in certain places, you know, you're making a statement to others too. I guess they are trying to say, 'Hey look, I have arrived or look at the hard work I did and where I am.' And I think it is...an ego boost"

Respondents also pointed out that Indians are apathetic to the social or environmental policies of the manufacturers and retailers in their fervent search for a good deal. As Nikita says, "Most Indians will not give a damn about the social policies of a store." Words such as frugal, price sensitive, looking for deals, and bargain hunting, all surfaced frequently. Eesha discloses that she buys name brands, but only if she can get them at a significant discounted rate. "I don't mind spending a little extra time...I would only shop at TJ Maxx or Marshalls. A lot of Indians won't say it." It is important to keep up the appearances of conspicuous consumption within the Indian community but is often done "on the sly" through outlets or off-price retailers. As Eesha explains, "It's a prestige issue. They want to talk about Neiman Marcus or Louis Vuitton but they don't want to talk about how they got a good deal. They want to pose superior financially for their peers, with everybody. It's in the culture." When asked to contrast Indian consumption behavior with that of mainstream American, price was a fairly common distinction.

Communal influence

Frequently, new immigrants are taken under the wing of large Indian groups and 'tutored' on the ways of American life, including what and how to consume. This process may start even before they arrive in the USA. Nikita points out that "most Indian students abroad usually enroll in these Indian community groups" which offer pick-up services for Indian students from airports and accommodations with Indian students or families for the first week or two. Participants talk about how Indians tend to stick together, travelling

together, socializing frequently and even making communal buying decisions. This trend is reflected in movies such as *The Namesake*, where the main character Nikhil tells his American girlfriend about his communal family vacations involving various Bengali (a subgroup based on language within the Hindu religion) families, riding together in mini-vans, stopping for eight course Indian lunches at rest stops. Similarly, the book of the same name discusses how the Bengali families often confer with each other before making any major purchases. Manpreet adds, "Within your little community... there are collaborative decisions made about what you would buy or where you would shop...if you go shop [elsewhere]...in some ways your loyalty in that community is threatened. So you would conform more towards that." As Rohan puts it, you are not pressured to conform to the group, "Instead of peer pressure [to conform to the group], it is peer influence." However, not everyone saw this influence in a positive light. For example, Manpreet felt forced to act "more Indian" to fit in among the Indian diaspora.

> When I came to (a particular city in US), I started socializing with all the Indians there. When I would go to all these parties and... the [elder Indians] were...shocked at what kind of clothes I was wearing. To the point that they said I should not be wearing such clothes. I was aghast. When I was in India, my parents were not so conservative, and then I went to school in Bombay and I wore all kinds of clothes. I'm sure when I came they expected me to be an Indian from India and to be and eat and wear a certain way. And I was forced to be more Indian than I ever was.

Faced with such pressure to conform, many decide to break away and choose their own path, often aligning themselves to the dominant white culture and as a result are typically referred to as *coconuts*.

Breaking away

Coconuts are those individuals viewed as betraying Indian culture by the larger Indian subculture. That is, someone who eschews expectations of the collectivist culture of a tightly knit Indian community to venture out on their own within the American consumption landscape. Manpreet explains that being a *coconut* is not about acting white as much as it is about rejecting the Indian community.

> I think it is more to do with the fact that you're not conforming to what you are first. Or dismissing your true identity to identify in the white culture. I think that for somebody, say for an Indian, it would mean maybe you're not proud to be an Indian or you're ashamed to be an Indian. You're trying your best to disassociate yourself from it. So that's why you would be termed a *coconut* by your community.

Sanjana adds, "[Coconuts] think Indians are inferior." *Coconuts* are seen as individuals who reject their Indian identity and embrace all things western, often white, and more specifically, liberal white. Nandini referred to the website and book, *Stuff White People Like* (SWPL) in her description of *coconuts*, "Every single thing on SWPL – I am. Camping in the woods? Check. Attending art exhibits and blithely discussing artists? Check. We are such a cliché, heading off to the farmer's market every week with our canvas bags and with our baby strapped to us"

According to the participants, *coconuts* prefer to hang out with Americans versus Indians and thus have more American friends than Indian friends. They are more brand conscious and less price conscious as compared to the average Indian immigrant. Moreover, they are more embedded in American politics and often make buying decisions not based on price, but on the social policies or reputation of a retailer of manufacturer. As Nikita explains,

> I think coconuts in general are more likely to care about politics, which translates into policies on a micro scale. I think coconuts don't view America as a "foreign country." There is some involvement even if it's passive in the countries policies/issues. And by default it trickles into how companies behave politically. For example, as a personal issue I care deeply about gay rights and will not enter a store that discriminates against gay people but most Indians I know will not give a damn because it is not something that affects them personally.

Both Nandini and Nikita have embraced the term *coconut*, however Sharmila sees it as a derogatory term. She feels that she is different from other Indians in that she focuses on "being independent…valuing privacy…not seeking out other Indians" as well as breaking away from stereotypical molds and expectations of Indian women such as pre-marital sex or going to bars, all of which makes her stand out among other Indian females.

Obviously there are several reasons why someone is labeled a *coconut* and why *coconut* behavior is understood as a contradiction to the more expected *desi*-like behavior. Indeed, there is a marked difference in consumption habits of *desis* and *coconuts*. From sports to music, language to travel, participants enumerated several examples of typical *desi* consumption habits vis-à-vis *coconuts*. These differences are illustrated in Table 1.

Evolution of an Indian immigrant's identity

Those participants who self-identify as *coconuts* also see themselves as Indians. As Nandini explains, "I still feel profoundly Indian. Carrying the baby close, shopping at an open air market with my own bags is so very Indian, when I think about it." Similarly Sharmila argued that even though she considered herself outside of the Indian community, "I don't consider myself less Indian." Manpreet says her brother was called a *coconut* by fellow Indian graduate students for playing soccer, including taking off his shirt on the field and having American friends. However, she attests that none of this was unusual behavior for her brother. "I've seen him play back in India. He would take his shirt off all the time." In the same vein, she explained that her brother made American friends while his roommates stuck to their own core Indian group and that this stems from their unique upbringing:

> The fact (is) that my father was in the army and we changed schools every two-years, we had to make new friends, new teachers, so you had to learn to adapt pretty quickly. That just became a part of life. And the fact is when you've travelled across India and don't grow up in a certain region; your level of comfort with new people is just there. So it makes it easier to blend in.

Allegations of being a *coconut* in such instances are a means of passing judgment on someone who is deemed not Indian enough. Nandini, Nikita, Manpreet, all lived in large cities in India and grew up in fairly liberal households which enabled them to blend in with the American fabric more easily once they immigrated.

Table 1: Consumption habits of Desis and Coconuts

	Desis	Coconuts
General Characteristics	Inquisitive. Share a lot of personal information within the Indian social circle.	Value privacy and independence
Food	Mostly Indian food. Sometimes they will eat other cuisines	Will eat various cuisines, will sometimes eat Indian food
Restaurants	Prefer restaurant chains	Prefer local restaurants and diners
Music	Indian music or mainstream American such as Kanye West and Lady Gaga	Indie or lesser known bands
Movies	Bollywood, Tollywood and mainstream American movies	Prefer indie movies, foreign films, documentaries
Retailers	Costco, Wal-Mart, TJ Maxx	Target, Thrift Stores, etc.
Friends	Mostly Indian friends	Mostly American friends
Ties to the community	Join Indian associations, go to temple/Gurdwara/mosque regularly, socialize mostly with Indians	Does not join Indian association, may go to the temple/Gurdwara, mosque sometimes or never, doesn't socialize with Indians
Sports	Play carrom, chess, cricket or badminton	Play tennis, soccer or other American sports
Shopping	Care mainly about price	Care mainly about fashion and style
Grocery Shopping	Prefer mainstream grocery stores	Prefer stores like Whole Foods, Trader Joe's and farmers markets
Travel	Prefer going to India. When traveling within USA will travel with other Indian families.	Prefer traveling by themselves or with American friends. Often engage in outdoor activities and adventures such as camping and hiking.
Language	Will talk mostly in the regional language at home.	Will talk almost exclusively in English.

The process of integrating or "becoming Americanized," as Gayatri puts it, is a slow process for most Indian immigrants. However, in the case of a *coconut*, because of their background, culture, upbringing or general willingness, this process may be fast-forwarded several years, thus making them not Indian enough in the eyes of the general Indian diaspora.

All participants felt that some identity issues were common among the immigrant population. Likewise, the tension between their Indian identity and their American identity was prevalent among all participants. Many of the participants said that when they were newly arrived, they felt their compatriot's accent or way of talking was a bit different, and that there was a marked difference between the newly immigrated Indian's accent and that of someone who had lived here for a long time. However, as years went by, the participants realized that they too had picked up the slight accent necessary to be better understood by Americans. Gayatri explains that being an Indian immigrant is a constant process where one changes little by little while adapting to American culture.

Discussion

Among the Indian immigrant community it is expected that each individual will go through the integration process. However, the *desi* community in the United States, in an attempt to seek control in a non-native land, sets up narrowly defined expectations as to how much and how quickly an Indian immigrant must integrate. Consequently, people on either extreme are frowned upon.

However, participants believe that some do a better job of integrating in the American culture than others depending on the region that they come from in India . For example, Sanjana, who is from North India contends, "I'm not being biased here, but I personally think that North Indians, they adapt. They look better, they adapt [more] easily than girls from South India." In contrast, Gayatri, who is from South India, argues, "It is not about the state, it is about the place that they come from…if you compare someone from a small village…possibly the girl might not be exposed to the city life." Nikhil, on the other hand, suggests that men do a better job of acculturating to the western way of dressing than women. Thus we see a North-South divide, a gender divide or even a rural versus urban lifestyle divide playing pivotal roles in immigrants' consumption habits.

Being too *desi* is a sign of failure. It implies that the person is incapable of adapting to American culture. However, being a *coconut* is also considered a negative as it implies that the person suffers from an inferiority complex, having internalized western values and chosen to disassociate from his or her *desi* identity. However, as is indicated by the participant responses, the person may not be acting contrary to their culture at all, especially if they grew up in a liberal environment and/or adapt easily to diverse cultures.

The participants indicated that the *desi* community prefers an in-between stage, defined by an acceptable degree of assimilation while retaining significant aspects of the native identity. This stage is a mix of being assimilated, yet still Indian enough, thus being "Properly Americanized." Due to the cornucopia of identities and the varying degrees of integration and/or assimilation that can be found in the diaspora at any given time, we have represented them in a continuum shown in Figure 1. A continuum that spans the two poles helps reflect the journey and the varying transformations immigrants go through when they are away from their homeland.

**Figure 1. From *desis* to *coconuts* –
the continuum of varying degrees of Indianness**

Too *desi*	Properly Americanized	Coconut

I--I--I

Each newly immigrated Indian can be placed on the continuum based on past experiences, travels, culture, upbringing, and so on. Each individual makes his or her own journey and stops where he or she feels most comfortable with their culture and identity. Those who are "properly Americanized" will have Indian as well as American friends and eat Indian as well as American food, but the longer they stay in the country, the more they gravitate toward *coconut* side of the Indianness continuum.

CONCLUSION

From *desis* to *coconuts*, immigrant identities are wrought with conflicting desires, and consumption choices often help people stitch together an identity that represents the self to themselves and others (Ahuvia, 2005). Today, a consumer with a fragmented identity or sense of self does not have to reconcile contradictions but can incorporate them using products to signify association (Ahuvia, 2005). Yet, by choosing different paths of consumption, individuals can align with or be alienated from their ethnic culture.

This paper uses Fanon's perspective on race discrimination and internalization to frame an understanding of the *coconut* subculture and overlay the politics of identity in the consumption context for this particular immigrant community. In the United States immigrants play a pivotal role in the creation of the national culture (Peñaloza, 1994), and while culture is a product of history (Burton, 2002) power structures between races are also a part of that history and serve to complicate matters of identity, especially within the diaspora. *Coconuts* are not just an Indian diasporic phenomenon; similar terms are also used within other ethnic sub-cultures. Insights from this study open the door for further research to understand how race relations, power structures and culture affect identity and consumption within various sub-cultures in a diaspora. The study adds value to the current body of consumption research by showcasing the intricate dynamics of consumption within a diaspora used to control, create and communicate identities and group identification. Moreover it posits that immigrant identities are in a state of constant flux, thereby making it impossible to fit them neatly into boxes. Instead these identities are better represented on a continuum.

REFERENCES

Ahuvia, A. C. (2005). Beyond the Extended Self: Loved Objects and Consumers' Identity Narratives. *Journal of Consumer Research*, *32*(1), 171-184.

Belk, R. (1988). Possessions and the extended self. *Journal of Consumer Research, 15*, 139-168.

Bhatia, S. (2007). *American karma: Race, culture, and identity in the Indian diaspora*. New York: New York University Press.

Burton, D. (2002). Towards a critical multicultural marketing theory. *Marketing Theory, 2*(2), 207-236.

Burton, D. (2009). "Reading whiteness in consumer research. *Consumption, Markets & Culture, 12*(2), 171-201.

Cardon, P. W. (2010). Using films to learn about the nature of cross-cultural stereotypes in intercultural business communication courses. *Business Communication Quarterly, 73*(2), 150-165.

Fanon, F. (1991). *Black skin, white masks*. New York: Grove Weidenfeld.

Jacoby, H. S., & Bal, A. S. (2007). *History of East Indians in America: The first half-century experience of Sikhs, Hindus and Muslims*. Amritsar, India: B. Chattar Singh Jiwan Singh.

Kates, S. M. (2002). The protean quality of subcultural consumption: An ethnographic account of gay consumers. *Journal of Consumer Research, 29*, 383-399.

Kibria, N. (2002). *Becoming Asian American: Second-generation Chinese and Korean American identities*. Baltimore: Johns Hopkins University Press.

Kozinets, R. V. (2002). Can consumers escape the market? Emancipatory illuminations from burning man. *Journal of Consumer Research, 29*(1), 20-38.

Lindridge, A. M., Hogg, M. K., & Shah, M. (2004). Imagined multiple worlds: How South Asian women in Britain use family and friends to navigate the "border crossings" between households and social contexts. *Consumption, Markets & Culture, 7*(3), 211-238.

Lindridge, A.M., & Dhillon, K. (2005). Cultural Role Confusion and Memories of a Lost Identity: How Non-Consumption Perpetuates Marginalisation. *Advances in Consumer Research, 32*(1), 408.

Lindridge, A. M., & Hogg, M. K. (2006). Parental Gate-keeping in Diasporic Indian Families: Examining the Intersection of Culture, Gender and Consumption. *Journal of Marketing Management, 22*(9/10), 979.

Lindridge, A. (2010). Are we fooling ourselves when we talk about ethnic homogeneity? : The case of religion and ethnic subdivisions amongst Indians living in Britain. *Journal Of Marketing Management, 26*(5/6), 441-472.

McCracken, G. (1986). Culture and consumption: A theoretical account of structure and movement of the cultural meaning of consumer goods. *Journal of Consumer Research, 13*, 71-83.

Meamber, Laurie A.. and Venkatesh, Alladi (2000) "Ethnoconsumerist Methodology for Cultural and Cross-Cultural Consumer Research", in Beckman, S. and Elliott, R. (Eds.) *Interpretive Consumer Research: Paradigms, Methodologies and Applications*, Copenhagen: Copenhagen Business School Press.

Mehta, R., & Belk, R. W. (1991). Artifacts, Identity, and Transition: Favorite Possessions of Indians and Indian Immigrants to the United States. *Journal of Consumer Research, 17*(4), 398-411

O'Guinn, T. O., & Belk, R. (1989). Heaven on earth: Consumption at Heritage Village, USA. *Journal of Consumer Research, 16*, 227-238.

Peñaloza, L. (1994). *Atravesando fronteras/* border crossings: A critical ethnographic exploration of the consumer acculturation of Mexican immigrants. *Journal of Consumer Research, 21*, 32-54.

Richwine, J. (2009, February 24). Indian Americans: The new model minority. *Forbes*, Retrieved from http://www.forbes.com/2009/02/24/bobby-jindal-indian-americans-opinions-contributors_immigrants_minority.html

Schouten, J. W., & McAlexander, J. H. (1995). Subcultures of consumption: An ethnography of the new bikers. *Journal of Consumer Research, 22*, 43-61.

Singh, H. (2007). Confronting colonialism and racism: Fanon and Gandhi. *Human Architecture: Journal of the Sociology of Self-Knowledge, 5*341-352

Sekhon, Y. K. (2007). 'From saris to sarongs' ethnicity and intergenerational influences on consumption among Asian Indians in the UK. *International Journal of Consumer Studies, 31*(2), 160

Sekhon, Y. K., & Szmigin, I. (2011). Acculturation and identity: Insights from second-generation Indian Punjabis. *Consumption, Markets & Culture, 14*(1), 79-98.

Spiggle, S. (1994). Analysis and interpretation of qualitative data in Consumer Research. *Journal of Consumer Research, 21*, 491-503.

Thompson, C. J., & Haytko, D. I. (1997). Speaking of fashion: Consumers' uses of fashion discourses and the appropriation of countervailing cultural meanings. *Journal of Consumer Research, 24*(1), 15-42.

U.S. Census Bureau. (2010). *2010 population distribution in the United States and Puerto Rico*. Washington, D. C.: US Census Bureau

Venkatesh, A. (1995) "Ethnoconsumerism: A New Paradigm to Study Cultural and Cross-Cultural Consumer Behaviour", in Costa, J. and Bamossy, G. (Eds.) *Marketing in a multicultural world-Ethnicity, Nationalism and Cultural Identity*, London: Sage Publications, 68-104.

Wallendorf, M. & Reilly, M. D. (1983). Ethnic migration, assimilation, and consumption. *Journal of Consumer Research, 10*, 292-302.

I Don't Need an Agreement on My Inconsistent Consumption Preferences: Multiple Selves and Consumption in Japan

Satoko Suzuki, Kyoto University, Japan
Akutsu Satoshi, Hitotsubashi University, Japan

ABSTRACT

This paper explores multiple selves and their inconsistent consumption preferences among East-Asians. The findings from 28 depth-interviews in Japan illustrate that East-Asians, contrary to Westerners, experience less psychological tension facing their inconsistent consumption preferences. They therefore have less need to find an agreement among inconsistencies. Dialectical thinking theory is employed to understand cultural differences towards contradictions. East Asian cultures tend to more tolerate psychological contradiction, whereas Western cultures are less comfortable with contradiction. Our research also suggests the absence of consumers' need for a coherent identity narrative in Japan, whereas in Western cultures, particularly in North America, consumers seek to reconcile identity contradictions. From the childhood, Japanese learn to shift between multiple selves. This norm is called *kejime*, the ability to make distinctions. Hence, Japanese consumers are culturally accustomed to shifting among multiple selves than to pursuing a consistent global self-concept.

Today, it has become common to view consumers' selves as involving multiplicity (Gergen 1981; Markus and Wurf 1987). We now have a great deal of information and choices about who we want to be. Multiple selves often involve inconsistent views and affect consumer behavior. Hence, many consumer studies have examined multiple selves and consumption (e.g., Ahuvia 2005; Bahl and Milne 2010; Firat and Shultz 2001; Firat and Venkatesh 1995; Schenk and Holman 1980; Schouten 1991; Tian and Belk 2005).

Yet, little attention has been focused on the issue of whether the findings apply to consumers around the globe. Although consumers from different cultures may vary in their response to inconsistent consumption preferences, the majority of research has been conducted in the U.S. Indeed, recent studies in cultural psychology have identified that cultures differ in the tolerance towards contradiction (Peng and Nisbett 1999). More particularly, East Asian cultures tend to more tolerate psychological contradiction (Spencer-Rodgers, Williams, and Peng 2010), whereas Western cultures are less comfortable with contradiction (Festinger 1957; Lewin 1951). In this article, we explore the various implications of multiple selves and consumption among Japanese.

This article is organized as follows. In the first section, we review the existing literature on the multiple selves and consumption; then we discuss synthetic versus dialectical thinking. In the second section, we describe our methodology used in this study. In the third section, based on the data gathered from the Japanese participants, we argue that Japanese consumers experience no significant psychological tension facing own inconsistent consumption preferences. In the fourth section, we discuss our findings. Finally in the fifth section, we provide limitations in our study and suggestions for future directions.

CONCEPTUAL FOUNDATIONS

Multiple Selves and Consumption

In the literature discussing multiple selves and consumption, the term 'conflict' has been used frequently. For example, Bahl and Milne (2010) state in their study on the dialogical self that navigates through inconsistent consumption preferences that "dialog is used to manage *conflict*…to avoid *conflict*" (190, emphasis added). Ahuvia (2005) also states in his study on the role of loved objects in the construction of a coherent identity narrative that "consumers attempt to reconcile identity *conflicts*" (181, emphasis added). The researchers seem to implicitly presume that consumers' inconsistent consumption preferences or inconsistencies among multiple selves are in conflict with each other.

Bahl and Milne (2010) define conflict using Janis (1959) and Emmons and King (1988). Janis (1959) defines conflict as "opposing tendencies within an individual, which *interfere with the formulation, acceptance, or execution of a decision*" (as cited in Bahl and Milne 2010, emphasis added). Emmons and King (1988) define it as "a situation in which one goal striving is *seen by an individual as interfering* with the achievement of other strivings in the individual's striving system" (as cited in Bahl and Milne 2010, emphasis added). Both definitions consider that in conflict, an individual regards the situation as interfering. Based on these two definitions, Bahl and Milne (2010) provide more nuanced understanding of conflict; however, they consider conflict as one *hindering* the other. Hence, there is an implied meaning of confrontation among consumers' inconsistent consumption preferences or inconsistencies among multiple selves.

However, the term 'inconsistent' does not necessary imply confrontations. According to the *Merriam-Webster Online Dictionary*, inconsistent is defined as "lacking consistency: as a) not compatible with another fact or claim; b) containing incompatible elements; c) incoherent or illogical in thought or actions: changeable; d) not satisfiable by the same set of values for the unknowns." We feel that the view towards inconsistency as conflicting may be culturally limited. This will be further explained in the next section.

Another common trait identified in the existing literature on multiple selves and consumption is that consumers usually seek to reconcile differences and achieve coherence in their identity. Although Firat and Venkatesh (1995) see the postmodern consumers as possessing multiple selves with no need to reconcile identity contradictions, researchers have not found many examples of consumers abandoning the desire for a coherent identity narrative. Thompson and Hirschman (1995) deny Firat and Venkatesh's claim as an "optimistic theoretical construction" (151). Thompson and Haytko (1997) and Murray (2002) find that young adults experience a tension in their sense of identity as they strive to be both unique individuals and part of a group, and they use fashion to resolve this tension. The plurality of fashion discourses allows diverse interpretive positions, enabling consumers to find meaning by contrasting opposing values and beliefs. These "countervailing meanings" are used by consumers to moderate tensions arising from their efforts to develop a sense of individual agency (i.e., distinction) and perceptions of social prescription (i.e., social integration). The study by Ahuvia (2005) also shows that consumers attempt to reconcile identity conflicts using three strategies labeled "demarcating," "compromising," and "synthesizing" solutions. However, this need for coherence in self-identity may also be culturally specific.

In extending multiple selves and consumption theory beyond the Western cultural realm, we question the view of consumers' navigation of inconsistent consumption preferences as management or avoidance of identity conflicts. We also question the view of consumers as having the desire for the coherent identity narrative. Cultural differences in the tolerance towards contradictions will be discussed next.

Synthetic versus Dialectical Thinking

Culturally shared folk epistemologies influence people's reasoning about contradiction and their tolerance for ambiguity (Peng and Nisbett 1999). Western psychology has largely assumed that individuals are uncomfortable with incongruity and that they possess a basic need to synthesize contradictory information (Festinger 1957; Lewin 1951; Thompson, Zanna, and Griffin 1995). Western cultures tend to be more linear or synthetic in their cognitive orientation. They consider both sides of an opposing argument and then they search for synthesis and the resolution of incongruity (Lewin 1951; Peng and Nisbett 1999). Western folk epistemologies are rooted in Aristotelian traditions, which emphasize three basic principles (Peng and Nisbett 1999): the law of identity (if A is true, then A is always true), the law of noncontradiction (A cannot equal not A), and the law of the excluded middle (all propositions must be either true or false). As a result, Westerners are generally less comfortable with contradiction, and attitudinal ambivalence is associated with psychological tension and conflict (Festinger, 1957; Lewin, 1951).

On the other hand, East Asian epistemologies tend to tolerate psychological contradiction. East Asian cultures tend to be more dialectic in their cognitive orientation. Recognizing and accepting the duality in all things is regarded as normative in East Asian cultures. Two central features of dialectical ways of knowing are moderation and balance: good is counterbalanced by evil, happiness is offset by sadness, and self-criticism is tempered by sympathy for the self (Kitayama and Markus 1999; Peng and Nisbett 1999). Dialectical thinking is rooted in East Asian philosophical and religious traditions, and is based on three primary tenets: the principle of contradiction (two opposing propositions may both be true), the principle of change (the universe is in flux and is constantly changing), and the principle of holism (all things in the universe are interrelated). Dialecticism also discourages the adoption of extreme positions. A principal consequence of dialectical thinking is that East Asians more comfortably accept psychological contradiction (Spencer-Rodgers et al. 2009).

Consequently, the Western and East Asian views of contradiction are fundamentally different (Peng and Nisbett 1999). Hence, we argue that consumer attitude towards inconsistent consumption preferences and the consumers' desire for the coherent identity narrative may differ between the West and East Asia.

METHODOLOGY

This study employed a phenomenological interviewing (Thompson, Locander, and Pollio 1989). Because the concept of self is complex, the study required a research method with the ability to delve into the thoughts, feelings, and behaviors of informants and to capture the social and situational contexts of those phenomena (Schouten 1991). The study was conducted in Japan, one of Asia's leading countries. Since the Japanese consumer market is mature as the one in Western counterparts such as the U.S, the selection of Japan allows us to control confounding. In-depth interviews with 28 Japanese informants (14 females and 14 males) were conducted. Our sample was composed of various age groups, from twenties to fifties. The informants were recruited using the research agency. They were given 10,000 yen (about $100) for their participation. The interviews lasted three hours and were audiotaped. The data collection process took place between April 27 and May 13, 2009. All interviews were conducted in the local language (Japanese).

To obtain a first-person description of consumers' experience, the goal of the phenomenological interview, the interview was intended to yield a conversation with the informants. During the interview, a concerted effort was made to allow informants freely describe their experiences in detail. Respondents were assured of anonymity (names are all pseudonyms). The questions and probes were aimed at bringing about descriptions of experiences and were not intended to confirm theoretical hypotheses. Such attempts were important to capture the true feelings of informants because Japanese people have a tendency to value social harmony and not to reveal their true inner feelings. In fact, one of the informants commented that "I'm talking a lot today. I can't talk about it [the topic] normally."

The luxury consumption was chosen as the specified domain of experience for this study. Luxury is nonessential that is closely associated with indulgence and hedonics (Kivetz and Simonson 2002). Consumers often show ambivalent attitudes towards luxury (Dubois and Laurent 1994). Furthermore, it is often associated with consumers' self-concepts (Vigneron and Johnson 1999). Hence, we assumed that the luxury consumption would be a good context to study consumers' multiple selves and consumption.

We used a hermeneutic process to analyze the text, first completing an emic analysis for each informant with regard to his/her multiple selves and luxury consumption experiences and then moving to an etic analysis by comparing our findings across the informants (Bahl and Milne 2010; Thompson, Locander, and Pollio 1989). Findings were interpreted using an iterative process of going back and forth between our findings and those in the literature. Concepts from the literature were compared and contrasted with our findings to arrive at new insights.

CREATING A NARRATIVE: MULTIPLE SELVES AND CONSUMPTION IN JAPAN

Excerpts from an Interview with Erika: Worker-Self versus Private-Self

Erika is 24 years old OL (office lady) who lives with her parents and siblings. Now working at a bank, she has two selves – one as a banker (worker-self) and another as a private. As a banker, she invests in fashion to look professional. She comments about wearing a manicure:

Interviewer (*I*): Why do you think it's important to take care of your fingers?

Erika (*E*): Well… I wonder… My mother doesn't wear the manicure. So… My mother thinks I don't need to wear it. But… when I started to work, I felt that those who can take care even of their fingers appear to do well in their work. So, well… I began to wear the manicure.

Erika wears the manicure because she thinks that women wearing it portray the successful women. In her view, those who can pay careful attention to the details (as represented in wearing manicures on fingers) do well in the work. She also thinks it is important to look nice at work. Hence, she spends money on fashion including the manicure.

On a contrary, as a private-self, Erika has no interest in investing in fashion. She feels that fashion is a waste of money. She speaks with confidence that she will never spend money on a house dress.

E: I never experienced this [buying an expensive house dress], so I'm not sure, but I think this dress really addresses only me and not others. It's like I want to look nice even if there's no one around.

I: Do you think you'll purchase one in the future?

E: Well, I really doubt it. Even if I became to wear something nicer, I don't think I'll spend money on this [house dress].

I: Why is that?

E: Why? Well, let's see... I can't think of spending money on something that I'm not going to wear outside.

As the private-self, Erika has no concern to look nice. This is perhaps because her family admires the spirit of simplicity and frugality.

Although Erika has seemingly inconsistent preferences towards the fashion consumption, she seems to have no need to reconcile them. During the three hours interview, she told numerous episodes about her fashion consumption such as the manicure, lash extensions, depilation, and luxury brand wallet, but also told about her thoughts on fashion how it is not a necessity in life. At one side, she feels spending money on fashion is important and fun, whereas on the other side, she feels fashion is unnecessary and should be avoided. She has mixed emotions towards the fashion consumption. Although her fashion consumption preferences are inconsistent, she accepts them without any psychological tension. It seems that she simply makes distinction between outside (*soto*) and home (*uchi*). She says that "I can't think of spending money on something that I'm not going to wear outside," which indicates that she would spend money for public but not for private.

Excerpts from an Interview with Keiko: Duality of Japanese Self (*Omote* and *Ura* Dimensions)

Keiko is 23 years old OL working in the financial industry. She has just graduated from a highly reputables university in Japan. Like Erika, she now has the worker-self and private-self. In addition, she also has the friend-self which surfaces when she is with her former classmates.

Keiko also has two dimensions of self, *omote* (public-self that she shows to others) and *ura* (private, inner-self that she does not show to others). With *omote*-self, she adjusts consumption preference to fit with her friends. Such consumption preference is seemingly inconsistent with the one of her *ura*-self. To give an example, Keiko talks about drinking Dom Pérignon Rosé at the party with her friends:

Keiko (K): I don't like a carbonated drink, so I don't like champagne. I don't want to drink, but [others want to order. They say] 'let's order because it's expensive,' or 'we're going to order *pin-don* (abbreviated word for pink Dom Pérignon) today.' [...] [People consider that *pin-don* is] a must-have item for the party. Speaking the truth, I don't understand its price [...] I prefer *shochu* (Japanese spirits) or sake. [...]

Interviewer (I): How do you feel when you're drinking *pin-don*?

K: [...] it's not tasty at all. It's carbonated. I don't want it. [...]

I: Why do you drink it if it's not tasty?

K: Well, I don't [want to] order it but others want to.

Keiko shows her *omote*-self to her friends and hides her *ura*-self. With the *omote*-self, she hides her real drinking preference and adjusts it to her friends. Although she does not like champagne, she orders it because her friends want it. She does not mention her dislike of champagne nor order the other preferred drink such as *shochu* or sake.

Keiko's two-tiered self is also apparent in her opinion towards possessions such as the luxury brand handbag and watch. She has the Chanel handbag and Piaget watch to which her *omote* and *ura* selves have different opinions.

K: To tell the truth, I'm not materialistic. For a watch, if I can tell the time, it's enough. In reality, I'm such person. Still, [I feel good] when people tell me 'Wow, you're wearing that watch [Piaget watch]! How nice!' It's really Japanese-like. So, I think it's better to have one. It's like wearing armor. [...] It's same for a handbag. Really, I want to walk around empty-handed. If I have my cigarettes, wallet, and mobile phone, I'm fine. I want to put them in my pockets. But I'm a female [so I should carry around some kind of bag]. I can't be walking around with the supermarket's shopping bag. If I have the handbag of this sort [Chanel handbag], people tell me 'That's nice.' And I learnt. So I think it's better to have one. That's why I want it.

Keiko's *ura*-self has no interest towards the luxury brand goods; however, her *omote*-self needs them. She feels a need in order to fit in with society and survive (as reflected in her use of the armor metaphor).

Like Erika, Keiko does not seem to feel psychological tension from these seemingly inconsistent opinions between her *omote* and *ura* selves. Rather, she accepts *omote* and *ura* as the characteristics of Japanese society. Comparing Japan and New York (from her experience of visiting NY), she recognizes that *omote* and *ura* do not exist at NY. She comments that people are more plain and natural at NY. Still, she does not have negative feelings towards Japan. When the interviewer asked Keiko where she prefers to live, she chose Japan without hesitation.

DISCUSSION

Western versus East Asian View towards Inconsistent Consumption Preferences

Erika and Keiko, like other informants, have multiple selves and inconsistent preferences towards consumption, but they don't seem to be uncomfortable with contradictions or attitudinal ambivalence. Is this uniquely Japanese? Westerners, like Japanese, also have multiple selves and are able to adjust to different social relationships and situations. The difference may be of the tolerance for holding apparently contradictory beliefs. Japanese, unlike Westerners, tend to tolerate psychological contradictions (Peng and Nisbett 1999). Whereas Westerners are uncomfortable with inconsistencies and perceive them as conflict (Ahuvia 2005; Bahl and Milne 2010), Japanese accept them without feeling much psychological tension. The model in figure 1 explains the differences between East Asia such as Japan and West on consumers' approach towards inconsistent consumption preferences.

We argue that the dialectical thinking allows East Asians to accept inconsistent consumption preferences without much psychological tension. Our informants show the tendency towards dialectical thinking. One of the characteristics of dialectical thinking is the acceptance of contradiction. For example, majority of participants speak about their contradicting view towards luxury consumption.

FIGURE 1
CULTURAL DIFFERENCES IN CONSUMER APPROACH TOWARDS INCONSISTENT CONSUMPTION PREFERENCES

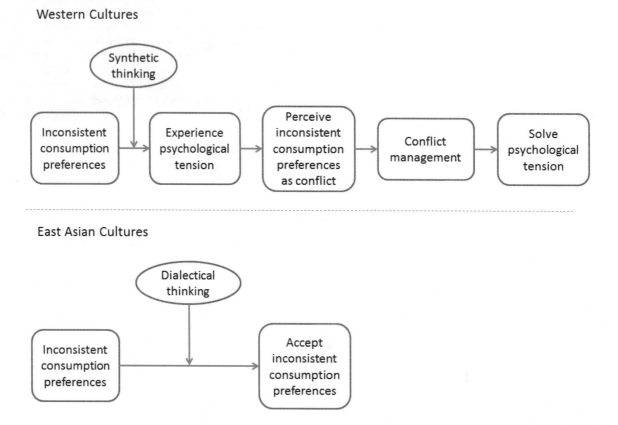

On the one hand, they feel that luxury consumption is unnecessary. However, on the other hand, they consume luxury to fulfill their desire. They recognize that there is a contradiction; however, they simply accept it. Consider how Koji (male, age 44) speaks on this issue.

Koji: Under original Buddhism [...], recognition itself brings perplexity. For example, we look at water; then we think is it tasty or not tasty. [...] From the sense, all fantasies emerge. Well...when you come to think of it, various things including desire are evoked. So I deny it. [...] I don't think about the unnecessary things, such as what I need to do tomorrow or about a beautiful lady. In a nutshell, I don't think about those noises; rather, I feel that just being there is of greatest happiness. Honestly speaking, I think such way of thinking is best for human beings. Then, there would be no perplexity. [...] But having said that, I'm a vulgar person who lives in a secular world. So, I enjoy eating nice foods and talking with beautiful ladies. I was happy when I bought good things.

Koji speaks about how his beliefs and actions towards consumption are contradicting. He does not seem to be irritated by his contradictory thoughts, however. The tone of his voice remains calm. His comment 'I'm a vulgar person' suggests that he considers a vulgar person to be contradictory. Indeed, East Asians do possess more contradictory self-beliefs, attitudes, and values (Campbell et al. 1996; Choi and Choi 2002; Spencer-Rodgers et al. 2009; Wong, Rindfleisch, and Burroughs 2003), compared with Westerners.

Dialectical thinking is also characterized by the acceptance of changes. Consider how some of the informants have shown such changes in attitude and behavior. Ichiro (male, age 52) shows attitudinal change towards brands. He says that "I don't like brands. I

have a perverse opinion towards brands." Hence, when purchasing the condominium, he didn't choose the famous developer. Still, he now has a desire for Ferrari. He says that Ferrari is "an ideal. It's my aspiration." He admits that Ferrari's premium price includes the cost for its brand name; however, he still desires it. Shizue (female, age 36), like Erika and Keiko, show behavioral changes depending on the situation. Her behavior with friends is quite different from her behavior in private. Since marrying to the owner of game software company, she has friends who come from the rich background. However, she spent her childhood in poverty. Hence, when she is in the gorgeous places, she feels ashamed. She thus pays a careful attention and makes an extra effort when she is with her current friends. For example, when she goes to the restaurant with her friends, she matches her clothing and accessories to them. She says,

Shizue (*S*): I don't want to be rude to my friends when eating at a restaurant. My friends have very nice fashion goods, so when we go to the restaurant, I feel that I cannot take the 3,980 yen handbag.

Shizue feels that taking 3,980 yen handbag is improper when meeting her rich friends. So, she brings an expensive Hermès handbag. On the other hand, when she goes to casual, cheap restaurants such as fast food restaurants, most often alone, she feels that the Hermès handbag is improper. Depending on the situation, she drastically changes her behavior (i.e., dressing in this case) without any hesitation.

Multiplicity of Self for Japanese

We also argue that multiplicity of self for Japanese is culturally embedded; therefore, the Japanese consumers have less need for the coherent identity narrative compared with Westerners. Anthropologists studying Japan have claimed that Japanese selves are multiple and changing (Rosenberger 1992). They demonstrate that the Japanese nurture multiple selves to reconcile what Westerners have viewed as oppositions in Japanese life such as public versus private life. The Japanese are multifaceted people who are subject to the influences that surround them, but shape selves creatively around a broad spectrum of social relationships and situations. They define and redefine themselves in relation to the social relationship. In addition to this shifting relational self, the Japanese also conceives the multiplicity of self in various dimensions such as in relation to objects, aspects of nature, and historical ideologies (Rosenberger 1992).

In the Japanese life, a series of antonyms, which include *soto* versus *uchi*, *omote* (in front; surface appearance) versus *ura* (in-back, what is hidden from others), and *tatemae* (the surface reality) versus *honne* (inner feelings), appears in every sphere (Bachnik 1992). The meanings of these sets of terms are related; aspects of public / social cluster at one pole (*soto, omote, tatemae*), while aspects of private / self cluster at one pole (*uchi, ura, honne*) (Doi 1986).

Japanese shift between two poles, adjusting their self to fit in a given social relationship and situation. From the childhood, Japanese learn to shift between two poles (Tobin 1992). Japanese select certain behavior, including choice, in consistency with social relationship and situation (Bachnik 1992). This is called *kejime*, the ability to make distinctions (Hendry 1986). *Kejime* indexes what kind of behavior or personality characteristic is appropriate; or how little emotion and self-expression is appropriate in a given situation (Bachnik 1992). Our informants also seem to be aware of *kejime*. For example, Keiko is very considerate of a social context. Consider the following comment that she speaks about living in a society:

K: After all, I'm not living alone. To live in a society, it's not okay that only I'm satisfied. For example, when walking in the city, I'm comfortable wearing sweatshirts and sneakers with my hairs loose. This may be okay to me, but [there are other people in the city and it may not be okay for them]. I need to worry about what others think of me and I can't live alone. At work, it's impolite if I'm not wearing a make-up.

Hence, Keiko accepts *omote* and *ura* dimensions of self, and shifts between the two according to the situations. Similarly, other informants also shift between social contexts of work and private, between the social group and the family, among friends, children, husbands or wives, and in-laws; among boss and staff; between the outer dimensions of self and inner self. Japanese consumers shift among multiple selves, instead of attempting to reconcile multiple selves and to construct a coherent identity narrative.

CONCLUSIONS

This study emphasizes the importance of redefining our understanding of multiple selves and consumption through data gathered in Japan. We argue that consumer approach towards inconsistent consumption preferences and the consumers' desire for the coherent identity narrative may differ between West and East Asia such as Japan. Our findings suggest that Japanese consumers experience less psychological tension facing their seemingly inconsistent consumption preferences. They therefore are accepting inconsistencies and have a less need for solving them. We also argue that the difference in consumer approach towards inconsistent consumption preferences may be due to the difference in tolerance toward contradictions. East Asians (including Japanese) have dialectical thinking and are more tolerant toward contradictions, whereas Westerners have synthetic

thinking and are less tolerant toward contradictions (Peng and Nisbett 1999). Findings also suggest the absence of consumers' need for a coherent identity narrative in Japan. We argue that shift among multiple selves are culturally embedded in Japan as reflected in the paired antonyms such as *soto* versus *uchi*, *omote* versus *ura*, and *tatemae* versus *honne*.

Our findings suggest the absence of consumers' need for a coherent identity narrative in Japan. While consistency of the self-concept across different social relationships and situations may be less important in Japan than West, Japanese consumers may still have a need to maintain consistency within a specific social relationship and situation (English and Chen 2011). For example, Erika may seek consistency in her worker-self over time; and Keiko in her *omote*-self over time. As such, as English and Chen (2011) claim, pursuit of a consistent self-concept may be important in East Asian cultures such as Japanese as in Western cultures. However, we suspect that in the degree of consumers' consciousness about consistency may be much smaller in this case than in the case of maintaining consistency in self-image across different social relationships and situations. The reason is that while global self-concept is created and actively managed by the individual, social self (i.e., socially appropriate person image) is defined by the community like a cultural norm and shared by its members. Therefore, Western consumers who pursue the consistency in the global self-concept are more apt to be conscious about consistency as they define the attributes themselves. In contrast, East Asian consumers who pursue the consistency in the social self may be less conscious about consistency as they may be simply following cultural norms defined by the community.

In any case, none of our informants seem conscious about inconsistency across different social relationships and situations; therefore feeling no significant psychological tension facing own inconsistent consumption preferences. Future research could explore conceptual distinctions between different types of self-concept consistency and consumers' consciousness about consistency.

Furthermore, there are still some unanswered questions on East Asians' tolerance toward contradictions. For example, do East Asians have tolerance toward inconsistencies even within a specific social self and/or inner self? It could be argued that inconsistency of the self-concept across different social relationships and situations among East Asians can also be explained by the interdependent self-construal theory (Markus and Kitayama 1991) besides dialectical thinking. Since the principal goal of the interdependent self-construal is to maintain connectedness and harmony with others, it may be natural for the individuals with interdependent self-construal to change their attitudes across different social relationships. Thus, by examining the tolerance towards inconsistencies within a specific social relationship yet across varying situations (e.g., with a professor in classroom vs. in cafeteria) or within a varying situations not involving social relationships (i.e., inner-self) (e.g., consistency in brand preference of a yogurt at home or at office), it would be possible to disentangle the effects of dialectical thinking from that of interdependent self-construal. These questions require further exploration and examination.

REFERENCES

Ahuvia, Aaron C. (2005), "Beyond the Extended Self: Loved Objects and Consumers' Identity Narratives," *Journal of Consumer Research*, 32 (June), 171-84.

Bachnik, Jane (1992), "*Kejime*: Defining a Shifting Self in Multiple Organizational Modes," in *Japanese Sense of Self*, ed. Nancy R. Rosenberger, Cambridge: Cambridge University Press, 152-72.

Bahl, Shalini and George R. Milne (2010), "Talking to Ourselves: A Dialogical Exploration of Consumption Experiences," *Journal of Consumer Research*, 37 (1), 176-95.

Campbell, Jennifer D., Paul D. Trapnell, Steven J. Heine, Ilana M. Katz, Loraine E. Lavallee, and Darrin R. Lehman (1996), "Self-Concept Clarity: Measurement, Personality Correlates, and Cultural Boundaries." *Journal of Personality and Social Psychology*, 70 (1), 141-56.

Choi, Incheol and Yimoon Choi (2002), "Culture and Self-Concept Flexibility," *Personality and Social Psychology Bulletin*, 28, 1508-17.

Doi, Takeo (1986), *The Anatomy of Self*, Tokyo: Kodansha.

Dubois, Bernard, Gilles Laurent, and Sandor Czellar (2001), "Consumer Rapport to Luxury: Analyzing Complex and Ambivalent Attitudes," Working Paper, HEC School of Management, Paris, France.

Emmons, Robert A. and Laura A. King (1988), "Conflict among Personal Strivings: Immediate and Long-Term Implications for Psychological and Physical Well-Being," *Journal of Personality and Social Psychology*, 54 (6), 1040–48.

English, Tammy and Serena Chen (2011), "Self-Concept Consistency and Culture: The Differential Impact of Two Forms of Consistency." *Personality and Social Psychology Bulletin*, 37 (6), 838-49.

Festinger, Leon (1957), *A Theory of Cognitive Dissonance*, Stanford, CA: Stanford University Press.

Firat, Fuat A. and Clifford J. Shultz (2001), "Preliminary Metric Investigations into the Postmodern Consumer," *Marketing Letters*, 12 (2), 189-203.

Firat, Fuat A. and Alladi Venkatesh (1995), "Liberatory Postmodernism and the Reenchantment of Consumption," *Journal of Consumer Research*, 22 (December), 239-67.

Gergen, Kenneth J. (1991), *The Saturated Self: Dilemmas of Identity in Contemporary Life*, New York: Basic.

Hendry, Joy (1986), *Becoming Japanese*, Honolulu: University of Hawaii Press.

Janis, Irving L. (1959), "Decisional Conflicts: A Theoretical Analysis," *Journal of Conflict Resolution*, 3 (1), 6–27.

Kitayama, Shinobu and Hazel Markus (1999), "The Yin and Yang of the Japanese Self: The Cultural Psychology of Personality Coherence," in *The Coherence of Personality: Social Cognitive Bases of Personality Consistency, Variability, and Organization*, ed. Daniel Cervone and Yuichi Shoda, New York: Guilford, 242-302.

Kivetz, Ran, and Itamar Simonson (2002), "Self-Control for the Righteous: Toward a Theory of Precommitment to Indulgence," *Journal of Consumer Research*, 29 (2), 199-217.

Lewin, Kurt (1951), *Field Theory in Social Science*, New York: Harper & Brothers.

Markus, Hazel Rose and Shinobu Kitayama (1991), "Culture and the Self: Implications for Cognition, Emotion, and Motivation," *Psychological Review*, 98 (2), 224-53.

Markus, Hazel and Elissa Wurf (1987), "The Dynamic Self-Concept: A Social Psychological Perspective," *Annual Review of Psychology*, 38, 299-337.

Murray, Jeff B. (2002), "The Politics of Consumption: A Re-inquiry on Thomson and Haytko's (1997) 'Speaking of Fashion,'" *Journal of Consumer Research*, 29 (December), 427–40.

Peng, Kaiping and Richard E. Nisbett (1999), "Culture, Dialectics, and Reasoning about Contradiction," *American Psychologist*, 54 (9), 741-54.

Rosenberger, Nancy. R. (ed.) (1992), *Japanese Sense of Self*, Cambridge: Cambridge University Press.

Schenk, Carolyn Turner and Rebecca H. Holman (1980), "A Sociological Approach to Brand Choice: The Concept of Situational Self Image," in *Advances in Consumer Research*, Vol. 7, ed. Jerry C. Olson, Ann Arbor, MI: Association for Consumer Research, 610-14.

Schouten, John W. (1991), "Selves in Transition: Symbolic Consumption in Personal Rites of Passage and Identity Reconstruction," *Journal of Consumer Research*, 17 (March), 412-25.

Spencer-Rodgers, Julie, Helen C. Boucher, Sumi C. Mori, Lei Wang, and Kaiping Peng (2009), "The Dialectical Self-Concept: Contradiction, Change, and Holism in East Asian Cultures," *Personality and Social Psychology Bulletin*, 35 (1), 29-44.

Spencer-Rodgers, Julie, Melissa J. Williams, and Kaiping Peng (2010), "Cultural Differences in Expectations of Change and Tolerance for Contradiction: A Decade of Empirical Research," *Personality and Social Psychology Review*, 14 (3), 296-312.

Thompson, Craig J. and Diana L. Haytko (1997), "Speaking of Fashion: Consumers' Uses of Fashion Discourses and the Appropriation of Countervailing Cultural Meanings," *Journal of Consumer Research*, 24 (1), 15–42.

Thompson, Craig J. and Elizabeth C. Hirschman (1995), "Understanding the Socialized Body: A Poststructuralist Analysis of Consumers' Self-Conceptions, Body Images, and Self-Care Practices," *Journal of Consumer Research*, 22 (2), 139–53.

Thompson, Craig, William B. Locander, and Howard R. Pollio (1989), "Putting Consumer Experience Back into Consumer Research: The Philosophy and Method of Existential-Phenomenology," *Journal of Consumer Research*, 16 (September), 133-46.

Thompson, Megan M., Mark P. Zanna, and Dale W. Griffin (1995), "Let's Not be Indifferent about (Attitudinal) Ambivalence," in *Attitude Strength: Antecedents and Consequences*, Vol. 4, ed. Richard E. Petty and & Jon A. Krosnick, Mahwah, NJ: Lawrence Erlbaum, 361-86.

Tian, Kelly and Russell W. Belk (2005), "Extended Self and Possessions in the Workplace," *Journal of Consumer Research*, 32 (September), 297-310.

Tobin, Joseph (1992), "Japanese Preschools and the Pedagogy of Selfhood," in *Japanese Sense of Self*, ed. Nancy R. Rosenberger, Cambridge: Cambridge University Press, 21-39.

Vigneron, Franck and Lester W. Johnson (1999), "A Review and a Conceptual Framework of Prestige-Seeking Consumer Behavior," *Academy of Marketing Science Review*, 1, 1-15.

Wong, Nancy, Aric Rindfleisch, and James E. Burroughs (2003), "Do Reverse-Worded Items Confound Measures in Cross-Cultural Consumer Research? The Case of the Material Values Scale," *Journal of Consumer Research*, 30 (1), 72-91.

Immersion in a New Commercial Virtual Environment:
The Role of the Avatar in the Appropriation Process

Ingrid Poncin, SKEMA - Univ Lille Nord de France, France
Marion Garnier, SKEMA - Univ Lille Nord de France, France

ABSTRACT

Building on the work by Carù and Cova (2003, 2006), we observe Internet users in front of a new virtual environment: a 3D commercial mall. A longitudinal study (4 visits on a 2-months period) allows studying the process that leads to the experience of immersion. Although individual differences are observed, the analysis of logbooks allow us to observe the realization of the three steps of the appropriation model (nesting, investigating and stamping) that lead to the experience of immersion. Our results also highlight the central role played by the avatar in the appropriation of that new commercial space.

INTRODUCTION

Since the seminal work of Hirshman and Holbrook (1982), consumer experience has been given great attention in literature. The postmodern approach considers that the consumer now looks for varied and if possible extraordinary experiences (Firat, 2001). The notion of experience has then become a key element in consumer behavior understanding (Carù and Cova, 2006). More specifically regarding online consumption, immersion (or flow as the ultimate immersion) is seen as fundamental outcome and stake for online consumption experiences (Hoffman and Novak, 1996; Tisseron, 2008). Developing enriching and immersive virtual experience is now a main issue for online marketers, be it on traditional 2D websites or in 3D life simulation, games or commercial virtual universes. Though being widely studied as a consequential state, immersion can also be presented as a process (Carù and Cova, 2003, 2006): these authors make the difference clear between the process of immersion and its result by proposing an appropriation operations model. Carù and Cova (2003) explored a specific context (artistic experience) and despite extended research on flow following Hoffman and Novak (1996)'s founding works, no research has studied this process of immersion in a virtual experience context from a longitudinal perspective yet.

Though, getting immerged on the Internet is not always easy, as for real. Among the various tools that may help creating an enriching and immersive experience online, the avatar has been identified as a key for immersion (Biocca, 1997; Taylor, 2002; Tisseron, 2009), as it reintroduces the body in a so-said "disembodied" experience (Vicdan and Ulusoy, 2008) and allows consumers to play an active role in the experience (Peng, 2008; Yee and Bailenson, 2009) that is favorable to immersion (Carù and Cova, 2003, 2006).

The first objective of this research is then to observe and analyze the process that leads to an immersion experience in a new virtual environment (a 3D shopping mall, see Appendix for illustrations). Moreover, our second aim is to assess the role the avatar can play in the appropriation operations process leading to immersion.

The conceptual framework first deepens the notion of experience and immersion on the web and presents the appropriation operations theory (Carù and Cova, 2003). The role the avatar might take in this experience and immersion process is then discussed. A longitudinal study, associating qualitative and quantitative data, allows analyzing and empirically validating the process that leads to immersion on the 3D shopping mall and the influence of the avatar. Results are presented and discussed and the paper concludes on contributions of the research and its perspectives.

CONCEPTUAL FRAMEWORK

Since Hoffman and Novak (1996)'s founding works, the experiential approach has be adopted by a great numbers of researchers to study what is lived by Internet users while visiting a website. Even if the Internet obviously offers wide utilitarian opportunities and value, some authors stated that the more immersive, hedonic aspects of Internet could play at least an equal role in predicting online attitudes and behaviours (Childers, Carr and Peck, 2001; Mathwick, Malhotra and Rigdon, 2001). Moreover, improving the experiential value of shopping on the Internet should lead to a better conversion rate, more satisfaction, stickiness and loyalty (Childers et al., 2001; Mathwick et al., 2001).

Pioneers in this area associated three main characteristics to the virtual experience: immersion, interactivity and possibility of real relationships (Tisseron, 2008). Regarding more specifically immersion, it is stated that as physical stores, commercial websites might induce emotional and affective reactions of Internet users, provoking immersion (Charfi and Volle, 2010).

The Immersion Process: The Appropriation Steps Theory

Immersion in computer-mediated environment is defined as "*the extent to which the computer displays are capable of delivering an illusion of reality to the senses of the human participant*" (Slater and Wilbur, 1997). On a broader scope, immersion appears in any case in which an individual is plunged, involved or absorbed in a totally different world (Fornerino, Helme-Guizon and Gotteland, 2006). This immersion - that can be partial or total, durable or temporary, wanted or undergone – or "feeling of" immersion of an individual in a physical or virtual universe consists in entering the universe and absorb/be absorbed by its atmosphere.

Nevertheless marketing literature, and especially in this experiential marketing area, is ambiguous toward the concept of immersion. Indeed, immersion is presented by some researchers as a process to reach the immersion experience (Ladwein, 2003; Carù and Cova, 2003, 2006) while for others, it is the final state itself, of being immerged in the environment or the experience (Sherry, 1998; Pine and Gilmore, 1998, 1999). This state of immersion is often related to the state of flow (Hoffman and Novak, 1996). Indeed, in computer-mediated environments, immersion is often considered through or seen as an antecedent of flow (Hoffman and Novak, 1996; Csikszentmihalyi, 1990; Novak, Hoffman and Yung, 2000). Flow is defined as "*the state occurring during network navigation which is characterized by a seamless sequence of responses facilitated by machine interactivity, intrinsically enjoyable, accompanied by a loss of self-consciousness and self-reinforcing*" (Novak et al. 2000). If immersion and flow share concentration and focus on the consumption object, flow also implies a high control of actions, due to a confrontation between high stakes and high skills (Fornerino et al., 2006) while this is not a basic condition for immersion to develop. Moreover, flow is a state and not a process.

On one hand, the idea of state of immersion relates to an immediate dive, abruptly going from a non-immerged state to an immerged final and ideal state (Firat, 2001; Goulding, Shankar and Elliot, 2002). On the other hand, the immersion process relates to and takes into account a series of steps that lead to the immersion experience. Carù et Cova (2003, 2006)'s works clearly separates the process of immersion from its results by proposing an appropriation operations model, composed of three operations: nesting, investigating and stamping. Understanding means and methods by which the consumer accesses the experience is essential, as this access is neither evident nor systematic (Ladwein, 2002). For Ladwein (2003), there will then be immersion when the distance between the experience and the consumer is reduced by those appropriation operations. Appropriation can be defined as *"a fundamental psychological process of action and intervention on a space to transform and personalize it; this influence system on places entails all forms and interventions on the space that translate into possession and attachment relationships"* (Fischer, 1992, p.91).

According to Carù and Cova (2003) on the basis of Fischer (1983)'s work, the first step, Nesting, is characterized by the set of perceptions and sensations felt by the consumer, on the basis of which the consumer is going to look for rooting points, so to *"feel at home"*. The individual isolates a part of the experience he's facing and sets into that part he's already familiar with. This step allows the individual to develop control on and stability within the experience, that are necessary for a forthcoming unwinding.

The second step, Investigating, is linked to observation of events and to the positive or negative evaluation of the experience. The individual will then develop his knowledge of the context he's facing and progressively extend his territory, by beginning to mark rooting and control points. According to that, the consumer will feel a more or less important distance toward the environment.

Finally, the third step, Stamping, is an imaginative activity characterized by the elaboration of impressions relative to the situation, the context and the attribution of a sense to that same situation. This sense will be specific according to the individual's own references and experiences.

The immersion will then be a *"strong moment that is felt by the consumer, and that results from a partial or complete appropriation process"* (Carù and Cova, 2003, p.80). Two important aspects should be given attention. First, the immersion is not necessarily total (unlike what is implied by the idea of an ideal final state): it can be partial and there can be ups and downs. Second, there can be a plurality of appropriation sequences within a single experience, like cyclic round-trips between the different operations, and sequences might not follow the presented hierarchy because of short-circuits between the operations.

Generating Immersion Online?

Experiential components of websites are then essential to reach the immersion experience and improving the virtual experience has become a major issue for e-marketers managing websites. Rich media technologies and web 2.0 concepts have considerably broadened the extent to which websites can be used in an experiential and entertaining way (Helme-Guizon, 2001; Jeandrain and Limbourg, 2002) and possibly generate immersion by going beyond the flat "inhuman" screen and display of traditional websites. Those techniques, such as high quality sound, video/audio streaming or 3D can lead to a decrease in the perception of the computer mediation. Jeandrain and Diesbach (2008) noticed that those technologies all follow the same pattern: reaching media transparency and generating immersion and so called feeling of (tele)presence (Steuer, 1992; Lombard and Ditton, 1997). As a matter of fact, virtual universes perfectly fit what consumers may look for to live extraordinary experiences, as Goulding et al. (2002, p.281) state that *"those immersions in hyperreal but reassuring settings contrast with everyday stress"*. Such universes then provide the thematized, enclosed and reassuring setting (Goulding et al., 2002) that is necessary to favour immersion

experience. Nevertheless, creating immersion is not that easy, even more in a virtual environment. Among the various possibilities, two solutions caught our attention.

First, 3D technology, by creating a hyperreal setting (Baudrillard, 1981), should be appropriate to generate immersion of online consumers. Indeed it provides an enriching and interactive environment, high visual stimulation and potentially reduces the distance with reality by reproducing it. Though, Garnier and Poncin (2009) revealed difficulties that Internet users can meet to immerge during the first and only one visit, in their case on a 3D commercial website. This was mainly due to the lack of familiarity with this very innovative environment. The frontier between real and virtual and the search for a rooting into reality seemed determining in the experience lived in such a setting (Poncin and Garnier, 2010). As a matter of fact, very little attention has been given to 3D shopping malls, despite their development and how they challenge virtual worlds, retail marketing and consumer online behavior (Burke, 1996; Garnier and Poncin, 2009, 2011, 2012).

The second feature, the avatar, has been identified as essential (Biocca, 1997; Tisseron, 2009) for immersion, as it reintroduces the body in a situation where it is not much solicited, contrary to "real life" consumption (Vicdan and Ulusoy, 2008).

Toward Re-Embodiment of the Virtual Experience and the Immersion Process

Immersion as an Embodied Experience. Immersion is seen throughout literature as a fundamentally embodied experience (Joy and Sherry, 2003), which may first seem inconsistent with virtual experience. Any experience is indeed embodied (Niedenthal, Barsalou, Winkielman, Krauth-Gruber and Ric, 2005) with the body being a processor of sensory stimuli and information (Lakoff and Johnson, 1980).

But online experience is usually seen as disembodied, as the physical body is not highly mobilized (as staying sat down on a chair in front of a screen), while cyberspace allows to free oneself from the physical constraints and the finiteness of the bodily incarnation (Turkle, 1995).

Though, the avatar allows individuals to have an online digital body that might impact the immersion experience.

Avatar and Immersion. In a computer-mediated environment, an avatar is defined as *"a pictorial representation of a human in a chat environment"* (Bahorsky, Jeffrey and Mason, 1998), *"a representation of the user as an animated character in virtual worlds"* (Loos, 2003), or *"graphic personifications of computers or processes that run on computers"* (Halfhill, 1996). Researches related to avatar use and influences are widely spread in Psychology, Information Systems or Human-Computer Interactions, in relation with learning, life-simulation or gaming virtual universes. Though, in the study of Consumer Behavior and Marketing, the subject of avatars in a direct (commercial websites, virtual models, virtual goods purchase) or undirect (brand communities, virtual worlds) commercial settings is still in its infancy (Crete et al., 2008 ; Kym and Forsythe, 2008, 2009; Malter, Rosa and Garbarino, 2008; Ulusoy and Vicdan, 2008; Vicdan and Ulusoy, 2008; Merle, St Onge et Sénécal, 2009, 2011; Garnier and Poncin, 2009, 2010, 2011).

Beyond debates on body and relationships between body and mind[1], the use of avatars questions the idea of disembodiment and more globally the role of the body in a virtual experience (Turkle, 1995; Biocca, 1997; Ulusoy et Vicdan, 2008; Vicdan et Ulusoy, 2008; Yee et al., 2009; Schultze, 2010). A whole range of researches

---

[1] See for example Descartes (1649) or Merleau-Ponty (1962)'s philosophical works on the topic.

also show that, as a real body would, strong emotional and physical reactions can be provoked by an experience that is mediated by an avatar (Turkle, 1994 ; Von der Pütten et al., 2010, among others).

As stated by Taylor (2002), the digital body anchors the self in the virtual and social space and the virtual body is then key to the experience (Biocca, 1997; Taylor, 2002; Tisseron, 2009). Practically speaking, creating the avatar is the first thing a new user will do: as such, it is clearly the first contact with and the entrance point in the universe. It can be considered as a mediator (Kolko, 1999), reconciliating Internet users with an inherent need for physicality in a virtual space (Meamber and Venkatesh 1999 ; Vicdan and Ulusoy 2008). Academic literature has then regularly demonstrated the positive effects of using an avatar on the virtual experience and its components, as a potential source of perceived presence, immersion and socialization (Taylor, 2002 ; Choi and Kim, 2004; Turkle, 2007; Smahel et al. 2008; Garnier and Poncin, 2009; Davis et al. 2009; Schultze, 2010). The digital body engages the individual in the virtual world (Biocca, 1997; Taylor, 2002; Tisseron, 2009), allow him/her to re-embody in the virtual experience and to engage in bodily practices (Schultze, 2010). The avatar also makes the individual producer and actor of the experience (Peng, 2008; Yee and Bailenson, 2009). Thanks to embodiment in the avatar, users can indeed play an active role, providing himself a nearly direct experience (enactive experience), more powerful than mere observation. This is particularly interesting as it has been demonstrated that being a producer and an actor favors an immersive experience (Carù and Cova, 2003, 2006).

In addition to the appropriation process study, this research then tackles the role an avatar can play to favor immersion by allowing embodiment, and more specifically how it could participate in the appropriation process leading to immersion (Carù and Cova, 2003).

METHODOLOGY

AuShopping 3D shopping mall

Access to Aushopping website can be found at the following URL: http://www.aushopping.com/galerie3d/aushopping/monde3D/login. This is the first integrally 3D shopping mall that is also associated with a price comparison website, a commercial social network and 3D apartments consumers can personalize with products from their purchases or wish lists. We focus on the main feature of the 3D shopping mall. As the website was a beta version when data were collected, some features, such as flats for example, were not accessible: they consequently do not appear in the data collection and are not dealt with in that study.

When using the 3D mall, the consumer enters a fully 3D commercial center (environment, shops, structures and shelves, product display) and is represented by an avatar he can personalize and uses it to navigate. He can also visualize (picture or 3D display) products and try them on, chat online with avatars of other consumers, participate to social or gaming activities within the virtual shopping mall and possibly ends his visit by purchasing. Again, it is to note

that some features (such as gaming activities) were not accessible to participants when data were collected. Illustrations of Aushopping can be found in Appendix.

Sample and Data Collection

32 students (22 women and 10 men, aged 19 to 22) were recruited on a voluntary basis (following a previous broader data collection on a related topic) to participate to a longitudinal study over a 2-months period. They visited the website at least 4 times over the 2-months period, with instructions for each visit (V1: open visit; V2: product retrieval; V3: shopping in a specific shop; V4: open shopping).

Data regarding the appropriation operations were collected following the methodology recommended by Carù and Cova (2003, 2006): appropriation operations can be identified in individuals' introspective narratives of their experience using written logbooks (Carù and Cova, 2003), as this kind of subjective experience is difficultly accessible in itself. This method is a form of guided introspection (Wallendorf and Brucks, 1993), with the specificity of being executed without any presence of the researcher. Respondents were then to fill a logbook directly after each visit to describe their experience through a series of open questions related to their feelings and thoughts on the experience they had just lived during the visit.

In order to deepen our understanding of the phenomenon, an online questionnaire was associated to logbooks. Respondents had then to fill the questionnaire right after filling the logbook, with items measuring immersion (Fornerino et al., 2008) and identification to the avatar (Van Looy et al., 2010). It is to note that immersion and identification measures are reported for V1, V3 and V4 only, as the questionnaire for V2 did not include them for parsimony purposes (linked to the specific focus of V2).

DATA ANALYSIS

A content analysis was conducted on textual data from logbooks by two independent coders on NVIVO9, based on logbook themes and identical coding units. Content was categorized according to the characteristics of each appropriation operation, as described by Carù and Cova (2003). Codings were then compared and discussed so to reach consensus.

Quantitative data were analyzed on SPSS18. Measures demonstrate good reliability and validity across visits (see table 1).

RESULTS AND DISCUSSION

The immersion appropriation process

Analyses of textual data (vocabulary, described process, description of feelings and thoughts...) extracted from logbooks allowed us to pinpoint the three appropriation operations of the immersion process (Carù and Cova, 2003).

First, during the Nesting phase, the consumer uses all perceptions and sensations felt to look for rooting points and "feel at home". Respondents are then looking for elements of proximity and safety with regard to reality and familiar experiences:

Table 1. Psychographics qualities of quantitative measures

Variables	Identification toward the avatar	Immersion
Initial scale	Van Looy et al. (2010) ; 8-item scale ; Unidimensional	Fornerino et al. (2008) ; 6-item scale ; Unidimensional
Final scale	8-item scale - Unidimensional	6-item scale - Unidimensional
Explained variance	58% V1; 74% V3; 75% V4	56% V1; 83% V3 ;77% V4
Cronbach α	0.90 V1; 0.95 V3; 0,96 V4	0.82 V1; 0.96 V3; 0.94 V4

"I had the feeling to be as in a video game, except that I am more used to action games thus this world appeared more "peaceful" and monotonous." (M, V1)

"The shops display really looks like real shops display." (F, V1)

"First I was surprised because I hadn't the impression that I was in a shopping mall!" (F, V1)

Nesting mainly appears during V1 but also later, particularly when facing elements not investigated yet. For example, it appeared during V3, as participants were to visit a specific shop they had never entered previously (as it was not available until that moment):

"The Willemshop looks like a botanical garden" (M, V3)

The Nesting operation can then reappear regularly when new things are to be discovered: respondents keep on looking for rooting points, especially though analogies and comparisons with reality.

Second, during the Investigating phase, starting "from the nest", exploration is expressed through the observation of events and new activities in order to evaluate the experience:

"I wandered around in other places of the mall to see if there were more shops than before." (F, V2)

"I tried to put products in the basket for the first time: the feeling was ok, it was easy" (M, V2)

This might happen since V2, but also previously during V1 for some participants. As Carù and Cova (2003) stated, cycles of appropriation operations can be faster for some individuals, depending on their previous experiences and specific familiarity areas. In that stage, consumers often refer to previously described elements and how they explore the environment:

"I discover at every visit the different and surprising universes by their realistic appearance. The application is then more and more stimulating: urge to see everything, to make everything!" (F, V4)

Finally, the Stamping phase is an imaginative and creative activity characterized by the elaboration of impressions on the situation, the context and the attribution of a specific meaning to this experience or to a part thereof. It is characterized, in narratives, by the meaning given either to the experience itself or to the virtual environment:

"I liked the feeling of controlling everything and the easiness of tasks. Making my avatar walk and calmly visit the gallery is enough." (F, V1)

"According to me, it could be a kind of trade for tomorrow." (F, V4)

As a matter of fact, immersion can be felt since V1 or appear later:

"I felt a total freedom! You can do your shopping with no one bothering you, you can go where you want – you are free of your direction, of your needs…" (F, V1)

"I really had the feeling to do my shopping in a real garden which was very pleasant." (F, V3)

"I had the impression to make shopping for real, in a real shopping mall." (F, V4)

Those differences in the appropriation process pace can be explained as immersion can be facilitated by familiarity with the material of the experience (Aurier and Passebois, 2002): preliminary knowledge about playful universes or shopping can help individuals to immerge more quickly, by recognizing rites and referents that favour the appropriation operations.

Quantitatively speaking, immersion scores significantly progress between V1 and V3 (V1=2.2, V2=2.45, V3=2.68), confirming the process identified in logbooks. However, it does not evolve positively anymore at V4. This seems quite normal, as Carù and Cova (2003, 2006) indicate that immersion is not perfectly linear: there can be ups and downs, across visits or within a single visit, with more or less immersive moments. The experience of immersion can be composed of a succession of strong moments (called small conquests by Carù and Cova, 2003) intersected with numerous moments that are lived far less intensely. In that perspective the third visit, in the Willenshop garden, was an important conquest for most of the participants.

So the immersion process has been identified thanks to logbooks analysis and confirmed with our quantitative results. Our second aim was to assess the role the avatar might take to favor immersion.

The avatar in the appropriation process

First, it is to state that in order to identify to that virtual self (Suh et al., 2011), respondents tend to create an avatar that physically look like themselves (Suh et al., 2011) or at least project part of their identity in the avatar (Vicdan and Ulusoy, 2008; Vasalou and Joinson, 2009), creating a sort of idealized self in the virtual character. This process of avatar personalization helps individuals in the Nesting phase by enhancing a cognitive connection with the digital body that represents them and consequently becomes a strong rooting point related to reality:

"I find it nice to be able to move with an avatar that looks like me as much as possible, it makes things more real." (M, V1)

The avatar also allows individuals to keep control of their first experience, which helps them facing and nesting into the new virtual environment:

"I like the fact to totally control the visit: to be able to move, to go where we want" (F, V1)

The avatar might then intervene by being adapted to various situations (hedonic *vs* utilitarian shopping, socialization with friends or other consumers) and shops during the Investigating phase:

"I've adapted my clothes to the situation of buying a waffle iron. It's just a bit of shopping. I would have dressed in a more elegant way if I had been to pounce about in the shopping mall as during my previous visit." (F, V2)

The avatar can also help exploring the environment by acting as a mediator:

"It is very nice to be able to change the viewing angle of the avatar. It helps feeling more immersed in the virtual world" (F, V1)

"My avatar already knows the place and how it works." (M, V3)

Finally, the avatar becomes a source of meaning for individuals in the Stamping phase. More specifically, they give meaning to the avatar by recognizing it as themselves, consequently stamping the experience as their own experience:

"I've discovered the website with him and I think he has become a mark in that virtual universe, as a well-known person. It helps me to absorb the website even better and to make one with my avatar. He's become me in the virtual universe." (M, V4)

"There is a great pleasure to wander around myself (as an extension of the avatar) in the shopping mall. The character is not important anymore because I feel like being her. There is no distinction between her and me anymore." (F, V4)

The correlation is very significant between identification toward the avatar and immersion (V3: 0.88**; V4: 0.87**). Embodiment in and identification to the avatar is then strongly linked with the ability to fully live the immersion experience. This is line with literature highlighting that one salient element of an experience is the active role of the consumer (Carù and Cova, 2003). Then, we clearly assess that the avatar is really key to immersion by making consumers feel actor (Peng, 2008; Yee and Bailenson, 2009) of the navigation into the 3D website and by making the virtual experience fundamentally (re-)embodied, as any other experience (Joy and Sherry, 2003).

Interestingly, a recursive process is also observed: the user starts by identifying with his avatar to be able to start the process of immersion, but after some visits or achieving a certain level of immersion, the process seems to reverse: the more the consumer is immersed, the more he identifies to his avatar.

CONCLUSION

Building on Carù and Cova (2003, 2006)'s work, we observed consumers facing a new commercial environment, a virtual 3D shopping mall, and we studied the process leading to the immersion experience. This is key, as the immersive properties of a commercial website can be an important element of differentiation among the thousands commercial websites consumers have access to (Charfi and Volle, 2011). Thanks to a longitudinal study – that is to our knowledge the first on the immersion process in a virtual environment and the impact of the avatar, we effectively observed the three operations of Nesting, Investigating and Stamping that lead to immersion. We also identified, both qualitatively and quantitatively, the central role of the avatar in the appropriation of this new commercial environment. Embodiment in the avatar appears as a crucial point for the experience, as it allows the individual to be an actor in the experience and as it reintroduces the body and the self in the virtual environment. Our analysis clearly links the avatar to each appropriation step. Table 2 synthesizes those findings.

Furthermore, the relationship between immersion and avatar throughout time had never been shown previously. Other interesting results lie in identifying that appropriation leading to immersion can be more or less fast, varying between individuals and in confirming that immersion is not a static linear process, but can fluctuate over time. As a matter of fact, it now seems clear that immersion should definitely be considered as a process studied from a longitudinal perspective, and not as a one-shot state with a linear strength increase.

Managerial consequences are multiples. As already suggested by other authors (Filser, 2002; Carù and Cova, 2006), it is necessary for the individual to be accompanied by firms all along the process of immersion, so to facilitate it. Environment design with tight relations to reality enhancing rooting and nesting, poly-sensorial elements that facilitate feeling of telepresence and embodiment, effective personalization of the avatar are possible assets that can be used by firms in such environments, beyond the usual experiential theatralization of the offer.

Some limits to this research can be highlighted, as the relatively small numbers of respondents, the use of a single 3D environment, and the limits inherent to the website that was not fully

Table 2. Results from the qualitative data analyses synthesis

Appropriation step	Verbatims linked to the appropriation process	Verbatims linked to the avatar in the appropriation process
Nesting Looking for rooting points	**References to familiar materials:** *"I had the feeling to be as in a video game, except that I am more used to action games thus this world appeared "peaceful" and monotonous."* (M, V1) *"The display in shops looks like so much that of the real shops."* (F, V1) **New nesting process in a newly discovered environment:** *"The Willemshop looks like a botanical garden"* (M, V3)	**Identification to the avatar linked to reality and familiarity:** *"I find it nice to be able to move with an avatar that looks like me as much as possible, it makes things more real."* (M, V1) **The avatar as a source of control of the first experience:** *"I like the fact to totally control the visit: to be able to move, to go where we want"* (F, V1)
Investigating Exploring	**Exploration of new elements:** *"I wandered around in other places of the mall to see if there were more shops than before."* (F, V2) *"I tried to put products in the basket for the first time: the feeling was ok, it was easy"* (M, V2) **References to previously described elements:** *"I discover at every visit the different and surprising universes by their realistic appearance. The application is then more and more stimulating: urge to see everything, to make everything!"* (F, V4)	**Situational adaptation of the avatar :** *"I've adapted my clothes to the situation of buying a waffle iron. It's just a bit of shopping. I would have dressed in a more elegant way if I had been to ponce about in the shopping mall as during my previous visit."* (F, V2) **Avatar as a mediator to explore:** *"It is very nice to be able to change the viewing angle of the avatar. It helps feeling more immersed in the virtual world"* (F, V1) *"My avatar already knows the place and how it works."* (M, V3)
Stamping Giving meaning	**Attribution of a meaning to the experience:** *"I liked the feeling of controlling everything and the easiness of tasks. Making my avatar walk and calmly visit the gallery is enough."* (F, V1) **Attribution of a meaning to the virtual environment:** *"According to me, it could be a kind of trade for tomorrow."* (F, V4)	**Attribution of a meaning to the avatar: the avatar is me, I'm the avatar** *"I've discovered the website with him and I think he has become a mark in that virtual universe, as a well-known person. It helps me to absorb the website even better and to make one with my avatar. He's become me in the virtual universe."* (M, V4) *"There is a great pleasure to wander around myself (as an extension of the avatar) in the shopping mall. The character is not important anymore because I feel like being her. There is no distinction anymore between her and me."* (F, V4)

accessible to participants. Some features such as the apartment or social activities could have been very interesting materials to study the immersion process and could enhance (or change) our results. Regarding analyses that were conducted on textual data, we were not able to formally demonstrate any temporal pattern of appropriation operations cycles within a single visit or across visits, as done by Carù and Cova (2003). Finally, our quantitative measure of immersion is obviously apprehending a state in an *a posteriori* declarative approach, as there is no scale, up to now, that may quantitatively assess the appropriation process, if this could be possible.

Research perspectives cover a wide area of confirmatory researches. First, the study of the appropriation process leading to immersion should be studied more deeply, in various virtual settings such as online games, life simulation universes or commercial websites, settings in which immersion is generally considered in existing researches as a final abrupt state. A deeper application of Carù and Cova (2003)'s methodology on virtual universes experience, in order to identify temporal sequences and various paces according to individual charactics, should lead to a better understanding of the virtual experience. Confirmatory and longitudinal researches also lack on the use of an avatar and its role in the immersion process and more globally in any virtual experience related to a consumption context.

REFERENCES

Aurier, Philippe and Juliette Passebois (2002), "Comprendre Les Experiences De Consommation Pour Mieux Gerer La Relation Client", *Décisions Marketing*, 28(Oct/Déc.), 43- 52.

Bahorsky, Russ, Graber Jeffrey and Steve Mason (1998), *Official Internet Dictionary: A Comprehensive Reference for Professionals Reviews*. Portland: ABS Consulting.

Baudrillard, Jean (1981), "*Simulacra and simulations*", University of Michigan Press.

Biocca, Franck (1997), "The Cyborg's Dilemma: Progressive Embodiment In Virtual Environments", *Journal of Computer-Mediated Communication*, 3(2), online.

Burke, Raymond (1996), "Virtual Shopping: Breakthrough in Marketing Research", *Harvard Business Review*, March-April, 120-131.

Carù, Antonella and Bernard Cova (2003), "Approche Empirique de l'Immersion Dans l'Experience de Consommation: Les Operations d'Appropriation", *Recherche et applications en marketing*, 18(2), 47-65.

Carù, Antonella and Bernard Cova (2006), "How to Facilitate Immersion in a Consumption Experience: Appropriation Operations and Service Elements", *Journal of Consumer Behaviour*, 1(5), Jan./Feb., 4-14.

Charfi, Ahmed Anis and Pierre Volle (2010), "L'Immersion dans les Environnements Expérientiels en Ligne : Rôle des dispositifs de la Réalité Virtuelle", *Actes de la 26ème Conférence de l'Association Française du Marketing*, Le Mans.

Childers, Terry, Chris Carr and Joan C. Peck (2001), "Hedonic and Utilitarian Motivations for Online Retail Shopping Behaviour", *Journal of Retailing*, 77(4), 511-35.

Choi, Donseong and Jinwoo Kim (2004), "Why People Continue to Play Online Games: In Search of Critical Design Factors to Increase Customer Loyalty to Online Contents", *CyberPsychology and Behavior*, 7(1), 11-24.

Crete, David, Anick Saint-Onge, Aurélie Merle, Nicolas Arsenault and Jacques Nantel (2008), "Personalized Avatar, a New Way to Improve Communication and E-Services", *Proceedings of the 37th EMAC Conference*, Brighton, UK (CD-Rom).

Csikszentmihalyi, Mihaly (1990), *Flow: The Psychology of Optimal Experience*, New York: H & Row.

Davis, Alanah, John Murphy, Down Owens, Deepak Khazanchi and Ilze Zigurs (2009), "Avatars, People, and Virtual Worlds: Foundations for Researches in Metaverses", *Journal of the Association for Information Systems*, 10(2), 90-117.

Firat, Fuat A. (2001), "The Meanings and Messages of Las Vegas: the Present of Our Future", *M@n@gement*, 4(3), 101-120.

Filser, Marc (2002), "Le Marketing de la Production d'Expérience. Statut Théorique et Implications Managériales", *Décisions Marketing*, 28(Oct), 13-22.

Fischer, Gustave-Nicolas (1983), "*Le travail et son espace : de l'appropriation à l'aménagement*", Paris: Dunod.

Fischer, Gustave-Nicolas (1992), "*Psychologie sociale de l'environnement*", Toulouse: Privat.

Fornerino, Marianela, Agnès Helme-Guizon and David Gotteland (2008), "Expériences Cinématographiques en Etat d'Immersion : Effets sur la Satisfaction", *Recherche et Applications en Marketing*, 23(3), 93-111.

Garnier Marion and Ingrid Poncin (2009), "To be or not to be ? Virtual experience and immersion on a 3D commercial website" *in Advances in Consumer Research*, Vol. 37, eds. M. C. Campbell, J. Inman, & R. Pieters, Pittsburgh, PA: Association for Consumer Research.

Garnier Marion and Ingrid Poncin (2012), " La dynamique d'identification à l'avatar dans un univers commercial en 3D ", *Actes de la 28ème Conférence de l'Association Française du Marketing (A.F.M.)*, Brest, Mai.

Goulding, Christina, Avi Shankar and Richard Elliott (2002), "Working Weeks, Rave Weekends: Identity Fragmentation and the Emergence of New Communities", *Consumption, Markets and Culture*, 5(4), 261-284.

Halfhill, Tom R. (1996), "Agents and Avatars", *Byte*, 21 (February), 69–72.

Helme-Guizon, Agnès (2001), "Le Comportement du Consommateur sur un Site Marchand est-il Fondamentalement Différent de son Comportement en Magasin ? Proposition d'un Cadre d'Etude de ses Spécificités", *Recherche et Applications en Marketing*, 16(3), 25-38.

Hirschman, Elizabeth C. and Morris B. Holbrook (1982), "Hedonic Consumption: Emerging Concepts, Methods and Propositions", *Journal of Marketing*, 46(3), 92-101.

Hoffman, Donna L. and Thomas P. Novak (1996), "Marketing in Hypermedia Computer-Mediated Environments: Conceptual Foundations", *Journal of Marketing Research*, 60(July), 50-68.

Jeandrain, Anne-Cécile and Brice-Pablo Diesbach (2008), "Immersion In An Online Merchant Environment: Are Consumers Ready To Feel Their Presence In Such Environment?", *Proceedings of the 37th EMAC Conference*, Brighton. (CD-Rom).

Jeandrain, Anne-Cécile and Quentin Limbourg (2002), "On Application of Virtual Environments to Marketing", *Proceedings of Virtual Reality Concept 2003 Symposium*, November, Biarritz, 325-32.

Joy, Annama S. and John F. Sherry (2003), "Speaking of Art as Embodied Imagination: a Multisensory Approach to Understanding Aesthetic Experience", *Journal of Consumer Research*, 30(2), 259-282.

Kim, Jiyeon and Sandra Forsythe (2008), "Adoption of Virtual Try-On Technology for Online Apparel Shopping", *Journal of Interactive Marketing*, 22(2), 45-59.

Kim, Jiyeon and Sandra Forsythe (2009), "Adoption of Sensory Enabling Technology for Online Apparel Shopping", *European Journal of Marketing*, 43(9/10), 1101-1120.

Kolko, Beth (1999), "Representing Bodies in Virtual Space: the Rhetoric of Avatar Design", *The Information society*, 15, 177-186.

Ladwein, Richard (2002), "Voyage à Tikidad : de l'Accès à l'Expérience de Consommation", *Décisions Marketing*, 28(Oct-Dec), 53-63.

Ladwein, Richard (2003), "Les Méthodes de l'Appropriation de l'Expérience de Consommation : le Cas du Tourisme Urbain", *Société, consommation et consommateurs*, Eds. E. Rémy, I. Gurubuau-Moussaoui, D. Desjeux et M. Filser, Paris, Paris : L'Harmattan, 85-98.

Lakoff, George and Mark Johnson (1980), *Metaphors we live by*, Chicago, IL: University of Chicago Press.

Lombard, Matthew and Theresa B. Ditton (1997), "At The Heart Of It All: The Concept Of Presence", *Journal of Computer-Mediated Communication*, 3(2), (online).

Malter Alan J., Rosa José Antonio, Ellen C. Garbarino (2008), "Using Virtual Models to Evaluate Real Products for Real Bodies", In *Advances in Consumer Research*, edited by Angela Y. Lee and Dilip Soman, vol. 35, Duluth, MN: Association for Consumer Research 35, 87-88.

Mathwick, Charla, Naresh Malhotra and Edward Rigdon (2001), "Experiential Value: Conceptualization, Measurement And Application In The Catalog And Internet Shopping Environment", *Journal of Retailing*, 77(1), 511-35.

Meamber, Laurie A. and Alladi Venkatesh (1999), "The Flesh is Made Symbol: an Interpretive Account of Contemporary Bodily Performance Art", in *Advances in Consumer Research*, eds. Eric J. Arnould and Linda M. Scott, Volume 26 : Association for Consumer Research, 190-194.

Merle, Aurélie, Annick St-Onge and Sylvain Senecal (2009), "Do I Recognize Myself in This Avatar? An Exploratory Study of Self-Congruity and Virtual Model personalization Level", *The 5th World Conference on Mass Customization and Personalization*, MCPC, Helsinki.

Merle, Aurélie, Annick St-Onge and Sylvain Senecal (2011), "Est-ce que je me reconnais dans cet avatar ? L'Influence de la Congruence de l'Avatar sur les Réponses des Consommateurs", *Actes de la 27ème Conférence de l'Association Française du Marketing*, Bruxelles.

Merleau-Ponty, Maurice (1962), Phenomenology of Perception, trans. Colin Smith. London: Kegan Paul.

Niedenthal, Paula .M., Lawrence W. Barsalou, Piotr Winkielman, Silvia Krauth-Gruber and François Ric (2005), "Embodiment in Attitudes, Social Perception and Emotion", *Personality and Social Psychology Review*, 9(3), 184-211.

Novak, Thomas P., Donna L. Hoffman and Yiu-Fai Yung (2000), "Measuring the Flow Construct in Online Environment: A Structural Modeling Approach", *Marketing Science*, 19(1), 22-44.

Peng, Wei (2008), "The Mediational Role of Identification in the Relationship between Experience Mode and Self-Efficacy: Enactive Role-Playing versus Passive Observation", *CyberPsychology and Behavior*, 11(6), 649-652.

Pine, B. Joseph and James H. Gilmore (1998), "Welcome to the Experience Economy", *Harvard Business Review*, 76(4), 97-105.

Pine, B. Joseph and James H. Gilmore (1999), *The experience economy: work is theatre and every business a stage*, Harvard: HBS Press.

Poncin Ingrid and Marion Garnier (2010), *"L'expérience sur un site de vente 3D. Le vrai, le faux et le virtuel : à la croisée des chemins", Management et Avenir*, 2, 32,173-191.

Poncin Ingrid and Marion Garnier (2011), "Avatar Identification on 3D Commercial Website: Gender Issues", *Informs Marketing Science Conference*, Houston, USA, June.

Schultze, Ulrike (2010), "Embodiment and Presence in Virtual Worlds: a Review", *Journal of Information Technolog*, 25, 434-449.

Sherry, John F. (1998), "The Soul of the Company Store: Nike Town Chicago and the Emplaced Brandscape", *Servicescapes: the concept of place in contemporary markets*, Eds J.F. Sherry, Lincolnwood: NTC Business Books, 109-150.

Slater, Mel and Sylvia Wilbur (1997), "A Framework for Immersive Virtual Environments (FIVE): Speculations on the Role of Presence in Virtual Environments", *Presence: Teleoperators and Virtual Environments*, 8, 560-65.

Smahel, David, Lukas Blinka and Ondrej Ledabyl (2008), "Playing MMORPGs: Connections between Addiction and Identifying with a Character", *CyberPsychology and Behavior*, 11(6), 715-718.

Steuer, Jonathan (1992), "Defining Virtual Reality: Dimensions Determining Telepresence", *Journal of Communication*, 42(4), 73-93.

Suh, Kil-Soo, Hongki Kim and Eung Kyo Suh (2011), "What if your Avatar Looks Like You? Dual-Congruity Perspectives for Avatar Use", *MIS Quarterly*, 35(3), 711-729.

Taylor, T.L. (2002), "Living Digitally: Embodiment in Virtual Worlds", in R. Schroeder (Ed.), *The social life of avatars: presence and interaction in shared virtual environments*, London: Springer-Verlag.

Tisseron, Serge (2008), *"Virtuel Mon Amour: Penser, Aimer, Souffrir, A l'Ere Des Nouvelles Technologies"*, Paris : Albin Michel.

Tisseron, Serge (2009), "L'Ado et ses Avatars", *Adolescence*, 27(3), 591-600.

Turkle, Sherry (1994), "Constructions and Reconstructions of Self in Virtual Reality: Playing in the MUDs", *Mind, Culture, And Activity*, 1(3), 158-167.

Turkle, Sherry (1995), "Life on the Screen: Identity in the Age of the Internet", Simon & Schuster.

Turkle, Sherry (2007), "Authenticity in the Age of Digital Companions", *Interaction Studies*, 8(3), 501-511.

Ulusoy, Ebru and Handan Vicdan (2009), "Bodily Experiences of Second Life Consumers (37:04)", in *Advances in Consumer Research*, 36.

Van Looy, Jan, Cédric Courtois and Mélanie De Vocht (2010), "Player Identification in Online Games: Validation of a Scale for Measuring Identification in MMORPGs ", *Proceeding of ACM*, May, online.

Vasalou, Asimina and Adam N. Joinson (2009), "Me, Myself and I: the Role of Interactional Context on Self-Presentation through Avatars", *Computers in Human Behavior*, 25, 510-520.

Vicdan, Handan and Ebru Ulusoy (2008), "Symbolic and Experiential Consumption of Body in Virtual Worlds: from (Dis)Embodiment to Symembodiment", *Journal of Virtual Worlds Research*, 1(2), online.

Von der Pütten, Astrid M., Nicole C. Krämer, Jonathan Gratch and Sin-Hwa Kang (2010), "It doesn't matter what you are!" Explaining Social Effects of Agents and Avatars", *Computers in Human Behavior*, 26, 1641-1650.

Wallendorf, Melanie and Merrie Brucks (1993), "Introspection in Consumer Research: Implementation and Implications, *Journal of Consumer Research*, 20(4), 339-359.

Yee, Nick and Jeremy N. Bailenson (2009), "The Difference between Being and Seeing: the Relative Contribution of Self-Perception and Priming to Behavioral Changes via Digital Self-representation", *Media Psychology*, 12, 195-209.

Yee, Nick, Jeremy N. Bailenson and Nic Ducheneaut (2009), "The Proteus Effect: Implications of Transformed Digital Self-Representation on Online and Offline Behavior", *Communication Research*, 36, 285-312.

APPENDIX
Illustrations of the 3D shopping mall

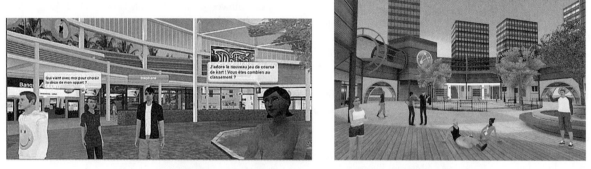

Avatars in the external space of the shopping mall

Avatar in a 3D shop

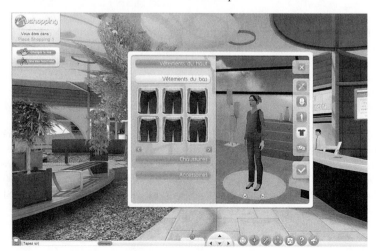

Avatar personalization tool

'Because I'm Worth It' - Luxury and the Construction of Consumers' Selves

Andrea Hemetsberger, University of Innsbruck, Austria
Sylvia von Wallpach, University of Innsbruck, Austria
Martina Bauer, University of Innsbruck, Austria

ABSTRACT

This study inquires how consumers' experiences of luxury relate to consumers' selves. The objective is to broaden our contemporary understanding of luxury experiences by departing from the traditional view of conspicuous luxury consumption as a marker of social class. Consumer diaries provide fundamental insights into the complex nature of luxury experiences as *moments of luxury,* which are an integral part of consumers' everyday lives. Luxury experiences are inextricably linked with states and processes of self that revolve around multifaceted experiences of *having* (materialistic self), *doing* (liberating, oscillating, integrating, and relating self), *being* (harmony), and *becoming* (achievement-oriented and self-transformational). Our findings relate to and extend current self theory and fundamentally change our understanding of luxury from its groundings in status consumption towards a transient and abstract concept.

INTRODUCTION

Consumer behavior literature inextricably ties luxury to demonstrative and conspicuous consumption, assuming that luxury derives meaning primarily from the luxury object (Vickers and Renand 2003) and the social context (Brückner 2008). Based on Veblen's (1902) seminal work, traditional luxury literature has a strong focus on social affiliation and social comparison, stressing consumers' social identity needs (Stets and Burke 2000; Tajfel 1982). Traditionally, functional characteristics such as high price, outstanding quality, uniqueness/scarcity, unnecessity, and aesthetics characterize luxury goods and brands (e.g., Keller 2009) that are produced as means for social distinction (e.g., Han, Nunes, and Drèze 2010).

Recently, authors have portrayed luxury from a more individual and abstract angle, framing the essence of luxury as a special treat that is out of the ordinary (Hansen and Wänke 2011). Additionally, recent studies increasingly acknowledge the primacy of the luxury experience over object (e.g., Tynan, McKechnie, and Chhuon 2009), as well as the tendency to view luxury consumption as predominantly inner-directed and inconspicuous (Bauer, von Wallpach, and Hemetsberger 2011). The present study picks up the thread and focuses on meaningful objects and moments consumers might experience as luxury.

We propose that luxury is not experienced in enclaved luxurious spaces and contexts but integrated in consumers' everyday lives. Building on the widely held belief of products and brands as supporters of the self (e.g. Belk 1988; Kleine, Kleine III, and Allen 1995), this study contributes to previous literature by showing how luxury experiences are inextricably linked to the self. Building on narratives reported in consumer diaries, this study illuminates the contribution of consumers' lived experiences of luxury to the states and processes of having, doing, being, and becoming that underlie consumers' selves. Our radically constructivist view implies that any material thing, or any consumer experience might be perceived as luxurious, if consumers attach luxurious meaning to it. This article, therefore, departs from conceptual presumptions and aims to enrich our understanding of luxury with fundamental consumer insights.

The subsequent sections review current conceptualizations of luxury first, describe the emerging view of luxury experiences as part of the self-narrative of consumers, elaborate on the study findings, and discuss their implications.

THEORY

Luxury experiences

Traditionally, premium image, high price, outstanding quality, uniqueness/scarcity, unnecessity, and aesthetics characterize luxury goods and brands, which are produced as means for social distinction (e.g., Han et al. 2010). Berthon et al. (2009, 47) characterize luxury as "amalgam of the material, the social, and the individual". Postmodernity has radically altered contemporary definitions of luxury, adding pastiche and democratized forms of luxury for the masses (Atwal and Williams 2009; Tsai 2005; Yeoman and McMahon-Beattie 2006). Additionally, recent postmodern theorizations in the field of consumption practices argue that most action is not directed towards communication with others but towards the fulfillment of self-regarding purposive projects (Joy et al. 2010; Warde 2005). Accordingly, research acknowledges the individual meaning of luxury consumption, focusing on the measurement of luxury perception (e.g., Christodoulides, Michaelidou, and Li 2009), the value of luxury brands for individuals (e.g., Tsai 2005), and individual consumption practices (e.g., Atwal and Williams 2009; Gistri et al. 2009). However, despite the recent prominence of experiential marketing (e.g., Brakus, Schmitt, and Zarantonello 2009), only few studies stress the importance of consumer experiences in the context of luxury brands (e.g., Atwal and Williams 2009; Berthon et al. 2009). Tynan et al. (2009) lay the foundation for a distinct experiential approach, and extract three main types of value consumers derive from luxury—symbolic/expressive, experiential/hedonic, and relational. Yet, classifications of luxury experiences into taxonomies of value have serious conceptual shortcomings from a constructionist perspective as they predetermine experiential categories, instead of focusing on luxury's essential meaning for consumers' selves. Hansen and Wänke (2011) maintain that the majority of consumers cannot afford indulging in luxury every day. As a consequence, luxury goods are psychologically more abstract and distant than everyday necessities. We assume that consumers' desire for luxury is independent from accessibility, which necessitates a re-definition of the meaning of luxury on the side of consumers. Consumers might exclude inaccessible luxury goods and include other, more achievable domains of luxury consumption experiences in their everyday lives. Bauer et al. (2011) have introduced an interesting perspective on everyday luxuries that are situation-specific, individual, and narrated. First empirical evidence shows that luxury experiences are much more self-related, private, and less materialistic than previously assumed in the context of traditional views of luxury. The authors find that from a consumer-experiential perspective luxury can be characterized as transient, which is reflected in its situation-specific, escapist nature, and its integration in consumers' everyday lived experiences.

Luxury experiences and the self

Relationships between products, special possessions, brands and the consumer's self have been widely discussed in literature (e.g. Belk 1988; Berger and Heath 2007; Kleine et al. 1995; Sirgy 1982; Sprott, Czellar, and Spangenberg 2009). Existing studies provide ample evidence of the supportive function of products/brands for identity construction and consumers' self-understanding. In his seminal work, Sirgy (1982) suggests that individuals have an "actual self"—a realistic view of how a person perceives herself—and an "ideal self", relating to how a person would like to be. The uncomfortable gaps between the real and the ideal selves respectively can be removed through consumption. As products and brands communicate symbolic meaning, their consumption potentially enriches a consumer's self-concept via the transfer of certain product or brand meanings to the self.

A more postmodern view has been introduced by Belk (1988), Ahuvia (2005), and Bahl and Milne (2010), who draw attention to the extended, fragmented and negotiable consumer self. Whereas Belk and others (1988; Tian and Belk 2005) introduce the deep meaning of possessions as part of individual's identity, Ahuvia (2005) supports a multiple selves view of consumers, who solve conflicting facets of their identities through consumption. Consumers appropriate specific objects for the purpose of self-transformation rather than self-extension as proclaimed by Belk (1988). In contrast to Ahuvia (2005), who discusses consumers' strategies in the formation of a coherent self-narrative, Bahl & Milne (2010) look at the constant dialogue of different selves to avoid or solve possible conflicts amongst them. Similarly, Obodaru (2012) emphasizes the importance of alternative selves for people's self-narratives, and the consequences for their lives. Studying self-representations of who a person could have been, she finds affective, self-knowledge, satisfaction and motivational effects on people's professional lives (Obodaru 2012). Other authors introduced the notion of transformative experiences and consciousness transformation to denote short-term and long-term self-changes that consumers undergo when consuming valued consumption objects (Hoppe et al. 2009; Mick 2006; Sussan, Hall, and Meamber 2012).

To sum up, the consumption of products/brands can help individuals to master their identity projects by transferring symbolic meaning to consumers' selves (Kleine and Schultz Kleine 2000). Identity construction through luxury consumption remained rather untouched, probably assuming that the conceptual underpinning of luxury is unambiguously related to social status, or remains a permanent desire (Belk, Ger, and Askegaard 2003) of the aspirational class. Following the assumption that consumers, themselves, define what they perceive as luxury, luxury might contribute in many ways to consumers' identity construction. This might encompass a broad array of actual, ideal, extended, multiple, alternative, and transformative self-experiences, eventually involving luxury products and brands. Luxury experiences help individuals to negotiate and construct their personal self-narrative (Bauer et al. 2011); luxury makes individuals feel unique and generates a multitude of potential self negotiations and constellations so as to create a coherent self-narrative. Our empirical study aims to contribute to this field of research and to uncover luxury experiences that go beyond traditional conceptualizations of luxury.

METHODOLOGY

This study applies an interpretative, exploratory approach to gain a detailed understanding of luxury experiences' contribution to consumers' selves. To achieve maximum variation of views on luxury experiences and the respective effect on the self, selected informants differed with regard to age group, job/educational background, and gender (Ritchie and Lewis 2003). We applied purposeful sampling, selecting German speaking informants who are in accord with our selection criteria. The number of informants amounts to 17 (7 male, 10 female; age range: 24-84, mean = 41; education: university degree: 8, high school degree: 4, no high school degree: 5; marital status: married: 7, in a relationship: 8, single: 2).

This study uses diary research for investigating consumers' personal luxury moments. Diaries are documents containing informants' regular records of events, observations, and thoughts as well as feelings, experiences and consequences (Bolger, Davis, and Rafaeli 2003, 580). Qualitative diary research is a method that enables the researcher to deeply understand processes, relationships and consumers in *their* world (Patterson 2005) and to gain intimate and personal insights in an unobtrusive way (Alaszewski 2006, 43). In the present research context, consumers wrote diaries on an everyday basis (Alaszewski 2006), providing introspective accounts of luxury moments, related experiences, and feelings (Bolger et al. 2003). The diaries provide in-depth insights into consumers' subjective perceptions of luxury experience and its contribution to consumers' selves. We analyzed consumer diaries, using an inductive categorization process (Kreiner, Hollensbe, and Sheep 2006; Spiggle 1994), and constant comparative method (Charmaz 2006).

FINDINGS

The findings of our diary study brought forward a myriad of everyday and 'grand' luxuries that range from materialistic, romantic notions of a life of luxury to metaphysical accounts of eudaimonic well-being and living a happy and fulfilling life. Consumers' perceptions of luxury embrace object- and experience-related, abstract and concrete notions of luxury. Our analysis of consumer diaries illustrates that consumers' luxury moments revolve around multifaceted experiences of *having* (materialistic self), *doing* (liberating, oscillating, integrating and relating self), *being* (harmony of selves), and *becoming* (achievement-oriented and self-transformational) (cf. Belk 1988). As Michael succinctly notes:

"There are little, everyday luxuries and the big ones, which is something extraordinary, something you have aspired to have, do, or be for a long time." (Michael, 28)

Having

Having strongly reflects traditional conceptualizations of luxury, highlighting the importance of luxury objects (Vickers and Renand 2003), and experiences (Tynan et al. 2009). Consumers define and express their materialistic self with strong accounts related to *precious possessions and places*, that is, luxury objects that are

Table 1: Sample characteristics

No.	Code Name	Gender	Age	Education	Marital Status
1	David	male	29	University	relationship
2	Michael	male	28	University	relationship
3	Eva	female	58	High school	single
4	Jennifer	female	26	University	relationship
5	Tina	female	51	No high school	relationship
6	Claudia	female	22	University	relationship
7	Sarah	female	34	University	married
8	Susanna	female	24	High school	relationship
9	Peter	male	30	University	single
10	John	male	25	High school	relationship
11	Philip	male	63	No high school	married
12	Patricia	female	42	No high school	married
13	Robert	male	48	University	married
14	Linda	female	32	No high school	married
15	Barbara	female	84	No high school	married
16	Elisabeth	female	27	High school	relationship
17	James	male	56	University	married

"mine" (Belk 1988; Goffman 1959; Mittal 2006). These special possessions and eventually multi-sensory experiences are typically related to convenience consumption of high-priced 'little luxuries'.

> *"I currently own a shampoo that I also used this morning. Whenever I use it I am excited because it smells so good, lasts much longer and I do only need tiny bits of it. And the bottles look really nice ☺. I should probably also mention that shampoo and conditioner cost around 80€ and that is pure luxury for me... but it is really good." (Elizabeth, 27)*

Traditional luxury objects often derive their value from the superfluous, or *unnecessity*. We do not need them but appreciate the fact that we can *indulge* whenever we want. Consuming these luxury objects reflects traditional luxury consumption at its best. It speaks to a "because I'm worth it" self, which is not to be confused neither with practices of "self-care", as discussed by Rindfleish (2005), nor with aesthetic consumption practices. As demonstrated in the diary excerpt of Patricia, the luxury of *having* reflects 'the special treat out of the ordinary', as suggested by Hansen and Wänke (2011).

> *"Today I bought a beautiful scarf in the berry colors that are currently en vogue. I saw it last week already and I really liked it. Even though it was not expensive I did not buy it because I actually own enough scarves. But then I could not stop thinking about it all week long and today I bought it – I was lucky that it was still there. I do not really need it but I treated myself and it feels great ☺!" (Patricia, 42)*

Doing

Apart from classical ownership of luxury goods, reports of luxury experiences comprise various states of a self released, liberated, and able to live out the most wanted facet of self. Consumers' narratives revolve around desires of *doing* and related moments of fulfillment. Diaries vividly illustrate how consumers pursue multiple selves that mutually co-exist, complement, or conflict with each other. Consumers constantly balance this multiplicity of selves through processes of self-negotiation (Bahl and Milne 2010). We found that these processes involve *liberating an aspired self* (i.e., striving for/actually achieving a desirable state of self), *oscillating between selves* (i.e., processes of switching between selves), (unexpected) relieving states of *self integration*, and *self-others relations*. The goal of *doing* is the achievement of an ideal state of liberation and integration, which is typically experienced as luxury.

Liberating an aspired self. Consumers often describe states of suspense that precede luxury moments, whose dissolution is experienced as self-release. Liberating an aspired self reflects a consumer's striving for or actual achievement of a desirable, often rare state of self. This process eventually involves self-experiences that are perceived as luxury moments. The liberation of one's self can consist of *disposing of unwanted parts of a self*, for instance, by having the possibility to partially externalize or completely overcome certain aspects/duties that are typically associated with a specific role.

> *"With Ms. X as a part-time office manager I have the luxury to free myself from bothersome administrative tasks and to concentrate on activities that I am qualified for." (James, 56)*

Many narratives illustrate a strong urge to *escape* the profanity of everyday life. Luxury lies in the possibility to do so by transforming common everyday situations into special moments. Similar to Atwal and William's (2009) description of escapist qualities of luxury brands, these luxury moments show qualities of high intensity and high involvement with the experience.

> *"During the day, I really have hardly any time for me, but on days, when I don't get around doing anything, there is at least tea for me. A cup of tea is then on that day a little island, on which I am. It is so small that nobody else can be there. I'm sitting on it with my tea. As soon as I've finished the tea, a pirate ship docks with a three-headed crew at the age of 10 months, 3 years, and 5 years." (Sarah, 34)*

Liberating one's self is further associated with "doing what I want", that is, the *freedom* to define one's ideal state of self, for instance, by choosing between two selves one could or should reside in. Freedom can manifest itself through indulgence in *forbidden pleasures*. This type of self- liberation eventually involves struggles between conflicting selves, before an ultimate decision is made that liberates a self, which is not dominated by moral obligations or, as denoted by Cialdini, Reno and Kallgren (1990), by injunctive and descriptive norms of doing/not doing. These acts of liberation put the "happy self" in the foreground, the self that is not constrained by considerations of boundary setting "other" (Joy et al. 2010).

> *"While looking at the flowerage in front of me, some exceptionally big blossoms attracted my attention. 'Come on, pick them and put them in a vase'. In this moment I felt like split half: One part of me said: 'Take some of these beautiful, golden branches of this spring bush. It would look beautiful in your vase with some blue flowers'. The other part of me admonished me: 'Let them here. Here they look most beautiful ... In your vase they are lovely but only for a short time and without fulfilling their actual purpose.' Guess what I did? My egotism won!" (Barbara, 84)*

Not all self-liberation can necessarily be attributed to an individual's free will. Self-liberation is in many cases only possible due to a force majeure, which *unleashes an aspired self* from social constraints and external circumstances. When externalities happen to liberate unexpected time for a more aspired self, these moments become like valuable gifts, experienced as moments of luxury.

> *"This afternoon I sat on my balcony for the first time this spring, although it was a workday. My customer cancelled the meeting and I had time for myself. I went cycling, had some coffee and was full of joy over the unexpected spare time—that's luxury." (Tina, 51)*

Oscillating between multiple selves. Oscillating between multiple selves denotes the process of switching between selves and accentuating different selves at different points in time. Both *factual oscillations* and related rituals, as well as *mental oscillations* are experienced as luxury. Factual oscillations involve actually switching between selves, that is, entering, residing in, and/or expressing a desirable self. Mental oscillations describe the process of imagining or mentally simulating to switch between selves.

> *"I love being with my family. I'm really looking forward to see my family and my cat every time I'm going home—it's like a safe haven for me. Yet, being with them all the time wouldn't be possible. I simply love being able to live in two worlds, my hometown and the town where I'm currently living." (David, 29)*

"Today I bought again the somewhat more expensive bio-bananas from the Dominican Republic. At home I ate them instantly with pleasure. Since my holidays in the Caribbean I do not eat bananas carelessly anymore. Whenever I eat them I'm mentally on the beach under palm trees enjoying the turquoise blue sea—pure endorphins!" (Patricia, 42)

Oscillation is not always based on a deliberate choice but dictated by external forces. While not being a voluntary endeavor, especially *oscillating with nature* is experienced as luxury. Consumers subordinate themselves to an external force that liberates them from the burden of making their own decision and allows them oscillating with a naturally recurring pattern.

"After the long winter, which was not really enjoyable, nature's awakening incited a need to stimulate my senses and to really pep myself up. And so I got started: first a thorough hot and cold shower with the bathroom window wide open. The prickling feeling of the stimulated blood circulation already generated a pleasant sensation. The ensuing extended body treatment added to this pleasant sensation. Finally also the choice of clothes had a touch of spring – I chose something extraordinary. Then I looked into the mirror and my smiling face told me that it was good". (Barbara, 84)

A phenomenon closely related to oscillation is the *integration of multiple selves*. Integration implies the temporary and often unexpected relieving state of *partial integration* of aspects appertaining to one self into another self, for instance, the integration of leisure aspects into a professional self. Integrated selves are not necessarily balanced. A specific facet of self dominates whereas another self—which is most wanted in a specific context—is permitted to squeeze in. These unexpected experiences are very much valued and perceived as luxury. On the other hand, consumers experience frustration and non-luxury when an aspired integration of selves fails, typically due to some external restriction.

"Today I was in our plant in Genk, Belgium, where the Mondeo, S-Max and Galaxy are built. This time my colleague had plenty of time and gave us a tour of the plant. Typically, plant visits are very stressful, since we have many problems to solve. But this time it was great." (Robert, 48)

Relations between one's self and others. Considering our self in relation to others indicates the relational value of luxury (Tynan et al. 2009). Others extend and complement our selves, evoking the feeling that they "are part of my self".

"It is a beautiful day. The sun is shining. We have a relaxed breakfast and decide to visit the zoo. Emma runs from time to time and sits on Christopher's shoulders. Her eyes are glowing with joy and she is laughing. It is so beautiful to see how she enjoys it." (Linda, 32)

Others also contribute to luxury experiences when consumers succeed to *demarcate* the 'I' (Mittal 2006) from the social self, for instance, by recognizing their current self's rareness and unattainability for others.

"My part-time job since October 2009 is a special luxury. It gives me the wonderful feeling of a new dimension of freedom and control over time. Having the time to enjoy a red traffic light and to consciously relax while other people are stressed out is quite luxurious". (James, 56)

Both, enjoying the social self and enjoying one's very personal self are luxury when we deliberately enact them.

Being

Unity of body, mind, and environment characterize being. Contrary to doing, being does not involve actions or activities but rather states of the self. Examples vary from simple bodily relaxations, realization of the state of health, stocking up energy or sensorial states of wholeness to feelings of unity with the natural or social environment. *Being* involves intense existential experiences, enjoying what consumers depict as pure existence, relating to what Belk (1988) and Mittal (2006) describe as the innermost core self. Here we find love, timelessness, and deep, intense feelings of wholeness that consumers describe as *Dasein* (Heidegger 1962), *harmony, the authentic self,* and *joy of living.* The luxury of *Dasein* (Heidegger 1962) is commonly portrayed as doing nothing but being.

"I meditated today. Being completely relaxed and the sense of delight afterwards is luxury to me." (Michael, 28)

Luxurious states of *harmony* can be reached if consumers are able to organize the interplay of selves and the extent to which they live out these selves freely; or when they feel perfect harmony of being and living. As harmony is a state of being it is independent of doing and merely a consciousness of self as enjoying, valuing what is. The harmonious self is not a category of its own but may be the sole self, the relational self, or the spiritual self amongst many others—all actual selves being harmoniously united. Consumers report states of harmony with themselves but also how enjoyable it is to share the joy of being with others:

"Today I'll stay in my apartment, and this is today's luxury: privacy. It's important for me to isolate myself and to enjoy time with myself from time to time. [...] sometimes I experience being alone as luxury, even though this may sound a bit strange." (Peter, 30)

"Desire, fun, amusement, recreation...and what's most important: To know and feel how great life can be! AND to be free to share this feeling!" (John, 25)

Authenticity is luxury for those consumers who sense the innermost need to simply be who they are and appreciate being free from role pressures. Consumer diaries portray the consciously contemplating individual, who is very aware of the emptiness of the materialistic self and the self being totally straitjacketed in societal constraints. Material consumption does not correlate with subjective well-being, nor does it capture consumers' spiritual motivations for consumption (Sussan et al. 2012). Consumer narratives illustrate that luxury is ultimately associated with *joy of living*, referring to pleasurable feelings, such as warmth, joy, amusement, and felicity.

"It's Sunday. The warm sun is shining through the window even though a cold borealis is blowing outside. I lie in my armchair and relax. I enjoy the 'dolce far niente' with all senses. As always, peace and satisfaction confirm that I'm really fine. Compared to politicians who depend on fighting and begging for everybody's favor to 'be someone' or better to 'appear to be someone' I have much more freedom. I enjoy this consciousness of being free and perceive it as luxury." (Barbara, 84)

Becoming

Becoming ultimately describes those moments when transformative processes, related to important life projects, are consciously perceived and valued as life achievements and self-realization.

"Being able to do a dissertation is luxury; it's hard work but definitely luxury; forget all about new fashion and other material goods. Simply knowing that you are getting closer to the great achievement feels great. What I mean is: being able to proof that I can do it. That's part of my self-realization process. And my company pays for it—that's luxury." (David, 29)

Becoming is a process rather than a state and relates to the goal-oriented achiever as well as to more spiritual processes of self-transformation, or self-transcendence. Becoming draws upon common imaginations of an ideal future self but is different from desire as it is more fulfilling the more it is close to its realization. Supporters of becoming, as for instance a financial sponsor, a supportive environment, family, or one's own capabilities are experienced as luxury.

DISCUSSION

This article illuminates how consumers' perceptions and experiences of luxury contribute to consumers' selves. Luxury, from a consumer perspective, is not characterized through boldly exhibited products and brands but rather constitutes exceptionally valuable, potentially hidden moments of luxury that serve as supporters of self in everyday living. These luxury experiences are more intimately related to different states and processes of self than traditionally assumed: Luxury experiences are much more than just a perceived extension of consumers' selves (Belk 1988) but rather an opportunity to live out different selves, reflected by symbolic consumption, indulgence in special moments and activities, moments of harmony, self-enhancement and self-transcendence.

Our findings suggest that respondents do not privilege any of these luxury experiences. *Having* and owning is as valuable in providing luxury experiences as *doing*, *being* and *becoming*. Figure 1 portrays how luxury moments are related to self theory.

Belk's seminal work on special possessions (1988), Daniel Miller's study about the importance of things (2009), or Klein and Hill's study into forced dispossessions (2008) demonstrate the importance of material things, and why they potentially qualify for moments of luxury. Owning and having per se is not a luxury moment; but the deep symbolic of possessions and how they relate to our selves and lives is. Research into motivation theories and autotelic activities (Csikszentmihalyi 1997) provides ample evidence of the importance of *doing*. Csikszentmihalyi (2000, 271) emphasizes that "…trying to avoid the mental chaos of everyday life by resorting to acquisitions and passive entertainment does not work very well". Our study strongly supports this critical finding, and extends this research by relating *doing* to the transient self. Doing is active and qualifies as everyday luxury, when we can freely choose what we want to do most in a specific situation. We enjoy doing different things at different times. Our study shows that moments of luxury emanate from meaningful activities of relating, liberating, oscillating, and integration of selves at specific times.

Our findings partly corroborate Ahuvia's (2005) findings that consumers are looking for a synthesis of conflicting selves, or harmonious states of being, respectively. However, oscillation as a way to switch between worlds and selves extends Ahuvia's (2005) findings. Similar to what Tian and Belk (2005) have coined self-shifting and oscillation, we also find that consumers switch among selves yet, moments of luxury are experienced only when individuals actually enact different selves, purposefully, or unexpectedly. Oscillation is an important principle and demonstrates the volatile character of luxury moments. One day we long for solitude, the other day we experience togetherness as luxury. It is these contradictions and desires (Belk et al. 2003) which are never perfectly fulfilled in life that seem to make luxury moments precious, and our lives interesting.

Our findings also clearly extend Bahl and Milne's (2010) meta-self theory in that they show that consumers not only avoid or manage conflicting selves, or accord with a dominating meta-self, but also indulge themselves in luxurious states of perfect harmony. In many ways states of perfect harmony liken moments of happiness. Harmony is not described as a perfect integration of different facets of self but rather acknowledges its facets. Perfect harmony unfolds as a metaphysical experience of oneness with nature, or humanness with a *Dasein*-like quality. This is exactly what *becoming* is about, sometimes as an imperfect striving for achievement, sometimes as

Figure 1: Luxury experiences and self

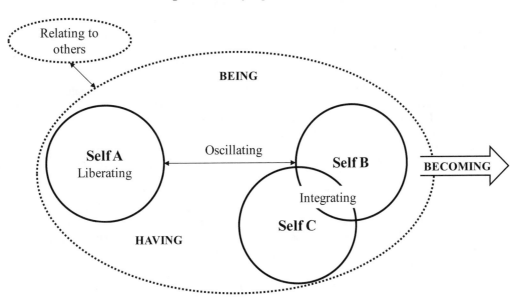

a self-developmental and self-transcending endeavor. Becoming is about the possibility to realize the alternative self that I might have become (Obodaru 2012). These spiritual motivations for (non-)consumption have recently been described by Skousgaard (2006) and Sussan et al. (2012). Our study further illuminates the immanent spiritual quality of luxury experiences.

Overall, this study suggests that luxury is not a permanent state but seems to be a *transient* concept that manifests in moments of luxury and thus, is inherently experiential. Luxury moments include the rare and precious. It is the moment when we unwrap the little silver spoons, when we look at the wonderful new painting, or when we brush our leather shoes with the glossy toecap. Luxury experiences in many ways are preceded by moments of suspense before the many little dramas in people's lives dissolve, and the most aspired self is finally liberated. Moments of luxury then comprise experiences of something extraordinary in ordinary life, integrating the demands of different roles, escaping, and oscillating between different selves. Luxury experiences are also *abstract*. Postmodern reflexivity of individuals and practices of "self-care" —becoming someone you were not at the beginning—permeate our search for happiness in life (Rindfleish 2005). This search, however, needs some harmonious ending. Ultimately, human beings are striving for self-transcendence, self-transformation, and engage in conscious contemplation resulting in deep feelings of gratitude and harmony, reflecting processes of becoming, and perfect states of being. In that sense, moments of luxury liken concepts of consumer happiness, eudaimonic well-being (Bauer, McAdams, and Pals 2008), joy of life, and other related constructs. Is it luxury, then?…What else?

REFERENCES

Ahuvia, Aaron C. (2005), "Beyond the Extended Self: Loved Objects and Consumers' Identity Narratives," *Journal of Consumer Research*, 32 (June), 171–84.

Alaszewski, Andy (2006), *Using Diaries for Social Research*, London: Sage.

Atwal, Glyn and Alistair Williams (2009), "Luxury Brand Marketing the Experience Is Everything!" *The Journal of Brand Management*, 16 (February), 338–46.

Bahl, Shalini and George R. Milne (2010), "Talking to Ourselves: A Dialogical Exploration of Consumption Experiences," *Journal of Consumer Research*, 37 (June), 176–95.

Bauer, Jack J., Dan P. McAdams, and Jennifer L. Pals (2008), "Narrative Identity and Eudaimonic Well-Being," *Journal of Happiness Studies*, 9 (January), 81–104.

Bauer, Martina, Sylvia von Wallpach, and Andrea Hemetsberger (2011), "'My Little Luxury': A Consumer-Centred, Experiential View," *Marketing - Journal of Research and Management*, 33 (January), 57–68.

Belk, Russell W. (1988), "Possessions and the Extended Self," *Journal of Consumer Research*, 15 (September), 139–68.

Belk, Russell W., Güliz Ger, and Søren Askegaard (2003), "The Fire of Desire: A Multisited Inquiry Into Consumer Passion," *Journal of Consumer Research*, 30 (December), 326–51.

Berger, Jonah A. and Chip Heath (2007), "Where Consumers Diverge from Others: Identity Signaling and Product Domains," *Journal of Consumer Research*, 34 (August), 121–34.

Berthon, Pierre, Leyland Pitt, Michael Parent, and Jean-Paul Berthon (2009), "Aesthetics and Ephemerality: Observing and Preserving the Luxury Brand," *California Management Review*, 52 (1), 45–66.

Bolger, Niall, Angelina Davis, and Eshkol Rafaeli (2003), "Diary Methods: Capturing Life as It Is Lived," *Annual Review of Psychology*, 54 (February), 579–617.

Brakus, Josko J, Bernd H Schmitt, and Lia Zarantonello (2009), "Brand Experience: What Is It? How Is It Measured? Does It Affect Loyalty?" *Journal of Marketing*, 73 (May), 52–68.

Brückner, Michael (2008), *Megamarkt Luxus: Wie Anleger von der Lust auf Edles Profitieren können*, Munich: FinanzBuch Verlag.

Charmaz, Kathy (2006), *Constructing Grounded Theory: A Practical Guide Through Qualitative Analysis*, London: Sage.

Christodoulides, George, Nina Michaelidou, and Ching Hsing Li (2009), "Measuring Perceived Brand Luxury: An Evaluation of the Bli Scale," *Journal of Brand Management*, 16 (January), 395–405.

Cialdini, Robert B., Raymond R. Reno, and Carl A. Kallgren (1990), "A Focus Theory of Normative Conduct: Recycling the Concept of Norms to Reduce Littering in Public Places," *Journal of Personality and Social Psychology*, 58 (June), 1015–26.

Csikszentmihalyi, Mihaly (1997), *Creativity: Flow and the Psychology of Discovery and Invention*, New York, NY: Harper Perennial.

_____ (2000), "The Costs and Benefits of Consuming," *Journal of Consumer Research*, 27 (September), 267–72.

Gistri, Giacomo, Simona Romani, Stefano Pace, Veronica Gabrielli, and Silvia Grappi (2009), "Consumption Practices of Counterfeit Luxury Goods in the Italian Context," *Journal of Brand Management*, 16 (February), 364–74.

Goffman, Erving (1959), *The Presentation of Self in Everyday Life*, New York: The Overlook Press.

Han, Young Jee, Joseph C. Nunes, and Xavier Drèze (2010), "Signaling Status with Luxury Goods: The Role of Brand Prominence," *Journal of Marketing*, 74 (July), 15–30.

Hansen, Jochim and Michaela Wänke (2011), "The Abstractness of Luxury," *Journal of Economic Psychology*, 32 (October), 789–96.

Heidegger, Martin (1962), *Being and Time*, Malden, MA: Wiley-Blackwell.

Hoppe, Melanie, Andrea Hemetsberger, Elisabeth Pichler, and Kurt Matzler (2009), "The Transformative Power of Brands - an Investigation into the Impact of Self-Transformation on Consumer Passion," *Proceedings of the 38th EMAC Conference, Nantes*.

Joy, Annamma, John F. Sherry, Gabriele Troilo, and Jonathan Deschenes (2010), "Re-Thinking the Relationship between Self and Other: Levinas and Narratives of Beautifying the Body," *Journal of Consumer Culture*, 10 (November), 333–61.

Keller, Kevin L. (2009), "Managing the Growth Tradeoff: Challenges and Opportunities in Luxury Branding," *Journal of Brand Management*, 16 (January), 290–301.

Klein, Jill G. and Ronald P. Hill (2008), "Rethinking Macro-Level Theories of Consumption: Research Findings from Nazi Concentration Camps," *Journal of Macromarketing*, 28 (September), 228–42.

Kleine, Robert E. and Susan Schultz Kleine (2000), "Consumption and Self-Schema Changes Throughout the Identity Project Life Cycle," in *Advances in Consumer Research*, Vol. 27, ed. Stephen J. Hoch and Robert J. Meyer, Provo, UT: Association for Consumer Research, 279–85.

Kleine, Susan, Robert E. Kleine III, and Chris T. Allen (1995), "How Is a Possession 'Me' or 'Not Me'? Characterizing Types and an Antecedent of Material Possession Attachment," *Journal of Consumer Research*, 22 (December), 327–43.

Kreiner, Glen E., Elaine C. Hollensbe, and Mathew L. Sheep (2006), "Where is the 'Me' Among the 'We'? Identity Work and the Search for Optimal Balance," *Academy of Management Journal*, 49 (October), 1031–57.

Mick, David G. (2006), "Meaning and Mattering Through Transformative Consumer Research," in *Advances in Consumer Research*, Vol. 33, ed. Cornelia Pechmann and Linda L. Price, Duluth, MN: Association for Consumer Research, 1–4.

Miller, Daniel (2009), *Stuff*, Malden, MA: Polity.

Mittal, Banwari (2006), "I, Me, and Mine—How Products Become Consumers' Extended Selves," *Journal of Consumer Behaviour*, 5 (November/December), 550–62.

Obodaru, Otilia (2012), "The Self Not Taken: How Alternative Selves Develop and How They Influence Our Professional Lives," *Academy of Management Review*, 37 (January), 34–57.

Patterson, Anthony (2005), "Processes, Relationships, Settings, Products and Consumers: The Case for Qualitative Diary Research," *Qualitative Market Research: An International Journal*, 8 (2), 142–56.

Rindfleish, Jennifer (2005), "Consuming the Self: New Age Spirituality as 'Social Product' in Consumer Society," *Consumption, Markets and Culture*, 8 (November), 343–60.

Ritchie, Jane and Jane Lewis (2003), *Qualitative Research Practice: A Guide for Social Science Students and Researchers*, London: Sage.

Sirgy, Joseph M. (1982), "Self-Concept in Consumer Behavior: A Critical Review," *Journal of Consumer Research*, 9 (December), 287–300.

Skousgaard, Heather (2006), "A Taxonomy of Spiritual Motivations for Consumption," in *Advances in Consumer Research*, Vol. 33, ed. Connie Pechmann and Linda Price, Duluth, MN: Association for Consumer Research, 294–96.

Spiggle, Susan (1994), "Analysis and Interpretation of Qualitative Data in Consumer Research," *Journal of Consumer Research*, 21 (December), 491–503.

Sprott, David, Sandor Czellar, and Eric Spangenberg (2009), "The Importance of a General Measure of Brand Engagement on Market Behavior: Development and Validation of a Scale," *Journal of Marketing Research*, 46 (February), 92–104.

Stets, Jan E. and Peter J. Burke (2000), "Identity Theory and Social Identity Theory," *Social Psychology Quarterly*, 63 (September), 224–37.

Sussan, Fiona, Richard Hall, and Laurie A. Meamber (2012), "Introspecting the Spiritual Nature of a Brand Divorce," *Journal of Business Research*, 65 (April), 520–26.

Tajfel, Henri (1982), "Social Psychology of Intergroup Relations," *Annual Review of Psychology*, 33 (February), 1–39.

Tian, Kelly and Russell W. Belk (2005), "Extended Self and Possessions in the Workplace," *Journal of Consumer Research*, 32 (September), 297–310.

Tsai, Shu-Pei (2005), "Impact of Personal Orientation on Luxury-Brand Purchase Value," *International Journal of Market Research*, 47 (July), 351–82.

Tynan, Carloine, Sally McKechnie, and Celine Chhuon (2009), "Co-Creating Value for Luxury Brands," *Journal of Business Research*, 63 (November), 1156–63.

Veblen, Thorstein (1902), *The Theory of the Leisure Class*, New York, NY: MacMillan.

Vickers, Jonathan S. and Franck Renand (2003), "The Marketing of Luxury Goods: An Exploratory Study-Three Conceptual Dimensions," *The Marketing Review*, 3 (December), 459–78.

Warde, Alan (2005), "Consumption and Theories of Practice," *Journal of Consumer Culture*, 5 (July), 131–53.

Yeoman, Ian and Una McMahon-Beattie (2006), "Luxury Markets and Premium Pricing," *Journal of Revenue and Pricing Management*, 4 (January), 319–28.

Social Curation in Consumer Communities
Consumers as Curators of Online Media Content

Mikko Villi, Aalto University, Finland

Johanna Moisander, Aalto University, Finland

Annamma Joy, University of British Columbia, Canada

INTRODUCTION

In contemporary consumer culture, the consumption of media content online is increasingly a shared social experience. In the US, for instance, as much as 75% of the online audience consumes news shared by peers (Purcell et al. 2010). As a result, the importance of consumer communities in distributing and marketing professional media content is growing (Newman and Dutton 2011). Online media and the particular applications designed for sharing media content enable and encourage the contemporary media consumers to share their media consumption experiences by providing links in e-mail messages or web pages, and increasingly by tweeting, using such social plugins as the Recommend Button on Facebook, or utilizing services like Pinterest and Storify. In the paper, our aim is to contribute to a better understanding of this phenomenon and Internet-based activity by theoretically elaborating on its nature as *social curation*.

In building our theoretical argument, we start from the idea that curation is essentially about people adding their qualitative judgement to whatever is being gathered and organized, as Rosenbaum (2011, 3-4) has argued. In the context of the media, curation is about consumers aggregating, sharing, ranking, juxtaposing and critiquing content on a variety of platforms (Clark and Aufderheide 2009, 6-7). In the literature on computer science (Ball, Whyte, and Donnelly 2010; Goble et al. 2010), curation is usually discussed in relation to data management. More explicitly, digital curation entails the management and preservation of digital material to ensure accessibility over the long-term (Higgins 2011, 79). We part ways with this data management approach in our study and rather focus on the aspects of sharing and dissemination when discussing social curation (Gaskill 2010; Liu 2010; Ammann 2011). More specifically, we set out to conceptualize social curation as a communal practice, similar to practices that characterize brand communities (Muniz and O'Guinn 2001; Schau, Muniz, and Arnould 2009). The discussion and elaboration of the concept of social curation enables to elucidate the role of consumer communities (Kozinets 1999, 259; Prahalad and Ramaswamy 2004, 8; Arvidsson 2005, 242) in the practices of distributing and marketing media content – imbuing media content with social significance – and to understand content sharing as consumption phenomena on the Internet (Belk 2010, 730).

From a technological perspective, social curation refers to the communication of media content (e.g. news and entertainment) in digital networks, in particular by using social media platforms and services. But since we are trying to contribute to a better conceptual understanding of social curation as consumption, we work towards a more sociological and cultural definition and conceptualization of social curation. On a very general level, we look into social curation as consumption of media content in online market environments. It can be viewed as a social and communicative activity through which people engage in appropriation, appreciation and mediation of digital media content, for various kinds of personal, social and political purposes (Warde 2005). Media content is put to use (appropriated and appreciated) in the course of engaging in the practice of social curation. In practice, this entails a set of sense-making and sense-giving activities that are grounded in individual and social activity (Weick 1995). These activities of the media consumers include browsing, reading, and watching interesting media content; making sense of the content by analyzing, evaluating, and categorizing; giving sense to the content by commenting, narrating, and tagging; and communicating and mediating the content by recommending, posting, and tweeting.

From the viewpoint of consumer research, the media audience cannot be regarded as a group of passive consumers, but as active participants in the processes through which value is created in the market (Potts et al. 2008; Cova and Dalli 2009, 315; Banks and Humphreys 2008; Merrin 2009). Personalized media consumption is experiencing a transition toward consumption as a networked practice (Jenkins 2006, 244). The transformations in the relationship between media producers and consumers may suggest a shift in which the frameworks of analysis and categories that worked well in the context of an industrial media economy are no longer helpful (Banks and Humphreys 2008, 402), as the consumption of media content is not restricted anymore to the reception of ready-made mass products (Chan-Olmstead 2006, 31; Livingstone 2008, 394; Merrin, 2009, 24). The industrial model of one-to-many mass consumption is giving way to an interactive model based on partnership and conversation with consumers (Hartley 2004, 6).

Despite the fact that social curation represents a strategically important change in the business environment for media companies, social curation as a phenomenon is currently inadequately understood and studied, particularly theoretically. Along with discussing the relevance and the implications of social curation for the media industry, we consider it to be important to critically refine and elaborate on social curation as a concept and a construct in consumer research. In the paper, we therefore set out to work towards a theoretically more sophisticated conceptualization of social curation, drawing firstly from the discussion on art curation.

ANALYSIS OF THE CONCEPT

The Element of Curation in Social Curation

In order to conceptualize social curation, it is necessary to pose two questions: (1) what is *curation* in social curation, and (2) what is *social* in social curation. Curation as a practice and concept has extended beyond galleries and museums into different fields of consumption in the creative industries, as the words curate and curator have become increasingly common in describing activities such as selecting and presenting (Schlatter 2010). In a sense, curation, both as a concept and practice, has gone viral.

We consider it to be important to question the rather loose use of the term curation. Conventionally, in the art world, curators have functioned as gate-keepers, as arbitrators of taste (Ames 1992), recognizing, and in some cases nurturing, emerging trends, celebrating a previously unknown artist as worthy of our attention, or delegating another to oblivion. As such, they carry a position of great trust and authority. Little wonder that the term curator, derived from the Latin word cuare, translates to *to care*. Curators care not only about a given art object, but also about how that object is perceived and experienced, and, equally important, whether and how it is remembered.

Through their exhibitions, collections, and catalogues (Lisus and Ericson 1999), art museums provide a particular vision of culture, one imbued with aesthetic value by the individual taste and knowledge of their curators, the linchpins within the inner workings of the art world. Museums' primary mission, to bring art to the public, is carried out through the efforts of curators, who serve as mediators between the artist and the observer as they select, organize, and display art objects, siting them within a cultural and historical continuum. Through special exhibits and related educational activities, curators target a diverse audience, ranging from artists and fellow connoisseurs, to dilettantes in search of an afternoon's diversion, to tourists eager to pose before an important object, documenting their visit with a souvenir photograph.

The curators' drive to capture their audience's attention, and to leave a lasting impression, has long depended on an array of skills both broad and finely honed, with a strong emphasis on writing. Curation writing, whether a simple identifying label or a complex discussion of an object's embodiment of a specific trend, or a mirroring of social mores, offers a context crafted to pique and sustain interest. For many museum attendees, words matter: they can shape a museum experience, providing a means for understanding a given display. Is an object a variation on a theme, a continuous innovation, or a breakthrough into completely new territory? Is it a simple reflection of, or a heartfelt response to, the political realities of its time and place? The more complex the narrative, the greater the importance accorded the object, and the higher its value (Morgan 1996).

Much as research and development are critical to the strategic thrust of an organization, so is the work of curators critical to success within the art world (Joy and Sherry 2003). The heart of any art museum from a curatorial perspective is its permanent collection, with curators bearing primary responsibility for precisely what is collected, how it is classified and interpreted, and how and when it is exhibited. Curators are knowledge brokers of a specific nature, taking culture created by others, and interpreting and publicizing it for the public good.

Historically, curators have had the cultural cache to make unknown objects both known and valuable, serving as a link between art production and consumption. They have had personal and scholarly reputations to develop and sustain; as professionals, they have had to be objective in their evaluation of art, as well as of the artists and movements on which they choose to focus. Often authors in their own rights, curators have exerted a powerful influence within not only the art world, but also within the general public—one need look no farther than the scholarly, painstakingly produced catalogues, mementos of the equally scholarly and painstakingly produced shows that they chronicled, to appreciate the cultural impact curators have wielded over the years.

That curatorial role is changing rapidly, however, and concurrently diminishing in gravitas, as museums have increasingly (and, one might argue, unavoidably), become a highly theatrical hybrid form of art commingled with commerce. The once scholarly catalogues have been replaced by glossy brochures (Sandler 1996). Blockbuster exhibits, necessitated by the realities of museum finances, are becoming more common. The curators themselves, once armed with graduate degrees in the Fine Arts or related disciplines and active researchers in niche subjects, have been increasingly superseded by those more involved in overtly commercial endeavours. How to appeal to an audience with a less leisurely style of consumption, with an expectation of constantly refreshed imagery? The pull between high art and low commerce, while age-old, has escalated since the 1980s, as the art market welcomed art writers committed to research, conservation, publication, and art exhibition within a strong market orientation. As museums increasingly lack the funds to acquire new art, they often must sell objects from their permanent collections before acquiring new pieces in a bid to stay current. The

job of curators now, by necessity, includes assessing and monitoring the financial worth of museum holdings. While curators once typically were employed solely as permanent members of a museum staff, or as freelancers working with an assortment of museums, today many under-employed curators routinely also work for private investors, galleries, or auction houses to supplement their incomes. Where once a curator's job was to, in essence, protect an object from becoming a commodity, today their job is, in no small measure, to ensure that it does become a commodity, and more specifically a brand – one ideally with resale value in the museum gift shop.

There are many similarities between art curation and content curation in social media. According to Rohit Bhargava (2009), Senior Vice President of Strategy and Marketing for Ogilvy 360 Digital Influence, "a content curator is someone who continually finds, groups, organizes and shares the best and most relevant content on a specific issue online." The New York Times, which curates blog posts from outside sources, is a good example of a content curator. As Steve Rosenbaum (2009) of the Silicon Valley Insider comments about the New York Times, "what the Times knows is that content that they validate with their brand and redistribution becomes more valuable, both to readers and to the content curators." The same could be said of important curators in the Metropolitan Museum of Art, or the Smithsonian. The job of a content curator is not to create more content, but to make sense of the best and most relevant content and thereby to add a voice and point of view about existing material.

In principal, anyone who has an opinion about the value of a product and means to inform others about this and also to distribute the product itself can be a curator. However, when comparing the use of curation in the popular discourse to how it is conceived in the art context, we confront several problems with the somewhat inflated use of curation in describing content sharing online. Those who curate content in social media are not expected to use professional skills when curating content. They are not presumed to conduct research around the specific topics that they curate. In addition, they do not necessarily organize content into collections and structures, although such curation services as Storify offer the possibility to arrange online content into specific collections and create narratives that highlight the importance of the selected articles. On the Storify website (http://storify.com/tour) it is proclaimed that "Storify lets you curate social networks to build social stories, bringing together media scattered across the Web into a coherent narrative. We are building the story layer above social networks."

Professional art curation is more of a top-down process than a participatory activity. Gaskill (2010) ties social and curation explicitly together and defines the social curator as "a practitioner who seeks to contextualise fully the potential of exhibitions as structures of communication and exchange, and aims to maximise social interaction and intervention across curatorial approach, process and outcome." However, in this definition the social curator is still a (professional) practitioner, somebody who is trained to curate, not just a layperson who informs others in social media about interesting content.

According to Rosenbaum (2011, 3-4), there can be both amateur and professional curation. Social curation is about amateur curation, where the curators are ordinary consumers. Social curation is about choosing from a group of content possibilities, however not necessarily making the choices based on expert skills in, for example, art or journalism. Yet, ranking, juxtaposing and critiquing content requires some kind of knowledge, it is not an arbitrary practice. The amateurs might not be experts but they often have an educated and informed opinion, involving some accountability. However, it is unclear what is the relevance of this element of selection and qualitative judgement in social curation from the perspective of media organizations. Does it matter if the choices made by the consumers on what to distribute entail knowledge and expertise or not? Do the media companies care, what of their content is curated as long as their content is distributed as extensively as possible? Do connections matter more than expertise? Put bluntly, a professional authority with 50 Facebook friends might be less valuable as a curator for a media company than a high school kid with 1000 Facebook friends.

Importantly, in an era of abundance of online content, amateur curation – the bottom-up or lay-curation – serves an important role in making contents both known and valuable, serving as a link between media production and consumption. Social curation is a vital filter in content consumption on the Internet. In art curation, the curator is the linchpin in a system that imbues art with aesthetic significance, and curatorial decisions can catapult an object from obscurity to public exposure (Joy and Sherry 2003, 163). In the same vein, social curation as a practice can imbue various kinds of online media content with social significance and extend the circulation of those contents.

Social curation shares characteristics with both sharing and word-of-mouth communication. According to Belk (2010, 715-720), sharing is a consumer behaviour that bears on a broad array of consumption issues ranging from sharing household resources to file sharing. In contrast to other acquisition and distribution mechanisms, such as gift giving and commodity exchange, which involve transfers of ownership, sharing is about joint ownership and mutuality of possession (ibid.). Similarly, social curation is not about the exchange or transfer of ownership, because the one who curates the digital content does not lose possession of it – she can still read the news article, for example, after having curated it. Importantly, and in contrast to sharing, social curation is pronouncedly about distribution. Curation is not about sharing the car with other family members, but distributing content forward. Curation does not represent the sharing of ownership but rather the provision of access to others.

Social curators are knowledge brokers that interpret, publicize and endorse content. Thus, there is always an aspect of recommendation involved. This links social curation with word-of-mouth (WOM) communication (Brown, Broderick, and Lee 2007; Kozinets et al. 2010). But again, the element of distribution marks the difference. In social curation, the access to the content itself is provided with the recommendation. In the online environment, it is much easier to share the (digital, Internet-based) content, not just provide verbal descriptions of it. By contrast, in WOM the content or product is not necessarily distributed, but rather only an awareness of its existence is acknowledged by means of expressing an opinion. This is comparable with how in the context of art the curator provides the content, as opposed to an art reviewer or art critic who only offers information about the content.

SOCIAL CURATION AS A SOCIAL PHENOMENON

Now we turn to discuss what is *social* in social curation. In a general sense, social curation is a social activity in that it entails communicative interactions and relationships between two or more individuals. People engage in social curation as members of particular social entities, that is, groups, communities and society, as part of a whole network of social relations. As such, social curation represents social action in the sense that it is intentional and rule governed: it is performed in order to achieve particular purposes and in conformity to some social rules, and it is this intentional content that specifies what sort of an action it is (Fay and Moon 1994, 21). Social curation becomes intelligible based on not only the intentions of the social agent who performs the activity (the intentional communica-

tion of the agent) but also based on the culturally shared or collective understandings (ideas, norms, and values) that give meaning to and thus regulate the activity (Moisander and Valtonen 2012).

As a result, the ways in which individuals engage in social curation always and inevitably reflect the social and cultural context in which they perform the activity. The cultural context in which social curation has emerged and is typically performed is the participatory media consumer culture. Social curation may thus be viewed as social and cultural practice. From this perspective, the analytical focus shifts from the particular activities and technologies to the symbolic significance and uses of social curation in consumers' everyday lives, as integral parts of consumers' everyday lives especially as members of the contemporary media culture.

As a social and communicative practice, social curation may be viewed as a discursive activity through which people make sense of themselves as individuals and members of groups, communities and society. Much like authoring personal blogs and status updates, social curation maybe be viewed as a self-defining and self-expressive behaviour: people share content that is self-relevant and help them to communicate particular ideas and images of themselves to their peers (Schau and Gilly 2003). This discursive activity may also be something that relates to people's civic engagement or political activity as citizens and members of the political society (Kozinets and Handelman 2004). The social curator thus engages in the activity of curation in the role of a consumer and citizen.

Social curation is a practice through which people construct their individual and collective identities: they engage in identity work and pursue their identity projects (Holt and Thompson 2004; Mikkonen, Moisander, and Firat 2011; Thompson and Tambyah 1999) using the complex repertoires of images, narratives, and accounts that the global mediascape (Appadurai 1990, 1996) offers as discursive resources. Through social curation, consumers thus author and elaborate on coherent "narratives of the self" both for themselves and also to their peers and social networks (Shankar 2001; Thompson 1997). Through this identity work, people not only make sense of themselves but also build and maintain their personal relationships and create a sense of belonging and community (companionship, friendship) as well as collective identity as members of their in-groups and communities (Cova 1997; Cova and Pace 2006; Muniz and O'Guinn 2001).

The purpose is to be social, in that by *curating content people maintain social contacts to other people*. Alike any form of sharing, social curation is a communal act that links people to others and creates feelings of solidarity and bonding; it is an expression of the desire for connection (Belk 2010, 716-717). In social curation, this personal connection plays an important part. It is significant that the curator is somebody familiar, with whom the audience has a personal relationship (e.g. by being friends). Alike word-of-mouth communication, social curation is based on interpersonal exchanges (Brown et al. 2007, 4). This idea is expressed well in the way Facebook stresses the social aspect of recommending: "Rather than seeing popular stories, products or reviews from people you don't know, you'll now see content that matters to you the most—from your friends" (Haugen 2010).

Recent research shows how the sharing of media content in communities leads often to the receivers actually reading, listening or watching that content (Purcell et al. 2010, 40). It can be assumed that the curated content is commonly consumed because of the personal connection between the curator and the receivers and not necessarily because of the significant content-related expertise possessed by the curating individual. As Kozinets (1999, 259) notes, in the online environment, consumers evaluate quality together and place great weight on the judgments of their fellows. Therefore, a lot of the expertise involved in social curation is social in nature – it entails skills in maintaining relationships and nurturing the collective identity and the sense of belonging together.

IMPLICATIONS FOR THE MEDIA INDUSTRY

Our conceptualization of social curation opens up a number of research questions concerning the role of social curation in contemporary marketplace and consumer culture, in particular in the context of the media industry. Media consumers share media content, but they also share their media consumption experiences and especially the choices concerning which content they have decided to consume. In our research, we are especially interested in the implications of social curation for media organizations.

The backdrop for social curation is that, because of digital networks, media contents are in constant flux. Manovich (2008, 203) uses the term media mobility to describe a state where media contents never arrive at some final destination, as in the mass communication model. Instead, they continue to move between sites, people and devices, and as they move, they accumulate comments and discussions (ibid.). Similarly, Jenkins (2009) uses the term spreadable media to describe how the digital networks facilitate the sharing of contents (see also Terranova 2004, 2). What the Internet-based social networks have had an effect on are precisely the abilities of people to distribute content; because of the new communication platforms and services, the audience can now have an audience (Napoli 2009, 2010). Social curation is well attuned to the nature of the Internet as an environment that enables efficient horizontal communication between consumers (Lüders 2007, 194-195).

According to Marshall (2009, 81), the successful operation of the media industry is in fact as much about media production, as it is about facilitating the maintenance of social connections though content sharing and communication among its consumers. Pre-existing social networks are becoming fundamental to the sustenance of media, and therefore the media companies need to acknowledge the convergence of media and communication, where the social and communicative (interpersonal) dimensions have invaded, informed and mutated the media elements. When in the traditional model of mass communication, a newspaper or a television company created the value to the product without consumer involvement, the value is now increasingly created as consequence of the process of nurturing the activities of media consumer communities (Bowman and Willis 2005, 10) and the careful cultivation of consumers' narrative networks (Kozinets et al. 2010, 87). This outlook is characterized in how, instead of audiences, media businesses today, indeed, talk about networks (Deuze 2009, 152).

Also Jensen (2010, 14) proposes a shift of focus from media to communication when studying the media consumption – an agenda emphasising the recombination and reconfiguration of one-to-one, one-to-many and many-to-many communication. Media consumer studies should shed more light on the links between consumption of mass media, interpersonal communication and networked communication. The significance of media use does not remain on the individual level alone but it flows from the personal media consumption toward more collective experiences and social sharing. (Heikkilä et al. 2011.)

With this progression as a setting, our argument is that social curation is an important means for media organizations to a) connect with consumers and b) utilize the interpersonal networks in consumer communities in distributing and marketing their content. Available research indicates that social media is already an important channel for obtaining more readers, listeners and viewers for the online content produced by the media companies (Guo and Chan-Olmstead 2011; Hermida et al. 2012). For instance, in Britain the BBC, Financial Times, Guardian and the Economist have seen a sharp rise in the number of referrals from Facebook, Twitter and other social networks. In fact, search engines are being partly replaced by the social media as a portal to news and other information. (Newman and Dutton 2011.) Media scholars (Domingo et al. 2008; Thurman 2008; Wardle and Williams 2010; Qing and Hollifield 2011; Lewis 2011; Hermida et al. 2012) have argued that for contemporary media corporations, engaging, encouraging and assisting consumers in the circulation and distribution of media content is more important than having them participate in content production with or for the companies. Thus, a key challenge for the media industry consists of tapping into the social and community dimensions of the participatory media culture.

REFERENCES

Ames, Michael (1992), *Cannibal Tours and Glass Boxes: The Anthropology of Museums*, Vancouver: UBC press.

Ammann, Rudolf (2011), "Reciprocity, Social Curation and the Emergence of Blogging: A Study in Community Formation," *Procedia - Social and Behavioral Sciences*, 22, 26-36.

Appadurai, Arjun (1990), "Disjuncture and Difference in the Global Cultural Economy," *Theory, Culture and Society*, 7, 295-310.

_____ (1996), *Modernity at Large. Cultural Dimensions of Globalization*, Minneapolis: Univestity of Minnesota Press.

Arvidsson, Adam (2005), "Brands: A critical perspective," *Journal of Consumer Culture*, 5(2), 235-58.

Ball, Alex, Angus Whyte and Martin Donnelly (2010), *Social networking tools for the DCC,* University of Edinburgh; UKOLN, University of Bath; HATII, University of Glasgow.

Banks, John and Sal Humphreys (2008), The Labour of User Co-Creators: Emergent Social Network Markets? *Convergence: The International Journal of Research into New Media Technologies,* 14(4), 401-18.

Belk, Russell (2010), "Sharing," *Journal of Consumer Research*, 36(5), 715-34.

Bhargava, Rohit (2009), "Manifesto For The Content Curator: The Next Big Social Media Job Of The Future?" http://rohitbhargava.typepad.com/weblog/2009/09/manifesto-for-the-content-curator-the-next-big-social-media-job-of-the-future-.html.

Bowman, Shayne and Chris Willis (2005), "The Future Is Here, But Do News Media Companies See It*?" Nieman Reports*, 6-10.

Brown, Jo, Amanda J. Broderick and Nick Lee (2007), "Word-of-mouth Communication within Online Communities: Conceptualizing the Online Social Network," *Journal of Interactive Marketing*, 21(3), 2-21.

Chan-Olmstead, Sylvia M. (2006), *Competitive Strategy for Media Firms: Strategic and Brand Management in Changing Media Markets*. Mahwah, New Jersey: Lawrence Erlbaum Associates.

Clark, Jessica and Patricia Aufderheide (2009), *Public media 2.0: Dynamic, engaged publics*, Washington DC: Center for Social Media.

Cova, Bernard (1997), "Community and Consumption," *European Journal of Marketing*, 31 (3/4), 297-316.

Cova, Bernard and Daniele Dalli (2009), "Working consumers: the next step in marketing theory?" *Marketing Theory*, 9(3), 315-39.

Cova, Bernard and Pace Stefano (2006), "Brand Community of Convenience Products: New Forms of Customer Empowerment - the Case 'My Nutella the Community'," *European Journal of Marketing*, 40 (9/10), 1087-105.

Cuno, James (1997), "Money, Power and the history of Art," *Art Bulletin*, 79(1), 6-9

Deuze, Mark (2009), "Convergence Culture and Media Work," in *Media Industries: History, Theory, and Method*, ed. Jennifer Holt and Alisa Perren, Chichester, UK: Wiley-Blackwell, 144-56.

Domingo, David, Thorsten Quandt, Ari Heinonen, Steve Paulussen, Jane Singer and Marina Vujnovic (2008), "Participatory Journalism Practices in the Media and Beyond: An international comparative study of initiatives in online newspapers," *Journalism Practice*, 2(3), 326-42.

Fay, Brian and J. Donald Moon (1994), "What Would an Adequate Philosophy of Social Science Look Like?" in *Readings in the Philosophy of Social Science*, ed. Michael Martin and Lee C. McIntyre, Cambridge: The MIT Press, 21-35.

Gaskill, Karen (2010), "In search of the Social – Toward an understanding of the Social Curator," dissertation, University of Huddersfield, UK.

Goble, Carole A., Bhagat Jiten, Sergejs Aleksejevs, Don Cruickshank, Danius Michaelides, David News, Mark Borkum et al. (2010), "myExperiment: a repository and social network for the sharing of bioinformatics workflows," *Nucleic Acids Research*, 38, 677-82.

Guo, Miao and Sylvia M. Chan-Olmstead (2011), "Building Online Relationship: Examining Social Media Utilization on Traditional Media Websites," paper presented at the 2011 International Communication Association Conference, Boston, USA, May 26-30th, 2011.

Hartley, John (2004), "The New Economy, Creativity and Consumption," *International Journal of Cultural Studies*, 7(1), 5-7.

Haugen, Austin (2010), "Answers to Your Questions on Personalized Web Tools," http://www.facebook.com/blog/blog.php?post=384733792130.

Heikkilä, Heikki, Laura Ahva, Jaana Siljamäki and Sanna Valtonen (2011), "What if everyday life is not that civic," paper presented at the 2011 International Communication Association Conference, Boston, USA, May 26-30th, 2011.

Hermida, A., Fred Fletcher, Darryl Korell, Donna Logan (2012), "Share, Like, Recommend: Decoding the social media news consumer," *Journalism Studies*, iFirst, March 22 2012.

Higgins, Sarah (2011), "Digital Curation: The Emergence of a New Discipline," *The International Journal of Digital Curation*, 6(2), 78-88

Holt, Douglas B. and Craig J. Thompson (2004), "Man-of-Action Heroes: The Pursuit of Heroic Masculinity in Everyday Consumption," *Journal of Consumer Research*, 31 (2), 425-40.

Jenkins, Henry (2006), *Convergence culture*, New York: NYU Press.

_____ (2009), "If It Doesn't Spread, It's Dead (Part One): Media Viruses and Memes," http://henryjenkins.org/2009/02/if_it_doesnt_spread_its_dead_p.html.

Jensen, Klaus Bruhn (2010), *Media convergence: The Three degrees of network, mass, and interpersonal communication*, Milton Park: Routledge.

Joy, Annamma and John F. Sherry (2003), "Disentangling the Paradoxical Alliances between Art Market and Art World," *Consumption, Markets and Culture*, 6(3), 155-81.

Kozinets, Robert V. (1999), "E-tribalized marketing?: the strategic implications of virtual communities of consumption," *European Management Journal*, 17(3), 252–64.

Kozinets, Robert V. and Jay M. Handelman (2004), "Adversaries of Consumption: Consumer Movements, Activism, and Ideology," *Journal of Consumer Research*, 31 (3), 691-704.

Kozinets, Robert V., Kristine De Valck, Andrea C. Wojnicki and Sarah J.S. Wilner (2010), "Networked Narratives: Understanding Word-of-Mouth Marketing in Online Communities," *Journal of Marketing*, 74(2), 71-89.

Lewis, Seth C. (2011), "The Sociology of Professions, Boundary Work, and Participation in Journalism: A Review of the Literature," paper presented at the 2011 International Communication Association Conference, Boston, USA, May 26-30th, 2011.

Lisus Nicola and Richard Ericson (1999), "Authorizing Art: The effect of Multimedia Formats on museum experience," *The Canadian Review of Sociology and Anthropology*, 36 (2), 199-216.

Liu, Sophia B. (2010), "Trends in Distributed Curatorial Technology to Manage Data Deluge in a Networked World," *Upgrade – The European Journal for the Informatics Professional*, 11(4).

Livingstone, Sonia (2008), "Taking risky opportunities in youthful content creation: teenagers' use of social networking sites for intimacy, privacy and self-expression," *New Media and Society*, 10(3), 393-411.

Lüders, Marika (2007), "Converging Forms of Communication?" in *Ambivalence towards Convergence: Digitalization and Media Change*, ed. Tanja Storsul and Dagny Stuedahl, Gothenburg: Nordicom, 179-98.

Manovich, Lev (2008), *"Software Takes Command,"* www.softwarestudies.com/softbook.

Marshall, David P. (2009), "New Media as Transformed Media Industry," in *Media Industries: History, Theory, and Method*, ed. Jennifer Holt and Alisa Perren, Chichester, UK: Wiley-Blackwell, 81-9.

Merrin, William (2009), "Media Studies 2.0: upgrading and open-sourcing the discipline," *Interactions: Studies in Communication and Culture*, 1(1), 17-34.

Mikkonen, Ilona, Johanna Moisander, and A. Fuat Firat (2011), "Cynical Identity Projects as Consumer Resistance: The Scrooge as a Social Critic?" *Consumption Markets and Culture*, 14 (1), 99-116.

Moisander, Johanna and Anu Valtonen (2012), "Interpretive Marketing Research: Using Ethnography in Strategic Market Development," in *Marketing Management: A Cultural Perspective*, ed. Lisa Penaloza, Luca Visconti and Nil Ozcaglar-Toulouse, London: Routledge, 246-60.

Morgan, Robert C. (1996), *Art Into Ideas: Essays on Conceptual Art,* London: Cambridge University Press.

Muniz, Jr., Albert M. and Thomas C. O'Guinn (2001), "Brand Community," *Journal of Consumer Research*, 27(4), 412-32.

Napoli, Philip M. (2009), *Navigating Producer-Consumer Convergence: Media Policy Priorities in the Era of User-Generated and User-Distributed Content*. New York: The Donald McGannon Communication Research Center, Fordham University.

_____ (2010), "Revisiting 'mass communication' and the 'work' of the audience in the new media environment," *Media, Culture and Society*, 32(3), 505-16.

Newman, Nick and William Dutton (2011), "Social Media in the Changing Ecology of News Production and Consumption: The Case in Britain," paper presented at the 2011 International Communication Association Conference, Boston, USA, May 26-30th, 2011.

Potts, Jason, John Hartley, John Banks, Jean Burgess, Rachel Cobcroft, Stuart Cunningham, and Lucy Montgomery (2008), "Consumer Co-creation and Situated Creativity," *Industry and Innovation*, 15(5), 459-74.

Prahalad, C.K. and Venkat Ramaswamy (2004), "Co-creation experiences: The next practice in value creation," *Journal of Interactive Marketing*, 18(3), 5-14.

Purcell, Kristen, Lee Rainie, Amy Mitchell, Tom Rosenstiel and Kenny Olmstead (2010), *Understanding the participatory news consumer: How Internet and cell phone users have turned news into a social experience*, Pew Internet and American Life Project, Washington DC: Pew Research Center.

Qing, Qingmei and Cheryl Ann Hollifield (2011), "Adopting the News Prosumer: User-Generated Content as a Strategic Resource for Local News Media," paper presented at the 2011 International Communication Association Conference, Boston, USA, May 26-30th, 2011.

Rosenbaum, Steve (2009), "Can 'Curation' Save Media?" http://www.businessinsider.com/can-curation-save-media-2009-4.

_____ (2011), *Curation nation: How to win in a world where consumers are creators*, New York: McGraw-Hill.

Sandler, Irving (1996), *Art of the Postmodern Era*, Icon editions, New York: Harper and Collins.

Schlatter, N. Elizabeth (2010), *A New Spin: Are DJs, rappers and bloggers 'curators'?* Washington DC: American Association of Museums.

Schau, Hope Jensen and Mary C. Gilly (2003), "We Are What We Post? Self-Presentation in Personal Web Space," *Journal of Consumer Research*, 30 (3), 385-404.

Schau, Hope Jensen, Albert M. Muniz, Jr. and Eric J. Arnould (2009), "How Brand Community Practices Create Value," *Journal of Marketing*, 73(5), 30-51.

Shankar, Avi (2001), "Understanding Consumption: Contributions from a Narrative Perspective," *Journal of Marketing Management*, 17 (3/4), 429-53.

Terranova, Tiziana (2004), *Network culture,* London: Pluto Press.

Thurman, Neil (2008), "Forums for citizen journalists? Adoption of user generated content initiatives by online news media," *New Media and Society*, 10(1), 139-57.

Thompson, Craig (1997), "Interpreting Consumers: A Hermeneutical Framework for Deriving Marketing Insights from the Texts of Consumers Consumption Stories," *Journal of Marketing Research*, 34 (Nov.), 438-55.

Thompson, Craig and Siok Kuan Tambyah (1999), "Trying to Be Cosmopolitan," *Journal of Consumer Research*, 26 (Dec.), 214-41.

Warde, Alan (2005), "Consumption and Theories of Practice," *Journal of Consumer Culture*, 5 (2), 131-53.

Wardle, Claire and Andrew Williams (2010), "Beyond user-generated content: a production study examining the ways in which UGC is used at the BBC, " *Media, Culture and Society*, 32(5), 781-99.

Weick, Karl E. (1995), *Sense-Making in Organizations*, Thousand Oaks, CA: Sage.

Cars for Sale! An Ethnography of the Collusion of Space and Consumption in Power and Agency Struggles

Helene de Burgh-Woodman, University of Notre Dame, Australia

INTRODUCTION

The importance of space and its "perception-shaping, behaviour-inducing properties" (Sherry 1998) has been long acknowledged by consumer researchers. Public spaces such as shopping malls (Sandicki and Holt, 1998), bridal salons (Otnes, 1998), and converted shopping centres (Maclaren and Brown, 2005) have all been investigated as spaces where meanings are unravelled, contested and entertained. Equally, spaces play out emotive experiences such as escape (Hewer, 2003), utopia and nostalgia (Maclaran and Brown, 2005). Adding to this important opus, the present paper investigates public space as a site of contested power and agency manifested through consumption. The use of public in this context means a "realm in which people define themselves as publics, through ongoing communication, definition and negotiation" (Sargeson 2002, 21).

Using the case of impromptu car yards where private cars for sale are illegally congregated in one space against local council laws and regulations, this paper theorises public space and consumption as interwoven in a larger discourse of power and agency (Visconti, Sherry Borghini and Anderson 2010). Space, in this instance, lays the ground for alternative consumption, sharing (Belk 2010) and exchange which defy the structures of the formal "marketplace" and contest the power held by legal and political entities (Campbell 2005; White 2007). While public space in modernity is ordered and managed by political and cultural entities such as councils, governments etc, space also "complicates the assumption of a collective experience of culture and its products" (de Burgh-Woodman and Brace-Govan 2010).

This paper uses the work of Henri Lefevbre (1974) to theorise the collusion of space and consumption to express power and agency struggles between people and formal structures. In this respect, the present study extends previous use of Lefebvre's (1974) work in consumer research (Houliez 2010a 2010b) and urban studies (McCann 1999, 1995). While previous work has illuminated the importance of spatial practices and negotiating processes by consumers, this paper advances on this use of Lefebvre by situating space and consumption as two collusive channels to agency and dissent. While space creates a context for an alternative site for consumption, more significantly it is the sense of political and social agency that space facilitates that concerns us here. In this respect, this paper draws on previous uses of Lefebvre's work in studies of the urban milieu and racial inequality (McCann 1999) where

"abstract space", - space represented by elite social groups as homogeneous, instrumental, and ahistorical in order to facilitate the exercise of state power and the free flow of capital – lends itself to a discussion of the manner in which downtown business spaces in major U.S. cities are exclusionary territories dominated by White, middle-class male (McCann 1999: 164).

By contrast with concrete space (or everyday life), abstract space is a hegemonic space, a space loaded with representations of control, power and domination. In the same fashion that Lefebvre's work has been used to dissect this construction of space and subvert abstract space in favour of agency over space, this paper looks at power and agency struggle in space. This paper aims, through the study of these self-fashioned "car yards", to show how space both contests and is contested (Lefebvre 1974), how consumption outside of the designated marketplace utilises space and finally what implications this has for embedded understandings of power and agency.

The paper commences with a conceptual framework that draws from Lefebvre's (1974) theorisation of space as an inhabited yet contested site which lays the ground for understanding how space is integral to consumption, contest and agency practices. This is followed by an outline of the method employed and a discussion of its implications. Finally, some concluding comments are made regarding how consumption and space collude to create the conditions for the expression of power and agency struggles.

CONCEPTUAL FRAMEWORK

The theoretical framework for this paper draws from the work of Henri Lefebvre (1974). Lefebvre's argument that space is socially constructed and thereby imbued with politically and socially meaningful values and symbolisms is resonant for the present study. As a French sociologist writing primarily in the mid-twentieth century, Lefebvre's identification with a Marxist perspective led to his conceptualisation of space as a social enactment of political and social ideologies (Stanek 2011) and thereby to his key distinctions between dominating (those with power) and dominated space (those over whom power is exerted). Echoing Marx's own distinction between the powerful and the powerless or bourgeois and worker, these categories of dominating and dominated found in social space are, Lefebvre argues, endemic to contemporary capitalist society.

Lefebvre outlines three different kinds of space operating in the contemporary environment. Implicit in his conceptualisation of space and his representational space triad of *perceived space* (spatial practice), *conceived space* (representations of space) and *lived space* (representational space) (Zhang 2006) is its positioning of space as a site of control and contestation (see Fig.1)

Fig. 1 The Spatial Triad Taken from Jensen 2011

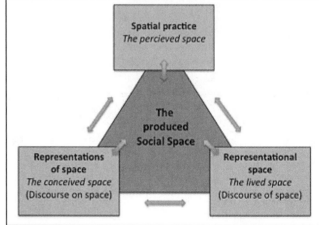

These different kinds of space should not be seen as discrete but rather as merged, iterative and free-flowing where "it is necessary for the interactions between the triadic elements to be appropriate and in balance if an [spatial] event was to be persuasive and effective" (Watkins 2005 220). Space is not passive or latent. It is inhabited (itself a consequence of modernity), constructed and produced or "seen as the site of ongoing interactions of social relations rather than

Advances in Consumer Research
Volume 40, ©2012

the mere result of such interactions" (Zhang 2006 219). In the process, it is controlled, manipulated and politicised:

> (Social) space is a (social) product... the space thus produced also serves as a tool of thought and of action... in addition to being a means of production it is also a means of control, and hence of domination, of power (1974, 26)

In many ways, Lefebvre's concern with agency and "central planning's ensuing depoliticization, fragmentation and segregation of 'possible communities', in other words, the very denial of every citizen's right to the city as ongoing communal project of co-habitation" (Knoll 2012) finds increasing relevance in contemporary consumer research. While Lefebvre's own consideration of how the dominated might resist or find legitimacy in the face of the dominating stemmed from his experience of the WWII, the May 1968 demonstrations and the reality of communist Russia, his fundamental insights into everyday life as the real battleground for the dominated and their expression through space are echoed in consumer research studies.

While space is not always discussed in such studies, research into areas such as consumer resistance, anti-consumption and subcultural appropriation illuminate similar concerns with the agency of the consumer and the effort to subvert or avoid perceived power structures. For instance, anti-consumption is frequently understood as an active ethical, social critique of, and dissent from, exploitative or excessive aspects of the marketplace and its accompanying consumer culture (Cherrier, 2009, 2005; Penaloza and Price, 2003; Zavestoski, 2002) that result from the capitalist logic that frames our modern world (Jameson, 1991). The situation of a mainstream capitalist culture as the point of critique and dissent implies the same issues that Lefebvre plays out through the dialectic of space. They share in a wariness of cultural meta-narratives, a desire to reclaim the social sphere and highlight the importance of community over structures. Lefebvre sees this contest unfolding through and in space.

Thus far, the canon of consumer research has seen this contest unfold through consumption and, by extension, community (Arnould, Price and Otnes 1999; Belk and Costa 1998; Hewer and Brownlie 2007; Holbrook 1993; McRobbie 1995; Penaloza 1994; Thornton 1995). These two axes, consumption and community, have direct relevance here too. While space may be the site of contestation, it is at the level of community that dissent is enacted *in* space. Just as community also resides at the centre of Lefebvre's work (Stanek 2011), the consumer research canon has illuminated the fine detail of how communities, and the social networks that underpin them, enable active dissent. This paper endeavours to bring these threads of space and consumption through community together, showing them to be linked in a shared outlook and agenda.

While there are many variations of this critical negotiation between people and the marketplace (Etzioni, 1998; Kingsnorth, 2003), which have also linked to other issues such as environmental sustainability (Dobscha and Ozanne, 2001; Leonard-Barton, 1981), excessive consumption (Craig-Lees and Hill, 2002; Shaw and Newholm, 2002), class inequality (Tomolilo and Shaw, 2003),ethical consumption (Borgmann, 2000; Cherrier, 2004) and space itself (de Burgh-Woodman and Brace-Govan 2010), the common thread is a fundamental emphasis on critique of the status quo and divergence through defiance. Taking these significations of critique, agency and dissent as definition and praxis, space and consumption collude to become a mode of expression and the context through which critique (both of structure and capitalist logic) is spoken. These significations underpin the point of dissent for geneses of alternate (cultural) consumption discourses.

In following this structuring of space and consumption as a collusion of critique and

dissent from the logic of late capitalism (Jameson, 1991), we move again towards Lefebvre's work that positions space as something that structures the mode of expression of structural domination and everyday consumer resistance. Space, consumption and consumer defiance intercept, since one speaks to another, and thus consolidate their connection. To this extent, this paper suggests that this mutual re-enforcement of space and consumption can be a pervasive, subtle tool for agency interpolated with the lived experience.

METHOD

The site of the impromptu car yard is at Forrester's Beach on the Central Coast, one hour north of Sydney, Australia. Forresters forms the site of analysis although it should be noted that these impromptu car yards are also emerging in Sydney itself and at other locations around the Central Coast. The Coast's demographics range from low socio-economic suburbs such as Toukley and Umina Beach through to very wealthy areas such as Pearl Beach and Daleys Point where homes sell for several million dollars. To this extent, the practice of curbside car selling takes in a spectrum of social groups and a range of cars. The cars for sale are found on the side of the road with "for sale" signs hung on their windscreens (see photo 1 and 2). Occupying large stretches of road, these impromptu car yards can go for several hundred metres. The cars themselves reflect the diverse socio-economic scale of the area with everything from old vehicles through to new SUVs appearing on the side of the road.

The method adopted for this research was an ethnographic field diary documenting shifts in the composition of cars combined with a photographic record (Penaloza and Cayla 2006). The synergy between the field diary and the photographic record was designed to enable a thick description (Geertz 1973) of the car selling phenomenon. The research commenced with a three month long field diary in Summer 2011, notating the number, type and price range of the cars for sale at Forresters. Along each of these dimensions, significant growth was observed over this period, thus indicating a growing civic swell around the impromptu car yard see Fig 2.

A visual record was maintained through photographic material. Secondary material was also consulted including media coverage of the issue since there has been reportage driven by local council and law enforcement. The response by law enforcement and council in popular press is significant in that, from the perspective of authority, this is not a neutral practice that goes unseen. Further material including council regulations and laws were also consulted.

Once the visual and secondary data was collected, the interpretive framework derived from Lefebvre's theoretical distinction between dominating and dominated space (1974) was applied to sift the political, agentic and power struggles that emerge out of the use of space.

The possibility of gathering first hand qualitative data was compromised by the unwillingness of both buyers and sellers to be interviewed. Given that this practice is essentially illegal, neither group was willing to comment on their involvement in curbside car trading. This is significant in itself in that participants are aware of the political, legal and social dimensions of their acts, realising that they are participating in a subversive act of defiance as much as the act of buying/selling a car. Hence, this adds further strength to the argument that the practice of curbside buying/selling can be seen as a symbolically and politically inflammatory act played out as the nexus of consumption and space. However, some degree of insight was offered through an online forum. This forum is interpreted and discussed below where the use of space and consumption to express agency and dissent are illuminated.

DISCUSSION

The use of a roadside to sell private cars seems an innocuous act but its political and cultural resonance is immense. In the first instance, the physical location of cars illegally placed on the roadside represents a being *in* space, an act of liminal physicality that locates objects in illicit space for exchange and consumption. The means of contacting the owner is by ringing the advertised phone number since being found on-site by police or council rangers would result in a fine. Sellers would also be required to remove their cars from the curb. The act of dissent against existing power structures is enacted physically - in space. But space also mediates, it acts as the intervening buffer between owner and authority and, in doing so, facilitates the dissenting act. To this extent, space is complicit in the contestation of power and agency.

Equally, space and consumption are linked where consumption occurs in space but also *through* space. The many acts of exchange that occur at the site are only made possible through a collective understanding and use of the space. By extension then, space makes possible an alternative marketplace that again challenges power and agency structures. The dynamics here are quite complex in that when space and consumption collude, this prompts commentary and re-action from councils and law enforcement. The New South Wales Government passed its Roadside Vehicle Sales Bill in 2011 outlawing the practice of roadside selling and imposing fines, removal and cautionary notes. Most local councils were quick to adopt the bill and galvanise it through local bylaws. This legislative act refracted an "official" responsiveness at the level of government (filtering down to local authorities), demonstrating an administrative or policy action against a "social problem". Yet, at the level of real spatial practice or lived space, there is no human body, no face to prosecute and the "rule of law" is rendered inert in and by space.

While it was challenging to collect interview data for this study (precisely because the one protection consumers have in this battle between dominating and dominated space is invisibility), this one trace of an online discussion (that will remain unidentified) illuminates the self-constructed tactics that these consumers enact. The thread also reveals the almost subcultural or guerilla community of illicit car sellers and the common concern with dissent. The thread starts by a forum discussant asking:

Is it legal to sell a car on the roadside in NSW? I am considering parking my car on a grassy verge beside a busy road (I'm guessing it is council land). Just checking to see if anyone else has experienced any issues doing this.

This initial inquiry releases a series of responses that show how the boundaries are tested, the parameters are deliberately left unclear and though forum members frequently advise one another to check with council, none of them do. The ambiguity of practice, ambiguity of governmental response in lived space and the latent tensions that underpin this practice propel dissent where to clarify the parameters potentially threatens action:

There used to be quite a few regular spots people did it all around it seemed years ago but alot of those are now fenced and signed by Council telling you not to. It was my understanding it wasn't actually legal to sell your car on the side of the road anymore but alot of people still do, you just have to pick a spot

Fig 2. Trajectory of car numbers over a three-month period

Date	Car details
4.12.2011	16 cars (mainly priced under 10000AUD) majority are small to medium sedans
16.12.2011	14 cars (mainly priced under 10000AUD majority are small to medium sedans)
22.12.2011	14 cars (mainly priced under 10000AUD majority are small to medium sedans)
27.12.2011	21 cars (slight increase in cars over 100000AUD and a more noticeable number of SUV/ute)
	* In general, the calibre of cars was basic. While there were some newer cars SUV/ute and sports models, the majority during the month of December were slightly older small to medium sedans and hatchbacks. The most expensive was a relatively recent Commodore (GM) priced at 18000AUD.
3.1.1.2012	23 cars (mainly priced under 10000AUD but with a steady number of SUV/ute along with small to medium sedan)
9.1.2012	28 cars (mainly priced under 10000AUD but with a steady number of SUV/ute along with small to medium sedan)
14.1.2012	29 cars (mainly priced under 10000AUD but with a steady number of SUV/ute along with small to medium sedan)
25.1.2012	31 cars (more priced over 10000AUD with steady number of SUV/ute, more sports and small/medium sedans)
30.1.2012	32 cars (more priced over 10000AUD with steady number of SUV/ute, more sports and small/medium sedans)
	*In general, the calibre of cars improved in January with a greater number of more recent models, SUVs and sports cars being placed on the side of the road. The most expensive car for sale was 41000AUD for a Nissan convertible.
3.2.2012	36 cars (a steady number priced over 10000AUD with a greater number of SUV/ute and steady sedan numbers)
10.2.2012	31 cars (a steady number priced over 10000AUD with a greater number of SUV/ute and steady sedan numbers)
14.2.2012	31 cars (same 31 cars as 14.2.2012)
22.2.2012	28 cars a steady number priced over 10000AUD with a greater number of SUV/ute and steady sedan numbers)
27.2.2012	33 cars a steady number priced over 10000AUD with a greater number of SUV/ute and steady sedan numbers)
	*In general, the caliber of cars stayed the same for February. The most expensive car for sale was a Toyota Prado priced at 53000AUD but this was unusually expensive. Every other car was under 35000AUD.

Picture 1

Picture 2

that isn't going to end up in peoples or the councils way. I could be wrong but…

When one forum member directly asks another whether they have called council, the response deliberately perpetuates this ambiguity, noting "I've been busy travelling interstate over the past few days, when I get a chance I'll call the local council and ask them what their policy is. Cheers!" The thread goes for several more days but no report back on the call to council is recorded.

While this question of clarifying goes deliberately untreated in the thread, the conversation about dissent and which spaces best facilitate dissent dominates the discussion.

> my local councils dont like it, but pretty much can only do something about it if you illegally park – for that it means not parallel to the roadway. If there is a spot that people use regularly, then you can bet they are not fining people for doing it at that spot. I sold mine on the side of the rd – it was parked parallel to the roadway without a big sign (there are signage by laws for council too). because of the spot – it was clearly a for sale car, and anyone interested could walk up to it and get the details. (stood for 2 weekends – 2 test drives, then sold).

A similar theme is reflected in the comment of "Not sure of its legal implication but I see cars parked on the side of road regularly with for sale sign + prices attached to the inside of the windscreen. I have even seen trucks and trailers." In both of these comments, the authors demonstrate an awareness of their resistance to local authorities that "don't like" these impromptu caryards but use space to mitigate the risk of prosecution. Forum members are aware of the potential consequences with several mentions of fines, towing and cautionary notices but employ a spatial strategy to elude prosecution. The "side of the road" in both comments represents a safe space as long as the space is organised strategically against legal structures. The comment from another discussant also captures this strategic use of space:

> It will all depend on local council, some care others don't. If its a place where many cars are sold every weekend then its probably safe to assume that they aren't booking people for it. If there are no other cars being sold in the suburb then it probably means they give tickets.

This comment is more explicit in showing the game or contest played out through space where both dominated and dominating utilise space in their struggle. Interestingly, at no point in the thread are actual people ever discussed as present at the impromptu caryards. The cars, their location and their strategic arrangement are all mentioned but the only reference made to real people using this space is the comment "anyone interested could walk up to it and get the details". Even in this remark, the physical presence of the consumer is only required to gather details. The seller is absent, waiting for the buyer to create a second space in which the sale takes place. However, this transactional space is separate from the curbside space of contest and dissent.

So, the car yard is a guerilla space, an alternative market that trades on collective agency or, to borrow Lefevbre, a reclamation of dominated space. Space then operates at several levels – as a site, as a facilitator for consumption and a field for contest. Equally, consumption acts in space, through space and colludes with it to enact contest. In this respect, while this struggle between dominating and dominated does not tangibly occur in lived space (only the cars are present), this power struggle is enacted through both perceived and conceived space in that this struggle is represented in and through space.

CONCLUSION

The aim of this paper is to theorise the collusion of space and consumption as implicated elements of contest, agency and power. Space contextualises consumption, provides it with tangible form and, in this case, allows alternative consumption acts and exchanges to take place. Our consideration of impromptu caryards as a means of analysing agency and power struggles through consumption takes a step towards expanding our understanding of how space and consumption collude as a strategy of critique and divergence and a modality for consumer resistance is animated. The most salient point to be taken from this study is that while consumption itself can be situated as a discursive strategy and practical tactic of resistance, the role of space becomes implicated as the context for such resistance too.

This paper shows one instance in which space is enlisted to articulate a specific political critique or show of consumer defiance. In the introductory remarks, space and consumption were identified as collusive elements in an active defiance of laws and regulations. By way of extension, this paper concludes that space and consumption provide a modality of critique or resistance and a consequent point of divergence. Seen in this way, space and consumption can be strategically enlisted as a broader critique of modern capitalist culture and its attendant restrictions, controls and politics.

Here, consumption provides the language of critique, a referential discursive frame upon which communities call to articulate their specific form of critique, resistance and divergence. If we expand our understanding to apprehend space as a framing logic and as critique's ordering effect (or as Lefebvre suggests, society produces its own specific space) we might also come to see space and consumption as mutually implicated in the articulation of various cultural interactions in a modern capitalist world. This potential of consumption to mediate, and be mediated by, social space specific to the cultural conditions of modernity makes it an exciting site for marketing investigation.

REFERENCES

Arnould, Eric, Linda Price and Cele Otnes (1999), "Making Consumption Magic: A Study of White-Water Rafting," *Journal of Contemporary Ethnography*, 28 (1), 33-68.

Belk, Russell, (2010), "Sharing," *Journal of Consumer Research*, 36 (February), 715-34.

Belk, Russell W., and Janeen Arnold Costa (1998), "The mountain man myth: A contemporary consuming fantasy," *Journal of Consumer Research*, 25 (December), 218-240.

Borgmann, Albert (2000), "The moral complexion of consumption," *Journal of Consumer Research*, 26 (March), 418-422.

Campbell, Kelly (2005), "Theorizing the Authentic: Identity, Engagement and Public Space," *Administration and Society,* 336 (6), 688-705.

Cherrier, Helene (2004), "The Construction of Meanings in Ethical Consumer Narratives: The Importance of Control, Social Integration, and Authenticity," in Harrison R., Newholm, T. and Shaw, D eds. *The Ethical Consumer*, Thousand Oaks: Sage.

-- (2005), "Becoming Sensitive to Ethical Consumption Behavior: Narratives of Survival in an Uncertain and Unpredictable World," in *Advances in Consumer Research Volume 32* eds. Geeta Menon and Akshay R. Rao, Duluth, MN: Association for Consumer Research, 600-604.

-- (2009), "Anti-consumption discourses and consumer-resistant identities," *Journal of Business Research*, 62 (2), 181–190.

Craig-Lees, Margeret, and Hill, Chris (2002), "Understanding voluntary simplifiers," *Psychology and Marketing*, 19 (2), 187-210.

Dobscha, Susan, and Ozanne, Julie (2001), "An ecofeminist analysis of environmentally sensitive women using qualitative methodology: The emancipatory potential of an ecological life," *Journal of Public Policy & Marketing*, 20 (2), 201-214.

Etzioni, Amitai (1998), "Voluntary simplicity characterization, select psychological implications, societal consequences," *Journal of Economic Psychology*, 19 (5), 619-43.

Hewer, Paul (2003), "Consuming gardens: Representations of paradise, nostalgia and postmodernism," *European Advances in Consumer Research Volume 6*, eds. Darach Turley and Stephen Brown, Provo, UT: Association for Consumer Research, 327-331.

Hewer, Paul and Douglas Brownlie (2007), "Cultures of consumption of car aficionados: Aesthetics and consumption communities," *International Journal of Sociology and Social Policy*, 27 (3/4), 106-119.

Holbrook, Morris (1993), "Nostalgia and consumption preferences: Some emerging patterns of consumer tastes," *Journal of Consumer Research*, 20 (September), 245-257.

Houliez, Chris (2010a), "When non-store meets in-store: mobile communications technology, servicescapes, and the production of servicespace," *Journal of Customer Behaviour*, 9 (Summer), 201-220.

Houliez, Chris (2010b), "When Mobile Shoppers Meet Immobile Retail," *Journal of Digital Marketing*, 1 (January), 15-40.

Jameson, Frederic (1991), *Postmodernism or the logic of late capitalism*, Durham, NC: Duke University Press.

Jensen, Jeppe Mikel (2011), *Velo-mobility in Copenhagen*, Copenhagen: Roskilde University.

Kingsnorth, Peter (2003), *One no, many yeses; A journey to the heart of the Global Resistance Movement*, London: Free Press.

Lefebvre, Henri (1974), *La production de l'espace*, Paris: Anthropos.

Leonard-Barton, Dorothy (1981), "Voluntary simplicity lifestyles and energy conservation," *Journal of Consumer Research*, 8 (December), 213-52.

Maclaran, Pauline and Stephen Brown (2005), "The Center Cannot Hold: Consuming the utopian marketplace," *Journal of Consumer Research* 32 (October), 311-323.

Maffesoli, Michel (1991), *The time of the tribes: The decline of individualism in mass society*, Thousand Oaks: Sage Press.

McCann, Eugene (1999), "Race, Protest and Public Space: Contextualizing Lefebvre in the US City", *Antipode* 31 (2), 163-184.

McCann, Eugene (1995), "Neotraditional developments: The anatomy of a new urban form," *Urban Geography* 16, 210-233.

McRobbie, Angela (1995), "Recent Rhythms of Sex and Race in Popular Music," *Media, Culture and Society*, 17 (2), 323-331.

Otnes, Celes (1998), "Friend of the Bride – and then some: Roles of the Bridal Salon during wedding planning," in ed. Sherry, John F. *Servicescapes: The concept of place in contemporary markets*. Lincolnswood, IL: NTC Business Books: 229-258.

Peñaloza, Lisa (2001), "Consuming the American west: Animating cultural meaning and memory at a stock show and rodeo," *Journal of Consumer Research*, 28 (October): 369-99.

Peñaloza, Lisa (1994), "Atravesando Fronteras/Border Crossings: A Critical Ethnographic Exploration of the Consumer Acculturation of Mexican Immigrants," *Journal of Consumer Research*, 21 (June), 32-54,

Peñaloza, Lisa and Julien Cayla (2006), "Writing pictures/taking fieldnotes: towards a more visual and material ethnographic consumer research," in *Handbook of Qualitative Research Methods in Marketing* ed. Russell Belk, London: Edward Elgar, 279-290.

Penaloza Lisa and Linda Price (2003), "Consumer resistance: a conceptual overview," in *Advances in Consumer Research Volume 20*, eds. Leigh McAlister and Michael L. Rothschild, Provo, UT: Association for Consumer Research, 123-128

Sandicki, Ozlem and Douglas Holt (1998), 'Malling Society: Mall, consumption practices and the future of public space." in *Servicescapes: The concept of place in contemporary markets,* ed. John F. Sherry, Lincolnswood, IL: NTC Business Books: 305-336.

Sargeson, Sally (2002), "The Contested Nature of Collective Goods in East and Southeast Asia," in *Collective Goods, Collective Futures in Asia*, ed. Sally Sargeson, New York: Routledge 1-24.

Stanek. Łukacz (2011), *Henri Lefebvre on Space. Architecture, Urban Research, and the Production of Theory,* Minneapolis, London. University of Minnesota Press.

Thornton, Sarah (1995), *Club Cultures: Music, Media and Subcultural Capital*, Cambridge: Polity Press.

Tomolillo, Dennis. and Shaw, Deidre (2003), "Undressing the ethical issues in clothing choice," *Journal of New Product Design and Innovation Management*, 15 (2), 99-107.

Visconti, Luca, John F. Sherry, Stefania Borghini and Laurel Anderson (2010), "Street Art, Sweet Art? Reclaiming the "Public in Public Place," *Journal of Consumer Research*, 37 (October), 511-529.

Watkins, Ceri (2005), "Representations of Space, Spatial Practices and Spaces of Representation: An Application of Lefebvre's Spatial Triad," *Culture and Organization*, 11 (3), 209-220.

White, Rob (2007), "Public Space, Consumption and the Social Regulation of Young People." in *Youth, Globalization and the Law*, eds. Sudhir Alladi Venkatesh and Ronald Kassimir, Palo Alto, CA: Stanford University Press, 223-48.

Zavestoski Stephen. (2002), "Guest editorial: anticonsumption attitudes," *Psychology and Marketing*, 19 (2), 121-26.

Zhang, Zhongyuan (2006), "What is Lived Space?," *Ephemera*, 6 (2): 219-223

In Pursuit of Being Different

Andrea Hemetsberger, University of Innsbruck, Austria
Ralf Weinberger, University of Innsbruck, Austria

ABSTRACT

This study assumes that individuals' desires for autonomy as well as concessions to conformity inform consumers' attempts to create consumption styles that are different. Our interpretive study investigates into male consumers' pursuit of being different and finds willful ignorance, non non-conformity (*provocative conformity, wearing the old and outdated, consuming the ugly*), and defamiliarization practices (*delocalization, delabeling, contrasting personal practice*) of individualization. We introduce the notion of *Anders-sein*—a hybrid but distinct form of identity construction via fashion and lifestyle that we interpret as existentialist.

INTRODUCTION

Consumers want to be unique. In seeking individuality, consumers use marketplace offers in various ways to pursue a distinct lifestyle (Arnould and Thompson 2005), including social status consumption (Thompson and Tambyah 1999; Bourdieu 1984,1986; Veblen 1899), uniqueness and counter-conformity (Nail 1986; Tian, Bearden and Hunter 2001), alternative (Arsel and Thompson 2011), and resistant forms of consumption (Thompson and Haytko 1997).

According to Tian et al. (2001) public recognition of taste drives the consumption of counter-conform items. Apart from demonstrating self-directedness, counter-conformity seeks to prevent pigeonholing (Thompson and Haytko 1997), or marking as one of a kind (Tian et al. 2001). Further theorizations on uniqueness have portrayed anti-conform behavior as individual authenticating acts. Lipovetsky (1994) argues that a multitude of fashion consumption practices are informed by a 'taste for autonomy' rather than social differentiation.

However, in pursuit of differentness and uniqueness, consumers oftentimes conspicuously end up in sameness, or worse, conformity (Arsel and Thompson 2011). Literature offers several explanations. First, society rewards conformity more than differentiation (Snyder and Fromkin 1977). Transgressions of boundaries of legitimate consumption choices and behaviors (Rinallo 2007) might lead to social sanctions, which consumers try to evade (Ourahmoune and Nyeck 2008). Second, critics of consumer sovereignty uncover independence as a myth arguing that consumers are hardly free from market influences (Caruana, Crane and Fitchett 2008, Holt 2002, Thompson and Hirschman 1995), and unable to adjust to fragmented styles and rapid fashion cycles (Rocamora 2002).

In the context of fashion consumption, Chan, Berger and Boven (forthcoming 2012) recently showed in seven experimental studies that consumers can satisfy desires for assimilation and differentiation, both, within a single choice context by satisfying different motives on different choice dimensions. Previous research has typically studied these assimilation and differentiation motives in isolation, or from a one-dimensional perspective, Chan, Berger and Boven (forthcoming 2012) rightly criticize. This study picks up the thread, and extends their claims from a micro- towards a meso- and macro perspective of social conformity versus the pursuit of individual autonomy within mass-marketed domains of consumption. Consequently, we assume that both, concessions to conformity as well as individuals' desire for autonomy, inform consumers' attempts to create unique consumption styles.

To support our assumption, we first review current theory on conformity and uniqueness, and discuss it against the background of the philosophy of human existence. We investigate into consum-

ers' pursuit of being different in the context of fashion consumption of male handbags, and interpret this consumption style as paradoxical, non non-conform. We introduce the notion of *Anders-sein* to denominate this phenomenon of a hybrid but distinct form of identity construction.

THEORY

Being different and being the same

Consumer attempts of differentiation and adapting to common fashion styles can be placed in a broader context of identity construction. In his seminal works on aesthetics, for instance, Simmel (1905/1995) asserted that people as social beings are driven by two oppositional forces—belongingness and differentiation. These sociological interpretations of identity construction are mirrored in social psychological concepts of conformity and uniqueness.

Literature differs in explanations of why individuals want to be unique. Berger and Heath (2008) succinctly summarize motives for divergence driven by low-status others, by disliked others, or even by similar others, when too much similarity leads to negative emotional reactions. Some people feel a stronger need for uniqueness than others, experience a decline in self esteem and feel bereft of their identity when similar to others (Tian et al., 2001; Snyder and Fromkin, 1980). Fromkin and Lipshitz (1976) characterized uniqueness prone people as independent, nonconforming, and inventive. In fashion contexts, particularly fashion innovators and opinion leaders rate high on uniqueness scales (Workman and Caldwell, 2007). Thompson and Haytko (1997) noted that the desire for consuming differing fashion items is rooted in the resistance to fashion conformity, which is deeply embedded in Western consumers' values of being a self-directed individual. Public recognition of taste drive the consumption of counter conform items. According to Tian et al. (2001) counter conformity relative to conventional behaviors, possessions and taste notions evince uniqueness and differentiation. The authors identified three dimensions of the pursuit of uniqueness—creative choice counter-conformity, unpopular counter-conformity, and avoidance of similarity. Creative choice counter-conformity refers to the consumption of novel, unique and original products to create social distinction. Such consumption bears comparatively low risk and is considered a good choice amongst others, eliciting positive evaluations by consumers' social environment (Snyder and Fromkin 1980). Unpopular choice counter-conformity, on the other hand, represents high risk consumption as it deviates from social norms and conventions. Consuming socially illegitimate objects may even elicit social sanctions. Nonetheless, consuming the unpopular also creates an enhanced self and social image. Avoidance of similarity refers to the discontinuation of items considered as mainstream or common on the account that these objects are no longer available to generating uniqueness. Fashion innovators dispose items attracting style copies or fashion followers as they violate their standards of individuality and uniqueness (Workman and Caldwell, 2007).

Further theorizations on uniqueness have portrayed anti-conform behavior as identity signaling and individual authenticating acts. Identity-signaling reflects individual's attempts to avoid sending undesired identity signal to others. People diverge from mainstream consumption patterns to ensure that others understand who they are (Berger and Heath 2007, 2008). Authenticity quests in con-

Advances in Consumer Research
Volume 40, ©2012

sumption refer to the generation of a genuine self. Strong quests result from authenticity threats emerging from a postmodern consumer society (Rose and Wood, 2005; Firat and Venkatesh, 1995). Thompson, Rindfleisch and Arsel (2006) assert that these threats for the authentic self are born out of the increasing homogenization of consumption in consumers' everyday lives. Authentication strategies in consumption thus reflect defense strategies against mass production and consumption, standardization, or popularization of consumption activities (Arsel and Thompson 2011, Beverland and Farelly 2010, Rose and Wood 2005). Arsel and Thompson (2011), for example, highlight how high status indie music consumers authenticate their music consumption through strategies of demythologization to protect themselves against popularization.

Counter-conform fashion consumption could also bear activist purposes of trying to change the moral and ethical conceptions of other consumers. Thompson and Haytko's study (1997), for example, shows that consumers resist particular fashion aesthetics and fashion brands so as to demonstrate what they are *not*. Goulding and Saren (2009)'s study exemplifies how self styling within the Goth subculture constructs individual aesthetic appearances through rebellious and provocative behavior as well as highlights differing individual aesthetic style projects within an aesthetic subculture.

Critics of consumer independence problematize independence as a myth arguing that consumers are hardly free from being subjected to any market influence, guidance, or control of other people (Caruana et al., 2008; Holt, 2002; Thompson and Hirschman, 1995). Consumers can only revert to the similar, limited, and increasingly globalized choice of market offerings in their consumption activities. Although independence from the market system is often thematized in the context of emancipatory and resistive consumer action (Kozinets and Handelman 2004, Kozinets 2002), researchers still assume only partial or temporal escapism until markets have re-conquered escapist consumptionscapes (Kozinets 2002, Holt 2002, Caruana et al. 2008). Caruana et al. (2008) and Schouten and McAlexander (1995) conclude that outcries for consumer autonomy and independence reflect market discourses, which, in the end, dictate how independence and differentiation from mainstream conventions need to be performed thus, contradicting independence.

Fromkin and Synder (1980) maintain that society, in general, rewards conformity and the refusal of differentiation more than differentiation and anti-conformity. On that account, conformity is the rule rather than the exception. Simmel (1905/1995) detects people's desire for being different relative to others in people's little, inconspicuous reworking and alterations of dresses to display the individual, differing character of personal fashion. Ourahmoune and Nyeck (2008) describe male's concealing and clandestine consumption of items considered as illegitimate for males. Males hide their boundary crossing consumption of lingerie due to fears of stigmatization. Rinallo (2007) discussed the oppression of individuality in favor of conformity and found that consumer's immediate environment sets boundaries of legitimate consumption choices and behaviors. Transgressing these boundaries leads to social sanctions from the immediate social environment, which consumers try to evade and mitigate by relapsing into conformity.

Human existence and individuality

When we critically review different strands of literature we necessarily come to the conclusion that what seems contradictory, might eventually be just two sides of a coin. While we see the importance for analytical distinctions and the need to investigate conformity as well as individuality, here we aim to re-integrate two theoretical concepts that belong together when viewed from a biographical perspective of identity construction. In our search for an integrated conceptualization, we review important philosophical notions of human existence and individuality.

Talking about identity construction necessitates an understanding of both, human identity, and how it is constructed. Sartre partly accords with Marx in that he views human creative acts as constituting element of human being (Sartre 1989/2011). In criticizing the traditional view of a single, coherent and stable individual subjectivity (the Cartesian cogito) in the 18th century, he accords with other existentialists (cf. Søren Kierkegaard, Karl Jaspers, Martin Heidegger, Friedrich Nietzsche, and Maurice Merleau-Ponty) on the superiority of existence (*Existenz*) over substance (*Wesen*). Hence, *becoming* is a life-long endeavor without end yet, accompanied by a never-ending search and pursuit of being (*Sein*). Whereas Merleau-Ponty (1945/1974), later, postulates that human existence is unthinkable without existence in the lifeworld (*Lebenswelt*), Sartre speaks of *pour-soi* of human consciousness, which is different from any notion of person or individual ego but simply *Sein*. The conscious being, as such, lives in a constant yearning for something which is not (yet) (Sartre 1943); human beings develop life projects, live for something to happen in the future or in relationship to their past. Human existence is everything that is possible; that I could eventually be. Human beings are never fully what they are and constantly desire for being. This is why and how we construct ourselves. Yet, human consciousness is not just *Sein* as *Sein* but radically complicated through the existence of the other (human being) through which the I becomes an object. We need the other existence in order to comprehend what we are. Similarly, Merleau-Ponty (1945/74) contends that we are in the world, there is no human existence except in the world around us, and we are as we perceive ourselves within the world.

For most people and for most of the time, people take for granted the conditions of their existence and their concomitant identities (Shankar, Elliott and Fitchett 2009). This implies that there are people and there are times when we consciously reflect on our existence, how the other views and influences our consciousness of being; we develop and pursue life projects, and different styles in an attempt to become what we aspire to be. Moving from Merleau-Ponty's Being-in-the-world to a Deleuzian Being-for-the-world, contemporary philosophers, such as for instance Schirmacher (1994) focus on the self-generative powers of the human being. His *homo generator* (the art of giving one's life a certain, distinct form) provides a model for the question of how the art of living could be envisioned; an art of living which makes use of different methods of self transformation and takes to heart Nietzsche's premonition that we need to "give style" to our existence (Koppensteiner 2009).

Based on these philosophical groundings two different explanations for the need of individuality permeate the literature. One is that we want others to understand who we are; the other is that we ourselves want to understand who we are (through ourselves and through others). Our main argument here is that we cannot pursue one without the other. We adopt a view that accepts the juxtaposition of both, the human existence and the other, not as a contradiction but as a paradox instead that needs no solution.

METHODOLOGY

In the present study we employed a variety of qualitative and interpretive methods. The data were collected with phenomenological interviewing (Thompson et al., 1989), participant observation, and diary research (Alazewski, 2006) among male fashion consumers in Central European cities. Our purposive sampling followed the principles of criterion sampling (Patton, 1991), which focused on the phenomenon of boundary-crossing male handbag consumption, where handbags are reflective of the aesthetics of female handbags. Aesthetic phenomena in urban areas, particularly fashion related ones, are subject to certain contemporaneity and similar emergence across different locations (Eicher and Sumberg, 1995), which allowed us to sample in different urban locations. We sampled in several cities in order to level out local occurrences endemic to a particular urban environment, such as local trends or local fashionistas. Respondents were sampled in smaller (from 130.000 inhabitants) and larger European cities (up to 1.3.mio inhabitants). Theoretical saturation (Goulding, 2005) was achieved with 14 respondents. The sample yielded a wide range of different fashion appearances, aesthetic understandings, interests and occupations, ranging from company owners, students, employees, designers, editors to social workers and teachers, thus demonstrating the demographic heterogeneity of the limited number of consumers engaging in male handbag consumption. Despite these vast differences, an astounding similarity of self reflection and consumption patterns underlie their different styles.

We developed our study in a two step process. The first step involved observation of handbag consumption in different locations so as to understand why and how this would be different from common male bags. We, then, approached male consumers either online or directly on the streets in urban areas. People, who agreed to participate in our study, were provided with a diary. We asked them to freely write report not just about their particular handbag consumption but also their fashion experiences and related thoughts for a period of two and a half to three weeks. In addition, we asked participants to take pictures of items they evaluated as aesthetic, and characterize their style.

In a second step we conducted phenomenological interviews (Thompson et al., 1989) with the participants at their homes or in their offices. The long interviews and the trips through their homes and offices informed us about the respondent's life biographies, the different aesthetic styles they developed, and their consumption patterns. We further included questions focused on societal changes and general opinions, specifically with regard to boundary-crossing topics. Diaries were used to identify additional important topics and stimulated stories and narrations about respondents' reflections and developments of aesthetic styles. Photoelicitation (Heisley and Levy, 1991) additionally supported our attempts to gather a rich data set on boundary-crossing aesthetic consumption.

Interviews accumulated to a total of approximately 30 hours of recorded information. The interviews were transcribed and subject to a hermeneutical interpretation (Thompson and Haytko 1997). The hermeneutic analysis proceeded from idiographic analyses to cross-case analysis and the development of themes that permeate the stories of our informants (Goulding 2002). We applied constant comparative method of interpretation (Charmaz 2006), based on literature in the area of gender-related consumption, aesthetics, fash-

ion, uniqueness and conformity, and philosophy. Additionally, diary entries helped us with the development of our interpretations in a constant discursive interaction among researchers.

FINDINGS

Some consumers are *anders*. Their style irritates. We present our findings according to three paradoxical practices of *willful ignorance*, *non non-conformity* and *defamiliarization* that aim at distancing themselves from societal conventions in various consumption domains; they reflect personal life projects and convictions about how to make sense of these domains in life.

Willful ignorance

Willful ignorance depicts the deliberate avoidance of signifiers of prevailing tastes and ideologies (Gould et al. 1997). Whereas willful ignorance characterizes various consumption cultures (Schouten and McAlexander 1995, Goulding and Saren 2009, Muniz and O'Guinn 2001), we found that our respondents ignore mainstream on a broader scope, which surfaces in a plenitude of life aspects that are subject to boundaries of legitimate consumption. Ignorance manifests, for instance, in fleeing from societal blueprints of gender, family life, relationships, or profession. One of these societal blueprints concerns common gender concepts and traditional lifestyles, which respondents strongly criticized. Respondents claimed that imposed conventions aim at restricting people's freedom. Ignoring these lifestyles, for Nico, means liberation.

> At the age of 23, this episode was over. I have been a little petty bourgeois, who thought at the age of 20 that something he needs to do is (.) to do it the way everyone else is doing it. Marry, having children, build a house, buy an apartment–like that. Now when I think of that, it is (...) stupid.

> Interviewer: What was changing?

> Well back then I thought that everything needs to be done away with. All the legacy of junk needed to be done away with. The beliefs and ah (...) expectations that I was talked into. All the suppression and the expectations of society, and the people, and so forth. I abandoned all and (.) what I also did was that I questioned all other things in my life. And set up new rules; one of these was not to wear what others want me to wear but to dress the way I want it. (Nico, 35, self employed)

Nico liberated himself from prevailing normative concepts through willfully ignoring them at a certain stage in life when he started questioning societal conventions. Nico's narrative also reveals that he applied willful ignorance in other life areas as well,

TABLE 1. Respondent characteristics

Interview 1: Daniel, teacher, 29	Interview 8: Patrick, designer, 30
Interview 2: Marcus, company owner, 28	Interview 9: Simon, editor, 31
Interview 3: Steve, student, 25	Interview 10: Marc, student, 25
Interview 4 : Robert, PhD student, 27	Interview 11: Oliver, make up artist, 24
Interview 5: Peter, hairdresser, 29	Interview 12: Richard, social worker, 27
Interview 6: Thomas, employee, 28	Interview 13: Nico, self employed, 35
Interview 7: Michael, employee, 42	Interview 14: Lukas, student/ marketer, 28

where he felt societal pressure. At the time of the interview, for instance, Nico reported being in an open relationship with a man, and living separately.

Ignorance frees consumers from predefined lifestyles and consumption patterns but requires elaborate consideration and critical reflection of own desires, needs and convictions that match the autonomous self. In doing that, consumers liberate themselves from societal blueprints, and localize themselves. Willful ignorance is commonly a first step in people's search for a self-determined identity and leaves consumers with a number of important decisions to be made in almost all areas of life. Yet, only after careful reflection—sometimes over years or even decades—when respondents found prevailing societal conventions not to fit their selves, they were apt to apply non non-conformity and defamiliarization practices.

Performing non non-conformity

Overall, respondents report about three main practices of non non-conformity, which is *provocative conformity*, *wearing the old and outdated*, and *consuming the ugly*. Whereas 'provocative conformity' displays fashion-consciousness, 'wearing the old and outdated', and 'consuming the ugly' is practiced in order to avoid being categorized as mainstream fashionable.

Provocative conformity. Respondents portray themselves as adjusted and as non-conformers at the same time. Although respondents clearly aim to set themselves apart from group think, they do however not construct themselves as oppositional to others. Such non non-conform behavior, which generally accords with contextual fashion rules, is commonly spiced with a provocative element, as for instance wearing a black suit and a pink baguette handbag in the opera, a suit with torn sneakers in a business meeting, or dressing in crème at a white party, as for instance Patrick reports.

" For example to a white party I won't go in white. Because I think it is stupid. Well I am not the revolutionary type, but it is stupid. I (...) I don't like white at all anyways and accordingly when I am invited to a white party I avoid that by simply wearing crème, ebony or similar and then some (.) something else, some other color. Yes." (Patrick, 30, designer)

By using misplaced objects, respondents distance themselves from the conventional style of social contexts and at the same time exhibit their connoisseurship of these social settings to ensure that they are accepted as knowledgeable. All of these provocations exhibit sophisticated, playful boundary transgressions without putting social acceptance in danger. It is these boundaries; the other; that which is not me that is used by respondents to reflect about what they aspire to be. The other is always different; a moving target that demands sophisticated differentiating aesthetic styles for different social environments. Fashion items, or life concepts are taken out of the situational and/or time context so as to break consumption rules.

Wearing the old and outdated. Wearing the old and outdated is not to be confused with nostalgia or retro consumption (Brown, Sherry and Kozinets 2003). Respondents rather apply specific practices to render recently bought consumption items as old and outdated thus negating the act of purchasing. Informants withdraw from the gaze of others through commoditization of the shiny and new; recognition is not their purpose and still, they become exactly recognized for that; because it is peculiar in a world of conspicuousness and gaze. In order to conceal newness, respondents report that they wash their new clothing items several times until they look regular and worn. They wear new shoes in the rain to make them look muddy and old. "All that jazz" supports consumers in creating a personalized, distinctive appearance. The worn and the old have a history and

bear the hallmarks of the owner. The item has thus lost its characteristics as a mass-marketed fashion item; it has lost the sameness of the newly bought item that is bought fresh from the rack.

Wearing the old and outdated is non non-conformal because consumers do not break with fashion conformities at all. Practicing the old and outdated is not restricted to fashion items. Nico for example, reported that he only went to cafés and restaurants which were once trendy, but have now been abandoned by the in-crowds. He evades being part of a crowd of people who chases after new trends. Practicing the old and outdated thus inverts conceptions of what is generally conceived as trendy and fashionable. The untrendy becomes fashionable, different and, most importantly, a statement of who we are/want to be.

Consuming the ugly. Another practice of creating the self as non non-conformal is the appraisal of objects or behaviors despite other people's negative evaluations and reactions. This practice resembles Tian et al.'s (2001) behavioral category of unpopular counter conformity. However, in contrast to Tian et al.'s (2001) findings, respondents, in their consumption narratives, referred to well known and even popular brands and consumption objects . Oliver, for example, reports about using an eau de cologne, which a lot of people do not like.

"One I like a lot is from Dior "Fahrenheit" but ah (...) but a lot of people hate that. I really like it because of that. So many people said "Boah, Oliver you are really smelling bad, like rotten moss" or something. I really like it a lot when people talk like that about my eau de Cologne" (Oliver, 24, Make-up artist)

Oliver's excerpt reveals that he uses a perfume, which produces social sanctions like ridicule. More accurately, for Oliver the appeal of wearing this eau de cologne results from its negative evaluation. Being a make-up artist and working with people in the aesthetic industries exposes Oliver to constant aesthetic evaluations. Being fashionably groomed yet, using objects that other people dislike sets Oliver apart from his peers, and even puts his own profession into question. Consuming the ugly very strongly resists common conventions of beauty and aesthetics. Therefore, it is non non-conformal. Respondents borrow from other people's negative evaluations. At the same time, respondents challenge others' conventional aesthetic evaluations. By turning things upside down, which is rendering ugly stuff beautiful, and vice versa, informants construct themselves as unconventional.

DEFAMILIARIZATION

Defamiliarization practices aim at altering popular consumption objects, behaviors and conventions in order to disguise their origin or primary purpose. Respondents report that they remove or add features to render consumption objects unusual. Similarly, familiar behavior is contrasted through its adoption in inappropriate contexts so as to render them unfamiliar. Defamiliarization practices comprise *delocalization*, *delabeling* and *contrasting personal practice*.

Delocalization. Delocalization strategies are related to the adoption of typical urban lifestyles which are unfamiliar to the places that respondents inhabit. These practices are straight forward attempts to consume the latest urban styles in small hometown contexts, and show dissent of local narrow-mindedness. Respondents report about their discontent with rural lifestyles and aesthetics:

"I am actually a country boy, who on the other hand is not. I have always been someone who (...) does not see [the respondent's home town] as the centre of the world and I am not like others (...) Last year in spring I have been to Hongkong for

two months. My last relationship has been abroad, too. I orient myself on other things. For me [the respondent's home town] is nice, but it's not that I think that I should stay here; people are very provincial here. Like what the local magazine reports about styling, that is, yes, well, that is for people who want to blend in. Those are people who are satisfied with what society tells them to do. I am different. I think "I want to try this and that – different things". I simply try things out and I am the only one in my peer group who does that." (Robert, 27, student)

Respondents delocalize themselves primarily through the adoption of urban and cosmopolitan aesthetics. They adopted specific aesthetic styles, which they encountered in metropolitan areas like Paris, London, or Berlin. As these aesthetic styles are unknown in their home cities, they serve them to display their distinctiveness, which, in an urban context, would blend smoothly into contemporary urban lifestyles. Examples of such urban aesthetics are skinny jeans before they became stylish a couple of years ago, male handbags, specific hairstyles, color combinations, or particular shoes. Apart from aesthetics, respondents also engage in activities they connect with urbanism. They listen to particular music, prefer ethnic food and try to escape to urbanities whenever possible. Delocalization practices liken typical cosmopolitan lifestyles (Thompson and Tambyah 1999) and could therefore be straightforwardly be misinterpreted as cultural capital accumulation. In addition to that, the urban lifestyle also exposes respondents to resentments from their local environment, and confronts them with two paradoxical ways of living and being.

Delabeling. Delabeling aims at detaching consumption objects, and lifestyles from their sources so as to decontaminate them from their mainstream origins. Practices range from ripping off labels to transgressions of gender boundaries.

"When I see an item with something sewn on the back, which you can get rid of, then I would consider it. But when it is ahm (...) like Dolce &Gabbana there is a big logo imprint on it; well I would not spend money on that."

Interviewer: "Because?"

"Because the thing would be worn by like a million other people and everyone would see what label it is. I am my own person and therefore I don't like that." (Patrick, 30, designer)

Patrick is very clear about his attitude towards mainstream labels and mass consumption. The deep resentment against depersonalization through mass marketed brands is noticeable here. His resentment resembles Tian et al.'s (2001) avoidance of marking as one of a kind and expresses a deep desire for developing a distinct personality, keeping some mystique, undefined facet of self. Such authentication acts (Lipovetsky 1994) become even more pronounced through cross-gender consumption. Through consumption of opposite gender styles, respondents renegotiate typical societal gender blueprints (Tuncay and Otnes, 2008, Holt and Thompson, 2004, Firat and Venkatesh, 1995). They engage in male and female performances and situate their self gender in between the extremes of maleness and femaleness. Contrasting, blending, and altering male and female aesthetics and performances supports the accomplishment of a unique gender.

Contrasting personal practices. Contrary to delocalizing and delabeling, which is directed towards others, contrasting personal practices aim at altering own behaviors and personal consumption habits in order not to become a prototype of oneself. These findings, specifically, moved our interpretive frame from nonconformity and gender-crossing concepts towards Lipovetsky's (1994) argument of the authenticating self, existentialist notions of *Sein*, and psychological notions of individuation, and self-transformation (Koppensteiner 2009). Whereas previous findings strongly point towards respondents' attempts to differentiate from the aesthetics- and gender-illiterate crowd, here, respondents seek to render themselves unfamiliar through alterations of styles, genders and related practices. According to the respondents, such style reworking is independent of life transitions but pursued regularly so as to keep style imitators out, and

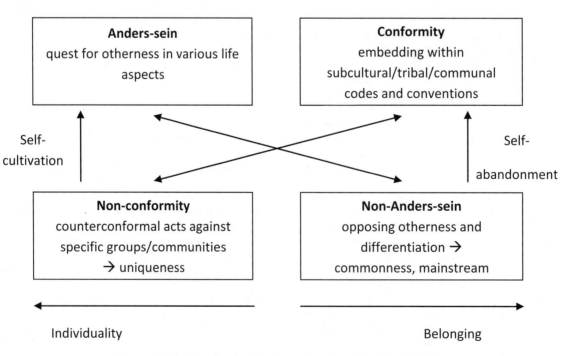

Figure 1. Semiotic square of Anders-sein and conformity distinctions

experience how they themselves change as their styles and behaviors change. By doing that, respondents continuously alter their selves— including gender—, reflecting an inner desire to better understand who they are. Strict consumption rules provide structure; contrasting personal practices provide the means for self-transformation.

DISCUSSION

Our study investigated into the lifestyle of young males for making an important theoretical point. We describe and interpret a lifestyle which is neither conform, nor non-conform; which is unique, yet only within specific social contexts. We introduce the notion of *Anders-sein* for this paradoxical, yet coherent life project. The term *Anders-sein* is rooted in German philosophy and literature (cf. Nietzsche 1969/1983, 1989). *Anders* depicts differentness and deviating behavior, or conception, whereas *sein* is related to an existentialist notion of self. Figure 1 presents a semiotic square that depicts how *Anders-sein* is related to common conceptualizations of conformity and non-conformity.

Anders-sein refers to a general quest for being different, relative to what is common and typical, in an attempt to ultimately cultivate one's self. We understand its opposite, non-Anders-sein, as the lack of differentiation desires in favour of generally accepted behaviours and conventions. Whereas non-Anders-sein reflects a deliberate individual decision, conformity refers to the concepts of belongingness and identity construction through and within communities, tribes, or subcultures (Wooten 2006, Kates, 2004). Counter conformity as the opposite of conformity willingly and explicitly diverts from group behaviour, while *Anders-sein* lacks this turn against a particular, defined group, or notion. Rather it tries to contrast what is generally perceived as normal in society.

Anders-sein is a concept that informs our understanding of individuals' pursuit of differentness in at least two ways. First, *Anders-sein* transcends uniqueness and conformity and remains inconspicuous and un-ideological. While uniqueness is infused by counter conformity (Tian et al. 2001), *Anders-sein* embraces practices that may be indeed popular. Second, consumer's small scale boundary transgressions in important life domains through practices of provocative conformity are neither bold social signals, nor unimportant subtleties. They confront consumers with reactions from their environment, which they reflect upon vis-á-vis their own critical conviction.

Respondents' accounts are reminiscent of critical and liberal discourse of the intellectual elite, spiced with a pretentious undertone. Still, critique is not a matter of public discourse and, through practices of non non-conformity, remains within the aesthetic domain. Respondents' styles could be interpreted as aestheticism. Just as dandyism came up during the 19th century as style "entrepreneurship" so as to gain deference in a period of cultural decay (Smith 1974), *Anders-sein* likens dandyism's refined aesthetics as a form of disregard of social structure, and willful ignorance of social conventions. Yet, in stark contrast to dandyism, *Anders-sein* is far from conspicuousness, and social competition. Rather, *Anders-sein* seeks to contrast other, contemporary forms of social conventions, as for instance, common understandings of beauty, for instance through *wearing the old and outdated* and *consuming the ugly*; gender definitions, and the localism-cosmopolitan dualism through practices of *delocalization*, and *delabeling*.

Gender crossing practices of informants, which are not overtly homosexual, remind of Marcel Proust's famous modern novel A la recherche du temps perdu (*In Search of Lost Time*), and its use of feminized masculine names for the portrayal of the novel's main character's desires (O'Brien, 1949). The gender-crossing practices

found in our study remain widely uncontested and liken contemporary, everyday popular media representations of boundary crossings that are legitimized as popular arts form. Similarly, critique on provincialism in local communities rather remains a still expression of dissent through practicing of different styles hence is non non-conform. By mimicking normality, practices of *Anders-sein* remain apolitical and un-ideological. Still, as normality is transposed in other contexts, their pursuit of being different gains a slightly provocative touch, which is sufficiently *anders*.

Apart from the distinct but mostly unspectacular outer-directedness of *Anders-sein*, its pursuit has a strong inner-directedness. Through defamiliarization and *contrasting personal practices*, in particular, males permanently oscillate among styles, geographical locations, genders, habits, and selves, so as to find out what they like, dislike, what kind of gender understanding they have, and have not, thereby developing self-understanding. Although less radical and less public, *Anders-sein* practices liken the "constantly changing chameleon persona" (Kelley 2000:7) of 20th century popular music culture. We interpret this permanent search for self-understanding as existentialist. The self, while not unconscious, is impossible to conceptualize, nor directly accessible (Sartre 1964). Instead, individuals engage in gradual rapprochement to their self, which they will probably never be able to denominate. While we are cautious with the notion of the authentic self, we nevertheless could also interpret practices of *Anders-sein* as practices of authentication towards an unknown self. Still, *Anders-sein* strategies help getting a glimpse of inner desires, (dis)likes, tastes, and particularities that commonly remain inexplicable.

REFERENCES

Alaszewski, Andy (2006), *Using diaries for Social Research*, London: Sage.

Arnould, Eric J. and Craig J. Thompson (2005), "Consumer Culture Theory (CCT): Twenty Years of Research," *Journal of Consumer Research*, 31 (March), 868–82.

Arsel, Zeynep and Craig J. Thompson (2011), "Demythologizing Consumption Practices: How Consumers Protect their field dependent Identity Investments from Devaluing Marketplace Myths" *Journal of Consumer Research*, 37 (February), 791–806.

Berger, Jonah and Chip Heath (2007), "Where Consumers Diverge from Others: Identity Signaling and Product Domains," *Journal of Consumer Research*, 34 (August), 121–34.

_____ (2008), "Who Drives Divergence? Identity Signaling, Outgroup Dissimilarity, and the Abandonment of Cultural Tastes," *Journal of Personality and Social Psychology*, 95 (September), 593–607.

Beverland, Michael B. and Francis J. Farrelly (2010), "The Quest for Authenticity in Consumption: Consumer's Purposive Choice of Authentic Cues to Shape Experiences Outcomes," *Journal of Consumer Research*, 36(December), 838–56.

Bordieu, Pierre (1984), *Distinction: A Social Critique of the Judgment of Taste* Harvard, MA: Harvard University Press.

_____ (1986), "The Forms of Capital," *Handbook of Theory and Research for the Sociology of Education,* ed. John Richardson, New York: Greenwood, 241–58.

Brown, Stephen, John F. Sherry Jr. and Robert V. Kozinets (2003), "Teaching Old Brands New Tricks: Retro Branding and the Revival of Brand Meaning" *Journal of Marketing*, 67 (July), 19–33.

Caruana, Robert, Andrew Crane and James A. Fitchett (2008), "Paradoxes of Consumer Independence: A Critical Discourse Analysis of the Independent Traveler," *Marketing Theory*, 8 (September), 253–72.

Chan, Cindy, Jonah Berger, and Leaf Van Boven (2012), "Identifiable but Not Identical: Combining Social Identity and Uniqueness Motives in Choice," *Journal of Consumer Research*, forthcoming.

Charmaz, Kathy (2006), *Constructing Grounded Theory: A Practical Guide through Qualitative Analysis*: Sage.

Eicher, Joanne B. and Barbara Sumberg (1995), "World Fashion, Ethnic, and National Dress," *Dress and Ethnicity. Change Across Space and Time*, (ed) Joanne B. Eicher, Oxford: Berg, 295-306.

Firat, A. Fuat and Alladi Venkatesh (1995), "Liberatory Postmodernism and the Reenchantment of Consumption," *Journal of Consumer Research*, 22 (June), 239-67.

Fromkin, Howard L. and Raanan Lipshitz (1976), *A Construct Validity Method of Scale Development: The Uniqueness Scale*, Institute for Research in the Behavioral, Economic, and Management Sciences, Krannert Graduate School of Management, Purdue University.

Gould, Stephen J., Franklin S. Houston and JoNel Mundt (1997), "Failing to Try to Consume: A Reversal of the Usual Consumer Research Perspective," in *Advances in Consumer Research* (24), ed. Merrie Brucks, Deborah J. MacInnis, Provo, STAAT: Association for Consumer Research, 211–16.

Goulding, Christina (2002), *Grounded Theory: A Practical Guide for Management, Business and Market Researchers*, London: Sage.

_____ (2005), "Grounded Theory, Ethnography and Phenomenology: A Comparative Analysis of Three Qualitative Strategies for Marketing Research," *European Journal of Marketing*, 39(3-4), 294–308.

Goulding, Christina and Michael Saren (2009), "Performing Identity: An Analysis of Gender Expression at the Whitby Goth Festival," *Consumption, Markets and Culture*, 12 (March), 27–46.

Heidegger, Martin (1962), *Being and Time*, Malden, MA: Wiley-Blackwell.

Heisley, Deborah D. and Sidney J. Levy (1991), "Autodriving: A Photoelicitation Technique," *Journal of Consumer Research*, 18 (December), 257-72.

Holt, Douglas B. (2002), "Why Do Brands Cause Trouble? A Dialectical Theory of Consumer Culture and Branding," *Journal of Consumer Research*, 29 (June), 70–90.

Holt, Douglas B. and Craig J. Thompson (2004), "Man-of-Action Heros: The Pursuit of Heroic Masculinity in Everyday Consumption," *Journal of Consumer Research*, 31 (September), 425–40.

Kates, Steven M. (2004), "The Dynamics of Brand Legitimacy: An Interpretive Study in the Gay Men's Community," *Journal of Consumer Research*, 31 (September), 455–64.

Kelley, Mike (2000), "Cross Gender/Cross Genre," *Journal of Performance and Art*, 22(1), 1–9.

Koppensteiner, Norbert (2009), *The Art of the Transpersonal Self – Transformation as Aesthetic and Energetic Practice*. Dresden: Atropos Press.

Kozinets, Robert V. (2002), "Can Consumers Escape the Market: Emancipatory Illuminations from Burning Man," *Journal of Consumer Research*, 29 (June), 20–38.

Kozinets, Robert V. and Jay M. Handelman (2004), "Adversaries of Consumption: Consumer Movements, Activism, and Ideology," *Journal of Consumer Research*, 31 (December), 691–704.

Lipovetsky, Gilles (1994), *The Empire of Fashion*, Princeton, STAAT: Princeton University Press.

Merleau-Ponty, Maurice (1945/1974), *Phänomenologie der Wahrnehmung*, 6th edition, translated by Rudolf Boehm, Berlin: Verlag Walter de Gruyter.

Muñiz, Albert M. and Thomas O'Guinn (2001), "Brand Community," *Journal of Consumer Research*, 27(March), 412–32.

Nail, Paul R. (1986), "Toward an Integration of Some Models and Theories of Social Response," *Psychological Bulletin*, 100 (September), 190–206.

Nietzsche, Friedrich (1969/1983), *Also sprach Zarathustra - Ein Buch für alle und keinen*, Stuttgart: Kröner.

_____ (1989), *Ecce Homo. How One becomes What One Is*, translated with Commentaries by Walter Kaufmann, in *On the Genealogy of Morals and Ecce Homo*, ed. Walter Kaufmann, New York, NY: Vintage Books.

O'Brien, Justin (1949), "Albertine the Ambiguous: Notes on Proust's Transposition of Sexes," PMLA *Publications of the Modern Language Association*, 64 (5), 933–52.

Ourahmoune, Nassima and Simon Nyeck (2008), "Male Consumers Entering the Private Sphere: An Exploratory Investigation of French Male Involvement, Practices and Interaction around Lingerie for Men Consumption," in *Proceedings of Latin American Advances in Consumer Research*, Vol.9, eds. Claudia R. Acevedo, Jose Mauro C.Hernandez, Tina M. Lowrey, 2, Association for Consumer Research.

Patton, Michael, Q. (1991), *Qualitative Evaluation and Research Methods*, Newbury Park: Sage Publications.

Rinallo, Diego (2007) "Metro/Fashion/Tribes of Men: Negotiating the Boundaries of Men's Legitimate Consumption", in *Consumer Tribes*, ed. Bernard Cova, Robert V. Kozinets, Avi Shankar, Oxford: Butterworth-Heinemann, 76–92.

Rocamora, Agnès (2002), "Fields of Fashion: Critical Insights into Bourdieu's Sociology of Culture," *Journal of Consumer Culture*, 2 (November), 341–62.

Rose, Randall L. and Stacy L. Wood (2005), "Paradox and the Consumption of Authenticity Through Reality Television," *Journal of Consumer Research*, 32 (September), 284-96.

Sartre, Jean-Paul (1943), *L'Être et le néant. Essai d'ontologie phénoménologique.* Paris: Librairie Gallimard.

_____ Jean-Paul (1964), *Die Transzendenz des Ego.* Reinbek/Hamburg: Rowohlt.

_____ Jean-Paul (1989/2011), *Wahrheit und Existenz*, 3rd edition, Reinbek/Hamburg: Rowohlt.

Schirmacher, Wolfgang (1994), "Homo Generator - Militant Media and Postmodern Technology," in *Culture on the Brink: Ideologies of Technology (Discussions in Contemporary Culture)*, ed. Gretchen Bender, Timothy Duckrey, NY: The New Press, 65-79.

Schouten, John and James H. McAlexander (1995), "Subcultures of Consumption: An Ethnography of the New Bikers," *Journal of Consumer Research*, 22 (June), 43–61.

Shankar, Avi, Richard Elliott and James A. Fitchett (2009), "Identity, Consumption and Narratives of Socialization," *Marketing Theory*, 9 (March), 75–94.

Simmel, Georg (1905/1995), *Philosophie der Mode*, in Georg Simmel Gesamtausgabe, Band 10, Frankfurt: Suhrkamp, 7–38.

Smith, Thomas S. (1974), "Aestheticism and Social Structure: Style and Social Network in the Dandy Life," *American Sociological Review*, 39 (5), 725–743.

Snyder, Charles A. and Harold L. Fromkin (1977), "Abnormality as a Positive Characteristic: The Development and Validation of a Scale Measuring Need for Uniqueness," *Journal of Abnormal Psychology*, 86 (October), 518–27.

_____ (1980), *Uniqueness. The Human Pursuit of Difference*, NY: Plenum.

Tian, Kelly T., William O. Bearden and Gary L. Hunter (2001), "Consumer's Need for Uniqueness: Scale Development and Validation," *Journal of Consumer Research*, 28 (June), 50–66.

Thompson, Craig J. and Elizabeth C. Hirschman (1995), "Understanding the Socialized Body: A Poststructuralist Analysis of Consumer's Self-Conceptions, Body Images, and Self-Care Practices," *Journal of Consumer Research*, 22 (September), 139–53.

Thompson, Craig J. and Diana L. Haytko (1997), "Speaking of Fashion: Consumers' Uses of Fashion Discourses and the Appropriation of Countervailing Cultural Meanings," *Journal of Consumer Research*, 24 (June), 15–42.

Thompson, Craig J., William B. Locander, and Howard R. Pollio (1989), "Putting Consumer Experience into Consumer Research: the Philosophy and Method of Existential-Phenomenology,"*Journal of Consumer Research*, 16 (September), 133–46.

Thompson, Craig J. and Siok K. Tambyah (1999), "Trying to be Cosmopolitan*", Journal of Consumer Research*, 26(December), 214–41.

Thompson, Craig J., Aric Rindfleisch and Arsel Zeynep (2006), "Emotional Branding and the Strategic Value of the Doppelgänger Brand Image," *Journal of Marketing*, 70(January), 50–64.

Tuncay, Linda and Cele Otnes (2008), "The Use of Persuasion Management Strategies by Identity Vulnerable Consumers: The Case of Urban Heterosexual Male Shoppers," *Journal of Retailing*, 84(December), 487–99.

Veblen, Thorstein (1899), *The Theory of the Leisure Class*, New York: MacMillan.

Wooten, David B. (2006), "From Labelling Possessions to Possessing Labels: Ridicule and Socialization among Adolescents," *Journal of Consumer Research*, 33 (September), 188–98.

Workman, Jane E. and Lark F. Caldwell, (2007), "Centrality of Visual Product Aesthetics, Tactile and Uniqueness Needs of Fashion Consumers," *International Journal of Consumer Studies*, 31 (November), 589–96.

Cultural Brand Innovation within Emerging Economies:
A Tale of Two Campaigns from Modernising India

Sudipta Das, University of Strathclyde, UK
Paul Hewer, University of Strathclyde, UK

ABSTRACT

In this paper we extend Holt's (2004) seminal Cultural Branding Model within emerging economies, namely India. By studying the genealogy of an iconic Indian brand – Bajaj – we reveal how a transforming political and socio-economic infrastructure supplies opportunities for building iconic brands in the age of fast-moving consumer culture.

THEORETICAL UNDERPINNINGS

The recent conjugation of traditional brand management and consumer culture research has transformed the way we used to interpret the winning stories of some of the most powerful iconic brands in the history (McCracken 2009; Holt 2004; Holt and Cameron 2010). In 2004, Holt noted "Brands become iconic when they perform identity myths: simple fictions that addresses cultural anxieties from afar, from imaginary worlds…[that reflect] expression of [consumers'] aspired identities [within a nation]" (ibid, p. 8). Conventional branding models have largely misinterpreted identity values as cognitive resources for branding. Instead brands that enjoy success emerge from their ability to inspire identity values as products of a nation's cultural brief - something Holt identified as *The Principles of Cultural Branding*. Holt believes that targeting a nationwide ideological demand with an authentic story-telling (myth) capability supplies a brand with intensive and pervasive societal meanings and catapults them into iconic status. For example, think about how the historical fit between the populist world of outlaw biking and the counter-cultural texts of alternative American masculinities had paved the raw materials for Harley Davidson's iconic constituencies (Holt 2004; Schouten and McAlexander 1995).

In this paper we analyse the iconic constituencies of an Indian two-wheeler brand – Bajaj – and reveal how cultural innovation has been achieved and sustained by constant (re)innovation of myth markets addressing anxieties and orthodoxies hidden within socio-cultural spheres of a transforming post-colonial society. The inspiration for such debate comes in the form India's changing social, economical, and political agendas that supplied widespread ideological resources for identity construction as India moved from a post-colonial to a modern society (Varma 2007; Desouza et al. 2009), and Thompson's (2011) call for increased research, following CCT conference 6, into a nation's dominant political ideologies and it's impact on consumer culture and identity politics. Our analysis reveals what we like to think of as a tale of two campaigns, one rooted in a nostalgic impulse for the past and the glory days of yesteryear. The other, forward-looking, aspirational, clad if you like in new clothes and new styles of riding fit for New Times.

In the past century India has experienced two different kinds of economy - first suffocated by slothful growth, multiculturalism, genocides, civil wars, and a conservative form of modernity; second, economic liberalisation and a land of surging growth and optimism which brought a significant transformation in consumption culture, identity, and class politics. Today with a projected 34% of youth population of the world by 2020, today's India is young, vibrant and restless. Its growing aspirations we suggest are no longer limited within the postcolonial discourse of *Swadeshi*[1] or multicultur-

alism as expressed through Nehru's ideology to achieve modernity. Contemporary India is thus a context of significant change, and such changes can be distilled in the ways material objects are advertised – the representations which surround such objects of desire – more so – we can suggest that such changes can be explored at the level of consumption practices.

To express this transformation, **we coin the phrase FMCCs to characterise consumer culture within economies such as India, Brazil and China to name but three**, as **Fast-Moving-Consumer-Cultures**. Such economies require objects for movement and transportation, objects that are rich in expressive and *intensive* potential (Miller 2010). Objects which can transcend tradition, nationhood, generation and local community; objects which are full of richer promises initiated we believe at the level of representation (the changing forms of advertising imagery employed); but also which herald and bring in their wake changes at the level of practice – in this case how to ride a motorbike with sufficient glamour and allure to stand out.

METHOD

Our analysis takes the forms of a case examination of Brand Bajaj, we initiated by investigating the historical development (*brand genealogy*) of brand Bajaj within the Indian marketplace. In doing so we scrutinised a number of secondary sources, i.e., Market Intelligence reports by McKinsey, company reports and case studies produced by Bajaj, the official website of Bajaj two-wheelers, and a number of influential business magazines and biking gazettes (Forbes India, India Today, Business World, Bike India etc.). To complement this analysis the first author travelled across India to experience the socio-political situation within the context and to collect a number of Bajaj two-wheeler advertisements (printed and television) released within the Indian mass market. In our efforts to develop a *brand genealogy* of Bajaj we moved back and forth between Holt's (2004) suggested 'three levels'. During the primary analysis we scoured the managerial archives to trace the history of Bajaj's marketing practice, while we interpreted the advisements to understand the "resonate or disconnect" between the brand and a transforming postcolonial society (Holt 2004, p.227). Our systematic comparison of cases reveals how the brand Bajaj acted as a 'cultural activist' by emulating the postcolonial models of 'desired Indian manhood' since 1980s (Cayla and Koops-Elson, 2006).

Finally, to add nuance to this textual analysis the first author conducted in depth interviews with a number of influential personalities within the Indian advertising industry with connections to the brand (Cf. Appendix 1). We only chose to participate in those agencies who are actively engaged in the creation and promotion of Bajaj two-wheeler brands in India, i.e., Lowe-Lintas, Ogilvy & Mather, Leo Burnett etc. On average the interviews lasted between 40 minutes to an hour. The interviews were further supplemented by additional observations, photographs, and field notes collected throughout India.

---

[1] Swadeshi is an anticonsumption ideology evolved during India's independence movement against British colonial rule. The key construct of this ideology stated: "indigenous goods should be preferred by consumerseven if they were more expensive and inferior in quality to their imported substitutes." (Sarkar 1973, p. 92)

The first cut: Hamara Bajaj

The company Bajaj Auto Production was established most significantly in 1945, one of the iconic years when India was at its final stage of negotiation for independence from British colonial rule. In this instance, from the outset it must be understood as one of India's first local brands that came into existence by celebrating the 'spirit of national independence' (Cayla and Koops-Elson, forthcoming). Initially the company sustained their business by selling imported Italian Vespa scooters under the name of brand Bajaj. In the 1970s however the two-wheeler market in India started to become increasingly competitive and Bajaj was forced to move into its own production category. The importation of Japanese motorbikes and increasing popularity of the British-made *Royal Enfield* made it increasingly harder for Bajaj to sustain their image on technological grounds alone. This was the time in our view when Bajaj turned their back on a 'better mousetrap' strategy (Holt 2010) and started to compete on the grounds of culture. With the release of their landmark advertising campaign 'Hamara Bajaj' (our Bajaj) in the 1980's Bajaj became so popular that they achieved widespread appeal in the national consciousness. Owning a Bajaj in the '80s appeared to be "similar to owning a station wagon in 1950's and 1960's America" (Pyssler 1992). People were happy to remain on the waiting list for seven years for their chance to purchase a Bajaj scooter (ibid).

In understanding the logic for the campaign and it's connection with the Indian nation, we reflect on our analysis along with the ex-director of Lowe-Lintus India, Alyque Padamsee's interview – the man who acted as the head of creative for the campaign:

Our analysis reveals that Bajaj's first landmark campaign depicted a picture of peace, unity, and most importantly Indian men from different religious community (Hindu, Muslim, Sikh, Parsi etc.) in the time of social turmoil, when the nation was struggling to deal with its post-colonial diversity, multiculturalism, and consequent civil wars. In this context the 'Hamara Bajaj' campaign reinforced the secular idea of different communities existing peacefully and collaborating with each other (Cayla and Koops-Elson 2006). The campaign name - 'Hamara Bajaj' (our Bajaj) - itself depicted a collectivist theme, a sense of Indian citizenship, where as the theme song symbolised Bajaj as a symbol of the nation - "our past..our present…the stronger India has a stronger picture - Hamara Bajaj (our Bajaj)… Hamara Bajaj (our Bajaj)".

Images from the campaign express how such sentiments were encapsulated within the visual iconography of the brand to add resonance and meaningfulness to its appeal:

In their efforts to supply extraordinary identity value to the brand, Padamsee inscribed Bajaj within the nation by depicting it as an old, reliable, and hardworking individual, just like the majority of Indian men. More so, the phrase 'Hamara Bajaj' (or the message of collectivism) received a warm reception because of its strong sentimental association with colonial movements and wars.

Therefore, the 1980s Hamara Bajaj campaign presented the scooters as an object of national consciousness and togetherness, powerful seeds to lay as they served to remind Indians of golden times when the Indians congregated together to reclaim their identity from a foreign power.

The second cut: shifting tales of masculinity, power and performance

A rich stream of research has explored how economic prosperity and the flow of global knowledge have increasingly educated the Indian middle class about global consumption patterns (Mish 2007; Varma 2007; DeSouza et al. 2009; Rajagopal 1998). With discretionary buying power middle class Indians have crucially started to reinvent their identity and class affiliations (Fernandes 2006; Varma 2007). Bajaj has managed to survive this widespread cultural shift by renewing their ties with the emerging consumer class. In the most recent embodiment of the brand, Bajaj reinvented their image by, scrapping scooter production and, introducing a range of motorbikes. The earlier versions of national iconic names (Bajaj Chetak[2] Scooters) have been replaced by Western versions of motorbikes (Pulsar, Discovery, Avenger, Eliminator etc.). The names seek to signify associations with power, experience and driving desire as suggested through the shift from 'everyday' scooters to a new generation of faster and sleeker motorbikes.

Central to the new brand imaginary, as we suggest, is not only the shedding of the previous national and collectivist ethos, but also what, we believe, is championed imagery of modernity, individualism, and *risk consumption* (Celsi et al. 1993). An image for a rebellious and cosmopolitan Indian Youth who lives for the autonomy and free spirit of the open road; an image at one with the fast-moving zeitgeist of Contemporary India. In such images the emphasis is

[2] The 'Chetak' was named after the famous horse of the Hindu ruler Maharana Pratap. The heroic performance of Chetak in the battle of Haldighati and his contribution in saving his master's life made him a heroic and iconic symbol of carrier in Indian history. Eliminator was a name used by Kawasaki in 1984.

upon standing out from the crowd, rather than being at one with the crowd. In explaining the shift, the regional manager of Ogilvy & Mather India, Abhijit Avasthi suggested:

> "Hamara Bajaj was a different era. In this case we were very clear from the beginning that we should position the bikes somewhere in the lines of rawness...something that captures the macho effect of youth."

Essential to this new imaginary was the revalorisation of Indian Manhood, but not draped in the religious traditional whiteness of Nehru and Gandhi, rather a new style of riding which is encapsulated in considering masculinity as an expression of ways of movement, embodied in deed and action. Essential to these changes are not simply those of representation, but also how the object affords a new style of travel, confident in its status and future potential. Not nostalgic, but driving fast into its anticipated future of possibilities.

Signing Off

Our point of departure for this study was Holt's (2004) explanation of cultural branding strategies within American societies. The aim of this study was to examine the cultural branding principles operating within transforming India. Our analysis reveals that what we like to think of as a tale of two campaigns, one rooted in a nostalgic impulse for the past and the glory days of yesteryear. The other, forward-looking, aspirational, clad if you like in new clothes and new styles of riding fit for New Times. A new ethic of consumption which appears to fit more snuggly with the confident days of the *here and now* in contemporary India and thereby find broader appeal with the rootless, forward looking, thrill seekers of youth in India.

REFERENCES

Appadurai, Arjun (1988), "How to Make a National Cuisine: Cookbooks in Contemporary India", *Comparative Studies in Society and History*, Vol.30, No.1, pp.3-24.

Cayla, Julien (2002), "A Passage to India: An Ethnographic Study of the Advertising Agency's Role in Mediating the Cultural Learning and Adaptation of Multinational Corporations", Unpublished Ph.D. Dissertation, University of Colorado.

Cayla, Julien and Koops-Elson, Mark (2006), "Global Men with Local Roots: Representation and Hybridity in Indian Advertising", *Advances in Consumer Research*, Vol. 8.

Cayla, Julien and Koops-Elson, Mark (forthcoming), "Between the Home and World: A Postcolonial Analysis of Indian Advertising", *Journal of Macromarketing*

Celsi, Richard, Randall Rose, and Thomas Leigh (1993), "An Exploration of High-Risk Leisure Consumption through Skydiving", *Journal of Consumer Research*, Vol. 20 (June), pp. 1–21

DeSouza, Peter R., Kumar, Sanjay, and Shastri, Sandeep (2009), *Indian Youth in a Transforming World: Attitudes and Perceptions*, Sage Publications: India.

Fernandes, Leela (2006), *India's New Middle Class: Democratic Politics in an Era of Economic Reform*, University of Minnesota Press: Minneapolis.

Ger, G. (1998), "Identity and Material Culture across Borders", *Advances in Consumer Research*, Vol. 25, pp. 45-47.

Ger, G. and Belk, R.W. (1996), "'I'd Like to Buy the World a Coke': Consumptionscapes of a Less Affluent World", *Journal of Consumer Policy*, Vol. 19 (3), pp. 271-304.

Hebdige, D. (1988), "Object as Image", In *Hiding in the Light - On Images and Things*, London: Comedia.

Holt, Douglas B. (2004), *How Brands Become Icons: The Principles of Cultural Branding*, Harvard Business School Press: Boston.

Holt, Douglas B. and Thompson, Craig. J. (2004), "Man-of-Action Heroes: The Pursuit of Heroic Masculinity in Everyday Consumption", *Journal of Consumer Research*, Vol. 31 (September), pp. 425–40.

Holt, Doulas and Cameron, Douglas (2010), *Cultural Strategy: Using Innovative Ideologies to Build Breakthrough Brands*, Oxford University Press: New York.

Jafari, Ali Akbar (2008), "The Impact of Cultural Globalisation on the Interrelatedness of Identity Construction and Consumption Practices of Iranian Youth", Unpublished Ph.D. Dissertation, University of Wolverhampton, UK.

Lash, Scott and Lury, Celia (2007), *Global Consumer Culture*. Polity: Cambridge.

Miller, Daniel (2010), "*Stuff*", Polity Press: Cambridge: UK

Mish, Jenny (2007), "A Heavy Burden of Identity: India, Food, Globalisation, and Women", in *Research in Consumer Behaviour*, ed. By Belk, Russell and Sherry, John, Vol. 11.

Nehru, Jawaharlal (1960), *The Discovery of India*, Pitman Press: Bath, UK

Padamsee, Alyque (1999), *A Double Life: My Exciting Years in Theatre and Advertising*, Penguin Books: India.

Pyssler, Bruce (1992), "The Cultural and Political Economy of the Indian Two-Wheeler", Advances in Consumer Research, Vol. 19, pp. 437-442.

Rajagopal, Arvind (1998), "Advertising, Politics and the Sentimental Education of the Indian Consumer," *Visual Anthropology Review*, 14 (2), pp.14-31.

Rajagopal, Arvind (1999), "Thinking through Emerging Markets," *Social text*, Vol. 17 (3), pp. 131-149.

Sarkar, Sumit (1973), *The Swadeshi Movement in Bengal*, New Delhi: People's Publishing House

Schouten, John and McAlexander, James (1995), "Subcultures of Consumption: An Ethnography of New Bikers," *Journal of Consumer Research*, 22 (June), pp. 43-61

Thompson, Craig (2011), "Understanding consumption as political and moral practice: Introduction to the Special Issue", Journal of Consumer Culture, Vol. 11, p. 139

Thompson, Craig and Tambyah, Siok (1999), "Trying to be Cosmopolitan", *Journal of Consumer Research*, Vol. 20 (3), pp. 214 -241

Ustuner, Tuba and Holt, Douglas B. (2010), Toward a Theory of Status Consumption in Less Industrialized Countries, *Journal of Consumer Research*, Vol. 37 (June), pp.

Varma, Paban K. (2007), *The Great Indian Middle Class*, Penguin Books: London

Varman, Rohit and Belk, Russell (2009), "Nationalism and Ideology in an Anticonsumption Movement", *Journal of Consumer Research*, Vol. 36 (December), pp. 686-700

Venkatesh, Alladi (1994), "India's Changing Consumer Economy: A Cultural Perspective", *Advances in Consumer Research*, Vol. 21, pp. 323-328

Wilk, R. (1995), "Learning to Be Local in Belize: Global Systems of Common Difference", *in* Miller, D. (ed.) *Worlds Apart: Modernity through the Prism of the Local*, London: Routledge, pp. 110-33.

Appendix 1: *List of Marketing/Advertising Officials Interviewed*

Name	Background	Designation	Agency
Alyque Padamshee	Theatre & Film	Ex – Director	Lowe - Lintas
Shantanu Sapre	Marketing Graduate	Account Manager	Lowe - Lintas
Abhijit Avasthi	Chemical Engineer	National Creative Director	Ogilvy & Mather India
Dharam Valia	Graduate	Client Services Director	Ogilvy & Mather India
Sumanto Chattopadhyay	Marketing Graduate	Executive Creative Director, South Asia	Ogilvy & Mather India
Rupali Bhat#	Marketing Graduate	Creative Director	Ogilvy & Mather India
Rajeev Sharma	Advertising professional	National Brand Planning Director	Leo Burnett, India
Prashant Godebole*	Art and Photography	------------	Lowe - Lintas
Rahul DaChunha*	Theatre & Film	Director	DaCunha Communications
Rajiv Samra#	Engineering and Marketing Graduate	Brand Relationship Manager	Bajaj Two-Wheelers (Core Company)

* Denotes the Interviewee didn't agree for their interview(s) to be recorded

\# pseudonym has been used for this respondent

- Alyque Padamshee – head of advertising Bajaj Scooters in 1980s and 1990s
- Abhijit Avasthi – head of adverting Bajaj Pulsar since 2000

An Exploratory Study of Collective Nostalgia

Faye Kao, Eastern Michigan University, USA

ABSTRACT

Collective nostalgia refers to the nostalgia originating from emotional attachment to collective cultural identities without earlier personal experience. This study shows that *collective nostalgia* is independent of *personal nostalgia, the nostalgia* originating from personal earlier experience. These two types of nostalgia exert independent influences on the formation of identity preferences.

AN EXPLORATORY STUDY OF COLLECTIVE NOSTALGIA

Nostalgia Literature Review

Nostalgia is an individual's propensity to seek emotional comfort from a familiar past. Individuals in a transition period, such as relocation, are particularly likely to experience nostalgic sentiment (Davis, 1979). In nostalgia formation, the attachment of strong and subjective emotion to past objects is a necessary factor (Holbrook & Schindler, 2003).

In consumer research, nostalgia can be traced to two origins. *Personal nostalgia* originates from direct earlier experience. *Personal nostalgia* formation takes place through a nostalgic bonding process, in which strong personal emotion is attached to a past experience or treasured objects owned in the past. The experience is direct (Holbrook 1993; Schindler & Holbrook, 2003). Holbrook (1993) developed a Nostalgia Proneness Index to measure personal nostalgia. The consequences of the personal nostalgia are profound. For example, personal nostalgia proneness is found to shape aesthetic tastes for cultural products and influence consumption preferences (Holbrook & Schindler, 1994). Personal nostalgia also influences donors' intention to contribute to charitable organizations (Ford & Merchant, 2010), alumni giving, and alumni relations (Merkel 2010).

Collective nostalgia originates from a group experience, such as stories passed down within a family, or learning from books or mass media about one's cultural heritage. The emotional bonding is formed through exposure to culturally created events for a prolonged period of time (Holak, Havlena & Matveev, 2006).

Personal nostalgia is oriented toward internalized cultural identities associated with the past and subjectively defined by individuals; *collective nostalgia* is oriented toward external collective cultural identities associated with the past and shared among the group. While *personal nostalgia* tends to be richer and more distinctive, *collective nostalgia* tends to be abstract and more consistent among individuals within the same generation of the cultural group.

Little research has been dedicated to the study of *collective nostalgia*. This study is an exploratory investigation of *collective nostalgia* and its influences on consumption. This study is interested in the following questions:

Study 1: What is the content of *collective nostalgia*?

Study 2: Are *collective nostalgia* and *personal nostalgia* related?

Study 3: What possible psychological traits are related to *collective nostalgia*?

Study 4: What are the behavior consequences of *collective nostalgia*?

METHODOLOGY

Ypsilanti is a town in Michigan with a population of 22,362 (2010 Census). Since the 1970s, it has been famous for its cultural preservation movement. However, residents who were born in the 1980s did not personally participate in this movement. They only learned about Ypsilanti culture from their parents or from the media. They experience *collective nostalgia*. Therefore, Ypsilanti was used as the cultural context in the study. Seventy-three students in a Midwest university with Michigan origin were recruited to participate in this study. Their average age was twenty-five.

To identify the content of shared Ypsilanti cultural identities, a focus group of two experts on Ypsilanti culture was formed to compose an *Ypsilanti Culturescape*. Ten themes emerged, and were used to design a ten-item *Ypsilanti Culturescape,* the collective nostalgia questionnaire.

Seventy-three subjects were asked to rate their preferences toward the ten-item *Ypsilanti Culturescape*. In addition, to measure *personal nostalgia*, this study used nine items selected from *Nostalgia Proneness Index* (Holbrook, 1993). This study also included measurements of *Consumer Cosmopolitan Motivation* (Kao, 2007) to examine the possible psychographic trait that might be related to collective nostalgia. For the behavior consequence measurements, this study used a dichotomy scale: "*Have you ever participated in any Ypsilanti cultural events in the past twelve months?*"

Study 1: What is the content of *collective nostalgia*?

Factor analysis was performed on the ten-item *Ypsilanti Culturescape* preference scores. It resulted in two dimensions: Heritage-Ypsi (pre-1960s), and Transforming-Ypsi (post-1960s) (Table 1). It is consistent with previous studies in that time is a primary factor in defining nostalgia content (Holbrook, Morris, and Robert, 1994). Heritage-Ypsi is the major component of collective nostalgia in this context. Heritage-Ypsi includes Depot Town and its associated railroad culture, auto industry, and airplane industry development history in the Ypsilanti area, Native American history, French exploration and trading history, frontier community culture, and the Ypsilanti heritage preservation projects since 1970. The second dimension is Transforming-Ypsi, which includes immigrants from the south, the increasing African American population, the development of a suburban community in 1960-1990, and the globalization of Ypsilanti in the past few years.

The factor scores were then subjected to cluster analysis and produced three clusters: Modern-Ypsi-Goers, Ypsi-Culture-Sponsors, and Don't-Like (Figure 1). The Modern-Ypsi-Goers are characterized by their mediocre scores on both dimensions. These people are indifferent to traditional and transformative identities. Some of them, however, show a slightly higher preference for transformative Ypsilanti cultural identity. This segment comprises the largest percentage of the sample. The second largest segment is The Ypsi-Culture-Sponsors, characterized by high Heritage-Ypsi scores regardless of their Transforming-Ypsi scores. This group is the traditional value sponsors although they may agree or disagree with the transformation of local cultural heritage. They are proud of and are interested in Ypsilanti culture. The smallest segment is the Don't-Like, who are not interested in either traditional or in transformative cultural identities.

Based on the analyses, the two dimensions of *collective nostalgia* are meaningful. In addition, *collective nostalgia* is a valid base to segment consumers. The construct has criteria validity.

Study 2: Are *collective nostalgia* and *personal nostalgia* related?

Personal nostalgia and *collective nostalgia* are of different origins; therefore, it is hypothesized to result in lower correlation between these two types of nostalgia. However, since Heritage-Ypsi and Transforming-Ypsi are two aspects of *collective nostalgia*, it is hypothesized that the two dimensions of *collective nostalgia* should have a higher correlation within themselves than with *personal nostalgia*. Pearson correlation coefficients were calculated to examine these correlations.

The result shows that *personal nostalgia proneness* is correlated with Heritage-Ypsi with a correlation coefficient of .243, but not with Transforming-Ypsi. However, Transforming-Ypsil and Heritage-Ypsi, which are the two dimensions of *collective nostalgia*, are highly correlated, .532 (Table 2). This result supports that *personal nostalgia* and *collective nostalgia* are two separate constructs. The result supports discriminant and convergent validities.

Study 3: What possible psychological traits are related to *collective nostalgia*?

To further investigate discriminant and convergent validities, the two types of nostalgia were compared to a different construct: *consumer cosmopolitan motivation*. *Consumer cosmopolitan motivation* is the emotional attachment to an out-group cultural identity. Since nostalgia bonding involves a strong emotional attachment toward one's original culture, it is hypothesized that both types of nostalgia may negatively correlate with *consumer cosmopolitan motivation*. Pearson correlation coefficients were calculated to examine the relationship between types of nostalgia and consumer cosmopolitan motivation.

The results show that only *personal nostalgia* is negatively correlated with *consumer cosmopolitan motivation* with a correlation coefficient of -.256; but the correlation between *collective nostalgia* and *consumer cosmopolitan motivation* is not significant (Table 3). The result suggests that *personal nostalgia* and *consumer cosmopolitan motivation* are related constructs. However, these two constructs

oriented from consumers' preferences toward opposite cultural identities: in-group vs. out-group. A consumer who develops a strong emotional attachment to his or her cultural identity through direct personal participation experience tends to abhor other out-group cultural identities. At the same time, the result suggests that *collective nostalgia* and *consumer cosmopolitan motivation* are independent constructs. Each construct exerts its own influence on the formation of consumers' preferences. In other words, people who develop nostalgic sentiment through collective group experience can develop a preference for an out-group culture. It allows for the concomitant development of positive emotional attachment to both in- and out-group cultural identities.

ANOVA was performed to compare the *consumer cosmopolitan motivation* scores among the three *collective nostalgia* segments. The ANOVA result shows that Ypsi-Culture-Sponsors have significantly higher *consumer cosmopolitan motivation* score than Don't-Like segment (Table 4). In other words, those who have higher preferences toward in-group heritage cultural identity tend to have higher preferences for out-group cultural identities. However, people who are indifferent to their collective cultural identity also tend to be indifferent to any out-group cultural identities. This finding is worthy of future research.

Study 4: What are the behavior consequences of *collective nostalgia*?

Personal nostalgia results in in-group cultural consumption behavior. Will *collective nostalgia* have a similar characteristic? If *collective nostalgia* can predict behavior as *personal nostalgia* does, *collective nostalgia* should be correlated with in-group cultural events participation.

To investigate this relationship, respondents were asked to indicate on a dichotomy scale: *"Have you ever participated in any Ypsilanti cultural events in the past twelve months?"* ANOVA was conducted to compare the *collective nostalgia* scores of those who answered "yes" and those who said "no." The result shows that the models are not significant (Table 5). *Collective nostalgia* does not

Table 1: Dimensions of Collective Nostalgia
Rotated Component Matrix[a]

	Component	
	Heritage-Ypsi	Transforming-Ypsi
Native American history in Ypsi area.	.797	.230
Frontier community culture, i.e. lumber mills, settler lifestyle.	.788	.166
French exploration and trading history.	.735	.055
Ypsi railroad cultural heritage-- Depot Town.	.663	.177
Auto industry development history in Ypsi.	.636	.434
Ypsi heritage preservation events since 1970.	.520	.516
Willow Run and the history associated with it.	.513	.355
Globalization of Ypsi/Ann Arbor: immigration from foreign countries.	.147	.784
Ypsi suburbia community in 1960-1990: highway, modern shopping centers.	.065	.727
Ypsi township community: immigrants from Southern states, and increasing African American population.	.352	.577
Variance Explained	33.23%	21.72%

Extraction Method: Principal Component Analysis.

Rotation Method: Varimax with Kaiser Normalization.

a. Rotation converged in 3 iterations.

Figure 1: Collective Nostalgia Segments

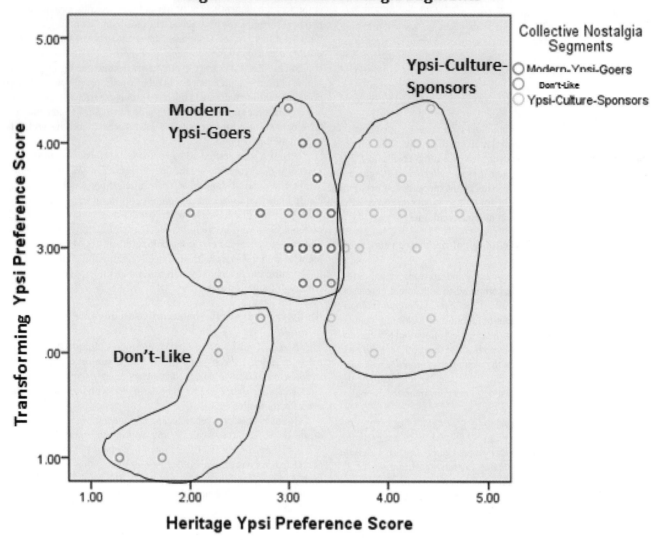

Table 2: Convergent vs. Discriminant Validity

		Nostalgic Proneness Index	Transforming Ypsi Preference Score	Heritage Ypsi Preference Score
Nostalgic Proneness Index	Pearson Correlation	1	.086	.243*
	Sig. (2-tailed)		.474	.040
	N	72	72	72
Transforming-Ypsi Preference Score	Pearson Correlation	.086	1	.532**
	Sig. (2-tailed)	.474		.000
	N	72	74	73
Heritage Ypsi Preference Score	Pearson Correlation	.243*	.532**	1
	Sig. (2-tailed)	.040	.000	
	N	72	73	73

*. Correlation is significant at the 0.05 level (2-tailed).

**. Correlation is significant at the 0.01 level (2-tailed).

Table 3: Correlations between Cosmopolitan Motivation and Types of Nostalgia

		Transforming Ypsi Preference Score	Heritage Ypsi Preference Score	Nostalgic Proneness Index	Consumer Cosmopolitan Motivation
Transforming Ypsi Preference Score	Pearson Correlation	1	.532**	.086	.196
	Sig. (2-tailed)		.000	.474	.095
	N	74	73	72	74
Heritage Ypsi Preference Score	Pearson Correlation	.532**	1	.243*	.127
	Sig. (2-tailed)	.000		.040	.285
	N	73	73	72	73
Nostalgic Proneness Index	Pearson Correlation	.086	.243*	1	-.256*
	Sig. (2-tailed)	.474	.040		.030
	N	72	72	72	72
Consumer Cosmopolitan Motivation	Pearson Correlation	.196	.127	-.256*	1
	Sig. (2-tailed)	.095	.285	.030	
	N	74	73	72	74

**. Correlation is significant at the 0.01 level (2-tailed).

*. Correlation is significant at the 0.05 level (2-tailed).

Table 4: Consumer Cosmopolitan Motivation Score

Tukey HSD[a,b]

Collective Nostalgia Segments		Subset for alpha = 0.05	
	N	1	2
Don't-Like	6	3.1250	
Modern-Ypsi-Goers	47	3.8138	3.8138
Ypsi-Culture-Sponsors	20		4.0125
Sig.		.153	.851

Means for groups in homogeneous subsets are displayed.

a. Uses Harmonic Mean Sample Size = 12.608.

b. The group sizes are unequal. The harmonic mean of the group sizes is used. Type I error levels are not guaranteed.

Table 5: ANOVA: Consequence of Collective Nostalgia

Have you ever participated in Ypsi cultural events? (Yes vs. No)		Sum of Squares	df	Mean Square	F	Sig.
Transforming Ypsi Preference Score	Between Groups	1.585	1	1.585	3.345	.072
	Within Groups	34.120	72	.474		
	Total	35.706	73			
Heritage Ypsi Preference Score	Between Groups	.301	1	.301	.682	.412
	Within Groups	31.290	71	.441		
	Total	31.591	72			

necessarily lead to in-group cultural event participation behavior as *personal nostalgia* does. The behavior consequences of *collective nostalgia* therefore merit further research.

CONCLUSION

This study shows that *collective nostalgia* and *personal nostalgia* are independent constructs that exert independent influences on consumers' culture consumption behavior. The nostalgia that is developed through personal participation tends to exert significant influence on consumers' preferences for their original culture, but has a negative impact on their preferences for out-group cultural identities. However, the nostalgia that emerges through a collective experience tends not to result in in-group cultural consumption behavior, nor does it prevent the development of preferences for out-group cultural identities. These two types of nostalgia exert independent influence on cultural consumption behavior and deserve additional research. Further study can investigate the interaction effects, and possible mediating or moderating factors that are involved in the formation of cultural identity preferences.

REFERENCES

Davis, Fred (1979), *Yearning for Yesterday: a Sociology of Nostalgia*. New York: The Free Press.

Ford, John B. and Altaf Merchant (2010), "Nostalgia Drives Donations: The Power of Charitable Appeals Based on Emotions and Intentions," *Journal of Advertising Research*, 50 (December), 4, 450-459.

Kao, Faye J. (2007), "Consumer Cosmopolitan and Acculturative Motivations: an Executive Function Aspect of Ethnic Identity," unpublished doctoral dissertation, City University of New York, Baruch College, 196 pages.

Holak, Susan L., William J. Havlena, and Alexei V. Matveev (2006), "Exploring Nostalgia in Russia: Testing the Index of Nostalgia-Proneness," *European Advances in Consumer Research*, 7, 195-200.

Holbrook, Morris B. and Robert M. Schindler (1994), "Age, Sex, and Attitude toward the Past as Predictors of Consumers' Aesthetic Tastes for Cultural Products," *Journal of Marketing Research*, 31 (August), 412-422.

Holbrook, Morris B. and Robert M. Schindler (2003), "Nostalgic Bonding: Exploring the Role of Nostalgia in the Consumption Experience," *Journal of Consumer Research*, 3 (December), 107-127.

Holbrook, Morris B. (1993), "Nostalgia and Consumption Preferences: Some Emerging Patterns of Consumer Tastes," *Journal of Consumer Research*, 20 (September), 245-256.

Merkel, Ryan Edward (2010), "Managing the Relationship Between the Students and the University, a Case Study in the Context of Development and Alumni Relations," unpublished doctoral dissertation, University of Maryland, College Park, 158 pages.

Schindler, Robert M. and Morris B. Holbrook (2003), "Nostalgia for Early Experience as a Determinant of Consumer Preferences," *Psychology & Marketing*, 20 (April), 4, 275-302.

'Granny Would be Proud': On the Labours of Doing Vintage, Practices and Emergent Socialities

Katherine Duffy, University of Strathclyde, UK
Paul Hewer, University of Strathclyde, UK
Juliette Wilson, University of Strathclyde, UK

ABSTRACT

This paper unpacks the ways in which consumer and seller practices construct the vintage marketplace. In this discussion the role of material objects and practices, the way that they intersect in vintage consumption, and how these vintage fashion objects are (re) used in this second-hand marketplace are explored. Discussion is based on ethnographic observations over a ten-month period at a twice monthly vintage market, 'Granny Would be Proud' in Glasgow, Scotland UK and in-depth interviews with key market practitioners. This was combined with visual analysis to explore the staging of the marketplace and the context of such practices. Our findings are organised in a number of themes that are important in understanding the practices of the vintage marketplace: vintage as a social practice, practicing the 'vintage look' and vintage as a skilled practice. In exploring these emergent themes the centrality of the practices in the construction of the marketplace is also illustrated.

The first outward sign that there is anything taking place in this side street restaurant is the crochet sign that hangs above the entrance exclaiming 'Granny Would be Proud Vintage market'. On the second level of the restaurant, in the eaves of this converted cinema, is a mixture of vintage clothes, jewellery, bags & briefcases, china & crockery. Rails of vintage furs, denim shorts and tea dresses fill the space, with tables laid out for stallholders with memorable finds, suitcases brimming over with silk scarves & neckties. People move from stall to stall and back again, excitedly chattering with friends. Vendors smile politely as people enter their area & try to engage with the people for a minute or two before they move on. There is a busy, bustling atmosphere, food smells waft from the restaurant below, stallholders drink tea & coffee from vintage china from the restaurant, 1940s and 50s music plays in the background and people wander about the stalls, rummaging, lifting, inspecting, coveting, new found treasures. (Fieldnotes, January 29th 2012)

INTRODUCTION

Vintage is a global phenomenon, from Decades in Los Angeles, Rellik in London to the Saint-Ouen markets of Paris. Vintage is often held as being in stark contrast to the perceived homogenised culture of mainstream fashion (Tungate 2008; Palmer 2005; Entwistle 2000 a) however through the rise in popularity and accessibility in the marketplace, vintage is changing the consumption landscape. In this paper vintage is conceptualised as a set of practices, of the actions of consumers that are tied to notions of belonging (Warde, 2005: Murphy & Patterson, 2011), of in essence the performance of 'doing vintage'. There has been much discussion of how practitioners mobilise knowledge, but far less focus on how this knowledge is apportioned into their practices (Magaudda 2011). This paper acknowledges this gap and explores the practices involved in producing and sustaining the vintage marketplace. Coming from the Consumer Culture Theory (Arnould and Thompson 2005; Schau et al. 2008) approach in which markets are seen as social and cultural constructs, the marketplace is unpacked with a focus on the collective effort needed in constructing the vintage market. The paper begins with a theoretical exploration of vintage and how it links to prior consumption studies and the materiality of the practice, before outlining the ethnographic methods employed in the marketplace: observation, visual analysis and depth semi-structured interviews with consumers and sellers, and then pro-

vides an empirical account of the 'doing' of vintage. Our findings and discussion highlight the emergent themes of the practices of vintage: the social nature, the skill involved and the enactment of vintage. These are explored and related to existing consumption theory.

Vintage is not new as a concept: second-hand markets and the trading of clothing has been a constant presence. It is a concept that has been explored in the consumption literature from flea markets (Belk et al, 1988; Sherry, 1990), charity shops and car boot sales (Gregson & Crewe 2002), ideas of thrift shopping (Bardhi 2003; Bardhi & Arnold 2003), to alternative spaces of consumption (Belk et al. 1999; Roux & Korchia 2006; McGrath et al. 1993). The vintage turn in consumer culture cannot be explained in terms of simple nostalgia, it must be perceived in conjunction with aesthetics, style, fashion and social collectives. One way to conceptualise vintage is to anchor it in terms of the postmodern experience, of consumers who are alienated and desire to return to a romantic, creative past (Campbell 2005). Vintage could also be depicted as a form of consumer politics, of "virtuous consumption" (Chatzidakis et al. 2004) or could be considered as a form of consumer resistance (Brownlie and Hewer 2009). With regards to history, vintage could be anchored quite neatly in discussions of nostalgia and a yearning for an idealised past, however nostalgia here is unpacked not with regards to Holbrook and Schindler's (1994) 'real' or 'stimulated' debate, but nostalgia as a learned emotion, of Goulding's 'vicarious' nostalgia (Goulding, 2002:542.) McRobbie asserts that the retro phenomenon is part of the nostalgia enthusiasm for bringing history into an 'ahistorical present' (1988). Similarly, vintage must give a nod to its retro predecessors and finds it's footing clearly in Brown and Sherry's (2003) 'Retroscapes.' This synthesis of past and present, the 'retro revolution', highlights that retro and vintage are related, they are both strategic ways of employing the past in the fast paced consumer present.

This paper adopts a material culture approach to the exploration of consumption practices as it emphasizes the intersection of cultural and social practices around vintage objects. Building on Miller's (1998) material culture approach to shopping and Dant's (2005) sociological perspective which argues for a more in-depth focus on the 'material stuff of life', this approach suggests a consideration of the social and cultural meanings of the object, rather than considering the meaning as inextricably linked to the object (Miller, 1998). The framing and the performance of the consumption sphere have been previously explored in marketing and in particular in the service landscape. However in these accounts the literature fails to discuss the role that objects play in the staging of the marketplace. Parsons' (2009) work on antiques moves this argument forward by positing that value is staged and that the presentation of objects and the narrative built around them is a key communicator in achieving this framing. In applying this material culture perspective, it is argued that the narrative of the object cannot be separated from the vintage object itself.

METHODOLOGY

This study used an ethnographic approach to attempt to capture how the practices of vintage consumption were undertaken in a market space and the materials, meanings and competences of the actors within that space. The findings presented reflect ten months absorption by the researcher in the vintage scene, specifically a vintage mar-

Advances in Consumer Research
Volume 40, ©2012

ket titled 'Granny Would be Proud' in Glasgow, Scotland UK. The market runs twice monthly in the upstairs of a converted old cinema, which now functions as a restaurant in the west-end of Glasgow[1]. The restaurant below has 1940s music playing in the background and serves food on mismatched vintage china (See Figure 1). The wider venue of the west-end of the city acts as a cultural hub and has a high student population. The market has been running for three years, selling vintage clothes, homeware, accessories, upcycled vintage and independent craft. It was one of the first of this format of 'pop-up' markets in the city. The sellers differ at every market, with the exception of a couple of longstanding stallholders. The market is run by a young couple that promote the market through the use of social media (https://www.facebook.com/GrannyWouldBeProud) and flyering on market day (See Figure 2).

Figure 1 Hillhead Bookclub Interior & Exterior (February 26th 2012)

[1] See http://www.hillheadbookclub.com/GrannyWouldBeProud. Here the website constructs its other-worldly non-mainstream delights in the following terms: The "Granny Would Be Proud!" fairs started as a small vintage and retro venture in mid 2009 and has now grown into a twice a month event, each holding 25 colourful stalls from a repertoire of over 80 sellers. Taking place in the almighty Hillhead Bookclub, GWBP is one of the biggest fairs in Glasgow that brings together some of the finest vintage and retro fashion stalls, and arts and crafts lovers. Offering from clothing and accessories to the handmade and homemade to present a heaven of all kinds. To keep things interesting each fair guarantees to be a bit of a surprising delight for the eyes and the purse! It is a shopping experience you will definitely not forget! From having your picture taken in its very own retro photo-booth to treating yourself to tea and brunch in the old fashion laced tearoom, GWBP never disappoints, the proof? Go and check us out on Facebook: Granny Proud Glasgow Fairs and see for yourself.

Figure 2: Granny Would be Proud Flyer (Aug – Nov 2011)

The ethnographic methods employed included observation over this ten-month period; photographic documentation, a research diary and six in-depth interviews with key practitioners in the vintage marketplace were conducted. As is discussed below, traditional market roles were less easy to define in this context, and this informs our understanding of the vintage practices and the market space. These approaches attempted to give an understanding of the practices of the vintage marketplace. Observation of the staging of the marketplace and of how the culture of vintage consumption was enacted in such spaces was central to the conduct and logic of the ethnographic research.

The researcher assumed a subjective position, being interested in the meanings and interpretations of vintage. These individual actors are assumed to have different cultural interpretations (Miles and Huberman 1994) within a 'shared social milieu' (Perren and Ram 2004: 90). All interviews were conducted in naturalistic contexts, either in situ at the market or in practitioners' homes. Discussions covered topics such as sourcing goods, the nature of vintage consumption, and the community around the vintage markets. All interviews were taped, transcribed and annotated with initial impressions and observations noted to crystallise the main themes emerging (Bryman and Bell 2007). Interpretation and analysis involved multiple iterations of coding, with the researcher repeatedly returning to the multiple forms of data to refine thematic codes. Three themes emerged as significant in highlighting the practices of the vintage collective: vintage as social practice, the practice of the vintage look and vintage as skilled practice.

The researcher gained access to the market through attending regularly and building relationships with key characters in the marketplace. The participants were identified through a snowballing technique. This sample features three stallholders, two vintage consumers, who are regular market visitors and, one vintage clothing storeowner who is also a regular visitor at the market. The ethnographic interviews (McCracken, 1988 b) were used to gain an emic perspective of vintage behaviours and practices through their stories and descriptions of their own and others behaviour. The interview data supplemented the observational data and provided practitioner perspectives on the actions and practices of 'doing vintage' in the marketplace.

VINTAGE AS A SOCIAL PRACTICE

Building on Gregson and Crewe's (1998, 50) perspective of consumption as never purely an economic endeavour but as "eminently social, relational and active, rather than private, atomic or passive," in the marketplace of Granny Would be Proud, the vintage transaction was seen to be a highly personalised exchange. This was echoed in the interviews with notions of 'being in the club' and 'community' permeating them. Vintage consumption from the observations was both an individualistic and collective act that enlivened the market space. The development of practices in the marketplace, similarly to Schau et al's (2008) brand communities, led to the exchange of collectively valued goods. From the observations, the building of relationships and these sharing practices formed a large portion of the interaction between consumer and stallholder and through this dialogue could be seen to grant status in the marketplace to both. In this way it was seen as testing emotional practices, such as commitment to vintage as a lifestyle. Acceptance by the collective meant that these sharing practices benefitted individuals and also created consumption opportunities: stallholders kept stock to the side for consumers that they knew or mentioned other items that they had that may interest returning customers. These notions were highlighted in the interviews Jess explained how this relationship even encouraged her to buy more:

"It definitely makes me go back there because I know she is nice …they will hold onto something while you go to the bank or they will give you advice or their opinion on something, they might be lying but you tend to feel like they are probably quite truthful."

This dynamic interaction seemed to aid both consumer and seller in the exchange. As Jess highlights the consumer receives personal attention adding to the experience of the exchange and the seller is able to sell their item and start to build a role of expert in the marketplace. The personal nature of this exchange was illuminated again by Louise who described how when selling her vintage homeware pieces she likes to "get a feel for the customer," and to "try and understand their vintage style and preferences" so as to make recommendations and know what they would be comfortable with. This role that is adopted in the exchange of expert and consumer unfolded across the interviews with the stallholders taking pride in this position of authority in the market. The building of a relationship between stallholders and consumers and the subsequent acceptance into the vintage community was marked by the time spend over the interactions around the exchange. This relationship and interaction of the stallholder and consumer were intrinsic as to how the objects would be viewed in their new lifecycle, as illustrated through our field notes:

"In most of the market stalls, the stallholder seems to acknowledge the consumer walking past or stopping to look at their items with a smile or a nod or looking up from what they are doing at least. Some don't look up or glance at consumers and it seems like unless the consumer has seen something that has caught their attention, they don't bother to stop." (Researcher field notes, March 25th 2012)

From this extract it is depicted that the interaction although apparently basic, seemed to set the norms for the possible exchange and group acceptance. Stallholders asked the consumer questions about their style and influences and where they normally find vintage objects. This dialogue provided a means for stallholders to present their objects to a consumer and enabled them to engage in a discussion around the object's history. This ultimately aided the stallholder in navigating a use value and potential in the mind of the consumer.

Stallholders often described their consumers as friends and these friendships seemed to be longstanding with some spanning years. They were relationships that although built around an exchange were spoken about in affectionate terms. This friendship in some instances seemed almost strategic, in that being friendly with a stallholder ensured that the consumer was able to find out about other stock that they had, when they would next be selling at the market and the stallholder acted as guide as to where to source the best vintage items. They appeared to be friendships based on a shared understanding of aesthetics and style similarities but also of gaining advantage and knowledge in the marketplace. In exploring this relationship with Tina, she spoke of building up almost familial relationships with the consumers she worked with:

"It is my business but I love working with people for months on creating something that will mean so much to them but it always shapes me as well…it is important that you have the same vision and share a vintage aesthetic…long afterwards I still like to have a drink with them as we have been so much part of each other's lives."

Tina conveys esteem around these relationships with consumers she highlights the time and involvement with each other, the idea that they both invest so much in each other around the exchange – in both a personal and a monetary way. She also illuminates the idea of the importance of the shared 'vintage aesthetic', that this similarity in how they view the world, their style preferences and appreciation of the vintage scene is key in the development of this relationship.

These basic exchanges in the marketplace were often followed up with encouragement to 'befriend' each other on Facebook. This move onto a further online connection enabled the consumer to obtain information about when the fairs were occurring, but it also more significantly represented a lasting, tangible social connection that resulted from this initial exchange. In this way the stallholders acted like gatekeepers to the vintage scene and community. Michael highlighted the idea that this online platform allowed for an interaction and acceptance of vintage tastes that was hard to find before the Internet provided ways of connecting with similar people:

"I think social networking has a lot to do with it, say you had a particular thing for vintage clothes, you would maybe meet other people who liked vintage clothes at the vintage clothes shop but the chances of hitting it off with them or going for a pint with them were pretty slim… because now people can express their interests up front on Facebook and places like that, there is more interaction with people, with groups that are like-minded…"

This extract conveys that social media acts as a coordinator of the marketplace; it connects tribes (Cova 2002) that may have been unable to connect without this medium. It also serves as a way to market the events of the marketplace to an interested audience. This is crucial as the 'Granny Would be Proud' market was not a permanent fixture: it occurred every two weeks. In this way social media facilitates the marketplace, this allows knowledge of the marketplace to reach a potentially interested audience. Molly comments on her use of social media to find out information about markets: *"Of a weekend I normally just look on Facebook to see what markets are on that day or I will have seen friends or the organisers posting about an event during the week and I will then remember to stop by."*

In this way, social media reaffirms the physical connection for Molly and also allows for the community to move online. It takes these notions of social exchanges and the desire to be part of 'the club' to a more visible, tangible state.

The importance placed on the practices of a shared aesthetic and the social demonstration of these practices around the exchange, portrayed a social investment in the object from both stallholder and consumer in which the value is constructed. The stallholder acts as gatekeeper to this vintage community and the friendliness of the interactions steers the exchange. Each practice encouraged deeper commitment to the vintage collective. The development of relationships and shared understandings suggested that the constitutive elements of vintage are social in character. In considering this, this paper demonstrates that 'vintage' in the Granny Would be Proud marketplace was a social construct. This can be seen in the meaning and subsequent value attached to individual possessions (Belk et al. 1988), the provision of this value and the concept of vintage could be argued to be a social practice.

PRACTICING THE 'VINTAGE LOOK'

The production of 'the look' of the vintage marketplace was seen to be key to practitioners and suggested concepts of authenticity, acceptance and stylisation. The marketplace was not permanent and the active process of creating the physical marketplace that took place every two weeks involved consideration of the staging of the event. The creation of 'the look' was produced critically as a way to create a feeling for the market. This well managed atmosphere was a mechanism for stallholders to show their own personality within the vintage context but also to act as a framing of their aesthetic vision. This striving for 'the look' also ties in with the consideration of the socialites of consumption, as the achievement of this was also crucial for the staging of the stall, but also significantly for both the stallholder and consumer. The creation of 'the look' was seen as key in gaining access and approval in the marketplace (see Figure 3).

Figure 3: 'Practicing the vintage look' in the marketplace

"The sellers arrive and are greeted with a brown table and a lamp, on returning an hour later, they bring the space to life with ornate, embroidered table cloths, rose adorned cake stand holders overflowing with costume jewellery, tweed suits and silk scarves hanging over the walls, suitcases brimming with goods at the foot of the table..." (Researcher notes, March 4th 2012)

Extending this notion further to the construction of the marketplace, the stall and the stallholder must also achieve a certain look

to gain credibility in the marketplace. The vintage look was seen to add to their reputation and either attracts or detracts consumers from engaging with them. This proposes that the personal nature of the transaction and the focus on the aesthetics was key and again stands in contrast to views of exchange as a simple process. This highly personal and social nature of the interaction can be seen to affect value construction as the excerpt above highlights, achieving acceptance and building a relationship, if even for the time that the interaction occurs, shapes both the consumer and the stallholder's views of vintage. Building on the idea that the object has a complex history or "social life" (Appadurai, 1986) that the consumer is not necessarily aware of but that through interaction with the exchange with the seller can be created, rather than diminishing potential value, appeared to add to the consumer desire for the object. The central concern of stylisation also highlights again the fluidity of vintage and that far from being fixed, the production of 'the look' can affect the way that the vintage objects are seen.

Practitioners spoke of the "camaraderie" and "community" of vintage, and this conveyed forms of sociality tied to their consumption practices. The vintage marketplace can be viewed therefore as a performance of community value, which is a collective and social undertaking and in which negotiations over objects, use and ultimately price, are intimately woven into the social. By this account, while appearing individualistic, vintage consumption must also be understood as a communal form of consumption whereby the reclamation of social relations and the enlivenment of social spaces are made possible through the marketplace. As expressed by Michael:

"There is no doubt about it, there is a community thing going on, I think this is what will keep the thing going..."

And further added to by Louise:

"Vintage is a lifestyle and not just how you choose to shop: it is about a way of seeing the world but also I suppose how you see your friendships. Yes, I sell at markets as my job, but it is something that I love, when I am up at 4 am to go to a house clearance or car boot sale on a rainy Glasgow November morning, what I think about is selling that object, discussing with the customer about the item, building a relationship with them and thinking about what new lease of life they will give it... I love those interactions...I have made so many friends in this line of work and I always thought that I was alone in how I valued vintage stuff over new things..."

Vintage here is considered as more than a consumption habit, it is a way of connecting and finding shared values in a busy consumer present. In this way it acts as a bridge to shared interests, values and practices. Consumption can therefore be viewed as a way to connect to others. In conceptualising consumption in this way it allows for an understanding of the complex emotional and social relations that unfold in the marketplace. The vintage marketplace can be perceived as a space for social relations and one in which the practices of 'self-fashioning' are used as a medium for self-differentiation and identification within the vintage collective (Rafferty, 2011).

Vintage as a skilled practice

The skills of vintage consumption have long lost their roots of necessity and the apparent stigmas of economic thrift. The act of vintage is tied to activities such as finding, examining, evaluating, haggling, socialising and interacting. In the vintage marketplace there was a cache and cultural capital in being able to uncover hidden 'treasures' that differed from the mass production approach of the high street. This talent for spotting potential treasures was heralded as a revered skill in the community. Sellers expressed the necessity of 'getting a feel for things', and of knowing what is wanted in the marketplace. Ideas of expertise and knowledge were mentioned frequently with regards to negotiating the marketplace. One of the key resources in the stallholders achieving acceptance and subsequently success is in their knowledge of the marketplace. This includes both where to source the items and also an understanding of what will be desired by the current marketplace audience. This skill is revered as Alice illustrated:

"What I love doing is raking through all the crap and finding, I mean sometimes you don't, it is not always there, but it is like finding gold when you do."

This idea that Alice personally finds each individual object that she sells, gives her great pride and for her it played an important role in the creation of vintage. She observes that this ability to find comes from years of experience. She is disparaging of newcomers to the marketplace that think it will be an easy way to make money. This highlights elements of communities of practice (Wenger 1998) as knowledge of rules and procedures must be present for acceptance into the vintage community. Alice highlights emotional elements of practice as she values the time spent on finding vintage objects as representative of their commitment to the vintage aesthetic. Her extract also highlights some of the ways in which vintage is achieved, of the importance of being able to 'see' something in an object that has been abandoned as potential stock and a worthy commodity. It also illustrates the notion that her finding is not necessarily driven by market demand, but that through this active process and knowledge, the stallholders create market demand. This notion was echoed throughout the interviews as stallholders expressed the necessity in the active processes of vintage: of 'missions', 'rummaging' and 'finding', illustrating the physicality and labours of 'doing vintage':

"It is a lot of work sourcing, going to car boot sales, jumble sales, auctions, house clearances. I mean often bidding on whole lots at auction with the hope of finding a couple of good things that can be used." (Tina)

Tina's excerpt highlights the active nature of searching and trawling through items to find something that she thinks is useable. In considering the objects of these processes, in order to become a thing of value, a transition in how the object is viewed must be achieved. This is an important consideration when considering a marketplace that is constructed on the basis of items being re-seen and re-evaluated. DeLong et al.'s work (2005, 24) moved this proposition forward and assert that being 'hooked on vintage' is not a haphazard process, but rather it is a complex process that involves the consumer possessing the relevant "aesthetics, taste, clever dressing, historical curiosity, and an ability to discriminate the authentic product, and revalue it in a new setting." Many of the stallholders revealed that the way to learn about finding objects and unearthing value in objects was through the practice of buying and selling. In this way vintage can be conceptualised as a doing process, one in which over time the necessary skills and values are developed.

By the very nature of the vintage markets, objects were seen as rare and hard to find, this uncovering of objects added social capital to the finding process. In introducing the discarded objects back into the consumption sphere, the stallholders had to undertake the practice of ascribing a value to the objects. For stallholders in the Granny Would be Proud marketplace this act of placing a monetary price on objects was difficult for all the interviewees to put into words, with Louise commenting it was "like a black art". Unlike a traditional marketplace, monetary prices were not highly visible in the vintage market.

When discussing the idea of value in the vintage marketplace, Michael suggests that by its very nature, vintage was fundamentally elusive:

"I've stopped so much valuing them on the age of them, its not like antique value, its not that, it is intrinsic, the quality, rarity and the look of them...it is the how unique or individual they are...how irreplaceable they are" (See Figure 4).

Figure 4: The Transience of value - Michael and his vintage glasses that he selects before each market

Michael's excerpt demonstrates that vintage far from being a fixed construct is open to active negotiation based on skill and knowledge practices. As a skilled practitioner he is able to unpack the contained value in the objects and present them again to the marketplace. In this way value can be seen as an embodiment of capital. The stallholders also demonstrated knowledge both of the network in which they functioned but also of particular objects and their origins. Vintage goods by their nature have characteristics that have merited their inclusion in a second or third cycle of exchange. The meaning attributed and value constructed around the object are created and manipulated by marketplace practitioners. Vintage consumption can be seen as culturally and socially shaped through practices as the object's status is created through a process of being withdrawn and introduced in a new setting (DeLong et al, 2005). This transition in how the item is viewed requires the skill of being able to perceive its possibilities in a new setting. This mirrors notions in McCracken's (1988) early work of the possibility of objects, of the "combination and recombination take place until a concept and an aesthetic emerge that help give substance to a group's wish to differentiate itself from the mainstream" (1988, 136). Vintage objects have a history to them, which could potentially be seen to add or detract from their value. The stallholder to increase the value, for example through nostalgia or styling, could elaborate these histories of previous consumption cycles on. Conversely they may attempt to rid the object of its history through rituals of mending and cleaning of the object (Parsons 2008, 2009). Vintage can be seen therefore not as an inherent characteristic of the object, but as a result of emotional and social relationship, in which consumption is the result of this engagement. In this way, vintage consumption is embedded within the objects and in the practices and also around being able to appreciate and see the potential in these objects which became key for acceptance in the collective.

CONCLUSIONS

As this paper sought to reveal, consumption spaces such as those devoted to vintage represent fields in which the conventions of the traditional marketplace are transformed and altered. Vintage here speaks of a form of making space: making space for oneself; making space for others; making space for *fun, fantasy and emotions* (Holbrook and Hirschmann 1982). Vintage social spaces speak of a longing for alternative worlds; alternative modes of consuming and exchanging. Drawing on the practice theory lens allowed a re-thinking of marketplace dynamics, comprehensions of knowledge application and understandings of vintage. This exploratory study of the vintage collective in Glasgow has depicted that the knowledge of the marketplace is central to in negotiating the boundaries of this marketplace. For a successful exchange there needs to exist a knowledge of the object, a competence on the part of the practitioners and also the performance of forms of intimacy with such objects and the social.

It is thus clear that the vintage marketplace is an intimate, personalised, lived experience that brings with it social and personal elements to the exchange. Vintage appeared to be a way of looking at objects, of interacting around these objects and building relationships based on shared appreciations for knowledge and skill. As demonstrated from the emergent themes, vintage consumption can be conceptualised as an embodied practice that is socially and contextually constructed.

Vintage is constructed as 'other', as an alternative to the mainstream, of being different and doing things differently. Vintage is thus the ultimate form of 'bricolage', of recycling styles; it allows the consumer to play with the stylistic norms, gender boundaries through fashion. Wearing vintage clothing can be seen as a way to escape the confines and dictates of the modern marketplace. Or as Reynolds (2011: 194) proclaims about vintage, the individual acts as a 'curator of their own life-in-style'. In accordance with Thompson and Haykto's (1997) work, vintage allows consumers to use fashion to self-define, to construct a personal discourse of their history and to negotiate the dynamics of the social. Finally, the concept of time and its appreciation is tied to vintage from the outset. By the very definition of vintage given at the start of the paper, the second-hand object is conceptualised as 'vintage' only through a certain amount of time passing. The discussion highlighted that the learning of 'doing vintage' is a social endeavour and is bound by the time commitment given to this learning. In this way vintage could be considered a form of 'learned nostalgia' (Goulding, 2003). Our analysis reveals that vintage must also be understood as a form of embodied practice. It is a preference for a time that has long since passed but that is brought back to the modern consumption sphere through the revival of interest around an object. Vintage in this way allows for an unlocking of an imagined past in every wear of an item. The marketplace has facilitated a community based on these shared ideals and aesthetics. It has created a consumption space in which the community's preference for the past, be it a 1950s china tea set or 1980s checked flannel shirt, has been cultivated through practices and their associated forms of understanding; that is a practice of finding and possessing a sensibility to the past and its elusive charms amidst a hectic and ever-changing consumer present.

REFERENCES

Appadurai Arjun (1986) *The Social Life of Things: Commodities in Cultural Perspective,* Cambridge UK: Cambridge University Press.

Arnould Eric J., Thompson Craig J. (2005), Reflections and Reviews: Consumer Culture Theory (CCT): Twenty Years of Research, *Journal of Consumer Culture,* Volume 31, 868-882.

Arsel, Zeynep, Thompson Craig J. (2011), "Demythologizing Consumption Practices: How Consumers Protect Their Field-Dependent Identity Investments from Devaluing Marketplace Myths," *Journal of Consumer Research*, Vol. 37, No. 5, 791-806.

Bardhi Fleura, Arnold Eric J. (2003) Thrift shopping: Combining Utilitarian thrift and hedonic treat benefits, *Journal of Consumer Behaviour,* Vol 4, 223-233.

Bardhi Fleura (2003) Thrill of the Hunt: Thrift Shopping for Pleasure, *Advances in Consumer Research,* Volume 30, 375-376.

Belk, Russell (1991a), "Collecting in a Consumer Culture." In Belk et al. Highways and Buyways: Naturalistic Research from the Consumer Behavior Odyssey, *Advances in Consumer Research*, 178-215.

Belk, Russell (1991b), "Possessions and a Sense of the Past." In Belk et al. Highways and Buyways: Naturalistic Research from the Consumer Behavior Odyssey *Advances in Consumer Research*, 114-130.

Belk Russell (1988) Possessions and the Extended Self, *Journal of Consumer Research,* 15: 139-168.

Belk Russell, Sherry John F., Wallendorf Melanie (1988) A Naturalistic Inquiry into Buyer and Seller Behaviour at a Swap Meet, *Journal of Consumer Research,* Vol 14, No 4, 449-470.

Bourdieu Pierre (1984) *Distinction: A Social critique of the judgement of taste*, Boston, USA: President & Fellows of Harvard College & Routledge & Kegan Paul Ltd.

Bourdieu Pierre (1985) The Social Space and the Genesis of Groups, *Theory and Society*, Volume 14, Number 6, 723-744.

Brown Stephen, Sherry John F Jr. eds (2003) *Time, Space and the Market: Retroscapes Rising,* London, UK: ME Sharpe.

Brownlie Douglas, Hewer Paul (2009) Cultures of Unruly Bricolage: Debadging and the Logic of Resistance, *Advances of Consumer Research*, Volume 36, 686-687.

Brownlie Douglas, Hewer Paul. (2011) Articulating consumers through practices of vernacular creativity, *Scandinavian Journal of Management*, 27, 243–253.

Bryman Alan, Bell Emma. (2007), *Business Research Methods*, Oxford, UK: Oxford University Press.

Campbell Colin (2005) *The Romantic Ethic and the Spirit of Modern Consumerism,* UK: Alcuin Academics.

Chatzidakis Andreas, Hibbert Sally, Mittusis Darryn, Smith Andrew (2004) Virtue in Consumption? *Journal of Marketing Management,* 20:5-6, 526-543.

Chua Beng Huat (1992) Shopping for Women's Fashion in Singapore, in Shields R. (ed) *Lifestyle Shopping: The Subject of Consumption,* London, UK: Routledge.

Clarke Allison, Miller Daniel (2002) Fashion and Anxiety, *Fashion Theory*, Volume 6, Issue 2, 191-214.

Cova Bernard, Cova Veronique (2002), Tribal Marketing: The Tribalisation of Society and its Impact on the Conduct of Marketing, *European Journal of Marketing*, Volume 36, Issue 5/6, 595-620.

Crewe Louise, Gregson Nicky, Brooks Kate (2003) The Discursivities of Difference: Retro retailers and the ambiguities of 'the alternative', *Journal of Consumer Culture,* 3:61.

Dant Tim (2005) *Materiality and Society*, Maidenhead, UK: Open University Press.

Davis Fred (1992) *Fashion, Culture, Identity,* Chicago IL: University of Chicago Press.

Delong Marilyn. R., Heinemann, Barbara, Reiley, Kathryn. (2005). Hooked on vintage! *Fashion Theory: The Journal of Dress, Body & Culture,* 9 (1), 23-42.

Entwistle Joanne (2000 a) *The Fashioned Body: Fashion Dress and Modern Social Theory,* Cambridge, UK: Polity Press.

Entwistle Joanne (2000 b) Fashion and the Fleshy Body: Dress as Embodied Practice, *Fashion Theory*, Volume 4, Issue 3, 323-348.

Goffman Erving, (1986) *Frame Analysis,* Boston MA: Northeastern University Press.

Goulding Christina (2002) An Exploratory Study of Age Related Vicarious Nostalgia and Aesthetic Consumption, *Advances in Consumer Research,* Volume 29, 542-546.

Goulding Christina, Shankar Avi, Elliott Richard, (2001) Dance Clubs, Rave, and the Consumer Experience: An Exploratory Study of a Sub-cultural phenomenon, *European Advances in Consumer Research,* Vol 5, 203-208.

Gregson Nicky, Crewe Louise (1998) Tales of the unexpected: exploring car boot sales as marginal spaces of contemporary consumption, *Transactions of the Institute of British Geographers,* Volume 23: 1, 39-53.

Gregson Nicky, Crewe Louise (2002), *Second-Hand Cultures*, Oxford: Berg Publishers.

Hewer Paul, Hamilton Kathy (2010) On Emotions and Salsa: some thoughts on dancing to rethink consumers, *Journal of Consumer Behaviour,* 9: 113-125.

Holbrook Morris B, Hirschman Elizabeth (1982), "The Experiential Aspects of Consumption: Consumer Fantasies, Feelings, and Fun," *Journal of Consumer Research*, Vol. 9, No. 2, 132-140.

Holbrook Morris B, Schindler Robert. M (1994) Age, sex and attitude toward the past as predictors of consumer's aesthetic tastes for cultural products, *Journal of Marketing Research,* XXX1 (August) 412-422.

McCracken Grant (1988 a), *Culture and Consumption: New Approaches to the Symbolic Character of Consumer Goods and Activities*, Bloomington, IN: Indiana University Press.

McCracken Grant (1988 b), *The Long Interview*, Newbury Park, CA: Sage, University Press.

McGrath Mary Ann, Sherry John F, Heisley Deborah D, (1993) An ethnographic study of an urban periodic marketplace: lessons from the Midville Farmer's market, *Journal of Retailing*, Vol 69, Issue 3, 280-319.

McRobbie Angela (1988), *Zoot Suits and Second Hand Dresses*, Boston, MA: Unwin Hyman.

Magaudda Paolo (2011) When Materiality 'bites back': Digital music consumption practices in the age of dematerialisation, *Journal of Consumer Culture,* 11:15.

Miles Matthew. B., Huberman, A. Michael (1994), *Qualitative Data Analysis: A Sourcebook of New Methods*, Beverly Hills, London: Sage Publications.

Miller Daniel (1998) *Material Cultures: Why some things matter*, University of Chicago: Chicago Press.

Murray Jeff (2002) The Politics of Consumption: A Re-Inquiry on Thompson and Haytko's (1997) Speaking of Fashion, *Journal of Consumer Research*, 29: 427-440.

Murphy Stephen, Patterson Maurice (2011) Motorcycling edgework: A Practice Theory Perspective, *Journal of Marketing Management*, Vol 27, Issue 13-14, 1322-1340.

Palmer Alexandra, Hazel Clark (ed) (2005) *Old Clothes, New Looks: Second Hand Fashion,* Oxford, UK: Berg Publishers.

Parsons Elizabeth (2009) 'What Things Do:' Examining Things that 'Matter' in Consumer Research, *Advances in Consumer Research,* Volume 36.

Parsons Elizabeth (2008) Thompson's Rubbish Theory: exploring the practices of value creation, *European Advances in Consumer Research,* Volume 8.

Parsons Elizabeth (2006) Dealing in Second-hand Goods: Creating meaning and value, *European Advances in Consumer Research,* Volume 7, 189-194.

Perren Lew, Ram Monder (2004), Case study methods in small business and entrepreneurial research: Mapping boundaries and perspectives, *International Small Business Journal*, Vol. 22 (1), 83-101.

Rafferty Karen (2011) Class based emotions and the allure of fashion consumption, *Journal of Consumer Culture,* 11:239.

Reckwitz Andreas (2002) Towards a Theory of Social Practices, *European Journal of Social Theory*, Vol 5, No 2.

Reynolds Simon (2011), *Retromania: Pop Culture's Addiction to Its Own Past,* New York: Faber and Faber Inc.

Roux Dominique, Korchia Michaël (2006), "Am I What I Wear? An Exploratory Study of Symbolic Meanings Associated with Second-hand Clothing," *Advances in Consumer Research*, Vol. 33, 29-35.

Schau Hope, Muñiz Albert, Arnould Eric Jr. (2009), "How Brand Community Practices Create Value," *Journal of Marketing*, Vol. 73, (5), 30-51.

Schatzki Theodore R, Cetina Karin Knorr, Savigny Eike von (Eds) (2001*) The Practice Turn in Contemporary Theory*, London, UK: Routledge.

Sherry John Jr. (1990) A Socio-cultural analysis of a Midwestern American Flea market, *Journal of Consumer Research*, Vol 17, No 1. 13-30.

Shove Elizabeth, Araujo Luis (2010) Consumption, materiality and markets, included in Araujo Luis, Finch John, Kjellberg Hans (Eds) (2010) *Reconnecting Marketing to Markets*, Oxford, UK: Oxford University Press.

Shove Elizabeth, Pantzar Mika (2005), Consumers, Producers and Practices: Understanding the invention and reinvention of Nordic walking, *Journal of Consumer Culture,* 5:43.

Simmel Georg (1957) Fashion, *The American Journal of Sociology*, LXII 6: 541-558.

Thompson Craig J, Haytko Diana L. (1997) Speaking of Fashion: Consumer's Uses of Fashion Discourses and the Appropriation of Countervailing Cultural Meanings, *Journal of Consumer Research*, 24: 15-42.

Tungate Mark (2008), *Fashion Brands: Branding Style from Armani to Zara*, 2nd Edition, London: Kogan Press.

Warde Alan (2005) Consumption and Theories of Practice, *Journal of Consumer Culture,* 5:131.

Warde Alan (2004) Practice and Field: revising Bourdieusian concepts, *CRIC Discussion Paper,* No 56, Centre for Research on Innovation and Competition, The University of Manchester.

Wenger Etienne (1998) *Communities of Practice: Learning, Meaning and Identity,* Cambridge,UK: Cambridge University Press.

Consumption-Related Values and Product Placement: The Effect of Cultivating Fashion Consciousness on the Appeal of Brands in Reality Television

Claire Sherman, Zayed University, UAE
Damien Arthur, Zayed University, UAE

ABSTRACT

By 2003, Baylor University's forensic science program had grown by ten times the 1999 intake and other universities across the US were scrambling to create forensic science courses to cater for new student demand (Johnston 2003). The reason? Since it aired on the 6th of October 2000, Crime Scene Investigation (CSI), a television (TV) series, had stimulated enormous interest in forensics and the science of solving crime. So much so that it was affecting student choice and behavior. These types of TV inspired phenomenon are not uncommon. Although much of the evidence is anecdotal, there are many instances where very specific consumption trends have been fueled by television programs. The Biggest Loser has generated an interest in boot camps, American Idol has created a resurgence of karaoke games and various home improvement programs have inspired their audience to renovate. These trends have become more acute with recent reality and lifestyle television focusing on particular behaviors that transform the real people on their programs. This paper examines how the cultivation of relevant consumption values generates these trends through increasing the viewer's desire for associated products and brands integrated within TV programs. Specifically, this longitudinal study explores the cultivation of fashion consciousness and its impact on the desire for brands that are implicitly endorsed within reality television programming.

LITERATURE REVIEW

Cultivation Theory

Cultivation theory suggests that increased exposure to television content creates a worldview, or a consistent picture of social behavior, norms, and structure, based on the stable view of society that television content portrays (Gerbner et al. 1994). Research in this area examines the idea that heavy television viewers will agree with the 'television view' more often than lighter television viewers. Studies of cultivation have examined a range of topics including the cultivation of violence, substance abuse, individualism, materialism and body image (Cohen and Weimann 2000; Harrison 2003; O'Guinn and Shrum 1997; Shrum, Burroughs, and Rindfleisch 2005), and, in general, have found cultivation effects exist. For example, women who watch more television perceive an ideal female body that is closer to the curvaceously thin woman depicted on television than females who do not watch as much television (Harrison 2003).

One notable consumer study by O'Guinn and Shrum (1997) explored the influence of television on peoples' perceptions of affluence. In particular, they studied consumers' perceptions of the prevalence of convertibles, car telephones, maids or servants, hot tubs/Jacuzzis and wine within the USA. One significant factor of this study, different to many other studies of cultivation effects, was the examination of direct experience with the product. As expected, direct experience enhanced estimates of affluence. That is, participants who had a maid, hot tub, sport car, etc, judged these items to be more prevalent in society than those who did not. This research found that both experience and television viewing were sources of information with which to build perceptions of affluence. In addition, it was posited, although not tested, that those who had no direct experience with the products would be more influenced by television as a source of information. This is interesting because it suggests that the level of television viewing influences consumer perceptions, particularly when there is no or little direct experience with the matter being cultivated.

O'Guinn and Shrum's (1997) study, like many of the early studies of cultivation effects focused on beliefs about the prevalence of phenomena within society (i.e. how much violence there is in society, how many people drive sports cars), however, more recent studies have focused on the cultivation of values, such as materialism (Shrum et al. 2005). The distinction is important, as cultivating beliefs of prevalence and cultivating values are inherently different processes that occur in different ways. Interestingly, unlike judgments of prevalence, which are formed at the time the judgment is made, consumer values are formed at the time of viewing. Known as online processing (Shrum et al. 2011), this formation of values may have particular implications for brands that are simultaneously presented within TV shows. If a relevant consumption value is formed during the viewing experience, when the brand is implicitly endorsed, desire for the brand should also be enhanced during viewing. However, this effect will depend on both the relatedness of the brand and value as well as the power of the television program to elicit a change in viewers' consumption-related values, a power reality television may hold.

The Power of Reality TV

In addition to being entertained, reality television viewers often examine the behavior of the participants and reflect on their own identity and whether they would behave in a similar way (Nabi et al. 2003). However, as the viewers observe how the various characters within the program approve and disapprove of certain behaviors, they are presented with opportunities to learn from these experiences. In this way, reality TV may shape viewer norms by allowing a vicarious experience of human interactions. This may be particularly relevant for what has been termed 'transformational' reality programming (Bratich 2006), where a transformation takes place during the program, such as the 'make-over' of a straight male on "Queer Eye for the Straight Guy" or the transformation of a participant's cars on "Pimp my Ride". The power of transformation was described by Bratich (2006) as a reason why reality television is more than a representation of society, but a mechanism through which society may be controlled or changed. Where a program is seen as an authority in transforming a participant from the everyday person to a desired self, those who identify or wishfully identify with the participants are likely to absorb the implications of certain behaviors, attitudes, reactions, styles and brands in achieving that aspirational goal, whether it be their inner self or their extended self, such as their home or car, that is enhanced. Hence, reality TV is a very powerful context for a brand to be promoted within since, on an individual level, the viewer is vicariously learning and changing. This individual connection to the program may be the mechanism that underpins the cultivation effect.

From a consumer behavior perspective reality television's ability to cultivate consumption values and instigate trends, such as fashion consciousness, is similar to stimulating primary demand. However, it may be one step removed, stimulating interest not in a specific product category (e.g. high heels) but in an area of interest (e.g. fashion). For example, a viewer of MasterChef, a competitive cooking show, may begin to value the art of home cooking and fine cuisine as a result of watching ordinary people create culinary masterpieces. Subsequently, this will then enhance the viewer's motivation to process information about how to cook, for instance, which types of knives are best, what ingredients are fashionable and what type of utensils are desirable. If a brand is then presented at the very time that this value is being generated (via online processing) there is a greater likelihood that the brand will be noticed and ultimately desired. Thus, the closer the brand's proximity to the cultivation of related consumption values, the more likely the brand will be desired. Unlike a viewer who is already interested in cooking and deliberately watches the program to feed this interest, a viewer that simply watches due to their interest in human interactions and competition, or to negate boredom may be even more susceptible to influence, as they are a clean slate, with no pre-existing knowledge and experience with the product category and associated brands. With this in mind, it may be important to focus product placement research not solely on those with prior product involvement or particular consumption values but those who experience a change in their consumption values.

The Link Between Brand and Program

The cultivation of consumption values that stem from a reality television program will have flow on effects for relevant products and brands. For the flow-on effects to be realized, some relationship between the brand and the program's theme or content is required. A match between the context and the product aids the acceptance of the brand within the program or scene as well as ensures a particular target audience, likely to be interested in the product. This thematic congruence differs from 'natural integration' in that it relates to the match with the theme rather than whether it is naturally depicted within a particular scene. For example, a toddler tantrum within a Subway store may seem to be natural and well integrated within the reality program Super Nanny, yet the brand Subway is not necessarily congruent with the theme. Alternately, a scene depicting contestants on the Biggest Loser eating low-fat Subway sandwiches is a more thematically congruent placement. In addition to transferring meaning from the program to the brand, a thematically congruent placement will also provide meaning to the program (Karrh 1998). From the viewers' perspective they will gain value from this brand because it may help to fulfill a new consumption value generated via the theme of the program.

A Proposed Test of Cultivation Effects on Brand Appeal

Previous research has often cited a significant association between television viewing and any particular 'television view' as the result of cultivation (Cohen and Weimann 2000; Gerbner et al. 1994; O'Guinn and Shrum 1997). However, this may be the result of correlation or indeed the reverse relationship may be true, where a particular attitude may cause greater TV viewing of a particular genre (Cohen and Weimann 2000). Therefore, to resolve this issue this study will test whether the change in fashion consciousness, rather than the absolute level of fashion consciousness, affects the desire for a thematically congruent brand. This is not to say that there may not be a prior relationship between those who have a high level of fashion consciousness and a change in brand appeal. Marketing communications theory tells us that those that are more involved with a product category (or in this case the surrounding theme of fashion) may be more motivated to pay attention to a product message (Petty and Cacioppo 1986). However, this effect would not be due to the cultivation effect of TV viewing. For this reason, we capture and include prior product involvement within our model, yet the independent variable of focus is the change in fashion consciousness. Denoting

cultivation, this change may even occur for those who initially have low levels of fashion consciousness.

In addition to product involvement, brand familiarity is also included within the model to avoid further specification error. Brand familiarity has been found to affect product placement outcomes perhaps due to greater perceptual fluency (Brennan and Babin 2004), which is viewers' superior ability to process a brand due to prior familiarity with its shape, meaning and context. Finally, the model also needs to account for the audiences' level of desire for the brand prior to viewing. For this reason, prior brand appeal is included in the model so that its effect is captured and we can ensure that the resultant brand appeal is not simply a factor of the viewer's previous desire for the brand. The resultant proposed model is depicted in Figure 1.

METHODOLOGY

A challenge faced by many researchers of cultivation effects is discerning between correlation and causation (Hughes 1980). Although it may be argued that causation cannot be proven, a longitudinal design was used to enable the capture of a stimulus effect and allow causal inferences to be made (Rindfleisch et al. 2008). To test for viewing effects, a panel study was undertaken. The procedure allowed for viewers to watch six episodes of a target program on an advert-free DVD (totaling four hours and 15 minutes of screen time). This was done within their own homes over a three-week period. This design is notably different from previous studies of product placement effects due to the length of the viewing situation. In particular, this design might afford the necessary time and exposure for the cultivation of fashion consciousness to take place. Viewers were asked to fill in a self-administered online survey both before and after viewing. To test whether pre-measurement had a priming effect, a small post-test only control group (n=45) also undertook the study and tests of significant differences between the control and main group responses were carried out with no significant differences in post brand appeal found.

As a typical example of transformational reality television, the program, Australia's Next Top Model was used as stimuli. It promoted the value of fashion consciousness. Specifically, it was centered on the fashion industry and was closely aligned with well-known fashion designers and models. Several brand-program relationships were also already established. Four brands were initially assessed for the strength of congruence via a pilot study: a small car, a body spray, a magazine and a cosmetics brand. The cosmetics brand, Napoleon Perdis Cosmetics, exhibited the greatest level of fit and was used for the final analysis.

The specific target population would usually comprise individuals who watch the target program (Neuman 2003). However, for this study, the aim was to capture a sampling frame that would best replicate the natural viewing audience of the series, whilst excluding existing viewers to avoid any prior cultivation effects. On consultation with the producers and brand managers responsible for the placements, the target audience for the program and brands was confined to Australian females aged 16 to 35. Considering the nature and content of the program, as well as the use of a cosmetics brand, this all female sample was necessary to uphold the ecological validity of the study. To capture a qualified sample, a filtering process was undertaken, where the initial invitation for participation was sent to a wider population and those outside of the target sample were gradually filtered out via questioning. The panel of viewers was recruited via an email, with a link to the preliminary online survey. The initiating email was sent to all staff at a large, South Australian, vocational training college. This sample was not a student sample and, if passed

Figure 1:
Proposed Model of the Effect of the Cultivation of Fashion Consciousness on Brand Appeal

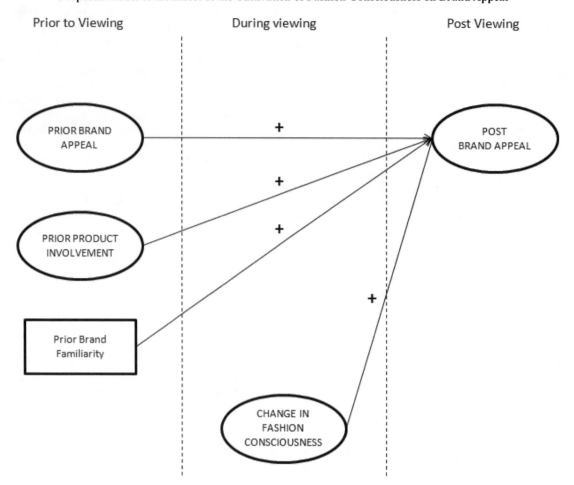

on to the college students, they would be a more generalisable, non-traditional student sample in any case (James and Sonner 2001). The email request outlined the television program to be viewed, the incentive of a $30 mall voucher, the necessary sample characteristics and encouraged forwarding of the email. Nineteen percent of the sample was recruited directly from the original email, whilst the remaining 80.7% were recruited via snowballing. From 663 responses, 234 eligible respondents were sent the DVD package. Of this, 203 completed the two surveys and viewing in full, yielding a retention rate of 86.76%.

Fashion consciousness was measured both before and after the viewing experience and a latent difference score model was developed (as outlined in Ferrer and McArdle 2003) that provided a three-item measure for change in fashion consciousness over the viewing experience. The measure for fashion consciousness was taken from the 'overall fashion consciousness' dimension of a 38 item 'fashion consciousness scale' developed by Gould and Stern (1989). Three of the dimension's items were deemed inappropriate and were removed as they related to specific behavioral changes that were unlikely to occur over a three-week period. The ten items included (see Table 1) were randomized and evaluated on seven-point Likert scales.

Confirmatory factor analysis was conducted on this dimension using AMOS software and three separate factors emerged, instead of the expected one (Gould and Stern 1989). These factors each related to slightly different aspects of fashion consciousness, specifically to reflections on the viewer's own fashion, their awareness of

fashion and how fashionable they are (see Table 1). Each of these factors were highly correlated (ρ = .86, .89, .91) and exhibited good fit as a three-factor higher order construct ($\chi2$ (78) =161.332, p=.056, GFI=.931). To reduce the item-to-subject ratio the composites of these factors were created and a three item higher-order factor was used to generate the difference score measuring the latent construct 'change in fashion consciousness'.

Brand appeal was measured both before and after the viewing experience. This enabled an evaluation of any resultant desirability for the brand to focus on the influence of a cultivation effect and not simply on a prior judgment of the brand. The 'brand appeal' construct was used rather than the possible alternatives (i.e. brand image) as it is a more universal measure and may apply to many different brand characteristics depending on what is appealing to the individual. Brand appeal was measured using a scale that has been validated in numerous studies investigating attitudes towards a brand (Bruner et al. 2001). The three particular items used in this study (see Table 1) were chosen for their generality and relatedness to appeal. Each of the items was randomized and measured on seven-point Likert scales. After several unprompted 'don't know' comments were reported during pre-testing, a 'don't know' response category was deemed necessary and included. This inclusion was especially important as the preexposure measure was taken at a time when viewers may not yet have been aware of the brand.

Both brand familiarity and product involvement were measured before the viewing experience to account for any intervening effects.

Table 1:
Measurement Scales and Items

Construct and Items	Factor
Fashion Consciousness (Gould and Stern 1989)	
1. I reflect about the fashions I wear a lot	Own Fashion
2. I am very involved with the clothes I wear	Own Fashion
3. I'm very conscious of the fashions related to my own gender	Fashion Awareness
4. I'm very alert to changes in fashion	Fashion Awareness
5. I would say I'm very fashion conscious	Fashion Awareness
6. I'm very involved with fashion	Fashionable
7. I'm more fashionable than the average person	Fashionable
8. I'm very fashionable	Fashionable
9. Other people think I'm very fashionable	Fashionable
10. Other people ask me what is fashionable	Fashionable
Brand Appeal (Bruner, James, and Hensel 2001)	
1. *Brand* is appealing	Brand Appeal
2. *Brand* is desirable	Brand Appeal
3. I like *Brand*	Brand Appeal
Brand Familiarity (Bruner et al. 2001)	
1. I am familiar with this brand	Brand Familiarity
Product Category Involvement (Bruner, James, and Hensel 2005)	
1. In general, I have a strong interest in *product category*	Product Involvement
2. This *product category* is important to me	Product Involvement
3. This *product category* is very relevant to me	Product Involvement

Brand familiarity was measured using a single-item seven-point Likert scale that has been validated in previous studies (Bruner et al. 2001) (see Table 1). Product involvement was measured similarly using three statements validated in previous studies with anchors of 'Not at all' to 'Very much', indicating the relevancy, importance and viewer interest in the product category (Bruner et al. 2001) (see Table 1).

Structural Equation Modeling (SEM) was used to test the effect of cultivation on brand appeal because it allows the impact of other variables to be accounted for, avoiding some of the specification error that may occur in single regressions. It also accounts for both measurement and structural error relating to latent variables (Kline 2005).

RESULTS AND DISCUSSION

The final model was tested and exhibited excellent fit based on all fit indices (χ^2 (33) = 32.417, *p*=.938; GFI=.938) and explained a good proportion of the variance in brand appeal (R^2 = 42.1%) (see Figure 2). As hypothesized, both product involvement (β_{PI}=.16, *p*=.024) and brand familiarity (β_{BF}=0.20, *p*=.011) have a significant positive influence on brand appeal. In addition to these established effects, the change in fashion consciousness also had a significant positive effect on brand appeal as hypothesized (β_{FC}=0.22, *p*=.000). That is, viewers who experienced a greater change in fashion consciousness after watching the program, Australia's Next Top Model, reported a greater desire for the cosmetics brand Napoleon Perdis. Hence, through the cultivation of a specific consumption–related value, reality television programming was found to increase viewers'

desires for a thematically congruent brand. Importantly, this relationship was found to exist while controlling for the effects of prior product involvement and the viewers' original desire for the brand. This is an important contribution as it demonstrates that the simultaneous cultivation of consumption-related values has the power to directly affect consumers' attitudes towards integrated brands, thus providing a better understanding of how product placement operates.

In contrast to previous studies that have focused on whether an overall cultivation effect exists, this study extends the current literature by demonstrating that viewers who experience a greater cultivation effect develop a greater desire for the brand; a second-order effect. Importantly, these results indicate that it is not just prior interests and values that dictate individuals' desire for the brands placed within the TV programs they watch. Via online processing, the development of consumption-related values also contributes to a desire for the brand. This finding is a significant contribution to the marketing literature as it demonstrates the worth of a malleable viewer. Furthermore, this malleability pertains to values, which are generally considered an influential yet stable consumer variable within the communication situation. This notion should now be rethought given the prolonged viewing of many forms of entertainment.

IMPLICATIONS, LIMITATIONS AND CONCLUSIONS

The major findings of this study suggest that, when considering brand placements, marketers should look beyond programs with an audience that is already interested in the product category or surrounding interests, and consider the potential of programs capable

Figure 2:
The Effect of a Change In Fashion Consciousness on Brand Appeal

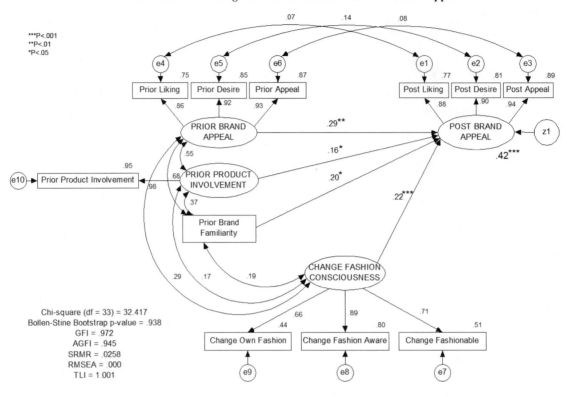

of cultivating a relevant consumption value. This notion challenges more traditional media planning techniques that use audience analytics, or even those that analyze the mood induced by various programs, and encourages analysis of a media vehicle's ability to cultivate relevant values. Product placement provides a benefit over traditional advertising through the embedded connection to viewers' online processing of consumption-related values. This provides marketers with an opportunity to increase their market share by gaining first access to new consumers at the moment they become interested, rather than attempting to steal existing customers from competitors.

Moreover, if brands realize this potential and fund the cultivation of particular consumption-related values through entertainment media, in particular reality TV, it may be possible for them to actively enhance the size of the entire market. If this occurs on a wide scale the entertainment landscape will be changed (or perhaps it already has). Based on the traditional funding model for entertainment, content may become skewed towards values that support consumption. For example, it would be highly useful for a cosmetics brand to fund shows on beautifying individuals or an SUV brand to fund programs that promote an outdoor lifestyle. In doing so, brand-funded programming has the ability to influence consumers by promoting a consumption agenda. Such directed or controlled agendas have been discussed in the media psychology literature, however, agenda-setting theory is most commonly based on the dissemination of information, rather than cultivating values, and it often focuses on the control that media has in influencing what society deems newsworthy (Weaver 2007). Nevertheless, this theory lends itself to the influence of advertiser-funded programming, where consumption related values are more likely to be at the centre of program content. This big picture view suggests a change in how society consumes television and has implications for debate regarding rational consumer choice.

A basic interpretation of brand-funded cultivation suggests that the viewer is a passive entity, however, critics may argue that viewers will not choose to watch a program if the content does not satisfy some underlying need. This is not disputed; however, viewers watch television programs to gratify many different needs simultaneously (Katz, Blumler, and Gurevitch 1974). While a viewer may be watching The Biggest Loser to fulfill their need for voyeurism, they may also come to value good exercise and a balanced diet, which in turn may generate a desire to attend a boot camp. Alternately, America's Next Top Model may be viewed because it satisfies the viewers' need for downward social comparison (Nabi et al. 2003). At the same time, the young women who watch it will begin to value appearance and materialism, which may fuel a desire to consume beyond their means. These examples suggest that a viewer may be both passive and active simultaneously: Active in pursing entertainment needs, yet passive to the cultivation of consumption values. These examples also highlight that cultivation of consumption values may have both positive and negative consequences for the viewer, raising questions regarding the responsibility of media and marketing practitioners who, while enhancing the desirability of brands, may change societal values.

It should be made clear that this study does not provide evidence of the dominance of cultivation over other effects on product placement. Furthermore, there is a need to reaffirm these results in a more controlled manner. In particular, including a control group of non-viewers would alleviate concerns of internal validity that may stem from the existence of external factors present over the extended viewing period. Despite these concerns, this study furthers our understanding of how cultivation affects more specific brand-related outcomes and the different ways in which individuals may be motivated to process product placements. Indeed, Petty and Cacioppo's (1986) Elaboration Likelihood Model purports that more lasting attitude change is enabled by a consumer's motivation to attend and process brand information, however, this study advances this extant knowledge by demonstrating that motivation itself can be enhanced by cultivating the underlying value that fuels this motivation. While this finding may seem intuitive, this is the first time it has been empirically confirmed in this context and thus advances our understanding of how product placement operates. Hence, this study moves the research agenda beyond questions relating to the validity of the now well-established cultivation theory, to questions of its role in effecting identifiable brand outcomes.

REFERENCES

Bratich, Jack Z. (2006), ""Nothing Is Left Alone for Too Long": Reality Programming and Control Society Subjects," *Journal of Communication Inquiry*, 30 (1), 65-83.

Brennan, Ian and Laurie A. Babin (2004), "Brand Placement Recognition: The Influence of Presentation Mode and Brand Familiarity," *Journal of Promotion Management*, 10 (1/2), 185-202.

Bruner, Gordon C., Karen E. James, and Paul J. Hensel (2001), *Marketing Scales Handbook : A Compilation of Multi-Item Measures*, Vol. III, Chicago, Illinois: American Marketing Association.

_____ (2005), *Marketing Scales Handbook: A Compilation of Multi-Item Measures for Consumer Behavior & Advertising*, Vol. IV, Chicago, Illinois: American Marketing Association.

Cohen, Jonathan and Gabriel Weimann (2000), "Cultivation Revisited: Some Genres Have Some Effects on Some Viewers," *Communication Reports*, 13 (2), 99-114.

Ferrer, Emillo and John J. McArdle (2003), "Alternative Structural Models for Multivariate Longitudinal Data Analysis," *Structural Equation Modeling*, 10 (4), 493-524.

Gerbner, George, Larry Gross, Michael Morgan, and Nancy Signorielli (1994), "Growing up with Television: The Cultivation Perspective," in *Media Effects: Advances in Theory and Research*, ed. J. Bryant & D. Zillman, Hillsdale, NJ: Lawrence Erlbaum, 17-41.

Gould, Stephen J. and Barbara B. Stern (1989), "Gender Schema and Fashion Consciousness.," *Psychology & Marketing*, 6 (2), 129-45.

Harrison, Kristen (2003), "Television Viewers' Ideal Body Proportions: The Case of the Curvaceously Thin Woman," *Sex Roles*, 48 (5-6), 255-64.

Hughes, Michael (1980), "The Fruits of Cultivation Analysis - a Reexamination of Some Effects of Television Watching," *Public Opinion Quarterly*, 44 (3), 287-302.

James, William L. and Brenda S. Sonner (2001), "Just Say No to Traditional Student Samples," *Journal of Advertising Research*, 41 (5), 63-71.

Johnston, Lauren (2003), "'CSI' Spurs Forensic Academics: Colleges Report Long Wait Lists for Crime Fighting Science Courses," in *CBS news*, Mansfield: The Associated Press.

Karrh, James A. (1998), "Brand Placement: A Review," *Journal of Current Issues and Research in Advertising*, 20 (2), 31-49.

Katz, Elihu, Jay G. Blumler, and Michael Gurevitch (1974), "Uses and Gratifications Research," *Public Opinion Quarterly*, 37 (4), 509-23.

Kline, Rex B (2005), *Principles and Practice of Structural Equation Modeling*, New York: The Guilford Press.

Nabi, Robin L., Erica N. Biely, Sara J. Morgan, and Carmen R. Stitt (2003), "Reality-Based Television Programming and the Psychology of Its Appeal," *Media Psychology*, 5 (4), 303 - 30.

Neuman, William Lawrence (2003), *Social Research Methods : Qualitative and Quantitative Approaches*, Boston ; London: Allyn and Bacon.

O'Guinn, Thomas C. and L. J. Shrum (1997), "The Role of Television in the Construction of Consumer Reality," *Journal of Consumer Research*, 23 (March), 278-94.

Petty, Richard E and John T Cacioppo (1986), "The Elaboration Likelihood Model of Persuasion," in *Advances in Experimental Social Psychology* Vol. 19, ed. L. Berkowitz, New York: Academic Press, 123-205.

Rindfleisch, Aric, Alan J. Malter, Shankar Ganesan, and Christine Moorman (2008), "Cross-Sectional Versus Longitudinal Survey Research: Concepts, Findings, and Guidelines," *Journal of Marketing Research (JMR)*, 45 (3), 261-79.

Shrum, L. J., Jaehoon Lee, James E. Burroughs, and Aric Rindfleisch (2011), "An Online Process Model of Second-Order Cultivation Effects: How Television Cultivates Materialism and Its Consequences for Life Satisfaction." *Human Communication Research*, 37, 34–57.

Shrum, L. J., James E. Burroughs, and Aric Rindfleisch (2005), "Television's Cultivation of Material Values," *Journal of Consumer Research*, 32 (December), 473-79.

Weaver, David H. (2007), "Thoughts on Agenda Setting, Framing and Priming," *Journal of Communication*, 57, 142-47.

Cyber-Jihad: Islamic Consumer Activism on the Web

Elif Izberk-Bilgin, University of Michigan-Dearborn, USA

ABSTRACT

This study explores Islamic cyber-activism and finds that activists pursue a virtual jihad against transnational brands as an economic and non-violent means of asserting Islamic values and identity in the marketplace. The study contributes to consumer activism literature by highlighting the role of religious discourse and authorities as market-structuring forces.

INTRODUCTION

While there is considerable research on religion and ideology in social sciences, consumer researchers have given little attention to how the interplay of these influential forces informs brand attitudes. Notably lacking are examinations of consumer activism fueled by religious ideology. This is concerning given that brand avoidance driven by fundamentalist beliefs is not always substantiated, unlike typical boycotting behavior (e.g., Nike protests following media exposes of labor abuse). Yet research shows that consumer activism, particularly in the form of boycotts, can have adverse effects on profits (Klein et al. 2004), tarnish brand image (Thompson et al. 2006), and may result in violent acts.

Compounding the dynamics of contemporary consumer activism is new media. Internet has changed the way individuals pursue social change, rendering activism convenient and, largely, anonymous. Further, viral activism has dramatically reduced the time in which boycott messages proliferate and reach mass audiences (Hollenbeck and Zinkhan 2006; Krishnamurthy and Kucuk 2009).

While the literature on consumer activism - also known as consumer resistance, anti-consumption, brand avoidance, political consumerism, and boycotting - is vast (Holt 2002; Kozinets 2002; Lee et al. 2009; Micheletti et al. 2004; Thompson and Arsel 2004; see special issues of *Consumption Markets and Culture* and *Journal of Business Research*), there is little theorizing on the interplays among religious ideology, activism, and new media. Considering that Internet is instrumental in social mobilization (e.g., Arab Spring, Occupy Wall Street) and dissemination of ideologies (Kahn and Kellner 2004), it is critical that consumer researchers explore the roles of religious ideology and new media on brand attitudes and consumer identity.

This study seeks to advance our theoretical understanding of these issues. Through a netnography of cyber-activism, this research investigates how Islamism informs consumption discourses. The data includes textual, visual, and audio material collected over two years on Islamic boycott websites, forums, and blogs in English. The study identifies two themes that underlie and distinguish Islamic consumer activism from other examinations of critical consumerism (Holt 2002; Kozinets 2002; Lee et al. 2009; Micheletti et al. 2004; Thompson and Arsel 2004): 1) tyrannization of the other – the discursive construction of non-Muslims as tyrants, and 2) formation of a cyber-*umma* (community of Muslims). The study also highlights religious authorities' role in mobilizing Islamic boycotts as unique to consumer activism driven by religious ideology.

THEORETICAL BACKGROUND

Consumer Activism

Recent research has identified a broad spectrum of contemporary forms of consumer activism. Consistent with a postmodern consumer culture, these newer forms of activism represent individualized quests for social change and range from consumer resistance (Holt 2002; Penaloza and Price 1993), culture jamming (Handelman 1999), anti-branding (Hollenbeck and Zinkhan 2010), brand avoidance (Lee 2007), anti-consumption (Lee et al. 2009) to political consumerism (Micheletti, Føllesdal, and Stolle 2004).

Among various forms of consumer activism, boycotting stands out as the oldest (Friedman 1999), the most prominent, and the most effective form of consumer expression of discontent (Pruitt and Friedman 1986). Friedman (1985, 87) defines a boycott as "an attempt by one or more parties to achieve certain objectives by urging individual consumers to refrain from making selected purchases in the marketplace." Often viewed as a 'vote in the marketplace,' or more dramatically as a 'weapon of resistance' in socio-political conflicts, boycotting commands powerless groups with authority to pursue social change. For example, consumer boycotts have played a fundamental role in labor unionization and the mobilization of the civil rights movements in America (Cohen 2003; Klein, Smith, and John 2004), while the Indian boycott of British salt and cloth propelled the British to withdraw from India.

While boycotting is a powerful tool consumers use to realize sociopolitical goals, recent research suggests that today's boycotts are less focused on political causes and civic objectives. For example, Klein, Smith, and John (2004, 93) state that contemporary boycotts "are more typically focused on corporate practices and marketing policy issues rather than on broader sociopolitical goals such as civil rights." Confirming this comment, a series of studies have identified brands' unethical business practices (Friedman 1985), 'hard-sell' tactics or overt commercialism (Micheletti et al. 2004), negative country of origin effects (Klein, Ettenson, and Morris 1998), and representation of undesired self-image (Hogg, Banister, and Stephenson 2009) as significant motivations underlying contemporary boycotts. While these studies highlight some of the important drivers of boycotting behavior, they inadvertently imply that contemporary consumer activism is divorced from ideology.

However, a close reading of the studies, particularly those emerging in the *Consumer Culture Theory* domain, suggests that consumers' anti-consumption (and consumption) practices are imbued with various ideological and moralistic narratives. For example, Thompson and Coskuner-Balli (2007, 150) find that a strong desire to redress "the ecological and socioeconomic problems fostered by economic globalization," while contesting the asymmetrical power relationships among transnational corporations, nations, and labor motivates some consumers to opt out of mainstream grocers and to participate in community supported agriculture (CSA) practices. In addition to these environmentalist, anti-industrialization, anti-globalization, and anti-corporate ideologies, Press and Arnould (2011) find that American pastoralist ideology is a prominent theme underlying CSA practices and discourses. Similar political and moral motives can also be found among the proponents of the fair-trade and green consumption movements (Connolly and Prothero 2008), not to mention the counter-cultural practices of high minded consumers concerned about the socio-economic and environmental implications of McDonaldization (Ritzer 1983) of global food production via agricultural bioengineering (Sassatelli and Davolio 2010). Lastly, Simon (2011) argues that consumers demand social justice and equality while demonstrating civic engagement through the politics of consumption. These examples show that boycotts, buycotts, or other articulations of consumer dissent, are not simply a contestation over "corporate practices and marketing policy issues" as Klein et al. (2004, 93) suggest. Rather, these studies suggest that such acts of consumer activism remain deeply infused with personal and shared ideologies.

Consumer activism and religious ideology

While the latest literature has addressed the role of political, nationalist, and competing marketplace ideologies in structuring consumer choice and identity works (Crockett and Wallendorf 2004; Dobscha and Ozanne 2001; Holt 2002; Kozinets 2002; Kozinets and Handelman 2004; Luedicke, Thompson, and Giesler 2010; Thompson 2003; Thompson 2004; Thompson and Coskuner-Balli 2007; Varman and Belk 2009), there is little theorizing on how religious ideology might foster consumer activism (see Friedman 1999 for boycotts organized by religious groups on moral concerns). This is concerning given that religious beliefs, when coupled with socio-political tensions and economic conflicts, may become significant ideological resources with which activist consumers contest the marketplace. One good example is Islamic consumer activism. Recent boycotts of Danish goods (and of global retailers like Carrefour or Tesco that carry Danish goods) by Muslims in response to the ill-perceived cartoon depictions of Prophet Mohammed powerfully demonstrate how religious sentiments may mobilize consumer resistance and result in financial damage to the targeted businesses (Jensen 2008; Knudsen, Praveen Aggarwal, and Maamoun 2008). Far from a reflexive response to what is perceived as an offense to one's faith, the Danish boycott is a reflection of Muslim ideological views about Western powers that are deeply rooted in the colonial history and the recent Western involvement in Muslim-majority countries such as Iraq, Afghanistan, and Palestine.

Islamic activism has been extensively examined as a new social movement with a political and militant agenda (Ayoob 2008; Roy 1994), yet little research has explored marketplace articulations of Islamic ideology (Izberk-Bilgin 2012a; Rudnyckyj 2009; Sandikci and Ger 2010; Wong 2007). Particularly missing is an understanding of how Islamic beliefs, coupled with consumers' political ideology and the socio-historical structures, shape brand attitudes and consumer activism in light of consumers' identity projects. Considering that consumers increasingly pursue social change and perform identity goals through the marketplace and that new forms of media has propelled this trend, an interesting area of research lies at the intersection of new media, consumer activism, and religious ideology.

Islamic activism and new media

Evolving new media environment has led to a profound restructuring of societies by enabling an unprecedented degree of interconnectivity among various social groups, cultures, and nations. New media has provided an alternative platform for 'other' voices, which has fostered new interpretations of taken for granted ideas and practices. This, in turn, has gradually led to the fragmentation of political and religious authorities in not only the democratic societies of North America or Europe, but also countries under totalitarian regimes. These profound changes are perhaps nowhere more visible than in the Islamic world. The proliferation of media has played a crucial role in amplifying the exchange of ideas, discourses, and practices among the Islamic communities in diaspora, homeland-Muslims, and converts, which led to a wide range of emerging discourses about Islam from fundamentalist to reformist (Eickelman and Anderson 2003; Oncu 1995). Dialoguing with Islamic communities in other cultures allowed Muslims to not only discover alternative articulations of belief and practice, but more importantly, question the authority of the religious scholars, who have traditionally served as the spokespersons for Islam. Accordingly, new media has

transformed the public space into "a marketplace of ideas, identities, and discourses" (Eickelman and Anderson 2003, xii). Indeed, the expansion of Islamic public sphere and identity politics fueled by the Internet is quite visible in the global rise of the halal industry (Izberk-Bilgin 2012b) and the formation of Islamic consumption-scapes (Pink 2009). Paralleling the growth of Islamic consumerism, interestingly, is a proliferation of discourses and practices of Islamic consumer activism. Particularly, in the aftermath of 9/11, there has been a wave of Islamic cyber-activism protesting anti-Muslim discourses as well as American and Israeli foreign policies involving Muslim-majority countries. This cyber-activism is most evident in the increasing number of websites, Islamic forum threads, blogs, Facebook boycott pages, and tweets that target transnational brands. This paper examines why multinational companies become key targets of Islamic cyber-activism as well as how religious discourse and authorities, combined with socio-historical factors, influence Muslim consumers' motivation to boycott.

METHODOLOGY

This study draws from a netnographic analysis of online Islamic forums (e.g., ummah, shiachat, islamicawakenings, turntoislam, muslimvillage, and islamicity) as well as websites (e.g., islamicinsights, muslimmatters.org, altmuslim, radioislam, missionislam, inminds, alqudsday.org) and Facebook pages that address issues relevant to Muslim audiences. Islamic forums were initially chosen among those awarded the "Top 40 Muslim Forums Award," which ranks Muslim forums based on "the page rank of the Forum, the number of visitors, the number of post threads, the number of viewers, the quality of the topics debated,..." (http://topmuslimforums.wordpress.com/). A smaller sample was then identified for closer analysis based on the number of forum members; for example, the analysed sites ummah.com and turntoislam.com have more than 58,000 and 93,000 members, respectively, with close to 5 million posts combined. The forums were also carefully chosen to reflect the diversity of sectarian views; shiachat.com and shiasisters.net were included in the analysis despite having fewer members than predominantly Sunni forums in order to incorporate Shia perspectives. A similar approach was taken with the identification of Islamic websites. For example, islamicinsights, which started out as a print magazine and later added a web portal that features news and various Muslim lifestyle topics, has garnered more than 8,000 likes on Facebook and 5,000 followers on Twitter.

Most of the Islamic forums are structured in a similar way. The main categories of discussion include religious topics, political news concerning Muslims, Islamic marriage, events, and boycott campaigns. The narratives chosen for analysis were identified from links that contained key words such as 'boycott', 'campaign', 'protest' and 'activism'. A total of 120 posts were analysed. Data was interpreted by moving back and forth individual postings and the entire discussion threads as suggested by Kozinets (2010). The findings are presented below.

FINDINGS

Tyrannization of the other

The Islamic activist rhetoric found online parallels that of the many anti-corporate, anti-globalization movements'. Corporate commitment to fair-trade wages, use of non-genetically modified organisms, and environmental sustainability are of concern to Islamic cyber-activists. However, one critical discourse, namely, 'tyrannization of the other' stands out as unique. Islamic boycott materials construe many multinational companies (MNCs) as tyrants and oppressors of Islamic faith and identity.

At the core of this criticism is the long standing Palestine-Israel conflict. A number of provocative images that mix corporate logos with rhetoric infused with religious ideology can be found on forums and blogs that appeal to a Muslim audience. One of these images (Figure 1) shows a Coca Cola bottle shaped like a missile with the texts "Where does our money go?" and "Don't buy your brother's blood".

Figure 1

Source: Islamicawakening.com

The image appears on one of a series of articles that Islamic Insights ran from January 2009 to November 2010 urging "god-conscious consumers" to boycott MNCs for allegedly providing financial support to Israel. The author of the article 'Boycotting for Justice' urges readers to reflect on the war in Gaza by evoking a verse from the Qur'an:

Remember the time when joining hands in murdering innocent people seemed atrocious? The time when "To kill one soul is as though you have killed the whole of humanity" of the Holy Qur'an actually meant something to most of us?... Because

these days ... murdering entire families and directing perfectly-targeted bullets in the chests of innocent babies in Gaza is habitually supported by Muslims... we continue to support those nations which take pride in the unwarranted death of the people of Palestine by purchasing and selling their products...

The author goes on to cite several *fatwa*s (religious decree) that have been issued by Muslim scholars such as Ayatollah Sayyid Ali Sistani and Khameni that deem the consumption of "any item which helps strengthen Zionism" impermissible. Based on these fatwas and other canonical evidence, the author then concludes that continuing to buy Coca Cola or other global brands would be "committing a great sin": "*For those of us who resent the boycott, news flash! We are not only committing a great sin, we are also helping the oppressors! In regards to the helpers of oppressors, the Messenger of Allah has said "On the Night of Ascension, I saw the following inscription on the doors of Hell: Do not be a helper of the oppressors."[emphasis original] ... what would be wiser is for us to actually act upon this narration of the Holy Prophet...Who would have thought buying a Nestle chocolate bar would be committing a major sin, and the negative du'as [prayers] of the oppressed ones would be directed towards us, as aiders of oppressors?*"

The provocative image of the Coca-Cola missile along with the religious rhetoric has attracted several reader comments, which echo the views that MNCs are oppressors of Muslim faith and boycotting these companies is a religious duty. For example Ahmad, dismissing skeptical remarks about boycott effectiveness, comments that: "*...participating in a boycott of companies that support slaughter and oppression is for our own benefit. ..you read up on the guilty companies. You then print out a list of the guilty companies and post it on the fridge. Now every time you walk by the fridge, you've got a small reminder of what our brothers and sisters are going through. Every time we go to the grocery store or to a restaurant, we remember that there are certain products or chains to avoid. We have a DAILY and INTIMATE (in your own kitchen) REMINDER about what our brothers and sisters are going through.*" Next, Ahmad posts a link to a boycott list (Figure 2), which conveniently narrows down the number of targeted companies to three: Starbucks, McDonald's, and Coca-Cola. The list displays these three logos next to a picture of a group of people, including children, running for their lives as a tank chases them. Ahmad ends his remarks by emphasizing that standing up to oppressors is a religious duty for Muslims: "*we should remember that a consumer boycott is just one small aspect of fulfilling our obligation to support the oppressed and reject the oppressor.*" Likewise, HiddenSoldier angrily responds to another forum member, who suggests political participation as an alternative to boycotting, by reminding this religious duty: "*Just because those strategies may be considered "easier" than boycotting the companies which support zionism, it doesn't mean it's not WAJIB [religious duty] to boycott. In other words it is still haram [religiously unlawful] if we do not boycott! There's no point in taking party of a political rally in front of government offices if we purchase Fanta or Sprite when we get thirsty...*"

Similar sentiments can be found on Islamic forums such as ummah.com, turntoislam.com, and shiachat.com. For example, on ummah.com's forum, a user nicknamed lonerider evokes what seems to be a common analogy within the Muslim community (Figure 3) by likening the consumption of McDonald's and Coke products to drinking the blood of Palestinians as s/he sends a call for boycott through this provocative post: "*Do you go to Marks and Spencer's cos their salad is just too good? Do you do McD's fish fillet? Do you drink Coca-Cola? Have you tried the blood of a Palestinian? All of*

Figure 2

Source: alqudsday.org

Figure 3

Source: iluvislam.com

these products have one thing in common: Israel. So the question is do you?" It is noteworthy how these cyber-activists collaborate in strategically combining graphic pictures of baby corpses, culture-jammed images of brand logos, and religious rhetoric to link MNCs to the Palestine-Israel conflict and portray these companies as "child killers" or "murderers" draining "the blood of Palestinians." Activist consumers use many tactics to sustain this discourse and the boycott efforts. For example, cyber-activists routinely share greeting cards and boycott pamphlets with images reportedly of suffering Palestinians (Figure 4), use subverted logos as avatars or signatures (Figure 5), circulate boycott lists, share links to youtube clips about the Palestinian resistance movement and boycott organizations, as well as sharing fatwas and Israel's barcode information to discourage buying Israeli products.

Figure 5

Source: ummah.com

Notably, the Islamic scholars' fatwas (and e-fatwas) play a key role in motivating the activists, but more importantly, presenting boycotting as a religious duty, thus equating the consumption of global brands with committing sin. Also, organizations such as Innovative Minds (the prominent face of the Boycott Israel Campaign online), the BIG Campaign (Boycott Israeli Goods Campaign), Boycott, Divestment, and Sanctions Movement, and Friends of Al-Aqsa (a UK based NGO) are instrumental in providing discursive material and paraphernalia such as books, clothing, badges, pins, key chains, boycott lists, and greeting cards to consumer activists, who then share these materials to create a global consciousness about the boycott and construe global brands as tyrants.

The conflict between Palestine and Israel and the concomitant Arab League's boycott of Israeli goods date back to 1948; both have been well documented in the media and literature (Jevtic 2009). Rather interesting is how quintessentially American or Western brands that clearly do not have Israeli origins are enwrapped in this conflict to be construed as tyrants and become key targets of consumer protest. From a socio-historical perspective this is partly due to the transformation of the Israel boycott from a state-led policy with a secular, Pan-Arab rhetoric to a consumer-driven campaign infused with religious ideology. The Arab League boycott of 1948 primarily targeted products with Israeli origin and secondarily sought to discourage foreign countries to invest in Israel. The boycott was largely carried out at a diplomatic level through limited trade relations, however, participation gradually dropped after Egypt withdrew its support in 1979 as a result of the Egypt-Israel Peace Treaty and other states followed suit to seek membership in WTO.

In the late 1990s, as the state support for the boycott was dwindling, a grassroots campaign was in the making. Interestingly, this consumer driven phase of the boycott targeted American and Western MNCs more aggressively than the earlier phase which focused on non-branded Israeli produce like dates. This strategic shift can be attributed to the growing involvement of American and Western nations in the Middle East following the 1991 Gulf War. While Muslim majority nations such as Egypt and Saudi Arabia participated in the Western coalition against Iraq's invasion of Kuwait, for the masses,

Figure 4

The companies listed here have a track record of supporting Israel.
Their economic support enables Israel to continue killing unarmed Palestinian children.
Stop supporting the murder of children
Boycott these companies today

L'ORÉAL
* Giorgio Armani Perfumes
* Redken 5th Avenue NYC
* Lancome Paris
* Vichy, Matrix
* Cacharel
* La Roche-Posay
* Garnier, Biotherm
* Helena Rubinstein
* Maybelline
* Ralph Lauren Perfumes
* Carson

ESTÉE LAUDER
* Aramis
* Clinique
* MAC cosmetics
* Bobby Brown essentials
* Tommy Hilfiger
* Donna Karan, DKNY
* Jo Malone

DANONE
* Actimel
* Evian/ Volvic Mineral Water
* Jacob's Biscuits
* Galbani Cheese
* Amoy, Lea-Perrins, HP Sauce

Kimberly-Clark
* Andrex
* Kleenex Tissues
* Kotex Sanitary towels
* Huggies Nappies

MARKS & SPENCER

Johnson & Johnson

Coca-Cola

RIVER ISLAND

SELFRIDGES&Cº

Disney

REVLON

Sara Lee
* Sanex, Ambi pur
* Just my size
* Picwick tea
* Pretty Polly
* Brylcream
* Radox, Bloom

Nestlé
* Kit Kat / Milkybar / Quality Street
* Perrier/ Vittel/ Pure Life water
* Maggi, Clusters cereal
* Nescafe Coffee
* Buitoni Pasta
* Crosse & Blackwell, Sarson's
* Carnation, Libby's

DELTA
GALIL INDUSTRIES LTD.
This Israeli company's products are
sold in the UK under the following
labels:
* Ralph Lauren
* Calvin Klein men's underwear
* Hugo Boss Clothing
* Marks & Spencer
* Gap, Hema
* Structure, Dim
* J.C.Penny, Lindex
* J.Crew, Tchibo

Full details of how each of these companies supports Israel are
available on the following web-site:
http://www.inminds.com/boycott-israel.html

BOYCOTT ISRAEL
http://www.inminds.com/boycott-israel.html

STOP SUPPORTING CHILD KILLERS

BOYCOTT ISRAEL
http://www.inminds.com/boycott-israel.html

Source: inminds.co.uk

the presence of foreign military forces on Arab lands was reminiscent of the colonial years. From the perspective of the consumer activists, adding to this bitter colonial past is a collective memory of perceived Western indifferences to Muslim suffering in Bosnia and Chechnya, not to mention the stigmatization of Muslim identity following the tragic events of 9/11 in the US and Europe (e.g., the minaret ban in Switzerland), the ensuing wars in Iraq and Afghanistan, and the Danish cartoon crisis.

Collectively, these developments are perceived as threats to Muslim identity and faith. From the cultural lenses of the cyberactivists examined in this study, MNCs with their ubiquity, immense financial power, and close ties to Western states, are viewed as the hallmarks of these threats to Islamic identity.

Cyber-ummah: forming a transnational Muslim community

Sharing the boycott discourse and paraphernalia is undoubtedly crucial for campaign success. To ensure that the boycott messages deeply resonate with the Muslim community, cyber-activists frequently borrow from the Quran and Sunnah (Prophet's practice) to urge fellow Muslims to demonstrate solidarity with the oppressed. Consider the religious referents used by the activists in the following quotes:

Our Prophet Muhammad (PBUH) was reported to have said, "The similitude of believers in regard to mutual love, affection,

fellow feeling is that of one body; when any limb of it aches, the whole body aches, because of sleeplessness and fever." In light of the above, I call you, all dear brothers and sisters to join hands with us in order to achieve our aims and to defend our main issues and primarily that of wronged and oppressed Palestine. It seems ironic and illogical that while Zionists in Israel and their supporters in the West are killing the innocent in Gaza we keep consuming the products of those aggressors and give them the price of the bullets they cold-bloodily use to kill our children in Palestine. Have our hearts turned into stone?! Have we stopped thinking?! (nosrat-sunna on Islamic-life.com)

…the Qur'an says, on the subject of trading/dealing with non-Muslims "you are not forbidden from trading fairly with those who do not seek to kill you or drive you from your lands"…well you can't say that for companies that support the occupation of Palestine, can you? So I'd question whether it's even halal [permissible] to buy from companies that support the state terrorism of Israel." (dhak1yya on ummah.com)

Interestingly, activists' highly emotional and religiously-laden language serve a more important purpose than merely summoning solidarity for the oppressed; such rhetoric latently allows consumer activists to pursue ummah, a global community of Muslims united around common causes. While the concept of ummah has been interpreted as merely a community of believers by Western scholars, Saunders (2008, 303-307) argues that ummah has political connotations as "the nation of Islamic creed" and suggests that *ummahism* is "a new form of postnational, political identity which is as profound as any extent nationalism." Indeed, this utopia of an imagined community (Anderson 1991) of Islam is reflected in the works of Islamist ideologues such as Sayyid Qutb and engrained in the leading Islamist movements' agenda (Ayoob 2008). While the Islamist organizations like Muslim Brotherhood and Jemaah Islamiah pursue ummah through political platforms and armed struggle, at the microlevel, ordinary Muslims, who want to seek this ideal and demonstrate solidarity around Muslim causes in a non-violent way, do so through boycotts and other forms of activism against transnational companies. The internet undeniably has facilitated the everyday Muslim consumers' pursuit of ummah by offering a transnational space that is relatively free of sectarian divisions and confining local power dynamics. Consider how two users utilize this space to create and sustain this utopian Muslim community through referents of imagined kinship ties in the following quotes:

In the absence of the possibility of Jihad, boycott has become in the opinions of many prestigious Muslim scholars, an obligation and not only a desirable action...boycott ...helps us to prioritize and give more importance to the issues of our *ummah* [emphasis original] and forget our selfish desires. Let us always remember the pictures of the innocent being bombed brutally by the Zionists... Let us always remember that ..., every Muslim has an obligation to support the Palestinian issue in every possible way until we free al-Madjid al-Aqsa [a Muslim holy site in Jerusalem] from the hands of the children-killing Zionists. (nosrat-sunna on Islamic-life.com)

Dear brothers and sisters - ...We urge the entire Ummah to desist from buying these "HARAM PRODUCTS" immediately. .. most of the profits from these large organizations are FUNDING The ISRAEL Military to MURDER & KILL the innocent Palestinians and ALSO to create chaos in this world. JUST Like you all made the DUTCH economy suffer by BOYCOTTING products from HOLLAND, NOW dear brothers and sisters be steadfast and committed and BOYCOTT ALL ISRAELI PRODUCTS. Dear Arab brothers, The Arab world is one of the BIGGEST MARKETS FOR THE FOLLOWING PRODUCTS: COKE, PEPSI, McDONALDS, STAR BUCKS, TOMMY HILFIGER, GIORGIO ARMANI, PERRIER WATER, JOHNSON & JOHNSON, MARKS & SPENCER, RALPH LAUREN, ARAMIS, CALVIN KLEIN, SPRITE...For the sake of your brother/sister/son/daughter/father/mother who are been [sic] SLAUGHTERED by the BLOOD THIRSTY KILLERS. PLEASE BOYCOTT NOW. !!! Please circulate this message all your contacts. (Murshid on Google Groups).

Noteworthy in the creation and performance of a virtual ummah is the role that Islamic scholars play. Among the prominent Muslim scholars is Sheikh Yousef Al-Qaradawi; his fatwas are widely circulated on Islamic forums, websites of Islamic organizations such as inminds.com, and even youtube. One of his fatwas that presents boycotting as an economic warfare encourages Muslims to unite in activism against transnational corporations by evoking the concept of ummah 18 times:

We must all be united against the aggressors. We are united in Islam, ...and also united in pain and hope. As Allah Almighty

says: "Verily this Ummah of yours is one Ummah." (Qur'an, 21:92)...Now we see our brothers and children in Al-Aqsa and the blessed land of Palestine generously sacrificing their blood, giving their souls willingly in the way of Allah...If people ask in the name of religion we must help them. The vehicle of this support is a complete boycott...The time has come for the Islamic Ummah to say "NO" to America, "NO" to its companies, and "NO" to its goods, which swamp our markets...The boycott is a demonstration of Muslim brotherhood and unity of the Ummah. It is our duty to say we are not going to betray our brothers...Our sisters and daughters, who control the houses, have a role to play in this matter, which may be more important than the role of the man, because women supervise the needs of the house, and buy what must go inside the house. She is on hand to guide the boys and girls. She... educates them in what they must do for their Ummah and its causes, ...especially in the area of boycott.

While many cyber-activists simply copy and paste the fatwa on discussion forums with no further input, it is also easy to find the fatwa's discursive motifs woven in users' personally crafted comments. For example, users allude to the notions of economic warfare and ummah as well as the role of 'sisters' or the 'fairer gender' in forging this economic crusade frequently: *"The economy is one of the major lifelines for this oppressive entity* [referring to Israel]. *Remember the Jahil* [ignorant/nonbeliever] *Quraish, with their trade routes to the north & south. The early Muslims cut the jugular of the northern markets, because the trade caravans had to pass Medina. It was this series of raids that led to the Jahil Quraish being bled white, thus curtailing their growing threat. As much as we are reasonably able, let us boycott the apartheid state & her major supporters. Even if it stops just one bullet being fired into the skull of a defenceless babe in arms on her way to school. Let's hit them where it hurts i.e. in the pocket! ... I know that the majority of the day to day household supplies are purchased by the female gender. It is important that the fairer gender is educated & made aware of their how the defence of the Ummah is in their hands as well...I feel it is incumbent on the more educated & aware of the fairer gender to gently proffer the pro-Ummah advice to their less aware peers."* (Ashfaq Bahman on hansot.com). Bibi's comments on onislam.net also resounds the discursive motifs of Sheikh's fatwa: *"Mothers, as you lovingly bathe your babies with Johnson & Johnson products, think of the Palestinian babies who died from Israeli bullets — courtesy of J & J, who support Israel. Next time we pop a Nestle's candy in our mouth, let us savor the taste of the pain of those who are oppressed by Israel, of those whose land was taken from them, of those who will never taste the olives they so lovingly grew.....It's important we don't ever forget. It's easy to become complacent and be seduced by the consumerist culture. Let this be our jihad. Let us strive in our efforts to speak out against oppression. Let us not fail in our duty toward our brothers and sisters. Let us boycott Israel."*

As these examples demonstrate, cyber-activism is a means through which Muslims seek the imagined community of ummah. This quest for ummah can be more comprehensively understood as an exercise to reconfigure Islamic identity in light of modernization in the post-colonial era. In the years following independence, the modernization movements in Muslim majority countries like Turkey, Iran, and Egypt, led by a small, authoritarian, and pro-Western elite class left the Islamic identity sidelined to a great extent in the nation formation process. Most notably, the abolishment of the Caliphate (religious and political leader of all Muslims) institution marked the dissolution of the ummah, which had traditionally represented a united Islamic society under the former Ottoman Empire. Losing their 'righteous' leader, seeing the erosion of ummah, falling behind Western powers in science and technology, and witnessing the incapacity of local regimes in finding a dignifying solution to the Palestinian conflict left the pious believing that they have fallen from grace for swaying away from Islam's path. Islamist movements' rhetoric of justice that promised to end Muslim suffering in the hands of 'infidel' powers, to reclaim Muslim dignity, and to revive the ummah fueled the perception that Islam was on assault, particularly among the economically disadvantaged and those discontent with the local regimes. Such sentiments were even more intense among the European Muslims who had difficulties assimilating to the host country and yearned for connecting with the ummah (Saunders 2008). This quest gained urgency as a crisis for unity among Muslims erupted post 9/11.

It is in this socio-historical context that many Muslims seek the ummah through the new platforms made possible by information and communication technologies. For many Muslims who do not want to associate with political or militant Islamist movements, waging a cyber-jihad against multinational brands through a rhetoric laden with religious ideology is the ideal means to forge an Islamic identity and connect with fellow Muslims on a global scale. Boycott websites and forums do not only provide a common cause around which a community of believers can be formed, but also offer a nonviolent and convenient form of ideological resistance, allowing users to create a space for Islamic identity and politics.

DISCUSSION

This study examines Islamic consumer activism at the nexus of religious ideology and new media. The findings suggest that the quest for a transnational community, coupled with the discursive construction of MNCs as icons of economic and social injustice, propels a cyber-jihad against transnational brands. Jihad, while generally associated with Islamist fanaticism, also means spiritual rejuvenation and self-defense (Ayoob 2008). In this sense, the cyber-jihad is an economic and non-violent means of asserting Islamic values and identity in the marketplace. These findings offer several interesting theoretical implications.

First of all, the study highlights the important role that religious discourse and authorities play as market-structuring forces. While prior studies have addressed how various ideologies motivate consumer activism (Varman and Belk 2009), the role of religious ideology in shaping consumption goals and brand attitudes has not been examined before. The findings indicate that transnational brands, which are perhaps the most conspicuous symbols of the secular, easily can get tangled in global webs of ideological conflicts and can be enwrapped in religious rhetoric to be construed as tyrants by consumer activists. The role of religious authorities such as Islamic scholars in this ideological construction of global brands is also noteworthy; sheiks and the fatwas they disseminate through the internet are instrumental in framing MNCs and Islamic activism as tyrants and a religious duty to defend sacrosanct values, respectively. In this sense, religious authorities represent a unique type of authority and market structuring force that previous consumer research literature has not sufficiently explored.

Secondly, this study contributes to our understanding of brands as symbolic devices by demonstrating the role that shared brand meanings inadvertently play in the formation of consumer identity projects and communities (Askegaard 2006; Cayla and Eckhardt 2008; Holt 2002; Muniz and O'Guinn 2001; Muñiz Jr. and Schau 2005). The cyber-jihad Muslim consumers discursively wage against tyrant brands facilitates virtual activists' assertion of a pan-Islamic

identity on a global scale. Moreover, cyber-activism allows these consumers to seek and perform a transnational community of Muslims. While this pursuit of ummah is similar to the postmodern quest for communal affiliation that has been addressed in detail in previous studies (Muniz and O'Guinn 2001; Muñiz Jr. and Schau 2005), it is important to note a few nuances. The ummah forged through cyber-activism against global brands, unlike other brand or anti-brand communities, is founded on a shared religious identity and ideological aspirations of Islam. As such, unlike the postmodern brand communities or evanescent hypercommunities, membership in the cyber-ummah cannot be established in an ad hoc fashion (Kozinets 2002; McAlexander, Schouten, and Koenig 2002; Muniz and O'Guinn 2001), purchased (Thompson and Coskuner-Balli 2007), or easily terminated. Future research should explore whether these types of market-mediated communities, in which religious identity is a sine qua non, are more effective in transforming the policies and practices of MNCs than other brand (anti-brand) communities.

The limitations of this study offer opportunities for future research. First, the study focuses on cyber-discourses of Islamic activism, however, to what extent, if any, these consumers practice the boycott remains unexplored. Also, non-boycotters views may not be equally represented in the forums since counter-boycott comments are effectively rebuffed and such commentators are stigmatized as "sinners" or "traitors" by fervent cyber-activists.

REFERENCES

Anderson, Benedict R. O'G (1991), *Imagined Communities : Reflections on the Origin and Spread of Nationalism*, London ; New York: Verso.

Askegaard, Søren (2006), "Brands as a Global Ideoscape," in *Brand Culture*, ed. Jonathan Schroeder and Miriam Salzer-Mörling, NY: Routledge.

Ayoob, Mohammed (2008), *The Many Faces of Political Islam : Religion and Politics in the Muslim World*, Ann Arbor: University of Michigan Press.

Cayla, Julien and Giana M. Eckhardt (2008), "Asian Brands and the Shaping of a Transnational Imagined Community," *Journal of Consumer Research*, 35 (2), 216-30.

Cohen, Lizabeth (2003), *A Consumer's Republic : The Politics of Mass Consumption in Postwar America*, New York: Knopf.

Connolly, John and Andrea Prothero (2008), "Green Consumption," *Journal of Consumer Culture*, 8 (1), 117-45.

Crockett, David and Melanie Wallendorf (2004), "The Role of Normative Political Ideology in Consumer Behavior," *Journal of Consumer Research*, 31 (3), 511-28.

Dobscha, Susan and Julie L. Ozanne (2001), "An Ecofeminist Analysis of Environmentally Sensitive Women Using Qualitative Methodology: The Emancipatory Potential of an Ecological Life," *Journal of Public Policy and Marketing*, 20 (2), 201-14.

Eickelman, Dale F. and Jon W. Anderson, eds. (2003), *New Media in the Muslim World: The Emerging Public Sphere*, Bloomington, IN: Indiana University Press.

Friedman, Monroe (1985), "Consumer Boycotts in the United States, 1970–1980: Contemporary Events in Historical Perspective," *Journal of Consumer Affairs*, 19 (1), 96-117.

--- (1999), *Consumer Boycotts: Effecting Change through the Marketplace and the Media*, New York: Psychology Press.

Handelman, Jay M. (1999), "Culture Jamming: Expanding the Application of the Critical Research Project," in *Advances in Consumer Research*, Vol. 26, ed. Eric J. Arnould and Linda M. Scott, Provo, UT: Association for Consumer Research, 399-404.

Hogg, Margaret K., Emma N. Banister, and Christopher A. Stephenson (2009), "Mapping Symbolic (Anti-) Consumption," *Journal of Business Research*, 62 (2), 148-59.

Hollenbeck, Candice R. and George M. Zinkhan (2010), "Anti-Brand Communities, Negotiation of Brand Meaning, and the Learning Process: The Case of Wal-Mart," *Consumption Markets & Culture*, 13 (3), 325-45.

Holt, Douglas B. (2002), "Why Do Brands Cause Trouble? A Dialectical Theory of Consumer Culture and Branding," *Journal of Consumer Research*, 29 (1), 70-90.

Izberk-Bilgin, Elif (2012a), "Infidel Brands: Unveiling Alternative Meanings of Global Brands at the Nexus of Globalization, Consumer Culture, and Islamism," *Journal of Consumer Research*, forthcoming.

--- (2012b), "Theology Meets the Marketplace: The Discursive Formation of the Halal Market in Turkey," in *Consumption and Spirituality*, ed. Diego Rinallo, Linda Scott and Pauline Maclaran, London: Routledge.

Jensen, Hans Rask (2008), "The Mohammed Cartoons Controversy and the Boycott of Danish Products in the Middle East," *European Business Review*, 20 (3), 275-89.

Jevtic, Jana (2009), "Global Muslim Boycott of Mncs as a Method of Economic Weakening of Israel," International Relations and European Studies, Central European University, Budapest, Hungary.

Klein, Jill Gabrielle , N. Craig Smith, and Andrew John (2004), "Why We Boycott: Consumer Motivations for Boycott Participation," *Journal of Marketing*, 68 (3), 92-109.

Klein, Jill Gabrielle, Richard Ettenson, and Marlene D. Morris (1998), "The Animosity Model of Foreign Product Purchase: An Empirical Test in the People's Republic of China," *Journal of Marketing*, 62 (1), 89-100.

Knudsen, Kjell , Praveen Aggarwal, and Ahmed Maamoun (2008), "The Burden of Identity: Responding to Product Boycotts in the Middle East," *Journal Of Business & Economics Research*, 6 (11), 17-25.

Kozinets, Robert V. (2002), "Can Consumers Escape the Market? Emancipatory Illuminations from Burning Man," *Journal of Consumer Research*, 29 (1), 20-38.

--- (2010), *Netnography: Doing Ethnographic Research Online*, Thousand Oaks, California: Sage Publications.

Kozinets, Robert V. and Jay M. Handelman (2004), "Adversaries of Consumption: Consumer Movements, Activism, and Ideology," *Journal of Consumer Research*, 31 (3), 691-704.

Lee, Michael (2007), "Brands We Love to Hate: An Exploration of Brand Avoidance," Dissertation, University of Auckland.

Luedicke, Marius K., Craig J. Thompson, and Markus Giesler (2010), "Consumer Identity Work as Moral Protagonism: How Myth and Ideology Animate a Brand-Mediated Moral Conflict," *Journal of Consumer Research*, 36 (6), 1016-32.

McAlexander, James H., John W. Schouten, and Harold F. Koenig (2002), "Building Brand Community " *Journal of Marketing*, 66 (1), 38-54.

Micheletti, Michele, Andreas Føllesdal, and Dietlind Stolle, eds. (2004), *Politics, Products, and Markets: Exploring Political Consumerism Past and Present*, New Jersey: Transaction Publishers.

Muniz, Jr., Albert M. and Thomas C. O'Guinn (2001), "Brand Community," *Journal of Consumer Research*, 27 (4), 412-32.

Muñiz Jr., Albert M. and Hope Jensen Schau (2005), "Religiosity in the Abandoned Apple Newton Brand Community," *Journal of Consumer Research*, 31 (4), 737-47.

Oncu, Ayse (1995), "Packaging Islam: Cultural Politics on the Landscape of Turkish Commercial Television.," *Public Culture*, 8 (1), 51-71.

Penaloza, Lisa and Linda L. Price (1993), "Consumer Resistance: A Conceptual Overview," in *Advances in Consumer Research*, Vol. 20, ed. Leigh McAlister and Michael L. Rothschild, Provo, UT: Association for Consumer Research, 123-28.

Pink, Johanna, ed. (2009), *Muslim Societies in the Age of Mass Consumption*, Newcastle upon Tyne: Cambridge Scholars Publishing.

Press, Melea and Eric J. Arnould (2011), "Legitimating Community Supported Agriculture through American Pastoralist Ideology," *Journal of Consumer Culture*, 11 (2), 168-94.

Pruitt, Stephen W. and Monroe Friedman (1986), "Determining the Effectiveness of Consumer Boycotts: A Stock Price Analysis of Their Impact on Corporate Targets," *Journal of Consumer Policy*, 9 (4), 375-87.

Ritzer, George (1983), "The "Mcdonaldization" of Society," *Journal of American Culture*, 6 (1), 100-07.

Roy, Olivier (1994), *The Failure of Political Islam*, Cambridge, Mass.: Harvard University Press.

Rudnyckyj, Daromir (2009), "Market Islam in Indonesia," *Journal of the Royal Anthropological Institute*, 15, S183-S201.

Sandikci, Özlem and Güliz Ger (2010), "Veiling in Style: How Does a Stigmatized Practice Become Fashionable?," *Journal of Consumer Research*, 37 (1), 15-36.

Sassatelli, Roberta and Federica Davolio (2010), "Consumption, Pleasure and Politics," *Journal of Consumer Culture*, 10 (2), 202-32.

Saunders, Robert A. (2008), "The Ummah as Nation: A Reappraisal in the Wake of the 'Cartoons Affair'," *Nations and Nationalism*, 14 (2), 303-21.

Simon, Bryant (2011), "Not Going to Starbucks: Boycotts and the out-Scouring of Politics in the Branded World," *Journal of Consumer Culture*, 11 (2), 145-67.

Thompson, Craig J. (2003), "Natural Health Discourses and the Therapeutic Production of Consumer Resistance," *The Sociological Quarterly*, 44 (1), 81-107.

Thompson, Craig J. (2004), "Marketplace Mythology and Discourses of Power," *Journal of Consumer Research*, 31 (1), 162-80.

Thompson, Craig J. and Gokcen Coskuner-Balli (2007), "Countervailing Market Responses to Corporate Co-Optation and the Ideological Recruitment of Consumption Communities," *Journal of Consumer Research*, 34 (2), 135-52.

Varman, Rohit and Russell W. Belk (2009), "Nationalism and Ideology in an Anticonsumption Movement," *Journal of Consumer Research*, 36 (4), 686-700.

Wong, Loong (2007), "Market Cultures, the Middle Classes and Islam: Consuming the Market?," *Consumption Markets & Culture*, 10 (4), 451 - 80.

How Do Social Capital-Driven Consumption Communities Conceal Their Economic Interests?

Katharina C. Husemann, University of Innsbruck, Austria

ABSTRACT

Consumption communities face the challenge of dealing with economic influences while staying true to their community values. Building on Bourdieu's theory of capital, this interpretive study addresses the intersection of social and economic capital production within social capital-driven consumption communities. The study explores the concealment strategies that consumers use to protect their communities from contamination through economic influences. Drawing on two data sources, the study reveals four distinct concealment strategies–from total denial, through re-articulation and partial appropriation, to teleological alignment–that differ to the degree to which consumers conceal economic capital production within the community. The study contributes new theoretical insights into consumers' concealment strategies and documents how pursuing these strategies allows social capital-driven consumption communities for incorporating economic activities under the primacy of social capital production.

INTRODUCTION

Social capital is a key notion in consumer culture theory. Social capital concerns "the aggregate of the actual or potential resources which are linked to (…) membership in a group" (Bourdieu 1986, 248). Consumer researchers have used this influential notion to illuminate for instance, how brand community members build social capital as part of their value-creating practices (Schau, Muñiz, and Arnould 2009), how virtual problem-solving community members produce social capital on both individual and group levels (Mathwick, Wiertz, and Ruyter 2008), or how subcultural consumers defend their field-dependent social capital against pejorative stereotypes (Arsel and Thompson 2011).

For Bourdieu (1986), individuals build social capital by establishing, maintaining, and defending long-term social relations and mutual obligations with their social peers. One particular characteristic of social capital is that it is a "disguised" (252) form of economic capital that paradoxically produces its most influential effects to the extent to which it hides economic roots. Therefore, for individuals to build social capital requires proactive 'concealment' of potential economic calculations. How does this concealment of economic activities work for consumption communities such as brand communities (Muniz and O'Guinn 2001) and subcultures of consumption (Schouten and McAlexander 1995) that draw their consumer appeal predominantly from social (rather than economic) exchanges? Which (if any) concealment strategies do members of these social capital-driven consumption communities use to protect the 'innocence' of their social relations.

Prior consumer research has occasionally addressed the intersection of social and economic production within consumption communities. Bonsu and Darmody (2008), for instance, find the rhetoric of "well-intentioned commercialism" (363) which Second Life residents use to justify commercial success. Kozinets (2002a) documents anti-market strategies such as the reinforcement of a "No Vending Rule" (24) within the Burning Man community. In the context of community-supported agriculture (CSA), Thompson and Coskuner-Balli (2007) report on consumers who defy "commodity fetishism" (142) through "practices of decommodification" (142) as a response to corporate co-optation. And Weinberger and Wallendorf (2012) explain how intracommunity gifting serves the post-Katrina New Orleans' community to rebuff undesired commercial influences.

These studies have produced important insights into the intersection of social and economic capital production in consumer research. However, prior research has not yet systematically addressed the strategies through which consumers' conceal potential economic activities within social-capital driven consumption communities.

To address this gap in knowledge and to reveal a comprehensive range of concealment strategies within social capital-driven consumption communities, I conducted an interpretive study drawing on two data sources. The first data set consists of netnographic data (Kozinets 2002b) from two social capital-driven online communities–the outdoorseiten.net community (www.outdoorseiten.net) and the veganelinke.antispe community (www.veganelinke.antispe.org). The second data set consists of eight academic articles that explicitly or implicitly address the intersection of social and economic capital production within consumption communities. I analyzed these data using a qualitative content analysis (Mayring 2002), through which I inductively built and iteratively refined categories of how these communities conceal economic influences (aspects of economic capital production such as self-interest, profit maximization, competition, private ownership, or wage labor (see also Bourdieu 1986)).

The study reveals four concealment strategies that social capital-driven consumption communities tend to use when confronted with economic capital production. I differentiate the strategies by the degree to which consumers conceal economic capital production– from total denial, through re-articulation and partial appropriation, to teleological alignment.

To best reveal these findings, I first review the notion of social capital in sociology and existing consumer research studies that directly address the intersection of social and economic capital within social capital-driven consumption communities. Then, I present a set of four concealment strategies and show how consumers use these strategies to manage economic capital production within the confines of their communities. Finally, I discuss these theoretical insights and conclude with outlining paths for future research.

THEORY ON SOCIAL CAPITAL

Bourdieu (1986) offers the first and most deliberate analysis of social capital. For him, social capital is "the aggregate of the actual or potential resources which are linked to (…) membership in a group" (Bourdieu 1986, 248). In contrast to other forms of capital (e.g. economic or human) social capital possesses an intangible character that resonates in structures of relationships (Bourdieu 1986; Coleman 1988; Portes 1998). Consequently, social capital is an influential asset that individuals accumulate through continuous investments in relationships to family, friends and associates (Putnam and Goss 2001; Woolcock and Narayan 2000). For Bourdieu (1986), individuals build social capital by establishing, maintaining, and defending long-term social relations and mutual obligations with their social peers. Social capital investments are associated with a high degree of uncertainty because of indefinite obligations, vague time horizons, and the potential danger of ingratitude or noncompliance to reciprocity expectations (e.g. exchanges of gifts or mutual visits) (Bourdieu 1986).

However, according to Bourdieu (1986), the notion of social capital, its inner structure and way of functioning is inseparable from that of economic capital. Economic capital "is immediately and directly convertible into money" (monetary capital) (Bourdieu 1986, 243). Economic theory has devoted itself to this (one-sided) interpretation of capital which constrains the universe of exchanges to commercial exchanges. Thus, today, economic capital is the most obvious and direct form of capital characterized by capitalist tenets such as self-interest, profit maximization, competition, private ownership, or wage labor (Bourdieu 1986).

Despite the ostensible independence between social and economic capital, Bourdieu systematically elaborates on the interplay between economic and social exchanges in appropriating capital. For Bourdieu (1986), all forms of capital, including economic, social and cultural, must be understood as "accumulated labor" (241). Thus, both forms of capital are highly related–even transferable into each other. Social capital, for instance, is converted into economic capital when members of a social network gain privileged access to special investment-tips or job offers by making use of previously established social obligations. Transferability is due to one particular characteristic of social capital–it is a "disguised" (Bourdieu 1986, 252) form of economic capital. Paradoxically, social capital produces its most influential effects only to the extent that it conceals its economic roots.

Although Bourdieu (1986) addresses the significance of 'concealment' in the accumulation social capital, he does not fully address how this dynamic unfolds.

CONSUMER RESEARCH ON THE INTERSECTION OF SOCIAL AND ECONOMIC CAPITAL WITHIN CONSUMPTION COMMUNITIES

Consumption community research also sheds a theoretical light on the intersection of social and economic capital, but with a focus on communal rhetorics and practices that protect the community from contamination through economic influences. Investigating the Web-based virtual world of Second Life, for instance, Bonsu and Darmody (2008) find evidence of residents that "traverse communal and commercial boundaries" (364) when they turn a communal idea of creating animal avatars into a commercial success story. However, facing the mingling of community-driven ideas and commercial agendas, Second Life residents frame commercial success as a communal enrichment. Bonsu and Darmody (2008) mark these rhetorical efforts as "well-intentioned commercialism" (363).

Kozinets (2002a) investigates the Burning Man festival, a community-oriented anti-market event which is specifically designed to offer participants a social space that is distanced from market logics. Burning Man's gift economy, the "No Vending Rule" (24) and the prohibition of brand names are illustrative mechanisms of how the Burning Man community frames the event as uncommercial. Although Kozinets concludes that the Burning Man community still "materially supports the market" (20), the set of communal-resistive practices and rhetorics demonstrates participants' perception of commercialism and economic exchanges as contaminating threat within the community.

Similarly, participants of the CSA market niche interpret commercialism, capitalist motifs, and modern "commodity fetishism" (Thompson and Coskuner-Balli 2007, 142) as threats that have the potential to pollute consumers' sacred alternative market system. Thus, CSA farmers and consumers jointly strive for controlling the commercial nature of their food products through decommodification practices which relate CSA food to "symbol[s] of natural splendor and ecological harmony" (142).

Weinberger and Wallendorf's (2012) multi-layered analysis within the context of the Mardi Gras festival reveals how intracommunity gifting serves the post-Katrina New Orleans' community to rebuff undesired commercial influences. The authors detail how post-Katrina New Orleans's geographic community repaves

the damaged "intersection of moral and market economies" (77) through traditional practices of intracommunity gifting. In particular they show how moral economy logics either harness or reject market economy logics in intracommunity gifting, depending on the giver's local cultural knowledge and community membership. The study reveals that commercial sponsorship–only to certain moral confines–is legitimated within communal boundaries.

Taken together, these studies suggest that the relationship between social and economic capital production is an important and delicate one for consumption communities. These consumption communities draw their appeal from social capital production (i.e. building relationships, pursuing social exchanges, freely sharing knowledge) and–to different degrees–from their denial of economic capital production. As the above authors show, consumers put much effort in protecting the community from contamination through economic influences. Seen through the lens of Bourdieuian capital theory, the appeal of such social capital-driven consumption communities largely thrives on the members' ability to conceal present and emerging economic interests and thus remain 'purely' social entities.

However, despite these important insights into the intersection of social and economic capital production in consumption communities, consumer researchers have not yet systematically explored the full range of consumers' concealment strategies–representing a potentially relevant endeavor for community perpetuation.

METHOD

This interpretive study draws on two data sources. The first data set comprises empirical data from an netnographic investigation (Kozinets 2002b) of two social capital-driven online communities - the outdoorseiten.net community (www.outdoorseiten.net) and the veganelinke.antispe community (www.veganelike.antispe.org). Online communities offer "a novel medium for social exchange between consumers" (Kozinets 2002b, 63) and allow unobtrusive access to consumers' discursive and interactive encounters at the intersections of social and economic capital production. Pursuing the goal of revealing a comprehensive range of communities' concealment strategies and assuming that online consumption communities with diverse (political-ideological) backgrounds might react differently to economic capital production, I searched for communities that have potentially divergent political orientations, but evolve particularly around social rather than exchanges.

The outdoorseiten.net community and the veganelinke.antispe community have different fields of interest and community goals, however, they both draw their appeal from social exchanges to experience and consume a "linking value" (Cova 1997, 297). Outdoorseiten.net has its roots in 1999 and since then the community has developed into a 20.000-member flourishing online community. It exhibits passionate discussions about nature, outdoor sports, and advances an independent and creative outdoor consumption. This community provides a fascinating environment to study the range of concealment strategies which consumers use to respond to economic influences since the community shows elements of both economic and social capital production. On the one hand, community members are engaged in testing commercial outdoor equipment, in jointly innovating and branding products; On the other hand, community members feel inspired by their social, communal network and their independence from corporate influence (Füller, Lüdicke, and Jawecki 2008). Veganelinke.antispe's 1,300 members are motivated to fighting capitalism. Since 2006, this forum has offered a dialogue platform for community members who discuss progressive movements against all sorts of oppressions such as capitalism, sexism, racism or speciesism. The official anti-capitalist orientation of the veganelinke.antispe community promises a fascinating context to study consumers' strategies to conceal economic influences.

Data collection within the online communities proceeded through screening and observing the fora's archives and resulted in a data set of 4.008 posts from 47 threads. I particularly included those discussions in which community members were confronted with aspects of economic capital (i.e. self-interest, profit maximization, competition, private ownership, or wage labor).

The second data set consists of eight published academic articles. These articles, explicitly or implicitly, deal with the intersection of social and economic capital production within consumption communities. Consumers within these communities primarily draw their appeal from social rather than economic exchanges. With the exception of Bonsu and Darmody (2008) all articles were published in the Journal of Consumer Research (Giesler 2008; Kozinets 2001, 2002a; Mathwick et al. 2008; Schouten and McAlexander 1995; Thompson and Coskuner-Balli 2007; Weinberger and Wallendorf 2012). The combination of empirical netnographic data and data from journal articles provided fruitful grounds to reveal consumers' concealment strategies within consumption communities.

I analyzed these two data sources using a qualitative content analysis (Mayring 2002). I identified concealment strategies through isolating consumers' efforts to conceal economic influences within social capital-driven consumption communities. These influences refer to (aspects of) economic capital production such as self-interest, profit maximization, competition, private ownership, or wage labor (see also Bourdieu 1986). I moved back and forth between the two data sets and exposed the inductively emerging categories (concealment strategies) to iterative refinement.

FINDINGS

Four focal concealment strategies emerge from my analysis. I differentiate these strategies with respect to the degree to which consumption communities conceal economic capital production. The degree of concealment varies according to consumers' level of refusal and legitimization of economic influences within the community. Figure 1 summarizes the findings followed by a detailed description of each concealment strategy.

Concealment Strategy One: Denial of Economic Capital Production

The strategy of denial of economic capital production is the most direct form of concealment. Community members use this strategy to demonize economic capital production and rhetorically frame corporate players as "industrial monsters" (Giesler 2008, 747) or legal community owners as "demigods" or "wizards" (Bonsu and Darmody 2008, 362). In my data, community members use three expressions of denial: 1) Actively repelling economic capital production; 2) waiting until the (economic) turbulence passes by; and 3) relocating the community into a new, uncontaminated realm.

Actively Repelling Economic Capital Production. The outdoorseiten.net community actively repels the capitalization of a community project in which community members plan, organize, and design the construction of an outdoor-cooker. The project starts out without any economic agenda. However, when individual community members suggest the idea of cooperating with a commercial investor to sell the outdoor-cooker to the mass market, an emotional discussion emerged. Does the community betray its spirit when converting a community project into profit-opportunities? The initiator of the outdoor-cooker project finally holds an arousing plea for the social benefits of the project to the community.

> *„I proposed a project herein, because of the idea of producing a low-priced and improved product that is currently not available in the market. And because I was convinced of the fact that one could even make this project better through challenging a community of enthusiast to develop a perfect product. With all the accumulated know-how and the ideas of a creative community…Beyond this original idea I had the idea that the community would profit from this product too: more members (product would serve as a promoter externally), more reputation for the community, more ideas… and so on and so on…Why do I write this? Because I perceive the idea of this project is endangered."* (community member, outdoorseiten.net)

The initiator perceives the commercialization of the communal project as a threat ("endangered") to the community. Finally, the community refuses capitalizing on the marketability of an improved outdoor-product and thus actively repels economic capital production. The community upholds the primacy of social capital production and community spirit, and consequently, conceals economic

Figure 1: Concealment Continuum

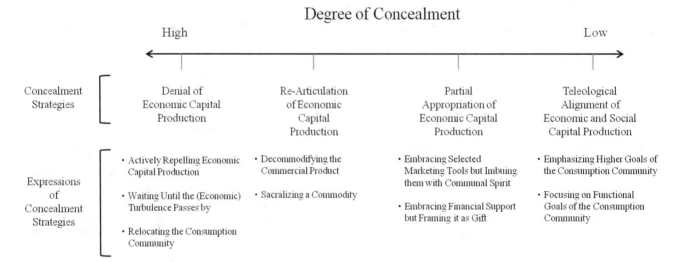

capital production. In a more general tone, community members of the veganelinke.antispe community debate the possibilities of how to consume best in an exploitative capitalist system. In favor of social capital production within and beyond the confines of their community, participants propose to actively repel economic capital production of cooperations through boycotting.

> *"For sure, our togetherness is improvable and as long as it is improvable I strive for improvements. I make a small contribution through my consumer behavior and boycotts."* (community member, veganelinke.antispe)

Similarly, Giesler (2008), Bonsu and Darmody (2008), Mathwick et al. (2008), Kozinets (2001, 2002a) and Schouten and McAlexander (1995) report on communities actively repelling economic capital production.

Waiting Until the (Economic) Turbulence Passes by. Community members that wait until the (economic) turbulence passes by practice a less aggressive expression of the concealment strategy of denial of economic capital production. In his investigation of the war on music downloading in which downloaders and representatives of the music industry negotiate the price of music downloads, Giesler (2008) introduces the notion of "outpeacing" (747) as a graceful exercise of passive consumer resistance. A similar form of concealment appears within the Second Life community. Bonsu and Darmody (2008) report on the prevailing inequality and hierarchical structures between the regular residents ("creative consumer masses" (362)) and the Lindens (corporate owner) of the virtual platform.

> *"Even though they [the residents] recognized this inequality in the world, many residents pointed to the fluid nature of this structure, believing that it was only a matter of time before the tables turned in their favor"* (Bonsu and Darmody 2008, 362).

Again, community members appear suspicious about economic influences within their community and perceive corporate power as contaminating. However, the community does not deny economic capital production by actively resisting the economic influence, but by sitting it out peacefully.

Relocating the Consumption Community. A third expression of denying economic capital production implies the relocation of the consumption community into a new, uncontaminated realm. The case of community-supported (CSA) agriculture investigated by Thompson and Coskuner-Balli (2007) serves as the most illustrative example. Agents of the originally anticorporate organic food movement respond to the economic contamination of corporate co-optation through relocating the communal realm of social capital production into a new CSA market–an "emotionally and existentially engaging communal project" (Thompson and Coskuner Balli 2007, 139). Similar to idea of relocating a consumption community into a pure social realm, community members in the veganelinke. antispe community discuss the idea of moving to and living on self-sufficient farms in an attempt to escape from capitalist market exchanges. Patterns of relocation emerge in Kozinets' (2002a) Burning Man festival which can be read as a community-oriented anti-market event, staged remote from civilization, specifically designed to offer participants a social space that is distanced from market logics.

Concealment Strategy Two: Re-Articulation of Economic Capital Production

Second, community members using the strategy of re-articulation of economic capital production also perceive economic influences as threat to the community. Yet, consumers do not repel, but rhetorically re-articulate aspects of economic capital production that are indirectly supportive of community members' interests and morals. Consumers re-articulate external service providers or commodities by 1) decommodifying them as artisan, creative or performative, or 2) sacralizing them through endowing it with transcendent meaning.

Decommodifying the Commercial Product. Decommodifying commodities constitutes a well-known practice in consumer research (Wallendorf and Arnould 1991). Members of the outdoorseiten.net community, for instance, decommodify commercial products as artisan. Some members are particularly enthusiast about Mr. Geiger, a manufacturer of hand-crafted hiking boots. Although Mr. Geiger is a regular participant in the marketplace, community members portray him as a do-gooder and artisan that manufactures genuine and sensually superior hiking boots.

> *"Something is notably nice: The man who is producing your shoes individually customizes them. He looks at your feet and you directly feel that he has lots of experience. He does not want a quick deal, but he wants to do his trade how he thinks that it is right. It is an adventure to meet someone like him these days."* (community member, outdoorseiten.net)

Community members refer to Mr. Geiger as an "artist" who takes his artistic license to create and improve details of his handmade hiking boots. In associating commercial commodities with arts, outdoorseiten.net community members deny market-players' commercial interest and conceal the transactions' economic character. Thus, community members prevent the community from economic contamination. Among the consumption communities analyzed patterns of decommodification are prevailing (Bonsu and Darmody 2008; Giesler 2008; Kozinets 2002a; Thompson and Coskuner-Balli 2007; Weinberger and Wallendorf 2012).

Sacralizing a Commodity. Sacralizing a product or service is a second expression of re-articulating economic capital production. Members of the Star Trek subculture, for example, identify with the anticapitalist nature of the Star Trek universe and appreciate its "utopian sense of the communalism" (Kozinets 2001, 72). However, the Star Trek universe is part of a multi-million dollar industry and Star Trek fen constitute active participants. In response to this overwhelming economic irritation which is, in effect, an inherent component of Star Treks subculture's existence, participants engage is sacralizing practices by framing Star Trek rhetorically as a religion. Kozinets (2001) reveals:

> *"Legitimizing articulations of Star Trek as a religion or myth underscore fans' heavy investment of self in the text. These sacralizing articulations are used to distance the text from its superficial status as a commercial product."*(Kozinets 2001, 67)

Kozinets' analysis of consumers that read Star Trek as religion or myth involves the idea of concealing an economic agenda that threatens to contaminate Star Treks subcultural "moral and inclusive community" (82). Members of the Harley-Davidson subculture of consumption are similarly engaged in sacralizing efforts as a response to economic influences.

Concealment Strategy Three: Partial Appropriation of Economic Capital Production

Consumers using the concealment strategy of partial appropriation of economic capital production deliberately embrace 1) selected marketing tools or 2) financial support to leverage their social capital production. Community members do not use tools and support unreflectedly, but take both out of their initial economic context and imbue them with communal spirit to conceal economic influences.

Embracing Selected Marketing Tools but Imbuing them with Communal Spirit. Consumption communities appropriate economic capital production through embracing and adjusting selected marketing tools. For instance, the outdoorseiten.net community organizes community competitions such as "best travel report", "wiki writing competition", and "best photo competition" or pursues a project in which community members design and create a community logo. Thus, the outdoorseiten.net community makes use of basic tools that are closely related to economic capital production, but appropriate them for the cohesive needs of their community. The playful competitions and logo development processes encourage social exchanges and foster bondings among community members. Following vignette from the logo development threat shows how community members within the outdoorseiten.net conceal the logo's economic character through imbuing it with communal spirit.

> *"Hm, everything is initiated from users. Nonone is making profit with the logo batches; it is something that is done by and for the community. It is just nice when the forum is showed to the world."* (community member, outdoorseiten.net)

The community does not conceal economic capital production in general as it draws on its equipment, however, community members cover the tools' inherent economic character and revitalize them with a social agenda. The embracement and adjustment of selected economic tools is empirically supported in the veganelinke.antispe community in which community members similarly discuss and organize the order of community stickers.

Embracing Financial Support but Framing it as Gift. Embracing financial support but framing it as gift constitutes a second expression of the strategy of partial appropriation of economic capital production. Communities take advantage of group members' financial resources accumulated in the external commercial market. Community members accept this economic encroachment in form of financial resources but rhetorically frame the financial support as gifts from insiders which provide opportunities to encourage social capital production. Thus, internal agents with financial resources, although strongly involved with commercialism, do not contaminate community. For instance, Kozinets (2002) reports on impressive art installations at the Burning Man festival which are essentially gifts from participating artists to the community:

> *"My fieldnotes capture a fireside conversation with "Giovanni Maximi," an artist (a millionaire businessman in his life outside Burning Man), late one evening... It is worthwhile to note that, as indicated by Giovanni's personal wealth, status at Burning Man is often constructed from conditions requiring considerable economic standing in the outside commercial realm".* (Kozinets 2002a, 28-29)

Empirical support of this concealment strategy can be found in Weinberger and Wallendorf's (2012) investigation of the Mardi Gras geographic community in which rich krewe members give - officially noncommercial - parades to the community. These gifts, although sponsored through crew members' real-life commercial involvements are not considered as stemming from the logic of economic capital production.

Concealment Strategy Four: Teleological Alignment of Economic and Social Capital Production

The strategy of teleological alignment of economic and social capital production shows the least degree of concealment. In these cases, community members show how certain economic activities are useful for relevant community goals and consequently for community perpetuation. Community members conceal detrimental side effects of such economic activities by 1) emphasizing the higher goals that they support (e.g. survival of the community) or by 2) focusing on functional goals (e.g. testing outdoor-material). Thus, the community conceals the flaring up of economic capital production through justifying it with a mutual goal-orientation.

Emphasizing Higher Goals of the Consumption Community. One expression of teleological alignment of economic and social capital production revolves around community members' effort to emphasize higher goals of the community. Goals are, for instance, the survival of the community or the maintenance of the community as a vibrant, inspiring and emotionally attracting space. If economic activities assist in accomplishing these goals, community members seem to refrain from framing them as threat. For instance, after Hurricane Katrina had destroyed parts of New Orleans in 2005, a public discussion emerged whether to hold or to skip the traditional Mardi Gras celebration that was set few month after the catastrophe. Local community members, personally strongly involved with the rituals and inherent meanings of the celebration, but generally skeptical towards commercial influences within the Mardi Gras, use the logic of social and economic capital to argue for the realization (survival) of the Mardi Gras communal festival:

> *"[Mardi Gras] is essential for the spirit of New Orleans, because..."* *"Plus it pumps a lot of money into the economy, which they need. A lot of jobs, all the people who build the floats and make the costumes, and sell all the junk you throw."* (Weinberger and Wallendorf 2012, 88)

Bonsu and Darmody (2008, 363) use the notion of "well-intentioned commercialism" to capture Second Life residents' rhetorical efforts to legitimize commercial success. Similarly, Burning Man participants justify high ticket fees through its contribution to the "good of the Burning Man community" (Kozintes 2002, 20).

Focusing on Functional Goals of the Consumption Community. Communities conceal economic capital production through teleologically aligning it with social capital production when they legitimize economic capital production efforts with functional goals of the community. They legitimize and even welcome the aspects economic capital production to the extent that it helps to reach functional goals of the community. For instance, members of the veganelinke.antispe community support an advertising campaign that follows the logic of economic capital production. However, community members conceal this economic influence by focusing on functional goals of the community–to spread the idea of vegan life and equality between humans and animals.

> *„United Creations has created a really interesting and professional advertisement campaign, together with the Austrian vegan society. The basic idea is that not all people that eat vegan live according to clichés."* (community member, veganeline. antispe)

Interestingly, the limits of unmolested concealment appear exhausted within the confines of this community. Some community members start reflecting on the campaign and complain about its lack of criticism on capitalism. Members of the outdoorseiten.net community who are primarily engaged in discussing, testing, and improving outdoor products appear to positively evaluate the fact that profit-driven outdoor manufacturers might read their test reports. Community members perceive themselves as outdoor experts and being used by corporate manufactures as "beta tester" is a meaningful step toward the goal of creating improved outdoor products.

DISCUSSION

This study illuminates the strategies that consumers in social capital-driven consumption communities use to manage the intersection of social and economic capital production. Grounded in Bourdieu's (1986) notion of capital, I investigated how these consumption communities face the challenge of dealing with economic influences while staying true to their community values.

The study contributes three insights to consumer (culture) theory. First, this research uncovers a set of four concealment strategies that social capital-driven consumption communities tend to use when confronted with economic capital production. These strategies range from total denial of economic capital production, through re-articulation and partial appropriation of economic capital production, to teleological alignment of economic and social capital production. Each concealment strategy manifests through different expressions, and differentiates to the degree to which consumers conceal economic influences. The degree of concealment varies according to consumers' level of refusal and legitimization of economic capital production within their community.

This comprehensive range of four concealment strategies integrates prior findings of consumption community research dealing with the intersection of social and economic capital production. For instance, the "No Vending Rule" (Kozinets 2002a, 24) within the Burning Man community is an illustration of the first, most direct, concealment strategy. This official rule can be read as an institutionalized mechanism that helps the community to actively repel economic capital production. CSA participants that are jointly engaged in rhetorically decommodifying CSA food products (Thompson and Coskuner-Balli 2007) make use of the strategy of re-articulation of economic capital to conceal the market niche's commercial nature. And "well-intentioned commercialism" (Bonsu and Darmody 2008, 363), which serves Second Life residents to justify commercial success, illustrates the concealment strategy of teleological alignment of economic and social capital production.

Two expressions of the isolated concealment strategies emerged exclusively from empirical netnographic data. First, social capital-driven communities embrace selected marketing tools such as playful competitions or creative logo development processes, imbue those with a communal spirit, and thus leverage the community's social capital production. Second, social capital-driven consumption communities legitimize aspects of economic capital production to the extent that it helps the community to reach functional goals (e.g. spreading the word of vegan life, testing outdoor material, etc.).

Although this study proposes a first step towards a comprehensive range of concealment strategies, depending on the context, other social capital-driven consumption communities might use slightly different strategies (or expressions). Locating the strategies on a concealment continuum implies the potential existence of further concealment strategies that differ in the degree to which communities conceal economic influences.

Second, this research contributes consumption-specific empirical evidence to Bourdieu's (1986) theory of concealment of social capital. The diversity of four concealment strategies exhibiting multiple degrees of concealment suggests that concealment is a more nuanced concept than previously assumed.

Third, the study empirically supports the idea that concealment is one focal strategy for managing social capital-driven consumption communities' various interfaces with economic capital production. Building on Bourdieu (1986), the study shows that social capital-driven consumption communities conceal economic capital production through moving back and forth between repelling and–to certain extents–legitimizing economic capital. Thus, the study suggests that engaging these concealment strategies allows consumption communities for incorporating economic influences under the primacy of social capital production–yielding a potentially important dynamic for community perpetuation.

To conclude, these insights are of particular interest for Western society that is said to suffer from a loss of community spirit (Putnam and Goss 2001). The pluralization of lifestyles and attitudes available within society hampers a joint value creation among people. Thus, Western society faces the danger of social dissolution (Dubiel 1998; Heitmeyer 2004; Putnam and Goss 2001). However, societal cohesions (or 'social capital'), solidarity, community spirit, and the ability to build community are central resources of healthy societies (Weidenfeld 2001). This study implies that cohesive forces still permeate Western society. But today, social capital might prevail in micro socio-cultural spaces such as (online) consumption communities and might comprise potentially new consumption-specific dynamics such as the necessity of concealing economic capital production on behalf of community perpetuation. Future research should address these new consumption-specific aspects of social capital production–conceding potentially relevant insights into the social glue of Western society.

REFERENCES

Arsel, Zeynep and Craig J. Thompson (2011), "Demythologizing Consumption Practices: How Consumers Protect Their Field-Dependent Identity Investments from Devaluing Marketplace Myths," *Journal of Consumer Research*, 37 (February), 791-806.

Bonsu, Samuel K. and Aron Darmody (2008), "Co-Creating Second Life: Market–Consumer Cooperation in Contemporary Economy," *Journal of Macromarketing*, 28 (December), 355-68.

Bourdieu, Pierre (1986), "The Forms of Capital," in *Handbook of Theory: Research for the Sociology of Education*, ed. John Richardson, New York: Greenwood, 241–58.

Coleman, James S. (1988), "Social Capital in the Creation of Human Capital," *American Journal of Sociology*, 94 (Supplement), 95-120.

Cova, Bernard (1997), "Community and Consumption: Towards a Definition of the 'Linking Value' of Product or Services," *European Journal of Marketing*, 31 (3/4), 297-316.

Dubiel, Helmut (1998), "Cultivated Conflicts," *Political Theory*, 26 (2), 209-20.

Füller, Johann, Marius K. Lüdicke, and Gregor Jawecki (2007), "How Brands Enchant: Insights from Observing Community Driven Brand Creation" in *Annual North American Conference*, ed. Association for Consumer Research, Memphis, USA.

Giesler, Markus (2008), "Conflict and Compromise: Drama in Marketplace Evolution," *Journal of Consumer Research*, 34 (April), 739-53.

Heitmeyer, Wilhelm (2004), „Einleitung: Auf dem Weg in eine Desintegrierte Gesellschaft," in *Was Treibt Die Gesellschaft Auseinander?*, Vol. 6, ed. Wilhelm Heitmeyer, Frankfurt am Main: Suhrkamp, 9-26.

Kozinets, Robert V. (2001), "Utopian Enterprise: Articulating the Meanings of Star Trek's Culture of Consumption," *Journal of Consumer Research*, 28 (June), 67-88.

_____ (2002a), "Can Consumers Escape the Market? Emancipatory Illuminations from Burning Man," *Journal of Consumer Research*, 29 (June), 20-38.

_____ (2002b), "The Field Behind the Screen: Using Netnography for Marketing Research in Online Communities," *Journal of Marketing Research*, 39 (1), 61-72.

Mathwick, Charla, Caroline Wiertz, and Ko D. Ruyter (2008), "Social Capital Production in a Virtual P3 Community," *Journal of Consumer Research*, 34 (April), 832-49.

Mayring, Philipp (2002), *Einführung in die Qualitative Sozialforschung: Eine Anleitung zu Qualitativem Denken*, Vol. 5, Weinheim: Beltz.

Muniz, Albert M. Jr. and Thomas C. O'Guinn (2001), "Brand Community," *Journal of Consumer Research*, 27 (March), 412-29.

Portes, Alejandro (1998), "Social Capital: Its Origins and Applications in Modern Sociology," *Annual Review of Sociology*, 24, 1-24.

Putnam, Robert D. and Kristin A. Goss (2001), „Einleitung," in Gesellschaft Und Gemeinsinn: Sozialkapital Im Internationalen Vergleich, ed. Robert D. Putnam, Gütersloh: Bertelsmann Stiftung, 15-44.

Schau, Hope J., Albert M. Muñiz, and Eric J. Arnould (2009), "How Brand Community Practices Create Value," *Journal of Marketing*, 73 (September), 30-51.

Schouten, John W. and James H. McAlexander (1995), "Subcultures of Consumption: An Ethnography of the New Bikers," *Journal of Consumer Research*, 22 (June), 43-61.

Thompson, Craig J. and Gokcen Coskuner-Balli (2007), "Countervailing Market Responses to Corporate Co-Optation and the Ideological Recruitment of Consumption Communities," *Journal of Consumer Research*, 34 (August), 135-52.

Wallendorf, Melanie and Eric J. Arnould (1991), "'We Gather Together': Consumption Rituals of Thanksgiving Day," *Journal of Consumer Research*, 18 (June), 13-31.

Weidenfeld, Werner (2001), „Vorwort," in *Gesellschaft und Gemeinsinn: Sozialkapital im Internationalen Vergleich*, ed. Putnam Robert D., Gütersloh: Bertelsmann Stiftung, 11-14.

Weinberger, Michelle F. and Melanie Wallendorf (2012), "Intracommunity Gifting at the Intersection of Contemporary Moral and Market Economies," *Journal of Consumer Research*, 39 (June), 74-92.

Woolcock, Michael and Deepa Narayan (2000), "Social Capital: Implications for Development Theory, Research, and Policy," *The World Bank Research Observer*, 15 (August), 225-49.

The Effect of Dual Anchors on Numeric Judgments: The Moderating Effects of Anchor Order and Domain Knowledge

Devon DelVecchio, Miami University, USA
Timothy B. Heath, HEC Paris, France

ABSTRACT

Anchoring is typically forwarded to explain how available numeric instances alter beliefs. The anchoring literature typically focuses on exposure to either single anchors or lengthy numeric sequences. We fill in the gap between single-anchor and large-series studies by assessing the effect of dual anchors on target judgments. We do so since individuals are often exposed to two numeric representations from a domain and the features of dual anchors and, in turn, likely processing of associated information, differ from the features of both single-anchor and longer-sequence anchor scenarios. Results of Experiment 1 indicate the low-knowledge participants exhibit a recency effect in which estimates are lower when a high anchor is presented first than when a low anchor is first. Conversely, high-knowledge participants display a primacy effect as estimates are higher when a high anchor is presented first than when a low anchor is first. Experiment 2, indicates that the effects of target knowledge on anchor order are moderated by anchor extremity. Practical advice for managers as they consider how they communicate dual pieces of numeric information such prices or attributes is offered.

THE EFFECT OF DUAL ANCHORS ON NUMERIC JUDGMENTS

Anchoring (Tversky and Kahneman 1974) is the process that is typically forwarded to explain how available numeric instances alter beliefs. Anchoring holds that numeric estimates are assimilated toward available anchors. A classic example of the anchoring effect is the estimation task employed by Tversky and Kahneman (1974) which asked participants to estimate the number of African nations in the United Nations. Prior to providing their estimates, participants were informed that a randomly generated estimate suggests that the number is either 10% or 65% (manipulated between subjects). Participants who were exposed to the 10% anchor estimated the percentage of African nations in the UN to be 25% while participants who were exposed to the 65% anchor estimated that 45% of African nations are in the UN. The effect of single numeric anchors on target estimates has been widely studied. Results across domains such as height, age, and temperature judgments (Mussweiler and Strack 1999; Wegner, Petty, Detweiler-Bedell, and Jarvis 2001), product purchase decisions (Wansink, Kent, and Hoch 1998), and real estate valuation (Northcraft and Neale 1987) consistently demonstrate that a numeric anchor influences numerical judgments toward the anchor (see Ku, Gallinsky, and Murnnghan 2006 for an exception).

As is the case with the United Nations example above, much of the anchoring literature focuses on exposure to a single anchor. Single exposures to a numeric instance of a domain are frequently encountered. For instance, a motorist may be exposed to several domain-specific individual instances of numeric domains. For instance, when driving a motorist may pass a single speed limit sign, take one glance at the speed readout on the speedometer, or notice one price for gas. Lengthy numeric series are also frequently encountered. For instance, the same driver may be exposed to a series of street addresses, speed limits, or gas prices. Similarly, shoppers observe many prices while shopping in any grocery category. Investors are exposed to stock returns over a number days, quarters, and years. Sports tickers inform fans of the scores of dozens of games. Fittingly, the effect of numeric sequences on subsequent target judg-

ments has also been widely explored. Research across contexts such as pricing (Monroe 1971, Janiszewski and Lichtenstein, 1999; Niedrich, Sharma, and Wedell, 2001), exam scores (Wedell, Parducci, and Roman 1989), gambling options (Lim 1995), and salary allocations (Mellers 1986) has studied the effect of exposure to fairly lengthy numerical sequences (e.g., sequences of ten or more numerical occurrences) on subsequent target judgments. The results of this research stream indicate that judgments following exposure to numeric sequences are a function of the range, median, mode, and order of the sequence.

The frequency with which numbers are encountered decreases nearly monotonically from one (Dehaene and Mehler 1992). That is, the most frequently written and verbally stated number is one, followed by two, and three, etc. Similarly, the frequency with which a domain-specific anchor series are encountered is likely a monotonically decreasing from zero. Given the mind-boggling array of domains in the world, most people are likely to go unexposed to most numeric target objects. People are next most likely to be exposed to a single numeric instance in a domain, followed by two instances, etc. We attempt to fill in a gap in extant literature, a gap between single-anchor studies and large series studies, by studying the effect of dual anchors. We do so due to a) the likelihood that individuals are, relatively speaking, often exposed to two numeric representations from a domain and b) the fact that the features of dual anchors and, in turn, likely processing of associated information, differ from the features of both single-anchor and longer-sequence-anchor scenarios. Assuming dual anchors are not of the same numerical value (e.g., that a person is not given two sources both estimating the number of African countries in the UN at 30%), dual-anchor scenarios differ from single-anchor scenarios in terms offering higher and a lower anchor values that may be conveyed in two orders. Dual anchor situations differ from longer numerical sequences in that instance frequency and sequence mode are not relevant and that any one anchor is likely to carry greater weight thereby magnifying order effects.

LITERATURE REVIEW AND HYPOTHESIS DEVELOPMENT

Despite their differences, the process by which single anchors affect such judgments sheds light on how dual anchors will likely affect numeric judgments. Evidence indicates that anchors affect target judgments via a selective accessibility process in which anchors prime anchor-consistent knowledge that is subsequently used to form the target judgment (e.g., Mussweiler and Strack 1999; Strack and Mussweiler 1997). Thus, an anchor that suggests that 65% of African nations are in the UN may prompt thoughts of relatively large African Nations (South Africa, Egypt) and the role of such nations in international relations – information that is consistent with the high anchor. However, while this process explains reactions to a single anchor, perhaps of greater import when considering dual anchors is the relative effect of each anchor. On one hand, accessibility of information that is consistent with the first anchor may suppress access to information that is consistent with the second anchor. In such a case, judgments will be more aligned with the first of the two anchors and a primacy effect will emerge. Conversely, if information consistent with the second anchor is accessed, judgments should be

Advances in Consumer Research
Volume 40, ©2012

more aligned with this information and judgments should reflect the second anchor value thereby demonstrating a recency effect.

Research on the order in which non-numeric arguments are presented (e.g., Haugtvedt and Wegener 1994; Lana 1961, 1963) provides further insight into how dual numeric anchors will be processed. Such research assesses how individuals integrate conflicting written arguments into attitude structures. For instance, participants may see arguments in favor and against topics such as senior comprehensive exams for college students, nuclear power, or animal experimentation. As an example, Haugtvedt and Wegener (1994) manipulated argument valence for senior exams via statements such as "students graduating from schools with comprehensive exams were more likely to be accepted into very good graduate schools" and "capturing the benefits of a four-year program on a single standardized exam would be difficult." This line of research indicates that the effect of the order of conflicting arguments is a function of an individual's motivation and ability to elaborate on the arguments. When individuals are able and motivated to process message arguments, a primacy effect emerges (Haugtvedt and Wegener 1994; Lana 1961, 1963). This primacy effect is driven by elaboration of the initial message in the form of greater message consistent thinking. In turn, greater integration of the message into existing schema occurs, resulting in greater attitude change toward the initial argument, and subsequent attitude resistance to the conflicting second argument presented (Haugtvedt and Wegener 1994). This process is consistent with selective accessibility. When motivated to process the initial message, participants accessed argument-consistent information that swayed attitudes toward the argument and insulated the attitude from subsequent counter argumentation.

When less able and/or motivated to process arguments, a recency effect emerges (Haugtvedt and Wegener 1994; Lana 1961, 1963). The recency effect is driven by the lack of elaboration in response to the initial argument leading to weak attitudes. In turn, when prompted to indicate an attitude toward the focal object, reliance on available information (i.e., the second argument) biases attitudes toward the latter of the two arguments presented (Haugtvedt and Wegener 1994).

The results described above lead to the question of what will determine people's anchor elaboration. Although many factors may affect anchor elaboration, we focus on target knowledge for two reasons. First, as opposed to environmental factors such as time constraints, the issue of the respondent's knowledge is omnipresent in responses to anchors. Second, as evidenced by the title of one of the first articles on the anchoring heuristic ("Judgment under Uncertainly: Heuristics and Biases"), the anchoring phenomena explains judgment under uncertainty (Tversky and Kahneman, 1974). The level of uncertainty surrounding a numeric judgment task will depend on the level of knowledge of the target object of the individual making the estimate. In some instances, people will have complete knowledge and thus no uncertainty. For instance, exposure to an anchor or multiple anchors is unlikely to have a significant effect on judgments of one's own age. Conversely, someone with some, but less than perfect, knowledge will have anchor-consistent aspects of that knowledge primed and demonstrate a bias toward the anchor. Although even experts in a domain may exhibit anchoring effects when primed with domain specific anchors (e.g., Joyce and Biddle 1981; Northcraft and Neal 1987), consistent with the role of knowledge in determining uncertainty, knowledge has been shown to affect anchor-driven judgments such that greater knowledge (i.e., less uncertainty) is associated with smaller anchor effects (Mussweiler and Strack 1999).

The selective accessibility and elaboration-based accounts of dual anchors hold that initial exposure to the first anchor may prompt recall of anchor-consistent information that reinforces the anchor's legitimacy. For instance, when asked to estimate the number of students at the University of Rhode Island, someone exposed to a high anchor may access knowledge of the general size of flagship state schools, past basketball successes for the University, and noted alumni (e.g., Christian Amanpour, Lamar Odom). One the other hand, someone exposed to a low anchor may consider the diminutive size of the state, that URI's football team competes at the FCS level (a level below the top level of competition), and that the basketball team is in a conference with relatively small schools. Assuming the two anchors are fairly discrepant, but not so discrepant as for one or both to be summarily dismissed, a scenario we refer to as low anchor extremity, generating anchor-consistent thoughts in response to the first anchor should interfere with generating thoughts that are consistent with the second anchor. As a result, dual-anchors should be subject to a primacy effect in which the first anchor has a stronger effect on numeric estimates than does the second anchor. However, this expectation assumes that the respondent has anchor-consistent knowledge to be primed by the first anchor. For people with little knowledge of the target object, elaboration is unlikely and the second anchor should carry more weight simply due to its more recent encoding. Thus, the effect of dual anchors on target estimates will be a function of anchor order and target knowledge such that responses to dual anchors will demonstrate a primacy effect when target knowledge is high and a recency effect when target knowledge is low.

Hypothesis 1: Target estimates following exposure to dual anchors of low extremity will demonstrate a primacy effect when target knowledge is high and a recency effect when target knowledge is low.

Given evidence that estimates display a greater anchoring effect in single anchor contexts when target knowledge is low than when it is high suggest the same might hold in a dual anchor scenario. If so, estimates of low-knowledge targets should display an overall greater anchoring effect than those of high-knowledge targets. As formalize in H2, a stronger anchoring effect for low-knowledge targets would result in estimates for such targets reflecting a larger recency effect than the corresponding primacy effect arising for high-knowledge targets.

Hypothesis 2: Target estimates following exposure to dual anchors of low extremity will demonstrate a greater recency effect when target knowledge is low than they will demonstrate a primacy effect when target knowledge is high.

Hypothesis 1 in founded upon the expected effect of target knowledge on individuals' ability to access anchor-consistent knowledge in response to anchors that are of low extremity. Knowledge should also affect individuals' perceptions of anchors as the anchors become more extreme. When subjected to a numeric judgment task, individuals access a mental model of the range of plausible responses (Epley and Gilvich 2006; Mussweiler and Strack 2000; Quattrone et al. 1981). When an anchor is within the range of plausibility, respondents engage in the anchor-consistent accessibility process described above and, in turn, bias judgments toward the anchor. Conversely, anchors outside the range of plausibility are either ignored or met with counter-argumentation (Mussweiler and Strack 2000). As a result, more extreme anchors often produce less of an anchoring effect than do less extreme anchors (e.g., Bochner and Inkso; Mussweiler and Strack 2000; Wegener et al. 2001).

Individuals with high target knowledge should produce a less variant range of plausible responses. As such, the likelihood that a given anchor value is judged to be outside the range of plausibility decreases. Thus, despite having more anchor-consistent knowledge to access, the likelihood that knowledgeable respondents access such knowledge decreases as anchor extremity increase. In turn, the failure to access anchor consistent information will mitigate the effect of extreme anchors. Conversely, individuals with lower knowledge of the target object will lack the ability to discern that an anchor is implausible and thus should produce more extreme target estimates in response to extreme anchors than in response to less extreme anchors. H3 reflects the resulting interaction between anchor extremity, anchor order, and target knowledge.

Hypothesis 3:   *Extreme anchor values a) attenuate dual-anchor order effects when target knowledge is high and b) magnify dual-anchor order effects when target knowledge is low.*

EXPERIMENT 1

Method

Experiment 1 is designed to test the effects of dual anchors across targets about which individuals have lower- and higher-knowledge (i.e., Hypotheses 1 and 2). Such a test may be undertaken in many ways. For instance, existing knowledge of a single target object can be measured or knowledge about the object may be imbued. In Experiment 1, we selected a pair of objects about which knowledge among the sample population differs. More specifically, the target objects are a pair of universities. The universities were selected via a pretest with participants (n = 25) from the same subject pool used to recruit subjects for Experiment 1. The pretest asked students to estimate the size of several universities and indicate their confidence that their estimate is within 20% of the actual enrollment. Confidence was measured on a one-to-ten scale in which 1 = not at all confident, 5 = moderately confident, and 10 = very confident. The two universities chosen as a result of the pretest are the university in which the participants are enrolled and the university of Rhode Island. The two universities differed as intended with respect to confidence with mean confidence of 2.64 for the University of Rhode Island and 8.52 for the participants' home university (t = 17.38, p < .001). Further, the pretest indicates that the two universities are perceived to be generally of the same size (Rhode Island mean = 14,100, home university mean = 15,483, t = 0.96, p > .30).

Experiment 1 called for participants (78 undergraduate students at a mid-sized Midwestern university) to estimate the number of students enrolled at either the high-knowledge target (i.e., the students' home university) or the low-knowledge target (i.e., University of Rhode Island) university. Experiment 1 features a 2 (anchor order – low first, high first) x 2 (target knowledge – low, high) design. Participants completed Experiment 2 via pencil and paper. On the cover page, participants were first informed of the general estimation task, and that to help them with the task, they would be provided two randomly selected estimates of student enrollment provided by students attending the target university. On the next page, participants were informed of the identity of the target university and were exposed to the first anchor. Participants then advanced to the second anchor. The low anchor was 13,600 and the high anchor was 18,400, values that are minus and plus 15% of a 16,000 midpoint. After viewing the

second anchor, participants advanced to a page that asked them to provide their estimate of the enrollment at the target university.

Results

Two focal estimates were in excess of three standard deviations of the mean and were removed from the analysis. ANOVA results of the remaining 76 data points Consistent with H1, a significant knowledge by anchor order interaction emerged (F(1,75) = 5.15, p < .05). As can be seen in Figure 1, when the low anchor is presented first, estimates do not differ across the high- and low-knowledge targets (F(1,35) = 0.78, p > .35). When the high anchor is presented first, estimates are higher when target knowledge is high and lower when target knowledge is low (F(1,38) = 10.16, p < .01); an outcome indicative of a recency effect when target knowledge is low and a primacy effect when target knowledge is high.

Figure 1
Target Estimates in Experiment 1

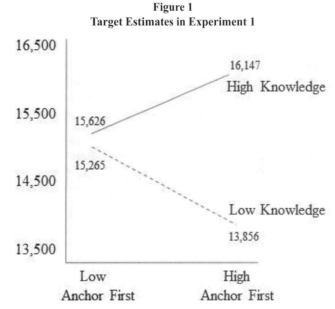

To test Hypothesis 2 we consider whether the change across anchor order conditions is greater for the lower-knowledge target than for the higher-knowledge target. Specifically, we created a variable that reflects the strength of anchor effect by subtracting the mean estimate in the high-knowledge, low anchor first task (M = 15,626) from participants' estimates of the high knowledge, high anchor first condition and by subtracting the mean estimate of the low-knowledge, high anchor first target (13,856) from participants' estimates of the low knowledge, low anchor first condition. While the result is directionally consistent with the belief that low-knowledge targets will be associated with greater differences across order conditions (M = 1439) than will high-knowledge targets (M = 521) the difference is not statistically significant (F(1,38) = 1.63, p > .20).

Discussion

Experiment 1 offers support for the belief that the effect of anchor order differentially affects estimates as a function of individuals' target knowledge. As noted, this hypothesis was based on the individuals assessing anchors that are of low extremity. Study 2 is designed to test the effect of more extreme anchors and the specific relationships between anchor order, target knowledge, and anchor extremity hypothesized in H3.

EXPERIMENT 2

Method

In Experiment 2, forty-four undergraduate students at a mid-sized Midwestern university provided estimates for nine target objects drawn from world events (states won by Barrack Obama in the 2008 election, deaths in the Mumbai terrorist attacks, closing Dow Jones average), pop culture (Grady Sizemore's career homerun total, number of Madonna studio albums, number of players in the World Series of Poker), and pricing (Honda Accord EL base price per honda.com, 8GB iPod Nano price on apple.com, 1.7 oz Obsession by Calvin Klein perfume price on calvinklein.com) domains. Anchor order (low first, high first) and anchor extremity (low, high) were randomized across questions. Question order was randomized across respondents. Anchor extremity was manipulated by varying the anchor distances from the correct response by either plus or minus 15% (low extremity, consistent with Study 1) or plus or minus 30% (high extremity). For example, anchor values for the number of homeruns hit by Grady Sizemore, who had hit 129 homeruns at the time of the study, were 110 and 148 in the low extremity condition and 90 and 168 in the high extremity condition.

The general method of Experiment 2 follows that of Experiment 1 except that anchors were supposedly the estimates of other students enrolled at the participants' university and participants responded to a set of four items measuring their subjective knowledge of the target objects (*alpha* = .854). The knowledge questions, which were tailored to each target object, asked participants the extent to which they a) know more about the topic than most people, b) know more about the topic than most students at their university, c) attend to the general domain (e.g., pop music, US politics, poker), and d) attend to the specific target object (e.g., Madonna, the 2008 election, the World Series of Poker).

Focal estimates were normed to the center of the anchor range (i.e., the actual value of the focal question). For instance, an estimate that is 5% above (below) the actual target value was coded as 1.05 (0.95). The effects of anchor order, anchor consistency, and target knowledge (median split) on normed estimates were assessed via mixed model ANOVA with the estimation task as a repeated factor.

Results

The mixed model ANOVA results indicate a significant three-way interaction between knowledge, anchor order, and anchor extremity ($F(1, 356) = 5.78, p < .05$). We investigate the nature of this relationship in two ways. First, looking at the data associated with the low anchor extremity condition allows us to retest Hypotheses 1 and 2. When anchors are less extreme, a significant anchor order by knowledge interaction emerges ($F(1, 93) = 12.11, p < .01$, see Figure 2). Consistent with H1, the form of the interaction is such that presenting the low anchor first is associated with higher estimates for lower-knowledge targets and lower estimates for higher-knowledge targets ($F(1, 21) = 5.41, p < .05$). This pattern reverses when the high anchor is presented first ($F(1, 62) = 7.40, p < .01$). Thus, in the case of low anchor extremity, estimates of low-knowledge targets display a recency effect while estimates of high- knowledge targets display a primacy effect.

Figure 2
Normed Target Estimates in the
Low Extremity Condition of Experiment 2

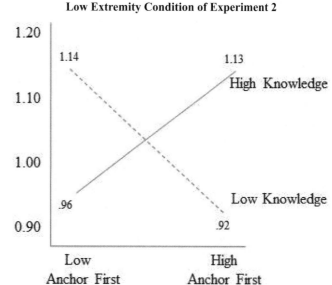

Value reflect estimates normed against the actual target value (e.g., an estimate 5% above the actual target value is coded as 1.05)

As with Study 1, we assess the possibility that the anchoring effects observed in the low extremity conditions of Study 2 are greater for low-knowledge than for high-knowledge targets (i.e., is the 0.22 difference across anchor orders in for low-knowledge targets greater than the .17 difference across anchor orders in the high-knowledge target?). Estimates were transformed as in Study 1 to form a measure of relative anchor strength. Subsequent mixed model ANOVA provides support for H2 as the difference in estimates across order conditions is greater for low-knowledge targets than for high-knowledge targets at $p < 001$ ($F(1,45) = 21.50$).

Testing Hypotheses 3 calls the inspection of estimates across levels of anchor extremity. As displayed in Figure 3, when target knowledge is high, anchor order and extremity interact ($F(1, 167) = 5.27, p < .05$). The form of the interaction is such that a primacy effect emerges for high-knowledge targets when there is low ($F(1, 45) = 6.89, p < .05$), but not high ($F(1, 54) = 0.22$), anchor extremity. This is consistent with H3a's prediction that anchor extremity will mitigate the effect of anchor order when target knowledge is high. For low-knowledge targets, there is a non-significant trend toward a recency effect in the low-extremity anchor condition that reverses toward a primacy effect for high-extremity anchors ($F(1,148) = 1.80, p > .15$). This outcome is inconsistent with H3b's prediction that greater anchor extremity will magnify the effect of anchor order when target knowledge is low. Thus, H3 is partially supported.

Figure 3
Normed Target Estimates in Experiment 2

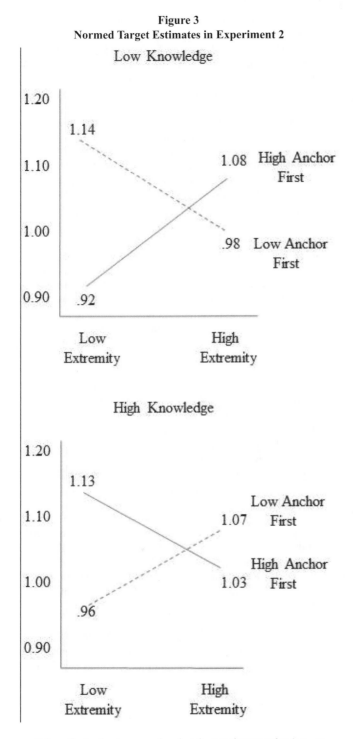

Value reflect estimates normed against the actual target value (e.g., an estimate 5% above the actual target value is coded as 1.05)

Discussion

This research advances knowledge of general anchoring effects by evaluating the specific context of dual anchors. Some of the results add confirming evidence to existing beliefs regarding anchoring in general that arise from single anchor studies. For instance, that anchors differentially affect people of greater and lesser knowledge has been established (e.g., Mussweiler and Strack 1999). This research adds to this research by demonstrating that, in the context of dual outcomes, the difference in reactions to anchors across lower- and higher-knowledge contexts is one driven by the relative weight

placed on the first versus the second anchor. Specifically, the results of the two experiments support the notion that anchors of moderate extremity exhibit a primacy effect when target knowledge is high, but a recency effect when target knowledge is low. The possibility that the recency effect associated with low-knowledge targets is stronger than the primacy effect observed for low-knowledge tasks received directional support in Study 1 and statistical support in Study 2.

Within a marketing context, consumers are often exposed to, and marketers can often control the order of, dual anchors. For instance, regular and sale prices may be conveyed in either order as can attributes such as highway and city miles per gallon. This research indicates that managers must consider their audience when ordering dual prices or numeric attributes. This suggests, for instance, that a retailer may reinforce the perception of low prices among its regular (high knowledge) customers by conveying sales prices before regular prices (i.e. "$2.99 was $4.09"). Conversely, an automobile company or salesperson would want to convey the lower city miles per gallon before the higher highway MPG when talking to an inexperienced car buyer. When in doubt, the possibility that anchor effects are stronger for lower-knowledge targets suggests erring on the side of presenting the less attractive numeric value first.

Limitations and Future Research

The effects of anchor order and anchor extremity were held to arise due to different levels of anchor elaboration across high- and low-knowledge targets. Although this is derived from existing research (e.g., Haugtvedt and Wegener 1994; Lana 1961, 1963), this process was not tested directly. This represents a theoretical limitation and the opportunity for additional research. In particular, one issue that arises from the current results that can benefit from process measurement involves the failure to find support for H3b. H3b hypothesized that more extreme anchors would magnify order effects when target knowledge is low. This expectation was based on the assumptions that (1) more extreme anchors would be viewed as falling within the bounds of reason when target knowledge is low, but (2) not be subject to diligent elaboration. The reason for the observed failure to support this hypothesis, which could be a function of a failure of either or both of the underlying assumptions, might be tested with process measures such as thought-listing tasks. Similarly, future research may want to investigate potential differences across targets low vs. high in need for cognition given that these groups have been found to differ in the care with which they process numerical information (Chatterjee et al. 2000). Moderation from need-for-cognition would be consistent with an elaboration-based explanation of H3b's failure, but a lack of moderation would be consistent with a perceptual explanation.

While providing an initial look at basic effect of anchor order across lower- and higher-knowledge targets, this research tests only one additional moderator, anchor extremity, and this moderator was assessed at only two levels. Regarding anchor extremity, just as a more extreme anchor mitigated order effects, so too could less extreme anchors. For instance, anchors of +/-5% of the actual target could be interpreted as indicators of agreement and precision.

From a marketer's perspective, research has explored how consumer responses to numeric information are affected by framing the information as percentages versus raw numbers (e.g., DelVecchio, Krishnan, and Smith 2007), as round versus sharp numbers (e.g., King and Janiszewski 2011), and as gains versus losses (e.g., Heath, Chatterjee, and France 1995). Each of these could moderate the extent to which the extremity and order of dual anchors affect target judgments. For instance, employing dual anchors in percentage terms (e.g., save 20% as opposed to save $2.00) or in sharp numbers (e.g., save $2.07 as opposed to save $2.00) makes the numeric information harder to interoperate. Greater difficulty in processing may mitigate elaboration and, in turn, magnify the effect of the second anchor. Similarly, potential gains may be scrutinized less than potential losses thereby exacerbating the effect of the second anchor value when dual anchors are framed as gains. Research on such moderators of dual anchor effects and the processes by which they occur is merited.

REFERENCES

Chatterjee, Subimal, Timothy B. Heath, Sandra J. Milberg, and Karen R. France (2000), "The Differential Processing of Price in Gains and Losses: The Effect of Frame and Need for Cognition," *Journal of Behavioral Decision Making,* 13 (1), 61-75.

DelVecchio, Devon, H. Shanker Krishnan, and Daniel C. Smith (2007), "Cents or Percent? The Effects of Promotion Framing on Price Expectations and Choice," *Journal of Marketing,* 71 (July), 158-70.

Dehaene, Stanislas and Jacques Mehler, (1992), "Cross-Linguistic Regularities in the Frequency of Number Words," *Cognition,* 43 (1), 1-29.

Epley, Nicholas and Thomas Gilovich (2006), "The Anchoring-and-Adjustment Heuristic: Why the Adjustments Are Insufficient," *Psychological Science,* 17 (April), 311-318.

Haugtvedt, Curtis P. and Duane P. Wegener (1994), "Message Order Effects in Persuasion: An Attitude Strength Perspective," *Journal of Consumer Research,* 21 (June), 205-218.

Heath, Timothy B., Subimal Chatterjee, and Karen Russo France (1995), "Mental Accounting and Changes in Price: The Frame Dependence of Reference Dependence," *Journal of Consumer Research,* 22 (1), 90-97.

Janiszewski, Chris and Donald R. Lichtenstein (1999), "A Range Theory Account of Price Perception", *Journal of Consumer Research,* 25 (March), 353-368.

Edward J. Joyce, and Gary C. Biddle (1981), "Anchoring and Adjustment in Probabilistic Inference in Auditing," *Journal of Accounting Research,* 19 (Spring), 120-145.

Kahneman, Daniel and Amos Tversky (1979), "Prospect Theory: An Analysis of Decision Under Risk", *Econometrica,* 47 (March), 263-291.

King, Dan and Chris Janiszewski (2011), "The Sources and Consequences of the Fluent Processing of Numbers," *Journal of Marketing Research,* 48 (2), 327-41.

Lim, Rodney G., (1995), "A Range-frequency Explanation of Shifting Reference Points in Risky Decision Making," *Organizational Behavior and Human Decision Processes,* 63 (July), 6-20.

Neyman, J. (1977), "Frequentist Probability and Frequentist Statistics", *Synthese,* 36 (September), 97-131.

Northcraft, Gregory B. and Margaret A. Neal (1987), "Experts, Amateurs, and Real Estate: An Anchoring and Adjustment Perspective on Property Pricing Decisions," *Organizational Behavior and Human Decision Processes,* 39 (February), 84-97.

Mellers, Barbara A. (1986), "'Fair' Allocations of Salaries and Taxes," *Journal of Experimental Psychology: Human Perception and Performance,* 12 (February), 80-91.

Monroe, Kent B. (1971), "Measuring Price Thresholds by Psychophysics and Lattitudes of Acceptance," *Journal of Marketing Research,* 8 (November), 460–64.

Mussweiler, Thomas and Fritz Strack (1999), "Hypothesis-Consistent Testing and Semantic Priming in the Anchoring Paradigm: A Slective Accessibility Model," *Journal of Experimental Social Psychology,* 35 (March), 136-164.

Mussweiler, Thomas and Fritz Strack (2000), "Numeric Estimates under Uncertainty: The Role of Knowledge in Anchoring," *Journal of Experimental Social Psychology,* 36 (September), 495-518.

Niedrich, R. W., Sharma, S., and Wedell, D. H. (2001), "Reference Price and Price Perceptions: A Comparison of Alternative Models", *Journal of Consumer Research,* 28 (December), 339-354.

Parducci, Allen (1965), "Category Judgment: A Range-frequency Model", *Psychological Review,* 72 (November), 407-418.

Strack, Fritz and Thomas Mussweiler (1997), "Explaining the Enigmatic Anchoring Effect: Mechanisms of Selective Accessibility," *Journal of Personality and Social Psychology,* 73 (September), 437-446.

Tversky, Amos and Daniel Kahneman, (1974), "Judgment Under Uncertainty: Heuristics and Biases," *Science,* 185 (4157), 1124–1131.

Volkman, John (1951), "Scales of Judgment and Their Implications for Social Psychology," in John H. Rohrer and Muzafer Sherif (Eds.), *Social Psychology at the Crossroads,* Oxford, England: Harper, 273-298.

Wansink, Brian, Robert J. Kent, and Stephen J. Hoch (1998), "An Anchoring and Adjustment Model of Purchase Quantity Decisions," *Journal of Marketing Research,* 35 (February), 71-81.

Wedell, Douglas H., Allen Parducci, and Diana Roman (1989), "Student Perceptions of Fair Grading: A Range-frequency Analysis," *American Journal of Psychology,* 102 (Summer), 233-248.

Collective Authentication

Sabrina Gabl, University of Innsbruck, Austria
Andrea Hemetsberger, University of Innsbruck, Austria

ABSTRACT

Our netnographic study of an open-source marketing community investigates collective practices of authentication. We find that the community embraces emerging contradictions—open closedness, professional amateurs, market logic of doing good, and a faceful mass—instead of solving them and thus constantly fuels collective authentication practices. Our study extends existing findings on authenticity in three ways: We see a high potential in the dynamic perspective of authenticity paradoxes, find additional paradoxes relevant to the marketing context, and point out the relevance of the individual, even against the backdrop of collective authentication.

INTRODUCTION

How come a collective that initially formed around a communal resentment to market hegemony is now so well integrated in the market that it becomes an award-winning brand? This is what happened to the online open-source community around Mozilla Firefox at the biggest computer fair in Germany in 2011, when they were elected brand of the year for their successful introduction of the Firefox brand ("Mozilla Awards" 2011).

In their beginnings, many consumer-producer communities followed a grassroots effort, distancing themselves from the profit motive, and, by thriving on values of openness and transparency, they were able to blur the boundaries between internal and external realities, granting consumers "the authority to walk backstage" (Holt 2002, 86). In doing so, they have been perceived and recognized as authentic, valuable cultural resources that were able to compensate for the perceived loss of a personalized self in mass society. Some well-established consumer-producer communities have given up parts of their anti-conformist and resistant aura and turned to gradual professionalization in favor of a more mainstream logic of market success. They have turned into "commercially viable" (Fitzgerald 2006, 587), entrepreneurial (Hemetsberger 2006, 2008) organizations and are so displaying characteristics of commercialization; factors which have been associated with a gradual loss of authenticity (Alexander 2009; Arsel and Thompson 2011; Baron 2004; Beverland 2005, 2006; Carroll and Swaminathan 2000; Holt 2002; Kozinets 2002a; Thompson and Arsel 2004).

A collision of two contradictory notions very often initiates a vast number of discussions displaying polarized either/or viewpoints (Lewis 2000). Likewise, researchers are raising concerns about the seeming commercialization of non-profit organizations, regarding it to be against a non-profit organization's nature to rely on commercial revenues (Child 2010).

This study wants to understand how entrepreneurial consumer-producer communities, which are similarly challenged by contradictory discourse, aim to balance the need to adapt to market conventions and, simultaneously, keep up their authenticity. In other words, this study aims to understand authentication practices of a collective. In the theory part, we aim to conceptualize the need for understanding collective authentication, drawing on authenticity and organization theory literature. Next, we present our specific research subject, the Mozilla marketing community, and provide details on our empirical study. We find four major contradictions arising from the community discourse that are enabling authentication—open closed-ness, professional amateurs, market logic of doing good, and a face-ful mass—and describe how the contradictions are fueling discourse and, simultaneously, authentication processes.

THEORY

Views on Authenticity

Authenticity has been discussed in various disciplines, grounding its relevance in the world's growing superficiality (Boyle 2004; Gilmore and Pine 2007; Grayson 2002; Leigh, Peters, and Shelton 2006). In conceptualizing authenticity, we identify three major viewpoints across disciplines; objective, constructivist, and existential views on authenticity (Wang 1999, Leigh et al. 2006, Alexander 2009).

According to an objective viewpoint, authenticity can be pinned down to absolute, objective criteria, leading to a definition of authenticity that is closest to genuineness and originality. While Grayson and Martinec's (2004) indexical authenticity can be compared to objective authenticity, the authors define an additional type, iconic authenticity, which denotes an authentic reproduction and is judged according to its similarity to something that is indexically authentic. Grayson and Martinec (2004) do not regard these two kinds of authenticity to be exclusive either and support the idea that authenticity is not inherent to an object, but rather a socially or individually constructed judgment. Rose and Wood (2005) further develop the constructivist understanding of authenticity by studying how the perception of reality television programming is negotiated. In line with Kozinets (2001) or Peñaloza (2001), Rose and Wood (2005) argue that—in postmodern times—consumers are blurring the boundaries between fiction and reality and so create their own "hyperreality" (Baudrillard 1983) in which they perceive a kind of "hyperauthenticity." Similar to Cohen (1988) and Arnould and Price (2000), Rose and Wood (2005) find that an "experience is not objectively real but rather endowed with authenticity by the individual" (295). Beverland's (2009) studies on brand authenticity follow a similar notion; however, he takes on a more management-oriented perspective when he suggests authenticity attributes (Beverland 2005, 2006) or habits of iconic brands (Beverland 2009) to contribute to authenticity claims.

Existential authenticity is deeply grounded in existential philosophy, with Kierkegaard, Sartre, and Heidegger among the representatives (Golomb 1995). In this tradition, authenticity takes a central role and describes the existential condition of being, in which an individual is "true to oneself, and acts as a counterdose to the loss of 'true self' in public roles and public spheres in modern Western society" (Berger 1973, as cited in Wang 1999, 359). The focus on the authentic self has been adapted in various other fields; management literature is vastly discussing the concept of the authentic leader (e.g., Special Issue of *The Leadership Quarterly*, 16, 2005) and tourism literature has recognized the potential of existential authenticity in tourism experiences (Wang 1999; Steiner and Reisinger 2006).

Although interested in self authentication, community research takes a quite different stance towards the self which is not existentialist but rather (social) constructivist. Subculture and community research identified means to authenticate the self within a collective (Arnould and Price 2000; Beverland, Farrelly, and Quester 2010; Widdicombe and Wooffitt 1990). Wang (1999) and Arnould and Price (2000) find as well individual and collective factors that influence the authentic self as a member of a group. Wang (1999) distinguishes between intra-personal authenticity, involving individual physical and psychological concerns, and inter-personal authenticity, which can only be reached in a social context and having relationships with others. Similarly, Taylor (1991) locates authenticity as part of a dialog between the individual and others of significance. Arnould and Price (2000) find self-authenticating acts, "self-referential behaviors actors feel reveal or produce the 'true' self" (138), and authoritative performances, "collective displays aimed at inventing or refashioning cultural traditions" (Arnould and Price 2000, 140) that situate the self within society.

These three literature streams leave us with diverging viewpoints and insights into various idiosyncratic research contexts, and the conclusion that authenticity can either be judged on objective/ existential grounds, or is rather co-constructed based on a specific frame of reference. Whereas the objective view emphasizes genuineness and originality, the authentic self is either self-referential/ existentialist, or other-referential, becoming an authentic group member through authoritative performances. An other-referential view implies that authenticity is not a question of being *true to self* for all time, but rather of being true to self-in-context or true to self-in-relationship (Erickson 1995), emphasizing the impossibility to *be* authentic but rather *act* authentically. Authenticity, then, is a transient concept, changing its system of reference across different situations, relationships, times, and places. Even historical objects can only be judged as authentic from the perspective of their origins; their use/display in museums is not authentic but rather constructed as appropriately authentic in a contemporary setting. For collectives representing social entities, their existence is inherently based on social institutionalization. As such, they are void of any essentialist character. The postmodern challenge of authenticity for collectives is that of many different possible authenticities that are contextually co-constructed.

But how do collectives cope with multiple possible authenticities? How can they authenticate their existence, not only vis-à-vis their members but also the "the outer world"? Authenticity literature offers insights into the role of the community as a means to authenticate the self; the authenticating collective remains an underresearched domain.

Authenticating Collectives

Some references to a collective form of authenticity are made in organizational theory. Authors like Carroll and Wheaton (2009), who take on an internal identity perspective, focus on the question of how authenticity can be effectively projected to an audience. Carroll and Wheaton do not regard authenticity construction as a collective endeavor but as features that are deeply grounded in the organization's identity. Similar to literature on authenticity, the authors back out of the perspective of the organization as an authenticating collective, and present authenticity as a bundle of characteristics, such as sincerity and "being true to one's self" and one's craft. Yet, the authors introduce an interesting perspective on authenticity as related to organizational identity.

Harrison and Corley (2011) offer a practice-oriented and more open attitude towards authenticity, when they employ an open-systems perspective. They define authenticity as a balancing act between practices of cultural infusing, importing and translating cultural material, and cultural seeding, exporting cultural material. In their model of cultural cultivation, the authors lay grounds for a circular view of organizational authentication. A circular view emphasizes the necessity to not just seed and propagate organizational ethos and style but simultaneously bring in new members, new knowledge, and ways of doing, thus keeping organizational structures flexible and open. Harrison and Corley's (2011) notion of authenticity as constructed through cultural cultivation explicitly integrates external parties as co-constructors of the organization. Through parallel processes of infusing and seeding, the authors claim, organizations

can solve the authenticity paradox of being unique as an organization and similar to interested external parties at the same time (Lewis 2000), thereby solving issues of authenticity with members, customers, and a larger social audience (Carroll and Swaminathan 2000). Similar to Harrison and Corley (2011), Driver (2006) argues that being connected is part of an authentic, relational organizational self-definition. Hence, collective authentication means connecting various actors and claims. By doing that, Driver (2006) and Liedtka (2008) argue, authentication also takes on a moral quality, exposing organizational action to public scrutiny.

In accordance with Driver (2006), Liedtka (2008), Harrison and Corley (2011), and other (social) constructivist approaches in authenticity literature (Beverland 2005; Leigh et al. 2006; Peterson 1997, 2002), we assume that authenticity is the result of an interplay between various actors and therefore, a dynamic process of authentication that resolves the paradox of multiple authenticity claims. We will focus on processes of authentication, thereby contributing to an understanding of the practices employed by actors involved in the authentication of a collective.

METHODOLOGY

Our investigation into collective authentication processes is based on the information-rich case of the Mozilla Foundation and Corporation. The Mozilla online marketing community is especially interesting, because it is the first one of its kind trying to combine all the contradictory assumptions of the open-source movement and marketing practice. In 2007, popular media was talking about the Mozilla paradox, praising Mozilla's successful way of operating (Freedman 2007). However, changes such as increasing market share and growing professionalization were perceived as a challenge for Mozilla's core values, thus endangering its claims of authenticity. The marketing community was identified as a kind of bottleneck where open-source collides with a business logic, and presumably leads to appropriation by the capitalist market system. The Mozilla Corporation is critically aware of these perils and therefore offers rich data on collective authentication discourses.

Our netnographic study (Kozinets 2002b, 2010) focuses on Mozilla's marketing community, taking into account data collected from the Mozilla mailing lists (the marketing and the community Drumbeat mailing list), respective Mozilla Wiki pages, 13 blogs, and eight interviews with key engagement staff and marketing volunteers. Before entering the online field, we tried to get to know more about how Mozilla is organized on- and offline. We, therefore, researched the web presence of Mozilla, tried to learn more about Mozilla's history and projects, and became familiar with the open-source phenomenon. We got into contact with local Mozillians (a common denomination of Mozilla community members) and attended two community meetings in Munich. We then entered the field by gathering data from the official Mozilla marketing mailing list. We selected posts for coding according to their relevance and the attention they attracted among community members (Kozinets 2010). The mailing lists and other central information websites helped us to identify key and most active participants within the field. Based on this observation, we gathered data from 13 blogs dealing with issues germane to our study—with a focus on blogs written by employees of the Mozilla Corporation or Foundation. Blogs hosted by well-known employees proved to be most relevant, as they were well frequented and most interactive. In many cases they served as information source for voluntary contributors, because staff reported on their projects and published professional or personal thoughts. In those first steps, we took a purely observational position (Kozinets 2006) and when necessary, checked the Mozilla Wiki for background information. The online observation covers a period of about one year, from August 2010 to August 2011—a time when tremendous changes, such as the hiring of a large number of new employees, were taking place within the Mozilla community. In order to complement the online data, we conducted four in-depth interviews with core engagement employees from different positions in the marketing field, one in-depth interview with a SUMO (Support Mozilla) employee, and three in-depth interviews with active volunteers selected according to their active participation on the marketing mailing list.

The transcript of more than eight hours of interview footage, the downloaded online material, and memos written during the data gathering and initial coding stages, were abstracted and coded according to grounded theory (Goulding 2002; Strauss and Corbin 1998) and constant comparative method (Charmaz 2006) by using open-source software for qualitative data analysis (TAMS analyzer). Most often, Mozillians referred to their mission and core values, towards the Mozillian way of doing things, and how to develop and safeguard it. We were able to gain a deeper understanding of the Mozilla community through the first author's attendance at a major European community meeting, MozCamp Europe 2011. This allowed her to meet some interview partners and bloggers face-to-face and engage in enlightening discussions with them.

FINDINGS

Our analytical journey from first categorization to an advanced understanding of Mozilla discourse around authenticity issues culminated in four fundamental contradictions—open closed-ness; professional amateurs; market logic of doing good, and a face-ful mass. These contradictory notions are not there to be resolved but are fueling discourse and initiate collective authentication processes. Figure 1 gives an overview of the various contradictions and respective authentication processes identified.

Figure 1: Collective Authentication Processes and Contradictions.

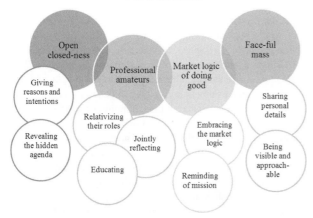

Open Closed-ness

The Mozilla marketing community translates its demands for openness and transparency, rooted in their open-source coding background, directly into the field of marketing. By doing so, they are often reaching the limitations of traditional marketing theories' assumptions of closed/internal development of marketing tactics. When openness and transparency is one of the key values, the surprise factor of a campaign launch can easily get lost. Pitt et al. (2006) refer to these opposing dimensions of brands, but predict that with rising demands of authentic brands traditionally closed brands will have to move along the continuum toward openness. Two authentication processes emerge from this contradiction and simultaneously expand the closed branding approach; *giving reasons and intentions* and *revealing the hidden agenda*.

Complete transparency within a community is difficult to accomplish, as communication among a large group of people increases complexity—even more so, if it is globally distributed as in the case of Mozilla. Despite a variety of communication tools available, information exclusivity is not unusual and can have different sources; though some information might be available, it does not necessarily mean that everyone receives it. Communication at Mozilla takes place on two levels. The first level conveys straightforward, informative content about what is done at Mozilla with regard to marketing efforts. The second level, which can be regarded as a kind of meta-level, serves to process this sober information content in a more subtle way and involves *giving reasons and intentions* and, sometimes, *revealing the hidden agenda*. Communication on this meta-level becomes essential when the marketing volunteers are not sufficiently integrated in a specific project, and thus, this kind of closed-ness needs to be balanced. The following passage taken from the Mozilla Wiki, illustrates best, how projects are presented to the whole community.

"Purpose

- Build on (and grow) brand affinity for Firefox: help people understand that we're about something bigger than just a browser.

- Grow a bigger base to back 50k Mozillians who donate time: millions of supporters backing our community.

- Raise funds for grants and programs like Mozilla Drumbeat that create new tools and drive innovation.

Anti-purpose

- *Join Mozilla is NOT a replacement for our existing contributor community*

  - *We already have programs to support Firefox and Thunderbird contributors, and plan to grow and improve them throughout 2011*

  - *We also have programs like Mozilla Drumbeat aimed at getting new kinds of contributors and projects into Mozilla..."*

("Join Mozilla" from the Mozilla Wiki)

The information provided by the initiators of this project, called "Join Mozilla," goes far beyond the key data that would usually be communicated to relevant stakeholders. Outlining the purpose, and even the anti-purpose, of the project, helps voluntary contributors to better understand why it is necessary to pursue this project—its existence becomes legitimated within a wider community and willingness to support it might rise.

Whenever the community still does not feel sufficiently enlightened and says so, it is critical that staff reacts, further explains the project, and *reveals* its *hidden agenda*. This goes even as far as laying marketing strategies completely bare. An extract from a discussion on one of the employee's blogs shows how such a hidden agenda might look like. This discussion was about whether a donator, without having contributed, should be able to become a Mozillian.

"All the best practices show that you need to give people a small and easy way to get involved first, and then slowly to help the most motivated amongst them dig into deeper contribution.

So, that's the thinking behind the $5 — based on what we've seen in other big nonprofits that use volunteers." (staff member, posted to his/her blog, January 6, 2011)

In this case, the employee reveals the hidden agenda by publicly stating online that the thought behind this idea was to drag more contributors into the project.

On other occasions, *closed-ness* is even created purposefully; when contributors need to sign up for project groups. This is how a voluntary contributor describes this situation:

"They have had you sign up for the launch campaigns. I have been too busy to sign up for those and those were purposely done secretly, so that... so anyone could be involved in the launch, but all the plans were happening close, so that it would be a surprise to people who weren't involved." (voluntary contributor, interview, June 23, 2011)

On the one hand, this quotation shows how easily community members feel excluded from the project, but on the other hand, the person is still aware of what is going on. Mozillians do not leave anyone in the dark. Though the contributor is not very happy about being excluded, he or she shows understanding. Within this exclusive group, however, unrestricted and targeted communication is possible. Interestingly, fully embracing the contradiction of open closed-ness, which means full information on demand but avoidance of complexity (Hemetsberger and Reinhardt 2009), leads to the highest level of transparency.

Professional amateurs

The contradiction of the professional amateurs derives from the heterogeneity within the marketing community consisting of both paid staff und voluntary contributors with different backgrounds and knowledge in marketing. Though this category might be reminiscent of what Beverland (2009, 63) refers to, when he writes about "appearing as artisanal amateurs," it is distinctive in several ways. It neither involves the element of "appearance" implying a kind of conceit, nor is it about downplaying their professionalism.

The question which arises in the context of Mozilla is who is the amateur and who the professional. Is it the fully trained and experienced marketer or is it the dedicatedly involved community member? Three processes transcending this contradiction of professional amateurs could be identified; *jointly reflecting, relativizing their roles,* and *educating.*

There are instances when the whole community is *jointly reflecting* on what Mozilla is and does, making concessions, *relativizing their roles,* and consequently embracing their disparities. The discussion forum but also blogs are vital sources for such discourses. Here an example where one of the basic qualities of Mozilla—openness—is revisited.

*"**Working open is a means to an end.** As [Ben] pointed out, the key question is not whether every itty bitty piece of communication or decision-making should be "open" or "closed." The key question is: **How does working in the open enable useful participation? How does it help us be more agile? How does it produce visible progress and momentum? How does it help us do good?"** (staff member, posted to his/her blog, April 6, 2011)

Here, voluntary contributors and employees are reflecting on what working in the open means. By referring to another person and raising questions, the author of this passage suggests that there is a

discussion on this central issue and that he would love others to join in on this discussion.

While marketing staff emphasizes that they are first and foremost community members, the distinct roles of staff and voluntary contributors become evident nevertheless. However, staff members are trying to work against such boundaries by giving each community member a voice and listening to these voices. Staff regularly asks the community for their feedback and so lessen power discrepancies. While staff might have a better knowledge about how marketing should look in theory, voluntary members are the acknowledged experts when it comes to localizing them. Voluntary contributors are explicitly consulted when it comes to local decisions; accordingly, their expert statuses are *relativized.* An interview partner, a Mozilla staff, put it best when he or she said that the voluntary contributors were their *"checks and balances"* (interview, June 16, 2011).

In another attempt, staff offers marketing tools to the whole community—*educating* them in doing marketing, enhancing their understanding of actions, and so helping them to digest marketing efforts. By doing so, they reduce knowledge differences and, at the same time, teach the community to spread Mozilla's message in a desirable way. One of the best examples for this is the Firefox Brand Toolkit, which, developed by marketing staff, should help the community to tell the Mozilla story as consistently as possible. By explaining theoretical marketing concepts, as shown in the following verbatim, professionalization of volunteer contribution is supported, too.

*"I've been asking myself recently: **what does effective social marketing look like in the internet era?** How could it improve internet literacy? The core of social marketing is extremely **simple messaging** that makes people care about seemingly hard to grok concepts. It's difficult to imagine millions of people getting excited about 'how to read a URL' — but this is what social marketing is about."* (staff member, posted to his/her blog, April 14, 2011)

Straightforwardly, this staff member explains the concept of *"social marketing"* in an easy language. The practice of asking for feedback and these processes of educating approve to the metaphor of infusing and seeding raised by Harrison and Corley (2011) and are signs for openness. The passage also implies that Mozilla staff does not aim to downplay or even hide its professional attitude towards marketing. Though the community is also striving for professionalism, their actions are still done in an amateurish style; especially local marketing efforts, aimed at spreading Mozilla's mission and gaining new community members, are organized by the local community, without following strict marketing rules. Neither are amateurs trying to mimic professionalism, nor are professionals mimicking amateurish action; Mozillians rather pursue both styles, depending on who is talking and who they are talking to. In order not to resolve this contradiction, it is crucial for Mozilla to keep up this element of amateurship which helps them to mitigate their alignment with the market and emphasizes their communal spirit.

Market logic of doing good

Though Mozilla does not base its decision-making on profit motives, as their corporation is fully owned by the foundation, its marketing is well-embedded in the market logic. This contradiction of working with means that are in line with the current market logic, but not striving for profit maximization, is balanced by the authentication process of *reminding themselves and others of their mission.*

Mozilla staff and volunteers *embrace the market logic* for pursuing their agenda and proudly discuss their marketing efforts and achievements—though they might not support the market ideology entirely. The following example is part of a discussion among staff and volunteers about whether to use or not to use non-free services for their viral marketing efforts. This volunteer clearly argues for making use of such market logic tools.

> *"The main focus that convinced me into joining Drumbeat is involving people to jump into a wider garden. If we deliberately ignore or just don't use such media like the "walled/non- free etc..." to communicate our goals, idèas and approach, we are putting ourselves into another walled garden. Probably more pure, better and cleaner. But it's walled same way. Given the fact that ppl just use them, and we want to reach out for new people to join open web approach, I don't really see any other option rather than using nonfree services in other to spread our ideas, projects and results."* (voluntary contributor, message posted to the community Drumbeat mailing list, February 17, 2011)

What this contributor impressively argues is that, as long as it is for reaching their goals, it is okay to use methods that might be opposed to their values because if they were avoiding them, they would also act against their principles. Implicitly, this contributor already balances the contradiction of a market-based logic of doing good when he or she implicitly refers to Mozilla's mission by claiming that *"we want to reach out for new people to join open web approach."* This process of *reminding themselves and others of their mission* to strive for the betterment of the Web is also visible in communication efforts. Here a quotation of what a Mozilla employee writes about the Mozilla Parks campaign, where Mozilla cooperated with several nature parks.

> *"Comparing the need to protect physical commons with the need to protect digital commons is showing promise as an effective way to talk about Mozilla's mission, so we wanted to refine the idea further with one more park (or in this case, beach) page."* (staff member, posted to his/her blog, April 9, 2010)

By cooperating with nature parks that aim to *"protect physical commons"* Mozilla wants to convey an impressive picture of their mission. As their Mozilla's mission is very much grounded in their history, reciting their evolution story and the reason the project came into existence is another powerful tool used to further legitimize Mozilla's actions, no matter how much they might be in line with the market logic. Only by embracing both ends of the continuum, Mozilla is able to balance this contradiction; a contradiction that reflects Holt's (2002) prediction that authenticity judgments will no longer depend on profit motives and simultaneously objects to current literature regarding commercialization to be a disauthenticating factor (Alexander 2009; Arsel and Thompson 2011; Baron 2004; Beverland 2005, 2006; Carroll and Swaminathan 2000; Holt 2002; Kozinets 2002a; Thompson and Arsel 2004).

A face-ful mass

Though it is the power of the community as a whole that empowers Mozilla, they nevertheless aim to single out the individual. This finding adds to Smith and Berg's (1987) notion that within successful groups, members must be able to express their individualities. Lewis (2000) lists three methods that help to manage such paradoxes: "maintaining a task focus, valuing differences, and reducing power discrepancies" (770). While the issue of power discrepancies supports our findings on professional amateurs, this study can add two processes at the Mozilla marketing community that are

transcending the contradiction of the face-ful mass: *sharing personal details* and *being visible and approachable.*

Staff members try not to be faceless decision makers responsible for a large number of people. They *share personal details* through various personal blogs, but also through social networks sites, where most Mozillians, both staff and volunteers, have signed up. Exhibit 1 shows a picture posted by a Mozilla employee on Facebook—a snapshot of a funny moment at the office. It reveals a lot about the character of both people in it and gives others a glimpse of how work life at Mozilla might sometimes look like.

Exhibit 1: Picture posted on Facebook (November 23, 2011)

Twitter is one of the main media in order to find out what is going on at Mozilla and has even been recommended as being the most effective tool in order to be up to date about Mozilla. On Flick'r, anyone can access pictures of community events and private, more intimate ones, as for example wedding photos. Mozilla even hosts an online video channel, Air Mozilla, where various videos and community meetings are aired. This format, which allows a globally dispersed community to get a feeling of intimacy and closeness, has been very well received. All those tools are basically there to foster practices of sharing—resembling Belk's (2010) concept of sharing in, thus "making extended self boundaries permeable to others" (726). Sharing in extends sheer expressions of individuality that differentiate the individual from the other (Smith and Berg 1987) and is more about letting others in. Simultaneously, sharing can lead to a higher visibility and a certain accountability of actors. An interviewee describes the importance of *being visible and approachable*:

> *"...assuming that you as an individual are close to the project's meaning and that you are accountable to the community and the people there... that they know you, that you're visible, that you are not faceless. That you are prepared to stand up for what you are doing."* (staff member, interview, June 8, 2011)

As staff and other community members *"stand up for what [they] are doing,"* actions are always linked to a certain person who is personally made responsible for what is going on. This kind of personification is very important, because when there is something wrong about a project, the person responsible can directly be addressed. However, personification at Mozilla goes even further, with a staff member describing Mozilla as a *"sea of smiling faces"* (staff member, interview, June 16, 2011) and a contributor who claims to think a lot about *"the Mozilla mission through [...] a person"* (voluntary contributor, interview, July 5, 2011). The extent of visibility and accessibility of Mozillians seems quite unmanageable to outsiders and paradoxical, considering their immense workload. Mozillians' solution to this paradox is quite counterintuitive. Visibility of the private side of Mozillians provides cultural and personal information, and accessibility increases trust, which both lead to less information needs. Again, contradictions are not tackled but naturalized through actions reviving their contradictory nature.

DISCUSSION

Contradictions are constructed (Lewis 2000). In the same manner as we accept harmony and consistency as being balanced and harmonious, we discursively construct contradictions and paradoxes as paradoxical and contradictory. The findings of our study not only show that we are able to find contradictory elements when we search for them, but that in successful producer-consumer communities contradictions fuel discourse in a positive way and so authenticate community action. Our study finds that authenticity is not plain and one-dimensional, but what is seemingly inauthentic is just the other side of the coin of authenticity. By showing that both sides can fruitfully complement each other instead of threatening authenticity, organizations can find positive paths of change without losing identity, hence authenticity.

Our findings also highlight in what ways contradictions contribute to authentication. We find nine collective authentication practices which constantly engage people in lively discourse. Yet, communication about tasks and daily activities is not sufficient. We found that community members engage in strategic thinking, formulating theses and anti-theses in accounts of *purposeful communication* and *revelations of the hidden agenda*. These findings also support the assumption that transparency is essential for authentication (Holt 2002). Similar to Harrison and Corley (2011), we also find a constant exchange of what they frame as ethos and style, however, we find no internal and external party but rather a flow of meta-communication among all members of the community. Infusing and seeding culture (Harrison and Corley 2011) comes from all members, facilitated by practices of *relativizing roles*. Relativizing roles critically depends on the paradox of professional amateurs that inspires the community to continuous *reflecting* and *educating* where it is not that professionals educate amateurs, but equally so vice versa (Hemetsberger and Reinhardt 2009; Kozinets, Hemetsberger, and Schau 2008; Schau, Muñiz, and Arnould 2009).

Embracing the market logic out of a former resentment against the hegemony of the market seems an adventurous, or at least a brave-hearted move. Yet, even marketers today claim that it is not the market logic that prevents positive and authentic organizational action but rather its misinterpretation as capitalism (Arnould 2007). The Mozilla case shows that producer-consumer communities ascribe a functional role to market mechanisms as enablers and multipliers of value-creating practices; value that is judged against the community's *mission*, which members constantly remind themselves of. The *market logic of doing good* reflects Holt's (2002) prediction that authenticity judgments will no longer depend on profit motives. Authentic consumer-producer brands seem to be prototypical citizen-artists, providing cultural resources for the community and beyond (Holt 2002).

These citizen artists have a face and share. Our findings underscore the importance of sharing (Belk 2010) as a collective authentication practice but also as an important theoretical concept for understanding producer-consumer communities. Community members impressively demonstrate that by *being visible and approachable*, they are able to reduce communication complexity and overload, corroborating findings from other open-source community research (Hemetsberger and Reinhardt 2009).

In order to enhance understanding of the functionality of collective authentication practices and its grounding in contradictions, we draw on organization theory and literature about paradoxes, in particular. Generally, organization literature maintains that we are used to think in a dialectical manner, and our language feeds the tendency to polarize (Lewis 2000). Westenholz (1993) juxtaposes the concept of paradox with other similar concepts, such as conflict, inconsistency, ambivalence, irony, or dialectic. "Paradoxes differ from...[*other*]...concepts in that no choice needs to be made (is possible) between the two contradictions constituting the paradox. The contradictory elements are present simultaneously and are accepted as such" (Westenholz 1993, 41). Westenholz (1993), Lewis (2000), Lüscher and Lewis (2008), and Smith and Lewis (2011) in their works on organizational change maintain that organizational change is at the same time hampered and enhanced by paradoxes, depending on how well organizations are able to reframe and reintegrate paradoxes into organizational processes. They outline three main paradoxes of learning, organizing, and belonging which liken our findings in many ways. Major commonalities in the resolution of these paradoxes are "open communications," "superordinate goals" (*reminding of mission*) (Lewis 2000, 765), and "reducing power discrepancies" (*relativizing roles*) (770). It seems that the majority of authenticity literature has largely overlooked this great potential to integrate inauthenticity into the authenticity paradox. Only Rose and Wood (2005) found that contradictions of reality television programming lead to the engagement of the consumer; an engagement which the authors interpreted as "a causal role for paradox in judgment of authenticity" (294). Harrison and Corley (2011) also recognize authenticating practices as a way of balancing organizational paradoxes such as the need to be similar and unique at the same time.

Our study contributes to a reframing of authenticity in three ways. Firstly, we see no positive end state of being authentic but rather high potential to learn from authenticity-inauthenticity paradoxes. Secondly, we contribute to organizational accounts of authenticity and organizational paradoxes in that we add two paradoxes that are relevant in a contemporary marketing context—the paradox of *professional amateurs* and *market logic of doing good*. Thirdly, we extend authenticity theorization beyond issues of the authenticating self (in society) and add a collective dimension of authentication practices. However, collective authentication does not go without inclusion of individual action, as demonstrated by our findings. Similarly, Liedtka (2008) and Driver (2006) argue that an organization is both an entity in and of itself and a collective of specific individuals, thus complicating the concept of organizational authenticity.

Collective authentication resembles the transcendence of paradoxes (Lewis 2000) as it implies the capacity to think and act paradoxically. It involves a leap in thinking and acting inauthentically authentic and authentically inauthentic.

REFERENCES

Alexander, Nicholas (2009), "Brand Authentication: Creating and Maintaining Brand Auras," *European Journal of Marketing*, 43 (3/4), 551–62.

Arnould, Eric J. (2007), "Should Consumer Citizens Escape the Market?" *The Annals of the American Academy of Political and Social Science,* 611 (May), 96–111.

Arnould, Eric J. and Linda L. Price (2000), "Authenticating Acts and Authoritative Performances: Questing for Self and Community," in *The Why of Consumption: Contemporary Perspectives on Consumer Motives, Goals, and Desires,* ed. Srinivasan Ratneshwar, David G. Mick, and Cynthia Huffman, London: Routledge, 140–63.

Arsel, Zeynep and Craig J. Thompson (2011), "Demythologizing Consumption Practices: How Consumers Protect Their Field-Dependent Identity Investments from Devaluing Marketplace Myths," *Journal of Consumer Research,* 37 (February), 791–806.

Baron, James N. (2004), "Employing Identities in Organizational Ecology," *Industrial and Corporate Change,* 13 (February), 3–32.

Baudrillard, Jean (1983), *Simulations,* New York: Semiotexte.

Belk, Russell (2010), "Sharing," *Journal of Consumer Research,* 36 (February), 715–34.

Beverland, Michael B. (2005), "Crafting Brand Authenticity: The Case of Luxury Wines," *Journal of Management Studies,* 42 (July), 1003–29.

_____ (2006), "The 'Real Thing': Branding Authenticity in the Luxury Wine Trade," *Journal of Business Research,* 59 (February), 251–58.

_____ (2009), *Brand Authenticity: Seven Habits of Iconic Brands,* New York: Palgrave Macmillan.

Beverland, Michael B., Francis Farrelly, and Pascale G. Quester (2010), "Authentic Subcultural Membership: Antecedents and Consequences of Authenticating Acts and Authoritative Performances," *Psychology and Marketing,* 27 (July), 698–716.

Boyle, David (2004), *Authenticity: Brands, Fake, Spin and the Lust for Real Life,* London: Harper Perennial.

Carroll, Glenn R. and Anand Swaminathan (2000), "Why the Microbrewery Movement? Organizational Dynamics of Resource Partitioning in the U.S. Brewing Industry," *American Journal of Sociology,* 106 (November), 715–62.

Carroll, Glenn R. and Dennis R. Wheaton (2009), "The Organizational Construction of Authenticity: An Examination of Contemporary Food and Dining in the US," *Research in Organizational Behavior,* 29 (January), 255–82.

Charmaz, Kathy (2006), *Constructing Grounded Theory: A Practical Guide through Qualitative Analysis,* London: Sage.

Child, Curtis (2010), "Whither the Turn? The Ambiguous Nature of Nonprofits' Commercial Revenue," *Social Forces,* 89 (1), 145–61.

Cohen, Erik (1988), "Authenticity and Commoditization of Tourism," *Annals of Tourism Research,* 15 (4), 371–86.

Driver, Michaela (2006), "Beyond the Stalemate of Economics Versus Ethics: Corporate Social Responsibility and the Discourse of the Organizational Self," *Journal of Business Ethics,* 66 (July), 337–56.

Erickson, Rebecca J. (1995), "The Importance of Authenticity for Self and Society," *Symbolic Interaction,* 18 (2), 121–44.

Fitzgerald, Brian (2006), "The Transformation of Open Source Software," *MIS Quarterly,* 30 (September), 587–98.

Freedman, David H. (2007), "Mitchell Baker and the Firefox Paradox," *Inc,* 29 (February), 104–11.

Gilmore, James H. and B. Joseph Pine II (2007*), Authenticity: What Consumers Really Want.* Boston, MA: Harvard Business School Press.

Golomb, Jakob (1995), *In Search of Authenticity,* London: Routledge.

Goulding, Christina (2002), *Grounded Theory: A Practical Guide for Management, Business and Market Researchers,* London: Sage.

Grayson, Kent (2002), "Telling the Difference: Consumer Evaluations of Authentic and Inauthentic Market Offerings," in *Advances in Consumer Research,* Vol. 29, ed. Susan M. Broniarczyk and Kent Nakamoto, Valdosta, GA: Association for Consumer Research, 44–5.

Grayson, Kent and Radan Martinec (2004), "Consumer Perceptions of Iconicity and Indexicality and Their Influence on Assessments of Authentic Market Offerings," *Journal of Consumer Research,* 31 (September), 296–312.

Harrison, Spencer H. and Kevin G. Corley (2011), "Clean Climbing, Carabiners, and Cultural Cultivation: Developing an Open-Systems Perspective of Culture," *Organization Science,* 22 (March), 391–412.

Hemetsberger, Andrea (2006), "When David Becomes Goliath: Ideological Discourse in New Online Consumer Movements," in *Advances in Consumer Research,* Vol. 33, ed. Connie Pechmann and Linda Price, Duluth, MN: Association for Consumer Research, 494–500.

_____ (2008), "Consumers' Changing Roles: From Creative Communities to Entrepreneurial Tribes," in *European Advances in Consumer Research,* Vol. 8, ed. Stefania Borghini, Mary Ann McGrath, and Cele Otnes, Provo, UT: Association for Consumer Research, 345–46.

Hemetsberger, Andrea and Christian Reinhardt (2009), "Collective Development in Open-Source Communities: An Activity Theoretical Perspective on Successful Online Collaboration," *Organization Studies,* 30 (September), 987–1008.

Holt, Douglas B. (2002), "Why Do Brands Cause Trouble? A Dialectic Theory of Consumer Culture and Branding," *Journal of Consumer Research,* 29 (June), 70–90.

Kozinets, Robert V. (2001), "Utopian Enterprise: Articulating the Meanings of *Star Trek*'s Culture of Consumption," *Journal of Consumer Research,* 28 (June), 67–88.

_____ (2002a), "Can Consumers Escape the Market? Emancipatory Illuminations from Burning Man," *Journal of Consumer Research,* 29 (June), 20–38.

_____ (2002b), "The Field Behind the Screen: Using Netnography for Marketing Research in Online Communities," *Journal of Marketing Research,* 39 (February), 61–72.

_____ (2006), "Netnography 2.0," in *Handbook of Qualitative Research Methods in Marketing,* ed. Russell W. Belk, Cheltenham: Edward Elgar, 129–42.

_____ (2010), *Netnography: Doing Ethnographic Research Online,* London: Sage.

Kozinets, Robert V., Andrea Hemetsberger, and Hope Jensen Schau (2008), "The Wisdom of Consumer Crowds: Collective Innovation in the Age of Networked Marketing," *Journal of Macromarketing,* 28 (December), 339–54.

Leigh, Thomas W., Cara Peters, and Jeremy Shelton (2006), "The Consumer Quest for Authenticity: The Multiplicity of Meanings within the MG Subculture of Consumption," *Journal of the Academy of Marketing Science,* 34 (October), 481–93.

Lewis, Marianne W. (2000), "Exploring Paradox: Towards a More Comprehensive Guide," *The Academy of Management Review*, 25 (October), 760–76.

Liedtka, Jeanne (2008), "Strategy Making and the Search for Authenticity," *Journal of Business Ethics*, 80 (June), 237–48.

Lüscher, Lotte S. and Marianne W. Lewis (2008), "Organizational Change and Managerial Sensemaking: Working Through Paradox," *Academy of Management Journal*, 51 (April), 221–40.

Mozilla Awards (2011), "CHIP's Brand of the Year 2011: Mozilla Firefox," http://www.mozilla.org/en-US/press/awards, accessed July 26, 2012.

Peñaloza, Lisa (2001), "Consuming the American West: Animating Cultural Meaning and Memory at a Stock Show and Rodeo," *Journal of Consumer Research*, 28 (December), 369–98.

Peterson, Richard A. (1997), *Creating Country Music: Fabricating Authenticity*, Chicago: Random House.

—————— (2005), "In Search of Authenticity," *Journal of Management Studies*, 42 (July), 1083–98.

Rose, Randall L. and Stacy L. Wood (2005), "Paradox and the Consumption of Authenticity through Reality Television," *Journal of Consumer Research*, 32 (September), 284–96.

Schau, Hope J., Albert M. Muñiz Jr., and Eric J. Arnould (2009), "How Brand Community Practices Create Value," *Journal of Marketing*, 73 (September), 30–51.

Smith, Kenwyn K. and David N. Berg (1987), *Paradoxes of Group Life*, San Francisco, CA: Josey-Bass.

Smith, Wendy K. and Marianne W. Lewis (2011), "Toward a Theory of Paradox: A Dynamic Equilibrium Model of Organizing," *Academy of Management Review*, 36 (2), 381–403.

Steiner, Carol J. and Yvette Reisinger (2006), "Understanding Authenticity," *Annals of Tourism Research*, 33 (2), 299–318.

Strauss, Anselm L. and Juliet M. Corbin (1998), *Basics of Qualitative Research: Techniques and Procedures for Developing Grounded Theory*, Thousand Oaks, CA: Sage.

Taylor, Charles (1991), *The Ethics of Authenticity*, Cambridge, MA: Harvard University Press.

Thompson, Craig J. and Zeynep Arsel (2004), "The Starbucks Brandscape and Consumers' (Anticorporate) Experiences of Glocalization," *Journal of Consumer Research*, 31 (December), 631–42.

Wang, Nina (1999), "Rethinking Authenticity in Tourism Experience?" *Annals of Tourism Research*, 26 (April), 349–70.

Westenholz, Ann (1993), "Paradoxical Thinking and Change in Frames of Reference," *Organization Studies*, 14 (January), 37–58.

Widdicombe, Sue and Rob Wooffitt (1990), "'Being' versus 'Doing' Punk: On Achieving Authenticity as a Member," *Journal of Language and Social Psychology*, 9 (December), 257–77.

CITED WEBSITES

http://commonspace.wordpress.com

http://davidwboswell.wordpress.com

http://openmatt.wordpress.com

https://fbcdn-sphotos-a.akamaihd.net/hphotos-ak-ash4/s720x720/385313_10100407084281658_328697975_n.jpg

https://groups.google.com/forum/#!topic/mozilla.community.drumbeat

https://wiki.mozilla.org/JoinMozilla

"A Coke is a Coke?" Interpreting Social Media Anti-Brand Rhetoric and Resolution

E. Taçlı Yazıcıoğlu, Bogazici University, Turkey
Eser Borak, Bogazici University, Turkey

ABSTRACT

The study offers a rich non-Western context for theorizing about co-creation and the ideological role of social media for global brands. This paper is the result of a netnography of six social media communities in Turkey focusing on the Coca Cola brand. Our findings suggest that some local rituals integrate the brand with the traditions of the local culture. Each culture has its own way of dealing with such tensions by daily consumption experiences and rituals. Resolutions are not the province of those produce anti-Coke rhetoric, as Holt's (2002) study of resistant brand activists suggests, but rather of the average consumer. Thus, this study offers insights on how local and global social media and online discussions co-create the meanings surrounding a brand. Global-local social media-based brand co-creation can be understood as an ideological element of consumption processes in people's daily lives.

INTRODUCTION

Social media and online communities have transformed the world of marketing as a source of ideas and insights for more than a decade. This transformation has also made the cultural contexts that influence the ideological and political sides of consumption more visible. Ideologies in consumer narratives trigger tensions and stand as both a threat and an information source for global brands that have to face varying cultural contexts. Ironically, global brands can both be a source of such tensions but also become successful at the same time, as with Thompson and Arsel's (2004) study of Starbucks. Brand meaning is produced collectively. The brand value co-creation process is social and continuous, and is a highly dynamic and interactive process between the firm, the brand, the community and all stakeholders. Thus, consumer narratives from social media sources are useful data to study such processes. Despite the importance of the anti-branding, the literature does not offer us an adequate explanation about the role of the social media in how such contrasts and tensions are resolved in different cultural settings, and about how a brand still remains a global sweetheart. Coca Cola is one such context.

Thus, the purpose of this research is to explore the ideological and cultural bases of how such tensions are resolved through the social media. To explore these issues, our research includes locating richly textured venues in the extensive user-generated content on the internet (Kozinets 2010).

Theoretical Foundations

Co-Creation and (Online) Brand Communities

Consumers are acting as creative agents in the co-production of value that alters our understanding of consumers as merely users of the value provided by firms or other organizations. Both the consumer and the producer as (operant) resource integrators co-create value (Vargo and Lusch 2004). Given this result, value depends on the context of complex and dynamic networks (Venkatesh, Peñaloza, and Fırat 2006) that comprise not only firms and customers but also the circumstances involving their communities and the other stakeholders (Merz, He, and Vargo 2009).

Others examine online communities under the contexts of collective consumer creativity because social interactions can trigger new interpretations that consumers cannot generate alone (Hargadon and Bechy 2006; Szmigin and Reppel 2004). Online collective creativity not only provides researchers a new field for understanding

the social phenomena, but also adds an alternative, free resource that the industry can exploit (Kozinets, Hemetsberger and Schau 2008). This, in effect, realizes the value creation (Schau, Muñiz, and Arnould 2009). There are also ideologically oriented cultural exceptions that we explore in this study.

Coke as the Context

Coke has been chosen as the context as first it is a part of the daily lives both in the *online* and *offline* worlds, and second, it is among the few brands that promote the creativity motives in consumers (Ives 2004). Coca-Cola's branding history also reflects the history of marketing (e.g., Hartley 1998). Hence the literature and marketplace mythologies (Thompson 2004) about Coke are relatively richer than any other global commodity (Ger and Belk 1996). As consumer cultures are continuing to evolve, the branding culture of Coke is a part of this evolution, giving it a value in marketing research in a variety of fields. The dynamism of Coke contains contrasts and contradictions; that is, it has held the top spot in the global rankings for each of the past nine years (Interbrand 2011).

Among global brands, Coke is always the subject of successful branding that creates emotional bonds even in the area of childhood memories (LaTour, LaTour, and Zinkhan 2009 and many others). It is also a symbol of globalization and Coca-Colanization (Askegaard and Csaba 2000), of consumer resistance and anti-consumption movements (Varman and Belk 2009; Yazıcıoğlu and Fırat 2007; Krishnamurthy and Kucuk 2009) and as one of the few demonizing agents of imperialism (Klein 1999). Coke can even encourage a rhetoric of the West versus Islam (Özkan and Foster 2005; Sandıkçı and Ekici 2009) in non-Western contexts.

Schroder (2005) refers to one of Andy Warhol's most famous quotes, "A Coke is a Coke. You can't buy a better Coke," and argues that it captures the core strategy of the world's most successful brand – its distribution power, marketing activities and emotional bonds with the consumers. Indeed, Coca-Cola does not segment its market based on quality or price, but remains a psychological entity as much as a physical product; its brand equity goes beyond mere material ingredients. Miller (1998: 171) refers to an advertiser who claims, "I don't think Coca-Cola projects. I think that Coca-Cola reflects" in the pursuit to explore the underlying corporate strategies for globalization. Yet the literature is relatively silent on how this reflection really takes place, that is, through the cultural elements of a global brand (Askegaard 2006) and the place of mass communication (Borak 1986) due to its wide segmentation.

RESEARCH METHOD

Netnography

This research deploys netnography as the method that enables us to examine the multifarious and multiplicative nature of consumer cultures through a sphere of networked communications that the internet illuminates (Kozinets 2002; 2006; 2010).

Data Collection

The data collection has taken place in six online communities and social media in Turkey. To start with, Eksisozluk (www.eksisozluk.com) is currently one of the biggest online communities in Turkey. Established in 1999, it is a collaborative hypertext dictionary on the web (i.e., a wiki) with over 220,000 members contributing to it. The dictionary attracted the most crowded online traffic in

Turkey a couple of years ago. Due to its vast public influence, new online dictionaries emerged, each of which generally represents an ideological group. Eksisozluk deliberately avoids being associated with any ideology, but rather defends the freedom of speech. Hence, the online community enables us to compare and contrast conflicting views in the same space. Despite competition, its online traffic currently ranks twenty-second in the country – even when Yahoo! (the twenty-fifth) is considered (alexa.com 2012). Unlike Wikipedia, eksisozluk is a de facto encyclopedia because each entry has to be written as a dictionary item that reflects subjective views containing experiences, rituals, discussions and critiques. They are like mini-blogs, but there are a hierarchy and collective norms in the group that make it one of a kind as compared to other global practices. That is, it does not belong to any online community categorizations in Western cultures (e.g., the classification of online communities by Kozinets, Hemetsberger and Schau 2008). From eksisozluk the study includes all 516 definitions of Coke, entered between 1999 and June 2011 and all 427 definitions of Rock'n Coke, a rock festival that has been organized by Coke since 2003. The number of entries shows the involvement of consumers with a topic (e.g., people, brands, political events). For example the number of entries for Pepsi is 181 and Nike is 202 since 2000 (publicly open statistics of www.eksizsozluk.com by July 2011). Due to its both textual and contextual diversity when compared with other social media, eksisozluk represents the richest resource in our study.

The yahoogroup called Coca-Cola Collectors Club (which appears as Coca-Cola Koleksiyoncular Kulubu in Turkish) constitutes the second community in the study. The group was established in 2001. In this online community, there are 170 members with 4693 posts and 56 photographs about their experiences with Coke as the collectors. Like eksisozluk, this group represents the initial versions of the online communities in the sense that some of the members still use nicknames. The membership is restricted. Hence, the researchers had to disclose their identities and purposes due to the ethical issues involved.

The data collection have included four Facebook groups on Coke in Turkish. Turkey represents one of the most crowded Facebook countries in the world with more than thirty million users; this puts it in sixth place globally (socialbakers.com 2012). This popular social networking is also the second top website in the country (alexa.com 2012). Anybody can join and post these groups. The subentries sometimes point to the degree of interaction among the group. But sometimes instead of a response, a new post is an answer.

The first Facebook group in the study is one for Coca-Cola fans called Those Who Say That They Don't Drink Any Other Cola But Coca-Cola (it appears as "Coca-Cola'dan Baska Kola Icmem Diyenler" in Turkish). The group was established in February 2008, and had 961 Coke fan members, 139 posts, 14 responses and 26 photos. The focus of this group (Facebook Coke Fans hereafter) is mainly socialization under the brand and to share their experiences. There are only a few negative remarks about Coke among the discussions. The group is open to the public and not moderated.

The second Facebook group is for Rock'n Coke (it appears this way in Turkish). It was established in April 2008 and it has 3937 members. The data contains 181 posts and 228 photographs from this group. The members are either the participants of previous Rock'n Coke festivals or those who plan to participate in that year's festival. The discussion topics are mostly about the performing bands or camping area in the festival or the tickets for sale. It is not moderated. There are a few posts which criticize the festival.

The third Facebook group is Coke Collectors (it appears as: "Coca-Cola Koleksiyonculari" in Turkish). Established in October 2007, it had 89 members. The data contains 44 posts and 75 photographs from this group. This community counts as a subgroup of the yahoogroup because one finds the same people there who are members mainly for sharing, exchanging and trading the Coke collection items. The posts are generally either announcements of meeting dates and places or for exchanging and trading collectible items.

The fourth Facebook group -- Coca-Cola - Continue the Boycott (it appears as: "Coca-Cola Boykota Devam" in Turkish) -- is focused on anti-Islamic Coke boycott. The group started in February 2009. There are discussions regarding the unhealthiness and pro-military activities of Coke, but these are leitmotivs. The content of the discussions as well as its jargon describe the religiously oriented ideological standpoint of over 73,000 group members. The data contains 614 posts and 1835 responses to these entries from this group. As the Coke boycott represents only a logo to attract those with the same ideological tendencies and discourses, the discussions are mostly about tangential topics (e.g., radical religious propaganda). This group has shown how Coke, as a logo, can become instrumental in attracting many people and for providing condensed anti-Coke discourses in a non-Western context.

Analysis

The qualitative data analysis and interpretation that this study undertakes is in line with those that are adopted by the mainstream methods (Fischer and Otnes 2006; Kozinets, de Valck, Wojnicki and Wilner 2010). The data collection includes 6793 entries and posts that are coded and grouped in terms of consumption meanings, daily life events and co-creation as will be discussed in the findings. The researchers code the data into initial categories so as to analyze them for themes relevant to the research questions. In-person discussions by the researchers and reiteratively visiting the data enable the achievement of a grounded interpretation. Revisiting and comparing the data continuously through multiple rounds of analysis provide sufficient interpretive convergence. At this stage the researchers constantly check for the mismatching cases in the data. Due to the limitations of space in this article the contextual richness and originality of eksisozluk entries is used as the main source of the intra-thematically consistent excerpts.

FINDINGS

Coke not only satisfies the criteria of a brand community (Muñiz and O'Guinn 2001; Schau, Muñiz and Arnould 2009) but beyond this provides an umbrella value universe of a commodity (Askegaard 2006) that collects alternative communities. The multi-dimensionality of Coke branding enables observation of such a strategically produced and disseminated commercial set of signs from different perspectives. The social media discourses revealed a number of both theoretical and methodological contributions to the literature that focus on the co-creation of meanings as will be discussed below.

Brand Meanings Causing Social Tensions: The Anti-Brand Rhetoric

In some parts of the world, non-western countries in particular, when there is a social movement against globalization and consumption Coke is among the first to provide the symbol for an attack (e.g., Varman and Belk 2009; Sandıkçı and Ekici 2009). In line with Klein's arguments (1999) it is often described as an agent of globalization and imperialism that is anti-union and anti-labor. In Turkey, Coke is the main target of those who are radical Islamists, an uncommon theme in the western contexts. The activists often choose the brand (Krishnamurthy and Kucuk 2009) to attract anti-Coke community members who discuss various topics not necessarily under the heading of Coke. While including such data into the findings, we were aware of the extreme emotions (Kozinets and Handelman 1998), that a brand triggers, particularly regarding anti-branding and addiction. Yet these play important roles in creating social tensions and in resolving them.

As the data suggests, those who oppose Coke describe it as a company capable of doing anything to promote the product, from murder to animal testing. The evolving constellation of such negative connotations seems to materialize in an *anti-Coke* rhetoric that not only activists who are against globalization, but also by those who ideologically belong to radical religious groups utilize:

> It is a company that sells sweetened water and makes millions of dollars by illegally treating workers in South America through anti-unionism and murderers. Because of this it is called "killer Coke" (www.killercoke.org). (tsan chan, posted on eksisozluk in 14.05. 2007)

The compulsion that Coke produces and the relevant health risks are among the favorite topics of the anti-Coke rhetoric as people often regard them as obvious facts that are not subject to discussion. Despite these, the pleasure it gives is also undeniable for many:

> It is a shitty drink whose formula is kept secret…It gives pleasure to everybody. If you ask me, with every sip, I only feel sorry remembering that the son of the pharmacist who invented it died of a morphine overdose. (melyus, posted on eksisozluk in 14.11.2009)

In a country where the majority of the population consists of Muslims (Izberk-Bilgin 2008; Sandıkçı and Ekici 2009), wherever necessary the theme of Israel under the leitmotiv of military action is used in the anti-Coke rhetoric. The perception of a pro-Israel company automatically implies opposing Islam and consequently, the Muslims in the local culture. Specifically, in the religiously oriented Facebook Coke Boycott group, such themes constitute one of the major topics that excite the group members:

> There cannot be anything dirtier. I got a friend who tells us not to drink it as they put cockroaches in it. The real purpose of my not drinking it is because of my Palestinian sisters. (Guher, posted in Facebook Coke Boycott group in 28.08. 2009)

> [Response] Oh, I don't believe that. Look at what we are drinking. Thank you very much for this information. (Filiz, posted in Facebook Coke Boycott group in 29.08. 2009)

The anti-Coke discourses contain comments on how the company is anti-union and anti-labor and against cultural values (i.e., including both local culture and rock culture). The narratives reveal the negative connotations with corporate communications like the sponsorship of a rock festival:

> [Rock'n Coke] is a festival where we see that the bands performing have nothing to do with rock. It is the organization that makes me furious because it qualifies rock'n roll as something governed by a power like Coca-Cola, like some cheap simulations. (kuyku, posted on eksisozluk in 06.07.2003)

Brand Meanings Potentially Resolving Social Tensions

The use of positive word-of-mouth techniques (Keller 1993) builds up brands by also providing a trustworthy resource for consumers. Yet it is rather difficult to capture all such processes due to the complexities of data collection in real-life settings. By using netnography as the methodology we have been able to observe these almost in vivo, yet in a condensed way.

This positive aspect is apparent in a number of discourse schemes that resolve the tensions from the anti-Coke rhetoric. First, some of them prefer to exemplify both the global and local corporate success and some act sarcastically on such negative claims so as to disparage the anti-Coke rhetoric. It seems that the corporate success is sufficient to prove that pro-religious discourses opposing Coke are wrong and to resolve tensions (Kozinets and Handelman 1998):

> I got a few words for those idiots who believe Coca-Cola is pro-Israel: Do you think the company is as stupid as you are?... Are those managers who are graduates of Harvard, Wharton as dumb as you are?… (vito Genovese, posted on eksisozluk in 03.01.2009)

Pointing to the company's employment rates, particularly in a country where unemployment represents a major social issue, also helps counter the anti-labor claims. Highly involved Coke fans focus on their personal experiences and tastes:

> When I look at these [anti-Coke] photos, I understand how ignorant a people we are once again. Just imagine how many people are being employed by them you idiots. If Coca-Cola offers you a job, you'll run to it. (yener, posted in Facebook Coke Fans in March 8, 2009)

Addictiveness is almost the only common theme that both Coke fans and adversaries accept. Interestingly, Coke fans convert this compulsion into a positive dependency, and the enjoyment of the consumption experience seems to override all other issues:

> Its only competitor is tap water. (jacqueline wilson, posted on eksisozluk in 31.10.2005)

> Let me also ask you. Have you ever seen anybody who got sick because of Coke????? Sugar, salt, fat, cigarettes, alcohol etc. etc. You must know lots of people who got sick because of these. I have always drunk it. I'll make my son drink it too. (Bernev, posted on Facebook Coke Fans in April 3, 2008)

Coke fans explicitly explain that they see Coke as a traditional/local soft drink by illustrating the consumption of it by the elderly and the poor segment of the society such as the construction workers. The local culture emphasizes the family values such as loyalty and respect for elderly people (Kağıtçıbaşı 1996). The poorer segment legitimizes the overall Coke experience because it does not constitute a consumption pattern that is privileged (like a luxury product), but rather is one that is accessible and democratized. It is the common people's drink:

> It is the official soft drink of construction workers. (orion ares, posted on eksisozluk in 23.01.2010)

> It is a soft drink that elderly people like my grandmother call 'black'. They call Fanta 'yellow'. (acme, posted on eksisozluk in 28.01.2010)

Despite the emergence of such local values that reinforce and legitimize Coke's presence, Coke fans also note how the global positioning of the brand seems to strengthen that of the local market.

Hence, both the global and local histories focus on the distinctiveness of the brand over time. Not only John Pemberton the founder, but also the first contractor of the Coca-Cola brand in Turkey are well-known within the brand community in Turkey. This retelling of history (Muñiz and O'Guinn 2001) completes the overall experience as it connects the Coke fans to both global and local brand cultures and their legacies:

> Its history is like this: In 1886, the pharmacist John Styth Pemberton starts selling a french coca wine he discovered with the slogan "the best tonic for the brain." (infe, posted on eksisozluk in 13.01.2003)

> It is a drink that first entered Turkey from the Incirlik base [a US military base]. At that time Kadir Has [a publicly known wealthy man] is a young guy and lives in Adana... Our young Kadir meets Coca-Cola there and buys cases to store at home... (alyoop, posted on eksisozluk in 11.11.2007)

Apparently, the mediation and developing use of commercial texts (Muñiz and O'Guinn 2001) and the advertisement of the products (i.e., brands, bottles, tastes, etc) and their rituals (McCracken 1987; Özkan and Foster 2005) play a part in transmitting such values of Coke branding. This will be further discussed in the next section.

Rituals, Collecting and Advertising: The Daily Co-creative Media of a Global Brand

Consumers can create possession rituals to relocate the brand in their daily lives (Rook 1985); to start collecting (Pearce 1999; Belk 2006) and even to create ads for the brand they are strongly attached to (Muñiz and Schau 2007). In other words they can act independently of marketers and advertisers. Among global brands, Coke stands at the center of such richly varied consumption experiences.

The role of advertising in the context of consumption puts it at the disposal of modern culture as an area of play, experimentation and innovation with which to fashion new cultural meanings. Consumers examine advertisements searching out meanings to use in their construction of new versions of the self, of the family, of a community (McCracken 1987). They even try to fill in the lack of advertising of a discontinued brand with the documents they write as Muñiz and Schau (2007) explore.

Other corporate communication schemes can work in line with that of advertising. McAlexander, Schouten, and Koenig (2002) show that participation in brandfests can lead to significant increases in feelings of integration into brand communities and to positive feelings about the brand and product category. Indeed, the opportunity to watch world-famous bands' performances enhanced Rock'n Coke's welcome. Despite the tensions coming from the ideological anti-Coke rhetoric that refuses to identify rock with Coke, there are people who enjoyed the festival experience and think that it has even criticized the system:

> It was a wonderful festival... I wished some of them [performing bands] would stay longer... We had fun. Let those who weren't able to come feel sad about it. (angelic purple, posted on eksisozluk in 08.09.2003)

> It is a festival that criticizes the existing system under the umbrella of Coca-Cola. (gothic evil, posted on eksisozluk in 29.11.2007)

Apparently, the community members created a variety of rituals such as exploring old and new ads, and collecting and sharing them with friends. These went beyond what the corporation had actually displayed and/or suggested. Despite a few studies (e.g., Mick and Buhl 1992; Muñiz and Schau 2007; Kozinets et al 2010) co-creative meanings involving advertising still expect different cases to fully capture the processes. Among the data sets, eksisozluk specifically showed how Coke fans share their consumption related rituals, even by referring to Milan Kundera:

> Coca-Cola Manifesto: ...You shouldn't consume it light unless you are obese. It has to be drunk cold as ice. It is never the same when you drink those kept 3-5 minutes in the fridge... You should never drink Coke with a standard straw. Wide straws are acceptable. The burning potential of carbon dioxide can decrease... It has to be consumed very quickly. It's not Turkish coffee. (alha, posted on eksisozluk in 19.03.2006)

> After a football game, the unbearable happiness of sharing the 2.5lt version with my friends, that's enough for me. (hmmm, posted on eksisozluk in 12.02.2002 00:31)

Advertising emerges as a medium for displaying their creativity as well as resistance and the will to become self-appointed promoters of the brand (Muñiz and Schau 2007). The community members open-heartedly share their experiences without minding about the exploitation of their views by corporate marketing or advertising agencies. Eksisozluk acts as an open forum that offers everybody access for reading its content that sometimes offer suggestions to Coke:

> The jingle was great. The film was taken with the correct visual planning. The success of the creative team is so obvious. When I see such work, I'd like to be a part of these campaigns. Although we weren't in the creative team, this work is highly admirable. (sir erdoquan, posted on eksisozluk in 01.09.2006)

In addition to daily life themes, collection rituals also emerge as a way to express not only people's attachment to the brand, but also as a way to become a part of the brand (Belk 1995). Forming a community to exchange and share the Coke collectibles manifests an alternative ritual for co-creation specifically in mundane consumption (e.g., Schau, Muñiz and Arnould 2009). As Danet and Katriel (1994) suggest, if the Coca-Cola collector concentrates on bottles, for example, a collector will want exemplars of all the shapes and colors produced by different factories and in different countries, etc. Collectors socialize among themselves and mostly exchange their duplicate materials, but the real challenge for them is catching the limited promotional material. Some of the collectors are highly involved with dressing or painting (e.g., knitted or dazzling) the cans and bottles and uploading to the website in both yahoogroup and Facebook. These all leverage emotional attachments towards the brand and customer-firm interaction. Thus semiotic analysis can support the existence of the collection rituals that point to different forms of consumption:

> Friends, how many of you were able to collect the new bottle? And would you please tell me how many of them are in the market now? I was able to obtain only 4 varieties and I know that there is the 5th. (sinem, posted on Facebook Coke Collectors in 21.01.2008)

Given all the rituals and experiences, the cultural facet explored by this study reveals the meanings inherent in consumers' daily lives related to Coke, in particular the desire to co-create it better.

Ice-cold Cokes were drunk by the glasses with the Coke logo. Can you get how such stuff is like luxury for a student house dear uncle Muhtar Kent [the global CEO of Coca-Cola Company who is Turkish]?... Would they know the newly met girlfriend can be made happy by taking out a polar teddy bear with a scarf from under the table and saying "I got a gift for you Mualla. Close your eyes" after the meal and that makes you her lover boy? How would you know these Uncle Muhtar Kent? Have you ever had a girlfriend who cried after receiving a ridiculous polar teddy bear? (nouma21, posted on eksisozluk in 11.08.2009)

CONCLUSION AND DISCUSSION

The findings of this netnography group brand meanings into three broad themes within the context described as above. First are the negative connotations of brand meanings that create tensions. Second are the positive connotations of brand meanings that have the potential to resolve such tensions. Third are a host of co-created meanings that symbolize openness, transformation, and change. Negative connotations materialize into an anti-brand rhetoric ideologically positioned against globalization and related to radical Islam. These radical Islamic discourses contain the most radical form of opposition to Coke's meanings. In the anti-brand communities, unrelated topics are used by participants to instrumentalize Coke in order to support their views. We found two core meanings in the anti-Coke online communities: anti-branding and addiction. These core meanings play important roles in creating social tensions and also in resolving them.

The study offers a valuable non-Western context for theorizing about co-creation and the role of the social media. Local and non-Western cultural contexts may deserve separate scrutiny despite the fact that the subject of study is a leading global brand with uniform global positioning. Coke's brand community reveals practices with intrathematically consistent discursive elements. Some local rituals integrate the brand with the traditions of the local culture. Interestingly, environmentalism did not emerge among the anti-branding discourses we studied. We might suggest that this flexibility of ideological orientation could be a further finding to investigate in research on the ethical aspects, particularly in an anti-brand context.

Through local social media contexts, self-appointed advertisers emerge as a type of agent of cultural resolution. Thus, this study offers insights on how local and global social media and online discussions co-create the meanings surrounding a brand. Each culture has its own way of dealing with such tensions by daily consumption experiences and rituals. Adding to a growing body of knowledge in this area (e.g., Cova and Pace 2006; Izberk-Bilgin 2008; Sandıkçı and Ekici 2009), our research suggests that global-local social media-based brand co-creation can be understood as an ideological element of consumption processes in people's daily lives. Nevertheless, resolutions are not the province of those produce anti-Coke rhetoric, as Holt's (2002) study of resistant brand activists suggests, but rather of the average consumer.

Finally, our study shows how branding evolves as cultures and marketing evolve. At a time when the literature points to the developments of social media collaborative co-creation, new research that studies the interaction of local and global meanings in these contexts offers potentially novel insights into these processes of marketing reception and the dynamic nature of brand ideology and sustainability.

A Coke is never a Coke, but an evolving product of its time and its relationship with consumers.

REFERENCES

alexa.com. http://www.alexa.com/topsites/countries;1/TR (2012) (Accessed at March 12, 2012).

Arvidsson, Adam (2006). *Brands: Meaning and Value in Media Culture*, London and New York: Routledge.

Askegaard, Søren and Fabian F. Csaba (2000). "The good, the bad and the jolly: taste, image and the symbolic resistance to the coca-colonisation of Denmark" in *Imagining Marketing: Art, Aesthetics and The Avant-Garde*, Stephen Brown and Anthony Patterson (ed), 121-136, London: Routledge.

Askegaard, Søren (2006). "Brands as a Global Ideoscape," in *Brand Culture,* Jonathan E. Schroeder and Miriam Salzer-Mörling (ed), 91–102, London: Routledge.

Belk, Russell W. (1995). *Collecting in a Consumer Society*. New York: Routledge.

_____ (2006). *Handbook of Qualitative Research Methods in Marketing*, Cheltenham, UK: Edward Elgar.

Bengtsson, Anders and Jacob Ostberg (2006). "Researching Cultures of Brands," in *Handbook of Qualitative Research Methods in Marketing*, Russell W. Belk (ed), 83-93. Cheltenham, UK: Edward Elgar.

Borak, Eser (1986), "Consumerism and Consumer Protection Issues in Turkey," in *The Role of Marketing in Development. Global, Consumer and Managerial Issues, Proceedings of the International Conference on Marketing and Development,* Erdogan Kumcu, and A. Fuat Fırat (ed), 188-198, Indiana: Ball State University Press.

Cova, Bernard and Stefano Pace (2006). "Brand Community of Convenience Products: New Forms of Customer Empowerment? The Case? My Nutella The Community?," *European Journal of Marketing*, 40(9): 1087-1105.

Danet, Brenda and Tamar Katriel (1994). "No Two Are Alike: Play and Aesthetics in Collecting," in *Interpreting Objects and Collections,* Susan M. Pearce (ed), 220-239. London: Routledge.

Fırat, A. Fuat and Nikhilesh Dholakia (2006). "Theoretical and Philosophical Implications of Postmodern Debates: Some Challenges to Modern Marketing," *Marketing Theory*, 6(2): 123-162.

Fischer, Eileen and Cele C. Otnes (2006). "Breaking New Ground: Developing Grounded Theories in Marketing and Consumer Behavior," in Handbook of Qualitative Research Methods in Marketing Russell W. Belk (ed), 19-30, Cheltenham, UK: Edward Elgar.

Ger, Guliz and Belk, Russell W. (1996). "I'd like to buy the world a Coke: Consumptionscapes of the Less Affluent World," *Journal of Consumer Policy*; 19(3): 271-304.

Hargadon, Anrew B. and Beth A. Bechky (2006). "When collections of creatives become creative collectives: A field study of problem-solving at work," *Organization Science*, 17(4): 484–500.

Hartley Robert F. (1998). "Coca-Cola's Classic Blunder: The Failure of Marketing research," *Marketing Mistakes and Successes*, 160-176, (7th Edition), New Jersey: John Wiley&Sons.

Holt, Douglas B. (2002). "Why do brands cause trouble? A dialectical theory of consumer culture and branding," *Journal of Consumer Research*, 29(June): 70-90.

Interbrand (2011). "Best Global Brands, 2011 Rankings,"

http://www.interbrand.com/en/best-global-brands/Best-Global-Brands-2011.aspx (accessed January 12, 2012).

Ives, Nat (2004). Unauthorized Campaigns Used by Unauthorized Creators to Show Their Creativity Become a Trend. New York Times. December 23, C3.

Izberk-Bilgin, Elif (2008). "When Starbucks Meets Turkish Coffee: Cultural imperialism and Islamism as "Other" Discourses of Consumer Resistance," in *Advances in Consumer Research,* Angela Y. Lee and Dilip Soman (eds), 808–9. Duluth, MN: Association for Consumer Research.

Kağıtçıbaşı, Ciğdem (1996). "Family and human development across cultures: A view from the other side," New Jersey: Lawrence Erlbaum Associates.

Keller, Kevin L. (1993). "Conceptualizing, measuring, and managing customer-based brand equity," *Journal of Marketing*, 57, 1–22.

Klein, Naomi (1999). *No Logo: Taking Aim at the Brand Bullies*, New York: Picador.

Kozinets, Robert V. (2002). "The Field Behind the Screen: Using *Netnography* for Marketing *Research* in Online Communities," *Journal of Marketing Research*, 39, 1 (February), 61-72.

———— (2006). "Netnography 2.0," in *Handbook of Qualitative Research Methods in Marketing*, ed. Russell W. Belk, 129-142. Cheltenham, UK: Edward Elgar.

———— (2008). "Technology/Ideology: How Ideological Fields Influence Consumers' Technology Narratives," *Journal of Consumer Research*, April(34), 865-881.

———— (2010). *Netnography*. London: Sage Publications Ltd.

Kozinets, Robert V. and Jay Handelman (1998). "Ensouling Consumption: A Netnographic Exploration of Boycotting Behavior," in *Advances in Consumer Research*, Joseph W. Alba and J. Wesley Hutchinson (eds), 475-480. Provo, UT: Association for Consumer Research.

Kozinets, Robert V., Andrea Hemetsberger, and Hope Jensen Schau (2008). "The Wisdom of Consumer Crowds: Collective Innovation in the Age of Networked Marketing," *Journal of Macromarketing*, 28, 339-354.

Kozinets, Robert V., Kristine de Valck, Andrea C.Wojnicki and Sarah J.S. Wilner (2010). "Networked Narratives: Understanding Word-of-Mouth Marketing in Online Communities," *Journal of Marketing*; 74(March): 71-89.

Krishnamurthy Sandeep and S. Umit Kucuk (2009). "Anti-branding on the Internet," *Journal of Business Research*, 62, 1119-1126.

LaTour, Kathryn, Michael LaTour and George M. Zinkhan (2010). "Coke is It: How stories in childhood memories illuminate an icon," *Journal of Business Research*, 63(3), 328-336.

McAlexander, James H., John W. Schouten, and Harold F. Koening (2002). "Building Brand Community," *Journal of Marketing*, 66(January), 38–54.

McCracken, Grant (1987). "Advertising: Meaning or Information," in *Advances in Consumer Research*, eds. Melanie Wallendorf and Paul Anderson, Vol.14, 121–24. Provo: UT.

Merz, Michael A., Yi He and Stephen L. Vargo (2009). "The evolving brand logic: a service-dominant logic perspective," *Journal of the Academy of Marketing Science*, 37: 328-344.

Mick, David Glen and Claus Buhl (1992). "A Meaning-Based Model of Advertising Experiences," *Journal of Consumer Research*, (19)3, 317–38.

Miller, Daniel (1998). "Coca Cola: a Black Sweet Drink from Trinidad," in *Material Cultures, Why Some Things Matter*, ed. Daniel Miller, 169-188, London: Taylor and Francis.

Muñiz, Albert M. Jr. and O'Guinn, T. C. (2001). "Brand Community," *Journal of Consumer Research*, 18(September): 129-144.

Muñiz, Albert M. Jr. and Hope J. Schau (2005). "Religiosity in the Abandoned Apple Newton Brand Community," *Journal of Consumer Research*, 31(March): 737-747.

Rook, Denis W. (1985). "The Ritual Dimension of Consumer Behavior," Journal of Consumer Research, 12(December), 251-264.

Özkan, Derya, and Robert J. Foster (2005). "Consumer Citizenship, Nationalism, and Neoliberal Globalization in Turkey: The Advertising Launch of Cola Turka," *Advertising and Society Review*, 6(3):1–34.

Sandıkçı, Ozlem and Ahmet Ekici (2009). "Politically motivated brand rejection," *Journal of Business Research* 62, 208–217.

Schroeder, J. E. (2005). The Artist and the Brand," *European Journal of Marketing*, 39: 1291–305.

socialbakers.com (2012), Turkey Facebook Statistics, http://www.socialbakers.com/facebook-statistics/turkey (accessed at March 12, 2012).

Szmigin, Isabelle and Alexander E. Reppel (2004). "Internet Community Bonding: The Case of Macnews.De," *European Journal of Marketing*, 38(5–6), 626–40.

Thompson, Craig (2004). "Marketplace Mythology and Discourses of Power," *Journal of Consumer Research*, 31(June), 162-180.

Thompson, Craig J. and Zeynep Arsel (2004). "The Starbucks brandscape and consumers' (anticorporate) experiences of glocalization," *Journal of Consumer Research*, 31(3), 631–42.

Vargo, Stephen L. and Lusch, Robert F. (2004). "Evolving to a New Dominant Logic for Marketing," *Journal of Marketing*, 68(January): 1-17.

Varman, Rohit and Russell W. Belk (2009). "Nationalism and Ideology in an Anticonsumption Movement," *Journal of Consumer Research*, 36(December), 686-700.

Venkatesh, Alladi, Lisa Peñaloza, and A. Fuat Fırat (2006), "The market as a sign system and the logic of the market," in *The service-dominant logic of marketing: Dialog, debate, and directions*, Robert F. Lusch and Stephen L. Vargo (eds), 279–285. Armonk, NY: M.E. Sharpe.

Yazıcıoğlu, E. Taçlı and Fırat A. Fuat (2007), "Glocal Rock Festivals as Mirrors to the Future of Culture(s)," in *Consumer Culture Theory, Research in Consumer Behavior*, Russell W. Belk and John Sherry (eds), Vol. 11: 85-102. Oxford: Elsevier.

Brand Authenticity:
Towards a Deeper Understanding of Its Conceptualization and Measurement

Manfred Bruhn, University of Basel, Switzerland
Verena Schoenmüller, University of Basel, Switzerland
Daniela Schäfer, University of Basel, Switzerland
Daniel Heinrich, Technische Universität Braunschweig, Germany

ABSTRACT

In times of increasing uncertainty, authenticity is an essential human aspiration, making it a key issue in contemporary marketing and a major factor for brand success. By conducting a literature review and several studies with different consumers and brands, we develop a scale for measuring the strength of consumers' perceived brand authenticity, where authenticity is analyzed as consisting of four dimensions identified as continuity, originality, reliability, and naturalness. We also demonstrate the discriminant validity of brand authenticity with regard to related marketing constructs such as brand involvement, brand image, and brand satisfaction. Finally, we conclude our paper by discussing the implications for marketing practice and by offering stimuli for further research.

INTRODUCTION

Nowadays, our society is increasingly characterized by a growing feeling of uncertainty due to events such as the global financial crisis, increasing political instability, or climate change. People try to relieve this uncertainty by seeking authenticity in their daily lives, even in the products they consume and the brands they own. Thus, authenticity is as an essential human aspiration, making it "one of the cornerstones of contemporary marketing" (Brown, Kozinets, and Sherry 2003, 21). Moreover authenticity is also defined as one of the key values of brand image (Ballantyne, Warren, and Nobbs 2006) and a major success factor for brands in being a characteristic of brand identity (Beverland 2005; Kapferer 2004).

However, academic research on brand authenticity is still in its infancy. The few studies that do exist are predominantly of a general nature, either in establishing theoretical foundations or analyzing manifestations of authenticity in the marketplace: "Yet, consumer research has not given considerable focused attention to authenticity" (Grayson and Martinec 2004, 296). Past research (Ballantyne et al. 2006; Beverland 2006; Brown et al. 2003; Grayson and Martinec 2004; Groves 2001) presents a differentiated understanding of authenticity in general, and of brand authenticity in particular. This is often enhanced by the studies' focus on a specific product category such as wine (Beverland 2006), tourist attractions (Grayson and Martinec 2004), or food production (Groves 2001). Therefore, there is no consensus on a general definition for brand authenticity as well as no agreement regarding its dimensional structure in consumer research. Thus, it is necessary to conceptualize brand authenticity using a "bottom-up approach" and to acquire a deep understanding of how consumers perceive authentic brands.

To address this research gap, we aim to conceptualize the phenomenon of brand authenticity. As with other brand research, the underlying dimensions of brand authenticity need to be identified by means of a conceptual analysis. We generate a scale to assess the intensity with which a brand elicits diverse authenticity dimensions. As the phenomenon cannot be attributed with any one specific basic discipline, we have to conceptualize our construct based on a variety of academic fields and develop scale items based on this comprehensively derived theoretical conceptualization.

In order to define, conceptualize, and analyze the construct of brand authenticity, we structure our paper as follows. We begin by classifying brand authenticity within the general authenticity concept and derive its particularities. Based on this, we distinguish brand authenticity from other branding concepts. We then provide a review of the literature to understand and differentiate several brand authenticity dimensions. Additionally, we conduct qualitative consumer interviews (study 1) to assess the consumer's understanding of brand authenticity. Combining the results from the literature review as well as the interviews, we derive the different brand authenticity dimensions. In study 2, we ask test-persons to review the identified items and complement the item list with further brand authenticity associations. Using standard procedures, we reduce the number of items. In study 3, we request students to evaluate brands on the elaborated item list and run an exploratory factor analysis to identify the dimensions of the brand authenticity construct. In study 4, we empirically validate the scale and expand its generalizability. Moreover, in study 5, we examine the scale's discriminate validity. We conclude our paper by discussing the implications for marketing practice and by offering stimuli for further research.

THEORETICAL AND CONCEPTUAL FRAMEWORK

The Concept of Brand Authenticity

The concept of authenticity is derived from the Latin word *authenticus* and the Greek word *authentikos* conveying the sense trustworthiness (Cappannelli and Cappannelli 2004, 1). Due to its pertinence to the humanities and social sciences, it covers a wide field of conceptual associations. Within marketing research, a definition of the concept of authenticity can only be rarely found. Thus, a variety of associations and denotations of the term are implemented by different researchers (Grayson and Martinec 2004; Leigh, Peters, and Shelton 2006). It has been defined as a positively connoted concept with semantic associations of "genuineness" (Stern 1996; see also Aaker and Drolet 1996), agelessness and tradition (Aaker and Drolet 1996), "positive valuation", "cultural" and "personal" aspect (Stern 1996), originality (Ballantyne et al. 2006; Holt 2002; Stark 2002), substantiveness (Ballantyne et al. 2006; Stark 2002), "uniqueness […]", "cultural or traditional associations", "characteristics of the production process", "presence of an authority" (Groves 2001, 251), "evidence and truth" (Grayson and Martinec 2004, 310), "heritage and pedigree, stylistic consistency, quality commitments, relationship to place, method of production" (Beverland 2006, 253), and dissociation from commercial motives (Beverland 2006; Holt 2002).

To sum up, the definitions of the general concept of authenticity differ. Nevertheless, the following conclusions can be drawn for the specific context of brand authenticity: (1) Authenticity in the context of brands deals with the authenticity of market offerings (objects and services) in contrast to the authenticity of human beings; (2) Brand authenticity is based on the evaluations of individuals rather than being solely related to the inherent attributes of the brand (for references on this topic cf. Beverland and Farrelly 2010); (3) Brand authenticity corresponds to a variety of attributes since there is no unique definition of the authenticity concept, particularly in the branding context.

Distinction Between Brand Authenticity and Further Brand-related Constructs

Although brand authenticity has conceptual commonalities with several other constructs within the branding context, it necessarily possesses its own distinctive features. It differs from brand involvement, brand image, and brand satisfaction. Brand authenticity differs from brand involvement in that the latter is defined as "A person's perceived relevance of the object [brand] based on inherent needs, values, and interests" (Zaichkowsky 1985, 342). In contrast to this definition, brand authenticity does not involve a motivational aspect. Consumers may perceive a brand to be authentic without being motivated to possess it or linking it to themselves in any way. Equally, brands that elicit a consumer desire for involvement need not possess any aspect of authenticity.

Brand authenticity is also not identical to brand image, but it could be seen as an aspect of brand image and thus as constituting characteristics that consumers associate with a brand. Brand image consists of the consumers' mental pictures of a brand which are linked to an offering (Dobni and Zinkhan 1990) and thus to a set of the consumers' perceptions about the brand, namely brand associations (Dobni and Zinkhan 1990; Keller 1993). This implies that brand authenticity can be regarded as one specific (positively connoted) brand association of consumers and thus a highly authentic brand could be assumed to have a positive effect on the overall image of a brand.

Brand authenticity can also be conceptually distinguished from brand satisfaction. Brand satisfaction can be defined as a positive emotional state of mind resulting from the fulfillment of a desire to consume a brand (cf. Hunt 1977 cited after Mano and Oliver 1993). It results from the perceived discrepancy between an initial reference point, the expectation, and the actual brand perception (Oliver 1980). Alternatively, brand authenticity need not be seen as depending on consumption of the brand. A consumer's judgement of a brand's authenticity then derives rather from an a priori notion of it. Moreover, brand authenticity is not the result of a perceived discrepancy, but instead is based on a single variable rooted in the consumer's brand mindset. Nevertheless, it could be expected that consumers who attribute a high degree of authenticity to a brand are more likely to be satisfied with that brand.

The Role of Authenticity in Other Scientific Disciplines

Considerable consensus exists on the meaning of authenticity among philosophers, sociologists, anthropologists, and psychologists. Within the field of philosophy, authenticity is related to the emancipation from conventional bonds as well as with originality (Taylor 1991). Moreover, the authentic individual is often defined as not being self-deceptive and thus being self-reliant as well as true-to-self (Steiner and Reisinger 2006). According to Heidegger (1996), authenticity is related to being oneself and thus implies that individuals who strive for conformity in their lives are inauthentic and risk losing their own identity (Steiner and Reisinger 1996). Sociologists investigate authenticity with regard to individuals, objects, their representation and/or performance. They denote authentic experiences or performances as being original, credible, sincere, genuine, natural, and unaffected (Carrol and Wheaton 2009; Fine 2003; Grazian 2003). In anthropology authenticity is often associated with the preservation of cultural values. Authentic experiences are comprehensively characterized as natural (e.g., unspoiled, untouched) (Handler 1986) and the opposite of being a fake, plastic, and kitschy imitation (Gable and Handler 1996). Anthropologists also understand authentic as being credible and convincing and at the same time closely related to distinctiveness (Bruner 1994; Cameron and

Gatewood 1994). Psychologists state that authentic individuals possess a strong and unique inner reality (Smelser and Baltes 2001). They regard the increasing orientation of the individual's behavior towards social expectations as the opposite of authenticity (Guignon 2004). Within psychology several researchers have proven an individual's authenticity to be a multidimensional construct (Goldman and Kernis 2002; Kernis 2003; Kernis and Goldman 2006; Lopez and Rice 2006; Wood et al. 2008).

Consistent with our conceptualization, the literature review of the different scientific disciplines reveals that authenticity is a rationally-created characteristic informing an individual's subjective perceptions and is thus not a characteristic interpreted as being immanent in objective reality. Combining these thoughts and results, authenticity seems to be related to and connected with terms such as stability, endurance, consistency, particularity, individuality, trustfulness, credibility, keeping promises, genuineness, and realness. In order to establish a holistic conceptualization of brand authenticity, we integrate the consumers' understanding of brand authenticity within the brand authenticity construct. Thus, we complement the results gained from the relevant research disciplines with an exploratory, qualitative study.

STUDY 1: ASSESSING THE CONSUMER'S NOTION OF BRAND AUTHENTICITY

As we aim to ensure that the consumer's notion of brand authenticity corresponds to the one we have developed so far, we ask 17 people to describe their perceptions of authentic brands by thinking of one brand of their choice. In a first step, using open-ended questions, we ask participants to select a brand which they perceive as highly authentic, to write down the brand name as well as the reasons why they perceive the brand as authentic. In a second step, we ask them to select a brand from an identical or closely related product category which they perceive as being hardly authentic or totally inauthentic. Contrary to the first case, participants in the second case are stimulated by words that we identified through the literature review as representing brand authenticity. This allowed us to establish whether consumers share our understanding of brand authenticity and investigate whether their perceptions of very authentic brands and hardly authentic brands differ (for the procedure of this study, cf. Brakus, Schmitt, and Zarantonello 2009). For a detailed analysis see table 1.

Later, we ask three raters to assign descriptions derived from the concept of authenticity to each brand identified as being authentic. For a better visualization of the descriptions, table 2 presents two characterizations selected by the raters for each of the strongly authentic brands. For Nivea and Porsche, we provide six descriptions and four descriptions, respectively, as these brands are named more than once. As displayed in table 2, respondents gave descriptions referring to stability, endurance, and consistency (e.g., "constant in its style," "offers consistent high quality," "was always like this"), a plethora of clues regarding particularity, individuality, and innovativeness (e.g., "novel ideas," "very innovative marketing campaigns," "satisfies exceptional needs," "witty creations"), descriptions about trustfulness, credibility, and keeping promises (e.g., "answers my product expectations," "trustworthy," "reliable," "confidence-building," "keep this promise"), and different indications regarding genuineness and realness (e.g., "it is what it is," "naturalness," "genuine," "uncontrived"). Participants situate their reminiscences of the brand in a commonly shared context (e.g., "I've been knowing it from my grandma's bathroom since I was little," "the company is still locally anchored in the area where it has its roots"). We also contrast the participants' descriptions of weakly and strongly authentic brands.

Table 1
Authentic and Inauthentic Brands

Strong Authentic Brands	Weak Authentic Brands
Number of Naming (in parentheses)	
Adidas (1)	Ariel (1)
Alnatura (1)	Balea (1)
American Apparel (1)	Bally (1)
Axe (1)	Crane Sports (1)
Calida (1)	Dove-Men (1)
Coca-Cola (1)	Fila (1)
Landliebe (1)	H&M (1)
Miele (1)	Jägermeister (1)
Nivea (3)	Müllermilch (2)
Nutella (1)	Nestlé (2)
Persil (1)	Opel (1)
Porsche (2)	P2-Cosmetics (1)
Tamaris (1)	Samsung (1)
66° North (1)	Snickers (1)
	Tata Motors (1)

Note: Some of the brands named in the studies were only known in the area where the study was conducted, and are therefore outlined in Appendix A.

Table 2
Description of Authentic Brands

Brand	Description
Adidas	Offers reliability regarding the quality and continuity of its products.
	Answers my product expectations.
Alnatura	Principles, promoted in marketing campaigns, are observed; i.e., employee satisfaction and organically produced.
	Always offers exceptional high-quality food.
American Apparel	American Apparel offers successfully reliable, beautiful, and consistent products.
	They've taken care of ecologically and socially sustainable production for a long time.
Axe	Very innovative marketing campaigns; they differ from one another but fundamentally have the same content.
	It's not a copy – it is what it is.
Calida	A confidence-building brand.
	A reliable brand that delivers what it promises; i.e., high quality and pleasant wearing comfort.
Coca-Cola	The advertisement is always modern and new but constant in its style.
	A classic beverage that hasn't changed over time.
Landliebe	Offers uncontrived and environment-friendly groceries.
	A natural-taste adventure.
Miele	Reliable, rich in tradition, and thereby constantly premium of quality.
	Longstanding success without aggressive advertising.
Nivea	Nivea offers consistent high quality in diverse product categories.
	Nivea is trustworthy and even abroad I can rely on its products being harmless.
	Nivea was always like this.
	It also satisfies exceptional needs.
	Stands for naturalness.
	I've known it from my grandma's bathroom since I was little.
Nutella	I buy it because it's delicious and I know what I get.
	Nutella promotes its brand with honest product claims.
Persil	Advertising messages are honest and appropriate.
	Persil has a long-standing market success and is always up-to-date.
Porsche	Genuine brand image of sportiness, exclusivity, and high quality.
	Company is still locally anchored in the area where it has its roots.
	Products are not very innovative, but the design still reminds me of nostalgic cars.
	Porsche is a brand with a long tradition.
Tamaris	I can trust in finding witty creations at Tamaris.
	The shoes are affordable and keep this promise, but are not made for eternity.
66° North	I can rely on the brand's quality even in extreme weather conditions.
	Products are created by experts who always have novel ideas.

This reveals that weakly authentic brands are perceived primarily in terms of their lack of an unambiguous brand image, which is not the case for strongly authentic brands.

Finally, additional findings that appear to be interesting were that all characterizations of strong authentic brands are positive, except for two. Moreover, many descriptions referring to authenticity are formulated in the same general terms that our conceptualization offered. The results of the first study indicate that all consumers have an idea of brand authenticity and that the descriptions assigned to brand authenticity by the respondents are mostly in line with the findings we derived from the literature review. Building on these results, it seems that the terms related to authenticity can be grouped into four overall categories representing a brand (1) to be stable and/or continuous over time; (2) to be creative, original and/or innovative; (3) to keep promises and/or be reliable; (4) to be genuine and/or natural. Thus, we anticipate brand authenticity to be a four-dimensional construct. We term the four dimensions comprehensively as (1) continuity, (2) originality, (3) reliability, and (4) naturalness.

STUDY 2: GENERATING AND SELECTING ITEMS FOR THE BRAND AUTHENTICITY SCALE

To capture the four elaborated dimensions of perceived brand authenticity, we develop a brand authenticity scale. The development of an appropriate scale presents specific methodological challenges. On the one hand, brand authenticity is a concept that has a very wide spectrum of reference. Therefore, we have to investigate several research disciplines in order to select items that are suitable in establishing its definition for our present investigation. On the other hand, the scale items should refer to the extent to which a consumer evaluates the brand as continuous, original, reliable, or natural; they should not measure the continuity, originality, reliability, or naturalness of the brand's specific components (e.g., whether the brand's advertisement is credible and likely to be true).

We conduct an extensive literature review to identify concepts associated with the four dimensions of authenticity that also prove to be transferable to the branding context. The literature demonstrates that continuity is an important concept, being often discussed in the context of relationships between individuals, consumers, and companies. However, research so far only defines and measures the continuity of relationships in terms of relationship duration (Anderson and Weitz 1989; Hess, Ganesan, and Klein 2003; Lusch and Brown 1996). For originality, we examine research on brand image, consumer, and advertising research (Lynn and Harris 1997; Netemeyer et al. 2004; Olney, Holbrook, and Batra 1991) and identify scales such as the originality scale, which assesses how a person views him- or herself as being creative, individual, and spontaneous (Im, Bayus, and Mason 2003). For reliability, we review the literature on branding, consumer, and advertising research (Goldsmith, Lafferty, and Newell 2000; Ohanian 1990; Rodgers 2004; Sengupta and Johar 2002) and find scales such as the brand trustworthiness scale (Erdem and Swait 2004), the brand trust scale (Delgado-Ballester, Munuera-Alemán, and Yagüe-Guillén 2003) and the ad believability scale (Beltramini 1988). Finally, for naturalness, only a limited number of literature streams that deal explicitly with the naturalness of products or brands are identified. The naturalness of products has recently become an important feature in the food sector, reflected in the huge demand for organic groceries. Thus, we review articles dealing with the naturalness of these and related products (Tenbült et al. 2005; Verhoog et al. 2003).

This literature review led to the identification of 31 terms. Although, we invested substantial effort in reviewing adequate scales and scale items, we cannot adopt these specific items and apply them to our four authenticity dimensions without reservation. One of the main reasons for their sometimes limited transferability often relates to their implementation within a non-branding context. Additionally, these identified items only refer to a partial aspect of brand authenticity and thus cannot comprehensively reflect whether and to what degree a consumer has a continuous, original, reliable, or natural perception of a brand.

Thus, to check the identified terms and to determine further items designed to capture the brand authenticity construct, we ask a sample of 10 students as well as marketing experts to name a brand which they perceive as highly authentic. Participants are then requested to specify on a seven-point Likert scale (ranging from 1 indicating 'not at all' to 7 indicating 'very much') the extent to which the 31 items describe the brand's authenticity. Additionally, respondents are asked to name further associations characterizing authentic brands that are missing in the initial list. Another 36 additional items are generated by this procedure, augmenting the total number to 67 items, which are then assigned to: (1) the continuity dimension covering items referring to stability, endurance, and consistency; (2) the originality dimension covering items referring to particularity, individuality, and innovativeness; (3) the reliability dimension covering items referring to trustfulness, credibility, and keeping promises, and (4) the naturalness dimension covering items referring to genuineness, realness, and non-artificiality.

For item purification, we ask a new sample of 20 students to name a brand they would classify as authentic and then ask them to point out the degree to which the 67 items describe the brand's authenticity using a seven-point Likert scale (ranging from 1 indicating 'describes poorly' to 7 indicating 'describes very well'). Building on the results of the participants' ratings, we remove items with a mean rating below four. We also reject the items that were not rated by more than 10% of respondents, supposing poor comprehensibility of these items (see Brakus, Schmitt, and Zarantonello 2009; Thomson, MacInnis, and Park 2005 for this approach). We also rephrased some items based on respondent's comments and conducted a face-validity check regarding the plausibility of the items as well as in order to examine whether the items' content overlap. After these validations, we finally retain 24 applicable items.

Next, another sample consisting of 10 test-persons complete a comparative rating task for our assessment of substantive-validity. In this item-sort task, the respondents are requested to ascribe each identified item to one of the four authenticity dimensions. Respondents are then asked to verify their assignment of items to the respective construct and to review their responses as well as to make – in their opinion – any necessary changes. Following Anderson and Gerbing (1991), we calculate the "substantive-validity coefficient". This value indicates "the extent to which respondents assign an item to its posited construct more than to any other construct" (Anderson and Gerbing 1991, 734). This conducted procedure confirms the validity of all included items, confirming the developed item structure for the four brand authenticity dimensions.

STUDY 3: REDUCING ITEMS AND ASSESSING THE DIMENSIONALITY OF THE SCALE

The aim of study 3 is to further reduce items and establish the number of constituent brand authenticity dimensions. We choose to conduct the study with brands from the sports apparel and the soft drinks industry for two reasons: (1) First the brands that were most often mentioned in study 1 belong to these two product categories; (2) Second these categories differ as sports apparel represents durables and soft drinks represent commodities supporting the generalizability of the results. Based on this, we conduct a survey asking 60 students to name one authentic brand within these two product categories. The stated authentic brands are Adidas, Boss, Burton, Capri Sonne, Carpe Diem, Coca-Cola, Diesel, Esprit, Fanta, Gatorade, Gazosa, Gucci, H&M, Lacoste, Levi's, Nike, Orangina, Red Bull, Rip Curl, Rivella, Schweppes, Sprite, Strellson, Tommy Hilfiger, Vittel, Volvic, and Zara.

In the main study, we ask a new student sample (n = 288) to judge how well the 24 items describe the authenticity of one of the brands listed above. We use a seven-point Likert scale (ranging from 1 indicating 'strongly disagree' to 7 indicating 'strongly agree') to capture the test-persons' evaluations of brand authenticity. As the literature review as well as the results of our empirical studies 1 and 2 lead to the assumption of four distinct brand authenticity factors, we conduct a factor analysis using varimax rotation limiting the number of factors to four. The factor analysis with a strict loading condition (> .7) reveals a solution with eigenvalues greater than 1 (the variance explained shows a value of 70.33%). Fifteen items out of 24 are found to fulfill this condition (cf. Table 3). The identified four factors confirm the theoretical assumption of a four-factor structure. This means in more detail that solely reliability items load on the first factor (4 items), merely continuity items load on the second factor (4 items), only originality items load on the third factor (4 items), and finally, just naturalness items load on the fourth factor (3 items). Additionally, we test the derived items regarding their reliability using Cronbach's alpha (Nunally 1978). The Cronbach's alphas are in line with the required minimum value regarding all items of the four factors: continuity (.90), originality (.90), reliability (.96), and naturalness (.95).

STUDY 4: VALIDATING THE DIMENSIONS OF BRAND AUTHENTICITY

In study 4, we aim at validating the four dimensions by conducting exploratory as well as confirmatory analyses. We employ again new group of participants and brands to verify the stability of our scale. By doing this, we ensure that the scale items do not depend on the participants and brands. This enables us to reveal a general brand authenticity. For pre-testing we conduct 27 interviews

Table 3
Exploratory Factor Analysis

Item	Factor			
	Reliability	**Continuity**	**Originality**	**Naturalness**
I think *brand* is consistent over time.	.29	**.81**	.20	.08
I think the brand *brand* stays true to itself.	.27	**.79**	.20	.30
Brand offers continuity.	.28	**.84**	.16	.24
The brand *brand* has a clear concept that it pursues.	.17	**.77**	.32	.17
The brand *brand* is different from all other brands.	.10	.23	**.86**	.15
Brand stands out from other brands.	.12	.35	**.83**	.15
I think the brand *brand* is unique.	.33	.07	**.79**	.13
The brand *brand* clearly distinguishes itself from other brands.	.21	.19	**.83**	.23
My experience of the brand *brand* has shown me that it keeps its promises.	**.81**	.31	.25	.27
The brand *brand* delivers what it promises.	**.84**	.30	.23	.29
Brand's promises are credible.	**.82**	.28	.19	.33
The brand *brand* makes reliable promises.	**.83**	.28	.21	.32
The brand *brand* does not seem artificial.	.33	.24	.17	**.79**
The brand *brand* makes a genuine impression.	.32	.20	.23	**.86**
The brand *brand* gives the impression of being natural.	.31	.22	.22	**.85**

Table 4
Model Fit Comparison

Model	χ^2	d.f.	NFI	CFI	GFI	RMSEA
Independence model	17531.13	105	–	–	–	–
One-factor model	5898.74	90	.66	.67	.46	.28
Four-factor model	457.63	84	.97	.98	.93	.07
Second-order with four subdimensions	457.97	86	.97	.98	.93	.07

by asking participants to name two brands they regard as authentic and one brand they would classify as inauthentic. We focus on the brands with the highest frequencies of mention, for example Nivea and VW (each 5 mentions as being authentic), BMW and Coca-Cola (each 4 mentions as being authentic) and Müller-Milch (2 mentions as not being authentic). Most of the mentioned brands belong to the following product category: automobile, sports apparel, beverages, and body care. Following explicit calls for research regarding the attribution of human characteristics to retail brands (Ailawadi and Keller 2004), we integrate retail brands as an additional product category into the subsequent study, leading to a total number of 15 brands (three per category). Based on this broad pool of authentic and inauthentic brands, we conduct a main study to validate the generalizability of our proposed scale.

The study has the purpose to verify the scale's stability and to compare the four-factor model with other possible models for further validation. Thus, we analyze three different models which are oulined in the following: (1) a four-factor model (continuity, originality, reliability, and naturalness) with correlated factors, (2) a one factor model assuming that the entirety of items load on one brand authenticity factor, (3) a second-order model with four subdimensions. We conduct structural equation modeling and employ confirmatory factor analyses in order to define the model that produces a fit which is better than the fit of the other two models. We generate

a sample of 857 participants with an age range of 34 to 69 and an average age of 49.6 years.

The results of the analysis demonstrate that the four-factor model fits the data very well: $\chi^2(84) = 457.63$, $p < .001$, normed fit index (NFI) = .97, the comparative fit index (CFI) = .98, the goodness-of-fit index (GFI) = .93, the root mean square error of approximation (RMSEA) = .07. The four-factor model shows a clear superior fit to the one-factor model. The comparison to the second-order model with four subdimensions demonstrates a very good fit of both models and can not reveal one model to demonstrate a superior fit (table 4). As our theoretical derivations support the four-factor model with correlated factors and as there is no theoretical foundation that would privilege the more complex second-order model, we approve the four factor-model with correlated factors as the most suitable model (figure 1).

STUDY 5: ASSESSING DISCRIMINANT VALIDITY OF BRAND AUTHENTICITY AND RELATED

The objective of study 5 is to test for discriminant validity of the brand authenticity scale, demonstrating its discriminability from other relevant latent variables. A new sample of 115 participants respond to the 15-item brand authenticity scale and scales relating to brand involvement, brand image, and brand satisfaction. These constructs are measured implementing measurements that have been

Figure 1
Confirmatory Factor Analysis: The Brand Authenticity Construct

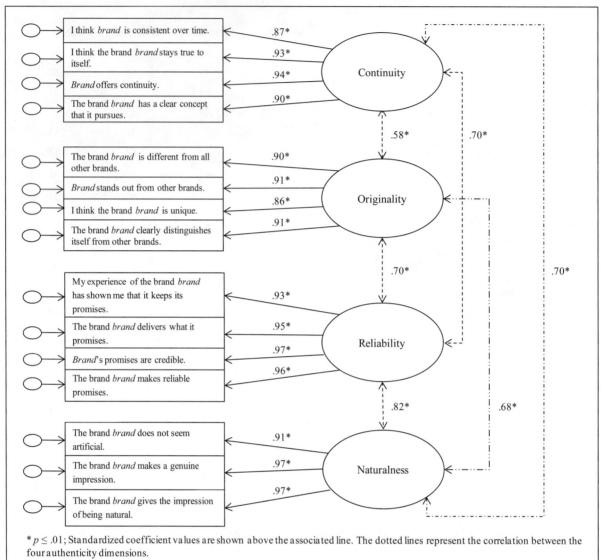

*$p \leq .01$; Standardized coefficient values are shown above the associated line. The dotted lines represent the correlation between the four authenticity dimensions.

already developed and approved in previous works (Appendix B). To create variation in brand authenticity values, we followed the procedure of Thomson, MacInnis, and Park (2005). We requested about one third of the participants to imagine a brand which they evaluate as "strongly," "moderately," or "not authentic" in order to fill out the questionnaire. For manipulation checks, we examined the consumers' reported brand authenticity. Results demonstrate that the scores average 3.03, 5.63 and 6.67 in the three manipulation conditions (weak, moderate, and strong). Moreover, the resulting means significantly differ from one another ($p < .01$).

Prior to the analysis of discriminant validity, we transform all semantic differential scales to Likert scales ranging from 1 to 7 and compute composite scores for the four brand authenticity dimensions. The discriminant validity of the brand authenticity scale is assessed using an exploratory factor analysis with varimax rotation that included the composite scores of the brand authenticity dimensions as well as the items indicating brand involvement, brand image, and brand satisfaction. The factor analysis reveals four factors. Table 5 reports the results of this analysis.

Factor one and two represent brand satisfaction and brand involvement, respectively, whereas the third factor that emerges reflects brand authenticity. The fourth factor is comprised of items from the brand image construct. These results demonstrate the discriminant validity of the brand authenticity scale compared to other related marketing constructs, and it also shows that continuity, originality, reliability, and naturalness load on a single brand authenticity factor.

DISCUSSION

This paper primarily aimed at the development of a measure reflecting the consumer's perception of a brand's authenticity. We identified brand authenticity as a construct consisting of four dimensions, namely continuity, originality, reliability, and naturalness – with the dimensions being differentially evaluated for various brands. The final brand authenticity scale (15-items) is reasonable regarding its length and therefore easy to implement. The existence of the four-factor model is consistent across different samples and studies and thus passes reliability and validity tests successfully. Moreover, evi-

Table 5
Exploratory Factor Analysis with Brand Authenticity, Brand Satisfaction, Involvement and Image

Table 5
Exploratory Factor Analysis with Brand Authenticity, Brand Satisfaction, Involvement and Image

Item	Factor			
	Satisfaction	Involvement	Authenticity	Image
Naturalness	.40	.31	.71	.28
Reliability	.47	.39	.72	.09
Continuity	.29	.16	.86	.04
Originality	.19	.34	.65	.41
Satisfaction 1	.76	.39	.21	.30
Satisfaction 2	.76	.32	.25	.35
Satisfaction 3	.83	.28	.32	.21
Satisfaction 4	.80	.31	.40	.10
Satisfaction 5	.78	.37	.39	.07
Satisfaction 6	.77	.42	.22	.27
Satisfaction 7	.79	.32	.17	.30
Involvement 1	.35	.80	.18	.22
Involvement 2	.34	.82	.19	.27
Involvement 3	.31	.84	.22	.23
Involvement 4	.33	.80	.23	.28
Involvement 5	.33	.63	.40	.02
Involvement 6	.35	.78	.27	.25
Image 1	.22	.26	.20	.83
Image 2	.15	.29	.21	.86
Image 3	.26	.11	-.01	.82

dence of discriminant validity is obtained in study 5, where brand authenticity is distinguishable from other branding concepts.

Several implications for brand managers can be drawn from the results of our studies. In order to positively influence a brand's continuity and thus its authenticity, it seems necessary to determine key facts (historically as well as over time) about the brand, such as its foundation and its circumstances, the features upholding its traditions, its anniversary, the values based on its traditions, and to implement these in the marketing mix. Implementations can take a variety of forms: a brand's permanent pledge to its roots, and the introduction of proxies (e.g., founders, innovations, stories) that symbolize a brand's heritage. Key facts about the brand can also be implemented within brand communications in order to promote positive brand features associated with its traditionalism. This can be achieved by presenting images of traditional elements on brand packaging and integrating these values visually in brand logos and verbally in slogans. Events can also be used to convey these key facts about the brand: traditional occasions and brand anniversary celebrations offer opportunities to animate such associations.

Brands which symbolically embody the image of the consumer's national identity benefit from epithets such as 'rich in culture and tradition', and are thereby attributed with authenticity. Moreover, brand's originality and naturalness can be positively influenced by stimulating local icon value, as this is unique for every single brand and part of its real self. Thus, brand managers firstly have to examine the values of a specific country and its culture, respectively. Secondly, they have to investigate the symbols (e.g., a logo, an image) that represent these values, which can be expected to vary widely between different countries and cultures. Numerous channels exist for conveying these identified values and integrating them within the company culture: They can be incorporated in symbols printed on the brand's packaging and, if possible, integrated in the product design; they can be transmitted graphically, verbally or actively using the media of the brand's communications (e.g., storytelling through advertising, events); they can be incorporated in rituals and artifacts designed to promote them and be reflected in a pricing strategy and distribution channels that serve to reinforce them.

To enhance a brand's authenticity, companies should also aim at creating a unified brand perception, using all internal and external communication sources in order to ensure its reliability. This implies a persistent presentation of the brand name, logo, and slogan through all communication media and communication tools. Additionally, marketers need to focus on a contextual, formal, and temporal integration of all these communication activities. Contextual integration can be achieved through a consistent implementation of messages, arguments, and statements which should particularly emphasize the different dimensions of a brand's authenticity. Formal integration can be attained by a consistent brand appearance. This entails establishing fixed brand references such as the brand name, logo and slogan as well as to the font, typography, layout, colors, and images. Finally, temporal integration demands an action plan regarding the implementation of the different communication activities. In addition, communication also needs to be consistent with regard to the different target groups (consumers, retailers, the public) and external communication activities need to be coordinated with internal brand management. This also enhances a brand's reliability. One specific example of how to create authenticity using an integrated brand presence would be to create a communication platform to address the topic of sustainability and thereby highlight the company's engagement in supporting this issue (e.g., advertising campaigns, sponsoring activities). This communication platform could then be implemented for external as well as internal communication purposes. In summary, in order to achieve an integrated brand presence, companies need to ensure consistency (consistent statements), congruence (between communication and behavior), and continuity (regarding the implementation of the different communication instruments) of brand communications.

Thus, the brand authenticity scale developed in this paper is not only theoretically relevant, but will find application in marketing practice. As marketers strive to satisfy the consumer's search for authenticity more than ever before and as companies try to understand and improve the authenticity of their brands by clearly communicating their brand's salient sale's features, both groups will be able to use the brand authenticity scale for assessment, planning, and tracking purposes. With regard to using brand authenticity for appraisal and planning purposes, the brand's positioning should be assessed, and brand authenticity should be integrated within the company-specific brand model as a major component of brand positioning. The application of brand authenticity to brand positioning is also a relevant factor in the context of brand repositioning in a competitive market. Moreover, the scale can be used to track changes in brand perception when implementing any kind of marketing action (e.g., communication campaign), and it can also be used to track and evaluate important competitors over time in terms of their brand authenticity.

Nevertheless, our study is not without limitations. Although, we have been successful in validating the generalizability of the brand authenticity scale across various product categories, we have not fully achieved the aim of capturing the respondents' reports on brands that reflect extreme levels of brand authenticity. One possible explanation for this might be the fact that respondents in German-speaking regions tend to tick less extreme response categories than respondents in southern European countries (Van Rosmalen, van Herk, and Groenen 2010). This implies that it is necessary to validate the scale in further countries by paying particular attention to the country-specific differences in response behavior. This leads to another interesting area for future research; namely, an intercultural comparison of brand authenticity. It can be assumed that certain characteristics of brand authenticity are differently evaluated depending on cultural background.

With regard to the authenticity levels, the findings also demonstrate that brands with low measures of authenticity are scarce. However, some brands show moderate levels of overall brand authenticity, while they show very low values for specific authenticity dimensions. This result indicates that managers who aim to enhance their brand's authenticity should pay attention to the specific authenticity dimensions and implement dimension-specific analysis. The sparseness of results on highly authentic brands may either indicate that such brands are rare in the general branding context or that managers still have a considerable distance to go in improving their brand's authenticity. This requires future research.

Additionally, further research should be undertaken using the brand authenticity scale. It is interesting that the brands chosen by the respondents tended to be consumer goods, as opposed to services or even industrial goods. It is possible that consumer goods' brands are more frequently mentioned, because they are more salient and memorable, irrespective of their authenticity level. However, future research must investigate whether the type of product is relevant to the level of brand authenticity perceived and required by the consumer.

Additionally, longitudinal research on the development of brand authenticity over time would also be useful in order to identify the changes in brand authenticity that are possibly connected with changes in society. In the context of these issues, it would also be interesting to investigate whether the often-stated assumption of an increased consumer quest for authenticity in times of uncertainty, for example in financial crises or periods of political instability, can be empirically proven. In this context, an investigation of the role that brand authenticity performs in critical corporate situations arising, for instance, from environmental scandals or public outcries against poor working conditions would present an interesting field for future research. Finally, an application of the authenticity concept to other contexts such as the authenticity of politicians would offer very promising research questions, particularly in view of the public's increasing political apathy today. Given the increasing relevance of brand authenticity in a constantly changing marketing environment, our findings provide a threshold to a wide area of future research.

APPENDIX A

Alnatura: Alnatura is a retail brand in the biological grocery sector. Alnatura offers groceries and textiles which are fabricated according to ecological standards and certified by an independent accredited institution for organic product testing.

Balea: Balea is a private body- and hair-care brand of a drugstore chain.

Calida: Calida is an underwear brand that specializes in day and night wear for men and women as well as on luxurious lingerie.

Landliebe: Landliebe is a dairy brand that emphasizes the naturalness of their products by claiming to guarantee that their animals are not fed on genetically modified food.

Lidl: Lidl is a discount chain for groceries.

Müllermilch: Müllermilch is a milky drink brand that is offered in a variety of basic flavors such as strawberry, vanilla, and chocolate, as well as special flavors such as pistachio-coconut.

Persil: Persil is a brand of laundry detergent.

P2-Cosmetics: P2-Cosmetics is the private make-up brand of a drugstore chain.

Rewe: Rewe is a retail chain for groceries.

Ryan Air: Ryan Air is a low-cost airline.

Tamaris: Tamaris is a shoe brand offered in their own outlets or in multibrand stores selling women's shoes at reasonable prices.

REFERENCES

Aaker, Jennifer L. and Aimee Drolet (1996), "To Thine Own Self Be True: The Meaning of "Sincerity" in Brands and Its Impact on Consumer Evaluations," *Advances in Consumer Research,* Vol. 23, Kim P. Corfman and John G. Lynch Jr., Provo, UT: Association for Consumer Research, http://www.acrwebsite.org/search/view-conference-proceedings.aspx?Id=7988 (accessed 3rd September 2012).

APPENDIX B

Author/Year	Construct	Scale
Based on Zaichkowsky (1985)	Brand Involvement	**Six items, seven-point semantic differential:** "unimportant to me/important to me," "of no concern to me/of concern to me," "irrelevant to me/relevant to me," "means nothing to me/means a lot to me," "useless to me/useful to me," "insignificant to me/significant to me".
Based on Laroche et al. (2005)	Brand Image	**Three items, seven-point Likert scale:** "It is easy to describe many features related to the brand," "I could easily explain many features associated with the brand," "It is not difficult to give a precise description of the brand".
Based on Brakus, Schmitt, and Zarantonello (2009); Hausman (2004), Oliver (1980); Westbrook and Oliver (1981) cited after Swan and Mercer (1982)	Brand Satisfaction	**Seven items, seven-point Likert scale:** "This brand is exactly what I need," "This is one of the best brands I could have bought," "My choice to buy this brand was a wise one," "I am satisfied with my decision to buy this brand," "I am satisfied with the brand and its performance," "I have truly enjoyed this brand," "Owning this brand has been a good experience".

Ailawadi, Kusum L. and Kevin L. Keller (2004), "Understanding Retail Branding: Conceptual Insights and Research Priorities," *Journal of Retailing,* 80 (4), 331–42.

Anderson, Erin and Barton Weitz (1989), "Determinants of Continuity in Conventional Industrial Channel Dyads," *Marketing Science,* 8 (4), 310–23.

Anderson, James C. and David W. Gerbing (1991), "Predicting the Performance of Measures in a Confirmatory Factor Analysis with a Pretest Assessment of Their Substantive Validities," *Journal of Applied Psychology,* 76 (5), 732–40.

Ballantyne, Ronnie, Anne Warren, and Karinna Nobbs (2006), "The Evolution of Brand Choice," *Journal of Brand Management,* 13 (4/5), 339–52.

Beltramini, Richard F. (1988), "Perceived Believability of Warning Label Information Presented in Cigarette Advertising," in *Journal of Advertising,* 17 (2), S. 26–32.

Beverland, Michael B. (2005), "Crafting Brand Authenticity: The Case of Luxury Wines," *Journal of Management Studies,* 42 (5), 1003–29.

——— (2006), "The "Real Thing": Branding Authenticity in the Luxury Wine Trade," *Journal of Business Research,* 59 (2), 251–58.

Beverland, Michael B., Francis J. Farrelly, (2010), "The Quest for Authenticity in Consumption: Consumers' Purposive Choice of Authentic Cues to Shape Experienced Outcomes," *Journal of Consumer Research,* 36 (5), 838–56.

Brakus, J. Josko, Bernd H. Schmitt, and Lia Zarantonello (2009), "Brand Experience: What Is It? How Is It Measured? Does It Affect Loyalty?" *Journal of Marketing,* 73 (3), 52–68.

Brown, Stephen, Robert V. Kozinets, and John F. Sherry Jr. (2003), "Teaching Old Brands New Tricks: Retro Branding and the Revival of Brand Meaning," *Journal of Marketing,* 67 (3), 19–33.

Bruner, Edward M. (1994), "Abraham Lincoln as authentic reproduction: A critique of Postmodernism," *American Anthropologist,* 96 (2), 397–415.

Cameron, Catherine M. and John B. Gatewood (1994), "The authentic interior: Questing Gemeinschaft in post-industrial society," *Human Organization,* 53 (1), 21–32.

Cappannelli, George and Cappannelli, Sedena (2004), *Authenticity: Simple Strategies for Greater Meaning and Purpose at Work and Home,* New York, NY: Emmis Books.

Carroll, Glenn R. and David Ray Wheaton (2009), "The organizational construction of authenticity: An examination of contemporary food and dining in the U.S.," *Research in Organizational Behavior,* 29, 255–82.

Delgado-Ballester, Elena, Jose L. Munuera-Alemán, and Marí J. Yagüe-Guillén (2003), "Development and Validation of a Brand Trust Scale," *International Journal of Market Research,* 45 (1), 35–53.

Dobni, Dawn and George M. Zinkhan (1990), "In Search of Brand Image: A Foundation Analysis," in *Advances in Consumer Research,* Vol. 17, eds. Marvin E. Goldberg, Gerald Gorn, and Richard W. Pollay, Provo, UT: Association for Consumer Research, 110–9.

Erdem, Tülin and Joffre Swait (2004), "Brand Credibility, Brand Consideration, and Choice," *Journal of Consumer Research,* 31 (1), 191–98.

Fine, Gary A. (2003), "Crafting Authenticity: The Validation of Identity in Self-Taught Art," *Theory and Society,* 32 (2), 153–80.

Gable, Eric and Richard Handler (1996), "After Authenticity at an American Heritage Site," *American Anthropologist,* 98 (3), 568–78.

Goldman, Brian M. and Michael H. Kernis (2002), "The Role of Authenticity in Healthy Psychological Functioning and Subjective Well-Being," *Annals of the American Psychotherapy Association,* 5 (6), 18–20.

Goldsmith, Ronald E., Barbara A. Lafferty, and Stephen J. Newell (2000), "The Impact of Corporate Credibility and Celebrity Credibility on Consumer Reaction to Advertisements and Brands," *Journal of Advertising,* 29 (3), 43–54.

Grayson, Kent and Radan Martinec (2004), "Consumer Perceptions of Iconicity and Indexicality and Their Influence on Assessments of Authentic Market Offerings," *Journal of Consumer Research,* 31 (2), 296–312.

Grazian, David (2003), *Blue Chicago: The Search for Authenticity in Urban Blues Clubs,* Chicago, IL: University of Chicago Press.

Groves, Angela M. (2001), "Authentic British Food Products: A Review of Consumer Perceptions," *International Journal of Consumer Studies,* 25 (3), 246–54.

Guignon, Charles B. (2004), *On Being Authentic,* London and New York: Routledge.

Handler, Richard (1986), "Authenticity," *Anthropology Today,* 2 (1), 2–4.

Hausman, Angela (2004), "Modeling the Patient-Physician Service Encounter: Improving Patient Outcomes," *Journal of the Academy of Marketing Science,* 32 (4), 403–17.

Heidegger, Martin (1996), *Being and Time,* Albany, NY: State University of New York Press.

Hess, Ronald L., Shankar Ganesan, and Noreen M. Klein (2003), "Service Failure and Recovery: The Impact of Relationship Factors on Customer Satisfaction," *Journal of the Academy of Marketing Science,* 31 (2), 127–45.

Holt, Douglas B. (2002), "Why Do Brands Cause Trouble? A Dialectical Theory of Consumer Culture and Branding," *Journal of Consumer Research,* 29 (1), 70–90.

Hunt, H. Keith (1977), "CS/D-Overview and Future Research Directions," in *Conceptualization and Measurement of Consumer Satisfaction and Dissatisfaction,* ed. H. K. Hunt, Cambridge: Marketing Science Institute, 455–88.

Im, Subin, Barry L. Bayus, and Charlotte H. Mason (2003), "An Empirical Study of Innate Consumer Innovativeness, Personal Characteristics, and New-Product Adoption Behavior," *Journal of the Academy of Marketing Science,* 31 (1), 61–73.

Kapferer, Jean-Noël (2004), *Strategic Brand Management: Creating and Sustaining Brand Equity Long Term,* London: Kogan Page.

Keller, Kevin L. (1993), "Conceptualizing, Measuring, and Managing Customer-Based Brand Equity, *Journal of Marketing,* 57 (1), 1–22.

Kernis, Michael H. (2003), "Toward a Conceptualization of Optimal Self-Esteem," *Psychological Inquiry,* 14 (1), 1–26.

Kernis, Michael H. and Brian M. Goldman (2006), "A Multicomponent Conceptualization of Authenticity: Theory and Research," *Advances in Experimental Social Psychology,* 38, 283–357.

Laroche, Michel, Yang Zhiyong, Gordon H. G. McDougall, and Jasmin Bergeron (2005), "Internet Versus Brick and Mortar Retailers: An Investigation into Intangibility and Its Consequences," *Journal of Retailing,* 81 (4), 251–67.

Leigh, Thomas W., Cara Peters, and Jeremy Shelton (2006), "The Consumer Quest for Authenticity: The Multiplicity of Meanings Within the MG Subculture of Consumption," *Journal of the Academy of Marketing Science,* 34 (4), 481–93.

Lopez, Frederick G. and Kenneth G. Rice (2006), "Preliminary Development and Validation of a Measure of Relationship Authenticity," *Journal of Counseling Psychology,* 53 (3), 362–71.

Lusch, Robert F. and James R. Brown (1996), "Interdependency, Contracting, and Relational Behavior in Marketing Channels," *Journal of Marketing,* 60 (4), 19–38.

Lynn, Michael and Judy Harris (1997), "The Desire for Unique Consumer Products: A New Individual Differences Scale," *Psychology and Marketing,* 14 (6), 601–16.

Mano, Haim and Richard L. Oliver (1993), "Assessing the Dimensionality and Structure of the Consumption Experience: Evaluation, Feeling, and Satisfaction," *Journal of Consumer Research,* 20 (3), 451–66.

Netemeyer, Richard G., Balaji Krishnan, Chris Pullig, Guangping Wang, Mehmet Yagci, Dwane Dean, Joe Ricks, and Ferdinand Wirth (2004), "Developing and Validating Measures of Facets of Customer-Based Brand Equity," *Journal of Business Research,* 57 (2), 209–24.

Nunally, Jum C. (1978), *Psychometric Theory,* New York, NY: McGraw-Hill.

Ohanian, Roobina (1990), "Construction and Validation of a Scale to Measure Celebrity Endorsers' Perceived Expertise, Trustworthiness, and Attractiveness," *Journal of Advertising,* 19 (3), 39–52.

Oliver, Richard L. (1980), "A Cognitive Model of the Antecedents and Consequences of Satisfaction Decisions," *Journal of Marketing Research,* 17 (4), 460–9.

Oliver, Richard L., and John E. Swan (1989), "Equity and Disconfirmation Perceptions as Influences on Merchant and Product Satisfaction," *Journal of Consumer Research,* 16 (3), 372–83.

Olney, Thomas J., Morris B. Holbrook, and Rajeev Batra (1991), "Consumer Responses to Advertising: The Effects of Ad Content, Emotions, and Attitude toward the Ad on Viewing Time," *Journal of Consumer Research,* 17 (4), 440–53.

Rodgers, Shelly (2003), "The Effects of Sponsor Relevance on Consumer Reactions to Internet Sponsorships," *Journal of Advertising,* 32 (4), 67–76.

Sengupta, Jaideep and Gitta V. Johar (2002), "Effects of Inconsistent Attribute Information on the Predictive Value of Product Attitudes: Toward a Resolution of Opposing Perspectives," *Journal of Consumer Research,* 29 (1), 39–56.

Smelser, Neil J. and Paul B. Baltes (2001), *International Encyclopedia of the Social and Behavioral Sciences,* Amsterdam: Elsevier.

Stark, Myra (2002), "The State of the U.S Consumer2002," *www.saatchikevin.com* (accessed 3rd September 2012).

Steiner, Carol J., and Yvette Reisinger (2006), "Understanding Existential Authenticity," *Annals of Tourism Research,* 33 (2), 299–318.

Stern, Barbara B. (1996), "Clarifying the Construct: What is Authenticity?" *Advances in Consumer Research,* Vol. 23, eds. Kim P. Corfman and John G. Lynch Jr., Provo, UT: Association for Consumer Research, http://www.acrwebsite.org/search/view-conference-proceedings.aspx?Id=7988 (accessed 3rd September 2012).

Swan, John E. and Alice A. Mercer (1982), "Consumer Satisfaction as a Function of Equity and Disconfirmation," in *Proceedings of the 1981 CS/D&CB conference. Conceptual and Empirical Contributions to Consumer Satisfaction and Complaining Behavior,* eds. H. Keith Hunt and Ralph L. Day, Bloomington, IN: Indiana University Press, 2–8.

Taylor, Charles (1991), *The Ethics of Authenticity,* Cambridge and London: Harvard University Press.

Tenbült, Petra, Nanne K. de Vries, Ellen Dreezens, and Carolien Martijn (2005), "Perceived Naturalness and Acceptance of Genetically Modified Food," *Appetite,* 45 (1), 47–50.

Thomson, Matthew, Deborah J. MacInnis, and Whan C. Park (2005), "The Ties That Bind: Measuring the Strength of Consumers' Emotional Attachments to Brands," *Journal of Personality and Social Psychology,* 15 (1), 77–91.

Van Rosmalen, Joost, Hester van Herk, and Patrick J. F. Groenen (2010), "Identifying Response Styles: A Latent-Class Bilinear Multinomial Logit Model," *Journal of Marketing Research,* 47 (1), 157–72.

Verhoog, Henk, Mirjam, Edith Lammerts van Bueren, and Ton Baars (2003), "The Role of the Concept of the Natural (Naturalness) in Organic Farming," *Journal of Agricultural and Environmental Ethics,* 16 (1), 29–49.

Westbrook, Robert A. and Richard L. Oliver (1981), "Developing Better Measures of Consumer Satisfaction: Some Preliminary Results," in *Advances in Consumer Research,* Vol. 8, ed. Kent B. Monroe, Ann Arbor, MI: Association for Consumer Research, 94–9.

Wood, Alex M., Alex P. Linley, John Maltby, Michael Baliousis, and Stephen Joseph (2008), "The Authentic Personality: A Theoretical and Empirical Conceptualization and the Development of the Authenticity Sale," *Journal of Counseling Psychology,* 55 (3), 385–99.

Zaichkowsky, Judith L. (1985), "Measuring the Involvement Construct," *Journal of Consumer Research,* 12 (3), 341–52.

Competitive Papers—Extended Abstracts

Judging by Appearances: The Effect of Goal Pursuit on Product Preferences

Tess Bogaerts, Ghent University, Belgium
Mario Pandelaere, Ghent University, Belgium

EXTENDED ABSTRACT

Self-determination theory (SDT) is a well-known theory of human motivation that explores both the process and the content of goal-directed behavior (Deci & Ryan, 1985; Sheldon, Ryan, Deci, & Kasser, 2004). Intrinsic goals are contrasted with extrinsic goals based on the extent to which they are directly satisfying one of three innate psychological needs - competence, relatedness and autonomy (Kasser & Ryan, 1993, 1996). The attainment of intrinsic aspirations such as personal growth, close relationships fostering or community involvement, is intrinsically rewarding because it directly fulfills the basic needs. In contrast, extrinsic goals, such as wealth, image or fame, are externally rewarding (e.g. result in praise) (Deci & Ryan, 2000; Sheldon et al., 2004). Accordingly, intrinsic motivations lead to behavior that is satisfying by itself, whereas extrinsic motivations result in instrumental behavior in order to reach outcomes extrinsic to the behavior itself.

Research has shown that placing relatively more importance on extrinsic rather than on intrinsic goals, is negatively associated with well-being (Kasser & Ryan, 1993, 1996; Ryan & Deci, 2000). An extensive body of research has demonstrated that intrinsic and extrinsic goals can affect how people feel, but, to our knowledge, no evidence has shown that intrinsic and extrinsic goals can influence consumer's product preferences. However, as consumers can incorporate product characteristics to their sense of self (Escalas & Bettman, 2005; Mc-Cracken, 1989), it seems plausible that they prefer product qualities that are appealing to them. Hence, we expect that people who pursue extrinsic goals will attach greater value to the aesthetic quality of a product, whereas people who pursue intrinsic goals will appreciate the inner quality of a product more.

In Study 1, 122 people participated (Mage=29.22; SDage=13.13) in an online survey. We presented them two alternative products for five product categories, one superior version with a bad-looking package and one inferior version with a good-looking package. The products were basic, low-involvement products that people often buy: laundry detergent, orange juice, shower gel, kitchen roll and chocolate biscuits. We told the participants that the products were tested by a well-known national consumer organization which is specialized in testing and evaluating consumer products. Based on the expertise of this consumer organization, each product scored points out of ten. The superior products scored between one and two points higher than the inferior alternatives. To distinguish between good-looking and bad-looking packages, we designed the packages so that the good-looking packages had a more colorful and superior graphical layout. Participants had to indicate for each product category which version they would rather buy by moving the slider to their favorite product (0=superior product with bad-looking package; 100=inferior product with good-looking package). To assess participant's aspirations, we administered the Aspiration Index developed by Kasser and Ryan (1996). Multilevel analysis revealed that the more people are extrinsically motivated, the more they are inclined to buy inferior products with a good-looking package (F1,119=5.36; p=.022). In contrast, the more people are intrinsically motivated, the more they prefer superior products with a bad-looking package (F1,119=3.41; p=.067). Figure 1 demonstrates that people with a

strong intrinsic motivation (M=30.00) are less inclined to buy products of superior package design compared to people with a strong extrinsic motivation (M=36.57). Additionally, people with a weak intrinsic motivation (M=35.83) would rather buy inferior products with superior package design compared to people with a weak extrinsic motivation (M=29.27).

Figure 1: The effect of extrinsic and intrinsic goal pursuit on intention to buy

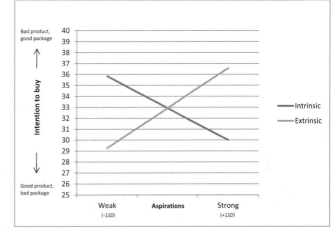

To find out why extrinsically motivated people would even consider buying an inferior product, we ran a second online study in which 125 people participated (Mage=41.15; SDage=14.24). We presented them two alternative products for six different product categories: chocolate chip cookies, body milk, olive oil, coffee, mascara for female participants and aftershave for male participants. We manipulated both the package design (good-looking versus bad-looking) and the product quality (superior versus inferior). Participants had to indicate to what degree each product appealed to them on a 7-point scale. Afterwards, all products were displayed separately and without quality information. The participants were asked to assess the quality of each product on a 7-point scale. To measure participant's aspirations, we used the Aspiration Index (Kasser & Ryan, 1996). In line with Study 1, we found that the more people are extrinsically motivated, the stronger their preference for products with an appealing package design (F1,121=8.69; p=.004). The more people pursue intrinsic goals, the more they opt for superior products with an unappealing package design (F1,126=5.67; p=.019). Moreover, as shown in Figure 2, we found that the more people want to attain extrinsic life goals, the more quality they assign to the products with an appealing package design (F1,122=7.29; p=.008). Current results suggest that extrinsically oriented people not only appreciate the aesthetic qualities of a product, but they actually infer from the nice exterior that the product itself should be of good quality too. Thus, even though they received objective information about the product quality, extrinsically oriented people derive information about the product quality from the package design. This might explain why extrinsically motivated people are more inclined than intrinsically motivated people to buy inferior products with an appealing package design.

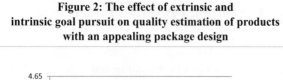

Figure 2: The effect of extrinsic and intrinsic goal pursuit on quality estimation of products with an appealing package design

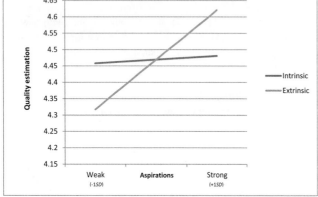

Taken together, we found that the extent to which people appreciate exterior over interior product qualities depends on the goals they pursue in their life. The contribution of this article is twofold. First, we contributed to self-determination theory. This research is the first to demonstrate that the aspirations people pursue in their life can affect which type of products they intend to buy. Second, current research adds new insights to the theory on product packaging. For people who strongly pursue image, fame and financial success in their life, product design can be of great importance, even for low-involvement products. Future research will be conducted to arrive at a better understanding of the effect of goal pursuit on the intention to buy inferior, but good-looking products. For now, we can conclude that people with a strong desire to attain extrinsic life goals, will be more inclined to judge products by their appearance.

REFERENCES

Deci, Edward L., and Richard M. Ryan (1985), Intrinsic Motivation and Self-Determination
in Human Behavior. Plenum Press.
Escalas, Jennifer E., and James R. Bettman (2005), "Self-Construal, Reference Groups, and
Brand Meaning," Journal of Consumer Research, 32(3), 378-389.
Kasser, Tim, and Richard M. Ryan (1993), "A dark side of the American dream: Correlates
of financial success as a central life aspiration," Journal of Personality and Social Psychology, 65 (2), 410.
Kasser, Tim, and Richard M. Ryan (1996), "Further Examining the American Dream:
Differential Correlates of Intrinsic and Extrinsic Coals," Personality and Social Psychology Bulletin, 22, 280–287.
McCracken, G. (1989), "Who is the celebrity endorser? Cultural foundations of the
endorsement process," Journal of Consumer research, 16(3), 310–321.
Ryan, Richard M., and Edward L. Deci (2000), "Self-determination theory and the
facilitation of intrinsic motivation, social development, and well-being," The American psychologist, 55 (1), 68-78.
Sheldon, Kennon M., Richard M. Ryan, Edward L. Deci, and Tim Kasser (2004), "The
independent effects of goal contents and motives on well-being: it's both what you pursue and why you pursue it," Personality and social psychology bulletin, 30 (4), 475-86.

Effects of Narrative Transportation on Persuasion: A Meta-Analysis

Tom van Laer, ESCP Europe, United Kingdom
Ko de Ruyter, Maastricht University, the Netherlands
Martin Wetzels, Maastricht University, the Netherlands

EXTENDED ABSTRACT

The impact of narrative transportation on persuasion continues to attract research attention (e.g., Escalas 2004; Escalas 2007; Green and Brock 2000, 2002; Slater and Rouner 2002). When consumers lose themselves in a story, their attitudes and intentions change to reflect that story (Green 2008). Since Green and Brock (2000) initiated quantitative transportation research, many studies have investigated narratives, how they transport consumers, and how they change consumers' views. Furthermore, recent developments have enhanced the significance of transportation effects, including interactive video games (Baranowski et al. 2008), narrative advertising (Chang 2009), and reality TV (Hall 2009). Thus, transportation demands theoretical and applied research attention (Singhal and Rogers 2002).

Despite notable strides, extant transportation literature remains fragmented, in terms of both its conceptual breadth and its empirical findings (e.g., Green, Brock, and Kaufman 2004; Moyer-Gusé 2008; Nabi and Krcmar 2004). A comprehensive synthesis that can unify and advance the field after a decade of transportation research is thus needed. Therefore, this research pursues three objectives: (1) develop a conceptual framework integrating the antecedents and consequences of the transportation effect; (2) empirically assess a model derived through a quantitative meta-analysis; and (3) uncover issues that deserve further attention.

We seek meaningful relationships of transportation with affective and cognitive responses, attitudes, and intentions. In line with the postulates of transportation theory (Green 2008; Green and Brock 2002), our meta-analytic model comprises the story, medium, and consumer attributes as the antecedents of the transportation effect. Finally, our model considers methodological factors in prior studies.

METHOD

To appear in our meta-analysis, a study must include transportation as a key variable. A vast array of experimental designs is acceptable. We limited our search to literature published after Green and Brock's (2000) empirical operationalization. Our search produced 12 unpublished and 187 published articles (including book sections) related to transportation.

We analyzed 287 effect sizes. To ensure the independence of the effect sizes, we applied Johnson and Eagly's (1989) technique. Two expert researchers classified the multitude of dependent variables reported in the identified studies, using four categories: affective response, cognitive response, attitude, and intention. These expert coders achieved acceptable agreement levels (Cohen's $\kappa = .74$, $p < .001$) but disagreed on 54 variables (18.8%).

For these 54 variables, 189 undergraduate students served as the coders. Each variable was summarized in several sentences and included on a questionnaire. The questionnaire instructed respondents to read each variable description carefully and decide which of the outcome categories it represented, as described at the top of the questionnaire. Respondents coded the variables and we entered the mode into the analysis.

The effect size statistic contrasts groups on their mean transportation and outcome scores. The Pearson correlation provides the effect size indicator. We calculated not only the sample-weighted, reliability-adjusted r but also the conservative random effect z (Hunter and Schmidt 2004). To determine the presence of heterogeneity, we used the QWithin statistic (Huedo-Medina et al. 2006). In addition, we determined the file drawer N, or the number of studies with a zero effect size required to reduce the mean effect size to a probability level of $\alpha = .05$ (Rosenthal 1991). The QBetween statistic tests whether the size of the effect differs across factor levels (Borenstein et al. 2009; Hedges and Olkin 1985).

RESULTS

Transportation had significant, positive on affective responses (file drawer $N = 2,955$), cognitive responses (file drawer $N = 330$), attitudes (file drawer $N = 8,001$), and intentions (file drawer $N = 3,304$). Because we determined positive main effects for all outcomes, we could merge the correlations of transportation with the four outcome variables into an overall persuasive transportation effect.

The transportation effect varied for chronology and intrusiveness. However, character similarity did not have an effect. The transportation effect was also greater with greater media readability. However, richness did not enhance the transportation effect. The transportation effect further differed depending on consumers' familiarity and transportability. However, no significant effect emerged for attention.

Finally, transportation occurs when a study uses participant distraction, simple observation, or in-story perspective manipulation; assigns participants randomly; focuses on a communication or marketing domain; provides incentives; and includes highly educated, young, male participants.

DISCUSSION

This research underscores the robustness of the effect of narrative transportation and builds on previous research to refine extant understanding. Transportation has a significant impact on each stage of narrative processing, from mental processing invested to empathize with story characters to changes in consumers' beliefs. Moreover, transportation's effect appears influenced by key variables, such as the consumer's familiarity with the story topic and chronic propensity to be transported. These findings have implications for not only persuasion research but communication practices overall—as demonstrated by the growing popularity of public narratives. As consumers increasingly experience transportation in their dealings with persuasive narratives, it becomes increasingly important to understand the processes underlying narrative communication. We have identified some research paths and thus hope to have enabled scholars and practitioners alike to see the way forward as well.

REFERENCES

Argo, Jennifer J, Rui Zhu, and Darren W Dahl (2008), "Fact or Fiction: An Investigation of Empathy Differences in Response to Emotional Melodramatic Entertainment," *Journal of Consumer Research*, 34 (5), 614-23.

Baranowski, Tom, Richard Buday, Debbe I. Thompson, and Janice Baranowski (2008), "Playing for Real: Video Games and Stories for Health-Related Behavior Change," *American Journal of Preventive Medicine*, 34 (1), 74-82.

Borenstein, Michael, Larry V Hedges, Julian P T Higgins, and Hannah R Rothstein (2009), *Introduction to Meta-Analysis*, Chichester: John Wiley & Sons.

Bracken, Cheryl Campanella (2006), "Perceived Source Credibility of Local Television News: The Impact of Television Form and Presence," *Journal of Broadcasting & Electronic Media*, 50 (4), 723-41.

Braverman, Julia (2008), "Testimonials Versus Informational Persuasive Messages: The Moderating Effect of Delivery Mode and Personal Involvement," *Communication Research*, 35 (5), 666-94.

Chang, Chingching (2008), "Increasing Mental Health Literacy Via Narrative Advertising," *Journal of Health Communication*, 13 (1), 37-55.

--- (2009), ""Being Hooked" By Editorial Content: The Implications for Processing Narrative Advertising," *Journal of Advertising*, 38 (1), 21-33.

Dal Cin, Sonya (2005), "The Use of Stories as Persuasive Tools," doctoral dissertation, University of Waterloo, Waterloo, ON.

Dal Cin, Sonya, Mark P. Zanna, and Geoffrey T. Fong (2004), "Narrative Persuasion and Overcoming Resistance," in *Resistance and Persuasion*, ed. Eric S Knowles and Jay A Linn, Mahwah, NJ: Lawrence Erlbaum, 175-91.

de Graaf, Anneke, José Sanders, Hans Beentjes, and Hans Hoeken (2007), "De Rol Van Identificatie in Narratieve Overtuiging," *Tijdschrift voor Taalbeheersing*, 29 (3), 237-50.

Escalas, Jennifer Edson (2004), "Imagine Yourself in the Product: Mental Simulation, Narrative Transportation, and Persuasion," *Journal of Advertising*, 33 (2), 37-48.

--- (2007), "Self-Referencing and Persuasion: Narrative Transportation Versus Analytical Elaboration," *Journal of Consumer Research*, 33 (4), 421-29.

Escalas, Jennifer Edson, Marian Chapman Moore, and Julie Edell Britton (2004), "Fishing for Feelings? Hooking Viewers Helps!," *Journal of Consumer Psychology*, 14 (1-2), 105-14.

Green, Melanie C. (2004), "Transportation into Narrative Worlds: The Role of Prior Knowledge and Perceived Realism," *Discourse Processes*, 38 (2), 247-67.

--- (2008), "Transportation Theory," in *International Encyclopedia of Communication*, ed. Wolfgang Donsbach, Oxford, UK: Wiley-Blackwell, 5170-75.

Green, Melanie C. and Timothy C. Brock (2000), "The Role of Transportation in the Persuasiveness of Public Narratives," *Journal of Personality and Social Psychology*, 79 (5), 701-21.

--- (2002), "In the Mind's Eye: Transportation-Imagery Model of Narrative Persuasion.," in *Narrative Impact: Social and Cognitive Foundations.*, ed. Melanie C. Green, Jeffrey J. Strange and Timothy C. Brock, Mahwah, NJ: Lawrence Erlbaum, 315-41.

Green, Melanie C., Timothy C. Brock, and Geoff F. Kaufman (2004), "Understanding Media Enjoyment: The Role of Transportation into Narrative Worlds," *Communication Theory*, 14 (4), 311-27.

Green, Melanie C., Sheryl Kass, Jana Carrey, Benjamin Herzig, Ryan Feeney, and John Sabini (2008), "Transportation across Media: Repeated Exposure to Print and Film," *Media Psychology*, 11 (4), 512-39.

Hall, Alice (2009), "Perceptions of the Authenticity of Reality Programs and Their Relationships to Audience Involvement, Enjoyment, and Perceived Learning," *Journal of Broadcasting & Electronic Media*, 53 (4), 515-31.

Hedges, Larry V and I Olkin (1985), *Statistical Methods for Meta-Analysis*, Orlando, FL: Academic Press.

Huedo-Medina, Tania B., Julio Sánchez-Meca, Fulgencio Marín-Martínez, and Juan Botella (2006), "Assessing Heterogeneity in Meta-Analysis: Q Statistic or I^2 Index?," *Psychological Methods*, 11 (2), 193-206.

Hunter, John Edward and Frank L Schmidt (2004), *Methods of Meta-Analysis: Correcting Error and Bias in Research Findings* Newbury Park, CA: Sage.

Johnson, Blair T. and Alice H. Eagly (1989), "Effects of Involvement on Persuasion: A Meta-Analysis," *Psychological Bulletin*, 106 (2), 290-314.

LaMarre, Heather L. and Kristen D. Landreville (2009), "When Is Fiction as Good as Fact? Comparing the Influence of Documentary and Historical Reenactment Films on Engagement, Affect, Issue Interest, and Learning," *Mass Communication and Society*, 12 (4), 537-55.

Landreville, Kristen D. and Heather L. LaMarre (2010), "Working through Political Entertainment: How Negative Emotion and Narrative Engagement Encourage Political Discussion Intent," *Communication Quarterly*.

Mar, Raymond A., Keith Oatley, Jacob Hirsh, Jennifer. dela Paz, and Jordan B. Peterson (2006), "Bookworms Versus Nerds: Exposure to Fiction Versus Non-Fiction, Divergent Associations with Social Ability, and the Simulation of Fictional Social Worlds," *Journal of Research in Personality*, 40 (5), 694-712.

Morgan, Susan E, Lauren Movius, and Michael J Cody (2009), "The Power of Narratives: The Effect of Entertainment Television Organ Donation Storylines on the Attitudes, Knowledge, and Behaviors of Donors and Nondonors," *Journal of Communication*, 59 (1), 135-U24.

Moyer-Gusé, Emily (2008), "Toward a Theory of Entertainment Persuasion: Explaining the Persuasive Effects of Entertainment-Education Messages," *Communication Theory*, 18 (3), 407-25.

Nabi, Robin L. and Marina Krcmar (2004), "Conceptualizing Media Enjoyment as Attitude: Implications for Mass Media Effects Research," *Communication Theory*, 14 (4), 288-310.

Rosenthal, Robert (1991), *Meta-Analytic Procedures for Social Research*, Newbury Park, CA: Sage.

Schlosser, Ann E. (2003), "Experiencing Products in the Virtual World: The Role of Goal and Imagery in Influencing Attitudes Versus Purchase Intentions," *Journal of Consumer Research*, 30 (2), 184-98.

Shrum, L. J. (2009), "Television Viewing, Materialism, and Life Satisfaction: Mediating and Moderating Processes in the Cultivation Effect," in *Cultivation and materialism*.

Shrum, L. J., James E. Burroughs, and Aric Rindfleisch (2005), "Television's Cultivation of Material Values," *Journal of Consumer Research*, 32 (3), 473-79.

Singhal, Arvind and Everett M Rogers (2002), "A Theoretical Agenda for Entertainment-Education," *Communication Theory*, 12 (2), 117–35.

Slater, Michael D. and Donna Rouner (2002), "Entertainment-Education and Elaboration Likelihood: Understanding the Processing of Narrative Persuasion," *Communication Theory*, 12 (2), 117-244.

van den Hende, Ellis A., Jan P. L. Schoormans, Kaj P. N. Morel, Tatiana Lashina, Evert van Loenen, and Erik I. de Boevere (2007), "Using Early Concept Narratives to Collect Valid Customer Input About Breakthrough Technologies: The Effect of Application Visualization on Transportation," *Technological Forecasting and Social Change*, 74 (9), 1773-87.

van Laer, Tom (2005), "How the Mechanisms Underlying Analytical and Narrative Persuasion Differ," master's thesis, Department of Business Communications, University of Nijmegen, Nijmegen.

Vaughn, Leigh Ann, Zhivka Petkova, Sarah J Hesse, Lindsay Trudeau, and Melahat Ozses (2007), "When It Feels Easy to Enter a Story: Processing Fluency and Mental Transportation Via Narratives," in *Processing fluency and transportation*, Ithaca, NY.

Wang, Jing and Bobby J Calder (2006), "Media Transportation and Advertising," *Journal of Consumer Research*, 33 (2), 151-62.

--- (2009), "Media Engagement and Advertising: Transportation, Matching, Transference and Intrusion," *Journal of Consumer Psychology*, 19 (3), 546-55.

West, Patricia M, Joel Huber, and Kyeong Sam Min (2004), "Altering Experienced Utility: The Impact of Story Writing and Self-Referencing on Preferences," *Journal of Consumer Research*, 31, 623-30.

Good Deeds, Risky Bids: Accessible Pro-Social Behavior Increases Monetary Risk Taking

Maria Blekher, Ben-Gurion University of the Negev, Israel
Shai Danziger, Tel-Aviv University, Israel
Amir Grinstein, Ben-Gurion University of the Negev, Israel

EXTENDED ABSTRACT

Pro-social behavior is common. A rich literature explains why people act pro-socially (e.g., Boezeman & Ellemers, 2007; Erez, Mikulincer, Ijzendoorn, & Kroonenberg, 2008), and documents positive consequences of pro-social behavior on well-being and health (Borgonovi, 2008; Post, 2005; Strahilevitz, 2011; Thoits & Hewitt, 2001; Van Willigen, 2000). Recent evidence suggests accessible pro-social decisions transiently influence self-perceptions and consequently choice. Khan and Dhar (2006) find that in a hypothetical-choice task, choosing among volunteering options transiently boosts a positive self-concept, thereby "licensing" the choice of a self-indulgent option in a subsequent task. Mazar and Zhong (2010) find people act less altruistically after purchasing green products than after purchasing conventional products. The authors propose that by boosting a person's moral self-concept, virtuous decisions "license" indulgence in self-interested and unethical behavior.

We suggest accessible pro-social behaviors may also increase risk taking. Specifically, we propose that in addition to making people feel virtuous, accessible pro-social behaviors may signal a safe environment (Mikulincer et al., 2001, and Mikulnicer & Shaver, 2005, for evidence that people tend to volunteer when they feel secure), increase one's feelings of interdependence (Borgonovi, 2008), prompt an optimistic outlook (Mellor, et al., 2008), and increase sense of control (Mellor, et al., 2008). We propose these outcomes either independently or jointly contribute to feelings of security, which, as we outline next, increase financial risk taking, presumably via a mechanism whereby decision makers gauge risk by how they feel at the time of choice (Loewenstein, Weber, Hsee, & Welch, 2001).

Hsee and Weber (1999) report the size of a person's social network is positively correlated with one's willingness to take financial risks. The authors suggest the network serves as a safety net should the risky financial decision fail. Mandel (2003) found that people primed to think about their friends and family increased their financial risk taking, acting as if they had a safety net. Last, Levav and Argo (2010) show that being lightly touched by another person increases one's feelings of security, which mediates preference for risky financial decisions.

In light of these findings, we propose that accessible volunteering behavior increases feelings of security, which promotes risky decision making. We test our prediction in four studies. In each study, we assessed risk taking by asking participants to make 14 choices between sure payoffs and risky gambles. Studies 1a and 1b demonstrate that an accessible act of volunteering increases risky monetary decision making, the mediating role of sense of security, and that the volunteering effect is not contingent on just-world beliefs. Study 2 shows that expressing volunteering intent increases monetary risk taking in participants primed to feel insecure, but not in participants primed to feel secure. This finding demonstrates the moderating role of feelings of security. Finally, study 3 shows the effect of volunteering intent on risky decision making can be eliminated when the reason for volunteering is attributed to an external source.

Study 1a tested whether an accessible pro-social act increases monetary risk taking. Participants were asked either before or after they engaged in a purportedly unrelated monetary risk-taking task whether they had volunteered in the past six months. The monetary risk taking task consisted of making 14 hypothetical choices between a sure cash payoff and a risky gamble (Hsee and Weber 1999). Participants were told they would participate in a lottery and the four winners would receive payment according to their decision in a randomly selected choice out of the 14. We also measured sense of security. Supporting our prediction, accessible pro-social activity increased risk taking and sense of security mediated this effect.

Study 1b replicated the initial effect, ruled out an alternative account, and showed the effect is not contingent on just-world beliefs

Study 2 examined whether feelings of security moderate the effect of pro-social intent on risky monetary choices. Participants were randomly assigned to one of four conditions of a 2 (secure/insecure) x 2 (volunteering/control) between-subjects design. Participants completed three purportedly unrelated tasks; first, participants were primed to feel insecure or secure. Then, they either chose a community services or a chair. Finally, participants made the same 14 monetary choices as in Study 1. Consistent with our prediction expressing virtuous intent led to increased risk taking (relative to the control condition) in participants primed to feel insecure but not in participants primed to feel secure.

Study 3 examined whether attributing pro-social intent to an external source attenuates the effect of virtuous intent on risky decision making. As in Study 1, choices were consequential.

As we predicted, when people felt the decision to volunteer was not their own, they did not infer a benign environment and therefore were not more willing to take risks.

Four studies demonstrate a link between accessible volunteering behavior, feelings of security, and monetary risk taking. Importantly, in the introduction, we were careful to note that accessible volunteering may also increase monetary risk taking via a boost in optimism, sense of control, and positive mood (all of which may also contribute to feelings of security).

For example, although our manipulations did not produce significant mood changes, a stronger effect on mood may be experienced while volunteering, which could also increase monetary risk taking (Mano, 1994). Also, although individual differences in just-world beliefs did not moderate the effects of an accessible act of volunteering on risk taking in Study 1b, priming just-world beliefs may have such a moderating effect.

In summary, our findings extend existing research on volunteering behavior and on risk taking. First, we demonstrate a relatively distant, and therefore seemingly unrelated, consequence of accessible volunteering behavior and intent, and second, we document yet another factor that can transiently influence risk-taking preferences. Critically, we demonstrate that an accessible act of volunteering increases feelings of security, which increase the willingness to choose risky options.

REFERENCES

Boezeman, Edwin J. and Naomi Ellemers (2007), "Pride and Respect in Volunteers' Organizational Commitment, " *European Journal of Social Psychology*, 38, 159-172.

Bem, Daryl J. (1972), "Self-Perception Theory," in *Advances in Experimental Social Psychology*, Vol. 6, ed. Leonard Berkowitz, New York, NY: Academic Press, 2-57.

Erez, Ayelet, Mario Mikulincer, Marinus Vanijzendoorn and Pieter Kroonenberg (2008), "Attachment, Personality, and Volunteering: Placing Volunteerism in an Attachment-Theoretical Framework," *Personality and Individual Differences*, 44 (1), 64-74.

Hsee, Christopher. K. and Elke U. Weber (1999), "Cross-National Differences in Risk Preference and Lay Predictions," *Journal of Behavioral Decision Making*, 12 (2), 165-179.

Khan, Uzma and Ravi Dhar (2006), "Licensing Effect in Consumer Choice," *Journal of Marketing Research*, 43 (2), 259-266.

Kouchaki, Maryam (2011), "Vicarious Moral Licensing: the Influence of Others' Past Moral Actions on Moral Behavior," *Journal of Personality and Social Psychology*, 101 (4), 702-15.

Levav, Jonathan and Jennifer Argo (2010), "Physical Contact and Financial Risk Taking," *Psychological Science*, 21 (6), 804-10.

Mandel, Naomi (2003), "Shifting Selves and Decision Making: The Effects of Self-Construal Priming on Consumer Risk-Taking," *Journal of Consumer Research*, 30 (1), 30-40.

Mazar, Nina and Chen Bo Zhong (2010), "Do Green Products Make Us Better People?" *Psychological Science*, 21 (4), 494-8.

McCoy, Kathleen, Mark E. Cummings and Patrick T. Davies (2009), "Constructive and Destructive Marital Conflict, Emotional Security and Children's Pro Social Behavior," *Journal of Child Psychology and Psychiatry*, 50, 270–279.

Mikulincer, Mario, Omri Gillath, Vered Halevy, Neta Avihou, Shelly Avidan and Nitzan Eshkoli (2001), "Attachment Theory and Reactions to Others' Needs: Evidence that Activation of the Sense of Attachment Security Promotes Empathic Responses," *Journal of Personality and Social Psychology*, 81 (6), 1205-1224.

Mikulincer, Mario and Phillip R. Shaver (2005), "Attachment Security, Compassion, and Altruism," *Current Directions in Psychological Science*, 14 (1), 34-38.

Musick, Mark and John Wilson (2003). "Volunteering and Depression: the Role of Psychological and Social Resources in Different Age Groups," Social *Science & Medicine*, 56 (2), 259-69.

Post, Stephen G. (2005), "It's Good to Be Good," *International Journal of Behavioral Medicine*, 12 (2), 66–77.

Thompson, Edmund R. (2007), "Development and Validation of an Internationally Reliable Short-Form of the Positive and Negative Affect Schedule (PANAS)," *Journal of Cross-Cultural Psychology*, 38 (2), 227-242.

Watson, David, Lee A. Clark and Auke Tellegen (1988), "Development and Validation of Brief Measures of Positive and Negative Affect: the PANAS Scales," *Journal of Personality and Social Psychology*, 54 (6), 1063-1070.

Van Willigen, Marieke (2000), "Differential Benefits of Volunteering Across the Life Course," *The Journal of Gerontology: Social Sciences,* 55B, S308–318

The Haefer Group Ltd. (2009). The younger generation and volunteering, http://www.regionalassociation.org/RAC.

When are Frugal Consumers NOT Frugal? It Depends on Who They Are With

Seung Hwan (Mark) Lee, Colorado State University, USA

EXTENDED ABSTRACT

When are frugal consumers not frugal? Increasing recognition by marketing researchers to understand non-consumption has sparked an interest in exploring the spending habits of frugal consumers (Bardhi and Arnould 2005; Lastovicka et al. 1999; Rick, Cryder, and Loewenstein 2008). By definition, frugality is a "unidimensional consumer lifestyle trait characterized by the degree to which consumers are both restrained in acquiring and in resourcefully using economic goods and services to achieve long-term goals" (Lastovicka et al. 1999, p. 88). It is the extent to which individuals exhibit self-restraint in their consumption behavior (Kasser 2005).

For the most part, literature on frugality has primarily focused on individual characteristics and behavior, ignoring the impact of individuals' network (and/or reference group) on their frugal behavior. Given that consumers are often influenced by how others will judge and perceive them (Calder and Burnkrant 1977), individuals' personal networks should play an influential force in one's frugal identity. Personal networks can also act as reference groups for consumers. Reference groups are important because it can be an influential force in establishing social norms (Fisher and Ackerman 1998). The normative pressures that the group exerts result in high levels of influence over a variety of individuals' decision (Feldman 1984). A major source of influence comes from consumers' belief about how others will perceive their decisions (Calder and Brunkrant 1977).

However, previous research suggests that frugality may be an exception; it is a trait that is considered not to be influenced by social factors. Lastovicka et al. (1999) suggest that frugal consumers are more independent than the average consumer, and thus they are less swayed by their interpersonal network. Since frugal consumers are disciplined in their spending, they are better able to withstand the social pressures to be engaged in money-spending activities (Lastovicka et al. 1999). However, this research will suggest that under certain conditions, the frugality trait is malleable to social influences, especially when they are consuming with individuals from high-spending networks. More importantly, frugality may be a relative trait, rather than a constant trait as people presumed it to be. Four studies were conducted to explore this inquiry.

Study 1 was a two-way between subjects design with two measured factors, average spending of their personal network (ASPN) and frugality (scale from Lastovicka et al. 1999) (n=110). High (low) ASPN indicates high (low) spending networks. Individuals were asked to list a close group of friends whom they see on a regular basis. Then participants rated each of their friends on three seven-point bi-polar items (Save Money / Spend Money, Thrifty / Spendthrift, Economical / Splurge). To calculate the degree of spending by their personal network, we averaged the scores of these three items (α = .89) for each person and then averaged the scores of friends listed (participant's social network) to get the ASPN index. Next, participants were asked to choose an ideal meal that they would have in their outing with their friends (the friends that they listed). The results show a significant interaction between individual's frugality and ASPN, β = .25, t = 2.76, p <.01, f^2 = .07. Simple slopes test confirmed that the effect of frugality on the amount ordered was significant for those in the low ASPN groups (one SD below the mean of ASPN), b = -4.17, t = -5.81, p < .001 and non-significant for those in the high ASPN groups (one SD above the mean), b = -1.20, t = .22, ns.

This study was replicated in a field setting using an actual social network (n=42). Instead of asking individuals to list their friends, network analysis was used to determine people's social network. The dependent variable for this study was average monthly spending (not including rent, groceries, and bills). Consistent with study 1's findings, there was a significant interaction between frugality and ASPN, β = .30, t = 2.03, p <.05, f^2 = .11. Simple slopes test confirmed that the effects of frugality on monthly spending was significant for those in low SN groups (one SD below the mean), b = -51.67, t = -2.50, p < .05, and non-significant for those in high SN groups (one SD above the mean), b = 7.80, t = .34, ns. More importantly, this study also revealed that frugal individuals in high spending networks have an inaccurate perception of their own level of frugality. Specifically, frugal individuals perceived that they were frugal, although they were not perceived to be frugal by their friends. This perhaps can explain why frugal individuals in high spending networks were willing to spend, because relatively, they may have perceived that they were spending less than their peers, thus believing that they were frugal.

The results from study 3 show that the effects of prior studies are limited to strong-tie networks, thus, introducing a boundary condition. When frugal individuals are consuming with high spending acquaintances (weak-tie ASPN), they behave according to their trait. However, when frugal individuals are consuming with high spending friends (strong-tie ASPN), they spent nearly as much as those who were non-frugal.

Finally, the results from study 4 show that the effects of prior studies are limited to publicly-consumed goods. Under the privately-consumed good (i.e. mattresses) condition, frugal consumers behaved according to their trait. However, under the publicly-consumed good condition (i.e., notebooks), frugal consumers spent more when they were primed to list a network of high spending friends.

In conclusion, findings from four studies (two experimental, two field-based studies) reveal that when frugal individuals consume with high spending networks, they spend more than those that consume with low spending networks (Study 1). These results are replicated in a field study, but also show that frugal consumers in high spending networks were not perceived to be frugal, even though they believed themselves to be frugal (Study 2). Next, the results demonstrate that these effects occur only in strong-tie networks (as opposed to weak-tie networks), introducing a boundary condition (Study 3). Finally, these effects apply only to publicly consumed products and not privately consumed products (Study 4).

REFERENCES

Bardhi, Fleura and Eric J. Arnould (2005), "Thrift Shopping: Combining Utilitarian Thrift and Hedonic Treat Benefits " *Journal of Consumer Behaviour*, 4 (4), 223-33.

Calder, Bobby J. and Robert E. Burnkrant (1977), "Interpersonal Influence on Consumer Behavior: An Attribution Theory Approach," *Journal of Consumer Research*, 4, 29-38.

Feldman, Daniel C. (1984), "The Development and Enforcement of Group Norms," *Academy of Management Review*, 9 (1), 47-53.

Kasser, Tim (2005), "Frugality, Generosity, and Materialism in Children and Adolescents," in *What Do Children Need to Flourish?: Conceptualizing and Measuring Indicators of Positive Development*, ed. Kristin Moore and Laura Lippman, New York: NY: Springer.

Lastovicka, John L., Lance A. Bettencourt, Renee S. Hughner, and Ronald J. Knutze (1999), "Lifestyle of the Tight and Frugal: Theory and Measurement," *Journal of Consumer Research*, 26 (1), 85-98.

Scott, Rick, Cynthia Cryder, and George Loewenstein (2008), "Tightwads and Spendthrifts," *Journal of Consumer Research*, 34 (6), 767-82.

From Bye-Bye to Buy Buy: Influence of Homophonic Primes on Judgment and Behavior

Derick F. Davis, Virginia Tech, USA
Paul M. Herr, Virginia Tech, USA

EXTENDED ABSTRACT

Can reading the word "bye" influence how much someone is willing to pay to "buy" a product? Or can telling consumers to "wait" influence their perceptions of a target object's "weight"? We investigate conditions where one homophone – a word that sounds the same as another but has different spelling and meaning –primes perceptions and behaviors related to the complementary homophone. We suggest that this priming effect is an outgrowth of the reading process and is more likely to occur when individuals experience cognitive load, as load suppresses a secondary corrective process (Gernsbacher and Faust 1991). This research represents the first demonstration of homophone behavioral and perceptual priming and contributes to our understanding of priming in general.

We argue the described effect is an outgrowth of an automatic process—wherein stimuli induce processing (Bargh 1994; Schneider and Shiffrin 1977). We also draw from research on homophones and their relationships from the cognitive psychology literature (Lesch and Pollatsek 1993; Lukatela and Turvey 1994; Van Orden 1987). This research finds that homophones are linked via their phonology and can influence subsequent tasks (e.g. lexical decision tasks, Pexman et al. 2001; stem completion tasks, Rueckl and Mathew 1999; and also induce memory errors, Azuma et al. 2004; Starns et al. 2006), however these investigations never extend to the behavioral realm—where homophones can prime behaviors and perceptions.

In four studies we investigate how one word in a homophone pair (i.e. wait, right, bye, or phew) can influence behaviors and/or alter perceptions related to the complementary homophone (weight, write, buy, and few, respectively). We find support for homophone priming, relative to control conditions, but only when participants experience cognitive load, suggesting participants suppress the influence of homophone primes with sufficient cognitive resources (Gernsbacher and Faust 1991).

In study 1, we test if reading, "wait" can influence perceptions of "weight". The experiment had eight conditions (Wait Type: No Wait, 30sec wait labeled "delay", 30sec wait labeled "wait", 30sec wait without labeling) x (cognitive load: load vs. no load). Participants were primed then completed the target task, wherein they viewed a grocery bag depiction and answered, "If you placed the bag on a scale, what is your guess for the readout in pounds?" and "To ask another way, how heavy is the bag above?" on a 7-point scale anchored by "not heavy at all" and "very heavy". Responses were combined into a composite measure of subjective weight (cronbach's alpha = .83). An ANOVA revealed a marginal main effect of wait type ($F(3, 223) = 2.5$, $p = .06$), and a significant wait type x load interaction ($F(3, 223) = 3.74$, $p < .05$). Planned contrasts revealed that subjective weights in the wait/wait load condition were significantly greater than in any other condition (all ps < .05). Indicating that participants who read "wait" perceived the grocery bag to weigh more, but only when under cognitive load.

In study 2, we test if reading, "right" elicits longer essays from participants (i.e. they "write" more). The experiment had five instruction conditions (two containing the word "right" and three controls) crossed with a load manipulation. The main task was to "tell us about" a recent grocery trip. Initial analyses confirmed that collapsing conditions into "right" vs. "control" was appropriate. An ANOVA revealed a main effect of condition ($F(1, 150) = 10.02$, $p < .01$) such that people who saw the word "right" wrote fourteen more words on average, a marginal effect of load ($p = .059$), which was qualified by a significant condition x load interaction ($F(1, 150) = 5.20$, $p < .03$). An inspection of the means revealed that participants wrote more (eighteen words more on average) when they read "right" under load. Control conditions did not significantly differ from each other.

In study 3, we test if reading "bye" influences "buying" behaviors. Participants read an ostensibly unrelated story about a vacationer's last day. The story either concluded with the writer saying "Bye Bye" or "So Long" to their vacation spot. These conditions were crossed with a load manipulation. Participants then read about a restaurant promotion and indicated their WTP for dinner for two, this was the dependent variable related to "buy". An ANOVA revealed a significant condition x load interaction ($F(1, 109) = 4.03$, $p < .05$) such that people under load who read "Bye Bye" were willing to pay the most for the restaurant deal. Planned contrasts revealed that WTP in this condition was significantly greater than in any other condition (all ps < .05).

In study 4, we test if reading "phew" can have a downward effect on behavioral intentions. Participants read a story that ended with the protagonist exclaiming "phew" or "close call". These conditions were crossed with a load manipulation. Participants then answered a behavioral intention question (9-point scale) about saving money in the next year (a socially desirable behavior). This served as the dependent variable. An analysis revealed a significant prime x load interaction ($F(1, 173) = 5.85$, $p < .02$) such that individuals who read "phew" while under load indicated that they intended to save less money than any other condition (planned contrasts, all ps <.05).

Taken together these studies provide initial evidence for how homophones can prime perceptions and behavior. It contributes to our understanding of how and when behavioral priming can occur, by identifying a new way to prime behavior and influence perceptions. Homophones can prime both "more" and "less" of a behavior, behavioral intention, and perceptions. Additionally, this research may contribute to a related stream of research on phonemes and the role of phonology in branding (Argo et al. 2010; Lowrey and Shrum 2007; Yorkston and Menon 2004) and marketing in general. Consider for instance, the case of the weight loss drug "Alli". It is a constructed or psuedohomophone designed to help consumers understand that the drug is their "ally" in weight loss.

REFERENCES

Argo, Jennifer J., Monica Popa, and Malcolm C. Smith (2010), "The Sound of Brands," *Journal of Consumer Research,* 74(July), 97-109.

Azuma, Tamiko, Erica J. Williams, and Juliet E. Davie (2004), "Paws + Cause = Pause? Memory Load and Memory Blends in Homophone Recognition," *Psychonomic Bulletin and Review,* 11(4), 723-28.

Bargh, John A. (1994), "The Four Horsemen of Automaticity: Awareness, Intention, Efficiency, and Control in Social Cognition," in *Handbook of Social Cognition,* ed. Robert S. Wyer Jr. and Thomas K. Srull, Hillsdale, NJ: Erlbaum, 1-40.

Gernsbacher, Morton Ann and Mark E. Faust (1991), "The Mechanism of Suppression: A Component of General Comprehension Skill," *Journal of Experimental Psychology: Learning, Memory, and Cognition,* 17(2), 245-62.

Higgins, Edward T. (1996), "Knowledge Activation: Accessibility, Applicability, and Salience," in *Social Psychology: Handbook of Basic Principles,* ed. E. Tory Higgins and Arie W. Kruglanski, New York, NY: Guilford Press, 133-68.

Lesch, Mary F., and Alexander Pollatsek (1993), "Automatic Access of Semantic Information by Phonological Codes in Visual Word Recognition," *Journal of Experimental Psychology: Learning, Memory, and Cognition,* 19(2), 285-94.

Lowrey, Tina M. and L.J. Shrum (2007), "Phonetic Symbolism and Brand Name Preference," *Journal of Consumer Research,* 34(October), 406-14.

Lukatela, Georgije, and M. T. Turvey (1994), "Visual Lexical Access is Initially Phonological: 1. Evidence from Associative Priming by Words, Homophones, and Pseudohomophones," *Journal of Experimental Psychology: General,* 123(2), 107-28.

Pexman, Penny M., Stephen J. Lupker, and Debra Jared (2001), "Homophone Effects in Lexical Decision," *Journal of Experimental Psychology: Learning, Memory, and Cognition,* 27(1), 139-56.

Rueckl, Jay G., and Shashi Mathew (1999), "Implicit Memory for Phonological Processes in a Visual Stem Completion", *Memory & Cognition,* 27 (1), 1-11.

Schneider, Walter, and Richard M. Shiffrin (1977), "Controlled and Automatic Human Information Processing: I. Detection, Search, and Attention," *Psychological Review,* 84(1), 1-66.

Starns, Jeffrey J., Gabriel I. Cook, Jason L. Hicks, and Richard L. Marsh (2006), "On Rejecting Emotional Lures Created by Phonological Neighborhood Activation," *Journal of Experimental Psychology: Learning, Memory, and Cognition,* 32(4), 847-53.

Van Orden, G.C. (1987), "A ROWS is a ROSE: Spelling, Sound and Reading," *Memory & Cognition,* 15, 181-98.

Yorkston, Eric, and Geeta Menon (2004), "A Sound Idea: Phonetic Effects of Brand Names on Consumer Judgments," *Journal of Consumer Research,* 31(June), 43-51.

Towards a Better Understanding of the Role of Social Media in the Processes of Independent and Interdependent Identity Construction

Gachoucha Kretz, ISC, Paris
Benjamin G. Voyer, ESCP Europe, UK

EXTENDED ABSTRACT

1. Introduction

With more than 520 million daily-active Facebook users (April 2012), social media have now become part of many customers' life. Individuals use social media to obtain information, entertain themselves, and fulfil mood-management needs (Shao, 2009). We argue and show here that social media also fulfil more profound identity construction needs, and can be used to communicate with brands about symbolic aspects of consumption. Using the example of consumers running weblogs about fashion and luxury products – which represent one of the most common types of weblogs on the Internet (Rickman & Cosenza, 2007) – we address one of the paradoxes of social media: namely, that despite the social nature of these media, many customers use them *primarily* for managing personal and symbolic aspects of their identity construction and relations with brands. The present paper contributes to the literature on social media and consumer identities, by offering a way of framing the existing literature and findings, combining both traditional literatures on symbolic consumptions (Levy, 1959) and more recent approaches to independent and interdependent identities and self-construals (Markus & Kitayama, 1991).

2. Methods

We carried out a netnography (Kozinets, 2010) from mid-2005 to end of 2011 on 30 popular fashion / luxury weblogs to research individual differences in self-construal and further corroborated our interpretations through in-depth interviews with 20 of these 30 bloggers.

3. Results & Discussion

Our findings – summarised in table 1 - suggest that fashion and luxury bloggers develop different types of independent and interdependent identities through personal branding, and carefully designed interaction strategies with others. The type of personal brand - or 'character'- construed differs on what we identified as the four dimensions of a blogger's identity: dominant mode of *self-construal*, type of '*others*' he/she interacts with, type of *relationship* he/she *aims a*t, and *dominant type of social media* used. Based on different combinations of these dimensions, consumers develop different characters, which they use to signal to others - and particularly to brands - the kind of communal activities bloggers would like to engage into and with what members.

Celebrity bloggers are bloggers who became very famous, regularly work for famous brands and designers, and post their work and stories on their weblog. Their primary motivation is to be recognized as a like of the people they admire (designers, photographers…), but not to belong to or interact with a community of bloggers. They thus hold a highly dominant independent *self-construal* - only making obvious bonds with the fashion and luxury people they have worked with - and low levels of interdependent self-construal. The '*others*' they interact with are mainly brands and brand representatives or fellow professionals. The '*type of relationship*' they aim at creating with brands is a worshipping one. Celebrity bloggers signal potential partner brands their willingness to work for them. Interestingly, we found that while these bloggers engage into active networking with professionals they want to become like, they mostly do so offline. Celebrity bloggers gather most of their online social media content on their weblogs and make scarce use of other social networks like Facebook or Twitter.

Character bloggers are those who became famous among a very dedicated audience and web marketing agencies, being occasionally mentioned in women's magazines. They are rather independent, while entertaining very close relationships with a few peer- bloggers and web-marketing representatives with whom the have become friends. These types of bloggers have a high level of independent *self-construal*, and a moderate level of interdependent *self-construal*. The '*others*' made obvious in their weblogs are their blogger friends and brands promoted by their web marketing agencies' connections. The *relationship* they aim for is a 'clique' one: sharing scarce resources, with limited access for new entrants. The *dominant social media* used are weblogs, where most of the brand narrative happens. Facebook, Twitter, Lookbook or Flickr are used for a public account of activities, serve as a recruitment platform for other readers, and also as a location for extended self-construal and personal branding.

Spokesperson bloggers are bloggers that became famous and received media coverage, eventually turning their blogging activities into a job (journalism, acting…). Spokespersons usually use their influence to speak up about causes such as fighting for larger sizes in fashion. By embracing issues that federate other bloggers, they display a high level of interdependent self-construal. Their status also contributes to moderate levels of independent *self-construal*. The '*others*' they like to introduce on their weblogs are fellow bloggers, most of whom are simple readers, with whom they want to share opinions and co-produce debates and discussions. Brands are not always present in these discussions, except if relevant to the cause being defended. The *type of relationship* Spokesperson bloggers want to create is a highly interactive and communal one. Thus, discussions happen on every platform possible (e.g. commenting on their weblog, Facebook page, professional website, Twitter account…).

Finally, **Buddy** bloggers are those who are not famous but who are liked by a strong loyal community of readers / followers. Their motivation to weblog is most of all about sharing their passion and ideas about fashion and luxury consumption with other passionate people. Consequently, Buddy bloggers display high levels of interdependent *self-construal*, and low levels of independent self-construal. The '*others*' they interact with are firstly their readers, then fellow bloggers. Buddy bloggers are organized in 'bastions' or subgroups of similar bloggers, who adore each other within the subgroups and hate each other outside those subgroups. Brands are also very present in their narratives. Buddy bloggers mainly promote them directly in accordance with what they feel their audience will like. The *relationship* built with the audience is about recommending and trusting, and Buddy bloggers therefore always try and balance branded narratives with readers' expectations and comments. Because interactions and recommendations are at the heart of Buddy weblogs, discussions happens on all possible *loci*, whether in the weblogs comments or on various social networks.

Overall, our paper is the first to investigate the relation between the use of social media and the development of different types of independent and interdependent identities, via self-construal.

REFERENCES

Kozinets, R. V. (2010). *Netnography. Doing ethnographic research online.* Thousand Oaks, CA: Sage Publications.

Levy, S. J. (1959). Symbols for Sale. *Harvard Business Review 37*(July-August), 117-119.

Markus, H. R., & Kitayama, S. (1991). Culture and the self: Implications for cognition, emotion, and motivation. *Psychological Review, 98*(2), 224-253.

Rickman, T. A., & Cosenza, R. M. (2007). The changing digital dynamics of multichannel marketing: The feasibility of the weblog: text mining approach for fast fashion trending. *Journal of Fashion Marketing and Management, 11*(4), 604-621.

Shao, G. (2009). Understanding the appeal of user-generated media: a uses and gratification perspective. *Internet Research, 19*(1), 7-25.

APPENDIX

Table 1: The four characters of bloggers' identities

	Type of Self-Construal		Type of communal tools used	Type of relationship aimed at	Types of "Others" bloggers interact with
	Independent Self-Construal	Interdependent Self-Construal			
Celebrity	High	Low	Weblog	Brand worshipping Professional networking	Brands Brand representatives
Character	High	Medium	Weblog Textual social networks Visual social networks	Implicit brand promotion Networking with friends & agencies	Brands Friend- bloggers
Spokesperson	Medium	High	Weblog Textual social networks Professional web resources	Co-production High communal activities	Fellow Bloggers Readers
Buddy	Low	High	Weblog Textual social networks Responding to comments	Bastion High Communal activities Recommendation & Trust	Friend- bloggers Readers

Time and Context Dependencies in Consumer Behavior

Euehun Lee, Korea Advanced Institute of Science and Technology, Korea
Anil Mathur, Hofstra University, USA
Choong Kwai Fatt, University of Malaya, Malaysia
George P. Moschis, Georgia State University, USA

EXTENDED ABSTRACT

Scholars have noted that many consumption phenomena are time and context-dependent, but have offered limited directions that would help researchers study consumers over the course of their lives. The life course paradigm, which is considered one of the most important achievements of social science in the second half of the 20th century and is widely used globally and across disciplines (Elder et al. 2003), can address time and context dependent consumer issues.

The life course approach focuses on examining gradual or abrupt changes in behavior of a unit (e.g., individual, family) that take place over time. These changes are assumed to be embedded with earlier life experiences, including earlier changes in behavior, and are studied as time- and context-dependent events, changes, or transitions. Behavior at any stage in life or given point in time is viewed as the product of responses to earlier life conditions and the way the individual or other units have adapted to various circumstances (Mayer and Tuma 1990). The purpose of this paper is to illustrate the life course approach. Theories and methods are presented, hypotheses based on theoretical life course perspectives are developed, and data from a national longitudinal study are used to test the proposed relationships. Implications of study findings for theory development and future research are also discussed.

According to the life course paradigm, biological and psychological changes during a person's life and social demands across the life course define typical life events and social roles that serve as turning points and affect a person's life; they create physical, emotional, and social demands and circumstances to which one must adapt by changing his or her thoughts and actions. Patterns of thought and action at a given stage in life are viewed as outcomes of one's adaptation to various demands and circumstances experienced earlier in life, with adaptation entailing the processes of (a) stress and coping responses, (b) socialization, and (c) development or growth and decline. These processes are the underlying change mechanisms of the three most widely-accepted life course perspectives: stress, normative, and human capital, respectively (Moschis 2007).

The rapid diffusion of the life course as a research framework across disciplines was largely because of the development of models collectively known as event history analysis (EHA) (Mayer and Tuma 1990). Most EHA models are defined by expressing the hazard rate of an event or change (or transition rate when a shift to one of several states is possible) as a specific function of relevant time dimension (e.g., duration, age), measured covariates, and unmeasured random disturbances (Mayer and Tuma 1990). When an event, transition, or change at any given point depends on how long an individual has been at a given state, it becomes duration-dependent; that is, it can be modeled as a probability in the rate of transition (change) with respect to time on the basis of how long (duration) a person has been in that state. In life course research, a change in behavior is equivalent to an event; it is viewed as a transition from one state to the next (e.g., from a nonuser to a user of a product). Movement from an original state to a destination state defines transitions. All people begin in the original state (e.g., nonusers) and are "at risk" of making the transition to the destination state. The risk of making a transition is defined as a function of time, and the dependent variable is expressed as a probability of change given the length of time a person has been at a given state.

We illustrate the application of life course paradigm by formulating our hypotheses based on the three theoretical perspectives to explain consumers' responses to two types of consumption choices (studied as events)—one first-time and another repeat choice. Acquiring membership in age-segmented associations that serve people over a certain age (ASAS) is a first time decision that requires age eligibility (age 50 that marks the beginning of the "risk" period and defines a person's membership in the "older-age" subculture (e.g., AARP). The second, changes in investments (CINV), which may involve both new investments and new allocation of existing assets, can be a repeated behavior (event) that requires no age eligibility; it is relevant to adult consumers regardless of their stage in life.

A stratified sample of 9500 household heads, heavily skewed toward older-age brackets received the first questionnaire, and exactly five years after the first survey was administered, the 709 identified respondents who agreed to participate in the second survey were mailed the second questionnaire. A total of 379 usable questionnaires were returned (53.4% of those who had agreed to participate), of which 318 could be matched to the first anonymous questionnaire by means of date of birth and other demographic information in rare cases. In our EHA models, the dependent variables were expressed as events that occurred after a consumer had entered the "risk" period of experiencing the specific consumer behavior change.

Among the study findings, results suggest that consumers change their behaviors in anticipation of specific life transition events, suggesting the importance of studying the timing of these changes in response to the expected transitions, and the types of consumers who change their behaviors earlier than others. The life course approach could make a useful contribution to research in consumer behavior because it because it makes time, context, and process more salient dimensions of theory and analysis.

REFERENCES

Elder, Glen H., Jr., Monica Kirkpatrick Johnson, and Robert Crosnoe (2003), "The Emergence and Development of Life Course Theory" in Handbook of the Life Course, ed. J. T. Mortimer and M. J. Shanahan, New York: Plenum Publishers, 3-19.

Mayer, Karl Urich and Nancy B. Tuma (1990), "Life Course Research and Event History Analysis: An Overview," in Event History Analysis in Life Course Research, eds. Karl Ulrich Mayer and Nancy B. Tuma, Madison, WI: University of Wisconsin Press, 3-20.

Moschis, George P. (2007), "Life Course Perspectives on Consumer Behavior," Journal of the Academy of Marketing Science, 35, 2, 295-397.

What Effect Does the Relationship Portfolio Have on Well Being?
Comparing the Impact of Brand, Service, and Interpersonal Relationships

Seung Hwan (Mark) Lee, Colorado State University, USA
Allison Johnson, University of Western Ontario, Canada
Matthew Thomson, University of Western Ontario, Canada

EXTENDED ABSTRACT

Extensive psychological research suggests that the quality and quantity of interpersonal relationships are linked with increased life satisfaction (Argyle 1999). For example, a meta-analysis of almost 300 empirical studies shows that elderly people who enjoy extensive or high quality social contacts report elevated well-being (Pinquart and Sorensen 2000). What is absent, though, is a simultaneous consideration of well-being in light of a person's *consumption* relationships (i.e., service and brand relationships). To explore this opportunity, we contemplate consumers' more broadly-construed relationship portfolios.

Relationships are dyadic enterprises with different types of interaction that may confer a variety of benefits and costs. Interpersonal relationships have myriad possible forms and features, including emotional support (e.g., providing reassurance of self-worth and concern), appraisal support (e.g., feedback and confirmation), information support (e.g., advice and information) and instrumental support (e.g., money or resources) (Wills 1991). These interpersonal relationships "have a powerful effect on happiness and other aspects of well-being, and are perhaps its greatest single cause (Argyle 2001, p. 71).

Likewise, research suggests service relationships have many of these same features and play a non-trivial role in consumer's lives. Indeed, "many services are almost exclusively based upon person-to-person interactions" (Gremler and Brown, p. 174) and service relationships may provide many of the same benefits as interpersonal relationships (Wellman and Gulia 1999).

They typically include the servicing of important human needs such as autonomy, security and belonging (McKenna and Bargh 1999; Wellman and Gulia 1999) that leads to higher life satisfaction both directly and through enhanced self-esteem (Diener and Diener 1995; Kwan, Bond and Singelis 1997).

Here, we explore that possibility that not all relationships are beneficial: Specifically, we investigate whether the number and strength of brand relationships has a negative impact on a person's well-being (e.g. life satisfaction and self-esteem). Consumers form meaningful relationships with brands – this has been amply demonstrated by decades of research (Belk 1988; Fournier 1998). We propose several reasons to believe brand relationships can be detrimental to consumers' well-being. First, brands cannot act on their own behalf. Compared to relationships that involve humans (e.g. interpersonal and service), consumer-brand relationships are less interactive: "Brands do not experience emotions and therefore [do] not return a person's love…" (Batra et al. 2011, p. 3). Since brands are unable to reciprocate in a similar fashion to the consumers who hold them dear, there will be ever-increasing chasm between partners representing a lack of social exchange that over time will erode self-esteem. Moreover, brands' relational 'toolkits' are barren. They are less capable of reassuring communications such as pledges of commitment, encouragement or intimate self-disclosure that are common in and form the foundation of interpersonal and service relationships (Price and Arnould 1999). There is consistent evidence that physical proximity affects the likelihood of communication between actors (Krackhardt 1994), presumably by increasing the probability of positive, serendipitous interactions (Monge et al. 1995). These qualities are lacking in brand relationships. Finally, having many strong brand relationships may be associated with devaluing importance of interpersonal relationships (Thomson, Whelan, and Johnson, in press). Such consumers may prefer to gain comfort and psychological support from their possessions rather than with actual people (Kasser and Ryan 1993). Thus, this may cause individuals to become socially lethargic, as brand relationships become central to their lifestyle (Kasser and Ryan 2001). In consequence, people who value brand-relationships may become less socially productive and exhibit greater numbers of antisocial behaviors (Burroughs and Rindfleisch 2002; Cohen and Cohen 1996; Kasser and Ryan 1993), thus contributing to their lower self-esteem and well-being.

We examine the effect of people's relationship portfolio on their general well-being (i.e. "life satisfaction'; see Table 1) both directly and through self-esteem. We recruited 323 respondents using a private research panel composed of adults. We collected the following variables: Life Satisfaction (Diener et al. 1985), Rosenberg's Self-Esteem scale (1965), people's current state of health, financial strength, and a trait-measure of worry (Stober and Joormann 2001), as well as gender and age. We then asked in random order for individuals to list relationships that "mean a lot to you" in the context of other people (i.e. interpersonal), service providers (i.e. service) and brands (i.e. brand). For each relationship, respondents answered a two-item metric of 'relationship strength' (e.g. 'This brand [person] is important to me'). Once all this information was provided, we calculated respondents' number and average strength of each respective type of relationship. Upon centering each variable, we also calculated the interaction terms.

Using structural equation modeling, we conducted and replicated the basic result that interpersonal relationships improve a person's well-being. We also show that while person-service provider relationships have a similar effect, person-brand relationships are associated with significantly diminished self-esteem and well-being, even after accounting for a person's tendency to worry, age, gender and financial and physical health. In model 1, we find that stronger interpersonal relationship predict life satisfaction and self-esteem. With respect to service relationships, neither the number of the strength matters, but the interaction is a positive predictor. However, more and stronger brand relationships are related to significantly lower life satisfaction and self-esteem.

Understanding how this portfolio behaves is a worthwhile exercise not only because integrating across domains has theoretical value, but also because relationships are centrally implicated in predicting people's general well-being. Thus, there are considerable managerial and public-policy implications of understanding what patterns of portfolios are most beneficial for people. It also allows us to address the issue of whether the variety of target objects involved in the portfolio are complementary or competing with respect to an individual's well-being.

Table 1: Structural Equation Model Results

From	To	Model 1* γ	Model 1* $p<$
Number$_{person}$		0.16	0.01
Strength$_p$		0.07	0.17
Interaction$_p$		0.01	0.90
Number$_{service}$		-0.10	0.13
Strength$_s$	Life Satisfaction	0.05	0.40
Interaction$_s$		0.10	0.09
Number$_{brand}$		-0.03	0.70
Strength$_b$		-0.04	0.50
Interaction$_b$		-0.10	0.10
Number$_p$		-0.07	0.37
Strength$_p$		0.20	0.01
Interaction$_p$		0.16	0.01
Number$_s$		0.00	0.96
Strength$_s$	Health	0.18	0.01
Interaction$_s$		0.14	0.05
Number$_b$		-0.07	0.43
Strength$_b$		-0.08	0.28
Interaction$_b$		-0.08	0.32
Number$_p$		0.28	0.01
Strength$_p$		0.09	0.13
Interaction$_p$		0.00	0.97
Number$_s$		-0.09	0.28
Strength$_s$	Financial Weakness	-0.02	0.82
Interaction$_s$		-0.15	0.05
Number$_b$		-0.05	0.64
Strength$_b$		0.06	0.43
Interaction$_b$		0.06	0.47
Number$_p$		0.01	0.93
Strength$_p$		0.19	0.01
Interaction$_p$		0.07	0.28
Number$_s$		0.05	0.53
Strength$_s$	Self Esteem	-0.11	0.11
Interaction$_s$		0.27	0.01
Number$_b$		-0.03	0.73
Strength$_b$		-0.10	0.17
Interaction$_b$		-0.20	0.01
Financial Weakness		-0.21	0.01
Health	Life Satisfaction	0.18	0.01
Self Esteem		0.43	0.01
	DF	25	
	Chi-Sq.	42.01	
	CMIN/DF	1.68	
	RMSEA	0.05	

*note: gender was not a significant covariate (p> .10) but increasing age (γ= .09, p< .05) and decreasing worry (γ= -.29, p< .05) **significantly predicted** higher life satisfaction.*

REFERENCES

Argyle, Michael (1999), "Causes and Correlates of Happiness," in *Well-Being: The Foundations of Hedonic Psychology*, ed. Daniel Kahneman, Ed Diener and Norbert Schwarz, New York: NY: Russell Sage Foundation, 353-73.

Batra, Rajeev, Aaron Ahuvia, and Richard P. Bagozzi (2011), "Brand Love," *Journal of Marketing*, 76 (2), 1-16.

Belk, Russell W. (1988), "Possessions and the Extended Self," *Journal of Consumer Research*, 15 (2), 139-68.

Burroughs, James E. and Aric Rindfleisch (2002), "Materialism and Well-Being: A Conflicting Values Perspective," *Journal of Consumer Research*, 29 (3), 348-70.

Cohen, Patricia and Jacob Cohen (1996), *Life Values and Adolescent Mental Health*, Mahwah, NJ: Erlbaum.

Diener, Ed and Marissa Diener (1995), "Cross-Cultural Correlates of Life Satisfaction and Self-Esteem," *Journal of Personality and Social Psychology*, 68, 851-64.

Diener, Ed, Robert A. Emmons, Randy J. Larsen, and S. Griffin (1985), "The Satisfaction with Life Scale," *Journal of Personality Assessment*, 49 (1), 71-75.

Fournier, Susan (1998), "Consumers and Their Brands: Developing Relationship Theory in Consumer Research," *Journal of Consumer Research*, 24, 343-73.

Gremler, Dwayne D. and Stephen W. Brown (1996), "Service Loyalty: Its Nature, Importance, and Implications," in *American Marketing Association*, ed. B Edvardsson, S.W. Brown, R. Johnston and E.E. Scheuing: American Marketing Association, 171-80.

Kasser, Tim and Richard M. Ryan (1993), "A Dark Side of the American Dream: Correlates of Financial Success as a Central Life Aspiration," *Journal of Personality and Social Psychology*, 65 (2), 410-22.

--- (2001), "Be Careful What You Wish For: Optimal Functioning and the Relative Attainment of Intrinsic and Extrinsic Goals," in *Life Goals and Well-Being: Towards a Positive Psychology of Human Striving*, ed. Peter Schmuck and Ken M. Sheldon, Goettingen, Germany: Hogrefe & Huber, 116-31.

Krackhardt, David (1994), "Constraints on the Interactive Organization as an Ideal Type," in *The Post-Bureaucratic Organization: New Perspectives on Organizational Change*, ed. Charles Heckscher and Anne Donnelan, Beverly Hills, CA: Sage Publications, 211-22.

Kwan, Virginia S., Michael H. Bond, and Theodore M. Singelis (1997), "Pancultural Explanations for Life Satisfaction: Adding Relationship Harmony to Self-Esteem," *Journal of Personality and Social Psychology*, 73 (5), 1038-51.

McKenna, Katelyn Y. and John A. Bargh (1999), "Causes and Consequences of Social Interaction on the Internet: A Conceptual Framework," *Media Psychology*, 1 (3), 249-69.

Monge, Peter R., Lynda W. Rothman, Eric M. Eisenberg, Katherine I. Miller, and Kenneth K. Kirste (1985), "The Dynamics of Organizational Proximity," *Management Science*, 31 (9), 1129-41.

Pinquart, Martin and Silvia Sorensen (2000), "Influences of Socioeconomic Status, Social Network, and Competence on Subjective Well-Being in Later Life: A Meta-Analysis," *Psychology and Aging*, 15 (2), 187-224.

Price, Linda L. and Eric J. Arnould (1999), "Commercial Friendships: Service Provider-Client Relationships in Context," *Journal of Marketing*, 63 (4), 38-56.

Rosenberg, Morris (1965), *Society and the Adolescent Self-Image*, Princeton, NJ: Princeton University Press.

Stober, Joachim and Jutta Joormann (2001), "A Short Form of the Worry Domains Questionnaire: Construction and Factorial Validation," *Personality and Individual Differences*, 4 (5), 591-98.

Wellman, Barry and Milena Gulia (1999), "Net Surfers Don't Ride Alone: Virtual Communities as Communities," in *Communities and Cyberspace*, ed. Peter Kollock and Marc Smith, New York, NY: Routledge.

Wills, Thomas A. (1991), "Social Support and Interpersonal Relationships," in *Review of Personality and Social Psychology*, Vol. 12, ed. Margaret S. Clark, Thousand Oaks, CA: Sage Publications, 265-89.

Figure 1: General Theoretical Model

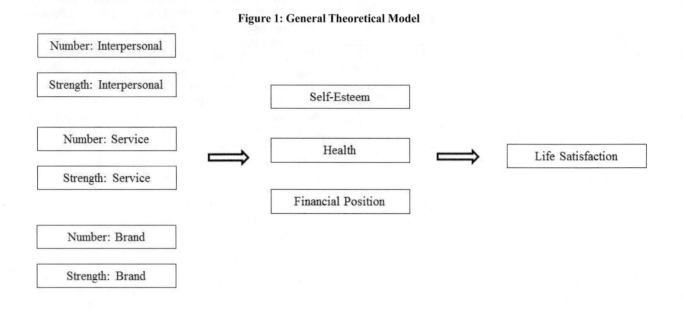

Market Mavens and Networking: Benefits and Costs of Network Participation

Seung Hwan (Mark) Lee, Colorado State University, USA
Gail Leizerovici, University of Western Ontario, Canada
Shuoyang Zhang, Colorado State University, USA

EXTENDED ABSTRACT

Market mavens are "individuals who have information about many kinds of products, places to shop, and other facets of markets, and initiate discussions with consumers and respond to requests from consumers for market information" (Feick and Price 1987, p.85). Previous research has suggested market mavens act as important social beings for the marketplace. Specifically, they have a desire to help others and have a sense of obligation to share their market knowledge with others in their social networks (Walsh, Gwinner, and Swanson 2004). Even though prior research has documented the links between market mavens and a variety of social traits, what remains underexplored is how it influences consumers within the domain of emerging social networks. Our work fills this gap by tracking market mavens longitudinally and observing their network growth and their personal outcomes over time.

Our findings contribute to the extant literature in three distinct ways. First, despite their social nature and desire to interact, market mavens have a lower rate of network growth over time. They tend to build a selective network, rather than a larger network. Second, market mavens occupying central positions experience both positive (satisfaction) and negative (stress) personal outcomes over time. Finally, we identify the importance of differentiating perceptual networks (vs. objective networks) as the primary driver of consumers' personal outcomes.

Method

We conducted a longitudinal field study at a large North American university. Participants filled out questionnaires at two different time-periods. Time 1 data was collected approximately five to six weeks after the start of the academic freshman year (early October) and Time 2 data was collected about five months after the initial data collection (early February). The final sample (N=71) included 37 females and 34 males.

Network data were collected using the roster method, a technique that is widely used in network research (Wasserman and Faust 1994). This method is consistent with previous network studies in marketing and is useful in identifying individuals' network positions (Iacobucci et al. 1996). Then, participants rated their relationship strength (1 – do not know or barely know; 2 – acquaintance; 3 – friend; 4 – close friend) with every other student on the floor (Lee et al., 2010). To identify one's friendship network, a rating of 3 or above was chosen to reflect individual's strong-tie network. Therefore, for every direct link (a rating of 3 or above), the focal actor received a score 1 and all other responses were given a rating of 0. Given that this was a longitudinal study, we were able to track the change in development of outgoing ties and incoming ties over time.

To analyze the effects of market mavenism on individuals' social network development, a stochastic actor-oriented model of network dynamics was assessed using the SIENA 3.14 software (Snijders et al. 2007). The actor-oriented model, when elaborated upon for application use, contains parameters that are estimated from the observed data by a statistical procedure (Snijders et al. 2010). The effects of market mavenism on the development of network ties are assessed by examining the parameter estimates of three selection effects: *ego effect, alter effect,* and *similarity effect* (Burk et al. 2007). A positive (negative) ego effect implies that market mavenism is positively (negatively) associated with an individual's ability to develop social ties and thus is likely to increase (decrease) the number of friendship nominations made over time. A positive (negative) alter effect implies that market mavenism is positively (negatively) associated with being attractive as a friend and thus is likely to result in an individual receiving more (fewer) friendship nominations over time. Lastly, a positive (negative) similarity effect implies that individuals prefer friendships with others that have similar (dissimilar) levels of market mavenism (i.e., homophilous selection). To test the interaction of market mavenism x centrality on stress and satisfaction, we analyzed the data using regressions. Market mavenism, out-degree ties (for out-degree models), in-degree ties (for in-degree models) were centered and entered into a regression, along with their respective interaction terms, as predictors of satisfaction and stress.

Results

Contrary to our expectations, we find that market mavenism is negatively associated with network growth (negative ego effect). This result is unexpected given the social nature of market mavens. We speculate that despite market mavens' desire to interact and to connect with others, their motivation for building relationships stems not from assembling a larger network (connection quantity), but from nurturing a selective network that can bring social benefits (connection quality, positive similarity effect).

Further, we find that market mavens occupying central positions experience both positive (satisfaction) and negative (stress) personal outcomes over time. While previous research has generally viewed market mavenism as a positive characteristic (e.g., Feick and Price 1987), we find that market mavens are prone to experiencing stress as a result of their network position. We suggest that greater satisfaction was generated by centrally-located market mavens through more strategic and active use of their network. While this did not create satisfaction immediately, the results of their network building efforts garnered them greater satisfaction over time. On the same token, we also found that the market maven role came at a personal cost. Based on the demands-resources model of stress (Bakker and Demerouti 2007), the relationship between market mavenism and high network centrality was found to be positively associated with stress. We believe this was due to their increased investment in the time and energy to respond to the demands, which thereafter faltered due to their inability to keep up with the resource requirements necessary to meet those demands. This presents a paradox for market mavens as their market knowledge and sharing behavior, when linked with network centrality, may beneficial and detrimental to their personal well-being.

Finally, we find that individuals' perception of their network position were more strongly associated with their personal outcomes than others' perceptions. This is an important finding because it reveals that how one perceives him/herself within their network acts as the primary driver of his or her psychological well-being.

REFERENCES

Bakker, Arnold and Evangelia Demerouti (2007), "The Job Demand-Resources Model: State of the Art," *Journal of Managerial Psychology*, 22 (3), 309-28.

Advances in Consumer Research
Volume 40, ©2012

Burk, William J., Christian Steglich, and Tom A. Snijders (2007), "Beyond Dyadic Interdependence: Actor-Oriented Models for Co-Evolving Social Networks and Individual Behaviors," *International Journal of Behavioral Development*, 31 (4), 397-404.

Feick, Lawrence F. and Linda L. Price (1987), "The Market Maven: A Diffuser of Marketplace Information," *Journal of Marketing*, 51 (1), 83-97.

Iacobucci, Dawn, Geraldine Henderson, Alberto Marcati, and Jennifer Chang (1996), "Network Analyses of Brand Switching Behavior," *International Journal of Research in Marketing*, 13, 415-29.

Lee, Seung Hwan (Mark), June Cotte, and Theodore J. Noseworthy (2010), "The Role of Network Centrality in the Flow of Consumer Influence," *Journal of Consumer Psychology*, 20 (1), 66-77.

Snijders, Tom A., Christian Steglich, Michael Schwinberger, and Mark Huisman (2007), *Manual for Siena Version 3.1*: University of Groningen: ICS / Department of Sociology; University of Oxford: Department of Statistics.

Walsh, Gianfranco, Kevin P. Gwinner, and Scott R. Swanson (2004), "What Makes Mavens Tick? Exploring the Motives of Market Mavens' Initiation of Information Diffusion," *Journal of Consumer Marketing*, 21 (2), 109-22.

Wasserman, Stanley and Katherine Faust (1994), *Social Network Analysis: Methods and Applications*, Cambridge, MA: Cambridge University Press.

Is More Always Better? Examining the Effects of Highly Attentive Service

Maggie Wenjing Liu, Tsinghua University, China
Hean Tat Keh, University of Queensland, Australia
Lijun Zhang, Peking University, China

EXTENDED ABSTRACT

The services marketing literature generally indicates that attentive, friendly, and personalized services can help improve customer satisfaction (Bitner, 1990; Bitner, Booms, & Mohr, 1994; Hui, Au, & Fock, 2004; Price, Arnould & Tierney, 1995; Surprenant & Solomon, 1987). Some researchers even suggest that firms should attempt to transcend customer expectations by delighting them (Oliver, Rust, & Varki, 1997; Rust & Oliver, 2000). Consequently, it has become imperative for many service firms to invest in customer-focused procedures or programs in order to create more competitive service offerings (Lemmink & Mattsson, 2002), and some of them are even willing to go the extra mile in serving customers. For example, the wait staff of many restaurants is trained to get to know their customers, frequently drop by customer tables and enquire if things were going well (Scanlon, 1998).

The underlying assumption is that such outwardly concern for consumers and personalization would be well received. Yet, some customers may find such efforts to be overwhelming and disruptive of their service experience. As observed by Solomon, Surprenant, Czepiel, and Gutman (1985, p. 107), "greater personalization of service does not necessarily result in a more positive service expectation." Indeed, there is considerable anecdotal evidence suggesting that, rather than increasing customer satisfaction, highly attentive service may lead to customer complaints, dissatisfaction, and even switching behavior. This raises the paradox that more attentive service is not always better. From the perspective of the organization, Schneider, Paul, and White (1998) suggest that an overemphasis on service quality for end users may be detrimental to the organization in the long-term as overemphasis on a single constituent will be in conflict with the expectations and demands of other constituents such as employees and shareholders.

The literature in related areas indicates that too much of a good thing may not always turn out well. For instance, in the context of product choices, Iyengar and Lepper (2000) challenge the popular notion that "the more choice, the better." They find that consumers faced with extensive choices may find them to be initially more appealing but are subsequently less satisfied with their choices compared with those in the limited-choice condition. Similarly, when manufacturers put too many features into a product, it can be overwhelming for consumers and result in "feature fatigue" (Thompson, Hamilton, & Rust, 2005). We expect the effects of highly attentive service to be analogous to such choice overload effects.

Our review of the literature yields surprisingly little insight into the paradox of highly attentive service (see Estelami & De Maeyer, 2002). Questions on how customers respond to highly warm or generous service attention, and to what extent should firms attend to their customers, have not been systematically addressed. Knowing the answers would be relevant and important for both managerial practice and marketing scholars. Accordingly, our objective in this research is to understand the nature of highly attentive service and how it affects customers' responses and evaluations of service providers. As little has been done in this area, we use a two-phase research design in conducting this study (Creswell, 1994). We first perform an exploratory qualitative research to define the concept of highly attentive service from the perspective of the customer. Based on the dimensions identified, we then proceed to conduct two experiments to better understand customers' response mechanisms. Specifically, we address the following research questions:

1. How do customers define or perceive highly attentive service?
2. How does highly attentive service influence customer affective response and evaluation of the provider?
3. Do customers' characteristics and situational factors influence their affective response and evaluation of highly attentive services?

Based on the related literature and content analysis of our qualitative study, we establish a conceptual model of highly attentive service and develop the relevant hypotheses. We conduct two experiments to test the model. Finally, we discuss the results, the theoretical and managerial implications, and conclude with the limitations of this study and directions for further research.

We contribute to the literature by expanding the scope of investigation beyond monetary generosity. As the literature is sparse on the "attentiveness fatigue" problem, our exploratory study on the nature and consequences of highly attentive service fills a major theoretical void. The main results of our empirical analysis are that highly attentive services have an inverted U-shaped relationship with customer satisfaction, and this relationship is partially mediated by customers' affect and moderated by customers' need for interaction. These findings are new to the literature, and impel us to reconsider the received wisdom of providing services that exceed the desired level (Zeithaml, Berry, & Parasuraman, 1993, 1996).

Specifically, our results confirm the affective satisfaction model (Oliver, 1993; Westbrook, 1987; Westbrook & Oliver, 1991); service attributes influence customer satisfaction both directly and indirectly via positive and negative affects. While past research highlights the effect of positive affect on satisfaction (Lemmink & Mattsson, 2002; Price, Arnould, & Tierney, 1995), our study reveals the crossover effects between service attributes and positive and negative affects simultaneously. Our factor analysis elicits one positive affect, "warmth," and two types of negative affects, "pressure" and "sadness/anger." This is in line with Russell's (1980) "circumplex model of affect," which posits two dimensions of affective structure, pleasure/displeasure and arousal/boredom.

In our three-factor affect model, "warmth" and "sadness/anger" are almost polar opposites on the same continuum, and are independent of (orthogonal to) "pressure." Additionally, we find that while both negative affects, "pressure" and "sadness/anger," are evoked by unfavorable service attentiveness conditions, the underlying mechanisms are different. Results show that "pressure" is more likely to be evoked by highly attentive services, but "sadness/anger" is not significantly different for either excessive or too little attention.

REFERENCES

Allen, C. T., Machleit, K. A., & Kleine, S. S. (1992). A comparison of attitudes and emotions as predictors of behavior at diverse levels of behavioral experience. *Journal of Consumer Research*, 18 (March), 493-504.

Arnould, E. J., & Price, L. L. (1993). River magic: extraordinary experience and the service encounter. *Journal of Consumer Research*, 20 (June), 24-45.

Baron, R. M., & Kenny, D. A. (1986). The moderator-mediator variable distinction in social psychological research: conceptual, strategic, and statistical considerations. *Journal of Personality and Social Psychology*, 51 (6), 1173-1182.

Bitner, M. J. (1990). Evaluating service encounters: the effects of physical surroundings and employee responses. *Journal of Marketing*, 54 (Apr.), 57-71.

---, Booms, B. H., & Mohr, L. A. (1994). Critical service encounters: the employee's viewpoint, *Journal of Marketing*, 58 (Oct.), 95-106.

---, ---, & Tetreault, M. S. (1990). The service encounter: diagnosing favorable and unfavorable incidents. *Journal of Marketing*, 54 (January), 95-106.

Creswell, J. W. (1994). *Research design: qualitative and quantitative approaches*. CA: Sage.

Dabholkar, P. A. (1996). Consumer evaluations of new technology-based self-service options: an investigation of alternative models of service quality. *International Journal of Research in Marketing*, 13, 29-51.

---, & Bagozzi, R. (2002). An attitudinal model of technology-based self-service: moderating effects of consumer traits and situational factors. *Journal of the Academy of Marketing Science*, 30(3), 184-201.

Dillon, W. R., & Goldstein, M. (1984). *Multivariate analysis: methods and applications*. New York: John Wiley and Sons.

Dubé-Rioux, L. (1990). The power of affective reports in predicting satisfaction judgments. *Advances in Consumer Research*, 17, 571-576.

Edell, J., & Burke, M. C. (1987). The power of feelings in understanding advertising effects. *Journal of Consumer Research*, 14 (December), 421-433.

Estelami, H., & De Maeyer, P. (2002). Customer reactions to service provider overgenerosity. *Journal of Service Research*, 4 (3), 205-216.

Havlena, W. J., & Holbrook, M. B. (1986). The varieties of consumption experience: comparing two typologies of emotion in consumer behavior. *Journal of Consumer Research*, 13 (December), 394-404.

Holsti, O. R. (1968). Content analysis. In G. Lindzey & E. Aronson (Ed.), *The handbook of social psychology: research methods*, Vol. 2, (pp. 596-692) MA: Addison-Wesley.

Hui, M. K., Au, K., & Fock, H. (2004). Reactions of service employees to organization–customer conflict: A cross-cultural comparison. *International Journal of Research in Marketing*, 21 (2), 107-121.

Iyengar, S. S., & Lepper, M. R. (2000). When choice is demotivating: can one desire too much of a good thing. *Journal of Personality and Social Psychology*, 79 (6), 995-1006.

Johnson, M. & Zinkhan, G. M. (1991). Emotional responses to a professional service encounter. *Journal of Services Marketing*, 5 (2), 5-16.

Kassarjian, H. H. (1977). Content analysis in consumer research. *Journal of Consumer Research*, 4 (June), 8-18.

Keaveney, S. M. (1995). Customer switching behavior in service industries: an exploratory study. *Journal of Marketing*, 59 (April), 71-82.

Lemmink, J. & Mattsson, J. (2002). Employee behavior, feelings of warmth and customer perception in service encounters. *International Journal of Retail & Distribution Management*, 30 (1), 18-33.

Liljander, V. & Strandvik, T. (1997). Emotions in service satisfaction. *International Journal of Service Industry Management*, 8 (2), 148-169.

Malhotra, N. K. (2007). *Marketing research: an applied orientation* (5th ed). Prentice Hall.

Meuter, M. L., Ostrom, A. L., Roundtree, R. J., & Bitner, M. J. (2000). Self-service technologies: understanding consumer satisfaction with technology-based service encounters," *Journal of Marketing*, 64 (3), 50-64.

Oliver, R. L. (1980). A cognitive model of the antecedents and consequences of satisfaction decisions. *Journal of Marketing Research*, 17 (November), 460-469.

--- (1981). Measurement and evaluation of satisfaction process in retail settings. *Journal of Retailing*, 57 (3), 25-48.

--- (1993). Cognitive, affective, and attribute bases of the satisfaction response. *Journal of Consumer Research*, 20 (December), 418-430.

--- (1994). Conceptual issues in the structural analysis of consumption emotion, satisfaction, and quality: evidence in a service setting," *Advances in Consumer Research*, (21), 16-22.

---, & Burke, R. R. (1999). Expectation processes in satisfaction formation: a field study. *Journal of Service Research*, 1 (3), 196-214.

---, Rust, R. T., & Varki, S. (1997). Customer delight: foundations, findings, and managerial insight. *Journal of Retailing*, 73 (3), 311-336.

Ostrom, A. L., & Iacobucci, D. (1995). Consumer trade-offs and the evaluation of services. *Journal of Marketing*, 59 (1), 17-28.

Phillips, D. M., & Baumgartner, H. (2002). The role of consumption emotions in the satisfaction response. *Journal of Consumer Psychology*, 12 (3), 243-252.

Price, L. L., Arnould, E. J., & Deibler. S. L. (1995). Customers' emotional responses to service encounters: the influence of the service provider. *International Journal of Service Industry Management*, 6 (3), 34-63.

---, ---, & Tierney, P. (1995). Going to extremes: managing service encounters and assessing provider performance. *Journal of Marketing*, 59 (April), 83-97.

Russell, J. A. (1980). A circumplex model of affect. *Journal of Personality and Social Psychology*, 39 (December), 1161-1178.

Rust, R. T., & Oliver, R. L. (2000). Should we delight the customer? *Journal of the Academy of Marketing Science*, 28 (1), 86-94.

Scanlon, N. L. (1998). *Quality restaurant service guaranteed: a training outline*, New York, NY: Wiley.

Schneider, B., Paul, M. C. & White, S. S. (1998). Too much of a good thing: a multiple-constituency perspective on service organization effectiveness. *Journal of Service Research*, 1 (1), 93-102.

Smith, A. K., & Bolton, R. N. (2002). The effect of customers' emotional responses to service failure on their recovery effort evaluations and satisfaction judgments. *Journal of the Academy of Marketing Science*, 30 (1), 5-23.

Soley, L., Teel, J. E. Jr., & Reid, L. N. (1980). A comparison of influences on fixed and grid radio advertising rates. *Journal of Advertising*, 9 (Fall), 15-19.

Solomon, M. R., Surprenant, C. F, Czepiel, J. A., & Gutman, E. G. (1985). A role theory perspective on dyadic interactions: the service encounter. *Journal of Marketing*, 49 (Winter), 99-111.

Surprenant, C. F., & Solomon, M. R. (1987). Predictability and personalization in the service encounter. *Journal of Marketing*, 51 (April), 73-80.

Thompson, D. V., Hamilton, R. W., & Rust, R. T. (2005). Feature fatigue: when product capabilities become too much of a good thing. *Journal of Marketing Research*, 42 (4), 431-442.

Westbrook, R. A. (1987). Product/consumption-based affective responses and postpurchase processes. *Journal of Marketing Research*, 24 (August), 258-270.

---, & Oliver, R. L. (1981). Developing better measures of consumer satisfaction: some preliminary results. *Advances in Consumer Research*, 94-99.

---, & ---. (1991). The dimensionality of consumption emotion patterns and consumer satisfaction. *Journal of Consumer Research*, 18 (June), 84-91.

Zeithaml, V. A., Berry, L. L., & Parasuraman, A. (1993). The nature and determinants of customer expectations of service. *Journal of the Academy of Marketing Science*, 21 (1), 1-12.

---, ---, & ---. (1996). The behavioral consequences of service quality. *Journal of Marketing*, 60 (2), 31-46.

---, Parasuraman, A., & Berry, L. L. (1985). Problems and strategies in service marketing. *Journal of Marketing*, 49 (Spring), 33-46.

"Shall We Share Our Clothes?":
Understanding Clothing Exchanges With Friends During Adolescence

Elodie Gentina, University Lille Nord de France, France
Marie-Hélène Fosse-Gomez, University Lille Nord de France, France

EXTENDED ABSTRACT

The concept of exchange has long been of interest to marketing researchers (e.g., Alderson 1957; Houston and Gassenheimer 1987). According to Bagozzi (1975), any type of human intercourse is a form of exchange. Such reflections have prompted a stream of research on exchange theory in marketing, from which two oppositional perspectives emerge. The economic perspective stipulates that exchanges are valued for their economic worth, as determined by factors outside the dyad, including the monetary price (Belk 2009). Thus, the term "exchange" implies that each party to the exchange gives and receives something simultaneously (Bagozzi 1979; Sahlins 1972). A more social view of the phenomenon points to the (mostly non-economic) benefits available to consumers who engage in exchanges. Scholars subscribing to this social perspective understand exchange as an expressive act, not an instrumental response (Belk and Coon 1993). They investigate, for example, emotional bonds enjoyed by consumers who engage in exchanges within their family network, such as parents and their children (Belk 2009; Ozanne and Ozanne 2011), siblings (Tinson and Nuttall 2007), or couples (Belk and Llamas 2011).

What is lacking from both perspectives though is a consumer-centric understanding of what people seek when they engage in exchanges outside the family, such as with friends. Consumer researchers thus far also have not sufficiently explored exchanges during a crucial time in consumers' lives: their adolescence (Belk and Llamas 2011). Research in this area is particularly necessary because exchange transactions pervade the everyday lives of modern adolescents and are woven tightly into the matrix of their social lives (Gianinno and Crittenden 2005). During adolescence, children emerge from their family setting and begin to achieve independence from parents (Youniss and Smollar 1985). To support this process, adolescents increasingly rely on their friends to help construct their social identity (Mangleburg, Doney, and Bristol 2004).

With this research, we examine whether and how different forms of exchanges with friends contribute to define adolescent identity and explain the dynamic interplay of individual, relational, and group identities. Accordingly, we study the experience of exchanges in a field particularly relevant to adolescents: clothing. Clothing symbolizes adolescents' connections to their peer group and enables them to "fit in" with this group (Auty and Elliott 2001). Moreover, we focus particularly on adolescent girls, for whom, relative to adolescent boys, exchanging clothes with friends is a common practice (Lurie 1981).

An interpretive study of 20 adolescent girls (ages 13–18 years) provided a stronger understanding of the experience of clothing exchanges between friends. We combined photographs of the most often exchanged clothes by adolescent girls with in-depth interviews, conducted in the adolescent girls' bedrooms, to ensure an appreciation for their intimate and living space. The data set includes 382 pages of interview transcripts and 60 pictures. Each interview was analyzed for thematic categories, following an emic and bracketing approach (Thompson, Locander, and Pollio 1989).

Why do adolescent girls exchange clothes so often with their friends? Clothing exchanges are a practical way to minimize costs and enlarge their wardrobes with no additional expenditures. Beyond these economic benefits, adolescent girls exchange clothes to interact with their friends and manage their multiple identity projects. Instead of defining a sharp distinction between economic exchange and social exchange though, our results call for a more gradational continuum of clothing exchange that highlights a social scale of friendship, from most to least intimate ("just friends," "good friends," and "close friends"). The clothing exchange continuum guides different forms of exchanges, including balanced reciprocal exchanges with just friends, loans without any expectation of a reciprocal act with good friends, and unbalanced exchanges with close friends. It also determines rules for exchanging (e.g., time periods, place) (Figure 1).

Figure 1: The clothing exchange continuum

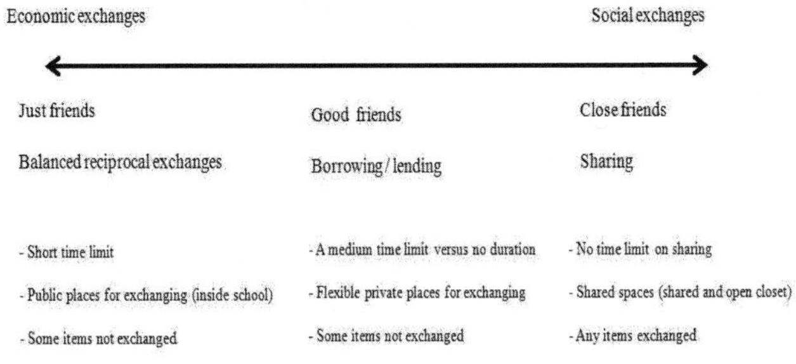

Three of the four metaphors identified by Holt (1995), namely, classification, integration, and play, provide a theoretical frame for understanding different processes that underlie the different forms of clothing exchanges. Our findings reveal that adolescent girls use clothing exchanges with just friends as classification, to build affiliations with some adolescent groups and enhance distinctions from others, in an instrumental way. With good friends, adolescent girls exchange clothes through an integration perspective: Clothes serve as resources to interact with significant others and mimic friends' behaviors or attitudes. The analysis further reveals that adolescent girls use clothes sharing with close friends as play, to socialize and preserve existing social bonds. These three consumption practices (following Holt's definitions) contribute to three dimensions of identity construction. That is, by exchanging clothes, adolescent girls define or enhance their individual identity, their group identity, and their relational identity.

Our discussion provides insightful accounts of the status of adolescents as materialistic consumers. Social scientists argue that modern adolescents are "the most brand-oriented, consumer-involved, and materialistic generation in history" (Schor 2004, p. 13). Consumer researchers also posit that materialistic values develop strongly in adolescence and that adolescents need to acquire material goods to develop positive social identities (Chaplin and John 2007, 2010). Concerns about the rising level of materialism in adolescents are thus increasing among consumer behavior researchers. Unlike previous accounts, our research revisits the very question of whether adolescents are materialistic beings in a marketplace that is increasingly oriented toward them as consumers. Because adolescents, who exist in a period of significant uncertainty, count on the symbolic property of clothes (Piacentini 2010), clothing exchanges offer a way to consume more. However, the social scale of friendship offers a different view that reveals how adolescent girls manage multiple identity projects, depending on the form of their clothing exchanges with friends.

Their purpose is not merely to "have" but rather to "be" or even to "become." Thus, adolescent girls seek, express, and ascertain a sense of being through the act of exchanging. With this finding, we provide a more nuanced conceptualization of materialism as a means to understand adolescents' world.

REFERENCES

Alderson, Wroe (1957), *Marketing Behavior and Executive Action, A Functionalist Approach to Marketing Theory,* Homewood, IL: Richard D. Irwin.

Auty, Susan and Richard Elliott (2001), "Being Like or Being Liked: Identity vs. Approval in a Social Context," in *Advances in Consumer Research*, Vol. 28, eds. Mary C. Gilly and Joan Meyers-Levy, Valdosta, GA: Association for Consumer Research, 235-241.

Bagozzi, Richard P. (1975), "Marketing as Exchange," *Journal of Marketing,* 39 (4), 32-39.

Belk, Russell W. (2009), "Sharing," *Journal of Consumer Research*, 36 (5), 715-734.

Belk, Russell W. and Gregory S. Coon (1983), "Gift-Giving as Agapic Love: An Alternative to the Exchange Paradigm Based on Dating Experiences," *Journal of Consumer Research*, 20 (3), 393-417.

Belk, Russell W. and Rosa Llamas (2011), "The Nature and Effects of Sharing in Consumer Behaviour," in *Transformative Consumer Research for Personal and Collective Well-Being: Reviews and Frontiers,* eds. David Glen Mick, Simone Pettigrew, Cornelia Pechmann, and Julie L. Ozanne, London: Taylor and Francis.

Chaplin, Lan Nguyen and Deborah Roedder John (2007), "Growing up in a Material World: Age Differences in Materialism in Children and Adolescents," *Journal of Consumer Research*, 34 (4), 480-493.

Chaplin, Lan Nguyen and Deborah Roedder John (2010), "Interpersonal Influences on Adolescent Materialism: A New Look at the Role of Parents and Peers," *Journal of Consumer Psychology*, 20 (2), 176-184.

Gianinno, Lawrence and Victoria L. Crittenden (2005), "Assessing Shared Understanding of Economic Exchange Among Children and Adults," *Psychology & Marketing,* 22 (7), 551-576.

Holt, Douglas B. (1995), "How Consumers Consume: A Typology of Consumption Practices," *Journal of Consumer Research,* 22 (1), 1-16.

Houston, Franklin S., and Jules B. Gassenheimer (1987), "Marketing and Exchange," *Journal of Marketing,* 51 (October), 3-18.

Lurie, Alison (1981), *The Language of Clothes,* New York: Random House.

Mangleburg, Tamara F., Patricia M. Doney, and Terry Bristol (2004), "Shopping with Friends and Teens' Susceptibility to Peer Influence," *Journal of Retailing,* 80 (2), 101-116.

Ozanne, Lucie K. and Julie L. Ozanne (2011), "A Child's Right to Play: The Social Construction of Civic Virtues in Toy Libraries," *Journal of Public Policy & Marketing,* 30 (2), 263-276.

Piacentini, Maria (2010), "Children and Fashion," in *Understanding Children and Consumers*, ed. Davis Marshall, London: Sage Publication, 202-217.

Sahlins, Marshall D. (1972), *Stone Age Economics,* Chicago: Aldine Atherton.

Schor, Juliet B. (2004), *Born to Buy*, New York: Scribner.

Thompson, Craig J., William B. Locander, and Howard R. Pollio (1989), "Putting Consumer Experience Back into Consumer Research: The Philosophy and Method of Existential-Phenomenology," *Journal of Consumer Research,* 16 (1), 77-91.

Tinson, Julie and Pete Nuttall (2007), "Insider Trading? Exploring Familial Intra-Generational Borrowing and Sharing," *The Marketing Review,* 7 (2), 185-200.

Youniss, James and Jacqueline Smollar (1985), *Adolescents' Relations with their Mothers, Fathers, and Friends*, University of Chicago Press: Chicago.

Alliteration Alters: Its Influence in Perceptions of Product Promotions and Pricing

Derick F. Davis, Virginia Tech, USA
Rajesh Bagchi, Virginia Tech, USA
Lauren G. Block, Baruch College, USA

EXTENDED ABSTRACT

Alliteration is the repetition of the initial sound in a word across two or more consecutive and/or adjacent words in a sentence or phrase. Alliteration is common in brand and organizational names (e.g. Best Buy, Coca-Cola, Better Business Bureau), is used extensively in advertising copy, political speeches, poetry and prose, and can facilitate memory and recall (Lea et al. 2008). Alliteration is one of many rhetorical devices, the main purpose of which is to persuade via effective communication (see McQuarrie and Mick 1996 for a framework). As noted by McQuarrie and Mick (1996), rhetoric is used widely, but little has been done (excluding the framework they present) to further theoretical understanding of how rhetorical devices influence consumers. Empirical research in this area is even more rare. Many questions remain in this field of research. Do rhetorical devices in the consumption domain truly exert influence on consumers? If so, in what way? Furthermore, what are some potential mental processes driving any observed effects? We present evidence that alliterative pricing presentations can positively influence price perceptions as well as process evidence for the observed effects.

In this paper we focus on the use of alliteration in communicating pricing for multiple items. We theorize that alliteration has a positive effect on evaluations such that alliterative prices (9 for $.90) are evaluated higher than objectively better nonalliterative prices, such as 9 for $.88, because the alliteration imparts a rhythm to the presentation that "sounds" better. Additionally, we theorize that if brand or product name is included in such pricing presentations, and whether than name is alliterative or not can also influence perceptions. For instance, we predict that "3 Threybles $30" will be rated higher than "3 Fables $30" because all components are alliterative in the former presentation and therefore "sounds" better. We present three studies that demonstrate this effect and provide evidence that supports our contention that the repetition of phonological units in alliterative prices "sounds" better, which in turn influences perceptions of the deal presented.

In study 1 ($n = 118$) we compared two types of price presentations for multiple items (a fictitious soap brand): one where the quantity, brand, and price were all alliterative, and one where quantity and brand where alliterative, the price was not (e.g. 10 Teven for $10 vs. 10 Teven for $9.70). Participants found the fully alliterative presentation (10 Teven for $10) to be a more attractive offer, more attention grabbing, had higher purchase intentions for the product, were happier with the deal, and thought the deal was a better value, than the alternate presentation (all $ps < .03$). In each case, the effects were fully mediated by participant's perceptions of whether the deal "had a ring to it" or "sounds right" (bootstrap mediation; Preacher and Hayes 2008).

In study 2 ($n = 244$) we used a different product (fictitious shirt brands) and compared the price presentations used in study 1 with two additional presentations, one where quantity and price were alliterative, but the brand was not (e.g. 3 Fables $30), and one where nothing was alliterative but the product was less expensive (e.g. 3 Fables $29). Planned contrasts revealed that participants who saw the fully alliterative presentation (e.g. 3 Threybles $30) were more likely to buy the product, thought the deal was more attention grabbing, were happier with the deal, and thought it was a better

deal than any other type of presentation (all $ps < .05$). As in study 1, all the effects were fully mediated by participant's perceptions of whether the deal "had a ring to it" or "sounds right" (bootstrap mediation; Preacher and Hayes 2008). Additionally, we rule out other potential process explanations including message recall, unit cost calculation difficulty, cost importance, attention, brand name typicality, and verbal/visual processing style (Childers, Houston, and Heckler 1985).

Study 3 was a 2 (Price/Quantity Presentation: Alliterative vs. Nonalliterative) x 2 (Cognitive Load: High vs. Low) full factorial between-subjects experimental design ($n = 108$). Nonalliterative price/quantity presentations (e.g. 2 for $19) always represented an objectively better deal than alliterative price/quantity presentations (e.g. 2 for $20). Cognitive load was achieved by asking participants to remember 7 words (high load) or 2 words (low load). We reasoned that rehearsal of the words in high load conditions would inhibit the positive effect of alliteration on price perceptions by disrupting the repetitive rhythm present in the price presentation. Therefore alliteration effects should persist under low load, but not high load conditions. Analysis of the data revealed significant two-way interactions for six dependent variables (all $ps < .05$). Planned contrasts revealed that the means were in the predicted direction, individuals who read alliterative price/quantity presentations while experiencing low cognitive load thought the offer was more attractive, were more likely to buy the product, thought the deal was more attention grabbing, had higher purchase intentions, and thought the deal was better and presented more value than in any other condition (all $ps < .05$).

In summary, this work presents the first (to the best of our knowledge) empirical demonstration that alliterative price presentations can influence perceptions of promotions. We contribute theoretically to the understanding of how rhetorical devices, such as alliteration, can influence consumers. More specifically, we provide process evidence supporting our contention that the rhythm-inducing effect of alliteration "sounds right" to consumers, which in turn influences perceptions. Furthermore, we can "turn off" this effect by interrupting the alliteration's repetitive rhythm via memorizing nonalliterative words. We situate this research at the intersection of phonological theories in marketing (e.g. Argo, Popa, and Smith 2010; Lowry and Shrum 2007; Yorkston and Menon 2004) and the use of rhetoric in marketing (McQuarrie and Mick 1996).

REFERENCES

Argo, Jennifer J., Monica Popa, and Malcolm C. Smith (2010), "The Sound of Brands," *Journal of Consumer Research,* 74(July), 97-109.

Lea, R. Brooke, David N. Rapp, Andrew Elfenbein, Aaron D. Mitchel, and Russell S. Romine (2008), "Sweet Silent Thought: Alliteration and Resonance in Poetry Comprehension," *Psychological Science,* 19(7), 709-16.

Lowrey, Tina M. and L.J. Shrum (2007), "Phonetic Symbolism and Brand Name Preference," *Journal of Consumer Research,* 34(October), 406-14.

Childers, Terry L., Michael J. Houston, and Susan E. Heckler (1985), "Measurement of Individual differences in Visual vs. Verbal Information Processing," *Journal of Consumer Research,* 12(September), 125-134.

McQuarrie, Edward F. and David Glen Mick (1996), "Figures of Rhetoric in Advertising Language," *Journal of Consumer Research,* 22(March), 424-438.

Preacher, Kristopher J. and Andrew F. Hayes (2008), "Asymptotic and Resampling Strategies for Assessing and Comparing Indirect Effects in Multiple Mediator Models," *Behavior Research Methods,* 40(3), 879-91.

Yorkston, Eric, and Geeta Menon (2004), "A Sound Idea: Phonetic Effects of Brand Names on Consumer Judgments," *Journal of Consumer Research,* 31(June), 43-51.

The Secondary Contamination Effect of Luck

Chun-Ming Yang, Ming Chuan University, Taiwan
Edward Ku, National Kaohsiung University of Hospitality and Tourism, Taiwan

EXTENDED ABSTRACT

The influences of superstition in consumer's daily life are prevalent. Superstition are peculiar beliefs which presumed to not be veridical (Berenbaum, Kerns, and Raghavan 2000) and do not have a rational, empirical, or scientifically established link to an outcome they are intended to influence (Kramer and Block 2011). Despite it may be denied on the conscious level, recent development in consumer psychology has demonstrated that consumers are affected by various superstition beliefs (Block and Kramer 2009; Jiang, Cho, and Adaval 2009; Kramer and Block 2008, 2011). Drawing on the research in social psychology, this research introduces the secondary contamination effect and demonstrates its influences on consumer's self-rated winning likelihood and risk-taking behavior.

In the current research, we define the secondary contamination effect as the consumer's responses affected by physically contacting with a contaminated vehicle. Originated from medical and social psychology literature (Hejmadi, Rozin, and Siegal 2004; Nemeroff and Rozin 2000; Rozin, Markwith, and McCauley 1994; Rozin and Nemeroff 1990; Rozin et al. 1989), the research stream on the law of contagion has indicated the possibility of the secondary contamination effect. Participants in these literatures consistently showed negative responses toward some contaminated objects (e.g., food or sweaters) because they believed that touching a contaminated object may make healthy people sick or catch some negative essences. In this research, the authors hypothesize that touching a contaminated vehicle may affect consumer's responses. More specifically, by either actually or virtually contacting with a source with different luck characteristic (lucky or unlucky), an originally neutral vehicle (e.g. a pen) is transformed into a contaminated vehicle, and a recipient's responses will be in turn affected by physically contacting with it. The authors conducted four experiments to test the hypothesis.

82 undergraduate students (42 male) participated in a hypothetical beverage taste evaluation study. They were randomly assigned to one of three different source characteristics (Lucky, Unlucky, or Control). When participants arrived at the research lab, they were asked to wait in a separate room for five more minutes because of the late arrival of another research assistant (i.e. our confederate). One minute later, the confederate appeared and explained why he was late.

We manipulated source characteristics by presenting different excuses for confederate's late arrival. In the (Un)Lucky condition, the confederate told the participant he was late because the local police station informed him that his lost wallet was found and his money were safe (were taken). In the control condition, the confederate was late because of traffic jam. After explaining the reason, our confederate poured drinks into a plain paper cup in front of the participants and told them to taste the drink as much as they want before reporting their evaluation. We measured participants' taste evaluation with three seven-point scales ($\alpha = .79$). Following the taste evaluation task the confederate informed our participants that they had a chance to win an additional $30 prize in order to appreciate their contribution. Participants were then asked to rate their likelihood of winning this lottery game with a seven-point scale. Results of an one-way ANOVA indicated that there were significant differences on self-rated winning likelihood between groups ($F(2, 79) = 10.47$, $p < .001$). A post-hoc analysis suggested that participants in the Lucky condition reported highest likelihood ($M = 4.85$), followed by the

control condition ($M = 3.92$), and lowest winning likelihood for participants in the Unlucky condition ($M = 2.79$). However, results of another ANOVA showed no significant difference on taste evaluation ($F(2, 79) = .45$, $p > .60$, $M = 5.31$). Experiment 1 provided initial evidence for the secondary contamination effect.

Experiment 2 examines the influences of consumer's trait superstition (Carlson, Moen, and Fang 2009). The authors argue that consumer's trait superstition will moderate the relationship between source luck characteristics and downstream responses. Specifically, the secondary contamination effect will be stronger for those high in trait superstition. 145 undergraduate students participated in Experiment 2.

The procedure and manipulations were identical with experiment 1 except two modifications. First, in the current experiment, before our confederate's arrival, participants completed an unrelated lifestyle questionnaire. In this questionnaire, we captured participant's trait superstition with seven items adopted from Carlson et al. (2009). Secondly, participants participated in another ostensibly unrelated task after the taste valuation task. They were invited to a bigger or smaller game, and they could bet any amount on with their participation fee ($5). The betted amount was recorded as the dependent variable.

Multiple regression was conducted to test our hypothesis. Source characteristics were coded as two dummy variables using control condition as the baseline. As we expected, results indicated that Lucky condition had a positive effect on betting amount ($\beta = .16$, $p < .05$) and Unlucky condition had a negative coefficient ($\beta = -.28$, $p < .01$). Trait superstition had no direct influence ($p > .60$), but its interactions with both dummy variables reached significance. More specifically, for high-trait-superstition participants, the influence of (Un)Lucky condition on the betting amount was stronger (Lucky: $\beta = .18$, $p < .05$; Unlucky: $\beta = .27$, $p < .01$), comparing with those of low trait superstition.

In another two experiments, the authors found that the secondary contamination effect was attenuated when the participants believed that luck is an indivisible personal resource (experiment 3). Moreover, by modifying our experiment procedure, experiment 4 demonstrated that participant's direct observation was not a necessary condition for the secondary contamination effect.

This research contributes to the literature in consumer psychology in several ways. First, we introduced the secondary contamination effect into consumer research context. Second, our research answers a recent call for more research on the synergistic effects of various forms of peculiar beliefs (Kramer and Block, 2011). Third, the current research also suggests that people may take more risk just because they incidentally touch a contaminated vehicle.

REFERENCE

Berenbaum, Howard, M. Tyler Boden, and John P. Baker (2009), "Emotional Salience, Emotional Awareness Peculiar Beliefs and Magical Thinking," *Emotion*, 9 (2), 197–205.
Block, Lauren and Thomas Kramer (2009), "The Effect of Superstitious Beliefs on Performance Expectations," *Journal of the Academy of Marketing Science*, 37 (2), 161-169.

Advances in Consumer Research
Volume 40, ©2012

Hejmadi, Ahalya, Paul Rozin, and Michael Siegal (2004), "Once in Contact, Always in Contact: Conceptions of Essence and Purification in Hindu Indian and American Children", *Developmental Psychology*, 40 (4), 467–476.

Jiang, Yuwei, Angela Cho, and Rashmi Adaval (2009), "The Unique Consequences of Feeling Lucky: Implications for Consumer Behavior," *Journal of Consumer Psychology*, 19(2), 171-184.

Kramer, Thomas and Lauren Block (2008), "Conscious and Nonconscious Components of Superstitious Beliefs in Judgment and Decision Making," *Journal of Consumer Research*, 34 (6), 783-793.

_____ (2011), "Nonconscious Effects of Peculiar Beliefs on Consumer Psychology and Choice," *Journal of Consumer Psychology*, 21 (1), 101-111

Nemeroff, Carol and Paul Rozin (2000), "The Makings of the Magical Mind: The Nature and Function of Sympathetic Magical Thinking," in *Imagining the Impossible: The Development of Magical, Scientific, and Religious Thinking in Contemporary Society*, ed. Karl S. Rosengren, Carol N. Johnson and Paul L. Harris, Cambridge: Cambridge University Press, 1–34.

Rozin, Paul, Maureen Markwith, and Clark Mccauley (1994), "Sensitivity to Indirect Contacts with Other Persons: AIDS Aversion as a Composite of Aversion to Strangers, Infection, Moral Taint, and Misfortune," *Journal of Abnormal Psychology*, 103 (3), 495-504.

Rozin, Paul and Carol Nemeroff (1990), "The Laws of Sympathetic Magic: A Psychological Analysis of Similarity and Contagion.," in *Cultural Psychology Essays on Comparative Human Development*, eds. James W. Stigler, Richard A. Schweder, Gilbert Herdt, Cambridge: Cambridge University Press, 205-232.

Rozin, Paul, Carol Nemeroff, Wane, M., and Sherrod, A. (1989), "Operation of the Sympathetic Magical Law of Contagion in Interpersonal Attitudes among Americans," *Bulletin of the Psychonomic Society*, 27 (3), 367-370.

Carlson, Brad D., John C Mowen, and Xiang Fang (2009), "Trait Superstition and Consumer Behavior: Re-Conceptualization, Measurement, and Initial Investigations," *Psychology and Marketing*, 26 (8), 689-713

Shifting Identities and Brand Preferences: How and When A Malleable Identity Helps Individuals Differentiate, and the Role of Brands

Sara Dommer, University of Pittsburgh, USA
Vanitha Swaminathan, University of Pittsburgh, USA
Rohini Ahluwalia, University of Minnesota, USA

EXTENDED ABSTRACT

Brand names enable consumers to express their self-identities in various ways (Fournier 1994; Swaminathan, Page, and Gürhan-Canli 2007). For instance, Vans shoes, whose slogan is "Off the wall," are likely to appeal to consumers who would like to exhibit their distinctiveness from the group. In contrast, Mercedes Benz's "Unlike any other" slogan will potentially attract consumers interested in demonstrating their superiority to others. Brands can also emphasize their power in helping consumers connect with others, such as AT&T's slogan, "Reach out and touch someone." While the symbolic use of brands has been an important topic in consumer behavior (Belk 1988), more recent research has been devoted to developing a greater understanding of *why* consumers use products and brands to express their identities.

According to symbolic self-completion theory, individuals use material possessions and other indicators to communicate aspects of the self, particularly when individuals feel insecure in such aspects (Braun and Wicklund 1989). Consumers have been known use brands to strengthen their belongingness to social groups (Escalas and Bettman 2005; Reed 2004; Swaminathan et al. 2007) or to cope with interpersonal rejection and social exclusion (Loveland, Smeesters, and Mandel 2010). While there is a lot of research suggesting that social exclusion and the need for belongingness can motivate consumers to use brands to blend in to their social surroundings, recent research has shifted the focus away from belongingness to understanding the role of distinctiveness (Chan, Berger and van Boven 2012).

The present research argues for two moderators that have not been examined previously: (1) need for belongingness; (2) self-esteem, which jointly create a preference for two types of differentiated brands (i.e., horizontally and vertically differentiated brands). In summary, this research suggests that there are two primary ways in which individuals (particularly those with low self-esteem) can differentiate themselves from others within their reference group: horizontal and vertical differentiation (Tafarodi, Marshall, and Katsura 2004). Horizontal differentiation implies achieving distinction by going against the norms of the reference group and distancing oneself from it. Second, individuals can achieve distinctiveness by being better (or superior) to others in a reference group, which is known as vertical differentiation. We argue that a preference for horizontal and vertical differentiated brands will be driven by an interaction of need for belongingness and self-esteem. Our hypotheses, which argue for an interaction of need for belongingness and self-esteem on preferences for horizontally and vertically differentiated brands as follows:

(1) When need for belongingness is high (i.e., social exclusion), preferences for horizontally differentiated brands will vary as a function of self-esteem such that: (a) Individuals high in self-esteem will seek to re-affirm their belongingness by increasing attachment to the in-group linked brand; (b) Individuals low in self-esteem will shift their identity and increase their preference for brands which are horizontally differentiated from the in-group brand, in order to reaffirm their belongingness elsewhere.

(2) When need for belongingness is low (i.e., social inclusion), preferences for vertically differentiated brands will vary as a function of self-esteem such that: (c) Individuals high in self-esteem will show no change in their preference for in-group linked brand; (d) Individuals low in self-esteem will increase their preference for brands which are vertically differentiated from the in-group.

METHOD

We used multiple approaches to test our hypotheses to establish the robustness of these results. In study 1, we identified a particular reference group (i.e., college students) and manipulated positioning strategies for a brand (i.e., Motorola cell phones) such that the same brand was positioned as in-group-consistent, exclusive, or counterconformity. In study 2, we allowed the reference group to vary by letting participants name both the reference group as well as the brands. Thus, both reference groups and brands were idiosyncratic to each individual. In study 3, we pre-selected both the reference group (i.e., business school student) as well as the brands using a pretest. Further, we utilized multiple dependent variables across studies ranging from purchase likelihood (study 1), to brand attachment (study 2), to brand choice (study 3). In Study 4, we changed the manipulation of social exclusion and used a Cyberball manipulation to demonstrate the effects. Results confirm our hypotheses.

FINDINGS

Taken together, the results from four studies provide strong support for the hypothesized conditions under which consumers use brands to either blend in or stand out. Our results make a few important contributions to the literature. First, much of the literature has shown how brands help fulfill belongingness needs (Loveland et al. 2010; Swaminathan, Stilley, and Ahluwalia 2009). We go beyond these findings to demonstrate that when belongingness is satiated or made temporarily unattainable, some individuals (i.e., those with low self-esteem) may seek differentiating counterconformity brands or exclusive brands.

Second, while the majority of the literature has focused on how brands can help consumers belong (Loveland et al. 2010), we extend this literature by showing that brands can also help consumers stand out, in line with recent research (Chan et al. 2012). We identify two moderators of the desire to seek brands that are differentiated from the reference group, i.e., need for belongingness and self-esteem. It is shown that when low self-esteem individuals' belongingness needs are thwarted, they shift their identity and increase their affiliation for brands that are distinct from the core brand. We show that when low self-esteem consumers' belongingness needs are attained via social inclusion their preference for exclusive brands increases. Because their belongingness needs have been attained, LSE consumers' focus most likely shifts to eliciting admiration from others in the in-group. An exclusive brand, which vertical differentiates one from the group, affords consumers the opportunity to be superior, or ideal, members of the group.

The present research demonstrates conditions under which consumers use brands for identity expression, be it group membership or differentiation. Reed (2004) supports the idea that identity expression can vary in importance based on contextual cues that may make identity more salient or important. An individuals' construal of self (Escalas and Bettman 2005; Swaminathan et al. 2007), and type of reference groups (White and Dahl 2007) also play roles in identity expression. We add to this stream by demonstrating that consumers use brands express various identities (individual or social) depending upon whether they feel social excluded or included. By highlighting the moderating role of self-esteem in the desire for horizontal and vertical differentiation, we build upon White and Argo (2009)'s findings regarding the role of collective self-esteem in exhibiting identity avoidance effects.

REFERENCES

Belk, Russell W. (1988), "Possessions and the Extended Self," *Journal of Consumer Research*, 15 (2), 139–68.

Braun, Ottmar L. and Robert A. Wicklund (1989), "Psychological Antecedents of Conspicuous Consumption," *Journal of Economic Psychology*, 10 (2), 161–87.

Brewer, Marilynn B. (1991), "The Social Self: On Being the Same and Different at the Same Time," *Personality and Social Psychology Bulletin*, 17 (5), 475–82.

Chan, Cindy, Jonah Berger, and Leaf Van Boven (2012), "Identifiable but Not Identical: Combining Social Identity and Uniqueness Motives in Choice," *Journal of Consumer Research*, forthcoming.

Escalas, Jennifer Edson and James R. Bettman (2005), "Self-Construal, Reference Groups, and Brand Meaning," *Journal of Consumer Research,* 32 (3), 378–89.

Fournier, Susan (1994), "A Consumer-Brand Relationship Framework for Strategic Brand Management," unpublished dissertation, Graduate School of Business, University of Florida, Gainesville, FL.

Loveland, Katherine E., Dirk Smeesters, and Naomi Mandel (2010), "Still Preoccupied with 1995: The Need to Belong and Preference for Nostalgic Products," *Journal of Consumer Research*, 37 (3), 393–408.

Reed, Americus, II (2004), "Activating the Self-Importance of Consumer Selves: Exploring Identity Salience Effects on Judgments," *Journal of Consumer Research*, 31 (2), 286–95.

Swaminathan, Vanitha, Karen L. Page, and Zeynep Gürhan-Canli (2007), "'My' Brand or 'Our' Brand: The Effects of Brand Relationship Dimensions and Self-Construal on Brand Evaluations," *Journal of Consumer Research*, 34 (2), 248–59.

Swaminathan, Vanitha, Karen Stilley, and Rohini Ahluwalia (2009), "When Brand Personality Matters: The Moderating Role of Attachment Styles," *Journal of Consumer Research*, 35 (6), 985–1002.

Tafarodi, Romin W., Tara C. Marshall, and Haruko Katsura (2004), "Standing Out in Canada and Japan," *Journal of Personality*, 72 (4), 785–814.

White, Katherine and Jennifer J. Argo (2009), "Social Identity Threat and Consumer Preference," *Journal of Consumer Psychology*, 19 (3), 313–25.

White, Katherine and Darren W. Dahl (2007), "Are All Out-Groups Created Equal? Consumer Identity and Dissociative Influence," *Journal of Consumer Research*, 34 (4), 525–36.

Resistance to Persuasion: Minimizing Cognitive Effort by Implicit Forewarning

Marieke L. Fransen, University of Amsterdam, The Netherlands

EXTENDED ABSTRACT

Almost constantly people try to convince others to change their behavior. To reinforce their persuasive attempt, senders often use heuristic cues, such as 'expensive is good' and 'if an expert says so, it must be true' (Chaiken, Liberman, and Eagly 1989; Kruglanski and Thompson 1999; Petty, Cacioppo, and Schumann 1983). Recipients' reliance on these heuristic cues as a decision rule has been described as an automatic and unintentional process (e.g., Bargh and Ferguson 2000; Devine 1989; Dovidio, Evans, and Tyler 1986; Janiszewski 1988). Persuasion thus often happens because consumers automatically rely on heuristic cues concealed in persuasive messages (e.g., Bargh 2004; Cialdini 1993; Langer 1992). This automaticity may subsequently result in biased judgment (Tversky and Kahneman 1974) potentially hurting personal benefits.

Research showed that even though the persuasiveness of heuristic cues is subtle and pervasive, people can correct for them by motivated effortful processing (e.g., Blair 2001, Forehand and Perkins 2005; Gorn, Jiang, and Johar 2008; but see Bargh 1999) which can be instigated by traditional resistance strategies like forewarning (Freedman and Sears 1965). Forewarning has been found to reduce the impact of persuasive messages by signaling risk, subsequently inducing effortful processing, counter-arguing, and attitude bolstering. Unfortunately, forewarning requires cognitive capacity (Freedman and Sears 1965; Hass and Grady 1975; Papageorgis 1968). In many situations, however, people lack the motivation and/or ability to devote their limited cognitive capacity (Baumeister et al. 1998; Baumeister, Vohs, and Tice 2007; Fennis, Janssen, and Vohs 2009; Vohs and Faber 2007) to the resistance of persuasive appeals.

Does this leave the consumer defenseless against the influence of persuasive messages that rely on subtle cues? Recent research suggests not. Laran, Dalton, and Andrade (2011) recently showed that consumers sometimes correct for the effects of subtle marketing tactics by relying on automatic responses. The advantage of these automatic responses is that they do not require cognitive capacity (see the 'smart unconscious' Dijksterhuis 2004; Dijksterhuis et al. 2006). In the present research, it is suggested that implicitly warning people by reminding (i.e., priming) them of a situation in which someone tried to influence their behavior may automatically activate the responses that are associated with explicit (traditional) forewarning and therefore exert similar effects (i.e., reduce persuasion).

In sum, it is expected that explicit and implicit forewarning both enhance resistance towards an advertisement that includes a heuristic cue (compared to a control condition). However, explicit forewarning will consume more energy than implicit forewarning.

Experiment 1 tested the hypothesis that explicit and implicit forewarning both reduce persuasion. We conducted a 3 (forewarning: explicit vs. implicit vs. control) x 2 (heuristic cue: present vs. absent) between-subjects design. In the explicit forewarning condition, participants were informed that they would be exposed to an advertisement trying to convince them that the advertised brand is the best in it's kind. Participants in the implicit forewarning condition were instructed to recall a situation in which someone had tried to influence their behavior. In the control condition participants recalled a situation in which they had travelled with public transport. Next, participants were exposed to an advertisement in which a heuristic cue ('scientifically proven') was present or not. Subsequently, the persuasiveness of the advertisement was measured.

The results demonstrated no main effects of forewarning and heuristic cue. However, we did find the expected interaction effect between forewarning and heuristic cue ($F(1, 162) = 3.26$, $p < .05$). Simple main effect analyses demonstrated that participants who were not forewarned rated the advertisement with the heuristic cue as more persuasive ($M = 2.8$, SD = .74) than the control advertisement ($M = 2.14$, SD = .78; $F(1, 162) = 8.38$, $p < .00$). This effect, however, was not observed in both the explicit ($F(1, 162) < 1$) and the implicit forewarning conditions ($F(1, 162) < 1$, see figure 1). This indicates that forewarning consumers (explicit and implicit) eliminates the impact of heuristics in advertisements.

Figure 1.
Persuasiveness as a function of heuristic cue and warning

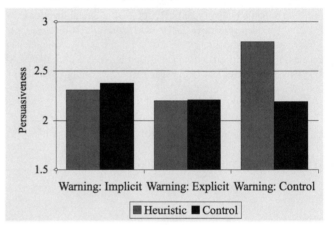

In a second experiment we included a depletion measure to assess whether implicit forewarning indeed consumes less energy than explicit forewarning. The design and method was exactly the same as in Experiment 1 although we used another heuristic cue (expert endorser). After participants evaluated the persuasiveness of the advertisement, the amount of energy consumption was measured. Participants responded to several cognitively demanding assignments. The idea behind this measure is that participants who provide more correct answers have more energy left and have thus spent less energy in resisting the message (Schmeichel et al. 2003; Fennis et al. 2009).

A main effect of heuristic cue was observed ($F(1, 135) = 6.12$, $p < .05$), such that the advertisement including the heuristic cue was observed as more persuasive ($M = 2.65$, SD = .70) than the control advertisement ($M = 2.36$, SD = .66). More importantly, the results yielded an interaction effect between forewarning and heuristic cue ($F(1, 135) = 3.64$, $p < .05$). Simple main effect analyses demonstrated that participants who were not forewarned rated the advertisement with the heuristic cue as more persuasive ($M = 2.90$, SD = .73) than the control advertisement ($M = 2.19$, SD = .64; $F(1, 135) = 13.32$, $p < .00$). This effect was not found in both the explicit ($F(1, 135) < 1$) and the implicit forewarning conditions ($F(1, 135) < 1$, see figure 2). This indicates that forewarning consumers (explicit and implicit) reduces the impact of heuristics in advertisements. However, participants in the explicit forewarning condition were more depleted, reflected in lower scores on the cognitive demanding assignments, ($M = 3.30$, SD = 1.56) than participants in both the implicit forewarning condition ($M = 4.04$, SD = 2.39; $p = 0.85$) and the control condition ($M = 4.33$, SD = 2.11; $p < .05$, see figure 3). These results demonstrate that although implicit and explicit forewarning both enhance resistance, participants in the implicit forewarning condition consume less energy in doing so than participants in the explicit forewarning condition.

These findings provide a first empirical demonstration of the working of implicit resistance strategies. The major advantage of this kind of strategy is that it limits energy consumption making it more useful in many real life situations.

Figure 2.
Persuasiveness as a function of heuristic cue and forewarning

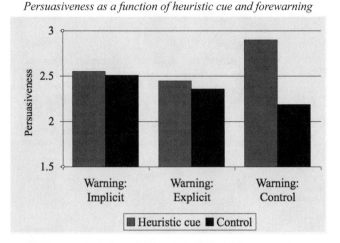

Figure 3.
Amount of correct answers as a function of forewarning

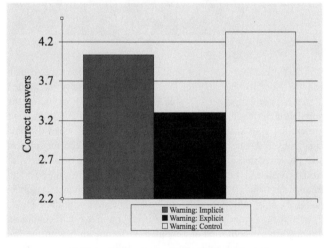

* Note: lower scores indicate more depletion

REFERENCES

Bargh, John A. (1999), "The cognitive monster: The case against the controllability of automatic stereotypes effects," in *Dual process theories in social psychology*, 361-82, ed. Shelly Chaiken and Yaacov Trope, New York, NY: Guilford press.

Bargh, John A. (2004), "Losing consciousness: Automatic influences on consumer judgment, behavior, and motivation," *Journal of Consumer Research*, 29, 280-85.

Bargh, John A. and Melissa J. Ferguson (2000), "Beyond behaviorism: On the automaticity of higher mental processes," *Psychological Bulletin*, 126, 925-45.

Baumeister, Roy F., Ellen Bratslavasky, Mark Muraven, and Dianne M. Tice, (1998), "Ego depletion: Is the active self a limited resource?," *Journal of Personality and Social Psychology*, 74, 1252-65.

Baumeister, Roy F., Kathleen D. Vohs, and Dianne M. Tice (2007), "The strength model of self-control," *Current Directions in Psychological Science*, 16, 351-55.

Blair, Irene V. (2001), "Implicit stereotypes and prejudice," in *Cognitive social psychology: The Princeton Symposium on the Legacy and Future of Social Cognition*, 361-82, ed. Gordon B. Moskowitz , New York: Guilford.

Cialdini, Robert B. (1993) Influence: *The psychology of persuasion*, New York: Morrow.

Devine, Patricia G. (1989), "Stereotypes and prejudice: Their automatic and controlled components," *Journal of Personality and Social Psychology*, 56, 5-18.

Dijksterhuis, Ap (2004), "Think different: The merits of unconscious thought in preference development and decision making," *Journal of Personality and Social Psychology*, 87, 586-98.

Dijksterhuis, Ap, Maarten W. Bos, Nordgren, Loran F. and Rick B. van Baaren (2006), "On making the right choice: The deliberation-without-attention effect," *Science*, 311, 1005-07.

Dovidio, John, Nancy Evans, and Richard B. Tyler (1986), "Racial stereotypes: The contents of their cognitive representations," *Journal of Experimental Social Psychology*, 22, 22-37.

Fennis, Bob M, Loes Janssen, and Kathleen D. Vohs (2009), "Acts of benevolence: A limited-resource account of compliance with charitable requests," *Journal of Consumer Research*, 35, 906-24.

Forehand, Mark R. and Andrew Perkins (2005), "Implicit assimilation and explicit contrast: A set/reset model of response to celebrity voice-overs," *Journal of Consumer Research*, 32, 435-41.

Freedman, Jonathan L. and David O. Sears (1965), "Warning, distraction and resistance to influence," *Journal of Personality and Social Psychology*, 1, 262-66.

Gorn, Gerald J., Yuwei Jiang, and Gita V. Johar (2008), "Baby-faces, trait inferences, and company evaluations in a public relations crisis," *Journal of Consumer Research*, 35, 36-49.

Hass, R. Glen and Kathleen Grady (1975), "Temporal delay, type of forewarning, and resistance to influence," *Journal of Experimental Social Psychology*, 11, 459-69.

Janiszewski, Chris (1988), "Preconscious processing effects: The independence of attitude formation and conscious thought," *Journal of Consumer Research*, 18, 223-35.

Kruglanski, Arie. W. and Erik P. Thompson (1999), "Persuasion by a single route: A view from the unimodel," *Psychological Inquiry*, 10(2), 83-109.

Langer, Ellen J. (1992), "Matters of mind: Mindfulness/ mindlessness in perspective," *Consciousness and Cognition*, 1(4), 289-305.

Papageorgis, Demetrios (1968), "Warning and persuasion," *Psychological Bulletin*, 70, 271-82.

Schmeichel, Brandon J. Kathleen D. Vohs and Roy Baumeister (2003), "Intellectual performance and ego-depletion: Role of the self in logical reasoning and other information processing," *Journal of Personality and Social Psychology*, 85, 33-46.

Tversky, Amos and Daniel Kahneman (1974), "Judgment under uncertainty: Heuristics and biases," *Science*, 185, 1124-31.

Vohs, Kathleen D. and Ronald Faber (2007), "Spent resources: Self-regulatory resource availability affects impulse buying," *Journal of Consumer Research*, 33, 537-47.

New Variables for the Brand Prominence Construct

Heather M. Schulz, University of Nebraska at Kearney, USA
Steven A. Schulz, University of Nebraska at Kearney, USA

EXTENDED ABSTRACT

Brand prominence is a new construct in the literature associated with status signaling. Brand prominence describes, "the conspicuousness of a brand's mark or logo on a product" (Han, Nunes, and Dreze 2010, p. 15). The current study was designed to extend the literature on brand prominence by supplying three new variables of brand prominence: 1) brand presence, 2) brand frequency, and 3) brand abbreviation. These variables break down conspicuousness into more quantifiably measurable categories. A survey was conducted where respondents were shown images of shirts with manipulations of each of these variables and were asked about their behavioral intentions towards these items. Results reveal several statistically significant differences between men and women in their approach to the process of brand prominence behavioral intentions.

Han, Nunes and Dreze (2010) introduced the construct of brand prominence and through content analyses found that for luxury brands, brand prominence decreases as the price of the luxury item increased. The researchers also developed a taxonomy that classifies consumers according to their level of personal wealth and their need for status. From this, four consumer lifestyles associated with the use of products with difference levels of brand prominence: 1) patricians, 2) parvenus, 3) proletarians, and 4) poseurs. Individuals in these groups engage in strategic behaviors through conspicuous consumption in order to associate or dissociate themselves from individuals in other social groups.

The conspicuous consumption literature is the study of status signaling by individuals in a community. Conspicuous consumption describes the displayed use of a brand or a product in a social atmosphere. Veblen (1899/1994) is one of the seminal authors on this subject, and is heavily cited in the literature. Contemporary conspicuous consumption researchers have studied the social meaning (O'Cass and Frost 2002), social utility (Thompson and Norton 2011), social value (Wiedmann, Hennings, and Siebles 2009), and social power (Crosno, Freling, and Skinner 2009) associated with the signaling of one's status through the conspicuous consumption of luxury brands.

Research by Schulz (2009; 2011) has uncovered several themes for brands that are consumed by individuals in the public atmosphere. The major themes include: brand visibility, brand distribution, brand frequency, and brand abbreviation. Each theme also has several sub-themes. For example, brand frequency is made up of: 1) individual unique brand frequency, 2) individual gross brand frequency, 3) product unique brand frequency, and 4) product gross brand frequency. Several of these sub-themes were adapted into behavioral intention variables for brand presence in this study.

A survey was administered to 300 participants in a nationally-representative sample of the U.S. adult population. The survey captured participants' demographics and behavioral intentions towards brand presence variable manipulations across four conditions. The photographic stimuli for the brand prominence conditions can be seen in figure 1. A cross-sectional analysis was conducted in order to see what connections exist among brand presence behavioral intentions.

Figure 1: Stimuli for Brand Presence Variables

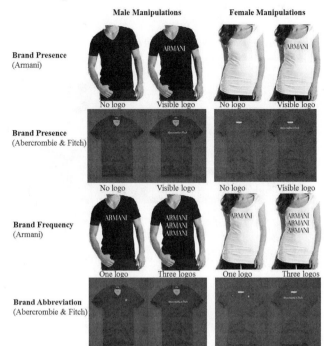

First, frequencies for the brand presence variable in the Armani and the Abercrombie & Fitch conditions show evenly distributed preferences among the aggregated consumer data. About half of the population prefers the shirt with the visible logo, while the other half prefers the shirt without the visible logo. However, when the data is split by sex, one can see that in both scenarios the majority of men preferred the shirt without the visible logo, while the majority of women preferred the shirt with the visible logo. In terms of the brand frequency (Armani) condition, the majority of both men and women prefer the shirt with only one logo versus the shirt with three logos. Finally, for the brand abbreviation (Abercrombie & Fitch) condition, the majority of both men and women prefer the shirt with the full logo rather than the abbreviated logo. Table 1 summarizes these results. Chi-square tests also reveal that gender differences produced significant effects in every condition. These results can be seen in table 2.

Overall, the results of this study show that on average, most consumers prefer the more subtle signal variations of brand prominence variables such as brand frequency. However, most consumers also prefer the fuller version of a brand signal rather than an abbreviated version. Plus, in relation to brand presence most men prefer clothes without branded signals, while most women prefer clothes with branded signals. Further testing of variables related to the brand prominence construct may aid in gaining a better understanding of consumer behavior related to status signaling and conspicuous consumption.

Table 1: Behavioral Intention Frequencies

Brand Prominence Variable	Condition	Women	Men	Total
Brand Presence	No logo (Armani)	31.5%	79.0%	53.3%
	Visible logo (Armani)	68.5%	21.0%	46.7%
Brand Presence	No logo (Abercrombie & Fitch)	23.5%	75.4%	47.3%
	Visible logo (Abercrombie & Fitch)	76.5%	24.6%	52.7%
Brand Frequency	One logo (Armani)	77.8%	93.5%	85.0%
	Three logos (Armani)	22.2%	6.5%	15.0%
Brand Abbreviation	Logo initials (Abercrombie & Fitch)	25.3%	15.2%	20.7%
	Full logo (Abercrombie & Fitch)	74.7%	84.8%	79.3%

Table 2: Behavioral Intention Chi-Square Tests for Gender

Brand Prominence Variable	df	Sample (N)	Pearson Value (X^2)	Significance (p)
Brand Presence (Armani)	1	300	67.57	< 0.001
Brand Presence (Abercrombie & Fitch)	1	300	80.54	< 0.001
Brand Frequency (Armani)	1	300	14.41	< 0.001
Brand Abbreviation (Abercrombie & Fitch)	1	300	4.63	< 0.05

REFERENCES

Crosno, Jody L., Traci H. Freling, and Steven J. Skinner (2009), "Does Brand Social Power Mean Market Might? Exploring the Influence of Brand Social Power on Brand Evaluations," *Psychology & Marketing*, 26 (February), 91-121.

Han, Young Jee, Joseph C. Nunes, and Xavier Dreze (2010), "Signaling Status with Luxury Goods: The Role of Brand Prominence," *Journal of Marketing*, 74 (July), 15-30.

O'Cass, Aron and Hmily Frost (2002), "Status Brands: Examining the Effects of Non-product-related Brand Associations on Status and Conspicuous Consumption," *Journal of Product and Brand Management*, 11 (2), 67-88.

Schulz, Heather M. (2009), "A Brand's Ability to Communicate: Ethnography of Self-extension Through Brand Use," in *Proceedings of the American Academy of Advertising*, ed. Glen Noward, Cincinnati, OH: American Academy of Advertising, 42.

_____ (2011), "The Prop Metaphor: How Consumers and Socially-visible Brands Connect," Unpublished doctoral dissertation, *University of Texas at Austin*, Austin, TX.

Thompson, Debora V., and Michael I. Norton (2011), "The Social Utility of Feature Creep," *Journal of Marketing Research*, XLVIII (June), 555-65.

Veblen, Thorstein (1899/1994), *The Theory of the Leisure Class*, Mineola, NY: Dover.

Wiedmann, Klaus-Peter, Nadine Hennings, and Astrid Siebels (2009), "Value-based Segmentation of Luxury Consumption Behavior," *Psychology & Marketing*, 26 (7), 625-51.

Preferred Persuasion:
How Self Construal Changes Consumer Responses to Persuasion Attempts

Wenxia Guo, University of Manitoba, Canada
Kelley J. Main, University of Manitoba, Canada

EXTENDED ABSTRACT

While the literature on self-construal (independent versus interdependent) has examined such topics as advertisement appeals (Aaker 2000) and values (Triandis 1995), no research so far has investigated how self-construal influences consumers' responses to persuasion attempts. An independent self-construal is oriented towards the self (Miller 1984). Thus, a consumer with a salient independent self-view may evaluate a salesclerk based on his/her prior view of salesclerks (e.g., dishonest, a negative stereotype, Babin et al. 1995) with less influence of the type of persuasion attempt used. An interdependent self-construal is oriented towards social contexts (Miller 1984) and is more likely to be influenced by others and situational information (Iyengar and Lepper 1999), which may make the type of persuasion attempt matter when evaluating salesclerks. Further, when an interdependent self-construal is activated, people's sense of uniqueness may be threatened, which may make them more sensitive to individually focused persuasion (e.g., messages focused on distinctiveness) during the interaction with salesclerks.

The following studies examine whether individuals with a dominant interdependent self-construal should have higher perceived trustworthiness in a salesclerk and a higher need for uniqueness when processing individually focused persuasion attempts than interpersonally focused persuasion attempts. This difference will be attenuated for individuals with a dominant independent self-construal.

STUDY 1

75 participants from a Chinese university in Beijing were randomly assigned to a 2 (persuasion attempt: individually vs. interpersonally focused) × 2 (primed self-construal: independent vs. interdependent) between-subjects design. A pronoun (first-personal singular vs. plural) circling task in a paragraph involving a trip to a restaurant (Oyserman et al. 2009) primed independent versus interdependent. Next, a scenario was used to manipulate the interpersonally vs. individually focused persuasion attempt. The dependent variables were salesclerk trustworthiness (Main et al. 2007) and need for unique choice (Tian et al. 2001).

Results showed that when participants were primed with an interdependent self-construal, individually focused persuasion attempts led to higher trustworthiness ($F(1, 71) = 5.21$, $p < 0.01$, $M_{interpersonally\ focused} = 4.04$, $M_{individually\ focused} = 4.58$) and need for unique choice ($F(1,71) = 3.14$, $p < 0.1$, $M_{interpersonally\ focused} = 2.98$, $M_{individually\ focused} = 3.42$) than interpersonally focused persuasion attempts. However, when participants were primed with an independent self-construal, these effects were attenuated.

STUDY 2

This was a field study where interdependent self-construal was measured (Singelis, 1994). 79 participants were randomly assigned to two conditions (persuasion attempt: individually vs. interpersonally focused) and received $7 compensation.

Two new product lines were created solely for the purpose of this research so that students would be unfamiliar with the products. Participants were instructed to visit a retail store and evaluate the new product lines that were on display. A female confederate in her mid forties was selected to act as a company representative. She was responsible for the administration of the persuasion attempt: a uniqueness focused statement (individually focused) or a connection focused statement (interpersonally focused).

Regression analysis was conducted with persuasion attempts (dummy code), level of interdependence (mean-centered score; Aiken and West 1991), and the interaction term included in the model as predictors. There was a significant interaction between persuasion attempt type and the level of interdependence on trustworthiness ($\beta = 0.36$, $p < 0.05$) and need for unique choice ($\beta = 0.31$, $p < 0.05$) respectively. Simple slope analysis at one standard deviation above the mean of interdependence indicated a significant difference such that participants with a high level of interdependence trusted the clerk more ($\beta = 0.75$, $t = 2.58$, $p < 0.01$) and had higher need for unique choice ($\beta = 0.63$, $t = 2.20$, $p < 0.05$) for individually focused as compared to interpersonally focused persuasion attempts. Simple slope analysis at one standard deviation below the mean of interdependence showed no significant difference.

STUDY 3

Study 3 was to test the underlying process for the effect observed in proceeding studies. Briley and Aaker (2006) suggest that cognitive load is an alternative way to examine the underlying process from cross cultural studies. We propose that under low cognitive load, persuasion knowledge mediates the relationship between the interaction of persuasion attempts and self-construal on trustworthiness.

156 participants were randomly assigned to a 2 (persuasion attempt: individually vs. interpersonally focused) × 2 (primed self-construal: independent vs. interdependent) × 2 (cognitive load: high vs. low) between-subjects design. First, participants were primed with either an independent or interdependent self-construal adapted from Mandel (2003). The persuasion attempt manipulation was the same as study 1. The manipulation of high (vs. low) cognitive load required (vs. did not require) participants to remember eight numbers presented in the scenario.

Results illustrated a significant three-way interaction ($F(1,148) = 12.8$, $p < 0.001$) that showed self-construal had impacts on processing persuasion attempts under low cognitive load. We bootstrapped the indirect effect of the different persuasion attempts and priming on trustworthiness (Hayes and Matthes 2009). The 95% CIs demonstrated that the indirect interaction between persuasion attempt type and priming through persuasion knowledge on trustworthiness was significantly different from zero under low cognitive load, but was not significant under high cognitive load.

DISCUSSION

The present research contributes to the literature from several perspectives. First, this research integrates self-construal into the Persuasion Knowledge Model (Friestad and Wright 1994). Second, we identify a counterintuitive result given current research in the advertising literature. Advertising appeals that are compatible with a salient independent (versus interdependent) self result in more positive effects than appeals that are incompatible (e.g., Han and Shavitt 1994). However, the current study finds that when an interdependent self-construal is made salient, individually rather than interpersonally focused persuasion attempts result in more positive consumer perceptions. That is, an incompatible effect occurs in a retailing context.

Third, we contribute to the psychological literature by showing that priming participants with an interdependent self-construal can threaten their fundamental need for distinctiveness and thus results in a higher need for uniqueness. Subsequently, this threat affects people's interactions with others. In a retailing context, consumers may be more sensitive to individually focused persuasion attempts (i.e. focusing on uniqueness) which may help them rebuild their sense of uniqueness.

REFERENCES

Aaker, Jennifer L. (2000), "Accessibility or Diagnosticity? Disentangling the Influence of Culture on Persuasion Processes and Attitudes," *Journal of Consumer Research*, 26(March), 340-357.

Aiken, Leona S and Stephen G. West (1991). *Multiple regression: Testing and interpreting interactions*. Newbury Park, CA: Sage Publications.

Babin, Barry J., James S. Boles, and Williams R. Darden (1995), "Salesperson Stereotypes, Consumer Emotions, and their Impact on Information Processing," *Journal of the Academy of Marketing Science*, 32(2), 94-105.

Briley, Donnel A. and Jennifer L. Aaker (2006), "When does Culture Matter? Effects of Personal Knowledge on the Correction of Culture-based Judgments," *Journal of Marketing Research*, August, 395-408.

Friestad, Marian R., and Peter Wright (1994), "The Persuasion Knowledge Model: How People Cope with Persuasion Attempts," *Journal of Consumer Research*, 21, 1-31.

Han, Sang and Sharon Shavitt (1994), "Persuasion and Culture: Advertising Appeals in Individualistic and Collectivistic Countries," *Journal of Experimental Social Psychology*, 30, 326-350.

Hayes, Andrew F. and J. Matthes (2009), "Computational Procedures for Probing Interactions in OLS and Logistic Regression: SPSS and SAS Implementations," Behavior Research Methods, 41, 924-936.

Iyengar, Sheena S. and Mark L. Lepper (1999), "Rethinking the value of choice: A cultural perspective on intrinsic motivation," *Journal of Personality and Social Psychology*, 76(3), 349-366.

Mandel, Naomi (2003), "Shifting Selves and Decision Making: The Effects of Self-construal Priming on Consumer Risk-taking," *Journal of Consumer Research*, 30 (June), 30-40.

Main, Kelley J., Darren W. Dahl, and Peter R. Darke (2007), "Deliberative and Automatic Bases of Suspicion: Empirical Evidence of the Sinister Attribution Error," *Journal of Consumer Psychology*, 17(1), 59-69.

Miller, Joan G. (1984), "Culture and the Development of Everyday Social Explanation," *Journal of Personality and Social Psychology*, 46, 961-978.

Oyserman, Daphna, Nicholas Sorensen, Rolf Reber, and Sylvia Chen (2009), "Connecting and Separating Mind-sets: Culture as Situated Cognition," *Journal of Personality and Social Psychology*, 97(2), 217-235.

Singelis, Theodore M. (1994), "The Measurement of Independent and Interdependent Self-Construals," *Personality and Social Psychology Bulletin*, 7, 233-269.

Snyder, C.R. and Howard L. Fromkin (1980). Uniqueness: The human pursuit of difference. New York: Plenum.

Tian, Kelly T., William O. Bearden, and Gary L. Hunter (2001), "Consumers' Need for Uniqueness: Scale Development and Validation," *Journal of Consumer Research*, 28(June), 51-65.

Triandis, Harry C. (1995). *Individualism and Collectivism*. Boulder, CO: Westview.

Consumer Propensity to Resist (CPR): Measurement and Validation

Annie Stéphanie Banikema, Groupe Sup de Co Amiens-Picardie, France
Dominique Roux, Université Paris Sud, France

EXTENDED ABSTRACT

This paper offers a valid measure of Consumer Propensity to Resist (CPR). A qualitative research helps define the construct. Then, a scale is developed through four samples from 1,476 individuals. A final model confirms the links between Self-Affirmation and Self-Protection, their antecedents and effects on various buying behavior.

THEORETICAL GAP AND RESEARCH QUESTIONS

Culturalist approaches have explored various forms of opposition in which people express their rejection of market structures (Peñaloza and Price 1993). However, from a micro-social perspective, research paradoxically presents a significant gap at the individual level. Thus, the aim of this paper is to provide a reliable and valid measurement tool of the consumer's propensity to resist (CPR), capable of predicting critical motivations and various buying behaviors in the marketplace. Its theoretical underpinnings rest on Mowen's (2000) hierarchical model of personality and motivation, where CPR is conceptualized as a situational trait i.e. resulting from the joint effects of elemental traits, compound traits and the situational context in which the behavior occurs.

LITERATURE REVIEW

Numerous qualitative approaches have focused on resistant behavior in various contexts (Close and Zinkhan 2009; Dobscha and Ozanne 2001; Giesler 2006; Holt 2002; Kozinets 2002; Kozinets and Handelman 2004; Romani, Grappi, and Dalli 2012; Sandikci and Ekici 2009; Thomson and Arsel 2004). Yet, although it is likely that people react differently to influences exerted on them, there has been very little research on capturing this individual trait. The anti-commercial consumer rebellion (ACR) measure proposed by Austin, Plouffe and Peters (2005) in fact focuses on resistant behavior rather than the propensity to adopt such behavior. The Iyer and Muncy (2009) anti-consumption measure is also mainly behavioral and noticeably different from resistance (Lee et al. 2011). Hence, a dispositional approach to consumer propensity to resist still has to be constructed.

METHOD

A two-step qualitative study provided an in-depth understanding of the dimensions of the construct and of its determinants and consequences. A measurement tool was then developed, covering four different market influence contexts—selling, advertising, retail and marketing—and replicated for the first two context. Finally, a structural equation model, including determinants and effects of CPR, was tested.

FINDINGS

The results of the qualitative study first show that CPR is an inherently volitional construct expressing the commitment and effort needed to enact a desired behavior (Bagozzi 1993; Perugini and Conner 2000). Two distinct orientations underpin informants' psychological orientation: for some, the wish to assert themselves, and for others, to protect themselves. Hence, CPR is conceptualized as a personality trait whose observable manifestations in an influence situation—self-affirmation and self-protection—echoes Higgins's (1997) regulatory focus. CPR is thus defined as *the consumer's conscious and voluntary psychological tendency to thwart market influ-*ence attempts, in order to self-regulate his consumer decisions and maintain self-control.

The qualitative study provided 31 items—15 for the "Affirmation" and 16 for the "Protection" dimension—that were then examined by five experts to assess their clarity and relevance. 26 remaining items were purified through two data collections, finally producing a reliable 7-item scale. In the "salespeople" context as well as in the "advertising" context, the scale shows good reliability and convergent validity, based on the observation of confirmatory factor loadings higher than 0.607. It meets the intra-construct discriminant validity condition as the root average variance extracted (AVE) indices for each dimensions exceed the correlation between the two CPR dimensions. Though, an alternative one-dimensional model (in which the two latent variables are regarded as measuring a single construct) was tested. It finally attests to the superiority of the two-dimensional model.

Furthermore, discriminant validity is successfully met since CPR is more highly correlated with its two dimensions than with other potentially similar constructs such as skepticism, metacognition, psychological reactance and cynicism. Finally, the relationships between the antecedents of CPR and its behavioral consequences are tested through structural equation modeling. Based on the theoretical indices that emerged from the qualitative study and the literature review, four antecedents are retained:

- Skepticism (Obermiller and Spangenberg 1988), with which a positive relationship is postulated on both CPR dimensions.
- Metacognition (Friestad and Wright 1994) and Self-confidence (Bearden, Hardesty, and Rose 2001) as antecedents of the "Affirmation" dimension, since persuasion knowledge and self-assurance in everyday life inherently protect the consumer against sources of influence.
- Psychological reactance as an antecedent of the "Protection" dimension, since avoidance behavior is likely to be response to the perceived threat of loss of freedom (Clee and Wicklund 1980).

Five effects variables are also considered for testing the predictive validity:

- Smart shopping (Mano and Elliott 1997), second-hand shoppers' critical motivations (Guiot and Roux 2010) and the tendency to engage in socially responsible consumption (SRC) (François-Lecompte and Roberts 2006). The "Protection" dimension, predisposing consumers to exit, is expected to favor smart shopping or secondhand shopping rather than SRC. Conversely, the "Affirmation" dimension, prompting consumers to openly engage in resistance to the market, would be positively correlated with the SRC dimensions and negatively with smart shopping or alternative channel solutions. However, because of the volitional character of CPR, deal proneness and impulsive buying should be negatively correlated with the two CPR dimensions.

As hypothesized, CPR-Affirmation is well predicted by skepticism, metacognition and the two self-confidence dimensions, while psychological reactance appears, in addition to skepticism, as a specific antecedent of CPR-Protection. Regarding the effects, CPR-Affirmation well predicts expected orientations—both SRC dimensions and critical motivations towards secondhand shopping. It is negatively linked to deal proneness and impulsive buying. Besides, CPR-Protection well predicts smart shopping and critical motivations toward secondhand shopping, but surprisingly, is positively linked to deal proneness and impulsive buying. Similarly, the postulated negative link between the CPR-Protection and SRC proves to be non-significant, showing that these consumers seem not to view responsible consumption as a relevant orientation to avoid market influence.

CONTRIBUTIONS

Ultimately, the CPR scale shows satisfactory psychometric properties. It has the advantage of being formulated so as to be adaptable to other contexts of market influence mechanisms. Overall, it captures consumers' tendency to resist, which reflects their dominant orientation in terms of regulatory focus (Higgins 1997). Finally, it shows that while CPR-Affirmation profiles are prone to oppose influence attempts, CPR-Protection consumers succumb to these more easily than first thought.

REFERENCES

Austin, Caroline G, Christopher R. Plouffe, and Cara Peters (2005), "Anti-commercial consumer rebellion: conceptualization and measurement," *Journal of Targeting, Measurement and Analysis for Marketing,* 14(1), 62-78.

Bagozzi, Richard P. (1993), "On the Neglect of Volition in Consumer Research: A Critique and Proposal," *Psychology & Marketing*, 10, 1993, 215-37.

Bearden, William O., David M. Hardesty, and Randall L. Rose. (2001), "Consumer Self-Confidence: Refinements in Conceptualization and Measurement," *Journal of Consumer Research*, 28(1), 121-34.

Clee, Mona A and Robert A Wicklund (1980), "Consumer Behaviour and Psychological Reactance, "*Journal of Consumer Research*, 6(4), 389-405.

Close, Angeline and George M. Zinkhan G. (2009), "Market-resistance and Valentine's Day events," *Journal of Business Research*, 62(2), 200-07.

Dobscha, Susan and Julie L. Ozanne (2001), "An ecofeminist analysis of environmentally sensitive women using qualitative methodology: findings on the emancipatory potential of an ecological life," *Journal of Public Policy and Marketing*, 20(2), 201-14.

François-Lecompte, Agnès and James A. Roberts (2006), "Developing a measure of socially responsible consumption in France," *Marketing Management Journal*, 16 (2), 50-66

Friestad, Marian and Peter Wright (1994), "The Persuasion Knowledge Model: How People Cope with Persuasion Attempts, "*Journal of Consumer Research*, 21(1), 1-31.

Giesler, Markus (2006), "Consumer gift system: netnographic insights from Napster," *Journal of Consumer Research*, 33(2), 283-90.

Guiot Denis and Dominique Roux (2010), "A Second-hand Shoppers' Motivation Scale: Antecedents, Consequences, and Implications for Retailers," *Journal of Retailing,* 86(4), 355-71.

Higgins, E. Tory (1997), "Beyond pleasure and pain," *American Psychologist,* 52(12), 1280-1300.

Holt, Douglas B (2002), "Why do brands cause trouble? A dialectical theory of consumer culture and branding," *Journal of Consumer Research*, 29(1), 70-90.

Iyer, Rajesh and James A. Muncy (2009), "Purpose and Object of Anti-Consumption," *Journal of Business Research*, 62(2), 160-68.

Kozinets, Robert V. (2002), "Can consumers escape the market? Emancipatory illuminations from burning man," *Journal of Consumer Research*, 29(1), 20-38

Kozinets, Robert V. and Jay M. Handelman (2004), "Adversaries of consumption: consumer movements, activism, and ideology," *Journal of Consumer Research*, 31(3), 691-704.

Lee, Mike, Dominique Roux, Hélène Cherrier and Bernard Cova (2011), "Anti-consumption and consumer resistance: concepts, concerns, conflicts and convergence, Guest Editorial," *European Journal of Marketing*, 45, 11/12, 1680-87.

Mano, Haim and Michael T. Elliott (1997), "Smart shopping: the origins and consequences of price savings," *Advances in Consumer Research*, 24(1), 504-10.

Mowen, John C. (2000), *The 3M model of motivation and personality: theory and empirical applications to consumer behaviour*, New York: Kluwer Academic Publishers.

Obermiller, Carl and Eric R. Spangenberg (1998), "Development of a scale to measure consumer scepticism toward advertising," *Journal of Consumer Psychology*, 7(2), 159-86.

Peñaloza, Lisa and Linda L. Price (1993), Consumer resistance: a conceptual overview, *Advances in Consumer Research*, 20, 123-28.

Perugini, Marco and Mark Conner (2000), "Predicting and understanding behavioral volitions: the interplay between goals and behaviors," *European Journal of social Psychology*, 30(5), 705-31.

Romani, Simona, Silvia Grappi, and Danielle Dalli (2012), "Emotions that drive consumers away from brands: measuring negative emotions toward brands and their behavioral effects," *International Journal of Research in Marketing*, 29(1), forthcoming.

Sandıkci, Özlem and Ahmet Ekici (2009), "Politically motivated brand rejection," *Journal of Business Research*, 62(2), 208-17.

Thompson, Craig J. and Zeynep Arsel (2004), "The Starbucks brandscape and consumers' (anticorporate) experiences of glocalization," *Journal of Consumer Research*, 31(3), 631-42.

Negative Consumption Episodes, Counterfactuals and Persuasion

Kai-Yu Wang, Brock University, Canada
Xiaojing Yang, University of Wisconsin-Milwaukee, U.S.A.
Shailendra P. Jain, University of Washington, U.S.A.

EXTENDED ABSTRACT

Consumption outcomes often induce different consumer post-purchase responses, with one of them being counterfactual thinking (CFT). CFT refers to the process of reflecting on past events and simulating alternative possible outcomes. For example, in a consumption context, imagine that a consumer finds her HDTV needs repair just after the warranty expires. This consumer may think to herself: "If only I had purchased a TV with an extended warranty, I would not have to incur so much cost on this repair." CFT impacts consumers' emotions, judgments and decision making, and occurs in a variety of contexts, regardless of the valence of purchase outcomes. However, negative purchase outcomes are more likely to evoke CFT (Wang, Liang, and Peracchio, 2011). CFT plays an important role in an individual's experience of emotions such as regret and disappointment (Zeelenberg, van Dijk, van der Pligt, Manstead, van Empelen, and Reinderman, 1998) and these emotions influence customer dissatisfaction and behavioral response (e.g., brand switching and complaint) (Zeelenberg and Pieters, 2004).

Only a handful of studies have explored the impact of CFT on information processing and persuasion in consumer settings. In their research, Krishnamurthy and Sivaraman (2002) view CFT as a problem-solving function and investigate its influence on future problem-solving behaviors. They find that CFT makes consumers scrutinize ad claims encountered subsequent to the CFT generating episode. Upward CFT makes consumers feel worse vis-a-vis their chosen product, making them examine incoming information more carefully to prepare for the future. If we think of CFT as a preparative (problem-solving) function, CFT may influence consumers' preferences for different types of advertising. To examine this possibility and identify how CFT impacts such ad receipt, this research focuses on ad persuasion processes that involve CFT. In specific, we investigate how CFT initiated by a negative purchase experience impacts consumers' subsequent receipt of comparative versus noncomparative ads. Such motivational priming processes are only beginning to be understood in social psychology (Roese, Hur, & Pennington, 1999), and have not received much attention in the consumer behavior literature. Expanding on prior research in counterfactual priming effects (Kray, Galinsky, & Wong, 2006), our investigation examines whether a counterfactual mind-set evoked by a negative consumption episode may influence information processing and persuasion in subsequent related as well as unrelated consumption contexts.

We argue that comparative ads evoke both, approach and avoidance motivations, whereas noncomparative ads induce mostly approach motivations (Jain, Agrawal, and Maheswaran, 2006). Further, we expect that when individuals engage in counterfactual comparisons, the advertised brand in a comparative ad will be judged more favorably than the one in a noncomparative ad. This will be so because motivations (approach and avoidance) evoked by counterfactual comparisons are consistent with the motivations engendered by comparative ads. In contrast, when consumers engage in past-temporal comparisons (fact-based comparisons as opposed to simulation-based counterfactual comparisons), the brand in a noncomparative ad will be evaluated more positively because of the motivational (approach) consistency between processing focus and ad frames.

We conducted two experiments examining the impact of CFT in response to a previous negative consumption experience on the effectiveness of subsequently encountered advertising appeals. Experiment 1's stimulus featured the same category in the consumption experience and the ad. Experiment 2 featured a different category in the consumption episode vis-à-vis the one featured in the ad. Varying the category enabled us to test the robustness of our findings.

In both experiments, counterfactual thinking (CFT and control) and ad format (comparative and noncomparative) were manipulated. We hypothesized that when presented with a comparative ad, respondents encouraged to think counterfactually (vs control respondents) will generate higher ad evaluations, brand evaluations, and purchase intentions. In contrast, when presented with a noncomparative ad, control (vs CFT) respondents will generate higher ad evaluations, brand evaluations, and purchase intentions. The results for the two experiments were consistent with our predictions. Examination and analysis of thoughts provided additional support for the hypotheses.

Taken together, these two studies support much of our proposed theorizing regarding the effect of CFT on consumers' processing of subsequently encountered messages. In addition, we identify the process underlying this pattern of response (matching of motivational focus). The findings suggest that CFT evokes both approach and avoidance motivation whereas past-temporal comparison induces largely approach motivation. This difference in motivation leads to a difference in the preference for different ad formats. To our knowledge, this is the first attempt to apply CFT to comparative advertising contexts and advances our understanding of the impact of CFT on ad related persuasion. This research also extends CFT priming effects research to subsequent information processing in unrelated consumption contexts.

REFERENCES

Higgins, E. T. (1997). Beyond pleasure and pain. *American Psychologist*, *52*, 1280-1300.

Kray, L. J., Galinsky, A. D., & Wong, E. M. (2006). Thinking within the box: The relational processing style elicited by counterfactual mind-sets. *Journal of Personality and Social Psychology*, *91*, 33-48.

Krishnamurthy, Parthasarathy and Anuradha Sivaraman (2002), "Counterfactual thinking and advertising responses," *Journal of Consumer Research*, 28 (March), 650-8.

Jain, S. P., Agrawal, N., & Maheswaran, D. (2006). When more may be less: The effects of regulatory focus on responses to different comparative frames. *Journal of Consumer Research*, *33*, 91-98.

Roese, N., Hur, T., & Pennington, G. L. (1999). Counterfactual thinking and regulatory focus: Implications for action versus inaction and sufficiency versus necessity. *Journal of Personality and Social Psychology*, *77*, 1109-1120.

Wang, K.-Y., Liang, M., & Peracchio, L. A. (2011). Strategies to offset dissatisfactory product performance: The role of post-purchase marketing. *Journal of Business Research*, *64*, 809-815.

Zeelenberg, M., van Dijk, W.W., van der Pligt, J., Manstead, A.S.R., van Empelen, P., & Reinderman, D. (1998). Emotional reactions to the outcomes of decisions: The role of counterfactual thought in the experience of regret and disappointment. *Organizational Behavior and Human Decision Processes*, 75, 117-141.

Zeelenberg, M. & Pieters, R. (2004). Beyond valence in customer dissatisfaction: A review and new findings on behavioral responses to regret and disappointment in failed services. *Journal of Business Research*, 57, 445-455.

The Mediating Role of the Built Environment in Family Consumption Practices

Margaret K. Hogg, Lancaster University Management School, England
Pauline Maclaran, Royal Holloway University of London, England
Carolyn Folkman Curasi, Georgia State University, University Plaza, USA

EXTENDED ABSTRACT

Our paper addresses two key questions: firstly how does the built environment, both public and private, mediate family relationships; and secondly, how are certain spaces used to re-create family life whereas others allow altered relationships between family members to emerge? We use empty nest families as our empirical site for investigating how consumption is employed in order to maintain a sense of family as family life moves increasingly outside its traditional setting of the domestic household to a variety of new places (e.g. children's new homes; wider urban spaces and consumptionscapes) as children move away from home.

This paper draws on two sets of literature: firstly about space and place; and secondly about the family. There are two main streams of research on place: firstly the servicescape literature about the built environment which includes studies on shopping malls (Sandikci and Holt 1998); flagship brand stores (Kozinets et al. 2002; Peñaloza 1999; Sherry 1998a); retail outlets (McGrath 1989; Otnes 1998; Maclaran and Brown 2005), and leisure venues (Kozinets et al. 2004). The second strand of literature on place relates to the built place of the home, for instance homes as part of the extended self (Belk, 1988); creating 'homeyness' (McCracken, 1989); and the material culture of the home (Miller 2001; Marcoux 2001a; 2001b; Gregson 2007). Alongside the literature on place and space we also draw on the family literature, most notably Epp and Price's (2008) work which identified that family identity comprises individual, relational and collective aspects.

In our study we concentrate particularly on the relational identities within families and, most notably, the mother/child dyad as an important site for generating relational identities within family via activities and consumption practices. We chose to track the changes in family life via mothers' perspectives because women have been identified as having the primary responsibility for the creation of family life in households via nurturance, socialization, relationality, and emotionality (De Vault 1991; Hochschild 1975; Hochschild and Machung 1989; Lorber 2000). It is women's relational identities as mothers that are particularly destabilized as they undergo dislocation and disruption in the context of empty nest households. The home traditionally represents the socio-spatial embeddedness of women's mothering identities; and this dislocation of their relational identities (as mothers) from its recognized spatial location (the home) is crucial to our examination of how space and place mediate the reconfiguration of social-spatial relationships.

For our data collection, accordingly, we focused on empty-nest mothers' experiences and feelings during the 18 months just after their adult child left the parental home, in order to study, first, how mothers work to recreate a sense of family life diffused from the fixed physical space of the original family household; and second, how both private and public spaces are appropriated (or re-appropriated) as family formation changes and relational mothering selves are reconfigured. We collected two data sets: firstly we undertook 27 in-depth interviews with women whose children have just left home (within the last 18 months); and secondly we used participant observation (netnography) on empty nester bulletin boards (this phase lasted for 6 months). As an interpretivist study that falls within the Consumer Culture Theory programme of research (e.g. identity projects, Arnould and Thompson 2005) we tacked back and forth between our qualitative datasets and the literature to analyze and interpret the data, identify themes and conceptualize our findings as an early stage in theory building.

Our conceptualization (Figure 1) flows from our findings which we map in relation to two main dimensions: spaces (firstly for wandering e.g. consumptionscapes; and secondly, for enclosing e.g. domestic places); and relational identities (firstly, maintaining the status quo and secondly, changing identities) into four quadrants. The first quadrant deals with reifying consumption practices where enclosing spaces are private, domestic & inward focused. Here there is a strong sense of rootedness and relational attachment; activities are directed at maintaining the status quo; children's bedrooms are used to freeze time and to tempt children to return home; and the materiality of the space physically anchors women's identities as mothers. The second quadrant mediates relational consumption practices, and here the child's new apartment/house acts also as a hestial space which means that it can exclude the parents and thus represent a threatening time for mothers. Mothers therefore seek to influence their children's strategic decisions about what to take from home and what to leave behind, and thereby try and emplace a sense of family life in the child's new space. The third quadrant is about reconfiguring relational consumption practices, and here there is a temporary appropriation of public spaces for family life. These are hermetic spaces that encourage temporary stays: dwelling by wandering versus dwelling by residing; they are outward rather than inward looking, de-centered rather than centered. These spaces tend to be unfamiliar, and invite exploration. In these spaces mothers seek ways of adjusting to different types of corporeal engagement and explore new ways of being with their children. The fourth and final quadrant relates to stabilising relational consumption practices by emplacing a continued sense of family life to reinforce the habitual, for instance by re-enacting familiar family routines away from home. Here we can see that consumptionscapes may have hestial qualities (cf. Sherry et al.'s work (2001) on American Girl; and Kozinets et al.'s (2002) paper on the ESPN zone). In this case, mothers look for more neutral environments in which to meet their children and stabilise existing relations.

Figure 1: Nature of Family Relational Consumption Practices Across Public & Private Spaces

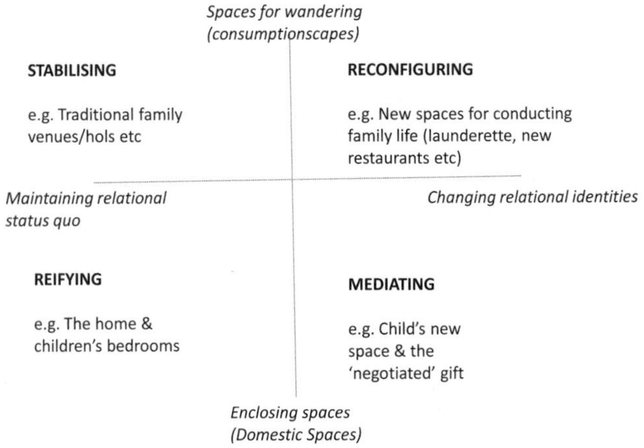

Spaces for wandering (consumptionscapes)

STABILISING	RECONFIGURING
e.g. Traditional family venues/hols etc	e.g. New spaces for conducting family life (launderette, new restaurants etc)

Maintaining relational status quo | *Changing relational identities*

REIFYING	MEDIATING
e.g. The home & children's bedrooms	e.g. Child's new space & the 'negotiated' gift

Enclosing spaces (Domestic Spaces)

In conclusion our study shows firstly, how relational identity changes over time and space, and the use of implacement practices (e.g. defending, maintaining or changing the relational self in dyads) by mothers to maintain a sense of family life; secondly the embedded nature of power relations and how they change over time and space, and how the balance tips between mother and child; and thirdly, how relational identities operate across public and private spheres and how space is used strategically with respect to relational identity.

REFERENCES

Arnould, Eric J. and Craig J. Thompson (2005), "Consumer Culture Theory (CCT) Twenty Years of Research" *Journal of Consumer Research,* 31, 868-882.

Belk , R.W. (1988), "Possessions and Extended Self," *Journal of Consumer Reseach,* 15, 139-168.

De Vault, Marjorie L. (1991), *Feeding the Family: The Social Organization of Caring as Gendered Work,* Chicago: University of Chicago Press.

Epp, A. and L. Price (2008), "Family Identity: A Framework of Identity Interplay in Consumption Practices*," Journal of Consumer Research,* 35, 50-70 .

Gregson, Nicky (2007), *Living with Things: Ridding, Accommodation, Dwelling*, Wantage, England: Sean Kingston Publishing.

Hochschild, Arlie Russell (1975), "The Sociology of Feeling and Emotion: Selected Possibilities," in *Another Voice,* ed. Marcia Millman and Rosabeth Moss Kanter, New York: Anchor, 280-307.

Hochschild, Arlie Russell and Anne Machung (1989), *The Second Shift: Working Parents and Revolution at Home,* New York: Viking.

Kozinets, Robert V., John F. Sherry, Jr., Diana Storm, Adam Duhachek, Krittinee Nuttavuthisit and Benét DeBerry-Spence (2002), "Themed Flagship Brandstores in the New Millennium: Theory, Practice, Prospects," *Journal of Retailing,* 78 (1), 17-29.

_____ (2004), "Ludic Agency and Retail Spectacle," *Journal of Consumer Research,* 31 (December), 658-72.

Lorber, Judith (2000), "Using Gender to Undo Gender: A Feminist Degendering Movement," *Feminist Theory,* 1 (1), 79-95.

Maclaran, Pauline and Stephen Brown (2005), "The Center Cannot Hold: Consuming the Utopian Marketplace," *Journal of Consumer Research,* 32 (September), 311-23.

Marcoux, Jean-Sebastien (2001a), "The '*Casser Maison*' Ritual': Constructing the Self by Emptying the Home," *Journal of Material Culture,* 6 (2), 213-35.

_____ (2001b), "The Refurbishment of Memory," in *Home Possessions*, ed. Daniel Miller, 69-86, Oxford, UK: Berg.

McCracken, Grant (1989), "Homeyness: A Cultural Account of One Constellation of Consumer Goods and Meanings," in *Interpretive Consumer Research,* ed. Elizabeth C. Hirschman, Provo, UT: Association for Consumer Research, 168-83.

McGrath, Mary Ann (1989), "An Ethnography of a Gift Store: Trappings, Wrappings, and Rapture," *Journal of Retailing,* 65 (4), 421-49.

Miller, Daniel (2001), "Possessions," *Home Possessions*, ed. Daniel Miller, Oxford, UK: Berg.

Otnes, Cele (1998), ""Friend of the Bride" – and Then Some: Roles of the Bridal Salon During Wedding Planning," *Servicescapes: The Concept of Place in Contemporary Markets*, Lincolnwood, IL: NTC Business Books .

Peñaloza, Lisa (1999), "Just Doing It: A Visual Ethnographic Study of Spectacular Consumption Behavior at Nike Town," *Consumption, Markets and Culture,* 2 (4), 337–400.

Sandikci, Ozlem and Douglas B. Holt (1998), "Malling Society: Mall Consumption Practices and the Future of Public Space," in *Servicescapes: The Concept of Place in Contemporary Markets,* ed. John F. Sherry, Jr., Chicago: NTC Business Books, 305-36.

Sherry, John F., Jr. (1998), *Servicescapes*, Lincolnwood, IL: NTC Business Books.

Store Personality as a Source of Customer Value

Kim Willems, Vrije Universiteit Brussel & Hasselt University, Belgium
Sara Leroi-Werelds, Hasselt University, Belgium
Sandra Streukens, Hasselt University, Belgium

ACKNOWLEDGEMENTS

The authors thank the Research Foundation - Flanders (FWO Vlaanderen) for a doctoral fellowship.

EXTENDED ABSTRACT

1. Literature Review

"What is the value of the different personality dimensions? Are certain personality dimensions more valuable at driving preference or loyalty than others?"

(Keller and Lehmann 2006, 741)

In the mature and highly competitive retailing environment, customers are more value conscious than ever before. Therefore, creating customer value is particularly vital for retailers to obtain satisfied and loyal customers (Sweeney and Soutar 2001). In line with Zeithaml's (1988, 4) definition that "perceived value is the consumer's overall assessment of the utility of a product based on perceptions of what is received and what is given", there has been a general consensus that customer value involves a trade-off between benefits and costs.

According to the utility theory which provides a theoretical underpinning for the value concept (He and Mukherjee 2007), customers do not buy products for their own sake, nor do they patronize retailers for merely functional benefits. We propose store personality as a potential source of value in retailing and define it as "the way in which the store is defined in the shopper's mind, partly by its functional qualities and partly by an aura of psychological attributes" (Martineau 1958, 47). Just as personality has been proven to serve as a viable metaphor to ascribe stable human characteristics to product brands, so can retail brands be expected to serve as symbolic devices (Caprara, Barbaranelli, and Gianluigi 1998). As such, the consumer's first, general impression of a store's personality may be positive and subsequently color further elaborative information processing on the store and its offerings (Freling, Crosno, and Henard 2011).

2. Research Objectives

This study examines the strategic role of store personality and the related construct self-congruity (i.e., the match between the customer's personality and store personality) by assessing their effect on customer value. Additionally, we investigate the potential interaction between store personality and self-congruity.

Figure 1 summarizes our hypotheses, with H1 and H2 as the focus of our research. Apart from unpleasantness, all store personality dimensions as well as self-congruity are hypothesized to positively impact customer value. Furthermore, the relationship between store personality and value is expected to be strengthened by perceived self-congruity (i.e., H10).

To obtain a full understanding of the impact of store personality and self-congruity on customer value, we take existing knowledge about the nomological web of these constructs into account (see Figure 1).

Figure 1
CONCEPTUAL MODEL

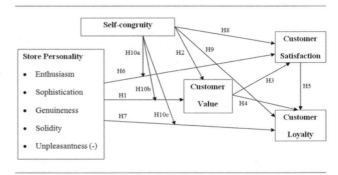

With these research objectives in mind, four unique aspects of this study differentiate it from previous studies. First, whereas the dominant focus in most customer value studies is on the consequences of customer value (Cronin, Brady, and Hult 2000), our focus is rather on the antecedent side. Second, rather than focusing on the most easily observable (and also the most straightforward to copy by competitors) store cues, such as price, merchandise quality or store design (Baker, Parasuraman, Grewal, and Voss 2002), the antecedents under study situate at a higher level of abstraction. Third, although customer value, personality, and self-congruity are extensively studied in a product context, these concepts are relatively scarcely studied in retailing (Sirgy, Grewal, and Mangleburg 2000). Fourth, we contribute to the research stream on the conceptualization and operationalization of both customer value and store personality. With regard to customer value, Holbrook's (1999) Typology is adapted to a retail setting, resulting in seven retail value types (i.e., efficiency, product excellence, service excellence, aesthetics, play, social-, and altruistic value), as opposed to the traditional dichotomous view on shopping value (i.e., utilitarian and hedonic value; Babin, Darden, and Griffin 1994). With respect to store personality, the robustness of d'Astous and Lévesque's (2003) operationalization is formally tested.

3. Methodology

We collected data from 206 visitors (61% female) of an international fashion retailer. The questionnaire consists of existing scales adapted to the setting at hand. As our conceptual model contains both reflective and formative constructs, we opted for PLS path modeling to estimate the relationships. We evaluated the statistical significance of the parameter estimates by using bootstrapping procedures based on 5000 samples.

Since customer value is a second-order construct, we used the two-stage approach to model it in PLS (Reinartz, Krafft, and Hoyer 2003; Ringle, Sarstedt, and Detmar 2012).

In order to prevent multicollinearity problems commonly associated with the product indicator approach, we tested the interaction effect between store personality and self-congruity by using the orthogonalizing approach (cf. Lance 1988; Little, Bovaird, and Widaman 2006).

4. Results

First, we examined the measurement model and conclude that all constructs display favorable psychometric properties.

With regard to the structural model, the R-squared values indicate that our model is very well supported by the data.

Regarding our main hypotheses, we can conclude that both store personality and self-congruity have a significant influence on customer value, supporting respectively H1 and H2. In order of decreasing (absolute) magnitude of coefficients, value is significantly influenced by self-congruity, solidity, unpleasantness, enthusiasm, and genuineness.

Turning to H10, related to the moderating influence of self-congruity on the relationship between store personality and the outcome variables, we fail to find any significant effect. Hence, H10 is not supported by our data.

5. Discussion and Further Research

Our findings indicate that store personality indeed can be considered as a source of customer value. Value has been recognized as one of the most significant factors in the success of organizations (Slater 1997), leading to satisfaction and loyalty (Cronin et al. 2000). Since the latter two constructs are widely acknowledged as antecedents of a firm's financial performance (e.g., Anderson, Fornell, and Lehmann 1994), investing in store personality potentially offers a good return on marketing.

Additionally, self-congruity is found to have a positive effect on customer value but the moderating effect was not supported. Although future research is needed to assess whether this particular finding indeed holds, our results are consistent with the notion that store personality and self-congruity are separate and complementary constructs (Helgeson and Supphellen 2004) and that store personality is valued regardless of whether there is a match with the self-concept (Zentes, Morschett, and Schramm-Klein 2008).

REFERENCES

Anderson, Eugene W., Claes Fornell, and Donald R. Lehmann (1994), "Customer Satisfaction, Market Share, and Profitability: Findings from Sweden," *Journal of Marketing,* 58 (July), 53-66.

Babin, Barry J., William R. Darden, and Mitch Griffin (1994), "Work and/or Fun: Measuring Hedonic and Utilitarian Shopping Value," *Journal of Consumer Research,* 20 (4), 644-56.

Baker, Julie, A. Parasuraman, Dhruv Grewal, and Glenn B. Voss (2002), "The Influence of Multiple Store Environment Cues on Perceived Merchandise Value and Patronage Intentions," *Journal of Marketing,* 66 (April), 120-41.

Caprara, Gian Vittorio, Claudio Barbaranelli, and Guido Gianluigi (1998), "Personality as Metaphor: Extension of the Psycholexical Hypothesis and the Five Factor Model to Brand and Product Personality Description." in *European Advances in Consumer Research,* Vol. 3, ed. Basil G. Englis and Anna Olofsson, Provo, UT: Association for Consumer Research, 61-9.

Cronin Jr., J. Joseph, Michael K. Brady, and G. Tomas M. Hult (2000), "Assessing the Effects of Quality, Value, and Customer Satisfaction on Consumer Behavioral Intentions in Service Environments," *Journal of Retailing,* 76 (Summer), 193-218.

d'Astous, Alain and Mélanie Lévesque (2003), "A Scale for Measuring Store Personality," *Psychology & Marketing,* 20 (May), 455-69.

Freling, Traci H., Jody L. Crosno, and David H. Henard. (2011), "Brand Personality Appeal: Conceptualization and Empirical Validation," *Journal of the Academy of Marketing Science,* 39 (June), 392-406.

He, Hongwei and Avinandan Mukherjee (2007), "I Am, Ergo I Shop: Does Store Image Congruity Explain Shopping Behavior of Chinese Consumers?," *Journal of Marketing Management,* 23 (5), 443-60.

Helgeson, James G. and Magne Supphellen (2004), "A conceptual and measurement comparison of self-congruity and brand personality," *International journal of Market Research,* 46 (2), 205-33.

Holbrook, Morris B. (1999), *Consumer Value: a Framework for Analysis and Research,* London: Routledge.

Keller, Kevin L. and Donald. R. Lehmann (2006), "Brands and Branding: Research Findings and Future Priorities," *Marketing Science,* 25 (6), 740-59.

Lance, Charles E. (1988), "Residual Centering, Exploratory and Confirmatory Moderator Analysis, and Decomposition of Effects in Path Models Containing Interactions," *Applied Psychological Measurement,* 12 (2), 163-75.

Little, Todd D., James A. Bovaird, and Keith F. Widaman (2006), "On the Merits of Orthogonalizing Powered and Product Terms: Implications for Modeling Interactions Among Latent Variables," *Structural Equation Modeling,* 13 (4), 497-519.

Martineau, Pierre (1958), "The Personality of the Retail Store," *Harvard Business Review,* 36 (1), 47-55.

Reinartz, Werner, Manfred Krafft, and Wayne D. Hoyer (2004), "The Customer Relationship Management Process: Its Measurement and Impact on Performance," *Journal of Marketing Research,* 41 (August), 293-305.

Ringle, Christian M., Marko Sarstedt, and Detmar W. Straub (2012), "A Critical Look at the Use of PLS-SEM in MIS Quarterly," *MIS Quarterly,* 36 (1), iii-xiv.

Sirgy, Joseph M., Dhruv Grewal, and Tamara Mangleburg (2000), "Retail Environment, Self-Congruity, and Retail Patronage: An Integrative Model and a Research Agenda," *Journal of Business Research,* 49 (2), 127-38.

Slater, Stanley F. (1997), "Developing a Customer Value-Based Theory of the Firm," *Journal of The Academy of Marketing Science,* 25 (March), 162-67.

Sweeney, Jill C. and Geoffrey N. Soutar (2001), "Consumer Perceived Value: The Development of a Multiple Item Scale," *Journal of Retailing,* 77 (2), 203-20.

Zeithaml, Valerie A. (1988), "Consumer Perceptions of Price, Quality, and Value: A Means-End Model and Synthesis of Evidence," *Journal of Marketing,* 52 (July) 2-22.

Zentes, Joachim, Dirk Morschett, and Hanna Schramm-Klein (2008), "Brand Personality of Retailers – An Analysis of its Applicability and its Effect on Store Loyalty," *The International Review of Retail, Distribution and Consumer Research,* 18 (2), 167-84.

Helping Others or Oneself: How Incidental Social Comparisons Affect Prosocial Behavior

Ann Schlosser, University of Washington, USA
Eric Levy, Cambridge University, UK

EXTENDED ABSTRACT

We propose that an important yet overlooked variable affecting individuals' willingness to be charitable is how the social context provides comparative information regarding being better (vs. worse) off than others. As a result, seemingly irrelevant social comparison situations--such as one's relative position in line at a store—can affect individuals' propensity to be charitable. Specifically, social comparisons can vary in terms of direction (Aspinwall and Taylor 1993; Taylor, Wayment and Carrillo 1996). For instance, comparisons can be with those in a relatively better position (i.e., upward comparisons) or worse position (i.e., downward comparisons). Direction of comparison is important because it can have different motivational effects. For instance, upward comparisons can motivate individuals to improve their relative position (i.e., a self-improvement motive), whereas downward comparisons can cause individuals to relax such motives (Taylor et al 1996). We build upon this literature by proposing that downward (vs. upward) comparisons cause individuals to feel a general sense of accomplishment, which in turn frees them to benefit from sharing their resources with others (e.g., to view themselves as kind and generous). Conversely, upward comparisons should cause individuals to feel less accomplished, thereby motivating them to devote their resources to improving themselves rather than helping others. In summary, downward (vs. upward) comparisons should cause individuals to be more receptive to subsequent charitable appeals (H1). We test this and the basis of H1 through moderation and mediation in four studies.

In study 1, we test H1 by giving participants a purchasing scenario in which they have spent less or more than a co-worker for the same product (a downward vs. upward comparison respectively), after which they are asked whether they would buy a candy bar with a charity incentive (i.e., part of the proceeds goes to charity). Because social comparison (SC) effects should be strongest among those less confident in their abilities in the domain being compared (Festinger 1954), we measured confidence in the compared domain (i.e., consumer self-confidence; Bearden, Hardesty and Rose 2001) and expected SC effects to be strongest when confidence is low (H2). Consistent with H1, downward (vs. upward) comparisons led to higher purchase intentions ($b = .95$, $p = .001$) and willingness-to-pay, or WTP ($b = .82$, $p = .01$). Furthermore, the SC x confidence interaction was significant for purchase intentions ($b = -1.52$, $p < .001$) and WTP ($b = -.92$, $p < .05$; see Figure 1). Consistent with H2, SC had a significant effect on intentions and WTP for those with less (vs. more) confidence in their purchasing decisions.

In study 2, we examine whether these SC effects are specific to the presence of a charitable incentive. If downward (vs. upward) comparisons free individuals to use their resources to view themselves positively by helping others, then downward (vs. upward) comparisons should cause individuals to be more receptive to products when they are bundled (vs. unbundled) with a charity incentive (H3). We tested H3 with a different manipulation of SC and product (a barbeque lunch) that either had a charitable incentive or not. Consistent with H3, a significant interaction emerged for purchase intentions ($F(1, 149) = 4.61$, $p < .05$) and WTP ($F(1, 149) = 6.40$, p =.01). When the product was bundled with a charity incentive, purchase intentions were higher among those in the downward than upward condition ($Ms = 1.17$ vs. $.59$, $F(1, 149) = 4.35$ $p < .05$), whereas when the product did not have a charity incentive, there was no significant

Figure 1
Interactive Effect of Confidence and Direction of Comparison on Willingness to Be Charitable

Figure 1A. Purchase Intentions (Mean Centered)

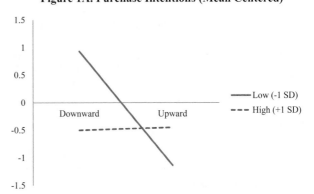

Figure 1B. Willingness to Pay (Mean Centered)

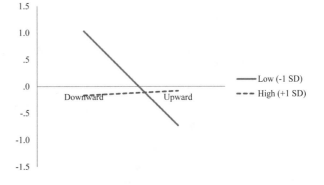

difference between conditions ($Ms = .18$ vs. $.53$, $F(1, 149) = 1.32$, NS). The results for WTP similarly supported our predictions.

If those making downward (vs. upward) comparisons are more receptive to charitable requests because such acts allow them to view themselves as kind and generous, then our predicted SC effects should be greatest among those who highly value such characteristics-- when individuals have a high (vs. low) moral identity (H4). Thus, in study 3, we measured moral identity (Aquino and Reed 2002) as well as used a SC manipulation using line queues (Zhou and Soman 2003), thereby making the compared resource time rather than money. Supporting H4, the interaction was significant for both purchase intentions ($b = .26$, $p < .05$) and WTP ($b = .95$, $p < .005$; see Figure 2). Downward comparisons led to higher purchase intentions and WTP than upward comparisons only when individuals had a high moral identity ($b = 1.07$, $p < .05$ and $b = 2.73$, $p < .05$ respectively). For those with a low moral identity, SC had no significant effect on purchase intentions ($b = -.67$, NS) or WTP ($b = -1.93$, NS).

The final study was designed to test personal accomplishment as a mediator (H5) in addition to measuring donation behaviors and donations of time. SC was manipulated by providing participants with false feedback on a performance test. As part of an ostensibly unrelated study on consumer decision making, participants had the opportunity to win $25. Similar to past measures of helping behavior (Cialdini and Kendrick 1976), participants were told that they had

Figure 2
Interactive Effect of Moral Identity and Direction of Comparison on Willingness to Be Charitable

Figure 2A. Purchase Intentions (Mean Centered)

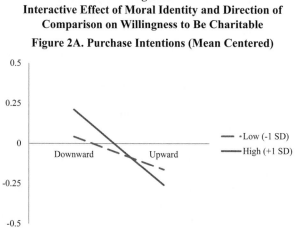

Figure 2B. Willingness to Pay (Mean Centered)

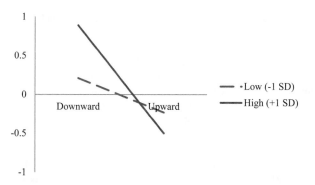

five raffle tickets that they could use all, some, or none of to enter themselves (vs. a charity) in the raffle. As predicted, those in the downward condition donated more tickets to charity than those in the upward condition did (Ms = 4.38 vs. 3.37; $F(1, 52)$ = 6.60, p = .01). In addition, a higher proportion of those in the downward than upward condition opted-in to a volunteering email list (35% vs. 7%; χ^2 = 6.58, p = .01). Furthermore, those in the downward (vs. upward) condition had a higher willingness to volunteer their time (Ms = 4.78 vs. 3.73; $F(1, 52)$ = 5.05, p < .05). Moreover, the mediation results using bootstrapping methods showed that the indirect effect from SC to prosocial behaviors and intentions through perceived accomplishment was significantly different from zero at p < .05. In conclusion, the results of these four studies provide support for our theory of the incidental effects of social comparison on prosocial behavior.

REFERENCES

Aquino, Karl F. and Americus Reed II (2002), "The Self-Importance of Moral Identity," *Journal of Personality and Social Psychology,* 83 (December), 1423-40.

Aspinwall, Lisa G., and Shelly E. Taylor (1993), "Effects of Social Comparison Direction, Threat, and Self-Esteem on Affect, Self-Evaluation, and Expected Success," *Journal of Personality and Social Psychology,* 64 (May), 708-22.

Bearden, William O., David M. Hardesty, and Randall L. Rose (2001), "Consumer Self-Confidence: Refinements in Conceptualization and Measurement," *Journal of Consumer Research*, 28 (June), 121-34.

Cialdini, Robert B., and Douglas T. Kenrick (1976), "Altruism as Hedonism: A Social Developmental Perspective on the Relationship of Negative Mood State and Helping," *Journal of Personality and Social Psychology*, 34 (November), 907-14.

Festinger, Leon (1954), "A Theory of Social Comparison Processes," *Human Relations*, 7 (January), 117-40.

Taylor, Shelly E., Heidi A. Wayment, and Mary Carrillo (1996), "Social comparison, self-regulation, and motivation," in *Handbook of Motivation and Cognition*, eds. R.M. Sorrentino and E.T. Higgins, New York: Guilford Press, 3-27.

Zhou, Rongrong, and Dilip Soman (2003), "Looking Back: Exploring the Psychology of Queing and the Effect of the Number of People Left Behind," *Journal of Consumer Research*, 29 (March), 517-30.

Becoming a Mindful Eater: Improving Food Choices through Emotional Ability Training

Blair Kidwell, Ohio State University, USA
Jonathan Hasford, University of Kentucky, USA
David Hardesty, University of Kentucky, USA
Terry Childers, Iowa State University, USA

EXTENDED ABSTRACT:

Poor food choices have far reaching negative consequences for consumers including obesity and decreased quality of life (Chandon and Wansink 2007) and have contributed to the burgeoning healthcare crisis (Cheema and Soman 2008). As a result, government programs and mandates to inform consumers of the caloric content of their food choices have been implemented across the United States (Rosenbloom 2010). However, we suggest an alternative to these programs by developing the mindfulness of consumers through emotional ability training. Emotional ability training has the potential to enable consumers to more systematically think about their choices and subvert underlying tendencies to engage in unhealthy, yet hedonically rewarding decisions.

In this research, we draw upon the emotional calibration framework to understand how emotions impact food choice. Emotional calibration involves the correspondence between one's emotional intelligence (EI, also known as emotional ability; Kidwell et al. 2008a) and consumers' confidence in their emotional ability (i.e., subjective emotional knowledge). Since emotions can have profound influences on daily decisions (Schwarz and Clore 1996), enhancing one's knowledge about emotions and how emotions can be used to make better quality decisions. Despite the potential importance of training people to more effectively use their emotions, research has yet to develop and implement an EI training program that not only can increase emotional abilities, but also show improvements in performance of trained individuals. In two studies, we utilize the default-interventionist framework (Evans 2008) to show that the development of emotional intelligence creates more emotionally calibrated consumers (Kidwell et al. 2008b), allows individuals to more analytically process their food decisions, and ultimately improves food choice. Conversely, individuals who lack emotional abilities are susceptible to heuristic processing of food choices (i.e. tasty = unhealthy heuristic; Raghunathan, Naylor, and Hoyer 2006) and subsequently make poorer food choices.

STUDY 1

Participants completed either EI training or training in nutrition knowledge (NK; mirroring current government mandates). One hundred and twenty-three students with high confidence and low emotional ability were selected from a prescreening survey that included the consumer EI scale (CEIS, Kidwell et al. 2008a) and related confidence items. Of the 123 individuals contacted, 49 signed up to participate in the study (Response Rate = 39.8%, 25 EI participants and 24 NK participants). Participants in both conditions completed a 45-minute training session described as equally informative (p > .05) and clear (p > .05) across training conditions.

After training, participants completed the CEIS and related confidence items. Participants also completed the unhealthy = tasty Implicit Association Test (IAT; Raghunathan et al. 2006). Upon leaving the lab session, participants completed the study by keeping a 24 hour food diary of all food and drinks consumed 48 hours after their training session. Calories were computed via independent raters. The diary also contained follow-up items measuring how analytically their food choices were made during the 24 hour period.

Results showed significantly higher emotional intelligence for EI trained participants (norm CEIS score = 109.83) relative to NK trained participants (87.98, p < .01). Furthermore, EI trained participants reported significantly lower caloric intake (M = 1823) relative to NK trained participants (M = 2388, p < .05). Lastly, PLS was used to demonstrate that emotional calibration was positively related to analytic processing (ß =.37, t44 = 2.37 p < .05), which was negatively related to caloric intake (ß = -.32, t44 = -2.45, p < .05). Conversely, emotional calibration was negatively related to heuristic processing (ß = -.39, t44 = -3.72 p < .05), which was positively related to caloric intake (ß = .28, t44 = 3.56, p < .05). Study 1 thus demonstrates the ability of emotional ability training to improve food choice. Study 2 investigated the impact of EI training on confidence, identified the underlying mechanism of positive arousal, and demonstrated the longitudinal effect of training on caloric intake.

STUDY 2

Participants completed either EI training or were in a no-training control condition. Two hundred and seventy students with low confidence and low emotional ability were selected from a prescreening survey. Of the 270 individuals contacted, 69 signed up to participate in the study (Response Rate = 39.8%, 34 EI trained participants and 35 control participants).

The design was similar to Study 1. However, after participants were (not) trained, they completed measures of positive arousal toward their food decisions in addition to the CEIS, confidence items, and the IAT. After the lab session concluded, participants again completed a food diary after training with similar explicit processing items.

Results provided additional support for the effects of training on emotional ability, confidence, analytic processing, and food choice. Individuals in the EI group following training scored higher on the CEIS than the control group (M = 108.5 vs. 91.1, t61 = 5.64, p < .01). Furthermore, individuals trained in EI had higher reported confidence in their emotional ability relative to individuals in the control group (M = 89% vs. 68.6%, t61 = 5.96, p < .01). PLS analysis demonstrated support for the proposed model. Emotional calibration was positively related to positive arousal (ß =.30, t59 = 2.90, p < .01), which was positively related to explicit processing (ß = .19, t59 = 2.13, p < .05). Explicit processing was negatively related to caloric intake (ß = -.17, t59 = -2.02, p < .05).

Approximately 3 months after completing the initial food diary, participants were again contacted to complete another 24 hour food diary. 17 EI trained and 20 control participants completed the follow up diary for 10 dollars. Results remained consistent as EI trained participants consumed significantly fewer calories relative to control participants (Ms = 1555 vs. 2173, t35 = 4.13, p < .01). These results provide support for the longitudinal effects of EI training on caloric intake.

The results of two studies demonstrate the ability of emotional ability training to increase the mindfulness of individual food choice and improve food decision making. These findings further develop the emotional calibration framework and provide implications for transformative research and government programs and mandates aimed at improving consumer health.

Figure 1. Theoretical Model of Emotional Calibration on Consumer Decision Quality

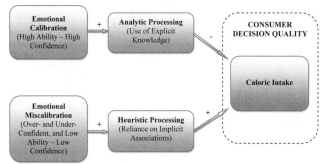

Figure 2. Path Models for Studies

Panel a: Study 1

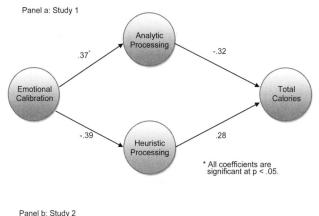

* All coefficients are significant at p < .05.

Panel b: Study 2

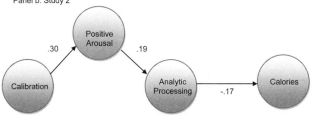

REFERENCES

Andrade, Eduardo B. and Joel B. Cohen (2007), "On the Consumption of Negative Feelings," *Journal of Consumer Research*, 34 (October), 283-300.

Barbalet, Jack M. (2001), *Emotion, Social Theory and Social Structure: A Microsociological Approach*, Cambridge, MA: Cambridge University Press.

Bearden, William O., David M. Hardesty, and Randall L. Rose (2001), "Consumer Self-Confidence: Refinements in Conceptualization and Measurement," *Journal of Consumer Research*, 28 (June), 121-34.

Brucks, Merrie (1985), "The Effects of Product Class Knowledge on Information Search Behavior," *Journal of Consumer Research*, 12 (1), 1-16.

Calder, Bobby J., Lynn W. Philips and Alice M. Tybout (1981), "Designing Research for Application," *Journal of Consumer Research*, 8 (Sept) 197-207.

Chaiken, Shelly (1980), "Heuristic Versus Systematic Information Processing and The Use of Source Versus Message Cues in Persuasion," *Journal of Personality and Social Psychology*, 39 (5), 752-66.

Chandon, Pierre and Brian Wansink (2007), "The Biasing Health Halos of Fast Food Restaurant Healthy Claims: Lower Calorie Estimates and Higher Side-Dish Consumptions Intensions," *Journal of Consumer Research*, 34 (October), 301-14.

Chartrand, Tanya L., Rick B. van Baaren, and John A. Bargh (2006), "Linking Automatic Evaluation to Mood and Information Processing Style: Consequences for Experienced Affect, Impression Formation, and Stereotyping," *Journal of Experimental Psychology: General*, 135 (1), 70-77.

Cheema, Amar and Dilip Soman (2008), "Effect of Partitions on Controlling Consumption," *Journal of Marketing Research*, 45 (6), 665-75.

Cherniss, Cary and Mitchel Adler (2000), *Promoting Emotional Intelligence in Organizations: Making Training in Emotional Intelligence Effective*, Alexandria, VA: ASTD.

Chin, Wynne W. (1998), "The Partial Least Squares Approach to Structural Equation Modeling," in *Modern Methods for Business Research*, ed. George A. Marcoulides, Mahwah, NJ: Lawrence Erlbaum Associates, 295-358.

Dasgupta, Nilanjana and Anthony G. Greenwald (2001), "On the Malleability of Automatic Attitudes: Combating Automatic Prejudice with Images of Admired and Disliked Individuals," *Journal of Personality and Social Psychology*, 81 (November), 800-14.

Daus, Catherine S. and Tiffani Cage (2008), "Learning to Face Emotional Intelligence: Training and Workplace Applications," in *Research Companion to Emotion in Organizations*, eds. Cary L. Cooper and Neal M. Ashkanasy, Edward Elgar Publishing Ltd.

Durlak, Joseph A. and Roger P. Weissberg (2005), *A Major Meta-Analysis of Positive Youth Development Programs*, Paper presented at the annual meeting of the American Psychological Association, August, Washington, D.C.

Ekman, Paul (1992), "Facial Expression of Emotion: New Findings, New Questions," *Psychological Science*, 3 (1), 34-38.

Evans, Jonathan St. B. T. (2006), "The Heuristic-Analytic Theory of Reasoning: Extension and Evaluation," *Psychonomic Bulletin and Review*, 13 (3), 378-95.

_____ (2008), "Dual-Processing Accounts of Reasoning, Judgment, and Social Cognition," *Annual Review of Psychology*, 59 (1), 255-78.

Fischhoff, Baruch, Paul Slovic, and Sarah Lichtenstein (1977), "Knowing With Certainty: The Appropriateness of Extreme Confidence," *Journal of Experimental Psychology: Human Perception and Performance*, 3 (November), 552-64.

Garg, Nitika, Brian Wansink, and J. Jeffrey Inman (2007), "The Influence of Incidental Affect on Consumers' Food Intake," *Journal of Marketing*, 71 (January), 194-206.

Glockner, Andreas and Cilia Witteman (2010), "Beyond Dual-Process Models: A Categorization of Processes Underlying Intuitive Judgment and Decision Making," *Thinking and Personality*, 16 (1), 1-25.

Greenwald, Anthony G., Debbie E. McGhee, and Jordan L. K. Schwartz (1998), "Measuring Individual Differences in Implicit Cognition: The Implicit Association Test," *Journal of Personality and Social Psychology*, 74 (6), 1464-80.

Henseler, Jorg, Christina M. Ringle, and Rudolf R. Sinkovics (2009), "The Use of Partial Least Squares Path Modeling in International Marketing," *Advances in International Marketing*, 20 (1), 277-319.

Isen, Alice M. (2000), "Positive Affect and Decision Making," in *Handbook of Emotions*, 2nd edition, eds. M. Lewis and J. M. Haviland-Jones, New York, NY: Guilford, 417-35.

Izard Carroll E. (1971), *The Face of Emotion*, New York, NY: Appleton-Century-Crofts.

Jacoby, Larry L. (1998), "Invariance in Automatic Influences of Memory: Toward a User's Guide for the Process-Dissociation Procedure," *Journal of Experimental Psychology: Learning, Memory, and Cognition*, 24 (1), 3-26.

Job, Veronika, Daniela Oertig, Veronika Brandstätter, and Mathias Allemand (2010), "Discrepancies between Implicit and Explicit Motivation and Unhealthy Eating Behavior," *Journal of Personality*, 78 (4), 1209-38.

Kahneman, Daniel and Shane Frederick (2002), "Representativeness Revisited: Attribute Substitution in Intuitive Judgment," in *Heuristics and Biases: The Psychology of Intuitive Judgment*, eds. Thomas Gilovich, Dale W. Griffin, and Daniel Kahneman, Cambridge: Cambridge University Press, 49-81.

Karmarar, Uma R. and Zakary L. Tormala (2010), "Believe Me, I Have No Idea What I'm Talking About: The Effects of Source Certainty on Consumer Involvement and Persuasion," *Journal of Consumer Research* 36 (6), 1033-49.

Kidwell, Blair, David M. Hardesty, and Terry L. Childers (2008a), "Consumer Emotional Intelligence: Conceptualization, Measurement, and the Prediction of Consumer Decision Making," *Journal of Consumer Research*, 35 (June), 154-66.

_____ (2008b), "Emotional Calibration Effects on Consumer Choice," *Journal of Consumer Research*, 35 (December), 611-21.

Ladhari, Riadh (2007), "The Effect of Consumption Emotions on Satisfaction and Word-Of-Mouth Communications," *Psychology and Marketing*, 24 (12), 1085-1108.

Loewenstein, George, Elke Weber, Christopher Hsee, and Ned Welch (2001), "Risk as Feelings," *Psychological Bulletin*, 127 (2), 267-86.

Lopes, Paulo N., Stephane Côté, and Peter Salovey (2006), "An Ability Model of Emotional Intelligence: Implications for Assessment and Training,' in *Linking Emotional Intelligence and Performance at Work: Current Research Evidence with Individuals and Groups*, eds. Vanessa Urch Druskat, Fabio Sala, and Gerald Mount, Mahwah, NJ: Lawrence Erlbaum Associates, 53-80.

Mano, Haim and Richard L. Oliver (1993), "Assessing the Dimensionality and Structure of the Consumption Experience: Evaluation, Feeling, and Satisfaction," *Journal of Consumer Research*, 20 (3), 451-66.

Matthews, Gerald, Richard Roberts, and Moshe Zeidner (2004), "Seven Myths About Emotional Intelligence," *Psychological Inquiry, 15 (3)*, 179-96.

Mayer, John D. and Peter Salovey (1997), "What is Emotional Intelligence?," in *Emotional Development and Emotional Intelligence: Implications for Educators*, eds. Peter Salovey and David Slusher, New York, NY: Basic Books, 3-31.

Mayer, John D., Peter Salovey, and David R. Caruso (2004), "Emotional Intelligence: Theory, Findings, and Implications," *Psychology Inquiry*, 15 (3), 197-215.

McEnrue, Mary Pat, Kevin S. Groves, and Winny Shen (2009), "Emotional Intelligence Development: Learning Individual Characteristics," *Journal of Management Development*, 28 (2), 150-74.

McFerran, Brent, Darren W. Dahl, Gavan J. Fitzsimmons, and Andrea C. Morales (2010), "I'll Have What She's Having: Effects of Social Influence and Body Type on the Food Choices of Others," *Journal of Consumer Research*, 6 (April), 915-29.

Moorman, Christine, Kristin Diehl, David Brinberg, and Blair Kidwell (2004), "Subjective Knowledge, Search Locations, and Consumer Choice," *Journal of Consumer Research*, 31 (December), 673-80.

Olson, Michael A., Russell H. Fazio, and Anthony D. Hermann (2007), "Reporting Tendencies Underlie Discrepancies between Implicit and Explicit Measures of Self Esteem," *Psychological Science*, 18 (4), 287-97.

Ortony, Andrew, Allen Collins, and Gerald L. Clore (1988), *The Cognitive Structure of Emotions*, New York: Cambridge University Press.

Payne, Keith B. (2001), "Prejudice and Perception: The Role of Automatic and Controlled Processes in Misperceiving a Weapon," *Journal of Personality and Social Psychology*, 81 (20), 181-92.

_____ (2005), "Conceptualizing Control in Social Cognition: How Executive Functioning Modulates the Expression of Automatic Stereotyping," *Journal of Personality and Social Psychology*, 89 (4), 488-503.

Raghunathan, Rajagopal, Rebecca Walker Naylor, and Wayne D. Hoyer (2006), "The Unhealthy = Tasty Intuition and Its Effects on Taste Inferences, Enjoyment, and Choice of Food Products," *Journal of Marketing*, 70 (October), 1-6.

Raju, Sekar, Priyali Rajagopal and Timothy J. Gilbride (2010), "Marketing Healthful Eating to Children: The Effects of Incentives, Pledges, and Competition," *Journal of Marketing*, 74 (May), 93-106.

Ringle, Christian M., Sven Wende, and Alexander Will (2005), Smart-PLS 2.0, University of Hamburg, Hamburg. [available at www.smartpls.de].

Salisbury, Linda Court and Fred M. Feinberg (2008), "Future Preference Uncertainty and Diversification: The Role of Temporal Stochastic Inflation," *Journal of Consumer Research*, 35 (August), 151-63.

Scherer, Klaus R. (1984), "On the Nature and Function of Emotion: A Component Process Approach," in *Approaches to Emotion*, eds. Klaus R. Scherer and Paul Ekman, Hillsdale, NJ: Erlbaum, 293-317.

Schwarz, Norbert (2002), "Situated Cognition and the Wisdom of Feelings: Cognitive Tuning," in *The Wisdom in Feeling*, eds. L. Feldman Barrett and Peter Salovey, New York, NY: Guilford Press, 144-66.

Schwarz, Norbert and Gerald L. Clore (1996), "Feelings and Phenomenal Experiences," in *Social Psychology: A Handbook of Basic Principles*, eds. E. Troy Higgins and Arie W. Kruglanski, New York, NY: Guilford Press, 433-65.

Scott, Maura L., Stephen Nowlis, Naomi Mandel, and Andrea Morales (2008), "Do Diet Foods Lead to Increased Consumption? The Effect of Reduced Food Sizes and Packages on the Consumption Behavior of Dieters and Non-Dieters," *Journal of Consumer Research*, 35 (October), 100-16.

Stanovich Keith E. (1999), *Who is Rational? Studies of Individual Differences in Reasoning*, Mahwah, NJ: Lawrence Elrbaum Associates.

Stewart, Brandon D., William von Hippel, and Gabriel A. Radvansky (2009), "Age, Race, and Implicit Prejudice," *Psychological Science*, 20 (2), 1640-68.

Sunghwan, Yi and Hans Baumgartner (2004), "Coping with Negative Emotions in Purchase-Related Situations," *Journal of Consumer Psychology*, 14 (3), 303-11.

Taylor, Shelley E. and Jonathon D. Brown (1994), "Positive Illusions and Well-Being Revisited: Separating Fact from Fiction," *Psychological Bulletin*, 116 (1), 21-27.

Vohs, Kathleen D. and Todd F. Heatherton (2000), "Self Regulatory Failure: A Resource Depletion Approach," *Psychological Science*, 11 (3), 249-54.

Wansink, Brian, James E. Painter, and Jill North (2005), "Bottomless Bowls: Why Visual Cues of Portion Size May Influence Intake," *Obesity Research*, 13 (January), 93-100.

Wansink, Brian (2006), *Mindless Eating – Why We Eat More Than We Think*, New York: Bantam-Dell.

Wood, Stacy (2010), "The Comfort Food Fallacy: Avoiding Old Favorites in Times of Change," *Journal of Consumer Research*, 6 (April), 950-63.

Zeidner, Moshe, Richard D. Roberts, and Gerald Matthews (2004), "The Emotional Intelligence Bandwagon: Too Fast to Live, Too Young to Die," *Psychological Inquiry, 15 (3)*, 239-48.

Zhao, Xinshu, John G. Lynch Jr., and Qimei Chen (2010), "Reconsidering Baron and Kenny: Myths and Truths About Mediation Analysis," *Journal of Consumer Research*, 37 (2), 197-206.

Political Ideology, Persuasive Appeals, and Sustainability

Blair Kidwell, Ohio State University, USA
Adam Farmer, University of Kentucky, USA
David Hardesty, University of Kentucky, USA

EXTENDED ABSTRACT:

At the forefront of the sustainability movement are efforts to increase environmental consciousness and promote sustainable consumption (McDonagh, Dobscha, and Prothero 2012). Yet, many consumers are either skeptical of or reluctant to embrace green marketing efforts (Luchs et al., 2010). Considerable research has been devoted to understanding and overcoming this reluctance through policy, regulatory, market, and technological innovations (Crittenden et al., 2011). However, very little progress has been made in actually changing behavior (Polonsky 2011; Prothero, et al. 2011). Given the sharp divide in attitudes toward many sustainability issues (e.g., climate change) between groups on different sides of the political aisle (Baumgartner and Jones 2009; Kim, Rao, and Lee 2009), surprisingly little attention has been paid to understanding how differences in political ideology might influence sustainable behaviors. For example, might conservatives and liberals be differentially likely to engage in specific sustainable behaviors like recycling or purchasing green products? Might different types of appeals targeted to these two groups of consumers, based on their underlying ideological differences, be more effective at persuading them to adopt environmentally conscious behaviors? If so, what process can inform us about how these consumers are influenced?

In this research, we investigate the impact political ideology has on sustainability practices and propose ways to appeal to liberals and conservatives based on their underlying moral foundations. In addition, we uncover the mechanism by which political appeals influence intentions and demonstrate how the behaviors of each ideology can ultimately be changed through tailored persuasive appeals.

In our efforts to address these issues, we make four main contributions. First, we examine the understudied area of how political ideology affects consumer behavior in order to understand its impact on sustainability. Second, we highlight the underlying moral foundations of each ideology and develop persuasive appeals based on these foundations to influence disposition behavior (recycling) as well as the spillover effects on acquisition (selection of sustainable products) and usage (conservation of resources) behaviors. Third, we examine the effectiveness of these persuasive appeals in a 113-household longitudinal field study on recycling behavior. Fourth, we offer practical implications for marketers, public policy officials, and environmental scientists interested in changing acquisition, consumption, and disposition-related behavior.

Matching Persuasion to Moral Foundations

We developed persuasive appeals that are congruent with conservative and liberal moral foundations to promote enhanced sustainable behaviors. Given that conservatives value duty, authority, self-discipline, and actions consistent with their in-group's social norms (Graham et al. 2009; McAdams et al. 2008), we created a persuasive appeal designed around the message to "joint the fight" to help the environment. This type of messaging incorporates adherence to social norms and in-group effects while promoting actions that will strengthen the social order (Janoff-Bulman et al. 2009). This is also consistent with a binding moral foundation in that this appeal uses terms like we, citizens, duty, and our as well as images of patriotism. Conversely, liberals value empathy, fairness, and individuality (McAdams et al. 2008; Morrison and Miller 2008). We developed a

message designed to appeal to liberals underlying moral foundation revolving around "making a difference." This type of messaging sets the individual apart as one who helps others while promoting behaviors or actions that improve overall social justice (Janoff-Bulman et al. 2009). This is consistent with an individualizing appeal through a call to individual action, images of helping and fairness, and relies on a caring nature.

Study 1

Eighty-two undergraduate business students completed measures of political ideology and moral foundations. Specifically, 40 participants saw a "Join the Fight" binding appeal while 42 participants saw the "Make a Difference" individualizing appeal. Next, participants completed a thought listing task and a manipulation check measure assessing the moral foundations associated with the appeals. Lastly, participants completed recycling intention measures.

A chi-square test of independence revealed a significant difference in the number of foundational thoughts generated by the different appeals. In addition, the full model was also significant ($F(3, 78) = 2.98$, $p < .05$). The results revealed a significant interaction of political ideology by appeal ($\beta = .82$, $t(78) = 2.37$, $p < .05$). The results of study 1 provided support that congruent moral foundation appeals affect intentions to recycle depending upon one's political ideology.

Study 2

Study 2 was conducted to examine the mediating effect of fluency on the relationship between the interaction of political ideology and appeal to recycling intentions. We also rule out two alternative possibilities that might reasonably result from message congruence.

Specifically, 73 participants saw the "Join the Fight" appeal while 69 participants saw the "Make a Difference" appeal. Next, participants completed process measures pertaining to fluency, involvement, and recycling efficacy related to the appeals, and finally their intentions to recycle, purchase compact fluorescent light bulbs, and to conserve water.

The indirect effect of the interaction onto recycling intentions through fluency revealed a positive and significant indirect effect ($\beta = .10$) as the 95% confidence interval did not include zero (CI: .02 to .26). Study 2 demonstrated that appeals congruent with moral foundations are more effective due to fluency than incongruent appeals. Enhanced fluency positively influenced intentions to recycle as well as have spillover effects on acquisition and usage disposition intentions.

Study 3

Study 3 was conducted to assess the effectiveness of our persuasive appeals on actual recycling behavior in a longitudinal field setting. Specifically, a 14-week field study was conducted to assess the effects of the two persuasive appeals on recycling behaviors of households from a typical southeastern U.S. city.

Study 3 provided an examination of persuasive appeals designed to initiate recycling behavior across 113 households. The congruent appeals resulted in greater recycling than the control conditions ($t = 2.04$, $p < .05$ and $t = 2.47$, $p < .05$). Appeals congruent with underlying moral foundations were found to influence actual recycling behavior for both liberals and conservatives over a 14-week period.

REFERENCES

Ahluwalia, Rohini, H. Rao Unnava, and Robert E. Burnkrant (2001), "The Moderating Role of Commitment on the Spillover Effect of Marketing Communications," *Journal of Marketing Research*, 38 (November), 458-70.

Aiken, Leona S. and Stephen G. West (1991), "Multiple Regression: Testing and Interpreting Interactions," Newbury Park, CA: Sage.

Baumgartner, Frank R. and Bryan D. Jones (2009), "Agendas and Instability in American Politics," 2nd ed. Chicago, IL: University of Chicago Press.

Bobbio, Norberto (1996), "Left and Right: The Significance of a Political Distinction," Cambridge, England: Polity Press.

Carney, Dana R., John T. Jost, Samuel D. Gosling, and Jeff Potter (2008), "The Secret Lives of Liberals and Conservatives: Personality Profiles, Interaction Styles, and the Things They Leave Behind," *Political Psychology*, 29 (6), 807-40.

Cesario, Joseph, Heidi Grant, and E. Tory Higgens (2004), "Regulatory Fit and Persuasion: Transfer from 'Feeling Right'," *Journal of Personality and Social Psychology*, 86 (3) 388-404.

Chandon, Pierre, Brian Wansink, and Gilles Laurent (2000), "A Benefit Congruency Framework of Sales Promotion Effectiveness," *Journal of Marketing*, 64 (4), 65-81.

Cohen, Geoffrey, L. (2003), "Party Over Policy: The Dominating Impact of Group Influence on Political Beliefs," *Journal of Personality and Social Psychology*, 85 (5), 808-22.

Crittenden, Victoria L., William F. Crittenden, Linda K. Ferrell, O.C. Ferrell, and Christopher C. Pinney (2011), "Market-Oriented Sustainability: A Conceptual Framework and Propositions," *Journal of the Academy of of Marketing Science*, 39 (1), 158-74.

Feldman, Stanley and Karen Stenner (2008), "Perceived Threat and Authoritarianism," *Political Psychology*, 18 (1), 741-70.

Friestad, Marian and Peter Wright (1994), "The Persuasion Knowledge Model: How People Cope with Persuasion Attempts," Journal of Consumer Research, 21 (June), 1-31.

Goel, Sharad, Winter Mason, and Duncan J. Watts (2010), "Real and Perceived Attitude Agreement in Social Networks," Journal of Personality and Social Psychology, 99 (4), 611-21.

Graham, Jesse, Jonathan Haidt, and Brian A. Nosek (2009), "Liberals and Conservatives Rely on Different Sets of Moral Foundations," *Journal of Personality and Social Psychology*, 96 (5), 1029-46.

Graham, Jesse, Brian A. Nosek, Jonathan Haidt, Ravi Iyer, Spassena Koleva, and Peter H. Ditto (2011), "Mapping the Moral Domain," *Journal of Personality and Social Psychology, 101 (2),* 366-85.

Griskevicius, Vladas, Michelle N. Shiota, and Stephen M. Nowlis (2010), "The Many Shades of

Rose-Colored Glasses: An Evolutionary Approach to the Influence of Different Positive Emotions," *Journal of Consumer Research*, 37 (2), 238-50.

Hanas, Jim (2007), "Environmental Awareness Has Not Only Tipped in the Media -- It's Hit Corporate Boardrooms as Well" http://adage.com/eco-marketing/article?article_id=117113.

Hatemi, Peter L., Nathan A. Gillespie, Lindon J. Evans, Brion S. Maher, Bradley T. Webb, Andrew C. Heath, Sarah E. Medland, David C. Smyth, Harry N. Beeby, Scott D. Gordon, Grant W. Montgomery, Ghu Zhu, Enda M. Byrne, and Nicholas G. Martin (2011), "A Genome-Wide Analysis of Liberal and Conservative Political Attitudes," *Journal of Politics*, 73 (1), 1-15.

Hunch.com (2011), "Mac vs. PC: A Hunch Rematch," http://blog.hunch.com/?p=45344.

Janakiraman, Narayan, Robert J. Meyer, and Andrea C. Morales (2006), "Spillover Effects: How Consumers Respond to Unexpected Changes in Price and Quality," *Journal of Consumer Research*, 33 (4), 361-9.

Janoff-Bulman, Ronnie, Sana Sheikh, and Sebastian Hepp (2009), "Proscriptive Versus Prescriptive Morality: Two Faces of Moral Regulation," *Journal of Personality and Social Psychology*, 96 (3), 521-37.

Jost, John T. (2006), "The End of the End of Ideology," *American Psychologist*, 61 (7), 651-70.

Jost, John T., Arie W. Kruglanski, Jack Glaser, and Frank J. Sulloway (2003), "Political Conservatism as Motivated Social Cognition," *Psychological Bulletin*, 129 (3), 339-75.

Kanai, Ryota, Tom Feilden, Colin Firth, and Geraint Rees (2011), "Political Orientations Are Correlated with Brain Structure in Young Adults," *Current Biology*, 21 (8), 677-80.

Kim, Hakkyun, Akshay Rao, and Angela Lee (2009), "It's Time to Vote: The Effect of Matching Message Orientation and Temporal Frame on Political Persuasion," *Journal of Consumer Research*, 35 (6), 877-89.

Kivetz, Ran (2005), "Promotion Reactance: The Role of Effort-Reward Congruity," *Journal of Consumer Research*, 31 (4), 725-36.

Kruglanski, Arie W. (1996), "Motivated Social Cognition: Principles of the Interface," in *Social Psychology: Handbook of Basic Principles*, ed. E. Troy Higgins and Arie W. Kruglanski, New York: Guilford Press, 493-520.

Kruglanski, Arie W. (1999), "Motivation, Cognition, and Reality: Three Memos for the Next Generation of Research," *Psychological Inquiry*, 10 (1), 54–8.

Kruglanski, Arie W., and Donna M. Webster (1991), "Group Members' Reactions to Opinion Deviates and Conformists at Varying Degrees of Proximity to Decision Deadline and of Environmental Noise," *Journal of Personality and Social Psychology*, 61 (2), 215–25.

Kruglanski, Arie W., and Donna M. Webster (1996), "Motivated Closing of the Mind: 'Seizing' and 'Freezing'," *Psychological Review*, 103 (2), 263–83.

Labroo, Aparna A.and Angela Y. Lee (2006), "Between Two Brands: A Goal Fluency Account of Brand Evaluation,"*Journal of Marketing Research*, 43 (4), 374-85.

Lee, Angela and Jennifer Aaker (2004), "Bringing the Frame into Focus: The Influence of Regulatory Fit on Processing Fluency and Persuasion," Journal of Personality and Social Psychology, 86 (2), 205-18.

Lee, Angela Y. and Aparna A. Labroo (2004), "Effects of Conceptual and Perceptual Fluency on Brand Evaluation," *Journal of Marketing Research*, 41 (2), 151-65.

Luchs, Michael G., Rebecca Walker Naylor, Julie R. Irwin, and Rajagopal Raghunathan (2010), "The Sustainability Liability: Potential Negative Effects of Ethicality on Product Preference," *Journal of Marketing*, 74 (5), 18-31.

McAdams, Dan P., Michelle Albaugh, Emily Farber, Jennifer Daniels, Regina L. Logan, and Brad Olson (2008), "Family Metaphors and Moral Intuitions: How Conservatives and Liberals Narrate Their Lives," *Journal of Personality and Social Psychology*, 95 (4), 978-90.

McDonagh, Pierre, Susan Dobscha, and Andrea Prothero (2012), "Sustainable Consumption and Production: Challenges for Transforming Consumer Research," in *Transformative Consumer Research: For Personal and Collective Well-Being*, ed. David G. Mick, Simone Pettigrew, Cornelia Pechmann, and Julie L. Ozane, New York: Routledge, 267-82.

Mitchell, Deborah J., Barbara E. Kahn, and Susan C. Knasko (1995), "There's Something in the Air: Effects of Congruent or Incongruent Ambient Odor on Consumer Decision Making," *Journal of Consumer Research*, 22 (2), 229-38.

Morrison, Kimberly Rios and Dale T. Miller (2008), "Distinguishing between Silent and Vocal Minorities: Not All Deviants Feel Marginal," *Journal of Personality and Social Psychology*, 94 (5), 871-82.

Nail, Paul R., Ian McGregor, April E. Drinkwater, Garrett M. Steele, and Anthony W. Thompson (2009), "Threat Causes Liberals to Think Like Conservatives," *Journal of Experimental Social Psychology*, 45 (4), 901-07.

Perreault, William D., Jr. and Laurence E. Leigh (1989), "Reliability of Nominal Data Based on Qualitative Judgments," *Journal of Marketing Research*, 26 (2), 135-48.

Polonsky, Michael J. (2011), "Transformative Green Marketing: Impediments and Opportunities," *Journal of Business Research*, 64 (2), 1311-9.

Prothero, Andrea, Susan Dobscha, Jim Freund, William E . Kilbourne, Michael G . Luchs, Lucie K. Ozanne, John Thøgersen (2011), "Sustainable Consumption: Opportunities for Consumer Research and Public Policy", *Journal of Public Policy & Marketing*, 30 (1) 31-38.

Raggio, Randle D. and Judith Anne Garretson Folse (2011), "Expressions of Gratitude in Disaster Management: An Economic, Social Marketing, and Public Policy Perspective on Post-Katrina Campaigns," *Journal of Public Policy and Marketing*, 30 (2), 168-74.

Rao, Akshay R., Lu Qu, and Robert W. Reukert (1999), "Signaling Unobservable Product Quality through a Brand Ally," *Journal of Marketing Research*, 36 (2), 258-68.

Reber, Rolf and Norbert Schwarz (1999), "Effects of Perceptual Fluency on Judgments of Truth," *Consciousness and Cognition*, 8 (3), 338–42.

Reber, Rolf, Norbert Schwarz, and Piotr Winkielman (2004), "Processing Fluency and Aesthetic Pleasure: Is Beauty in the Perceiver's Processing Experience?," *Personality and Social Psychology Review*, 8 (4), 364-82.

Schwarz, Norbert (2004), "Meta-Cognitive Experiences in Consumer Judgment and Decision Making," *Journal of Consumer Psychology*, 14 (4), 332-48.

Schwarz, Norbert and Gerald L. Clore (1983), "Mood, Misattribution, and Judgments of Well-Being: Informative and Directive Functions of Affective States," *Journal of Personality and Social Psychology*, 45 (3), 513-23.

Thompson, Debora V. and Rebecca W. Hamilton (2006), 'The Effects of Information Processing Mode on Consumers' Responses to Comparative Advertising," *Journal of Consumer Research*, 32 (4), 530-40.

Wansink, Brian, James E. Painter, and Jill North (2005), "Bottomless Bowls: Why Visual Cues of Portion Size May Influence Intake," *Journal of Consumer Research*, 13 (1), 93-100.

White, Katherine, Rhiannon MacDonnell, and Darren W. Dahl (2011), "It's the Mindset that Matters: The Role of Construal Level and Message Framing in Influencing Consumer Efficacy and Conservation Behaviors," *Journal of Marketing Research*, 48 (3), 472-85.

Wu, Bob T.W. and Susan M. Petroshius (1987), "The Halo Effect in Store Image Measurement," *Journal of the Academy of Marketing Science*, 15 (3), 44-51.

Wu, Amery D. and Bruno D. Zumbo (2007), "Understanding and Using Mediators and Moderators," *Social Indicators Research*, 87 (3), 367-92.

Zhao, Xinshux, John G. Lynch, and Qimei Chen (2010), "Reconsidering Baron and Kenny: Myths and Truths about Mediation Analysis," *Journal of Consumer Research*, 37 (2), 197-206.

Zhu, Rui (Juliet) and Joan Meyers-Levy (2007), "Exploring the Cognitive Mechanism that Underlies Regulatory Focus Effects," *Journal of Consumer Research*, 34 (1), 89-96.

Putting Your Eggs in One Basket: Sex Ratio Effects on Bet-Hedging

Joshua Ackerman, Massachusetts Institute of Technology, USA
Vladas Griskevicius, University of Minnesota, USA

EXTENDED ABSTRACT

Human populations, from towns to regions to countries, vary in their distributions of men and women. These differences in operational sex ratio, the relative number of sexually mature men to women, can produce marked changes in various cognitions and actions, such as modulating tendencies toward aggression, parenting style, and long-term vs. short-term romantic proclivities (e.g., Barber 2001). The same is also true in a wide variety of animal species (e.g., Kvarnemo and Anhesjo 1996). Differences in population sex ratios index the availability of potential mates and can produce competitive behaviors even in individuals not actively seeking romance. Recent research has shown that, in addition to real skews in sex ratios, perceptions of sex ratio skew can also lead people to change their behavior. For instance, male students who believed their school was populated by more men than women (an unfavorable ratio for heterosexual males) were less likely to save income and more likely to spend to the point of debt (Griskevicius et al. 2012). In the current paper, we expand on this research by investigating how changes in sex ratios affect the more general process of decision-making under uncertainty. We do so by asking whether perceptions of increased and decreased potential mate availability directly influence preferences for option variability in situations where choice entails risk. Specifically, we test whether sex ratio skew affects bet-hedging behavior.

Bet-hedging refers to the notion that individuals often gain long-term utility by lowering the variance of their decisions and spreading risk over possible outcomes (Slatkin 1974). A specific form of bet-hedging, diversified bet-hedging, involves an individual investing resources in several (possibly competing) strategies simultaneously (Olofsson, Ripa and Jonzén 2009). That is, not "putting all your eggs in one basket." Diversified bet-hedging is often considered to be a safer strategy than investing resources in single-options and thus is more often employed by individuals with a relatively short time-horizon (Olofsson et al. 2009). In contrast, we predict the perceptions of decreased mate availability that accompany an unfavorable sex ratio will produce a competitive mindset through which people (implicitly) presume that success necessitates risk-taking (cf., Kunreuther and Wright 1979). Further, we predict that this mindset can generalize to other decision-contexts. Thus, we expect that exposure to unfavorable sex ratios will produce decreases in diversified bet-hedging behavior.

Study 1 investigated this idea in the context of gambles. Participants took part in a study labeled "accuracy in interpersonal perception and memory." Participants were briefly shown multiple arrays of face photographs ostensibly taken from the local area (e.g., campus, websites) and were told they would complete a memory test on these faces later in the study. After each array, participants recalled the number of men and women in each set as a measure of "accuracy." These arrays varied in the ratio of female to male faces, and were either female-biased or male-biased between-participants (from 68-78% of the more numerous sex). As an interlude before a (non-existent) final memory test, participants completed several supposed distracter items, beginning with the primary dependent measure. This task required participants to imagine playing a lottery and choosing between one of two options, either 1 $10 ticket with a possible $10,000 prize or 10 $1 tickets for a possible $1,000 prize. Analyses revealed that, consistent with predictions, people who viewed unfavorable ratios (men + male-biased, women + female-biased) were more likely to choose the single ticket, high-payoff/high-risk option—to put their eggs in one basket—than people who viewed favorable ratios.

Study 2 expanded on this finding by testing outcomes that allowed for a greater degree of decision diversification. Participants received a similar cover story, and after completing the face array tasks, were told that they would complete several tasks prior to a face memory test. These two tasks included a retirement account investment procedure and a public funds investment procedure. The retirement procedure involved making allocation decisions regarding the percentage of one's investment that should be assigned to stocks (described as higher risk, higher return), bonds (lower risk, lower return) and cash (no risk, little if any return). The public funds procedure asked participants to imagine that four companies were working on a disease vaccine to prevent a possible future epidemic, and to decide how the government should allocate research funding support between the four (with funding described as increasing a company's research speed, but not necessarily success). For each procedure, decision variance (spread of allocations across the options) was used as the dependent measure. Both measures showed similar patterns: People who viewed unfavorable sex ratios invested more money into fewer options, again putting their eggs into fewer baskets.

In summary, two studies show that perceptions of environmental variation in the relative numbers of men and women can influence whether people choose to diversify their decision outcomes or not. "Unfavorable" sex ratios led to less diversification and more high-risk/high-reward decisions, consistent with the interpretation that success under such conditions necessitates risk-taking. This work contributes to our understanding of the incidental factors that elicit risky behavior and highlights how decision domains with quite important long-term relevance (e.g., retirement accounts, research funding) are susceptible to seemingly irrelevant situational cues. Future research will investigate particular mediating mechanisms and individual differences that may play a role in these decision strategies.

REFERENCES

Barber, Nigel (2001), "On the relationships between marital opportunity and teen pregnancy: The sex ratio question," Journal of Cross-Cultural Psychology, 32, 259–267.

Griskevicius, Vladas, Joshua M. Tybur, Joshua M. Ackerman, Andrew W. Delton, Theresa E. Robertson and Andrew E. White (2012), "The Financial Consequences of Too Many Men: Sex Ratio Effects on Saving, Borrowing, and Spending," Journal of Personality and Social Psychology, 102, 69-80.

Kunreuther, Howard and Gavin Wright (1979), "Safety-First, Gambling, and the Subsistence Farmer," In Risk, Uncertainty and Agricultural Development, ed. by James A. Roumasset, Jean-Marc Boussard, and Inderjit Singh, Philippines: Searca.

Kvarnemo, Charlotts and Ingrid Anhesjo (1996), "The dynamics of operational sex ratios and competition for mates," Trends in Ecology & Evolution, 11, 404–408.

Olofsson, Helen, Jörgen Ripa and Niclas Jonzén (2009), "Bet-hedging as an evolutionary game: the trade-off between egg size and number," Proceedings of the Royal Society London B, 276, 2963-2969.

Slatkin Montgomery (1974), "Hedging one's evolutionary bets," Nature, 250, 704–705.

"How About Giving My Things Away Over The Internet?"
When Internet Makes It Easier To Give Things Away

Valérie Guillard, Paris Dauphine University, France
Céline Del Bucchia, Audencia Business School, Nantes, France

EXTENDED ABSTRACT

Many studies have explored the way people dispose of items they no longer want (Jacoby, Berning and Dietvorst 1977; Cherrier 2009; Arsel and Dobsha 2011) either through the market economy (Chu and Liao 2009; Sherry 1990), the kith and kin gift economy (Price, Arnould and Curasi 2000), charities (Bendapudi, Singh and Bendapudi 1996) or online (Nelson, Rademacher and Paek 2007; Arsel and Dobsha 2011). Studies investigating online recycling have generally looked at the trend from a community perspective, concluding that giveaway websites are underpinned by a mechanism of generalised reciprocity. However, these websites have a specific feature that makes it interesting to analyse the online giving process from an individual slant since, unlike giving possessions to charities, free recycling websites enable the giver to *meet* the unknown recipient and, unlike gifts to close friends or family, they allow the giver to meet a *stranger*. In short, free recycling websites offer a new channel whereby individuals can give things away to a stranger in person, a factor that is likely to change the way givers perceive gift-giving. Underpinned by research on the difficulties inherent to giving (Price, Arnould and Curasi 2000; Lastovika and Fernandez 2005; Marcoux 2009), our paper illustrates how recycling websites resolve the tensions that the giver may otherwise be confronted with when giving, by offering an encounter with an alien recipient.

REVIEW OF THE LITERATURE

Many studies have highlighted the romantic aspects of giving (Belk and Coon 1993; Joy 2001), but the process also has a darker side (Sherry, McGrath and Levy 1993; Ruth, Otnes and Brunel 1999; Marcoux 2009). Gifts to kith and kin can lead to unease in both the giver and the recipient. The giver is not entirely free when giving, but is trapped in a web of constraints and norms. Giving to friends and family not only means that the giver gives, but also that the recipient must receive (Gouldner 1960) or must reciprocate (Godbout and Caillé 1992). Giving to charities, on the other hand, presents fewer constraints, and is underpinned by a notion of solidarity (Frémeaux and Michelson 2011). However, it can also be a source of frustration for the givers who have no idea what happens to their donations. In effect, some people need to meet the future beneficiary in order to be able to detach themselves from their possessions (Roster 2001; Lastovicka and Fernandez 2005). While previously, only the market enabled two strangers to meet in the circulation of second-hand goods (Herrmann, 1997), today free recycling websites also offer this possibility. Our aim is to explore what this encounter means to the online giver.

METHODOLOGY

To understand how givers experience online recycling and what it means to them as individuals, we conducted 27 long interviews (McCracken 1986), adopting a phenomenological approach (Thompson, Locander and Pollio 1989). The respondents were recruited through the managers of the free recycling websites www.recupe. net, www.donnons.org and www.recupe.fr, who put us in touch with givers. The interviews began with the question "*Can you tell me about the different options you choose when you decide to get rid of something?*" and then focused on online recycling and how this is experienced by the giver.

FINDINGS

In addition to the practical and environmentally-friendly nature of the practice (Nelson, Rademacher and Paek 2007; Arsel and Dobscha 2011), our analysis led us to identify two central factors that give insights into the meaning of the online recycling experience: first, givers experience it as spontaneous gift-giving rather than just an opportunity to get rid of unwanted clutter. Second, the gesture is given its full sense through the encounter with the unknown recipient. This specific feature of online recycling removes the obstacles inherent to the three-way gift-giving process that arise in other forms of gift-giving (Mauss 1924): i.e. the giving, the receiving and the return.

With regard to *giving*, online recycling means that the giver does not run the risk of a refusal as may be the case when giving to friends or family, or to a charity. A refusal is often painful for the giver: by refusing an object, individuals signal a rejection of the relationship. Refusal is very rare in online recycling as recipients are aware of the state of the items they will find at the givers' beforehand. Consequently, givers are able to give 'everything away as they are not worried about being judged for the 'poor' quality of their objects. With regard to *receiving*, the giver chooses the future beneficiary he or she will meet in order to give them the object, along with its history, its wear and tear and its special way of working. In listening to the giver, the recipient implicitly makes a promise to take care of the object, thereby reassuring the former (Lastovicka and Fernandez 2005). Finally, with regard to the *return*, the interaction with the recipient makes the giver feel (s)he exists and is recognised. Online recycling fulfils the need of givers for recognition, without necessarily creating a bond of dependence: the meeting is a brief, one-off situation, and reciprocity is immediate. The desire not to get involved with the recipient, that is also reflected in other studies (Bajde 2009), can be seen in the way the items are passed on: some givers will place the items in a neutral space like the hallway or the corridor (Korosec Serfaty 1988) to ensure that the recipient does not trespass on the giver's privacy.

CONCLUSION

This article adds to current research on the circulation of second-hand goods (Lucas 2002; Cherrier 2009) in several ways. The study contributes to our understanding of the topic by analysing online recycling websites from the perspective of the individual. This is interesting in view of one specific feature of such websites, namely the *encounter* with an unknown recipient.

The article also illustrates how free recycling websites remove the difficulties inherent in giving to kith and kin or to charities. Such sites offer givers the potential for rewarding interaction with the recipient that is also liberating. It is rewarding since they are recognised for their gesture, unlike giving objects to charities. At the same time, it liberates the giver as, even if there is a meeting with the recipient, it is brief, reciprocity is immediate and it does not create a relationship or a bond of dependence in the same way as a gift to family or friends. At the same time, the study enriches the model proposed by Marcoux (2009): by removing the obstacles linked to giving, free recycling websites offer individuals the possibility to remain in the gift economy. The gift economy and the market economy are two options that free individuals from the obligations inherent to other forms of giving, although they are not mutually exclusive.

The article has implications with regard to three pillars of sustainable development: i.e. economic, as the free flow of objects facilitates the decision to replace them (Roster and Richins 2009); social, as free recycling websites help people to find what they need at less cost, while developing social links, and finally, environmental, as free recycling websites contribute to reducing the volume of waste.

Finally, our research opens up several potential avenues for further research to enhance our understanding of online recycling. While our study focuses on givers, an investigation of the recipients could raise some interesting questions: what signals does the recipient put out that the giver picks up as recognition for his or her gesture, for instance? How does the recipient receive a gift via the Internet? Why does the recipient use free recycling websites apart from the obvious reason of getting something for free?

RESEARCH FUNDING

This research is funded by Ademe (Agence de l'Environnement et de la Maîtrise de l'Energie; appel à projet 2010, Déchets et Sociétés, projet Rechange)

REFERENCES

Arsel, Zeynep and Susan Dobsha (2011), "Hybrid Pro-social Exchange Systems: The Case of Freecycle," in *Advances in Consumer Research*, forthcoming.

Bajde, Domen (2009), "Rethinking the Social and Cultural Dimensions of Charitable Giving," *Consumption, Markets and Culture*, 12 (1), 65-84.

Belk, Russell W. and Gregory S. Coon (1993), "Gift Giving and Agapic Loves: An Alternative to the Exchange Paradigm Based on Dating Experiences," *Journal of Consumer Research*, 20 (December), 393-417.

Bendapudi, Neeli, Surendra N. Singh, and Venkat Bendapudi (1996), "Enhancing Helping Behavior: An Integrative Framework for Promotion Planning," *Journal of Marketing*, 60 (July), 33-49.

Cherrier, Hélène (2009), "Disposal and Simple Living: Exploring the Circulation of Goods and the Development of Sacred Consumption," *Journal of Consumer Behavior*, 8 (6), 327-39.

Chu, Hsunchi and Shuling Liao (2009), "Buying While Expecting to Sell: The Economic Psychology of Online Resale," *Journal of Business Research*, 63 (9-10), 1073-78.

Frémeaux, Sandrine and Grant Michelson (2011), "No Strings Attached: Welcoming the Existential Gift in Business," *Journal of Business Ethics*, 99 (Springer), 65-75.

Godbout, Jacques T., and Alain Caillé (1992), *L'esprit du don*, Paris: La Découverte.

Gouldner, Alvin W. (1960), "The Norm of Reciprocity: A Preliminary Statement," *American Sociological Review*, 25 (April), 176-77.

Herrmann, Gretchen M. (1997), "Gift or Commodity: What Changes Hands in the U.S. Garage Sale ?" *American Ethnologist*, 24 (4), 910-30.

Jacoby, Jacob, Carol K. Berning, and Thomas F. Dietvorst (1977), "What About Disposition?," *Journal of Marketing*, 2, 22-28.

Joy, Annamma (2001), "Gift Giving in Honk Kong and the Continuum of Social Ties," *Journal of Consumer Research*, 28 (September), 239-56.

Korosec-Serfaty, Perla (1988), "La sociabilité publique et ses territoires - Places et espaces publics urbains," *Architecture et Comportement*, 4 (2), 111-32.

Lastovicka, John L. and Karen V. Fernandez (2005), "Three Paths to Disposition: The Movement of Meaningful Possessions to Strangers," *Journal of Consumer Research*, 31 (March), 813-23.

Lucas, Gavin (2002), "Disposability and Dispossession in the Twentieth Century," *Journal of Material Culture*, 7 (5), 5-22.

Marcoux, Jean-Sébastien (2009), "Escaping the Gift Economy," *Journal of Consumer Research*, 36 (December), 671-85.

Mauss, Marcel (1923-24/2000), *The Gift: The Form and Reason for Exchange in Archaic Society*, trans. W.D. Halls, New York: Norton.

McCracken, Grant (1986), "Culture and Consumption: A Theoretical Account of the Structure and Movement of Cultural Meaning of Consumer Goods," *Journal of Consumer Research*, 13 (June), 71-84.

Nelson, Michelle R., Mark Rademacher, and Hye-Jin Paek (2007), "Downshifting Consumer: Upshifting Citizen? An Examination of a Local Freecycle Community," *The Annals of the American Academy of Political and Social Science*, 611 (1), 141-56.

Price, Linda L., Eric J. Arnould, and Carolyn F. Curasi (2000), "Older Consumers' Disposition of Special Possessions," *Journal of Consumer Research*, 27 (September), 179-201.

Roster, Catherine A. (2001), « Letting go, » in *Advances in Consumer Research*, Vol. 28, ed. Mary C. Gilly and Joan Meyers-Levy, Provo, UT: Association for Consumer Research, 425-30.

Roster, Catherine A. and Marsha L. Richins (2009), "Ambivalence and Attitudes in Consumer Replacement Decisions," *Journal of Consumer Psychology*, 19, 48–61.

Ruth, Julie A., Cele C. Otnes, and Frederic F. Brunel (1999), "Gift Receipt and the Reformulation of Interpersonal Relationships," *Journal of Consumer Research*, 25 (March), 385-402.

Sherry, John F., Jr. (1990), "A Sociocultural Analysis of a Midwestern American Flea Market," *Journal of Consumer Research*, 17 (June), 13-30.

Sherry, John F., Mary Am McGrath, and Sidney J. Levy (1993), "The Dark Side of the Gift," *Journal of Business Research*, 28, 225-44.

Thompson, Craig J., William B. Locander, and Howard R. Pollio (1989), "Putting Consumer Experience Back into Consumer Research: The Philosophy and Method of Existential-Phenomenology", *Journal of Consumer Research*, 16, 133-46.

From Luxury Counterfeits to Genuine Goods: Why Would Consumers Switch?

Anne-Flore Maman Larraufie, INSEEC & SemioConsult, France

EXTENDED ABSTRACT

Counterfeiting of luxury goods is a key issue for all major luxury industries. Some conglomerates such as LVMH have even set up some kind of fighting force to identify, to arrest and to sue counterfeiters. However, little attention has been paid to those consumers who occasionally or on a regular basis do mix legal and illegal purchases of luxury goods (Ha and Lennon 2006; Wilcox, Kim, and Sen 2009). Various reasons have been advanced as triggers, from demographics characteristics (Safa and Jessica 2005) to postmodern ethics (Maman 2009), including rational price-saving strategies. This article aims at providing a different view to the issue: instead of focusing on the reasons why people buy fake luxuries, it has a look at what would make these consumers turn to the purchase of their genuine versions.

To our knowledge, no past research has been conducted to investigate how consumers of non-deceptive luxury counterfeits (knowingly buying a counterfeit good) perceive the worlds of luxury and hence which kind of arguments could be used by luxury companies to convince those people to switch from the fake to the genuine item. Therefore, the present research will be exploratory by nature, in a discovery-oriented perspective. This is to pave the way for future more confirmatory research, by reducing the chance of beginning with an inadequate, incorrect or misleading set of research objectives.

Hence, we defined on purpose quite broadly our research questions: How do consumers of non-deceptive luxury counterfeits perceive the worlds of luxury and of counterfeiting? What makes them stay away from luxury houses? How could marketers use such knowledge to capture these consumers?

To answer these questions, we relied upon a qualitative methodology, as it looked like the most appropriate way to really get insights and understandings from the consumers. The selected research method was in-depth interviews, for they "are much the same as psychological, clinical interview" (Zikmund and Babin 2007). This method suits our needs in understanding the various values associated with the luxury/counterfeiting world or the consumption of luxury goods. Attitudes are mentally-driven, and since we are interested in getting the 'why' of their existence, and not only identifying them, in-depth interviews would really enable us to uncover underlying motivations, beliefs, attitudes and feelings.

More specifically, 21 in-depth interviews were conducted with MBA students from two French Business Schools (13), high-school pupils (3) and grown-ups with job activity (5). Students from Western business schools are usually said as having as having more purchasing power and as being more sensitive to the consumption of conspicuous goods, such as luxury or luxury-looking goods, than other types of students. Besides, they have been found as regular consumers of non-deceptive luxury counterfeits. High-school pupils are usually considered as having no or low purchasing power, as they only get a limited amount of pocket money but might in the future be able to buy luxury goods. Working adults dispose of a regular income they can spend the way they want.

The interviews lasted between 40 minutes to one hour and a half and were unstructured. The first part of the interview dealt with the topic of luxury. Respondents were asked to describe past experience and express feelings about luxury consumption. Their ultimate luxury was also touched upon. The second part of the interview dealt with counterfeiting. Past experience about its consumption and vari-

ous thoughts were under investigation in this part. It also included a projective drawing to elicit deeper feelings of the respondents. For the analysis, the interviews were transcribed and coded, with a goal to identify the key dimensions emerging from the discourse (see Spiggle 1994 and Strauss and Corbin 2008 for a discussion of the procedures used in this stage). Coding schemes were modified as analysis progressed and new concepts were uncovered.

As previously mentioned, the objective of the analysis was to be able to identify potential connections in-between how people view the world of luxury, and their view of the world of counterfeiting. This was achieved in three steps.

Step 1: What's in the World of Luxury

A content analysis of what the interviewees mentioned about luxury goods ended up in the identification of six specificities related to Luxury, potentially leading to purchase intents.

Table 1 sums up the characteristics and identification 'labels' of these faces.

Step 2: What's in the World of Counterfeiting?

A content analysis of the discourses regarding counterfeiting isolated four actors in the consumption process of counterfeits: the brand, the context, the consumer and the product per se. These four actors are no surprise but what is more interesting is the various characteristics associated with them and how they interact. Figure 1 sums up the overall findings.

Step 3: What Incentives to Switch Consumption from Fakes to Real Goods?

A comparison of the two previous steps helped us identify three necessary conditions that must be met to allow consumers of non-deceptive counterfeits to switch to the purchase of real goods. These are: an exigency of quality, both in terms of product and of sales forces' competencies; a retail environment "smelling luxury" (quoted from one respondent); and a service experience without any flaw. Table 2 exhibits this comparison.

ANALYSIS AND CONCLUSION

The two content analyses give a better understanding of how people develop an initial attitude toward luxury, toward counterfeiting and potentially how one attitude may impact another one. For instance, seeing the luxury world as a superficial/artificial world is very much connected with the idea that some people engage in the consumption of counterfeits to display artificial symbolic codes of belonging to a potential social class.

A discourse analysis leading to a semiotic analysis of the discourses hold by the respondents was thus conducted (see Figure 2). Out of four types of consumers, three would be eligible for switching from fake consumption to genuine one. The reasons why (consumption values) are represented on a semiotic square.

With such better knowledge of deep consumption motives, capturing some counterfeit consumers appears feasible if proper marketing strategies are undertaken.

Friends Show the Forest Beyond the Trees:
Friendship Enhances Consumer Self-Control by Facilitating Global Processing

Eline L.E. De Vries, University of Groningen, The Netherlands
Debra Trampe, University of Groningen, The Netherlands
Bob M. Fennis, University of Groningen, The Netherlands, and Norway Business School BI, Norway

EXTENDED ABSTRACT

While years ago consumers' potential shopping activities were limited to eight hours a day, the 24/7 economies of today's society present a never-ending stream of consumption opportunities. Notwithstanding the positive effects, the ever-present consumption temptations pose a serious challenge to consumer self-control (Faber and Vohs 2011; Hoch and Loewenstein 1991; Vohs and Faber 2007).

Whether or not consumers succumb to consumption temptations depends on their processing style (Fujita, Trope, and Liberman 2010; Fujita et al. 2006). Self-control failure has been associated with *low-level construals:* a focus on the local, subordinate and secondary features of an entity or event, whereas *high-level construals* (i.e., a focus on the global, superordinate or primary features) have been associated with effective self-control (Fujita and Han 2009; Fujita and Roberts 2010; Fujita and Sasota 2011; Fujita et al. 2010). For instance, Fujita et al. (2006) showed that activation of high-level construals results in less positive evaluations of consumption temptations and in decreased preference for immediate over delayed consumption. Hence, increasing consumers' construal level (i.e., promoting ones global, as opposed to local, processing; Förster and Dannenberg 2010; Förster, Liberman, and Shapira 2009) entails an interesting opportunity to promote consumer self-control.

In the present research we hypothesize that reminding consumers of friendship promotes consumer self-control by increasing global (conceptual or perceptual) processing. We expected that reminding individuals of an abstract, superordinate and long-term goal such as friendship (Baumeister and Leary 1995) would broaden consumers' processing style. This, in turn, would allow consumers to transcend and see beyond the alluring but subordinate features of consumption temptations, resulting in enhanced self-control.

Findings reported by Förster, Özelsel and Epstude (2010) provided initial support for our hypothesis. In their studies, individuals were primed with either love or lust. The authors reasoned that whereas love is generally associated with a long-term perspective, lust is associated with the short-term. Indeed, their studies showed that love priming enhanced global perceptual processing, while lust priming induced a more local processing style. Consistent with our hypothesis that friendship increases self-control by enhancing global processing, the authors suggested that friendship, like love, is related to long-term goals. Moreover, a number of defining characteristics of love (i.e., caring for and identifying with a person, and emotional bonding) also apply to friendship. Hence, reminding consumers of friendship may engender global processing.

Three experiments tested our hypothesis that friendship increases global processing and subsequently, self-control. In the first experiment, participants were either reminded of friendship by writing a short essay about a situation in which they experienced friendship or they were not reminded of friendship and wrote about the manufacturing process of a table. They then completed the Behavior Identification Form (BIF) as a measure of (conceptual) processing style (Förster et al. 2009; Vallacher and Wegner 1989). Results showed that participants who were reminded of friendship construed situations at higher construal levels than participants in the control condition. In all three studies reported here, the friendship manipulation did not influence positive or negative affect. Experiment 1 shows

that reminding participants of friendship broadens their (conceptual) processing style.

In the second experiment, we used a 3 (friendship: friend vs. peer vs. control) × 2 (self-regulatory resource depletion: depletion vs. no-depletion) between-subjects factorial design and aimed to disentangle the friendship effect from a mere social presence effect. In addition to a friend condition, in which participants wrote about their relationship with a good friend, and a non-social control condition, we added a condition where participants wrote about their relationship with a fellow student they knew but were not friends with (peer condition). The next task consisted of the manipulation of self-regulatory resource depletion (Baumeister et al. 1998). We then measured participants' global (perceptual) processing with the Kimchi-Palmer task (Gasper and Clore 2002; Kimchi and Palmer 1982), asking participants to indicate which of two sample figures looked most like a target figure (e.g., a triangle made up of small squares). Choice of local sample figures indicates a local processing style, whereas choice of global sample figures reflects global processing. Finally, we added a measure of self-control by asking participants to indicate their willingness-to-pay for a cupcake. Results showed that under conditions of susceptibility to consumption temptations (i.e., self-regulatory resource depletion), being reminded of a friend, but not of a peer in general, enhanced global processing and reduced willingness-to-pay relative to the control condition. Moreover, in line with our hypothesis, a significant bootstrap analysis (Zhao, Lynch, and Chen 2010) showed that the effect of friendship and depletion on willingness-to-pay was mediated by enhanced global processing.

In the third experiment, we used a 2 (processing style: local vs. global) × 3 (friendship: friend vs. peer vs. control) between-subjects factorial design, to provide converging evidence that friendship enhances self-control in consumers prone to self-control failure (i.e., participants with a local processing style). We directly manipulated processing style with the Navon task (Navon 1977), showing participants a series of composite letters (a global letter made up of local letters), and asked them to report either the global or local letters, dependent on condition. We used the same friendship manipulation as in experiment 2. We subsequently showed participants photos of six hedonic products and, following Fujita et al. (2006), measured participants' self-control by measuring their preference for immediate versus delayed consumption of these products. In line with our expectations, reminding participants with a local processing style of friendship significantly enhanced their self-control (i.e., reduced their preference for immediate over delayed consumption) relative to both the control and peer conditions. Unsurprisingly, friendship did not influence the self-control of participants in the global processing condition.

In sum, employing multiple validated tasks to assess or manipulate local versus global processing, we demonstrate the facilitative effect of friendship on self-control and the mediating role of global processing. By broadening consumers' (conceptual or perceptual) processing style, friends show consumers the proverbial forest beyond the trees and as such substantially enhance consumer self-control.

REFERENCES

Baumeister, Roy F., Ellen Bratslavsky, Mark Muraven, and Dianne M. Tice (1998), "Ego Depletion: Is the Active Self a Limited Resource?" *Journal of Personality and Social Psychology,* 74 (5), 1252-65.

Baumeister, Roy F. and Mark R. Leary (1995), "The Need to Belong: Desire for Interpersonal Attachments as a Fundamental Human Motivation," *Psychological Bulletin,* 117 (3), 497-529.

Faber, Ronald J. and Kathleen D. Vohs (2011), "Self-Regulation and Spending: Evidence from Impulsive and Compulsive Buying," in *Handbook of Self-Regulation: Research, Theory, and Applications,* ed. Kathleen D. Vohs and Roy F. Baumeister, New York, NY: Guilford Press, 537-50.

Förster, Jens and Laura Dannenberg (2010), "GLOMO^sys: A Systems Account of Global Versus Local Processing," *Psychological Inquiry,* 21 (3), 175-97.

Förster, Jens, Nira Liberman, and Oren Shapira (2009), "Preparing for Novel Versus Familiar Events: Shifts in Global and Local Processing," *Journal of Experimental Psychology: General,* 138 (3), 383-99.

Förster, Jens, Amina Özelsel, and Kai Epstude (2010), "How Love and Lust Change people's Perception of Relationship Partners," *Journal of Experimental Social Psychology,* 46 (2), 237-46.

Fujita, Kentaro and H. A. Han (2009), "Moving Beyond Deliberative Control of Impulses: The Effect of Construal Levels on Evaluative Associations in Self-Control Conflicts," *Psychological Science,* 20 (7), 799-804.

Fujita, Kentaro and Joseph C. Roberts (2010), "Promoting Prospective Self-Control through Abstraction," *Journal of Experimental Social Psychology,* 46 (6), 1049-54.

Fujita, Kentaro and Jo A. Sasota (2011), "The Effects of Construal Levels on Asymmetric Temptation-Goal Cognitive Associations," *Social Cognition,* 29 (2), 125-46.

Fujita, Kentaro, Yaacov Trope, and Nira Liberman (2010), "Seeing the Big Picture: A Construal Level Analysis of Self-Control," in *Self Control in Society, Mind, and Brain.* ed. Ran R. Hassin, Kevin N. Ochsner and Yaacov Trope, New York, NY: Oxford University Press, 408-27.

Fujita, Kentaro, Yaacov Trope, Nira Liberman, and Maya Levin-Sagi (2006), "Construal Levels and Self-Control," *Journal of Personality and Social Psychology,* 90 (3), 351-67.

Gasper, Karen and Gerald L. Clore (2002), "Attending to the Big Picture: Mood and Global Versus Local Processing of Visual Information," *Psychological Science,* 13 (1), 34.

Hoch, Stephen J. and George F. Loewenstein (1991), "Time-Inconsistent Preferences and Consumer Self-Control," *Journal of Consumer Research,* 17 (4), 492-507.

Kimchi, Ruth and Stephen E. Palmer (1982), "Form and Texture in Hierarchically Constructed Patterns," *Journal of Experimental Psychology: Human Perception and Performance,* 8 (4), 521-35.

Navon, David (1977), "Forest before Trees: The Precedence of Global Features in Visual Perception," *Cognitive Psychology,* 9 (3), 353-83.

Vallacher, Robin R. and Daniel M. Wegner (1989), "Levels of Personal Agency: Individual Variation in Action Identification," *Journal of Personality and Social Psychology,* 57 (4), 660-71.

Vohs, Kathleen D. and Ronald J. Faber (2007), "Spent Resources: Self-Regulatory Resource Availability Affects Impulse Buying," *Journal of Consumer Research,* 33 (4), 537-47.

Zhao, Xinshy, John Lynch Jr G., and Qimei Chen (2010), "Reconsidering Baron and Kenny: Myths and Truths about Mediation Analysis," *Journal of Consumer Research,* 37 (2), 197-206.

The Perception of Two Types of Corporate Social Responsibility on the Consumer-brand Relationship

Lei Huang, Dalhousie University, Canada

EXTENDED ABSTRACT

The research identifies two categories corporate social responsibility information – corporate operational performance (COP) and social performance (CSP) – to test their respective impact on consumer brand advocacy and brand trust. Results from two empirical studies suggest that product involvement has a moderating effect on COP/CSP and brand advocacy and brand trust.

LITERATURE REVIEW

Corporate Social Responsibility (CSR) has been an important area of research in brand equity. Consumers may associate CSR with a positive product and its evaluations, brand recommendations, and brand choice (Drumwright, 1994; Brown and Dacin, 1997; Osterhus, 1997; Handelman and Arnold, 1999; Sen and Bhattacharya, 2001). On the other hand, negative CSR, or Corporate Social Irresponsibility (CSI), can impair brand equity by weakening consumers' brand evaluations and purchase intentions (Dawar and Pillutla, 2000; Armstrong, 1977). However, the debate about the nature of CSR has been debating for decades. The purpose of this article is to examine a fundamental, yet unexplored, question: Do consumers respond differently to CSR information?

RESEARCH TOPIC

In answering to the above proposed question, I define two major dimensions of CSR – corporate operational performance (COP) and corporate social performance (CSP) – to test and predict their respective impact on consumer brand advocacy and brand trust. The former captures a company's publicly released information regarding product quality and innovativeness capability (Gatignon and Xuereb, 1997; Rust, Moorman, and Dickson, 2002); the latter includes a company's activities and status related to its perceived societal or stakeholder obligations (Varadarajan and Menon, 1988). The assumption is that successful relationship marketing requires trust as the cornerstone (Morgan and Hunt, 1994) and relies on advocacy to flourish (Berens, van Riel, and van Bruggen, 2005).

Furthermore, as an unobservable state of motivation, arousal, or interest toward consumption (activity) of a product or object (Olsen, 2007), the role of product involvement on the relationship between CSR and brand trust has not, to this author's knowledge, been tested empirically. The objective of this study is to add to the body of theoretical and empirical research in CSR by demonstrating that COP and CSP information can be applied to a consumer–brand relationship context.

HYPOTHESES

In the consumer-brand continuum, we expect that the exposure of CSR-COP may strengthen consumer brand advocacy (i.e., purchase intention, and evaluation of the corporation, and WOM communications, etc.), especially when the brand is in the high involvement product categories. Consumers will rely more on this diagnostic information for judgment. That is, when consumers look at low involvement products, CSR-CSP/ CSR-COP has a stronger effect on brand advocacy than CSR-COP/ CSR-CSP, whereas CSI-COP/ CSI-CSP has a stronger effect on brand advocacy than CSI-CSP/ CSI-COP (H1a/b). Similar postulations are held for brand trust (H2a/b).

METHODOLOGY

Study 1 is a 2 (COP-CSR vs. COP-CSI) × 2 (CSP-CSR vs. CSP-CSI) × 2 (high- vs. low- involvement) between-subject design. Fictitious companies producing juices and manufacturing TV sets were used as the low and high involvement product categories, respectively. All the experimental stimuli and the valence of messages were pretested. A total of 326 commerce major undergraduate students were randomly assigned to eight experimental conditions and asked to finish a questionnaire including COP and CSP ratings after reading the scenarios. Then, subjects were told that this company had recently introduced a new juice drink/a new model of TV set, with the product descriptions, and asked to provide a purchase intention rating with the assumption that they were interested in buying a juice for their breakfast/buying a TV set for their apartment. Finally, subjects were quizzed on whether they had guessed the purpose of the experiment before debriefing.

Study 2 is similar to Study 1 but using actual brand names instead of fictitious ones.

FINDINGS

Study 1 presents a significant three-way interaction ($F = 35.24$, $p < .05$). Results from further two-way ANOVAs suggested significant interaction effects between COP and CSP under low ($F = 15.12$, $p < .01$) and high ($F = 17.36$, $p < .01$) product involvement situations, respectively. Simple effects tests showed that in the low involvement circumstance (H1a), CSR-CSP had a stronger effect on brand advocacy than CSR-COP ($F = 11.78$, $p < .01$), whereas CSI-COP had a stronger effect on brand advocacy than CSI-CSP ($F = 7.13$, $p < .05$). As H1b predicted, COP and CIP presented opposite patterns in the high product involvement circumstance. Results from Study 2 indicate the similar patterns.

For brand trust, although the three-way interaction among COP, CSP and product involvement is significant ($F = 28.87$, $p < .05$), only the conditional two-way interactions between COP and CSP in the high ($F = 14.57$, $p < .05$), but not low ($F = 2.03$, $p > .3$) involvement (Study 1 and 2). However, CSR-CSP has a stronger effect on brand trust than CSR-COP, whereas CSI-COP has a stronger effect on brand trust than CSI-CSP for low involvement products in Study 2. Thus, both H2a and H2b are supported.

CONTRIBUTIONS

This study suggests that individuals have different WOM preferences in positive/negative CSP and negative/positive COP information for low/high involvement products. These findings can further contribute to the everlasting WOM information valence research as well as the relatively infertile cause-related marketing areas.

By extending the expectancy value theory that posits overall brand attitude through the formation of brand associations held in consumer's memories (Ajzen and Fishbein, 1980), results from the current study add that for low involvement products (e.g., juice), consumers associate a company's CSP information as more diagnostic information compared with COP in brand evaluation and consequent advocacy behavior intentions while for high involvement products COP is viewed more diagnostic and valuable. These findings can also contribute to clarifying how consumers perceive and react to distinctive CSR information and how firms can design communication strategies to utilize these effects. Finally, the lack of empirical research on brand trust in CSR could be explained by the fact that applying interpersonal relationship theories such as trust is not well-understood because the brand is an inanimate object. In a marketing context it is impossible to completely detach trust from the nature of its object. These empirical results shed some light on the moderating effect of product involvement in this CSR-trust consumer and brand relationship.

REFERENCE

Armstrong, J. Scott (1977), "Social Irresponsibility in Management," *Journal of Business Research*, 5 (September), 185–213.

Ajzen, Icek and Martin Fishbein (1980), *Understanding Attitudes and Predicting Social Behaviour. Englewood Cliffs*, NJ: Prentice-Hall.

Berens, Guido, Cees B.M. van Riel, and Gerrit H. van Bruggen (2005), "Corporate Associations and Consumer Product Responses: The Moderating Role of Corporate Brand Dominance," *Journal of Marketing*, 69 (3), 35–48.

Brown, Tom J. and Peter A. Dacin (1997), "The Company and The Product: Corporate Associations And Consumer Product Responses," *Journal of Marketing*, 61 (1), 68–84.

Dawar, Niraj and Madan M. Pillutla (2000), "The Impact of Product-Harm Crises on Brand Equity: The Moderating Role of Consumer Expectations," *Journal of Marketing Research*, 37 (5), 215–226.

Drumwright, Minette E. (1994), "Socially Responsible Organizational Buying: Environmental Concern as a Non-Economic Buying Criterion," *Journal of Marketing*, 58 (3), 1–19.

Gatignon, Hubert and Jean-Marc Xuereb (1997), "Strategic Orientation of the Firm and New Product Performance," *Journal of Marketing Research*, 34 (1), 77–90.

Handelman, Jay M. and Stephen J. Arnold (1999), "The Role of Marketing Actions with a Social Dimension: Appeals to the Institutional Environment," *Journal of Marketing*, 63 (3), 33–48.

Morgan, Robert M. and Shelby D. Hunt (1994), "The Commitment Trust Theory of Relationship Marketing," *Journal of Marketing*, 58 (4), 20–38.

Olsen, Svein O. (2007), "Repurchase Loyalty: The Role of Involvement and Satisfaction," *Psychology & Marketing*, 24 (4), 315–341.

Osterhus, Thomas L. (1997), "Pro-Social Consumer Influence Strategies: When and How Do They Work?" *Journal of Marketing*, 61 (4), 16–29.

Rust, Roland T., Christine Moorman, and Peter R. Dickson (2002), "Getting Return on Quality: Cost Reduction, Revenue Expansion, or Both," *Journal of Marketing*, 66 (4), 7–24.

Sen, Sankar and C.B. Bhattacharya (2001), "Does Doing Good Always Lead to Doing Better? Consumer Reactions to Corporate Social Responsibility," *Journal of Marketing Research*, 38 (2), 225–243.

Varadarajan, P. Rajan and Anil Menon (1988), "Cause-Related Marketing: A Coalignment of Marketing Strategy and Corporate Philanthropy," *Journal of Marketing*, 52 (4), 58–74.

All Numbers are Not Created Equal: Price Points, Price Processing and Price Rigidity

Haipeng (Allan) Chen, Texas A&M University, USA
Avichai Snir, Bar-Ilan University, Israel
Daniel Levy, Bar-Ilan University, ISRAEL, Emory University, USA, and Rimini Center for Economic Analysis, Italy
Alex Gotler, Open University, Israel

EXTENDED ABSTRACT

One common type of price points is *9-ending prices*, also known as *psychological prices* (Kashyap 1995; Levy et al. 2011; Knotek 2010). In the current research, we use data from a lab experiment, a field study, and a large Midwestern US supermarket chain to study the rigidity of 9-ending prices. Our results demonstrate a hitherto undocumented asymmetry in rigidity associated with 9-ending prices, and provide a link between consumers' cognitive costs and pricing policies that have significant effects on demand and inflation.

TESTABLE HYPOTHESES

Empirical evidence suggests that individuals usually process multi-digit numeric information, including numbers and prices, from left to right (Poltrock and Schwartz, 1984, Stiving and Winer 1997). The marketing literature also suggests that consumers often use 9-endings as a signal for low prices (Schindler 2001, 2006; Thomas and Morwitz 2005). We therefore expect that while consumers will process *numbers* digit by digit, they will use 9-endings as a signal when comparing *prices*. Since relying on 9-endings as a signal interferes with left-to-right processing, we predict that consumers will be less accurate in comparing prices and in judging price changes. We also predict that retailers are likely to respond strategically to these consumer perceptions in setting prices. Specifically, retailers will tend to set 9 ending prices after price increases because the consumers are less likely to recognize a price increase when the new price is 9-ending. Retailers are less likely, however, to set 9-ending prices after price decreases, because price decreases are often promoted by alternative signals of low prices, such as shelf signs and leaflets. Thus, we predict an asymmetry in the price rigidity of 9-ending prices, with 9-ending prices being less likely to increase than, but as likely to decrease as, non 9-ending prices.

3. DATA AND ANALYSIS

3.1. Evidence from a Laboratory Experiment

Participants compared 300 pairs of numbers or prices on lab computers. They were instructed to respond as quickly and as accurately as possible. In addition, they were told that 10 percent of them would be selected at random and paid according to their performance. The results suggest that 9-endings reduce participants' accuracy only for price comparisons but not for number comparisons. In addition, we find that 9-endings reduced accuracy only when the greater of the two prices ended with 9 but not when the smaller of the two prices ended with 9, consistent with our premise that consumers oftentimes mistaken a 9-ending price as being smaller.

3.2. Evidence from a Field Study

We recruited 365 shoppers at three supermarkets located in different cities in Israel. Consumers exiting the three supermarkets were approached, and only those who shopped in the same supermarket also in the previous week were given a questionnaire. The questionnaire was composed of a list of 52 goods in 12 categories. For each good, respondents were asked whether the good's price had increased, decreased or remained the same from the previous week to the current week.

Recall data suggest that 9-ending is associated with a higher probability that a consumer thought that a price had decreased, but does not affect the probability that a consumer thought that the price had increased. We also find that consumers are more likely to associate changes from 9-endings to non-9-ending prices with price increases, and associate changes from non 9-ending prices to 9-ending prices with price decreases.

Analysis of recall accuracy revealed that consumers are less likely to recognize price increases when the new price is 9-ending. At the same time, 9-ending prices do not increase the probability that the consumers correctly recognized a price decrease. This might be because many price decreases are sale prices that are promoted by shelf signs, leaflets, etc., regardless of whether the new prices are 9-ending or not.

3.3. Evidence from a Large U.S. Supermarket Chain

Finally, we use data on price changes in Dominick's Finer Food, a large Midwestern US supermarket chain, to test our predictions concerning retailer's pricing behaviors. We find that retailers are more likely to set 9-endings after price increases than after price decreases. Moreover, the likelihood that the prices will be 9-endings is even lower for sale prices than for regular price decreases, confirming our speculation that price decreases are oftentimes promoted by shelf signs, flyers, etc. rather than by the 9-ending. In addition, when the old price is 9-ending, the retailers are more likely to change it to another 9-ending price than when the old price is non 9-ending.

Addition analyses showed that the right-most digits were less likely to adjust if the previous prices ended with 9, more so following a price increase than following a price decrease; 9-ending prices are significantly less likely to increase than, but as likely to decrease as, non 9-ending prices; non 9-endings transitioned to 9-ending with higher probabilities for price increases than for price decreases; and 9-ending prices, when they did change, had a larger average magnitude of change than non 9-ending prices for increases but not for decreases. These results combined depict a clear pattern for an asymmetry in rigidity, with 9-ending prices being more rigid than non 9-ending prices upward but not downward.

CONCLUSION

We use data from a lab experiment, a field study, and a large Midwestern US supermarket chain to study the rigidity of 9-ending prices. We find that consumers often interpret 9-endings as a signal for low prices and therefore, they are more likely to make mistakes in price comparisons if the greater prices end with 9, and are less accurate in recalling price increases from non 9-ending prices to 9-ending prices. Retailers respond to these consumer perceptions by setting prices at 9-endings more often after price increases than after price decreases.

Thus, it seems that 9-endings as an outcome of retailers' response to consumers' cognitive bias might have significant effects on pricing policies and consequently on market structure, demand and inflation (Basu, 1996, Kehoe and Midrigan, 2008, Knotek, 2010, Eichenbaum et al., 2011).

REFERENCES

Akelrof, George A. and Janet M. Yellen (1985), "Can Small Deviations from Rationality Make Significant Differences for Economic Equilibria?," *American Economic Review*, 75(4), 708 – 720.

Anderson, Eric T. and Duncan I. Semester (2003), "Effects of $9 Price-endings on Retail Sales: Evidence from Field Experiments," Quantitative Marketing and Economics 1(1), 93 – 110.

Ball, L. and D. Romer (2003), "Inflation and the Informativeness of Prices," 35(2), 177–196.

Barsky, R., et al. (2003), "What Can the Price Gap between Branded and Private Label Products Tell Us about Markups?" In R. Feenstra and M. Shapiro, Eds., *Scanner Data and Price Indexes* (Chicago, IL: University of Chicago Press), pp. 165–225.

Basu, K. (1997), "Why Are So Many Goods Priced to End Nine? And Why This Practice Hurts Producers," 54(1), 41–44.

Basu, K. (2006), "Consumer Cognition and Pricing in the Nines in Oligopolistic Markets," 15(1), 125–141.

Bergen, M., et al. (2008), "On the Inefficiency of Item Pricing Laws: Theory and Evidence," 51(2), 209–250.

Bils, M. and P. Klenow (2004), "Some Evidence on the Importance of Sticky Prices," 112(5), 947–985.

Bergen, Mark, Robert J. Kauffman and Dongwon Lee (2005), "Price Points and Price Rigidity on the Internet: A Massive Qusi Experimental Data Mining Approach," Working paper.

Blinder, A., et al. (1998), *Asking about Prices* (NY, NY: Russell Sage Foundation).

Carlton, D. (1986), "The Rigidity of Prices," 76, 637–658.

Chen, H., et al. (2008), "Asymmetric Price Adjustment in the Small," 55(4), 728–737.

Cecchetti, S. (1986), "The Frequency of Price Adjustment: A Study of the Newsstand Prices of Magazines," 31(3), 255–274.

Chevalier, J., et al. (2003), "Why Don't Prices Rise during Peak Demand Periods? Evidence from Scanner Data," 93, 15–37.

Danziger, L. (1999), "A Dynamic Economy with Costly Price Adjustments," 89(4), 878–901.

Dutta, S., et al. (1999), "Menu Costs, Posted Prices, and Multiproduct Retailers," 31(4), 683–703.

Dutta, S., et al. (2002), "Price Flexibility in Channels of Distribution: Evidence from Scanner Data," 26(11), 1845–1900.

Eichenbaum, M., N. Jaimovich, and S. Rebelo (2011), "Reference Prices, Costs and Nominal Rigidities," 101, 234–262.

Kahneman, D. and S. Frederick (2002), "Representativeness Revisited: Attribute Substitution in Intuitive Judgment," in Gilovich, T. et al. (Eds.), *Heuristics and Biases* (UK: Cambridge University Press), pp. 49–81.

Kashyap, A. (1995), "Sticky Prices: New Evidence from Retail Catalogs," 110(1), 245–274.

Kalayanaram, G. and R. Winer (1995), "Empirical Generalization from Reference Price Research," 14(3), G161–G169.

Kehoe, P. and V. Midrigan (2008), "Temporary Price Changes and the Real Effects of Monetary Policy," NBER WP No. 14392.

Kehoe, P. and V. Midrigan (2010), "Prices Are Sticky After All," RSR 413, Fed of Mpls.

Klenow, P. and O. Kryvtsov (2008), "State-Dependent vs. Time-Dependent Pricing: Does it Matter for Recent US Inflation?" 123, 863–904.

Klenow, P. and B. Malin (2011), "Microeconomic Evidence on Price-Setting," in B. Friedman and M. Woodford (Eds.), *Handbook of Monetary Economics*, 3A-B (NY, NY: North Holland), pp. 231–284.

Knotek, E. (2010), "The Roles of Menu Costs and Nine Endings in Price Rigidity," RWP No. 10-18, Fed of Kansas City.

Knotek, E. (2011), "Convenient Prices and Price Rigidity: Cross-Section Evidence," , forthcoming.

Konieczny, J. (1993), "Variable Price Adjustment Costs," 31, 488–98.

Lach, S. and D. Tsiddon (1992), "The Behavior of Prices and Inflation: An Empirical Evidence of Disaggregate Price Data," 100, 349–89.

Lach, S. and D. Tsiddon (1996), "Staggering and Synchronization in Price Setting: Evidence from Multiproduct Firms," 86, 1175–1196.

Lachman, R., et al. (1979), *Cognitive Psychology and Information Processing: An Introduction* (Hillsdale, NJ: Lawrence Erblaum Associates).

Levy, D., et al. (1997), "The Magnitude of Menu Costs: Direct Evidence from Large U.S. Supermarket Chains," 112, 791–825.

Levy, D., et al. (2010), "Holiday Price Rigidity and Cost of Price Adjustment," 77, 172–198.

Levy, D., et al. (2011), "Price Points and Price Rigidity," (forthcoming).

Levy, D. and A. Young (2004), "The Real Thing: Nominal Price Rigidity of the Nickel Coke, 1886–1959," 36, 765–799.

Macé, Sandrine (2011), "The impact and Determinants of 9-Ending Pricing in Grocery Stores," *Journal of Retailing*.

Mankiw, N.G. (1985), "Small Menu Costs and Large Business Cycles: a Macroeconomic Model of Monopoly," 100, 529–539.

Mazumdar, T. and P. Papatla (2000), "An Investigation of Reference Price Segments," 38, 246–258.

Midrigan, V. (2011), "Menu Costs, Multi-Product Firms, and Aggregate Fluctuations," 79, 1139–1180.

Nakamura, E. and J. Steinsson (2008), "Five Facts about Prices: A Reevaluation of Menu Cost Models," 123(4), 1415–1464.

Nakamura, E. and J. Steinsson (2009), "Price Setting in Forward-Looking Customer Markets," manuscript.

Nevo, A. (2002), "Measuring Market Power in the Ready to Eat Cereal Industry," 69, 307 – 342.

Peltzman, S. (2000), "Prices Rise faster than They Fall," 108, 466–502.

Poltrock, S. and D. Schwartz (1984), "Comparative Judgments of Multidigit Numbers," 10, 32–45.

Ray, S., et al. (2006), "Asymmetric Wholesale Pricing: Theory and Evidence," 25, 131–54.

Rotemberg, J. (1982), "Sticky Prices in the United States," 90, 1187–1211.

Rotemberg, J. (1987), "The New Keynesian Microfoundations," , 69–104.

Rotemberg, J. (2005), "Customer Anger at Price Increases, Changes in the Frequency of Price Adjustment, and Monetary Policy" , 829-52.

Rotemberg, J. (2010), "Altruistic Dynamic Pricing with Customer Regret," 112(4), 646-672.

Ruffle, B. and Z. Shtudiner (2006), "99: Are Retailers Best Responding to Rational Consumers?" 27, 459–75.

Schindler, R. (1984), "Consumers Recognition of Increases in Odd and Even Prices," 11, 459–462.

Schindler, R. (2001), "Relative Price Level of 99-Ending Prices: Image Vs. Reality," 12(3), 239–247.

Schindler, R. (2006), "The 99 Price-ending as a Signal of a Low-Price Appeal," 82(1), 71–77.

Schindler, R. and R. Chandrashekaran (2004), "Influence of Price-endings on Price Recall: a by-Digit Analysis," 13, 514–524.

Schindler, R. and P. Kirby (1997), "Patterns of Right Most Digits Used in Advertised Prices," 24, 192–200.

Snir, A. and D. Levy (2011), "Shrinking Goods and Sticky Prices: Theory and Evidence," WP No. 11-04, Emory University.

Stiving, M. (2000), "Price-endings When Prices Signal Quality," 46(12), 1617–1629.

Stiving, M. and R. Winer (1997), "An Empirical Analysis of Price-endings with Scanner Data," 24(1), 57–67.

Thomas, M. and V. Morwitz (2005), "Penny Wise and Pound Foolish: The Left- Digit Effect in Price Cognition," 32, 54–64.

Warner, E. and R. Barsky (1995), "The Timing and Magnitude of Retail Store Markdowns," 110(2), 321–352.

Willis, J. (2003), "Implications of Structural Changes in the US Economy for Pricing Behavior and Inflation Dynamics," , (1st Q.), 5–26.

Wolman, A (2007), "The Frequency and Costs of Individual Price Adjustment: A Survey," 28(6), 531–552.

Zbaracki, M., et al. (2004), "Managerial and Customer Costs of Price Adjustment: Direct Evidence from Industrial Markets," 86, 514–33.

In the Aftermath of an Earthquake: Interactive Effects of Self-construal and Victim Group-Status on Charitable Behavior

Rod Duclos, Hong Kong University of Science and Technology, Hong Kong
Alixandra Barasch, University of Pennsylvania, USA

EXTENDED ABSTRACT

When a natural disaster strikes, consumers often face numerous requests to help devastated communities. Only a small percentage of people who view these ads, however, wind up contributing resources to aid rescue and rebuilding efforts. What factors influence consumers' decision to help victims of natural disasters and other disadvantaged populations? The present research tackles this question by investigating the interactive effects of self-construal and victim origin on prosocial behavior.

Fundamental to people's emotional and cognitive responses, *self-construal* characterizes the extent to which one considers oneself separate from versus connected with others (Markus and Kitayama 1991). Not surprisingly, one's mental representation of personhood activates quite distinct mindsets. Whereas individualism (i.e., independence) highlights the personal and centralizes individuals as the unit of analysis, collectivism (i.e., interdependence) highlights the social and contextualizes individuals as parts of socially-connected units (Oyserman et al. 1998). Because the *interdependent* self focuses on social roles and relations, one might expect interdependents to be more generous than independents with needy others. Consistent with this view, several studies found positive correlations between interdependence and charitable behavior (Moorman and Blakely 2006; Eckstein 2001; Skarmeas and Shabbir 2011).

Drawing from work in psychology, however, we nuance the above view and argue that interdependents may not necessarily be more connected to and generous toward others. Indeed, recent self-construal research underscores the importance of group status (*in* vs. *out*) for the interdependent self (Iyengar and Lepper 1999; Kitayama et al. 1997). That is, whereas interdependents are generally motivated to integrate themselves with and meet the expectations of others, they do so mostly when these "others" are considered *relevant* (e.g., family members, peers; Heine and Lehman 1997).

Accordingly, the present research investigates the interaction of self-construal and victim group-status on donation behavior. In three experiments run in both America and China, we manipulated participants' self-construal before observing their prosocial dispositions toward victims of natural disasters. Our central proposition is that victim group-status (in vs. out) influences more heavily interdependents' willingness to help than independents' (since the latter see themselves as more separate from others, regardless of group-status).

To test this hypothesis, our three studies adopted a similar 2 (Self-construal: Independent/Interdependent) by 2 (Victim group-status: In/Out) between-subjects design. To manipulate self-construal, we asked participants to complete an alleged "emotional empathy questionnaire" (Gardner et al.1999) which required reading a story written either in the first person (e.g., I, my, me) or in the inclusive plural form (e.g., we, our, us) before completing manipulation checks. Next, participants viewed an appeal from "Global Relief", a fictitious charity collecting money to help victims of natural disasters. Vivid in nature, the advertisement featured death toll statistics (e.g., "hundreds dead and millions homeless"), a description of victims' needs (e.g., "food and medicine for vulnerable children and devastated families"), and the pictures of suffering victims underneath the text. The ad concluded by asking participants to visit the charity's website to make a donation. Of note, the photographs featured within each study were identical in every aspect (e.g., content;

victims' age, gender, apparent suffering) except race. Extensive pretests further ensured the pictures differed in neither mood nor arousal (e.g., nervous, excited, bad, good, depressed, relaxed).

Study 1 recruited online 292 Americans (all-White sample; average age = 35) before randomly assigning them to one of four conditions (cf. design and procedure above). Upon completing the self-construal manipulation and its manipulation checks, participants reviewed an ad from "Global Relief" depicting recent tornado victims in the southern U.S. To manipulate group-status, the ad portrayed either White (i.e., in-group) or Black (i.e., out-group) victims. Our analyses revealed no main effects but a significant crossover interaction (cf. table). On average, independents were neither more nor less likely to donate than interdependents. Similarly, White victims elicited neither more nor less donations than their Black counterparts. As expected, however, contrast analyses confirmed our central hypothesis. Whereas independents were just as likely to make a donation regardless of victims' origin, interdependents donated significantly more to in-group (i.e., White) than out-group (i.e., Black) victims.

Study 2 replicated these findings with 148 Chinese undergraduates. After being induced to think individually vs. collectivistically, participants reviewed an ad by "Global Relief" asking them to support rebuilding efforts following the Sichuan (i.e., in-group) vs. Haiti (i.e., out-group) earthquake. Once again, independents were neither more nor less likely to donate than interdependents. Similarly, Chinese victims elicited neither more nor less donations than their Haitian counterparts. As predicted, however, independents were just as likely to donate regardless of victims' origin whereas interdependents donated significantly more to in-group (i.e., Sichuan) than out-group (i.e., Haitian) victims. A look at our mood (i.e., PANAS) and self-esteem measures further revealed that neither affect- nor esteem-based explanations could account for our findings.

To articulate these results, study 3 re-enacted the above procedure with 171 Chinese undergraduates but added attitude measures intended to capture consumers' lay beliefs about happiness and prosocial behavior (Duclos et al. 2012; Oyserman et al. 1998). The same pattern of results emerged (i.e., no main effects but a significant interaction). Whereas independents were just as likely to donate regardless of victims' origin, interdependents donated significantly more to in-group (i.e., Sichuan) than out-group (i.e., Haitian) victims. Once again, mood (i.e., PANAS) and self-esteem measures remained incapable of explaining our results. The extent to which participants believed that "helping others promotes happiness", however, did mediate the self-construal by victim group-status interaction on donation intentions (mediated moderation; Sobel test: z = 2.349, p = .019).

By uncovering the interactive effects of self-construal orientation and victim group-status on prosocial behavior in both Western and Eastern cultures, the present paper offers novel insights for both psychology and consumer research. Moreover, by articulating the mediating role of cognitions (vis-à-vis affect and self-esteem) in charitable decisions, our findings provide charities actionable insights into the psychology of donors (e.g., matching recipients of help to donors' profile in *interdependent* contexts, stressing the happiness derived from helping others). Hence, for its contributions to both theory and practice, we believe this research would be of interest to a wide audience at ACR.

REFERENCES

Baron, R.M. & Kenny, D.A. (1986), "The Moderator-Mediator variable distinction", in Social Psychological research: Conceptual, strategic, and statistical considerations. *Journal of Personality and Social Psychology*, 51, 1173-1182.

Duclos, Rod, J. Bettman, P. Bloom, and G. Zauberman (2012), "Charitable Giving: How Ego-Threats Impact Donations of Time and Money," Working Paper.

Eckstein, Susan (2001), "Community as gift-giving: Collectivistic roots of volunteerism," *American Sociological Review*, 66 (Dec), 829-851.

Gardner, W. L., Gabriel, S., & Lee, A. Y. (1999), "I" value freedom but "we" value relationships: Self-construal priming mirrors cultural differences in judgment. *Psychological Science*, 10, 321-326.

Heine, Steven J. and Darrin R. Lehman (1997), "The cultural construction of self-enhancement: An examination of group-serving biases," *Journal of personality and social psychology*, 72 (6), 1268-1283.

Iyengar, Sheena S. and Mark R. Lepper (1999), "Rethinking the Value of Choice: A Cultural Perspective on Intrinsic Motivation," *Journal of Personality and Social Psychology*, 76 (3), 349-366.

Kitayama, Shinobu, Hazel Rose Markus, Hisaya Matsumoto, and Vinai Norasakkunit (1997), "Individual and collective processes in the construction of the self: Self enhancement in the United States and self-criticism in Japan," *Journal of Personality and Social Psychology*, 72 (6), 1245-67.

Markus, Hazel Rose and Shinobu Kitayama (1991), "Culture and the self: Implications for cognition, emotion, and motivation," *Psychological Review*, 98 (2), 224-53.

Moorman, Robert H. and Gerald L. Blakely (2006), "Individualism-collectivism as an individual difference predictor of organizational citizenship behavior," *Journal of Organizational Behavior*, 16 (2), 829-851.

Oyserman, Daphna, Izumi Sakamoto, and Armand Lauffer (1998), "Cultural Accommodation: Hybridity and the Framing of Social Obligation," *Journal of Personality and Social Psychology*, Vol. 74, No. 6, 1606-1618.

Singelis, Theodore M. (1994), "The Measurement of Independent and Interdependent Self-Construals," *Personality and Social Psychology Bulletin*, 20 (5), 580-591.

Skarmeas, Dionysis and Haseeb Shabbir (2011), "Relationship quality and giving behaviour in the UK fundraising sector: Exploring the antecedent roles of religiosity and self-construal," *European Journal of Marketing*, 45 (5).

Do Open Hands (Always) Open Wallets: The Influence of Gestures on Generosity

Ellen Garbarino, University of Sydney, Australia
En Li, Central Queensland University, Australia

EXTENDED ABSTRACT

Emerging research on embodied cognition (Glenberg 2010), explores the influence of the body on the mind. We contribute to this literature by examining the influence of hand gestures on generosity. Two recent studies provide evidence that generosity can be embodied in certain hand processes. Williams and Bargh (2008) found that participants whose hands experienced physical warmth (vs. coldness) displayed higher generosity. Hung and Labroo (2011) demonstrated that participants who firmed their hand muscles were more likely to make monetary donations to an earthquake relief appeal. However, hand firming did not affect the amount participants donated. To extend this hand processes research, we focus on two gestures that are metaphorically related to generosity: "open-hand" (which relates to the idiom open-handed, or generous) and "tight-fist" (which relates to tightfisted, or stingy). We hypothesize and demonstrate that holding an "open-hand" (vs. "tight-fist") gesture increases consumers' generosity and that this embodied generosity effect is moderated by consumers' idiom knowledge (study 1), gesture timing (study 2), and self-monitoring (study 2).

STUDY 1

The embodied cognition literature suggests that perceptual-motor patterns are an integral part of the representation of concepts (Barsalou 2008). Hence, making a gesture related to a concept should increase the accessibility of the concept, which should shape thoughts and behaviors to which the concept is applicable. From this logic, we propose that consumers who hold "open-hand" (vs. "tight-fist") gestures should be more (vs. less) generous. Furthermore, as knowledge availability is a necessary condition for its accessibility (Higgins 1996), consumers' idiom knowledge should increase their susceptibility to this embodied generosity effect.

Online panel participants were asked to hold certain body position, including the key gesture manipulation (randomly assigned to hold palm or fist gestures with both hands). To maintain such gestures for a sufficient amount of time, they were asked to complete some online tasks (e.g., watching and evaluating a tv commercial) before releasing the required body position. Afterwards, they completed a spendthrift-tightwad scale (Rick, Cryder, and Loewenstein 2008) and a survey of their knowledge of English idioms (including open-handed and tight-fisted idioms). It was expected that those cued for generosity (open-hand) would report higher spendthrift scores. We find participants who had held palm gestures reported marginally higher spendthrift scores ($p = .10$). This generosity effect was more pronounced among participants who knew the correct meanings of both idioms ($p < .01$) than those who didn't ($p = .40$); thus, supporting the moderating role of awareness of the concepts on generosity.

STUDY 2

"Effector dependency" theory suggests that embodiment effects should only be driven by activation of relevant muscles (Glenberg 2010). As people use their dominant hand to perform skilled actions, the dominant hand, rather than the non-dominant hand, could be the more critical effector involved in hand related embodiment effects (Borghi and Scorolli 2009). Hence, the proposed generosity effect could be driven by the gesture on one's dominant hand. To probe this possibility, we manipulated gesture timing, some participants

holding the requested gesture then released both hands to complete a donation task (i.e., prior gesture condition), and others kept holding the gesture with the non-dominant hand while using the dominant hand to respond (i.e., simultaneous gesture condition). We predict the prior gesture condition would be more likely to activate generosity concepts among participants holding an open-hand (vs. tight-fist) gesture, leading to higher generosity in a donation task (as it did in study 1). While the simultaneous gesture condition should lead to the opposite effect; holding an open-hand (vs. tight-fist) in the non-dominant hand would make the dominant hand seem more (less) constricted by comparison and could consequently lead to activation of "less generous" (vs. "less stingy") responses.

Another potential moderator lies in individual differences in self-monitoring. Existing research shows that individuals who are high (vs. low) in self-monitoring are more sensitive to external cues (vs. internal states) (DeMarree, Wheeler and Petty 2005). As the prior gesture condition does not provide present external cues for the donation task, low (vs. high) self-monitoring consumers would be more likely to make their donation decisions based on their internal states, including bodily sensations carried over from prior gesture. Therefore, the proposed embodied generosity effect should be more prevalent among low (vs. high) self-monitoring consumers under the prior gesture condition. The simultaneous gesture condition, provides the still gesturing hand as a salient external cue, rendering high (vs. low) self-monitoring consumers more susceptible to the proposed effect.

Participants were assigned to one of four conditions: 2 (gesture: tight-fist vs. open-hand) × 2 (gesture timing: prior gesture vs. simultaneous gesture). They completed a questionnaire including the Revised Self-Monitoring scale (Lennox and Wolfe 1984). They then reset their body position including the manipulated hand gesture. After holding the gesture for 60 seconds, those in the prior gesture condition released both hands and proceed with the donation task, those in the simultaneous gesture condition were only allowed to release their dominant hand. Participants were told that one out of every 100 participants would receive $100. They indicated, by writing with their dominant hand, how much of their $100 they wanted to donate to a charity, if selected.

The results indicated a significant gesture × gesture timing interaction ($p < .05$). In the simultaneous gesture condition, contrasts revealed more generous donations from participants who held a tight-fist than from those who held an open-hand ($p < .05$). In contrast, a reversed pattern was found among participants in the prior gesture condition, though the level fell short of significance ($p < .18$). Spotlight analyses (Fitzsimons 2008) shows the predicted effects of gestures among high self-monitoring participants in the simultaneous gesture condition ($p < .05$) but not among low self-monitors ($p > .50$) and the predicted effects among low self-monitoring participants in the prior gesture condition ($p < .05$) but not among high self-monitors ($p > .70$).

The current study illustrates that generosity can be embodied in subtle hand gestures. Further, this embodiment effect is moderated by consumer idiom knowledge, gesture timing, and self-monitoring. Future research could seek support for this effect in other consumption domains (e.g., product purchase decisions).

REFERENCES

Barsalou, L. W. (2008), "Grounded Cognition," *Annual Review of Psychology*, 59, 617-645.

Borghi, A. M. and C. Scorolli (2009), "Language Comprehension and Dominant Hand Motion Simulation," *Human Movement Science*, 28, 12-27.

DeMarree, K. G., S. C. Wheeler, and R. E. Petty (2005), "Priming a New Identity: Self-monitoring Moderates the Effects of Nonself Primes on Self-judgments and Behavior," *Journal of Personality and Social Psychology*, 89 (5), 657-671.

Fitzsimons, G. J. (2008), "Death to Dichotomizing," *Journal of Consumer Research*, 35(June), 5-8.

Glenberg, A. M. (2010), "Embodiment as a Unifying Perspective for Psychology," *Wiley Interdisciplinary Reviews: Cognitive Science*, 1 (July/August), 586-596.

Higgins, E. Tory (1996), "Knowledge Activation: Accessibility, Applicability, and Salience," in *Social Psychology: Handbook of Basic Principles*, ed. E. Tory Higgins and A. Kruglanski, New York: Guilford, 133-68.

Hung, I. W. and A. A. Labroo (2011), "From Firm Muscles to Firm Willpower: Understanding the Role of Embodied Cognition in Self-regulation," *Journal of Consumer Research*, 37 (April), 1046-1064.

Lennox, R. D. and R. N. Wolfe (1984), "Revision of the Self-monitoring Scale," *Journal of Personality and Social Psychology*, 46 (June), 1349-1364.

Rick, Scott I., Cynthia E. Cryder, and George Loewenstein (2008), "Tightwads and Spendthrifts," *Journal of Consumer Research*, 34 (April), 767-782.

Williams, L. E. and J. A. Bargh (2008), "Experiencing Physical Warmth Influences Interpersonal Warmth," *Science*, 322 (5901), 606-607.

Leisure Consumption as Conspicuous Work

Andre F. Maciel, University of Arizona, USA
Melanie Wallendorf, University of Arizona, USA

EXTENDED ABSTRACT

One characteristic of postmodernity that is of central interest for marketing scholars is the reversal and interpenetration of production and consumption (Firat and Venkatesh 1995). This altered relation between the two is encountered in distinctive practices such as those addressed in the growing literature on co-creation (Prahalad and Ramaswamy 2000; Schau et al. 2009; Vargo and Lusch 2004). Beyond practices, this altered relation between production and consumption also generates the co-existence of sometimes conflicting ideologies (Ritzer and Jurgenson 2010; Zwick et al. 2008) that are regarded as incompatible when viewed through a modernist lens (Campbell 1987; Gelber 1999; Weber 1958). Our research addresses this cultural condition in a consumer-centric study that asks: what are the personal and cultural meanings of consumer practices that emerge from contemporary interpenetration of production and consumption in leisure?

This ethnographic project was implemented in two empirical contexts of productive leisure (Gelber 1999) where individuals intertwine production and consumption both voluntarily and consistently across time. That is, they do not engage in productive activities because of financial need, as with low income people for whom producing may sometimes be cheaper than buying. Further, they are not occasional customizers of products or assemblers of do-it-yourself kits. In productive leisure, individuals (called *productive consumers*) acquire domain-specific skills to enact a continuous cycle of production-consumption in which they buy supplies, infuse labor and creativity to make a final product, and eventually choose the intended user. The formative stage of the research pointed to the importance of including both a female-dominated and a male-dominated context to understand the gendered nature of production-consumption. Ethnographic fieldwork has been conducted among knitters and beer homebrewers to enhance the depth and the conceptual nuance of the project (Pyett 2003; Whittemore et al. 2001).

Fieldwork indicates a key outcome of the interpenetration of work and consumption in leisure is the cultural re-signification and repositioning of manual, slow-paced labor. With contemporary late capitalism's emphasis on efficiency and intellectual work, manual labor has been devalued in the realm of production (Sennett 2008). With regards to consumption, however, we argue that late capitalism has created the cultural and economic conditions for the assertion of social status through leisure activities that are particularly compatible with American production-oriented values of work and self-reliance (Gelber 1999; McClelland 1961; Weber 1930). Unlike the privileged classes' historical practice of marking status through conspicuous consumption of luxury items produced by others as well as through non-productive leisure (Veblen 1899), productive consumers build distinction in their social circles (Bourdieu 1987) by dedicating leisure time to productive manual activities that are inefficient as compared with capitalist mass-manufactures.

We find three practices that productive consumers of both genders employ to conspicuously display their work-like leisure and its handmade output to demonstrate distinctiveness. First, they find ways to take this activity beyond the realm of domestic production to also engage in the slow production of their crafts in public settings. When they do so with other hobbyists in places where the practice of productive leisure is expected (e.g., homebrewing clubs), they find recognition for creativity that is often scarce in their middle-class jobs. Productive consumers value this aesthetic feedback based on the emergent standards of the group, inasmuch as they operate in craft fields that tend not to have well-defined aesthetic standards (Becker 1978). When productive consumers take their activities to places where it is somewhat unexpected (e.g., knitting in the airplane), they commonly command admiration from others who show appreciation for the time and labor productive consumers apply to manually produce things in a society oriented towards convenience and efficiency.

Second, productive consumers engage in practices that ensure high visibility for the handmade origin of their output. In gift-giving, a common outlet for their handmade production, they draw the recipient's attention to the handmade character of the gift through cards or commentaries to ensure that the time and effort invested in it will be converted into higher esteem (symbolic capital) from the recipient (Bourdieu 1987). Moreover, productive consumers from both genders often create products to insert in special social events (e.g., a homebrewer making beer for Christmas or a knitter making a *huppah* for her wedding) to signal their commitment to the occasion and enhance others' esteem for them.

Third, in a subtle demonstration of their labor, productive consumers enact a self-presentation strategy (Goffman 1959) that downplays mass-manufactured items to emphasize both the quality and the handmade-ness of the item. Productive consumers use mass-produced items as a background for the display of the handmade, as with knitters who often favor relatively plain outfits that make a colorful handmade shawl stand out. Productive consumers thus relegate mass-produced items to an inferior position to draw attention to what is much more central to their identities and much more socially distinctive: their capability to produce things manually and inefficiently.

Strikingly, productive consumers invest a substantial amount of time and labor that is not remunerated in order to craft products that do not necessarily comply with current taste standards. The process through which the handmade items acquire value relies less on aesthetic and financial criteria than on the distinctiveness they convey when delivered in the context of the larger culture's transition from modernity to postmodernity. This research unpacks a particular dynamic between time, leisure, and labor that emerges from a contemporary reencounter of work and consumption during leisure. In this dynamic, which is interestingly consistent across genders, relatively privileged classes emulate the work practices of lower classes to build distinctiveness and prestige. Unlike non-productive leisure, this strategy is validated by the centrality of work, time, and self-reliance in contemporary American culture. Productive consumers use unpaid, time-consuming, and labor-intensive activities to reassert and display their control over scarce, valuable resources, thereby acquiring and communicating symbolic capital.

REFERENCES

Becker, Howard S. (1978), "Arts and Crafts," *American Journal of Sociology,* 83 (4), 862-89.

Bourdieu, Pierre (1987), *Distinction: A Social Critique of the Judgment of Taste,* Cambridge: Harvard University Press.

Campbell, Colin (1987), *The Romantic Ethic and the Spirit of Modern Consumerism,* Great Britain: Blackwell Publishers.

Firat, A. F., and Alladi Venkatesh (1995), "Liberatory Postmodernism and the Reenchantment of Consumption," *The Journal of Consumer Research,* 22 (3), pp. 239-267.

Gelber, Steven M. (1999), *Hobbies: Leisure and the Culture of Work in America,* New York: Columbia University Press.

Goffman, Erving (1959), "Performances," in *The Presentation of Self in Everyday Life,* New York; London; Toronto; Sydney; Auckland: Anchor Books, 17-76.

McClelland, David C. (1961), *The Achieving Society,* Princeton, N.J.: Van Nostrand.

Prahalad, C. K., and Venkatram Ramaswamy (2000), "Co-Opting Customer Competence," *Harvard Business Review,* 78 (1), 79-87.

Pyett, P. M. (2003), "Validation of Qualitative Research in the "Real" World," *Qualitative Health Research,* 13 (8), 1170-9.

Ritzer, George, and Nathan Jurgenson (2010), "Production, Consumption, Prosumption: The Nature of Capitalism in the Age of the Digital 'Prosumer,'" *Journal of Consumer Culture,* 10 (1), 13-36.

Schau, Hope J., Albert Muñiz M., and Eric J. Arnould (2009), "How Brand Community Practices Create Value," *Journal of Marketing,* 73 (5), 30-51.

Sennett, Richard (2008), *The Craftsman,* New Haven & London: Yale University Press.

Vargo, Stephen L., and Robert F. Lusch (2004), "Evolving to a New Dominant Logic for Marketing," *The Journal of Marketing,* 68 (1), pp. 1-17.

Veblen, Thorstein (1899), *The Theory of the Leisure Class,* New York: Mcmillan

Weber, Max (1958), *From Weber: Essays in Sociology,* In Gerth H., Mills C. W. (Ed.), Oxford.

Weber, Max (1930), *The Protestant Ethic and the Spirit of Capitalism,* New York: Routledge.

Whittemore, R., S. W. Chase, and C. L. Mandle (2001), "Validity in Qualitative Research," *Qualitative Health Research,* 11 (4), 522-37.

Zwick, Detlev, Samuel K. Bonsu, and Aron Darmody (2008), "Putting Consumers to Work 'Co-Creation' and New Marketing Govern-Mentality," *Journal of Consumer Culture,* 8 (2), 163-96.

Influence of Future Time Perspective on Involvement:
An Approach with two Studies

Stefanie Scholz, Otto-Friedrich-University Bamberg, Germany
Yvonne Illich, Friedrich-Alexander-University Erlangen-Nuremberg, Germany
Björn S. Ivens, Otto-Friedrich-University Bamberg, Germany
Martina Steul-Fischer, Friedrich-Alexander-University Erlangen-Nuremberg, Germany

EXTENDED ABSTRACT

Both marketers and scholars have recognized the growing economic relevance of older consumers (Yoon, 1997; Yoon et al., 2005). While demographic change alone cannot justify research on older individuals' consumer behaviour, this field is nevertheless important as there is a great deal of evidence regarding age differences in consumer behaviour (see e.g. Yoon & Cole, 2008). The aim of this research is to extend current knowledge of older consumers' behaviour, focusing on involvement and future time perspective (FTP). Furthermore, older consumers face new challenges in daily life, for instance in the realm of medical decision-making (Wood, Shinogle, & McInnes, 2010). We propose recommendations for the development of customer approaches in the context of colon cancer prevention.

INVOLVEMENT

Involvement is defined as "a person's perceived relevance of the object based on inherent needs, values and interests" (Zaichkowsky, 1985, p. 342), and has an affective and a cognitive dimension (Zaichkowsky, 1985, 1987, 1994). It affects the cognitive effort people put into decision-making processes (Bienstock & Stafford, 2006; Mittal, 1995). Research mostly focuses on product involvement (Laurent & Kapferer, 1985; Michaelidou & Dibb, 2006, 2008; Mittal, 1995). This paper extends research in the area of services (Bienstock & Stafford, 2006; Varki & Wong, 2003) and health services in particular (Shaffer & Sherrell, 1997).

FTP

FTP, a construct embedded in the socioemotional selectivity theory (SST), describes a person's subjective perception of time left to live. FTP can vary depending on life situation (Bouffard, Lens, & Nuttin, 1983; Carstensen & Fredrickson, 1998) and lifestyle (Lang & Carstensen, 2002), and can be influenced through framing in advertisements (Fung & Carstensen, 2003; Fung, Carstensen, & Lutz, 1999; Williams & Drolet, 2005).

SST provides a comprehensive approach to explaining age related differences in consumer behaviour (Drolet, Lau-Gesk, Williams, & Jeong, 2010). For example, consumers with a more limited FTP prefer more positive information in a health context, and avoid negative information (Löckenhoff & Carstensen, 2007). Yet, ignoring information is an important issue in the health care context (Löckenhoff & Carstensen, 2004). Furthermore, older adults' focus on emotions has been identified in many different studies (for a commentary see Drolet, Lau-Gesk, Williams, & Jeong, 2010). SST holds that this focus on emotions is due to older individuals' limited FTP (Carstensen, 2006).

HYPOTHESES

Health is of emotional relevance, especially for older adults. According to SST, emotionally relevant goals are prioritized by adults with a limited FTP. We therefore derive the following hypothesis:

Hypothesis 1: *Adults with a limited (vs. expansive) FTP have a high (vs. low) affective/ cognitive involvement in colon cancer prevention.*

In order to prove that the FTP-involvement link is not mainly based on a cohort effect, we hypothesize that FTP manipulation influences involvement as follows:

Hypothesis 2: *Affective/ cognitive involvement can be increased (vs. reduced) through limited (vs. expansive) FTP framing.*

METHOD

To test H1, study 1 was carried out among 538 younger (mean age: 25.03) and 482 older adults (mean age: 57.89). After reading a text containing information about colon cancer prevention, participants answered a questionnaire including an involvement (Hagendorfer, 1992; Zaichkowsky, 1994) and an FTP scale (Carstensen & Lang, 1996; Lang & Carstensen, 2002). Cronbach's alphas were good for involvement (.913) and FTP (.905).

In Zaichkowsky's involvement concept and in SST, the emotional component is a substantial part (Zaichkowsky, 1987). Therefore we checked for the influence of emotions. Furthermore we included questions regarding lifestyle (cf. Reitzler, 2001; Hess, 2001).

In order to test H2, for study 2 we added an FTP frame (based on Williams & Drolet, 2005) in the text about colon cancer prevention. A 2 (older vs. younger adults) x 3 (limited vs. expansive vs. control condition) between-subjects design resulted. 160 younger (mean age: 23.58) and 127 older adults (mean age: 64.38) participated in this experimental study.

STUDY 1

Our results confirm that FTP influences involvement. Analyses relied on structural equation modeling using AMOS 19. The fit indices show the acceptable model fit (χ^2/d.f.=7.439, RMSEA=.079, IFI=.852, CFI=.851). The paths from FTP to affective involvement (–.17, p<.001) and cognitive involvement (–.26, p<.001) were significant. Thus, H1 is supported. The results (see figure 1) show that the path from FTP to lifestyle is significant (.55, p<.001). Furthermore, lifestyle is related to cognitive involvement (.10, p<.001). As expected, emotions have an impact both on affective (.87, p<.001) and cognitive (.84, p<.001) involvement. Findings are consistent with the assumptions of SST and earlier research on involvement.

STUDY 2

A 2 x 3 ANOVA on the FTP index found a significant effect for framing group (F(5, 280)=28.582; p<.000). Although this effect is attributed to differences between age groups rather than framing (see table 1), data encourages the view that FTP framing can influence involvement. Two 2 x 3 ANOVAs on the affective involvement (F(5, 268)=6.539; p<.000) and cognitive involvement (F(5, 278)=8.491; p<.000) indices found significant effects. Differences exist between age groups: younger participants have a more expansive FTP and are less involved than older participants. Thus, we again find support for H1. Furthermore, older individuals are less involved in the limited frame than in the expansive frame and in the control condition. For the young, the results do not show clear framing effects (see table 1).

Figure 1
The relationship between FTP and Involvement: Structural Equation Model Results

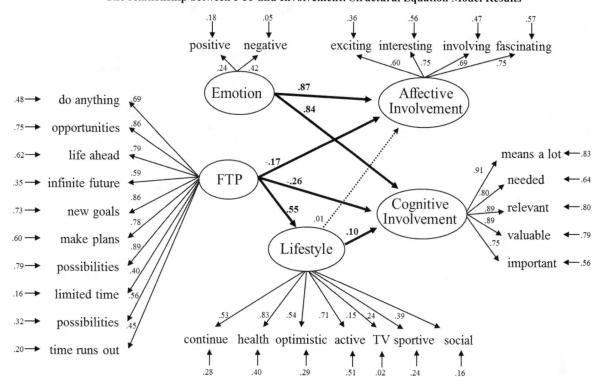

Table 1
Study 2 Results

	Younger adults		
Frame	Expansive	Limited	Control
FTP	2.35 (.69)	2.19 (.63)	2.31 (.66)
Affective involvement	4.02 (1.35)	4.04 (1.09)	4.22 (1.17)
Cognitive involvement	2.98 (1.28)	3.13 (1.07)	3.24 (1.30)
	Older adults		
Frame	Expansive	Limited	Control
FTP	3.63 (1.17)	3.63 (1.38)	3.73 (1.16)
Affective involvement	3.06 (1.59)	3.62 (1.22)	3.05 (1.37)
Cognitive involvement	2.10 (1.52)	2.51 (1.55)	1.77 (1.21)

Results imply that older and younger adults react differently to FTP framing. While a limited FTP frame seems to alienate the elderly from screenings, merely mentioning life time seems to provoke positive reactions towards prevention among the young. Although H2 is not supported, results indicate that the FTP-involvement link is independent from cohort effects.

CONTRIBUTIONS

FTP affects involvement in the context of health care services. Furthermore, involvement can be influenced through FTP manipulation. These findings provide players in the health care sector with the possibility of adopting FTP-based approaches for successfully addressing older customers. Concerning the participation in medical screenings, consumers could be activated more efficiently. Future research should verify if the relationship between FTP and involvement exists for other services.

REFERENCES

Barak, B., Mathur, A., Lee, K. and Zhang, Y. (2001), "Perceptions of age-identity: A cross-cultural inner-age exploration," *Psychology and Marketing*, 18(10), 1003-1029.

Bienstock, C. and Stafford, M. (2006), "Measuring Involvement With the Service: A Further Investigation of Scale Validity and Dimensionality," *The Journal of Marketing Theory and Practice*, 14(3), 209-221.

Bouffard, L., Lens, W. and Nuttin, J. R. (1983), "Extension de la Perspective Temporelle Future en Relation avec la Frustration," *International Journal of Psychology*, 18(5), 429-442.

Carstensen, L. L. (2006), "The influence of a sense of time on human development," *Science*, 312(5782), 1913-1915.

Carstensen, L. L. and Fredrickson, B. L. (1998), "Influence of HIV status and age on cognitive representations of others," *Health Psychology*, 17(6), 494-503.

Carstensen, L. L. and Lang, Frieder R. (1996), "Future Time Perspective Scale - English," *unpublished manuscript. Stanford University*. Retrieved from http://www-psych.stanford.edu/~lifespan/doc/FTP_english.pdf

Drolet, A., Lau-Gesk, L., Williams, P. and Jeong, H. G. (2010), "Socioemotional selectivity theory: Implications for consumer research," In A. Drolet, N. Schwarz and C. Yoon (Eds.), *The Aging Consumer - Perspectives from Psychology and Economics* (1st ed., pp. 51-72). New York London: Routledge.

Fung, H. H. and Carstensen, L. L. (2003), "Sending memorable messages to the old: Age differences in preferences and memory for advertisements," *Journal of Personality and Social Psychology*, 85(1), 163-178.

Fung, H. H., Carstensen, L. L. and Lutz, A. M. (1999), "Influence of time on social preferences: Implications for life-span development," *Psychology and Aging*, 14(4), 595-604.

Hagendorfer, A. (1992), „Meßtheoretische Überprüfung des Zaichkowsky Personal Involvement Inventory in Österreich," *der markt*, 31(121), 86-93.

Hess, T. M. (2001), "Ageing-related influences on personal need for structure," *International Journal of Behavioral Development*, 25(6), 482-490.

Krugman, H. E. (1965), "The impact of television advertising: learning without involvement," *Public Opinion Quarterly*, 29(3), 349-356.

Krugman, H. E. (1967), "The measurement of advertising involvement," *Public Opinion Quarterly*, 30(4), 583-596.

Lang, F.R. and Carstensen, L. L. (2002), "Time counts: Future time perspective, goals, and social relationships," *Psychology and Aging*, 17(1), 125-139.

Laurent, G. and Kapferer, J.-N. (1985), "Measuring Consumer Involvement Profiles," *Journal of Marketing Research*, 22(1), 41-53.

Löckenhoff, C. E. and Carstensen, L. L. (2004), "Socioemotional selectivity theory, aging, and health: the increasingly delicate balance between regulating emotions and making tough choices," *Journal of Personality*, 72(6), 1395-1424.

Löckenhoff, C. E. and Carstensen, L. L. (2007), "Aging, emotion, and health-related decision strategies: motivational manipulations can reduce age differences," *Psychology and Aging*, 22(1), 134-146.

Michaelidou, N. and Dibb, S. (2006), "Product involvement: an application in clothing," *Journal of Consumer Behaviour*, 5(5), 442-453.

Michaelidou, N. and Dibb, S. (2008), "Consumer involvement: a new perspective," *The Marketing Review*, 8(1), 83-99.

Mittal, B. (1995), "A comparative analysis of four scales of consumer involvement," *Psychology and Marketing*, 12(7), 663-682.

Reitzler, R. (2001), *Versicherungen für Senioren: Perspektiven für das Zielgruppen-Marketing*. Wiesbaden: DUV Deutscher Universitätsverlag.

Shaffer, T. R. and Sherrell, D. L. (1997), "Consumer satisfaction with health-care services: The influence of involvement," *Psychology and Marketing*, 14(3), 261-285.

Varki, S. and Wong, S. (2003), "Consumer Involvement in Relationship Marketing of Services," *Journal of Service Research*, 6(1), 83-91.

Williams, P. and Drolet, A. (2005), "Age-related differences in responses to emotional advertisements," *Journal of Consumer Research*, 32(3), 343-354.

Wood, S. L., Shinogle, J. A. and McInnes, M. (2010), "New Choices, New Information: Do Choice Abundance and Information Complexity Hurt Aging Consumers' Medical Decision Making?," In A. Drolet, N. Schwarz and C. Yoon (Eds.), *The Aging Consumer - Perspectives from Psychology and Economics* (1st ed., pp. 131-147). New York London: Routledge.

Yoon, C. (1997), "Age Differences in Consumers' Processing Strategies: An Investigation of Moderating Influences," *Journal of Consumer Research*, 24(3), 329-342.

Yoon, C. and Cole, C. A. (2008), "Aging and consumer behavior," In C. P. Haugtvedt, P. M. Herr and F. R. Kardes (Eds.), *Handbook of consumer psychology*. (1st ed., pp. 247-270). New York: Lawrence Erlbaum Associates.

Yoon, C., Laurent, G., Fung, H. H., Gonzalez, R., Gutchess, A. H., Hedden, T., Lambert-Pandraud, R., et al. (2005), "Cognition, Persuasion and Decision Making in Older Consumers," *Marketing Letters*, 16(3-4), 429-441.

Zaichkowsky, J. L. (1985), "Measuring the Involvement Construct," *Journal of Consumer Research*, 12(3), 341-352.

Zaichkowsky, J. L. (1987), "The emotional aspect of product involvement," *Advances in Consumer Research*, 14(1), 32-35.

Zaichkowsky, J. L. (1994), "Research Notes: The Personal Involvement Inventory: Reduction, Revision, and Application to Advertising," *Journal of Advertising*, 23(4), 59-70.

Differential Discounting of Hedonic and Utilitarian Rewards: The Effect of Outcome Related Affect on Time-Sensitivity

Selcuk Onay, University of Waterloo, Canada
Valeria Noguti, University of Technology Sydney, Australia

EXTENDED ABSTRACT

Hyperbolic discounting has been proposed as an explanation for impulsive, time-inconsistent behavior (Ainslie 1975; Ainslie and Haslam 1992; Strotz 1955). Although previous research on intertemporal choice has consistently demonstrated that hyperbolic discounting can explain time preferences better than exponential discounting (for a literature review see Frederick, Loewenstein, and O'Donoghue 2002), the underlying psychological mechanisms involved in this process are not well understood. More importantly, the explanations for hyperbolic discounting proposed so far in the literature either focused solely on affective motives and visceral factors (Loewenstein 1996; Metcalfe and Mischel 1999) or only on perceptual and cognitive factors such as time-sensitivity (Ebert and Prelec 2007; Zauberman et al. 2009). We argue that while each of these two approaches can successfully explain a wide array of consumer behaviors, affective and perceptual factors are not independent of each other and the interaction between them gives rise to the discount function's shape. More specifically, we propose that affect toward delayed rewards reduces sensitivity to time in intertemporal decisions leading to differential discounting of hedonic and utilitarian rewards.

We operationalize time sensitivity using Ebert and Prelec's (2007) *constant-sensitivity discount function* which separates impatience (parameter a) from time-sensitivity (parameter b). Ebert and Prelec (2007) have argued that hyperbolic discounting can be explained by insufficient sensitivity to prospective delays and that time-sensitivity can be heightened or reduced experimentally. We propose that positive affect toward hedonic outcomes reduces time-sensitivity giving rise to more hyperbolic discounting of affect-rich, hedonic rewards compared to affect-poor, utilitarian ones (Dhar and Wertenbroch 2000; Hirschman and Holbrook 1982; Khan, Dhar, and Wertenbroch 2004). A similar effect has been demonstrated in the domain of risky choice. Rottenstreich and Hsee (2001) found that sensitivity to probabilities is reduced for affect-rich rewards.

We report three studies in which we demonstrate: (a) lower time-sensitivity for hedonic than for utilitarian rewards, and (b) a decrease in time sensitivity as a function of an increase in positive affect. In all studies we used two categories of rewards (between subjects): hedonic and utilitarian. In study 1 participants were asked to suppose that they had won a contest and could choose to receive a reward valued today at $100 or to receive a higher value reward in the future. Indifference points were elicited by using sets of six matching questions, each relative to a different future time (one day, one week, one month, six months, one year, and two years) and to a given category. Questions were worded as follows: "what is the minimum value of the [reward] in [future time] that would make you choose to receive the [reward] in [future time] instead of receiving the $100 [reward] today?" Participants also indicated the intensity of their feelings when receiving each reward type. Following Ebert and Prelec's constant-sensitivity function (2007), the parameter b was estimated for each individual. Higher b indicates more sensitivity to the time dimension. We obtained a significant category effect ($\beta = .32$, $t(57) = 2.54$, $p < .05$). In the utilitarian category b was significantly higher ($M = .39$, $SD = .14$) than in the hedonic category ($M = .31$, $SD = .11$). Positive affect mediated this relationship.

In study 2 we demonstrate that an increase in positive affect towards rewards leads to decreased time sensitivity. A choice task was used instead of matching. Positive affect conditions were created by introducing the word 'excitement' in the options. For example, each question read: "Option 1: I prefer *the excitement of* getting a $100 [reward] gift certificate now" or "Option 2: I prefer *the excitement of* getting a $x [reward] gift certificate in [future time]". In the neutral condition b was higher for utilitarian ($M = .59$, $SD = .24$) than for hedonic rewards ($M = .51$, $SD = .21$; $\beta = .24$, $t(122) = 1.97$, $p = .05$), but in the positive affect condition b was at the same level for utilitarian ($M = .52$, $SD = .17$) and hedonic rewards ($M = .54$, $SD = .24$; $\beta = .12$, $t(122) = .91$, $p > .10$).

In study 3 we develop an imagery-based manipulation of positive affect and demonstrate that cognitive reflection moderates the impact of positive affect on b. An iterative choice task was used. In both conditions a picture was introduced in the choice screens. In the neutral conditions the pictures were factual, e.g., an electricity meter to represent bills (example in the utilitarian category). The pictures in the positive affect conditions depicted happy people, for example, a smiling lady holding coins and a bill to represent bills. The positive affect conditions involved an additional task before the choice questions in which participants were asked to imagine that they won a contest and the prize was a $100 [reward] gift certificate. They were then asked to visualize themselves when receiving the certificate and the excitement and joy they would feel on the occasion. Next, participants responded to the CRT (Cognitive Reflection Test) questions (Frederick 2005). We found a main effect of category ($M_{util} = .60$ vs. $M_{hed} = .51$; $\beta = .23$, $t(126) = 2.65$, $p < .01$) and the two-way interaction between positive affect and CRT ($\beta = .22$, $t(126) = 2.54$, $p < .05$). The predicted effect of positive affect decreased b for low CRT participants ($M_{positive} = .48$ vs. $M_{neutral} = .61$; $\beta = -.46$, $t(125) = -2.78$, $p < .01$) but did not change b for high CRT participants ($M_{positive} = .58$ vs. $M_{neutral} = .54$; $\beta = -.06$, $t(125) = -.36$, $p > .10$).

In conclusion, we propose that positive affect reduces sensitivity to time, and hence enhances hyperbolic discounting, and demonstrate that time sensitivity is indeed reduced when positive affect increases. This argument provides a significant contribution to the literature as so far little has been published on how the interaction between hedonic motives and "time perception gives rise to the discounting function's shape. We also provide an explanation for why discounting is more hyperbolic for affect-rich, hedonic goods than affect-poor, utilitarian goods.

REFERENCES

Ainslie, George (1975), "Special Reward: A Behavioral Theory of Impulsiveness and Impulse Control," *Psychological Bulletin*, 82 (4), 463-96.

Ainslie, George and Nick Haslam (1992), "Hyperbolic Discounting," in *Choice over Time*, ed. George Loewenstein and Jon Elster, New York: Russell Sage Foundation, 57-92.

Dhar, Ravi and Klaus Wertenbroch (2000), "Consumer Choice between Hedonic and Utilitarian Goods," *Journal of Marketing Research*, 37 (1), 60-71.

Ebert, Jane E. J. and Drazen Prelec (2007), "The Fragility of Time: Time-Insensitivity and Valuation of the near and Far Future," *Management Science*, 53 (9), 1423-38.

Frederick, Shane (2005), "Cognitive Reflection and Decision Making," *Journal of Economic Perspectives*, 19 (4), 25-42.

Frederick, Shane, George Loewenstein, and Ted O'Donoghue (2002), "Time Discounting and Time Preference: A Critical Review," *Journal of Economic Literature*, 40 (2), 351-401.

Hirschman, Elizabeth C. and Morris B. Holbrook (1982), "Hedonic Consumption: Emerging Concepts, Methods and Propositions," *Journal of Marketing*, 46 (3), 92-101.

Khan, Uzma, Ravi Dhar, and Klaus Wertenbroch (2004), "A Behavioral Decision Theoretic Perspective on Hedonic and Utilitarian Choice," in *Inside Consumption: Frontiers of Research on Consumer Motives, Goals, and Desires*, ed. S Ratneshwar and David Glen Mick, NY: Routledge.

Loewenstein, George (1996), "Out of Control: Visceral Influences on Behavior," *Organizational Behavior & Human Decision Processes*, 65 (3), 272-92.

Metcalfe, Janet and Walter Mischel (1999), "A Hot/Cool-System Analysis of Delay of Gratification: Dynamics of Willpower," *Psychological Review*, 106 (1), 3-19.

Rottenstreich, Yuval and Christopher K. Hsee (2001), "Money, Kisses, and Electric Shocks: On the Affective Psychology of Risk," *Psychological Science*, 12 (3), 185-90.

Strotz, R. H. (1955), "Myopia and Inconsistency in Dynamic Utility Maximization," *Review of Economic Studies*, 23, 165-80.

Zauberman, Gal, B. Kyu Kim, Selin A. Malkoc, and James R. Bettman (2009), "Discounting Time and Time Discounting: Subjective Time Perception and Intertemporal Preferences," *Journal of Marketing Research*, 46 (4), 543-56.

Cooling Down or Heating Up with Emotions:
How Temperature Affects Customer Response to Emotional Advertising Appeals

Pascal Bruno, University of Cologne, Germany
Valentyna Melnyk, University of Waikato, New Zealand
Franziska Völckner, University of Cologne, Germany

EXTENDED ABSTRACT

Target's heartwarming mascot-puppy Bullseye, the adorable Pillsbury-Doughboy, the cute Gerber-Baby – emotional advertising appeals are prevalent and are even considered as more influential on purchase decisions than reason (Binet and Field 2009; Wood 2012). Advertising particularly frequently arouses emotional warmth (Fam 2008; Smit, van Meurs, and Neijens 2006), that is, a positive, mild, volatile emotional construct triggered by experiencing a love, family or friendship relationship (Aaker, Stayman, and Hagerty 1986). Despite the prevalence of warmth in advertising, empirical research on the effectiveness of such a strategy has been scarce (Vanden Abeele and MacLachlan 1994). So far, it is unclear whether and under which conditions emotionally warm (e.g., joy) or cold advertising appeals (e.g., disgust) are effective.

Recent embodied cognition research proposes that cognition is grounded in the physical context (Barsalou 2010), and emotional and physical warmth are interrelated (e.g., Williams and Bargh 2008). Drawing on this interrelation, we introduce and test in an advertising context the moderating influence of physical temperature on consumers' responses to emotional warmth versus coldness. We demonstrate in a lab experiment that physical coldness enhances consumers' attitudes towards emotionally warm ads; physical warmth decreases consumers' responses to emotionally warm ads and instead enhances attitudes towards emotionally cold ads. Our findings have implications for seasonal and international advertising campaigns.

THEORETICAL BACKGROUND

Embodied cognition research proposes that cognitive activity is grounded in the environment (Barsalou 2010). Put simply, it suggests that mind and body are closely related. Studies found, that respondents experiencing physical warmth considered a person's personality as warmer (Williams and Bargh 2008) and socially closer (IJzerman and Semin 2009). In contrast, people feeling physically cold were willing to pay more to watch romantic movies (Hong and Sun 2012), or felt lonelier (Bargh and Shalev 2012) and vice versa (Zhong and Leonardelli 2008).

From a biological perspective, humans urge to keep themselves warm to survive (Austin and Vancouver 1996). Hence, feeling physically cold should lead to an increased desire for warmth. Given the apparent link between physical and emotional warmth, an anxiety for emotional warmth could channel this desire to warm up under physical coldness.

As emotional warmth is predominant in advertising (Fam 2008), this study focuses on the ad context, analyzing the relation of physical temperature with *ad-induced warmth* in contrast to *ad-induced coldness*. We predict that *physical* coldness (warmth) activates a need for *psychological* warmth (coldness) and thus should increase consumers' response to advertising triggering emotional warmth (coldness).

METHODOLOGY

In total, 299 students (46.8 % females) were randomly assigned to one of the four conditions of the 2 (cold vs. warm physical temperature) x 2 (cold vs. warm advertising) between-subjects design experiment. In the warm (cold) temperature condition, we held room temperature constant at around 30 °C/86 °F (14 °C/57.2 °F). The emotional temperature was manipulated by pretested emotionally warm (cold) advertisements.

Participants evaluated the ads on six 7-point scales: ad liking, ad interest, convincingness of the ad, ad appeal, the ad's potential to be remembered, and ad effectiveness. Next, participants indicated the ad's perceived emotional warmth and the perceived physical room temperature (on 7-point scales, respectively).

We conducted a 2 (physically cold vs. warm) x 2 (emotionally cold vs. warm) between-subjects ANOVA. As our dependent variable, we calculated an index for attitude towards the ad (A_{ad}) as the mean of our six consumer response items (Cronbach's α = .836).

We find a significant main effect of emotional warmth of the advertisements on A_{ad} ($F(1, 290)$ = 13.52, p = .000, η^2 = .045). The main effect of physical temperature on A_{ad} ($F(1, 290)$ = .06, p = .800, η^2 = .000) was not significant. However, as predicted, the interaction effect of emotional warmth and physical temperature on A_{ad} was significant ($F(1, 290)$ = 8.37, p = .004, η^2 = .028). This result implies that respondents' physical temperature moderated the effect of emotional warmth (see figure 1).

To better understand the interaction effect, we conducted planned comparisons. Respondents in the cold temperature condition indicated for emotionally warm advertisements a significantly higher A_{ad} (M = 3.68) than for emotionally cold advertisements (M = 2.70; $F(3, 290)$ = 7.42, p = .000). Thus, under the influence of cold temperatures our results indicate a positive effect of emotional warmth (vs. emotional coldness) on consumers' responses to advertising. Moreover, the attitude towards an emotionally warm ad is higher in the physically cold condition (M = 3.68) than in the physically warm condition (M = 3.29; $F(3, 290)$ = 7.42, p = .072). Hence, the results indicate that cold temperature enhances attitude towards emotionally warm ads.

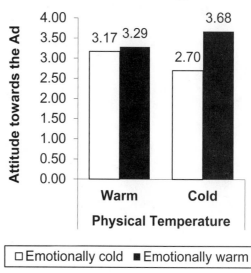

Figure 1
Moderating Effect of Temperature on the Effect of Warm/Cold Appeals

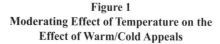

Furthermore, as expected, attitude towards the ad arousing emotional coldness is significantly higher in the physically warm condition ($M = 3.17$) than in the physically cold condition ($M = 2.70$; $F(3, 290) = 7.42$, $p = .022$). However, once people feel physically warm, they show no significant difference in attitude towards emotionally cold ($M = 3.17$) and warm advertising ($M = 3.29$; $F(3, 290) = 7.42$, $p = .581$). Hence, while consumers use, as suggested by embodied cognition theory, warm appeals to warm themselves up in a physically cold environment, they do not seem to make a difference between either cold or warm emotional stimulation when they are physically warm.

DISCUSSION AND IMPLICATIONS

Drawing on embodied cognition research, we introduce and empirically test the environmental context moderator of physical temperature on the effectiveness of emotionally warm versus cold advertising campaigns. We find that while cold physical temperature enhances consumers' responses to emotionally warm ads, warm physical temperature decreases consumers' responses to emotionally warm ads and instead enhances consumers' attitudes towards emotionally cold ads.

Our findings have important implications for the execution of seasonal and international marketing campaigns. Managers might, for instance, employ either warm or cold appeals in advertising during the summer months or in countries with warm climates, while they should prefer warm appeals over cold ones in winter or in colder regions.

REFERENCES

Aaker, David A., Douglas M. Stayman, and Michael R. Hagerty (1986), "Warmth in Advertising: Measurement, Impact, and Sequence Effects," *Journal of Consumer Research*, 12 (4), 365–81.

Austin, James T. and Jeffrey B. Vancouver (1996), "Goal Constructs in Psychology: Structure, Process, and Content," *Psychological Bulletin*, 120 (3), 338–75.

Bargh, John A. and Idit Shalev (2012), "The Substitutability of Physical and Social Warmth in Daily Life," *Emotion*, 12 (1), 154–162.

Barsalou, Lawrence W. (2010), "Grounded Cognition: Past, Present, and Future," *Topics in Cognitive Science*, 2 (4), 716–24.

Binet, Les and Peter Field (2009), "Empirical Generalizations About Advertising Campaign Success," *Journal of Advertising Research*, 49 (2), 130–133.

Fam, Kim-Shyan (2008), "Attributes of Likeable Television Commercials in Asia," *Journal of Advertising Research*, 48 (3), 418–32.

Hong, Jiewen and Yacheng Sun (forthcoming), "Warm It Up with Love: The Effect of Physical Coldness on Liking of Romance Movies," *Journal of Consumer Research*, electronically published October 7, 2011.

IJzerman, Hans and Gün R. Semin (2009), "The Thermometer of Social Relations: Mapping Social Proximity on Temperature," *Psychological Science*, 20 (10), 1214–20.

Smit, Edith G., Lex van Meurs, and Peter C. Neijens (2006), "Effects of Ad Likeability: A 10-Year Perspective," *Journal of Advertising Research*, 46 (1), 73–83.

Vanden Abeele, Piet and Douglas L. MacLachlan (1994), "Process Tracing of Emotional Responses to TV Ads: Revisiting the Warmth Monitor," *Journal of Consumer Research*, 20 (4), 586–600.

Williams, Lawrence E. and John A. Bargh (2008), "Experiencing Physical Warmth Promotes Interpersonal Warmth," *Science*, 322 (5901), 606–07.

Wood, Orlando (2012), "How Emotional Tugs Trump Rational Pushes: The Time Has Come to Abandon a 100-Year-Old Advertising Model," *Journal of Advertising Research*, 52 (1), 31–39.

Zhong, Chen-Bo and Geoffrey J. Leonardelli (2008), "Cold and Lonely: Does Social Exclusion Literally Feel Cold?" *Psychological Science*, 19 (9), 838–42.

The Specificity Heuristic: Consumer Evaluation of Expert Recommendation

Mauricio Palmeira, Monash Unviersity, Australia
Gerri Spassova, Monash Unviersity, Australia

EXTENDED ABSTRACT

This research investigates how consumers evaluate expert advice in the presence of little diagnostic information. Consumers often seek recommendations from a range of sources, referred to as consumer agents (Solomon 1986; West 1996). Such advice represents an important component of the decision-making process and the offering (Beatty and Smith 1987; Solomon 1986; Urbany, Dickson, and Wilkie 1989).

THEORETICAL BACKGROUND

Prior research has identified several factors that influence perceptions of the diagnosticity of agent advice, such as expertise and past performance (Feick and Higie 1992; Gershoff, Broniarczyk, and West 2001), or perceived similarity of the source to the self (Brown and Reingen 1987; MacKie, Gastardo-Conaco, and Skelly 1992; Reingen and Kernan 1986). In many cases, however, consumers have little access to such information (Gershoff et al. 2001) and resort to heuristics in judging the soundness of the advice (Yaniv 2004). For example, they may judge the expertise of the agent based on his confidence (Karmarkar and Tormala 2010; Keren and Teigen 2001; Price and Stone 2004; Sniezek and Van Swol 2001) or the extremity of the claims (Gershoff et al. 2003; Goldberg and Hartwick 1990). In this research we propose another heuristic that consumers use when evaluating advice – the specificity heuristic.

Individuals who use the specificity heuristic infer that the expertise of an agent is positively correlated with the level of specificity of his recommendation. Specificity can take various forms, from excluding particular options from a recommended set, to specifying the manner in which a recommended option should be taken. It is not driven by the amount of detail provided, but rather by how restricted the recommended course of action is. The specificity heuristic cannot be explained through a negativity bias either – it is equally effective when it takes the form of including a specific behavior, as it is when taking the form of excluding a specific behavior.

We propose that people seeking advice employ the specificity heuristic because they overweigh the importance of differences among available choice options or courses of action. While expertise allows one to perceive both more similarities and more differences among options, to the person seeking advice the latter ability is more important. This is because individuals seeking advice typically lack the depth of knowledge necessary to discern between available options and actions and identify superior one(s) – to the novice eye, "they all look the same." The more specific the advice that an agent provides, then, the more knowledgeable he is judged to be.

While the use of the specificity heuristic may seem as a reasonable inferential process, specificity per se does not determine the accuracy or validity of a recommendation. A recommendation can be unnecessarily restrictive – for example, the Dukan diet prescribes that the daily dose of protein be taken with "no more than 1.5 tablespoons of oat bran." While this specification is most likely random, consumers may infer that taking their protein with more or less than the prescribed amount would affect the success of their diet. Thus agents aware of the specificity bias can deliberately include random specific restrictions, similar to the manner in which confidence, extremity, or over criticism can be misused to influence impression of expertise.

We report the results of six studies that document the use of the specificity heuristic and identify boundary conditions.

METHOD AND FINDINGS

Studies 1 and 2 demonstrate the use of the specificity heuristic when specificity takes the form of excluding particular options from a choice set. A travel agent advising a customer on places to visit in Brazil, receives more favorable evaluations ($M_{restr.}$ = 4.66 vs. $M_{control}$ = 3.88, $t(81)$ = 2.39, $p < .05$) and is perceived as more knowledgeable ($M_{restr.}$ = 4.51 vs. $M_{control}$ = 3.74, $t(81)$ = 2.32, $p < .05$) when she excludes specific destinations or modes of transport from her recommendation. Similarly, in Study 2, a waiter recommending wine receives higher evaluations ($M_{restr.}$ = 5.68 vs. $M_{control}$ = 4.94, $t(83)$ = 3.06, $p < .005$) and knowledge ratings ($M_{restr.}$ = 5.62 vs. $M_{control}$ = 5.02, $t(83)$ = 2.11, $p < .05$) when he excludes particular wines from a set of recommended wines.

Studies 3 and 4 document the use of the specificity heuristic in the context of medical decision making and demonstrate that it cannot be explained with a negativity bias. In study 3 a doctor who recommends that the patient *include* dairy food while taking the prescribed medication is evaluated just as favorably as one who recommends that the patient *exclude* dairy food from their diet ($F < 1$). In both scenarios, which represent specificity cases, the doctor is evaluated more positively, on average (M = 4.75) than a doctor who prescribes the same medication but states that dairy intake does not impact its effectiveness (M = 4.14, $t(150)$ = 2.40, $p < .05$). In study 4, a doctor who advises a patient to take three dietary supplements is evaluated more favorably ($M_{restriction}$ = 4.90 vs. $M_{control}$ = 4.38; $F(1, 125)$ = 4.42, $p < .05$) and is perceived as more knowledgeable ($M_{restriction}$ = 4.90 vs. $M_{control}$ = 4.33; $F(1, 125)$ = 4.58, $p < .05$) when he recommends that the supplements be taken in a particular order (versus a control condition, in which he states that the order makes no difference).

Studies 5 and 6 demonstrate that the use of the specificity heuristic is moderated by the availability of other diagnostic information. Individuals are less likely to rely on the heuristic when they are familiar with the recommended option (study 5) or when they have access to diagnostic information about the agent's expertise (study 6).

CONTRIBUTION

This research contributes to the literature on advice taking by expanding our understanding about factors which impact the perceived expertise of agents. The research contributes, more broadly, to the literature on information source evaluation, by documenting a heuristic that people use when they have access to little diagnostic information. Such situations represent a significant proportion of real-life decision making, especially given the increased use of online recommendations whose sources are often anonymous.

REFERENCES

Beatty, Sharon E. and Scott M. Smith (1987), "External Search Effort: An Investigation across Several Product Categories," *The Journal of Consumer Research*, 14 (1), 83-95.

Brown, Jacqueline Johnson and Peter H. Reingen (1987), "Social Ties and Word-of-Mouth Referral Behavior," *The Journal of Consumer Research*, 14 (3), 350-62.

Feick, Lawrence and Robin A. Higie (1992), "The Effects of Preference Heterogeneity and Source Characteristics on Ad Processing and Judgements About Endorsers," *Journal of Advertising*, 21 (2), 9-24.

Gershoff, Andrew D., Susan M. Broniarczyk, and Patricia M. West (2001), "Recommendation or Evaluation? Task Sensitivity in Information Source Selection," *The Journal of Consumer Research*, 28 (3), 418-38.

Goldberg, Marvin E. and Jon Hartwick (1990), "The Effects of Advertiser Reputation and Extremity of Advertising Claim on Advertising Effectiveness," *The Journal of Consumer Research*, 17 (2), 172-79.

Karmarkar, Uma R and Zakary L Tormala (2010), "Believe Me, I Have No Idea What I'm Talking About: The Effects of Source Certainty on Consumer Involvement and Persuasion," *The Journal of Consumer Research*, 36 (6), 1033-49.

Keren, Gideon and Karl Teigen (2001), "Why Is P = .90 Better Than P = .70? Preference for Definitive Predictions by Lay Consumers of Probability Judgments," *Psychonomic Bulletin & Review*, 8 (2), 191-202.

MacKie, Diane M., M. Cecilia Gastardo-Conaco, and John J. Skelly (1992), "Knowledge of the Advocated Position and the Processing of in-Group and out-Group Persuasive Messages," *Personality and Social Psychology Bulletin*, 18 (2), 145-51.

Price, Paul C. and Eric R. Stone (2004), "Intuitive Evaluation of Likelihood Judgment Producers: Evidence for a Confidence Heuristic," *Journal of Behavioral Decision Making*, 17 (1), 39-57.

Reingen, Peter H. and Jerome B. Kernan (1986), "Analysis of Referral Networks in Marketing: Methods and Illustration," *Journal of Marketing Research*, 23 (4), 370-78.

Sniezek, Janet A. and Lyn M. Van Swol (2001), "Trust, Confidence, and Expertise in a Judge-Advisor System," *Organizational Behavior and Human Decision Processes*, 84 (2), 288-307.

Solomon, Michael R. (1986), "The Missing Link: Surrogate Consumers in the Marketing Chain," *The Journal of Marketing*, 50 (4), 208-18.

Urbany, Joel E., Peter R. Dickson, and William L. Wilkie (1989), "Buyer Uncertainty and Information Search," *The Journal of Consumer Research*, 16 (2), 208-15.

West, Patricia M. (1996), "Predicting Preferences: An Examination of Agent Learning," *The Journal of Consumer Research*, 23 (1), 68-80.

Yaniv, Ilan (2004), "Receiving Other People's Advice: Influence and Benefit," *Organizational Behavior and Human Decision Processes*, 93 (1), 1-13.

Yeung, Catherine W. M. and Dilip Soman (2007), "The Duration Heuristic," *The Journal of Consumer Research*, 34 (3), 315-26.

Regulating Consumer Behavior by Refraining From Action

Anneleen Van Kerckhove, Ghent University, Belgium
Maggie Geuens, Ghent University, Belgium

EXTENDED ABSTRACT

In face of positive stimuli, people generally activate approach motivation, whereas avoidance motivation is activated in face of negative stimuli (Elliot and Thrash 2002). Embodied cognition research has shown that engaging in approach/avoidance-related motor actions also activates the corresponding motivational system, and as such has a profound influence on consumers' judgments and choices (Cacioppo et al. 1993; Friedman and Förster 2000). Performing approach motor actions increases both preference for vices over virtues (Van den Bergh, Schmitt, and Warlop 2011) and attractiveness ratings of generally positively evaluated consumer goods (Förster 2004). Likewise, engaging in avoidance motor actions leads to a devaluation of generally negatively evaluated stimuli (Förster 2004), and is suggested to increase insurance adoption (Van den Bergh et al. 2011).

We propose that refraining from engaging in approach/avoidance motor action may be embodied as well, as people often encounter situations that require them to override impulsive approach/avoidance tendencies (Kühn et al. 2009). For example, a person who passes a stall selling fresh lemonade may experience the urge to buy some, and may yet choose to walk by and avoid consuming the calories. Similarly, medicines often evoke an avoidance reaction because of their bad taste, yet consuming them is indispensable when ill (Hung and Labroo 2011).

Hence, people often benefit from overriding initial approach and avoidance impulses by refraining from executing an impulsive motor action. Therefore, we investigate whether experiencing the retraction of a reflexive approach/avoidance movement leads to decreased activation of approach/avoidance systems. The former should manifest in the devaluation of positively evaluated stimuli and a decreased preference for vices over virtues, as these consumption-related variables have been shown to be influenced by differential activation of approach motivation (Förster 2004; Van den Bergh et al. 2011). The latter should be apparent in a more positive evaluation of negative stimuli, and decreased likelihood to purchase insurance products.

As people's behavioral approach and behavioral inhibition systems may exhibit differential sensitivity (Carver and White 1994), the effect of refraining from an approach (avoidance) motor action should be moderated by BAS (BIS) sensitivity, such that only people with a highly sensitive BAS (BIS) likely experience the influence of exercising restraint in the face of positively (negatively) evaluated stimuli.

Study 1 investigates the consequences of refraining from action on the evaluation of positive and negative stimuli and addresses the moderating role of BIS/BAS sensitivity. 284 students were randomly assigned to one of five conditions; arm positions (flexion vs. extension) and the amount of exercised pressure (slight pressure vs. refraining from exercising pressure) varied between subjects, and a control condition provided no instructions on arm movements. Subjects were presented with consumer goods with either positive and negative valences.

First, the participants completed the Sensitivity to Punishment/Sensitivity to Reward Questionnaire (Torrubia et al. 2001) as a self-reported index of BIS/BAS functioning (Caseras, Avila, and Torrubia 2003). Next, while adopting the required hand positions, participants indicated how much they liked each consumer good on a 9-point scale by pressing the appropriate number on the keyboard. Most in-

terestingly, the results indicate that engaging in and refraining from avoidance motor actions had opposite effects on the evaluation of generally negatively evaluated consumer goods. While the former resulted in a devaluation, the latter increased the evaluation of negative goods (figure 1a). In addition, the more negative evaluation after performing an avoidance movement and the more positive evaluation after refraining from an avoidance movement reached its highest level among participants with a highly sensitive BIS (figure 1b). Evaluations of positive consumer goods improved when participants performed approach behavior and worsened when they refrained from performing approach behavior (figure 2a). This difference in liking reached its highest levels among participants with a highly sensitive BAS (figure 2b).

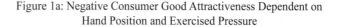

Figure 1a: Negative Consumer Good Attractiveness Dependent on Hand Position and Exercised Pressure

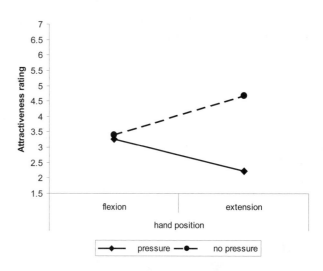

Figure 1b: Negative Consumer Good Attractiveness for People Engaging in Arm Extension, Dependent on Exercised Pressure and BIS Sensitivity

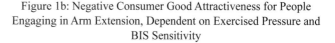

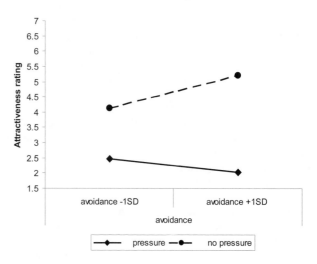

Figure 2a: Positive Consumer Good Attractiveness Dependent on Hand Position and Exercised Pressure

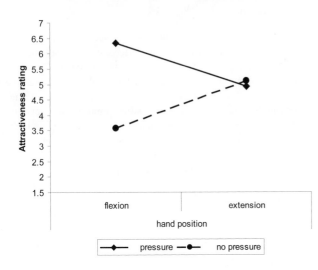

Figure 2b: Positive Consumer Good Attractiveness for People Engaging in Arm Flexion, Dependent on Exercised Pressure and BAS Sensitivity

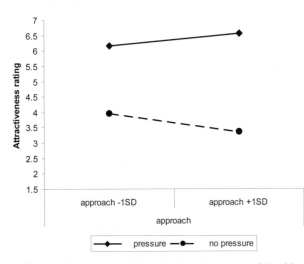

These findings suggest that refraining from approach/avoidance behavior likely decreases the activation of an approach/avoidance motivation. If so, refraining from approach/avoidance motor action should also lower preference for vices/decrease preference for insurance. This is tested in Studies 2 and 3 with data gathered from, respectively, 183 and 165 students, and a design similar to study 1. A 2 × 2 between-subjects design, plus a control, manipulating participants' right-hand position and the amount of exerted pressure. While keeping their right hand in place, participants chose between pairs of vice/virtue products (study 2),or indicated their willingness to pay for insurance (study 3) by checking an "include" or "do not include" box for several car insurance options at a certain price.

In both studies the interaction of hand position and exercised pressure appeared significant. Among participants engaged in arm flexion, those who exercised pressure were significantly more likely to select vice products than those instructed not to exercise pressure, but no significant difference emerged for those engaged in arm extension. Among participants engaged in arm extension, those who exercised pressure were significantly more inclined to obtain insurance options than those instructed to refrain from exercising pres-

sure, but no significant difference in insurance adoption emerged for those engaged in arm flexion. Studies 2 and 3 yield further confirmation for the influence of refraining from approach/avoidance motor actions in consumer choices that reflect the activation of the motivational approach/avoidance system.

Overall, this research adds to a body of consumer research on strategies to increase self-control (Hoch and Loewenstein 1991; Mukhopadhyay and Johar 2005). People are often shortsighted and easily tempted by hedonic "sins", such as overbuying, splurging on tasty but unhealthy food, and indulging in luxuries (Baumeister 2002; O'Guinn and Faber 1998). As these impulsive behaviors result from an impulsive approach/avoidance response, they often contradict with long-term goals (Baumeister 2002). From a consumer well-being perspective it is valuable to gain insight in elements underlying increased willpower.

REFERENCES

Baumeister, Roy F. (2002), "Yielding to Temptation: Self-Control Failure, Impulsive Purchasing, and Consumer Behavior," *Journal of Consumer Research*, 28 (March), 670–76.

Cacioppo, John T., Joseph R. Priester, and Gary G. Berntson (1993), "Rudimentary Determinants of Attitudes. II: Arm Flexion and Extension Have Differential Effects on Attitudes" *Journal of Personality and Social Psychology,* 65 (1), 5-17.

Carver, Charles S. and Teri L. White (1994), "Behavioral Inhibition, Behavioral Activation, and Affective Responses to Impending Reward and Punishment: The BIS/BAS Scales," *Journal of Personality and Social Psychology,* 67 (2), 319-33.

Caseras, Xavier, César Avila, and Rafael Torrubia (2003), "The Measurement of Individual Differences in Behavioural Inhibition and Behavioural Activation Systems: A Comparison of Personality Scales," *Personality and Individual Differences*, 34 (6), 999-1013.

Elliot, Andrew J. and Todd M. Thrash (2002), "Approach-Avoidance Motivation in Personality: Approach and Avoidance Temperaments and Goals," *Journal of Personality and Social Psychology,* 82 (5), 804-18.

Förster, Jens (2004), "How Body Feedback Influences Consumers' Evaluation of Products," *Journal of Consumer Psychology,* 14 (4), 416-26.

Friedman, Ronald S. and Jens Förster (2000), "The Effects of Approach and Avoidance Motor Actions on the Elements of Creative Insight," *Journal of Personality and Social Psychology,* 79 (4), 477-92.

Hoch, Steve and George Loewenstein (1991), "Time-Inconsistent Preferences and Consumer Self-Control," *Journal of Consumer Research*, 17 (March), 492–507.

Hung, Iris W. and Aparna A. Labroo (2011), "From Firm Muscles to Firm Willpower: Understanding the Role of Embodied Cognition in Self-Regulation," *Journal of Consumer Research,* 37, 1046-64.

Kühn, Simone, Wim Gevers, and Marcel Brass (2009), "The Neural Correlates of Intending Not to Do Something," *Journal of Neurophysiology*, 101 (4), 1913-20.

Mukhopadhyay, Anirban and Gita Venkataramani Johar (2005), "Where There Is a Will, Is There a Way? Effects of Lay Theories of Self-Control on Setting and Keeping Resolutions," *Journal of Consumer Research*, 31 (March), 779–86.

O'Guinn, Thomas C. and Ronald J. Faber (1989), "Compulsive Buying: A Phenomenological Exploration," *Journal of Consumer Research*, 16 (2), 147–57.

Torrubia, Rafael, César Avila, Javier Molto, and Xavier Caseras (2001), "The Sensitivity to Punishment and Sensitivity to Reward Questionnaire (SPSRQ) as a Measure of Gray's Anxiety and Impulsivity Dimensions," *Personality and Individual Differences,* 31 (6), 837-62.

Van den Bergh, Bram, Julien Schmitt, and Luk Warlop (2011), "Embodied Myopia," *Journal of Marketing Research*, 48(6), 1033-44.

When Lower is Better: The Impact of Activated Magnitude Interpretation Frames on Reactions to Alpha-numeric Brand Names

Anneleen Van Kerckhove, Ghent University, Belgium
Hendrik Slabbinck, Ghent University, Belgium
Mario Pandelaere, Ghent University, Belgium

EXTENDED ABSTRACT

Brand names play a vital role in the construction of a brand image that can affect the consumers' purchase decisions (Kohli and LaBahn, 1997). As brand names frequently comprise numerical components, resulting in alpha-numeric brand names, number liking should be an important consideration of marketers interested in creating effective brand names. Besides associations with specific, often culturally determined, meanings (e.g., the number 7 is lucky) (Battig and Spera 1962), structural characteristics of numbers (e.g., magnitude) may affect their liking. As people exhibit a general tendency to rely on magnitude information in their judgments, even when non-diagnostic (Silvera et al. 2002), this research investigates whether brand name conveyed magnitude information affects alpha-numeric brand preferences.

It is not clear how the magnitude of the numerical part is evaluated. Often when relying on magnitude information people endorse the idea that "bigger is better". People often favor bigger objects (Silvera et al. 2002); Larger assortments are evaluated better (Broniarczyk et al. 1998) and increasing the number of attributes accompanying a brand increases its favorability (Carpenter et al. 1994). Similarly, people also prefer larger numbers and this translates to object preference; colors are perceived as better when labeled with larger versus smaller numbers (Fias and Fischer 2005). Of particular relevance, Gunasti and Ross (2010) show that consumers' preference for alpha-numeric brands increases when the magnitude of the numerical part increases.

Situations in which small objects are highly valued are also prevalent. In today's society it is a challenge to build the smallest microchip, cellular phone or laptop computer. Body weight is typically evaluated more favorably when it is lower (Meier et al. 2008). In addition, lower numbers are better for many health indicators, golf scores, product grades, etc. As such, two opposing magnitude interpretation frames may exist and color people's judgments. Consumers may exhibit a preference for higher versus lower level alpha-numeric brand names dependent on whether they adopt a "bigger-is-better" versus a "smaller-is-better" frame. On which frame consumers rely may be influenced by external cues. Priming research has shown that people's interpretation of information depends on concepts that are currently active. In addition, priming cues may not only activate specific conceptual information, but also information processing procedures (Meyers-Levy 1989).

That both concepts and procedures can be primed suggests interpretation frames (i.e., procedures by which meaning is attached to concepts) can also be primed. As such, contextual information may affect alpha-numeric brand preferences dependent on whether it evokes a "larger is better" or "smaller is better" magnitude interpretation frame. Three studies yield evidence for this proposition.

Studies 1a (n = 122) and 1b (n = 122) rely on attribute specification to cue magnitude interpretation frames. Participants were presented with two printer (Study 1a) or refrigerator (Study 1b) brands and chose one of both. Each choice set varied along 2 dimensions (Tables 1a and 1b). The brands were described by units of expression representing a higher is better or smaller is better logic. In addition, brands were described by neutral terms (Brand A and Brand B) or by alpha-numeric brand names (CR-P-9 and CR-P-91 for printers; DMB-4 and DMB-96 for refrigerators).

Most importantly, when brands are described by a neutral label, changing the logic of the attribute units does not affect brand preferences. However, when brands are described by alpha-numeric brand names, changing the logic of the attribute units flips brand choices. When expression mode represents a "lower is better" ("higher is better") logic brands including a small (large) number are chosen more often compared to when expression mode represents a "higher is better" ("lower is better") logic (Tables 2a and 2b). These results demonstrate the importance of matching the number of an alpha-numeric brand name to the contextually evoked magnitude interpretation frame.

Study 2 (n=122) demonstrates that magnitude interpretation frames may also be evoked by brand slogans and that these frames may also guide absolute evaluations of alpha-numeric brand names including numbers that are generally judged as small (e.g., 1) or large (e.g., 100). In this study, participants inspected an advertisement of a new soda can 'Valens' (see Figure 1 for an example), which varied along two dimensions: the magnitude of the number included in the alpha-numeric brand name (No Number = 'Valens' vs. Small = 'Valens 1' vs. Large = 'Valens 100') and the slogan that was used to promote the product (Lower-is-better interpretation frame = 'Leave everyone behind' vs. Higher-is-better interpretation frame = 'Take it all'). Next, participants rated the attractiveness of the can they had been exposed to on a one-item 101-point scale.

Table 1a: Attribute Scores of the Printer Choice Options in Study 1a

Attribute Expression logic	Attributes	Brand A CR-P-9	Brand B CR-P-91
Higher is Better	Printing Speed # pages per minute	12	19
	Ink Price # pages for 1€	25	17
Lower is Better	Printing Speed # seconds to print 1 page	5	3
	Ink Price # cents to print 1 page	4	6

Table 1b: Attribute Scores of the Refrigerator Choice Options in Study 1b

Attribute Expression logic	Attributes	Brand A DMB-4	Brand B DMB-96
Higher is Better	CO_2 Emission # seconds to emit 100 gr	53	61
	Price Expenditure # minutes for 1€	353	286
Lower is Better	CO_2 Emission # grams per hour	114	98
	Price Expenditure # cents per hour	17	21

Figure 1:Example of a Fictitious Soda Can Used in Study 2

Figure 2: Mean Attractiveness Ratings of Brands Including No Number, aSmall or a Large Number Depending Evoked Magnitude Interpretation Frame

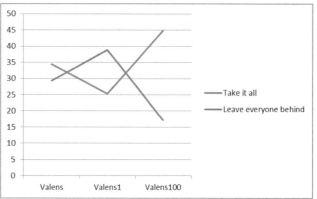

Most importantly, matching number magnitude onto the magnitude interpretation frame generated higher brand attractiveness ratings, whereas mismatching decreased the attractiveness ratings (see Figure 2).

This finding shows that not only relative preferences, but also absolute evaluations of brands may be influenced by activated magnitude interpretation frames. Studies 1 and 2 activated magnitude interpretation frames by changing brand-related information which is important, as these elements are under control of brand managers. Though, study 3 assesses whether contextual information, unrelated to the target brands, also affects alpha-numeric brand preferences, by using a different cue. Participants (n=103) rated the attractiveness of brand promotions, either announcing a price discount or a package premium (see Figure 3 for an example). Next, participants indicated their preferences for three pairs of printers. Each choice option was presented with a picture and an alpha-numeric brand name.

Figure 3: Example of Brand Promotions used in Study 3

The pictures and the left-right presentation of brand names were counterbalanced within pairs across participants. Priming different types of brand promotions significantly influenced participants' brand choices (see Table 3). Evaluating a price promotion (package

Table 2a: Choice Shares of the Printer Choice Options in Study 1a

	Neutral Brand Name		Alpha-Numeric Brand Name	
Attribute Expression logic	**Brand A**	**Brand B**	**CR-P-9**	**CR-P-91**
Higher is Better	76.3%	23.7%	61.3%	38.7%
Lower is Better	72.4%	27.6%	91.7%	8.3%

Table 2b: Choice Shares of the Refrigerator Choice Options in Study 1b

	Neutral Brand Name		Alpha-Numeric Brand Name	
Attribute Expression logic	**Brand A**	**Brand B**	**DMB-4**	**DMB-96**
Higher is Better	59.4%	40.6%	27.3%	72.7%
Lower is Better	45.7%	54.3%	72.7%	27.3%

premium) leads participants to prefer a printer comprising the lowest (highest) numerical portion.

The current paper contributes to research investigating how alpha-numeric brand names' numerical part affects their appeal. We focused on the impact of the conveyed magnitude. While Gunasti and Ross (2010) demonstrated alpha-numeric brands to benefit from including a higher number, our research demonstrates that this depends on the activated magnitude interpretation frame.

REFERENCES

Battig, William F. and Annette J. Spera (1962), "Rated association values of numbers from 0-100," *Journal of Verbal Learning and Verbal Behavior,* 1, 200-2.

Broniarczyk, Susan M., Wayne D. Hoyer, and Leigh McAlister (1998), "Consumers' perceptions of the assortment offered in a grocery category: The impact of item reduction," *Journal of Marketing Research,* 35, 166-176.

Carpenter, Gregory S., Glazer, Rashi, and Kent Nakamoto (1994), "meaningful brands from meaningless differentiation: The dependence on irrelevant attributes," *Journal of Marketing Research,* 31, 339-350.

Fias, Wim and Martin H. Fischer (2005), "Spatial representation of numbers," In *Handbook of Mathematical Cognition,* Campbell, Jamie I. D. eds., New York: Psychology Press, 43-54.

Gunasti, Kunter and William T. Ross (2010), "How and when alphanumeric brand names affect consumer preferences," *Journal of Marketing Research,* 47, 1177-92.

Kohli, Chiranjeev and Douglas W. LaBahn (1997), "Observations: Creating effective brand names: A study of the naming process," *Journal of Advertising Research,* 37, 67-75.

Meier, Brian P., Michael D. Robinson and Andrew J. Caven (2008), "Why a big mac is a good mac: Associations between affect and size," *Basic and Applied Social Psychology,* 30, 46-55.

Meyers-Levy, Joan (1989), "Priming effects on product judgments: A hemispheric interpretation," *Journal of Consumer Research,* 16, 76-86.

Silvera, David H., Robert A. Josephs and Brian Giesler (2002), "Bigger is better: The influence of physical size on aesthetic preference judgments," *Journal of Behavioral Decision Making,* 15, 189-202.

Table 3: Choice Shares of the Printer Choice Options in Study 3

Promotion Logic	3-WS-Epson	97-WS-Epson	Canon 3 KFS	Canon 7 KFS	Canon 73 LGD	Canon 77 LGD
Higher is Better	34.0%	66.0%	34.6%	65.4%	38.5%	61.5%
Lower is Better	64.0%	36.0%	66.0%	34.0%	66.7%	33.3%

In or Out of Focus? Subcategories Trigger In-group Heterogeneity and Out-group Homogeneity Effects in Product Assortments

Erica van Herpen, University of Wagening, The Netherlands
Anick Bosmans, Tilburg University, The Netherlands

EXTENDED ABSTRACT

Ever since organic, fair trade, and other 'special' products have entered the conventional supermarket channel, retailers face "a dilemma as to where such products should be shelved" (Dahm, 2005). The retailer can place, for example, a line of organic products separately from conventional products, and devote part of the total shelf space for a product category to these products. Retail managers often believe that this will attract new consumers by drawing their attention to products they might not otherwise have considered (Lazarus, 2010). However, it also entails the risk that consumers ignore these products when they browse the shelf. Alternatively, the retailer may integrate an organic product line into the mainstream shelf. This may increase the chance that consumers will notice the organic products when browsing through the regular products, but also decreases the visibility of the organic product line as a whole.

Whereas previous studies have focused on how assortment organization affects consumers' variety perception of the total assortment (Hoch, Bradlow, & Wansink, 1999; Mogilner, Rudnick, & Iyengar, 2008), little is known about if and how the use a specific subcategory affects the variety perceptions of the products placed inside and outside that subcategory. Whereas the perceived variety of the total assortment might increase as a function of the amount of subcategories available, as suggested by previous studies (Kahn & Wansink, 2004; Mogilner et al. 2008), the perceived variety of the products presented in a specific subcategory may not. We argue that variety perceptions can increase and decrease simultaneously, and that whether consumers perceive less or more variety within a subcategory crucially depends on their intrinsic interest in the subcategory. People have a natural tendency to selectively attend to categories that are important to them, which affects their similarity perceptions (Goldstone 1998). Ample psychological studies have provided evidence for in-group heterogeneity and out-group homogeneity effects in people perception (Boldry & Kasy 1999; Judd, Ryan & Park 1991), and we expect that similar effects are present in product perception. That is, when a subcategory is of interest to consumers, they will focus more on these products and attempt to differentiate between them, while at the same time giving less attention to the products in another subcategory. These other products are perceived as more similar to one another, because they all share a common product attribute. As a result, perceived variety is high for products presented in the category of interest (i.e., in-group heterogeneity) but low for products presented outside this category (i.e., out-group homogeneity).

In two studies we investigate the effects of assortment organization (i.e. product presented in subcategories vs. products presented in a mixed display) and consumers' intrinsic interest (as an externally induced shopping goal in experiment 1 and as a measured individual difference variable in experiment 2) on perceived variety of products presented in the subcategories. In both experiments, organic products (teas and wines, respectively) are presented either mixed with regular products or in a separate subcategory in a computer-based experiment. Choice is recorded, as well as which products are clicked on for closer examination. The proportion of organic product examined is investigated as a mediator to test whether assortment organization allows consumers to better focus on the products they are interested in, which should drive variety perceptions.

Results for both experiments show that assortment organization can indeed trigger in-group versus out-group effects, such that variety perceptions for one subcategory increase and variety perceptions for another subcategory decrease simultaneously. Hence, we show that the presence of subcategories does not uniformly increase variety perceptions, but that it can even decrease variety perceptions for a specific subcategory. As expected, these effects are moderated by consumers' intrinsic interest in the subcategory: consumers pay attention to the subcategory of interest, leading to an increase in perceived variety of the subcategory of interest (i.e., an in-group heterogeneity effect), but ignore the subcategory that is not of interest (i.e., an out-group homogeneity effect). Moderated mediation analyses suggest that these effects are indeed mediated by the attention that consumers allocate to the different subcategories. In addition, our effects carry-over to consumers' product choice.

Our results extend prior research in several ways. In particular, whereas previous studies have shown that the use of subcategories can increase variety perceptions of the total assortment (Hoch et al. 1999; Kahn and Wansink 2008; Mogilner et al. 2008; Morales et al. 2005), we show that subcategories can affect variety perceptions of products presented inside and outside the subcategory of interest differently. These effects cannot be explained by processes proposed in prior research. For instance, whereas prior research has indicated that larger assortments are processed differently from smaller assortments (Iyengar & Lepper 2000; Broniarczyk et al. 1998), this alone cannot explain why two subcategories of equal size receive different variety ratings.

Our results have important implications for retailers who want to promote sustainable (e.g., organic or fair trade) or otherwise 'special' products (e.g., private labels). Whereas the use of a separate display might increase the salience of the attribute (e.g., sustainability), it may not necessarily increase the perception of variety and choice for these products. In fact, when many of the store's customers are not interested in the subcategory, devoting a separate section to these products may decrease sales levels. Contrary to current practices (Dahm 2005), when consumers' initial interest in the product category is low, retailers may be better off to integrate these products in the existing assortment, instead of presenting them in a separate product category.

REFERENCES

Boldry, J. G. & Kashy, D. A. (1999). Intergroup perception in naturally occurring groups of differential status: A social relations perspective. *Journal of Personality and Social Psychology, 77,* 1200-1212.

Broniarczyk, S. M., Hoyer, W. D. & McAlister, L. (1998). Consumers' perceptions of the assortment offered in a grocery category: The impact of item reduction. *Journal of Marketing Research, 35,* 166-176.

Dahm, L. (2005). Where to put the healthy stuff: opinions differ on optimal shelf placement for natural and organic products. *Private Label Buyer*, November 1, 2005, http://www.allbusiness.com/retail-trade/clothing-clothing-accessories-stores-stores/846009-1.html

Goldstone, R. L. (1998). Perceptual Learning. *Annual Review of Psychology, 49,* 585-612.

Hoch, S. J., Bradlow, E. T., & Wansink, B. (1999). The variety of an assortment. *Marketing Science, 18,* 527-546.

Iyengar, S. S. & Lepper, M. R. (2000). When choice is demotivating: Can one desire too much of a good thing? *Journal of Personality and Social Psychology, 79,* 995-1006.

Judd, C. M., Ryan, C. S. & Park, B. (1991). Accuracy in the judgment of in-group and out-group variability. *Journal of Personality and Social Psychology, 61,* 366-379.

Kahn, B. E. & Wansink, B. (2004). The influence of assortment structure on perceived variety and consumption quantities. *Journal of Consumer Research, 30,* 519-533.

Lazarus, E. (2010). Even in hard times, organics is hot. *Canadian Grocer,* November 4, 2010, http://www.canadiangrocer.com/categories/natural-selection-249

Mogilner, C., Rudnick, T. & Iyengar, S. S. (2008). The mere categorization effect: How the presence of categories increases choosers' perceptions of assortment variety and outcome satisfaction. *Journal of Consumer Research, 35,* 202-215.

Morales, A., Kahn, B. E., McAlister, L. & Broniarczyk, S. M. (2005). Perceptions of assortment variety: The effects of congruency between consumers' internal and retailers' external organization. *Journal of Retailing, 81,* 159-169.

Tajfel, H., & Wilkes, A. L. (1963). Classification and quantitative judgment. *British Journal of Psychology, 54,* 101-114.

Together or Alone: How The Social Setting of Experiences Impacts Preferences For Improving Versus Declining Sequences.

Rajesh Bhargave, University of Texas at San Antonio, USA
Nicole Votolato Montgomery, College of William and Mary, USA

EXTENDED ABSTRACT

People experience consumption episodes either in the presence of others or individually. For instance, a consumer may tour a museum as part of a group or only by himself. To date, little is understood about the impact of social context on how an experience unfolds over time or the subsequent effects on experience evaluations. We find that people's preference for improving vs. declining trends depends on whether the experience is consumed together or alone. This effect stems from differences in how consumers process and incorporate early versus later parts of the experience in evaluations.

Past research has demonstrated both direct and indirect social influence during experiences. Consumers communicate their reactions to others verbally (Raghunathan & Korfman 2006) or through subtle signals, such as facial expressions (Ramanathan & McGill 2007). We argue that social influence operates on another subtle dimension: consumers' processing style. Research on culture and self-construal has found that people embedded in social relations process information holistically, whereas those less embedded in these relations process analytically (Nisbett et al. 2001; Monga and John 2007). We predict that these differences will also emerge when comparing social and isolated hedonic experiences.

Processing style has been shown to moderate how people integrate sequences. In a person perception task, Forgas (2011) showed that participants who processed holistically (analytically) exhibited judgments that were more impacted by early (later) presented personality traits, consistent with a primacy effect (recency effect). Under holistic processing the initial information was weighted more in summary judgments and also provided an overarching frame to which later information was assimilated. Conversely, analytical processing suppressed such top-down perception, facilitating recency effects.

Extending Forgas' findings to consumption episodes, we identify a preference reversal that emerges due to differences in the processing style that the social setting promotes. We hypothesize that when people experience episodes alone, they prefer improving (vs. declining) sequences of events (i.e., those beginning with the worst event and ending with the best event), consistent with past research on hedonic experiences (Kahneman et al., 1993; Redelmeier & Kahneman 1996). However, when an experience occurs in the presence of others, the improving trend preference will be attenuated or even reversed, because such social experiences promote holistic processing, As such, we expect evaluations of later parts of the sequence to assimilate to earlier parts of the sequence, leveling the slope of the experienced trend. Moreover, when processing holistically, greater weighting of early events can produce higher evaluations for experiences that begin with the best event (declining sequences) versus the worst event (improving sequence).

Study 1 was a 2 (analytical vs. holistic processing prime) x 2 (improving vs. declining vacation experience trend) between-subjects design. Participants were either asked to find embedded images in a presented scene (analytical prime), or write about what they saw in the scene (holistic prime) (Monga and John 2008). Subsequently, they read about a vacation with events presented in either improving or declining order of pre-tested liking. Finally, participants rated their willingness to pay for the vacation. Consistent with past research (Kahneman et al. 1993), we found a main effect of trend,

showing a preference for the improving sequence (F(1,89) = 3.95, p =.05). Supporting our hypothesis, we also found a processing style X trend interaction (F(1,89) = 4.09, p <.05). Under analytical processing, participants preferred the improving sequence (Mimproving = $1642.86 vs. Mdeclining = $766.67, t(43) = 2.10, p < .05), but there was no trend preference under holistic processing (Mimproving = $722.68 vs. Mdeclining= $715.38, t(46) < 1).

Study 2 utilized the same design, but differed in two important ways. First, we used an actual experience (not simulated) with trend (improving vs. declining) manipulated using a sequence of 15 pre-tested art images. Second, we manipulated processing style using the presence or absence of others during the experience (vs. the processing style prime in study 1). Participants in the isolated condition wrote about themselves prior to viewing the images. Participants in the social condition were asked to introduce themselves to another person and were told that others in the lab would experience the same episode, prior to viewing the images. A pre-test confirmed that participants in the isolated versus the social condition exhibited a less holistic style of thinking (M = 4.45 vs. 4.86, F(1,74) = 5.20, p < .05) (Choi et al. 2007). After viewing the images, participants indicated their willingness to pay for the experience using a scale with different payment levels. Supporting our hypothesis, there was a significant social setting X trend interaction (F(1, 178) = 6.69, p = .01). Participants in the isolated condition exhibited a preference for the improving sequence (Mimproving = 2.95 vs. Mdeclining= 2.04, t(90) = 2.35, p = .02), whereas participants in the social condition directionally preferred the declining sequence (Mimproving = 2.39 vs. Mdeclining= 2.93, t(88) = 1.33, p = .18). Participants also rated each art image. Analyzing the slope of their ratings over the sequence's duration, we found a main effect of manipulated trend condition (F(1, 178) = 201, p < .001) and a social setting X trend interaction (F(1, 178) = 8.65, p <.01). Slopes were steeper in the isolated condition compared to the social condition (see figure 1). These results are consistent with our explanation that people undergoing the social experience anchor on earlier events in the sequence when reacting to later events.

Three unreported studies examine other operationalizations of the social vs. isolated distinction. Combined, this research advances our knowledge of the role of social context on consumption experiences, offering several contributions. Foremost, we demonstrate that social context influences hedonic experiences even without direct social interaction, and we show how these effects emerge over the course of the episode. Second, we reveal how processing style differences emerge due to variations in the social context of experiences, whereas past research on processing style focused on individual differences and cultural factors. Finally, we find an important boundary condition to the common preference for improving trends. These findings have implications for how marketers present experiences under different social situations.

REFERENCES

Choi, I., Koo, M., and Choi, J.A. (2007). Individual Differences in Analytic versus Holistic Thinking. *Personality and Social Psychology Bulletin, 33*, 691-705.

Forgas, J. (2011). Can negative affect eliminate the power of first impressions? Affective influences on primacy and recency effects in impression formation. *Journal of Experiemental Social Psychology, 47,* 425-429.

Kahneman, D., Fredrickson, B. L., Schreiber, C. A. and Redelmeier, D. A. When more pain is preferred to less: adding a better end. *Psychological Science, 4* (1993), 401-405.

Monga, A. & John, D. R. (2007). Cultural differences in brand extension evaluation: The influence of analytic versus holistic thinking. *Journal of Consumer Research, 33,* 529-536.

_____(2008). When does negative brand publicity hurt? The moderating influence of analytical versus holistic thinking. *Journal of Consumer Psychology, 18,* 320-332.

Nisbett, R. E., Peng, K., Choi, I., & Norenzayan, I. (2001). Culture and Systems of Thought: Holistic versus Analytic Cognition. *Psychological Review, 108,* 291–310.

Raghunathan, R. & Korfman, K. (2006). Is happiness shared doubled and sadness shared halved? Social influence on enjoyment of hedonic experiences. *Journal of Consumer Research, 33,* 386-394.

Ramanathan, S. & McGill, A. (2007). Consuming with others: Social influences on moment-to-moment and retrospective evaluations of an experience. *Journal of Consumer Research, 34,* 506-524.

Redelmeier, D. A. and Kahneman, D. Patients' memories of painful medical treatments: real-time and retro-spective evaluations of two minimally invasive procedures. *Pain, 66* (1996), 3-8.

Figure 1: Moment-to-moment evaluations of art images

Mean moment-to-moment evaluations of art images in the second study described in the extended abstract. The left hand panel depicts evaluations for these images in the isolated experience conditions, and the right hand panel depicts these evaluations for the social experience conditions. Ratings for each image were on a 7-point scale of enjoyment, as reflected by the vertical axis in each panel. The sequence consisted of 15 images. The dashed lines indicate mean evaluation for each image in the declining (blue) and improving (red) trend conditions separately. The darker lines depict the trendline for each trend condition.

On Higher Ground: Moral Thinking Leads to Abstract Processing

Eugene Chan, University of Toronto, Canada
Eunice Kim Cho, University of Toronto, Canada

EXTENDED ABSTRACT

We often describe people who do the "right" thing as being "on a moral high ground", or we say that they are "taking the high road". There are also other similar sayings that refer to people behaving morally as "high-minded" or "upstanding" individuals. All of these images suggest a metaphorical connection between the concept of morality and the spatial orientation of vertical height. Specifically, they suggest that people who behave morally hold a position that is higher above ground than those who behave less morally. But are there cognitive consequences of being so high above ground – and thus, so *distant* to the world "down below" – that they would process their world differently?

Recent research on metaphorical thinking adopts an embodied cognition view, suggesting that people use their concrete physical sensations to describe abstract psychological experiences (Bargh 2006; Boroditsky and Ramscar 2002). For example, metaphors involving vertical height often have an embodied basis. In contexts of social power, powerful people are said to be "up high", such that individuals with social authority attend to high spatial locations quicker than low ones (Moeller, Robinson and Zabelina 2008). In many religions, "God is most high", and people perceive others as being more religious when their pictures are displayed at the top of a page rather than the bottom (Chasteen, Burdzy, and Pratt 2009). And people often give "thumbs up" to communicate positive feedback, stemming from the perception that anything "up" is good but "down" is bad (Meier and Robinson 2004). These findings suggest that moral metaphors referring to vertical height or the physical sensation of being high above ground may also have a similar embodied basis.

We posit that a consequence of behaving morally is that the vertical height increases the *distance* to the world down below, affecting how people high above ground would cognitively process their world. According to construal level theory, as distance (vs. closeness) increases, so does abstract processing (Trope and Liberman 2003). Consider spectators sitting in the highest rows of a sports stadium, and hence are vertically high from where the main action is located. They describe their experiences as "squinting to see ant-sized players", and only see the broader aspects of the game, not its finer details. Building on these links between metaphorical thinking, embodied cognition, and construal level theory, we thus hypothesize and find in four experiments that people who do the right thing process their world abstractly.

Experiment 1 demonstrated the main effect that moral thinking leads to abstract processing. To prime moral or less moral thinking, we had undergraduate students write about an instance in their lives in which they did the "right" or "wrong" thing, respectively. They then completed the Behavioral Identification Form (BIF; Vallacher and Wegner 1989). As predicted, participants who recalled behaving morally selected more abstract descriptions on the BIF than those who recalled behaving less morally. We also ruled out mood as an alternative explanation for our findings.

Experiments 2 and 3 aimed to explore how moral thinking may influence specific cognitive consequences of abstract thinking. In Experiment 2, we reason that people who process abstractly pay little attention to details, and so they should be worse at analytical reasoning than those who process concretely (Friedman and Förster 2011). To prime moral or less moral thinking, we had undergraduates write stories about themselves using either positively- or negative-ly-valenced words, such as kind or greedy, respectively. They then completed the Cognitive Reflection Test (CRT; Frederick 2005). As expected, participants in the moral prime scored lower on the CRT than those in the less moral prime. Mood had no effect. Meanwhile, in Experiment 3, we hypothesized that people who do the right thing are more creative than those who do the wrong thing (Förster, Epstude, and Özelsel 2009). Undergraduates received the same prime as Experiment 1, in addition to a control condition. They then generated as many creative ways of using a brick as possible. Planned contrasts revealed that participants in the moral prime generated more ways to use a brick creatively than those in the control, who generated more than those in the less moral prime.

Finally, Experiment 4 examined how moral thinking may influence consumer preferences. Mechanical Turk participants received the same moral or less prime as Experiment 1. They then saw an ad for the "Simply Orange" brand of orange juice that emphasized either the brand's abstract, future benefits or its concrete, immediate benefits. Participants who recalled behaving morally had more favourable attitudes toward Simply Orange when the ad was in an abstract than a concrete frame. Conversely, participants who recalled behaving less morally had more favourable attitudes toward the ad in a concrete than an abstract frame.

Across four experiments, this research demonstrates that metaphors like "on a high ground" and "taking the high road" are linked to embodied cognitions. More specifically, this link can cause people doing the right thing to subsequently process their world abstractly. Our findings may also offer another explanation for other consequences of moral thinking, such as licensing. Furthermore, our present findings encourage future research to understand morality not in isolation, but in terms of physically-grounded concepts.

Table 1
Experiment 2: Correct responses on the CRT.

	Ball/Bat	**Widgets**	**Lily Pads**	**Total**
Moral Thinking ($N = 100$)	42.7%	39.2%	36.8%	.81
Less Moral Thinking ($N = 112$)	58.3%	60.8%	63.2%	1.14
p-level	.241	.059	.008	.027

REFERENCES

Bargh, John A. (2006), "What Have We Been Priming All These Years? On the Development, Mechanisms, and Ecology of Nonconscious Social Behavior", *European Journal of Social Psychology*, 36 (March/April), 147-68.

Boroditsky, Lera and Michael Ramscar (2002), "The Roles of Body and Mind in Abstract

Thought", *Psychological Science*, 13 (March), 185-9.

Chasteen, Alison L., Donna C. Burdzy, and Jay Pratt (2010), "Thinking of God Moves Attention", *Neuropsychologia*, 48 (January), 627-30.

Förster, Jens, Kai Epstude, and Amina Özelsel (2009), "Why Love Has Wings and Sex Has Not: How Reminders of Love and Sex Influence Creative and Analytic Thinking", Personality and Social Psychology Bulletin, 18 (August), 1479-91.

Frederick, Shane (2005), "Cognitive Reflection and Decision Making", *Journal of Economic Perspectives*, 19 (Fall), 25-42.

Friedman, Ronald S., and Jens Förster (2001), "The Effects of Promotion and Prevention Cues on Creativity," *Journal of Personality and Social Psychology*, 81 (6), 1001-1013.

Lakoff, George and Mark Johnson (1980), *Metaphors We Live By*, Chicago: University of Chicago Press.

Meier, Brian P. and Michael D. Robinson (2004), "Why the Sunny Side is Up : Associations

between Affect and Vertical Position", *Psychological Science*, 15 (April), 243-7.

Moeller, Sara K., Michael D. Robinson, and Darya L. Zabelina (2008), "Personality Dominance and Preference Use of the Vertical Dimension of Space: Evidence from Spatial Attention Paradigms", *Psychological Science*, 19 (April), 355-61.

Nelson, Leif D. and Joseph P. Simmons (2009), "On Southbound Ease and Northbound Fees: Literal Consequences of the Metaphoric Link between Vertical Position and Cardinal Direction", *Journal of Marketing Research*, 46 (December), 715-24.

Trope, Yaacov and Nora Liberman (2010), "Construal-Level Theory of Psychological Distance", *Psychological Review*, 117 (April), 440-63.

Vallacher, Robin R. and Daniel M. Wegner (1987), "What Do People Think They're Doing?

Action Identification and Human Behavior", *Psychological Review*, 94 (January), 3-15.

The Role of Gender Congruity for Anthropomorphized Product Perception

Ellis van den Hende, University of Amsterdam, The Netherlands
Ruth Mugge, Delft University of Technology, The Netherlands

EXTENDED ABSTRACT

Anthropomorphism refers to the tendency to attribute human-like characteristics, intentions, and behavior to non-human artifacts, such as products (Epley, Waytz, and Cacioppo 2007). When consumers anthropomorphize products, this will enhance their evaluation and reduce their willingness to replace these products (Aggarwal and McGill 2007; Chandler and Schwarz 2010).

Prior research has used product-schema congruity to explain consumers' evaluation of anthropomorphized products (Aggarwal and McGill 2007). They suggested that only if there is congruity between the activated human schema and the product's features (e.g., two same-sized bottles with a primed twin schema), consumers are able to humanize the product, and anthropomorphism will increase product evaluation. Such product-schema congruity is thus considered to be crucial for anthropomorphism to be effective. However, for many products the opportunities to add schema-congruent product features are limited (Delbaere et al. 2011). Accordingly, the present research seeks to broaden our understanding of anthropomorphism by investigating when and why priming a human schema will encourage consumers to perceive the product as human, thereby positively affecting product evaluations, even when there is no product-schema congruity. Extending the anthropomorphism literature on twins and salespersons that are generally self-incongruent, this research uses self-congruity theory (Sirgy 1982) to explain the effects of humanizing a product through self-congruent gender primes (i.e., describing the product as male/female) on product evaluations.

This research focuses on gender because gender is a central part of consumers' self-concept (Cross and Markus 1993), As a consequence, consumers prefer products that are associated with their own gender and avoid those associated with the other (White and Dahl 2006, 2007; Worth, Smith, and Mackie 1992). We propose that because of the importance of gender to the self-concept, consumers can readily see the human analogy suggested by the marketer if the human gender schema that is primed, is congruent to their own gender, regardless of the presence/absence of schema-congruent product features. Furthermore, the human gender schema that is primed contributes to the product's symbolic image and will affect consumers' product evaluations. We thus hypothesize a gender-schema congruity effect: when primed with a human gender schema that is congruent (vs. incongruent) to consumers' own gender, consumers show more preferential evaluations (H1). In contrast, when a human gender schema is primed that is incongruent to a person's own gender, (s)he may not readily see the analogy. Then, schema-congruent features of the product will help consumers to anthropomorphize the product successfully. Consequently, we hypothesize that product-schema congruity moderates the effect of gender anthropomorphism on product evaluations (H2). Finally, we hypothesize that the extent to which consumers perceive the product as human mediates the effects of gender-schema congruity and product-schema congruity on consumers' product evaluations (H3).

Two experimental studies tested the hypotheses. Study 1 tested our basic premise that consumers' evaluation of anthropomorphized products are more positive when the human gender schema that is primed is congruent to their own gender. The study used a 2(human gender schema: male vs. female schema) × 2(participants' gender: men vs. women) between-subjects design. To prime the human gender schemas, we created product descriptions of a bottle perfume with either a male or female focus (e.g., "This little guy/girl is the decidedly young scent [...] He/She has a family of 30ml, 50ml, and 100ml bottles"). This resulted in conditions of either low or high gender-schema congruity, depending on the gender of the participant. Participants read the product description, and subsequently, completed a multi-item product evaluation measure. The results revealed only a significant human gender schema by participant's gender interaction. Comparing contrasts showed that male participants evaluated the product more positively when a male schema was primed, that is congruent to their own gender, than when an incongruent, female schema was primed. This gender-schema congruity effect on product evaluation was also identified for female participants. Specifically, female participants evaluated the product more positively when a congruent, female schema (vs. incongruent, male schema) was primed, supporting hypothesis 1.

In study 2, we extended these findings by investigating the gender-schema congruity effect alongside the effect of product-schema congruity. Furthermore, Study 2 provided insights in the underlying process of the gender-schema congruity effect by investigating perceived anthropomorphism as a mediator. The study used a 2(human gender schema) × 2(product features: black/blue vs. yellow/purple) × 2(product replicate: camera, car) mixed design and used male subjects. Product replicate was a within-subjects variable. Different colors were pretested to select products with masculine (black/blue color) and feminine (yellow/purple color) features (Grossman and Wisenblit 1999), resulting in products with features that were either congruent or incongruent to the activated human gender schema. Participants read the product description, in which a human gender schema was primed, together with a product picture, and subsequently, completed multi-item product evaluation and perceived anthropomorphism measures. Results revealed a main effect for human gender schema, providing additional support for the hypothesized gender-schema congruity effect (H1). Furthermore, a significant two-way interaction was found. Comparing contrasts showed that when primed with a human gender schema that is congruent to the participant's gender (i.e., male schema), the presence of product-schema (in)congruent features in the product did not affect product evaluations or perceived anthropomorphism. However, when primed with a human gender schema that is incongruent (i.e., female schema), participants evaluated the product more positively and were more likely to perceive it as human when the product is endowed with a feature that is congruent with that human gender schema, than when it is endowed with a feature that is incongruent. Finally, regression analyses and Sobel tests showed that perceived anthropomorphism mediated the effects of gender-schema congruity and product-schema congruity on product evaluations. Together, these results support our hypotheses.

Our research contributes to the literature by demonstrating that product-schema congruity can only partly explain consumer response towards anthropomorphized products. Specifically, we demonstrate that products do not necessarily need to be endowed with schema-congruent features for product anthropomorphism to be effective. If a human gender schema is primed that is congruent to consumers' gender, gender-schema congruity will positively influence product evaluations, even when there is no product-schema congruity.

REFERENCES

Aaker, Jennifer (1997), "Dimensions of Brand Personality," *Journal of Marketing Research*, 34 (August), 347-56.

--- (1999), "The Malleable Self: The Role of Self-Expression in Persuasion," *Journal of Marketing Research*, 36 (February), 45-57.

Aggarwal, Pankaj and Ann L. McGill (2007), "Is That Car Smiling at Me? Schema Congruity as a Basis for Evaluating Anthropomorphized Products," *Journal of Consumer Research*, 34 (December), 468-79.

--- (2012), "When Brands Seem Human, Do Humans Act Like Brands? Automatic Behavioral Priming Effects of Brand Anthropomorphism," *Journal of Consumer Research*, 39 (August), http://www.jstor.org/stable/10.1086/662614.

Alreck, Pamela L., Robert B. Settle, and Michael A. Belch (1982), "Who Responds to "Gendered" Ads, and How?," *Journal of Advertising Research*, 22 (2), 25-32.

Baron, Reuben M. and David A. Kenny (1986), "The Moderator-Mediator Variable Distinction in Social Psychological Research: Conceptual, Strategic, and Statistical Considerations," *Journal of Personality and Social Psychology*, 51 (6), 1173-82.

Burgoon, J. K., J. A. Bonito, B. Bengtsson, C. Cederberg, M. Lundeberg, and L. Allspach (2000), "Interactivity in Human-Computer Interaction: A Study of Credibility, Understanding, and Influence," *Computers in Human Behavior*, 16 (553-574).

Chandler, Jesse and Norbert Schwarz (2010), "Use Does Not Wear Ragged the Fabric of Friendship: Thinking of Objects as Alive Makes People Less Willing to Replace Them," *Journal of Consumer Psychology*, 20 (2), 138-45.

Cowart, Kelly O., Gavin L. Fox, and Andrew E. Wilson (2008), "A Structural Look at Consumer Innovativeness and Self-Congruence in New Product Purchases," *Psychology & Marketing*, 25 (12), 1111-30.

Cross, Susan E. and Hazel R. Markus (1993), "Gender in Thought, Belief, and Action: A Cognitive Approach," in *Psychology of Gender*, ed. Anne E. Beall and Robert J. Sternberg, New York: Guilford, 55-98.

Cunningham, Sheila J. and C. Neil Macrae (2011), "The Colour of Gender Stereotyping," *British Journal of Psychology*, 102 (3), 598-614.

Delbaere, Marjorie, Edward E. McQuarrie, and Barbara J. Phillips (2011), "Personification in Advertising," *Journal of Advertising*, 40 (1), 121-30.

Epley, Nicholas, Scott Akalis, Adam Waytz, and John T. Cacioppo (2008a), "Creating Social Connection through Inferential Reproduction: Loneliness and Perceived Agency in Gadgets, Gods and Greyhounds," *Psychological Science*, 19 (2), 114-20.

Epley, Nicholas, Adam Waytz, Scott Akalis, and John T. Cacioppo (2008b), "When We Need a Human: Motivational Determinants of Anthropomorphism," *Social Cognition*, 26 (2), 143-55.

Epley, Nicholas, Adam Waytz, and John T. Cacioppo (2007), "On Seeing Human: A Three-Factor Theory of Anthropomorphism," *Psychological Review*, 114 (4), 864-86.

Ericksen, Mary K. and M. Joseph Sirgy (1992), "Employed Females' Clothing Preference, Self-Image Congruence, and Career Anchorage," *Journal of Applied Social Psychology*, 22 (5), 408-22.

Freimuth, Marylin J. and Gail A. Hornstein (1982), "A Critical Examination of the Concept of Gender," *Sex Roles*, 8 (5), 515-32.

Fugate, Douglas L. and Joanna Phillips (2010), "Product Gender Perceptions and Antecedents of Product Gender Congruence," *Journal of Consumer Marketing*, 27 (3), 251-61.

Gainer, Brenda (1993), "An Empirical Investigation of the Role of Involvement with a Gendered Product," *Psychology & Marketing*, 10 (4), 265-83.

Gould, Stephen J. and Barbara B. Stern (1989), "Gender Schema and Fashion Consciousness," *Psychology & Marketing*, 6 (2), 129-45.

Grohmann, Bianca (2009), "Gender Dimensions of Brand Personality," *Journal of Marketing Research*, 46 (February), 105-19.

Grossman, Randi Priluck and Joseph Z. Wisenblit (1999), "What We Know About Consumers' Color Choices," *Journal of Marketing Practice: Applied Marketing Science*, 5 (3), 78-88.

Guthrie, Stewart (1993), *Faces in the Clouds: A New Theory of Religion*, New York: Oxford.

Janiszewski, Chris, Tim Silk, and Alan D. J. Cooke (2003), "Different Scales for Different Frames: The Role of Subjective Scales and Experience in Explaining Attribute-Framing Effects," *Journal of Consumer Research*, 30 (December), 311-25.

Keaveney, Susan M., Andreas Herrman, Rene Befurt, and Jan R. Landwehr (2012), "The Eyes Have It: How a Car's Face Influences Consumer Categorization and Evaluation of Product Line Extensions," *Psychology & Marketing*, 29 (1), 36-51.

Kim, Sara and Ann L. McGill (2011), "Gaming with Mr. Slot or Gaming the Slot Machine? Power, Anthropomorphism, and Risk Perception," *Journal of Consumer Research*, 38 (June), 94-107.

Landwehr, Jan R., Ann L. McGill, and Andreas Herrman (2011), "It's Got the Look: The Effect of Friendly and Aggressive "Facial" Expressions on Product Liking and Sales," *Journal of Marketing*, 75 (May), 132-46.

Levy, Sidney J. (1959), "Symbols for Sale," *Harvard Business Review*, 37 (July-August), 117-24.

Morris, George and Edward W. Cundiff (1971), "Acceptance by Males of Feminine Products," *Journal of Marketing Research*, 8 (August), 372-74.

O'Cass, Aron and Debra Grace (2008), "Understanding the Role of Retail Store Service in Light of Self-Image-Store-Image Congruence," *Psychology & Marketing*, 26 (6), 521-37.

Orth, Ulrich R. and Denisa Holancova (2004), "Men's and Women's Responses to Sex Role Portrayals in Advertisement," *International Journal of Research in Marketing*, 21 (1), 77-88.

Palan, Kay M. (2001), "Gender Identity in Consumer Behavior Research: A Literature Review and Research Agenda," *Academy of Marketing Science Review*, 10, 1-31.

Sirgy, M. Joseph (1982), "Self-Concept in Consumer Behavior: A Critical Review," *Journal of Consumer Research*, 9 (December), 287-300.

--- (1985), "Using Self-Congruity and Ideal Congruity to Predict Purchase Motivation," *Journal of Business Research*, 13 (June), 195-206.

Sobel, Michael E. (1982), "Asymptotic Confidence Intervals for Indirect Effects in Structural Equation Models," in *Sociological Methodology*, ed. Samuel Leinhardt, Washington, DC: American Sociology Association, 290-312.

Swann, William J., Alan Stein-Seroussi, and R. Brian Giesler (1992), "Why People Self-Verify," *Journal of Personality and Social Psychology*, 62 (3), 392-401.

Waytz, Adam, Carey K. Morewedge, Nicholas Epley, George Monteleone, Jia-Hong Gao, and John T. Cacioppo (2010), "Making Sense by Making Sentient: Effectance Motivation Increases Anthropomorphism," *Journal of Personality and Social Psychology*, 99 (3), 410-35.

White, Katherine and Darren W. Dahl (2006), "To Be or Not Be? The Influence of Dissociative Reference Groups on Consumer Preferences," *Journal of Consumer Psychology*, 16 (4), 404-14.

--- (2007), "Are All out-Groups Created Equal? Consumer Identity and Dissociative Influence," *Journal of Consumer Research*, 34 (December), 525-36.

Windhager, Sonja, Fred L. Bookstein, Karl Grammer, Elisabeth Oberzaucher, Hasen Said, Dennis E. Slice, Truls Thorstensen, and Katrin Schaefer (2012), ""Cars Have Their Own Faces": Cross-Cultural Ratings of Car Shapes in Biological (Stereotypical) Terms," *Evolution and Human Behavior*, forthcoming.

Worth, Leila T., Jeanne Smith, and Diane M. Mackie (1992), "Gender Schematicity and Preference for Gender-Typed Products," *Psychology & Marketing*, 9 (1), 17-30.

Zhang, Shi and Sanjay Sood (2002), ""Deep" and "Surface" Cues: Brand Extension Evaluations by Children and Adults," *Journal of Consumer Research*, 29 (June), 129-41.

Disclosure in Word-of-Mouth Marketing: The Role of Prior Agent Experience

Lisa J. Abendroth, University of St. Thomas, USA

EXTENDED ABSTRACT

Recent research on marketer-incented word-of-mouth (WOM) finds that disclosing an agent-brand relationship can make the recommendation more effective (Carl 2008; Tuk, Verlegh, Smidts, and Wigboldus 2009). Abendroth and Heyman (2012) further found that disclosure increased product attitudes and feeling informed, which mediated the effect of disclosure on purchase consideration. The present research looks deeper into why this positive effect occurs. Further, as the growing prevalence of incented WOM increases the likelihood that a WOM recipient has experience as an agent, this research also examines how past experience affects perceptions of the technique and its effectiveness.

Abendroth and Heyman (2012) argue that voluntary disclosure, which goes against relationship norms (Tuk et al. 2009), makes the agent seem more credible, in turn allowing the recipient to feel more informed. If this is true, then adding a disclaimer that disclosure is federally mandated (per the Federal Trade Commission) should eliminate the effect. An alternative explanation is that recipients feel a closer connection to the brand when the agent discloses a relationship with the brand. This should occur regardless of any legal disclaimer and is consistent with feeling more informed. An additional consideration is whether the message recipient has been an agent in another campaign, in which case their reaction to disclosure may be different. They know how receiving incentives affected the nature of their own WOM, and in turn may respond to other incented recommendations less positively.

First, a survey (N=102) was conducted to understand how current undergraduates perceive incented WOM. After explaining the difference between incented and organic WOM, 65% of respondents thought marketers use incented WOM "quite often" or "very often" on college campuses. If asked to be an agent, only 56% indicated they were likely to disclose receiving incentives, despite being informed of the FTC disclosure guidelines. Although concerning, these results are consistent with Ahuja, Michels, Walker, and Weissbuch (2007). When asked who is at fault if the relationship is not disclosed, 26% indicated the company is more at fault and 39% indicated the recommender is more at fault. Finally, looking at the impact of disclosure, 43% thought it would help and 29% thought it would hurt product attitudes, while 28% thought it would help and 24% thought it would hurt attitudes toward the recommender. The remainder expected no impact from disclosure. While 28% of those surveyed had experience as a WOM agent, this did not significantly alter their responses.

Second, an experiment (N=148) was conducted that manipulated WOM (disclosure, disclosure plus legal disclaimer, organic/no disclosure) between-subjects and measured agent status (agent, non-agent). The manipulation was embedded into a scenario about a friend recommending a winter jacket. Participants responded to several 7-point semantic differential scales that measured purchase consideration (6 items, e.g. I would consider purchasing this brand), product attitude (3 items, e.g. good/bad), agent credibility (5 items, e.g. credible/not credible), feeling informed (3 items, e.g. I feel knowledgeable) and brand connection (3 items, e.g. I can relate to this brand). All cronbach's alphas were greater than 0.88. Lastly, they were asked whether "a company had previously given (them) products, cash, or other incentives to talk about their products with other people," to which 26% answered yes.

An interaction between agent status and WOM type was found for purchase consideration (F(2,142) = 4.3, p<.05), product attitude (F(2,142) = 3.6, p<.05), and feeling informed (F(2,142) = 3.7, p<.05), along with a marginal interaction for brand connection (F(2,142) = 2.6, p<.08). Meanwhile, agent credibility only showed a main effect of WOM type (F(2,142) = 7.9, p<.01) with greater credibility in the organic condition versus both the disclosure (F(1,142) = 11.2, p<.01) and disclosure plus disclaimer (F(1,142) = 11.9, p<.01) conditions. Interestingly, adding a legal disclaimer to the disclosure had no effect (F<1) on the agent's credibility.

Next we look more closely at the effect of WOM type by agent status, beginning with non-agents. Compared to organic WOM, when the agent discloses their relationship to the brand along with a legal disclaimer, purchase consideration increased (F(1,142) = 4.1, p<.05) as did feeling informed (F(1,142) = 4.9, p<.05) and feeling connected to the brand (F(1,142) = 4.0, p<.05), while attitude toward the product remained unchanged (F=0). Comparing the two disclosure conditions, adding a disclaimer made the message recipient feel more informed (F(1,142) = 4.5, p<.05) and feel marginally more connected to the brand (F(1,142) = 2.7, p<.10), but had no effect on product attitudes (F<1.1) or purchase intentions (F<1.3).

In contrast, agents had the opposite response to disclosure. Compared to organic WOM, disclosing a brand relationship decreased purchase consideration (F(1,142) = 7.3, p<.01), product attitudes (F(1,142) = 12.7, p<.01) and brand connections (F(1,142) = 4.6, p<.05), along with a marginal decrease in feeling informed (F(1,142) = 3.3, p<.07). Adding a legal disclaimer led to mean results between disclosure and no disclosure, but lacked the power necessary to find significance for all variables.

This research makes several contributions to the WOM literature. First, the survey indicates that undergraduates are aware of the prevalence of incented WOM on college campuses with over a

Table 1: Means for Experiment

	Non-Agent			Agent		
	Organic	Disclose + Disclaimer	Disclose	Organic	Disclose + Disclaimer	Disclose
Purchase Consideration	4.3	4.9	4.6	5.2	4.7	3.9
Attitude toward Product	5.7	5.7	5.4	6.0	5.2	4.5
Feeling Informed	4.5	5.0	4.6	5.4	4.7	4.6
Brand Connection	3.9	4.6	4.1	4.8	4.4	3.6
Agent Credibility	5.4	4.8	4.8	5.6	4.6	4.5

quarter of respondents in both the survey and the experiment having acted as an incented WOM agent. Second, despite knowledge of FTC disclosure guidelines, the issue of non-disclosure of the agent-brand relationship remains, and both agent and brand carry blame for this non-disclosure. Third and more interesting, most undergraduates cannot accurately predict the impact disclosure has on WOM effectiveness. Fourth, while agent status had no effect on WOM perceptions, experimental results suggest that it does impact WOM effectiveness; organic WOW was more effective for past agents, while knowledge of an agent-brand relationship was more effective for non-agents. Fifth, feeling connected to the brand is introduced as a new factor that is impacted by disclosure. Results surrounding the addition of a legal disclaimer as the reason for disclosure were less conclusive.

REFERENCES

Abendroth, L.J. and J.E. Heyman. 2012. Honesty is the best policy: The effects of disclosure in word-of-mouth marketing. *Journal of Marketing Communications,* http://www.tandfonline.com/doi/abs/10.1080/13527266.2011.631567

Ahuja, R.D., T. A. Michels, M.M. Walker, and M. Weissbuch. 2007. Teen perceptions of disclosure in buzz marketing. *Journal of Consumer Marketing* 24: 151-159.

Carl, W.J. 2008. The role of disclosure in organized word-of-mouth marketing programs. *Journal of Marketing Communications* 14: 225-241.

Tuk, M.A., P.W.J. Verlegh, A. Smidts, and D.H.J. Wigboldus. 2009. Sales and sincerity: The role of relational framing in word-of-mouth marketing. *Journal of Consumer Psychology* 19: 38-47.

Exploring the Mythology of Viral Videos and the Epic Fail: Why Video Communications Capture the Market's Imagination

Dante M. Pirouz, Ivey Business School, Western University, Canada
Allison Johnson, Ivey Business School, Western University, Canada
Raymond Pirouz, Ivey Business School, Western University, Canada
Matthew Thomson, Ivey Business School, Western University, Canada

EXTENDED ABSTRACT

There are few rewards more exhilarating to marketers than the exponential increase in reach, awareness, and word-of-mouth from communications gone 'viral'. Marketers strive for the viral success of communications across a number of channels, but recent developments in online video (i.e., YouTube's emergence in 2005) offer a means of tracking audience responses in a manner not previously possible. Video also affords a tremendous opportunity for people to engage others with emotion and information. We focus on online video and examine content and audience response features that predict the video going viral.

It might be assumed that any interesting content that generates a strong emotional response is enough to achieve viral status. Indeed, research (Berger 2011; Berger and Milkman 2011) has identified emotional arousal intensity as the motivation for news content sharing, with higher arousal emotions more strongly linked to sharing (Berger 2011). Berger and Milkman (2011) also find that the emotional responses of positivity, awe, anger, sadness, and anxiety all predict sharing.

Logically preceding this strong emotional response, we predict that video content features will also explain viral success. Based on the Incongruity-Resolution theory of humor (Mulder and Nijholt 2002), videos with *elements of incongruity* should be more successful. This incongruity might take the form of juxtaposition (i.e., unexpected combinations) or exaggeration (i.e., hyperbole of basic facts). Though the implication of humor might seem to suggest that such videos would be perceived positively, we also investigate the role of negative reactions, such as sadness and anger because Benign Violation theory (McGraw and Warren 2010) suggests that negative reactions may also lend explanatory power.

We compiled a dataset of over six-hundred English-language videos hosted by YouTube across 15 categories (e.g., Auto, Comedy, Education). Four research assistants blind to the hypotheses coded the videos. One was exclusively tasked with collecting data on the outcomes while the remaining were responsible for coding all the videos according to a scheme we provided. The inter-rater reliability (PRL) scores for each coded variable exceed .80.

Predictors: Many videos contain highly exaggerated content, such as those that make hyperbolic claims or show extravagant or over-the-top behavior. We code this variable (*exaggeration*) on a three point scale ('none', 'modest exaggeration', to 'extensive exaggeration'). Second, we code to what extent videos put together two or more elements whose joining seemed incongruous (*juxtaposition*) also on a three point scale ('none', 'moderately incongruous' to 'highly incongruous'). The correlation between the two predictors was weak ($r = .10, p < .01$).

Mediators: Each content coder also included ratings on a 5-point scale ('none/very weak' to 'very strong') of how a 'typical viewer' would respond emotionally to the video in terms of 6 basic emotions: joy, love, sadness, fear, anger, and surprise (Shaver et al. 1987).

Outcomes: All five outcomes measures are based on statistics provided by YouTube: Under each video, viewers are able to press one of two buttons: '*like*' and '*dislike*', a likely indicator of positive and negative attitudes; the number of '*comments*' made by viewers and the number of times a viewer added the video to a personal page ('*favorites*');

and '*video views*', the number of times a video has been seen overall. The five variables are positively correlated ($r = .51-.77, p < .01$).

We conducted our analysis using Structural Equation Modeling and a series of covariates (e.g. dummies to reflect the category from which we harvested the video, length of video, interactive component, presence of a call to action). Our first model (without mediators) suggests that Exaggeration predicts Comments ($\gamma = .08, p < .05$), Dislikes ($\gamma = .15, p < .01$), Favorites ($\gamma = .07, p < .05$) and Likes ($\gamma = .10, p < .01$) while Juxtaposition predicts Comments ($\gamma = .08, p < .05$), Favorites ($\gamma = .08, p < .05$) and Video Views ($\gamma = .08, p < .05$).

Model 2, including only significant emotional mediators (all were initially included but only significant paths are retained), shows that Exaggeration influences Anger ($\gamma = .16, p < .01$), which in turn impacts both the number of Dislikes ($\gamma = .07, p < .05$) and Favorites ($\gamma = -.07, p < .05$). Also, Juxtaposition predicts Surprise ($\gamma = .45, p < .01$), which in turn leads to increased Comments ($\gamma = .11, p < .01$) and Video Views ($\gamma = .10, p < .01$). With the mediators included, the direct path between Exaggeration and each of Comments ($\gamma = .09, p < .05$), Dislikes ($\gamma = .14, p < .01$), Favorites ($\gamma = .08, p < .05$) and Likes ($\gamma = .10, p < .01$) remain significant while the impact of Juxtaposition on Comments ($\gamma = .03, p > .10$) and Video Views ($\gamma = .04, p > .10$) disappears. We also assessed each emotional mediator one at a time in order to guard against the possibility that two or more mediators were accounting for the same variance in the outcomes, but this revealed that none of Joy, Love, Sadness or Fear individually predicted any of the outcomes regardless of the method of analysis. Based on our data, only Anger and Surprise offered explanatory power.

The findings of this research show that indeed there are two strategic ways that video content goes viral: Exaggerated content has a direct positive effect of the number of favorites, likes, and dislikes but at the cost of inspiring anger. Juxtaposed content has a direct positive effect on the number of comments and video views, an effect that is fully mediated by surprise. These findings open the door to additional exploration and theorizing as well, such as what is the role of specific video features (e.g. use of humor versus disgust versus sexual imagery) in driving virality by virtue of differentially impacting juxtaposition, exaggeration, anger and surprise?

REFERENCES

Berger, Jonah (2011), "Arousal Increases Social Transmission of Information", *Psychological Science*, 22 (7), 891-893.

Berger, Jonah and Katherine L. Milkman (2011), "What Makes Online Content Viral?", *Journal of Marketing Research*, forthcoming.

McGraw, A. Peter and Caleb Warren (2010), "Benign Violations: Making Immoral Behavior Funny", *Psychological Science*, 21 (8), 1141-1149.

Mulder, M. P. and A. Nijholt (2002), "Humour Research: State of the Art" *Internal Report at http://doc.utwente.nl/63066/1/0000009e.pdf*

Shaver, Phillip, Judith Schwartz, Donald Kirson and Cary O'Connon (1987), "Emotion Knowledge: Further Exploration of a Prototype Approach," *Journal of Personality and Social Psychology*, Vol. 52, No. 6, 1061-1086.

When Excuses Backfire: The Ironic Effect of Excuses on Consumer Perceptions

Elise Chandon Ince, Virginia Tech, USA
Nora Moran, Virginia Tech, USA
Rajesh Bagchi, Virginia Tech, USA

EXTENDED ABSTRACT

He who excuses himself, accuses himself.
Gabriel Meurier

In any service setting, failures are likely to happen, and fallout is often significant. Consequently there is considerable literature assessing how providers can recover from failures. We study the role of one noncontroversial strategy: we investigate whether providing an excuse (vs. not) can have a detrimental effect on consumer service perceptions, specifically looking at minor versus major failures.

Service providers believe that after any failure, proper recovery is essential for maintaining customer satisfaction (Hart, Heskett, and Sasser 2000). Likewise, after failures, consumers appreciate communications from firms (Tax, Brown, and Chandrashekaran 1998), and personnel feel compelled to provide information to alleviate guilt, manage impressions, and distance themselves from failure (Bies and Shapiro 1987; Snyder and Higgins 1988; Schlenker 1982; Schlenker and Weigold 1992).Although extensive, past literature has not addressed how failure severity affects inferences—in particular, how consumers evaluate minor failures, which are more common and require prompt responses from personnel.

First, we argue that expectations regarding responses from firms depend on failure severity (H1). While those experiencing a major failure might expect a reason for the transgression, those experiencing a minor failure may not —consumers may not wonder about the reason for the minor failure unless it is made explicit. However, once an excuse is offered, recipients elaborate and focus more on the failure, even when an excuse is considered valid. Specifically, we predict that customers' critical evaluations of a minor failure increase when an excuse is provided (H2), thus decreasing customer satisfaction (H3). We then identify a boundary condition, level of suspicion, and show that individuals primed with suspicion of negative ulterior motives are less satisfied after a minor failure when given no excuse (H4), as priming suspicion prompts individuals to seek out causes for failures (Fein, 1996; Fein, Hilton, and Miller, 1990).

We test these predictions in three studies, using different failure contexts and excuses. In study 1, we used a 2 failure (major/minor) x 2 excuse (yes/no) between subjects design. The scenario indicated that participants were getting their car's battery replaced. We manipulated failure by varying the actual price for the replacement from its prior estimate ($120): $125 for minor, and $170 for major failure. In the excuse condition, the mechanic offered an apology and excuse ("We did not have the right kind of battery for your car and had to order it and that is why your price is higher"), whereas in the no-excuse condition, the mechanic only apologized for the price increase. In addition to main effects, we obtained the predicted significant failure x excuse interaction. In the minor failure condition, providing an excuse elicited lower satisfaction ratings relative to when an excuse was not provided. No difference emerged in the major failure condition.

In study 2, we investigated the process in detail. We used a 2 failure (major/minor) x 2 excuse (yes/no) between subjects design. The scenario was identical to that of study 1, except we manipulated delivery delay. At pickup, either the mechanic showed up after a 5 minute-delay (minor failure) or a 30 minute-delay (major failure). In the excuse condition, the mechanic apologized for the delay and offered an excuse ("We did not have the right kind of battery for your car"), but only offered the apology in the no-excuse condition. In addition to main effects, a significant failure by excuse interaction also emerged. When failure was minor, satisfaction was lower with an excuse (vs. no-excuse). In the major failure condition, no differences emerged as a function of excuse presence. A marginal two-way failure x excuse interaction also emerged for critical evaluations; in the minor failure condition, participants were more critical when an excuse was offered relative to when it was not. No differences emerged in the major failure condition. Furthermore, critical evaluations mediated the effect of excuses on satisfaction.

In study 3, we manipulated suspicion by asking participants to either read an article on the potential for unethical behavior among employees (suspicion condition) or a neutral article (control condition) before completing the mechanic scenario from study one. We only considered the minor failure condition. As expected, the suspicion x excuse interaction was significant for satisfaction. In the control group, participants were less satisfied when an excuse was offered relative to when it was not. However, when primed with suspicion, participants were more satisfied when an excuse was offered relative to when it was not.

While prior research suggests that valid excuses lead to positive evaluations (Hill, Baer, and Morgan 2000), we find that provider-relevant valid excuses can be problematic (we conducted several pretests to ensure that excuses were considered valid). Our findings also suggest different processes for evaluating minor versus major failures. By studying service failures from the consumer perspective, our findings provide a fuller understanding of consumers' immediate reactions to service failures, and enriches both services and excuse-making literature in new ways.

While past research has focused extensively on what wrongdoers can say and do to recover from failures, our results suggest that doing nothing can be advantageous. Thus, there appears to be a significant asymmetry between what both researchers and firms think increases satisfaction and what actually occurs, particularly after minor failures. At a time when the ethos of service is to go above and beyond the call of duty to keep consumers happy, we suggest that omission of information can do more to improve satisfaction and firm perceptions. Our findings thus are consistent with a quote attributed to Gabriel Meurier that "He who excuses himself, accuses himself."

REFERENCES

Bies, Robert J., and Debra L. Shapiro (1987), "Interactional Fairness Judgments: The Influence of Causal Accounts," *Social Justice Research*, 1 (2), 199–218.

Fein, Steven, James L. Hilton, and Dale T. Miller (1990), "Suspicion of Ulterior Motivation and the Correspondence Bias," *Journal of Personality and Social Psychology*, 58 (May), 753–64.

Fein, Steven (1996), "Effects of Suspicion on Attributional Thinking and the Correspondence Bias," *Journal of Personality and Social Psychology*, 70, 1164–1184.

Hart, Christopher W., James L. Heskett, and W. Earl Sasser Jr. (1990), "The Profitable Art of Service Recovery," *Harvard Business Review*, 68 (July/August), 148–56.

Hill, Donna J., Robert B. Baer, and Amy J. Morgan (2000), "Excuses: Use 'Em If You Got 'Em," *Advances in Consumer Research,* 27, 87-91.

Schlenker, Barry R., and Mark R. Leary (1982), "Social Anxiety and Self-Presentation: A Conceptualization and Model," *Psychological Bulletin*, 92, 641-669

Schlenker, Barry R., and Michael F. Weigold (1992), "Interpersonal Processes Involving Impression Regulation and Management," *Annual Review of Psychology*, 43, 133-168.

Snyder, C. R., and Raymond L. Higgins (1988), "Excuses: Their Effective Role in the Negotiation of Reality," *Psychological Bulletin*, 104, 23-35.

Tax, Stephen S., Stephen W. Brown, and Murali Chandrashekaran (1998), "Customer Evaluations of Service Complaint Experiences: Implications for Relationship Marketing," *Journal of Marketing*, 62 (April), 60-76.

When Losing Hurts Less:
How Spending Time versus Money Affects Outcome Happiness

Subimal Chatterjee, Binghamton University, USA

Chien-Wei (Wilson) Lin, Binghamton University, USA

EXTENDED ABSTRACT

When consumers engage in an activity, they are likely to invest both time and money in that activity to ensure a desirable outcome. However, research recognizes that thinking about spending time or spending money on an activity evokes distinctly different consumer mindsets (Liu and Aaker 2007). Thinking about spending time evokes real and imagined experiences that are invariably tagged with deep feelings and emotions (Schwarz and Clore 1996), whereas thinking about spending money triggers less emotional and more concrete thoughts about the rewards that consumers can expect in return (Vohs, Mead, and Goode 2006). The current paper builds upon these existing theories to suggest that spending time on an activity may reduce the sting of an ultimate loss, relative to spending a commensurate amount of money on the same activity.

When individuals spend money (relative to time) on an activity, they are more likely to regard the spent money as an investment that should give them a tangible benefit or a return (Soman 2001; Okada and Hoch 2004; Vohs, Mead, and Goode 2006). A subsequent loss, then, is likely to trigger thoughts that the money has gone to waste. However, when individuals spend time on the same activity, the time spent strengthens their personal connections to the activity, and focuses them more on the activity experience (Mogilner and Aaker 2009; Schwarz and Clore 1996; Van Boven and Gilovich 2003). A subsequent loss, then, may not sting as much, as the thoughts that are triggered may focus more on how the time spent helped the individuals to develop (gain) their potential (Ryan and Deci 2000).

Study 1 tests the above proposition in a 2 (spending time/spending money) by 2 (win/lose) between subjects scenario-based study. One hundred and twenty undergraduates (52 females) imagine that they are preparing in different ways to win a tennis tournament. For the time/money manipulations, we calibrated the exchange rate between the two currencies in a pretest ($n = 30$) and found that the tradeoff rate to be \$12.50 per hour (see Okada and Hoch, 2004, for similar results). Accordingly, half of the participants imagined that they had spent 40 hours (practicing with friends) and \$25 (buying equipment) preparing for the tournament, whereas the other half of the participants imagined that they had spent \$500 and 2 hours, doing the same. The win/lose manipulation had half of the sample imagine that they ultimately won the tournament, and the other half imagine that they lost.

We measured outcome happiness on a 7-point scale (unhappy/happy scale; see Van Boven and Gilovich 2003), and the extent to which our participants felt pressured for time (Andrews and Smith 1996) and pressured for money (Mittal 1994) in their lives. In all analyses, we treated the latter two variables as statistical covariates. Figure 1 shows the means of outcome happiness across all four experimental conditions. As expected, in the loss condition, participants were less unhappy, if they had spent more time, relative to spending more money ($F(1, 55) = 4.9$, $p < .05$). The time/money manipulation did not affect outcome happiness in the win condition ($F(1, 57) = 1.45$, $p > .10$).

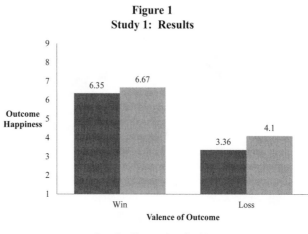

Figure 1
Study 1: Results

In Study 2, we made two changes relative to Study 1. First, we use a different scenario (an investments competition); the change in context was promoted by a pretest ($n = 23$), which showed that while participants are more predisposed towards spending time to prepare for a tennis tournament, they are more inclined to spend money to prepare to win an investments competition. Second, Study 2 tests for a potential mediator of the time/money effect on outcome happiness. Specifically, we argue that spending time on an activity makes a person focus more on the experience of personal striving and social connection (Mogilner and Aaker 2009; Mogilner 2010). This experience allows individual to get closer to attaining his/her potential, thereby enhancing that person's feelings of psychological well-being (Ryan and Deci 2000), and buffering the sting of the ultimate failure. Spending money on an activity, however, makes a person focus on external rewards that fail to satisfy needs for self-actualization (Van Boven and Gilovich 2003). An ultimate loss, then, only highlights that the reward was not obtained and the money spent was wasted.

One hundred and forty-eight undergraduates (61 females) participated in Study 2, and were randomly assigned to one of four conditions in a 2 (time/money: spending \$500, spending 40 hours) by 2 (outcome: winning, losing) between subjects experiment. In addition to outcome happiness, and the tendencies to feel pressured for time and money (see Study 1), we measured psychological well-being by tapping into the three main elements of that construct: autonomy, competence, and relatedness (Deci et al. 2001; La Guardia et al. 2000, $\alpha = .81$). The Appendix reports the scales, as adapted to the study context.

Figure 2 shows the means of outcome happiness across all four experimental conditions. As expected, in the loss condition, participants were less unhappy, if they had spent more time, relative to spending more money ($F(1, 70) = 3.69$, $p = .06$). The time/money manipulation did not affect outcome happiness in the win condition ($F(1, 70) < 1$). Preacher and Hayes's (2008) SAS macro with 5,000 bootstrapped samples revealed indirect-only mediation (Zhao, Lynch, and Chen 2010), in which psychological well-being mediates the effect of spending on outcome happiness (95% confidence interval between 0.03, and 1.18; Figure 3).

Advances in Consumer Research
Volume 40, ©2012

Figure 2
Study 2: Results

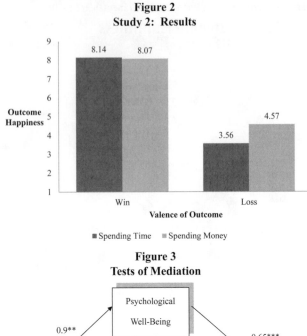

Figure 3
Tests of Mediation

Note: * = significant at the .1 level;
** = significant at the .05 level;
*** = significant at the .01 level;
NS = not significant

Our research shows that spending time (as opposed to a commensurate amount of money) on an activity reduces the sting of an ultimate loss as consumers may think of the time spent as enhancing their psychological well-being in their goal pursuit. Future research may wish to investigate how such enhanced psychological well-being could engage consumers to continue pursue their goals when substantial effort has already been invested (Fishbach, Dhar, and Zhang 2006) and/or prevent them from disengaging from goal pursuit after encountering some initial failure (Fishbach and Dhar 2005). A second direction would be to investigate, how enhanced feelings of well-being could potentially elevate the desirability of the ultimate goal (Zhang et al. 2011) and assist in goal pursuit.

APPENDIX
MEASURE FOR PSYCHOLOGICAL WELL-BEING*

1. I feel that I have become a better investor (*competence*)
2. I feel that I have been able to learn new investing skills (*competence*)
3. I do not regret, for one moment, the amount of time (money) that I put into preparing for the competition (*autonomy*)
4. I do not care what other people think about the amount of time (money) that I put into the competition (*autonomy*)
5. I feel more connected to the bank (*relatedness*)
6. I feel more close to the other interns/professionals in the bank (*relatedness*)

* All measures on a 1 = *Not agree at all* to 9 = *Very strongly agree* scale

REFERENCE

Andrew, Jonlee and Daniel C. Smith (1996), "In Search of Marketing Imagination: Factors Affecting The Creativity of Marketing Programs for Mature Products," *Journal of Marketing Research*, 33 (May), 174-87.

Deci, Edward L., Richard M. Ryan, Marylène Gagné, Dean R. Leone, Julian Usunov, and Boyanka P. Kornazheva (2001), "Need Satisfaction, Motivation, and Well-being in the Work Organizations of a Former Eastern Bloc Country," *Personality and Social Psychology Bulletin, 27 (February)*, 930-42.

Fishbach, Ayelet and Ravi Dhar (2005), "Goals as Excuses or Guides: The Liberating Effect of Perceived Goal Progress on Choice," *Journal of Consumer Research*, 32 (December), 370–77.

Fishbach, Ayelet, Ravi Dhar, and Ying Zhang (2006), "Subgoals as Substitutes or Complements: The Role of Goal Accessibility," *Journal of Personality and Social Psychology*, 91 (August), 232–42.

La Guardia, Jennifer G., Richard M. Ryan, Charles E. Couchman, and Edward L. Deci (2000), "Within-Person Variation in Security of Attachment: A Self-Determination Theory Perspective on Attachment, Need fulfillment, and Well-being," *Journal of Personality and Social Psychology, 79 (September)*, 367-84.

Liu, Wendy and Jennifer L. Aaker (2008), "The Happiness of Giving: The Time-Ask Effect," *Journal of Consumer Research*, 35 (October), 543-57.

Mittal, Banwari (1999), "An Integrated Framework for Relating Diverse Consumer Characteristics to Supermarket Coupon Redemption," *Journal of Marketing Research*, 31 (November), 533-44.

Mogilner, Cassie (2010), "The Pursuit of Happiness: Time, Money, and Social Connection," *Psychological Science*, 21 (September), 1348-54.

_____ and Jennifer Aaker (2009), "The "Time vs. Money Effect": Shifting Product Attitudes Through Personal Connection," *Journal of Consumer Research,* 36 (August), 277-91.

Okada, Erica Mina and Stephen J. Hoch (2004), "Spending Time versus Spending Money," *Journal of Consumer Research*, 31(September), 313-23.

Preacher, Kristopher J. and Andrew F. Hayes (2008), "Asymptotic and Resampling Strategies for Assessing and Comparing Indirect Effects in Multiple Mediator Models," *Behavior Research Methods*, 40 (August), 879–91.

Ryan, Richard M. and Edward L. Deci (2000), "Self-Determination Theory and the Facilitation of Intrinsic Motivation, Social Development, and Well-Being," *American Psychologist*, 55 (January), 68-78.

Schwarz, Norbert and Gerald Clore (1996), "Feelings and Phenomenal Experiences," in *Social Psychology: Handbook of Basic Principles*, ed. Tory Higgins and Arie Kruglanski, New York: Guilford, 433–65.

Soman, Dilip (2001), The Mental Accounting of Sunk Time Costs: Why Time is Not Like Money," *Journal of Behavioral Decision Making*, 14 (July), 169-85.

Van Boven, Leaf and Thomas Gilovich (2003), "To Do or To Have? That Is the Question," *Journal of Personality and Social Psychology*, 85 (December), 1193–1202.

Vohs, Kathleen D., Nicole L. Mead, and Miranda R. Goode (2006), "The Psychological Consequences of Money," *Science*, 314 (November), 1154-56.

Zhang, Ying, Xu Jing, Jiang Zixi, and Szu-Chi Huang (2011), "Been There, Done That: The Impact of Effort Investment on Goal Value and Consumer Motivation," *Journal of Consumer Research*, 38 (June), 78–93.

Zhao, Xinshu, John G. Lynch Jr., and Qimei Chen (2010), "Reconsidering Baron and Kenny: Myths and Truths about Mediation Analysis," *Journal of Consumer Research*, 37 (August), 197–206.

Matching The Words to the Features in Persuasive Advertising:
A Construal-Matching Hypothesis

Karthik Easwar, Ohio State University, USA
Lifeng Yang, University of Mississippi, USA

EXTENDED ABSTRACT

Recently, a number of journal articles have examined the effects of construal on consumer behavior. Construal level has been shown to influence voting, self-control, saving, social influence, conservation and perceptions of complementarity or promotion value (Cheema & Patrick, 2008; Ülkümen & Cheema, 2011). Our research finds evidence that matching the construal level of advertising copy to that of the focal product can improve product attitudes by facilitating processing fluency, a finding that has significant implications for attitude and advertising research.

Construal level theory (CLT), has found evidence that, as abstraction increases, psychological distance increases and as psychological distance increases processing of abstract events is facilitated (Liberman and Trope 1998). This research has shown that desirability is more abstract than feasibility, idealistic values (respect, honesty, etc.) are more abstract than pragmatic and functional concerns (uses, extrinsic benefits) and hedonic products (music, chocolate) are also more abstract than utilitarian products (glue stick, ball point pen). CLT has also discovered that psychological distance can be affected by temporal, geographical and social distance in such a way that objects that are farther away on these dimensions are construed more abstractly. In other words, a computer that comes out in a year, or was made in Europe, or is owned by an out-group member is construed at a higher level than one that is coming out next week, made in the US or owned by a close friend.

While social psychology has found differences in attitudes, perceptions, and behavior depending on the level of construal, psycholinguists have also studied the idea of abstract vs. concrete. Research on linguistic categories finds that words with the same semantic definitions can be grouped into different levels of abstractness. The Linguistic Category Model developed by Semin and Fiedler (1988) provides 5 categories of words that have different degrees of cognitive functions in interpersonal communications and vary in their level of abstraction. It is found that adjectives are generally governed by abstract, semantic relations rather than be governed by the contingencies of contextual factors; verbs, in contrast, are generally governed by concrete relations.

We apply these speech classifications to marketing messages in print ads and propose a construal-matching effect. We hypothesize that an effective match facilitates a fluency that results in increased persuasiveness of the matched messages. Using verbs (concrete) to advertise utilitarian (concrete) products (e.g. glue stick), due to matching, will make the message more effective. In the same vein, using adjectives (abstract) to advertise hedonic (abstract) products (e.g. music) will create positivity.

Study 1 examines the matching hypothesis by examining two different products with either matched or unmatched messages. Study 2 examines the matching hypothesis by priming the same product to be either hedonic or utilitarian. Finally, in study 3, to provide more evidence of the construal-matching hypothesis, we alter the release date of the iced coffee to be distal or proximal, manipulating a different dimension of psychological distance and still see the positive effects of construal-matching.

A pretest revealed a glue stick to be primarily utilitarian and an mp3 to be primarily hedonic. Therefore, these were taken as the two focal products in study 1. Two versions of ads for each of the two products were developed for the experiment and pretested to be semantically equivalent. One version of the ads use concrete verb words, the other version of the ads use abstract adjective words. After reading the ads, subjects reported their brand attitude, message believability and desirability, cognitive involvement when reading the ad, and cognitive responses.

The results of study 1 support the construal-matching hypotheses. Ads framed in concrete words were perceived to be more believable and persuasive when they were used to describe the utilitarian product. In contrasts, ads framed with abstract words were perceived to be more convincing and more effective when used to describe the hedonic product.

The initial pretest also revealed that iced coffee was considered to be a hybrid product consisting of hedonic and utilitarian attributes. Therefore, this product was used in study 2. In study 2, subjects were primed to either view iced coffee as hedonic or utilitarian. Consistent with traditional methods of priming, subjects were given a word search in which they were either asked to find words that related to utility (function, aim, objective, function, etc.) or to hedonicity (love, enjoy, fun, pleasure, etc). They were then shown an ad promoting a new iced coffee drink at a university café. This ad either used verbs to promote the product and café or adjective (e.g. tastes great vs. tasty).

Results from this study also support our construal-matching hypothesis. Those who viewed ads that matched their primed mindset had more positive attitudes towards the iced coffee, the café, and the advertisement itself.

Finally, to test the generalizability of our matching hypothesis, in a third study, we change the dimension of psychological distance that influences construal of our focal product. In study 3, we use the same iced coffee, but alter the opening day of the café to be either this coming fall or one year from now. Again, even using a different manipulation, we see the same construal-matching. Over all three studies, we see that using adjectives (verbs) to advertise abstract (concrete) products is the most effective.

This research adds to the steam of research examining the positive effects of matching. Work in frame matching (Cheema and Patrick, 2008; Yan and Sengupta 2011) demonstrates that when message frames match an individual's mindset, consumers are more likely to develop positive attitudes. Consistent with these positive matching effects, this research finds matching the construal level of advertisement language to product features creates positivity. Using adjectives (verbs) to advertise abstract (concrete) products leads to the most positive product attitudes.

REFERENCES

Cheema, Amar, and Patrick, Vanessa M. (2008), "Anytime Versus Only: Mind-Sets Moderate the Effect of Expansive Versus Restrictive Frames on Promotion Evaluation," *Journal of Marketing Research*, 45 (August), 462-72.

Liberman, Nira and Yaacov Trope (1998), "The Role of Feasibility and Desirability Considerations in Near and Distant Future Decisions: A Test of Temporal Construal Theory," *Journal of Personality and Social Psychology*, 75 (1), 5–18.

Semin, G.R., & Fiedler, K. (1988). The cognitive functions of linguistic categories in describing persons: Social cognition and language. *Journal of Personality and Social Psychology*, 54, 558–68.

Ulkumen, Gulden, Amar Cheema (2011) "Framing Goals to Influence Personal Savings: The Role of Specificity and Construal Level," *Journal of Marketing Research.*

Yan, D., & Sengupta, J. (2011). Effects of Construal Level on the Price-Quality Relationship. *Journal of Consumer Research*, 38, 376-389.

The Influence of Discrete Emotions on Strategic Goal-Setting

Karthik Easwar, Ohio State University, USA
Patricia M. West, Ohio State University, USA

EXTENDED ABSTRACT

People regulate affect when they choose options and behaviors specifically for their affect-related consequences (Cohen et al. 2008). Generally, people prefer to experience positive affect, a desire that manifests itself in two different affect regulation motivations; protection and lifting (Zillman 1988). When mood protecting, people attempt to remain in a positive affective state by avoiding tasks that may produce negative outcomes (Andrade and Cohen 2007; Isen and Means 1983). When mood-lifting, people approach various tasks in hopes of an affective boost.

People in a positive affective state tend to exhibit a mood protection motivation. They engage in more enjoyable behaviors, avoid painful experiences, take fewer risks, and help less, in order to maintain their positivity (Andrade 2005; Andrade and Cohen 2007; Forest et al. 1979; Isen and Geva 1987; Isen and Means 1983).

Those in a negative affective state worry less about the affective consequences of their choices, seek more variety and are more helpful than those experiencing positive affect (Cialdini and Fultz 1990; Cohen et al. 2008; Drolet and Luce 2004; Wegener and Petty 1994). However, when experiencing negative affect people's focus on mood-lifting differed depending on their beliefs about the transience and controllability of their affective state (Labroo and Muhkopadhyay 2009; Shen and Wyer 2008; Tice, Bratslavsky, and Baumeister 2001). Norem and Cantor (1986) argue for two regulation strategies: defensive pessimism, in which people prepare for the worst, and optimism in which they hope for the best. However, they provide little insight into what underlying process leads to the selection of a strategy.

Our research identifies regulatory focus as the process by which affective states influence affect regulation motivation. Regulatory focus theory argues that there are two separate and independent self-regulatory orientations: prevention and promotion (Higgins, 1997). A prevention focus emphasizes safety, responsibility, and security needs, is concerned with losses, and is especially sensitive to failure. A promotion focus emphasizes hopes, accomplishments, and advancement needs, is concerned with gains, and is especially sensitive to attainment. Thus, someone who is either chronically, or situationally, prevention-focused generally prefers a "vigilant strategy", and someone who is either chronically, or situationally, promotion-focused generally prefers an "eager strategy" (Crowe and Higgins, 1997; Higgins et al., 2001).

We hypothesize that one's current affective state will directly impact their motivational state, which in turn will affect goal-setting, but that this impact will depend on one's regulatory focus. We also expect that the affect regulation motivation of an individual will drive their goal-setting strategy; a protection motivation will lead to low goal-setting while a lift motivation will lead to higher goal-setting. In other words, participants who are protection motivated will set goals lower than those who are lift motivated, regardless of their affective state.

Study 1 utilized a 3 × 3 between subjects, factorial design where affective state (positive, neutral or negative) was induced using previously tested videos (Cohen and Andrade 2004) and regulatory focus was manipulated by having participants write about their hopes and aspirations (promotion focus) or their duties and obligations (prevention focus) or daily routine (Freitas and Higgins 2002).

The dependent variable was the goal set in an anagram task. After setting a goal, participants evaluated their level of agreement with two key statements intended to capture their affect regulation motivation ("I chose this goal because I wanted to improve my state of mind" and "I chose this goal because I wanted to keep the same state of mind"; Cohen and Andrade 2004). Using these two items, we created a Motivation Score to capture the degree of one's affect regulation motivation. This index ranged from -6 to 6, where -6 indicates a strong protection motivation and 6 indicates a strong lift motivation.

Results from study 1 (see table 1) indicate that participants in a positive affective state who were promotion focused, displayed a greater lift motivation than either those who were prevention focused or had no induced regulatory focus. In a negative affective state, participants who were prevention focused were the most protection oriented when compared to those who were promotion focused or had no induced regulatory focus. These results demonstrate that regulatory focus is moderating the effect of affective state on affect regulation motivation for people experiencing negative affect.

We expect that one's affective regulation motivation will mediate the relationship between the current affective state by regulatory focus interaction and the goal-set. We support this hypothesis using Preacher and Hayes (2008) bootstrapping procedure to test for mediation (see figure 1). This mediation analysis shows that, regardless of their affective state, protection motivated participants set lower goals than participants that are lift motivated.

Table 1

Study 1: Affect Regulation Motivation and Goal-Setting by Affective State and Regulatory Focus

Regulatory Focus	Affective State		
	Positive	**Neutral**	**Negative**
	Motivation Score		
Promotion	-.19	-.08	-1.07
Prevention	1.70	-.13	1.15
No Focus	1.35	.31	-.09
	Goal-Setting		
Promotion	30.0	31.4	34.6
Prevention	23.5	31.1	25.5
No Focus	25.6	30.5	31.2

Figure 1

Study 1: Affect Regulation Serving as Mediator of Goal

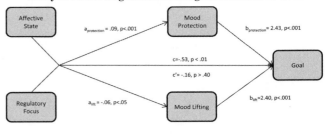

In a second study, we extend the literature on affect regulation by studying the role of specific emotions in strategic goal-setting. Previous research has indicated that while happiness and calm are both positive affective states, they have very different regulatory focuses. Specifically, calmness is associated with a prevention focus, while happiness is associated with a promotion focus. Similarly, anxiety is associated with a prevention focus, while sadness is associated with a promotion focus. Based on the results from study 1, we expect that regardless of affective state, those who are prevention focused will set lower goals than those who are promotion focused. Supporting this general hypothesis, we find that those who were in an anxious mood (prevention focused) set lower goals than those who were sad (promotion focused). While not as strong an effect, those who were calm (prevention focused) also set lower goals than those who were happy (promotion focused).

Our research expands the affect regulation literature in three key ways. First, we extend this work by demonstrating that goal-setting – because it divides the outcome space into success and failure (Heath, Larrick, and Wu 1999) – is a tailor-made way to strategically regulate affect. Second, we identify the role of regulatory focus in affect regulation, in the process, explaining some of the contradictory results previously seen in the literature. Finally, we use regulatory focus to identify how different emotions, not general affect, influence affect regulation motivation and strategic goal-setting.

REFERENCES

Andrade, Eduardo B. (2005), "Behavioral consequences of affect: Combining evaluative and regulatory mechanisms," *Journal of Consumer Research,* 32 (3), 355-62.

Andrade, Eduardo B., and Joel B. Cohen (2007), "On the consumption of negative feelings," *Journal of Consumer Research,* 34 (3), 283-300.

Cohen, Joel B., and Eduardo B. Andrade (2004), "Affective intuition and task-contingent affect regulation," *Journal of Consumer Research,* 31 (2), 358-67.

Cohen, Joel B., Michel T. Pham and Eduardo B. Andrade (2008), "The Nature and Role of Affect in Consumer Behavior," *Handbook of Consumer Psychology,* Ed. Curt Haugtvedt, Frank Kardes, and Paul Herr. Mahwah, NJ: Erlbaum, 297–348.

Crowe, Ellen, and E. T. Higgins (1997), "Regulatory focus and strategic inclinations: Promotion and prevention in decision-making," *Organizational Behavior & Human Decision Processes,* 69 (2), 117-32.

Forest, Duncan, Margaret S. Clark, Judson Mills, and Alice M. Isen (1979), "Helping as a function of feeling state and nature of the helping behavior," *Motivation and Emotion,* 3 (2), 161-9.

Freitas, Antonio L., and E. T. Higgins (2002), "Enjoying goal-directed action: The role of regulatory fit," *Psychological Science (Wiley-Blackwell),* 13 (1), 1.

Heath, Chip, and Richard P. Larrick (1999), "Goals as reference points," *Cognitive Psychology,* 38 (1), 79.

Higgins, E. T. (1997), "Beyond pleasure and pain," *American Psychologist,* 52 (12), 1280.

Higgins, E. T., Friedman, R. S., Harlow, R. E., Idson, L. C., Ayduk, O. N., & Taylor, A. (2001). Achievement orientations from subjective histories of success: Promotion pride versus prevention pride. *European Journal of Social Psychology,* 31, 3-23.

Isen, Alice M., and Nehemia Geva (1987), "The influence of positive affect on acceptable level of risk: The person with a large canoe has a large worry," *Organizational Behavior and Human Decision Processes,* 39 (2), 145-54.

Isen, Alice M., and Barbara Means (1983), "The influence of positive affect on decision-making strategy," *Social Cognition,* 2 (1), 18-31.

Labroo, Aparna A., and Anirban Mukhopadhyay (2009), "Lay theories of emotion transience and the search for happiness: A fresh perspective on affect regulation," *Journal of Consumer Research,* 36 (2), 242-54.

Norem, Julie K., and N. Cantor (1986), "Anticipatory and post hoc cushioning strategies: Optimism and defensive pessimism in 'risky' situations". *Cognitive Therapy and Research,* 10, 347-62.

Preacher, K. J., & Hayes, A. F. (2008), "Asymptotic and resampling strategies for assessing and comparing indirect effects in multiple mediator models." *Behavior Research Methods,* 40, 879-91.

Shen, Hao, and Robert S. Wyer (2008), "The impact of negative affect on responses to affect-regulatory experiences," *Journal of Consumer Psychology (Elsevier Science),* 18 (1), 39-48.

Tice, Dianne M., Ellen Bratslavsky, and Roy F. Baumeister (2001), "Emotional distress regulation takes precedence over impulse control: If you feel bad, do it!" *Journal of Personality & Social Psychology,* 80 (1), 53-67.

Zillman, Dolf (1988), "Mood management: Using entertainment to full advantage," in *Communication, social cognition, and affect,* Edited by L. Donohew, H. E. Sypher and E. T. Higgins. Hillsdale, NJ: Erlbaum, 147-71.

When the Message "Feels Right": When and How does Source Similarity Enhance Message Persuasiveness?

Ali Faraji-Rad, Columbia University, USA

Luk Warlop, KU Leuven, Belgium and BI Norwegian Business School, Norway

Bendik M. Samuelsen, BI Norwegian Business School, Norway

EXTENDED ABSTRACT:

We study how momentary subjective experiences (feelings) caused by a characteristic of a message source contribute to message persuasiveness. Specifically, we focus on message recipients' perceived similarity with the message source and argue that similarity enables higher self/other merging (Aron et al. 1991), which is turn yields to a "feels right" experience driven from receiving and processing that message. This feeling is then incorporated, as information (Schwarz & Clore 1983), into judgment about the target of the message – increasing message persuasiveness.

We used a similar paradigm in all our studies. In all studies we asked participants to read a scenario describing them trying to book a hotel online and to read a reviews of an unknown hotel and then evaluate the hotel based on the review. Similarity was manipulated through reviewer profiles. Other than the review(s), we gave no information regarding the hotel to the participants. In studies 1A-B we tested our basic assumption that feelings are responsible for a similar source's higher persuasiveness. We manipulated our participants' reliance on feelings versus logic by either instructing (1A) or priming (1B) them to use either their feelings or logic while evaluating the hotel. Specifically, in study 1A we adopted the instructions from Pham and colleagues (2001) and in study 1B, under the disguise of an open-ended study about different decision-making strategies, we told the participants to write down why they think using emotion (logic) in decision making is more beneficial than using logic (emotions). Then, in both studies we asked participants, to read the scenario and evaluate the hotel based on a negative review from an MBA student. Then participants reported their perceived similarity to the reviewer. In both studies we hypothesized that similarity enhances message persuasiveness only when participants are induced to rely on their feelings while evaluating the hotel, and not when they are made to use their logic. Results from both studies supported our hypothesis.

In studies 2 and 3, we built on research that shows that compared to experiential motives, if people have functional motives they will make less use of their feelings (Pham 1998; Adaval 2001). In both studies, we hypothesized and showed that similarity enhances message persuasiveness only when the motive of booking a hotel is experiential (vacation), and not when it is functional (work). Study 2 was different from studies 1A-B in that we manipulated similarity instead of measuring it. In this study we used a sample of student participants and ask them to imagine planning a trip for experiential or functional purposes. However, one group saw a profile of a reviewer who was an MBA student and the other group saw a profile of a researcher in a major chemical company. As expected, results showed that similarity influenced message persuasiveness only when motive was experiential, and not when it was functional. In study 3 we used scenarios similar to study 2. However, we ran the study on a sample similar to studies 1A-B and we measured (instead of manipulating) similarity. We also used two different profiles similar to study 2 in this study, with the goal of showing that the profiles per se do not have any effect on persuasiveness. Replicating results of study 2 we showed that higher message persuasiveness was associated with higher perceived similarity, but only when participants had experiential motives. Our effects held for both reviewer profiles, generalizing our findings.

In study 4, we built on research suggesting that the affective system is a decision-making system of the present (Chang & Pham 2012) to show that similarity increases message persuasiveness more if people are making a judgment about the near future, versus distant future. Here all participants had to first read a scenario that asked them to imagine that they would go on the trip in a week (near-future), or a year from now (distant-future) and then complete the procedure similar to study 3, except that they only saw the profile of an MBA student. The results supported our hypothesis. We based study 5 on the notion that people use feeling more for more reachable and immediate decisions (Mischel & Shoda 1995). Here the scenarios either told participants that they are participating in a lottery to win the trip and chances of winning are either 1-in-5 (high-probability) or 1-in-5000 (low probability). As predicted, the association between perceived similarity and message persuasiveness was higher if participants had higher probability of winning the hotel (compared to lower probability).

In study 6, we built on the literature that shows that assessment of relevance of feelings requires substantial cognitive resources (Avnet, Pham, & Stephen 2012) and showed that even when people have functional motives, a similar source is more persuasive if participants have only limited cognitive resources. Here, as in study 2 we manipulated similarity instead of measuring it. Student participants had to first memorize a two-digit (low-cognitive-load group) or a seven-digit (high-cognitive-load group) number. Then they all read the functional scenario identical the one used in study 2. We manipulated similarity same as study 2. As expected, similarity enhanced message persuasiveness if participants did not have cognitive resources, but not when they had cognitive resources available. In all our studies, controlling for reviewer expertise, credibility, and trustworthiness did not affect the results. Also, in studies 3, 4, and 5, we measured participants' self-reported "feels right" sensation towards the message. Mediated moderation analysis in all studies supported the notion that similarity makes the message "feel right" but people do not use this feeling when they do not see feelings relevant, thus lack of persuasiveness of a similar source in conditions where we expect less use of feelings.

REFERENCES

Adaval, R. (2001). Sometimes it just feels right: The differential weighting of affect-consistent and affect-inconsistent product information. Journal of Consumer Research, 28(1), 1-17.

Aron, Arthur, Aron, Elaine N., Tudor, M., & Nelson, G. (1991). Close relationships as including other in the self. Journal of Personality and Social Psychology, 60(2), 241-253

Avnet, T., Pham, M. T., & Stephen, A. T. (2011). Consumers' Trust in Feelings as Information. Yeshiva University.

Chang, H.H., & Pham, M.T. (2012). "Affect as a Decision Making System of the Present," Columbia University

Mischel, W. & Shoda, Y. (1995). A cognitive-affective system theory of personality: Reconceptualizing situations, dispositions, dynamics, and invariance in personality structure. Psychological Review, 102, 246-268.

Pham, M. T. (1998). Representativeness, relevance, and the use of feelings in decision making. Journal of Consumer Research, 25(2), 144-159.

Pham, M. T., Cohen, J. B., Pracejus, J. W., & Hughes, G. D. (2001). Affect monitoring and the primacy of feelings in judgment. Journal of Consumer Research, 28(2), 167-188.

Schwarz, N., & Clore, G. L. (1983). Mood, misattribution, and judgment of well-being: Informative and directive functions of affective states. Journal of Personality and Social Psychology, 45(3), 513-523.

Using Construal-Level Theory to Deter Social Desirability Responding

Scott Wright, Providence College, USA

EXTENDED ABSTRACT

Social desirability responding (SDR) is the tendency of respondents to adjust their responses or behavior in such a way as to present themselves in socially acceptable terms (Maccoby and Maccoby 1954). The systematic bias introduced by SDR threatens the legitimacy of empirical research by confounding a phenomenon of interest with impression management behavior, thus obscuring research results and potentially triggering false conclusions (see Fisher 1993; Ganster, Hennessey, and Luthans 1983). When SDR is a concern (e.g., when asking socially sensitive, embarrassing, or private questions), researchers commonly use techniques such as indirect questioning to avoid the bias introduced by SDR. By asking respondents how *most* or the *typical* person would respond (i.e, referring to a third party target) the respondent transcends from an egocentric focus on his or her own unflattering attitudes or behavior onto that of an ambiguous target. Given the target's indistinctness, respondents project their own feelings, attitudes, behaviors, or beliefs when responding while remaining psychologically distanced from the true, yet socially undesirable response (Calder and Burnkrant 1977; Grubb and Stern 1971; Haire 1950).

According to construal-level theory (CLT) this process of "*transcendence*" is made possible because individuals are able to form abstract mental construals (Liberman and Trope 1998; Trope and Liberman 2003; Trope and Liberman 2010). This mental construal process is essential to recalling the past, empathizing with others, imagining what could have been, and visualizing future events. As mental construals increase, individuals refocus from detailed, incidental features to central, fundamental characteristics (Trope and Liberman 2010). Consequently, we propose that indirect questioning prompts respondents to deemphasize the contextual demand to engage in impression management behavior through an increase in construal-levels.

In our project, we apply CLT to develop and explain novel techniques deterring SDR. To test the effectiveness of our techniques, we chose two contexts known to exhibit SDR (consumer surveys and consumer choices). In study 1 we demonstrate that increasing construal-levels through psychological distances decreases SDR within a survey context. To gain deeper insights into the cognitive mechanism, we directly manipulated construal-levels in study 2, and found that increasing construal-levels directly decreased SDR on a subsequent choice task. In study 3, we examined a mediational model establishing relationships between psychological distance, impression management, and choice.

STUDY 1

To investigate whether increasing construal-levels through psychological distances might attenuate SDR within a survey we had 453 participants complete seven marketing scales shown or suspect to elicit SDR: Materialism (Richins 2004), Impulsive Buying Tendency (Martin, Weun, and Beatty 1994), CSR (Sen and Bhattacharya 2001), Green Orientation (Dunlop and Van Liere 1978), Frequency of Healthy Preventative Behaviors (Jayanti and Burns 1998), Television Viewing Frequency, and Regulation of Alcohol Consumption, while manipulating the questioning format according to the dimensions of psychological distance (i.e., temporal, spatial, or social distance). Participants also completed a measure of SDR using Paulhus' (1991) BIRD scale.

To detect the presence of SDR, we implemented Steenkamp et al.'s (2010) substance versus style approach and regressed the two dimensions of SDR onto each marketing scale. In support of our hypotheses, when using direct questioning, five of the seven constructs exhibited a non-negligible relationship with one of SDRs two factors. We hypothesized that indirect questioning increasing social or spatial distance would attenuate SDR, while temporal distance would enhance SDR given research on the future optimism effect (see Regan, Snyder, and Kassin 1995; Weinstein 1980). Results indicate that whereas indirect questioning increasing social or spatial distance reduced the number of scales demonstrating a non-negligible relationship with SDR (compared to direct measures), indirect questioning increasing temporal distance increased this number, thus lending preliminary support to our hypotheses.

STUDY 2

Previous research demonstrates a bidirectional relationship between the psychological distance dimensions and construal-level, such that as construal-levels increase, inferred psychological distances increase, and vice versa (Trope and Liberman 2010). In study 2 we explored the mediational role of construal-levels and extended our findings to a consumer choice context. Consumers construe sustainable actions, products, and attitudes as pro-social in nature (i.e., beneficial to society), as a result, there exists a social pressure to display behaviors endorsing sustainability (see Luchs et al. 2010). Consistent with our hypothesis that increasing construal-levels will decrease SDR we found that when we increased contrual-levels through an obstensably unrelated mind-set task (Freitas, Gollwitzer, and Trope 2004), the share of choice for a non-sustainable (vs. sustainable) laundry detergent increased from 10% to 27% in a subsequent choice task ($\chi^2(1,97) = 4.48, p < .05$).

STUDY 3

To provide additional clarity into the underlying mechanism, in study 3, we manipulated self-presentation demand and the psychological distance of the choice task while incorporating a measure of SDR ($N=406$). Self-presentation demand was manipulated by asking participants to present themselves as favorably as possible during the experiment (see Paulhus 2002). To test the generalizability of our results we incorporated two choice tasks each between a sustainable and non-sustainable option. The results provide evidence of an indirect-only moderated mediation model (see figure 1). When the demand to engage in impression management behavior was high, increasing the psychological distance of the choice task successfully deterred respondents from engaging in deliberate SDR. We also report a significant relationship between the impression management dimension of SDR and choice, whereby the impression management tendency increased the likelihood of selecting the sustainable (vs. non-sustainable) laundry detergent ($\beta = .37$, Wald $\chi^2 = 8.63, p < .004$) and hand sanitizer ($\beta = .34$, Wald $\chi^2 = 5.67, p < .02$). A significant indirect effect between our interaction term and choice through impression management provided evidence of the mediational process and identified the distortion as deliberate for both laundry detergents ($\beta = .18, p < .05$) and hand sanitizers ($\beta = .16, p < .05$).

Figure 1
Study 3: Indirect-Only Mediated Moderation Model For Choice

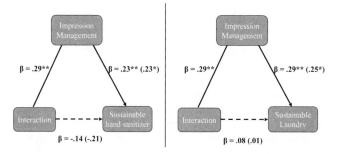

Note: Betas outside parenthesis represent standardized regression coefficients for the direct relationships between the variables; betas inside parentheses represent regression coefficients for the strength of relationships between to variables after statistically adjusting for the other variable in the model. Asterisks indicate level of significance (* *p* < .05, ** *p* <.01).

The results support our hypothesis that increasing construal-levels directly or through psychological distances deters SDR by deemphasizing contextual demands to engage in impression management behavior, thus, encouraging respondents to report accurate responses. This research has important methodological and substantive implications for marketers, researchers, and consumer psychologists.

REFERENCES

Calder, Bobby J. and Robert E. Burnkrant (1977), "Interpersonal Influence on Consumer Behavior: An Attribution Theory Approach," *The Journal of Consumer Research*, 4 (1), 29-38.

Dunlop, Riley E. and Kent. D. Van Liere (1978), "The New Environmental Paradigm," *Journal of Environmental Education*, 9 (4), 10-19.

Fisher, Robert J. (1993), "Social Desirability Bias and the Validity of Indirect Questioning," *Journal of Consumer Research*, 20 (2), 303-15.

Freitas, Antonio L., Peter Gollwitzer, and Yaacov Trope (2004), "The Influence of Abstract and Concrete Mindsets on Anticipating and Guiding Others' Self-Regulatory Efforts," *Journal of Experimental Social Psychology*, 40 (6), 739-52.

Ganster, Daniel C., Harry W. Hennessey, and Fred Luthans (1983), "Social Desirability Response Effects: Three Alternative Models," *The Academy of Management Journal*, 26 (2), 321-31.

Grubb, Edward L. and Bruce L. Stern (1971), "Self-Concept and Significant Others," *Journal of Marketing Research*, 8 (3), 382-85.

Haire, Mason (1950), "Projective Techniques in Marketing Research," *The Journal of Marketing*, 14 (5), 649-56.

Jayanti, Rama K. and Alvin C. Burns (1998), "The Antecedents of Preventive Health Care Behavior: An Empirical Study," *Journal of the Academy of Marketing Science*, 26 (1), 6-15.

Liberman, Nira and Yaacov Trope (1998), "The Role of Feasibility and Desirability Considerations in near and Distant Future Decisions: A Test of Temporal Construal Theory," *Journal of Personality and Social Psychology*, 75, 5-18.

Luchs, Michael G., Rebecca Walker Naylor, Julie R. Irwin, and Rajagopal Raghunathan (2010), "The Sustainability Liability: Potential Negative Effects of Ethicality on Product Preference," *Journal of Marketing*, 74 (5), 18-31.

Maccoby, Eleanor E. and Nathan Maccoby (1954), "The Interview: A Tool of Social Science," *Handbook of social psychology*, 1, 449-87.

Martin, Wendy K., Seungoog Weun, and Sharon E. Beatty (1994), "Validation of an Impulse Buying Tendency Scale," in *The 1993 annual conference of the Association for Consumer Research*, Nashville, TN.

Paulhus, Delroy L. (1991), "Measurement and Control of Response Bias," in *Measures of Personality and Social Psychological Attitudes, Measures of Social Psychological Attitudes*, Vol. 1, ed. John P. Robinson, Phillip R. Shaver and Lawrence S. Wrightsman, San Diego, CA: Academic Press, 17-59.

——— (2002), "Socially Desirable Responding: The Evolution of a Construct," *The role of constructs in psychological and educational measurement*, 49–69.

Regan, Pamela C., Mark Snyder, and Saul M. Kassin (1995), "Unrealistic Optimism: Self-Enhancement or Person Positivity?," *Personality and Social Psychology Bulletin*, 21 (10), 1073.

Richins, Marsha L. (2004), "The Material Values Scale: Measurement Properties and Development of a Short Form," *Journal of Consumer Research*, 209-19.

Sen, Sankar and C.B. Bhattacharya (2001), "Does Doing Good Always Lead to Doing Better? Consumer Reactions to Corporate Social Responsibility," *Journal of Marketing Research*, 38 (2), 225-43.

Steenkamp, Jan-Benedict E.M., Martijn G. de Jong, and Hans. Baumgartner (2010), "Socially Desirable Response Tendencies in Survey Research," *Journal of Marketing Research*, 47 (2), 199-214.

Trope, Yaacov and Nira Liberman (2003), "Temporal Construal," *Psychological Review*, 110 (3), 403-20.

——— (2010), "Construal-Level Theory of Psychological Distance," *Psychological Review*, 117 (2), 440.

Weinstein, Neil D. (1980), "Unrealistic Optimism About Future Life Events," *Journal of Personality and Social Psychology*, 39 (5), 806.

Conservative When Crowded: How Social Crowding Leads to Safety-Oriented Choices

Ahreum Maeng, University of Wisconsin - Madison, USA
Dilip Soman, University of Toronto, Canada
Robin Tanner, University of Wisconsin - Madison, USA

EXTENDED ABSTRACT:

While extant research on crowding in retail contexts indicates that it can reduce shopper satisfaction and precipitate an earlier departure from the store (Eroglu et al., 2005; Hui and Bateson 1991), relatively little research has examined whether being crowded might influence the actual choices consumers make. Thus, despite the fact that many socially crowded locations (e.g., stores or offices) are actually places where highly consequential decisions are made, our understanding of the potential effects of crowding on decision making is rather incomplete (e.g., Epstein and Karlin, 1975).

The most germane concept in developing our theoretical framework is the notion of personal space, as violations of personal space are particularly likely to occur in crowded public settings. Personal space is defined as a moveable boundary around the human body, primarily functioning as a buffer protecting individuals from potential threats (Graziano and Cooke, 2006). Research shows that violations of this personal space lead individuals to experience feelings of anxiety and psychological unease (Hall, 1966). Further, recent neurological research has shown that personal proximity activates the amygdala, the structure known to be involved in social approach and avoidance response (Kennedy et al., 2009). Indeed, crowding leads to physiological outcomes such as increased skin conductance, high arousal, and low experienced pleasure (Worchel and Teddlie, 1976). From an approach-avoidance motivation perspective, all these findings are consistent with social crowding leading to the avoidance motivation system being activated as part of a broader self-protection mechanism (Lang and Bradley, 2008).

Substantial empirical evidence demonstrates that an avoidance motivation is associated with prevention goals (Forster, Higgins, and Idson, 1998). Consequently, we propose that if social crowding leads to the activation of the avoidance system, then a greater prevention focus is likely to result. Therefore, we propose crowded individuals are more likely to seek objects with connotations of personal safety as these objects are instrumental in achieving the activated prevention goal (Markman and Brendl, 2000). Similarly, from a regulatory fit perspective, individuals experience regulatory fit when they choose objects with safety implications because those alternatives align with their goal orientation (i.e., a prevention goal). As such, individuals may more readily choose these options because it feels appropriate to them to choose an option that fits their regulatory focus (Higgins, 2000; Lee and Aaker, 2004). Three studies explore the relationship between social crowdedness and risk oriented choice.

Study 1 (N=49) was an initial investigation as to whether being socially crowded increases the accessibility of safety oriented constructs. Social crowdedness was manipulated directly by having participants complete the task in a laboratory room that was either crowded (24 participants per session) or uncrowded (3-4 participants per session). Participants were presented with a word search grid and were given 3 minutes to write down as many words as they could find. The grid contained 10 neutral words (e.g., speaker, coffee) and 10 safety related words (e.g., insurance, helmet). While participants found a similar number of words in each condition, participants in the crowded room uncovered a greater number of safety-related words than those in the less crowded room (F(1, 47) = 9.23, p=0.004).

Study 2 (N=75) was designed to build on Study 1 by exploring if this apparent crowding driven increase in safety-orientation would influence product decisions, and whether this effect would be mediated by a greater prevention focus. To generalize the results from Study 1, social crowdedness was manipulated via picture priming. Specifically, participants were exposed to one of three images: a crowded scene, an uncrowded scene, or a no picture control. Next, participants completed two preference tasks designed to explore their preference toward making choices with prevention orientated benefits. These were presented as scenarios requiring participants to indicate their relative preference between two places to visit while their flight was delayed (pharmacy vs. convenience store) and between two free gifts at a local store (first aid products vs. a box of cookies). Finally, we administered a questionnaire designed to measure participants' incidental regulatory focus. This questionnaire followed Higgins and colleagues (1994) approach and required participants to rate the importance to them of 14 different issues on a nine-point scale anchored from 1 ("extremely important") to 9 ("extremely unimportant"). Half of the items reflected a promotion focus (e.g., "doing well in work") and half a prevention focus (e.g., "avoiding unsafe sexual practices"). The summed importance scores for the promotion items were subtracted from the equivalent summed prevention item scores to create a measure of net prevention focus (see Lockwood, Jordan, and Kunda 2002).

Results showed that, participants in the crowded condition illustrated a dramatically stronger net prevention focus than did those in the uncrowded and control conditions (F(2,72) = 11.9, p<.001). Similarly, both rating tasks also indicated a stronger preference for the safety oriented options (i.e., pharmacy and first-aid kit) in the crowded conditions. More importantly, mediation analysis using 5,000 bootstrap samples revealed that these safety-oriented preferences were mediated by the net-prevention focus scores. For a detailed description of these results.

Study 3 (N=114) aimed to further generalize our findings by examining if the crowdedness of the environment would enhance receptivity towards persuasive messages presented with a prevention-oriented frame. After completing the same picture priming task from Study 2 (control vs. crowded vs. uncrowded conditions), participants were presented with an oral-hygiene message presented with either a prevention or promotion focus and were asked to rate the importance of the message in various ways. Results revealed the expected Crowding X Message framing interaction on the message importance rating (F(2, 108) = 11.9, p < .001) with participants primed with crowdedness rating the prevention oriented message as (a) more convincing (p = .013), (b) more appealing (p = .03), and (c) as saying something important to them (p < .01). For detailed analysis.

In sum, our research provides the first demonstration of the important finding that the crowdedness of the choice environment can significantly influence the choices we make in that environment.

APPENDIX

A) How You Can Prevent Gingivitis

Gingivitis is a serious and very common dental condition, but it is 100 per cent preventable and easily treated if you have it diagnosed early. So if you begin to notice the signs of gingivitis, then you need to pay a visit to you dentist for a recommended treatment plan.

The condition is caused by an overgrowth of bacteria inside the mouth that converts into plaque and leads to bad breath, bleeding gums and often sore or swollen gums. If you leave the condition for too long, it can cause more serious conditions such as tooth loss, periodontal disease and even heart disease.

You can easily prevent the condition from occurring by combining good home dental practices with regular dentist visits. By brushing, flossing and rinsing twice a day at home using the correct technique and then having a professional clean twice a year at your dentist, the instance of gingivitis is drastically reduced.

Before you brush, you should floss your teeth and get all the bacteria and food particles that get trapped between the teeth out. Brushing with then help to get rid of the bacteria on the tooth surface and get rid of plaque. Using a natural toothpaste that is based on mint oil is the best choice as it is both effective and gentle on your body. Mint oil is a naturally powerful antibacterial agent and also has anti-fungal properties. In contrast commercial toothpastes contain detergents, which can act as allergens for many people.

Mouthwash is another essential part of a good dental routine. It is able to kill bacteria left over in the mouth, particularly the bacteria that gets stuck around the gum line. Additionally, scraping your tongue can also get rid of a lot of bacteria that can lead to gingivitis. You can buy tongue scrapers, or alternatively, use your regular tooth brush.

Protecting your dental health from the onslaught of gingivitis is relatively easy, but the key is consistency. You have to ensure that you are brushing, flossing and rinsing twice a day to prevent the buildup of harmful bacteria in the mouth. When you visit your dentist you should discuss how you can best prevent gingivitis and other dental conditions and ask them to show you how to most effectively brush your teeth as many people do not use the right technique.

B) How You Can Get Brighter Smiles

Everyone loves a bright white smile. Fortunately there are a variety of procedures and products available today that can improve the look of yours. When exploring these options it's wise to know the difference between "teeth whitening" and "teeth bleaching" and familiarize yourself with cosmetic dentistry and its terminology. With so many companies offering their magical teeth whitening treatments, it's easy to feel overwhelmed. To counteract the influx of these potentially bogus programs, several websites have recently popped up with accurate and easy to digest information regarding your teeth.

Whitening one's teeth is the process of restoring teeth to their natural color. This is done by removing the build-up and dirt collected on the tooth's surface. You can achieve these results with toothpastes that boast a whitening agent. Having your teeth cleaned regularly is an excellent way to keep your teeth free of debris.

Bleaching one's teeth actually whitens teeth beyond their natural state to produce its desired result. The use of a bleach-containing agent will draw out the stain and color leaving them clean and whiter than before. There are two types of bleach used in this process. Hydrogen peroxide is used by your dentist in a controlled environment and contains a high level of peroxide. Take-home kits use carbamide peroxide which has a lower percentage of peroxide and is therefore safer to use on your own.

Over-The-Counter teeth bleaching products can be purchased at your local drugstore for the most affordable prices. A good choice would be one that uses a tray (as a dentist would) that covers the teeth and holds the peroxide-based gel in place over your teeth. Other options include strips and "paintable" teeth whitening gel. Many toothpaste brands incorporate peroxide as a way to bleach teeth while brushing.

Professional take-home teeth bleaching kits are slightly more expensive but are dentist-approved and therefore more reliable. They utilize the tray process and are custom fitted for your teeth. This makes them more effective than over-the-counter brands. Custom molded trays may take several weeks to receive so plan accordingly.

The long and the short of it is that teeth whitening works. Virtually everyone who opts for this cosmetic treatment will see moderate to substantial improvement in the brightness and whiteness of their smile. However, teeth whitening is not a permanent solution and requires maintenance or "touch-ups" for a prolonged effect.

REFERENCES

Epstein, Yakov M., and Robert A. Karlin (1975), "Effects of Acute Experimental Crowding," *Journal of Applied Social Psychology,* 5, no. 1: 34-53.

Eroglu, Sevgin A., Karen Machleit, and Terri Feldman Barr (2005), "Perceived Retail Crowding and Shopping Satisfaction: The Role of Shopping Values," *Journal of Business Research* 58, no. 8: 1146-1153.

Förster, Jens, E. Tory Higgins, and Lorraine Chen Idson (1998), "Approach and Avoidance Strength During Goal Attainment: Regulatory Focus and the 'Goal Looms Larger' Effect." *Journal of Personality and Social Psychology*, 75, no. 5: 1115-1131.

Graziano, Michael S. A., and Dylan F. Cooke (2006), "Parieto-Frontal Interactions, Personal Space, and Defensive Behavior," *Neuropsychologia,* 44, no. 6: 845-859.

Hall, E. T. (1966). *The Hidden Dimension.* Anchor Books.

Higgins, E. Tory (2000), "Making a Good Decision: Value from Fit*,"* *American Psychologist* 55, no. 11: 1217-1230.

Higgins, E. Tory, Christopher J. R. Roney, Ellen Crowe, and Charles Hymes (1994), "Ideal Versus Ought Predilections for Approach and Avoidance Distinct Self-Regulatory Systems," *Journal of Personality and Social Psychology,* 66, no. 2: 276-286.

Hui, Michael K., and John E. Bateson (1991), "Perceived Control and the Effects of Crowding and Consumer Choice on the Service Experience," *Journal of Consumer Research,* 18, no. 2: 174-184.

Kennedy, Daniel P., Jan Gläscher, J. Michael Tyszka, and Ralph Adolphs (2009), "Personal Space Regulation by the Human Amygdala." *Nature Neuroscience,* 12, no. 10: 1226-1227.

Lang, Peter J., and Margaret M. Bradley (2008), "Appetitive and Defensive Motivation is the Substrate of Emotion," *In Handbook of approach and avoidance motivation*, 51-65. New York, NY US: Psychology Press, 2008.

Lee, Angela Y., and Jennifer L. Aaker (2004), "Bringing the Frame Into Focus: The Influence of Regulatory Fit on Processing Fluency and Persuasion*," Journal Of Personality And Social Psychology* 86, no. 2: 205-218.

Lockwood, Penelope, Christian H. Jordan, and Ziva Kunda (2002), "Motivation by Positive or Negative role Models: Regulatory Focus Determines Who Will Best Inspire Us," *Journal of Personality and Social Psychology,* 83, no. 4: 854-864.

Markman, Arthur B., and C. Miguel Brendl (2000), "The Influence of Goals on Value and Choice," In *The psychology of learning and motivation: Advances in research and theory*, Vol. 39, 97-128. San Diego, CA US: Academic Press, 2000.

Worchel, Stephen, and Charles Teddlie (1976), "The Experience of Crowding: A Two-Factor Theory," *Journal of Personality and Social Psychology* 34, no. 1: 30-40.

When the Accessible Global Identity Leads to Unfavorable Evaluations of Global Products? The Roles of Consumers' Lay Theory on Global and Local Cultures

Yinlong Zhang, University of Texas at San Antonio, USA
Ying-Yi Hong, Nanyang Technological University, Singapore

EXTENDED ABSTRACT

In today's increasingly globalized world, many consumers tend to have both global and local identities (Arnett 2002; Benet-Martinez et al. 2002; Zhang and Khare 2009). A global identity refers to mental representations in which consumers are interested in global cultures and identifying with people around the world. A local identity refers to consumers' mental associations of their faith in and respect for one's local traditions and cultures as well as identifying with people in one's local community (Arnett 2002; Zhang and Khare 2009).

How will consumers respond to marketing efforts targeted at their global and local identities? Recent research (Benet-Martinez et al., 2002; Hong et al., 2009) suggests that this may be dependent on consumers' view of their two cultural identities; specifically their subjective perceptions of their two identities as compatible with or oppositional to each other. Consumers who believe that their two cultural identities are compatible with each other tend to show assimilative responses to the identity prime, while those who believe that their two cultural identities are opposite each other tend to show the contrastive response. Based on Hong and her colleagues (2009), this happens because consumers who believe that their two identities are compatible with each other tend to hold separate knowledge about these two identities, and activation of one identity via prime will not activate the other identity. Since consumers tend to rely only on the accessible identity to form their evaluations, they provide identity consistent evaluations (i.e., assimilative identity effect). Consumers who believe that their two identities are oppositional to each other will experience activation of both identities in response to a prime. These two identities are conceptually opposite each other and as a result, consumers provide identity inconsistent evaluations (i.e., contrastive identity effect).

Earlier studies have shown that consumers' view on global and local cultures determines their global and local identities (Arnett 2002). As a result, their lay theory of the relationship between global and local cultures can have similar effects as their lay theory of the global and local identities on product evaluations. Applying this framework to the global-local context, the bi-cultural identity lay theory predicts that the global-local identity will lead to an assimilative identity effect for consumers who believe that global and local cultures are compatible with each other. For consumers who believe that the two cultures are oppositional to each other, a contrastive identity effect will be observed. We ran three studies to test this hypothesis as well as the underlying process.

Study 1 was an identity primed (local vs. global) x lay theory (compatible vs. oppositional) x product version (local vs. global) mixed design, in which we measured consumers' lay theory on global and local cultures. A total of 134 undergraduate students from a large southwestern U.S. university took part in this study for extra course credit. In this study, we found that the identity prime lead to an assimilative identity effect when participants believed that global and local cultures could be compatible with each other, and that the identity prime lead to a contrastive identity effect when participants believed that global and local cultures were opposite each other.

Study 2 was a lay theory prime (compatible vs. oppositional) x identity measured (local vs. global) x product version (local vs. global) mixed design, in which consumers' lay theory of global and local cultures was manipulated. A total of 164 undergraduate students

from a large southwestern U.S. university took part in this study for extra course credit. In this study, through directly manipulating the lay theory, we showed that the measured global-local identity lead to an assimilative identity effect when participants believed that global and local cultures could be compatible with each other. Further, the measured global-local identity lead to a contrastive identity effect when participants believed that global and local cultures were oppositional or conflicting each other.

Study 3 was run to further test the possible process underlying this effect. A total of 152 undergraduate students from a large southwestern U.S. university took part in this globalization prime (positive vs. negative) x oppositional lay theory measured x product version (local vs. global) mixed design study for extra course credit. This study provided a test of the counter-arguing mindset, the explanation for the contrast effect observed in the first two studies. Because the oppositional lay theory prime tends to make people believe that the two cultures are conflicting, they seem to engage in a counter-arguing mindset when they process the global-local stimuli, and as a result they have the exact opposite associations in response to the stimuli.

Our results have several important theoretical implications. First, we provide boundary conditions for the identity accessibility effect in the context of global-local products. While earlier studies (Arnett 2002; Zhang and Khare 2009) tended to focus on the assimilative accessibility effect, we found that when the global or local identity is made accessible it does not always lead to the assimilative identity effect.

Second, our results have important implications for understanding the assimilation vs. contrast debate in the literature (Förster & Liberman 2007; Reed 2004). While the earlier debate tended to focus on the diagnosticity of the accessible identity to determine if the evaluation is assimilative or contrastive (Zhang & Khare 2009), our results showed that the consumers' view about the relationship between global and local cultures is another key to understanding the exact nature of product evaluation.

Third, we provide a theoretical explanation for the contrasting findings about differential preference for local and global products. While earlier studies (Arnett 2002; Zhang and Khare 2009) showed that it is important to specify consumers' accessible global or local identity, we replicated the identity accessibility effect but also showed that it will happen only when consumers view their two identities as compatible with each other. Thus, our study provides a more comprehensive theoretical explanation for reconciling earlier reported divergent preference patterns for local and global products.

REFERENCES

Aaker, Jennifer L. (2000), "Accessibility or Diagnosticity? Disentangling the Influence of Culture on Persuasion Processes and Attitudes," *Journal of Consumer Research*, 26 (March), 340-57.

Alden, Dana L., Jan-Benedict E.M. Steenkamp, and Rajeev Batra (1999), "Brand Positioning Through Advertising in Asia, North America, and Europe: The Role of Global Consumer Culture," *Journal of Marketing*, 63 (1), 75-87.

Arnett, Jeffrey J. (2002), "The Psychology of Globalization," *American Psychologist*, 57 (10), 774-83.

Batra, Rajeev, VenkatramRamaswamy, Dana L. Alden, Jan-Benedict E.M. Steenkamp, and S. Ramachander (2000), "Effects of Brand Local and Nonlocal Origin on Consumer Attitudes in Developing Countries," *Journal of Consumer Psychology*, 9 (2), 83-95.

Benet-Martinez, Veronica, JanxinLeu, Fiona Lee, and Michael W. Morris (2002), "Negotiating Biculturalism: Cultural Frame Switching in Biculturals with Oppositional Versus Compatible Cultural Identities," *Journal of Cross-Cultural Psychology*, 33 (5), 492-516.

Benet-Martinez, Veronica, and Jana Haritatos (2005)."Bicultural Identity Integration (BII): Components and Psychosocial Antecedents,"*Journal of Personality. 73*, 1015-1050.

Brewer, Marilynn B. (1991), "The Social Self: On Being the Same and Different at the Same Time," *Personality and Social Psychology Bulletin*, 17 (5), 475-82.

Dijksterhuis, Ap, Russel Spears, Tom Postmes, Diederik A. Stapel, Willem Koomen, Ad van Knippenberg, and DaanScheepers (1998), "Seeing One Thing and Doing Another: Contrast Effects in Automatic Behavior," *Journal of Personality and Social Psychology*, 75 (4), 862–71.

Feldman, Jack M., and John G. Lynch Jr. (1988), "Self-Generated Validity and other Effects of Measurement on Belief, Attitude, Intention, and Behavior," *Journal of Applied Psychology*, 73 (3), 421-35.

Forehand, Mark R., RohitDeshpandé, and Americus Reed II (2002), "Identity Salience and the Influence of Differential Activation of the Social Self-Schema on Advertising Response," *Journal of Applied Psychology*, 87 (6), 1086-99.

Förster, Jens and Nira Liberman (2007), "Knowledge Activation," in Kruglanski A. and Higgins E. (eds), *Social Psychology: Handbook of Basic Principles*, 2nd ed, New York, London: Guilford Publications.

Higgins, E. Tory (1996), "Knowledge Activation: Accessibility, Applicability, and Salience," in Higgins E. and Kruglanski A. (1996), *Social Psychology: Handbook of Basic Principles*. New York, London: Guilford Publications.

Hong, Ying-yi, Melody Chao, and Sun No (2009), "Dynamic Interracial/Intercultural Processes: The Role of Lay Theories of Race."*Journal of Personality, 77,* 1283-309.

Hong, Ying-yi, Michael W. Morris, Chi-yue Chiu, and Veronica Benet-Martinez (2000), "Multicultural Minds: A Dynamic Constructivist Approach to Culture and Cognition," *American Psychologist*, 55(7), 709-20.

Ledgerwood, Alison, and Shelly Chaiken (2007), "Priming Us and Them: Automatic Assimilation and Contrast in Group Attitudes," *Journal of Personality and Social Psychology*, 93 (6), 940-56.

No, Sun, Ying-yi Hong, Hsin-Ya Liao, Kyoungmi Lee, Dustin Wood, and Melody Manchi Chao (2008), 'Lay Theory of Race Affects and Moderates Asian Americans' Responses Toward American Culture," *Journal of Personality and Social Psychology*, 95 (4), 991-1004.

Oyserman, Daphna and Spike W. S. Lee (2008), "Does Culture Influence What and How We Think?" *Psychological Bulletin,* 134 (March), 311-42.

Rigby, Darrell, K., and Vijay Vishwanath (2006), "Localization: The Revolution in Consumer Markets," *Harvard Business Review,* 84 (4), 82-92.

Shimp, Terence A., and Subhash Sharma (1987), "Consumer Ethnocentrism: Construction and Validation of the CETSCALE," *Journal of Marketing Research*, 24 (3), 280-89.

Srull, Thomas K., and Robert S. Wyer, Jr. (1980), "Category Accessibility and Social Perception: Some Implications for the Study of Person Memory and Interpersonal Judgments," *Journal of Personality and Social Psychology*, 38 (6), 841-56.

Steenkamp, Jan-Benedict E.M., Rajeev Batra, and Dana L. Alden (2003), "How Perceived Globalness Creates Brand Value," *Journal of International Business Studies*, 34 (1), 53-65.

Swaminathan, Vanitha, Karen L. Page, and Zeynep Gürhan-Canli (2007), "'My' Brand or 'Our' Brand: The Effects of Brand Relationship Dimensions and Self-Construal on Brand Evaluations," *Journal of Consumer Research*, 34 (August), 248-59.

Tu, Lingjiang, Adwait Khare and Yinlong Zhang (2012), "A short 8-item scale for measuring consumers' local–global identity," *International Journal of Research in Marketing***.**

Van Ittersum, Koert and Wong, Nacy (2010), "The Lexus or the Olive Tree? Trading Off Between Global Convergence and Local Divergence," *International Journal of Research in Marketing,* 27(2), 107-118.

Zhang, Yinlong, and Adwait Khare (2009), "The Impact of Accessible Identities on the Evaluation of Global versus Local Products," *Journal of Consumer Research***,** 36 (October), 524-37**.**

Moving On and Away: Closure Increases Psychological Distance Through Emotion

Jae-Eun Namkoong, University of Texas at Austin, USA
Andrew Gershoff, University of Texas at Austin, USA

EXTENDED ABSTRACT

Psychological closure is the feeling of completeness of an experience, providing a feeling of *pastness* or distance between an experience and the current time (Beike, Adams et al. 2007). A same event can feel like it happened yesterday or like ancient history (Van Boven, Kane et al. 2010), and the notion of closure is important to consumer researchers because it may influence evaluations of the time since a product or service failure, or the likelihood that similar negative events will reoccur. In turn, this could affect the likelihood of consumers retaliating against a brand, likelihood of re-trying or reconsidering a brand, as well as decisions about insurance to protect from similar outcomes.

In this research, we examine how closure influences evaluations of psychological distance from negative product experiences. We propose and test the role of emotional intensity as a mediating mechanism. Prior research has shown that closure alleviates negative emotion (Beike and Wirth-Beaumont 2005; Li, Wei et al. 2010) and that emotional intensity and psychological distance have a negative relationship (Van Boven, Kane et al. 2010). In the present research we link these constructs to demonstrate that psychological closure is a significant determinant of psychological distance, both perceived temporal distance in Studies 1 and 2, and perceived probabilistic distance in Studies 3 and 4. Further, we explore the role of emotional intensity as both mediator (Study 1 to 4) and moderator (Study 3 & 4) of this process.

Our findings show that, when people experience closure on a negative event, they feel as if the event happened a longer time ago and that a similar problem is less likely to reoccur. This perception was reflected in perceived product quality, purchase intention, and willingness to purchase insurance.

Study 1 was conducted in a university with a top ranked football team. The negative consumer experience was the team's previous football season, which was one of the worst in the school's history. All participants first read a short news clip reminding them of the overall abysmal performance of the team during the season. Next, depending on condition, participants were instructed to provide reasons why they would consider the prior year's football season as "closed" or "not closed." This manipulation task has been successfully used in previous literature (Beike, Adams et al. 2007; Beike, Adams et al. 2010) and was used in all 4 studies of this research. After the closure manipulation, participants reported on 11-point scales their felt emotions (i.e. frustrated, upset) when thinking about the football season. Finally, using measures from previous research (Van Boven, Kane et al. 2010), participants provided perceived temporal distance from the previous football season (0 = *Feels like yesterday*, 10 = *Feels far away*; 0 = *Feels very close*, 10 = *Feels very distant*). As predicted, participants in the high (vs. low) closure condition reported greater temporal distance (M = 7.2 vs. 5.4; p = .003), which was mediated by a significant reduction in emotional intensity (n boots = 5,000; 95% CI(.095, .822)). Study 2 further examined the mechanism by manipulating both closure and emotionality of the experience, and by looking at embarrassment rather than a loss as the negative experience (Dahl, Manchanda et al. 2001). Participants first recalled an embarrassing moment from the past and described it in either an emotional or emotionless manner depending on condition. Next, participants completed the closure manipulation as in study 1. As predicted, there was a significant interaction between closure and description emotionality. Those in the emotional description condition reported significantly higher perceived temporal distance in the high (vs. low) closure condition (M = 6.78 vs. 5.19; p = .004) while there was no significant effect of closure in the low emotion condition. The moderated mediation was also significant. In the emotional description conditions, emotional intensity significantly mediated the effect of closure on perceived temporal distance (n boots = 5,000; 95% CI(.234, .75)), but no effect or mediation was found in the low emotion description condition.

Study 3 and 4 further expanded these results by examining closure on probabilistic distance. In study 3 participants read a negative product review and were instructed to write about why the experience could be thought of as closed or not closed, depending on condition. Participants in the high (vs. low) closure condition thought the likelihood of the problem reoccurring was lower which was also reflected in their evaluations of product quality and purchase intention (M = 3.85 vs. 3.37; p = .032). This was mediated by significant changes in emotional intensity (n boots = 5,000; 95% CI(.015, .213)).

Study 4, like study 2, manipulated both closure and emotionality on participants' own negative product experiences, by manipulating whether participants wrote about it in either an emotional or pallid style, and by whether or not the experience could be considered closed or not. The predicted interaction revealed that, when participants described the event in an emotional manner, high (vs. low) closure led to a lower willingness to purchase insurance that would protect them from that problem in the future (M = 3.86 vs. 5.81; p = .001). The same moderated mediation pattern as Study 2 emerged. In the emotional description conditions, emotional intensity significantly mediated the effect of closure on probabilistic distance (n boots = 5,000; 95% CI(-.486, -.003)), but no effect or mediation was found in the emotionless description condition.

To summarize, our results demonstrate how closure increases psychological distance as mediated though emotional intensity. With closure participants feel events happened longer ago (Study 1 & 2) and were less likely to reoccur (Study 3 & 4). Manipulation of emotionality and mediation analysis shows how emotional intensity underlies this effect. The findings contribute to the literature on psychological closure and psychological distance by finding it a new consequence and determinant, respectively.

REFERENCES

Beike, D. and E. Wirth-Beaumont (2005). "Psychological closure as a memory phenomenon." *Memory* 13(6): 574-593.

Beike, D. R., L. P. Adams, et al. (2010). "Closure of autobiographical memories moderates their directive effect on behaviour." *Memory* 18(1): 40-48.

Beike, D. R., L. P. Adams, et al. (2007). "Incomplete inhibition of emotion in specific autobiographical memories." *Memory* 15(4): 375-389.

Dahl, D. W., R. V. Manchanda, et al. (2001). "Embarrassment in consumer purchase: The roles of social presence and purchase familiarity." *Journal of Consumer Research* 28(3): 473-481.

Li, X., L. Wei, et al. (2010). "Sealing the Emotions Genie." *Psychological Science* 21(8): 1047.

Van Boven, L., J. Kane, et al. (2010). "Feeling Close: Emotional Intensity Reduces Perceived Psychological Distance." *Journal of Personality and Social Psychology* 98(6): 872.

Powerlessness-induced Compensatory Consumption: The Preference for Experiential vs. Material Luxury Products

Ayalla Ruvio, Temple University, USA
David Dubois, INSEAD, France

EXTENDED ABSTRACT

Despite the lasting financial crisis, the commerce of luxury goods and services has enjoyed a continuous growth, reaching $276 billion in sales in 2011 worldwide (Bain 2011). To better understand the reasons of this success, recent work has started to examine more specifically the motives underlying individuals' motivation to consume luxury products. In particular, recent work suggested that states of powerlessness can increase consumers' preference for status products, because these products help them to alleviate the aversive feelings associated with powerlessness (Rucker and Galinsky 2008).

The present work builds on a key distinction between two types of luxury offerings: experiences (e.g., a luxurious vacation or dining in a high-end restaurant) and products (e.g., a status car or designer piece of furniture). Interestingly, while some offerings might be uniquely categorized as experiences or products, a luxury brand might choose to frame its offering (e.g., a car) either as an experience (by emphasizing driving the car) or a material product (by emphasizing its features). As a first step, we investigate how one pervasive factor – consumers' sense of power – will affect consumers' preferences for experiential vs. material luxury. By power, we refer to people's perceived or actual asymmetric control over valued resources in social relations (Rucker, Galinsky and Dubois 2012). Past work showing that powerless consumers are more willing to spend on a luxury product than powerful and power-neutral consumers (Rucker and Galinsky 2008) might predict that states of powerlessness equally foster preferences for material and experiential products, but little is known about whether the powerless' preference might vary based on whether luxury is experiential or material. Yet, recent research argued that experiences can be more rewarding than products (Carter and Gilovich 2010; Van Boven and Gilovich 2003). Thus, we make the novel proposition that states of powerlessness would foster greater preference for experiential luxury than for material luxury. In support for this proposition, the powerless' sensitivity to their environment might increase the value derived from experiential products (Galinsky et al 2008).

We conducted two experiments to test these hypotheses. Results were analyzed using ANOVAs, regressions and t-tests, as appropriate.

EXPERIMENT 1

The Powerless' Preference for Experiential vs. Material Luxury. One hundred and sixty four undergraduates filled out an online survey in exchange for extra course credit. They were randomly assigned to conditions in a 3 (power: low, high, control) × 2 (status: low, high) × 2 (product type: experience, possession) mixed design with status and object serving as a within-participants factor. Participants were asked to recall a time they had or lacked power (Galinsky et al. 2003). Subsequently, participants were told they would participate to the evaluation of different consumer products. More specifically, participants were shown four different products associated with high and low levels of status, two of which were experiences (high-status: a luxury vacation; low-status: a massage; Van Boven and Gilovich 2003) and two of which were material objects (high-status: luxury car; low-status: a fabric sofa; Rucker and Galinsky 2008). Participants were asked to indicate how much they would be willing to pay for each of the products. Consistent with past research, results re-vealed a main effect for power, status and type of product, replicating both Rucker and Galinsky's (2009) and Van Boven and Gilovich's (2003) findings. Participants were willing to pay significantly more for a product under the low power (p< .05), for high status products (p < .001), and for experiential products (p < .001). Of key importance, there was he significant interaction of power × status × product type (p < .05). Low-power participants indicated a higher willingness to pay for experiential luxury than for material luxury, p <.01. Overall, these results support both Rucker and Galinsky (2008) and Van Boven and Gilovich (2003) assertions. Under the aversive state of powerless, consumer will pay more for high status material products, but will pay even more for high status experiential products.

EXPERIMENT 2

Framing Luxury as Experience or Material. One hundred and twenty eight undergraduates filled out an online survey in exchange for extra course credit. They were randomly assigned to conditions in a 2 (power: low, high) × 2 (status: low, high) × 2 (product characteristics: experiential, material) between-participants design. Power was manipulated through the recall task as in experiment 1. Next, participants took part to a consumer product experience. Participants were exposed to a high-status (Ferrari car) or low-status (Mini-van) framed as experiential ("the perfect driving experience") or material luxury ("the perfect car to own"). Our dependent variable was participants' willingness to pay for the product, in percent of the retail price. Results revealed significant main effects for status and for product type, similar to experiment 1 (p < .05). Of most importance, there was a significant power × status × product interaction (p < .01). That is, our participants were willing to pay the most under a low power condition and for the high status car when highlighting its experiential attribute than when highlighting its material attribute (p <.01).

Thus, overall consumers will be willing to pay more for material products when they are thinking of the in experiential terms. Nevertheless, once again, state of low power forester greater attractiveness to high status experiential purchases in the form of willingness to pay for them.

CONCLUSION AND CONTRIBUTIONS

Overall, our results successfully both replicated and integrated classic findings from the power literature (Rucker and Galinsky 2008; 2009) and the literature on experiential purchases (Carter and Gilovich 2010; Van Boven and Gilovich 2003) assertions, and supported our novel proposition: powerless consumers paid more for high status luxury products overall, and indicated a higher preference for experiential purchases over material ones. These results suggest that experiential purchases have a greater compensatory power than material ones, and multiply the possibilities for future research. Implications for power, and luxury marketing practices are discussed.

SELECTED REFERENCES

Bain (2010), Luxury Goods Worldwide Market Study, 7th ed., Boston: Bain.

Carter, Travis J., and Thomas Gilovich (2010), "The relative relativity of experiential and material purchases", *Journal of Personality and Social Psychology, 98,* 146-159.

Rucker, Derek D. and Adam Galinsky (2008), "Desire to Acquire: Powerlessness and Compensatory Consumption," *Journal of Consumer Research*, 35, 257-67.

Van Boven, Leaf and Thomas Gilovich (2003), "To do or to have: That is the question", *Journal of Personality and Social Psychology, 85,* 1193-1202.

Can Brands Move In from the Outside:
How Moral Identity Enhances Out-group Brand Evaluations

Woo Jin Choi, Texas A&M University, USA
Karen Page Winterich, Pennsylvania State University, USA

EXTENDED ABSTRACT:

Consumers tend to evaluate out-group brands less favorably than in-group brands. Though in-group favoritism and out-group hostility are well-established in the literature, little is known about how out-group brand evaluations can be improved. However, as the number of niche brands with small customer segments expand (Aaker 1991; Erdem and Sun 2002), brands that are perceived as the outgroup or are seeking to increase their customer base by appealing to more customer segments will need to overcome the less than favorable attitudes toward their brands. As such, marketers need to understand how consumers' out-group brand evaluations can be improved. To address this issue, we theorize that moral identity (hereafter, MI) will aid marketers of out-group brands in overcoming out-group hostility by enhancing brand evaluations.

MI is a self-regulating construct that fosters one's moral actions (Aquino and Reed 2002). Prior research on MI suggests that individuals with high self-importance of MI have more expansive group boundaries (Reed and Aquino 2003). However, this expansive effect of MI has focused on prosocial and moral behavior toward outgroups (Hardy et al. 2010; Reed and Aquino 2003) without considering whether these psychological characteristics of MI may extend to brands. Recognizing the role that morality may play in personal relationships (Hart et al. 1998; Reed and Aquino 2003) and the relationships that consumers have with brands (Aaker 1997) suggests that MI can be extended beyond moral behavior. Specifically, MI may influence consumers' responses to brands, which hold important social and reference group associations for consumers.

We theorize that MI will act as a conduit that reduces the perceived distance between a consumer and his or her out-group brands, thereby enhancing out-group brand evaluations. More specifically, consumers with high MI will more favorably evaluate their out-group brands compared to those with low MI such that MI moderates the effect of group membership on brand evaluations. Given the existing tendency to favor in-group brands (Escalas and Bettman 2005; White and Dahl 2007), we propose that MI will not influence in-group brand evaluations. Furthermore, we theorize that this effect will be mediated by the psychological distance, the "subjective" perception regarding how close or far an object is from the self (Trope and Liberman 2010), between consumers and their out-group brands.

We conducted four studies to test our theorizing. Study 1 examined the moderating effect of MI on brand evaluations by measuring the chronic self-importance of MI. First, participants self-identified one ingroup and one outgroup and then listed a brand associated with each group, which followed Escalas and Bettman's (2005) procedure. After a 20 minute unrelated task, participants evaluated (using 4 items; e.g., unfavorable/favorable on a 7-point scale) the two brands that they identified earlier among several other filler brands and completed the Self-Importance of Moral Identity Scale (Aquino and Reed 2002). As theorized, the results revealed that consumers' MI enhanced attitudes toward out-group brands but did not affect attitudes for in-group brands.

To assess whether this effect occurred due to MI rather than related constructs, study 2 replicated these results using temporarily salient MI (Aquino et al., 2009). We primed participants with either MI or a student identity (SI, hereafter). Those primed with MI should temporarily have MI salient and those primed with SI should tem-

porarily have their SI salient, and thus temporarily low salience for MI, such that those in the MI condition would evaluate out-group brands more favorably than those in the SI condition, but identity prime would have no effect on in-group brand evaluations. Results were consistent with this theorizing.

Studies 3 and 4 investigated the underlying process by examining the mediating role of the psychological distance between the consumer and the brand. To measure the psychological distance between a consumer and a brand, we utilized the Inclusion of Others in Self scale (IOS; Aron et al. 1992). In study 3, a 2 (brand group membership: in-group vs. out-group) within-subjects design was used with MI measured continuously. All participants evaluated the pre-designated in-group (i.e., Nike, Polo) and out-group (i.e., TOMS, Old Navy) brands, which were pretested and presented in random order. The findings of Study 3 replicated the results of the first two studies, demonstrating the positive influence of consumers' MI on out-group brand evaluations but no effect of MI on in-group brand evaluations. More importantly, the effect of MI was mediated by the psychological distance such that consumers with high MI were more likely to expand their boundaries to outgroups than where those with low MI.

Study 4 sought to demonstrate the practical implications of these findings for out-group brands seeking to improve their brand evaluations. Thus, we primed MI versus business identity (BI) in an advertisement for a hypothetical brand. Though previous studies on MI (e.g., Reed et al. 2007) manipulated participants' MI through priming tasks, to the best of our knowledge, this study is the first attempt to show that MI can be temporarily primed through an advertisement. A 2 (brand group membership: in-group vs. out-group) X 2 (primed identity: BI vs. MI) between-subjects design was used. The results replicated the moderating effect of MI on brand group membership on brand evaluations as well as the mediating role of psychological distance such that brand evaluations of a hypothetical out-group brand were more favorable when participants were exposed to the brand with an advertisement eliciting temporarily accessible MI.

This research extends both the marketing and MI literature by addressing the role of MI in consumers' brand evaluations. First, we identify the role of MI in everyday consumer judgments that do not regard moral decision-making. Though it may be obvious that MI would influence prosocial behavior and brand evaluations for brands engaging in CSR or other moral behaviors, we demonstrate that the effects of MI extend beyond prosocial behavior to marketplace judgments such as brand evaluations irrespective of the moral behaviors of the firm. Furthermore, brand managers seeking to overcome the less favorable perceptions associated with out-group brands may benefit from drawing upon consumers' MI in their marketing communications.

REFERENCES

Aaker, David A. (1991), *Managing Brand Equity*. New York: The Free Press.

Aaker, Jennifer L. (1997), "Dimensions of Brand Personality," *Journal of Marketing Research*, 34 (August), 347-56.

Aquino, Karl and Americus Reed II (2002), "The Self-Importance of Moral Identity," *Journal of Personality and Social Psychology*, 83 (December), 1423-40.

Aquino, Karl, Dan Freeman, Americus Reed II, Vivien K. G. Lim, and Will Felps (2009), "Testing a Social-Cognitive Model of Moral Behavior: The Interactive Influence of Situations and Moral Identity Centrality," *Journal of Personality and Social Psychology*, 97 (1), 123-141.

Aron, Arthur, Elaine N. Aron, and Danny Smollan (1992), "Inclusion of the Other in the Self Scale and the Structure of Interpersonal Closeness," *Journal of Personality and Social Psychology*, 63 (October), 596-612.

Erdem, Tűlin and Baohong Sun (2002), "An Empirical Investigation of the Spillover Effects of Advertising and Sales Promotions in Umbrella Branding," *Journal of Marketing Research*, 39 (November), 408-20.

Escalas, Jennifer E. and James R. Bettman (2005) "Self-Construal, Reference Groups, and Brand Meaning," *Journal of Consumer Research*, 32 (December), 378-89.

Hardy, Sam A., Amit Bhattacharjee, Americus Reed II, and Karl Aquino (2010), "Moral identity and Psychological Distance: The Case of Adolescent Parental Socialization," *Journal of Adolescence*, 33, 111-23.

Hart, Daniel, Robert Atkins, and Debra Ford (1998), "Urban America as a Context for the Development of Moral Identity in Adolescence," *Journal of Social Issues*, 54 (3), 513-30.

Reed, Americus II (2004), "Activating the Self-Importance of Consumer Selves: Exploring Identity Salience Effects on Judgments," *Journal of Consumer Research*, 31 (Sept), 286-95.

_____ and Karl Aquino (2003), "Moral Identity and the Expanding Circle of Moral Regard toward Out-Groups," *Journal of Personality and Social Psychology*, 84 (June), 1270-86.

_____, _____, and Eric Levy (2007), "Moral Identity and Judgments of Charitable Behaviors," *Journal of Marketing*, 71 (January), 178-93.

Trope, Yaacov and Nira Liberman (2010), "Construal Level Theory and Psychological Distance," *Psychological Review*, 117 (2), 440-463.

White, Kate and Darren Dahl (2007), "Are All Out-Groups Created Equal? Consumer Identity and Dissociative Influence," *Journal of Consumer Research*, 34 (December), 525-36.

The Influences of Social Power on Social and Physical Distance

Yanli Jia, Chinese University of Hong Kong, China
Robert S. Wyer, Chinese University of Hong Kong, China
Hao Hu, Chinese University of Hong Kong, China

EXTENDED ABSTRACT

Social power refers to the ability to control others' resources and outcomes (e.g., Fiske, 1993). However, there is a metaphorical relationship between social power and social distance. This relation is often conveyed symbolically. When a picture of a company hierarchy is drawn, for example, the CEO is at the top, with less powerful individuals at increasing distances away. This relationship may extend to physical distance as well. Construal level theory (e.g., Liberman, Trope and Wakslak, 2007) suggests that activating concepts of distance along one dimension can potentially influence judgments and overt behavior along other dimensions of distance to which these concepts are metaphorically related. The present research examined implications of this possibility.

The notion that "power equals distance" pervades many societies. Socially powerful individuals typically possess substantial material/social resources and do not need to depend on others for survival. Therefore, they may be disposed to see themselves as separate and distinctive. By the same token, individuals with little power are more likely to depend on others to survive. Consequently, they are more likely to be motivated to maintain social closeness to others. These differences in social distance could generalize to physical distances.

This relation may not hold for the particular individuals involved in a power relationship. Powerful people might be motivated to be close to their powerless counterparts in order to successfully exert their influence, whereas low-power individuals might resist being influenced against their will and find others' imposition on them to be aversive. To this extent, they may be motivated to keep distance from those who have power over them. This, therefore, leads to our main hypothesis:

Hypothesis 1   *People who perceive themselves to have high power in a particular relationship will judge themselves to be closer to the other person involved in this relationship, but more distant from people in general, than people who perceive themselves to have low power.*

Three studies examined the possibility. In one study, participants wrote about a personal experience in which they either had power over another or another had power over them. Then, they indicated both how close they felt to the other person in the situation they recalled and to other college students in general (adopted from Aron, Aron and Smollan, 1992). Participants perceived their distance from the person they wrote about to be less, but their distance from people in general to be greater, when they had written about a powerful experience than when they had described a powerless one.

A second study showed that individuals' perception of themselves as socially distant from people in general affected the *physical* distance from others at which they feel comfortable. After performing the same recall task we used in Study 1 to manipulate power status, participants were told that "because other persons are going to use this room, you will have to complete the second part of the experiment in a different room" and on this pretext, participants moved to a different room for completing a questionnaire that assessed their conformity (adopted from Shen, Wan and Wyer, 2011). Seven chairs were lined up in the middle of this room, and a schoolbag had been left on the chair next to the extreme right, suggesting the pres-

ence of another person (Snyder and Endelman, 1979). Participants chose to sit further away from the chair occupied by unknown other if they had previously described a powerful experience than if they described a powerless experience. Furthermore, they showed less willingness to conform to others' product preferences in the former condition than in the latter.

Finally, people's perceptions of their social distance from others may affect their subsequent behavior. We examined this possibility under a gift-exchange situation. Gift-giving has been interpreted as a confirmation of the giver's desire to establish a connection to the recipient (Sherry, 1983). When accepting a gift, however, people may take reciprocity norms into consideration and feel indebted if they accept a gift from someone they feel close to (Shen, Wan and Wyer, 2011). Therefore, we hypothesized that people who perceived themselves to be close to another would be more willing to give than to accept a gift, whereas people who perceived themselves to be distant from others might show the reverse pattern.

In a third study, participants first completed the same power-manipulation task employed in other studies. Then, they were asked to imagine a situation in which they shared a taxi with either (a) the person they recalled interacting with in the power-manipulation task or (b) a casual acquaintance. Finally, some participants indicated the likelihood that they would accept the other's offer to pay the fare for both of them, whereas others estimated the likelihood that they would personally offer to pay the fare for both of them. As expected, participants were more willing to offer to pay the fare for the person they had written about, but were less willing to accept the other's offer to pay, if they had had power over this person than if the person had had power over them. However, priming feelings of power slightly *decreased* their willingness to pay for a casual acquaintance, but increased their willingness to accept an offer from this person, than priming feelings of low power.

To conclude, although individuals who feel powerful are motivated to be close to the specific individuals over whom they have power, they prefer to be distant from people in general. Moreover, this tendency generalizes to actual behavior, leading them to sit further away from others, decreasing their tendency to conform to others' preferences in a product choice situation, and affecting their tendency to give and accept gifts.

REFERENCES

Fiske, Susan T. (1993), "Controlling Other People: the Impact of Power on Stereotyping", *American Psychologist*, 48, 621-628.

Liberman, Nira, Trope, Yaacov and Wakslak, Cheryl (2007), "Construal Level Theory and Consumer Behavior", *Journal of Consumer Psychology*, 17(2), 113-117

Aron, Arthur, Aron, Elaine N. and Smollan, Danny (1992), "Inclusion of Other in the Self Scale and the Structure of Interpersonal Closeness", *Journal of Personality and Social Psychology*, 63 (4), 596-612.

Snyder, C. R. and Endelman, Janet R. (1979), "Effects of Degree of Interpersonal Similarity on Physical Distance and Self-reported Attraction: A Comparison of Uniqueness and Reinforcement Theory Predictions", *Journal of Personality*, 47 (3), 492-505.

Shen, Hao, Wan, Fang and Wyer, Robert S. (2011), "Cross-Cultural Difference in the Refusal to Accept a Small Gift: The Differential Influences of Reciprocity Norms on Asians and North Americans", *Journal of Personality and Social Psychology*, 100 (2), 271-281.

Sherry, John F. (1983), "Gift Giving in Anthropological Perspective", *Journal of Consumer Research*, 10 (2), 157-168.

The Effect of Package Shape on Consumer's Calorie Estimation

Jieun Koo, Korea University, Korea
Kwanho Suk, Korea University, Korea

EXTENDED ABSTRACT

People are becoming more conscious about health and weight control and as a consequence, calorie intake is an important concern for many consumers. However, people's calorie estimation is shown to be vulnerable to various biases associated with the influence of nutrition labels (e.g., low fat) and package sizes (Chandon and Wansink 2007; Scott et al. 2008). This research investigates another source of bias in calorie estimation, namely, the shape of the package containing food.

According to the well-known elongation bias, container shape affects perception of spatial volume. People perceive the volume of a taller container as larger than that of a shorter and wider container (Raghubir and Krishna 1999). Extant research has also shown that the shape of the container affects perceived consumption and product choice (Chandon and Ordabayeva 2009; Folkes and Matta 2004; Krishna 2006; Raghubir and Krishna 1999; Wansink and Van Ittersum 2003). However, little attention has been directed to the influence of container shape on calorie estimation, which may be partially caused by the common belief that calorie is a direct function of volume. This lay belief would suggest that when the two containers are equal in their actual volume, foods will be estimated to have more calories when they are contained in a taller container than a wider container due to the elongation bias.

We propose the idea contradictory to this belief. Specifically, we hypothesize that food is perceived to have *lesser* calories when it is contained in a taller than in a wider container. This counterintuitive effect is assumed to arise from different psychological processes underlying the estimation of spatial volume and that of calories. Volume estimation is based on perceptual judgment and a taller container is perceived to be more voluminous because human perception emphasizes height as the most salient dimension (visual prominence effect) (Krider, Raghubir, and Krishna 2001). In contrast, calorie estimation is conceptually driven. Because calorie is ambiguous and intangible, calorie judgment relies on inferences based on cognitive associations. This is reason why consumer's calorie estimation has been shown to be influenced by situationally activated concepts (Chandon and Wansink 2007; Chernev 2010; Scott et al. 2008; Kardes, Posavac, and Cronley 2004, Wansink and Chandon 2006).

We hypothesize that package shape affects calorie estimation due to different conceptual associations activated by different shape. We propose that taller and thinner packages activate the concepts relating to slimness and lightness, whereas shorter and wider packages activate concepts relating to fatness and heaviness. Further, consumers use concepts brought to their mind to infer calories, resulting in biases in judgment. The slimness and lightness activated by an elongated container will lead to underestimation of calories. By contrast, fatness and heaviness associated with a shorter and wider container will lead to overestimation of calories.

Hypothesis 1: *Food will be perceived to have lower calories when it is contained in a taller container than when it is contained in a wider container even though the actual volume is made constant.*

In Study 1, 40 participants estimated the calories of milk placed in a tall or a wide glass. The two glasses had equal volumes. The estimated calorie of milk in the wider glass was higher than that in the taller glass (M_{taller} = 140.0 vs. M_{wider} = 163.3; $F(1, 38)$ = 20.75, $p <$ .001). The results were consistent with our hypothesis.

Study 2 demonstrates the opposite effect of package shape on volume estimation and calorie estimation. We expect a taller container to be perceived to have more volume but lesser calories than a wider glass. Participants were presented with orange juice placed in a tall or wide glass. The participants estimated either the calories or the volume of the contained orange juice. Consistent with the elongation bias, the juice in the taller glass was perceived to be greater in volume than that in the wider glass (M_{taller} = 947.9 vs. M_{wider} = 917.6; $F(1, 143)$ = 5.42, p = .021). However, the juice in the taller glass was judged to have lower calories than that in the wider glass (M_{taller} = 461.3 vs. M_{wider} = 485.6; $F(1, 144)$ = 7.92).

Study 3 extends our findings to the package display orientation. In this study, the same rectangular-shaped package is displayed either vertically or horizontally. Vertical display would make the product look slimmer and lighter, whereas horizontal display would make the product look fatter and heavier. Accordingly, perceived calorie would be lower when the same package is presented vertically instead of horizontally. In the study, participants were presented with five food products, each of which is contained in a rectangular-shaped package. The packages were then presented either vertically (i.e., height is greater than width) or horizontally (i.e., width is greater than height). A 2 (package display: vertical vs. horizontal) × 5 (products) ANOVA on estimated calories showed the significant main effect of package display, indicating that participants estimated lower calories when the packages were presented vertically, rather than horizontally ($M_{vertical}$ = 334.7 vs. $M_{horizontal}$ = 475.2; $F(1, 53)$ = 11.27, p = .001). Separate test for each product category showed the significant effect of display direction for all five products (all $t(53) >$ 2.12, all p's < .046).

In conclusion, the results of the current research demonstrate the relationship between shape of product package and consumer's calorie estimation. Contradicting to the belief that calorie estimation is a positive function of volume estimation, our findings from three studies show that a taller package perceived to have more volume was judged to contain lesser calories. We believe our research contributes to the existing literature on consumer calorie estimation and spatial perception by separating the psychological mechanisms underlying these two seemingly related judgments.

REFERENCES

Chandon, Pierre and Brian Wansink (2007), "The Biasing Health Halos of Fast-Food Restaurant Health Claims: Lower Calorie Estimates and Higher Side-Dish Consumption Intentions," *Journal of Consumer Research*, 34 (October), 301-14.

Chandon, Pierre and Nailya Ordabayeva (2009), "Supersize in One Dimension, Downsize in Three Dimensions: Effects of Spatial Dimensionality on Size Perceptions and Preferences", *Journal of Marketing Research*, 46 (December), 739-53.

Chernev, Alexander (2010), "The Dieter's Paradox," *Journal of Consumer Psychology*, 21 (April), 178-83.

Folkes, Valerie and Shashi Matta (2004), "The Effect of Package Shape on Consumers' Judgments of Product Volume: Attention as a Mental Contaminant," *Journal of Consumer Research*, 31 (September), 390-401.

Kardes, Frank R., Steven S. Posavac, and Maria L. Cronley (2004), "Consumer Inference: A Review of Processes, Bases, and Judgment Contexts," *Journal of Consumer Psychology*, 14 (3), 230-56.

Krider, Robert E., Priya Raghubir, and Aradhna Krishna (2001), "Pizzas: π or square? Psychophysical Biases in Area Comparisons," *Marketing Science*, 20 (Fall), 405-25.

Krishna, Aradhna (2006), "Interaction of Senses: The Effect of Vision versus Touch on the Elongation Bias," *Journal of Consumer Research*, 32 (March), 557-66.

Raghubir, Priya and Aradhna Krishna (1999), "Vital Dimensions in Volume Perception: Can the Eye Fool the Stomach?" *Journal of Marketing Research*, 36 (August), 313-26.

Scott, Maura L., Stephen M. Nowlis, Naomi Mandel, and Andrea C. Morales (2008), "The Effects of Reduced Food Size and Package Size on the Consumption Behavior of Restrained and Unrestrained Eaters," *Journal of Consumer Research*, 35 (October), 391-405.

Wansink, Brian and Koert Van Ittersum (2003), "Bottom Up! The Influence of Elongation on Pouring and Consumption Volume," *Journal of Consumer Research*, 30 (December), 455-63.

Wansink, Briand and Pierre Chandon (2006), "Can "Low-Fat" Nutrition Labels Lead to Obesity?" *Journal of Marketing Research*, 43 (November), 605-17.

Anti-Consumption Lifestyles and Personal Debt

Marcelo Nepomuceno, ESCP Europe, France
Michel Laroche, Concordia University, Canada

EXTENDED ABSTRACT

This study examines if the scores on anti-consumption lifestyles correlate with account balance and balance due. In a sample of Brazilians customers, it was found that voluntary simplicity, but not frugality and tightwadism, correlate negatively with balance due. In addition, none of the lifestyles correlates significantly with account balance.

The adoption of anti-consumption lifestyles results in the voluntary reduction of consumption by individuals. This study investigates the impact of adopting such lifestyles on the banking behavior of Brazilian customers. Arguably, an individual who reduces consumption will naturally spend less money, and have more resources. Therefore, we test if frugal consumers (Lastovicka et al. 1999), tightwad consumers (Rick, Cryder, and Loewenstein 2008), and voluntary simplifiers (Iwata 1999; Zavestoski 2002) are less susceptible to debt.

Testing this susceptibility to credit is important for two reasons. First, financial institutions should be particularly interested about customers who adopt such lifestyles. Banks that attract such customers are able to use their credit to provide loans to other customers. Second, policy makers concerned with reducing the rate of personal indebtedness in a given population might promote anti-consumption lifestyles that correlate with lower debt levels.

This study looks at other factors that might affect one's personal debt. Antecedents included in the model are income, self-control, long-term orientation and materialism. Additionally, the interactions between these antecedents are also considered in the model.

A partnership between a Brazilian financial institution and the authors made the study possible. In this agreement, the financial institution supported the data collection by recruiting their customers for the study. The sample includes 502 customers with bank accounts in Cuiaba, in one of the major rural areas of Brazil. A special effort was dedicated to recruit participants with a wide range of income levels. To increase customer participation, the financial institution created a raffle with an Ipad2. The participants answered an online survey composed of several scales, presented in random order. To measure frugality, we used Lastovicka's et al. (1999) frugality scale, as translated by Castilhos and Petersen-Wagner (2009). To measure materialism, we used Garcia's (2009) adapted version of Richins' (2004) materialism scale. Tightwadism was measured with a back translated version of the tightwad-spendthrift scale (Rick, Cryder, and Loewenstein 2008). Voluntary simplicity was measured with a back translated version of the adapted Iwata's (1999) scale. Self-control was measured with a back translated version of the self-control scale (Tangney, Baumeister, and Boone 2004). Long-term orientation was measured with a back translated version of the long-term orientation measure (Bearden, Money and Nevins 2006). In addition, we used a translated version of an instructional manipulation check (Oppenheimer, Meyvis, and Davichenko 2009) to identify and remove inattentive participants. This resulted in the exclusion of 45 participants (or roughly 9%), and a final sample of 457 customers.

The financial institution provided information on the income, account balances and balance due for each of the 457 participants. Income, participants' scores on these scales and the interaction terms were considered as independent variables in two different analyses. First, a linear regression was performed using account balances as the dependent variable. It was found that account balances do not corre-

late significantly with income, anti-consumption lifestyles, materialism, self-control or long-term orientation. Therefore, the adoption of an anti-consumption lifestyle does not affect one's account balance. This occurs probably because the money saved through the adoption of an anti-consumption lifestyle is directed to savings accounts. However, the interaction between the materialism dimensions with income, self-control and long-term orientation significantly affects the scores on account balances. Most notably, it was found that a person who believes that acquisition is a central goal in life will have larger account balances to deal with the temptation of consuming. In addition, low-income individuals have larger account balances when they think that possessions are a source of happiness.

In the second analysis, a regression was run only with the 172 participants who had balances due. Financial institutions in Brazil offer pre-approved credit to its customers, without the need to sign a loan. However, a high-income is a necessary condition to have access to this service. Therefore, low-income individuals are considerably less likely to have balances due, as financial institutions do not offer them this service. To deal with this bias, the variable balances due was transformed into a new variable, which considers participants' incomes. This new variable, named "weighted balances due", is the mathematical result of the division of balances due by income. When analyzing the impact of the independent variables on weighted balances due, it was found that voluntary simplifiers own less debt (β=-.283, p=.006), whereas frugality and tightwadism do not shield one from having larger balances due. Also interestingly, high-income individuals who score high on self-control have large balances due, probably because they are fooling themselves into believing that they are more self-controlled that they actually are. Finally, we found a negative correlation between the success dimension of materialism and "weighted balances due" (β=-.214, p=.05), indicating that individuals who use possessions to signal success are more prone to own larger debt. On the other hand, the centrality and happiness dimensions of materialism do not correlate significantly with balances due.

The current results show that not all anti-consumption lifestyles reduce one's balances due. The adoption of a simple lifestyle is the best shield that one has against owning larger debts. Furthermore, the belief that possessions signal success also leads one to have larger balances due. Therefore, at least in Brazil, policy makers concerned with the citizens' debt level should promote anti-materialistic values and a simple lifestyle, particularly to groups of individuals with high indebtedness. Finally, future studies should evaluate participants' saving accounts to test which anti-consumption lifestyles lead to more saving behavior. The current study showed that none of the lifestyles correlates with account balances significantly. However, this result might be particular to Brazil, where individuals are significantly motivated to invest any outstanding money. That is because, Brazil is a country with high inflation, and a place where investing in financial institutions is highly profitable.

REFERENCES

Bearden, William O., Money, R. Bruce and Nevins, Jennifer L. (2006), "A Measure of long-term orientation: development and validation", *Journal of the Academy of Marketing Science,* 34 (3), 456-467.

Castilhos, Rodrigo B., and Petersen-Wagner, Renan (2009), "Frugalidade, avaliacao de precos e clases sociais no varejo de calcados", *Revista Alcance - Eletrônica*, 16 (2), 162-180.

Garcia, Patricia A.O. (2009), "Escala Brasileira de Valores Materiais - EBVM - Elaboração e validação de um escala para materialismo como valor de consumo", *unpublished thesis*, Universidade de Brasilia, Brasilia - DF, 87 pages.

Iwata, Osamu (1999), "Perceptual and behavioral correlates of voluntary simplicity lifestyles", *Social Behavior and Personality: an International Journal,* 27 (4), 379-386.

Lastovicka, John L., Bettencourt, Lance A., Hughner, Renee S., and Kuntze, Ronald J. (1999), "Lifestyle of the tight and frugal: theory and measurement", *Journal of Consumer Research*, 26 (1), 85-98.

Oppenheimer, Daniel M., Meyvis, Tom, and Davidenko, Nicolas (2010), "Instructional manipulation checks: Detecting satisficing to increase statistical power", *Journal of Experimental Social Psychology*, 45 (4), 867-872.

Richins, Marsha L. (2004), "The Material Values Scale: Measurement Properties and Development of a Short Form", *Journal of Consumer Research*, 31 (1), 209-219.

Rick, Scott I., Cryder, Cynthia E., and Loewenstein, George (2008), "Tightwads and spendthrifts", *Journal of Consumer Research,* 34 (6), 767-782.

Tangney, June P., Baumeister, Roy F., and Boone, Angie L. (2004), "High self-control predicts good adjustment, less pathology, better grades, and interpersonal success", *Journal of Personality,* 72 (2), 271-324.

Zavestoski, Stephen (2002), "The Social-Psychological Bases of Anticonsumption Attitudes", *Psychology & Marketing,* 19 (2), 149-165.

Rebels Without a Clue:
Nonconscious Motivation for Autonomy Preservation Moderates Social Decision Biases

Randy Stein, University of California-Riverside, USA
Joshua Ackerman, Massachusetts Institute of Technology, USA
John A. Bargh, Yale University, USA

EXTENDED ABSTRACT

Consumer judgment and decision making is often shaped in unwanted ways by unconscious and uncontrollable processing, a phenomenon known as mental contamination (Wilson & Brekke, 1994). However, when consumers believe that contaminating influences threaten their judgments, they engage several resistance strategies. For instance, several lines of research converge on the idea that consumers prefer to make judgments that are self-generated and free from the influence of others, thus satisfying a basic need for autonomy (Ryan & Deci, 2006). When consumers perceive that communications threaten their freedom of belief, they become resistant to those communications and endorse their original positions more (Brehm 1966). Consumers also generally consider themselves better decision makers than others and devalue the thoughts and feelings others use to make decisions (Pronin et al., 2007; Pronin, 2008; Pronin & Kugler, 2007).

This line of thinking suggests that (at least from a lay perspective), when active, a motive to protect judgments from exogenous social influence might be an effective means of decreasing mental contamination. But is this accurate? Here, we confront the veracity of this idea by examining whether nonconscious autonomy preservation motivation reduces or, perhaps counterproductively, amplifies several decision biases that may result from contaminating social information.

Many decision biases might occur because individuals fail to properly regulate how social information is used. For example, incidentally heightened accessibility of another person can influence self-directed judgments via an automatic comparison process (e.g., Dijksterhuis et al., 1998). Here, an exogenous agent (the exemplar) taints views of the self because individuals fail to reject irrelevant social information. Since mental contamination is often caused by processing outside of conscious awareness, we reasoned that corrective processes need to be operating nonconsciously as well.

Thus, here we examine the effects of nonconsciously priming autonomy preservation (using a scrambled sentence test) across a wide range of decision biases. The current research adds to our understanding of mental contamination by addressing the broad sense in which the social environment contributes to biases, by showing how social perception processes can both increase and decrease bias (contrary to the lay belief that exogenous social influence is generally bad), and by examining how biases can be reduced without conscious awareness (previously thought to be impossible; Wilson & Brekke, 1994).

In Study 1, we demonstrated how autonomy preservation priming attenuates the usual effects of exemplar priming. Indeed, consistent with prior research (Dijksterhuis et al., 1998), in a neutral scrambled sentence prime condition, participants primed with Einstein considered themselves less intelligent than those primed with Britney Spears. However, in line with our hypothesis, when initially primed with autonomy preservation, this tendency actually reversed, $[F(3,27) = 7.87, p = .01]$.

In Study 2 we demonstrated that resistance priming also attenuates exemplar priming effects that usually cause assimilation. Following Gollwitzer et al. (2011) we utilized the exemplar prime of Mother Teresa and assessed its influence on judgments of prosocial values. In a control condition, participants tended to assimilate to the Mother Teresa prime; however, this tendency was reversed when initially primed with autonomy preservation $[F(3, 71) = 8.26, p = .005]$.

In Study 3 we tested whether autonomy preservation priming attenuates the halo effect, the robust tendency to evaluate attractive people more positively than unattractive people on a number of dimensions unrelated to attractiveness (Nisbett & Wilson, 1977). This effect is due at least in part to perceived similarity between attractive others and the self (Horton, 2003). Based on our earlier findings, we hypothesized that resistance priming should reduce the expression of this bias. We had participants rate two women (one relatively more attractive, one less attractive) on several interpersonal attributes. We found that resistance priming attenuated the tendency to evaluate the more attractive woman more positively, $[F(1, 113) = 6.76, p = .04]$.

The initial studies spotlight decision biases that result from a failure to reject social influence. However, it is also possible that some biases result from a too great an emphasis on autonomy preservation. For example, egocentric biases can occur when people fail to properly discount their own knowledge and take into account another person's knowledge and beliefs (e.g., Keysar, Ginzel, & Bazerman, 1995). Here, outside influence (i.e., other people's knowledge and beliefs) would help to mitigate such biases, but resisting influence would theoretically aggravate such biases.

In Study 4, we hypothesized that resistance priming would increase the "curse of knowledge" error (Keysar, Ginzel, & Bazerman, 1995). Participants completed Converse et al's (2008) adaption of the Birch & Bloom (2007) false belief task. In this task, participants make probability estimates about the likelihood that person A will look for an object (a violin) in a specific container when person B has either moved the object to a new container without person A's knowledge (privileged knowledge condition) or not (no privileged knowledge condition). We found that autonomy preservation-primed participants were more likely to use privileged knowledge (and hence, make a curse of knowledge error) when it was available, $[F(3, 96) = 4.15, p = .044]$.

In study 5 we examine how autonomy preservation priming increases the correspondence bias, an egocentric bias because of a failure to properly consider why someone might make a judgment that is disposition-inconsistent. Following Jones and Harris's (1967) classic paradigm participants were given an essay about the legalization of marijuana, with instructions indicating that the author's position was assigned by the experimenter. Participants estimated the author's actual attitude towards marijuana. Autonomy preservation-primed participants made stronger dispositional attributions than control participants $[t=2.18, p = .03]$.

These five studies highlight how autonomy preservation motivation reduces decision biases involving over-reliance on social information but increases biases involving under-reliance on social information, all without conscious awareness. These results highlight the broad influence of the social environment on mental contamination by strengthening while also alleviating specific biases. Thus, due to the nonconscious and autonomous operation of social resistance goals, consumers' presumption that resisting social influence will improve decision quality is not always accurate.

REFERENCES

Birch, Susan A.J. and Paul Bloom (2007). "The curse of knowledge in reasoning about false belief," *Psychological Science,* 18 (May), 382–386.

Brehm, Jack W. (1966). *A Theory of Psychological Reactance,* New York: Academic Press.

Converse, Benjamin A., Shuhong Lin, Boaz Keysar, and Nicholas Epley (2008). "In the mood to get over yourself: Mood affects theory-of-mind use," *Emotion,* 8 (October), 725-730.

Dijksterhuis, Ap, Russell Spears, Tom Postmes, Diederik Stapel, William Koomen, Ad van Knippenberg, Daan Scheepers (1998). "Seeing One Thing and Doing Another: Contrast Effects in Automatic Behavior," *Journal of Personality and Social Psychology*, 75 (October), 862-71.

Gilbert, Daniel T, Brett W. Pelham, and Douglas S. Krull (1988). "On cognitive busyness: When person perceivers meet persons perceived," *Journal of Personality and Social Psychology,* 54 (May), 733-740.

Gollwitzer, Peter M., Paschal Sheeran, Roman Trötschel, and Thomas Webb (2011). "Self-regulation of behavioral priming effects," *Psychological Science,* 22 (July) , 901-907.

Horton, Robert S. (2003). "Similarity and attractiveness in social perception: Differentiating between biases for the self and the beautiful," *Self & Identity,* 2 (April-June), 137–152.

Jones, Edward E., and Victor A. Harris (1967). "The attribution of attitudes," *Journal of Experimental Social Psychology,* 3 (May), 1–24.

Keysar, Boaz, Linda E. Ginzel, and Max H. Bazerman (1995). "States of Affairs and States of Mind: The Effect of Knowledge about Beliefs." *Organizational Behavior and Human Decision Processes,* 64 (December), 283-293.

Nisbett, Richard E. and Timothy D. Wilson, (1977). "The halo effect: Evidence for unconscious alteration of judgments," *Journal of Personality and Social Psychology,* 35 (April), 250-256.

Pronin, Emily (2008). "How we see ourselves and how we see others," *Science,* 320 (May), 1177-1180.

Pronin, Emily, Jonah Berger, and Sarah Molouki (2007). "Alone in a Crowd of Sheep: Asymmetric Perceptions of Conformity and Their Roots in an Introspection Illusion," *Journal of Personality and Social Psychology*, 92 (April), 585-95.

Pronin, Emily and Matthew B. Kugler (2007). "Valuing thoughts, ignoring behavior: The introspection illusion as a source of the bias blind spot," *Journal of Experimental Social Psychology,* 43 (July), 565-578.

Ryan, Richard M and Edward L. Deci (2006). "Self-Regulation and the Problem of Human Autonomy: Does Psychology Need Choice, Self-Determination, and Will?" *Journal of Personality,* 74 (December), 1557-1586.

Wilson, Timothy D and Nancy Brekke (1994). "Mental Contamination and Mental Correction: Unwanted influences on Judgments and Evaluations," *Psychological Bulletin*, 116 (July), 117-42.

The Difference Novelty Makes:
Incidental Exposure to Unfamiliar Stimuli Primes Exploratory Behavior

Gerri Spassova, Monash Unviversity, Australia
Alice M. Isen, Cornell University, Ithaca, USA

EXTENDED ABSTRACT

Understanding what makes consumers more likely to explore new products is of crucial importance to marketers. Prior research on consumer innovativeness has focused on identifying stable individual characteristics that determine the propensity of consumers to try new offerings. The present research takes a different perspective by investigating the role of contextual factors on consumer innovativeness. We propose that situational exposure to novelty primes exploratory behavior that carries over to subsequent unrelated choice tasks. Three studies demonstrate these effects and investigate their consequences.

THEORETICAL BACKGROUND

At the individual consumer level, innovativeness has been operationalized primarily as a stable trait, a "predisposition to buy new and different brands rather than remain with pervious choices" (Steenkamp, ter Hofstede, and Wedel 1999) and has been measured using various personality scales (Mehrabian 1978; Raju 1980; Zuckerman 1978).

There is some evidence, however, that innovativeness may be a malleable construct. For example, innovativeness is influenced by socio-behavioral variables, such as age, education, and income (Steenkamp and Gielens 2003), and by prior knowledge (Moreau, Lehmann, and Markman 2001). The amount of change in a person's life can also affect consumers' likelihood of trying less familiar products (Wood 2009) and contextual factors, such as positive mood, can enhance consumers' propensity to adopt brand extensions (Barone, Miniard, and Romeo 2000) or try less familiar products (Kahn and Isen 1993; Menon and Kahn 1999). In this research, we investigate the possibility that exposure to contextual novelty also promotes innovativeness, by priming exploratory behavior.

Context can have powerful effects on behavior (Bargh, Chen, and Burrows 1996; Bargh et al. 2001; Fitzsimons, Chartrand, and Fitzsimons 2008). Subtle environmental cues can activate mental constructs related to traits or goals that subsequently prompt construct-consistent behavior. Behavior can be automatically guided by the presentation of semantic associates (e.g., Bargh et al. 2001; Chartrand and Bargh 1996; Chartrand, Huber, Shiv and Tanner 2008), by the presence of other people (Bargh et al. 1996; Shah 2003), or by situations or objects associated with the behavior (e.g., Aarts and Dijksterhuis 2003; Chen, Lee-Chai, and Bargh 2001; Kay and Ross 2003). Even stimuli that have no prior associations but from which people extract meaning, such as visual arrays, can be a source of non-conscious construct activation (Maimaran and Wheeler 2008).

In this research we argue that behavior can also be influenced by stimuli that carry different semantic meanings but share a common property, such as being novel. We propose that this common property prompts property-consistent behavior, which carries over to unrelated situations. Specifically, we argue that exposure to novel stimuli primes subsequent exploratory behavior. It has been established that novel stimuli attract attention and promote exploration (Berlyne 1960; Fiske and Maddi 1961; Hirshman 1980; Venkatesan 1973). We build on this research and propose that exposure to novel stimuli prompts exploration in an unrelated subsequent situation, similar to the way in which exposure to a cue activating a semantic concept primes behavior consistent with this concept. We investigate the implications of the proposed effect for consumer behavior by testing the hypothesis that presentation of novel contextual stimuli prompts consumers to choose less familiar and more diverse products in a subsequent choice task.

METHOD AND FINDINGS

Study 1 shows that people who have been exposed to novelty choose a broader range of products in an unrelated subsequent choice task, but only when the available options are relatively unfamiliar. Novelty is operationalized as exposure to either new or familiarized neutral images. The subsequent consumer task involves choice of snacks from a set containing either very familiar options or less familiar options. A 2 x 2 ANOVA reveals a significant interaction between novelty prime and choice set familiarity ($F(1, 97) = 6.43$; $p < .05$). Novelty-primed participants choose a broader range of options than controls, indicating a greater propensity to explore, but only when the available options are relatively unfamiliar ($M_{novelty} = 4.97$ vs. $M_{control} = 4.35$, $t(58) = 2.39$, $p = .01$). When choosing from the more familiar set, novelty participants do not differ from controls ($M_{novelty} = 4.44$ vs. $M_{control} = 4.92$, $t(41) = 1.32$, $p = .10$).

Studies 2a and 2b test the effect of novelty on exploration in the context of choice of jam, using presentation of unfamiliar (vs. familiar) words as a manipulation of novelty. In Study 2a, where participants can choose as many options as they want from an assortment of 45 jams, novelty participants select a broader range of jams than controls ($M_{novelty} = 7.11$ vs. $M_{control} = 4.61$; $F(1, 35) = 5.21$, $p < .05$) and also choose a higher number of unusual flavors ($M_{novelty} = 4.08$ vs. $M_{control} = 1.89$, $F(1, 35) = 8.51$, $p = .006$). In study 2b, where participants can choose one out of a set of 30 jams, novelty-primed participants again choose more unusual and unfamiliar flavors ($N_{novelty} = .54$ vs. $M_{control} = .15$; $F(1, 47) = 10.91$, $p = .002$).

Study 3 replicates the previously observed effects in the context of real product choice. Novelty participants choose more unusual and unfamiliar jams, relative to controls ($M_{novelty} = .61$ vs. $M_{control} = .31$; $F(1, 38) = 4.13$, $p = .05$). After sampling their chosen jam, however, novelty participants report lower satisfaction with the chosen option ($M_{novelty} = 4.83$ vs. $M_{control} = 5.86$; $F(1, 38) = 4.65$, $p < .05$). Mediation analysis reveals that the effect of novelty exposure on post-sampling satisfaction is mediated by the unusualness of their choice.

CONTRIBUTION

This research contributes to the literature on consumer innovativeness by studying the ability of novelty exposure – a contextual factor that to some extent is controllable by retailers and manufacturers – to enhance exploratory behavior. We also contribute to the priming literature by showing that behavior can be influenced by exposure to stimuli that reference different semantic concepts but share a common property. This property primes related behavior that can carries over to unrelated tasks. Finally, we build on the literature on novelty by documenting downstream effects of novelty exposure that have not been shown before.

REFERENCES

Aarts, Henk and Ap Dijksterhuis (2003), "The Silence of the Library: Environment, Situational Norm, and Social Behavior," Journal of Personality and Social Psychology, 84 (1), 18-28.

Bargh, John A., Mark Chen, and Lara Burrows (1996), "Automaticity of Social Behavior: Direct Effects of Trait Construct and Stereotype Activation on Action," Journal of Personality and Social Psychology, 71 (2), 230-44.

Bargh, John A., Peter M. Gollwitzer, Annettee Lee-Chai, Kimberly Barndollar, and Roman Trotschel (2001, "The Automated Will: Nonconscious Activation and Pursuit of Behavioral Goals," Journal of Personality and Social Psychology, 81 (6), 1014-27.

Barone, Michael J., Paul W. Miniard, and J. B. Romeo (2000), "The influence of positive affect on brand extension evaluations," *Journal of Consumer Research*, 26 (March), 386-400.

Berlyne, Daniel E. (1960), "Conflict, Arousal and Curiosity," New York: McGraw-Hill.

Fiske, Donald W. and Salvatore R. Maddi (1961), *Functions of Varied Experience*, Homewood, IL: Dorsey Press.

Chartrand, Tanya L. and John A. Bargh (1996), "Automatic Activation of Impression Formation and Memorization Goals: Nonconscious Goal Priming Reproduces Effects of Explicit Task Instructions," Journal of Personality and Social Psychology, 71 (3), 464-78.

Chartrand, Tanya L., Joel Huber, Baba Shiv, and Rob Tanner (2008), "Nonconscious Goals and Consumer Choice," Journal of Consumer Research, 35 (August), 189-201.

Chen, Serena, Annette Y. Lee-Chai, and John A. Bargh (2001), "Relationship Orientation as a Moderator of the Effects of Social Power," Journal of Personality and Social Psychology, 80 (2), 173-87.

Fitsimons, Grainne, M., Tanya L. Chartrand, and Gavan J. Fitzsimons (2008), "Automatic Effects of Brand Exposure on Motivated Behavior: How Apple Makes You 'Think Different,'"Journal of Consumer Research, 35 (June), 21-35.

Hirschman, Elizabeth C. (1980), "Innovativeness, Novelty Seeking, and Consumer Creativity," *Journal of Consumer Research*, 7 (December), 283-95.

Kahn, Barbara E., and Alice M. Isen (1993), "Variety Seeking among Safe, Enjoyable Products," *Journal of Consumer Research*, 20 (September) 257 – 70.

Kay, Aaron C. and Lee Ross (2003), "The Perceptual Push: The Interplay of Implicit Cues and Explicit Situational Construals on Behavioral Intensions in the Prisoner's Dilemma," Journal of Experimental Social Psychology, 39 (6), 634-43.

Maimaran, Michal and J. Christian Wheeler (2008), "Circles, Squares, and Choice: The Effect of Shape Arrays on Uniqueness and Variety Seeking," *Journal of Marketing Research*, 45 (December), 731-40.

Mehrabian, Albert (1978), "Characteristic Individual Reactions to Preferred and Unpreferred Environments," *Journal of Personality*, 46 (December), 717-31.

Menon, Satya and Barbara E. Kahn (1995), "The Impact of Context on Variety Seeking in Product Choices, "*Journal of Consumer Research*," 22 (December), 285-295.

Moreau, C. Page, Donald R. Lehmann, and Arthur B. Markman (2001), "Entrenched Knowledge Structures," *Journal of Marketing Research*, 38 (February), 14-29.

Raju, P.S. (1980), "Optimum Stimulation Level: Its Relationship to Personality, Demographics, and Exploratory Behavior," *Journal of Consumer Research*, 7 (December), 272-82.

Shah, James (2003), "Automatic for the People: How Representations of Significant Others Implicitly Affect Goal Pursuit," Journal of Personality and Social Psychology, 84 (4), 661-81.

Steenkamp, Jan-Benedict E. M. and Katrijn Gielens (2003), "Consumer and Market Drivers of the Trial Probability of New Consumer Packaged Goods," *Journal of Consumer Research*, 30 (December), 368-82.

Steenkamp, Jan-Benedict, Frenkel ter Hofstede, and Michel Wedel (1999), "Antecedents of Consumer Innovativeness," *Journal of Marketing*, 63 (April), 55-69.

Venkatesan, M. (1973), "Cognitive Consistency and Novelty Seeking," in *Consumer Behavior: Theoretical Sources*, ed. Scott Ward and Thomas S. Robertson, Englewood Cliffs, NJ: Prentice Hall, 55-384.

Wood, Stacy (2010), "The Comfort Food Fallacy: Avoiding Old Favorites in Times of Change," Journal of Consumer Research, 36 (April), 950-63.

Zuckerman, Marvin, Sybil Eysenck, and Hans J. Eysenck (1978), "Sensation Seeking in England and America: Cross-cultural, Age, and Sex Comparisons," *Journal of Consulting and Clinical Psychology*, 46 (1), 139-49.

Guilt Appeals as a Blessing or a Curse?
Influences of Sponsorship Identity and Sponsor-Issue Fit on Guilt Appeals in Charity-Related Advertising

Chun-Tuan Chang, National Sun Yat-sen University, Taiwan
Ya-Ting Yu, National Sun Yat-sen University, Taiwan
You Lin, National Sun Yat-sen University, Taiwan

EXTENDED ABSTRACT

Nowadays as companies experience increasing competition, social cause efforts become a prominent role in the profit-seeking efforts of the corporation domain. Two types of societal marketing programs are common: (1) social sponsorship through explicit donation to a cause and (2) cause-related marketing (CRM) through consumer purchases. Because advertising determines the success of societal marketing programs (e.g., Chang, 2008), many advertising persuasion techniques are adopted. Emotional appeals are widely used to "cut through the clutter" in crowded media environment. Among them, guilt appeals are identified as popular to arouse persuasive communication, especially in prosocial and charitable contexts (e.g., Basil, Ridgway, and Basil, 2006 and 2008; Hibbert et al., 2007). Chang (2011) suggested the importance of exploring potential moderating variables in explaining the effects of guilt appeals.

Although societal marketing programs with charitable causes become popular among corporations, consumers may respond differently to corporate-sponsored social messages than they do to the similar ads sponsored by a non-profit. A corporate sponsor in association with a social message is likely to make ulterior motives accessible, which lead consumers to question the reasons behind sponsorship (Szykman, Bloom, and Blazing, 2004). People possess stereotypes of organizations merely based on the knowledge that a firm is a for-profit or non-profit (Aaker, Vohs, and Mogilner, 2010). Therefore, we predict that sponsorship identity will matter in consumer information processing and moderate the effects of guilt appeals.

Selecting the "right" cause by a company is a key to a successful societal marketing program. Nevertheless, the results of previous studies are inconsistent and contradictory regarding the influences of fit on advertising persuasion, e.g. whether high fit can be an asset or liability. A good fit between prior expectations, knowledge, and competencies of a firm and a promoted social cause can be more easily integrated into the consumers' existing cognitive structure and lead to favorable evaluation of the company (Becker-Olsen, Cudmore, and Hill, 2006; Menon and Kahn, 2003; Pracejus and Olsen, 2004; Rifon et al,. 2004; Sen and Bhattacharya, 2001; Simmons and Becker-Olsen, 2006). However, highly fitting relationships may raise consumer skepticism about company motives and lead consumers to respond more positively to non-fitting relationship (Barone, Norman, and Miyazaki, 2007; Bloom et al., 2006). The intriguing questions of whether and how different sponsorship contexts (who the ad sponsor is and what the sponsorship fit is) may enhance or disrupt consumer guilt perceptions and evaluation are addressed in this paper.

An experiment with 3 (sponsorship identity: corporate social sponsorship vs. CRM vs. non-profit) X 2 (sponsor-issue fit: high fit vs. low fit) X 2 (ad appeal: guilt vs. non-guilt appeals) factorial design was conducted. Prior to the experiment, the treatment booklets were randomized. Administration of the experiment was performed via a shopping mall intercept method. 429 participants were recruited over a 2-week period during mall operating hours. After successful manipulation checks, a series of analysis of variance were conducted to examine proposed hypotheses. Analyses on maladaptive responses were further conducted to test the mediator of maladaptive responses

on the effect of guilt appeal on purchase intention for the condition of corporate social advertising and CRM. Univariate results with dependent measures of attitudes toward the ad, attitudes toward the sponsor, and behavioral intentions are summarized in Table 1. Table 2 presents related descriptives across experimental conditions. Three main findings are noteworthy.

First, guilt appeals are found more effective than non-guilt appeals when the ad sponsor is a non-profit. The findings are consistent with previous studies (anti-alcohol: Becheur et al., 2008; bone marrow donation: Lindsey, 2005; charity donation: Basil et al., 2006 and 2008; Hibbert et al., 2007; condom promotion: Alden and Crowley, 1995; mammogram promotion: Turner et al., 2009). Social responsibility guilt has been identified as one of the major forms of consumer guilt (Burnett and Lunsford, 1994). The findings also echoes the charity donation literature that the guilt may be viewed as an awareness of the difference in well-being between oneself and others (Ruth and Faber, 1988) and guilt feelings can be used as a method of gaining compliance (Lindsey, Yun, & Hill, 2007).

Second, guilt appeals backfire when the sponsors-issue fit in a corporate social ad (i.e., explicit donation) is high. Maladaptive responses to charity appeals occur when an individual feels he or she is being manipulated, causing the individual to respond in a negative manner (Coulter and Pinto, 1995). Such responses make sense in that they seek to protect a consumer's balanced (homeostatic) state. In ads using guilt appeals, consumers may evaluate the degree to which the advertiser is attempting to manipulate their attitudes. Consumers will resist the message when they perceive the message as manipulative (Wood and Eagly, 1981). When guilt appeals are used to promote a corporate social ad, consumers are likely to interpret the ad as an explicit placement and view the advertising message as manipulative. Promotion with a high-fit social cause may be viewed as opportunistic and the sponsored company as merely seeking commercial gain for itself. Consumers thus counterargue the message and discount the sponsor to protect themselves from the persuasion attempt.

Third, guilt appeals have boomerang effects when the sponsor-issue fit in a CRM ad is low. When consumers could not find the link between the brand and the cause, they might not understand why they should give away a small fraction of the price they pay to a social cause. Consumers may also feel skeptical why the company "sells" such a low-fit cause to them. Due to people's fiscal associations with the for-profit's motive, the suspicion may negatively influence guilt appeals on sponsor evaluation.

The main goal of the present study was to extended earlier work on guilt appeals by identifying boundary conditions associated with the role of guilt appeals in consumer perceptions and attitudes. Findings from this investigation are informative both theoretically and pragmatically, and underscore the importance for marketers to learn more about when guilt appeals work, and in turn describe how practitioners can avoid negatively toward guilt appeals.

REFERENCES

Aaker, J., Vohs, K., and Mogilner, C. (2010), "Non-Profit Are Seen as Warm and For-Profits as Competent: Firm Stereotypes Matter" *Journal of Consumer Research,* 37 (August), 277-291.

Alden, D. L., and Crowley, A. E. (1995), "Sex Guilt and Receptivity to Condom Advertising," *Journal of Applied Social Psychology*, 25(16), 1446-1463.

Barone, M. J., Norman, A. T., and Miyazaki, A. D. (2007), "Consumer Responses to Retailer Use of Cause-Related Marketing: Is More Fit Better?" *Journal of Retailing*, 83(4), 437-445.

Basil, D. Z., Ridgway, N. M., and Basil, M. (2006), "Guilt Appeals: The Mediating Effect of Responsibility," *Psychology and Marketing*, 23(12), 1035-1054.

Basil, D. Z., Ridgway, N. M., and Basil, M. (2008), "Guilt and Giving: A Process Model of Empathy and Efficacy," *Psychology and Marketing*, 25(1), 1-23.

Becker-Olsen, K. L., Cudmore, B. A., and Hill, R. P., (2006), "The Impact of Perceived Corporate Social Responsibility on Consumer Behavior," *Journal of Business Research*, 59(1), 46-53.

Bloom, P. N., Hoeffler, S., Keller, K. L., and Meza, C. E. B., (2006), "How Social-cause Marketing Affects Consumer Perceptions," *MIT Sloan Management Review*, 47(2), 49-55.

Burnett, M. S., and Lunsford, D., (1994), "Conceptualizing Guilt in the Consumer Decision-Making Process," *Journal of Consumer marketing*, 11(3), 33-43.

Chang, C. (2008), "To Donate or Not to Donate? Product Characteristics and Framing Effects of Cause-Related Marketing on Consumer Purchase Behavior," *Psychology and Marketing*, 25(12), 1089-1110.

Chang, C. (2011), "Guilt Appeals in Cause-Related Marketing: The Subversive Roles of Product Type and Donation Magnitude," *International Journal of Advertising*, 30(4), 587-617.

Coulter, R. H., and Pinto, M. B., (1995), "Guilt Appeals in Advertising: What are Their Effects?" *Journal of Applied Psychology*, 80(6), 697-705.

Hibbert, S., Smith, A. D., and Ireland, F. (2007), "Guilt Appeals: Persuasion Knowledge and Charitable Giving," *Psychology and Marketing*, 24(8),723-742.

Lindsey, L. L. M., (2005), "Anticipated Guilt as Behavior Motivation: An Examination of Appeals to Help Unknown Others through Bone Marrow Donation," *Human Communication Research*, 31(4), 453-481.

Lindsey, L. L. M., Yun, K. A., and Hill, J. B., (2007), "Anticipated Guilt as Motivation to Help Unknown others," *Communication Research*, 34(4), 468-480.

Menon, S. and Kahn, B. E., (2003), "Corporate Sponsorships of Philanthropic Activities: When Do They Impact Perception of Sponsor Brand?" *Journal of Consumer Psychology*, 13(3), 317-327.

Pracejus, J. W., and Olsen G. D., (2004), "The Role of Brand/cause Fit in the Effectiveness of Cause-related Marketing Campaigns," *Journal of Business Research*, 57(6), 635-640.

Rifon, N., Choi, S. M., Trimble, C. S., and Li, H. (2004), "Congruence Effects in Sponsorship: The Mediating Role of Sponsor Credibility and Consumer Attributions of Sponsor Motive," *Journal of Advertising*, 33(1), 29-42.

Ruth, J. A., and Faber, R., (1988), "Guilt: An Overlooked Advertising Appeal," In J. D. Leckenby (ed.) *Proceedings of the Conference of the American Academy of Advertising* (83-89). TX: American Academy of Advertising.

Sen, S., and Bhattacharya, C. B. (2001), "Does Doing Good Always Lead to Doing Better? Consumer Reactions to Corporate Social Responsibility," *Journal of Marketing Research*, 38(2), 225-243.

Simmons, C. J., and Becker-Olsen, K. L. (2006), "Achieving Marketing Objectives through Social Sponsorships," Journal of Marketing, 70(4), 154–169.

Szykman, L. R., (2004), "Who are You and Why are You Being Nice? Investigating the Industry Effect on Consumer Reaction to Corporate Societal Marketing Efforts," in *Advances in Consumer Research*, 31, B. E. Kahn and M. F. Luce (eds.), Valdosta, GA: Association for Consumer Research, 306-315.

Turner, M., Xie, X., Lanmm, E., and Southard, B., (2009), "Encouraging Mothers to Get a Mammogram: A Cross-cultural Examination of Guilt Appeals," Paper presented at the annual meeting of the *International Communication Association*, New York.

Wood, W., and Eagly, A. H., (1981), "Stages in Analysis of Persuasive Messages: The Role of Causal Attributions and Message Comprehension," *Journal of Personality and Social Psychology*, 40(2), 246-259.

Brand-Related Background Music and Consumer Choice

Arnd Florack, University of Vienna, Austria
Claudiu Dimofte, San Diego State University, USA
Karin Rössler, University of Vienna, Austria
Susanne Leder, Zeppelin University, Germany

EXTENDED ABSTRACT

Previous studies have shown that background music associated with a product category can have positive effects on related sales in a retail environment (North et al. 1999). However, the mechanism by which this effect occurs has not been clearly explained, nor has the effect been shown at lower categorical levels of representation (e.g., the brand). The fact that many marketers select particular songs for use in brand advertising in order to strengthen their brand image raises the question of whether exposure to such brand-related auditory cues affects consumer behavior toward the brand.

In this research, we propose that consumer exposure to a brand-related song enhances the accessibility of the brand attitude in memory and consequently the reliance on that brand attitude. Hence, we expect positive effects of exposure to brand-related music on the choice of brand products when consumers' brand attitudes are positive and when the specific product evaluated (and not others in the brand's portfolio) is associated with the music.

In 3 studies, the impact of the incidental presentation of a brand-related song on product choice is examined in both field and laboratory settings. Study 1 shows that a song used in prior advertising for a brand influences brand sales when played within background music, but only for the brand product directly associated with the music. Study 2 demonstrates that exposure to a brand-related song increases the reliance on the brand attitude and examines fluency perceptions as the underlying mechanism resulting from the exposure to brand-related music. Finally, study 3 looks at possible negative effects of the exposure to brand-related music for brand products that are not directly associated with the respective music.

STUDY 1

The study was conducted in a grocery store in Germany and aimed to assess whether the inclusion of a brand associated song (*Beck's Pils* beer advertising tune) within the background music leads to an increase of sales for the product. It was expected that the presence of this song would lead to an activation of the associated product, making its choice more likely. We found that Beck's Pils sales increased significantly, but we also observed a marginally significant reduction of sales in other beers in the Beck's line. Thus, the brand song had a clear effect on consumers who favored Becks' brands, but induced them to switch from other Beck's products back to the traditional, leading product (Pils) in the brand portfolio.

STUDY 2

The results above suggest that exposure to brand-related music is most likely to increase brand choice for consumers who already favor the brand. We assume that the exposure to a brand-related song increases the accessibility of the associated brand attitude, rendering consumers more likely to rely on their brand attitude when exposed to a brand-related song. Hence, one objective of study 2 was to examine whether the exposure to brand-related music (*Merci* chocolate song) increases the correlation between brand attitudes and brand choice. However, we hold more specified assumptions about how attitude accessibility shapes choice. We expect that enhanced accessibility leads to higher perceived fluency that is attributed to the attitude's "rightness." To test this hypothesis, we included a misattri-

bution manipulation in study 2. In one condition, participants could attribute their perceived fluency to an alternative, exogenous source (a merely perceivable smell of chocolate in the room). Hence, we applied a 2x2 design with the music manipulation (brand-related song played/not played) and the misattribution manipulation (misattribution source mentioned/not mentioned). In order to provide incidental processing of music similar to a shopping context, we applied the guise of a memory test: participants were told that background music was being played to distract them during the memory test. In the experimental condition, the background music included short pieces of the brand-related song. In the control condition, alternative songs were played. The brand attitude was measured outside of the lab with an online-questionnaire.

The results support our hypotheses. We found significantly higher correlations of the brand attitude with brand choice and faster choice latencies when participants were exposed to the brand-related music than when they were not. Importantly, the difference in correlations and the effect on choice latencies disappeared when participants could attribute the felt fluency to an exogenous source. Thus, the perceived fluency resulting from exposure to the brand-related song seems to be critical for effects on choice to occur. In line with study 1, the results imply that positive effects of exposure to brand-related music are less likely for target groups with negative brand attitudes.

STUDY 3

The aim of this experiment was to build on study 1 and assess the effects of a song related to a particular brand product line on the evaluation of other product lines sold under the same brand. We hypothesized that the positive effect of brand-related background music on choice for specific product lines results in negative effects for other product lines in the same brand portfolio. Participants completed a memory task while music was played. In the treatment condition, the music included the famous Oscar Mayer wiener jingle, associated with Oscar Meyer hot dogs. Afterwards, participants were exposed to five ads that included either an ad for Oscar Meyer hot dogs (matching ad) or an ad for another product of the Oscar Meyer line (bologna; non-matching ad). The results provided support for the formulated hypotheses. Exposure to the Oscar Mayer wiener jingle had a positive effect on the evaluation of the matching ad, but negative effects on the evaluation of the non-matching ad. Process measures revealed that the wiener song enhanced (inhibited) responses toward Oscar Mayer hot dogs (bologna).

CONCLUSIONS

The present research supports the assumption that brand-related music used in the background has direct effects on consumer attitudes and choices, despite being limited to incidental processing that is not explicitly acknowledged by consumers. However, negative effects of brand-related music can be expected when negative attitudes are activated and when alternative products in the brand portfolio (not directly associated with the music) are evaluated.

REFERENCE

North, A. C., Hargreaves, D. J., & McKendrick, J. (1999). The influence of in-store music on wine selections. *Journal of Applied Psychology, 84*, 271–275.

Using Consumption in Everyday Resistance Practices to Contest Negative Stereotypes: The Case of Teenage Mothers

Emma N. Banister, University of Manchester, United Kingdom
Margaret K. Hogg, Lancaster University, United Kingdom
Mandy Dixon, Lancaster University, United Kingdom

EXTENDED ABSTRACT

Media representations of younger mothers often allude to their inexperience and lack of preparedness for motherhood, and in particular, target young working class mothers for derision (Tyler 2008).

We pose three questions: firstly what do young mothers *do* with this stereotype of the teenage mother (and its associated discourses); secondly what role do the everyday practices of consumption play in young mothers' attempts to distance themselves from the negative aspects of this stereotype and contest these discourses; and thirdly how do they manage an inconsistency between two aspects of their identity (age versus parental status) and what role does the marketplace play?

DISCOURSES AND MOTHERHOOD

Expectations of motherhood are socially embedded, emphasized via prevailing discourses (Miller 2007) and include a variety of publicly and privately-generated messages regarding good mothering and its reverse, bad mothering. The main culturally pervasive discourse that affects women's identity projects as new mothers relates to self-management (Fischer et al 2007:433) and taking on the responsibilities of parenthood. Planned parenthood is one of the markers of 'responsible parenting' generated by societal and life-framing discourses. Motherhood when entered into at the 'correct' time is positioned as "women's supreme achievement" (Phoenix et al. 1991:9) but young mothers are contradictorily positioned because they reach the same landmark which then becomes devalued because of their age. Children and adults are seen as separate categories, so instead of an achievement, motherhood is seen by many as a challenge to morality and the role of the family (Hunt et al. 2005).

CONSUMPTION, RESISTANCE AND MOTHERHOOD

We focus on individual (Penaloza and Price 1993), everyday (Reissman 2000) acts of resistance, rather than the political and collective action that has provided the focus for many consumer research studies (e.g. Kozinets and Handelman (2004). Resistance can be identity-based, focused on the resister's "expected or attributed identity" (Hollander and Einwohner 2004:537). In this context, the expected and attributed identity reflects the expectations of teenage motherhood, informed by societal and life-framing discourses, what it means to be a good mother. We examine the ways in which young mothers use consumption as a tool with which to resist the life-framing negative discourses surrounding the negative imagery associated with the teenage motherhood stereotype, and explore the ways in which young women use consumption to help provide alternative positive mothering identities.

METHOD

We use empirical data collected from a sample of teenage mothers to explore how resistance is deployed via consumption to contest negative stereotypes, and to achieve splitting i.e. separation of *teenage* [age status, negative imagery] from mother [parental status, positive imagery] in the identity frame. Qualitative data was collected via two phased interviews (prior and post birth) with seventeen new mothers who became pregnant between the ages of 17 and 19. We recruited participants via a National Health Service (NHS) antenatal service for younger women. Interviews were analyzed by the three authors: emergent themes were coded and then compared, along with the exchange of detailed notes and memos. An agreed interpretation of the data was written up.

FINDINGS

Our findings support recent research that suggests that early motherhood can help some women from relatively disadvantaged backgrounds to develop a stronger and more mature identity (Duncan 2007; Wilson and Huntingdon 2005). In their attempts to be seen as a 'good mum' or 'just a mum' our informants abandon many of their previous notions of what it means to be young and use consumption as a means to demonstrate a 'responsible' approach to parenting. Participants produce a counter position, a positive young mothering identity that incorporates positive aspects of younger mothering. Participants were aware of the communicative properties of goods, particularly clothing, and sought to manage their identity via the consumption process. This concern with appearance also extends to participants' babies. A recurring theme was the importance of *not* dressing the baby in particular fashions that participants saw as associated with stereotyped out-groups (White and Dahl 2007). Through their marketplace knowledge, women sought to differentiate themselves from the kind of person who would dress their baby in particular ways (Tyler 2008).

Participants turn to the market as a means to prepare for motherhood (Davies et al. 2010) and to demonstrate that they are good mothers and understand the important ingredients of good, 'responsible', mothering (being careful planners; systematic allocation of resources; thoughtful care of their new babies). A clear theme was the challenge of providing and preparing for motherhood on a limited budget, often through second hand items and hand me downs, which were interpreted in two ways. Some mothers positioned second hand items as an inexpensive means to prepare appropriately for the arrival of a baby within financially limited circumstances. For these young women, second hand items reinforced a positive image of prepared motherhood and thus reflected an adult approach to managing the allocation of limited resources. Second-hand goods were sometimes repositioned as 'gifts for the baby'. For other participants accepting second hand goods was seen as an admission of failure; an acknowledgement of truth in the discourses surrounding young motherhood about a lack of responsibility in either planning to have the baby, or how to cope once the baby is born. Our mothers also made important associations between being a 'good mother' and consuming certain branded products (e.g. diapers).

DISCUSSION

This research contributes to understandings of the role of consumption in identity formation (Arnould and Thompson 2005). Consumption played an important role in our participants' contestation of undesired identities as they turned to the market for assistance in resisting negative associations with being a young mother. However, in resisting the teenage mother stereotype, participants risked upholding a dominant discourse (that there is an appropriate time at which women should have children) or at least recognising its existence. Our study demonstrates that every day practices of resistance to the stereotypical negative images associated with an undesired self (i.e. teen mother = bad mother) are important components in the creation, appropriation and maintenance of identity projects as our informants embrace the positive imagery of motherhood and distance themselves from their teenage status.

REFERENCES

Arnould, E., and C. Thompson (2005) "Consumer culture theory (CCT): Twenty years of research" *Journal of Consumer Research,* 31(March), 868–82.

Davies, Andrea, Susan Dobscha, Susi Geiger, Stephanie O'Donohue, Lisa O'Malley, Andrea Prothero, Elin B Sørensen and Thyra U Thomsen (2010) "Motherhood, Marketization, and Consumer Vulnerability: Voicing International Consumer Experiences" *Journal of Macromarketing,* 30, 384-392.

Duncan, Simon (2007) "What's the problem with teenage parents? What's the problem with policy? "*Critical Social Policy,* 27, 3: 307-334

Fischer, Eileen and Gainer, Brenda (1993) "Babyshowers: a rite of passage in transition" in *Advances in Consumer Research* 20, 320-324

Hollander, Jocelyn A and. Einwohner, Rachel L (2004) "Conceptualizing Resistance," *Sociological Forum,* 19, 4, 533-554

Hunt, Geoffrey, Joe-Laidler, Karen and Mackenzie, Kathleen (2005) "Moving into Motherhood. Gang girls and controlled risks," *Youth and Society*, 36, 333-373.

Kozinets, R.V and Handelmann, J.M (2004) "Adversaries of Consumption: Consumer Movements, Activism, and Ideology" *Journal of Consumer Research*; 31, 691-704

Miller, T. (2007) "Is this what motherhood is all about? Weaving experiences and discourse through transition to first-time motherhood" *Gender & Society,* 21,337-358.

Penaloza, Lisa and Linda L. Price (1993) "Consumer Resistance: A Conceptual Overview," *Advances in Consumer Research*, 20: 123-128

Phoenix, A., Woollett, A. and Lloyd, E. (eds) (1991) *Motherhood: Meanings, Practices and Ideologies*, London, Sage.

Reissman, C. K. (2000). "Stigma and everyday practices: Childless women in south India" *Gender & Society,* 14, 1: 111-135.

Tyler, Imogen (2008) "Chav Mum Chav Scum", *Feminist Media Studies*,8, 1: 17-34.

White, Katherine and Darren W. Dahl (2007), "Are all Outgroups Created Equal? Consumer Identity and Dissociative Influence", *Journal of Consumer Research*, 34 (4), 525-536.

Wilson, H. and Huntington, A. (2005) "Deviant Mothers: The Construction of Teenage Motherhood in Contemporary Discourse" *Journal of Social Policy* 35, 1: 59–76.

(Arnould and Thompson 2005).

Should I Get in Shape or Get Closer to "Mr. Health"?
The Effects of Goal Anthropomorphization on Goal Pursuit

Frank May, University of South Carolina, USA

EXTENDED ABSTRACT

Extant research on anthropomorphism has exclusively focused on the anthropomorphization of either physical objects (Aggarwal and McGill 2007) or the representation of physical objects (i.e., brands; Aggarwal and McGill 2012). Given that anthropomorphism entails endowing non-human agents with human-like qualities (Epley et al. 2007), it makes sense to extend the notion of anthropomorphism to the abstract concept of goals—goals can be thought of as agentic forces in the lives of the people who possess them (Patrick and Hagtvedt 2012). This research explores the consequences of goal anthropomorphization.

First, goal anthropomorphization must be defined—goal anthropomorphization occurs whenever humanlike qualities are assigned to a goal. For example, a student may possess the goal of graduating with honors. If the student were to anthropomorphize her goal as "Mrs. Academics", the goal representation would take on human characteristics. If this occurs, as the student closes in on her goal, instead of approaching the goal representation of "graduating with honors," which lacks human qualities, she will instead be approaching the anthropomorphized entity "Mrs. Academics".

Do people actually anthropomorphize goals? Two preliminary studies were conducted to explore this notion. A prudent first step in the study of goal anthropomorphization would be to determine if established antecedents of physical entity-based anthropomorphism apply to goals as well. Research has shown that need for control positively predicts the tendency to anthropomorphize physical entities (Epley et al. 2008), and the first pretest tested whether this relationship holds for goals. Indeed, need for control (Burger and Cooper 1979) positively predicted the anthropomorphization of a financial goal (as measured by an anthropomorphism scale adapted for financial goals; Waytz et al. 2010). That is, individuals who have the tendency to anthropomorphize physical entities also direct this natural tendency to imbue goals with human-like attributes. The second pretest involved measuring the natural tendency to anthropomorphize goals (Waytz et al. 2010) and eight other items (e.g., dogs, cars, brands, insects, robots, computers, mountains, and phones) using an established scale that measures the tendency to anthropomorphize in general and adapting it for all of the items. The results revealed that the average goal anthropomorphism score was significantly lower than those of the two living items, but it was higher than those of all other items. These results suggest that, when left to their own devices without external stimuli provided by researchers or prodding from marketers, individuals anthropomorphize goals to a greater degree than they do entities that are more traditionally considered able to be anthropomorphized

The results from these two initial studies provide encouraging evidence that goals can be anthropomorphized and that an investigation into the consequences of goal anthropomorphization is warranted. Given that a goal is a desired end state (Bagozzi and Dholakia 1999) that one approaches or makes progress toward (Fishbach et al. 2005), conceptualizing a goal as possessing human qualities should have differential effects depending on the degree to which the person setting the goal desires the company of others. People who are high (low) in sociability regularly approach (avoid) people in their everyday lives (McAdams 1988). Therefore, it is hypothesized that goal anthropomorphization will help (hurt) individuals who are high (low) in sociability when the goal is anthropomorphized as a person to be approached (study 1, 2 and 3), but this relationship will reverse when the goal is anthropomorphized as a person to be avoided (studies 2 and 3). Furthermore, perceptions of goal fit will mediate this interaction (study 2).

Study one tested the notion that goal anthropomorphization would help (hurt) those who are high (low) in sociability using a 2 (anthropomorphism: high vs. low) X 2 (sociability: high vs. low) between subjects design. Participants first described their health goals. Next, they indicated how motivated they were to achieve their health goals. Afterward, the goal anthropomorphism scale used in the second preliminary study was completed. Finally, participants completed a sociability scale (Cheek and Buss 1981). For participants high (low) in sociability, as the tendency to anthropomorphize goals increased (decreased), so did goal motivation. Additionally, it was shown that sociability and the tendency to anthropomorphize goals were not related.

While the first study demonstrated the effects of natural goal anthropomorphization, study two demonstrates the effects of completely active goal anthropomorphization. A 3 (Goal conceptualization: Anthropomorphized goal-inconsistent outcome, Non-anthropomorphized goal, Anthropomorphized goal) x 2 (sociability: high vs. low) between subjects design was utilized. In the non-anthropomorphized goal condition, participants merely described their health goals. In the anthropomorphized goal (anthropomorphized goal-inconsistent outcome) condition, participants described their goals as personified by a third person character named Mr./Mrs. Health (Mr./Mrs. Anti-Health). Sociability was measured as it was in study one. For people who were high (low) in sociability, motivation was higher in the goal anthropomorphization (goal-inconsistent outcome anthropomorphization) condition than in the non-anthropomorphized goal condition. Additionally, for people who were high (low) in sociability, motivation was lower in the goal-inconsistent outcome anthropomorphization (goal anthropomorphization) than it was in the non-anthropomorphized goal condition. A similar pattern emerged for purchase intentions toward a goal related item (i.e., a book on healthy living). Finally, goal fit mediated the interactive effects of anthropomorphization and sociability.

In the third study, it is demonstrated that the effects of goal anthropomorphization extend to actual goal-related behavior. A 2 (Anthropomorphism: absent vs. present) x 2 (goal framing: goal vs. goal-inconsistent outcome) x 2 (sociability: high vs. low) design was utilized. In this study, participants were asked to solve anagrams. Before solving the anagrams, the participants were asked to either describe the goal of solving puzzles, or the exact opposite of the goal of solving puzzles, in an anthropomorphized or non-anthropomorphized manner (as was done in study two). Afterward, the participants were directed to a screen that contained 80 anagrams and were told that they could exit the anagram solving task at any time. However, they were automatically exited from the task after 5 minutes. Sociability was measured as it was in previous studies. In the goal condition, people high (low) in sociability persisted longer on the puzzle task in the anthropomorphized (non-anthropomorphized) condition. In the goal-inconsistent outcome condition, people low (high) in sociability persisted longer on the puzzle task in the anthropomorphized (non-anthropomorphized) condition.

REFERENCES

Aggarwal, Pankaj and Ann McGill (2007), "Is That Car Smiling at Me? Schema Congruity as a Basis for Evaluating Anthropomorphized Products," *Journal of Consumer Research,* 34(December), 468-479.

Aggarwal, Pankaj and Ann McGill (2012), "When Brands Seem Human, Do Humans Act Like Brands? Automatic Behavioral Priming Effects of Brand Anthropomorphism," *Journal of Consumer Research*, DOI:10.1086/662614.

Burger, Jerry and Harris Cooper (1979), "The Desirability of Control," *Motivation and Emotion*, 3 (4), 381-93.

Cheek, Jonathan and Arnold Buss (1981), "Shyness and Sociability," *Journal of Personality and Social Psychology*, 41 (2), 330-39.

Epley, Nicholas, Adam Waytz, and John Cacioppo (2007), "On Seeing Human: A Three Factor Theory of Anthropomorphism," *Psychological Review,* 114(4), 864-886.

Epley, Nicholas, Adam Waytz, Scott Akalis, and John Cacioppo (2008), "When We Need a Human: Motivational Determinants of Anthropomorphism," *Social Cognition*, 26 (2), 143-55.

McAdams, Dan P. (1988), "Personal Needs and Personal Relationships," in *Handbook of Personal Relationships*, ed. Steve Duck, New York, NY: John Wiley and Sons, 7-22.

Patrick, Vanessa M. and Henrik Hagtvedt (2012), ""I Don't" Versus "I Can't": When Empowered Refusal Motivates Goal-Directed Behavior," *Journal of Consumer Research*, 39 (August), DOI: 10.1086/663212.

Happiness from Actions versus Inactions

Priyali Rajagopal, Southern Methodist University, USA
Sekar Raju, Iowa State University, USA
Rao Unnava, Ohio State University, USA

EXTENDED ABSTRACT

Happiness is an important goal for consumers, and an understanding of how happiness can be enhanced may therefore be beneficial. In this article, we focus on a subtle but important distinction between experiencing happiness by doing something (actions) versus not doing something (inactions). We find that actions are attributed internally whereas inactions are attributed externally and therefore actions elicit greater happiness than inactions. Thus, people believe that greater happiness is associated with actions because they perceive actions as more intentional than inactions, even though not acting may be a volitional decision.

Research finds that attributing positive outcomes to one's own effort yields greater happiness than attributing such outcomes to external sources (Nurmi 1991). Similarly, literature in subjective wellbeing shows that willful actions yield greater wellbeing than non-autonomous actions (Deci & Ryan 2000). We extend these findings and suggest that actions evoke greater dispositional attributions than inactions, and elicit greater happiness than inactions.

In Study 1 (N = 34), we provided an example of happiness elicited by actions versus inactions and asked respondents to choose whether they experienced greater happiness from their actions or inactions over the course of their lifetime. Subsequently, we asked respondents to rate the extent to which they experienced happiness from their actions and inactions.

A majority of the respondents (85%) reported experiencing greater happiness from their actions than their inactions ($\chi^2 = 16.9$, $p < 0.01$). Further, respondents reported experiencing greater happiness from their actions (5.64) as compared to their inactions (3.88, t (33) = -4.85, $p < 0.01$).

In Study 2 (N = 15), we used a free response measure for happiness. Respondents were asked to recall and write down events that elicited happiness over the course of their lifetime. A significantly larger number of actions (4.4) than inactions (0.27, t (14) = 7.75, $p < 0.01$) were recalled. Further, a chi-square analysis revealed that a majority of respondents (87%) listed an action as the first item on their list ($\chi^2 = 8.06$, $p < 0.01$) suggesting that actions are more accessible in memory than inactions.

In Study 3 (N = 47), we randomly assigned respondents into either an action or inaction condition. Respondents in the action condition were asked whether they agreed or disagreed with the statement "I am happy about things that I have done in my life" while respondents in the inaction condition were shown the statement "I am happy about things that I have not done (my inactions) in my life"). We found that respondents were faster at agreeing with the action statement (4.1s) than the inaction statement (7.57s, F (1, 43) = 14.86, $p < 0.05$), suggesting greater accessibility for actions. Further, a chi-square analysis of the agreement with the statements revealed that a more respondents (77%) in the action condition agreed with the statement than respondents in the inaction condition (48%, $\chi^2 = 4.24$, $p < 0.05$,).

One potential explanation for the results of studies 1-3 is that actions are more impactful than inactions, i.e. they have greater consequences, which leads to greater accessibility and happiness and not the action- inaction distinction per se. To test this explanation, we used scenarios with identical consequences in study 4 (N = 55).

Respondents were shown two scenarios adapted from previous research (Gilovich & Medvec 1994) that contained two protagonists, one who acted to obtain a positive outcome (e.g. switched schools) and the second who did not act (e.g. did not switch schools) but also obtained the same positive outcome. Respondents were asked to choose which of the two characters would experience greater happiness. A majority of respondents expected the person who acted to experience greater happiness than the one who decided not to act in the first (76% vs. 24%, $\chi^2 = 15.29$, $p < 0.01$) and second scenarios (62% vs. 38%, $\chi^2 = 3.07$, p = 0.08). Thus, even when the outcomes of actions and inactions were held equal, respondents associated greater happiness with actions than inactions.

We tested our attribution explanation in study 5, i.e. people believe that they will experience greater happiness from their actions than inactions because actions are more amenable to internal attribution (dispositional attributions) than inactions.

Fifty-five respondents were asked to recall either actions or inactions that had given them happiness during the course of their entire life and then asked to rate how much happiness they experienced. They were then asked to rate the frequency with which they thought of their actions/inactions and the impact of their actions/inactions on their life. Two different measures were used to measure the impact of actions and inactions. The first measure required respondents to list all the consequences of their actions/inactions. The second measure required respondents to select all the areas of their life (from a set of 13 categories) that had been impacted by their actions/inactions (Rajagopal et al 2006). We also included a four item, 7-point scale (Dube, Jodoin, and Kairouz 1998) to measure respondents' attributions of their decisions.

As expected (Table 1), we found a larger number of actions listed as compared to inactions (F (1, 44) = 6.7, $p < 0.05$). Actions were also reported to elicit greater intensity of happiness (F (1, 44) = 4.86, $p < 0.05$), and greater frequency of thought than inactions (F (1, 44) = 6.09, $p < 0.05$). There were no differences in either of the two impact measures (F's < 1). Thus, neither the number of consequences nor the areas of life affected were different for actions as compared to inactions. These results suggest that actions are not perceived to have greater impact or consequences than inactions (similar to the results from study 4), but are nonetheless thought about more than inactions. In line with our expectations, actions evoked greater internal attributions than inactions (F (1, 44) = 5.02, $p < 0.05$).

Table 1
Results Of Study 5

Variable	Actions	Inactions
Mean number	7.08 (4.06)	4.55 (2.24)
Mean happiness intensity	6.33 (.64)	5.68 (1.28)
Mean frequency of thought	5.13 (1.59)	3.95 (1.62)
Net internal attributions	5.84 (.50)	5.37 (.88)
Mean number of consequences	4.56 (2.51)	3.94 (2.98)
Mean number of areas of life impacted	7.39 (2.13)	6.93 (3.23)
N	24	22

Note: Numbers in parentheses indicate standard deviations

Across 5 studies we find that actions elicit greater happiness than inactions because they are attributed internally and thought about more frequently. We did not find support for a larger network of consequences for actions versus inactions. Thus, the impact of actions and inactions appears to be no different, but the motivation to take credit for actions and hence, think about them more frequently appears to underlie the perceived differences in happiness.

REFERENCES

Deci, E. L., & Ryan, R. M. (2000). The "what" and "why" of goal pursuits: Human needs and the self-determination of behavior. *Psychological Inquiry, 11*, 227-268

Dube, L., Jodoin, M., & Kairouz, S. (1998). On the Cognitive Basis of Subjective Well-Being Analysis: What do Individuals Have to Say About it? *Canadian Journal of Behavioral Science*, 30(1), 1-13.

Gilovich, T., & Medvec, V. H. (1994). The temporal pattern to the experience of regret. *Journal of Personality and Social Psychology, 67*, 357-365.

Nurmi, J. (1991). The effect of others' influence, effort, and ability attributions on emotions in achievement and affiliative situations. *Journal of Social Psychology*, 131(5), 703-715.

Rajagopal, P., Raju, S., & Unnava, H. R. (2006). Differences in the cognitive accessibility of action and inaction regrets. *Journal of Experimental Social Psychology*, 42 (3), 302-313.

Bonding Through Service Friendliness: A Potential Double-Edged Sword

Elison Ai Ching Lim, Nanyang Technological University, Singapore
Yih Hwai Lee, National University of Singapore, Singapore
Maw-Der Foo, University of Colorado, Boulder, USA

EXTENDED ABSTRACT

Amidst growing interest in the engineering of positive emotions in commercial interactions (e.g., Tan, Foo, and Kwek, 2004), research underscores the need to consider both employee and customer characteristics when it comes to the appreciation for nonverbally- expressed emotion (Rafaeli and Sutton 1990). We posit that strong employee-customer bonds are formed when the affective style (i.e., expressiveness) of employees aligns closely with the customer's preference for nonverbally- expressed emotions. Support comes from research suggesting that rapport (i.e., quality interpersonal interactions characterized by a connection among the interactants) can be established using nonverbal cues (Harrigan, Oxman, and Rosenthal 1985).

Given that the quality of consumers' interaction with the service provider predicts customer (dis)satisfaction (Mohr and Bitner 1995), we expect a more rapportful employee-customer interaction to enhance consumers' satisfaction. Paradoxically, we predict that a dissatisfying event will appear more negative to consumers from high-rapport conditions, as it poses as a greater contrast to the initial enjoyable interaction. We further examine how low-/high-rapport employee-customer interactions affect the way in which customers vocalize felt (dis)satisfaction. Besides positive (e.g., compliments) and negative (e.g., complaints) voice, we further differentiate between customer voice that is directed inward (to the organization) and outward (to the public). Despite key differences between inward and outward voice, no research has yet examined consumers' relative tendency to use them. We predict that when there is a rapportful exchange due to affective match (i.e., low expressiveness-low receptivity, high expressiveness-high receptivity), consumers will behave in a way that enhances or protects the well-being of the service employee. This is expressed either by a higher tendency to direct positive voice inward (vs. outward) after a positive encounter, or a lower likelihood to voice negatively inward (vs. outward) after a negative encounter.

OVERVIEW OF STUDIES 1 AND 2

Two experiments (featuring a satisfying or dissatisfying service context respectively) were conducted to test our predictions. Both studies used a 2 (emotional expressiveness: low vs. high) x 2 (emotional receptivity: low vs. high) factorial design whereby emotional expressiveness was manipulated and emotional receptivity was measured. Data collection was completed over two sessions. In the first session, participants' emotional receptivity (Lee and Lim 2010) was assessed. A week later, they watched a video showing an employee-customer exchange in a holiday resort. The employee was actually a confederate actor who was trained to deliver low-, or high-, expressiveness by varying the use of smiling, voice intonations, and hand gestures hand gestures[1]. The dependent variables were rapport, customer satisfaction, and participants' proclivity to use inward and outward positive voice (see Appendix).

Key findings from Studies 1 and 2

In Study 1, we found that less emotionally receptive participants reported less rapport with a more (vs. less) expressive employee, whereas high receptivity respondents perceived higher rapport with the more (vs. less) expressive employee. In terms of satisfaction, the more expressive employee condition produced lower satisfaction for low receptivity levels. For high emotional receptivity, conversely, participants were more satisfied with high (vs. low) expressiveness. Further, low receptivity participants in the less (vs. more) expressive employee condition indicated a higher relative tendency to voice inward than outward. At high receptivity levels, a higher relative tendency to voice inward than outward was observed in the more (vs. less) expressive employee condition.

In Study 2, we observed that low receptivity participants indicated less rapport with a more expressive (vs. a less expressive) employee, whereas high receptivity respondents reported higher rapport with the more (vs. less) expressive employee. While the less receptive participants were more dissatisfied in the less (vs. more) expressive condition, high receptivity participants felt more dissatisfied in the high (vs. low) expressive employee condition. In terms of customers' voice intentions, for low receptivity, participants in the less (vs. more) expressive employee condition indicated a lower relative tendency to voice inward than outward. At high emotional receptivity level with high (vs. low) expressiveness, the relative inward-to-outward voice tendency was lower.

Discussion

Our work supports the common belief that strong relationships with customers can be beneficial (e.g., Ganesan, Brown, Mariadoss, and Ho 2010), but cautions that they can backfire in service failures. Theoretically, this research expands the voice literature by delineating positive and negative customer voice, as well as its direction (inward vs. outward). Since rapport can be formed even in service encounters (as we show in this research), firms should coach service employees about how to leverage the use of nonverbal cues to enhance customers' overall service experience.

Moving forward, we conjecture that the amplification effects due to strong employee-customer bonds may diminish for senior employees (e.g., the general manager) as they are seen to be more representative of the organization. Future research may investigate if the strength of employee-organization affiliation, as communicated via overt or subtle cues (e.g., employee's uniforms or corporate artifacts; Rafaeli and Pratt 1993), moderates the observed in this current research.

REFERENCES

Ganesan, Shankar, Steven Brown, Babu John Mariadoss, and Dixon Ho (2010), "Buffering and Amplifying Effects of Relationship Commitment in Business-to-Business Relationship," *Journal of Marketing Research*, 47 (2), 361-373.

Gremler, Dwayne D. and Kevin P. Gwinner (2008), "Rapport-Building Behaviors Used by Retail Employees," *Journal of Retailing*, 84 (3), 308-24.

Harrigan, Jinni A., Thomas E. Oxman, and Robert Rosenthal (1985), "Rapport Expressed Through Nonverbal Behavior," *Journal of Nonverbal Behavior*, 9 (2), 95-110.

---

1 Across both studies, manipulation checks indicate that the actor displayed appropriately lower (higher) levels of expressiveness in the low- (high-) expressiveness conditions respectively.

Lee, Yih Hwai and Elison A. C. Lim (2010), "When Good Cheer Goes Unrequited: The Moderating Role of Consumer Emotional Receptivity," *Journal of Marketing Research*, 47 (6), 1151-61.

Maxham III, James G. and Richard G. Netemeyer (2002), "Modeling Customer Perceptions of Complaint Handling Over Time: The Effect of Perceived Justice on Satisfaction and Intent," *Journal of Retailing*, 78 (4), 239-52.

Mohr, Lois A. and May Jo Bitner (1995), "The Role of Employee Effort in Satisfaction with Service Transactions," *Journal of Business Research*, 32, (3), 239-52.

Rafaeli, Anat and Robert I. Sutton (1990), "Busy Stores and Demanding Customers: How Do They Affect the Display of Positive Emotion?" *Academy of Management Journal*, 33 (3), 623-37.

_____, and Michael G. Pratt (1993), "Tailored Meanings: On the Impact and Meaning of Organizational Dress," *Academy of Management Review*, 18 (1), 32-55.

Tan, Hwee Hoon, Maw Der Foo, and Min. H. Kwek (2004), "The Role of Customer Personality Traits on the Display of Positive Emotions," *Academy of Management Journal,* 47 (2), 287-96.

Tickle-Degnen, Linda and Robert Rosenthal (1990), "The Nature of Rapport and Its Nonverbal Correlates," *Psychological Inquiry*, 1 (4), 285-93.

APPENDIX
Dependent Measures Used In Studies 1 and 2

STUDY 1

Emotional receptivity
(1 = strongly disagree, 7 = strongly agree; Lee and Lim 2010)

1. The use of hands and other body movements is very helpful in facilitating communication
2. It is not necessary to show too much facial expressions (reverse-coded item).
3. People should show a lot of facial expressions when talking.
4. When communicating, a person should use a lot of variation in his/her voice tone, pitch, and loudness.

Rapport
(1=strongly disagree, 7=strongly agree; Gremler and Gwinner 2000)

1. In thinking about my relationship with the service employee.
2. I would enjoy interacting with this employee.

3. I would look forward to seeing the service employee when I visit this resort again.
4. The service employee relates well to me.
5. I care for the service employee.
6. I am comfortable interacting with the service employee.
7. The service employee has my personal interest in mind.

Satisfaction
(1=strongly disagree, 7=strongly agree; adapted from Maxham and Netemeyer 2002)

1. I am satisfied with my overall experience with the resort.
2. As a whole, I am happy with the resort.
3. Overall, I am pleased with the service experience at the resort so far.

Positive Voice
(1 = not at all, 7 = very likely; adapted from Maxham and Netemeyer 2002).

Inward voice. How likely are you to send your compliments to the resort manager?

Outward voice. How likely are you to recommend this resort to my friends if there were looking for a vacation in the same area as (name of resort)?

STUDY 2
The items used to measure emotional receptivity and rapport are identical to those used for Study 1.

Dissatisfaction
(1=strongly disagree, 7=strongly agree; adapted from Maxham and Netemeyer 2002)

1. I am dissatisfied with my overall experience with the resort so far.
2. As a whole, I am not happy with the resort.
3. Overall, I am displeased with the service experience at the resort.

Negative Voice
(1 = not at all, 7 = very likely; items adapted from Maxham and Netemeyer 2002).

Inward voice. How likely are you to complain to the resort manager?

Outward voice. How likely are you to discourage your friends from the resort if there were looking for a vacation in the same area as (name of resort)?

Over and Over Again: Negative Emotions, Consumer Rumination and Post-Service Failure Outcomes

Yuliya Strizhakova, Rutgers University, USA
Julie A. Ruth, Rutgers University, USA

EXTENDED ABSTRACT

With social networking, youtubing, and twittering, consumers are gaining power to express publicly their discontent with products and services (Grégoire, Tripp and Legoux 2009). Yet, consumer research has largely ignored internal processes that prompt or hinder consumers' public display of thoughts and emotions toward companies at fault in service failures. We investigate consumer rumination as a psychological process through which consumers' negative emotions influence three service failure outcomes: complaining, negative word-of-mouth, and repatronage intentions. Rumination is defined as recurrent thoughts instigated by a discrepancy between one's current position versus a goal (Martin and Tesser 1996; Porath, MacInnis and Folkes 2010). Although extensively studied in psychology, rumination has received sparse attention in the consumer domain. By conceptualizing and testing rumination as a mediator within the consumer's experience of a service failure, we contribute to knowledge of consumer emotions and show that rumination has important implications for service providers.

CONCEPTUAL MODEL AND HYPOTHESES

Building upon emotion (Bagozzi, Baumgartner and Pieters 1998; Lazarus and Folkman 1984) and attribution theories (Weiner 1986), we posit that in service failures, contextual factors shape consumers' negative emotions that contribute to rumination and service failure outcomes (see Figure 1). Specifically, contextual factors – locus of control (internal/external), extent of controllability (under someone's /beyond anyone's control), failure severity, and outcome certainty – are systemically linked to negative emotions such as anger and anxiety (Smith and Ellsworth 1985; Roseman, Wiest, and Swartz 1994). Rumination is believed to be an involuntary response elicited in response to such emotion-provoking situations (Salovey et al. 2002; Martin and Tesser 1996). Research in non-business contexts shows that, when activated, rumination facilitates negative and hinders positive behaviors toward transgressors. Accordingly, because service failures provoke negative emotions such as anger and anxiety (e.g., Bougie et al. 2003; Gelbrich 2010), we hypothesize rumination as an involuntary response mediating the relationship between negative emotions and service failure outcomes such as complaining, negative word-of-mouth and repatronage intentions.

METHODS AND ANALYSIS APPROACH

Three experiments were conducted. In each study, adult participants were presented with an experimentally manipulated scenario regarding a service failure. Participants then responded to measures of emotions, rumination, complaining, negative word-of-mouth (WOM), and patronage intentions. Conceptual mediation models were analyzed via SEM with bootstrapping bias-corrected procedure. Measurement and hypothesized models achieved satisfactory model fits (Bagozzi and Yi 2012); detailed results are available from authors.

Study 1 manipulated three contextual factors: locus of control (external/internal), controllability (high/low), and frequency (high/low). Results show that anger and anxiety have significant positive direct effects on rumination. Rumination has significant positive direct effects on complaining and negative WOM intentions as well as a significant negative direct effect on patronage intentions. Consumer rumination about the service failure fully mediates effects of anger on complaining and negative WOM and partially mediates effects of anger on patronage; rumination fully mediates effects of anxiety on the three outcomes. Anger and anxiety only partially mediate effects of controllability on rumination, but they fully mediate effects of external locus of control and frequency on rumination. The results sug-

Figure 1
Conceptual Framework

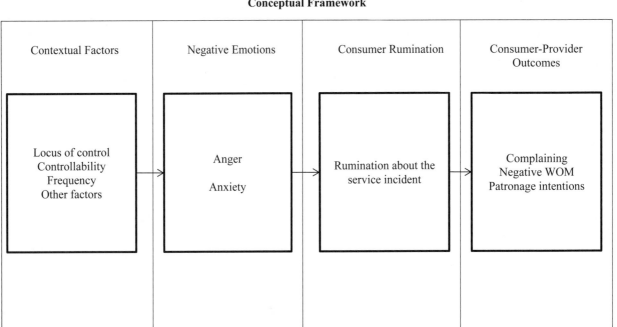

Contextual Factors	Negative Emotions	Consumer Rumination	Consumer-Provider Outcomes
Locus of control Controllability Frequency Other factors	Anger Anxiety	Rumination about the service incident	Complaining Negative WOM Patronage intentions

gest that effects of consumer anger and anxiety on outcomes may be underestimated if the internal process of consumer rumination about the service failure incident is not taken into consideration. Studies 2 and 3 examine the effects of other contextual factors. Results are available from the authors.

DISCUSSION

Our research expands understanding of an internal process – consumer rumination – that mediates effects of anger and anxiety on outward manifestations of service failures: consumer complaining, negative word-of-mouth and repatronage intentions. We adapted a measure of rumination to the service failure context, demonstrating its validity and reliability across studies. Our research contributes to emotion theory by showing that rumination is an important mediator, adding explanatory power across contextual conditions that elicit anger and anxiety. Our research also contributes by showing that rumination not only has damaging effects when providers are at fault, consumer rumination decreases patronage intentions and increases negative WOM when consumers are responsible for the failure. Given that only a small percentage of dissatisfied customers actually complain, consumer rumination may provide an explanation for the loss of customers and greater negative publicity that accompany service failures.

REFERENCES

Bagozzi, Richard P., Hans Baumgartner, and Rik Pieters (1998), "Goal-directed Emotions," *Cognition & Emotion,* 12, 1-26.

Bagozzi, Richard P. and Youjae Yi (2012), "Specification, Evaluation, and Interpretation of Structural Equation Models," *Journal of the Academy of Marketing Science, 40,* 8-34.

Bougie, Roger, Rik Pieters, and Marcel Zeelenberg (2003), "Angry Customers Don't Come Back, They Get Back: The Experience and Behavioral Implications of Anger and Dissatisfaction in Services," *Journal of the Academy of Marketing Science,* 31, 377-393.

Gelbrich, Katja (2010), "Anger, Frustration, and Helplessness after Service Failure: Coping Strategies and Effective Informational Support," *Journal of the Academy of Marketing Science,* 38 (5), 567-85.

Grégoire, Yany, Thomas M. Tripp, and Renaud Legoux (2009), "When Customers Love Turns into Lasting Hate: The Effects of Relationship Strength and Time on Customer Revenge and Avoidance," *Journal of Marketing,* 73 (6), 18-32.

Lazarus, Richard S. and Susan Folkman (1984), *Stress, Appraisal, and Coping.* New York: Springer.

Macho, Siegfried and Thomas Ledermann (2011), "Estimating, Testing, and Comparing Specific Effects in Structural Equation Models: The Phantom Model Approach," *Psychological Methods, 16,* 34-43.

Martin, Leonard L. and Abraham Tesser (1996), "Some Ruminative Thoughts," in Robert S. Wyer (Eds.), *Advances in Social Cognition.* Hillsdale, NJ: Lawrence Erlbaum, 1-48.

Porath, Christine, Debbie MacInnis, and Valerie Folkes (2010), "Witnessing Incivility Among Employees: Effects on Consumer Anger and Negative Inferences about Companies," *Journal of Consumer Research*, 37 (August), 292-303.

Roseman, Ira J., C. Wiest, and T. S. Swartz (1994), "Phenomenology, Behaviors, and Goals Differentiate Discrete Emotions," *Journal of Personality & Social Psychology,* 67, 206-221.

Salovey, Peter, Laura R. Stroud, Alison Woolery, and Elissa S. Epel (2002), "Perceived Emotional Intelligence, Stress Reactivity, and Symptom Reports: Further Explorations Using the Trait Meta-Mood Scale," *Psychology and Health,* 17 (5), 611-27.

Smith, Craig A. and Phoebe Ellsworth (1985), "Patterns of Cognitive Appraisal in Emotion," *Journal of Personality & Social Psychology*, 48, 813-838.

Weiner, Bernard (1986), *An Attributional Theory of Motivation and Emotion.* New York: Springer.

Seeking the Coherent Moral Self: A Process of Alignment

Michal J. Carrington, La Trobe University, Australia
Benjamin A. Neville, University of Melbourne, Australia
Robin Canniford, University of Melbourne, Australia

EXTENDED ABSTRACT

Can a manageable sense of self-coherency co-exist with identity multiplicity and internal fragmentation? Through immersive/interpretive research, we discover multiplicity extending to life projects and themes; ideological fragmentation resulting in a sense of incoherent moral self; and a compelling meta-life project directed towards a coherent moral self.

Prior CCT research conceptualizes the 'self' as an integration of many aspects, including multiple identities, relationships, possessions and other various symbols that enable the individual to construct themselves in ongoing processes (Bardhi, Eckhardt, and Arnould 2012; Schouten 1991). In this state of identity multiplicity, the consumer is constantly assessing (consciously or subconsciously) which identity should be activated in a given situation to guide their behavior (Brewer 2001; Schouten 1991). The multiple identities coalescent in the construction of self, however, are not always in alignment, and this divergence results in a self that is fragmented (Ahuvia 2005; Bahl and Milne 2010; Firat and Venkatesh 1995; Tian and Belk 2005). Fragments of self that are in conflict are expressed in contradictory consumption choices when influenced by competing identities that are momentarily clashing in the marketplace (Ahuvia 2005; Bahl and Milne 2010; Ustuner and Holt 2007).

In prior research, we discover two dominant framings of identity multiplicity: liberated multiplicity and manageable multiplicity. One perspective, liberated multiplicity, takes an optimistic view of the fragmented self (Goulding, Shankar and Elliott, 2002), arguing that consumers are "content to live with the paradoxes" (Firat and Venkatesh 1995) arising from multiplicity (Firat, Dholakia, and Venkatesh 1995; Firat and Venkatesh 1995). Indeed, that postmodern consumers have been liberated from the constraints of a unified sense of self, and are free to weave multiple identities into the complex tapestry of their life's narratives (Firat and Dholakia 2006; Schau, Gilly, and Wolfinbarger 2009). This optimistic view, however, is not the only lens through which multiplicity and fragmentation are viewed (Goulding, Shankar, and Elliott 2002). A second perspective acknowledges the tension created by conflicting identities and takes the view that fragmented consumers manage this tension by deploying coping strategies such as compartmentalizing the discordant fragments of self (Ahuvia 2005; Goulding et al. 2002) or engaging in dialogue between competing identities (Bhal and Milne, 2010).

We note, however, that these consumer studies are predominantly contextualized within the domains of the *aesthetic* and *hedonic* – such as high-end automobile purchases (Luedicke et al. 2010; Bahl and Milne, 2010), weekend rave parties (Goulding et al. 2002; Goulding et al. 2009), cherished possessions (Ahuvia, 2005), and global elites (Bardhi et al. 2012). Moreover, though many studies of consumer identity projects and communal consumption contexts recognize the ideologically charged nature of consumers' life worlds (Canniford and Shankar 2012; Kozinets 2002; Luedicke, Thompson, and Giesler 2010), fewer explore the personal, internal, tensions that consumers experience from contradictions when the ideological frameworks guiding their consumption experiences clash. Thus, we argue that existing theory has stopped short of exploring the identity conflict that is played out in *ideologically* charged consumption arenas.

Our primary research question, therefore, asks whether consumers are less willing to tolerate discordant multiplicity when the resulting conflict is waged on ideologically charged consumption stages in which contradictory choices impinge on their moral frameworks. In this sense, moral values are inherently ideological, informing the consumer's worldview and filtering their perceptions of acceptable choice (Luedicke et al. 2010; Monroe 2009). Second, to what layers or levels of abstract self does multiplicity and conflict extend? Consumer research has tended to present a disjointed account of multiplicity (e.g. Belk 1988; Gould 2010). Third, what processes of transformation enable consumers to dynamically re-align their multiple identities with their integrated moral beliefs and transition to an ideologically coherent self? The context specificity of current consumer multiplicity research limits our understanding of the contingencies of liberated fragmentation and related consumer struggles.

The contradictory consumption of ethically-minded consumers is a well documented site of *ideologically* charged consumption (e.g. Chatzidakis, Hibbert and Smith, 2007; Carrington, Neville and Whitwell, 2010), presenting a potent context from which to develop theory about the multiplicity of identity and discordant selves in transition. Taking an ethnographic approach, we immersed in the daily lives of 13 ethical consumers over a nine month study to explore the construction of the ethical-self in the midst of everyday consumption practices (Newholm and Shaw 2007). We employed multiple methods including semi-structured interviews, photographic and written diaries, video interviews, projective interviews, and extended participant observation in a range of personal and social activities.

TABLE 1
Data Summary

Activity/Data Format	Details/Volume
Duration of Study	Nine Months
Transcribed Material	445 pages
Photographic Material	34 images
Video Footage	63 minutes
Field Notes	49 pages
Coded Observations	2605

Aligned with the aims of the study, the data were analyzed using an interpretive, grounded approach (Corbin and Strauss 2008). To enhance trustworthiness of the study, we strategically combined triangulation of methods, sources and data; member checks; persistent immersion; and regular researcher debriefing sessions (Wallendorf and Belk 1989).

In contrast to previous researchers' suggestions that identity multiplicity may be liberating (Firat and Venkatesh 1995) or manageable (Bahl and Milne 2010), our data analysis reveals that multiplicity becomes an unmanageable problem for some consumers when the conflict is ideological. We discover that the presence of a *dominant moral life theme* compels these consumers to seek coherent moral selves. We also discover that multiplicity and conflict extend beyond identity to the clashing of life themes reflected in conflicting life projects. Finally, we reveal a dynamic and purposive overarching consumer transition to a more coherent ideological self, a process of alignment that we call a *meta life project*. Meta life projects are guided by a single dominant moral life theme that act as a pathway to moral coherence. We show that through meta life project work, fragmented life projects and identities, discordant extended selves and inconsistent consumption choices are progressively aligned with informants' sense of moral self. Our study integrates and develops multiple threads of extant consumer research – multiplicity (Belk 1988; Goulding et al. 2002; Luna, Torsten, and Peracchio 2008; Schau and Gilly 2003; Thompson 1996), fragmentation (Bahl and Milne 2010; Firat and Venkatesh 1995; Goulding et al. 2002), moral conflicts (Luedicke et al. 2010), and identity conflict resolution (Ahuvia 2005; Bahl and Milne 2010; Murray 2002). – to offer an alternative lens through which to view the consumption contradictions and purposive life transitions of fragmented selves in the ideological domain.

REFERENCES

Ahuvia, Aaron C. (2005), "Beyond the Extended Self: Loved Objects and Consumers' Identity Narratives," *Journal of Consumer Research*, 32 (1), 171-84.

Bahl, Shalini and George R. Milne (2010), "Talking to Ourselves: A Dialogical Exploration of Consumption Experiences," *Journal of Consumer Research*, 37, 176-95.

Bardhi, Fleura, Giana M. Eckhardt, and Eric J Arnould (2012), "Liquid Relationships to Possessions," *Journal of Consumer Research*, 39.

Belk, Russell (1988), "Possessions and the Extended Self," *Journal of Consumer Research*, 15, 139-68.

Brewer, Marilynn B (2001), "The Many Faces of Social Identity: Implications for Political Psychology," *Political Psychology*, 22 (1), 115-25.

Canniford, Robin and Avi Shankar (2012), "Purifying Practices: How Consumers Assemble Romantic Experiences of Nature," *Journal of Consumer Research*, NA (NA), NA.

Corbin, Juliet and Anselm Strauss (2008), *Basics of Qualitative Research*, Thousand Oaks, California: SAGE Publications.

Firat, A.Fuat. and Nikhilesh Dholakia (2006), "Theoretical and Philosophical Implications of Postmodern Debates: Some Challenges to Modern Marketing," *Marketing Theory*, 6 (2), 123-62.

Firat, A.Fuat., Nikhilesh Dholakia, and Alladi Venkatesh (1995), "Marketing in a Postmodern World," *European Journal of Marketing*, 29 (1), 40-56.

Firat, A.Fuat. and Alladi Venkatesh (1995), "Liberatory Postmodernism and the Reenchantment of Consumption," *Journal of Consumer Research*, 22 (3), 239-67.

Gould, Stephen J. (2010), ""To Thine Own Self(Ves) Be True": Reflexive Insights for Etic Self Theory from Consumer's Emic Constructions of the Self," *Consumption, Markets and Culture*, 13 (2), 181-219.

Goulding, Christina, Avi Shankar, and Richard Elliott (2002), "Working Weeks, Rave Weekends: Identity Fragmentation and the Emergence of New Communities," *Consumption, Markets and Culture*, 5 (4), 261-84.

Goulding, Christina, Avi Shankar, Richard Elliott, and Robin Canniford (2009), "The Marketplace Management of Illicit Pleasure," *Journal of Consumer Research*, 35 (5), 759-71.

Kleine, Robert E, Susan Schultz-Kleine, and Jerome B Kernan (1992), "Mundane Everyday Consumption and the Self: A Conceptual Orientation and Prospects for Consumer Research," *Advances in Consumer Research*, 19, 411-15.

Kozinets, Robert (2002), "Can Consumers Escape the Market? Emancipatory Illuminations from Burning Man," *Journal of Consumer Research*, 29, 20-38.

Luedicke, Marius K, Craig J Thompson, and Markus Giesler (2010), "Consumer Identity Work as Moral Protagonism: How Myth and Ideology Animate a Brand-Mediated Moral Conflict," *Journal of Consumer Research*, 36, 1016-32.

Luna, David, Ringberg Torsten, and Laura A Peracchio (2008), "One Individual, Two Identities: Frame Switching among Biculturals," *Journal of Consumer Research*, 35 (August), 279-93.

Monroe, Kristen Renwick (2009), "The Ethical Perspective: An Identity Theory of the Psychological Influences on Moral Choice," *Political Psychology*, 30 (3), 419-44.

Murray, Jeff B. (2002), "The Politics of Consumption: A Re-Inquiry on Thompson and Haytko's (1997) "Speaking of Fashion"," *Journal of Consumer Research*, 29 (3), 429-40.

Newholm, Terry and Deirdre Shaw (2007), "Studying the Ethical Consumer: A Review of Research," *Journal of Consumer Behaviour*, 6, 253-70.

Schau, Hope Jensen and Mary C. Gilly (2003), "We Are What We Post? Self Presentation in Personal Web Space," *Journal of Consumer Research*, 30 (3), 385-404.

Schau, Hope Jensen, Mary C. Gilly, and Mary Wolfinbarger (2009), "Consumer Identity Renaissance: The Resurgence of Identity-Inspired Consumption in Retirement," *Journal of Consumer Research*, 36 (2), 255-76.

Schouten, John W. (1991), "Selves in Transistion: Symbolic Consumptions in Personal Rites of Passage and Identity Reconstruction," *Journal of Consumer Research*, 17, 412-25.

Thompson, Craig J (1996), "Caring Consumers: Gendered Consumption Meanings and the Juggling Lifestyle," *Journal of Consumer Research*, 22, 388-407.

Tian, Kelly and Russell W. Belk (2005), "Extended Self and Possessions in the Workplace," *Journal of Consumer Research*, 32 (2), 297-310.

Ustuner, Tuba and Douglas B. Holt (2007), "Dominated Consumer Acculturation: The Social Construction of Poor Migrant Women's Consumer Identity Projects in a Turkish Squatter," *Journal of Consumer Research*, 34, 41-56.

Wallendorf, Melanie and Russell W Belk (1989), "Assessing Trustworthiness in Naturalistic Consumer Research," in *Interpretive Consumer Research*, ed. Elizabeth C Hirschman, Provo, UT: Association for Consumer Research, 69-84.

Family Quality Time and the Techno-Culture Food Environment

Pepukayi Chitakunye, University of KwaZulu-Natal, South Africa
Amandeep Takhar, University of Bedfordshire, United Kingdom

EXTENDED ABSTRACT

More than ever, new technologies are demonstrating their potential for transforming society. Although we know much about consumption of technology (Vandewater and Lee 2009; Kozinets 2008; Sorenson 2006), interplay between technology and family quality time still needs further investigation. Within the social sciences, attention to family time has been more attuned to differences across men and women in terms of time spent at work (Fiese, Foley and Spagnola 2006), lack of family time driven by consumption desires (Mestdag and Vandeweyer 2005), how mothers and fathers balance work and home responsibilities (DeVault 2000; Hochschild 1997), and the role of homemade food in the construction of family identity (Moisio, Arnould and Price, 2004). Despite the noteworthy contributions of these studies, we have virtually no understanding of how family quality time is changed and altered in form particularly when media devices such as iphones, ipads, and cell phones encroach on the mealtime context.

Whilst prior research explores the role of technology in consumer lives (Kozintets 2008; Ventantesh 2006; Jackson 2002; Mick and Fournier 1998), there is silence on how technology impacts on parent-child mealtime interactions, and family routines. What we need to understand is whether the purpose and meanings of quality time changes when new technologies become an inseparable part of family mealtimes. Gutierrez, Price and Arnould (2008: 189) observe that time spent over family dinner, is positively correlated with benefits such as reduced childhood obesity, aiding literacy development and reduced speech impairments, language socialization, lower levels of behavioral problems, higher academic achievement and reduced drug and alcohol use among teens. And yet, media devices such as iPods, iPads, smart phones, encroach on daily family life and transform the meanings of time spent over family dinner. Further, technology, in the form of TV programs and their characters can become an obsession with which viewers constantly interact and around which they model their lives (Chitakunye and Maclaran 2012; Russell, Norman and Heckler 2004; Russell and Puto 1999; O'Guinn and Shrun 1997). Although these new technologies continue to mediate family relationships and are progressively more embedded in everyday practices, our knowledge is still limited as to how these are changing the form and meaning of family quality time.

Given this background, the purpose of this study is to explore how the techno culture environment is transforming family quality time in the domestic context of food consumption. In particular, we are interested in children's naturalistic practices when they come into contact with media devices at mealtimes. Unlike previous research, this study takes everyday mealtime practices as the unit of investigation.

This study uses an interpretive research strategy. Informants were children aged between 13 and 17 who provided insights through visual diaries that generated 360 photographs, and 13 in-depth interviews, which was supplemented by immersing ourselves in four families on five different occasions. These constant repetitive visits to the families, over a period of two years, were vital in deepening our experience of action, conversations and the mealtime context. Prior to, during, and subsequent to our immersion into mealtimes, we kept detailed written fieldnotes.

Consistent with previous research, we find that technology transforms family relations in different ways (Venkatesh, Stolzkoff, Shih, and Mazumdar 2001; Mick and Fournier 1998). In line with previous research, our findings also show how, in some families, the essence of quality time has been reorganised around specific television programmes. For example, the *X-factor*, *East Enders*, and *Coronation Street*, were popular programmes around which families communed. However, this presented a paradox that resulted to assimilation and isolation effects (Mick and Fournier 1998), particularly in families with conflicting viewing interests.

Prevalent across the families visited, we observed an array of multitasking practices at mealtimes, not only with the television, but with other with media devices such as iPods, iPads, smart phones, cellphones, and laptops. Similarly, photographs generated by the children reveal the continued presence of these media devices at the dinner table, indicating a willingness to use them whilst eating. Although it is becoming increasingly rare that families eat together, at times, family members stay connected through interplay with technology. For example, in Hayley's household (female, 16), the father worked away from home, and through media devices, he stayed connected to family members at different times, including mealtimes. In this sense, mediated communications during family dinner are sometimes with family members who are not present, and not just friends, and other non-family members. Within this context, we argue that interplay with technology contribute to the construction of both family and individual identity.

In some families, children felt that media devices were intertwined with family interactional processes. On the contrary, some parents saw these media devices as disruptive to family togetherness. However, examples from our study include some parents using these media devices at the dinner table. For example, during one mealtime observation, a mother could be seen using the cordless phone more frequently than the children. In another family, the father always took the cordless phone to the dinner table. Agreeing with Mick and Fournier (1998), we found that technology presents a paradox that leads to both assimilation and isolation effects. Within this context, we align assimilation effects with the construction of a collective family identity, and isolation effects with the construction of individual identity. For example, when the children were connected to the outside world, parents felt more isolated, and vice versa. Here, it emerged that different communication technologies are preferred by family members. In one family, the children preferred to use their smartphones whilst the parents preferred to use the cordless phone. When the cell phone or cordless phones were answered, at times, the family members would leave the table, and continued talking whilst in another part of the house. This behaviour reduced family quality time.

One contribution of this study is that it shifts the focus of the interplay between family quality time and technology from the television and its contents (Chitakunye and Maclaran 2012; Russell et al 2004; Schau and Muniz 2004; O'Guinn and Shrun 1997) and instead considers the construction of collective and individual identities within a mix of mealtime multitasking practices, in particular, in relation to media devices that encroach on the mealtime context. These devices include iphones, ipads, cordless phones, laptops; cell phones and other related devices. Within this context, we argue that, family quality time is changed and altered in form, but not ultimately abandoned.

REFERENCES

Chitakunye, Pepukayi and Pauline Maclaran (2012), "Materiality and family consumption: the role of the television in changing mealtime rituals," *Consumption, Markets and Culure* (in press).

DeVault, Marjorie L. (2000), "Producing Family Time: Practices of Leisure Activity Beyond the Home," *Qualitative Sociology*, 23(4), 485-503.

Fiese, Barbara H., Kimberly P. Foley, and Mary Spagnola (2006), "Routine and ritual elements in family mealtimes: Contexts for child well-being and family identity," *New Directions for Child and Adolescent Development*, 2006 (111), 67-89.

Gutierrez, Kullie., Linda, L. Price and Eric J. Arnould (2008), "Consuming Family Dinner Time," in *Advances in Consumer Research*, Volume 35, eds. Angela Y. Lee and Dilip Soman, Duluth, MN : Association for Consumer Research.

Hochschild, Arlie R. (1997), *The time bind: When work becomes home and home becomes work.* New York: Metropolitan Books.

Jackson, Maggie (2002). *What's Happening to Home? Balancing Work, Life and Refuge in the Information Age*, Notre Dame, IN:Sorin Books.

Kozinets, Robert V. (2008), "Technology/Ideology: How Ideological Fields Influence Consumers' Technology Narratives," *Journal of Consumer Research*, 34 (6), 864-881.

Mestdag, Inge and Jessie Vandeweyer (2005), "Where Has Family Time Gone? In Search of Joint Family Activities and the Role of the Family Meal in 1966 and 1999," *Journal of Family History* 30 (3), 304-323.

Moisio, Risto, Eric J. Arnould, and Linda L. Price (2004), "Between mothers and markets:

Constructing family identity through homemade food", *Journal of Consumer Culture*, 4 (3), 361–384.

Mick, David and Susan Fournier (1998), "Paradoxes of Technology: Consumer Cognizance, Emotions, and Coping Strategies," *Journal of Consumer Research,* 23(3), 123-143.

O'Guinn, Thomas C., and L.J. Shrun (1997), "The role of television in the construction of consumer reality", *Journal of Consumer Research,* 23 (4), 278–294.

Russell, Cristel A., Andrew T. Norman, and Susan E. Heckler (2004), "The consumption of

television programming: Development and validation of the connectedness scale", *Journal of Consumer Research* 31 (1), 150–161.

Russell, Cristel A.,and Christopher P. Puto (1999), "Rethinking television audience measures: An exploration into the construct of audience connectedness," *Marketing Letters,* 10 (4), 387–401.

Schau, Hope J., and Albert M. Muniz Jr. (2004). If you can't find it, create it: An analysis of consumer engagement with Xena: Warrior Princess. In *Advances in consumer research*, vol. 31, ed. Kahn Barbara E. and Luce Mary Frances, 545–7. Toronto: Association for Consumer Research.

Sørenson, Knut H. (2006), "Domestication: the Enactment of Technology," in *Domestication of Media and Technology,* eds., Thomas Berker, Maren Hartmann, Yves Punie, and Katie J. Ward, Berkshire, England: Open University Press, 40-57.

Vandewater, Elizabeth A., and Sook-Jung Lee (2009), "Measuring children's media use in the digital age: Issues and challenges". *American Behavioural Scientist* 52 (8), 1152–1176.

Venkatesh, Alladi, Stolzoff Norman, Eric Shih King, and Mazumdar Sanjoy (2001). The home of the future: An ethnographic study of new information technologies in the home. In *Advances in consumer research,* ed. Mary Gilly and Joan Meyers-Levy, 88–96. Valdosta, GA: Association for Consumer Research.

The Best and the Bizarre:
Prototype and Exemplar-based Retrospective Evaluations of Experiences

Robert Latimer, New York University, USA
Priya Raghubir, New York University, USA

EXTENDED ABSTRACT

Consumers evaluate past experiences based on overall impressions (prototypes) and specific remembered components (exemplars). The prototype-based memory system converts experience components into an "abstracted representation" (Shreiber and Kahneman, 2000) or "gestalt" (Ariely and Carmon, 2003), which leads to retrospective evaluations based on a limited number of key components, such as trend, peak, and end. The prototype system draws from prototype theories in the categorization literature (e.g. Rosch and Mervis, 1975). Prototypes influence evaluations immediately after an experience and are robust to delay. Distinctive experience components – components that share few features with their surroundings – should have little influence on the prototype.

The exemplar-based memory system represents experience components individually, which leads to retrospective evaluations based on the most contextually accessible components (Montgomery and Unava, 2009). The exemplar system draws from the memory literature which suggests that distinctive information (Hunt, 1995, Hunt and Worthen, 2006) and experiences (Berntsen, 1996, 1998) are more accessible than typical information and experiences. Critically, the privileged accessibility of distinctive components increases with delay.

Four studies test a framework integrating prototype and exemplar models, focusing on the ability of retrieved exemplars (Studies 1 and 2) and the presence of a distinctive peak (Studies 3 and 4) to predict participants' overall retrospective evaluations, immediately after the experience and after a delay. We predict and find that when exemplars are contextually accessible, their ratings flow through to the overall evaluation that remains the same after a delay. However, when the peak component (the most pleasant component of a pleasant experience) is a distinctive one, this particular component does not change the prototype, but becomes an accessible exemplar, which is used to form an overall evaluation. Further, as this distinctive peak is even more easily recalled after a delay, its weight in evaluations increases over time, leading to improved overall evaluations after a delay. These predictions are tested by examining the weight (ß) and overall predictive power (R^2) of models including the ratings of prototypical and distinctive components of the experience on overall evaluations of the experience.

STUDIES 1 AND 2

Study 1 demonstrates in a field setting that distinctive experience components are more likely to be spontaneously recalled and used as inputs to overall evaluations, especially if they are made contextually accessible. Attendees of a large theatre festival (n = 46) completed a short survey while waiting in line for a show. They indicated the overall quality of the festival either before or after listing and rating six shows that they had seen. Finally, participants rated the distinctiveness of the first and last shows on their list on a three item 7-point scale (afirst = 0.83, alast = 0.88) and reported the total number of shows they had seen. Ratings of the six listed shows better predicted the overall evaluation when participants listed the shows before evaluating the festival overall. Festival attendees were more likely to base their overall evaluations on retrieved exemplars (listed shows) when those exemplars were contextually accessible.

Study 2 (n = 98) replicates the results of Study 1 for evaluations of films released in 2011 using a different manipulation for exemplar accessibility: cognitive load. Specific films recalled under load were worse predictors of participants' overall ratings for films released during 2011 when they were recalled under load, as compared to when there was no load.

Studies 3 and 4 go on to examine the role of delay in increasing the accessibility of distinctive peaks that become inputs to overall retrospective evaluations.

STUDIES 3 AND 4

Study 3 examined the role of a distinctive peak before and after a delay. Fifty-five participants viewed fifteen pieces from the Museum of Modern Art's collection and rated their enjoyment of each. Participants viewed either three paintings and twelve sculptures (paintings distinctive) or twelve paintings and three sculptures (sculptures distinctive). Participants then rated their overall enjoyment of the set of pieces, both immediately and after a delay of three to six weeks. A linear regression model tested the predictive power of components extracted from individual ratings: the peak, end, mean of non-distinctive pieces, mean of distinctive pieces, and whether or not the peak was one of the distinctive pieces.

Without a delay, only the mean of non-distinctive components) and peak ratings were significant predictors of the overall liking of the set. After the delay, the mean non-distinctive rating failed to predict retrospective liking of the set, but the peak remained important. Critical to my hypothesis, the presence of a distinctive peak increased overall evaluations, but only after the delay. Study 3 confirms the importance of the peak-dominated prototype, even after a delay, but suggests that distinctive exemplars may amplify the peak effect through a separate, exemplary-based memory system.

Study 4 replicates (4a, n = 82) and reverses (4b, n = 85) the results of Study 3 for experiences with music and jelly beans respectively. A pretest revealed that music was well suited to retrieval of specific exemplars, while jelly beans tended to be thought of in generic, prototypical terms. In both 4a and 4b, we manipulated the presence or absence of a distinctive component in a five part experience. In Study 4a, a distinctive peak increased overall evaluations after a two week delay, supporting the exemplar system. In Study 4b, a distinctive peak decreased overall evaluations immediately after the experience, supporting the prototype system.

SUMMARY

People rely on exemplars when they are contextually accessible (Studies 1 and 2), leading to a disproportionate influence for distinctive peaks on overall evaluations after a delay (Studies 3 and 4a). Non-distinctive peaks remain important with and without delay however (Studies 3 and 4a), and may produce increased overall evaluations in contexts well suited to prototype formation (Study 4b). These findings are of interest to researchers concerned with how consumers represent experiences and construct evaluations, or managers who wish to design experiences that consumers will remember as enjoyable.

REFERENCES

Ariely, D., & Carmon, Z. (2003). In Loewenstein, G., Read, D., Baumeister, R (Eds). *Time and decision: Economic and psychological perspectives on intertemporal choice*, (pp. 323-349). New York, NY, US: Russell Sage Foundation.

Bernsten, D. (1996). Involuntary autobiographical memories. *Applied Cognitive Psychology, 10, 435-454.*

Bernsten, D. (1998). Voluntary and involuntary access to autobiographical memory. *Memory, 6*(2), 113-141.

Fredrickson, B. L., & Kahneman, D. (1993). Duration neglect in retrospective evaluations of affective episodes. *Journal of Personality and Social Psychology, 65*(1), 45-55.

Hunt, R. R. (1995). The subtlety of distinctiveness: What von Restorff really did. *Psychonomic Bulletin & Review, 2*(1), 105-112.

Hunt, R. R., & Worthen, J. B. (2006). *Distinctiveness & Memory,* pp. 3-25. Oxford University Press: New York, NY.

Johansen, M. K., & Palmeri, T. J. (2002). Are there representational shifts during category learning? *Cognitive Psychology, 45,* 482-553.

Kemp, S., Burt, C. D. B., & Furneaux, L. (2008). A test of the peak-end rule with extended autobiographical events. *Memory & Cognition, 36*(1), 132-138.

Knowlton, B. J., & Squire, L. R. (1993). The learning of categories: parallel brain systems for item memory and category knowledge. *Science, 262,* 1747-1749.

Montgomery, N. V., & Unnava, H. R. (2009). Temporal sequence effects: A memory framework. *Journal of Consumer Research, 36*(1), 83-90.

Rosch, E., & Mervis, C.B. (1975). Family resemblances: Studies in the internal structure of categories. *Cognitive Psychology, 7*(4), 573-605.

Shreiber, C. A., & Kahneman, D. (2000). Determinants of the remembered utility of aversive sounds. *Journal of Experimental Psychology: General, 129*(1), 27-42.

Social Context as Price Information:
Social Density, Status Inferences, and Object Valuations

Ahreum Maeng, University of Wisconsin - Madison, USA
Thomas O'Guinn, University of Wisconsin - Madison, USA
Robin Tanner, University of Wisconsin - Madison, USA

EXTENDED ABSTRACT:

It has been widely demonstrated that the context in which an object appears influences its evaluation. One way in which such context effects have been shown to occur is by automatically altering the internal comparative standards consumer use when evaluating products (Mazumdar, Raj, and Sinha, 2005). To date, the majority of the research on context effects has examined them in terms of product attributes (e.g. Adaval and Monroe, 2002; Simonson, 1989). However, in this research we explore an example of how the broader social context of the choice environment may provide a meaningful context. In particular, we propose that the crowdedness of a retail store can spontaneously evoke a set of stored representations such as the social status or disposable income of the people frequenting the store. Furthermore, these representations of social class can lead to distortions in perceptions of price and willingness to spend. For example, we propose that a highly crowded store environment activates lower class representations (e.g., that shoppers have lower disposable income) which in turn alters consumers' expectations about the prices of products in the store. Three studies explore this hypothesis.

In a pilot study, we wanted to demonstrate that different levels of social density have historically been associated with different expectations about social class. Thus we performed Google image searches for the terms "upper class Americans" and "working class Americans". For the first 100 images retrieved in each search we counted the number of people portrayed in each image. This analysis revealed that working class images contained a higher number of people (M= 5.4) than did images associated with the upper class (M = 1.6; t(198) = -5.80, p <0.001). Thus, as far as historical imagery is concerned, there does appear to be a clear visual relationship between class and social density.

Study 1 (N=75) was designed to test whether this apparent relationship between class expectations and social density could actually influence the class inferences individuals make from social density cues. All participants were shown a picture which they were told was a stylistic representation of an actual social scene, and which consisted of human stick figures on a white background. The scene was either crowded (36 stick figures) or uncrowded (2 stick figures). Stick figures were used to ensure no inferences could be drawn from specific social cues such as clothing. Participants were asked to estimate both the average social class of the individuals in the scene (1=upper class to 5=lower class) and their average annual income. Results revealed that participants rated the figures in the low-density context as being from a higher class (Msparse = 2.1) than those in the high-density condition (Mdense = 3.7; F(1,73) = 64.9, p < 0.001). Furthermore, figures in the low-density context were also rated as having a higher annual income (Msparse = $114K) than those in the high-density condition (Mdense = $49K; F(1,73) = 51.6, p < 0.001).

Study 2 (N=84) was designed to explore if a similar social density manipulation would influence inferences of price of products in a store. To do this, we created three images of a clothing store, which contained 35 to 4 human silhouettes depending on the level of crowdedness. Participants, who were once again told the image was adapted from a real picture, were asked to make an inference for the price of a typical pair of shoes in the store. Ratings of the expected income of a typical customer were collected in the same manner as

Study 1. Results showed that participants estimated shoe price highest at the low-density store (M= $207), lowest at the high-density store (M= $131; F(2, 81) = 3.62, p=0.03), and in-between at the medium-density store (M = $171). Furthermore, the expected income findings from Study 1 replicated and mediated the effect of social density on expected price of the given product. Thus, perceived value of products in the store, seemed to be determined by their beliefs about other shoppers incomes, which were themselves driven by how crowded the store was.

By examining if the mere crowdedness of a store could influence how products are subsequently recalled, Study 3 (N=180) was provides differential evidence that the social density of a store can influence how consumers codify the relative prices of products in the store. Study 3 built on prior research demonstrating that consumer's abstract recollections of the expensiveness of a particular product presented in a specific context are influenced by the prices of the other products viewed in that context. Specifically, consumers subsequently remember products as being relatively more expensive/(cheap) if they were originally presented in the context of other products which were themselves relatively lower/(higher) in price. Thus we predicted that individuals who considered a product in an uncrowded/(crowded) store context should subsequently remember the product to be relatively more cheap/(expensive).

The study was carried out in two stages: First, participants were asked to choose between two similar pairs of dress shoes at a pictured store which was uncrowded, moderately crowded, or crowded. While we were ultimately interested in memories of the expensiveness of the product chosen, not the choice itself, we had participants make a choice between two similar products to ensure they considered them in as naturalistic a way as possible. 24 to 36 hours later participants were asked to rate the expensiveness of the shoes they had previously chosen on an 11-point scale anchored from very inexpensive to very expensive. As predicted, results showed that participants recalled the chosen product to be less expensive when previously presented in an uncrowded context (Msparse= 6.05), versus the crowded context (Mdense= 6.57) with the moderate density context in-between the other two (M = 6.14; F(2, 177) = 2.98, p=0.05).

Taken together, these data provide the first evidence of the important finding that the social density of the choice environment can act as a context effect and influences how consumers process price information in the store.

REFERENCES

Adaval, Rashmi, and Kent B. Monroe (2002), "Automatic Construction and Use of Contextual Information for Product and Price Evaluation," *Journal of Consumer Research,* 28, no. 4: 572-588.

Mazumdar, Tridib, S. P. Raj, and Indrajit Sinha (2005), "Reference Price Research: Review and Propositions," *Journal of Marketing*, 69, no. 4: 84-102.

Simonson, Itamar (1989), "Choice Based on Reasons: The Case of Attraction and Compromise Effects," *Journal of Consumer Research*, 16, no. 2: 158-174.

An Examination of Social Collective Decision-Making

Julie Tinson, University of Stirling, UK
Pete Nuttall, University of Bath, UK

EXTENDED ABSTRACT

Decision-making by a social entity is a universal experience yet virtually overlooked in consumer research (Ward and Reingen, 1990). A recent call for research to consider affiliation and separation in a social group decision-making setting supports the assertion that this area is under-researched (see Tinson and Nuttall, 2011). Exploring group as opposed to individual decision-making is of particular interest as it provides an opportunity to understand both the social context and social interaction that occurs when making consumption decisions. Although there are a plethora of studies examining the phenomena of family decision-making (e.g. Beatty and Talpade, 1994; Palan and Wilkes, 1997; Lee and Collins, 2000; Chaplin and John, 2010), exploring group consumption and consumer behaviour in an alternate social environment (e.g. amongst colleagues or peers) will generate insight and provide marketing implications for social collective decision-making. Collective decisions made by social groups can be for low or high involvement products and may include, for example, friends deciding which film to see at the cinema, which night club or restaurant to go to, or which holiday to choose. The purpose of this paper, employing a qualitative approach, is to explore the decision-making of an adolescent collective, their social interactions (including conflict and conflict resolution) and to propose an original model based on influencing strategies for social collective decisions.

As such, the objectives of the study are as follows:

- To explore the experience of adolescent social collective decision-making and to establish how adolescents influence one another in a group to make decisions with consequences for the collective
- To understand how social collective decision-making is influenced by the social environment as well as the group dynamics
- To propose an original model based on influencing strategies for social collective decisions

RESEARCH DESIGN

A two stage qualitative approach, employing a longitudinal single embedded case study (Yin, 2009) followed by in-depth interviews, was designed to meet the proposed objectives of this investigation. This involved conducting four focus groups with the committee throughout the year and four individual interviews with the 'Services Captain' with overall responsibility for the high-school prom. She was an "embedded unit of analysis" (Yin, 2009: 46). That is, discussions with the Services Captain would allow a more holistic understanding of the way in which social collective decision-making was shaped. There were six members of the committee. Permission to meet with the members of the high-school prom organising committee was given by the school and on-going consent was provided by the pupils (see Tinson, 2009).

Following analysis of the case study material 12 in-depth interviews were arranged with young adults (18-20 years of age) who were members of a high-school prom organising committee within the last three years (see **Table 1**). All the interviewees attended school in Scotland and each respondent contributed to social collective decisions about the high-school prom e.g. venue, menus, photographer, band etc. The respondents were recruited via email through the use of university class lists to send invites. A semi-structured interview guide was developed for this phase of data collection. Questions ranged from an initially broad approach with questions such as 'tell me about your prom organising committee' with later questions addressing the specific aspects of social collection decision-making such as negotiation within the group and how was any conflict resolved to did decisions change over time.

DATA ANALYSIS

An interpretive analytic stance was adopted that drew on the transcriptions (see Bryman and Burgess, 1994) and the constant comparative method described by Glaser and Strauss (1967) was employed. Emerging insights and prior assumptions allowed interpretations to develop (Spiggle, 1994). The data was examined by considering social collective decision-making behaviour and changes to decisions and the associated negotiations and context.

FINDINGS

The findings established that adolescents influence one another in a group using a variety of influencing techniques (e.g. coalition formation, reasoning, bargaining and playing on emotion) and that the group is subject to conflict and conflict resolution (e.g. yielding, dominating, compromising and avoiding). Coalition formation (see

Table 1: Respondent Profiles

Pseudonym	Gender	Age	Location of prom	Time elapsed since prom attendance	No. of organising committee members
Jill	Female	19	Central Scotland	8 months	30→11
Felicity	Female	21	Central Scotland	3 years	5→6
Jon	Male	19	Dumfries and Galloway	10 months	10
Steve	Male	20	Highlands	20 months	6
Ruby	Female	19	Edinburgh & the Lothians	9 months	12→4
Catriona	Female	20	Aberdeenshire	18 months	10→8
Kerry	Female	20	Glasgow	14 months	12→8
Rosie	Female	19	Glasgow	9 months	10→6
Darren	Male	19	Central Scotland	8 months	11→8
Megan	Female	20	Edinburgh & the Lothians	2 years	15→7
Lily	Female	18	Glasgow	6 months	12→8
Suzanne	Female	19	Central Scotland	18 months	8→5

Lee and Collins, 2000) was not only evident within the group but externally between teachers and/or venue liaisons. This allowed for an exploration of the inter-relationship between the macro and micro environment (see Bamaca and Umana-Taylor, 2006). These external coalitions were significant not only because they were recognised as being credible but as a consequence of how the perceptions of these coalitions changed over time. Over the period of event preparation (typically nine months) the external coalitions became more important and were able to appreciably impact on the dynamics and related decision-making of the social collective. Intra coalitions were more likely to use bargaining or emotional appeals (e.g. guilt) to influence decisions whilst inter coalitions and their subsequent position/s on issues were often used as leverage within the social decision-making collective. Dominant roles adopted by intra coalitions typically materialised in (potential) conflict. Noticeably, those who appeared most dominant within the social group either disassociated from decisions made within the collective that they did not agree with or exited the group 'on principal' to preserve their perceived integrity (and more effectively manage their individual goals and identity ambitions).

CONCLUSIONS

This paper responds to the need for greater consideration of separation and affiliation in a social group context. This research has not only identified influencing strategies employed to influence choice but has also established how these strategies are used variably over time. The inter-relationship between the macro and the micro environment has also been explored within the context of social collective decision-making and has furthered our knowledge of adolescent social interaction e.g. inclusion and exclusion. A novel theory has been produced here and can be tested in other contexts.

REFERENCES

Bamaca, M.Y. and Umana-Taylor, A.J. (2006) "Testing a model of resistance to peer pressure among Mexican-origin adolescents", *Journal of Youth and Adolescence*, 35(4), pp. 631-645

Beatty, S.E. and Talpade, S. (1994) "Adolescent Influence in Family Decision Making: A Replication with Extension", *Journal of Consumer Research*, 21 (2) pp. 332-341

Bryman, A. and Burgess, R.G. (1994), *Analyzing Qualitative Data*, London: Routledge

Chaplin, L.N. and John, D.R. (2010) "Interpersonal influences on adolescent materialism: A new look at the role of parents and peers", *Journal of Consumer Psychology,* 20 (2), pp.176-184

Glaser, B and Strauss, A. (1967), *The Discovery of Grounded Theory: Strategies for Qualitative Research*, Chicago: Aldine

Lee, K.C.C. and Collins, B.A. (2000), "Family Decision Making and Coalition Patterns", *European Journal of Marketing*, 34 (9/10), pp.1181-1198

Palan, K.M. and Wilkes, R.E. (1997) "Adolescent-Parent Interaction in Family Decision Making", *Journal of Consumer Research*, 24 (2), pp.159-169

Spiggle, S. (1994) "Analysis and Interpretation of Qualitative Data in Consumer Research", *Journal of Consumer Research*, 21, pp.491-503

Tinson J. (2009) *Conducting Research with Children & Adolescents: Design, Methods and Empirical Cases* Oxford:Goodfellow

Tinson, J. and Nuttall, P. (2011) "Performing the High School Prom in the UK: Locating Authenticity through Practice", *Journal of Marketing Management*, 27 (9-10), pp.1007-1026

Ward, J.C. and Reingen, P.H. (1990) "Sociocognitive Analysis of Group Decision Making among Consumers", *Journal of Consumer Research*, 17 (3) pp. 245-262

Yin, R.K. (2009) *Case Study Research: Design and Methods*, 4th Edition, California:Sage

The Dead People Bias in Disaster Aid

Ioannis Evangelidis, Erasmus University Rotterdam, The Netherlands
Bram Van den Bergh, Erasmus University Rotterdam, The Netherlands

EXTENDED ABSTRACT

"In Peru, the rainy weather and flooding have caused 15 deaths across the country, and affected another 30,000 residents".

Natural disasters often result in severe death tolls and economic damage. In an effort to help those who require immediate assistance, fund-raising activities often follow such catastrophes. In this paper we investigate how numerical information (i.e., the number of dead and the number of affected people) influences decision-making about disaster aid.

When the United Nations compile a Humanitarian Action Plan to support victims of a disaster, they estimate the appropriate amount of donation by multiplying the number of affected with a minimum amount. Indeed, the ideal size of donation depends on the number of people affected, and not on the number of dead people, since the affected people represent the beneficiaries of disaster aid.

Nevertheless, past work on prosocial behavior has documented numerous biases in decision-making, such as the identifiable victim effect (Kogut and Ritov 2005; Small and Loewenstein 2003), psychophysical numbing (Friedrich et al. 1999; Slovic 2007), and scope insensitivity (Desvousges et al. 1993). This evidence suggests that decision-making is subjected to inherent limitations in the way we process information (Kahneman 2003). As a consequence, donors may not always react in the way the United Nations hopes. Indeed, donors may use the number of dead, rather than the number of affected people, to determine the extent to which financial aid must be provided.

In our first study, we analyzed real disaster relief data about 381 natural disasters using a two-stage model. We find that the number of dead, and not the number of people affected in a disaster, is a significant predictor of the probability to grant financial aid (Heckman $z = 3.54$, $p < .001$), as well as of the size of the financial aid (Heckman $z = 13.25$, $p < .001$). Donors are both more likely to donate and more likely to donate more money to a natural disaster as the number of dead people increases, whereas they are insensitive to the number of affected.

Because correlational studies are not always reliable and do not allow causal inferences, we experimentally manipulated the number of affected (Study 2A) and the number of dead (Study 2B). Using an imaginary earthquake in Asia, we found that people donate more money when the number of dead people increases [$t(47) = -2.45$, $p = .018$], but remain insensitive to the number of people affected in a disaster [$t(35) = -.38$, NS].

We place the dead people bias in the category of one-reason heuristic decision-making (Gigerenzer and Gaissmaier 2011) in which a single cue (e.g., number of affected people, number of dead people) drives decisions. The validity rule asserts that the use of a cue is based on its validity, that is, the relative frequency with which the cue allows for correct inferences (Gigerenzer and Goldstein 1996). Other work highlights the importance of a cue's reliability. This account suggests that individuals are more likely to rely on a cue when they perceive its values as reliable regardless of cue validity (York et al. 1987). We argue that although the number of affected is a more "valid" driver of financial donations, the number of dead is more "reliable". Further studies provide evidence that individuals do not consider cue validity, but use a cue as long as it is seen as reliable.

In a third experiment, we test whether people's sensitivity to the number of dead is attenuated when they are primed to think in terms of validity. In addition to manipulating the number of dead and the number of affected, we also manipulated validity (control vs. primed). In the primed validity condition, respondents were instructed to "think about who will receive the donation" prior to deciding on how much should be donated. We found a significant two-way interaction between the number of dead and validity [$F(1, 228) = 4.32$, $p < .04$]. At the control level of validity, we replicate the dead people bias: People donated more to a fictitious earthquake in Asia when the number of dead people is high rather than low [$F(1, 228) = 4.01$, $p < .05$]. However, this bias is eliminated when validity is primed [$F(1, 228) = .77$, NS]. This study provides evidence for the use of a discrimination rule in responses to disasters and that priming validity of cues eliminates the dead people bias.

The final study consisted of two parts. In the first part, we manipulate the number of dead and affected people between-subjects and replicate the dead people bias: People feel that more money should be donated when the number of dead people due to a tropical cyclone in the Caribbean was high rather than low (Heckman $z = 2.87$, $p = .004$), but not when the number of affected is high rather than low ($p > .16$). In the second part, we manipulated the number of dead and affected people within-subjects and asked participants to rank-order four disasters in terms of appropriate size of donation. We predicted that when people are forced to use one cue at the expense of the other, such as when rank-ordering, cue usage would be based on validity rather than discrimination ability. Confirming our predictions, we found that the majority of the participants used a validity rule, thus ranking a disaster with a high number of affected higher than a disaster with a high number of dead (Friedman's $\chi^2 = 200.42$, $p < .001$).

Our research contributes to theory on heuristic decision-making by showing how cue selection critically depends on the decision context. In addition, we examined event severity, and attribute evaluability as potential alternative explanations, but none of these mechanisms seemed to drive donation decisions. The potential implications of the present research are broad and important as we provide novel insights on how communications of fund raising agencies, journalists or humanitarian organizations should be optimally designed. Our ultimate goal is to improve aid towards future disaster victims.

REFERENCES

Desvousges, William H., Reed F. Johnson, Richard W. Dunford, Sara P. Hudson, Nicole K. Wilson, and Kevin J. Boyle (1993), "Measuring Natural Resource Damages With Contingent Valuation: Tests of Validity and Reliability," in *Contingent Valuation: A Critical Assessment,* ed. Jerry A. Hausman, Amsterdam: North-Holland, 91-164.

Friedrich, James, Paul Barnes, Kathryn Chapin, Ian Dawson, Valerie Garst, and David Kerr (1999), "Psychophysical Numbing: When Lives are Valued Less as the Lives at Risk Increase," *Journal of Consumer Psychology,* 8 (3), 277-99.

Gigerenzer, Gerd and Wolfgang Gaissmaier (2011), "Heuristic Decision Making," *Annual Review of Psychology,* 62, 451-82.

Gigerenzer, Gerd and Daniel G. Goldstein (1996), "Reasoning the Fast and Frugal Way: Models of Bounded Rationality," *Psychological Review,* 103 (4), 650-69.

Kahneman, Daniel (2003), "Maps of Bounded Rationality: Psychology for Behavioral Economics," *The American Economic Review,* 93 (5), 1449-75.

Kogut, Tehila and Ilana Ritov (2005), "The "Identified Victim" Effect: An Identified Group, or Just a Single Individual?" *Journal of Behavioral Decision Making,* 18, 157-67.

Penner, Louis A., John F. Dovidio, Jane A. Piliavin, and David A. Schroeder (2005), "Prosocial Behavior: Multilevel Perspectives," *Annual Review of Psychology,* 56, 365-92.

Slovic, Paul (2007), ""If I Look at the Mass I Will Never Act": Psychic Numbing and Genocide," *Judgment and Decision Making,* 2 (2), 79-95.

Small, Deborah A. and George Loewenstein (2003), "Helping a Victim or Helping the Victim: Altruism and Identifiability," *Journal of Risk and Uncertainty,* 26 (1), 5-16.

York, Kenneth M., Michael E. Doherty, and Joseph Kamouri (1987), "The Influence of Cue Unreliability on Judgment in a Multiple Cue Probability Learning Task, " *Organizational Behavior and Human Decision Processes,* 39, 303-317.

"Happiness Ain't Always Material Things" (Destiny by Michael Jackson) -- Or, Is It?

Lan Nguyen Chaplin, Villanova University, USA
Tina M. Lowrey, University of Texas at San Antonio, USA
Kristin Trask, University of Texas at San Antonio, USA
Ayalla Ruvio, Temple University, USA

EXTENDED ABSTRACT:

Children love getting presents. In fact, children today are deemed the most materialistic and brand conscious generation (Schor 2005). Research on materialism, which has been conducted with adult samples, has found a link between materialism and less happiness (Carter and Gilovich 2010). If we simply apply adult findings to children, this would mean that children are the least happy. Yet, studies have shown that there are no significant differences in happiness by age (see Myers and Diener 1995). Thus, the findings from the adult literature cannot simply be applied to children. In fact, children might find more happiness in objects than experiences. If so, a related question emerges – when might children begin to resemble adults in favoring experiences over objects?

We propose that young children (3-5 years old) appreciate and prefer objects over experiences. Because young children notice and give their attention to concrete features of their world more so than abstract features, they are likely going to connect with concrete aspects of their world (e.g., objects) more so than abstract aspects (e.g., experiences). By late childhood (6-12 years old), children are beginning to think more abstractly, opening up the possibility of defining themselves in more complex and abstract terms (e.g., I like spending time with my family doing yard work), and therefore, intangible experiences may begin to gain recognition as useful devices for characterizing the self more for older children compared to their younger counterparts. However, the intangible abstract nature of experiences will still likely make it too hard for even older children to appreciate experiences over objects. By late adolescence (16-17 years old), we expect a reversal of this relative preference, in that older adolescents will prefer experiences over objects. Thus, we propose that relative preferences will change over time (age) for all children and adolescents, such that objects are preferred the most in the earliest years (ages 3-5), that this relative preference will decline for older children (ages 6-12), and reverse for older adolescents (16-17).

Figure 1
Happiness Collage: Developmental Changes in Children's Preference for Objects vs. Experiences

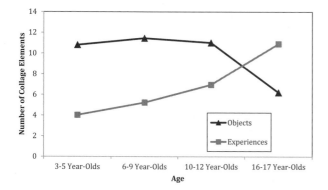

We also propose that age moderates the effect of memory and theory of mind on children's preferences for objects over experiences. Specifically, young children simply do not have sufficiently developed knowledge structures to think about details of prior experiences (Justice 1985). Moreover, young children have not collected enough memorable experiences. In other words, to appreciate experiences, one must first collect memorable experiences, or develop what Keinan and Kivetz (2010; p.937) call an "experiential check list or experiential CV." Clearly this experiential CV is underdeveloped during early childhood and develops with age.

An underdeveloped theory of mind is also likely to contribute to children's preferences for objects over experiences. Without the ability to understand theirs' or others' emotions/feelings that result from an experience [dining out together] or to be able to predict others' behaviors or feelings based on an experience, it will be difficult for children to fully appreciate the value of experiences in building successful social relationships, which is one reason why adults prefer experiences over objects (Diener and Seligman 2004). We suspect that as children grow older and develop into more socially aware individuals (Piaget 1932; Turiel 2006), develop better memories for experiences, and begin to make more disadvantageous comparisons between objects, that experiential purchases will begin to make them happier than objects. But, until all of the above-mentioned develops, we would expect children to look more to objects to make them happy.

We test these predictions in three studies. In Study 1, we used unstructured interviews to ensure that children do indeed think of objects and experiences when they think about what makes them happy. Providing participants with an unstructured, open-ended task, as opposed to asking them to tailor their responses to narrowly focus on experiences and objects, allowed us to let children reveal what specific experiences and objects are meaningful to them. Results from Study 1 were used to develop age and gender appropriate stimuli for Studies 2a, 2b, and 3. In Study 2a, children ages 3-12 were asked to construct collages using pictures of objects (e.g., toys, clothes) and experiences (e.g., birthday parties, playing sports) to answer the question, "What makes you happy?" . In Study 2b, we examined further age differences by sampling 16-17 year olds. In Study 3, we used a reaction time experiment with the full age range of children and adolescents, ages 3-17, to determine whether objects or experiences were most accessible to children and adolescents.

Our research provides evidence that the preference for objects over experiences is quite strong from early to middle childhood (ages 3-9). Although the preference for objects over experiences exists throughout childhood (ages 3-12), by late childhood (ages 10-12), the preference is significantly weaker. By late adolescence, the preference reverses and adolescents find more happiness in experiences than objects, resembling findings in the adult literature. Finally, we offer a process explanation (memory and theory of mind), for the developmental change observed—moving from preference for objects in childhood to preference for experiences by adolescence.

In conclusion, happiness emanates from many sources. People derive happiness from objects (a luxury handbag, a large house, a nice car) and from experiences (an exotic vacation, an exquisite dinner). However, research suggests that objects and experiences are not valued equally. People tend to derive more happiness from experiences than from objects. Our research confirms these findings, but with a very important caveat. A preference for experiences over objects is not an innate characteristic, but a child developmental process that unfolds over time. The thrill of objects during childhood is a phase that all children go through. When they have acquired a sufficient "experiential CV" and their memory and theory of mind have matured, the stage will be set for them to appreciate the intangible benefits of experiences— they will indeed prefer experiences over objects similar to adults.

REFERENCES

Carter, Travis J. and Thomas Gilovich (2010), "The Relative Relativity of Material and Experiential Purchases," *Journal of Personality and Social Psychology*, 98 (1), 146-46-59.

Diener, Ed and Martin E. P. Seligman (2004), "Beyond Money: Toward an Economy of Well-Being: Toward an Economy of Well-Being," *Psychological Science in the Public Interest*, 5 (1), 1-31.

Justice, Elaine M. (1985), "Categorization as a Preferred Memory Strategy: Developmental Changes During Elementary School," *Developmental Psychology*, 21 (6), 1105-10.

Keinan, Anat and Ran Kivetz (2011), "Productivity Orientation and the Consumption of Collectable Experiences," *Journal of Consumer Research*, 37 (6), 935-50.

Myers, David G. and Ed Diener (1995), "Who Is Happy?" *Psychological Science*, 6 (1), 10-19.

Piaget, Jean (1932), *The Moral Judgment of the Child*, London, UK: Routledge.

Schor, Juliet (2005), *Born to Buy*, New York, NY: Scribner.

Turiel, Elliot (2006), "Thoughts, Emotions, and Social Interactional Processes in Moral Development," in *Handbook of Moral Development*, ed. Melanie Killen and Judith G. Smetana, Mahwah, N.J: Erlbaum, 7-35.

My Heart Longs for More: The Role of Emotions in Assortment Size Preferences

Aylin Aydinli, London Business School, UK
Yangjie Gu, London Business School, UK
Michel Tuan Pham, Columbia University, USA

EXTENDED ABSTRACT

Past research has documented the factors that influence consumer choice among assortments, such as the decision flexibility (McAlister and Pessemier 1982), the probability of a match between consumers' preferences and the available alternatives (Lancaster 1990), availability of ideal point (Chernev 2003), the anticipated cognitive effort in making a choice (Huffman and Kahn 1998) and the nature of decision process (Chernev 2006). This research has mainly focused on the cognitive processes used in the construction of assortment size preferences.

In this paper, we investigate the role of emotions in influencing consumers' assortment size preferences. In particular, we investigate how feeling-based (compared with reason-based) decisions may influence preferences for assortment size. Prior research has shown that emotional system is holistic (Epstein 1994). Accordingly, while evaluating the assortment, people who engage in such holistic processing may focus more on judging the global features of the choice set. Research suggests that people who search at a global (vs. local) level tend to have larger consideration sets (Pham and Chang 2010). In addition, it has been shown that global evaluations favour varied sequences (Ratner, Kahn and Kahneman 1997). Therefore, people who perform global evaluations might desire for more variety and compared to small assortments, large assortments provide greater fit to the desire for more variety. Hence, we posit that people who make feeling-based choices would be more satisfied with a large assortment than a small assortment. In contrast, people who rely on their feelings less may experience less fit from the large assortment. As a consequence, the difference in preferences for large and smaller assortments is mitigated. The predicted effect of feeing-based decision on preferences for large assortments versus smaller assortments was tested in four studies.

The first three studies aimed to test the predicted effect by using different approaches to manipulate how much participants relied on their feelings. Study 1 was a 2 (assortment size: small vs. large) x 2 (product type: hedonic vs. functional) between-subjects design. Participants were asked to imagine going to a supermarket to purchase either detergent (functional) or jam (hedonic) from a selection of either 12 (small-set) or 36 options (large-set). Research shows that hedonic products elicit greater affective response in consumers than functional ones (Okada 2005). We measured participants' satisfaction with the selection. Results showed that participants evaluating the jam selection were more satisfied with the large assortment than the small assortment. However, this difference was mitigated when they evaluate the detergent selection.

Study 2 employed a 2 (assortment size: small vs. large) x 2 (trust in feelings (TF): high vs. low) between-subjects design. Participants, either in high-TF or low-TF conditions, were asked to imagine purchasing a coffee from a menu that either provided a selection of 12 (small-set) or 36 coffees (large-set). Before the choice task, supposedly in an unrelated study, we manipulated participants' momentary trust in their feelings and thus their reliance on feelings using a procedure called the *trust-in-feelings manipulation* (Avnet, Pham, and Stephen 2012). Participants were asked to describe either two (high-TF) or 10 (low-TF) situations where they trusted their feelings to make a decision and it turned out to be the right decision. It has been shown that recalling two (vs. 10) instances of successful reliance on feelings induce higher (vs. lower) reliance on feelings. Results showed that in the high-TF condition, satisfaction with the large assortment was higher than the small assortment. However, this difference was not significant in the low-TF condition.

Study 3 was a 2 (assortment size: small vs. large) x 2 (cognitive load: high vs. low) between-subjects design. Participants were asked to imagine selecting a coffee from a selection of 12 (small-set) or 36 options (large-set). ROF was operationalized through a cognitive load manipulation (Shiv and Fedorikhin 1999), where participants were asked to memorize either a 2-digit code (low-load) or a 10-digit code (high-load) and to reproduce the code at the end of the study. Prior research has demonstrated that choice under cognitive load limits cognitive capacity, thus generating a greater degree of reliance on feelings than choice under low cognitive load (Lieberman et al. 2002). Accordingly, we expected participants who memorized 10-digit (vs. 2-digit) code to rely more on their feelings while making decisions. Results showed that participants in the high-load condition were more satisfied with the large (vs. small) assortment. However, this difference was not significant for low-load participants.

Study 4 aimed to test the process driving the observed effect. Study 4 employed a 2 (assortment size: small vs. large) x 2 (cognitive load: high vs. low) between-subjects design. The procedure of study 4 was similar to study 3, except that this time participants were asked to imagine considering purchasing a snack from a vending machine that contained a selection of 12 (small-set) or 36 snacks (large-set). To test the process, we measured whether participants would like to have had greater variety in the selection they were given. Results showed that in the high-load condition, the desire for more variety was less for participants who were confronted with the large assortment than for those who were faced with the small assortment. Therefore, in the high-load condition, participants liked the large assortment more than the small assortment, because the former provided a better "fit" to their need for variety. However, in the low-load condition, the difference in desire for greater variety was not significant. Consequently, there was no difference in satisfaction with large and small assortments. Mediation analysis further supported that desire for greater variety mediated the observed effect only in the large-set condition.

To summarize, four studies documented the impact of reliance on feelings on consumers' assortment size preferences. We found that greater reliance on feelings boosts individuals' preference for larger assortments as opposed to smaller assortments. First three studies have demonstrated the effect of reliance on feelings on satisfaction with the assortment. Study 4 has provided the process evidence: A large assortment provides a better "fit" to the desire for variety that is triggered by the feeling-based process.

REFERENCES

Avnet, Tamar, Michel Tuan Pham, and Andrew T. Stephen (2012), "Consumers' Trust in Feelings as Information," unpublished manuscript.

Chernev, Alexander (2003), "When More Is Less and Less Is More: The Role of Ideal Point Availability and Assortment in Consumer Choice," *Journal of Consumer Research*, 30 (September), 170-183.

Advances in Consumer Research
Volume 40, ©2012

_____ (2006), "Decision Focus and Consumer Choice among Assortments," *Journal of Consumer Research*, 33 (June), 50-59.

Epstein, Seymour (1994), "Integration of the Cognitive and the Psychodynamic Unconscious," *American Psychologist*, 49 (August), 709–24.

Huffman, Cynthia and Barbara E. Kahn (1998), "Variety for Sale: Mass Customization or Mass Confusion?" *Journal of Retailing*, 74 (Winter), 491-513.

Lancaster, Kelvin (1990), "The Economics of Product Variety: A Survey," *Marketing Science*, 9 (Summer), 189-206.

Lieberman, Matthew D., Ruth Gaunt, Daniel T. Gilbert, and Yaacov Trope (2002), "Reflexion and Reflection: A Social Cognitive Neuroscience Approach to Attributional Inference," in *Advances in Experimental Social Psychology*, Vol. 34, ed. Mark P. Zanna, San Diego: Academic Press, 199–249.

McAlister, Leigh (1982), "A Dynamic Attribute Satiation Model of Variety-Seeking Behavior," *Journal of Consumer Research*, 9 (September), 141-151.

Okada, Erica Mina (2005), "Justification effects on Consumer Choice of Hedonic and Utilitarian Goods," *Journal of Marketing Research,* 42 (February), 43-53.

Pham, Michel Tuan and Hannah H. Chang (2010), "Regulatory Focus, Regulatory Fit, and the Search and Consideration of Choice Alternatives," *Journal of Consumer Research*, 37 (December), 626-40.

Ratner, Rebecca K., Barbara E. Kahn, and Daniel Kahneman (1999), "Choosing Less Preferred Experiences for the Sake of Variety," *Journal of Consumer Research*, 26 (June), 1-15.

Shiv, Baba and Alexander Fedorikhin (1999), "Heart and Mind in Conflict: The Interplay of Affect and Cognition in Consumer Decision Making," *Journal of Consumer Research*, 26 (December), 278–92.

Me, Myself, and Ikea: Qualifying the Role of Implicit Egotism in Brand Judgment

Jacob H. Wiebenga, University of Groningen, the Netherlands
Bob M. Fennis, University of Groningen, the Netherlands, and Norwegian Business School BI, Norway

EXTENDED ABSTRACT

We frequently like occupations, partners, cities, streets, birthdays, and a host of other objects, events and entities because, essentially, we like ourselves (Pelham et al. 2005). This intriguing phenomenon is known as 'implicit egotism' – the unconscious attraction to things that are linked to the self (Pelham et al. 2002). Although abundant research in numerous contexts has shown its pervasive existence (Jones et al. 2004; Pelham et al. 2002), research in the consumer sphere is surprisingly scarce (but see Brendl et al. 2005). This is all the more surprising given that recent trends indicate that the use of personal pronouns in branding such as 'I' and 'my' (e.g., iTunes and MySpace) shows a marked surge in recent years (BOIP 2012). The present research extends previous findings and examines whether and when such self-referencing brand names affect brand judgment, and under which conditions the self-referencing effect might turn from positive into negative.

To understand the possible impact of pronouns in brand names, we draw from work on the disproportionate liking of people for things that are associated with the self (Greenwald and Banaji 1995). Most notably in this regard is the finding that people even like their own names to such an extent that they like the letters that comprise it over other letters in the alphabet (Nuttin 1985). Recent research has found that this so-called 'name letter effect' extends to the liking of people, places, and products with similar name letters (Brendl et al. 2005; Pelham et al. 2005). The underlying rationale is that name letters produce a link between the self and the target which subsequently leads to a transfer of self-evaluations to the self-associated target (Gawronski et al. 2007).

It is striking to note that most studies have limited themselves to examining the effects of implicit egotism by assessing name letters as proxies for self-referencing. We, however, posit that self-associations can also be created by more generic self-referencing stimuli. More in particular, we propose that also first person pronouns like 'I' and 'my' may function as persuasion cues in eliciting a bias toward the self-associated target. Hence, we expect that brands featuring self-referencing pronouns in their name will be liked better than brand names without such pronouns.

Implicit egotism is thought to be a self-enhancement mechanism which enables people to preserve their positive self-view (Pelham et al. 2002). Research on self-enhancement has shown that people often respond to self-threat in ways to reaffirm their sense of self-worth (Tesser 2000). One way in which people compensate for this threat is by enhancing the value of external targets that are associated with the self (Jones et al. 2002). We posit that if pronouns in brand names create a self-target association, these brands might also function as a source for self-affirmation. More specifically, we propose that the positive effect of self-referencing brands on brand name liking will be more pronounced under conditions of self-threat, i.e., when the need for self-affirmation is high.

To date, research on implicit egotism has found that the bias resulting from the self-target association is generally positive because the 'default' evaluation of the self is mildly positive (Greenwald and Banaji 1995; Yamaguchi et al. 2007). Hence, self-referencing stimuli are assumed to enhance the favorability of practically anything even when the self-associated target itself is undesirable (Nelson and Simmons 2007). But what if people's self-evaluations are not positive but negative? If the self-referencing effect hinges on the valence of people's self-evaluations, and if the positive bias is the result of a transfer of positive self-evaluations to the target, then, by implication, also negative self-evaluations can spill over to the target resulting in a negative bias. It follows that attraction can turn into avoidance or at least an unfavorably valenced brand judgment when consumers' self-evaluations are negative. We tested these notions in three studies.

Study 1 showed that, while controlling for brand familiarity, existing brand names with a generic self-referencing pronoun (e.g., iPhone, iDeal) were evaluated more positive than non-self-referencing brand names (e.g., X-Box, X-Travel) or brand names without any prefix (e.g., Blackberry, Paradigit). Interestingly, this study also showed that references to the self that are less specific than 'I' (i.e., brand names starting with 'you' or 'u') did not yield the implicit egotism effect.

Study 2 ruled out the alternative account that the previous effects were driven by other, existing brand name associations than with the self. More in particular, in Study 2 we used fictitious instead of existing brand names and were able to replicate the effects found in Study 1 while using 'I' and 'my' as self-referencing stimuli. Moreover, we tested whether the self-referencing effect was more pronounced when the self-concept was threatened. As hypothesized, we found that the preference for generic self-referencing (vs. non-self-referencing) brand names only increased after self-threat but not when the self was affirmed.

Study 3 sought to provide converging evidence for our notions, and to directly test the role of negative self-evaluations in implicit egotism while using a consumer sample representative of the population. That is, Study 3 tested the hypothesis that under conditions of negative self-evaluations the attraction effect turns into an avoidance effect. As expected, results showed reduced (instead of increased) liking of generic self-referencing brand names when consumers' self-evaluations were negative. In contrast, we found that positive self-evaluations led to increased liking of brands that referred to the self.

The present findings extend previous research on implicit egotism by taking into account the valence of the consumer's self-evaluations. Moreover, the present work showed that implicit egotism is not limited to such incidental instances where (brand) names and name letters match, but extends to more generic references to the self, and particularly when the consumer is in need of self-affirmation. Simply referring to the consumer's self by using personal pronouns in brand names may therefore influence a host of consumption decisions and hence account for the stunning marketing success of such brands as Ipod, Ikea and MySpace.

REFERENCES

BOIP (2012) "Benelux office for intellectual property," http://www.boip.int.

Brendl, C. Miguel., Amitava Chattopadhyay, Brett W. Pelham, and Mauricio Carvallo (2005), "Name letter branding: Valence transfers when product specific needs are active," *Journal of Consumer Research,* 32 (3), 405-15.

Gawronski, Bertram, Galen V. Bodenhausen, and Andrew P. Becker (2007), "I like it, because I like myself: Associative self-anchoring and post-decisional change of implicit evaluations," *Journal of Experimental Social Psychology,* 43 (2), 221-32.

Greenwald, Anthony G., and Mahzarin R. Banaji (1995), "Implicit social cognition: Attitudes, self-esteem, and stereotypes," *Psychological Review,* 102 (1), 4-27.

Jones, John T., Brett W. Pelham, Matthew C. Mirenberg, and John J. Hetts (2002), "Name letter preferences are not merely mere exposure: Implicit egotism as self-regulation," *Journal of Experimental Social Psychology,* 38 (2), 170-7.

Jones, John T., Brett W. Pelham, Mauricio Carvallo, and Matthew C. Mirenberg (2004), "How do I love thee? Let me count the Js: Implicit egotism and interpersonal attraction," *Journal of Personality and Social Psychology,* 87 (5), 665-83.

Nelson, Leif D., and Joseph P. Simmons (2007), "Moniker maladies: When names sabotage success," *Psychological Science,* 18 (12), 1106-12.

Nuttin, Jozef M. (1985), "Narcissism beyond gestalt and awareness: The name letter effect," *European Journal of Social Psychology,* 15 (3), 353-61.

Pelham, Brett W., Mauricio Carvallo, and John T. Jones (2005), "Implicit egotism," *Current Directions in Psychological Science,* 14 (2), 106-10.

Pelham, Brett W., Matthew C. Mirenberg, and John T. Jones (2002), "Why Susie sells seashells by the seashore: Implicit egotism and major life decisions," *Journal of Personality and Social Psychology,* 82 (4), 469-87.

Tesser, Abraham (2000), "On the confluence of self-esteem maintenance mechanisms," *Personality and Social Psychology Review,* 4 (4), 290-9.

Yamaguchi, Susumu, Anthony G. Greenwald, Mahzarin R. Banaji, Fumio Murakami, Daniel Chen, Kimihiro Shiomura, Chihiro Kobayashi, Huajian Cai, and Anne Krendl (2007), "Apparent universality of positive implicit self-esteem," *Psychological Science,* 18 (6), 498-500.

Trading off Health for Thrift in a Supersized World

Kelly L. Haws, Texas A&M University, USA
Karen Page Winterich, Pennsylvania State University, USA

EXTENDED ABSTRACT

Have you ever found yourself holding a larger dish of ice cream or mega-size latte because though you only intended to get the small, you couldn't seem to pass up the value as getting nearly twice as much for only a few cents more? Such behavior corresponds to the classic effect of nonlinear pricing in the form of increasing purchase quantity in the presence of quantity discounts (Dolan 1987; Gu and Yang 2010). However, in this case, the increased quantity is consumed immediately by one person rather than in multiple servings over time, potentially negatively impacting health. In such situations, consumers may experience conflict between their desire to obtain a good value (Grewal, Monroe, and Krishnan 1998) and their desire to consume food in moderation (Wansink, Payne, and Chandon 2007). We examine conflict and goal tradeoff processes as well as whether the supersized effect holds when a health goal is salient (e.g., encountering messages about healthy behaviors) to provide insight into the consumer processes that lead to the effects of nonlinear pricing. Such understanding may be particularly important given the prevalence of such pricing strategies for unhealthy fast foods and snacks coupled with America's obesity epidemic.

Consumers tend to focus on achieving one goal at a time, often at the expense of other goals (Baumeister, Heatherton, and Tice 1994). Generally, whichever goal is made more salient by the environment will take priority over conflicting goals (Shah and Kruglanski 2003). However, most research focuses on tradeoffs between goals within the same general domain of consumption (Dhar and Simonson 1999; Soman and Zhao 2011) whereas we examine inter-domain goal conflict and the tradeoff of health goals for thrift goals in the presence of supersized pricing. In doing so, we demonstrate that supersized pricing engenders a thrift goal as consumers experience pleasure from the discount offered by supersized pricing.

Moreover, immediate financial consequences are likely to be far more concrete than are potential health consequences. That is, while consumers, even those with numerical illiteracy, may realize that getting 24-ounces for $3.00 versus 12-ounces for $2.00 is a better deal consumers are likely unable to grasp the consequences of the extra (often unknown quantity of) calories or the financial costs of obesity (Close and Schoeller 2006). Thus, consumers may focus on the thrift goal due to the clear and immediate gratification of saving and the corresponding discounting of ambiguous, delayed health benefits (Frederick, Loewenstein, and O'Donoghue 2002).

Our studies focus on products consumed immediately following purchase (e.g., candy bars, movie popcorn, milkshakes, and snack chips). We show supersized pricing leads to larger size choice and greater consumption and demonstrate the intervention of health goal salience to retain focus on health goals and overcome the effects of supersized pricing.

In study 1, participants in an online study were randomly assigned to one of four conditions in a 2 (consumption: immediate vs. delayed) x 2 (price: linear vs. nonlinear) between-subjects design. Participants were asked to imagine choosing between two sizes of their favorite candy bar. Results from a logistic regression showed that nonlinear pricing increases purchase size relative to linear unit pricing. Additionally, the increase in size choice is significantly larger for immediately consumed purchases rather than those consumed over a period of time. More importantly, we show that size choice is influenced by more importance on thrift (vs. health) goals for immediately consumed goods offered at nonlinear pricing, which is accompanied by greater conflict.

In study 2, participants in a behavioral lab study were offered the opportunity to purchase popcorn and were either given supersized or linear pricing options for 3 sizes of popcorn. Again, the presence of supersized pricing led consumers to choose larger sizes as compared to linear pricing for immediately consumed goods. Process evidence showed that an increased emphasis on the importance of thrift relative to health drove the differences in size choice. This study replicated the main findings of study 1 for real choice and consumption.

Study 3 examines a potential intervention as a moderator: increasing health goal salience. A 2 (price: linear vs. supersized) x 2 (goal salience: health vs. control) between-subjects design revealed an interaction between the factors such that salient health goals attenuate the effect of supersized pricing on purchase quantity. Process evidence shows that the shifts in the salience of health importance in the purchase environment impacts responses to supersized pricing.

Studies 4 and 5 provide further evidence of health goal salience interventions. In a field study (study 4) examining purchase size for 1 and 2 ounce bags of potato chips offered with supersized pricing, we find that the presence (vs. absence) of a nutrition poster as a health cue overrides the effects of supersized pricing on purchase size. Similar to study 2, study 5 was conducted in a lab examining effects for real food and real money. Results reveal that a health salience prime again reduces the effect of supersized pricing. In addition, consumption quantity is found to be closely related to size choice, such that once a larger size is purchased, consumption quantity increases.

In conclusion, we demonstrate that supersized pricing leads to an increase in the quantity of food purchased and consumed. This occurs because supersized prices cause thrift to become a more focal goal than health, particularly for immediately consumed goods, unless a health goal is made salient. This focus on thrift when supersized pricing is offered may give the struggling consumer justification to achieve their thrift goal while inadvertently increasing their waistline. Substantial practical implications, including the consequences of increased consumption quantity, relate to both individual consumers and society at large.

REFERENCES

Baumeister, Roy F., Todd F. Heatherton, and Dianne M. Tice (1994), *Losing Control: How and Why People Fail at Self-Regulation*, San Diego, CA: Academic Press.

Close, Rachel N. and Dale A. Schoeller (2006), "The Financial Reality of Overeating," *Journal of the American College of Nutrition,* 25 (3), 203–9.

Dhar, Ravi and Itamar Simonson (1999), "Making Complementary Choices in Consumption Episodes: Highlighting Versus Balancing," *Journal of Marketing Research*, 36 (1), 29-44.

Dolan, Robert J. (1987), "Quantity Discounts: Managerial Issues and Research Opportunities," *Marketing Science,* 6 (1), 1–22.

Frederick, Shane, George Loewenstein, and Ted O'Donoghue (2002), "Time Discounting and Time Preference: A Critical Review," *Journal of Economic Literature*, 40 (June), 351–401.

Grewal, Dhruv, Kent B. Monroe, and R. Krishnan (1998), "The Effects of Price-Comparison Advertising on Buyers' Perceptions of Acquisition Value, Transaction Value, and Behavioral Intentions," *Journal of Marketing*, 62 (2), 46-59.

Gu, Zheyin and Sha Yang (2010), "Quantity-Discount-Dependent Consumer Preferences and Competitive Nonlinear Pricing," *Journal of Marketing Research*, 47 (December), 1100-13.

Shah, James Y. and Arie W. Kruglanski (2003), "When Opportunity Knocks: Bottom-up Priming of Goals by Means and Its Effects on Self-Regulation," *Journal of Personality and Social Psychology*, 84 (6), 1109–22.

Soman, Dilip and Min Zhao (2011), "The Fewer the Better: Number of Goals and Savings Behavior," *Journal of Marketing Research*, 48 (6), 944-57.

Would You Purchase From A Seller in Alaska?
Preference for Differently Located Sellers in Online Marketplaces

Sae Rom Lee, Pennsylvania State University, USA
Margaret G. Meloy, Pennsylvania State University, USA

EXTENDED ABSTRACT

With the advent of new technology, especially the Internet and the Web, consumers today can purchase what they need from multiple sellers around the world. As a result, many have argued that the issue of the sellers' physical distance is "dead" (Cairncross, 2001). However, we argue that distance should not be dismissed as a factor affecting consumers' preferences for sellers. Based on real transaction data from two large online stores, eBay and MercadoLibre.com, Hortaçsu et al. (2009) found that distance is still an important deterrent to transactions between geographically distant buyers and sellers. The locations of sellers can be an important factor influencing consumers' purchase decisions. Understanding what drives perceptions of distance is thus an important issue given that sellers are competing to attract consumers' attention in the online marketplace.

We propose that consumers will prefer a near seller over a distant seller despite holding the costs associated with distance constant. We also propose that preference for a distant seller can be increased if the psychological distance of that distant seller is reduced. To establish a baseline for consumer preference for near over far sellers, we conducted a pilot study. When both near and far sellers provided an identical computer monitor at the exactly same price, free insured shipping, and same delivery time, participants preferred the near seller over the far seller, regardless of whether the difference in distance was large or small between the locations. We attribute this finding to not only physical distance but psychological distance as well.

Psychological distance is a "subjective experience that something is close or far away from the self, here and now (Trope and Liberman 2010, p.440)." We suggest that greater psychological distance, normally associated with greater physical distance, will negatively influence the preference for the far seller. This greater distance will lead to an abstract mental representation of the product and uncertainty in online shopping. Thus we predict that if the psychological distance of the near seller is not shorter than the far seller, preference for the near seller will be attenuated. We test this prediction in study 1.

In study 1, participants located in Pennsylvania were asked to imagine that they were spending their summer in Arizona and were purchasing a new backpack online. In the two cell design, two differently located sellers were selling the exact same backpack, all else equal. The far seller was always located in Pennsylvania, physically far from Arizona but socially near to participants. In one condition, the near seller was located in Arizona, a location both socially and physically nearer. In the second condition, the near seller was located in Colorado, physically closer to Arizona but not socially closer to the participants than Pennsylvania. The results revealed that participants clearly preferred the near seller over the far seller when the near seller was both socially and physically closer to them. However, when the seller was physically closer to the participants but not socially closer to them, participants preferred the physically distant seller in Pennsylvania (Figure 1). Mediation analysis revealed that the difference in preference for the far seller relative to the near seller was mediated by psychological distance.

What can far sellers do to reduce psychological distance in online marketplaces? We propose that sellers can overcome the disadvantages associated with physical distance by changing the perception of psychological distance through their product presentations.

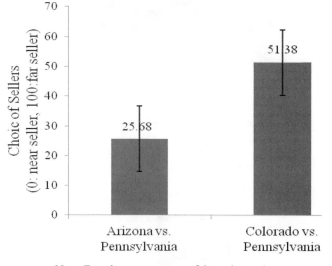

Figure 1. Study1. Choice of Near Seller versus Far Seller

Note. Error bars represent confidence intervals.

Past research suggested that information processing fluency increases liking of an object (Alter and Oppenheimer, 2008). In particular, information with distance-congruent levels of construal increases fluent evaluations of objects (Trope et al. 2007; Nussbaum et al. 2006). As such, to enhance fluency, the far seller should present their product information with descriptions in abstract terms denoting far distance while the near seller should present their product information with descriptions in concrete terms, denoting near distance. In contrast, we propose that using descriptions denoting near distance that help consumers to envision the product more concretely will always increase preference for a product in an online marketplace. When people easily and vividly envision a product experience, purchase intentions increase (Elder and Krishna 2011; Petrova and Cialdini 2005; Schlosser 2003). Thus, we propose that to increase preference for far sellers, these sellers should present their product information with distance-incongruent descriptions (i.e. far sellers should provide concrete product descriptions denoting near distance).

We tested this prediction in study 2. We created product advertisements using a product picture and words denoting different levels of distance (Bar-Anan et al. 2007) (Figure 2). Participants were assigned to one of the four conditions in a 2 (near seller: proximal vs. distal product descriptions) by 2 (far seller: proximal vs. distal product descriptions) between-subjects design. Participants were asked to select which of two sellers (near vs. far) they wished to purchase a new computer monitor from. The study revealed that the interaction between the description of near seller and far seller was significant. When the near seller's product was described in proximal terms, the near seller was always preferred relative to the far seller, regardless of whether the far seller's product was described proximally or distally. However, when the near seller's product was described distally, the choice of the far seller increased significantly, especially when the far seller's product was described proximally rather than distally. Mediation analysis revealed that psychological distance underlies the interaction effect.

Figure 2. Study 2. Proximal and Distal Product Information

Proximal Presentation

This LCD monitor surely is perfect for you if you are looking for a monitor with high quality. It is a must-have for you who love watching movies on your computers. Its fast response time also ensures you great gaming experience everyday from today.

Distal Presentation

This LCD monitor may be perfect for people if they are looking for a monitor with high quality. It would be a want-to-have for people who love watching movies on their computers. Its fast response time may also provide people great gaming experience for years to come.

This research contributes to our understanding of how the distance between consumers and sellers influences consumer choice in online marketplaces. Consumers prefer near sellers to distant sellers, even when the costs associated with physical distance are held constant. When the seller was nearer physically but not socially closer, preference for that near seller diminished. The far seller who was socially closer became more attractive due to the reduced psychological distance. Presentation of product information denoting near distance could also reduce psychological distance associated with physical distance and increase preference for the far seller. The managerial implications of the research will be discussed.

Figure 3. Study 2. Choice of Near Seller versus Far Seller

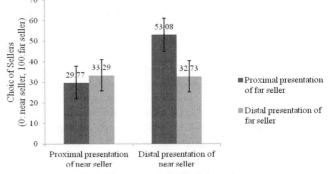

Note. Error bars represent confidence intervals.

REFERENCES

Alter, Adam L. and Daniel M. Oppenheimer (2008), "Effects of Fluency on Psychological Distance and Mental Construal (or Why New York Is a Large City, but New York Is a Civilized Jungle)," *Psychological Science*, 19 (2), 161-67.

Bar-Anan, Yoav, Nira Liberman, Yaacov Trope, and Daniel Algom (2007), "Automatic Processing of Psychological Distance: Evidence from a Stroop Task," *Journal of Experimental Psychology: General*, 136 (4), 610-22.

Cairncross, Frances (2001), *The Death of Distance 2.0: How the Communications Revolution Will Change Our Lives*, New York: Norton.

Elder, Ryan S. and Aradhna Krishna (2012), "The "Visual Depiction Effect" in Advertising: Facilitating Embodied Mental Simulation through Product Orientation," *Journal of Consumer Research, 38(6),* 988-1003.

Hortaçsu, Ali, F., Asís Martínez-Jerez, and Jason Douglas (2009), "The Geography of Trade in Online Transactions: Evidence from Ebay and Mercadolibre," *American Economic Journal: Microeconomics*, 1 (1), 53-74.

Nussbaum, Shiri, Nira Liberman, and Yaacov Trope (2006), "Predicting the near and Distant Future," *Journal of Experimental Psychology: General*, 135 (2), 152-61.

Petrova, Petia K. and Robert B. Cialdini (2005), "Fluency of Consumption Imagery and the Backfire Effects of Imagery Appeals," *Journal of Consumer Research*, 32 (3), 442-52.

Schlosser, Ann E. (2003), "Experiencing Products in the Virtual World: The Role of Goal and Imagery in Influencing Attitudes Versus Purchase Intentions," *Journal of Consumer Research*, 30 (September), 184-98.

Trope, Yaacov and Nira Liberman (2010), "Construal-Level Theory of Psychological Distance," *Psychological Review*, 117 (2), 440-63.

Trope, Yaacov, Nira Liberman, and Cheryl Wakslak (2007), "Construal Levels and Psychological Distance: Effects on Representation, Prediction, Evaluation, and Behavior," *Journal of Consumer Psychology*, 17 (83-95).

The Thrifty Meal: Re-creating Value in the Kitchen

Benedetta Cappellini, Royal Holloway, University of London, UK
Elizabeth Parsons, Keele University, UK

EXTENDED ABSTRACT

This paper looks at the localised control of value within the household and the intersection of practices of thrift and accommodation with familial relations in the household. Its focus on food leftovers is significant in that it foregrounds the varying creative practices through which food is re-ordered, transformed and reused, and the resulting travels and circularities of food. Leftovers are theorised as 'thrifty meals' using Miller's (1998) work on thrift and sacrifice. As such they might be viewed as a form of saving by spending. However what is saved in relation to leftovers is not only money, but also importantly time and effort in the kitchen. Using up leftovers saves not only financial resources (ingredients) but also time and effort in preparing the food. These resources can then be invested elsewhere.

Instead of viewing food leftovers as the negative or non-present end point of production this paper explores possibilities of their return, renewal and reuse. Taking inspiration from theorists who have explored the ways in which we classify, manage and value household durables through practices of storing and sorting (Cwerner and Metcalfe, 2003; Daniels, 2009) hoarding (Maycroft, 2009; Cherrier & Ponnor, 2010) and accommodating (Gregson, 2007), this paper shows an intimate relation between decisions to rid, the channels and conduits chosen for disposal and relationships indicated or made present by these practices. These practices have received scant attention in domestic food consumption contexts (although see Evans, 2011).

This paper emerges from an interpretive study looking at discourses and practices surrounding the everyday meal in the Midlands (UK). Fieldwork consisted of observations of meal times of 20 households and semi-structured interviews of the person in the family responsible for the food provision. Data were analysed following the general guides of qualitative research and a thematic analysis was conducted following common practices in interpretive consumer research (Silverman, 2006).

Despite having different routines and standards of judging a meal as quick, easy or cheap just about all of the participants' selection of their everyday meal was driven by saving resources. For example, in a manner similar to Miller's (1998) mothers, Margaret plans her meal in order to save her scarce resources which are time, effort and money. She customises her 'spag bol' in such a way that it becomes a dish in which leftovers can be reused. Margaret and the other participants' focus on thrift does not necessarily mean that they save resources, but rather that they are motivated by saving resources in order to spend them elsewhere. It is here that leftovers become significant for our participants, considered a strategic means of saving resources in the kitchen.

A second finding was the degree of skill and knowledge employed in using up leftovers. For example David who keeps parts of his Sunday roast chicken to make a salad for lunch on Monday. He prepares a stock with the bones which he freezes along with any leftover vegetables in order to make a risotto during the week. David applies a significant amount of knowledge to his meal leftovers he breaks it down into its constituent parts each with different characteristics and thinks creatively about how each part might be reused and re-valued in the context of a new meal. This process of revaluation also has a geography attached to it. In describing his conduits of disposal of the meal, David divides the leftovers into various parts and moves them into different places (such as the bin, the fridge, the freezer and the lunchbox). Here David's differing placings of the food shows how disposal is not simply a matter of moving things away but rather moving things along (Gregson et al. 2007) according to their possible re-use.

People spent a considerable amount of time changing the look of their leftovers. In some cases they become a completely new dish, like the Thursday night chicken and pea risotto that Tim prepared from what was left from his Sunday roast dinner. Tim deliberately cooks an over generous portion of risotto giving him enough to feed his family and leaving enough for his own lunch on Friday. On such occasions meals might be composed of the leftovers of leftovers. As such food might travel through a range of conduits before it is finally fully disposed of. In the case of Tim the chain goes from Sunday roast dinner to his Friday lunch box, from the bone china serving plates in his dining room with his family to the more modest plastic container which will be opened at lunch time on his office desk.

To conclude we see value in theorising the consumption of leftovers as thrifty meals. These thrifty meals contribute to the control of the flow of value within the home just as much as thrifty practices of shopping. Drawing on Miller's (1998) concept of thrift we observe that it is likely that the resources saved in thrifty meals are then spent in more extravagant meals in the longer term. Preparing and eating Sunday dinner everyday simply would not be possible or practical given the resources of time and effort required. Thus we see a longer run cycle of spending to save and saving to spend in mealtime practices.

However these meals are not only a means of saving resources they are also a means of value creation, food is literally revived and re-valued once more as 'meal'. This process takes both skill in planning meals with re-use in mind, but also knowledge of the material elements of food ingredients (i.e. the length of their reusable lifetime and the likely contexts of their reuse). Value is therefore created through creative acts of transforming and re-framing food. The framing or placing of food is important here in understanding its value considering the bone china plate in the dining room against the plastic lunchbox in the office. Therefore food provision and in this case the consumption of leftovers in order to make sense must be located within everyday household routines wherein the social context of (re)valuation is vital.

REFERENCES

Cherrier, H. and Ponnor, T., (2010), 'A study of Hoarding Behavior and Attachment to Material Possessions', *Journal of Qualitative Market Research*, special issue on video-ethnography, 13 (1): 8-23.

Cwerner, S.B. and Metcalfe, A., (2003), 'Storage and Clutter: Discourses and Practices of Order in the Domestic World', *Journal of Design History*, 16(3): 229-239.

Daniels, I., (2009), 'The 'Social Death' of Unused Gifts Surplus and Value in Contemporary Japan', *Journal of Material Culture*, 14(3): 385-408.

Evans, D., (2011), 'Beyond the Throwaway Society: Ordinary Domestic Practice and a Sociological Approach to Household Food Waste', *Sociology*, forthcoming.

Gregson N., Metcalfe A. and Crewe L., (2007) 'Moving Things Along: the Conduits and Practices of Divestment in Consumption', in *Transactions of the Institute of British Geographers*, 32(2), 187-200.

Gregson, N., (2007), *Living with things: Ridding, accommodation, dwelling*, Wantage: Sean Kingston Publishing.

Maycroft, N., (2009), Not Moving Things Along; Hoarding, Clutter and Other Ambiguous Matter, *Journal of Consumer Behaviour,* 8(6): 354-364.

Miller, D., (1998), *A Theory of Shopping*, New York : Cornell University Press.

Silverman, D., (2006), *Interpreting qualitative data; methods for analysing talk, text and interaction,* London: Sage.

Virtually Unhappy:
How Probability Neglect in Social Comparison Biases Judgments of Satisfaction with Life

Mudra Mukesh, IE University, Spain
Dilney Goncalves, IE University, Spain

EXTENDED ABSTRACT

Our perception of how great (or not!) our lives are is often based on comparisons with others' lives (Corcoran, Crusius, and Mussweiler 2011; Festinger 1954). With the proliferation of social networking sites, our ability to get a glimpse of others' lives is magnified, with vast information available at our fingertips. However, the representativeness of this information is contentious since people have a tendency to selectively share information that is self-enhancing (Manago et al. 2008) while observers tend to underestimate the prevalence of misery among others (Jordan et al. 2011). When individuals read the information provided by friends online, they may compare facets of their life to the vivid content posted, to assess how well they are doing (Wood 1996; Wood, Taylor, and Lichtman 1985).

Whilst the dominant paradigm used in social comparison literature acknowledges that cues used to make social comparisons are subjective, it doesn't remedy the fact that people don't have perfect information about others (Prentice and Miller 1993). When judging life satisfaction, people need to make inferences about the others' life satisfaction based on sampled pieces of information, however these inferences are likely to be subject to cognitive biases. Probability neglect—ignoring actual probability of events (Rottenstreich and Hsee 2001; Sunstein 2002) is one such bias. On social networking sites, people with large number of friends would be likely to encounter a larger sample of ostentatious information each time they visit the site. Probability neglect would thus result in people not accounting for probability of observing ostentatious information and, consequently assuming that the *amount* of ostentatious information viewed on a social networking site reflects *how good* the lives of their connections are. Thus, people would rely on the *number* of informational cues ignoring the probability of observing such cues given the number of friends. So even if research (Ellison, Steinfield, and Lampe 2007; Helliwel and Putnam 2004) and popular wisdom might favor having more friends for a better life, we hypothesize that reading others' posts on social networking sites will have a negative (positive) impact on life satisfaction for people with a large (small) number of friends. Furthermore, probability neglect in this domain could be a result of accessibility bias since information that is implicit is often ignored or underweighted by people (Tversky and Koehler 1994). Thus, we hypothesize that making the relationship between number of friends and ostentatious posts accessible will reduce the bias.

We conducted two studies to test our hypotheses. In the first study (N = 158), the participants, recruited online, were randomly assigned to one of the two conditions: *Updates* or *Control*. In the *Updates* condition the participants viewed the first five updates on their homepage on Facebook. They then categorized the updates and indicated the number of updates in each category. Subsequently, participants completed the Satisfaction with Life Scale (SWLS; Diener et al. 1985) and the Social Comparison Orientation (CO) scale (Gibbons & Buunk 1999). The *Control* group only responded to the scales. Information relating to number of Facebook friends and demographics was collected.

We found a significant positive correlation between the number of ostentatious updates (operationalized as sum of purchase, travel related and professional achievements updates) and the number of Facebook friends. More importantly, we found a significant interaction of number of Facebook friends with *Updates* Condition (t(152) = -2.59; p < .05) where CO was included as a control variable. A spotlight analysis compared the effect of reading updates (vs. control) on participants' life satisfaction at large and small (one SD above and below mean) number of Facebook friends. When the number of friends was small, viewing updates increased life satisfaction (B = 0.554; t(152) = 2.089; p < .05). However, when the number of friends was large, viewing updates decreased life satisfaction (B = -0.554; t(152) = -2.103; p <.05). Thus the results provided support for our hypothesis.

The second study was undertaken to examine if individuals can correct their judgments when provided information about the correlation between number of Facebook friends and the number of ostentatious updates. Moreover we wanted to test the hypothesis that the bias occurs because of low accessibility of the aforementioned correlation (Accessibility Hypothesis) at the time of assessing life satisfaction. To rule out alternate explanations we also test if the bias occurs because people have no knowledge about the phenomenon (Knowledge Hypothesis). Participants (N = 204) were recruited online and assigned to one of the three conditions: *debias-before-update*, *debias-after-updates* or *no-debias*. In the *debias-before-update* condition, the debiasing information that related the correlation between number of friends and number of ostentatious information was presented before the participants read updates. In the *debias-after-update* condition the debiasing information was presented after the participants read updates but just before the SWLS. No information regarding the correlation was presented in the *no-debias* condition. In the end, all participants completed the SWLS.

Planned contrasts showed that the difference between *no-debias* and the two *debias* conditions was not statistically significant (F(1, 201) = 0.530; p = .468). Thus, we found no support for the knowledge hypothesis. Supporting the accessibility hypothesis, the difference between *debias-before-updates* and *no-debias* conditions to the *debias-after-updates* condition was statistically significant (F(1, 201) = 5.115; p = .025).

The contribution of this article is twofold. Firstly, we show how ignoring the probability of available information used to make social comparisons can impact the outcome of those comparisons. Thus, this research represents one of the first studies to focus on the nature of informational cues people use to make social comparisons. By introducing the concept of probability neglect in the domain of social comparisons, this research paves the way for seamless integration of social comparison literature with decision-making literature. Secondly, we demonstrate, within the powerful context of Facebook, that a large friend network on social networking sites may be detrimental to the well-being of users. With more than 845 million users and 50% of them logging on to Facebook everyday (Facebook 2012), this research has resounding practical implications for the life satisfaction of millions.

REFERENCES

Corcoran, Katja, Jan Crusius, & Thomas Mussweiler, (2011), "Social comparison: Motives, Standards, and Mechanisms," in *Theories in social psychology*, ed. D. Chadee , Oxford, UK: Wiley-Blackwell, 119-139.

Diener, Ed, Robert A. Emmons, Randy J. Larsen, and Sharon Griffin (1985), "The Satisfaction With Life Scale," *Journal of Personality Assessment, 49,* 71–75.

Ellison, Nicole B., Charles Steinfield, and Cliff Lampe (2007). "The benefits of Facebook "Friends:" Social Capital and College Students' Use of Online Social Networks Sites," *Journal of Computer Mediated Communication,* 12(*4*), 1143-1168.

Facebook Statistics (2012) http://newsroom.fb.com/content/default.aspx?NewsAreaId=22

Festinger, Leon (1954), " A Theory of Social Comparison Processes," *Human Relations, 7,* 117-140.

Gibbons Frederick X. and Bram P. Buunk (1999), "Individual Differences in Social Comparison: Development and Validation of a Measure of Social Comparison Orientation," *Journal of Personality and Social Psychology, 76,* 129-142.

Helliwell, John F. and Robert D. Putnam (2004), "The Social Context of Well-Being," *Philosophical Transactions of the Royal Society,* 359(1449*),* 1435–1446.

Jordan, Alexander H., Benoit Monin, Carol S. Dweck, Benjamin J. Lovett, Oliver P. John, and James J. Gross (2010), "Misery Has More Company than People Think: Underestimating the Prevalence of Others' Negative Emotions," *Personality and Social Psychology Bulletin,* 37(1), 120-135.

Manago, Adriana M., Michael B. Graham, Patricia M. Greenfield, & Goldie Salimkhan (2008), "Self-presentation and Gender on MySpace," *Journal of Applied Developmental Psychology,* 29, 446–458.

Prentice, Deborah A., & Dale T. Miller (1993), "Pluralistic Ignorance and Alcohol Use on Campus: Some Consequences of Misperceiving the Social Norm," *Journal of Personality and Social Psychology,* 64, 243–256.

Rottenstreich, Yuval and Christopher K. Hsee (2001), "Money, Kisses, and Electric Shocks: On the Affective Psychology of Risk*," Psychological Science,* 12(3*),* 185–190.

Sunstein, Cass R. (2002), "Probability Neglect: Emotions, Worst cases, and Law," *Yale Law Journal,* 112, 61-66.

Tversky, Amos and Derek J. Koehler (1994), "Support Theory: A Nonextensional Representation of Subjective Probability," *Psychological Review,* 101 (4), 547–67.

Wood, Joanne V. (1996), "What is Social Comparison and How Should We Study it?" *Personality and Social Psychology Bulletin,* 22, 520-537.

Wood, Joanne V., Shelley E. Taylor, and Rosemary R. Lichtman (1985), "Social Comparison in Adjustment to Breast Cancer," *Journal of Personality and Social Psychology,* 49, 1169-1183.

Slow Sinkers Are the Real Stinkers:
Why a Plummeting Stock Price Can Be Better for Investors Than a Gradual Decline

Neil Brigden, University of Alberta, Canada
Gerald Häubl, University of Alberta, Canada

EXTENDED ABSTRACT

Choosing to sell a poorly performing financial asset can be difficult. Indeed, prior research has shown that investors tend to hold flagging assets for too long (Odean 1998; Shefrin and Statman 1985; Weber and Camerer 1998). This is in line with prospect theory (Tversky and Kahneman 1979) in that an asset that has lost value relative to a reference price is coded as a loss. Decision makers are risk seeking for losses, and therefore hold losing assets hoping they will recover.

However, investors do not hold sinking assets indefinitely. In particular, they do tend to respond to large price changes (Andreassen 1988). We hypothesize that an asset that declines rapidly can actually be better for the investor than one that declines slowly or stagnates. This occurs because the investor holding a rapidly declining asset is more likely to sell it quickly, while the investor holding a slowly declining or stagnating asset is more likely to continue to hold that poor asset. Compounding the effect, investors may become less likely to sell a poor asset the longer they hold it because of inaction inertia (Tykocinski, Israel, and Pittman 2004; Tykocinski, Pittman, and Tuttle 1995).

Inaction inertia refers to the decreased likelihood of taking an attractive course of action when a similar and superior course of action has been previously foregone (Tykocinski and Pittman 1998; Tykocinski et al. 1995). If investors do not sell a poorly performing asset initially, they are less likely to sell it in the future, because they compare the opportunity to sell with previous, superior opportunities.

We hypothesize that "slowly sinking" assets can be more costly to investors than assets that decline rapidly. However, the risk of sinking slowly can be reduced by preventing investors from maintaining their asset allocations via mere inaction – using an "forced-selling" intervention, whereby investors must actively choose how to invest their capital afresh each period.

To test these hypotheses, we conducted an experiment in which 152 participants played a consequential investment game. Participants were initially endowed with an investment portfolio worth $40,000 to invest over the course of the game. Upon completion of the experiment, all participants were paid 0.0005% of the final value of their portfolio.

The portfolio was initially divided evenly among four assets. In each of 20 periods, participants saw updated price information and could then reallocate the value of their investments across the four assets. Participants could not keep money out of the market as cash, nor could they borrow additional funds to invest.

All participants had one asset in their portfolio that was inferior to the other three in performance. The severity of the inferior asset's poor performance was manipulated as either dramatically inferior (averaging -6% per period) or moderately inferior (averaging 0% per period). The other three assets were common to all participants and averaged returns of 1%, 3%, and 5% per period. All prices were determined individually for each participant and subject to random variations of plus or minus 3% per period.

In the standard-trading condition, participants continued to hold the same number of shares of each investment by default, unless they chose to sell. By contrast, in the forced-selling condition, all shares

were sold at the end of each period, and participants had to allocate their entire capital across assets afresh.

As predicted, there was a significant two-way interaction between asset performance and condition $F(3, 148) = 8.346$, $p < .01$ (see figure 1). In the standard-trading condition, participants earned less money when their portfolio initially included the moderately inferior asset $(M=\$77,834)$ than if it included the dramatically inferior asset $(M=\$82,264)$, $t(75)=2.05$, $p<.05$. By contrast, in the forced-selling condition, participants earned more when their portfolio initially contained the moderately inferior asset $(M=\$85,514)$ than if it included the dramatically inferior asset $(M=\$81,209)$, $t(73)=2.04$, $p<.05$.

Figure 1: Final Portfolio Value (After 20 Periods) by Experimental Condition

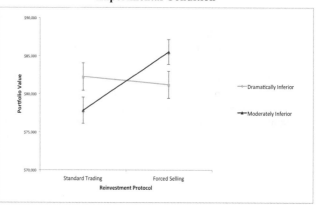

We predicted that these effects would be driven by how investors respond to the inferior asset. When that asset declines rapidly, investors respond quickly, regardless of the selling manipulation, and sell those shares. By contrast, when the lowest performing asset has zero growth, investors' responses depend on the selling manipulation. Under standard trading conditions, investors are slow to sell. The lack of growth does not attract much attention, and several periods may pass before investors realize that the asset is dragging their portfolio down. By that point, they have already missed several, more attractive, opportunities to sell the asset. Therefore, although selling now is still the normative action, it may appear relatively unattractive because it is being compared to superior, previously foregone opportunities.

Forced selling overcomes this inaction inertia trap because it requires investors to make an active asset allocation decision each period. Rather than deciding whether to retain an asset that has not increased in value, investors must decide whether to buy this poorly performing asset instead of an asset that has increased in value. Although these decisions are economically equivalent, they are very different psychologically and, as a result, they lead to different wealth states.

Figure 2 shows the number of inferior asset shares investors hold across all 20 periods. For both dramatically inferior conditions, and the moderately inferior, automatic selling condition, the pattern of results is almost identical. Participants sold most of their shares in the lowest performing asset within the first three periods. By contrast, in the moderately inferior, standard-trading condition, participants still had most of their shares in the inferior asset at the end of the fifth period. Over time, compounding growth amplifies the importance of these early decisions.

Figure 2: Units of the Inferior Asset Held

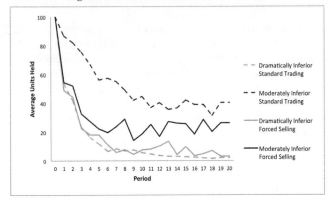

The present research identifies a previously unidentified threat to investors – "slow sinkers" that perform moderately poorly, don't attract attention, and tend to be held for too long, dragging down the value of consumers' investment portfolios. The results of the forced-selling intervention pinpoint inaction inertia as the key psychological mechanism leading investors to hold "slow sinkers" for too long, and also identify an intervention that enhances consumer welfare by expediting the sale of investments that perform poorly without being spectacular losers.

REFERENCES

Andreassen, P. B. (1988). Explaining the price-volume relationship: The difference between price changes and changing prices. *Organizational Behavior and Human Decision Processes, 41*(3), 371-389.

Kahneman, D., & Tversky, A. (1979). Prospect theory: An analysis of decision under risk. *Econometrica, 47*(2), 263.

Odean, T. (1998). Are investors reluctant to realize their losses? *The Journal of Finance, 53*(5), 1775-1798.

Shefrin, H., & Statman, M. (1985). The disposition to sell winners too early and ride losers too long: Theory and evidence. *The Journal of Finance, 40*(3), 777.

Tykocinski, O. E. and Pittman, T. S. (1998), "The Consequences of Doing Nothing: Inaction Inertia as Avoidance of Anticipated Counterfactual Regret," *Journal of Personality and Social Psychology, 75*, 607-615.

Tykocinski, O., Israel, R., & Pittman, T. (2004). Inaction inertia in the stock market. *Journal of Applied Social Psychology, 34*(6), 1166-1175.

Tykocinski, O. E., Pittman, T.S., & Tuttle, E.E. (1995). Inaction inertia – Forgoing future benefits as a result of an initial failure to act. *Journal of Personality and Social Psychology, 68*(5), 793-803.

Weber, M., & Camerer, C. (1998). The disposition effect in securities trading: An experimental analysis. *Journal of Economic Behavior & Organization, 33*(2), 167-184.

Shape Matters: How does Logo Shape Inference Shape Consumer Judgments

Yuwei Jiang, Hong Kong Polytechnic University, Hong Kong
Gerald J. Gorn, University of Hong Kong, Hong Kong
Maria Galli, HKUST, Hong Kong
Amitava Chattopadhyay, INSEAD, Singapore

EXTENDED ABSTRACT

Brand logos, are important components of any company's identity. Previous empirical research on brand logos (e.g. Henderson and Cote 1998; Henderson et al. 2003; Janiszewski and Meyvis 2001) has primarily focused on measures related to its aesthetic appeal (e.g., how beautiful a particular logo is) and on ease of recognition. How different logo shapes influence consumers' perceptions of the company and its products is still largely unknown. This is the focus of our research.

Broadly speaking, logo designs can be classified as angular, circular, or a combination of the two. Angular shapes are those consisting of straight lines and sharp corners (e.g. a rectangle); whereas circular shapes are curved and without sharp angles (e.g. an oval). According to Berlyne (1976), angular shapes induce confrontational associations such as energy, toughness, and strength. In contrast, circular shapes induce compromise associations such as approachableness and friendliness (e.g. Liu and Kennedy 1994). We expect that the associations that a person has with an angular vs. round shape, will transfer to consumers' perceptions of objects with that shape. Regarding brand logos, we expect the associations to transfer to the brand associated with the logo. Specifically, we predict that circular brand logos have a symbolic meaning of "soft", and angular brand logos have a symbolic meaning of "hard" and hence that the symbolic meaning of "soft" and "hard" will influence consumers' perceptions of the brand and its product characteristics. We test this hypothesis in four experiments.

In experiment 1, participants were asked to give us their initial reactions towards a company and its products after viewing either a circular logo or an angular logo. As expected, participants judged the brand using a circular logo to: 1) be less tough/hard than the brand using an angular logo, and 2) more likely to be in an industry associated with softness (e.g. *Daycare Center* or *Pet Shop*) than the brand using an angular logo; the brand using an angular logo was perceived to be more likely in an industry associated with toughness (e.g. *Construction Company* or *Law Firm*) than the brand using a circular logo.

Several important product attributes are closely connected with the concept of "soft" vs. "hard/tough". Products made of soft materials are usually perceived to be more comfortable to use, for example. In contrast, products made of hard materials are usually perceived to be capable of lasting longer. Thus the second experiment examined whether different logo shapes can influence consumers' beliefs about a product's comfortableness and durability. We also tested whether the observed logo inference effect occurs through a process of misattribution, akin to the HDIF heuristic (Schwarz and Clore 1988). After seeing a shoe ad with either a circular or an angular logo, participants were either asked to explicitly report their logo-shape inferences (e.g. "The logo gave me the impression that the shoe is very comfortable/durable") before they reported their beliefs of the comfortableness/durability of the shoe, or report the shape inferences after reporting their product beliefs. We found that participants believed the product is more comfortable when the brand had a circular logo, and believed that the product is more durable when the brand has an angular logo. Moreover, consistent with the misattribution hypothesis, the effect of logo shape on product beliefs disappeared when participants were

explicitly asked about their logo inferences before measuring their product beliefs.

Experiment 3 built on the first two studies by exploring the relationship between explicit verbal claims and the logo. We examine whether the consistency between the inference drawn from logo and the verbal claims leads to more favorable outcomes than when the logo shape and verbal claims are not matched. Participants were shown a shoe ad with either a circular or an angular brand logo. Also the verbal information contained in the shoe ad focused either on the comfortableness of the shoe or its durability. Consistent with expectations, the results showed a matching effect. Consumers liked the shoe more and were willing to pay more for the shoe if the logo shape inferences were consistent with the verbal information in the advertisement.

Experiment 4 attempted to expand the generalizability of our findings by showing that brand logo shapes not only influence consumer inferences about specific product attributes, but also inferences about general brand characteristics, including the behavior of company employees. Extending the idea that circular logos lead to inferences of softness to the notion that soft also implies caring, we examined whether consumers expected companies with circular logos to be more responsive to consumer needs. Participants were shown a consumption scenario– a passenger has an over-weight luggage when trying to board an airplane operated by an airline company with either a circular logo or an angular logo—and asked how likely the passenger was to be allowed to board without some penalty. As expected, participants predicted that the airline company would be more likely to allow the passenger to bring their bag on board without penalty if the company has a circular brand logo. Participants also thought that the airline company was more willing to respond to consumer needs/demands, and cared more about its customers if the brand used a circular logo.

Summarizing, we find that brand logo shapes impact both specific product attribute judgments and overall product evaluations. We show that this impact is due to a misattribution of the inference elicited by the logo shape and that it is stronger when the explicit claims are in line with the inference elicited by the logo, inferences which seem to be outside the consumers' awareness. These findings are novel and contribute to our theoretical understanding of how brand logos can influence consumers' responses to a brand. Our research has practical implications, in suggesting that companies should choose logos that have aesthetic properties that reinforce the desired image of the brand.

REFERENCES

Berlyne, Daniel E. (1976), "Psychological aesthetics," *International Journal of Psychology*, 11, 43-55.

Henderson, Pamela W., and Joseph A. Cote (1998), "Guidelines for selecting or modifying logos," *Journal of Marketing*, 62, 14-30.

Henderson, Pamela W., Joseph A. Cote, Siew Meng Leong, and Bernd Schmitt (2003), "Building strong brands in Asia: Selecting the visual components of image to maximize brand strength," *International Journal of Research in Marketing*, 20, 297-313.

Janiszewski, Chris, and Tom Meyvis (2001), "Effects of brand logo complexity, repetition, and spacing on processing fluency and judgment," *Journal of Consumer Research*, 28, 18-32.

Liu, Chang Hong, and John M. Kennedy (1994), "Symbolic forms can be mnemonics for recall," *Psychonomics Bulletin & Review*, 29, 494-498.

Schwarz, Norbert, and Gerald L. Clore (1988), "How do I feel about it? Informative functions of affective states," in K. Fiedler & J. Forgas (Eds.), *Affect, Cognition, and Social Behavior*, 44-62, Toronto: Hogrefe International.

Predicting Consumer Preference:
Prediction Strategy and Data Presentation

Jaewoo Joo, Kookmin University, Korea

EXTENDED ABSTRACT

When designers predict consumer preference using market information, they often base their predictions on consumer preferences for similar products. This categorization-based strategy, however, can result in biased predictions because similar products are not liked equally by an individual consumer. We propose that designers should use a sequential learning strategy – making a sequence of predictions and receiving feedback after each prediction – and, for further improvement in prediction accuracy, they should make predictions with multiple data sets rather than with a single data set.

Psychologists have long argued that categorization shapes the way people use cross-category information and make predictions (Medin et al. 1993; Osherson et al. 1990). However, marketing studies suggest that these categorization-based strategies can introduce prediction bias (Shocker et al. 1990). Following a significant body of research on Multiple Cue Probability Learning (MCPL), we propose that designers make predictions more accurately when employing a sequential learning strategy (Klayman 1984; West et al. 1996). This strategy will be of particular benefit to designers when their implicit rule of categorization is incongruent with the target rule of data (West 1996).

Hypothesis 1: Prediction accuracy is greater when designers employ sequential learning strategy than when employ categorization-based strategy.

Psychologists also claim that data presentation affects learning. Research shows that when classifying randomly provided items, people often fail to form coherent abstract categories, whereas they succeed in doing so when inferring the rules that govern pre-classified items. This is because inference learners are more likely to understand the fundamental similarities among items than are classification learners (Markman and Ross 2003; Rehder and Ross 2001).

Hypothesis 2: Prediction accuracy of sequential learning strategy is greater when data are presented in multiple sets than when presented in a single set.

We applied a typical Multiple Cue Probability Learning experiment to a designer's preference learning task and conducted two studies to test whether prediction accuracy is the function of prediction strategy and data presentation.

STUDY 1

We created 69 preference profiles by simulating the preferences of 64 hypothetical consumers. In particular, we randomly distributed two colors, silver and black, to the six products to create 64 preference profiles ($2^6 = 64$), randomized their order, and repeated the initial five preference profiles after the end of the preference profiles, creating a set of 69 preference profiles (Figure 1).

Figure 1. An Example of Preference Profile

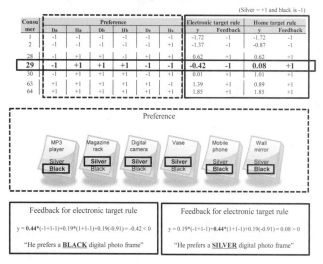

Subjects were instructed to select the color for a target product by predicting consumers' color preferences. They went through 69 iterations of prediction trials. They (1) were provided with one preference profile; (2) predicted which color the target consumer would prefer for a digital photo frame; and (3) were provided with feedback whether their prediction was correct.

This study consisted of a 2 (category of the target product: electronic vs. home) x 2 (target rule of data: electronic vs. home) between-subjects design. First, we manipulated the category of the digital photo frame by emphasizing its different attributes. Subjects in the electronic category condition read about the electronic attributes of a digital photo frame (e.g., supporting JPEG and BMP photo formats). Subjects in the home category condition read about its home accessory attributes (e.g., placed on a table top or hung on a wall). Next, we manipulated the target rule of data by developing two

Table 1. Prediction Accuracy Between Seqeutnial Learning Strategy and Categorization-Based Strategy (Study 1)

	When Two rules are congruent		When two rules are incongruent	
Categorization	*DIGITAL*	*HOME*	*DIGITAL*	*HOME*
Target rule	*DIGITAL*	*HOME*	*HOME*	*DIGITAL*
64 trials	80.25 (90.63)	81.35 (90.63)	80.92 (59.38)	79.58 (59.38)
Random 40 trials	79.82 (90.00)	81.33 (92.50)	81.43 (57.50)	79.83 (60.00)
Random 32 trials	75.89 (84.38)	77.08 (90.63)	75.22 (43.75)	73.75 (50.00)
Random 24 trials	77.08 (87.50)	78.61 (79.17)	80.36 (58.33)	80.56 (50.00)
Random 16 trials	83.48 (93.75)	75.83 (87.50)	72.32 (56.25)	76.67 (50.00)
Random 8 trials	78.57 (87.50)	74.17 (75.00)	74.11 (50.00)	79.17 (37.50)
Initial 8 trials	75.89 (100)	79.17 (100)	70.54 (62.50)	65.83 (62.50)

* Scores in the parentheses are the simulated prediction accuracies of the categorization-based strategies

different data sets. We placed greater weight on the preference of the electronic products than of the home accessories for the electronic target rule, and a greater weight was assigned to the home accessories than to the electronic products for the home target rule.

We found that the sequential learning strategy is better than the categorization-based strategy (Table 1). When the two rules were congruent, the sequential learning strategy performed slightly poorly compared to the categorization-based strategy (electronic category + electronic target rule: sequential learning = 78.57% vs. categorization-based = 87.50%, $t(13) = 2.69$, $p < .05$; home category + home target rule: sequential learning = 74.17% vs. categorization-based = 75.00%, $t(14) = 0.29$, $p > .05$). However, it dominated the categorization-based strategy when the two rules were incongruent (electronic category + home target rule: sequential learning = 74.11% vs. categorization-based = 50.00%, $t(13) = 6.74$, $p < .01$; home category + electronic target rule: sequential learning = 79.17% vs. categorization-based = 37.50%, $t(14) = 12.34$, $p < .01$). Since designers are unable to predict whether the two rules are congruent or not, we conclude that prediction accuracy increases by 14% on average when employing the sequential learning strategy instead of the categorization-based strategy.

STUDY 2

We employed the same stimuli and the same procedures in study 1. This study consisted of a 2 (rule congruency: congruent vs. incongruent) x 2 (data presentation: single vs. multiple) between-subjects design. We manipulated rule congruency in the same way as Study 1. We manipulated data presentation by providing the identical data in different formats. Subjects in the single data set condition were asked to complete 32 prediction trials without break. In the multiple data set condition, subjects were provided with four sets of the 32 preference profiles and asked to take a break every eight prediction trials.

We found that predictions were more accurate when data were presented in multiple sets (69%) than when in a single set (59%, $F(1,154) = 20.12$, $p < .01$). This suggests that breaking down a single data set into multiple sets benefits the sequential learning strategy.

CONTRIBUTIONS

Our research contributes to the existing body of knowledge on market research and MCPL. First, previous work on market research pays significant attention to data collection without discussing data analysis (Urban and Hauser 2004; Zaltman 1997). Our work addresses this issue by demonstrating and correcting designers' mistakes when analyzing data. Secondly, a significant body of research on MCPL has found that the performance of the sequential learning strategies may depend on contextual variables (Karelaia and Hogarth 2008; Klayman 1984, 1988). We add data presentation to the list of the contextual variables.

REFERENCES

Karelaia, Natalia and Robin Hogarth (2008), "Determinants of Linear Judgment: A Meta-Analysis of Lens Model Studies," *Psychological Bulletin*, 134 (3), 404–426.

Klayman, Joshua (1984), "Learning from Feedback in Probabilistic Environments," *Acta Psychologica*, 56 (1-3), 81-92.

Klayman, Joshua (1988), "Cue Discovery in Probabilistic Environments: Uncertainty and Experimentation," *Journal of Experimental Psychology: Learning, Memory, and Cognition*, 14 (2), 317-330.

Markman, Arthur B. and Brian H. Ross (2003), "Category Use and Category Learning," *Psychological Bulletin*, 129 (4), 592-613.

Medin, Douglas, Robert Goldstone, and Dedre Gentner (1993), "Respects For Similarity," *Psychological Review*, 100 (2), 254-278.

Osherson, Daniel N., Edward E. Smith, Ormond Wilkie, Alejandro Lopez, and Eldar Shafir (1990), "Category-Based Induction," *Psychology Review*, 97 (2), 185-200,

Rehder, Bob and Brian H. Ross (2001), "Abstract Coherent Categories," *Journal of Experimental Psychology: Learning, Memory, and Cognition*, 27 (5), 1261-1275.

Shocker, Allan D., David W. Stewart, and Anthony J. Zahorik (1990), "Determining the Competitive Structure of Product-Markets," working paper, Carlson School of Management, University of Minnesota, Minneapolis.

Urban, L. Glen and John R. Hauser (2004), "Listening-in to Find and Explore New Combinations of Customer Needs," *Journal of Marketing*, 68 (April), 72-87.

West, Patricia M. (1996), "Predicting Preferences: An Examination of Agent Learning," *Journal of Consumer Research*, 23 (June), 68-80.

West, Patricia M., Christina L. Brown, and Stephen J. Hoch (1996), "Consumption Vocabulary and Preference Formation," *Journal of Consumer Research*, 23 (September), 120-135.

Zaltman, Gerald, "Rethinking Market Research: Putting People Back In," *Journal of Marketing Research*, 34 (November), 424-437.

Should Birds of a Feather Flock Together? Navigating Self-Control Decisions in Dyads

Hristina Dzhogleva, University of Pittsburgh, USA
Cait Poynor Lamberton, University of Pittsburgh, USA

EXTENDED ABSTRACT

While the bulk of research in consumer behavior focuses on self-control tasks undertaken independently, our tendency to exercise self-control is often socially-determined. For example, a pair of friends may decide together whether to study or go to a movie. Similarly, a couple may go grocery shopping or create a household budget together. Moreover, individuals in work environments may have little choice about the self-control levels of the people with whom they need to make decisions. How will different types of dyads make these decisions together, and how can these patterns be altered?

To answer this question, we examine how different dyad types, formed on the basis of different combinations of partners' self-control levels, perform on joint self-control tasks. We examine the following dyad types: dyads containing two low self-control individuals (homogeneous low self-control), dyads composed of one low self-control and one high self-control individual (mixed self-control), and dyads of two high self-control partners (homogeneous high self-control). Our objective is to determine which dyads would lead to better self-control and what can be done to improve self-control outcomes for non-optimally-constructed dyads.

We predict that homogeneous high self-control dyads will perform better on joint self-control tasks than both homogeneous low self-control and mixed dyads. However, we propose that there will be no difference in the self-control performance of the latter two dyad types. The rationale for this proposition is based on past research that conceptualizes working with other people on a shared task as an activity that requires self-regulatory resources since it involves sacrificing individual to group interests (Baumeister and Exline 2000; Glance and Huberman 1994). Since forgoing individual for collective interests demands self-control, high self-control individuals will be more likely to do this than will low self-control individuals, for whom this would be too demanding. Therefore, within a mixed dyad, the low self-control individual will play a more determining role in the dyad's decisions, which would cause the dyad's self-control performance to be comparable to that of a homogeneous low self-control pair. However, if primed to maintain their independent mindset, we would expect high self-control individuals to decrease their likelihood to capitulate to the low self-control individuals' preference. In such cases, mixed dyads should perform like homogeneous high self-control pairs rather than homogeneous low self-control pairs.

In Experiment 1, couples (married for 1-60 years) completed a brief questionnaire. The outcome of interest was the extent to which the couple was successful at meeting long-term goals. We also asked both spouses to respond individually to the Tangney et al. self-control scale. Based on the partners' self-control levels, we categorized the couples into three types: homogeneous low self-control, mixed, and homogeneous high self-control couples. Results demonstrated that homogeneous high self-control couples were more successful at achieving long-term goals than both homogeneous low self-control and mixed couples (p=.03; p=.02). However, there was no difference between the long-term goal performance of the latter two dyad types (p=.98), which reveals that one high-self-control spouse might not be enough to ensure a couple's long-term success.

Experiment 2 replicated these findings using artificially-created dyads working on a self-control task in the lab. In this study, individuals first completed the Tangney et al. self-control scale and several filler tasks. Then the experimenter paired participants to create the three dyad types. All dyads worked on a menu selection task. The self-control measures were the amount of calories and fat in each pair's menu. Results revealed that homogeneous high self-control dyads chose menus that contained fewer calories and fewer grams of fat than did both homogeneous low self-control (p=.03; p=.02) and mixed self-control dyads (p=.06; p<.05). Nevertheless, there was no difference in the amount of calories and fat in the menus of homogeneous low self-control and mixed dyads (p =.74; p=.76). Both pairs chose equally unhealthy menus and exhibited poorer self-control than did homogeneous high self-control pairs.

Experiment 3 tested the proposed mechanism. Participants were paired based on their responses to the Tangney et al. self-control scale, included in a prescreening questionnaire. On arriving at the lab, participants were primed with independence using a sentence unscrambling task. Then, working in pairs, participants planned together their time for the upcoming week, by allocating 84 hours to time for studying, fun, and errands. The percentages of hours allocated to fun and studying were our DVs. Results showed that priming independence switched the pattern of effects observed in our first two studies, such that mixed dyads now exhibited self-control comparable to that of homogeneous high self-control pairs (p's>.70 for the two DVs). Specifically, both mixed and homogeneous high self-control dyads allocated less time for fun than homogeneous low self-control pairs (p=.01; p=.02). Similarly, these two dyad types allotted more time to studying than did homogeneous low self-control dyads (p=.02; p=.03). This experiment provides support for our proposed mechanism by showing that making high self-control individuals more individualistic led them to be the driving person of the mixed dyad's decision-making and elevated the mixed pairs' self-control performance to that of homogeneous high self-control dyads.

The present work contributes to our understanding of both dyad decision-making and self-regulation. Theoretically, we build on findings by Rick, Small and Finkel (2011), who suggest that a tendency toward mixed tightwad/spendthrift combinations in marriage leads to conflict and marital unhappiness. While our first study similarly focuses on married couples, we generalize this investigation beyond financial outcomes. Moreover, we demonstrate that mixed dyads also show general self-control lapses when created artificially and in the short-term. Finally, we illustrate the mechanism underlying these effects and how they can be reversed. These findings are also of practical importance. Many individuals who struggle with self-control place themselves in groups or "accountability pairs" in an effort to improve their behaviors. For example, Weight Watchers encourages individuals to sign up in a "buddy system," and Alcoholics Anonymous pairs recovering individuals with those who have already completed treatment. These strategies, however, may only work in certain circumstances, with appropriate reminders to maintain one's independent goals, or given a certain combination of partners' self-control levels in the dyad.

REFERENCES

Baumeister, Roy F. and Julie Juola Exline (2000), "Self-Control, Morality, and Human Strength," *Journal of Social and Clinical Psychology*, 19 (1), 29-42.

Glance, Natalie S. and Bernardo A. Huberman (1994), "The Dynamics of Social Dilemmas," *Scientific American*, 270 (3), 58-63.

Rick, Scott I., Deborah A. Small, and Eli J. Finkel (2011), "Fatal (Fiscal) Attraction: Spendthrifts and Tightwads in Marriage," *Journal of Marketing Research*, 48 (2), 228-237.

How do Adolescents Define Consumer Vulnerability? Toward A Youth-Centric Approach

Wided Batat, University of Lyon 2, France

EXTENDED ABSTRACT

Young consumer vulnerability is today regarded as an important social issue to analyze in marketing and consumer behavior literature. Researchers have focused on this topic by studying the behaviors and the main features of vulnerable groups such as homeless consumers (Hill and Stamey 1990), poor consumers (Lee et al. 1999), older consumers (Moschis 1992), disabled consumers (Adkins and Ozanne 2005), immigrant (Baker et al. 2001), low-literacy consumers (Peñaloza 1995) and younger consumers (Martin and Gentry 1997; Pechmann et al. 2005; Pechmann et al. 2011). Baker et al. (2005) have defined consumer vulnerability as "*a state of powerlessness that arises from an imbalance in marketplace interactions*". In their consumer vulnerability conceptual framework, they distinguish between actual and perceived vulnerability. However, the concept of consumer vulnerability has not been studied widely and the field lacks studies on who experiences vulnerability and what is the consumer perception of his vulnerability within the consumption context. In this perspective, today's adolescents represent an important at-risk group to focus on by consumer researchers and public policy (Pechmann et al. 2011). Because adolescents' perception of their own risks is larger than adult's reality, they do not always behave in ways that serve their own interest. Thus, they may experience vulnerability as they face difficult situations where they loose control. In other cases, adolescents underestimate the risks and engage in risky behaviors because of their perception of invulnerability. Therefore, it is important for researchers to focus more on teenage consumers who underestimate the consequences of their risky behavior. Following this logic, Transformative Consumer Researchers (TCR) suggested that future research should explore the "dark-side" of adolescent behavior by focusing on his limitation related to his inaccurate perception of invulnerability. Despite this attention, few consumer researchers have explicitly defined consumer vulnerability from the youth perspective. This has allowed the term of vulnerability to be used in different ways according to the adult perception and with a direct inadequate application to the youth subculture. The purpose of this paper is to understand on the "dark-side" of adolescent's definition of consumer vulnerability.

RESEARCH QUESTIONS

Using a youth-centric approach to consumer vulnerability in this research leads us to understand deeply through a bottom-up strategy the domains and the dimensions of consumer vulnerability as defined by adolescents aged 11-15. A comprehensive approach of the perception of vulnerability within today's adolescent subculture seems to be an urgent issue to be taken into consideration. In this study, consumer vulnerability will be studied from the adolescent's perspective through an immersion within the youth subculture. To accomplish this purpose, the objective of this research is to define the dimensions related to young consumer perception of vulnerability within the consumer society. This definition might enable Transformative Consumer Researchers and public policy to address the "dark-side" of adolescent's vulnerability via a bottom-up approach based on youth subculture rather than adult's perception.

METHOD

To investigate these aspects of youth vulnerability within the consumption context, we conducted a longitudinal ethnographic research (Wolcott 1994) for six months with a group of 20 adolescents. This ethnographic approach allowed us to delve deeply into vulnerability's meanings emerging within youth consumption subculture. Methods included participant and non-participant observations, document reviews, photographs, drawings, informal conversations and formal interviews. A grounded theory method (Strauss and Corbin 1990; Glaser and Strauss 1967) was used to explore and analyze data collected from in-depth interviews with the 20 teenagers aged 11-15 both male and female, followed by Wolcott's (1994) ethnographic conventions to interpret the data emerging from specifics transcripts, artefacts and observations of teenage subculture and youth social environment. The first approach based on grounded theory led the researcher to define themes, concepts and behaviors that were indicative of young consumer vulnerability. The second analysis method with respect to analysis and interpretation as defined by Wolcott's framework allowed us to developed patterned regularities in the data on adolescents' perceptions of consumer vulnerability and the behaviors associated with the risky behaviors.

FINDINGS

The key findings illustrate the domains and the behaviors related to teenage consumer vulnerability in a youth subculture. The results revealed six categories related to young consumer's perception of vulnerability within their youth subculture: 1) impulsivity and self-conscious, 2) incapacity of making independent and confident decisions, 3) incapacity to resist peer group pressure, 4) lack of knowledge and consumption experiences, 5) the paradox of the digital society, and 6) using risky online communities as a confident source of information. Furthermore, adolescents can experience a vulnerable situation on the basis of their consumption experiences and the way others view them in social or community settings. The teenage consumer vulnerability concept appears to be more reflexive and irrational than adult consumer vulnerability. Thus, the experience of consumer vulnerability with the youth subculture might be a <u>deliberate</u> as well as an <u>imposed</u> experience. In the first posture "<u>deliberate vulnerability</u>" determined by experiencing vulnerability through a risky behavior such as surfing porn websites is a desired behavior. Indeed, the main purpose of such a practice for adolescents is to transgress the rules established by adults by showing their independence and their resistance to adults' rules and policy makers. In the second case "<u>imposed vulnerability</u>" characterized by experiencing consumer vulnerability within the youth subculture such as purchasing brands that they can't afford is a stage within the young consumer socialization process. Consumption items are then considered as facilitator objects because they might help the adolescent to belong to a peer group by wearing the same brand. In this case, the young consumers are vulnerable because they can't control or resist the peer group pressure and consequently they involve their parents in debt problems.

CONTRIBUTIONS

This research contributes to the comprehension of explicit "imposed" and implicit "desired" dimensions of youth vulnerability within the consumption context. These ideas might change the way researchers are studying at-risk groups such as young consumers (Pechmann et al. 2011) and have several implications for both public policy and marketers targeting young consumers. Therefore, understanding the peer group influence (positive/negative) within youth consumption culture can help public policy makers to adapt their policy to the youth target by using the peer group as a communication medium and as a tool to empower young consumers through a bottom-up approach based on youth subculture.

REFERENCES

Adkins, N., & Ozanne, J. (2005). Critical consumer education: empowering the low-literate consumer. *Journal of Macromarketing, 25*(2), 153–162.

Baker, S. M., & Kaufman-Scarborough, C. (2001). Marketing and public accommodation: a retrospective on the Americans with Disabilities Act. *Journal of Public Policy & Marketing, 20*(Fall), 297–304.

Baker, S. M., Gentry, J.W., & Rittenburg, T. L. (2005). Building understanding of the domain of consumer vulnerability, *Journal of Macromarketing, 25*(2), 128–139.

Barker, V., Giles, H., Noels, K., Duck, J., Hecht, M., & Clément, R. (2001). The English-only movement: a communication analysis of changing perceptions of language vitality. *Journal of Communication, 51*, 3–37.

Glaser, B., & Strauss, A. (1967). *The discovery of grounded theory.* Chicago: Aldine.

Hill, R. P., & Stamey, M. (1990). The homeless in America: An examination of possessions and consumption behaviors. *Journal of Consumer Research, 17*(December), 303–321.

Lee, R. G., Ozanne, J. L., & Hill, R. P. (1999). Improving service encounters through resource sensitivity: the case of health care delivery in an Appalachian Community. *Journal of Public Policy and Marketing, 18*(2), 230–248.

Martin, M. C., & Gentry, J. W. (1997). Stuck in the model trap: The effects of beautiful models in ads on female pre-adolescents and adolescents, *Journal of Advertising, 26* (Summer), 19–34.

Moschis, G. P. (1992). *Marketing to older consumers.* Westport CT: Quorum Books.

Pechmann, C., Levine, L., Loughlin, S., & Leslie, E. (2005). Impulsive and self-conscious: adolescents vulnerability to advertising and promotion. Journal of Public Policy & Marketing, *24*, 202–221.

Pechmann, C., Moore, E. S., Andreasen A. R. Connell P. M., Freeman, D., Gardner, M. P., Heisley, D., Lefebvre, R. C., Pirouz, D. M., & Soster, R. L. (2011). Navigating the central tensions in research on consumers who are at risk: challenges and opportunities, *Journal of Public Policy and Marketing. 30*(1), Spring, 23–30.

Peñaloza, L. (1995). Immigrant consumers: Marketing and public policy considerations in the global economy. *Journal of Public Policy & Marketing, 14*(Fall), 83–94.

Strauss, A., & Corbin, J. (1990). *Basics of qualitative research: grounded theory procedures and techniques.* Sage Publications.

Wolcott, H. F. (1994). *Transforming qualitative data: description, analysis and interpretation.* Thousand Oaks: Sage.

Focusing Attention on the Hedonic Experience of Eating and the Changing Course of Hunger and Pleasure

Jordan LeBel, Concordia University, Canada
Ji Lu, Dalhousie University, Canada
Laurette Dubé, McGill University, Canada

EXTENDED ABSTRACT

With a comparison of low- versus high-external eaters, this research examines the influence of attention focus to hedonic experience (compared to a distraction) on the change in hunger feeling and hedonic experience, as two important motivational forces, over the course of a food consumption episode.

LITERATURE REVIEW

For consumers in current sensation-rich marketing environment, various food-related, hedonic cues often override hunger and other homeostatic signals and motivate overconsumption (Loewenstein 1996; Paquet et al. 2010). Furthermore, the pleasure brought by food consumption can be enhanced/weakened by external factors, which direct/distract the attention toward/away-from the hedonic experience (Nowlis and Shiv 2005; Shiv and Nowlis 2004; Tal 2008), such as the cognitive information about food (Lee, Frederick, and Ariely 2006; Siegrist and Cousin 2009), the package image (Mizutani et al. 2010), and expectation on taste (Wansink et al. 2000). Also, the subjective experience of hunger, although is closely tied to the homeostatic signals, does not necessarily reflect the diminishing need for food during eating (de Castro and Elmore 1988). Being exposed to food-related cues, be it visual, taste or smell, can turn one's attention to the hedonic experience of consumption (Stroebe, Papies, and Aarts 2008), and can increase the hunger feeling (Nederkoorn, Smulders, and Jansen 2000).

An individual propensity that eating is easily triggered by hedonic rather than homeostatic cues is identified as external eating (Rodin and Slochower 1976), and was found to be associated with food overconsumption and obesity (Burton, Smit, and Lightowler 2007). The vulnerability to hedonic cues and the maladaptive eating behaviors demonstrated among external eaters certainly showcase the importance of "uncontaminated" hunger signals in keeping healthy eating pattern.

HYPOTHESES

Statically, enhancing one's hedonic experience can increase the hunger feeling; therefore we hypothesize that an attention focus on hedonic experience during an eating episode will translate in sustained feeling of hunger, compared to the decline expected under a distraction condition. Moreover, we expect that external eaters intrinsically tune themselves into a hedonic experience focus states during the course of food consumption. Hence, the externally imposed hunger-sustaining effects of hedonic focus should not be particularly salient for them. By the same token, we expect that a cognitive distraction compared to a hedonic focus can at least initially suppress the pleasure rating, but the pleasure suppression effect of cognitive distraction is relatively smaller for external eaters than others. We also predict that external eaters are less sensitive to hunger feeling for the motivation to continue eating, compared to low-external eaters.

METHOD

Two studies were conducted to examine the hypotheses. The procedure for these two studies is similar, except in field study ($n=52$), each participant received a 100 grams of chocolate bar, and they were invited to eat as much or as little of the chocolate at home within a 20 minutes period; while in laboratory study ($n=85$), participants were informed that they had to eat one 5-gram-square chocolate at regular intervals (for a total intake of 30g) in our laboratory. In both studies, Participants were randomly assigned to one of two attention focus conditions; one is distraction condition, and the other is hedonic-focus condition. In both conditions, participants worked on a word puzzle while eating the stimulus. In the hedonic-focus condition, participants were prompted to "set the puzzle aside momentarily. Eat the chocolate and focus exclusively on the sensations and feelings it produces in your mouth." In the distraction condition, participants were asked to keep working on the word while eating.

Before the chocolate-eating begins, participants rated their current feeling of hunger. Analyses revealed no differences on pre-consumption hunger between two conditions. Participants rated their pleasure right after the first bite of chocolate and completed the same measure again after the last bite. When they were done eating, participants rated their hunger once again. Participants also reported how much they would like to eat (desire) another piece of chocolate after their last bite. Participants were identified as high- or low-external eaters based on the median split on their external eating score, which was obtained from their responses to the Dutch Eating Behavior Questionnaire (van Strien et al. 1986).

FINDINGS

Both studies revealed that the hedonic-focus manipulation slowed down the decreasing speed of hunger feeling, compared to the condition that participants were distracted by cognitive task (interactions: $ps<.03$). Furthermore, results show that such hunger-sustaining effect of hedonic-focus was only salient for low-external eaters, whose homeostatic signals are less "contaminated." Also, low-external eaters' desire to continue eating was significantly predicted by self-reported hunger and pleasure ($ps<.01$), while high-external eaters' desire was only associated with pleasure ($p<.01$).

The laboratory study, which strictly controlled the consumption environment, volume, and speed, clearly demonstrated that the "immunity" to attention focus manipulation demonstrated on high-external eaters' self-reported hunger may be largely due to high-external eaters' predisposition of hedonic experience focus, which imposed a similar influence as sensory-focus experimental condition. As shown in figure 1; first, the initial impact of attention focus on pleasure was significant for low-external eating group ($p<.001$), whereas hedonic-focus/distraction manipulation did not impact high-external eaters first-bite pleasure. This implies that high-external eaters' predisposition effectively directs their attention to the hedonic signals therefore insensitive to the externally imposed attention focus. Second, in terms of the changing course of pleasure, high-external eaters did not experience pleasure decrease as low-external eaters did ($p<.001$). This suggests that the hedonic-experience focus predisposition makes high-external eaters enjoyed more hedonic experience during the food consumption than low-external eaters did.

Figure 1: First- and Last Bite Pleasure Ratings by Attention Condition and External Eating Group - Lab Study

Panel A: Low-external Eating Participants

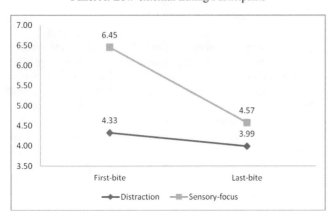

Panel B: High-external Eating Participants

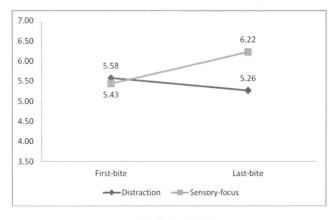

CONTRIBUTIONS

To our knowledge, this research is the first analyses on the impact of conditions that direct attention to or distract from hedonic experience on changes in hunger feeling over the course of a consumption episode. The results highlight the individual difference in the responsiveness on attention focus; external eaters tend to be more sensitive to hedonic signals rather than other internal and external signals. This pattern reveals that distracting people from hedonic experience of food, as a strategy to decrease the motivation to eat unhealthy (often palatable) food, does not necessarily work for all.

REFERENCES

Burton, Pat, J. Hendrik Smit, and J. Helen Lightowler (2007), "The Influence of Restrained and External Eating Patterns on Overeating," *Appetite*, 49 (1), 191-97.

de Castro, John M. and Dixie K. Elmore (1988), "Subjective Hunger Relationships with Meal Patterns in the Spontaneous Feeding Behavior of Humans: Evidence for a Causal Connection," *Physiology & Behavior*, 43 (2), 159-65.

Lee, Leonard, Shane Frederick, and Dan Ariely (2006), "Try It, You'll Like It," *Psychological Science*, 17 (12), 1054-58.

Loewenstein, George (1996), "Out of Control: Visceral Influences on Behavior," *Organizational Behavior and Human Decision Processes*, 65 (3), 272-92.

Mizutani, Nanami, Masako Okamoto, Yui Yamaguchi, Yuko Kusakabe, Ippeita Dan, and Toshimasa Yamanaka (2010), "Package Images Modulate Flavor Perception for Orange Juice," *Food Quality and Preference*, 21 (7), 867-72.

Nederkoorn, C., F. T. Smulders, and A. Jansen (2000), "Cephalic Phase Responses, Craving and Food Intake in Normal Subjects," *Appetite*, 35 (1), 45-55.

Nowlis, Stephen M. and Baba Shiv (2005), "The Influence of Consumer Distractions on the Effectiveness of Food-Sampling Programs," *Journal of Marketing Research*, 42 (2), 157-68.

Paquet, Catherine, Mark Daniel, Bärbel Knäuper, Lise Gauvin, Yan Kestens, and Laurette Dubé (2010), "Interactive Effects of Reward Sensitivity and Residential Fast-Food Restaurant Exposure on Fast-Food Consumption," *The American journal of clinical nutrition*, 91 (3), 771-76.

Rodin, Judith and Joyce Slochower (1976), "Externality in the Nonobese: Effects of Environmental Responsiveness on Weight," *Journal of Personality and Social Psychology*, 33 (3), 338-44.

Shiv, Baba and Stephen M. Nowlis (2004), "The Effect of Distractions While Tasting a Food Sample: The Interplay of Informational and Affective Components in Subsequent Choice," *Journal of Consumer Research*, 31 (3), 599-608.

Siegrist, Michael and Marie-Eve Cousin (2009), "Expectations Influence Sensory Experience in a Wine Tasting," *Appetite*, 52 (3), 762-65.

Stroebe, Wolfgang, Esther K. Papies, and Henk Aarts (2008), "From Homeostatic to Hedonic Theories of Eating: Self-Regulatory Failure in Food-Rich Environments," *Applied Psychology*, 57, 172-93.

Tal, Aner (2008), "It Tastes Better Conscious: Attention and Information in Hedonic Consumption Experience," *The Proceedings of the Society for Consumer Psychology*, 283-85.

van Strien, Tatjana, Jan E. R. Frijters, Gerard P. A. Bergers, and Peter B. Defares (1986), "The Dutch Eating Behavior Questionnaire (DEBQ) for Assessment of Restrained, Emotional, and External Eating Behavior," *International Journal of Eating Disorders*, 5 (2), 295-315.

Wansink, Brian, Se-Bum Park, Steven Sonka, and Michelle Morganosky (2000), "Ingredient Disclosure and Product Acceptance," *International Food and Agribusiness Management Review*, 3, 85-94.

The Distributed Spirit of Consumerism:
How Consumers Inform and Defend Themselves in a Fragmented World

Dominique Roux, Université Paris-Sud, France
Corinne Chevalier, Université Paris-Sud, France
Lydiane Nabec, Université Paris-Sud, France

EXTENDED ABSTRACT

Research groups such as Macromarketing, Marketing Ethics, Consumer Economics, Public Policy and Marketing, Social Marketing, and more recently Transformative Consumer Research (Wilkie and Moore, 2012) frequently address issues related to consumer protection. However, though consumer education and rights constitute hot topics and common concerns, the way consumers inform and defend themselves in a more complex multi-actors environment remains understudied. Thus, we aim at exploring how mainstream consumers proceed, what representations they hold and types of relationships they maintain with non-profit consumer organizations (NCOs) and other competing new market actors who now contribute to the "consumerism industry" (Smith and Bloom 1984, 369). We also seek to investigate the links between individual and collective actions when addressing consumers' demands of legal remedy. This objectives take place in a context where NCOs are experiencing a decline in their influence, while social media offer new opportunities for consumer empowerment and social change (Josefsson and Ranerup 2003; Kozinets, Belz, and McDonagh 2011; Rezabakhsh et al. 2006; Umit Kucuk and Krishnamurthy 2007).

LITERATURE REVIEW

The many regulations in terms of consumer protection policy and lobbying by activist groups have led to major advances in consumer protection (Aaker and Day 1972; Barksdale and Darden 1972; Brobeck, Mayer, and Herrmann 1997; Buskirk and Rothe 1970; Day and Aaker 1970; Herrmann 1970; Rao 1998; Smith and Bloom 1984). However, the outcomes of excessive consumption as well as the recent threats of failure of the financial system have exposed the frailty of consumers faced with the corporate power of big businesses. In this gloomy context, the desired or implemented responses of the public authorities accompany growing questioning as to the state of consumerism and consumer well-being (Cohen 2010; Mick et al. 2011; Rotfeld 2010). At the same time, literature on online communities and social media (Kozinets et al. 2011), consumer resistance and empowerment (Kozinets 2002) opens more optimistic avenues as to the ability for individuals to share problems and educate one another.

METHOD

Two sets of data were used. First, in-depth interviews were conducted with 29 consumers to analyze the way they orient themselves among various informational channels and how they deal with post-purchase dissatisfaction. Informants were selected through a snow-balling technique, with age, gender, socio-professional standing, and prior experience with NCOs taken into account (Lincoln and Guba 1985). The interviews focused on four themes: the types of actors and pre-purchased sources consulted; reactions to problems encountered with a company and types of actions undertaken; knowledge and representations of NCOs as well as other consumerist actors; and overall expectations in terms of information and defence. A second set of data then sought to provide a broader view of collective actions. Though class action is not legally valid in France, we conducted interviews with the main protagonists of four 'collective actions' against big firms. By 'collective actions', we mean groups of similarly situated individuals represented by the same lawyer, simultaneously bringing their case to court and sharing litigation costs. The three authors jointly developed a coding scheme for analyzing informants' discourses. This inductive process helped illuminate the various strategies consumers deploy, with whom and how.

FINDINGS

The consumers' individual discourses shed light on two main themes. The first shows the erosion of the preventive role of NCOs in a situation of informational excess and consumers' ability to orient themselves alone. Regarding NCOs, several informants question their independence, largely ignoring their way of operating. Major contradictions also emerge around possible ways of correcting NCOs image deficit. Their need to communicate to make themselves more visible implies the use of marketing techniques but comes up against the idea of the possible confusion with market actors. Regarding difficulties encountered in marketplace relationships, the findings also stress the ability of mainstream consumers to deal with companies by their own. Again, informants do not rely upon NCOs to solve their problems but, instead, try to find direct arrangements with merchants. Turning to NCOs thus appears to be a "last resort" solution when the "seriousness" of problems requires seeking help to restore equity.

The second theme finally highlights the dominant idealized view of NCOs' problem-solving capacity, ex post facto, for collective defence and prevention of abuses. Their perceived residual role consists of regulating the balance of power and defending an ideal of justice against big market actors. However, this federative role in protecting "little people" is mainly accounted by informants who never faced severe situations or who accepted to cope with poor performances of products and services. Conversely, those who decided to sue defaulting companies where not so prone to idealize NCOs' power. The second set of data illustrates how mainstream consumers become entrepreneurs of consumerism by deploying new skills to defend themselves and others.

Findings pertaining to collective actions show that hard core members of these transient defence communities first problematize the unfair situation and generate interest from other "victims". They then provide the arguments, moral support, skills and material devices to build support-based networks through communal websites (Kozinets et al. 2011). The second stage illuminates how they subsequently succeed in enrolling additional agents such as media, lawyers, private or institutional ombudsmen, political leaders, and NCOs. It shows that larger networks prove to be more successful in spreading influence far beyond the online community.

CONTRIBUTIONS

Our research challenges the more or less pessimistic predictions as to the survival of consumerism (Cohen 2010; Rotfeld 2010) in showing that it spirit and practices are distributed on multiple actors and enacted by new means that bring empowerment to isolated individuals. In line with Kozinets et al. (2011), the findings bring evidence of the emergence of support-based online communities that organize collective defence and actively struggle against unbalanced marketplace power. But they extend previous research in showing that these communities overstep their own limits by enrolling new actors and building powerful though ephemeral networks.

REFERENCES

Aaker, David and George S. Day (1972), "Corporate Response to Consumerism Pressures," *Harvard Business Review*, 50 (November-December), 114-124.

Barksdale, Hiram C. and William D. Darden (1972), "Consumer attitudes toward marketing and consumerism," *Journal of Marketing*, 36 (October), 28-35.

Brobeck, Stephen, Robert E. Mayer and Robert O. Herrmann (eds.) (1997), *Encyclopedia of the consumer movement*, Santa-Barbara:ABC – CLIO.

Buskirk, Richard H. and James T. Rothe (1970), "Consumerism. An interpretation," *Journal of Marketing*, 34 (October), 61-65.

Cohen, Lizabeth (2010), "Colston E. Warne Lecture: Is it Time for Another Round of Consumer Protection? The Lessons of Twentieth-Century U.S. History," *The Journal of Consumer Affairs*, 44 (1), 234-246.

Day, George S. and David Aaker (1970), "A guide to consumerism," *Journal of Marketing*, 34 (3), 12-19.

Herrmann, Robert O. (1970), "Consumerism: Its Goal, Organizations and Future," *Journal of Marketing*, 34, 55-60.

Josefsson, Ulrika and Agneta Ranerup (2003), "Consumerism revisited: The emergent roles of new intermediaries between citizens and the public sector," *Information Polity: The International Journal of Government & Democracy in the Information Age*, 8, 3/4, 167-80.

Kozinets, Robert V. (2002), "Can Consumers Escape the Market: Emancipatory Illuminations from Burning Man," *Journal of Consumer Research*, 29 (June), 20-38.

Kozinets, Robert V., Frank-Martin Belz, and Pierre McDonagh (2011), "Social Media for Social Change," in *Transformative Consumer Research to Benefit Global Welfare*, David Glen Mick, Simone Pettigrew, Cornelia Pechmann, and Julie L. Ozanne, eds., 205-23.

Lincoln, Yvonna S. and Egon G. Guba (1985), *Naturalistic Inquiry*, Beverly Hills, CA: Sage Publications.

Mick, David Glen Simone Pettigrew, Cornelia (Connie) Pechmann, and Julie L. Ozanne (2011), Origins, Qualities, and Envisionments of Transformative Consumer Research, in *Transformative Consumer Research to Benefit Global Welfare*, Simone Pettigrew, Cornelia Pechmann, and Julie L. Ozanne, eds., 3-24..

Rao, Hayagreeva (1998), "Caveat emptor: the construction of nonprofit consumer watchdog organizations," *American Journal of Sociology*, 103 (4), 912-61.

Rezabakhsh, Behrang, Daniel Bornemann, Ursula Hansen, and Ulf Schrader (2006), "Consumer Power: A Comparison of the Old Economy and the Internet Economy," *Journal of Consumer Policy*, 29 (1), 3-36.

Rotfeld, Herbert Jack (2010), "A pessimist's simplistic historical perspective on the fourth wave of consumer protection," *Journal of Consumer Affairs*, 44 (2), 423-29.

Smith, Darlene B. and Paul N. Bloom (1984), "Is consumerism dead or alive? Some new evidence," *Advances in Consumer Research*, 11, 1, ed. Thomas Kinnear, Provo, UT: Association for Consumer Research, 369-73.

Umit Kucuk S. and Sandeep Krishnamurthy (2007), "An analysis of consumer power on the Internet," *Technovation*, 27 (1/2), 47-56.

Wilkie, William L. and Elizabeth S. Moore (2012), "Expanding our understanding of marketing in society," *Journal of the Academy of Marketing Science*, 40 (1), 53-73.

The Red Sneakers Effect: Inferring Status from Signals of Nonconformity

Silvia Bellezza, Harvard Business School, USA
Francesca Gino, Harvard Business School, USA
Anat Keinan, Harvard Business School, USA

EXTENDED ABSTRACT

We examine the inferences observers make based on individuals' nonconforming behaviors (e.g., not complying with a certain dress code). Research in social psychology, sociology, and consumer behavior demonstrates the benefits of conforming to group norms and expectations (Dittes and Kelley 1956; Phillips and Zuckerman 2001; Wang et al. 2012)2 different norms were developed: one concerning a social value judgment; the other, a simple perceptual judgment. The Ss were experimentally made to feel different degrees of being accepted by the other members and were then given opportunities and incentives to deviate from the norms. Subsequent conformity, participation, and attitudes toward the group were studied in relation to the different conditions of acceptance. The results point to 2 contrasting patterns of conformity evolved by different conditions of acceptance. The first appears to consist of a high degree of genuine adherence to the norms\u2026 . The second pattern is marked by high conformity only under public conditions.\"'"", "author" : [{ "family" : "Dittes", "given" : "James E." }, { "family" : "Kelley", "given" : "Harold H." }], "container-title" : "The Journal of Abnormal and Social Psychology", "id" : "ITEM-3", "issue" : "1", "issued" : { "date-parts" : [["1956"]] }, "page" : "100-107", "title" : "Effects of different conditions of acceptance upon conformity to group norms", "type" : "article-journal", "volume" : "53" }, "uris" : ["http://www.mendeley.com/documents/?uuid=459ecb6e-f9ef-4f2d-b1b7-bc23eb26531a"] }], "mendeley" : { "previouslyFormattedCitation" : "(Dittes and Kelley 1956; Phillips and Zuckerman 2001; Wang et al. 2012. In this research we argue that under certain conditions, nonconforming behaviors, such as entering a luxury boutique wearing gym clothes rather than an elegant outfit, or wearing red sneakers in a professional setting, can be beneficial and signal a higher status.

High-status individuals generally feel confident about their social acceptance. Unlike lower status individuals, high-status people are more likely to deviate from conventional behavior and common expectations about appropriate responses other people might have (Hollander 1958). For instance, CEOs of major corporations, such as Bill Gates (Microsoft) or Mark Zuckerberg (Facebook), often appear without ties or wear sweatshirts at interviews or formal gatherings like the World Economic Forum. In this research, we focus on the perspective of external observers and investigate when nonconforming behaviors may lead to inferences of higher status.

We propose that inferences of status demand that the observer is aware of the norms of appropriate behavior in the group to which the individual belongs and that the context is prestigious. Our investigation of underlying mechanisms reveals that the inference of status from signals of nonconformity is mediated by perceived intentionality and moderated by individual differences in need for uniqueness (Snyder and Fromkin 1977).

A series of lab and field studies explore responses to a variety of nonconforming behaviors in different settings. In an effort to ensure high external validity of our findings, all our studies are preceded by interviews and pilots to explore the expected behavioral norms in specific environments and to confirm that higher status individuals in these contexts tend to deviate from such norms.

Study 1 examines responses to descriptions of potential prospects by shop assistants in luxury boutiques in downtown Milan. As was confirmed in interviews with store managers of luxury boutiques in Italy, the accepted norm for shoppers at these high-end stores is an elegant outfit that fits the store's atmosphere. In this study, we manipulated between-subjects the descriptions of a client (non-conforming vs. conforming) entering the store, and compared reactions of shop assistants to those women not familiar with the norm who were recruited in Milan's central station. Shop assistants in luxury boutiques have an economic incentive to learn how to interpret the unconventional behavior of their prospects. Thus, we predict they will infer higher status from signals of nonconformity.

In particular, in study 1a the prospect entering the store was described as wearing gym clothes and a jacket (non-conforming), or wearing an elegant dress and a fur (conforming). We find that shop assistants of luxury boutiques perceive a client as wealthier and more likely to buy when she is wearing gym clothes, rather than elegant dresses. Respondents indicated that these poorly dressed shoppers are often "playing a role and doing it on purpose." They mentioned that "wealthy people sometimes dress very badly to demonstrate superiority", and that "if you dare enter these boutiques so underdressed, you are definitely going to buy something". In contrast, women recruited in Milan's central station perceived the shopper with the elegant outfit as a higher-status individual.

In study 1b we operationalize nonconformity through usage of well-known brand names. The prospect entering the store was described as wearing flip-flops and a Swatch watch on her wrist (nonconforming), or elegant sandals with heels and a Rolex (conforming). Again, we find that boutique assistants attribute higher status to the nonconforming individual, whereas people not acquainted with these boutique shoppers attribute higher status to the conforming individual.

In studies 2 and 3, we examine the effect of non-conforming on another dimension and test students' responses to the nonconforming dress-style of their professors. In these studies, we recruited students who could ensure that our sample is familiar with the experimental stimuli manipulated (i.e. descriptions of professors). In a pre-test with students we confirmed that participants perceive the majority of their professors to dress more formally (i.e. professional / business attire), rather than informally (i.e. wear t-shirts). Furthermore, in a pilot study conducted at the ACR conference in 2011, we provided evidence that in this environment high status individuals tend to deviate from the norm. We find a significant negative correlation between formality in clothing style and the number of publications in top journals. Individuals who are well-published were more likely to wear an informal or unusual outfit or clothing item (e.g., wearing jeans, red sneakers, or t-shirts) rather than a professional / business attire (e.g., a button-down shirt).

In study 2 we demonstrate that undergraduate students perceive a male professor who wears a t-shirt and is not shaven as having higher status than a professor who wears a tie and is shaven, but only when the professor teaches at a top school, i.e. the context is prestigious. These inferences of status are mediated by participants' perceived intentionality of the individual's nonconforming behavior. Participants who judged the professor to have higher status when his behavior was nonconforming rather than conforming also believed that the nonconforming professor was purposely deviating from the accepted norm of appropriate behavior in an attempt to distinguish himself.

In study 3, we find that when a specific nonconforming behavior becomes the norm, then the inference of higher status disappears. Participants did not infer higher status when they were told that wearing a t-shirt to school was the accepted norm in the professor's department.

Finally, in study 4 we examine nonconformity in the presentation style of participants in an entrepreneurship competition. We show that inferences of status are moderated by need for uniqueness (Snyder and Fromkin 1977).

Taken together, these results identify a counterintuitive strategy for gaining status in the eyes of others: rather than dressing up and adhering to norms, one may instead need to adopt nonconforming behaviors.

REFERENCES

Dittes, James E., and Harold H. Kelley (1956), "Effects of different conditions of acceptance upon conformity to group norms," *The Journal of Abnormal and Social Psychology*, 53(1), 100–107.

Hollander, E. P. (1958), "Conformity, Status, and Idiosincratic Credit," *Psychological review*, 65(2), 117–27.

Phillips, Damon J., and Ezra W. Zuckerman (2001), "Middle-Status Conformity : Theoretical Restatement and Empirical Demonstration in Two Markets," *American Journal of Sociology*, 107(2), 379–429.

Snyder, C. R., and L. Howard Fromkin (1977), "Abnormality as a Positive Characteristic: The Development and Validation of a Scale Measuring Need for Uniqueness," *Journal of Abnormal Psychology*, 86(5), 518–27.

Wang, Jing, Rui (Juliet) Zhu, and Baba Shiv (2012), "The Lonely Consumer: Loner or Conformer?" *Journal of Consumer Research*, 38(6), 1116–28.

Growing with Love:
Priming Attachment Security Enhances Exploratory Consumer Behaviors

Yuan-Yuan Li, KU Leuven, Belgium
Sabrina Bruyneel, KU Leuven, Belgium
Luk Warlop, KU Leuven, Belgium

EXTENDED ABSTRACT

Love is one among very few topics that have fascinated people across all times and cultures. Marketers often use reminders of love to decorate their stores, to package products, and to organize promotion campaigns. We know very little, however, about how cueing loving relationships might affect consumer behavior. In this paper we explore the impact of a specific consequence of love primes, namely feelings of attachment security, on exploratory consumer behavior.

Attachment is the innate tendency to form strong emotional bonds with particular individuals and to seek proximity to these individuals when distressed (Feeney and Van Vleet 2010). Attachment security is developed early in life, through initial interactions with significant others who are available and supportive in times of need (Bowlby 1973). It guarantees that offspring will maintain proximity to caring attachment figures in times of need, and thus enhances chances of survival, reproduction, and parenting (Bowly 1982). Feelings of attachment security become internalized in a working model of attachment, and generalize to other important relationships that come into existence later in life (Bowlby 1973).

Attachment and exploration are believed to be tightly intertwined (Bowlby 1988), but empirical evidence has been lacking (Shaver and Mikulincer 2010). Exploration is the urge to go out in the world to work, play, discover, and create (Feeney and Van Vleet 2010). It has been argued that being securely attached gives individuals the confidence and courage to explore the environment, accept challenges, and take risks (Bowlby 1988; Feeney and Van Vleet 2010). As risk taking and variety seeking are two prominent manifestations of exploratory tendencies in consumer behavior (Raju 1980; Steenkamp and Baumgartner 1992), the present paper aims to explore whether priming consumers with attachment security enhances financial risk taking and variety seeking.

In Study 1, we demonstrated that attachment security enhanced variety seeking. 43 participants (Mage=18.42, SDage=.59; 22 males) were randomly assigned to one of two story writing conditions, and were instructed to imagine and describe an interaction with "someone who takes good care of you and who is there for you whenever necessary" (attachment security condition) or "a mere acquaintance" (control condition). Then they chose four scoops of ice-cream out of five flavors. Choosing more flavors indicates more variety seeking. Attachment security indeed increased variety seeking (F(1, 38)=4.75, p<.05).

In Study 2, we replicated the effect of attachment security on another exploratory consumer behavior, namely risk taking. Participants (N=54; Mage=21.76, SDage=2.03; 17 males) were randomly assigned to one of two story writing conditions, and were instructed to imagine and briefly describe a walk with someone they felt attached to (attachment security condition) or alone (control condition). Afterwards, all participants completed two sets of seven monetary risk preference questions, one small-stake and one large-stake set (Hsee and Weber 1999). For example, they indicated their preference between "receiving €30 for sure" and "flipping a coin; receiving €100 if Heads or €0 if Tails". The risk preference index for each participant ranged from 1 (extremely risk-aversive) to 8 (extremely risk-taking). We found a significant interaction between attachment security priming and stake size on financial risk taking (F(1, 51)=6.24, p=.02).

Specifically, when stakes were small, risk taking was higher in the attachment security (MRP=4.04, SDRP=.28) compared to the control condition (MRP=3.26, SDRP=.29; see Figure 1).

Figure 1: Study 2

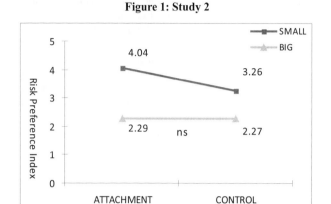

In Study 3, we replicated the effect of attachment security on financial risk taking for small financial gains, but not for large gains or losses. Participants (N=115; Mage=21.38, SDage=2.33; 49 males) were randomly assigned to one of three picture evaluation conditions. They evaluated ten pictures of mothers holding babies (attachment security condition), babies (baby condition), or landscapes (control condition). Afterwards, they provided certainty equivalents for various uncertain gambles (50% chance of gaining [losing] €4 [€2000] or 50% chance of gaining [losing] €0) (Abdellaoui, Bleichrodt et al. 2008). In the gain domain, the interaction between stake size and attachment security was replicated (F(2, 56)=2.92, p=.06). When the risk was small, participants primed with attachment security stated larger certainty equivalents than those in the baby priming (p=.03) and control condition (p=.05), meaning they were more risk taking. However, when the risk became larger, the effect disappeared (ps>.48)(See Figure 2). We found no significant effects in the loss domain.

Figure 2: Study 3

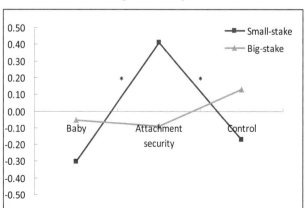

Advances in Consumer Research
Volume 40, ©2012

It has been shown that decision-makers prefer options with 100% of winning $W over uncertain options with P% of winning a higher prize $J and (1-P)% of winning $0, even if these two options have the same expected utility (U=W=P*J) (Tversky and Kahneman 1992). Both feelings of security (captured by the size of $W) and optimism (captured by the probability to win) may drive risk taking behavior. In Study 4, we employed two decision tasks to explore the underlying mechanism. Participants (N=44; Mage=21.82, SDage=5.69; 22 males) were randomly assigned to either the same attachment security or control treatments as in Study 2. Then they engaged in two decision tasks (p-game & w-game) in a random order (Demaree, Dedonno, Burns, and Everhart 2008). In the p-game, the wager was fixed, and the probability to win was changeable to participants (0-100%). The lower probability to win was accompanied by a higher prize. In the w-game, the probability was fixed, and participants could decide on the wager (0-50€). A higher wager was accompanied by a higher prize. Both small and large risks were included. We found a significant interaction between stake size and attachment security in both w-game (F(1, 42)=3.59, p=.065) and p-game (F(1, 42)=5.09, p=.03) (See Figure 3). When stakes were of a moderate size, attachment security enhanced risk taking in both p-game (p=.001) and w-game (p=.06). However, we found no effect when stakes were extremely small.

Figure 3: Study 4

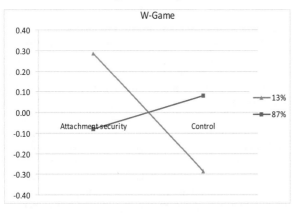

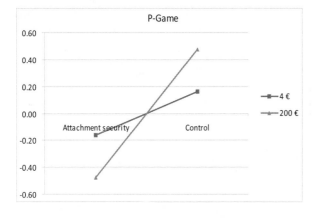

In conclusion, we demonstrate that attachment security enhances exploratory consumer behaviors in the form of variety seeking and risk taking for financial gains at acceptable levels of risk. Preliminary evidence suggests that both optimism towards the environment and feelings of security drive this effect.

REFERENCES

Abdellaoui, Bleichrodt and L'Haridon (2008), "A tractable method to measure utility and loss aversion under prospect theory," *Journal of Risk and Uncertainty,* 36(3): 245-266.

Bowlby (1973), "Attachment and loss: Vol. 2. Separation: Anxiety and anger," New York, NY: Basic Books.

Bowlby (1982), "Attachment and loss: Vol. 1," Attachment (2nd ed.). New York: Basic Books.

Bowlby (1988), "A secure base," New York: Basic Books.

Demaree, DeDonno, Burns and Erikeverhart (2008), "You bet: How personality differences affect risk-taking preferences," *Personality and Individual Differences,* 44(7): 1484-1494.

Feeney, B. C. and M. Van Vleet (2010), "Growing through attachment: The interplay of attachment and exploration in adulthood," *Journal of Social and Personal Relationships,* 27(2): 226-234.

Hsee and Weber (1999), "Cross-national differences in risk preference and lay predictions," *Journal of Behavioral Decision Making,* 12(2): 165-179

Raju (1980), "Optimum Stimulation Level: It's relationship to personality, demographics, and exploratory behavior," *Journal of Consumer Research,* 7, 272-282.

Shaver and Mikulincer (2010), "New directions in attachment theory and research," *Journal of Social and Personal Relationships,* Vol. 27(2): 163–172.

Steenkamp and Baumgartner (1992), "The Role of Optimum Stimulation Level in Exploratory Consumer Behavior," *Journal of Consumer Research,* Vol. 19, No. 3 (Dec., 1992), pp. 434-448.

Tversky and Kahneman (1992), "Advances in prospect theory: Cumulative representation of uncertainty," *Journal of Risk and Uncertainty,* 5, 297–323

Low Batteries Make You Greedy: The Effect of Product States on Human Behavior

Zoey Chen, Georgia Institute of Technology, USA
Nicholas H. Lurie, University of Connecticut, USA

EXTENDED ABSTRACT

Humans depend on resources to survive and reproduce. Historically, those who successfully competed for resources thrived while those who failed languished. Although most residents of developed economies no longer struggle for basic resources, such as food and shelter, they are increasingly reliant on technological products such as cell phones and laptop computers for work and maintaining social relationships. An important characteristic of these products is that they take on different transitory states as they are used. For example, a cell phone will be in a full state after charging overnight but will lose its charge after usage.

We propose that product states act as resources that affect human behavior. Specifically, we predict that exposure to a low product state (i.e., a low battery) leads to behavior consistent with resource scarcity. Building on research showing that scarcity in one resource domain increases resource seeking behavior in other domains (Briers et al. 2006; Nelson and Morrison 2005), we theorize that exposure to a low product state will increase acquisition of other, more basic, resources such as money and food. In addition, since resource scarcity precipitates coping behaviors to boost self-concept (Hobfoll 1989), we predict that exposure to a low product state will also increase performance on cognitive tasks since this boosts self-concept (e.g., I did well, therefore I'm smart, Skaalvik and Hagtvet 1990). However, when a low product state is actively being restored (i.e., by plugging the product in) thereby removing the threat to resources, the effect of a low product state on enhancing cognitive performance should diminish.

STUDY 1: MONEY HOARDING

In Study 1, we exposed people to low versus full product states and measured money hoarding behavior using the dictator game (Bolton, Katok, and Zwick 1998; Fehr and Camerer 2007).

Participants from an online forum completed the study for pay. They were told the study was about attitudes towards cell phones. Participants were asked to imagine they owned an iPhone and were presented with two images of "their iPhone." The first image showed either a fully charged (i.e., full product state) or nearly drained (i.e., low product state) iPhone battery and the second image showed an iPhone home screen displaying different iPhone applications (see Figure 1). Consistent with the cover story, participants were asked questions about the iPhone's design (e.g., design, readability, etc.). Then, participants were told that there was a fixed bonus to be split with another participant, and were asked to indicate how much of the bonus they would keep for themselves. Participants were then debriefed and paid both the fixed fee and the bonus they requested.

Confirming our predictions, participants exposed to a low product state took more of the bonus money for themselves than those exposed to a full product state.

STUDY 2: FOOD HOARDING

Study 2 examines whether a product's state also affects food hoarding. Participants from an online forum completed the study for pay. The first half of the study was identical to Study 1, in which participants viewed screenshots of an iPhone (that was either in a full or low product state) and rated the iPhone on design. Participants were then asked to imagine a shopping scenario in which they were offered chocolate biscuit samples. They were then asked how many samples they would take.

Consistent with Study 1, those exposed to a low product state took more biscuit samples than those exposed to a full product state.

Figure 1
Product State Manipulation in Studies 1 and 2

Full Product State

Low Product State

STUDY 3: COGNITIVE PERFORMANCE

In Studies 3 and 4, we test the idea that exposure to low product state will increase cognitive performance, since resource scarcity increases the desire for positive self-view (Hobfoll 1989) which—in turn—can be enhanced through superior performance on cognitive tasks (Newman 1984).

Undergraduate students completed the study for course credit. In the first part of the study, participants played a game on iPod Touches where we manipulated product state by placing a translucent image of a battery icon into the background of the game. The battery icon either stayed full or started off full and then slowly drained throughout the game, ending in a low product state. Then, iPods were taken up by the experimenter and participants participated in a

Advances in Consumer Research
Volume 40, ©2012

seemingly unrelated study that involved solving anagram puzzles on desktop computers.

Supporting our predictions, those who interacted with an iPod in a low product state showed higher cognitive performance (i.e., solved more anagrams) than those who interacted with an iPod in a full product state.

STUDY 4: RESTORING PRODUCT STATES

Restoring a product that's in a low product state (i.e., plugging in a low battery product) should reduce the need to compensate for low resources by enhancing self-concept (Hobfoll 1989). This should, in turn, lower cognitive performance relative to being unable to restore a low-state product.

Undergraduate students completed the study for course credit. As in Study 3, participants first played a game on the iPod Touch. Since the manipulation of product state in Study 3 may be perceived by some as too heavy handed, in Study 4 we relied on the iPod's default battery display. All iPod Touches were in a low product state condition (i.e., charged to 1/3 full) and half of the participants were asked to charge their iPods during the game. After playing the game, participants completed an ostensibly unrelated proofreading task. Cognitive performance was measured as the number of errors correctly identified.

Supporting our prediction, those who were not able to charge their iPods showed significantly better performance on the proofreading task than their charging counterparts. In addition, there was no significant difference in the false detection rates or mood for the two groups, suggesting that difference in performance was not driven by differences in the criteria participants used to identify errors.

GENERAL DISCUSSION

To our knowledge, this is the first study that looks at how dynamically changing product characteristics affect consumer behavior. Our research suggests a broader definition and interaction of resources relevant to human behavior.

REFERENCES

Bolton, Gary E., Elena Katok, and Rami Zwick (1998), "Dictator Game Giving: Rules of Fairness Versus Acts of Kindness," *International Journal of Game Theory*, 27 (2), 269-99.

Briers, Barbara, Mario Pandelaere, Siegfried Dewitte, and Luk Warlop (2006), "Hungry for Money," *Psychological Science*, 17 (11), 939-43.

Fehr, Ernst and Colin F. Camerer (2007), "Social Neuroeconomics: The Neural Circuitry of Social Preferences," *Trends in Cognitive Sciences*, 11 (10), 419-27.

Fitzsimons, Grainne M., Tanya L. Chartrand, and Gavan J. Fitzsimons (2008), "Automatic Effects of Brand Exposure on Motivated Behavior: How Apple Makes You "Think Different"," *Journal of Consumer Research*, 35 (1), 21-35.

Gino, Francesca, Michael I. Norton, and Dan Ariely (2010), "The Counterfeit Self," *Psychological Science*, 21 (5), 712-20.

Hobfoll, Stevan E. (1989), "Conservation of Resources: A New Attempt at Conceptualizing Stress," *American Psychologist*, 44 (3), 513-24.

Nelson, Leif D. and Evan L. Morrison (2005), "The Symptoms of Resource Scarcity," *Psychological Science*, 16 (2), 167-73.

Newman, Richard S. (1984), "Children's Achievement and Self-Evaluations in Mathematics: A Longitudinal Study," *Journal of Educational Psychology*, 76 (5), 857-73.

Skaalvik, Einar M. and Knut A. Hagtvet (1990), "Academic Achievement and Self-Concept: An Analysis of Causal Predominance in a Developmental Perspective," *Journal of Personality and Social Psychology*, 58 (2), 292-307.

Measuring Arousal in Consumer Research: A New EDA Signal Processing Method

Mathieu Lajante, University of Rennes 1, and Center for Research in Economics and Management, France
Olivier Droulers, University of Rennes 1, and Center for Research in Economics and Management

EXTENDED ABSTRACT

A careful reading of the literature has identified several processing methods of the EDA signal in consumer research. Recommendations are proposed and illustrated in an empirical study which shows that the application of new EDA signal processing techniques improves the valuation of work in consumer research.

For thirty years now, research in consumer behavior has included the measurement of skin conductance response (SCR) in the evaluation of « activation » component of an emotional episode (arousal) (Kroeber-Riel 1979). This electrophysiological index is commonly used in marketing (Micu and Plummer 2010; Ohme et al. 2009 ; Peacock, Purvis, and Hazlett 2011) since its recording technique is reachable, provided you follow some basic rules and have the proper equipment. Furthermore, electrodermal activity (EDA) is an electrophysiological signal like EEG or EMG which requires a rigorous processing before any data interpretation. However, if the interest of marketing researchers in EDA seems certain, what about the processing and interpretation of the signal?

The review of marketing literature identifies three methods for SCR measurement, which is understood as the physiological index of arousal. The first method is based on comparing the overall level of EDA according to experimental conditions (Peacock et al. 2011). This approach is unsatisfactory because it ignores the signal properties of the EDA, which are composed of a tonic activity (baseline) and a phasic activity (SCR). Indeed, measuring the overall level of EDA does not distinguish the tonic activity from the phasic activity, nor identify significant SCR following the occurrence of a stimulus. The second method is based on comparing the average level of EDA before stimulus presentation (baseline) and the average level of EDA during the stimulus presentation (Lang et al. 1999). This approach is problematic because it ignores the SCR time course, thereby causing confusion with the tonic activity and the phasic activity, depleting the information by removing the number of SCR appeared during stimulus presentation, and most importantly removing the spatial (amplitude) and temporal (duration) information of SCR. The third method is based on comparing of the EDA baseline with the sum of the SCR peak amplitudes (Groeppel-Klein 2005). This approach is questionable because it focuses solely on the spatial dimension of SCR and ignores its temporal dimension. However, two of the same SCR amplitude may have different time values.

Moreover, the main focus should be placed on the inherent limitation on the temporal properties of SCR. These properties are characterized by a deflection (1/3sec), followed by a steep slope to a peak (1/3sec) which thereafter slowly declines in the recovery phase (Boucsein 2012). Due to the fact that the rise time of SCR is always shorter than the recovery time, the appearance of several SCR in restricted time interval generates an overlapping phenomenon. Furthermore, this overlapping phenomenon results in an underestimation of the latency and amplitude of subsequent SCR, thus biasing the interpretation of results. To our knowledge, the marketing literature to date has ignored this phenomenon.

However, recent authors in psychophysiology have presented several significant methodological advances in the field of EDA signal processing. For example, the toolbox Ledalab (www.ledalab.de) developed by Benedek and Kaernbach (2010a, 2010b) is based on a signal deconvolution that responds to enacted issues. This method treats the waning asymmetric SCR, fixes the overlapping phenom-enon and optimizes the accuracy of SCR time markers calculation (start/end). Several indices of EDA property can be calculated; most importantly the integral of SCR (ISCR). This index should be emphasized because many authors consider that the calculation of the integral as an optimal solution for evaluating the arousal. With that said, it integrates both the spatial and temporal dimensions of SCR (Benedek and Kaernbach 2010a, 2010b).

Therefore, we created a study to assess arousal caused by exposure to seven national brand television commercials (Coca-Cola, McDonald, Nikon, Spa, Pantoloc, Philadelphia, Bose; t=30sec) using the toolbox Ledalab for the first time in marketing. 30 right-handed subjects (22 women) participated in the study in exchange for a fee (15 euros). Each subject had two 10mm Ag-AgCl electrodes prepared with an isotonic paste, which were placed on the medial phalanges of digits II and III of the non-dominant hand. Electrodes were connected to a wireless preamplifier which then forwarded the signal to an amplifier coupled to data acquisition software (MP150, Biopac System, Inc., Goleta, CA). The signal downsampled offline at 10Hz was analyzed with Ledalab V3.2.3 (Benedek and Kaernbach 2010a, 2010b).

We observed a significant variability of results based on the evaluation index of arousal. With our observations, we realized that the first index (mean EDA) does not distinguish a significantly different level of arousal of a commercial to another. The second index (SCR amplitude) distinguishes a significantly different level of arousal between the commercials "Spa" versus "Nikon" (p=.01) and "Spa" versus "Bose" (p=.03). Finally, the third index (ISCR) can distinguish a significantly different level of arousal between the commercials "Spa" versus "Nikon" (p<.01), "Spa" versus "Bose" (p=.002), "Spa" versus "Philadelphia" (p=.01) and "Spa" versus "Pantoloc" (p=.02).

In conclusion, we show that the choice of the evaluation index of arousal leads to different results. Most importantly, our study highlights the importance of the signal processing phase to reach major academic conclusions, as well as robust managerial recommendations in marketing research which mobilizes the EDA recording. Based on our observations, we advocated more transparency in the methodological choices made in terms of EDA signal processing. Additionally, it seems essential to communicate the three indices – mean, amplitude, ISCR – and justify the choice of index used for data interpretation. Overall, beyond identifying the methodological limitations inherent of EDA signal processing, our results demonstrates the usefulness of both the signal deconvolution method by Benedek and Kaernbach (2010a, 2010b), and the ISCR as a robust index for evaluating arousal.

REFERENCES

Benedek, Mathias, and Christian Kaernbach (2010a), "Decomposition of Skin Conductance Data by Means of Nonnegative Deconvolution," *Psychophysiology*, 47 (March), 647-58.

Benedek, Mathias, and Christian Kaernbach (2010b), "A Continuous Measure of Phasic Electrodermal Activity," *Journal of Neuroscience Methods*, 190 (April), 80-91.

Boucsein, Wolfram (2012), *Electrodermal Activity* (2nd ed.), New York, NY: Springer.

Groeppel-Klein, Andrea (2005), "Arousal and Consumer In-Store Behavior," *Brain Research Bulletin*, 67 (June), 428-37.

Kroeber-Riel, Werner (1979), "Activation Research: Psychobiological Approaches in Consumer Research," *Journal of Consumer Research*, 5 (March), 240-50.

Lang, Annie, Paul Bolls, Robert F. Potter, and Karlynn Kawahara (1999), "The Effects of Production Pacing and Arousing Content on the Information Processing of Television Messages," *Journal of Broadcasting & Electronic Media*, 43 (November), 451-75.

Micu, Anca C. and Joseph T. Plummer (2010), "Measurable Emotions: How Television Ads Really Work? Patterns of Reactions to Commercials Can Demonstrate Advertising Effectiveness," *Journal of Advertising Research*, 50 (June), 137-53.

Ohme, Rafal, Dorota Reykowska, Dawid Wiener, and Anna Choromanska (2009), "Analysis of Neurophysiological Reactions to Advertising Stimuli by Means of EEG and Galvanic Skin Response Measures," *Journal of Neuroscience, Psychology, and Economics*, 2 (February), 21-31.

Peacock, James, Scott Purvis, and Richard L. Hazlett (2011), "Which Broadcast Medium Better Drives Engagement? Measuring the Powers of Radio and Television with Electromyography and Skin-Conductance Measurements," *Journal of Advertising Research*, 51 (December), 578-85.

When Making it Easy Leads to Working Harder:
The Effects of Popularity Cues on Consumer Decision Making

Erin Younhee Ha, University of Illinois at Urbana-Champaign, USA
Tiffany Barnett White, University of Illinois at Urbana–Champaign, USA
Robert S. Wyer, Chinese University of Hong Kong, Hong Kong

EXTENDED ABSTRACT

Consumers are often assumed to use consensus cues (e.g., cues indicating a product's popularity) as a heuristic to reach conclusions about products' desirability without carefully considering specific information about a product's attributes (Burnkrant and Alain 1975; Salganik et al. 2006; Shugan 1980; West and Broniarczyk 1998). Moreover, decision complexity is typically assumed to increase the use of consensus information and, correspondingly, to decrease attention to product attribute information (Gino and Moore 2007; Johnson et al. 1988; Shugan 1980).

In fact, however, these assumptions may not always hold. We investigated the circumstances under which product popularity *increases* the tendency to process product attribute information and consequently leads to more confident decisions and a higher likelihood of purchasing unpopular as well as popular items. We propose that product popularity can increase consumers' consideration of attribute information when they perceive a gap between what they know about the product category in general and what others seem to know about the specific product being promoted. This gap in their knowledge increases the consumers' epistemic curiosity (Loewenstein 1994) and consequently increases their attention to attribute information and the influence of this information on judgments.

We further show that consumers' epistemic curiosity (and thus their attention to attribute information) is greater when a large number of unfamiliar options are presented with popularity cues, and thus the gap in their knowledge is more apparent. It also depends on consumers' perceptions of their expertise in the product domain in question. If consumers consider themselves to be novices in this domain, they may use popularity cues to reduce their uncertainty about their decision, leading to greater conformity and less attention to the available attribute information. When people believe that they are knowledgeable about a product, however, they tend to be sensitive to the gap between their general knowledge and others' knowledge about the particular product. Consequently, they are curious about the reasons for the others' judgments when consensus cues are provided, and are more motivated to process attribute information in this condition, leading the information to have greater influence on their judgments than it would in the absence of consensus cues.

EXPERIMENT 1

Experiment 1 used a 2 (assortment size: large vs. small) × 2 (presence of cue: no-cued vs. popularity-cued) between-subjects design. Relatively unfamiliar cheesecakes were used to construct two sizes of assortment (6 vs. 24 options). The names and descriptions of each cake were provided in all conditions. In *popularity-cue* conditions, however, half of the items in each assortment size condition were cued with three people-shaped icons. After viewing the product list, participants chose the option they would be most likely to buy and reported their intention to purchase it, the extent to which they had considered the descriptions, their choice confidence, and choice difficulty.

As we expected, the effect of popularity cues depended on the assortment size. When the size of the assortment was large, participants were significantly more willing to purchase the item they had chosen when popularity cues had been provided than when they had

not (6.20 vs. 5.48, respectively). In addition, they reported giving relatively more consideration to product descriptions (6.40 vs. 5.70) although their decision difficulty and level of confidence did not differ. When the assortment size was small, however, no effects of popularity information were evident.

EXPERIMENT 2

The design and procedure used in Experiments 2 and 3 were similar to those in Experiment 1, but the focal product category was wine in Experiment 2 and beer in Experiment 3. Experiment 2 focused on the effect of popularity cues on participants' level of deliberation. Consistent with Experiment 1, participants who were confronted with a large assortment reported greater intentions to purchase the product they had chosen when popularity cues were provided than when they were not (4.78 vs. 4.48, respectively) and were more confident of their choice in the former condition (7.54 vs.6.56, respectively). More important, however, they reported deliberating over the wine descriptions to a significantly greater extent when popularity cues were provided than when they were not (6.57 vs. 5.56, respectively) and spent more time making choices in the former condition (102.45 vs. 81.65, respectively). None of these differences were evident when the assortment size was small.

EXPERIMENT 3

Experiment 3 provided more direct evidence of the mediating influence of curiosity and also the moderating role of perceived product knowledge. Participants were classified as having high or low perceived knowledge about beer based on their self-reports (5.21 vs. 1.80, respectively). As expected, knowledgeable participants who had been exposed to a large assortment reported being more curious when popularity cues were provided than when they were not (3.07 vs. 2.65, respectively). Moreover, they reported considering attribute information to a significantly greater extent (8.64 vs. 7.33, respectively) and wanted additional product descriptions (7.64 vs. 6.92). When the assortment size was small, however, the opposite was true: these participants felt *less* curious when popularity cues were provided than when they were not (2.65 vs. 3.35, respectively), were less likely to consider attribute information (7.92 vs. 8.46, respectively) and were less likely to want more product information (5.46 vs. 7.38, respectively).

In contrast, less knowledgeable participants who received a large assortment showed *less* curiosity when popularity cues were provided than when they were not (2.06 vs. 2.70, respectively) and considered less attribute information in the former condition than in the latter (6.89 vs. 9.90).

Taken together, the results confirm that when participants are knowledgeable about the product domain, popularity cues lead to deliberative processing of attribute information. That is, popularity cues lead to heuristic processing only when participants have little knowledge about the type of products they are considering (word count: 936).

REFERENCES

Burnkrant, Robert, and Alain (1975), "Informational and normative social influence in buyer behavior," *Journal of Consumer Research,* 2, 206-15.

Gino, Francesca, and Don A. Moore (2007), "Effects of task difficulty on use of advice," *Journal of Behavioral Decision Making,* 20 (1), 21-35.

Johnson, E., J. Payne, and J. R. Bettman (1988), "Information displays and preference reversals," *Organizational Behavior and Human Decision Processes,* 42, 1-21.

Loewenstein, George (1994), "The psychology of curiosity: A review and reinterpretation." *Psychological Bulletin,* 116 (1), 75-98.

Salganik, Matthew, Peter S. Dodds, and Duncan J. Watts (2006), "Experimental study of inequality and unpredictability in an artificial cultural market," *Science,* (311), 854-6.

Shugan, Steve (1980), "The cost of thinking," *Journal of Consumer Research,* 7, 99-111.

West, Patricia M., and Susan M. Broniarczyk (1998), "Integrating multiple opinions: The role of aspiration level on consumer response to critic consensus," *Journal of Consumer Research,* 25 (1), 38-51.

How does Power Affect the Evaluations of Luxury Brand Extensions?

Youngseon Kim, Central Connecticut State University, USA
Yinlong Zhang, University of Texas at San Antonio, USA

EXTENDED ABSTRACT

Existing research on brand extensions indicates that luxury brands have a greater extendibility than non-luxury brands (Monga and John 2010; Park, Milberg, and Lawson 1991). For example, luxury brands such as Rolex can be more successfully extended into dissimilar categories than non-luxury, functional brands such as Timex (Park et al. 1991). Little research has been devoted to explaining the differential extendibility across luxury brands. For instance, luxury brands such as Louis Vuitton have been successful in the market through brand extensions, whereas luxury brands such as Pierre Cardin have failed after brand extension efforts. How can we explain this variation of brand extendibility within luxury brands? The current research aims to provide an answer to this question.

Past brand extension researchers have investigated the role of a variety of brand-related factors that affect an extension success (e.g., perceived fit with the parent brand, Ahluwalia 2008; Keller 2002); however, the role of consumers' power states has never been explored. Given the central role that power states play in determining consumer attitudes toward luxury products (Rucker and Galinsky 2008, 2009), we argue that power states will affect consumer evaluations of luxury brands' extensions. Following Rucker and Galinsky (2008, 258), we define power as "the capacity to control resources and outcomes, both one's own and that of others." We define broad extensions as a large range of extended products, that is, brand extensions into different categories from a parent brand regardless of the level of fit. We define narrow extensions as a small range of extended products, that is, brand extensions into similar categories from a parent brand. A pretest indicated that broad versus narrow extensions are independent from vertical versus horizontal extensions.

Powerful consumers have a desire to communicate their relatively exclusive association with status symbols (Berger and Ward 2010; Han, Nunes, and Drèze 2010). Because luxury brands with narrow (vs. broad) extensions are perceived as relatively scarce and exclusive (Kirmani, Sood, and Bridges 1999), we propose that:

Hypothesis 1: *Powerful consumers (vs. powerless consumers) will show a stronger preference for luxury brands with narrow (vs. broad) extensions.*

If the effect of power on luxury brand extension preference is due to powerful consumers' desire to show their exclusive association with scarce resources as a status symbol, this effect will be stronger when consumers are in a competitive (vs. non-competitive) mindset. This tendency occurs because a competitive mindset induces a desire for a higher status (Kawada et al. 2004). In other words, people try to maximize position gains and compete for a higher status when social competition goals are activated (Griskevicius et al. 2009; Ordabayeva and Chandon 2011). Therefore, powerful consumers' desire to communicate their exclusive social position tends to be stronger. Formally:

Hypothesis 2: *The impact of power on luxury brand extension preference will be significant only when consumers are in a competitive (vs. non-competitive) mindset.*

To further test the underlying process, we investigated the role of public vs. private consumption. Public (vs. private) consumption induces a strong desire for self-presentation (Goffman 1959). Consumers are more likely to engage in variety seeking behavior to show other consumers that they are interesting to be with when their consumption is public (vs. private) (Ratner and Kahn 2002). In addition, individuals with fashion knowledge show a stronger preference for subtle signals in public consumption than in private consumption (Berger and Ward 2010). Accordingly, we propose that the two-way interaction between power and a competitive mindset will be stronger under public (vs. private) consumption because one's status should be noticed by others. More specifically:

Hypothesis 3: *Public (vs. private) consumption will make the interactive effect of power and a competitive mindset stronger.*

Experiment 1 was a one factor between-subjects design in which we manipulated power by asking participants to recall a past event in which they were powerful or powerless (Galinsky, Gruenfeld, and Magee 2003). After reading a description of luxury brands with narrow, vs. broad, extensions, participants indicated their attitudes toward two different brand extensions. The results showed that powerful participants preferred brands with narrow (vs. broad) extensions more than powerless participants ($p < .05$). A meditational analysis indicated that the power effect was driven by the association between high status and narrow luxury brand extensions.

Experiment 2 was a 2 (powerful vs. powerless) x 2 (competitive vs. non-competitive mindset) between-subjects design. The power manipulation was the same as experiment 1. Following the power manipulation, we manipulated a competitive or a non-competitive mindset (Griskevicius et al. 2009). After that, participants were asked to report their attitude toward luxury brands with narrow, vs. broad, extensions. We found that powerful participants liked the narrow (vs. broad) extensions more than powerless participants only when they were in a competitive (vs. non-competitive) mindset ($p < .05$); however, a difference was not found in the non-competitive mindset condition ($p = .27$).

Experiment 3 was a 2 (powerful vs. powerless) x 2 (competitive vs. cooperative mindset) x 2 (public vs. private consumption) between-subjects design. The manipulations of power and competitive mindset were the same as those in experiment 2, but the manipulation of non-competitive mindset was replaced with cooperative mindset for a cleaner contrast. The public vs. private consumption was based on Berger and Ward (2010). We found a significant three-way interaction: the two-way interaction between power and competitive mindset was significant for the public consumption ($p < .05$), but not for the private consumption ($p = .42$). The two-way interaction of power and competitive mindset was of the same nature as that in experiment 2: powerful participants preferred luxury brands with narrow extensions more than powerless participants; this effect was significant for the competitive mindset but not for the cooperative mindset.

Our results provide a possible theoretical explanation for the inconsistent results of brand extensions of luxury brands: Consumers' power states influence the range of extensions that luxury brands can achieve.

REFERENCES

Ahluwalia, Rohini (2008), "How Far Can A Brand Stretch? Understanding the Role of Self-Construal," *Journal of Marketing Research*, 45 (June), 337-50.

Berger, Jonah and Morgan Ward (2010), "Subtle Signals of Inconspicuous Consumption," *Journal of Consumer Research*, 37 (December), 555-69.

Galinsky, Adam D., Deborah H. Gruenfeld, and Joe C. Magee (2003), "From Power to Action," *Journal of Personality and Social Psychology*, 85 (3), 453-66.

Goffman, Erving (1959), *The Presentation of Self in Everyday Life*, New York, NY: Doubleday.

Griskevicius, Vladas, Joshua M. Tybur, Steven W. Gangestad, Elaine F. Perea, Jenessa R. Shapiro, and Douglas T. Kenrick (2009), "Aggress to Impress: Hostility as an Evolved Context-Dependent Strategy," *Journal of Personality and Social Psychology*, 96 (5), 980-94.

Han, Young Jee, Joseph C. Nunes, and Xavier Drèze (2010), "Signaling Status with Luxury Goods: The Role of Brand Prominence," *Journal of Marketing*, 74 (July), 15-30.

Kawada, Christie L. K., Gabriele Oettingen, Peter M. Gollwitzer, and John A. Bargh (2004), "The Projection of Implicit and Explicit Goals," *Journal of Personality and Social Psychology*, 86 (4), 545-59.

Keller, Kevin Lane (2002), *Branding and Brand Equity*, Cambridge, MA: Marketing Science Institute.

Kirmani, Amna, Sanjay Sood, and Sheri Bridges (1999), "The Ownership Effect in Consumer Responses to Brand Line Stretches," *Journal of Marketing*, 63 (January), 88-101.

Monga, Alokparna B. and Deborah Roedder John (2010), "What makes brand elastic? The Influence of Brand Concept and Styles of Thinking on Brand Extension Evaluation," *Journal of Marketing*, 74 (May), 80-92.

Ordabayeva, Nailya and Pierre Chandon (2011), "Getting Ahead of the Joneses: When Equality Increases Conspicuous Consumption among Bottom-Tier Consumers," *Journal of Consumer Research, 38 (June), 27-41.*

Park, C.Whan, Sandra Milberg, and Robert Lawson (1991), "Evaluation of Brand Extensions: The role of Product Feature Similarity and Brand Concept Consistency," *Journal of consumer research*, 18 (September), 185-93.

Ratner, Rebecca and Barbara E. Kahn (2002), "The Impact of Private versus Public Consumption on Variety-Seeking Behavior," *Journal of Consumer Research*, 29 (2), 246-57.

Rucker, Derek D. and Adam D. Galinsky (2009), "Conspicuous Consumption versus Utilitarian Ideals: How Different Levels of Power Shape Consumer Behavior," *Journal of Experimental Social Psychology*, 45 (3), 549-55.

_____ (2008), "Desire to Acquire: Powerlessness and Compensatory Consumption," *Journal of Consumer Research*, 35 (August), 257-67.

Modelling Everyday Consumer Behavior: The Case of Restricted Consumption

Justine Rapp, University of San Diego, USA
Ronald Paul Hill, Villanova University, USA
Donald Lehmann, Columbia University, USA

EXTENDED ABSTRACT

Despite our needs and desires, many consumers face a number of restrictions to acquisition and consumption of marketed commodities. While a majority of the restriction literature highlights subsistence populations (see Andreasen 1975; 1993; Hill 2002; Hill and Gaines 2007), marketplace restrictions also arise from nonfinancial sources, such as illiteracy and physical impairment (see Baker et al. 2005; Viswanathan, Rosa, and Harris 2005). Yet, little has been done to understand everyday consumer behavior based on the premise of restricted consumption as part of our material landscape. Thus, we seek to comprehend how consumers recognize restrictions, their subsequent affective reactions, and any behavioral aftermath, emphasizing support for theory development on our everyday decision making and consideration of the larger sociopolitical context.

RESTRICTED CONSUMPTION

Our model of restricted consumption (Figure 1) is composed of three parts in a sequential and interrelated order – recognition, reaction, and behavioral intentions. First, recognition of restriction is evaluated as either self- or other-imposed. A dichotomy exists in extant literature between self-imposed restriction (e.g., vegetarianism) and other-imposed restrictions (e.g., product discontinuation). As self-imposed restrictions place a strong focus on individual autonomy, we expect that such restrictions remain either unnoticed or recognized as beneficial. Contrarily, other-imposed constraints generate a more dynamic array of outcomes – from frustration and inconvenience to malice and personal harm (Hill and Gaines 2007), thus posing roadblocks to successful navigation of the marketplace and increasing negative emotional states.

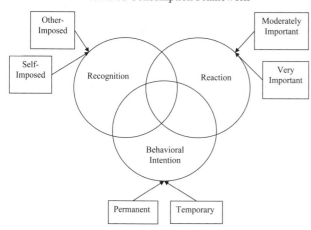

Figure 1
Restricted Consumption Framework

Secondly, we observe cognitive and affective reactions, understood through the subjective importance (moderate versus very) of the restricted object at hand. Defined as "the extent to which a consumer links a product to salient enduring or situation-specific goals" (Bloch and Richins 1983, 71), we surmise that product importance is the primary determinant of consumer reactions to restrictions, and limitations in access to very important products may produce greater emotional reactions due to stronger product-consumer connections (Laurent and Kapferer 1985). Such reactions range from active defiance (e.g., fighting restriction) to positive sense of autonomy.

The third facet of our argument explores behavior of restricted consumers through time (permanent versus temporary). As some consumers revolt against typical consumption behaviors by refusing ownership, curtailing product use, and giving possessions away (Mick 2008), we expect converse reactions in subsistence populations. Potentially positive effects may occur, however, through development of business frameworks termed microenterprises (Viswanathan, Rosa, and Ruth 2010) that allow the poor to become change agents in their consumptive lives.

METHOD

Our empirical work entails both qualitative and quantitative measurement using a sample of 145 participants. Each participant was asked to reflect on a time they were faced with a restrictive situation based on a combination of the following: (1) the source of restriction (i.e., self- or other-imposed), (2) time length of restriction (i.e., temporary or permanent), and (3) importance of the restricted object (i.e., very or moderately). The qualitative component required identification of restricted items, while the quantitative portion developed composite scores for individual feelings towards the restriction, as well as measurement of resultant behavioral reactions based on seven dependent measures.

FINDINGS

As seen in Table 1, three themes emerged through this qualitative assessment, allowing for a richer perspective. Our first quantitative assessment finds that consumers felt better about restrictions when based on their volition. Further, an interaction showed respondents in the moderately (very) important product condition expressed more positive feelings about restriction when the constraint was permanent (temporary) $(F(1,117) = 4.221, p < .05)$.

Next, we evaluate how our three independent variables contribute to the restricted consumption model. Addressing consumer recognition, our participants more easily accepted restriction and were more willing to find a substitute when caused by one's volition. Counter intuitively, participants were more willing to fight and attempt to get around restrictions when products were moderately important to them. Further, individuals believed they were unable to get products they wanted/needed when restricted from an item of only moderate importance. Finally, we found that permanent restrictions led to higher substitution rates and feelings of greater ability to acquire goods and services. An interaction occurs between importance and time in relation to participant's perceived ability to obtain goods $(F(1,117) = 4.43, p < .05)$, as respondents in the moderately (very) important product condition expressed greater inability to obtain products when restriction is permanent (temporary).

Exploring multidimensionality, factor analysis performed on the seven dependent variables revealed two distinct behavioral patterns: (1) lack of acceptance (comprised of fighting, not accepting, trying to get around the restriction, and believing the restriction to be negative), and (2) autonomy (comprised of finding a substitute, feeling in control of one's own destiny, and feeling able to obtain needed/wanted products). We found individuals experiencing restriction of moderately important products were less accepting of the restriction ($F(1,116) = 6.76$, $p < .05$), while individuals felt greater sense of autonomy if restriction is permanent ($F(1,118) = 4.48$, $p < .05$) or self-imposed ($F(1,118) = 14.61$, $p < .001$).

DISCUSSION

The findings presented set the stage for deeper discovery into restricted consumption domains. It is clear that self-imposed restrictions produce greater behavioral nuances, through more positive attitudes and greater autonomy. Presence of autonomy among consumers highlights potential inherent motivations within their reactions to unexpected changes in the marketplace. Greater autonomy suggests one's likelihood to seek alternative product options and maintain a more positive outlook, which more accurately supports the presented hypotheses. Accordingly, action is based on empowerment rather than dissatisfaction or frustration. This finding encourages additional research to understand subjective valuation processes consumers use with goods and services.

We also find both confirmatory market reactions, as well as intriguing results for future analysis. More detailed and prescriptive methodological designs are need, perhaps utilizing directed restriction situations to systematically eliminate subjective valuation. Such knowledge may allow for greater ease predicting consumer response patterns, thus enabling increased customer support processes and/or product search tools. Further, the two-factor solution among our original seven dependent variables helps strengthen theoretical contribution to marketing scholarship enabling progress towards a more holistic interpretation of consumer decision making within restrictive situations.

REFERENCES

Andreasen, Alan R. (1975), *The Disadvantaged Consumer,* New York: The Free Press.

Andreasen, Alan R. (1993), "Revisiting the Disadvantaged: Old Lessons and New Problems," *Journal of Public Policy & Marketing*, 12 (2), 270-275.

Baker, Stacey Menzel, James W. Gentry, and Terri L. Rittenburg (2005), "Building Understanding of the Domain of Consumer Vulnerability," *Journal of Macromarketing*, 25 (December), 128-139.

Bloch, Peter H. and Marsha L. Richins (1983), "A Theoretical Model for the Study of Product Importance Perceptions," *Journal of Marketing*, 47 (Summer), 69-81.

Hill, Ronald Paul (2002), "Stalking the Poverty Consumer: A Retrospective Examination of Modern Ethical Dilemmas," *Journal of Business Ethics*, 37 (May), 209-219.

Hill, Ronald Paul and Jeannie Gaines (2007), "The Consumer Culture of Poverty: Behavioral Research Findings and Their Implications in an Ethnographic Context," *Journal of American Culture*, 30 (March), 81-95.

Laurent, Gilles and Jean-Noel Kapferer (1985), "Measuring Consumer Involvement Profiles," *Journal of Marketing Research*, 22 (February), 41-53.

Mick, David Glen (2008), "Degrees of Freedom of Will: An Essential Endless Question in Consumer Behavior," *Journal of Consumer Psychology*, 18, 17-21.

Viswanathan, Madhu, Jose Antonio Rosa, and James Edwin Harris (2005), "Decision Making and Coping of Functionally Illiterate Consumers and Some Implications for Marketing Management," *Journal of Marketing*, 69 (January), 15-31.

Viswanathan, Madhu, José Antonio Rosa, and Julie A. Ruth (2010), "Exchanges in Marketing Systems: The Case of Subsistence Consumer-Merchants in Chennai, India," *Journal of Marketing*, 74, 1-17.

Table 1
Qualitative Themes

Theme	Characterization	Examples
Short-run need for monetary savings	Temporary restriction	Future purchase of car or house
Product discontinuations	Permanent restriction Other-imposed	Type of shampoo Restaurant dressing Brand of cereal
Negative product qualities and product failure	Permanent restriction Self-imposed	Brand of television Brand of alcohol

Consuming the Dead: Symbolic Exchange in Thai 'Hungry Ghost' Festivals

Rungpaka Amy Tiwsakul, Queen Mary, University of London, UK
Chris Hackley, Royal Holloway University of London, UK

EXTENDED ABSTRACT

This study contributes to the theoretical and conceptual understanding of death and consumption in two main ways. Firstly, it describes and interprets a ritual context that has not previously been the subject of published consumer research: 'hungry ghost' festivals in the Thai Theravāda Buddhist tradition. Previous consumer research studies have touched upon the hungry ghost cosmology, but within the rather different Tibetan Mahāyāna Buddhist tradition (e.g. Gould, 1991; 1992) and without the focus on the dead as the nexus of relational consumption. Secondly, we use this cultural context to move towards a dyadic conceptualisation of ritual death consumption, expanding the focus on the management of death *by* the living to embrace the symbolic exchange *between* living and dead. We follow Bonsu and Belk's (2003) ethnographic work on death ritual in Ghana, Africa, in seeking to move from the predominant Western assumption of death as end point for consumption and identity toward a relational perspective on death, using the interactions between living and the ghosts at the festival. This perspective is facilitated by the belief in this tradition that ghosts are literally present in, and interact with, corporeal life. These interactions are engaged with in ritual form in various aspects of hungry ghost festivals.

LITERATURE

Ritual and death remain two relatively neglected topics in consumer research. Since Rook (1985) first introduced ritual into the field, various commentators (e.g. Arnould, 2001) have remarked on the relatively small number of follow-up studies that elaborate on the importance of ritual to consumption, and of consumption to ritual. Death, similarly, has been neglected, partly perhaps it is assumed to be beyond the scope of corporeal consumer researchers since, in Western philosophy and the Judaeo-Christian-Islamic eschatology, death is assumed to mark the end of earthly identity, and of consumption (Bauman, 1998; Giddens, 1991; Riley, 1983). For the living, material possessions have symbolic meanings (Belk et al., 1989; Gentry et al., 1995) but there are instances where possessions and their meanings invoke the dead, for example where items symbolise the relationship with the deceased. The closeness of life to death has been commented upon by some Western philosophers (Baudrillard, 1993; Hegel, 1977) but the consumption issues surrounding death remain relatively under explored. Exceptions include some social scientific studies that explore the links between consumption and death (Turley, 1998; Metcalf and Huntington, 1991; Davies, 1997). Within consumer research, the link between secular immortality and consumer affluence has been explored (Hirschman, 1990) as have the ways in which the living dispose of the possessions of the dead (Kates, 2001; Price et al., 2001). More recently, consumer researchers have explored the interplay of death with identity (Bonsu and DeBerry-Spence, 2008; Bonsu and Belk, 2003; O'Donohoe and Turley, 2005; Wattanasuwan, 2005; Langer, 2007). Three consumer culture studies in particular look into death rituals and death consumption in a non-Western context: Bonsu and Belk (2003) (and a subsequent work by Bonsu and DeBerry-Spence in 2008); Zhao and Belk's (2008) study of Chinese death ritual consumption; and Wattanasuwan's (2005) research on the paper burning ritual in Thailand. Our study draws on and extends this line of work into a previously uncharted cultural context, developing a dyadic conceptualisation of death consumption and informing understanding of how death is produced and consumed in different cultural contexts.

METHOD

We use a multi-method approach to interpret the cultural meanings of this festival, bearing in mind the complexity, depth and variability of the Thai Theravāda Buddhist tradition and the consequent impossibility of achieving a single definitive reading. We employ a cultural semiotic analysis (Buckingham, 2009; Pink, 2006) focusing mainly on the centre piece of the 'Pee Ta Khon' festival, in which the living re-enact the mythical journey back from exile in the forest, of the tenth and last incarnation of the Buddha, Prince Mahavejsandon. According to legend, the Buddha was escorted on this journey by hungry ghosts. The hungry ghost figure varies in different traditions of Buddhist mythology but a common feature is that the ghosts are dead relatives seeking to move to the next stage in the wheel of life. The ghosts are perpetually hungry because they yearn for earthly gratifications, and in their liminal state they need the intercession of the living to transition to become ancestors. In the festival procession, the bizarrely costumed ghost figures indulge in ribald humour, giving the proceedings a carnivalesque air, in contrast to the more pious and solemn parts of the ritual. We set this within a local cultural context by drawing on the first author's cultural knowledge as a Thai national, on informal conversations with Thais supplemented by other internet and literary sources of information, and through interviews, conducted in Thai and translated, with festival organisers. In addition, we also draw for our frame of understanding on our first hand ethnographic investigations of other Theravāda Buddhist death rituals in Thailand. We choose to focus this study on the world famous 'Pee Ta Khon' festival (also known under different Anglicised spellings) because of its unique mythology and the visual flamboyance which makes tangible the presence of ghosts in Thai cultural life.

FINDINGS/DATA

The findings offer an ethnographically-informed description of the hungry ghost phenomenon in Thailand. Observation and analysis of the ritual underlines the immanence of ghosts in Thai religious life and the centrality of consumption to this death ritual. We focus on 'Pee Ta Khon' as one of the most important and visually striking merit-making 'hungry ghost' festivals in the highly spirit-infused Thai Theravāda Buddhist tradition (McDaniel, 2006). Originally known as 'Pee Tam Khon', which is literally translated as 'ghosts follow the living', Pee Ta Khon also doubles as a fertility ritual, and has, in recent years, evolved into an important tourist attraction for the Dansai district of Loei province in North-Eastern Thailand. It has major economic implications for the region, both in terms of the cash it generates from visiting tourists and from the success it may bring to the growth of crops if the spirits are suitably placated. A striking feature of the festival is the combination of evil, represented by the grotesque and fearsome masks, and the joyous irreverence of the hungry ghost figures as they poke fun at the crowds with their huge phalluses during the procession. Profanity is highly unusual in Thai public life and especially so in religious ritual, yet the ghosts of Pee Ta Khon revel in their ribaldry. In return for giving the hungry ghosts assistance, in the form of prayers, food or other ritual forms of respect and holy celebration, the living will receive blessings which can increase their spiritual and material wellbeing in this life, through the benevolent intercession of the duly placated ancestors. It is the manifest reality of ghosts in this tradition as liminal beings capable of great evil a well as good which bring into relief the tangibility of symbolic exchanges between living and dead in hungry ghost rituals. In Pee Ta Khon and other hungry ghosts festivals, the living, in a sense, symbolically consume the dead in ways that have implications for the identities of the living, as well as for the dead.

REFERENCES

Arnould, Eric J. (2001), Ritual three gifts and why consumer researchers should care, *Advances in Consumer Research*, Vol. 28, p.384-386.

Baudrillard, Jean (1993), *Symbolic Exchange and Death*, (I. H. Grant Trans.), London: Sage (original work published in 1976).

Bauman, Zygmunt (1998), *Postmodernity and its discontents*, Cambridge: Polity Press.

Belk, Russell. W., Wallendorf, Melanie and Sherry, John F. JR. (1989), The sacred and the profane in consumer behaviour: Theodicy on the Odyssey, *Journal of Consumer Research*, Vol. 16, Iss. June, p.1-38.

Bonsu, Samuel K. and Belk, Russell W. (2003), Do not go cheaply into that good night: death-ritual consumption in Asante, Ghana, *Journal of Consumer Research*, Vol. 30, Iss. June, p.41-55.

Bonsu, Samuel K. and DeBerry-Spence, Benét (2008), Consuming the dead: identity and community building practices in death rituals, *Journal of Contemporary Ethnography*, Vol. 37, Iss. 6, p. 694-719.

Buckingham, David (2009), Creative visual methods in media research: possibilities, problems and proposals, *Media Culture Society*, Vol. 31, Iss. 4, p. 633-652.

Davies, Douglas J. (1997), *Death ritual and belief: rhetoric of funerary rites*, London: Continuum.

Gentry, James W., Kennedy, Patricia F., Paul, Catherine, and Hill, Ronald P. (1995), Family transitions during grief: discontinuities in household consumption patterns, *Journal of Business Research*, Vol. 34, Iss. September, p.67-79.

Giddens, Anthony (1991), *Modernity and self-identity: self and society in the late modern age*, Cambridge: Cambridge Polity Press.

Gould, Stephen J. (1991), An Asian approach to the understanding of consumer energy, drives and states, in Hirschman, Elizabeth C., *Research in Consumer Behaviour: A Research Annual*, Vol. 5, London: Jai Press Inc., p. 33-59.

Gould, Stephen J. (1992), Consumer Materialism as a Multilevel and Individual Difference Phenomenon - An Asian-Based Perspective, in *Special Volumes – Meaning, Measure and Morality of Materialism*, Association for Consumer Research, p. 57-62.

Hegel, Georg Wilhelm Friedrich (1977), *The Phenomenology of Spirit*, (A.V. Miller Trans.) Oxford: Clarendon Press (original work published in 1807).

Hirschman, Elizabeth C. (1990), Secular immortality and American ideology of affluence, *Journal of Consumer Research*, Vol. 17, Iss. June, p. 31-42.

Kates, Steven M. (2001), Disposition of possessions among families of people with AIDS, *Psychology and Marketing*, Vol. 18, Iss. 4, p. 365-387.

Langer, Rita (2007), *Buddhist rituals of death and rebirth: Contemporary Sri Lankan Practice and its origins*, New York: Routledge.

McDaniel, Justin (2006), *The map and the world in Buddhism*, Thai digital monastery, Available at http://tdm.ucr.edu/index.html.

Metcalf, Peter and Huntington, Richard (1991), *Celebrations of death: anthropology of mortuary practices*, New York: Cambridge University Press.

O'Donohoe, Stephanie and Turley, Darach (2005), Till death us do part? Consumption and the negotiation of relationships following a bereavement, *Advances in Consumer Research*, Vol. 32, p. 625-626.

Pink, Sarah (2006), *Doing Visual Ethnography*, 2nd ed. London: Sage.

Price, Linda, Arnould, Eric J. and Curasi, Carolyn F. (2000), Older consumers' disposition of special possessions, *Journal of Consumer Research*, Vol. 37, Iss. September, p.179-201.

Riley, John W. (1983), Dying and the meaning of death: sociological inquiries, *Annual Review of Sociology*, Vol. 9, p.191-216.

Rook, Dennis (1985), The ritual dimension of consumer behaviour, *Journal of Consumer Research*, Vol. 12, Iss. December, p. 251-264.

Turley, Darach (1998), A postcard from the very edge: mortality and marketing, in *Consumer research: postcards from the edge*, S. Brown and D. Turley (eds.), London: Routledge, p. 350-377.

Wattanasuwan, Kritsadarat (2005), Remembering you, remembering your brands: Immortalising the decreased through the paper-burning ritual in Thailand, *3rd workshop on interpretive consumer research, Copenhagen Business School, Denmark.*

Zhao, Xin and Belk, Russell W. (2008), Desire on fire: a naturalistic inquiry of Chinese death ritual consumption, *European Advances in Consumer Research*, Association for Consumer Research conference proceedings, Vol. 8, p.245.

The Crossmodal Effect of Attention on Preferences

Hao Shen, Chinese University of Hong Kong, Hong Kong
Jaideep Sengupta, Hong Kong University of Science and Technology, Hong Kong

EXTENDED ABSTRACT

Consumers often have to decide between two products located adjacent to each other – as for example, on a supermarket shelf. How are such decisions, which are based on visually processing the two products, influenced by unrelated, non-visual stimuli that may emanate from either lateral direction? Suppose, for example, that you are standing in a supermarket aisle, trying to decide between two packets of cookies, one placed nearer your right side and the other nearer your left. While you are trying to decide, you hear an in-store announcement, on your left, about store closing hours. Will this unrelated announcement influence your cookie decision?

This research seeks to answer such questions by demonstrating what we believe is a novel phenomenon: namely, an enhancement in product evaluations that are based on visual processing, as a result of a spatial match between the product's location along a lateral dimension and the location of an external, non-visual stimulus. Thus, in the example above, the store announcement from the left (an auditory stimulus) should increase the preference for the cookie packet on the left.

According to our theorizing, such phenomena are driven by crossmodal links in spatial attention (see Driver and Spence 1998a, 1998b for a review). Because of such links, when attention in one sensory mode is drawn in a particular direction, people find it easier to direct attention in another sensory modality towards that direction. Thus, an auditory stimulus from a particular direction makes it relatively easier for consumers to process products that are more aligned with that general direction. The consequent fluency of processing, we argue, should directly influence product evaluations and choice.

In study 1, participants were asked to listen to a news broadcast while simultaneously being exposed to pictures of two hotel rooms that either appear on the left or right side of a computer screen. The key manipulation involved the location of the loudspeaker from which the news was broadcast. This speaker was placed either towards the left or right corner of the room. We found that participants paid more visual attention to the hotel room on the left (right) of their screen if the auditory signal came from their left (right), and that this attention bias was reflected in fluency of processing as well as actual preference for the room on the corresponding side.

Study 2 aimed to illustrate the applied implications of our findings by documenting them in a field setting. The study was conducted in the context of choosing a product from one of two adjacent vending machines, both selling soft drinks. A research assistant placed a speaker on the top of each vending machine and linked the speakers to a notebook computer that was broadcasting a local news bulletin. The assistant also adjusted the speaker's volume control to ensure that at any moment in time, only one of the speakers (either the one on the right or on the left) was playing at normal volume, while the other was muted. We found that consumers were more likely to purchase a drink from the machine placed on the right when the broadcasting speaker was placed on top of that machine, than when it was placed on the one on the left.

We assumed that consumers might either passively attend to any voice or actively choose which voice to attend to. Study 3 aimed to investigate whether the latter possibility is true by manipulating the valence of voice. Participants either listened to positive or annoying music while making an impression of two pictures of restaurants on a computer screen. The music, which lasted for 1.5 minutes, either came from their left or right side. In positive music condition, we replicated the findings of study 1. In annoying music condition, however, participants paid more visual attention to the restaurant on the opposite side to the music and prefer that restaurant to more extent than the restaurant on the same side of the music. These results suggested that participants had avoided listening to annoying music and that this shift in audio attention had affected their visual attention accordingly.

We assumed that even when participants listen to annoying music, they might initially attend to it passively and then consciously avoid it in order to cope with their negative feelings elicited by the music. If this is the case, their visual attention should also first be shifted toward and then away from the music. Study 4 sought to examine this process. Participants listened to annoying music that either came from their left or right side. At the same time, they sequentially examined product options of two categories on a computer screen. In each category, they examined two options, one on the left and the other on the right side of the screen. Participants examined options of the first category while listening to music for 20 seconds. Then the music stopped, and participants reported their preference and relative attention toward each option. After that, the experimenter continued to play music, Participants examined options of the second category while listening to music for another 20 seconds. Consistent with our assumption that participants would first attend to annoying music and then avoid it, we found that participants paid more attention to the option of the first category on the same side of music but to the option of the second category on the opposite side to the music. Their actual preference for option was affected accordingly.

This research represents the first investigation of how attention shifts in one sensory mode can influence preferences in another. In doing so, not only does this research add to the literature on attention, but also to the small but growing body of work illuminating the vital role of the senses in shaping product preferences (Elder and Krishna, 2010; Krishna and Morrin, 2008).

REFERENCES

Driver, Jon, and Spence, Charles (1998a), "Attention and the Crossmodal Construction of Space," *Trends in Cognitive Science*, 2, 254–62.

——— (1998b), "Crossmodal Links in Spatial Attention," *Proceedings and the Royal Society of London, Series B*, 353, 1319-331.

Elder, Ryan S. and Aradhna Krishna (2010), "The Effects of Advertising Copy on Sensory Thoughts and Perceived Taste," Journal of Consumer Research, 36 (5), 748–56.

Krishna, Aradhna and Maureen Morrin (2008), "Does Touch Affect Taste? The Perceptual Transfer of Product Container Haptic Cues," Journal of Consumer Research, 34 (April), 807–18.

Insights into Decisions from Neuroscience and Choice Experiments:
The Effect of Eye Movements on Choice

Barbara E. Kahn, University of Pennsylvania, USA
Jordan J. Louviere, University of Technology Sydney, Australia
Claudia Townsend, University of Miami, USA
Chelsea Wise, University of Technology Sydney, Australia

EXTENDED ABSTRACT

Discrete Choice Experiment (DCE) research has predominately been used to observe choice outcomes. However a better understanding of the underlying choice process can help improve our ability to predict choices. Prior work examining choice processes has traditionally used methods such as concurrent or retrospective reporting (verbal protocols), information boards, mouse-tracing methods, or eye-tracking and click stream analysis in computer-based environments. However, these methods face issues of internal and external validity. For example, concurrent reporting consumes mental resources and forces serial processing, limiting external validity. Moreover, many of these measures are unable to capture emotional or automated processes, base state (engagement), or conviction, resulting in compromised internal validity. Thus, there is a need for a better process measurement system for experimental decision making environments that offers both externally and internally valid data.

We proffer that the combination of eye-tracking measures and discrete choice experiments fulfills that need. Eye-tracking has been used to study decision processes in various tasks including probabilistic inference, risky decisions, and advertisements. Indeed, if visual attention and eye movements are coupled, attentional shifts should be related to changes and patterns of eye movements (Hoffman 1998; Rayner 1998). However, eye-tracking observes only information acquisition behavior and not internal cognitive processes. Instead, one must infer underlying cognitive strategies from eye-tracking data. Alternatively, process may be inferred through the experimental design by maximizing the resultant statistical information on cognitive factors influencing choice. For example, choice experiments (Louviere and Woodworth 1983) using full factorial designs allow one to infer certain types of decision rules (Anderson 1971). In this paper we use eye-tracking measures in discrete choice experiments to exploit the benefits these methods offer in understanding preference and choice processing. The broad purpose of our research is to identify empirical generalizations that can be integrated with neuroscience and other literatures.

RESEARCH HYPOTHESES

Consistent with research suggesting individuals are selective in information search (e.g., Bettman, Johnson, and Payne 1991), we hypothesize that individuals quickly look for features and/or feature levels of choice options that best help them discriminate and they focus fixations in areas of a scene that most likely contain information to shorten search length (Rayner and Castelhano 2008).

Hypothesis 1: *The time to first fixate on important features is shorter than that for less important features.*

Hypothesis 2: *Fewer fixations should occur before an individual looks at an important feature compared with the number occurring before looking at an unimportant feature.*

In familiar choice contexts, individuals have the ability to isolate that which is most important and task relevant (Alba and Hutchinson 1987). Thus, individuals may focus their visual attention more on choice options or features that require deliberation or a second look than choice options or features that individuals have quickly identified as important.

Hypothesis 3: *Individuals spend more time looking at less discriminating features than more discriminating features.*

Hypothesis 4: *We expect fewer fixations or unique visits for chosen options than for unchosen options. Similarly, we expect fewer fixations or unique visits to attractive, more discriminating features/levels than for less attractive, less discriminating features/levels.*

STUDY 1: VISUAL ATTENTION AND CHOICE

In study 1 we a) design, implement and execute a choice experiment that incorporates eye-tracking, b) obtain meaningful eye-tracking measures and c) relate eye-tracking measures to choices.

Method

We used a Tobii X60 eye tracker. The experiment focused on choices of cracker options described by combinations of three features: shape (circle, square, triangle), flavor (wheat, dark rye, plain) and topping (salt, poppy, no topping). We selected nine cracker descriptions from the 3^3 factorial using a main effects design. Following Louviere et al. (2008) we used a balanced incomplete block design to assign the crackers to 12 choice sets, each containing three crackers. The 12 sets of crackers were displayed one set at a time, and 14 participants chose their most and least preferred cracker for a party they would host.

Results

Table 1 gives the results from stacking all the participants' choices (Horsky and Rao 1984) and estimating an aggregate conditional logit model (McFadden 1974) including the effects of eye-tracking measures as covariates. Although preliminary, the results are promising, suggesting the visual attention measures are systematically associated with choices.

Specifically, 'time to first fixation' was significant ($B_{time to first fixation}$ = -.3190, $p < .05$), implying the longer to fixate on a choice option, the less likely it is chosen. 'First fixation duration' also was significant ($B_{first fixation duration}$ = 2.100, $p < .001$), implying the longer one initially fixates on a choice option the more likely it is chosen. The latter result supports the notion that individuals quickly look for features/feature levels of choice options that help discriminate choice options. Finally, 'visit count' was significant ($B_{visit count}$ = -.408, $p < .05$), implying fewer unique visits to more attractive than less attractive choice options. Thus, the results suggest eye movements play a non-trivial role in choice.

TABLE 1
Study 1 Results, Aggregate Conditional Logit Model

	est. b	s.e.	t-stat	p-value	
Attribute effects					
Round	0.1821	0.1507	1.2100	0.2270	
Square	-0.1005	0.1668	-0.6000	0.5470	
Wheat	0.7835	0.1553	5.0400	0.0000	**
Dark rye	0.0573	0.1434	0.4000	0.6890	
Salt	0.4476	0.1603	2.7900	0.0050	**
Poppy	0.2118	0.1447	1.4600	0.1430	
The Effect of Visual Attention					
Time to first fixation	-0.3109	0.1279	-2.4300	0.0150	*
Fixation duration	-0.1210	0.2366	-0.5100	0.6090	
Fixation count	0.1977	0.1147	1.7200	0.0850	
First fixation duration	2.1004	0.7592	2.7700	0.0060	**
Visit count	-0.4076	0.1411	-2.8900	0.0040	**

* p < .05   ** p < .01,   results based on the exploded approach to coding
  the dependent variable, choice
The effect of visual attention variables are mean centered
Reference for the estimate of shapes round and square is triangle
Reference for the estimate of flavors wheat and dark rye is plain
Reference for the estimate of toppings salt and poppy is no topping

Summary Statistics			
Number of observations	500	Log-likelihood intercept	-183.063
LR chi^2(11)	89.88	Log-likelihood full model	-138.121
prob > chi^2	0.0000	AIC	1.786
Mcfaddens r^2	0.2460	BIC	-522.165

STUDY 2: GREATER NUMBER OF CHOICE SETS AND VISUAL ATTENTION

Study 2 builds on study 1 by using a greater number of choice sets to insure participants evaluate each cracker relative to all 27 possible crackers.

Method

The stimuli, design and procedure was identical to study 1, except for 18 participants evaluated 57 choice sets. Observing most and least preferred choices in each set provides a complete preference ranking of the three, and allows extrapolation to non-tested choice sets. This method ensures participant-level estimation of the conditional logit choice model (Louviere et al. 2008) required to test hypotheses 1-4. For brevity, individual-level model results are not reported.

Results

Consistent with study 1, both 'time to first fixation' and 'visit count' were significant ($B_{\text{time to first fixation}}$ = -.953, $p < .001$; $B_{\text{visit count}}$ = -.552, $p < .001$) and offer the same implications as study 1. There also are fewer unique visits to more attractive cracker features than less attractive features.

CONCLUSION

This research provides an innovative manner for examining the processing behind choice without the pitfalls of limited external and internal validity implicit in other methods. Moreover, our findings offer strong support that there is, in fact, a strong relationship between eye movements and choice.

REFERENCES

Alba, Joseph W. and Wesley J. Hutchinson (1987), "Dimensions of Consumer Expertise," *Journal of Consumer Research*, 13 (4), 411-54.

Anderson, Norman H. (1971), "Integration Theory and Attitude Change," *Psychological Review*, 78 (3), 171-206.

Bettman, Jim R., Eric J. Johnson, and John W. Payne (1991), "Consumer Decision Making," in *Handbook of Consumer Behavior*, ed. Thomas S. Robertson and Harold H. Kassarjian, Englewood Cliffs, NJ: Prentice-Hall, 50-84.

Hoffman, J.E. (1998), "Visual Attention and Eye Movements," in *Attention*, ed. H. Pashler, East Sussex, United Kingdom: Psychology Press, 119-53.

Horsky, Dan and M. R. Rao (1984), "Estimation of Attribute Weights from Preference Comparisons," *Management Science*, 30 (7), 801-22.

Louviere, Jordan J., Deborah J. Street, Leonie Burgess, Nada Wasi, Towhidul Islam, and Anthony A. J. Marley (2008), "Modeling the Choices of Individual Decision-Makers by Combining Efficient Choice Experiment Designs with Extra Preference Information," *Journal of Choice Modelling*, 1 (1), 128-63.

Louviere, Jordan J. and George Woodworth (1983), "Design and Analysis of Simulated Consumer Choice or Allocation Experiments: An Approach Based on Aggregate Data," *Journal of Marketing Research*, 20 (4), 350-67.

McFadden, Daniel L. (1974), "Conditional Logit Analysis of Qualitative Choice Behaviour," in *Frontiers in Econometrics*, ed. P. Zarembka, New York: Academic Press, 105-42.

Rayner, Keith (1998), "Eye Movements in Reading and Information Processing: 20 Years of Research," *Psychological bulletin*, 124 (3), 372-422.

Rayner, Keith and Monica S. Castelhano (2008), "Eye Movements During Reading, Scene Perception, Visual Search, and While Looking at Print Advertisements," in *Visual Marketing: From Attention to Action*, ed. M. Wedel and R. Pieters, New York: Lawrence Erlbaum Associates, 9-42.

Uncertainty Increases People's Reliance on Their Feelings

Ali Faraji-Rad, Columbia University, USA
Michel Tuan Pham, Columbia University, USA

EXTENDED ABSTRACT

Imagine sitting in your office in a normal day, trying to make an important decision. Suddenly, a colleague of yours passes by your office door and says "congratulations!" and quickly vanishes. You have not received any good news recently so you do not know why the colleague congratulated you. This creates a momentary (positive in this case) feeling of uncertainty. How is this feeling of uncertainty likely to influence your subsequent, and unrelated decision? People usually think of uncertainty as a state of lack of information about the actual decision at hand, yet, uncertainty can be due to a feeling of not knowing, or activation of the concept of uncertainty in the mind. This feeling could be related or unrelated to the decision at hand (Bar-Anan, Wilson, and Gilbert 2009). In this paper we propose that a general feeling of uncertainty increases people's propensity to rely on their feelings.

This proposition has not been tested before, yet, prior research in psychology is suggestive of such an effect. For example, using fMRI, Berns et al (2001) showed that the response of human reward region to rewarding stimuli (i.e., juice) was greatest when the stimuli were unpredictable. Also, Grupe and Nitzchke (2011) showed that people's aversion towards negative stimuli is heightened with cues related to uncertainty. Research in experimental psychology too has documented that uncertainty elevates people's responses to both positive and negative stimuli (Bar-Anan et al 2009; Lee and Qiu 2009; Wilson et al 2005). But could these findings, at least partly, be due to a general reliance on feelings in face of uncertainty? We report 4 studies that are designed to test this question.

In study 1, we first asked participants to recall and write down the thoughts and feelings they experienced in a situation where they felt uncertain (uncertain condition), certain (certain condition), or went shopping (control condition). Then as a "second" task, we asked them to make a choice between an apartment that was superior on logical dimensions (e.g., more spacious closet space) and an apartment that was superior on affective dimensions (e.g., better view). In support of our hypothesis, compared to participants in the certain condition (42.5%), or the control condition (50%), participants in the uncertain condition (68%) chose the affectively superior apartment more than the cognitively superior apartment ($?2 = 6.28$, $p < .05$).

In studies 2A-B, we replicated the results of study 1, with a different, and novel, manipulation of uncertainty. In both of these studies, first, under the disguise of a study on the effects of length of measurement-scales on people's reporting of their emotions, we asked participants to answer a question ("How do you feel right now?") 5 times. The end-point of the scales where used to manipulate uncertainty, or certainty. Specifically, in the uncertain condition the end-points where "somewhat uncertain" and "totally uncertain", and in the certain condition, the end-points were "somewhat certain" and "totally certain". Participants had to answer the question five times using 5, 9, 11, 15, and 19-point scales. The logic behind this manipulation was that the use of half of the range of the scale (i.e., scales starting with "somewhat uncertain", instead of "not uncertain") would create a momentary feeling of uncertainty/certainty in the participants. After completing this task, participants went on to participate in an ostensibly separate task, which in study 2A was to

make a choice between apartments similar to study 1, and in study 2B was to make a choice between 2 laptops. One of the laptops used in study 2 was superior on the cognitive dimensions (e.g., performance), and the other was superior on the affective dimensions (e.g., aesthetics). As predicted, in both studies, compared to participants in the certain conditions (38% in 2A and 51% in 2B), participants in the uncertain conditions (61% in 2A and 68% in 2B) chose the affectively superior options more than the cognitively superior options.

In study 3 we tried to rule out the alternative explanation that a feeling of uncertainty, compared to certainty, creates a negative mood and thus encourages people to regulate their mood by opting for more affective (i.e., hedonic) options. Here, we first asked participants to recall and write down a situation where they were certain in a positive way (positive certain condition), certain in a negative way (negative certain condition), uncertain in a positive way (positive certain condition), or uncertain in a negative way (negative uncertain condition). Then under the disguise to a second task, participants had to choose between the two apartments as in study 1. Results revealed a main effect of uncertainty such that compared to certain participants, uncertain participants chose the affectively superior apartment more than the cognitively superior apartment ($B=0.361$, Wald $?2=3.88$, $p<.05$). Also a main effect of valence was found such that compared to the positive condition, those in the negative condition chose the affectively superior apartment more than the cognitively superior one ($B=-.367$, Wald $?2=4.02$, $p<.05$). But importantly, we observed no interaction between uncertainty and valence (Wald $?2=.373$, $p>.89$), suggesting that the effect of uncertainty works independent from the effect of mood.

Collectively these results are suggestive of the fact that a feeling of uncertainty increases people's reliance on their feelings. A shortcoming of our research is that in all studies only one paradigm was used to test people's reliance on their feelings (i.e., people opting for more affective options, compared to more cognitive ones). Using other paradigms, such as testing a higher effect of people's incidental mood states on their evaluations in uncertain situations (compared to certain situations), are possibilities for further research.

REFERENCES

Bar-Anan, Y., Wilson, T.D., Gilbert, D.T., (2009). The Feeling of Uncertainty Intensifies Affective Reactions, Emotion, Vol. 9, No. 1, 123-127

Berns, G.S., McClure, S.M., Pagnoni, G., Montague, P.R. (2001). Predictability Modulates Human Brain Response to Reward, The Journal of Neuroscience, April 15, 2001, 21(8):2793–2798

Grupe, D.W., Nitschke, J.B. (2011). Uncertainty Is Associated With Biased Expectancies and Heightened Responses to Aversion, Emotion, Vol. 11, No. 2, 413–424

Lee, Y.H., Qiu, C., (2009). When Uncertainty Brings Pleasure: The Role of Prospect Imageability and Mental Imagery, Journal of Consumer Research, Vol. 36, No. 4, pp. 624-633

Wilson, T.D., Centerbar, D.B., Kermer, D.A., Gilbert, D.T. (2005). The Pleasures of Uncertainty: Prolonging Positive Moods in Ways People Do Not Anticipate, Journal of Personality and Social Psychology, Vol. 88(1), 5-21.

"Seeing" the Consumer-Brand Relationship:
How Relative Physical Position Influences Relationship Perceptions

Irene Xun Huang, The Chinese University of Hong Kong, Hong Kong
Xiuping Li, National University of Singapore, Singapore
Meng Zhang, The Chinese University of Hong Kong, Hong Kong

EXTENDED ABSTRACT

Consumers can form various relationships with brands similar to those that they form with other human beings (Aggarwal, 2004; Fournier, 1998). Despite the relevance and rich implications of brand relationship research, few studies to date have investigated the antecedent factors associated with different types of brand relationships. In this paper, we examine the possibility that the physical positioning of brands in relation to the customer influences brand relationship perception and brand evaluation. Specifically, we start this line of investigation by focusing on two kinds of relationships (brands as leaders, or as friends), and examining the effects of relative physical location (horizontal vs. vertical) and distance (close vs. distal) between a brand and its customer in print ads. We draw on the following two lines of research on metaphors to propose our theory.

Horizontal distance and social distance perception. Spatial distance has a direct influence on judgments of interpersonal connectedness and emotional attachment (Williams & Bargh, 2008; Zhang & Wang, 2009). This line of research suggests that there is a positive correlation between horizontal closeness and social closeness. The closer the horizontal distance between two individuals the stronger the intimacy felt between them. Indeed, in our daily languages, we tend to use "closest friend" to describe a person who cares about us the most, or with whom we have a mutually strong and enduring relationship.

Vertical positions and power perception. Studies from a different stream of research, however, show that vertical location is associated with power perception (Meier & Dionne, 2009; Schubert, 2005). For instance, Schubert (2005) finds that people tend to judge an animal (e.g., a wolf) as being more powerful if its picture is physically positioned in a higher place versus a lower place. In addition, there is a negative correlation between vertical closeness and power perception: the closer the vertical distance between a leader and his followers, the less the power inferred on the leader (Giessner & Schubert, 2007). Looking again at linguistic cues, we "look up" to a leader, and admire or are inspired by someone "above" ourselves.

Our proposition. Based on research on location metaphors, we make three predictions. First, we posit that consumers are more likely to represent relationships involving power differences (i.e., brand-as-a-leader; e.g., The Times "When the Times speaks, the World listens") in a vertical manner, and those involving no power differences (i.e., brand-as-a-friend; e.g., Hyundai "Always there for you") in a horizontal manner. Second, we hypothesize that for friend-like brands, physical closeness could lead to social closeness and intimacy, strengthening the relationship (Aaker, Fournier, & Brasel, 2004; Fournier, 1998). However, this dynamic might be reversed for leader-like brands. Finally, we predict that location metaphors will influence consumers' evaluations of brands. When promoting a new brand, if the promoted relationship matches its physical position (i.e., location and distance) relative to its customers, consumers will evaluate the brand more favorably, than when the promoted relationship mismatched physical position.

We tested our predictions in two experiments. In Experiment 1 (N=54), we collected 40 real ads: half of them had brand image and consumer image horizontally to each other, whereas the other half had the brand image being located "up" to the consumer image. Par-

ticipants viewed both groups of ads with the order of the group counterbalanced. They were asked to infer the kind of relationship that the brand has with its customers (i.e., as a leader or a friend). Their familiarity and attitudes towards each brand were included as covariates. As predicted, controlling for familiarity and prior attitudes, leader-like relationship was more frequently inferred by participants in the "up" group ($M = 8.89$) than in the "horizontal" group ($M = 7.44$; $F(1, 50) = 4.84, p < .05$); On the contrary, friend-like relationship was more frequently inferred in the "horizontal" group ($M = 11.11$) than in the "up" group ($M = 12.56$; $F(1, 50) = 4.84, p < .05$).

Experiment 2 (N=323) used a fictitious new watch brand, and had a 2(promoted relationship: leader, friend) × 2(position: up, right) × 2(distance: close, distant) between subject design. Participants were asked to view the ad carefully. The ad had a tagline, an image of customer in the center, and an image of a watch, either to the up, or to the right of the customer image. We manipulated the promoted relationship by different taglines of the ad (leader: "A leader always inspires you"; friend: "A friend you can trust". After viewing the ad, participants reported their evaluations of the brand. As expected, consumers evaluated the brand more favorably in the matched conditions. For leader-like brand, participants had the highest evaluation of it in the *up-distant* condition ($M = 5.43$), as compared to other conditions ($M_{up-close} = 4.70$; $M_{right-close} = 4.60$; $M_{right-distant} = 4.53$; $F(1, 315) = 8.45, p < .01$). For friend-like brand, participants expressed the most favorable attitudes toward it in the *right-close* condition ($M = 5.41$), as compared to all the other conditions of mismatch conditions ($M_{up-close} = 4.79$; $M_{up-distant} = 4.55$; $M_{right-distant} = 4.64$; $F(1, 315) = 8.22, p < .01$).

Taken together, results from our research provide new insights as to bring physical positioning metaphors – both relative location and relative distance – into the literature of consumer-brand relationships.

REFERENCES

Aaker, Jennifer, Susan Fournier, and S. Adam Brasel (2004), "When Good Brands Do Bad," *Journal of Consumer Research,* 31, 1-16.

Aggarwal, Pankaj and Ann L. McGill (2007), "Is That Car Smiling at Me? Schema Congruity as a Basis for Evaluating Anthropomorphized Products," *Journal of Consumer Research,* 34(4), 468-79.

Aron, Arthur, and Tracy McLaughlin-Volpe (2001), "Including Others in the Self: Extensions to Own and Partner's Group Memberships," In M. Brewer & C. Sedikides (Eds.), *Individual self, relational self, and collective self: Partners, opponents, or strangers* (pp. 89–108). Mahwah, NJ: Erlbaum.

Fournier, Susan (1998), "Consumers and Their Brands: Developing Relationship Theory in Consumer Research," *Journal of Consumer Research,* 24(4), 343-73.

Giessner, Steffen R., and Thomas W. Schubert (2007), "High in the Hierarchy: How Vertical Location and Judgments of Leaders' Power are Interrelated," *Organizational Behavior and Human Decision Processes,* 104, 30-44.

Lakoff, George and Mark Johnson (1980). *Metaphors we live by.* Chicago: University of Chicago Press.

Advances in Consumer Research
Volume 40, ©2012

Landau, Mark J., Brian P. Meier, and Lucas A. Keefer (2010), "A Metaphor-Enriched Social Cognition," *Psychological Bulletin,* 136, 1045-67.

Liberman, Nira, Yaacov Trope, and Elena Stephan (2007), "Psychological Distance," In E. T. Higgins & A. Kruglanski (Eds.), *Social psychology: Handbook of basic principles* (2nd ed.). New York: Guilford.

Meier, Brian P., and Sarah Dionne (2009), "Downright Sexy: Verticality, Implicit Power, and Perceived Physical Attractiveness," *Social Cognition,* 27(6), 883-92.

Schubert, Thomas W. (2005), "Your Highness: Vertical Positions as Perceptual Symbols of Power," *Journal of Personality and Social Psychology,* 89(1), 1-21.

Swaminathan, Vanitha, Karen L. Page, and Zeynep Gürhan-Canli (2007), "'My' Brand or 'Our' Brand: The Effects of Brand Relationship Dimensions and Self-Construal on Brand Evaluations," *Journal of Consumer Research*, 34, 248–59.

Williams, Lawrence E. and John A. Bargh (2008), "Keeping One's Distance: The Influence of Spatial Distance Cues on Affect and Evaluation," *Psychological Science,* 19(3), 302-8.

Zhang, Meng and Jing Wang (2009). "Psychological Distance Asymmetry: The spatial Dimension vs. Other Dimensions," *Journal of Consumer Psychology,* 19, 497-507.

Mere-Alignability of Alphanumeric Brand Names:
How Exposure To Mercedes C350 Affects The Choice Between BMW 335I and BMW 330I

Kunter Gunasti, University of Connecticut, USA
Berna Devezer, Michigan State University, USA

EXTENDED ABSTRACT

The use of numbers along with letters in brands—in other words, alphanumeric brand names (ABs) —became pervasive in many product categories (Boyd 1985). In a retail setting, consumers often encounter numbers not only as a part of attribute values (e.g., 10 vs. 14 megapixel resolution) but also as a part of brand names (e.g., Canon SD3500 and SD4500 cameras). While research on ABs has examined different types of associations between brands and attributes, the possibility that ABs themselves can function as independent attributes and get traded off has not been explored. Current research aims to address this gap, proposing three major contributions.

First, drawing on the numerology literature, we develop a *mere-alignability* hypothesis to explain how ABs can function as regular attributes—even when they do not convey meaningful product information—and get traded off against objectively diagnostic attributes. For instance, a choice between Canon SD3500 with14MP vs. Canon SD4500 with 10MP potentially involves brand-attribute tradeoffs. Second, we show that even mere exposure to merely aligned competitor ABs can affect the choices of focal ABs (e.g., exposure to Nikon S6000 affecting the choice between Canon SD4500 and SD3500). Lastly, we identify competitive categorization as a boundary condition for the mere-alignability effect such that only the ABs that are viewed as competitors affect the focal choices.

The processing of numbers requires a different type of knowledge compared to the processing of nonnumeric information. Dehaene (2001) refers to this as "number sense" and defines it as a combination of biologically, socially, and culturally developed knowledge that enables us to understand numbers. As a result, individuals can process numbers and compare their magnitudes almost effortlessly. ABs are semi-quantitative in nature and have a tendency to form trends; as a result, they can trigger consumers' number sense. We introduce the term *mere-alignability*, to refer to the conception that when exposed to multiple ABs that include easily comparable numbers (e.g., XC100, XK200), consumers engage in comparisons and tradeoffs among ABs as well as other numerical information.

If ABs function as regular product attributes due to their mere-alignability, well known context effects (e.g., compromise and attraction effects) should arise, leading consumers to give up higher attribute values in favor of ABs with higher numbers. These preference shifts occur when making a choice among options within the same brand as well as across competitor ABs, even when the options introduced in the context are not available for choice.

Categorization theories (e.g., Schwarz and Bless 1992) suggest that at least some type of similarity between two exemplars is needed in a decision making to group them together. Accordingly, we propose that consumers will engage in comparisons of ABs only if they are perceived as competitors. We tested our hypotheses with three empirical studies.

Study 1 examined how the mere-alignability of ABs leads attribute-brand tradeoffs resulting in preference shifts. The study involved a two-way between-subjects design where participants were presented with a choice task involving either a binary or a trinary choice set of e-readers of the same brand (i.e., Nook). Control conditions were given the same binary set which involved a tradeoff between the AB and the screen size (Table 1). Treatment conditions received a trinary set, which included an extreme third option. E-

reader B had a smaller screen than e-reader A and was the inferior option. Participants' choice for e-reader B doubled when it became a compromise option.

Table 1*
Study 1 - Compromise Effect – Choice Stimulus

	A	B	C
Attributes	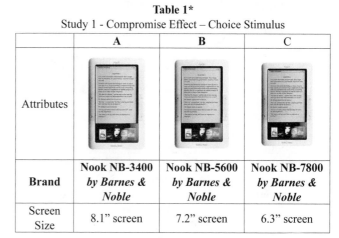		
Brand	**Nook NB-3400** *by Barnes & Noble*	**Nook NB-5600** *by Barnes & Noble*	**Nook NB-7800** *by Barnes & Noble*
Screen Size	8.1" screen	7.2" screen	6.3" screen

Study 2 – Competitor Brand Name Stimulus

	A	B	C
Attributes	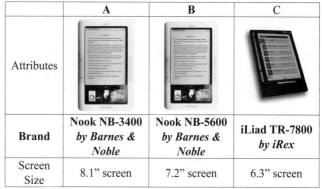		
Brand	**Nook NB-3400** *by Barnes & Noble*	**Nook NB-5600** *by Barnes & Noble*	**iLiad TR-7800** *by iRex*
Screen Size	8.1" screen	7.2" screen	6.3" screen

* **Various filler attributes including**: *Micro-USB 2.0 cable*, *AC adapter*, *Rechargeable battery*, **15 books** *Storage capacity, Wi-Fi (802.11 b/g)...etc. were also presented. Since these did not differ among the options, they are not shown in the above table.*

The letter labels are only presented in this table for ease of representation. In the actual experiments the options were presented in random order with no letter labels. The binary set consisted of options A and B depicted above and trinary sets also included options C or D.

Study 2 closely resembled study 1 with the exception that the third option in the treatment condition belonged to a competitor brand, iLiad (Table 1). We replicated the findings of study 1 within this across-brand context, where participants' preference for the inferior Nook option doubled when it became a compromise option.

Study 3 tested competitive categorization as the boundary condition for the mere-alignability effect. We used a one-way design with four conditions where participants were introduced to a used luxury sedan purchase scenario. The control condition consisted of a binary choice set of two Mercedes brands with different mileage (Table 2). In all three treatment conditions, a third, phantom AB was added to the choice set. This third option was a BMW 350i in the competitor brand condition, a Ford Explorer 350 in the non-competitor brand condition, and a Mercedes M350 in the non-competitor product condition (all established with pretests). In the competitor brand condition, exposure to BMW 350i significantly increased the choice of C340. On the other hand, in the non-competitive brand and non-competitor product conditions, the presence of the phantom option did not affect the choice of C340.

Table 2
Study 3 – Competitor and Non-Competitor Choice Sets

Focal Choices In The Binary Set – Control Condition

Brand-Model	Mercedes C340	Mercedes C330
Year	2008	2008
Transmission	Auto	Auto
Upholstery	Leather	Leather
Mileage	14,300 miles	12,900 miles
Options	Heated Seats	Heated Seats

Third Brand Options Included In Trinary Sets*

Competitor Brand	Non-Competitor Product by Same Brand	Non-Competitor Product by Different Brand
BMW 350i	Mercedes M350	Ford Explorer 350
OUT OF STOCK	*OUT OF STOCK*	*OUT OF STOCK*

* In each treatment condition one of these third options was added to the binary choice set. No Attribute information was shown for any of the third options - only the "OUT OF STOCK" label

Overall, these three studies show how and when ABs can be traded off against objective attribute values. In Study 1, we demonstrated that consumer preferences can be shifted easily through introducing new ABs in the choice context. Although the numbers had no diagnostic value, consumers treated them as regular attributes and engaged in AB–attribute tradeoffs that prompted normative violations. Second, Study 2 extended the mere-alignability effect to different competitor ABs by showing that consumers' mere exposure to competitor ABs affects their focal choices. Third, Study 4 revealed that preference shifts disappear when the nonfocal brand appears incomparable with the focal options, whether it represents a noncompetitive brand or a different product category, establishing competitive categorization as a boundary condition.

REFERENCES

Ang, Swee Hoon (1997), "Chinese Consumers' Perception of Alpha-Numeric Brand Names," *Journal of Consumer Marketing*, 14 (3), 220–33.

Ariely, Dan, George Loewenstein, and Drazen Prelec (2003), "Coherent Arbitrariness: Stable Demand Curves Without Stable Preferences", *Quarterly Journal of Economics*, 73-105.

Boyd, Colin W. (1985), "Point of View: Alpha-Numeric Brand Names," *Journal of Advertising Research*, 25 (5), 48–52.

Cacioppo, John T. and Richard E. Petty, (1982), "The need for cognition," *Journal of Personality and Social Psychology, 42*, 116–131.

Dehaene, Stanislas (1997). The number sense. New York: Oxford University Press.

_____ (2001), "Précis of The Number Sense", *Mind & Language*, 16 (1), February, 16-36.

Goldstein, E. Bruce (1999), *Sensation and Perception,* Pacific Grove, CA: Brooks/Cole.

Gunasti, Kunter and William T. Ross, Jr. (2010), "How and When Alphanumeric Brand Names Affect Consumer Preferences," *Journal of Marketing Research*, 47(December), 1177-92.

Hamilton, Ryan, Jiewen Hong, and Alexander Chernev (2007), "Perceptual Focus Effects in Choice," *Journal of Consumer Research*, 34 (August), 187-99.

Heath, Timothy B., Subimal Chatterjee, and Karen Russo France (1990), "Using the Phonemes of Brand Names to Symbolize Brand Attributes," in William Bearden and A. Parasuraman (eds.), *The AMA Educators' Proceedings: Enhancing Knowledge Development in Marketing*, Chicago: American Marketing Association.

Higgins, E. Tory, William S. Rholes, and Carl R. Jones, (1977), "Category Accessibility and Impression Formation," *Journal of Experimental Social Psychology*, 13, 141-154.

Hsee, Chritopher K., Yang Yang, Yangjie Gu, and Jie Chen (2009), "Specification seeking: How product specifications influence consumer preferences," *Journal of Consumer Research*, 35 (April), 952-66.

Huber, Joel, John Payne and Christopher Puto (1982), "Adding Asymmetrically Dominated Alternatives: Violations of Regularity and the Similarity Hypothesis," *Journal of Consumer Research*, 9 (June), 90-8.

Johnson, Michael D. (1984), "Consumer Choice Strategies for Comparing Noncomparable Alternatives," *Journal of Consumer Research*, 11 (December), 741-53.

_____ (1988), "Comparability and Hierarchical Processing in Multialternative Choice," *Journal of Consumer Research*, 15 (December), 303-14.

_____ (1989), "The Differential Processing of Product Category and Noncomparable Choice Alternatives," *Journal of Consumer Research*, 16 (December), 300-9.

Keller, Kevin L., Susan E. Heckler, and Michael J. Houston (1998), "The Effects of Brand Name Suggestiveness on Advertising Recall," *Journal of Marketing,* 62 (January), 48-57.

King, Dan and Chris Janiszewski (2011), "The Sources and Consequences of the Fluent Processing of Numbers, *Journal of Marketing Research*, 48 (April), 327-341.

Klink, Richard R. (2000), "Creating Brand Names With Meaning: The Use of Sound Symbolism," *Marketing Letters,* 11 (1), 5-20.

_____ (2003), "Creating Meaningful Brands: The Relationship between Brand Name and Brand Mark," *Marketing Letters*, 14 (3), 143-57.

_____ and Gerard A. Athaide (forthcoming), "Creating Brand Personality with Brand Names," *Marketing Letters*.

Maheswaran, Duaraj, Diane M. Mackie, and Shelly Chaiken (1992), "Brand Name as a Heuristic Cue: The Effects of Task Importance and Expectancy Confirmation on Consumer Judgments," *Journal of Consumer Psychology*, 1 (4), 317–36.

Markman, Arthur B. and Douglas Medin (1995), "Similarity and Alignment in Choice," *Organizational Behavior and Human Decision Making Processes*, 63 (August), 117–30.

McCabe, Deborah Brown, and Stephen Nowlis (2003), "The Effect of Examining Actual Products or Product Descriptions on Consumer Preference," *Journal of Consumer Psychology*, 13 (4), 431–39.

Medin, Douglas L. and Brian H. Ross (1992), Cognitive psychology. Fort Worth: Harcourt Brace Johanovich.

Nowlis, Stephen M. and Itamar Simonson (1997), "Attribute-Task Compatibility as a Determinant of Consumer Preference shifts," *Journal of Marketing Research*, 34 (May), 205-18.

Park, C. Whan and Daniel C. Smith (1989), "Product-Level Choice: A Top-Down or Bottom-Up Process?," *Journal of Consumer Research*, 16 (December), 289-99.

Pavia, Teresa A. and Janeen Arnold Costa (1993), "The Winning Number: Consumer Perceptions of Alpha-Numeric Brand Names," *Journal of Marketing*, 57 (July), 85–98.

Paul, Annie Murphy (2012), "10 Ideas: Your Head is in the Cloud," *Time Magazine,* (March 12), 64-65

Peterson, Robert A. and Ivan Ross (1972), "How to Name New Brands," *Journal of Advertising Research*, 12, (December), 29-34.

Richardson, Paul S., Alan S. Dick, and Arun K. Jain (1994), "Extrinsic and Intrinsic Cue Effects on Perceptions of Store Brand Quality," *Journal of Marketing,* 58 (October), 28-36.

Rosch, Eleanor (1978), "Principles of Categorization," in *Cognition and Categorization*, ed. Eleanor Rosch and Barbara B. Lloyd, Hillsdale, NJ: Erlbaum.

Russo, J. Edward and Barbara Dosher (1983), "Strategies for Multiattribute Binary Choice," *Journal of Experimental Psychology: Learning, Memory and Cognition*, 9 (4), 676-96.

Schwarz, Norbert and Herbert Bless (1992), "Constructing Reality and Its Alternatives: Assimilation and Contrast Effects" in Leonard L. Martin and Abraham Tesser (Eds.), *The Construction of Social Judgments*, Hillsdale, NJ: Lawrence Erlbaum Associates, 217-245.

Sen, Sankar (1999) "The Effects Of Brand Name Suggestiveness And Decision Goal On

The Development Of Brand Knowledge," Journal of Consumer Psychology, 8(4), 431-455

Simonson, Itamar and Amos Tversky (1992), "Choice in Context: Tradeoff Contrast and Extremeness Aversion," *Journal of Marketing Research*, 29 (August), 281–95.

Sullivan, Mary W. (1998), "How Brand Names Affect the Demand for Twin Automobiles," *Journal of Marketing Research,* 35 (May), 154-65.

Taylor, Shelley E. (1981), "A Categorization Approach to Stereotyping," in *Cognitive Processes in Stereotyping and Intergroup Behavior*, ed. David L. Hamilton, Hillsdale, NJ: Erlbaum, 88–114.

Tversky, A. & Kahneman, D. (1974), "Judgment under uncertainty: Heuristics and biases," *Science*, 185, 1124-1130.

Wänke, Michaela, Herbert Bless and Eric R. Igou (2001), "Next to a Star: Paling, Shining or Both? Turning Interexemplar Contrast Into Interexemplar Assimilation," *Personality and Social Psychology Bulletin*, 27, 14-29.

Yorkston, Eric and Geeta Menon (2004), "A Sound Idea: Phonetic Effects of Brand Names on Consumer Judgments," *Journal of Consumer Research,* 31 (June), 43-51.

Two-sided Messages for Health Risk Prevention:
The Role of Argument Type, Refutation and Issue Ambivalence

Erlinde Cornelis, Ghent University, Belgium
Veroline Cauberghe, Ghent University, Belgium
Patrick De Pelsmacker, University of Antwerp, Belgium

EXTENDED ABSTRACT

A variety of studies suggests that commercial advertising can include some negative information along with the positive product information, and still be more effective than when only positive information is provided (Crowley and Hoyer 1994; Pechmann 1992). For instance, when selling a product, it might pay off to also mention a few shortcomings (Eisend 2006). Such two-sided messages are found to generate attitudinal resistance to counter-persuasion (Kamins and Assael 1987).

However, the two-sided message strategy has not been tested in a reversed way (e.g., to prevent unhealthy behavior) (Eisend 2006). What if health prevention campaigns not only emphasize the negative aspects of, for instance, binge drinking, but also mention the perceived benefits of that behavior? Two experimental studies were set up to address this research gap. The effectiveness of two-sided anti binge drinking and anti marijuana messages was investigated in relation to argument type, refutation, and issue ambivalence.

Study 1 serves as a baseline study in which the principle of message sidedness (one- versus two-sided) is tested in combination with argument type (rational versus affective). Previous message sidedness literature mainly focused on rational arguments (Eisend 2007), neglecting the role of affective arguments, despite the importance of affect in consumer persuasion processes (Ray and Batra 1983; Pham 1998). Affective arguments are especially relevant for health issues, as affect plays a crucial role in health-related decisions (Agrawal, Menon, and Aaker 2007). The results of study 1 show that two-sided messages have superior effects on attitude toward the ad over one-sided messages, but only when the argument is affective (see figure 1). The reason is that affective arguments are more issue-relevant for consummatory motivated behavior (such as binge drinking) than rational arguments (Pham 1998; Ricciardelli, Williams, and Finemore 2001).

Figure 1: The Interaction Effect Between Message Sidedness and Argument Type on Attitude Toward the Message

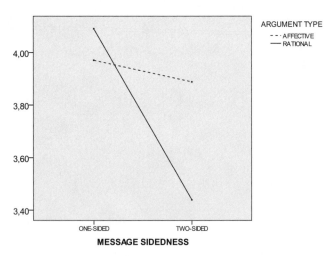

Study 2 therefore builds on the results of the first study by focusing solely on affective two-sided messages. In order to investigate two-sided messages more profoundly, a distinction is made between two different subtypes of two-sided messages: a refutational versus a non-refutational two-sided message. In a non-refutational two-sided message, advertisers simply present positive and negative information. In a refutational two-sided (commercial) message, advertisers subsequently refute or discount the negative information in an attempt to 'inoculate' the audience against possible counterclaims by competitors afterwards (Eisend 2007). In our study of binge drinking prevention, a two-sided refutational message would refute the positive argument (instead of the negative one), in order to bolster teenagers' attitudes when they are subsequently exposed to peer pressure. After receiving one of the two stimuli (a refutational or a non-refutational two-sided message), the participants were exposed to peer pressure. Peer pressure was conceptualized as a printed online chat conversation between two peers who explicitly promoted binge drinking.

Using a physiological analogy, inoculation theory (McGuire 1961) states that offering mild counterarguments in a message and afterwards refuting them enhances attitudes in the preferred direction (Eisend 2007). In immunology, to build resistance to a disease, people are often injected with a solution that contains a mild form of the disease itself (Etgar and Goodwin 1982). One of the main tenets of inoculation theory is the need for including a refutation of the counterargument(s) within the message (Crowley and Hoyer 1994). However, many researchers also found beneficial effects for two-sided advertising without refutation (Crowley and Hoyer 1994; Golden and Alpert 1987; Kamins and Assael 1987). These mixed findings indicate that refutation is not always necessary, but rather depends on certain moderating variables.

Study 2 explains the inconsistent findings of previous literature concerning the effectiveness of refutional versus non-refutational two-sided messages by including a moderating variable: issue ambivalence. The reason why some previous studies report no different effect for a refutational versus non-refutational two-sided message, could be due to the nature of the issue itself. For instance, the issue we used in study 1 (i.e., binge drinking) is not a very ambivalent issue in that most people would consider it as undesirable behavior. Binge drinking is characterized by strong contra-arguments and (relatively) weak pro-arguments, making it easy for individuals to mentally refute the pro-argument themselves. So, in the case of a unambivalent issue, refutation of the (weak) pro-argument within the message would offer little added value, as refutation can easily be done by the consumers themselves. Conversely, for a more ambivalent issue, characterized by relatively stronger pro-arguments besides the contra-arguments, it might be more difficult for consumers to mentally refute the pro-argument themselves. Consumers in an ambivalent condition need a stronger direction in the message (e.g., a refutational statement) in order to resolve the ambivalence (Zemborain and Johar 2007). Hence, in this case, refutation of the pro-argument within the message might be more necessary. We therefore expected to find a positive persuasive effect of refutational over the non-refutational two-sided message only when the topic is more ambivalent. Based on the results of a pretest, in which seventeen different issues were questioned within-subjects among 20 respondents, we selected marijuana use as an ambivalent issue and binge drinking as a unambivalent issue.

The results of study 2 reveal that for the ambivalent issue (marijuana use), refutation of the positive argument within the two-sided message is more effective than when the argument is not refuted. In other words, for an ambivalent issue, teenagers' attitudes toward the issue are significantly more negative when they were inoculated by a two-sided refutational message prior to exposure to peer pressure, than when they had received a two-sided non-refutational message before. In the case of the unambivalent issue (binge drinking), however, the results show that refutation is not necessary, hence, no different effect between the refutational and the non-refutational two-sided message was found for a unambivalent issue (see figure 2).

Figure 2: The Interaction Effect Between Refutation and Issue Ambivalence on Attitude Toward the Issue After Exposure to Peer Pressure

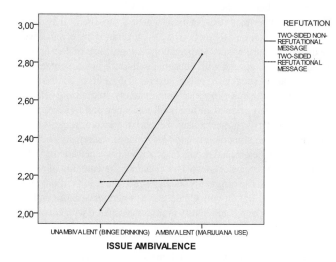

The theoretical added value of this research is threefold. First, it extends message sidedness literature to a health prevention context. Second, our study addresses not only rational, but also affective two-sided messages. Third, our research explains a gap in message sidedness literature by addressing the effect of a crucial moderator, namely issue ambivalence, on the impact of refutational versus non-refutational two-sided messages.

REFERENCES

Agrawal, Nidhi, Geeta Menon, and Jennifer L. Aaker (2007), "Getting Emotional About Health," *Journal of Marketing Research*, 64 (1), 100-13.

Crowley, Ayn E. and Wayne D. Hoyer (1994), "An Integrative Framework for Understanding Two-sided Persuasion," *Journal of Consumer Research*, 20 (4), 561-74.

Eisend, Martin (2006), "Two-sided Advertising: A Meta-analysis," *International Journal of Research in Marketing*, 23 (2), 187-98.

Eisend, Martin (2007), "Understanding Two-sided Persuasion: An Empirical Assessment of Theoretical Approaches," *Psychology and Marketing,* 24 (7), 615–40.

Etgar, Michael and Stephen A. Goodwin (1982), "One-sided versus Two-sided Comparative Message Appeals for New Brand Introductions," *Journal of Consumer Research*, 8 (4), 460-65.

Golden, Linda L. and Mark I. Alpert (1987), "Comparative Analysis of the Relative Effectiveness of One-and Two-sided Communication for Contrasting Products," *Journal of Advertising,* 16 (1), 18-25.

Kamins, Michael A. and Henry Assael (1987), "Two-sided versus One-sided appeals: A Cognitive Perspective on Argumentation, Source Derogation, and the Effect of Disconfirming Trial on Belief Change," *Journal of Marketing Research*, 24 (1), 29–39.

McGuire, William J. (1961), "Resistance to Persuasion Conferred by Active and Passive Prior Refutation of the Same and Alternative Counterarguments," *Journal of Abnormal and Social Psychology*, 63, 326-32.

Pechmann, Cornelia (1992), "Predicting When Two-sided Ads will be More Effective than One-sided Ads: The Role of Correlational and Correspondent Inferences," *Journal of Marketing Research,* 29 (November), 441-53.

Pham, Michel T. (1998), "Representativeness, Relevance, and the Use of Feelings in Decision Making", *Journal of Consumer Research*, 25 (2), 144-59.

Ray, Michael L. and Rajeev Batra (1983), "Emotion and Persuasion in Advertising: What We Do & Don't Know About Affect," *Advances In Consumer Research*, 10 (1), 543-8.

Ricciardelli, Line A., Robert J. Williams, Jennifer Finemore (2001), "Restraint as misregulation in drinking and eating", *Addictive Behaviors,* 26 (5), 665-75.

Zemborain, Martin R. and Johar Gita Venkataramani (2007), "Attitudinal ambivalence and openness to persuasion: A framework for interpersonal influences," *Journal of Consumer Research*, 33 (4), 506-15.

Decrease or Enhance?
Assessment of the Effect of Shanzhai on the Original Products

Liangyan Wang, Shanghai Jiao Tong University, Shanghai
Cornelia Pechmann, University of California, USA
Yitong Wang, Tsinghua University, Beijing

EXTENDED ABSTRACT

As a term connoting copycat manufacturing, "Shanzhai" has become a significant market phenomenon in many economies. Shanzhai has grown into a major industry segment in China. The number of people involved in the Shanzhai industry is estimated to be up to one million, and the annual total capital flow can reach as much as 100 billion yuan (Zhu and Shi 2010).

Shanzhai products are indeed based on imitation, which is an infringement of copyright to some extent. However, putting legal issues aside, the ubiquity of Shanzhai products in the market deserves attention. Investigating the effect of Shanzhai products on the original products from a consumers' perspective will benefit both marketers and manufacturers. The expected effect of Shanzhai on incumbent business players in mature industries is almost one-sided: companies with famous brands worry that imitators will eat up their market share and cause huge losses in profits. This issue is frequently discussed in the media, but surprisingly, there is scant academic research on it especially from the perspective of consumer behavior. The existing research examines this phenomenon either from a sociological or from an anthropological point of view, and the results are mostly qualitative. There has been a lack of research on the role that Shanzhai products play in consumers' perceptions and evaluations of leading brands.

Attempting to fill the gap from consumers' perspective, our study aims to examine the effect of Shanzhai on original products in China. Specifically, by applying and extending the General Evaluability Theory (Hsee 1996; Hsee and Leclerc 1998; Nowlis and Simonson 1997; Hsee and Zhang 2010) and the Expectancy Disconfirmation Model of Satisfaction (Wirtz and Bateson 1999; Spreng, MacKenzie and Olshavsky 1996), we address the following questions using both laboratory and field experiments: Do Shanzhai products have a positive or negative effect on the original products? Are there variables moderating this effect? Finally, what underlying mechanism accounts for this effect?

The General Evaluability Theory predicts that, apart from noticing the categorical differences (i.e., Shanzhai vs. Original, in our case), people will be more sensitive to the incremental differences (i.e., low-quality vs. high-quality differences, in our case) in the joint evaluation mode. Therefore, the juxtaposition of a low-quality Shanzhai product and the original product should make the quality difference more salient, thus increasing the evaluation of and the intent to purchase the original products, and indicating a contrast effect. The Expectancy Disconfirmation Model of Satisfaction focuses on the process of evaluation and emphasizes the comparison between attribute-based expectations and perceived performance, which is also called expectations congruency (Wirtz and Bateson 1999; Spreng, MacKenzie and Olshavsky 1996). Thus when Shanzhai and the original products are juxtaposed, the quality of Shanzhai product matters and serves as a baseline or starting point for people to form their expected performance of the original product. Viewing and evaluating high-quality Shanzhai may unintentionally lead consumers to expect the performance of the original product to be above the actual level of performance. Subsequently, the original product performs at the actual level but falls short of their inflated expectations. Thus, consumers would likely be less satisfied with their overall experience with the original product than if they had not been shown and allowed to view and evaluate the high-quality Shanzhai (i.e., single evaluation mode). Accordingly, we propose that the quality level of Shanzhai may moderate the effect of Shanzhai products on the original products, and the expectations congruency toward the original may mediate the effects of Shanzhai quality level on the original products.

In Experiment 1, we found that compared with the single evaluation of the original, the joint presence of low-quality Shanzhai and the original enhanced consumers' evaluation of and intent to purchase the original. In Experiment 2, which was conducted among real consumers, we replicated the findings in Experiment 1 with low-quality Shanzhai (Experiment 2a) and found that the pattern observed earlier reversed with the comparison of the high-quality Shanzhai (Experiment 2b). In Experiment 3, we found that the effects of Shanzhai on satisfaction and evaluation of the original were mediated by participants' expectations congruency of the original when it was juxtaposed with Shanzhai with differing quality levels.

We have sought to make several substantive contributions through this research. First, we quantitatively studied the effect of Shanzhai on the original in terms of consumer preference and explored its underlying mechanism. Second, the results suggest that if there is no contrasting quality and performance discrepancy between Shanzhai and the original products, Shanzhai has a detrimental effect on the original because it decreases consumers' evaluation of and intent to purchase the original products. Third, the results of our study indirectly help explain why Chinese consumers have more enthusiasm for leading brand and luxury products compared with consumers from western countries where Shanzhai or counterfeits are not available, aside from the existing explanation of status signaling (Han, Nunes and Drèze 2010) and social motivations (Wilcox et al. 2009).

ACKNOWLEDGEMENT:

This research was funded by the National Natural Science Foundation of China Grant (71072059), the Ministry of Education of China Grant (09YJC630156) and PuJiang Science and Technology Program Grant (10PJC060) to Liangyan Wang.

REFERENCES

Han, Young Jee, Joseph C. Nunes, Xavier Drèze (2010), "Signaling Status with Luxury Goods: The Role of Brand Prominence," *Journal of Marketing*, 74(4), 15-30.

Hsee, Chrisopher K. (1996), "The Evaluability Hypothesis: An Explanation for Preference Reversals Between Joint and Separate Evaluations of Alternatives," *Organizational Behavior and Human Decision Processes*, 67 (3), 247-57.

Hsee, Christopher K. and Jiao Zhang (2010), "General Evaluability Theory," *Perspectives on Psychological Science*, 5 (4), 343-55.

Hsee, C. K. & Leclerc, F. (1998), "Will products look more attractive when evaluated jointly or when evaluated separately?" *Journal of Consumer Research*, 25, 175-186.

Nowlis, Stephen M. and Itamar Simonson (1997), "Attribute-Task Compatibility as a Determinant of Consumer Preference Reversals," *Journal of Marketing Research*, 34 (2), 205-18.

Spreng, Richard A., Scott B. MacKenzie and Richard W. Olshavsky (1996), "A Reexamination of the Determinants of Consumer Satisfaction," *Journal of Marketing*, 60(July), 15-32.

Wilcox, Keith, Hyeong Min Kim, Sankar Sen (2009), "Why Do Consumers Buy Counterfeit Luxury Brands?" *Journal of Marketing Research*, 247-59.

Wirtz, Jochen. and John, E. Bateson (1999), "Consumer Satisfaction with Services: Integrating the Environment Perspective in Services Marketing Into the Traditional Disconfirmation Paradigm," *Journal of Business Research*, 44(1), 55-66.

Zhu, Sheng and Yongjiang Shi (2010), "Shanzhai Manufacturing - An Alternative Innovation Phenomenon in China: Its Value Chain and Implications for Chinese Science And Technology Policies", *Journal of Science and Technology Policy in China*, 1(1), 29-49.

Actors Conform, Observers Counteract:
The Effects of Interpersonal Synchrony on Conformity

Xianchi Dai, The Chinese University of Hong Kong, Hong Kong
Ping Dong, University of Toronto, Canada
Robert S. Wyer Jr., The Chinese University of Hong Kong, Hong Kong

EXTENDED ABSTRACT

Synchrony is an integral part of our daily life: chorus, dancing, and marching are just a few examples that we experience or see every day. Given the ubiquity of these behaviors, it is surprising that little is known about how synchrony may affect consumers' judgments and decisions. Our research shows that not only engaging in this behavior but also observing it can influence people's later judgments in quite unrelated choice domains. Moreover, the effects of actual and observed behavior can often be diametrically opposite.

Our conceptualization of these effects distinguishes between (a) the cognitions that govern behavior and (b) the motivation that is elicited as a result of performing or observing it. Performing goal-directed behavior can activate concepts that, once accessible in memory, elicit conceptually similar behavior in a later situation (Wyer, Xu, and Shen 2012). Prior research has documented that interpersonal synchrony can give rise to a sense of group cohesiveness (Ehrenreich 2006; see also Haidt 2007; Haidt, Seder, and Kasebir 2008), stronger cooperation and greater social attachment in later situations even at the expense of monetary rewards (Hove and Risen 2009; Wiltermuth and Heath 2009). To this extent, actively engaging in synchronous behavior may activate more general concepts associated with behaving like others and that these concepts might influence the likelihood of conforming to others' behavior in a later situation.

At the same time, however, individuals who are consciously aware of the requirement to copy others' actions might often feel that their freedom of behavior is restricted and experience psychological reactance (Brehm 1966). Thus, they may attempt to assert their freedom by making judgments and decisions that deviate from others' and confirm their uniqueness and individuality. For instance, Andreoli, Worchel and Folger (1974) showed that after seeing another person's freedom being restricted, participants' ratings of the desirability of normatively popular stimuli declined. This was true regardless of whether the observers expected to interact with the person who imposed the threat, the person who was threatened, or neither. We therefore expected that in the conditions we investigated, observers of interpersonal synchrony would experience threat to their freedom and that the reactance induced by this threat would decrease their disposition to conform to others' preferences in a product choice task.

These cognitive and motivational factors could both exert an influence and their effects on conformity could partially offset one another. However, the relative impact of these factors may differ. This difference is suggested in part by research on actor-observer differences in attributions and judgment (Jones and Nisbett 1971; for a review, see Fiske and Taylor 1991). Moreover, the differences in actor and observer perspectives could influence other things, including the intensity of emotions (Hung and Mukhopadhyay 2011), the reliance on concrete versus abstract information (Yan and Sengupta 2011) and expectations for a service encounter (Cowley 2005). In the present context, actors who engage in synchronous behavior are likely to focus their attention primarily on the goal toward which their behavior is directed (i.e., matching the actions of others). To this extent, general concepts associated with this goal may become salient and influence later behavior for reasons suggested by Wyer et al. (2012). In contrast, observers' attention may be directed primarily to the actors' behavior per se (Nisbett and Wilson 1977). Conse-quently, observers may be relatively more sensitive to the restrictions on freedom exemplified by this behavior than to the goal to which the behavior is directed and may be more likely to experience reactance.

We conducted four studies to examine these predictions and the underlying mechanisms. In Study 1, participants either first engaged in, or first saw others engage in synchronous or non-synchronous exercise, and then were asked to make brand choice for several product categories. Consistent with our prediction, participants were more likely to conform to others' preferences in a product choice task after engaging in synchronous behavior than after behaving non-synchronously, whereas observers of this behavior were less likely to conform to others' product choices when the behavior they observed was synchronous than when it was not. In Study 2, actors in some conditions were given a free choice over whether to perform the behavior or not, and this choice was made salient to observers. As expected, giving actors freedom to choose whether to engage in synchronous behavior increased both actors' and observers' conformity relative to conditions in which actors were required to perform the behavior. Also, we found that situational reactance mediated the effect of choice freedom on conformity.

Studies 3 and 4 evaluated further implications of our conceptualization. In Study 3, actors were told that they would compete with other groups for a reward to be given to the group that was most successful in behaving synchronously. Moreover, in some conditions, observers were told that they would share the reward with the actors, thus tying their own outcomes to the actors' success. In other conditions, observers believed that their reward would be independent of the actors' success. Results in this study showed that stimulating observers to imagine that the persons they observed were in-group members, which increased their sensitivity to the restrictions imposed on their behavior, decreased their likelihood of donating to unique charity organizations in a subsequent unrelated donation task. Study 4 showed that stimulating actors to anticipate engaging in synchronous behavior rather than actually doing so, thus inducing them to imagine the behavior from the perspective of an observer, decreased their conformity relative to conditions in which they actually performed the behavior. In combination, the four studies provided converging evidence for the dual effects of interpersonal synchrony that we proposed.

This research, to our best knowledge, is the first to test the implications of engaging and observing synchronous behavior on individuals' disposition to subscribe to popular courses of actions in the context of consumer choice. In addition, our paper shows that cognitive processes, such as mindset, can interact with motivational processes (e.g., reactance) to jointly affect subsequent unrelated behaviors. These results suggest the importance of considering the relative impact of cognition and motivation in studying consumer behavior.

REFERENCES

Andreoli, Virginia A., Worchel Stephen, and Folger Robert (1974), "Implied Threat to Behavioral Freedom," *Journal of Personality and Social Psychology*, 30 (6), 765-71.

Brehm, Jack W. (1966), *A Theory of Psychological Reactance*, Academic Press.

Cowley, Elizabeth (2005), "Views From Consumers Next in Line: The Fundamental Attribution Error in a Service Setting", *Journal of the Academy of Marketing Science*, 33 (2), 139-52.

Ehrenreich, Barbara (2006), *Dancing in the Streets: A History of Collective Joy*, New York: Metropolitan.

Fiske, Susan T. and Shelley E. Taylor (1991), *Social Cognition* (2nd ed.), New York: McGraw-Hill.

Haidt, Jonathan (2007), "The New Synthesis in Moral Psychology," *Science*, 316, 998–1002.

Haidt, Jonathan, J. Patrick Seder, and Selin Kesebir (2008), "Hive Psychology, Happiness, and Public Policy," *Journal of Legal Studies*, 37, S133-S156.

Hove, Michael J. and Jane L. Risen (2009), "It's All in the Timing: Interpersonal Synchrony Increases Affiliation," *Social Cognition*, 27, 949-61.

Hung, Iris W. and Anirban Mukhopadhyay (2011), "Lenses of the Heart: How Actors' and Observers' Perspectives Influence Emotional Experiences," *Journal of Consumer Research*, forthcoming.

Jones, Edward E. and Richard E. Nisbett (1971), *The Actor and the Observer: Divergent Perceptions of the Causes of Behavior*, New York: General Learning Press.

Nisbett, Richard E. and Timothy D. Wilson (1977), "Telling More than We Can Know: Verbal Reports on Mental Processes," *Psychological Review*, 84 (3), 231–59.

Wiltermuth, Scott S. and Chip Heath (2009), "Synchrony and Cooperation," *Psychological Science*, 20 (1), 1-5.

Wyer, Robert S., Alison Jing Xu, and Hao Shen (2012), "The Effects of Past Behavior on Future Goal-Directed Activity," In *Advances in Experimental Social Psychology*, ed. Mark P. Zanna and James M. Olson, Vol. 46, San Diego, CA.: Academic Press.

Yan, Dengfeng and Jaideep Sengupta (2011), "Effects of Construal Level on the Price-Quality Relationship," *Journal of Consumer Research*, 38 (2), 376-89.

Intertwined Destinies: How Subsistence Entrepreneurs and Consumers Harness Social Capital to Overcome Constraints and Uncertainties

Srinivas Venugopal, University of Illinois at Urbana-Champaign, USA
Madhu Viswanathan, University of Illinois at Urbana-Champaign, USA
Raj Echambadi, University of Illinois at Urbana-Champaign, USA
Srinivas Sridharan, Monash University, Australia

EXTENDED ABSTRACT

Consumer research has significant potential for contributing unique insights into the human experience of poverty and mechanisms for poverty alleviation (Chakravarthi, 2006). Reaching this potential, however, will require CB research to explore some of the distinct and unique consumption experiences that occur in the lives of the poor. One such phenomenon is the duality of consuming and engaging in entrepreneurial activity, both with the goal of survival. The consumption-entrepreneurship interface is inadequately explored in the consumer literature, especially in contexts of poverty. Entrepreneurship involves the detailed study of the sources and exploitation of entrepreneurial opportunities and the set of individuals who discover, evaluate, and exploit them (Shane and Venkataraman, 2000). Despite the burgeoning body of research in entrepreneurship, the study of entrepreneurial action in poverty contexts has received limited attention. Consequently, little is known theoretically regarding the entrepreneurial process in these contexts (Webb et al., 2009). In this article, we attempt to fill this gap by focusing on subsistence entrepreneurs, also referred to as subsistence consumer-merchants, who operate within the informal economy (Viswanathan et al., 2010). Subsistence entrepreneurs are those who a) live in poverty themselves, b) are embedded within the social milieu of their customers and c) engage in entrepreneurial action with the goal of economic survival (Viswanathan et al., 2010). Past literature brings to light the duality of roles of subsistence entrepreneurs. Viswanathan and colleagues (2010) maintain that, in subsistence contexts, the consumer and entrepreneur roles are two sides of the same coin. Further, the subsistence entrepreneur is seen as being a hub of an interdependent and self-sustaining system of relationships with vendors, consumers and family members (Viswanathan et al., 2010). We draw from this systemic view of the subsistence entrepreneur's relational ecosystem and focus specifically on the entrepreneur-consumer dyad. We employ a nuanced view of social capital, namely, structural, relational and cognitive social capital as a theoretical lens. We use this theoretical lens to explain the mechanisms thorough which the subsistence entrepreneur-consumer dyad harnesses different dimensions of social capital to overcome constraints and uncertainty and co-create unique value in contexts of poverty.

Figure 1: Model

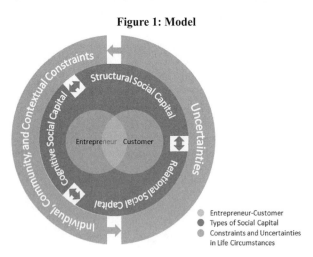

- Entrepreneur-Customer
- Types of Social Capital
- Constraints and Uncertainties in Life Circumstances

Our field research was conducted in Chennai, South India. We conducted 11 in-depth interviews, beginning with informant's life circumstances and then focusing on consumer and entrepreneurial activities (see Moustakas, 1994). Interviews were analyzed in accordance with guidelines for constructing grounded theory (Goulding, 1998).

Life in poverty is marked by constraints and uncertainty at multiple levels. As reviewed, individual-level constraints include low literacy and low income. Community level constraints include such factors as limits to interactions and opportunities across gender lines or social hierarchies, the lack of recourse in the face of exploitation by more powerful community members. Further, subsistence individuals face larger environmental-level constraints relating to physical infrastructure, institutional mechanisms, and labor and capital markets (Khanna and Palepu, 2005). Constraints at multiple levels contribute to a mix of uncertainties that leave individuals vulnerable. In the face of poverty and limited survival prospects, entrepreneurial action is seen as the primary source of earning income, thereby managing uncertainty and ensuring immediate survival.

Despite extreme constraints, subsistence entrepreneurs survive and overcome daunting challenges and possess both strengths and vulnerabilities to navigate these trying environments. Entrepreneurs are "experts" at survival but, at the same time, they are also constrained at individual and marketplace levels. Learning about the marketplace stems from face-to-face interactions between buyers and sellers. Sharing adversity and empathizing with each other leads to greater understanding of the two roles. Interestingly, these relationships with consumers help entrepreneurs learn about and navigate the marketplace. In the following section, we highlight how the entrepreneur-consumer dyad harnesses cognitive, relational and structural social capital to co-create mutual value.

The cognitive dimension, i.e. shared life circumstances and common life goals, forms the platform for the development of social capital. Both the entrepreneurs and their customers live in poverty and hence the level of empathy for one another's life circumstances is inordinately high (Viswanathan et al., 2009). Subsistence entrepreneurs share adversity with their customers and they tend to identify with each other being members of the same group, as noted in literature in other contexts (Tajfel, 1982). They tend to possess a shared narrative of living and subsisting in poverty which enables them to comprehend, process, and exchange rich sets of deeper meanings that literature in other contexts has highlighted (Nisbet, 1969). Both entrepreneurs and their customers perceive themselves to be part of a larger community and hence are both bound by community-level expectations, norms, and obligations to help each other in times of need.

Owing to the nature of, and the frequency, of interactions between the entrepreneurs and the customers, trust is developed which, in turn, leads to commitment to each other (Morgan and Hunt, 1992) and enduring relationships. Trust becomes the mechanism by which entrepreneurs and their customers become open and willing to share information, co-operate, and invest in each other. Trust is a by-product of the interactional environment that has been characterized as having enduring relationships and being empathetic (Viswanathan et al., 2011). Relational social capital emphasizes the primary purpose of subsistence entrepreneurship, i.e. to survive at a basic human level and to help "similar" others. Over time, the history of repeated fruitful interactions begets more trust and renewed commitment thereby leading to enhanced levels of social capital.

Subsistence entrepreneurs live in close proximity with their customers and their lives are interdependent. Interdependence marks social ties between entrepreneurs and their customers and reflects structural social capital referred to as the "impersonal configuration of linkages between people" (Nahapiet and Ghoshal, 1998; p244). As physical proximity is positively related to greater interpersonal communications (Ganesan et al., 2005), by virtue of being in the same community, subsistence entrepreneurs and their customers can engage in frequent face-to-face communications. Information benefits occur to these subsistence entrepreneurs in all three forms of access, timing, and referrals (Burt, 1992). Apart from the access and timing benefits that arise of these embedded social connections, these rich relationships also provide referral opportunities to other customers within the same community.

REFERENCES

Burt, R. S., 1992. Structural holes: The social structure of competition. Cambridge, MA: Harvard University Press.

Corbin, J., Strauss, A., 2008. Basics of qualitative research. Sage, Los Angeles, CA.

Ganesan, S., Malter, A.J., Rindfleisch, A., 2005. Does Distance Still Matter? Geographic Proximity and New Product Development. Journal of Marketing, 69 (October), 44-60.

Goulding, C., 1998. Grounded theory: the missing methodology on the interpretivist agenda. Qualitative Marketing Research: An International Journal, Vol. 1 No. 1, pp. 50-7.

Khanna, T., Palepu, K.G., 2005. The evolution of concentrated ownership in India: broad patterns and the history of the Indian software industry, in Randall Morck (ed.) The History of Concentrated Corporate Ownership, NBER, University of Chicago Press, pp 283-324.

Morgan, R.M., Hunt, S.D., 1994. The commitment-trust theory of relationship marketing. Journal of Marketing, Vol. 58, July, pp. 20-38.

Moustakas, C., 1994. Phenomenological research methods. Thousand Oaks, CA: Sage.

Nahapiet, J., Ghoshal, S., 1998. Social capital, intellectual capital, and the organizational advantage. Academy of Management Review, 23: 242-266.

Nisbet, R. A., 1969. Social Change and History. New York: Oxford University Press.

Shane, S., Venkataraman, S., 2000. The promise of entrepreneurship as a field of research. Academy of Management Review 25(1):217-226.

Tajfel, H., 1982. Instrumentality, identity and social comparisons. In H. Tajfel (Ed.), Social identity and intergroup relations (pp. 483-507). Cambridge, England: Cambridge University Press.

Viswanathan, M., Sridharan, S., Gau, R., Ritchie, R., 2009. Designing Marketplace Literacy Education in Resource-Constrained Contexts: Implications for Public Policy and Marketing. Journal of Public Policy and Marketing, 28 (1), 85–94.

Viswanathan, M., Rosa, J.A., Ruth, J., 2010. Exchanges in Marketing Systems: The Case of Subsistence Consumer Merchants in Chennai, India, Journal of Marketing, 74 (May), 1-18.

Viswanathan, M., Sridharan, S., Ritchie, R., Venugopal, S., Jung, K., 2011. Marketing Interactions in Subsistence Marketplaces: A Bottom-Up Approach to Designing Public Policy, Forthcoming.

Webb, J., Tihanyi, L., Ireland, D., & Sirmon, D. 2009. You say illegal, I say legitimate: Entrepreneurship in the informal economy. Academy of Management Review, 34(3), 492–510.

The Product-agnosia Effect: How Increased Visual Scrutiny Reduces Distinctiveness

Jayson Jia, Stanford University, USA
Sanjay Rao, Stanford University, USA
Baba Shiv, Stanford University, USA

EXTENDED ABSTRACT

A picture is said to be worth a thousand words. But does that mean two pictures are worth two thousand words? And what about seven pictures? Situations abound where consumer decisions are based on visual appeal, whether we are looking at cars, shoes, or birthday cakes. When comparing objects visually, our intuition suggests that more visual scrutiny should aid information processing. However, this simple intuition does not consider the possibility that acquiring more visual information may alter the structure and style of visual information processing – with potentially detrimental effects. Thus, looking more can end up yielding less if it changes *how* we look.

Specifically, increased viewing of choice objects leads to more local-level processing and less global-level processing. Since products are often distinguished through global-level features such as style and brand, increased focus on a product's local-level features can result in a relative decline in uniqueness and attractiveness. Conceptually, such a shift in perceptual focus is akin to comparing brush strokes in a painting rather than the overall picture, or contrasting individual trees instead of entire forests. Across four studies, we explored how more visual exposures can generate product-agnosia (the loss of ability to distinguish between products) through shifts in perceptual focus.

STUDY 1

To demonstrate the basic effect, participants (n=105) in Study 1 were randomly assigned to one of three conditions to evaluate two pairs of shoes. In the single picture condition, subjects were exposed to one picture of each shoe. In the multiple-repeated picture condition, subjects were exposed to seven of the same picture of each shoe. In the multiple-unique picture condition, subjects were exposed to seven unique pictures of each shoe (see Figure 1). To simulate a real purchasing context, the pictures were obtained from a leading online retailer (zappos.com), which like many other retail websites has the option of viewing more pictures of products from "additional views".

We found that similarity ratings of the shoes were higher in the multiple-unique picture condition than in the single and multiple-repeated picture conditions ($p < .05$). There was no significant difference between the single and multiple-repeated picture conditions. In other words, the products became relatively less distinct after multiple visual scrutiny to new visual images.

STUDY 2

Study 2 expanded the findings of Study 1 to another product category (duffel bags) and contained a thought listing task to explore the mechanism driving product-agnosia. Participants (n=102) were randomly assigned to the single-picture or multiple-picture condition using the same experimental paradigm as Study 1. At the end of the survey, participants were also asked to list their thoughts about the products presented. The thoughts were coded for perceptual focus (local vs. global-level) by two independent coders (alpha = .98).

Consistent with Study 1, we found that perceptions of product uniqueness ($p < .05$) and predicted liking ($p < .1$) was lower in the multiple picture condition. The thought listing task showed a higher proportion of local-level thoughts ($p < .05$) in the multiple exposure condition, and no difference in total number of thoughts between the two conditions ($p = .39$). Thus, in addition to providing a further demonstration of the main effect, Study 2 yielded evidence that increased visual exposure can lead to a shift to more local and less global –level processing

STUDY 3

In Study 3, we demonstrated the causal link between local and global –level processing and the product-agnosia effect by directly manipulating perceptual scope using a 2 (global, local processing) X 2 (single, multiple visual exposures) ANOVA design. In Part 1, we induced global versus local processing using a procedure similar to Friedman et al (2003). Participants (n = 124) were shown seven maps of different American states sequentially, each on a different page. In the global condition, subjects were asked to look at the overall features of each state map, whereas in the local condition, subjects were asked to focus their attention on a marker that pointed to a city near the center of the map. In Part 2, we used the same single versus multiple exposures experimental paradigm as in Study 1 (as well as the same products and images).

We found significant interactions for perceptions of uniqueness (Figure 2), attention-grabbing, predicted liking, and choice strategy (p's < .05). Under induced- local processing, increased visual exposures resulted in an analogous pattern of results as Study 1, where the shoes became less distinct, attention-grabbing, and attractive, and participants were less likely to engage in a global-level choice strategy ('focus on style'). But under induced global processing, we found the opposite trend, and that increased visual exposures resulted in the shoes being rated as more distinct, attention-grabbing, and attractive, and a global-level choice strategy was more prevalent.

STUDY 4

In Study 4 (n = 84), we found an analogous reversal of the product-agnosia effect under different memory conditions. The intuition for such an effect is that when evaluating from memory, we recall gestalt (global) features more than details (local). Under stimulus-evaluations (not memory based), we find that the multiple picture condition induces product-agnosia (less distinctiveness, lower willingness to pay, p's < .05). However, under recall-evaluation (memory based), we find that the multiple picture condition increases perceived distinctiveness and willingness to pay (Figure 3, Figure 4, p's < .05).

Overall, the persistence of the effect after inducing local processing but its reversal after inducing global processing provides evidence that the product-agnosia effect is driven by perceptual scope. When one's perceptual scope is local and focused on narrow details, new information through multiple observations were disadvantageous for ratings of distinctiveness and predicted liking. However, when one takes a metaphorical step back under global processing, increased visual exposures begin to have benefits for a product's perceived distinctiveness and predicted liking. These effects have numerous implications for marketing strategy, product positioning, and optimal consideration set construction: For example, generic or entry brands may seek to induce product-agnosia to better compete with premium brands, while brands that desire to maintain unique positioning would do best to carefully manage the perceptual scope of their own advertising.

Exploding Turkeys and Shattered Reporters:
Comparative Ads and Their Unintended Affective Consequences

Ozge Yucel-Aybat, Pennsylvania State University at Harrisburg, USA
Thomas Kramer, University of South Carolina, USA

EXTENDED ABSTRACT

Comparative ads, in which marketers "identify their competitors directly or by clear implication," are becoming more popular in media (Roggeveen, Grewal and Gotlieb 2006). Frequently, when marketers compare their brands to others, they show comical situations in which misfortunes befall those consumers who are using competitors' brands instead of theirs. For instance, in AT&T's "Exploding Turkey" commercial, we see a house destroyed by an exploding deep-fried turkey since the owner who did not have AT&T service could not be reached on time to be notified of the danger. In another commercial, misfortunes befall reporters, who do not have AT&T service and could not be warned that they were standing in a blast zone. We propose that when marketers show unfortunate events happening because of using the wrong or a competitor's product, they may incidentally invoke "schadenfreude," defined as a malicious pleasure at the misfortunes of others, which in turn will impact consumers' purchase intentions and attitudes.

Comparative (vs. noncomparative) ads have been shown to generate positive consumer responses (Grewal et al. 1997). Moderators, such as comparative valence of framing (Jain et al. 2007) and consumer-related variables such as need for cognition (Polyorat and Alden 2005) have been identified. Surprisingly, research to date has examined the impact of comparative ad appeals without taking consumers' affective reactions into account. However, persuasive messages used in advertisements have been shown to elicit affective reactions that may mediate consumers' attitudes and behaviors (Holbrook and Batra 1987). Schadenfreude appears particularly relevant in comparative advertisements because these ads often depict the unfortunate failures of competitors' brands. Thus, in the current research, we examine schadenfreude as an incidental emotional response elicited by comparative ads and investigate its impact on attitudes and purchase likelihood. Further, we suggest that the effects of schadenfreude may not be uniform for everyone and an individual's competitiveness is an important antecedent of incidental schadenfreude.

In study 1, participants were presented with the storyboard of a digital camera (XYZ) and their competitiveness level was measured. In the comparative ad condition, brand XYZ compared itself to a cheaper brand by showing the competitor brand fail; in the noncomparative ad condition no competitor was mentioned. Results revealed a significant two-way interaction between ad type and competitiveness on schadenfreude ($\beta = .500$, $t = 2.335$, $p < .05$). More competitive individuals were likely to feel greater levels of incidental schadenfreude when exposed to comparative versus noncomparative ads ($M_{comparative} = 3.67$, $M_{noncomparative} = 2.87$, $t = 2.128$, $p < .05$). Also, more (vs. less) competitive participants experienced greater levels of schadenfreude in the comparative ad condition ($M_{more\_competitive} = 3.67$, $M_{less\_competitive} = 2.77$, $t = 2.287$, $p < .05$). Moreover, ad type did not have any significant effect on schadenfreude for less competitive participants.

Study 2 introduced a boundary condition by investigating the impact of brand status and shows that higher- (vs. lower-) status brands invoke greater levels of incidental schadenfreude in their comparative (vs. noncomparative) ads. Brand status was manipulated by portraying Mercedes (vs. Kia) as the advertiser in the higher-status (vs. lower status) brand condition. Results showed that more competitive participants felt more schadenfreude when they saw the comparative (vs. noncomparative) ad of the higher-status brand ($M_{comparative} = 4.44$, $M_{noncomparative} = 1.73$, $t = 4.358$, $p < .01$). However, level of schadenfreude of less competitive participants did not significantly differ according to ad type. Consistent with study 1, more (vs. less) competitive participants felt more schadenfreude in the higher-status brand condition ($M_{more\_competitive} = 4.44$, $M_{less\_competitive} = 3.43$, $t = 1.7564$, $p = .08$). There were no significant results in the lower-status brand condition ($\beta = 0.281$, $t = 0.674$, $p > .50$).

In study 3, we explored the effect of incidental schadenfreude on the downstream implications of attitudes and purchase likelihood. Participants in the comparative ad condition were presented with the storyboard for a deodorant in which a higher-status (vs. lower-status) brand compared itself to another brand by showing the misfortunes happening to the person who bought the competitor brand. No comparisons were used in the noncomparative ad condition. The analysis revealed a significant three-way interaction on purchase likelihood ($\beta = 1.510$, $t = 3.396$, $p = .001$). Consistent with the results of study 2, more competitive individuals experienced greater schadenfreude when exposed to the comparative ad of the higher-status brand. As a result, they were more likely to buy the advertised product ($M_{comparative} = 4.93$, $M_{noncomparative} = 3.76$, $t = 2.63$, $p < .01$). However, purchase likelihood of less competitive individuals did not significantly differ according to ad type. A moderated mediation analysis demonstrated that schadenfreude was the mediator on purchase likelihood for the higher-status brand. Moreover, the mediating effect was valid for more competitive but not for less competitive participants. Incidental schadenfreude also mediated brand and ad evaluations such that more competitive individuals had more positive attitudes towards the brand and the ad when exposed to the comparative ad of the higher-status brand.

Study 4 manipulated level of competitiveness and investigated a way to persuade less competitive consumers to buy the advertised product in a comparative ads. Research has indicated that schadenfreude may heighten individuals' anticipation of misfortunes happening to them (Kramer, Yucel-Aybat and Lau-Gesk 2011). Therefore, in this study, we reassure participants that the misfortunes shown in the ad will not happen to them if they buy the advertised brand, and thus encourage them to feel higher levels of schadenfreude. An ANOVA on purchase likelihood revealed a three-way interaction among the predictor variables ($F(1, 126) = 7.222$, $p < .01$). As expected, reassurance encouraged less competitive participants to buy more in the higher-status brand condition ($M_{reassurance} = 4.56$, $M_{no\_reassurance} = 3.50$, $F(1, 126) = 9.393$, $p < .01$). However, the purchase likelihood of more competitive participants did not significantly differ whether reassurance was present or absent. Moreover, schadenfreude mediated purchase likelihood for less competitive participants and not for more competitive participants when reassurance was present.

REFERENCES

Grewal, Dhruv, Sukumar Kavanoor, Edward F. Fern, Carolyn Costley, and James Barnes (1997), "Comparative versus Noncomparative Advertising: A Meta-Analysis," *Journal of Marketing*, 61 (4), 1-15.

Holbrook, Morris B. and Rajeev Batra (1987), "Assessing the Role of Emotions as Mediators of Consumer Responses to Advertising," *Journal of Consumer Research*, 14 (3), 404-20.

Jain, Shailendra P., Charles Lindsey, Nidhi Agrawal, and Durairaj Maheswaran (2007), "For Better or For Worse? Valenced Comparative Frames and Regulatory Focus," *Journal of Consumer Research*, 34 (1), 57-65.

Kramer, Thomas, Ozge Yucel-Aybat, and Loraine Lau-Gesk (2011), "The Effect of Schadenfreude on Choice of Conventional versus Unconventional Options," *Organizational Behavior and Human Decision Processes*, 116 (1), 140-47.

Polyorat, Kawpong and Dana L. Alden (2005), "Self-Construal and Need for Cognition Effects on Brand Attitudes and Purchase Intentions in Response to Comparative Advertising in Thailand and the United States," *Journal of Advertising,* 34 (1), 37-48.

Roggeveen, Anne L., Dhruv Grewal, and Jerry Gotlieb (2006), "Does the Frame of a Comparative Ad Moderate the Effectiveness of Extrinsic Information Cues?" *Journal of Consumer Research*, 33 (1), 115-22.

What Did You Do To My Brand?
Consumer Responses to Changes in Brands Towards Which They are Nostalgic

Alison B. Shields, Kent State University, USA
Jennifer Wiggins Johnson, Kent State University, USA

EXTENDED ABSTRACT

Marketers often make changes to brands to make the brand seem current or exciting. Some updates are successful while others are spectacular failures. This research establishes a connection between consumer acceptance or rejection of updated brands and the consumer's reported nostalgia towards the brand. We develop and measure a new construct, Nostalgia Towards the Brand, defined as "an individual's positive affect towards a brand due to the brand's associations with the individual's lived past." We show that consumers' affective and attitudinal responses to changes in a brand are moderated by Nostalgia Towards the Brand.

Nostalgia has been defined as "a positively toned evocation of a lived past" (Davis 1979), and "a fondness for possessions and activities associated with days of yore" (Holbrook 1993). Consumers have been observed to engage in nostalgic behaviors, from re-watching favorite old movies (Holbrook, 1993) to reminiscing about favorite cars from their youth (Brown, Kozinets and Sherry 2003) to consuming specific foods as a way to reconnect with the past (Loveland, Smeesters and Mandel, 2010). Consumers have also reported nostalgic feelings for particular brands or items (Holbrook and Schindler 2003).

When individuals recall nostalgic memories, they recall affect and brand information stored in their schema for the target brand (Collins and Loftus 1975). Nostalgia is "not a true recreation of the past but rather a combination of many different memories, all integrated together and in the process, all negative emotions filtered out" (Hirsch 1992). Thus, the individual's memory trace will be biased, leading the individual to recall the brand as being better than it actually was. Once the individual experiences the updated brand, he will compare the new experience to his biased memory and attempt to assimilate the new stimuli into his existing schema. The individual's ability to assimilate the new experience into their schema built on the biased memory will depend on the degree of change to the brand as well as the individual's level of nostalgia towards the brand.

Therefore, we predict that when the change to the brand is small, individuals will be able to assimilate the change regardless of their nostalgia toward the brand because the update will fit smoothly into their existing schema without significant cognitive effort. Individuals' affective response and attitudes toward the changed brand are expected to reflect their feelings towards the original brand, leading higher nostalgia individuals to exhibit more positive attitudes toward the changed brand than lower nostalgia individuals. However, as the degree of change to the brand increases, individuals who are more nostalgic towards the brand will engage in higher levels of cognitive effort when making assimilation/contrast judgments because of their increased schema complexity and resulting attribute-based processing. This increase in cognitive effort will lead to a smaller latitude of acceptance, causing nostalgic individuals to reject the change more readily than individuals who are not nostalgic towards the brand.

Hypothesis 1: *When the change to the brand is small, individuals with higher nostalgia towards the brand will exhibit more positive affective response and attitudes toward the brand than individuals with lower nostalgia toward the brand.*

Hypothesis 2: *As the change to the brand becomes larger, individuals with higher nostalgia towards the brand will exhibit more negative affective responses and attitudes toward the brand, while individuals with lower nostalgia towards the brand will not exhibit a change in affect and attitudes.*

The hypothesized effects were tested in two experiments, one using two distinct brands with perceived small and large degrees of change (based on pretests) and the second using a single brand with two levels of manipulated changes. Subjects were assigned to low, moderate, and high nostalgia clusters based on their response to the Nostalgia to the Brand scale and their affective responses, attitudes toward the original and changed brand, and purchase intentions toward the changed brand were measured.

Across both studies, attitudes towards the original brand were more positive when nostalgia towards the brand was greater. Consistent with the proposed positive memory bias, highly nostalgic participants in the small change condition also reported more positive affective and attitudinal responses to the updated brand than did low or moderately nostalgic participants, supporting Hypothesis 1. In the large change condition, highly nostalgic individuals rejected the change and showed a significantly greater magnitude in the drop of their affective and attitudinal responses than did individuals in the moderate nostalgia cluster. In the low nostalgia cluster, conversely, individuals reported similar levels of attitude and affect in both the high and low change conditions, suggesting more attitude based processing and wider latitudes of acceptance, supporting Hypothesis 2. Interestingly, moderately nostalgic individuals exhibited a negative change in affect and attitudes in Study 1, but not in Study 2, suggesting that there is a threshold level of nostalgia before these changes are observed.

These findings suggest that when confronted with changes to a brand, consumer responses will be influenced by nostalgia towards the brand. Brands with nostalgic consumers should be wary of making changes to their brands and risking negative consumer responses.

REFERENCES

Brown, Stephen, Robert V. Kozinets and John F. Sherry, Jr. (2003) "Teaching Old Brands New Tricks: Retro Branding and the Revival of Brand Meaning," *Journal of Marketing*, 67, 19-33.

Collins, Allan M., and Elizabeth F. Loftus, (1975) "A Spreading-Activation Theory of Semantic Processing," *Psychological Review*, 6, 407-428.

Davis, Fred (1979), Yearning for Yesterday: A Sociology of Nostalgia, New York: Free Press.

Hirsch, Alan R. (1992), "Nostalgia: A Neuropsychiatric Understanding" *Advances in Consumer Research*, 19, 390-395.

Holbrook, Morris B. (1993), "Nostalgia and Consumption Preferences: Some Emerging Patterns of Consumer Tastes," *Journal of Consumer Research*, 20, 245-256.

Holbrook, Morris B. and Robert M. Schindler (2003), "Nostalgic Bonding: Exploring the Role of Nostalgia in the Consumption Experience," *Journal of Consumer Behavior*, 3 (2), 107–27.

794 / **What Did You Do To My Brand? Consumer Responses to Changes in Brands Towards Which They are Nostalgic**

Loveland, Katherine, E., Dirk Smeesters and Naomi Mandel, (2010) "Still Preoccupied with 1995: The Need to Belong and Preference for Nostalgic Products," *Journal of Consumer Research*, 37, 393-408.

Schindler, Robert M. and Morris B. Holbrook, (2003), "Nostalgia for Early Experience as a Determinant of Consumer Preferences," *Psychology & Marketing*, 20(4), 275-302.

Zaichkowsky, Judith Lynne, (1985), "Measuring the Involvement Construct," *Journal of Consumer Research*, 12 (December), 341-352.

The Mere Presence of Money Motivates Goal Achievement

Gülen Sarial-Abi, Koç University, Turkey

Kathleen D. Vohs, University of Minnesota, USA

People's relationship with money is inherently tied to goal pursuit. When people use money, they do so as an act that serves to reach a desired end-point (Baumeister, 1998; Carver & Scheier, 1990). Likewise, people also obtain money for performing jobs and tasks that meet a standard, which also links the idea of money to goal pursuit. Consider the act of going to dinner at a restaurant. The diner who is hungry and wants to be full (i.e., this is the goal) pays money to the restaurateur as compensation for providing the means to achieve the goal. Hence, money enables the means by which people reach myriad commonplace goals. The current work tested whether people reminded of money become particularly attuned to the presence of a goal in that they show enhanced motivation in the presence of goals.

We do not posit that reminders of money enhance motivation without the presence of a goal. The concept of money has many connotations, including greed, fair trade, free markets, and so on. In other words, the construct of money does not wholly overlap with goal pursuit, but is proposed to have such deep motivational connections that the construct of money will potentiate the psychological system to be ready for goal pursuit. Hence we predicted that in the presence of goal pursuit cues, reminders of the concept of money would stimulate motivation, relative to non-money reminders. In contrast, when goal pursuit cues were absent, we predicted that reminders of the concept of money would not change motivation relative to non-money reminders. We tested these hypotheses in 5 experiments. Using contexts ranging from financial, health, performance, and fun goals, we saw robust support for our predictions.

In study 1 (N = 108), we tested whether participants reminded of money, relative to others, would report lower purchase intentions if they had been given a goal of curbing their spending. An ANOVA with money prime and goal condition factors as predictors of spending intentions revealed the predicted interaction effect, $F(1, 104) = 5.21, p < 0.05$. Planned comparisons showed that participants in the money condition who were given an explicit goal (versus no goal) reported lower spending intentions, $F(1, 104) = 7.17, p < .05$. Participants in the no money condition, however, did not differ in their spending intentions as a function of goal condition, $F < 1$.

In study 2 (N = 90), we studied goal pursuit in the domain of limiting caloric intake. An ANOVA with money prime and goal condition as predictors of healthy attitude scores revealed the predicted interaction effect, $F(1, 86) = 4.68, p < .05$. Planned comparisons revealed that participants in the money condition who were presented with a goal to restrain their eating had more favorable attitudes toward the healthy words than did participants who were not reminded of money, $F(1, 86) = 13.81, p < .001$. Furthermore, in the absence of being given a goal, whether participants earlier had been reminded of money did not affect their attitudes toward the healthy words, $F < 1$.

In study 3 (N= 108), participants were once again reminded of money or not. They were given a lengthy set of mathematical problems to solve by hand. Some of them were told that their goal was to solve as many as possible, whereas others were not given a goal. Time spent on the problems was our dependent measures of motivation. An ANOVA with money prime and goal condition as predictors revealed the predicted significant interaction effect, $F(1,104) = 18.85, p < .001$. When given a goal, participants who had been primed with money, relative to their non-money primed counterparts, spent more time trying to solve the math problems (39.69 min vs. 29.64, $F(1,104) = 17.20, p < .001$). Without being given a goal, though, duration was equivalent among participants primed with money or fish (25.86 vs. 30.76, $F(1,104) = 3.98, p > .05$).

Study 4 (N = 113) adopted a new context in which to study the effects of money cues and goals. Because people's exposure to money is largely utilitarian, it could be that reminding people of the concept of money simply activates hard work but not goal pursuit per se. We tested this alternative explanation in a study in which participants' goal was to have fun and enjoy themselves. An ANOVA on intentions to do fun things revealed a significant money (vs. no money) and goal (vs. no goal) interaction, $F(1, 109) = 4.25, p < .05$. Specifically, when participants in the money (vs. no money) condition had a goal, they were more likely to have intentions to do fun things (6.47 vs. 5.56, $F(1,109) = 6.09, p < .05$). Furthermore, when participants in the money (vs. no money) condition did not have a goal, intentions to do fun things did not differ significantly (5.61 vs. 5.76, $F(1,109) = .19, p > .67$).

Finally, results of Study 5 (N = 96) showed that duration spent to solve the puzzles revealed a significant money (vs. no money) and task framed as fun (vs. no fun) interaction, $F(1, 92) = 6.29, p < .05$. Specifically, when participants in the money (vs. no money) condition had a task framed as fun, they spent more time on solving the puzzles (50.14 vs. 41.31, $F(1,92) = 8.02, p < .05$). Furthermore, when participants in the money (vs. no money) condition had a task that is not framed as fun, time spent on solving the puzzles did not differ significantly (37.35 vs. 39.56, $F(1,92) = .51, p > .48$).

The findings of this research contribute to the literature in several ways. First, we demonstrate money as a tool for goal-achievement. Second, we integrate the literature in psychology of money and self-regulation to highlight the underlying mechanism under the influence of money on goal-achievement. In sum, our data, for the first time, shows that money can be used as a facilitator for goal-achievement.

REFERENCES

Baumeister, Roy F. (1998). The self. In D.T. Gilbert, S.T. Fiske, & G. Lindzey (Eds.), *Handbook of social psychology* (4th ed.; pp. 680-740). New York: McGraw-Hill.

Carver, Charles S. and Michael F. Scheier (1990), "Origins and functions of positive and negative affect: a control-process view," *Psychological Review*, 97, 19-35.

Power Distance Belief, Status, and Charity Giving

DaHee Han, Indiana University, USA

Ashok K. Lalwani, Indiana University, USA

Adam Duhachek, Indiana University, USA

EXTENDED ABSTRACT

Power distance belief-the tendency to accept and expect inequalities in society- is a central construct in cross-cultural research (Hofstede 2001). Although limited research has examined the effects of PDB on consumer behavior, there is growing recognition that PDB is an important construct with significant implications on varied facets of consumer behavior (Winterich and Zhang 2011; Zhang et al. 2010). The current research is concerned with the effects on PDB and charitable giving. Some research shows that people in high PDB contexts are less likely to donate to maintain the status quo (Winterich and Zhang 2011).

Although this finding provides initial evidence that individual beliefs about inequalities in power affect charitable giving, we argue that charitable giving depends not only on individual beliefs toward power disparity but also on their own perceived power within the system. Prior research suggests that power held by individuals affects prosocial behaviors (e.g., Goetz et al. 2010; Piff et al. 2010). Therefore, we propose that the extent of charitable giving across PDB contexts depends on the power (i.e.,"perceived asymmetric control over valued resources [Keltner, Gruenfeld, and Anderson 2003; Rucker, Galinsky, and Dubois, 2011, p.8]").

In particular, we propose that among high PDB consumers, high power people will be more likely to donate to charity than low power people because in high PDB contexts low power people owe high power people respect and obedience whereas high power people in turn owe low power people protection, help, and support (i.e., the reciprocity principle; Carl et al. 2004). In contrast, we argue that in low PDB contexts, high power people will be less likely to donate to charity than low power people because low PDB consumers believe that it takes a lot of effort, persistence, and energy to become a member of the high power group as the government and society have rules to protect equality in society. Given the difficulties involved, high power people in low PDB contexts tend to be careful with money at best and miserly at worst (Stanley and Danko 1998).

We further posit that the mechanism underlying these effects relates to differences in empathy, defined as "an other-oriented emotional response congruent with the perceived welfare of another" (Batson 1990, p.399) felt by high and low power people in the two types of systems. Specifically, we hypothesize that in high PDB contexts, high (vs. low) power people will feel greater empathy toward people in need because of the reciprocity principle outlined earlier (de Waal 2008; Fisher et al. 2008), thus leading to greater charitable giving. Conversely, in low PDB contexts, low (vs. high) power people will feel greater empathy toward people in need because low power people in low PDB contexts have been found to pay more attention to others' needs (van Kleef et al. 2008) and behave in ways that enhance social engagement and connection with others (Piff et al. 2010), thus leading them to be more prosocial (i.e., greater charitable giving).

Study 1. We manipulated participants' perception of their power using the role playing scenario (Anderson and Berdahl 2002) and power distance belief by following the procedure of Zhang et al. (2010). Next, we showed the brief description of charities and then measured the amount of money participants would donate to charities. Results revealed a significant power by PDB interaction (p<.003) such that in the high PDB condition, participants with high power donated more than those with low power (p<.033) whereas among participants in the low PDB condition, those with high power donated less than those with low power (p<.042), supporting our hypotheses.

Study 2. PDB was manipulated by asking participants to complete a scrambled sentences task (see Zhang et al. 2010). We manipulated power by asking participants to recall the incident that they felt powerful or powerless (Rucker and Galinsky 2008). Donation intention and empathy were measured (Stürmer et al. 2006). A 2-way interaction results (p<.001) revealed that in the high PDB condition, those with high power reported greater intentions to donate money to the charity than those with low power (p<.001) whereas within the low PDB condition, those with low power reported greater intentions to donate money to the charity than those with high power (p<.001). In addition, a 2-way interaction results (p<.001) indicated that in the high (low) PDB condition, those with high (low) power reported greater empathy than those with low (high) power (ps<.03). Finally, we performed mediation analyses (Muller et al. 2005) and found that empathy mediated the proposed relationship (Sobel test:z=3.01,p<.002).

Study 3. We experimentally manipulated empathy to provide further evidence of the process underlying our effects. We manipulated empathy (Batson et al. 1997, study 1) and power as in study 2 and measured PDB using the scale developed by Zhang et al (2010). We also used a different charity and measured donation intention. We measured perceived similarity to rule out the alternative explanation. Results indicated that the three-way interaction was significant for donation intention (p<.001). In the high empathy condition, the results replicated such that for participants high in PDB, power was positively associated with charitable giving (ß=3.44,p<.001), whereas for participants low in PDB, power was negatively associated with charitable giving (ß=-2.86,p<.001). These relationships were not observed in the low empathy condition. The three-way interaction for perceived similarity was not significant (p>.79), ruling out the alternative explanation.

Our research makes a number of contributions. First, it shows that charitable giving depends on not only individual beliefs about inequalities in society, but also on their own power within the system. Second, prior research suggests that empathy based charitable donations stem from perceived similarity between the donor and the recipient. In sharp contrast to this perspective, our framework highlights the role of differences based on inequalities within the system. Hence, empathy does not always result from perceived similarity, but strong differences in power and inequality can promote empathy and lead to charitable giving.

REFERENCES

Anderson, Cameron and Jennifer L. Berdahl (2002), "The Experience of Power: Examining the Effects of Power on Approach and Inhibition Tendencies," *Journal of Personality and Social Psychology*, 83 (6), 1362- 1377.

Batson, C. Daniel (1990), "How Social is the Animal? The Human Capacity for Caring," *American Psychologist*, 45 (March), 336-346.

Carl, Dale, Vipin Gupta, Mansour Javidan (2004). "Power Distance," in *Culture, Leadership, and Organizations: The GLOBE Study of 62 Societies*, House Robert et al., eds. Thousand Oaks, CA: Sage Publications, 513-559.

de Waal, Frans B. M. (2008), "Putting the Altruism Back into Altruism: The Evoluation of Empathy," *Annual Review of Psychology*, 59, 279-300.

Fisher, Robert J., Mark Vandenbosch, and Kersi D. Antia (2008), "An Empathy-Helping Perspective on Consumers' Responses to Fund-Raising Appeals," *Journal of Consumer Research*, 35 (3), 519-531.

Goetz, Jennifer L., Dacher Keltner, and Emiliana Simon-Thomas (2010), "Compassion: An Evolutionary Analysis and Empirical Review," *Psychological Bulletin*, 136 (3), 351-374.

Hofstede, Geert (2001), *Culture's Consequences: Comparing, Values, Behaviors, Institutions, and Organizations Across Nations*, 2d ed. Thousand Oaks, CA: Sage Publications.

Keltner, Dacher, Deborah H. Gruenfeld, and Cameron Anderson (2003), "Power, Approach, and Inhibition," *Psychological Review*, 110 (2), 265-284.

Muller, Dominique, Charles M. Judd, and Vincent Y. Yzerbyt (2005), "When Moderation Is Mediated and Mediation Is Moderated," *Journal of Personality and Social Psychology*, 89 (December), 852–63.

Piff, Paul K., Michael W. Kraus, Stephane Côté, Bonnie Hayden Cheng, and Dacher Keltner (2010), "Having Less, Giving More: The Influence of Social Class on Prosocial Behavior," *Journal of Personality and Social Psychology*, 99 (5), 771-784.

Rucker, Derek and Adam D. Galinsky (2008), "Desire to Acquire: Powerlessness and Compensatory Consumption," *Journal of Consumer Research*, 35 (2), 257–67.

Rucker, Derek D., Adam D. Galinsky, and Davide Dubois (2011), "Power and Consumer Behavior: How Power Shapes Who and What Consumers Value," *Journal of Consumer Psychology*, doi:10.1016/j.jcps.2011.06.001.

Stanley, Thomas J. and William D. Danko (1996), *The Millionaire Next Door: The Surprising Secrets of America's Wealthy*, New York: Simon & Schuster.

Sturmer, Stefan, Mark Snyder, Alexandra Tropp, and Birte Siem (2006), "Empathy-Motivated Helping: The Moderating Role of Group Membership," *Personality and Social Psychology Bulletin*, 32 (7), 943-956.

van Kleef, Gerben A., Christopher Oveis, Ilmo van der Löwe, Aleksandr LuoKogan, Jennifer Goetz, and Dacher Keltner (2008), "Power, Distress, and Compassion: Turning a Blind Eye to the Suffering of Others," *Psychological Science*, 19, 1315-1322.

Winterich, Karen and Yinlong Zhang (2011), "When Accepted Inequality Deters Responsibility for Helping Others," in *Advances in Consumer Research*, Vol. 39, Duluth, MN : Association for Consumer Research.

Zhang, Yinlong, Karen P. Winterich, Vikas Mittal (2010), "Power Distance Belief and Implusive Buying," *Journal of Marketing Research*, 47 (5), 945-954.

When Does Personalization Really Pay Off?

Isabelle Kes, TU Braunschweig, Germany
David M. Woisetschläger, TU Braunschweig, Germany

EXTENDED ABSTRACT

Personalized advertising is seen as THE mean to increase advertisement effectiveness and efficiency by selecting ad content being relevant to the customer and by answering the need for convenience of customers at the same time (Milne and Bahl, 2010). Especially regarding the depreciative opinion of many users on personalized advertisement it is important to know whether personalized advertisement is really worth the effort and costs it bears. Although in practice it seems to be common sense that personalization is more effective than standardization, little knowledge exists about circumstances that affect its performance outcomes. Therefore, this study questions the effectiveness of personalization in different conditions and attempts to identify success factors of personalized advertising. In particular we test the effect of personalization intensity, frequency of exposure, and the time since a customer's last action on the probability of a click. Additionally we control for differences in customer history.

CONCEPTUAL BACKGROUND

Several studies report that personalization in general is more effective than standardized mass communication (e.g., Lambrecht and Tucker, 2011). Beneath this, other studies focus on negative impacts of personalization, especially on customer reactions regarding the use of personal information (e.g., Pavlou and Stewart, 2000). As to the authors best knowledge no research exists that analyzes different intensities of personalization and its effectiveness and, surprisingly, no elaborate research stream exists that concentrates on circumstances under which different levels of personalization are effective. Our study tries to fill this gap by analyzing various intensities of personalization as well as the influence of the advertising strategy on its effectiveness.

Personalized banners use information about a customer to choose banner content the customer is highly involved with and that fit his interests. Thus, banners showing complementary products to a formerly bought one are seen as highly personalized, while those banners referring to a category of formerly visited products are slightly personalized. So, generally personalized banners are expected to be clicked more often than standardized ones, that show randomly chosen products unrelated to the customer. Moreover, higher personalization goes along with higher likelihood of a click (H1a/b).

After the consideration of this general coherency we focus on the different circumstances that determine varying potential for personalization. Our conceptual model includes hypothesis (H2-H5) regarding advertising strategy and its interactions with personalization intensity: While it is without controversy that frequency of exposure is a crucial determinant of banner success, no consensus exists about the optimal number of ad impressions (e.g., Manchanda et al., 2006). A high frequency goes along with the fear of oversaturation but it is also a mean to avoid banner blindness (Chatterjee, 2005). But even more critical is whether the effect on click likelihood is really linear: there are two opposing psychological processes operating simultaneously in the case of banner exposures (Lee and Cho, 2010): "Positive habits" lead to increasing effects with diminishing returns of each additional exposure, while "tedium" starts as result of repetitive exposure and decreases the effects gradually (Berlyne 1970). Referring to this discordance whether frequency has a linear or non-linear effect, we formulate rivaling hypothesis (H2a1-H2b). Moreover, time since the customer's last observed action is supposed to negatively influence click behavior. Structuration Theory sees interactions as recurring events that are embedded in a structure (Giddens, 1984). Hence past transactions influence future ones and are responsible for a decision to click (H3).

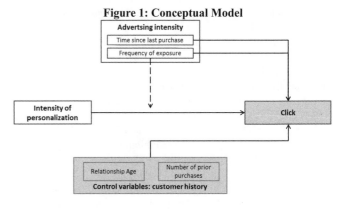

Figure 1: Conceptual Model

Furthermore, interactions between frequency of exposure and personalization are anticipated. As highly personalized advertising, using high involvement of a customer with banner content, is recognized faster, we expect that customers need to be contacted less often, to increase the likelihood of a click. (H4).

DATA AND METHOD

To answer our research questions, we used a real experimental design, that contained 1,939,939 adimpressions showed to 98.984 customers of whom 7,450 customers clicked on a banner. Five types of banners were sent out, including a standardized (click-through-rate .1%), two slightly personalized (.3%) and two highly personalized banners (.2%).

We take a binary logistic regression approach for testing our conceptual model. An often overlooked characteristic of logistic regression is that in case of an imbalanced sample it produces biased logit coefficients that underestimate rare events (King and Zeng, 2001). To take this as well as the huge amount of data into account we used bootstrapping. Thus, 1000 control samples are taken to control for the stability of the estimates. To adress the class imbalance between clicks and non-clicks within the data a stratified sampling is used to ensure a balanced sample of clicks and non-clicks (Nigam and Rao, 1996).

RESULTS

The analysis is separated in two steps: firstly the general advantageousness of personalization is tested, followed by a more detailed look on the differently personalized ads.

Personalized advertisement is clicked more often than standardized banners, confirming H1a. Surprisingly, with increasing levels of personalization the likelihood of clicking is reduced. Banners based on the product category of visited products had a stronger positive effect as those that contain products complementary to formerly bought ones. Hypothesis H2 and 3 could not be confirmed. Contrary to H4, sending out less personalized banners more frequently affects the probability of a click just slightly positive. But a slight increase of frequency for strongly personalized advertisement results in a considerably higher click probability. Besides, controlling among others for number of prior purchases shows that with more past purchases more information about a customer can be collected and the more efficient is the advertising.

CONCLUSION AND IMPLICATIONS

First and foremost, companies need to realize that personalization is no universal remedy. Personalized banners are more effective than standardized while using high involvement content is not always the most effective personalization. Furthermore, weaker personalization is easier to realize and can be used with new customers that only visited a shop once. Regarding the frequency of exposure an increase is only effective in case of highly personalized banners. Although highly personalized banners seem to be inferior when considered isolated, in combination with a high frequency of exposure the probability of a click increases considerably.

Two Paths from Boredom to Consumption

Soo Kim, Northwestern University, USA
C. Miguel Brendl, Northwestern University, USA

EXTENDED ABSTRACT

Boredom is prevalent in today's society. Naturally in this era, one of the behaviors oriented towards escaping boredom is consumption (Spacks 1995). Indeed, it is not difficult to imagine our bored selves mindlessly reaching for the bowl of jellybeans or perhaps the long-neglected Dostoevsky on the table. However, what is yet unknown is when bored individuals would reach out for either the jellybeans or the Dostoevsky and why one over the other.

Although scarce, past literature has suggested that it is possible for individuals to attribute their experience of boredom either to the situation (Mikulas and Vodanovich 1993) or to the self (Svendsen 2005). Given these viewpoints, we propose that differences in to which source the experience of boredom is attributed would lead to a different consumption means for escape.

Specifically, we propose that when consumers attribute their boredom to the situation they would be drawn to vices, because vices (e.g., snacks) offer sensory pleasures that can reconcile the inadequately stimulating nature of the situation (Wertenbroch 1998). On the other hand, we propose that when consumers attribute their boredom to the self they may be looking for something that can help them restore the sense of meaningfulness (cf., van Tilburg and Igou 2011), known to be achievable by investing one's resources into attaining higher-order goals (King et al. 2006). In consumption context, one means to perceive that one is investing to achieve a higher-order goal (e.g., becoming a healthy person) would be to consume virtues (Khan et al. 2004), because, by consuming virtues (e.g., healthy foods) consumers can restore the sense of meaningfulness that they are engaging in purposeful actions ("I am investing to be healthy.").

Hence, we propose and test in three experiments that, whereas consumers under the influence of situation-attributed boredom would display a vice-preference, those under the influence of self-attributed boredom would display the opposite pattern: a virtue-preference.

EXPERIMENT 1

Experiment 1 tested whether consumers under situation-attributed boredom would increase evaluation of a vice whereas those attributing their experience of boredom to the self would increase evaluation of a virtue.

Participants were randomly assigned in a 3 (boredom-attribution: situation vs. self vs. baseline) x 2 (product: vice vs. virtue). Participants in the situation-attributed boredom condition read the description of boredom that drew their attention to the environment as the source whereas participants in the self-attributed boredom condition read the description of boredom that drew their attention to the self as the source. They also elaborated on how it felt/would feel to experience the respectively described boredom. Then, they indicated willingness-to-pay for either a vice (sundae) or a virtue (asparagus salad) on a $0-$10 scale. Baseline participants only completed the product evaluation.

Experiment 1 found that participants who attributed boredom to the situation increased evaluation of a vice whereas those who attributed boredom to the self increased evaluation of a virtue, compared to those in the other two conditions.

EXPERIMENT 2

Experiment 2 tested whether consumers under situation- or self-attributed boredom would still exhibit a preference for either a vice or a virtue, even when both options are available.

Participants were randomly assigned in a 3 (boredom-attribution: situation vs. self vs. baseline) and were instructed to write about their personal experience of boredom. Additionally, those in the situation-attributed boredom condition were asked to describe which aspect of the environment caused boredom whereas those in the self-attributed boredom condition were asked to describe which aspect of their character caused boredom. Baseline participants wrote about their rooms. Then, participants in the two boredom conditions waited 90 seconds on a blank screen for the "second" study to load. Baseline participants moved on without waiting. Then, all participants indicated willingness-to-pay ($0-$10) for both a vice (cake) and a virtue (salad). Participants' vice- versus virtue-preference was computed by subtracting their willingness-to-pay for a virtue from that for a vice.

Experiment 2 demonstrated that even when participants were provided with both a vice and a virtue, those under situation-attributed boredom paid more for a vice than a virtue (vice-preference). On the other hand, participants under self-attributed boredom paid more for a virtue than a vice (virtue-preference), even when both options were available.

EXPERIMENT 3

Experiment 3 tested whether the virtue-preference of consumers under self-attributed boredom was driven by their need to restore meaningfulness rather than by their need to boost their self-worth after attributing boredom to the self.

Participants were randomly assigned in a 2 (boredom-attribution: situation vs. self) x 3 (buffer: life-meaning, self-worth, no-buffer). As in experiment 2, participants first either wrote about their situation-attributed or self-attributed boredom. They then waited 90-seconds for a "second" task, where they had to write about their important possession (Dalton 2008) that either reflected their meaningful purpose in life (life-meaning buffer) or makes them feel good about themselves (self-worth buffer). Participants in the no-buffer conditions did not buffer via writing. Then, participants indicated willingness-to-pay ($0-$10) for both a vice (cookies) and a virtue (asparagus salad). Again, participants' vice- versus virtue-preference was computed by subtracting their willingness-to-pay for a virtue from that for a vice.

Experiment 3 found that participants who attributed boredom to the self but restored the sense of meaningfulness via a life-meaning buffer no longer exhibited a virtue-preference. However, the virtue-preference persisted for participants under self-attributed boredom who restored their self-worth (self-worth buffer) or those who did not buffer the self. Additionally, the vice-preference of participants under situation-attributed boredom persisted regardless of whether they buffered and what type of buffering they engaged in, indicating that it is the external environment, rather than aspects of the self, that must change for one to resolve situation-attributed boredom.

CONCLUSION

In sum, this work provides empirical evidence that bored individuals' consumption patterns differ depending on whether they attribute boredom to the situation or to the self. Also, by demonstrating that individuals under situation-attributed boredom prefer vices to virtues and vice versa for those under self-attributed boredom, we extend the field's understanding of why consumers experiencing boredom might be more drawn to one type of product over another.

REFERENCES

Dalton, Amy N. (2008), "Look on the Bright Side: Self-Expressive Consumption and Consumer Self-Worth," Duke University.

Khan, Uzma, Ravi Dhar, and Klaus Wertenbroch (2004), "A Behavioral Decision Theoretic Perspective on Hedonic and Utilitarian Choice " in *Inside Consumption: Frontiers of Research on Consumer Motives, Goals, and Desires,* ed. S. Ratneshwar and David Glen Mick, Eds. New York: Routledge.

King, Laura A., Joshua A. Hicks, Jennifer L. Krull, and Amber K. Del Gaiso (2006), "Positive Affect and the Experience of Meaning in Life," *Journal of Personality and Social Psychology*, 90 (Jan), 179-96.

Mikulas, William L. and Stephen J. Vodanovich (1993), "The Essence of Boredom," *Psychological Record*, 43 (Win), 3-12.

Spacks, Patricia M. (1995), *Boredom: The Literary History of a State of Mind*. Chicago: University of Chicago Press.

Svendsen, Lars (2005), *A Philosophy of Boredom*. London: Reaktion Books Ltd.

van Tilburg, Wijnand A. P. and Eric R. Igou (2011), "On Boredom and Social Identity: A Pragmatic Meaning-Regulation Approach," *Personality and Social Psychology Bulletin*, 37, 1679-91.

Wertenbroch, Klaus (1998), "Dynamic Aspects of Hedonic Experience: Where Experimental and Interpretive Approaches Meet," *Advances in Consumer Research, Vol. Xxv*, 25, 216-18.

Consumers' Search Intentions in Response to Conditional Promotions

Atul Kulkarni, University of Missouri, USA
Hong Yuan, University of Illinois, USA

EXTENDED ABSTRACT

Online retailers often offer conditional promotions such as a cash reward or free shipping, which shoppers can avail when their order sizes reach a threshold dollar value, e.g., $100. In this research, we examine consumers' search behavior in response to the conditional promotions.

Presumably, sellers' objective of offering a conditional promotion is to encourage shoppers to increase their basket sizes (Zhou, Katehakis, and Zhao 2009). If so, it would be useful to understand the effects that a free shipping promotion may have on consumer response, as compared to a cash reward promotion. We hypothesized that consumers perceive cash reward promotions as gains to be obtained, whereas free shipping promotions as losses to be avoided. Therefore, in accordance with the psychological value function (Kahneman and Tversky 1979; Thaler 1985) that is steeper in loss domain than in gain domain, we expected consumers to value free shipping promotion more than cash reward promotion. Study 1 tested this hypothesis.

Study 1. A 2-factorial (promotion type: free shipping versus cash reward) between-subjects design was used. In response to a hypothetical shopping scenario, participants were asked to imagine that they had to visit an online store to purchase a gift item for their niece's birthday. Further, they were asked to imagine that they found the gift item for $75, and proceeded to the checkout. At the time of checkout, the store reminded them of the promotion -free shipping or a cash reward- if their total basket size exceeds $100. They were also informed that the shipping charges (or, the cash reward) were flat $10. After reading this scenario, the participants were asked to report the likelihood that they will search for additional items in order to increase the basket size to be over $100. In line with our expectations, the search likelihood was significantly higher ($F_{(1, 59)} = 5.44$, $p<.023$) when the promotion was free shipping ($M_{sh} = 4.45$) as compared to cash reward ($M_{cr} = 3.42$). Therefore, study 1 results support the conjecture that consumers encode different promotion types differently such that free shipping (cash reward) incentive is perceived as a loss (gain) to be avoided (obtained).

In study 2, we tested whether conditional promotions act as goals for consumers. If conditional promotions serve as shopping goals (e.g., Lee and Ariely 2006), then in accordance with the goal gradient hypothesis, consumers are more likely to search when they are relatively near to (vs. farther from) the goal (e.g., Hull 1932). Further, previous research has suggested that goal framing may interact with perceived distance to goal such that people may value positively (negatively) framed goals more when they perceive to be relatively far from (close to) the goal (e.g., Mogilner, Aaker, and Pennington 2008). Therefore, we hypothesized an interaction between promotion type (i.e., goal framing) and the relative distance to threshold basket sizes.

Study 2. A 2 (promotion type: free shipping vs cash reward) X 2 (original basket size: $25 vs $75) between-subjects design was used. A scenario similar to the study 1 was presented, and participants' search likelihood reports were obtained. As expected, the interaction between promotion type and original basket size was significant ($F_{(1, 55)} = 29.70$, $p<.001$). In response to the threshold order size of $100 and the original basket size of $25, participants reported higher search likelihood for cash reward promotion ($M_{cr} = 2.54$) than for free shipping promotion ($M_{sh} = 1.39$). When the original basket

size was $75, participants reported higher search likelihood for free shipping promotion ($M_{sh} = 5.03$) than for cash reward ($M_{cr} = 3.27$). Further, as expected the effect of original basket size on search likelihood was also significant ($F_{(1, 55)} = 66.71$, $p<.000$) with participants in the $75 ($M_{75} = 4.15$) condition reporting higher search likelihood as compared to $25 ($M_{25} = 1.96$). Thus, study 2 results support the conjecture that conditional promotions serve as shopping goals, and that promotion type interacts with relative distance to the threshold order size to influence search intentions.

In study 3, we examined whether consumers' search behavior is influenced specifically by their relative distance to a threshold order size or by a general sense of psychological distance experienced due to incidental objects/events. Previous research has implied that a sense of distance caused by an object or event (stimulus A) may influence individuals' subsequent evaluations, judgments, and behaviors toward another object or event (stimulus B) even when stimulus B may be unrelated to stimulus A (e.g., Brown and Levinson 1987). Trope and Liberman (2010) have argued that people access a common meaning underlying the different dimensions of psychological distance even when it is not directly related to their current goals.

Study 3. A 2 (promotion type: free shipping vs cash reward) X 2 (psychological distance: far vs close) between-subjects design was used with the experimental scenario similar to studies 1 and 2. The objective difference between the original basket size ($50 for all) and the threshold order size ($100) was kept the same for all participants. Following Liberman, Trope, and Stephan's (2007) postulation that psychological distance can be represented in terms of subjective perception of spatial distance, we manipulated spatial distance to prime participants with psychological proximity/remoteness. After reading the conditional promotions scenario, participants were asked to read a scenario about the city of Sydney (Chicago) for priming psychological remoteness (proximity), and then were asked report their search likelihood in response to the conditional promotions scenario. The interaction effect of psychological distance and promotion type on search likelihood was significant ($F_{(1, 50)} = 35.11$, $p<.006$). When primed with psychological remoteness (proximity), participants reported higher search likelihood for cash reward ($M_{cr} = 4.63$) (free shipping ($M_{sh} = 4.86$)) promotion than for free shipping ($M_{sh} = 2.59$) (cash reward ($M_{cr} = 3.58$)). Thus, study 3 results suggest that not only perceived distance from the threshold order size, but completely irrelevant cues priming a sense of psychological distance can also interact with promotion type to influence consumers' search behavior in response to conditional promotions.

REFERENCES

Lewis, Michael, Vishal Singh, and Scott Fay (2006), "An Empirical Study of the Impact of Nonlinear Shipping and Handling Fees on Purchase Incidence and Expenditure Decisions," *Marketing Science,* 25 (1), 51-64.

Tyagi, Rajeev (2004), "Technological Advances, Transaction Costs, and Consumer Welfare," *Marketing Science,* 23 (3), 335-44.

Zhou, Bin, Michael N. Katehakis, and Yao Zhao (2009), "Managing Stochastic Inventory Systems with Free Shipping Option," *European Journal of Operational Research,* 196 186-97.

Kahneman, D., & Tversky, A. (1979). Prospect theory: An analysis of decision under risk. *Econometrica, 47,* 263-291.

Thaler, Richard (1985), "Mental Accounting and Consumer Choice," *Marketing Science,* 4 (3), 199-214.

Lee, Leonard and Dan Ariely (2006), "Shopping Goals, Goal Concreteness, and Conditional Promotions," *Journal of Consumer Research,* 33 (June), 60-70.

Hull, C. L. (1932), "The Goal Gradient Hypothesis and Maze Learning," *Psychological Review,* 39 25-43.

Mogilner, C., Aaker, J. L., & Pennington, G. L. (2008). Time will tell: The distant appeal of promotion and imminent appeal of prevention. *Journal of Consumer Research, 34*(5), 670-681.

Brown, P., & Levinson, S. C. (1987). *Politeness: Some universals in language usage.* Cambridge, England: Cambridge University Press.

Trope, Y., & Liberman, N. (2010). Construal level theory of psychological distance. *Psychological Review, 117,* 440-463.

Liberman, N., Trope, Y., & Stephan, E. (2007). Psychological distance. In A. W. Kruglanski, & E. T. Higgins (Eds.), *Social psychology: Handbook of basic principles* (pp. 353-383). New York: Guilford Press.

Fujita, K., Henderson, M. D., Eng, J., Trope, Y., & Liberman, N. (2006). Spatial distance and mental construal of social events. *Psychological Science, 17*(4), 278-282.

When White Obscures Evaluations: The Influence of Automatic Color Preferences on Product, Race and Spokesperson Evaluations

Ioannis Kareklas, Washington State University, USA
Frédéric F. Brunel, Boston University, USA
Robin A. Coulter, University of Connecticut, USA

EXTENDED ABSTRACT

Visual characteristics contribute greatly to the formation of initial evaluations of products and people (Bloch 1995). In this research, we focus on one visual element, color, and investigate how automatic color preference is linked to automatic product and spokespeople preferences. Building on color theory research, we argue that an automatic preference for the color white impacts consumers' automatic evaluations of products and people and may explain the lack of automatic in-group favoritism previously reported for African-Americans.

Research suggests that preference for white over black (1) can be traced to ancient tribal fears for darkness, the night and the unknown, versus the fondness for light, fire and the sun (Mead and Baldwin 1971), and (2) is acquired during early childhood and culturally reinforced through the learning of color symbolism (Duckitt, Wall, and Pokroy 1999). For example, in religion, literature and the media white often symbolizes "goodness," whereas black connotes "badness" (Williams, Tucker, and Dunham 1971). Because of this deeply rooted preference, and based on cross-cultural findings of an explicit white color preference across socio-cultural and ethnic backgrounds (Adams and Osgood 1973), we expect that Caucasian and African-Americans will automatically prefer the color white (vs. black) (H1) and white products over otherwise identical black products (H2).

The potential impact of automatic color preference becomes more complex as we consider evaluations of advertising spokespeople. Although skin color is a readily noticeable visual characteristic, its impact on automatic preferences is multifaceted. On one hand, building on an automatic preference for white and research showing a positive relationship between color and racial preferences (Neto and Williams 1997), one would expect that everyone would prefer light skinned (i.e., white) people and advertisements featuring light-skinned spokespeople (H3). On the other hand, because skin color can serve as a basis for in-group identification (Spira and Whittler 2004), and people evaluate members of their own group more favorably than people from other groups (in-group favoritism; Tajfel, Billig, Bundy, and Flament 1971), we would expect that both Caucasian and African-Americans would prefer in-group spokespeople (H4). However, H3 and H4 would lead to conflicting predictions for African-Americans.

These conflicting theoretical predictions for systematic color-based versus in-group-based preferences are echoed in previous studies. Although past findings support that consumers favor spokespeople from their in-group, the effects are mixed when race is the salient basis for identification. Research using explicit (i.e., self-report) measures has demonstrated that African and Caucasian-Americans respond more favorably to messages by spokespeople from their racial in-group (Schlinger and Plummer 1972; Whittler 1989). Yet, studies utilizing implicit measures have found that while Caucasian-Americans exhibit automatic in-group preferences, African-Americans do not exhibit automatic in-group preferences (Brunel, Tietje, and Greenwald 2004; Nosek, Banaji, and Greenwald 2002).

System justification theory provides an explanation for the lack of automatic in-group preference among African-Americans (Jost and Banaji 1994). It posits that a long history of discrimination can lead individuals to internalize negative attitudes toward their own group as a means of justifying the status quo (Rudman, Feinberg, and Fairchild 2002). Notwithstanding, we propose that a universal automatic white color preference is an even more fundamental explanation for these contradictory results. We expect that automatic preference for white will strengthen (weaken) automatic in-group favoritism for Caucasian-Americans (African-Americans). In other words, observed automatic in-group preference is the combined cumulative effect of an automatic color preference plus a "unique" in-group effect. In particular, we argue that ignoring the effect of an automatic white color preference might have prevented previous studies from showing that African-Americans favor their in-group. Therefore, by removing the color effect, one can disentangle the two underlying effects and uncover a unique in-group preference for both African and Caucasian-Americans (H5).

METHOD

We administered a series of Implicit Association Tests (IAT; Greenwald, McGhee, and Schwartz 1998) to explore African and Caucasian-Americans' implicit color preferences (ICP, studies 1&2), implicit product preferences (IPP, study 1), implicit racial preferences (IRP, study 2), and implicit attitudes toward advertisements featuring African and Caucasian-American spokespeople (IAad, study 2). See Appendix for stimuli examples.

FINDINGS

In study 1 (see figure 1), we support H1 and H2 and show that African-American (N = 96) and Caucasian-American (N = 123) adults exhibit automatic pro-white color (ICP_MeanD = .23 and .68 respectively) and pro-white product preferences (IPP_MeanD = .17 and .48 respectively). Additionally, ICP significantly predicted IPP $(F(1,217) = 59.67, \beta = .46, p < .001)$.

Figure 1
Mean D Scores for IAT Measures in Study 1

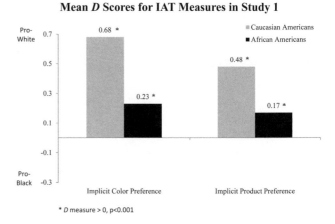

* D measure > 0, p<0.001

In study 2 (see figure 2), we provide additional support for H1 by showing that African-Americans (N = 81) and Caucasian-Americans (N = 245) exhibit an automatic pro-white color preference (ICP_MeanD = .36 and .58). We also show that Caucasian-Americans exhibit racial (IRP_MeanD = .46) and advertising preferences (IAad_Mean$D$ = .40) consistent with a color or in-group preference explanation (H3 and H4). But, African-Americans do not exhibit significant racial (IRP_Mean$D$ = -.02) or advertising preferences (IAad_Mean d = -.03) (no support for H3 or H4). In addition, we show that across groups, ICP is linked to IRP ($F(1,324)$ = 52.56, β = .37, p < .001), and IAad ($F(1,324)$ = 31.41, β = .30, p < .001), and that IRP mediates the effect of ICP on IAad.

Figure 2
Mean *D* Scores for IAT Measures in Study 2

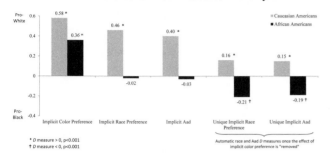

* *D* measure > 0, p<0.001
† *D* measure < 0, p<0.001

We then regressed IRP (IAad) on ICP and saved the unstandardized residuals which represent the portion of IRP (IAad) that is not explained by ICP. Once this is done, both racial groups exhibit in-group racial and advertising preferences. Specifically, African-Americans exhibit both a Unique Implicit Racial Preference (UIRP_Mean$D$ = -.21) and a Unique Implicit Attitude toward the Ad (UIAad_Mean$D$ = -.19) in favor of their in-group.

CONTRIBUTION

Our research extends color theory into the consumer behavior area. In particular, it shows that there are automatic and predictable underlying color associations that impact automatic product, racial, and advertising preferences. Also, our findings suggest the need to take into account the potential effect of automatic color preference in order to avoid overestimating (underestimating) automatic in-group preferences of Caucasian-Americans (African-Americans). Accounting for automatic color preference allows us to show that Africans-Americans have underlying automatic pro-in-group attitudes, thereby providing an alternative viewpoint to system justification theory. Instead of offering a socio-historical explanation for a "lack of in-group preference" among African-Americans, we show that a more fundamental explanation based on automatic color preference may explain past results.

APPENDIX
Examples of IAT Stimuli used in Studies 1 And 2

Color IAT (Studies 1 and 2)	Product IAT (Study 1)	Race IAT[1] (Study 2)	Advertising IAT[1] (Study 2)

Note: All stimuli were presented at a resolution of approximately 250 x 250 pixels, and the background color was gray (RGB color code 127 127 127).

[1]An equal number of women and men from each racial group photographed in similar poses were depicted in both the race and advertising IATs.

REFERENCES

Adams, Francis M. and Charles E. Osgood (1973), "A Cross-Cultural Study of the Affective Meanings of Color," *Journal of Cross-Cultural Psychology*, Vol. 4 (2), 135-56.

Bloch, Peter H. (1995), "Seeking the Ideal Form: Product Design and Consumer Response," *Journal of Marketing*, 59 (July), 16-29.

Brunel, Frédéric F., Brian C. Tietje, and Anthony G. Greenwald (2004), "Is the Implicit Association Test a Valid and Valuable Measure of Implicit Consumer Social Cognition?," *Journal of Consumer Psychology*, 14 (4), 385-404.

Duckitt, John, Carolyn Wall, and Barry Pokroy (1999), "Color Bias and Racial Preference in White South African Preschool Children," *Journal of Genetic Psychology*, 160 (2), 143-54.

Greenwald, Anthony G., Debbie E. McGhee, and Jordan L. K. Schwartz (1998), "Measuring Individual Differences in Implicit Cognition: The Implicit Association Test," *Journal of Personality and Social Psychology*, 74 (6), 1464-80.

Jost, John T. and Mahzarin R. Banaji (1994), "The Role of Stereotyping in System-Justification and the Production of False Consciousness," *British Journal of Social Psychology*, 33 (1), 1-27.

Mead, M. and J. Baldwin (1971), *A Rap on Race*, New York: J.B. Lippincott.

Neto, Felix and John E. Williams (1997), "Color Bias in Children Revisited: Findings from Portugal," *Social Behavior and Personality*, 25 (2), 115-22.

Nosek, Brian A., Mahzarin Banaji, and Anthony G. Greenwald (2002), "Harvesting Implicit Group Attitudes and Beliefs from a Demonstration Web Site," *Group Dynamics: Theory, Research, and Practice*, 6 (1), 101-15.

Rudman, Laurie A., Joshua Feinberg, and Kimberly Fairchild (2002), "Minority Members' Implicit Attitudes: Automatic Ingroup Bias as a Function of Group Status," *Social Cognition*, 20 (4), 294-320.

Schlinger, Mary J. and Joseph T. Plummer (1972), "Advertising in Black and White," *Journal of Marketing Research*, Vol. 9 (2), 149-53.

Spira, Joan Scattone and Tommy E. Whittler (2004), "Style or Substance? Viewers' Reactions to Spokesperson's Race in Advertising," in *Diversity in Advertising: Broadening the Scope of Research Directions*, ed. Jerome D. Williams, Wei-Na Lee and Curtis P. Haugtvedt, Mahwah, New Jersey: Lawrence Erlbaum Associates.

Tajfel, Henri, M. G. Billig, R. P. Bundy, and Claude Flament (1971), "Social Categorization and Intergroup Behaviour," *European Journal of Social Psychology*, 1 (2), 149-78.

Whittler, Tommy E. (1989), "Viewers' Processing of Actor's Race and Message Claims in Advertising Stimuli," *Psychology & Marketing*, 6 (4), 287-309.

Whittler, Tommy E. and Joan Scattone Spira (2002), "Model's Race: A Peripheral Cue in Advertising Messages?," *Journal of Consumer Psychology*, 12 (4), 291-301.

Williams, John E., J. Kenneth Moreland, and Walter L. Underwood (1970), "Connotations of Color Names in the United States, Europe, and Asia," *Journal of Social Psychology*, 82 (1), 3–14.

Williams, John E., Richard D. Tucker, and Frances Y. Dunham (1971), "Changes in the Connotations of Color Names among Negroes and Caucasians: 1963-1969," *Journal of Personality and Social Psychology*, 19 (2), 222-28.

Sticking to Plan: How Concrete Mindsets Increase Reliance on Mental Budget

Sonja Prokopec, ESSEC Business School, France
Francine Espinoza, ESMT, Germany
Vanessa M. Patrick, University of Houston, USA

EXTENDED ABSTRACT

Our research aims to contribute to the extant literature on mental budgets as self control devices by demonstrating: 1) that mental budgets are temporally unstable in that consumers do not rely on them for future consumption decisions, and 2) that concrete mindsets can enhance reliance on mental budgets over time. We present a set of three studies to investigate these notions.

Making the decision to exert self-control is not enough. Monitoring or keeping track of relevant behavior is an important aspect of the self-regulatory process (Baumeister 2002). Little research, however, has investigated the factors that impact the *efficacy* of the monitoring devices and control strategies that consumers rely upon to monitor goal-directed behavior *after* the decision to exert self-control has been made. This is the impetus for the current research.

Mental budgets have been shown to be effective self-control devices because they allow consumers to monitor their behavior around an active self-control goal (Krishnamurthy and Prokopec 2010). We conceptualize mental budgets as concrete plans of action or specific intentions framed in terms of explicit quotas that an individual uses to execute and monitor a particular behavior (e.g., "I can drink two small glasses of wine per day"). The extant research has found that mental budgets are effective, but have only investigated them in the short-run. The assumption is that mental budgets will be similarly effective self-regulatory tools *in the long run*. The current research invalidates this assumption to illustrate that while mental budgets are effective for implementing a self-control goal when decisions are made for present consumption, their efficacy decreases for future consumption decisions.

The question then becomes, how can we increase the efficacy of mental budgets in making future consumption decisions? We argue that mindsets determine whether consumers align their consumption with the mental budget. Our argument draws on the role of construal in the execution or implementation of the goal (Bayuk, Janiszewski, and Leboeuf 2010). We argue that mindsets moderate the efficacy of mental budgets. Specifically, a concrete mindset facilitates the execution of the self-control goal, increasing the reliance on the mental budget while an abstract mindset permits competing information to be accessible, decreasing this reliance. In sum, this research aims to contribute to the extant literature on mental budgets as self control devices by demonstrating: 1) that mental budgets are temporally unstable in that consumers do not rely on them for future consumption decisions, and 2) that concrete mindsets can enhance reliance on mental budgets over time. We present a set of three studies to investigate these notions.

Study 1 employed a 2 (Mental budget: Yes/No) x 2 (Decision: Present/Future) between-subjects design (N = 179). The design of this experiment was adapted from previous work on the relationship between mental budgeting and self-regulation (Krishnamurthy and Prokopec, 2010). A pre-test revealed that European students struggle with over-consumption of alcohol. To manipulate mental budget, participants in the mental budget condition were asked to type in the number of small wine glasses that they planned to consume during the wine tasting event (part of the cover story); after this, participants saw pictures of 10 different wines and indicated the number of small glasses of wine they would like to drink immediately (present deci-

sion condition) or a week later (future decision condition). Results revealed a significant interaction between mental budget and decision time frame (F $(1,175)$ = 6.16, $p < .02$). Planned contrasts suggest that participants drank less wine when they had set a mental budget for the present ($M_{no\ mb}$ = 6.77, M_{mb} = 5.12, F $(1,175)$ = 3.79, $p < .05$), than for the future ($M_{no\ mb}$ = 5.88, M_{mb} = 7.26, F $(1,175)$ = 2.46, $p = .11$).

Study 2 employed a 2 (Mental budget: Yes/No) x 2 (Decision: Present/Future) x 2 (Mindset: Concrete/Abstract) mixed design (scenario as Study 1), where mental budget and decision time frame were between-subjects and mindset was measured using the behavioral identification form (Vallacher and Wegner 1989) (N = 296). Results revealed a main effect of mental budget (F $(1, 284)$ = 25.41, $p < .001$) and a tree-way interaction between mental budget, decision time frame, and mindset (F $(1, 284)$ = 3.98, $p < .05$). When mindset was concrete, a main effect of mental budget (F $(1, 284)$ = 14.07, $p < .05$) suggests that presence of mental budget reduces consumption for both present ($M_{no\ mb}$ = 7.55, M_{mb} =4.10, F $(1, 284)$ = 3.51, $p < .06$) and future decisions ($M_{no\ mb}$ =9.07, M_{mb} =4.54, F $(1, 284)$ = 9.94, $p < .01$). When mindset was abstract, a main effect of mental budget (F $(1, 284)$ = 11.41, $p < .01$) that was qualified by a 2-way interaction (F $(1, 284)$ = 4.35, $p < .05$) suggests that mental budget reduces consumption for present decisions ($M_{no\ mb}$ =9.09, M_{mb} =3.95, F $(1, 284)$ = 13.18, $p < .01$) but not for future decisions ($M_{no\ mb}$ =7.86, M_{mb} =6.65, F $(1, 284)$ = .94, $p > .33$).

Study 3 employed a 2 (Mental budget: Yes/No) x 2 (Decision: Future vs. Implementation of future) x 2 (Mindset: Concrete/Abstract) mixed design (N = 63) (scenario as study 1). Mental budget was a between-subjects factor, decision time frame was a within-subjects factor, and mindset was measured with the behavioral identification form (Vallacher and Wegner, 1989). A repeated-measures ANOVA revealed a 3-way interaction (F $(1,59)$ = 5.55, $p < .02$). This interaction suggests that when consumers operate under a concrete mindset, mental budgets help self-control when they decide on their future consumption ($M_{no\ mb}$ = 7.25, M_{mb} = 4.37, F $(1, 59)$ = 27.73, $p < .01$) and remain an effective self-control tool when, a week later, they implement their consumption decision ($M_{no\ mb}$ = 6.39, M_{mb} = 4.87, F $(1, 59)$ = 7.71, $p < .01$). In contrast, when consumers operate under an abstract mindset, mental budgets do not help self-control for future decisions ($M_{no\ mb}$ = 6.37, M_{mb} = 7.85, F $(1,59)$ = 4.84, $p < .04$) and when the time of the event comes, mental budgets remain an ineffective self-control tool ($M_{no\ mb}$ = 7.25, M_{mb} = 7.20, F $(1,59)$ = .01, $p > .92$).

Taken together, our three studies support the proposition that mental budgeting is a temporally unstable self-regulatory strategy, in that it is effective for implementing a self-control goal when decisions are made for present consumption (but not for future consumption). Further, while the existing research shows that high-level construals (e.g., an abstract mindset) are better for self-regulation (Fujita and Han 2009; Labroo and Patrick 2009) we demonstrate that low-level construals (e.g., a concrete mindset) can also enhance self-control. We argue and find support for the notion that a concrete mindset facilitates the stability of a mental budget in the long-run because it helps consumers to implement their self-control decision.

REFERENCES

Baumeister, Roy F. (2002), "Yielding to Temptation: Self-Control Failure, Impulsive Purchasing, and Consumer Behavior," *Journal of Consumer Research,* 28 (March), 670–76.

Bayuk, Julia Belyavsky, Chris Janiszewski and Robyn A. LeBoeuf (2010), "Letting Good Opportunities Pass Us By: Examining the Role of Mindset during Goal Pursuit," *Journal of Consumer Research*, 37, 570-83.

Fujita, Kentaro and H. Anna Han (2009), "Moving Beyond Deliberative Control of Impulses: The Effect of Construal Levels on Evaluative Associations in Self-Control Conflicts," *Psychological Science*, 50 (7), 799-804.

Krishnamurthy, Parthasarathy and Sonja Prokopec (2010), "Resisting That Triple-Chocolate Cake: Mental Budgets and Self-Control, *Journal of Consumer Research*, 37 (June), 68-79.

Labroo, Aparna and Vanessa M. Patrick (2009), "Why Happiness Helps You See the Big Picture," *Journal of Consumer Research,* 35 (February), 800-809.

Vallacher, Robin R. and Daniel M. Wegner (1989), "Levels of Personal Agency: Individual Variation in Action Identification," *Journal of Personality and Social Psychology*, 57 (4), 660-671.

Center of Shelf Attention: Understanding the Role of Visual Attention on Product Choice

A. Selin Atalay, HEC Paris, France
H. Onur Bodur, Concordia University, Canada
Dina Rasolofoarison, Aston University, UK

EXTENDED ABSTRACT

When choosing from an array of products, consumers are more likely to choose the option located in the center (*horizontal centrality effect*). This effect is demonstrated in various contexts, when choosing among highlighters, chairs, bathroom stalls and products in a shelf display (Christenfeld 1995; Shaw et al. 2000). This is a relevant phenomenon for marketers; using eye tracking methodology van der Lans et al. (2008) demonstrated that competitive advantage on the shelf is generated mostly by in-store factors rather than out-of-store factors with a ratio of 2:1. In this research, a positive effect of horizontal centrality on choice was found across three studies and product categories (vitamins, meal replacement bars, and energy drinks). Findings from two eye tracking studies (1 and 2) support a visual attention based explanation of horizontal centrality on choice. Study 3 further demonstrated that the central option in the product category is chosen even when the product is not in the center of the visual field.

What derives the horizontal centrality effect? In recent eye-tracking studies, Chandon et al. (2007, 2009) found that brands located in the (vertical and horizontal) center of a shelf are noted more and chosen more often, supporting an attention based explanation. Valenzuela and Raghubir (2009) proposed *center-stage effect* as an explanation: Consumers hold the lay belief that in retail contexts the products placed in central positions are more popular, reflecting the overall quality of the product, which leads consumers to systematically prefer items in the center. Note that, Chandon et al. (2007, 2009) focused only on visual attention, did not measure inferences made about the chosen brand, whereas Valenzuela and Raghubir

(2009) reported an indirect effect through brand inferences, but not through memory based attention.

Research in visual perception identified a crucial role of visual attention in the final moments of the choice task that shapes individual's preference for the eventually chosen alternative, *independent* of the effects of memory or prior preferences (Shimojo et al. 2003; Simion and Shimojo 2006). Shimojo et al. (2003) conducted gaze pattern analyses in a binary choice task, and found that the role of attention on preference for the chosen option is rapid and concentrated in the final moments of the choice task (*gaze cascade effect*).

This project provides an investigation of consumer search and choice process. Using eye-tracking methodology, in study 1 (N=63), participants were presented with a 3x3 shelf display. The brands were organized in columns such that the effect of horizontal position was isolated. Brands were rotated such that each brand was presented in left, center, or right. Each brand had equal number of facings (3). Other contextual effects (e.g., brand names, background color, readability) were pretested and ruled out prior to study 1.

Participants reviewed each product on the screen as if they were on the store shelf and indicated their brand choice. Next, they were asked to complete a survey that assessed their inferences about the brands, memory based attention, product familiarity and demographics. The product categories were repeated within participants.

Overall, horizontal centrality increased choice by 18.0%. A brand located in the center had a choice frequency of 45.3%, whereas a brand that was not in the center had a choice frequency of 27.3%. An ANOVA revealed a significant effect of horizontal centrality on visual attention captured by eye tracking measures and choice ($p <$

Figure 1

Study 1: Likelihood of Looking at Each Column During the Initial and Final Five Seconds

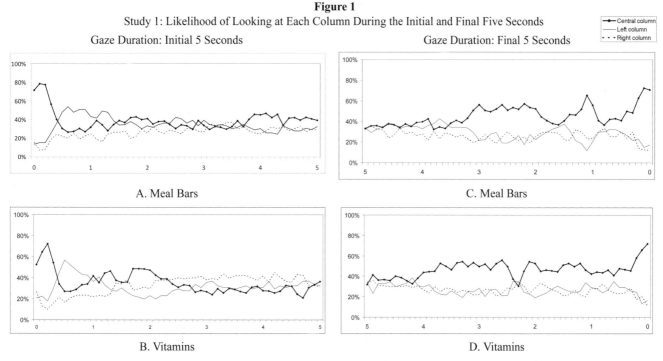

A. Meal Bars

C. Meal Bars

B. Vitamins

D. Vitamins

Note that the likelihood to look at the central, left, and right columns are represented by the bold, solid, and dashed line, respectively.
Sampling bins are 100 milliseconds.

.05), but not on brand inferences or memory based attention measures ($p > .10$). A multiple mediation analysis revealed that the indirect effect of horizontal centrality on choice through visual attention is significant ($p < .05$). The indirect effects of horizontal centrality on choice through brand inferences and memory based attention were not significant.

Next, gaze analyses explored: (1) Is there a greater tendency to focus on the horizontal center in the *initial* few seconds or *final* 5 seconds of the gaze? (2) Does the higher visual attention on the horizontal center in the initial or final 5 seconds of the gaze duration drive the effect of attention on brand choice? As in Shimojo et al. (2003), gaze likelihood curves were plotted for the initial 5 seconds and final 5 seconds of the choice task (see Figure 1). Although there was a higher likelihood to focus on the central brand in the initial and final 5 seconds, this pattern was consistently significant only in the final 5 seconds. A multiple mediation analysis using visual attention in the initial and final 5 seconds also revealed that visual attention in the final 5 seconds mediated the impact of central location on choice.

Study 2 (N=64) investigated whether the horizontal centrality effect is explained by horizontal centrality of the brand or by centrality on the computer screen. Study 2 extended the design of study 1 by introducing displays that were shifted off the center of the computer screen. Results were similar to study 1 and ruled out screen-based presentation as the possible explanation for the centrality effect ($p <.05$).

In retail contexts, the centrally located product in the array of products in a particular product category may not necessarily be in the center of the shelf space and the consumers' visual field. Would a product placed in the center of an array of products within a category, but to the right or left side of the shelf, still be chosen more often? Study 3 (N=84) addressed this question with tangible products (3D) presented on a shelf. Results showed that the centrally located brand is chosen more often, even when it is not placed in the center of the shelf or the visual field ($p <.05$).

The effect of horizontal centrality on visual attention and choice was demonstrated, and the process of visual attention was explored.

The findings suggest that in the context of choice between unfamiliar yet similar options, horizontal centrality and increased visual attention drives choice. Interestingly the effect of centrality on choice is not due to favorable evaluations of the chosen option. The findings point to horizontal central shelf location as premium location.

REFERENCES

Chandon, Pierre, J. Wesley Hutchinson, Eric T. Bradlow, and Scott Young (2007), "Measuring the Value of Point-of-Purchase Marketing with Commercial Eye-Tracking-Data," in *Visual Marketing: From Attention to Action*, ed. Michel Wedel and Rik Pieters, New York, NY: Erlbaum, 225-58.

_____ (2009), "Does In-Store Marketing Work? Effects of the Number and Position of Shelf Facings on Brand Attention and Evaluation at the Point of Purchase," *Journal of Marketing*, 73 (November), 1-17.

Christenfeld, Nicholas (1995), "Choices from Identical Options," *Psychological Science*, 6 (January), 50-5.

Shaw, Jerry I., Jon E. Bergen, Chad A. Brown, and Maureen E. Gallagher (2000), "Centrality Preferences in Choices among Similar Options," *Journal of General Psychology*, 127 (April), 157-64.

Shimojo, Shinsuke, Claudiu Simion, Eiko Shimojo, and Christian Scheier (2003), "Gaze Bias Both Reflects and Influences Preference," *Nature Neuroscience*, 6 (December), 1317-322.

Simion, Claudiu and Shinsuke Shimojo (2006), "Early Interactions Between Orienting, Visual Sampling and Decision Making in Facial Preference," *Vision Research*, 46 (October), 3331-335.

Valenzuela, Ana and Priya Raghubir (2009), "Position-based Beliefs: The Center-Stage Effect," *Journal of Consumer Psychology*, 19 (April), 185-96.

van der Lans, Ralf, Rik Pieters, and Michel Wedel (2008), "Competitive Brand Salience," *Marketing Science*, 27 (September), 922–31.

Spatio-Temporal Dimensions in Consumer-Oriented Activism

Andreas Chatzidakis, Royal Holloway, University of London, UK
Pauline Maclaran, Royal Holloway, University of London, UK
Alan Bradshaw, Royal Holloway University of London, UK

EXTENDED ABSTRACT

Research on the interface between politics, ethics and consumer culture has grown substantially since the 1990s (e.g. Arnould 2007; Shah et al. 2007). Encapsulated in terms such as anti-consumption (e.g. Iyer and Muncy 2008), consumer resistance (e.g. Penaloza and Price 1993), radical consumption (Littler 2009) and consumer-oriented activism (Barnett et al. 2011), the extant studies have followed two main paradigmatic traditions. The first takes a more socio-cognitive perspective and attempts to understand instances of consumer activism in terms of individual attitudes and decision-making processes (see Harrison, Newholm and Shaw 2005). The second, paralleling developments within consumer culture theory (Arnould and Thompson 2005), attempts to provide a more contextualised understanding, focusing on themes such as identity projects, consumption communities and socio-economic factors that determine the scope and nature of consumer-oriented activism. Yet, despite significant advancements, the temporal and spatial elements of consumption remain largely unexplored and under-theorised. In fact more generally, researchers have only recently started to explore the spatio-temporal parameters of all consumption activity (e.g. Visconti et al. 2010). Accordingly, in this research we attempt to develop a more nuanced understanding of the role of space and time in consumption, by acknowledging both objectivist and relativist dimensions.

The empirical site of our analysis is Exarcheia, an anarchist neighbourhood in Athens that has been the birthplace of the 2008 Greek riots and is renowned for its anti-capitalist, anti-consumerist ethos. We draw on data that includes field notes, participant observation and interviews, to illustrate how this turbulent area provides a rich site for exploring the relationship of space and time with consumer activism.

Figure 1: Conceptual Framework

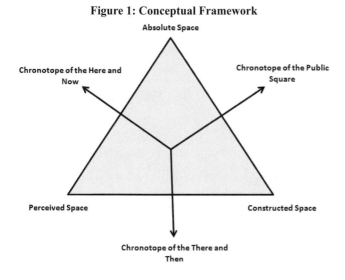

Our findings point to a conceptualisation of consumption spaces that moves beyond conventional understandings of actual-material space as simply 'a kind of container in which . . . entities are found and . . . events take place' (Abbott 2008 cited in Hones 2011, 686). In resonance with seminal contributions to spatial studies by Lefebevre, Soja and Harvey, we propose a triadic view of space as *absolute*, *perceived* and *constructed*. For instance, whereas *absolute* space in our data included the built environment and its various facets, from street art and graffiti-covered walls to frequent intersections that enable the spread of riots (Makrygianni and Tsadvaroglou 2011), *perceived* space included the more experiential-phenomenological aspects, such as "a sense of tension and urgency" that almost all of our informants mentioned when visiting the area. Finally our notion of *constructed* space includes place as the ever-contested product of social relations (Lefebvre, 1991). Within Exarcheia, this becomes evident in Exarcheia residents' ongoing struggles against the comnmodification of their city, from throwing bricks and firebombs at Apple stores and Starbucks, to occupying squares and constructing guerrilla parks.

Subsequently, we attempt to theorize the intersection of space with time that is beyond the linear-chrononological (Kern 2003), by drawing on Bahktin's (1981) notion of the chronotope (literally meaning time-space). In analyzing our informants' narratives in relation to (anti-)consumption practices, we identify three key chronotopes, the Bakhtinian *Public Square*, the *Here and Now* and the *There and Then,* that although distinct, they are also interlinked. The chronotope of the public square reflects informants' pride in their communal spaces where many of the anti-consumption practices take place and are shared. For instance one of the Exarcheian public squares used to be a deserted parking lot earmarked for (commercial) redevelopment by the mayor and city planners until it was occupied and bulldozed by locals. It is now transformed into a very impressive park and public space that operates on the basis of anti-commercialisation and gift economy. In talking about the park, many of our older informants mentioned how it reminded them, somewhat nostalgically, the spirit of past Athens, a period in which community living and social interaction around squares was common. Concurrently, residents' attempts to fight against the commodification of their public space, point to that space can be not only the context but also the object of (anti-)consumption; consumption as *in* and *of* space and place (cf. Goodman, Goodman and Redclift 2010). The here and now chronotope relates to experimentations with doing things differently, of creating societies within society and moments of "cracks" (Holloway 2010), as opposed to waiting for mass insurrection and total overthrow of free market capitalism. It is mainly this chronotopic logic that fed into various forms of consumer-oriented activism in Exarcheia, including, among others, various alternative food networks and forums for the exchange of knowledge and services; collectives who contribute to an economy of solidarity by supporting ethical producers and importing coffee from the Zapatistas, collective cooking events, self-managed squats and "no ticket" cinema screenings, music and artistic events. Finally, the there and then chronotope includes residents' utopic visions of an ideal society that makes them continuously question the current socio-economic system, of which consumer culture is a key part.

The third part of our analysis examines the intersection of different spaces and chronotopes. As the surrounding city deeps further into recession and increasingly faces the "there and then" of the past, we observe moments of explosion (solidarity trading events and occupy movements in other neighbourhoods in Athens; cf. Vradis and Dalakoglou 2011) but also of implosion (dramatic fall of living standards and explosion of violence) that (among others) have redefined the types and nature of consumer-oriented activism. For instance, in some collectives the notion of anti-consumption has become redundant as it has quickly given way to solidarity for all those that now have to live below the poverty line.

In the final part of the article we consider the spatial and chronotopic parameters of alternative consumption spaces and practices. For instance, more conventional forms of consumer activism, such as Fair Trade purchasing and boycotting, are still embedded within a chronotope of a here and now, albeit in spaces that are far less lived and contested (e.g. supermarkets), whereas the chronotope of the public square is to some extent recreated in anti-consumerist festivals (Kozinets 2002) and in frequenting coffee establishments (Thompson and Arsel 2004). Implications and avenues for future research are discussed.

REFERENCES

Arnould, Eric J. (2007), "Should Consumers Escape the Market?", *The Annals of the American Academy of Political and Social Science,* 611 (May), 96-111.

Arnould, Eric J. and Craig J. Thompson, (2005), "Consumer Culture Theory (CCT): Twenty Years of Research." *Journal of Consumer Research,* 31, 868-882.

Bakhtin, Mikhail (1981), *The Dialogic Imagination – Four Essays.* Austin, TX: University of Texas Press.

Barnett, Clive, Paul Cloke, Nick Clarke, and Alice Malpass (2011), *Globalising Responsibility: The Political Rationalities of Ethical Consumption.* Oxford: Wiley-Balckwell.

Goodman, Michael K., David Goodman, and M. Redclift (2010), *Consuming Space – Placing Consumption in Perspective,* Burlington, VP: Ashgate.

Harrison, Rob, Terry Newholm and Deirdre Shaw (2005), *The Ethical Consumer.* London: Sage.

Holloway, John (2010), *Crack Capitalism.* London: Pluto Press.

Hones, Sheila (2011), "Literary Geography: Setting and Narrative Space", *Social & Cultural Geography,* 12 (7), 685-699.

Iyer, Rajesh and James A. Muncy (2009), "Purpose and Object of Anti-consumption.", *Journal of Business Research,* 62(2), 160–168.

Kozinets, V. Rob (2002), "Can Consumers Escape the Market? Emancipatory Illuminations from Burning Man, *Journal of Consumer Research,* 29, 20-38.

Kern. Stephen (2003), *The Culture of Time and Space, 1880-1918: with a New Preface,* Harvard: Harvard University Press.

Lefebvre, Henri (1991), *The Production of Space,* Cambridge, MA: Blackwell.

Littler, Jo (2009), *Radical Consumption: Shopping for Change in Contemporary Culture,* Open University Press.

Makrygianni, Vaso and Haris Tsadvaroglou, (2011), "Urban Planning and Revolt: A Spatial Analysis of the December 2008 Uprising in Athens.", In Vradis, Antonis and Dimitris Dalakoglou, (Eds). *Revolt and crisis in Greece – Between a present yet to pass and a future yet to come.* London: AK Press, (29-57).

Peñaloza, Lisa and Linda Price (1993), "Consumer Resistance: A Conceptual Overview.", *Advances in Consumer Research,* 20 (1), 123-128.

Shah, Dhavan V., Douglas M. McLeod, Lewis Friedland, L. and Michelle R. Nelson, (2007), "The Politics of Consumption/ The Consumption of Politics", *The Annals of the American Academy of Political and Social Science,* 611, 6-15.

Thompson, Craig J and Zeynep Arsel, (2004). "The Starbucks Brandscape and Consumers' (Anticorporate) Experiences of Glocalisation." *Journal of Consumer Research,* 31, 631-642.

Visconti, Luca M, John F. Sherry Jr, Stefania Borghini, and Laurel Anderson, (2010), "Street Art, Sweet Art? Reclaiming the "Public" in Public Space, *Journal of Consumer Research,* 37, 511-529.

Vradis, Antonis and Dimitris Dalakoglou, (2011). *Revolt and Crisis in Greece – Between a Present Yet to Pass and a Future Yet to Come.* London: AK Press.

Zizek, Slavoj (2010), *Living in the End of Times.* London: Verso.

Navigating the Waters: Regulating versus Using Feelings Toward Risky Choices

Eugene Chan, University of Toronto, Canada
Najam Saqib, Qatar University, Qatar

EXTENDED ABSTRACT

Research on how people's feelings toward risky choices affect such choices has been of interest in the past 30 years (Loewenstein et al. 2001; Slovic et al. 2004). We draw upon two streams of research on affect regarding non-risky choices and apply them to risky ones. One stream suggests that people take actions to balance or repair their feelings, known as "affect regulation" (Manucia, Baumann, and Cialdini 1984; Isen 1987), while another stream suggests that people use their feelings as informational input, known as "affect-as-input" (Mayer et al. 1992; Schwarz and Clore 1983). We extrapolate these two streams' predictions regarding *non-risky* choices to make predictions regarding *risky* choices.

People who regulate their feelings make choices that produce a favourable affective outcome. They thus aim to avoid negative outcomes. Over risky gains, which produce positive feelings about possible benefits from taking risks, they avoid risks to prevent losses from accruing and to keep their feelings "in check". Similarly, over risky losses, which produce negative feelings about possible dangers, they would avoid risks for the same reason. By taking risks but losing, the counterfactual that they could have won with certainty would be unfavourable. As such, we predict that people who regulate their feelings *fear* the worst possible outcome that could come from taking risks – over both gain and loss domains. Meanwhile, people who use their feelings use them as a sign about possible directions to take. Positive feelings signal that "everything is okay" but negative ones signal that "something is wrong". Over risky gains, they consider positive feelings toward possible benefits as a sign that they can accrue possible gains, suggesting risk-seeking. Over risky losses, they consider their negative feelings toward possible dangers as a sign that something needs to be done to avoid possible losses, again suggesting risk-taking. As such, we predict that people who use their feelings *hope* for the possible outcome that could come from taking risks – over both gain and loss domains.

Five experiments support our hypothesis. In Experiments 1A and 1B, we primed participants to regulate or use their feelings by having them think affectively or analytically, respectively (Hsee and Rottenstreich 2004). Participants primed to regulate their feelings preferred the certain option in the Asian disease problem (Experiment 1A; Tversky and Kahneman 1981) and were more likely to sell their shares in a hypothetical stock scenario in the disposition effect (Experiment 1B) than participants primed to use their feelings. These findings were consistent over both gain and loss domains (Experiment 1A; Figure 1) and whether the stock portfolio increased or decreased (Experiment 1B; Figure 2).

In Experiment 2, we used a different manipulation of regulating and using feelings. People thinking concretely regulate their feelings, while people thinking abstractly use them, due to the affective feedback loop that exists in concrete but not abstract mindsets (Kivetz and Kivetz, *forthcoming*). We thus primed participants with a concrete or abstract mindset. In a hypothetical gamble between winning $500 and a 50% chance of winning $1,000, or between losing $500 and a 50% chance of losing $1,000, participants primed to regulate their feelings prefer the certain option more over both gain and loss domains than participants primed to use their feelings (Figure 3).

Experiments 3 and 4 shed light on the hypothesized emphasis on fear and hope from regulating or using feelings, respectively. In Experiment 3, we measured participants' tendencies to regulate or use their feelings using the Negative Mood Regulation scale (NMR; Catanzaro and Mearns 1990). Participants took part in a hypothetical lottery similar to Experiment 2. However, before they made their choices, they wrote about what they would do and feel if they either "win" or "lose" by taking the risky option. Findings replicated those from Experiment 2. Participants who regulated their feelings wrote about the worst possible outcome, while those who used their feelings wrote about the best possible outcome – again, over both gain and loss domains. This suggests an emphasis on fear and hope, respectively.

Finally, Experiment 4 used a word-association task to measure participants' tendencies to regulate or use their feelings. First, participants wrote down the first word that came to mind in response to negatively-valenced words such as *cancer*. Then, they wrote down words in response to neutral words such as *chair*. We coded responses on this second task as either positive or negative, as a proxy for regulating or using feelings. Participants indicated their subjective happiness towards winning or losing a series of money from $100 to $1,000. We fitted a regression model in each gain/loss domain for participants who regulated/used their feelings, and included the squared subjective happiness to assess the second-order curvature of participants' utility curves (Figure 4). Participants who regulated their feelings had concave curves, while those who used their feelings had convex curves. These findings suggest risk-aversion and risk-seeking, respectively, over both gain and loss domains.

This research suggests that people who regulate their feelings are risk-averse while those who use them are risk-seeking over both gain and loss domains. This is likely due to the emphasis on fear or hope from taking risks, as Experiments 3 and 4 suggest. We offer an implication for prospect theory: people are risk-averse over gains because they regulate their feelings, but people are risk-seeking over losses because they use those feelings. Our findings bridge research distinguishing between affect regulation and affect-as-input, with that on risky decision-making. Our findings also encourage future research to focus more on anticipated than current feelings. That is, they should emphasize the "prospect" in prospect theory.

REFERENCES

Catanzaro, Salvatore J. and Jack Mearns (1990), "Measuring Generalized Expectancies for Negative Mood Regulation: Initial Scale Development and Implications," *Journal of Personality Assessment*, 54 (Summer), 546-63.

Hsee, Christopher K. and Yuval Rottenstreich (2004), "Music, Pandas, and Muggers: On the Affective Psychology of Value," *Journal of Experimental Psychology: General*, 133 (March), 23-30.

Isen, Alice M. (1987), "Positive Affect, Cognitive Processes, and Social Behavior," in *Advances in Experimental Social Psychology*, vol. 20, ed. Leonard Berkowitz, San Diego: Academic Press, 203-53.

Kivetz, Ran and Yifat Kivetz (forthcoming), "Reconciling Mood congruency and Mood Regulation: The Role of Psychological Distance," *Journal of Personality and Social Psychology*.

Loewenstein, George, Elke U. Weber, Christopher K. Hsee, C. K., and Ned Welch (2001), "Risk as Feelings," *Psychological Bulletin*, 127 (March), 267-86.

Manucia, Gloria K., Donald J. Baumann, and Robert B. Cialdini (1984), "Mood Influences on Helping: Direct Effects or Side Effects?" *Journal of Personality & Social Psychology*, 46 (February), 357-64.

Mayer, John D., Yvonne N. Gaschke, Debra L. Braverman, Temperance W. Evans (1992), "Mood-Congruent Judgment is a General Effect," *Journal of Personality and Social Psychology*, 63 (July), 119-32.

Schwarz, Norbert and Gerald L. Clore (1983), "Mood, Misattribution and Judgments of Well-Being: Informative and Directive Functions of Affective States," *Journal of Personality and Social Psychology*, 45 (September), 513-23.

Slovic, Paul, Melissa Finucane, Ellen Peters, and Donald G. MacGregor (2004), "Risk as Analysis and Risk as Feelings: Some Thoughts about Affect, Reason, Risk, and Rationality," *Risk Analysis*, 24 (April), 1-12.

Tversky, Amos and Daniel Kahneman (1981), "The Framing of Decisions and the Psychology of Choice," *Science*, 211 (January), 453-58.

The Impact of Goal (Non)attainment on Behavior through Changes in Regulatory Focus.

Danielle Mantovani, Federal University of Parana, Brazil
Paulo Prado, Federal University of Parana, Brazil
Eduardo B. Andrade, University of California Berkeley, USA

EXTENDED ABSTRACT

Based on the regulatory fit phenomenon, the authors examined how goal (non)attainment of a particular goal can influence subsequent behavior through changes in regulatory focus (experiments 1 and 2). Experiment 3 shed light into the boundary conditions of this phenomenon and how emotions play a role into the process.

Feedback about goal progress or goal attainment represents a mundane experience in consumers' lives. A lot has been done to understand how performance feedback impacts motivational aspects such as goal pursuit, commitment and goal revision (Finkelstein and Fishbach 2012). Much less is known, however, on how performance feedback influences people's specific mindsets, and particularly, regulatory focus. Despite the huge literature in the area (Crowe and Higgins 1997; Shah, Higgins and Friedman 1998; Higgins et al 2003), the role of previous success and failure on state regulatory focus, and subsequent behavior is yet to be systematically investigated.

According to the classic psychological theories of motivation, it is possible to suggest that success feedback induces approach motivation, whereas failure feedback raises avoidance motivation (Atkinson 1974; Carver and Sheier 1998). Therefore, we hypothesize (H1) that promotion (vs. prevention)-focused message in a subsequent task will be more persuasive after people have *succeeded* in a previous unrelated task whereas a prevention (vs. promotion)-focused message in a subsequent task will be more persuasive after people *failed* in a previous unrelated task.

Achieving (vs. not achieving) a goal, not surprisingly, triggers meaningful emotional reactions (Carver, 2006). People feel happy and proud after accomplishing a task (Higgins et $al.$ 2001), whereas disappointment and frustration arise when the goal is not attained (Bosmans and Baumgartner 2005). An open question is the extent to which these emotions contribute to the previously predicted interaction or if a simple cognitive priming of goal (non)attainment suffices to impact regulatory focus. We hypothesize (H2) that emotions play a major role into the process and that the feeling of disappointment and/or frustration (rather than the sheer priming of goal non-attainment) is critical into making people more sensitive to a prevention focus message. Similarly, the feelings of joy and/or pride (rather than the sheer priming of goal attainment) are critical into making people more persuaded by a promotion focus message.

Experiment 1 (n = 148) used a 2 (goal: attained vs. unattained) by 2 (message frame: promotion focus vs. prevention focus) between subjects design to test H1. Participants were informed that the goal of the study was to analyze individual's problem solving skills. The goal (solve the problems) was either attainable or not and participants were randomly assigned to one of the conditions (Puca and Schmalt 1999, Shah and Kruglanski 2002). In the second part of the experiment, participants read one of two advertisements for a brand juice, framed in a promotion or prevention focus manner (adapted from Aaker and Lee 2001). Finally, they evaluated the target product. As expected, participants showed stronger attitude toward the ad and higher willingness to buy the product when being exposed to promotion frame message after having *attained* a goal in previously unrelated task, whereas the opposite was true when participants had *failed to attain* the goal in previously unrelated task. In that case, the prevention focus message dominated. H1 was supported (Attitude; F

$(1, 144) = 18.58, p < .001; \eta_p^2 = .114$; WTB; $F (1, 144) = 12.9, p < .001, \eta_p^2 = .082$).

Experiment 2 (n = 120) was designed to replicate the previous findings and to test the robustness of the effect using a more consequential dependent variable. The procedure followed was similar to the one used in experiment 1, but participants, who had received a U\$3.00 fee, could use the money to purchase the product (the grape juice). Results confirm the evidence that when the goal was attained in a previous irrelevant task, participants paid on average more for the product when the ad message was framed in a promotion (vs. prevention) focus manner. The opposite pattern was observed when the goal was not attained ($F (1, 116) = 12.78, p < .001, \eta_p^2 = .099$). As expected, a two-way interaction between goal and message frame emerged both for the, supporting H1.

Experiment 3 (n = 240) tested H2 - the role of emotions - and employed a 2 (goal: attained vs. unattained) x 2 (message frame: promotion focus vs. prevention focus) x 2 (task: real vs. hypothetical) between subjects design. In the hypothetical task condition, participants were given instructions about the task and were asked to quickly imagine going through it and attaining (vs. non-attaining) the goal. In the real condition, like in the previous experiments, participants went through the actual task and either attained or not the goal. Participants were then exposed to a promotion vs. prevention message frame in a subsequent unrelated study. In the actual task condition, where participants did feel significantly prouder (frustrated) for having attained (not attained) the goal, the findings replicate the 2 previous studies. In the hypothetical goal condition, however, where participants did not experience stronger feelings of pride or frustration, the interaction went way. Study 3 sets an important boundary condition. Simply priming people with hypothetical goal (non)attainment manipulation is not enough to generate the regulatory fit phenomenon observed in experiments 1 and 2. It requires that people experience the pleasures and pains associated with goal (non)attainment for the effect to emerge.

REFERENCES

Aaker, Jennifer L., and Angela Lee (2001), ""I" Seek Pleasures and "We" Avoid Pains: The Role of Self-regulatory Goals in Information Processing and Persuasion," *Journal of Consumer Research, 28*(June), 33–49.

Atkinson, John W. (1974), Strength and Motivation and Efficiency of Performance. In J. W. Atkinson & J. O. Raynor (Eds.), *Motivation and achievement* (pp. 193-218). New York: Wiley.

Bosmans, Anick, and Hans Baumgartner (2005), "Goal-Relevant Emotional Information: When Extraneous Affect Leads to Persuasion and When It Does Not," *Journal of Consumer Research*, 32 (December), 424-434.

Carver, Charles S. (2006), "Approach, Avoidance, and the Self-Regulation of Affect and Action," *Motivation and Emotion,* 30 (September), 105-110.

Carver, Charles S., and Michel F. Scheier (1998), *On the Self-Regulation of Behavior.* New York: Cambridge University Press.

Crowe, Ellen and E. Tory Higgins (1997), "Regulatory Focus and Strategic Inclinations: Promotion and Prevention in Decision-Making," *Organizational Behavior and Human Decision Processes*, 69 (February), 117-132.

Finkelstein, Stacey R., Ayelet Fishbach (2012), "Tell Me What I Did Wrong: Experts Seek and Respond More to Negative Feedback," *Journal of Consumer Research,* 39 (June), p.1-17.

Higgins, E. Tory, Antonio L. Freitas, Lorraine Chen Idson, Scott Spiegel and Daniel C. Molden (2003), "Transfer of Value From Fit," *Journal of Personality and Social Psychology,* 84 (Junho),1140–1153.

Higgins, E. Tory, Ronald S. Friedman, Robert E. Harlow, Lorraine Chen Idson, Ozlem N. Ayduk, and Amy Taylor (2001), "Achievement Orientation from Subjective Histories of Success: Promotion Pride Versus Prevention Pride," *European Journal of Social Psychology*, 31(January), 3-23.

Puca, Rosa M., Heinz-Dieter Schmalt (1999), "Task Enjoyment: A Mediator Between Achievement Motives and Performance," *Motivation and Emotion*, 23, 15-29.

Shah, James Y., and Arie W. Kruglanski (2002), "Priming Against Your Will: How Accessible Alternatives Affect Goal Pursuit," *Journal of Experimental Social Psychology*, 38(July), 368-383.

Shah, James; Higgins, E. Tory and Ronald S. Friedman (1998), "Performance Incentives and Means: How Regulatory Focus Influences Goal Attainment," *Journal of Personality and Social Psychology*, 74 (February), 285-293.

The Ghosts of Information Past and Future:
Effects of Memory and Motivation on Reference Price

Jolie M. Martin, University of Minnesota, USA
Tomas Lejarraga, University of the Balearic Islands, Spain
Cleotilde Gonzalez, Carnegie Mellon University, USA

EXTENDED ABSTRACT

In recent years, reference-dependence has gained acceptance as a conceptual framework for understanding the way that consumers compare outcomes of their choices to other salient outcomes in their environment. Kahneman and Tversky's Prospect Theory (1979) formalized the idea that consumption utility is determined by the difference of an outcome from a reference point rather than by its absolute value. There exist many real-world examples where reference points accurately describe behavior (Camerer, 2000). Within the domain of finance, for instance, empirical evidence demonstrates robust loss aversion in the reluctance of stock holders to sell below their purchase price (Shefrin and Statman, 1985). However, there is little consensus among researchers about the *ex ante* specification of an individual's reference point in various decision contexts (Klein and Oglethorpe, 1987). Reference points are purported to derive from a range of disparate sources including a consumer's past experiences (Wathieu, 1997), immediate social comparisons (Novemsky and Schweitzer, 2004), and expectations about the future (Koszegi and Rabin, 2006).

The goal of the present research is to explore the contextual factors that impact consumers' formation of reference points so that, ultimately, reference points can be isolated to serve as better predictors of behavior. Here, we focus on reference *prices*, which are the salient dollar amounts to which consumers compare other potential buying or selling prices. Because prices fall along a single quantifiable dimension of money, this narrowed scope eliminates confounds of multi-dimensional comparisons (e.g., "reference points" for vacations). Specifically, we assess how reference prices for stocks are affected by two contextual factors: (1) whether decision-makers have the history of price information available versus relying on memory alone, and (2) whether decision-makers are motivated to adopt a high reference price as sellers or a low reference price as buyers. We hypothesized these factors to influence the use of information in reference price formation in several ways. First, primacy and recency memory effects suggest that the first and most recent pieces of information, respectively, will be recalled most readily (Ebbinghaus, 1913; Hogarth and Einhorn, 1992). We predicted that these memory effects would play a greater role when historical price information was unavailable to decision-makers. Second, both subconscious emotions and deliberative reasoning about prices tend to reflect consumers' motivations (Heath, Larrick, and Wu, 1999: Kunda, 1990). We thus expected decision-makers to focus on favorable reference prices when several were available.

Our methodology was based on that of Baucells, Weber, and Welfens (2011). In several laboratory studies, these authors showed participants the evolution of stock prices over time (revealed on the screen one-by-one), and then elicited reference prices by asking participants the price at which they would feel neutral (neither happy nor unhappy) about selling the stock in the next time period. Every participant did this for the same 60 randomly ordered price sequences, which were designed to differ on five informational variables: first price (*first*), last price (*last*), average intermediate price (*average*), high price (*high*), and low price (*low*). We extended this paradigm by testing how the effects of these variables on reference price differed according to contextual factors of memory and motivation. In

an online experiment conducted in the laboratory, we used the same price sequences and reference price elicitation procedure, but with a 2x2 between-subjects design varying both the presence or absence of the stock history (i.e., a list of previous prices) when participants reported their reference price (*history* = 1 or 0, respectively), and the role of participants as stock seller or buyer (*seller* = 1 or 0, respectively). Eighty participants (35 female; M_{age} = 23.1) completed the study for a flat payment of $10.

Our results show that both memory and motivation interact with objective information to influence reference prices. There are no three-way interactions, so our regression analysis includes main effects of the five informational variables (*first*, *last*, *average*, *high*, and *low*), main effects of the two contextual factors (*history* and *seller*), and the 10 two-way interactions between each of the five informational variables and the two contextual factors (R^2=.11, $F(17, 4782)$=36.3, $p<.0001$). We find a significant main effect of each of the five informational variables except *low*. The coefficient is positive for *first* (β=0.088, p=.008), *last* (β=0.40, $p<.0001$), and *average* (β=0.41, $p<.0001$), which indicates that increasing any of these variables while holding the others constant raises reference prices. However, the coefficient is negative for *high* (β=-0.17, p=.0006), which suggests – less intuitively – that a higher maximum stock price lowers reference price. We attribute this to overcompensation by participants in ensuring that peak information is not weighted too heavily, particularly in light of the recent stock market crisis.

More central to the present analysis are the effects of contextual factors which differ across the four experimental conditions. Although neither main effect of *history* or *seller* is significant, their interactions with the informational variables partially support our hypotheses. Each has a positive interaction with *first* (*history* x *first*: β=0.096, p=.01; *seller* x *first*: β=0.21, $p<.0001$), a negative interaction with *last* (*history* x *last*: β=-0.10, p=.05; *seller* x *last*: β=-0.11, p=.04), and a negative interaction with *average* (*history* x *average*: β=-0.12, p=.05; *seller* x *average*: β=-0.18, p=.005). Taken together, these results demonstrate a stronger effect of primacy than of recency when the price history is available (compared to decay over time during reliance on memory alone), and when individuals are motivated to recoup their purchase price as sellers (compared to buyers who place more emphasis on recent prices). In addition, we observe positive interactions between *history* and *high* (β=0.16, p=.005), and between *seller* and *high* (β=0.15, p=.008), meaning that the availability of historical prices and the motivation to transact at a higher price, respectively, increase weight on the sequence peak as a reference point. We suspect that both factors make this "one-off" piece of information more salient.

We conclude by discussing the role of memory and motivation in shaping reference prices across a range of consumer choices. We also highlight other features of a decision context that might alter information processing, and in turn, reference point formation.

REFERENCES

Baucells, Manel, Martin Weber, and Frank Welfens (2011), "Reference-Point Formation and Updating," *Management Science*, 57(3), 506-519.

Camerer, Colin F. (2000), "Prospect Theory in the Wild: Evidence from the Field," in D. Kahneman and A. Tversky (Eds.), *Choices, Values, and Frames* (pp. 288-300), Cambridge, UK: Cambridge University Press.

Ebbinghaus, Hermann (1913), *Memory: A Contribution to Experimental Psychology*, New York, NY: Teachers College, Columbia University.

Heath, Chip, Richard P. Larrick, and George Wu (1999), "Goals as Reference Points," *Cognitive Psychology*, 38(1), 79-109.

Hogarth, Robin M., and Hillel J. Einhorn (1992), "Order Effects in Belief Updating: The Belief-Adjustment Model," *Cognitive Psychology*, 24(1), 1-55.

Kahneman, Daniel, and Amos Tversky (1979), "Prospect Theory: An Analysis of Decision Under Risk," *Econometrica,* 47(2), 263–292.

Klein, Noreen H., and Janet E. Oglethorpe (1987), "Cognitive Reference Points in Consumer Decision Making," in M. Wallendorf and P. Anderson (Eds.), *Advances in Consumer Research Volume 14* (pp. 183-187), Provo, UT : Association for Consumer Research.

Koszegi, Botond, and Matthew Rabin (2006), "A Model of Reference Dependent Preferences," *Quarterly Journal of Economics*, 121(4), 1133-1165.

Kunda, Ziva (1990), "The Case for Motivated Reasoning," *Psychological Bulletin*, 108(3), 480-498.

Novemsky, Nathan, and Maurice E. Schweitzer (2004), "What Makes Negotiators Happy? The Differential Effects of Internal and External Social Comparisons on Negotiator Satisfaction," *Organizational Behavior and Human Decision Processes*, 95(2), 186–197.

Shefrin, Hersh, and Meir Statman (1985), "The Disposition to Sell Winners Too Early and Ride Losers Too Long: Theory and Evidence," *Journal of Finance*, 40(3), 777-790.

Wathieu, Luc (1997), "Habits and the Anomalies in Intertemporal Choice," *Management Science*, 43(11), 1552–1563.

Thank You for the Music! A Working Memory Examination of the Effect of Musical Elements on Verbal Learning

Esther Kang, State University of New York, USA
Arun Lakshmanan, State University of New York, USA

EXTENDED ABSTRACT

Past research examining the effect of music on learning have presented mixed findings. Music in advertisements may attract attention, enhance excitement, or act as mnemonic aids (Seashore 1967). Sometimes, music may reduce memory (Oakes and North 2006; Tavassoli and Lee 2003). This paper extends past research by examining the interactive effect of musical *elements* on learning. Specifically, we focus on musical elements that affect the flow of phonological processing when visual learning of verbal information is of interest. While prior research examines the effect of presence or absence of music and its tempo on memory, to the best of our knowledge, the current research is the first to examine (a) how different characteristics of music – lyrics, tempo and repetitiveness – *interact* to affect learning, and, (b) the *process* underlying this interaction. Substantively, given that music is multi-faceted and complex, an understanding of how individual elements interact to shape learning is pertinent for constructing more effective marketing communications.

STUDY 1:
THE IRRELEVANT SPEECH EFFECT IN MUSIC

Music may be classified into two varieties – purely instrumental or vocal, which typically includes lyrics along with instrumentation. According to Salamé and Baddeley (1982), irrelevant speech inhibits encoding of verbal material on account of the limited capacity of the phonological store – a component of working memory. During learning, visually presented verbal information accesses this store via the process of articulation. Auditory elements also directly access this store (Baddeley 2001). Thus, when music containing lyrics is heard while observing visuo-verbal information, (a) the dual load on the phonological store and (b) articulatory suppression leads to reduced learning of verbal information. Formally,

Hypothesis 1:   *Verbal learning will be lower when background music is vocal (vs. instrumental).*

Our experiment followed a single-factor (music: vocal vs. instrumental) design. All participants saw a screen containing product information about a fabric softener on computer while identical music clips (either vocal or purely instrumental) was played in the background. Seventy five undergraduate students participated in exchange for course credit. Supporting H1, a one-way ANOVA on participants' recall of product information revealed a significant main effect ($p<.05$). Specifically, vocal music led to significantly *poorer* recall (Minstru=1.90, Mvocal=1.42; $t(73) = 2.18$, $p<.05$). Study 1 presents initial evidence that vocal music interferes with verbal learning.

STUDY 2: MUSICAL TEMPO AND MUSIC TYPE

According to the theory of changing state effects (Jones, Madden, and Miles 1992), faster music distracts the learner more due to the greater number of changes in 'states' per unit time. Consequently, when tempo is fast, interference from lyrics in vocal music should be more pronounced due to the greater opportunity of sub-vocal repetition of the lyrics themselves, thereby reducing the 'space' available in the phonological store to rehearse visually presented verbal information (Baddeley 2001). Thus,

Hypothesis 2:   *Verbal learning will be poorer for vocal music (versus instrumental) when tempo is fast but not when tempo is slow.*

One hundred undergraduate students participated in a 2 (tempo: fast/slow) × 2 (type: instrumental/vocal) laboratory experiment in which they viewed a product information screen with background music. Tempo was manipulated by using two versions of a song (20% slower vs. 20% faster than the original). Manipulation checks revealed that our tempo manipulation was successful (Mfast=4.28, Mslow=2.94; $t(97)=4.66$, $p<.01$). An ANOVA on verbal learning revealed a two-way interaction ($F (1,95) = 4.36$, $p<.05$). Specifically, when tempo was fast, vocal music led to significantly poorer recall (Mfast-instru =3.27, Mfast-vocal= 2.37; $p<.05$) but when tempo was slow, there were no significant differences (Mslow-instru =2.89, Mslow-vocal= 2.80; $p>.05$). Study 2 demonstrates that fast background music with lyrics interferes more with visuo-verbal learning.

STUDY 3: REPETITIVENESS AND MUSIC TYPE

Repetitive patterns readily awaken 'collaborative expectancy' (Burke 1969). Once listeners grasp the trend of a form, they infer how it is destined to develop and they "collaborate to round out its symmetry". Thus, repetitive music should induce attention to and learning of the musical pattern (as opposed to visually observed verbal information). However, when repetitive music is vocal, individuals' tendency to round out the lyrical pattern should lead to greater interference with verbal content learning. In turn, it should lead to lower verbal recall but correlate with greater attention to music. Formally,

Hypothesis 3:   *Recall will be lower for repetitive (vs. non-repetitive) music when music is vocal (but not instrumental).*

Hypothesis 4:   *Attention to the music will be greater for repetitive (vs. non-repetitive) music when background music is vocal (but not instrumental).*

One hundred and eighteen students participated in a 2 (repetitiveness: repetitive/non-repetitive) × 2 (type: instrumental/vocal) laboratory experiment. We manipulated repetitiveness by reiterating a phrase thrice (once) in the music. Participants' judgments of the music's repetitiveness revealed that our manipulation was successful (Mrepeat= 6.18, Mnon-repeat= 5.23; $t (116) = 3.571$, p<.01). Analyses of variance revealed significant two-way interactions for verbal recall ($F (1,114) = 4.38$, $p<.05$) as well as attention to music ($F (1,114) = 4.62$, $p<.05$). Supporting H3, we found that repetitive music led to poorer recall when music is vocal (Mvocal-repeat=2.26, Mvocal-non repeat=2.96; $p<.05$) but not instrumental (Minstru-repeat=2.63, Minstru-non repeat=2.37; $p>.05$. Supporting H4, repetitiveness also elicited greater attention to music when vocal (Mvocal-repeat=5.44, M vocal-non repeat=4.24; $p<.05$) but not when it was instrumental (Minstru-repeat=4.60, Minstru-non repeat=4.62; $p>.05$). These results further support our conjecture that interference appears to be greatest when *vocal* background music is repetitive.

Further, study 3 presents evidence supporting our theory that interference from lyrical elements diminish verbal learning and recall.

CONTRIBUTION

Our research explores the interactive effect of lyrics, tempo and repetitiveness on verbal learning and finds that lyrical content in music often inhibits verbal learning. Importantly, this is more likely under faster tempos and for repetitive music. We also show that attention to music has an opposite pattern vis-à-vis verbal learning. Thus, while vocal background music may inhibit learning of visually presented product information, it also presents the opportunity for increased learning by drawing attention towards the lyrical content. (994 words).

REFERENCES

Baddeley, Alan D. (2001), "Is Working Memory Still Working?," *American Psychologist*, 56 (11), 851-64.

Burke, Kenneth (1969), *A Rhetoric of Motives*, Berkeley, CA: University of California Press.

Jones, Dylan, Clare Madden, and Chris Miles (1992), "Privileged Access by Irrelevant Speech to Short-Term Memory: The Role of Changing State," *The Quarterly Journal Of Experimental Psychology. A, Human Experimental Psychology*, 44 (4), 645-69.

Oakes, Steve and Adrian C. North (2006), "The Impact of Background Musical Tempo and Timbre Congruity Upon Ad Content Recall and Affective Response," *Applied Cognitive Psychology*, 20 (4), 505-20.

Salamé, Pierre and Alan D. Baddeley (1982), "Disruption of Short-Term Memory by Unattended Speech: Implications for the Structure of Working Memory," *Journal of Verbal Learning and Verbal Behavior*, 21 (2), 150-64.

Seashore, Carl (1967), *Psychology of Music*, New York, NY: Dover Publications.

Tavassoli, Nader T. and Yih Hwai Lee (2003), "The Differential Interaction of Auditory and Visual Advertising Elements with Chinese and English," *Journal of Marketing Research*, 40 (4), 468-80.

Culture, Relationship Norms, and Perceived Fairness of Asymmetric Pricing

Haipeng (Allan) Chen, Texas A&M University, USA
Lisa Bolton, Pennsylvania State University, USA
Sharon Ng, Nanyang Technological University, Singapore

EXTENDED ABSTRACT

According to the principle of dual entitlement (DE), buyers are entitled to a reference price and sellers are entitled to a reference profit. In a series of studies, Kahneman et al. (1986a 1986b) provide evidence that consumers deem it fair for a seller to 1) increase its price when its costs increase (to protect its reference profit), and 2) maintain its price when its costs decrease (because doing so does not violate the buyer's entitlement to a reference price). This pioneering work naturally begs the question: To what extent is DE a *global* standard of fairness?

Although such a question is not readily answered in one research endeavor, prior research has tended to conclude that DE is relatively robust across consumers (e.g., Frey and Pommerehne 1993, Shiller, Boycko, and Borokov 1991, Bian and Keller 1999, Gao 2009, Urbany et al. 1989). Some intriguing differences have emerged in within-subject testing of DE (Kalapurakal et al. 1991) and in across-country testing (e.g., Kimes and Wirtz 2003, Gao 2009). However, the latter has produced mixed evidence by relying upon direct cross-country comparisons that are confounded and do not readily allow conclusions regarding cultural differences (nor psychological mechanism). The present research addresses this issue by priming culture (and corresponding relationship norms) in order to investigate the effects on consumer fairness response within a DE context.

Cultural differences in social relationships and self-definitions, such as independence/interdependence, are one of the myriad dimensions along which cultures vary (e.g., Hofstede 1980; Markus and Kitayama 1991). Although not without its critics (e.g., Brewer and Chen 2007; Oyserman, Coon, and Kemmelmeier 2002; Shavitt et al. 2006), the distinction between independent and interdependence has received robust support, and has been linked to relationship norms that are exchange- and communal-oriented, respectively (Kim et al. 1995; Triandis 1996, 2001a, 2001b). Indeed, Triandis (1995) argues that an emphasis on communal versus exchange relationships is one of the key defining attributes of interdependence and independence. Communal norms emphasize taking others' welfare and interests into account whereas exchange norms endorse the seeking of benefits in the pursuit of self-interest—and these social norms may serve as the standard by which behavior is judged (e.g., Clark and Mills 1993, 1979; Mills and Clark 1982).

Within a DE context, what are the implications of salient norms driven by culture for fairness response? Consider first the case of asymmetric pricing. Asymmetric pricing appears inconsistent with the communal norms of interdependent consumers. The firm passes on cost increases but does not pass on costs decreases to customers—suggesting that the firm is not emphasizing the welfare and interests of its customers, a violation of communal norms salient among interdependent consumers. In contrast, when practicing asymmetric pricing the firm is acting in a manner consistent with pursuit of the firm's self-interest—and independent consumers guided by exchange norms should be relatively more accepting of such behavior. Accordingly,

Hypothesis 1: *Interdependent (independent) consumers will a) be guided by communal (exchange) norms and b) judge asymmetric pricing as relatively unfair (fair).*

When considering the two components of asymmetric pricing separately, however, it becomes relatively difficult to judge whether firm's pricing actions are consistent with social norms. Put simply, when consumers know *either* the give *or* the take but do not know the give-and-take in the relationship, as when considering each pricing action separately, cultural differences in fairness response arising from social norms are not expected to emerge as strongly. Formally:

Hypothesis 2: *Price fairness response for cost-increase and cost-decrease pricing actions (compared to asymmetric pricing) will be relatively insensitive to cultural differences and corresponding communal/exchange norms.*

H1 and H2 together predict an interaction of culture and pricing and mediation by relationship norms (communal/exchange) that are salient as a function of culture.

A series of experiments investigate the impact of culture and corresponding relationship norms on price fairness. In each study, culture/norms are primed using established techniques. Participants rate price fairness after reading a scenario (adapted from Kahneman et al. 1986a, 1986b) in which a firm i) increases prices to cover cost increases (cost-increase); ii) maintains prices when costs decrease (cost-decrease); or iii) practices both (i.e., asymmetric pricing).

To briefly summarize findings: In Study 1, priming Chinese (vs. American) culture among bi-cultural Singaporean participants (Chen et al. 2005) reduces price fairness perceptions for asymmetric pricing (but not cost-increase and cost-decrease pricing), an effect that is mediated by relationship norms. To provide additional evidence for the underlying process, Studies 2 and 3 examine the role of norms more directly (Spencer et al. 2005). Priming communal (vs. exchange) norms (Aggarwal and Law 2005) or manipulating norms through the use of different industries mimics the effects of priming culture: It reduces price fairness perceptions for asymmetric pricing (but not cost-increase and cost-decrease pricing). Finally, study 4 focuses on asymmetric pricing and manipulates perspective taking (Galinsky, Wang, and Ku 2008) as well as culture. Adopting an other (vs. self) perspective increases perceived fairness among bi-cultural Singaporean participants primed with the Chinese culture, but perspective does not affect fairness perceptions when the U.S. culture is primed. That is, when communal (but not exchange) norms are primed via culture, adopting an other versus self perspective shifts emphasis to the needs of others (i.e., the firm).

In summary, our research provides converging evidence that culture makes salient relationship norms that guide consumer fairness perceptions of firms' pricing actions, especially asymmetric pricing. Our contributions are three-fold. First, we add to the emerging literature on cultural differences in price fairness (e.g., Bolton et al. 2010) by examining the role of culture and corresponding relationship norms, thereby answering Xia et al.'s (2005) call for research on the role of social norms in price fairness. Second, we examine the robustness of the pioneering work on DE in two ways: by comparing consumer fairness perceptions of pricing actions based on DE (i) between joint and separate evaluations, and (ii) across culture and corresponding salient relationship norms. Third, we shed light on the 'economics puzzle' of asymmetric pricing (cf. Peltzman 2000) from the perspective of consumer fairness perceptions.

REFERENCES

Aggarwal, Pankaj and Sharmistha Law (2005), "Role of Relationship Norms in Processing Brand Information," *Journal of Consumer Research*, 32 (December), 453-64.

Bian, Wen-Qiang and L. Robin Keller (1999), "Patterns of Fairness Judgments in North America and the People's Republic of China," *Journal of Consumer Psychology*, 8 (3), 301-20.

Bolton, Lisa, Hean Tat Keh and Joseph Alba (2010), "How Do Price Fairness Perceptions Differ Across Culture?" *Journal of Marketing Research*, 47 (June), 564-76.

Brewer, Marilynn B., and Ya-Ru Chen (2007), "Where (Who) Are Collectives in Collectivism? Toward Conceptual Clarification of Individualism and Collectivism," *Psychological Review*, 114 (1), 133-51.

Chen, Haipeng, Daniel Levy, Sourav Ray, and Mark E. Bergen (2008), "Asymmetric Price Adjustment in the Small", *Journal of Monetary Economics*, 55 (4), 728-37.

Clark, Margaret and Judson Mills (1979), "Interpersonal Attraction in Exchange and Communal Relationships," *Journal of Personality and Social Psychology*, 37, 12-24.

---- and ---- (1993), "The Difference Between Communal and Exchange Norms: What it is and is not," *Personality and Social Psychology Bulletin*, 19 (6), 684-691.

Frey, Bruno and Werner Pommerehne (1993), "On the Fairness of Pricing — An Empirical Survey Among the General Population," *Journal of Economic Behavior and Organization*, 20, 295-307.

Galinksy, Adam D., Cynthia S. Wang and Gillian Ku (2008), "Perspective-Takers Behave More Stereotypically," *Journal of Personality and Social Psychology,* 95 (2), 404-419.

Gao, Yue (2009), "A Study of Fairness Judgments in China, Switzerland and Canada: Do Culture, Being a Student, and Gender Matter," *Judgment and Decision Making*, 4 (3), 214-226.

Kahneman, Daniel, Jack L. Knetsch, and Richard Thaler (1986a), "Fairness as a Constraint on Profit Seeking: Entitlements in the Market," *American Economic Review*, 76 (4), 728-41.

----, ---- and ---- (1986b), "Fairness and the Assumptions of Economics," *Journal of Business*, 59 (4), S285-300.

Kalapurakal, Rosemary, Peter R. Dickson and Joel E. Urbany (1991), "Perceived Price Fairness and Dual Entitlement," *Advances in Consumer Research*, 18 (1), 788-93.

Kim, Uichol, Harry C. Triandis, Çiğdem Kâğitçibaşi, Sang-Chin Choi and Gene Yoon (1995), *Individualism and Collectivism: Theory, Method and Applications*, Volume 18, Cross-Cultural Research and Methodology Series, Sage: Thousand Oaks

Kimes, Sheryl and Jochen Wirtz (2003), "Has Revenue Management Become Acceptable? Findings from an International Study on the Perceived Fairness of Rate Fences," *Journal of Service Research*, 6 (2), 125-135.

Mills, Judson and Margaret Clark (1982), "Communal and Exchange Relationships," *Review of Personality and Social Psychology*, 3, 121-144.

Oyserman, Daphna, Heather M. Coon, and Markus Kemmelmeier (2002), "Rethinking Individualism and Collectivism: Evaluation of Theoretical Assumptions and Meta-Analyses," *Psychological Bulletin*, 128 (1), 3-72.

Peltzman, Sam (2000), "Prices Rise Faster Than They Fall," *Journal of Political Economy*, 108(3), 466–502.

Shavitt, Sharon, Ashok K. Lalwani, Jing Zhang, and Carlos J. Torelli (2006), "The Horizontal/Vertical Distinction in Cross-Cultural Consumer Research," *Journal of Consumer Psychology*, 16 (4), 325-56.

Shiller, Robert, Maxim Boycko and Vladirmie Korobov (1991), "Popular Attitudes toward Free Markets: The Soviet Union and the United States Compared," *American Economic Review*, 81(3), 385-400.

Triandis, Harry (2001a), *Individualism and Collectivism*, Boulder, CO: Westview Press.

---- (2001b), "Individualism-Collectivism and Personality," *Journal of Personality*, 69 (6), 907-24.

---- (1996), "The Psychological Measurement of Cultural Syndrome," *American Psychologist*, 51 (4), April, 407-15.

Urbany, Joe, Thomas Madden and Peter Dickson (1989), "All's not Fair in Pricing: An Initial Look at the Dual Entitlement Principle," *Marketing Letters*, 1, 17-25.

Xia, Lan, Kent Monroe and Jennifer Cox (2004), "The Price is Unfair! A Conceptual Framework of Price Fairness Perceptions," *Journal of Marketing*, 68 (October), 1-15.

Effects of Timing of Purchase and Perceived Proximity of Climate Change on Green Product Purchase

Kiju Jung, University of Illinois at Urbana-Champaign, USA
Madhu Viswanathan, University of Illinois at Urbana-Champaign, USA
Robert S. Wyer, Jr., Chinese University of Hong Kong, Hong Kong
Dolores Albarracin, University of Pennsylvania, USA

EXTENDED ABSTRACT

Despite concerns about the adverse consequences of climate change, sustainable consumption practices have not increased correspondingly (Bonini, Hintz, and Mendonca 2008). To understand the factors that influence green product purchase and other sustainable consumption practices, we consider three temporal factors, timing of green product purchase, temporal proximity of climate change and temporal order of information presentation. We draw upon construal level theory (Trope and Liberman 2003, 2010), environmental psychology (Gifford 2011) and information integration theory (Anderson 1981; Fishbein and Hunter 1964). Three experiments show consumers' willingness to purchase green products depends on (a) whether they contemplate making the purchase immediately or in the future, (b) the urgency of doing so, and (c) the order in which the purchase consideration and the urgency are called to their attention.

Experiment 1 investigated the effect of the time that consumers consider purchasing green products under conditions in which the possibility of climate change is not called to their attention. Drawing upon construal level theory (Trope and Liberman 2003), we predicted that consumers' intentions to purchase green products would be greater in the distant future than in the near future. Sixty-four participants were randomly assigned to two conditions that differed in terms of timing of purchase (one week later vs. one year later). Specifically, half of the participants were asked to imagine buying green products "a week from now," whereas the other half were asked to imagine buying them "a year from now." Then, in each case, they reported their intentions and attitudes toward green product purchase. As predicted, participants reported greater intentions to purchase green products in the distant future than in the near future. Although participants' attitudes toward purchasing the products also differed, the difference was much less pronounced.

If consumers perceive climate change to not be imminent, they will be more willing to purchase green products in the future than to do so immediately. If they perceive climate change to be imminent, however, they will be willing to purchase green products immediately as well because making the immediacy of climate change salient to consumers at the time they contemplate a purchase decision may motivate them to purchase green products immediately. However, this may be the case only when information of proximity of climate change is already called to attention before considering purchase (climate-change-before order). When the threat of climate change is called to attention later, they may simply adjust the intentions to take this threat into account rather than completely ignoring the threat of climate change, generating piecemeal information integration.

Experiment 2 examined these contingencies by employing a 2 (information presentation order: climate-change-before vs. climate-change-after) × 2 (timing of green product purchase: near future, distant future) × 2 (proximity of climate change: immediate, future) between-subjects design. One hundred seventy-six participants were asked to consider the purchase of green products either "a week from now" or "a year from now." Before considering the purchase of green products, however, participants in *climate-change-before* conditions read a news article in which climate change was described as either an immediate threat or a future one. In *climate-change-after* con-

ditions, however, they did not read the article until after they had considered the purchase. All participants then reported their intentions and attitudes along the scales employed in experiment 1. Participants were generally more inclined to purchase green products in the distant future than in the near future. Three-way interaction of these variables was marginally significant. Supplementary analyses were performed under each order condition separately. When climate change was not an immediate threat, participants reported greater intentions to purchase green products in the future than in the near future. When climate change was imminent, however, this difference was not apparent. When participants were not informed of proximity of climate change until after they had considered the purchase (climate-change-after order), they were more willing to make a purchase in the distant future than in the near future, and this was true regardless of whether climate change was imminent or not. Proximity of climate change had a marginally significant main effect, with participants more willing to make the purchase when climate change is immediate than when it is not. In contrast, attitudes toward purchasing green products did not depend on either the time of purchase or the immediacy of climate change, regardless of presentation order.

Experiment 3 ($N = 275$) replicated these contingencies providing further insight into the processes that underlie them, employing a 3 (information presentation conditions: climate-change-before vs. climate-change-after vs. climate-change-after with integration) x 2 (time of purchase: near future, distant future) × 2 (proximity of climate change: immediate, future) between-subjects factorial design. The procedure employed in this experiment was identical to that employed in experiment 2 with the addition of the integration condition. In this condition, participants were first asked to consider purchasing green products either a week from now or a year from now and then reminded of proximity of climate change, as in climate-change-after conditions. Before doing so, however, they were given instructions that were designed to lead them to postpone making a definite purchase decision until after learning about the climate change information. The effects of experimental variables on purchase intentions in climate-change-before and climate-change-after conditions replicated the results of experiment 2. Of particular interest, however, are the effects obtained when participants were asked to consider a purchase at the outset but were encouraged to integrate the information of proximity of climate change they received afterwards (climate-change-after with integration). The effects in this condition were virtually identical to the effects obtained in climate-change-before conditions, revealing that information integration was the key to the order effect.

In summary, to our knowledge, this article is the first to show how and why both a cause temporality (i.e., proximity of climate change) and a behavior temporality (i.e., timing of purchase) combine to influence purchase intentions. Our findings provide important theoretical and practical insights about the framing and sequencing of climate change information in order to maximize consumers' engagement in sustainable consumption behavior.

REFERECES

Anderson, Norman H. (1981), *Foundations of Information Integration Theory*, New York: Academic Press, Inc.

Bonini, Sheila M. J., Greg Hintz, and Lenny T. Mendonca (2008), "Addressing Consumer Concerns About Climate Change," *The McKinsey Quarterly*, https://www.mckinseyquarterly.com/Addressing_consumer_concerns_about_climate_change_2115.

Fishbein, Martin and Ronda Hunter (1964), "Summation versus Balance in Attitude Organization and Change*," Journal of Abnormal and Social Psychology*, 69 (5), 505–10.

Gifford, Robert (2011), "The Dragons of Inaction: Psychological Barriers That Limit Climate Change Mitigation and Adaptation," *American Psychologist*, 66 (May–June), 290–302.

Trope, Yaacov and Nira Liberman (2003), "Temporal Construal," *Psychological Review*, 110 (3), 403–21.

———— (2010), "Construal-Level Theory of Psychological Distance," *Psychological Review*, 117 (2), 440–63.

Looking For Answers in the Forest Rather than the Trees: Causal Uncertainty Increases Attraction to Abstraction

Jae-Eun Namkoong, University of Texas at Austin, USA
Marlone Henderson, University of Texas at Austin, USA

EXTENDED ABSTRACT

One of the first questions people spontaneously ask themselves in unexpected circumstances is why such things happen (Wong and Weiner 1981). A sudden loss of electricity or internet connection, for instance, will naturally cause consumers to wonder the cause of these events. Three experiments in the present research demonstrate that people seek abstraction (i.e., prefer abstract visual and verbal stimuli) when they lack causal understanding because this process helps extract similarities or the essence across contexts.

People's intrinsic desire to understand causal relationships may come from the fact that understanding causality leads to greater predictability, one of the key antecedents of perceived control (Rothbaum, Weisz et al. 1982). Understanding what caused the previous blackout would help one prevent the next blackout, or at least predict and prepare for it. This leads to a greater control over the situation. Some theorists speculate that predictability or informational control can be gained by creating a constant, eventless environment (Rothbaum, Weisz et al. 1982); this can be challenging if not impossible. One way to deal with this challenge is to extract similarities across different situations and as a result, recover something constant (i.e. a pattern) within the ever-changing environment. Abstraction is an effective way to achieve this goal because when people think about things in more abstract terms, they tend to focus less on temporary, incidental, and contextual information, and instead focus more on central and cross-situationally consistent information (Wakslak, Nussbaum et al. 2008; Ledgerwood and Trope 2010).

We test the idea that when lacking causal understanding about a problem, people seek abstraction and more specifically, similarity across problems to understand what is essential. Study 1 confirms that high causal uncertainty leads people to focus on similarities across problems. Study 2 and 3 demonstrate that high causal uncertainty leads people to prefer abstract (vs. concrete) pictures and advertising message, respectively. In study 3, the effect on preference is diminished after participants engage in abstract thinking. This suggests that causal uncertainty creates a need or goal to think abstractly, which is reflected in their preference for abstract stimuli. By satisfying this need, we found that causal uncertainly no longer influences preference.

In Study1, all participants first recalled a specific relationship conflict and answered some basic questions about it. In the next page, they were asked to write about this conflict with different focuses depending on the condition; In the high (low) understanding condition they focused on causal aspects of the conflict that they understand (do not understand) very well. The dependent measure was a 7-point scale evaluating participants' relative preference for writing an essay about similarities (vs. differences) across other relationship conflicts that they had. As predicted, participants in the low (vs. high) under-standing condition reported greater desire to write about similarities than differences (M = 4.35 vs. 3.56; p = .025).

Study 2 examined the effect of causal uncertainty when a consumer problem (i.e., an Internet service failure) was being experienced at the moment rather than recalled from the past. Specifically, we inserted computer network glitches that significantly interrupted what was supposed to be the main survey - a memory test with a cash prize on the line. After experiencing these frustrating glitches, participants were presented with an "important update" screen notifying them about the Internet problem. In the high causal understanding condition, participants read information about the reason why the problem was happening, while in the low understanding condition the message said the reason was unclear. Both conditions were told that the problem was not resolved. Then, in an allegedly separate survey, they were asked to rate a set of six pictures – three global (abstract stimuli) and three local (concrete stimuli). Results showed that participants in the low understanding condition liked the global (relative to local) pictures more compared to those in the high under-standing condition (M = 1.01 vs. 0.60; p = .029).

Study 3 uncovers the mechanism by satisfying the need for abstraction for some participants before asking about their preferences. The initial procedure of this study was the same as study 1. Participants first recalled a relationship conflict and wrote about certain or uncertain causal aspects. Subsequently, we gave participants either a broad or narrow categorization task to induce abstract or concrete thinking, respectively. The dependent measure was people's relative preference for an abstract (vs. concrete) advertising message. As predicted, a significant Understanding X Categorization interaction emerged (F(1,85) = 4.093; p = .046). In the narrow categorization condition we replicated the finding of study 2; Participants in the low (vs. high) understanding condition showed higher relative preference for the abstract advertising message (M = 4.75 vs. 3.66; p = .029). In the low understanding condition, a broad (vs. narrow) categorization task significantly reduced participants' relative preference for the abstract ad (M = 3.64 vs. 4.75; p = .012). In the broad categorization condition, lack of understanding did not increase participants' prefer-ence for the abstract ad message, as their need for abstract thinking was supposedly fulfilled by the categorization task (M = 3.64 vs. 3.79; p = .739).

The present research demonstrates that low causal understand-ing activates the need for abstraction and more importantly, the need for similarity or essence extraction. We also show that this need is a general motivation that goes beyond the specific problem that acti-vated the need in the first place. Because of this, the need for abstrac-tion can be observed even in unrelated contexts such as evaluating pictures and advertising messages.

Love it or Leave it?
Diverging from Others Depends on Attachment

Yajin Wang, University of Minnesota
Deborah Roedder John, University of Minnesota

EXTENDED ABSTRACT

Consumers use brands to communicate their self-image and reference group membership (Escalas and Bettman 2005). And, consumers also express their identities by avoiding items used by dissimilar groups (Berger and Heath 2008; White and Dahl 2006). White and Dahl (2006), for example, found that men were less likely to choose a 10-oz. steak when it was branded as a "ladies' cut" versus a "chef's cut." Berger and Heath (2008) report that individuals will even abandon products they own if they are adopted by a dissimilar group. After distributing Livestrong wristbands to students in a campus dorm, and asking them to wear the wristbands to support cancer awareness, they sold the same wristbands to "geeky" students a week later. Once "geeks" adopted the wristbands, students in the target dorm abandoned their wristbands.

In this paper, we ask the question: What happens when consumers who have formed a strong attachment to a brand face this situation? Consumers can form strong attachments to brands, especially when the brand is closely connected to one's sense of self (Park et al. 2010). When consumers feel a strong attachment to a brand, will they abandon the brand when a dissimilar group adopts the brand, consistent with prior research?

Across three studies, we find that strongly attached consumers respond differently than prior research would suggest. These consumers do not abandon brands when they are adopted by a dissimilar group. Instead, they respond by expressing a greater interest in the brand, especially purchasing "special products" (such as limited editions and new collections) from the brand. In contrast, consumers with a weak attachment to the brand are more likely to abandon the brand, consistent with prior research.

Our first study replicates the Berger and Heath (2008) field experiment with Livestrong wristbands, including attachment as a moderator variable. Wristbands were distributed to a group of "talented students"—athletes, artists, and musicians—attending a private high school in China. Students were asked to wear the wristbands in support of cancer awareness. A week later, the same wristbands were distributed to a dissimilar group of students at the high school—the campus geeks. After the wristbands were adopted by the geeks, 63% of the talented students with a weak attachment to the Livestrong wristband abandoned it, while only 14% of talented students with a strong attachment did so.

In a second study, we extended these findings by manipulating rather than measuring brand attachment, and examining diverging responses other than abandonment. In the strong attachment group, participants (female business undergraduates) read an article highlighting "Burberry totes" as the perfect accessory for young career women. They were then given the opportunity to use a real Burberry tote to complete several tasks. In the weak attachment group, participants read an article about another tote brand and used this tote to complete the same tasks. Finally, all participants read an article about chic alternatives to diaper bags, which mentioned Burberry totes as a favorite of working moms (dissimilar group). After reading this article, participants in the weak attachment group were more likely to say they would abandon the Burberry brand (e.g., avoid using it), replicating results from study 1. In contrast, participants in the strong attachment group were more likely to say that they would purchase "special products" from Burberry, particularly limited editions and

new collections, which presumably would allow them to differentiate themselves from dissimilar brand users. Thus, weak attachment participants distanced themselves from the brand (saying they would abandon it), whereas strong attachment participants favored distancing themselves from the dissimilar users (saying they would buy special products from Burberry).

In study 3, we examined these patterns with a different brand (Under Armour) and different threat conditions. In prior studies, we compared a threat (dissimilar other using the brand) with a no threat (no one else using the brand) condition. This comparison raises the question of whether the source of the threat is a dissimilar other using the brand *or* just anyone else using the brand (less exclusivity in general). To answer this question, we compared a low threat condition (similar other using the brand) versus a high threat condition (dissimilar other using the brand) in study 3. After brand attachment was measured, participants read a scenario about a day on campus, which included seeing a similar group member (business school student) or dissimilar group member (geeky computer science student) wearing the same Under Armour sweatshirt they were wearing. Comparing these different users, we found the same pattern of results reported for study 2, indicating that it is the dissimilarity of other brand users that drives the abandonment response for weak attachment consumers and the "special product" purchase response for strong attachment consumers.

These findings provide a deeper understanding of how consumers diverge from others. In particular, we show that attachment affects the way consumers diverge. Although we might expect consumers who are strongly attached to a brand to be very distressed when dissimilar users adopt the same brand, and to respond by abandoning the brand, our results are counter to this intuition. These consumers do not abandon the brand and are even willing to purchase new and limited edition items as a way to diverge from others. In contrast, consumers with a weak attachment to a brand are more likely to abandon the brand, consistent with prior research.

REFERENCES

Berger, Jonah and Chip Heath (2008), "Who Drives Divergence? Identity Signaling, Outgroup Dissimilarity, and the Abandonment of Cultural Tastes," *Journal of Personality and Social Psychology*, 95(3), 593-607.

Escalas, Jennifer Edison and James R. Bettman (2005), "Self-Construal, Reference Groups, and Brand Meaning," *Journal of Consumer Research*, 32 (December), 378-89.

Park, C. Whan, Deborah J. MacInnis, Joseph Priester, Andreas B. Eisingerich, and Dawn Iacobucci (2010), "Brand Attachment and Brand Attitude Strength: Conceptual and Empirical Differentiation of Two Critical Brand Equity Drivers," *Journal of Marketing*, 74 (November), 1-17.

White, Katherine and Darren W. Dahl (2006), "To Be or *Not* Be? The Influence of Dissociative Reference Groups on Consumer Preferences," *Journal of Consumer Psychology*, 16(4), 404-14.

When Do Consumers Forgive? A Causal Attribution Model of Marketer Transgression and the Moderating Effects of Self-Construal

Jayati Sinha, University of Arizona, USA
Fang-Chi Lu, University of Iowa, USA
Narayan Janakiraman, University of Arizona, USA

EXTENDED ABSTRACT

Even well-respected, high-reputation brands sometimes fail their customers. For example, the automobile market leader at the time, Toyota, announced three recalls from 2009 to 2010 because of pedal problems. How did the public, especially Toyota's recent and old customers, react to the recent recalls or similar information, what we refer to as brand transgressions in this research? Toyota's plight is not uncommon and the role that consumer-brand relationships play is likely to be of great interest to marketers and researchers.

Prior research on brand transgressions suggests that positive relationships buffer consumer responses to transgressions, such that brands with which consumers have positive relationships are less affected by transgressions, than brands with which consumers have weak or negative relationships. However, recent research identified many boundary conditions for this buffer effect such as emotional bonding with the service provider (Mattila 2001), perceived brand personalities (Aaker, Fournier and Brasel 2004), and relationship norms (Wan et al. 2011).

While we know that some brands take a lesser hit after a transgression than others do, we know little about what drives consumers to either react very or less negatively towards brand transgression. In this research, we use attribution theory (Folkes 1984) to suggest that the reaction to brand transgressions depends on the underlying causal properties of transgressions—stability and controllability. While there is extensive research applying attribution theory to service failures, we believe that our paper, apart from using attribution theory to succinctly explain brand transgressions, extends the theory in two important ways. Firstly, based on construal level theory (looking at the *global trend*, the history of previous experiences with the brand, versus a *local deviation*, the current transgression; Henderson et al. 2006), we suggest that an individual's stability attributions depend on the relationship strength s/he has formed with the brand (H1). These attributions about stability of transgressions in turn influence likelihood of *brand forgiveness*, extent to which an individual is willing to forgive a brand transgression. Secondly, we draw on an emerging doctrine in interpersonal relationship research, suggesting that an individual's reaction to a personal relationship violation is dependent on the extent to which the individual is willing to forgive the violation and the violator (Tsarenko and Gabbott 2006). We show that in a brand context too brand forgiveness is a key mediator (H2).

In order to repair their relationship with consumers after transgressions, in practice, companies usually make some recovery attempts, such as apology and compensations. The use of such recovery methods is fairly widespread in service failure, however, only recently research has focused on the effect of recovery efforts and the role of compensation types (brand-related vs. unrelated; Mogilner and Aaker 2008) in the context of brand transgressions. In this paper, we try to understand whether matching type of compensation with consumers' self-construal explains why some brand transgression recovery efforts succeed while others don't. Building on the cultural differences in attribution tendency (independent/interdependent people refer to controllability/stability of a wrongdoing in deciding to forgive an offender; Takaku, Weiner and Ohbuchi 2001), we suggest that independent (interdependent) consumers will be more forgiving (H3) and prefer brand-unrelated (brand-related) compensations (H4)

when transgressions are perceived controllable (they share positive relationship with the brand).

Study 1, to examine H1, used a 2 (brand relationship: strong vs. weak) × 2 (transgression: controllable vs. non-controllable) between-participants design. We manipulated participant's brand relationship by asking them to list an airline which they have become attached to (strong relationship) or not attached to (weak relationship), and manipulated transgression type by presenting participants with a transgression scenario where the airline they listed cancels a flight due to either flight overbooking (controllable) or weather (non-controllable). Analyses revealed that participants were more likely to think the transgression as temporary when they had strong versus weak relationship with the airline (F (1,118) = 24.56, p<.001).

Study 2, examining brand forgiveness as a mediator (H2), used the same design as Study 1, but replaced the dependent measures with (1) brand forgiveness (likelihood to forgive) (2) passive (likelihood to stay away), and (3) active (negative WOM) behavioral intentions. Results showed that when controllability was low, consumers with strong brand relationships were more likely to forgive the brand as they were relatively uninfluenced by an unintentional transgression and were more likely to adopt a passive than active strategy. Conversely, when controllability was high, consumers with strong and weak brand relationships were less likely to forgive the brand because they might feel deceived by the brand and were more likely to disseminate negative WOM. Mediation analyses confirmed that brand forgiveness explained the joint effects of brand relationship and transgression type on consumers' post-transgression behavioral intentions.

Study 3, using a product failure and manipulating self-construal by activating a "I" versus "We" construal, showed a significant three-way interaction among brand relationship, transgression type, and self-construal (F (1,218) = 5.04, p<.03). Specifically, participants with interdependent self-construal were more likely to forgive the brand when they had strong prior brand relationship. However, participants with independent self-construal, irrespective of their brand relationships, were more likely to forgive when the transgression was non-controllable versus controllable. These effects remained significant after controlling for consumers' tendency to forgive (TTF) and attitude toward forgiveness (ATF) (Brown 2003). Consistently with Study 2, brand forgiveness predicted the active versus passive behavioral intentions in circumstances involving different brand relationship strength and controllability of transgression.

Study 4, examining the effectiveness of brand-related (i.e., voucher for a future free flight on the Airline) and versus brand-unrelated (i.e., voucher for a free meal at an upscale restaurant) compensations after brand transgressions, demonstrated that regardless of controllability of transgression, interdependent consumers who had strong brand relationships preferred brand-related compensation, and interdependent consumers who had weak prior brand relationships preferred brand-unrelated compensations. However, independent consumers preferred brand related compensation only when transgression was non-controllable and they had strong brand relationships. Moreover, consumers' negative attitudes towards the company were improved by their choice of compensation.

REFERENCES

Aaker, Jennifer, Susan Fournier, and S. Adam Brasel (2004), "When Good Brands Do Bad," *Journal of Consumer Research*, 31(1), 1-16.

Brown, Ryan P. (2003), "Measuring Individual Differences in the Tendency to Forgive: Construct Validity and Links with Depression," *Personality and Social Psychology Bulletin*, 29, 759-71.

Folkes, Valerie S. (1984), "Consumer Reactions to Product Failure: An Attributional Approach," *Journal of Consumer Research*, 10(4), 398-409.

Henderson, Marlone D., Kentaro Fujita, Yaacov Trope, and Nira Liberman (2006), "Transcending the "Here": The Effect of Spatial Distance on Social Judgment," *Journal of Personality and Social Psychology*, 91(5), 845-56.

Mattila, Anna S. (2001), "The Impact of Relationship Type on Customer Loyalty in a Context of Service Failures," *Journal of Service Research*, 4(2), 91-101.

Mogilner, Cassie, and Jennifer Aaker (2008), "Forgiving by Not Forgetting: The Effect of Compensations following Brand Transgressions," *Advances in Consumer Research*, 35, 149-50.

Takaku, Seiji, Bernard Weiner, and Ken-Ichi Ohbuchi (2001), "A Cross-Cultural Examination of the Effects of Apology and Perspective Taking on Forgiveness," *Journal of Language and Social Psychology*, 20, 144-66.

Tsarenko, Yelena, and Mark Gabbott (2006), "Forgiveness: A New Insight into Business Relationships," in *AMA Educators' Proceedings: Enhancing Knowledge Development in Marketing*, ed. Dhruv Grewal, Michael Levy, and R. Krishnan, Chicago: American Marketing Association, 30-6.

Wan, Lisa C., Michael K. Hui, Robert S. Wyer Jr. (2011), "The Role of Relationship Norms in Responses to Service Failures," *Journal of Consumer Research*, 38(2), 260-77.

Talking About the Ad Vs. Talking About The Product: What Works And When

Rashmi Adaval, Hong Kong University of Science and Technology, Hong Kong
Maria Galli, Hong Kong University of Science and Technology, Hong Kong
Robert S. Wyer Jr., Chinese University of Hong Kong, Hong Kong

EXTENDED ABSTRACT

When introducing a product with which consumers are unfamiliar, there are various strategic options a company can follow to advertise it. The advertising can be fairly product-centric with the goal of getting consumers to form impressions of the product. Alternately it might focus on drawing attention to the ad to get people to talk about it – the assumption being that this "much talked about" advertising will have a positive effect on product evaluations. To understand how consumers react to such strategies, we examine how the processing goals they have (impression formation vs. communication) interact with their chronic styles of processing (tendency to process information visually vs. verbally) to affect responses to advertising.

Television commercials contain both visual and auditory components. The visual component typically conveys a temporal sequence of events intended to grab attention and, sometimes, portrays conditions in which the advertised product might be used. The auditory component typically describes the product's benefits. We hypothesized that individuals' chronic tendency to process information visually or verbally (see Childers, Houston and Heckler 1985) can influence their evaluations of the products being advertised. However, the nature of this influence depends on their familiarity with the product being advertised and their goal in viewing the commercial. If the goal is to form an "impression," verbalizers (who are naturally predisposed to attend to the auditory portion of the commercial that describes the product's benefits) are likely to evaluate the product more favorably than visualizers. However, if the goal is to "communicate" and tell others about the ad, visualizers, (given their natural predisposition to form a detailed nonverbal representation of the sequence of events observed) are likely to make more favorable product evaluations than verbalizers. We expect these differences to hold only when the product being advertised is relatively unfamiliar, because with familiar products individuals are more likely to base their judgments on their a priori knowledge about its attributes. Such knowledge would obscure any differences in their responses to a commercial promoting the product.

Experiment 1 evaluated this hypothesis. We asked participants to view four TV commercials, two for familiar products and two for unfamiliar products. Some participants were told to form an impression of the products in the commercials and were told that they would be asked to describe these impressions after viewing them. Others were told that we were interested in how people communicate information to others and that after viewing the commercials, they would be asked to describe the events they observed. After viewing the commercials, all participants wrote down either their impression of the product or a description of the events. Finally, they evaluated the products advertised and completed a style of processing scale that was used to categorize them as visualizers or verbalizers.

We expected that the interactive effects of processing goal and processing style implied by our hypothesis would be more evident when the products being advertised were unfamiliar than when they were familiar. Product evaluations were analyzed as a function of processing goal, processing style, and the familiarity of the product being advertised. The data confirmed the implications of our hypothesis. Specifically, the effects of processing style and processing goal on product evaluations depended on product familiarity, as evidenced by a 3-way interaction of these variables, $F(1, 140) = 4.16$, p $< .05$. Verbalizers evaluated *unfamiliar* products more favorably than visualizers under impression formation conditions (0.41 vs. -.06), but less favorably than visualizers in communication goal conditions (0.62 vs. 1.37). The interaction of processing style and processing goal implied by these differences was significant, $F(1, 140) = 4.03$, $p < .05$. However, the corresponding differences in evaluations of *familiar* products were negligible ($F < 1$).

In a second experiment, we examined whether the time at which the goal is induced matters. Suppose individuals know at the time they view a commercial that they will later be asked to do something that requires a verbal encoding of it (e.g., write down their impressions of the product or verbally describe what they saw). Likely, they will try to code both auditory and visual features of the commercial linguistically at the time of viewing it, in a way consistent with the specific objective. If verbalizers are better able to encode things verbally than visualizers are, and if they use this coding as a basis for their later evaluations of the product, their evaluations may end up being relatively more favorable. On the other hand, suppose individuals view a commercial without any specific objective in mind. Likely, they will pay less attention to the auditory description of the product's features (which is not intrinsically interesting) relative to the visual images, and will form a nonverbally coded episodic model like that assumed by Wyer and Radvansky (1999). In this case, because visualizers should be better able to construct a detailed representation than verbalizers, if they are unexpectedly called upon to evaluate the product, and if they base their judgment on the implications of this representation, they should evaluate the product more favorably than verbalizers.

To assess this, experiment 2 manipulated the order in which the processing goals were induced. Participants were shown a commercial for a familiar product and were given the impression formation or communication goal, either before or after seeing the ad. After providing the corresponding descriptions, they evaluated the product and completed a style of processing scale. The results support the hypothesis: Verbalizers evaluated products more favorably than visualizers when they were given a processing objective at the outset (2.35 vs. 1.34, respectively), but less favorably than visualizers when they had viewed the commercial with no particular goal in mind (1.31 vs. 2.05). The interaction implied by this pattern of differences was significant, $F(1, 106) = 4.30$, $p < .05$, and did not depend on whether participants had a communication objective or an impression formation objective, $F < 1$.

Collectively our results suggest that the strategy (getting people to talk about the ad vs. the product) that is optimal might depend very much on whether the audience consists of verbalizers or visualizers.

REFERENCES

Childers, Terry L., Michael J. Houston, and Susan E. Heckler (1985), "Measurement of Individual Differences in Visual Versus Verbal Information Processing," *Journal of Consumer Behavior*, 12 (September), 125-134.

Wyer, Robert S., & Radvansky, Gabriel A. (1999), "The comprehension and validation of social information," *Psychological Review*, 106, 89-118.

Competing Consumers and the Valuation of Products

Gerald Häubl, University of Alberta, Canada
Christian Schmid, University of Alberta, Canada
Hua (Olivia) Lian, University of Alberta, Canada

EXTENDED ABSTRACT

While a vast amount of research has examined competition between sellers vying for market share (e.g., Hildebrandt and Klapper 2001; Peattie, Peattie, and Emafo 1997; Zhu, Singh, and Manuszak 2009), competition among consumers is not well understood. This gap in the literature is particularly striking given the increasing prevalence of market mechanisms – such as auctions – that require consumers to compete against each other as they seek to buy products.

We propose that the experiences consumers have in the process of acquiring products affects their subsequent attachment to these possessions. In particular, we hypothesize that the experience of competing against other individuals during product acquisition increases consumers' valuation of a product.

The notion that the experience consumers have when obtaining a product through a particular acquisition mode can affect how highly they value that product is consistent with prior research indicating that consumers construct their value assessments and preferences during the decision making process (Ariely and Simonson 2003; Johnson, Häubl, and Keinan 2007).

We propose that obtaining a product by competing against other consumers differs from typical (non-competitive) means of product acquisition in terms of the following key aspects: First, competing against others to obtain a product requires *effort*. Second, it implies *product scarcity* – i.e., demand for the product exceeds supply. Finally, when there is competition among consumers, not everybody who wishes to acquire the product is able to do so, invoking *social comparison* between those who were and those who were not successful at acquiring the product (Figure 1).

Figure 1:
Conceptual Framework - The Effect of Competition Experience During Product Acquisition on Consumers' Product Valuation

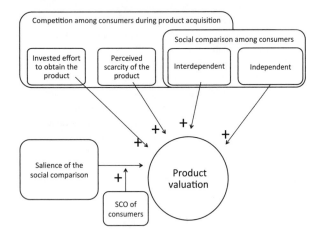

In studies 1 and 2, we disentangle these three aspects of the experience of competing against other consumers – effort, product scarcity, and social comparison – and examine the role of each in consumers' construction of product value. Study 3 focuses on the social comparison (SC) aspect of competition and investigates the moderating roles of competition salience and consumers' social comparison orientation.

STUDY 1

A 2 (SC: yes vs. no) x 2 (effort: high vs. low) between-subjects design was used. SC was manipulated by whether two participants (believed they) had to compete for a single mug based on their performance at solving puzzles (SC) or everyone received the mug irrespective of their performance (no-SC condition). In fact, all participants received a mug. Effort was manipulated via the duration of the puzzle task. The dependent variable – in all three studies – was participants' monetary valuation of the object they obtained, measured via an incentive-compatible BDM procedure.

The results show that both social comparison and effort had significant positive effects on product valuations, and that these were independent (rather than interactive).

STUDY 2

A 2 (SC: yes vs. no) x 2 (scarcity of the object: high vs. low) x 2 (object: mug vs. notice-board) mixed-design was used. Participants were instructed either to compete on a task to win the object (SC) or to simply complete the task to obtain it (no-SC). The probability of getting the object was purportedly either 10% (high scarcity) or 50% (low scarcity). Each participant completed two rounds of the task (one for each object).

The results reveal that both social comparison and scarcity had significant positive effects on product valuations, and that these were independent (rather than interactive).

STUDY 3

This study examines whether competitive social comparison has to be of an interdependent nature, where winning by one consumer implies losing by another (such as within an auction), to increase product valuations. If social comparison is independent, such that winning by one consumer has no implications for the outcome of another (e.g., when they bid in different auctions for the same product), does this effect still hold? We also examine the interplay between the salience of social comparison and consumers' chronic social comparison orientation (SCO). People vary in the degree to which they engage in social comparison. Individuals high in SCO compare themselves more with others and are more affected by the outcomes of social comparisons (Gibbons and Buunk 1999). Thus, high SCOs may value a product more highly if its acquisition involved high salience of SC than if its acquisition involved less SSC, while low SCOs should respond less to the salience of SC.

A 2 (salience of SC: high vs. low) x 2 (nature of SC: independent vs. interdependent) x 2 (SCO: high vs. low, measured factor) between-subjects design was used. Participants completed the study in pairs, with each participant independently solving a number of puzzles as quickly as possible. The two participants in a pair were either introduced face-to-face (high salience of SC) or merely connected via their computers (low salience of SC). In the interdependent condition, participants (believed they) had to outperform their partner at the puzzle task to win a mug. By contrast, in the independent condition, participants believed that each member of the pair completed a separate random draw with an independent 50% chance of winning the mug. In fact, all participants received a mug.

The results reveal no significant difference between the interdependent and independent SC conditions, indicating that both positively contribute to product valuations. Importantly, there is a highly significant 2-way interaction between salience of SC and SCO ($p<0.01$). Spotlight analysis (Fitzsimons 2008) reveals that, for consumers high in SCO, high (vs. low) salience of SC leads to higher product valuations, whereas it does not affect the product valuations of consumers low in SCO (Figure 2).

Figure 2:
Product Valuation as a Function of the Salience of Social Comparison and Consumers' Social Comparison Orientation

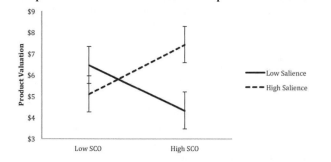

This research enhances our understanding of how the manner in which products are acquired influences how highly consumers value them. It also provides a framework for understanding the implications of competition among consumers that identifies effort, product scarcity, and social comparison as the essential distinct aspects of this type of competition.

REFERENCES

Allport, Floyd H. (1924), *Social Psychology*, Boston: Houghton Mifflin.

Ames, Carole and Russell Ames (1984), "Goal Structures and Motivation," *Elementary School Journal*, 85 (1), 39-50.

Ariely, Dan, George Loewenstein, and Drazen Prelec (2006), "Tom Sawyer and the construction of value," *Journal of Economic Behavior & Organization*, 60 (1), 1-10.

Ariely, Dan and Itamar Simonson (2003),"Buying, Bidding, Playing, or Competing? Value Assessment and Decision Dynamics in Online Auctions," *Journal of Consumer Psychology*, 13(1&2), 113-123.

Aronson, Elliot and Judson Mills (1959), "The Effect of Severity of Initiation on Liking for a Group," *The Journal of Abnormal and Social Psychology*, Vol. 59(2), 177-181.

Axsom, Danny and Joel Cooper (1985), "Cognitive Dissonance and Psychotherapy: the Role of Effort Justification in Inducing Weight Loss," *Journal of Experimental Social Psychology*, Vol. 21(2), 149-160.

Becker, Gordon M., Morris H. DeGroot, and Jacob Marschak (1964), "Measuring Utility by a Single-Response Sequential Method," *Behavioral Science*, 9, 3, 226-232.

Belk, Russell W. (1988), "Possessions and the Extended Self," *Journal of Consumer Research*, 15 (June), 139-168.

Belk, Russell W. (1991a), "The Ineluctable Mysteries of Possessions," in Floyd W. Rudmin (Ed.), *To Have Possessions: A Handbook on Ownership and Property*, Corte Madera, CA: Select Press, 17-55.

Belk, Russell W. (1991b), "Possessions and the Sense of Past," in Russell W. Belk (Ed.), *Highways and Buyways: Naturalistic Research From the Consumer Odyssey*, Provo, UT: Association for Consumer Research, 114-130.

Bem, Daryl J. (1972), "Self-Perception Theory," in L. Berkowitz (Ed.), *Advances in Experimental Social Psychology*, Vol. 6, New York: Academic Press.

Bettman, James R., Mary Frances Luce, and John W. Payne (1998), "Constructive Consumer Choice Processes," *Journal of Consumer Research*, 25 (December), 187-217.

Bloch, Peter H. and Marsha L. Richins (1983), "A Theoretical Model for the Study of Product Importance Perceptions," *Journal of Marketing*, 47 (Summer), 69-81.

Brenner, Lyle, Yuval Rottenstreich, Sanjay Sood, and Baler Bilgin (2007), "On the Psychology of Loss Aversion: Possession, Valence, and Reversals of the Endowment Effect," *Journal of Consumer Research*, 34 (September), 369-376.

Brock, Timothy C. (1968), "Implications of Commodity Theory for Value Change," in A. G. Greenwald, T. C. Brock, and T. M. Ostrom (Eds.), *Psychological Foundations of Attitudes*, New York: Academic Press.

Brown, Stephen (2001), "Torment Your Customers (They'll Love it)" *Harvard Business Review*, 79(9), 82-88.

Butler, Ruth (1989), "Interest in the Task and Interest in Peers' Work in Competitive and Noncompetitive Conditions: A Developmental Study," *Child Development*, 60, 3, 562-570.

Buunk, Bram P. (1994), "Social Comparison Processes under Stress: Towards an Integration of Classic and Recent Perspectives," in W. Stroebe and M. Hewstone (Eds.), *European Review of Social Psychology*, Vol. 5, Chichester: Wiley, 211-241.

Buunk, Bram P. and Frederick X. Gibbons (2006), "Social Comparison Orientation: A New Perspective on Those Who Do and Those Who Don't Compare with Others," In S. Guimond (Ed.), *Social Comparison and Social Psychology: Understanding Cognition, intergroup relations and culture*, Cambridge, England: Cambridge University Press, 15-32.

Buunk, Bram P. and Frederick X. Gibbons (2007), "Social Comparison: The End of a Theory and the Emergence of a Field," *Organizational Behavior and Human Decision Processes*, 102, 3-21.

Cardozo, Richard. N. (1965), "An Experimental Study of Customer Effort, Expectation, and Satisfaction," *Journal of Marketing Research*, Vol. II, 244-249.

Carmon, Ziv and Dan Ariely (2000), "Focusing on the Forgone: How Value Can Appear So Different to Buyers and Sellers," *Journal of Consumer Research*, 27 (December), 360-370.

Cialdini, Robert B. (1985), *Influence: Science and Practice.* Glenview, IL: Scott, Foresman.

Connell, Joseph H. (1983), "On the Prevalence and Relative Importance of Interspecific Competition: Evidence from Field Experiments," *American Naturalist*, 122 (November), 661-696.

Cox, Tom and John H. Kerr (1990),"Self-Reported Mood in Competitive Squash," *Personality and Individual Differences*, 11 (February), 199-203.

Csikszentmihalyi, Mihaly and Eugene Rochberg-Halton (1981), *The Meaning of Things: Domestic Symbols and the Self*, Cambridge: Cambridge University Press.

Diener, Carol I. and Carol S. Dweck (1978), "Analysis of Learned Helplessness – Continuous Changes in Performance, Strategy, and Achievement Cognitions Following Failure," *Journal of Personality and Social Psychology*, 35(1), 451-62.

Dittmar, Helga (1992), *The Social Psychology of Material Possessions: To Have Is to Be*, New York: St. Martin's Press.

Dweck, Carol S. and Ellen L. Leggett (1988), "A social-cognitive approach to personality," *Psychological Review*, **95**, 256–273.

Dye, Renee (2000), "The Buzz on Buzz," *Harvard Business Review,* 78(6), 139-146.

Engelbrecht-Wiggans, Richard and Elena Katok (2009), "A Direct Test of Risk Aversion and Regret in First Price Sealed-bid Auctions," *Decision Analysis,* 6(2), 75-86.

Fenigstein, Allan, Michael F. Scheier, and Arnold H. Buss (1975), "Public and Private Self-Consciousness: Assessment and Theory," *Journal of Consulting and Clinical Psychology,* 43 (4), 522-527.

Festinger, Leon (1954), "A Theory of Social Comparison Processes," *Human Relations*, 7, 117-140.

Festinger, Leon (1957), "Cognitive Dissonance," Stanford, Calif.:Stanford University Press.

Gardner, Wendi L., Shira Gabriel, and Angela Y. Lee (1999), "'I' Value Freedom, But 'We' Value Relationships: Self-Construal Priming Mirrors Cultural Differences in Judgment," *Psychological Science*, 10 (July), 321-326.

Gibbons, Frederick X. and Bram P. Buunk (1999), "Individual Differences in Social Comparison: Development of a Scale of Social Comparison Orientation," *Journal of Personality and Social Psychology,* 76 (January), 129-142.

Grayson, Kent and David Shulman (2000), "Indexicality and the Verification Function of Irreplaceable Possessions: A Semiotic Analysis," *Journal of Consumer Research*, 27 (March), 17-30.

Grenci, Richard T. and Charles A. Watts (2007), "Maximizing Customer Value via Mass Customized E-customer Services," *Business Horizons,* 50(2), 123-132.

Heyman, Gail D., Dweck, Carol S. (1992), "Achievement goals and achievement motivation: Their relation and their role in adaptive motivation," *Motivation and Emotion*, **16**, 231–247.

Higgins E. Tory, Lorraine Chen I., Antonio L. Freitas, Scott Spiegel, and Daniel C. Molden (2003), "Transfer of Value From Fit," *Journal of Personality and Social Psychology,* 84 (June), 1140-1153.

Higgins, E. Tory (2006), "Value from Hedonic Experience and Engagement," *Psychological Review*, 113 (3), 439-460.

Hildebrandt, Lutz and Daniel Klapper (2001), "The Analysis of Price Competition Between Corporate Brands," *International Journal of Research in Marketing*, 18(1/2), 139-159.

Holbrook, Morris B. and Elizabeth C. Hirschman (1982), "The Experiential Aspects of Consumption: Consumer Fantasies, Feelings, and Fun," *Journal of Consumer Research*, 9 (September), 132-140.

Janiszewski, Chris (2009), "The Consumer Experience," Association for Consumer Research 2009 Presidential Address.

Jellison, Jenny L. (2003), "Justification of Effort in Rats: Effects of Physical and Discriminative Effort on Reward Value," Psychological Reports, vol. 93(3), 1095-1100.

Johnson, Eric J., Gerald Häubl, and Anat Keinan (2007), "Aspects of Endowment: A Query Theory of Value Construction," *Journal of Experimental Psychology: Learning, Memory, and Cognition*, 33 (May), 461-474.

Kerr, John H. and Peter van Schaik (1995), "Effects of Game Venue and Outcome on Psychological Mood States in Rugby," *Personality and Individual Differences,* 19 (March), 407-410.

Kim, Sara and Aparna A. Labroo (2011), "From Inherent Value to Incentive Value: When and Why Pointless Effort Enhances Consumer Preference," *Journal of Consumer Research,* Vol. 38(4), 712-742.

Kruger, Justin, Derrick Wirtz, Leaf van Boven, and T. William Altermatt (2004), "The Effort Heuristic," *Journal of Experimental Social Psychology,* 40 (January), 91-98.

Ku, Gillian, Deepak Malhotra, and J. Keith Murnighan (2005), "Towards a Competitive Arousal Model of Decision Making: A Study of Auction Fever in Live and Internet Auctions," *Organizational Behavior and Human Decision Processes*, 96, 89-103.

Laird, J. D. (2007), *Feelings: The Perceptions of Self,* New York: Oxford University Press.

Li, Sheng, Joshua R. Foulger, and Peter W. Philips (2008), "Analysis of the Impacts of the Number of Bidders upon Bid Values: Implications for Contractor Prequalification and Project Timing and Bundling," *Public Works Management & Policy,* 12(3), 503-514.

Lichtenstein, Sarah and Paul Slovic (2006), The Construction of Preference, Cambridge University Press.

Loewenstein, George and Samuel Issacharoff (1994), "Source Dependence in the Valuation of Objects," *Journal of Behavioral Decision Making*, 7, 157-168.

Lydall, Emma. S., Gary Gllmour, and Dominic M. Dwyer (2010), "Rats Place Greater Value on Rewards Produced by High Effort: An Animal Analogue of the 'Effort Justification' Effect," *Journal of Experimental Social Psychology,* 46(6), 1134-1137.

Lynn, Michael. (1991), "Scarcity Effects on Value: A Quantitative Review of the Commodity Theory Literature," *Psychology & Marketing,* 8(1), 43-57.

Ma, Yan, Jianxun Ding, and Wenxia Hong (2010), "Delivering Customer Value Based on Service Process: The Example of Tesco.com," *International Business Research,* 3(2), 131-135.

McAuley, Edward, Dan Russell, and John B. Gross (1983), "Affective Consequences of Winning and Losing: An Attributional Analysis," *Journal of Sport Psychology*, 5 (Summer), 278-287.

Mussweiler, Thomas (*2003*), "Comparison processes in social judgment: Mechanisms and consequences," *Psychological Review*, 110, 472-489.

Mussweiler, Thomas, and F. Strack (2001), "The 'Relative Self': Information and Judgmental Consequences of Comparative Self-evaluations," *Journal of Personality and Social Psychology*, 79, 23-38.

Nayakankuppam, Dhananjay and Himanshu Mishra (2005), "The Endowment Effect: Rose-Tinted and Dark-Tinted Glasses," *Journal of Consumer Research*, 32, 3, 390-395.

Nicholls, John G. (1989), *The competitive ethos and democratic education*, Cambridge, MA: Harvard University Press.

Peattie, Ken, Sue Peattie, and E. B. Emafo (1997), "Promotional Competitions as a Strategic Marketing Weapon," *Journal of Marketing Management,* 13(8), 777-789.

Pepitone, Emmy (1980), *Children in cooperation and competition*, Lexington , MA: Lexington.

Pham, Michel T. (1998), "Representativeness, Relevance, and the Use of Feelings in Decision Making", Journal of Consumer Research, 25(September), 144-159.

Richins, Marsha L. (1994), "Valuing Things: The Public and Private Meanings of Possessions," *Journal of Consumer Research,* 21 (December), 504-521.

Rosenfeld, Paul, Robert A. Giacalone, and James T. Tedeschi (1984), "Cognitive Dissonance and Impression Management Explanations for Effort Justification," *Personality and Social Psychology Bulletin,* Vol. 10(3), 394-401.

Rosenkranz, Stephanie and Patrick W. Schmitz (2007), "Reserve Prices in Auctions as Reference Points," *Economic Journal,* 117(520), 637-653.

Scheier, Michael F. and Charles S. Carver (1985), "Optimism, Coping, and Health – Assessment and Implications of Generalized Outcome Expectancies," *Health Psychology*, 4 (May), 219-247.

Schoener, Thomas W. (1983), "Field Experiments on Interspecific Competition," *American Naturalist*, 122 (August), 240-285.

Schwarz, Norbert and Gerald L. Clore (1983), "Mood, Misattribution, and Judgments of Well-being: Informative and Directive Functions of Affective States," *Journal of Personality and Social Psychology,* 45(3), 513-523.

Slovic, Paul (1995), "The Construction of Preference," *American Psychologist,* 50(5), 364-371.

Stapel, Diederik A. and Willem Koomen (2001), "I, We, and the Effects of Others on Me: How Self-Construal Moderates Social Comparison Effects," *Journal of Personality and Social Psychology*, 80 (May), 766-781.

Strahilevitz, Michal A. and George Loewenstein (1998), "The Effect of Ownership History on the Valuation of Objects," *Journal of Consumer Research*, 25 (December), 276-289.

Stock, Axel and Subramanian Balachander (2011), "The Making of a 'Hot Product': A Signaling Explanation of Marketers' Scarcity Strategy," *Management Science,* 51(8), 1181-1192.

Tassi, Fulvio and Barry H. Schneider (1997), "Task-Oriented Versus Other-Referenced Competition: Differential Implications for Children's Peer Relations," *Journal of Applied Social Psychology*, 27 (17), 1557-1580.

Taylor, Shelley E. and Marci Lobel (1989), "Social Comparison Activity Under Threat: Downward Evaluation and Upward Contacts," *Psychological Review,* 96 (October), 569-575.

Tesser, Abraham (1988), "Toward a Self-Evaluation Maintenance Model of Social Behavior," in L. Berkovitz (Ed.), *Advances in Experimental Social Psychology*, Vol. 20, 181-227. New York: Academic Press.

Thaler, Richard (1980), "Toward a Positive Theory of Consumer Choice," *Journal of Economic Behavior and Organization*, 1 (March), 39-60.

Tilman, David (1982), *Resource Competition and Community Structure*, Princeton University Press.

Vallerand, Robert J., Lise I. Gauvin, and Wayne R. Halliwell (1986), "Effects of Zero-Sum Competition on Children's Intrinsic Motivation and Perceived Competence," *Journal of Social Psychology,* 126 (August), 465-473.

Van der Zee, Karen, F. Oldersma, B. Buunk, D. Bos (1998), "Social Comparison Preferences Among Cancer Patients as Related to Neuroticism and Social Comparison Orientation," *Journal of Personality and Social Psychology,* 75(3), 801-810.

Watson, David, Lee A. Clarke, and Auke Tellegen (1988), "Development and Validation of Brief Measures of Positive and Negative Affect: The PANAS Scales," *Journal of Personality and Social Psychology*, 54, 1063-1070.

Wood, Joanne V. (1996), "What is Social Comparison and How Should We Study It?" *Personality and Social Psychology Bulletin*, 22 (May), 520-537.

Yu, Hueju and Wenchang Fang (2009), "Relative Impacts from Product Quality, Service Quality, and Experience Quality on Consumer Perceived Value and Intention to Shop for the Coffee Shop Market," *Total Quality Management & Business Excellence,* 20(11), 1273-1285.

Zhu, Ting, Vishal Singh, and Mark D. Manuszak (2009), "Market Structure and Competition in the Retail Discount Industry," *Journal of Marketing Research,* 46(4), 453-466.

Humorous Consumer Complaints

A. Peter McGraw, University of Colorado, USA
Christina Kan, University of Colorado, USA
Caleb Warren, Universita Commerciale Luigi Bocconi, Italy

EXTENDED ABSTRACT

"I should have flown with someone else or gone by car... 'cause United breaks guitars."

When United Airlines refused to compensate David Carroll for his damaged guitar, the musician parodied his negative experience with the company in a YouTube music video. His humorous complaint became a media sensation, leading United to apologize and offer Carroll compensation (Deighton and Kornfeld 2010).

Although complaints typically document dissatisfaction, some complaints intentionally include a positive element: humor. Drawing on marketing and humor research, we introduce the concept of *humorous complaining* and differentiate it from non-humorous (i.e., serious) complaining.

We define a humorous consumer complaint as a behavioral expression of dissatisfaction about a product or service that elicits humor in others. As compared to serious complaints, we hypothesize that:

Consumers enjoy humorous complaints. People pursue and enjoy humorous experiences (Martin 2007). People often dislike attending to others' complaints (Kowalski 1996), but humor can help improve people's attitudes towards experience they would otherwise find annoying and unpleasant, such as advertisements (Alden, Mukherjee, and Hoyer 2000; Eisend 2009).

Consumers judge humorous complainers more favorably. Complainers are often considered annoying or grumpy and may be ostracized by their audience (Kowalski 1996). Conversely, a sense of humor is generally seen as an admirable trait (Cann and Calhoun 2001; Martin 2007).

Consumers pay more attention to humorous complaints. Research in advertising shows that humor attracts attention (Madden and Weinberger 1982; Weinberger and Gulas 1992). Humorous content is remembered better than non-humorous content (Schmidt 1994).

Consumers are more likely to share humorous complaints. Content that elicits positive emotions is more likely to be shared with others (Berger and Milkman 2011). A recent study finds that the perceived humor in a *YouTube* video predicts its number of views (Warren and Berger 2011).

THREE STUDIES SUPPORT OUR HYPOTHESES:

In Study 1, based on random assignment, we asked undergraduates ($N=75$) to create and post a serious or humorous complaint as a status update on Facebook. In the 24 hours following the posting, participants recorded the number of people who 'liked' the update. Humorous complaints generated significantly more likes than serious complaints ($M_{Humor}=9.07$, $SD_{Humor}=7.16$, $M_{Serious}=5.59$, $SD_{Serious}=4.68$; $F(1,71)=5.67$, $p<.05$). Subsequently, we asked another group of undergraduate students ($N=50$) to read through the complaints. Half of the participants rated the perceived humor in the complaints and the other half rated how likely they would be to 'friend' a person who posted the update and also how likely they would be to share the update with others. Consistent with our hypotheses, participants were significantly more likely to 'friend' people who posted more humorous complaints ($r=.30$, $p<.01$) and significantly more likely to share more humorous complaints with others ($r=.52$, $p<.001$).

Study 2 explored enjoyment, likelihood of sharing, attitude towards the complainer and attitude towards the firm using complaint letters. The study used a 2(humorous vs. serious) x 2(bank vs. feminine product) between-subjects design. To obtain the stimuli, we asked a sample of mTurk workers ($N=50$) to send us the most humorous consumer complaint they could find on the internet. A research assistant blind to the hypotheses screened the complaints for validity and selected the two most humorous complaints. Another research assistant (also blind to the hypotheses) rewrote the complaints to be strictly serious in nature.

Depending on random assignment, undergraduates ($N=165$) read either a humorous or a serious letter complaining about one of two possible products, and assessed on seven-point scales their enjoyment of the letter, likelihood of sharing the letter, attitude towards the writer of the complaint and attitude towards the firm. Consistent with our hypotheses and the results of our previous study, we find that compared to the serious complaints, participants reported greater enjoyment of the humorous complaints ($M_{Humorous}=4.60$, $M_{Serious}=3.00$, $F(1,163)=27.25$, $p<.01$), reported being more likely to share the humorous complaints ($M_{Humorous}=3.65$, $M_{Serious}=2.87$, $F(1,163)=5.66$, $p<.05$) and had a more positive attitude towards the complainer when the complaint was humorous ($M_{Humorous}=4.52$, $M_{Serious}=3.65$, $F(1,163)=8.69$, $p<.01$). Interestingly, brand attitudes did not differ depending on whether the complaint was humorous or serious ($M_{Humorous}=3.33$, $M_{Serious}=3.17$, $F(1,163)=.38$, $p=.54$).

Study 3 explored the influence of humorous complaints on brand choice, using online product reviews. If consumers attend more to humorous complaints, then humorous complaints may be more influential when making choices. We used a between-subjects design with 3 conditions (serious complaint and two humorous complaint replicates). To obtain the stimuli for this study, we first randomly selected a negative product review regarding a pair of earphones from Amazon.com. To create the humorous versions of the review, we asked 30 mTurk workers to rewrite the review in a humorous way, and then had a second sample of 39 mTurk workers rate how humorous they found each humorous rewrite. We selected two of the funniest reviews for the study.

mTurk workers ($N=148$) first read a product description for Brand X, followed by one positive and one negative Brand X review. Next, participants read the description for Brand Y, followed by one positive and one negative Brand Y review. Depending on random assignment, the negative Brand Y review was either serious or humorous in tone (two humor replicates). Participants were informed that they would have the opportunity to win one of the two pairs of headphones and were asked to indicate which brand they preferred.

As hypothesized, participants were less likely to select Brand Y when a negative consumer review of the product was humorous (21.8%) than when it was serious (42.6%; $\chi^2(1)=6.61$, $p=.01$). Participants exposed to the first humorous review were just as likely (20.9%) to select Brand Y as those who were exposed to the second humorous review (22.4%; $\chi^2(1)=.03$, $p>.85$).

In summary, the use of humor in consumer complaints can significantly alter the responses of other consumers exposed to them. Because humorous complaints are more enjoyable, attention getting, and more likely to be shared than serious complaints, we suggest that, as was the case with Dave Carroll's complaint, they can be a source of empowerment to consumers who have been wronged by brands.

REFERENCES

Alden, Dana L., Ashesh Mukherjee and Wayne D. Hoyer (2000), "The Effects of Incongruity, Surprise and Positive Moderators on Perceived Humor in Television Advertising," *Journal of Advertising,* 29 (2), 1-15.

Berger, Jonah and Katherine L. Milkman (2012), "What Makes Online Content Viral?" *Journal of Marketing Research,* 49 (2), 192-205.

Cann, Arnie and Lawrence G. Calhoun (2001), "Perceived Personality Associations With Differences in Sense of Humor: Stereotypes of Hypothetical Others with High or Low Senses of Humor," *Humor,* 14 (2), 117–30.

Deighton, John and Leora Kornfeld (2010), *United Breaks Guitars (Case Study),* Boston: Harvard Business Publishing.

Eisend, Martin (2009), "A Meta-Analysis of Humor in Advertising," *Journal of the Academy of Marketing Science,* 37, 191-203.

Kowalski, Robin M. (1996), "Complaints and Complaining: Functions, Antecedents, and Consequences," *Psychological Bulletin,* 119 (2), 179-96.

Madden, Thomas J. and Marc G. Weinberger (1982), "The Effects of Humor on Attention in Magazine Advertising," *Journal of Advertising,* 11 (3), 8-14.

Martin, Rod A. (2007), *The Psychology of Humor – An Integrative Approach,* Burlington, MA: Elsevier Academic Press.

Schmidt, Stephen R. (1994), "Effects of Humor on Sentence Memory," *Journal of Experimental Psychology,* 20 (4), 953-67.

Warren, Caleb and Jonah Berger (2011), "The Influence of Humor on Sharing," poster presented at the Association for Consumer Research conference, St. Louis, MO.

Weinberger, Marc G. and Charles S. Gulas (1992), "The Impact of Humor in Advertising: A Review," *Journal of Advertising,* 21 (4), 35-59.

Improving Associative and Item Memory for Brands Among Elderly Consumers

Praggyan (Pam) Mohanty, Governors State University, USA
S. (Ratti) Ratneshwar, University of Missouri, USA
Moshe Naveh-Benjamin, University of Missouri, USA

EXTENDED ABSTRACT

Prior research in cognitive psychology has found important differences between associative memory and item memory (Clark 1992; Clark and Burchett 1994; Gronlund and Ratcliff 1989; Hockley 1991). While item memory is memory for individual items present in a stimulus episode, associative memory is memory for a combination of two or more items together. Especially germane to the present research is the prior finding that *aging* affects item and associative memory differently. Larger age-related impairments are seen in associative memory than item memory (for a review refer to Old and Naveh-Benjamin 2008; Spencer and Raz 1995).

Item memory and associative memory for brand information are both important for brand building. Memory for item information such as individual brand names or brand logo graphics helps increase brand awareness and keeps the brand salient in the minds of consumers. Associations between the brand and favorable and distinct attributes and benefits work towards the creation of a positive brand image (Aaker 1996, 25; Broniarczyk and Alba 1994; Keller 1993). Overall, brand equity and marketplace success of brands depend upon the creation of high levels of brand awareness as well as positive and distinctive brand images (Warlop, Ratneshwar, and van Osselaer 2005).

Despite the importance of item and associative memory for effective brand building, there has been very little consumer research on how these constructs are different from one another. Further, to the best of our knowledge, there is not even a single published study in consumer research on the effects of aging on item versus associative memory for brand information. This dearth of research is perplexing, given the importance of the elderly consumer to marketers (Yoon et al. 2005). Indeed, current demographic trends suggest that the age segment of 65 and above will increase dramatically over the next two decades, growing to nearly 20 percent of the total U.S. population by 2030. The growth of the elderly consumer segment makes a compelling argument for studying memory issues in this age group.

The aim of this paper is therefore to address an important research gap by studying the effects of aging on item and associative memory for brand elements. We focus not only on memory deficits in elderly versus younger consumers in a branding context, but also investigate how marketers can alleviate such deficits in the elderly. For doing so, we build on prior research in cognitive psychology which has shown that "schematic support" in terms of schemas or prior semantic knowledge within a domain should aid encoding and retrieval of information (Craik and Bosman 1992). Two different forms of schematic support are examined in regard to item and associative memory for brand information among elderly consumers. In study 1, the main question of interest is whether using more versus less meaningful brand elements (i.e., brand logo graphics) will improve item and associative memory for brand information in elderly (vs. younger) consumers. *Meaningfulness* of a brand element is the extent to which an individual has pre-existing semantic knowledge of the element in memory. In study 2, the same type of question is explored in regard to the degree of *relatedness* between brand elements (i.e., brand logo graphics and brand names).

Study 1 (N = 50) used a 2 (elderly vs. younger consumer, between-subjects) x 2 (associative memory for brand information vs. item memory for brand logo graphics, within-subject) x 2 (more vs. less meaningful brand logo graphics; within-subject) mixed factorial design. The dependent variable was recognition accuracy as measured by the proportion of hits minus false alarms (Law, Hawkins, and Craik 1998; Morrin and Ratneshwar 2003). The stimuli were pairs of brand logo graphics and brand names. While brand logo graphics were manipulated to be more vs. less meaningful, the brand names were meaningful ones that were counterbalanced across the more and less meaningful brand logo graphics conditions.

Study 1 results showed that meaningfulness of brand logo graphics helped elderly consumers in remembering brand logo graphics better. Further, there was a two-way interaction between meaningfulness of logo graphics and age in the case of brand logo graphics (i.e., item) memory. Thus, the deficit in brand logo graphics memory between elderly (vs. younger) consumers in the less meaningful brand logo graphics condition was actually eliminated in the more meaningful brand logo graphics condition. In addition, meaningfulness of brand logo graphics enhanced associative memory for brand logo graphics and brand names in elderly consumers. Some interesting results were also obtained in subsequent follow-up analyses where we examined hit rates and false alarm rates separately.

Study 2 (N = 48) used a similar design and procedure as study 1. Results showed that relatedness between brand logo graphics and brand names helped elderly consumers remember the individual brand elements better (i.e., improved item memory). Interestingly, there was also a significant two-way interaction between age and relatedness between brand logo graphics and brand names for item memory. Specifically, elderly (vs. younger) consumers benefited more from relatedness between brand logo graphics and brand names in boosting their item memory performance. Further, relatedness between brand logo graphics and brand names also helped elderly consumers improve associative memory for brand information. Finally, in accord with past research, both studies 1 and 2 demonstrated that in the case of novel brand information, elderly (vs. younger) consumers display a larger deficit in associative memory than item memory, i.e., there was a significant two-way interaction between age and type of memory.

To Think or Not to Think: The Pros and Cons of Thought Suppression

Natalina Zlatevska, Bond University, Australia
Elizabeth Cowley, University of Sydney, Australia

EXTENDED ABSTRACT

Consumers are often faced with failure. They buy things that are never worn. They buy items the day before the item goes on sale. They find out after a negotiation that a friend got a better price than they did. Thinking about failure can be unpleasant. Is trying not to think about the failure a good coping strategy?

Actively suppressing thoughts about the failure may seem like a viable short-term strategy because avoiding the unwanted thoughts means the individual faced with the failure might also avoid the negative feelings associated with the unsuccessful outcome. Thought suppression requires two mechanisms; an operating process to promote the suppression by finding distracting thoughts and a monitoring system to search consciousness for signals of suppression failure (Wegner 1987; 1994). The irony of thought suppression is that the monitoring process causes hyperaccessibility of the unwanted thought. For example, in Wegner's famous white bear studies, not thinking of a white bear requires continuous activation of the thought to ensure it has not come to mind. This monitoring process leads to increased accessibility of the unwanted thought after thought suppression has been discontinued (the rebound effect). If the unwanted thought is not a benign white bear thought, but is instead related to poor consumption, the rebound effect may have important consumption ramifications including poor consumption decisions (Erskine, Georgiou and Kvavilashvili 2010). Independent of rebound effects, thought suppression has been shown to result in poor consumption decisions when suppressing benign white bear thoughts. Vohs and Faber (2007) demonstrate that not thinking about white bears can result in suboptimal consumption decisions because of a reduction in self-regulatory resources. Although we know that depleting self-regulatory resources can be detrimental to subsequent behavior (Baumesiter 2002), it is not clear which of the two processes causes poor decision making when consumers suppress thoughts about their own past failures. In order to understand when the detrimental effects of thought suppression can be eliminated, it is important to determine which of the two processes is depleting. The monitoring process always occurs and cannot be eliminated, while the distracting process can be more or less difficult. We propose that it is not the monitoring process, but the process of finding a distraction that is resource depleting.

In three studies, we show that depletion during thought suppression is not caused by monitoring for the presence of an unwanted thought or the negative affect associated with thinking about failure. We show that it is the process of looking for a distracting thought. In each study, participants work on an unsolvable puzzle task and are given failure feedback. In study one, we manipulate the motivation to thought suppress. In studies two and three, thought suppression is instructed.

The aim of study one (N=61) was to establish that after acknowledging failure, participants engaging in an activity that did not provide sufficiently distracting thoughts, had fewer self-regulatory resources than participants that did not acknowledge the failure (t =2.63, p =.01). Consistent with previous measures of depletion, the volume of food consumed was a proxy for the level of remaining self-regulatory resources (more 'sinful tempting' food consumed = fewer remaining resources: Vohs and Heatherton 2000; Fedorikhin and Patrick 2010). Thought protocols and scales show that participants did try to suppress thoughts after acknowledging the failure.

To more directly test for the depleting effects of thought suppression, we instructed thought suppression and manipulated the effort required to find distracting thoughts by providing cues (vs. not providing cues) reminding participants of the unwanted thought (poor performance) in study two (N =98). The number of times a distraction had to be found during thought suppression was measured by counting the intrusions in the participants' speak-aloud recordings. Hopelessness was measured after the suppression task. Finally, during an unrelated task, participants were told to help themselves to M&Ms. If it's the effort involved in finding a distracting thought drives depletion, then the number of times a distraction had to be found (intrusions), not hopelessness, should mediate the cue/resource depletion relationship.

As expected, participants in the cued condition were more depleted than participants in the no-cue condition (t =-2.41, p =.018). Importantly, the number of intrusions fully mediated the cue/depletion relationship (Figure 1). To eliminate the monitoring process as the explanation for depletion, we manipulated monitoring in study three (N =81). We introduced a control condition where participants were not told to thought suppress, but instead to think about the failure and improvement strategies. They, therefore, didn't need to activate the monitoring process. In two thought suppression conditions, we manipulated the difficulty of finding a distraction following an intrusion by offering (vs. not offering) distracting thoughts. To test the effect across contexts, a more general measure of resource depletion was used; attentional control on a dichotic listening exercise.

Figure 1

Study 2 – Mediation of Cue Manipulation on Consumption via Thought Intrusions

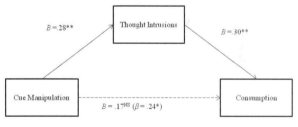

*=p<.05; ** =p<.01

If monitoring, and the subsequent rebound effect, explained the depletion found in studies one and two, then participants in the thought suppression condition should always be less able to perform on a resource demanding dichotic listening task compared to participants in a 'no thought suppression' (control) condition. Instead, we found that thought suppression was only depleting, compared to the control condition, when the distracting thoughts had to be found (t =2.27, p =.03), not when they were offered (Figure 2).

Advances in Consumer Research
Volume 40, ©2012

Figure 2
Study 3 – Remaining Self-Regulatory Resources

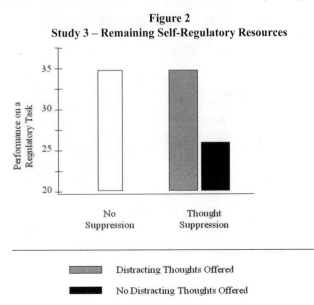

Distracting Thoughts Offered

No Distracting Thoughts Offered

This research demonstrates that the short-term benefit of suppressing thoughts to avoid the negative feelings associated with failure depletes self-regulatory resources and causes poor consumption decisions. Importantly, we explore reasons for the depletion. We demonstrate that the conscious act of finding a distraction, causes depletion and sub-optimal consumption behavior in a domain completely unrelated to the failure itself.

The findings shed light on a trade-off for consumers dealing with a failure. Either try to feel better now by suppressing thoughts at the risk of a breakdown in behavioral regulation later or wallow in the negative thoughts now, knowing that better consumption decisions will be made in future.

REFERENCES

Alexander Fedorikhin and Vanessa M. Patrick (2010). Positive Mood and Resistance to Temptation: The Interfering Influence of Elevated Arousal. *Journal of Consumer Research*, 37(December), 698-711.

Erskine, James A. K., George J. Georgiou and Lia Kvavilashvili (2010), "I Suppress, Therefore I Smoke : Effects of Thought Suppression on Smoking Behavior," *Psychological Science.* 21(9) 1225–30.

Finkelstein, S. R. & Fishbach A (2012) Tell Me What I Did Wrong: Experts Seek and Respond to Negative Feedback. *Journal of Consumer Research.*

Lyubomirsky, S. & S. Nolen-Hoeksema (1995). Effects of Self-Focused Rumination on Negative Thinking and Interpersonal Problem Solving. *Journal of Personality and Social Psychology.* 69(July), 176-190.

Meyvis, T. & A. D. J. Cooke (2007). Learning from Mixed Feedback: Anticipation of the Future Reduces Appreciation of the Present. *Journal of Consumer Research.* 34(August) 200-211.

Najmi, S. & D. M. Wegner (2008). The Gravity of Unwanted Thoughts: Asymmetric Priming Effects in Thought Suppression. *Consciousness and Cognition, 17(March),* 114-124.

Vohs, K. D. & R. J. Faber (2007). Spent Resources: Self-Regulatory Resource Availability Affects Impulse Buying. *Journal of Consumer Research.* 33 (March), 537-547.

Wegner, D. M. (1994). Ironic Processes of Mental Control. *Psychological Review.* 101(January), 34-52.

-----------; David J. Schneider; Samuel R. Carter; & Teri L. White (1987). Paradoxical Effects of Thought Suppression. *Journal of Personality and Social Psychology.* 53(July), 5-13.

Zhang, Yinlong & L. J. Shrum (2009).The Influence of Self-Construal on Impulsive Consumption. *Journal of Consumer Research.* 35(February), 838-850.

Self-Affirmation Can Backfire For Experts: The Case Of Product Warning Messages

Valeria Noguti, University of Technology Sydney, Australia

EXTENDED ABSTRACT

Protecting self-worth and integrity is a central human motivation (Steele 1988). However, it can lead people to resist threatening information which could otherwise improve their decisions (Sherman and Cohen 2002). Self-affirmation provides one way to overcome this kind of resistance (Steele 1988). As the self-concept is formed by multiple selves which get differentially activated at different moments (Markus and Kunda 1986), affirming one of these selves, for example, 'the benevolent self', activates evidence of self-worth, so the need for self-integrity protection can be relaxed, decreasing resistance to threatening information.

Although affirmation generally eases the acceptance of threatening information, it can result in higher resistance as well. For example, higher resistance is observed when the threat occurs in the same domain as the affirmation (Blanton et al. 1997) because affirmation highlights a person's commitment to the issue and the identity at stake (Sherman and Cohen 2006). As self-affirmation turns one's attention to the adequacy of the self, strengthening the pursuit of self-esteem, people feel threatened by criticism in domains in which they have staked self-worth, and feel pressure to succeed in that domain (Crocker and Park 2004). Therefore, we propose that resistance to threat is triggered by affirmation when consumers have expertise in a domain, as individuals often take pride in learning while experiencing products, and form internal attributions about personal efficacy (Hoch and Deighton 1989).

Surprisingly the role of expertise on self-affirmation effects has been absent from the literature. We start to fill this gap by investigating this question in the domain of warning labels. Product warning labels are used to communicate potential risks of product usage and/ or to persuade individuals to behave in a particular manner (Stewart and Martin 1994)w. In this context, one way to accomplish self-protection is to reassure that products with warning labels in one's domain of expertise are valuable. Hence, self-affirmation for experts who are threatened is predicted to lead to more positive product perceptions.

Further, while high self-esteem individuals respond to threats through dominance and competence, low self-esteem people pursue self-esteem by seeking acceptance, for example by looking for reassurance from others or becoming more interdependent (Crocker and Park 2004; Vohs and Heatherton 2001). Evaluating products per se cannot address the social needs that low self-esteem individuals pursue. Therefore, if self-affirmation triggers the self-esteem system, we would expect increases in product perceptions only for high self-esteem consumers because boosting these perceptions can help ascertain the importance of their competence which was threatened.

We report three studies, all with two conditions: affirmed vs. control. In study 1 participants were members of an online panel. The study started with the manipulation (Steele and Liu 1983) in which participants ranked values then explained either why their first ranked value was important to them (affirmed condition) or why their fifth ranked value was important to others (control condition). Next, participants were presented with a can of an unknown energy drink containing a label: "Warning: May cause heart palpitations in caffeine sensitive people. Usage: Max 2 cans daily", and indicated their attitudes toward the drink (α = .89) (unfavorable/favorable, negative/positive, bad/good, nonattractive/attractive). Participants then indicated their expertise (α = .86) on a 7 point scale: "I am knowledgeable regarding energy drinks" and "I have a lot of experience with energy drinks". Given length constraints, we report only the results for those who reported having seen the warning and who were more expert (estimated by mixed models using the continuous expertise measure). More expert, affirmed participants reported more positive (M = 3.98) attitudes than more expert, non-affirmed participants (M = 3.03; F(1, 79) = 5.62, p < .05).

Study 2 was run with students and used a high-involvement product category. After the affirmation manipulation, participants were presented with information about a 3D TV, including a picture of 3D glasses with the label: "Warning: Do not view images too closely or for a long period of time as it may harm your eyesight". Attitudes toward the product (α = .89) were measured, in addition to purchase intentions, and perceptions that the product would sell well. Expertise (α = .77) questions followed: "I am knowledgeable regarding 3D viewing", and "Compared to most other people, I have a lot of experience with 3D viewing (this includes time spent watching movies in 3D)". To measure category effects, participants filled out an attractiveness scale (Boyd and Mason 1999) toward 3D TVs (α = .88). Compared to control participants, for more expert consumers self-affirmation resulted in marginally more positive product attitudes (4.83 vs. 5.43; F(1, 175) = 3.20, p = .08), significantly higher perceptions that the product would sell well (4.20 vs. 4.90; F(1, 175) = 4.01, p < .05) and greater attractiveness of 3D TVs (3.39 vs. 4.43; F(1, 175) = 15.74, p < .001). Although purchase intentions did not significantly increase with affirmation (4.07 vs. 4.56; NS), this is understandable as participants were students.

In study 3, ran with members of an online panel, in the affirmed condition participants were asked to describe two situations in which they acted kindly towards someone else. In the control condition they listed 10 cities in their state. The remaining part was identical to study 2, followed by a measure of implicit self-esteem (ISE), namely a name letters evaluation task (Koole, Dijksterhuis, and Van Knippenberg 2001). The results replicate the previous findings, except that purchase intentions also increased from the control to the affirmed condition (3.94 vs. 5.00; F(1, 219) = 5.89, p < .05). Furthermore, when considering ISE, these results replicate again but only for those high in ISE (except for attitudes, which did not reach significance), not for those low in ISE.

In conclusion, we identify expertise as a significant factor in self-affirmation effects. When expertise is high, self-affirmation may lead threats to become more (rather than less) aversive, in consequence leading consumers to evaluate a product more (rather than less) positively when it contains a warning label. Self-esteem appears as a moderator: affirmation backfires only for high self-esteem experts who perceive a warning label threat.

REFERENCES

Blanton, Hart, Joel Cooper, Ian Slkurnik, and Joshua Aronson (1997), "When Bad Things Happen to Good Feedback: Exacerbating the Need for Self-Justification with Self-Affirmations," *Personality and Social Psychology Bulletin*, 23 (7), 684-92.

Boyd, Thomas C. and Charlotte H. Mason (1999), "The Link between Attractiveness of 'Extrabrand' Attributes and the Adoption of Innovations," *Journal of the Academy of Marketing Science*, 27 (3), 306-19.

Crocker, Jennifer and Lora E. Park (2004), "The Costly Pursuit of Self-Esteem," *Psychological Bulletin*, 130 (3), 392-414.

Hoch, Stephen J. and John Deighton (1989), "Managing What Consumers Learn from Experience," *Journal of Marketing*, 53 (2), 1-20.

Koole, Sander L., Ap Dijksterhuis, and Ad Van Knippenberg (2001), "What's in a Name: Implicit Self-Esteem and the Automatic Self," *Journal of Personality & Social Psychology*, 80 (4), 669-85.

Markus, Hazel and Ziva Kunda (1986), "Stability and Malleability of the Self-Concept," *Journal of Personality and Social Psychology*, 51 (4), 858-66.

Sherman, David K. and Geoffrey L. Cohen (2002), "Accepting Threatening Information: Self-Affirmation and the Reduction of Defensive Biases," *Current Directions in Psychological Science*, 11 (4), 119-23.

--- (2006), "The Psychology of Self-Defense: Self-Affirmation Theory," *Advances in experimental social psychology*, 38, 183-242.

Steele, Claude M. (1988), "The Psychology of Self-Affirmation: Sustaining the Integrity of the Self," *Advances in experimental social psychology*, 21, 261-302.

Steele, Claude M. and Thomas J. Liu (1983), "Dissonance Processes as Self-Affirmation," *Journal of Personality and Social Psychology*, 45 (1), 5-19.

Stewart, David W. and Ingrid M. Martin (1994), "Intended and Unintended Consequences of Warning Messages: A Review and Synthesis of Empirical Research," *Journal of Public Policy & Marketing*, 13 (1), 1-19.

Vohs, Kathleen D. and Todd F. Heatherton (2001), "Self-Esteem and Threats to Self: Implications for Self-Construals and Interpersonal Perceptions," *Journal of Personality and Social Psychology*, 81 (6), 1103-18.

Transformational Solutions of Self through Companion Animals

Jill Mosteller, Portland State University, USA

EXTENDED ABSTRACT

How consumers manage the dynamics between love and money can be intertwined in a myriad of ways. Based upon the growing presence of companion animals in U.S. households (now estimated at 62%) and related financial spend (over $50 billion in 2011) (APPA 2011), understanding consumers' identity dynamics relating to companion animals may be theoretically insightful. The things we love exert a strong influence on our sense of self (Ahuvia 2005). Companion animals may be classified as extensions of oneself in addition to being associated with significant life events or experiences (Belk 1988; Ahuvia 2005). By understanding the meanings companion animals serve related to a person's self-concept and integration within society may serve as "relationship climate canaries" (Brownlie 2008). Given fundamental human need for social relatedness (Baumeister and Leary 1995) and assertions of decline in one's sense of community (Cushman 1990), do the roles one adopts as it relates to companion animals serve as adaptive solutions for social relatedness?

Consumers' motives for consumption and possession stem in large part from the "meaning of consumption objects and the value that meaning provides" (Richins 1994, 519). In North America, the freedom to create one's identity comes with the consumer responsibility to self-define, suggesting that the "goods" one acquires may be particularly meaningful because they may serve to help construct and communicate one's identity (McCracken 1986). Identities represent self-concepts because they reflect internalized role expectations within social relationships; the goal being to understand and explain how social structures affect self and self affects social behaviors (Stryker 2007).

Noting that "an adequate understanding of human behavior must begin with an exploration of how people define the situation, selves, and others that compose the social worlds they inhabit" (Sanders and Hirschman 1996, 112-113), a phenomenological approach was employed. Depth interviews ranging from one to three hours in length with continued documented conversations and observations covering a five-year period provide the basis for the emergent findings. People who engaged in a variety of animal related roles provided the foundation for this purposeful sample. Observations and conversations with other informants engaged in animal related roles, and people who knew the informants, were added to triangulate and enhance data credibility (Patton 2002).Two selected cases highlight how animal-related roles serve to create a self-conceptual fit within one's community under varying degrees of resource (e.g. money, housing) and social support (e.g. community, family, professional). These two cases depict role trajectories that start, progress, and end on opposite ends of the perceptual map spectrum (social conflict/social support on the x-axis and access to resources draining/gaining on the y-axis). The emotional and financial trade-offs each makes within their respective social structures, inform identity project outcomes.

Role Abandonment to Role Acquisition: Transformative Synthesized Solution: Al

Al's story 'begins' when he was 9 years old with his "own" dog. Due to Al not spending enough time caring for and fulfilling his dog responsibility duties, his parents facilitated the abandonment of his dog caretaker role by returning the dog to the 'pound'. He had no control over the outcome; parents exerted control over resources. Al expressed conflict in terms of love and money, stating how the lack of money causes "love" to go away. To resolve this conflict, Al later worked to become Superintendent of an animal shelter, responsible for hundreds of animals. This role, a symbol of his animal stewardship achievement, helped to resolve his earlier childhood conflict, seeing himself as being a bad dog caretaker. The path from role abandonment to role acquisition illustrates a synthesized solution (Ahuvia 2005) predicated on his love "for all things natural." He constructed a desired self-concept by forcefully going after the roles that developed his animal caretaker ability and enabling him to exert control over animal life and death outcomes through the resources he responsibly managed. Al's identity transformation required him to confront his dark side, as well as others' dark sides concerning animal caretaking. This role acquisition enabled him to exert control over necessary resources so he could manage when and how love would go away.

Role Acquisition to Role Abandonment: Transformative Dysfunctional Solution: Deb

Deb began breeding dogs as a means to earn money while she cared for her mother. Over time she acquired more dogs than she sold. Rising food and care costs related to the growing number of dogs depleted her financial resources. She worked as a vet tech in a nearby city, a role she acquired role from the vet who vaccinated and treated the puppies she bred. Initially, being a vet tech and breeder helped her financially, but Deb's motivations shifted over time. To combat feelings of social isolation and reduced emotional intimacy she experienced after moving from the city back to the country, her animal family became her social surrogate. Social conflict emerged with community members calling the department of agriculture about the growing number of dogs. The sudden death of Deb's mother, a critical source of social and financial support, overwhelmed Deb emotionally and financially. She voluntarily relinquished the dogs to authorities. Deb's case illustrates how one's need for money transformed into a need for love and social connectedness not fulfilled within her community. Deb's sense of alienation and resulting identity emptiness after losing the animals is attributed in part by her inability to manage resources needed to sustain the identity project and confronting her own dark side in the process.

Findings suggest that one's perceived degree of conflict or support within one's social structure influences the construction and evolution of identities and related role behaviors as a means of creating synthesized solutions. These two cases contribute to symbolic interaction by illustrating how social relations (e.g. love) and resources (e.g. money) shape consumers' identity projects with companion animals adding social dimension. For Deb, companion animals were a social surrogate, signaling her growing alienation and distrust of others within her community. For Al, companion animals were a social conduit that enabled a personal transformation, signaling integration and support from others.

REFERENCES

APPA (2011). Industry Statistics and Trends, American Pet Products Association, http://www.americanpetproducts.org/press_industrytrends.asp. Accessed May 29, 2011

Ahuvia, Aaron C. (2005), "Beyond the Extended Self: Loved Objects and Consumers' Identity Narratives," *Journal of Consumer Research*, Vol. 32, (June), 171-84.

Baumeister, Roy F. and Mark R. Leary (1995), "The Need to Belong: Desire for Interpersonal Attachments as a Fundamental Human Motivation," *Psychological Bulletin*, Vol. 1 7 (3), 497-529.

Belk, Russell W. (1988), "Possessions and the Extended Self," *Journal of Consumer Research*, 15 (2), 139-68.

Brownlie, Douglas (2008), "Relationship Climate Canaries: A Commentary Mosteller (2007) inspires," *Journal of Business Research*, Vol. 61 (5), May, 522-24.

Cushman, Philip (1990), "Why the Self Is Empty: Toward a Historically Situated Psychology," *American Psychologist*, Vol. 45 (5), May, 599-611.

Markus, Hazel (1977), "Self-Schemata and Processing of Information about the Self," *Journal of Personality and Social Psychology*, Vol. 35, 63-78.

McCracken, Grant (1986), "Culture and Consumption: A Theoretical Account of the Structure and Movement of the Cultural Meaning of Consumer Goods," *Journal of Consumer Research*, Vol. 13, (June), 71-84.

Patton, Michael Q. (2002), *Qualitative Research and Evaluation Methods*, 3rd edition, Sage Publications, Thousand Oaks, CA.

Richins, Marsha L. (1994), "Valuing Things: The Public and Private Meaning of Possessions," *Journal of Consumer Research*, Vol. 21, (December), 504-521.

Sanders, Clinton R. and Elizabeth C. Hirschman (1996), "Guest Editors' Introduction: Involvement with Animals as Consumer Experience," *Society and Animals*, Vol. 4 (2), 111-9.

Stryker, Sheldon (2007), "Identity Theory and Personality Theory: Mutual Relevance," *Journal of Personality*, Vol. 75, (6), December, 1083-1102.

Increasing Serving-Size Increases Amount Consumed: A Catch-22

Natalina Zlatevska, Bond University, Australia
Chris Dubelaar, Bond University, Australia
Stephen Holden, Bond University, Australia

EXTENDED ABSTRACT

The effect of serving-size on consumption is well-established (Chandon and Wansink 2011). The larger the serve, the greater the amount consumed. However, what is not clear is the size of the effect, the processes driving the effect, and the conditions under which the effect is stronger or weaker.

The present research used a meta-analysis to quantify the effect of serving-size on amount consumed. We also test two alternate views in the literature for why the effect occurs. The view that the influence of serving-size on consumption volume is a perceptual effect is compared to the view that the effect is a function of a unit-bias.

Extant research shows that people's estimations of serving-size changes tend to be inelastic (Chandon and Wansink 2006; Chandon and Ordabayeva 2009; van Ittersum and Wansink 2012). Generally, the size of the increase is underestimated (100% increase in serving-size leads to a perceived increase of only 50-60%). These published results describe a standard diminishing psychophysical function as described by Weber's Law (1834). Meaning that, although there is a constant linear effect for the ratio of change in serving-size to amount consumed, the change in perceived serving-size does not equate to the actual change in serving-size.

An alternative view suggests a unit-bias drives the serving-size effect (Geier et al. 2006). Individuals generally base consumption around a single unit or serving (e.g. we consume a bowl of soup or a plate of pasta). However, focusing on the consumption of one unit (or even part of one unit) leaves individuals susceptible to variations in the size of that unit (100% increase in serving-size leads to a 100% increase in consumption).

In the present study, we expect that if the serving-size effect results from a unit-bias, consumption would change linearly in direct proportion to serving-size. Conversely, if the serving-size effect results from a perceptual influence the ratio of change in consumption will not directly equate to the actual change in serving-size.

A meta-analysis using 67 separate studies with a combined sample of 2792 respondents, revealed a substantial and significant effect of serving-size on consumption (d=.469,CI95=[.376,.562]). To test for the underlying process of the effect, we regressed the absolute measures provided within each study for both amounts served and amounts consumed. If the serving-size effect is due to a unit-bias, the relationship between amount served and amount consumed should be linear and approaching a slope of one. However, the results show that there is a diminishing impact of serving-size on amount consumed as the size of the serving increases.

While this shows that unit-bias is not the source of the size effect, it does not conclusively show that the source is perceptual. To test whether the process is perceptual, we created a metric that relates the size of change in consumption to the change in serving-size. The change in amount consumed was regressed on the change in amount served.

Our results show that the change in serving-size significantly predicts the change in consumption. Importantly, the regression coefficient tells us that if the serving-size doubles (i.e., the large serve is 100% larger than the small serve), consumption is 22% greater than in the small serve condition. In addition to providing an absolute measure of the serving-size effect, the result suggests that perceptual processes, rather than a unit-bias, drive the effect.

Finally, in an effort to identify conditions under which the effect is stronger or weaker we conducted a moderator analysis. A moderator analysis shows that although the effect varies under a range of conditions, the effect is significantly smaller for children relative to adults. The effect is also stronger when participants were distracted while eating.

To examine how the serving-size effect varies by the significant moderators we entered a dummy variable for children into our regression based on changes in consumption and serving-size. For adults the serving-size effect coefficient is .296 (t=4.88,p<.001) while the coefficient for the dummy variable for children was negative and significant (B =-.110, t=-2.49,p=.005) implying that the coefficient for children is .186. That is, children will increase consumption by 19% if the serving-size is doubled, while adults will increase their consumption by 30%. We also included a dummy variable for food focus, where 1 is no food focus and 0 is food focus. Results revealed a significant coefficient for food focus (B=0.113, t=15.62, p<0.001), implying that when eaters are distracted, and there is a doubling of the serving-size, the amount consumed will increase by 33%.

The results make a number of important contributions. The meta-analysis provides the relative size of the serving-size effect. However, the development of ratio measures of change in serving-size and consumption allows for the absolute quantification of this effect. Consumption can be expected to increase by 22% when the serving-size is doubled. The result shows consumption to be a constant ratio of serving-size and supports the notion that the serving-size effect is perceptual rather than resulting from a unit-bias. And finally, while the effect is fairly reliable and general, it is found to be stronger when consumers are distracted and among adults. The effect is weaker among children.

Some clear public policy implications may be drawn from the findings. First, the size of the serving-size effect should encourage a move away from super-sizing promotions. It might also encourage the adoption of smaller sizes – although to get a 22% reduction in consumption requires a halving of current serving-sizes. The perceptual nature of the effect means that introducing extrinsic benchmarks for appropriate sizing portions (e.g. serving size charts) into the consumption episode should be a more effective strategy in monitoring consumption than adopting rules such as 'always eat half of what you are given'. And finally, as it is encouraging to see that children are less susceptible to the serving-size effect than adults, attention needs to be given to sustaining the apparently natural resistance of children to serving-size manipulations.

In summary, there is a Catch-22 to larger serving-sizes. Serve twice as much; you will eat 22% more!

REFERENCES

Chandon, Pierre and Brian Wansink (2011), "Is Food Marketing Making us Fat? A Multi-disciplinary Review," *Foundations and Trends in Marketing*, 5(3), 113-196.

Chandon, Pierre and Brian Wansink (2006), "Is Obesity caused by calorie Underestimation? A psychophysical Model of Meal Size Estimation," *Journal of Marketing Research*, 44(February), 84-99.

Chandon, Pierre and Nailya Ordabayeva (2009), "Supersize in One Dimension, Downsize in Three Dimensions: Effects of Spatial Dimensionality on Size Perceptions and Preferences," *Journal of Marketing Research*, 46(December), 739-753.

Geier, Andrew B., Paul Rozin, and Gheorghe Doros (2006), "Unit Bias. A New heuristic That Helps Explain the Effect of Portion Size on Food Intake," *Psychological Science*, 17(6), 521-525.

Krider, Robert E., Priya Raghubir and Aradhna Krishna (2001), "Pizzas: π or Square? Psychophysical Biases in Area Comparisons, *Marketing Science*, 20(4), 405-425.

Van Ittersum, Koert and Brian Wansink (2012), Plate Size and Colour Suggestibility: The Delboeuf Illusion's Bias on Serving and Eating Behavior," *Journal of Consumer Research*

Wansink, Brian and Koert Van Ittersum (2003), "Bottoms Up! The Influence of Elongation on Pouring and Consumption Volume," *Journal of Consumer Research*, 30(December), 455-463.

Exploring African-American Women's
Lived Experiences with Stigma, Identity, and Consumption

Elizabeth Crosby, University of Wisconsin La Crosse, USA

EXTENDED ABSTRACT

A stigma "refers to an attribute that is deeply discrediting" (Goffman 1963, 3). The stigmatized characteristic labels the possessor as different from what is considered "normal" in some way. Furthermore, in order for stigmatization to occur, the attribute must be connected with a negative stereotype. This paper explores African-American women's lived experiences with stigmatization. More specifically, I address the following research questions: (1) How does stigmatization affect African-American women's identities? and (2) How do African-American women manage stigma? Specifically, how do African-American women use consumption to manage stigma?

I employed qualitative data collection methods to tap into African-American women's experiences with stigma. I conducted 23 depth interviews. Informants also constructed collages depicting their identity as African-American women. All informants live in a small city in the Midwest. They come from a variety of social classes and are between the ages of 19 and 56. All interviews were audiotaped and transcribed, yielding more than 650 pages of text. In analyzing both the collages and the written text from the depth interviews, I searched for emergent themes while also engaging in dialectical tacking (Strauss and Corbin 1998).

I argue that stigma significantly affects African-American women's identities and can create identity gaps. The Communication Theory of Identity (CIT) argues that there are four frames of identity: (1) personal, (2) enacted, (3) relational, and (4) communal (Hecht, Collier, and Ribeau. 1993). The personal identity frame is how individuals view themselves while the enacted frame is how people communicate their identity to those around them. The relational frame is others' perceptions of an individual's identity. In the communal frame, society ascribes individuals an identity based on group membership. Because different discourses govern the various identities, discrepancies among the frames can occur, which results in an identity gap (Hecht et al. 1993). Hecht et al. (1993) identify 11 potential identity gaps between frames. Research shows that identity gaps can lead to increased feelings of depression (Jung and Hecht 2008). Identity gaps can also engender feelings of perceived discrimination (Wadsworth, Hecht, and Jung 2008).

In this study, the first identity gap to emerge is the personal-communal gap. None of my informants believe they personify the stereotypes associated with their race and gender. As these women reject the stereotypes society attempts to impose on them, there is a disconnect between their personal identity frame and the communal identity that society ascribes to them. These informants also describe experiencing a communal intra-frame identity gap. While Hecht et al. (1993) explore inter-frame identity gaps (gaps occurring between frames), they fail to consider intra-frame identity gaps (gaps occurring within one identity frame). African-American women can be subjected to two opposing communal identities—one by mainstream society and the other by the African-American community. Intra-frame gaps can be just as problematic for African-American women to manage as inter-frame gaps.

In order to eliminate or reduce the identity gap, individuals can manipulate one of the four frames of identity.

PERSONAL IDENTITY FRAME

One way to eliminate an identity gap is for African-American women to accept the stereotype. The existence of the ascribed communal identity actually results in its internalization into the personal identity frame. This coping strategy is one of the biggest dangers of stereotypes. While none of my informants feel that they fit the stereotypes, they note that constantly fighting stereotyping is difficult and they have been tempted to just accept the identity society ascribes to them. They also discuss how other African-American women they know have internalized the stereotypes. While consumption is not generally used as a management strategy when changing this identity frame, it can be used to facilitate the process. For example, one informant discusses that she has considered if she should accept the gold-digger stereotype and travel to professional basketball games to try to find a rich husband.

COMMUNAL IDENTITY FRAME

African-American women can also attempt to eliminate an identity gap through the communal frame. With these strategies individuals are trying to eliminate the stereotype, thus changing the communal identity. Generally, in order for this to be effective, multiple people must work together to change the stereotype. A notable example of this is the Civil Rights Movement. Attempts to change this frame can be made at the local and national levels. Similar to the personal identity frame, while consumption is generally not the main focus of this management strategy, it can be a part of the strategy. Informants discuss organizing events to educate people on African-American culture in hopes of eradicating stereotypes.

RELATIONAL IDENTITY FRAME

The strategies associated with this frame allow African-American women to distance themselves from the stereotypes associated with their race and gender. The dominant strategy that informants discuss is letting people get to know them as an individual. Through this process those around the individual will realize that she does not fit the stereotype. Individuals can use consumption to help this process. For example, they might have coffee with others while becoming acquainted. However, it is important to note that is not always possible for individuals to get to know every person who may stereotype them. Furthermore, in some cases, an individual might not have the time to get to know the person stereotyping her because of the short duration of the encounter (e.g., during a job interview).

ENACTED IDENTITY FRAME

The strategies associated with the enacted identity frame are consumption laden. African-American women deliberately use consumption to disassociate themselves from particular stereotypes. For example, a common stereotype is that if African-American women have natural hair, they are militant or anti-white. In order to combat this, informants report either processing their hair or wearing a wig, especially in professional contexts. Other women report dressing a particular way to distance themselves from stereotypes.

In this paper I present a theoretical model of how stigma affects identity. I explore how stigmatization affects identity and how consumption is utilized as a management strategy. I hope this paper encourages scholars to revisit the construct of stigma and its importance to the field of consumer behavior.

REFERENCES

Goffman, (1963), *Stigma: Notes on the Management of Spoiled Identity*, New York, NY: Touchstone.

Hecht, Michael L., Mary Jane Collier, and Sidney A. Ribeau (1993), *African-American Communication: Ethnic Identity and Cultural Interpretation*, Thousand Oaks, CA: Sage.

Jung, Eura and Michael L. Hecht (2004), "Elaborating the Communication Theory of Identity: Identity Gaps and Communication Outcomes," *Communication Quarterly*, 52 (3), 265–83.

Strauss, Anselm and Juliet Corbin (1990), *Basics of Qualitative Research: Grounded Theory Procedures and Techniques*, Newbury Park, CA: Sage.

Wadsworth, Brooke Chapman, Michael L. Hecht, and Eura Jung (2008), "The Role of Identity Gaps, Discrimination, and Acculturation in International Students' Educational Satisfaction in American Classrooms," *Communication Education*, 57 (1), 64-87.

Don't Put All Your Green Eggs in One Basket:
Examining Self-monitoring and Environmentally Friendly Sub-branding Strategy

Jayoung Koo, University of Minnesota, USA
Barbara Loken, University of Minnesota, USA

EXTENDED ABSTRACT

Motivation

Sustainability concerns in the United States and worldwide have gained much attention in recent years, and companies are jumping on the bandwagon trying to understand strategies to best promote environmentally friendly brand images to consumers. A variety of sub-brand strategies, for example, are found in the marketplace. Toyota entered the hybrid market by introducing the sub-brand Toyota Prius as eco-friendly.

Research is needed to understand whether some sub-branding strategies are more effective than others in influencing consumers' perceptions of eco-friendliness of the overall parent brand. In two studies, we examine whether a strategy in which eco-friendly products are concentrated within a sub-brand is different from a strategy in which eco-friendly products are dispersed across sub-brands. We also examine how the sub-branding strategy interacts with the consumer's level of self-monitoring and variability (similarity or dissimilarity) between the sub-brands.

Hypotheses

Prior research in stereotyping and schematic processing (e.g. Weber and Crocker 1983) finds that when information about one category member is novel or different from the others, it will have less effect on the overall category when it is concentrated within a sub-category than when the same information is dispersed across different sub-categories. The present studies compare concentrated and dispersed sub-branding strategies and their effect on eco-friendly beliefs about the brand. Consistent with previous research, we predicted that the dispersed sub-branding strategy would have a greater impact on consumers' beliefs about the parent brand than the concentrated strategy.

We also predicted that these effects would be reinforced when differences between the sub-brands is high (versus low). Spillover from a brand extension to parent brand beliefs and attitudes (e.g., Lei, Dawar, and Lemmink 2008, John, Loken, and Joiner 1998, Loken and John 1993) has been previously documented. Based on prior research (Weber and Crocker, 1983) we expect that when a parent brand's architecture includes several sub-brands, eco-friendly products of the sub-brands should lead to greater eco-friendly beliefs for the parent brand when the products are dispersed across the different sub-brands than concentrated within a single sub-brand. Low self-monitors may be particularly attuned to differences between these strategies, whereas high self-monitors may be attuned more to other cues as well as strategies. Consumers high (low) in the trait of self-monitoring judge products by their image-enhancing properties more (less) than product performance (Snyder and DeBono 1985), and focus more (less) on behaving appropriately to the situation, they should be more receptive to any attempts by the company to develop an eco-friendly "green" image.

Hypothesis 1: When green products are dispersed across several sub-brands (vs. concentrated within one sub-brand), consumers will be more likely to infer that the parent brand is environmentally friendly.

Hypothesis 2: Low (versus high) self-monitors will be more influenced by concentrated versus dispersed strategies.

Hypothesis 3: When sub-brands are dissimilar (vs. similar) to one other, consumers will be more likely to infer that the parent brand is environmentally friendly.

Method

Study 1 (N=244) was conducted online using MTurk. Participants were shown a catalog of a hypothetical brand of automobiles (CarMak) with four sub-brands (CarMak S, T, V, and R) and four products within each sub-brand. Photos and specifications (e.g., type, horsepower, seats) of all sixteen cars were provided, and eco-friendly CO_2 emission hybrids were indicated. Participants were randomly assigned to either a concentrated strategy (all green brands shown within a single sub-brand) or dispersed strategy (each sub-brand included one green brand). Participants then completed three 1-7 scales (subsequently averaged) about whether the parent brand, CarMak, is environmentally friendly, an 18-item Self-monitoring Scale (Snyder and Gangestad 1986), and participants overall concern for the environment, the latter of which was used in analyses as a covariate. In Study 1, participants were asked to answer questions from the perspective of the consumer.

Study 2 (N=164) used the same procedure as in Study 1, with two differences. First we also manipulated the variability of products by asking participants to write either three similarities or dissimilarities of the four sub-brands (i.e., sedans, trucks, minivans, and SUVs). Second, we did not specify that participants should take the perspective of the average consumer. The latter change was made in case results were affected by participants thinking about what other consumers (rather than themselves) might infer.

Findings

In Study 1, we found support for the first hypothesis. In particular, consumers were more likely to infer that the parent brand was environmentally friendly when the green products were dispersed across sub-brands rather than concentrated ($F(1, 236) = 16.70$, $p < .001$). Second, results supported the second hypothesis. We found a marginally significant interaction effect ($F(1, 236) = 3.14$, $p = .07$) between strategy and self-monitoring such that low self-monitors were more attuned to strategy differences than high self-monitors.

The results of study 2 supported the first hypothesis, replicating Study 1 ($F(1, 155) = 4.05$, $p < .05$). Second, in support of Hypothesis 3, participants were more likely to infer the parent brand was environmentally friendly when they were primed with dissimilarities between the sub-brands than when they were primed with similarities ($F(1, 155) = 13.03$, $p < .001$). Finally, we found a significant three-way interaction of strategy, variability, and self-monitoring. Interestingly, we found mixed support for the second hypothesis. Specifically, compared to high self-monitors, low self-monitors were less influenced by variability (similar vs. dissimilar) than by strategy (concentrated vs. dispersed; $F(1, 155) = 7.75$, $p < .01$).

Contributions

First, the current research provides insights about how to promote a brand's environmentally friendly image by using sub-branding strategies. In particular, dispersed strategies were superior to concentrated strategies. In addition, prior research in stereotyping and schematic processing was successfully applied to the study of green branding, an emerging topic in consumer research. Finally, it proposes a possible extension of self-monitoring to green branding. For example, marketers who are engaged in global branding might want to place different type of advertisement depending on the target consumer (e.g. the Asian culture may have chronically lower self-monitoring compared to Americans, Fuglestad and Snyder 2009).

REFERENCES

Fuglestad, Paul. T. and Mark Snyder (2009), "Self-monitoring," in *Handbook of Individual Differences in Social Behavior,* ed. Mark. R. Leary and Rick. H. Hoyle, New York: Guilford, 574-591.

John, Deborah R., Barbara Loken, and Christopher Joiner (1998), "The Negative Impact of Extensions: Can Flagship Products Be Diluted?" *Journal of Marketing,* 62 (January), 19-32.

Lei, Jing, Niraj Dawar, and Jos Lemmink (2008), "Negative Spillover in Brand Portfolios: Exploring the Antecedents of Asymmetric Effects," *Journal of Marketing*, 72 (May), 111-123.

Loken, Barbara and Deborah R. John (1993), "Diluting Brand Beliefs: When Do Brand Extensions Have a Negative Impact?" *Journal of Marketing*, 57 (July), 71-84.

Snyder, Mark and Kenneth G. DeBono (1985), "Appeals to Image and Claims about Quality: Understanding the Psychology of Advertising," *Journal of Personality and Social Psychology*, 49 (3), 586-597.

Snyder, Mark and Steve Gangestad (1986), "On the Nature of Self-monitoring: Matters of Assessment, Matters of Validity," *Journal of Personality and Social Psychology,* 51(1), 125-139.

Weber, Reneé and Jennifer Crocker (1983), "Cognitive Processes in the Revision of Stereotypic Beliefs," *Journal of Personality and Social Psychology,* 45(5)*,* 961-977.

Food Customization: How Decision Frame Influences Choice

Anish Nagpal, The University of Melbourne, Australia
Jing Lei, The University of Melbourne, Australia
Adwait Khare, The University of Texas Arlington, USA

EXTENDED ABSTRACT

Nowadays, restaurants and food outlets increasingly allow consumers to customize their food, which often involves either a selection or a rejection decision. For example, shop A might allow you to build a food platter by asking you to *choose* from a range of healthy (e.g., carrots, celery) and/or unhealthy (e.g., fried spring rolls, fries) options. Alternatively, shop B might offer a pre-prepared platter consisting of healthy/unhealthy options, but then asks you to customize it by *rejecting* the ones that you don't like. Although prior research has examined the effect of choose versus reject decision frames on the 'quantity' of items selected, (e.g., Dhar and Wertenbroch 2000; Huber, Neale, and Northcraft 1987; Park, Jun, and MacInnis 2000; Shafir 1993, Yaniv and Schul 1997), it has been surprisingly mute on the 'quality' of the choice. What we mean is that although a choose frame may appear to be the 'correct' frame to adopt because it leads to a smaller quantity of items as indicated by past research, it can lead to the false conclusion that a healthier choice has been made. In fact, the opposite might be true because the items selected might be unhealthy. Alternatively, the reject decision frame might appear to be inappropriate as it leads to a larger number of items, hence more calories, but the opposite might be true as the nature of items selected might be healthy.

We draw upon three theoretical frameworks to predict the impact of decision fame on food customisation decisions. First, hedonic attributes (e.g., taste) are weighted more under a reject decision whereas the utilitarian attributes (e.g., calories) are weighted more under a choose decision frame (Bohm and Pfister 1996; Dhar and Wertenbroch 2000). Second, the goal progress literature (Fishbach and Dhar 2005; Fishbach and Zhang 2008) suggests that upon seeing a healthy item, people may feel a sense of vicarious fulfilment that they have progressed towards the health goal, thus permitting them to indulge in unhealthy food (Martin 2007; Wilcox et al. 2009). Third, activation of the long-term health goal upon being exposed to temptations occurs more spontaneously than vice-versa (Fishbach, Friedman, and Kruglanski 2003). Across three studies, we show that the decision frames of choosing versus rejecting have important consequences for food customisation decisions.

In study 1, half of the participants were shown a randomised list of 5-healthy and 5-unhealthy items and asked to check the items they wanted to add to their customisable platter (choose decision frame). The other half were told that a pre-selected platter already included the 5-healthy and 5-unhealthy items, which could be removed by un-checking the items they did not want (reject decision frame). We found that a greater number of unhealthy versus healthy items were included when rejecting (3.82 vs. 3.21; $F (1, 37) = 5.29, p < .05$) but there was no difference in the number of unhealthy versus healthy items when choosing (2.24 vs. 2.68), $F (1, 37) = 1.16$, ns.

In study 1, healthy and unhealthy items were presented mixed together on one page. However, we often select from two separate lists. For example, when customising a sandwich, we may first select from a list of salads (healthy) and then move on to select meats and sauces (unhealthy). In study 2, half of the participants were first shown the healthy list followed by the unhealthy list and the order was reversed for the other half of the participants. Interestingly, we observed a significant Decision Frame x Item Type x Order three-way interaction on the number of items included in the food platter

$(F (1, 246) = 4.65, p < .05)$. Specific contrasts revealed that under the choose decision frame, although a greater number of healthy (versus unhealthy) items were included (2.90 vs. 2.10; $F (1, 127) = 35.16, p < .05$) under both UH-H and H-UH orders, this difference was marginally greater in the UH-H order than the H-UH order (1.02 vs. 0.58; $t (246) = 1.70; p < .1$). Under a reject decision frame, a greater number of healthy (versus unhealthy) items were included in the food platter (3.80 vs. 2.95; $t (121) = 6.13, p < .05$) in both UH-H and H-UH order. The key takeaway is that consumers should choose sequentially – unhealthy followed by healthy items.

In study 3, we varied the valence of the food platter (in studies 1 and 2, the food platter had a neutral valence) by asking participants to customise a salad (healthy valence) versus a pizza (unhealthy valence). Our results indicated that that a greater number of toppings were selected under rejecting than choosing when customising a salad (6.70 vs. 5.24; $F (1, 174) = 9.55, p < .001$), but not when customising a pizza (5.95 vs. 6.06, ns). Second, in terms of quality, a greater number of healthy (versus unhealthy) toppings were selected when choosing (3.14 vs. 2.42; $t (91) = 3.10, p < .05$), but not under rejecting (3.15 vs. 3.20, ns). Third, when customising a salad, both the decision frames of choosing and rejecting led to an equal number of healthy versus unhealthy toppings. However, when customising a pizza, a greater number of healthy (vs. unhealthy) items were included when choosing (3.50 vs. 2.45; $t (41) = 3.10$, p < .05), but not under rejecting (3.04 vs. 3.02 ($t (45) = .075$, ns).

Our research has several implications. First, it adds to the understanding of how decision frames of choosing versus rejecting influence consumer choices. We show that decision frames not only influence the quantity but more importantly, the quality of the decision. Second, our research suggests that by presenting food choices in the 'right' format (e.g., presenting unhealthy and healthy options separately in the order of unhealthy followed by healthy options), businesses in the food industry can aid the consumer in making healthier choices. Third, and most important, we suggest that consumers have an important role to play in the battle against rising obesity levels. By having the right frame of mind, they can certainly make healthier choices.

REFERENCES

Bohm, Gisela and Hans-Riidiger Pfister (1996), "Instrumental or Emotional Evaluations: What Determines Preferences?" *Acta Psychologica*, 93 (1-3), 135-48.

Dhar, Ravi and Klaus Wertenbroch (2000), "Consumer Choice Between Hedonic and Utilitarian Goods," *Journal of Marketing Research,* 37 (1), 60-71

Fishbach, Ayelet, Ronald S. Friedman, and Arie W. Kruglanski (2003), "Leading Us Not unto Temptation: Momentary Allurements Elicit Overriding Goal Activation," *Journal of Personality and Social Psychology*, 84 (2), 296–309.

Fishbach, A., and Ravi Dhar (2005), "Goals as Excuses or Guides: The Liberating Effect of Perceived Goal Progress on Choice," *Journal of Consumer Research*, 32 (3), 370–77.

Fishbach, Ayelet and Ying Zhang (2008), "Together or Apart: When Goals and Temptations Complement versus Compete," *Journal of Personality and Social Psychology*, 94 (4), 547–59.

Huber, V. L., Margaret A. Neale, and Gregory B. Northcraft (1987), "Decision Bias and Personnel Selection Strategies," *Organizational Behavior & Human Decision Processes*, 40, 136-147.

Martin, Andrew (2007), "Did McDonald's Give In to Temptation?" *New York Times*, July 22

Park, C. Whan, Sung Y. Jun, and Deoborah J. MacInnis (2000), "Choosing What I Want Versus Rejecting What I Do Not Want: An Application of Decision Framing to Product Option Choice Decisions," *Journal of Marketing Research*, 37, 187-202.

Shafir, E. (1993), "Choosing Versus Rejecting: Why Some Options are Both Better and Worse than Others," *Memory and Cognition*, 21, 546-556.

Wilcox, K., Beth Vallen, Lauren Block, and Gavin J. Fitzsimons (2009), "Vicarious Goal Fulfilment: When the Mere Presence of a Healthy Option Leads to an Ironically Indulgent Decision," *Journal of Consumer Research*, 36 (October), 380-393.

Yaniv, I. and Yaniv Schul (1997), "Elimination and Inclusion Procedures in Judgment," *Journal of Behavioral Decision Making*, 10, 211-220.

Social Support Style and Risky Behaviors in Everyday Life

Lili Wang, Zhejiang University, China
Tanya L. Chartrand, Duke University, USA
Linyun Yang, University of North Carolina, USA

EXTENDED ABSTRACT

The findings of four studies showed that the impact of receiving social support on risky behaviors depends on the style in which the support is provided. Encouraging social support inhibits risky behaviors while controlling social support triggers risky behaviors. We find that the negative relationship between encouraging social support and risky behaviors is moderated by relational concerns and mediated by increased support-based self-esteem. In contrast, the positive relationship between controlling social support and risky behaviors is moderated by independence concerns and mediated by support-triggered reactance.

SOCIAL SUPPORT STYLES

Those who receive encouraging social support are given the opportunity to set their own goals. Support providers serve an ancillary role and offer assistance and moral support when needed (Harber et al. 2005). Examples of encouraging support include encouraging independent problem solving (Grolnick and Ryan 1989), providing reassurance and comfort, and providing options for the recipient to choose from (Overall, et al. 2010). In contrast, controlling social support can be overbearing and intrusive and is characterized by attempts to impose solutions or views on recipients. These behaviors include interfering with the recipient's choices (Lewis and Rook 1999), dictating corrective actions (Cohen and Lichtenstein 1990) and determining how much effort recipients should exert (Taylor et al. 1985).

IMPLICATIONS FOR RISKY BEHAVIORS

From an interpersonal relationship perspective, research suggests that individuals respond positively to encouraging social support and are less likely to engage in risky behaviors (Davison et al. 2003; Reblin and Uchino 2008). From a self-control perspective, research suggests that encouraging social support can enhance self-regulation (Grolnick and Ryan 1989; Fizsimons and Shah 2008). Furthermore, cognitive neuroscience studies find that the brain areas associated with self-control are also tied to regulating risk-taking behaviors (Cohen and Lieberman 2010). Thus, we assume that:

Hypothesis 1: *Encouraging social support inhibits risky behaviors.*

However, Ryan et al. (1983) found that a controlling context or relationship can compromise emotional control (Ryan et al. 1983) and exacerbate problem behaviors in children. Similarly, Petti et al. (2001) found that increased parental control increases the likelihood that adolescents will engage in risky, delinquent and antisocial behavior. More direct evidence is that Landsford et al. (2003) found that children engage in more risky, maladaptive behaviors when their parents make all their decisions for them. Thus, we assume that:

Hypothesis 2: *Controlling social support induces risky behaviors.*

MODERATING ROLE OF RELATIONAL CONCERNS AND INDEPENDENT CONCERNS

Research has found that individuals with high relational concerns value their interpersonal relationships and put much effort into maintaining them (Cross et al. 2000; Swap and Rubin 1983). In contrast, individuals with high independence concerns are more concerned with maintaining their personal rights and autonomy (Cross et al. 2000).

According to our conceptualization, the extent to which support behaviors are helpful depends on the needs and desires of the recipient. Since the benefits of receiving encouraging social support involve enhancement of the relationship between the recipient and provider, recipients for whom personal relationships are important should respond most favorably to encouraging social support and be less likely to engage in risky behaviors. In contrast, the costs of controlling social support stem from diminished feelings of self-reliance and independence, so those who particularly value their autonomy should be especially likely to respond with increased risky behavior. We hypothesize that:

Hypothesis 2a: *Relational concerns strengthen the negative relationship between encouraging social support and risky behaviors.*

Hypothesis 2b: *Independent concerns intensify the positive relationship between controlling support style and risky behaviors.*

UNDERLYING PROCESSES

We propose that encouraging social support will bolster individual perceptions of self-esteem (Dubois et al. 1994; Short et al. 1996), resulting in enhanced self-control (Fitzsimons and Shah 2008; Dubois et al. 2002) and reduced maladaptive, risky behaviors (e.g., delinquency).Implicit bargain theory also provides support for this notion and suggests that people (particularly those high in self-esteem) are reluctant to approach desirable outcomes if doing so will compromise close relationships (Bartz and Lydon 2008; Baumeister et al. 2005; Baumeister and Stillman 2007). Therefore, we hypothesize that:

Hypothesis 3a: *Support-based self-esteem will mediate the effect of encouraging social support on risky behaviors.*

Research has found that when significant others are perceived as controlling or authoritative (Deci and Ryan, 2000), individuals might respond with "reactance" and do the exact opposite of what the significant others want them to do (Brehm and Brehm 1981). We propose that taking risky behaviors is one way to for individuals' to regain their freedom from those offering controlling social support. Given that people view potential gains (such as money) as a source of personal control (Johnson and Kruger 2006), we posit that increased reactance will increase the appeal of risky behaviors because the potential gains of such behaviors become more attractive. Taken together, we hypothesize that:

Hypothesis 3b: *Support-triggered reactance will mediate the effect of controlling social support on risky behaviors.*

EXPERIMENTS AND RESULTS

Using a survey method, study 1 found that while encouraging support inhibited risky behaviors, controlling support enhanced risky behaviors. In study 2, we replicated the findings in study 1 by directly manipulating encouraging and controlling social and measuring risky behaviors with self-report measures and real lab-based behaviors. Study 3 demonstrated that relational concerns strengthened the impact encouraging support had on risky behaviors while independence concerns enhanced the influence of controlling support on risky behaviors. In study 4, we explored possible reasons for the divergent effects of encouraging and controlling support. Results indicated that encouraging support enhances individuals' self-esteem, which in turn facilitate their behavioral adjustments and decrease likelihood they will engage in risky behaviors. In contrast, we found that controlling social support induces reactance in individuals, which in turn increases the likelihood they will engage in maladaptive, risky behaviors in attempt to regain their personal autonomy.

CONCLUSIONS

In sum, this research provides a more nuanced understanding of social support by demonstrating that the specific style in which social support is provided can have divergent effects on maladaptive, risky behaviors. We believe that our research extends the research on social support and interpersonal relationships and provides a new perspective for understanding risky behaviors.

REFERENCES

Ayers, T. S Sandler, I. N., & Twohey, J. L. (1998). Conceptualization and measurement of coping in children and adolescents. Advances in Clinical Child Psychology, 20, 243–301

Brehm, S. S. and Brehm, J. W. (1981). Psychological reactance: a theory of freedom and control. New York: Academic Press.

Chartrand, T.L., Cheng, C.M., Dalton, A.N, and Tesser, A. (2010). Nonconscious goal pursuit: Isolated incidents or adaptive self-regulatory tool? Social Cognition, 28, 569-588.

Compas, B. E., Hinden, B. R., and Gerhardt, C. A. (1995). Adolescent development: Pathways and processes of risk and resilience. Annual Review of Psychology, 46(1), 265–293.

Cross, S. E., Bacon, P.L and Morris, M. L (2000). The relational-interdependent self-construal and relationships. Journal of Personality and Social Psychology, 78(4): 791-808

Deci, E. L. and Ryan, R. M. (2000). The 'What' and 'Why' of Goal Pursuits: Human Needs and the Self-Determination of Behavior. Psychological Inquiry 11(4): 227-268

Dubois, D. L., Burk-Braxton, C., Swenson, L. P., Tevendale, H. D., Lockerd, E. M., and Moran, B. L. (2002). Getting by with a little help from self and others: self-esteem and social support as resources during early adolescence. Developmental Psychology, 38(5), 822-839.

Dubois, D. L., Felner, R. D., Meares, H., and Krier, M. (1994). Prospective investigation of the effects of socioeconomic disadvantage, life stress, and social support on early adolescent adjustment. Journal of Abnormal Psychology, 103(3), 511–522.

Fitzsimons, G. M., and Shah, J. (2008). How goal instrumentality shapes relationship evaluations. Journal of personality and social psychology, 95 (2), 319-337.

Hirsch, B. J. (1980). Natural support systems and coping with major life changes. American Journal of community psychology, 8 (2), 159-172

Hsee, C. K., and Weber, E. U.(1999). Cross-national differences in risk preference and lay predictions. Journal of Behavior Decision Making, 12(2), 165-179

Kahn, R. L. (1979). Aging and social support. In M. W Riley (Ed.), Aging from birth to death: Interdisciplinary perspectives (pp. 77-91).Boulder, CO: Westview Press

Kaplan, B. H., Cassel, J. C., and Gore, S. (1977).Social support and health. Medical Care, 15(5), 47-58.

Kashima, Y., Yamaguchi, S., Kim, U., Choi, S. C, Gelfand, M. J., and Yuki,M. (1995). Culture, gender, and self: A perspective from individualism collectivism research. Journal of Personality and Social Psychology, 69(5), 925-937.

Krantz, D. Z., Grunberg, N. E and Baum, A. (1985). Health Psychology. Annual Review of Psychology, 36: 349-383

Mandel, N. (2003). Shifting Selves and Decision Making: The effects of self-construal priming on consumer risk-taking. Journal of Consumer Research, 30(1): 30-40.

Mitchell, R. E. (1982) Social networks and psychiatric clients: The personal and environmental context. American Journal of Community Psychology, 10(4), 387-401.

Petersen, A. C., Kennedy, R. E., and Sullivan, P. A. (1991). Coping with adolescence. In M. E. Colten and S. Gore (Eds.), Adolescent stress: Causes and consequences (pp. 93–110). New York: Aldine de Gruyter

Bartz, A. Jennifer and John E. Lydon (2008), "Relationship-Specific Attachment, Risky Regulation, and Communal Norm adherence in Close Relationships", *Journal of Experimental Social Psychology*, 44, 655-663

Baumeister, F. Roy and Tyler F. Stillman (2007), "Self-Regulation and Close Relationship," in *The self and Social Relationships*, eds. Joanne V. Wood, Abraham Tesser, and John Grenville Holmes. Philadelphia, PA; Psychology Press.

Baumeister, F. Roy, Nathan C. Dewall, Natalie J. Ciarocco and Jean M. Twenge (2005), "Social Exclusion Impairs Self-Regulation," *Journal of Personality and Social Psychology*, 88(4): 589-604.

Brehm, S. Sharon and Jack W. Brehm (1981). *Psychological reactance: A theory of*

Cohen, R. Jassica and Matthew D. Liberman (2010) "The Common Neural Basis of Exerting Self-Control in Multiple Domain," in *Self Control in Society, Mind and Brain*, ed Ran R. Hassin, Kevin N. Ochsner and Yaacov Trope. New York, NY: Oxford University Press, 141-162.

Cohen, Sheldon and Edward Lichtenstein (1990), "Partner Behaviors that Support Quitting Smoking," *Journal of Consulting and Clinical Psychology*, 58(3): 304-309.

Cross, Susan E., Pamela L. Bacon and Michael L. Morris (2000), "The Relational-Interdependent Self-construal and Relationships," *Journal of Personality and Social Psychology*, 78(4), 791-808

Davison, Kirsten Krahnstoever, Tanja M. Cutting and Leann L. Birch (2003), "Parents' Activity-Related Parenting Practices Predict Girls' Physical Activity," *Medicine and Science in Sports and Exercise*,35 (9),1589-1595.

Deci, L. Edward and Richard M. Ryan (2000). "The 'What' and 'Why' of Goal Pursuits: Human Needs and the Self-Determination of Behavior," Psychological Inquiry, 11(4), 227-268.

Dubois, David L., Carol Burk-Braxton, Lance P. Swenson, Heather D. Tevendale, Erika M. Lockerd, and Benjamin L. Moran(2002), " Getting by with a Little Help from Self and Others: Self-esteem and Social Support as Resources during Early Adolescence," *Developmental Psychology*, 38(5), 822-839.

Dubois, David L., Robert D. Felner, Henry Meares, and Marion Krier(1994) , "Prospective Investigation of the Effects of Socioeconomic Disadvantage, Life Stress, and Social Support on Early Adolescent Adjustment," *Journal of Abnormal Psychology*, 103(3), 511–522.

Fitzsimons, Gráinne M. and James Y. Shah(2008) , "How Goal Instrumentality Shapes Relationship Evaluations," Journal of personality and social psychology, 95 (2), 319-337.

freedom and control. New York: Academic Press.

Grolnick, Wendy S.and Richard M. Ryan (1989), "Parent Styles Associated with Children's Self-Regulation and Competence in School," *Journal of Educational Psychology*, 81(2), 143-154.

Harber, D. Kent, Joanne Kraenzle Schneider, Kelly M. Everard and Edwin B. Fisher (2005), "Directive support, Nondirective Support, and Morale," *Journal of Social and Clinical Psychology*, 24(5): 691-722

Johnson, Wendy and Robert F. Krueger (2006), "How Money Buys Happiness: Genetic and Environmental Processes Linking Finances and Life Satisfaction," *Journal of Personality and Social Psychology*, 90(4), 680-691.

Lansford, E. Jennifer, Michael M. Criss, Gregory S. Pettit, Kenneth A. Dodge and John E. Bates (2003), "Friendship Quality, Peer Group Affiliation, and Peer Antisocial Behavior as Moderators of the Link Between Negative Parenting and Adolescent Externalizing Behavior", *Journal of Research on Adolescence*, 13(2), 161-184

Lewis, A. Megan and Karen S. Rook (1999), "Social Control in Personal Relationship: Impact of Health Behaviors and Psychological Distress," *Health Psychology*, 18(1):63-71

Pettit, S. Gregory, John E. Bates, Kenneth A. Dodge and Darrel W. Meece (2003), "The Impact of After-School Peer Contact on Early Adolescent Externalizing Problems Is Moderated by Parental Monitoring, Perceived Neighborhood Safety, and Prior Adjustment", *Child Development*, 70(3), 768-778

Rebin, Maija and Bert N. Uchino (2008), "Social and Emotional Support and Its implication for health," Current Opinion in Psychiatry, 21(2), 201-205.

Ryan, M. Richard, Valerie Mims and Richard Koestner (1983), "Relation of Reward Contingency and Interpersonal Context to Intrinsic Motivation: A Review and Test Using Cognitive Evaluation Theory", *Journal of Personality and Social Psychology*, 45(4), 736-750.

Short, Jerome L., Irwin N. Sandler and Mark W. Roosa (1996), "Adolescents' Perceptions of Social Support: The Role of Esteem Enhancing and Esteem Threatening Relationships," *Journal of Social and Clinical Psychology*, 15(4), 397–416.

Swap, Walter C. and Jeffrey Z. Rubin (1983). "Measurement of Interpersonal Orientation," *Journal of Personality and Social Psychology*, 44 (1), 208-219.

Taylor, B. Craig, Albert Bandura, Craig K. Ewart, Nancy H. Miller and Robert F. DeBusk (1985), "Exercise Testing to Enhance Wives' Confidence in Their Husbands' Cardiac Capabilities Soon After Clinically Uncomplicated Myocardial Infarction," *American Journal of Cardiology*, 55(6), 635-638.

Is Consumer Culture Good for Women?
A Study of the Role of Consumer Culture in Disadvantaged Women's Gender Role Negotiation

Zuzana Chytkova, University of Economics, Czech Republic
Dannie Kjeldgaard, University of Southern Denmark, Denmark

EXTENDED ABSTRACT

The category of gender, a "filter, through which individuals experience their social world" (Bristor and Fischer 1993) is recognized as an important aspect of consumer behavior. Yet, it has been noted elsewhere that it tends to be overlooked in the mainstream consumer research (Schroeder 2003). Particularly, we argue that there is not enough understanding of the role of consumer culture in women's gender negotiation and their emancipation from traditional gender roles, especially so in the case of minority, non-middle class, non-Western women (Catteral, McLaren and Stevens 2005). The lack of these women's viewpoint is increasingly significant, as consumer culture logic is spreading and becoming the dominant ideology in an ever larger part of the world. Furthermore, an increasing number of female immigrants from developing countries are integrated in first world households as they are engaged in paid care work and the ensuant consumption opportunities (however meager) oftentimes lead them to experience emancipation from home culture's traditional gender roles. These renegotiations of gender roles emerging from global cultural flows remain relatively unexplored and the study of this promises further conceptual development of the role and inter-relationship of gender and consumption within consumer culture.

LITERATURE REVIEW

With relation to gender, consumer culture has been traditionally seen by the second-wave feminists as an overpowering force that drives the perpetuation of patriarchy both in feminist and consumer research literature. It is often criticized for picturing women in stereotypical roles or as sexual subjects, creating unattainable beauty myths serving to keep women under patriarchal domination (Bordo 1993; Wolf 2002; Faludi 2006). Such critique, however, reproduces the dichotomy found by feminist deconstructions of marketing literature, i.e. the active, controlling, male marketer/creator and the passive, controlled, female consumer/desctructor (Hirshman 1991, Bristor and Fisher 1993). In this way, this view of market and gender thus reproduces this dichotomy by picturing women as passive consumers uncritically taking over the market representations of herself (Scott 2000, 2005).

Another view has been offered by postmodern feminism that draws inspiration from the liberatory postmodern view of consumption (Firat and Venkatesh 1995), suggesting that through consumption choices women in the postmodern era can escape the construction of femininity imposed upon them (Caterall, Maclaran and Stevens 2005). Critics of this stream, however, draw attention to the fact that such claims do not hold for non-white, non-middle class women not originated in Western countries (McDonald 2000, McRobbie 2000, 2004). Yet, the role of marketplace in these women's gender negotiation has not been explored. There is thus a need to address these issues and study the role of consumer culture in disadvantaged women's emancipation from traditional gender roles. However, the traditional emancipation theories are based on the notion of production: emancipation through participation in the workforce, while we concentrate on the role of consumer culture that favors consumption.

RESEARCH QUESTIONS

Our research question seeks to uncover if and under what circumstances can gender become a resource rather than constriction. In particular, we want to explore if the conditions of late modern consumer culture, precisely because of its accent on consumption rather than production, can act as a facilitator for these processes, offering it potential for disadvantaged women to perform alternative (to traditional) gender roles. In this paper, we investigate if and how exactly do these women use conceptions of gender as a resource on day-to-day basis, altering their gender roles through consumption practices.

METHOD

In order to answer the research questions, we have carried out interviews with fourteen Romanian female immigrants to Italy between June 2008 and February 2009. Two of the respondents were then interviewed again July 2011, which allowed to follow up on processes of gender negotiation individuated in the first round of data collection. Our respondents were 23 to 51 years old and had low-status jobs in Italy. The interviews were transcribed verbatim. Parts of our analysis that deal with the general accounts of gender roles in Romania and Italy concentrate on the interviews with all fourteen respondents, while the two specific informants' accounts are used where we treat the long-term effects of consumer culture on gender construction.

FINDINGS

The respondents have shown to be acculturated into traditional gender role centered on notions of self sacrifice, care and passive endurance of hardships. Such gender role is an evidence of a culture historically centered heavily around production. As Ceaucescu strived to level out the national debt, the whole country revolved around producing as much as possible and the ideal of a woman reflected this trend in that women were expected to sacrifice their own aspirations in order to produce and reproduce (to produce more labor force). Traditional gender roles were enforced without an alternative and gender in this setting thus represented a constriction in self definition.

Our respondents moved to a setting with advanced consumer culture, which is centered on consumption and which offers a different gender discourse, part of which is constructed in and by the marketplace. In the accounts of the informants we have individuated gender resources, some offered by consumer culture, that immigrant women use in their gender role negotiation. Namely, the (global) modern woman discourse found in the marketplace offered individualism, active self-help, free (consumption) choices and the focus on hedonistic and self-enhancement consumption.

Our informants made use of these resources in their gender role negotiation. For instance, for both Georgeta and Elisabeta, our long term respondents, hedonistic consumption has proved to be instrumental in the negotiation of their perception of themselves as women. This perception they had of themselves as women, or their gender, then became a resource in their everyday lives, enabling them to overcome the constrictions of the traditional gender role.

CONTRIBUTIONS

We show that different contexts are gendered in a different way, depending on their focus on either consumption or production. Contexts favoring production (such as those presented by communist regimes) do not offer alternative resources for women to draw on in their gender negotiation and gender thus becomes a constriction. Consumer culture, on the other hand, with its focus on consumption (constructed as feminine), allows for more gender negotiation space.

We argue that the second wave feminist critique of consumer culture reproduces the same dichotomy it criticizes, i.e. the active producer/passive consumer. Furthermore, the criticism of certain aspects of consumer culture, such as hedonistic consumption, can be seen as instantiation of Western thought, in which what is on the surface is superficial.

REFERENCES:

Bordo, Susan (1993), "Hunger as Ideology," in *The Consumer Society Reader*, eds. J.B. Schor and D.B. Holt, New York: The New Press, 99-114.

Bristor, Julie M., and Eileen Fischer (1993), "Feminist thought: Implications for consumer research," *Journal of Consumer Research,* 19, 518-36.

Catterall, Miriam, Pauline Maclaran, and Lorna Stevens (2005), "Postmodern paralysis: The critical impasse in feminist perspectives on consumers." *Journal of Marketing Management* 21: 489-504.

_____ (2006), "The Transformative Potential of Feminist Critique in Consumer Research," in: *Advances in Consumer Research,* Vol. 33, eds. C. Pechmann and L. L. Price, Provo: Association for Consumer Research, 222-226.

Faludi, Susan (2006), *Backlash: the undeclared war against American women*, New York: Crown Publishing.

Firat, Fuat and Alladi Venkatesh (1995), "Liberatory Postmodernism and the Reenchantment of Consumption," *Journal of Consumer Research,* 22, 239-67.

Hirschman, Elizabeth C. (1993), "Ideology in Consumer Research, 1980 and 1990 : A Marxist and Feminist Critique," *Journal of Consumer Research*, 19, 537-555.

McDonald, Mary G. (2000), "Association and the making of postfeminism: The marketing of the women's national basketball," *International Review for the Sociology of Sport,* 35, 35-47.

McRobbie, Angela (2000), "A New Kind of Rag Trade?" in: *The Consumer Society Reader*, eds. J.B. Schor and D.B. Holt, New York: The New Press, 433-445.

_____ (2004), "Post-feminism and popular culture." *Feminist Media Studies*, 4(3), 255-264.

Scott, Linda M. (2000), "Market feminism: the case for a paradigm shift," in: *Marketing and Feminism: Current issues and research*, eds. M. Catterall, P. Maclaran, and L. Stevens, New York: Routledge, 16-38.

_____ (2005), *Fresh Lipstick: Redressing Fashion and Feminism*, New York: Palgrave.

Schroeder, Jonathan (2003), "Guest Editor's Introduction: Consumption, Gender and Identity," *Consumption Markets & Culture*, 6(1), 1-4.

Wolf, Naomi (2002), *The Beauty Myth: How images of beauty are used against women*, New York: HarperCollins Publishers.

Brand Perception: Influence of Gender Cues on Dimensions of Warmth and Competence

Alexandra Hess, the University of Waikato, New Zealand
Valentyna Melnyk, the University of Waikato, New Zealand
Carolyn Costley, the University of Waikato, New Zealand

EXTENDED ABSTRACT

Today's challenge for advertisers is to increase positive brand perception and influence consumers with increasingly low attention spans. Advertisers must find ways to convey the right brand image in a short time and with the restricted mental resources of the consumer. One potential solution is to utilize stereotypes because people activate stereotypes in less than milliseconds, almost automatically (Bargh 1997). Hence, activating stereotype knowledge may influence desired brand perceptions automatically and effectively.

Most stereotypes fall between two robust fundamental dimensions: warmth and competence (Fiske, Cuddy, Glick, and Xu 2002; Fiske et al. 2007). Aaker, Vohs and Mogilner (2010) examined these dimensions and found that people perceive non-profit organizations as warmer than for-profit, but as less competent. Furthermore, perceived competence, rather than warmth influences purchasing behavior.

Aaker et al.'s (2010) research shows that the warmth and competence dimensions influence marketplace decision making. Our study therefore aims to find ways to increase warmth/competence of a brand via subtle cues. Towards this we investigate whether utilizing gender stereotypes in the product description influences the warmth/competence perception of a brand. Further, we investigate how the perception of warmth/competence influences purchasing behavior depending on a product's gender (Fugate and Phillips, 2010). Specifically, we seek conditions where warmth influences purchasing behavior.

THEORETICAL BACKGROUND

The stereotypical woman is viewed as warm, whereas men as competent (Eagly and Mladinic 1994; Eagly, Mladinic, and Otto 1994). What's more, we activate gender stereotypical knowledge on the basis of cues associated to gender stereotypes (e.g. occupation, physical appearance etc.; Banaji and Hardin 1996; Deaux and Lewis 1984). Consequently, those cues could take the form of colors and symbols which are associated with a gender (Fagot, et al. 1997; Leinbach, Hort, and Fagot 1997) and which we believe are triggers for activating gender stereotype knowledge. Therefore, we assume that gender cues incorporated with product descriptions influence brand perceptions along the warmth and competence dimensions. In addition, consumers automatically assign a gender to most products (e.g. hair spray is feminine whereas coffee is masculine; Fugate and Phillips 2010). Hence, in our first study, we estimate the effect of (in) congruence between the perceived gender of the product category and the gender of the subtle cues in the product's description on the product's purchase likelihood.

METHODOLOGY

We first test the effect of gender primes on purchasing intention for masculine versus feminine typed products. Second, we investigate the role of warmth and competence as the mediator for gender prime and purchasing likelihood.

In an online experiment, 204 participants (110 female) were randomly assigned to one of the six conditions of the 2 (masculine vs. feminine product) x 3 (masculine vs. feminine vs. no prime) between-subjects design throughout 3 different product categories within-subject. The gender typed products were chosen on the basis

of a pre-test. The gender primes were symbols and colors which are previously identified as male-typed or as female-typed (Fagot et al. 1997; Leinbach et al. 1997).

Participants evaluated advertisements via seven 7-point scales: purchasing likelihood as well as warmth, kindness, and generosity which comprises the warmth index (Cronbach's $\alpha = .85$) and competence, effectiveness and efficiency which comprises the competence index (Cronbach's $\alpha = .90$; Aaker et al. 2010; Grandey et al., 2005; Judd et al., 2005).

We conducted a 2 (masculine vs. feminine product) x 2 (masculine vs. feminine prime) between-subjects ANOVA with purchase likelihood as the dependent variable throughout all product categories. The main effects of product gender and gender prime were insignificant (both $ps > .10$). However, we found a significant positive interaction effect between product gender and gender prime ($F(1,407) = 5.513, p < .02$), suggesting that gender primes moderate the effect of gender typed products (see figure 1).

Figure 1
Purchasing Likelihood of Gender Typed Products, Primed with Feminine Cues, Masculine Cues or No Prime

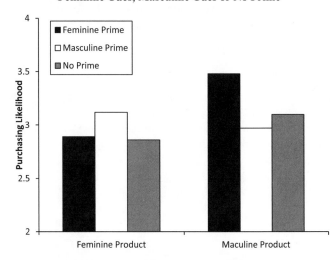

The follow-up planned comparisons reveal for the masculine products that feminine primes lead to a higher purchase likelihood than masculine primes ($t(605) = 2.326, p = .02$). For the feminine products, masculine primes were not significantly higher compared to feminine primes ($t(605) = -1.041, p > .05$). Thus, the results indicate that feminine primes increase purchase likelihood significantly when combined with a masculine product.

To test the role of perceived warmth and competence of a brand we conducted two separate mediation analyses between gender primes and purchasing likelihood (Zhao, Lynch Jr., and Chen 2010). The result indicates that warmth mediates the effect of gender primes on purchase likelihood. Namely, the indirect effect from the conducted bootstrap analysis is negative and significant (a x b = -.1415), with a 95% confidence interval excluding zero (-0.2819 to -0.0104). In the indirect path, the masculine prime decreases warmth by a = -0.2499, and holding constant the prime, each unit increase in warmth increases purchasing likelihood by b = 0.5663. We conducted the same analysis with competence as the mediator and found it to be insignificant with a 95% confidence interval including zero (-0.2549 to 0.0285). Therefore, the results suggest that feminine primes enhance purchase likelihood via increased warmth of the product. Interestingly, we do not find the same effect for masculine primes.

To understand the underlying process of warmth and competence more thoroughly, we are currently conducting further studies, where we manipulate the baseline (warmth/competence) of a brand as well as gender cues.

DISCUSSION AND IMPLICATIONS

Our results indicate that feminine primes enhance perceived warmth which increases purchase likelihood for masculine products. Interestingly, perceived warmth serves as a mediator between prime and purchasing likelihood, yet competence does not.

With our study we directly address Aaker et al.'s (2010) call to investigate conditions under which perceived warmth drives purchasing likelihood. Further, we demonstrate that feminine symbols and colors can trigger feminine gender stereotype knowledge which can be utilized to influence brand perception and consumer behavior.

From a practical viewpoint, our results provide important implications for companies and their marketplace decisions. Thus, companies that sell masculine products are able to utilize female advertising cues to increase their brands perception of warmth, which in turn, translates to a higher purchasing likelihood.

REFERENCES

Aaker, Jennifer., Kathleen D. Vohs, and Cassie Mogilner (2010), "Nonprofits are Seen as Warm and For-Profits as Competent: Firm Stereotypes Matter," *Journal of Consumer Research, 37* (August), 224-237.

Banaji, Mahzarin R. and Curtis Hardin (1996), "Automatic Stereotyping," *Psychological Science, 7* (May), 136-41.

Bargh, John A. (1997), "The Automaticity of Everyday Life," in *Advances in Social Cognition,* Vol. 10, ed. Robert S. Wyer, Jr., Mahwah, NJ: Erlbaum, 1-61.

Deaux, Kay and Laurie L. Lewis (1984), "Structure of Gender Stereotypes: Interrelationship among Components and Gender Label," *Journal of Personality and Social Psychology, 46* (May), 991-1004.

Eagly, Alice. H. and Antonio Mladinic (1994), "Are People Prejudiced Against Women? Some Answers from Research on Attitudes, Gender Stereotypes, and Judgments of Competence" in *European Review of Social Psychology,* Vol. 5 ed. Wolfgang Stroebe and Miles Hewstone, New York: Wiley, 1-35.

Eagly, Alice. H., Antonio Mladinic, and Stacey Otto (1994), "Cognitive and Affective Bases of Attitudes toward Social Groups and Social Policies," *Journal of Experimental Social Psychology, 30* (March), 113-37.

Fagot, Beverly I., Mary D. Leinbach, Barbara E. Hort, and Jennifer Strayer (1997), "Qualities Underlying the Definitions of Gender," S*ex Roles, 37* (July), 1-17.

Fiske, Susan T., Amy J. C. Cuddy, and Peter Glick (2007), "Universal Dimensions of Social Cognition: Warmth and Competence," *Trends in Cognitive Sciences, 11* (February), 77-83.

Fiske, Susan T., Amy J. C. Cuddy, Peter Glick, and Jun Xu (2002), "A Model of (often Mixed) Stereotype Content: Competence and Warmth Respectively Follow from Perceived Status and Competition," *Journal of Personality and Social Psychology, 82* (June), 878-902.

Fugate, Douglas. L. and Joanna Phillips (2010), "Product Gender Perceptions and Antecedents of Product Gender Congruence," *Journal of Consumer Marketing, 27* (3), 251-61.

Grandey, Alicia, Glenda Fisk, Anna Mattila, Karen Jansen, and Lori Sideman (2005), "Is 'Service with a Smile' Enough? Authenticity of Positive Displays During Service Encounters," *Organizational Behavior and Human Decision Processes, 96* (January), 38-55.

Judd, Charles M., Hawkins, Laurie James-Hawkins, Vincent Yzerbyt, and Yoshihisa Kashima, (2005), "Fundamental Dimensions of Social Judgment: Understanding the Relations between Judgments of Competence and Warmth," *Journal of Personality and Social Psychology, 89* (December), 899-913.

Leinbach, Mary Driver, Barbara E. Hort, and Beverly I. Fagot (1997), "Bears are for Boys: Metaphorical Associations in Young Children's Gender Stereotypes," *Cognitive Development, 12* (March), 107-30.

Zhao, Xinshu., John G. Lynch Jr., and Qimei Chen (2010), "Reconsidering Baron and Kenny: Myths and Truths about Mediation Analysis," *Journal of Consumer Research, 37* (August), 197-206.

Self-Control Spillover:
Impulse Inhibition Facilitates Simultaneous Self-Control in Unrelated Domains

Mirjam A. Tuk, Imperial College Business School, UK, INSEAD, France
Kuangjie Zhang, INSEAD, France
Steven Sweldens, INSEAD, France

EXTENDED ABSTRACT

Imagine participating in an important meeting. Despite the fact that the meeting already took for hours, there is still a list of decisions to be made. Keeping your attention focused on the discussion requires a significant amount of self-control. Notably, there is a bowl filled with chocolates on the table. How likely would you be to over-indulge on the chocolates during this meeting?

One of the most influential theories of self-control predicts overindulgence on the chocolates. According to the strength model (Baumeister 2002), human ability to exert self-control relies on a limited energy resource. Consequently, each act of self-control (e.g., controlling attention) temporarily depletes this resource, resulting in a deteriorated performance on subsequent self-control tasks (e.g., resisting chocolates), termed an 'ego depletion effect'.

Recent findings in (neuro)psychology suggest an alternative outcome. This research suggests that various forms of response inhibition which seem very different on the surface, all originate from the same neurological areas, also referred to as a general inhibitory network (Cohen and Lieberman 2010). Importantly, Berkman, Burklund and Lieberman (2009) show that a consequence of such a general inhibitory network is that inhibitory signals are not completely task specific, but can spill over to unrelated domains and result in unintentional inhibition of unrelated responses, termed an 'inhibitory spillover effect'. Tuk, Trampe and Warlop (2011) show that a physiological form of inhibition (bladder control), can result in more impulse control in the behavioural domain (intertemporal patience). These findings suggest that intentional acts of self-control (of which response inhibition is a crucial property) could actually *facilitate* self-control in unrelated domains.

In the current research, we argue that a crucial determinant for whether one act of self-control deteriorates (ego depletion) or facilitates (inhibitory spillover) self-control ability on unrelated tasks is the timing of the control tasks. Inhibitory signals required for one task are only present *during* execution of this task, and should only facilitate self-control performance on *simultaneously* executed tasks. Conversely, when the self-control tasks are sequential to each other, we expect the ego depletion effect to occur, consistent with a large body of research supporting the strength model (see Hagger et al. 2010, for a meta-analysis). In the first four studies, we test the inhibitory spillover effect in simultaneous self-control tasks, using tasks that are well-known to be susceptible to ego depletion effects when sequentially administered. In a fifth study, we directly manipulate the sequential versus simultaneous nature of the self-control tasks.

STUDY 1

In study 1, participants engaged in a thought listing task. Only participants in the inhibition condition were instructed not to think of a white bear during this task (Vohs and Faber 2007). This was followed by an intertemporal choice task (Li 2008), in which respondents made eight choices between a smaller, but sooner (SS) and a larger but later (LL) reward. Crucially, respondents in the inhibition condition were instructed to *continue* not to think of a white bear during this task. In line with the inhibitory spillover hypothesis, respondents made less impulsive choices in the inhibition condition.

STUDY 2

In study 2, participants engaged in an attention regulation task while watching a movie of an interview. On the bottom of the screen, a series of words appeared. Only participants in the inhibition condition were instructed to ignore these words and focus on the interviewee. Simultaneously, participants received a bowl of crisps to consume *during* the movie. In line with our hypothesis, participants in the inhibition condition consumed less of the crisps.

STUDY 3

In study 3, food consumption formed our self-control manipulation. Respondents engaged in a taste test, and were instructed to consume one crisp from a bowl of crisps. This was followed by the Stroop task. Only participants in the inhibition condition were explicitly instructed to resist further crisp consumption during the Stroop task. Results showed that participants in the inhibition condition made fewer errors on the self-control requiring (incongruent) trials of the Stroop task.

STUDY 4

In order to provide stronger evidence for the inhibitory spillover hypothesis, we examined whether the inhibitory spillover effect is moderated by an interpersonal difference in sensitivity of the Behavioral Inhibition System (BIS; Carver and White 1994; Tuk et al. 2011). In study 4, respondents engaged in the same thought suppression task as in study 1, and continued with this thought suppression during the next task. This was a short self-control scenario (Labroo and Patrick 2009), measuring whether respondents opt for an impulsive or self-controlled option. Results showed that participants in the inhibition condition had a greater preference for the self-controlled option, especially when they have a sensitive BIS.

STUDY 5

In study 5, we manipulated the simultaneity of the self-control tasks. Participants in the inhibition condition were instructed not to feel/express emotions during an emotional movie clip, whereas participants in the control condition could watch this movie freely. In the simultaneous condition, respondents received a bowl of crisps together with this first clip. In the sequential condition, respondents continued with a second movie (where they could feel/express their emotions freely) and received the crisps during this second clip. In line with our predictions, inhibition of emotions resulted in decreased food consumption in the simultaneous condition (inhibitory spillover), but resulted in increased food consumption in the sequential condition (ego depletion), relative to the control conditions. Hence, study 5 provides strong evidence for the crucial role of timing of the control tasks for inhibitory spillover versus ego depletion to occur.

CONCLUSIONS

In five studies, we used a variety of the most well-known paradigms from the ego-depletion literature, but changed the timing of the self-control tasks such that they occurred simultaneously. Consistent with the inhibitory spillover hypothesis we found a self-control boost for simultaneously occurring tasks. Our results suggest that deliberative acts of self-control can facilitate self-control ability on unrelated tasks, when both tasks occur together. These findings provide support for the existence of an inhibitory network, susceptible to inhibitory spillover, and suggest that the predictions of the strength model cannot easily be translated to simultaneous control tasks.

REFERENCES

Baumeister, Roy F. (2002), "Yielding to Temptation: Self-Control Failure, Impulsive Purchasing, and Consumer Behavior," *Journal of Consumer Research*, 28 (4), 670-76.

Berkman, Elliot T., Lisa Burklund, and Matthew D. Lieberman (2009), "Inhibitory Spillover: Intentional Motor Inhibition Produces Incidental Limbic Inhibition Via Right Inferior Frontal Cortex," *NeuroImage*, 47 (2), 705-12.

Carver, Charles S. and Teri L. White (1994), "Behavioral-Inhibition, Behavioral Activation, and Affective Responses to Impending Reward and Punishment - the Bis Bas Scales," *Journal of Personality and Social Psychology*, 67 (2), 319-33.

Cohen, Jessica R. and Matthew D. Lieberman (2010), "The Common Neural Basis of Exerting Self-Control in Multiple Domains," in *Self-Control in Society, Mind, and Brain*, ed. R. R. Hassin, K. N. Ochsner and y. Trope, New York: Oxford University Press, 141-60.

Hagger, Martin S., Chantelle Wood, Chris Stiff, and Nikos L. D. Chatzisarantis (2010), "Ego Depletion and the Strength Model of Self-Control: A Meta-Analysis," *Psychological Bulletin*, 136 (4), 495-525.

Labroo, Aparna A. and Vanessa M. Patrick (2009), "Psychological Distancing: Why Happiness Helps You See the Big Picture," *Journal of Consumer Research*, 35 (5), 800-09.

Li, Xiuping P. (2008), "The Effects of Appetitive Stimuli on out-of-Domain Consumption Impatience," *Journal of Consumer Research*, 34 (5), 649-56.

Tuk, Mirjam A., Debra Trampe, and Luk Warlop (2011), "Inhibitory Spillover: Increased Urination Urgeny Facilitates Impulse Control in Unrelated Domains," *Psychological Science*, 22 (5), 627-33.

Vohs, Kathleen D. and Ronald J. Faber (2007), "Spent Resources: Self-Regulatory Resource Availability Affects Impulse Buying," *Journal of Consumer Research*, 33 (4), 537-47.

Exploration vs. Exploitation Mindsets in Consumer Search

Valerie Trifts, Dalhousie University, Canada
Gerald Häubl, University of Alberta, Canada

EXTENDED ABSTRACT

Much attention has been devoted to the importance of mindsets in consumer decision making. A mindset is characterized by the persistence of cognitive processes and judgmental criteria activated in the course of performing a task that generalize to other situations (Xu and Wyer 2007). Much research builds on work by Gollwitzer, Heckhausen, and Steller (1990), examining the influence of deliberative versus implemental mindsets in areas such as sales promotions (Cheema and Patrick 2008), consumer expectations regarding the demands of future tasks (Bosmans, Pieters, Baumgartner 2009), and shopping momentum (Dhar, Huber, and Khan 2007). More recent research has focused on the impact of construal-level (i.e., high-level abstract versus low-level concrete mindsets) to explain various phenomena – e.g., purchase intentions (Goldsmith, Xu, and Dhar 2010), perceived truthfulness of ad claims (Wright et al. 2012), and consumer recycling behavior (White, MacDonnell, and Dahl 2012).

Yet, the role of mindsets in the domain of consumer *product search* is not well understood. The present work introduces and tests the hypothesis that providing initial exposure to multiple products, as opposed to as single product, inhibits consumer search for additional alternatives and results in stronger preference for initially presented products. While some recent work on comparative mindsets (e.g., Xu and Wyer 2007; 2008) has provided insights into how making initial comparative judgments evokes a "which to buy" mindset in subsequent choice tasks, this paper examines how a comparative context can induce an *exploitative mindset*, which renders consumers more likely to search fewer products when making purchase decisions.

Hills, Todd, and Goldstone (2008; 2010) argue that problem solving is often characterized as a search process, involving a trade-off between exploiting old solutions and exploring new ones. They found that exploitation- and exploration-inducing spatial-foraging tasks can prime corresponding exploitation and exploration strategies during subsequent abstract search tasks. In the context of consumer search, we propose that initially presenting consumers with multiple products (vs. only a single product) activates an exploitation (vs. exploration) mindset. Compared to an exploration mindset, an exploitation mindset drastically reduces the number of products that consumers choose to discover through search. Thus, we hypothesize that consumers consider fewer products overall if they initially see two products rather than one, and this in turn increases the probability of a given initially presented alternative to be chosen eventually.

These hypotheses were tested in two computer-based experiments. Study 1 examined the effect of viewing one versus two initial alternative(s) on subsequent search and preference. Participants from an online panel were initially shown either one or two products, described as typical examples randomly selected from a product database. They were then asked to search as many additional products as they wished prior to making choices, across four randomly ordered product categories. Only 55% percent of participants who initially viewed two products engaged in further search, compared to 97% of those who initially viewed one product (85% searched at least two additional products). Poisson regression revealed that, across the four product searches, participants who initially viewed two products searched fewer alternatives (including those initially presented) ($M_{view1} = 7.77$ vs. $M_{view2} = 4.85$; Wald = 5.45, $p < .05$), and spent less time searching ($M_{view1} = 106.41$ sec. vs. $M_{view2} = 82.36$ sec.; Wald= 6.21, $p < .05$) than those who initially viewed only one prod-uct. Separate Poisson regression analyses for each product category support these effects. Participants who initially viewed two products were also significantly less likely to choose one of the subsequently searched alternatives than those who initially viewed only a single product (see Appendix A for detailed results).

In Study 2, a spatial-foraging task (see Hills, Todd, and Goldstone 2008; 2010) was used to more directly test the mindset account of the results from Study 1. Participants from an online panel were randomly assigned to one of six conditions in a 3 (priming task: exploration vs. exploitation vs. no prime) x 2 (number of products presented initially: 1 vs. 2) full-factorial experimental design. Participants in the prime conditions first completed five 2-minute tasks where their objective was to uncover as many of the 580 red dots in a search space consisting of 5,625 squares by moving the cursor throughout the search space. After that, they completed a product search and choice task for a coffee maker. In the exploitation conditions, the red dots were clustered into 4 diamond shapes, whereas in the exploration conditions, they were diffused randomly in the search space (see Appendix B). Participants were shown the time remaining for each search task and the number of red dots they had uncovered, and a monetary incentive based on the number of red dots found was used to make the priming task consequential.

Manipulation check measures for the mindset prime showed that this manipulation was effective. As expected, participants in the exploitation prime condition found more red dots and, critically, navigated the space in more locally concentrated manner, than those in the exploration prime condition (see Appendix B for details). Results for the no prime condition replicate those of Study 1 for all dependent measures (see Appendix C for details). Poisson regression analysis reveals that participants in the exploration mindset searched significantly more products (including the initially viewed ones) than those in the exploitation mindset ($M_{explore} = 6.26$ vs. $M_{exploit} = 4.16$; Wald = 9.52, $p < .01$). Comparison of the control condition to the exploration condition reveals a significant interaction between the priming task and the number of initially presented products for both the number of products searched (Wald = 9.57, $p < .01$) and the amount of time spent searching (Wald = 6.39, $p < 0.05$). Moreover, participants in the exploration mindset condition were significantly less likely to choose the first product listed than participants in the exploitation mindset.

Taken together, the results of Studies 1 and 2 suggest that initially presenting consumers with multiple products activates an exploitation mindset, resulting in a drastic reduction in additional search. In turn, this effect on the total number of alternatives inspected influences which product is ultimately chosen.

REFERENCES

Bosmans, Anick, Rik Pieters, and Hans Baumgartner (2010), "The Get Ready Mind-Set: How Gearing Up for Later Impacts Effort Allocation Now," *Journal of Consumer Research*, 37 (June), 98-107.

Cheema, Amar, and Vanessa M. Patrick (2008), "Anytime versus Only: Mind-Sets Moderate the Effect of Expansive versus Restrictive Frames on Promotion Evaluation," *Journal of Marketing Research*, 45 (4), 462-472.

Dhar, Ravi, Joel Huber, and Uzma Khan (2007), "The Shopping Momentum Effect," *Journal of Marketing Research*, 44 (August), 370-378.

Goldsmith, Kelly, Jing Xu, and Ravi Dhar (2010), "The Power of Customers' Mindset, "*Sloan Management Review*, 52, 19-20.

Gollwitzer, Peter M., Heinz Heckhausen, and Birgit Steller (1990), "Deliberative and Implemental Mind-Sets: Cognitive Tuning Toward Congruous Thoughts and Information," *Journal of Personality and Social Psychology*, 59 (6), 1119-1127.

Hills, Thomas T., Peter M. Todd, and Robert L. Goldstone (2008), "Search in External and Internal Spaces: Evidence for Generalized Cognitive Search Processes," *Psychological Science*, 19 (8), 802-808.

_____(2010), "The Central Executive as a Search Process: Priming Exploration and Exploitation Across Domains," *Journal of Experimental Psychology: General*, 139 (4), 590-609.

White, Katherine, Rhiannon MacDonnell, and Darren W. Dahl (2011), "It's the Mind-Set that Matters: The Role of Construal Level and Message Framing in Influencing Consumer Efficacy and Conservation Behaviors," *Journal of Marketing Research*, 48 (June), 472-485.

Wright, Scott, Chris Manolis, Drew Brown, Xiaoning Guo, John Dinsmore, C.-Y. Peter Chiu, and Frank R. Kardes (2012), Construal-Level Mind-Sets and the Perceived Validity of Marketing Claims," *Marketing Letters*, 23, 253-261.

Xu, Alison Jing and Robert S. Wyer Jr. (2007), "The Effect of Mind-Sets on Consumer Decision Strategies," *Journal of Consumer Research*, 34 (December), 556-566.

_____(2008), "The Comparative Mind-Set," *Psychological Science*, 19(9), 859-864.

For Fun or Profit: How Shopping Orientation Influences the Effectiveness of Monetary and Nonmonetary Promotions

Oliver B. Büttner, University of Vienna, Austria
Arnd Florack, University of Vienna, Austria
Anja S. Göritz, University of Freiburg, Germany

EXTENDED ABSTRACT

Different types of promotions have different pros and cons. Monetary promotions (e.g., discounts) can be very effective in producing short-term effects on sales (Alvarez-Alvarez and Vázquez-Casielles 2005), but have negative effects on price sensitivity and brand equity (Yi and Yoo 2011). Nonmonetary promotions (such as sweepstakes or free gifts) do not show these negative effects, but their influence on attractiveness of the offer and marketing share is often lower than that of monetary promotions (Alvarez-Alvarez and Vázquez-Casielles 2005). Thus, to effectively use promotions as a tool, marketers and retailers need to know when and how which type of promotion is the most effective.

The present research examines whether consumer shopping orientation influences how consumers react towards monetary and nonmonetary promotions. In line with research on fit and congruency effects (Chernev 2004; Lee and Higgins 2009), we posit that promotions are more effective when the promotional benefits match a consumer's motivational orientation. Consumers' shopping orientation can be narrowed down to two fundamental motivational orientations: a task-focused and an experiential shopping orientation (Kaltcheva and Weitz 2006). According to the benefit-congruency model of sales promotion effectiveness, monetary and nonmonetary promotions differ in the benefits they provide (Chandon, Wansink, and Laurent 2000). Nonmonetary promotions provide primarily hedonic benefits. This should meet experiential shoppers goals for hedonic stimulation during shopping. Task-focused shoppers should be insensitive to these hedonic benefits, because they focus on efficiency during shopping. Monetary promotions provide primarily utilitarian benefits. This should meet the goals of task-focused shoppers, who focus on maximizing utilitarian shopping value. In addition, experiential shoppers may experience hedonic benefits in terms of pleasure when hunting for price promotions.

Thus, nonmonetary promotions are congruent only with the goals of experiential shoppers, but not with the goals of task-focused shoppers. By contrast, monetary promotions are congruent with the goals of both task-focused and experiential shoppers. This implies that nonmonetary promotions are more attractive to experiential shoppers than to task-focused shoppers. Furthermore, this difference should be less pronounced for monetary promotions.

We examined these hypotheses in two experiments. Study 1 (N = 217) applied a 2 x 2 mixed design. Promotion type (monetary vs. nonmonetary) was a within-subject factor. Shopping orientation (task-focused vs. experiential) was a continuous between-subject predictor and was measured using eight items (Reynolds and Beatty 1999). Participants evaluated a number of monetary and nonmonetary promotions for fast moving consumer goods from existing national brands. The results supported the hypotheses. The more experiential a consumer's shopping orientation, the more positive was the evaluation of promotions. This positive relationship was more pronounced for nonmonetary than for monetary promotions.

Thus, Study 1 found that shopping orientation influences how consumers evaluate promotions, and that this influence is moderated by promotion type. Study 2 sought to extend this finding in a number of ways. First, Study 2 examined whether the different reactions to promotions transfer on the retailers offering nonmonetary or monetary promotions. Second, the study included a control condition with a retailer offering no promotions. Third, Study 2 experimentally manipulated shopping orientation, whereas study 1 measured consumers' chronic shopping orientation. Finally, Study 2 used a different and more hedonic product category (entertainment DVD) than study 1 (FMCG).

Study 2 applied a 2 x 3 mixed design (N = 120). Shopping orientation (task-focused vs. experiential shopping orientation) was a between subject factor and was manipulated by a scenario (Kaltcheva and Weitz 2006). Promotional strategy (monetary vs. nonmonetary vs. no promotion) was a within-subject factor: Each participant read descriptions of three stores with a DVD department that differed in their promotional strategy. For each store, participants indicated the store attractiveness on three items. The results supported the hypotheses. The store with the nonmonetary promotions was evaluated as more attractive by experiential than by task-focused shoppers. For the store with the monetary promotions, the store evaluation did not differ between the experiential and the task-focused shoppers. Finally, the store evaluation of the store offering no promotions received the lowest attractiveness ratings and these ratings did not differ between experiential and task-focused shoppers.

In sum, the present research supports the assumption that promotions are more effective when they support a consumer in pursuing his or her goals during shopping. Across two experiments, we found that shopping goals as reflected in consumer shopping orientation influenced evaluations of promotions and evaluations of retailers offering promotions. Nonmonetary promotions were more attractive for experiential shoppers than for task-focused shoppers. This influence of shopping orientation was moderated by promotion type: The differences in the attractiveness of promotions between task-focused and experiential shoppers were more pronounced for nonmonetary than for monetary promotions.

The present research extends the benefit congruency framework of sales promotion effectiveness (Chandon et al. 2000) in two ways. First, Chandon et al. (2000) found a congruency effect between promotion type and product type (hedonic vs. utilitarian). We found that there are also positive consequences of a congruency between promotion type and shopping orientation. Second, Chandon et al. (2000) examined the influence of the congruency effect on the market share of brands. We demonstrated that the positive effect of congruency also transfers to the evaluation of a retailer that adopts a monetary versus a nonmonetary promotion strategy. The latter finding suggests that the decision of whether to use monetary or nonmonetary promotions also has consequences for a retailer's image and for consumers' patronage intentions.

The results have also implications for the design of promotions. The results imply that retail and marketing managers can enhance the effectiveness of promotions by customizing promotion type to customers' shopping orientation. Task-focused shoppers should be given monetary promotions because these promotions are more successful with this type of shopper. Experiential shoppers should be given nonmonetary promotions: They react favorably to both nonmonetary and monetary promotions, and nonmonetary promotions do not bring the dangers of lowering expectations regarding prices and increasing price sensitivity. Such an approach offers a trade-off between the positive effects of promotions (increased sales) and the negative effects of promotions (increased price sensitivity from monetary promotions).

REFERENCES

Alvarez-Alvarez, Begoña and Rodolfo Vázquez-Casielles (2005), "Consumer Evaluations of Sales Promotion: The Effect on Brand Choice," *European Journal of Marketing*, 39 (1/2), 54-70.

Chandon, Pierre, Brian Wansink, and Gilles Laurent (2000), "A Benefit Congruency Framework of Sales Promotion Effectiveness," *Journal of Marketing*, 64 (4), 65-81.

Chernev, Alexander (2004), "Goal-Attribute Compatibility in Consumer Choice," *Journal of Consumer Psychology*, 14 (1/2), 141-50.

Kaltcheva, Velitchka D. and Barton A. Weitz (2006), "When Should a Retailer Create an Exciting Store Environment?," *Journal of Marketing*, 70 (1), 107-18.

Lee, Angela Y. and E. Tory Higgins (2009), "The Persuasive Power of Regulatory Fit," in *Social Psychology of Consumer Behavior*, ed. Michaela Wänke, New York: Psychology Press.

Reynolds, Kristy E. and Sharon E. Beatty (1999), "A Relationship Customer Typology," *Journal of Retailing*, 75 (4), 509-23.

Yi, Youjae and Jaemee Yoo (2011), "The Long-Term Effects of Sales Promotions on Brand Attitude across Monetary and Non-Monetary Promotions," *Psychology and Marketing*, 28 (9), 879-96.

This Number Just Feels Right:
The Impact of Roundness of Numbers on Reliance on Feelings versus Cognition

Monica Wadhwa, INSEAD, France
Kuangjie Zhang, INSEAD, France

EXTENDED ABSTRACT

Consider two consumers who are on the market to buy a camera for an upcoming family vacation. While one of them comes across a camera priced at $200.00, the other comes across the same camera at another store, but priced at $198.76. Given that the camera has all the features required by these two consumers, how would the mere roundedness of the price number impact their preference for the camera? Further, could the price number (200 vs. 198.76) impact the consumers' preference for the camera differently if they were buying it for a class project (a purchase decision that is primarily driven by cognition) instead of a family vacation (a purchase decision that is primarily driven by feelings)? In the current research, we examine the impact of the roundedness of the numbers on consumers' decision making, given the basis of the purchase decision—that is whether the purchase decision is driven by feelings or cognition.

Emerging research on number cognition suggests that rounded numbers are easier to process and therefore are more fluent as compared to non-rounded numbers (McClure 2011). Further, research on fluency and dual processing theories suggest that targets that are fluently processed lead one to rely more on feeling-based inputs while making evaluative judgments, whereas targets that are not fluently processed lead one to rely more on cognitive inputs while evaluating the target (Alter et al. 2007). Drawing upon these perspectives, we hypothesize that rounded prices are likely to facilitate the use of feelings and thereby lead to more favorable product evaluations when the purchase decision is based on feelings. However, non-rounded prices are likely to facilitate the use of cognition and thereby lead to more favorable product evaluations when the purchase decision is based on cognition.

We tested the aforementioned rounded number hypotheses in a series of five studies. Study-1 examined the main hypothesis related to the rounded-number effect. In this study, participants were asked to indicate their purchase intentions for either a bottle of champagne for a friend's birthday (purchase decision based on feelings) or a calculator (purchase decision based on cognition), which was priced at either a rounded number ($40.00) or a non-rounded number ($39.72 or $40.29). Consistent with our hypotheses, rounded price ($40.00) led to enhanced purchase intentions for the champagne compared with either of the two non-rounded prices ($39.72 or $40.29). In contrast, both the non-rounded prices ($39.72 and $40.29) led to enhanced purchase intention for the calculator compared with the rounded price ($40.00)

In Study-2, keeping the product constant, we manipulated the consumption goal the product was stated to achieve. Specifically, participants were asked to imagine buying a camera for a family vacation (hedonic-consumption goal) or for a photography class (utilitarian-consumption goal), with the price tag randomly displayed at either a rounded number ($200.00) or a non-rounded number ($203.96). To make the camera evaluation procedure more realistic, two sample pictures purportedly taken from the camera were presented. Participants first evaluated the sample pictures and then reported their anticipated satisfaction with the camera. A significant price by consumption goal interaction emerged. When buying a camera for a family vacation, rounded price (vs. non-rounded price) led to greater anticipated satisfaction with the camera. In contrast, when buying a camera for a photography class, non-rounded price

(vs. rounded price) led to greater anticipated satisfaction with the camera. The same pattern of results was observed on perceived quality of the sample pictures.

In Study-3, we examine the impact of rounded versus non-rounded prices on product choices. Further, we provide support for our underlying conceptualization by examining the role of one's reliance on feelings versus cognition in mediating participants' product choices. All participants first engaged in a shopping survey and were then informed that they could choose one out of the two equally priced displayed food items as a free gift. The choice set consisted of a food item relatively superior on affective dimension (a chocolate bar) and a food item relatively superior on cognitive dimension (a cereal bar). Both the items were displayed with the same price tag, which was either a rounded-number ($2.00) or a non-rounded number ($1.83). Subsequently participants indicated the basis of their choice on three nine-point items that were presented after the following statement—"My decision about which food option to choose was driven by." These items were anchored by "My thoughts (1)/My feelings (9)", "My prudent self (1)/My impulsive self (9)", and "My calculative judgment (1)/My affective judgment (9)" (adapted from Shiv and Fedorikhin 1999). Responses to these three items were averaged to form a single variable-"decision basis". Our findings show that consumers were more likely to choose the chocolate bar when the food items were displayed at a rounded (vs. non-rounded) price. More importantly, this rounded-number effect was mediated by participants' decision basis. Specifically, rounded (vs. non-rounded) price enhanced participants' reliance on feelings (vs. cognition), and thereby led to greater preference for the chocolate bar over the cereal bar.

In Study-4, we provide stronger support for our reliance on feelings versus cognition conceptualization by examining the role of cognitive resources in moderating the rounded number effects. Prior research suggests that when the processing resources are constrained, relative reliance on feeling-based inputs is enhanced (Greifeneder, Bless and Pham 2010). Drawing upon this research, we argue that rounded prices should lead to more favorable product evaluations when processing resources are constrained. On the other hand, when the processing resources are available, relative reliance on cognitive inputs should be enhanced and thus non-rounded prices should lead to more favorable product evaluations. Participants evaluated a digital camera-binocular either priced at a rounded number ($80.00) or a non-rounded number ($81.43). However, prior to the evaluation task, we manipulated the availability of cognitive resources by asking participants to memorize either a string of seven English letters (high cognitive load) or one English letter (low cognitive load). Our results revealed a significant interaction between price and cognitive load. Specifically, participants in the high (low) cognitive load condition indicated higher purchase intention with the product when it was priced at a rounded (non-rounded) number.

Finally, Study-5 sought to provide further support for our conceptualization by directly manipulating one's reliance on feelings versus cognition before product evaluation. Participants evaluated a digital camera-binocular either priced at a rounded number ($80.00) or a non-rounded number ($81.43). However, prior to the evaluation task, participants were either primed to rely on feelings or cognition (adapted from Hsee and Rottenstreich 2004). Our results revealed a significant price by priming interaction. Specifically, those in the feeling-prime (cognition-prime) condition indicated higher purchase intention and anticipated satisfaction with the product when it was priced at a rounded number (non-rounded number).

Together, these results suggest that rounded number (non-rounded) prices enhance consumer product evaluations when the purchase decision is based on feelings (cognition), and these effects are moderated by consumers' reliance on feelings versus cognition.

Easy Like a Sunday Morning:
How The Fluency of Analogies Affects Innovation Liking

Antonia Erz, Copenhagen Business School, Denmark
Bo T. Christensen, Copenhagen Business School, Denmark
Torsten Tomczak, University of St. Gallen, Switzerland

EXTENDED ABSTRACT

In the search of successful communication strategies for innovations, authors have identified analogies (Feiereisen, Wong, and Broderick 2008). An analogy compares the novel with the familiar and helps people to utilize pre-existing knowledge to understand the unfamiliar (Gregan-Paxton and Roedder John 1997). The optimal analogy was suggested to allow the consumer to map existing knowledge from a base (e.g., diary) to a target analog (e.g., tablet-PC) to understand the key benefits of an innovation (Hoeffler 2003).

However, people may be rarely able to match each correspondence between a base and a target (Day and Gentner 2007). Instead they may also draw information from how fluent they can process the analogy and interpret these meta-cognitive experiences (Schwarz 2004) in the light of the consumption context (Pocheptsova, Labroo, and Dhar 2010).

In an online-experiment with 503 German consumers, we investigated 1) the processing fluency of analogies, and 2) its effect on innovation liking and purchase intention, testing the usual fluency-liking link and its reversal.

Findings from analogy research indicate a good and sound–and therefore fluent–analogical match as based on relational similarities as well as surface similarities (Gentner and Markman 1995). We therefore hypothesize that *participants will judge an analogy as being more fluent when the base and the target are perceived as similar* (H_1).

In a second step, we aimed at investigating the phenomenon of naïve beliefs which determine how individuals interpret their meta-cognitive experiences. Research found that stimuli which are processed fluently are perceived as familiar and elicit a positive affect in contrast to disfluently processed stimuli (Schwarz 2004). However, think of yourself at the rollercoaster park. Do you go for the well-known and slightly boring or the latest and most exciting ones? Are you better 'safe than sorry' or is your motto 'no risk, no fun'? Authors found that, dependent on the consumption context which may activate a specific naïve belief, consumers prefer a disfluent stimulus, if the disfluent experience is, for example, attributed to adventure (Song and Schwarz 2009), product exclusivity (Pocheptsova et al. 2010) or quality (Galak and Nelson 2010). A similar effect may be true when consumers make decisions about innovative products based on marketing information. On the one hand, they may prefer fluency and like the product better if no additional information is given about the innovative degree of the product, relying on the common naïve belief 'If it is familiar, it must be good.' On the other hand, when an advert clearly indicates the product as an innovation, individuals might prefer disfluency, attributing the feeling of novelty to the innovative degree of the product. We therefore hypothesize that *participants will show increased innovation liking when the analogy is fluent (vs. disfluent)* (H_{2a}). However, *if the advert clearly indicates the product as an innovation, participants will show increased innovation liking when the analogy is disfluent (vs. fluent)* (H_{2b}). The same hypotheses were formulated for purchase intention (H_{3a-b}).

In an online-experiment with a 2 (analogy: similar vs. dissimilar) × 2 (innovativeness claim: without vs. with) between-subjects design, 503 German consumers, consisting of 44.5 % females between 19 and 40 years, were randomly assigned to one of the advertisements and asked to fill in the questionnaire.

A tablet-PC and all-in-one media player device were chosen based on a round of experts (n = 10). Two analogical bases for each product were selected, one similar, containing relational as well as surface similarities (tablet-PC: diary; player: DVD-player), and one dissimilar, containing only relational similarities (tablet-PC: storage room; player: distribution room). An advert with a picture and a one-sentence copy text used the analogy (e.g., "like a diary") as a claim. To manipulate the indication as an innovation, we chose a realistic setting by using the word "innovative" in the copy text ("innovativeness claim"). The manipulation of analogy similarity was deemed successful across conditions ($ps < .05$).

Fluency was measured on a two-item scale. The scale for innovation liking was adapted from Boyd and Mason (1999), and purchase intention was measured by one item.

To test the hypotheses, several 2 (Analogy) × 2 (Innovativeness Claim) ANOVAs were performed followed by planned contrasts.

For fluency, there was a significant main effect of the type of analogy ($F(1, 499) = 27.8$, $p < .001$) but no effect of innovativeness claim or a significant interaction effect. Results of planned contrasts for the single products revealed that the dissimilar analogy was perceived as more disfluent across conditions and products ($ps < .05$). H_1 could be supported.

For innovation liking, a significant interaction across products was found ($F(1,499) = 4.38$, $p < .05$). A series of planned contrasts revealed that H_{2a} and H_{3a} could only be supported for the Tablet PC but not for the Media Player.

A significant interaction was also found for purchase intention ($F(1,499) = 5.06$, $p < .05$). Performing a series of planned contrasts, H_{2b} and H_{3b} could again only be supported for the Tablet-PC but not for the Media Player.

Our study supports the idea that analogies have an effect beyond the content they convey, and, at the same time, adds to the consistency of findings in fluency research. Furthermore, the partial reversion of the fluency effect by using a relatively realistic manipulation contributes to its current theoretical discussion (Galak and Nelson 2010). It further illustrates an important practical insight: explicitly claiming that a product is innovative might interfere with other parts of an advertisement.

We aimed at a somewhat realistic setting by testing true innovations, which had several drawbacks: The selection of stimuli was limited, and confounding variables, such as the visual complexity of the products, may have caused the inconsistent results in reversing the fluency effect. A replication in a more controlled setting with a stronger manipulation in indicating the consumption context and activating a naïve belief will help to produce more consistent results and define a mediating variable for a more profound explanation of the reversal.

REFERENCES

Boyd, Thomas C. and Mason, Charlotte H. (1999), "The Link between Attractiveness of 'Extrabrand' Attributes and the Adoption of Innovation". *Journal of the Academy of Marketing Science,* 27(3), 306-19.

Day, Samuel B. and Gentner, Dedre (2007), "Hidden Structure: Indirect Measurement of Relational Representation". Paper presented at the Twenty-ninth Annual Meeting of the Cognitive Science Society.

Feiereisen, Stephanie, Wong, Veronica, and Broderick, Amanda J. (2008), "Analogies and Mental Simulations in Learning for Really New Products: The Role of Visual Attention". *Journal of Product Innovation Management,* 25(6), 593-607.

Galak, Jeff and Nelson, Leif D. (2010), "The Virtues of Opaque Prose: How Lay Beliefs About Fluency Influence Perceptions of Quality". *Journal of Experimental Social Psychology,* in press.

Gentner, Dedre and Markman, Arthur B. (1995), Similarity Is Like Analogy: Structural Alignment in Comparison. In C. Cacciari (Ed.), *Similarity in Language, Thought and Perception* (pp. 111-47). Brussels: BREPOLS.

Gregan-Paxton, Jennifer and Roedder John, Deborah (1997), "Consumer Learning by Analogy: A Model of Internal Knowledge Transfer". *Journal of Consumer Research,* 24(3), 266-84.

Hoeffler, Steve (2003), "Measuring Preferences for Really New Products". *Journal of Marketing Research,* 40(4), 406-20.

Pocheptsova, Anastasiya, Labroo, Aparna A., and Dhar, Ravi (2010), "Making Products Feel Special: When Metacognitive Difficulty Enhances Evaluation". *Journal of Marketing Research,* 47(6), 1059-69.

Schwarz, Norbert (2004), "Metacognitive Experiences in Consumer Judgment and Decision Making". *Journal of Consumer Psychology,* 14(3), 332-48.

Song, Hyunjin and Schwarz, Norbert (2009), "If It's Difficult to Pronounce, It Must Be Risky". *Psychological Science,* 20(2), 135-38.

The Impact of Flow on Memory and Attitudes For In-Game Brand Placements: The Moderating Role of Brand Congruence and Placement Prominence

Iris Vermeir, University College Ghent and Ghent University, Belgium
Snezhanka Kazakova, Ghent University, Belgium
Tina Tessitore, Ghent University, Belgium
Veroline Cauberghe, Ghent University, Belgium
Hendrik Slabbinck, Ghent University, Belgium

EXTENDED ABSTRACT

The substantial growth of the video gaming industry has provided advertisers with a 'new' medium to effectively exploit the product placement technique. Academic interest into consumers' reactions to persuasive messages in videogames is increasing (e.g., Cauberghe and De Pelsmacker 2010; Farrar et al., 2006; Mau et al., 2008). However, previous studies scarcely take into account the specific characteristics of the gaming environment (Lee and Faber, 2007). Inherent to videogames is their capacity to force the player into a cognitive state, which approximates a state of *flow*, an intrinsically motivated optimal enjoyable mental state (e.g. Csikszentmihalyi and Lefevre 1989, Cowley et al., 2008). Few studies have examined the influence of game-evoked flow on the cognitive and affective outcomes of in-game product placements (Grigorovici and Constantin 2004; Mau et al. 2008; Nelson et al. 2006). Previous research has produced mixed results, suggesting the presence of moderating variables. Moreover, in previous research flow has often been investigated by measuring telepresence (Grigorovici and Constantin 2004; Nelson et al. 2006), while the latter incorporates only one aspect of flow.

In two studies, we investigate the relationship between *game-evoked flow* and *brand memory and brand attitudes toward brands placed within a video game* and the potential moderating influence of two important dimensions of brand placements i.e. brand congruence and brand prominence. Flow focuses the gamer's attention on the interactive game content (Hoffman and Novak, 1996) resulting in higher memory of this interactive content. This enhanced attention to the central game action is beneficial in terms of memory for congruous (H1a) and prominent (H2) brands, probably because congruous/prominent brands fit better into this central game action. Conversely, incongruous/subtle placements do not benefit from a flow experience, since they are not central to the game action due to their misfit with the game/subtlety. Furthermore, incongruous product placements do not add realism to the game, since they do not match with the game. Conversely, they might even disrupt the sense of realism experienced while playing a video game. Consequently, its ulterior motive (i.e., an attempt to persuade) becomes accessible to gamers, making both gamers experiencing flow versus not experiencing flow, who equally attend to incongruous placements, also equally resist the placement (Campbell and Kirmani, 2000). Therefore, we hypothesize that flow has no effect on attitudes toward incongruous placements (H1b). For subtle placements, increased enjoyment due to flow simply transfers to the brand. Counter argumentation is out of question here, due to the subtleness of the placements. By contrast, previous literature has shown that prominent product placements could entail persuasion knowledge activation and hence, counterarguments (e.g., van Reijmersdal, 2009). However, flow can deplete players' limited cognitive resources in a gaming context (Lang, 2000). Additionally, we could presume that our use of *congruous*[1] prominent placements makes the persuasion motive less accessible, due to their fit with

the game. We could then assume that gamers experiencing flow, for whom only limited cognitive resources remain, are less likely to resist the placement (cf. Campbell & Kirmani, 2000). We hypothesize that flow has a favorable effect on brand attitudes for *congruous* prominent placements (H3).

To test the proposed hypotheses we performed two studies. In study one, brand congruence of the in-game advertised brand was manipulated as either congruous or incongruous (Adidas and Visa were identified as the 'congruous' and 'incongruous' brand in a pretest); participants rated both congruous and incongruous brands. In study two, brand prominence of the in-game advertised brand was manipulated as either high or low. Two versions were created with the same congruous brand (i.e., Audi) presented either in a prominent or subtle way. Participants were randomly assigned to either the prominent or the subtle placement condition. In both studies, game-evoked flow was measured after game play (Refiana et al., 2000) and was used as a continuous variable. The participants were asked to play the video game; afterwards, they completed a questionnaire containing game-evoked flow, recognition (study 1) and implicit memory (study 2) and brand attitude measures. Brand congruence, brand prominence, brand knowledge an socio-demographic variables were also included. Participants (N = 120; N=227) were in the age group of 12 to 59 years (Mean age = 26.57; Mean age= 20) and included both males and females.

An estimated a multilevel logistic regression model shows a marginally significant interaction between brand congruence and flow ($F (1,234) = 2.91, p = .08$). Simple slope tests revealed that participants recognized the congruous brand more frequently as flow increased ($F (1,117) = 3.98, p < .05$), but no such relationship could be established for the incongruous brand ($F (1,117) =.15, p > .05$) confirming H1a. The interaction between brand congruence and flow significantly predicted brand attitudes ($F (1,234) = 8.90, p < .01$). Simple slope tests revealed that flow significantly influenced brand attitudes for the congruous brand ($F (1,117) = 4.79, p < .05$) but not for the incongruous brand ($F (1,117) =.62, p > .05$) supporting H1b.

A binary logistic regression model (study 2) showed a significant interaction effect with placement prominence ($b = 1.15$, Wald $\chi^2 = 14.24$, df = 1, $p < .01$). Simple slopes tests revealed that flow was positively related to implicit memory rates for prominent brand placements ($b = 1.11$, Wald $\chi^2 = 11.13$, df = 1, $p < .01$), while flow does not influence implicit memory rates for subtle brand placements ($b = -.36$, Wald $\chi^2 =.02$, df = 1, $p > .10$) confirming hypothesis two.

Ann ordinary least squares (OLS) regression model showed no significance for either prominence ($\beta = -.043, p > .05$), or the interaction between flow and prominence ($\beta = -.047, p > .05$) confirming hypothesis three. Our results confirm that experiencing flow while playing a computer game can, in some situations, have a positive effect on memory and attitudes for brands presented during game play.

---

[1]   Since we expect that congruence is a moderating variable of the flow-outcome relation (cfr. Hypotheses 1a and 1b), we chose one level of congruence (i.e. high congruence) to explore the moderating influence of prominence on the flow-outcome relation.

REFERENCES

Campbell, Margaret and A. Kirmani (2000), "Consumers' Use of Persuasion Knowledge: The Effects of Accessibility and Cognitive Capacity on Perceptions of an Influence Agent," *Journal of Consumer Research*, 27 (1), 69-83

Cauberghe, Verolien, and Patrick De Pelsmacker (2010), "Advergames: The Impact of Brand Prominence and Game Repetition on Brand Responses," *Journal of Advertising,* 39(Spring), 5-18.

Cowley, Ben, Darryl Charles, Michael Black, and Ray Hicke, (2008), "Toward an understanding of flow in

Csikszentmihalyi, Mihaly, and Judith Lefevre (1989), "Optimal experience in work and leisure," *Journal of Personality and Social Psychology*, 56 (5), 815–22.

Farrar, Kristie M., Marina Krcmar, and Kristine L. Nowak (2006), "Contextual Features of Violent Video Games, Mental Models and Aggression," *Journal of Communication,*56(2), 387-405.

Grigorovici, Dan, and Corina Constantin (2004), " Experiencing interactive advertising beyond rich media: impacts of ad type and presence on brand effectiveness in 3D gaming immersive virtual environments," *Journal of Interactive Advertising,* 5 (Fall), available at http://jiad.org/article53 (accessed January 09, 2012).

Hoffman, Donna L., and Thomas P. Novak (1996), "Marketing in Hypermedia Computer-Mediated Environments: Conceptual Foundations," *Journal of Marketing*, 60(July), 50-68.

Lang, Annie. (2000), "The limited capacity model of mediated message processing," *Journal of Communication*, 50, 46–70.

Lee, Mira, and Ronald J. Faber (2007), "Effects of product placement in on-line games on brand memory: A Perspective of the Limited-Capacity Model of Attention*," Journal of Advertising*, 36(Winter), 75-90.

Mau, Gunnar, Günter Silberer, and Christoph Constien (2008), "Communicating Brands Playfully: Effects of in-game advertising for familiary and unfamiliar Brands," *International Journal of Advertising*, 27(5), 827-51.

Nelson, M.R., Ronald A. Yaros, and Heejo Keum (2006), "Examining the influence of telepresence on spectator and player processing of real and fictitious brands in a computer game," Journal of Advertising, 35(Winter), 87-99.

Refiana, Lailay, Dick Mizerski, and Jamie Murphy, J. (2005), "Measuring The State of Flow In Playing Online Games," in Proceedings of ANZMAC 2005 Conference, Marketing Research and Research Methodologies (quantitative), Sharon Purchase, ed., Freemantle, Australia: School of Business, University of Western Australia, 108-13.

van Reijmersdal, P. Neijens & E.G. Smit (2009). A new branch of advertising: reviewing factors that influence reactions to product placement. *Journal of Advertising Research, 49*(4), 429-449.

Segmenting Consumer Reactions to Social Network Advertising

Colin Campbell, Monash University, Australia
Carla Ferraro, Monash University, Australia
Sean Sands, Monash University, Australia

EXTENDED ABSTRACT

Marketers and advertisers have been quick to respond to the shift in online social media activity in a bid to facilitate consumer engagement. In order to optimise social media and social network advertising investments, and the potential to generate online social WOM, knowledge of how consumers interact with the medium is necessary. Fundamental is an understanding of the type of consumers that use social media and social network platforms. Several studies (e.g., Foster, West, and Francescucci, 2011; Ip and Wagner, 2000; Li and Bernoff, 2008; Riegner, 2007; Wiertz and DeRuyter, 2007) provide a basic understanding through segmentations of usage or motivation to participate. This paper offers a more nuanced understanding of how consumers engage with social media by specifically examining response to social network advertisements, which are "a new, rapidly growing, substantively important, and largely unexplored frontier," (Taylor, Lewin, and Strutton, 2011, p. 260). Likewise, instead of a single segmentation base as is common to many previous studies, we employ three segmentation bases: brand engagement, purchase intention and WOM. This paper therefore contributes to existing knowledge through a unique social media segmentation analysis predicated on the behavior a social network advertisement has the potential to engender.

Literature highlights the growing significance of social media in shaping consumer engagement online. Specifically, social media and social network sites have attracted the attention of researchers investigating marketing opportunities (e.g., Fournier and Avery, 2011; Hanna, Rohm, and Crittenden, 2011; Kaplan and Haenlein, 2011a; Kietzmann, Hermkens, McCarthy, and Silvestre, 2011; Weinberg and Pehlivan, 2011), consumer usage and influence (e.g., Katona, Zubcsek, Pal, and Miklos, 2011; Kozinets, de Valck, Wojnicki, and Wilner, 2010; Trusov, Bodapati, and Bucklin, 2010) and the related impact on consumer preferences (Narayan, Rao, and Saunders, 2011; Taylor, Lewin, and Strutton, 2011). Research has also looked at what causes social network advertising avoidance (Kelly, Kerr, and Drennan, 2010) and acceptance (Taylor, Lewin, and Strutton, 2011), as well as consumer-generated conversations and brand engagement (Fournier and Avery, 2011; Muniz and Schau, 2011). However, the literature has not yet fully explored the consumer behaviour effects of social network advertising.

A common thread running through the online and social media segmentation literatures is a focus on general behavior or motivation segmentation bases (e.g., Aljukhadar and Senecal 2011; Sung and Jeon, 2009) rather than specific responses to marketing stimuli. Researchers examining consumers' online social behavior have similarly focused on general segmentation bases such as WOM (Riegner, 2007; Foster, West, and Francescucci 2011), usage (Ip and Wagner, 2000; Taylor, Lewin, and Strutton, 2011) and motivation (Wasko and Faraj, 2000a, 2000b; Wiertz and DeRuyter, 2007; Foster, West, and Francescucci, 2011). This stream of research sheds light on organic consumer behavior online, but provides only tangential knowledge of consumer response to social media advertising. The present study attempts to fill this gap and specifically responds to the need to better understand online social community advertising (Zeng, Huang and Dou, 2009) and user engagement with brands (Foster, West and Francescucci, 2011). In doing so, we explore whether segments of consumers exist based on their level of brand engagement, WOM referral behavior, and purchase intention, all following exposure to a social network advertisement, and profile resulting consumer segments along dimensions of both theoretical and practical importance.

Using survey data from 883 consumers, we identify five segments of response to social network advertising – Passive, Talkers, Hesitant, Active, and Averse – and significant covariates such as information search, convenience, entertainment, age and gender that predict segment membership. Two segments are highly impacted by social network advertising in terms of all behavioural outcomes: brand engagement, purchase and WOM intentions. The larger of these two segments (Talkers, 28%) is relatively high on all behavioural outcomes and information motivation, but weaker in terms of purchase intentions, while the other (Active, 10%) is impacted highly on all outcomes. A third segment reveals a relative level of indifference across the behavioral outcomes (Passive, 29%), but relatively high entertainment motivation and a low convenience motivation. The remaining two segments held low levels of behavioral intention and information motivation.

This paper thus expands current understanding of how consumers respond to social network advertising through a focus on how they are impacted by advertisements in this channel. The findings highlight that two segments, Actives and Talkers (representing 38% share of the market), are highly impacted by social network advertising in terms of brand engagement, purchase and WOM referral intention. Our results also reveal that social network advertising segment membership is associated with psychographic variables such as information motivation and entertainment motivation, as well as age. Specifically, information motivation is a strong determinant of segment membership for Actives and Talkers. While this makes intuitive sense, in that positive effects from social network advertising interactions are therefore linked to consumer's desire for information, it also supports prior theory that those consumers who desire information explore and use new alternatives (e.g., Steenkamp and Baumgartner 1992). We also find that entertainment motivation is a significant predictor of membership for Actives, the segment most engaged in and responsive to social network advertising.

To sum up, our research reinforces that it is problematic to collapse all social network users into one grouping (Hargittai and Hsieh, 2010) and that advertising is more effective for some consumer segments (based on variation in response). Importantly, we identify a large (and likely growing) proportion of consumers (38%) who can be influenced by social network advertising, but also a majority who are not 'in tune' with social networks as an advertising m edium. Nonetheless, given the existence of different segments, there is a need for firms to tailor their social media marketing strategies accordingly. We find that those consumers most engaged with social network advertising also have a high information and entertainment motivation, and therefore informative and entertaining content is most effective.

REFERENCES

Aljukhadar, M., and Senecal, S. (2011), "Segmenting the online consumer market", *Marketing Intelligence and Planning*, Vol. 29 No. 4, pp. 421–435.

Allred, C.R., Smith, S.M., and Swinyard, W.R. (2006), "E-shopping lovers and fearful conservatives: a market segmentation analysis", *International Journal of Retail and Distribution Management*, Vol 34 No 4/5, pp. 308–333.

Bhatnagar, A., and Ghose, S. (2004a), "A latent class segmentation analysis of e-shoppers", *Journal of Business Research*, Vol. 57 No. 7, pp. 758–767.

Bhatnagar, A., and Ghose, S. (2004b), "Segmenting consumers based on the benefits and risks of Internet shopping", *Journal of Business Research*, Vol. 57 No. 12, pp. 1352–1360.

Blackshaw, P. and Nazzaro, M. (2004), "Consumer generated media (CGM) 101: Word-of-mouth in the age of the web-fortified consumer," available at: http://www.nielsenbuzzmetrics. com/downloads/whitepapers/ISwp_CGM.pdf (accessed 7 November 2011).

Boyd, D.M., and Ellison, N.B. (2007), "Social network sites: Definition, history, and scholarship", *Journal of Computer-Mediated Communication*, Vol. 13 No. 1, pp. 210-230.

Brown, J., Broderick, A., and Lee, N. (2007), "Word of mouth communication within online communities: Conceptualizing the online social network", *Journal of Interactive Marketing*, Vol. 21 No. 3, pp. 2-20.

Cheng, J., Wong, S.H.Y., Yang, H. and Lu, S. (2007), "SmartSiren: Virus Detection and Alert for Smartphones", MobiSys'07, San Juan, Puerto Rico, USA.

Chevalier, J. and Mayzlin, D. (2006), "The effect of word of mouth on sales: Online book reviews", *Journal of Marketing Research*, Vol. 43 No. 3, pp. 345–354.

De Bruyn, A. and Lilien, G. (2008), "A multi-stage model of word-of-mouth influence through viral marketing" *International Journal of Research in Marketing*, Vol. 25, pp. 151–163.

Deighton, J. and Kornfeld, L. (2009), "The effect of word of mouth on sales: Online book reviews", *Journal of Interactive Marketing*, Vol. 43 No. 3, pp. 345-354.

Deloitte (2010), "A new bread of brand advocates: Social networking refines consumer engagement", available at: http://www.deloitte.com/assets/Dcom-UnitedStates/Local%20Assets/Documents/Consumer%20Business/US_CP_BrandAdvocatesStudy_020910.pdf (accessed 10 December 2011).

Donthu, N and Garcia, A. (1999), "The Internet Shopper", *Journal of Advertising Research*, Vol. 39 No. 3, pp. 52-58.

Duan, W., Gu, B. and Whinston, A. (2008), "Do online reviews matter? An empirical investigation of panel data", *Decision Support Systems*, Vol. 45 No. 4, pp. 1007-1016.

Foster, M., West, B. and Francescucci, A. (2011), "Exploring social media user segmentation and online brand profiles", *Journal of Brand Management*, Vol. 19 No. 1, pp. 4–17.

Fournier, S., and Avery, J. (2011), "The uninvited brand", *Business Horizons*, Vol. 54 No. 3, pp. 193–207.

Godes, D. and Mayzlin, D. (2009), "Firm-created Word-of-Mouth communication: Evidence from a field test", *Marketing Science*, Vol. 28 No. 4, pp. 721–739.

Gupta, A., Su, B-C. and Walter, Z. (2004), "An empirical study of consumer switching from traditional to electronic channels: A purchase-decision process perspective", *Journal of Electronic Commerce*, Vol. 8 No. 3, pp. 131-161.

Hanna, R., Rohm, A. and Crittenden, V.L. (2011), "We're all connected: The power of the social media ecosystem", *Business Horizons*, Vol. 54 No. 3, pp. 265–273.

Hargittai, E. and Hsieh, Y.P. (2010), "Predictors and consequences of differentiated social network site uses", *Information, Communication and Society*, Vol. 13 No. 4, pp. 515-536.

Ignatius, A. (2011), "Shaking things up at Coca-Cola", available at: http://hbr.org/2011/10/shaking-things-up-at-coca-cola/ar/1 (accessed 18 October 2011).

Inman, J.J., Shankar, V. and Ferraro, R. (2004), "The roles of channel-category associations and geodemographics in channel patronage decision", *Journal of Marketing*, Vol. 68, pp. 51-71.

Ip, R.K.F. and Wagner, W. (2008), "Weblogging: A study of social computing and its impact on organizations", *Decision Support Systems*, Vol. 45, pp. 242–250.

Kaplan A.M. and Haenlein M. (2010), "Users of the world, unite! The challenges and opportunities of social media", *Business Horizons*, Vol. 53 No. 1, pp. 59-68.

Kaplan, A.M. and Haenlein, M. (2011a), "Two hearts in three-quarter time: How to waltz the social media/viral marketing dance", *Business Horizons*, Vol. 54 No. 3, pp. 253–263.

Kaplan, A. and Haenlein, M. (2010b), "The early bird catches the news: Nine things you should know about micro-blogging", *Business Horizons*, Vol. 54, pp. 105–113.

Zsolt K., Zubcsek, P. and Sarvary, M. (2011), "Network effects and personal influences: Diffusion of an online social network", *Journal of Marketing Research*, Vol. 48 No. 3, pp. 425-443.

Keller, K.L. (2001), "Building customer-based brand equity: A blueprint for creating strong brands", Marketing Science Institute, Working Paper Series.

Kelly, L., Kerr, G. and Drennan, J. (2010),"Avoidance of advertising in social networking sites: The teenage perspective", *Journal of Interactive Advertising*, Vol. 10 No. 2, pp. 16–27.

Kietzmann, J., Hermkens, K., McCarthy, I. and Silvestre, B. (2011), "Social media? Get serious! Understanding the functional building blocks of social media", *Business Horizons*, Vol. 54 No. 3, pp. 241–251.

Ko, H., Cho, C-H. and Roberts, M.S. (2005), "Internet uses and gratifications: A structural equation model of interactive advertising", *Journal of Advertising*, Vol. 34 No. 2, pp. 57-70.

Konus, U., Verhoef, P.C. and Neslin, S.A. (2008), "Multichannel shopper segments and their covariates," *Journal of Retailing*, Vol. 84 No. 4, pp. 398-413.

Korgaonkar, P.K. and Wolin, L.D. (1999), "A multivariate analysis of web usage", *Journal of Advertising Research*, Vol. 39, pp. 53-68.

Kozinets, R., De Valck, K., Wojnicki, A. and Wilner, S. (2010), "Networked narratives: Understanding word-of-mouth marketing in online communities", *Journal of Marketing*, Vol. 74, pp. 71–89.

Li, C. and Bernoff, J. (2008), *Groundswell: Winning In A World Transformed By Social Technologies*, Harvard Business Press, Boston, MA.

Mangold, W. and Faulds, D. (2009), "Social media: The new hybrid element of the promotion mix", *Business Horizons*, Vol. 52 No. 4, pp. 357–365.

Muniz, A.M. and Schau, H.J. (2011),"How to inspire value-laden collaborative consumer-generated content", *Business Horizons*, Vol. 54 No. 3, pp. 209–217.

Narayan, V., Rao, V.R. and Saunders, C. (2001), "How peer influence affects attribute preferences: A Bayesian updating mechanism", *Marketing Science*, Vol. 30 No. 2, pp. 368-384.

Nielson. (2009), Global Online Consumer Survey, Nielson Consumer Research. Available at: http://blog.nielsen.com/nielsenwire/wp-content/uploads/2009/07/pr_global-study_07709.pdf (accessed 18 October 2011).

Nielson. (2011), State of the Media: The Social Media Report, Nielson Consumer Research. Available at: http://blog.nielsen.com/nielsenwire/social/ (accessed 18 October 2011).

Par, B. (2011), Twitter CEO: Promoted Tweets Working "Better Than We Could Have Ever Hoped. Available at: http://mashable.com/2011/10/17/twitter-ceo-advertising/ (accessed 18 October 2011).

Parent, M., Plangger, K. and Bal, A. (2011), "The new WTP: Willingness to participate", *Business Horizons*, Vol. 54 No. 3, pp. 219–229.

Rheingold, H. (2002), *Smart Mobs: The Next Social Revolution*. Basic Books: Cambridge, MA.

Riegner, C. (2007), "Word of mouth on the web: The impact of Web 2.0 on consumer purchase decisions", *Journal of Advertising Research*, Vol. 47 No. $, pp. 436-437.

Smith, T., Coyle, J.R, Lightfoot, E. and Scott,A. (2007), "Reconsidering models of influence: The relationship between consumer social networks and word-of-mouth effectiveness", *Journal of Advertising Research*, Vol. 47 No. 4, pp. 387-397.

Sprott, D. and Czellar, S. (2009), "The importance of a general measure of brand engagement on market behavior: Development and validation of a scale", *Journal of Marketing*, Vol. 46 No. 1, pp. 92–104.

Steenkamp, J-B.E.M. and Baumgartner, H. (1992), "The role of optimum stimulation level in exploratory consumer behavior", *Journal of Consumer Research*, Vol. 19, pp. 434-448

Strebel, J., Erdem, T. and Swait, J. (2004), "Consumer search in high technology markets: exploring the use of traditional information channels", *Journal of Consumer Psychology*, Vol. 14, pp. 96-104.

Sung, H., and Jeon, Y. (2009), "A profile of Koreans: who purchases fashion goods online", *Journal of Fashion Marketing and Management*, Vol. 13 No. 1, pp. 79–97.

Sweeney, J., Soutar, G., and Mazzarol, T. (2008), "Factors influencing word of mouth effectiveness: receiver perspectives", *European Journal of Marketing*, Vol. 42 No 3/4, pp. 344–364.

Taylor, D.G., Lewin, J.E., and Strutton, D. (2011), "Friends, fans, and followers: Do ads work on social networks", *Journal of Advertising Research*, pp. 1–19.

The Economist (2007), Conversational marketing. Word of mouse: Will Facebook, MySpace and other social-networking sites transform advertising?, accessed at: http://www.economist.com/NODE/10102992?STORY_ID=10102992 (accessed 14 December 2011).

Trusov, M. and Bucklin, R. (2009), "Effects of word-of-mouth versus traditional marketing: Findings from an Internet social networking site", *Journal of Marketing*, Vol. 73 No. 5. pp. 90-102.

Trusov, M., Bodapati, A. and Bucklin, R. (2010), "Determining influential users in Internet social networks", *Journal of Marketing*, Vol. 47 No. 4, pp. 643–660.

Vermunt, J.K. and Magidson, J. (2003), *Latent GOLD Choice User's Guide*. Statistical Innovations Inc: Boston, MA.

Vermunt, J.K. and J. Magidson (2005), *Latent GOLD 4.0 User's Guide*. Statistical Innovations Inc: Boston, MA.

Wasko, M.M. and Faraj, S. (2000a), "It is what one does: Why people participate and help others in electronic communities of practice", *Journal of Strategic Information Systems*, Vol. 9, pp. 155–173.

Wasko, M.M. and Faraj, S. (2000b), "Why should I share? Examining social capital and knowledge contribution in electronic networks of practice", *MIS Quarterly*, Vol. 29 No. 1, pp. 35–57.

Wedel M. and Kamakura, W. (2002), "Introduction to the special issue on market segmentation", *International Journal of Research in Marketing*, Vol. 19 No. 3, pp. 181-183.

Wedel, M. and Kamakura, W. (1999), *Market segmentation: Conceptual and methodological foundations*. Kluwer Academic Publishers: Boston, MA.

Weinberg, B.D. and Pehlivan, E. (2011), "Social spending: Managing the social media mix", *Business Horizons*, Vol. 54 No. 3, pp. 275–282.

Wiertz, C. and DeRuyter, K. (2007), "Beyond the call of duty: Why consumers contribute to firm-hosted commercial online communities", *Organization Studies*, Vol. 28 No. 3, pp. 347–376.

Yellavali, B., Holt, D. and Jandial, A. (2004), *Retail multi-channel integration, delivering a seamless customer experience*. Infosys Technologies Ltd: Dallas, TX.

Zeng, F., Huang, L. and Dou, W. (2009), "Social factors in user perceptions and responses to advertising in online social networking communities", *Journal of Interactive Advertising*, Vol. 10 No. 1, pp. 1-13.

Zhang, N.L. (2004), "Hierachical Latent Class Models for Cluster Analysis", *Journal of Machine Learning Research*, Vol. 5, pp. 697–723.

Producing & Consuming Public Space: A 'Rhythmanalysis' of the Urban Park

Morven McEachern, Lancaster University, UK
Gary Warnaby, University of Liverpool, UK
Fiona Cheetham, University of Salford, UK

EXTENDED ABSTRACT

Over 2.5 billion visits are made to UK parks each year (Greenspace, 2007). Hence, there is, unsurprisingly, an abundance of literature dedicated to parks, especially within the context of urban regeneration (Inroy 2000). However, little attention has been given to how these forms of social space are produced/consumed (Arsel and Bean 2010; Brace-Govan 2010; Costa and Bamossy 2003; Ozalp and Belk 2009; Sherry 2000), or about the temporality of these consumption experiences (Arnould and Thompson 2005). Calls to develop a more detailed understanding of the nature and meanings of consumption-related practices associated with park users have recently been made (Lee, Shepley, and Huang 2009), which suggests an opportunity to offer a more comprehensive analysis of the temporal consumption experiences encountered by urban park users, and the subsequent contribution to a perceived 'sense of place'.

For many industrialised cities, the creation of urban parks in the mid nineteenth century was seen to provide "lungs to the inhabitants of densely populated districts" (Latimer 1987, 7) and a place where the general public could take exercise. Thus, giving rise to a strong correlation between the quality of green space/accessibility to public parks and quality of life (Barbosa et al. 2007). Accordingly, changes were also made to the way that urban park spaces are being produced and managed, moving from city councils merely fulfilling the function of park caretaker to a more strategic and actively 'managed' role whereby planned marketing activities are created to differentiate experience of the locale and (co-)create consumer value (Warnaby 2009).

Public parks and green spaces are "by their nature multifunctional and analysis falls between different academic areas" (CABE Space 2010, 42). Therefore, drawing from sociology's view that "space and the duality production/consumption are thus dynamic concepts based on practices" (Styhre and Engberg 2003, 116), de Certeau's (1984) and Lefebvre's (1991) notion of space as a "practiced place" is employed here. Moreover, as social practice is composed from daily, monthly and annual rhythms as well as natural rhythms, Lefebvre's (2004) concept of 'rhythmanalysis' helps to capture more fully the embodied everyday experience of those who use or pass through the urban park space. Lefebvre suggests that rhythm exists when there is an interaction between a place, a time and an expenditure of energy, and which will incorporate repetition (in time and space), interferences of linear processes (originating from human activity/social practices) and cyclical processes (originating in nature/the cosmos), and a cycle of birth, growth, peak, decline and end. Lefebvre notes the existence of numerous rhythms (i.e. polyrhythmia), which can "unite with one another in a state of health, in normal (which is to say normed!) everydayness" (i.e. eurhythmia), or can be discordant (i.e. arrthymia), which he perceives as "a pathological state" (2004, 16).

The study focuses on parks in the north west of England, UK. To help capture the diversity and complexity of human and non-human interaction in this socio-cultural context, we employ visual ethnography (Pink 2007) and walking interviews with users (Clark 2009). Compared to interviews alone, the use of photographs and film arguably help to capture more fully, the "lived realities of everyday consumption" (Belk and Kozinets 2005, 128). Rather than merely recording movement or repetition of rhythms, our mode of analysis attends to moods, atmospheres and reciprocal interactions

between humans as well as between non-human pulses of life, in other words, the ways in which rhythms *animate* the urban and facilitate the creation of a 'sense of place'.

The visual and aural narratives produced as a result of these complimentary methods have helped us to make sense of the temporality of the urban park as a consumption experience. A constant and dominant rhythm identified at all parks is the ebb and flow of user traffic, echoing the linear rhythms of travelling to work or school as well as serving as a constant reminder of the surrounding industrialisation. Unsurprisingly, cyclical rhythms are extremely pronounced in the urban park context, separated by days, nights and seasonal events. Early morning, weekend rhythms are dominated by harmonic non-human interactions between swaying trees and birdsong which later become muffled as the park gates give way to the everyday 'commercial rhythms' of the fast food vendors preparing for the day ahead. From mid-morning to early afternoon, the urban park attracts a diverse range of individuals and groups. As the rhythmic pace intensifies, the exchanges between humans appear organized and amicable.

For the most part, the user's mood is of enjoyment and appreciation - "*Heaton Park would be my favourite...it's a lovely space. It really used to lift my spirits and clear my head especially going for an early morning walk...it was lovely*". However, tensions were evident at times (perhaps in a manifestation of arrthymia), with certain users indicating their annoyance at the intrusions and lack of respect for their space - *"Every time I go to the park jogging I have dogs chase me. A few make contact with my feet and I have no idea if they are going to bite or something"*. Social relations brought about by interactions between non-humans and other non-humans were also spoken of by dog walkers – *"the dogs stop and say hello to each other and you kind of naturally speak to the owner and ask them about their dog...so you build up a rapport based on dog ownership"*. While recognising the role of urban park managers in 'managing' the aesthetics of the park space and organising seasonal events such as summer concerts and charity 'fun-runs', it is clear that it is the users who are instrumental in co-creating the overall image, ambience and consumption experience of the urban park.

The multiple (poly)rhythms brought about by interactions between place, time and human (and non-human) action, help to illustrate more fully the temporal nature of urban park users' consumption experiences. The paper concludes by discussing how our study helps distance our analysis from wholly textual accounts of park usage as well as providing management and policy recommendations regarding the essence of urban park space.

REFERENCES

Arnould, Eric J. and Craig J. Thompson (2005), "Consumer Culture Theory (CCT): Twenty Years of Research," *Journal of Consumer Research,* 31 (March), 868-82.

Arsel, Zeynep and Jonathan Bean (2010), "Making and Consuming Places: From Discrete Things to the Big Picture," in *Advances in Consumer Research,* Vol. 38, ed. Darren W. Dahl, Gita V. Johar and Stijn M.J. van Osselaer, Duluth, MN: Association for Consumer Research, 1-8.

Barbosa, Olga., Jamie A. Tratalos, Paul R. Armsworth, Richard G. Davies, Richard A. Fuller,

Pat Johnson and Kevin J. Gaston (2007), "Who Benefits from Access to Green Space? A Case Study from Sheffield, UK," *Landscape and Urban Planning,* 83(2-3), 187-95.

Belk, Russell W. and Robert Kozinets (2005), "Videography in Consumer Research," *Qualitative Market Research,* 8(2), 128-41.

Brace-Govan, Jan (2010), "Where to From Here? A Comparison of the Meanings Designed into Three Public Spaces," in *Advances in Consumer Research,* Vol. 38, ed. Darren W. Dahl, Gita V. Johar and Stijn M.J. van Osselaer, Duluth, MN: Association for Consumer Research, 1-8.

CABE Space (2010) *"Urban Green Nation: Building the Evidence Base,"* London: Commission for Architecture and the Built Environment.

Clark, Andrew (2009), *Visualising Connected Lives: Qualitative Techniques for Mapping the Social and Spatial Landscapes of Community*, Proceedings from 1st International Visual Methods Conference, Leeds.

Costa, Janeen A. (2003), "Becoming A "Where" B Constructing and Consuming Space," ," in *Advances in Consumer Research,* Vol. 6, ed. Darach Turley and Stephen Brown, Provo, UT: Association for Consumer Research, 312-15.

de Certeau, Michel (1984), *Practices of Everyday Life,* Translated by S. Rendall, Berkeley: University of California Press.

Greenspace (2007), *The Park Life Report: The First Ever Public Satisfaction Survey of Britain's Parks and Green Spaces,* June, Berkshire: Greenspace.

Inroy, Neil M. (2000), "Urban Regeneration and Public Space: The Story of An Urban Park," *Space and Polity,* 4(1), 23-40.

Latimer, C. (1987), *Parks for the People: Manchester and its Parks 1846-1926*, Manchester City Art Galleries, Leeds: Maney and Son Ltd.

Lee, Hyung-Sook, Mardelle Shepley and Chang-Shan Huang (2009), "Evaluation of Off-leash Dog Parks in Texas and Florida: A Study of Use Patterns, User Satisfaction and Perception," *Landscape and Urban Planning,* 92(3-4), 314-24.

Lefebvre, Henri (1991) *The Production of Space*, Translated by D. Nicholson-Smith, Oxford: Blackwell.

Lefebvre, Henri (2004) *Rhythmanalysis: Space, Time and Everyday Life*, Translated by S. Elden and G. Moore, London & New York: Continuum.

Ozalp, Yesim and Russell W. Belk (2009), "The Role of Consumption in the Organization of Urban Space: The Case of Neo-Bohemia," in *Advances in Consumer Research,* Vol. 36, ed. Ann L. McGill and Sharon Shavitt, Duluth, MN: Association for Consumer Research, 1-8.

Pink, Sarah. (2007), *Doing Visual Ethnography: Images, Media and Representation in Research*, 2nd Edition, London: Sage Publications.

Sherry Jr., John F. (2000), "Place, Technology and Representation," *Journal of Consumer Research,* 27(2), 273-78.

Styhre Alexander and Tobias Engberg (2003), "Spaces of Consumption: From Margin to Centre," *Ephemera: Critical Dialogues on Organization,* 3(2), 115-25.

Warnaby, Gary (2009), "Towards a Service-Dominant Place Marketing Logic," *Marketing Theory,* 9(4), 403-23.

Trajectories of the Self: A Phenomenological Study of Women's Changing Faces Reflected in Cosmetics Consumption

Chihling Liu, University of Manchester, UK
Debbie Keeling, University of Manchester, UK
Margaret K. Hogg, Lancaster University, UK

EXTENDED ABSTRACT

Past literature indicates the importance of changes in appearance in helping the individual define herself (McAlexander and Schouten, 1989) or cope with problems during liminal states (McAlexander, Schouten et al., 1992). For example, by undergoing plastic surgery, individuals emphasize their role transitions and set out upon a trajectory of identity reconstruction (Schouten, 1991). Nevertheless, plastic surgery is considered to be an extraordinary event, which lies outside individual realms of everyday experience. Therefore, we argue that studies on plastic surgery, whilst useful as setting boundaries for the study of the self, have limited insights in the unfolding drama of the self and the subtle sensitivity of 'individual' in daily life. Paradoxically, 'cosmetics' are a necessity of daily life for many women and for centuries have been utilized to modify or enhance physical appearance. The systems of everyday consumer consumption, e.g. cosmetics, that make us human – appear to be easily overlooked and hide potential meanings from us (Crotty, 1998). This study addresses this opportunity for examining selves in daily transition and cosmetics use across key developmental stages of everyday life (Markus and Wurf, 1987; Schembri, Merrilees et al., 2010; Aguirre-Rodriguez, Bosnjak et al., 2011). We aim to provide a holistic understanding of changes in the issues of sense of self and how cosmetics consumption is used to strategically reflect, protect and impact on the trajectories of the self over the lifetime.

A sample of twenty-six women, aged between 19 and 62, who wore makeup on a daily basis, was recruited for this study. Verbatim transcriptions were generated via phenomenological interviews (Thompson, Locander et al., 1989; Smith, Flowers et al., 2009), regarding their feelings, perceptions and experiences of cosmetics use. The interviews ranged from 1-2 hours. Fictitious names were assigned to all informants, guaranteeing confidentiality. Each interview began with the question, *"when you think about a cosmetics brand, what comes to your mind?"* This question was used to initiate a dialogue on an understandable domain, however, exerted little influence upon the overall course of the dialogue (Thompson, Locander et al., 1990). All other questions emerged spontaneously from the informants' narratives, therefore ensuring restricted influence from the interviewer and allowing informants to make sense of their experiences at their own pace. A hermeneutic approach was adopted to discern the constellation of past-present-future relations that underlies intentionality (Husserl, 1970), e.g., consumer consumption goals, and individual reflections on everyday experiences (Heidegger, 1960; Gadamer, 1993). Consumer depictions about their everyday experiences create temporal trajectories in which a past event is relived in relation to present concerns and used in shaping an envisioned image of the future self (Thompson, 1997). The interview focused on descriptions of consumers' lived experiences in terms of changes in the self over time and the role cosmetics consumption plays in facilitating this experiential journey.

THE TRAJECTORY OF CONTRADICTORY SELVES

This study showed how contradictory selves conflict in the different time frames of past, present and future (See figure 1). Our findings suggest cosmetics consumption is used dynamically as an instrument to enable views of the self and manage changes in priorities over the life course.

Past-present Conflict

For example, Abbie was constantly battling signs of aging. She was at times almost denying this fact and spoke as if she was still young and her complexion was still perfect. At the same time she was torn between two cultures, i.e. Africa (her family roots) and Europe (brought up), and changing society's expectations from the 'old days' to the present, e.g. conform to a certain look.

Present-future Conflict

She anticipated that her future self would be wearing fewer cosmetics, for example, due to the importance of passing the 'right' values to her children, e.g. beauty comes from inside. Nonetheless, she envisaged having more dramatic makeup at night for herself as a woman; and for her husband, in order to feel sexy and attractive as a wife.

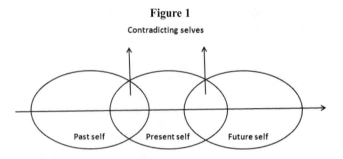

Figure 1

Contradicting selves

Past self   Present self   Future self

THE TRAJECTORY OF CONFLICTING SELVES

Furthermore, in Isobel's set of realities, cosmetics enabled her to have multiple selves, particularly in terms of her conflicting selves; when she wears makeup (e.g., 'demanding', 'tougher' and 'argumentative') compared to when she wears no makeup (e.g. 'timid', 'caring' and 'vulnerable'). Her obsession with cosmetics grew out of childhood issues she faced in the family and at school. She used makeup as a 'shield' to keep people from getting close; and as a 'sword' to be ready to fight back. She was caught in a struggle between wanting to be different and yet be the same, especially during childhood (See figure 2).

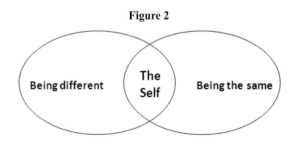

Figure 2

Being different   The Self   Being the same

As she grew older, she pictured changes in the reasons for wearing cosmetics. She used to wear makeup to hide her problems but in the future, she would hope to only utilize cosmetics to boost her confidence. As she aged, she became more confident and grew more tolerant within herself, like most of our informants.

COSMETIC COMMUNICATION BETWEEN THE SELVES

Cosmetics are used as a mechanism to communicate between the contrasting selves, particularly during major life events. For instance, Nancy was re-applying makeup in a constant manner to communicate between her 'hopeless self' and her 'hopeful self' post-breakup. She strove to depart from the hopeless depressing self and pick herself up as makeup allowed her to be that strong, confident and attractive woman.

Consumption is more than skin deep. Beyond cosmetics consumption, we provide a more enlightened perspective on this very complicated area – how does consumption potentially reflect and impact on issues of sense of self? Our findings offer intriguing insights into changes in the trajectories of the self and identity projects (Arnould and Thompson, 2005). They inform the challenges individuals face to define the self and how cosmetics are used as tools for coping with these challenges in a deeper, more dramatic way. Following on from enhancing understanding of the trajectories of the self, we conclude that the self changes over time and cosmetics consumption provides instrumental values to manipulate and attack others; and to create, re-define and protect the self, responding to transition phases during life.

REFERENCES

Aguirre-Rodriguez, Alexandra, Michael Bosnjak and Joseph M. Sirgy (2011). "Moderators of the Self-Congruity Effect on Consumer Decision-Making: A Meta-Analysis." *Journal of Business Research,* 65 (8), 1179-1181.

Arnould, Eric J. and Craig J. Thompson (2005). "Consumer Culture Theory (CCT): Twenty Years of Research." *Journal of consumer research,* 31 (4), 868-882.

Crotty, Michael (1998). *The Foundations of Social Research: Meaning and Perspective in the Research Process,* Sage Publications Ltd.

Gadamer, Hans-Georg (1993). *Truth and Method 2nd Edition,* New York: Continuum International Publishing Group Ltd.

Heidegger, Martin (1960). *Being and Time,* New York: Harper & Row.

Husserl, Edmund (1970). *Logical Investigations,* English trans, John N. Findlay, Routledge, London.

Markus, Hazel and Elissa Wurf (1987). "The Dynamic Self-Concept: A Social Psychological Perspective*." Annual review of psychology,* 38 (1), 299-337.

McAlexander, James H. and John W. Schouten (1989). "Hairstyle Changes as Transition Markers*." American Psychologist,* 74 (1), 58-62.

McAlexander, James H., John W. Schouten and Scott D. Roberts (1992). "Consumer Behavior in Coping Strategies for Divorce." *Advances in consumer research,* 19 (1), 155-157.

Schembri, Sharon, Bill Merrilees and Stine Kristiansen (2010). "Brand Consumption and Narrative of the Self." *Psychology and Marketing,* 27 (6), 623-637.

Schleiermacher, Friedrich and Andrew Bowie (1998). *Hermeneutics and Criticism and Other Writings,* Cambridge University Press.

Schouten, John W. (1991). "Selves in Transition: Symbolic Consumption in Personal Rites of Passage and Identity Reconstruction." *Journal of consumer research,* 17 (4), 412-425.

Smith, Jonathan A., Paul Flowers and Michael Larkin (2009). *Interpretative Phenomenological Analysis: Theory, Method and Research,* Sage Publications Ltd.

Thompson, Craig. J. (1997). "Interpreting Consumers: A Hermeneutical Framework for Deriving Marketing Insights from the Texts of Consumers' Consumption Stories." *Journal of Marketing Research,* 34 (4), 438-455

Thompson, Craig J., William B. Locander and Howard R. Pollio (1989). "Putting Consumer Experience Back into Consumer Research: The Philosophy and Method of Existential-Phenomenology." *Journal of consumer research,* 16 (2) 133-146.

Thompson, Craig J., William B. Locander and Howard R. Pollio (1990). "The Lived Meaning of Free Choice: An Existential-Phenomenological Description of Everyday Consumer Experiences of Contemporary Married Women." *Journal of Consumer Research,* 17 (3), 346-361.

The BOP Metanarrative: A Critical Exploration

Suparna Chatterjee, Xavier University, USA

EXTENDED ABSTRACT

Stemming from the work of C.K. Prahalad (2006) market development at the bottom of the economic pyramid has emerged as one of the viable alternatives for dealing with the challenge of global poverty. In the present paper, I contend that the "Bottom of the Pyramid" (henceforth BOP) approach is fast emerging as a meta-narrative[1] (a grand synthesizing framework) providing business practitioners and scholars with a template for future research and action aimed at creating market based solutions for poverty eradication (Anderson & Markides, 2007; Hammond & Prahalad, 2004; Karamchandani, Kubzansky & Lawani, 2011; Kasturi Rangan et al., 2007; London & Hart, 2004; Prahalad, 2006; Prahalad & Hart, 2002; Seelos & Mair, 2007; and Vachani & Smith, 2008). As a meta-narrative, the BOP proposition provides a limited set of interpretative frameworks within which a whole host of issues ranging from globalization, poverty, partnerships to markets, enterprise, and development, are understood, represented, and analyzed. Like all meta-narratives, the BOP meta-narrative opens up some kinds of debates and discussions while silencing those that lie outside its interpretative frameworks. Taking an interdisciplinary approach which involves drawing on recent developments in the in fields such as marketing, management, economic geography, anthropology, sociology, and development studies, I subject this emergent meta-narrative to a close scrutiny by highlighting the implicit and tacit assumptions, motivations, and commitments that are mobilized to construct the BOP proposition. With the help of examples drawn from Prahalad's definitive work, "Fortune at the Bottom of the Pyramid," (2006), the present paper attempts to explore the fundamental conceptual and theoretical issues at stake in the BOP proposition, and in so doing, illuminate some of the larger socio-cultural, political, and ethical implications of the project.

Broadly, the paper argues that the BOP project presents an inadequately contextualized and, in many instances, dehistorized understanding of processes and practices that affect the lives of the people at the bottom of the economic pyramid. For instance, the BOP proposition draws on a thin understanding of globalization which compartmentalizes and fragments processes and relations that are, in fact, interconnected and interlinked. Large private firms (one of the principle agents of globalization) are cast as distant and neutral players who somehow remain above and beyond the processes and relations that sustain and energize them. Such a sanitized reading of

the large private sector's involvement in global economy not only exonerates them from taking any responsibility for the uneven and contradictory consequences of their operations; but it also restricts us from thinking about newer ways of building coalitions and solidarities connecting different positions, interests, and stakes in the spirit of mutual recognition and responsibility.

The BOP proposition rests on an essentialist understanding of human nature as reflected in the arguments related to the "enterprising consumers" where the entrepreneurial trait is seen as natural and intrinsic to the consumers at the BOP. Further, the focus on entrepreneurialism as a panacea for all forms of social problems leads to depoliticization of social issues as it rests on an implicit understanding that the locus of "problems" (poverty, jobless, dispossession, environmental degradation, so forth) lies not in institutional, social, political and economic dysfunctions but rather in the individual themselves (Giroux, 1980, pp. 338).

The BOP proposition takes a purely instrumental view of knowledge which leads to abstractions and generalizations about the conditions of life at the bottom of the pyramid. Indeed, the BOP project, as Charusheela and Zein-Elabdin, 2004, in a different context (critique of economics as a hegemonic discourse of modernity) put it, is "epistemologically comfortable" with generating disembodied, context free and value-neutral knowledge. Thus, the BOP program presents economic distress and socio-spatial marginalization of the poor (for example; high population densities in slums in developing countries) as "exploitable observations" (Wilson, 1977 quoted in Giroux, 1980, pp. 334) which is then used as "knowledge" for market development at the bottom of the economic pyramid. This purely instrumental view of knowledge becomes part of the expert vocabulary (expertise) of business disciplines be it management or marketing which ultimately (although unwittingly) desensitizes poverty. It hides more than it reveals about the condition the life at the BOP as it normalizes acute economic upheavals and instabilities by making "the crisis" appear as a normal condition of life at the BOP. The claim of equal partnership between the poor and the large private sector, a central idea in the BOP proposition, is criticized for obfuscating how power works to shape interactions among differentially (hierarchically) located entities in ways which limits the field of possible actions that can be initiated by the more vulnerable "partner." Thus, given the productive capacity of power (to create individuals who are self-directed toward "certain" goals) how can firms and the people from poor communities collaborate?

The paper argues that by glossing over the conceptual and theoretical implications of ideas and concepts mobilized to study people at the bottom of the economic pyramid, the BOP project ends up resurrecting the very biases and prejudices which it allegedly set out to challenge, in the first place. While taking issue with many of the central arguments of the BOP project, the paper is not about a wholesale rejection of the idea of large private sector participation in poverty alleviation; rather the purpose is to confront the blind spots and omissions in the BOP project which serves to undermine its own potential, and in so doing recover in some measure, the emancipatory thrust of the BOP approach. In the concluding section, I maintain that the BOP project will be well served if it remains reflexive (self critical) about its own theories, perspectives, and positions. I contend that an introspective stance would make the BOP project sensitive to the uncertainties and contingencies arising from diverse historical, political, and socio-economic contexts thereby making it

---

[1]   Meta-narratives can be thought of as dominant paradigms that provide conceptual frameworks and tools to arrive at an understanding and analysis of processes and phenomena under consideration. Colonialism, modernization, development theory, under-development theory are some of the meta-narratives that have structured and shaped our knowledge of colonization, modernity, and development in contemporary times. In his brilliant essay calling for a reconsideration of the claim of value neutrality in social sciences and humanities, renowned African Studies specialist, Allen Issacman (2008) raises an important question about meta-narratives. Following a critique of meta-narratives surrounding the continent of Africa which silences and renders invisible alternative or local knowledge, he writes: "This is not to say that the meta-narratives, paradigms, or chronologies prevalent in the scholarly literature are inconsequential or wrong, but rather that they necessarily constitute only one set of intellectual conventions and representations of reality" (8). Also, it must be recognized that we often use the concepts and tools made permissible by the meta-narrative to critique the meta-narratives. So, instead of claiming a ground outside meta-narratives, the point is to highlight the fault lines that hold together the dominant logic that underwrites meta-narratives.

more circumspect (and less celebratory) about the possibilities and perils of business innovations and ventures aimed to generate profits as well as reduce poverty.

REFERENCES

Anderson, J., & Markides, C. 2007. Strategic Innovations at the Base of the Pyramid. *Sloan Management Review*, 49 (1): 83-88.

Arnould, E., & Mohr, J. 2005. Dynamic Transformations for the Base-of-the-Pyramid Market Clusters. *Journal of the Academy of Marketing Science*, 33(3): 254-274.

Charusheela, S. 2004. Postcolonial Thought, Postmodernism, and Economics. In E. O. Zein-Elabdin & S. Charusheela, eds., *Postcolonialism Meets Economics*. 40-58. New York: Routledge.

Karamchandani, A., Kubzansky, M and Lawani, N., 2011. Is the Bottom of the Pyramid Really for you? Harvard Business Review, March 11, 107-111.

Kasturi Rangan. V. et al. eds. *Business Solutions for the Global Poor, Creating Social and Economic Value*. San Francisco: John Wiley and Sons, Inc.

London, T., & Hart, S. 2004. Reinventing Strategies for Emerging Markets: Beyond the Transnational Model. *Journal of International Business Studies*. 35(1): 1-21.

Prahalad, C.K., & Hart, S. 2002. The Fortune at the Bottom of the Pyramid. *Strategy+Business*, January issue: 1-14.

Prahalad, C.K. and Hammond, A. 2002. Serve the World's Poor Profitably. *Harvard Business Review*, September issue: 48-57.

Prahalad, C. K. 2006. *The Fortune at the Bottom of the Pyramid, Eradicating Poverty Through Profits*. NJ: Wharton School Publishing.

Prahalad, C. K. 2007. Forward. In Kasturi Rangan. V., et. al., eds. *Business Solutions for the Global Poor, Creating Social and Economic Value*. San Francisco: John Wiley and Sons, Inc.

Seelos, C. & Mair, J. 2007. Profitable Business Models and Market Creation in the Context of Deep Poverty; A Strategic View. *Academy of Management Perspectives*, 21 (4): 49-63.

Vachani, S., & Smith, N. 2008. Socially Responsible Distribution: Distribution Strategies for Reaching the Bottom of the Pyramid. *California Management Review,* 50(2): 52-84.

The Effect of Social Networking Orientation on Risk Preference:
The Risk-Taking Capacity Hypothesis

Hakkyun Kim, Concordia University, Canada
Kyoungmi Lee, Yonsei University, Korea
Kiwan Park, Seoul National University, Korea

EXTENDED ABSTRACT

Will consumers' social networking orientations influence their psychological functioning on subsequent tasks in seemingly remote, unrelated domains? Prior research on social capital (Putnam 2000) suggests the distinction between a *bonding* orientation, with which people seek to cement connectedness among exclusive and relatively homogeneous groups, and a *bridging* orientation, with which people focus on creating new contacts with different groups, resulting in spanning diverse social cleavages. We propose that an individual's primary orientation associated with social networking affects subsequent risk-related decisions.

Building on the resource depletion paradigm that suggests that people who engage in an initial self-regulation task perform worse on a subsequent task demanding self-regulation resources (e.g., Baumeister et al. 1998; Baumeister, Vohs, and Tice 2007), we posit that humans have a limited amount of risk-taking resources. Thus, once their risk-taking resources are drained, individuals will act more conservatively in subsequent tasks. Specifically, given that bridging-versus bonding-oriented activities are involved with a higher level of social risk, thereby depleting more resources, we hypothesize that consumers may become more risk-averse after performing bridging-versus bonding-oriented social networking activities. We conducted three experiments to examine this hypothesis.

In study 1, we manipulated social networking orientation by asking participants to perform different types of activities on Facebook. Specifically, participants in the bridging condition were asked to log in to their Facebook accounts, choose some people on their friend lists with whom they had not personally interacted (e.g., someone from a class or friends' friends), and visit each person's Wall. The participants were then asked to spend about 10 minutes reading their friends' recent events and leaving Wall posts. In contrast, those in the bonding condition were asked to choose some people to whom they felt close (e.g., best friends or family members). Then, participants were asked to indicate how much they would consume each of the two food items, GMO (genetically-modified organism) foods or imported vegetables (study 1a) or how much they would engage in a high-risk leisure activity (i.e., Jet Ski; study 1b), on seven-point scales. In study 1a, a 2 (Orientation) × 2 (Food) mixed ANOVA with food as a within-subject factor revealed that people who performed the Facebook task with bridging (vs. bonding) orientation were less likely to consume risky food items ($F(1, 18) = 13.61, p < .01$; GMO foods: 3.13 vs. 4.17; imported vegetables: 2.83 vs. 5.00). Similarly, results from study 1b showed that participants who completed bridging-oriented activities reported lower intentions to try Jet Skiing than those in the bonding condition (5.03 vs. 5.98, $F(1, 38) = 4.50, p < .05$).

In study 2, we examined whether merely recalling previous networking activities participants had performed would produce similar effects (Usta and Häubl 2011). Thus, we manipulated social networking orientation by having participants recall and write about activities that they had done on social networking sites in the recent past. In the bridging condition, participants wrote about activities intended to newly link them with others, whereas participants assigned to the bonding condition performed the same tasks, but about activities intended to deepen their bonds with close friends. A 2 (Orientation) × 3 (Food) mixed ANOVA with three high-risk food items (raw meat, GMO corns, and fatty pork belly) replicated the findings of study 1a, showing that regardless of food items, people recalling bridging-related episodes were less likely to consumer risky food items than those recalling bonding-related episodes ($F(1, 66) = 17.28, p < .001$; raw meat: 4.58 vs. 5.94; GMO corns: 2.27 vs. 2.83; pork belly: 5.45 vs. 6.09), echoing the notion of people's risk-taking resource regulation.

In study 3, we examined the role of resource depletion as the underlying mechanism to understand the effect of social networking orientation. We used the same Facebooking manipulation as in study 1. For the risk-preference task for our dependent measure, we presented a series of seven scenarios in which participants had to choose whether to write a term paper on either a provocative topic (a risky option) or a conservative topic (a sure option), a modification of Hsee and Weber's (1999) stimulus. On the basis of each participant's choice pattern in the seven scenarios, we assigned the risk-preference index (0 – 7; higher scores indicate more risk-seeking) and used it as our focal dependent measure. We also asked participants to rate how socially risky and stressful they perceived the assigned Facebook activities, on seven-point scales (1 = not risky at all, not stressful at all, 7 = very risky, very stressful). A composite index was formed to operationalize the degree of depletion of risk-taking resources by averaging the two items ($\alpha = .76$). This index served as a mediator to the effect of social networking orientation.

We found that people reported lower scores on the risk-preference index after completing bridging versus bonding task on Facebook (2.81 vs. 3.70, $F(1, 56) = 7.19, p < .01$). We also observed that the bridging task was perceived as riskier than the bonding one, suggesting that participants spent more resources completing the bridging versus bonding task (3.55 vs. 2.59, $F(1, 56) = 6.22, p < .01$). More importantly, a bootstrapping confirmed the depletion of risk-taking resources as the underlying process by showing its mediating role between social networking orientation and risk preference (a 95% CI: .0080, .3251). We ruled out alternative explanations, such as perceived support from others, self-competence, and self-liking (all F's < 1).

Combined together, these results provide converging evidence that bridging-oriented (versus bonding-oriented) experiences on social networking or even merely recalling such experiences lead consumers to behave in a more risk-averse fashion, be it food selection, leisure activities, or academic decisions. Theoretically, we propose and find that this effect is driven by depletion of risk-taking resources induced by bridging versus bonding social networking task. Given the popularity of online social networking and its potential influence on a variety of unrelated decision domains, the present research promises to advance our understanding of consumers' implicit decision-making processes.

REFERENCES

Baumeister, Roy F., Ellen Bratslavsky, Mark Muraven, and Dianne M. Tice (1998), "Ego Depletion: Is the Active Self a Limited Resource?" *Journal of Personality and Social Psychology*, 74 (5), 1252-65.

Baumeister, Roy F., Kathleen D. Vohs, and Dianne M. Tice (2007), "The Strength Model of Self-Control," *Current Directions in Psychological Science*, 16 (6), 351-55.

Hsee, Christopher K. and Elke U. Weber (1999), "Cross-National Differences in Risk Preferences and Lay Predictions for the Differences," *Journal of Behavioral Decision Making*, 12 (2), 165-79.

Putnam, Robert D. (2000), *Bowling Alone: The Collapse and Revival of American Community*, New York: Simon and Schuster.

Usta, Murat and Gerald Häubl (2011), "Self-Regulatory Strength and Consumers' Relinquishment of Decision Control: When Less Effortful Decisions Are More Resource Depleting," *Journal of Marketing Research*, 48 (April), 403-12.

Minority Matters:
The Influence of Minority And Majority Descriptive Norms on Product Choice

Erica van Herpen, Wageningen University, The Netherlands
Hans C. M. van Trijp, Wageningen University, The Netherlands
Mariette van Amstel, Schuttelaar & Partners and Vrije Universiteit, The Netherlands

EXTENDED ABSTRACT

Social norms often have a substantial impact on human behavior (Cialdini et al. 1990; Melnyk et al. 2010). In fact, the influence of descriptive norms is much higher than that of other types of information, even though consumers themselves rate descriptive norms as least important in energy conservation behavior and campaigns using these norms as least motivating (Nolan et al. 2008). Such descriptive norms communicate what is typical in a situation and thereby provide "social proof" of what is effective behavior (Jacobson et al. 2011). They have been successfully applied in marketing campaigns to improve health and safety (e.g., www.mostofus.org).

Studies on these descriptive norms have examined campaigns communicating the behavior of a majority of others. In their study on the reuse of hotel towels, Goldstein et al. (2008) communicated that 75 % of guests participate in the resource saving program, and in a study on energy saving, Nolan et al. (2008) used doorhangers communicating behavior of 99 % of people in the community. These are powerful descriptive norms changing consumer behavior. Yet, sometimes an advocated behavior is performed by only a minority of people: the market share of organic products is low (www.ota.com) and most people fail to eat enough fruit and vegetables according to dietary guidelines (www.cdc.gov). Communicating that most people fail to perform an advocated behavior typically undermines this behavior (Cialdini 2003; Stok et al. 2011). So are descriptive social norms never effective in advocating a desired behavior when this behavior is performed only by a minority of people?

Ample research on minority influence shows that sources advocating minority options can exert influence, albeit less strong and less direct (Horcajo et al. 2010; Wood et al. 1994). Applying this to descriptive norms, this would suggest that descriptive norms of minorities might be able to initiate the desired behavior when the emphasis is not on the failure to perform this behavior by the majority ("people should eat two pieces of fruit each day but only a minority does so") but instead on the advocated behavior itself ("some people eat two pieces of fruit each day"). The latter could activate personal norms and stimulate consumers to focus on the desirability of the behavior. The effectiveness of minority norms could be further enhanced when consumers perceive that the group performing the behavior is growing. After all, economic research on information cascades suggests that the tendency to follow the behavior of others is stronger when the group who is performing a behavior grows (Banerjee 1992; Bikhchandani et al. 1998).

In contrast, the effectiveness of majority norms might not be enhanced by information that the group performing the behavior is growing. A message involving a growing majority may be perceived as 'pushy' and evoke the perception of social pressure. This perceived pressure can undermine the effectiveness of the norm: when consumers perceive a persuasion attempt they tend to counteract this attempt (Clee and Wicklund 1980; Laran et al. 2011).

The two main objectives of the current study are thus to determine (a) whether weak descriptive norms (minority norms) can nonetheless enhance an advocated behavior, and (b) whether especially strong descriptive norms (a growing majority) are indeed less effective in stimulating behavior. We expect that information that a growing group of people are performing a behavior will enhance the influence of minority norms but weaken the influence of majority norms. This is tested in three experiments.

The first experiment (n = 91 students) employed a taste test. Participants chose between organic and regular orange juice, in a 3-group design with no information, majority, or minority norm information (e.g., 20 % of students in a prior study chose the organic juice). Results showed that choice for organic juice was significantly higher for both norms than in the control condition, indicating that minority norms can indeed stimulate behavior.

In the second experiment, students (n = 245) were asked to pick rewards for a series of unrelated studies. They could choose between more or less healthful options (e.g. Vitamin Water vs. Coca Cola). In a 2 by 2 design plus control condition, it was indicated that either a majority or a minority picked healthy snacks, and that this group was growing versus no trend information. Compared to the control condition, all norm conditions raised the number healthy options that were chosen. Additionally, the growing minority and majority norms raised the number of healthy options chosen more than the minority and growing majority norms, as expected. There was no difference between conditions in perceptions of how clear, reliable, and realistic the information was.

Experiment 3 employed a virtual environment with a train station stand of snacks and a quota sample of the general population to validate results. Additionally, time pressure was manipulated. Participants made three store visits, the first without norm information and the latter two with a shelf advertisement promoting fruit and using a similar 2 x 2 between subjects design as in experiment 2. Time pressure was applied in the instructions for one of the two latter visits. Results showed that choice of healthy products was higher for visits with the descriptive norm present rather than absent. Additionally, we found a significant three-way interaction between the type of norm, trend, and time pressure. With time pressure, all norms increased healthy choice, but without time pressure participants returned to unhealthy choices when the shelf advertisement featured a growing majority.

These results have important implications for norm theory. When ability to process information is low, descriptive norms appear to be a heuristic cue triggering behavior (c.f. Jacobson 2010), but when ability to process information is high, the formulation of the descriptive norm matters. Specifically, our results indicate that the band width in which descriptive norms are effective is both more extensive than previously assumed (i.e., minority norms can advocate a desired behavior) and more restrictive (i.e., norms using a growing majority are ineffective).

REFERENCES

Banerjee, A. V. (1992), "A Simple Model of Herd Behavior," *The Quarterly Journal of Economics*, 107, 797-817.

Bikhchandani, S., D. Hirshleifer, and I. Welch (1998), "Learning from the Behavior of Others: Conformity, Fads, and Information Cascades," *Journal of Economic Perspectives*, 12(3), 151-170.

Cialdini, Robert B. (2003), "Crafting Normative Messages to Protect the Environment," *Current Directions in Psychological Science*, 12, 105-109.

Cialdini, Robert B., Raymond R. Reno, and Carl A. Kallgren (1990), "A Focus Theory of Normative Conduct: Recycling the Concept of Norms to Reduce Littering in Public Places," *Journal of Personality and Social Psychology*, 58, 1015-1026.

Clee, Mona A. and Robert A. Wicklund (1980), "Consumer Behavior and Psychological Reactance," *Journal of Consumer Research*, 6, 389-405.

Goldstein, Noah J., Robert B. Cialdini, and Vladas Griskevicius (2008), "A Room with a Viewpoint: Using Social Norms to Motivate Environmental Conservation in Hotels," *Journal of Consumer Research*, 35, 472-482.

Horcajo, Javier, Richard E. Petty, and Pablo Briñol (2010), "The Effects of Majority Versus Minority Source Status on Persuasion: A Self-Validation Analysis," *Journal of Personality and Social Psychology*, 99, 498-512.

Jacobson, Ryan P., Chad R. Mortensen, and Robert B. Cialdini (2011), "Bodies Obliged and Unbound: Differentiated Response Tendencies for Injunctive and Descriptive Social Norms," *Journal of Personality and Social Psychology*, 100, 433-448.

Laran, Juliano, Amy N. Dalton, and Eduardo B. Andrade (2011), "The Curious Case of Behavioral Backlash: Why Brands Produce Priming Effects and Slogans Produce Reverse Priming Effects," *Journal of Consumer Research*, 37, 999-1014.

Melnyk, Vladimir, Erica van Herpen, and Hans van Trijp (2010), "The Influence of Social Norms in Consumer Decision Making: A Meta-Analysis," *Advances in Consumer Research*, 37, 463-464.

Nolan, Jessica M., P. Wesley Schultz, Robert B. Cialdini, Noah J. Goldstein, and Vladas Griskevicius (2008), "Normative Social Influence is Underdetected," *Personality and Social Psychology Bulletin*, 34, 913-923.

Stok, F. Marijn, Denise T. D. de Ridder, Emely de Vet, and John B. F. de Wit (2011), "Minority Talks: The Influence of Descriptive Social Norms on Fruit Intake," *Psychology and Health*, 1-15.

Wood, Wendy, Sharon Lundgren, Judith A. Ouelette, Shelly Busceme, and Tamela Blackstone (1994), "Minority Influence: A Meta-Analytic Review of Social Influence Processes," *Psychological Bulletin*, 115, 323-345.

Fashion Sense:
Chinese Women's Response to Feminine Appeals in Transnational Advertising

Jie Gao Fowler, Valdosta State University, USA
Aubrey R. Fowler III, Valdosta State University, USA

EXTENDED ABSTRACT

Women are, in large part, responsible for the growth in retail sales in China (Rein 2009) and are becoming much more fashion conscious in this dawning consumer culture (China in Focus 1995). According to Rein (2009), Chinese women are spending as much as men on luxury consumption, accounting for 50% of luxury purchases from companies like Louis Vuitton and Gucci. Additionally, Chinese women are becoming much more focused on buying clothing and beauty products and are becoming much more concerned with looking good and looking fashionable.

As such, international fashion magazines and advertising agencies have entered into the Chinese market, helping to usher in a new fashion culture within the country. Much of the images portrayed in these media are simply adapted from Western sources, involving the modification of title, imagery, or copy in advertisements used in different cultures (Buzzell 1968; Reichal 1989; Ricks et al. 1974). Such modification ranges from a nearly complete transformation of an existing ad involving all three aspects or simply translating the copy language that appears in the ads. However, the Western advertisements in fashion magazines often do not change the model for their counterparts in China, leaving many idealized and European-looking (i.e. blonde, and blue-eyed) women in these ads.

As such, a few studies are beginning to look at the impact of fashion advertising on women and women's assessment of that advertising. For instance, Hung, Li, and Belk (2005; 2007) examined images of women in Chinese magazine advertising and developed a typology of the modern woman as portrayed in that advertising, and also examined the response strategies women used to interpret those images. Their study focused on the target audiences for those ads, essentially recruiting women who came of age well after the advent of the open-door policy. We seek to advance their study, examining the responses for feminine appeals in advertising for both the target audience as well as that target audiences' mothers, women who came of age before the open door policy when advertising was still viewed as a suspect aspect of capitalism.

Scholars such as Hirschman and Thompson (1997) and Hung et al. (2006) have conducted research on consumers' response to media images. Hirschman and Thompson (1997) identified three self-referencing responses that consumers employed to describe their relationship with media icons: aspiring/inspiring, deconstructing/rejecting, and identifying/individualizing, which were adapted by Hung et al. (2007). According to Hirschman and Thompson (1997), inspiring and aspiring occurs when a media image is interpreted as representing an ideal self to which the consumer can aspire. Media icons are read as inspirational goals or ideals that the consumer chooses to work towards. In this motivational relationship, many potential sources of disbelief are suspended. Rejecting/deconstructing occurs when the consumer's relationship with the mass media is expressed through overt criticism of the artificial and unrealistic quality of the media representation. Identifying/individualizing describes distinct ways by which consumers negotiate their self-perceptions and personal goals in relation to the idealized images presented in the mass media.

Little is known about how women from a different culture respond to similar advertising within the global marketplace. As such, the purpose of the following paper is to examine the response that Chinese and American women have for such ads found in the pages of their fashion magazines and the inter-generational differences that occur with these responses. To do so, we took a focus group interview approach to address the research purpose. Focus groups are a useful method for gathering ideas and insights for a variety of purposes such as obtaining consumer impressions of advertising copy (Iacobucci and Churchill 2005) or determining the impact of gender on the consumption of advertising (Hogg and Garrow 2003).

Given the purpose of our research concerns how different generations of women in a different culture respond to the feminine appeals in ads, we conducted a variety of dyadic focus group interviews where mother (age between 45 to 60) and daughter (age between 21 to 34) were shown advertising images taken from fashion magazines in both the U.S. and China. Based upon previous research (Chang 2004), the magazines we chose for the study share primary target audiences and are consistent in each country with each ranging between the ages of 21 and 35 (Cosmopolitan 2011; Elle 2011). The participants were recruited through a regional Chinese University and a regional American university of approximately the same size (between 11,000 and 13,000 students.

The results demonstrate that both generational and cross-cultural differences exist in terms of the interpretative strategies that were applied by these consumers. For instance, our American informants very much liked the nurturer appeal present in the advertisements with the U.S. daughters tending to associate the nurturer type with their families and/or mothers and the U.S. mothers identifying with the images in the ads. Conversely, both the Chinese daughters and their mothers rejected the ads outright, claiming that they did not represent their idea of the Chinese nurturer type. In addition, both the American mothers and daughters rejected the professional appeal in these ads, viewing them as fake and unrealistic. On the other hand, Chinese mothers and daughters both appreciated the ad with the daughters often aspiring to be like the image in the ad or, at the very least, aspiring to the professional role in which the image made the most sense.

Our study extended Hirschman and Thompson (1997)'s findings. Women not only can compare the self with the media images but also seeking solutions (e.g., comparing the media icon with friends, relatives, and even strangers). In addition, culture plays a significant element to shape how female consumers perceived the femininity in ads. Finally, there appears to be an authenticity gap in relation to the advertisements. Chinese women saw the nurturer in the ads as inauthentic whereas American women viewed the professional women as inauthentic. This authenticity gap is, of course, culturally bound; however, it also indicates the degree to which femininity and feminine appeals may not be universal in regards to fashion and consumption.

REFERENCE

Buzzell, Robert D (1968), "Can You Standardize International Marketing?" *Harvard Business Review,* 46, 103-113.

Chang, Jui-Shan (2004), "Refashioning Womanhood in 1990s Taiwan: An Analysis of the Taiwanese Edition of Cosmopolitan Magazine," *Modern China*, 30 (3), 361-97.

Cosmopolitan (2012), Demographic Profile, http://www. cosmomediakit.com/r5/showkiosk.asp? listing_ id=360482&category_id=27810&category_code=, Retrieved 3/10/2012

Elle (2012), Demographic Profile, http://web.archive.org/ web/20071028130827/http:// www.hfmus.com/ HachetteUSA/ page.asp?site=elle, Retrieved 3/10/2012

Hogg, Margaret K. and Jade Garrow (2003), "Gender, Identity, and the Consumption of Advertising," Qualitative Market Research: An International Journal, 6(3), 160-174.

Iacobucci, Dawn and Gilbert A. Churchill, Jr. (2005), *Marketing Research: Methodological Foundations,* OH: Cengage Learning.

Hirschman, Elizabeth C. and Craig J. Thompson (1997), "Why Media Matter: Toward a Richer Understanding of Consumers' Relationships with Advertising and Mass Media," *Journal of Advertising*, 26 (1), 43-60.

Hung, Kineta H., Stella Yiyan Li, and Russell W. Belk (2007), "Global Understandings: Female Readers' Perceptions of the New Woman in Chinese Advertising," *Journal of International Business Studies*, 38 (6), 1034-51.

Reichal, Jurgen (1989), "How Can Marketing Be Successfully Standardized for the European Marketing?" *European Journal of Marketing*, 23 (7): 60-67.

Reid, T.R. (1999), *Confucius Lives Next Door: What Living in the East Teaches Us about Living the West*. New York: First Vintage Books.

Ricks, David A., J. S.Arpan, and M.Y. Fu (1974), "Pitfalls in Advertising Overseas," *Journal of Advertising Research*, 4 (6), 47-51.

When and How Price-Dropping Serves as a Coping Mechanism for Price-Jolts

Aaron M. Garvey, The Pennsylvania State University, USA
Simon J. Blanchard, Georgetown University, USA
Karen Page, The Pennsylvania State University, USA

EXTENDED ABSTRACT

Imagine you just bought a new designer jacket that you are quite pleased with despite its high price—that is, until you hear that someone else purchased the exact same jacket at a different store for a lower price. We refer to this experience of realizing *post*-purchase that a lower price than the price paid was available as a *price-jolt*. In such situations, how do you feel? To date, and perhaps not surprisingly, research has indicated that such price-jolts significantly decrease satisfaction (Oliver and DeSarbo 1988) and likely result in negative feelings and attributions given the extent to which paying a lower price than retail results in positive affect (Schindler 1998). Building on this research, we consider how consumers cope with such price-jolts. Specifically, we examine how consumers may casually mention to others that they overpaid, which we term *price-dropping,* as a way to cope with price-jolts.

Previous research has shown that name-dropping, where an individual mentions a name in a conversation, is used to manage impressions and enhance self-presentation. For example, individuals that name-drop may be perceived as more likeable and competent when signaling a distant and casual connection with the person whose name was invoked (Lebherz, Jonasa, and Tomljenovic 2009). Similarly, we propose that sharing overpayment through price-dropping may signal pecuniary strength and status that aids in consumer coping with price-jolts (e.g., increased product satisfaction).

This theorizing is supported by recent empirical literature, which indicates that the appeal of many products is due to status needs rather than material needs (Amaldoss and Jain 2005), and that dearth of discounted payment may be perceived as a status signal (Argo and Main 2008). Furthermore, heightened sensitivity to status cues due to individual differences (Lichtenstein, Ridgway, and Netemeyer 1993) or situations (Rucker and Galinsky 2008) may increase signaling tendencies. Thus, consumers experiencing the negative consequences of a price-jolt may obtain psychological status benefits from telling others about their overpayment (i.e., price-dropping).

The results of three studies demonstrate that i) consumers choose to engage in price-dropping if they are naturally sensitive to status or if they are in a status-relevant context, ii) satisfaction with the product is improved when price-dropping, and iii) consumers perceive themselves as wealthier and more popular after price-dropping.

Study 1 explored whether consumers choose to engage in price-dropping after a price-jolt based upon perceived importance of status cues. After imagining purchasing an iPad2 for a given price, participants in the price-jolt (no price-jolt) condition were informed that the product was readily available at a nearby store for a higher (lower) price. Participants then indicated their likelihood to share the price paid if asked. To investigate whether willingness to price-drop depends on consumers' perceived importance of status cues, a multi-item measure of individual prestige sensitivity was recorded (Lichtenstein, Ridgway, and Netemeyer 1993). A significant three-way interaction between price-jolt condition and prestige sensitivity (analyzed continuously) emerged. As predicted, highly prestige sensitive consumers were more likely to price-drop when they experienced a price-jolt than those who did not. In contrast, low prestige sensitive consumers were less likely to price-drop when they were price-jolted than when they were not. Product quality assessments

did not differ between conditions, thus precluding a price-quality inference explanation. Consistent with predictions, the desire among prestige sensitive consumers to price-drop suggests that negative effects of unintentional overpayment may be offset by signaling (and thus self-perceiving) heightened status. Subsequent studies examine whether the value obtained from price-dropping is reflected in product satisfaction.

Study 2 was conducted to determine whether product satisfaction is influenced by price-dropping. A 2 (price-jolt: yes/no) x 2 (price-drop: yes/no) between-subjects design with a continuous measure of prestige sensitivity was employed. After reading about their (lack of) price-jolt for the purchase of an Armani jacket, participants in the "no price-drop" condition indicated their product satisfaction. In contrast, participants in the "price-drop" condition were told they shared the actual price paid and the market price with a colleague prior to being asked about satisfaction. A three-way interaction supported our predictions. First, the effect of price-dropping on satisfaction differed by perceived importance of status cues: price-dropping increased satisfaction for high prestige sensitive consumers experiencing a price-jolt whereas low prestige sensitive consumers were less satisfied after a price-jolt regardless of price-dropping. All consumers experiencing a price-jolt (vs. no jolt) without price-dropping were dissatisfied. Notably, the level of satisfaction for price-dropping consumers rivals the level of satisfaction of other consumers who were unexpectedly delighted by under-paying for the same product. Study 2 thus demonstrates that price-dropping following a price-jolt recovers satisfaction for status-concerned consumers.

Study 3 investigated whether price-dropping can aid in coping with a price-jolt (i.e., increase satisfaction) among consumers not perpetually concerned with prestige if a status-relevant context arises. A 2 (price-jolt: yes/no) x 2 (status relevance: important/unimportant) between-subjects design was employed. Specifically, after learning of the same (lack of) price-jolt for the Armani jacket from study 2, the requestor of the jacket price paid was described as either high or low in receptivity to status cues ("…shops at high-end stores…recently vacationed at the Ritz-Carlton" vs. "…shops at discount stores…recently hiked and camped the local Appalachian trail"). Jacket satisfaction and self-ratings on several characteristics were then recorded. A significant two-way interaction confirmed our predictions. Consumers reporting to an audience low in receptivity to status cues were less satisfied in the case of a price-jolt. In contrast, and as predicted, those reporting to an audience receptive to status cues demonstrated full satisfaction recovery (i.e., satisfaction equal to those not experiencing a price-jolt). Mediation analysis suggested that individuals engaging in price-dropping in status-relevant conditions perceived themselves to be wealthier and more popular. Thus, price-dropping provides direct psychological benefits in addition to improving satisfaction.

In summary, this work introduces the theoretically novel concept of price-dropping and explicates how consumers may engage in this behavior to overcome the otherwise negative effects of price jolts. Beyond theoretical contributions to pricing and status literatures, this work has substantive implications, particularly given the abundance of price communications among consumers in social media.

REFERENCES

Amaldoss, Wilfred and Sanjay Jain (2005), "Conspicuous Consumption and Sophisticated Thinking," *Management Science*, 51 (10), 1449–67.

Argo, Jennifer. J., and Main, Kelley J. (2008). "Stigma by association in coupon redemption: Looking cheap because of others." *The Journal of Consumer Research*, *35*(4), 559-572.

Chandon, P., Wansink B., & Laurent, G. (2000). "A benefit congruency framework of sales promotion effectiveness." *Journal of Marketing*, 64, 65–81.

Lebherz, Carmen, Klaus Jonas, and Barbara Tomljenovic (2009), "Are we known by the company we keep? Effects of name-dropping on first impressions," *Social Influence,* 4 (1), 62-79

Lichtenstein, Donald R., Ridgway, Nancy M., and Netemeyer, Richard G. (1993). "Price perceptions and consumer shopping behavior: a field study." *Journal of Marketing Research*, 234-245.

Oliver, Richard L. and Wayne S. DeSarbo (1988), "Response Determinants in Satisfaction Judgments," *Journal of Consumer Research*, 14 (4), 495-507.

Rucker, Derek D., and Adam D. Galinsky (2008), "Desire to Acquire: Powerlessness and Compensatory Consumption," *Journal of Consumer Research*, 35(2), 257–267.

Schindler, R. M. (1998). "Consequences of perceiving oneself as responsible for obtaining a discount: Evidence for smart-shopper feelings." *Journal of Consumer Psychology*, 371-392.

You Might not Get what You Ask for:
Evidence for and Impact of Non-WTP Reporting in Willingness-to-Pay Surveys

Reto Hofstetter, University of St. Gallen, Switzerland
David Blatter, University of Bern, Switzerland
Klaus M. Miller, University of Bern, Switzerland

EXTENDED ABSTRACT

Knowing consumers' willingness-to-pay (WTP) is fundamental to managers engaging in consumer-oriented pricing strategies and tactics. To gauge consumers' WTP, marketing researchers frequently prefer, and rely on, direct WTP measurement approaches such as the open-ended (OE) question format. The OE question format is widely used by various professional market research firms and compared to indirect approaches to measure WTP (e.g., conjoint analysis) direct approaches have the advantage of simplicity, which explains their enduring popularity with practitioners. They are simple to explain, easy to implement, and never fail to generate timely information at a low cost. In addition, recent research has found that the external validity of direct approaches is not always necessarily inferior to indirect approaches (Miller et al. 2011).

With the OE question format, respondents are directly asked to state their maximum WTP for the specific product under consideration (Arrow et al. 1993; Mitchell and Carson 1989). As this format does not provide respondents with a selection of answering options, the respondents have unlimited degrees of freedom to come up with an estimate of their maximum WTP. This is why the OE question format is also referred to as "price-generation task" (Chernev 2003). These price-generation tasks are very flexible and allow consumers to precisely articulate their willingness to pay. Viewed from an economics standpoint, this flexibility is one of the reasons why price-generation tasks are potentially superior to price-selection tasks as a way to determine WTP if one assumes that consumers have established preferences that can easily be translated into monetary terms (Varian 1999). From a behavioral perspective this, however, is not necessarily the case as respondents have to go through a cognitively demanding multi-stage process to generate the answer (Krosnick 1991). In such situations, when optimally answering a survey question would require substantial cognitive effort, Krosnick (1991) argues that some respondents are tempted to shorten the cognitive route and simply provide a reasonably satisfactory answer instead, a behavior coined as "satisficing". The likelihood of engaging in such satisficing behavior is seen to be regulated by three factors: task difficulty, ability, and motivation. Given that price-generation tasks are generally perceived as difficult because consumers are not used to name their own price, and that some respondents potentially lack ability or motivation to perform this particular task, satisficing behavior is likely to occur in price-generation tasks.

In this paper, we propose that satisficing behavior in price-generation task can lead to a reporting of other price-types than WTP, which are more salient to the respondent and thus require less cognitive effort to generate. In a first study, we test whether the theoretical framework of satisficing can explain this observed behavior. For this purpose, we elicit WTP using both a price-generation and an incentive-aligned task for an innovative digital camera prior to market introduction. We find that 40.71 percent of the test persons indeed do not report their WTP and also find clear evidence that satisficing is more likely to happen among consumers who lack ability and motivation to perform the fully cognitive process of the price-generation task. In addition, expertise can explain the reporting of internal-reference prices instead of WTP. This effect is u-shaped, such that consumers with a low or high level of expertise are the most likely to report internal-reference prices. For consumers with high levels of expertise, this result is intuitive as for them it will require little cognitive effort to come up with an internal reference price relative to the cognitive effort needed to construct WTP. These results are in line with theory and suggest that not all respondents are equally capable of performing the price-generation task. We also find that satisficing has an effect of the external validity of the WTP statements. If a price-type different from WTP is reported, prices are substantially biased. If WTP is reported, this bias was significantly lower. This result is confirmed in both between- and within-subjects data.

In a second study, we replicate the external validity test for a lower-priced product. Again, a large proportion of the respondents report other price-types than WTP (55.72 percent). We find that if all elicited data is used for further analysis, measures that we calculate based on these data were all significantly biased. In contrast, if we focus on data from optimizing respondents, the bias was not only significantly lower, but it fully vanishes. This result holds for a number of statistical tests, such as comparing means or distributions, and also for a managerial relevant test, such as the outcome of a pricing decision based on these data. Interestingly, this group of optimizing respondents does not differ from the sample population in terms of demographics.

We believe that our study is among the first to offer a plausible explanation for the frequently reported hypothetical bias in empirical WTP studies. Our results suggest that consumer responses to price-generation tasks cannot always be interpreted as WTP. Intriguingly, the behavior that leads to this result can come from unlikely sources as experts are more likely to suffer from it. Experts are more likely to have stored internal reference prices. As reporting reference prices requires much less cognitive effort compared to coming up with WTP, they are more prone to engage in satisficing behavior.

Our research is limited in that the price-type selection task does not account for possible uncertainty at the individual level. We do not know if the chosen price-type was the only one that reflected the stated price. However, we would assume that respondents would select the price-type that best reflects the type of the stated price. A second limitation is that it is not guaranteed that the price the respondents state and later identify as WTP truly reflects WTP. Study 1 suggests that even this value can still be biased. This indicates that also other possible explanations besides satisficing may explain the hypothetical bias. It could be worthwhile to take a more holistic approach and test various competing explanations for the bias in one single research setting. We leave this endeavour to future research.

REFERENCES

Arrow, Kenneth, Robert Solow, Paul R. Portney, Edward E. Leamer, Roy Radner, and Howard Schuman (1993), "Report from the NOAA Panel on Contingent Valuation," *Federal Register*, 58 (10), 4601-14.

Chernev, Alexander (2003), "Reverse Pricing and Online Price Elicitation Strategies in Consumer Choice," *Journal of Consumer Psychology*, 13 (1/2), 51-62.

Krosnick, Jon A. (1991), "Response strategies for coping with the cognitive demands of attitude measures in surveys," *Applied Cognitive Psychology*, 5 (3), 213-36.

Miller, Klaus M., Reto Hofstetter, Harley Krohmer, and Z. John Zhang (2011), "How Should Consumers' Willingness to Pay Be Measured? An Empirical Comparison of State-of-the-Art Approaches," *Journal of Marketing Research*, 48 (1), 172-84.

Mitchell, Robert C. and Richard T. Carson (1989), *Using Surveys to Value Public Goods: The Contingent Valuation Method*. Washington, DC: Resources for the Future.

Varian, Hal R. (1999), "Commentary on 'Economic Preferences or Attitude Expressions: An Analysis of Dollar Responses to Public Issues' by Kahneman et al.," *Journal of Risk and Uncertainty*, 19 (1-3), 241-42.

When Good Things Come to an End: Mispredicting Motivation for Unavailable Goods

Yang Yang, Carnegie Mellon University, USA
Carey Morewedge, Carnegie Mellon University, USA
Jeff Galak, Carnegie Mellon University, USA

EXTENDED ABSTRACT

Many, if not all, good things come to an end, and consumer products are generally no exception. Consumers frequently deal with not only acquiring goods and services, but also losing access to them for various reasons. Consumers are not indifferent to loss. When anticipating losing access to a desirable item, consumers' motivation to keep it increases when the loss becomes closer (Kurtz 2008; Shu and Gneezy 2010; Worchel, Lee, and Adewole 1975).

In the current research, we explore the anticipated and actual trajectory of the desire for a good to which one has already lost access. How much will one crave another few days on the beach, for example, a week after returning to work? Is the longing that one anticipates realized, or does the desire to lie in the sun quickly fade when it is replaced by the glow of the computer monitor?

Study 1 examined NFL fans' desire to watch more NFL football games after the end of the 2011 season. The Monday after SuperBowl 46, forecasters reported their desire to watch another NFL football game on that day, and predicted their desire to watch another NFL football game on the subsequent three Mondays. Experiencers reported their desire to watch another NFL football game on each of those Mondays. Whereas forecasted wanting remained constant across the month, experienced wanting significantly decreased over the course of the month. Reported liking for the NFL, however, did not change.

Study 2 examined consumers desire to consume a food after losing access to it. Experiencers watched a 45-minute video. To whet their appetite, experiencers were allowed to eat M&M's ad libitum during the first 5 minutes of the video. They then lost access to the candy for the remainder of the video. At the end of the video, experiencers indicated how many M&M's they would eat if they could right then. Forecasters predicted their desire for M&M's across the course of the video, and predicted the number of M&M's they would want to eat at its end. Whereas forecasters predicted that their desire for M&M's would remain constant over the course of the video, experiencers' reported wanting for M&M's decreased linearly with time. Experiencers also desired fewer M&M's at the end of the video than forecasters anticipated they would desire.

Study 3 examined which of the two possible accounts of the discrepancy between forecasted and reported wanting explains this difference. An attentional account suggests that wanting requires attentional resources, and thus wanting for a stimulus will decrease when attention is directed toward other experiences; a process that forecasters may not anticipate. A motivated reasoning account sug-

gests that experiencers derogate the option that they cannot have due to their own internal self-justification, but forecasters do not anticipate engaging in motivated reasoning. Whereas the attentional account predicts that the degree to which the subsequent experience consumes attention should determine whether wanting remains constant or decreases, the motivated reasoning account suggests that a change in liking should determine whether wanting remains constant or decreases.

In Study 3, all participants first ate ten M&M's and played Whac-A-Mole on a computer for one minute. As a manipulation of attentional resources, participants were randomly assigned to play one of two versions of Whac-A-Mole that were identical in all aspects except for the level of engagement. Experiencers then lost access to the M&M's and played Whac-A-Mole for 20 minutes and reported their wanting, liking, and the extent to which they were thinking about M&M's over those 20 minutes. Forecasters predicted their wanting, liking, and thoughts about M&M's on the same scales.

The attention manipulation had a significant impact on the actual trajectory of desire for M&M's. Experiencers who played the unengaging game reported a lesser decrease in their desire for M&M's than those who played the engaging game. In contrast, forecasters were insensitive to this manipulation. They predicted that their desire for M&M's would remain constant in both conditions. A mediated moderation model showed that the change in attention allocated to M&M's, rather than the change in liking of M&M's, mediated the change in their wanting.

To conclude, we examine consumers' desire for goods to which they lose access in the domains of sports and food, and find that in contrast to their predictions, desires for those goods decrease due to consumers' allocation of attention to alternative experiences. This research should be of interest to marketers interested in consumption, cravings, and more general processes of motivation.

REFERENCES

Kurtz, Jaime L. (2008), "Looking to the Future to Appreciate the Present," *Psychological Science*, 19 (12), 1238.

Shu, Suzanne B. and Ayelet Gneezy (2010), "Procrastination of Enjoyable Experiences," *Journal of Marketing Research*, 47 (5), 933-44.

Worchel, S, J Lee, and A Adewole (1975), "Effects of Supply and Demand on Ratings of Object Value," *Journal of Personality and Social Psychology*, 32 (5), 906-14.

Forced Transformations and Consumption Practices in Liquid Times

Andres Barrios, Lancaster University, UK and Universidad de los Andes, Colombia
Maria Piacentini, Lancaster University, UK
Laura Salciuviene, Lancaster University, UK

EXTENDED ABSTRACT

Literature Review

Throughout life, consumers experience many changes that can impact on and transform their identities. Some of these changes occur naturally as individuals move through their lives (e.g. becoming an adult), while others are the result of more conscious decisions made by individuals (e.g. getting married). From a consumer behaviour perspective, studies have analyzed the support that possessions and consumption practices offer individuals (functionally and/or emotionally) during these changes that are associated with fairly defined points in consumers' lives (McAlexander, 1991, Ozanne, 1992, Curasi et al., 2004, Schouten, 1991b)

An analysis of consumer behaviour studies examining individuals' transformations highlights the prominence of Van Gennep's model of Rites of Passages as a framework to describe and understand these transitions (see for example Curasi et al., 2004, Ozanne, 1992, Young, 1991, Schouten, 1991a). While these studies have provided useful insights into the consumption practices associated with identity transitions, in our understanding Van Gennep's framework does not reflect the evolution of individuals' identity development and performance. Specifically, the framework is not suitable for situations where transformational outcomes are uncertain and/or forced, i.e. where transformations do not have a clearly defined end-state.

Bauman (2000, 2007) has suggested that society has reached a postmodern ('liquid') era in which the social forms cannot keep their shape for long (Bauman, 2007, p. 1). As a result, there is higher uncertainty surrounding individuals' transformations (McCracken, 2008). Building on Hill's work on individual's experiences of homelessness (Hill and Stamey, 1990, p. 96) and extended periods of poverty (Hill, 2001) as triggers of a reconfiguration of the sense of self, this paper focuses on the homeless experience, in which forced and uncertain changing events disrupt individuals' entire life. In so doing, this paper proposes an alternative framework that takes into account the uncertainty that accompanies forced transformations, and the role of consumption during the transformation pathways.

Method

A phenomenological study was adopted, focussing on the specific events that led informants into a state of homelessness. The study was developed as a two-stage process. First, a twelve-month quasi-ethnographical study (Elliott and Jankel-Elliott, 2003) where the lead author volunteered for a charity that supports homeless individuals. Second, long interviews were conducted and focused on homeless people's *retrospective biographical narratives* about the events that led them into a homeless state. The combined database (16 interviews with homeless individuals, and a research journal of the quasi-ethnography study) was analyzed and interpreted using existential phenomenological procedures (Thompson, 1997, Thompson et al., 1989).

FINDINGS AND CONTRIBUTIONS

The study findings reveal a four-stage process of forced self-transformation that takes place across two stressful situations: the triggering events that led informants to lose their home, and their further survival in a homeless state (Figure 1).

Figure 1. Process of Forced Self- Transformation

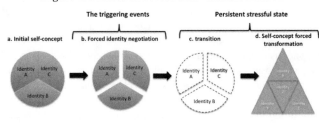

Source: the authors

a. Initial self-concept

This initial stage refers to the informants' state before the triggering events occurred. All informants' narratives of their lives before entering the pathway to homelessness reflect them as being relatively stable, comprising multiple identifications that together comprised their dominant initial self-concept.

b. Forced identity negotiation

This stage relates to the reactions individuals had while the triggering events occurred, as well as the changes that their identities went through. According to informants' narratives when the trigger events occurred, they initially believed it was a transient situation. Therefore, and despite the uncertainty that surrounded those moments, their initial reaction was to: a) use their remaining economic and social resources (e.g. savings, friends, family) to avoid losing their home, and b) manage the meaning of their possessions to continue performing their identities (Black, 2011).

However, informants realized their homeless situation was not transient and this created a major identity continuity disruption. Informants' narratives reflect a forced identity negotiation processes associated with the identities they wanted to perform and ones they could actually perform. This in turn was related to the props (i.e. possessions and/or practices) they had to support those identities including: the meaning of the remaining possessions, how they supported their identities, and what they could do with them in their current situation.

c. Transition

This stage relates to the individuals' confrontation with the consequences of the triggering events. Individuals realized that homelessness was an enduring state and the props they had imagined would assist them to cope with their situation were no longer reliable or available. Their narratives reflect they entered in a transitional state, in which they felt grief for their past; doubts about who they were at that time; and uncertainty about what they would become in the future. In order to cope with the situation, individuals' activities focused on their day-to-day survival including: where to find food (e.g. scavenging), how to obtain money (e.g. begging) and where to spend the night (e.g. sleeping on benches).

Authors have highlighted how consumption activities and possessions help individuals address the ambiguity during transitional times (Noble and Walker, 1997, Fischer and Gainer, 1993, Banister and Piacentini, 2008, Schouten, 1991b). In this specific context, informants relied on different adaptive strategies that helped them to relieve their anxiety. These strategies include compulsive consumption behaviours and/or certain routines that help informants to escape from their current conditions (e.g. walking, reading, drinking).

d. Self-concept transformation

This stage relates to the individuals' reinvention of their self-concept, based on their past experience and their current situation. The informants' narratives reveal how their experience on the streets, and the consumption practices they were forced to perform to survive, helped them to develop new identities. Individuals experience tensions between their past and present self, whose solution can be characterized using Ahuvia's (2005) synthesizing strategy. Both new identities and previous ones evolved, forcing individuals to reinterpret their past, present, and envision lives based on their homelessness experience (Figure 2).

Figure 2. Effect of the trigger event as reflected through informants' past and present narratives

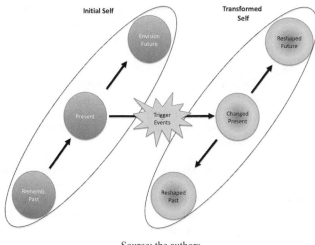

Source: the authors

CONCLUSION

Our study describes the forced self-transformation process individuals experience in their pathway to homelessness. This process represents a framework to facilitate the navigation of this type of transformation and to understand how at times of uncertain life changes consumption practices become key elements in individuals' self-development. Consumption practices served initially as symbols during the forced identity negotiation process. Subsequently, and although these practices did not emerge as identity-laden (day to day survival), they became with time the source for constructing a new self.

REFERENCES

Banister, E. N. & Piacentini, M. G. 2008. Drunk and (Dis) Orderly: The Role of Alcohol in Supporting Liminality. *In:* Lee, A. Y. & Soman, D. (eds.) *Advances in Consumer Research, Vol 35.*

Bauman, Z. 2000. *Liquid Modernity,* Cambridge, Policy Press.

Bauman, Z. 2007. *Liquid Times: Living in an Age of Uncertainty,* Cambridge, Polity Press.

Black, I. 2011. Sorry Not Today: Self and Temporary Consumption Denial. *Journal of Consumer Behaviour.*

Curasi, C. F., Hogg, M. K. & Maclaran, P. 2004. Identity, consumption and loss: The impact of women's experience of grief and mourning on consumption in empty nest households. *In:* Kahn, B. E. & Luce, M. F. (eds.) *Advances in Consumer Research, Volume Xxxi.*

Elliott, R. & Jankel-Elliott, N. 2003. Using Ethnography in Strategic Consumer Research. *Qualitative Market Research,* 6, 215-233.

Fischer, E. & Gainer, B. 1993. Baby Showers: A Rite of Passage in Transition. *In:* Mcalister, L. & Rothschild, M. L. (eds.) *Advances in Consumer Research, Vol 20.*

Hill, R. P. 2001. Surviving in a material world - Evidence from ethnographic consumer research on people in poverty. *Journal of Contemporary Ethnography,* 30, 364-391.

Hill, R. P. & Stamey, M. 1990. The Homeless in America: An Examination of Possessions and Consumption Behaviors. *Journal of Consumer Research,* 17, 303-321.

Mcalexander, J. 1991. Divorce, the Disposition of the Relationship, and Everything. *In:* Research, A. F. C. (ed.) *Advances in Consumer Research.* Provo, UT.

McCracken, G. 2008. *Transformations: Identity Construction in Contemporary Culture,* Bloomington, IN, Indiana University Press.

Noble, C. H. & Walker, B. A. 1997. Exploring the relationships among liminal transitions, symbolic consumption, and the extended self. *Psychology & Marketing,* 14, 29-47.

Ozanne, J. L. 1992. The Role of consumption and Disposition During Classic Rites of Passage. - The Journey of Birth, Initiation, and Death. *In:* Sherry, J. F. & Sternthal, B. (eds.) *Advances in Consumer Research, Vol 19 - Diversity in Consumer Behavior.*

Schouten, J. W. 1991a. Personal Rites of Passages and the Reconstruction of the Self. *In:* Holman, R. H. & Solomon, M. R. (eds.) *Advances in Consumer Research, Vol 18.*

Schouten, J. W. 1991B. Selves in Transition: Symbolic Consumption in Personal Rites of Passage and Identity Reconstruction. *The Journal of Consumer Research,* 17, 412-425.

Thompson, C., Locander, W. & Polio, H. 1989. Putting Consumer Experience Back into Consumer Research: The Philosophy and Method of Existential-Phenomenology. *Journal of Consumer Research,* 16.

Thompson, C. J. 1997. Interpreting Consumers: A Hermeneutical Framework for Deriving Marketing Insights from the Texts of Consumers' Consumption Stories. *Journal of Marketing Research,* 34, 438-455.

Young, M. M. 1991. Disposition of Possessions During Role Transitions. *Advances in Consumer Research,* 18, 33-39.

Dispositional Greed: Scale Development and Validation

Goedele Krekels, Ghent University, Belgium
Mario Pandelaere, Ghent University, Belgium
Bert Weijters, Vlerick Leuven Gent Management School, Belgium

EXTENDED ABSTRACT

Greed is often invoked to explain non-cooperative behavior in economic games (Stanley & Ume, 1998), resource exploitation (Ludwig et al, 1993) and is considered intrinsic to a materialistic lifestyle (Belk, 1985). Despite this view of greed as a fundamental motive for behavior, no empirical research has investigated individual differences in greed. The current paper aims to contribute by developing a dispositional greed scale.

In layman's terms, greed is commonly defined as "the excessive desire to accumulate more than one needs or deserves". However, this definition is not value-free and uses an external perspective. In academic research greed has been used in varied contexts, from anthropological to psycho-analytical research, leading to a diverse array of definitions. What is important to note is that in many definitions of greed, a key aspect is insatiability: no amount of a given commodity is ever sufficient. Similar to greed, insatiability is more likely to be observed for goals for which no satiation can occur and with no natural upper bound. Hence, the best starting point for this scale development was to equate greed with insatiability. An advantage of such a definition is that it might broaden the contexts as it is applicable to non-monetary outcomes as well.

1. SCALE DEVELOPMENT STUDIES

Based on literature and focus groups, an initial item pool of 60 items was generated. In the first study these greed items were administered to 318 Caucasian Americans (144 males, M age = 44.5, SD = 12.4). An EFA was conducted for trimming and retaining items for the final scale. Items which violated the standard criteria were eliminated from the factor solution, after which three expert judges reviewed the remaining items (Netemeyer et al, 2003). In this process certain items were deleted and others were reformulated.

To further refine the scale, 211 fully employed US citizens (106 males, M age = 45.6, SD = 11.7) responded to the 25 remaining items. The EFA model pointed at two factors but the second factor existed only of reversed items. Following Marsh (1996), a one factor model with method effect (9 items, 3 reversed, α = .81) was found to be the best fit: the χ^2/Df ratio was 2.84, the CFI was 0.98, the TLI was 0.97, the SRMR was 0.028 and the RMSEA was 0.051.

A third study was conducted using the final 9 items (317 fully employed US citizens; 151 males, M age = 44.8, SD = 11.9). The CFA confirmed the one-factor model. Thus, the final greed scale consists of 9 items (including 3 reversed items), with a Cronbach's Alpha of .87 and explaining 72.1% of variance[1].

To check for nomological validity, the greed scale was correlated with other measures. The highest correlation[2] was observed with Richins and Dawson's (1992) materialism (r = .73), but discriminant validity analysis clearly showed greed to be a different construct (Fornell & Larcker, 1981). The correlation with Belk's (1985) materialism was more moderate (r = .43). Furthermore we found correlations of -.34 with gratitude and of .24 with dispositional envy.

2. VALIDITY STUDIES

The results of a fourth study (185 fully employed US citizens; 89 males, M age = 44.5, SD = 12.3) indicate that dispositional greed might be a reaction to personal and resource insecurity. A greedy disposition might be a way to cope with this insecurity. This suggests that greedy people focus on themselves and their own needs. Moreover they feel entitled to more and are focused on achieving. However, a link with social comparison indicates that greedy people are not entirely self-focused. 9 Behavioral items were also added in the questionnaire. The scale showed a high predictive validity (r = .16 to .56), thereby indicating that dispositional greed predicts behaviors generally considered as greedy.

The last study was distributed to respondents that had previously participated in the third study (184 fully employed US citizens; 91 males, M age = 44.9, SD = 11.8). Test-retest reliability proved to be good: the correlation between both studies (three weeks apart) was .83 and the Spearman-Brown coefficient was .91. Also known group validity was tested. We found that men are more greedy than women, t(182) = 2.71. Furthermore, greed was negatively related to religiosity (r = -.22). Finally, respondents working in financial or management sectors were significantly greedier than those working in agriculture, services or arts, t(63) = 2.98.

As the third study found a high correlation with materialism, further analyses were set up to thoroughly investigate the relation between dispositional greed and materialism. We conducted multiple regression analyses with both constructs as predictors to account for a possible overlap with materialism. These analyses show that the established relation between materialism and uncertainty (measured as childhood insecurity and need for control and power) might be mediated by greed. Further, controlling for materialism, greed is not related to well-being. This implicates materialism as more of a dark trait than greed is. Possibly, this may be explained by the fact that materialism is more strongly related to social comparison than greed is. Also while greed is positively related to need for achievement, materialism is negatively related to it. When looking at the behavioral effects of both constructs, we find materialism to be predictive for behavior towards regulation and dispositional greed to be predictive for behavior towards products. Thus, while materialism is known to be connected to a value system focusing on social status and affluence as shown through conspicuous consumption of luxury, dispositional greed is an inner desire to gain more of all kinds of goals and is less focused on others.

3. DISCUSSION

The current research constructed a 9 item dispositional greed scale. Analyses showed greed to be related yet different from materialism. Future research will examine cultural differences and real-life consequences. More specifically, we will look for moderators between dispositional greed and behavioral greed and experiments will be conducted to see how greed affects consumer and economic decisions.

REFERENCES

Belk RW (1985) Materialism: Trait Aspects of Living in the Material World. *Journal of Consumer Research, 12*, 265–80.

---

1   For details, please contact the first author.

2   For reasons of brevity, all p-values are at least below .01 unless otherwise indicated.

Cozzolino, P.J., Sheldon, K.M., Schachtman, T.R. & Meyers, L.S. (2009). Limited time perspective, values, and greed: Imagining a limited future reduces avarice in extrinsic people. *Journal of Research in Personality, 43*, 399–408

Fornell, C. & Larcker, D.F. (1981) Evaluating Structural Equation Models with Unobservable Variables and Measurement Error, *Journal of Marketing Research, 18*, 39-50.

Kasser, T. & Sheldon, K.M. (2000). Of wealth and death: Materialism, mortality salience, and consumption behaviour. *Psychological Science, 11*, 348–351.

Kasser, T. (2002). Sketches for a self-determination theory of values. In E. L. Deci & R. M. Ryan (Eds.), *Handbook of self-determination research* (pp. 123-140). Rochester, NY: University of Rochester Press.

Ludwig, D., Hilborn, R. & Walters, C. (1993) Uncertainty, resource exploitation and conservation: lessons from history. *Ecological Applications, 4*, 548-549.

Marsh, H.W. (1996). Positive and negative self-esteem: A substantively meaningful distinction or artifactors? *Journal of Personality and Social Psychology, 70*, 810-819.

Mazar, N., Caruso, E. & Zhong, C.-B. (2011). Greed or green? The impact of the colour green on the conservation of monetary and natural resources. Conference presentation at SCP Winter conference Atlanta, Georgia, 25/02/2011

Netemeyer, R.G., Bearden, W.O. & Sharma, S. (2003) *Scaling procedures : Issues and applications.* Thousands Oaks, CA: Sage Publications, Inc.

Richins, M.L. & Dawson, S. (1992) A consumer values orientation for materialism and its measurement: scale development and validation. *Journal of Consumer Research, 19*, 303–316.

Smith, R.H., Parrot, W.G., Diener, E., Hoyle, R.H. & Kim, S.H. (1999). Dispositional envy. *Personality and Social Psychology Bulletin, 25*, 1007-1020.

Spielberger, C.D. (1989). *State–Trait Anxiety Inventory: a comprehensive bibliography.* Palo Alto, CA: Consulting Psychologists Press.

Stanley, T.D. & Ume, T. (1998). Economics Students Need Not Be Greedy: Fairness and the Ultimatum Game. *Journal of Socio-Economics, 27* (6), 657-664

Stones, M.J., Hadjistavopoulos, T., Tuuko, H. & Kozma, A. (1995). Happiness has traitlike and statelike properties: a reply to Veenhoven. *Social Indicators Research, 36*, 129–144.

From Commitment to Detachment:
A Historical Analysis of Gift Advertisements by Department Stores in Japan, 1963-2008

Takeshi Matsui, Hitotsubashi University, Japan
Yuko Minowa, Long Island University, USA
Russell W. Belk, York University, Canada

EXTENDED ABSTRACT

This paper analyzes 1,308 gift related advertisements by Japanese department stores in newspapers collected in every five years from 1963 to 2008. Our goal is to understand the dynamics of the shared meaning of seasonal gifts in Japanese society. In Japan, there is a tradition to send gifts to people to whom one is indebted, such as superiors, clients, matchmakers, parents, and relatives on both summer (*ochūgen*) and winter (*oseibo*) gift occasions. Starting in 1964, Japanese department stores opened temporary "gift centers" in their premises for these seasonal gifts, and they have played a pivotal role in developing and maintaining such gift giving rituals in post war Japanese society (Mitsukoshi Honsha 2005).

Gift giving has been an important research topic within the Consumer Culture Theory tradition (Arnold and Thompson 2005). However, contemporary Japanese gift culture has rarely been explored in spite of its importance in the society, with some exceptions (Ito 2011; Minami 1998; Minowa and Gould 1999; Minowa, Khomenko, and Belk 2011; Rupp 2003). Also, while most of the extant research in consumer research has been at a micro level, there is a paucity of research on commercially constructed representation of gift giving at a macro level. This paper tries to open this line of inquiry.

The advertisements were collected from the *Newspaper Advertisement Small Edition*, which compiles the advertisements by industry published in major newspapers each month. We checked every page of the *Small Editions* from 1963 to 2008, every five years, and collected all the gift related advertisements by department stores. There were 581 *ochūgen* and 522 *oseibo* advertisements. Other gift occasion promoted by department stores include Christmas, Fathers' Day, and Mothers' Day. These advertisements were also compared to examine the distinctiveness of the seasonal gift advertisements.

We also conducted interviews about gift-related marketing with store personnel of the eight major national chain department stores in Tokyo in order to check the plausibility of our interpretations of the advertisements. We asked questions concerning the meaning of gift giving culture for Japanese society over the past fifty years. This helped to place the findings from our analysis of advertising within the broader context of societal change.

Two main findings emerged from our historical analysis. First, there has been a coexistence of Japanese and Western cultural references in the advertisements, regardless of year, although seasonal gift giving is deeply rooted in Japanese culture. The apparent reason is that department stores in Japan have been important gatekeepers introducing Western things to Japanese consumers (Creighton 1992). The items introduced in the advertisements have been both from Japan (e.g., Kikkoman soy sauce) and from the West (e.g., Twinings black tea). Also, the advertisements sometimes use both Japanese and Western cultural elements (e.g., a Japanese woman costumed in *kimono* with pasta and ham).

Second, some of the gift items appearing in the advertisements until the 1970s are durable gifts for adult men, such as socks, underwear, and shirts, which then began to be replaced by nondurable gifts for anybody, such as sweets, coffee, and canned foods. Men's wear was popular due to the economic needs of consumers for such "necessity" gifts during the 60s and 70s. Then there was a resurgence of food items as dominant seasonal gifts, while food has generally been regarded as the important gift item throughout Japan's history (Ito 2011). The change may imply that the symbolic meaning of the seasonal gift giving ritual has shifted from commitment to detachment. Sending durables for seasonal gifts requires givers to expend efforts to carefully consider the recipients' needs and tastes because it is possible that the recipients do not like the gifts but cannot abandon them easily as they feel guilty. On the other hand, food gifts are called *kiemono*, defined as "gifts that will disappear after consumption -- such as food, seasonings, detergents, and bathing powder" in Japanese dictionary. *Kiemono* gifts carry a smaller psychological burden than durable gifts for both givers and recipients. If the recipient does not like these things, he or she can give them to somebody else as *osusowake* (sharing with others what has been given) or discard them because they are expected to disappear by virtue of their perishable nature. The decline of communal values as a result of urbanization, the shift of family structures from extended to nuclear, the decline of corporate culture, and the abundance and accumulation of material objects at home contributed to a decrease in the amount of obligatory seasonal gift giving and allowed people to revert to *kiemono* gifts rather than durables. This is strikingly evident in seasonal gift advertisements. The progressive dominance of such *kiemono* gifts is markedly different from other gift giving occasions like Christmas, Mother's Day, Father's day, and Valentine's Day. Our interpretation complements that of Daniels (2001) who interpreted the practicality of consumable gifts in Japan merely due to limited space.

REFERENCES

Arnould, Eric J. and Craig J. Thompson (2005), "Consumer Culture Theory (CCT): Twenty Years of Research," *Journal of Consumer Research*, 31 (March), 868-82.

Creighton, Mille R. (1992), "The Depāto: Merchandising the West While Selling Japaneseness," in *Re-made in Japan: Everyday Life and Consumer Taste in a Changing Society*, ed. Joseph J. Tobin, New Haven: Yale University Press, 42-57.

Daniels, Inge Maria (2001), "The 'Unitidy' of Japanese House," *Home Possessions: Material Culture behind Closed Doors*, edited by Daniel Miller, Oxford : Berg, 201-29.

Ito, Mikiharu (2011), *Zōtō no nihonbunka* [Japanese culture with gift giving], Tokyo: Chikuma shobō.

Minami, Chieko (1998), *Gifuto māketingu: gireitekishōhi ni okeru shōchō to goshūsei* [Gift Marketing: Symbols and Reciprocity in Ritual Consumption], Tokyo: Chikurashobo.

Minowa, Yuko and Stephen J. Gould (1999), "Love My Gift, Love Me or is it Love Me, Love My Gift: A Study of The Cultural Construction of Love and Gift-Giving among Japanese Couples," in *Advances in Consumer Research*, Vol. 26, ed. Eric J. Arnould and Linda M. Scott, Provo, UT: Association for Consumer Research, 119-24.

Minowa, Yuko, Olga Khomenko, and Russell W. Belk (2011), "Social Change and Gendered Gift-Giving Rituals: A Historical Analysis of Valentine's Day in Japan," *Journal of Macromarketing*, 31 (1), 41-56.

Mitsukoshi Honsha (Mitsukoshi Headquarter) (2005) ed., *Kabushiki kaisha mitsukoshi 100 nen no kiroku: 1904-2004: depātomento sutoa sengen kara 100 nen* [Mitukoshi Corporation, Record of 100 Years: 1904-2004: One Hundred Years since the Department Store Declaration], Tokyo: Mitsukoshi.

Rupp, Katherine (2003), *Gift-Giving in Japan: Cash, Connections, Cosmologies*, Stanford, CA: Stanford University Press.

When Hopes are Dashed: Sour Grapes or Searching for Greener Pastures?

Aaron M. Garvey, Pennsylvania State University, USA
Margaret G. Meloy, Pennsylvania State University, USA
Baba Shiv, Stanford University, USA

EXTENDED ABSTRACT

Dashed hopes are powerful experiences in which an overwhelmingly attractive and attainable choice option is dangled in front of a consumer and then yanked away. What impact do dashed hopes have on subsequent preferences? On the one hand, individuals may cling to familiar status quo options (i.e., "sour grapes") as suggested by the robustness of the status quo bias (Knutson et. al. 2008; Samuelson and Zeckhauser 1988) and dissonance research (Festinger and Carlsmith 1959). On the other hand, individuals may abandon the status quo and search for hopeful alternatives (i.e., "searching for greener pastures").

Our research proposes that dashed hopes will lead to abandonment of the status quo under predictable circumstances. Specifically, research examining cognitive hope and outcome-oriented motivation indicates that the denial of a highly desirable outcome may increase pursuit of that outcome (Carver, Sutton, and Scheier 2000; Clee and Wicklund 1980; Fitzsimons 2000; Litt, Khan, and Shiv 2010) and facilitate substitution attempts (Kruglanski et al. 2002; Kruglanski and Jaffe 1998; Snyder 2002; Snyder, Cheavens, and Michael 1999). Moreover, research indicates that individuals may engage in motivated reasoning when hope is threatened (deMello, MacInnis, and Stewart 2007), which may positively bias the interpretation of alternatives to the status quo. Thus, we propose that in the presence of a status quo option, the introduction and subsequent removal of a hoped-for alternative (i.e. a dashed hope) will increase status quo abandonment (H1). Furthermore, this effect will be driven by denigration of the status quo during consideration of the hoped-for option (H2). Finally, motivated reasoning increases when option information consistent with the desired outcome is ambiguous (Mishra, Mishra, and Shiv 2011; Russo, Carlson, and Meloy 2006; Sloman, Fernbach, and Hagmayer 2010). As such, if motivated reasoning underlies the basic effect, abandonment of the status quo due to dashed hopes should increase (decrease) as the ambiguity of alternatives to the status quo option increases (decreases) (H3).

We contribute to the literature by introducing the novel dashed hope effect and explicating its underlying processes. We also provide insights into consumer decision biases. The dashed hope effect is substantively important for a range of consumer-related behaviors (e.g., product launch delays, stock outs, romantic relationships, career management). Four empirical studies provide support for the preceding hypotheses. For brevity, studies 1 and 3 are presented in detail.

Study 1 employed a field setting to determine whether the experience of dashed hopes decreases bias toward a status quo option. H1 was evaluated entirely in the context of real behavior, from endowment and product evaluation, to the experience of dashed hopes, and finally to option selection.

Participants were 43 university staff members. A 2 (Dashed hopes vs. No dashed hopes) x 2 (Status quo: Wine brand A vs. Wine brand B) between subjects design was employed. Volunteers personally evaluated a real bottle of wine (two comparable brands unfamiliar to participants, counterbalanced between dashed hope conditions) with the promise of receiving that bottle of wine upon leaving the building for the day (to establish a status quo option). Later, participants received an email detailing the pick-up location and containing the dashed hopes manipulation; for the dashed hope (control) condition, extra bottles of a fine French chardonnay (wine comparable to the status quo) were to be available. Upon pickup, those in the dashed hopes condition were told that the fine French wine was already gone, and offered the choice between the status quo and a comparable alternative. The control condition simply chose between the status quo and the comparable alternative.

As predicted, selection of the status quo was significantly higher in the control versus the dashed hopes condition (M = 88%; M = 57%; $\chi^2 = 3.87$, $p < .05$), with no effect of wine brand ($\chi^2 < 1$). These findings are consistent with dashed hopes mitigating the status quo bias, and directly support H1.

Study 2 examined the effect in a second domain (automobiles) and provided insights into the underlying process. Both H1 and H2 were supported.

Study 3 was conducted to evaluate the motivated interpretation of ambiguous information as further evidence of the underlying mechanisms leading to the dashed hopes effect (H3). Specifically, we assess whether abandonment of the status quo is more likely when the ultimate choice set contains an ambiguous (rather than unambiguous) alternative to that status quo.

Participants were 335 undergraduate students in a 2 (Dashed hopes: Present vs. Absent) x 2 (Status quo: Present vs. Absent) x 2 (Option ambiguity: High vs. Low) between subjects design. The choice context involved winning a gift certificate to a fine dining restaurant. A target option was manipulated to be either the status quo or non-status quo (see Sen and Johnson 1997). A choice set of multiple certificates (containing the target option) was then introduced. In the dashed hopes condition, the second option was a world class restaurant; in the non-dashed hopes condition, the second option was comparable to the target option. The second option was then removed for everyone, leading to (not) dashed hopes. In the final choice set, the unambiguous condition described the target option and its alternative in detail, whereas the ambiguous condition described the target option in detail and provided ambiguous information about the alternative. Choice was then recorded.

Binary logistic regression for choice share of the target option revealed the predicted three-way interaction ($\chi^2 = 4.19$, $p < .05$). Within the ambiguous choice condition, when hopes were not dashed, a significant status quo bias was observed; choice share of the target option was 21% higher when framed as the status quo ($\chi^2 = 5.92$, $p < .01$). However when hopes were dashed, the status quo bias was non-existent ($\chi^2 = 1.29$, $p = .25$). For the unambiguous choice condition, a significant status quo bias existed regardless of whether hopes were dashed ($\chi^2 = 12.31$, $p < .01$). These results directly support H3 and support a process explanation of motivated reasoning for the dashed hopes effect.

Study 4 replicated the overall findings and provided evidence ruling out alternative explanations of anger and simple reactance.

REFERENCES

Carver, Charles S., Stephen K. Sutton, and Michael F. Scheier (2000), "Action, Emotion, and Personality: Emerging Conceptual Integration," *Personality and Social Psychology Bulletin*, 26 (June), 741-751.

Clee, Mona A. and Robert A. Wicklund (1980), "Consumer Behavior and Psychological Reactance," *Journal of Consumer Research,* 6 (March), 389-405.

deMello, Gustavo, Deborah J. MacInnis and David W. Stewart (2007), "Threats to Hope: Effects on Reasoning about Product Information," *Journal of Consumer Research,* 34 (August), 153-161.

Festinger, Leon and James M. Carlsmith (1959), "Cognitive Consequences of Forced Compliance," *The Journal of Abnormal and Social Psychology,* 58 (March), 203-210.

Fitzsimons, Gavan J. (2000), "Consumer Response to Stockouts," *Journal of Consumer Research,* 27 (September), 249-266.

Knutson, Brian, G. Elliott Wimmer, Scott Rick, Nick G. Hollon, Drazen Prelec, and George Loewenstein (2008), "Neural Antecedents of the Endowment Effect," *Neuron*, 58 (June), 814-822.

Kruglanski, Arie W., and Yorum Jaffe (1988), "Curing by Knowing: The Epistemic Approach to Cognitive Therapy," in *Social Cognition and Clinical Psychology*, ed. Lyn Y. Abramson, New York, NY: Guilford, 254-291.

Kruglanski, Arie W., James Y. Shah, Ayelet Fishbach, Ronald S. Friedman, Woo Chun, and David Sleeth-Keppler (2002), "A Theory of Goal Systems," in *Advances in Experimental Social Psychology*, Vol. 34, ed. Mark P. Zanna, San Diego, CA: Academic Press, 331-378.

Litt, Ab, Taly Reich, Senia Maymin and Baba Shiv (2011), "Pressure and Perverse Flights to Familiarity," *Psychological Science,* 22 (April), 523-531.

Mishra, Himanshu, Arul Mishra and Baba Shiv (2011), "In Praise of Vagueness: Malleability of Vague Information as a Performance Booster," *Psychological Science,* 22 (June), 733-738.

Russo, J. Edward, Kurt A. Carlson, and Margaret G. Meloy (2006), "Choosing an Inferior Option," *Psychological Science*, 17 (October), 899-904.

Samuelson, William, and Richard Zeckhauser (1988), "Status Quo Bias in Decision Making," *Journal of Risk and Uncertainty*, 1 (January), 7-59.

Sen, Sankar and Eric J. Johnson (1997), "Mere-Possession Effects without Possession in Consumer Choice," *Journal of Consumer Research,* 24(June), 105-117.

Sloman, Steven A., Philip M. Fernbach and York Hagmayer (2010), "Self-Deception Requires Vagueness," *Cognition,* 115 (May), 268-281.

Snyder, C. R. (2002), "Hope theory: Rainbows in the mind," *Psychological Inquiry*, 13 (October), 249-275.

Snyder, C. R., Cheri Harris, John R. Anderson, Sharon A. Holleran, Lori M. Irving, Sandra T. Sigmon, Lauren Yoshinobu, June Gibb, Charyle Langelle and Pat Harney (1991), "The Will and the Ways: Development and Validation of an Individual-Differences Measure of Hope," *Journal of Personality and Social Psychology,* 60 (April), 570-585

Consumer-Created Advertising:
Does Awareness of Advertising Co-Creation Help or Hurt Persuasion?

Debora Thompson, Georgetown University, USA
Prashant Malaviya, Georgetown University, USA

EXTENDED ABSTRACT

Marketers increasingly are involving consumers to co-create advertising (Moskowitz 2006), presumably because they expect that consumers who were not involved in the co-creation process would find that a message crafted by a fellow consumer resonates with their needs and will respond positively to it. While the message content may well resonate with consumers, what is so far untested is the influence, if any, on message recipients of awareness that a message was created by another consumer. Communicating information about the ad creator to enhance ad effectiveness is a potential opportunity that marketers might be overlooking. In this research, we examine whether knowledge that an ad was created by another consumer affects its persuasiveness.

A priori, it is unclear if awareness that a consumer is the creator of an ad would enhance or undermine ad effectiveness. The literature on source effects suggests that to the extent consumers are perceived as more trustworthy than professional persuaders, disclosing that a target ad is consumer-created should increase message persuasiveness (Wilson and Sherrell 1993). In contrast, regular consumers may be perceived as lacking the skills and expertise needed to create persuasive messages, leading viewers to question the ad's quality and persuasiveness. Consequently, awareness that a consumer created an ad could prompt message counter-argumentation and a decrease in persuasiveness. Across four studies, we examine which of these effects – trust and identification with the ad creator versus questioning of ad creator expertise – is more likely to emerge. In addition, we examine the underlying mechanism and two moderators of the effect: cognitive distraction and source identification.

Study 1 establishes the core effect of awareness that an ad was created by a consumer. One hundred and twenty-five undergraduate students were randomly assigned to a 2 ad creator disclosure (control vs. consumer-created) x 2 ad replicates between subjects design. Participants watched one of two ads for a target product and evaluated the ad and the advertised brand. Before watching the ad, half the participants were informed that the ad they were about to see was created by a consumer. Participants in the control condition were not given any ad creator information. Results reveal a negative effect of disclosing that the ad was consumer-created: Awareness that the ad was created by a consumer lowered ad evaluation ($F(1,114)=4.89$, $p<.05$) and brand evaluation ($F(1,114)=19.27$, $p<.001$), a pattern consistent with heightened skepticism as opposed to trust or identification.

The goal of study 2 was to examine the mechanism by which disclosure of the consumer source may lead to negative responses to the ad and brand. If this negative effect is the result of an effortful judgment correction process prompted by critical thoughts towards the ad creator, the effect should be mitigated when consumers' cognitive resources are constrained (Grant, Malaviya and Sternthal 2004). Findings show that when cognitive resources are unconstrained the outcomes obtained in study 1 are replicated, but under cognitive load, disclosure that a consumer created the ad increased ad evaluation, and mitigated the negative effect on brand evaluation, relative to the control condition. These findings support the notion that the negative response to the disclosure of consumer as ad creator is an effortful process of message correction, which is mitigated or even reserved under distracted viewing conditions.

Studies 3 and 4 explore additional conditions that moderate the negative effect of ad creator disclosure. Both these studies fo-

cus on perceived similarity between the respondent and ad creator, with the expectation that when respondents perceive greater similarity between themselves and the ad creator, they would also perceive greater affiliation, leading to lower skepticism and more favorable ad and brand evaluations. Study 3 manipulates similarity by including a condition where the ad creator was a business-school student. Three hundred and sixteen undergraduate students were randomly assigned to a 3 ad creator (control, consumer-created, student-created) x 2 ad replicate between subjects design. Ad creator information was provided in the same manner as in study 1. The results show that informing respondents that the ad was created by a consumer had no effect on perceived similarity between the ad creator and the respondent, and as in previous studies, decreased ad and brand evaluations. In contrast, informing respondents that the ad creator was a business-school student, increased perceived similarity, enhancing ad ($F(2,304)=18.15$, $p<.0001$) and brand evaluation ($F(2,304)=6.75$, $p<.001$). Analysis of open-ended thoughts suggests that the consumer as ad creator makes viewers more critical of the ad and its content compared to the student as ad creator.

Study 4 examines the effect of perceived similarity with the ad creator via respondents' self-reported brand loyalty. Our expectation was that brand loyal respondents would perceive greater affiliation to the creator of the ad, leading to a positive effect of disclosing the consumer source, whereas low loyalty consumers would show a negative effect of the consumer source. One hundred and twenty-three participants were randomly assigned to a 2 ad creator (control vs. consumer) by 2 (high vs. low loyalty) between subjects ANOVA. Analysis revealed a significant ad creator by brand loyalty interaction for both ad ($F(1, 119)=8.74$, $p<.004$) and brand evaluation ($F(1, 119)=8.43$, $p<.004$). For non-loyal respondents we replicate the negative effect of disclosing ad creator information on ad and brand evaluation, while for loyal respondents, a positive effect of ad creator disclosure is observed.

Taken together, our findings challenge the view that consumer-created ads are processed as word-of-mouth communications from a trustworthy source. Our studies show that (1) awareness that an ad is consumer-created undermines persuasion by triggering a critical mindset towards the ad creator because consumers question the ability of regular consumers to develop effective advertising; (2) the presence of distractions during ad exposure mitigates, and could reverse, this negative effect; and (3) making consumers aware that the ad creator is a member of the same social community (another student) or of the same psychographic community (shared brand loyalty) as the message recipient reverses this effect.

REFERENCES

Grant, Susan Jung, Prashant Malaviya and Brian Sternthal (2004), "The Influence of Negation on Product Evaluations," *Journal of Consumer Research*, 31 (December), 583-591.

Moskowitz, Robert (2006), "Are Consumer-Generated Ads Here to Stay," *iMedia Connection*, May 10, accessed on 02/28/11 (http://www.imediaconnection.com/content/9521.asp).

Wilson, Elizabeth J. and Daniel L. Sherrell (1993), "Source Effects in Communication and Persuasion Research: A Meta-Analysis of Effect Size," *Journal of the Academy of Marketing Science*, 21 (2), 101-112.

Pictures Versus Words in Changing Implicit Attitudes in Ambush Marketing Disclosure: The Role of Valence of Mental Images

Olivier Trendel, Grenoble Ecole de Management, France
Marc Mazodier, University of South Australia, Australia
Kathleen D. Vohs, University of Minnesota, USA

EXTENDED ABSTRACT

The study of attitude change has for long depended solely on self-reported (explicit) measures of attitudes (i.e. on explicit attitudes). Yet, the development of implicit measures of attitude has challenged the classic view of attitude change that assumes that the old attitude is replaced with a new one (Petty et al., 2006). Implicit measures of attitudes are specialized techniques that rely on respondents' non-declarative responses, instead reflecting particular evaluative associations automatically activated when encountering a relevant stimulus. Because implicit attitudes often diverge from explicit attitudes and because both attitudes independently predict different types of behaviors (Rydell and McConnell, 2006) it is essential to understand the antecedents of both explicit and implicit attitudes change. In this research we compare the effectiveness of counterattitudinal pictures versus text in changing explicit and, more importantly, implicit attitudes in the case of ambush marketing disclosure (a specific case of corrective advertising).

Pictures seem effective to change implicit attitudes (Dasgupta and Greenwald, 2001) and results concerning the impact of textual information on implicit attitude change are mixed (Gregg et al., 2006; Petty et al., 2006; Rydell and McConnell, 2006). Yet, no study directly compares the influence of pictures and text. Dual process models (Gawronski and Bodenhausen, 2006; Sloman, 1996) suggest that explicit attitudes are the result of rule-based processes relying in particular on verbal representations whereas implicit attitudes are the results of associative processes. Moreover, Sloman (1996) suggests that the associative system, hence implicit attitude, should be particularly sensitive to concepts encoded in concrete forms such as concrete images or metaphors (see also the CEST model of Epstein and Pacini, 1999). Therefore, we hypothesize that the relative effectiveness of pictures versus text in changing implicit attitudes resides in the valence of mental images produced by the counterattitudinal information. Concerning explicit attitude change, pictures and text conveying the same information should have the same effectiveness.

We test our hypotheses in the case of ambush marketing, which is the clear intent by a brand to mislead consumers (usually through advertising using event-related elements) into thinking the brand is sponsoring the event (Sandler and Shani, 1989; Meenaghan, 1996). It is perceived as a major threat by event organizers who have therefore undertaken to disclose ambushers to the general public using either press releases or advertisements (Humphreys et al., 2010; International Olympic Committee, 2010).

Because consumers almost never identify ambushers as such (Sandler and Shani, 1989; Meenaghan, 1998), they will form the same often positive attitude toward sponsors and ambushers. We study the change of implicit and explicit attitude toward an ambusher after disclosure of the ambush tactic in the context of the Beijing 2008 Olympics. We specifically compare the effectiveness of disclosure strategies based on text versus pictures.

We conducted 3 pretest-posttest between-subject experiments that used the same underlying procedure. First participants (students) were exposed to pictures of the 2008 Olympic Games and to ads related to this event (including 3 ads for Beifa, the target ambusher brand). The ads for Beifa aimed to deceive participants by giving the impression that Beifa was an Olympic sponsor. Then participants reported their attitudes towards Beifa with an implicit measure based on the Fazio et al. (1986) evaluative priming paradigm and also with a set of rating scales. Next participants were either informed or not about the existence of ambush marketing and about the fact that Beifa was an ambusher. Finally, we measured again implicit and explicit attitude toward Beifa. The different disclosure strategies used were pretested for equivalence in meaning (both explicitly and implicitly using a semantic priming task) and in persuasiveness.

In the first experiment (N=84) with 3 conditions (no disclosure using a neutral article, disclosure with a press article, immediate disclosure at the beginning of the experiment with a press article) we obtained that disclosure using a press article explicitly reporting Beifa's ambush marketing activities, is effective to change explicit attitude toward the ambusher but ineffective to change implicit attitude. This was the case even though respondents had to provide a summary of the article.

In the second experiment (N=70) with 3 conditions (no disclosure, disclosure with 3 drawings, disclosure with 6 drawings) we show that both implicit and explicit attitudes can be changed when drawings (representing the visual parts of rough print ads) are used instead of a press article. Ad copies used brand personification and represented the ambusher stealing money from the IOC. We also obtained that whereas explicit attitude toward the ambusher changed quickly and were not sensitive to the number of ad repetitions (3 versus 6), implicit attitude changed more slowly and decreased from 3 to 6 ad repetitions.

We then performed a pretest (N=113) to identify the characteristics of the mental images that participants had in mind after the different disclosure conditions. We also included a new condition in which we asked participants to visualize Beifa after having read the press article. As expected, valence of mental images differed between disclosure conditions, such as mental images were more negative in the disclosure with drawings conditions and disclosure with news article followed by verbal imagery instruction condition compared to the disclosure with news article condition. All the other characteristics of mental images (e.g. quantity, ease…) did not differ between the disclosure conditions.

In the third experiment (N=103) with 4 conditions (no disclosure, disclosure with a press article, disclosure with 6 drawings, disclosure with a press article followed by verbal imagery instructions) we replicate previous findings and, most importantly, found that valence of mental images mediates the relationship between type of disclosure and implicit attitude change but not explicit attitude change (Zhao et al., 2010).

Overall, our results suggest that pictures are superior to text in changing implicit attitudes. Yet textual information that is imagery-provoking can also lead to a change in implicit attitude. These results could explain some of the discrepant findings concerning the effectiveness of textual information in changing implicit attitudes (Gregg et al., 2006).

REFERENCES

Dasgupta, Nilanjana and Anthony G. Greenwald (2001). On the Malleability of Automatic Attitudes: Combating Automatic Prejudice with Images of Admired and Disliked Individuals. *Journal of Personality and Social Psychology, 81,* 800–814.

Epstein, Seymour and Rosemary Pacini (1999), "Some Basic Issues Regarding Dual-process Theories from the Perspective of Cognitive-experiential Self-theory," in *Dual-Process Theories in Social Psychology*, Shelly Chaiken and Yaacov Trope, eds. New York: Guilford Publishers, 462- 82.

Fazio, Russell H., David M. Sanbonmatsu, Martha C. Powell and Frank R. Kardes (1986), "On the Automatic Activation of Attitudes", *Journal of Personality and Social Psychology*, 50 (2), 229-38.

Gawronski, Bertram and Galen V. Bodenhausen (2006), "Associative and Propositional Processes in Evaluation: An Integrated Review of Implicit and Explicit Attitude Change", *Psychological Bulletin*, 132 (5), 692-731

Gregg, Aiden P., Beate Seibt, and Mahzarin R. Banaji (2006), "Easier Done Than Undone: Asymmetry in the Malleability of Implicit Preferences", *Attitudes and Social Cognition*, 90 (1), 1-20.

Humphreys, Michael S., Bettina T. Cornwell, Anna R. McAlister, Sarah J. Kelly, Emerald A. Quinn, and Krista L. Murray (2010), "Sponsorship, Ambushing, and Counter-Strategy: Effects Upon Memory for Sponsor and Event", *Journal of Experiential Psychology: Applied*, 16 (1), 96-108.

International Olympic Committee (2010), Marketing Fact File 2010, Lausanne, IOC.

Meenaghan, Tony (1996), "Ambush Marketing – A Threat to Corporate Sponsorship", *Sloan Management Review*, 38 (1), 103-13.

Meenaghan, Tony (1998), "Ambush marketing: corporate strategy and consumer reaction." *Psychology and Marketing*, 15 (4), 305-22.

Petty, Richard E, Zakary L. Tormala, Pablo Brinol and W. Blair G. Jarvis (2006), "Implicit Ambivalence from Attitude Change: An Exploration of the PAST Model", *Journal of Personality and Social Psychology*, 90, 21-41.

Rydell, Robert J. and Allen R. McConnel (2006), "Understanding Implicit and Explicit Attitude Change: A Systems of Reasoning Analysis", *Journal of Personality and Social Psychology*, 45 (6), 995-1008.

Sandler, Dennis M. and David Shani (1989), "Olympic sponsorship vs. ambush marketing: who gets the gold?", *Journal of Advertising Research*, 29(4), 9-14.

Sloman, Steven A. (1996), "The Empirical Case for Two Systems of Reasoning", *Psychological Bulletin*, 119 (1), 3-22.

Zhao, Xinshu, John G. Lynch Jr., and Qimei Chen (2010), "Reconsidering Baron and Kenny: Myths and Truths about Mediation Analysis," Journal of Consumer Research, 37 (2), 197-206.

"I Would Want a Magic Gift":
Desire for Romantic Gift Giving and the Cultural Fantasies of Baby Boomers in Japan

Yuko Minowa, Long Island University, USA
Takeshi Matsui, Hitotsubashi University, Japan
Russell W. Belk, York University, Canada

EXTENDED ABSTRACT

Age and consumer identity are inseparable. Age cohorts, who grow up with the same sociohistorical context, experience the consequences of historical events in similar ways (Jaworski and Sauer 1985). The Baby Boomers in Japan, called *Dankai no Sedai*, or the nodule generation, is defined as the people born from 1947 to 1949. Having grown up in the zeitgeist of the post-war economic miracle, they are often characterized as self-expressive and individualistic consumers (Tsuda 1987). They were the first generation who enjoyed American consumer culture such as blue jeans and rock' n' roll music at a mass level, and were considered as the liberated generation who did not experience the economic problems their parents faced after the World War II (Iwama 1995). Influenced by the Western cultures, some of the Baby Boomers revealed these new values through gift giving practices. They experienced such consumer choice dilemmas for the first time. Among the choices they have faced, we examine their gift-giving behaviors with opposite sex, because identity projects are not atomized but social in nature. As such, gift-giving rituals are considered the appropriate context to understand how they create their identity as women or men through consumption.

In the Consumer Culture Theory tradition (Arnold and Thompson 2005), gift giving has been an important research topic. Most of the prior research has dealt with the North American context (e.g., Belk and Coon 1993; Fischer and Arnold 1990), and Japanese gift culture has not been much explored in spite of its heightened importance in Japan (Minowa and Gould 1999; Rupp 2003). Investigating the gift giving rituals of aging Japanese Baby Boomers is significant for at least three reasons. First, there has not been a study that explored romantic gift giving of aging consumers in Japan. Second, this study investigates the changing meaning of romantic gift giving and the factors that affect changing gift giving orientations throughout the consumer's life. By focusing on the Baby Boomers who have accumulated memories of gift giving over the longer life span, we investigate sociohistorical influences on gift giving practices instead of single gift giving occasions. Third, this study explores whether aging and romanticism are considered incompatible in Japan, because older people's roles are often focused on being grandparents (Kinly and Sivils 2000).

Based on depth interviews with 30 Baby Boom participants, we generated narratives about their experiences of romantic gift giving, gender socialization, memorable gift giving from their youth, and the zeitgeist of historical moments shared by their cohort. All participants were residents of Metropolitan Tokyo. They consisted of 15 males and 15 females, ranging in age from 60 to 65. Occupations varied from a retired former office worker to a taxi driver, a business owner, a college student, and housewives. We also conducted depth interviews with the eight Baby Boom Jr., (age from 37 to 40, four males), and with eight teens (17 and 18 years old, four males) to shed light on the Baby Boomer cohort's characteristics. Interviews lasted between 60 and 75 minutes. The analysis of the verbatim interview transcripts involved an iterative strategy (Spiggle 1994). Repeated ideas and similarities across the transcripts were analyzed by the research team. We developed a holistic understanding that yielded two factors affecting the gift giving orientations of the informants, resulting in taxonomy of four gift orientation types.

Gift giving orientations were influenced by the genealogy of gender domination – whether participants are from patriarchal or matriarchal families of origin– and whether they had euphoric or traumatic gift-giving experience and gender socialization in their youth. A two-by-two cross-classification yielded four types of gift giving orientations: reality adaptor, nostalgia indulger, fantasy seeker, and fantasy avoider (Figure 1). Reality Adapters, who are from matriarchal families who grew up having euphoric gift giving experiences, indicated that they adapt to the changing norms and practices of gift rituals in Japanese society. Nostalgia Indulgers are those from patriarchal families who had euphoric gift giving experiences. Because of the recent post-retirement economic depression, their future prospects are not optimistic and seem to regress toward the past. Fantasy Seekers are those from matriarchal families and who had traumatic socialization experiences. They expressed a strong desire for their dreams to come true through gifts from her romantic partners. Fantasy Avoiders are those from patriarchal families who had traumatic experiences and avoid gift practices that would lead to passionate romantic relationship.

Figure 1: Gift Giving Orientations of Baby Boomers in Japan Genealogy of Gender Domination

		Matrilineal/Matriarchal	Patrilineal/Patriarchal
Nature of Gift Experience	Euphoric	**Reality Adapter** "My daughter is dry and practical... no gift exchange, but it's her generation." Commensal experience important. Reflection of gender role in gift giving. Similarity of female givers and recipients to mother.	**Nostalgia Indulger** "I would like to have a magic gift... go back to my teens ... express my appreciation to the girl who gave me the scarf." Women in the past were virtuous givers.
Nature of Gift Experience	Traumatic	**Fantasy Seeker** "He remembers everything I say...and makes things into reality [by giving her as gifts]." Giving away gifts is like festival. Materialism emphasized.	**Fantasy Avoider** "I would hate a magic gift." "My father told me not to be obligated to men by not giving them a return gift." Gifts for steady communication. Gives social gifts to multiple men.

Our study reveals that the intra-cohort variation in romantic gift giving orientations for aging consumers is related to factors beyond historical change. While the fundamental components of romantic love – attraction and attachment - are primarily, panhuman rather than Western emotions, behavioral manifestations of love and emotional expressions are socially cultivated and culturally construed (Jankowiak 2008). As Jaworski and Sauer (1984) argue, cohorts carry the imprint of early socialization forward in time. We found that in regard to romantic gift giving, the socialization factors consist of gender and gift giving socializations. The meanings of romance and romantic gift giving are not static but changing, reflecting transformations in the consumer's life course (Otnes, Zolner, and Lowrey 1994).

Another significant finding from the present study is that intra-cohort variation in gift giving orientations is strongly associated with the genealogy of gender domination of the family in which the consumer grew up. The socially structured nature of family life has a lasting impact on consumption patterns. Japanese consumers from patriarchal families observed their fathers' domination as a reflection of *amae* or emotional dependency. A married woman may allow her husband to behave like *teishu kanpaku*, or "petty tyrant" but demand that he indulge them with gifts, services, and attention. From these women's perspective, performing as an inferior wife is insulting by today's standards and seems to have left them resentful as manifested in their giving practices. Finally, the conceptual link between romantic gift giving practice and sociohisorically constructed emotions is partly explained by the deployment of cultural fantasies for aging consumers while the meanings of gift giving rituals are renewed and have evolved through the cultural media (Bell 1997).

REFERENCES

Arnould, Eric J. and Craig J. Thompson (2005), "Consumer Culture Theory (CCT): Twenty Years of Research," *Journal of Consumer Research*, 31 (March), 868-82.

Belk, Russell W. and Gregory Coon (1993), "Gift Giving as Agapic Love: An Alternative to the Exchange Paradigm Based on Dating Experiences," *Journal of Consumer Research*, 20 (December), 393-417.

Bell, Catherine (1997), Ritual: Perspectives and Dimensions, New York: Oxford University Press.

Fischer, Eileen and Stephen J. Arnold (1990), "More than a Labor of Love: Gender Roles and Christmas Gift Shipping," *Journal of Consumer Research*, 17 (December), 333-45.

Iwama, Natsuki (1995), *Sengo wakamono sedai no kōbō: dankai, shinjinrui, dankai junia no kiseki* [The splendar of the post-war youth culture: The locus of the Baby Boomers, the new breed, and the Baby Boomer Juniors], Tokyo: Nihon Keizai Shinbunsha.

Jankowiak, William R., ed. (2008), *Intimacies: Love and Sex Across Cultures*, New York: Columbia University Press.

Jaworski, Bernard and William J. Sauer (1985), "Cohort Variation," in *Advances in Consumer Research* Volume 12, eds. Elizabeth C. Hirschman and Morris B. Holbrook, Provo, UT: Association for Consumer Research, 32-36.

Kinley, Tammy and Linda Sivils (2000), "Gift Giving Behavior of Grandmothers," *Journal of Segmentation in Marketing*, 4 (1), 53-70.

Minowa, Yuko and Stephen J. Gould (1999), "'Love My Gift, Love Me or is it Love Me, Love My Gift': A Study of The Cultural Construction of Love and Gift-Giving among Japanese Couples," in *Advances in Consumer Research*, Vol. 26, ed. Eric J. Arnould and Linda M. Scott, Provo, UT: Association for Consumer Research, 119-24.

Otnes, Cele, Kyle Zolner, and Tina M. Lowrey (1994), "In-laws and Outlaws: The Impact of Divorce and Remarriage Upon Christmas Gift Exchange," in *Advances in Consumer Research* Vol. 21, ed. Chris T. Allen and Deborah Roedder John, Provo, UT: Association for Consumer Research, 25-29.

Rupp, Katherine (2003), *Gift-Giving in Japan: Cash, Connections, Cosmologies*, Stanford, CA: Stanford University Press.

Spiggle, Susan (1994), "Analysis and Interpretation of Qualitative Data in Consumer Research," *Journal of Consumer Research*, 21 (3), 491-503.

Tsuda, Masumi (1987), *Shinsedai sararīman no seikatsu to iken: "Dankai no sedai" kara "shin jinrui" made* [The life and opinion of the new generation of salaried men: From "the Baby Boomers" to "new breed"], Tokyo: Tōyō Keizai.

My LV bag is a Counterfeit:
The Role of Regulatory Focus on Consumer Deceptive Behavior

So Hyun Bae, Nanyang Technological University, Singapore
Sharon Ng, Nanyang Technological University, Singapore

EXTENDED ABSTRACT

Imagine that you are carrying a counterfeit Louis Vuitton bag and you run into someone you know. She starts asking about your bag. Will you tell her that your bag is a counterfeit? Admitting that the bag is a counterfeit would defeat the signaling purpose of using a counterfeit product, but not admitting that the bag is a counterfeit might lead to a potentially embarrassing situation when the deceit is uncovered. This poses a dilemma to most people and prediction of how one would react is far from straight forward.

The consumption of counterfeit luxury brands is a frequently used deceptive strategy to signal status (Van Kempen 2003). People who have a need for status but cannot afford or are not willing to purchase genuine goods are prone to buy counterfeit products (Han, Nunes, and Drèze 2010). However, why are some consumers more likely to admit the truth to others about their counterfeit luxury goods? What situational factors drive consumers to admit or deceive others? On a broader level, how do consumers manage such deceptive behavior? This research aims to address a small slice of this question by examining the impact of regulatory goals and relationship status on consumers' propensity to engage in deceptive behavior.

Regulatory focus theory proposes two systems of self-regulation: a prevention focus that involves security needs, strong oughts and minimizing losses, and a promotion focus that involves nurturance needs, strong ideals and maximizing gains (Higgins 1997). Therefore, prevention-focused people emphasize their obligations and duties to fulfill their needs for security and safety whereas promotion-focused people emphasize hopes and aspirations to fulfill their needs for advancement and gains (Higgins 1997). Furthermore, promotion-focused people are more willing to take risks whereas prevention-focused people are more risk averse (Righetti, Finkenauer, and Rusbult 2011). In this research, we suggest that regulatory focus will interact with relationship status (i.e., in-group vs. out-group) to influence whether consumers will engage in deceptive behavior.

Prior research shows that people have fewer tendencies to engage in deceptive behavior toward in-group members compared to out-group members. According to DePaulo and Kashy (1998), people are less likely to lie in close relationships than in casual relationships for several reasons. First, deceptive behavior undermines close relationship ideals (e.g., openness). Second, since people in close relationships know each other and meet frequently, they may fear that close people will discover the truth more easily (Neziek 1995). Third, people have less confidence about lying to familiar people than to unfamiliar people. Though this is generically true, we argue that promotion and prevention focused consumers will react quite differently to deception to in-group (versus out-group).

Recall from the discussion that prevention-focused people focus on their duties, responsibilities, and ought-self. In the interpersonal context, they should be honest and truthful to their friends because it is an interpersonal duty and obligation. Lying and deceptive behavior is undesirable because it threatens respect and trust, thereby negatively impacting interpersonal relationships (Tyler, Feldman, and Reichert 2006). Therefore, we propose that prevention-focused consumers are likely to admit to their friends (in-group members) that they are using counterfeits in order to fulfill their obligations to their friends. Furthermore, since they are risk averse, they are also less likely to lie to their friends whom know them well and they interact frequently as there is a higher probability that the deceit is uncovered. However, since they do not feel the same duties and obligations to acquaintances (out-group members) and do not interact with them frequently, they are less likely to admit the truth to them.

What about promotion-focused consumers? Since they emphasize achievement and accomplishment, and are generally more willing to take risks to achieve gains, they are less likely to admit the truth, even when there is a chance of their deception being detected by friends. Therefore, regardless whether a target person is a friend or an acquaintance, promotion-focused consumers are less likely to admit the truth. Thus, we propose that prevention-focused consumers are more likely to admit that they are using counterfeit luxury goods to a friend than to an acquaintance, while promotion-focused consumers are less likely to admit regardless of the type of target person. Two studies were conducted to test the hypothesis.

Experiment 1 had a 2(regulatory focus: prevention focus vs. promotion focus) x 2 (target person: friend vs. acquaintance) between-subject design, with 79 female participants. First, regulatory focus was manipulated by using an anagram task. Following this, participants read a scenario whereby a target person (either friend or acquaintance) saw their counterfeit bags and asked them about it. Participants were asked to indicate the extent to which they would admit to the target person that the bag is a counterfeit. Findings showed that prevention-focused consumers were more likely to admit that they were using a counterfeit product to a friend than to an acquaintance. On the other hand, promotion-focused consumers showed no difference in their propensity to admit that the bag was a counterfeit to a friend or an acquaintance.

The design of experiment 2 was similar to that of experiment 1, except that culture was primed instead of regulatory focus. Extensive research (e.g., Lee, Aaker, and Gardner 2000) has shown that people living in Western (independent) cultures are promotion-focused, while people living in Eastern (interdependent) cultures are prevention-focused. To test if the same pattern of results may be obtained using a different form of regulatory focus manipulation, culture was used as a proxy for regulatory focus. The experiment had a 2 (culture priming: US vs. China) x 2 (target person: friend vs. acquaintance) between-subject design, with 79 female participants. Culture was primed by using 12 cultural icons. Experiment 2 found that participants primed by Chinese icons were more likely to admit to a friend than to an acquaintance that the bag was a counterfeit. On the other hand, participants primed by US pictures showed no difference in the likelihood of admission between the friend and acquaintance conditions.

In summary, our two studies demonstrate that regulatory focus is a key factor in understanding consumer deceptive behavior.

REFERENCES

DePaulo, Bella M., and Deborah A. Kashy (1998), "Everyday Lies in Close and Casual Relationships", *Journal of Personality and Social Psychology*, 74 (1), 63-79.

Han, Young Jee, Joseph C. Nunes, and Xavier, Drèze (2010), "Signaling Status with Luxury Goods: The Role of Brand Prominence", *Journal of Marketing*, 74 (4), 15-30.

Higgins, E. Tony (1997), "Beyond Pleasure and Pain", *American Psychology*, 52 (12), 1280-1300.

Lee, Y. Angela, Jennifer L. Aaker, and Wendi L. Gardner (2000), "The Pleasures and Pains of Distinct Self-Construals: The Role of Interdependence in Regulatory Focus", *Journal of Personality and Social Psychology*, 78 (6), 1122-34.

Neziek, John B. (1995), "Social Construction, Gender/ Sex Similarity and Social Interaction in Close Personal Relationships", *Journal of Social and Personal Relationships*, 12 (4), 503-20.

Righetti, Francesca, Catrin Finkenauer, and Caryl Rusbult (2011), "The Benefits of Interpersonal Regulatory Fit for Individual Goal Pursuit", *Journal of Personality and Social Psychology*, 101 (4), 720-36.

Tyler, M. James, Robert S. Feldman, and Andreas Reichert (2006), "The Price of Deceptive Behavior: Disliking and Lying to People who Lie to Us", *Journal of Experimental Social Psychology*, 42 (1), 69-77.

Van Kempen, Luuk (2003), "Fooling the Eye of the Beholder: Deceptive Status Signaling among the Poor in Developing Countries", *Journal of International Development*, 15 (2), 157-77.

Implicit Measures of Motivation: Convergent, Discriminant and Predictive Validity

Alexandra Kraus, Aarhus University, Denmark
Joachim Scholderer, Aarhus University, Denmark

EXTENDED ABSTRACT

The incentive salience theory (Berridge, 1996, 2009; Berridge & Robinson, 1995, 2003) and the differentiation between two neurophysiological separate reward components – motivational wanting (incentive salience of the reward) and evaluative liking (hedonic pleasure associated with the reward) – provides an elegant account for food reward, at least in animal studies. The rather counterintuitive idea that it is sometimes possible to "want" something that is not "liked" or the other way around has inspired many scholars in developing different measures to disentangle both components of food reward in man. Recently, that movement has been criticised as unnecessary and impossible (Havermans, 2011), whereas others replied that it is possible to distinguish both components in human (Finlayson & Dalton, 2012). In the past decade different, rather implicit motivational measures were developed (e.g., Ebstein et al., 2003; Finlayson, King, & Blundell, 2008; Giesen, Havermans, & Jansen, 2010), however, none completely tested under "fair" conditions (i.e., stimuli that do not evoke different social desirability; implicit measures for wanting and liking components).

The aim of this research was to develop and validate implicit measures of motivation that could meet that criticism and that could finally be used as valid measures in consumer research. Therefore, we started out with two existing implicit measures – the implicit association test (IAT; Greenwald, McGhee, & Schwartz, 1998) and a recent published procedural variation, the recoding free IAT (IAT-RF; Rothermund, Teige-Mocigemba, Gast, & Wentura, 2009). The latter test is argued to prevent recoding strategies of the IAT; however, its predictive validity has only been examined in one further study (Houben, Rothermund, & Wiers, 2009). Both paradigms were originally designed to measure the relative strength of associations between two evaluative (e.g., positive, negative) and two target concepts (e.g., two products) to finally asses implicit attitudes. In order to develop measures of implicit motivation both paradigms needed slight modifications. Hence, the two opposing evaluative concepts were replaced with two motivational tendencies (approach, avoidance) and consequently both implicit motivation tests shall be named M-IAT and M-IAT-RF to address this modification. Furthermore, two target products were chosen that would create strong preferences but that would not evoke biases through social desirability or self presentation. Therefore, we decided on wine gum and liquorice – both belonging to the same product category, are equally unhealthy, sized, priced, and nevertheless, only differ in sensory dimensions. The final four concepts were represented by verbal and visual stimuli and reaction-times were recorded as dependent variables. Three studies were conducted.

The aim of Study 1 was to test and validate both measures, whereas Study 2 focused specifically on the discriminant validity of motivational versus evaluative versions of both paradigms. The M-IAT-RF was further validated with different stimuli material in Study 3. All three studies included explicit measures of wanting and liking (visual analogue scales) and a relative behavioural preference was measured as a predictive validation criterion. In Study 1 and 3 this was based on unobtrusive observation of the amount of target products consumed during the session. In Study 2 it was based on simple choices of the two products.

Study 1. 132 native Danish speakers were tested in a two-group between-subjects design (M-IAT vs. M-IAT-RF) with random alloca-tion. The experimental sessions were divided into three parts: first a pre-test (paper-pencil), then the computer-based implicit motivation test (either M-IAT or M-IAT-RF), and finally a post-test (paper-pencil). All experimental sessions were held individually. Difference scores were calculated from reaction-times in the same way as is usually done in IAT studies (Greenwald et al., 1998; Greenwald, Nosek, & Banaji, 2003). In addition, a latent-difference bifactor model was fitted to the log-transformed, error-corrected reaction-times to obtain a more stringent psychometric representation of the measures. The model was a refined version of the model used by Blanton, Jaccard, Gonzales, and Christie (2006), separating the latent true difference in implicit motivation from common method-variance. The model-fit was excellent for both implicit tests. The M-IAT-RF was highly predictive of behaviour (D-score: $r = .32$; latent-true-difference: $\beta = .58$) and showed strong convergent validity with explicit measures of wanting (D-score: $r = .29$; latent-true-difference: $\beta = .54$). Furthermore, its discriminant validity with explicit measures of liking was satisfactory (D-score: $r = .19$; latent-true-difference: $\beta = .37$). In comparison, the M-IAT was also strongly related to explicit measures of wanting (D-score: $r = .50$; latent-true-difference: $\beta = .53$) but only weakly related to behaviour (D-score: $r = .24$; latent-true-difference: $\beta = .26$). Its discriminant validity with respect to explicit measures of liking was only partially satisfactory (D-score: $r = .48$; latent-true-difference: $\beta = .50$).

Study 2. To test the discriminant validity of implicit measures of motivation (M-IAT and M-IAT-RF) versus implicit measures of evaluation (E-IAT and E-IAT-RF that are commonly used in attitude research), a two-group between-subjects design with random allocation was used. Participants ($N = 181$) either completed two IATs (M-IAT and E-IAT) or two IAT-RFs, respectively. Test order was counterbalanced between subjects. The discriminant validity of the IAT-RF procedures was excellent. The D-score calculated from the M-IAT-RF did not correlate significantly with the D-score calculated from the E-IAT-RF ($r = .23$, *n.s.*). Furthermore, the M-IAT-RF was predictive of behaviour (D-score: $r = .28$; latent-true-difference: $\beta = .70$) whereas the E-IAT-RF was less (D-score: $r = .26$; latent-true-difference: $\beta = .47$). In comparison, the discriminant validity of the IAT procedures was less satisfactory ($r = .40$, $p < .01$) and both IATs were also not predictive of behaviour.

Study 3. To further validate the M-IAT-RF different stimulus material was applied in Study 3 ($N = 40$): wine gum and liquorice were replaced by broader concepts of fruit and chocolate and the behavioural criterion was based on the consumed amount of offered fruit (pieces of banana, apple, and grapes) and chocolate (milk, dark, and hazelnut). Corroborating the result of Study 1 and 2, the M-IAT-RF procedure was highly predictive of behaviour, and showed strong convergent as well as satisfying discriminant validities.

Taken together, it is possible to develop implicit measures of motivation with convergent validities that were as high as those commonly found for implicit measures of evaluation (for a meta-analysis, see Greenwald et al., 2009) and excellent psychometric characteristics. Remarkable, the recently published and slightly modified M-IAT-RF was always superior to the M-IAT, with high predictive validities and clearly distinguishable from implicit measures of evaluation.

REFERENCES

Berridge, K. C. (1996). Food reward. Brain substrates of wanting and liking. *Neuroscience & Biobehavioral Reviews, 20,* 1-25.

Berridge, K. C. (2009). 'Liking' and 'wanting' food rewards. Brain substrates and roles in eating disorders. *Physiology & Behavior, 97,* 537-550.

Berridge, K. C., & Robinson, T. E. (2003). Parsing reward. *Trends in Neurosciences, 26,* 507-513.

Berridge, K. C., & Robinson, T. E. (1995). The mind of an addicted brain. Neural sensitization of wanting versus liking. *Current Directions in Psychological Science, 4,* 71-76.

Blanton, H., Jaccard, J., Gonzales, P., & Christie, C. (2006). Decoding the implicit association test: Implications for criterion prediction. *Journal of Experimental Social Psychology, 42,* 192-212.

Epstein, L. H., Truesdale, R., Wojcik, A., Paluch, R. A., & Raynor, H. A. (2003). Effects of deprivation on hedonics and reinforcing value of food. *Physiology & Behavior, 78,* 221-227.

Finlayson, G., & Dalton, M. (2012). Current progress in the assessment of 'liking' vs. 'wanting' food in human appetite. Comment on '"You say it's liking, I say it's wanting...". On the difficulty of disentangling food reward in man'. *Appetite, 58,* 373-378.

Finlayson, G., King, N., & Blundell, J. (2008). The role of implicit wanting in relation to explicit liking and wanting for food: Implications for appetite control. *Appetite, 50,* 120-127.

Giesen, J. C. A. H., Havermans, R. C., & Jansen, A. (2010a). Substituting snacks with strawberries and sudokus. Does restraint matter? *Health Psychology, 29,* 222-226.

Greenwald, A., McGhee, D.E., & Schwartz, J.L.K. (1998). Measuring individual differences in implicit cognition: The implicit association test. *Journal of Personality and Social Psychology, 74,* 1464-1480.

Greenwald, A., Nosek, B., & Banaji, M. (2003). Understanding and using the Implicit Association Test: I. An improved scoring algorithm. *Journal of Personality and Social Psychology, 85,* 197-216.

Greenwald, A., Poehlman, T., Uhlmann, E., & Banaji, M. (2009). Understanding and using the Implicit Association Test: III. Meta-analysis of predictive validity. *Journal of Personality and Social Psychology, 97,* 17-41.

Havermans, R. C. (2011). "You Say it's Liking, I Say it's Wanting...". On the difficulty of disentangling food reward in man. *Appetite, 57,* 286-294.

Houben, K., Rothermund, K.,& Wiers, R. W. (2009). Predicting alcohol use with a recoding-free variant of the Implicit Association test. *Addictive Behaviors, 34,* 487-489.

Rothermund, K., Teige-Mocigemba, S., Gast, A., & Wentura, D. (2009). Minimizing the influence of recoding in the Implicit Association Test: The Recoding-Free Implicit Association Test (IAT-RF). *The Quarterly Journal of Experimental Psychology, 62,* 84-98.

Exposure to Food Temptation Improves
Children's Resistance to Similar Food Temptations

Aiste Grubliauskiene, KU Leuven, Belgium
Siegfried Dewitte, KU Leuven, Belgium
Luk Warlop, KU Leuven, Belgium and BI Norwegian Business School, Norway

EXTENDED ABSTRACT

If sweets are present at home, do people consume more of them? The intuitive answer is yes (Chandon and Wansink 2002; Painter, Wansink, and Hieggelke 2002). This expectation is even stronger for children because they are thought to lack elaborative self-regulation strategies and may have not yet developed a clear long-term goal (Mischel and Underwood 1974). We will show, however, how pre-exposure to food temptation actually decreases the consumption of attractive but unhealthy products in children. Being exposed to food temptation without consuming it has been already shown to reduce adults' desire and consumption in a subsequent tempting situation (Dewitte, Bruyneel, and Geyskens 2009; Geyskens, Dewitte, Pandelaere, and Warlop 2008). So far, there has been little research into the effect of pre-exposure in children. Demonstrating the pre-exposure effect in children would suggest that self-control strategies during the exposure are more basic. It also would have important implications for theories on the emergence of self-regulation (e.g. Egan, Santos, and Bloom 2007) and for public policy, which often assumes that restricting access to unhealthy food is the best way to curb obesogenic consumption (Wardle 1990).

So far, conflicting results have been revealed regarding exposure to temptation. Earlier studies (Mischel, Ebbesen, and Zeiss 1972; Mischel and Ebbesen 1970) have demonstrated that food temptation availability reduces self-control in children by decreasing their willingness to wait for a larger reward. More recent findings suggest that self-control improves when a temptation is present (Myrseth, Fishbach, and Trope 2009; Zhang, Huang, and Broniarczyk 2009). A possible explanation for this might be that when exposed to a temptation, people (at least adults) feel conflict and invest efforts to resist a temptation. Another possible explanation for self-control enhancement is that a temptation may be perceived in a different way. A symbolic mode of presentation encouraged children to think more about cognitive rather than affective qualities (Metcalfe and Mischel 1999) and thus facilitated self-control by increasing children's willingness to wait (Mischel and Moore 1973).

Obviously, the way temptation is constructed in the mind influences self-control (Mischel and Moore 1973). After pre-exposure to temptation in a situation where consumption is not appropriate, people seem to activate their self-control operations and facilitate the repetition of these operations when another similar tempting opportunity is present. In one study, after being exposed to a sweet temptation, people reduced the importance of sweetness (Grubliauskiene, Dewitte, and Warlop, in prep.). Thus re-construction of essential temptation dimensions may support the subsequent resistance to temptation. These self-control strategies are less likely in young children. Aiming to resist a temptation, 7 – 11 year old children have been shown to employ simple distraction strategies, such as covering their eyes, but they still do not use cognitive distractions that transform a temptation (Demetriou 2000). Lack of cognitive skills should not prevent successful self-control after pre-exposure if self-control processes are rather simple and automatic. Indeed, it has been shown that pairing positive pictures with a no-go task lowers picture evaluations (Veling, Holland, and Knippenberg 2008). Even 4-year-olds decrease preferences for an unchosen option (Egan et al. 2007). This paper attempts to show that children, while still lacking sophisticated

self-regulation skills, are able to automatically change the meaning of products and thus resist a temptation after pre-exposure to it.

In two experiments, we exposed participants to temptation in two successive phases. We manipulated the availability of the temptation (physical or symbolic or not available) during pre-exposure in the first phase. To ensure a self-control conflict, children had to construct a flower from candy (physical pre-exposure condition) or construct a flower from Lego® bricks while a photo with a child happily eating chocolate was present (symbolic pre-exposure condition). In the control condition, children had to construct a flower from Lego® bricks. The second task differed across studies. In Study 1, children (7 – 11) tasted a different type of candy for evaluation, and the quantity consumed served as a measure of children's self-control. In Study 2, children (7 – 8) had a choice between a healthy product (strawberry) and an unhealthy product (chocolate) that were presented in pictures. We investigated differences in total fixation duration (Sutterlin, Brunner, and Opwis 2008) as a measure of preference.

In Study 1, the effect of gender was marginally significant ($F (1, 51) = 3.26, p < 0.1$) which is common in eating experiments, with boys eating more than girls. As expected, there was an effect of pre-exposure to temptation ($F (2, 50) = 3.42, p < .05$) on candy consumption. Simple effects showed that both physical ($M = 1.02$) and, to a lesser extent, symbolic ($M = 1.05$) temptation reduced the consumption as compared to a control condition ($M = 1.34$). These results show that pre-exposure to temptation enhances self-control in children. Study 2 used eye tracking to explore the preference construction process after pre-exposure effect. Findings from Study 2 suggest that pre-exposure to a temptation affects automatic preference. In the physical and in the symbolically presented temptation conditions, fixation duration on a healthy product was longer ($M = 1.42, M = 1.39$ respectively) than in the control condition ($M = 1.07$, physical: $F (1, 69) = 11.49, p < .05$, symbolic: $F (1, 69) = 7.8, p < .05$). Results suggest that healthy food gains attractiveness after exposure to temptation. There were no significant effects for unhealthy products.

Children's self-control increases after pre-exposure to a real or symbolically presented temptation, thereby replicating findings in adults, and suggesting that this type of self-regulation emerges early on in life. Eye-tracking measures show that pre-exposure to a real or symbolically presented temptation increases the attractiveness of healthy options whereas it does not affect the attractiveness of unhealthy options. This pattern may explain why pre-exposure leads to low vice consumption in pre-exposure condition.

REFERENCES

Chandon, Pierre and Brian Wansink (2002), "When Are Stockpiled Products Consumed Faster? A Convenience-Salience Framework of Postpurchase Consumption Incidence and Quantity," *Journal of Marketing Research*, 39 (3), 321-335.

Demetriou, Andreas (2000), "Organization and development of self-understanding and self-regulation", in Monique Boekaerts, Paul Pintrich and Moshe Zeidner (Eds.), *Handbook of self-regulation*, San Diego, CA, Academic press, 209 – 251.

Dewitte, Siegfried, Sabrina Bruyneel, and Kelly Geyskens (2009), "Self-Regulation Enhances Self-Regulation in Subsequent Consumer Decisions Involving Similar Response Conflicts," *Journal of Consumer Research*, 36 (3), 394 – 405.

Egan, Louisa C., Laurie R. Santos, and Paul Bloom (2007), "The Origins of Cognitive Dissonance. Evidence from Children and Monkeys," *Psychological Science*, 18 (11), 978 – 983.

Geyskens, Kelly, Siegfried Dewitte, Mario Pandelaere, and Luk Warlop (2008), "Tempt Me Just a Little Bit More: The Effect of Prior Food Temptation Actionability on Goal Activation and Consumption," *Journal of Consumer Research*, 35 (4), 600-610.

Grubliauskiene, Aiste, Siegfried Dewitte, and Luk Warlop, "Self-Inferred Norms reduce Desire and Consumption through Changing Product Perceptions," in preparation.

Metcalfe, Janet and Walter Mischel (1999), "A Hot/Cool-System Analysis of Delay of Gratification: Dynamics of Willpower," *Psychological Review*, 106 (1), 3 – 19.

Mischel, Walter, and Ebbe B. Ebbesen (1970), „Attention in Delay of Gratification," *Journal of Personality and Social Psychology*, 16 (2), 329 – 337.

Mischel, Walter, Ebbe B. Ebbesen, and Antonette R. Zeiss (1972), "Cognitive and Attentional Mechanisms in Delay of Gratification," *Journal of Personality and Social Psychology*, 21 (2), 204 – 218.

Mischel, Walter and Bill Underwood (1974), "Instrumental Ideation in Delay of Gratification," *Child Development*, 45 (4), 1083 – 1088.

Mischel, Walter and Bert Moore (1973), "Effects of Attention to Symbolically Presented Rewards on Self-Control," *Journal of Personality and Social Psychology*, 28 (2), 172 – 179.

Myrseth, Kristian O. R., Ayelet Fishbach, and Yaacov Trope (2009), "Counteractive Self-Control. When Making Temptation Available Makes Temptation Less Tempting," *Psychological Science*, 20 (2), 159 – 163.

Painter, James E., Brian Wansink, and Julie B. Hieggelke (2002), "How visibility and convenience influence candy consumption," *Appetite*, 38, 237 – 238.

Sutterlin, Bernadette, Thomas A. Brunner and Klaus Opwis (2008), "Eye-tracking the cancelation and focus model for preference judgments," *Journal of Experimental Psychology* 44, 904 – 911.

Veling, Harm, Rob W. Holland, and Ad van Knippenberg (2008), "When approach motivation and behavioral inhibition collide: Behavior regulation through stimulus devaluation," *Journal of Experimental Social Psychology*, 44, 1013 – 1019.

Wardle, J. (1990), "Overeating: A regulatory behavior in restrained eaters," *Appetite*, 14, 133 – 136.

Zhang, Ying, Szu-Chi Huang, and Susan M. Broniarczyk (2010), "Counteractive construal in Consumer Goal Pursuit," *Journal of Consumer Research,* 37(June), 129 – 142.

Negative Scope Sensitivity:
The Collapse of Feeling-Based Valuation for Multiple Desirable Objects

Kuangjie Zhang, INSEAD, Singapore
Steven Sweldens, INSEAD, France
Monica Wadhwa, INSEAD, Singapore

EXTENDED ABSTRACT

Dual-process theories have identified two distinct consumers' valuation processes, distinguishing between a feeling-based valuation process and a calculation-based valuation process (Epstein 1994; Hsee and Rottenstreich 2004; Metcalfe and Mischel 1999). A calculation-based valuation process relies on a rational and rule-based assessment of the target products, and displays normal scope sensitivity such that more products are valued more. A feeling-based valuation process, on the other hand, is crucially dependent on consumers' integral affective response towards the products and can be surprisingly insensitive to the scope of appetitive objects. For example, consumers display the same willingness-to-pay for five versus 10 Madonna CDs and donate the same amount to save one versus four panda(s) (Hsee and Rottenstreich 2004), a phenomenon termed *scope insensitivity*.

Extending the scope of this stream of research, we argue that increasing numbers of different desirable objects can ironically reduce consumers' feeling-based valuation for these objects. We derive our conceptualization from research on the role of mental imagery in feelings. Specifically, prior research suggests that consumers' affective responses towards the objects is crucially determined by the concreteness and vividness of mental imagery related to these objects (Metcalfe and Mischel 1999; Pham 2007), which form the basis of consumers' feeling-based valuation. However, mental imagery requires processing resources, which are limited in nature and thereby restrain consumers' ability to form concrete and vivid mental images of multiple different objects simultaneously (MacInnis and Price 1987; Shiv and Huber 2000). Therefore, we propose that the degree of concreteness and vividness of the mental images that consumers can generate deteriorates as the number of different objects increases. This leads to our hypothesis that consumers' feeling-based valuation of multiple different desirable objects can be lower than the feeling-based valuation of a single object from that set, a phenomenon we term as *negative scope sensitivity*.

We examined our negative scope sensitivity hypothesis in five studies. In Study-1, we used an implicit measure (adapted from Custers and Aarts 2005) to assess whether consumers are more motivated and thus work harder to acquire a single desirable reward (vs. two equally desirable rewards). After completing several unrelated questionnaires, participants learned that the experiment was almost over and would be followed by one more task (a mouse-click task). They were further told that subsequent to this last task they would receive a lottery ticket entitling them to win a reward. Half of the participants were told that the reward was a movie ticket (single-reward condition), whereas the other half learnt that the reward was a movie ticket plus a music CD (two-reward condition). The movie ticket and the music CD were pretested to be equally desirable. Participants then completed the mouse-click task, wherein they had to click on the computer screens according to a specified pattern. Our dependent variable was the speed with which participants completed this mouse-click task. Consistent with our hypothesis, participants in the single-reward condition were more motivated and worked significantly faster on the mouse-click task than participants in the two-reward condition, even though the total monetary value of the two rewards is twice as high as the value of the single reward.

In Study-2, we examine whether negative scope sensitivity is indeed restricted to feeling-based valuations and does not occur when consumers engage in a calculation-based valuation process. Specifically, we employed a priming task (Hsee and Rottenstreich 2004) to manipulate consumers' reliance on feelings versus calculation. Subsequently, participants were asked to imagine that a local museum was holding an art exhibition, which featured, among others, one painting (vs. two paintings) from the celebrated artist Salvador Dalí. In the single-painting condition, one of the two paintings (pretested to be equally attractive) was randomly chosen and displayed, whereas in the two-painting condition, both paintings were displayed. Our results show that participants who were primed to rely on feelings (vs. calculation) reported higher intention and greater willingness-to-pay for attending the exhibition that featured only one painting (vs. two paintings). However, we observed an opposite effect for participants who were primed to rely on calculation.

Further, prior research suggests that consumers are more likely to use mental imagery to "see how it feels" when they have a hedonic consumption goal rather than a utilitarian consumption goal (Pham 1998). This logic formed the basis of Study-3. Employing the art exhibition scenario in the previous study, we manipulated the consumption goal by asking participants to imagine they wanted to enjoy themselves after a week of hard work (hedonic goal) or they wanted to enrich their knowledge of art history (utilitarian goal). We show that participants with a hedonic (vs. utilitarian) consumption goal reported higher intention and greater willingness-to-pay for attending the exhibition that featured only one painting (vs. two paintings).

In the next two studies, we provide direct support for the role of mental imagery in negative scope sensitivity. Specifically, we argue that consumers who have a greater reliance on mental imagery are more likely to exhibit negative scope sensitivity. In Study-4, we examine the individual differences related to the reliance on mental imagery. Participants first evaluated a vacation package highlighting either one or two appealing vacation experience(s). In the single-vacation-experience condition, the vacation package featured either a picture of snorkeling in the tropical seascapes or a picture of a beautiful ancient temple; whereas in the two-vacation-experience condition, both pictures were featured in the vacation package. Next, participants responded to a Style-of-Processing Scale (Childers, Houston, and Heckler 1985), which distinguishes between individuals with a disposition to construct mental images when processing information (visualizers) and individuals with a disposition to process information semantically without forming images (verbalizers). We show that participants reported higher willingness-to-pay for the vacation package featuring only one vacation experience (vs. two vacation experiences). More importantly, this effect was only observed for visualizers but not for verbalizers.

In Study-5 we directly manipulate the reliance on mental imagery and show that participants who were encouraged to rely on mental imagery reported higher willingness-to-pay for the vacation package featuring only one vacation experience (vs. two vacation experiences). However, this effect disappeared when participants were discouraged from using mental imagery.

In summary, our findings demonstrate that consumers' feeling-based valuation can exhibit negative scope sensitivity, according to which the valuation of a set of multiple different desirable objects can ironically be lower than the valuation of a single object from that set. We discuss the theoretical and practical importance of our findings.

REFERENCES

Childers, Terry L., Michael J. Houston, and Susan E. Heckler (1985), "Measurement of Individual Differences in Visual versus Verbal Information Processing," *Journal of Consumer Research,* 12 (2), 125-34.

Custers, Ruud and Henk Aarts (2005), "Positive Affect as Implicit Motivator: On the Nonconscious Operation of Behavioral Goals," *Journal of Personality and Social Psychology,* 89 (2), 129-42.

Hsee, Chris K. and Yuval Rottenstreich (2004), "Music, Pandas, and Muggers: On the Affective Psychology of Value," *Journal of Experimental Psychology: General,* 133 (1), 25-30.

MacInnis, Deborah and Linda Price (1987), "The Role of Imagery in Information Processing: Review and Extensions," *Journal of Consumer Research,* 13 (4), 473-91.

Metcalfe, Janet and Walter Mischel (1999), "A Hot/Cool-System Analysis of Delay of Gratification: Dynamics of Willpower." *Psychological Review,* 106 (1), 3-19.

Pham, Michel Tuan (1998), "Representativeness, Relevance, and the Use of Feelings in Decision Making," *Journal of Consumer Research,* 25 (2), 144-60.

Pham, Michel Tuan (2007), "Emotion and Rationality: A Critical Review and Interpretation of Empirical Evidence," *Review of General Psychology,* 11 (2), 155-78.

Shiv, Baba and Joel Huber (2000), "The Impact of Anticipating Satisfaction on Consumer Choice," *Journal of Consumer Research,* 27 (2), 202-16.

A Penny Saved is Another Penny Spurned
The Effect of Promotions on Consumer Impatience

Franklin Shaddy, Columbia University, USA
Leonard Lee, Columbia University, USA

EXTENDED ABSTRACT

Consumers enjoy receiving discounts, and retailers frequently appeal to their desire to save money by offering promotions. The present work investigates a potential consequence of exposure to promotions: impatience. Specifically, we propose that promotions heighten consumers' desire for rewards (Wadhwa, Shiv, and Nowlis 2008); such a reward-seeking tendency in turn generates the desire for instant gratification and thus, impatience (Li 2008). Consequently, promotions increase impatience in consumers such that they are both more willing to spend money to avoid waiting and less willing to wait to obtain additional money.

Our proposed account for the impatience consequence of promotions, based on the reward-seeking mindset that promotions trigger, suggests that people with higher predisposed sensitivity toward reward cues should react more intensely to promotions, which possess high incentive value (Chandon, Wansink, and Laurent 2000). In particular, one relevant measure is the behavioral activation system (BAS) scale, which has been linked to affective response tendencies for impending rewards (Carver and White 1994; Gray 1994). We therefore expect any relationship between promotions and impatience to be moderated by BAS sensitivity; that is, the effect should be stronger for people who are high, rather than low, on the BAS scale.

In **Experiment 1**, we tested whether exposure to promotions yields greater impatience by examining willingness-to-pay (WTP) to avoid waiting. We employed a single-factor (prime: *promotions* or *control*) between-subjects design with 72 participants from a national online pool. Participants were first asked to evaluate a poster, which displayed a collection of common products for sale (e.g., candy, chips, gum, etc.), according to several criteria (e.g., products, prices, informational content, etc.). While both posters included the names, prices, and images of the same set of 10 products, participants in the *promotions* condition were also shown the regular undiscounted prices alongside each product; this additional information increased the salience of the price discounts. Next, in a purportedly unrelated follow-up questionnaire, all participants answered a series of questions in response to a hypothetical scenario describing an opportunity to avoid a wait time by paying more (Leclerc, Schmitt, and Dube 1995). Specifically, participants were asked to imagine that while waiting for a bus, they could save waiting time if they were willing to pay extra money. Participants were then asked how much money they were willing to spend to avoid wait times of 30, 60, and 90 minutes, respectively.

Consistent with our hypothesis, higher WTP values for participants in the *promotions* condition were observed. An analysis of variance (ANOVA) revealed a significant main effect of the poster version on overall WTP to save time ($p = .012$). WTP was higher in the *promotions* condition than the *control* condition at each of the 30-minute wait time increments ($p = .023$, $p = .005$, and $p = .038$, respectively).

The next experiment was designed to test the hypothesized reward-seeking account for the observed effect in Experiment 1. Based on this account, while exposure to promotions might generate impatience and induce greater WTP in order to avoid waiting, the relationship between promotions and impatience may also vary by BAS sensitivity, given the high incentive value of promotions (Chandon et al. 2000). Therefore, in **Experiment 2**, besides attempting to conceptually replicate the results in Experiment 1 by utilizing a more subtle experimental manipulation and a different measure for impatience, we also captured BAS sensitivity to assess its moderating effect on the causal relationship between promotions and impatience.

Ninety-three participants from a national online pool were randomly assigned to either a *promotions* or *control* condition. All participants were then instructed to evaluate the technical qualities (composition and lighting) of each of 15 photographs. Those in the *promotions* condition were shown 10 photographs that included signs or labels with promotions-related messages (e.g., discounted prices, limited-time offers, clearance sales, etc.), in addition to five other filler photographs, while *control* participants were shown 10 photographs that included signs or labels with non-promotions-related messages (e.g., biking directions, subway station name, bookshelf filing number, etc.) and the same five fillers. Next, in a purportedly unrelated follow-up questionnaire, participants were asked to make eight binary choices between a smaller-sooner and a larger-later payoff (e.g., $10 tomorrow vs. $12 in 25 days), which were used to measure impatience (Li 2008). Finally, all participants completed the BAS questionnaire (Carver and White 1994), which presented 13 statements (e.g., "When I see something I want, I usually go all out to get it"; "When I go after something, I use a 'no holds barred' approach") assessed on four-point scales anchored by "strongly disagree" and "strongly agree."

Random-effects logistic regression revealed that the difference in the choice outcome (smaller-sooner vs. larger-later) between the two conditions was, indeed, moderated by BAS sensitivity ($p = .037$). Consistent with our prediction, participants with higher BAS sensitivity selected more smaller-sooner payoffs in the *promotions* condition, as compared to those in the *control* condition.

Our work contributes new insights to the literature on the psychological effects of promotions. While promotions provide numerous immediate monetary and nonmonetary benefits for consumers (Chandon et al. 2000), an important consequence of promotions that may undermine longer-term consumer welfare is the impatience that exposure to promotions can generate. More broadly, despite the existence of much prior work that has cast doubt on the adage "time is money" (e.g., Leclerc et al. 1995; Zauberman and Lynch 2005), our findings suggest that consumers' valuation of time can be implicitly influenced by a pervasive monetary factor (i.e., price promotions). Paradoxically, although consumers seek out and take advantage of promotions as opportunities to save money, exposure to promotions may "backfire" such that consumers are worse off financially. In other words, the bargain itself may be more than consumers bargain for. (940 words)

REFERENCES

Carver, Charles S. and Teri L. White (1994), "Behavioral Inhibition, Behavioral Activation, and Affective Responses to Impending Reward and Punishment: The BIS/BAS Scales," *Journal of Personality and Social Psychology*, 67 (February), 319–33.

Chandon, Pierre, Brian Wansink, and Gilles Laurent (2000), "A Benefit Congruency Framework of Sales Promotion Effectiveness," *Journal of Marketing*, 64 (October), 65–84.

Gray, Jeffrey A. (1994), "Framework for a Taxonomy of Psychiatric Disorder," in *Emotions: Essays on Emotion Theory*, Joseph A. Sergeant, Nanne E. Van De Poll, and Stephanie H.M. Van Goozen, eds. Hillsdale, NJ: Lawrence Erlbaum Associates, 29–59.

Leclerc, France, Bernt H. Schmitt, and Laurette Dube (1995), "Waiting Time and Decision Making: Is Time Like Money?" *Journal of Consumer Research*, 22 (June), 110–19.

Li, Xiuping (2008), "The Effects of Appetitive Stimuli on Out of Domain Consumption Impatience," *Journal of Consumer Research*, 34 (February), 649-656.

Wadhwa, Monica, Baba Shiv, and Stephen Nowlis (2008), "A Bite to Whet the Reward Appetite: The Influence of Sampling on Reward-Seeking Behaviors," *Journal of Marketing Research*, 45 (August), 403-413.

Zauberman, Gal, and John G. Lynch, Jr. (2005), "Resource Slack and Propensity to Discount Delayed Investments of Time Versus Money," *Journal of Experimental Psychology: General*, 134(1), 23-37.

The Role of Personal Relevance in the Effect of Ad Repetition on Attitudes and Choice

Ann Kronrod, MIT, USA
Joel Huber, Duke University, USA

EXTENDED ABSTRACT

The most common reason for an ad that is frequently repeated to become annoying is that ads are not an integral part of the audience's activities, and more specifically, of the audience's communicational activity (e.g. *Edwards*, *Li* and *Lee* 2002). This may also reduce evaluations of the advertised brand (Wang and Calder 2006). But not in all situations is ad repetition irritating to the same extent. Aaker and Bruzzone (1985) found that the most irritating ads were those that featured women's hygiene products or underwear, and hemorrhoid/laxative products, while the least irritating categories were shampoo, snacks, and cold remedies. This finding can be explained in terms of personal relevance: Women's products are relevant only to the female part of the sample, and so the male part of the sample finds them irritating. By contrast, snacks, shampoo and cold remedies are relatively often consumed by both men and women, and therefore are much more relevant to the sample as a whole. Taking a communicational approach, we define an advertisement as a conversational element in the communication between advertiser and consumer. Grice's Cooperativeness Principle (1975) assumes that, being cooperative, the speaker makes an effort to be relevant, and the addressee assumes the speaker does so. When an ad interferes with a consumer's activity, a non-cooperative mode of conversation may emerge between the consumer and the advertiser, generating justified annoyance. However, when faced with a need to make a consumption choice, the consumer's attitude towards the ad changes if the ad is relevant to the decision. The consumer becomes a cooperative conversation partner and also sees the ad as such. Consequently the ad is no longer annoying and the same attributes which were deemed annoying when no choice was to be made, not only cease to be irritating but also come to be seen as conversationally contributing. Based on this logic we suggest that personal relevance of a product moderates the effect of ad repetition, such that when a product is irrelevant, repetition causes irritation, but when a product is relevant, the otherwise annoying effect of repetition turns into familiarity and liking and results in higher choice of products that are more frequently advertised.

METHOD

We tested our hypothesis in two experiments. Three products, pretested for personal relevance and familiarity, were used: Apples (high in both personal relevance and familiarity), baby formula (low in personal relevance and high in familiarity), and beets (moderate in personal relevance and low in familiarity). Two fictional ads were prepared for each product, resulting in six ads. Ad repetition rate was manipulated, for each product, by making one of the ads pop up frequently (7 times) and the other one infrequently (3 times) during an article reading task.

STUDY 1

In Study 1, participants read an online article while ads repeatedly popped up. Personal relevance of the ads was manipulated within subject (all participants were exposed to ads for apples (personally relevant) and baby formula (personally irrelevant)) and between subjects (the personal relevance of beets, which was ambiguous due to its low level of familiarity, was manipulated between subjects by warning half of the participants that they will have to choose a brand of beets to prepare "*the famous Russian Svekolnik Soup, which is mainly made of beets*"). After reading the article with the popping

ads, participants reported their annoyance with as well as their preferences for the six fictitious brands. The results showed that for irrelevant products (baby formula and the low relevance condition of beets), the brands with frequently repeating ads were deemed more annoying (M=4.7) as well as less preferable (M=1.4) than the brands with infrequently repeating ads. However, this result flipped for relevant products (apples and the high relevance condition of beets): In this case, brands that were frequently repeated were less annoying (M=3.7), and participants preferred them more in a choice task (M=1.8, F(1,78)=18.6,p<.001). See figure 1 below.

Figure 1: The Moderating Effect of Relevance on Positive Attitudes towards high and low frequency repetition of Ads for Apples, Baby Formula and Beets brands

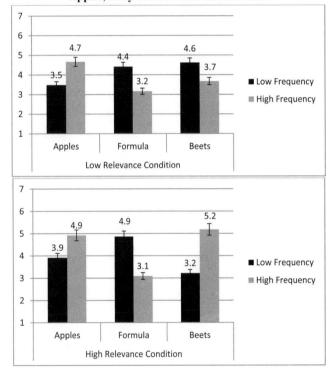

STUDY 2

Using the same stimuli, in Study 2 we manipulated relevance within subjects in a two-stage experiment, with a three-week interval between the stages. In stage 1, all participants read an article while being exposed to the six ads with varying frequencies, and expressed their attitudes toward the six brands. The relevance manipulation came three weeks later, in stage 2. Half of the participants read an introduction inviting them to **a Russian Folklore Party, to which they were asked to bring a Russian dish.** They also saw a picture and a short recipe for the famous **Russian "Svekolnik" Soup.** Participants then had to choose one of the brands of beets they had seen in Stage 1. Following this they answered recall and attitudinal questions regarding all six products. The results showed that whereas in the first stage the beets brand that had been frequently repeated led to higher annoyance (M=4.64) than the infrequent beets ad (M=3.25), on Stage 2, choices of the same brand depended on the relevance manipulation. Namely, participants who did not read the invitation indicated lower choice of the more frequently advertised brand, consistent with their indications of annoyance regarding these brands in the first stage. However, participants exposed to the Russian folklore party invitation chose more the brand that had been more frequently advertised in stage 1 (Chi^2=11.8,p<.03), that is, the same brand for which they had indicated higher annoyance in Stage 1.

Our results are consistent with research showing that it matters little if consumers instantly like or dislike an ad (Henderson 2007). One past pundit accurately phrased it: "It doesn't matter what they say about you in the press, as long as they spell your name right." The current work presents a new way of looking at advertising as a conversation: An ad is annoying when it violates the conversational norm of relevance, but when it becomes pertinent to consumer needs, attitudes, or intentions, it becomes a piece of fruitful conversation between the consumer and the marketer.

REFERENCES

Aaker, David A. and Bruzzone, Donald E. (1985). Causes of Irritation in Advertising. Journal of Marketing, 49(2), 47-57.

Grice, H.P. (1975). Logic and Conversation. In: Cole, P. and Morgan, J. (eds.) *Syntax and Semantics: Speech Acts*, Vol. 3, Academic Press, New York.

Edwards, Steven M., Hairong Li, and Joo-Hyun Lee (2002), "Forced Exposure and Psychological Reactance: Antecedents and Consequences of the Perceived Intrusiveness of Pop-Up Ads," *Journal of Advertising*, 31(Fall), 83-95.

Henderson, Naomi (2007), "Beyond Likes and Dislikes," *Marketing Research*, 19(2), 34-39.

Wang, Jing and Bobby J. Calder (2006), "Media Transportation and Advertising", *Journal of Consumer Research*, 33(2), 151-162.

Is Extremeness Aversion Driven by Loss Aversion?
Contrasting Reference-Point Models of Durable Product Choice

Nico Neumann, University of New South Wales, Australia
Ashish Sinha, University of New South Wales, Australia
Ulf Böckenholt, Northwestern University, USA

EXTENDED ABSTRACT

Prospect theory, which introduced the notions of loss aversion and reference-dependent choice (Kahneman and Tversky 1979; Tversky and Kahneman 1991), has gained wide acceptance among scholars in marketing, psychology, management science, and economics. However, as Bell and Lattin (2000, p. 187) note: "it is silent with respect to the origin of the reference points." A great deal of research investigates reference-points in product choice scenarios and finds that the reference point tends to be some adaptive function of past information (Baucells, Weber, and Welfens 2011). However, these findings are almost exclusively based on choice studies of nondurable product categories, such as FMCG-goods (Niedrich et al. 2009) or financial products (Baucells, Weber, and Welfens 2011). In comparison to nondurables, durable products have much longer interpurchase-cycles (Mazumdar, Raj, and Sinha 2005), often coupled with rapid technological progress that makes comparing attribute levels of new alternatives with the previously bought product impractical or impossible. Therefore, we need to understand which reference-point mechanisms appear feasible and most likely in the background of durable product choice.

Furthermore, it is well known that context-effects often influence consumer choice (Bettman, Luce, and Payne 1998). One robust context-effect is extremeness aversion, which refers to the tendency of consumers to avoid products with extreme attribute values, often leading to preference for the middle option(s) in choice sets (Simonson 1989; Simonson and Tversky 1992). Probably the most popular account offered to explain the extremeness aversion phenomenon has been loss aversion: individuals may evaluate the options of a choice set relative to the other options, resulting in the extreme values having the biggest disadvantages (Simonson and Tversky 1992). However, while conclusive in theory, we lack empirical evidence on whether loss aversion actually may cause extremeness aversion.

In this work, we pit various choice models that are based on different underlying reference-point theories against each other to shed light on how consumers form and utilize reference point(s) when choosing from durable products. Within this reference-point analysis framework, we further explore whether framing options as losses and gains accounts for extremeness aversion and whether any potential interplay of loss and extremeness aversion depends on the choice set size. To be able to incorporate individual-specific information, we study choice data from an experimental setting using two durable product categories: laptops and digital cameras. The number of options and positions of extreme products were systematically manipulated to provide a wide range of stimuli for potential loss and extremeness aversion. Following the choice tasks, participants rated the perceived overall quality, the product importance, as well as the individual attribute levels of each presented choice option, using the self-explicated approach (Kivetz, Netzer, and Srinivasan 2004).

Our base model (base) includes only partworth utilities of the attribute levels and product relevance (these variables are part of all models). The base model is benchmarked with various models that include additional parameters to accommodate reference-dependent choice. For instance, the context-dependent reference point model (CRP) employs the mean of the presented options as reference point based on adaptation-level theory (Helson 1964). Evidently, the reference point of the CRP-model varies for each choice set, but is the same for all individuals. In contrast, the expectations model (ERP) uses the same reference point, measured for each individual through the procedure suggested by Janiszewski and Lichtenstein (1999), for all choice sets. The two RP-models are contrasted with a model based on range-frequency theory (Parducci 1965). According to range-frequency theory (RFT), perceptions of stimuli depend on the distance of the range of options and the rank of the option within a set. Thus, the RFT-model represents a multiple reference-points model as RFT implies that consumers compare one option against all options in the contextual set (Niedrich, Sharma, and Wedell 2001).

Finally, we explore extensions of all models (base, RPs and RFT) by additionally including utility components that capture extremeness aversion (models: baseE, CRPE, ERPE, and RFTE). Using hierarchical Bayes, we estimate mixed logit models that allow the impact of context-dependent components (RFT, losses, gains, and extremeness aversion) and other parameters to differ for each individual (Train 2003).

The choice model results indicate that incorporating reference-dependence parameters leads to improvement in both fit and predictive validity, which can be even further increased through the inclusion of extremeness aversion variables. Overall, the CRPE-models outperform the other models for the two tested product categories. These findings suggest that consumers use a single reference point that is adjusted to the presented choice set and stimuli in each choice situation. This reference point mechanism provides strong support for the view that preferences are often constructed rather than recalled (Bettman, Luce, and Payne 1998).

For the CRPE-model, we find significant loss-parameters (taking a classical interpretation of the Bayesian estimates) as well as significant loss aversion for both quality and price for laptops and digital cameras. Moreover, the CRPE-models provide empirical evidence for extremeness aversion, which seems to strongly depend on the size of the assortment: sometimes individuals actually appear to prefer high-end extremes in smaller choice sets according to our data. This is consistent with the notion of the polarization effect that was observed in many choice scenarios involving price-quality trade-offs (Simonson and Tversky 1992). However, when increasing the number of options in the choice sets, we find significant extremeness aversion towards both low- and high-end alternatives. We would like to highlight that these findings on the extremeness aversion patterns were fairly similar across all tested models. This implies that extremeness aversion can be present even when fully accounting for loss aversion (i.e., loss- and gain-framing) and various context mechanisms. We interpret these findings as evidence that loss and extremeness aversion are two independent behavioral phenomena and conclude with a discussion of which other accounts might provide a better explanation of extremeness aversion behavior.

REFERENCES

Baucells, Manel, Martin Weber, and Frank Welfens (2011), "Reference-Point Formation and Updating," *Management Science,* 57(3), 506-519.

Bell, David R., and James M. Lattin (2000), "Looking for Loss Aversion in Scanner Panel Data: The Confounding Effect of Price Response Heterogeneity," *Marketing Science,* 19(2), 185-200.

Bettman, James R., Mary Frances Luce, and John W. Payne (1998), "Constructive Consumer Choice Processes," *Journal of Consumer Research,* 25(3), 187-217.

Helson, Harry (1964), *Adaptation-Level Theory*, New York: Harper and Row.

Janiszewski, Chris, and Donald R. Lichtenstein (1999), "A Range Theory Account of Price Perception," *Journal of Consumer Research*, 353-368.

Kahneman, Daniel, and Amos Tversky (1979), "Prospect Theory: An Analysis of Decision Under Risk," *Econometrica: Journal of the Econometric Society,* 47(2), 263-291.

Kivetz, Ran, Oded Netzer, and V. Seenu Srinivasan (2004), "Alternative Models for Capturing the Compromise Effect," *Journal of Marketing Research,* 41(3), 237-257.

Mazumdar, Tridib, S. P. Raj, and Indrajit Sinha (2005), "Reference Price Research: Review and Propositions," *Journal of Marketing,* 69(4), 84-102.

Niedrich, Ronald W., Subhash Sharma, and Douglas H. Wedell (2001), "Reference Price and Price Perceptions: A Comparison of Alternative Models," *Journal of Consumer Research,* 28(3), 339-354.

Niedrich, Ronald W., Danny Weathers, R.Carter Hill, and David R. Bell (2009), "Specifying Price Judgments with Range-Frequency Theory in Models of Brand Choice," *Journal of Marketing Research,* 46(5), 693-702.

Parducci, Allen (1965), "Category Judgment: A Range-Frequency Model," *Psychological Review,* 72(6), 407.

Simonson, Itamar (1989), "Choice Based on Reasons: The Case of Attraction and Compromise Effects," *Journal of Consumer Research,* 16(2), 158.

Simonson, Itamar, and Amos Tversky (1992), "Choice in Context: Tradeoff Contrast and Extremeness Aversion," *Journal of Marketing Research,* 29(3), 281-295.

Train, Kenneth (2003), *Discrete Choice Methods with Simulation*, New York: Cambridge University Press.

Tversky, Amos, and Daniel Kahneman (1991), "Loss Aversion in Riskless Choice: A Reference-Dependent Model," *The Quarterly Journal of Economics,* 106(4), 1039-1061.

Effects of Set Size, Scarcity, Packaging, and Taste on the Marketing Placebo Effect

Scott Wright, Providence College, USA
José Mauro da Costa Hernandez, Centro Universitário da FEI, Brazil
Aparna Sundar, University of Cincinnati, USA
John Dinsmore, University of Cincinnati, USA
Frank Kardes, University of Cincinnati, USA

EXTENDED ABSTRACT

The marketing placebo effect is defined as *"the influence of consumers' beliefs and expectations, shaped by experiences in their daily lives, on product judgments and services"* (Shiv, Carmon, and Ariely 2005). Shiv, Carmon, and Ariely (2005) demonstrated that consumer expectations mediate the relationship between product beliefs and product efficacy. In three studies, participants consumed an energy drink purported to increase mental acuity followed by a series of word-jumble puzzles. Participants were told either they would be charged $1.89 for the energy drink (i.e., the regular priced condition) or 89 cents (i.e., the discounted priced condition). Not only did participants anticipate that the full priced (vs. discounted priced) energy drink would be more (vs. less) effective, but they also completed more (vs. fewer) puzzles subsequent to consuming the drink.

Participants completed more puzzles because the naïve theory associating price with quality increased nonconscious performance expectancies that the energy drink would improve mental acuity (see Rao and Monroe 1989). Within this stream of research, we investigate how other elements of the marketing mix (beyond price) affect product efficacy. In doing so, we extend theory on the marketing placebo effect and related naïve theories.

STUDY 1: SET SIZE

In a *pilot study*, we manipulated price to replicate the aforementioned marketing placebo effect. This study served to test the stimuli and efficacy measures used in three subsequent experiments. Study 1 investigated the impact of set size on efficacy. It is commonly held that persuasiveness increases as the number of items supporting an argument increases (i.e., the length-implies-strength heuristic; Chaiken, Liberman, and Eagly 1989; Anderson 1967). Given this naïve theory, we hypothesized that a product's efficacy would increase as the number of its positive attributes increases (H1). To test our hypothesis, we experimentally manipulated the number of active ingredients contained in an energy drink and asked participants to consume the beverage before completing a word puzzle (adapted from Shiv et al. 2005). In support of H1, we found that participants randomly assigned to the condition featuring six active ingredients outperformed participants assigned to the condition featuring three active ingredients.

STUDY 2: SCARCITY

Study 2 investigated the impact of product availability on efficacy. According to Cialdini (2009) an item's availability is often used to infer quality or value. This association is so fundamental to human cognition, it is observed in children as young as two (Brehm and Weintraub 1977; Caplan et al. 1991; Cialdini 2009) and for products as diverse as cafeteria food (West 1975), shoes (Tan and Chua 2004), messages (Worchel 1992), wine (van Herpen, Pieters, and Zeelenberg 2009), and cookies (Worcliel, Lee, and Adewole 1975). Limited availability rouses interest in a product, increasing the likelihood of either supply- or demand- side inference formation (Kardes 1993; Kardes, Posavac, and Cronley 2004; Kardes et al. 2008; Kruglanski and Webster 1996). Hence, when consumers encounter a scarce product they often attribute its limited availability to inferred demand, which in turn is associated with quality inferences (Parker and Lehmann 2011). Given this naïve theory linking scarcity with increased quality perceptions, we hypothesized that a product's efficacy would increase as its availability decreases (H2). To test our hypothesis, we experimentally manipulated the shelf availability of an energy drink and asked participants to consume the beverage before completing a word puzzle (adapted from Shiv et al. 2005). In support of H2, we found that participants randomly assigned to the limited availability condition outperformed participants in the abundant availability condition.

STUDY 3: TASTE AND PACKAGING

Study 3 investigated the impact of taste and packaging on efficacy. Several studies demonstrate the influence of contextual inputs on subjective consumption experiences of foods and drinks (Lee, Frederick, and Ariely 2006; McClure et al., 2004; Wansink et al., 2000). For example, Raghunathan, Naylor, and Hoyer (2006) found that consumers rated foods labeled "healthy" as worse tasting than foods labeled "unhealthy" and concluded that hedonic pleasures like taste are construed as lacking in virtue compared to objects like health. Moreover, Eccles (2006) suggested that the taste of a cough syrup is likely to influence the occurrence or magnitude of a placebo effect. Consistent with these lines of research, we hypothesized that efficacy would increase as a food item's tastiness decreases (H3). This hypothesis is also consistent with classical conditioning theory. Since the flavor of most medicines is unpleasant (Sharma and Chopra 2010), the repeated association of medicines with unpleasant flavors pairs substandard taste with efficacy expectations.

Similarly, several studies document the influence of product packaging on consumption experiences (Raghubir and Greenleaf 2006). Compared to congruent designs, product designs incongruent with consumer expectations are perceived as more risky (Campbell 1999) and evaluated more negatively (Mandler 1982). Given this naïve theory, we hypothesized that efficacy would increase as a product's packaging typicality increases (H4). To test our hypotheses, we experimentally manipulated the taste and packaging typicality of an energy drink that purportedly relaxed the user and enhanced memory. We asked participants to consume the beverage before completing a memory task. Manipulation checks confirmed that we successfully manipulated taste and packaging typicality. In support of H3, we found that participants randomly assigned to the substandard taste condition outperformed participants assigned to the superior taste condition. Moreover, in support of H4, we found that participants randomly assigned to the typical product packaging condition outperformed participants assigned to the atypical product packaging condition.

In conclusion, this research contributes to the literature by demonstrating that there are unique features beyond price that moderate the marketing placebo effect. Overall, we conclude that any element increasing expectancies of performance should magnify the marketing placebo effect. We have demonstrated that set size, scarcity, packaging, and taste all influence this effect (see table 1). Future researchers can continue to advance our understanding of the marketing placebo effect by exploring additional factors affecting expectancies. This work is vital given the association of product performance with post consumption satisfaction, WOM, brand loyalty, and repeat purchasing behavior (Phillips, Chang Buzzell 1983; Westbrook 1987; Dwyer 1989; Oliver 1993; Day 1994; De Matos et al. 2008).

Table 1: **Performance as a function of expectancies**

Study	Experimental Conditions (N = 400)	
	Low Expectancy	*High Expectancy*
Pilot Study (*n* = 58)		
Price	16.9 (6.2)	22.3 (6.8)
Study 1 (*n* = 58)		
Set Size	20.0 (5.4)	24.4 (7.8)
Study 2 (*n* = 109)		
Scarcity	13.6 (7.12)	16.6 (8.5)
Study 3 (*n* = 175)		
Taste	11.5 (3.0)	13.1 (3.0)
Product Packaging	11.1 (2.6)	13.5 (3.1)

Note: For each row, the means across expectancy conditions differ at the $p < .05$ level. Standard deviations are reported in parentheses.

REFERENCES

Anderson, Norman H. (1967), "Averaging Model Analysis of Set-Size Effect in Impression Formation," *Journal of Experimental Psychology*, 75 (2), 158-65.

Brehm, Sharon S. and Marsha Weintraub (1977), "Physical Barriers and Psychological Reactance: 2-Year-Olds' Responses to Threats to Freedom," *Journal of Personality and Social Psychology*, 35 (11), 830-36.

Campbell, Margaret C. and Ronald C. Goodstein (2001), "The Moderating Effect of Perceived Risk on Consumers' Evaluations of Product Incongruity: Preference for the Norm," *Journal of Consumer Research*, 28 (3), 439-49.

Caplan, Marlene, JoEllen Vespo, Jan Pedersen, and Dale F. Hay (1991), "Conflict and Its Resolution in Small Groups of One- and Two-Year-Olds," *Child Development*, 62 (6), 1513-24.

Chaiken, Shelly, Akiva Libermanand, and Alice H. Eagly (1989), "Heuristic and Systematic Information Processing Within and Beyond the Persuasion Context," in Uleman, J. S. and Bargh, J. A. (Eds.), *Unintended Thought*, New York: Guilford, 212-252.

Cialdini, Robert B. (2009), *Influence: Science and Practice*: Pearson Education, Inc.

Day, George S. (1994), "The Capabilities of Market-Driven Organizations," *Journal of Marketing*, 58 (4), 37-52.

De Matos, Celso A. and Carlos A.V. Rossi (2008), "Word-of Mouth Communications in Marketing: A Meta-Analytic Review of the Antecedents and Moderators," *Journal of Academy of Marketing Science*, 36 (4), 578-96.

Dwyer, F. Rorbert (1989), "Customer Lifetime Valuation to Support Marketing Decision Making," *Journal of Direct Marketing*, 3 (4), 8-15.

Eccles, Ronald (2006), "Mechanisms of the Placebo Effect of Sweet Cough Syrups," *Respiratory Physiology & Neurobiology*, 152 (3), 340-48.

Kardes, Frank R. (1993), "Consumer Inference: Determinants, Consequences, and Implications for Advertising," *Advertising Exposure, Memory and Choice*, 163–91.

_____, Steven S. Posavac, and Maria L. Cronley (2004), "Consumer Inference: A Review of Processes, Bases, and Judgment Contexts," *Journal of Consumer Psychology*, 14 (3), 230-56.

_____, _____, _____, and Paul M. Herr (2008), "Consumer Inference," in Haugtvedt P. Curtis, Paul M. Herr and Frank R. Kardes. (Eds,), *Handbook of Consumer Psychology*, 165–92, New York: Lawrence Erlbaum Associates.

Kruglanski, Arie W. and Donna M. Webster (1996), "Motivated Closing of the Mind: "Seizing" and "Freezing,"" *Psychological Review*, 103 (2), 263-83.

Lee, Leonard, Shane Frederick, and Dan Ariely (2006), "Try It, You'll Like It: The Influence of Expectation, Consumption, and Revelation on Preferences for Beer," *Psychological Science*, 17 (12), 1054-58.

Mandler, George (1982), "The Structure of Value: Accounting for Taste," in *Affect and Cognition: The Seventeenth Annual Carnegie Symposium on Cognition*, eds. Margaret S. Clarke, and Susan T. Fiske, Hillsdale NJ: Erlbaum, 3-36.

McClure, Samuel. M., Jian Li, Damon Tomlin, Kim S. Cypert, Latane M. Montague, and P. Read Montague (2004), "Neural Correlates of Behavioral Preferences for Culturally Familiar Drinks," *Neuron*, 44, 379-87.

Oliver, Richard L. (1993), "Cognitive, Affective, and Attribute Bases of the Satisfaction Response," *Journal of Consumer Research*, 20 (3), 418-30

Parker, Jeffrey R. and Donald R. Lehmann (2011), "When Shelf-Based Scarcity Impacts Consumer Preferences," *Journal of Retailing*, 87 (2), 142-55.

Phillips, Lynn W., Dae R. Chang, and Robert D. Buzzell (1983), "Product Quality, Cost Position and Business Performance: A Test of Some Key Hypotheses," *Journal of Marketing*, 47 (2), 26-43.

Raghubir, Priya and Eric A. Greenleaf (2006), "Ration in Proportion: What Should the Shape of the Package Be," *Journal of Marketing*, 70 (2), 95-107.

Raghunathan, Rajagopal, Rebecca W. Naylor, and Wayne D. Hoyer (2006), "The Unhealthy = Tasty Intuition and Its Effects on Taste Inferences, Enjoyment, and Choice of Food Products," *Journal of Marketing*, 70 (4), 170-84.

Rao, Akshay R. and Kent B. Monroe (1989), "The Effect of Price, Brand Name, and Store Name on Buyers' Perceptions of Product Quality: An Integrative Review," *Journal of Marketing Research*, 26 (3), 351-57.

Sharma, Vijay and Himanshu Chopra (2010), "Role of Taste and Taste Masking of Bitter Drugs in Pharmaceutical Industireies- An Overview," *International Journal of Pharmacy and Pharmaceutical Sciences*, 2 (4), 14-18.

Shiv, Baba, Ziv Carmon, and Dan Ariely (2005), "Placebo Effects of Marketing Actions: Consumers May Get What They Pay For," *Journal of Marketing Research*, 42 (4), 383-93.

Tan, Soo-Jiuan and Seow Hwang Chua (2004), ""While Stocks Last!" Impact of Framing on Consumers' Perception of Sales Promotions," *Journal of Consumer Marketing*, 21 (5), 343-55.

van Herpen, Erica, Rik Pieters, and Marcel Zeelenberg (2009), "When Demand Accelerates Demand: Trailing the Bandwagon," *Journal of Consumer Psychology*, 19 (3), 302-12.

Wansink, Brian, Se-Bum Park, Steven Sonka, and Michelle Morganosky (2000), "How Soy Labeling Influences Preference and Taste," *International Food and Agribusiness Management Review*, 3, 85-94.

West, Stephen G. (1975), "Increasing the Attractiveness of College Cafeteria Food: A Reactance Theory Perspective," *Journal of Applied Psychology*, 60 (5), 656-58.

Westbrook, Robert A. (1987), "Product/Consumption-Based Affective Responses and Postpurchase Processes," *Journal of Marketing Research* , 24 (3), 258-270.

Worchel, Stephen (1992), "Beyond a Commodity Theory Analysis of Censorship: When Abundance and Personalism Enhance Scarcity Effects," *Basic and Applied Social Psychology*, 13 (1), 79-92.

_____, Jerry Lee, and Akanbi Adewole (1975), "Effects of Supply and Demand on Ratings of Object Value," *Journal of Personality and Social Psychology*, 32 (5), 906-14.

From the Hands to the Mind: Haptic Brand Signatures

Mathias Streicher, University of Innsbruck, Austria

EXTENDED ABSTRACT

Many consumption situations connect consumers to brands in a physical sense by touch. A famous example is Coca-Cola's contour bottle, which has become the brand's haptic signature and part of consumers' brand knowledge. Here, I address the question of how closely brands are linked to their haptic signatures. In four experiments I show brand-specific knowledge activation from haptic primes with implications for sensory marketing.

Touch is the first sense to develop in the womb presumably providing an early matrix for self-awareness in the absence of the external world (Gallace and Spence 2010) and it is the only proximal sense that connects the percipient directly to the source of experience (Peck 2010). Touch-orientated consumers feel more frustrated and less confident when making product evalu-ations if touch is unavailable (Peck and Childers 2003a) and simply holding products in the hands can promote a sense of psychological ownership (Peck and Shu 2009). While some com-panies already brand haptic sensations very successfully (Lindstrom 2005), research on brand-related touch thus far has received no attention at all, perhaps because the touch sense is still the most underappreciated sense in marketing (Peck and Childers 2007). Previous studies have ad-dressed effects from inter-personal touch (Hornik 1992), touch as chronic need (Peck and Childers 2003b), effects from haptic imagery on psychological owner-ship (Peck and Berger 2009), or cross-modal carry-over effects from nondiagnostic tactile sensations to gustatory judgments of products (Krishna and Morrin 2009).

In the domain of social psychology there is increasing evidence that haptic experience is directly linked to mental concepts in a met-aphorical way such as touching a warm cup activates concepts of social warmth (Williams and Bargh 2008), tactile roughness carries over to the eval-uation of a social interaction (Ackerman, Nocera, and Bargh 2010), or lying in an email increases preference for hand sanitizers to purify the dirty body part (Lee and Schwarz 2010). These mo-dality-specific pathways between haptic sensations and mental concepts suggest a physical-to-mental scaffolding which grist the mills of embodied theorists suggesting higher-order concepts to be ontogenetically scaffolded by concrete bodily experience (Williams, Huang, and Bargh 2009) and grounded in perceptual systems (Barsalou 1999; 2008).

Here, I hypothesize that exposing participants to haptic primes from beverage containers automatically activates the corresponding brand knowledge structures promoting perceptual pro-cessing in other modalities, cognitive accessibility, and prime-congruent brand choices.

To carve out the effects from brand-related haptic input with-out interference from other modalities I conducted four experiments where I exposed participants blindfolded for 1 second under cog-nitive load within an ostensible weight-judging task to beverage containers from dif-ferent brands. Afterwards, they were asked to participate in another unrelated study that was the actual dependent variable. Finally, participants were debriefed whether they had rec-ognized the prime in the weight-judging task to exclude their data if necessary.

In experiment 1 I randomly assigned participants to Coca-Cola glass bottles, Red Bull cans, or a group without treatment followed by an unrelated task that visually presented the tar-get name Red Bull with increasing clarity on a computer screen. Participants were significantly faster to identify the brand name Red Bull if they had been previously exposed to a Red Bull can compared to the other groups (MRedBull = 2.85 sec vs. Munprimed = 3.04 vs. MCoca-Cola = 3.05; F (2, 111) = 5.244, p = .007; Tukey post hoc p < .05). Ex-periment 2 replicated the results but this time I used the brand name Coca-Cola as visual target and compared Coca-Cola versus Römer-quelle bottles that share basic characteristics such as surface material (glass), container type (bottle), girth, and weight. As expected, the Coca-Cola group was significantly faster to identify the visu-al target Coca-Cola compared to the other groups (MCoca-Cola = 3.09 sec vs. MRömerquelle = 3.27 vs. Munprimed = 3.34; F (2, 177) = 6.294, p = .002; Tukey post-hoc test p < .05). The results show that brand-related haptic sensations automatically increase perceptual fluency cross-modally for the corresponding brand. It seems noteworthy that these effects occurred outside of people's aware-ness. Although the experience of perceptual fluency can influence affective judgments in a posi-tive direction (Reber, Winkielman, and Schwarz 1998) it remains unclear whether this lifts a brand top-of-mind in consumers' consideration set when thinking about brands of a certain prod-uct category.

In experiment 3 I therefore primed participants with either Co-ca-Cola bottles, Römerquelle bottles, or Red Bull cans. In a subse-quent task, I asked them to list brands for the category of beverages. The ANOVA for Red Bull shows that the ratio the brand was listed first (top-of-mind) was significantly higher in the Red Bull condition compared to all other groups (MRedBull = 26% vs. MCoca-Cola = 6% vs. MRömer = 6% vs. Mcontrol = 12 %; F (3, 227) = 5.134, p = .02; Tukey post-hoc p < .05).

Experiment 4 analyzed whether brand-related haptic sensations can actually influence consumption choices. Containers from Coca-Cola, Red Bull, and Römerquelle served as stimuli. After the priming task participants were offered either a Coca-Cola or a Red Bull bev-erage as reward. The ANOVA of a dummy variable (1= Coca-Cola vs. 0 = Red Bull) shows that partici-pants primed with Coca-Cola bottles chose most often Coca-Cola (MCoca-Cola = 64%) while those primed with Römerquelle bottles chose almost equally from the two brands (MRömer = 52%) and those primed with Red-Bull cans chose Coca-Cola least frequently (MRedBull = 39 %) but the most Red Bull (F (2, 167) = 4.160 p = .017; Dunnett-C post-hoc p < .05).

This is the first study to show how brand-related haptic sen-sations automatically activate brand knowledge and how this influ-ences a brand's cognitive accessibility or brand choices. In times of diminishing product life cycles with frequent visual face-liftings, the retention of haptic signatures could perpetuate the bond between consumers and brands and help to reduce commu-nication costs to familiarize consumers with new products or product changes. New products that use established haptic signatures have a greater chance to do better simply because they feel more familiar, facilitate per-ceptual processing, and automatically activate existing brand knowl-edge.

REFERENCES

Ackerman, Joshua M., Christopher C. Nocera, and John A. Bargh (2010), „Incidental Haptic Sensations Influence Social Judgments and Decisions," *Science*, 328 (5986), 1712–15.

Barsalou, Larence W. (1999), "Perceptual Symbol Systems," *Behavioral and Brain Sciences,* 22, 577–609.

——————— (2008), "Grounded Cognition," *Annual Review of Psychology*, 59 (1), 617–45.

Gallace, Alberto and Charles Spence (2010), "Touch and the Body: The Role of the Somatosensory Cortex in Tactile Awareness," *Psyche: An Interdisciplinary Journal of Research on Consciousness*, 16 (1), 2010, 30–67.

Hornik, Jacob (1992), "Haptic Stimulation and Consumer Response," *Journal of Consumer Research*, 19 (December), 449–58.

Krishna, Aradhna and Maureen Morrin (2008), „Does Touch Affect Taste? The Perceptual Transfer of Product Container Haptic Cues," *Journal of Consumer Research,* 34 (April), 807–18.

Lee, Spike W. and Norbert Schwarz (2010), "Dirty Hands and Dirty Mouths: Embodiment of the Moral-Purity Metaphor is Specific to the Motor Modality Involved in Moral Transgression," *Psychological Science, 21*, 1423–25.

Lindstrom, Martin (2005), *BRAND sense - How to Build Powerful Brands through Touch, Taste, Smell, Sight, and Sound*, London: Kogan Page.

Peck, Joann (2010), "Does Touch Matter? Insights From Haptic Research in Marketing," in *Sensory Marketing: Research on the Sensuality of Products*, ed. Aradhna Krishna, New York, NY: Routledge, 17–31.

Peck, Joann and Victor Barger (2009), „In Search of a Surrogate for Touch: The Effect of Haptic Imagery on Psychological Ownership and Object Valuation," in *Advances in Consumer Research,* 36, eds. Ann L. McGill and Sharon Shavitt, Duluth, MN : Association for Consumer Research, 127–130.

Peck, Joann and Terry L. Childers (2003b), "Individual Differences in Haptic Information Processing: The 'Need for Touch' Scale," *Journal of Consumer Research*, 30 (December), 430–42.

——————— (2003a) "To Have and To Hold: The Influence of Haptic Information on Product Judgments," *Journal of Marketing*, 67 (April), 35–48.

——————— (2007), "Effects of Sensory Factors on Consumer Behaviors," in *Handbook of Consumer Psychology*, ed. Frank Kardes, Curt Haugtvedt, and Paul Herr, Mahwah, NJ: Erlbaum.

Peck, Joann and Suzanne B. Shu (2009), "The Effect of Mere Touch on Perceived Ownership," *Journal of Consumer Research*, 36 (October), 434–47.

Reber, Rolf, Piotr Winkielman, and Norbert Schwarz (1998), "Effects of perceptual fluency on affective judgments," *Psychological Science*, 9, 45-48.

Williams, Lawrence. E. and John A. Bargh (2008), "Experiencing Physical Warmth Promotes Interpersonal Warmth," *Science*, 322, 606–7.

Williams, Lawrence E., Julie Y. Huang, and John A. Bargh (2009), "The scaffolded mind: Higher mental processes are grounded in early experience of the physical world," *European Journal of Social Psychology*, 39, 1257–67.

Getting (Ex)cited: The Role of Herding in Driving Citations

Simon Quaschning, University College Ghent/Ghent University, Belgium
Mario Pandelaere, Ghent University, Belgium
Iris Vermeir, University College Ghent/Ghent University, Belgium

EXTENDED ABSTRACT

Citations play a role of ever increasing importance in the academic world. Publishing in top journals and establishing a considerable citation record has become essential for a successful academic career. However, most scientific work never gets noticed (Surowiecki 2005). As many as 20% of all articles are never cited at all, while only a limited number of articles are cited hundreds of times (Mingers and Burrell 2006). Existing literature has argued that the quality of an article is the primary driver of the difference between successful and unsuccessful articles (Mingers and Xu 2010). Moreover, past research has identified other, more quantifiable factors, such as the domain, visibility and personal promotion of an article (Stremersch, Verniers, and Verhoef 2007). In contrast, this paper proposes an alternative explanation: herding behavior.

When selecting sources for their research, academics are often confronted with a seemingly endless amount of information. Moreover, while some articles are clearly better than others, often it is rather difficult to compare their quality. Under such circumstances of uncertainty, people have the tendency to rely on heuristics to filter the abundance of information. According to the Matthew effect, the number of citations itself serves as a cue of quality for researchers. A large number of citations will accordingly lead to a good reputation, which then attracts even more citations (Nederhof and van Raan 1987). Correspondingly we propose that due to herding, articles get cited increasingly more often when they have been cited heavily in the past.

Our prediction is based on theory related to herding behavior and information cascades. When herding occurs, people ignore their own knowledge and instead look at the actions of others (Surowiecki 2005). As such, the number of citations does serve as a cue of quality for researchers. Researchers may believe that the persons before them had better information on the quality of the article than they themselves do and therefore may include the articles in their own research (Bonabeau 2004). However, when this imitation occurs in large numbers, informational cascades are formed (Banerjee 1992; Bickchandani, Hirshleifer and Welch 1992). People will mainly focus on articles with an already established citation count, and the limited number of articles that are already heavily cited tends to accumulate citations rapidly, while a large set of initially uncited articles tends to be (virtually) ignored.

The current paper is the first to illustrate empirically how herding has an effect on the citation record of scientific articles. We tested this idea with a sample of all articles published in five major marketing journals from 1985 to 2001 (*JM, JMR, JCR, MKS* and *IJRM; JCP* has been excluded since articles were only available from 2000), resulting in 2,227 articles. Also, we excluded all editorial content, books- and software reviews and comment sections, because of a significantly different citation profile. For each article, we tallied the number of citations made in each of the 10 years following its year of publication (excluding self-citations).

Consistent with the idea of herding, the results show that a large number of articles barely get cited, while a limited number of articles are cited very often. Interestingly, a multilevel regression analysis indicates that on average, the times that an article gets cited is a concave function of the age of the article: the increase in citations diminishes over time. We tested three models in which we tested if the difference in citation behavior can be explained by herding or by quality.

A first model tested the herding hypothesis, by including the number of times an article got cited in the year before (*autocorrelation*) into our model. The results illustrate that the number of citations in year t is positively related to the number of citations in year $t-1$. Moreover, we find a steeper increase in citations over the years for articles that have been cited heavily in the year before. Rarely cited articles, in contrast, will be cited only sporadically in future years. These findings support the herding hypothesis.

With a second model we tested an alternative explanation. According to the existing literature, the differences in citation behavior can be explained by the articles' quality. Since inherent quality is hard to measure, we relied on the quality assessments of editors and editorial boards (Stremersch et al. 2007). As such, we included *article order* (considered as the editors' assessment of quality and contribution), the journals' *best article awards* and the *article length* (articles with a higher contribution are often allowed to be longer). The results partly confirm the role of quality. While there were no significant effects for article order, we find that article length and awards moderate the increase in citations in the years after publication. In particular, high quality articles will show a steeper increase in citations over the years as opposed to articles of lower quality.

A third model was estimated in which both herding and quality were included simultaneously. The results support both the quality and the herding hypotheses. However, the highly concave function for high quality articles indicates that the number of citations will decrease again after some years. In contrast, the increase in the number of citations over the years is more linear for articles that have been cited more heavily in year $t-1$. Therefore, the findings suggest that, while quality is important in the first years, herding is responsible for the accumulation of citations over a longer period of time.

The current research sheds new light on an often discussed topic: the difference in citations of academic articles. The existing knowledge is challenged and extended by illustrating that the difference between highly and rarely cited articles cannot only be explained by differences in quality, but also by herding. We found that articles that got cited heavily in the past will be cited even more in the future. Next to theoretical contributions, this research also has practical implications. We hope this paper encourages a more careful use of citations as an indicator of article quality.

REFERENCES

Banerjee, Abhijit V. (1992), "A Simple Model of Herd Behavior," *The Quarterly Journal of Economics,* 107 (3), 797-817.

Bikhchandani, Sushil, David Hirshleifer and Ivo Welch (1992), "A Theory of Fads, Fashion, Custom, and Cultural Change as Informational Cascades," *Journal of Political Economy,* 100 (5), 992-1026.

Bonabeau, Eric (2004), "The Perils of the Imitation Age," *Harvard Business Review,* 82 (6), 45-54

Mingers, John and Quentin L. Burrell (2006), "Modeling Citation Behavior in Management Science Journals," *Information processing and Management,* 42 (6), 1451-64.

Mingers, John and Fang Xu (2010), "The Drivers of Citations in Management Science Journals," *European Journal of Operational Research,* 205 (2), 422-30.

Nederhof, A. J., and Anthony F.J. van Raan (1987), "Peer-Review and Bibliometric Indicators of Scientific Performance – A Comparison of Cum Laude Doctorates with Ordinary Doctorates in Physics," *Scientometrics,* 11 (5-6), 333-50.

Stremersch, Stefan, Isabel Verniers and Peter C. Verhoef (2007), "The Quest for Citations: Drivers of Article Impact," *Journal of Marketing,* 71(3), 171-93.

Surowiecki, James (2005). *The Wisdom of Crowds.* New York: Anchor.

Unintended Effects of Implementation Intentions on Goal Pursuit Initiation vs. Persistence: Substitution and Acceleration

Jelena Spanjol, University of Illinois at Chicago, USA
Leona Tam, University of Wollongong, Australia
José Antonio Rosa, University of Wyoming, USA

EXTENDED ABSTRACT

When trying to achieve a goal (such as losing five pounds), people run into problems with getting started (begin controlling one's diet), keeping at it (continue cutting out the sugar), or both. Failure at either initiation or persistence in goal striving reduces goal attainment significantly. One way to overcome these challenges is to form implementation intentions (i.e., make detailed plans on when, where, and how to enact goal-directed behaviors, Gollwitzer 1999). Implementation intentions improve action initiation under cognitive load (Brandstaetter, Lengfelder, and Gollwitzer 2001), and shield goal pursuit behaviors from distractions (Bayer, Gollwitzer, and Achtziger 2010). Most implementation intentions research focuses on the outcome (i.e., goal attainment), not distinguishing between initiation and persistence or examining them independently (Gollwitzer and Sheeran 2006). It is unclear if planning out goal-directed behaviors is equally effective for starting and persisting in goal pursuit and what the underlying mechanisms are. The present research addresses this gap.

RESEARCH QUESTIONS

One important condition to the effectiveness of implementation intentions is the perceived level of difficulty of the goal being pursued. The greater the perceived difficulty, the more effective implementations are in improving goal attainment (e.g., Bagozzi and Edwards 2000; Chasteen et al. 2001). Importantly, the same goal can be perceived as more difficult to attain when it is being pursued under regulatory nonfit (Tam and Spanjol 2012), which occurs when a person's regulatory focus (promotion or prevention; Higgins 1997) does not match the goal pursuit strategy employed (eager or vigilant; Higgins 2000). Under regulatory fit, however, implementation intentions do not appear to have any incremental value on goal attainment (Tam and Spanjol 2012).

What is unknown is whether the type of regulatory fit matters to implementation intention effectiveness. The present research examines the impact of implementation intentions under regulatory fit more closely and aims to answer this research question: Do implementation intentions work differently for action initiation vs. action persistence in goal pursuit, and are those effects conditional upon the type of regulatory fit?

LITERATURE REVIEW

When implementation intentions are formed under regulatory fit the effectiveness of implementation intentions is reduced (Tam and Spanjol 2012), due to a ceiling effect, in which the fluency or "feeling right" of a regulatory fit situation provides a boost to goal attainment, leaving little room for the incremental impact from implementation intentions. An alternative explanation is that implementation intentions have opposite effects on goal striving under promotion fit vs. prevention fit conditions, in essence cancelling each other out. Based on the regulatory focus and fit literatures, we propose two unintended effects from implementation intentions under promotion vs. prevention fit: substitution and acceleration.

Substitution effect. Prevention-focused consumers are motivated by obligations and tend to see an adopted goal as a necessity (Liberman et al. 1999) or a minimal goal that needs to be satisfied (Freitas et al. 2002). When goals are construed as obligations or minimal standards to be met, goal-directed behaviors are initiated more quickly (Freitas et al. 2002). Thus, under prevention fit (when prevention-focused individuals pursue goals with vigilant strategies), the salience of minimal goals will be heightened and people will seek to satisfy the need for initiating goal striving as quickly as possible. When asked to form specific plans regarding when, where, and how goal striving will be enacted (via forming implementation intentions), individuals might interpret the act of developing such detailed goal pursuit plans as actual goal-directed behaviors. By forming implementation intentions, prevention-fit individuals then substitute cognitive goal striving for behavioral goal striving, delaying the initiation of goal-directed behaviors.

Acceleration effect. Promotion-focused consumers are motivated by hopes and tend to see an adopted goal as one of many opportunities for accomplishment (Liberman et al. 1999) or a maximal goal that one hopes to fulfill (Freitas et al. 2002). As a result, promotion-focused individuals tend to initiate goal-directed behaviors later (Freitas et al. 2002) but show greater persistence once started. By forming implementation intentions, promotion-fit individuals might accelerate or intensify their goal-directed behaviors to achieve the goal more quickly or more thoroughly and then desist from continuing the goal striving since they might feel they have "done enough."

METHOD AND FINDINGS

We conduct two longitudinal studies to assess whether implementation intentions affect initiation vs. persistence in goal striving differently under prevention vs. promotion fit. Study 1 asked 175 participants (83 females, 92 males) that reported having recently formulated financial goals (reducing debt or increasing savings) when they planned to start working on those goals (initiation). After two months, participants were asked about their likely continuation (persistence) of goal striving. Half of the participants were asked to form implementation intentions. We expected implementation intentions to boost initiation only under promotion fit, and persistence only under prevention fit. As shown in figure 1, initiation was enhanced for promotion-fit participants, as expected. Moreover, in support of our proposed substitution effect, prevention-fit participants delayed starting their goal striving when forming implementation intentions.

We also expected that promotion-fit participants would not benefit from forming implementation intentions to boost their likely continuation of goal striving. We find that promotion-fit individuals report lower persistence when forming implementation intentions.

Since the perceptual forward-looking measure of persistence did not allow us to test the acceleration effect, we conduct study 2, where 183 undergraduate students (112 females, 71 males) participated in a 7-day healthy snacking study. We find that promotion-fit participants do not benefit from forming implementation intentions, as expected.

A third study examining flossing behavior in a month-long time frame is under way to investigate both substitution and acceleration effects in a longer time frame within the same context. Results of this study will be ready for presentation at the conference.

REFERENCES

Bagozzi, Richard P. and Elizabeth A. Edwards (2000), "Goal-Striving and the Implementation of Goal Intentions in the Regulation of Body Weight," *Psychology and Health*, 15, 255-270.

Bayer, Ute C., Peter M. Gollwitzer, and Anja Achtziger (2010), "Staying on Track: Planned Goal Striving is Protected from Disruptive Internal States," *Journal of Experimental Social Psychology*, 46 (3), 505-14.

Brandstätter, Veronika, Angelika Lengfelder, and Peter M. Gollwitzer (2001), "Implementation Intentions and Efficient Action Initiation," *Journal of Personality and Social Psychology*, 81 (5), 946-60.

Chasteen, Alison L., Denise C. Park, and Norbert Schwarz (2001), "Implementation Intentions and Facilitation of Prospective Memory," *Psychological Science*, 12 (6), 457-61.

Freitas, Antonio L., Nira Liberman, Peter Salovey, and E. Tory Higgins (2002), "When to Begin? Regulatory Focus and Initiating Goal Pursuit," *Personality and Social Psychology Bulletin*, 28 (1), 121-30.

Gollwitzer, Peter M. (1999), "Implementation Intentions: Strong Effect of Simple Plans," *American Psychologist*, 54 (7), 493-503.

Gollwitzer, Peter M. and Paschal Sheeran (2006), "Implementation Intentions and Goal Achievement: A Meta-Analysis of Effects and Processes," *Advances in Experimental Social Psychology*, 38, 69-119.

Higgins, E. Tory (1997), "Beyond Pleasure and Pain," *American Psychologist*, 52 (12), 1280-1300.

_____ (2000), "Making a Good Decision: Value from Fit," *American Psychologist*, 55 (11), 1217-30.

Liberman, Nira, Lorraine Chen Idson, Christopher J. Camacho, and E. Tory Higgins (1999), "Promotion and Prevention Choices between Stability and Change," *Journal of Personality and Social Psychology*, 77 (6), 1135-45.

Tam, Leona and Jelena Spanjol (2012), "When Impediments Make You Jump Rather Than Stumble: The Beneficial Effects of Regulatory Nonfit on Forming Implementation Intentions to Attain Goals," *Marketing Letters*, 23 (1), 93-107.

Do Higher Stakes Lead to Better Choices?

Traci Freling, University of Texas - Arlington, USA
Ritesh Saini, University of Texas - Arlington, USA
Zhiyong Yang, University of Texas - Arlington, USA

EXTENDED ABSTRACT

Imagine a situation where a decision maker has to choose from two alternate preventive medications to ward off a threatening disease: one medication is supported by hearsay and anecdotal information, while rigorous statistical evidence favors the other. Common sense suggests that when the threat of such a disease is miniscule, either of the medications may be taken, but when vulnerability to the disease is perceived to be high, the choice is no longer inconsequential. Then, better sense should prevail and the statistically proven medication would usurp the one which is merely supported by anecdotal evidence. Higher stakes would therefore lead to better choices. In this paper, we provide evidence to the contrary. We demonstrate that greater likelihood of an event can lead to more visceral decision-making which can in turn lead to sub-optimal choices.

Normative decision-making models propose that anecdotal information—which describes a specific instance of a phenomenon or event—should be ideally ignored in the presence of contradicting statistical information—provides a numerical summary of a series of instances (Hornikx 2005). This is because the latter is based on a larger sample and should be objectively more reliable in decision making than an isolated anecdote (Ragubir and Menon 1996). However, a substantial stream of literature suggests that such rational disregard rarely occurs, and that anecdotal evidence often overwhelms statistical information (Bar-Hillel 1980; Hamill, Wilson, and Nisbett 1980). Such anecdotal biases have largely been attributed to the greater vividness and ease of processing that characterizes stories, as compared to statistical forms of data which tend to be more pallid and require more cognitive effort to process (Hamill et al. 1980).

In four studies, we investigate how contextual cues influence consumers' reliance on anecdotal information. We propose that the anecdotal bias should be less salient in high- versus low-involvement conditions, based upon the Elaboration Likelihood Model (ELM; Petty and Cacippo 1986). However, high-involvement does not always reduce the anecdotal bias. In situations where high-involvement induces a high level of perceived vulnerability among consumers, high-involvement can in fact increase the anecdotal bias, a phenomenon we call the "visceral compatibility effect" (study 1). We propose that emotional engagement underlies the visceral compatibility effect, mediating consumers' reliance on anecdotal information when involvement is enhanced by increasing vulnerability—and effect we test in study 2. We also examine the moderating role of consumers' holistic-analytical thinking style. Holistic thinking encourages context-dependence, which we believe will make people more cognizant of the visceral nature of the decision context, and therefore be more susceptible to its influence. As such, we expect that holistic (vs. analytic) thinking participants will display greater variance in anecdotal bias as a function of perceived vulnerability. Studies 3 and 4 provide consistent findings in support of our expectations, using chronic and situationally primed thinking styles, respectively.

Study 1 (N=293) featured a 2 (Involvement Type: non vulnerability-based vs. vulnerability-based) × 2 (Involvement Level: low vs. high) between-subjects design. We designed a decision scenario in which participants were asked to choose between two different automobile insurance policies for an extended travel in a foreign country: one option was statistically superior, while the other was anecdotally superior. In the vulnerability-based condition, participants' involvement level was manipulated through the information about the destination's ranking on automobile accidents in that country. In the non vulnerability-based condition, vulnerability was maintained at a moderate level. Participants assigned to the high-involvement condition were asked to provide reasons for their choice, whereas those in the low-involvement condition were prompted to make a choice without being asked to provide reasons. Immediately following the involvement manipulation, participants chose one of the two insurance policies.

Consistent with our expectations, we found that increasing involvement did not always result in reduced anecdotal bias (see Table 1). When involvement was enhanced by engaging in reasoning, it indeed did reduce this bias, as predicted by ELM. But when involvement was enhanced by increasing perceived vulnerability, anecdotal bias in fact increased, thereby confirming our visceral compatibility hypothesis.

Table 1: Study 1 Results: Choice of Anecdotally Superior Insurance Option

Involvement Type	Involvement Level	
	Low	High
Non vulnerability-based manipulation	49%	36%
Vulnerability-based manipulation	38%	50%

Study 2 (N=199) used the same research design, but provided further evidence for our principal hypothesis using a different choice scenario (i.e., participants were asked to choose between two different medications for a stomach virus that sometimes affects tourists in a particular foreign country) and measured emotional engagement (a potential mediator). As expected, Involvement Type moderated the effect of Involvement Level on anecdotal bias and on the level of emotional engagement elicited by high vulnerability (see Table 2). Further, under the vulnerability-based condition of Involvement Type, the effect of Involvement Level on consumers reliance on anecdotal information is mediated by emotional engagement.

Table 2: Study 2 Results: Choice of Anecdotally Superior Drug Option

Involvement Type	Involvement Level	
	Low	High
Non vulnerability-based manipulation	35%	15%
Vulnerability-based manipulation	27%	42%

Study 3 examined how individuals' chronic thinking style influences susceptibility to the visceral compatibility effect using a 2 (Vulnerability: low vs. high) x 2 (Thinking Style: analytic vs. holistic) between-subjects design. Results confirmed our expectation that vulnerability causes greater susceptibility to the anecdotal bias in holistic- versus analytic-thinking participants (see Table 3). Study 4 was similar to Study 3, except that we manipulated analytic-holistic thinking. Again confirmed our expectations about the moderating role of holistic-analytic thinking style (see Table 4).

Table 3: Study 3 Results: % Choice of Anecdotally Superior Drug Option

Chronic Thinking Style	Perceived Vulnerability	
	Low	High
Holistic	31%	53%
Analytic	44%	45%

Table 4: Study 4 Results: % Choice of Anecdotally Superior Drug Option

Manipulated Thinking Style	Perceived Vulnerability	
	Low	High
Holistic	23%	57%
Analytic	29%	31%

Our findings demonstrate a counterintuitive result (i.e., that higher involvement can lead to greater susceptibility to anecdotal evidence, seemingly in contradiction to the ELM framework) and provide consistent support for the proposed visceral compatibility hypothesis. Study 1 reconciles contradictory predictions, demon-strating that high-involvement can decrease or enhance the anecdotal bias, depending on whether it is accompanied by high-vulnerability. Study 2 replicates this finding in a different decision context and identifies emotional engagement as the mechanism underlying the visceral compatibility effect. Studies 3 and 4 reveal that holistic-analytic thinking style constitutes a boundary condition for the visceral compatibility effect.

REFERENCES

Bar-Hillel, Maya. (1980), "The Base-Rate Fallacy in Probability Judgments," *Acta Psychologica*, 44 (3), 211-233.

Hamill, Ruth, Timothy D. Wilson, and Richard E. Nisbett (1980), "Insensitivity to Sample Bias: Generalizing from Atypical Cases," *Journal of Personality and Social Psychology*, 39 (4), 578-589.

Hornikx, Jos (2005), "A Review of Experimental Research on the Relative Persuasiveness of Anecdotal, Statistical, Causal, and Expert Evidence," *Studies in Communication Sciences*, 5 (1), 205-216.

Petty, Richard E., and John T. Cacioppo (1986), *Communication and Persuasion: Central and Peripheral Routes to Attitude Chang*, New York: Springer-Verlag.

Remembering Better or Remembering Worse: Age Effects on False Memory

Priyali Rajagopal, Southern Methodist University, USA
Nicole Votolato Montgomery, College of William & Mary, USA

EXTENDED ABSTRACT

Research in memory has focused on understanding the origins, characteristics and consequences of false memory (Rajagopal and Montgomery 2011). However, there has been little focus on variables that moderate false beliefs about past experiences. In this paper, we examine one such variable – age.

Research suggests that older adults are more prone to memory deficits. For example, Skurnik et al (2005) found that older adults were more likely to forget the context of a claim over time (true vs. false) and therefore were more likely to mistakenly believe it to be true. Consistent with this research, our expectation was that false memories would be more pronounced for older versus younger adults. That is, older adults would be more likely to report having tried a product that they had not in reality tried.

Study 1 was a 2 (age: old vs. young) x 2 (imagery: high vs. low) between subjects study (n = 104). Thirty-four respondents were students (M_{age} = 20.5 years), while seventy were older adults (M_{age} = 62.2 years). All respondents read a set of 10 advertisements (1 target, 9 fillers) for different products that utilized a real brand name with a fictitious variant name (e.g., Gatorade Zoom). The target product was for Orville Redenbacher's Blue Corn microwave popcorn. The high and low versions of this ad were pretested to ensure that the two versions of the ad varied only in terms of their imagery-evoking ability and not dimensions such as meaningfulness, believability etc.

After reading all the ads, respondents reported their task involvement on a 3-item scale (α = .87) to ensure that differences in involvement could not explain our results (p's > .05). One week later, they completed an online survey that contained the dependent measures.

Our key dependent measures were false memory and attitude strength. False memory was assessed using two different measures. The first measure was a dichotomous measure wherein respondents selected all the products that they thought they had ever tried from a list of fifty different products including the target brand. Our second measure was a set of four statements about the target product, from which respondents were asked to choose all the statements that applied to them. The statements attempted to delineate false memory about the product (e.g., "I have purchased this product", "I have seen this product in local grocery stores" and "I have heard about this product from friends or family members") from accurate memory about the product ("I have seen an advertisement for this product in another study"). For reporting purposes, we summed the first three statements as our measure of false memory. We collected responses to the statements for three filler brands in addition to the target product.

We used attitude predictiveness as our measure of attitude strength. Attitudes were measured using a four-item scale (bad-good, negative-positive, unfavorable-favorable, undesirable-desirable, α = .88). Purchase intentions were measured using a single item scale ("How likely are you to purchase Orville Redenbacher's blue corn popcorn the next time you are purchasing microwave popcorn?").

RESULTS

False Memory. We found a significant interaction between age and imagery on the product usage memory measure ($\chi2$ (3) = 8.91, p < .05) and the false statements (F (1, 100) = 4.12, p < .05), with the older adults reporting a lower incidence of false memory as compared with the younger respondents. Thus, a larger number of younger respondents selected the target product when they viewed the high imagery ad (28.5%) as compared to the low imagery ad (10%), but there was no significant difference between the high (5.5%) and low imagery (2.9%) ad conditions for the older respondents. Similarly, younger respondents choose a larger number of false memory statements when they viewed the high imagery ad (M = .86) as compared to the low imagery ad (M = .30; t (100) = 2.66, p < .05), with no differences between the two conditions for the older respondents (M_{high} = .30, M_{low} = .26, t (100) < 1). There were no differences in the selection of the correct memory statement ($\chi2$ (3) = 1.03, p > .1). These results suggest that age moderates the creation of false memories such that older respondents are *less* susceptible to the creation of false memories through advertising.

Attitude strength. Regression analyses revealed that attitudes significantly predicted purchase intentions for the young respondents who viewed the high imagery ad (β = .59, p < .05), but not the other experimental conditions ($\beta_{young,low\ imagery}$ = .29, p > .1, $\beta_{old,high\ imagery}$ = -.22, p > .1, $\beta_{old,low\ imagery}$ = .17, p > .1). Thus, consistent with the results for memory, we find that attitude-intent correlations are significant only when false memory is reported. This further suggests that the false memory effect is found only for the younger respondents.

These results suggest that age moderates the creation of false memories such that older respondents are *less* susceptible to the false experience effect than younger respondents. This is contrary to our predictions and is a very interesting finding because it is also contrary to the findings from past research that has consistently documented a memory disadvantage with age.

We propose that our findings occur because older adults may suffer from a decline in the ability to image, which decreases the creation of false memories via high imagery advertising. To that end, we have two unreported studies that further examine the moderating effect of age using different techniques to instantiate false memory (e.g., repetition, writing detailed experiences), consistent with past research (Garry et al. 1996). In study 2, respondents are asked to write detailed information about erroneous autobiographical experiences. In study 3, we test whether repeating ads can attenuate the differences in false memory between the two age groups since research has shown that repetition can aid memory for older adults more than younger adults. In addition, we also collect information on frequency of consumption, product familiarity and knowledge to rule out the possibility that differences in these variables may underlie the findings.

REFERENCES

Garry, Maryanne, Charles G. Manning, Elizabeth F. Loftus, and Steven J. Sherman (1996), "Imagination Inflation: Imagining a Childhood Event Inflates Confidence that it Occurred," *Psychonomic Bulletin and Review*, 3 (2), 208-214.

Rajagopal, Priyali and Nicole Votolato Montgomery (2011), "I Imagine, I Experience, I Like: The False Experience Effect," *Journal of Consumer Research*, 38 (3), 578-594.

Skurnik, Ian, Carolyn Yoon, Denise C. Park and Norbert Schwarz (2005), "How Warnings about False Claims Become Recommendations," *Journal of Consumer Research*, 31 (4), 713-724.

Dynamic Patterns of Intra-Shopping Spending for Budget and Non-Budget Shoppers

Daniel Sheehan, Georgia Institute of Technology, USA
Koert van Ittersum, Georgia Institute of Technology, USA

EXTENDED ABSTRACT

Much of our current understanding about how consumers shop for goods and services is based on a cross-sectional analyses of end-of-trip variables (e.g., basket composition, spending). However, research increasingly examines intra-shopping decision-making processes to gain an understanding about how spending unfolds during a single shopping trip. Dhar et al. (2007), for example, study the impact of an initial purchase on subsequent decisions. Stilley and colleagues (2010), in turn, examine how shoppers shift their spending between planned and unplanned items. Following this paradigm, the present research examines how shoppers' spending decisions, pertaining to each individual product choice, change as a function of their cumulative spending during a single shopping trip. Building on recent research that shows the differentiating effects of budget constraints on shopping behavior (Van Ittersum et al. 2010, 2011), we examine this for budget versus non-budget shoppers.

Intrigued by the idea of whether cumulative spending during a shopping trip influences subsequent purchase decisions (spending $2.25 vs. $3.75 on eggs), we conducted a simple exploratory lab experiment where participants were asked to make sixteen subsequent choices from one of two products (for different product categories). The results revealed a U-shaped relationship between the cumulative amount of money spent and the relative spending on an individual item. Shoppers are more inclined to purchase more expensive items early and towards the end of the shopping trip, but are more inclined to purchase less expensive items halfway through their shopping trip. Interestingly enough, this relationship takes on an inverted U-shape when shoppers are budget constrained. Halfway through the shopping trip, budget shoppers actually spend relatively more on individual items than their non-constrained counterparts (F(1,59)=5.4, p<.05).

To explain the origin of these unique relationships between cumulative spending and the relative spending on an individual item, we build on research on the pain of payment (Prelec & Loewenstein 1998) and regulatory resources (Baumeister 2002), both of which have shown to influence shopper decision making (Thomas et al. 2011). The literature on the pain of payment suggests that pain of payment increases with spending. We extend this to propose that for non-budget shoppers, the pain of payment evolves concavely throughout a shopping trip (as the relative pain of payment of the last $1 spent is less compared to the first $1 spent). For budget shoppers, however, we hypothesize an S-shaped relationship, as the money left in their budget reduces the pain of payment early in the shopping trip (Heath & Soll 1996). We further expect to find differences in the speed with which budget versus non-budget shoppers deplete their regulatory resources. While both groups of shoppers are expected to deplete resources in a convex manner, the resource depletion of budget shoppers is expected to occur more quickly due to the additional need of monitoring the spending (Van Ittersum, et al. 2010). Both sets of unique patterns help explain the differences in the relationship between the cumulative amount of money spent and the relative spending on an each purchase between budget and non-budget shoppers. We conducted two independent studies to provide evidence for the proposed mechanism.

STUDY 1: PAIN OF PAYMENT

To observe how shoppers' pain of payment evolves during a single shopping trip, we asked participants to complete a simulated shopping task containing 30 randomized purchase decisions. For each decision, participants selected one out of four choice options. After randomly assigning participants to a budget or non-budget condition, we measured each participant's pain of payment (Thomas et al. 2011) after 5, 10, 15, 20, 25, or 30 decisions (between-subjects). Consistent with expectations, the pain of payment evolves concavely during the shopping trip (ßdecision=.09, p<.01; ßdecision2=-.02, p<.05). Furthermore, budget shoppers experience significantly less pain than non-budget shoppers halfway during the trip (3.4 vs. 4.5, F(1, 53)=4.57, p<.05), but not at the beginning or end of the shopping trip.

STUDY 2: REGULATORY RESOURCES

The setup of this study was similar to that of Study 1, with the exception of the measurement task within each shopping trip. In study 2, participant's resources were measured by observing their persistence on an anagram task (Vohs et al. 2008) after a specified number of purchase decisions (identical to Study 1). Consistent with expectations, the regulatory resources deplete during the shopping trip (p<.05) and slightly quicker for budget shoppers (p<.10). Furthermore, by the end of the shopping experience, there are significant differences in the persistence of budget and non-budget shoppers (252 vs. 140 secs., F(1, 27)=5.57, p<.05).

STUDY 3: ONLINE SHOPPING EXPERIMENT

As the exploratory lab study was a small controlled laboratory experiment, we conducted a final field experiment in a mock online grocery store. Subjects were randomly assigned to a budget conditions (budget vs. non-budget) and asked to shop with a pre-tested shopping list. This online grocery store contains more than 3000 products, and for items on the shopping list, subjects were able to choose from between five and fifteen product alternatives (e.g., blueberry bagels, plain bagels) from between two and eight different store and national brands. We coded the relative spending of each subjects decisions throughout the experiment. A repeated measures analysis reveals the predicted quadratic interaction between budget and purchase decision (F(1,92)=11.53, p<.01). Furthermore, consistent with the pilot study, the conventional wisdom that non-budget shoppers always spend more than budget shoppers is only found in the beginning and end of the shopping trip. In the middle of the shopping trip, budget shoppers actually spend slightly more (1.08 vs. 0.98, F(1,92)=3.48, p<.10).

Our research makes three important contributions. First, this research is among the first to examine shoppers' intra-shopping trip decision-making and its subsequent spending consequences. Second, significantly extends literature on pain-of-payment (Prelec & Loewenstein 1998) by demonstrating the evolution of pain of payment within a shopping trip for budget and non-budget shoppers, as well highlighting a point in a shopping trip when pain experienced by budget shoppers actually decreases. Finally, this research provides insights on both the rate and consequences of regulatory resource depletion for budget and non-budget shopper

REFERENCES

Baumeister, R. F. (2002). Yielding to temptation: Self-control failure, impulsive purchasing, and consumer behavior. *Journal of Consumer Research*, 670-676.

Dhar, R., Huber, J., & Khan, U. (2007). The shopping momentum effect. *Journal of Marketing Research, 44*(3), 370-378.

Heath, C., & Soll, J. B. (1996). Mental budgeting and consumer decisions. *Journal of Consumer Research*, 40-52.

Prelec, D., & Loewenstein, G. (1998). The red and the black: Mental accounting of savings and debt. *Marketing Science*, 4-28.

Stilley, K. M., Inman, J. J., & Wakefield, K. L. (2010). Planning to Make Unplanned Purchases? The Role of In-Store Slack in Budget Deviation. *Journal of Consumer Research, 37*(2), 264–278.

Thomas, M., Desai, K. K., & Seenivasan, S. (2011). How Credit Card Payments Increase Unhealthy Food Purchases: Visceral Regulation of Vices. *Journal of Consumer Research, 38*(1), 126-139.

Van Ittersum, Pennings, & Wansink. (2010). Trying Harder and Doing Worse: How Grocery Shoppers Track In-Store Spending. *Journal of Marketing, 74*(2), 90-104.

Van Ittersum, Pennings, & Wansink. (2011). *Budget Shoppers' Spending Biases.* Paper presented at the Society of Consumer Psychology Winter Conference, Atlanta, GA.

Vohs, K. D., Baumeister, R. F., Schmeichel, B. J., Twenge, J. M., Nelson, N. M., & Tice, D. M. (2008). Making choices impairs subsequent self-control: A limited-resource account of decision making, self-regulation, and active initiative. *Journal of Personality and Social Psychology, 94*(5), 883.

Effective Substitution: The Drawback of High Similarity

Zachary G. Arens, Jesse H. Jones Graduate School of Business, USA
Rebecca W. Hamilton, Robert H. Smith School of Business, USA

EXTENDED ABSTRACT

Consumers frequently substitute for products that are out-of-stock (Emmelhainz, Stock, and Emmelhainz 1991; Peckham 1963), too expensive (Bucklin and Srinivasan 1991), too unhealthy (Tuorila, Kramer, and Cardello 1997) or otherwise unattainable. Despite the prevalence of substitution, there is little research on what makes a replacement product an effective substitute. This research investigates the relationship between product similarity and substitution. We show that although consumers believe that highly similar products are better substitutes, in fact moderately similar products more effectively satisfy the consumer's desire for the original. For example, if a consumer is looking forward to a Coca-Cola but finds it unavailable, our data suggest that another brand of cola (a highly similar product) will be a worse substitute than a lemon-lime soda (a moderately similar product), although the consumer believes the opposite.

Substitutes are defined as products that fulfill the same goal (Kruglanski et al. 2002; Lewin 1935). The degree of substitutability between products is not a fixed property but can vary depending on the particular goal at hand (Ratneshwar, Pechmann, and Shocker 1996; Ratneshwar and Shocker 1991). Typically substitutability is measured by examining the change in quantity demanded of one product in response to a change in the price of another (Hicks 1963; Slutsky 1960) or by the likelihood of consuming one product after consuming another (Lattin and McAlister 1985). In this research, we operationalize effective substitution as the degree to which a replacement product fulfills the consumer's desire for the unattained product.

Because a replacement product is intended to fulfill the goal associated with an unattained product, consumers often choose replacements that share features with the unattained product (e.g., Yelp Review 2012). Thus we propose that consumers will predict that highly similar products will be better substitutes than moderately similar ones. However, in contrast to consumers' beliefs, we predict that moderately similar products will serve as more effective substitutes than highly similar ones. While earlier work on substitution using the task-interruption paradigm (Child and Grosslight 1947; Lissner 1933) suggests that similar substitutes will be more effective than dissimilar substitutes, we focus on the difference between highly similar and moderately similar products.

We propose that moderately similar substitutes will be more effective because they prompt an abstract view. The goal that motivates consumption of a product can be viewed at different levels of abstraction (Huffman, Ratneshwar, and Mick 2000; Vallacher and Wegner 1987). If a dissimilar (versus similar) replacement encourages consumers to think about the motivation for consumption abstractly (e.g., drinking soda instead of drinking cola), this could make the replacement seem better suited to fulfill the goal. Following this logic, a moderately similar replacement will appear less satisfactory and, as a result, be a less effective substitute than a moderately similar one.

Our first study demonstrates these effects by comparing consumer's beliefs about substitution with their experiences. Participants were led to believe that they would eat Cheerios, but instead were given Merry-O's, a fictitious brand of breakfast cereal. Some participants, the forecasters, imagined eating Merry-O's, and predicted how effectively it would substitute for Cheerios, while the others, the experiencers, actually ate Merry-O's (which in reality was Cheerios) and then rated how well it substituted for Cheerios. In the highly similar condition, Merry-O's shared a number of features with Cheerios (e.g., similar packaging and both are "a good source of fiber") and in the moderately similar condition, Merry-O's had more distinct features (e.g., dissimilar packing and "a good source of vitamins and minerals" compared with Cheerios which was "a good source of fiber"). As shown in figure 1, the forecasters predicted that Merry-O's would be a more effective substitute in the highly similar condition than in the moderately similar condition whereas experiencers showed the opposite pattern. Notably, these effects cannot be explained by participants negatively characterizing Merry-O's as a copycat brand.

Figure 1. Substitution Effectiveness

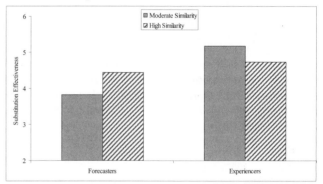

Our second study extends the first by demonstrating that satisfaction with the replacement product mediates the effect. As part of an ostensible taste test participants were given a choice between drinking Coke and Pepsi in one condition and Sprite and 7up in another condition. Later, participants were told that the soda they had selected was out of stock and were given one of two replacement beverages: a store brand of cola or a store brand of lemon-lime soda. Thus, all participants either received a moderately similar beverage (lemon-lime when they expected cola or cola when they expected lemon-lime) or a highly similar beverage (e.g., cola when they expected cola). The results showed that the moderately similar replacement beverage was consistently a more effective substitute than the highly similar beverage. For instance, lemon lime soda was a better substitute for Coke than for Sprite. This effect of similarity on substitution effectiveness was mediated by satisfaction with the replacement.

Our third study provides support for the underlying mechanism: the degree to which participants think abstractly or concretely about their consumption goal. Participants evaluated 16 classic songs and were told that they would get to listen to their favorite. However they were later told that their favorite song was unavailable and listened to a replacement song that was either moderately or highly similar based on their similarity ratings. Replicating our previous results, a moderately similar song was more satisfying and a better substitute than a highly similar one. Providing support for our predictions about the abstractness of participants' thinking, the result was mediated by the specificity of the purpose, suggesting that a moderately similar replacement prompts an abstract view, making the replacement more satisfying and a more effective substitute.

In summary, our research suggests that the lay theory that highly similar products make the best substitutes is incorrect. Instead, moderately similar replacements encourage consumers to adopt an abstract view, making the replacement a more effective substitute. By improving our understanding of the determinants of effective substitution this research offers insights to help consumers make better choices and help firms design products to better suit their needs.

REFERENCES

Bucklin, Randolph E. and V. Srinivasan (1991), "Determining Interbrand Substitutability through Survey Measurement of Consumer Preference Structures," *Journal of Marketing Research*, 28 (February), 58-71.

Child, Irvin L. and Joseph H. Grosslight (1947), "The Effect of Substitute Activity as Depending Upon the Nature of the Similarity between Substitute and Original Activity," *The American Journal of Psychology*, 60 (April), 226-39.

Emmelhainz, Margaret A., James R. Stock, and Larry W. Emmelhainz (1991), "Consumer Responses to Retail Stock-Outs," *Journal of Retailing*, 67 (Summer), 138-47.

Hicks, John Richard (1963), *Theory of Wages*, London: Macmillan.

Huffman, Cynthia, S. Ratneshwar, and David Glen Mick (2000), "Consumer Goal Structures and Goal-Determination Processes: An Integrative Framework," in *The Why of Consumption: Contemporary Perspectives on Consumer Motives, Goals and Desires*, ed. S. Ratneshwar, David Glen Mick and Cynthia Huffman, New York: Routledge, 9-35.

Kruglanski, Arie W., James Y. Shah, Ayelet Fishbach, Ron Friedman, Woo Young Chun, David Sleeth-Keppler, and Mark P. Zanna (2002), "A Theory of Goal Systems," in *Advances in Experimental Social Psychology*, Vol. 34, ed. Mark P. Zanna, San Diego, CA: Academic Press, 331-78.

Lattin, James M. and Leigh McAlister (1985), "Using a Variety-Seeking Model to Identify Substitute and Complementary Relationships among Competing Products," *Journal of Marketing Research*, 22, 330-39.

Lewin, Kurt (1935), *A Dynamic Theory of Personality: Selected Papers*, New York: McGraw Hill.

Lissner, Käte (1933), "Die Entspannung Von Bedürfnissen Durch Ersatzhandlungen," *Psychologische Forschung*, 18, 218-50.

Peckham, James O. (1963), "The Consumer Speaks," *Journal of Marketing*, 27 (October), 21-26.

Ratneshwar, S., Cornelia Pechmann, and Allan D. Shocker (1996), "Goal-Derived Categories and the Antecedents of across-Category Consideration," *Journal of Consumer Research*, 23 (December), 240-50.

Ratneshwar, S. and Allan D. Shocker (1991), "Substitution in Use and the Role of Usage Context in Product Category Structures," *Journal of Marketing Research*, 28 (August), 281-95.

Slutsky, Eugen E. (1960), "On the Theory of the Budget of the Consumer," in *Readings in Price Theory*, ed. Kenneth E. Boulding and George J. Stigler, London: George Allen and Unwin, 27-56.

Tuorila, Hely, F. Matthew Kramer, and Armand V. Cardello (1997), "Role of Attitudes, Dietary Restraint, and Fat Avoidance Strategies in Reported Consumption of Selected Fat-Free Foods," *Food Quality and Preference*, 8, 119-23.

Vallacher, Robin R. and Daniel M. Wegner (1987), "What Do People Think They're Doing? Action Identification and Human Behavior," *Psychological Review*, 94, 3-15.

Y., Susan (2012), "Tuck Shop Review," http://www.yelp.com/biz/tuck-shop-manhattan-2#hrid:3TDi4jKNuRa6_Gh5j7h1IQ.

The Effect of Message Credibility, Need for Cognitive Closure, and Information Sufficiency on Thought-Induced Attitude Change

Bruce E. Pfeiffer, University of New Hampshire, USA
Hélène Deval, Dalhousie University, Canada
David H. Silvera, University of Texas at San Antonio, USA
Maria L. Cronley, Miami University, USA
Frank Kardes, University of Cincinnati, USA

EXTENDED ABSTRACT

Substantial research on self-generated persuasion has demonstrated that simply thinking about an attitude object can result in more extreme attitudes toward the object (e.g., Tesser, 1978; Tesser, Martin, & Mendolia, 1995). This mere thought effect suggests that when people think about attitude objects, they generate additional attitude-consistent thoughts leading to greater attitude polarization. Although research in this area has investigated several moderating factors (e.g., Judd & Lusk, 1984; Linville, 1982; Millar & Tesser, 1986; Tesser & Leone, 1977), most of the research looks at constraints that attenuate but not reverse the effect. It has been suggested, however, that under some situations people may generate attitude inconsistent thoughts resulting in a depolarizing effect (e.g., Marsh & Wallace, 2005). Further, it has been shown that if people have too much time to think, they may lose the motivation or ability to generate additional attitude-consistent thoughts, leading to a loss in thought confidence and resulting in attitude depolarization (Clarkson, Tormala, & Leone, 2011).

This research investigates source effects as another depolarizing variable and two additional moderating variables, need for cognitive closure and information sufficiency. Consumers have many resources for gathering information about products that vary in perceived objectivity. Source effects play an important role in consumer attitude formation and product evaluations and have been shown to operate at varying levels of processing (Kang & Herr, 2006) depending on ability and motivation (e.g., Petty & Cacioppo, 1986). Whether consumers view an ad as informative and accurate or persuasive depends on the ambiguity of the information and the motivation to think about the implications of the ad (Hung & Wyer, 2008). Consumers generally expend little cognitive effort when presented with advertisements (Hung & Wyer, 2008). When people are motivated to consider an advertisement, they are likely to consider that the advertiser's claims are generally exaggerated and designed to persuade (Persuasion Knowledge Model; Friestad & Wright, 1994).

Need for cognitive closure (NFCC) (Kruglanski & Webster, 1996) refers to a desire to form a definite opinion ("seize") and to maintain the opinion once it is formed ("freeze"). Since people high in NFCC are more likely to "seize" and "freeze" on an evaluation, they should be less likely to adjust an evaluation once it is formed. Low NFCC consumers should be more likely to draw additional inferences, allowing for attitude polarization. Further, it is possible that enough diagnostic information may override a source effect. The "set-size effect" (Anderson, 1967, 1981; Yamagishi & Hill, 1981, 1983) has demonstrated that as the number of attributes used to describe a person or object increases, the overall evaluation becomes more extreme. If enough positive information is provided, it may not matter as much whether the source is credible or not.

Experiment 1 was designed to investigate source effects in relation to attitude change. Participants were asked to imagine that they were shopping for a new cell phone plan and were provided with a brief description of a plan. Participants were informed that the information was either taken from an advertisement (low credibility) or from an article in Consumer Reports Magazine (high credibility).

Participants then rated their attitudes toward the plan. Next, participants were asked to either think about the plan (thought task) or work on a crossword puzzle (distraction task) for 90 seconds. They then rated their attitude toward the plan a second time. A polarization score was computed using the difference between the attitude score at time 1 and time 2. A 2 (thought vs. distraction) X 2 (source credibility) ANOVA revealed a significant two-way interaction. As expected, participants in the thinking condition adjusted their attitude from time 1 to time 2, while those in the distraction condition did not. When the source was credible a polarization effect was found. When the source was less credible, a depolarized effect was found.

Experiment 2 further investigated the depolarizing effect, while including NFCC as a potential moderator. This study was identical to experiment 1 except only the low credibility source (advertisement) was used, and participants completed the 42-item NFCC scale (Webster & Kruglanski, 1994). A regression analysis revealed a significant two-way interaction. As expected, a depolarizing effect was found in the thinking condition, but only when NFCC was low. No change was found in the distraction condition regardless of NFCC.

Experiment 3 extended the findings of experiment 2 by manipulating NFCC while also considering the potential moderating effect of set-size on polarization. Participants were asked to imagine that they were shopping for a new laptop computer and were presented with a description. They were informed that the information was taken from a recent advertisement. The amount of descriptive information varied (four vs. eight pieces of information). NFCC was manipulated via an accountability manipulation (e.g., Tetlock, 1985). The attitude measure and thought/distraction task were the same as the previous studies. A 2 (thought vs. distraction) X 2 (set size: large vs. small) X 2 (NFCC: high vs. low) ANOVA revealed a significant three-way interaction. We found the same depolarizing effect in the small set-size condition as in experiment 2. A thought-induced depolarization effect was found but only for those low in NFCC. No change was found in the distraction condition regardless of NFCC. In contrast, we found a marginally polarizing effect in the large set-size condition. A thought-induced polarization effect was found but only for those low in NFCC. No change was found in the distraction condition regardless of NFCC. Apparently the larger set-size doesn't just attenuate the source effect, but also reverses it.

This research provides important new insight into self-generated persuasion. Source effects can result in polarizing effects if the source is credible but depolarizing effects if the source is less credible. Further, thought-induced attitude change depends on varying levels of NFCC and information sufficiency.

REFERENCES

Anderson, Norman H. (1967), "Averaging Model Analyses of Set-Size Effect in Impression Formation," *Journal of Experimental Psychology*, 75 (2), 158-165.

Anderson, Norman H. (1981), *Foundations of Information Integration Theory*; New York: Academic Press.

Clarkson, Joshua J., Zakary L. Tormala, and Christopher Leone (2011), "A Self-Validation Perspective on the Mere Thought Effect," *Journal of Experimental Social Psychology,* 47, 449-454.

Friestad, Marion and Peter Wright (1994), "The Persuasion Knowledge Model: How People Cope With Persuasion Attempts," *Journal of Consumer Research,* 21, 1–31.

Hung, Iris W. and Robert S. Wyer (2008), "The Impact of Implicit Theories on Responses to Problem-Solving Print Advertisements," *Journal of Consumer Psychology,* 18, 223-235.

Judd, Charles M. and Cunthia M. Lusk (1984), "Knowledge Structures and Evaluative Judgments: Effects of Structural Variables on Judgment Extremity," *Journal of Personality and Social Psychology,* 46 (6), 1193-1207.

Kruglanski, Arie W. and Donna M. Webster (1996), "Motivated Closing of the Mind: 'Seizing' and 'Freezing'," *Psychological Review*, 103 (2), 263-83.

Linville, Patricia W. (1982), "The Complexity-Extremity Effect and Age-Based Stereotyping," *Journal of Personality and Social Psychology,* 42 (2), 193-211.

Marsh, Kerry L. and Harry M. Wallace (2005), "The Influence of Attitudes on Beliefs: Formation and Change," In Dolores Albarracín, Blair T. Johnson, and Mark P. Zanna (Eds.), *The Handbook of Attitudes*; Mahwah, NJ: Erlbaum.

Millar, Murray G. and Abraham Tesser (1986), "Thought-Induced Attitude Change: The effects of Schema Structure and Commitment," *Journal of Personality and Social Psychology,* 51 (2), 259-269.

Petty, Richarcd E. and John T. Cacioppo (1986), *Communication and Persuasion: Central and Peripheral Routes to Attitude Change*; New York: Springer-Verlag.

Tesser, Abraham (1978), "Self-Generated Attitude Change," *Advances in Experimental Social Psychology,* 11, 289-338.

Tesser, Abraham and Christopher Leone (1977), "Cognitive Schemas and Thought as Determinants of Attitude Change," *Journal of Experimental Social Psychology,* 13, 340-356.

Tesser, Abraham, Leonard Martin, and Marilyn Mendolia (1995), "The Impact of Thought on Attitude Extremity and Attitude-Behavior Consistency," In Richard E. Petty and Jon A. Krosnick (Eds.), *Attitude Strength: Antecedents and Consequences*; Mahwah, NJ: Erlbaum.

Webster, Donna M. and Arie W. Kruglanski (1994), "Individual Differences in Need for Cognitive Closure," *Journal of Personality and Social Psychology,* 67 (6), 1049-62.

Yamagishi, Toshio and Charles T. Hill (1981), "Adding Versus Averaging Models Revisited: A Test of a Path Analytic Integration Model," *Journal of Personality and Social Psychology*, 41, 13-25.

Yamagishi, Toshio and Charles T. Hill (1983), "Initial Impression Versus Missing Information as an Explanation of the Set-Size Effect," *Journal of Personality and Social Psychology,* 44 (5), 942-51.

Diversity Appreciated?
A Visual Longitudinal Analysis of Ukraine's Nation Branding Campaigns

Luca M. Visconti, , ESCP Europe, France
Mine Üçok Hughes, Woodbury University, USA
Ruben Bagramian, Woodbury University, USA

EXTENDED ABSTRACT

This paper discusses the nation branding efforts of Ukraine, a post-communist country, since gaining its independence from the Soviet Union in 1991. In detail, our study aims at: i) highlighting the specifics of nation branding campaigns for Ukraine, whose communist past fuels a nation image problematic to promote; and ii) grounding future research that will analyze the power dynamics between Ukrainian citizens and international tourists who are the main audience for these campaigns.

Nation branding falls within the field of place branding (Fan 2009; Gnoth 2002; Hanna and Rowley 2008) that covers an array of studies differing in terms of: i) unit of analysis (city versus nation), ii) stakeholders (local and national governments, citizens, companies, and the media), and iii) objectives of enhancing exports, protecting local/national production, attracting tourists and investors, and facilitating international relations (Papadopoulos 2004). It also shows differences from the country-of-origin research. While the latter holds companies' perspective and leverages the place to improve the attractiveness of other products designed/assembled/produced in that place, place branding literature fosters the perspective of governments and individuals (tourists and local dwellers) and considers the place as the main object of market exchange (Anholt 2004; 2011).

Existing research on place branding can be divided into managerially or conceptually driven studies. Managerial projects explore the application of marketing to improve the economic development of the place (Anholt 2004; 2011; Fan 2009; 2006; Giannopoulos, Piha and Avlonitis 2011; Jaffe and Nebenzhal 2001; Kotler and Gertner 2002). More conceptual projects investigate connections between place, city and nation branding (Hanna and Rowley 2008), the boundary between place branding and country-of-origin (Papadopoulos 2004) or between nation brand and nation branding (Fan 2006) and the differences between corporate and place branding (Kavaratzis 2005).

Our research analyzes longitudinally the nation branding campaigns of Ukraine. With a population of around 45 million, Ukraine has been developing an increasingly tight relationship with the EU (http://eeas.europa.eu/ukraine/index_en.htm). Several reasons justify the choice of our empirical setting: i) the country is transitioning from a central economy to a market economy, thus striving to develop a nation brand far from Soviet associations (Nordbeg and Kuzio 1998), ii) the difference of this nation brand from Western nation brands makes it an intriguing case in studying the specificities of nation branding in transitioning economies, iii) longitudinal analysis of Ukraine's nation branding campaigns is made possible by its twenty years of independence, and iv) more recently the UEFA 2012 Football Championship supports the economic and managerial relevance of this research.

Our data set includes five major nation branding campaigns that Ukraine has conducted over the last 11 years. We collected Ukrainian short promotional videos, logos, press articles and press releases, and other broadcast materials as well as monitored web sites, blogs and forums. Data analysis is consistent with established procedures of interpretive research in general (Spiggle 1994) and of visual analysis in particular (Schroeder 2002; Scott 1994). The research team is comprised of three researchers, one from the USA, one from Western Europe, and a third from Ukraine, thus facilitating a derived etic approach to data analysis (Berry 1989).

Our findings show two main drivers steadily directing Ukraine's nation branding efforts. Firstly, Ukraine has built its new identity by *stating what it is not*—a communist country—instead of conveying a clear, assertive image of what it is. In an attempt to distance itself from its communist past, its campaigns try to reassure local and international audiences of the "modernization" undertaken by Ukraine. This finding is also supported by other studies focusing on nation branding in post-communist countries (Anholt 2007; Kaneva 2012; Kaneva and Poescu 2011; Kemming and Sandikci 2007). Secondly, Ukraine's nation branding campaigns portray a wide range of visual information that is at times incongruous with each other. Ukrainian nation brand is a collection of folkloristic, architectural, natural, economic, urban, and social elements. The promotional videos illustrate the appeal of clean cities, happy people, a healthy life style, elegant architectural landmarks, and beautiful nature. Catchy slogans such as "Switch on Ukraine" or "High Time to See Ukraine" were created to show the attractiveness of Ukraine, primarily to foreign tourists. However, these all result in a string of campaigns where a lot is shown but nothing is clearly said. These two findings demonstrate that the stigma for Ukraine's past reverted traditional principles guiding nation branding campaigns from an assertive communication approach (what the nation is) to an avoiding approach (what the nation is not), and from a frontal positioning (a few key nation identifiers) to a smokescreen of overlapping elements, which—we argue—are due to the willingness to divert audience's attention from the communist past and an enduring uncertainty about extant national identity. However, despite its multiple nation branding efforts ever since its independence, Ukraine's perceived difference from other Western nations presents a disvalue to both its government and international audiences. In the Brand Index ranking provided by Future Brand, out of 110 nations Ukraine dropped from position 75 in 2009 to position 99 in 2010.

With reference to the second research objective, our analysis indicates that the sense of superiority for the market economy of the Western world has been transferred to *a sense of superiority of international visitors toward local citizens*. The campaign "Ukraine. All about U" may appear as an innocent attempt to attract tourists. However, looking at it from a different perspective, we argue that tourists are given the power to consume, modify, and divert the meanings grounding Ukraine's national identity, thus turning power dynamics to their advantage.

Our work advances nation branding literature by showing that this literature is not culturally neutral and embeds deep post-colonial, Western, capitalistic values and norms, which post-communist countries have problems to elaborate when transitioning toward the market economy. Paradoxically their adherence to capitalism maintains these countries in a state of subjection and helps twist the application of nation branding principles, thus maintaining their gap even further.

REFERENCES

Anholt, Simon (2004), "Branding places and nations," in *Brands and Branding,* Rita Clifton and John Simmons, eds. New Jersey: Bloomberg Press, 213-226.

Anholt, Simon (2011), "Beyond the Nation Brand: The Role of Image and Identity in International Relations," in *Brands and Branding Geographies*, Andy Pike, ed. UK: Edward Elgar Publishing, 289-301.

Berry, John W. (1989), "Imposed Etics-Emics-Derived Etics: The Operationalization of a Compelling Idea," *International Journal of Psychology*, 24 (6), 721-35.

Fan, Ying (2006), "Branding the nation: What is being branded?" *Journal of Vacation Marketing*, 12 (January), 5-14.

Fan, Ying (2009), "Branding the nation: Towards a better understanding," (accessed January 5, 2012), [available at http://bura.brunel.ac.uk/handle/2438/3496]

Giannopoulos, A. Antonios, P. Lamprini Piha, and J. George Avlonitis, (2011), "Desti–Nation Branding: what for? From the notions of tourism and nation branding to an integrated framework," paper presented at the 2011 Berlin International Economics Congress, Berlin, Germany (March 15).

Gnoth, Juergen (2002), "Leveraging export brands through a tourism destination brand," *Journal of Brand Management,* 9 (April), 262-280.

Hanna, Sonya and Jennifer Rowley (2008), "An analysis of terminology use in place branding," *Place Branding and Public Diplomacy,* 4, 61-75.

Jaffe, Eugene D. and D. Israel Nebenzahl (2001), *National Image and Competitive Advantage: The theory and practice of country-of-origin effect.* Copenhagen Business School Press.

Kaneva, Nadia (2012), "Nation Branding in Post-Communist Europe: Identities, Markets, and Democracy," in *Branding Post-Communist Nations: Marketing National Identities in the New Europe*, ed. Nadia Kaneva, New York, NY: Routledge, 3-22.

Kaneva, Nadia and Delia Popescu (2011), "National Identity Lite: Nation Branding in Post-Communist Romania and Bulgaria," *International Journal of Cultural Studies*, 14 (2): 191-207.

Kavaratzis, Mihilis (2005), "Place Branding: A Review of Trends and Conceptual Models," *The Marketing Review*, 5, 329-342.

Kemming Jan Dirk and Özlem Sandikci (2007), "Turkey's EU Accession as a Question of Nation Brand Image," *Place Branding and Public Diplomacy*, 3 (1): 31-41.

Kotler, Philip and David Gertner (2002), "Country as brand, product, and beyond: a place marketing and brand management perspective," *Journal of Brand Management*, 9 (April), 249-261.

Nordberg, Mark and Taras Kuzio (1998), "Nation and State Building, Historical Legacies and National Identities in Belarus and Ukraine: A Comparative Analysis," in *Belarus and Russia: Societies and States*, Dmitry Furman ed. Moscow: Parava Cheloveka, 376-392.

Papadopoulos, Nicolas (2004), "Place branding: Evolution, meaning and implications," *Place Branding*, 1, 36-49.

Schroeder, Jonathan (2002), *Visual Consumption*, London: Routledge.

Scott, Linda (1994), "Images of Advertising: The Need for a Theory of Visual Rhetoric," *Journal of Consumer Research*, 21 (September), 252-273.

Spiggle, Susan (1994), "Analysis and Interpretation of Qualitative Data in Consumer Research," *Journal of Consumer Research*, 21 (December), 491-503.

Should You or Could You? The Effect of Social Influence in Text Warnings Against Product Placement and the Moderating Role of Self-Monitoring

Tina Tessitore, Ghent University, Belgium
Maggie Geuens, Ghent University, Belgium

EXTENDED ABSTRACT

Product placement (pp) is a paid inclusion of brands in mass-media programming (Balasubramanian 1994), for which persuasion knowledge (PK) (i.e., the knowledge people rely on to deal with a persuasion attempt) is not always activated (Friestad and Wright 1994; Wei, Fischer, and Main 2008). The European Union (2009) authorized pp on the condition that this covert practice is clearly identified to viewers. Hence, research on warnings for pp becomes important in the marketing and public policy domain. In this respect, it is essential to test *which types of warnings* are most effective (for *which types of persons*). Moreover, resistance is a conscious process, requiring cognitive resources (Campbell and Kirmani 2000). Hence, consumers must consciously recall/recognize the brand for resistance to occur. Moreover, brand recall reflects attention to the placed brand, which might increase its accessibility in viewers' minds, increasing their likelihood of choosing the brand (Van Kerckhove, Vermeir, and Geuens 2011). Consequently, we hypothesize that purchase intent is higher with than without brand recall, when no (effective) warning is provided. Therefore, we also consider brand recall in this research.

A number of researchers has proven the importance of explicitness in warnings (i.e., "the specificity or detail with which potential injury consequences are described" (Laughery et al. 1993, p.598) to increase warning effectiveness, mostly in the context of product hazards (e.g., Trommelen 1997; Frantz 1994). In the subtle and less dangerous context of pp, explicitness in a warning can perhaps counterbalance the subtleness of pp as a persuasion tactic, making the tactic's ulterior motive more salient. As such, a text warning, containing information about pp, may be effective to activate PK and hence, to enable resistance.

In Study 1 (*N*=119), we investigated the effectiveness of a text warning to enable viewers to counteract pp influence on their purchase intent. We manipulated warning presence (text warning: yes vs. no) and measured brand recall. A two-way ANOVA revealed two significant main effects, which were qualified by an interaction effect. Specifically, when the brand is recalled, purchase intent is significantly lower in case of a text warning versus no warning. When the brand is not recalled, no resistance is found. Furthermore, only in the control group, brand recall led to higher purchase intent than no recall.

In some occasions, warnings can lead to reactance against the warning itself (Bushman 1998; Bushman and Stack 1996). Reactance theory (Brehm 1966) states that when a person feels obliged to adopt an opinion or certain behavior, he could perceive his freedom to be constrained, making him more likely to react against the communicator. In our case, a warning that is perceived as more stringent, would then be less effective. Consequently, it seems important to identify a potential moderator of the effectiveness of text warnings that drives potential reactance.

To this end, we investigated in Study 2 (*N*=86) whether the type of social influence comprised in a warning (i.e., informational versus normative warning) can moderate the effectiveness of text warnings. Normative warnings can be perceived as more stringent, since they contain norms and expectations of a certain group, compared to informational warnings, which contain pure objective information. Consequently, we hypothesize that normative warnings are less effective than informational warnings to counteract pp influence.

A between-subjects design with three conditions (no vs. informational vs. normative warning) was set up. An ANOVA (warning x

brand recognition) revealed a significant interaction effect. In case of brand recognition, an informational warning significantly deteriorated purchase intent compared to no warning. No significant differences were found between the other conditions. So, although there is an indication that an informational warning is more effective than a normative warning in comparison with no warning, no direct difference between both warnings is found. Without brand recognition, we found no significant differences. Again, only in the control group, brand recognition entailed more purchase intent than no recognition. Moreover, an ANOVA on PK-activation revealed only two significant main effects. Brand recognition led to more PK than no recognition. Moreover, both warnings entailed more PK-activation than no warning. No significant difference is found between both warnings. Furthermore, we wanted to explore whether PK-activation drives the effectiveness of these warnings to resist pp influence compared to a situation without warning. Since no direct difference was found between both warnings on purchase intent and PK-activation, we constructed a new variable, coded as warning - including both the informational and normative warning - versus no warning. Bootstrap analysis (Preacher and Hayes 2004) shows evidence for mediation by PK-activation of the diminishing effect of warnings (versus no warning) on purchase intent in case of brand recognition.

A last issue that we consider, is which type of social influence in a warning is most effective for which type of person? With regard to social influence, self-monitoring is a relevant personality variable to contemplate. High self-monitors are more sensitive to others' expectations and norms (Snyder 1974), making us assume that they will be less likely to react against a normative warning than low self-monitors. Hence, for high self-monitors, a normative warning is expected to be more effective than an informational warning.

In Study 3 (*N*=109), we manipulated social influence (informational vs. normative warning), measured self-monitoring (Lennox and Wolfe 1984) and only considered those people who recalled the brand. A two-way ANOVA revealed a significant interaction effect. For high self-monitors, a normative warning seems to be more effective than an informational warning to resist pp influence on purchase intent, whereas no difference is found between the two warnings for low self-monitors.

This research has both theoretical and practical contributions. First, it reveals the important role of brand recall/recognition in both persuasion as well as resistance processes of pp. Second, resistance can be triggered by a text warning. However, we recommend to consider both the type of social influence comprised in the warning and the type of group the warning is targeted to. Popular blockbusters could for example attract more high self-monitors than alternative movies.

REFERENCES

Balasubramanian, Siva K. (1994), "Beyond Advertising and Publicity: Hybrid Messages and Public Policy Issues," *Journal of Advertising*, 23 (4), 29-46.

Brehm, Jack W. (1966), "A Theory of Psychological Reactance," New York: Academic Press.

Bushman, Brad J. (1998), "Effects of Warning and Information Labels on Consumption of Full-Fat, Reduced-Fat, and No-Fat Products," *Journal of Applied Psychology*, 83 (1), 97-101.

Bushman, Brad J. and Angela D. Stack (1996), "Forbidden Fruit Versus Tainted Fruit: Effects of Warning Labels on Attraction to Television Violence," *Journal of Experimental Psychology: Applied*, 2 (3), 207-226.

Campbell, Margaret C. and Amna Kirmani (2000), "Consumers' Use of Persuasion Knowledge: The Effects of Accessibility and Cognitive Capacity on Perceptions of an Influence Agent," *Journal of Consumer Research*, 27 (1), 69-83.

European Union (2009), "Audiovisual Media Services Directive: Product Placement," (accessed February 9, 2012), [available at http://ec.europa.eu/avpolicy/reg/tvwf/advertising/product/index_en.htm].

Frantz, J. Paul (1993), "Effect of Location and Presentation Format on Attention to and Compliance with Product Warnings and Instructions," *Journal of Safety Research*, 24, 131-154.

Friestad, Marian and Peter Wright (1994), "The Persuasion Knowledge Model: How People Cope with Persuasion Attempts," *Journal of Consumer Research*, 21 (1), 1-31.

Laughery, Kenneth R., Kent P. Vaubel, Stephen L. Young, John W. Brelsford Jr. and Anna L. Rowe (1993), "Explicitness of Consequence Information in Warnings," *Safety Science*, 16, 597-613.

Lennox, Richard D. and Raymond N. Wolfe (1984), "Revision of the Self-Monitoring Scale," *Journal of Personality and Social Psychology*, 46 (6), 1349-1364.

Preacher, Kristopher J. and Andrew F. Hayes (2004), "SPSS and SAS Procedures for Estimating Indirect Effects in Simple Mediation Models," *Behavior Research Methods, Instruments, & Computers*, 36 (4), 717-731.

Snyder, Mark (1974), "Self-Monitoring of Expressive Behavior," *Journal of Personality and Social Psychology*, 30 (4), 526-537.

Trommelen, Monica (1997), "Effectiveness of Explicit Warnings," *Safety Science*, 25, 79-88.

Van Kerckhove, Anneleen, Iris Vermeir, and Maggie Geuens (2011), "Combined Influence of Selective Focus and Decision Involvement on Attitude–Behavior Consistency in a Context of Memory-Based Decision Making," *Psychology & Marketing*, 28 (6), 539-60.

Wei, Mei-Ling, Eileen Fischer, and Kelley J. Main (2008), "An Examination of the Effects of Activating Persuasion Knowledge on Consumer Response to Brands Engaging in Covert Marketing," *Journal of Public Policy & Marketing*, 27 (1), 34-44.

"I Apologize. I Understand Your Concerns": When an Empathetic Apology Works

Kyeong Sam Min, University of New Orleans, USA
Jae Min Jung, California State Polytechnic University at Pomona, USA
Kisang Ryu, Sejong University, Korea

EXTENDED ABSTRACT

An apology is a powerful tool to repair broken relationships among individuals. However, we know very little about *when* and *why* some apologies are more effective than others because academic research on apology has mainly focused on examining a victim's reaction to an apology relative to no apology (Brown, Wohl, and Exline 2008; Wooten 2009). This research addresses these two important questions. Specifically, we explore how an apology works when it is offered after (i.e., delayed apology), rather than before (i.e., immediate apology), victims have their concerns heard. Services marketing researchers have shown that an immediate apology has a more favorable impact on consumer satisfaction than a delayed apology (Smith, Bolton, and Wagner 1999; Wirtz and Mattila 2004). Yet, there is contradictory evidence that a delayed apology can be more persuasive than an immediate apology. According to Frantz and Bennigson (2005), victims are likely to be ready to accept an apology after they have their concerns expressed and heard. Such a delayed apology is viewed as more empathetic and sincere and less superficial than an immediate apology. To resolve the apparently conflicting findings in the literature, we examine the situations that influence the apology timing effect.

LITERATURE REVIEW AND HYPOTHESES

Building on Fehr and Gelfand (2010), we predict that the relative advantage of a service person's delayed (vs. immediate) apology exists only when consumers know that they are likely to interact with the same service person in the future. According to Fehr and Gelfand (2010), the effectiveness of an apology depends on whether an offender's apology is consistent with the way victims view their relationship with the offender. They show that victims with a relational self-view are more likely to forgive an offender when the apology focuses on empathic concerns. As a result, we hypothesize that, for those who have a high expectation to interact with the same service person, the service person's apology will be more effective if it is offered after consumers have their concerns heard, compared to if it is immediately offered. In contrast, for those who have a relatively low interaction expectation, the service person's empathic apology will not be matched with their view on the relationship. For them, it will be more forgiving to get a prompt apology instead of a delayed apology.

According to Zhao, Hoeffler, and Zauberman (2011), individuals whose main focus is on the process of consuming a hedonic product tend to rely more on cognitive and effortful processing, whereas individuals whose primary focus is on the outcome are more likely to rely on affective and effortless processing. By the same token, we argue that consumers in the high interaction expectation situation will focus more on a process of their service experience than those in the low interaction expectation situation. Unlike the latter, the former are likely to believe that their relationship with the same service person will continue. Thus, we predict that the relative effectiveness of a delayed (vs. immediate) apology in the high expectation condition will be predominantly driven by a cognitive process (e.g., "The service person understand my concerns"), whereas the relative effectiveness of an immediate (vs. delayed) apology in the low expectation condition will be mainly guided by an affective process (e.g., "I do not feel angry").

METHOD AND FINDINGS

In the first three scenario-based experiments, we used a 2 (apology timing: immediate vs. delayed) x 2 (interaction expectation: high vs. low) between-subjects design. We tested how the timing of a service person's apology operates when the consumer described in the scenario received services that were slower than did other consumers. Experiment 1 examined the moderating role of interaction expectation at a restaurant. We manipulated the apology timing based on whether a service person apologized either before (i.e., immediate apology) or after consumers had their concerns heard (i.e., delayed apology). Additionally, in the high (low) expectation condition, participants were led to believe that they were likely (unlikely) to interact with the same service person. As predicted, we found that the delayed apology produced greater post-apology satisfaction than the immediate apology in the high expectation condition, whereas the apology timing effect was reversed in the low expectation condition.

Experiments 2 and 3 replicated and extended previous findings in the context of hotel and hair salon services, respectively, by testing underlying processes and ruling out alternative accounts. As in experiment 1, we found the same interaction effect on post-apology satisfaction between apology timing and interaction expectation. Next, we observed that the apology timing effect was differentially mediated by cognitive and affective reactions, depending on interaction expectation. Using bootstrapping methods with two mediators (Preacher and Hayes 2008), we consistently showed that for the high (low) expectation condition, the apology timing effect was mediated only by cognitive (affective) reactions.

In experiment 4, we employed a 2 (apology timing: immediate vs. delayed) x 2 (interaction expectation: high vs. low) x 2 (expression of empathy: yes vs. no) between-subjects design in a hair salon service scenario. We investigated whether the apology timing effect would be weaker when a service person's empathy is removed from the apology. We varied the presence of a service person's expression of empathy, and also used tip size as a new dependent variable. As expected, we found the joint effect on consumers' post-apology tip size between apology timing and interaction expectation only when the service person expressed empathy, but not when the service person did not express any empathy.

CONTRIBUTIONS

The main contribution of this research is its novel findings that the apology timing effect depends on whether the consumer expects to interact with the same offender in the future. We extend Frantz and Bennigson (2005) and Fehr and Gelfand (2010) by documenting boundary conditions for the apology timing effect (experiments 1 to 4) and identifying the underlying processes (experiments 2 and 3). Particularly, we confirm that empathy is a key ingredient for success of a delayed apology (experiment 4).

REFERENCES

Brown, Ryan P., Michael J. A. Wohl, and Julie Juola Exline (2008), "Taking Up Offenses: Second-hand Forgiveness and Identification with Targets of Transgressions," *Personality and Social Psychology Bulletin*, 34, 1406-19.

Fehr, Ryan and Michele J. Gelfand (2010), "When Apologies Work: How Matching Apology Components to Victims' Self-Construals Facilitate Forgiveness," *Organizational Behavior and Human Decision Processes,* 113, 37-50.

Frantz, Cynthia McPherson and Courtney Bennigson (2005), "Better Later Than Early: The Influence of Timing on Apology Effectiveness," *Journal of Experimental Social Psychology*, 41, 201-7.

Preacher, Kristopher J. and Andrew F. Hayes (2008), "Asymptotic and Resampling Strategies for Assessing and Comparing Indirect Effects in Multiple Mediator Models," *Behavior Research Methods*, 40, 879-91.

Smith, Amy K., Ruth N. Bolton, and Janet Wagner (1999), "A Model of Customer Satisfaction with Service Encounters Involving Failure and Recovery," *Journal of Marketing Research*, 39, 356-72.

Wirtz, Jochen and Anna S. Mattila (2004), "Consumer Responses to Compensation, Speed of Recovery and Apology After a Service Failure," *International Journal of Service Industry Management*, 15, 150-66.

Wooten, David B. (2009), "Say the Right Thing: Apologies, Reputability, and Punishment," *Journal of Consumer Psychology*, 19, 225-35.

Zhao, Min, Steve Hoeffler, and Gal Zauberman (2011), "Mental Simulation and Product Evaluation: The Affective and Cognitive Dimensions of Process Versus Outcome Simulation," *Journal of Marketing Research*, 48 (October), 827-39.

Monetary Incentives and Pro-Social Behavior in Idea Co-creation

Christoph Ihl, RWTH Aachen University, Germany
Alexander Vossen, RWTH Aachen University, Germany

EXTENDED ABSTRACT

Instead of solely using in house R&D, the use of external ideas has become popular and accepted among organizations in various industries. Prevalent examples for this are firm-initiated innovation or ideation contests, which can be defined as a competitive activity hosted by an organization in order to gather external ideas from consumers with respect to specific topics (Piller and Walcher 2006). Typically, the hosts incentivize consumers' contribution by offering a monetary reward.

Within this paper, we show that the decision to offer such a monetary incentive greatly influences consumers' exerted effort. For showing this, we incorporate three different aspects that play a key role in how monetary incentives are perceived, namely the amount of monetary incentives offered (low vs. high), the organizational stereotype of the host (for-profit vs. non-profit) and the task domain (commercial ideas vs. pro-social ideas).

Concerning the role of monetary incentives, prior research shows ambiguous findings. Since ideation resembles a creative task, it profits from high levels of intrinsic motivation (Burroughs et al. 2011). Many authors therefore highlight the negative impact of monetary incentives, since they lower intrinsic motivation (Ryan and Deci 2000) and lead to a crowding out (Frey and Oberholzer-Gee 1997). However, marketing literature proves evidence for the opposite showing that awarding participants can indeed be beneficial (Toubia 2006; Burroughs et al. 2011). These ambiguous results show that it seems beneficial to further explore the role of monetary rewards as an incentive for participation in idea co-creation.

Regarding the organizational stereotype of the host, the predominant examples of ideation contests consist of many large companies, like for example Dell (Bayus 2011). However, more recently non-profit organizations have also begun to host ideation contests for pro-social topics. Contrarily to all for-profit examples, many of them do not provide a monetary incentive to the participants. Hence, the question arises if this is the right choice.

For for-profit hosts, Harhoff and Mayrhofer (2010) argue that monetary incentives are mandatory, since ideation contests resemble a form of innovation, where the host is capable of systematically utilizing the outcome of an innovative community. However, it remains questionable if this is also valid for non-profit organizations, since consumers perceive non-profits differently from for-profits (Aaker, Vohs, and Mogilner 2009).

Finally, we examine the impact of the task domain. Heyman and Ariely (2004) find that monetary incentives have an ambiguous effect depending on for what they are offered. They explicitly differ between money markets, where relations among actors are based on the basis of economic principles, and social markets, where relations among actors are based on social exchange. Consequently, the impact of monetary rewards in money markets, where people intend to earn money, is positive, while it has a negative impact in social markets, where people intend to engage socially. This is closely related to the task the hosts ask for, since the actual perception of the relevant market could change, when, for example a for-profit firm asks for a pro-social task or the non-profit host asks for a commercial task. When outside their original activity domain, consumers could perceive a lack of competence for both kinds of organizations. Following Vohs, Mead, and Goode (2006), who find that monetary incentives have a strong signalling effect, Aaker et al. (2009) find that monetary rewards can be used to signal competence, which could also be the case for monetary incentives offered for idea co-creation participation.

Hence, we postulate the following research questions: (1) Is the effect of monetary rewards different for non-profit and for-profit organizations? (2) Is the effect of monetary rewards different, when organizations ask for tasks outside their original domain?

For testing our assumptions, we choose to run an online scenario based choice experiment with different scenarios of idea contests. For data collection, 537 participants are recruited by an online panel. All participants are shown four different possible idea contest scenarios dealing with cars and mobility. This leads to a total of 2148 observations. For the scenarios, we use a reduced design that includes the three main factors of interest and additionally factors that are included as controls. Two of these factors are within factors, namely the host (non-profit vs. for-profit) and the monetary incentive (low amount vs. high amount), and one is a between factor, namely the task domain (pro-social vs. commercial).

Due to the nested nature of our data (four observations per participant), we use a Random Coefficients Zero-Inflated Negative Binominal Model with the hours participants would invest in the contest as a dependent variable. Following the procedure for interaction terms in non-linear models suggested by Greene (2010), all interaction effects are plotted in order to interpret their effect.

Results show that indeed monetary rewards play an important, yet ambiguous role as an incentive for participation in idea co-creation. Whether this role is positive strongly depends on who offers the monetary rewards (the host's organizational stereotype) and for what they are offered (the task domain). For both organizational stereotypes, monetary incentives work as suggested by literature—they are beneficial for for-profits (Harhoff and Mayrhofer 2010) and negative for non-profits (confirming literature on crowding out). However, when outside their original activity domain (when for-profits ask for pro-social tasks and a non-profit asks for commercial tasks) both need to introduce monetary rewards in order to signalize competence and the willingness to utilize the consumer generated ideas.

Our study contributes to theory by showing that monetary rewards for a pro-social task do not necessarily lead to a crowding out. Moreover, it shows that monetary rewards can indeed fortify pro-social behavior, if they are used by the for-profit host to show competence and willingness to utilize the idea. Further, we contribute to motivational theory by giving further examples for the fact that the efficiency of monetary incentives is contingent not only on the traits and preferences of individuals, but also on the circumstances under which they are provided, in this case for what and by whom they are offered.

REFERENCES

Aaker, J., Vohs, K. , and Mogilner, C. (2010), "Nonprofits Are Seen as Warm and For-Profits as Competent: Firm Stereotypes Matter," *Journal of Consumer Research*, 37(2), 224-37.

Bayus, B. (2011), "Crowdsourcing New Product Ideas Over Time: An Analysis of Dell's IdeaStorm Community," Working Paper, University of North Carolina.

Burroughs, J. E., Dahl, D. W., Moreau, C. P., Chattopadhyay, A., and Gorn, G. J. (2011), "Facilitating and Rewarding Creativity during New Product Development," *Journal of Marketing*, 75(July), 53-67.

Frey, B. S., and Oberholzer-Gee, F. (1997), "The cost of price incentives: An empirical analysis of motivation crowding-out," *American Economic Review*, *87*(4), 746–55.

Greene, W. (2010), "Testing hypotheses about interaction terms in nonlinear models," *Economics Letters*, *107*(2), 291-96.

Harhoff, D., and Mayrhofer, P. (2010), "Managing User Communities and Hybrid Innovation Processes: Concepts and Design Implications," *Organizational Dynamics*, *39*(2), 137-44.

Heyman, J., and Ariely, D. (2004), "Effort for payment. A tale of two markets," *Psychological Science*, *15*(11), 787-93.

Piller, F. T., and Walcher, D. (2006), "Toolkits for idea competitions: a novel method to integrate users in new product development," *R & D Management*, *36*(3), 307-18.

Ryan, R. M., and Deci, E. L. (2000), "Self-determination theory and the facilitation of intrinsic motivation, social development, and well-being," *American Psychologist*, *55*(1), 68.

Toubia, O. (2006), "Idea Generation, Creativity, and Incentives," *Marketing Science*, *25*(5), 411-25.

Vohs, K. D., Mead, N. L., and Goode, M. R. (2006), "The psychological consequences of money," *Science, 314*, 1154-56.

Targeted Marketing and Customer Search

Nathan Fong, Temple University, USA

EXTENDED ABSTRACT

Can personalized marketing efforts inhibit customer exploration? It has become common practice for retailers to personalize direct marketing offers based on customer transaction histories. Targeted email offers featuring products similar to a customer's previous purchases generate higher response rates, but also have the potential to affect customer search behavior. A closely matched offer may encourage a customer to start the search process, leading to increased search activity. Alternatively, providing customers with closely matched offers may weaken their propensity to search beyond the targeted items. In a field experiment using email offers sent by an online wine retailer, targeted offers result in less search activity on the retailer's website. In a second study, transaction data from an online ticket exchange shows that, after receiving targeted offers, customers are less likely to broaden their purchasing to new genres. These findings indicate that targeted offers carry a hidden cost: a decrease in customer exploration and discovery.

PREDICTIONS AND BACKGROUND

The trend towards increased personalization in electronic environments has the potential to affect the dissemination of new ideas. This could affect citizens learning about different perspectives or scientists learning about new research (Van Alstyne and Brynjolfsson, 1996, 2005); it could also affect how consumers learn about new products. Online retailing has provided better access to a wide range of niche products, which has necessitated tools to help manage the time and effort of search (Brynjolfsson, Hu, and Smith, 2003). Retailers have quickly adopted various forms of personalization that aim to improve the efficiency of a retailer's communications to its customers. One of the most common tactics is to use targeted offers that send customers information on products that a retailer believes the recipients will be interested in. As targeted offers have become increasingly prevalent in online retailing, it is important to understand all of the consequences, such as the potential effect on customer information search behavior.

Are customers more or less inclined to search when you offer them something they have bought in the past? One hypothesis is that an appeal that is aligned with a customer's revealed interests may secure the customer's attention, and encourage them to explore the retailer's other offerings. Dhar, Huber, and Khan (2007) showed that an offer that is more likely to be purchased can create shopping momentum, which makes additional purchasing more likely. Alternatively, by emphasizing products from a familiar category, a targeted offer could result in quick evaluation and curtailed search for other products. In a sequential search model, considering a higher-valued option is more likely to terminate the search process (Weitzman, 1979). Intuitively, by providing something interesting to look at, a targeted offer makes it harder to find something more interesting, lowering the value of continued search. The primary empirical contribution of this article is to examine how these factors play out in the context of targeted offers.

Previous research has examined how the Internet and information technology have affected search behavior. Häubl and Trifts (2000) looked at how recommendation agents (algorithms that provide personalized lists of recommended products) and comparison matrices (which typically line up alternatives in columns, and attributes in rows) affect online shopping behavior. They found that these tools allowed customers to search more efficiently, making better purchase decisions while reducing the number of alternatives they viewed. Research has also looked at how retailer actions affect customer exploration; for example, the visual layout of product information can affect the intensity of exploratory search (Janiszewski, 1998). The studies in this article find that targeted offers result in less search activity, but this is not simply saving time; there is less of the exploratory search that can expose customers to a broader range of products.

METHOD AND FINDINGS

The first study is a field experiment run with the cooperation of an online wine retailer. Customers in a targeted group were randomly assigned to receive offers for wine from two different regions, one of which (the targeted offer) matched the regional preferences revealed by their purchase histories. Their activity was compared to that of an untargeted control group, whose purchase histories did not match either offer. Detailed web browsing data for these customers was collected over a several day period. Unsurprisingly, the targeted customers were more likely to click through to the offer, and were more likely to purchase the offer. However, page views and similar metrics show that targeted emails decreased customer search activity for other products (see figure 1). This supports the hypothesis that targeted offers result in decreased information search.

Figure 1. Wine Retailer Information Search Response

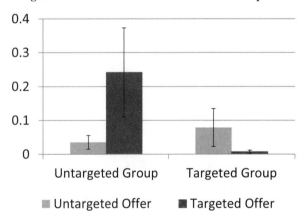

Note: Depicts the average number of page views categorized as customer search for products other than the offer, such as browsing product categories and product pages (interaction is significant $p<.05$)

The second study used data on experimental email marketing campaigns run by an online ticket exchange. The firm sent emails promoting different genres of events, to groups of customers who either had (targeted) or had not (untargeted) previously bought tickets to the genre. Their behavior was compared to that of a holdout (no offer) group. Analysis of the ticket sales data shows that, after receiving targeted offers, customers are more likely to purchase from the target genre. However, they are also less likely to buy tickets for events in new categories, excluding the target genre and any other genres they had previously purchased in (see figure 2). This suggests that the curtailed search following targeted offers is not simply saving customers time, but it reduces exploratory search that could affect future purchasing.

Advances in Consumer Research
Volume 40, ©2012

Figure 2. Online Ticket Exchange Sales Response

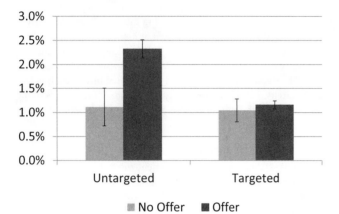

Note: Depicts the proportion of customers purchasing from a new genre during the 28 day observation period following the offer (interaction is significant $p<.05$)

CONTRIBUTIONS

These field studies demonstrate how targeted offers result in decreased search activity and narrower subsequent purchasing activity. Conversely, less targeted offers can expose customers to a broader range of products, and lead to consideration of new products. Broader awareness could generate cross-selling opportunities and increase sales diversity, improving customer retention and lifetime value. If relying heavily on targeted offers, the retailer sacrifices opportunities to bring attention to products for which a customer has low awareness. Thus, retailers should balance the need for immediate sales response with measures that encourage exploration and sustain customer interest.

REFERENCES

Brynjolfsson, E., Hu, Y. (Jeffrey), & Smith, M. D. (2003), "Consumer surplus in the digital economy: Estimating the value of increased product variety at online booksellers," *Management Science*, 49(11), 1580–1596.

Dhar, R., Huber, J., & Khan, U. (2007), "The Shopping Momentum Effect," *Journal of Marketing Research*, 44(3), 370-378.

Häubl, G., & Trifts, V. (2000), "Consumer decision making in online shopping environments: The effects of interactive decision aids," *Marketing Science*, 4–21.

Janiszewski, C. (1998), "The Influence of Display Characteristics on Visual Exploratory Search Behavior," *Journal of Consumer Research*, 25(3), 290-301.

Van Alstyne, M., & Brynjolfsson, E. (1996), "Could the Internet Balkanize Science?" *Science*, 274(5292), 1479-1480.

_____ (2005). Global Village or Cyber-Balkans?, "Modeling and Measuring the Integration of Electronic Communities," *Management Science*, 51(6), 851-868.

Weitzman, M. (1979), "Optimal search for the best alternative," *Econometrica*, 47(3), 641-654.

The Traffic Light Colors Red and Green in the Context of Healthy Food Decision-Making

Joerg Koenigstorfer, Pennsylvania State University, USA
Andrea Groeppel-Klein, Saarland University, Germany
Friederike Kamm, Saarland University, Germany
Michaela Rohr, Saarland University, Germany
Dirk Wentura, Saarland University, Germany

EXTENDED ABSTRACT

Traffic light-colored nutrition labeling may help consumers make healthy food choices (FSA 2009). The underlying assumption is that the colors green and red automatically activate the associated meanings ('go' for green, 'no-go' for red) when assigned to more or less healthful foods, thereby implying automatic approach-avoidance reactions. However, there is evidence that the meanings of colors change with contexts (Maier et al. 2009). Although traffic light colors have been learned in traffic (Bargh 1992), it is unknown whether this automaticity transfers to food contexts.

RED (GREEN) AND AVOIDANCE (APPROACH) BEHAVIOR OF FOODS

Evaluative connotations of attitudes to foods are activated automatically and linked bi-directionally to the motor behavior of individuals (De Houwer and De Bruycker 2007; Van den Bergh, Schmitt, and Warlop 2011). Pulling or pushing movements toward or away from one's body are indicators of innate motor behavior (Chen and Bargh 1999; Solarz 1960). Individuals' tendency to approach healthy food (pull) and avoid unhealthy food (push) may be affected by the traffic light colors red and green–i.e., complementary colors in the color wheel. Red carries the negative meaning of danger or failure, while green is less arousing and represents safety (Elliot et al. 2009). However, individuals may react more strongly to red-unhealthy (vs. green-healthy) pairings, because they are more sensitive to negative (vs. positive) product attributes (here: unhealthiness) providing greater information diagnosticity (Balasubramanian and Cole 2002; Moorman 1996).

Hypothesis 1 *Red (vs. green) intensifies automatic avoidance reactions towards unhealthy foods; for healthy foods, green (vs. red) does not intensify approach reactions.*

APPROACH-AVOIDANCE TASK STUDIES

Laboratory study 1 used a 2 (food: healthy vs. unhealthy) × 2 (color: green vs. red) × 2 (movement: toward vs. away) repeated-measures design to test hypothesis 1. Twenty black-and-white drawings of pre-tested healthy and unhealthy foods were presented on a white background within a red- or green-colored circle. Participants ($n = 179$) were asked to categorize each food as either healthy or not by moving a PC mouse toward or away from themselves.

Reaction times were recorded and used as dependent variable in a repeated-measures ANOVA yielding the proposed three-way-interaction of food category × color × movement, $F(1, 178) = 6.05$, $p < .05$, $\eta^2 = .033$. The two-way interaction effect between color and movement is only present in unhealthy foods, not in healthy foods. A relative index of the automatic approach-avoidance tendency was calculated to describe this effect. Follow-up study 2 ($n = 95$) using the same approach-avoidance task with the colors pink and blue–they are analogous to red and green and have the same chroma and value–finds that the enforcing avoidance effect is unique to red, and that this effect cannot be attributed to a mere increase in attention to the colors. Thus, hypothesis 1 is supported; the implicit meaning

of red (danger) transfers to food contexts and reinforces avoidance of unhealthy foods, whereas green (representing safety) does not increase approach towards healthy foods.

TRAFFIC LIGHT-COLORED NUTRITION LABELS

Uncertainty remains about whether the implementation of traffic light colors on nutrition labels guides consumers' actual buying behaviors, and which consumers profit most. The goal conflict theory of eating (Stroebe et al. 2008) proposes that self-control conflicts between indulgence and healthy eating impact consumers' reactions to food items. Tasty foods (indulgences) trigger hedonic thoughts in low self-control consumers (Papies, Stroebe, and Aarts 2007). The salience of traffic light colors, in particular red on unhealthy food items, may inhibit this tendency, inducing avoidance reactions (Fishbach and Shah 2006), and thus lead to healthier decisions. We expect that high self-control consumers do not respond to the colors, because their decision-making is affected less by self-regulatory primes (Fishbach, Friedman, and Kruglanski 2003).

Hypothesis 2 *Low self-control consumers make healthier in-store choices when traffic light colors are implemented on front-of-pack nutrition labels; for high self-control consumers, no differences are found.*

IN-STORE STUDIES

Study 3 was conducted in a supermarket to test hypothesis 2. A one-way factorial (nutrition label with traffic light colors vs. without coloring) between-subjects design was applied. A retailer allowed us to manipulate product packages of one category (pasta and sauce). An expert rating of the products' healthiness based on their nutrient profiles with 162 dieticians reveals varying degrees of healthiness. Colored labels were implemented accordingly (FSA 2009): the unhealthiest (healthiest) products showed three macronutrients labeled red (green), the second unhealthiest (healthiest) products two macronutrients labeled red (green), and so on.

Participants ($n = 184$) were asked to buy four products for the purpose of the study (cover story: orientation in supermarkets during shopping). A shopping list was given to them that included one pasta meal of their choice. Self-control was measured using Giner-Sorolla's (2001) scale ($\alpha = .72$).

The unhealthiness of the product choice according to the mean expert ratings (*1 = very healthy, 20 = very unhealthy*) was used as dependent variable in a moderated regression analysis including the manipulation (traffic light colors = 1, no coloring = -1), mean-centered self-control, and their interaction as independent variables. The proposed interaction between the labeling and self-control emerged ($b = 0.76$, $p < .05$). Among low self-control consumers (-1 SD), the traffic light-colored labels led to healthier choices ($b = -0.51$, $SE = 0.20$, $p < .05$), whereas there was no effect on high self-control consumers ($+1$ SD; NS). Follow-up study 4 ($n = 152$) replicates these findings for a different product category (cereal bars).

CONTRIBUTIONS

This study extends research into automatic approach-avoidance behaviors, introducing the notion that colors–particularly red–affect individuals' motor behavior not only in cognitive tasks (Mehta and Zhu 2009), but also in food contexts. It may be considered positive that approach behavior is not enhanced when green is related to healthy food, because this may indicate a mechanism of protection against the feeling of pre-commitment and, hence, overconsumption. This research also contributes to the goal conflict theory of eating (Stroebe et al. 2008) showing that low self-control consumers, despite close physical distance to food temptations, are affected by traffic light-colored nutrition labeling.

REFERENCES

Balasubramanian, Siva K. and Catherine A. Cole (2002), "Consumers' Search and Use of Nutrition Information: The Challenge and Promise of the Nutrition Labeling and Education Act," *Journal of Marketing*, 66 (3), 112-27.

Bargh, John A. (1992), "The Ecology of Automaticity: Toward Establishing the Conditions Needed to Produce Automatic Processing Effects," *The American Journal of Psychology*, 105 (2), 181-99.

Chen, Mark and John A. Bargh (1999), "Consequences of Automatic Evaluation: Immediate Behavioral Predispositions to Approach or Avoid the Stimulus," *Personality and Social Psychology Bulletin*, 25 (2), 215-24.

De Houwer, Jan and Els De Bruycker (2007), "The Implicit Association Test Outperforms the Extrinsic Affective Simon Task as a Measure of Interindividual Differences in Attitudes," *British Journal of Social Psychology*, 46 (2), 401-21.

Elliot, Andrew J., Markus A. Maier, Martin J. Binser, Ron Friedman, and Reinhard Pekrun (2009), "The Effect of Red on Avoidance Behavior in Achievement Contexts," *Personality and Social Psychology Bulletin*, 35 (3), 365-75.

Fishbach, Ayelet, Ronald S. Friedman, and Arie W. Kruglanski (2003), "Leading Us Not to Unto Temptation: Momentary Allurements Elicit Overriding Goal Activation," *Journal of Personality and Social Psychology*, 84 (2), 296-309.

Fishbach, Ayelet and James Y. Shah (2006), "Self-control in Action: Implicit Dispositions toward Goals and away from Temptations," *Journal of Personality and Social Psychology*, 90 (5), 820-32.

FSA (2009), *Comprehension and Use of UK Nutrition Signpost Labelling Schemes*, London: Food Standards Agency.

Giner-Sorolla, Roger (2001), "Guilty Pleasures and Grim Necessities: Affective Attitudes in Dilemmas of Self-control," *Journal of Personality and Social Psychology*, 80 (2), 206-21.

Maier, Markus A., Petra Barchfeld, Andrew J. Elliot, and Reinhard Pekrun (2009), "Context Specificity of Implicit Preferences: The Case of Human Preference for Red," *Emotion*, 9 (5), 734-8.

Mehta, Ravi and Rui (J.) Zhu (2009), "Blue or Red? Exploring the Effect of Color on Cognitive Task Performance," *Science*, 323 (February), 1226-9.

Moorman, Christine (1996), "A Quasi Experiment to Assess the Consumer and Informational Determinants of Nutrition Information Processing Activities: The Case of the Nutrition Labeling and Education Act," *Journal of Public Policy & Marketing*, 15 (1), 28-44.

Papies, Esther K., Wolfgang Stroebe, and Henk Aarts (2007), "Pleasure in the Mind: Restrained Eating and Spontaneous Hedonic Thoughts about Food," *Journal of Experimental Social Psychology*, **43 (5),** 810-7.

Solarz, Andrew K. (1960), "Latency of Instrumental Responses as a Function of Compatibility with the Meaning of Eliciting Verbal Signs," *Journal of Experimental Psychology*, 59 (4), 239-45.

Stroebe, Wolfgang, Wendy Mensink, Henk Aarts, Henk Schut, and Arie W. Kruglanski (2008), "Why Dieters Fail: Testing the Goal Conflict Model of Eating," *Journal of Experimental Social Psychology*," 44 (1), 26-36.

Van den Bergh, Bram, Julien Schmitt, and Luk Warlop (2011), "Embodied Myopia," *Journal of Marketing Research*, 48 (6), 1033-44.

The Importance of Warmth and Competence in the Acquisition and Retention of New Customers

Iana A. Castro, San Diego State University, USA

Scott Thompson, University of Georgia, USA

James Ward, Arizona State University, USA

EXTENDED ABSTRACT

According to the stereotype content model (SCM), humans evaluate others along two fundamental dimensions, warmth and competence. Warmth is an assessment of others' intent to help us or harm us, and is tapped by our perceptions of others' honesty, sincerity, trustworthiness, and helpfulness. Competence is an assessment of others' ability to carry out their intentions and is tapped by our perception of others' intelligence, skillfulness, determination, and industry. Thus, the SCM argues that people are strongly disposed to evaluate others' warmth and competence, and that such judgments have strong links to emotional reactions and action tendencies. Supporting the SCM, a growing oeuvre of studies show that warmth and competence underlie our perception of and behavior toward other human groups, and that warmth judgments are "primary" – that is, the first judgment made and the perception most strongly related to emotional reaction and behavior toward others (Fiske, Cuddy, and Glick 2007).

Although studies of social perception have typically found judgments of warmth to be more influential than judgments of competence (e.g., Cuddy, Fiske, and Glick 2007), studies of customer purchasing decisions have found the opposite. For example, Aaker, Vohs, and Mogilner (2010) found that consumer purchase intentions are better predicted by competence perceptions than warmth perceptions. In the services literature, warmth related perceptions have been shown to be critical in judgments of service quality and satisfaction (e.g., Parasuraman, Zeithaml, and Berry 1985). Nevertheless, in a service encounter study, Grandey and colleagues (2005) found that service provider warmth impacted customer satisfaction only when the service provider performed competently.

In summary, past studies of the impact of warmth and competence perceptions on consumer choice and satisfaction have found results in conflict with the larger body of work in social psychology that identifies warmth as more influential than competence in determining behavior toward a group. How might the discrepancy be explained? First, consumer anticipation of the length of a relationship with a firm could impact the relative importance of the firm's warmth versus competence. Second, a consumer's degree of experience with a brand should impact the relative influence of firm warmth versus competence on purchase decisions. Warmth is a primary judgment because it is important to gauge others' intentions, so once intent has been revealed by action, the importance of judging intent for the next round of interaction should wane, as the importance of gauging competence waxes. Across three studies, we find support for our predictions.

Study 1 determined the role of warmth judgments versus competence judgments in deciding which company to hire and asked participants to rate a list of competence and warmth traits on how important they would be when selecting a company. The results supported the prediction that competence plays a more important role when selecting a company, contrary to the presumed primacy of warmth. However, the decision involved a one-time transaction. It is possible that warmth may play a larger role in decision-making if consumers are anticipating an ongoing relationship.

To address this question, in Study 2 we conducted an experiment in which participants were presented with a company description that manipulated the warmth and competence dimensions. The experiment used a 2 (warmth: low, high) x 2 (competence: low, high) between-subjects design. Participants were then asked to determine their likelihood of hiring the company for an ongoing relationship. Our results suggest that warmth is consistently valued over competence when an ongoing relationship is anticipated (interaction effect: $F(1, 118) = 16.14$, $p < .001$; $M_{\text{High Warmth High Competence}} = 5.47$, $M_{\text{High Warmth Low Competence}} = 3.26$, $M_{\text{Low Warmth High Competence}} = 1.93$, $M_{\text{Low Warmth Low Competence}} = 1.71$). Specifically, participants were most likely to hire the company when it was high on warmth and competence, with second preference being a company that was high on warmth and low on competence. Furthermore, when the company was low on warmth, differences did not emerge between the competence dimensions, suggesting that in the absence of warmth, level of competence did not matter.

In Study 3, we examined how the role of warmth and competence changes as consumers acquire experience with a firm. We followed the same procedure as in Study 2 and measured their attitudinal loyalty toward the company, word of mouth intentions, purchase intentions, and stability during the course of an interaction that included a service failure. The results indicate that prior to a service experience, warmth was consistently valued over competence. Furthermore, given a choice between either warmth or competence, customers will forgo competence in favor of warmth (attitudinal loyalty interaction effect: $F(1, 368) = 10.36$, $p < .01$; $M_{\text{High Warmth High Competence}} = 3.91$, $M_{\text{High Warmth Low Competence}} = 2.45$, $M_{\text{Low Warmth High Competence}} = 2.08$, $M_{\text{Low Warmth Low Competence}} = 1.38$; other measures followed the same pattern).

Next, participants were shown a description of a service failure in which participants ordered a product from the company, received a different product than the one ordered, and then wrote the firm to ask for a correction of the problem. The scenario ended as the consumer awaited the firm's response. Following this service failure, the importance and impact of warmth begins to fade. The only measure that warmth plays a larger role on than competence is stability, or the probability that a failure will occur again (interaction effect: $F(1, 364) = 8.18$, $p < .01$; $M_{\text{High Warmth High Competence}} = 4.23$, $M_{\text{High Warmth Low Competence}} = 2.91$, $M_{\text{Low Warmth Low Competence}} = 2.57$, $M_{\text{Not Warm Not Competent}} = 2.10$). This suggests that warmth judgments are dominant over competence judgments prior to service interactions. However, once customers have an experience with the company, the information from the event begins to upstage these perceptions of warmth, and competence becomes increasingly important. Nonetheless, companies that are high on warmth *and* competence still benefit on the key outcomes of word of mouth and purchase intentions compared to those who are not, which suggests that brand personality can buffer the impact of an initial service failure, but only for those that have both a warm and competent brand personality.

REFERENCES

Aaker, J., K. Vohs and C. Mogilner (2010), "Non-Profits Are Seen as Warm and For-Profits as Competent: Firm Stereotypes Matter," *Journal of Consumer Research,* 37 (August), 277-291.

Cuddy, A. J. C., S. T. Fiske, and P. Glick (2007), "The BIAS Map: Behaviors from Intergroup Affect and Stereotypes," *Journal of Personality and Social Psychology*, 92(4), 631-648.

Fiske, S. T., A. J. C. Cuddy and P. Glick (2007), "Universal Dimensions of Social Cognition: Warmth and Competence," *Trends in Cognitive Science*, 11(2), 77-83.

Grandey, A. A., G. M. Fisk, A. S. Mattila, K. J. Jansen and L. A. Sideman (2005), "Is 'Service with a Smile' Enough? Authenticity of Positive Displays During Service Encounters," *Organizational Behavior and Human Decision Processes*, 96, 38-55.

Parasuraman, A., V. A. Zeithaml and L. L. Berry (1985), "A Conceptual Model of Service Quality and Its Implications for Future Research," *Journal of Marketing*, 49(4), 41-50.

Gift Cards and the Social Relationship

Kunter Gunasti, University of Connecticut, USA
Michelle F. Weinberger, Northwestern University, USA

EXTENDED ABSTRACT

Through selection and presentation, gift givers communicate to the recipient about the strength and nature of the relationship (Caplow 1982; Joy 2001) and ultimately reinforce or reformulate the social tie (Ruth, Otnes, and Brunel 1999). Most research examines gifts given from a giver to the recipient in a relatively usable, final form (see Sherry 1983). Yet a gift card is different; the recipient must take additional action to finish the gift and make it symbolically successful. Despite pervasive use of gift cards in the marketplace, little research has looked at the role of the social relationship in card use.

Imagine that John receives a bookstore gift card. Will he buy videogames, what he really wants, even though the giver clearly wants him to buy books? Would he re-gift it for his sister? What if the giver is his close friend, or someone rarely seen? Our research focuses on the different ways in which gift card recipients finish the gifting process and the social drivers of their actions.

We hypothesize that gift recipients will be more affected by the intentions of the givers (communicated via visual cues on the gift card: card merchant, overall theme, giving occasion) when the giver and recipient are in a close relationship. When completing the gift, close (vs. distant) recipients will try harder to subtly ascertain and fulfill the giver's intentions, at times overriding their own desires and making less economically rational decisions by spending more. Our theorization suggests that in the case of the gift card, relationship reformulation does not fully occur on gift receipt (Sherry 1983); instead, the process is extended while recipients finish the gift physically and symbolically.

In study 1, participants read a scenario about a girl receiving a bookstore gift card with a book picture on it from a close vs. distant giver. It indicated that the girl did not have time to read but she enjoyed music. Then participants described how she should spend the gift card. When it came from a distant giver, none of participants thought the recipient should buy books (vs. the intended gift). When it came from someone close, 14% indicated that she should buy books, even though it wasn't what she wanted. Participants were more likely to use moral language as guiding their imperative for her to use the card on herself when it was from a close giver.

In study 2, a 2 Relationship (Close vs. Distant) x 2 Store Theme on Gift Card (Generic Store/No Picture vs. Sports Store) design was used. Participants identified either a close friend or someone with whom they were not close who then ended up giving them a $75 gift card for Kleine's, a new store. The gift card either displayed no picture or a sports theme. Participants were taken to Kleine's store website to choose among 9 products, 3 categories (sports, cameras, luggage) x 3 three price levels (high, equal, low). For close givers, the sports themed card led to significantly higher preferences for sports goods; for distant givers, the card format did not affect the choice of sports goods. When the givers were close (vs. distant), more recipients spent above the value of the gift card out of pocket.

In study 3, students were given a $50 Generic vs. Birthday Theme Target gift card by their "significant other" and told that they go the store to use the card. However, the jacket they wanted to buy is $57 at Target and available for $45 elsewhere. Participants were further informed that they also needed to purchase a grill for a friend. When the gift card had a birthday theme, participants were more likely to pay the premium, purchasing themselves the jacket as a birthday gift. The non-birthday themed card almost doubled the number of recipients who chose not to fulfill their significant others' intentions, using the gift card for someone else.

In sum, over the course of three experiments, we revealed that implicitly recipients take on additional relational work to fulfill the giver's intentions when they feel close to the giver. To do this, recipients use three visual cues to interpret the givers' intentions for the gift cards' use: store/merchant of the card, general theme, and gift occasion. Although some might claim that economically the gift card is only a vehicle for transferring funds, this study shows that in certain cases the card becomes infused with meaning and becomes a symbolic vehicle. Yet only recipients who feel close to the giver feel a moral obligation to do additional relational work to ascertain and fulfill the givers wishes even when it is incongruent with the recipient's own desires and is the less economically rational use of the funds.

REFERENCES

Aron, Arthur, Elaine N. Aron, and Danny Smollan (1992), "Inclusion of Other in the Self Scale and the Structure of Interpersonal Closeness," *Journal of Personality and Social Psychology*, 63 (4), 596-612.

Caplow, Theodore (1982), "Christmas Gifts and Kin Networks," *American Sociological Review*, 47 (June), 383-92.

Cheal, David (1988), *The Gift Economy*, London: Routledge.

Joy, Annamma (2001), "Gift Giving in Hong Kong and the Continuum of Social Ties," *Journal of Consumer Research*, 28 (September), 239-56.

Ruth, Julie A., Cele C. Otnes, and Frederic F. Brunel (1999), "Gift Receipt and the Reformulation of Interpersonal Relationships," *Journal of Consumer Research*, 25 (March), 385-402.

Sherry, John F., Jr. (1983), "Gift Giving in Anthropological Perspective," *Journal of Consumer Research*, 10 (September), 157-68.

Wooten, David B. (2000), "Qualitative Steps Towards an Expanded Model of Anxiety in Gift-Giving," *Journal of Consumer Research*, 27 (June), 84-95.

The Construction of Cosmetics-Consuming Women Through Generational Families in Brazil's "New Middle Class" Context

Roberta Dias-Campos, Federal University of Rio de Janeiro, Brazil
Leticia Moreira Casotti, Federal University of Rio de Janeiro, Brazil

EXTENDED ABSTRACT

Theory on consumer socialization has described the cognitive aspects of consumer formation (Roedder, 1999), coupled with extensive measurement developments on family influence on individual decisions (Moschis, 1985, 1988; Commuri, Gentry, 2000; Thompson, Laing, Mckee, 2007; Götze, Prange, Uhrovks, 2009). Nevertheless, less attention has been made to the social context to consumer formation (Ward, Klees and Wackman, 1990). Besides, the socialization field has been historically based on a positivistic perspective, which could benefit from contributions of an interpretative and cultural approach (Hirschman, 1986; Holbrook and O'Shaugnessy, 1988; Arnould and Thompson, 2005; 2007) and from social sciences theory itself, as new form of lens to consumer socialization studies (Bourdieu, 1979; Rocha-Coutinho, 2006; Darmon, 2006; Foucault, 1984; Dubar, 2009).

This study aims to provide a social and cultural perspective to the theoretical domain of socialization of consumer (Ward, 1974; Moschis, 1985, 1988), through the use of interpretative tools to investigate beauty consumption in the Brazilian middle class. It seeks to understand beauty consumption itineraries among three generations from the same family – grandmother, mother and daughter. A both social and generational approach (Shah and Mittal, 1997; Bertaux, 1997; Alberti, 2005; Atkinson, 1998; Lins e Barros, 2006) was adopted to investigate family transmission dynamics, which constitute rich laboratories to consumer socialization, within the chosen micro-social scale of a qualitative and interpretative research design (Desjeux, 2004; Cova and Cova, 2002).

Different qualitative methods were considered to allow data triangulation and the emergence of natives' point of view (Geertz, 1979): in-depth life story interviews (McCracken, 1988; Bertaux, 1997) combined with in-home observations (Rodhain, 2008; Alami; Desjeux; Garabuau-Moussaoui, 2009). Fifteen families were selected by a professional recruiter, and 30 interviews were carried, totalizing a 6 hours minimum interview per family. For the third generation, children aged from 4 to 10, data was gathered in informal conversations, interview with adults and observation of their living space. Social-economic sample definition was inspired by the emergence of a new Brazilian "middle class", result of an uprising within the social pyramid. This new large group rapidly conquered its space in "cold" statistic studies, but remains largely unknown due to lack of research capable of describing its diversity.

The family life stories enabled the identification of a socialization process from a social point of view. Based on Bourdieu's social perspective on socialization, the analysis pointed out to four different construction moments of the beauty consumer: the development of taste, the rehearsal by mimicking, the consumption premiere and the adjustments phase.

In the development of taste, rules and judgment are incorporated to form consumers' values, sense of taste and femininity. Even before girls can understand the meaning of daily care rituals, they begin to incorporate a silent group of values that will shape their appreciation of themselves and others. Manicure and hair treatments such as straitening (for the curly hair), for example, are internalized as basic practices and values for displayed femininity in adult life in Brazil.

The rehearsal by mimicking marks the beginning of concrete action, even if still in the form of childish games. Girls are often observed playing with makeup or giving themselves a "manicure", from the frequent observation of their mothers and sisters. At this moment, they are not yet consumers, but they are playing as one.

The consumption premiere moment is identified not only by the use of beauty products as a full consumer, but also by the emergence of shopping habits and new use occasions. This premiere may be prompted by events such as the 15th birthday (a still important tradition in Brazilian middle class), the first job, the beginning of going-out with friends without parental supervision, and a first romantic relationship.

After a while, consumers get to know better their consumption needs as well as products, brands and services available. At this moment they enter the last stage, where adjustments are made to their childhood practices, and they start searching solutions, better suited for their grown-up needs. At this moment, the consumer seems to start his adult consumption phase, and the socialization process finds its end.

Particularly in Brazil, an important generational gap seems to indicate uneven family influence, according to different product categories. Life story of interviewed consumers shows a large distance between grandmothers and mother social roles. While the first ones were centered on the household and family activities, the next generation tries to make room for career and education. They get married later and have fewer children, on one side, and strike for gathering more educational degrees, on the other. This gap determines different forms of family influence in operation. While the older generation (grandmothers) relied more on maternal counseling for consumption decisions, the mothers' generation combines both pairs and family as source of consumption guidance. Depending on the category analyzed, the family influence will be greater or diminished. The most striking example is the consumption of makeup products as means to build a more professional presentation. For this category, interviewees indicated friends and colleagues as the main consumption reference. Nevertheless, for hair treatments, family is still the central unit of influence, determining patterns for volume control standards.

Finally, in order to reduce risk in adopting unknown treatments that, for instance, may affect hair structure - such as the "progressive brushing" – consumers adopt a strategy of triangulating opinions from three particular influence groups: specialists (that provide technical expertise), the media (that guarantee the wide use of the treatment) and the family (that confirm the treatment adaptability to a particular kind of hair). These three sources are continuously confronted in a confirmatory cycle that tries to reduce the risk of adopting new hair solutions. This strategy has not been identified on previous research with upper class consumers in Brazil (Casotti, Suarez and Campos, 2008).

This paper aimed to contribute to consumer socialization research, by offering a social and interpretative perspective. It proposes four stages for consumer socialization from a contextual and social standpoint. Additionally, it discusses specifics aspects of Brazilian middle class consumption, determined by generational changes and particular social network dynamics.

REFERENCES

Alami, Sophie, Dominique Desjeux and Isabelle Garabuau-Moussaoui (2009), *Les méthodes qualitative* (Collection que-sais je? n. 2591), Paris: PUF.

Alberti, Verena (2005), *Manual de história oral*, Rio de Janeiro: FGV.

Arnould, Eric J. and Craig Thompson (2007)*,* "Consumer culture theory (and we really mean theoretics): dilemmas and opportunities posed by an academic branding strategy." in *Consumer Culture Theory*, ed. Russel W. Belk and John F. Sherry Jr., Oxford: Elsevier, 3-22.

Arnould, Eric J. and Craig J. Thompson (2005), "Consumer culture theory (CCT): twenty years of research," *Journal of Consumer Research* 31 (4), 868-82.

Atkinson, Robert (1998), *The life story interview (Qualitative Research Methods 4)*. Newbury Park: Sage.

Bertaux, Daniel (1997), *Les récits de vie*, Paris: Nathan.

Bourdieu, Pierre (1979), *La distinction: critique sociale du jugement*, Paris: Les Editions de Minuit.

Casotti, Leticia, Maribel Suarez and Roberta Campos (2008), *O Tempo da Beleza: consumo e comportamento feminino, novos olhares*, Senac: Rio de Janeiro.

Commuri, Suraj and James W. Gentry, (2000). "Opportunities for family research in marketing". *Academy of Marketing Science Review*, 8.

Cova, Bernard and Véronique Cova (2002), "Tribal Marketing: the tribalization of society and its impact on the conduct of marketing," *European Journal of Marketing* 36 (5), 595-620.

Darmon, Muriel, (2006) *La socialisation*, Paris: Armand Collins.

Desjeux, Dominique (2004), *Les sciences sociales*. Paris: PUF.

Dubar, Claude. (2009)*, La socialisation*, Paris: Armand Collins.

Geertz, Clifford. (1979), *The interpretation of cultures: selected essays*, NY: Basic Books.

Götze, Elisabeth; Christiane Prange and Iveta Uhrovks, (2009), "Children's impact on innovation decision making: a diary study", *European Journal of Marketing*, 43, 1/2, 264-295.

Hirschman, Elizabeth C. (1986), "Humanistic inquiry in marketing research: philosophy, method, and criteria," Journal *of Marketing Research* 23(August), 237-49.

Holbrook, Morris B. and John O'Shaugnessy. (1988) "On the scientific status of consumer research and the need for an interpretive approach to studying concumption behavior," *Journal of Consumer Research* 15(December), 398-402

Lins e Barros, Myriam (org) (2006), *Família e gerações*, Rio de Janeiro: Editora: FGV.

McCracken, Grant. (1988) The *long interview (Qualitative research methods series, v.13)*, Newbury Park: Sage.

Moschis, George P. (1985), "The role of family communication in consumer socialization of children and adolescents," *Journal of Consumer Research,* 11(4), 898-913.

Moschis, George P. (1988), "Methodological issues in studying intergenerational influences on consumer behavior". *Advances in Consumer Research*, 15, 569-573.

Rocha-Coutinho, Maria Lúcia. (2006), "Transmissão geracional e família na contemporaneidade" in *Família e gerações*, org. Myriam Lins de Barros, Rio de Janeiro: Editora FGV, 91-106.

Rodhain, Angélique. (2008) "L'observation directe," in *A la recherche du consommateur: nouvelles techniques pour mieux comprendre le client*, Paris: Dunod, 5-28.

Roedder John, Deborah. (1999), "Consumer Socialization of Children: A Retrospective Look at Twenty-Five Years of Research". *Journal of Consumer Research,* 26, 3, 183-213.

Shah, Reshma H. and Banwari Mittal, (1997), "Toward a theory of intergenerational influence in consumer behavior: an exploratory essay". *Advances in Consumer Research,* 24, 55-60.

Thompson, Elizabeth S.; Angus W. Laing and Lorna McKee, (2007), "Family purchase decision making: exploring child influence behavior". *Journal of Consumer Behavior.* 6, 4, 182-202.

Ward, Scott. (1974), "Consumer socialization". *Journal of Consumer Research* 1(2), 1-14.

Ward, Scott; Donna M. Klees and Daniel B. Wackman, (1990), "Consumer Socialization Research: Content Analysis of Post-1980 Studies, and Some Implications For Future Work". *Advances in Consumer Research*, 17, 798-803.

Cruising the Unadulterated Terrain of Consumption:
Rural Snowmobilers' Interpellation through Collective Simplicity

Soonkwan Hong, Michigan Technological University, USA

EXTENDED ABSTRACT

Consumer research has thus far been virtually taciturn about poor consumers in rural areas who have less access to, or interests in what has been normalized as mainstream lifestyles in urban, suburban, or exurban areas. Bourdieu's (1984) cultural and symbolic capital that embodies tastes (consumption practices) and configures the consumer's ideological position has instead been the focus of various analyses of contemporary status consumption phenomena (Holt 1997; Ustuner and Holt 2010; Ustuner and Thompson 2012). Nonetheless, the economic capital, as a boundary condition of consumption, needs to be considered more essential rather than tangential when exploring marketplace performances by the poor (Bauman 2007).

The current literature employing discourses about the intersection between consumption and social status explains that cultural capital operates as a determinant of lifestyle choices (Holt 1997), a basis for aesthetic and ideological claims (Holt 1998), a catalyst for socially stratified consumption (Ustuner and Holt 2010), and a requisite for a smoother acculturation process (Ustuner and Holt 2007). The listed research, however, has not documented how consumers with low economic capital in a highly developed country carry on their identity projects and execute their ideological positioning in the immensely hierarchical field of consumption. Therefore, this research aims to explicate the process in which relatively deprived consumers build social capital, cultivate cultural capital, and potentially rearticulate the meaning of symbolic capital.

The interwoven and thus inseparable connections among social status, interpellation, and consumer identity have been illuminated (e.g., Kozinets 2008). However, the social aspect of the dynamics does not necessarily address the plasticity of social constraints (i.e., habitus), made possible by individual consumers' agentic endeavors (see Bourdieu1990a). While different kinds and degrees of capital constitute habitus, it is not totally predestined boundary of individual ideological positioning. Bourdieu is never a determinist (Bourdieu1990b). Nor are consumers. The sociocultural backdrop for an individual is also reflexively malleable insofar as one empowers oneself as an ideologically autonomous agent, rather than incapacitating him/herself based on the notion of habitus' reproduction of itself (Calhoun et al. 1993; Henry 2005). Interpellation imposes personal and social identity (status) upon an individual and concomitantly sets limits that make individual desubjugation possible (Butler 1997, 2002). Social power relations, norms, dominant ideologies, mainstream consumer culture, and episteme together create an arena wherein consumers can stylize themselves as agents at the limits of their socially interpellated being, as long as they espouse critical mode instead of obedient mode (cf. Foucault 2003). Critical resistance to what orthodox interpellation process inculcates is witnessed in the context of rural snowmobilers, especially when consumers with low economic capital collectively governmentalize not only their identities, but what governmentalizes them as well.

In order to unpack the "critical interpellation" process embraced by rural snowmobilers, a snowmobilers' club in the Upper Peninsula of Michigan was contacted for participatory observation and unstructured depth interviews. Twelve members participated in the interviews at their homes and outdoors as the weather permits. The interviews ranged from 45 minutes to 150 minutes, and observation was conducted as often as possible at such places as bars, gas stations, grocery stores, hotel lobbies, and other local shops that the snowmobilers frequented. The author also participated in road trips and rallies to different places. Fieldnotes, photographs, and videos were kept. Based upon the conventions of hermeneutic approach (Thompson, Pollio and Lacander 1994), the informants' narratives and lived experiences were explicated, employing semiotic clustering method (Feldman 1995).

Rural snowmobilers rearticulate the meaning of social stratification of consumption and dismantle the relevant sociocultural fields in which players are expected to comply with the logic of "foreclosure (subordination)." Six distinct thematic manifestations of rural snowmobilers' ontological positions were identified, three of which contrast the other three with respect to ethics, social status, and ideology (see Figure 1). Owing to the harsh conditions (cultural, economic, and climatic) of rural life, snowmobilers subordinate their desires and aspirations as contemporary consumers to self-discipline and self-preservation. Simultaneously, the mirror images of such hardship, as postmodern lifestyles, and the subsequent pragmatic positioning of rural snowmobilers' sociocultural statuses are also uncovered as rearticulation and reconfiguration of their own styles of being, or emerging statuses. Such highly agentic repositioning and transformation of their personal and social identities take place in a collective setting, in which constant interactions with other snowmobilers enhance the camaraderie amongst them, as "narrowcasted" and "enclaved" social capital.

Ethical consumption practices facilitate snowmobilers' interpellation, as they subscribe to Nietzschean notion of indebtedness, which determines the degree of ethicality. Abnegation of extensive use of credit cards, excessive domestic wastes, gluttony, and materialistic worldview in general is what stylizes their statuses as ethical consumers whom relatively affluent consumers seeking new statuses emulate and simulate. The reflexivity between their consumption practices and the newly developed lifestyles in mainstream consumer culture also creates an ideological niche where poor consumers find a new status that is both subsistent and stylish.

A simple life is what rural snowmobilers collectively pursue, and it signifies environmental consciousness, human ecology, communal harmony, and cultural preservation. The nuanced dissimilitude between their everyday practices and the movement of responsible consumption in the mainstream consumer culture caused by varied levels of economic capital is sublimated into a new source of cultural and symbolic capital. The bases for the novel type of cultural capital comprise habits, skills, and knowledge about thrifty living and self-sustainability. By the same token, rural snowmobilers rewrite the prescribed recipe for symbolic capital, as they earn socio-politically high-ranked position of conscientious consumers.

The reflexive interpellation process brought out in the context provides a platform for researchers to enunciate how poor rural consumers maintain ontological security (Giddens 1991). The received view of inherited and institutionalized cultural and symbolic capital is not necessarily applicable to the context where upward sociocultural mobility can be collectively achieved through agentic appropriation of highly stylized and politicized consumer movements. Avenues for future research extend to the theoretical and empirical junction between anti-consumption and conscientious consumption where both practices bestow unique ideological positions on consumers. Perhaps poor conscientious consumers co-opt socioculturally distanced simulacra to glamorize their lifestyle.

REFERENCES

Bauman, Zygmunt (2007), "Collateral Casualties of Consumption," *Journal of Consumer Culture*, 7 (1), 25-56.

Bourdieu, Pierre (1984), *Distinction: A Social Critique of the Judgment of Taste*, Cambridge, MA: Harvard University Press.

——— (1990a), *The Logic of Practice*, Stanford, CA: Stanford University Press.

——— (1990b), *In Other Words: Essays Towards a Reflexive Sociology*, Stanford, CA: Stanford University Press.

Butler, Judith (1997), *The Psychic Life of Power: Theories in Subjection*, Stanford, CA: Stanford University Press.

——— (2002), "What is Critique? An Essay on Foucault's Virtue," in *The Political*, ed. David Ingram, Malden, MA: Blackwell.

Calhoun, Craig, Edward LiPuma, and Moshie Postone (1993), *Bourdieu: Critical Perspectives*, Chicago: University of Chicago Press.

Feldman, Martha S. (1995), *Strategies for Interpreting Qualitative Data*, Thousand Oaks, California, Sage Publications.

Foucault, Michel (2003), *Society Must Be Defended*, New York, NY: Picador.

Giddens, Anthony (1991), *Modernity and Self-Identity*, Stanford, CA: Stanford University Press.

Henry, Paul C. (2005), "Social Class, Market Situation, and Consumers' Metaphors of (Dis)Empowerment," *Journal of Consumer Research*, 31 (March), 766-778.

Holt, Douglas B. (1997), "Poststructuralist Lifestyle Analysis: Conceptualizing the Social Patterning of Consumption," *Journal of Consumer Research*, 23 (March), 326–50.

Kozinets, Robert V. (2008), "Technology/Ideology: How Ideological Fields Influence Consumers' Technology Narratives," *Journal of Consumer Research*, 34 (April), 865-881.

Thompson, Craig J., Howard R. Pollio, and William B. Locander (1989), "The Spoken and the Unspoken: A Hermeneutic Approach to Understanding the Cultural Viewpoints Than Underlie Consumers' Expressed Meanings," *Journal of Consumer Research*, 21 (December), 432-452.

Üstüner, Tuba and Douglas B. Holt (2007), "Dominated Consumer Acculturation: The social Construction of Poor Migrant Women's Consumer Identity Projects in a Turkish Squatter," *Journal of Consumer Research*, 34 (June), 41-56.

——— (2010), "Toward a Theory of Status Consumption in Less Industrialized Countries," *Journal of Consumer Research*, 37 (June), 37-56.

Üstüner, Tuba and Thompson, Craig J. (2012), "How Marketplace Performances Produce Interdependent Status Games and Contested Forms of Symbolic Capital," *Journal of Consumer Research*, 38 (February), 796-814.

Eat to Be Fit or Fit to Eat?
Restrained Eaters' Food Consumption in Response to Fitness Cues

Joerg Koenigstorfer, Pennsylvania State University, USA
Hans Baumgartner, Pennsylvania State University, USA

EXTENDED ABSTRACT

It is recommended that individuals exercise regularly (Haskell et al. 2007). However, today's environment provides many apparent substitutes for physical activity. This research investigates whether and how fitness cues – both cues that are incidentally present in the environment and cues that are integral to food products (e.g., as part of the packaging) – affect food consumption volumes and whether the relationship is moderated by individual differences and product perceptions.

CONCEPTUAL FRAMEWORK

We propose that both dietary restraint and the perception of food as 'good' or 'bad' impact the relationship between fitness cues and consumption. Dietary restraint refers to chronic eating patterns by individuals who are guided less by their internal feelings of hunger and more by external factors and a constant concern with weight control and dieting (Bublitz, Peracchio, and Block 2010). Restrained eaters often experience conflicts between the goal of eating enjoyment and the goal of weight management (Stroebe et al. 2008). Furthermore, restrained eaters tend to think heuristically about food and view food as either more (allowed) or less (forbidden) suitable for achieving long-term goals (Oakes and Slotterback 2005). If product categories are perceived as dietary-forbidden, both incidental and integral fitness cues should inhibit restrained eaters' tendency to approach tasty but unhealthy food and *decrease* consumption relative to when the concept of fitness is not salient (Anschutz, van Strien, and Engels 2011; Fishbach and Shah 2006).

In contrast, when product categories are perceived as dietary-allowed, we expect the opposite effect. In this case, the compatibility of eating with long-term health benefits reduces the conflict between eating enjoyment and weight management and may liberate restrained eaters from pursuing their dieting goals (Fishbach and Dhar 2005). Therefore, both incidental and integral fitness cues are hypothesized to *increase* consumption for restrained eaters when the product category is dietary-allowed.

Previous research has implicated a variety of mechanisms that may increase or decrease food consumption, including biased product perceptions (calorie under- or over-estimation; Wansink and Chandon 2006) and biased self-perceptions (the extent to which consuming a food affects the perceived closeness to desired fitness or body weight; Geyskens et al. 2007). We examine which of these accounts is most consistent with the effect of fitness cues on consumption for restrained eaters.

EMPIRICAL STUDIES AND MATERIALS

We conducted four studies to test these hypotheses. Studies 1a and 1b assessed the consumption of dietary-forbidden (potato chips) and dietary-allowed (yogurt and granola) foods (both pre-tested, 150 kcal per serving) in response to incidental fitness cues. Study 1a (n = 132) used a two-group design in which either fitness or neutral concepts were primed supraliminally via a scrambled sentence task. After the priming task, participants had a chance to sample a dietary-forbidden food (potato chips) and their consumption was assessed unobtrusively. Dietary restrained eating was assessed via Herman and Polivy's (1980) scale (α = .78). A moderated regression analysis with prime (neutral = 0, fitness = 1), mean-centered dietary restraint,

their interaction, gender, BMI, perceived tastiness, and hunger as independent variables and the number of calories consumed as the dependent variable revealed the expected two-way interaction between prime and dietary restraint ($b = -7.74, p < .05$, model $R^2 = .15$). There was no effect of the prime on consumption for unrestrained eaters, but restrained eaters consumed significantly less when they were primed with fitness ($b = -7.60, p < .01$).

Study 1b (n = 166) was similar in design to study 1a, except that the product category was dietary-allowed (yogurt and granola). As expected, there was a significant interaction between prime and dietary restraint ($b = 5.83, p < .05$, model $R^2 = .22$). The fitness prime had no effect for unrestrained eaters, but restrained eaters consumed significantly more when they were primed with fitness ($b = 4.57, p = .01$).

Study 2 (n = 162) investigated the effect of integral fitness cues on consumption of dietary-allowed food (trail mix) using a two-group design in which participants had a chance to sample (under the pretence of a taste test) either a Fitness Trail Mix or simply a Trail Mix. Consumption was measured unobtrusively, and dietary restraint was measured with Van Strien et al.'s (1986) scale (α = .91). As expected, there was a significant interaction between fitness cue and dietary restraint ($b = 68.33, p < .05$, model $R^2 = .19$). The fitness cue had no effect on unrestrained eaters, but restrained eaters consumed significantly more trail mix when it was labeled Fitness Trail Mix ($b = 85.90, p < .01$).

Study 3 (n = 104) examined potential mediators of this effect. The design was similar to study 2, except that we asked participants to rate the perceived calorie content per serving (150 kcal, presented in bowls) and their perceived closeness to desired fitness and desired body weight (0 = *far away*, 100 = *fully reached*). The results of moderated regression analyses showed that a fitness cue on the product did not have a differential effect on calorie estimates of restrained and unrestrained eaters ($b = -1.98, p = .85, NS$). However, the interactions of dietary restraint with closeness to both desired fitness ($b = 1.65, p < .05$) and body weight ($b = 2.54, p < .001$) were significant. Spotlight analyses showed that restrained eaters saw themselves as closer to their desired fitness and body weight in the Fitness Trail Mix condition.

CONTRIBUTIONS

Our research shows that fitness cues primarily influence the amount of food consumed by restrained eaters, and that the direction of the effect depends on whether (isocaloric) food is perceived to be dietary-forbidden or dietary-allowed. Although liberation processes in restrained eaters have previously been shown for diet- and health-related primes (Papies and Hamstra 2010) and for certain food attributes (e.g., 'haloes' associated with low-fat; Wansink and Chandon 2006), we demonstrate that they also occur in response to fitness cues. Despite the fact that the focal goal of becoming more fit is actually not fulfilled by eating food associated with fitness, consumption of dietary-permitted food increased for restrained consumers.

REFERENCES

Anschutz, Doeschka J., Tatjana van Strien, and Rutger C. M. E. Engels (2011), "Exposure to Slim Images in Mass Media: Television Commercials as Reminders of Restriction in Restrained Eaters," *Psychology of Popular Media Culture*, 1 (S), 48-59.

Bublitz, Melissa G., Laura A. Peracchio, and Lauren G. Block (2010), "Why Did I Eat That? Perspectives on Food Decision Making and Dietary Restraint," *Journal of Consumer Psychology*, 20 (3), 239-58.

Fishbach, Ayelet and Ravi Dhar (2005), "Goals as Excuses or Guides: The Liberating Effect of Perceived Goal Progress on Choice," *Journal of Consumer Research*, 32 (3), 370-7.

Fishbach, Ayelet and James Y. Shah (2006), "Self-control in Action: Implicit Dispositions toward Goals and away from Temptations," *Journal of Personality and Social Psychology*, 90 (5), 820-32.

Geyskens, Kelly, Mario Pandelaere, Siegfrid Dewitte, and Luk Warlop (2007), "The Backdoor to Overconsumption: The Effect of Associating 'Low Fat' Food with Health References," *Journal of Public Policy & Marketing*, 26 (1), 118-25.

Haskell, William L., I-Min Lee, Russell R. Pate, Kenneth E. Powell, Steven N. Blair, Barry A. Franklin, Caroline A. Macera, Gregory W. Heath, Paul D. Thompson, and Adrian Bauman (2007), "Physical Activity and Public Health: Updated Recommendation for Adults from the American College of Sports Medicine and the American Heart Association," *Medicine & Science in Sports & Exercise*, 39 (8), 1423-34.

Herman, Peter C. and Janet Polivy (1980), "Restrained Eating," in Albert J. Stunkard (ed.), *Obesity*, New York, NY: Raven Press, 208-25.

Oakes, Michael E. and Carole S. Slotterback (2005), "Too Good to Be True: Dose Insensitivity and Stereotypical Thinking of Foods' Capacity to Promote Weight Gain," *Food Quality and Preference*, 16 (8), 675-81.

Papies, Esther K. and Petra Hamstra (2010), "Goal Priming and Eating Behavior: Enhancing Self-regulation by Environmental Cues," *Health Psychology*, 29 (4), 384-8.

Stroebe, Wolfgang, Wendy Mensink, Henk Arts, Henk Schut, and Arie W. Kruglanski (2008), "Why Dieters Fail: Testing the Goal Conflict Model of Eating," *Journal of Experimental Social Psychology*, 44 (1), 26-36.

Van Strien, Tatjana, Jan E. R. Frijters, Gerard P. A. Bergers, and Peter B. Defares (1986), "The Dutch Eating Behavior Questionnaires (DEBQ) for Assessment of Restrained, Emotional, and External Eating Behavior," *International Journal of Eating Disorders*, 5 (2), 295-315.

Wansink, Brian and Pierre Chandon (2006), "Can 'Low-fat' Nutrition Labels Lead to Obesity?" *Journal of Marketing Research*, 43 (4), 605-17.

How Accidents Can Be Good For the Brand: The Role of Accident-Brand Stereotype Match and Self-Brand Congruity in User Accidents

Tarje Gaustad, BI Norwegian Business School, Norway
Jakob Utgård, BI Norwegian Business School, Norway
Gavan J. Fitzsimons, Duke University, USA

EXTENDED ABSTRACT

Bad things happen, even to good brands. Sometimes brands get involved in negative events that they could do little to avoid. Cars are crashed, knives used to kill, alcohol abused, and firms cannot always influence these events. In 2008, there were almost four million serious road accidents in Europe and North America combined (UNECE 2011). Consumers are frequently exposed to these accidents in the media or on the road. Car accidents are negative events with sometimes tragic consequences, but they also have interesting branding implications. How does exposure to a car accident affect attitudes to the car brand?

When the brand is little to blame for a negative outcome, consumers tend to judge the brand lightly (Klein and Dawar 2004). Research shows that consumers with strong brand commitment react less negatively when presented with negative information about the brand (Ahluwalia, Burnkrant, and Unnava 2000). Aaker, Fournier, and Brasel (2004) demonstrate that mistakes and transgressions have less negative impact for exciting brands than for sincere brands. This indicates a relationship between expectations based on brand personality and how consumers respond to transgressions.

Building on this, we hypothesize that match between the accident and brand associations (stereotypical accident) increase fluency of the currently held brand associations and polarize attitudes. We base this on the availability-valence hypothesis (Kisielius and Sternthal 1986) which argues that judgments depend on the valence of information available in memory. If the accident's characteristics match consumers' associations of the brand, the accident will increase fluency for those associations and lead to a valence polarization of the existing brand attitudes (positive attitudes becoming more positive and negative attitudes becoming more negative). We use self-brand congruity as a proxy for the valence of the existing associative network available in memory. For consumers who feel congruency between their own self-image and the brand (self-brand congruity), a stereotypical accident confirms pre-existing brand associations and strengthens positive attitudes. For consumers who do not feel congruent with the brand, a stereotypical accident confirms existing negative associations and strengthens negative attitudes.

Study 1 investigates how match/mismatch between the accident and brand associations influence consumers' judgments. Undergraduate students (n=103) participated in a 2 (stereotypical vs. non-stereotypical accident) × self-brand congruity (measured) between-subjects experiment. First, we measured participants' attitude and self-brand congruity (Sirgy 1982) to BMW. Next, respondents read a newspaper article about a BMW car crash. The article was similar for both conditions except from the description of *how* the accident happened. We manipulated the accident to be stereotypical (racing in high speed) or not stereotypical (crossing over into the wrong lane) of BMW. Pretests had confirmed that the speeding accident was significantly more typical for BMW than the other accident ($p = .03$), but that they were equally serious ($p = .4$). Last, we measured perception of the accident and change in attitude to BMW.

We conducted multiple regression with change in attitude to BMW after reading the newspaper article as a dependent measure, and experimental condition (not stereotypical accident=0, stereotypical accident=1), self-brand congruity (continuous variable), and their interaction as independent variables.

The results showed a negative effect of type of accident ($\beta = -2.02$, $t = -3.26$, $p < .01$), meaning that participants evaluated BMW more negatively after reading about the stereotypical accident (versus non-stereotypical), even though the two accidents are equally serious. As expected, the interaction between type of accident and self-brand congruity was significant ($\beta = .51$, $t = 3.32$, $p < .02$), also after controlling for pre-attitude to BMW. Investigation of the interaction confirmed the predicted significance and non-significance of slopes, as well as contrasts at low and high levels of self-brand congruity.

The results confirm our hypothesis. Participants who do not feel congruent with the brand decrease their brand evaluation after learning about an accident that confirms their brand associations, while participants who feel congruent with the brand increase their evaluation when an accident confirms their brand associations.

In study 2, we seek to replicate the findings by including a condition with a car brand that is not strongly associated with high speed and racing (Toyota), and to rule out the alternative explanation of "high speed" as a signal of high performance. To explain the results, high speed needs to be a positive performance signal for those feeling congruent with any car brand (whether or not the accident matches brand associations) and similarly negative for those who do not feel congruent.

Online respondents (n =287) participated in a 2 (high speed accident vs. wrong lane accident) × 2 (BMW vs. Toyota) × self-brand congruity (measured) design. The procedure was similar to study 1, except for the "Toyota-condition".

We conducted multiple regression and the three-way interaction (brand, accident type, and self-brand congruity) yielded the expected result ($\beta = .016$, $t = 2.01$, $p < .05$). Separate analysis of the BMW condition and the Toyota condition also show the expected results, with a significant two-way interaction between accident type and self-brand congruity ($\beta = .16$, $t = 2.90$, $p < .01$) in the BMW condition and no interaction in the Toyota condition ($\beta = .00$, $t = -.053$, $p =.96$).

The results replicate the findings from study 1, and confirm that the effect is dependent on a match between the user accident and brand associations.

This research suggests that accident "stereotypicality" influence brand evaluations. Participants evaluate the brand more negatively after learning about an accident that matches brand associations than an accident that does not match brand associations. However, this effect interacts with participants' felt self-brand congruity, suggesting that stereotypical accidents polarize brand evaluations. Those participants who feel that the brand is "like them" increase their brand attitudes if the accident is stereotypical, whereas those participants who feel that the brand is not "like them", decrease their attitude if the accident is stereotypical of the brand.

REFERENCES

Aaker, Jennifer, Susan Fournier, S. Adam Brasel, David Glen (Ed.) Mick, and Donald R. (Ed.) Lehmann (2004), "When good brands do bad," *Journal of Consumer Research*, 31 (January), 1-16.

Ahluwalia, Rohini, Robert E. Burnkrant, and H. Rao Unnava (2000), "Consumer response to negative publicity: The moderating role of commitment," *Journal of Marketing Research*, 37 (Februar), 203-214.

Klein, Jill and Niraj Dawar (2004), "Corporate Social Responsibility and Consumers' Attributions and Brand Evaluations in a Product-Harm Crisis," *International Journal of Research in Marketing*, (March), 203-217.

Kisielius, J. & Sternthal, B., 1986. Examining the Vividness Controversy: An Availability-Valence Interpretation. *Journal of Consumer Research*, 12 (April), 418-431.

Sirgy, M. Joseph (1982), "Self-concept in consumer behavior: A critical review," *Journal of Consumer Research*, 9 (March), 287-300.

UNECE, United Nations Economic Commission for Europe. (2011). Statistics of Road Traffic Accidents in Europe and North America. http://www.unece.org/trans/main/wp6/publications/stats_accidents2011.html

Tell Me What to Do When I am in a Good Mood, Show Me What to Do When I am in a Bad Mood: Mood as a Moderator of Social Norm's Influence

Vladimir Melnyk, Maastricht University, The Netherlands
Erica van Herpen, Wageningen University, The Netherlands
Arnout Fischer, Wageningen University, The Netherlands
Hans C. M. van Trijp, Wageningen University, The Netherlands

EXTENDED ABSTRACT

Social norms are an influential driver of consumers' preferences in different domains of everyday life (Cialdini et al., 2006; Melnyk et al., 2009) and are extensively used in marketing campaigns. The influence of social norms may depend on the mood that consumers experience while being exposed to them (Bless et al., 1990), but also on the formulation of the social norm. Social norms can be formulated as descriptive or injunctive norms (Cialdini et al. 1990). Descriptive norms describe the typical behavior of others, and set behavioral standards from which people may not want to deviate (Schultz et al. 2007). Injunctive norms prescribe a behavior, and refer to what people should do in a given situation.

Despite a large body of research on social norms (see Goldstein & Cialdini, 2009) and on the role of mood in consumer behavior (see Gardner, 1985) little is known about the effect of mood on social norms' influence. This paper argues and shows that each norm formulation can be differently affected by mood due to mood-protection and the mood-repair mechanisms. That is, individuals are motivated to maintain the mood when they are already in positive mood, but engage in mood repair when they are in negative mood (Hirt & McCrea, 2000).

Importantly, because of these mechanisms, positive and negative moods can result in different effects on the amount of cognitive effort that people exert (Isen et al., 1985). When in positive mood, individuals avoid investing cognitive effort unless doing so promises to enhance their positive mood (Bohner et al., 1992; Wegener et al., 1995), and they show more compliance with requests, compared to negative mood (Forgas, 1998). In contrast, when in negative mood mood-repair mechanism stimulates individuals to invest cognitive effort to find ways of improving their mood (Clore et al., 1994; Hirt & McCrea, 2000).

This difference in the amount of cognitive deliberation under positive and negative mood can lead to different perceptions of injunctive compared to descriptive social norms. Previous research has shown that injunctive norms have a smaller influence on the advocated behavior, when consumers cognitively deliberate upon them (Melnyk et al., 2011). This is because injunctive norms by conveying an explicit and straightforward request can be perceived by consumers as a limitation to their freedom and can therefore trigger them to counter-argue (Mann & Hill, 1984). In contrast, in positive mood the mood-protection mechanism should decrease the likelihood of thoughts against such a request (Batra & Stayman, 1990). Therefore we expect a higher responsiveness towards injunctive norms in positive mood compared to negative mood.

Hypothesis 1:   Injunctive norms have a greater influence on attitudes, behavioral intentions and behavior under positive than under negative mood.

For descriptive norms negative mood should not decreases their influence, because due to the mood-repair mechanism consumers are more likely to cognitively deliberate upon the messages (Clore et al., 1994), and this can increase the influence of descriptive norms (Melnyk et al., 2011). The mood-repair mechanism also simulates consumers to think about solutions to improve their mood. Descriptive norms can present such a solution, by providing "social proof" of what is likely to be effective behavior (Cialdini, 2006; Reno et al., 1993) and beneficial behavior (Schultz et al., 2007). Furthermore, Griskevicius et al. (2009) showed that a descriptive norm message with a social proof appeal ("most popular"), was persuasive when people experienced negative feelings (fear), but was counter persuasive when people experienced pleasant feelings (romantic desire). This can make descriptive norms more influential under negative than positive mood.

Hypothesis 2:   Descriptive norms have a greater influence on attitudes, behavioral intentions and behavior under negative than under positive mood.

These hypotheses are tested in two experiments.

Experiment 1 ($N = 140$) had a 2 (mood induction: negative vs. positive) × 3 (norm formulation: descriptive vs. injunctive vs. no norm) between subjects design. For *mood manipulation*, participants were asked to recall either a negative life event (negative mood condition), or a positive life event (positive mood condition). *Norm formulation* was manipulated by a short statement on the background of a neutral picture with chocolate: "Did you know that nowadays most WUR students buy fair trade chocolate?" (descriptive norm condition), "Did you know that nowadays most WUR students think you should buy fair trade chocolate?" (injunctive norm condition), and "Did you know that nowadays there is a possibility to buy fair trade chocolate in any supermarket?" (no norm condition). At the end of the experiment participants were offered an opportunity to make a donation to a well-known fair trade organization "Oxfam-Novib" from their monetary reward for participation.

Experiment 2 ($N = 160$) examines the proposed underlying mechanism of cognitive deliberation by testing if preventing people from deliberating decreases the moderating effect of mood. It had a 2 (mood induction: negative vs. positive) × 2 (norm formulation: descriptive vs. injunctive) × 2 (cognitive load: high vs. low) between subjects design. The manipulations of mood and norm formulation were similar to Experiment 1. *Cognitive load* was manipulated by asking participants to either remember a 7-digit number (high cognitive load) or a 1-digit number (low cognitive load).

Consistent with our expectation the results obtained from the two experiments show a fundamental difference between injunctive and descriptive norms. Injunctive norms lead to more positive attitudes and intentions under positive (vs. negative) mood, whereas descriptive norms lead to more positive attitudes and intentions under negative (vs. positive) mood. Furthermore, we show that this effect translates to actual (donations) behavior. Experiment 2 shows that the effect is due to cognitive deliberation, as the effects disappear when cognitive deliberation is hindered.

Our results indicate that social norms should be carefully chosen, and used depending on the context in which the information supported by the norm is processed by the consumer. The study has theoretical implications as well. Previously, negative mood was shown to decrease consumer's evaluations of received information and persuasive messages (Miniard et al., 1992). This paper shows that mood not only changes the responsiveness of consumers to social norms for attitudes and intentions, but it does so differently for the two norm formulations. In particular, the negative effect of bad mood on responsiveness to persuasive information can be reversed by using descriptive norm formulations rather than injunctive norms.

This research contributes to our understanding of the influence of social norms on decision making by showing how mood affects the influence of descriptive compared to injunctive norm formulations on consumers' attitudes, purchase intentions, as well as on real behavior.

REFERENCES

Batra, R., & Stayman, D. M. (1990). The role of mood in advertising effectiveness. *Journal of Consumer Research, 17*(2), 203-214.

Bless, H., Bohner, G., Schwarz, N., & Strack, F. (1990). Mood and Persuasion: A Cognitive Response Analysis. *Personality and Social Psychology Bulletin, 16*(2), 331-345.

Bohner, G., Crow, K., Erb, H.-P., & Schwarz, N. (1992). Affect and persuasion: Mood effects on the processing of message content and context cues and on subsequent behaviour. *European Journal of Social Psychology, 22*(6), 511-530.

Cialdini, R. B. (2006). *Influence: The Psychology of Persuasion*. New York: Collins Business Essentials.

Cialdini, R. B., Demaine, L. J., Sagarin, B. J., Barrett, D. W., Rhoads, K., & Winter, P. L. (2006). Managing social norms for persuasive impact. *Social Influence, 1*(1), 3 - 15.

Cialdini, R. B., Reno, R. R., & Kallgren, C. A. (1990). A focus theory of normative conduct: Recycling the concept of norms to reduce littering in public places. *Journal of Personality and Social Psychology, 58*(6), 1015-1026.

Clore, G. L., Schwarz, N., & Conway, M. (1994). Cognitive causes and consequences of emotion. In E. R. S. Wyer and T. K. Srull (Ed.), *Handbook of social cognition.* (2nd ed., pp. 323-418). Hillsdale: Erlbaum.

Forgas, J. P. (1998). Asking nicely? The effects of mood on responding to more or less polite requests. *Personality and Social Psychology Bulletin, 24*(2), 173-185.

Gardner, M. P. (1985). Mood states and consumer behavior: a critical review *Journal of Consumer Research, 12*(3), 281-300.

Goldstein, N. J., & Cialdini, R. B. (2009). Using social norms as a lever of social influence. In A. R. Pratkanis (Ed.), *The science of social influence* (pp. 167-192). New York: Psychology Press.

Griskevicius, V., Goldstein, N. J., Mortensen, C. R., Sundie, J. M., Cialdini, R. B., & Kenrick, D. T. (2009). Fear and Loving in Las Vegas: Evolution, Emotion, and Persuasion. *Journal of Marketing Research, 46*(3), 384-395.

Hirt, E. R., & McCrea, S. M. (2000). Beyond hedonism: Broadening the scope of affect regulation. *Psychological Inquiry, 11*(3), 180-183.

Mann, M. F., & Hill, T. (1984). Persuasive communications and the boomerang effect: some limiting conditions to the effectiveness of positive influence attempts. *Advances in Consumer Research, 11*, 66-70.

Melnyk, V., Van Herpen, E., Fischer, A., & Van Trijp, H. (2011). To Think or Not to Think: The Effect of Cognitive Deliberation on the Influence of Injunctive versus Descriptive Social Norms. *Psychology and Marketing, 28*(7), 709-729.

Melnyk, V., Van Herpen, E., & Van Trijp, H. (2009). The Influence of Social Norms in Consumer Decision Making: a Meta-analysis. In M. C. Campbell, J. Inman & R. Pieters (Eds.), *Advances in Consumer Research* (Vol. 37). Duluth, MN: Association for Consumer Research.

Reno, R. R., Cialdini, R. B., & Kallgren, C. A. (1993). The transsituational influence of social norms. *Journal of Personality and Social Psychology, 64*(1), 104-112.

Schultz, P. W., Nolan, J. M., Cialdini, R. B., Goldstein, N. J., & Griskevicius, V. (2007). The constructive, destructive and reconstructive power of social norms. *Psychological Science, 18*(5), 429-434.

Wegener, D. T., Smith, S. M., & Petty, R. E. (1995). Positive mood can Increase or decrease message scrutiny: The hedonic contingency view of mood and message processing. *Journal of Personality and Social Psychology, 69*(1), 5-15.

Consuming the Cyborg

Arundhati Bhattacharyya, York University, Canada
Richard Kedzior, Bucknell University, USA

EXTENDED ABSTRACT

Pace-makers have been placed in the body for the last 50 years. Abilities enhancing micro-chips have been grafted into the human body for the last 15 years (Naam 2005; Warwick 2004). Despite these identity-problematizing developments (Williams 1997), extant consumer research on individuals' engagement with *active*-technology (stimuli-responsive technology like micro-processors, as opposed to inert Silicone implants) remains limited to contexts where such technology is external to the body. The current study seeks to correct this oversight by examining the lay discourses surrounding active-technology embedded bodies. Specifically, we ask:

1. What are the discourses surrounding active-technology embedded human bodies?
2. When would such bodies be construed as threatening?
3. What discourses facilitate the acceptance of such bodies?

LITERATURE REVIEW

Extant consumer research exploring consumers' reactions to technology (Mick and Fournier 1998, Kozinets 2008) is rooted in contexts where active-technology is physically external to the body. The exceptions that discussed the Cyborg (an active-technology embedded human), have used the term either as a metaphor (Giesler and Venkatesh 2005), or an image (Campbell, O'Driscoll and Saren 2006), thus overlooking actually existing active-technology embedded bodies. The "leaky" figure (Haraway 1991) of the Cyborg is an apt context for studying consumer interpretations about technology embedded bodies since, by dissolving several body-oriented boundaries (Haraway 1991), the Cyborg problematizes the West's maximal privileging of the body (Johnston 2001). While cyber-theologians have hailed boundary-dissolving technologies as the route to humans' technological salvation (Wertheim 1999; Haraway 1991), their assumption has been based on Futurists' views, not on actual lay discourses. While the body in recent consumer studies has received a lot of attention (Hung and Labroo 2011; Labroo and Neilsen 2010; McFerran, Dahl, Fitzsimons and Morales 2010; Thompson and Hirschman 1995; Schouten 1991), the body embedded with technology has remained under-researched. This paper seeks to examine lay discourses around active-technology embedded human body, here termed the Cyborg.

METHODOLOGY

For the purpose of this study we conducted a netnographic investigation of an online discussion forum which was formed around a YouTube video documenting lived experiences of an active-technology embedded body. The naturally occurring discussion, generating 730 posts, extended across 3 years (2009-2012). Concomitant to our research questions, we adopted a discourse analytical approach to explore the dataset.

FINDINGS

The initial data explorations revealed a technological continuum of acceptance where certain forms of technological enhancements were desirable and approved of (e.g. pacemakers), whereas others (e.g. implanted chips enabling extra experiences and abilities) were approached as dangerous and threatening. We next investigated the reasons why technology was construed as threatening in the con-

text of an enhanced body. Our analysis unearthed the following three predominant discourses that framed threat as:

1) **the ability of technology to take control over human beings**: The fear of humans giving up control of their thoughts, actions and feelings to the embedded artificial processor is palpable in the following representative excerpt:

"*... Like that, **we will eventually become biological masses who have everything done for them by machines**. It sickens me to think there is a chance it becomes real.*"

2) **the ability to use technology to control other humans**: The concept of the cyborg is feared as an elitist way of gaining control over "the masses", as the following comment exemplifies:

"**The only sector that matters in this issue is the rich elite... No technocrat or anything of the sort will be above the secret societies that remain in charge,** and ill (sic) die with a weapon on hand before i (sic) let those new world order a******* **ever get my mind and soul into their matrix of evil.**"

3) **the loss of human identity and selfhood**: As underscored by the following comment, being a cyborg is equated with losing the essence of what it means to be human, and crucially, losing what one perceives as one's self.:

"*... the only thing i fear is ...before u know it the entire brain has been completely replaced with synthetic parts to "improve" man. **it's at that point u'd have comitted** (sic) **suicide (in a sense) because it is now a machine that has copies of your memories, mannerisms, and personality... but it's not u** anymore...*"

Additionally, our data revealed the existence of three discourses which facilitate the acceptance of technologically enhanced bodies. They can be summarized as:

1) **problematizing the natural**: What is considered natural, including earlier species, is positioned as something that has existential flaws, with the Cyborg conceived as the route to transcend extermination. For example:

"*Ever heard of the Neanderthal? Take a guess why Homo Sapiens won out in that evolutionary competition.(If you guessed better technology and willingness/ability to adapt you guessed right, a **Sapiens for Sapiens sake is the Neanderthal of the future.**)*"

2) **naturalizing the technology**: An alternative discourse offers the Cyborg as an inevitable, part of the natural order of things, only faster, as is underscored by the following:

"*Going cyborg is just like **advancing naturally. The difference is that it is a million times faster .... I think it is inevitable** and one day everybody will have some enchantments.*"

3) **sacralizing the cyborg**: In response to "*We shouldn't play to be God.*", one of the responses was, " *Why not? **We invented God in the image of what we aspired to be, so let's become that image.** :)*"

CONTRIBUTION

The study sought to examine the lay discourses around consumption of body-embedded active-technology. In doing so, it added to the growing literature on consumers' engagement with active technology which has hitherto overlooked the phenomenon of technology internal to the body and also to the research on consumer bodies which has neglected technology-enhanced body. The study revealed that contrary to cyber-theologians' theorizations, lay interpretations of active-technology embedded in the body ranged from acceptance of certain active-technology that helps individuals function as humans (for eg,the pacemaker) to utter rejection of active-technology that enhances humans' normal abilities (for eg, in the case of the cyborg). While a few deployed certain acceptance strategies, the majority's rejection stemmed from fear and threat centred around a perceived loss of control across various domains.

REFERENCES

Campbell, Norah, Aidan O'Driscoll, and Michael Saren (2006), "Cyborg Consciousness: A Visual Culture approach to the Technologised Body," *European Advances In Consumer Research,* 7, 344-51.

Giesler, Markus and Alladi Venkatesh (2005), "Reframing the Embodied Consumer as Cyborg A Posthumanist Epistemology of Consumption," *Advances In Consumer Research,* 32, 661

Haraway, Donna J. (1991), *Simians, Cyborgs, and Women: The Reinvention Of Nature,* New York: Routledge

Hung, Iris W. and **Aparna Labroo** (2011), "From Firm Muscles To Firm Willpower: Understanding the role of Embodied Cognition in Self-Regulation", *Journal of Consumer Research,* 37(6), 1046-64.

Johnston, Jessica R. (2001), "The American Body in Context : An Anthology," in *American Visions, No. 3,* Ed: Jessica R. Johnston, Wilmington: Scholarly Resources, xiii-ix.

Kozinets, Robert V. (2008), "Technology/Ideology: How Ideological Fields Influence Consumers' Technology Narratives," *Journal of Consumer Research,* 34 (6), 865-81.

Labroo, Aparna and Jesper H. Nielsen (2010), "Half the Thrill is in the Chase: Twisted Inferences from Embodied Cognitions and Brand Evaluation", *Journal of Consumer Research,* 37 (1), 143-58

McFerran, Brent, Darren W Dahl, Gavan J. Fitzsimons and Andrea C Morales (2010), "I'll have what she's having: Effects of Social influence and Body type on the food choices of others," *Journal of Consumer Research,* 36 (6), 915-29

Mick, David. G., and Susan Fournier (1998), "Paradoxes of Technology: Consumer Cognizance, Emotions, and Coping Strategies," *Journal of Consumer Research,* 25 (2), 123-43

Naam, Ramez (2005), *More Than Human: Embracing the promise of Biological Enhancement,* New York: Broadway Books, Random House

Schouten, John W. (1991), "Selves in Transition: Symbolic Consumption in Personal Rites of Passage and Identity Reconstruction," *Journal of Consumer Research,* 17(4), 412-25

Thompson, Craig J. and Elizabeth C. Hirschman (1995), "Understanding The Socialized Body: A Poststructuralist analysis of Consumers' Self-Conceptions, Body Images, And Self-Care Practices," *Journal of Consumer Research,* 22(2), 139-53

Warwick, Kevin (2004), *I, Cyborg,* Urbana And Chicago: University Of Illinois Press

Wertheim, Margaret (1999), *The Pearly Gates of Cyberspace: A History of Space from Dante to the Internet,* New York: WW Norton.

Williams, Simon J. (1997), "Modern Medicine and the 'Uncertain Body' -From Corporeality to Hyperreality?", *Social Science & Medicine,* 45 (7), 1041-9.

Infectious Counterfeiting:
Labeling Products as Fakes can Contaminate Perceived & Actual Efficacy

Moty Amar, OAC, Israel
Ziv Carmon, INSEAD, Singapore
Dan Ariely, Duke University, USA

EXTENDED ABSTRACT

Counterfeiting is a rampant worldwide phenomenon with substantial economic and societal consequences. Whereas macro level consequences have been extensively studied, customer-level consequences of this phenomenon—the focus of this paper –are not well understood. Our research suggests that merely presenting products as counterfeits can contaminate them psychologically. Importantly, this can result in poorer perceptions and lower actual efficacy. Briefly, the notion is that counterfeiting is a moral offense, affecting perceptions & efficacy. This is because the moral offense causes a sense of moral disgust (Schnall et al.,2008), which like physical disgust follows sympathetic magic laws (Greene et al., 2001) of contagion and similarity (Frazer 1890/1959). Labeling a product as counterfeit can thus contaminate both that product and similar non-fake products. The results of three experiments support the predicted effect and its explanation.

The goal of Experiment 1 was to study our ideas in the field. In this experiment, 61 experienced-golf players were presented with 2 identical putters (a golf club used to hit the ball into the last hole) and were told that one of them was real and the other one a fake. They were then asked to determine, to the best of their ability, which putter was real and which a fake. Next, they were randomly placed in one of two experimental conditions: putt with the non-fake club first, or putt with the "fake" club first. Their goal in both conditions was to sink the ball in the hole, or get it as close as possible to the hole if they missed it. As predicted, participants played better with the non-fake club than with the "fake" one. Specifically, participants playing with the non-fake club sunk the ball in the hole more than those who played with the "fake" club (14 times versus 7 times; $t(59) = -5.89$, $p <.05$), and brought it closer to the hole when failing to sink it ($M=24$ versus $M=32$; $t(59) = 2.58$, $p< .01$).

In Experiment 2, 42 participants were presented with two different Parker fountain pens, and were told that one of them was real and the other a fake. They were asked to use each pen to trace a line from the start of a maze to its end, trying to avoid touching the contours. After completing the task with both pens, participants were asked to evaluate each pen. As predicted, across different measures, pens were rated less favorably when they were said to be fake than when they were said to be non-fake. Specifically, compared to the non-fake pen participants rated the "fake" as significantly less comfortable, of lower quality, and as less appealing. Furthermore, results of the maze task, suggest that deleterious effects of believing that a product is fake may not limited to participants' reported evaluations, and also affect efficacy. Participants who completed the task using the "fake" pens performed significantly worse than those who used the non-fake pens, touching the lines of the maze more frequently. This effect was, in turn, was mediated by participants' attitudes towards using the fake pen, per the procedure recommended by Zhao, Lynch, and Chen (2010).

In experiment 3, we examined whether fake products negatively affect similar non-fake products. Eighty three participants were randomly allocated to one of two conditions. In the first condition, participants were presented with 2 different pairs of Chloe (a prestigious designer brand) sunglasses and were told that one of them was real and the other a fake. Participants then tried on the sunglasses, exam-ined them, and compared them to another (third) pair of sunglasses that the experimenter presented. In the second condition participants followed same procedure except that they were told that both sunglasses were non-fake. Results show that participants who first saw a "fake" product rated the subsequent non-fake product lower than participants who first saw a non-fake product. Specifically, compared to participants who first had a non-fake pair of sunglasses, those who first had the "fake pair" reported that they saw significantly less well with the non-fake sunglasses, and rated them significantly lower on comfort, perceived quality and liking. Note that the non-fake product being rated more poorly when it was tested after the "fake" product versus when it was tested after a non-fake one, conflicts with prediction of an alternative account whereby differences in ratings are an artifact of participants' tendency to compare the second pair of sunglasses to the first.

Altogether, this paper illustrates harmful effects that counterfeiting can have from consumers' perspective. We show that merely presenting a products as a counterfeit can hurt perceptions and even objective efficacy. Theoretically, this work adds to the emerging research streams on psychological contamination, on marketing effects of disgust, and on placebo effects of marketing actions. Practically, our

findings, suggest that counterfeiting may be more damaging than previously believed, due to effects we document, and in particular effects on non-fake versions of the product.

REFERENCES

Allison, R.I. and Uhl, K. P. (1964), "Influence of beer brand identification on taste perception," *Journal of Marketing Research*, 36–39.

Colloca, L., Petrovic, P., Wager, T. D., Ingvar, M and Benedetti, F. (2010), "How the number of learning trials affects placebo and nocebo responses," *Pain*151, 2, 430-439.

Chapman, H, A., Kim, D. A., Susskind, J, M. and Anderson, A, k., (2009), "In bad taste: Evidence for the oral origins of moral disgust," *Science*, 323, 5918, 1222.

Fullerton, R. A. and Punj, G. (1993), "Choosing to misbehave: A structural model of aberrant consumer behavior," *Advances in Consumer Research*, 1, 570–574.

Frazer, J. G. (2003), "The golden bough: A study in magic and religion" *Kessinger Publishing*.

Frazer, J. G. (1959), "The golden bough: A study in magic and religion," New York: Macmillan. (reprint of 1922 abridged edition, edited by T. H. Gaster. Original work published 1890).

Greene, J. D., Sommerville, R. B., Nystrom, L, E., Darley, J, M., Cohen, J, D. (2001), "An fMRI investigation of emotional engagement in moral judgment," *Science* 293, 5537, 2105.

Gerstner, E. (1985), "Do higher prices signal higher quality?," *Journal of Marketing Research*, 209–215.

Huber, J and McCann, J. (1982), "The impact of inferential beliefs on product evaluations," *Journal of Marketing Research*, 324–333.

Hahn, R. A. (1997), "The Nocebo Phenomenon: Concept, Evidence, and Implications for Public Health," *Preventive medicine* 26, 5, 607–611.

Johnson, M, Wilson, A, Kline C, Blumberg, B, Bobick A. (1999) "Sympathetic interfaces: using a plush toy to direct synthetic characters," in *Proceedings of the SIGCHI conference on Human factors in computing systems: the CHI is the limit, ,* 152–158.

Kohlberg, L. (1969), "Stage and sequence: The cognitive-developmental approach to socialization," *Chicago, IL.*

Levin, I. P. and Gaeth, G. J. (1988), "How consumers are affected by the framing of attribute information before and after consuming the product," *Journal of Consumer Research,* 374–378.

Muncy, J.A. and Vitell, S. J. (1992), "Consumer ethics: an investigation of the ethical beliefs of the final consumer," *Journal of Business Research,* 24, 4, 297–311.

McClure, S. M., Li, J., Tomlin, D., Cypert, K.S., Montague, L.M., Montague, P.R. (2004) , "Neural correlates of behavioral preference for culturally familiar drinks," *Neuron* 44, 379–387.

Penz, E. and Stottinger, B. (2005), "Forget the'real' thing-take the copy! An explanatory model for the volitional purchase of counterfeit products," *Advances in consumer research,* 32, 568.

Rozin, P. and Nemeroff, C. (1990), "The laws of sympathetic magic," *Cultural psychology: Essays on comparative human development,* 205–232.

Rozin, P. and Nemeroff, C. (1990), "The laws of sympathetic magic," *Cultural psychology: Essays on comparative human development,* 205–232.

Rao, A.R. and Monroe, K. B. (1989), "The effect of price, brand name, and store name on buyers' perceptions of product quality: An integrative review," *Journal of Marketing Research,* 351–357.

Shiv, B., Carmon, Z., and Ariely, D. (2005), "Placebo effects of marketing actions: Consumers may get what they pay for," *Journal of Marketing Research* 42, 383–393.

Schnall, S., Haidt, J., Clore, G and Jordan, A. H. (2008), "Disgust as embodied moral judgment," *Personality and Social Psychology Bulletin* 34, 8, 1096.

Turiel, E., Killen, M., and Helwig, C.C. (1987), "Morality: Its structure, functions, and vagaries," *The emergence of morality in young children,* 155–243.

Wilcox, K., Kim, H.M., and Sen, S. (2009), "Why do consumers buy counterfeit luxury brands?" *Journal of Marketing Research* 46, 2: 247–259.

Zhao, X., Lynch, J. G. Jr. and Chen, Q. (2010), " Reconsidering Baron and Kenny: Myths and Truths about Mediation Analysis," *Journal of Consumer Research,* Vol. 37, No. 2 (August 2010), pp. 197-206

Zeithaml, V.A. (1988), "Consumer perceptions of price, quality, and value: a means-end model and synthesis of evidence," *The Journal of Marketing,* 2–22.

Recovering From Ethical Failures:
Role of External Attribution and Monetary Compensation

Sekar Raju, Iowa State University, USA
Priyali Rajagopal, Southern Methodist University, USA

EXTENDED ABSTRACT

Research has found that denying ethical failures elicits more favorable attitudes than accepting them (Ferrin et al 2007) due to the differential inferences people draw from the failure (Reeder and Brewer 1979). An ethical failure is more diagnostic in judging moral character and hence likely to have greater informational value and impact on judgment. This suggests that the effect of accepting ethical failures is difficult to overcome. However, the literature on moral disengagement (White, Bandura and Bero 2009) provides insight into recovery strategies from ethical transgressions. We focus on two such alternatives that are often observed in a marketing context – external attribution and monetary compensation.

Attributing a failure to outside sources is commonly adopted by firms (e.g. Ford/Firestone). External attribution shifts the culpability of the unethical act away from the firm. By attributing the failure to an outside party, firms can restrict the negative association of having committed an unethical act and consequently reduce the future likelihood of repeating the act. In other words, the diagnostic value of the ethical failure for consumers is reduced. Thus, when the failure is attributed externally, consumers will have more favorable attitudes and intentions towards the firm, greater trust in the firm and be less likely to believe that the firm will make similar errors in the future, as compared to when the firm accepts the failure. Finally, there will be no differences in attitudes, intentions, future likelihood estimates or trust in the firm when the firm externally attributes the failure as compared to when the firm denies the failure.

Monetary compensation, however, attempts to shift the focus away from the failure and its consequences to resolution of the failure. Therefore, we expected to find that this response would improve consumer attitudes but would not improve intentions or reduce the future failure likelihood.

In real life, consumers often hold varying levels of trust in a company. We therefore also hypothesize that under conditions of low prior trust, there will be no differences in consumer responses towards the firm between offering monetary compensation, accepting, externally attributing or denying the failure.

STUDY 1 (N = 154)

Design: 2 (prior trust: high versus low) x 3 (recovery: accept, deny, external attribution) between subjects study. The dependent measures included attitudes towards the firm, trust in the firm, likelihood of future transgressions by the firm and behavioral intentions towards the firm (7-point scales).

We found a significant interaction between prior trust and company responses on attitudes (F (1, 147) = 7.62, p < .01), intentions (F (1, 147) =10.3, p < .01, post-failure trust (F (1, 147) = 4.89, p < .01) and future likelihood of failure (F (1, 147) = 2.73, p = .06). Planned contrasts revealed that when trust was high, externally attributing the failure led to results that were no different from denying the failure (p's > .1). However, when trust was low, externally attributing the failure did not improve any of the dependent measures as compared to accepting the failure.

In addition, a mediation analysis revealed that the response significantly predicted post-failure trust in the company (F (1, 71) = 7.14, p < .01) and likelihood of future failures (F (1, 71) = 6.97), p < .01); the likelihood of future failures significantly predicted post-

recovery trust in the company (β = .68, p < .05), and when both the type of response and likelihood of future failures were included as predictors of post-recovery trust, only likelihood of future failures remained a significant predictor (F (1, 70) = 19.85, p < .01) and the type of response was non-significant (F (1, 70) = 2.33, p > .1). Thus, external attribution reduces the diagnosticity of the ethical failure and thereby improves consumer perceptions of the firm.

STUDY 2 (N = 147)

In study 2, we varied the failure context (environmental damage) and conducted a 2 (prior trust: high versus low) x 3 (response: accept, deny, external attribution) between subjects study. We replicated the findings from study 1 and found a significant interaction between prior trust and type of response on consumer attitudes (F (2, 140) = 3.57, p < .05) and post-recovery trust (F (2, 140) = 3.49, p < .05). Under high trust, external attribution elicited responses that were no different as compared to denying the failure (p's > .1) but were significantly higher than when the failure was accepted (p's < .05) but under low trust, external attribution elicited results that were no different from accepting the failure.

STUDY 3 (N = 200)

Design: 2 (prior trust: low versus high) x 4 (responses to failure: accept, deny, monetary compensation, external attribution) between subjects study. We used the same scenario and dependent measures used in study 1.

We found the expected interaction between prior trust and company responses on attitudes towards the firm (F (3, 192) = 3.0, p < .05), intentions towards the firm (F (3, 192) = 4.39, p < .05) and post-failure trust in the firm (F (3, 192) = 2.29, p = .07). We replicated the pattern of results for external attribution that was found in study 1. Thus, external attribution improved attitudes and intentions and lowered future likelihood of failure when trust was high.

When prior trust was high, monetary compensation improved attitudes, but not intentions, trust or future failure likelihood, as compared to accepting the failure. Thus, externally attributing the failure was better than offering monetary compensation in terms of future intentions and diagnosticity. Also as predicted, there were no differences between any of the four conditions on attitudes, intentions, post-failure trust in the firm or the likelihood of future failures when prior trust in the firm was low (all p's > .1). Thus, any response to an ethical failure appears to require a modicum of trust in the firm in order to be successful.

CONTRIBUTION

While prior research has shown that denying ethical failures is the only option to retain favorable consumer attitudes and intentions, we identify exceptions to this finding. We show that external attribution reduces the perceived diagnosticity of ethical failures, leading to more favorable attitudes/intentions towards the firm while monetary compensation can improve attitudes, but not future intentions. We also identify an important moderator to these effects – prior trust in the company.

REFERENCES

Ferrin, Donald, L., Peter H. Kim, Cecily D. Cooper and Kurt T. Dirks (2007), "Silence Speaks Volumes: The Effectiveness Of Reticence In Comparison To Apology And Denial For Repairing Integrity- And Competence-Based Trust Violations," *Journal of Applied Psychology*, 92(4), 893-908.

Reeder, Glenn D. and Marilynn B. Brewer (1979), "A schematic model of dispositional attribution in interpersonal perception," *Psychological Review*, 86 (Jan), 61-79.

White, Jenny, Albert Bandura and Lisa A Bero (2009), "Moral Disengagement in the Corporate World," *Accountability in Research: Policies & Quality Assurance*, 16(1), 41-74.

Cultural Effects on Perception and Cognition:
Integrating Recent Findings and Reviewing Implications for Consumer Research

Minas N. Kastanakis, ESCP Europe, UK
Benjamin G. Voyer, ESCP Europe, UK

EXTENDED ABSTRACT

Research increasingly suggests that cultural differences may account for variation in cross-cultural consumer reactions to several phenomena of interest to marketing scholars and practitioners, including consumer expectations, evaluations and reactions to service (Zhang, Beatty and Walsh 2008), or attitudes to consumerism in general (Tse, Belk and Zhou 1989). Despite the growing interest – focusing mainly on consumers' behaviors – relatively little research has examined cross-cultural differences or similarities in pre-behavioral processes such as perception and cognition – with little attempt aiming at explaining, synthesizing and extending existing evidence, especially in the light of the latest developments. Given the central role played by perception and cognition in subjective human experience and eventual behavior (Varela, Thompson, and Rosch 1999), studying cross-cultural differences in pre-behavioral domains is important in order to ultimately understand differences in cross-cultural consumer behaviors.

LITERATURE REVIEW AND CONCEPTUAL FRAMEWORK

Drawing upon the literature on cross-cultural, social, and cognitive psychology, as well as neuroscience, we offer a review of the role played by cultural environments and stimuli in shaping individual perception and processing of information (i.e. cultural conditioning effects). The idea of culturally-conditioned behavior emerges from recent developments in several cross-cultural disciplinary fields. Culture, acting as a "lens", affects the basic sensory perceptions and modes of information processing by providing to humans sets of values, life expectations, modes of living, and codes of conduct (Markus and Kitayama 1991) through which people experience the world around them. Although perceptions and cognitions are mainly dependent on sensory inputs, they also involve a variety of top-down processes that are automatically recruited from cultural artifacts to actively construct a conscious percept from the input (Kitayama, Duffy, Kawamura, and Larsen 2003). Hence, basic exogenous sensory inputs (colours, sounds or other stimuli) cannot fully account for the emerging percept: they are modified by factors endogenous to the perceiver such as cultural expectations, values, or needs (Bruner 1957). However similarities also exist: for example the meaning of certain percepts (like the degree of symmetry of a human face) is universal across cultures.

We incorporate in our review – as a guiding conceptual framework – two recent trends reflecting a fast moving field. Firstly, we highlight new findings in the relationship between culture and self-construal (Markus and Kitayama 1991), a culturally-shaped individual difference variable in terms of independent and interdependent self-perception, which appears to be a key conveyor of cross-cultural values on individual perceptions, cognitions, and behaviors (Kastanakis and Balabanis 2011). Secondly, we introduce recent research evidence (Nisbett and Masuda 2003) suggesting that the physical environment and other culture-specific stimuli such as language (e.g. alphabetic vs. ideographic/phonetic languages) can – in conjunction with processes of cultural learning – affect both information perception and processing, as a result of brain plasticity.

Our review (key highlights in Table 1) uncovers cross-cultural differences in terms of sensory, environment/aesthetic, and perception of emotions. We also find differences in self- and group/other-perception. In addition, we find a number of cognitive differences in information processing, categorization, memory, and the processing of persuasion messages; as well as in decision-making, self-esteem, attributions and perspective-taking.

Table 1
Culturally-conditioned perceptual & cognitive orientation(s): Individualistic/Independent vs. Collectivist/Interdependent

		Individualistic/independent orientation	Collectivist/interdependent orientation
Perception	*Self-perception*	Autonomous, detached, differentiated	Inseparable, connected, non-differentiated
	Perception of others/groups	Group exists to serve individual needs	Individuals exist to serve group needs
	Perception of emotions	Individual-orientation, de-contextualized, non-relational	Group-orientation, contextual, relational
	Perception of the environment and aesthetic preferences	Analytical, focal	Holistic, contextual
	Sensory perception	Several differences between the two orientations across sensory channels	
Cognition	*Perspective-taking*	Low perspective-taking ability, egocentric errors, insider perspective	High perspective-taking ability, less egocentric errors, outsider perspective
	Attributions & causal judgments	Tendency for dispositional attributions	Tendency for situational, contextual attributions
	Self-esteem	High need for self-enhancement	Low need for self-enhancement
	Information processing	Field-independent, focal, analytical	Field-dependent, contextual, holistic
	Categorization	Rule-based, categorical	Relational
	Memory	Self-related memories	Other-related, relational memories
	Processing of persuasion messages and decision-making	Central-orientation (content of message), uncomfortable with contradictory information	Peripheral-orientation (how is the message delivered), comfortable with contradictory information

We encounter a series of striking findings that, taken together, consistently point towards two distinctive perceptual/cognitive orientations. We, therefore, suggest that there are two types of culture-dependent (or "culturally-conditioned", in accordance with existing terminology) perceptual and cognitive orientations which we define as the overall, culture-specific, processes by which sensations are selected, organized and interpreted (culturally-conditioned perceptual orientation); as well as the overall, culture-specific, mental processes involved in gaining knowledge and comprehension – including thinking, knowing, remembering, judging and problem-solving (culturally-conditioned cognitive orientation). These are the "individualistic/independent", mostly encountered in the Western world; and the "collectivist/interdependent", mostly in the East (however, we also include studies on non-Asian collectivist cultures, such as Africa).

IMPLICATIONS AND DIRECTIONS FOR CONSUMER RESEARCH

As global consumer psychology research is in its infancy (Shavitt, Lee, and Johnson, 2008), we propose an agenda for future research along the lines of this review. We need to explore in more depth the propositions that natural environments (Nisbett and Masuda 2003) and language (Ji, Zhang, and Nisbett 2004; Ross, Xun, and Wilson 2002) are cultural factors that directly affect human perception and cognition. Nisbett and Masuda (2003) suggest that environments influence perception; and, more convincingly in our opinion, the resulting perceptual preferences prompt people to (re-) produce different environments. For example, because Asians tend to focus broadly on the field and attend to a large number of elements, they seem to (re-) construct environments with a large number of elements; Westerners focus, more narrowly, on a smaller number of elements and seem to prefer (and build) environments with a smaller number of elements. Hence, research could examine the relationship between different retailing environments and perceptual preferences. In addition, there is evidence that language can trigger a culture-bound view of the self and that East-Asian and Western identities may be stored in knowledge structures activated by their associated language (Ji et al. 2004; Ross et al. 2002). Research could explore related questions, such as how this phenomenon could affect the cultural consumer identities of multilingual new generations.

Another promising avenue for research opens from recent developments in neuroscience – suggesting cross-cultural differences in terms of neural correlates of various consumption-related mechanisms (Ames and Fiske 2010). For example, Gutchess, Welsh, Boduroğlu, and Park (2006) found that, when looking at pictures, Americans used more regions of the brain typically involved in the processing of objects, compared with Chinese. Other cross-cultural neural differences in information processing and perception, that invite interesting questions, include the taste of branded vs. non-branded products (McClure, Li, Tomlin, Cypert, Montague, and Montague 2004) and perception of colors (Davidoff 2001).

Overall, despite the youngness of the field of cross-cultural neuroscience, recent findings appear promising and need better integration in the consumer psychology literature. In this review we show how consumer research can benefit from embracing innovative approaches in viewing the world and appreciating the diversity offered by multiple perspectives originating outside the mainstream consumer psychology domains.

REFERENCES

Ames, D., and Fiske, S. (2010), "Cultural neuroscience," *Asian Journal of Social Psychology, 13*(2), 72-83.

Bruner, J. S. (1957), "On perceptual readiness," *Psychological Review, 64*(2), 123-152.

Davidoff, J. (2001), "Language and perceptual categorization," *Trends in Cognitive Science*, 5(9), 382-387.

Gutchess, A. H., Welsh, R. C., Boduroğlu, A., and Park, D. C. (2006), "Cultural differences in neural function associated with object processing," *Cognitive, Affective, & Behavioral Neuroscience*, 6(2), 102-109.

Ji, L. J., Zhang, Z., and Nisbett, R. E. (2004), "Is it Culture, or is it language? Examination of language effects in cross-cultural research on categorization," *Journal of Personality and Social Psychology, 87*(1), 57-65.

Kastanakis, M. N., and Balabanis, G. (forthcoming 2012, online 2011), "Between the mass and the class: Antecedents of the "bandwagon" luxury consumption behavior," *Journal of Business Research*, doi: 10.1016/j.jbusres.2011.10.005.

Kitayama, S., Duffy, S., Kawamura, T., and Larsen, J. T. (2003) "Perceiving an object and its context in different cultures: A cultural look at New Look," *Psychological Science, 14*(3), 201-206.

Markus, H. R., and Kitayama, S. (1991), "Culture and the self: Implications for cognition, emotion, and motivation," *Psychological Review, 98*(2), 224-253.

McClure, S. M., Li, J., Tomlin, D., Cypert, K. S., Montague, L. M., and Montague, P. R. (2004), "Neural correlates of behavioral preference for culturally familiar drink," *Neuron, 44*(2), 379–387.

Nisbett, R. E., and Masuda, T. (2003), "Culture and point of view," *Proceedings of the National Academy of Sciences of the United States of America, 100*(19), 11163-11175.

Ross, M., Xun, W. Q., and Wilson, A. E. (2002), "Language and the bicultural self," *Personality and Social Psychology Bulletin, 28*(8), 1040-1050.

Shavitt, S., Lee, A., and Johnson, T. P. (2008), *Cross-cultural consumer psychology*, in C. Haugtvedt, P. Herr and F. Kardes (eds.), *Handbook of Consumer Psychology* (p. 1103-1131), Mahwah, N.J: Erlbaum.

Tse, D. K., Belk, R. W., and Zhou, N. (1989), "Becoming a consumer society: A longitudinal and cross-cultural content analysis of print ads from Hong Kong, the People's Republic of China, and Taiwan," *Journal of Consumer Research, 15*(4), 457-472.

Varela, F. J., Thompson, E., and Rosch, E. (1999), *The embodied mind: Cognitive science and human experience*: MIT press.

Zhang, J., Beatty, S. E., and Walsh, G. (2008), "Review and future directions of cross-cultural consumer services research,' *Journal of Business Research, 61*(3), 211-224.

An Exclusionary or Integrative Approach to Goal Conflict: The Moderating Role of Mindset Abstraction

Fang-Chi Lu, University of Iowa, USA
Jooyoung Park, University of Iowa, USA
Dhananjay Nayakankuppam, University of Iowa, USA

EXTENDED ABSTRACT

Pursuit of a certain goal (i.e., managing weight) is often challenged by the presence of alternative goals (i.e., enjoying a tasty chocolate cake). How individuals solve this goal conflict and manage multiple goals has been an important topic of self-regulation (Emmons King & Sheldon 1993; Shah 2005).

Because multiple goals compete for one's available resources, the classic approach to resolving goal conflict usually involves a tradeoff. An individual has to exercise a goal choice through (1) *goal prioritization*: focusing on more important goals and temporarily withdrawing alternative goals (Shah 2005; Simon 1967) or (2) *goal shielding*: cognitively inhibiting alternative goals that compete for one's resources (Kuhl 1984; Shah Friedman & Kruglanski 2002). Recently, Kopetz et al. (2010) propose an alternative solution to goal conflict, quest for multifinal means which afford simultaneous pursuit of several goals. For example, one can attain the goals of maintaining slim figure and food enjoyment at the same time by choosing tasty, low-calorie foods. They further argue that a quest for multifinal means should be preferred over the goal-choice approach because individuals intend to maximize the return on their investment.

The current research proposes that the approach to goal conflict resolution differs depending on one's mindset. Construal level theory posits that individuals can represent an object at different levels of abstraction, where abstract mental representations are schematic and extracting the gist from available information and concrete representations are relatively unstructured and including contextual features (Liberman Trope & Wakslak 2007). It has been shown that abstract (vs. concrete) construal enhances searching for similarities (vs. dissimilarities) of given stimuli (Förster 2009). Building on construal level theory, we argue that concrete thinkers, adopting an exclusionary approach, will use a goal-choice strategy. They will shield the focal goal from alternative goals (Hypothesis1) or prioritize their goals (Hypothesis2) when a focal goal is highlighted. However, abstract thinkers, adopting an integrative approach, will search for multifinal means when facing goal conflicts (Hypothesis3). Three studies were conducted to examine these hypotheses.

Study1, to examine Hypothesis1, used a 2 (mindset: abstract vs. concrete)×2 (goal commitment: strong vs. weak) between-participants design. Participants first performed a mindset manipulation task, either comparing a traditional camera with a digital camera or comparing two digital cameras (Malkoc Zauberman & Bettman 2010). They then listed a personality characteristic which they had a slight (vs. strong) desire to attain. After that, they listed other personality characteristics that you were also trying to attain in addition to the one previously listed. We measured the extent of goal shielding by counting the number of alternative personality characteristics listed. Results showed a significant mindset-goal commitment interaction ($F(1, 147)=6.76$; $p=.01$). Specifically, participants with concrete mindset listed fewer alternative characteristics when the focal goal commitment was strong ($M_{strong}=2.86$ vs. $M_{weak}=4.9$); however, participants with abstract mindset listed similar numbers of alternative characteristics regardless of goal commitment ($M_{strong}=4.7$ vs. $M_{weak}=4$).

Study2, testing Hypothesis2, measured perceived importance of alternative goals after the introduction of a focal goal. We recruited participants who had not had lunch and had intention to have lunch later that day. We enhanced focal goal (having lunch) importance by using a fictitious scientific report discussing the importance of lunch. After that, participants were asked to list three activities they had planned for the rest of that day. Then, they completed the same mindset manipulation task in Study 1. Finally, they rated the importance of having lunch and each of the three planned activities. Regardless of the mindset manipulation, participants listed similar activities, such as "doing homework," "going to class," and "exercising." Also, participants perceived having lunch equally important across conditions ($M_{abstract}=5.31$, $M_{concrete}=4.47$, $p=.1$). More importantly, abstract thinkers perceived the first and the second alternative goals ($M_{1st-alternative}=6.69$, $M_{2nd-alternative}=6.63$) more important than concrete thinkers did ($M_{1st-alternative}=5.07$, $M_{2nd-alternative}=5.67$) ($p's<.05$), suggesting that concrete thinkers tended to prioritize goals. Study1 and 2 provide supporting evidence for the goal-choice behavior of concrete thinkers.

To test Hypothesis3, Study3 used a 2 (mindset: abstract vs. concrete)×2 (focal goal importance: high vs. control) between-participants design. We first activated two eating goals, food enjoyment and weight control, by asking participants to what extent they chose foods based on their taste or caloric content. Then, we manipulated the importance of a focal goal (food enjoyment) by asking participants to list either three advantages and three disadvantages of choosing tasty foods (high focal goal importance) or three advantage of choosing tasty foods and three advantages of choosing low-caloric foods (control condition where both goals are equally important). After that, participants performed the same mindset manipulation task as Studies1&2. Finally, participants were asked to list the foods they desired to have for dinner that day. We followed a similar procedure used by Kopetz et al. (2010) to compute two separate scores for each participant, representing the instrumentality of their listed foods to the goal of food enjoyment and weight control, respectively. A significant two-way interaction ($F(1, 123)=4.9$, $p<.03$) demonstrated that the expansion effect of goal importance on mean set size found in previous research (Kopetz et al. 2010) mainly occurred in concrete mindset, but not in abstract mindset condition. Concrete thinkers listed more foods in the condition of high focal goal importance ($M_{highimportance}=5.06$) than in the control condition ($M_{control}=3.69$); while abstract thinkers listed similar numbers of foods ($M_{highimportance}=4.27$ vs. $M_{control}=5.32$, n.s.). Further examining the instrumentality of food items listed by abstract versus concrete thinkers in the control condition, we found that the foods listed by abstract thinkers were equally instrumental to both goals (*evidence of a quest for multifinal means*); whereas, concrete thinkers listed food items which were more instrumental to the food enjoyment goal (*evidence of goal shielding*).

The current research has both theoretical and managerial contributions. First, it contributes to the goal conflict literature by identifying mindset abstraction as a key moderator. Second, it implies that mindset abstraction matters if marketers want consumers to see the benefits of a hybrid product, a product satisfying multiple goals. Marketers can better communicate multiple benefits of their products using abstract mindset framing.

REFERENCES

Emmons, Robert A., Laura A. King, and Ken Sheldon (1993), Goal conflict and the self-regulation of action. In D. M. Wegner & J. W. Pennebaker (Eds.), *Handbook of Mental Control* (pp. 528-51). Englewood Cliffs, NJ: Prentice-Hall.

Kopetz, Catalina, Tim Faber, Ayelet Fishbach, and Arie W. Kruglanski (2010), "The Multifinality Constraints Effect: How Goal Multiplicity Narrows the Means Set to a Focal End," *Journal of Personality and Social Psychology*, 100 (5), 810-26.

Kuhl, Julius (1984), Volitional aspects of achievement motivation and learned helplessness: Toward a comprehensive theory of action control. In B. A. Maher & W. A. Maher (Eds.), *Progress in Experimental Personality Research* (pp. 99-171). New York, NY: Academic Press.

Förster, Jens (2009), "Relations between Perceptual and Conceptual scope: How Global versus Local Processing Fits a Focus on Similarity versus Dissimilarity," *Journal of Experimental Psychology: General*, 138(1), 88-111.

Liberman, Nira, Yaacov Trope, and Cheryl Wakslak (2007), "Construal Level Theory and Consumer Behavior," *Journal of Consumer Psychology*, 17 (2), 113-17.

Malkoc, Selin A., Gal Zauberman, and James R. Bettman (2010), "Unstuck from the Concrete: Carryover Effects of Abstract Mindsets in Intertemporal Preferences," *Organizational Behavior and Human Decision Processes*, 113, 112–26.

Shah, James Y. (2005), "The Automatic Pursuit and Management of Goals," *Current Directions in Psychological Science*, 14, 10–13.

Shah, James Y., Ron Friedman, & Arie W. Kruglanski (2002), "Forgetting All Else: On the Antecedents and Consequences of Goal Shielding," *Journal of Personality and Social Psychology*, 83, 1261-80.

Simon, Herbert A. (1967), "Motivational and Emotional Controls of Emotion," *Psychological Review*, 74, 29–39.

Compliments Made Me Bolder: The Role of Self Construal and Brand Status in Brand Attachment and Product Evaluation

Fang Wan, University of Manitoba, Canada
Letty Kwan, Nanyang Technological University, Singapore
Amitava Chattopadhyay, INSEAD, France
Hesham Fazel, University of Manitoba, Canada
CY Chiu, Nanyang Technological University, Singapore

EXTENDED ABSTRACT

Compliments are conducive to social interactions and communications. Little research has been done to examine the psychological underpinnings of the observed cultural differences in response to social and brand compliments. Even more scarce attention has been given to extend research on compliments to study the impact of brand compliments on consumers' evaluations and preferences of the focal brand as well as subsequent product evaluation. Our work set out to study cultural difference in compliment appreciation (Study 1) and further investigate its implications in brand usage contexts (Study 2 and 3). In these three studies, we use self-construal as a proxy to cultural differences in the interdependent and independent culture. In the last two studies, we recruited participants from Asia and North America and studied the cultural difference in the brand attachment associated with brand compliment and in effect of compliment on the subsequent product evaluation.

Self construals are often used as a proxy to uncover cultural differences: how individuals classify or perceive themselves according to the constituted cultural values they follow (Singles & Brown, 2001). In North American culture, the normative imperative is to become independent from others and to determine and convey one's unique attributes (Markus & Kitayama, 1991). However, Asians cultures have interdependent self-concepts stressing on connectedness between themselves and others (Morris & Peng, 1994; Hong et al., 2000).

North Americans, who typically have independent self-construals, are likely to view social compliments as a matter of personal choice, indicative of compliment givers' genuine liking of self, therefore, are more likely to appreciate social compliments. Individuals with interdependent self construals view compliment givers as more likely to have ulterior motives (Park, 1998). Therefore we propose that individuals with independent self construals are more likely to appreciate social compliments than those with interdependent self construals. We further propose that brand status moderates the relationship of self construal and compliment appreciation. Interdependent individuals will feel less appreciative than self interdependent individuals when receiving a compliment about their usage of a low status brand (Study 2).

We further attempt to study how culture specifies the effect of compliments on high status brand usage. Research on status and power (Galinsky, Gruenfeld, and Magee 2003, Rucker, Galinsky, and Dubois 2011) suggest that these extrinsic cues can affect consumers' motivations of brand and product usage. We argue that the Interdependents (vs. independents) are more sensitive to brand status as it signifies the perceived popularity of the brand among others in the social group. Therefore, compliment of a high status brand usage makes the interdependent (vs. independents) appreciate the brand more (Study 3 and 4). However, we argue that for the interdependent (vs. independents), this brand attachment is driven by other-focused brand perceptions such as perceived popularity of the brand among one's social group, instead of ego-centric brand perceptions such as the fit between brand and self image (Study 4). And lastly, we propose that once complimented by the usage of high status brand, the need for seeking status and approval is satiated (Galak, Redden and Kruger 2009), Asians (the Interdependents) are less likely to seek social approval and more likely to make norm-inconsistent evaluations and favour products with less dominant status (Study 5).

Study 1 examined the impact of self construal on social compliment appreciation. Participants were asked to read a scenario where their product usage is compliment "I like your sweater." Then they filled out a survey measuring their appreciation of the compliment with 2 items (appreciation & grateful α = .73), and their cultural orientations with 24 items self-construal scale (Singelis, 1994), self-independent 12 items (α = .76) and self-interdependent 12 items (α = .79). We eliminated participants who score higher (lower) than the average score on both independents and interdependent scale. This procedure enabled us to use data from 79 participants, 41 independent, 38 interdependent. ANOVA test confirmed our expectation that the interdependent were less likely than the independents to feel appreciative of a social compliment appreciated when receiving a compliment (F = 2.915, p = .09).

Study 2 examined the moderator effect of brand status in the relationship between self construal and on compliment appreciation. Self construal was constructed similarly as in Study 1. Brand status was manipulated via varying a scenario where compliment was made about Gucci, high status (vs. Joe, low status) sunglasses (manipulation successful). As expected, ANOVA test on appreciation yielded only the significant interaction effect of brand status and self construal (F=5.85, p<.05), suggesting the interdependents (vs. independents) appreciated compliments on high status brand; the pattern was reversed when brand status was low.

Study 3 adopted the same design as in Study 2 but shifted gear towards examining participants' attachment with the brand (7-point scales such as feeling connected, loyal and attached, alpha=.89). Regression analysis with brand attachment as dependent variable yielded a significant effect of brand status (b=4.22, t=1.98, p<.05), significant effect of self construal (b=1.40, t=2.13, p<.05) and a significant but negative interaction (b=-.88, t=-1.95, p<.05). To uncover the interaction pattern, we dichotomized self construal and ran an ANOVA test, yielding a significant interaction effect (F=3.23, p<.05). As expected, the Interdependents (vs. independents) were more bonded with the brand when status was high, whereas the reverse was true for low status brand.

Study 4 intended to replicate findings in Study 3 with culture as the independent variable. We focused on high status brand (perception of Gucci is consistent across culture, mean of prestige in Asia=5.79 vs. in North America=5.77 out of 7 point scale, t<1). Study 4 found that when complimented on a high status brand usage, Asians feel more indebted to brand compliments (F=8.51, p<.001) and bonded with the brand more than North Americans (F=7.69, p<.01) as Asians would be more likely to perceive that high status brand is favoured by others in their social group than North Americans (F=3.68, p<.05). On the other hand, North Americans were more likely to attribute compliments of brand usage to ego-centric reasons such as brand and self image fit (F=6.87, p<.01) and tended

Advances in Consumer Research
Volume 40, ©2012

to think users of high status brand were more materialistic (F=13.21, p<.001), explaining their low endorsement of the high status brand.

Study 5 examined the impact of compliment of high status brand usage on motivations and subsequent product evaluation. We found that when given the brand compliments, compared to North Americans, Asians tended to be less likely to seek for social approval (mean=3.46 vs. 3.86, F=3.62, p<.05), less likely to view high status brand users to be materialistic (mean=3.79 vs. 4.57, F=15.66, p<.001). Satiation of status via brand compliments made Asians favour minority-status painting (liked by fewer people), a preference-reversal given that the Interdependents focus on group harmony and endorse less unique options (Markus and Kitayama 1991).

REFERENCES

Chen, R. (1993). Responding to compliments: a contrastive study of politeness strategies between American English and Chinese speakers. *Journal of Pragmatics*, 20 (1), 49–75.

Fong, M. (1998). Chinese immigrant's perceptions of semantic dimensions of direct/indirect communication in intercultural compliment interactions with North Americans. *The Howard Journal of Communications*, 9, 245-262.

Galak, Jeff, Joseph Redden, and Justin Kruger (2009), "Variety Amnesia: Recalling Past Variety Can Accelerate Recovery From Satiation," *Journal of Consumer Research, 36 (December), 575-584.*

Higgins, E. T. (1997). Beyond pleasure and pain. *American Psychologist, 52*, 1280-1300.

Holmes, Janet. (1986). Compliments and compliment responses in New Zealand English. *Anthropological Linguistics* 28, 485–508.

Hong, Y., Morris M., Chiu C.Y., & Benet-Martinez V. (2000). Multicultural minds: A dynamic constructivist approach to culture and cognition. American Psychologist, 55, 709–720.

Koshik, Irene A. (2002). A conversation analytic study of yes/no questions that assert their reverse polarity. *Journal of Pragmatics.* 547–571 569.

Nelson, Gayle L., Waguida, El Bakary, Mahmoud, Al-Batal. (1993). Egyptian and American compliments: a cross-cultural study. International Journal of Intercultural Relations 17, 293–313.

Manes, J . (1983). Compliments : A mirror of cultural values. In N. Wolfson & E. Judd (Eds.) , *Sociolinguistics and language acquisition* (pp . 96-102) . Rowley, MA: Newbury House.

Markus, H., & Kitayama S. (1991). Culture and the self: Implications for cognition, emotion and motivation. Psychological Review, 98, 224–253.

Morris, M. W., & Peng K.P. (1994). Culture and cause: American and Chinese attributions for social and physical events. Journal of Personality and Social Psychology, 67, 949–971.

Park, S. Y. (1998). A comparison of Korean and American gift-giving behaviors. Psychology and Marketing, 15, 577-593.

Rucker, Derek, David Dubois and Adam Galinsky (2011), Generous Paupers and Stingy Princes: Power Drives Consumer Spending on Self versus Others, *Journal of Consumer Research, 37(6), 1015-1029.*

Ruth, J. A. (1996). It's the feeling that counts: Toward a framework for understanding emotion and its influence on gift-exchange processes. In C. Otnes, & R. F. Beltramini (Eds), Gift-giving: An interdisciplinary anthology (pp. 195-214). Bowling Green, OH: Bowling Green University Popular Press.

Shen, H, Wan F. and Wyer, R.S. (2010), "Cross-Cultural Differences in the Refusal to Accept a Small Gift: The Differential Influence of Reciprocity Norms on Asians and North Americans," Journal of Personality and Social Psychology.

Singelis, T. M. (1994). The measurement of independent and interdependent self-construals. Personality and Social Psychology Bulletin, 20, 580–591.

Triandis, H. C. (1995). Individualism and collectivism. Boulder, CO: Westview Press.

Tang, C. H.. Zhang, G. Q. (2009). A contrastive study of compliment responses among Australian English and Mandarin Chinese speakers. Journal of Pragmatics, Volume 41, Issue 2, Pages 325-345.

Wolfson, Nessa. (1981). Compliments in cross-cultural perspective. *TESOL Quarterly* 15, 117–124.

Ying, Y.W. (1996). Immigration satisfaction of Chinese Americans: An empirical examination. *Journal of Community Psychology,* 24, 3-16.

Yu, M. (2004). Interlinguistic variation and similarity in second language speech act behaviour. *The Modern Language Journal*, 88 (1), 102–119.

Mythologized Glocalization of Popular Culture: A Postcolonial Perspective

Soonkwan Hong, Michigan Technological University, USA
Chang-Ho Kim, Nam-Seoul University, South Korea

EXTENDED ABSTRACT

Over the past decade, Korean popular culture (KPC hereafter) has increasingly gained enormous recognition in East and Southeast Asian countries, and the popularity currently extends to the Middle East, former Soviet Union countries in Central Asia, and even European countries. Previously dominated by American and Japanese popular cultures, Asian popular culture is currently transforming itself into a "neo-cultural imperialism" mode.

Popular culture has been one of the topics in consumer culture theory for its function as a transmitter of marketplace ideologies (Belk and Pollay 1985; Hirschman 1988, 1990), an indispensable element of local identity construction (Kjeldgaard and Askegaard 2006), and a portrayal of hegemonic brand culture (Thompson and Arsel 2004). However, it is rarely studied in its entirety, as a symbolic and ideological product that one cannot simply reject, and its globalization process has been understudied.

In recognition of popular culture's theoretical significance as a key driver of current consumer culture in Asia, this study will delve into two main research questions: 1) What are the cultural connotations of KPC, as opposed to American or Japanese popular culture, for Asian consumers with respect to their identity, lifestyle, and ideology? In other words, why do Asian consumers superannuate the almost "orthodox" representation of today's culture (American pop culture) and choose to fetishize a new ideology? 2) How is the globalization process of KPC discernible from that of hitherto predominant popular cultures?

One particular characteristic of cultural pluralism in popular culture is that it necessitates multi-directional, rather than top-town, or unidirectional movement of cultural elements among several cultures (Appadurai 1990). As a result, cultural hybridization is intensified by the perpetual tension between acceptance and resistance, as well as amid the "triumphantly universal and resiliently particular" (Appadurai 1990, p. 308). That is, the hybridized cultural products undergo a serious, long-term ideological process, which might be seen as a series of fads and trends (Figure 1). KPC's globalization is in accordance with Lévi-Strauss' (1963) understanding of the mythological structure of paradoxical resolution of binary oppositions.

Postassimilationist discourse contests the idea that the acculturation process is linear, easily traceable, and mostly characterizable (Askegaard et al., 2005; Oswald 1999; Peñaloza 1994). KPC's cultural outlook resonates with postassimilationists' standpoint as it facilitates heterogeneous, nondeterministic, and liberatory cultural enterprise among consumers of the new acculturation agent (Iwabuchi 2001; Ryoo 2005). The unique patterns and characteristics of KPC engender *third space* as the term BhaBha (1994) used to describe the challenge of explicating a new phenomenon in which alternatives or an indigenous mixture of discourses epitomize and texturize the hybridity.

A netnographic study combined with critical discourse analysis is conducted due to the unique discursive and reflexive ground of KPC that absorbs counteracting perspectives and manifests in harmony with the particular cultural landscape. One of the most popular Korean TV dramas, *Dae Jang Geum* (DJG), is chosen in the context of Hong Kong. Newspaper articles (417) were collected from Hong Kong and Mainland China between 2004 and 2005. From the articles, three characteristics of each report were identified: executional style, main theme, and sociocultural influence. Concurrently, textual data from six websites based in Hong Kong, including fan forums, discussion boards, and the main actress' fan-site, were collected from the same period of time. This attempt is to trace the relationship between discursive movements observed in newspapers and the grassroots practices.

The glocalization of KPC in Hong Kong underwent a cyclical formation process, in which the discursive drives of newspaper articles triggered tensions and development of particular social discourses. The first discursive phase detailed a taste-based class discourse among Hong Kong audiences, consistent with the main theme of the drama that depicts some elements of social stratification. In the second discursive stage (late 2004), changes in the newspaper discourses activated public sensibility of ethnic identity as a crucial discursive aspect of glocalization. In the following period (early 2005), a more pertinent discourse to postassimilationists' critique was galvanized. As fans of DJG started to fantasize about the characters and the story line on the websites due to the drama's novelty and cultural kinship, discussions of its positive and negative implications also took place. The last phase (late 2005) of the glocalization process of KPC in Hong Kong can be portrayed as a reflexive and yet transient ideology (*zeitgeist*). KPC was normalized and instilled in everyday life of Hong Kong consumers because the newspapers begun featuring interviews of the celebrities about their personal lives and heralded normal activities (e.g., cooking, shopping, and night life in Korea) practiced in Korea, as though the culture needed not be kept exotic any longer and became a part of daily life in Hong Kong. In each phase, observed tensions among consumers were resolved as the newspaper discourses redirected the public attention to a new discourse. However, concurrently, critical voices about class, ethnicity, and cosmopolitanism existed amid the discursive movements. The cultural pendulum of rejection and acceptance of the foreign popular culture is omnipresent and self-perpetuating, but not as the momentum of glocalization. Rather, the driving force of glocalzation is the continuing dynamics between the institutional reality-engineering practices on newspapers and grassroots responses to the new socio-politico-cultural episodes.

Glocalization process of popular culture cannot be reduced to a "uni-discursive" thesis that immortalizes the themes of cultural imperialism. Future research opportunities include juxtaposition of the ascent movement of KPC with the "demise of the imperial," witnessed in Asia. It is uncertain whether the cultural plurality that has been inculcated means coexistence of new ideologies with the dogmatic, or overthrow of Hollywood and MTV. The reaction from the losing party is of special interest because it may attempt to turn the temporarily calmed popular cultural outbreak upside down. Globalization of popular culture necessitates hybridity that uses the same traditional ingredients but transforms into a new taste based on a new cultural recipe. The paradoxical nature of KPC appears to be the same as the self-perpetuating theme of globalization, but the very paradox is what makes it "popular."

REFERENCES

Appadurai, Ajun. (1990), "Disjuncture and Difference in the Global Cultural Economy," *Public Culture*, 2 (Spring), 1-24.

Askegaard, Soren., Eric J. Arnould, and Dannie Kjeldgaard (2005), "Postassimilationist Ethnic Consumer Research: Qualifications and Extensions," *Journal of Consumer Research*, 32 (June), 160-170.

BhaBha, Homi K. (1994), *The Location of Culture*, New York: Routledge

Belk, Russell W. and Richard W. Pollay (1985), "Images of Ourselves: The Good Life in Twentieth Century Advertising," *Journal of Consumer Research*, 11 (March), 887-897.

Hirschman, Elizabeth C. (1988), "The Ideology of Consumption: A Structural-Syntactical Analysis of 'Dallas' and 'Dynasty'," *Journal of Consumer Research*, 15 (December), 344-359.

———— (1990), "Secular Immortality and the American Ideology of Affluence," *Journal of Consumer Research*, 17 (June), 31-42.

Iwabuchi, Koichi (2002), *Recentering Globalization: Popular Culture and Japanese Transnationalism*, Durham, NC: Duke University Press.

Kjeldgaard, Dannie and Soren Asekgaard (2006), "The Glocalization of Youth Culture: The Global Youth Segment as Structures of Common Difference," *Journal of Consumer Research*, 33 (September), 231-247.

Lévi-Strauss, Claude. (1963), *Structural Anthropology*, New York: Basic Books.

Oswald, Laura (1999), "Culture Swapping: Consumption and the Ethnogenesis of Middle-Class Haitian Immigrants," *Journal of Consumer Research*, 25 (March), 303–18.

Peñaloza, Lisa (1994), "Atravesando Fronteras/Border Crossings: A Critical Ethnographic Study of the Consumer Acculturation of Mexican Immigrants," *Journal of Consumer Research*, 21 (June), 32–53.

Ryoo, Woongjae. (2005), "Local Modes of Practice in an Age of Globalization: Renegotiating National Identity as Enacted in South Korean Advertising," *International Journal of Media and Cultural Politics*, 2 (September), 199-215.

Thompson, Craig J. and Zeynep Arsel (2004), "The Starbucks Brandscape and Consumers' (Anticorporate) Experiences of Glocalization," *Journal of Consumer Research*, 31 (December), 631-642.

Different Ways of Saying Goodbye:
Outlining Three Types of Abandonment of A Product Category

Maribel Suarez, Federal University of Rio de Janeiro / COPPEAD, Brazil
Marie Agnes Chauvel, Federal University of São João del Rei, Brazil

EXTENDED ABSTRACT

Creation of meaning via consumption involves positive and negative choices, but several scholars and practitioners' efforts have been devoted to positive aspects (Lee, Fernandez and Hyman 2009). In the context of the recent interest in anti-consumption, various studies have focused on more extreme and thus more "visible" manifestations of anti-choice such as, for example, actions involving boycotts or aversion to companies and brands (Hoffman and Muller 2009; Sandikci and Ekici 2009; Cromie and Ewing 2009; Yuksel and Mryteza 2009). However, little attention has been directed to investigating abandonment which refers to the deliberate choice of giving up something previously consumed. (Hogg, Banister and Stephenson 2009).

Some authors relate abandonment behaviors to social transition, that is, changes in the life-cycle or status of individuals (Young 1991; Roster 2001; Hogg et al. 2009). Hogg and Banister (2001) propose that in order to maintain a positive self-image – or at least a normative self-standard - consumers avoid risks, rejecting products, brands or suppliers that are associated with undesirable or negative stereotypes or reference groups. Hogg et al. (2009) present abandonment, aversion or avoidance behavior as the desired reaction to protect self-esteem and avoid self-concept humiliation.

In this paper, we look into meanings that motivate the abandonment of a product category and also the meanings abandonment gives rise to. The research used a qualitative methodology to collect and analyze data obtained from in-depth interviews with 16 Brazilian consumers who gave up automobile ownership. This category was chosen due to its intense symbolic dimension, with previous studies evidencing its relation with self-concept (Grubb and Hupp 1968; Belk 2004), capacity to engender life-style and social class stereotypes (Belk, Bahn and Mayer 1982; Dalli and Gistri 2006) and potential to tangibilize ideologies (Hirschman 2003; Brown, Kozinets and Sherry 2003; Luedicke and Giesler 2008). Interviews lasted between 60 and 240 minutes and were taped and transcribed (around 450 pages of text). This analysis sought to find, refine and develop concepts, themes and events that could be codified and inter-related in order to construct theoretical proposals (Strauss and Corbin 1998).

In the literature, abandonment is described as the act of giving up something previously consumed, thus presupposing that a deliberate choice was made (Hogg 1998; Hogg et al. 2009). The interviews, however, suggest that, rather than being a discrete event, an action or decision that is circumscribed by a given moment, abandonment is in fact a process. The accounts of former automobile owners revealed that various informants kept the same vehicle for long periods of time (in some cases years), even without using it, before selling it. Standing idle in the street or garage, without an effective functionality, the car ended up contradicting the prevailing social view that it is an indispensable product, thus signaling the possibility of life without a car. The promise of autonomy and mobility expressed in the product's advertising is erased little by little by a practice that shows that life is possible without it. Whether consciously perceived by the consumer or not, this period characterizes abandonment, a kind of discarding ritual (McCracken, 1986), which allows the meanings that motivated the purchase to be "cooled" and legitimizes the decision to sell.

The analysis also outlines three types of abandonment: contingent, positional and ideological:

CONTINGENT

In this kind of abandonment the consumer is forced to leave the category due to a conflict between objectives or practical and material limitations. Although they value the functional and/or symbolic benefits that the product confers, matters related to money, health, access to the product, space, family pressure, may lead the consumer to abandon it. This is the case of Jorge, an informant that still takes part in an on-line community of car owners which he never abandoned even after selling his car. Jorge does not identify himself with the abandonment of the category and describes his abandonment as provisional and situational.

POSITIONAL

This is motivated by the demarcation of a symbolic distance in relation to consumers of the category. Thus, the decision expresses a difference and generates a sense of distinct identity for individuals. Leonard, one informant, has a good salary and job stability, but preferred to sell the car and recognizes that he is different from most people: "I have a tendency to question things a lot. I'm critical about everything. Several people think I disagree just for the sake of it." Leonard does not consider the symbolic benefits that a car could confer on its owner, valuing only its transportation function. "Because if you have a car and don't use it, but think that it provides you with some kind of benefit, you're not rational".

IDEOLOGICAL

It is different from other types on account of its collective perspective. Consumers believe that society (and not just themselves individually) should abandon or rethink that consumption. This is the case of Eurico, an informant that advocates the use of the bicycle as a solution for the problems generated by motorized transport. In his interview he associates the car with individualism, with private space and isolation, to the detriment of the collective space. The philosophy of a more sustainable form of consumption helps Eurico to construct a differentiated and positive identity that Cherrier (2009) describes as the "hero identity": a way of acting that requires dedication and commitment to redefine and restructure daily life, articulating new meanings for consumption. Eurico seems to adopt this role and indeed he prides himself on already having convinced "various people to adopt the bicycle as a means of transport".

Analysis suggests that abandonment can operate affirmative and positive differentiation and reinforce self-esteem, helping individuals to constitute identities and signal important changes in their lives. In abandonment, the individual foregoes the functionality related to the product. The symbolic associations, however, continue to be used, created and manipulated even after abandonment happens. When they speak of the benefits and advantages of abandonment, consumers "make use" and "take advantage" of the meanings of the discarded category.

REFERENCES

Belk, Russell W. (2004), "Men and Their Machines," *Advances in Consumer Research* 31, 273-78.

Belk, Russel. W., Bahn, Kenneth D. and Mayer, Robert N (1982), "Developmental Recognition of Consumption Symbolism," *Journal of Consumer Research* 9, 4-17.

Brown, Stephen., Robert V. Kozinets and John F. Jr. Sherry (2003), "Teaching Old Brands New Tricks: Retro Branding and the Revival of Brand Meaning," *Journal of Marketing* 67, 19-33.

Cherrier, Helene (2009), "Anti-consumption discourses and consumer-resistant identities," *Journal of Business Research* 62 (2), 181-90.

Close, Angeline G. and George M. Zinkhan, (2009), "Market-resistance and Valentine's Day events," *Journal of Business Research* 62 (2), 200-7.

Cromie, John G. and Mike T. Ewing (2009), "The rejection of brand hegemony," *Journal of Business Research* 62(2), 218-30.

Dalli, Daniele and Giacomo Gistri (2006), "Consumption Symbols at the Cinema: Italian Masters' Movies (1945-1975)," *European Advances in Consumer Research* 7, 586-92.

Grubb, Edward L. and Gregg Hupp (1968), "Perception of Self, Generalized Stereotypes, and Brand Selection," *Journal of Marketing Research* 5 (1), 58-63.

Hirschman, Elizabeth C. (2003), "Men, Dogs, Guns and Cars," *Journal of Advertising* 32 (1), 9-22.

Hoffman, Stefan and Stefan Müller (2009), "Consumer boycotts due to factory relocation," *Journal of Business Research* 62 (2), 239-47.

Hogg, Margaret K. (1998) "Anti-constellations: exploring the impact of negation on consumption," *Journal of Marketing Management* 14 (April): 133-58.

Hogg, Margaret K. (2006), "Approach and avoidance behaviors in the symbolic consumption of clothes," in *Advances in Consumer Research* 7, 453-54.

Hogg, Margaret K. and Emma N. Banister (2001), "Dislikes, distastes and the undesired self: conceptualizing and exploring the role of the undesired end state in consumer experience," *Journal of Marketing Management* 17 (1), 73-104.

Hogg, Margaret K., Emma N. Banister and Christopher A. Stephenson (2009), "Mapping symbolic (anti)-consumption," *Journal of Business Research* 62 (2), 148-59.

Lee, Mike. S., Karen V. Fernandez and Michael R. Hyman. (2009), "Anti-consumption: an overview and research agenda," *Journal of Business Research* 62 (2): 145-47.

Lee, Mike. S., Judy Motion and Denise Conroy (2009), "Anti-consumption and brand avoidance," *Journal of Business Research* 62(2), 169-80.

Luedicke, Marius K. and Markus Giesler (2008), "Contested Consumption in Everyday Life," *Advances in Consumer Research* 35, 812-13.

McCracken, Grant C. (1986), "Culture and Consumption: A Theoretical Account of the Structure and Movement of the Cultured Meaning of Consumer Goods", *Journal of Consumer Research*, v. 13 (June), 71-84.

Roster, Catherine A. (2001) "Letting Go: The Process and Meaning of Dispossession in the Lives of Consumers," *Advances in Consumer Research* 28: 425-30.

Sandikci, Özlem and Ahmet Ekici (2009), "Politically motivated brand rejection," *Journal of Business Research* 62(2), 208-17.

Strauss, Anselm L. and Juliet Corbin (1998), *Basics of Qualitative Research 2.e., London: Sage Publishers.*

Young, Melissa M. (1991), "Disposition of Possessions During Role Transitions," *Advances in Consumer Research* 18, 33-39.

Yuksel, Ulku and Victoria Mryteza (2009), "An evaluation of strategic responses to consumer boycotts," *Journal of Business Research* 62 (2), 248-59.

Marketplace Performances in Emerging Economies:
Eliciting the Asymmetric Interactions Between Service Providers and Western Tourists

Nacima Ourahmoune, Reims Management School, France

EXTENDED ABSTRACT

While tourism is presented as virtuous for the developing countries in general, it is argued in this paper that it also generates social exclusion, gender asymmetry and that it perpetuates ethnic tensions. An ethnographic inquiry into Punta Cana's All-inclusive resort hotels in the Dominican Republic allows the author to interpret the disciplinary policies implemented by the transnational tourism industry that impedes cultural hybridity and exacerbates social, gender and ethnic hierarchies and stigmas. In particular, the narratives that emerge from the field rely on day - night / outside - inside the resort logics as spatio-temporal landmarks which rhythm the activities of visitors and locals. They are materialized by two locations: the beach and the disco, where power struggles are in play.

The author proposes a socio-spatial analysis that accounts for the tourism industry's attempt to frame a specific script or experience for the transnational tourists and to control and discipline the locals privatizing Dominican land. Far from the cultural hybridity promoted in its brochures, the transnational tourism management policies tend to reinforce power structures variously in terms of gender, ethnicity and social positions. However, the findings also account for the temptation for tourists and locals to contest those boundaries; in particular a sense of agency is manifest in constructing Caribbean identities within this context.

Dominican development policies

Emerging economies are insufficiently researched compared to western contexts (Jafari, Suerdem, Firat, Askegaard, Dalli, 2012), this study is a contribution to the thin body of research that tackles marketplace performances that occur and involve non-western consumers. Also, Askegaard and Linnet (2011) appeal for a broader understanding of consumption phenomena studying not only the micro-context as it is mostly the case in consumer research but enlarging the spectrum eliciting the findings within what the authors called "The context of the context". Understanding the meanings of the relationships between service providers and tourists calls a deep attention to the development policies in the Dominican Republic.

The Dominican Republic is the second largest country in the Caribbean; it covers two-thirds of *La Isla Hispaniola* that is shared with Haiti. Like many developing countries, the Dominican Republic was an agricultural exporter. Tremendous shifts in the DR's economy have recently occurred. The service sector has largely overtaken other activities, mainly due to the development of tourism as the result of a governmental effort since the early 1970s. Transitional economies often recognize that tourism is a good way to bring foreign investment and currency into the domestic market. It also diminishes the dependency on agricultural products and or natural resources, which are subject to market fluctuations. Foreign investment before the 60s (Trujillo Era) was very limited in an unstable economy seen as risky by investors. Now, with the booming tourism industry, investment is rather seen as attractive by foreigners and it is no surprise that they own most of DR's resorts. This is especially so since all the governments starting in the 1970s, and in light of the IMF recommendations, offered them many tax benefits (Haggerty, 1989). On the other hand, the island has become a favorite destination for westerners due to its inexpensiveness (many devaluations of the Dominican Peso), proximity to Canada and the US, and not least its 800 miles of beautiful beaches and the variety of aquatic activities and landscapes it

offers. In twenty years, the number of visitors increased by 15 times reaching over 3.7 million in 2010 (From Banco Central de la Republica Dominicana).

METHODOLOGY

By focusing on tourism in terms of consumption, commodification, and the political and cultural economy, the relationships between tourism, globalization, people and place are explored in an empirically grounded but theoretically informed analysis. The marketplace performances under-investigation are embedded in the broader socio-historic realm described earlier. However, unlike a body of research in Anthropology (Kempadoo, 1999, Brennan 2004) that tackled specifically sex workers' representations in the Caribbean, I locate this study in the context of crowded, close, safe, family resorts in Punta Cana as an apparent quiet and impersonal transnational place. I specifically investigate Local workers at large/ Western Tourists interactions in the context of holidays. Escaping usual images of female sex workers or the interactions of young male "beach boys" with aged female tourists allows the author to shed light on other forms of interactions between service providers and consumers in the Caribbean.

I conducted a four-year ethnographic study, with over 20 weeks in the field. I met a group of Dominican people, some of the Animation staff in a resort representative of the local offer, *Ifa Villas Bavaro Hotel,* several times during different stays, enriching the data collection. Some informants stayed in contact with the author via social media allowing on-going discussions. I did share activities with informants (local dance, disco, visit of native towns/family…). I performed observations, informal/formal interviews; hundreds of photographs were also taken to perform a semiotic analysis (Floch, 1989). In depth Interviews took place in Punta Cana, lasted 40min-2h. I interviewed Dominican men and women working in Punta Cana's resorts , male and female tourists, neophytes and connoisseurs of the Dominican Republic and, Haitians working in a resort or on the *Playa Bavaro* Beach. These interviews followed McCracken's (1988) recommendations and allowed a maximum of freedom to the informants to tell their stories without setting a structured agenda for the interview. The role of the interviewer was to ask for descriptions and details while the major themes under investigation appeared spontaneously during a "natural conversation" (Thompson, Locander and Pollio 1989).

FINDINGS AND DISCUSSION

In this section I discuss the themes and observations that emerged from the field as regard the socio-spatial organization of a transnational space in a third world country. I pay particular attention to the interactions between the diverse social actors involved. I will insist on the role played by the tourism industry in conveying dialectics of power, ethnic, and gender stigma in the Dominican Republic.

At the beach…

Usually All-Inclusive resorts enable guests to travel between the hotel and the enclosed beach facilities without entering public space or encountering local inhabitants. The beach is often the place where public vs. private space mediates the opposition between tourists and locals. There is a tendency among the resort hotels to privatize the public beach, and therefore to exclude locals at the margins. *Chaises longues* and private guards ensure the boundaries between them. But sometimes locals and tourists contest those boundaries: on Sundays sometimes some Dominican attempt to sit just next to some hotel chaises longues and argue with the private guard that *"this is Dominican land!"* they should not be forbidden to stay there. And the security guard answers, *"Sorry my friend, I am doing my job!"* Also, some tourists go for a walk on the beach, trying to find a part of the beach that is more "authentic" and often find at the end of it, -this is to say the liminal space- an informal or improvised Haitian market. Here tourists enter in contact with the population at the margins of Dominican society, offering mainly Haitian paintings and cheap beauty services (such as hair braiding...Dominicans do not braid their hair as Haitians do, as a denial of their African origins...).

The beach is then clearly a space of social and race power struggles. The sociospatial dialectics of power involve 4 types of populations on Dominican beaches, transnational tourists, Dominicans and Haitians officially paid by the resort hotels as service providers for tourists who apply transnational management rules, the inhabitants of *La Comunidad* and beach visitors on their day-off, illegal Haitian workers who propose services and goods (hair braiding, paintings...) at a lower price than hotel gift shops and Beauty services. All hotel employees invoke crime and danger when leaving the official hotel beach area. The same partitioning of the beach is observed in many Dominican regions.

> "It is very dangerous for you to leave the beach hotel that is safeguarded by our security team and also to buy any items from *Haitianos*, they are dangerous and known for crime ...and anyway the items you buy there are cheap souvenirs, those people are really involved in crime and drugs, and HIV...stay away from them for your own security" (Hotel concierge, April, 2009)

The lead agency in this policing of difference is the *Policia Turistica* (POLITUR), specialized tourism police under the aegis of the state secretary for tourism. Beyond law enforcement, the POLITUR's role is to ensure licensed vendors do not annoy tourists, and that unlicensed vendors, beggars or sex workers and largely those who work in the informal economy are excluded from the *Zona turistica*. The POLITUR often engage in cleaning campaigns (*limpiar la calle*) to clean the tourist zone from rubbish and exclude undesirable social elements such as Haitian migrants. These cleaning campaigns are often conducted with the sponsoring of Punta Cana Tourism Development Association.

As a young Haitian working informally with tourists on the beach put it:

> "The POLITUR are our nightmare, a constant stress for us, even if I have lived here for 10 years I feel the hate from everywhere. *Don't stay here* is the sentence I have certainly heard one million times in my life...this is why I try my best to find a solution to join my relatives in the Bronx... Dominicans hate us because we are smart, we speak languages and we are not lazy like them, if the POLITUR were not there and we had documents to work, there would be no jobs for them but you know the POLITUR and the resort managers it's the same racists!...The tourists, I mean the ones who aren't afraid of us, they like me because I am educated, I can spend a nice time with them speak English and French fluently, we (Haitians), we are different from the Latinos you know" (François, 29)

Actually, the POLITUR do not only deny Haitians access to touristic zones but also all informal workers. There are several issues here: the price of the license is high; no license is issued without birth certificates that many Haitians and Dominicans of Haitian descent fail to obtain, but also poor Dominicans from rural regions whose birth was not officially declared and who even seem to be threatened with expulsion to Haiti if they fail to prove their citizenship.

> "I know a woman, a cleaning lady, she was fired after 3 months in the resort as she failed showing her documents, she paid people to help her produce those documents but she never managed to obtain a birth certificate...It's better for her to go back to the countryside otherwise she might be mistaken as an illegal Haitian!" (Claudio, 34)

Citizenship is here a key element for securing a job and the traffic of documents among Haitians is quite a common story. Not only are the poor marginalized but as Playa Bavaro is treasured by the government -being ranked among the 10 most beautiful beaches in the World- and because of other regions' reputations regarding prostitution (e.g. Sosuà; Bocca Chica), "a zero sex workers on Playa Bavaro" policy is enforced by the POLITUR to guarantee the family atmosphere that is targeted by the tourism industry. Doing so, this does not discourage diverse forms of prostitution or "sex romances" that are very difficult to untangle and that often start at resort nightclubs.

At The Disco...

At night, tourists and locals gather in all-inclusive resorts discos. For the tourism industry it is the only way to fabricate a tropical Latino fantasy in this transnational space. Latino music and local dancers serve as a mean of differentiation from other destinations. Dominicans are often allowed to join tourists in the resort's disco, changing status from employees (with uniforms that are used to discipline their behavior) during the day to clients (displaying personal fashion codes) as they pay for their drinks. Nevertheless once again management rules impede tourists/locals interactions: close physical contact between clients and employees is forbidden, entering a client or employee's room is impossible. The strict surveillance from managers and security guards is obvious and feared by employees who can loose their job instantly if they do derogate to those rules. This context is the most difficult aspect of the job mentioned by the employees as they live in the resort sharing rooms with co-workers without any intimacy and getting two days off out of nine or ten days of hard work. Their family usually lives three to five hours away from the hotel, which means they spend most of their day off traveling by bus. Most of the hotel workers are young single parents who provide for their babies and families by accepting better-paid jobs in the tourism industry. This isolation is in particular experienced as somehow emasculating by the young men; although they also report satisfaction from being in contact with tourists in a beautiful environment, many of them use the term *progresar* to refer to their hope of upward social mobility by interacting with foreigners which echoes Ustuner and Thompson service providers' discourses in Istanbul (2012).

Yet, some Locals/ tourists contest those rules. Dominican male agency is emphasized through romances with young tourists. Competition to enhance their status within the employee peer group is as important as the rivalry over seduction with male tourists. Bodies, possessions and brands are manipulated as signs to convey specific discourses on sex, gender, ethnicity and social status. At a microlevel, intimate interactions between tourists and locals reveal the reproduction of power relations while male locals also show a sense of agency trying to take advantage of this situation both emulating white male consumers and exaggerating stereotypes of hyper-masculinity.

In this context, Dominican men literally take possession of the space - the disco floor - as a response to the emasculating tourism management. They reverse the situation by appearing very confident asserting their skills/competencies: easy contact with women; showing off by dancing and inviting women; display of bad boys fashion codes emulating hip hop celebrities; display of muscular bodies and a "cosmeticized" appearance.

These young female/ young male Caribbean interactions shed light on a reality ignored in previous ethnographies in the Dominican Republic (Kempadoo 1999, Brennan 2004, Gregory 1997) that analyze young Caribbean men with older White women and often presented by the popular media. Escaping those clichés makes it possible to account for a much complex gender game in a transnational context. For the female tourists encountered, those men represent a way to escape everyday narratives, and insert liberating, differentiating social discourses. They are aware of their agency as citizen of the western world but still state that they are attracted by what some informants term the "beauty", "sexiness", "manliness", and even the "machismo" of those men, who also pay them so much "attention" which is not the case of western men, who use "pseudo-egalitarian" schemes to avoid being "involved" and "gentle". These quite naïve assertions fuel idealized images of the foreign, exotic other who, via possessions (global tech, fashion brands and music), seems even closer. On the other hand, different strategies are at play for male hotel employees, some just want to have fun and forget tough working conditions, some (a minority) try to get a western girlfriend to settle abroad, some would like to have a nice time and hope for presents and/or money. However, most of them state they would not go with any women if she is "too old", "unattractive". Such behavior remained an exception during my several weeks there. For some men, it is an opportunity to express their "personality" through clothing and less controlled behavior than during the day, for instance some Haitians keep their long braided hair that is often forbidden by the management and confide about their cultural specificities while they are told not to voice they are Haitian it in the hotel. Meeting tourists - as seeming equals - helps reduce vivid internal tensions and reinforce self-esteem according to various informants.

"I don't have the possibility to share a meal with the tourists, all day I smell pizza and I can't get any unless some tourists hide some and bring me a slice, do you think this is normal? But when the night comes, it is like in Hector Acosta's song, I don't have money, I can't bring you to Europe and all the stuff but I am sure with me you feel happy... (big laughs)" (Melvin, 29)

In this context, complex representations of relationships which are forbidden by the management increase the sense of transgression by all actors transforming their initial representations and displaying seemingly opposite desires- the desire for the seductive foreign and the desire for the authentic local (Wilk, 1995). On the other hand, logics of co-dependencies (Ustuner and Thompson, 2012) disrupt traditional social status games and hierarchies and object/subject dialectics. Here especially hybrid identities are experienced as various capital games are emphasized. Seduction assets in a holiday resort are more valued than anywhere else. The mastery of Latino dance also empowers Locals over tourists although power structures are still at stake as Locals remain under surveillance. The only way they can escape it is leaving the resort for the night which can cause money issues as they depend on the female tourists to follow them

and, obviously, pay the expenses. In a sense, impeding close Locals/Tourist interactions ends up encouraging informal prostitution.

Interesting are the reactions of some young male tourists that either admire the successes of Locals with female tourists or often express a frustration while facing female tourists consuming the racialized fantasy of Latin hyper-masculinity.

"I will never come back to the Dominican Republic, it is my third and last time here... it's not possible to meet nice girls I mean tourists, they are all with the Dominicans, they don't pay attention to us. The worst of it is ...those people in Spain, the girls would never look at them! Anyway they would not be even able to enter the disco I am used to going to...I don't know what's wrong with these girls, I am sure they know those men have 15 girlfriends at the same time" (Ricardo, 32, Spanish, Wholesaler)

Here some informants activate classist and/or colonial discourses; it is also representative of other tourists' behaviors that avoid any particular contacts with locals except getting the best service for a minimum price. Especially during slack season weekends, some resorts are filled with Dominican families, NGOs or companies paying for their stay. Many tourists report they wish this did not happen as *it disrupts the whole thing!"* as a woman put it, or *"Dominican Rep. without the Dominicans is much better: I will never come back to this hotel!"*

It is noteworthy that skin-capital and citizenship become in this context socio-economic capital that blurs habitual social taxonomies (and the marginalized citizenship issues mentioned earlier). Some tourists from lower classes feel superior and are viewed as rich by employees, while some service providers are much more educated (doctors without jobs for instance), speaking several languages and trying to interact with western middle-class women whose financial independence is seen as a potential liberation.

CONCLUSION

As we have seen, the cultural hybridity that is a consequence of mass-tourism is nevertheless perceived as a threat to the seamless atmosphere of tourism and the principle of social exclusion. This unruly hybridity risks disrupting the binary oppositions undergirding the industry's symbolic economy between "guests" and "hosts", between subjects and objects of consumption and between cosmopolitan contemporaneity and the charm of, in this case, virgin beachtown tropical island. It is this subversive hybridity, a symbolic as much as an economic threat that the tourism industry tends to exclude.

The thick descriptions of the context organized in spatio-temporal landmarks help to convey the experience of different sets of actors interrelated in a network of performances leading to experiences of transformation in transnational places. The research contributes to three areas: global service providers/consumers' interactions, acculturation processes and social class deployment in less industrialized consumer cultures.

REFERENCES

Albuquerque K. (1998). Sex, Beach Boys, and Female Tourists in the Caribbean. *Sexuality and Culture*, 2:87-111.

Askegaard S. (1991). Toward a semiotic structure of cultural identity. In Larson et al. : 11–30

Askegaard S., Kjeldgaard D. (2006). The Glocalization of Youth Culture: The Global Youth Segment as Structures of Common Difference. *Journal of Consumer Research*, vol. 22 : 231-247.

Askegaard S, Kjeldgaard D & Arnould E (2009), Reflexive Culture's Consequenses in Cheryl Nakata (ed) Beyond Hofstede: Culture Framework for Global Marketing and Management, Macmillan/Palgrave: 101-122

Askegaard S., Linnet J. (2011). Towards an Epistemology of Consumer Culture Theory: Phenomenology and the Context of Context. Marketing Theory, Vol. 11 : 381-404

Belk R. W. (1994). Prostitution and AIDS in Thailand: sexual consumption a time of crisis, in *Asia Pacific Advances in Consumer Research*, 1 : 288-290.

Brennan D. (2004). *What's Love Got to Do With It? Transnational Desires and Sex Tourism in the Dominican Republic*, Durham and London: Duke University Press.

Cabezas A. L. (2004). Between Love and Money: Sex, Tourism, and Citizenship in Cuba and the Dominican Republic. *Signs,* 29(4) : 987-1015.

Campbell Sh., Perkins A., and Mohammed P. (1999), "Come to Jamaica and Feel All Right": Tourism and the Sex Trade. In *Sun, Sex, and Gold: Tourism and Sex Work in the Caribbean.* Kemala Kempadoo, Ed. Lanham, MD: Rowman and Littlefield Publishers.

Canterbury D. (2005), Globalization, Inequality and Growth in the Caribbean, *Canadian Journal of Development Studies*, 26(4), 847-866.

Clarke C. (1983), Review: Colonialism and Its Social and Cultural Consequences in the Caribbean, *Journal of Latin American Studies*, 15(2), 491-503.

Henshall M. (2005) Uncertain Images: Tourism Development and Seascapes of the Caribbean, In *Seductions of Place: Geographical Perspectives on Globalization and Touristed Landscapes.* Carolyn Cartier and Alan A. Lew, Eds. New York: Routledge.

Floch J-M (1989), La contribution d'une sémiotique structurale à la conception d'un hypermarché, *Recherche et Applications en Marketing*, 4, 37-49

Herold E., Garcia R., DeMoya T. (2001), Female Tourists and Beach Boys: Romance or Sex Tourism?, *Annals of Tourism Research*, 28(4).

Henry P. C. (2005), Social Class, Market Situation, and Consumers' Metaphors of (Dis) Empowerment, *Journal of Consumer Research*, 31, 766-78

Jafari A. and Firat A. F., Suerdem A., Askegaard S. and Dalli D. (2012) Non-western contexts: the invisible half. *Marketing Theory*, 12 (1). pp. 3-12

Kaur Puar J. (2002), Circuits of Queer Mobility: Tourism, Travel, and Globalization, *GLQ,* 8(1-2), 101-137

Kamala K. (1999), *Sexing the Caribbean: Gender, Race and Sexual Labor*, New York: Routledge.

Kjeldgaard D. and Askegaard S. (2006), The Glocalization of Youth Culture: The Global Youth Segment as Structures of Common Difference,‖ Journal of Consumer Research, 33, 231-47

Kozinets R. V. (2008), Technology/Ideology: How Ideological Fields Influence Consumers' Technology Narratives, *Journal of Consumer Research*, 34 (April), 864-881

Lowry L. L. (1993) Sun, Sand, Sea & Sex; A Look at Tourism Advertising Through the Decoding and Interpretation of Four Typical Tourism Advertisements. Society of Travel and Tourism Educatiors Annual Conference, Miami, Florida, *Proceedings of Research and Academic Papers*, V, 183-204.

MacClaran, P. and Brown S. (2005), The Center Cannot Hold: Consuming in the Utopian Marketplace, *Journal of Consumer Research*, 32, 311-24

Mullings B. (1999), Globalization, Tourism, and the International Sex Trade, In *Sun, Sex, and Gold: Tourism and Sex Work in the Caribbean*, Kamala Kempadoo, Ed. Lanham, MD: Rowman and Littlefield Publishers.

O'Connell D., Sanchez Taylor J. J. (1999), Fantasy Islands: Exploring the Demand for Sex Tourism, In *Sun, Sex, and Gold: Tourism and Sex Work in the Caribbean*, Kamala Kempadoo, Ed. Lanham, MD: Rowman and Littlefield Publishers.

Opperman, Martin 1999 Sex Tourism, *Annals of Tourism Research,* 26(2), 251-266

Pattullo P. (2005), *Last Resorts: The Cost of Tourism in the Caribbean*, 2nd Edition, New York: Monthly Review Press.

Ourahmoune N., Ozçaglar-Toulouse (2012), Exogamous weddings and fashion in a rising consumer culture: Kabyle minority dynamics of structure and agency, *Marketing Theory*, 12, 78-96

Payne S., Tourism in the Dominican Republic: Social and Economic Effects, Gatton Student Research Publication, 3, 1, 1-20

Pruitt D. and LaFont S. (1995), For Love and Money: Romance Tourism in Jamaica, *Annals of Tourism Research,* 22, 422-40

Price L.and Eric J. Arnould E. J. (1999), Commercial Friendships: Service Provider-Client Relationships in Context,‖ Journal of Marketing, 63, 38–56

Sanchez Taylor J. (2000), Tourism and 'Embodied' Commodities: Sex Tourism in the Caribbean, In *Tourism and Sex: Culture, Commerce and Coercion*, Stephen Clift and Simon Carter Eds. London; New York: Pinter.

Sassen S. (2002), Cities and Communities in the Global Economy,‖ in The City: Critical Concepts in the Social Sciences, ed. Michael Pacione, New York: Routledge, 382–92

Sanchez Taylor J. (2001), Dollars are a Girl's Best Friend? Female Tourists' Sexual Behavior in the Caribbean. *Sociology,* 35(3), 749-764

Shankar G. (1999), Where the Present is Haunted by the Past: Disarticulating Colonialism's Legacy in the Caribbean, *Cultural Dynamics*, 11, 57-87.

Shawe, R. (2001), Fantasy Voyages: An Exploration of White Males' Participation in the Costa Rican Sex Tourism Industry, *the Berkeley McNair Research Journal*, 81-91.

Sharpe J., Pinto S. (2006) The Sweetest Taboo: Studies of Caribbean Sexualities; A Review Essay, *Signs: Journal of Women in Culture and Society*, 32(1), 247-274

Sheller M. (2004), Natural Hedonism: the Invention of Caribbean Islands as Tropical Playgrounds, In *Tourism in the Caribbean*, Timothy Duval ed. London: Routledge.

Thompson, C., & Ustuner, T. (2012). How Marketplace Performances Produce Interdependent Status Games and Contested Forms of Symbolic Capital. *Journal of Consumer Research*, 38, 796-814

Wilk R. (1995), Learning to Be Local in Belize: Global Systems of Common Difference, in Worlds Apart: Modernity through the Prism of the Local, ed. Daniel Miller, London: Routledge, 110–31.

Wonders N. A. and Michalowski R. (2001), Bodies, Borders, and Sex Tourism in a Globalized World: A Tale of Two Cities - Amsterdam and Havana, *Social Problems,* 48(4):545-71.

Uppers and Downers: Conveying Product Activity Level with Diagonals

Ann Schlosser, University of Washington, USA
Ruchi Rikhi, University of Washington, USA

EXTENDED ABSTRACT

Perrier recently changed its packaging by orienting its horizontal logo to an upward diagonal, while Snapple has done the reverse. Although such changes may be part of routine brand updating, we propose that the direction of diagonals can have a significant influence on product judgments. Prior research has proven that the visual aspect of ads can convey semantic information and thus have important persuasive effects (Peracchio and Meyers-Levy 2005; Scott and Batra 2003). We contribute to this literature in at least three ways: by demonstrating that the direction of diagonals can (1) convey different amounts of activity, and thus differentially influence (2) product expectations, and (3) both pre- and post-consumption judgments.

Although conveying activity in a logo has been identified as an important design element, what makes a logo more or less active has yet to be specified (Henderson and Cote 1998). There exists initial evidence that diagonal (vs. vertical) orientations reflect dynamism (Peracchio and Meyers-Levy 2005). We extend this research by proposing that the direction of diagonals can convey different degrees of activity and effort, and thus differentially affect persuasion. Specifically, a line that slopes from the lower left to the upper right is an upward diagonal, whereas a line that slopes from the upper left to the lower right is a downward diagonal. The art literature suggests that the orientation of objects can convey movement. Specifically, whereas a horizontal line has been likened to an object lying flat (Gaffron 1956) and being static (Arnheim 1974; Wofflin 1950), diagonal lines differ in their direction, thereby conveying movement (Arnheim 1974; Gaffron 1956; Wolfflin 1950). Because visual information is processed from left to right (Deng and Kahn 2009), we argue that an upward (vs. downward) diagonal will convey greater movement/activity and thus be less relaxing. Indeed, upward (downward) diagonals are often described as ascending (descending; Gaffron 1956).

We test our account across three studies. In study 1, we test whether individuals process images from left to right, and infer that upward (vs. downward) diagonals convey more activity and success. To test this, 143 participants were randomly assigned to a 2 (orientation: upward vs. downward) x 3 (order: heatmap, activity items, or rest item measured last) design. After being shown an upward diagonal or downward diagonal, participants clicked on where the line starts. As predicted, an orientation main effect was nonsignificant for the x-coordinate ($F(1, 165)<1$), but was significant on the y-coordinate ($F(1,165)=1028.80$, $p<.001$) with values indicative of the left region of the grid. Participants also rated the line on a number of attributes. Consistent with the art literature and our theorizing, activity perceptions were greater for upward than downward diagonals ($M = 4.84$ vs. 4.00, $F(1, 137)=5.20$, $p < .05$), whereas at rest perceptions were greater for downward than upward diagonals ($M = 4.13$ vs. 3.25, $F(1,137)=4.23$, $p < .05$).

In studies 2 and 3, we varied whether individuals' goals favor activity or rest. If upward (vs. downward) diagonals convey greater activity, then they should lead to higher product expectations and evaluations with active (vs. relaxation) goals. In study 2, 108 participants were randomly assigned to a 2 (goal: adventure vs. relaxation) x 2 (diagonal: upward vs. downward) design. Participants were told they were planning an adventure or relaxation vacation before viewing an ad, in which the text and images emphasized either an upward or downward diagonal. For attitudes toward the resort, a goal x diagonal interaction was significant ($F(1,105) = 15.31$, $p<.001$). When adventure was primed, attitudes were higher in the upward than downward condition, whereas when relaxation was primed, attitudes were lower in the upward than downward condition ($Fs(1,103)> 5.81$, $ps<.05$). A similar pattern emerged for purchase intentions (PI) toward the vacation package ($F(1,103) = 6.35$, $p = .01$). As before, when adventure was primed, PI was higher in the upward than downward condition ($F(1,103)=5.79$, $p<.05$), and when relaxation was primed, PI was lower in the upward than downward condition, although this difference was not significant ($F(1,103) = 1.12$). Still, PI was higher for those in the downward/relaxation than downward/adventure condition ($F(1,103)=8.59$, $p<.005$). Furthermore, willingness to pay (WTP) was higher in the downward/relaxation than upward/relaxation condition ($F(1,103)=4.37$, $p<.05$). In contrast, WTP was somewhat (but not significantly) higher in the upward/adventure than downward/adventure condition ($F(1,103)=1.45$, NS).

Study 3 used a 2 (claim: energizing vs. relaxing) x 2 (diagonal: upward vs. downward) design for a hypothetical beverage claiming to either promote energy or relaxation. This product category was selected because energy and relaxation drinks are popular among this generation (Stacy 2011). Based on prior research (Shiv, Carmon and Ariely 2005), we predict that if diagonal orientation influences activity-level expectations, then activity-level experiences (i.e., feeling energized or relaxed) should vary depending on whether the claim is congruent. To test this, 141 participants viewed the beverage packaging that varied in claim and diagonal orientation, and then drank a purported sample of the beverage, which was the same water for everyone. For all of the dependent variables, goal x diagonal was significant ($Fs(1, 134)>4.41$, $ps< .05$). As predicted, in the relaxed condition, satisfaction was higher when the diagonal was downward than upward, whereas in the energized condition, satisfaction was higher when the diagonal was upward than downward ($Fs(1, 138)>4.11$, $ps<.05$). Moreover, participants in the relaxation condition reported feeling more relaxed when the diagonal was downward than upward ($F(1, 138)=5.59$, $p<.05$), whereas there was no significant difference in the energizing condition ($F(1,138)<1$). In contrast, participants in the energizing condition reported feeling more energized when the diagonal was upward than downward ($F(1, 138)=6.11$, $p<.05$). However, in the relaxation condition, participants reported feeling more energized when the diagonal was congruent—that is downward than upward ($F(1, 138)=6.91$, $p=.01$). Bootstrapping methods support that feeling relaxed (and energized) mediated the effect of diagonals on satisfaction in the relaxing condition, whereas feeling energized was the mediator in the energizing condition.

In summary, this is the first empirical research demonstrating that upward and downward diagonals convey different degrees of activity, and thus differentially influence product expectations and pre- and post-consumption judgments.

REFERENCES

Arnheim, Rudolf (1954), *Art and Visual Perception: A Psychology of the Creative Eye*, Berkeley: University of California Press.

Deng, Xiaoyan and Barbara E. Kahn (2009), "Is Your Product on the Right Side? The 'Location Effect' on Perceived Product Heaviness and Package Evaluation," *Journal of Marketing Research*, 46(6), 725-738.

Advances in Consumer Research
Volume 40, ©2012

Gaffron, Mercedes (1956), "Some New Dimensions in the Phenomenal Analysis of Visual Experience," *Journal of Personality*, 24(3), 285-307.

Henderson, Pamela W. and Joseph A. Cote, "Guidelines for Selecting or Modifying Logos," *Journal of Marketing*, 62 (2), 14-30.

Peracchio, Laura A. and Joan Meyers-Levy (2005), "Using Stylistic Properties of Ad Pictures to Communicate with Consumers," *Journal of Consumer Research*, 32, 29-40.

Scott, Linda M. and Rajeev Batra (2003), *Persuasive Imagery: A Consumer Response Persepctive*, Mahwah: Lawrence Erlbaum Associates, Publishers.

Shiv, Baba, Ziv Carmon, and Dan Ariely (2005), "Placebo Effects of Marketing Actions: Consumers May Get What They Pay For," Journal of Marketing Research, 42 (4), 383-93.

Stacy, Sylvie (2011), "Relaxation Drinks and Their Use in Adolescents," *Journal of Child and Adolescent Psychopharmacology*, 21(6), 605-10.

Wolfflin, Heinrich (1950), *Principles of Art History: The Problem of the Devleopment of Style in Later Art*, Mineola: Dover Publications, Inc.

Who Made This Thing? How Designer Identity and Brand Personality Impact Consumers' Evaluations of New Product Offerings

Matt O'Hern, University of Oregon, USA
Lan Jiang, University of Oregon, USA

EXTENDED ABSTRACT

Today, companies across a wide range of fields (e.g., Procter and Gamble, YouTube, Threadless.com) are adopting *external innovation* programs that allow individuals outside the firm to directly participate in the new product development (NPD) process. Although interest in customer involvement in NPD is increasing among marketing scholars (e.g., Franke, Keinz, and Steger 2009; Moreau and Herd 2010), much of the research has focused only on the mass-customization context and has explored how consumers' active participation in personalizing their own products influences their subsequent evaluations. The current study extends existing research by focusing not on customers who are actively involved in NPD, but on the broader segment of customers that simply consumes new product offerings. More specifically, this research explores whether consumers' product evaluations depend on the identity of an external designer (i.e., a fellow customer or an independent professional designer) and examines the role that brand personality may play in influencing consumers' reactions.

We propose that consumers will prefer customer-created new products when an exciting brand personality is present, but that this preference will be reversed in the presence of a sincere brand personality. This is due to the different focuses elicited by these two distinctive brand personalities, whereby excitement shifts consumers' focus toward the process used to create a product but sincerity draws the focus toward the outcome. When the focus is on the NPD process, firms that encourage customers to create new product concepts are seen as more democratic and customer-oriented (Fuchs and Schreier 2011). However, when the focus is on the outcome/product, consumers will be more likely to link the designer's professional status with the expertise necessary to create an innovative, highly effective product.

Study 1 adopts a 2 (Designer Identity: Customer vs. Professional) x 2 (Brand Personality: Sincere vs. Exciting) between-subjects design. A fictitious new product was created as the stimulus. In the customer condition, we introduce the product creator as a loyal customer, while in the professional condition the creator is a professional. Personality is manipulated through text, taglines, logos and website visuals, following Aaker et al. (2004). The key measure is consumer liking and participants were also asked whether they viewed the focal product / the process used to create the product as innovative and effective. The 2 x 2 ANOVA showed a two-way interaction ($F(1,141) = 6.68$, $p < .05$). When an exciting personality was present, subjects who were told that the creator was a fellow customer indicated a higher liking for the product. In contrast, when evaluating the sincere version, participants preferred the professionally created product.

When asked to evaluate the innovativeness and effectiveness of the NPD process, participants rated the process as being more innovative and effective when the designer was a customer. However, when asked about the innovativeness and effectiveness of the product itself, participants who learned that the product was created by a professional designer rated it as being more innovative and effective. Follow-up mediation analysis revealed that consumers prefer professionally designed products, because they view the end product as more innovative and effective and that consumers exhibit greater liking for customer creation, because they perceive the NPD process as more innovative and effective.

Study 2 further identifies the role of process vs. outcome orientation by directly manipulating consumers' focal orientation to concentrate on either process or outcome. This study adopts a 2 (Designer Identity) x 2 (Brand Personality) x 2 (Focal Orientation) between-subjects design. Another fictitious new product was used to increase generalizability. Results revealed an interactive effect of identity and personality ($F(1,134) = 9.13$, $p < .005$) and an interaction between designer identity and focal orientation, (i.e., process vs. outcome) ($F(1,134) = 11.02$, $p < .05$). The pattern showed that the moderating role of focal orientation is in parallel with the role of brand personality, such that a focus on process leads to a preference for customer creation as the exciting personality does, while a focus on outcome results in increased liking for professional creation as the sincere personality does.

Study 3 examines the timing of consumption as a boundary condition. We expect that if the product is to be consumed in the immediate future, attention will shift from brand personality and focus on more tangible product attributes, thus limiting the impact of personality. Study 3 adopted a 2 (Designer Identity) x 2 (Brand Personality) x 2 (Consumption Timing) between-subjects design. In the near future condition, participants were told to imagine that they have a time-critical project, i.e., to remodel their room before the coming weekend. In the distant future condition, they were told to imagine remodeling their room several months in the future. A 2 x 2 x 2 ANOVA on liking revealed a three-way interaction ($F(1,165) = 5.70$, $p < .005$). In the distant future condition, the results replicated the previous findings. Interestingly, when the time constraint was imposed, only a main effect of designer identity emerged, so that participants in both the sincere and exciting conditions indicated a greater liking for the professionally created product ($Mc = 4.21$ vs. $Mp = 5.17$; $F(1, 159) = 5.01$, $p < .01$).

Across three studies, our research makes three important contributions. First, we show that brand personality plays a significant role in determining whether customers respond more positively to products designed by fellow customers or by professional designers. Second, our research sheds light on the mechanism through which designer identity impacts consumers' new product evaluations and demonstrates that this relationship depends on whether customers are process-oriented or outcome-oriented. Finally, this study identifies a boundary condition in the form of consumption timing and demonstrates that the interaction effect between designer identity and brand personality is attenuated when customers contemplate making an immediate purchase.

Managerially, our research provides important insights for marketers. Our findings suggest that exciting brands could benefit from highlighting the active role that customer designers play in the external innovation process. Conversely, managers of sincere brands may wish to highlight the expertise of professional designers when mentioning an external innovation program in their marketing communications.

REFERENCES

Aaker, Jennifer, Susan Fournier and S. Adam Brasel (2004), "When Good Brands Do Bad," *Journal of Consumer Research*, 31 (June), 1-16.

Franke, Nikolaus, Peter Keinz, and Christoph J. Steger (2009), "Testing the Value of Customization: When Do Customers Really Prefer Products Tailored to Their Preferences?" *Journal of Marketing*, 73 (September), 103-21.

Fuchs, Christoph and Martin Schreier (2011), "Customer Empowerment in New Product Development," *Journal of Product Innovation Management*, 28 (1), 17-32.

Moreau, C. Page and Kelly B. Herd (2010), "To Each His Own? How Comparisons with Others Influence Consumers' Evaluations of Their Self-Designed Products," *Journal of Consumer Research,* 36 (April), 806-19.

I Think I Can, I Think I Can: Brand Use, Self-Efficacy, and Performance

Ji Kyung Park, University of Delaware, USA
Deborah Roedder John, University of Minnesota, USA

EXTENDED ABSTRACT

When individuals struggle with a difficult and challenging task, can using a brand with a strong image related to the task's domain empower them to perform better? For example, can individuals perform better when engaging in strenuous physical exercise if they wear Under Armour accessories (athletic image) while exercising? Our answer is yes. We propose that using brands with strong images while performing a difficult task can enhance feelings of self-efficacy (beliefs in one's capabilities; Bandura 1995) in a domain related to the brand's image, and this heightened sense of self-efficacy can lead to better task performance.

Further, we propose that the self-efficacy effect is not experienced by everyone—it depends on the implicit self-theory held by individuals (Dweck 2000). Individuals who endorse entity theory ("entity theorists"), who view their personal qualities as something they cannot improve through their own direct efforts, will rely on feelings of self-efficacy that using brands can trigger to perform better on difficult tasks. In contrast, individuals who endorse incremental theory ("incremental theorists"), who view their personal qualities as something they can develop through their own direct efforts at self-improvement, will be less reliant on the self-efficacy effect of brands. Thus, we predict that brand use will result in a heightened sense of self-efficacy and better task performance for entity, but not incremental theorists.

We examine these propositions in three studies. In a first study, we examined the effect of using an MIT pen on performance for a challenging GRE test. The MIT brand is strongly associated with the image of "intelligence", and we expected that using a pen embossed with the MIT name would enhance GRE test performance for entity, but not incremental theorists. Undergraduate students were given 30 minutes to take a GRE test that consisted of 15 difficult and 15 easy math problems. Implicit self-theory was measured prior to taking the test. As expected, *entity theorists* who used the MIT pen (vs. regular pen) *performed better* on the 15 difficult GRE problems, where test takers tend to struggle the most and the beneficial effects of using the MIT pen should be most pronounced. In contrast, the performance of incremental theorists did not vary across pen conditions. Additionally, incremental theorists performed more poorly than entity theorists using the MIT pen. Simply using the MIT pen without having training opportunities to directly improve their intelligence did not enhance performance among incremental theorists.

In a second study, we extended our findings using a different brand (Gatorade) associated with a different brand image (athletic) and a different type of task (strenuous athletic task). Also, we manipulated beliefs in entity versus incremental theory (Chiu, Hong, and Dweck 1997) prior to brand usage. Participants were invited to evaluate a new bottled water from Gatorade (athletic brand) or Ice Mountain (control brand). In the Gatorade condition, participants drank cold tap water in a cup featuring the Gatorade brand name and logo; in the Ice Mountain condition, they drank the same water in a plain cup. They were asked to drink water continuously while exercising with a hand-grip, which had a counter to record the number of times the hand-grip was pressed. This athletic task is initially easy, but gets harder (due to fatigue) as the hand-grip is pressed more times. As expected, participants in the *entity theory* condition *performed better* on hand-gripping (higher hand grip count) when drinking Gatorade (vs. Ice Mountain) water. In contrast, those in the incremental theory condition performed similarly regardless of the water they drank.

Additionally, their performance was lower than that of entity theorists who drank water from the Gatorade cup.

In a third study, we examined the mechanism underlying increases in task performance for entity theorists observed in the first two studies. Participants read several articles, including one about Gatorade that presented evidence that Gatorade increases athletic performance (high brand effectiveness) or does not increase athletic performance (low brand effectiveness). Next, participants completed the hand-grip task while drinking the tap water in the Gatorade cup. Finally, participants rated the degree of confidence they had about their ability during the hand-grip exercise (self-efficacy measure). If entity theorists (but not incremental theorists) derive a sense of self-efficacy from using brands such as Gatorade, which allows them to perform better on strenuous athletic endeavors, only entity theorists should be affected by the manipulation that Gatorade can (vs. cannot) make you a better athlete. Our results supported this line of reasoning. Entity theorists showed a heightened sense of *self-efficacy and performance* on the hand-grip task in the high (vs. low) brand effectiveness condition. However, incremental theorists did not show such a difference. More importantly, results from a *mediation analysis* showed that using Gatorade in the high (vs. low) brand efficacy condition enhanced self-efficacy among entity theorists, which led to better performance on the hand-gripping exercise.

Our findings show, for the first time, that using brands can be beneficial for consumers who find it difficult to believe that they can improve their abilities through their own direct efforts at self-improvement (entity theorists). Using a brand with a strong image empowers entity theorists to perform better on difficult and challenging tasks in a domain related to the brand's image. Using an MIT pen empowered entity theorists to perform better on difficult GRE questions (study 1) and drinking tap water from a Gatorade cup empowered them to perform better on a physically challenging athletic exercise (study 2 & 3). Brands can activate goals (Fitzsimons, Chartrand, and Fitzsimons 2008), but when tasks are difficult and challenging, simply possessing a goal to perform well may not be sufficient. A cognitive appraisal of personal efficacy is required to increase the level of challenge that individuals are willing to undertake and to encourage them to mobilize effort to perform well (Zimmerman, Bandura and Martinez-Pons 1992). For people (entity theorists) who need an external cue to enhance appraisals of one's capabilities, using brands provides the needed boost.

REFERENCES

Bandura, Albert (1982), "Self-Efficacy Mechanism in Human Agency," *American Psychologist*, 37, 122-47.

Dweck, Carol S. (2000), *Self-Theories: Their Role in Motivation, Personality and Development*, Philadelphia: Psychology Press.

Chiu, Chi-yue, Ying-yi Hong, and Carol S. Dweck (1997), "Lay Dispositionism and Implicit Theories of Personality," *Journal of Personality and Social Psychology*, 73 (1), 19-30.

Fitzsimons, Grainne M., Tanya L. Chartrand, and Gavan J. Fitzsimons (2008), "Automatic Effects of Brand Exposure on Motivated Behavior: How Apple Makes You Think Different," *Journal of Consumer Research*, 35 (June), 21-35.

Zimmerman, Barry J., Albert Bandura, and Manuel Martinez-Pons (1992), "Self-Motivation for Academic Attainment: The Role of Self-Efficacy Beliefs and Personal Goal Setting," *American Educational Research*, 29 (3), 663-76.

Beyond Seeing McDonald's Fiesta Menu:
The Role of Accent in Brand Sincerity of Ethnic Products and Brands

Marina Puzakova, Oregon State University, USA
Hyokjin Kwak, Drexel University, USA
Monique Bell, Drexel University, USA

EXTENDED ABSTRACT

The ascent of Hispanic-Americans as the largest U.S. minority has encouraged firms to start utilizing ethnic brand crossovers (e.g., McDonald's "Fiesta" menu). One effective way of engaging ethnic groups has been the use of ethnic accent in firms' branding messages (McDonald's use of Hispanic-accented spokespersons to tout its "Fiesta" menu). Indeed, accent induces enduring personality impressions (e.g., sincerity; Bresnahan et al. 2002; DeShields, Kara, and Kaynak 1996). Despite the powerful impact of accent in communicating personalities, scholarly research investigating the role of accent in brand communications has been limited. Understanding whether and under what circumstances a spokesperson's accent is likely to affect brand sincerity can provide marketers of domestic and ethnic brands with another marketing tool to strategically manage their brands' personalities.

Relying on a prosodic theory of accents, we propose that Hispanic accent's specific prosodic features (i.e., the acoustic language features such as pitch, rhythm, and intonation; Ramus et al. 2000) are perceived as more sincere (Ray 1986). Given that a spokesperson's accent is evaluated in part by the prosodic characteristics of the speaker's native language and that those prosodic features uniquely influence sincerity evaluations, our first hypothesis is that an advertisement using a Hispanic accent will be perceived as more sincere than a brand advertised using an American (standard) accent.

In Study 1, we used a 30-second radio advertisement for a fictitious brand of chocolate that included a verbal message discussing product characteristics and void of salient brand personality cues. As predicted, the results of a 2 (gender of the spokesperson) x 2 (spokesperson's accent: Hispanic vs. American) between-subject ANOVA (n = 60) revealed that Hispanic accent leads to higher brand sincerity perceptions. Consistent with previous literature, brand sincerity also predicted consumers' attitudes toward the brand.

Furthermore, while it seems sensible to employ a Hispanic-accented speaker to evoke brand sincerity impressions for an ethnic brand (e.g., Chipotle Mexican Grill), might there be greater advantages of using an American-accented speaker to enhance brand sincerity perceptions of a brand with American roots, however, in a traditionally ethnic product category (e.g., McDonalds' burritos)? We define brand ethnicity as consumers' perceptions that the brand originated from a specific ethnic culture. In accord with the dynamic constructivist theory of culture (Torelli and Ahluwalia 2012), people develop representations of what trait characteristics are associated with certain cultures. For American consumers, the associations of warmth and sincerity of Hispanic cultures are highly accessible and consensually shared (Cuddy, Fiske, and Glick 2008). Such group stereotypes are transferred to products, brands, and people originating from the cultures (Chattalas, Kramer, and Takada 2008). As prosodic features of Hispanic accent create greater perceptions of brand sincerity (Study 1), and as Hispanic "brand ethnicity" alone induces sincerity perceptions, our second hypothesis is that a match or mismatch between the spokesperson's accent and brand ethnicity is likely to play a significant role in either boosting or inhibiting brand sincerity inferences. Hypothesis 2 was tested in Study 2 (n = 60). We recorded 30-second radio commercials featuring a fictitious American brand, Joe's Burgers, and a fictitious Hispanic brand, Carlos' Tacos (both

identified though a pretest as ethnically salient), using either American- or Hispanic-accented spokespersons. Respondents rated brand sincerity (α = .88), brand attitude (α = .96), strength of their American identity (covariate was insignificant), and the ad's realism (no differences across conditions). No main effects of accent or brand ethnicity were detected. However, a significant interaction effect between brand ethnicity and accent emerged. That is, a spokesperson's Hispanic (American) accent created enhanced perceptions of brand sincerity for ethnic (domestic) brands.

Will the moderation effect of brand ethnicity hold when brand ethnicity is incongruent with product ethnicity? Product ethnicity associations are highly accessible, deeply embedded in consumers' interpretations of brands, are not easily affected by local branding efforts (Eckhardt 2005), and may become an important factor in evaluations of an unfamiliar brand (Nebenzahl and Secunda 1993). In addition, consumers show low levels of brand origin recognition for frequently purchased goods because this information is deemed non-diagnostic for purchasing decisions (Samiee, Shimp, and Sharma 2005). Thus, as product ethnicity is more likely to dominate brand ethnicity perceptions, our third hypothesis is that product ethnicity-accent congruity is likely to induce stronger effect on brand sincerity than brand ethnicity-accent congruity.

In Study 3 (n = 94), 30-second radio commercials for an American (Hispanic) product category and Hispanic (American) brand name, Carlos' Burgers (Joe's Tacos) were used. A significant interaction effect between incongruent product-brand ethnicity and accent emerged. Planned contrasts showed that in the commercial about the American (Hispanic) product with a Hispanic (American) brand name, an American (Hispanic)-accented spokesperson induced higher brand sincerity than when a spokesperson had a Hispanic (American) accent. In support of hypothesis 3, these results demonstrate that a congruity of an accent with a product ethnicity, versus brand ethnicity, drives brand sincerity perceptions.

Our research contributes to the literature by demonstrating how the use of Hispanic versus American accent affects the way consumers perceive brand sincerity. In resonance with source congruity theory, we find that a match between an accent and a product ethnicity boosts brand sincerity perceptions. Finally, this research deepens our understanding of the interaction effect of brand and product ethnicities that both determine more effective selection of a spokesperson accent. Overall, our findings have significant implications for brand managers as they consider using accented spokespersons to engender sincerity perceptions for brands that cross ethnic boundaries.

REFERENCES

Bresnahan, M.J., R. Ohashi, R. Nebashi, W.Y. Liu, and S. Moringa Shearman (2002), "Attitudinal and Affective Response toward Accented English," *Language and Communication*, 22, 171–86.

Chattalas, Michael, Thomas Kramer, and Hirokazu Takada (2008), "The Impact of National Stereotypes on the Country of Origin Effect: A Conceptual Framework," *International Marketing Review*, 25 (1), 54-74.

Cuddy, Amy J. C., Susan T. Fiske, and Peter Glick (2008), "Warmth and Competence as Universal Dimensions of Social Perception: The Stereotype Content Model and the BIAS Map," in *Advances in Experimental Social Psychology*, Vol. 40, ed. Mark P. Zanna. New York, NY: Academic Press, 61-149.

DeShields, Oscar W., Jr., Ali Kara, and Erdener Kaynak (1996), "Source Effects in Purchase Decisions: The Impact of Physical Attractiveness and Accent of Salesperson," *International Journal of Research in Marketing*, 13, 89-101.

Ramus, F., Hauser M.D., Miller C., Morris D., and Mehler J. (2000), "Language Discrimination by Human Newborns and by Cotton-Top Tamarin Monkeys," *Science*, 288, 349–51.

Ray, George B. (1986), "Vocally Cued Personality Prototypes: An Implicit Personality Theory Approach," *Communication Monographs*, 53 (September), 266-76.

Torelli, Carlos J. and Rohini Ahluwalia (2012), "Extending Culturally Symbolic Brands: A Blessing or a Curse?," *Journal of Consumer Research*, 38 (February), forthcoming.

For Love of Brand and Community: Why Self-Brand Connection Changes the Nature of Social Comparisons Involving Prestige Brands.

Jill Sundie, University of Texas at San Antonio, USA
Daniel Beal, Rice University, USA
Andrew Perkins, University of Western Ontario, Canada
James Ward, Arizona State University, USA

EXTENDED ABSTRACT

Nearly all consumers have coveted at least one prestige branded product (Taylor and Harrison 2008). Imagine a boy infatuated with Ferrari automobiles since age 8, displaying Ferrari posters on his bedroom wall, and reading any car magazine that featured the Ferrari. Unable to afford one himself, how would this now grown man respond when confronted with a peer who owns and drives his beloved vehicle? Such upward social comparisons are often emotionally laden, prompting feelings of inferiority and envy (Smith and Kim 2007). Sundie et al. (2009) demonstrated that envy generated by possession of a prestige product can quickly transmute into hostile, aggressive emotions. While the rapid transmutation of envy into hostility is conceptualized as a self-protective response, aimed at alleviating the self-threat posed by the upward comparison (Smith and Kim 2007), these feelings can prompt attitude change and behaviors that may ultimately be damaging to the prestige brand (Sundie et al. 2009).

Must the aspiration to obtain a prestige product always transform envy into hostility during social comparison? In the present research, we examine how, and why, strong connections between the self and the brand (Escalas and Bettman 2003) can change the emotional experience of social comparisons involving those brands. In the first study, we examine whether implicit self-brand connections can reduce the threatening nature of an upward comparison involving a prestige branded product. Study two examines a potential mediator of the effect of self-brand connection on hostile responses to envy in social comparison--felt connection between the self and other owners of the prestige brand. A summary of our findings is: To the extent that people feel a strong *self*-connection to the prestige *brand*, envy is less likely to transmute into other hostile emotions during an upward social comparison involving that brand. A key variable accounting for *why* a strong self-brand connection weakens the envy-hostility link during social comparison is the felt connection between the self and other *owners* of the prestige brand.

Study 1 examined how self-brand connection (assessed with a self-brand implicit association test or IAT; Perkins and Forehand 2012) affected the emotions experienced when making an upward social comparison based on a prestige brand (Lexus). After completing a self-Lexus IAT, 125 participants read a short social comparison scenario about someone fairly similar (another college student) who owned a sporty Lexus (price and picture of vehicle were provided). They then were asked about their emotional responses to this scenario (e.g., happy, envious; instructions and measures taken from Sundie et al. 2009). Finally, dispositional envy was measured as a control variable (Smith et al. 1999). We anticipated and found that implicit self-brand connection moderated the link between envy and hostility, such that stronger self-brand connections reduced the transmutation of envy into other hostile emotions (β for interaction = -.15, $p<.05$). Because self-brand connection was measured implicitly, it is highly unlikely that it influenced responses to the subsequent emotional measures (i.e., reducing the potential for demand effects). The fact that a range of emotions (very positive to very negative) were assessed after the presentation of the social comparison scenario also reduces the possibility of any demand effects (Sundie et al. 2009).

In research examining *antecedents* of self-brand connection (Escalas and Bettman 2003; 2005), consumption of a brand by reference group members, or brand associations consistent with the in-group, predicted developing a self-brand connection. Here, we examine *consequences* of self-brand connection for emotions experienced in a status consumption context, where social comparisons routinely occur. Intergroup emotions theory (Mackie et al. 2000) posits group identification (Turner 1991) will encourage positive emotional responses to group members possessing social advantages. Thus, the more individuals see another who possesses an envied product as a part of the self, the less inclined they should be to experience negative emotions. We hypothesized that felt connections between the self and *brand owners* may account for the dampening effect of self-brand connection on the envy-hostility link common to social comparisons involving status products.

Study 2 was designed to replicate study 1 findings, but extend upon it in two key ways: by using a validated *explicit* measure of self-brand connection (Escalas and Bettman 2003), and by examining a potential mediator of the moderating influence of self-brand connection on the envy-hostility link during social comparison (i.e., testing for mediated moderation). 305 participants completed the study for course credit. Participants selected a desirable luxury car from eight options, then reported their connection with that brand, α = .91. Next participants read a social comparison scenario featuring a peer who owned that prestige vehicle. Participants then reported their emotional responses to the scenario (as in study 1) and the extent to which they felt connected to owners of that prestige vehicle--this connection measure depicted increasingly overlapping circles (e.g., Tropp and Wright 2001); one circle represented "Me"; the other circle represented "Owners" of the luxury car. Dispositional envy was again measured as a control. Mediated moderation was tested using a path-analytic framework, consistent with the most recent published recommendations (Edwards and Lambert 2007). As anticipated, the interaction effect of self-brand connection and envy on hostility was mediated by the same interaction involving the overlap-with-brand-owners measure (see Figure 1). The indirect effect linking SBCx-Envy to Hostility is significant at p = .05, using Mplus' bootstrapped standard errors.

This research contributes to the envy literature, helping to clarify when envy will transmute into hostility during social comparison. Our studies also contribute to the literature on self-brand connection by showing that felt connection with brand owners (not just connection between self and the brand) changes the nature of social comparisons involving prestige brands; dampening hostile reactions to envy evoked by a similar other who owns a coveted brand. We also demonstrate this effect of self-brand connection in social comparison is driven by felt overlap with prestige brand owners. Our results imply that to the extent luxury good marketers can encourage brand coveters to feel connected to brand owners (e.g., through clubs, discussion forums, reality television), they may succeed in dampening hostile envy.

Advances in Consumer Research
Volume 40, ©2012

Figure 1. Moderating effects of self-brand connection (SBC; Panel A) and overlap with brand owners (Overlap; Panel B) on the Envy-Hostility link.

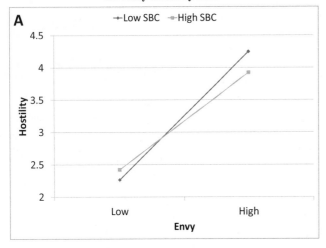

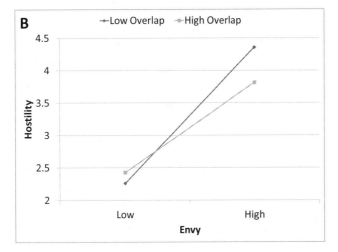

REFERENCES

Edwards, J. R. and L. S. Lambert (2007), "Methods for Integrating Moderation and Mediation: A General Analytical Framework Using Moderated Path Analysis," *Psychological Methods*, 12, 1-22.

Escalas, Jennifer E. and James R. Bettman (2003), "You Are What They Eat: The Influence of Reference Groups on Consumers' Connections to Brands," *Journal of Consumer Psychology*, *13*(3), 339-348.

Escalas, Jennifer E. and James R. Bettman (2005), "Self-Construal, Reference Groups, and Brand Meaning," *Journal of Consumer Research*, 32(3), 378-389.

Mackie, D. M., T. Devos and E. R. Smith (2000), "Intergroup Emotions: Explaining Offensive Action Tendencies in an Intergroup Context," *Journal of Personality and Social Psychology*, 79, 602-616.

Perkins, Andrew W. and Mark R. Forehand (2012), "Implicit Self-Referencing: The Effect of Non-Volitional Self-Association on Brand and Product Attitude," *Journal of Consumer Research* 39 (June), 142-156.

Smith, R. H., W. G. Parrott, E. F. Diener, R. H. Hoyle and S. H. Kim (1999), "Dispositional Envy," *Personality and Social Psychology Bulletin*, 25(8), 1007-1020.

Smith, R. H., and S. H. Kim (2007), "Comprehending Envy," *Psychological Bulletin*, 133(1), 46-64.

Sundie, Jill M., James C. Ward, Daniel J. Beal, Wynne W. Chin and Stephanie Geiger-Oneto (2009), "Schadenfreude as a Consumption-Related Emotion: Feeling Happiness about the Downfall of Another's Product," *Journal of Consumer Psychology*, 19(3), 356-373.

Taylor, J. and D. Harrison (2008), *The New Elite: Inside the Minds of the Truly Wealthy*, New York, NY: AMACOM.

Tropp, L. R. and S. C. Wright (1996), "Ingroup Identification as the Inclusion of Ingroup in the Self," *Personality and Social Psychology Bulletin*, 27(5), 585-600.

Turner, J. C. (1991), *Social Influence*, Milton Keynes, UK: Open University Press.

Do You Believe in Love at First Sight? I Do: Implicit Self-Theories and Attitude Strength

JaeHwan Kwon, University of Iowa, USA
Dhananjay Nayakankuppam, University of Iowa, USA

EXTENDED ABSTRACT

A consistent finding in the attitude literature is that strong attitudes are products of effortful cognitive elaboration (Petty and Cacioppo 1984; Petty and Wegener 1999). We argue that the link between elaboration and attitude strength could be more complicated.

Dweck, Chiu and Hong (1995) have identified two distinct implicit self-theories—entity vs. incremental theory—and have shown that each theory has a variety of influences on the theory holders' information processing and judgments. People who endorse entity theory (entity theorists) believe that their personal traits (i.e., personality, intelligence, and morality) are fixed, while people who endorse incremental theory (incremental theorists) view their personal traits as malleable. This line of research has found that individuals can extend their implicit self-theories: individuals apply their beliefs in personal traits not only to themselves, but also to other individuals.

We propose that individuals can extend their implicit-self theories, even to products or brands, and that implicit self-theories will affect individuals' attitude formation processes. Specifically, entity theorists will form attitudes toward products or brands more quickly (i.e., with less elaboration), but the strengths associated with the attitudes will be stronger than incremental theorists. That is, depending on implicit self-theories, individuals may form strong attitudes without elaboration.

STUDY 1: THE RELATIONSHIP BETWEEN IMPLICIT SELF-THEORY AND ATTITUDE FORMATION TIME AND ATTITUDE STRENGTH

We investigate whether entity theorists take less time than incremental theorists to form attitudes toward brands, and whether the strengths associated with the attitudes formed by entity theorists are stronger than those by incremental theorists. Attitude formation time was measured using Media Lab software while each participant viewed a computer screen showing a print ad for a new brand and indicated his or her attitude on a like-dislike dichotomous scale. After a thirty-minute lag, attitude strength was assessed both by metacognitive measures (direct responses; e.g., "How certain are you about your opinion?") and by attitude accessibility (indirect responses: response latency to access and express an attitude).

The results support our prediction that an individual's dispositional implicit self-theory orientation affects his/her attitudes, attitude formation time, and attitude strength. The results illustrate that, compared with incremental theorists, entity theorists quickly form attitudes that are congruent with the position of a persuasive message (β = -.37, t (62) = -2.99, p < .01). Further, even though they formed attitudes quickly, they held the attitudes more strongly than incremental theorists (β = .26, t (62) = 2.09, p < .05).

STUDY 2: THE CAUSAL IMPACT OF IMPLICIT SELF-THEORY ON ATTITUDE FORMATION TIME AND ATTITUDE STRENGTH

We validate the causal relationships between implicit self-theory and attitudes. In Study 1, we did not address the question of causality. In Study 2, we manipulate an individual's implicit self-theory orientation using the generalized implicit self-theory manipulation technique (Chiu, Hong, and Dweck, 1997).

The results replicated those of Study 1: entity theory priming reduced the time taken to form attitudes (F (1, 105) = 18.12, p < .001), but increased the strength associated with the attitudes (F (1, 105) = 6.71, p < .025).

STUDY 3: COGNITIVE ELABORATION—THE DIFFERENCE IN ATTITUDE FORMATION PROCESS BETWEEN ENTITY AND INCREMENTAL THEORISTS

Next, we manipulate the argument quality of a persuasive message (strong vs. weak argument) and examine if the level of cognitive elaboration is different between entity and incremental theorists when forming attitudes.

The results support the idea that the strong attitudes formed by entity theorists are not the results of effortful cognitive elaboration. The two-way, implicit self-theory by argument quality interaction on attitude demonstrates that only incremental theorists were affected by argument quality manipulation, whereas entity theorists were not. Incremental theorists formed more message-congruent attitudes under the strong argument condition and less message-congruent attitudes under the weak argument condition (F (1, 77) = 10.52, p < .001). In contrast, attitudes formed by entity theorists did not differ by argument quality manipulation (F (1, 77) = .20, NS). These results demonstrate that entity theorists exerted low levels of cognitive elaboration, whereas incremental theorists exerted high levels of elaboration. Nevertheless, attitude strengths of entity theorists were significantly greater than those of incremental theorists (p < .025). Taken together, although they did not exerted effortful cognitive elaboration when forming attitudes, entity theorists formed stronger attitudes than incremental theorists. These findings contradicts with the prior notion that strong attitude is a product of effortful cognitive elaboration.

STUDY 4: WHAT THEN MAKES ENTITY THEORISTS FORM STRONGER ATTITUDES THAN INCREMENTAL THEORISTS?

We prepared four consumer reviews on the 3D-TV (two positive and two negative) and then made four different combinations: positive-to-positive, positive-to-negative, negative-to-positive, and negative-to-negative. Participants read only one of the four combinations.

The results reveal that entity theorists are likely to stick to the attitude formed based on first reviews, and they are not be willing to adjust it after second reviews are provided, while incremental theorists put more weight on second reviews. The purpose of Study 5 was to explore how and why entity theorists form and hold strong attitudes without elaboration. Our results give us an interesting explanation: entity theorists believe that everything is fixed, so that they do not need to adjust their attitudes once formed. As a result, they do not need to process all of the information available; they focus on only the first few pieces of information when forming attitudes, while incremental theorists focus on more recent pieces of information.

SUMMARY

The present study extends our understanding of the effect of implicit self-theory on the attitude formation process. Entity theorists form strong attitudes without effortful cognitive elaboration. Specifically, entity theorists form attitudes more quickly toward products and brands, and they hold these attitudes more strongly than incremental theorists. Our findings contribute to both the implicit self-theory and attitude strength literature.

REFERENCES

Cacioppo, John T. and Richard E. Petty (1982), "The Need for Cognition," *Journal of Personality and Social Psychology*, 42, 116-31.

Chiu, Chi-yue, Ying-yi Hong, and Carol S. Dweck (1997), "Lay Dispositionism and Implicit Theories of Personality," *Journal of Personality and Social Psychology*, 73 (1), 19–30.

Dweck, Carol S., Chi-yue Chiu, and Ying-yi Hong (1995), "Implicit Theories and Their Role in Judgments and Reactions: A World from Two Perspectives," *Psychological Inquiry*, 6 (4), 267–85.

Erdley, C.S., and Carol S. Dweck (1993), "Children's Implicit Theories as Predictors of Their Social Judgments," *Children Development*, 64, 863-78.

Jarvis, W. Blare G. and Richard E. Petty (1996), "The Need to Evaluate," *Journal of Personality and Social Psychology*, 70, 172–194.

Petty, Richard E. and John T. Cacioppo (1984), "Source Factors and the Elaboration Likelihood Model of Persuasion," in L. Berkowitz (ed.), Advances in Experimental Social Psychology (vol. 19, pp. 123-205), San Diego, CA: Academic Press.

Petty, Richard E. and Duane T. Wegener (1999), "The Elaboration Likelihood Model: Current Status and Controversies," in Chaiken, Shelly and Trope Yaacov (Eds.), *Dual-Process Models in Social Psychology* (pp. 41-72), New York: Guilford.

Pomerantz, Eva M., Shelly Chaiken, and Rosalind S. Tordesillas (1995), "Altitude Strength and Resistance Process," *Journal of Personality and Social Psychology,* 69 (3), 408-19.

Visser, Penny. S., and Joel Cooper (2003), "Attitude change," in M. A. Hogg & J. Cooper (Eds.), *The Sage handbook of social psychology* (pp. 211–31), Thousand Oaks, CA: Sage.

Good or Bad, We Want It Now:
Resolution Theory Explains Magnitude Reversal in Intertemporal Choice

David Hardisty, Stanford University, USA
Kirstin Appelt, Columbia University, USA
Elke U. Weber, Columbia University, USA

EXTENDED ABSTRACT

Across four studies, outcome magnitude has opposite effects on intertemporal choice for gains and losses: consumers discount small gains more than large gains, but discount small losses *less* than large losses. Thought listings show that this is mediated by consumers' desire to resolve gains and losses as soon as possible.

Consumers often discount future consequences, for multiple reasons (Lynch and Zauberman 2006). The "magnitude effect" describes the fact that large gains are discounted more than small gains (Chapman and Elstein 1995; Estle et al. 2006; Thaler 1981). For example, someone might choose $10 today versus $11 in a year, yet prefer to wait for $11,000 in a year rather than take an immediate $10,000, even though in both cases the later amount is 10% larger than the sooner amount. In these earlier studies, the choice options always paired a smaller, sooner amount with a larger, later amount, so it was impossible for participants to express zero or negative discount rates. Thus, although some people might rather pay $10 immediately rather than $9 in a year (to get the loss over with), this preference could never be expressed. A pilot study we ran suggests that when negative discount rates are allowed, losses may show a *reverse* magnitude effect: Consumers considering small losses were indifferent between paying $10 today and $9.70 in six months (a -6% discount rate), whereas those considering large losses were indifferent between paying $1,000 today and $1,070 in six months (a 13% discount rate).

Although several models have been proposed to explain the magnitude effect (al-Nowaihi and Dhami 2009; Benhabib, Bisin, and Schotter 2010; Loewenstein and Prelec 1992; Scholten and Read 2010), none predict the interaction of magnitude and sign. To fill this gap, we propose *resolution theory*: Consumers have a psychological desire to resolve both gains *and* losses immediately, and this desire is combined with multiple other factors (such as uncertainty, see Table 1) to ultimately predict time preference. In the case of gains, people want the gain immediately to satisfy their desire for positive outcomes and to avoid feelings of deprivation while waiting (Hoch and Loewenstein 1991). When combined with other factors, which also favor the immediate gain, the resulting discount rate is high. In the case of losses, people want to get the loss over with immediately to close their mental books on the loss and avoid having to allocate attention and emotional capacity (e.g., dread) to looming future losses (Harris 2010; Loewenstein 1987). When balanced against other factors, which instead favor the delayed loss, the resulting discount rate is low. In both cases, the desire to resolve gains and losses is relatively insensitive to magnitude; it is a constant that is added to other attractions of the immediate reward (an assumption supported by Benhabib et al., 2010, for the domain of gains), rather than a parameter that multiplies the immediate reward's utility.

Importantly, resolution theory makes the prediction that *negative* discounting of losses will occur when amounts are small enough, because the cost of waiting is a constant that is added to the disutility

Table 1. *Summary of major factors hypothesized to determine intertemporal choices for gains and losses.*

Motivational Factor	Description	Makes people prefer to have...	Scales with magnitude?
Opportunity cost and investment (Franklin 1748; Samuelson 1937)	Resources can be invested and earn interest or otherwise grow over time	Gains now and losses later	Yes
Uncertainty (Patak and Reynolds 2007; Takahashi, Ikeda, and Hasegawa 2007)	Delayed gains and losses may never be realized	Gains now and losses later	Yes
Resource slack (Zauberman and Lynch 2005)	Expecting to have more resources in the future means that immediate resources are more dear than future resources	Gains now and losses later	Yes
Resolution (Benhabib et al. 2010; Harris 2010; Loewenstein 1987; O'Donoghue and Rabin 1999)	Psychological desire to resolve events immediately	Both gains and losses now	No
Other factors, such as social norms and ideals (Krantz and Kunreuther 2007)	Variable, but often suggest that individuals ought to delay gratification	Variable, but often postponing gains and attending to losses immediately	Variable

of the larger later loss. Negative discounting implies that outcome values intensify (i.e., positives become more positive and negatives become more negative) the further they lie in the future; in the case of losses, negative discounting means a preference to have losses sooner rather than later. For example, some people might rather pay $10 immediately rather than $9 in a year, to satisfy their desire to get the loss over with. In this case, a full *reversal* of the magnitude effect when comparing small and large losses is understandable.

METHOD

In four separates studies (total $N = 856$), participants made a series of choices between immediate and future gains and losses of different amounts. Three of these studies were run online with national samples and hypothetical outcomes, and one study was run in the lab with a student sample and real intertemporal gains and losses (in the range of $5 to $100). In two studies participants used an established type-aloud protocol (Hardisty, Johnson, and Weber 2010; Weber et al. 2007) to record their thoughts before making their decisions. Participants subsequently categorized their own previously recorded thoughts according to the factors listed in Table 1.

RESULTS

In all four studies, participants discounted small gains more than large gains, replicating the magnitude effect, and discounted small losses less than large losses, reliably establishing the reverse effect of magnitude on losses. Zero and negative discount rates were quite common when considering small losses; 78% of participants expressed this preference. In contrast, only 23% of those considering large losses, 2% of those considering small gains, and 2% of those considering large gains showed zero or negative discount rates.

Prior to making their choices, participants listed an average of 3.4 thoughts. As predicted by Resolution Theory, the proportion of resolution thoughts was significantly lower for large magnitude outcomes than for small magnitude outcomes. In other words, when participants considered $10, they frequently mentioned their psychological desire to resolve the situation as soon as possible, whereas when participants considered $10,000, other concerns were more prominent. Also as predicted, the proportion of resolution thoughts mediated the effect of magnitude on discount rates for gains and losses.

DISCUSSION

Our findings may offer some guidance to policy-makers hoping to encourage future-oriented decision making (i.e., low discount rates). As suggested by both previous research and the present findings, patience for gains may be encouraged by focusing on large magnitude outcomes. For example, an individual may be encouraged to save for retirement if the benefits of saving are aggregated over ten years of savings, rather than one year or one month. As the present research shows, however, the same strategy should *not* be applied to losses; consumers are motivated to take care of small losses immediately, but large losses are likely to be postponed until later. Therefore, a strategy of aggregating credit card debt or other debt into one large lump sum may be counterproductive, and lead consumers to delay paying off the large debt. Rather, breaking the problem down into smaller pieces that can be taken care of immediately should be more effective. Consumers will often choose to get losses over with immediately, but only if they are small and manageable.

REFERENCES

al-Nowaihi, A. and S. Dhami (2009), "A Value Function That Explains the Magnitude and Sign Effects," *Economic Letters*, 105, 224-29.

Benhabib, J., A. Bisin, and A. Schotter (2010), "Present-Bias, Quasi-Hyperbolic Discounting, and Fixed Costs," *Games and economic behavior*, 69 (2), 205-23.

Chapman, Gretchen B. and A. S. Elstein (1995), "Valuing the Future: Discounting Health and Money," *Medical Decision Making*, 15, 373-86.

Estle, S. J., L. Green, J. Myerson, and D. D. Holt (2006), "Differential Effects of Amount on Temporal and Probability Discounting of Gains and Losses," *Memory & Cognition*, 34, 914-28.

Franklin, Benjamin (1748), "Advice to a Young Tradesman."

Hardisty, D. J., E. J. Johnson, and E. U. Weber (2010), "A Dirty Word or a Dirty World? Attribute Framing, Political Affiliation, and Query Theory," *Psychological Science*, 21 (1), 86-92.

Harris, Christine R. (2010), "Feelings of Dread and Intertemporal Choice," *Journal of Behavioral Decision Making*.

Hoch, Stephen J. and George Loewenstein (1991), "Time-Inconsistent Preferences and Consumer Self-Control," *Journal of Consumer Research*, 17 (4), 492-507.

Krantz, David H. and Howard C. Kunreuther (2007), "Goals and Plans in Decision Making," *Judgment and Decision Making*, 2, 137-68.

Loewenstein, George (1987), "Anticipation and the Valuation of Delayed Consumption," *Economic Journal*, 97, 666-84.

Loewenstein, George and Drazen Prelec (1992), "Anomalies in Intertemporal Choice: Evidence and Interpretation," *The Quarterly Journal of Economics*, 107 (2), 573-97.

Lynch, J. G. and G. Zauberman (2006), "When Do You Want It? Time, Decisions, and Public Policy," *Journal of Public Policy & Marketing*, 25 (1), 67-78.

O'Donoghue, Ted and M. Rabin (1999), "Doing It Now or Later," *American Economic Review*, 89, 103-24.

Patak, M. and B. Reynolds (2007), "Question-Based Assessments of Delay Discounting: Do Respondents Spontaneously Incorporate Uncertainty into Their Valuations for Delayed Rewards?," *Addictive Behaviors*, 32, 351-57.

Samuelson, P (1937), "A Note on Measurement of Utility," *Review of Economic Studies*, 4, 155-61.

Scholten, M. and Daniel Read (2010), "The Psychology of Intertemporal Tradeoffs," *Psychological Review*, 117 (3), 925-44.

Takahashi, T., Koki Ikeda, and Toshikazu Hasegawa (2007), "A Hyperbolic Decay of Subjective Probability of Obtaining Delayed Rewards," *Behavioral and Brain Functions*, 3, 52.

Thaler, Richard (1981), "Some Empirical Evidence on Dynamic Inconsistency," *Economics Letters*, 8, 201-07.

Weber, E. U., E. J. Johnson, K. F. Milch, H. Chang, J. C. Brodscholl, and D. G. Goldstein (2007), "Asymmetric Discounting in Intertemporal Choice," *Psychological Science*, 18 (6), 516-23.

Zauberman, G. and J. J. G. Lynch (2005), "Resource Slack and Propensity to Discount Delayed Investments of Time Versus Money," *Journal of Experimental Psychology: General*, 134 (1), 23-37.

Accentuate the Positive: How Identity Affects Customer Satisfaction

Tilottama G. Chowdhury, Quinnipiac University, USA
Kalpesh K. Desai, State University of New York, Binghamton, USA
Lisa Bolton, Penn State University, USA

EXTENDED ABSTRACT

Consumers use products to create and communicate their identities (Kleine, Kleine, and Allen 1995; Sirgy 1982). As self-relevant social categories (e.g., male, college student), identities can appropriate associations belonging to brands and form connections between brands and consumer self-concepts (Escalas and Bettman 2003). Past research has shown that salient identities guide thinking, judgment, and behavior (Tajfel and Turner 1979), including brand preference (Escalas and Bettman 2005) and choice (Berger and Heath 2007). Compared to analytic thinking, identity-driven thinking leads to judgment that resists change (Bolton and Reed 2004). Surprisingly, prior research has not yet examined the robustness of identity-driven judgment to direct product experience—an issue that Swaminathan, Page, and Gurhan-Canli (2007) exhort academics to investigate. Specifically, the present research asks: How will identity-based thinking affect (dis)satisfaction with an experience?

Research in the disconfirmation paradigm of product satisfaction suggests that post-choice satisfaction is based on the performance of the product relative to a comparison standard, typically, pre-choice expectations (e.g., Cadotte, Woodruff, and Jenkins 1987; Oliver 1989). That is, performance above (below) expectations leads to satisfaction (dissatisfaction). Prior research has also provided evidence that cognitive cues, such as brand name (Richardson, Dick and Jain 1994) and product category (Stayman, Alden, and Smith 1992), can alter satisfaction. For example, the match/mismatch between expectations engendered by product category and product taste (in the fruit juice category) influenced satisfaction, independent of product taste (Stayman et al. 1992).

While brand and category labels are cognitive cues that influence evaluations through expectations, we argue that identity is a motivational cue that will operate primarily through performance perceptions. Prior research (Oyserman (2009) suggests that consuming identity-linked products imbues choice with more meaning, that is, expressive rather than utilitarian. Thus, a positive experience with the product will enable identity-primed consumer to enjoy both the expressive and utilitarian "components" of the product, resulting in greater satisfaction compared to non id-primed consumers who will avail only of the utilitarian element of product consumption. In contrast, a negative experience fails to deliver on functionality but also denies identity-expression to identity-primed consumers; if so, then identity-priming may exacerbate dissatisfaction following a negative experience. However, Oyserman (2009) proposes an opposite effect suggesting when products are identity-congruent they are preferred despite negative performance: "once a product is identity-congruent, it becomes what 'we' use, separate from utilitarian concerns". Given these two opposing effects, no net effect of identity on satisfaction with a negative experience may emerge.

Hypothesis 1: *Identity-based marketing will moderate the impact of product experience on customer satisfaction such that a) customers will be more satisfied following a positive experience when the product primes identity (versus not); and b) dissatisfaction with a negative experience will not differ as a function of identity.*

In contrast to category schema and brand names which are cognitive cues that evoke specific product expectations, identity is a motivational cue. Thus, the impact of identity on satisfaction is posited to occur via performance perceptions rather than expectations. That is, identity-based thinking will lead consumers to perceive performance as more superior when positive. Inasmuch as negative experience is unambiguously inconsistent with identity, then no identity-driven 'bias' is expected to emerge for a negative experience.

Hypothesis 2: *Performance perceptions will mediate the effects of identity and experience on satisfaction.*

Because the positive experience hypothesis is primarily driven by the motivational element of using the identity-linked product, we expect this effect to manifest only when consumers feel comfortable expressing or using their identity-driven interpretation of product performance. Specifically, we expect the effect posited in H1a to be stronger when consumption is either private or in the company of others who share the same identity (versus others who do not share the identity or who are of unknown identity). That is, identity enhances satisfaction with positive experiences when the setting favors identity-expression; otherwise, identity effects will not emerge.

Hypothesis 3: *Identity effects on satisfaction with a positive experience will emerge when consumption is private or the audience shares the same identity (vs. unknown or different).*

Six experiments were conducted to investigate these hypotheses. Across all experiments, identity was primed (vs. not) via an advertisement. Participants were then asked to imagine themselves as a customer and reported expectations. Participants then experienced (either real or imagined) the product, and experience valence was manipulated (along with other factors germane to hypotheses). After experience, satisfaction and perceived product performance were measured.

Study 1 examined real experience. Analyses revealed a significant identity by experience interaction on customer satisfaction ($F(1, 68) = 4.94$, $p < .05$) such that identity increases satisfaction with a positive but not negative experience. Study 2 replicated this interaction for an imagined product experience ($F(1,159) = 6.2$, $p = .01$) and demonstrated mediation by perceived product performance. These results support H1 and H2.

Studies 3 and 4 test boundary conditions on the phenomenon. Specifically, the identity effect was enhanced i) for private (vs. public-identity unknown) consumption [($F(1,160) = 5.09$, $p < .05$] and ii) when the purchase decision was made by another (vs. self) [($F(1, 52) = 9.80$, $p < .01$]. Finally, studies 5 and 6 test generalizability of our findings to i) another identity and to ii) service recovery (vs. a negative experience). (Details omitted for brevity's sake.) These results support H1—H3.

Together, these findings make four contributions. First, prior research has tended to investigate identity effects on judgment and choice and has not, to our knowledge, examined identity effects on satisfaction. We find that identity effects emerge for positive experience but do not emerge for negative experience—suggesting an important constraint on the 'power' of identity posited in prior research.

Second, our results point to mediation by performance perceptions. That is, identity-based thinking influences satisfaction through motivated interpretation of the experience (versus expectations). Third, our research identifies a boundary condition for the positive effects of identity on satisfaction: private or public consumption in which identity-expression is not constrained. Finally, these findings contribute to the satisfaction literature by investigating the role of identity in consumption and as a driver of customer satisfaction.

REFERENCES

Berger, Jonah and Chip Heath (2007), "Where Consumers Diverge from Others: Identity-Signaling and Product Domains," *Journal of Consumer Research*, 34(2), 121-134.

Bolton, Lisa E. and Americus Reed II (2004), "Sticky Priors: The Perseverance of Identity Effects on Judgment," *Journal of Marketing Research,* 41 (November), 397-411.

Cadotte, Ernest R., Robert B. Woodruff, and Roger L. Jenkins (1987), "Expectations and norms in models of consumer satisfaction," *Journal of Marketing Research*, 24, 305-314.

Escalas, Jennifer Edson and James R. Bettman (2005), "Self-Construal, Reference Groups, and Brand Meaning," *Journal of Consumer Research,* 32 (December), 378-389.

------------------------ (2003), "You Are What They Eat: The Influence of Reference Groups on Consumer Connections to Brands," *Journal of Consumer Psychology*, 13 (3), 339-348.

Kleine, Susan Schultz, Robert E. Kleine, III, and Chris T. Allen (1995), "How is a Possession 'Me' or 'Not Me'? Characterizing Types and an Antecedent of Material Possession Attachment," *Journal of Consumer Research*, 22 (December), 327-343.

Oliver, Richard L. (1989), "Processing of the Satisfaction Response in Consumption: A Suggested Framework and Research Propositions," *Journal of Consumer Satisfaction, Dissatisfaction and Complaining Behavior*, 2, 1-16.

Oyserman, Daphna (2009), "Identity-based motivation: Implications for action-readiness, procedural-readiness, and consumer behavior," *Journal of Consumer Psychology*, 19, 250-260.

Richardson, Paul S., Alan S. Dick, and Arun K. Jain (1994), "Extrinsic and Intrinsic Cue Effects on Perceptions of Store Brand Quality," *Journal of Marketing*, 58 (October), 28-36.

Sirgy, M. J. (1982), "Self-Concept in Consumer Behavior: A Critical Review," *Journal of Consumer Research,* 9 (December), 287-300.

Stayman, Douglas M., Dana L. Alden, and Karen H. Smith (1992), "Some Effects of Schematic Processing on Consumer Expectations and Disconfirmation Judgments," *Journal of Consumer Research*, 19 (September), 240-255.

Swaminathan, Vanitha, Karen Page, and Zeynep Gurhan-Canli (2007), "My Brand or Our Brand: Individual-and Group-Based Brand Relationships and Self-Construal Effects on Brand Evaluations," *Journal of Consumer Research*, 34(2), 248-259.

Tajfel, Henri and Turner, John C. (1979), An Integrative Theory of Intergroup Conflict, In W. G. Austin & S. Worchel (Eds.), *The Social Psychology of Intergroup Relations*. Monterey, CA: Brooks-Cole .

Cultures of Caring Consumption: Social Support and the Self in the Myeloma Community

Susan Dunnett, University of Edinburgh Business School, UK
Paul Hewer, University of Strathclyde, UK
Douglas Brownlie, University of Stirling, UK

EXTENDED ABSTRACT

"You just don't get the pros and cons and things with your doctor, you don't understand treatment options, what's coming down the pipe... I was at one of the support group meetings and we were just going around the room talking about things and [the group leader] mentions "XXX is thinking about [getting] a transplant". So they kinda went around the room, and as you know in these groups um, it's just a great big pot of everything you can think of, every combination of something that people have gone through... So that group is real important. I come back with stuff from the group that I bring to my doctor: "Why aren't we looking at this or that? When are we going to be testing for this? You know, what's the future treatment plan?" (Interview Data).

This study explores the ways in which the collective practices of consumption community formation and sustainment can be understood as a *technology* (Foucault, 1988) employed in the *caring for oneself* (Foucault, 1986). Taking inspiration from studies which have broadened out the domain of consumer research to include diverse groups living with serious illness (Adelman 1993; Kates, 2002; Pavia and Mason, 2004; Wong and King, 2008), the context for this investigation is the U.S. Myeloma community[1]. Through a phenomenological approach, utilising non-participant observation and depth interviews (Thompson et al., 1989; Turner and Wainwright, 2003; Forss et al 2004), attention is drawn to the importance of collective practices which emerge from community-based, patient-led support groups; particularly a network of 3 patient-led, community-based support groups in the Mid-west, accessed through a group leader who acted as gatekeeper. A period of contextualisation, drawing on informal interviews with community members and community-produced secondary data, was followed by non-participant observation at support group meetings over a period of 4 months. Subsequently 20 face-to-face depth interviews were carried out with 15 Myeloma patients and their spouses or family members - "carers", as they are known.

We employ a consumer research lens (Lupton, 1997; Henwood et al, 2003; Kates, 2002; Pavia and Mason, 2004; Wong and King, 2007), to explore the co-creation of social resources within such groups. As our interview data reveals (see above), the support groups are discursively positioned as receptacles of first-hand market information, with much of the narrative exchange within the group being concerned with navigating and (re)calibrating one's relationship with the healthcare, pharmaceutical and health insurance industries. Crucially this culture of information-exchange fosters a sense of belonging through the care for oneself and others. Or, as Foucault would have preferred: "The care of the self – or the attention one devotes to the care that others should take of themselves – appears then as an intensification of social relations." (Foucault, 1986: 53). The support groups operate as consumption communities where culturally accepted self-care practices deemed necessary to 'living with myeloma', are shared amongst patients and their carers (Whelan 2007).

Through our analysis we reveal a range of collective practices which emerge from this 'intensification of social relations' (Foucault, 1986). Crucial amongst these are the sharing and mediating of information, helping, storytelling and the fostering of personal responsibility and obligation. Such practices serve to sustain, replicate and energise the collective, but also to intensify the responsibilities of individual members through their participation. Carrying out the business of *identity work*[2], informants report being empowered with a sense of self-confidence and a new-found ability to negotiate various healthcare systems (Lo and Stacey 2008). The Myeloma community, through its cultivation of social and agentic practices, thus provides a space for members to 'forge new meanings and incorporate these meanings into changing self-conceptions' (Kates 2002: 636).

The medical marketplace is a realm where high-stakes decisions - concerning treatment, care, quality of life or insurance and other administrative matters - are made (Wong and King 2008; Botti et al 2009). We find that support groups function to provide patients with the emotional, social and knowledge resources to carry out complex decision making. Such is the focus on marketplace knowledge that we conceptualise support groups as a consumer-led solution to the dark side of consumer/patient empowerment – the burden of personal responsibility (Lupton 1997; Davies and Elliott 2006; Shankar et al 2006; Markus and Schwartz 2010). The study at hand is a demonstration not only of the ways in which community is (to use Foucault's term, 1988) a *technology* employed to develop the self and navigate the medical marketplace, but how a consumption collective – in its mutual disclosures, trust, shared hope, sense of belonging and other-centred ethos – can produce valuable emotional bonds and social resources. The extant literature has identified that consumption communities provide social support to members (Shouten and McAlexander 1995; Fournier and Lee 2009) but has been slow to explore this helping behaviour. By doing so, we answer Kozinets' (2002) call for consumption communities to be characterised as an 'ameliorative' to the effects of the marketplace (ibid: 34).

The study concludes that the robust and flexible culture of these support groups is crucial for understanding the transformation of the patient. The personal movement revealed is from a position of passivity, fear and objectification to one of *perceived* control, understanding and skilled navigation of the healthcare market. The resources constructed by such community-based support groups thus offer members access to and participation in a wealth of social practices for self-enhancement which transform the patient into an agent. Lupton noted (1997) that where the patient as consumer is examined, the privileged representation is that of 'dispassionate, thinking, calculating subject'; a depiction which draws heavily on models of consumer behaviour where consumers are seen as rational, economic decision-makers who benefit from sovereignty of choice.

---

1 Myeloma is an incurable, chronic form of bone marrow cancer. It is estimated that there are 75,000 – 100,000 myeloma patients at any one time in the USA, and upwards of 15,000 in the UK. Patients may have the disease for several years and it is characterised by periods of active disease and remission (Durie, 2003). Symptoms of this disease include pain, bone loss, anaemia and immune system suppression. Treatment is usually in the form of chemotherapy and/or stem cell transplantation.

---

2 Here we rely upon Schwalbe and Mason-Schrock: "anything people do, individually or collectively, to give meaning to themselves or others. Identity work is thus largely a matter of signifying, labelling, and defining. It also includes creation of the codes that enable self-signifying and the interpretation of others' signifying behavior." (1996: 115).

The archetypal counterpart to the consumerist patient is the passive or dependent patient, a model of unquestioning compliance (Lupton 1997). The study at hand unearths the lived experience beyond these simple conceptualisations; its contribution lies in the foregrounding of an under-researched aspect of communal consumption – the sharing of social support resources in order to realise agency within service interactions.

REFERENCES

Adelman, A. (1992) Rituals of Adversity and Re-membering: The Role of Possessions for persons living with AIDS, *Advances in Consumer Research*, Vol. 19. pp. 401-403.

Botti, S. Orfali, K. and Iyengar, S. (2009), Tragic Choices: Autonomy and Emotional Response to Medical Decisions, *Journal of Consumer Research*, Vol. 36, October, pp. 337-352.

Davies, A. and Elliott, R. (2006), The evolution of the empowered consumer, *European Journal of Marketing*, Vol. 40, No. 9/10, pp. 1106-1121.

Forss, A. Tishelman, C. Widmark, C. And Sachs, L. (2004), Women's experiences of cervical cellular changes: an unintentional transition from health to liminality?, *Sociology of Health and Illness*, Vol. 26 No. 3, pp. 306-325.

Foucault (1986), *The Care of Self: Volume 3 The History of Sexuality*, London, Allen Lane.

Fournier, S. and Lee. L. (2009), Getting Brand Communities Right, *Harvard Business Review*, April, pp. 105-111.

Henwood, F. Wyatt, S. Hart, A. and Smith, J. (2003), 'Ignorance is bliss sometimes': constraints on the emergence of the 'informed patient' in the changing landscapes of health information, Vol. 25, No. 6, pp. 589-607.

Kates, S.M. (2002), AIDS and community-based organizations: the marketing of therapeutic discourse, *European Journal of Marketing*, Vol. 36, No. 5/6, pp. 621-641.

Kozinets, R.V. (2002), Can Consumer Escape the Market? Emancipatory Illuminations from Burning Man, *Journal of Consumer Research*, Vol. 29 June, pp. 20-38.

Lo, M.M. and Stacey, C.L. (2008), Beyond cultural competency: Bourdieu, patients and clinical encounters, *Sociology of Health and Illness*, Vol. 30 No.5, pp. 741-755

Lupton, D. (1997), Consumerism, Reflexivity and the Medical Encounter, *Social Science and Medicine*, Vol. 45, No.3, pp. 373-381.

Markus, H.R. and Schwartz, B. (2010), Does Choice Mean Freedom and Well-Being?, *Journal of Consumer Research*, Vol. 37, August, pp. 344-355.

Pavia, T.M. and Mason, M.J. (2004), The Reflexive Relationship between Consumer Behaviour and Adaptive Coping, *Journal of Consumer Research*, Vol.31, September, pp. 441-454.

Schouten, J.W. and McAlexander, J.H. (1995), Subcultures of Consumption: An Ethnography of the new Bikers, *Journal of Consumer Research*, Vol. 22, June, pp 43-61.

Schwalbe, M.L. and Mason-Schrock, D. (1996), "Identity Work as Group Process", *Advances in Group Processes*, Vol.13, pp.113-147.

Shankar, A., Cherrier, H., and Canniford, R. (2006), Consumer Empowerment: A Foucauldian Interpretation, *European Journal of Marketing*, Vol. 40, No. 9/10, pp. 1013-1030.

Thompson, C.J., Locander, W.B., Pollio, H.R. (1989), Putting Consumer Experience Back into Consumer Research: The Philosophy and Method of Existential-Phenomenology, *Journal of Consumer Research*, Vol. 16, September, pp. 133-146.

Turner, B.S. and Wainwright, S.P. (2003), Corps de Ballet: the case of the injured ballet dancer, *Sociology of Health and Illness*, Vol. 25 No. 4, pp 269-288.

Whelan, E. (2007), 'No one agrees except those of us who have it': endometriosis patients as an epistemological community, *Sociology of Health and Illness*, Vol. 29 No. 7, pp, 957-982.

Wong, N. and King, T. (2008), The Cultural Construction of Risk Understandings Through Illness Narratives, *Journal of Consumer Research*, Vol. 34, February, pp. 579-594.

Everyday Objects of Desire:
Dimensions of Design Innovation and the Centrality of Product Aesthetics

Harold Cassab, University of Auckland, New Zealand
Claudiu Dimofte, San Diego State University, USA

EXTENDED ABSTRACT

It is commonly accepted that response to design novelty is influenced by perceptual fluency, either directly via affective evaluation of visual stimuli (cf. Winkielman et al. 2006), or indirectly via increased satisfaction generated by resolving a moderate challenge in stimulus evaluation (Reber, Schwarz, and Winkielman 2004). In addition, expertise facilitates the identification of sources of novelty and the efficient processing of product information (Alba and Hutchinson 1987). The link between novelty and consumer attitudes, however, is not entirely determined by perceptual fluency. Central to the response to design innovation are individuals' inferences about what the product affords (Hoegg and Alba 2011) and the importance of novelty in general for the user.

We propose that consumer preference for high versus low product novelty is jointly explained by the level of aesthetic infusion and its congruency with the perceived core value of the product (i.e., hedonic or utilitarian benefits). Yet previous research is ambivalent about the direction of the congruency effect. It is possible that products featuring high levels of design innovation will garner more favor if consumers find the aesthetic infusion congruent with the hedonic value they derive from the product (cf. Creusen and Schoormans 2005). In other words, hedonic products provide aesthetic design as a typical benefit, and presumably more thereof enhances the offer. However, it is also possible that design infusion into incongruent, utilitarian categories creates an unexpected consumer benefit through spillover inferences and thus more design innovation preference (cf. Hagtvedt and Patrick 2008). In other words, utilitarian products do not provide aesthetic design as a typical benefit, and presumably its additional inclusion enhances the offer. Research by Bertini, Ofek, and Ariely (2009) is informative and suggests that "non-alignable innovations" (i.e., utilitarian products featuring improvements in form and hedonic products with functional improvements) will garner more consumer preference. Thus, we posit that *consumer preference will be stronger for hedonic (utilitarian) products featuring innovation in function (form)*.

Differences in consumer response to innovative products are also related to individual traits such as need for uniqueness, variety seeking, or design sensitivity (Bloch 1995). The latter has been captured in consumer research via the *centrality of visual product aesthetics* (CVPA) construct (Bloch, Brunel, and Arnold 2003). Yet consumers generally find it hard to articulate the reasons why they prefer specific designs (Creusen and Schoormans 2005), and a much consumer research (e.g., Chartrand 2005) has been arguing for the role of automaticity in information processing and decision-making. In further support for the importance of automatic cognition, there may also be a disconnect between consumers' explicit responses and nonconscious reactions to innovation (see Wilson, Lindsey, and Schooler 2000). Thus, individuals may [claim to] like novel designs more in their explicit evaluations than their automatic responses would suggest, perhaps in order to appear more sophisticated. Conversely, they may erroneously argue that product innovativeness is not an important factor in their product assessments, when that is in fact very much the case (perhaps because they see themselves as reflective and not impulsive processors, cf. Strack, Werth, and Deutsch 2006). We examine the role that consumers' innate automatic preference for innovation plays in explaining CVPA effects on innovative product evaluations. We thus hypothesize that *automatic reactions to novelty mediate the effect of CVPA on consumer attitudinal response to innovative new products*.

STUDY 1

The first study assesses the extent to which there are different marketplace reactions to innovation based on two specific dimensions of design innovativeness (i.e., focus on function or form). In addressing H1, we evaluate the conditions under which design innovation in form is more or less likely to be attractive relative to functional innovation. We also evaluate the extent to which complementary improvements are better received by consumers faced with innovative products. Participants were randomly exposed to the picture of a purportedly new, innovative product and subsequently asked their opinions about it. Two product categories were employed: one pretested to be utilitarian (toothbrushes) and one hedonic (sunglasses). The design was a 2 (product value: utilitarian or hedonic) X 2 (dimension of innovativeness: functionality or aesthetics) X 2 (CVPA: low or high) factorial with the first two variables manipulated and the latter measured. The results (see Table 1) argue for a basic consumer preference for innovation in function for hedonic products and in form for utilitarian products. Innovative products are preferred more strongly by consumers high on CVPA. These consumers seem to universally prefer functional enhancements, whereas those low on CVPA seem to react more positively to nonalignable enhancements to both product types.

STUDY 2

This study evaluates the hypothesis that consumer attitudinal responses toward innovative products are generally spontaneous and automatic (see Veryzer 1999 for a related point). This argument suggests that the effect of CVPA is fully mediated by automatic, implicit responses to novelty. Results support the claim that consumers of high CVPA are more likely to appreciate innovative marketplace products. Their explicit liking for such products is based on an automatic, instinctive attraction to innovation and novelty (measured via the Implicit Association Test – Greenwald, McGhee, and Schwartz 1998), explaining why they like innovation in terms of both design and function, as well as for both utilitarian and hedonic products. The implicit appreciation of innovative designs explains the connection between CVPA and explicit attitudes.

STUDY 3

The final study assesses the effect of dimension of design innovativeness (i.e., function or form) for a more complex product category that is not disposable and thus entails more risk and requires more careful processing. We therefore extend the generalizability of our conceptual framework and also improve on the previous studies in two important ways. First, we evaluate the extent to which innovation enhances perceived value by including a control (i.e., no innovation condition) as the critical benchmark. Second, we replicate the automatic mediation effect of study 2 by having subjects perform IATs that involve actual product pictures as stimuli, as opposed to generic innovation-related words. Results are once again supportive of both hypotheses (see Table 2).

Table 1: Product Attitudes In Study 1

Product Value:	Utilitarian				Hedonic			
Improved:	Function		Form		Function		Form	
	Mean	S.E.	Mean	S.E.	Mean	S.E.	Mean	S.E.
Low CVPA Attitudes	3.50	.41	4.14[a]	.19	3.67	.30	3.07[b]	.23
High CVPA Attitudes	4.76	.28	4.42[a]	.28	5.23[b]	.27	3.75[c]	.29

Means within *the same* row with different *superscripts are significantly different* at $p < .05$ or lower.

Table 2: Product Attitudes In Study 3

Improved:	Nothing		Function		Form	
	Mean	S.E.	Mean	S.E.	Mean	S.E.
Low CVPA Attitudes	3.40[a]	.29	4.32[b]	.21	4.99[c]	.19
High CVPA Attitudes	2.79[a]	.20	4.95[b]	.23	5.41[b]	.18

Means within *the same* row with different *superscripts are significantly different* at $p < .05$ or lower.

REFERENCES

Alba, Joseph W. and J. Wesley Hutchinson (1987), "Dimensions of Consumer Expertise," *Journal of Consumer Research*, 13 (4), 411-454.

Bertini, Marco, Elie Ofek, and Dan Ariely (2009), "The Impact of Add-On Features on Consumer Product Evaluations," *Journal of Consumer Research*, 36 (2), 17-28.

Bloch, P. H. (1995). Seeking the Ideal Form: Product Design and Consumer Response. *Journal of Marketing*, 59 (3) 16-29.

------, Frederic. F., Brunel, and Todd J. Arnold (2003), "Individual Differences in the Centrality of Visual Product Aesthetics: Concept and Measurement," *Journal of Consumer Research*, 29 (4), 551-565.

Chartrand, Tanya (2005), "The Role of Conscious *Awareness* in Consumer Behavior," *Journal of Consumer Psychology*, 15 (3) 203-210.

Creusen, Marielle E. H. and Jan P. L. Schoormans (2005), "The Different Roles of Product Appearance in Consumer Choice," *Journal of Product Innovation Management*, 22 (1), 63-81.

Greenwald, Anthony G., Debbie E., McGhee, and Jordan L. K. Schwartz (1998), "Measuring Individual Differences in Implicit Cognition: The Implicit Association Test," *Journal of Personality and Social Psychology*, 74 (6), 1464-1480.

Hagtvedt, Henrik, and Vanessa M. Patrick (2008), "Art Infusion: The Influence of Visual Art on the Perception and Evaluation of Consumer Products," *Journal of Marketing Research*, 45 (2), 379-389.

Hoegg, JoAndrea, and Joseph W. Alba (2011), "Seeing is Believing (Too Much): The Influence of Product Form on Perceptions of Product Performance," *Journal of Product Innovation Management*, 28 (3), 346-359.

Reber, Rolf, Norbert Schwarz, and Piotr Winkielman (2004), "Processing Fluency and Aesthetic Pleasure: Is Beauty in the Perceiver's Processing Experience?" *Personality and Social Psychology Review*, 8 (4), 364-382.

Strack, Fritz, Lioba Werth, and Roland Deutsch (2006), "Reflective and Impulsive Determinants of Consumer Behavior," *Journal of Consumer Psychology*, 16 (3) 205-216.

Veryzer, Robert W. (1999), "A Nonconscious Processing Explanation of Consumer Response to Product Design," *Psychology and Marketing*, 16 (6), 497-522.

Wilson, Timothy D., Samuel Lindsey, and Tonya Y. Schooler (2000), "A Model of Dual Attitudes," *Psychological Review*, 107 (1) 101-126.

Winkielman, Piotr, Jamin Halberstadt, Tedra Fazendeiro, and Steve Catty (2006), "Prototypes Are Attractive Because They Are Easy on the Mind," *Psychological Science*, 17 (9), 799-806.

Inter-Racial Couples, Household Decision-Making and Contextual Influences on Consumer Acculturation

Wakiuru Wamwara-Mbugua, Wright State University, USA

EXTENDED ABSTRACT

This research examines household decision-making among inter-racial couples where one or both of the partners is an immigrant. Spousal decision-making is a culturally situated phenomena (Webster 2000) and it is increasingly clear that household decision making models developed for western "deciders" are inadequate when the "deciders" are non-western. (cf. Webster 2000; Wamwara-Mbugua 2007). Additionally, contextual influences (Schwartz et al. 2010) on immigrant acculturation highlight the need for research on spousal decision-making in non-western cultural contexts. Gendered patterns of behavior are extremely important in household decision-making. Qualls (1987) noted the impact of sex role orientation in household decision-making, while Webster (1994) highlighted the general consensus by researchers of the traditional role specialization in decision-making. For example, males were found to be dominant in decisions such as automobile purchase (Green et. al 1983), insurance (Davis and Rigaux 1974), while female dominant decisions included appliances (Green et al. 1983); groceries (Davis and Rigaux 1974) and washing machines (Woodside and Motes 1979). The female dominant decisions have been associated with the women's role as homemakers.

Prior research (Green et. al 1983) suggested that as nations become developed, that household decision-making becomes less-husband dominant. However, in the case of grocery shopping (a predominantly female preserve), a country's increased development should result in increased husband involvement in grocery shopping. In a study of Singaporean husbands, Piron (2002) found that husbands had lower levels of involvement with grocery shopping and that the wives were the principal deciders. This was attributed to Asian males and families being more traditional and less open to modern behaviors than their western counterparts (Piron 2002). Ethnicity has been found to be an important influencer of decision-making (Maldonaldo and Tansuhaj 1999; Webster 1994). Immigration presents immigrants with numerous decision-making opportunities and Berry (1980) has suggested that the immigrant experience is influenced by whether the immigrant wants to retain his/her culture of origin or whether s/he desires to have positive relations with the host culture. Answers to this yes/no questions results in a typology with four outcomes: integration, separation, marginalization and assimilation: with integration being the best strategy for immigrants' mental health. Food is central to our identity and oftentimes displays our cultural heritage. Consequently, food consumption and acquisition is an excellent area in which to investigate immigrant household decision-making processes among inter-racial couples in a non-western context.

Method: The data for this study is drawn from a larger study of thirty-three immigrants. Twenty one of these immigrants were married and eleven individuals were in interracial marriages. Research informants were recruited using the snowball method. The informants are from many different regions of the world, namely: Europe, North and South America, Africa, Asia, Australia and the Middle East. Consistent with research practices in Kenya, a government research permit was obtained before the research commenced. All interviews were conducted in English, in Nairobi, Kenya. Informants were assured of confidentiality and anonymity. The interviews were audio-taped, transcribed and analyzed by means of coding patterns and the constant comparative method (Glazer and Strauss 1967).

Findings: In most cultures, women have primarily been responsible for food acquisition and preparation. Therefore, it would likely follow that since the women were doing most of the food preparation that they would have a strong influence on the type of food consumed within the home. Nonetheless, in our research we found that with one exception, all food consumption and acquisition decisions were husband dominant. Berry (1980) suggested that for the best mental health that immigrants should integrate aspects of their own culture with that of their host culture. In this case we see an integration of the dominant culture in Kenya by making this decision husband dominant. In general, in Kenya, (a patriarchal society) women are overly concerned with ensuring that their husbands' food needs are met.

Six out of the ten informants were married to Kenyan men; two respondents were married to Kenyan women and three were in inter-racial-inter-country marriages while eleven were in same-race-same-country marriages. With one exception, informants ate food aligned with the husband's culture and more often than not completely ignored the "food culture" of the woman. The women adjusted and learned how to consume the food associated with the husbands' cultures while the men in general did not learn how to eat or appreciate the food associated with the women's cultures. One explanation for the observed findings is that the immigrants have integrated the "male dominance" culture evident in Kenya. Although a country's level of development has been shown to be correlated with increased wife dominance in decision-making, our research suggests that the reverse can happen. We find that when individuals from highly developed countries immigrate to a less developed country, they begin to adopt the behaviors and attitudes of those around them. Another possible explanation for the "husband dominance" in food consumption can be attributed to the availability of cheap labor. In Kenya, most middle-class families have "live-in house-help. Consequently, in spousal dyads where the husband was Kenyan, then the "cook/maid" would prepare the local foods. In instances where the husband was non-Kenyan, then the couples hired and trained a maid to cook the non-Kenyan foods. Nonetheless, the preferred non-Kenyan food was aligned with the husband's culture.

Conclusion: This research highlights some important issues: a) the development of a nation can indeed influence gendered patterns of decision-making. While researchers have demonstrated the movement of decisions towards less husband dominance as the nations develop, we demonstrate that when immigrants from more developed countries immigrate to less developed countries, their decision making patterns may return to more husband dominant decision-making. We attribute the return to husband dominance to the following: a) the integration of dominant culture's values and decision making patterns; b) the existence of cheap labor in these countries may mitigate these decisions and may facilitate the dominance of one decision-making pattern over another. Additionally, this research highlights the need to engage in research outside of western cultural contexts particularly with non-western deciders.

REFERENCES

Berry, John W. (1980), "Acculturation as Varieties of Adaptation," in *Acculturation: Theory, Models and Some New Findings*, ed. Amado M. Padilla, Boulder, CO: Westview, 9-26.

Davis, Harry L.and Benny P. Rigaux (1974), "Perception of Marital Roles in Decision Processes," *Journal of Consumer Research*, 1 (June), 51-62.

Ganesh, Gopala (1997), "Spousal Influence in Consumer Decisions: A Study of Cultural Assimilation," *Journal of Consumer Research*, 14 (April), 132-155.

Glaser BG, Strauss AL. *The discovery of grounded theory*. Chicago: Aldine; 1967.

Green, Robert T., Jean-Paul Leonardi, Jean-Louis Chandon, Isabella C. M. Cunningham, Bronis Verhage, and Alain Stratzzieri (1983), " Societal Development and Family Purchasing Roles : A Cross-national Study," *Journal of Consumer Research, 9* (March), 436-442.

Maldonado, Rachel and Patriya Tansuhaj (1999), "Transition Challenges in Consumer Acculturation: Role Destabilization and Changes in Symbolic Consumption," *Advances in Consumer Research*, 26, 134-140.

Piron, Francis (2002), "Singaporean Husbands and Grocery Shopping: An. Investigation into Claims of Changing Spousal Influence," in *Singapore Management Review,* Vol. 24, (1), 51-66.

Schwartz, Seth J., Jennifer B. Unger, Byron L. Zamboanga and José Szapocznik (2010), "Rethinking the Concept of Acculturation: Implications for Theory and Research," *American Psychologist,* (May-June), 237-251.

Qualls, William J. (1987), "Household Decision Behavior: The Impact of Husbands' and Wives' Sex Role Orientation," *Journal of Consumer Research*, 14 (September), 264-279.

Wamwara-Mbugua, L. Wakiuru, (2007), "An Investigation of Household Decision Making Among Immigrants." *Advances in Consumer Research*, Volume 34, 180-186.

Webster, Cynthia (2000), "Is Spousal Decision Making a Culturally Situated Phenomenon?," *Psychology & Marketing*, 17 (December), 1035-1058.

Webster, Cynthia (1994), "Effects of Hispanic Ethnic Identifica- tion on Marital Roles in the Purchase Decision Process," *Journal of Consumer Research*, 21 (September), 319-331.

Woodside, Arch G. and William H. Motes (1979), "Perceptions of Marital Roles in Consumer Decision Processes for Six Products," in *American Marketing Association Proceedings,* ed. Neil Beckwith et al., Chicago, IL: American Marketing Association, 214-219.

Something to Chew on:
Mastication based on Food Haptics and its Impact on Calorie Estimation

Dipayan Biswas, University of South Florida, USA
Courtney Szocs, University of South Florida, USA
Aradhna Krishna, University of Michigan, USA
Donald Lehmann, Columbia University, USA

EXTENDED ABSTRACT

Can haptics influence calorie perceptions? We focus on haptic properties of food and suggest that since food haptics directly impact mastication (chewing), they can also impact calorie estimation. Higher mastication (based on rougher versus smoother and harder versus softer foods) is proposed and demonstrated to reduce calorie estimation. Focusing on calorie estimation is relevant given rising obesity and need for healthy eating (Chandon and Wansink 2011). While emerging work on haptics has examined other factors (Peck and Wiggins 2006), hardness and texture properties of objects remain uninvestigated within the consumer behavior literature.

FOOD TEXTURE, MASTICATION, AND ASSOCIATIVE LEARNING

Typically, high-calorie/high-fat foods like butter, cream, and cheese, tend to have smooth, soft, and/or creamy textures. In contrast, lower calorie foods like raw vegetables, crackers, and cereals, tend to be rougher and harder. We propose that repeated exposure to this pattern of experience whereby unhealthier (healthier) food items tend to be smooth (rough) or soft (hard) results in learned associations between the haptic properties of the food and the level of healthiness of the food. Research in the domain of associative learning theories suggests that the co-occurrence of two stimuli results in the formation of an associative link (Van Osselaer and Alba 2000). When the two stimuli are repeatedly juxtaposed, the link strengthens, and over time can become a predictive rule that consumers apply to other stimuli or new contexts (McSweeney and Bierly 1984). Hence, we hypothesize:

Hypothesis 1:   *The Food Haptics – Perceived Calorie Effect, whereby consumers will perceive foods with soft (vs. hard) or smooth (vs. rough) textures as being higher in calories.*

When consuming food under high cognitive load, consumers pay less attention to all the senses (Elder and Krishna 2010). As such,

Hypothesis 2:   *With less attention paid to eating (e.g., greater time pressure), the food haptics-perceived calories effect is attenuated.*

BMI AND CALORIE PERCEPTION

Prior research suggests that BMI is an important factor in food choices and influences consumers' perceptions of foods (Irmak et al. 2011). Studies show that consumers with high BMIs are more sensitive to the hedonic properties of foods (Chandon and Wansink 2011), and more likely to inaccurately estimate nutritional properties of foods (Carels et al. 2006). Consistent with this, studies also suggest that consumers with high BMIs focus less attention on high calorie foods (Graham et al. 2011) and are less sensitive to the attributes of unhealthy foods because they consume these foods frequently (Stewart et al. 2010). Hence, the learned associations between food haptics and calories are less likely to form for high BMI consumers. In fact,

the desire to eat high calorie foods may even reverse this associative learning if it does occur. We propose:

Hypothesis 3:   *BMI will moderate the food haptics-perceived calorie effect so that the "higher mastication-lower calorie" perception will be reversed for higher BMIs.*

STUDIES

We tested our hypotheses in three experiments. Study 1 had two manipulated conditions (carrot texture: rough vs. smooth). Consistent with H1, participants rated the smooth (vs. rough) textured carrots as higher in calories. Taste perception measures revealed similar values across both conditions, ruling out perceived taste as the underlying process for perceived unhealthiness (Raghunathan et al. 2006).

Study 2 tested H2 with a 2 (hard vs. soft chocolates) X 2 (time pressure: low vs. high) between subjects design experiment. We manipulated time pressure based on prior studies (Siemer and Reisenzein 1998). The results support H2; under low time pressure, calorie estimation was higher for the soft (vs. hard) chocolate but the effects got attenuated under high time pressure.

Finally, a field experiment at a restaurant (Study 3) tested H3, with a 2 (hard vs. soft cookies) X 2 (BMI: normal weight vs. overweight) between subjects design. BMI was manipulated as in previous studies (Chandon and Wansink 2007). Consistent with H3, calorie perception was higher (lower) for the soft (vs. hard) cookie for normal weight (overweight) participants.

Collectively, the results of the three experiments reveal interesting theoretical and practical insights regarding the effects of mastication and food haptics on calorie estimations.

REFERENCES

Carels, Robert A., Jessica Harper, and Krista Konrad (2006), "Qualitative Perceptions and Caloric Estimations of Healthy and Unhealthy Foods by Behavioral Weight Loss Participants," *Appetite*, 46 (2), 199-206.

Chandon, Pierre and Brian Wansink (2007), "The Biasing Health Halos of Fast-Food Restaurant Health Claims: Lower Calorie Estimates and Higher Side-dish Consumption Intentions," *Journal of Consumer Research*, 34 (3), 301-314.

Chandon, Pierre and Brian Wansink (2011), "Is Food Marketing Making Us Fat? A Multi-disciplinary Review," *Foundations and Trends in Marketing*, 5 (3), 113-196.

Elder, Ryan S. and Arhadna Krishna (2010), "The Effects of Advertising Copy on Sensory Thoughts and Perceived Taste," *Journal of Consumer Research*, 36 (5), 748-756.

Graham, Reiko, Alison Hoover, Natalie A. Ceballos, and Oleg Komogortsev (2011), "Body Mass Index Moderates Gaze Orienting Biases and Pupil Diameter to High and Low Calorie Food Images," *Appetite*, 56 (3), 577-586.

Irmak, Caglar, Beth Vallen, and Stefanie Rosen Robinson (2011), "The Impact of Product Name on Dieters' and Nondieters' Food Evaluations and Consumption," *Journal of Consumer Research*, 38 (2), 390-405.

McSweeney, Frances K. and Calvin Bierley (1984), "Recent Developments in Classical Conditioning," *Journal of Consumer Research*, 11 (2), 619-631.

Peck, Joann and Jennifer Wiggins (2006), "It Just Feels Good: Customers' Affective Response to Touch and Its Influence on Persuasion," *Journal of Marketing*, 70 (4), 56-69.

Raghunathan, Rajagopal, Rebecca W. Naylor, and Wayne D. Hoyer (2006), "The Unhealthy =

Tasty Intuition and its Effects on Taste Inferences, Enjoyment, and Choice of Food Products," *Journal of Marketing*, 70, 170-184.

Siemer, Matthias and Rainer Reisenzein (1998), "Effects of Mood on Evaluative Judgments: Influence of Reduced Processing Capacity and Mood Salience," *Cognition and Emotion*, 12 (6), 783-805.

Stewart, Jessica E., Christine Feinle-Bisset, Matthew Golding, Conor Delahunty, Peter M. Clifton and Russell S. J. Keast (2010), "Oral Sensitivity to Fatty Acids, Food Consumption and in Human Subjects," *British Journal of Nutrition*, 104 (1), 145-152.

Van Osselaer, Stijn M. J. and Joseph W. Alba (2000), "Consumer Learning and Brand Equity," *Journal of Consumer Research*, 27 (1), 1-15.

Lies, Damned Lies, and Statistics:
Risk Reduction Framing and the Power of Prominent Brands

Robert Madrigal, University of Oregon, USA
Catherine Armstrong Soule, University of Oregon, USA
Leslie Koppenhafer, University of Oregon, USA

EXTENDED ABSTRACT

Would you be more persuaded to purchase a medication that advertises a 50% reduction in your risk of suffering a side effect or one that advertises a reduced risk from 2 (i.e., starting risk) to 1 (i.e., modified risk) case per 100,000? The former represents a conditional probability referred to as a relative risk reduction, whereas the latter is a natural frequency called an absolute risk reduction. Both estimates are correct, as the 1 per 100,000 is an absolute difference that represents a 50% reduction in risk. The two presentations differ in how they are framed.

Understanding how consumers process risk perceptions matters not only from a managerial perspective because it is necessary for good decision-making, it also matters because it provides theoretical insights that have implications for consumer welfare and public policy (Menon, Raghubir, and Agrawal 2008). Despite how helpful statistical information might be, consumers are often unable to discern the meaning of such information. This is especially problematic when information is presented in a way that at best doesn't tell the whole story and, at worst, is deceptive (Boush, Friestad, and Wright 2009).

Research has shown that a relative frame is more persuasive because it has a larger magnitude than its corresponding absolute frame (Gigerenzer 2002). It is therefore not surprising that marketers frequently use relative framing in product claims. Yet, without baseline information that allows for its calculation, a relative frame offers little diagnostic insight. Unfortunately, consumers often suspend their natural skepticism and do not counter-argue when presented with a statistic because of its apparent precision. Instead, consumers trust the presumed authority of the source (Sowey 2003).

Our research considers the moderating effect of brand prominence on responses to risk reduction framing. A brand's prominence may be derived from factors such as market share, brand awareness, visibility, and share of voice. Research has shown that consumers make numerous inferences based on market prominence (Johar and Pham 1999; Kirmani 1990; Kirmani and Wright 1989; Pham and Johar 2001). Prominent brands represent knowledge structures that function as judgmental heuristics. Such structures contain learned associations linking the brand to product quality and therefore provide the basis for a judgment without the need for extensive processing of specific attribute information (Maheswaran, Mackie, and Chaiken 1992).

Four studies are reported that test eight hypotheses. Study 1 finds that consumers prefer options framed in relative (vs. absolute) terms. Study 2 results speak to the heuristic power of brand prominence. For both actual and generic brands, prominence superseded risk framing in that no framing effect was found when the new product was associated with a prominent brand. However, given a non-prominent brand, consumers used risk framing as a basis for forming new product performance expectations and likelihood of recommending. Also, the direct effect of prominence on judgments was mediated by brand trust. Moreover, after accounting for prominence, trust moderated the effect of framing for an actual brand. Risk framing had no effect when trust was high. When trust was low, however, relative (vs. absolute) framing elicited higher expectations and greater likelihood of recommending.

Hypothesis 1: A product option framing risk reduction in relative (vs. absolute) terms will be preferred regardless of whether baseline information is presented.

Hypothesis 2: A new product claim framing risk reduction in relative (vs. absolute) terms will elicit (a) increased performance expectations, (b) greater consumer understanding, and (c) less purchase anxiety.

Hypothesis 3: An ordinal interaction is expected such that (a) product expectations and (b) recommendation likelihood will be reduced in response to a new product claim by a less prominent brand that uses absolute framing compared to a less prominent brand using relative framing or a more prominent brand that uses either absolute or relative framing.

Hypothesis 4: Brand trust will mediate the direct effect of brand prominence on (a) performance expectations and (b) recommendation likelihood.

Hypothesis 5: A new product claim framed in relative (vs. absolute) terms will elicit greater (a) performance expectations and (b) recommendation likelihood when brand trust is low. No such difference is expected when brand trust is high.

Hypothesis 6: In contrast to the lack of a risk framing effect on new product expectations for a prominent brand found in study 2 (see H3a), a risk framing main effect is expected such that an absolute (vs. relative) frame will elicit lower product expectations for a prominent brand when numeric information is presented graphically.

Hypothesis 7: Given a text only presentation, low numerates' performance expectations will be greater when (a) the new product claim is presented in relative (vs. absolute) terms, and (b) brand trust is high (vs. low). No such differences are expected for high numerates.

Hypothesis 8: Compared to those receiving instruction only about how absolute and relative risk reductions are calculated, respondents who receive additional instruction as to marketers' intent will perceive greater deception following exposure to a marketing claim that uses a relative risk reduction frame.

A boundary condition of presentation vividness was investigated in study 3. We found that brand prominence was ignored in favor of relative (vs. absolute) framing when risk information was presented graphically. In contrast, study 2 results were replicated when the same information was presented textually. Also explored was the individual difference variable of numeracy (Peters et al. 2006). Study 3 indicates that respondents – especially low numerates – place greater emphasis on brand prominence than risk framing when information is presented textually. However, given a graphical presentation, a brand's prominence is ignored in favor of how the risk reduction is framed.

Our final study explores whether consumers view the use of relative framing to be deceptive. Even though a relative frame with no baseline information provides no diagnostic insight, consumers may simply expect marketers to present their products in the best possible light. However, the use of relative framing is in fact an attempt to mislead because it deliberately omits important information that may have otherwise affected the consumer's decision and is therefore deceptive (Boush et al. 2009).

In order to understand the stimulus, respondents were told they must first read a passage that explained how baseline information is used to calculate absolute and relative risk reductions. In the "absolute frame only" condition, respondents were then shown the starting and modified risks used to calculate the relative risk reduction included in the stimulus. The same information was given to the "absolute frame plus instruction" condition, but they were also told that marketers use relative (vs. absolute) framing because the number appears larger. No mention was made as to the ethics of the tactic. All respondents were then presented with a product claim using a relative frame with no baseline information. No differences were found for performance expectations ($p = .91$) or recommendation likelihood ($p = .18$). However, those receiving additional instruction found the tactic more deceptive than did those who did not ($p < .02$).

In sum, direct-to-consumer advertising for products designed to reduce risk relies on consumers' ability to understand statistical information. Yet, our results suggest that consumers instead rely on heuristics when forming judgments. If faced with just a risk reduction ratio in a new product claim, consumers make their assessment on the basis of a relative frame, even though it is of little diagnostic value. In contrast, risk framing is ignored altogether when the new product is introduced by a prominent brand. This effect is obviated when risk reduction is communicated graphically. Finally, consumers do not view the use of a relative frame to be misleading even if they are aware of how it is calculated. Its use is viewed as deceptive only after they learn marketers' intent for using the tactic.

REFERENCES

Boush, David M., Marian Friestad, and Peter Wright (2009), *Deception in the Marketplace: The Psychology of Deceptive Persuasion and Consumer Self Protection*, New York: Routledge.

Gigerenzer, Gerd (2002), *Calculated Risks: How to Know When Numbers Deceive You*, New York: Simon & Schuster.

Johar, Gita Venkataramani and Michel Tuan Pham (1999), "Relatedness, Prominence, and Constructive Sponsor Identification," *Journal of Marketing Research*, 36 (3), 299-312.

Kirmani, Amna (1990), "The Effect of Perceived Advertising Costs on Brand Perceptions," *Journal of Consumer Research*, 17 (2), 160-71.

Kirmani, Amna and Peter Wright (1989), "Money Talks: Perceived Advertising Expense and Expected Product Quality," *Journal of Consumer Research*, 16 (3), 344-53.

Maheswaran, Durairaj, Diane Mackie, and Shelly Chaiken (1992), "Brand Name as a Heuristic Cue: The Effects of Task Importance and Expectancy Confirmation on Consumer Judgments," *Journal of Consumer Psychology*, 1 (4), 317-36.

Menon, Geeta, Priya Raghubir, and Nidhi Agrawal (2008), "Health Risk Perceptions and Consumer Psychology," in *Handbook of Consumer Psychology*, ed. Curtis Haugtvedt, Paul M. Herr and Frank R. Kardes, New York: Lawrence Erlbaum, 981-1010.

Peters, Ellen, Daniel Vastfjall, Paul Slovic, C.K. Mertz, Ketti Mazzocco, and Stephan Dickert (2006), "Numeracy and Decision Making," *Psychological Science*, 17 (5), 407-13.

Pham, Michel Tuan and Gita Venkataramani Johar (2001), "Market Prominence Biases in Sponsor Identification: Processes and Consequentiality," *Psychology & Marketing*, 18 (2), 123-43.

Sowey, Eric R. (2003), "The Getting of Wisdom: Teaching Statisticians to Enhance Their Clients' Numeracy," *The American Statistician*, 57 (2), 89-93.

Will Power Lead to Variety Seeking in Sexually Related Consumer Choices?

Duo Jiang, University of Illinois at Urbana-Champaign, USA
Sharon Shavitt, University of Illinois at Urbana-Champaign, USA

EXTENDED ABSTRACT

People who have power have often been observed (or caught) seeking sexual variety (e.g. President Bill Clinton, Italian Prime Minister Silvio Berlusconi). Indeed, power and sex are closely linked (Buss 1994). For example, people with power are evaluated as sexier (Martin 2005), males primed with power-related stimuli evaluate opposite-sex subordinates as more sexually attractive (Bargh, Raymond, Pryor, and Strack 1995), and having power over an opposite sex person activates sexual concepts that persist over time, indicating the activation of a mating goal (Kunstman and Maner 2010).

How will this link between power and sex impact choices in the consumption domain? We explore how feelings of power (powerfulness or powerlessness) affect variety seeking for consumer choices that are sexually relevant -- i.e., choices involving cues that could activate sexual or mating goals (Dahl, Sengupta, and Vohs 2009; Janssens, et al. 2011; Lin 1998). We predict that either powerfulness or powerlessness could shift attention towards sexual cues, but because powerful people expect access to a variety of mates, powerless people may engage in compensatory efforts in the consumption arena. Specifically, they may seek variety in daily product choices that are sex-relevant. In three studies, we examine how feelings of [not] having power influence consumer variety seeking and consistently find that people feeling low in power (LP) versus high in power (HP) preferred more variety, but only for choices that were sex-relevant.

Power feelings were primed using the same episodic recall task in all studies (Galinsky, Gruenfeld & Magee 2003). In Study 1, after recalling a past experience of either being powerful ($n = 23$) or powerless ($n = 24$), participants chose between magazines with either a single model or multiple models pictured on the cover. Each participant made binary choices for eight pairs of magazines among which four pairs had attractive human models on the cover (sex-relevant condition: female or male pop stars) and four pairs had attractive non-human models (sex-irrelevant condition: animals, buildings). The dependent measure of variety seeking was the total number of times one chose the magazine with multiple models, with a separate index (from 0 to 4) for human-model and non-human-model magazines. Results showed that LPs chose multiple models more often for the human-model magazines ($M = 1.83$, $SD = 1.20$) than HPs did ($M = 1.17$, $SD = 1.11$), $F (1, 45) = 3.79$, $p <.06$, but did not differ in variety seeking for non-human-model magazines (LP: $M = 2.00$, $SD = 1.10$; HP: $M = 2.39$, $SD = 1.37$). $F (1, 45) = 1.16$, $N.S.$ Hence, Study 1 suggests that when choices were potentially sexually relevant, LPs compared to HPs chose a greater variety (of cover models), whereas this pattern disappeared when choices were presumably not sexually related. Results for a separate no-power prime group (n = 24) fell between LP and HP results, though not significantly different from either.

Because the magazine covers in this study may not necessarily have activated sexually relevant thoughts, we addressed sex relevance directly in Study 2 by framing the same product choice as either relevant or irrelevant to dating. After recalling a powerful ($n = 50$) or powerless ($n = 48$) experience, participants imagined themselves in a scenario in which they ordered dessert for either a party or reception they are hosting. The event was described either as a party in which they might meet attractive people to date (sex-relevant) or as a reception in which they might meet recent grads who could offer internship opportunities (sex-irrelevant). Participants ordered 12 desserts out of five different options (cakes, pies) to serve at this event. When the choice was framed as sex-relevant, LP participants ordered more types of desserts ($M = 3.54$, $SD = 1.06$) than did HP participants ($M = 2.73$, $SD = 0.83$), $F (1, 94) = 7.08$, $p <.05$. However, when the choice was framed as sex-irrelevant, LPs and HPs ordered a similar amount of variety (LP: $M = 2.96$, $SD = 1.20$; HP: $M = 3.04$, $SD = 1.20$), $F (1, 94) = .07$, $N.S.$ Thus, consistent with the prior study, when the choice was sexually relevant, powerless versus powerful people chose more variety, but when the choice was not sexually relevant, this difference disappeared.

Next, we addressed whether the effects were due to LPs engaging in enhanced variety seeking or to HPs being less interested in variety compared to baseline feelings of power. In Study 3, after recalling a powerless ($n = 37$), powerful ($n = 40$), or neutral experience ($n = 42$), participants were asked to customize a box of Godiva chocolates as a birthday gift either for their significant other (sex-relevant) or their important co-worker (sex-irrelevant). As before, when the gift was for a significant other (sex-relevant), LPs chose more kinds of chocolates ($M = 6.41$, $SD = 1.73$) than HPs ($M = 4.59$, $SD = 1.44$) or controls did ($M = 4.68$, $SD = 1.46$), $F (2, 113) = 6.13$, $p <.05$. Post-hoc results showed that LPs significantly differed from HPs, $F (1, 113) = 12.066$, $p <.05$, and controls, $F (1, 113) = 9.312$, $p < .05$, but HPs did not differ from controls, $N.S.$ However, when the gift was for an important co-worker (sex-irrelevant), LPs did not differ from HPs and controls (LP: $M = 6.35$, $SD = 2.06$; HP: $M = 6.44$, $SD = 1.65$; Control: $M = 6.26$, $SD = 2.07$), $F (2, 113) = .05$, $N.S.$ The same pattern emerged in a separate replication study (N = 89) in which people made a binary choice between a high-variety and low-variety box of chocolates. Thus, in addition to replicating Study 1 and 2, Study 3 revealed that when choices were sex-related, feeling powerless led to choosing more variety than would normally occur.

In sum, across three studies, LPs chose more variety than HPs and control people did when choices were sex-relevant, but not when they were sex-irrelevant. This was observed across a number of products and ways of manipulating sex-relevance such as magazines with attractive human models (Study 1), foods to serve possible dating partners (Study 2), and gifts for a long-term significant other (Study 3). The findings suggest that compared with high power people who might have ready access to a variety of real mates, low power people have to settle for variety in their chocolates and magazines.

References

Bargh, J. A., Raymond, P., Pryor, J., and Strack, F. (1995), "Attractiveness of the Underling: An Automatic Power Sex Association and Its Consequences for Sexual Harassment and Aggression", *Journal of Personality and Social Psychology*, 68, 768-781.

Buss, D. M. (1994), *The Evolution of Desire*, New York: Basic Book.

Dahl, D. W., Sengupta, J. and Vohs, K. D. (2009), "Sex in Advertising: Gender Differences and the Role of Relationship Commitment", *Journal of Consumer Research*, 36 (August), 215-231.

Janssens, K., Pandelaere, M., Van den Bergh, B., Millet, K., Lens, I., and Roe, K. (2011), "Can buy me love: Mate attraction goals lead to perceptual readiness for status products", *Journal of Experimental Social Psychology*, 47(1), 254-258.

Kunstman, J. W., and Maner, J. K. (2010), "Sexual Overperception: Power, Mating Motives, and Biases in Social Judgment", *Journal of Personality and Social Psychology*, 100(2), 282-294.

Lin, C. A. (1998), "Uses of Sex Appeals in Prime-Time Television Commercials", *Sex Roles*, 38 (5/6), 461-475.

Martin, J. L. (2005), "Is Power Sexy?" *American Journal of Sociology*, 11(2), 408-446.

Galinsky, A. D., Gruenfeld, D. H., and Magee, J. C. (2003), "From Power to Action," *Journal of Personality and Social Psychology*, 85, 453–466.

Influenced by the Context: The Role of Thinking Systems in the Use of Contextual Cues

Ryan Rahinel, University of Minnesota, USA
Rohini Ahluwalia, University of Minnesota, USA

EXTENDED ABSTRACT

Consumer decisions are often influenced by the context within which they are made. For example, exposure to colors (Berger and Fitzsimons 2008), products (Lee and Labroo 2004), and brands (Ferraro et al., 2009) can systematically shift consumer choices. Although we know much about the contextual features that may influence choices, we know little about who is more likely to be influenced by which type of contextual cues. In this paper, we use Cognitive-Experiential Self-Theory (CEST) to understand how individual differences in thinking systems lead to decisions that are influenced by the decision context.

CEST (see Epstein 1994) suggests that humans have both a rational system and an experiential system. Whereas the rational system is slow, rule-based, contemplative, and deliberative, the experiential system is rapid, affect-based, action-oriented, and associative. Past work suggests that the two modes operate according to a dominance model, whereby one mode is likely to dominate thinking – typically the experiential system, unless the rational system is activated (temporally or chronically), in which case it tends to take over (Kahneman and Frederick 2005; Shiv and Fedorikhin 1999). This model implies that experiential and rational thinking are bipolar constructs, such that a higher activation of one system indicates a lower activation of the other. However, scale development studies by Pacini and Epstein (1999) found no relationship between the two thinking modes, suggesting that the two systems are independent. Therefore, contrary to the dominance model, we argue for a balance model which, in addition to the dominance cases where the activation of one system exceeds that of the other, also considers conditions of balanced thinking modes or simultaneous activation of both systems (either both relatively low or both relatively high). We posit that it is these latter two groups of individuals who tend to be more influenced by contextual cues.

The rationale for this prediction differs across the two balanced groups (i.e., low-lows and high-highs). Low-lows are likely to lack internally generated inputs for guiding a decision, given low activation of both the experiential and rational systems which account for the majority of decision inputs. Therefore, they are likely to turn to the decision context for cues. Conversely, high-highs, with two highly activated systems, are faced with the dilemma of choosing a system when faced with a decision, especially since the two systems often produce diverging outputs (Kirkpatrick and Epstein 1992). Therefore, compared to the dominant system groups, high-highs will also be more likely to turn to the decision context for cues. These differing rationales also allow us to predict the types of cues in the decision context that will influence their decisions. Low-lows, who do not have the cognitive resources for assessing the relevance of a cue, will be likely to turn to contextual cues that are highly accessible, for making their decisions. Conversely, high-highs, who have ample resources to assess the relevance of a cue, will be likely to focus on the most diagnostic contextual cues.

We tested these predictions in a series of studies. Across the studies, we measured experiential and rational system activation using the REI-40 (Pacini and Epstein 1999). In Study 1, we tested the basic prediction that low-lows and high-highs make decisions influenced by the contextual cues. We used the context of grocery shopping, where the items placed in the shopper's basket are likely to function as a contextual cue, making complementary products not only more accessible (Lee and Labroo 2004) but also more diagnostic (i.e., situation-appropriate), calling for increased purchase likelihood of complementary products for both these groups (as compared to their one-system dominant counterparts). Participants (n = 118) completed a simulated grocery shopping task in which they made a series of choices in the given product categories, subsequent to which they were asked to name three additional items they would buy on their shopping trip. The complementarity of these items to the target basket items was assessed. Regression analyses yielded the expected interaction and simple-slope analyses confirmed the prediction that low-lows and high-highs listed more complementary items than their dominant-system counterparts.

In the next two studies, we tested the predictions relating to differential cues and their underlying mechanism by manipulating the accessibility and diagnosticity of the contextual cues. Study 2 (n = 104) replicated Study 1 with one exception. The relative accessibility of the shopping basket was lowered, while keeping its diagnosticity high, by introducing an alternative high accessibility/low diagnosticity cue in the context (via a short story immediately after the product choices). The regression analyses revealed that, as expected, only the high-highs were influenced by the diagnostic contextual cue (shopping basket), demonstrating an increased level of complementary purchases. In Study 3 (n = 98), we took the opposite approach by using a contextual cue that operated on accessibility, but not diagnosticity, processes. We accomplish this by using a perceptual fluency paradigm adapted from Berger and Fitzsimons (2008). Participants completed a short questionnaire on product preferences using either a green or purple pen. They were then asked to choose two options in two different categories (candy and pop) of eight options each. There were two green options and two purple options in each category. We predicted that the pen color would make other similar-colored products more accessible and therefore chosen more often by low-lows, who rely on accessibility-based processes; however, such an effect would not emerge for high-highs. Our expectations were supported, with the low-lows choosing more color-consistent options than the other three groups.

These findings contribute to the consumer behavior literature in several ways. First, they enrich the theory of thinking systems by examining the decision making for low-lows and high-highs and demonstrating that these groups merit further attention and examination in the literature. Second, we identify consumer groups who are most likely to use contextual cues as inputs in their decision making. Finally, our findings distinguish between different types of contextual cues and demonstrate how their usage may differ based on individual differences in thinking systems. Future research can build on this work by investigating the implications of conceptualizing thinking systems and decision cues in these ways.

REFERENCES

Berger, Jonah and Gráinne Fitzsimons (2008), "Dogs on the Street, Pumas on Your Feet: How Cues in the Environment Influence Product Evaluation and Choice," Journal of Marketing Research, 65 (February), 1-14.

Epstein, Seymour (1994), "An Integration of the Cognitive and Psychodynamic Unconscious," *American Psychologist, 49,* 709 - 724.

Ferraro, Rosellina, James R. Bettman, and Tanya L. Chartrand (2009), "The Power of Strangers: The Effect of Incidental Consumer-Brand Encounters on Brand Choice," *Journal of Consumer Research*, 35 (February), 729-741.

Kahneman, Daniel and Shane Frederick (2005), "A Model of Heuristic Judgment," In K.J. Holyoak & R.G. Morrison(Eds.), *The Cambridge Handbook of Thinking and Reasoning* (pp. 267-293). New York: Cambridge University Press.

Lee, Angela Y. and Aparna A. Labroo (2004), "The Effect of Conceptual and Perceptual Fluency on Brand Evaluation," *Journal of Marketing Research*, 41 (May), 151–165.

Pacini, Rosemary and Seymour Epstein (1999), "The Relation of Rational and Experiential Information Processing Styles to Personality, Basic Beliefs, and the Ratio-Bias Phenomenon," *Journal of Personality and Social Psychology*, 76(6), 972 – 987.

Shiv, Baba and Alexander Fedorikhin (1999), "Heart and Mind in Conflict: The Interplay of Affect and Cognition in Consumer Decision Making," *Journal of Consumer Research*, 26(3), 278 – 292.

In The Mood for Special Experiences:
The Impact of Day-to-day Changes On Consumers

Jiska Eelen, University of Amsterdam, The Netherlands
Kobe Millet, VU University Amsterdam, The Netherlands
Luk Warlop, KU Leuven, Belgium and Norwegian Business School (BI), Norway and BI Norwegian Business School, Norway

EXTENDED ABSTRACT

When you find yourself in a novel situation, would you engage in novel consumption experiences, or would you prefer stable ground and stick to what you know? Empirical research has proved both ways for consumers who experienced large changes in life. Severe changes in people´s environment seem to enhance preference for familiarity. Oishi and colleagues (2012) studied residential mobility and showed that it led to anxiety and increased familiarity liking. However, it is also well-known that moderate levels of novelty lead to curiosity and exploration (Berlyne 1950). Consistent with this reasoning, Wood (2010) found that students who first moved to campus were more likely to be attracted to new or unfamiliar products. Therefore, different life changing events may lead to both familiarity-seeking (Oishi et al. 2012) and variety-seeking (Wood 2010). Nevertheless, literature is remarkably silent about the impact of day-to-day changes on consumer decisions. Therefore, the focus of the present project is on the impact of day-to-day changes on consumption.

Contrary to experiencing large changes in life, consumers frequently find themselves in unexpected situations. Hence we seek to find out how such novel environmental cues affect consumer behavior. We propose that subtle changes in the environment make people feel more special and choose more special consumption experiences, whereas more blatant changes in the environment make people choose comforting familiar consumption experiences. In five experimental studies we find that subtle unusual or novel circumstances (i.e., environmental changes, and unusual actions) boost unique consumption experiences, like the preference for scarce products and uncommon holiday destinations, and the willingness to try out new products. Moreover, we show that blatant changes in the environment reset familiarity-seeking. These studies are in line with priming literature documenting that subtle primes lead to assimilation effects, and blatant primes lead to contrast effects (Martin 1986). In particular, novelty gives rise to special and unique feelings. Subtle novelty leads participants to consumptions in line with primed feelings of uniqueness, whereas intrusive novelty leads consumers to choose familiar options. Alternative explanations driven by difficulty, mood regulation, increased self-awareness, lower self-confidence, and self-efficacy are discussed and ruled out.

OVERVIEW OF STUDIES

In five experimental studies we showed that subtle novel situations prime special consumption. Different manipulations and dependent variables were used to show the robustness of the effect. In four studies, subtle novelty was induced by having participants engage in a usual or unusual task (different tasks across studies), in one study the environment itself was changed. Whereas the first three studies focused on subtle novelty, and the process of priming feelings of uniqueness, the last two studies explicitly measured and manipulated subtle versus blatant novelty, and explored the differential impact on consumption.

In the first study, subtle task unusualness (i.e., right-handers performed a task with the right or left hand) affected novel consumption experience. We found that participants in a subtle unusual situation expressed a higher interest in trying out new products than participants in a usual situation. The second study showed that subtle

task unusualness (similar task to study 1) increased the likelihood of choosing a scarce, and hence more unique, product for consumers with a low need for uniqueness to the level of those that were high in need for uniqueness showing a chronic interest in novel and special products (Tian, Bearden, and Hunter 2001). This suggests that novel circumstances prime the drive to be special. Indeed, study 3 provided evidence that participants in the unusual condition showed a momentary drive to feel unique in comparison with those in the usual condition (similar task to study 1).

In two additional studies we showed that only subtle but not blatant environmental changes led to special consumption experiences. In study 4, participants described their ideal holiday destination while being in a usual or unusual environment (i.e., seated on a common or uncommon ergonomic chair). We found that participants in the unusual situation described more unique holidays than participants in the usual situation. Importantly, within the unusual condition, those that found the unusual situation disturbing described more common holidays. This indicates that more intrusive novelty leads to increased familiarity-seeking. In study 5, we manipulated, rather than measured, the impact of subtle and blatant changes. Participants performed a choice task by means of the computer mouse (usual) or by touching the screen (unusual). As expected, we found that the task affected choice for uncommon holiday destinations. Only when novelty was subtle did participants choose more uncommon destinations. When novelty was made explicit at the start of the task, preferences were reset to common destinations, similar to the level of the usual condition. Interestingly, the impact of subtle novelty was mainly driven by participants who were not habituated to touch screens and experienced the situation as truly novel.

DISCUSSION

We studied the impact of temporary and subtle deviations from common experience on consumers, and found that these cues led to more special and novel consumption experiences. By breaking the daily grind, marketers can evoke feelings of uniqueness among consumers and make them more likely to enjoy temporary offers or try out new products. It is especially interesting that the unusual experience can be subtle and entirely unrelated to the consumer choices that follow. Our research suggests that day-to-day changes can be a powerful tool to change habitual behavior, unless novelty becomes too intrusive. Our results help interpreting the seemingly opposite findings for the impact of different life events on consumption (Oishi et al. 2012; Wood 2010), as they may have been more or less intrusive for consumers. Future research should investigate whether the phenomenon described relies on a concept prime (i.e., activation of novelty), a goal prime (i.e, be unique), or a mindset prime (i.e., explore the environment).

REFERENCES

Berlyne, Daniel E. (1950), "Novelty and Curiosity as Determinants of Exploratory Behavior," *British Journal of Psychology: General Section*, 41 (1/2), 68-80.
Martin, Leonard L. (1986), "Set/Reset: Use and Disuse of Concepts in Impression Formation," *Journal of Personality and Social Psychology*, 51 (3), 493-504.

Oishi, Shigehiro, Felicity F. Miao, Minkyung Koo, Jason Kisling, and Kate A. Ratliff (2012), "Residential Mobility Breeds Familiarity-Seeking," *Journal of Personality and Social Psychology*, 102 (1), 149-62.

Tian, Kelly Tepper, William O. Bearden, and Gary L. Hunter (2001), "Consumers' Need for Uniqueness: Scale Development and Validation," *Journal of Consumer Research*, 28 (1), 50-66.

Wood, Stacy (2010), "The Comfort Food Fallacy: Avoiding Old Favorites in Times of Change," *Journal of Consumer Research*, 36 (6), 950-63.

Self-Construal and the Identifiable Victim Effect

Tatiana M. Fajardo, University of Miami, USA
Jiao Zhang, University of Miami, USA

EXTENDED ABSTRACT

Past research has established that victims who arouse stronger affective reactions have a higher chance of being helped. In general, identifying a victim increases emotional arousal and consequently a donor's willingness to contribute. This phenomenon has become known as the identifiable victim effect (Jenni and Loewenstein 1997; Small and Loewenstein 2003; Kogut and Ritov 2005; Small, Loewenstein, and Slovic 2007). We examine how self-construal moderates the effect of victim identification. The concept of self-construal originates from research on cross-culture differences. According to Markus and Kitayama (1991), Western cultures construe the self as separate from their social context, emphasizing autonomy (i.e. an independent self-construal). Whereas, eastern cultures typically consider the self part of the broader social context (i.e. an interdependent self-construal). Research on self-construal suggests that although independents rely on their feelings in making decisions, interdependents may suppress their emotions (Markus and Kitayama 1991). Therefore, our central premise is that compared to individuals with an independent self-construal, individuals with an interdependent self-construal will not be motivated by victim identification. Furthermore, we propose that the moderating effect of self-construal will be mediated by individuals' feelings of empathy.

We tested our propositions in four studies. In Study 1, participants were recruited to participate in an unrelated study. Participants were informed they would receive $2 in exchange for their participation. At the end of this unrelated survey participants completed a self-construal manipulation; they were asked to read a paragraph describing a trip. In the independent self-construal condition, all pronouns referred to the singular *I, me,* or *my*. In the interdependent self-construal condition, pronouns referred to the plural *we, us,* or *our* (Brewer and Gardner, 1996). Following this manipulation, participants were told that they had completed their task and earned the $2. On this same screen, participants were told that the experimenters were collecting donations and presented a donation appeal featuring either a group of 100 unidentified children, one unidentified child, or one child identified by name, age, and picture. Participants were given the opportunity to donate a portion of their payment. A significant two-way interaction emerged. Participants in the independent self-construal condition donated a higher portion of their payment when presented one identified child than when presented either one unidentified children or 100 unidentified children. Participants in the interdependent self-construal condition donated a lower portion of their payment when presented one identified child than when presented one unidentified child. There was no difference in the amount these participants donated to 100 unidentified children and one identified child. These results provide support for our premise that the identifiable victim effect is stronger among independents than among interdependents.

In Study 2, participants were shown a product positioned to prime either an independent or interdependent self-construal (Aaker and Lee 2001). They were then informed that sales of the product would benefit a charity concerned with protecting endangered wildlife; descriptions randomly included or omitted the picture of an endangered animal. Participants were asked their willingness to pay for the product. A self-construal by victim identifiability two-way interaction emerged. When the product primed an independent self-construal inclusion of the picture increased participants' willingness

to pay. In contrast, when the product primed an interdependent self-construal inclusion of the picture did not increase participants' willingness to pay. The results of Study 2 indicate that the basic finding documented in Study 1 applies to cause-related marketing contexts and to animal victims as well as human victims.

In Study 3, we examined the mechanism underlying the impact of self-construal on the identifiable victim effect. We propose that self-construal moderates the effect of victim identification on individuals' willingness to donate by influencing the effect of victim identification on individuals' empathic feelings toward the victim. We tested this prediction by measuring participants' empathic feelings (empathetic concern and empathetic distress) and showing that they mediated the findings documented in Study 1. Several other potentially relevant factors (perceived closeness of the victim, sense of urgency, etc.) were measured but none of these additional measures could serve as a mediator.

Study 4 further examined the mechanism underlying the impact of self-construal on the identifiable victim effect by testing the moderating effect of cognitive load. Based on the previous research showing that individuals rely more on their affective reactions when under high cognitive load (Shiv and Fedorikhin 1999; Small and Verrochi 2009), we expected that the impact of self-construal on the identifiable victim effect would be weaker when individuals are under high load. Participants were randomly assigned to the eight conditions of a 2 x 2 x 2 design. The first factor was self-construal. The second factor was cognitive load. We adopted the manipulation used in Shiv and Fedorikhin (1999); immediately after the self-construal manipulation, participants were presented and asked to hold either a two-digit or a seven-digit number in their heads throughout the remainder of the study. The third factor was victim identifiability. Results revealed a significant three-way interaction effect between cognitive load, self-construal, and victim identification. When cognitive load was low, we see a similar pattern to what was shown in earlier studies. Under high cognitive load neither the independent self-construal nor the interdependent self-construal participants favored an identifiable victim.

The results of these experiments indicate that the positive effect of victim identification is seen only among those with an independent self-construal. As we have shown, victim identification can end up having a negative impact on interdependents. An implication of our research is that providing potential donors with a picture of a victim to try to appeal to their emotions and enhance donation intent is not always a good idea. Charitable organizations and companies engaging in cause-related marketing ought to consider the characteristics of their target consumers when deciding whether to provide vivid, personal information about the victims who need help.

REFERENCES

Aaker, Jennifer L. and Angela Y. Lee (2001), "'I' Seek Pleasures and 'We' Avoid Pains: The Role of Self-Regulatory Goals in Information Processing and Persuasion," *Journal of Consumer Research*, 28 (June), 33–49.

Brewer, Marilynn B., and Wendi Gardner (1996), "Who Is This "We"? Levels of Collective Identity and Self Representations," *Journal of Personality and Social Psychology*, 71 (July), 83-87.

Jenni, Karen E. and George Loewenstein (1997), "Explaining the Identified victim Effect," *Journal of Risk and Uncertainty*, 14 (May), 235-57.

Kogut, Tehila, and Ilana Ritov (2005), "The Singularity Effect of Identified Victims in Separate and Joint Evaluations," *Organizational Behavior and Human Decision Processes*, 97 (July), 106-116.

Markus, Hazel R. and Shinobu Kitayama (1991), "Culture and the Self: Implications for Cognition, Emotion, and Motivation," *Psychological Review*, 98 (April), 224-253.

Shiv, Baba and Alexander Fedorikhin (1999), "Heart and Mind in Conflict: The Interplay of Affect and Cognition in Consumer Decision Making", *Journal of Consumer Research*, 26 (December), 278-92.

Small, Deborah A. and George Loewenstein (2003), "Helping *a* Victim or Helping *the* Victim: Altruism and Identifiabilty," *Journal of Risk and Uncertainty*, 26 (January), 5-16.

Small, Deborah A., George Loewenstein and Paul Slovic (2007), "Sympathy and Callousness: The impact of Deliberative Thought on Donations to Identifiable and Statistical Victims," *Organizational Behavior and Human Decision Processes*, 102 (March), 143-153.

Small, Deborah A., and Nicole M. Verrochi (2009), "The Face of Need: Emotional Expression on Charity Advertisements," *Journal of Marketing Research*, 46 (December), 777-787.

When Empathic Managers Become Consumers: A Self-Referential Bias

Johannes Hattula, University of St. Gallen, Switzerland
Walter Herzog, WHU – Otto Beisheim School of Management, Germany
Darren W. Dahl, University of British Columbia, Canada
Sven Reinecke, University of St. Gallen, Switzerland

EXTENDED ABSTRACT

How do managers predict consumer preferences? Over the past decades, numerous studies on this topic have been published (e.g., Gershoff, Mukherjee, and Mukhopadhyay 2008; Hoch 1987, 1988; West 1996). In this line of research, it has been argued that cognitive empathy, defined as the mental process of putting oneself into the shoes of consumers to understand their needs, supports managers in their construal of consumer preferences (Dahl, Chattopadhyay, and Gorn 1999). The present research, however, reveals an adverse effect of cognitive empathy in this context. Our findings suggest that cognitive empathy makes salient managers' personal consumption preferences, thereby biasing their prediction of consumer preferences.

THEORY

It seems reasonable to assume that managers have two identities: their professional identity as managers and their personal identity as consumers (Ashforth and Johnson 2001). In this research, we hypothesize that cognitive empathy increases the salience of a manager's consumer identity. Empathic managers put themselves into the shoes of consumers which means that they play the role of a consumer, imagine to act and feel as a consumer, and they simulate consumers' product and service experiences (Dahl et al. 1999; Stotland 1969). That is, empathic managers assume the mental processes of a consumer, which in turn is likely to activate the manager's consumer identity.

With an increasing salience of the manager's identity as a consumer, personal consumption preferences might become accessible (Zhang and Khare 2009), thereby influencing the manager's construal processes and decisions. Hence, we argue that cognitive empathy increases the impact of a manager's personal consumption preferences on predicted consumer preferences.

Hypothesis: Cognitive empathy increases the influence of a manager's personal consumption preferences on predicted consumer preferences.

Note that in general, it is expected that empathic persons are able to abstract from their personal preferences (Decety and Jackson 2004; Preston and de Waal 2002). In this context, however, the opposite might be true. We test our hypothesis in two empirical studies.

STUDY 1

Ninety-three marketing managers (mean age: 41.44) were recruited to take part in a case study on a product development process in the automotive industry. Participants first indicated their personal preferences for car attributes by assigning importance weights to six product features. Specifically, they were asked to assign 100 points to the following car attributes: design, performance, dependability, comfort, sustainability, and prestige (Horsky and Nelson 1992). By using a constant sum scale, we explicitly capture trade-offs between the product features (Krosnick and Alwin 1988).

Subsequently, participants were asked to assume the role of a manager of a hypothetical car manufacturer and steer the development process of a new car model. They were then provided with recent market research data on consumer preferences for each product feature. Moreover, participants were asked to define the character of the new model by assigning 100 points to the six product features. In particular, we asked participants to define the character of the new model in line with the preferences of a typical consumer in the market. Finally, we measured their degree of cognitive empathy during the case study (Davis 1980).

Assigned weights in the management task were then regressed on managers' personal importance weights, cognitive empathy, and the interaction of both variables. For each product feature, we find a positive effect of managers' personal importance weights and a positive interaction effect, supporting our hypothesis that cognitive empathy increases the influence of managers' personal consumption preferences on predicted consumer preferences.

STUDY 2

Since the findings of study 1 are based on self-selection into high/low empathy groups, we experimentally manipulated cognitive empathy in study 2. To enhance generalizability, study 2 is based on a case study on communications management.

For this study, we recruited 231 marketing managers (mean age: 45.31). In a first part, framed as a consumer study on personal identity and advertising effectiveness, participants watched two real ads of the luxury watch manufacturer Rolex and indicated their personal liking of each ad on an 11-point Likert-scale. In the second part, they were asked to assume the role of the head of marketing of Rolex. They were randomly assigned to either the "cognitive empathy" or "no cognitive empathy" condition. Participants in the cognitive empathy group were asked to describe a typical target consumer of Rolex, to imagine the target consumers' thoughts when watching the two ads, and to anticipate potential reactions to the ads. We assumed that participants had a clear impression of a prestige-oriented target consumer of Rolex (Puligadda, Ross, and Grewal 2012). Participants in the "no cognitive empathy" condition did not receive such instructions (Galinsky, Wang, and Ku 2008). Finally, participants estimated target consumers' evaluations of each ad on an 11-point scale. None of the participants was able to infer the true goal of the study.

The manipulation of cognitive empathy was successful (the cognitive empathy measures from study 1 were used as manipulation check). To test our hypothesis, we regressed predicted consumer evaluations on managers' personal liking scores, the cognitive empathy manipulation, and the interaction of both variables. For both ads, we find a positive effect of managers' personal liking scores and a positive interaction effect. Overall, study 2 replicates the findings of study 1 and supports the hypothesis that cognitive empathy increases the influence of managers' personal preferences on predicted consumer preferences.

CONCLUSIONS

This paper investigates an empathy-caused self-referential bias in managerial predictions of consumer preferences. The findings of two studies in distinct contexts and using different preference measures demonstrate that cognitive empathy increases the influence of managers' personal consumption preferences on predicted consumer preferences.

Our research makes a number of contributions. First, it extends previous research on managerial predictions of consumer preferences by showing the counterintuitive influence of cognitive empathy. Second, we introduce an identity-based perspective arguing that cognitive empathy increases the salience of a manager's consumer identity. Third, it underlines the importance of investigating managers' consumer identity and their personal consumption preferences.

REFERENCES

Ashforth, Blake E. and Scott A. Johnson (2001), "Which Hat to Wear? The Relative Salience of Multiple Identities in Organizational Contexts," in *Social Identities Processes in Organizational Contexts*, ed. Michael A. Hogg and Deborah J. Terry, Philadelphia: Psychology Press, 31-48.

Dahl, Darren W., Amitava Chattopadhyay, and Gerald J. Gorn (1999), "The Use of Visual Mental Imagery in New Product Design," *Journal of Marketing Research*, 36 (1), 18-28.

Davis, Mark H. (1980), "A Multidimensional Approach to Individual Differences in Empathy," *JSAS Catalog of Selected Documents in Psychology*, 10, 85.

Decety, Jean and Philip L. Jackson (2004), "The Functional Architecture of Human Empathy," *Behavioral and Cognitive Neuroscience Reviews,* 3 (2), 71-100.

Galinsky, Adam D., Cynthia S. Wang, and Gillian Ku (2008), "Perspective-Takers Behave More Stereotypically," *Journal of Personality and Social Psychology*, 95 (2), 404-19.

Gershoff, Andrew D., Ashesh Mukherjee, and Anirban Mukhopadhyay (2008), "What's Not to Like? Preference Asymmetry in the False Consensus Effect," *Journal of Consumer Research*, 35 (1), 119-25.

Hoch, Stephen J. (1987), "Perceived Consensus and Predictive Accuracy: The Pros and Cons of Projection," *Journal of Personality and Social Psychology*, 53 (2), 221-34.

--- (1988), "Who Do We Know: Predicting the Interests and Opinions of the American Consumer," *Journal of Consumer Research*, 15 (3), 315-24.

Horsky, Dan and Paul Nelson (1992), "New Brand Positioning and Pricing in an Oligopolistic Market," *Marketing Science*, 11 (2), 133-53.

Krosnick, Jon A. and Duane F. Alwin (1988), "A Test of the Form-Resistant Correlation Hypothesis," *Public Opinion Quarterly*, 52 (4), 526-38.

Preston, Stephanie D. and Frans B. M. de Waal (2002), "Empathy: Its Ultimate and Proximate Bases," *Behavioral and Brain Sciences*, 25, 1-72.

Puligadda, Sanjay, William T. Ross, and Rajdeep Grewal (2012), "Individual Differences in Brand Schematicity," *Journal of Marketing Research,* 49 (1), 115-30.

Stotland, Ezra (1969), "Exploratory Investigations of Empathy," *Advances in Experimental Social Psychology,* Vol. 4, ed. Leonard Berkowitz, New York: Academic Press, 271-314.

West, Patricia M. (1996), "Predicting Preferences: An Examination of Agent Learning," *Journal of Consumer Research*, 23 (1), 68-80.

Zhang, Yinlong and Adwait Khare (2009), "The Impact of Accessible Identities on the Evaluation of Global Versus Local Products," *Journal of Consumer Research,* 36 (3), 524-37.

How to Persuade 100,000 Friends? Understanding Blogs as One-to-One Mass Media

Soyean (Julia) Kim, Boston University, USA
Seema Pai, Boston University, USA
Frédéric F. Brunel, Boston University, USA
Barbara A. Bickart, Boston University, USA

EXTENDED ABSTRACT

Rumi: "It's a day of errands for me.. wearing vintage collar, Ralph Lauren blazer, Zara skirt, Céline bag, and Rag & Bone boots."

Comment: "I remember that blazer! It's super old, right? It's neat to see how it still fits into your style like 5 years later haha."

Comment: "You always look great when things get hectic. And I've told you before how well you wear Céline."

This posting by famous fashion blogger Rumi (fashiontoast. com) along with two of the many comments that she received on that day illustrates how Rumi has successfully created a communication environment where brands are discussed and celebrated but also one where friendships and intimate relationships might prevail. Although it is unlikely that Rumi has a meaningful relationship with each of her 133,672 readers, it is clear that many of them believe they have a relationship and close friendship with her. They relate to and connect with her at an interpersonal level, sharing slice of life stories, remembering past events, and engaging in brand level discussions. This level of closeness is rather counterintuitive especially if we consider that blogs are, by definition, a form of broadcast media in which a blogger shares his or her views with a large audience. In this paper, we examine how bloggers like Rumi develop different communication strategies that allow them to achieve specific objectives.

BLOGS AS ONE-TO-ONE MASS MEDIA

Blogs are "frequently updated web pages with a series of archived posts, typically in reverse-chronological order" (Nardi et al., 2004, p.1). Blog content can be provided by an individual writer or can be curated from a variety of sources (Blood 2002; Herring et al. 2005). In either case, blogs function as a mass communication medium in which content provided by a particular source is distributed to a large audience (Hoffman and Novak 1996). As such, we would expect blogs to function similarly to other mass media (Katz and Lazarsfeld 1955). We find, however, that the rules that govern one-to-many media do not apply to blogs and in fact, these rules are adjusted to create a personal and intimate relationship between bloggers and readers. Thus, drawing from persuasion theory and observation of a variety of blogs, we develop a theoretical framework that explains how blogs can be categorized based on audiences' perceptions and how bloggers use different strategies to shape or shift their audiences' perceptions and increase the persuasiveness of their messages.

Specifically, we propose a categorization scheme for blogs based on *the perceived target audience (mass versus one-to-one)* and *the perceived level of the blogger's commercial interest (explicit commercial interests versus no explicit commercial interests).* Our proposed scheme provides insights to marketers looking to leverage social media marketing strategies as well as to bloggers attempting to maximize the persuasiveness and reach of their communication. Using this scheme, we categorize blogs into four types: *Commercial, Market Maven, Commercial Friendship*, and *Community-Based Friendship.*

BLOGGERS' COMMUNICATION STRATEGIES

Our qualitative research suggests that bloggers can implement two key communication strategies: (a) *illusion of relationship* and (b)

ambiguity in commercial interests to shift their audiences' perceptions and thus make their messages more effective and persuasive. *Illusion of relationship* refers to a strategy that bloggers use to shift readers' perceptions of the blog away from a mass audience toward a one-to-one audience. The strategy creates a feeling of intimacy and personalized relationship between bloggers and their audience. *Ambiguity in commercial interests* refers to a strategy that bloggers use to deemphasize the presence of commercial interests. It disguises or hides the bloggers' commercial motives behind the communication.

By using the *illusion of relationship* strategy, bloggers can shift audiences' perception of their blogs from *Commercial* to *Commercial Friendship* and *Market Maven* to *Community-Based Friendship.* This perceptual shift from mass to one-to-one may create a feeling of intimacy, increase the level of trust, and enhance the quality of the blogger-audience relationship. As illustrated by our data, such a shift can be achieved through increases in: (i) the depth and breadth of self-disclosures (Cozby 1973; Derlega and Berg 1987; Jourard 1971), (ii) the frequency and duration of interactions (Altman and Taylor 1973; Delia and O'Keefe 1979; Little 1972; Werner 1957), and (iii) the perception of shared common interests (Morry 2005; Rose 1985; Weiss and Lowenthal 1975).

The use of the *ambiguity in commercial interests* strategy can shift audiences' perceptions of blogs from *Commercial* to *Market Maven* and *Commercial Friendship* to *Community-Based Friendship.* This perceptual shift from commercial to non-commercial creates a feeling of benevolence and care and increases audiences' trust towards the blogger, thus reducing the likelihood that persuasion knowledge is activated and that consumers invoke strategies to resist persuasive attempts. Because bloggers may want to avoid such resistance, they may try to hide or obfuscate their commercial interests. Ambiguity in commercial interests can be attained through: (i) hiding commercial interests (Boush, Friestad, and Rose 1994; Campbell and Kirmani 2000; Ford, Smith, and Swasy 1990; Friestad and Wright 1994, (ii) stressing benevolent communal interests (Kozinets et al. 2010), and (iii) mixing diverse topics and content types (Simon 1996). We present examples of each of these tactics drawn from our qualitative research.

CONCLUSION

In sum, this research presents a conceptual framework to explain how persuasion works in blogs. This framework is based on qualitative data and theory from persuasion knowledge (Friestad and Wright 1994), mass communication (Katz and Lazarsfeld 1955), word-of-mouth (Dichter 1966; Henning-Thurau et al. 2004), communication norms/motives (Rubin, Perse and Barbato 1988; Sundaram et al. 1998), relationship (e.g., self-disclosure (Cozby 1973; Derlega and Berg 1987), and intimacy (Jamieson 1998; Reis and Shaver 1988). Our work provides a broad view of how blogs operate, which should apply to many situations. For example, we expect that these ideas hold both when blog content is seeded by marketers (e.g., Kozinets et al. 2010) as well as when content is self-generated by the blogger. Thus, this framework extends the persuasion and WOM literature to address current changes in the structure of communication.

REFERENCES

Altman, I., and D. A. Taylor (1973), *Social penetration: The development of interpersonal relationships*. Oxford, England: Holt, Rinehart & Winston.

Blood, R. (2002), *The Weblog Handbook: Practical Advice on Creating and Maintaining Your Blog*, Cambridge, MA: Perseus Pub.

Boush, D. M., M. Friestad, and G. M. Rose (1994), "Adolescent Skepticism toward TV Advertising and Knowledge of Advertiser Tactics," *Journal of Consumer Research*, 21(1), 165-175.

Campbell, M.C. and A. Kirmani (2000), "Consumers' Use of Persuasion Knowledge: The Effects of Accessibility and Cognitive Capacity on Perceptions of an Influence Agent," *Journal of Consumer Research*, 27(1), 69-83.

Cozby, P. C. (1973), "Self-Disclosure: A Literature Review," *Psychological Bulletin*, 79(2), 73-91.

Delia, J. G., and B. J. O'Keefe (1979), Constructivism: The Development of Communication in Children. In E. Wartella (Ed.) *Children Communicating: Media and Development of Thought, Speech, Understanding*, (pp.157-185). Beverly Hills, CA: Sage.

Derlega, V. J. and J. H. Berg (1987), *Self-Disclosure: Theory, Research, and Therapy*, New York, NY: Plenum Press.

Dichter, E. (1966), "How Word-of-Mouth Advertising Work," *Harvard Business Review*, 44(Nov-Dec), 147-157.

Ford, G. T., D. B. Smith, and J. L. Swasy (1990), "Consumer Skepticism of Advertising Claims: Testing Hypotheses from Economics of Information," *Journal of Consumer Research*, 16(4), 433-441.

Friestad, M. and P. Wright (1994), "The Persuasion Knowledge Model: How People Cope with Persuasion Attempts," *Journal of Consumer Research*, 21(1), 1-31.

Hennig-Thurau, T., K. P. Gwinner, G. Walsh, and D. D. Gremler (2004), "Electronic Word-of-Mouth via Consumer-Opinion Platforms: What Motivates Consumers to Articulate Themselves on the Internet?" *Journal of Interactive Marketing*, 18(1), 38-52.

Herring, S., L. Scheidt, E. Wright and S. Bonus (2005), "Weblogs as a Bridging Genre," *Information Technology and People*, 18(2), 142-171.

Hoffman, D. L. and T. P. Novak (1996), "Marketing in Hypermedia Computer-Mediated Environments: Conceptual Foundations," *Journal of Marketing*, 60(3), 50-68.

Jourard, S. M. (1971), *Self-Disclosure: An Experimental Analysis of the Transparent Self*. New York: Wiley-Interscience.

Katz, E. and P. F. Lazarsfeld (1955), *Personal Influence: The Part Played by People in the Flow of Mass Communications*. Glencoe, IL: Free Press.

Kozinets, R. V., K. De Valck, A. Wojnicki, and S. S. Wilner (2010), "Networked Narratives: Understanding Word-of-Mouth Marketing in Online Communities," *Journal of Marketing*, 74(2), 71-89.

Little, B. R. (1972), "Psychological Man as Scientist, Humanist and Specialist," *Journal of Experimental Research in Personality*, 6(2), 95-118.

Morry, M. M. (2005), "Relationship Satisfaction as a Predictor of Similarity Ratings: A Test of the Attraction-Similarity Hypothesis," *Journal of Social and Personal Relationships*, 22(4), 561-584.

Nardi, B. A., D. J. Schiano, M. Gumbrecht, and L. Swartz (2004), "Why We Blog," *Communications of the ACM*, 47(12), 41-46.

Rubin, R. B., E. M. Perse and C. A. Barbato (1988), "Conceptualization and Measurement of Interpersonal Communication Motives," *Human Communication Research*, 14(4), 602-628.

Rose, S. M. (1985), "Same- and Cross-sex Friendships and the Psychology of Homosociality," *Sex Roles*, 12(1), 63-74.

Simon, G. K. (1996), *In Sheep's Clothing: Understanding and Dealing with Manipulative People*. Little Rock, AR: A. J. Christopher & Co.

Sundaram, D. S., K. Mitra, and C. Webster (1998), "Word-of-Mouth Communications: A Motivational Analysis," *Advances in Consumer Research*, 25, 527-531.

Weiss, L., and M. F. Lowenthal (1975), Life-course Perspectives on Friendship. In M. F. Lowenthal, M. Thurnher, & D. Chiriboga (Ed.), *Four Stages of Life: A Comparative Study of Women and Men Facing Transitions* (pp. 48-61). San Francisco, CA: Jossey-Bass.

Werner, H. (1957), The Concept of Development from a Comparative and Organismic Point of View. In D. Harris (Ed.), *The Concept of Development: An Issue in the Study of Human Behavior*. Minneapolis, MN: University of Minnesota Press.

Street Credibility:
What is it? Who has it? Why is it so Appealing to Diverse Consumer Groups?

Delancy Bennett, University of Massachusetts, USA
William Diamond, University of Massachusetts, USA

EXTENDED ABSTRACT

Celebrity endorsers are featured in 10 to 20 percent of commercials in the United States (Agrawal and Kamakura 1995). While firms have invested significant capital in celebrity endorsers, they traditionally shy away from those who have been involved in illegal or immoral acts (Briggs 2009; Creswell 2008). However, the rules of endorser selection appear to be changing. Recently, a new type of endorser whose celebrity is built in part upon criminal activity or violent history has emerged. These celebrities, often rappers, successfully endorse major brands such as Vitamin Water and Chrysler. They are often described as having another form of credibility—street credibility (Spiegler 1996). Patrick (2005) suggests that these street credible celebrities will replace athletes as the most important product endorsers. Therefore, it is important to determine the nature of street credibility, who has it, and how is it gained. As well, we need to understand how diverse consumer groups relate to these endorsers.

This paper will define the emergent construct of street credibility, delineate its antecedents, provide exemplars, and assess the attraction to street credible endorsers by diverse consumer groups. We will use Kohli and Jaworski's (1990) framework for developing emerging constructs. We begin by reviewing the literature on celebrity endorser credibility and integrating insights from research in anthropology and sociology relevant to the construct of street credibility. Next, we report findings from a series of field interviews exploring street credibility.

LITERATURE REVIEW

Early scholarly work on endorser credibility focuses on the moderators of source effectiveness. These studies suggest that trustworthiness, expertise and attractiveness are the most important elements of endorser credibility (Friedman, Santeramo, and Traina 1978; Hovland and Weiss 1951; McGuire 1985; Ohanian 1990).

McGuire (1985) suggests that similarity is an antecedent of attractiveness. Thus inner city consumers may be attracted to street credible endorsers based on their similar personal histories. However, this neglects to explain the popularity of street credible endorsers with other consumers. Before addressing this issue, we next will explore the literature on street credibility.

Researchers in the areas of marketing, sociology, and criminology use the term street credibility to refer to a reputation gained through acts of street crime and adherence to street codes in poor urban settings (Brunson and Stewart 2006; Grint and Case 1998). However, they stop short at providing a concrete definition of street credibility.

METHOD

To develop a definition of street credibility, we consulted existing ethnographic, anthropological and sociological studies regarding street culture (i.e. Bourgois 2003; LeBlanc 2003). Following the works of Burton, Cherlin, Winn, Estacion, and Holder-Taylor (2009) and Charmaz (2006), our approach was not completely inductive grounded theory. Rather we employed a modified form of grounded theory using "extant theory and ethnographic studies" to build a foundation for an emerging construct (Burton et al. 2009, 1107-1124).

This analysis resulted in our discovery of five areas producing respect within street culture: (1) ability to thrive, (2) acquisition of street smarts, (3) displayed toughness, (4) acquisition of material possessions and sexual conquest, and (5) the ability to achieve "cross-over dreams." Following the work of Kohli and Jaworski (1990) we next looked for commonalities between these studies and our fieldwork.

We used theoretical sampling (Glaser and Strauss 1967) to select 34 interview respondents in two U.S. communities. The first community represented inner-city consumers and the second represented consumers outside the inner-city.

The first author interviewed 21 African-American and Latino college students who grew up and attended high school in Harlem. While the interviews allowed for new questions to be generated based on respondents' feedback, all respondents were asked to define street credibility, and asked how it was gained, lost, transferred, used, and differentiated from other constructs such as "cool."

The second set of interviews built upon our findings by developing an understanding of how mainstream, non-inner-city consumers thought about street credibility. We interviewed 13 Caucasian and Asian students who grew up in mid- to small-sized towns from middle class to upper class families in the northeast.

To define street credibility, we followed the work of Kohli and Jaworski (1990) and Burton et. al. (2009) on construct development and used data from both the ethnographic studies on street culture and our field work to identify the antecedents of street credibility and produce an empirically grounded definition.

FINDINGS

This synthesis resulted in a definition of street credibility based on the identification of three main factors: "authentic origins in street life", "the acquisition of power", and the "width of the gap between the one's origin and one's current level of power." Our research further suggests that the diminishment of street credibility will occur when it is publically known that the street credible person has undergone a significant decrease or reversal in the elements of power.

Finally, while both groups show evidence of attachment to the endorsers and their histories, the inner-city consumer's view is more in line with traditional literature. These consumers see the endorser more through the lens of an aspiration reference group. However, the non-inner-city consumer is drawn to the street credible endorser as a form of entertainment. That is, as (Gilroy, Grossberg, and McRobbie 2000) posit, these consumers are drawn to street credible endorsers as their world provides an interesting form of exoticism and fantasy.

CONTRIBUTIONS

We contribute to the work on celebrity endorsement by empirically defining the construct of street credibility and by explaining the attraction that street credibility affords celebrities in diverse consumer groups. Contrary to traditional theories of endorsement and source persuasion, for many consumers street credibility is not related to trustworthiness or similarity. This insight challenges the current body of endorsement literature and leads to better understanding of credibility. Further research is needed to learn what product categories benefit most from street credible endorsers. In addition, research must focus on the development of scales to measure the aspects of street credibility.

REFERENCES

Agrawal, Jagdish, and Wagner A. Kamakura. 1995. The Economic Worth of Celebrity Endorsers: An Event Study Analysis. 07; 2012/3.

Bourgois, Philippe I. 2003. *In search of respect: Selling Crack in El Barrio*. Structural Analysis in The Social Sciences. 2nd ed. Vol. 10. Cambridge ; New York: Cambridge University Press.

Briggs, Bill. When a Celebrity Endorsement Deal Sours . 2009 [cited 4/30 2011]. Available from http://www.msnbc.msn. com/id/29433200/ns/business-sports_biz/t/when-celebrity-endorsement-deal-sours/.

Brunson, Rod K., and Eric A. Stewart. 2006. Young African American Women, The Street Code, and Violence: An exploratory analysis. *Journal of Crime & Justice* 29 (1) (05): 1-19.

Burton, Linda M., Andrew Cherlin, Donna-Marie Winn, Angela Estacion, and Clara Holder-Taylor. 2009. The Role of Trust In Low-Income Mothers' Intimate Unions. *Journal of Marriage and Family* 71 (5) (Dec 2009): 1107-24.

Charmaz, Kathy. 2006. *Constructing Grounded Theory*. London ; Thousand Oaks, Calif.: Sage Publications.

Creswell, Julie. 2008. Nothing Sells Like Celebrity. , 06/22; 2012/3, 2008, sec 157.

Friedman, Hershey H., Michael J. Santeramo, and Anthony Traina. 1978. Correlates of Trustworthiness for Celebrities. *Journal of the Academy of Marketing Science* 6 (4) (Fall78): 291-9.

Gilroy, Paul, Lawrence Grossberg, and Angela McRobbie. 2000. *Without Guarantees: In Honour of Stuart Hall*. London New York: Verso.

Glaser, Barney G., and Anselm L. Strauss. 1967. *The Discovery of Grounded Theory; Strategies for Qualitative Research*. Observations. Chicago: Aldine Pub. Co.

Grint, Keith, and Peter Case. 1998. The violent Rhetoric of Re-Engineering: Management Consultancy on the Offensive. *The Journal of Management Studies* 35 (5) (Sep 1998): 557-77.

Hovland, Carl I., and Walter Weiss. 1951. The Influence of Source Credibility on Communication Effectiveness. *Public Opinion Quarterly* 15 (4) (December 21): 635-50.

Kohli, Ajay K., and Bernard J. Jaworski. 1990. Market orientation: The Construct, Research Propositions, A. *Journal of Marketing* 54 (2) (Apr 1990): 1.

LeBlanc, Adrian Nicole. 2003. *Random Family: Love, Drugs, Trouble, and Coming of Age in The Bronx*. New York: Scribner.

McGuire, William J. (1985) Attitudes and Attitude Changes, Handbook of Social Psychology, (Eds.)   Gardner Linzey and Elliot Aronson, vol. 2, NY: Random House, pp. 233-346.

Ohanian, Roobina. 1990. Construction and Validation of a Scale to Measure Celebrity Endorsers' Perceived Expertise, Trustworthiness, and Attractiveness. *Journal of Advertising* 19 (3) (09): 39-52.

Patrick, Aaron O. 2005. Moss Proves Too Edgy For Retailer. , 09/21; 2012/3, 2005.

Spiegler, Marc. 1996. Marketing Street Culture; Bringing Hip-Hop Style to The Mainstream. 11; 2012/3.

Taking the Complexity Out of Complex Product Customization Decisions

Christian Hildebrand, University of St. Gallen, Switzerland
Jan R. Landwehr, Goethe University Frankfurt, Germany
Andreas Herrmann, University of St. Gallen, Switzerland
Gerald Häubl, University of Alberta, Canada

EXTENDED ABSTRACT

The customization of products based on consumers' idiosyncratic preferences has significant potential in terms of providing consumers with offers that match their personal preferences, as well as increasing their product satisfaction, loyalty, and willingness-to-pay (Alba et al. 1997, Ansari and Mela 2003, Franke et al. 2010). Recent research suggests that each of the two most common modes of product customization – (1) the "by alternative" mode of having consumers choose from a pre-specified set of alternatives and (2) the "by attribute" mode of asking consumers to customize every attribute and attribute level of the product (Valenzuela et al. 2009) – has distinct limitations from the consumers' perspective.

On one hand, the "by attribute" customization mode can reduce choice complexity and increase consumers' satisfaction with their product choices (Valenzuela et al. 2009). On the other hand, however, such comparisons among attribute levels can increase perceived tradeoff difficulty among attributes (Dhar 1997, Nordgren and Dijksterhuis 2009) as well as such customization systems may be challenging to consumers, requiring them to process an increased number of attribute information in parallel (Huffman and Kahn 1997).

Inspired by past research on multi stage decision processes by which consumers typically reduce the number of possible alternatives first, before applying more compensatory or non-compensatory decision rules on the remaining alternatives (Beach 1993, Häubl and Trifts 2000), we propose a two-step customization mode which is intended to reduce difficulties in current customization formats. Similarly to typical two-stage decision processes for information effort reduction (Bettman and Park 1980), the proposed customization mode is based on a two-step decision process in which consumers first select one of a small number of pre-specified prototypes, and then create their final customized product by further refining their initially selected product. Thus, instead of choosing from a large set of attributes and simultaneous tradeoffs among attribute levels, consumers choose from a smaller set of alternatives first, before conducting local tradeoffs in a subsequent customization task.

Evidence from three experiments shows that this two-step model of customization (TMC) outperforms the two predominant customization modes on a number of important outcome dimensions (e.g., reduced choice complexity, increased preference certainty, greater satisfaction with the self-designed product, etc.) and how the effectiveness of the TMC is moderated by the number of pre-specifications and different information formats.

In experiment 1, we examined whether the TMC mode results in higher preference certainty, greater product satisfaction, and reduced choice complexity, compared to the two predominant customization formats of an either "by attribute" or "by alternative" customization. Participants in the TMC condition were presented with a randomly chosen set of nine pre-specified prototypes and asked to select their preferred one, and then had the opportunity to customize the selected product in a second step. We recruited 126 participants from an online consumer panel for the experiment. As predicted, participants in the TMC condition were significantly more satisfied with their customized product, more certain about their preference, and perceived the process of customization as less complex. Furthermore, two multiple mediation models tested the TMC mode against each of the two predominant customization modes and revealed additional evidence that the TMC mode outperformed both of these through the mediating role of preference certainty, satisfaction, and process complexity on consumers' ultimate probability to buy the customized product.

In experiment 2, we examined the moderating role of different pre-specification descriptions to increase consumers' degree of certainty during the customization process. In particular, we manipulated the number of pre-specifications (4 vs. 15) and type of attribute descriptions (quantitative vs. qualitative), and examined how these factors influenced participants' preference certainty. We expected that consumers only navigate through quantitative attribute descriptions effectively if they need to make a small number of comparisons. In line with our prediction, quantitative attribute descriptions were only beneficial in the case of a small number of pre-specifications and less beneficial in the case of a large number of pre-specifications. Furthermore, we uncovered the influence of a novel moderator regarding the influence of a large number of alternatives on preference certainty: although we found that more alternatives do not necessarily reduce certainty directly (in line with Scheibehenne et al. 2010), our results reveal that this effect is moderated by consumers' need for cognition (NFC), such that low NFC consumers were less certain when choosing from a larger set of alternatives, adding an important new facet to our understanding of choice overload and its consequences.

Finally, experiment 3 was conducted to investigate the influence of different TMC procedures for generating pre-specifications. In particular, we examined the influence of different sources of pre-specifications (chosen by other consumers vs. no information; learning task of the mass customization system vs. no learning task) on the degree of deviation from pre-specifications. The learning task was manipulated by asking participants to make five domain-related choices, which were used to select the optimal bundle of pre-specifications. Building on previous research in the area of identity signaling (Berger and Heath 2007), we predicted that consumers would diverge from their initial choice if they conducted the learning task and believed that pre-specifications were chosen by other consumers. In line with our prediction, participants in the preference learning condition deviated significantly from their pre-specification if they believed that pre-specifications were based on what other consumers have chosen. Furthermore, this increased deviation (measured by the Euclidean distance between pre-specification and customized product) resulted in a significant decrease in final product satisfaction ($b_{deviation} = -.26, p < .001$; $R^2 = .08$, N = 331).

Our findings contribute to the literature in three ways: First, we provide empirical evidence that the TMC mode outperforms current customization modes, resulting in beneficial effects from a consumer perspective when navigating through mass customization systems. Secondly, we revealed that qualitative in contrast to quantitative attribute descriptions may help consumers to navigate through a large number of attributes in such systems. Finally, we provide additional evidence for backfire effects of preference learning tasks when providing subsequent information that alternatives were based on previous choices of other consumers, making distinction motives for self-designable products increasingly salient.

REFERENCES

Alba, Joseph, John Lynch, Barton Weitz, Chris Janiszewski, Richard Lutz, Alan Sawyer, and Stacy Wood (1997), "Interactive Home Shopping: Consumer, Retailer, and Manufacturer Incentives to Participate in Electronic Marketplaces," Journal of Marketing, 61 (July), 38–53.

Ansari, Asim and Carl F. Mela (2003), "E-Customization," Journal of Marketing Research, 40 (May), 131–45.

Beach, Lee Roy (1993), "Broadening the Definition of Decision Making: The Role of Prechoice Screening of Options," Psychological Science, 4 (4), 215–20.

Berger, Jonah and Chip Heath (2007), "Where consumers diverge from others: Identity signaling and product domains," Journal of Consumer Research, 34 (2), 121–34.

Bettman, James R. and C. Whan Park (1980), "Effects of Prior Knowledge and Experience and Phase of the Choice Process on Consumer Decision Processes: A Protocol Analysis," Journal of Consumer Research, 7 (December), 234–48.

Dhar, Ravi (1997), "Consumer Preference for a No-Choice Option," Journal of Consumer Research, 24 (September), 215–31.

Franke, Nikolaus, Martin Schreier, and Ulrike Kaiser (2010), "The "I Designed It Myself" Effect in Mass Customization," Management Science, 56 (1), 125–40.

Häubl, Gerald and Valerie Trifts (2000), "Consumer Decision Making in Online Shopping Environments: The Effects of Interactive Decision Aids," Marketing Science, 19 (1), 4–21.

Huffman, Cynthia and Barbara E. Kahn (1998), "Variety for Sale: Mass Customization or Mass Confusion?" Journal of Retailing, 74 (4), 491–513.

Nordgren, Loran F. and Ap Dijksterhuis (2009), "The Devil Is in the Deliberation: Thinking Too Much Reduces Preference Consistency," Journal of Consumer Research, 36 (June), 39–46.

Scheibehenne, Benjamin, Rainer Greifeneder, and Peter M. Todd, "Can There Ever Be Too Many Options? A Meta-Analytic Review of Choice Overload." Journal of Consumer Research, 37 (October), 409–25.

Valenzuela, Ana, Ravi Dhar, and Florian Zettelmeyer (2009), "Contingent Response to Self-Customization Procedures: Implications for Decision Satisfaction and Choice," Journal of Marketing Research, 46 (6), 754–63.

Two wrongs CAN make a right:
The influence of salient self-attribution on self-image and subsequent goal pursuit

Nina Gros, Maastricht University, The Netherlands
Kelly Geyskens, Maastricht University, The Netherlands
Caroline Goukens, Maastricht University, The Netherlands
Ko de Ruyter, Maastricht University, The Netherlands

EXTENDED ABSTRACT

Consider yourself indulging in your delicious warm popcorn in the movie theater: will the subsequent exposure to thin models in the commercials or movie influence your self-perception? How will this exposure to a goal related cue (i.e. thin model = dieting) immediately after having engaged in goal-inconsistent behavior (i.e. eating popcorn ≠ dieting) influence your self-image?

Based on previous research showing that negative affect that is attributed to the self will motivate behavior (Duval & Lalwani, 1999), we expect that a confrontation with a goal related cue (e.g. a thin model) after having engaged in goal-inconsistent behavior (e.g. eating an unhealthy snack) can drive goal motivation. More specifically, we conjecture that the increased salience of one's own goal failure (e.g. diet failure), triggered by the combination of these events, will lead people to attribute the resulting negative affect to themselves, which in turn will motivate them to change the self (Dana, Lalwani, & Duval, 1997; Duval, Silvia, & Lalwani, 2001). This implies that individuals will not only try to restore/enhance their self-esteem but they will also strive to change the self in order to match the violated goal. Counter intuitively, this entails that individuals that encounter a goal related cue after having engaged in goal inconsistent behavior end up feeling better about themselves compared to individuals that encountered only one or none of these events. Interestingly, this even leads to enhanced goal performance in subsequent, unrelated, situations.

Study 1 (N=120) investigates how exposure to a goal related cue after engagement in goal-inconsistent behavior influences individuals' self-image. We hypothesize that exposure to a goal related cue right after having engaged in goal-inconsistent behavior stresses the attribution of the failure to the self. Consequently, emotion regulation processes will be triggered in order to cope with this negative affect, resulting in enhancement of one's self-image.[1] A 2 (goal-inconsistent behavior: eat complete muffin, no eating) x 2 (goal reminder: thin models, control[2]) experimental design tested the isolated effects of goal-inconsistent behavior (eating a muffin) or goal reminder (being exposed to thin models in advertisements) against the condition in which participants engaged in goal-inconsistent behavior prior to being exposed to the desirable end-state. We measured self-image in a series of 16 self-image dichotomies (e.g. strong-weak, in control-out of control) (adjusted from McFarlane, Polivy, & Herman, 1998). The resulting interaction effect on self-image (F(16, 93) = 2.340, p < 0.01) indicates that, in line with previous research (e.g. Henderson-King, Henderson-King, & Hoffmann, 2001), the single exposure to thin models negatively affects self-image. Interestingly, however, these negative effects were suppressed when participants engaged in goal-inconsistent behavior prior to the exposure to the thin models.

In Study 2 (N=58) we test whether the failure attribution to the self and the resulting attempt to amplify and restore the self-esteem is reflected in an increased signature size, as an implicit measure of self-esteem (Zweigenhaft, 1977; Zweigenhaft & Marlowe, 1973). The results of a 2 (goal inconsistent behavior: eat complete muffin, no eating) x 2 (goal reminder: thin models, control) experimental design indicate a significant interaction effect (F(1,53)=11.272, p < .01). More specifically, participants who engaged in goal-inconsistent behavior (ate a muffin) before being exposed to the goal related cue (thin model) significantly increased their signature size compared to participants that either were only exposed to the thin model or only engaged in goal-inconsistent behavior. The results of Study 2 support the hypothesis that exposure to a goal related cue right after having engaged in goal inconsistent behavior triggers self-enhancement strategies.

In the third study (N=51), we investigate whether this increased self-enhancement has a positive effect on goal performance in subsequent unrelated situations and we generalize the previous findings to a studying context. A 2 (goal inconsistent behavior: above average leisure activity, average leisure activity) x 2 (goal reminder: attractive job advertisements, control) between subjects design was conducted, measuring signature size and amount of M&M's consumed in a subsequent taste test. The results indicate a significant interaction effect (F(1,47)=6.13, p < .01) for signature size. More specifically, participants who were told that they engaged in goal-inconsistent behavior (i.e. spend more time than average on leisure activities) before being exposed to the desired end-state (i.e. attractive job advertisements) significantly increased their signature size compared to participants in the other conditions. Additionally, we find a significant interaction effect on the consumed amount of M&M's (F(1,47)=4.97, p < .05), showing that participants that engaged in goal-inconsistent behavior before being exposed to the desired end-state consumed less M&M's during a subsequent taste test, indicating that they are better at controlling themselves in an unrelated domain. A mediated moderation model (Muller, Judd, & Yzerbyt, 2005; Preacher, Rucker, & Hayes, 2007) showed that signature size partially mediated the effect of consumption, implying that the self-enhancement leads participants to actually perform better on a goal task in a different domain.

Taken together our results indicate that, counter intuitively, encountering a goal related cue subsequently to having engaged in goal inconsistent behavior (=goal failure) triggers self-enhancement strategies to restore self-esteem which even has a positive effect on subsequent goal performance. Coming back to our movie example, this implies that seeing a thin model in the movies after having indulged in popcorn will make you feel better than the person next to you seeing the thin model without having indulged in an unhealthy snack. More interestingly, this will even enable you to outperform your neighbor on subsequent goal pursuits even in unrelated domains. (Word count: 959)

---

[1]   Important to note is that participants who engaged in eating the muffin before exposure to the thin models in the advertisements did not differ in the self-image ratings from the control condition.

[2]   The control condition that is influenced by neither the goal inconsistent behavior nor the goal reminder provides a baseline measure of individuals' self-image.

REFERENCES

Dana, Edward R., Neal Lalwani & T. Shelley Duval (1997), Objective self-awareness and focus of attention following awareness of self-standard discrepancies: Changing self or changing standards of correctness, *Journal of social and clinical psychology, 16*(4), 359-380.

Duval, T. Shelley & Neal Lalwani (1999), Objective self-awareness and causal attributions for self-standard discrepancies: Changing self or changing standards of correctness, *Personality and Social Psychology Bulletin, 25*(10), 1220-1229.

Duval, T. Shelley, Paul J. Silvia & Neal Lalwani (2001), *Self-awareness & causal attribution: A dual systems theory*, Springer.

Henderson-King, Donna, Eaaron Henderson-King & Lisa Hoffmann (2001), Media images and women's self-evaluations: Social context and importance of attractiveness as moderators, *Personality and Social Psychology Bulletin, 27*(11), 1407.

McFarlane, Traci, Janet Polivy & C. Peter Herman (1998), Effects of false weight feedback on mood, self-evaluation, and food intake in restrained and unrestrained eaters, *Journal of Abnormal Psychology, 107*(2), 312-318.

Muller, Dominique, Charles M. Judd & Vincent Y. Yzerbyt (2005), When moderation is mediated and mediation is moderated, *Journal of Personality and Social Psychology, 89*(6), 852-863.

Preacher, Kristpher J., Derek D. Rucker & Andrew F. Hayes (2007), Addressing Moderated Mediation Hypotheses: Theory, Methods, and Prescriptions, *Multivariate Behavioral Research, 42*(1), 185-227.

Zweigenhaft, Richard L. (1977), *Social Behavior & Personality: An International Journal, 5*(1), 177.

Zweigenhaft, Richard L. & D. Ross Marlowe (1973), Signature size: Studies in expressive movement, *Journal of Consulting and Clinical Psychology, 40*(3), 469-473.

The Sleeper Framing Effect: The Influence of Frame Valence on Immediate and Retrospective Experiential Judgments

Mathew S. Isaac, Seattle University, USA
Morgan Poor, University of San Diego, USA

EXTENDED ABSTRACT

One of the most pervasive findings in framing research is the valence-consistent shift (Levin et al. 1998, 160); that is, positively valenced frames are preferred over equivalent negatively valenced frames. For example, ground beef labeled as 75% lean (positive valence) has been shown to receive more favorable evaluations than ground beef labeled as 25% fat (negative valence), even though the two alternatives are identical (i.e., 75% lean = 25% fat) (Levin 1987; Levin et al. 1985). Most of the framing research documenting valence-consistent shifts has explored how labels influence judgments of prospective or hypothetical consumption (e.g., LeBoeuf and Shafir 2003; Levin et al. 1985; Levin, Schnittjer, and Thee 1988).

In contrast, the present research examines how frames interact with actual consumption episodes to influence not only immediate judgments (i.e., judgments made during or immediately after a consumption episode) but also retrospective judgments (i.e., judgments made when reflecting back on a consumption episode). Unlike judgments of prospective or hypothetical consumption, we find evidence that exposure to a positive or a negative frame has little effect on judgments that are made immediately after an identical consumption experience. However, following a short delay, we demonstrate that the valence-consistent shift reemerges when consumers make retrospective judgments about their consumption experience, which we term the *sleeper framing effect*.

We attribute the sleeper framing effect to differences in how consumers integrate experiential information (e.g., taste, smoothness) and frame information when making immediate versus retrospective judgments. For immediate judgments, we believe that consumers emphasize their actual experience over framing because experiential information is particularly vivid (Paivio 1971) and may therefore be preferentially active in working memory. Our claim is supported by the results of a single study conducted by Levin and Gaeth (1988), which showed that the lean/fat frame effect described earlier had no effect on taste judgments when respondents were able to actually sample the beef immediately beforehand.

However, for retrospective judgments, when both experiential information and frame information would have shifted into long-term memory, we expect that experiential information may have less impact than non-experiential information (such as frames) on retrospective judgments made after a short delay. This prediction is based on prior research documenting the extreme fragility and distorted recall of experiential information (Galin 1994; Robinson and Clore 2002; Snodgrass 1997). In sum, our theorizing predicts that the valence-consistent shift found in the framing literature will disappear when consumers are asked to make experiential judgments immediately after being exposed to a valenced frame and consuming a product, but will reemerge when consumers are asked to make retrospective experiential judgments. Across three experiments, we provide evidence of a robust sleeper framing effect and demonstrate that it occurs because of variation in how consumers use different informational inputs (i.e., experiential vs. frame) when making judgments.

In experiment 1, we provided an initial demonstration of the sleeper framing effect on experiential judgments. Participants were first exposed to one of two logically equivalent frames, either positive or negative in valence, and subsequently engaged in the same sensory experience (i.e., listening to an unfamiliar song). Frame valence was manipulated by telling participants that recent market research had found that 50% of college students either liked (positive frame) or disliked (negative frame) the song that they would be hearing. Timing of evaluation was manipulated by having half of the participants provide an evaluation of the song immediately after the listening task, whereas the other half provided a retrospective evaluation 40 minutes later (following an unrelated filler task). Results were in line with our theorizing; frame valence had no influence on immediate experiential judgments but had a significant impact on retrospective judgments.

Although the results of experiment 1 were consistent with our theory, a rival explanation might attribute our results to an interaction between the timing of the evaluation and the order of information presentation, irrespective of whether either input was experiential or non-experiential. For example, one might argue that the sleeper framing effect observed in experiment 1 was caused by a *recency effect* for immediate judgments (where the sensory experience influenced evaluations the most since it was the last informational input received) and a *primacy effect* for retrospective judgments (where frame valence influenced evaluations the most since it was the first informational input received). This rival explanation is consistent with research showing that recent items in a list are better recalled immediately after exposure to the list because the recent items are still present in working memory, but that the primacy effect prevails when the entire list has shifted to long-term memory.

In experiment 2, we aimed to show that the sleeper framing effect could not be attributed to an interaction between the timing of the evaluation and the order of information presentation. We did this by reversing the order of information presentation so that all participants received experiential information before encountering our framing manipulation. If the serial order explanation was more parsimonious, we should have obtained a data pattern opposite to the one observed in experiment 1. However, even when using a different experiential domain (the visual experience of watching a black-and-white film clip), we found the same pattern of results as in experiment 1.

In experiment 3, we provided more direct process evidence for our proposal that the sleeper framing effect arises because of differences in the processing of experiential information versus frame information. Using a new sensory dimension (taste), we were able to eliminate the valence-consistent shift observed in earlier studies for retrospective judgments by encouraging participants to mentally relive their earlier experience. Furthermore, we collected thought listings to show that experiential information becomes more salient when retrospective judgments are made while mentally reliving an experience as compared to merely recalling a recent experience.

In addition to enriching our understanding of framing effects and experiential consumption, the sleeper framing effect has important implications for consumer choice, since immediate and retrospective judgments routinely influence the subsequent decisions and behaviors of consumers.

REFERENCES

Galin, David (1994), "The Structure of Awareness: Contemporary Applications of William James' Forgotten Concept of 'the Fringe'," *Journal of Mind and Behavior*, 15 (4), 375-400.

LeBoeuf, Robyn A. and Eldar Shafir (2003), "Deep Thoughts and Shallow Frames: On the Susceptibility to Framing Effects," *Journal of Behavioral Decision Making*, 16 (2), 77-92.

Levin, Irwin P. and Gary J. Gaeth (1988), "How Consumers Are Affected by the Framing of Attribute Information before and after Consuming the Product," *Journal of Consumer Research*, 15 (3), 374-78.

Levin, Irwin P., Richard D. Johnson, Craig P. Russo, and Patricia J. Deldin (1985), "Framing Effects in Judgment Tasks with Varying Amounts of Information," *Organizational Behavior and Human Decision Processes*, 36 (3), 362-77.

Levin, Irwin P., Sara K. Schnittjer, and Shannon L. Thee (1988), "Information Framing Effects in Social and Personal Decisions," *Journal of Experimental Social Psychology*, 24 (6), 520-29.

Paivio, Allan (1971), *Imagery and Verbal Processes*, New York: Holt, Rinehart & Winston.

Robinson, Michael D. and Gerald L. Clore (2002), "Belief and Feeling: Evidence for an Accessibility Model of Emotional Self-Report," *Psychological Bulletin*, 128 (6), 934-60.

Snodgrass, Gay (1997), "The Memory Trainers," in *Mind and Brain Sciences in the Twenty-First Century*, ed. Robert L. Solso, Cambridge, MA: MIT Press.

An Examination of the Effects of Market Returns and
Market Volatility on Investor Risk Tolerance and Investment Allocation Decisions

Courtney M. Droms, Butler University, USA
Kurt Carlson, Georgetown University, USA
William G. Droms, Georgetown University, USA

EXTENDED ABSTRACT

The 2008 credit market debacle and subsequent "Great Recession" accompanied by the stock market crash of 2008 has caused many investors and their advisors to reevaluate their risk tolerance and investment asset allocation choices (McCarthy 2009). In light of the so-called "Black Swan" events of 2008, many financial institutions and investment advisors are rethinking the advice they give to both individual and corporate clients about the level of risk that is appropriate to meet their investment objectives. There is now an effort underway by many financial institutions to overhaul the advice they give to both individual and corporate clients about the level of risk suggested for their portfolios (Mannes 2009).

One way in which investment advisors attempt to do this is by assessing an investor's risk tolerance and advising that the individual make certain portfolio choices based on their amount of risk tolerance. Risk tolerance is a term that has been used repeatedly in the financial literature to describe how much risk an individual or family is willing to undertake (or tolerate) in their account portfolio. In the current literature, risk tolerance is considered to be a trait that individual's possess and as such is not susceptible to market conditions and market movement (Bateman et. al. 2010; Corter and Chen 2006; Dulebohn 2002).

There is one study that we are aware of that demonstrates based on an analysis of secondary data that investment risk tolerance moves with the direction of the market. However, it is our belief that the movement of risk tolerance of an individual is more complex than solely increasing when the market increases and decreasing when the market decreases (Yao, Hanna, and Lindamood 2004). In this research, we see to contribute to the risk tolerance literature by examining if tolerance depends on market volatility and market returns. The literature suggests two possibilities for how these two factors might interact to determine risk tolerance.

The first possibility, the *variance as risk hypothesis*, suggests that greater variance produces greater risk (Harlow and Rao 1989). The idea here is that when variance is high, investors perceive risk. Thus, their tolerance for risk depends on what that risk did for them recently. If recent returns were positive, then the risk was good. However, if recent returns were negative, the risk was bad. The second possibility is the semi-variance as risk hypothesis, which suggests that investors only perceive risk when losses result (Estrada 2007; Fama and French 2010). The idea here is that market volatility will only matter for risk tolerance when recent returns were negative because when returns are positive, investors don't perceive risk.

If risk tolerance responds to changes in market volatility and recent returns, then the variance as risk hypothesis predicts that recent returns will influence risk tolerance when there is a lot of risk (i.e., when volatility is relatively high) in the market. Specifically, under high volatility, positive recent returns will increase risk tolerance and negative recent returns will decrease risk tolerance, but when volatility is low, recent returns will not alter risk tolerance. In contrast, the semi-variance account suggests that when returns are positive, there will be no difference in risk tolerance across market volatility levels because no risk will be perceived. In contrast, when returns are negative, the semi-variance hypothesis predicts that risk tolerance will

be lower for high variance than low variance because that is where perceived risk will be greatest.

To test between these two hypotheses, we used a 2 (Market Volatility: Low vs. High) x 2 (Market Returns: Increasing Market Returns vs. Decreasing Market Returns) between-participants design with 177 individuals (104 males, 73 females) between the ages of 18 and 83. Participants saw one of four graphical depictions of the market and a brief description of the market returns and market volatility conditions and were then asked a series of questions about their tolerance for risk in their investment decisions.

Results revealed a significant interaction between market volatility and market returns on risk tolerance ($F(1, 173) = 4.328$, $p < .04$). Decomposition of this interaction provided support for the risk and variance hypothesis because there was no difference in risk tolerance across positive and negative market returns when market volatility was low. Specifically, market investors were equally tolerant of risk regardless of whether the market was rising or falling ($M_{up} = 30.45$, $M_{down} = 30.91$, $t(87) = -.282$, ns, See Figure 1), so long as there was little volatility in the market. In contrast, when the market was volatile, investors' risk tolerance depended on recent market returns. Specifically, participants were more tolerant of risk when the market was going up than when the market was going down ($M_{up} = 32.95$, $M_{down} = 28.45$, $t(86) = 2.574$, $p < .02$).

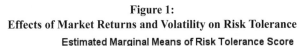

Figure 1:
Effects of Market Returns and Volatility on Risk Tolerance

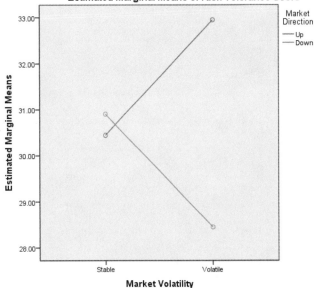

When these results are generalized to a large number of investors, this data may explain investor behavior during stock market "bubbles." As volatile markets move up, investor risk tolerance increases resulting in investors accepting increasing risk and contributing to the expansion of the bubble. In fact, it is likely that investors perceive accepting higher levels of risk as the key to success in a volatile and rising market. But when the volatile market turns down, risk tolerance plummets and investors begin to "de-risk" their portfolios by selling volatile assets and moving to less volatile assets, thus driving prices ever lower as the bubble bursts.

In addition to providing a new account for bubbles, this research shows that an investor's risk tolerance is not as stable as it has been portrayed previously. Practically, this research suggests how to examine investors' "true" risk tolerance. Namely, risk tolerance could be examined for low and high volatility markets with recent positive and recent negative returns and then averaged across all of these conditions to obtain a relatively general measure of risk tolerance for each investor. In addition, this research could assist government agencies and public policy groups in forecasting how individual investors may act as markets change.

REFERENCES

Bateman, Hazel, Jordan Louviere, Susan Thorp, Towhidul Islam, and Stephen Satchell (2010), "Investment Decisions for Retirement Savings," *The Journal of Consumer Affairs,* 44 (3), 463-482.

Corter, James E. and Yuh-Jia Chen (2006), "Do Investment Risk Tolerance Attitudes Predict Portfolio Risk?," *Journal of Business and Psychology*, 20 (3), 369-381.

Dulebohn, James H. (2002), "An Investigation of the Determinants of Investment Risk Behavior in Employer-Sponsored Retirement Plans," *Journal of Management*, 28 (1), 3-26.

Estrada, Javier (2007), "Mean-semivariance behavior: Downside risk and capital asset pricing," *International Review of Economics and Finance*, 16, 169-185.

Fama, Eugene F. and Kenneth R. French (2010), "Q&A: Semi-Variance: A Better Risk Measure?," *Fama/French Forum*, [available at http://www.dimensional.com/famafrench/2010/04/qa-semi-variance-a-better-risk-measure.html] (Accessed February 2012).

Harlow, W.V. and Ramesh K. S. Rao (1989), "Asset Pricing in a Generalized Mean-Lower Partial Moment Framework: Theory and Evidence," *Journal of Financial and Quantitative Analysis*, 24 (September), 285-311.

Mannes, Albert E.(2009), "Are we wise about the wisdom of the crowds? The use of group judgments in belief revision," *Management Science*, 55 (8), 1267-79

McCarthy, Ed (2009), "Time for Another Look at Client Risk Tolerance?" *Journal of Financial Planning*, February, 22 (2), 18–24.

Yao, Rui, Sherman D. Hanna, and Suzanne Lindamood (2004), "Changes in Financial Risk Tolerance, 1983-2001," *Financial Services Review*, 13, 249-266.

Shifting Away From Discomfort:
Managing Decision Difficulty Through Emotion Regulation

Stephanie M. Carpenter, University of Michigan, USA
J. Frank Yates, University of Michigan, USA
Stephanie D. Preston, University of Michigan, USA
Lydia Chen, University of Michigan, USA

EXTENDED ABSTRACT

Consumers are faced on a daily basis with difficult decisions in complex choice environments, and many of these decisions involve the careful weighing of options before a choice can be made. Research on pre-decisional coherence shifting (Simon, Krawezyk, and Holyoak 2004; pre-decisional distortion; Russo, Meloy and Medvec 1998) indicates that changes in the desirability and importance of choice alternative features begins prior to making a choice, rather than following the choice. Proposed mechanisms for why coherence shifting occurs, however, have been limited. Research suggests difficult decisions that are likely to create cognitive dissonance (Cooper 2007) are associated with a heightened arousal state or a feeling of discomfort. One method for measuring physiological arousal is with the skin conductance response (SCR), which is measured by attaching electrodes to the palm of the hand to detect slight changes in skin perspiration that reflect sympathetic activation. A seminal study on cognitive dissonance and skin conductance response (Croyle and Cooper 1983) indicated that cognitive dissonance increased SCR, and that resolving cognitive dissonance weakened the high arousal state.

The research described here sought to determine whether feature conflict arising from lacking a clearly dominant option produces a feeling of discomfort, which, in turn, leads some individuals to regulate this discomfort. We propose that coherence shifting reduces decision conflict, which in turn aids in the management of discomfort. We predicted that individuals who coherence shift would feel less of the discomfort that is often experienced when an individual must make a difficult choice between two competing alternatives, each of which includes both positive and negative attributes. In each of three studies, individuals who exhibited high levels of coherence shifting were hypothesized to do so as a consistent strategy for regulating feelings of discomfort, as reflected in lower physiological arousal and decreased perceived decision difficulty.

In Study 1, fifty-nine university undergraduates participated individually in a computerized procedure using an established coherence shift paradigm (Simon et al. 2004). Individuals were informed that they would be participating in a physiological study on decision making, and skin conductance response electrodes were attached to the palm of each participant's non-dominant hand. All participants rated the desirability of a number of possible job attributes, and then weighted how important these attributes were in a typical decision context. Participants were then shown the attributes of two specific job offers that varied on the dimensions of commute time, salary, office space, and vacation package. After viewing the offers, participants rated the desirability of the attributes and weighted attribute importance a second time. Participants then indicated their choice leanings. An interim task was given prior to participants making their final choices, followed by a third rating of attribute desirability and weighted importance.

In the studies conducted by Simon et al. (2004), coherence shifting was measured as a change in the attribute desirability and importance ratings at each time point to be consistent with the eventually chosen option. We replicated these general findings that individuals shift their desirability and importance ratings toward their final choice leanings. Analyses were conducted using a median split on the degree of coherence shifting, with the dependent variables representing SCR during the maximal decision window of 2000ms–3000ms. Results indicated that participants with high levels of coherence shifting on importance weightings also had significantly lower SCR (p < .05) across study blocks. Analyses were conducted to measure coherence shifting with respect to the specific study blocks. These revealed that participants who changed their importance weights the most also had significantly lower SCR (p < .05) across blocks. Further, the degree of coherence shifting with respect to the job offer attributes correlated significantly with perceived difficulty for both the desirability ratings (r = -.36, p = .005) and the importance weightings (r = -.53, p < .05), indicating that high coherence shifting was associated with less perceived decision difficulty.

In Study 2, one hundred and thirteen university undergraduates were recruited to participate individually in a laboratory study. Feelings of discomfort were manipulated to determine whether experiencing discomfort would lead to decreased coherence shifting among individuals who self-report less emotion regulation (Gross 1998). Using a difficult anagram procedure, participants were induced into a high discomfort, low discomfort, or baseline (no anagram task) condition. Following the discomfort manipulation, participants completed the job offer coherence shifting paradigm (Simon et al. 2004) described in Study 1. Results indicated that those who were induced to experience high discomfort and did not self-report emotion regulation tendencies shifted significantly less than those in a low discomfort or baseline condition (p < .05), supporting our argument that coherence shifting is a strategy used to regulate feelings of discomfort.

In Study 3, thirty-three university undergraduates were recruited to participate in a two-part study. Participants were brought back to the study for two separate sessions, held one week apart, to make two separate difficult decisions involving feature conflict. Decision tasks were counterbalanced across weeks. One task was the same job offer choice used in Studies 1 and 2, and the other task was a consumption choice involving selecting an apartment to rent. As predicted, some individuals consistently shifted more often than others across different decision occasions (p < .01), and this coherence shifting was correlated with self-reported emotion regulation tendencies (p < .05).

This research suggests that difficult decisions involving feature conflict are capable of producing feelings of discomfort, which some individuals manage via pre-decisional coherence shifting. These data are consistent with our proposed model of feature conflict leading to feelings of discomfort, which some individuals regulate through coherence shifting. Additional research is being conducted to further establish the proposed causal sequencing. These findings shed light on the basic mechanisms underlying decision making and provide important implications for why people use different choice strategies in complex consumption environments.

REFERENCES

Cooper, Joel (2007), *Cognitive Dissonance: Fifty Years of a Classic Theory,* London: Sage.

Croyle, Robert T. and Cooper, Joel (1983), "Dissonance Arousal: Physiological Evidence," *Journal of Personality and Social Psychology,* 45, 782-791.

Russo, J. Edward, Meloy, Margaret G. and Medvec, Victoria H. (1998), "Predecisional Distortion of Product Information," *Journal of Marketing Research,* 35, 438-452.

Simon, Dan, Krawezyk, Daniel C. and Hoyoak. Keith J. (2004), "Construction of Preferences by Constraint Satisfaction," *Psychological Science,* 15, 331-336.

"That Ad's Been Retouched? – That Can Be Me!":
The Persuasive Impact of Advertising Disclosure and Body-Image Idealization

Rania W. Semaan, American University of Sharjah, UAE
Stephen J. Gould, Baruch College/CUNY, USA
Bruno Kocher, HEC Paris, France

EXTENDED ABSTRACT

A common advertising tactic is to digitally manipulate models' images to enhance their looks. Research has found that exposure to media images depicting the thin-ideal body affects one's self-concept and product evaluations. However, despite their impact on advertising effectiveness, (Hafner and Trampe 2009) there is limited research that considers that the thin ideal is not only heightened through using slender models but also through their digital manipulation (Hitchon and Reaves 1999). Research on eating disorders suggests that mass media should be required to inform consumers of these computer-modified images, though without examining the consequences (Thompson and Heinberg 1999).

The present research looks at the exposure to digitally manipulated thin-idealized body images on consumers' product and self-evaluations. It also highlights the effects of disclosing such manipulation. We investigate the effects of such disclosure in terms of one-sided versus two-sided advertisements (ads featuring only positive appeals versus those with both positive and negative content, Etgar and Goodwin 1982). We posit that a disclosed retouched ad would be perceived as less honest than a disclosed un-retouched ad indicating that consumers perceive it as two-sided. This leads to higher preference for disclosed retouched ads and more favorable brand evaluations.

We also explore social comparison theory in explaining the ads' effects on consumers' self-evaluation. When individuals are exposed to comparison targets, they selectively compare themselves to these targets and evaluate their own performance where (dis)similarity generates (contrast) assimilation effects (Mussweiler 2003). Moreover, comparison targets affect people only when they are perceived as more inspirational and their achievement is attainable (Lockwood and Kunda 1997). Thus, we predict that when exposed to retouched advertisements depicting thin-attractive models, consumers will experience a contrast in their self-evaluation. However, this dissimilarity will dissipate once they are told that this advertisement has been digitally enhanced, thus leading them to experience assimilative self-evaluation and that perceived attainability of the model's attractiveness mediates this effect.

STUDY 1

Study 1 investigates whether when consumers are informed of digital manipulation, their brand evaluations for an imagined perfume brand, Espoire, will be higher after exposure to a retouched (vs. un-retouched) ad and whether this effect is mediated by perceptions of ad honesty. A 2 (Ad: (Un)retouched) x 2 (Disclosure: (No) Disclosure) between-subjects design was applied to a sample of 143 females.

Results revealed a significant two-way interaction on attitude towards the ad (A_{ad}) F (1, 138) = 5.946, $p < .01$), where consumers evaluate the retouched ad ($M_{No\ Disclosure}$ = 3.700, $M_{Disclosure}$ = 5.649) more favorably than the un-retouched ad ($M_{No\ Disclosure}$ = 2.686, $M_{Disclosure}$ = 3.129) whether they were told that the ad has (has not) been digitally-enhanced or not. Results also show a significant two-way interaction on brand evaluations (F (1, 139) = 4.118, $p < .05$) where participants evaluated the brand in the retouched ad more favorably (M = 5.108) than in the un-retouched ad (M = 3.724) when told the ad has (has not) been digitally enhanced. However, when no such disclosure was provided, consumers' brand evaluations did not differ. Planned contrasts revealed that, within the retouched ad, participants like the retouched ad and brand more when told the ad has been digitally-enhanced versus when no such disclosure is provided.

Following Zhao, Lynch, and Chen (2010) a mediated-moderation was performed. The analysis revealed that ad honesty significantly mediates the effect of ad × disclosure on A_{ad}, brand evaluations, and purchase intentions, such that participants perceive the disclosed retouched ad as less honest (two-sided) and therefore prefer it, evaluate the brand better, and have higher purchase intentions than for the one-sided advertisements.

STUDY 2

Study 2, using the same brand as in Study 1, explores the moderating effect of disclosure of thin-idealized body images on females' self-evaluation as a form of social comparison. We also examine the mediating effects of perceived attainability of the ad × disclosure interaction on self-evaluation.

Concerning product evaluations and ad honesty as a mediator, the results replicate Study 1. We also found a significant ad × disclosure interaction effect on participants' self-evaluation (F (1, 172) = 6.731, $p < .01$). Participants had higher self-evaluation when exposed to a disclosed retouched ad (M = 5.142) than a disclosed un-retouched ad (M = 4.407) or an undisclosed retouched ad (M = 4.365). When no disclosure was provided, participants' self-evaluation was not significantly different when exposed to a retouched or un-retouched ad.

Perceived attainability mediates the effect of image × disclosure interaction on self-evaluation such that participants who were exposed to the retouched ad and were told that it was retouched perceived that the model's looks are more attainable than all others thereby increasing their self-evaluations. However, attainability is not a significant mediator for the ad × disclosure interaction on A_{ad}, brand evaluations, and purchase intentions.

STUDY 3

In Study 3 we aim to investigate a boundary condition for the effects found in study 2. We employed a 2 (Disclosure: No(Disclosure) x 2 (Product: Problem-solving vs. beauty-enhancing) between-subjects design using only the retouched ad. Problem solving is a product that fixes a beauty problem (body lotion) whereas beauty-enhancing products do not necessarily hide a beauty problem (perfume).

Results reveal a significant two-way interaction (p < .05) such that participants have a higher ad and brand preference and higher purchase intentions for body lotion than for perfume when it is disclosed that the ad has been retouched. However when no such disclosure is provided, their preferences are not significantly different across the two types of product ads.

DISCUSSION

This research suggests that disclosure of digital-enhancement generates higher brand evaluations. Two studies show that consumers prefer retouched ads especially when told these ads have been digitally enhanced. Contrary to prior research, we demonstrate that even though consumers judge the digitally enhanced advertisement to be less honest, they evaluate brands more favorably and are more willing to buy them when displayed in retouched ads. Analysis also revealed that consumers' perceived attainability explains the effect of disclosed enhancement on self-evaluation. Research, managerial and public policy implications which incorporate not only the more conventionally perceived, negative effects, but also the more counterintuitive, positive effects of retouching may be drawn for these findings.

REFERENCES

Etgar, Michael and Stephen A. Goodwin (1982), "One-Sided versus Two-Sided Comparative Message Appeals for New Brand Introductions," *Journal of Consumer Research,* 8 (4), 460 – 65.

Hafner, Michael and Debra Trampe (2009), "When Thinking is Beneficial and When it is Not: The Effects of Thin and Round Advertising Models," *Journal of Consumer Psychology,* 19 (4), 619 – 28.

Hitchon, Jacqueline and Sheila Reaves (1999), "Media Mirage: The Thin Ideal as Digital Manipulation," in *Sexual Rhetoric: Media Perspectives on Sexuality, Gender, and Identity,* eds. Meta G. Castarphen and Susan Zavoina, Westport, CT: Greenwood, 65 – 76.

Lockwood, Penelope and Ziva Kunda (1997), "Superstars and Me: Predicting the Impact of Role Models on the Self," *Journal of Personality and Social Psychology,* 73 (1), 91 – 103.

Mussweiler, Thomas (2003), "Comparison Processes in Social Judgment: Mechanisms and Consequences," *Psychological Review,* 110 (July), 472 – 89.

Thompson, Kevin J. and Leslie J. Heinberg (1999), "The Media's Influence on Body Image Disturbance and Eating Disorders: We've Reviled Them, Now Can We Rehabilitate Them?" *Journal of Social Issues,* 55 (2), 339 – 53.

Zhao, Xinshu, John G. Lynch JR., and Qimei Chen (2010), "Reconsidering Baron and Kenny: Myths and Truths about Mediation Analysis," *Journal of Consumer Research*, 37 (2), 197-206.

On the Impact of Prior Ideas on Ideation Performance in Ideation Contests

Suleiman Aryobsei, University of St.Gallen, Switzerland
Reto Hofstetter, University of St.Gallen, Switzerland
Andreas Herrmann, University of St.Gallen, Switzerland

EXTENDED ABSTRACT

Ideation contests are increasingly held among employees and consumers (solvers) to support the innovation process particularly during the early stages of new product development (Boudreau, Lacetera, & Lakhani, 2011). In such contests, solvers generate ideas for how to solve innovation problems and hereby compete for financial rewards that will be granted to the best ideas, which are chosen by the idea seeker (Terwiesch & Ulrich, 2009). Frequently, such contests are held publicly and the whole solution space of ideas is accessible to all solvers at any time (Dell's IdeaStorm, 99designs). While prior literature mainly focuses on privately held or "parallel search" contests (Kornish & Ulrich, 2011), little is known about the optimal design of publicly held contests. In this project, we investigate how solvers behave in public ideation contests and how the contest outcome depends on prior information on the content and the context of the ideas.

THEORY AND HYPOTHESES DEVELOPMENT

Theory is mixed in predicting the impact of prior ideas on ideation performance. According to the recombinant growth theory, the creation of new ideas is commonly defined as the new recombination of existing ideas (Hadamard, 1949; Jeroen, 2008; Koestler, 1964; Weitzman, 1998). In ideation contests, solvers are able to further develop and recombine existing ideas. Though, we hypothesize that allowing for recombination of prior ideas improves the overall ideation performance and the specific nature of the prevalent information (degree of quality and novelty) influences the nature of the newly developed ideas.

Reversely, knowledge of the solution space can impede creativity to the extent that solvers seek conformity with existing ideas instead of generating new ideas (Smith, Ward, & Schumacher, 1993; Smith & Tindell, 1997). In a contest situation, we hypothesize that solvers will especially build upon existing ideas with high quality ratings. Building upon ideas that are presumed to have a higher chance of winning is in line with a behavior that aims at maximize the odds of winning the reward of the contest when a seeker's tastes are difficult to observe. We argue that such behavior can be counterproductive since the diversity of the solution space will ultimately be reduced, with negative impact on the overall quality of the contest outcome (Terwiesch & Xu, 2008).

ANALYSIS OF FIELD DATA

We analyzed a large-scale dataset of an online ideation platform, including 100 contests, 2,300 active solvers, and over 40,000 ideas. By using a text-mining approach we detect the number of similar words as an indicator for the similarity of the content of any pair of two submitted ideas. A high overlap of similar words between ideas is an indicator for a high degree of confirmation.

On the analyzed platform, submitted ideas are presented in a chronological order to the solvers. Though, very recent submitted ideas are more prevalent than earlier submitted ideas. We found that new submitted ideas had a high similarity to recent prior ideas. Figure 1 indicates that there is a significantly higher similarity of new ideas to very recent submitted ideas than to older ideas (β = -.00059, $t(1057)$ = -93.29, $p < .001$). Furthermore, solvers were more likely to build upon highly rated ideas compared of lower rated ideas (β =

.01313, $t(29)$ = 2.80, $p < .01$). Figure 2 shows the average similarity of ideas depending on the rating by the community of the previous submitted ideas. Highly rated ideas were more likely to be used as a basis compared to lower rated ideas.

Figure 1: Average similarity of ideas depending on their distance in their chronological order (R^2 = .90, $F(1, 1057)$ = 8703.62, $p < .001$).

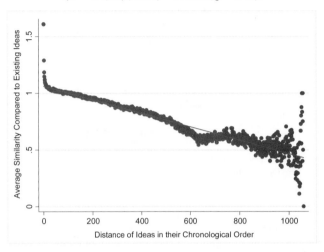

Participants rather confirmed ideas very recent submitted ideas than more early sent ideas. Very recent sent ideas were mere prevalent to the solver than more early send ideas.

Figure 2: Average similarity to new developed ideas depending on the number or rate ups (community rating) of the existing ideas (R^2 = .21, $F(1, 29)$ = 7.84, p < .01).

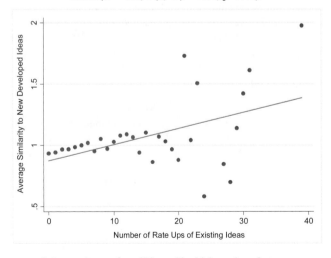

Solvers rather confirmed ideas with a high number of rate ups than ideas with a low number of rate ups.

In addition, we found that recombining existing ideas has positive influence on the quality the new developed ideas (β = .018079, $t(29)$ = 3.07, $p < .01$). Figure 3 shows the average similarity to previous submitted ideas depending on the rating of the new developed ideas. Ideas with high similarity to previous submitted ideas were rated higher than ideas with a low similarity to existing ideas.

Figure 3: Average similarity to previous submitted ideas depending on the number or rate ups of the new ideas ($R^2 = .24$, $F(1, 29) = 9.45$, $p < .01$).

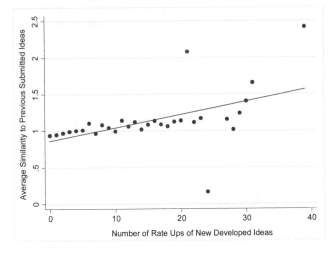

Ideas with a high number of rate ups are more similar to previous submitted ideas than ideas with a low number of rate ups.

EXPERIMENT

We further conducted an experiment with a 2x2 full-factorial between-subjects design. Each solver was asked to generate novel ideas to the same ideation problem. Before entering an own idea, he saw three existing ideas that varied by their quality and the novelty. 272 participants took part in this study and delivered ideas. After the experimental contest was held, the novelty and quality of the submitted ideas were evaluated by 265 judges using a web-based interface (similar to Girotra, 2010). The ideas were presented independently in a random order and each idea was evaluated by about 30 judges. We found significant main effects: The quality of the submitted ideas was higher, if solvers had seen high quality example ideas ($M_{LowQ} = 3.51$; $M_{HighQ} = 3.67$; $F(1, 272) = 1.65$; $p = 0.029$). Furthermore, the degree of novelty of submitted ideas was higher if solvers had seen more novel example ideas ($M_{LowN} = 3.62$; $M_{HighN} = 3.81$; $F(1, 272) = 4.21$; $p = 0.041$).

CONCLUSION

Our results show that solvers are indeed influenced by the nature of the extant ideas in open ideation contests. We found that in line with recombinant-growth theory, ideas that build upon existing ideas tend to be better evaluated. Our results suggest that this is due

to the self-organizing behavior of the community reacting sensitive to quality signals in a situation of high uncertainty about a seeker's tastes. Newly entering solvers look out for these signals that can guide their ideation effort into a direction that ensures maximization of the odds to win the contest. Community ratings, which are also publicly available, can provide such guidance when seeker feedback is missing. As a result, the ratings guide new users to high quality ideas which can then be further recombined for even better ideas. While increasing quality of the good ideas, such behavior ultimately leads to increased conformity with existing ideas.

In conclusion, our findings suggest that seekers that ought to maximize the quality of the best ideas should perform public ideation contests and allow for quality signaling during the contest. Seekers that intend to maximize the variance of the solution space, however, might be better off to keep their contests privately.

REFERENCES

Boudreau, Kevin J., Nicola Lacetera, and Karim R. Lakhani (2011), "Incentives and Problem Uncertainty in Innovation Contests: An Empirical Analysis," *Management science,* 57(5), 843-863.

Girotra, Karan, Christian Terwiesch, and Karl T. Ulrich (2010), "Idea Generation and the Quality of the Best Idea," *Management science,* 56, 591-605.

Hadamard, Jacques (1949), *The Psychology of Invention in the Mathematical Field.* Princton, NJ: Princeton University Press.

Koestler, Arthur (1964), *The Act of Creation.* New York: Macmillan.

Kornish, Lauro J. and Karl T. Ulrich (2011), "Opportunity Spaces in Innovation: Empirical Analysis of Large Samples of Ideas," *Management Science,* 57, 107-128.

Smith, Steven M. and Deborah R. Tindell (1997), "Memory blocks in word fragment completion caused by involuntary retrieval of orthographically related primes," *Journal of Experimental Psychology: Learning, Memory, and Cognition,* 23(2), 355-370.

Smith, Steven M., Thomas B. Ward, and Jay S. Schumacher (1993), "Constraining effects of examples in a creative generation task," *Memory & Cognition,* 21, 837-845.

Terwiesch, Christian and Karl T. Ulrich (2009), *Innovation Tournaments: Creating and Selecting Exceptional Opportunities.* Boston: Harvard Business School Press.

Terwiesch, Christian and Xu, Yi (2008), "Innovation contests, open innovation, and multiagent problem solving," *Management Science,* 54(9), 1529-1543.

Van den Bergh, Jeroen C.J.M (2008), "Optimal diversity: Increasing returns versus recombinant innovation," *Journal of Economic Behavior & Organization,* 68(3-4), 565-580.

Weitzman, Martin L. (1998), "Recombinant Growth," *The Quarterly Journal of Economics, 113*(2), 331-360.

When the Crowd is Divided: Perceptions of Dispersion in Word-of-Mouth

Stephen He, Georgia Institute of Technology, USA
Samuel Bond, Georgia Institute of Technology, USA

EXTENDED ABSTRACT

Empowered by information technology to seek the opinions of others, consumers are more likely than ever to encounter a mixture of positive and negative word-of-mouth for the same product or service. Given that consumers generally prefer certainty to uncertainty, intuition suggests that they will favor products with consistent WOM (Matz and Wood 2005; Urbany, Dickson, and Wilkie 1989). However, a survey of online platforms reveals that the distribution of customer ratings is often highly disperse or bimodal (Hu, Pavlou, and Zhang 2009), connoting substantial uncertainty and decision risk (Meyer 1981). Greater dispersion of WOM has been shown to lower sales and satisfaction in certain contexts (Moon, Bergey, and Iacobucci 2010; Zhu and Zhang 2010), but findings in other contexts have been mixed (Clemons, Gao, and Hitt 2006; Martin, Barron, and Norton 2008).

Drawing on research in social perception (Boldry and Kashy 1999; Nisbett and Kunda 1985) and attribution (Folkes 1988; Kelley 1973), we propose that WOM dispersion often stem from two general sources: 1) uncertainty in product performance, and 2) idiosyncrasy in preferences across reviewers (taste variability). Prior research using expert ratings and online reviews has focused primarily on the first of these sources. For products characterized by low taste variability, WOM can be viewed as a proxy for product quality; hence, high dispersion indicates inconsistent performance and is aversive (Price, Feick, and Higie 1989; West and Broniarczyk 1998; Sun 2011). We propose that for products characterized by high taste variability (e.g., art, restaurants), variation in WOM may also be attributed to idiosyncrasy among reviewers, or 'mixed opinions.' In these cases, high dispersion may be acceptable if consumers are both aware and tolerant of divergence in taste (Berger and Heath 2007; Cheema and Kaikati 2010).

To summarize, we predict that the influence of WOM dispersion on liking and choice will be moderated by taste variability: when perceived taste variability is low, greater dispersion will be detrimental, but this effect will be attenuated when perceived taste variability increases. Our hypotheses were examined in four studies involving hypothetical decision scenarios. In all studies, subjects were given displays of WOM distributions that included both an overall 'average' rating and the distribution of ratings around that average (using a horizontal bar chart). In terms of expected utility, this format allowed us to vary both the expected outcome of choosing the product (its average rating) and the risk of a obtaining a worse outcome (its dispersion).

Study 1 used a mixed factorial design including perceived taste variability, WOM average, and WOM dispersion. Taste variability was manipulated through product category: based on pretesting, we selected desk lamps and framed paintings for the low- and high-variability conditions, respectively. For each product, a set of sixteen scenarios was presented within-subjects. Each scenario described one focal product and its reviews. The scenarios crossed four levels of average rating (4 through 7 out of 10) with four levels of dispersion (high: $var > 8.00$, medium: $var \approx 2.00$, low: $var < 1.00$, and zero: $var = 0$). Participants (189 undergraduate students) evaluated all scenarios, one at a time, and reported their purchase intention.

In the analyses, purchase intention was mean-centered to allow comparisons between product categories. ANOVA revealed the predicted interaction between dispersion and product category

($F(3, 1349) = 2.55$, $p = .05$), and follow-up comparisons were consistent with our hypotheses. When dispersion was low, participants expressed similar purchase intention for lamps and paintings; when dispersion was high, they were less likely to buy lamps than to buy paintings.

Study 2a and 2b expanded the investigation to consumer choices. In study 2a, 61 paid participants made a series of choices based on WOM information. The choice scenarios included two target categories (lamps and paintings) separated by various fillers. For the two target categories, participants were asked to choose from a pair of similarly attractive options with distinct mean and variance. Analyses were conducted by comparing the relative shares of each option. As expected, choices differed reliably across taste variability ($\chi^2(1) = 3.97$, $p = .05$), such that the high-average / high-dispersion option (A) was chosen more often for paintings than for lamps.

Study 2b included 79 paid participants and was similar to Study 2a, with two major differences. First, two product categories were added: flash drives (low taste variability) and downloadable music albums (high taste variability). Second, the stimuli were constructed so that Option A 'dominated' Option B. Analyses of participant choices again revealed a reliable difference across taste variability conditions ($\chi^2(1) = 25.51$, $p < .001$). Moreover, despite having lower expected value and higher variance, the 'dominated' option was chosen by almost half of participants (43%) in categories with high taste variability.

Study 3 (132 paid students) removed potential confounds by holding constant the focal product category (hotels). Taste variability was manipulated directly, by telling participants that the WOM was posted by either a diverse group of reviewers or a group of college students. Dispersion was manipulated between-subjects: high ($var = 3.59$) or low ($var = 0.95$). Participants observed the WOM information and reported their intention to purchase a coupon for the hotel. In addition, they completed an attribution measure designed to collect evidence for our hypothesized process (see below).

Analyses revealed both a main effect of dispersion and a dispersion * taste variability interaction ($F(1, 128) = 4.60$, $p < .05$). Although more dispersion reduced purchase intention in general, the effect was smaller when WOM was provided by a diverse group of reviewers than by college students alone. The attribution measure provided further support for our model: when dispersion was high, participants were more likely to attribute dispersion to 'something about the hotel' if they believed the ratings came from a homogenous group of reviewers.

Taken together, our results demonstrate that consumers' reaction to dispersion in product WOM depends on the way that dispersion can be attributed. These findings have important implications for researchers exploring the impact of WOM and the processing of statistical information, as well as practitioners facing divided consumer opinions of their offerings.

REFERENCES

Averill, James R. (1973), "Personal Control over Aversive Stimuli and Its Relationship to Stress," *Psychological Bulletin*, 80 (4), 286-303.

Berger, Jonah and Chip Heath (2007), "Where Consumers Diverge from Others: Identity Signaling and Product Domains," *Journal of Consumer Research*, 34 (2), 121-34.

Boldry, Jennifer G. and Deborah A. Kashy (1999), "Intergroup Perception in Naturally Occurring Groups of Differential Status: A Social Relations Perspective," *Journal of Personality and Social Psychology*, 77 (6), 1200-12.

Cheema, Amar and Andrew M. Kaikati (2010), "The Effect of Need for Uniqueness on Word of Mouth," *Journal of Marketing Research*, 47 (3), 553-63.

Clemons, Eric K., Guodong Gordon Gao, and Lorin M. Hitt (2006), "When Online Reviews Meet Hyperdifferentiation: A Study of the Craft Beer Industry," *Journal of Management Information Systems*, 23 (2), 149-71.

Folkes, Valerie S. (1988), "Recent Attribution Research in Consumer Behavior: A Review and New Directions," *Journal of Consumer Research*, 14 (4), 548-65.

Fried, Lisbeth S. and Keith J. Holyoak (1984), "Induction of Category Distributions: A Framework for Classification Learning," *Journal of Experimental Psychology: Learning, Memory, and Cognition*, 10 (2), 234-57.

Hu, Nan, Paul A. Pavlou, and Jie Zhang (2009), "Overcoming the J-Shaped Distribution of Product Reviews," *Communications of the ACM*, 52 (10), 144-47.

Hui, Michael K. and John E. G. Bateson (1991), "Perceived Control and the Effects of Crowding and Consumer Choice on the Service Experience," *Journal of Consumer Research*, 18 (2), 174-84.

Kahneman, Daniel and Amos Tversky (1979), "Prospect Theory: An Analysis of Decision under Risk," *Econometrica*, 47 (2), 263-91.

Kelley, Harold H. (1973), "The Processes of Causal Attribution," *American Psychologist*, 28 (2), 107-28.

Laczniak, Russell N., Thomas E. DeCarlo, and Sridhar N. Ramaswami (2001), "Consumers' Responses to Negative Word-of-Mouth Communication: An Attribution Theory Perspective," *Journal of Consumer Psychology*, 11 (1), 57-73.

Martin, Jolie M., Gregory M. Barron, and Michael I. Norton (2008), "Response to Variance in the Opinions of Others: Preferable in Positive Domains, Aversive in Negative Domains," *Society for Consumer Psychology Conference Proceedings*, New Orleans, LA.

Matz, David C. and Wendy Wood (2005), "Cognitive Dissonance in Groups: The Consequences of Disagreement," *Journal of Personality and Social Psychology*, 88 (1), 22-37.

Meyer, Robert J. (1981), "A Model of Multiattribute Judgments under Attribute Uncertainty and Informational Constraint," *Journal of Marketing Research*, 18 (4), 428-41.

Moon, Sangkil, Paul K. Bergey, and Dawn Iacobucci (2010), "Dynamic Effects among Movie Ratings, Movie Revenues, and Viewer Satisfaction," *Journal of Marketing*, 74 (1), 108-21.

Mudambi, Susan M. and David Schuff (2010), "What Makes a Helpful Online Review? A Study of Customer Reviews on Amazon.Com," *MIS Quarterly*, 34 (1), 185-200.

Nisbett, Richard E. and Ziva Kunda (1985), "Perception of Social Distributions," *Journal of Personality and Social Psychology*, 48 (2), 297-311.

Parkes, K. R. (1984). "Locus of control, cognitive appraisal, and coping in stressful episodes." *Journal Of Personality and Social Psychology*, 46(3), 655-668.

Price, Linda L., Lawrence F. Feick, and Robin A. Higie (1989), "Preference Heterogeneity and Coorientation as Determinants of Perceived Informational Influence," *Journal of Business Research*, 19 (3), 227-42.

Sun, Monic (2011), "How Does Variance of Product Ratings Matter?," *Management Science*, forthcoming.

Urbany, Joel E., Peter R. Dickson, and William L. Wilkie (1989), "Buyer Uncertainty and Information Search," *The Journal of Consumer Research*, 16 (2), 208-15.

West, Patricia M. and Susan M. Broniarczyk (1998), "Integrating Multiple Opinions: The Role of Aspiration Level on Consumer Response to Critic Consensus," *Journal of Consumer Research*, 25 (1), 38-51.

Zhu, Feng and Xiaoquan Zhang (2010), "Impact of Online Consumer Reviews on Sales: The Moderating Role of Product and Consumer Characteristics," *Journal of Marketing*, 74 (2), 133-48.

Consuming 'Media Trash:' When "Bad" Becomes "Good"

Björn Bohnenkamp, University of Muenster, Germany
Caroline Wiertz, City University London, UK
Thorsten Hennig-Thurau, University of Muenster, Germany

EXTENDED ABSTRACT

Using a multi-method approach, we explore the concept of "media trash" and investigate why consumers with different levels of cultural capital seek the consumption of these particular media offers despite or even because of their questionable quality.

RESEARCH TOPIC AND QUESTION

Media consumption is one of today's most important consumption activities, with U.S. citizens spending more than 11 hours a day engaging with various media offerings (eMarketer 2011). The question of what constitutes "quality" in such offerings has been hotly debated among media scholars ever since the rise of reality TV formats and more recently user-generated content platforms (e.g., McCabe and Akass 2007). In consumer research, Holbrook (1999) states that the success of media offerings is grounded in popular appeal as opposed to "good taste" –and the commercial success of certain TV formats, movies, and books that are the opposite of 'critically acclaimed' seems to support his theory. While some studies identify general reasons for consuming reality TV shows (e.g., Papachrissi and Mendelson 2007) and particularly the quest for authenticity through the consumption of these shows (Rose and Wood 2005), they fail to address the startling question of why "bad taste" can be attractive. The aim of this study is to investigate what consumers mean when they refer to "media trash" and why consumers sometimes prefer the consumption of products of lower quality *purposefully because of* this lower quality (e.g., watching a "bad" reality TV show such as 'Wife Swap' just because it is so "bad").

LITERATURE REVIEW

In the popular press, the expression "media trash" is used frequently but without a clear definition or explanation. As an academic concept, the term "trash" is used in media studies for popular or pulp fiction (e.g., Bloom 1996), for a specific kinds of visual style in television (e.g., Caldwell 1995), or specific genres like soap operas, talk shows or B-movies (e.g., Kael 1969). In consumer research, the startling purposeful consumption of lower quality products has not been discussed, with the exception of Holbrook (1999, see above). However, a small body of research has investigated the consumption of special TV formats that fall into this category, namely soap operas (Russell, Norman, and Heckler 2004) and reality TV (Rose and Wood 2005). Russel et al. (2004) show that consumers develop a relationship with TV programs and their characters, and that the intensity of this "connectedness" how their behavior is influenced. Rose and Wood (2004) comment on the rise of reality TV formats and argue that consumers seek authenticity through the consumption of these particular TV formats. The question of why consumers seek the consumption of certain media offerings *despite* or even *because of* their questionable quality remains unanswered.

METHOD

We opted for an inductive multi-method approach to collect our data. First, we collected 1520 articles in relevant German newspapers and magazines that mentioned the word "trash" in the context of media. Second, we collected survey data from a representative sample of the German population (n=580) to understand which particular media offers were consumed regularly and how they were rated on a variety of quality and content dimensions.

The core data are semi-structured depth interviews with 38 consumers about one media offering that we selected based on the survey results: the German version of the reality TV show "I'm a Celebrity... Get Me Out of Here!" This TV show was one of the most relevant media offerings mentioned in German newspapers and magazines; it was known by nearly all consumers, and consensually described as "trash." The interviews took on average one hour and focused on when, how and why participants watched this show. Moreover, we also asked questions about our participants' general taste in media and their media consumption rituals.

FINDINGS

Based on a content analysis of the newspaper articles and the survey results, we developed an overview of current (German) media offerings which are commonly evaluated as trash, both by experts and by consumers. The term is most often used in association with television shows, but also newspapers, music, books and movies. We identified eight markers of "media trash" based on how consumers distinguish between offerings that they would describe as trash or non-trash. At least one of the markers presented in Table 1 has to be present for a media offering to be considered "trash."

Table 1: Eight Markers of Media Trash

Marker of "Media Trash"	Representative Quotes (translated from German)
Intellectually undemanding content	"It's just entertainment TV without any educational background." "Superficial person, who benefits from the stupidity of the people."
Low formal quality	"Cheap production, bad actors, pointless scenarios."
Low authenticity	"Nothing is real; everything is fake but touted as true." "It's completely posed."
Repeated emotion-seeking patterns	"Always the same – the Cobra team manages all situations and saves the world for us." "All songs are the same."
Absurd and unrealistic content	"The story is absolute wacky." "Absolute nonsense, but more than just funny."
Exaggerated content	"The gonzo headlines above badly researched articles."
Inappropriate content	"Distasteful and degrading to people and animals." "Sold voyeurism."
Arousal-seeking content	"Explicit description of sexual practices." "Exorbitant presentation of violence and blood."

An important finding is that the valence of these markers, despite appearing negative on first sight, is in fact dependent on each consumer and each media offering. For example, the newspaper "Bild"—comparable to the "Daily Mail"—was described by many consumers as being a favorite newspaper *because of* its low intellectual demand and its absurd and unrealistic content. In this sense, "bad" can indeed become "good" and the consumption of media trash is enjoyable for consumers.

This enjoyment, however, creates a conflict for consumers with high cultural capital when defining their social identity. They develop a number of arguments which "justify" trash consumption to reshape their own self-concept and to re-emphasize their cultural capital.

Furthermore, beyond the general notion of cultural capital, consumers display a media-specific capital. Consumers who have both a high involvement and a deep knowledge of a medium often watch bad taste offerings to reflect on the media-specific genre conventions on a meta-position.

Finally, consumers integrate trash media in a hypermedia consumption experience: During trash consumption they post their feelings and attitudes via Facebook, Twitter, and other social networking services. Not the actual media offering itself, but the communication among a subculture of consumers (Kates 2002, Schouten and McAlexander 1995) is the main reason for consumption.

CONTRIBUTIONS

Our project contributes to consumer research by shedding light on the markers of "media trash" and the reasons why consumers choose to consume these specific media offerings. We pay special attention to the social and cultural background of this consumption practice, and structure our understanding of the phenomenon with Bourdieu's theory of practice (Bourdieu 1977, 1984) and a broad range of media theories (e.g., Adorno and Horkheimer 1973; Hall 1973).

REFERENCES

Adorno, Theodor W. and Max Horkheimer (1973): *Dialectic of Enlightenment*, New York: Continuum.

Arnould, Eric J. and Craig J. Thompson (2005), "Consumer Culture Theory: Twenty Years of Research," *Journal of Consumer Research,* 31 (March), 868-82.

Bloom, Clive (1996): *Cult Fiction. Popular Reading and Pulp Theory,* London: MacMillan Press.

Bourdieu, Pierre (1984): *Distinction: a Social Critique of the Judgment of Taste,* Cambridge: Harvard University Press.

Bourdieu, Pierre. (1977): *Outline of a Theory of Practice,* Cambridge: Cambridge University Press 1977.

Caldwell, John Thornton (1995): *Televisuality - Style, Crisis, and Authority in American Television,* New Brunswick: Rutgers University Press.

eMarketer (2011), "TV, Mobile See Gains in Viewing Time" *eMarketer Digital Intelligence,* (accessed March 19, 2012), [available online at http://www.emarketer.com/Article.aspx?R=1008728].

Hall, Stuart (1973): "Encoding/Decoding", CCCS Stenciled Paper No.7.

Holbrook, Morris B. (1999): "Popular appeal versus expert judgments of motion pictures," *Journal of Consumer Research,* 26 (September), 144-55.

McCabe, Janet and Kim Akass (2007): *Quality TV: Contemporary American Television and Beyond,* London: I. B. Tauris.

Kael, Pauline (1969): "Trash, Art, and the Movies," *Harper's,* 238 (February).

Kates, Steven M. (2002): "The Protean Quality of Subcultural Consumption: An Ethnographic Account of Gay Consumers," *Journal of Consumer Research*, 29 (December), 383–99.

Papacharissi, Zizi and Andrew L. Mendelson (2007): "An Exploratory Study of Reality Appeal: Uses and Gratifications of Reality TV Shows," *Journal of Broadcasting & Electronic Media,* 51 (June), 355-70.

Rose, Randall L. and Stacy L. Wood (2005), "Paradox and the Consumption of Authenticity through Reality Television," *Journal of Consumer Research*, 32 (September), 284-96.

Russell, Cristel Antonia, Andrew T. Norman, and Susan E. Heckler (2004), "The Consumption of Television Programming: Development and Validation of the Connectedness Scale," *Journal of Consumer Research*, 31 (June), 150-61.

Schouten, John and James H. McAlexander (1995), "Subcultures of Consumption: An Ethnography of the New Bikers," *Journal of Consumer Research*, 22 (June), 43–61.

But How Did You Expect To Feel?: The Motivated Misremembering of Affective Forecasts

Mathew S. Isaac, Seattle University, USA
Alexander Fedorikhin, Indiana University, USA
David Gal, Northwestern University, USA

EXTENDED ABSTRACT

Following an event, people often reflect on how it compared to their expectations. For example, after a political election, people might consider whether they had correctly predicted the winner, the winning margin, or even their own feelings about the result. Extant research has shown that when actual forecasts and experiences are discrepant, people attempt to resolve this dissonance by recalling their forecast as being closer to the experience than it actually was. Although this hindsight bias (Fischoff 1975) occurs when experiences diverge from actual forecasts, little is known about how people recall their forecasts when their experience is similar to the actual forecast.

In the present research, we demonstrate that when experiences are concordant with actual forecasts, a novel bias may occur. Across three studies, we show that people tend to recall their affective forecast as being less favorable than both their actual forecast and their experience. We claim that people misremember their forecasts in this way so as to make their experience feel more surprising to them, which we describe as "illusory surprise." Since surprising outcomes are often more elating than expected outcomes (Mellers et al. 1997, Filipowicz 2006), we hypothesize that people derive affective benefits from misremembering their forecasts. Specifically, we demonstrate that people report greater affective arousal at the time of recall when they misremember their forecasts, which has implications for subsequent choices that they make.

Experiment 1 was a field study where movie theater patrons forecasted what their enjoyment of a movie was likely to be before seeing it. Afterwards, participants noted their actual enjoyment of the movie and then recalled their affective forecast. Subsequently, participants read the description of another movie from the same genre and indicated their intention to see it. We reasoned that participants experiencing greater illusory surprise when recalling the prior movie would be more inclined to watch another movie. In line with our theorizing, recalled forecasts of participants were significantly less favorable than both their experience and the actual forecasts they made earlier. Furthermore, experiences and actual forecasts did not differ; that is, participants actually enjoyed their movie as much as they had anticipated but reported recalling that they would not enjoy it as much as they had. We also found that that illusory surprise predicted participants' likelihood to watch another movie, such that those who misremembered being surprised by the movie they had seen were also more likely to watch the new film. Thus, illusory surprise appears to affect subsequent choices.

In Experiment 2, participants watched and evaluated an identical, neutral film clip. Expectations were manipulated beforehand, such that some participants were induced to believe that the clip would be positive, negative, or neutral. When participants' actual forecasts deviated significantly from their experience, we found strong evidence of the hindsight bias; that is, people tended to recall their forecast as being closer to the experience than it actually was. However, when actual forecasts matched their experience, participants misremembered their forecasts as being less favorable than both their experience and their actual forecasts. Irrespective of whether their surprise was real or illusory, participants who reported being surprised by the clip experienced greater affective arousal at the time of recall.

Experiment 3 provides evidence that the illusory surprise effect has a motivational basis. Participants who were given financial incentives to accurately recall their forecasts did not exhibit illusory surprise; however, we replicated our illusory surprise effect when accuracy incentives were not provided.

In sum, the present research shows that when experiences converge with expectations, the hindsight bias is unlikely to occur. However, even when experiences and expectations align, people may not recall their affective forecasts accurately. People evidently are motivated to convince themselves that a good-as-expected experience was unexpectedly good. Furthermore, this illusory surprise effect can actually alter the choices that participants subsequently make.

REFERENCES

Filipowicz, Allan (2006), "From Positive Affect to Creativity: The Surprising Role of Surprise," *Creativity Research Journal*, 18(2), 141-152.

Fischhoff, Baruch (1975), "Hindsight ≠ Foresight: The Effect of Outcome Knowledge on Judgment under Uncertainty," *Journal of Experimental Psychology: Human Perception and Performance*, 104, 288-299.

Geers, Andrew L. and G. Daniel Lassiter (2002), "Effects of Affective Expectations on Affective Experience: The Moderating Role of Optimism-Pessimism," *Personality and Social Psychology Bulletin*, 28 (8), 1026-39.

Mellers, Barbara A., Alan Schwartz, Katty Ho, and Ilana Ritov (1997), "Decision Affect Theory: Emotional Reactions to the Outcomes of Risky Options," *Psychological Science*, 8 (6), 423-429.

You Can't Always Forget What You Want:
Social Identity and Memory for Identity-based Advertising

Amy N. Dalton, Hong Kong University of Science and Technology, Hong Kong
Li Huang, City University of Hong Kong, Hong Kong.

EXTENDED ABSTRACT

Sigmund Freud's (1915) notion of memory repression, or motivated forgetting, suggests that people cope with unwanted memories by burying them deep in the mind, where they can lie dormant for weeks, years, or even a lifetime. Although Freud's theory has intrigued the world and stimulated fascinating research, it also has been fraught with controversy and empirical challenges. We draw on research on social identity and threat-induced coping to examine motivated forgetting in the context of memory for social identity-linked advertising.

Part of the difficulty in demonstrating motivated forgetting lies in isolating it. Memories people are motivated to forget are often threat-provoking memories they neglect to encode in the first place, so forgetting can be attributed to encoding processes rather than retrieval processes (Sedikides, Green and Pinter 2004). In contrast, consider cases where an intervening event makes otherwise neutral or positive memories difficult to confront. The death of a loved one, for example, makes retrieving fond memories of that person painful. Such contexts allow for a clean test of motivated forgetting because the threat is separated from the learned content. A similar separation can be achieved in a social identity threat paradigm that presents relatively neutral identity-linked content, facilitates its encoding, and then introduces social identity threat to motivate its forgetting.

The identity-linked content we use is identity-linked sales promotions, which target consumers based on an aspect of social identity, like gender, race, or nationality. Identity-linking occurs when firms strategically offer deals like "10% discount for senior citizens" or "Ladies receive 1 free drink." Because our participant population is comprised of HKUST students, our experiments used sales promotions offering 10% discounts to HKUST students. To facilitate encoding of the identity-linked promotions, we first prime students' university identity and then present the identity-linked promotions (mixed in with identity-neutral promotions). After viewing the promotions, participants are exposed to a social identity threat, a fictitious news article indicating that HKUST is underperforming relative to other local universities. After the threat, we measure memory for the identity-linked promotions in a standard old-new recognition task that presents the 20 old promotions along with 20 new ones (some identity-linked and some identity-neutral).

Using this basic framework, we test the hypothesis that even relatively neutral content can be forgotten if the content is identity-related, the identity to which that content relates is subject to threat, and consumers are motivated to protect against threat. We propose that the motivation to protect against threat depends on consumers' sense of connection to the threatened social identity, with high identifiers being more motivated to protect against threat and therefore more likely to forget identity-linked content when threatened.

Study 1 shows that priming a social identity has a positive effect on memory for identity-linked promotions. If, however, the primed identity is threatened, then the effect is reversed (i.e., consumers forget the promotions). As predicted, this effect is moderated by strength of identification, with high identifiers exhibiting better memory for identity-linked promotions when the relevant identity is primed, but worse memory for identity-linked promotions when the primed identity is threatened.

Study 2 tests the hypothesis that identity-linked content is not forgotten, it is simply not explicitly retrieved when the identity is threatened. In support of this theorizing, measuring memory implicitly reveals good memory performance even under threat. Again, this effect is moderated by strength of identification, with high identifiers exhibiting better implicit memory for the promotions under threat.

Study 3 tests the hypothesis that mitigating the threat via an identity affirmation task restores memory for otherwise forgotten identity-linked promotions. Moreover, this study shows that affirming the university identity restores memory for identity-linked promotions, but affirming aspects of self identity or other social identities does not have this effect. Again, the results are moderated by strength of identification, with high identifiers exhibiting better memory for identity-linked promotions when the threatened aspect of identity has been affirmed, but worse memory for identity-linked promotions in the absence of identity affirmation.

This research documents an elusive memory phenomenon, motivated forgetting, and offers a theoretical framework that predicts situations in which it is likely to occur, what memories are forgotten, and who is motivated to forget. This study also contributes to research on identity-linked marketing. With mass marketing on the decline, firms increasingly rely upon targeted marketing tactics like identity-linking, but despite its widespread use, the efficacy of identity-linking remains unclear. By examining motivated forgetting in the context of identity-linked promotions, we hope to not only advance theory about motivated forgetting, but also address factors that cause consumers to remember or forget identity-linked promotions.

REFERENCES

Freud, Sigmund (1915), "Repression," In *The Standard Edition of the Complete Psychological Works of Sigmund Freud*, Volume XIV (1914-1916): On the History of the Psycho-Analytic Movement, Papers on Metapsychology *and* Other Works, ed. James Strachey, The Hogarth Press and the Institute of Psychoanalysis: London, 141-58.

Sedikides, Constantine, Jeffrey D. Green, and Brad T. Pinter (2004), "Self-Protective Memory," In, *Memory and the Self*, ed. Beike, Denise R., James M. Lampinen, and Douglas A. Behrend, Philadelphia, PA: Psychology Press, 161-79.

The Individual Propensity to Take a Smell at Products

Monika Koller, WU Vienna, Austria
Thomas Salzberger, WU Vienna, Austria
Alexander Zauner, WU Vienna, Austria
Arne Floh, University of Surrey, UK
Maria Sääksjärvi, Delft University of Technology, The Netherlands
Hendrik Schifferstein, Delft University of Technology, The Netherlands

EXTENDED ABSTRACT

Although the importance of the olfactory system for animals is well understood, its importance for humans is still underresearched. In terms of the sense of smell, marketing research has predominantly investigated effects of product-specific scents as well as effects of in-store aromas on decision-making (e.g., Bosmans 2006). The issue of consumers actively using their olfactory modality in purchase decision-making has largely been neglected. It seems plausible that consumers differ in terms of their individual need for taking a smell at products given the observed variation in sensory needs and habits. Peck and Childers (2003) have shown that such individual differences do exist in the preference for haptic information ("Need for Touch"). Previous consumer research has disregarded the question whether "Need for Smell" exists as a personality trait. The present paper contributes to the exploration of the proposed construct of "Need for Smell" (NFS) in two ways. In a first step, we aim at conceptualizing NFS giving rise to the development of a measurement scale. As a second step, the proposed instrument is tested empirically. We present the first results of the development of a measurement scale for the "Need for Smell" construct (NFS scale) based on the Rasch model for measurement.

The definition of NFS as a personality variable follows the conceptualization of "Need for Touch", that is, the preference for haptic cues suggested by Peck and Childers (2003). Thus, we define NFS as an individual's propensity to gain and utilize information obtained through the olfactory system during the assessment of a product in a purchase decision. If a high NFS cannot be satisfied, the consumer is expected to experience discomfort and uncertainty about the product. In the worst case, the consumer refrains from buying the product. Obstacles that impede olfactory sensations are manifold. The packaging of products, for example plastic wrapping of fruits, may interfere with the consumer's intention to take a smell. Online shopping rules out the possibility of smelling altogether.

Hence, investigating the differential role of the need for olfactory cues among consumers promises to contribute to a more comprehensive understanding of consumer behavior. Building upon different streams of literature from multiple scientific disciplines resulted in initial assumptions about the dimensionality of the construct. We expect NFS to be a multidimensional construct, comprising instrumental (cognitively-toned) and autotelic (hedonically-toned) facets. In the behavioral domain, experiments suggest odour being related to associative learning, emotion and decision-making (Cupchik and Phillips, 2005). The olfactory system has direct anatomical linkages to the limbic system, making it the sensory modality most closely related to brain regions associated with emotions (Wrzesniewski, McCauley, and Rozin, 1999). Moreover, a good sense of smell is capable of eliciting positive emotions (Bosmans, 2006), suggesting the existence of an affectively-(hedonically)-toned dimension. Regarding the assumption of a cognitive dimension, evolutionary biology informs us that odour perception controls domains such as regulation of mood and cognition or food selection (Li, Moallem, Paller, and Gottfried, 2007). Hence, the instrumental dimension refers to pre-purchase smell that serves as an indicator for product evalua-

tion (e.g., quality assessment or expected functional and economic value). Moreover, it is goal-oriented (e.g., making a good choice). Product assessment based on olfactory input can also have an evolutionary foundation, as the smell of a potential food item informs us about its being toxic or distasteful.

Item generation for the NFS scale followed the process utilized by Peck and Childers (2003) and Richins and Dawson (1992). An extensive literature review and three focus group discussions led to the generation of 72 items referring to three different aspects of NFS. A subsequent quantitative pre-study administering an online questionnaire (n=165; convenience sample) aimed at a first empirical investigation of the psychometric properties of these items. The items were presented with a seven-point rating scale, ranging from 'strongly agree' to 'strongly disagree'. By means of traditional scale analysis using exploratory and confirmatory factor analysis as well as modern test theory (Rasch model for polytomous items), unsuitable items were identified and omitted. The majority of the items deleted at that stage either showed ambiguity or poor wording. A set of 35 items was retained representing three different but correlated dimensions of NFS: an instrumental dimension of NFS (11 items referring to a general instrumental facet in terms of "taking a smell facilitates choice and/or adds another informational cue"); an evaluative dimension (12 items) capturing the need for checking the product quality, which is at least partly rooted in evolution, in terms of "using olfaction to prevent negative or even harmful consequences"; and an autotelic dimension which covers the idea that taking a smell at products can be an enjoyable end in itself.

The second quantitative study utilized a representative sample (n=552) and served the purpose of cross-validating the findings of the quantitative pre-study as well as identifying redundant items. The psychometric assessment was based on the Rasch model for measurement using RUMM 2030 (Andrich, Sheridan, and Lou 2010). The three anticipated dimensions were widely confirmed, while several items showed a clear indication of redundancy. Their omission led to a set of 21 items, 8 of which measure the instrumental NFS dimension, 7 items capture the evaluative dimension, while 6 items quantify the autotelic dimensions of NFS. The three dimensions are correlated between 0.74 and 0.85.

So far the proposed existence of a latent variable NFS finds positive evidence in the data. Further studies are needed in order to reinvestigate the suitability of the suggested conceptualization, the dimensionality, and the validity the scale. In particular, discriminant and nomological validity of the NFS scale are to be investigated. Since the sense of smell is subject to individual biological differences as well as to changes related to for instance ageing (Milotic, 2003), biological factors might determine the individual level of NFS. In terms of consequences of NFS, the predictive power of NFS in the context of purchase-related phenomena is to be assessed in experimental settings. In all likelihood, the perceived importance of sensory modalities will vary between types of products (Schifferstein, 2006) and depend on the phase of product usage (Fenko, Schifferstein, and Hekkert, 2010). Ultimately such studies will reveal the relevance of NFS compared to other explanatory constructs.

REFERENCES

Andrich, David, Sheridan, Berry S. and Guanzhong Luo (2010), *Rumm 2030: Rasch Unidimensional Measurement Models,* RUMM Laboratory Perth, Western Australia.

Bosmans, Anick (2006), "Scents and sensibility: when do (in) congruent ambient scents influence product evaluations?" *Journal of Marketing*, 70 (July), 32-43.

Cupchik, Gerald and Krista Phillips (2005), "The scent of literature," *Cognition and Emotion*, 19 (1), 101-119.

Fenko, Anna, Schifferstein, Hendrik N. J. and Paul Hekkert (2010), "Shifts in sensory dominance between various stages of user-product interactions," *Applied Ergonomics*, 41, 34-40.

Li, Wen, Moallem, Isabel, Paller, Ken A. and Jay A. Gottfried (2007), "Subliminal smells can guide social preferences," *Psychological Science*, 18 (12), 1044-1049.

Milotic, Daniel (2003), "The impact of fragrance on consumer choice," *Journal of Consumer Behaviour*, 3 (2), 179-191.

Peck, Joann and Terry L. Childers, (2003), "Individual differences in haptic information processing: the "need for touch" scale," *Journal of Consumer Research*, 30 (December), 430-442.

Richins, Marsha L. and Scott Dawson (1992), "A consumer values orientation for materialism and its measurement: scale development and validation," *Journal of Consumer Research*, 19 (December), 303-316.

Schifferstein, Hendrik N. J. (2006), "The perceived importance of sensory modalities in product usage: a study of self-reports," *Acta Psychologica*, 121, 41-64.

Wrzesniewski, Amy, McCauley, Clark and Paul Rozin (1999), "Odor and affect: individual differences in the impact of odor on liking for places, things and people," *Chemical Senses*, 24, 713-721.

When Status Pulls You One Way and Another: A Dilemma for Sustainable Investments

Hannah Winkler von Mohrenfels, Frankfurt University, Germany
Corinne Faure, Grenoble Ecole de Management, France
Daniel Klapper, Humboldt University Berlin, Germany

EXTENDED ABSTRACT

According to the Forum for Sustainable and Responsible Investment (US SIF 2012), Sustainable and Responsible Investments (SRIs) roughly account for 3 trillion dollars, that is, about 12% of the total US investment market. Compared to traditional investments, SRIs are not only focusing on financial performance but also on ethical and environmental considerations. Our purpose in this research is to investigate whether status motives, which have been shown to foster pro-social behavior, are also effective in convincing consumers to invest in SRIs.

Griskevicius, Tybur, and Van den Bergh (2010) show that activating status motives is an effective mechanism in making consumers choose pro-social goods. They explain this phenomenon through costly signaling theory: individuals willingly incur the cost of purchasing a product that shows their care about others (or the environment) and use this cost as a signal to increase their status in society (their ability to incur altruistic costs is a signal of their superior status). Activating status motives therefore favors pro-social behaviors. Our focus in this research is to test whether this theory, applied so far to material products, can be extended to SRIs.

Costly signaling theory implies that an altruistic action can be used as signal to others. Because investments are private (unlike the products studied in previous research so far, investments are not potentially visible after the purchase), we suggest that status motives are not sufficient to trigger costly signaling activities; in fact, we argue that status motives are only functioning when the purchase is visible, so that it has some signaling value (Glazer and Konrad, 1996; Harbaugh, 1998); Milinski, Semmann, Krambeck, and Marotzke, 2006).

Consumers have been shown to behave quite differently for material goods and for money. As shown by Morewedge, Holtzman, and Epley (2007), simply thinking about financial accounts is enough to activate wealth considerations in consumer minds. In a recent paper, Goldstein, Johnson, and Sharpe (2008) explore consumer preferences for retirement products; they show that when confronted to financial products, consumers weigh in their expected future wealth with the costs incurred for each product. Furthermore, previous research suggests that individuals acquire wealth not only for the consumption that can be derived from it, but because of the status inducing effect of the money itself: individuals who care a lot about their (financial and social) status in comparison to others are especially interested in maintaining their wealth by gaining money (Bakshi and Chen, 1996); in contrast, persons with a lower income help others more, even if it is harder for them to afford (Piff, Kraus, Côté, Cheng, and Keltner, 2010; Rucker, Dubois, and Galinsky 2011)greater exposure to threat, and a reduced sense of personal control. Given these life circumstances, one might expect lower class individuals to engage in less prosocial behavior, prioritizing self-interest over the welfare of others. The authors hypothesized, by contrast, that lower class individuals orient to the welfare of others as a means to adapt to their more hostile environments and that this orientation gives rise to greater prosocial behavior. Across 4 studies, lower class individuals proved to be more generous (Study 1. In general, caring about status should make investors more averse to poverty and therefore make them choose investments that promise to increase their wealth quickly.

For the purchase of SRIs, we suggest that these two phenomena occur concurrently and we therefore expect consumers to face a dilemma. On one hand, according to costly signaling theory, status motives (and visibility) should make SRIs attractive. On the other hand, to the extent that SRIs are typically less attractive financially than traditional investments, consumers are likely to concentrate on lost future wealth, and therefore on the associated loss in future status associated with a lower investment yield. We therefore predict that when status motives are activated, SRI purchase will only improve in the case where the purchase is made visible; when the purchase is private, we expect status motives to activate concerns about future status loss and therefore to be counterproductive for the purchase of SRIs. We test these predictions in an experimental context.

Our main study consists of a (2 by 2) between-subject experiment, in which we manipulate status motives and decision visibility. 566 individuals (218 women, average age of 30.3 years) participated in the experimental study in exchange for the chance to win some Amazon vouchers. Status motives were manipulated using the scenario developed by Griskevicius et al (2009), in which participants are asked to project themselves in their first day on the job at a new company, with a detailed description focusing on high status features. To manipulate visibility, participants in the public condition were asked to imagine making their investment decision in the presence of an investment consultant and told that they would receive an email containing an evaluation of their performance in comparison to other participants; they were asked for their e-mail address. Participants in the private situation received no such instructions. After receiving background instructions about investment decisions, participants were asked to choose between a conventional investment and a pro-social one (SRI); the conventional product slightly outperformed the SRI. Demand checks at the end of the study revealed that no participant correctly guessed the purpose of the experiment.

We predicted that status activation would hurt SRI choice when choices are kept private and would only benefit SRI choice when choices are made public. Indeed, our results show that making choices public when status motives are active (and this, even though our visibility manipulation actually focused on performance) systematically increased SRI choice ($\chi^2(1) = 22.447$, $p < .01$). Moreover, as predicted, for private choices, status manipulations hurt the probability to choose SRIs over traditional investments ($\chi^2(1) = 5.036$, $p = .025$).

In further analyses, we replicated these patterns of results for a higher performance gap between conventional investments and SRIs and also investigated personality difference factors such as participants' income and experience with investment products.

Our research contributes to the growing literature on pro-social consumption. Our results are consistent with costly signaling theory: we show that visibility increases the likelihood of pro-social behaviors. Compared to recent literature in this area however, our results indicate that for private decisions, status activation can be counterproductive for products such as SRIs where status also activates concerns about potential future wealth loss. This study therefore provides a refined perspective on the effects of status and visibility on pro-social consumption, and offers first policy implications for SRI promotion.

Figure - Percentage of respondents choosing SRI over conventional investment as a function of active motive (status, control) and visibility (private, public)

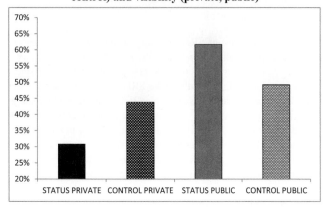

REFERENCES

Bakshi, Gurdip S. and Zhiwu Chen (1996). The Spirit of Capitalism and Stock-Market Prices. *American Economic Review*, 86(1), 133–157.

Glazer, Amihai and Kai A. Konrad (1996). A Signaling Explanation for Charity. *American Economic Review*, 86(4), 1019–1028.

Goldstein, Daniel G., Eric J. Johnson, and William F. Sharpe (2008). Choosing Outcomes versus Choosing Products: Consumer-Focused Retirement Investment Advice. *Journal of Consumer Research*, 35(October), 440-456.

Goldberg, Tony L. (1995). Altruism Towards Panhandlers: Who Gives? *Human Nature*, 6, 79-90.

Griskevicius, Vladas, Joshua M. Tybur, and Bram Van den Bergh (2010). Going Green to Be Seen: Status, Reputation, and Conspicuous Conservation. *Journal of Personality and Social Psychology*, 98(3), 392-404.

Griskevicius, Vladas, Joshua M. Tybur, Steven W Gangestad, Elaine F. Perea, Jenessa R. Shapiro, and Douglas T. Kenrick (2009). Aggress to Impress: Hostility as an Evolved Context-Dependent Strategy. *Journal of Personality and Social Psychology*, 96(5), 980-994.

Harbaugh, William T. (1998). What Do Donations Buy? A Model of Philanthropy Based on Prestige and Warm Glow. *Journal of Public Economics*, 67(2), 269-284.

Milinski, Manfred, Dirk Semmann, Hans-Jürgen Krambeck, , and Jochem Marotzke (2006). Stabilizing the Earth's Climate is not a Losing Game: Supporting Evidence from Public Goods Experiments. *PNAS Early Edition*, 103(11), 3994-3998.

Morewedge, Carey K., Leif Holtzman, and Nicholas Epley (2007). Unfixed Resources: Perceived costs Consumption, and the Accessible Account Effect. *Journal of Consumer Research*, 34(December), 459-467.

Piff, Paul K., Michael W. Kraus, Stéphane Côté, Bonnie Haiden Cheng, and Dacher Keltner (2010). Having Less, Giving More: The Influence of Social Class on Prosocial Behavior. *Journal of Personality and Social Psychology*, 99(5), 771-784.

Rucker, Derek D., David Dubois, and Adam D. Galinski (2011). Generous Paupers and Stingy Princes: Power Drives Consumer Spending on Self versus Others. *Journal of Consumer Research*, 37(April), 101561029.

When More Leads to Less: Greater Attentional Bias for Emotional Information is Negatively Associated with Self-Reported Feelings

Daniel Fernandes, Erasmus University Rotterdam, The Netherlands

Bart de Langhe, University of Colorado, USA

Stefano Puntoni, Erasmus University Rotterdam, The Netherlands

EXTENDED ABSTRACT

Social scientists often rely on self-reports to assess emotional experiences. Self-reports of emotional experience are an important tool for understanding and predicting judgment and behavior (Schwarz, 1999). A crucial assumption is that individual difference variables that are positively correlated with the intensity of emotional experience are also positively correlated with self-reports designed to measure that experience. This manuscript documents a violation of this assumption. Individuals who display greater attentional bias for emotional information—and hence experience emotional stimuli as more intense—report to be affected less by emotional stimuli.

Individuals automatically assess the emotional significance of stimuli in their environment (Ochsner & Feldman Barret, 2001). This default, low-road emotional sensitivity drives attention. Individuals who perceive a stimulus as more emotionally intense pay more attention to it (Phelps, 2006). Attentional bias is often assessed by measuring how performance on a focal task suffers as a result of automatically attending to task-irrelevant emotional information.

It seems reasonable to assume that people who display greater attentional bias also report feeling more intense emotions when explicitly asked. For example, greater attentional bias is associated with more intense cardiovascular reactivity to emotional stimuli (Jamieson, Nock, & Mendes, in press) and predicts changes in anxiety (Osinsky et al., in press). However, self-reported feelings are not only determined by the intensity of the to-be-rated emotional experience (i.e., true score) but also by the interpretation of the instrument used to probe it (i.e., measurement error). Respondents typically report their experienced emotions by selecting a response option on a rating scale (e.g., a seven-point scale ranging from "not at all happy" to "very happy"). Besides automatically assessing the emotional intensity of the target stimulus, respondents also assess the emotional intensity of the rating scale anchors. The perceived emotional intensity of rating scale anchors is negatively associated with self-reported feelings (Ostrom, 1966). This is because people who perceive a verbal anchor as more emotionally intense are less likely to endorse it, thus providing lower ratings of emotionality (De Langhe, Puntoni, Fernandes, & van Osselaer, 2011). Thus, greater attentional bias may show a negative correlation with self-reported feelings.

In sum, we propose two countervailing forces. Individuals with greater attentional bias should experience target stimuli as more emotionally intense, but should also perceive emotional verbal anchors on the scale as more intense. The first mechanism should lead to a positive association between attentional bias and self-reported feelings; whereas the second should lead to a negative one. Which of these effects dominate is an empirical question. We conducted six studies to assess the relationship between individual differences in attentional bias and self-reported feelings using a variety of target stimuli (e.g., textual vs. pictorial) and of positive and negative emotions. We assessed participants' attentional bias for emotional information using the emotional Stroop task (Williams Mathews, & MacLeod, 1996), the most frequently used paradigm to assess attentional bias. In this task, participants are asked to indicate as quickly as possible the color of emotional and neutral words. Because emotional words grab attention, performance on the color naming task tends to be worse when the word displayed is emotional. The comparison between reaction times for emotional and neutral words thus reflects one's level of attentional bias for emotional information (i.e., the emotional Stroop score).

In our studies, participants completed the emotional Stroop task and either before or after indicated their feelings after seeing an emotional target stimulus. In study 1, we find a negative correlation between participants' emotional Stroop score and self-reported feelings. In studies 2A and 2B, we also measured self-reported emotional sensitivity (using the Emotional and Interpersonal Sensitivity Measure, EISM; Bloise & Johnson, 2007). The EISM assesses people's beliefs about how sensitive they are to emotional events. It should therefore not be surprising to find a positive correlation between EISM and self-reported feelings triggered by an emotional stimulus. Consistent with our predictions, whereas the emotional Stroop score is negatively associated with self-reported feelings, EISM is positively associated with self-reported feelings. In studies 3A and 3B, we manipulated the amount of elaboration on scale anchors to test whether the negative correlation between attentional bias and self-reported feelings indeed stems from an automatic emotional reaction to scale anchors. In study 3A, half of participants were asked to elaborate on the meaning of the scale anchors before rating, whereas the other half did not receive these instructions. The negative effect of attentional bias to emotional information is attenuated when participants are asked to elaborate on the anchors. In study 3B, we asked half of participants to rate their emotional reactions using large font anchors and the other half to rate using normal font anchors. We find that, when participants use large font anchors (and elaborate more on them), the negative correlation between attentional bias and self-reported feelings is attenuated.

Marketing researchers often study people's emotional experiences by asking them how they feel. But do people who report feeling more emotional really experience more intense emotions? Researchers have criticized the use of self-reports in emotion research because of their low correlation with actual experiences (e.g., due to socially desirable responding). We highlight a different problem. People who display greater attentional bias for emotional information report feeling less intense emotions, implying a negative correlation between actual and reported feelings.

REFERENCES

Bloise, S. M., & Johnson, M. K. (2007). Memory for emotional and neutral information: Gender and individual differences in emotional sensitivity. *Memory, 15*, 192-204.

De Langhe, B., Puntoni, S., Fernandes, D., & Van Osselaer, S.M.J. (2011). The anchor contraction effect in international marketing research. *Journal of Marketing Research, 48*, 366-380.

Jamieson, J. P., Nock, M. K., & Mendes, W. B. (in press). Mind over matter: Reappraising arousal improves cardiovascular and cognitive responses to stress. *Journal of Experimental Psychology: General.*

Ochsner, K. N., & Feldman Barrett, L. (2001). A multiprocess perspective on the neuroscience of emotion. In T. J. Mayne and G. Bonnano (Eds.), *Emotion: Current Issues and Future Directions* (pp. 38-81). Guilford Press: New York .

Osinsky, R., Lösch, A., Henning, J., Alexander, N., & MacLeod, C. (in press). Attentional bias to negative information and 5-HTTLPR genotype interactively predict students' emotional reactivity to first university semester. *Emotion*.

Ostrom, T. M. (1966). Perspective as an intervening construct in the judgment of attitude statements. *Journal of Personality and Social Psychology, 3*, 135-144.

Phelps, E.A. (2006). Emotion and cognition: Insights from studies of the human amygdala. *Annual Review of Psychology, 24*, 27-53.

Quirin, M., Kazén, M., & Kuhl, J. (2009). When nonsense sounds happy or helpless: The implicit positive and negative affect test (IPANAT). *Journal of Personality and Social Psychology, 97*, 500-516.

Schwarz, N. (1999). Self-reports: How the questions shape the answers. *American Psychologist, 54*, 93-105.

Williams, J. M. G., Mathews, A., & MacLeod, C. (1996). The emotional Stroop task and psychopathology. *Psychological Bulletin, 120*, 3-24.

Emotional Marketing:
How Pride and Compassion Impact Preferences for Underdog and Top Dog Brands

Mark Staton, Western Washington University, USA
Neeru Paharia, Georgetown University, USA
Christopher Oveis, University of California San Diego, USA

EXTENDED ABSTRACT

In this research we investigate the impact of the emotions of compassion and pride on both brands that are viewed as strong or weak ("top dogs" versus underdogs), on marketing actions that are compassion-oriented or pride-oriented, in addition to investigating individual differences of people who perceive themselves as high on socioeconomic status (strong) versus those who are lower on socioeconomic status (weak). Participants primed with feelings of compassion show a preference for weaker underdog brands; however when primed with pride they show a preference for stronger top dog brands. In study 2, those with lower socioeconomic status prefer underdog compassion appeals more than underdog pride appeals to a higher degree than people of high socioeconomic status. Taken together, these studies provide promising evidence on the interaction of compassion and pride on strong or weak brands, valence of marketing actions, and personal feelings of power.

Compassion enhances perceived self-other similarity, in particular to those vulnerable and weak. Conversely, pride elicits feelings of being different from vulnerable others, and more similar to those that are considered strong (Oveis, Horberg and Keltner 2010). By extension we propose that feelings of compassion and pride can enhance feelings of similarity, and therefore purchase interest, for brands that exhibit qualities of being strong or weak. Research on top dog and underdog brands has explored how brands can be perceived as strong or weak based on their market position (Hoch and Deighton 1989), or on their brand origin story.

We hypothesize that primed compassion will result in preferences for underdog brands over top dog brands and conversely, primed pride will result in preferences for top dog brands over underdog brands. We also hypothesize that cause-related marketing emphasizing compassion for vulnerable others will be more impactful than pride related appeals for underdog brands, especially for those of low socioeconomic status.

STUDY 1: COMPASSION AND PRIDE INFLUENCE UNDERDOG/TOPDOG BRAND PREFERENCES

Participants were recruited through Amazon.com's Mechanical Turk, and were randomly assigned to one of 4 experimental conditions in a 2 (compassion v. pride) x 2 (underdog v. top dog) between-subjects design.

Participants were induced to feel compassion or pride, read a brand biography for an underdog or top dog company, and then rated their preference for the company on the following dimensions: how much do you identify with the brand (1=very little, 7=very much), how much do you like the brand (1=very little, 7=very much), and how likely are you to purchase the brand (1=very unlikely, 7=very likely). These three ratings were summed to create a brand preference composite (alpha=.84).

RESULTS

A 2x2 ANOVA revealed a significant interaction of induced emotion (compassion vs. pride) and brand status (underdog vs. top dog) on brand preference, $F(1, 95)=8.54$, $p<.01$. Consistent with our hypotheses, simple effects analyses revealed that participants induced to feel compassion preferred the underdog brand (M=14.88,

SD=3.15) significantly more than the top dog brand (M=11.52, SD=4.83), $t(47)=2.87$, $p<.01$, whereas participants induced to feel pride preferred the top dog brand (M=13.40, SD=4.20) more than the underdog brand (M=11.44, SD=5.52); however, this latter effect did not meet conventional levels of significance, $t(48)=1.41$, $p=.16$.

STUDY 2: HOW PRIDE AND COMPASSION CAUSE-RELATED MARKETING APPEALS INTERACT WITH SOCIOECONOMIC STATUS

In Study 2, rather than priming compassion or pride, we aimed to show that an ad that elicited feelings of compassion would be viewed more favorably for those with a low socio economic status. We used cause-related marketing ads and predicted that individuals with low subjective SES would respond more positively to compassion-inducing appeals than pride-inducing appeals due to their personal weaker status.

Participants were recruited through Amazon.com's Mechanical Turk service, and were randomly assigned to one of four conditions in a 2 (compassion vs. pride-inducing ad) x 2 (underdog vs. top dog brand) between-subjects design.

Participants first completed the McArthur subjective SES measure (Kraus, Piff and Keltner 2009), wherein participants place themselves on one of ten "rungs of a ladder" representing their place in their community, and then their place in the United States (alpha=.87). Next, participants read either one of two brand biographies and then viewed either a Compassion CRM advertisement or a Pride CRM advertisement for that brand.

Participants then indicated their preference for the brand as follows: how much do you identify with the brand and how much do you like the brand. These items were summed to form a composite brand preference measure (alpha=.83).

We examined separately how brand preferences interacted with consumers' subjective SES in the top dog and underdog condition by regressing brand preference onto ad condition (compassion vs. pride), subjective SES, and their interaction (ad condition*subjective SES).

Consistent with our hypothesis, a significant interaction was observed such that low-SES and high-SES participants responded differently to compassion- and pride-inducing ads from underdogs, $b=.91$, $t(99)=2.06$, $p=.04$. Simple slope analyses revealed that both low-SES, $b=-3.51$, $p<.01$, and high-SES participants, $b=-1.69$, $p<.01$, preferred underdogs significantly more with a compassion-inducing ad versus a pride-inducing ad. The interaction shows that the low-SES slope was significantly steeper than the high-SES slope suggesting that the effect was stronger for those of low-SES.

DISCUSSION

In two experiments, we have shown that compassion and pride can impact attitudes towards "top dog" and "underdog" brands. In Study 1, we illustrated how incidental feelings of compassion will lead to higher attitudes for underdog brands, while incidental feelings of pride will lead to higher attitudes for top dog brands. In Study 2 we, illustrated that for underdog brands, compassion appeals are preferred by low SES participants, however this effect is muted for those with high SES.

Theoretically, we believe that this line of research is important by illustrating that the sense of similarity to strong or weak others found in pride and compassion respectively are not just in play with people, but with brands as well. Managerially, we believe that we are further uncovering the information perceived by consumers through relative market position. Also, we show that there are personal factors that influence the impact of cause-related marketing messages.

REFERENCES

Costa, P.T.,Jr. & McCrae, R.R. (1992). *Revised NEO Personality Inventory (NEO-PI-R) and NEO Five-Factor Inventory (NEO-FFI) manual.* Odessa, FL: Psychological Assessment Resources.

Eisenberg, N. (2002). Empathy-related emotional responses, altruism, and their socialization. In R. J. Davidson & A. Harrington (Eds.), *Visions of compassion: Western scientists and Tibetan Buddhists examine human nature* (pp. 131–164). New York, NY: Oxford University Press.

Gomez, A., Brooks, M.L., Buhrmester, M.D., Vazquez, A., Jetten, J. & Swann, W.B. Jr. (2011). *Journal of Personality and Social Psychology 100*(5), 918-933.

Hoch, Stephen J. and John Deighton (1989), "Managing What Consumers Learn from Experience," *Journal of Marketing*, 53 (2), 1–20.

Isen, A. M., Shalker, T. E., Clark, M., & Karp, L. (1978). Affect, accessibility of material in memory, and behavior: A cognitive loop? *Journal of Personality & Social Psychology, 36*, 1–12.

Johnson, E. J., & Tversky, A. (1983). Affect, generalization, and the perception of risk. *Journal of Personality & Social Psychology, 45*, 20–31.

Kraus, M. W., Piff, P. K., & Keltner, D. (2009). Social class, the sense of control, and social explanation. *Journal of Personality and Social Psychology, 97*, 992–1004. doi:10.1037/a0016357

Han, S., Lerner, J.S. & Keltner, D. (2007) Feeling and consumer decision making: The appraisal-tendency framework. *Journal of Consumer Psychology, 17*(3), 158-168.

Lazarus, R. S. (1991). *Emotion and adaptation.* New York: Oxford University Press.

Lerner, J. S., & Keltner, D. (2000). Beyond valence: Toward a model of emotion-specific influences on judgment and choice. *Cognition and Emotion, 14*, 473–493.

Lerner, J. S., & Keltner, D. (2001). Fear, anger, and risk. *Journal of Personality & Social Psychology, 81*, 146–159.

Lerner, J. S., & Tiedens, L. Z. (2006). Portrait of the angry decision maker: How appraisal tendencies shape anger's influence on cognition. *Journal of Behavioral Decision Making, 19*, 115–137.

Oveis, C., Horberg, E.J. and Keltner, D. (2010). Compassion, pride and social ntuitions of self-other similarity. *Journal of Personality and Social Psychology , 98* (4), 618-630.

Oveis, C., Cohen, A. B., Gruber, J., Shiota, M. N., Haidt, J., & Keltner, D. (2009). Resting respiratory sinus arrhythmia is associated with tonic positive emotionality. *Emotion, 9*, 265–270.

Paharia, N., Keinan, A., Avery, J. and Schor, (2011). The underdog effect: The marketing of disadvantage and determination through brand biography. *Journal of Consumer Research, 37*(5), 775-790.

Shariff, A. F., & Tracy, J. L. (2009). Knowing who's boss: Implicit perceptions of status from the nonverbal expression of pride. *Emotion, 9,*

631–639.

Slovic, P. (1987). Perception of risk. *Science, 236*, 280–285.

Smith, C. A., & Ellsworth, P. C. (1985). Patterns of cognitive appraisal in emotion. *Journal of Personality & Social Psychology, 48*, 813–838.

Tracy, J. L., & Robins, R. W. (2004b). Show your pride: Evidence for a discrete emotion expression. *Psychological Science, 15*, 194–197.

Varadarajan, P.R. & Menon, A. (1988). Cause-related marketing: A coalignment of marketing strategy and corporate behavior. *Journal of Marketing, 52*(3) 58-74.

Wright, W. F., & Bower, G. H. (1992). Mood effects on subjective probability assessment. *Organizational Behavior & Human Decision Processes, 52*, 276–291.

Zahn-Waxler, C., Radke-Yarrow, M., Wagner, E., & Chapman, M. (1992). Development of concern for others. *Developmental Psychology, 28*, 126–136.

Ridiculing the Working Class and Reinforcing Class Boundaries:
The Chav Myth and Consumption in the Night Time Space

Hayley L. Cocker, Lancaster University, UK
Maria Piacentini, Lancaster University, UK
Emma N. Banister, University of Manchester, UK

EXTENDED ABSTRACT

Prior CCT research has investigated marketplace myths that "permeate consumer culture" (Thompson 2004, 162), and has understood these myths as "cultural resources that attract consumers to a consumption activity or brand" (Arsel and Thompson 2011 791). Research on identity myths however, has focused on devaluing and undesirable myths such as the southern white identity myth (Thompson and Tian 2008) and the hipster myth (Arsel and Thompson 2011). Whilst Arsel and Thompson's (2011) study enriched our understanding of how consumers' branded by an undesirable marketplace myth attempt to demythologize, further research is needed to explore how and why consumers use marketplace myths to ridicule and stigmatize others. In a separate stream of research, consumer researchers have applied and extended the work of Bourdieu (1984) and the concepts of habitus, field and capital to stress the continuing relevance of social class as an analytic category and advance our understanding of the relationship between social class and consumption (e.g. Holt 1997, Allen 2002, Henry 2005). We bring together recent streams of research on social class and identity myths to explore the link between class-based identity myths and consumption and the role of such myths in reinforcing social class boundaries. In order to demonstrate how young middle-class consumers mobilize the 'Chav' myth, we focus on a specific consumption context where this process is particularly visible - consumption in the nighttime space (e.g. bars, clubs).

Whilst we didn't initially set out to explore the 'Chav' myth, the young participants in our study frequently relied on this myth when discussing their identity (who NOT to be) and framing their consumption behavior (how NOT to consume). The wider study of which this data is a part, explored young people's alcohol consumption in relation to different aspects of the self (positive and negative). A total of 91 participants (aged 16-18) were recruited via four different educational institutions. Data was collected in five phases, drawing from Bahl and Milne's (2010) multi-method approach to identifying multiple selves in participants and exploring consumption from the lens of different selves. We used a combination of written answer booklets, projective techniques and visual research methods (e.g. qualitative clustering task and 3D avatar creation) to elicit young people's constructions of the self. This was followed by individual, paired and group interviews to explore alcohol consumption in relation to different aspects of self.

The term 'Chav' emerged in the UK around 2004, replacing the term 'underclass' and various regional terms (e.g. 'Townies' and 'Scallies') as a way of describing the white working-class. The 'Chav' myth incorporates highly stereotypical notions of the working-class and rests on the belief that there are "entire communities around Britain crawling with feckless, delinquent, violent and sexually debauched no-hopers" (Jones 2011, 80), airbrushing the reality of the working-class lifestyle "out of existence in favor of the chav caricature" (Jones 2011, 11). 'Chavs' have been referred to as a youth 'subculture' (Hollingworth and Williams 2009) and a 'phenomenon' (Hayward & Yar 2006) and similar to the working-class youth subcultures studied by the Center for Contemporary Cultural Studies (CCCS) in the 1970's, such as Teddy Boys, Mods, Skinheads and Punks (see Hall and Jefferson 1976 and Hebdige 1979), the 'Chav'

identity has developed around "particular activities, focal concerns and territorial spaces" (Clarke 1976, 14). CCT literature has focused its attention almost exclusively on "self-selecting or achieved (vs. ascribed) subcultures" (Schouten and McAlexander 1995, 43) and subcultures where "membership is usually conscious" (Kates 2002, 397), such as the Gay subculture (Kates, 2002), 'New Bikers' Harley-Davidson enthusiasts (Schouten and McAlexander 1995), Star Trek Fans (Kozinets 2001) and Goths (Goulding and Saren, 2009). In contrast, 'Chav' is tied to an ascribed class-based identity, is a collective label attached to members of the working-class by the dominant class and is used to ridicule (Wooten 2006) and demonize. Membership is often unconscious, in the sense that the majority of so-called 'Chavs' do not readily identify as such, and whilst it may be relatively easy for most people to become a Star Trek Fan or a Goth, it's extremely difficult for middle-class consumers to become a 'Chav' given the strong ties to locality and social class.

Findings from our study emphasize the ways in which young middle-class consumer's draw from the 'Chav' identity myth to construct, support and enhance the self. More specifically, the 'Chav' myth provides these young consumers with a concrete idea of who not to be and is used to reinforce the divide between the 'Chavs' and the 'Chav-Not's'. Similar to Ustuner and Holt (2010) who stressed the importance of the Western Lifestyle myth in relation to status consumption in Turkey, we highlight the relationship between myths and class-based consumption in a Western context. Whereas Ustuner and Holt's (2010) study looked at HCC consumers approaching a desirable marketplace myth, our study focuses on young consumers' avoiding an undesirable marketplace myth. We discuss in detail how young middle-class consumers in the UK mobilize the 'Chav' myth and how this serves to create and reinforce social class boundaries, within the context of the nighttime space. We found that young middle-class consumers draw from various aspects of the 'Chav' myth (e.g. particular dress styles, music preferences and demeanor) to identify, label and ridicule members of the working-class and to inform their consumption choices in the nighttime space (e.g. certain brands of alcohol, clothing styles, music genres as well as certain places and spaces were closely tied to the 'Chav'). Whilst certain aspects of the 'Chav' myth (e.g. violent behavior) played a role in creating boundaries, other aspects of the 'Chav' myth (e.g. clothing styles and brands) were used as a form of identity play and ridicule (e.g. chav-themed fancy dress parties). Additionally, we found that nightlife providers play a role in creating 'divisions in the dark' and reinforcing class boundaries (e.g. door policies refusing entry to those wearing brands associated with the 'Chav'). Our research offers valuable theoretical insights by enriching our understanding of how class-based identity myths are mobilized by consumers and serve to reinforce social class boundaries.

REFERENCES

Allen, Douglas E. (2002), "Toward a Theory of Consumer Choice as Sociohistorically Shaped Practical Experience: The Fits-Like-a-Glove (FLAG) Framework," *Journal of Consumer Research*, 28 (March), 515-33.

Arsel, Zeynep and Craig J. Thompson (2011), "Demythologizing Consumption Practices: How Consumers Protect Their Field-Dependent Identity Investments from Devaluing Marketplace Myths," *Journal of Consumer Research,* 37(5), 791-806.

Bahl, Shalini and George R. Milne (2010), "Talking to Ourselves: A Dialogical Exploration of Consumer Experiences," *Journal of Consumer Research,* 37 (1), 176-95.

Bourdieu, Pierre (1984), *Distinction: A Social Critique of the Judgement of Taste*, Cambridge, MA: Harvard University Press.

Clarke, John (1976), "The Skinheads and the Magical Recovery of Community" in S. Hall and T. Jefferson (eds), *Resistance Through Rituals: Youth Subcultures in Post-War Britain*, London: Hutchinson, London.

Goulding, Christina and Michael Saren (2009), "Performing Identity: An Analysis of Gender Expressions at the Whitby Goth Festival," *Consumption, Markets and Culture,* 12(1), 27-46.

Hall, Stuart and Tony Jefferson (1976), *Resistance Through Rituals: Youth Subcultures in Post-War Britain*, Hutchinson, London.

Hayward, Keith and Majid Yar (2006), "The 'Chav' Phenomenon: Consumption, Media and the Construction of a New Underclass," *Crime, Media, Culture*, 2 (1), 9-28.

Hebdige, Dick (1979), S*ubculture: The Meaning of Style,* Methuen, London.

Henry, Paul. C. (2005), "Social Class, Market Situation, and Consumers' Metaphors of (Dis) Empowerment," *Journal of Consumer Research,* 31(4), 766-78.

Hollingworth, Sumi and Katya Williams (2009), "Constructions of the Working-Class 'Other' among Urban, White, Middle-Class Youth: 'Chavs', Subculture and the Valuing of Education," *Journal of Youth Studies*, 12 (5), 467-82.

Holt, Douglas B. (1997), "Poststructuralist Lifestyle Analysis: Conceptualizing the Social Patterning of Consumption in Postmodemity," *Journal of Consumer Research,* 23 (March), 326-50.

Jones, Owen (2011) *Chavs: The Demonization of the Working Class,* Verso.

Kates, Steven. M. (2002), "The Protean Quality of Subcultural Consumption: An Ethnographic Account of Gay Consumers," *Journal of Consumer Research*, 29 (3), 383–99.

Kozinets, Robert. V. (2001), "Utopian Enterprise: Articulating the Meanings of Star Trek's Culture of Consumption," *Journal of Consumer Research,* 28 (1), 67-88.

Schouten, John. W and James. H. McAlexander (1995), "Subcultures of Consumption: An Ethnography of the New Bikers," *Journal of Consumer Research,* 22 (1): 43-61.

Thompson, Craig J. (2004), "Marketplace Mythology and Discourses of Power," *Journal of Consumer Research*, 31 (June), 162–80.

Thompson, Craig J and Kelly Tian (2008), "Reconstructing the South: How Commercial Myths Compete for Identity Value through the Ideological Shaping of Popular Memories and Countermemories," *Journal of Consumer Research*, 34 (5), 595-613.

Tyler, Imogen (2008), "'Chav Mum, Chav Scum": Class Disgust in Contemporary Britain," *Feminist Media Studies*, 8(1), 17–34.

Üstüner, Tuba and Douglas B. Holt (2010), «Toward a Theory of Status Consumption in Less Industrialized Countries,» *Journal of Consumer Research,* 37 (1), 37-56.

Wooten, Daniel. B. (2006), "From Labelling Possessions to Possessing Labels: Ridicule and Socialization among Adolescents," *Journal of Consumer Research*, 33 (September), 188-198.

When Soft Drink Taxes Don't Work: A Comparative Study

Andrew Hanks, Cornell University, USA
Brian Wansink, Cornell University, USA
David Just, Cornell University, USA

EXTENDED ABSTRACT

Taxes on energy-dense foods and beverages have been proposed to address the growing obesity problem (e.g. IOM, 2009; Brownell and Frieden, 2009; Jacobson 2004). Average daily sugar consumption, estimated at 11.1 teaspoons per person (Smith, Lin, and Lee, 2010) prompted the Institute of Medicine, the Center For Disease Control and Prevention and several State and local governments to propose a tax on sugar-sweetened beverages, such as full calorie soft drinks (Patterson 2008; IOM Report 2009; Roehr 2009; Rudd Report 2009; Smith, Lin, and Lee 2010). The aim of such a tax would be to reduce calorie intake, improve diet and health, and generate revenue that governments could use to further address obesity-related health problems (Brownell and Frieden 2009; Duffey et al. 2010; Jacobson and Brownell 2000; Powell and Chaloupka 2009, Smith, Lin, and Lee 2010).

Unfortunately, whether taxes on sugar-sweetened beverages have significant impacts on weight is not well understood. Recent estimates regarding the sensitivity of demand for sugar-sweetened beverages to changes in its own price suggest that a 1% increase in the price of sugar-sweetened beverages leads to a decrease in demand for these beverages from 0.8% to 1.2% (see Andreyeva et al. 2009; Brownell et al. 2009). Yet, there are negligible impacts on BMI for adults (Fletcher et al. 2011). This could be due to substitution towards other energy dense goods or a lack of tax saliency at the time of purchase. Finally, much of the previous research has relied on observational data and the effects of state wide sugar-sweetened beverage taxes on aggregate demand, or even BMI. Thus, while these studies are extremely useful, they impose strong assumptions on consumer preferences and data may lack sufficient variation to identify behavior.

Our objective is to compare the results from a controlled field experiment (List 2011; List 2009; Levitt and List 2009; Harrison and List 2004) to previous findings and demonstrate the impact that a tax on full calorie beverages has on the volume purchased of full calorie soft drinks and diet soft drinks. In the experiment, we imposed a 10% tax on full-calorie beverages, and other foods with few nutrients per calorie, on a randomly selected subset of our study's 113 participating households. Individual household purchases at a participating national grocery chain were recorded from August 2010 through February 2011. In August prices remained the same but in September through February, those in the tax group paid an additional 10% for low-nutrient and high-calorie foods and beverages. Although the tax included all foods and beverages with few nutrients per calorie, we focus on purchases of full calories soft drinks and its closest substitute, diet soft drinks.

Compared to data used in previous research, a controlled field experiment allows us to identify how individual households respond to the tax, identify differences in behavior between the tax and control groups, and makes the tax much more salient than the state imposed tax. To analyze the data we collected from the participants, we relied on a random effects panel regression technique with robust standard errors. With this estimation technique we estimate the impact that the tax had on purchases of full calorie soft drinks and its natural substitute, diet soft drinks.

In Figure 1, we plot the average monthly fluid ounces of full calorie soft drinks purchased form Aug-Feb, where fluid ounces in each month were differenced from fluid ounces purchased in August. Even though those in the tax group decreased fluid ounces purchased of full calorie soft drinks, those in the control group did as well. Yet over time, the impact of the tax diminished, though there is some evidence of seasonal variation.

Figure 1: A Tax on Full calorie soft drinks has No Impact on Fluid Ounces Purchased

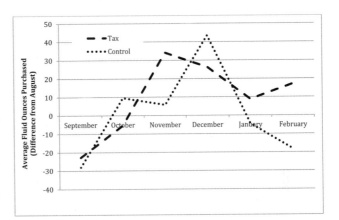

This similarity in tax and control group behavior is illustrated in Figure 2. The tax appears to have an affect on fluid ounces of full calorie soft drinks purchased between August and September (the first and second bars in the figure for the tax and control treatments), but this behavior is not much different than what we observed in the control group. If purchases for September through November, or even for September through February, are averaged, it is clear that any effect that may have occurred eventually diminished.

Figure 2: Plots of Averages over the Course of the Experiment Demonstrate that the Effect of a Full Calorie Soft Drink Tax Wears Off Over Time

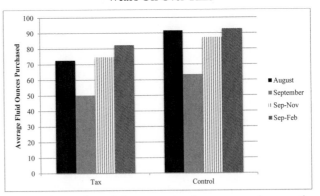

We then estimated the parameters in our regression equation, using either fluid ounces of full calorie or diet soft drinks purchased as the dependent variable. In Table 1, we report that over the course of the study, the tax had no statistically significant impact on fluid ounces of full calorie soft drinks purchased, which is consistent with the unconditional data presented in Figures 1 and 2. Even though we do find a marginally significant result in purchases of full calorie soft drinks by households in December, an increase of 39.2 fluid ounces, (unreported) regression results demonstrate that the tax has no significant impact in the holiday months. We do find, however, that families with at least two children purchased 52.4 more fluid ounces per month after the tax was imposed, which is approximately equal to four additional 12 oz cans. This could be attributed to resistance to a tax, especially in families with several children who have a strong demand for full calorie soft drinks. This finding still warrants further investigation into the behavior of households with multiple children.

Diet soft drinks, the most intuitive substitute for full calorie soft drinks, were not affected at all by the tax. This, along with our previous results, suggests that a salient tax of 10% on full calorie beverages is insufficient to reduce consumption of full calorie soft drinks, and in larger families, actually increases purchases. Furthermore, households did not substitute towards the next best alternative, diet soft drinks. These findings contribute to the current literature by presenting results from a study where the salience of a tax is not in question and a change in behavior related to the tax is identified by the experimental design. Second, these results uphold the notion that similar taxes on full calorie beverages have no impact on overall health outcomes.

Table 1: A Tax on Sugar-Sweetened Beverages Has no Significant Impact on Fluid Ounces of Full calorie soft drinks or Diet Soft Drinks Purchased

Independent Variables	Dependent Variables	
	Full calorie soft drinks	Diet Soft Drinks
Tax	-6.8	6.5
September	-24.6	-20.9
October	6.0	-32.9
November	21.3	-11.7
December	39.2*	4.2
January	4.2	-2.7
February	0.1	2.8
Married	-1.5	-22.0
No Response (marital)	-37.6	-2.5
$10K-40$K	-3.3	-59.3
> $70K	-1.1	-8.1
No Response (income)	31.3	-5.3
> 1 Child	54.5**	-3.6
Constant	73.9***	151.2**

Results are coefficients from two separate panel regressions of fluid ounces of soft drinks purchased on dummy variables for the tax treatment, months in the experiment, and other household characteristics.

*** $p < 0.01$. ** $p < 0.05$. * $p < 0.1$.

A Weight On Your Shoulders Makes You Pull Your Weight

Minkyung Koo, University of Illinois at Urbana Champaign, USA
Mina Kwon, University of Illinois at Urbana Champaign, USA
Sharon Shavitt, University of Illinois at Urbana Champaign, USA

EXTENDED ABSTRACT

Research on metaphorical thinking has shown that physical experiences are linked to one's thoughts and feelings (e.g., Lakoff & Johnson, 1980, 1999; Landau, Meier, & Keefer, 2011). For instance, physically experiencing a heavy (vs. light) weight increases judgments of importance (Ackerman, Nocera, & Bargh, 2010; Jostman, Lakens, & Schubert, 2009; Zhang & Li, 2011). We argue that the way in which weight is borne can also activate metaphorical thinking. People often use the metaphor "weight on the shoulders" to mean a burden or responsibility for something, which suggests that a heavy burden on the shoulders can increase willingness to take responsibility for a joint effort.

Study 1 demonstrated that merely imagining the experience of a heavy (versus light) weight on one's shoulders has this effect. Participants ($N = 36$) were randomly assigned to imagine wearing either a heavy or a light backpack. They then ostensibly prepared to work with other students in a group project simulation and indicated their willingness to contribute and amount of effort they would put into the project. Imagining wearing a heavy (vs. light) backpack increased feelings of responsibility for and willingness to contribute to the upcoming project ($M_{Heavy} = 5.18$; $M_{Light} = 4.49$), $F(1, 34) = 5.37$, $p < .05$. The results support the effect of the metaphor "weight on the shoulders." Yet, it is possible that actually carrying a heavy (vs. light) weight would result in burden and fatigue that may dampen these effects.

Study 2 was designed to test whether physically experiencing a heavy weight exerts the same effect as imagination did in Study 1. We also sought to support more directly the role of metaphorical thinking by examining whether this effect depends on where the weight is borne. Participants ($N = 184$) were randomly assigned to wear either a heavy or a light backpack on their shoulders, or to hold either a heavy or a light folder on their forearm. Because the same weight is experienced as heavier when carried on the arm (vs. shoulders), we calibrated the actual weight in order to equate subjective weight experiences across the two conditions. Participants reported their perceived weight of the backpack they were wearing or the folder they were holding (1 = very light; 7 = very heavy). There were no differences between the two heavy conditions ($M_{arm} = 3.93$; $M_{backpack} = 4.04$), $F < 1$, or the two light conditions ($M_{arm} = 1.67$; $M_{backpack} = 1.68$), $F < 1$. As before, the study was ostensibly a group project simulation. Participants indicated their willingness to contribute to the group and amount of effort they would put into the project. All participants completed these ratings while standing and carrying the weight on their shoulders [forearm]. Supporting the role of metaphorical thinking, the heavy (vs. light) weight effect was observed only when people carried the weight on their shoulders ($M_{Heavy} = 5.06$; $M_{Light} = 4.42$), not when they held a similar weight on their forearm ($M_{Heavy} = 4.76$; $M_{Light} = 4.82$), $F(1,180) = 4.01$, $p < .05$.

Study 3 addressed a closely a closely related metaphor, "a weight *off* one's shoulders" in order to provide more evidence for the role of metaphorical thinking. If a heavy burden increases felt responsibility to the team, the opposite should be the case when the burden is removed from one's shoulders, according to a metaphorical account. In other words, it is expected that those who take off a heavy backpack will be less willing to contribute to a group than those still wearing a heavy backpack. An alternative account is that the weight effect observed in the previous studies is the result of semantic prim-

ing of "hard work" that is associated with a heavy backpack. If the results reflect semantic priming activated by a heavy backpack, there should be no difference in willingness to contribute between those still wearing and those who just took off a heavy backpack. However, if the effect is due to metaphorical thinking, there should be a difference between these two groups.

Participants ($N = 91$) were randomly assigned to one of the three conditions: heavy backpack on, heavy backpack off, no backpack control. Participants in the first two backpack conditions were asked to wear a heavy backpack. After filling out a short survey and therefore experiencing the heavy weight on their shoulders for a few minutes, one group of participants were asked to take off the backpack (backpack off) while the other group kept it on (backpack on). Those in the control condition were asked to complete the study while standing as in other conditions. We found that people felt less willing to contribute to an upcoming group project after taking off the heavy backpack (i.e., taking a weight off their shoulders) than while wearing the backpack ($M_{on} = 5.55$; $M_{off} = 5.07$), $F(1,62) = 3.89$, $p < .05$. Neither group differed from the control condition ($M_{control} = 5.23$) in willingness to contribute. These findings support the role of metaphorical thinking and suggest that this effect is not an outcome of semantic priming.

CONCLUSION AND FUTURE DIRECTIONS

Supporting the role of metaphorical thinking, imagining or experiencing a heavy weight on one's shoulders increases felt responsibility and intentions to contribute. This effect does not emerge when weight is on one's forearm. Finally, taking weight off one's shoulders apparently has an unburdening effect. Our findings are counterintuitive in that one may expect people to be less willing to contribute effort when they are burdened and fatigued by carrying a heavy weight. This research has novel implications for understanding the drivers of felt responsibility in other contexts. For instance, consumers experiencing a product failure might assign more responsibility to themselves when carrying a heavy versus light weight on their shoulders. Future research can shed light on the underlying processes of this metaphorical effect and its generality to other consumer judgments.

REFERENCES

Ackerman, Joshua. M., Christopher C. Nocera, and John. A. Bargh (2010), "Incidental Haptic Sensations Influence Social Judgments and Decisions." *Science,* 328(5986), 1712-1715.

Jostmann, Nils B., Daniel Lakens, and Thomas W. Schubert (2009), "Weight as an Embodiment of Importance," *Psychological Science,* 20(9), 1169-1174.

Lakoff, George, and Mark Johnson (1980), *Metaphors We Live By,* Chicago: University of Chicago Press.

— 1999. *Philosophy In The Flesh: The Embodied Mind And Its Challenge To Western Thought.* New York: Basic Books.

Landau, Mark J., Brian P. Meier, and Lucas. A. Keefer (2010), "A Metaphor-Enriched Social Cognition," *Psychological Bulletin* 136(6), 1045-1067.

Zhang, Meng and Xiuping Li (2012), "From Physical Weight to Psychological Significance: The Contribution of Semantic Activations," *Journal of Consumer Research,* 38(6), 1063-1075.

A Meta-Analytic and Psychometric Investigation of the Effect of Financial Literacy on Downstream Financial Behaviors

Daniel Fernandes, Erasmus University Rotterdam, The Netherlands
John G. Lynch, Jr., University of Colorado, USA
Richard Netemeyer, University of Virginia, USA

EXTENDED ABSTRACT

Consumers' financial world used to be more forgiving. Consumers face increasing demands to ensure their own financial security via borrowing, saving, and managing their day-to-day budgets (Boshara et al. 2010). A generation ago, one did not need to know as much to avoid large financial mistakes that are now much more common. These increasing demands on consumers have led many analysts to point to the importance of financial literacy. Many nations around the world have calls for building financial literacy as a capability in the citizenry, spending billions of dollars worldwide to improve financial behavior. Financial literacy is a specialized kind of consumer expertise or knowledge pertaining to how one manages one's financial affairs (Remund 2010). Prior qualitative literature reviews had reached starkly different conclusions about whether financial literacy had "inconsistent" effects or effects so small that government policy promoting financial literacy was misguided.

We scrutinize the effect of financial literacy on downstream financial behaviors via rigorous meta-analysis of 137 papers and 164 studies published in a broad array of disciplines. We include studies of the effects of consumers' measured financial literacy and of financial education interventions. We grouped the types of dependent variables in eight different categories: 1) "Save" (amount saved for retirement), 2) "Plan" (level of planning for retirement), 3) "Debt" (level of debt for each respondent), 4) "Stock Ownership" (how much is invested in stocks), 5) "Investment" (amount invested or return), 6) "Cash Flow Management" (ability to perform healthy financial behaviors in a day-to-day basis), 7) "Plan Activity" (participation and contribution to retirement plans) and 8) "Inertia" (the likelihood to choose default options rather than choosing actively).

The integrated effect size (corrected for sample weighting) is "small" and significant ($r = .066$, $p < .001$). (By convention, $r \leq .10$ is small; $.10 < r < .40$ is medium; and $r \geq .40$ is large.) These results were based on 165 independent studies and 558,208 cases. Critically, we found significant heterogeneity in effect sizes obtained ($Q = 2,784$, $p < .001$), indicating that moderating variables might help explain the variance in the effect sizes. Our primary hypothesis was that this heterogeneity could be explained by larger effect sizes for studies measuring financial literacy rather than manipulating some financial education intervention. Results supported this conjecture: average effect-size was on the low end of "medium" for measured financial literacy ($r^2 = .013$ for 83 effect-sizes, $r = .116$, $CI_{95} = 0.112$ to 0.12) and quite "small" for manipulated financial literacy ($r^2 = .001$ for 82 effect-sizes, $r = .033$, $CI_{95} = 0.029$ to 0.036). As expected, the effect-size of manipulated financial literacy on downstream financial behaviors increases with more hours of instruction and shorter time delay between the intervention and the measurement of financial behavior. But even semester length classroom instruction explained only about 0.3% of the variance in later financial behavior. One explanation is that, interventions produced only small improvements in financial knowledge that serve as a manipulation check for the interventions in 12 studies (sample-weighted $r = .056$, $CI_{95} = 0.043$ to 0.068). We conclude that correlational and econometric studies that measure literacy find moderate connections to subsequent financial behaviors, but studies of the effects of financial literacy interventions show weak and almost null effects.

If it is so difficult to intervene to improve downstream financial behaviors, why is measured literacy such a potent predictor of healthy financial behaviors? We thought that the stronger effects of measured financial literacy may be due to either problems of measurement of financial literacy or to the omission of other traits that are correlated with, but distinct from, financial literacy. We follow up our meta-analysis with two primary research studies investigating the psychometric properties of measured financial literacy, its discriminant validity in relation to other constructs, and its nomological validity in predicting downstream financial behaviors. We develop from published items a brief, unidimensional measure of financial literacy from a pool of items used in prior work. We reproduce a number of published findings wherein measured literacy predicts financial behaviors when entered along with demographics. However, we find that the predictive effects weaken dramatically when we include measures of other correlated traits. We discuss the implications of our findings for research on financial literacy and for public policy and private investment in financial education.

In conclusion, forces in the legal, business, and social environment make today's financial world a much more dangerous place for consumers than what their parents faced a generation ago. This observation and a large literature connecting financial literacy to downstream financial behavior has been the impetus for a broad examination of financial literacy and efforts to improve it by governments, employers, and NGOs. Literally billions of dollars are being spent to promote financial literacy. We conducted a meta-analysis to evaluate whether, across all studies, financial literacy is connected to financial behavior. We found a large split between econometric or correlational studies that related measured literacy to financial behavior and experiments or quasi-experiments where there was some manipulation of an educational program intended to improve financial literacy, and thus, downstream financial behaviors. This dissociation occurs in part because financial interventions targeted at changing financial literacy are not effective (especially those with only a few hours of intervention and a long delay between intervention and behavior). Is the solution then to increase the effort towards financial interventions and invest more money on financial education? The answer is no. This is because the effect of financial literacy on financial behaviors is explained by other psychological traits that are not easily changed. In sum, financial interventions often don't work and the effect financial literacy on behavior seems to be explained by correlates of financial literacy. This poses a challenge for financial educators and policy makers about how best to foster healthy financial behaviors.

REFERENCES

Boshara, Ray, John Gannon, Lewis Mandell, John W. R. Phillips, and Stephen Sass (2010), "Consumer Trends in the Public, Private, and Nonprofit Sector." National Endowment for Financial Education Quarter Century Project.

Remund, David L. (2010), "Financial Literacy Explicated: The Case for a Clearer Definition in an Increasingly Complex Economy," *Journal of Consumer Affairs*, 44 (2), 276-295.

Gleaning Signals from Soldout Products

Xin Ge, University of Northern British Columbia, Canada
Paul R. Messinger, University of Alberta, Canada
Yuanfang Lin, University of Alberta, Canada

EXTENDED ABSTRACT

This article examines one type of market signal — a soldout product — and the inferences that purchasers make when they observe a soldout product. The notion that preferences of some consumers can shape those of others has been studied in the literature on social influence involving word of mouth, opinion leaders, reference groups, and herd behavior (Godes and Mayzlin 2004; Summers 1970). But inter-personal influence can emerge even without explicit communication or direct observation of other people's behavior. We argue that a soldout condition (when a certain product is sold out) is a market signal that accompanies an indirect mechanism of inter-personal influence on consumer choice.

We consider consumers who are initially uncertain about their preferences for a product, perhaps because they have never tried the product before. A soldout condition is interpreted as a signal that other consumers find the soldout product desirable. We develop and test a model whereby consumers (positively) update their expected preferences for the remaining products that are similar to the soldout product. We call the inference arising from a soldout product, the "preference signaling" effect.

The change in perceived desirability of a product, arising from observed market factors, is consistent with the concept of constructive preferences (Bettman, Luce and Payne 1998; Lichtenstein and Slovic 2006; Tversky and Thaler 1990). According to this view, preference is an evolving, context-dependent process. In the current article, the mechanism of preference construction is modeled as Bayesian updating; and a soldout condition constitutes a signal upon which an update is formed. The current research, thus, demonstrates how Bayesian thinking can underlie preference construction.

To motivate our hypotheses, we develop two Bayesian models: an attribute-free benchmark model and an attribute-based model. Both models require assumptions about consumer beliefs about previous store inventory levels and traffic/visits of other consumers to the store. In the former model, we derive the basic "preference signaling effect" and a boundary condition (whereby the market segment that gave rise to the soldout condition is unrepresentative of the focal consumer's preferences). In the attribute-based model, we demonstrate that soldout alternatives can give rise to the well-known attraction effect (Huber, Payne and Puto 1982; Huber and Puto 1983), which we distinguish from the preference signaling effect. We further demonstrate that a soldout condition can induce attribute weight shifts along the key attribute dimensions of products. We derived four hypotheses from these models.

Hypothesis 1: A soldout condition will cause increased consumer preference for an available option similar to the soldout product.

Hypothesis 2: The soldout condition increase consumer preference for an available option (similar to the soldout product) only when the decision maker perceives him/herself to be similar to those who have purchased the soldout product. When a decision maker perceives him/herself to be different from those who purchased the soldout prod-

uct, the soldout condition will not influence the decision maker's choice.

Hypothesis 3: The soldout condition will lead consumers to accord more importance to the attribute dimension on which the soldout product (and the target product) has a high value relative to the rival.

Hypothesis 4: The combined influence of a preference signaling effect and an attraction effect for a similar available option in a soldout condition will be the strongest when the soldout product is inferior to the available option, followed by the case when the soldout product is equal to the available option, and the weakest when the soldout product is superior to the available option.

These hypotheses were substantiated by with three experiments involving children's toys, exercise classes, and hotels for Hawaii beach vacations. Experiment 1 demonstrated a preference signaling effect, whereby the presence of a soldout product induced a greater choice share for a similar remaining option (H1). Experiment 2 supported a boundary condition whereby, if the soldout condition is attributable to consumers in a segment very different from the focal consumer, then the preference signaling effect does not occur (H2). Experiment 3 provided support for an attribute weight-shift effect (H3) and also showed that an inferior soldout product adds to the preference signaling effect whereas a superior soldout product lessens the preference signaling effect, consistent with H4 concerning the positive and negative attraction effects triggered by soldout products.

To the best of our knowledge, this research is the first to illustrate how Bayesian thinking can constitute a behavioral theory that explains "preference construction" in the face of market signals. This article illustrates an example of preference construction — where consumer preferences are formed or reformed, on the fly, by factors in the purchase environment. We show that a preference signaling effect is an outcome of Bayesian inference-making from soldout product signals. It would be desirable for future research to examine whether other forms of preference construction can be supported with models of Bayesian inference-making.

In particular, Lichtenstein and Slovic (2006, p. 1) argued that preference construction may arise when (1) some of the decision elements are unfamiliar; (2) preferences are unclear and it is difficult to make tradeoffs; or (3) positive and negative feelings are difficult to translate into a numerical response. Lichtenstein and Slovic (2006) also argued that the first situation (unfamiliarity) is rarely studied. This article implicitly restricts attention to such situations where consumers are considering unfamiliar decision options. It would be desirable to extend Bayesian models of thinking to other types of situations where preference construction is commonly employed — involving either tradeoffs between conflicting attributes or numerical quantification of preferences or probabilities. The literature has framed preference construction as a criticism of classical utility theory. From a conceptual perspective, we look forward to application of Bayesian thinking, along the lines illustrated in this article, to help begin to reconcile classical utility theory with the idea of preference construction.

REFERENCES

Bettman, James R., Mary Frances Luce, and John W. Payne (1998), "Constructive Consumer Choice Processes," *Journal of Consumer Research*, 25 (3), 187–217.

Godes, David and Dina Mayzlin (2004), "Using Online Conversation to Study Word-of-Mouth Communication," *Marketing Science*, 23 (4), 545-560.

Huber, Joel, John W. Payne, and Christopher Puto (1982), "Adding Symmetrically Dominated Alternatives: Violations of Regularity and the Similarity Hypothesis," *Journal of Consumer Research*, 9 (1), 90–98.

Huber, Joel and Christopher Puto (1983), "Market Boundaries and Product Choice: Illustrating Attraction and Substitution Effects," *Journal of Consumer Research*, 10 (1), 31–41.

Lichtenstein, Sarah and Paul Slovic (2006), "The Construction of Preference: An Overview," in Sarah Lichtenstein and Paul Slovic (eds.), *The Construction of Preference*, Cambridge University Press: Cambridge, England, pp 1–40.

Summers, John O. (1970), "The Identity of Women's Clothing Fashion Opinion Leaders," *Journal of Marketing Research*, 7 (2), 178-185.

Tversky, Amos and Richard H. Thaler (1990), "Anomalies: Preference Reversals," *The Journal of Economic Perspectives*, 41(2), 201-211.

Taking Dogs to Tourism Activities:
Examining a Pet-Related Constraints Negotiation Model

Annie Chen, University of Westminster, UK
Norman Peng, University of Westminster, UK

EXTENDED ABSTRACT

As modern individuals place more value on tourism and become more attached to their pets, growing business opportunities and challenges exist for the tourism industry. Pet-related products (including services) were a US $41 billion industry in 2007, which was ten times more than in 1997 (Chen, Hung, and Peng, 2011). Because the majority of pet owners (75%) consider their pets to be their children (Serpell, 2003, p.84), a large number of owners purchase luxury pet goods, such as pet beds that cost $700-$800 (Cavanaugh, Leonard, and Scammon, 2008; Ridgway, Kukar-Kiney, Monroe, and Chamberlin, 2008). When owners begin to treat their pets better and become more attached to their pets, they also place more value on tourism activities (e.g., American, the British, and Germans). Because of these trends, it is more likely that animal companions will influence owners' tourism participation intention and that some owners will consider taking their pets to tourism activities (Carr, 2010; Chen et al., 2011). This development could have significant implications for marketers and for the literature on tourism participation.

To date, consumer and tourism literature have not fully addressed this issue beyond a general analysis that taking pets to activities is difficult, requires extensive planning, and is more challenging than not taking pets (American Veterinary Medical Association, 2009; Chen et al., 2011). To contribute to the literature and further investigate a pet's influence on its owner's participation of tourism activities (Carr, 2010), this study examines the following question: 'What are the factors that influence an owner's intention to take pets to tourism activities?' To examine this question, this study modified the model of leisure constraints by focusing on a pet's tourism constraints (Jackson, 1993; Hung and Petrick, 2010; Son, Mowen, and Kerstetter, 2008). In addition to pet constraints, this research also tested how an owner's motivation to take a pet to tourism activities and his/her ability to negotiate for needed resources (e.g., time, money, transports) would affect his/her tourism intention (White, 2008; Wilhelm Stanis, Schneider, and Russell, 2009). The following are this research's hypotheses and framework (Figure 1).

Hypothesis 1: *A pet's specific constraints will negatively influence its owner's intention to take the pet along for tourism activities.*

Hypothesis 2: *A pet's interpersonal constraints will negatively influence its owner's intention to take pets when undertaking tourism activities.*

Hypothesis 3: *A pet's structural constraints will negatively influence an owner's intention to take the pet on tourism activities.*

Hypothesis 4: *An owner's negotiation ability/strategy will positively influence his/her intention to take pets on tourism activities.*

Hypothesis 5: *An owner's motivation to take pets on a tourism activity will positively influence his/her negotiation ability and/or strategy.*

To examine this study's hypotheses, qualitative and quantitative exploratory pilot test were conducted. After these steps, survey for the main research was finalized and five tourism activities were selected (Chen et al., 2011; Nyaupane, Morais, and Graefe, 2004; Son et al., 2008; White, 2008). The activities were nature sightseeing, visiting cultural sites, recreation, participating in events, and participating in other tourism activities that lasted four hours or more. 251 British adult dog owners were recruited through an on-site purposive sampling method. The sampling areas included the Greater London area, the Southwest, the Midlands, and the Northeast. From the results, 203 surveys were deemed effective, resulting in a valid return rate of 80.8%. All variables in this study's model were measured with multiple items. After examination, all variables are reliable

SPSS 17 and AMOS 5.0 were used to analyse the data. As recommended by Anderson and Gerbing (1988), a two-step approach to structural equation modelling (SEM) was used. After the overall measurement model was found acceptable, the structural model was again tested with the entire sample (N=203). The model fit was good (χ^2=368.961, df=187, RMSEA=0.072, CFI=0.917). According to Fornell and Larcker (1981) and Bogozzi and Yi (1988), composite reliability (CR) should be greater than 0.6 and AVE should be above 0.5 to achieve discriminant validity. Base on result of this research, both of these validities are achieved.

The structure estimate of −0.286 (t=−1.673, p<0.1), −0.789 (t=−6.063, p<0.001), and −0.286 (t=−1.673, p<0.1) show that pet specific constraints, interpersonal constraints and structural constraints have a significant and negative effect on an owner's intention to take pets on tourism activities. As a result, H1, H2, and H3 are supported. In other words, the more constraints the pets have, the less likely it is that their owners will take them to tourism activities. For H4, this study's finding supports the hypothesis that the owner's negotiation ability/strategy will positively affect the owner's intention to take pets on tourism activities. H4's structure estimate was 0.311 (t=2.212, p<0.05), indicating that the more negotiation ability/

Figure 1. Research Framework

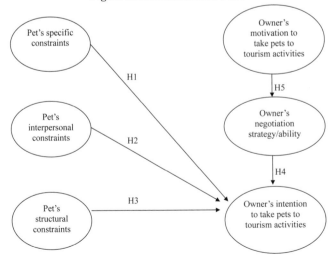

strategy the owner possesses, the more likely it is that he/she will have the intention to take pets along for tourism activities. Lastly, H5, which states that the owner's motivation to take pets along for tourism activities will positively affect his/her negotiation ability/ strategy, is significantly supported. The structure estimate for H5 was 0.625 (t=5.869, p<0.001). A pet owner is more likely to have a higher negotiation ability/strategy if he/she is highly motivated to take pets along for tourism activities. To test the mediating effects of motivation on negation ability/strategy, a Sobel test was performed (Sobel, 1982). Because the Z value was found to be greater than 1.96 (Z=5.955), negotiation strategy/ability was determined to fully mediate the relationship between motivation and participation.

In conclusion, this study identified and examined the factors that can affect an owner's intention to take pets to tourism activities. The results confirmed that a pet's associated constraints (i.e., pet-specific constraints, interpersonal constraints, and structural constraints) could negatively influence an owner's intention to take pets to tourism activities that they want to attend. In particular, a pet's interpersonal constraints (e.g., other participants do not like pets) will affect an owner's intention most significantly. Despite pets having constraints, if the owner is motivated and has the requisite negotiation ability/strategy, he/she will still plan to undertake tourism activities with his/her pet.

REFERENCES

American Veterinary Medical Association (2009), "Traveling with Your Pet," Retrieved March 15, 2011, from American Veterinary Medical Association Web site: https://ebusiness. avma.org/EBusiness50/files/productdownloads/traveling_ brochure.pdf

Anderson, James C. and David W.Gerbing (1988), "Structural Equation Modelling in Practice: A Review and Recommended Two-step Approach," *Psychological Bulletin*, 103(3), 411-423.

Bagozzi, Richard P. and Youjae Yi (1988), "On the Evaluation of Structural Equation Model," *Journal of Academy of Marketing Science*, 16(1), 74-94.

Carr, Neil (2009) "EDITORIAL Animals in the Tourism and Leisure Experience," *Current Issues in Tourism*, 12(5/6), 409-411

Cavanaugh, Lisa A., Hillary A. Leonard and Debra L. Scammon (2008), "A Tail of Two Personalities: How Canine Companions Shape Relationships and Well-being," *Journal of Business Research*, 61(5), 469-479.

Chen, Annie Huiling, Kuang-peng Hung, and Norman Peng (2011), "Planned Leisure Behaviour and Pet Attachment," *Annals of Tourism Research*, 38(4), 1657-1662.

Fornell, Claes and Larcker, David F. (1981), "Evaluating Structural Equation Models with Unobservables and Measurement Errors," *Journal of Marketing Research*, 18(3), 39-50

Jackson, Edgar L. (1993), "Recognizing Patterns of Leisure Constraints: Results from Alternative Analysis," *Journal of Leisure Research*, 25, 129-140.

Hung, Kam and James F. Petrick (2010), "Developing a Measurement Scale for Constraints to Cruising," *Annals of Tourism Research*, 37(1), 206-228.

Nyaupane, Gyan P., Duarte B. Morais and Alan R. Graefe (2004), "Nature Tourism Constraints A Cross-activity Comparison," *Annals of Tourism Research*, 31(3), 540-555.

Ridgway, Nancy M., Monika Kukar-Kinney, Kent B. Monroe and Emily Chamberlin (2008), "Does Excessive Buying for Self Relate to Spending on Pets?," *Journal of Business Research*, 61(5), 392-396.

Serpell, James A. (2003), "Anthropomorphism and Anthropomorphic Selection- Beyond the 'Cute Response'," *Society and Animals*, 11(1), 83-100.

Sobel, Michael E. (1982), "Asymptotic Confidence Intervals for Indirect Effects in Structural Equation Models," in *Sociological Methodology,*ed. Samuel Leinhardt, Washington, DC: American Sociological Association, 290-312.

White, Dave D. (2008), "A Structural Model of Leisure Constraints Negotiation in Outdoor Recreation," *Leisure Sciences*, 30, 342-359.

Wilhelm Stanis, Sonja A., Ingrid E. Schneider and Keith C. Russell (2009), "Leisure Time Physical Activity of Park Visitors: Retesting Constraint Models in Adoption and Maintenance Stages," *Leisure Science*, 31, 287-304.

Consuming Branded Stories:
A Netnography of Fashion and Luxury Blog Consumption

Gachoucha Kretz, ISC Paris School of Management, France

EXTENDED ABSTRACT

Blogs have grown rapidly in the last six years. A Mc Kinsey study has reported consumers growing interest in blogs: nearly four in five active Internet users visit social media including blogs to look for product information (NM Incite 2011). Blogs thus contribute to online consumption culture and processes, which justifies better understanding of blog content and impact on consumers.

Blogs offer consumer-generated content and particularly brand and product narratives that can bring "targeted, precise, influential comments and feedback" (Kozinets 2006, 138) both to readers and brands. In particular, fashion and luxury blogs provide consumption or branded narratives helping blogger's identity (Kretz 2010; Zhao and Belk 2007) construction while cultivating consumerist values and consumer culture through conspicuous consumption or brand mentioning. These narratives can be regarded as branded stories told by real characters that sometimes attract large audience.

How people consume stories has been quite substantially studied. Levy (2006) presents a detailed review of scholars of our field who have explained how people consume stories. Particularly, commercials or TV programs have been studied as persuasive stories with effects on consumers. Audience response to stories has been measured through attitude toward ads (McQuarrie and Mick 1999) or perceptions of the surrounding material world (O'Guinn and Shrum 1997) or described through gendered interpretation processes (Stern 1993). Levy (2006, 453) comes up with a breaking new approach of story consumption by exploring how stories are 'consumed, that is, taken up, internalized and transformed'. Outside the consumer research field, media research has addressed long unanswered questions about what the audience 'does' with stories with Katz and Liebes (1986), Ang (1985), Radway (1984) and Hobson (1982).

Overall, existing research shows that readers make use of stories to keep informed; entertain; create and update identities; settle life projects; socialize and communicate and train imagination and emotion. The stories underlying such results, however, are mostly fictional, related to myths or to historical facts. But what happens in the case of blogs that provide branded narratives from real consumers?

How consumers internalize and transform marketing content through branded stories published in blogs is a relevant question for marketers. It raises the issue of a blog's influence toward its audience, particularly regarding the readers' subsequent behavior, while escaping the strict cases of the 'typical endorser' (Friedman and Friedman 1976) or of the 'market maven' (Feick and Price 1987). While no precise short-term action is expected from fiction or myth readers, blog readers should at least better know and like the mentioned brands and at best, purchase them. Therefore, we are here focusing on the effect of branded narratives on blogs' audience and particularly on how they impact consumers' everyday lives.

We have explored audience behavior through Netnography (Kozinets 2010) from 2005 to December 2011, focusing on specific dimensions including: types of blog reading behavior; motivations to read and integration of blog reading in everyday life occupations. Twenty popular (A-list) fashion and luxury blogs – that is blogs attracting the most readers – have been identified to 'thickly describe' and interpret (Erlandson et al. 1993) reader behavior dimensions in commenting, interactiong and linking. The selected A-list fashion blogs mostly mention luxury fashion brands, which explains why we address them as luxury ones. Twenty readers of those popular blogs have been simultaneously selected for member checks through in-depth interviews (Kozinets 2010) and further explanation of their reading behavior and blog reading everyday life consequences. Readers consisted of people who commented or not.

We found that consumers read fashion and luxury blogs like any other story and for the same reasons mentioned by existing research. Blog reading becomes part of an everyday self-indulgence routine sometimes without any goal except for entertainment or discussion with peers and authors and sometimes focused on information search or brand and product recommendation. Readers take up blog stories differently from 'regular' stories because they come from real mundane people they feel are more trustworthy, passionate and thus knowledgeable about specific topics. Like for (auto)biography, bloggers are easier to identify with, to inspire from and model after and thus are more influential in triggering purchase behavior.

Theoretically speaking, we have observed an overall shift in the dynamics between brands and consumers in the marketplace, regarding involving brands and products like luxury and fashion ones. Specifically, we have discovered that purchase decision depends not anymore on the brands advertised but on the quality of the relationship held between the blogger and the readers. Readers who experience parasocial or social interactions with their favorite bloggers more often transform reading into purchase when the product is affordable. Bloggers, however, are expected to abide by a tacit initial contract, that is to remain true their initial content and to their relationships with their audience, if they want to maintain that influence. The present research extends Kozinets et al. (2010)'s findings on consumer-brand relationships to end readers and consumers who internalize the marketing content already filtered by the bloggers.

Our contribution is also empirical. Readers follow blog consumption strategies: they read many blogs every day, but do not internalize them the same way. Depending on the type of popular blog considered ('Celebrity', 'Character', 'Spokesperson' or 'Buddy') they will respectively seek for 'Initiation', 'Inspiration', 'Information' or 'Imitation'. With 'Initiation' they look for backstage and secret insights from the luxury world; with 'Inspiration', they look for atmospheres and creative ideas to take away and adapt for themselves; with 'Information', they merely want to gain knowledge about the luxury world and with 'Imitation', they expect recommendation and products and brands to purchase to construct identities.

Better knowledge of such reading strategies will lead brand managers to avoid mistakes in addressing bloggers and to identify potential spokespeople more efficiently. Indeed, blogs offer access to a wide audience through the blogger as an influencer. However, managers should check the audience reading strategies and expectations: Initiation and Inspiration can only lead to brand awareness building and image bolstering while Information can initiate shopping trips and Imitation can trigger actual purchase.

REFERENCES

Ang, Ien (1985), Watching Dallas: Soap Opera and the Melodramatic Imagination, Methuen &Co Ltd.

Erlandson, David A., Edward L. Harris, Barbara L. Skipper and Steve D. Allen (1993), Doing Naturalistic Inquiry: A Guide to Methods, Newbury Park, CA: Sage.

Feick, Lawrence F. and Linda L. Price (1987), "The Market Maven: A Diffuser of Marketplace Information", Journal of Marketing, 51 (January), 83-97.

Friedman, Hershey H. and Linda Friedman (1976), "Endorser Effectiveness by Product Type", Journal of Advertising Research, 19 (October), 63-71.

Hobson, Dorothy (1982), Crossroads: the Drama of a Soap Opera, Methuen &Co Ltd.

Katz, Elihu and Tamar, Liebes (1986), "Mutual Aid in the Decoding of Dallas: Preliminary Notes from a Cross-Cultural Study", in Television in Transition, eds. P. Drummond & R. Patterson, London, UK: British Film Institute, 187-198.

Kozinets, Robert V. (2006), "Netnography 2.0.", in Handbook of Qualitative Research Methods in Marketing, ed. R.W. Belk, Cheltenham, UK: Edward Elgar Publishing Ltd, 129-142.

Kozinets, Robert V. (2010), Netnography, Thousand Oak, CA: Sage.

Kozinets, Robert V., Kristine de Valck, Andrea C. Wojnicki, and Sarah J. S. Wilner (2010), "Networked Narratives: Understanding Word-of-Mouth Marketing in Online Communities," Journal of Marketing, 74 (2), 71-89.

Kretz, Gachoucha G. (2010), "Pixelize me! A semiotic approach of self-digitalization in fashion blogs", Advances in Consumer Research, Vol. 37, Association for Consumer Research, Duluth, MN: 393-399.

Levy, Sidney J. (2006), "The Consumption of Stories", in Handbook of Qualitative Research Methods in Marketing, ed. R.W. Belk, Cheltenham, UK: Edward Elgar Publishing Ltd, 453-464.

McQuarrie, Edward F. and David G. Mick (1999). "Visual rhetoric in advertising: Text-interpretive, experimental, and reader-response analyses", Journal of Consumer Research, 26 (January), 37-54.

O'Guinn, Thomas C. and L. J. Shrum (1997), "The role of television in the construction of consumer reality", Journal of Consumer Research, 23 (March), 278-294.

Radway, Janice (1984), "Interpretive Communities and Variable Literacies: The Functions of Romance Reading", Daedalus, 113 (Summer), 49-73.

Stern, Barbara B. (1993), "Feminist literary criticism and the deconstruction of ads: A postmodern view of advertising and consumer responses", Journal of Consumer Research, 19 (March), 556-566.

Zhao, Xin and Russell W. Belk (2007), "Live From Shopping Malls: Blogs and Chinese Consumer Desire", Advances in Consumer Research, Association for Consumer Research, Valdosta, GA: 131-137.

False but Persuasive Information: The Automatic Success of Infomercials

Claudiu Dimofte, San Diego State University, USA
Richard Yalch, University of Washington, USA
Kyra Wiggin, University of Washington, USA

EXTENDED ABSTRACT

Infomercials exemplify promotional messages wherein extraordinary claims abound. Given their reputation for exaggeration, the persuasion knowledge model (Friestad and Wright 1994) would suggest that consumer skepticism would render them ineffective. However, their continued existence and success indicate that infomercials influence many consumers. Explaining the popularity of an industry employing claims that are "too good to be true" challenges traditional persuasion models (e.g., Petty and Cacioppo 1981). This research presents a novel perspective based on a dual processing framework and experimental support for it.

Conceptual Framework. Infomercial producers employ an intuitive approach to selling that is universally alluring (Donthu and Gilliland 1996). They appeal to basic human needs related to consumers' hopes and desires – an effective way to influence people (MacInnis and de Mello 2005). Visually demonstrating the product claims (as incredible as some may be) makes infomercials more difficult to refute than reading information about these claims. FTC rules against deception may actually benefit infomercials, as consumers might erroneously assume a de facto approval, following the "if it is on TV, it must be true" fallacy that would not extend to print versions.

We propose that the infomercial paradox (persuasion without explicit product claim acceptance), occurs because the claims are also not completely rejected. This state of neither belief nor disbelief motivates consumers to satisfy their curiosity by trying the product and hoping for performance as claimed. In a consumer research classic, Maloney (1962) proposed that the disbelief most people experience when encountering exaggerated product claims is often overwhelmed by an innate curiosity. When advertising information conflicts with extant beliefs, the resulting dissonance must be somehow appeased, often by yielding to the message and trying out the product in an attempt to re-adjust personal brand attitudes (Maloney 1963). His results suggest that advertising that causes consumers to not believe the message claims but arouses their curiosity may be the most effective form of new product advertising.

We propose a two-factor model for explaining the persuasive effects of infomercial-type messages that is derived from "illusion of truth" research that distinguishes between information learning (an explicit process) and truth judgments (often an implicit process). This research (e.g., Gilbert, Krull, and Malone 1990) demonstrates that individuals often accept information as true unless they explicitly evaluate it as false. In the case of infomercials, it is possible that curiosity about the claims and difficulty in directly refuting them because of their convincing visual presentation inhibits the rejection process, especially at an implicit level. Consumers' explicit assessments of the veracity of infomercial claims based on the source may be consistent with their desire to portray themselves as not gullible and naïve (Chapman and Beltramini 2000). However, research on implicit associations often shows an inconsistency between how individuals respond explicitly and implicitly (Greenwald, McGhee, and Schwartz 1998) and their automatic tendencies to link thoughts (even rejected or conflicting beliefs) in memory (Dimofte and Yalch 2011).

Methods for minimizing the appeal of infomercials are suggested by findings (e.g., DiFonzo and Bordia 2002) that inducing skepticism in consumers when they view claims made in doubtful com-munications reduces their effectiveness. This can be implemented by providing consumers with discounting cues about the infomercial message that highlight the falsity of the claims made therein. However, timing of the discounting cues is important. In the context of demonstrating a sleeper effect, Pratkanis et al. (1998) reported that providing a credibility undermining discounting cue before message exposure eliminates the sleeper effect whereas presenting it after the message results in one. The before presentation alters how the information is processed and stored, whereas the after presentation does not. Thus, if consumers are forearmed with easily retrieved explanations for the deceptive visuals, the infomercials should not be persuasive. On the other hand, once false beliefs have been learned and implicit associations created, they are often difficult to extinguish. Information undermining the credibility of the infomercials will not be effective when presented after exposure to the infomercial.

Study 1. To address the curious nonbelief phenomenon, a first experiment was run that involved exposing subjects to a video excerpt from an infomercial for the Ultimate Chopper or the same information content in a textual presentation format. The infomercial was presented alone or preceded / followed by a discounting cue (an excerpt from an investigative report highlighting the product's false claims). Explicit measures were collected (brand rating, believability, curiosity, etc.) after the presentation. Finally, participants performed one of two Implicit Association Tests (Greenwald et al. 1998) looking at novel automatic associations created for the Chopper and a competing brand (Henckels). The items used in the IATs assessed the relative association between the brands and truthfulness attributes (believable/ unbelievable in IAT$_1$) or curiosity attributes (boring/interesting in IAT$_2$).

Results (see Table) showed that presenting the infomercial by itself was the most persuasive at both explicit and implicit levels, suggesting that the specific format of this marketing communication is indeed conducive to attitude change. Interestingly, the same information presented in a text format was deemed most believable but performed the worst in terms of eliciting curiosity and attaining persuasion. Exposure to the discounting cues either before or after the infomercial was successful in eliciting suspicion and hurt both explicit believability and curiosity, but only the pre-exposure cue lowered the infomercial's persuasive impact (in line with Pratkanis et al. 1988). Despite the explicit effects of the postexposure discounting cue, the infomercial was nevertheless perceived as relatively believable and elicited curiosity at implicit levels.

Conclusion. In summary, it appears that infomercials are successful because they stimulate a curious nonbelief that operates differently at the explicit and implicit levels. Explicitly, consumers are curious but reject the product claims as unbelievable. However, at an implicit level, consumers are both curious and more accepting of the product claims (i.e., they now have a stronger implicit association between the claims and the advertised brand compared to a nonadvertised brand). The implicit effects are most critical because they seem resistant to efforts to undermine the credibility of the infomercial by providing discounting cues.

Table 1: Means for main dependent variables in Study 1

	Infomercial	Discounting Cue + Infomercial	Infomercial + Discounting Cue	Text
Believability	4.45	3.71[a]	3.59[b]	4.78[a,b]
Curiosity	4.48	3.98	4.19	4.32
Attitudes	7.65[a,b]	5.93[a]	6.48	5.98[b]
Implicit Curiosity	.23[a,d]	.11[b,d,e]	.20[c,e]	-.29[a,b,c]
Implicit Believability	.31[a,b,c]	.01[a,d,e]	.16[b,d]	-.19[c,e]

9-point scale for attitude, 7-point scales for believability and curiosity; IAT means are D-measure. Values with shared superscripts are significantly different at $p < .05$ or lower

REFERENCES

Chapman, Patricia S. and Richard F. Beltramini (2000), "Infomercials Revisited: Perspectives of Advertisers and Advertising Agencies," *Journal of Advertising Research*, 40 (5), 24-31.

DiFonzo, Nicholas and Prashant Bordia (2002), "Corporate Rumor Activity, Belief, and Accuracy," *Public Relations Review, 28* (1), 1-19.

Dimofte, Claudiu V. and Richard F. Yalch (2011), "The Mere Association Effect and Brand Evaluations," *Journal of Consumer Psychology*, 20 (3), 24-37.

Donthu, Naveen and David Gilliland (1996), "The Infomercial Shopper. (Observations)," *Journal of Advertising Research*, 36 (2), 69-76.

Friestad, Marian and Peter Wright (1994), "Persuasion Knowledge Model: How People Cope with Persuasion Attempts," *Journal of Consumer Research*, 21 (1), 1-31.

Gilbert, Daniel T., Douglas S. Krull, and Patrick S. Malone (1990), "Unbelieving the Unbelievable: Some Problems in the Rejection of False Information," *Journal of Personality and Social Psychology*, 59 (4), 601-613.

Greenwald, Anthony G., Debbie E. McGhee, and Jordan L.K. Schwartz (1998), "Measuring Individual Differences in Implicit Cognition: The Implicit Association Test," *Journal of Personality and Social Psychology*, 74, 1464-1480.

MacInnis, Deborah and Gustavo de Mello (2005), "The Concept of Hope and Its Relevance to Product Evaluation and Choice," *Journal of Marketing*, 69 (1), 1-14.

Maloney, John C. (1962), "Curiosity Versus Disbelief in Advertising," *Journal of Advertising Research*, 2 (2), 2-8.

Maloney, John C. (1963), "Is Advertising Believability Really Important?" *Journal of Marketing*, 27 (4), 1-8.

Petty, Richard E. and John T. Caccioppo (1981). *Attitudes and Persuasion: Classic and Contemporary Approaches*. Boulder, CO: Westview Press.

Pratkanis, Anthony R., Anthony G. Greenwald, Michael R. Leippe, and Michael H. Baumgardner (1988), "In Search of Reliable Persuasion Effects: III. The Sleeper Effect is Dead. Long Live the Sleeper Effect," *Journal of Personality and Social Psychology*, 54 (2), 203-218.

Social Power and Financial Risk Taking: The Role of Agency-Communion

Didem Kurt, Boston University, USA

EXTENDED ABSTRACT

Often described as individuals' ability to control resources of their own and others without social interference, power has been shown to impact different aspects of human behavior. Recently, researchers have begun to explore the effects of power on individuals' consumption and spending patterns. This stream of literature documents that experiencing a state of powerlessness versus powerfulness leads consumers to spend more money on status related items (Rucker and Galinsky 2008), as well as on the items they purchase for others versus themselves (Rucker et al. 2011). In the present research, I investigate an alternative channel through which social power can influence consumers' welfare, namely financial risk taking.

Consumers often face risky monetary decisions such as investing in a stock versus bond fund, buying a lottery ticket or making a bet in a gamble. These decisions, in turn, have important implications for their welfare and well-being. However, little is known how individuals' interactions with others influence their financial risk taking. A recent study by Levav and Argo (2010) demonstrates that an interpersonal touch (i.e., a comforting pat on the shoulder by a female experimenter) increases individuals' propensity to make risky financial decisions. In this study, I focus on the link between financial risk taking and a more prevalent social force that generally has negative connotations, i.e., social power.

I propose that having power versus lacking power over others does not unconditionally affect people's risky financial decisions. Rather its impact depends on individuals' agency-communion orientation. Agency refers to a tendency to reflect on one's individuality and emphasizes the self and its separation from other organisms, while communion refers to the merging of an individual in a larger organism and social connections with others (Bakan 1966). I argue that feeling powerful versus powerless leads to greater financial risk taking only for agentic individuals. I built my prediction on Chen et al.'s (2001) relationship-orientation based conceptualization of power's effects, which proposes that self-focused individuals associate social power with self-interest goals, whereas other-focused individuals link power with responsibility goals. That is, agentic individuals experiencing a state of power take greater financial risk since increased wealth can fortify their powerful position and help them maintain their status. On the other hand, taking risk to enhance wealth and maintain the status associated with power is inconsistent with communal goals. Thus, agentic individuals with high (versus low) power are expected to make riskier financial decisions, whereas communal individuals with high (versus low) power are predicted to refrain from taking higher financial risk.

Study 1 employs a 2 (power: high vs. low) x 2 (orientation: agency vs. communion) between-subjects design (N = 94). Power was manipulated using an episodic priming task adapted from Galinsky et al. (2003) and agency-communion orientation was measured. Following previous research (e.g., Kurt et al. 2011), I created a measure to assess relative agency orientation, "ACDIF", by subtracting each respondent's communion score from his/her agency score. Participants were asked to imagine that they were given $100 and told that they could participate in a 50-50 gamble in which they could win an additional $100 or lose $10, $20,…, or $100. They indicated whether they would accept each of these offers. Among the offers accepted by a participant, the highest amount s/he is willing to risk to earn additional $100 is the dependent variable. As predicted, I found a significant interaction between power and ACDIF ($\beta = 3.56$, $p < .05$). Post-hoc analysis reveals that the slope for high ACDIF (i.e., agentic) participants is positive and significant ($b = 5.031$, $p < .05$), indicating that the experience of power increases agentic individuals' tendency to take financial risk. However, the slope for low ACDIF (i.e., communal) participants is negative and insignificant ($b = -3.575$, ns). The next study tests the underlying mechanism for this effect. Specifically, I argue that high power leads agentic individuals to take more financial risk only when self-benefit obtained from the risky decision is high.

Study 2 employs a 2 (power: high vs. low) x 2 (orientation: agency vs. communion) x 2 (self benefit: high vs. low) between-subjects design (N = 307). Power and self-benefit were manipulated, whereas agency-communion orientation was measured. Participants were asked to imagine that they have participated in a charity event where they can play "Odd-Even?", which is a game of chance based on correctly guessing whether the winning number is odd or even, and that they have $100 to bet. Participants assigned to the high (low) self-benefit condition were told that they can keep 75% (25%) of their winnings, whereas 25% (75%) of their winnings are automatically donated to the charity. I found a significant three-way interaction among power, self-benefit, and ACDIF ($\beta = 2.25$, $p < .05$). More important, the slope for high ACDIF and high self-benefit is positive and significant ($b = 6.495$, $p < .05$), suggesting that agentic individuals with high power take higher financial risk when the positive outcome of the risky decision benefits mostly themselves. In contrast, they take less risk when self-benefit is low ($b = -5.421$, $p < .05$). However, having power versus lacking it does not have any impact on financial risk taking of communal individuals regardless of the level of self-benefit.

Study 3 tests the underlying process via mediation analysis (as outlined in Zhao et al. 2010) and employs a 2 (power: high vs. low) x 2 (orientation: agency vs. communion) between-subjects design (N = 84). Participants were asked to imagine that they would allocate their $5,000 between a stock fund and a bond fund. Again, there was a significant interaction between power and ACDIF ($\beta = 6.00$, $p < .05$). As expected, agentic individuals with high power take more risk and invest a higher percentage in the stock fund ($b = 10.274$, $p < .05$). More important, this effect is mediated by the extent to which participants associate power with self-interest goals measured using a two-item scale (e.g., "Power should be used to benefit the self"). Specifically, the estimated 95% confidence interval around the indirect effect of power on % allocated to the stock fund through self-interest goals does not contain zero (0.12 to 4.40), supporting mediation.

Overall, the present research demonstrates the asymmetric impact of social power on financial risk taking of agentic and communal individuals and contributes to the literature in several important ways. First, this research adds to the growing body of work examining the role of social power in consumer behavior. Second, it furthers our understanding of how consumers' interactions with those around them influence their financial risk taking. Finally, it contributes to the recent literature on the link between consumers' agency-communion orientation and their monetary decisions.

REFERENCES

Bakan, David (1966), *The Duality of Human Existence*, Chicago: Rand McNally & Company.

Chen, Serena, Annette Y. Lee-Chai, and John A. Bargh (2001), "Relationship Orientation as a Moderator of the Effects of Social Power," *Journal of Personality and Social Psychology*, 80 (2), 173-187.

Galinsky, Adam D., Deborah H. Gruenfeld, and Joe C. Magee (2003), "From Power to Action," *Journal of Personality and Social Psychology*, 85 (3), 453-466.

Kurt, Didem, J. Jeffrey Inman, and Jennifer J. Argo (2011), "The Influence of Friends on Consumer Spending: The Role of Agency-Communion and Self-Monitoring," *Journal of Marketing Research*, 48 (August), 741-754.

Levav, Jonathan and Jennifer J. Argo (2010), "Physical Contact and Financial Risk Taking," *Psychological Science*, 21 (6), 804-810.

Rucker, Derek D. and Adam D. Galinsky (2008), "Desire to Acquire: Powerlessness and Compensatory Consumption," *Journal of Consumer Research*, 35 (August), 257-267.

Rucker, Derek D., David Dubois, and Adam D. Galinsky (2011), "Generous Paupers and Stingy Prices: Power Drives Consumer Spending on Self versus Others," *Journal of Consumer Research*, 6 (April), 1015-1029.

Zhao, Xinshu, John G. Lynch Jr., and Qimei Chen (2010), "Reconsidering Baron and Kenny: Myths and Truths about Mediation Analysis," *Journal of Consumer Research*, 37 (August), 197-206.

When Up Is Down: Natural Height Congruency in Product Evaluation

Michael Giblin, University at Buffalo, USA
Aner Tal, Cornell University, USA
Brian Wansink, Cornell University, USA

EXTENDED ABSTRACT

Despite the endless variety of products and customization options that saturate the world's markets in nearly every domain, marketing campaigns have a tendency to be one minded about certain beliefs, such as the superiority of high shelving space over low shelving space. This view is supported by metaphor research. However, situations may arise in which items shelved high up are at a disadvantage due to a violation of consumer expectations of "natural height".

Contemporary metaphor research suggests that metaphorical constructs become deeply rooted in our basic understanding of a phenomenon, forming a solid way of conceptualizing such abstract phenomena using physical concepts. With the vertical height metaphor, height is presented as the concrete infrastructure that metaphorically orders clusters of abstract ideas, such as good and bad, sophisticated and simplistic, and powerful and powerless (Lackoff and Johnson, 1980). However, what if item placement violates our expectations of where the item should naturally appear? In those cases, could up be bad and down good?

The benefits of congruency have been shown in a wide array of domains. Consumers weigh dimensions of a product more heavily when it is compatible with their goal (Tversky, Sattath, &Slovic, 1988). Extensive research on expectation congruency has given rise to theories of a confirmation bias (Watson, 1960), as well as disconfirmation processes (Cohen & Goldberg, 1970) leading to positive and negative affect. Congruency has proven an important factor in consumer responses to products (Chandon et al., 2010, Olshavsky and Miller, 1972, Spangenberg et al., 2005).

Congruency effects have been demonstrated in the realm of vertical height (see Landau et al., 2010, Meier et al. 2006, 2007, 2009 2011). Participants performed a musical task more quickly and efficiently when the vertical orientation of three keys was congruent with pitch (high key=high pitch, low key=low pitch) (Keller & Koch, 2008). Meier and Robinson (2004) found that participants were able to evaluate positive and negative words more quickly if the words were presented in congruent positions to valence (positive up, negative down). Across four studies, we demonstrate how natural-height congruency affects evaluations, overriding a general up=good tendency.

In study 1, four fruit that grow either high (apples, bananas) or low (melons, tomatoes) were placed on high or low displays, such that one each of the high and low fruit was in its proper position, and one each was in an incongruent position (e.g., lower shelf for bananas). Participants (N = 69) were instructed to take each fruit from its place and rate how tasty the fruit would be on a scale of 1 to 9 (not at all to very much). Fruit taste was rated higher for fruit placed in a position matching their natural growth height (6.68) than for fruit placed in a mismatched position (6.02) : $F(1, 62) = 15.71$, $p = .0002$.

In study 2 (N=50) we sought to replicate the findings of study 1 in the realm of consumer products, eliminating alternate explanations for study 1 that may claim that natural fruit height is in direct correlation with freshness (an apple on a tree vs. on the ground). Here, women's clothing was evaluated as more attractive (9-point scale) when placed at a position matching their natural height. Upper clothes (blouse, sports-bra) were rated more highly on upper shelves, but lower clothes (skirt, panties) were rated higher on lower shelves. No such effect was found for men's clothing. Thus, in a joint model

containing both types of clothes there was a significant interaction between condition and gender of clothing: $F(1, 49) = 7.27$, $p = .01$. In this joint model the effect was non-significant (p>.1). However, a contrast for women's clothing only was significant: $F(1, 49) = .546$, $p = .02$. This finding suggests that while natural order congruency tends to lead to higher ratings, the underlying force driving this effect is susceptible to subtle differences such as preconceived notions of clothing gender.

Consequently, study 3 examined a less gender-specific domain: sports balls. While our previous studies have focused on natural height in the sense of where one general sees an item, study 3 turns its focus to utility, or where an item would naturally be most readily accessible and usable. One naturally high (volleyball) and one naturally low (soccer ball) sports item was used. Items were chosen to be as similar as possible in size, function, and familiarity. Participants (N=96) rated their willingness to buy each item. Participants had higher willingness to buy for volleyballs when placed on a higher shelf (5.02 vs. 3.91), but lower willingness to buy for soccer balls placed on a higher shelf (3.81 vs. 4.57): $F(1, 88) = 5.25$, $p = .02$.

To support the idea that it is learned natural height associations underlying our effect, in study 4 we plan to use ambiguous items with no obvious natural height and assign participants randomly to natural height conditions. By manipulating what participants believe to be the natural height of items, we can examine what role preconceived notions play in perceived congruency and subsequent affect. Participants will be given surveys that begin with a paragraph about each item that includes its natural height. We expect more favorable evaluations for highly shelved items for which we create an "up" expectation, and lower evaluations for upper shelved items for which we create a "down" expectation.

Rather than finding a dominant up = good effect, the current research found that items may be evaluated better when placed on lower shelves if they are naturally associated with lower height. We find a reversal of the positive associations elicited by increased vertical height when up is an unnatural position for an item. Collectively, these results argue against the generality of the up = good metaphor, arguing that instead up is good when up is natural, whereas down can be good when down is natural. Theoretically, such findings indicate metaphorical mappings may not be as general as once thought. Pragmatically, they indicate the limitation of the general belief that upper shelves are better shelves.

REFERENCES

Chandon, Pierre, Brian Wansink, and Gilles Laurent (2000). "A Benefit Congruency Framework of Sales Promotion Effectiveness," *Journal of Marketing*, 64 (October), 65–84.

Cohen, Joel B., & Goldberg, Marvin E. (1970). The Dissonance Model in Post-Decision Product Evaluation. *Journal of Marketing Research*, **7** (3), 315–321.

Keller, P. E., & Koch, I. (2008). Action planning in sequential skills: Relations to music performance. *Quarterly Journal of Experimental Psychology*, 61, 275–291.

Lakoff, G. & Johnson, M. (1980). *Metaphors We Live By*, The University of Chicago Press, Chicago, IL, 1980.

Landau, M. J., Meier, B. P., & Keefer, L. A. (2010). A metaphor-enriched social cognition. *Psychological Bulletin, 136,* 1045-1067.

Meier, B. P., Moller, A. C., Chen, J., & Riemer-Peltz, M. (2011). Spatial metaphor and real estate: North-south location biases housing preference. *Social Psychological and Personality Science, 2,* 547-553.

Meier, B. P., & Dionne, S. (2009). Downright sexy: Verticality, implicit power, and perceived physical attractiveness. *Social Cognition, 27,* 883-892.

Meier, B. P., & Robinson, M. D. (2004). Why the sunny side is up: Associations between affect and vertical position. *Psychological Science, 15,* 243-247.

Meier, B.P., & Robinson, M.D. (2006). Does "feeling down" mean seeing down? Depressive symptoms and vertical selective attention. *Journal of Research in Personality,* 40, 4, 451-461.

Meier, B. P., Hauser, D. J., Robinson, M. D., Friesen, C. K., & Schjeldahl, K. (2007). What's "up" with God?: Vertical Space as a representation of the divine. *Journal of Personality and Social Psychology, 93,* 699-710.

Olshavsky, Richard W., & Miller, John A. (1972). Consumer Expectations, Product Performance, and Perceived Product Quality. *Journal of Marketing Research,* 9, 19-21

Spangenberg, Eric R., Grohmann, Bianca, & Sprott, David E. (2005). It's beginning to smell (and sound) a lot like Christmas: the interactive effects of ambient scent and music in a retail setting, *Journal of Business Research,* 58, 11, 1583-1589.

Tversky, Amos, Shmuel, Shattath, Slovic, Paul. (1988). Contingent Weighting in Judgement and Choice. *Psychological Review,* 95 (July), 204-217.

Wason, Peter C. (1960). On the failure to eliminate hypotheses in a conceptual task. *Quarterly Journal of Experimental Psychology,* 12 (3): 129–140.

Weger, U. W., Meier, B. P., Robinson, M. D., & Inhoff, A. W. (2007). Things are sounding up: Affective influences on auditory tone perception. *Psychonomic Bulletin and Review,* 14, 517-521.

Sadder, but Not Wiser: The Myopia of Misery

Jennifer S. Lerner, Harvard University, USA
Ye Li, Harvard University, USA
Elke U. Weber, Columbia University, USA

EXTENDED ABSTRACT

Intertemporal choices, which require a decision between a sooner (usually smaller) reward and a later (usually larger) reward, are pervasive in daily life and have important consequences. Given the choice between a sooner reward and a later reward, people typically choose the sooner reward, exhibiting in economic terms irrationally high discount rates, which have been linked to a multitude of undesirable consequences including insufficient savings, drug use, and obesity.

Although emotion is often posited as the main driver for irrationally high discount rates (Bazerman and Moore 1990; Loewenstein, Read, and Baumeister 2003), no studies have tested for their causal role, except for some recent research finding that positive emotion reduces the preference for present over future outcomes (Ifcher and Zarghamee 2011; Pyone and Isen 2011). On the other hand, the appraisal-tendency framework (Lerner and Keltner 2000, 2001) posits that sadness is characterized by appraisals of experiencing irrevocable loss and thus is accompanied by action tendencies to change one's circumstances, perhaps by seeking immediate rewards (Lerner, Small, and Loewenstein 2004). Consistent with this view, research has found that individuals induced to feel sad spend more to purchase items and demand less to sell their possessions than do neutral individuals (Lerner et al. 2004). Sadness has been shown to trigger a generalized devaluation of the self (Cryder et al. 2008), which creates an implicit desire to enhance what William James (1890) called the "material self."

Three incentivized experiments randomly assigned decision-makers to emotional states to test the hypothesis that sadness, but not other negative emotions, would increase impatience in intertemporal choices. Experiment 1 induced 202 participants (57% female; ages 18 to 63) to feel neutral, sad, or disgusted using standard protocols including watching a video and writing an essay. The emotion-induction procedure was effective in both magnitude and specificity. Sad-condition participants reported feeling more sad than feeling neutral, or any other measured negative emotion, including anger and fear. Comparable specific effects were found for the neutral and disgust conditions.

Participants then made 27 choices between receiving cash today (between \$11-\$80) or more cash (between \$25-\$85) in the future, ranging from 1 week to 6 months (Kirby, Petry, and Bickel 1999). We used maximum-likelihood estimation to fit choices to an exponential discounting function, $D(t) = \delta^t$, where *smaller* values of δ (the annual discount factor) indicate more impatience. Results for hyperbolic discounting were similar. Even though induced sadness should be irrelevant to these decisions, it exerted strong, unique effects on discounting. Sadness significantly increased preference for immediate rewards. In monetary terms, whereas the median sad participant accepted \$37 today rather than wait 3 months to receive \$85, the median neutral participant required \$56 today. Importantly, disgusted participants discounted about the same as neutral participants did and less than sad participants did.

Experiment 2 applied Query Theory (Weber et al. 2007), a cognitive process model of preference construction, by asking 189 participants (70% female; ages 19 to 69) to list their thoughts before making intertemporal choices between receiving \$50 today or amounts between \$55 and \$105 (in \$5 increments) in 3 months. Par-ticipants provided their thoughts on this choice, made their decision, and subsequently coded their thoughts on whether each one favored receiving the money now, later, both, or neither. Sad participants were again more impatient than neutral and disgusted participants, valuing \$50 in a year's time \$6.50 less. Moreover, Experiment 2 identified a mechanism for how sadness affected discounting: reasons for the immediate reward came to mind sooner and more frequently when participants had been made sad.

Experiment 3 introduced a new question. Does sadness produce a general increase in impatience or is its effect limited to choices offering an immediate payoff? A key innovation in modeling discounting distinguishes between two types of processes that are represented in the quasi-hyperbolic discounting function, $D(t)=\beta\delta^t$, for $t > 0$ (Laibson 1997; O'Donoghue and Rabin 1999). One process (δ) reflects economically rational—i.e., time-consistent—exponential discounting of rewards that is sensitive to the length of delay, t. The other process, "present bias" (β), discounts all future rewards when there is *any* delay (regardless of its length) and therefore cannot be strictly rational. We tentatively hypothesized that sadness would increase the desire to get something *now*, not just sooner, and should therefore increase present bias (β) more so than it increases time-consistent discounting (δ). Experiment 3 asked 203 participants (66.5% female, ages 19 to 68) to make 42 choices between A) immediate rewards versus later rewards; or B) later rewards versus even later rewards. As predicted, sadness resulted in greater impatience for A choices, but not B choices. Sad participants preferred immediate rewards to later rewards more strongly than neutral participants, but were no more generally impatient. That is, sad participants were more *present-biased* (Laibson 1997).

Sadness may make people wiser in some contexts (Alloy and Abramson 1979), but in our experiments, it made them more impatient, not an attribute associated with wisdom. Across three experiments, the median sad participant valued future rewards (i.e., delayed by three months) 13% to 34% less than the median neutral-state participant. Moreover, sadness increased present bias, consistent with the idea that immediate rewards can be self-bolstering.

These experiments demonstrated the causal effects of sadness on impatient intertemporal choices. For ethical reasons we could not induce high-intensity emotion. Observed effects arose from low-intensity, experimentally-induced feelings of sadness that would undoubtedly be dwarfed by the real-life sadness people may experience after the death of a loved one or after a devastating natural disaster. Strong feelings of sadness over the loss of a family member can thus be expected to show far greater effects on the many high-stake intertemporal decisions involved in settling the deceased person's estate. Sadness and depression are also common experiences for people who have been laid off. Our results suggest that such individuals might exacerbate their financial hardship by making intertemporal consumption decisions that favor immediate consumption more than is warranted or wise.

REFERENCES

Alloy, Lauren B. and Lyn Y. Abramson (1979), "Judgment of Contingency in Depressed and Nondepressed Students: Sadder but Wiser?," *Journal of Experimental Psychology: General*, 108 (4), 441-85.

Bazerman, M.H. and D.A. Moore (1990), *Judgment in Managerial Decision Making,* New York: Wiley.

Cryder, C.E., J.S. Lerner, J.J. Gross, and R.E. Dahl (2008), "Misery Is Not Miserly: Sad and Self-Focused Individuals Spend More," *Psychological Science*, 19 (6), 525-30.

Ifcher, John and Homa Zarghamee (2011), "Happiness and Time Preference: The Effect of Positive Affect in a Random-Assignment Experiment," *American Economic Review*, 101 (7), 3109-29.

James, W (1890), *Principles of Psychology*, New York: Holt.

Kirby, K.N, N.M Petry, and W.K Bickel (1999), "Heroin Addicts Have Higher Discount Rates for Delayed Rewards Than Non-Drug-Using Controls," *Journal of Experimental Psychology: General*, 128 (1), 78-87.

Laibson, D (1997), "Golden Eggs and Hyperbolic Discounting," *Quarterly Journal of Economics*, 112 (2), 443-77.

Lerner, J.S and D Keltner (2000), "Beyond Valence: Toward a Model of Emotion-Specific Influences on Judgement and Choice," *Cognition and Emotion*, 14 (4), 473-93.

Lerner, J.S and D Keltner (2001), "Fear, Anger, and Risk," *Journal of Personality and Social Psychology*, 81 (1), 146-59.

Lerner, J.S, D.A Small, and G Loewenstein (2004), "Heart Strings and Purse Strings: Carryover Effects of Emotions on Economic Decisions," *Psychological Science*, 15 (5), 337-41.

Loewenstein, G., D. Read, and R. Baumeister (2003), *Time and Decision: Economic and Psychological Perspectives on Intertemporal Choice*, New York: Russell Sage Foundation Press.

O'Donoghue, Ted and Matthew Rabin (1999), "Doing It Now or Later," *The American Economic Review*, 89 (1), 103-24.

Pyone, Jin Seok and Alice M. Isen (2011), "Positive Affect, Intertemporal Choice, and Levels of Thinking: Increasing Consumers' Willingness to Wait," *Journal of Marketing Research (JMR)*, 48 (3), 532-43.

Weber, Elke U., Eric J. Johnson, K.F. Milch, H. Chang, J.C. Brodscholl, and D.G. Goldstein (2007), "Asymmetric Discounting in Intertemporal Choice: A Query-Theory Account," *Psychological Science*, 18 (6), 516-23.

Walk A Mile In *My* Shoes: Psychological Ownership And Psychological Distance

Bart Claus, Iéseg School of Management, France
Wouter Vanhouche, Lessius University College, Belgium
Siegfried Dewitte, KU Leuven, Belgium
Luk Warlop, KU leuven, Belgium/ Bi Oslo, Norway

EXTENDED ABSTRACT

Ownership is a key concept to set consumer behavior apart from related disciplines. Nevertheless, the psychological nature of this construct has been grossly understudied. Our studies use CLT to show that ownership is related to psychological closeness, and conversely, low construal levels facilitate seeing objects as one's possessions.

INTRODUCTION

Ownership of products and its transactions has recently been highlighted as one of the core topics unique to consumer research (MacInnis & Folkes, 2010). While extensive research has reported on effects of ownership – e.g. the endowment effect (Thaler, 1980), the mere ownership effect (Beggan, 1992), – much of this literature takes a transactional perspective where ownership is acquired or lost in a "legal", objective way. This approach has banned the difficult to measure psychological state of ownership to a 'black box' between its antecedents and consequences. Only recently, consumer literature has begun to look at psychological ownership as a distinct phenomenon (Morewedge, Shu, Gilbert, & Wilson, 2009; Peck & Shu, 2009). The perspective of psychological ownership allows to think about ownership as a continuum (to what extent do your children feel the house they live in is theirs, although legally they probably have no claim?) and also permits a distinction between an affective and an ownership component in the study of ownership transactions (Shu & Peck, 2011).

However, this understanding is far from complete, and it is here that we aim for a contribution, by relating psychological ownership to the well-established concepts of psychological distance and Construal Level Theory (CLT) (Trope & Liberman, 2010). Many authors discussed the importance of "an association" between a person and objects in the genesis and perception of ownership (Beggan & Brown, 1994; Friedman, 2008). in terms of Here we test the hypothesis that the "(strength of) association" underlying psychological ownership can be seen as psychological closeness, with effects as predicted by CLT. The studies reported below test this hypothesis.

OWNERSHIP AND CONSTRUAL LEVEL

These studies aimed at testing whether owners think about objects in a more concrete way, a prediction based on CLT that should hold if owned objects are indeed lower in psychological distance than non-owned ones.

Study 1a used scenario's (Wakslak, Trope, Liberman, & Alony, 2006) to find that, when asking participants to classify objects in groups, professional movers made fewer categories (M = 1.97, SE = .059) than the owners of the objects to move (M = 2.15, SE = .063; t(85) = 2.07, p < .05). The same difference was observed between insurance brokers (M = 1.98, SE = .059) and the owners of objects (M = 2.17, SE = .065; t(85) = 2.12, p < .05).

Study 1.b. omitted the third person perspective present in 1.aa., showing an interaction effect (F(1,71)=10.14; p<0,005) indicating that participants were quicker to detect a detail-change between two near-identical pictures of a cup they were asked to imagine was theirs, relative to non-owners (t(71) = 2.18, p < .05). The opposite was true for global, contextual changes (t(71) = -2.35, p < .05).

Study 2 elaborated on the previous results by showing how typical endowment studies can be explained in terms of changes in construal level (CL): participants were asked to evaluate an owned [nonowned] flat and list all places of significance in it (could be rooms or parts of rooms). This measure was used to assess the level of detail participants used in their thinking as a proxy for their construal level. Results showed an indirect effect of the ownership manipulation on valuation of the apartment, mediated by the number of places mentioned (M = 9641.63, SE = 5119.59, LL99% = 1676.18, UL99% = 22224.50). Actually, the same is true when we replace valuation with a scale of perceived ownership (Peck & Shu, 2009) (M = .16, SE = .10, LL95% = .0013, UL95% = 0.39).

CONSTRUAL LEVEL AND OWNERSHIP

Mirroring the previous studies, we also tested whether a concrete mindset would instigate effects that are usually the result of ownership manipulations.

In study 3.a., a cup was shown and participants were asked to list reasons either why or how a cup can be used. We then gauged participants' perceived ownership and valuation of this cup, finding an indirect effect where perceived ownership functioned as a mediator between the manipulation and valuation (M = .30, SE = .16, LL95% = .050, UL95% = 0.63).

Study 3.b. again used a manipulation of psychological distance, i.e. physical distance (Fujita, Henderson, Eng, Trope, & Liberman, 2006), where by means of perspective in a picture, an object (in this case a parker pen in an ad) is represented as close or far. Again, we found that manipulating psychological distance is related to ownership, as we found an indirect effect of this manipulation on valuation of this pen, mediated by perceived ownership (M = .62, SE = .32, LL95% = .095, UL95% = 1.37).

DISCUSSION

In several studies, we show that ownership is associated with lower levels of construal, and that in turn, lower construal level facilitates feelings of ownership. We consider our contribution to be twofold. First, we demonstrate that psychological distance is an important driver of psychological ownership. We start building a more explicit and comprehensive theoretical account of psychological ownership in which earlier studied idiosyncratic drivers of ownership effects can be embedded. Second, we use that framework to make new predictions about effects that further help our understanding of the nature of psychological ownership. Obvious implications might be found in store atmosphere design, in research that investigates the modalities of (psychologically) long-distance shopping (i.e. internet, mail order, future delivery, etc.) or perceptual effects in advertising. As the proposed framework allows for clear hypotheses about the processes that relate owners to their possessions, other future research could deal with the investigation of characteristics that loop back and forth between owners and their possessions. It would for instance be easy to imagine that self-worth affects the importance we attach to our possessions, and our findings could shed new light on the well-established idea that we derive status from certain types of possessions. In short, we are convinced that the theoretical step our work makes can spur future research in a host of domains.

REFERENCES

Beggan, J. K. (1992). On the social nature of nonsocial perception: The mere ownership effect. *Journal of personality and social psychology, 62*, 229.

Beggan, J. K., & Brown, E. M. (1994). Association as a psychological justification for ownership. *Journal of Psychology, 128*, 365-380.

Friedman, O. (2008). First possession: An assumption guiding inferences about who owns what. *Psychonomic Bulletin & Review, 15*, 290-295.

Fujita, K., Henderson, M. D., Eng, J., Trope, Y., & Liberman, N. (2006). Spatial Distance and Mental Construal of Social Events. *Psychological Science, 17*, 278-282.

Morewedge, C. K., Shu, L. L., Gilbert, D. T., & Wilson, T. D. (2009). Bad riddance or good rubbish? Ownership and not loss aversion causes the endowment effect. *Journal of Experimental Social Psychology, 45*, 947-951.

Peck, J., & Shu, Suzanne B. (2009). The Effect of Mere Touch on Perceived Ownership. *Journal of Consumer Research, 36*, 434-447.

Shu, S. B., & Peck, J. (2011). Psychological ownership and affective reaction: Emotional attachment process variables and the endowment effect. *Journal of Consumer Psychology, 21*, 439-452.

Thaler, R. (1980). Toward a positive theory of consumer choice. *Journal of economic behavior & organization, 1*, 39.

Trope, Y., & Liberman, N. (2010). Construal-Level Theory of Psychological Distance. *Psychological Review, 117*, 440-463.

Wakslak, C. J., Trope, Y., Liberman, N., & Alony, R. (2006). Seeing the forest when entry is unlikely: Probability and the mental representation of events. *Journal of Experimental Psychology-General, 135*, 641-653.

Reducing Majority Customers' Prejudiced Behavior in Inter-Ethnic Service Encounters - Applying a Stress and Coping Framework.

Simon Brach, Friedrich-Schiller-University of Jena, Germany
Gianfranco Walsh, Friedrich-Schiller-University of Jena, Germany
Arne Albrecht, Friedrich-Schiller-University of Jena, Germany
Patrick Hille, Friedrich-Schiller-University of Jena, Germany
David Dose, Friedrich-Schiller-University of Jena, Germany
Mario Schaarschmidt, Friedrich-Schiller-University of Jena, Germany

EXTENDED ABSTRACT

Research on prejudiced behavior in services has largely focused on discriminative actions committed by majority employees towards minority co-workers (e.g. Cortina 2008) or customers (e.g. Crockett, Gier, and Williams 2003; Walsh 2009). With few exceptions (Bendick 2007; Cocchiara and Quick 2004; Etgar and Fuchs 2011; Hekman et al. 2010), the investigation of customers' prejudiced behavior towards minority service employees has been largely neglected. These studies show that customers' discriminative behavior towards minority service employees has several negative effects on employees' health and motivation (Bendick 2007; Cocchiara and Quick 2004). Furthermore, racial bias negatively affects majority customers' evaluations of minority service employees' performance, the service setting and the overall company (Etgar and Fuchs 2011; Hekman et al. 2010).

We based our research on the stress and coping framework by Trawalter and colleagues (2009). The framework suggests that behavior within inter-ethnic contact situations, like inter-ethnic service encounters, depends on the outcome of the comparison of two appraisal processes—situational demands and available (physical, cognitive and social) resources. If the relevant resources available are sufficient to meet the situational demands, positive behavior will result. If the demands are higher than the resources available, negative or discriminative behavior will result. As inter-ethnic contact situations are perceived as more demanding for the parties involved compared to same-ethnic contact (e.g. Page-Gould, Mendoza-Denton and Tropp 2008) the stress and coping framework predicts that inter-ethnic service encounters are likely to be characterized by negative (e.g. discriminative) behavior of majority customers towards minority service employees. The stress and coping framework further predicts that by increasing relevant (e.g. social) resources, negative behavior in situations with higher demands like inter-ethnic service encounters can be neutralized.

METHOD

We employed an experimental video-based paradigm from research on inter-ethnic contact situations (Vorauer and Turpie 2004). Videotaped inter-ethnic compared to same-ethnic service interactions between majority participants and confederate service employees are analyzed by independent raters to test the predictions derived from the stress and coping framework. Raters' codings of participants' behavior served as the dependent variable in the analyses. During the interaction participants rated their perception of the social resources provided by the employee.

FINDINGS

The results show that majority participants' discriminate against minority service employees. This supports the first prediction from the stress and coping framework. Further, the results indicate that majority participants' discriminative behavior towards a minority service employee is influenced by the level of social resources, provided by the service employee during the inter-ethnic service encounter. The results reveal that if majority participants perceive the level of relevant resources provided by the minority service em-

ployee as being high, discriminative behavior towards minority service employees is neutralized. This finding is in agreement with the second prediction from the stress and coping framework.

CONTRIBUTIONS

Our findings suggest that discrimination toward minority service employees in inter-ethnic contact situations is not a forgone conclusion. By drawing on the stress and coping framework we provide a theoretical basis for discrimination in inter-ethnic contact situations which emphasizes the importance of resources; therefore, there is scope for influencing the occurrence of discrimination towards minority service employees.

REFERENCES

Bendick, Marc (2007), "Situation Testing for Employment Discrimination in the United States of America," *Horizons stratégiques*, 3 (5), 17-39.

Cocchiara, Faye K. and James C. Quick (2004), "The Negative Effects of Positive Stereotypes: Ethnicity-Related Stressors and Implications on Organizational Health," *Journal of Organizational Behavior*, 25 (6), 781-85.

Cortina, Lilia (2008), "Unseen Injustice: Incivility as Modern Discrimination in Organizations," *The Academy of Management Review ARCHIVE*, 33 (1), 55-75.

Crockett, David, Sonya A. Grier, and Jacqueline A. Williams (2003), "Coping with Marketplace Discrimination: An Exploration of the Experiences of Black Men," *Academy of Marketing Science Review*, 4, 1-18.

Etgar, Michael and Galia Fuchs (2009), "Why and How Service Quality Perceptions Impact Consumer Responses," *Managing Service Quality*, 19 (4), 474-85.

Hekman, David R., Karl Aquino, Bradley P. Owens, Terence R. Mitchell, Pauline Schilpzand, and Keith Leavitt (2010), "An Examination of Whether and How Racial and Gender Biases Influence Customer Satisfaction," *The Academy of Management Journal*, 53 (2), 238-64.

Page-Gould, Elizabeth, Rodolfo Mendoza-Denton, and Linda R. Tropp (2008), "With a Little Help from My Cross-Group Friend: Reducing Anxiety in Intergroup Contexts through Cross-Group Friendship," *Journal of Personality and Social Psychology*, 95 (5), 1080-94.

Trawalter, Sophie, Jennifer A. Richeson, and J. Nicole Shelton (2009), "Predicting Behavior During Interracial Interactions: A Stress and Coping Approach," *Personality and Social Psychology Review*, 13 (4), 243-68.

Vorauer, Jacquie D. and Cory A. Turpie (2004), "Disruptive Effects of Vigilance on Dominant Group Members' Treatment of Outgroup Members: Choking Versus Shining under Pressure," *Journal of Personality and Social Psychology*, 87 (3), 384-99.

Walsh, Gianfranco (2009), "Disadvantaged Consumers' Experiences of Marketplace Discrimination in Customer Services," *Journal of Marketing Management*, 25 (1-2), 143-69.

Inter-Consumer Competition:
When Consumers Compete in the Marketplace for Products, Services, and Prizes

Derick F. Davis, Virginia Tech, USA
Kimberlee Weaver, Virginia Tech, USA

EXTENDED ABSTRACT

Consumers must compete among themselves for a variety of goods, services, discounts, and prizes available in the marketplace. For instance, consumers compete with one another when they enter a sweepstakes, contest, or lottery, they also compete when bidding in an auction, making dinner reservations on Saturday night, when waiting in line for black Friday deals, or when submitting an offer on a house or rental application in a tight market. Here we are interested in factors that influence consumers' motivation to engage in competition with other consumers. Our investigation builds upon a recent finding from social psychology referred to as "The N-effect" which states that as the number of competitors increases, competitive motivation decreases, even when the rewards and outcomes are held constant (Garcia and Tor 2009).

The current studies advance this theory by assessing whether the features of two types of common contests where consumers compete, lotteries where contestants simply enter their names in a drawing, and competitions where contestants must submit a skill-based work, will moderate the effects of group size on consumers' motivation to engage in consumer competition in the marketplace.

Past work on competition in marketing has focused almost exclusively on the firm-perspective of competing for customers or pioneering/competitive advantage (e.g. Day and Wensley 1983; Golder and Tellis 1993; Hunt and Morgan 1995; Schmalensee 1982) or utilizing a game theoretic approach (e.g. Moorthy 1985). One exception is auction theory (see Klemperer 1999) and the use of auctions as a context for consumer research (e.g. Ariely and Simonson 2003; Hoffman, Menkhaus, Chakravarti, Field, and Whipple 1993). Auctions are an interesting context to examine consumer competition, but differ fundamentally in several theoretically relevant ways. First, to win an auction one can always spend more, but in some consumer contests – such as those involving skill – consumers are bound by their abilities or effort and an increasing outlay of money will not guarantee success. Second, auctions are dynamic, and bidders can observe other bids and update accordingly. Most consumer contests are static, or include several static steps – consumers cannot see other submissions and update their own, for instance. Other work on competition has examined it in terms of payoffs, decisions, and strategies. Here, we are interested in the internal motivational forces that impel consumers to compete in the marketplace. We are interested in how one-shot consumer contests of different formats and sizes affect the likelihood of consumers to compete. To the best of our knowledge, very little research has been conducted on these topics.

Liu et al. (2007) utilize a game-theoretic approach to suggest optimal designs of consumer contests. They draw a distinction between "lottery-like" contests where the winner is determined by chance, and contests where the winner is determined by who performed the best on a specific skilled task. Here we compare skilled consumer contests to "lottery-like" contests and assess how consumers' motivation to participate is affected by the number of competitors involved in the contest. Skill is not systematically varied in the original N-effect paper; however, we examine this variable in the present research because it is relevant to participation in consumer contests. If social comparison drives the N-effect (Garcia and Tor 2009) effect than we should observe it more in skilled than non-skilled contexts, because people will be more likely to compare to others in situations involving skill. On the other hand, if the N-effect is driven by a simple diffusion of competition, a psychological situation that may occur if people simply become less interested in competing when there are more people, than we should observe the N-effect in both types of contests.

In Study 1, participants imagined they were entering an essay contest (skilled) or a random lottery drawing (non-skilled) sponsored by an online travel booking service. The prize was an all inclusive travel package. Participants' competitors were either other students in their experimental session (about 10) or all students completing experiments that semester (about 1,000). The top 20% of entrants would win the prize.

Participants were more likely to enter the lottery than the skilled contest, ($F(1, 40) = 18.09$, $p < .001$). This main effect was qualified by an interaction, ($F(1, 40) = 4.98$, $p < .04$). Participants were less likely to enter the essay contest when the group was large ($M = 3.0$) than when it was small ($M = 4.73$), $t(1,20) = 2.67$, $p < .015$), the N-effect. This difference did not materialize for participants entering a lottery ($M_{large-lottery} = 5.8$ vs. $M_{small-lottery} = 5.6$; ns). These results suggest that the size of the competition group affects consumers' participation in skill-based contests but not non-skilled ones.

Based on Langer's work on the illusion of control, we predicted that consumers selecting their own number in a lottery-like contest may treat it like a skilled task compared to those assigned a number. To test how this would affect consumer motivation, consumers in study 2 imagined competing in a contest with 100 [1,000] other consumers to win a $100 prepaid debit card. Half chose [were assigned] their raffle number. Tickets to enter the contest cost $5 and 2% of the entrants would win the prize. There was an interaction between the size of the competition group and choice versus assigned numbers on likelihood to enter the raffle, $F(1, 100) = 6.27$, $p < .02$. Consumers choosing their number ("skilled" condition) were more likely compete when faced with a small group ($M = 4.0$) than when faced with a large group ($M=2.8$), $t(1, 52) = 2.60$, $p < .02$. In contrast, the competitive motivation of consumers assigned a number were not affected by group size ($M_{large} = 3.6$; $M_{small} = 3.2$, ns). Results from a third study conceptually replicated study 2 in a more realistic context with consumers from the general population.

This initial investigation begins to identify some of the conditions under which the size of the competition group affects consumers' motivation to compete in the marketplace. This work has implications not only for consumer contests but for other areas where consumers compete amongst each other.

REFERENCES

Ariely, Dan, and Itamar Simonson (2003), "Buying, Bidding, Playing, or Competing? Value Assessment and Decision Dynamics in Online Auctions," *Journal of Consumer Psychology,* 13(1/2), 113-23.

Day, George S., and Robin Wensley (1983), "Marketing Theory with a Strategic Orientation," *Journal of Marketing,* 47(4), 79-89.

Garcia, Stephen M., and Avishalom Tor (2009), "The *N*-Effect: More Competitors, Less Competition," *Psychological Science,* 20(7), 871-77.

Golder, Peter N., and Gerard J. Tellis (1993), "Pioneer Advantage: Marketing Logic or Marketing Legend?" *Journal of Marketing Research,* 30(2), 158-70.

Hoffman, Elizabeth, Dale J. Menkhaus, Dipankar Chakravarti, Ray A. Field, and Glen D. Whipple (1993), "Using Laboratory Experimental Auctions in Marketing Research: A Case Study of New Packaging for Fresh Beef," *Marketing Science,* 12(3), 318-38.

Hunt, Shelby D., and Robert M. Morgan (1995), "The Comparative Advantage Theory of Competition," *Journal of Marketing,* 59(2), 1-15.

Liu, De, Xianjun Geng, and Andrew B. Whinston (2007), "Optimal Design of Consumer Contests," *Journal of Marketing,* 71 (October), 140-55.

Moorthy, K. Sridhar (1985), "Using Game Theory to Model Competition," *Journal of Marketing Research,* 22(3), 262-82.

Schmalensee, Richard (1982), "Product Differentiation Advantages of Pioneering Brands," *The American Economic Review,* 72(3), 349-65.

The Category Size Bias and Consumers' Perceptions of Risk

Mathew S. Isaac, Seattle University, USA
Aaron R. Brough, Pepperdine University, USA

EXTENDED ABSTRACT

When judging the likelihood of an event, decision makers are often influenced by irrelevant categorical information. For example, prior research finds evidence of a border bias in which people perceive a disaster as less severe when it originates from another state rather than from an equidistant origin in the same state (Mishra and Mishra 2010). Other findings show that probability judgments of a focal outcome are sensitive to the number of categories into which alternative outcomes are classified, even when such categorization is irrelevant to the judgment (Koehler 2000; Tversky and Koehler 1994; Windschitl and Wells 1998).

In contrast to prior research, we examine how the *size* of a category into which a particular outcome is classified influences consumers' probability judgments and corresponding perceptions of risk. Specifically, we argue that an outcome will be perceived as more likely to occur when it is part of a large (versus small) set of potential outcomes. For example, due to the fact that there are more black pockets on a roulette wheel than green pockets, novice gamblers may perceive a higher probability that the ball will land on the "black two" pocket rather than the adjacent "green zero" pocket. This constitutes a decision bias because the odds are identical that the ball will land on each individual pocket regardless of its color. This bias in probability judgments is likely to influence a gambler's perceptions of risk and the corresponding amount he would be willing to bet on each option.

We attribute this category size bias to a transference process whereby people believe that characteristics of a category (e.g., its propensity of being randomly selected) apply not only to the category as a whole, but also individually to each member of the category. In the roulette example, where individual pockets are categorized by color, people mistakenly overestimate the probability of the ball landing on any individual pocket that happens to be black because of their accurate impression that the ball is more likely to land on a black pocket than a green pocket. This erroneous assumption that each individual member of a category is infused with the overall category's characteristics can cause people to overestimate the probability of outcomes classified into large groups and underestimate the probability of outcomes classified into small groups.

Three studies test our prediction and theory. In Study 1, we demonstrate the category size bias by asking participants to judge the probability of selecting a particular ball (#8) from an urn containing 15 numbered balls. Participants judged the probability of selecting ball #8 to be higher [lower] if it was the same color as many [few] other balls in the urn, even though this color-based categorization was unrelated to the selection likelihood of a particular ball. The observed category size bias was consistent with our theorizing.

Study 2 shows that the category size bias is a function of our proposed transference process. We asked participants to estimate the odds of a particular team winning the NCAA college basketball tournament; lower odds denote higher probabilities and vice versa. Before providing their odds estimate, participants were informed that the team's mascot was either part of a large category (e.g., one of many animal mascots) or part of a small category (e.g., one of few human mascots). Importantly, the basis of categorization was non-diagnostic of the team's likelihood of success in the college basketball tournament. Furthermore, unlike Study 1, our dependent measure in Study 2 was such that lower numerical values suggest higher probabilities of occurrence. This design allowed us to test whether the category size bias is driven by transference or anchoring because each explanation makes opposite predictions. An anchoring account would suggest that participants anchor on category size and respond with a large number (which signifies a lower probability of winning) when the team's mascot is part of a large category. In contrast, a transference account suggests that respondents would be sensitive to what the category size implies about probabilities, such that they should respond with a small number (which signifies a higher probability of winning) when the team's mascot is part of a large category. The results of Study 2 are consistent with our proposed transference explanation but inconsistent with an anchoring account.

Study 3 provides further evidence of transference in the category size bias by showing that variation in the salience of the category moderates the magnitude of the category size bias. Specifically, participants were asked to judge the probability that rolling a die would result in a particular outcome. We found that participants inflated the probability of rolling a 'T' on a die with 26 letters when its membership in the relatively large category 'consonant' was more (vs. less) salient. Conversely, when the small category 'vowel' was more (vs. less) salient, participants underestimated the probability of rolling the vowel 'A'. This suggests that category salience influences the extent to which transference occurs and therefore, the degree to which consumers are biased by category size.

Overall, this research contributes to our understanding of how categorization can influence consumers' probability judgments and perceptions of risk. Furthermore, our findings suggest that healthy behaviors may be promoted through the strategic presentation of risk-related information. For example, policy-makers may contribute to cancer prevention and early detection by grouping lung cancer with a large (vs. small) number of other potential health risks in messages targeted at consumers. A higher perceived risk of contracting lung cancer may encourage consumers to visit their doctor for regular screenings and avoid risky behaviors such as smoking. Future research may further examine the process underlying the category size bias, including whether categorical information influences probability judgments during encoding, retrieval, or both.

REFERENCES

Koehler, D. J. (2000). "Probability judgment in three-category classification learning," *Journal of Experimental Psychology: Learning, Memory, and Cognition, 26*(1), 28-52.

Mishra, A., & Mishra, H. (2010). "Border Bias: The Belief that State Borders can Protect against Disasters," *Psychological Science,* 21, 1582-1586.

Tversky, A., & Koehler, D. J. (1994), "Support theory: A nonextensional representation of subjective probability," *Psychological Review, 101*(4), 547-567.

Windschitl, P. and Wells, G. (1998), "The Alternative-Outcomes Effect," *Journal of Personality and Social Psychology*, 75 (6), 1411-1423

Choosing an Experience Over a Product:
Uncertainty, Holistic Processing and Price Sensitivity

Iñigo Gallo, University of California Los Angeles, USA
Sanjay Sood, University of California Los Angeles, USA

EXTENDED ABSTRACT

Recent research in consumer behavior is paying increasing attention to differences between experiences – "events that one lives through" – and products or material possessions – "tangible objects, kept in one's possession" (Van Boven and Gilovich 2003). These authors propose that experiences are better at advancing happiness, and investigate the reasons why. Nevertheless, we do not yet have a clear understanding of how consumers choose between a product and an experience. We propose that, because consumers find a significant degree of uncertainty when evaluating an experience, there are important differences in how they evaluate and choose an experience versus a product. First, consumers evaluate experiences holistically and products analytically; second, consumers rely on price as a cue for the quality of the experience. We present support for our theory along three studies.

VALUE OF ADDITIONAL INFORMATION

Nelson defined experiences as goods for which most qualities cannot be determined prior to purchase (Nelson 1970). Additionally, intangibility makes experiential aspects of consumption difficult to evaluate (Zeithaml 1981), and experiences in general difficult to compare (Carter and Gilovich 2010). Indeed, traditional marketing models have difficulty capturing experiential aspects of consumption (Holbrook and Hirschman 1982). We suggest that even if consumers have access to additional information on an experience, this will not reduce their uncertainty and lack of confidence in their ability to make a good choice. This is because many experiential attributes must be "seen, heard, tasted, felt, or smelled to be appreciated properly" (Holbrook and Hirschman 1982).

INFORMATION PROCESSING

Second, we propose that holistic processing is more compatible with experiences and helps consumers' uncertainty. This is due to different characteristics of experiences. Consumers shift to holistic processing as the comparability of objects decreases (Bertini, Ofek, and Ariely 2009). This matches with experiences, which are difficult to compare (Carter and Gilovich 2010). Also, holistic processing is used by consumers who lack knowledge on a specific category (Sujan 1985). This seems appropriate for experiences, for which consumers find evaluation difficult without inspection (Nelson 1970). Finally, holistic thinkers look for multiple relevant causes and factors in a decision (Nisbett et al. 2001), which fits another characteristic of experiences: an attribute space that is less defined and more subjective (Holbrook and Hirschman 1982).

PRICE AS A QUALITY CUE

Finally, we propose that a second way in which consumers deal with uncertainty when evaluating an experience is by using price as a quality cue. This parallels research showing that, in situations where other information is not available, price becomes an indicator of quality (Zeithaml 1981). We propose that this is specific to experiences, and not to products.

STUDY 1

Participants are asked to consider a 3D TV that is framed as either a product or an experience (Carter and Gilovich 2012). We manipulate the number of attributes that participants can consider (three or six). Those evaluating the product-framed TV report being better informed and more confident in making a good decision when they consider more attributes. On the other hand, for those considering the experience-framed TV, increasing the attribute information has no effect. Both interactions were significant: confidence ($F(3, 217)$ = 4.77, $p < .05$) and product explanation ($F(3, 217)$ = 4.11, $p < .05$).

STUDY 2

Study 2 tests our hypotheses regarding the compatibility of holistic processing and experiences, and the use of price as a quality cue for experiences. We manipulate the price and the composition of the choice set. Participants were assigned to one of eight conditions: 2 (processing style: analytic/holistic) x 2 (choice set: product vs. product/product vs. experience) x 2 (price: same/different [20% increase]). Processing style was manipulated according to Monga and John (2008). Consistent with our hypotheses, there is a significant main effect of holistic processing on the choice of experiences ($X^2(1, N = 154)$ = 4.89, $p < .05$). Holistic processers chose the experience more often ($M_{experience}$ = 67%) than analytic processers ($M_{experience}$ = 49%). Also, price increase influenced choice share for analytic processers. In a product vs. experience choice set, the share of the experience increased when its price increased. This effect was specific to experiences: in a product vs. product choice set the share of the product decreased when its price increased. The interaction of price with type of choice set was significant ($F(1, 167)$ = 13.23, $p < .001$). We propose that consumers rely on price as a quality cue for the experience, and therefore choose the experience more often when its price increases. We test this explanation in study 3.

STUDY 3

Study 3 tests our process explanation based on uncertainty. We focus on the analytic conditions from study 2. We manipulate the degree of uncertainty in the choice by supporting the product and experience information with endorsements. Participants in the control condition continue to choose the experience more often when its price increases (consistent with study 2). On the other hand, participants do not show this effect when their uncertainty has been reduced. In line with basic economic intuition, they choose the experience less often when its price is increased. This interaction was significant ($F(1, 279)$ = 4.22, $p < .05$). This is consistent with our explanation based on uncertainty.

This research offers insight on how consumers evaluate and choose experiences differently from products. Because consumers' evaluation of experiences is uncertain, consumers rely on holistic processing and use price as a quality cue for experiences. Also, due to the experiential nature of the attributes, having access to more information does not heighten consumers' confidence or their perceived level of information.

REFERENCES

Bertini, Marco, Elie Ofek, and Dan Ariely (2009), "The Impact of Add-On Features on Consumer Product Evaluations," *Journal of Consumer Research*, 36 (June), 17-28.

Carter, T., and Thomas Gilovich (2010), "The Relative Relativity of Experiential and Material Purchases," *Journal of Personality and Social Psychology*, 98(2), 146-159.

_____ (2012), "I am What I Do, Not What I Have: The Differential Centrality of Experiential and Material Purchases to the Self," *Journal of Personality and Social Psychology*, 102(6), 1304-1317.

Holbrook, Morris B. and Elizabeth C. Hirschman (1982), "The Experiential Aspects of Consumption: Consumer Fantasies, Feelings, and Fun," *Journal of Consumer Research*, 2 (September), 132-140.

Monga, Alokparna B. and Deborah R. John (2008), "When Does Negative Brand Publicity Hurt? The Moderating Influence of Analytic Versus Holistic Thinking," *Journal of Consumer Psychology*, 18 (October), 320-332.

Nelson, Phillip (1970), "Information and Consumer Behavior," *Journal of Political Economy*, 78 (March–April), 311–29.

Nisbett, Richard E., Kaiping Peng, Incheol Choi, and Ara Norenzayan (2001), "Culture and Systems of Thought: Holistic vs. Analytic Cognition," *Psychological Review*, 108 (March), 291-310.

Sujan, Mita (1985), "Consumer Knowledge: Effects on Evaluation Strategies Mediating Consumer Judgments", *Journal of Consumer Research*, 12 (June), 31-46.

Van Boven, Leaf and Thomas Gilovich (2003), "To Do or to Have? That is the Question," *Journal of Personality and Social Psychology*, 85 (December), 1193–1202.

Zeithaml, Valarie A. (1981), "How Consumer Evaluation Processes Differ Between Goods and Services," In *Marketing of Services*. Eds. James H. Donnelly and William R. George. Chicago: American Marketing Association, 186-189.

Order Effects of Sampling Sequential Products with Similar Versus Dissimilar Sensory Cues

Dipayan Biswas, University of South Florida, USA
Lauren I. Labrecque, Loyola University Chicago, USA
Donald Lehmann, Columbia University, USA
Ereni Markos, Quinnipiac University, USA

EXTENDED ABSTRACT

Experiential products such as food/beverages and fragrances tend to be rich on sensory cues, such as color, taste, and smell (Morrin and Ratneshwar 2003; Krishna 2012). In addition, these types of products often facilitate sampling opportunities for consumers before they make purchase decisions. While consumers often sample a single product, they also on other occasions sample a sequence of experiential products before making a purchase decision. Importantly, sometimes these sampled products are similar to each other on sensory aspects, such as on taste/color (e.g., Diet Pepsi and Diet Coke) and sometimes the products are dissimilar to each other on sensory aspects (e.g., Diet Pepsi and Sprite Zero).

Despite the existence of such sampling practices, it is not clear as to how the order in which different types of experiential products (similar versus dissimilar) are sampled influences consumer choices. There has been very limited research examining order effects of sampling products that are high on sensory and experiential aspects (Biswas et al.[2010] and Mantonakis et al. [2009], being the notable exceptions). Interestingly, these two studies report different results in terms of order effects of sampling a limited number of experiential products. For instance, Mantonakis et al. (2009) examined the order effects of sequential sampling of wines and found that the participants demonstrated primacy effects, whereby they often preferred the wine sampled first. In contrast, Biswas et al. (2010) found recency effects, whereby experiment participants indicated stronger preference for the experiential product (e.g., beverages/music) sampled last. The findings of our research help resolve the apparent inconsistency in the findings of these prior studies. We test our hypotheses with the help of three experimental studies.

We propose that in a sequence of two products, when the sequentially sampled products are similar to each other on sensory aspects (e.g., taste, color or smell), there will be a more favorable evaluation of the product sampled first. In contrast, when the sequentially sampled products are dissimilar, there will be more favorable evaluation of the product sampled last.

This is because, when sampling sensory-rich products in a sequence, the experience of sampling the immediately preceding product will influence the evaluation of the subsequent product (Chernev 2011). Thus, in a two product sequence, the first product would serve as a reference point for the evaluation of the second (Chernev 2011; Novemsky and Ratner 2003). In essence, we examine order effects of sampling experiential products and the moderating effects of similarity of the products in the sequence. We propose that when the sampled products have sensory similarity, there will be an assimilation effect in terms of memory trace formation for the second sampled product. However, when the sampled products have sensory dissimilarity, there will be a contrast effect while forming the memory trace for the second product. In order to further investigate the underlying process, we also examine the effects of distraction and the effects of an induced goal in the form of hunger. We hypothesize that these effects will hold under low hunger, but under high hunger, consumers will have more favorable evaluation of the product sampled first. These propositions are consistent with findings in prior studies conducted across different domains (e.g., Chernev 2011; Mussweiler 2007; Zhu and Meyers-Levy 2009) and to the best of our knowledge, this is the first research to examine these issues.

We test our hypotheses with the help of three experimental studies. We use food products (beverages and chocolates) because these products are experiential in nature and are high on sensory aspects (Shiv and Nowlis 2004). Study 1 examines how the level of similarity/dissimilarity between experiential products in a sequence influences order effects of sampling. The results show that when the products are dissimilar, there are recency effects; however, when the products are similar to each other, there are primacy effects. Study 2 examines how reduced processing motivation might affect the results observed in Study 1. The results of Study 2 show that the effects observed in Study 1 are moderated by consumers' distraction levels; that is, distraction attenuates the effects observed in Study 1. Finally, Study 3 examines the effects of an induced situation where processing motivation is likely to be higher. Specifically, Study 3 examines the effects of hunger on evaluation of sequential experiential products in a restaurant setting. The results of this study reveal that the effects observed in Study 1 hold under low levels of hunger but there are only primacy effects when consumers are very hungry.

In conclusion, the results of two laboratory experiments an one field experiment show that the order in which consumers sample experiential products and the level of similarity between the products influence consumers' choices. When sampling a sequence of two experiential products such as flavored beverages or chocolates, consumers prefer the first product in the sequence when they are similar, but prefer the second product when they are dissimilar. The order effects of sampling similar versus dissimilar products are attenuated when consumers are highly distracted due to reduced cognitive capability. Also, when the sequential products are sampled under high levels of hunger, consumers prefer the first sampled product.

A key theoretical contribution of this research is that it potentially reconciles differences in recent research findings on order effects in the context of experiential products (Biswas et al. 2010; Mantonakis et al. 2009). This research also has managerial implications, especially in the area of product testing. Order effects such as those illustrated here can bias testers' evaluations of products since the assimilation or contrast effects produced when tasters are asked to sample and compare multiple test products may result in poor product performance when the product goes to market.

REFERENCES

Biswas, Dipayan, Dhruv Grewal, and Anne Roggeveen (2010), "How the Order of Sampled Experiential Products Affects Choice," *Journal of Marketing Research*, 47 (3), 508-519.

Chernev, Alexander (2011), "Semantic anchoring in sequential evaluations of vices and virtues," *Journal of Consumer Research*, 37 (February), 761-774.

Krishna, Aradhna (2012), "An integrative review of sensory marketing: Engaging the senses to affect perception, judgment, and behavior," *Journal of Consumer Psychology*, forthcoming.

Mantonakis, Antonia, Pauline Rodero, Isabelle Lesschaeve, and Reid Hastie (2009), "Order in Choice: Effects of Serial Position on Preferences," *Psychological Science*, 20 (11), 1309-1312.

Morrin, Maureen and S. Ratneshwar (2003), "Does It Make Sense to Use Scents to Enhance Brand Memory?" *Journal of Marketing Research*, 40 (1), 10-25.

Mussweiler, Thomas (2007), "Assimilation and Contrast as Comparison Effects: A Selective Accessibility Model," in *Assimilation and Contrast in Social Psychology*, D.A. Stapel and J. Suls, eds. New York, Psychology Press, 165-185.

Novemsky, Nathan and Rebecca K. Ratner (2003), "The Time Course and Impact of Consumers' Erroneous Beliefs about Hedonic Contrast Effects," *Journal of Consumer Research*, 29 (4), 507–516.

Shiv, Baba and Stephen Nowlis (2004), "Effects of Distraction while Tasting a Food Sample: The Interplay of Informational and Affective Components in Subsequent Choice," *Journal of Consumer Research*, 31 (December), 599-608.

Zhu, Rui and Joan Meyers-Levy (2009), "The Influence of Self-View on Context Effects: How Display Fixtures Can Affect Product Evaluations," *Journal of Marketing Research*, 46 (1), 37-45.

Carrying the Torch for the Brand: Inferring Brand Attachment From Logo Signals

Ted Matherly, Oklahoma State University, USA
Amna Kirmani, University of Maryland, USA

EXTENDED ABSTRACT

Brands frequently support advertising strategies through promotional items, such as hats, t-shirts, or stickers with the brands' logo. When consumers use these items, they build awareness for the brand and provide information to observers about their relationship with the brand. We consider the inferences observers draw from signalers' use of a brand's core products to those drawn from signals not requiring the individual to own or use these products. For example, an individual who does not own one of Apple's core products (e.g. a computer or smart phone) can still wear an Apple t-shirt. We refer to these as product signals and logo signals, respectively. Specifically, we propose individuals using logo signals will be viewed as attached to the brands they signal with.

Considerable research has examined consumer signaling through brands (Berger and Heath 2007; Escalas and Bettman 2003; Han, Nunes and Dreze 2010; Kirmani 2009), but work has largely focused on product signals. We consider how differences in the attitude functions that observers associate with the use of logo and product signals impact inferences about consumers' relationships with the brand. Consumers frequently use branded products for their utilitarian functionality and to satisfy value expressive attitude functions; that is, they allow consumers to affirm their attitudes, values and personality (Grewal, et al. 2004), and to communicate their self-view to others (Wilcox, Kim and Sen 2009). An observer may utilize these choices to learn about the signaler. For product signals, observers may infer utilitarian and value expressive attitude functions guide signaler behavior. However, because logo signals possess little marginal functional utility compared to a similar unbranded product (Heath, Ho and Joshi 2011), it is signalers using logo signals would do so because of utilitarian attitude functions. Instead, they will be seen to do so in service of a value expressive function.

An inference that a signaler is value expressing through a logo signal suggests the brand is an important part of her self-concept and that she is attempting to communicate about her relationship to the brand, which is consistent with high brand attachment. Brand attachment is defined as "the strength of the bond connecting the brand with the self" (Park, et al. 2010). Attachment contains both cognitive and emotional components reflecting the extent to which the brand reflects the self (Thomson, MacInnis and Park 2005; Swaminathan, Stilley and Ahluwalia 2009). Because logo signals are associated with value expression, we expect individuals using logo signals will be viewed as attached to the brands they signal with. In contrast, product signals, used for utilitarian or value expressive reasons, would be less likely to lead to an inference of brand attachment. We propose that individuals using logo signals will be viewed as more attached to brands compared to those using product signals, and that this process is mediated by inferences about signalers' value expressive behavior.

Prior literature reveals that individuals expend resources to develop relationships with brands to which they are attached (Park et al. 2010), and observers infer that when actors expend resources on something that the thing is meaningful to the actor (Kirmani 1990; Morales 2005). These expenditures are costs to the signaler, including monetary, opportunity and social costs (Park, et al. 2010). We propose that when observers determine individuals have incurred costs to acquire their logo signals, observers will infer that the signaler is more attached to the brand, and to be doing so in service of value expressive functions at greater rates compared to those using less costly logo signals. These inferences about value expression will drive attachment inferences.

In our first study, we considered the effects of signal type and logo signal costs on inferences of value expression and attachment for two different brands. Participants viewed images of an individual using a product signal (the brand's core product), low cost logo signal (a t-shirt) or high cost logo signal (a brand logo tattoo). Attachment inferences were higher for the low cost logo signal compared to the product signal, and similarly higher for the high cost logo signal compared to the low cost logo. This effect was mediated by inferences of value expression. The second study replicated these findings using two different brands within a different category (coffee shop coffee), as well as a more direct manipulation of logo signal costs by comparing \$20 and \$85 t-shirts.

In our third and fourth studies, we considered potential differences between brands in terms of the brand's self-expression potential (SEP); that is, the extent the brand's products is seen as having an intrinsic value expressive function. For example, a Rolex watch would be viewed as more self-expressive than a cup of coffee. For brands higher in SEP, attachment inferences for product signals should increase and the differences observed between product and logo signals in the prior studies may be eliminated. In the third study, we employed a similar design to prior studies, using two high SEP brands identified in pretests. Consistent with expectations, higher attachment inferences for product signals eliminated the difference between product and low cost logo signals, while attachment inferences for high cost logo signals were higher. In the final study, we employed a single brand, and used participants' ratings of the brand's SEP as a continuous independent factor. Participants were shown an image of a person using a product or low cost logo signal. For participants who viewed the brand's SEP as low, spotlight analysis indicated the signaler using the logo signal was viewed as more attached compared to one using a product signal. For those who viewed the brand's SEP as high, this difference was eliminated.

The results of our studies suggest that logo signals can be used by individuals to convey attachment to brands, and further identify the role of value-expression as a mediator of these inferences. We show that as individuals invest resources in their logo signals, they are viewed as more attached to their brands, and we also identify a boundary condition for the observed differences in the form of a brand's self-expression potential.

REFERENCES

Berger, Jonah, Benjamin Ho, and Yogesh Joshi (2011), "Identity Signaling with Social Capital: A Model of Symbolic Consumption," *Marketing Science Institute Working Paper Series*.

Berger, Jonah, and Chip Heath (2007), "Where Consumers Diverge from Others: Identity Signaling and Product Domains," *Journal of Consumer Research*, 34(2), 121-34.

Escalas, Jennifer, and James R. Bettman (2003), "You Are What They Eat: The Influence of Reference Groups on Consumers' Connections to Brands," *Journal of Consumer Psychology*, 13(3), 339-48.

Grewal, Rajdeep, Raj Mehta, and Frank R. Kardes (2004), "The Timing of Repeat Purchases of Consumer Durable Goods: The Role of Functional Bases of Consumer Attitudes," *Journal of Marketing Research,* 41(1) 101-15.

Han, Young Jee, Joseph C. Nunes, and Xavier Dréze (2010), "Signaling Status with Luxury Goods: The Role of Brand Prominence," *Journal of Marketing,* 74(4), 15-30.

Kirmani, Amna (1990), "The Effect of Perceived Advertising Costs on Brand Perceptions," *Journal of Consumer Research*, 17(2), 160-71.

Kirmani, Amna (2009), "The self and the brand," *Journal of Consumer Psychology,* 19(3), 271-5.

Morales, Andrea C. (2005), "Giving Firms an 'E' for Effort: Consumer Responses to High-Effort Firms," *Journal of Consumer Research*, 31(4), 806-812.

Park, C. Whan, Deborah J. Macinnis, Joseph Priester and Andreas B. Eisingerich (2010), "Brand Attachment and Brand Attitude Strength: Conceptual and Empirical Differentiation of Two Critical Brand Equity Drivers," *Journal of Marketing,* 74 (November), 1-17.

Swaminathan, Vanitha, Karen M. Stilley, and Rohini Ahluwalia (2009), "When Brand Personality Matters: The Moderating Role of Attachment Styles," *Journal of Consumer Research,* 35(6), 985-1002.

Thomson, Matthew, Deborah J. MacInnis, and C. Whan Park (2005), "The Ties That Bind: Measuring the Strength of Consumers' Emotional Attachments to Brands," *Journal of Consumer Psychology*, 15(1), 77-91.

Wilcox, Keith, Hyeong Min Kim, and Sankar Sen (2009), "Why Do Consumers Buy Counterfeit Luxury Brands?," *Journal of Marketing Research,* 46(2), 247-59.

Balancing the Basket:
The Role of Shopping Basket Composition in Embarrassment

Sean Blair, Northwestern University, USA
Neal J. Roese, Northwestern University, USA

EXTENDED ABSTRACT

Mellish: "I'll get a copy of Time magazine. And I think I'll take Commentary and the Saturday Review. And let's see, Newsweek. I'll just… grab one of these… *[slyly picks up a pornographic magazine]* I'll take 'em all."

Cashier: "Hey, Ralph, how much is a copy of Orgasm?"

Mellish: "…Just put 'em in a bag, will you?"

In this exchange from the film "Bananas," Woody Allen's character, Fielding Mellish, is in a store to purchase a pornographic magazine. Fearing that others will observe his purchase, he grabs several additional magazines in an attempt to hide his true shopping objective. Unfortunately, the strategy fails when the cashier's request for a price check makes the embarrassing product painfully salient to everyone within earshot.

The traditional explanation for this strategy is that additional purchases mitigate embarrassment because they reduce the salience of the embarrassing product (Brackett 2004; Lewittes and Simmons 1975). According to this *product prominence hypothesis*, products are either embarrassing to buy or they are not, and embarrassment results to the extent that an embarrassing product is salient in the context of the shopping basket. From this argument follows the intuitively appealing prediction that purchasing any additional product that is not itself embarrassing to buy will mitigate embarrassment relative to purchasing the embarrassing product alone.

Indeed, this prediction is consistent with the conventional wisdom, as reflected in a survey in which we asked consumers about their intuitions regarding this strategy. The data showed that the majority (81%) believed that purchasing a non-embarrassing product in addition to an embarrassing product would always be less embarrassing than purchasing the embarrassing product alone. When these respondents were asked why they believed the additional product would attenuate embarrassment, the majority (88%) provided a response implicating a shift in focus away from the embarrassing product.

Contrary to the conventional wisdom, we show that embarrassment does not decrease monotonically with additional purchases. Moreover, we show that these additional purchases, which are not embarrassing in and of themselves, can paradoxically exacerbate embarrassment, such that consumers expect purchasing non-embarrassing products in addition to an embarrassing product to be *more* embarrassing than purchasing the embarrassing product alone.

In this context, we argue that the impact of an additional purchase on embarrassment is a function of the extent to which it balances against the undesired persona communicated by the embarrassing product, such that the more it counterbalances (vs. complements) the undesired persona, the more it will attenuate (vs. exacerbate) embarrassment. We label this proposition the *balanced basket hypothesis* and attribute the effect to embarrassment being a function of the impression made by the shopping basket as a whole rather than by its constituent products. We test this hypothesis in a series of four experiments.

In experiments 1A and 1B, we sought to demonstrate that embarrassment is not monotonically decreasing with additional purchases but is instead a function of shopping basket composition such that additional purchases attenuate (vs. exacerbate) embarrassment when they are unrelated (vs. complementary) to the embarrassing

product. Respondents were told to imagine that they were purchasing either *The Complete Idiot's Guide to Improving Your IQ* or *The Complete Idiot's Guide to Handling a Breakup* and were asked to rate how embarrassed they would feel. Half of the respondents were told that they were buying the book by itself whereas the other half were told that they were also purchasing a box of tissues and a pint of cookie dough ice cream (unrelated to the book on IQ but complementary to the book on handling a breakup). Results revealed the predicted interaction ($F(1, 91) = 8.03, p < .01$) such that the additional items attenuated embarrassment for respondents purchasing the book on improving IQ ($M = 2.87, SD = 1.66$ vs. $M = 4.88, SD = 1.45; F(1, 91) = 13.34, p < .001$) but not for respondents purchasing the book on handling a breakup ($M = 4.80, SD = 1.79$ vs. $M = 4.64, SD = 2.16$, respectively; $F(1, 91) < 1, NS$). Experiment 1B used joint evaluation to show that the additional products significantly exacerbated embarrassment in the breakup book condition where the additional purchases were complementary ($M = 5.23, SD = 2.34$ vs. $M = 4.08, SD = 2.18; F(1, 38) = 13.06, p < .001$). Thus, purchasing complementary products that would not be embarrassing to buy separately made the purchase of an embarrassing product even more embarrassing than purchasing the embarrassing product alone.

Experiment 2 sought to demonstrate that an additional purchase is more (vs. less) effective at attenuating anticipated embarrassment when it is perceived to be more (vs. less) effective at counterbalancing the undesired persona communicated by the embarrassing product. Respondents were told to imagine they were purchasing a Justin Bieber album and were asked to rate both how embarrassed they would feel to purchase the album by itself and how embarrassed they would feel to purchase the album along with an Adele album. We measured counterbalance perception by asking respondents to rate the extent to which buying the Adele album (vs. the Justin Bieber album) would accurately reflect who they are. A significant interaction between shopping basket composition and counterbalance perception emerged ($B = -.15, \beta = -.09, p < .05$). Spotlight analysis (Aiken and West 1991; Fitzsimons 2008) at 1.5 standard deviations below the mean of counterbalance perception indicated that purchasing the Adele album in addition to the Justin Bieber album had no impact on anticipated embarrassment relative to purchasing the Justin Bieber album alone ($B = -.18, \beta = -.04, p > .35$). In contrast, the corresponding analysis at 1.5 standard deviations above the mean of counterbalance perception revealed the Adele album significantly decreased anticipated embarrassment ($B = -1.10, \beta = -.24, p < .001$). Thus, the same additional purchase was more effective at attenuating anticipated embarrassment when it was perceived to be more effective at counterbalancing the undesired persona, independent of its effect on the perceptual salience of the embarrassing product.

To provide evidence for the robustness of the balanced basket hypothesis to scenarios involving real behavior, experiment 3 employed a field study to demonstrate that shopping basket composition can cause embarrassed consumers to strategically alter their purchase decisions even when doing so is economically disadvantageous. Participants in this experiment were required to go to a drug store to purchase either condoms or anti-gas medicine. They were given the option of purchasing the product by itself or of purchasing the product along with a box of tissues and a bottle of lotion (unrelated to anti-gas medicine but complementary to condoms).

The experimenters paid for the purchases and participants were allowed to keep whatever products they purchased, thus providing an economic incentive for all participants to purchase the additional products. We measured participants' level of public self-consciousness (PSC; Fenigstein, Scheier, and Buss 1975) and predicted that individuals would be more likely to avoid additional complementary (vs. unrelated) purchases when they were higher in PSC than when they were lower in PSC, because avoiding embarrassment is a more compelling motive for these individuals. Supporting our predictions, a logistic regression predicting choice of purchasing the additional items revealed a significant interaction between the assigned product and PSC ($B = -.39$, $\beta = -.41$, $p < .05$) after controlling for purchase familiarity (Dahl, Manchanda, and Argo 2001). Spotlight analysis 1.5 standard deviations below the mean of PSC indicated an equivalent likelihood of choosing the larger basket regardless of which product was assigned for purchase ($B = -.17$, $\beta = -.04$, $p > .90$), indicating that individuals lower in PSC were likely to purchase the additional products regardless of whether they were unrelated or complementary. In contrast, the corresponding analysis at 1.5 standard deviations above the mean of PSC revealed a reduced likelihood of choosing the larger basket when condoms were assigned for purchase as compared to when anti-gas medicine was assigned for purchase ($B = -4.34$, $\beta = -1.11$, $p < .05$, one-tailed). Thus, individuals higher in PSC were more likely to sacrifice their own economic self-interest when the additional items were complementary in order to avoid embarrassment.

Across these four studies, we find consistent support for our hypotheses regarding the role of shopping basket composition in embarrassment.

REFERENCES

Aiken, Leona S. and Stephen G. West (1991), *Multiple Regression: Testing and Interpreting Interactions*. Newbury Park, CA: Sage Publications.

Brackett, Kimberly P. (2004), "College Students' Condom Purchase Strategies," *The Social Science Journal*, 41 (3), 459-64.

Dahl, Darren W., Rajesh V. Manchanda, and Jennifer J. Argo (2001), "Embarrassment in Consumer Purchase: The Roles of Social Presence and Purchase Familiarity," *Journal of Consumer Research*, 28 (December), 473-81.

Fenigstein, Allan, Michael F. Scheier, and Arnold H. Buss (1975), "Public and Private Self-Consciousness: Assessment and Theory," *Journal of Consulting and Clinical Psychology*, 43 (August), 522-27.

Fitzsimons, Gavan J. (2008), "Death to Dichotomizing," *Journal of Consumer Research*, 35 (June), 5-8.

Lewittes, Don J. and William L. Simmons (1975), "Impression Management of Sexually Motivated Behavior," *Journal of Social Psychology*, 96 (June), 39-44.

Reading Smiles to Read Minds: Impact of Positive Facial Affective Displays on Perceptions

Ze Wang, University of Central Florida, USA
Fan Liu, University of Central Florida, USA
Huifang Mao, University of Central Florida, USA

EXTENDED ABSTRACT

Emotions may influence the judgments and behaviors of both people who feel emotions and people who observe the expressions of emotions. There have been extensive research on consumers' emotional experience, yet we know considerably less about consumers' perception of emotional expressions (Andrade and Ho 2009), let alone the role of facial affective displays in social interactions. This is surprising, because marketers and even consumers ubiquitously use strategic modification of the emotional expressions in an attempt to influence a third party.

In this research, we attempt to contribute to this under-researched area about consumers' perception of facial affective displays. We focus on positive affective displays (PADs) for their ubiquity in the public display of emotions. In presenting oneself in social interactions, people deliberately report higher levels of happiness relative to their internal affective states, because people intuit that the intensity of PAD is associated with how likeable a person is (Clark, Pataki and Carver 1996). However, perceivers' reactions can be complex and may not fulfill displayers' intentions. Will PAD intensity always enhance perceptual ratings? Which factors may moderate the relationship between PAD intensity and perceptions? Under what conditions will a maximal PAD boomerang? This research addresses these questions.

The ecological view of emotion research (Fridlund 1994) suggests that emotional expressions are communicating signals serving social functions. Emotional expressions communicate rich and important information about displayers' attitudes, goals, and intentions to the observers. Deighton and Hoch (1993) suggest that consumers, even as quite dispassionate observers, can be aware of the feelings of another and understand the intention and meaning of the affective displays. Judging facial expressions of positive emotions alone, higher intensity of positive emotion displays have been found to associate with more favorable perceptual ratings of the expresser being more willing to affiliate, competent, confident, or more trustworthy (McGinley et al. 1987; Mueser et al. 1984).

Consumers often do not judge facial affective displays in a vacuum. They rely on two pieces of information to make inferences: the information derived from facial emotional cues and the information about expresser's situation (Carroll and Russell 1996). When PADs are presented in a positive context (e.g. with positively-framed verbal content), PAD intensity enhances perceptual ratings or behavioral intention of the observers. However, when PADs are presented in a negative context, perceives may find the two sources of information incompatible. A high-intensity positive expression activates negative ascriptions of the displayers' intentions and goals (e.g., ulterior motives to manipulate or impress perceivers) and may be perceived as inappropriate. Moreover, because perceivers' inferences about the perceivers' mental states on the basis of the PAD intensity and differentiate the implication of medium or maximal smiles in light of other informational cues are effortful and entail deliberation. Constraints on perceivers' cognitive capacity will decrease the likelihood for accurate differentiation based on PAD intensity.

We test the aforementioned hypotheses in a series of three experiments. We conducted a pilot study (N=347) with a 6 (smiling strength: 0%, 20%, 40%, 60%, 80%, 100%) × 2 (displayer's gender; male or female) between-subjects design. The experimental stimuli were facial portraits from MSFDE database and coded using FACS as muscle configuration of 0, 12, 12+25, 6+12+25, 6+12B+25, and 6+12C+25. The results elucidate that perceivers do differentiate different types of PADs and only a main effect of smiling strength on perceptual ratings was found.

In Study 1, we examine how contextual cues moderate the impact of PAD intensity on perceptions. The experimental stimuli consist of a flyer advertising a public health seminar offered by a local university. 178 local residents were recruited and interviewed to complete a short questionnaire in public areas. A 2 (Smiling strength: 40%, and 100%) × 2 (ad valence: positive and negative) ANOVA on attitude toward the ad showed a significant interaction effect. Supporting our hypothesis, when the contextual valence is positive, PAD intensity positively impacts the perceivers' reactions. When the contextual valence is negative, maximal PADs boomerang, leading to lower perceptual ratings and less favorable attitudinal or behavioral responses. Study 2 examines the psychological mechanisms underlying the effect, whether it is due to perceivers' strategic inferences or emotional contagion. We assessed changes in participants' positive and negative feelings and their cognitive inferences about PAD appropriateness. We used the bootstrapping procedures (Preacher, Rucker, and Hayes 2007) to test the multiple-mediator mediated moderation models and found support that perceivers' cognitive inferences about the emotional appropriateness, but not changes in perceivers' feelings, mediate the interaction effect of PAD intensity × information valence on perceptual ratings. Study 3 further explores the boundary conditions of moderation effects in previous studies by manipulating participants' cognitive load. We found that even a lower level of cognitive load (a memory task of 2-digits number) prohibits the activation of the deliberative mind-set of cognitive inferences based on PAD intensity.

Our findings make several theoretical contributions. The present research is the first to systematically investigate the impact of PADs of different levels of intensity on perceptions. This expands the prior research on facial emotional expressions in still image (Knutson 1996; Small and Verrochi 2009) from valence contrast (positive, neutral, versus negative) to a fine-grained differentiation with the positive realm. More importantly, this research highlights that PADs are not always perceived favorably and highlight the importance of congruence between the emotional intensity and situational cues. The well-intended maximal PADs may boomerang when perceived as inappropriate. We also shed light on the psychological drivers and boundary conditions of these effects.

These findings are also important for practitioners. Smiling is easily perceptible and influential. If effectively manipulated, it can favorably impact customers' judgment of the displayers' dispositional traits, as well as the evaluative judgment of the related objects (attitude toward the ad). By understanding the boundary conditions and factors that moderate the impact of facial affective displays, marketers can tailor their affective display to optimal level and avoid the situations when the well-intended positive display goes unrequited or even backfire.

REFERENCES

Andrade, Eduardo b., and Teck-hua ho (2009), "Gaming emotions in social interactions," *Journal of Consumer Research,* 36 (4), 539-52.

Carroll, James M., and James A. Russell (1996), "Do Facial Expressions Signal Specific Emotions? Judging Emotion from the Face in Context," *Journal of Personality and Social Psychology,* 70 (2), 205-18.

Clark, Margaret S., Sherri P. Pataki, and Valerie H. Carver (1996), "Some thoughts and findings on self-presentation of emotions in relationships," in *Knowledge structures in close relationships: A social psychological approach,* Edited by J. Fitness, and G. J. O. Fletcher. NJ: Erlbaum, 247-74.

Fridlund, A. J. (1994). *Human facial expression: An evolutionary view.* San Diego, CA: Academic Press.

Deighton, John and Stephen J. Hoch (1993), "Teaching Emotion with Drama Advertising," in *Advertising Exposure, Memory, and Choice*, ed. Andrew A. Mitchell, Hiilsdale, NJ: Lawrence Erlbaum Associates, 261-82.

McGinley, H., McGinley, P., and Nicholas, K. (1978), "Smiling, Body Position, and Interpersonal Attraction," *Bulletin of the Psychonomic Society*, 12, 21-24.

Mueser, K.T., Grau, B.W, Sussman, S., and Rosen, A.J. (1984), "You're only as Pretty as You Feel: Facial Expression as a Determinant of Physical Attractiveness," *Journal of Personality and Social Psychology*, 46, 469-78.

Knutson, Brain (1996), "Facial Expressions of Emotion Influence Interpersonal Trait Inferences", *Journal of Nonverbal Behavior*, 20(3), 165-82.

Small, Deborah A., and Nicole M. Verrochi (2009), "The Face of Need: Facial Emotion Expression on Charity Advertisements," *Journal of Marketing Research,* 46 (6), 777-87.

Film Festival 2012

Same Same but Even Better!

Marylouise Caldwell, University of Sydney
Paul Henry, University of Sydney

This year The Annual USA ACR Film Festival showcased films of particularly high quality, regardless of the level of experience and the technology used. Some researchers/film-makers just starting out, used I-Pads and web-cams to collect footage and thereafter edited their clips using Windows Movie-maker or Apple I-movie. The results were very professional, suggesting that sophisticated equipment and high level skills are not necessary to create great consumer research films and win acceptance to ACR film festivals. Rather the key to successful submission remains a compelling story about consumers expressed clearly. Others who'd been in the film-making game a bit longer with greater access to funding, used high-definition cameras and Final Cut Pro to edit their films as well as create animated graphics. The resulting film festival program was one of wide diversity in terms of both content and style. The juror's first prize *The Pere-Lachaise Cemetery: Between tourist experience and heterotopic consumption* by Stephanie Toussaint and Alain Decrop explored how tourists and Parisian residents make use of the cemetery, significantly showing that many use attendance as a means of paying homage to modern-day celebrities such as Jim Morrison who have been laid to rest there. Others see it as a means of maintaining a rich spiritual life that allows them to say connected with tradition, history and human kind more broadly. This film impressed both judges and reviewers because of its ability to capture the atmosphere of the cemetery and the emotion-laden yet varied responses of consumers. In contrast The People's Choice Awards *Differing Everydays: Planning and Emergence in Mundane Routines* by Karolus Viitala and Joel Hietanen looked at how young affluent Finnish consumers negotiate everyday life, a topic of deservedly increasing fascination to consumer researchers. The judges considered this work remarkable due to its sophisticated theorization and cool stylistic. The remaining films covered topics such as the impact of Middle Eastern culture on hospitality consumption, how consumers proactively rejuvenate and/or use public spaces, the impact of age on consumption, how competing sub-cultures engage in intra-brand community conflict, the re-adaptation processes of consumers upon returning home after living abroad, the impact of physical space and time on everyday on consumer behavior, what motivates high risk sport and consumers' perceptions of music authenticity. Finally we are glad to say that ACR film festivals are thriving, being hosted all over the world, thereby providing a highly distinct and stimulating addition to the word and numeric based scholarly output otherwise found at ACR conferences. We remain indebted to Russ Belk and Rob Kozinets for founding this noble enterprise and facilitating the presentation of a huge body of filmic works that continue to inspire ACR film-makers. We wish the very best to all ACR members. Please continue to submit your best work the ACR film festivals. See you in Barcelona next July or otherwise it's "Chicago Chicago our kind of town," October 2013. Best wishes, Marylouise and Paul.

Perceptions of Music Authenticity

Paul Barretta, University of Texas - Pan American, USA
Yi-Chia Wu, University of Texas - Pan American, USA

Perceptions of music authenticity are important to both evaluation of music, and word-of-mouth in today's socially networked world. The producers present the results of two studies through examples and evidence of an authentication process that consumers use to evaluate music and musicians.

Aging and the Changing Meaning of Consumption Experiences

Raquel Castano, Tecnológico de Monterrey, EGADE Business School, Mexico
Claudia Quintanilla, Tecnológico de Monterrey, EGADE Business School, Mexico
Maria Eugenia Perez, Tecnológico de Monterrey, EGADE Business School, Mexico

Like all major life transitions, aging and retirement produce new self-identities that are reflected in the way consumers give meaning to their lives. These findings highlight differences related to age on the goals accomplished through consumption and also show how temporal orientation affects the meaning of consumption experiences.

Co-Creation and Co-Production of Value: The Emergence of Competing Brand Subcultures

Jacob Hiler, Louisiana State University, USA

What happens when different subcultures both love a brand, but for very different and often mutually exclusive reasons? This research investigates what happens when these subcultures acknowledge each other's presence, interact and influence each other's enjoyment of the product, and ultimately attempt to influence the evolution of the product.

Parklife

Morven McEachern, Lancaster University, UK

The concept of space and place is central to understanding everyday life. Using an ethnographic approach, this film explores the consumption experiences encountered by park users. The interconnectivity of space, rhythm and consumption help to co-create the consumption experience, thus, helping to transform the everyday into something special.

Differing Days - Planning and Emergence in Contemporary Mundane Routines

Karolus Vittala, Aalto University, Finland
Joel Hietanen, Aalto University, Finland

This videography illustrates how our everyday life is a flux of emergent relations—one in which our conventional notion of cognitive agency may have much less to do with than we tend to allow. It seems that we plan ahead only to become swept away by the moment.

The Père-Lachaise Cemetery: Between Touristic Experience and Heterotopic Consumption

Alain Decrop, University of Namur, Belgium
Stéphanie Toussaint, Université Catholique de Louvain, Belgium

This videography offers an ethnographic analysis of the Père-Lachaise cemetery, a major tourist site of Paris. The film shows how the sacred and profane dimensions of consumption are entangled in the visiting experience through a series of symbolic behaviors and rituals that make the cemetery a heterotopia.

Living Abroad and Coming Back to Brazil: Analysis of the Acculturation and Re-adaptation Process of Brazilian Consumers

Simone Vedana, UFRGS, Brazil
Teniza da Silveira, UFRGS, Brazil

This study investigates the effects of the consumer acculturation process during and after an experience of living abroad. The 21 consumers surveyed showed changes in eating habits, in purchase decision processes, in cultural identity, and in their satisfaction with products and services in Brazil, among other results.

Arab Hospitality

Russell W. Belk, York University, Canada
Rana Sobh, University of Qatar, Qatar

We examine contemporary Arab Hospitality in Qatar and UAE at three levels: home hospitality, commercial hospitality, and hospitality toward the foreigners who comprise the majority of the populations in both countries. We find that divergences in these practices unify some and alienate others within Arab Gulf cultures.

Spaces and Temporarility

Joel Hietanen, Aalto University, Finland
Elina Koivisto, Aalto University, Finland
Pekka Mattila, Aalto University, Finland
Anastasia Seregina, Aalto University, Finland

In this video, we adapt the radical humanist non-representational perspective in order to bring about new ways of thinking and to question both the conventional social constructivist perspective and what video can epistemologically express as a spatio-temporally situated medium.

Labour of Love: Reforging Community Ownership and Identity

Matthew Alexander, University of Strathclyde, UK
Kathy Hamilton, University of Strathclyde, UK

This film focuses on consumer adoption of train stations and demonstrates how local communities can work with market forces to retain a sense of place through environment enhancements. In contrast to guerrilla community activity studies, we demonstrate how firm involvement can legitimize community actors and co-create mutual benefits.

Fear and Flow: Climbing the Bugaboos, British Columbia

Tommy Chandler, Backcountry.com, Utah, USA
Jeff Foreman, North Georgia College and State University, USA
Aditi Grover, Plymouth State University, USA
Karen Hood, University of Arkansas at Little Rock, USA

Rock climbing is often featured as a metaphoric illustration in business instructional and inspirational materials. As in business, rock climbing involves a balance of flow and fear. We capture the combination of the two in our short video exploring rock climbers doing what they love in the Bugaboos, British Columbia.

Roundtable Summaries

Roundtable
Different Methodological Approaches to Studying Transformative Consumer Research: What Can We Learn from Each Other?Participants:

Chair
Julie L. Ozanne, Virginia Tech, USA

Organizers:
Ekant Veer, University of Canterbury, New Zealand
Paul M. Connell, City University London, UK
Michal Ann Strahilevitz, Golden Gate University, USA

Participants
Ekant Veer, University of Canterbury, New Zealand
Paul M. Connell, City University London, UK
Michal Ann Strahilevitz, Golden Gate University, USA
Cornelia Pechmann, University of California Irvine, USA
Stacey Mezel Baker, University of Wyoming, USA
Punam Anand Keller, Dartmouth University, USA
Linda Price, University of Arizona, USA
Alan Andreasen, Georgetown University, USA
Laura Peracchio, University of Wisconsin-Milwaukee
Rebecca Ratner, University of Maryland
Carlos J. Torelli, University of Minnesota, USA

During David Mick's ACR Presidential Address TCR was coined as "consumer research in the service of quality of life" (Mick 2006, p. 3). By focusing on how consumer research can actively look to improve the lives of consumers, TCR has gained prominence as a field in both academia and practice. Since this time, a number of initiatives have been undertaken to further encourage TCR, including special issues in journals, such as the Journal of Consumer Research, Journal of Business Research, Journal of Research for Consumers, and the Journal of Public Policy and Marketing. TCR has also supports a bi-annual TCR conference, an edited volume (Mick et al. 2011), a dedicated list-serv for TCR researchers, special sessions and roundtables at North American and Regional ACR conferences, and an increasing number of competitive papers presented at ACR conferences that have a TCR focus. All this resonates with the overall health of the TCR field, but does not give us reason to be complacent in advancing its cause, particularly as TCR's growth has signalled an increasing diversity of research paradigms and methodologies actively engaging in the field.

It is believed that if TCR is to maximize its service to consumers, then a more connected effort is needed to avoid fragmentation of the field. This roundtable proposes to bring scholars operating within different methodological frameworks together to see what can be done to create greater understanding as well as better research that serves consumers through a collective effort.

Roundtable Motivation

Previous roundtables have often included scholars from differing methodological stances, but none have primarily addressed the means by which diverse research methods can be used synergistically to encourage higher quality TCR and an improvement in consumers' quality of life. For example, Baker, Hunt, and Mick (2007) discussed various means of advancing the field, but not specifically on methodological biases. Strahilevitz (2010) included researchers conducting research with diverse methods as part of a prior ACR roundtable, but the issue of methodological divide was not overtly discussed. Similarly, Veer and Hunt (2008), Veer and Austin (2010) and all engaged with large groups of academics, but the diversity of the group was not addressed as part of the roundtables. Furthermore, published papers in top-tier journals using both qualitative and quantitative data, such as Botti, Orfali, and Iyengar (2009) are rare, but have the potential to provide significant advances in TCR thinking. Thus, this roundtable will not engage in an ontological debate of whether one paradigm is better than the other (Weber 2004), but focus more on how collaboration and integration of differing perspectives can be used to benefit the field.

Roundtable Purpose and Aims

By drawing together TCR scholars to specifically discuss the value of methodological diversity in the field, it is expected that former research connections will be strengthened and that new ones will be formed, creating a closer community with a better understanding of the diverse ways that different paradigms are addressing mission and purpose of TCR. This will be achieved through:
1. An increased understanding and appreciation of the diversity in the TCR field.
2. Greater dissemination of TCR related work currently being undertaken by ACR members.
3. Greater communication of the goals of TCR, and how these goals can be achieved through multiple approaches.

Simply by engaging in this an open dialogue, it is expected that transformation would occur. This is not a forum to discuss which stance is more valid than the other, but to discuss how collective action can be taken to benefit consumers. This is the overarching aim of TCR and will continue to be at the heart of this roundtable.

Roundtable Structure and Content

By proposing a forum based on open dialogue it is more likely that the purpose of the roundtable are achieved. The discussion will be led and facilitated by the roundtable discussant, Prof. Julie Ozanne. The roundtable will propose the following questions but also allow the discussion to naturally evolve as necessary. The questions have been designed to specifically drive forward appreciation of the value of diverse research approaches, as well as collaboration. A critical lens will be taken to the field with an aim to enhance the development of TCR as a field. The proposed questions are:

1. Beyond ontological differences, what successes and failures have established TCR scholars had with conducting and disseminating their work from multiple research paradigms?
2. How have established TCR researchers from both research paradigms overcome issues with IRB and other Ethics approval processes?
3. How can collaborations and networks best be formed that encourage increased appreciation for diverse approaches to carrying out TCR? Should the two methodological stances simply stay separate and only address research questions that fit with their own research paradigms and techniques?
4. What steps need to be taken in order to ensure the longevity and relevance of TCR in the coming years?
5. Has there been resistance to carrying out TCR from within one's business school? What advice do panellists have for framing TCR work, regardless of its methodological approach, for a promotion and tenure committee?

Contributions and Implications

Although it is, for the most part, accepted that different research methods offer value depending on the aims and assumptions of the research, a greater integration and understanding of how researchers can work together to promote TCR is needed. This roundtable aims to explicitly discuss the differences and work more to increase synergies by bringing together prominent TCR scholars and interested participants. Having an appreciation for how methodological biases can be both beneficial and detrimental to TCR will aid in the development of the field, as well as better prepare new TCR scholars embarking in this area. The roundtable could also allow for discussion of how to collaborate more effectively with other diverse groups, such as TCR scholars internationally, or the importance of engaging persons from multiple backgrounds in a TCR project, such as academics, practitioners, public policy makers and consumers. It is hoped that by facilitating this discussion, this round table will be transformative for the participants, attendees and the field. Pre-conference discussion will be facilitated through online forums, such as the TCR Facebook page, dedicated email lists and the TCR Google resource page, which was recently set up by the TCR advisory committee.

References

Baker, Stacey Menzel, David M. Hunt, and David Glen Mick (2007), "Disseminating Transformative Consumer Research: Getting Research Results out of the Tower and into Consumers' Lives," in Advances in Consumer Research, Vol. 34, ed. Gavan Fitzsimons and Vicki Morwitz, Duluth, MN: Association for Consumer Research, 83.

Botti, Simona, Kristina Orfali, and Sheena S. Iyengar (2009), "Tragic Choices: Autonomy and Emotional Responses to Medical Decisions," Journal of Consumer Research, 36 (October), 337-52.

Mick, David Glen (2006), "Presidential Address: Meaning and Mattering through Transformative Consumer Research," Advances in Consumer Research, 33, 1-4.

Mick, David Glen, Simone Pettigrew, Cornelia Pechmann, and Julie L. Ozanne (2011), Transformative Consumer Research for Personal and Collective Well-Being, New York, NY: Routledge.

Strahilevitz, Michal (2010), "Roundtable Session : Understanding Prosocial Behavior among Consumers and Organizations " in Advances in Consumer Research, Vol. 38, ed. Darren W. Dahl, Gita V. Johar and Stijn M. J. van Osselaer, Duluth, MN Association for Consumer Research, Forthcoming.

Veer, Ekant and Graham C. Austin (2010), "Transformative Consumer Research: Postcards from Europe," in European Advances in Consumer Research, Vol. 9, ed. Pauline Maclaran, Alan Bradshaw and Chris Hackley, Duluth, MN: Association for Consumer Research, Forthcoming.

Veer, Ekant and David M. Hunt (2008), "Transformative Consumer Research: Getting Research out of the Tower and into Consumers' Lives," in European Advances in Consumer Research, Vol. 8, ed. Stefania Borghini, Mary Ann McGrath and Cele C. Otnes, Duluth, MN: Association for Consumer Research, 220.

Weber, Ron (2004), "Editor's Comments: The Rhetoric of Positivism Versus Interpretivism: A Personal View," MIS Q., 28 (1), iii-xii.

ROUNDTABLE
Consumption Addiction: Developing a Research Agenda to Understanding How Consumers Progress from Normal to Maladaptive Consumption and Addiction

Chairs
Dante M. Pirouz, Western University, Canada
Hieu Nguyen, California State University Long Beach, USA
Ingrid M. Martin, California State University Long Beach, USA

Participants
Merrie Brucks, University of Arizona, USA
Paul M. Connell, City University London, UK
June Cotte, Western University, Canada
Scott Davis, Texas A&M University, USA
Kelly L. Haws, Texas A&M University, USA
Michael Kamins, Stonybrook, USA
Ingrid M. Martin, California State University Long Beach, USA
Ann Mirabito, Baylor, USA
Hieu Nguyen, California State University Long Beach, USA
Dante M. Pirouz, Western University, Canada
Justine Rapp, University of San Diego, USA
Maura Scott, University of Kentucky, USA
Allison Johnson, Western University, Canada

What is the broad topic?

Although most work on addiction has focused on substance abuse such as drugs, alcohol, and tobacco, there is a growing recognition that addiction is manifested in domains beyond substance abuse, suggestive of common underlying causes leading to varying maladaptive responses (Martin et al. 2012). For example, the fifth edition of the Diagnostic and Statistical Manual on Mental Disorders (DSM-5) recognizes disorders such as pathological gambling as a new category of "behavioral addiction" alongside substance abuse (American Psychiatric Association 2013). However, for many consumption behaviors, such as shopping, technology use, hoarding, overeating, plastic surgery, use of pornography, kleptomania, dietary supplement usage, religious convictions, and exercise, there is an ongoing debate as to whether they fit the clinical definition of addiction. The diversity of potentially addictive consumption behaviors raises an important question that we need to address: how do individuals move on a continuum from engaging in seemingly normal consumption behaviors to engaging in potentially addictive behaviors characterized by uncontrolled use and frequency of the behavior?

What is the motivation for organizing roundtable around this topic?

The notion that addiction is a temporal process and that one should take a holistic view (across all consumption phases) underlies this roundtable discussion. The power of marketing cues is believed to have the potential to heavily influence the path that individuals take both towards becoming addicted as well as moving away from maladaptive consumption and addiction. Marketing cues can make salient the rewards of an increase in frequency of the behavior as well as highlight the potentially dysfunctional nature of that same increase in consumptive behavior. However, to understand the role of marketing cues in the process of becoming addicted, we first need to explore the meaning of addiction as well as the meaning of "not being addicted" to a behavior or a substance.

Our key focus is to explore the marketing cues that act as catalysts to influence this movement toward and away from potentially harmful behaviors that result in addictions, and to present some research directions (see Figure). Consumer research has a long tradition of examining how consumers react differentially to both subtle and not so subtle cues in their environments that may influence behavior. Indeed, marketing cues could easily facilitate the development and entrenchment of addictive consumption behaviors or, alternatively, inhibit them.

Our premise begins with the non-use and normal consumption phases. Most consumers remain in these two stages without progressing to the pre-addiction or addiction phases. The pre-addiction phase begins with an increase in frequency and time spent in a consumption behavior evolving into a dependence on the consumption behavior as a vital part of the individual's life leading to negative consequences. There is an adaptive part, where the behavior is manageable, and a maladaptive part, where the behavior begins to be problematic but still controllable, to the pre-addiction stage through which consumers can cycle through without ever moving into the addiction stage. However when consumers begin to lose the ability to control consumption, the shift from maladaptive to addictive consumption begins. This final phase is characterized by movement into physical and psychological addiction. Even while in the addiction stage, there is the possibility through warnings, willpower, therapeutic interventions and treatment, for consumers to exhibit restraint or possibly rehabilitation which may move them back down the continuum towards adaptive or normal consumption, or even non-use.

Numerous individual differences are likely to influence how consumers react to marketing cues that may facilitate movement towards addiction in the pre-addiction phase. Because many forms of consumption that may lead to harmful behavioral patterns are unavoidable (for example, eating, shopping, exercising), relevant marketing cues are also difficult to escape. And yet not all consumers are equally susceptible to marketing cues, particularly those cues that may influence behaviors associated with the pre-addiction phase.

At what point do marketing cues begin to negatively influence consumption behaviors that result in harmful outcomes. Moreover, what marketing approaches and theories are best in triggering contrast effects (where intake is perceived negatively) leading to less consumption, as opposed to assimilation effects where more consumption is perceived as optimal. While marketing cues can be indicted as the culprit in possibly facilitating if not causing addictive behaviors, they can also serve as the first line of defense in the prevention of such harmful behaviors.

Understanding how and when exposure to marketing cues progresses or even impedes individual consumer's movement along the adaptive-maladaptive consumption continuum is a critical research area where a gap in the knowledge remains. Uncovering the determinants of this process has significant implications for both public policy and marketing management. It is imperative that consumer behavior researchers continue to investigate the phases of and the mechanisms that drive consumption behavior toward addiction in order to develop a more holistic and efficacious view of consumption overall.

Who is likely to benefit from attending the roundtable?

This roundtable will be of interest to both experienced researchers who have been working in the area of extreme, maladaptive or addictive consumption and new researchers who are looking to incorporate a conceptual framework as they consider future research. We also believe that researchers studying goal related behaviors in some pervasive areas as food consumption and financial decision making may be interested in the relevant addictive underpinnings of these often impulsive or compulsive behaviors. We believe the dialogue developed in preparation for and during this roundtable discussion is an imperative for consumer behavior researchers as we strive to develop research that not only helps firms but also helps transform consumers and their experience to a more adaptive and proactive level.

ROUNDTABLE
Evolutionary Consumption:
Methodological Pluralism, Interdisciplinarity, and Consilience (Unified Knowledge)

Chair
Gad Saad, Concordia University, Canada

Participants
Joshua Ackerman, MIT, USA
Sarah E. Hill, Texas Christian University, USA
Kristina Durante, University of Texas at San Antonio, USA
Jill Sundie, University of Texas at San Antonio, USA
Eric Stenstrom, Concordia University, Canada
Tripat Gill, Wilfred Laurier University, Canada
Bram Van den Bergh, Erasmus University Rotterdam, The Netherlands
Gad Saad, Concordia University, Canada

Broad topic for discussion and enquiry?

A growing number of consumer scholars are becoming interested in the application of evolutionary psychology and related biological formalisms to the study of consumer behavior. The infusion of evolutionary principles in consumer behavior affords many benefits including increased consilience (unified knowledge) and the generation of novel hypotheses and research questions that would have otherwise been difficult to posit void of an evolutionary lens (Saad, 2007, 2011; Saad & Gill, 2000). In addition to the latter two epistemological advantages, evolutionary psychology promotes methodological pluralism as well as a strong ethos of interdisciplinarity (Garcia et al., 2011). Accordingly, the theme of the roundtable discussion will be to highlight each of these valuable benefits by drawing on numerous examples from the participants' research streams. This will then be followed by an exploration of future avenues of research at the nexus of evolutionary psychology and consumer behavior.

Motivation/purpose for organizing the round-table on this topic?

The purpose of the roundtable discussion is to highlight the integrative capacity of evolutionary psychology in the study of consumer behavior along both the methodological and epistemological fronts. In describing the state of the field of psychology, Sternberg and Grigorenko (2001) argued that many psychologists suffer from methodological and field fixation. Methodological fixation is well captured by Abraham Maslow's famous statement: "When the only tool you have is a hammer, every problem begins to resemble a nail." Field fixation refers to the trepidation with which psychologists venture outside (if at all) of their designated sub-disciplines (e.g., social psychology, cognitive psychology, clinical psychology, etc.). These forms of fixation happen in many disciplines including consumer behavior. For example, marketing scholars will often define themselves via the methodological approaches that drive their research streams (e.g., "I am an experimentalist," "I am a modeler"), or via the main cognate disciplines in which they received their training (e.g., cultural anthropology, social psychology, etc.).

By the very nature of its integrative meta-framework, evolutionary psychology engenders a plurality of methodological approaches (and dependent measures) as well as interdisciplinary pursuits, and as such reduces the likelihood of succumbing to methodological fixation. Furthermore, evolutionary psychology is antithetical to field fixation, as its epistemological tenets allow for its application across all of the behavioral sciences. Hence, consumer psychology, social psychology, cognitive psychology, clinical psychology, and cultural psychology can all be tackled from an evolutionary perspective. Evolutionary principles are not constrained by any disciplinary or sub-disciplinary boundaries, and in this sense offer consumer scholars the capacity to easily traverse across numerous areas of inquiry.

The participants of this roundtable have each tackled topics that would have been very difficult to broach void of a physiological/evolutionary lens. How does the menstrual cycle affect women's consumption (Durante et al., 2011; Saad & Stenstrom, 2012)? Does conspicuous consumption affect men's testosterone levels (Saad & Vongas, 2009)? How do evolutionarily relevant primes (e.g., mating motives) affect individuals' proclivity to engage in conspicuous consumption (Griskevicius et al., 2007; Sundie et al., 2011)? What are the neuronal activation patterns implicit to brand categorization (Yoon et al., 2006)? Does the sex ratio in a population affect financial decisions (Griskevicius et al., 2012)? How extensively do men and women search for information prior to making a mate choice (Saad, Eba, & Sejean, 2009)? Do products of popular culture (e.g., song lyrics or movie plotlines) reveal a shared and universal human nature (Saad, 2012)? Do consumers' decision making styles possess genetic underpinnings (Saad & Sejean, 2010)? Does the digit ratio affect men's proclivity for risk taking (Stenstrom et al., 2011)? Does the viewing of scantily clad women affect men's discounting rates (Van den Bergh, Dewitte, & Warlop, 2008)?

These innovative research questions, all of which are rooted in evolutionary/biological realities, have necessitated the use of novel methodological approaches and dependent measures including functional magnetic resonance imaging, hormonal/salivary assays, panel data across a full menstrual cycle, naturalistic experiments using Porsches and decrepit sedans, content analyses of cultural products, a twins registry, a process-tracing computer interface, historical economic data, and anthropomorphic measurements. This methodological diversity is perfectly congruent with this year's ACR theme of "appreciating diversity."

To reiterate, the goal is to have attendees walk away from the roundtable discussion with an appreciation of the epistemological and methodological pluralism afforded by an evolutionary approach. In doing so, this will hopefully encourage ACR scholars to explore how evolutionary-level theorizing might complement their individual research streams.

Who is likely to benefit from attending the round table?

Given that the driving theme of the roundtable is methodological pluralism, consilience, and interdisciplinarity, it is hoped that this inclusive message will resonate with many ACR attendees. This is precisely the point of the roundtable, namely that all consumer scholars stand to benefit from knowing how evolutionary principles might complement their various research streams. Saad (2007, chapter 2) offered ways by which areas that consumer scholars have typically been interested in including perception, attitude formation, decision making, learning, motivation, emotions, personality, and culture, can each be tackled from an evolutionary perspective. Hence, the raison d'être of the roundtable is to create a discussion centered on breaking down otherwise rigid disciplinary, methodological, and epistemological boundaries.

Facilitation of pre-conference discussions

The organizer of the roundtable (Gad Saad) will ask each participant to prepare a few examples from their research streams that highlight instances of methodological pluralism/diversity, consilience, and/or interdisciplinarity that were uniquely driven by the evolutionary lens. These will be collated into a working document that will then be passed around among all of the participants via email for comments and further suggestions. Once a clear outline of the session emerges, the organizer will post this tentative agenda at the ACR Facebook group site and the ACR Knowledge Exchange forum as a means of generating interest among the larger community. Schedule permitting, a get-together at the conference will be organized (prior to the roundtable) to go over key points to be discussed at the session.

References

Available upon request

ROUNDTABLE
Journal of Consumer Research (JCR) Reviewer Workshop

Chairs
Darren W. Dahl, University of British Columbia, Canada
Eileen Fischer, York University, Canada

Participants
Rashmi Adaval, Hong Kong University of Science and Technology, China
Søren Askegaard, University of Southern Denmark, Denmark
Hans Baumgartner, Pennsylvania State University, USA
Lauren G. Block, Baruch College/CUNY, USA
James Burroughs, University of Virginia, USA
Margaret C. Campbell, University of Colorado, USA
Darren W. Dahl, University of British Columbia, Canada
Aimee Drolet, University of California, Los Angeles, USA
Jennifer Edson Escalas, Vanderbilt University, USA
Eileen Fischer, York University, Canada
Gavan J. Fitzsimons, Duke University, USA
Kent Grayson, Northwestern University, USA
Rebecca W. Hamilton, University of Maryland, USA
Joel Huber, Duke University, USA
Gita Johar, Columbia University, USA
C. Page Moreau, University of Colorado, USA
Brian Ratchford, University of Texas at Dallas, USA
Rebecca Ratner, University of Maryland, USA
Jaideep Sengupta, Hong Kong University of Science and Technology, China
Baba Shiv, Stanford University, USA
Craig Thompson, University of Wisconsin, USA

The Editors and Associate Editors of the Journal of Consumer Research (JCR) will be conducting a roundtable to train reviewers and discuss the review process in general. They will explain what makes a great review, discuss how reviews are advisory to the editors, review the trainee program, and answer any questions.

Conversations on the Sacred and Spirituality in Consumer Behavior

Chairs
Diego Rinallo, Bocconi University, Italy
Pauline Maclaran, Royal Holloway, University of London, UK

Participants
Pauline Maclaran, Royal Holloway, University of London, UK
Russell W. Belk, York University, Canada
Stephen J. Gould, Baruch College, USA
Elif Izberk-Bilgin, University of Michigan, USA
Richard Kedzior, Hanken School of Economics, Finland
Robert Kozinets, York University, Canada
Hope Jensen Schau, University of Arizona, USA
Linda Scott, University of Oxford, UK
John F. Sherry, University of Notre Dame, USA
Eric J. Arnould, University of Bath, UK

Spirituality, once considered one and the same as religion, has attracted significant attention in the social sciences that, in the decades after the counterculture of the 1960s, have examined the secularization of society and the postmodern behavior of spiritual seekers, who mix and match from different sources to customize their spiritual beliefs and practices. In consumer research, spirituality per se has attracted limited explicit attention (for notable exceptions, see Hirschman, 1985; Holbrook, 1999; Gould, 1991; Moisio and Beruchashvili, 2010). Spirituality is however an element of the liberatory postmodernist quest to re-enchant human life (Fuat Firat and Venkatesh, 1995) and magical thinking in consumer behavior (Dion and Arnould, 2011; Fernandez and Lastovicka, 2011; St. James, Handelman and Taylor, 2011). Moreover, it is implicitly inherent in two influential streams of consumer research: (1) materialism, and (2) the sacred (as opposed to profane) aspects of consumer behaviour.

Materialism

Materialism is the idea that everything is made of matter. Most religions see the Divine as transcendent rather than immanent, that is, the creator is separated from the physical creation, which is often considered a distraction to the soul's spiritual journey, when not intrinsically evil. Accordingly, excessive pursuit of material goods is criticized as a hindrance to spiritual pursuits (see Belk, 1983). Materialism and spirituality do not, however, oppose each other. Religious/spiritual beliefs are reified in material culture (McDannell, 1995; Morgan, 1999; Moore, 1995), in the form of sacred images, devotional and liturgical objects, buildings and other places of worship, works of art, mass-produced consumption goods and entertainment products, and the practices surrounding these material objects (rituals, ceremonies, prayer, mediation, display, pilgrimage, worship, magic, study, etc.). Such consumption is not however exempt from critiques, ranging from bad taste (e.g., Catholic kitsch) to the more extreme accusation of spiritual materialism (Rindfleish, 2005; Trungpa, 1973).

Gould (2006) warns against conflating spirituality with spiritual materialism. He defines the latter as "the coopting of spiritual meanings and practices in the service of the material life of the self and then conflating them by rationalising that one is engaging in spirituality. For instance, one may use spiritual practices to reduce tension so one can get along better in the world as opposed to using them to seek some sort of spiritual fulfilment or enlightenment" (Gould, 2006: p. 65). Based on a Buddhist perspective, Gould (1992, 2006) suggests that spirituality can fruitfully engage with matter in ways different from asceticism. For example, alcohol, whose abuse is condemned by ascetic religious paths, may be employed under the right circumstances for spiritual transformation, like experiencing altered states of consciousness that might accelerate one's spiritual pursuits. From this perspective, consumption of goods, services and experiences can indeed provide the material means to achieve spiritual goals.

Sacred and Profane

In 1989, Belk, Wallendorf and Sherry argued that consumption may be a vehicle for experiencing the sacred, proposing that two processes are evolving in contemporary societies. One is the increased secularization of society and institutional religions. The other is the sacralization of the secular in the spheres of politics, science, art and consumption. Since Belk et al.'s (1989) publication, the sacred has become a frequently invoked conceptual category to refer to those aspects of consumer behavior that go beyond the satisfaction of functional needs, including those that do not necessarily involve transcendent or ecstatic experiences.

For example, Fournier (1998) draws on theories of animism to develop brand-consumer relationship theory; others have conceived certain types of brand-consumer relationship as based on devotion (Pimentel and Reynolds, 2004; Pichler and Hemetsberger, 2007). Reference to the sacred, re-enchantment and transcendence is also frequent in studies of extraordinary consumer experiences as different as river rafting (Arnould and Price, 1993; Arnould et al., 1999), consumer gatherings such as the mountain men rendezvous (Belk and Costa, 1998) and the Burning Man event (Kozinets, 2002; Kozinets and Sherry, 2003; Sherry and Kozinets, 2003, 2007), skydiving (Celsi et al., 1993), and mountain climbing (Tumbat and Belk, 2011). Spiritual elements are present not only in experiences that immerse consumers in nature, but also in those referred to as artificial, marketer-made consumptionscapes, such as disco clubs (Goulding et al., 2002, 2009), art exhibitions (Chen, 2009) and retail spaces (Borghini et al., 2009; Dion and Arnould, 2011; Kozinets et al., 2002, 2004; Sherry, 1998; Sherry et al., 2009).

Brands are also sometimes conceived in spiritual or even religious ways. In their ethnography of Harley Davidson bikers, Schouten and McAlexander (1995) observe that the "Harley consumption experience has a spirituality derived in part from a sense of riding as a transcendental departure from the mundane" (p. 50). Muñiz and Schau (2005), in their analysis of the abandoned Apple Newton community, identify several supernatural, religious and magic motifs in their informants' narratives. Belk and Tumbat (2005) develop the notion of brand cult and identify the sustaining myths that underlie the religious aspect of Macintosh consumption. Also popular management books provide guidance on how to create brand cults and turn customers into "true believers" (Atkin, 2004; Ragas and Bueno, 2002).

Spiritual elements are perhaps even more prominent in entertainment brands based on science fiction, fantasy and horror genres (e.g., X-Files, Kozinets, 1997; Star Trek, Kozinets, 2001; Star Wars, Brown et al., 2003). By introducing "fantastic" elements, these brands familiarize their audiences with supernatural beings (e.g., angels, vampires, fairies, aliens) and phenomena (e.g., magic, miracles) that are not supposed to exist from a secular, atheist standpoint.

Starting a conversation on the sacred and spirituality in consumer behavior

The idea of this roundtable session is to reflect again on the sacred in consumer culture, disentangle the different typologies of the sacred, and put spirituality back in. To facilitate pre-conference discussion, and as a tribute to the conference's theme of "appreciating diversity", we will circulate articles exploring different theoretical perspectives on the sacred, spirituality and spiritual diversity, including some written for a forthcoming book entitled Spirituality and Consumption edited by Rinallo, Scott and Maclaran. We will also create a Facebook group, to be widely promoted, to ensure the conversation extends beyond roundtable participants.

ROUNDTABLE

Market System Dynamics: The Value of and the Open Questions Associated with Studying Markets in Consumer Culture Theory

Chairs
Anton Siebert, Witten/Herdecke University, Germany
Anastasia Thyroff, University of Arkansas, USA

Participants
Ashlee Humphreys, Northwestern University, USA
Eminegul Karababa, Middle East Technical University, Turkey
Gokcen Coskuner-Balli, Chapman University, USA
Ela Veresiu, Witten/Herdecke University, Germany
Dannie Kjeldgaard, University of Southern Denmark, Denmark
Melea Press, University of Bath, UK
Eric J. Arnould, University of Bath, UK
John W. Schouten, Aalto University, Finland
Jeff B. Murray, University of Arkansas, USA
Anastasia Thyroff, University of Arkansas, USA

A thriving and diverse body of research that explicitly explores the creation, formation, and reshaping of markets has recently emerged in the consumer literature. This research places markets as social systems at the center of their analysis and examines how they are created and/or change through the discursive negotiations and the practices of various market stakeholders. As a nascent research area that has not yet been captured by overviews, however, it is still conceptually underdeveloped, lacks an agreed upon label and has no clear research agenda. To change this and facilitate the interaction among scholars, a roundtable provides an excellent opportunity.

Studying markets as social systems that are shaped by multiple actors and constitute specific forms of social reality is of increasing interest to consumer culture theorists (Giesler 2008; Humphreys 2009, 2010a, 2010b; Karababa and Ger 2011; Press and Arnould 2011; Zwick, Cayla, and Koops-Elson 2002; Penaloza and Venkatesh 2006; Thompson and Coskuner-Balli 2007). For example, Giesler (2008) illustrates how consumers and producers variously interpret the salient narrative of intellectual property in order to construct legitimacy for their activities in the cultural creative sphere. In his theorization, cultural conflict among opposing market stakeholders drives the formation of market structures. Employing institutional theory from sociology, Humphreys (2010a) shows the rhetoric and strategic efforts used by leading members of the casino gambling industry in cooperation with multiple stakeholders to create and maintain the industry. Humphreys portrays market creation as a political and social process of legitimation. Karababa and Ger (2011) investigate how struggles between the pursuit of pleasure and religious morality composed a coffeehouse culture and an active consumer subject in the early modern Ottoman era. Illustrating the alliance and transgressions of consumers and marketers against the enforcements of the state and the religious authority over time, the authors demonstrate that market formation is a sociocultural, political, and moral phenomenon located in the broader public sphere.

However, as in every research area in its nascent state, several questions remain to be explored, linkages need to be interrogated and established, and definitions have to be found. To explore what needs to be done in the area of market system dynamics, we conducted email exchanges and a Facebook discussion with key players. Several issues emerged:

What is the relationship between market system dynamics research and other areas of study?

Some participants brought up that other social sciences have already developed very interesting approaches to studying markets as social systems. Kjeldgaard listed work from sociology (Slater and Tonkiss 2001; Callon 1998), anthropology (Applbaum 2003; Lien 1997; Garsten and de Montoya 2004), economic sociology (Granovetter 1985, as referenced by Shankar), history (Schwarzkopf 2009), and interdisciplinary work such as Friedland and Robertson 1990. Furthermore, in the marketing landscape there is macromarketing work (Layton 2011; as mentioned by Arnould), market managerial scholarship, and work by researchers in the strategy realm (e.g. Peter Dickson and Bob Lusch; as mentioned by Rindfleisch). Do we contextualize, enrich, embed, and pattern their findings, or do we actually deviate from some of the more established economic and sociological concepts?

How should this research be defined?

The terms market formation (Press and Arnould 2011) and formations (Zwick et al. 2002), market creation (Humphreys 2010a), and market system dynamics (Giesler 2008) have been used recently. Although systemic thinking is increasingly supported in the marketing field (e.g. Layton 2011), Giesler noted that "[c]alling something a system is, in very consequential ways, looking for organization, meaning, harmony, purposeful structure, functionality, wholeness, etc. while de-emphasizing externalities, problems, leakages, and contradictions."

What are some of the unintended consequences of studying markets?

One participant said that we usually assume that markets are producers of value (e.g. identity value, economic value, structural value, technological innovations). What falls off of the analytic radar when assuming this primary role of markets? Adopting a more critical perspective, Giesler said that markets could also be regarded as agents or strategic consumers: "[H]ow do markets actively reconfigure social and cultural spheres in ways that maximize their economic and ideological returns?" How should market-focused CCT research in the future pick these consequences up?

What are future research directions?

For example, the current market legitimation theorization draws mainly upon institutional theory from sociology. Veresiu said that assemblage theory or actor-network theory provide alternate perspectives that have yet to be fully employed by consumer researchers. Giesler added that a historical understanding of how our own views of the market emerge and evolve over time relative to political, social, and economic events and broader institutional transformations could be worth future exploration. Critical work could address the role that humanistic researchers play in giving markets authenticity, meaning, integrity, and the ability to function and regulate effectively. Given the great work on markets outside of the consumer literature, however, Shankar noted that we were coming late to this game. So what can we as consumer researchers contribute?

These and other questions should be the focus of our roundtable. We hope that by finding answers and finding new questions we help develop this research agenda, which we consider to be an important source of innovation in the ACR and CCT vicinity.

The organizers will continue to facilitate pre-conference interaction among researchers with an interest in market system dynamics. Discussions on Facebook have proven to be useful in raising greater interest in the topic and the event of the round table. Complemented by email exchanges, these (and other) forms of pre-conference interaction helped to co-create this proposal and will be very important for the success of the roundtable.

As market system dynamics is a fundamentally interdisciplinary and diverse research stream that stretches across the vast field of consumer research as well as the social sciences more broadly, we aim at bringing together scholars with diverse theoretical and methodological backgrounds, not only CCT researchers. This is needed to look at what consumer research focusing on markets has done in the past, where it stands in the present, and what needs to be done to make this a fruitful exercise of scholarly activity in the future.

ROUNDTABLE
"Death and All His Friends":
The Role of Identity, Ritual, and Disposition in the Consumption of Death

Chair
Susan Dobscha, Bentley University, USA

Participants
Jenna Drenten, John Carroll University, USA
Kent Drummond, University of Wyoming, USA
Terrance Gabel, University of Arkansas, Fort Smith, USA
Chris Hackley, Royal Holloway, University of London, UK
Sidney J. Levy, University of Arizona, USA
Jeffrey Podoshen, Franklin and Marshall College, USA
Dennis Rook, University of Southern California, USA
Katherine Sredl, University of Notre Dame, USA
Rungpaka Amy Tiwsakul, Durham University, UK
Ekant Veer, University of Canterbury, NZ

This roundtable examines death as a topic with almost endless potential for consumer research projects with different foci and various methodologies. Death studies is an emergent subfield in other disciplines, notably sociology and history, as researchers are beginning to discover its many complexities and layers. This roundtable comfortably reflects the diversity theme of the conference because death is inherently cultural and governed by local, national, and global norms and customs, and is subject to consumer cultural forces. .

The purpose of this roundtable is to begin a discussion on the broad connections between death and consumption and to foster research linkages among members of the ACR community. Given the strong interest in the topic by researchers at all stages of their careers (doctoral students to full professors) and the inescapable amount of diversity built into the topic, it is clear that this roundtable will be of interest to a wide variety of scholars across content and methodological paradigms. .

Attitudes toward death change slowly over time. Until the Romantic era, death was treated as a banal, expected experience, often taking place at home with all family members present, including children (Aries 1974). Religious, especially eschatological concerns, shifted the conduct of death. What started as an experience organized by the dying person himself evolved into emotional expressions by the living and with modernity a need to hide the inevitability of death to the dying person, to spare him "the ugliness of dying" (Aries 1974).

The management of death has legal, ethical, financial, environmental, commercial, and social implications., including the disposition of possessions through wills, the implications of cryogenic storage, the environmental consequences of burial practices and the emerging 'natural burial' industry. The commercial enterprises focused on death-related consumption continue to grow and are placed squarely at the center of consumers' preparation for or reaction to the death of a loved one.

There seems to be two broad research domains when thinking about death. The first domain encompasses the ritual aspects of death. Turley and O'Donohoe's work on consumption during bereavement (2005) and Bonsu and Belk's work on death rituals in Ghana (2003) are excellent examples of the relationship between consumption and death rituals.

The second domain appears to relate to identity and meaning made of death by the dead, the dying, and the living. . Death impacts the identities of the living, as well as those of the dead. As Davies stated, "at death, identity is altered not only through the loss of figures who have served as sources of identity but also by the new responsibilities which the living must take on themselves."

The members of this roundtable have projects in various phases that encompass some aspect of death. The work can be loosely categorized across five broad themes. Jeffrey Podoshen, Kent Drummond, and Dennis Rook are examining the consumption of death in two radically different contexts. Podoshen is looking at death tourism in the black metal subculture while Drummond examines the blockbuster museum exhibit BodyWorlds, which places highly stylized cadavers in life-like positions. Rook has gathered data about longevity trends, changes in the leading causes of death, and actuarial statistics about the percent of any age cohort who are living (dead), which provide a basis for further study of the salience and anticipation of death.

Rungpaka Amy Tiwsakul and Chris Hackley, and Susan Dobscha are looking more broadly at the role of consumption in death rituals. Tiwsakul and Hackley are looking at death rituals in Asian culture while Dobscha is looking at the emerging consumption phenomenon of "green", "sustainable", or "natural" burials.

Katherine Sredl's work is focusing on death as a metaphor for transition in her exploration of the Museum of Broken Relationships whereby jilted partners leave artifacts from failed relationships as a way of finding closure.

Ekant Veer is looking at disposition activities when death is imminent. His research examines how people who know they are dying give away their possessions. And finally, Terrance Gabel and Jenna Drenten study post-mortem rituals among the living. In particular, Gabel looks at how online memorialization practices reflect a new approach to mourning by an almost reversion to medieval rituals that were more social and communal vs. the current way of mourning that is more private and affect-minimizing. He also differentiates between the idea of physical death, which is typically immediate, and social death, which can continue for many years. Drenten looks at the practice of gift-giving to the dead by the living in her study of consumers who continue to buy gifts for loved ones well after their death.

This roundtable serves to ask 3 key questions related to death and consumption:
1. Are current conceptualizations of death sufficient? Do these conceptualizations hinder future research on the topic?
2. What ethical concerns are raised when doing research in this area?

3. What is the role of material goods and their consumption in understanding (a) the evolving meaning of death, and (b) the evolving meaning and practice of mourning and memorialization?

The session organizer will provide a synopsis of the session for publication in the proceedings.

References

Bonsu, S.K., and R.W. Belk (2003), "Do Not Go Cheaply into That Good Night: Death-Ritual Consumption in Asante, Ghana," Journal of Consumer Research 30:41-55.

Hallam, Elizabeth and Jenny Hockey (2001), Death, Memory and Material Culture. New York: Berg.

Neimeyer, Robert A., Holly G. Prigerson, and Betty Davies (2002), "Mourning and Meaning," The American Behavioral Scientist, 46 (Oct.), 235-251.

O'Donohoe, S., and D. Turley (2005), "To Death Do Us Part? Consumption and the Negotiation of Relationships Following a Bereavment." Advances in Consumer Research 32: 625-626.

Sofka, Carla J. (1997), "Social Support 'Internetworks,' Caskets for Sale and More: Thanatology and the Information Superhighway," Death Studies, 21, 553-574.

Walter, Tony (1996), "A New Model of Grief: Bereavement and Biography," Mortality, 1 (1), 7-25.

Walter, Tony, Rachid Hourizi, Wendy Moncur, and Stacey Pitsillides (2011), "Does the Internet Change How We Die and Mourn? Overview and Analysis," Omega: Journal of Death & Dying, 64 (4), 275-302.

ROUNDTABLE
Think Outside the Lab: Using Field Data in Behavioral Research

Chair
Jonah Berger, University of Pennsylvania, USA

Participants
J. Jeffrey Inman, University of Pittsburgh, USA
Darren W. Dahl, University of British Columbia, Canada
Leslie John, Harvard University, USA
Ayelet Gneezy, University of California San Diego, USA
Uri Simonsohn, University of Pennsylvania, USA
Leif D. Nelson, University of California Berkeley, USA
Joe Simmons, University of Pennsylvania, USA
Sarah Moore, University of Alberta, Canada
Michael I. Norton, Harvard University, USA

The world has changed. We are now surrounded by a wealth of data in ways never before imagined. Loyalty cards record purchase, scanner panel data records basket size, and shopping cart trackers record movement through the store. Blogs record thoughts and opinions, Facebook tracks what topics are discussed, and search data records what people are interested in learning more about. With a couple of mouse clicks we can find everything from sports scores and stock prices to newsgroups and which baby names are popular.

How can consumer behavior researchers use these new data sources to enrich their research? How can we get access to this data? What are its benefits compared to lab experiments? What are some of the issues researchers face when moving outside the lab?

This roundtable will bring together a diverse group of behavioral researchers to discuss using field data in behavioral research. The group is a mix of senior and junior researchers, both more and less quantitatively inclined, all of which have figured out creative ways to use field data to enrich their research programs. They have conducted field experiments at Disney World, scraped sports score from the web, and coded customer service calls. They've measured the collective mood using blogs, had employees work while walking on treadmills, and examined student's report card to measure academic performance. Building on these experiences, they will share insights with the audience and exchange ideas about how to better incorporate these alternate sources of data into our research programs.

Detailed Description and Format

The laboratory experiment has always been the behavioral researcher's fruit fly. The relatively sterile environment allows for careful manipulation and measurement. You can tightly manipulate one key factor, holding everything else constant, and examine its causal impact on a dependent variable. The internal validity and experimental control lab experiments provide are ideal for teasing out complex psychological mechanisms.

But exactly because the lab environment is so simplified, people often wonder about the strength or importance of effects shown there. The real world is a noisy and complicated place. Lots of things are going on at once. Do the effects we've observed in the lab really hold in the field? And do they have a consequential impact on real behavior?

The session will answer these, and related questions, as it enriches the audience's understanding of how to use field data in behavioral research. The format will be as follows:

1)Concrete Examples: To give the audience a concrete sense of the breadth of what is possible, each roundtable participant will provide one short example of how they have used field data to enrich their work (approximately 3-4 minutes, 1-2 PowerPoint slides at most). This will include:

a)A brief overview of the project
b)Why they felt field data was useful (better than the lab or just valuable in a different way)
c)How they got the data
d)How they used the data

The point of these presentations will be to provide a breadth of concrete experiences to help the audience get a better sense of the space.

2)Broader Themes: The groups will then have a broader discussion regarding some key questions.

a)How do you get field data? We'll talk about different approaches to acquiring data including contacting companies, using Webcrawlers or scraping data from the web, and archival research.

b)What are the benefits of field data? We'll talk about external validity, the ability to compute effect sizes, and how such data can help communicate your effects to a broader audience.

c)But can we show causation? Many people may have already thought about field experiments, but for most experimentalists datasets are less common. But are datasets only good for showing correlations or can more be done? We'll start by talking about some of the ways that field data can provide correlational support for behavioral theories. Then we'll talk about methods like regression discontinuity and natural experiments that allow researchers to make causal inference from correlational data

d)How will reviewers react? We'll talk about experiences in the review process, complications involving showing experimental and non-experimental data, and how editors feel about such data (roundtable members Darren Dahl, Jeff Inman, and Uri Simonsohn are all Associate Editors)

e)But I'm not good with statistics! We'll talk about how to analyze field data and whether and when it is useful to bring in more quantitatively minded colleagues

Who is likely to benefit: Given the wide-range of types of data that are available, and the clear benefits of using such data to augment one's research program, this roundtable should benefit all consumer behavior researchers. It should be particularly valuable for doctoral students and junior researchers who are thinking of novel ways to test their research questions.

In summary, this roundtable will bring diverse perspectives together to shed light on how to use field data in behavioral research. Pre-conference discussion has already begun and will be facilitated through emails and discussion among the group of participants. The session is particularly relevant to ACR's theme of appreciating diversity, because it showcases diverse ways to test research hypotheses.

Reading the Mind of the Consumer:
Promises and Challenges of Predictive Methods in Consumer Neuroscience

Chair
Ming Hsu, University of California, Berkeley

Participants
Ming Hsu, University of California Berkeley, USA
Uma Karmarkar, Harvard Business School, USA
Karim Kassam, Carnegie Mellon, USA
Tom Meyvis, New York University, USA
Hilke Plassmann, INSEAD, France
Akshay Rao, University of Minnesota, USA
Baba Shiv, Stanford University, USA
Monica Wadhwa, INSEAD, France
Carolyn Yoon, University of Michigan, USA
Drazen Prelec, Massachusetts Institute of Technology, USA
William Hedgcock, University of Iowa, USA
Adam Craig, University of South Florida, USA
Mili Milosavljevic, Stanford University, USA
Angelika Dimoka, Temple University, USA
Nina Mazar, University of Toronto, Canada

Topic and Motivation

"Mind Reading" and Predicting Cognitive States: Can we predict behavior of consumers from their brain activity? Can we generalize predictions about behavior, generated from the brain activity in our subject samples, to the population at large? In short, are we able to "mind read"? These are provocative questions that may seem to be squarely in the realm of science fiction, but progress in the intersection of neuroscience, psychology, and machine learning is making this an increasingly likely proposition. Early examples have demonstrated how neuroimaging data can be used to predict the cognitive states, including whether participants were viewing faces versus non-faces, tools versus non-tools, and, more ambitiously, the contents of natural scenery images. More recently, these studies have scaled up to more complex and abstract constructs, including the contents of specific scenes that participants were watching, or the efficacy of social marketing campaigns.

Not surprisingly, these studies have been widely reported in the popular press, and have fueled expectations that we will soon be able to probe into the mind of consumers and predict when, where, and what they will buy. This leap from reconstructing our perception of the physical world to our inner thoughts and feelings, however, is a formidable one, and only recently are we starting to grasp the conceptual and technical hurdles. To use an analogy, this would be akin to predicting not only what moviegoers are watching, but also what they are thinking and feeling.

Bridging Neuroscience and Consumer Behavior: In essence, these so-called "decoding" studies have taken the traditional approach in neuroimaging and turned it upside down. Historically, neuroimaging studies have sought to map the set of brain regions that respond systematically to experimental manipulations of cognitive states and/or behavior. In consumer neuroscience, for example, there have been several studies that have investigated brain regions that respond differentially to branded vs. unbranded items, or when making inferences about brands vs. about people.

In contrast, decoding studies ask the question, "Are there patterns of brain activity that can be used to identify, or reconstruct, the outputs of the experiment, either in terms of the cognitive states, or the elicited behavior?" In particular, two new areas in cognitive neuroscience raise the provocative possibility of being able to do just what consumer researchers have sought for years: to be able to look into the mind of a consumer, by-pass socially desirable responses, and predict a consumers decisions based on patterns of neural data alone. The first area involves the prediction of individual level behavior based on patterns of neural data. Using machine learning techniques that allow for multivariate statistical analysis, algorithms can be developed which classify behaviors based on prior behavioral exemplars. The second area involves neural "focus groups" which seek to utilize neural data to inform population level inferences beyond the ability of behavioral approaches alone.

Goal of the Current Roundtable

Despite the similarities in purpose between these new techniques, however, many differences exist that make it difficult for researchers with diverse backgrounds to initiate collaborative efforts: first, these methods make different assumptions regarding the relationship between neural structures. Second, the data required for machine learning analyses necessitates novel experimental design compared to traditional neuroimaging designs. Third, the two methods require substantially different levels of neurocognitive theory.

This roundtable will serve as the starting point for discussion and collaboration between researchers interested in utilizing neuroscientific data for predictive studies and those behavioral researchers interested in merging neural study data with secondary data. We have drawn together a diverse panel of experts in neuroscience and decision research to explore the strengths and limitations of each emerging technique. Several specific issues to be discussed are:

1. Conceptual and technical background of predictive methods.
2. Discussion of past experiences of panel members who have researched worked with multivariate imaging data.

3. The most promising conceptual and methodological frontiers for applying predictive methodologies.

Interested and Likely-to-Benefit Audiences

This roundtable should be of interest to all consumer researchers, including both those who use biological methods and those who do not. Those interested in prediction of individual level neural data would find this roundtable stimulating and informative regarding the application of emerging techniques to address existing consumer research issues. For traditional consumer researchers, the discussion of existing and emerging techniques from the intersection of neuroimaging, machine learning, and decision-making, would provide a broader scope which would allow more nuanced discussion about appropriate analysis techniques.

A primary challenge to wider adoption of these approaches in consumer behavior is the complexity of the tools involved, and requires considerably more technical expertise than traditional neuroimaging approaches. However, despite their interest in predicting behavior, consumer researchers in each area are only infrequently exposed to the key assumptions and existing limitations of the other. Hence this roundtable's key contribution lies in actively addressing the assumptions and limitations of each predictive method.

Facilitating Pre-Conference Discussions

In order to facilitate pre-conference discussion that is both provocative and informal, we plan to utilize the ACR knowledge exchange forum and moderated emails between participants. Participants will be encouraged to provide informal summaries of existing research efforts along with discussion points focused on the challenges faced in applying predictive methodologies. These materials will be collected by the organizers and distributed to the finalized list of participants. Thus, these preconference efforts should maximize the value and vigor of the session itself.

Working Papers

1. Better Together or Alone? Joint vs. Individual Goal Pursuit

Lauren Trabold, Baruch College/CUNY, USA
Stephen J. Gould, Baruch College/CUNY, USA

We examine the commonly held lay theory that pursuing a goal with a partner will have a positive influence on goal pursuit. We aim to establish whether collaborating with someone with the same goal positively influences perceptions of the goal, and also examine its objective effect on goal progress.

2. Planning to Fail? The Role of Implementation Intentions in Emotional Responses to Goal Failures

Jason Stornelli, University of Michigan, USA
J. Frank Yates, University of Michigan, USA

We explore the role of planning in emotional responses to goal failure and demonstrate that forming detailed implementation plans makes post-failure regret more likely and intense. Further, we show this process is associated with subjective feelings of closeness to the desired outcome, independent of the objective distance to the goal.

3. Knowing What I Want: Alignability, Attentional Focus, and the Identification of Consumption Goals

Michael Hair, Georgia Institute of Technology, USA
Samuel Bond, Georgia Institute of Technology, USA

Our research addresses the direct benefits of goal identification on decision outcomes. In three studies, we demonstrate how conscious consideration of one's consumption can be beneficial or harmful. We explore the effects when non-alignable attributes are the basis for choice, or when goal-relevant attributes have limited influence on decision quality.

4. Lay Theories in Consumer Goal Setting and Striving: The Case of Weight Loss

Mariam Beruchashvili, California State University, Northridge, USA
Risto Moisio, California State University. Long Beach, USA
James Gentry, University of Nebraska-Lincoln, USA

Although consumer goals and lay theories have been examined separately in prior research, no studies investigate whether implicit theories of personality influence the goals consumers set and how they strive to attain those goals. In the context of Weight Watchers, we address this theoretical oversight.

5. From Apples to Alcopops: The Forbidden Fruit Effect on Supersized Alcoholic Beverages

Cassandra Davis, University of Arkansas, USA
Elizabeth Howlett, University of Arkansas, USA

The increasingly dangerous consequences of alcopops have led policy makers and health advocates to champion warning labels and restrictions for these products. This research examines the potential consequences of these actions and posits that these regulations will create a forbidden-fruit effect, such that consumers will find alcopops more desirable.

6. Knowing When to Assimilate and When to Contrast: Self-Control and the Influence of Contextual Order

Kelly L. Haws, Texas A&M University, USA
Joseph P. Redden, University of Minnesota, USA
Scott Davis, Texas A&M University, USA

We explore the role of self-control in consumption contexts where assimilation and contrast effects emerge. This research reveals that the presentation order of food stimuli (healthy vs. indulgent or ambiguous) has a striking impact on both consumer evaluations of healthiness and the amount consumed.

7. All Things Considered: When the Budgeting Process Promotes Consumers' Savings

Min Jung Kim, Texas A&M University, USA
Haipeng (Allan) Chen, Texas A&M University, USA

We examine when the budgeting process can promote consumers' savings. Results show that when consumers consider spending and savings goals to the same extent, the budgeting process makes them perceive savings goals as being more important, which in turn increases the amount of money saved.

8. Implementation Intentions as Self-Regulation Tool for Low- and High-Level Impulsive Buyers: A Behavioral and Neurophysiological Investigation

Isabella Kopton, Zeppelin University, Germany
Bruno Preilowski, Zeppelin University, Germany
Peter Kenning, Zeppelin University, Germany

In postmodern societies, impulsive buying has become increasingly prevalent and can even transition to pathological compulsive buying with negative consequences on consumers' well-being. This paper analyses the effectiveness of self-regulatory implementation intentions to control impulsive buying behavior. Results suggest that implementation intentions are a valuable tool for decreasing impulsive buying tendencies.

9. Joe vs. joe: Turning to One's Partner vs. Favorite Product in Emotion Regulation

Danielle J. Brick, Duke University, USA
Hannah Honey, Duke University, USA
Gráinne M. Fitzsimons, Duke University, USA
Gavan J. Fitzsimons, Duke University, USA

We compare negative emotion regulation strategies of support from partner vs. the consumption of a favorite beverage. When the negative emotion is irritation (vs. sadness or anxiety) a larger number turn to their product. Furthermore, those who imagine product consumption (vs. partner support) in the irritation condition report more reduced feelings of irritation.

10. The Influence of Social Relationships on Self-regulatory Focus in Buying for Others

Huimin Xu, The Sage Colleges, USA
Paul M. Connell, City University London, UK
Ada Leung, Pennsylvania State University Berks, USA
Cuiping Chen, University of Ontario Institute of Technology, Canada

Existing research often treats self-regulatory focus as a situational variable that can be made temporarily salient by task framing. Our research posits self-regulatory focus as an inherent characteristic of social relationships. Making purchase decisions for a particular social tie elicits a certain self-regulatory focus.

11. When Self-Serving Does Not Serve the Self: The Role of Serving-Style in Food Consumption

Anna Linda Hagen, University of Michigan, USA
Brent McFerran, University of Michigan, USA
Aradhna Krishna, University of Michigan, USA

Consumers increasingly consume food that is prepared and served by others. Three studies establish that self-serving a chosen food (re)instigates feelings of responsibility for the food, that consumers assume responsibility in a self-serving manner depending on the food's health-value, and that health-value and serving-style together shape consumers' self-conscious feelings after consumption.

12. When Do Consumers Compromise on Calories? Exploring the Attraction and Compromise Effects in Food Choice

Ryall Carroll, St. John's University, USA
Beth Valen, Fordham University, USA

Prior research shows that providing calorie information on menus leads to changes in consumer choice. We explore whether attraction and compromise effects occur when consumers are presented with calorie information on menus.

13. Changing Implicit Beliefs through Advertising: Exploring One of the Origins of the "Unhealthy=Tasty" Intuition

Carolina Werle, Grenoble École de Management, France
Olivier Trendel, Grenoble École de Management, France

Unhealthy foods are implicitly associated with good taste and this intuition influences taste perceptions, favoring the consumption of unhealthy options and contributing to obesity epidemics. In two studies we show that this intuition is culture dependent and that advertising images can change the implicit belief in the intuition.

14. Toward a Gender-Specific Emotional Eating Model: The Role of Self-Esteem and Emotional Intelligence

Paula C. Peter, San Diego State University, USA
Sukumarakurup Krishnakumar, North Dakota State University, USA

With a first empirical study, we show that males are more susceptible to emotional eating when their self-esteem and emotional intelligence (EI) are low. These findings provide initial support for a gender-specific emotional eating model, where males might benefit from an EI-specific intervention in order to reduce emotional eating.

15. The Effect of Pictorial Cues of Food on Restrained vs. Unrestrained Eaters

Nguyen Pham, Arizona State University, USA
Maureen (Mimi) Morrin, Rutgers University, USA
May Lwin, Nanyang Technological University, Singapore
Melissa G. Bublitz, University of Wisconsin Oshkosh, USA

This research represents a preliminary exploration of how exposure to highly craved but forbidden food pictures impacts hunger and guilt among restrained and unrestrained eaters, providing insight into the mechanisms associated with overeating via abandonment of long-term health goals.

16. Ironic Effects of Food Commercials: When More Food-Related Mental Images Make You Eat Less

Carolina Werle, Grenoble École de Management, France
Mia Birau, Grenoble École de Management, France

Food ads allowing imagining high-caloric foods consumption may increase feelings of fatness, characterizing the thought-shape fusion (TSF) phenomenon. Study 1 shows that a food advertisement inducing TSF increases food restriction intentions. Study 2 explores the TSF mechanism and shows that a high imagery-evoking food advertisement reduces subsequent food consumption.

17. Consumers' Alternative Dietary Lifestyles – A Narrative Approach

Anniina Luukkonen, Aalto University, Finland
Ilona Mikkonen, Aalto University, Finland
Elina Koivisto, Aalto University, Finland

The present study reports preliminary findings from a project on consumers' alternative dietary choices. It takes a narrative approach to explore how consumers make sense of their decision to reject official nutrition recommendations, and why they choose to follow a diet not generally accepted as healthy.

18. Happy Fat or Staying Thin? Evolutionary Motives Underlying Consumer Food Choice

Rob Richerson, University of Kentucky, USA
Blair Kidwell, Ohio State University, USA
Virginie Lopez-Kidwell, University of Kentucky, USA

We propose a new perspective for understanding healthy eating that explores social factors and the underlying evolutionary motives that influence eating behaviors. Specifically, we explore how evolutionary motives for affiliation in social groups and mate retention in personal relationships drive consumers to match the unhealthy or healthy eating styles of others.

19. Food in Motion

Michael Giblin, University at Buffalo, USA
Aner Tal, Cornell University, USA
Brian Wansink, Cornell University, USA

The current research examines the implications of product motion on consumer evaluations of attributes such as weight and overall appeal. We argue and demonstrate that a product shown moving will be evaluated more favorably. These effects might be due to associations of freshness with movement.

20. Oh Dear, I'm So Confused: Cognitive and Affective Coping Strategies to Deal with Consumer Confusion in the Food Market

Inga Wobker, Zeppelin University, Germany
Peter Kenning, Zeppelin University, Germany

In complex markets, poorly-informed consumers use different strategies to reduce information asymmetries. They may use cognitive mechanisms such as screening to acquire information and affective mechanisms such as trust for complexity reduction. This paper presents an analysis of these strategies in food distribution. Results suggest consumers with affective strategies use less cognitive coping.

21. It's Not Just Numbers: Nutrition Information Disclosure is Perceived as a Social Identity Threat by French Consumers

Pierrick Gomez, Reims Management School and Université Paris Dauphine, France

This research examines whether nutrition information disclosure can threaten the national identity of French consumers. Results of an experiment reveal that nutrition information disclosure impairs information processing of participants for whom French identity is made salient. Two additional experiments will investigate the influence of social identity threat induced by nutrition information disclosure on dietary choices.

22. When Dieting in Your Mind Brings Cake in Your Mouth

Jiah Yoo, Yonsei University, South Korea
Youngwoo Sohn, Yonsei University, South Korea

This study examines whether activating a dieting goal in the mind can induce a potential problem in regulating eating behaviors. The results reveal that for consumers who see themselves as unsuccessful dieters, activating dieting goals in their minds actually increases the desire to consume tempting foods, compared to consumers in the neutral condition.

23. Self-Construal and Self-Affirmation Effects in Effortful Customer Experiences

Prakash Das, University of Calgary, Canada
James Agarwal, University of Calgary, Canada

Across two studies, we show that primed self-construals have differential effects on company and self attributions, and judgments about the effortful tasks. In difficult tasks, those primed with an independent self-construal blame the company more than those primed with an interdependent self-construal. Further, self-affirmation moderates these effects more for independents than interdependents, suggesting self-affirmation produces greater self-threat reduction for the former compared to the latter.

24. The Persuasiveness of Abstract vs. Concrete Language in Commercial and Non-Commercial Settings

Peeter Verlegh, University of Amsterdam, The Netherlands

The present studies examine how the impact of language on persuasiveness is moderated by the context in which the language is used. We focus on one particular aspect of language (language abstraction), and show how its impact differs between non-commercial contexts like word of mouth, and commercial contexts like advertising.

25. Better in the (Near) Future: Biased Temporal Conceptions of Team Identification

Jesse S. King, Oregon State University, Cascades, USA
Colleen C. Bee, Oregon State University, Cascades, USA

The current research investigates temporal self and other biases among fans' evaluations of sports teams. Our findings suggest that fans appreciate a home team more for their future potential than for what they have been in the past. Additionally, our results demonstrate an increased optimism for one's own team.

26. The Moderating Role of Construal Level on Effectiveness of Purchase-Contingent Donations

Nara Youn, Hongik University, South Korea
Yun Lee, Virginia State University, USA

We document that the effectiveness of purchase-contingent donations moderated by customers' construal level differs by product type. Specifically, abstract thinkers evaluate the product more favorably when the donation is linked with a hedonic product, and the guilt of consuming the hedonic product is alleviated significantly more for abstract thinkers than concrete thinkers.

27. Activating Multiple Facets of the Self: Identity-Signaling and Brand Personality

Marilyn Giroux, Concordia University, Canada
Bianca Grohmann, Concordia University, Canada
Frank Pons, Université Laval, Canada

Using a multi-method approach consisting of qualitative and quantitative studies, the authors examine the impact of identity salience on preferences for the different dimensions of brand personality. Results from those studies demonstrate that consumers' motivations to express parts of their identities influence their preferences for brands.

28. Impression Management Practices of Stigma-Conscious Communities: The Case of an Online Pro-Smoking Forum

Navin Bahl, University of Hawaii, USA
Namita Bhatnagar, University of Manitoba, Canada
Rajesh V. Manchanda, University of Manitoba, Canada
Anne Lavack, Kwantlen Polytechnic University, Canada

We integrate literatures from consumption communities, stigmatization, and tobacco control to understand how smokers engage in impression-management practices to counteract stigma. Results of a netnography unearth impression-management practices (namely, enabling, compromising, and curing) inherent within an online pro-smoking community. We propose implications for theory and practice.

29. Putting Myself in your Shoes: The Role of Identification in Persuasion

Anne Hamby, Virginia Tech, USA
Meghan Pierce, Pontificia Universidad Católica de Chile, Chile
Kim Daniloski, University of Scranton, USA

While source characteristics contribute to persuasion in informational messages, identification with characters is more influential in a narrative context. The results of two studies indicate that level of identification with an author has a positive impact on attitude toward the focal subject in the narrative context.

30. Self-Construal as a Cultural Mindset and its Relevance for Automatic Social Behavior

Geetanjali Saluja, HKUST, Hong Kong
Rashmi Adaval, HKUST, Hong Kong

Past research has looked at how a context cues cultural mindsets. These mindsets, in turn, trigger cognitive procedures that help collectivists connect and integrate, and individualists pull apart and separate. This paper explores how such cognitive procedures impact automatic social behavior upon exposure to a member of a social category.

31. Self-Construal Moderates the Effect of Fear of Failure on Donation Likelihood

Lale Okyay-Ata, Koç University, Turkey
Baler Bilgin, Koç University, Turkey
Zeynep Gürhan-Canli, Koç University, Turkey

This research shows that self-construal moderates the effect of fear of failure on donation likelihood. An independent self-construal decreases and an interdependent self-construal increases donation likelihood. The effects are expected to be mediated by the perceived distance from others, via perceived uncertainty and loss of control.

32. Dynamic Co-Creation: Moving Beyond Foucault to Understand the Ideological Field of Parenting

Alexander S. Rose, University of Arkansas, USA
Robin L. Soster, University of Arkansas, USA
Kelly Tian, University of Wyoming, USA
Randall L. Rose, University of South Carolina, USA

Data from eight depth interviews reveal a dynamic formation process of parental ideology, contrasting sharply with previous mechanistic conceptualizations. The hegemonic discourse of therapeutic culture commodifies familial relations and parental know-how, bringing the parent-child relationship into the market. Both endorsements of, and resistance to, the discourse grant it legitimacy.

33. Children's Preferences of Package Design

Dan Zhang, City University of New York, USA
James Hunt, Temple University, USA
C. Anthony Di Benedetto, Temple University, USA
Richard Lancioni, Temple University, USA

This research explores children's preferences of package design on shape (straight or rounded), figurativeness, and complexity. Analysis of data from 766 children 3-12 years of age reveals children generally prefer rounded package shapes and realistic, figurative package designs. Furthermore, preferences for complex package shapes increase with age.

34. Innovation for Your Parents? The Impact of Lay Theories of Innovativeness on Upward Intergenerational Gift Giving

Jianping Liang, Sun Yat-sen University, China
Hongyan Jiang, China University of Mining & Technology, China

Little work explicitly considers the determinant factors for adult offspring acting as innovation influences on their parents. This paper investigates an ignored but important phenomenon; i.e., upward intergenerational gift giving of innovation, and examines the interplay of two dimensions of lay theories of innovativeness. We offer counterintuitive results.

35. Who Spends More on Children's Education: "I" or "We"?

Lingjiang Tu, University of Texas at San Antonio, USA
Yinlong Zhang, University of Texas at San Antonio, USA

Three studies show that interdependent self-construal induces more parental education spending than independent self-construal, and this effect is reversed when parent's feeling of failure is primed. Furthermore, the moderating role of failure on a self-construal effect is mediated by parental identity salience.

36. Ethno-Culturally Diverse Social Ecosystems

Esi Abbam Elliot, University of Illinois at Chicago, USA
Joseph Cherian, George Washington University, USA

This study seeks to explore how cultural diversity influences social networking behaviors in consumer communities. We administer a survey to various racial groups in five communities in the Lake County district in Chicago. The findings demonstrate cultural diversity in dynamic social networks -- a phenomenon we name ethno-culturally diverse social ecosystems (EDSO).

37. Cultural Identity and Brand Relationships: Negotiating Brand Meanings in a New Cultural Context

Anna Jansson Vredeveld, University of Connecticut, USA
Robin A. Coulter, University of Connecticut, USA

As consumers move across geographic spaces, they encounter culturally and contextually dependent meanings of brands. Findings from semi-structured interviews with nineteen sojourn consumers provide insights into how these consumers interpret brand meanings across cultures. We explore the implications of consistent and incongruent brand meanings for new and existing brand relationships.

38. Style Reimagined: Exploring Fashion and Identity among South African Smarteez

Kevin Thomas, University of Texas at Austin, USA
Guillaume Johnson, University of the Witwatersrand, South Africa
Marike Venter, University of the Witwatersrand, South Africa
Kristin Stewart, University of Texas at Austin, USA

This paper explores style and identity among the Smarteez, a youth subculture in South Africa. Using several ethnographic techniques, we demonstrate that the Smarteez use elements of style to reify nonconformist aspects of self, aid in the performativity of identity factors, and promote a uniquely cosmopolitan worldview.

39. A Cross-Cultural Comparison of the Impact of Consumers' Conspicuous Consumption Orientations on Brand Attitude and Purchase Intention

Xia (Linda) Liu, Louisiana State University, USA
Alvin C. Burns, Louisiana State University, USA
HongYan Yu, Sun Yat-Sen University, China

This research compares the impact of conspicuous consumption orientation on brand attitude and purchase intention across individualistic and collectivistic cultures.

40. Does Accent Matter? The Impact of Ethnic Similarity and Product Congruence on Spokesperson Credibility and Purchase Intention

Aarti S. Ivanic, University of San Diego, USA
Kenneth Bates, University of San Diego, USA
T. Somasundaram, University of San Diego, USA

This research examines whether and when firms should use accented spokespersons in radio ads. A 2 x 2 between-subjects experiment finds spokespeople are evaluated more positively and have greater perceived credibility when there is high listener-spokesperson similarity. Purchase likelihood is highest when there is high listener-spokesperson similarity and spokesperson-product congruence.

41. Acculturation, Brand Personality and Brand Preferences

Umut Kubat, University of Pittsburgh, USA
Vanitha Swaminathan, University of Pittsburgh, USA

The present research examines the relationship between acculturation, brand personality and brand preferences, in the context of bilingual advertising. We hypothesize that biculturals will not demonstrate a strong affinity to any particular brand. We further test how bilingual advertising can enhance biculturals' brand preferences, and how brand personality moderates this relationship.

42. Decoding BE-Commerce: The Invisible Hand of National Culture

Lei Song, Drexel University, USA
Srinivasan Swaminathan, Drexel University, USA
Rolph E. Anderson, Drexel University, USA

A lab experiment reveals significant differences between Chinese and U.S. consumers in their reactions to deviations between the actual service delivered and the service level promised. We find that Chinese consumers exhibit more tolerance to negative disconfirmation, and less reactions to positive disconfirmation than U.S. consumers.

43. Disentangling Two Types of Country of Origin: The Interactive Effects of Brand Origin and Product Origin on Persuasion

Sangwon Lee, Ball State University, USA
Xin He, University of Central Florida, USA

This research examines the joint effects of brand origin and product origin on persuasion. Through two experiments, we show that brand origin moderates the effect of product origin on consumer attitudes. Further, we demonstrate the mechanism underlying the interactive effects of brand origin and product origin through consumer involvement.

44. Exposure to Chicken-Abuse Images Has More Impact than that of Cows on Targeted Meat Consumption among a Sample of Japanese Consumers

Douglas Trelfa, Tamagawa University, Japan
Carolina Werle, Grenoble École de Management, France

This research examines denial and meat preferences among Japanese consumers exposed to disturbing images of animal abuse on factory farms. Findings suggest that consumers react differently to targeted animal products (chicken vs. beef) and may even increase consumption of targeted meat after viewing these images.

45. Gender Identity Politics and Consumption: Mobilizing Scottish Masculinities through Relational Consumption Practices

Wendy Hein, University of London, UK

Invigorated by recent debates about nationalism in consumer research, this paper presents findings from an ethnographic study that explored young Scottish male consumers. Depicting participants' mobilizations and manifestations of national identifications through gendered consumption, it seeks to contribute to an understanding of how gender relations interact with identity politics.

46. Constructing Ethnic Identity through Mealtime Rituals and Practices

Amandeep Takhar, University of Bedfordshire, UK
Pepukayi Chitakunye, University of KwaZulu-Natal, South Africa

This research examines the significance of mealtime rituals and food consumption practices in constructing individual ethnic identity. Using the third generation of the British Sikh community as the research context, I seek to understand how the acculturative and re-acculturative characteristics of mealtime rituals impact their individual identity projects.

47. Hey Y'all: Exporting Southern Food Culture, Implications for Brand Meaning and Local Consumer Identity

Catherine Coleman, Texas Christian University, USA

Through in-depth interviews and archival data, this research uses an interpretive case method at the intersection of food meaning, cultural identity, person branding and authenticity to examine the meanings ascribed to brand, community and self by local communities when their identities are exported globally through cultural brands.

48. The Making of an Everyday Concubine: Accounting for Simultaneous Love of Modernity and the Recently (Re-)Discovered Ottoman Heritage

Cagri Yalkin, Kadir Has University, Turkey

The aim of this paper is to explore how Turkish female consumers negotiate opposing ideologies in soap operas. Self-identified secular consumers are interviewed about the Ottoman-era based soap-opera *Muhtesem Yuzyil*. I identify empowered female characters as embodying the modernist ideal. Furthermore, consumers experience guilty pleasure when watching the sexualized Ottoman harem as it opposes the Islamist ideal.

49. Power over When: If Time is Human, Humans Act When They Want

Frank May, University of South Carolina, USA
Ashwani Monga, University of South Carolina, USA

In this research, we explore the humanness of time and demonstrate that consumers can exhibit a "power over when." Specifically, when time is perceived to be human, high-power (vs. low-power) individuals perceive a power over when to do something, and show little concern for the time dimension of intertemporal options.

50. Gifting Lightly When Feeling Powerful: Self-Construal, Power, and Gifting Anxiety

Fang Wan, University of Manitoba, Canada
Mehdi Akghari, University of Manitoba, Canada
Annika Sun, University of Manitoba, Canada
Yuwei Jiang, Hong Kong Polytechnic University, Hong Kong

Results of two experiments illustrate that high Interdependents experience more gifting anxiety than low Interdependents. The effect disappears when a feeling of higher psychological power is induced.

51. Will Purchasing from Groupon Make A Lonely Consumer Feel Empowered? Loneliness and Preference for Group-Buying Purchase Experiences

Hangeun Lee, Yonsei University, South Korea
Junyoung Lee, Yonsei University, South Korea
Kyoungmi Lee, Yonsei University, South Korea
Hakkyun Kim, Concordia University, Canada

We find that lonely consumers prefer group-buying experiences to individual-buying experiences because they obtain feelings of consumer empowerment by participating in group-buying. This research provides insights for understanding how consumers cope with their feelings of loneliness in the marketplace, and how they restore better self-views.

52. The Identifiable In-Group: Group Status Moderates the Identifiable Victim Effect

Alixandra Barasch, University of Pennsylvania, USA
Rod Duclos, HKUST, Hong Kong
Emma Edelman, University of Pennsylvania, USA

We investigate an important moderator of the identifiable victim effect: victim group status. While most studies focus on the out-group (e.g., victims of a foreign crisis), we build on previous work on identifiable vs. statistical victims by investigating the effectiveness of appeals that highlight in-group vs. out-group victims.

53. The Effect of Significant Others' Perceived States on the Evaluation of Relevant Products

Kiwan Park, Seoul National University, South Korea
Jiyoung Lee, Seoul National University, South Korea
Jerry Jisang Han, University of Texas-Austin, USA

The present research examines the effect of significant others' positive or negative states on the consumer's subsequent purchase intensions. We propose that individuals will exhibit compensatory attitudes toward certain products depending on their significant other's behavior, or on the situation prior to such a product assessment task.

54. Mark of Popularity or Distrust? The Role of "Peer Purchase Number" as a Cue Affecting Consumer Attitudes in the Web-Based Retail Context

Eun-Jung Lee, Kent State University, USA
Robert D. Jewell, Kent State University, USA

This study explores the role of peer purchase number (PPN) as a social cue affecting consumer attitudes online. In our experiment, increased PPN positively affected company/product evaluations, trust, and affirmation. Compared to the control condition where no PPN information was indicated, however, exposure of the small PPN negatively affected attitudes.

55. Network Coproduction: The Role of Self-Presentational Persona in Electronic Word-Of-Mouth

Shuling Liao, Yuan Ze University, Taiwan
Crystal Tzuying Lee, National Cheng-Chi University, Taiwan
Tzu Han Lin, Yuan Ze University, Taiwan

Consumers are regarded as active network co-producers to present their self-concepts though constructing eWOM. However, research that documents the link between self-presentational persona and eWOM is scant. We study show that consumers' self-presentational persona responds differently to their motives to post-eWOM.

56. Examining Consumer Response to Preferential Treatment Practices

Lan Xia, Bentley University, USA
Monika Kukar-Kinney, University of Richmond, USA

The practice of preferential treatment (i.e., treating and serving some customers better than other customers) is popular but involves both philosophical controversies and empirical inconsistencies. This research systematically examines characteristics of preferential treatment, its impacts on emotions and cognitions, and the underlying mechanisms of these effects.

57. Burger or Yogurt? The Effect of Private vs. Public Consumption Contexts on Indulgent Behavior

Shih-Chieh Chuang, National Chung Cheng University, Taiwan
Yin-Hui Cheng, National Taichung University of Education, Taiwan
Chien-Jung Huang, National Chung Cheng University, Taiwan
Yun Ken, National Yunlin University of Science and Technology, Taiwan

We conducted three studies and find that individuals tend to make choices other than those they favor privately when they anticipate that others will form impressions of them based on the decisions they make. Research findings support our basic prediction that people are more indulgent in private than in public.

58. Marketplace Metacognition in Consumer-to-Consumer Inferences: I Buy for Quality, You Buy for Status

Meghan Pierce, Pontificia Universidad Catolica de Chile, Chile
Kimberlee Weaver, VirginiaTech, USA
Kim Daniloski, University of Scranton, USA
Norbert Schwarz, University of Michigan, USA

Across three studies, participants identify quality reasons for their own and status reasons for others' purchases. These findings occur in recollected purchases (Study 1), when holding the products constant across condition, and when controlling for social desirability (Study 2). Consumers appear to be unaware of these consumer-to-consumer differences in metacognition (Study 3).

59. Dressed to Impress: When Images of Financial Success in Advertising Have an Inspirational vs. Detrimental Effect on Men

Abigail Schneider, University of Colorado, USA
Ethan Pew, Purdue University, USA
Susan Jung Grant, University of Colorado, USA

Although prior literature suggests that images of financial success in advertising are detrimental to men's self-esteem, the current paper posits a moderator of this condition: mating-motives. Specifically, we find that mate-seeking men desire to associate themselves with men who possess resources that aid in attracting members of the opposite sex.

60. Who Cares If It Is Deceptive, I Like It: The Effect of Social Exclusion on Advertising Deception

Hamed Aghakhani, University of Manitoba, Canada
Kelley J. Main, University of Manitoba, Canada

Research shows that advertising deception not only has a negative effect on subsequently encountered similar products and sources, but also has effects on people's attitudes towards advertising and marketing as an abstract concept. We show that social exclusion attenuates this carryover effect.

61. Speed and Social Connection

Melanie Thomas, University of Pennsylvania, USA
Cassie Mogilner, University of Pennsylvania, USA

This research examines the effect of speed on social connection. We examine how thinking about the benefits of time being slow, rather than the benefits of time being fast, increases desire for social connection and feelings of connectedness. We incorporate two different manipulations of speed and three measures of social connection.

62. Opening the Black Box: An Exploration of Consumer Production Influence on Marketplace Dynamics

Henri Weijo, Aalto University, Finland
Daiane Scaraboto, Pontificia Universidad Católica de Chile, Chile
Saara Könkkölä, Aalto University, Finland

Our study advances consumer researchers' understanding of consumer production. Through a meta-analysis of existing studies on consumers' value-creating activities, we identify three ways consumer production influences marketplace dynamics: through marketplace creation, actualization and reproduction of the marketplace, and marketplace destruction.

63. True Comeliness or Fake Beauty: Cosmetic Surgery as Mating Strategy

Sunyee Yoon, University of Wisconsin-Madison, USA
Nancy Wong, University of Wisconsin-Madison, USA

We explore the role of cosmetic surgery as a strategy to increase mating success from an evolutionary perspective. Cosmetic surgery is favored by females who are less sexually restricted and who possess stronger mating desires. However, men do not prefer women who have had cosmetic surgery because it does not improve reproductive values.

64. Classification of the Factors Influencing Ethical Consumer Choice: The Framework

Natalia Maehle, Institute for Research in Economics and Business Administration, Norway
Nina Iversen, Institute for Research in Economics and Business Administration, Norway
Leif Hem, Norwegian School of Economics, Norway

In the current study we explore the existing literature on ethical consumption and develop a framework classifying the main factors influencing ethical consumer choice. To our knowledge, this framework is the first one structuring the research in the field of ethical consumption and therefore represents an important theoretical contribution.

65. Whom to Trust? The Impact of Peer vs. Expert Opinions on Consumption Experiences

Travis Hancock, Brigham Young University, USA
Ryan Elder, Brigham Young University, USA

We demonstrate the differential impact of peer vs. expert reviews on pre-purchase attitudes and post-purchase consumption experience. We show that consumers use experts' opinions to a greater extent than peers', such that attitude change following a consumption experience is greater when consumers read peer (vs. expert) reviews.

66. The effect of Vertical Individualism on Status Consumption and Advertising Response

Michelle Nelson, University of Illinois at Urbana-Champaign, USA
Jing Zhang, San Jose State University, USA

Going beyond cultural differences in Individualism -Collectivism, we disentangle the Vertical (V) from Horizontal (H) aspects of Individualism (I) to illuminate its distinct effects in consumption and persuasion in three studies. We found that VI values affect consumers' brand consciousness, brand buying behavior, and their responses to status advertising appeals.

67. Emotional Intelligence, Giving, and Life Satisfaction: Some New Data and Conclusions

Rajani Ganesh Pillai, North Dakota State University, USA
Doug Rymph, North Dakota State University, USA
Sukumarakurup Krishnakumar, North Dakota State University, USA

In this paper we show that Emotional Intelligence (EI) may play a significant and unique role in the way people spend money on others (e.g., on gifts vs. donations). EI impacts the relationship between spending on others and life satisfaction differently, depending on whether individuals spend on gifts or donations.

68. It's All About Me: Effects on Product Samples for Self vs. Other

Chelsea Johnson, University of Illinois at Urbana-Champaign, USA
Brittany Duff, University of Illinois at Urbana-Champaign, USA

A promotional product sample high in incentive value may lead to general reward-seeking behavior. This study introduces the idea that reward seeking may be self-directed, with the effect driven by an increase in purchases for self. Implications for advertising and point-of-purchase incentives are discussed.

69. The Effect of Face Pressure on Chinese Consumer Decision-Making

Karthik Easwar, Ohio State University, USA
Robert Burnkrant, Ohio State University, USA

This research links two areas of research that suffer from minimal exploration, cross-cultural decision-making and face. We demonstrate that face is a crucial determinant of Chinese consumer behavior that explains behavior over and above the standard components of the TRA model.

70. Sense and Cents: Collective Consumer Sensemaking in an Online Investment Community

Andrew N. Smith, York University, Canada

Through an investigation of 241 blog posts, and all related comments in an online investment community, this study elaborates on the collective consumer sensemaking process. It finds that sensegiving plays an important role in shaping this process.

71. Consumer Creativity in Co-Creation: The Interaction between Default Product and Design Goal

Bo Chen, ESSEC Business School, France
Niek Althuizen, ESSEC Business School, France

Providing a default product in the co-creation process may influence the creativity of consumers' outcome, and this effect may be dependent on their design goal. This paper explores the interaction effect between the provided default product and the activated design goal on consumer creativity in co-creation.

72. Bidirectional Consumer Friends' Knowledge Calibration —Overestimated or Underestimated? A Two-Stage Model

Joicey Jie Wei, National University of Singapore, Singapore
Iris Hung, National University of Singapore, Singapore
Gita Johar, Columbia University, USA

The knowledge calibration process has been considered as a one-stage process in which people over-project their own self-knowledge to predict how much others know about them, leading to overestimation in friends' knowledge calibration. However, we suggest that the estimated accuracy should be a two-stage process.

73. What Drives Individual Purchase Decisions in a Network? A Consumer-Motivation Approach

Dongwoo Ko, University of Iowa, USA
Sanguk Jung, University of Auckland, New Zealand

Empirically, the center of the network has been regarded as a crucial component in marketing strategies; however, as the previous literature suggests, the center of network does not directly connect to revenue generation. This research pinpoints people who are more likely to follow others' opinions.

74. Assimilation and Contrast in Web Product Reviews: Devaluing the Recommendation of a Proficient but Dissimilar Reviewer

Michael Dorn, University of Bern, Switzerland
Claude Messner, University of Bern, Switzerland

Little is known about how the social information on the reviewer influences consumers' evaluation of the reviewed product. This experimental study applies the paradigm of social comparison and measures the product-evaluation. Contrasting the social information leads to a devaluation of the products recommended by a proficient but dissimilar reviewer.

75. A Typology of Crowdsourcing Participation Styles

Eric Martineau, Concordia University, Canada
Zeynep Arsel, Concordia University, Canada

What motivates individuals to participate in crowdsourcing, and what ends do they seek? We propose a typology of participation styles through a study of two prosumption communities: Threadless.com and Montreal Couture. We then provide guidelines for managers who wish to implement a crowdsourcing project.

76. Exploring Consumer Attitudes toward Social-Network Advertising

Cuauhtemoc Luna-Nevarez, New Mexico State University, USA
Jennifer Zarzosa, New Mexico State University, USA

Drawing upon the Theory of Reasoned Action, we develop a theoretical framework to explain the antecedents (perceived utility, attitude toward advertising, and advertisement intrusiveness) and consequences (intention to engage in online word-of-mouth and purchase intention) of social network advertising. A structural equation modeling analysis confirms the hypothesized causal relationships.

77. It's Not All About Coffee: A Netnography of the Starbucks Brand Page on Facebook

Heejin Lim, University of Tennessee, USA
Jewon Lyu, University of Tennessee, USA

This study aims to discover the nature and meanings of brand social networking on Facebook. A Netnography of the Starbucks Page on Facebook unveils a spatial meaning of the brand page, and the multifold meanings of the brand shared through the platform. Findings of this study support the postmodern consumption theory.

78. Changing Consumption Habits: Does Personalization Really Work?

Kirsikka Kaipainen, VTT Technical Research Centre, Finland
Brian Wansink, Cornell University, USA

Most dietary programs fail to produce sustainable behavior changes, since participants soon return to their old habits. Small changes based on simple behavioral heuristics have the best chance to be maintained. This study suggests that effectiveness of small habit changes is improved through personalization to circumstances and psychological needs.

79. Getting Lucky: When Loyalty Status Makes You Feel Lucky

Rebecca Walker Naylor, Ohio State University, USA
Kelly L. Haws, Texas A&M University, USA
Christopher Summers, Ohio State University, USA

Might loyalty status spillover into expectations about outcomes that should not be affected by membership (i.e. random events)? We suggest loyalty fosters a sense of deservingness that transfers to randomly determined outcomes, and propose that loyalty can lead consumers to feel lucky.

80. Feeling Lucky while Feeling Good: The Relative Impacts of Superstitious Beliefs and Affect on Consumer Judgment and Choice

Thomas Kramer, University of South Carolina, USA
Meredith David, University of South Carolina, USA

We examine the moderating role of superstitious beliefs on the established relationship between affect and preferences for a hedonic vs. utilitarian product. Two studies show that luck primes are more important than affect in influencing preferences, but they are less influential among consumers who have a high chronic belief-in-good-luck.

81. Shame on You! Motivating Consumer Behavior with Shame Appeals

Jennifer Jeffrey, University of Western Ontario, Canada
Juan Wang, University of Western Ontario, Canada
Dante M. Pirouz, University of Western Ontario, Canada
Matthew Thomson, University of Western Ontario, Canada

Social marketers use emotion-invoking appeals as a frequent persuasion technique but discount shame due to its association with avoidance behaviors and withdrawal. This research provides initial support that the intensity and self-focused nature of shame make it a helpful emotion to elicit in contexts aimed at changing a target's behavior.

82. Corporate Communications in Uncertain Times: Messages of Hope or Pride?

Anne Roggeveen, Babson College, USA
Anirban Mukhopadhyay, HKUST, Hong Kong
Dhruv Grewal, Babson College, USA

Hope and pride are two widely used positive emotions in corporate communications. Building on appraisal theory, four studies demonstrate that messages of pride result in more positive evaluations in situations of certainty, and messages of hope results in more positive evaluations in situations of uncertainty.

83. Affect and Consumer Behavior: A Meta-Analytic Review

Nancy M. Puccinelli, Oxford University, UK
Dhruv Grewal, Babson College, USA
Scott Motyka, Brandeis University, USA
Susan A. Andrzejewski, Franklin and Marshall College, USA

We report the results from a meta-analysis examining the influence of affect on evaluation and behavior, seeking to resolve discrepancies in findings by identifying mechanisms underlying affect-congruent vs. affect-incongruent outcomes (i.e., analytical bias and affect regulation). Conducted moderator analyses include involvement, transparency of affect manipulation, and social normative effects.

84. Hoarding and Consumer Anxiety: Understanding When Consumption Becomes Dysfunctional

Gail Leizerovici, University of Western Ontario, Canada
Dante M. Pirouz, University of Western Ontario, Canada
Samantha Cross, Iowa State University, USA

Hoarding is defined as the acquisition of and failure to discard large numbers of possessions and affects an estimated 6-15 million Americans. Our work shows that hoarding is related to OCD, anxiety and need for cognition. Future research will study what types of anxiety provoking events trigger hoarding.

85. All Kidding Aside: Humors Lowers Propensity to Remedy a Problem

A. Peter McGraw, University of Colorado, USA
Philip Fernbach, University of Colorado, USA
Julie Schiro, University of Colorado, USA

Although humor increases attention and liking, humorous appeals may lower people's propensity to remedy a problem because humor is associated with non-serious situations. Young adults viewed humorous and non-humorous PSAs that highlighted people's ignorance about birth control. We find the humorous PSA resulted in less search behavior for sexual health information.

86. Asymmetries in the Impact of Action and Inaction Regret: When and Why Do They Occur?

Atul Kulkarni, University of Missouri-Kansas City, USA
Rashmi Adaval, HKUST, Hong Kong

Through a set of three studies, we explore the conditions under which action vs. inaction regret may have an asymmetric effect on risk taking, and examines the underlying role of affective vs. cognitive drivers of the effect of regret on risk taking.

87. The Effect of Aging on Consumer Regret

Li Jiang, University of California Los Angeles, USA

This research investigates the moderating role of decision justifiability on age-related differences in the experience of regret. Older (vs. young) adults express more regret in response to a scenario in which a justifiable option is clearly defined, but not in the absence of a readily justifiable option.

88. Not Immediately Stupid: The Moderating Effects of Purchase Immediacy and the Mediating Effects of Regret on Self-Perceptions of Consumer Incompetence

Matthew Philp, Queen's University, Canada
Laurence Ashworth, Queen's University, Canada

Individuals feel like incompetent consumers after post-purchase discovery of a lower available price. This effect is attenuated when purchase immediacy is high, where the purchase was made out of immediate necessity. We present a model showing that consumer incompetence is moderated by purchase immediacy and mediated by regret.

89. Assessment of Heterogeneity of Compulsive Buyers Based on Affective States Preceding Buying Lapses

Sunghwan Yi, University of Guelph, Canada
Joowon Jung, Dongguk University, South Korea

We examine the heterogeneity of compulsive buyers based on the frequency of affective states preceding buying lapses. Contrary to the mood-repair view of compulsive buying, we identify two subtypes of compulsive buyers: one whose buying is mainly triggered by negative affect, and the other that is triggered by boredom.

90. Do Hedonic Benefits Always Create "Hedonic" Feeling? The Impact of Two Factors on Consumer's Response to Hedonic Rewards Design of Loyalty Program

Sidney Su Han, University of Guelph, Canada
Lefa Teng, University of Guelph, Canada
Yiqiu Wang, Northeastern University, China

Hedonic rewards do not always appeal to customers as marketers expect. Through two experiments, the authors propose that one scheme of loyalty program design (i.e. magnitude of rewards medium) and one consumer dispositional characteristic (i.e. self- regulatory concern) can influence consumers' affective and cognitive responses to the hedonic benefits of a loyalty program.

91. Compulsive Buyers Show an Attentional Bias in Shopping Situations

Oliver B. Büttner, University of Vienna, Austria
Matthew Paul, University of Vienna, Austria
Arnd Florack, University of Vienna, Austria
Helmut Leder, University of Vienna, Austria
Anna Maria Schulz, University of Vienna, Austria

This research used eye tracking to examine attentional processes that underlie compulsive buying. The results demonstrate an attentional bias. That is, compulsive (vs. noncompulsive) buyers are more likely to get distracted by products unrelated to their goal. The effect emerges only when the task is framed as a shopping situation.

92. Physical Temperature Effects on Consumer Decision Making

Tingting Wang, HKUST, Hong Kong
Rongrong Zhou, HKUST, Hong Kong

The present research explores the influence of temperature experiences on consumers' decision-making. The experiments reveal that physical coldness vs. hotness enhances consumers' tendency to buy, but decreases the inclination to sell products. These effects are moderated by the strength of belief in the association between temperature and abundance.

93. "It's Cold in Here. I Need a Bowl of Soup to Warm Me Up!" The Effects of Incidental Sensory Frames on Conflicting Sensory Inputs

Sydney Chinchanachokchai, University of Illinois at Urbana-Champaign, USA
Rashmi Adaval, HKUST, Hong Kong

Two studies show that sensory frames activate semantic concepts applied to judgment. However, when the attention is drawn to incidental cues, it triggers a motivation to think of the desirability of the focal object. The desirability increases only when there is a lack of it in the salient sensory frame.

94. "Size Matters!" The Effect of Floor Tile Size on Consumer Behavior in a Retail Environment

Nico Heuvinck, Ghent University and University College Ghent, Belgium
Iris Vermeir, Ghent University and University College Ghent, Belgium
Simon Quaschning, Ghent University and University College Ghent, Belgium

In this study, we show that although customers do not have the feeling of walking faster in small-tile aisles, they actually spent less time walking along small-tile aisles compared to big-tile/no-tile aisles, leading to lower brand recall and brand recognition.

95. Will People Express More or Less Conformity When They Feel Warm? The Moderating Role of Self-Construal

Xun (Irene) Huang, Chinese University of Hong Kong, Hong Kong
Meng Zhang, Chinese University of Hong Kong, Hong Kong
Michael K. Hui, Chinese University of Hong Kong, Hong Kong
Robert S. Wyer, Chinese University of Hong Kong, Hong Kong

We propose that high ambient temperature can either increase or decrease consumers' conformity tendency, depending on people's default level of perceived social closeness between self and others. Specifically, independent people conform more, and interdependent people conform less in the warm condition.

96. I Can Feel Your Pain: The Influences of Haptic Input on Donation Amount

Chun-Ming Yang, Ming Chuan University, Taiwan
Rong-Da Liang, National Kaohsiung University of Hospitality and Tourism, Taiwan

Three experiments test the influences of touch element on donation amount. The results showed that touching a victim's photo leads to higher donation amount, perceived sympathy mediates this effect, and seeing a victim's face is not a necessary condition, and this effect is stronger for high-NFT individuals.

97. Chi Ku: Bitter Taste Preferences and Responses to Unpleasant Experiences

Chun-Ming Yang, Ming Chuan University, Taiwan

"Eating bitterness" is a common Chinese metaphor but has received limited research attention. Five studies test the metaphorical link between bitter taste preference and responses to unpleasant experiences. Based on the embodied cognition literature, this research finds that individuals who prefer bitter taste reported higher distress tolerance and have different responses to unpleasant experiences.

98. Detaching the Ties of Ownership: The Effects of Hand Washing on the Exchange of Endowed Products

Arnd Florack, University of Vienna, Austria
Janet Kleber, University of Vienna, Austria
Romy Busch, University of Vienna, Austria
David Stoehr, University of Vienna, Austria

Research on the endowment effect shows owners usually exhibit more positive evaluations and a stronger preference for an object than non-owners. In three studies, we demonstrate that the action of hand washing can reduce these effects of endowment.

99. The Magic Touch: Psychological Drivers of the Discrepancy Between Traditional and Touchscreen Equipment

Ying Zhu, The University of British Columbia, Canada
Jeffrey Meyer, Bowling Green State University, USA

The research aims to advance knowledge in the touch literature to enable academic theory to keep up with the new technology. It builds on the literature of tactile functions and emotion, and incorporates new technology phenomena to predict consumer behavior on two devices: traditional and touchscreen equipment.

100. The Effect of Tangibility on Desire

Katrien Meert, Ghent University, Belgium
Mario Pandelaere, Ghent University, Belgium

This paper investigates the effect of tangibility on desire. Touching a product might increase product evaluations; however, consumers view items as appealing when they have to overcome obstacles to obtain them. Hence, we investigate whether displaying a product in a way that it cannot be touched might enhance desire.

101. Visceral Vigor: The Effects of Disgust on Goal Pursuit

Sachin Banker, MIT, USA
Joshua Ackerman, MIT, USA

Visceral states such as hunger, thirst, and sexual arousal are commonly shown to induce impulsive behaviors. We consider whether visceral states can instead result in long-term goal directed behavior. We present evidence that suggests induced-disgust states promote the pursuit of previously active goals.

102. Do We Judge a Book by its Cover? Unwrapping the Role of Visually-Appealing Packaging in Product Evaluation

Tanuka Ghoshal, Indian School of Business, India
Peter Boatwright, Carnegie Mellon University, USA
Jonathan Cagan, Carnegie Mellon University, USA

We find that aesthetically appealing packaging (AAP) positively impacts product attitudes and valuations for hedonic products but not for utilitarian products. We propose that evaluating a hedonic (utilitarian) product puts consumers in a promotion (prevention) orientation, making them more (less) likely to place weight on attractiveness factors like AAP.

103. Implied Sensory Experiences in Product Designs Makes People Think Global

Christophe Labyt, Ghent University, Belgium
Mario Pandelaere, Ghent University, Belgium

This paper examines the influence of exposure to products with an implied sensory design on a person's cognitive processing mode. Two studies indicate that exposure to sensory design triggers global processing. This finding is particularly true for participants who attach greater value than average to a product's appearance.

104. We're Gonna Need a Bigger Spoon: Spoon Size Effects on Product Perception

Aner Tal, Cornell University, USA
Brian Wansink, Cornell University, USA

Spoon size has been shown to lead to increased consumption. The current study examines whether this may be due to a distortion of product quantity where people see less food when holding a bigger spoon. We discuss potential explanations for this phenomenon.

105. The Effects of Physical Constraints on Creativity

Ke (Christy) Tu, University of Alberta, Canada
Jennifer A. Argo, University of Alberta, Canada

We investigate the effects of physical constraints on creativity in this paper. The results from one study show that when wearing a tight hat (vs. a loose hat), males are more creative, while females are less creative. We will test the theoretical framework in a serious of follow-up studies.

106. Multi-sensory Perception in Servicescapes: A Typology and Avenues for Future Research

Bernd Frederik Reitsamer, University of Innsbruck, Austria
Nicola Stokburger-Sauer, University of Innsbruck, Austria

The aim of this paper is to provide a conceptual framework that classifies existing research on environmental stimulus processing in management and marketing into four major dimensions. We highlight ample opportunities for further research in the multi-sensory realm.

107. The Sweet Taste of Charity: Cause Branding Affects Product Experience

Alyssa Niman, Cornell University, USA
Aner Tal, Cornell University, USA

Cause-branding is a wide and spreading marketing strategy. We demonstrate that part of the efficacy of cause-branding may lie in its alteration of product experience: products that do good taste good. We also explore possible underlying mechanisms such as conceptual consumption, the "halo" effect, and evolutionary psychology.

108. The Perils of an Expansive Posture: The Effect of Everyday, Incidental Posture on Stealing, Cheating and Parking Violations

Andy Yap, Columbia University, USA
Abbie Wazlawek, Columbia University, USA
Brian Lucas, Northwestern University, USA
Amy Cuddy, Harvard Business School, USA
Dana Carney, University of California Berkeley, USA

Three studies test the hypothesis that expansive postures lead to unethicality. A field experiment demonstrates that expansive postures induce stealing. Experiment 2 finds that incidentally expanded postures (e.g. forced upon by one's workspace) increase cheating. A third observational study finds that vehicles with larger cockpit-sizes are more likely to violate parking laws.

109. Hormones and Prosocial Behavior: The Influence of the Menstrual Cycle on Gift-Giving Propensity

Eric Stenstrom, Concordia University, Canada
Gad Saad, Concordia University, Canada

Can the menstrual cycle influence not only what women buy, but also for whom? Utilizing a 35-day panel study, we find that women allocate significantly more money towards gift-giving during the luteal phase than during the fertile phase. Our findings suggest that women's affiliative goals fluctuate across the menstrual cycle.

110. What Are Consumers Afraid Of? Perceived Risk toward Environmentally Sustainable Consumption

Jiyun Kang, Texas State University, USA
Sang-Hoon Kim, Seoul National University, South Korea

In this research, we investigate perceived risk in consumers' decision making specifically related to environmentally sustainable products, considering the multi-dimensional nature of perceived risk. This research provides marketers with implications to promote the adoption of socially-desirable products and further enables the broader diffusion of such products in the marketplace.

111. Sustainable Luxury: Oxymoron or Pleonasm? How Scarcity and Ephemerality Affect Consumers' Perceptions of Fit between Luxury and Sustainability

Catherine Janssen, Université Catholique de Louvain, Belgium
Joëlle Vanhamme, EDHEC Business School, France
Adam Lindgreen, University of Cardiff, UK
Cécile Lefebvre, IESEG School of Management, France

Sustainability may be key to luxury. Through a field experiment, we investigate the influence of two defining characteristics of luxury products—scarcity and ephemerality—on the perceived fit between luxury and sustainability, as well as how this perceived fit affects consumers' attitudes toward luxury products.

112. Born Out There: The Discursive Creation of Harmony between Humans and Nature

Joachim Scholz, Queen's University, Canada
Jay M. Handelman, Queen's University, Canada

This paper analyzes how the myth of living in harmony with nature is discursively constructed via the representation of nature in ads. Differentiating between Arcadian and Dynamic images of nature, we explore the complexities of the harmony myth, and how this myth relates to divergent meanings of "sustainable consumption."

113. Doing Good While Looking Good: Consumer Perceptions of Sustainability in the Fashion Industry

Rishtee Batra, Indian School of Business, India
Tonya Boone, College of William and Mary, USA

The present study uses the ZMET technique to examine consumers' general perceptions about sustainably manufactured products and also focuses more specifically on consumer perceptions of sustainably manufactured fashion items.

114. The Greening of Consumers: An Assimilation-Contrast Perspective for Product Sustainability Labeling

Yoon-Na Cho, University of Arkansas, USA
Scot Burton, University of Arkansas, USA

Despite an increase in consumers' interest in sustainable products, few studies focus on disclosures of sustainability levels for consumer packaged goods. We find that the type and amount of sustainability information disclosed interacts with the sustainability levels in influencing product evaluations.

115. Going Green, Going Feminism: Stereotype about Green Consumption and Social General Role

Yunhui Huang, Nanjing University, China
Echo Wen Wan, University of Hong Kong, Hong Kong

Green consumption is perceived to be related to the feminine gender role both implicitly (Study 1, through Implicit Association Test) and explicitly (Study 2). And engaging in green consumption will improve the judgment about the social status of male consumers but not for female consumers (Study 3).

116. Consumer Emotional Intelligence: Exploring Shades of Green and Grey

Sukumarakurup Krishnakumar, North Dakota State University, USA
Sonakshi Garg, North Dakota State University, USA
Christopher Neck, Arizona State University, USA

The role of consumer emotional intelligence (EI), or the ability to deal with emotions, has been much ignored in ethical and green consumer behaviors. We study the associations between EI, Machiavellianism, and ethical and recycling beliefs. Findings indicate that EI predicts ethical and environmental beliefs positively, even after controlling for Machiavellianism.

117. The Moderating Role of Situational Consumer Skepticism towards Sustainability Claims in the Effectiveness of Credibility Signals

Bonnie Simpson, University of Calgary, Canada
Scott Radford, University of Calgary, Canada
Mehdi Mourali, University of Calgary, Canada

This research explores boundary conditions of credibility signals in skeptical environments. The impact of situational skepticism is examined on the credibility of information source and message origin. We show that when the message originates internally, situational skepticism moderates source credibility and attitude certainty, resulting in less certainty in product attitudes.

118. The Moderating Role of Perceived Consumer Effectiveness and Consumer Involvement on the Effect of Message-Framing on Intention to Purchase Organic Food Products

Courtney Briggs, Purdue University, USA
Sejin Ha, Purdue University, USA
Richard Feinberg, Purdue University, USA

This study examines the effects of different label-message formats (positively- vs. negatively-framed message) on intention to purchase organic food, and the influence of two individual-difference moderators (involvement and perceived consumer effectiveness) on the performance. Using a Web-based experimental method, hierarchical moderated regression analyses confirmed the hypotheses.

119. From General vs. From Specific: Effects of Overestimating Future Engagement in General vs. Specific Green Behavior on Immediate Within-Domain and Across-Domain Green Behaviors

Kiju Jung, University of Illinois at Urbana-Champaign, USA
Dolores Albarracin, University of Pennsylvania, USA
Madhu Viswanathan, University of Illinois at Urbana-Champaign, USA

In two experiments, we find that consumers are more likely to immediately engage in various green behaviors after they are asked to engage in a general green behavior (green product purchase) in the distant future (vs. tomorrow). However, this is not case if they are requested to engage in a specific green behavior (e.g., compact fluorescent lamp purchase).

120. Mitigating Climate Change: The Role of Reasoning Errors, Ecological Knowledge, and Moral Positions

Christian Weibel, University of Bern, Switzerland
Ralph Hertwig, University of Basel, Switzerland
Sidonia Widmer, University of Basel, Switzerland

To explain inter-individual differences in pro-environmental behavior, we pitted the following predictors against each other: reasoning errors, environmental knowledge, and moral positions. We find little evidence that reasoning errors or environmental knowledge is strongly related to environmentally unfriendly behavior. Moral positions were far more predictive of pro-environmental behavior.

121. In the Name of Environmental Friendliness: Effects on Attitudes toward the Service

Ronnie (Chuang Rang) Gao, Drexel University, USA
Rajneesh Suri, Drexel University, USA

Environmental friendliness does not always offer consumers immediate benefits. For instance, many hotels no longer replace guest-bed linens daily. We empirically demonstrate that consumers high in environmental concern react more favorably towards reduced services, and more favorably when provided with a choice. We also found no effects when such consumers were merely exposed to environmental messages.

122. The Restorative Nature of Nature: Improving Consumer Decision Making

Merrie Brucks, University of Arizona, USA
Kevin Newman, University of Arizona, USA
Caitlin Nitta, University of Arizona, USA

This study provides evidence that natural environments improve self-regulation abilities, translating into healthier food choices and fewer items ordered. Given statistics related to the overconsumption of food, this research holds public policy implications affecting millions of Americans and provides them with a self-regulation resource that is free, safe, and plentiful - nature.

123. Risky Decisions: Citing Sources in Print Advertisement Claims

Catherine Armstrong Soule, University of Oregon, USA
Leslie Koppenhafer, University of Oregon, USA

The research investigates whether source citation of print advertisement claims can be beneficial to consumers by providing information that aids in accurate deception detection. Studies in different risk domains find the type and level of risk leads to differential processing of the presence or absence of advertising claim source information.

124. "Is it Risky or Beneficial?" Analysis of Supplement-Type and Dosage Preferences in Terms of Risk-Benefit Tradeoffs and Epistemological Beliefs

Zoe Rogers, Baruch College/CUNY USA
Stephen J. Gould, Baruch College/CUNY, USA

This research considers the effect of risk and benefit assessments on evaluations of health supplements. Familiar supplements lead to more thoughts about benefits and more positive evaluations, while unfamiliar supplements lead to more thoughts about risks and less positive evaluations. Epistemic beliefs are shown to underpin these assessments.

125. Personal Death-Thought Accessibility: A Mediating Mechanism between Self-Esteem and Risky Consumer Behaviors?

Sandor Czellar, University of Lausanne, Switzerland
Charles Lebar, HEC Paris, France
Christian Martin, University of Lausanne, Switzerland
Russell H. Fazio, Ohio State University, USA

Research investigating the relationship between self-esteem and mortality salience provides initial evidence that self-threats increase accessibility of death-related thoughts. We focus on the nature of those thoughts and investigate whether self-threats enhance accessibility of thoughts related to one's own death or death in general, bearing important implications for marketing communications.

126. Optimizing Targeting Effectiveness: The Reversed U-Shape Relationship between Target Market and Consumer Attitude

Shuoyang Zhang, Colorado State University, USA
Ishani Banerji, Indiana University, USA
Eliot Smith, Indiana University, USA

In the current research we propose a reversed U-shape effect of targeting strategy. Our findings show that compared with mass marketing and personal targeting, optimal consumer attitude is achieved when product recommendations are provided to a small group of similar people. This implies that extreme personalization can actually backfire.

127. Vice vs. Virtue: How Compromise Phantom Alternatives Can Increase Indulgence

Yuanyuan Liu, ESSEC Business School, France
Timothy B. Heath, HEC Paris, France
Ayse Önçüler, ESSEC Business School, France

The current study proposes that a compromise-but-unavailable "phantom" alternative can increase indulgence in vices. Three experiments examine this effect as well as the mediating roles of anticipatory guilt/regret and the moderating role of preference strength.

128. Scare an Optimist and Reassure a Pessimist: Message Frames Adjusted to Individual Coping Styles Enhance Breast Cancer Screening Participation

Laure Weckx, Katholieke University Leuven, Belgium
Anouk Festjens, Katholieke University Leuven, Belgium
Sabrina Bruyneel, Katholieke University Leuven, Belgium

We study (1) the relationship between individual coping styles and breast-cancer screening participation, and (2) the impact of message frames adjusted to these coping styles on participation intentions. Women who are optimistic about the outcome of the screening benefit from scaring invitations, whereas anxious women benefit from reassuring invitations.

129. To Trade or Not? Removing Trading Motivation Eliminates the Endowment Effect

Laurence Ashworth, Queens University, Canada
Lindsay McShane, Queens University, Canada
Tiffany Vu, Queens University, Canada

The current work suggests that owner/non-owner discrepancies can exist because consumers typically are required to specify prices at which they would trade. Consequently, we predict that owners/non-owners likely set prices sufficiently above/below perceived worth, to motivate trade. When ownership and trading are separated we find that the endowment effect disappears.

130. Why Preference Stability of Certain Product Attributes are More Than Others: Disaggregating Stability (Instability) into Core and Supplementary Attributes

Fangzhou Xu, University of Guelph, Canada
Juan Wang, Western University, Canada
Towhidul Ialam, University of Guelph, Canada

To reconcile the debate between stable and constructed preferences, we suggest an alternative view of decomposing product preference into attribute preference. Specifically, we argue that consumer preferences for core attributes of a product should be largely stable across time, while supplementary attributes should be largely unstable.

131. The Effect of the Change-Matching Heuristic on Consumer Purchase Decision Making

Yin-Hui Cheng, National Taichung University of Education, Taiwan
Chia-Jung Chang, National Chung Cheng University, Taiwan
Shih-Chieh Chuang, National Chung Cheng University, Taiwan
Che-Hung Lin, Cheng Shiu University, Taiwan

Based on the perspective of processing fluency, this study demonstrates the "change-matching heuristic," whereby people select a choice option that matches the amount of change in their wallets with the price of a product. We find that the compromise effect and the attraction effect will weaken the influence of the change-matching heuristic.

132. The Effects of Consumption Goals and Assortment on Cross-Price Sensitivity

Kiwan Park, Seoul National University, South Korea
Joonkyung Kim, Seoul National University, South Korea

We propose that activating a consumption goal makes people more sensitive to the price discounts of competing products in the same goal-derived category as the target product. Also, we propose that when one of two products is on sale, including a third option that highlights the similarity of the first two options would make people more sensitive to the price discount.

133. The Effect of Price Discounts and Quantity Restrictions on Consumption Enjoyment

Zhenfeng Ma, Wilfrid Laurier University, Canada
Guanfu Wang, University of International Business and Economics, China

Two experimental studies investigate the joint effect of price discounts and quantity restriction on consumption enjoyment. Findings suggest that price promotion can either enhance or dampen consumption enjoyment of the promoted product, depending on the form of quantity restriction (e.g., quantity ceiling vs. quantity flooring).

134. Letting Go of Meaningful Goods: How the Voluntary vs. Involuntary Nature of Disposition Impacts Seller Pricing

Kapitan Sommer, University of Texas at San Antonio, USA
David H. Silvera, University of Texas at San Antonio, USA

In this research, we show that voluntary sellers demand non-significantly different prices than buyers. However, involuntary sellers of prized goods, such as those selling in the face of foreclosure, layoff, divorce or death, demand higher prices than both involuntary sellers of non-prized goods and voluntary sellers of prized goods.

135. The Effects of Stackable Discounts on Consumers' Retail Price Image Perception

Shan Feng, William Paterson University, USA
Jane Cai, Independent, USA

This paper examines the impact of stackable discounts on retailers' price image. We compare stackable discounts to a single discount format in terms of the value perceived by consumers, and find that stackable discounts are superior in creating a more favorable retail image.

136. Presentation of Comparative Prices: Role of Working Memory

Rajneesh Suri, Drexel University, USA
Shan Feng, William Patterson University, USA
Rajesh Chandrashekran, Farleigh Dickinson University, USA

Comparative price promotions produce favorable consumer value perceptions and stimulate sales. This research suggests that the mental effort required when deciding about a price affects perceptions of discounts presented in vertical and horizontal formats. Three studies show that constraints on working memory resources favors computation of vertically vs. horizontally presented prices.

137. Virtual Endowment: How Location and Duration of Virtual Ownership Influence Valuation

Elisa K. Chan, Cornell University, USA
Aner Tal, Cornell University, USA

We examine the endowment theory in an online context and with virtual ownership. We find that simply placing an online product on a webpage vs. in an online shopping cart triggers a different willingness to pay. Our study suggests that general and personal virtual shopping carts elicit different perceived values.

138. The Effects of Scarcity Claims on Consumers' Willingness to Pay

Doreen Pick, Freie Universität, Germany
Peter Kenning, Zeppelin Universität, Germany
Felix Eggers, Zeppelin Universität, Germany

According to scarcity theory, time-limited offers can have positive effects on consumers' purchase intentions. We examine the impact of several scarcity claims on consumers' willingness to pay. Our results show mixed findings regarding different claims and product categories, which provides a basis for further investigation.

139. Don't Think Twice: The Effects of Decision Confidence on the Experienced Utility of Incidental Rewards

Aaron Snyder, Stanford University, USA
Maya Shankar, Stanford University, USA
Baba Shiv, Stanford University, USA

Research has shown that confidence in one's choice can increase satisfaction with the chosen outcome. We extend these findings to show that decision confidence can have downstream consequences on perceptions of incidentally-acquired rewards as well.

140. Your Cheating Heart: The Negative Impact of Sales Promotions on Loyalty

Olga (Olya) Bullard, University of Manitoba, Canada
Kelley J. Main, University of Manitoba, Canada
Jennifer J. Argo, University of Alberta, Canada

We examine the impact of consumers' use of sales promotions on service providers. Study1 reveals that service providers see consumers who redeem coupons and free gifts/service as disloyal. Study 2 identifies two moderators: size of sales promotion and existence of the relationship between consumer and service provider.

141. My Brand and I, and Others between Us: The Influence of Interpersonal Relationships on Consumer-Brand Relationships

Marina Carnevale, Fordham University, USA
Lauren G. Block, Baruch College/CUNY, USA

Despite their contextual nature, consumer-brand relationships are assumed to be independent of external interpersonal relationships (e.g., significant others). Across three studies, we show that when a product symbolizes an external relationship (e.g., it was a gift), changes in that relationship may impact consumers' feelings of self-brand connection and consequently their brand evaluations.

142. Revelatory Experiences: The Brand Backstory and its Impact on Consumers' Experience of Brand Narratives

Vanisha Narsey, University of Auckland, New Zealand
Cristel Russell, University of Auckland, New Zealand
Hope Jensen Schau, University of Arizona, USA

The "making-of" or "behind the scenes" activities of media brands are increasingly made available to consumers, often revealing the artifices of a brand. We explore consumers' experience of the brand backstory and the impact this experience has on personal brand narratives.

143. Who is the Brand Creator? The Effect of Different Brand Biographies on the Perception of Brand Personality

Marc Linzmajer, Zeppelin University, Germany
Jana Hauck, Zeppelin University, Germany
Marco Hubert, Zeppelin University, Germany
Reinhard Prügl, Zeppelin University, Germany

Based on the relationship model, this paper investigates the role of different brand biographies and hypothesizes that they lead to different consumer perceptions of brand personality. The results of our exploratory experimental study show there are significant differences between both brand creators and the perception of brand personality dimensions.

144. Consumer Persuasion Knowledge in Non-Conventional Marketplaces: The Case of Branded Prescription Drugs

Marjorie Delbaere, University of Saskatchewan, Canada
Mei-Ling Wei, Saint Mary's University, Canada

We argue that consumers are beginning to recognize the physician-prescribing situation as a potential persuasion attempt and that the onslaught of Direct-to-Consumer (DTC) advertising has brought about this change in meaning. We investigate the prescribing situation as a mixed-motive situation with high levels of ambiguity; in other words, as persuasion within a non-persuasion environment.

145. The Magic of Numbers and Letters in Alphanumeric Brand Names

Selcan Kara, University of Connecticut, USA
Kunter Gunasti, University of Connecticut, USA

This research explores the effect of number and letter changes in alphanumeric brand names (ABs) on consumers' reactions to brand extensions. Based on two experiments, we show that processing of number vs. letter changes in ABs lead to a variance in the perceived differences between the new and existing brands.

146. What is Brand Authenticity? An Exploration of the Concept

Amélie Guèvremont, Concordia University, Canada
Bianca Grohmann, Concordia University, Canada

This research focuses on understanding the concept of brand authenticity from a consumer perspective, a topic characterized by a lack of consensus in the literature. Following fifteen individual interviews, we identify eight common characteristics of authentic brands, revealing that some form of objectivity is found in consumers' authenticity perceptions.

147. Brand Happiness: Scale Development and Validation

Sunmyoung Cho, Yonsei University, South Korea
Ae-Ran Koh, Yonsei University, South Korea

This study develops a scale to measure the brand happiness construct and demonstrates that it captures consumers' feelings of happiness with their selves and lives as their happiness is related to brands. Through four different phases, we establish internal and nomological validity and explore various predictions.

148. Primacy of Acculturation Categories over Demographic Variables as Differentiators of Brand Preference

Rohini Vijaygopal, University of Bedfordshire, UK
Sally Dibb, Open University, UK
Maureen Meadows, Open University, UK

The literature highlights the importance of demographic variables and acculturation categories in consumer behavior involving ethnic minorities. This paper considers the primary differentiators of consumer behavior among British Indians by examining the relationships between acculturation categories, demographic variables and preferences for a range of ethnic and host brands.

149. Why Are Consumers Fans of Counterfeit Branded Products? Consumers' Psychological Motivations in Counterfeit Consumption

Xuemei Bian, University of Nottingham, UK
Natalia Yannopoulou, University of Newcastle, UK
Kai-Yu Wang, University of Brock, Canada
Shu Liu, University of Nottingham, UK

This research examines the psychological motivations of different consumer categories when counterfeits are consumed, while considering different quality levels of such products. Our findings reveal consumers' enjoyment during the shopping experience and satisfaction of securing a good deal as the main psychological motivations of such purchases. We offer guidelines to practitioners.

150. Is Social Responsibility Beneficial for Private-Label Brands?

Maryam Tofighi, Concordia University, Canada
H. Onur. Bodur, Concordia University, Canada

Integrating two research streams of corporate social responsibility in marketing and retail branding, this paper suggests that social responsibility initiatives are more beneficial for both national (or manufacturer) brands and high-quality private-label brands (i.e., brands owned, controlled and sold exclusively by a retailer), whereas social responsibility initiatives are detrimental for low-quality private-label brands.

151. The Impact of Luxury Brand-Retailer Co-Branding Strategy on Consumers' Evaluation of Luxury Brand Image: The Case of the U.S. vs. Taiwan

Shih-Ching Wang, Temple University, USA
Primidya K. Soesilo, Temple University, USA
Dan Zhang, City University of New York, USA
C. Anthony Di Benedetto, Temple University, USA

This study investigates whether co-branding of luxury brands and retailers negatively affects attitudes toward the luxury brands, and whether solutions can mitigate the negative effect. We empirically test our hypotheses using samples of consumers from Taiwan and the U.S.

152. My Brand and I: The Influence of Personal Pronouns on Brand Name Preference

Nicole Palermo, Fordham University, USA
Luke Kachersky, Fordham University, USA

In recent years, brand names that include the personal pronouns "I" and "my" have established a unique prevalence in consumer culture. The present research examines if, how, and under which circumstances the usage of "I" and "my" in brand names influences brand perceptions.

153. The Influence of Logo Design Elements on Perceptions of Brand Personality

Aditi Bajaj, Georgia Tech, USA
Samuel Bond, Georgia Tech, USA

Addressing a void in research on logos in consumer behavior, our research focuses on the connections between logo design elements and brand personality inferences. Basing our ideas in literature on branding and design, we suggest that specific logo design elements can be utilized to convey specific brand personality traits.

154. The Impact of Phonetic Symbolism on Stock Performance: Stocks with Stop-Consonant Ticker Symbols Perform Better Than Stocks with Fricative-Consonant Ticker Symbols during First Year of Trading

L.J. Shrum, University of Texas at San Antonio, USA
Tina M. Lowrey, University of Texas at San Antonio, USA
Sarah Roche, University of Texas at San Antonio, USA

The current research extends the notion of phonetic symbolism to stock performance. Because stop (vs. fricative) consonants and back (vs. front) vowels are associated with larger and stronger concepts, we expected that tickers with stop consonants would outperform those with fricatives, and so too would back vs. front vowel tickers. The hypotheses were supported for consonant effects but not vowel effects.

155. Phonetic Symbolism and Children's Brand Name and Brand Logo Preference

Stacey Baxter, University of Newcastle, Australia
Tina M. Lowrey, University of Texas at San Antonio, USA
Min Liu, University of Texas at San Antonio, USA

Phonemes can provide a cue for brand attributes with consumers preferring congruency between a brand's name-logo and attributes. However, because children do not possess adult-level language skills, they may not attach similar meaning to phonemes. In three experiments, we examine the meanings children draw from phonemes and the implications for branding.

156. Should Firms Apologize After a Crisis? The Moderating Role of Negative Publicity

Zack Mendenhall, McGill University, Canada
Ashesh Mukherjee, McGill University, Canada

Firms often apologize to consumers after product crises. Prior work suggests apologies improve customers' attitudes towards the firm. The present research shows apologies only work when negative publicity surrounding the crisis is low. When negative publicity is high, firm apologies do not improve attitude towards the firm.

157. Does Identifying Ambushers as Non-Sponsors Help or Hurt Legitimate Sponsors? Memory and Attitudinal Consequences

Clinton S. Weeks, Queensland University of Technology, Australia

Two experiments examine outcomes for sponsor and ambusher brands within sponsorship settings. It is demonstrated that although making consumers aware of the presence of ambusher brands can reduce subsequent event recall to competitor cues, recall to sponsor cues can also suffer. Attitudinal effects are also considered.

158. The Bad Side of Good: When More Experience Hurts Brands and Marketplace Agents

Jungim Mun, State University of New York Buffalo, USA
Charles Lindsey, State University of New York Buffalo, USA
Mike Wiles, Arizona State University, USA

Our framework asserts that for an omission error, observers penalize experienced brands/agents (in the form of decreased trust perceptions) more severely than inexperienced brands/agents. The mechanism responsible for this effect is that such errors are more likely to be viewed as intentional attempts to deceive when committed by experienced brands/agents.

159. Hot Brands, Hot Cognition: The Effects of Incumbency and Negative Advertising on Brand Preference and Choice—A Longitudinal Field Experiment

Joan Phillips, Loyola University Chicago, USA
Joel Urbany, University of Notre Dame, USA

The World Cup and the battle between Nike and Adidas to secure leadership of the world soccer market presented an opportunity to examine the impact of negative advertising in a natural setting, to identify the conditions under which an attack-brand might use negative advertising to capture leadership from the incumbent-brand.

160. The Company or the Crowd? The Impact of Customer-Led Service Recovery on Satisfaction

Lan Jiang, University of Oregon, USA
Matt O'Hern, University of Oregon, USA
Sara Bahnson, University of Oregon, USA

This research explores the impact of identity on service recovery satisfaction. Study 1 shows that when recovery fails, consumers prefer customer-provided solutions. Community connectedness mediates this effect. Study 2 shows that consumers' pursuit of individualistic goals attenuates this effect. Study 3 proposes that increasing participants' effort mitigates the community- connectedness effect.

161. Don't Care about Service Recovery—Inertia Effects Buffer the Impact of Complaint Satisfaction

Christian Brock, Zeppelin University, Germany
Markus Blut, University of Dortmund, Germany
Heiner Evanschitzky, Aston University, UK
Peter Kenning, Zeppelin University, Germany
Marco Hubert, Zeppelin University, Germany

Service recovery has received considerable attention in the marketing literature. The impact on purchase behavior has been largely neglected. However, intentions and purchase behavior are not necessarily highly correlated. We contribute to research analyzing service recovery effects on purchase behavior after recovery, as well as research assessing the role of inertia during service recovery.

162. Doing Worse and Feeling Better: Why Low Performance Can Increase Satisfaction

Dilney Goncalves, IE Business School, Spain
Antonios Stamatogiannakis, IE Business School, Spain
Jonathan Luffarelli, IE Business School, Spain

When average performance is low, high social-comparison orientation individuals infer that the task at hand is difficult. Subsequently, if relative performance is constant, they are more satisfied with a lower (vs. a higher) individual performance level, because they think that they outperformed more people in a difficult (vs. an easy) task.

163. New Insights on the Moderating Role of Switching Costs on the Satisfaction-Loyalty Link

Thomas Rudolph, University of St. Gallen, Switzerland
Liane Nagengast, University of St. Gallen, Switzerland
Heiner Evanschitzky, Aston University, UK
Markus Blut, TU Dortmund, Germany

Existing studies on the moderating role of switching costs on the satisfaction-loyalty relationship are inconclusive. Based on a meta-analysis and two studies, we show that switching costs moderate this relationship in a nonlinear (inverted u-shaped) way. Explaining existing inconsistencies, our results contribute to a better understanding of the satisfaction-loyalty link.

164. An Interruption Effect on Service Recovery

Fan Liu, University of Central Florida, USA

This paper attempts to advance the model of customer satisfaction in service-failure contexts and integrates interruption as a moderator and an enhancement on customer satisfaction.

165. Customer Satisfaction and Overall Rating: The Influence of Judgment Certainty

Eugene Sivadas, University of Washington, Tacoma, USA
John Kim, Oakland University, USA
Norman Bruvold, University of Cincinnati, USA

The objective of this research is to understand how rating magnitude and rating uncertainty and its interplay with satisfaction affects stated customer experience. We utilize the Judgment Uncertainty and Magnitude Parameters (JUMP) model to empirically examine consumer judgments of their overall experience.

166. Investigating the Positive Impact of Unexpected CSR

H. Onur Bodur, Concordia University, Canada
Bianca Grohmann, Concordia University, Canada
Ali Tezer, Concordia University, Canada

In this research, we investigate particular conditions in which consumers' elaborations of a CSR activity leads to more favorable motivations regarding the firm's involvement and more favorable brand evaluations.

167. A Research Paper on Process of Complaint Behavior Towards Social Commerce, Based on Attribution Theory

Yaeeun Kim, Korea Advanced Institute of Science and Technology, South Korea
Younghoon Chang, Korea Advanced Institute of Science and Technology, South Korea
Myeong-Cheol Park, Korea Advanced Institute of Science and Technology, South Korea

Through surveys, we find that the attributions consumers find themselves affect their post-purchase behavior. This study has implications in the social commerce area, because social commerce is based on the social network in which the consumers who are dissatisfied tend to complain.

168. The Difference of Satisfaction with the Second-Best Choice between Hedonic and Utilitarian Consumption

Yoonji Shim, University of British Columbia, Canada
Jinhyung Kim, Texas A&M University, USA
Incheol Choi, Seoul National University, South Korea

Two studies were conducted to investigate the difference of satisfaction with the second-best choice between hedonic and utilitarian consumption. Our results demonstrate that the gap of satisfaction between the best and the second-best choices is greater when the consumption goal is hedonic rather than utilitarian.

169. The Role of Self-Congruence in Consumers' Responses to Service Failures

Shuqin Wei, Southern Illinois University Carbondale, USA
Tyson Ang, Southern Illinois University Carbondale, USA

Using an experiment, we investigate an overlooked factor, consumers' self-congruence, in understanding consumers' emotional responses to service failures. Self-conscious emotions (e.g., embarrassment) and basic emotions (e.g., betrayal) are studied. Since distinct emotions require different service recovery strategies, distinguishing between different emotions is important. A moderator, service failure type, is explored.

170. Does Complaining Really Ruin a Relationship? Effects of the Propensity to Complain on Positive Consumer-Brand Relationships

Hongmin Ahn, West Virginia University, USA
Yongjun Sung, University of Texas at Austin, USA
Minette Drumwright, University of Texas at Austin, USA

This study suggests that when encountering relationship conflicts, consumers characterized by a high propensity to complain (PTC) are more likely to response destructively than are those with a low PTC. It further demonstrates that appraisals of a company's intention in regard to conflicts mediate such positive association between PTC and destructive responses.

171. Grotesque Imagery in Fashion Advertising

Jennifer Zarzosa, New Mexico State University, USA
Cuauhtemoc Luna-Nevarez, New Mexico State University, USA

The study investigates the grotesque genre of representation in luxury fashion advertising. In doing so, both the art and marketing literature is synthesized in order to identify distinct types of grotesque. In particular, we examine advertisements for Marc Jacobs. As such, the study further expands the theoretical parameters of the grotesque.

172. A Meta-Analysis of Nonverbal Accuracy Outcomes in Consumer Research Settings

Susan A. Andrzejewski, Franklin & Marshall College, USA

This meta-analysis quantitatively summarizes the literature on the relationship between nonverbal accuracy and consumer response in retail and service settings. In addition, this meta-analysis explores several potential moderators of the relationship between nonverbal accuracy and consumer response (i.e., domain, type of nonverbal cue decoded, channel of nonverbal cue).

173. (Illusory) Distance of Exposure as a Moderator of the Mere Exposure Effect

Anneleen Van Kerckhove, Ghent University, Belgium
Maggie Geuens, Ghent University, Belgium

Two studies demonstrate that (illusory) distance of exposure moderates the mere exposure effect, such that distant rather than nearby stimuli are more likely to generate liking after initial exposure. This advantage for distant stimuli levels off after multiple exposures; both distant and nearby stimuli then generate liking.

174. The Effects of Perceived Product-Association Incongruity on Consumption Experiences

Sarah Clemente, Brock University, Canada
Eric Dolansky, Brock University, Canada
Antonia Mantonakis, Brock University, Canada
Katherine White, University of British Columbia, Canada

The level of congruity between an object and its attribute is determined by the degree of match. Products with moderately incongruent associations enhance evaluations–this is the moderate schema incongruity effect. We investigate the influence of (in)congruity between an extrinsic cue (sponsor) and a product (wine) on consumers' product evaluations.

175. The Effect of Menu Presentation Characteristics on Consumer Food Choices

Jing Lei, University of Melbourne, Australia
Ying Jiang, University of Ontario Institute of Technology, Canada
Catharinna Cao, Mars Australia, Australia

This research examines how menu presentation characteristics such as the number of healthy vs. unhealthy options, separate vs. mixed presentation of healthy and unhealthy options, and text vs. picture presentation format influence consumers' food choices. We discuss the results from an experimental study and its implications.

176. The Impact of Category Labels on Perceived Variety

Tamara Ansons, University of Michigan, USA
Aradhna Krishna, University of Michigan, USA
Norbert Schwarz, University of Michigan, USA

We examine how different category labels influence viewers' perceptions of variety of a set by impacting visual imagery. Perceptions of variety increase when category labels sponsored the generation of mental imagery specifically related to the attributes of the set, but not when the labels merely increase imagery.

177. Illusion of Variety: The Effect of Metacognitive Difficulty on Variety Judgment

Zhongqiang (Tak) Huang, Chinese University of Hong Kong, Hong Kong
Y.Y., Jessica Kwong, Chinese University of Hong Kong, Hong Kong

In this research, we study variety judgment from a metacognitive perspective. Based on prior research on variety judgment, choice difficulty and metacognitive experience, we predict that higher-variety judgment in an assortment can result from metacognitive difficulty. We offer experimental evidence for this prediction.

178. Coffee without Overchoice

Claude Messner, University of Bern, Switzerland
Michaela Wänke, University of Mannheim, Germany

After choosing from simultaneously presented options, a coffee tastes less chosen from a large assortment than a small one. However, this effect reverses when consumers decide among attributes sequentially. Apparently, sequential choice is an effective strategy to retain the benefits of a large assortment without suffering from the costs.

179. Hmm…What Did Those Ads Say? Reducing the Continued Influence Effect in Political Comparison Ads

Rebecca E. Dingus, Kent State University, USA
Robert D. Jewell, Kent State University, USA
Jennifer Wiggins Johnson, Kent State University, USA

Comparative ads provide contradictory information and corrections. The impact this finding has on consumers' decisions is unknown because it is difficult to know what will be recalled. The continued influence effect (CIE) occurs when original information prevails in memory, although a correction is acknowledged. This paper aims to reduce the CIE.

180. Holistic vs. Analytic Thinkers in the West: Differential Reliance on Logos in Cognition- and Feelings-Based Product Evaluations

Alexander Jakubanecs, Institute for Research in Economics and Business Administration, Norway
Magne Supphellen, Norwegian School of Economics and Business Administration, Norway

Our research focuses on the effects of analytic-holistic information processing and product logos on cognitive and feelings-based product evaluations in France. One finding is that for lesser-known products, logos have effects on cognitive evaluations only for holistic thinkers. The research offers several contributions to the extant studies of processing styles.

181. The Relative Importance of Advertising Elements and the Roles of Sex (Gender) and Involvement

Even J. Lanseng, Norwegian Business School, BI, Norway
Maarten L. Majoor, Norwegian Business School, BI, Norway and University of Groningen, The Netherlands

This study examines men and women's reactions to models, number of product arguments, and claim type in advertising. We find that men process models as cues and hence prefer female models, whereas women process models as product arguments and hence prefer female or couple models. Sex differences are moderated by involvement.

182. Trivial Gets Central

Charan Bagga, Western University, Canada
Niraj Dawar, Western University, Canada

Our paper studies whether exemplar (non-exemplar) brands gain choice share and improve evaluations by differentiating on the basis of trivial attributes (TA). We focus on scenarios that disclose (do not disclose) the irrelevance of TAs. Finally, we investigate if the first-mover TA strategy of exemplars (non-exemplars) is sustainable.

183. Deception in Marketing: How the Source Influences Consumers' Responses to Deception and Its Contagious Effect on Unrelated Immoral Behavior

Marijke Leliveld, University of Groningen, The Netherlands
Laetitia Mulder, University of Groningen, The Netherlands

This study shows that perceptions of deceptive marketing strategies can be influenced by situational factors, like the source of the deception. Moreover, deception can be contagious to other (im)moral behavior, both related to the source, as well as unrelated to a consumer context.

184. Compassion for Evil but Apathy for Angels: The Interactive Effects of Mortality Salience and Just-World Beliefs on Donation Behavior

Fengyan Cai, Shanghai Jiao Tong University, China
Robert S. Wyer Jr., Chinese University of Hong Kong, Hong Kong

The present research examines the interplay of mortality salience and just-world beliefs in helping behavior. When mortality is not salient, individuals are more willing to help victims for whom they have much sympathy (little sympathy) when the need for help is low (great). Mortality salience qualifies these effects, however.

185. All Types of Mortality Salience Are Not Equal: The Effect of Contemplating Natural vs. Unnatural Death on Materialism Behavior

Zhi Wang, Chinese University of Hong Kong, Hong Kong

While previous research on Terror Management Theory (TMT) argues that Mortality Salience drives individuals to behave differently than they would otherwise, the literature has not differentiated behaviors caused by contemplations of death in different ways (e.g., unnatural vs. natural). This research aims to fulfill this gap by synthesizing TMT and Just-World Theory.

186. How Product Information Shapes Purchase Decisions: Behavioral and Functional Magnetic Resonance Imaging Studies

Sargent Shriver, Temple University, USA
Uma Karmarkar, Harvard University, USA
Michael I. Norton, Harvard University, USA
Angelika Dimoka, Temple University, USA

The authors use behavioral and functional neuroimaging methods to explore the mechanisms that underlie the evaluation of product information, and how this evaluation impacts purchasing behavior.

187. New Notion of Nostalgia

Keiko Makino, Seijo University, Japan

This study proposes a new notion of nostalgia and offers propositions by critically reviewing the previous literature. The propositions concern positive/ negative feelings evoked by nostalgic experiences, continuity/ discontinuity between the past and the present, and warmth as emotion/ aesthetic quality.

188. Constructing the Citizen-Consumer through Political Discourse in the U.S.

Gokcen Coskuner-Balli, Chapman University, USA
Gulnur Tumbat, San Francisco State University, USA

As political discourses denote a profound way that consumer subjectivities are constructed in the marketplace, this study explores the conceptualization of consumerism through political discourse in the US. Through historical analysis of American presidential speeches, we explore the myths that underlie the construction of consumer-citizens and their relations with the government.

189. When Nothing Means Everything: Consumer Evaluations of Specialized and Unspecialized Products

Gabriela Tonietto, Washington University in St. Louis, USA
Brittney Dalton, Washington University in St. Louis, USA
Stephen M. Nowlis, Washington University in St. Louis, USA

There are a number of strategies that companies can use when positioning products. This research focuses on three such strategies that vary in their degree of specialization. We propose that consumers infer that unspecialized products will fulfill all of their specific needs, leading to greater preferences for unspecialized than specialized products.

190. Can't Finish What You Started? Consumption Following Climactic Interruption

Daniella Kupor, Stanford University, USA
Taly Reich, Stanford University, USA
Baba Shiv, Stanford University, USA

We examine the important unanswered question of whether interruptions engender a quest for a resolution through the pursuit of closure-associated behaviors. We explore and demonstrate the possibility that interruptions trigger a need for a resolution that emerges in the choice of behaviors, even in totally unrelated domains. This is the case when the interruption disrupts an activity or task at its climactic moments (e.g., just before delivery of the punch line of a comedy act) rather than at non-climactic moments. We demonstrate that resolution-inducing behaviors will occur even if associated with a personal cost.

191. Monotonous Forests and Colorful Trees

Hyojin Lee, Ohio State University, USA
Xiaoyan Deng, Ohio State University, USA
Rao Unnava, Ohio State University, USA

We examine the effects of color on information processing style. We find that color makes people focus more on the details presented in a picture, while black and white makes people focus more on the overall meaning of the picture. The differential focus is then shown to affect product choice.

Author Index

A

Aaker, Jennifer L.. . . . . 13, 121
Abendroth, Lisa J. 670
Ackerman, Joshua . . . 178, 629, 701, 1091, 1123
Adaval, Rashmi 829, 1093, 1110, 1120, 1122
Adler, Jonathan M.. 276
Agarwal, James 1109
Aggarwal, Pankaj. 66
Aghakhani, Hamed 1116
Agrawal, Nidhi. 66
Ahluwalia, Rohini 604, 1007
Ahn, Hongmin 1136
Akghari, Mehdi 1114
Aknin, Lara B.. 13
Akpinar, Ezgi.. . . . . 228, 232
Albarracin, Dolores 823, 1126
Albrecht, Arne 1069
Alexander, Matthew. 1084
Alquist, Jessica L. 9
Althuizen, Niek 1118
Alvarez, Claudio 313
Amar, Moty 962
Amaral, Nelson 76
Amstel, Mariette van 881
Anderson, Rolph E. 1112
Andonova, Yana. 85
Andrade, Eduardo B.. 815
Andrea, Tonner. 357
Andreasen, Alan. 1087
Andrews, J. Craig. 85
Andrews, Steven 342
Andrzejewski, Susan A.. . . . . 1120, 1137
Ang, Tyson 1136
Ansons, Tamara 1137
Appelt, Kirstin 991
Arens, Zachary G. 931
Argo, Jennifer A. 209, 1124
Argo, Jennifer J.. . . . . 178, 1130
Ariely, Dan. 53, 219, 962
Arnould, Eric J. 1094, 1096
Arsel, Zeynep.. . . . . 28, 1118
Arthur, Damien 526
Aryobsei, Suleiman 1031
Ashton-James, Claire. 13
Ashworth, Laurence. 1121, 1128
Askegaard, Søren. 1093
Atalay, A. Selin 809
Avery, Jill. 313
Avnet, Tamar 168
Aydinli, Aylin. 195, 293, 731
Aydinoglu, Nilufer. 76

B

Baca-Motes, Katie 219
Bae, So Hyun. 903
Bagchi, Rajesh 280, 600, 673
Bagga, Charan 1138
Bagramian, Ruben 935
Bahl, Navin 1110
Bahnson, Sara 1134

Bajaj, Aditi. 1133
Baker, Stacey Mezel. 1087
Bambauer-Sachse, Silke. 319, 334
Banerji, Ishani 1128
Banikema, Annie Stéphanie 612
Banister, Emma N.. . . . . 708, 1047
Banker, Sachin 1123
Barasch, Alixandra. 640, 1114
Bargh, John A.. 701
Barraclough, Susan 298
Barretta, Paul 1083
Barrington-Leigh, Chris P.. 13
Barrios, Andres 101, 890
Bart, Yakov.. 228
Baskin, Ernest 134
Bastos, Wilson 255
Batat, Wided.. 751
Bates, Kenneth. 1112
Batra, Rishtee. 1125
Bauer, Martina 483
Baumeister, Roy F.. . . . . 9, 9, 121
Baumgartner, Hans. 954, 1093
Baxter, Stacey 1133
Beal, Daniel 70, 987
Bean, Jonathan. 28
Bee, Colleen C. 1109
Belk, Russell W.. . . 5, 327, 894, 901, 1084, 1094
Bell, Monique 985
Bellezza, Silvia 76, 757
Benedetto, C. Anthony Di 1111, 1133
Bennett, Delancy 1017
Berger, Jonah 203, 228, 228, 232, 288, 1100
Bergh, Bram Van den. 195, 727, 1091
Berman, Jonathan Z. 125
Bertini, Marco 195, 241, 293
Beruchashvili, Mariam. 1105
Bettany, Shona M. 117
Bettman, James R.. . . . . 76, 121, 182
Bhargava, Saurabh. 298
Bhargave, Rajesh 32, 663
Bhatnagar, Namita 1110
Bhattacharjee, Amit 125, 288
Bhattacharyya, Arundhati 960
Bian, Xuemei 1132
Bickart, Barbara A. 1015
Bilgin, Baler. 1110
Billeter, Darron 308
Birau, Mia 1108
Biswas, Dipayan 236, 1001, 1075
Biswas-Deiner, Robert. 13
Blair, Sean 1079
Blanchard, Simon J.. 885
Blatter, David. 887
Blekher, Maria 582
Block, Lauren G. . 42, 168, 173, 600, 1093, 1131
Blocker, Chris 101
Blut, Markus 1135, 1135
Boatwright, Peter. 1123
Böckenholt, Ulf 915
Bodur, H. Onur.. . . . . 809, 1132, 1136
Boer, Cara de 143, 198
Bogaerts, Tess 577

Bohnenkamp, Björn. 1035
Bolton, Lisa 821, 993
Bond, Samuel. 1033, 1105, 1133
Bonezzi, Andrea. 266
Boone, Tonya 1125
Borak, Eser.. 561
Borelli, Fernanda 379
Bosmans, Anick 661
Botti, Simona 266
Boven, Leaf Van. 134
Brach, Simon 1069
Bradford, Tonya Williams 28
Bradshaw, Alan 811
Brendl, C. Miguel 800
Brick, Danielle J.. . . . . 48, 1106
Brigden, Neil 743
Briggs, Courtney 1126
Brinberg, David 191
Brock, Christian 1135
Broderick, Amanda J 427
Broniarczyk, Susan 271
Brough, Aaron R. 266, 1072
Brown, Amber 219
Brownlie, Douglas 995
Brucks, Merrie 85, 255, 1089, 1127
Bruhn, Manfred 567
Brunel, Frédéric F. 804, 1015
Bruno, Pascal 651
Bruvold, Norman 1135
Bruyneel, Sabrina. 759, 1128
Bublitz, Melissa G. 1107
Bublitz, Mellisa G.. 236
Bucchia, Céline Del 630
Buechel, Eva 203
Bullard, Olga (Olya) 1130
Burgh-Woodman, Helene de 496
Burnkrant, Robert 1117
Burns, Alvin C. 1112
Burroughs, James 70, 1093
Burson, Katherine 241, 280
Burton, Scot 85, 1125
Busch, Romy 1123
Busselle, Rick 191
Butterfield, Max E.. 163
Büttner, Oliver B.. . . . . 862, 1121

C

Cagan, Jonathan. 1123
Cai, Fengyan 1139
Cai, Jane.. 1129
Caldwell, Marylouise. 1083
Camilleri, Adrian 298
Campbell, Colin. 870
Campbell, Margaret C.. . . . . 85, 1093
Campbell, Troy H.. . . . . 37, 134
Canniford, Robin 718
Cantu, Stephanie 163
Cao, Catharinna 1137
Cappellini, Benedetta 739
Caprariello, Peter A.. 255
Carlson, Kurt 1025

Carmon, Ziv 106, 962
Carnevale, Marina 1131
Carney, Dana 1124
Carpenter, Stephanie M. 213, 1027
Carrington, Michal J. 718
Carroll, Ryall 1107
Carter, Travis J. 106, 255
Caruso, Eugene M. 58
Casotti, Leticia Moreira 379, 950
Cassab, Harold 997
Castano, Raquel 1083
Castro, Iana A. 947
Cauberghe, Veroline 782, 868
Cavanaugh, Lisa 261
Cerf, Moran 158
Cesarini, David 22
Chae, Boyoun (Grace) 90
Chan, Elisa K. 1130
Chan, Eugene 665, 813
Chandler, Jesse 112
Chandler, Tommy 1085
Chandon, Pierre 143, 173
Chandrashekran, Rajesh 1130
Chang, Chia-Jung 1129
Chang, Chun-Tuan 705
Chang, Younghoon 1136
Chaplin, Lan Nguyen 213, 729
Chartrand, Tanya L. 48, 851
Chatterjee, Subimal 675
Chatterjee, Suparna 877
Chattopadhyay, Amitava 213, 745, 970
Chatzidakis, Andreas 811
Chauvel, Marie Agnes 974
Cheema, Amar 42, 112
Cheetham, Fiona 873
Chen, Annie 1055
Chen, Bo 1118
Chen, Cuiping 1106
Chen, Fangyuan 90
Chen, Haipeng (Allan) 637, 821, 1106
Chen, Lydia 1027
Chen, Yu-Jen 228
Chen, Zoey 228, 761
Cheng, Shirley Y. Y. 48
Cheng, Yin-Hui 1115, 1129
Cherian, Joseph 1111
Cherkassky, Vladimir 158
Chernev, Alexander 95, 266
Chevalier, Corinne 755
Childers, Terry 236, 622
Chinchanachokchai, Sydney 1122
Chitakunye, Pepukayi 720, 1113
Chiu, CY 970
Cho, Cecile 187
Cho, Eunice Kim 665
Cho, Sunmyoung 1132
Cho, Yoon-Na 1125
Choi, Incheol 1136
Choi, Woo Jin 693
Chong, Chiao Sing 236
Chowdhury, Tilottama G. 993
Christensen, Bo T. 866
Chuang, Shih-Chieh 1115, 1129
Chugani, Sunaina 255
Chytkova, Zuzana 854
Cillo, Paola 213
Clair, Julian Saint 288
Claus, Bart 1067

Clemente, Sarah 1137
Cocker, Hayley L. 1047
Cohen, Taya 22
Coleman, Catherine 1113
Coleman, Nicole Verrochi 261
Combe, Ian 442
Connell, Paul M. 85, 117, 1087, 1087, 1089, 1106
Cornelis, Erlinde 782
Corus, Canan 18
Coskuner-Balli, Gokcen 1096, 1139
Costley, Carolyn 856
Cotte, June 117, 1089
Coulter, Robin A. 804, 1111
Cowley, Elizabeth 837
Craig, Adam 1102
Critcher, Clayton R. 125
Crockett, David 117
Cronley, Maria L. 933
Crosby, Elizabeth 845
Cross, Samantha 236, 1120
Cryder, Cynthia E. 112
Cuddy, Amy 1124
Curasi, Carolyn Folkman 616
Cutright, Keisha M. 182
Czellar, Sandor 1128

D

Dahl, Darren W. 37, 95, 173, 178, 178, 209, 209, 1013, 1093, 1093, 1100
Dai, Xianchi 786
Dalton, Amy N. 1038
Dalton, Brittney 1140
Dang, Yan 81
Daniloski, Kim 191, 1110, 1115
Danziger, Shai 582
Das, Prakash 1109
Das, Sudipta 510
David, Meredith 1119
Davis, Brennan 37
Davis, Cassandra 1105
Davis, Derick F. 280, 585, 600, 1070
Davis, Scott 1089, 1106
Dawar, Niraj 1138
Dawes, Christopher 22
Debenedetti, Alain 28
Debevec, Kathleen 85
Decrop, Alain 1084
Delbaere, Marjorie 1131
DelPriore, Danielle J. 163
DelVecchio, Devon 547
Denburg, Natalie 158
Deng, Xiaoyan 1140
Denton, Esta 143
Desai, Kalpesh K. 993
Deval, Hélène 933
Devezer, Berna 779
Dewitte, Siegfried 143, 198, 907, 1067
Dhar, Ravi 106, 246
Diamond, William 1017
Dias-Campos, Roberta 950
Dibb, Sally 1132
Dimofte, Claudiu 707, 997, 1059
Dimoka, Angelika 1102, 1139
Ding, Min 313
Ding, Ying 95
Dingus, Rebecca E. 1138

Dinsmore, John 917
Dixon, Mandy 708
Dobscha, Susan 1098
Dolansky, Eric 1137
Dolbec, Pierre-Yann 81
Dommer, Sara 604
Dong, Ping 786
Dorn, Michael 1118
Dose, David 1069
Downs, Julie S. 112
Drenten, Jenna 1098
Drèze, Xavier 213
Drolet, Aimee 1093
Droms, Courtney M. 1025
Droms, William G. 1025
Droulers, Olivier 763
Drummond, Kent 1098
Drumwright, Minette 1136
Dubé, Laurette 753
Dubelaar, Chris 843
Dubois, David 143, 691
Duclos, Rod 640, 1114
Duff, Brittany 1117
Duffy, Katherine 519
Duguid, Michelle M. 303
Duhachek, Adam 62, 796
Dunn, Elizabeth W. 13
Dunnett, Susan 995
Dupuy, Angélique 334
Durante, Kristina 70, 1091
Dzhogleva, Hristina 9, 749

E

Easwar, Karthik 678, 680, 1117
Echambadi, Raj 788
Edelman, Emma 1114
Eelen, Jiska 1009
Eggers, Felix 1130
Eilert, A. Meike 62
Elbel, Brian 219
Elder, Ryan 1117
Elliot, Esi Abbam 1111
Ellsworth, Phoebe C. 134
Emile, Renu 363, 371
Emontspool, Julie 427
Engeler, Isabelle 293
Epp, Amber M. 18
Erdem, Tülin 182
Erz, Antonia 866
Escalas, Jennifer Edson 76, 191, 1093
Espinoza, Francine 403, 807
Etkin, Jordan 90, 246
Evangelidis, Ioannis 727
Evanschitzky, Heiner 442, 1135, 1135

F

Fajardo, Tatiana M. 250, 308, 1011
Fang, Xiang 153
Faraji-Rad, Ali 682, 776
Farmer, Adam 626
Faro, David 168
Farrell, Andrew 442
Fatt, Choong Kwai 589
Faure, Corinne 1041
Fazel, Hesham 970
Fazio, Russell H. 1128

Fedorikhin, Alexander 1037
Feinberg, Richard. 1126
Feng, Shan 1129, 1130
Fennis, Bob M. 13, 633, 733
Fernandes, Daniel 1043, 1052
Fernbach, Philip. 1120
Ferraro, Carla 870
Festjens, Anouk 1128
Finkelstein, Stacey. 195
Firat, Fuat. 417
Fischer, Arnout. 958
Fischer, Eileen 81, 1093, 1093
Fishbach, Ayelet. 223, 246
Fitzsimons, Gavan J. 37, 48, 48,
    182, 182, 261, 956, 1093, 1106
Fitzsimons, Gráinne M. 37, 1106
Floh, Arne 1039
Florack, Arnd 707, 862, 1121, 1123
Fong, Nathan 943
Foo, Maw-Der 714
Ford, John B. 32
Forehand, Mark 288
Foreman, Jeff 1085
Fosse-Gomez, Marie-Hélène 454, 598
Fournier, Susan 313
Fowler, Jie Gao 883
Fransen, Marieke L. 606
Frederick, Shane 271
Freling, Traci 926
Fujita, Kentaro 66

G

G.Voyer, Benjamin. 587, 966
Gabel, Terrance 1098
Gabl, Sabrina 553
Gal, David 187, 1037
Galak, Jeff 889
Galinsky, Adam D. 303
Galli, Maria 745, 829
Gallo, Iñigo 1073
Gao, Ronnie (Chuang Rang) 1127
Garbarino, Ellen. 422, 642
Garbinsky, Emily N. 13
Garg, Sonakshi. 1126
Garnier, Marion 475
Garvey, Aaron M.. . . . . 885, 896
Gaustad, Tarje 48, 956
Ge, Xin 1053
Gentina, Elodie 598
Gentry, James. 1105
Gershoff, Andrew 271, 690
Geuens, Maggie 655, 937, 1137
Geyskens, Kelly 173, 288, 1021
Ghoshal, Tanuka. 1123
Giblin, Michael 1063, 1108
Giesler, Markus 129
Gill, Tripat 1091
Gilovich, Thomas. 106, 255
Ginena, Karim 5
Gino, Francesca 5, 5, 757
Giroux, Marilyn 1109
Gneezy, Ayelet 121, 219, 1100
Gneezy, Uri 121
Godefroit-Winkel, Delphine 454
Godes, David 228
Goldenberg, Jacob 232, 232, 241
Goldsmith, Kelly 178

Goldstein, Daniel G. 112, 284
Gomez, Pierrick 1108
Goncalves, Dilney 228, 741, 1135
Gonzalez, Cleotilde 817
Goodman, Joseph K. 112
Göritz, Anja S. 862
Gorn, Gerald J. 745
Gosline, Renée Richardson 95
Goswami, Indranil 298
Gotler, Alex 637
Goukens, Caroline 173, 288, 1021
Gould, Stephen J. . . 417, 1029, 1094, 1105, 1127
Grant, Susan Jung 1116
Grayson, Kent 209, 1093
Greenleaf, Eric 158
Grewal, Dhruv 1120, 1120
Grinstein, Amir 582
Griskevicius, Vladas 70, 163, 178, 629
Groeppel-Klein, Andrea. 945
Grohmann, Bianca 1109, 1132, 1136
Gros, Nina 173, 173, 1021
Grover, Aditi 1085
Grubliauskiene, Aiste. 907
Gu, Yangjie 266, 731
Guèvremont, Amélie 1132
Guillard, Valérie 630
Gunasti, Kunter 779, 949, 1131
Guo, Wenxia. 610
Gürhan-Canli, Zeynep 48, 76, 1110

H

Ha, Erin Younhee. 765
Ha, Sejin 1126
Hackley, Chris 771, 1098
Hadi, Rhonda 42
Hagen, Anna Linda 1107
Hagtvedt, Henrik 198
Hair, Michael 1105
Haji, Iftakar 442
Halfman, Kameko 158
Hall, Crystal 58
Hamby, Anne 191, 1110
Hamerman, Eric 125
Hamilton, Kathy 101, 1084
Hamilton, Rebecca W. 931, 1093
Hamilton, Ryan 95
Han, DaHee 796
Han, Jerry Jisang 1114
Han, Sangman 232
Han, Sidney Su. 1121
Hancock, Travis 1117
Handelman, Jay M. 1125
Hanks, Andrew 1049
Hardesty, David 622, 626
Hardisty, David 991
Hasford, Jonathan 622
Hattula, Johannes. 1013
Häubl, Gerald. 187, 743, 830, 860, 1019
Hauck, Jana 1131
Haws, Kelly L. . . . 9, 163, 735, 1089, 1106, 1119
He, Stephen 1033
He, Xin. 250, 1113
Heath, Timothy B. 547, 1128
Hedgcock, William 158, 1102
Hein, Wendy. 1113
Heinrich, Daniel. 567
Helliwell, John F. 13

Helzer, Erik G. 125
Hem, Leif 1117
Hemetsberger, Andrea 483, 502, 553
Hende, Ellis van den 667
Henderson, Marlone. 825
Hennig-Thurau, Thorsten. 1035
Henry, Paul 1083
Herd, Kelly B. 53
Hernandez, José Mauro da Costa. 917
Herpen, Erica van. 661, 881, 958
Herr, Paul M. 585
Herrmann, Andreas 1019, 1031
Hershfield, Hal E.. . . . . 22, 276
Hertwig, Ralph. 1127
Herzenstein, Michal. 13
Herzog, Walter 1013
Hess, Alexandra 856
Heuvinck, Nico 1122
Hewer, Paul 510, 519, 995
Hietanen, Joel. 1084, 1084
Hildebrand, Christian. 1019
Hiler, Jacob 1083
Hill, Ronald Paul 769
Hill, Sarah E. 163
Hill, Sarah E. 1091
Hille, Patrick 1069
Hirschman, Elizabeth. 327
Hodges, Nancy 462
Hoegg, JoAndrea (Joey). 209, 209
Hoffman, Donna L. 203
Hofstetter, Reto 887, 1031
Hogg, Margaret K. 117, 616, 708, 875
Holbrook, Mandy B. 112
Holden, Stephen 843
Honey, Hannah. 1106
Hong, Jiewen 66
Hong, Soonkwan 952, 972
Hong, Ying-Yi 688
Hood, Karen. 1085
Horen, Femke van 58
Hosey, Christine. 5
Howlett, Elizabeth 85, 1105
Hsee, Christopher K. 53
Hsu, Ming 1102, 1102
Hu, Hao 695
Hu, Miao 303
Huang, Chien-Jung 1115
Huang, Irene Xun. 777
Huang, Lei 635
Huang, Li 1038
Huang, Szu-chi. 90
Huang, Xun (Irene) 42, 1122
Huang, Yanliu. 241
Huang, Yunhui 1126
Huang, Zhongqiang (Tak) 1138
Huber, Joel 913, 1093
Hubert, Marco 1131, 1135
Huff, Aimee Dinnin 117
Hughes, Mine Üçok 148, 935
Hui, Michael K. 42, 1122
Hui, Sam K. 241
Humphreys, Ashlee 1096
Hung, Iris 276, 1118
Hunt, James 1111
Husemann, Katharina C. 540
Hyde, Kenneth F. 371

I

Ialam, Towhidul 1129
Ihl, Christoph 941
II, Americus Reed 125, 288
III, Aubrey R. Fowler 883
Illich, Yvonne 646
Ilyuk, Veronika 168
Ince, Elise Chandon 673
Inman, J. Jeffrey 1, 241, 308, 1100
Irwin, Julie 255
Isaac, Mathew S. 1023, 1037, 1072
Isakman, Elif 261
Isen, Alice M. 106, 703
Ittersum, Koert van 929
Ivanic, Aarti S. 143, 1112
Ivens, Björn S. 646
Iversen, Nina 1117
Iyengar, Sheena 266
Izberk-Bilgin, Elif 532, 1094

J

Jain, Shailendra P. 614
Jakubanecs, Alexander 1138
Janakiraman, Narayan 827
Janiszewski, Chris 198
Janssen, Catherine 1125
Jayachandran, Satish 62
Jeffrey, Jennifer 1119
Jewell, Robert D. 349, 1115, 1138
Jia, Jayson 790
Jia, Yanli 695
Jiang, Duo 1005
Jiang, Hongyan 1111
Jiang, Lan 209, 982, 1134
Jiang, Li 1120
Jiang, Ying 1137
Jiang, Yuwei 303, 745, 1114
Johannesson, Magnus 22
Johar, Gita 1093, 1118
John, Deborah Roedder 826, 984
John, Leslie 219, 1100
Johnson, Allison 590, 672, 1089
Johnson, Chelsea 1117
Johnson, Eric 298
Johnson, Guillaume 1112
Johnson, Jennifer Wiggins 349, 793, 1138
Joo, Jaewoo 747
Joy, Annamma 490
Jr., Robert S. Wyer 786, 829, 1139
Jung, Jae Min 939
Jung, Joowon 1121
Jung, Kiju 823, 1126
Jung, Minah H. 121
Jung, Sanguk 1118
Just, David 1049
Just, Marcel 158

K

Kachersky, Luke 1133
Kahn, Barbara E. 223, 308, 774
Kaipainen, Kirsikka 1119
Kaiser, Ulrike 53
Kalaignanam, Kartik 153
Kamins, Michael 1089
Kamm, Friederike 945

Kan, Christina 834
Kang, Esther 819
Kang, Jiyun 1125
Kao, Faye 514
Kara, Selcan 1131
Karababa, Eminegul 1096
Kardes, Frank 917, 933
Kareklas, Ioannis 804
Karmakar, Uma 1102, 1139
Kassam, Karim 158, 1102
Kastanakis, Minas N. 966
Kazakova, Snezhanka 868
Kedzior, Richard 960, 1094
Keeling, Debbie 875
Keenan, Elizabeth 219
Keh, Hean Tat 595
Keinan, Anat 76, 757
Keller, Punam Anand 1087
Kelting, Katie 62
Kemeza, Imelda 13
Ken, Yun 1115
Kenning, Peter 1106, 1108, 1130, 1135
Kerckhove, Anneleen Van 655, 658, 1137
Kerrane, Ben 117
Kes, Isabelle 798
Kettle, Keri 187
Khare, Adwait 849
Kidwell, Blair 622, 626, 1108
Kim, Chang-Ho 972
Kim, Hakkyun 879, 1114
Kim, Jinhyung 1136
Kim, John 1135
Kim, Joonkyung 1129
Kim, Min Jung 1106
Kim, Sang-Hoon 1125
Kim, Soo 800
Kim, Soyean (Julia) 1015
Kim, Yaeeun 1136
Kim, Youngseon 767
King, Dan 42
King, Jesse S. 1109
Kipnis, Eva 427
Kirmani, Amna 1077
Kjeldgaard, Dannie 854, 1096
Klapper, Daniel 1041
Kleber, Janet 1123
Klesse, Anne 173, 288
Ko, Dongwoo 1118
Kocher, Bruno 198, 1029
Koehler, Derek 246
Koenigstorfer, Joerg 945, 954
Koh, Ae-Ran 1132
Koivisto, Elina 1084, 1108
Koller, Monika 1039
Könkkölä, Saara 1116
Koo, Jayoung 847
Koo, Jieun 697
Koo, Minkyung 1051
Koppenhafer, Leslie 1003, 1127
Kopton, Isabella 1106
Kozinets, Robert 1094
Kramer, Thomas 223, 276, 791, 1119
Kraus, Alexandra 905
Krekels, Goedele 892
Kretz, Gachoucha 587, 1057
Kreuter, Matthew 191
Krishna, Aradhna 1001, 1107, 1137
Krishnakumar, Sukumarakurup . 1107, 1117, 1126

Kristofferson, Kirk 178
Kronrod, Ann 913
Ku, Edward 602
Kubat, Umut 1112
Kukar-Kinney, Monika 1115
Kulkarni, Atul 802, 1120
Kulow, Katina 223
Kunchamboo, Vimala 395
Kunz, Daniella 1140
Kurt, Didem 1061
Kuruoğlu, Alev 129
Kwak, Hyokjin 985
Kwan, Letty 970
Kwon, JaeHwan 989
Kwon, Mina 1051
Kwong, Y.Y.,Jessica 1138

L

Labrecque, Lauren I. 236, 1075
Labyt, Christophe 1123
Laer, Tom van 579
Laesser, Christian 293
Lai, Ai-Ling 386
Lajante, Mathieu 763
Lakshmanan, Arun 819
Lalwani, Ashok K. 153, 796
Lamberton, Cait Poynor 9, 178, 749
Lancioni, Richard 1111
Landwehr, Jan R. 1019
Langhe, Bart de 195, 280, 284, 1043
Lanseng, Even J. 1138
Laran, Juliano 90, 198, 308
Laroche, Michel 699
Larraufie, Anne-Flore Maman 632
Larrick, Richard 280, 298
Larsen, Hanne Pico 28
Latimer, Robert 722
LaTour, Kathryn 32
LaTour, Michael S. 32
Laufer, Romain 101
Lau-Gesk, Loraine 276
Lavack, Anne 1110
Lebar, Charles 1128
LeBel, Jordan 753
Leder, Helmut 1121
Leder, Susanne 707
Lee, Christina K.C 395
Lee, Crystal Tzuying 1115
Lee, Euehun 589
Lee, Eun-Jung 1115
Lee, Hangeun 1114
Lee, Hyojin 1140
Lee, Hyun Jung 349
Lee, Jangyuk 232
Lee, Jeffrey K. 95
Lee, Jiyoung 1114
Lee, Junyoung 1114
Lee, Kyoungmi 879, 1114
Lee, Leonard 168, 241, 911
Lee, Mike 363, 371
Lee, Sae Rom 737
Lee, Sangwon 1113
Lee, Seung Hwan (Mark) 584, 590, 593
Lee, Yih Hwai 714
Lee, Yong Kyu 280
Lee, Yun 1109
Lefebvre, Cécile 1125

Lehmann, Donald. 232, 236, 313, 769, 1001, 1075
Lei, Jing 849, 1137
Leizerovici, Gail 593, 1120
Lejarraga, Tomas 817
Leliveld, Marijke 1139
Lemon, Katherine 313
Lens, Inge. 70, 182
Leonard, Bridget 85
Lerner, Jennifer S. 1065
Leroi-Werelds, Sara 618
Leung, Ada. 1106
Levin, Irwin 158
Levy, Daniel. 637
Levy, Doug. 298
Levy, Eric. 620
Levy, Sidney J. 139, 1098
Li, En 642
Li, Xiuping. 777
Li, Ye 1065
Li, Yuan-Yuan 830
Lian, Hua (Olivia) 1111
Liang, Jianping. 1122
Liang, Rong-Da 1115
Liao, Shuling 714
Lim, Elison Ai Ching. 1119
Lim, Heejin 1119
Lin, Chien-Wei (Wilson). 675
Lin, Che-Hung 1129
Lin, Lily 37, 178
Lin, Meng-Hsien (Jenny) 236
Lin, Tzu Han 1115
Lin, You 705
Lin, Yuanfang. 1053
Linder, Nicolas. 173
Lindgreen, Adam 1125
Lindridge, Andrew 148
Lindsey, Charles. 1134
Linnet, Jeppe Trolle 28
Linzmajer, Marc. 875
Liu, Chihling 875
Liu, Fan 1081, 1135
Liu, Maggie Wenjing. 595
Liu, Min 1133
Liu, Peggy J. 37
Liu, Shu 1132
Liu, Xia (Linda) 1112
Liu, Yuanyuan 1128
Loewen, Peter J. 22
Loewenstein, George 158
Loken, Barbara. 76, 847
Lopez-Kidwell, Virginie 1108
Louviere, Jordan J. 774
Lowrey, Tina M. 729, 1133, 1133
Lu, Fang-Chi 827, 968
Lu, Ji 753
Lucas, Brian. 1124
Luffarelli, Jonathan 1135
Luna-Nevarez, Cuauhtemoc 1119, 1137
Lurie, Nicholas H. 761
Luukkonen, Anniina. 1108
Lwin, May 236, 236, 1107
Lwin, May O. 22
Lynch, John G. 1052
Lyu, Jewon 1119

M

Ma, Jingjing 95, 106
Ma, Zhenfeng. 1129
MacDonnell, Rhiannon 250
MacGregor, Karen 66
Maciel, Andre F. 644
MacInnis, Deborah J. 261
Maclaran, Pauline 616, 811, 1094, 1094
Madrigal, Robert 1003
Madzharov, Adriana V. 173
Maehle, Natalia 1117
Maeng, Ahreum 686, 724
Magnusson, Patrik K. E. 22
Maheswaran, Durairaj 62
Maille, Virginie 22
Maimaran, Michal 223
Main, Kelley J. 610, 1116, 1130
Majoor, Maarten L. 1138
Makino, Keiko 1139
Malaviya, Prashant. 898
Malkoc, Selin A. 266, 303
Manchanda, Rajesh V. 1110
Mandel, Naomi 261
Mann, Traci 163
Manning, Kenneth C. 85
Manoli, Day 298
Mantonakis, Antonia 32, 1137
Mantovani, Danielle. 815
Mao, Huifang. 1081
Marcoux, Jean-Sébastien 81
Markey, Amanda 158
Markos, Ereni. 1075
Martin, Christian 1128
Martin, Ingrid M. 1089, 1089
Martin, Jolie M. 817
Martineau, Eric 1118
Mason, Winter 112
Massey, Cade 246
Matherly, Ted 1077
Mathur, Anil. 589
Matsui, Takeshi 894, 901
Mattila, Pekka 1084
May, Frank. 153, 710, 1114
Mazar, Nina 22, 1102
Mazodier, Marc 899
McEachern, Morven 873, 1084
McFerran, Brent. 37, 37, 209, 1107
McGraw, A. Peter. 834, 1120
McQuarrie, Edward 342
McShane, Blake 187
McShane, Lindsay 1128
Mead, Nicole L. 58, 121
Meadows, Maureen 1132
Meert, Katrien 182, 1123
Mehta, Ravi 58
Meilleur, Louise 280
Meise, Valerie. 173
Melnyk, Valentyna 651, 856
Melnyk, Vladimir. 958
Meloy, Margaret G. 737, 896
Mende, Martin 313
Mendenhall, Zack 1134
Menon, Geeta. 288
Merchant, Altaf 32
Mérigot, Philippe. 28
Messinger, Paul R. 1053
Messner, Claude. 1118, 1138
Meyer, Jeffrey 1123

Meyvis, Tom 158, 1102
Mikkonen, Ilona. 1108
Miller, Elizabeth G. 85
Miller, Klaus M. 887
Millet, Kobe 1009
Milosavljevic, Mili. 1102
Min, Kyeong Sam 939
Minowa, Yuko 894, 901
Minson, Julia 271
Mirabito, Ann. 1089
Mittal, Vikas. 22
Mochon, Daniel 53, 219
Mogilner, Cassie 121, 1116
Mohanty, Praggyan (Pam) 836
Mohrenfels, Hannah Winkler von 1041
Moisander, Johanna 436, 490
Moisio, Risto 1105
Molander, Susanna. 148
Moldovan, Sarit 232
Monga, Alokparna (Sonia). 153
Monga, Ashwani 1114
Montgomery, Nicole Votolato 32, 663, 928
Moore, Sarah 1100
Morales, Andrea C. 22, 37, 261
Moran, Nora 673
Moreau, C. Page. 53, 1093
Morewedge, Carey 889
Morrin, Maureen (Mimi) 22, 236, 236, 1107
Morwitz, Vicki G. 158, 293
Moscato, Emily 18
Moschis, George P. 589
Mosteller, Jill 841
Motyka, Scott. 1120
Mourali, Mehdi 303, 1126
Mourey, James A. 182
Mueller, Pam 112
Mugge, Ruth 667
Mukesh, Mudra 741
Mukherjee, Ashesh. 1134
Mukherjee, Sayantani 223, 276
Mukhopadhyay, Anirban 276, 1120
Mulder, Laetitia 1139
Mun, Jungim 1134
Murray, Jeff B. 1096
Mussweiler, Thomas 58
Mwiti, Fredah G. 101
Mykerezi, Elton 163

N

Nabec, Lydiane 755
Nagengast, Liane 1135
Nagpal, Anish. 849
Namkoong, Jae-Eun 690, 825
Narsey, Vanisha 1131
Naveh-Benjamin, Moshe 836
Nayakankuppam, Dhananjay 968, 989
Naylor, Rebecca Walker. 62, 1119
Neck, Christopher 1126
Nelson, Leif D. 121, 219, 1100
Nelson, Michelle 1117
Nenkov, Gergana 22, 187
Nepomuceno, Marcelo 699
Netemeyer, Richard 1052
Neumann, Nico 915
Neville, Benjamin A. 718
Newman, Christopher L. 85
Newman, George 121

Newman, Kevin 1127
Ng, Sharon 821, 903
Nguyen, Hieu 1089, 1089
Nielsen, Jesper H. 85
Niman, Alyssa 1124
Nitta, Caitlin. 1127
Noguti, Valeria 649, 839
Norton, Michael I. . . 5, 5, 13, 53, 213, 219, 1100, 1139
Novak, Thomas P. 203
Novemsky, Nathan 134
Nowlis, Stephen M. 261, 1140
Nunes, Joseph C. 143, 213
Nuttall, Pete 725
Nyende, Paul 13

O

O'Brien, Ed 134, 134
O'Guinn, Thomas. 139, 724
O'Hern, Matt 982, 1134
Ofen, Shlomit. 232
Ofir, Chezy. 53
Ohk, Kyung Young 232
Okyay-Ata, Lale. 1110
Olson, Jenny. 37, 70, 182
Onay, Selcuk 649
Önçüler, Ayse 1128
Ordabayeva, Nailya 143
Orhun, Yesim 271
Oromulu, Nelly 422
Ourahmoune, Nacima 976
Oveis, Christopher. 1045
Overbeck, Jennifer R. 143
Oza, Shweta 250
Ozanne, Julie L. 18, 1087
Özçaglar-Toulouse, Nil 454

P

Page, Karen 885
Paharia, Neeru 1045
Pai, Seema 1015
Palermo, Nicole 1133
Palmeira, Mauricio. 653
Pandelaere, Mario 70, 182, 577, 658, 892, 922, 1123, 1123
Paniculangara, Joseph 250
Paolacci, Gabriele 112
Park, C.W. 308
Park, Ji Kyung 984
Park, Joowon 293
Park, Jooyoung. 158, 968
Park, Kiwan 879, 1114, 1129
Park, Myeong-Cheol 1136
Parker, Jeffrey R. 125, 313
Parmentier, Marie-Agnès. 81
Parsons, Elizabeth 739
Passerard, Françoise. 101
Patrick , Vanessa M. 42
Patrick, Vanessa M. 807
Paul, Matthew 1121
Paulson, Erika 139
Pavlicek, Beth 158
Payne, John 121
Pechmann, Cornelia 784, 1087
Peel, Emily. 112
Peloza, John 62

Pelsmacker, Patrick De 782
Peñaloza, Lisa 129
Peng, Norman 1055
Peracchio, Laura 1087
Pereira, Beatriz. 241
Perez, Maria Eugenia. 1083
Perkins, Andrew. 987
Peter, Paula C. 1107
Peters, Ellen 280
Pew, Ethan 1116
Pfeiffer, Bruce E. 933
Pham, Michel Tuan 731, 776
Pham, Nguyen 236, 1107
Phillips, Barbara. 342
Phillips, Joan 1134
Philp, Matthew. 1121
Piacentini, Maria 890, 1047
Pick, Doreen 1130
Pierce, Meghan 1110, 1115
Pillai, Rajani Ganesh 1117
Pirc, Mitja 241
Pirouz, Dante M. . . 672, 1089, 1089, 1119, 1120
Pirouz, Raymond 672
Pizarro, David A. 125
Plassmann, Hilke 158, 173, 1102
Plessis, Christilene Du 228
Pocheptsova, Anastasiya 246
Podoshen, Jeffrey. 1098
Pol, Gratiana 308
Poncin, Ingrid. 475
Pons, Frank 303, 1109
Poor, Morgan 1023
Prado, Paulo. 815
Prandelli, Emanuella 213
Preilowski, Bruno 1106
Prelec, Drazen 1102
Press, Melea 1096
Preston, Stephanie D. 1027
Price, Linda 1087
Prokopec, Sonja 807
Prügl, Reinhard 1131
Puccinelli, Nancy M. 1120
Puntoni, Stefano. 280, 284, 1043
Puzakova, Marina 985
Pyone, Jin Seok 106

Q

Quaschning, Simon 922, 1122
Quintanilla, Claudia 1083

R

Radford, Scott 1126
Raghubir, Priya 722
Raghunathan, Rajagopal 198
Rahinel, Ryan. 1007
Rajagopal, Priyali. 32, 712, 928, 964
Raju, Sekar. 712, 964
Ramanathan, Suresh. 173
Rank, Tracy 209
Rao, Akshay. 1102
Rao, Sanjay 790
Rapp, Justine 769, 1089
Rasolofoarison, Dina 809
Ratchford, Brian. 1093
Ratner, Rebecca 1087, 1093
Ratneshwar, S. (Ratti) 836

Redden, Joseph P. 70, 163, 1106
Reich, Taly 1140
Reicks, Marla 163
Reimann, Martin 308
Reinecke, Sven. 1013
Reis, Harry T. 255
Reitsamer, Bernd Frederik 1124
Richerson, Rob. 1108
Rick, Scott 70, 241
Riis, Jason 219, 298
Rikhi, Ruchi. 980
Rinallo, Diego 1094
Ringler, Christine. 261
Rios, Kimberly. 195
Risen, Jane L. 5
Robinson, Stefanie Rosen 62
Roche, Sarah 1133
Rodeheffer, Christopher D. 163
Roese, Neal J. 106, 1079
Rogers, Zoe 1127
Roggeveen, Anne. 1120
Rohr, Michaela. 945
Rook, Dennis 1098
Rosa, José Antonio. 924
Rose, Alexander S. 1110
Rose, Randall L. 1110
Rosenzweig, Emily 106
Rössler, Karin. 707
Rothschild, David 284
Roux, Dominique 612, 755
Rozenkrants, Bella 288
Rucker, Derek D. 143, 303, 303
Rudolph, Thomas. 1135
Ruedy, Nicole E. 271
Russell, Cristel. 117, 1131
Ruth, Julie A. 716
Ruvio, Ayalla 327, 691, 729
Ruyter, Ko de 173, 288, 579, 1021
Rymph, Doug. 1117
Ryu, Kisang 939

S

Saad, Gad 1091, 1091, 1124
Sääksjärvi, Maria 1039
Saatcioglu, Bige. 18
Saini, Ritesh 926
Salciuviene, Laura 890
Salerno, Anthony 198
Salisbury, Linda Court 187
Saluja, Geetanjali 1110
Salzberger, Thomas 1039
Samper, Adriana 182
Samuelsen, Bendik M. 48, 682
Sandıkcı, Özlem 129
Sands, Sean 870
Sanghvi, Minita 462
Santana, Shelle 293
Saqib, Najam 813
Sarial-Abi, Gülen 48, 795
Satoshi, Akutsu 469
Savignac, Benoit-Mykolas. 81
Sayin, Eda 76
Scaraboto, Daiane 1116
Schaarschmidt, Mario 1069
Schäfer, Daniela. 567
Schau, Hope Jensen . . . 81, 117, 117, 1094, 1131
Schifferstein, Hendrik 1039

Schiro, Julie 1120
Schlosser, Ann 620, 980
Schmeichel, Brandon J. 9
Schmid, Christian. 830
Schneider, Abigail 1116
Schoenmüller, Verena 567
Scholderer, Joachim. 905
Scholz, Joachim. 1125
Scholz, Stefanie 646
Schouten, John W. 1096
Schreier, Martin 53
Schulz, Anna Maria 1121
Schulz, Heather M. 608
Schulz, Steven A. 608
Schwartz, Janet 219
Schwarz, Norbert 134, 1115, 1137
Schweitzer, Maurice E. 271
Scopelliti, Irene 213
Scott, Linda 18, 1094
Scott, Maura. 313, 1089
Sela, Aner. 223, 266
Sellier, Anne-Laure 168
Semaan, Rania W. 1029
Sengupta, Jaideep. 66, 90, 773, 1093
Seregina, Anastasia 1084
Sevilla, Julio. 308
Shachar, Ron 182
Shaddy, Franklin 911
Shafir, Eldar 58, 134
Shah, Avni 121
Shankar, Maya 1130
Shapira, Daniel. 232
Shavitt, Sharon 1005, 1051
Sheehan, Daniel 929
Shen, Hao. 773
Shen, Luxi 246
Sherman, Claire 526
Sherry, John F. 28, 1094
Shields, Alison B.. 793
Shim, Yoonji. 1136
Shiv, Baba 158, 288, 790,
    896, 1093, 1102, 1130, 1140
Shriver, Sargent 1139
Shrum, L.J. 1133
Siebert, Anton 1096
Silveira, Teniza da 1084
Silvera, David H. 933, 1129
Simmons, Joe 1100
Simonsohn, Uri 1100
Simonson, Itamar. 266
Simpson, Bonnie 1126
Sinha, Ashish 915
Sinha, Jayati. 827
Sirianni, Nancy J.. 261
Sivadas, Eugene 1135
Slabbinck, Hendrik 658, 868
Small, Deborah 13
Smith, Andrew N. 81, 1118
Smith, Eliot 1128
Snir, Avichai. 637
Snyder, Aaron. 1130
Sobh, Rana. 5, 1084
Soesilo, Primidya K. 1133
Sohn, Youngwoo 1109
Soman, Dilip 168, 203, 246, 686
Somasundaram, T.. 1112
Sommer, Kapitan 1129
Song, Lei 1112

Sonnenberg, Lillian 298
Sood, Sanjay 1073
Soster, Robin L. 1110
Soule, Catherine Armstrong. 1003, 1127
Spanjol, Jelena 924
Spassova, Gerri 653, 703
Sredl, Katherine 1098
Sridharan, Srinivas. 788
Stamatogiannakis, Antonios. 1135
Stamboli-Rodriguez, Celina. 148
Staton, Mark. 1045
Steffel, Mary 125, 134
Stein, Randy. 701
Steinhart, Yael 232
Stenstrom, Eric. 1091, 1124
Stephen, Andrew 203, 228, 232
Steul-Fischer, Martina 646
Stevens, Gillian 139
Stewart, Kristin 1112
Stich, Alexander. 408
Stoehr, David 1123
Stokburger-Sauer, Nicola. 1124
Stone, Tim 417
Stornelli, Jason 1105
Strahilevitz, Michal Ann 1087, 1087
Streicher, Mathias 920
Streukens, Sandra. 618
Strizhakova, Yuliya 716
Suarez, Maribel 974
Suher, Jacob A.. . . . . 198, 241
Suk, Kwanho 697
Summers, Christopher 1119
Sun, Annika 1114
Sundar, Aparna. 917
Sundie, Jill 70, 987, 1091
Sung, Yongjun 1136
Supphellen, Magne 1138
Suri, Rajneesh 1127, 1130
Suri, Siddharth 112
Suzuki, Satoko 469
Swaminathan, Srinivasan. 1112
Swaminathan, Vanitha 604, 1112
Sweldens, Steven 858, 909
Szocs, Courtney 1001

T

Takhar, Amandeep 720, 1113
Tal, Aner. 1063, 1108, 1124, 1124, 1130
Tam, Leona. 924
Tan, Su Xia 236
Tannenbaum, David 125
Tanner, Robin 686, 724
Teng, Lefa 1121
Tessitore, Tina 868, 937
Tezer, Ali 1136
Thomas, Kevin. 1112
Thomas, Manoj 293
Thomas, Melanie 1116
Thompson, Craig 1093
Thompson, Debora. 898
Thompson, Leigh 22
Thompson, Scott 313, 947
Thomson, Matthew 590, 672, 1119
Thorndike, Anne 298
Thyroff, Anastasia 1096, 1096
Tian, Kelly 1110
Tice, Dianne M.. 9

Tinson, Julie. 725
Tiwsakul, Rungpaka Amy 771, 1098
Tofighi, Maryam 1132
Tolstikova, Natalia 148
Tomczak, Torsten 866
Tong, Luqiong 42
Tonietto, Gabriela. 1140
Torelli, Carlos J.. . . . . 153, 1087
Toussaint, Stéphanie. 1084
Townsend, Claudia. 223, 250, 250, 308, 774
Trabold, Lauren 1105
Trampe, Debra 633
Trask, Kristin 729
Travis, Alyssa. 139
Trelfa, Douglas. 1113
Trendel, Olivier 899, 1107
Trifts, Valerie 860
Trijp, Hans C. M. van 881, 958
Trope, Yaacov 134
Trudel, Remi 62, 187
Tsai, Claire I.. . . . . 168, 203
Tu, Ke (Christy). 1124
Tu, Lingjiang 1111
Tu, Yanping 223
Tuk, Mirjam A.. 858
Tumbat, Gulnur 1139

U

Ubel, Peter A.. 134
Ülkümen, Gülden 261, 266
Ungemach, Christoph 298
Unnava, Rao 712, 1140
Urbany, Joel. 1134
Urminsky, Oleg 271, 284, 298
Utgård, Jakob. 956

V

Valck, Kristine De 101
Valen, Beth. 1107
Valenzuela, Ana 241
Vallen, Beth 37
Valtonen, Anu. 436
Vanhamme, Joëlle 1125
Vanhouche, Wouter 143, 1067
Vargas, Patrick 32
Vedana, Simone 1084
Veer, Ekant 1087, 1087, 1098
Velagaleti, Sunaina R. 18
Venkatesh, Alladi 129
Venter, Marike 1112
Venugopal, Srinivas 788
Veresiu, Ela 129, 1096
Verlegh, Peeter 1109
Vermeir, Iris 868, 922, 1122
Vickers, Zata 163
Vijaygopal, Rohini 1132
Villi, Mikko 490
Visconti, Luca M.. . . . . 148, 935
Viswanathan, Madhu 788, 823, 1126
Vittala, Karolus 1084
Vohs, Kathleen D. . . 5, 9, 13, 121, 121, 795, 899
Völckner, Franziska 651
Vossen, Alexander 941
Vredeveld, Anna Jansson 1111
Vries, Eline L.E. De 633
Vu, Tiffany 1128

W

Wadhwa, Monica 173, 864, 909, 1102
Wagner, Tillmann. 408
Wakslak, Cheryl J. 134
Wallendorf, Melanie. 139, 644
Wallpach, Sylvia von 483
Walsh, Gianfranco 1069
Wamwara-Mbugua, Wakiuru. 999
Wan, Echo Wen 66, 95, 1126
Wan, Fang 970, 1114
Wang, Chen 209
Wang, Guanfu 1129
Wang, Jessie J. 153
Wang, Jing 191
Wang, Juan. 1119, 1129
Wang, Kai-Yu. 614, 1132
Wang, Liangyan 784
Wang, Lili. 851
Wang, Shih-Ching 1133
Wang, Tingting. 1121
Wang, Xiaoyu. 153
Wang, Xuehua 153
Wang, Yajin 5, 153, 178, 826
Wang, Yiqiu 1121
Wang, Yitong 784
Wang, Ze 1081
Wang, Zhi 1139
Wänke, Michaela 1138
Wansink, Brian. 37, 1049, 1063,
 1108, 1119, 1124
Ward, James 947, 987
Ward, Morgan K. 95
Warlop, Luk 48, 70, 682,
 759, 907, 1009, 1067
Warnaby, Gary 873
Warren, Caleb. 834
Wazlawek, Abbie 1124
Weaver, Kimberlee. 1070, 1115
Weber, Bernd 173
Weber, Elke U. 298, 991, 1065
Weckx, Laure. 1128
Weeks, Clinton S. 1134
Wei, Joicey Jie 1118
Wei, Mei-Ling 1131
Wei, Shuqin 1136
Weibel, Christian 1127
Weijo, Henri 1116
Weijters, Bert 892
Weinberger, Michelle F. 949
Weinberger, Ralf 502

Weingarten, Evan 58
Wentura, Dirk. 945
Werle, Carolina 1107, 1108, 1113
West, Patricia M. 680
Wetzels, Martin 579
Wheeler, S. Christian 288
White, Andrew 178
White, Andrew E. 70
White, Katherine 250, 1137
White, Tiffany Barnett 48, 765
Widmer, Sidonia. 1127
Wiebenga, Jacob H. 733
Wiertz, Caroline. 1035
Wiggin, Kyra 1059
Wilcox, Keith. 198, 203
Wiles, Mike 1134
Willems, Kim 618
Williams, Elanor F. 125
Williams, Patti 261
Wilson, Jonathan 5
Wilson, Juliette. 519
Winterich, Karen Page 22, 153, 693, 735
Wise, Chelsea. 774
Wobker, Inga 1108
Woisetschläger, David M. 798
Wong, Nancy 1116
Wright, Scott 684, 917
Wu, George 284
Wu, Xiaochang. 121
Wu, Yi-Chia 1083
Wyer, Robert S. 42, 695, 765, 823, 1122

X

Xia, Lan 1115
Xie, Guang-Xin 209
Xu, Alison Jing. 48
Xu, Fangzhou 1129
Xu, Huimin 1106
Xu, Jing 95

Y

Yalch, Richard 1059
Yalkin, Cagri 1113
Yan, Dengfeng 66
Yang, Adelle. 168, 284
Yang, Chun-Ming. 602, 1122, 1122
Yang, Haiyang 106, 213
Yang, Lifeng. 678

Yang, Linyun 851
Yang, Qing. 121
Yang, Xiaojing 614
Yang, Yang 889
Yang, Zhiyong 926
Yannopoulou, Natalia. 1132
Yap, Andy. 1124
Yates, J. Frank 1027, 1105
Yazıcıoğlu, E. Taçlı 561
Ye, Christine. 62
Yeomans, Michael 284
Yi, Sunghwan. 1121
Yoo, Jiah. 1109
Yoon, Carolyn 182, 213, 1102
Yoon, Sunyee 1116
Youn, Jin 178
Youn, Nara 1109
Yu, HongYan 1112
Yu, Ya-Ting 705
Yuan, Hong 802
Yucel-Aybat, Ozge 791

Z

Zarzosa, Jennifer 1119, 1137
Zauner, Alexander 1039
Zemack-Rugar, Yael. 9
Zhan, Lingjing 303
Zhang, Dan. 1111, 1133
Zhang, Jiao. 1011
Zhang, Jing. 1117
Zhang, Kuangjie. 858, 864, 909
Zhang, Lijun. 595
Zhang, Meng 42, 777, 1122
Zhang, Shuoyang 593, 1128
Zhang, Yan 5
Zhang, Ying 90
Zhang, Yinlong. 153, 688, 767, 1111
Zhang, Yulei 81
Zhao, Min. 66, 168, 203
Zhao, Ping 42
Zheng, Yuhuang 42
Zhou, Rongrong 1121
Zhu, Meng 58, 308
Zhu, Rui (Juliet). 42, 90
Zhu, Ying 1123
Zlatevska, Natalina 837, 843
Zubcsek, Peter 232
Zwebner, Yonat 241